The New Comprehensive A-Z Crossword DICTIONARY

(REVISED EDITION)

The New Comprehensive A-Z Crossword DICTIONARY

(REVISED EDITION)

compiled by

EDY GARCIA SCHAFFER

G. P. PUTNAM'S SONS
NEW YORK

G. P. Putnam's Sons
Publishers Since 1838
200 Madison Avenue
New York, New York 10016

BOOK DESIGN BY DEBORAH KERNER

ISBN   0-399-14097-2

Printed in the United States of America

This book is printed on acid-free paper. ∞

To my Liebling,

whom I cannot thank enough
for his endless patience
and moral support,

AND TO MY EDITOR,
IRENE PROKOP

I am grateful
for your faith and
belief in my work.

List of
Abbreviations Used

abbr.	*abbreviation*		Mex.	*Mexican*
Austral.	*Australian*		myth.	*mythology*
Brit.	*British*		N.	*North*
colloq.	*colloquial*		naut.	*nautical*
comb. form	*combining form*		obs.	*obsolete*
dial.	*dialectal*		poet.	*poetic*
Eccles.	*Ecclesiastical*		S.	*South*
e.g.	*for example*		Russ.	*Russian*
Eng.	*English*		Scot.	*Scottish*
Fr.	*French*		sl.	*slang*
Ger.	*German*		Sp.	*Spanish*
Gr.	*Greek*		US/U.S.	*United States*
Ital.	*Italian*		var.	*variant*
Lat.	*Latin*			

A

A .... A, AN, AY, PER, EACH
  Greek .... ALPHA
  Hebrew .... ALEPH
à bas .... DOWN, OPPOSE
à la mode .... STYLISH,
  FASHIONABLE
  mort .... MORTALLY,
  MELANCHOLY
aa .... LAVA
aardvark .... ANTBEAR, ANTEATER
  eating place .... ANTHILL,
  FORMICARY
Aaron's ally .... HUR
  brother .... MOSES
  death mount .... HOR
  father .... AMRAM
  miracle worker .... ROD
  mother .... JOCHEBED
  rod .... MULLEIN
  sister .... MIRIAM
  son .... ABIHU, NADAB,
  ELEAZAR, ITHAMAR
  wife .... ELISHEBA
aba .... ROBE, GARMENT
abaca .... HEMP, FIBER, LUPIS,
  LINAGA
  product .... ROPE
aback .... BEHIND
  taken .... CONFUSED,
  STARTLED, SURPRISED
abacus .... SLAB, SOROBAN,
  ADDER, CALCULATOR
Abaddon .... HELL, ABYSS,
  HADES, SATAN
  angel .... APOLLYON
abaft .... AFT, REAR, ASTERN,
  BEHIND
abalone .... NACRE, ORMER,
  SNAIL, ASSEIR, MOLLUSK,
  EARSHELL
abandon ...... DROP, QUIT, DITCH,
  LEAVE, WAIVE, DESERT,
  VACATE, DISCARD, FORSAKE,
  ABDICATE
abandoned .... LEFT, LOST,
  FORLORN, DEPRAVED,
  DERELICT, DESOLATE,
  FORSAKEN, UNBRIDLED
abandonment .... DEFECTION,
  DESERTION, DESOLATION
abase .... LOWER, SHAME,
  DEMEAN, HUMBLE, DEGRADE,
  DISHONOR
abasement .... SHAME,

DEGRADATION, HUMILIATION
abash .... DAUNT, SHAME,
  CONFUSE, CONFOUND,
  DISCOMFIT, EMBARRASS
abate .... EASE, WANE, QUASH,
  DEDUCT, LESSEN, LOOSEN,
  SUBSIDE, DECREASE, DIMINISH
abatement .... LETUP, EASEMENT,
  REDUCTION
abatis ...... OBSTACLE, BARRICADE
abbatoir .... SHAMBLES,
  SLAUGHTERHOUSE
abb .... WOOL, YARN
abba .... BISHOP, FATHER
abbe .... MONK, ABBOT, PRIEST
  domain .... ABBACY,
  MONASTERY
abbess .... AMMA
  domain .... CONVENT,
  NUNNERY
  who loved Abelard
  .... HELOISE
abbey .... PRIORY, CONVENT,
  CLOISTER, MONASTERY
  head .... ABBOT, PRIOR,
  ABBESS
  of an .... ABBATIAL
abbot .... ABBE, ABBAS, COARB,
  HEGUMEN
  assistant .... PRIOR
  hero .... ROLLO
abbreviate .... CUT, CLIP, REDUCE,
  ABRIDGE, SHORTEN,
  CONTRACT
ABC, et al. .... NETWORKS
  Power .... CHILE, BRAZIL,
  ARGENTINA
abdicate .... QUIT, RESIGN,
  RENOUNCE, SURRENDER
abdication .... DEMISSION,
  (SE)CESSION
abdomen .... BELLY, PAUNCH,
  VENTER, STOMACH
  colloquial .... GUT
  fluid in .... ASCITES
  of the .... ALVINE
abdominal .... VENTRAL
  limb, crustacean ...... PLEOPOD
  pain .... COLIC, PYROSIS,
  COLLYWOBBLES
  region .... PUBES
  swelling .... BLOAT
abduct .... KIDNAP, CAPTURE
  slang .... SNATCH, SHANGHAI

Abdul the Bul Bul .... AMIR
abeam .... BY, ASIDE, BESIDE,
  ABREAST
abecedarian .... TYRO, NOVICE,
  AMATEUR, LEARNER,
  BEGINNER, NEOPHYTE
abed ...... SICK, NAPPING, RESTING,
  RETIRED, SLEEPING
Abelard's love .... HELOISE
abele .... PINE, POPLAR
Abel's brother .... CAIN, SETH
  parent .... EVE, ADAM
aberrant .... ASTRAY, DEVIANT,
  MISTAKEN, WANDERING
  slang .... OFF BASE
aberration ...... LAPSE, DELIRIUM,
  INSANITY, DEVIATION,
  DERANGEMENT
abet .... AID, EGG, HELP, BOOST,
  COACH, ASSIST, FOMENT,
  INCITE, SECOND, SUCCOR,
  UPHOLD
abettor .... BACKER, ADVOCATE,
  EXPONENT, PROMOTER
abeyance .... PENDENCY,
  SUSPENSION
abhor .... HATE, SHUN, DETEST,
  LOATHE, DESPISE
abhorrence ...... ODIUM, HATRED,
  DISGUST, AVERSION,
  DETESTATION
abide .... LIVE, STAY, (A)WAIT,
  DWELL, TARRY, ENDURE,
  REMAIN, SUBMIT
abiding .... LASTING, ENDURING
Abi's father .... ZECHARIAH
  husband .... AHAZ
  mother .... HEZEKIAH
Abie's loved one .... ROSE
abigail .... MAID
Abigail's husband .... DAVID,
  NABAL
  son .... AMASA
Abihail's daughter .... ESTHER
  father .... HURI, ELIAB
  husband .... ABISHUR,
  REHOBOAM
  son .... ZURIEL
Abijah's son .... ASA
ability .... FLAIR, POWER, SKILL,
  TALENT, CALIBER, FACULTY,
  PROWESS
  to borrow .... CREDIT
  to feel .... (A)ESTHESIA,

1

SENSATION
to read and write
.... LITERACY
Abimelech's brother ...... JOTHAM
father .... GIDEON, ABIATHA
friend .... AHUZZATH
Abital's husband .... DAVID
son .... SHEPHATIAH
abject ...... LOW, BASE, HANGDOG,
PITIFUL, SERVILE, WRETCHED
abjectly afraid .... CRAVEN
abjure .... DENY, SPURN, RECANT,
REJECT, DISAVOW, RENOUNCE,
REPUDIATE
ablation .... SURGERY
ablaze ...... AFIRE, AGLOW, EAGER,
AFLAME, BURNING, EXCITED
able .... CAN, ADEPT, HABILE,
SKILLED, SKILLFUL,
COMPETENT, QUALIFIED
bodied .... STRONG, HEALTHY
to be totaled .... ADDABLE
to pay .... SOLVENT
to read and write
.... LITERATE
to reason .... SANE
willing and ____ ...... READY,
SET
ablegate .... ENVOY
abluent .... SOAP, DETERGENT
ablution .... BATH(ING), WASHING,
CLEANSING
abnegation .... DENIAL
Abner, brother of .... KISH
cousin of .... SAUL
epithet/character LIL
father of .... NER
slayer of .... JOAB
son of .... JAASIEL
wife of .... RIZPAH
abnormal .... ODD, QUEER,
UNUSUAL, IRREGULAR,
UNNATURAL
eye condition .... MYOPIA
mental condition
.... DEMENTIA
Abo .... TURKO
abode ...... HOME, NEST, HABITAT,
DOMICILE, DWELLING,
QUARTERS, RESIDENCE
colloquial .... CONDO, ROOST
of animals ..... DEN, STY, ZOO,
LAIR, HUTCH, WARREN
birds .... COTE, NEST, NIDE,
AERIE, AVIARY
giants .... UTGARD
gods .... MERU, ASGARD,
OLYMPUS
humans .... MIGARD
paradise .... EDEN
sinners' souls .... LIMBO,

PURGATORY
the dead ..... ARALU, HADES,
ORCUS, SHEOL, HEAVEN,
NIRVANA, PARADISE
the Muses .... PARNASSUS
slang .... PAD, DUMP, JOINT
abolish .... END, ANNUL, KILL,
ERASE, CANCEL, REPEAL,
REVOKE, DISCARD, NULLIFY,
RESCIND
aboma ...... BOA, SNAKE, SERPENT
abominable .... VILE, ODIOUS,
HATEFUL, HEINOUS,
OFFENSIVE, UNPLEASANT
Abominable Snowman ...... YETI
abominate .... HATE, ABHOR,
DETEST, LOATHE, EXECRATE
abomination .... HATRED,
PLAGUE, AVERSION, LOATHING
aboriginal .... FIRST, NATAL,
ORIGINAL, PRIMITIVE,
INDIGENOUS
weapon ..... NULLA, BLOWPIPE,
WO(O)MERA, BOOMERANG
aborigine ..... NATIVE, INDIGENE
world boxing champ
.... (LIONEL) ROSE
abort .... CHECK, THWART
abortion .... FIASCO, FAILURE,
MISCARRIAGE
illegal .... FETICIDE,
ABORTICIDE
abortive .... FUTILE, FRUITLESS,
UNSUCCESSFUL
abound .... TEEM, SWARM
abounding .... RIFE, COPIOUS,
TEEMING, ABUNDANT,
PLENTIFUL
suffix .... FUL, ULANT
about ...... OF, RE, ANENT, CIRCA,
ALMOST, AROUND, NEARLY,
REGARDING, CONCERNING
face .... REVERSAL,
REVULSION, TURNABOUT,
SOM(M)ERSAULT
above .... ATOP, PAST, OVER,
UPON, ALOFT, BEYOND,
HIGHER, SUPERIOR
board .... FAIR, OPEN, LEGIT,
HONEST, BLAMELESS
poetic .... O'ER
prefix .... HYPER, SUPER,
SUPRA
reproach ...... PURE, INNOCENT,
BLAMELESS
the ear .... EPIOTIC
zero .... PLUS
abra .... PASS, DEFILE
abracadabra ...... SPELL, JARGON,
GIBBERISH
abrade .... RUB, RASP, GRATE,

SAND, WEAR, CHAFE, GRAZE,
ERODE, GRIND, SCRAPE
abrading tool .... FILE, RASP,
GRATER, SANDER, GRINDER
material .... EMERY,
CORUNDUM, ERODENT,
SAND(PAPER)
Abraham's birthplace .... UR
brother .... HARAN, NAHOR
burial place .... MACHPELAH
CAVE
concubine .... HAGAR
father .... TERAH
grandfather .... NAHOR
grandson .... ESAU, JACOB
nephew .... LOT
shrine .... C(K)AABA
son .... ISAAC, MEDAN, SHUAH,
MIDIAN, ZIMRAN, ISHBAK,
JOKSHAN, ISHMAEL
wife .... SARAH, SARAI,
KETURAH
abramis .... CARP, FISH, BREAM
abrasion .... BRUISE, SCRAPE
abrasive .... BORT(Z), EMERY,
QUARTZ, ERODENT, TRIPOLI,
SAND(PAPER)
abraxas ...... GEM, CHARM, STONE
abreast ...... EVEN, EQUAL, LEVEL
of the times .... MODERN,
TRENDY
abri .... DUGOUT, SHELTER
abridge .... EDIT, DIGEST, REDUCE,
SHRINK, CURTAIL, SHORTEN,
CONDENSE
abridg(e)ment .... DIGEST,
SKETCH, EPITOME, SUMMARY,
SYNOPSIS, COMPEND(IUM)
abroad .... AWAY, DISTANT,
OUTSIDE, OVERSEAS
abrogate .... ANNUL, CANCEL,
REPEAL, ABOLISH, RESCIND
abrogation .... ABOLITION,
CESSATION, RESCISSION
abrupt .... CURT, RUDE, GRUFF,
HASTY, STEEP, SUDDEN,
BRUSQUE, UNEXPECTED
abruptly .... SPANG, SUDDENLY
Absalom's captain/cousin
.... AMASA
father .... DAVID
mother .... MAACHAH
sister .... TAMAR
slayer .... JOAB
abscess ...... BOIL, ULCER, FESTER,
PUSTULE
on gums .... GUMBOIL
on skin .... PIMPLE, BLISTER
abscond .... FLEE, ELOPE,
DECAMP, ELOINE, ESCAPE,
LEVANT

absence .... HOOKY, TRUANCY
  from one's country ...... EXILE
  leave of .... EXEAT, PERMIT,
    FURLOUGH
  of feeling .... COLD, NUMB,
    INSENSATE
  government .... ANARCHY
  hair .... ACOMIA, ALOPECIA
  light .... NIGHT, DARKNESS
  money .... BANKRUPT
  motion .... REST, INERTIA
  shame .... BRAZEN
  taste .... AGEUSIA
absent .... OUT, AWAY, GONE
  minded .... LOST, RAPT,
    DREAMY, BEMUSED,
    ABSORBED, DISTRAIT
  without leave .... AWOL
absentee, a kind of ...... TRUANT,
    MALINGERER
  colloquial .... NO-SHOW
absinthe .... GENIPI, LIQUEUR,
    WORMWOOD
absolute .... FULL, PURE, VERY,
    SHEER, STARK, TOTAL, UTTER,
    CERTAIN, PLENARY, SUPREME,
    COMPLETE, DEFINITE
  independence .... ALOD
  rule .... AUTARCHY, DESPOTISM
  ruler .... CZAR, SHAH, TSAR,
    DESPOT, SULTAN
  superlative .... ULTRA, ELATIVE
absolutely ...... SIMPLY, UTTERLY,
    ENTIRELY, DEFINITELY,
    CERTAINLY
  certain .... COCKSURE
  not allowed .... FORBIDDEN
absolution .... PARDON,
    ACQUITTAL, CLEANSING,
    CLEARANCE, REMISSION
absolve .... FREE, CLEAR, PARDON,
    ACQUIT, REMIT, EXONERATE
  in law .... VESTED
  sin .... SHRIVE
absorb .... EAT, BLOT, SUCK,
    DRINK, ENGULF, CONSUME,
    ENGROSS, SWALLOW,
    ASSIMILATE
absorbed .... LOST, (W)RAPT,
    ENRAPT, MERGED
absorbent .... POROUS, SPONGY,
    BIBULOUS
  material .... GAUZE, SPONGE,
    BLOTTER
absquatulate .... FLEE, DECAMP
abstain ...... DENY, AVOID, DESIST,
    FORGO, FORBEAR, REFRAIN
  from .... ESCHEW
  from eating ...... FAST, STARVE
abstainer of a kind .... DRY,
    TEETOTALER

abstemious .... SOBER,
    MODERATE, TEMPERATE
absterge .... WIPE, PURGE,
    CLEAN(SE)
abstinence .... SELF-DENIAL, SELF-
    RESTRAINT
  from alcoholic drinks
    .... SOBRIETY, TEETOTALISM
  sexual .... CELIBACY,
    CHASTITY, CONTINENCE
  total .... TEMPERANCE
abstract .... BRIEF, STEAL, DIGEST,
    PRECIS, REMOVE, RESUME,
    COMPEND, EPITOME,
    SUMMARY
  being .... ENS, ESSE
abstraction .... NOTION,
    PREOCCUPATION
abstruse .... DEEP, HIDDEN,
    SUBTLE, ESOTERIC, RECONDITE
absurd .... WILD, INEPT, SILLY,
    FATUOUS, FOOLISH,
    RIDICULOUS, NONSENSICAL
  colloquial .... RICH
  slang .... COCKEYED
absurdity .... PARADOX,
    NONSENSE
  colloquial .... POPPYCOCK
abundance ...... FOISON, GALORE,
    WEALTH, OPULENCE,
    AFFLUENCE, PLENITUDE
  colloquial .... SCADS
abundant .... RIFE, AMPLE,
    TEEMING, AFFLUENT,
    PLENTIFUL
abuse .... RAIL, SCOLD, INSULT,
    MALIGN, MISUSE, REVILE,
    SLANDER, VIOLATE,
    MALTREAT(MENT), MISTREAT
  a confidence .... BETRAY
abusive .... FOUL, INSOLENT,
    INSULTING, OFFENSIVE
abut .... JOIN, ADJOIN, BORDER
abysmal .... GAPING, YAWNING,
    CAVERNOUS, BOTTOMLESS,
    FATHOMLESS
abyss .... PIT, GULF, HOLE, CHASM,
    CLEFT, CAVITY, DEPTH,
    HOLLOW, TRENCH
  Babylonian mythology
    .... APSU
  below Hades .... TARTARUS
Abyssinia .... AXUM, ETHIOPIA
  ancient capital of .... MEROE
  capital of .... ADDIS ABABA
Abyssinian .... KAF(F)A,
    ETHIOPIAN
  animal ..... KUDU, LION, ORYX,
    ZEBRA, BABOON, GELADA,
    IMPALA, JACKAL, MONKEY,
    GAZELLE, GIRAFFE

  area .... AMHARA, ERITREA
  banana .... ENSETE
  battleground .... ADOWA
  bishop .... ABUNA
  Catholic .... CUSH, GEEZ,
    UNIAT(E)
  city/town .... ADWA, GORE,
    ASSAB, HARAR, JIMMA,
    GONDAR, GAMBELA, NAZRET,
    DESSYE, ASMARA, MAKALE,
    MAGDALA, SODDU, WALDIA
  coin/money .... BESA, HARF,
    AMOLE, GIRSH, SANTIM,
    KHARAF, TALARI, BIRR,
    ASHRAFI, PIASTER
  dialect .... GEEZ, GHESE
  drink .... MESE, BOUSA
  emperor ...... NEGUS, MEMNON,
    MENELIK, SELASSIE
  fly .... ZIMB
  garment .... CHAMMA
  governor .... RAS
  grain/plant .... TEFF
  Hamite ...... AFAR, AGAO, BEJA
  herb .... RAMTIL
  island .... DAHLAK
  lake .... TANA, ABAYA,
    CHAMO, ASSALE, RUDOLF,
    ZWAI, TURKANA, STEFANIE
  language .... GEEZ, ARABIC,
    AMHARIC, SOMALI, TIGRINYA
  lyre .... KISSAR
  measure .... TAT, KUBA,
    SINJER, TANICA, FARSAKH,
    FARSANG
  mountain .... BALE, GUGHE,
    RAS DASHAN
  ox .... GALLA, SANGA
  peninsula .... BURI
  people .... KALA, BEJAS,
    ETHIOP, SOMALIS
  primate .... ABUNA
  prince .... RAS
  princess .... AIDA, ANDROMEDA
  province .... ARUSI, BALE,
    TIGRE, WALLO, SHOA, GOJJAM,
    ERITREA, GONDER, GAMU-
    GOFA, SIDAMO, KAFFA,
    HARAR, WALLAGA
  pygmy .... DOKO
  queen .... CANDACE
  river .... OMO, ABAY, WABI,
    BARO, DAWA, FAFAN, AWASH,
    AKOBO, MAREB, ATBARA,
    BARAKA, TAKKAZE
  rock salt money .... EMOL
  title .... RAS, ABUNA, NEGUS
  tree .... KOSO, CUSSO
  tribe .... AFAR, AGOWS, GALAS,
    TIGRES, DONAKUS, SOMALIS
  tribesman .... SHOA

violin .... MASINKO
weight .... PEK, KASM, NATR,
OKET, ALADA, NETER, RATEL,
WAKEA, WOGIET, FARASULA
wolf .... KABERU
acacia .... BABUL, MYALL, SHRUB,
LOCUST, MIMOSA, WATTLE,
SHITTAH
astringent .... CATECHU
academe .... GROVE
academic ...... CLASSIC, ERUDITE,
LEARNED, PEDANTIC,
SCHOLASTIC
achievement .... DEGREE,
DOCTORATE
costume appendage
.... LIRIPIPE
degree, kind of .... LICENTIATE
paper .... THESIS
academy .... LYCEUM, SCHOOL,
COLLEGE, INSTITUTE
Acadia .... NOVA SCOTIA
acaleph .... JELLYFISH, SEA
NETTLE
acarid ...... MITE, TICK, ARACHNID
acaudal/acaudate .... TAILLESS
accede .... AGREE, YIELD, ASSENT,
COMPLY, CONSENT
accelerant .... CATALYST
accelerate .... REV, RACE, HURRY,
SPEED, HASTEN, QUICKEN,
STEP UP, ADVANCE
accelerator .... GUN, THROTTLE
accent ...... BEAT, BURR, MARK,
TONE, DRAWL, ICTUS, PULSE,
TWANG, BROGUE, DIALECT,
STRESS, EMPHASIS
accenting syllable .... ARSIS
accentuate .... STRESS,
EMPHASIZE, HIGHLIGHT,
UNDERLINE, UNDERSCORE
accept .... TAKE, ADMIT, ADOPT,
ALLOW, GRANT, EMBRACE,
RECEIVE, SWALLOW
as true .... ADMIT, CREDIT
eagerly .... LEAP, POUNCE
readily .... DEVOUR, BELIEVE,
SWALLOW
with indulgence ..... CONDONE
without question .... ABIDE,
ENDURE, SUBMIT, TOLERATE
accepted .... APPROVED
not .... OUTCAST, UNWANTED
standard .... PAR, NORM, TYPE,
MODEL
access .... WAY, ROAD, ENTRY,
AVENUE, ENTREE, APPROACH,
ADMISSION
accessible .... OPEN, HANDY,
AVAILABLE, OBTAINABLE
accessory .... AIDE, ALLY, EXTRA,

ADJUNCT, ASSISTANT,
ACCOMPLICE
accident .... CHANCE, HAZARD,
MISHAP, CASUALTY
accidental ...... CASUAL, RANDOM,
FORTUITOUS
accipiter ...... OWL, HAWK, EAGLE
acclaim .... HAIL, LAUD, EXTOL,
PRAISE
acclamation .... CRY, SHOUT,
OVATION, PLAUDIT
word of .... HAIL, AVE, OLE,
RAH, HEIL, BRAVO, BANZAI,
MABUHAY
acclimate .... INURE, ENURE,
SEASON, ACCUSTOM
acclivity .... SLOPE, TALUS,
INCLINE
accolade .... AWARD, HONOR,
PRAISE, LAURELS, TRIBUTE
accommodate .... FIT, LEND,
ADAPT, GRANT, LODGE,
ADJUST, BILLET, OBLIGE
accommodation .... BERTH,
FAVOR, AMENITY, QUARTERS,
LOAN, CONCORD, CONCESSION
accompaniment .... ESCORT,
SPOUSE, SQUIRE, CONSORT
slang .... PARD
accompany .... JOIN, CONVOY,
ESCORT, CHAPERON(E)
accomplish .... DO, ATTAIN,
EFFECT, ACHIEVE, FULFILL,
PERFORM, COMPLETE
accomplished .... ADEPT, EXPERT,
GIFTED, SKILLED, POLISHED,
TALENTED
accomplishment .... DEED, FEAT,
SKILL, TALENT, FRUITION,
REALIZATION
accord ...... GIVE, UNITY, BESTOW,
CONCERT, CONFORM, UNISON,
HARMONY
according to .... PER, ALLA,
PURSUANT
good form .... DE RIGUEUR
law/rule .... FORMAL,
LEGAL(LY), DE REGLE,
LEGITIMATE
morals .... ETHICAL
regulations .... BY THE BOOK
usage .... CUSTOMARY
accordion-like instrument
...... MELODEON, CONCERTINA
accost .... CALL, HAIL, STOP,
GREET, SALUTE, WAYLAY,
ADDRESS
account .... TAB, SAKE, TALE,
SCORE, STORY, REPORT,
COMPUTE, EXPLAIN, NARRATE,
STATEMENT

accountant .... BEAN COUNTER
accounting .... AUDIT, COSTING,
BOOKKEEPING
entry .... ITEM, ASSET, DEBIT,
CREDIT, LIABILITY
form .... LEDGER, JOURNAL
accouter .... ARRAY, DRESS,
EQUIP, OUTFIT
accouterment .... TRAPPING(S),
HABILIMENT
Accra is capital of .... GHANA
accredit .... DEPUTE, APPOINT,
CERTIFY, LICENSE, AUTHORIZE
accrue ...... GROW, AMASS, ENSUE,
ISSUE, RESULT, COLLECT,
INCREASE
accumulate .... BANK, AMASS,
HOARD, STORE, ACCRUE,
GARNER, GATHER, COLLECT
accumulation .... FUND, HEAP,
PILE, HOARD, COLLECTION
accuracy .... TRUTH, PRECISION
of reproduction .... FIDELITY
accurate .... TRUE, EXACT,
CORRECT, PRECISE
accursed .... FEY, CURSED,
DAMNED, DOOMED
accusation .... RAP, BLAME,
CHARGE, INDICTMENT
slang .... FRAME
accuse ...... CITE, BLAME, ALLEGE,
IMPUTE, INDICT, ARRAIGN,
IMPEACH
accustom .... ENURE, INURE,
ADDICT, TOUGHEN,
ACCLIMATE, HABITUATE
accustomed .... USED, WONT,
USUAL, INURED, TRAINED
ace ...... TIB, ONE(R), HERO, TOPS,
STAR, FLYER, EXPERT,
ONESPOT
of clubs .... BASTO
of spades .... SPADILLE
queen combination
.... TENACE
to ten in poker .... STRAIGHT
to ten, same suit
.... (ROYAL)FLUSH
acephalous .... HEADLESS,
LEADERLESS
acerate .... NEEDLELIKE
acerb .... ACID, TART, HARSH,
SHARP, BITTER
acerbate .... VEX, EMBITTER,
IRRITATE
aces, two .... AMBSACE, AMESACE
acetic acid .... ESTER, ACETATE,
VINEGAR
acetone .... ACETOL, KEYSTONE
acetose .... ACID, SOUR
acetum .... VINEGAR

acetylene .... ETHIN(E), TOLANE
ache .... HURT, PAIN, PINE, SMART,
                THROB, YEARN
Acheron .... HADES, RIVER
   tributary .... COCYTUS
achieve .... WIN, GAIN, REACH,
     ATTAIN, COMPASS, REALIZE,
              ACCOMPLISH
achievement .... DEED, FEAT,
     END, RESULT, EXPLOIT,
    COMPLETION, ATTAINMENT
Achilles .... PELIDES
   adviser .... NESTOR
   captive .... BRISEIS
   charioteer .... AUTOMEDON
   friend .... PATROCLUS
   horse .... XANTHUS
   parent .... PELEUS, THETIS
   slayer .... PARIS
   teacher .... CHIRON
   victim .... HECTOR, TROILUS
   vulnerable spot .... HEEL
   warrior .... MYRMIDON
achira .... CANNA
achromatic substance ...... LININ
acicular .... SPINY, BRISTLY
acid .... SOUR, TART, ACERB,
     SHARP, BITING, CAUSTIC,
              CUTTING
   base indicator .... LITMUS
   etching .... MORDANT
   kind of .... AMINO, BORIC,
    NITRIC, OLEATE, MURIATIC,
     PECTIC, SALYCYLIC
   neutralizer .... ALKALI
   nicotinic .... NIACIN
   slang .... LSD
   tanning .... CATECHIN
acidity .... ACOR, ACERBITY,
              SOURNESS
acidulous .... TART
acinus .... RASPBERRY
ack-ack fire .... FLAK
   gun .... POMPOM
acknowledge .... OWN, AVOW,
     SIGN, ADMIT, CONFESS,
           RECOGNIZE
acknowledgment .... CREDIT,
            ADMISSION
   of liability .... COGNOVIT
acle .... IRONWOOD
acme .... TOP, APEX, PEAK,
       SUMMIT, PINNACLE
acolyte .... NOVICE, ALTARBOY,
            THURIFER
acolyte's garb .... COTTA
acomia .... BALDNESS
aconite .... ATIS, WOLFSBANE,
          MONKSWOOD
acor .... ACIDITY
acorn .... OVEST, FRUIT, MAST,

            NUT, CAMATA
barnacle .... SCUTA
   cup .... VALONIA
   dried .... CAMATA
   edible .... BALLOTE
   shaped .... BALANOID
acoustic equipment .... SIRENE
   vase .... ECHEA
acoustics .... SONICS, PHONICS
acquaint .... TELL, BRIEF, TEACH,
    VERSE, INFORM, REVEAL,
              APPRISE
acquainted .... FAMILIAR,
    (CON)VERSANT, KNOWN
acquiesce .... BOW, AGREE, YIELD,
    ACCEDE, ASSENT, CONCUR,
             CONSENT
acquire .... BUY, GET, GAIN,
    EARN, REAP, OBTAIN, SECURE
   in advance .... PREEMPT
   knowledge .... LEARN
acquired knowledge
              EDUCATION
acquisitiveness .... GREED,
             AVARICE
acquit ...... FREE, PARDON, CLEAR,
    EXCUSE, ABSOLVE, RELEASE
   colloq. .... WHITEWASH
   oneself .... BEHAVE
acquittance .... RELEASE,
           CLEARANCE
acre .... LAND, FIELD
   ¼ of .... ROOD
acres, 2.47 .... HECTARE
acrid .... SOUR, HARSH, NASTY,
     SHARP, BITING, BITTER,
     PUNGENT, VITRIOLIC
acrimonious .... CAUSTIC, BITTER,
    CUTTING, PEEVISH, SPITEFUL,
            STINGING
acrimony .... ANGER, SPITE,
    RANCOR, SPLEEN, ASPERITY
acrobat ...... GYMNAST, TUMBLER,
    STUNTMAN, AERIALIST,
         DAREDEVIL
   high-wire .... AERIALIST
   of India .... NAT
acrobat's equipment .... BARS,
   POLE, TIGHTROPE, TIGHTWIRE,
        TRAMPOLINE
   forte .... STUNTS,
     SOM(M)ERSAULTS
   net .... TRAMPOLINE
   risk .... FALL, SLIP
   wear .... TIGHTS, LEOTARD,
          FLESHINGS
acrogen .... FERN
acrolith .... STATUE
acropolis .... HILL, CADMEA,
     CITADEL, LARISSA
across .... ON, OVER, BEYOND,

      ASTRIDE, ATHWART,
    TRAVERSE, CROSSWISE,
         ASTRADDLE
combining form ..... DIA, TRA,
            TRANS
the board .... BLANKET,
    OMNIBUS, TOTALLY
acrostic .... AGLA, TELESTIC(H),
           WORDPLAY
act .... DO, DEED, FEAT, PLAY,
    SKIT, EMOTE, EDICT, EXERT,
    MODEL, BEHAVE, PERFORM
   according to rules
              CONFORM
   against morality .... SIN
   as chairperson .... PRESIDE
   before .... FORESTALL,
    PRECEDE, ANTICIPATE
   dishonestly: sl. .... FUDGE
   for .... REPRESENT, SUBSTITUTE
   helpful .... GOOD TURN
   in the interest of
          ADVANCE, PROMOTE
   insincerely .... FAKE, POSE,
           PRETEND
   like .... APE, IMITATE,
          SIMULATE
   of pretending .... FEIGN
   of prudence .... CAUTION
   of regret .... APOLOGY
   official .... LAW, BILL, EDICT,
            DEGREE
   out .... ENACT, MIMIC,
           PORTRAY
   over .... EMOTE, PLAYACT
   prima donna's .... TANTRUM
   regrettable .... CRIME
   silly .... CLOWN
   the idler .... LAZE
   up .... PRISS
   with exaggeration .... HAM,
            EMOTE
acting by turns ...... ALTERN(ATE)
   pertaining to .... THESPIAN,
         HISTRIONIC
   trophy .... OSCAR, EMMY,
            TONY
action .... DEED, EDICT, WORK,
    FIGHT, STEP, ACTIVITY,
    COMBAT, PRACTICE,
    BEHAVIOR, SUIT, PROCESS,
          FUNCTION
   court .... LAWSUIT
   melodramatic .... HEROICS
   put into .... ACTUATE,
           ACTIVATE
   put out of .... KO, MAIM,
       CRIPPLE, DISABLE
   symbolic .... CHARADE
   to outwit another .... PLOY,
           BLUFF

to recover property .... TROVER, REPLEVIN
violent .... RIOT, AFFRAY
where it is ..... ARENA, STAGE, OVAL, DIAMOND, SCENE, TABLE, COURT, STADIUM, (COCK)PIT, RING, FIELD, COLISEUM
with ridiculous end .... FIASCO
word .... VERB
activate .... SPARK, TRIGGER
activator .... DYNAMO, CATALYST
active .... BUSY, SPRY, ABOUT, BRISK, AGILE, ASTIR, MOVING, LIVELY, READY, NIMBLE, WORKING
one .... DOER
place .... HUB, HIVE
activity .... ADO, STIR, LIFE, BUSINESS, ACTION, BUSTLE, EXERCISE, OPERATION
after guessing wrong .... EATING CROW
forbidden .... NO-NO
actor .... LEAD, HERO, STAR, MIME, PLAYER, ARTIST, HISTRIO(N), THESPIAN, MUMMER, PERFORMER
in farces .... FARCEUR
last line(s) of .... TAG
many-faced .... MUNI, (LON)CHANEY
minor role .... WALK-ON
mythical .... SPELVIN
of a thousand faces .... (LON)CHANEY
overacting .... MUGGER
second-rate .... HAM, BARNSTORMER
veteran .... TROUPER
with speaking part ...... SUPER
actors' aid .... (PRESS)AGENT, STAND-IN, DRESSER, PROMPTER
apers .... ZANIES
association .... AEA, AAAA
group .... CAST, TROUPE
hint to .... CUE
improvisation .... AD LIB
in dramatics .... AMATEURS
offstage place .... GREEN ROOM
part ...... ROLE, LEAD, VILLAIN, COMIC, HEAVY, STAR(RING)
pest .... HECKLER
actress. See also **actor** ...... DIVA, STAR
"blond bombshell" .... HARLOW
from Brooklyn .... (MAE)WEST
in farces .... FARCEUSE

role sometimes .... INGENUE
with "it" .... (CLARA)BOW
with "oomph" .... (ANN)SHERIDAN
actual ...... REAL, TRUE, POSIT, DE FACTO, FACTUAL, GENUINE, CONCRETE
being .... ESSE
actuality .... FACT, TRUTH, VERITY, REALITY
actually .... TRULY, IN FACT, REALLY
actuate .... EGG, MOVE, STIR, URGE, DRIVE, IMPEL, ROUSE, START, INCITE, AGITATE, ACTIVATE, MOTIVATE
acuity .... WIT, EDGE, KEENNESS
acumen ...... WIT, FLAIR, WISDOM, INSIGHT, KEENNESS, SAGACITY
acute ...... SHARP, FIERCE, SEVERE, SHREWD, URGENT, CRUCIAL, INTENSE, CRITICAL
ad .... NOTICE, INSERTION, PUBLICITY, ADVERTISEMENT
hoc .... MAKESHIFT, TEMPORARY, TENTATIVE, PROVISIONAL
in tennis .... ADVANTAGE
infinitum .... FOREVER, ENDLESSLY, WITHOUT END
interim .... MEANTIME, MEANWHILE, TEMPORARY
lib .... INVENT, IMPROVISE, EXTEMPORIZE
sum .... PRESENT
type of .... COVER, INSIDE, DISPLAY, COLOR(ED), CLASSIFIED
valorem .... WORTH, VALUATION
verbum .... LITERAL, VERBATIM
verse .... JINGLE
A.D., part of .... ANNO, DOMINI
adage .... SAW, MAXIM, MOTTO, SAYING, PROVERB
subject .... TIDE, TIME
adagio .... SLOW, BALLET(DANCE)
Adam-and-Eve .... ORCHID, PUTTYROOT
Smith is pseudonym of .... GOODMAN
adamant .... SET, FIRM, RIGID, SOLID, UNMOVED
Adamite .... NUDIST
Adam's ale .... WATER
apple .... GUZZLE, LARYNX
flannel .... MULLEIN
grandson .... ENOS, ENOCH
mate of legend .... LILITH
needle .... YUCCA

second mate/rib .... EVE
son .... ABEL, CAIN, SETH
teacher .... RAISEL
adapt .... FIT, MOLD, SUIT, APPLY, ADJUST, ORIENT, CONFORM
add .... EKE, SUM, TOT, JOIN, PLUS, TOTAL, UNITE, COMBINE
carbon dioxide .... CHARGE
dash of liquor/spirits .... LACE, SPIKE
details .... SPELL OUT, ELABORATE, EMBROIDER
fuel to the flame .... STOKE, EXCITE, INCITE
insult to injury .... WORSEN, PROVOKE, AGGRAVATE
member to a board ..... COOPT
on .... AFFIX, RIDER, ATTACH
sugar .... SWEETEN
to .... PLUS, ADORN, ENRICH, EXPAND, AUGMENT, INCREASE
up ..... SUM, TOT, JIBE, COUNT, TALLY, TOTAL, CALCULATE
up to .... MEAN, SIGNIFY
adda .... LIZARD
addax .... ANTELOPE
added to .... AND, EKE, PLUS, ADDITIVE, SUPPLEMENT
addendum .... SEQUEL, ADJUNCT, APPENDIX, EPILOGUE
adder .... ASP, SNAKE, VIPER, COUNTER, REPTILE
addict .... FAN, USER, SLAVE, DEVOTEE
slang .... BUG, NUT, DOPE, HEAD, FIEND, HOUND, JUNKIE
addicted .... PRONE, HOOKED, BIBULOUS, DEPENDENT
addiction .... WONT, HABIT, ALCOHOLISM, DEPENDENCE
adding machine ...... TOTALIZER, CALCULATOR
Addis Ababa is capital of .... ABYSSINIA, ETHIOPIA
Addison and _____ ...... STEELE
poet .... CLIO, JOSEPH
addition .... AND, ALSO, ELSE, CODICIL, INCREASE, ADDEND(A) (UM), APPENDIX
to a bill .... RIDER
to a building .... ELL, ANNEX
to a letter ...... PS, NOTA BENE, POSTSCRIPT
additional .... MORE, EXTRA, (AN)OTHER, FURTHER
appearance of a performer .... ENCORE
name .... ALIAS, PSEUDONYM
pay .... TIP, BONUS
addle .... CONFUSE, FLUSTER, STUMP, BAFFLE, PERPLEX

slang .... BUFFALO
addlebrained .... STUPID, MUDDLED
addled .... FOGGED, MUDDLED, EMPTY, DAZED, FLOORED
addlepated .... IDIOTIC, PINHEAD, PEABRAIN
address .... HOME, TACT, TALK, ABODE, GREET, ACCOST, DIRECT, SPEECH, ORATION, PETITION, RESIDENCE
army .... APO
navy .... FPO
President's .... WHITE HOUSE
Secretary of Defense's
.... PENTAGON
to someone .... DEDICATE
adduce ...... CITE, INFER, PRESENT, ALLEGE, QUOTE, ADVANCE
adeem .... CANCEL, REVOKE
Adelina, singer .... PATTI
Adenauer's sobriquet
.... (DER)ALTE
adept .... ACE, DEFT, EXPERT, ADROIT, MASTER, SKILLED, VERSED, DEXTEROUS
adequate .... AMPLE, EQUAL, ENOUGH, SUITABLE, ACCEPTABLE, SUFFICIENT
Adhem _____ .... (BEN)ABOU
adhere .... GLUE, HOLD, ABIDE, CLING, STICK, ATTACH, CLEAVE
adherent .... ITE, IST, ALLY, VOTARY, ZEALOT, DEVOTEE, BELIEVER, DISCIPLE, FOLLOWER, PARTISAN, RETAINER, SERVITOR
adhesive .... GUM, GLUE, TAPE, EPOXY, PASTE, CEMENT, STICKY, PLASTER
adhibit ...... ADMIT, AFFIX, APPLY
adieu .... GOODBY(E), TATA, FAREWELL
adipose .... FAT(TY), OBESE, LARDY, FLESHY, SUETY
slang .... BLIMP, FATSO
adit .... INLET, STULM, INGRESS, ACCESS, PASSAGE, ENTRANCE
adjacent ...... NEAR, NEXT, CLOSE, ADJOINING, CONTIGUOUS
adjective ...... ADNOUN, MODIFIER
ending .... IC, ENT, IAL, IL, ISH, INE, ILE, IST, ITE, IVE, OUS, ICAL, ULAR
verbal .... GERUNDIVE
adjoin ...... ABUT, TOUCH, APPEND
adjourn ...... END, CEASE, CLOSE, RECESS, RETIRE, SUSPEND, PROROGUE
adjudge .... DEEM, AWARD,

DECIDE, DECREE, SETTLE, CONDEMN, SENTENCE
unfit .... CONDEMN, DISQUALIFY, RULE OUT
adjudicate ...... TRY, HEAR, RULE, JUDGE, DECIDE
adjunct .... ANNEX, APPENDAGE
adjust ...... FIT, FIX, SUIT, ADAPT, ALIGN, ATTUNE, ORIENT, SETTLE
adjutant .... AIDE, ALLY, HELPER, ASSISTANT
bird .... STORK, ARGALA, HURGILA, MARABOU
adman .... HUCKSTER, PR MAN, PITCHMAN, PROMOTER, PUBLICIST, COPYWRITER
slang .... FLACK, BARKER, PLUGGER, SPIELER, BALLYHOOER
Admetus' wife .... ALCESTIS
administer ...... RUN, DEAL, GIVE, MANAGE, CONDUCT, HUSBAND, DISPENSE
administration ...... RULE, REIGN, MINISTRY, REGIME(N), MANAGEMENT
administrative .... MANAGING, EXECUTIVE, MINISTERIAL
body .... JUNTA, BOARD, COUNCIL, ASSEMBLY
admiral .... NAVARCH, OFFICER, COMMODORE
of fame .... BYRD, KING, LEAHY, DEWEY, HALSEY, NIMITZ, NELSON, PORTER, FARRAGUT
rank .... VICE, REAR, FLEET, FOUR-STAR
winged .... BUTTERFLY
admire .... LOVE, ESTEEM, REGARD, REVERE, IDOLIZE
admissible .... OK, OKAY, LICIT, ACCEPTABLE
in law .... LIE
admission .... FEE, ACCESS, ENTREE, ADMITTANCE, CONFESSION, CONCESSION
ticket: sl. .... DUCAT
admit ...... OWN, ALLOW, ACCEDE, ACCEPT, CONCEDE, GRANT, PROFESS, RECEIVE
colloquial .... FESS
admitted fact .... DATUM, TRUTH, TRUISM
admixture .... ALLOY, BLEND, SHADE, FLAVOR, COMPOUND
admonish .... WARN, CHIDE, ADVISE, REBUKE, CAUTION, REPROVE, SERMON(IZE)
admonisher .... MENTOR,

ADVISER, MONITOR
admonition .... ADVICE, REPROOF, WARNING, SCOLDING, REPRIMAND
first word of, sometimes
.... DON'T
ado .... FUSS, STIR, TO-DO, BUSTLE, EFFORT, POTHER, TROUBLE
adobe .... MUD, CLAY, DOBY, BRICK
adolescence .... TEENS, YOUTH, TEENAGE, NONAGE, PUBERTY
adolescent, designating one
.... HIPPIE, TEENAGER, BOBBYSOXER
Adonais, per Shelley ...... KEATS
Adonis' beloved .... APHRODITE
parent ..... CINYRAS, MYRRH(A)
slayer .... (WILD)BOAR
adopt .... ACCEPT, ASSUME, CHOOSE, TAKE ON, ESPOUSE
adore .... DOTE, LOVE, ADMIRE, HONOR, IDOLIZE, REVERE, GLORIFY, WORSHIP
adorn ...... DIGHT, DRESS, GRACE, (BE)DECK, BEAUTIFY, EMBELLISH, DECORATE
with diamonds .... BEGEM
with rich clothing
.... CAPARISON
adorner .... DECORATOR, DRESSER, ORNAMENTIST
adrenal hormone .... CORTISONE
Adriana's servant .... LUCE
Adriatic city .... TRIESTE
island .... LAGOSTA
peninsula .... ISTRIA
port .... FIUME, TRIESTE, RIJEKA, RIMINI
resort .... LIDO
seaport .... VALONA, AVLONA
wind .... BORA
adrift .... ASEA, LOST, LOOSE, AWAFT, AFLOAT, UNTIED, FLOATING, DERELICT
adroit .... APT, DEFT, NEAT, ADEPT, HANDY, CLEVER, HABILE, CUNNING, SKILLFUL
adularia .... FELDSPAR, MOONSTONE
adulate .... PRAISE, FLATTER
adulation .... HONOR, GLORY, KUDOS
object of .... HERO, STAR, VICTOR, WINNER, CONQUEROR
slang ...... SWEET TALK, SWEET NOTHINGS
adulator, kind of .... FAN, YESMAN, TOADY, FAWNER, FLATTERER, COURTIER,

BOOTLICKER
adult .... MATURE, NUBILE, OF
AGE, GROWN(UP)
insect .... IMAGO
person .... MAN, WOMAN
tadpole .... FROG
wriggler .... MOSQUITO
adulterant, common .... FIZZ,
WATER
adulterate .... MIX, TAINT, CUT,
DEBASE, DEFILE, DILUTE,
DOCTOR, WEAKEN, CORRUPT,
DENATURE
slang .... BAPTIZE
adulterated .... MIXED,
THINNED(OUT), IMPURE,
WATERED(DOWN)
adultery .... TRIANGLE, HANKY-
PANKY, CUCKOLDRY,
INFIDELITY
adumbrate .... HINT, IMPLY,
SKETCH, OBSCURE, FIGURE,
SUGGEST, PREDICT
adust .... BURNT, SCORCHED,
SALLOW, PARCHED
advance ...... LOAN, RISE, MARCH,
PUSH, LEND, MOVE, FOSTER,
PROCEED, PROMOTE, FURTHER,
PROGRESS, ATTACK, INCREASE
man .... AGENT, PLAYBROKER
man: sl. .... TEN-PERCENTER
money .... (IM)PREST
notice .... WARNING
payment .... ANTE, ARLES
slowly .... INCH, CREEP
to prospector .... GRUBSTAKE
unit .... VAN(GUARD)
word .... TIP, CLUE
advanced .... OLD, AGED,
MODERN, REFINED,
PERFECTED, FAR(GONE)
in years ..... SENIOR, ELDERLY,
WRINKLED
advancement .... GROWTH,
PROGRESS, HEADWAY,
PROMOTION
advantage .... EDGE, PROFIT, USE,
ODDS, GAIN, BENEFIT,
AMENITY, FOOTHOLD,
LEVERAGE
kind of, in tennis .... AD IN,
AD OUT
take ...... ABUSE, CHEAT, TRICK
advent .... COMING, ARRIVAL,
APPROACH, IMMINENCE
adventitious ...... CASUAL, FLUKY,
ALEATORY, ACCIDENTAL,
EPISODIC
lung sound .... RALE
adventure .... HAP, GEST(E),
MISSION, ESCAPADE, FEAT,

EVENT, QUEST, EXPLOIT,
ARISTEIA
adventurer .... SPECULATOR,
PICAROON, TREKKER,
SPORTSMAN, EXPLORER,
FORTUNE HUNTER
of chance .... GAMBLER
of old .... MERCENARY,
KNIGHT, FREEBOOTER
of speculation .... PLUNGER,
GUNSLINGER, SCALPER,
STOCKBROKER
reckless .... DAREDEVIL,
HELLCAT, FIRE-EATER
upstart .... PARVENU,
TUFTHUNTER, NAME DROPPER
adventurous .... DARING, BOLD,
RASH, RECKLESS, DYNAMIC,
FOOLHARDY
slang .... WILD-ASS
adversary .... FOE, RIVAL, ENEMY,
OPPONENT, FOEMAN,
ANTAGONIST
adverse .... HOSTILE, COUNTER,
OPPOSED, CLASHING,
PERVERSE, CONTRARY,
INIMICAL, UNTOWARD
criticism: sl. .... PAN(NING)
opinion .... CENSURE
reaction, show of .... BOO,
HISS, HOOT, POUT, SCOWL,
RASPBERRY
adversity .... DISASTER, HARDSHIP,
CALAMITY, BLIGHT, MISHAP,
TRAGEDY, GRIEF, MISERY,
POVERTY
slang .... BUMMER, WHAMMY
advertisement .... AD, BLURB,
NOTICE, INSERTION, MESSAGE,
PLACARD, POSTER, AFFICHE,
COMMERCIAL
abbreviation .... AD, ADVT
book jacket .... BLURB
interpolate .... PLUG
make-up .... LAYOUT
outdoor .... POSTER, FLYER,
BILLBOARD, MARQUEE,
HANDBILL, LEAFLET,
SIGNBOARD
radio/television
.... COMMERCIAL
slang .... PLUG, DODGER
advertiser ...... PLUGGER, SPIELER,
HAWKER
kind of .... BARKER
advertising client .... ACCOUNT
colloquial .... BALLYHOO
contract .... ACCOUNT
handbill: sl. .... DODGER
man: colloq. .... PITCHMAN,
HUCKSTER

medium .... NEWSPAPER,
FLYER, TV, MAGAZINE, RADIO,
MARQUEE, BROCHURE,
BILLBOARD
on book jacket .... BLURB
poster .... BILL
praise in .... PUFFERY
statuette .... CLIO
text .... COPY
advice .... COUNSEL, REDE,
PROPOSAL, BRIEFING, REPORT,
AVISO, CAVEAT, MESSAGE,
GUIDANCE
in 1835 .... GO WEST
seek .... CONSULT
to stockholders in 1933
.... SELL, UNLOAD
advise .... COACH, TELL, WARN,
INSTRUCT, INFORM, GUIDE,
DIRECT, APPRISE, CAUTION,
ACQUAINT
and _____ .... CONSENT
colloquial .... KIBITZ
adviser .... MENTOR, MONITOR,
ORIENTER, NESTOR, EGERIA,
CONFIDANT, COUNSELOR
colloquial .... KIBITZER,
BACKSEAT DRIVER
slang .... BUTTINSKY
advisory .... DIRECTIVE,
MONITORY
on weather .... WARNING
advocate .... SIDER, BACKER,
LAWYER, ABETTOR, ESPOUSE,
PLEAD(ER), CHAMPION,
DEFENDER, PREACHER,
APOLOGIST, PROPONENT
colloquial .... FAN, BUFF
of majority rule
.... DEMOCRAT
slang ...... ANGEL, MOUTHPIECE
adytum ...... SANCTUARY, SHRINE,
SANCTUM
adz .... AX(E), HATCHET, CUTTING
TOOL
Aeetes' daughter .... MEDEA
Aegean gulf/sea .... SAROS
inhabitant .... SAMIOTE,
LELEGE
island .... MELOS, LESBOS,
PATMOS, SAMOS, IOS, NIO,
TENOS, MYTILENE
river .... STRUMA
Aegeon's wife .... AEMILIA
Aegir's wife .... RAN
aegis .... SHIELD, ARMOR,
AUSPICES, SAFEGUARD,
PATRONAGE
Aello .... HARPY
Aeneas follower .... ACHATES
great grandson .... BRUT

parent .... VENUS, ANCHISES
son .... ASCANIUS
wife .... CREUSA
Aeneid author .... VERGIL, VIRGIL
first word .... ARMA
hero .... AENEAS
Aengus' mother .... BOANN
Aeolian lyricist .... SAPPHO
Aeolus' brother .... DORUS,
XUTHUS
daughter .... CANACE,
HALCYONE
parent .... ORSEIS, HIPPOTES
son .... ATHAMAS, CRETHEUS,
SALMONEUS
aeon .... AGE, ERA, EON, CYCLE,
PERIOD, ETERNITY, LIFETIME
aeonian .... LASTING, ETERNAL,
AGELESS, INFINITE,
PERPETUAL
aerate .... GASIFY, DISTILL,
WINNOW, FLUIDIZE
aerial .... LOFTY, AIRISH, UNREAL,
ETHEREAL, ANTENNA,
IMAGINARY, TOWERING,
VAPOROUS
battle .... DOGFIGHT
bomb: sl. .... EGG,
BREADBASKET
bombardment .... BLITZ
bombing, describing one
.... SATURATION, CARPET
car suspended from cables
.... TELPHER
navigation aid .... TELERAN
stunt ..... BARREL, ROLL, LOOP,
AEROBATIC, LOOP-THE-LOOP
aerialist ...... ACROBAT, GYMNAST,
BALANCER, WIREWALKER
aerie .... NEST, NIDUS, APIARY,
BEEHIVE
aerobatics .... LOOP, ROLL, TURN,
STUNTS, IMMELMANN
aerobe .... BACTERIUM
aerolite .... METEORITE
aeronaut .... PILOT, AIRMAN,
AVIATOR, SPACEMAN
aeronautics .... AVIATION
aerosol .... SPRAY, ATOMIZER,
CLYSTER, ASPERGIL
aerostat .... BLIMP, BALLOON,
DIRIGIBLE, ZEPPELIN
aerugo .... RUST, PATINA,
VERDIGRIS
aes .... COIN, BRONZE
Aesculapian .... DOCTOR,
MEDICAL, PHYSICIAN
Aesculapius' father .... APOLLO
teacher .... CHIRON
Aesir ...... TYR, LOKI, ODIN, THOR,
VALI, DONAR, FREYA, WODEN,

BALDER
Aesop .... WRITER, FABULIST
home of .... SAMOS
story .... FABLE
aesthete .... GOURMET, VIRTUOSO,
DILETTANTE, CONNOISSEUR
aesthetic ...... ELEGANT, ARTISTIC,
CLASSIC(AL), TASTEFUL,
BEAUTIFUL
slang .... ARTY-CRAFTY
aestival .... SUMMER
aestivate, opposed to
.... HIBERNATE
Aether's father .... EREBUS
Aetolian prince .... TYDEUS
afar .... OFF, AWAY, HAMITE,
REMOTE, DISTANT
affable .... KIND, CIVIL, SUAVE,
BENIGN, GENIAL, DECENT,
POLITE, AMIABLE, URBANE,
CORDIAL, FRIENDLY,
GRACIOUS, OBLIGING,
SOCIABLE
affair .... AMOUR, PARTY,
MATTER, SOIREE, CONCERN,
LIAISON, ROMANCE, BUSINESS,
GATHERING, RECEPTION
afternoon .... MATINEE
class/family .... REUNION
illicit ..... ADULTERY, INTRIGUE
love .... ROMANCE, TRIANGLE
of high school juniors
.... PROM
of honor, usually .... DUEL
of seniors .... HOP
affect .... HIT, SMITE, MOVE,
TOUCH, POSE, STRIKE, SWAY,
FEIGN, PRETEND, IMPRESS,
INFLUENCE
emotionally .... TRAUMATIZE
with pity .... SOFTEN
affectation .... AIRS, POSE, SHAM,
FACADE, CONCEIT, FAKERY,
PRETEXT, PRETENSE, ARTIFICE
of elegance .... FRIPPERY
of prudery .... STUFFINESS
affected .... LURID, POSEY,
MOVED, GARISH, FLASHY,
SHOWY, FEIGNED, FALLAL,
STAGY, AFFLICTED
elegance .... FROUFROU
slang .... PHONY
affecting .... BLEAK, MOVING,
PATHETIC, PITIFUL,
WRETCHED, TOUCHING,
DISMAL, RUEFUL
affection .... LOVE, AMOUR,
RAPTURE, ECSTASY, PASSION,
REGARD, FEELING, ESTEEM,
EMOTION, DISEASE, CHARITY,
FONDNESS

affectionate .... KIND, FOND,
WARM, TENDER, LOVING,
FILIAL, DEVOTED
afferent .... SENSORY
affiance .... ENGAGE, PLIGHT,
PLEDGE, PROMISE, TRUST,
BETROTH(AL)
affianced ...... FIANCE(E), SWORN,
ASSURED, ENGAGED,
PLIGHTED, BETROTHED
slang .... INTENDED
affiant ...... DEPONENT, VOUCHER,
SWEARER, ATTESTER,
TESTATOR
affidavit .... DEPOSITION,
STATEMENT, TESTIMONY
addendum .... JURAT
maker .... AFFIANT, DEPONENT,
TESTATOR
taker .... NOTARY
affiliate .... JOIN, MERGE, ARM,
WING, BAND, UNITE, MEMBER,
CHAPTER, DIVISION, BRANCH,
ASSOCIATE, OFF-SHOOT,
INSIDER
affinity ...... BOND, LINK, KINSHIP,
RELATION(SHIP), RAPPORT,
ATTRACTION, LEANING,
ALLIANCE
slang .... BAG, CUP OF TEA
affirm .... AVER, AVOW, SWEAR,
VOUCH, ASSERT, POSIT,
RATIFY, CONFIRM, NOTARIZE
affirmation .... DICTUM,
SUMPTION, ASSERTION,
SANCTION, CONFIRMATION,
THEOREM, DECLARATION
slang .... SAY-SO
affirmative .... AYE, YES, YEA,
YEP, AMEN, YEAH, NOD,
POSITIVE
consent .... BLESSING
expression .... THUMBS-UP
side of controversy .... PRO
voice/vote .... AYE
affix .... SEAL, GRAFT, ANNEX,
APPEND, ATTACH, STAMP,
FASTEN
afflatus .... IMPULSE, INSPIRATION
afflict .... AIL, VEX, PAIN,
DISTRESS, HARM, HURT,
PINCH, STING, SCATHE,
SICKEN, BURDEN, GRIPE,
TORMENT, TROUBLE,
INDISPOSE
afflicted .... BESET, SOUSED,
RACKED, HURTING, CONFUSED,
WOUNDED, PLASTERED,
TORTURED, STEWED,
DISTRESSED
affliction .... PAIN, GRIEF, WOE,

AILMENT, MALADY, CURSE, SCOURGE, SICKNESS, PLAGUE, ILLNESS, CALAMITY, DISORDER, SUFFERING

affluence .... WEALTH, RICHES, LUCRE, MONEY, OPULENCE, SECURITY, GOLD, PLENTY, ABUNDANCE

slang .... EASY STREET

afflux .... FLOW, DRIFT

afford .... GIVE, BEAR, GRANT, SUPPLY, STAND, SPARE, YIELD, ENABLE

affray .... RIOT, BRAWL, FIGHT, MELEE, SCUFFLE, ASSAULT

affright .... SCARE, ALARM, DAUNT, DISMAY, DREAD, TERRIFY, HORRIFY

affront .... DARE, FACE, MOCK, SNUB, HARASS, INSULT, OFFEND, SLIGHT, OFFENSE, CHALLENGE

affronter .... DARER, INSULTER

affusion .... BAPTISM

affy .... BETROTH, ESPOUSE

Afghan(istan) .... PATHAN, HOUND, SHAWL, DURANI, BLANKET

ameer .... SHERE

capital .... KABUL

carpet/rug .... BUKHARA

city/town .... HERAT, FARSI, BALKH, AYBAK, MOQOR, KALAT, FARAH, KHOLM, TAGAB, TULAK, GARDEZ, GHAZNI, QONDUZ, KUNAR, ZARANJ, BAGHLAN, KANDAHAR, MEYMANEH, CHARIKAR, JALALABAD, TALOQAN, SHEBERGHAN

coin .... PUL, AMANIA

desert .... MARGOW-DASHT-E

garment .... CHADRI

king .... SHAH, ZAHIR

lake .... HELMAND

language .... PASHTO, DARI, PUSHTU, UZBEK, BALUCHI

measure .... JERIB, KAROH

monetary unit .... AFGHANI

mountain .... KOH, SAFEO, SULAIMAN, PAMIRS, HIMALAYAS, HINDU KUSH

native .... SISTANI

nomad .... KUCHI

parliament .... SHURA, JIRGA, WOLESI

pony .... YABU, YABOO

prime minister .... YUSUF

prince .... AMIR, AMEER

range .... PAROPAMISUS

religion .... ISLAM

river .... KABUL, KONAR, TARNAK, HARIRUD, LURAH, HELMAND, FARAHRUD

ruler .... SHER SHAH

salt lake .... NAMAKSAR

sea .... DARYA

title .... KHAN

tribe .... SAFI, ULUS, TURK, KAFIR, TAJIK

tribesman .... PATHAN

valley .... WAKHAN

aficionado .... FAN, DEVOTEE, FOLLOWER, ENTHUSIAST

aflame .... AFIRE, ABLAZE, GLOWING, BURNING

afloat .... ASEA, AWEIGH, RIFE, ADRIFT, UNMOORED, AIRBORNE, CURRENT, UNFIXED, UNSTABLE, RUMORED, IN THE NEWS

afoot .... ASTIR, ABROAD, MOVING, UNDERWAY

aforesaid .... PRIOR, NAMED, FORMER, PREVIOUS, ANTECEDENT

aforethought .... PREPENSE, PREMEDITATED

afoul .... (EN)TANGLED, IN COLLISION

afraid .... COWED, SCARED, TERRIFIED, FRIGHTENED, FEARED, DAUNTED, FEARFUL, PANICKY, TIMOROUS, COWARDLY, DISMAYED

slang .... YELLOW, CHICKEN

afreet .... DEMON, JINNI, JINNEE

afresh .... NEW, NEWLY, OVER, AGAIN, DITTO

French .... BIS, ENCORE

Italian .... DA CAPO

slang .... FROM SCRATCH

African ...... IBO, BANTU, BLACK, HAUS(S)A, KAFFIR, NUBIAN, YORUBA, ETHIOP(IAN), SWAHILI, MANDINGO, HOTTENTOT

American dance .... CAKEWALK

American folksong .... SPIRITUAL

and mulatto offspring .... GRIFF(E)

and white offspring .... MESTEE, MUSTEE, MULATTO

antelope .... ELAND, KOB, ASSE, GEMSBOK, KUDU, IMPALA, ORIBI, GNU, BLESBUCK, BLESBOK, BONGO, ADDAX, PEELE, BUBAL(IS), BUSHBACK, BONTEBOK, BOS(C)HBOK, DUIKER(BOK), KOODOO

ape .... BABOON

ash .... ATAR

ass .... QUAGGA

aunt .... TANTA

baboon .... DRILL, MANDRILL

bass .... IYO

bat .... HAMMERHEAD

bean .... CALABAR

beer .... POMBE

bird .... LORY, LOURI, TAHA, COLY, UMBER, UMBRETTE, TURAKOO

boat .... DHOW

boss/master .... BAAS

bread .... KISRA

buffalo .... NIARE

burrowing animal .... SURICATE, GERBIL(LE)

bushman .... NEGRILLO

bustard .... KORI, PAAUW

caffeine/nut tree .... KOLA, COLA

camp .... BOMA

canal .... SUEZ

canoe ...... ALMADIA, ALMADIE

cape ...... BON, BLANC, VERDE, PALMAS, AGULHAS, RASASER, BABAOMBY, GOOD HOPE

capital .... ACCRA, LAGOS, PRAIA, RABAT, CAIRO, DAKAR, TUNIS, LOME, BANJUL, NIAMEY, MONROVIA, PORTO NOVO, PRETORIA, CAPE TOWN, MORONI, HARARE, TRIPOLI, FREETOWN, PORT LOUIS, KHARTOUM, BRAZZAVILLE, VICTORIA, ADDIS ABABA, BISSAU, DAR ES SALAAM, LUANDA, KAMPALA, MAPUTO, CONAKRY, LIBREVILLE, KINSHASA, LILONGWE, LUSAKA, KIGALI, BAMAKO, YAOUNDE, DJIBOUTI, MALABO, NAIROBI

carnivore ..... CANNIBAL, LION, RATEL, HYENA, CHEETAH, LEOPARD

catfish .... SHAL

cattle .... NIATA

channel .... MOZAMBIQUE

charm .... GRIGRI, GREEGREE

chief .... KAID, CABOCEER

city/town ...... FES, ORAN, EDE, ADO, ABA, SALE, IWO, ARUSHA, SFAX, TANGIER, ABIDJAN, ILESHA, ILLORIN, ENUGU, JOHANNESBURG, DOUALA, FRANCISTOWN, TABORA, CASABLANCA, BLANTYRE, CONSTANTINE,

MANZINI, GERMISTON,
MOMBASA, MARRAKECH,
CALABAR, ABEOKUTA, KIKWIT,
AZROU, TANGA, CHINGOLA,
KIMBERLEY, KUMASI,
ROADEPORT, NDOLA, KITWE,
KABWE, COTONOU, DURBAN,
JINJA
civet .... NANDINE
cloak .... JELAB
coin ...... PESA, TOQUE, OKIA,
RIAL, GIRSH, RUPIE, TALARI
colonist .... BOER
cony .... DAS, DASSIE
corn .... MEALIE
council .... BAAD, INDABA
country ...... ALGERIA, GHANA,
DENIN, GAMDIA, GUINEA,
IVORY COAST, LIBERIA,
MAURITANIA, NIGERIA, MALI,
MOROCCO, EGYPT, NIGER,
SENEGAL, CHAD, LIBYA,
TUNISIA, TOGO, DJIBOUTI,
ETHIOPIA, CONGO, SUDAN,
ANGOLA, KENYA, GABON,
CAMEROON, ZAIRE, UGANDA,
SOMALIA, ZIMBABWE,
TANZANIA, ZAMBIA,
MADAGASCAR, COMOROS,
MOZAMBIQUE, SWAZILAND,
MAURITIUS, BOTSWANA,
SEYCHELLES
dance .... JUBA, N'GOMA
deity .... NYAMBE, NZAMBI
desert ...... KALAHARI, LIBYAN,
SAHARA, GRAND ERG,
TANEZROUFT
dialect ..... SAHO, TAAL, FANTI,
BANTU, GEEZ, SWAHILI
disease .... NENTA
dish .... COUSCOUS
district .... NUBIA, RAND,
RUANDA, NYASSA
dog .... BASENJI
drink .... OMEIRES
eagle .... BERGHAAN
explorer .... AKELEY
falls .... BOYOMA, STANLEY,
VICTORIA
ferryboat .... PONT
fish .... CHARACIN
fly .... KIVU, TSETSE
food .... CASSAVA
fox .... ASSE, CAAMA
fruit .... TERFA, TERFEZ
fugitive .... MAROON
gangster .... TSOTSIS
garden .... SHAMBA
garment .... TOBE, KAROSS
gazelle .... ADMI, CORA, NORA,
ARIEL

giraffe-like animal .... OKAPI
gold district .... RAND
gorge .... KLOOF
grass .... ALFA, FUNDI,
ESPARTO
grass country .... VELD(T)
greenhorn .... IKONA
grivet .... WAAG
groundnut .... GOBBE
guard .... ASKAR
gulf .... ADEN, GABES, SIDRA,
GUINEA
gun .... ROER
harp .... NANGA
hartebeest .... TORA
headland .... RAS
helmet .... TOPI, TOPEE
hemp .... IFE
hill .... KOP
hog .... BOSCHVARK
hornbill .... TOCK
horse .... BARB
horse disease .... SURRA
Hottentot .... NAMA
house .... TEMBE
hunting party .... SAFARI
hut .... KRAAL
instrument .... BALAFO,
NANGA, REHAB, ZANZE
iris .... IXIA
Islamic sect .... ALMOHADES
island .... AZORES, PEMBA,
BIOKO, ANNOBON, MAYOTTE,
ST. HELENA, BOURBON,
ASCENSION, CAPE VERDE,
ZANZIBAR
islands ...... CANARY, MADEIRA
jackal .... DIEB
javelin .... ASSEGAI
lake .... CHAD, ASSALE,
NASSER, KARIBA, EDWARD,
TANA, TURKANA, VICTORIA,
NVASA, VOLTA, NYAS(S)A,
LIFU, DEMBEL, RUDOLF,
ALBERT, TANGANYIKA
language .... BANTU, TAAL,
BERBER, FULANI, MENDE,
MOSSI, ARABIC, BALE, SENUFU,
SWAHILI, YORUBA
lemur .... MACACO
lily .... ALOE, AGAPANTHUS
livestock .... FE
lynx .... CARACAL
mint plant .... COLEUS
money(shell) .... COWRY,
COWRIE
monkey .... GRIVET, MONA,
MACAQUE, COLOBUS, GUENON
mortar .... SWISH
Moslem .... BERBER
mountain .... ELGON, KENYA,

TOUBKAL, NATAL,
KILIMANJARO
mountain pass .... NEK
mountains ...... ATLAS, TIBESTI
musical instrument .... NANGA
narcotic .... DAGGA
native .... IBO, BARI, ASHA,
KOPI, FELUP, FULAH, ZULU,
SOTIK, MAUMAU, DAMARA,
ASHANTI, WATU(T)SI,
DAHOMAN, GABUNESE
nurse .... AYAH
palm .... DOOM, DOUM
peasant .... KOPI
pigeon .... NAMAQUA
pine .... RONIER
pirate .... ALGERINE
plant .... ALOE, IXIA, OCRA,
CALLA, CALABAR, COLEUS
plateau .... KAROO
poisonous tree .... SASSY
polecat .... MUSANG, ZORIL
port .... ORAN, DAKAR
Portuguese colony
.... ANGOLA
pygmy .... ITA, AKKA,
NEGRILLO, HOTTENTOT
race .... SOMALI
region .... CONGO, NUBIA,
SAHARA, SUDAN, SOUDAN
rhinoceros .... KEITLOA
river ...... NILE, CONGO, KASAI,
BLUE NILE, NIGER, WHITE
NILE, VAAL, ORANGE,
LIMPOPO, RUFIJI, OKOVANGO,
VOLTA, UBANGI, ZAIRE,
ZAMBEZI
river bed .... DONGA
rosewood .... MULOMPI
rug .... KAROSS
ruminant .... CAMEL
scrub .... BITO
seaport .... ORAN, LAGOS,
TUNIS, CASABLANCA
secret society .... MAU-MAU
sect .... COPTIC, ABELITE
servant .... VOLK
sheep .... ZENU
snake .... BOA, ELAP,
CERASTES
soldier .... SPAHI, ASKARI
songbird .... LINNET
sorcery .... OBE, OBI, OBEAH
soup powder .... LALO
spear .... ASSAGAI, ASSEGAI
spiritual power .... NGAI
squirrel .... XERUS
stockade .... BOMA, KRAAL,
ZAREBA
stork .... ARGALA, MARABOU
tableland .... KAROO

"telegraph" .... TOM-TOM
tick .... TAMPAN
title .... AGA, RAS, AGHA,
BWANA, NEGUS
tree .... COLA, ARTAR, KOLA,
TARFA, BAOBAB, BAKU, SHEA,
BUMBO, SASSY, NJABE,
COPAIBA, AKEE, MOLI,
SAMANDURA
tribal conference ..... PALAVER
tribe .... ABO, KUA, AKAN,
ALAR, BONI, DOMA, GOGO,
HABE, KALI, MAKA, KETU,
NUBA, TIBU, VACA, KAFFIR,
WARI, KREPI, ZULU, BANTU,
KABONGA
trip .... TREK, SAFARI
U.N. president
.... (MONGI)SLIM
valley .... WADI, KLOOF
village .... DORP, STAD, KRAAL
wading bird .... IBIS
war dance .... CALINDA
weasel .... ZORIL(A)
weasel-like animal
.... ICHNEUMON
wheat .... IMPHEE
whip .... KOORBASH
wild cat .... SERVAL
wild hog .... BOAR,
BOSCHVARK, WART(HOG)
wild sheep .... ARUI, UDAD,
AOUDAD
wind .... SAMIEL, SIMOOM,
SIMOON
witchcraft .... OBI, OBEAH
wolf .... AARD
wood .... TEAK, EBONY
worm .... LOA

African-Americans,
discrimination against
.... JIM CROW(ISM)
Africa's ancient name .... LIBYA
Afrikaans .... BOER, TAAL
afro .... HAIRDO, NATURAL,
HAIRSTYLE, COIF(FURE),
HEADDRESS
aft .... TAIL, ABAFT, (A)STERN,
POSTERN
after .... NEXT, PAST, POST,
LATER, SINCE, BEHIND
a fashion ..... MERELY, SIMPLY
a while .... ANON, LATER,
SHORTLY
dinner treat .... CORDIAL
expenses .... NET
the style of .... A LA
afterbirth .... SECUNDINE
afterdeath .... POSTHUMOUS
after-effect .... WAKE, TRACK,
TRAIL, SIDE EFFECT

afterglow .... FLUSH, GLEAM,
GLINT, GLOSS, LUSTER,
SHEEN, SKYLIGHT
afterimage .... SPECTRUM
afterlife .... THE BEYOND, THE
HEREAFTER
aftermath .... EFFECT, RESULT,
ROWEN, SEQUEL, LINEAGE,
SUCCESSOR
afternoon .... POST-MERIDIAN
nap .... SIESTA
party .... TEA
show .... MATINEE
afterpiece .... EPODE, EXODE
of a sort .... ENCORE
aftersong .... EPODE
afterthought .... REGRET, REVIEW,
REMORSE, RETHINKING
French ...... ESPRIT D'ESCALIER
in a letter .... POSTSCRIPT
slang .... FLIPFLOP
afterward .... THEN, LATER,
SUBSEQUENTLY
Aga .... TURK
Agag's slayer .... SAMUEL
again ...... ANEW, MORE, ENCORE,
BESIDES
appear/happen .... RECUR
do/say .... REPEAT
against .... CON, ANTI, CONTRA,
OPPOSED, VERSUS
a person/thing .... HOSTILE,
UNFRIENDLY
a thing, in law .... IN REM
morals .... WICKED, RIBALD,
ILLICIT, OBSCENE, UNETHICAL
prefix .... ANTI, CONTRA
slang .... ASS-BACKWARDS
the current .... UPSTREAM
the grain .... AT ODDS
the law .... ILLEGAL,
UNLAWFUL
the state .... SEDITIOUS,
TREASON(OUS)
agalite .... TALC
agalloch wood .... AGAR, ALOE,
GAROO
agama .... LIZARD, CHAMELEON
Agamemnon rescued her
.... BRISEIS
Agamemnon's brother
.... MENELAUS
children .... ELECTRA,
ORESTES, IPHIGENIA
father .... ATREUS
agamic .... ASEXUAL
Agana is capital of .... GUAM
agape .... HOLE, AJAR, CHASM,
YAWNING, OPENING
agaric .... FUNGUS, MUSHROOM,
TOADSTOOL

agate .... ONYX, RUBY, ACHATE,
MARBLE, TYPE, QUARTZ
agave .... ALOE, PITA, AMOLE,
DATIL, ISTLE, MAGUEY, SISAL,
HENEQUEN
juice drink .... MESCAL,
PULQUE
age .... EON, ERA, TIME, RIPEN,
YEARS, MATURE, EPOCH,
CENTURY, MELLOW, LIFETIME
designating one ...... ICE, OLD,
IRON, STONE, ATOMIC,
BRONZE, GOLDEN, SILVER,
TEEN(S), PUBERTY,
ADOLESCENCE
modern .... JET, SPACE,
ATOMIC, COMPUTER,
ELECTRONIC
of moon on June 1st
.... EPACT
old .... DOTAGE, SENESCE,
SENILITY
pertaining to an .... ERAL,
EVAL, HEYDAY, INNOCENCE
same .... COEVAL
when mammals developed
.... NEOCENE
aged .... RIPE, ANILE, OLD(EN),
SENILE, ELDERLY
agee .... AWRY, ASKEW
Agena .... ATLAS
agency .... MEANS, MEDIUM,
HAND, PROXY, SERVICE,
TRADING, BROKERAGE
news .... UPI, AP, TASS,
REUTERS, DOMEI, MENA,
NCNA, HAVAS
agendum .... RITUAL
Agenor's daughter .... EUROPA
agent .... ENVOY, FACTOR, PROXY,
DEPUTY, BROKER, EMISSARY,
MIDDLEMAN, FACIENT,
LEGMAN, PROCTOR
business .... MANAGER
chemical .... ACID, ALKALI,
REAGENT
cleansing .... SOAP,
TOOTHPASTE, DETERGENT,
ENEMA, PURGATIVE
007 .... BOND
foreign firm .... COMPRADOR
freight/shipping
.... FORWARDER
insurance .... UNDERWRITER
intermediary .... JOBBER,
LIAISON, MIDDLEMAN,
DISTRIBUTOR
legal .... LAWYER, ATTORNEY
narcotics .... FED, NARC
real estate .... BROKER,
REALTOR

Treasury .... T-MAN, REVENUER
undercover .... SPY
undercover work .... ESPIONAGE
agglomerate .... MASS, LUMP, HEAP, GATHER, CLUSTER
agglomeration .... COHERENCE
aggrandize .... ENLARGE, EXPAND, INCREASE
aggravate ...... TWIT, ANGER, IRK, WORSEN, INTENSIFY
aggregate ... SUM, MASS, TOTAL, GATHER, WHOLE, COMBINED
fruit of strawberry .... ETAERIO
aggress .... ATTACK, INVADE, PROVOKE
aggression .... WAR, RAID, ASSAULT, ATTACK, INVASION, ONSLAUGHT, HOSTILITY
aggressive .... MILITANT, PEPPY, PUSHY, WARLIKE, DYNAMIC, COMBATIVE, PUSHING, SPIRITED, ZESTFUL, ASSERTIVE
slang .... GO-GO, TRIGGER-HAPPY
aggressor .... RAIDER, INVADER, ATTACKER, OFFENDER, PROVOKER, ASSAILANT
slang .... MUGGER
aggrieve .... WRONG, CRUSH, INJURE, OFFEND, SLIGHT, OPPRESS
aghast .... AMAZED, STUNNED, APPALLED, BEWITCHED, TERRIFIED, ENTRANCED, FROZEN, HORRIFIED
slang .... SCARED SHITLESS
agialid .... BITO
agile .... FAST, KEEN, SPRY, QUICK, PERT, ALERT, FLEET, SHARP, SWIFT, ACTIVE, NIMBLE, LISSOM(E), LIVELY, CHIPPER
aging .... SENESCENT
agio .... PREMIUM, REBATE, SETOFF, EXCHANGE, DISCOUNT, DEDUCTION
slang .... KICKBACK, ROLLBACK
agitate ...... STIR, ALARM, CHURN, ROUSE, EXCITE, WORRY, F(E)AZE, FEEZE, UPSET, SHAKE, INCITE, ROIL, DISTURB, FLUSTER
agitation .... DITHER, RUMPUS, POTHER, TUMULT, TURMOIL, FLURRY, ANXIETY, UPHEAVAL, TEMPEST, CACOPHONY
French .... BROUHAHA

Italian .... FURORE
slang .... HEEBIE-JEEBIES
state of .... AGOG, BOILING, SEETHING, STORMY, TUMULTUOUS
agitator .... INCITER, URGER, RIOTER, EXCITER, MUTINEER, PROVOKER, FIREBRAND, RABBLE-ROUSER, DEMAGOG(UE), ANARCHIST, INCENDIARY
French .... PROVOCATEUR
Aglaia .... GRACE
aglet .... TAG, LACE, SPANGLE
agley .... AWRY
aglow .... ALIT, SHINING, MOONLIT, RADIANT, STARLIT, BLUSHING, BURNING, TINSELED
agnail .... HANGNAIL
agname .... NICKNAME, PET NAME, MONICKER
agnate .... KIN, ALLIED, RELATIVE
Agnew's negativists .... NATTERING NABOBS
agnomen .... ALIAS, (NICK)NAME, COGNOMEN
agnostic .... CYNIC, NESCIENT, ATHEIST, DOUBTER, SCOFFER, SKEPTIC
Agnus Dei .... HYMN, LAMB, PRAYER
ago ...... BACK, ERST, GONE, PAST, SINCE
agog .... ASTIR, EAGER, MORBID, AQUIVER, CURIOUS, YEASTY, EXPECTANT
agonize .... RACK, FESTER, RANKLE, SUFFER, STRAIN, GRIEVE, TORTURE, TORMENT, WRITHE, STRUGGLE
agonizing struggle .... THROES
agony .... WOE, PAIN, THROE(S), SORROW, DESPAIR, PASSION, DISTRESS, ANGUISH, SUFFERING
"agony ____" of newspaper .... COLUMN
agora .... ASSEMBLY, MARKETPLACE
coin .... OBOL
agouti .... PACA, RODENT
agrafe .... CLASP, BRACKET
Agram .... ZAGREB
Agra's pride .... TAJ MAHAL
agree .... JIBE, GRANT, MATCH, TALLY, CONCUR, YIELD, ASSENT, APPROVE, COINCIDE, CORRESPOND
agreeable .... PLEASING, SUITABLE, PLEASANT,

WILLING, AMENABLE
odor .... SCENT, AROMA, PERFUME, FRAGRANCE
old style .... AMENE
taste .... SWEET, SAVORY, TOOTHSOME, PALATABLE
agreeableness of letter .... EUTONY
agreement .... PACT, DEAL, CARTEL, ACCORD, TREATY, MISE, ENTENTE, CONCORD, AMEN, CONTRACT, COVENANT
in opinion .... CONSENSUS
to rent .... LEASE
with conditions .... ESCROW
agrestic .... RURAL, RUSTIC, CRUDE, PASTORAL
agricultural .... FARM, RURAL, BUCOLIC, RUSTIC, AGRARIAN
overseer .... AGRONOME
worker .... OKIE, RYOT, PEASANT
agriculture, goddess of .... CERES, DEMETER
Agrippa's temple ...... PANTHEON
Agrippina's son .... NERO
agua .... TOAD, WATER
ague .... CHILL, FEVER
Ahab's cabin boy .... PIP
daughter .... ATHALIAH
father .... OMRI
royal palace ..... IVORY HOUSE
ship .... PEQUOD, WHALER
son .... AHAZIAH, JEHORAM
wife .... JEZEBEL
Ahasuerus' minister ...... HAMAN
wife .... ESTHER
Ahaz's father .... JOTHAM
grandson .... MANASSEH
son .... HEZEKIAH
ahead .... FIRST, EARLY, FRONT, BEFORE, FORWARD, WINNING, LEADING
forge .... LEAD, ADVANCE, PROGRESS
French .... A LA MODE
of its time ...... ULTRAMODERN
ahem sound .... COUGH
ahuehuete .... CYPRESS
ai .... SLOTH
aid .... ABET, HELP, SUCCOR, ASSIST, REMEDY, FAVOR, RESCUE, FURTHER
Aida's lover .... R(H)ADAMES
rival .... AMNERIS
aide .... ADJUTANT, DEPUTY, ORDERLY, ASSISTANT, SUBALTERN, LIEUTENANT
memoire .... MEMORANDUM
aiglet .... TAG, POINT
aigrette .... EGRET

ail .... PAIN, BOTHER, SUFFER
aileron part .... TAB
ailing .... ILL, SICK, HURTING,
    UNDER THE WEATHER
ailment .... ILLNESS, DEFECT,
    MALADY, DISEASE, DISORDER,
    COMPLAINT
    minor .... PIP
aim .... END, GOAL, POINT, ASPIRE,
    TARGET, SIGHT, INTENT,
    PURPOSE, DIRECTION,
    AMBITION, OBJECT(IVE)
aimless .... FUTILE, USELESS,
    POINTLESS, DESULTORY,
    HAPHAZARD
    scribble .... DOODLE
    wanderer of sorts .... JEW,
    NOMAD, ROVER, TRAMP
ain .... OWN
air .... ARIA, MEIN, SONG, TUNE,
    MANNER, MELODY, CARRIAGE,
    ATMOSPHERE
    apparatus .... FAN, SCUBA,
    BLOWER, AERATOR
    bends .... AEROEMBOLISM
    boundary .... FRONT
    castle .... (DAY)DREAM,
    AUTISM, FANTASY, REVERIE,
    STARGAZE
    combining form .... AERO,
    AER(I)
    current .... EDDY, STREAM
    currents, rising ...... ANABATIC
    expose to .... AERATE
    fear of .... AEROPHOBIA
    fill with .... AERATE, GAS UP
    filled film of liquid
    .... BUBBLE
    force girl .... WASP, WREN
    fresh/pure .... OZONE
    friction .... WINDAGE
    gauge .... AEROMETER
    group .... RAF, USAF, WING,
    ESCADRILLE
    hero .... ACE
    in motion .... WIND, BREEZE,
    ZEPHYR
    in violent agitation .... STORM,
    TORNADO, CYCLONE, TEMPEST,
    TYPHOON, WHIRLWIND
    mass .... ISOTHERM
    navigation officer
    .... AVIGATOR
    navigation system
    .... SHORAN, TELERAN
    of .... AERIAL
    open .... ALFRESCO
    passage/pipe .... FLUE,
    NOSTRIL, VENT(IDUCT)
    pertaining to .... AURAL,
    AERIAL

    pipe .... FLUE, VENTIDUCT
    plant .... ORCHID, EPIPHYTE
    pocket .... TURBULENCE
    poisonous/unwholesome
    .... MIASMA, MALARIA
    race marker .... PYLON
    raid ..... BLITZ(KRIEG), STRAFE,
    BOMBARDMENT
    route .... SKYWAY
    shaft ..... BLOWHOLE, NOSTRIL,
    SPIRACLE
    show .... FLYING CIRCUS
    spirit .... SYLPH, ARIEL
    stream producer .... FAN,
    BELLOWS, PROPELLER
    taxi .... SHUTTLE
    tight .... HERMETIC
    unhealthfulness .... POLLUTION
    upper .... OZONE, ETHER
aircraft .... SPAD, AIRPLANE,
    AUTOGIRO, TRIMOTOR,
    GLIDER, HELICOPTER,
    ZEPPELIN, DIRIGIBLE,
    HYDROPLANE
    abrupt climb .... CHANDELLE
    air from propeller ...... DOWN-
    WASH, SLIPSTREAM
    altitude controller .... BALLAST
    altitude indicator
    .... ALTIMETER, STATOSCOPE
    attack with gunfire .... STRAFE
    battle .... DOGFIGHT
    body .... FUSELAGE
    bombs .... EGGS
    carried by another
    .... PICKABACK
    carrier ..... FLAT-TOP, HORNET,
    YORKTOWN, SARATOGA,
    LEXINGTON, AMERICA,
    ENTERPRISE
    climb, sudden .... ZOOM
    commercial .... LINER, AIRLINE
    delivery of sold .... FERRY
    designer ..... FOKKER, CURTISS,
    SIKORSKY
    detector .... RADAR
    dome .... BLISTER
    enclosed part .... NACELLE
    engine cover .... COWLING
    engineless .... GLIDER,
    SAILPLANE
    flapping .... FLUTTER,
    ORTHOPTER, ORNITHOPTER
    flight .... HOP, TRIP,
    BARNSTORM
    flight record .... LOG
    formation .... FLIGHT,
    ECHELON
    front .... NOSE
    fuel, antiknock .... TRIPTANE
    group .... WING, ECHELON,

    SQUADRON, ESCADRILLE
    gun turret shield .... DOME,
    BLISTER
    heavier than air .... AERODYNE
    idle propeller of ...... FEATHER
    landing position ...... PANCAKE
    landing/take-off strip
    .... RUNWAY
    launcher on ship
    .... CATAPULT
    lever .... (JOY)STICK
    maneuver on ground ..... TAXI
    manufacturer .... BOEING,
    CESSNA, DOUGLAS, LOCKHEED
    military scouting
    .... GRASSHOPPER
    movable flap .... GILL,
    RUDDER, AILERON
    navigation aid .... LORAN,
    BEACON, SHORAN, TELERAN
    notice to pilots .... NOTAM
    obsolete .... CANARD
    opening for missile ..... BOMB
    BAY
    pilotless .... DRONE
    pilot's place .... COCKPIT
    propeller .... PROP, ROTOR,
    AIRSCREW
    recovery from a dive
    .... PULLOUT
    runner for landing .... SKID
    shed/shelter .... HANGAR,
    AIRDROME, AERODROME
    small .... FLIVVER
    stabilizer .... FIN, AIRFOIL,
    EMPENNAGE
    struts arrangement
    .... CABANE
    stunts .... AEROBATICS, SPIN,
    (BARREL)ROLL, LOOP (-THE-
    LOOP), IMMELMAN (TURN)
    tail part .... FIN, RUDDER,
    ELEVATOR, STABILIZER
    towed target .... DROGUE
    throttle .... GUN
    turn .... BANK, LOOP, BARREL
    LOOP
    twisting force .... TORQUE
    type .... JET, LINER, FIGHTER,
    AMPHIBIAN, TWOSEATER,
    MONOPLANE, BOMBER,
    COMMERCIAL
    war .... MIG, SPAD, ZERO,
    STUKA, BOMBER, FIGHTER,
    SABREJET, SUPERCOBRA,
    MIRAGE, SPITFIRE, CORSAIR,
    SUPERFORT
    water landing gear
    .... PONTOON
    window .... BOMB BAY

wing section for banking .... AILERON
wing support .... STRUT, CABANE
airdrome. See **airport**
airedale .... TERRIER
airfoil .... TAB, PLANE
airing .... OUTING, REVEALING, EXPRESSION, VENTILATION
airline schedule .... TIMETABLE
airmail, by .... PAR AVION
airman .... PILOT, AVIATOR, BARNSTORMER
mythological .... ICARUS
non-flying .... KIWI
would-be .... DODO
airplane. See **aircraft**
airport .... (AIR)DROME, HANGAR, AERODROME
busiest .... O'HARE
marker .... PYLON
part .... APRON, TOWER, RUNWAY, LANDING FIELD
paving .... TARMAC
queue .... TAXIS
air-raid shelter .... ABRI, BUNKER, DUGOUT
airs, given to .... VAIN, PRISSY, SNOOTY, SNOBBISH
airship .... AERO, BLIMP, BALLOON, ZEPPELIN, DIRIGIBLE
airsick .... QUALMY, QUEASY, NAUSEOUS
slang .... PUKY, PUKISH
airtight .... FOOLPROOF, HERMETIC(AL)
airy .... GAY, LIGHT, BREEZY, JAUNTY, ETHEREAL
aisle .... LANE, NAVE, PATH, ALLEY, CHANNEL, CORRIDOR, PASSAGEWAY
tread the middle .... WED, MARRY
treader of the middle .... BRIDE(GROOM)
ait .... EYOT, HOLM, ISLE(T)
Aix-la-Chapelle .... AACHEN
Ajaccio is capital of .... CORSICA
Ajax, father of .... TELEMON
the _____ .... LESS
akin .... SIB, LIKE, AGNATE, GERMANE, RELATED
Al Smith character .... JEFF, MUTT
ala .... WING
Alabama bay .... MOBILE, PERDIDO, BON SECOUR
capital .... MONTGOMERY
channel .... GRANTS PASS
city/town .... PELL, TROY, SELMA, LINDEN, MOBILE, GADSDEN, DECATUR, ANNISTON, CORONA, FLORENCE, HUNTSVILLE, BIRMINGHAM, PRICHARD, TUSCALOOSA
county .... LEE, BIBB, CLAY, DALE, BLOUNT, LAMAR, COFFEE, DALLAS, MOBILE, MORGAN, SHELBY, ELMORE, WALKER, WILCOX, BALDWIN, CALHOUN, COLBERT, DE KALB, HOUSTON, JACKSON, MADISON, MARSHALL, JEFFERSON, LAUDERDALE, LIMESTONE, MONTGOMERY
creek .... SANDY, PIGEON, ESCAMBIA, MULBERRY
island .... HERBES
lake .... LAY, WEISS, JORDAN, HARDING, WHEELER, BANKHEAD, PICKWICK, GREAT ROCK
mountain .... SAND, CHEAHA, LOOKOUT
river .... ELK, PEA, COOSA, CAHABA, LITTLE, MOBILE, SIPSEY, TENSAW, ALABAMA, PERDIDO, SEPULGA, CHATTOOGA, TENNESSEE, TOMBIGBEE
state bird ..... YELLOWHAMMER
state flower .... CAMELLIA
state nickname .... COTTON, HEART OF DIXIE
alabaster .... SILK, SATIN, IVORY, GYPSUM, VELVET, MINERAL, GRAPHITE
alackaday .... ALAS, WOE IS ME
alacrity .... ZEAL, AGILITY, CELERITY, VITALITY, RAPIDITY, RASHNESS, QUICKNESS, READINESS
Aladdin's lamp .... WISH-BRINGER
servant .... GENIE, JINNI
alamandite .... GARNET
alameda .... WALK, PROMENADE
alamo .... POPLAR
Alamo hero .... BOWIE, CROCKETT
in Texas .... SHRINE, MISSION
Alamogordo county .... OTERO
Alan, actor .... ALDA, LADD
author .... PATON
aland .... DOG
alange .... DRAB, DULL, DREARY
alantin .... INULIN
alar .... PTERO, WINGED, WINGLIKE, WINGSHAPED
Alaric's men .... GOTHS
alarm .... CALL, ALERT, PANIC, SCARE, SIREN, AROUSE, SIGNAL, WARN(ING)
bell .... TOCSIN
poetic .... ALARUM
system for short .... DEWS
whistle .... BLAST, SIREN(E), FOGHORN
alarming .... AWING, FAZING, SERIOUS, CHILLING, CRITICAL, MENACING
alarmist .... SCAREMONGER
slang .... WORRY WART
alas .... ALACKADAY, WOE (IS ME)
Alaska capital .... JUNEAU
former capital .... SITKA
Purchase in 1867, to some .... FOLLY
Alaskan auk .... ARRIES
bay .... DRY, ICY, HAZEN, MUZON, NORTON, TOGIAK, BRISTOL, CHIGNIK, PAVLOF, CORDOVA, GLACIER, TWO ARM, YAKUTAT
bear .... KODIAK
blizzard .... PURGA
canal .... SEYMOUR
cape .... ICY, HALKETT, LISBURNE, MENDENHALL, WRANGELL, FAIRWEATHER, CONSTANTINE, KRUSENSTERN
city/town .... NOME, KENAI, SITKA, BETHEL, KODIAK, SEWARD, VALDEZ, COLLEGE, CORDOVA, SKAGWAY, WRANGELL, ANCHORAGE, FAIRBANKS, KETCHIKAN
garment .... PARKA
glacier .... MUIR, GUYOT, BERING, COLUMBIA, MALASPINA
highway .... ALCAN
Indian .... TLINGIT, TLINKIT
inlet .... COOK, DEASE, PORT WELLS, PORT HEIDEN
island .... HALL, KING, KUIU, UNGA, KAYAK, KISKA, OTTER, SANAK, UMNAK, AGATTU, AKUTAN, KNIGHT, KODIAK, MARMOT, WALRUS, ETOLIN, MITKOF, STUART, BARANOF, YAKOBI
islands ..... FOX, RAT, SEMICHI, ALEUTIAN, PRIBILOF, ANDREANOF
lake .... CLARK, MUYAKUK, SELAWIK, BECHAROF
mining town .... NOME
monument .... KATMAI
mountain .... ADA, BEAR, BONA, COOK, HAYES, KENAI, DOUGLAS, FORAKER, SANFORD, MCKINLEY, MICHELSON,

VANCOUVER, DEVILS PAW, WEST POINT, FAIRWEATHER, KATES NEEDLE
mountains .... BAIRD, COAST, TAYLOR, WARING, CHUGASH, ENDICOTT
native .... DENE, ALEUT, ESKIMO
peak .... MCKINLEY
peninsula .... UNGA, KENAI, SEWARD
range .... BROOKS, ALEUTIAN
river ..... TAKU, FIRTH, KOBUK, MEADE, STONY, WHITE, YUKON, COPPER, INNOKO, NOATAK, TANANA, NOWITNA, SUSITNA, TAZLINA, COLVILLE, CHANDALAR, MATANUSKA, PORCUPINE
seaport .... KETCHIKAN
state bird .... WILLOW PTARMIGAN
state flower .... FORGET-ME-NOT
state nickname .... THE LAST FRONTIER
tree .... SPRUCE
valley .... MATANUSKA
vehicle .... SLED
volcano .... KISKA, KATMAI, PAVLOF, TANAGA, REDOUBT, MAKUSHIN, SHISHALDIN
alb .... ROBE, VESTMENT
alba .... SONG, AUBADE
albacore .... FISH, TUNNY, BONITO, MACKEREL
Albanese, soprano .... LICIA
Albanian .... GHEG
capital .... TIRANA, TIRANE
city/town .... FIER, BERAT, KORCE, VLORE, DURRES, KAVAJE, ELBASAN, SHKODER
dialect .... GEG, CHAM, TOSK
king .... ZOG
island .... SAZAN
lake .... OHRID, PRESPA, SCUTARI
money .... LEK, QUINTAR
mountain .... KORAB
river .... DRIN, VIJOSE
sea .... ADRIATIC
seaport .... SCUTARI
soldier .... PALIKAR
spy .... CICERO
strait .... OTRANTO
Albany is capital of .... NEW YORK
albatross .... GONY, NELLY, MALLEMUCK
Albee's Alice .... TINY
albeit .... YET, STILL, EVEN IF,

ALTHOUGH
Alberta resource .... OIL
scenery .... BANFF
albinism .... ALPHOSIS, BLONDNESS, WHITENESS
Albion .... ENGLAND
adjective for .... PERFIDIOUS
albite .... FELDSPAR
album .... RECORD, REGISTER, SCRAPBOOK
albumen .... GLAIR
alburnum .... SAPWOOD
alcaide .... JAILER, WARDEN
Alcestis' husband ...... ADMETUS
alchemical .... HERMETIC
alchemist, pioneer .... THOTH
alchemy, work on .... ALMAGEST
alchitran .... TAR, PITCH
Alcides .... HERCULES
Alcinous' garden .... SCHERIA
alcohol ...... BREW, GROG, LOTUS, LIQUOR, SPIRITS, BEVERAGE, SCHNAPPS, INTOXICANT
antiseptic .... IODINE, PEROXIDE, MERTHIOLATE
chemical .... BORAX, ACETONE, AMMONIA, BROMIDE, BENZOATE
crystal .... TALITOL
depressant .... OPIUM, CODEINE, MORPHINE
fuel .... GAS, ETHANOL, PROPELLANT
ingredient .... AMYL, ETHYL, METHYL
slang .... BOOZE
solid .... STEROL
alcoholic .... WINY, ADDICT, VINOUS, DRUNKARD
drink .... GIN, RUM, TOT, MEAD, WINE, VODKA, POSSET, WHISKEY
drink from rice/molasses .... SAKE, ARRACK
drunkard .... WASSAILER, DIPSOMANIAC
haunt of .... SKIDROW
liquor .... MESCAL, TIPPLE
liquor, craving for ...... THIRST
liquor from wine/fruit .... BRANDY, COGNAC
liquor smuggler .... RUMRUNNER
liquor to an Indian .... FIREWATER
slang .... LUSH, WINO, BOOZER, SPONGE
sugar .... TROSSE
Alcoran .... KORAN
Alcott heroine .... JO, AMY, MEG, BETH

alcove .... BAY, NOOK, BOWER, NICHE, ORIEL, RECESS
Alda, Frances .... DIVA, SOPRANO
aldehyde, liquid .... CITRAL
alder .... ROSE, ARN, SAGE, ALNUS
alderman .... REEVE, SOLON, SENATOR, LEGISLATOR
ale .... MOM, NOG(G), BEER, BOCK, FLIP, YILL, ALEGAR, LAGER, STOUT, STINGO, PORTER
flavor .... HOPS
ingredient .... HOPS, MALT, YEAST
measure .... GILL, PINT, NOGGIN
mug .... TOBY, STEIN
sour/vinegar .... ALEGAR
strong .... NAPPY, STINGO
alec .... (FISH)SAUCE
Alecto .... FURY
alee, opposite of .... STOSS, AWEATHER
alehouse .... BAR, INN, PUB, BISTRO, SALOON, TAVERN
slang .... SPEAKEASY
alembic .... STILL, RETORT, DISTILLER
Alencon is capital of .... ORNE
product .... LACE
Aleppo native .... SYRIAN
alert .... GLEG, KEEN, AWAKE, AWARE, READY, WARNING, VIGILANT, ON THE BALL
Aleut .... UNUNGUN
Aleutian fish .... GREENLING
isle .... ADAK, ATKA, ATTU
alewife .... FISH, HERRING, POMPANO, WALLEYE
Alexander .... KING, POPE, SEROV, FLEMING, THE GREAT, ARCHIPELAGO
Hamilton's downfall ..... DUEL
the Great's battle site .... ISSUS, GRANICUS, HYDASPES, GAUGAMELA
eastern conquest .... SIWA, SUSA, BABYLON, SAMARIA, PARSEPOLIS
enemy .... BATIS, PORUS, DARIUS
father .... PHILIP
general .... ANTIPATER
kingdom .... MACEDONIA
southern conquest .... ACCO, GAZA, TYRE, AZOTUS, ASHKELON, STRATO'S TOWER
Alexandria, patriarch ...... PAPA
Alexandrian courtesan ...... THAIS
mathematician .... PTOLEMY
theologian .... ARIUS
writer .... ORIGEN

alfalfa .... PEA, MEDIC, FODDER, LUCERN(E), SATIVA
alforja .... SADDLEBAG
alfresco .... OPEN-AIR, OUTDOOR(S), OUTSIDE
alga .... NORI, SCUM, DESMID, DIATOM, SEAWEED, NOSTOC, CONFERVA, ANABAENA, SPYROGYRA
filament .... TRICHOMA
algae genus .... ALARIA
like .... ALGOID
algarroba .... TREE, CAROB, CALDEN, LOCUST, (HONEY)MESQUITE
Algebar .... ORION
Algeria, Roman name .... POMARIA
Algerian cape .... BOUGAROUN
capital .... ALGIERS
cavalryman .... SPAHI
city/town .... BONE, ORAN, MEDEA, SAIDA, SETIF, BISKRA, BOUGIE, TIEMCEN, GHARDALA, TOUGGOURT, CONSTANTINE
city section .... CASBAH
desert .... IGUIDI, SAHARA, GRAND ERG, TANEZROUFT
governor .... DEY
grass .... ESPARTO
guerrilla chieftain .... ZBIRI
infantryman .... TURCO
lagoon .... AURES
minority group .... BERBERS
money .... DINAR
mountain .... TAHAT, CHELIA
native .... BERBER, KABYLE
native quarters .... CASBAH, KASBAH
port ..... BONE, ORAN, ALGIERS
president .... BELLA, BOUMEDIENNE
river .... CHELIF, MEDJERDA
ruler .... BEY
salt lake .... CHERGUI, MEIRHIR
soldier .... SPAHI, TURCO, SPAHEE
weight .... ROTL
algesis .... ACHE, PAIN
algia, as suffix .... PAIN
algid .... COLD, CHILLY
algolagnia .... SADISM, MASOCHISM
Algonquian friend .... NETOP
Indian .... SAC, CREE, MIAMI, LENAPE, OTTAWA, ARAPAHO(E), SHAWNEE
Indian money .... SEAWANT, SE(A)WAN
algor .... CHILL
algum ...... ALMUG, SANDALWOOD

Ali Baba .... WOODCUTTER
brother of .... CASSIM
helper of .... MORGIANA
word(s) of .... (OPEN)SESAME
alias .... ANONYM, HANDLE, PSEUDONYM, ALSO KNOWN AS, OTHERWISE KNOWN
letters before .... AKA
alibi .... PLEA, FEINT, DEVICE, EXCUSE, REFUGE, COVER(-UP), PRETEXT
slang .... COP-OUT
alible ...... NUTRITIVE, NOURISHING
Alice's cat .... DINAH
alidade .... DIOPTER
alien .... METIC, EXOTIC, ADVERSE, FOREIGN(ER), OUTSIDER, STRANGER, OUTLANDER
from outer space .... MARTIAN, SAUCERMAN
alienate .... WEAN, MADDEN, DIVIDE, SUBVERT, DISUNITE, ESTRANGE, TRANSFER, BRAINWASH, DISAFFECT
alienist .... PSYCHIATRIST
slang .... HEADSHRINKER
alight .... LAND, DEBUS, PERCH, ROOST, DEPLANE, DESCEND, DISMOUNT, STEP DOWN
align .... TRUE, ALINE, ARRAY, LEVEL, STRAIGHTEN
alignment .... UNION, FUSION, LINAGE
slang .... HOOKUP, CAHOOTS
alike ...... AKIN, SAME, MATCHED, SIMILAR
aliment .... PAP, FOOD, PABULUM, NUTRITION
alimentary canal .... ENTERON
motion .... PERISTALSIS
alimony .... AID, PENSION, SUBSIDY, SUPPORT
aliped creature .... BAT
aliquot .... PRIME, DIGITAL, NUMERAL
alit .... AGLOW, LANDED, RADIANT, DISMOUNTED
alive .... PERT, SPRY, ALERT, QUICK, LIVELY, LIVING, ANIMATED
and kicking .... HEALTHY
to .... COGNIZANT, IN THE KNOW
alkali .... LYE, SALT, SODA, POTASH, ANTACID, SALTWORT
alkaline .... LIME, OXIDE
solution .... LYE
alkaloid .... ARICIN, CAFFEIN(E), ESERINE, ARABINE, CODEINE, DITAMIN, SINAPIN, CAPSAICIN, QUININ(E), MORPHINE,

BERBERIN(E), MESCALINE
bean .... ESERIN
hemlock .... CONIN(E)
mushroom .... MUSCARINE
poison(ous) .... CONIN, CURARE, BRUCIN(E), TROPIN(E), THEBAINE, MUSCARIN(E)
sedative .... CODEIN(E)
tea .... THEINE
alkanet .... DYE, ANCHUSA, BUGLOSS
alkene .... OLEFIN
all .... ANY, SUM, FULL, WHOLE, ENTIRE, PLENARY, PLENUM, EVERY(ONE), TOTAL(ITY)
aboard .... ALOFT, ANCHORS AWEIGH
around ..... HANDY, VERSATILE
at once .... SUDDENLY
but .... ALMOST, NEARLY
clear .... SAFE, UNINDEBTED
combining form .... PAN, OMNI
comprehensive .... OMNIBUS, UNIVERSAL
consuming .... STIFLING, SILENCING
creating .... OMNIFIC
creation .... UNIVERSE
ears .... RAPTLY, ATTENTIVE
embracing .... WHOLE, THOROUGH
fired .... FANATIC(AL)
fours .... SEVEN UP
in .... TIRED, WEARY, FATIGUED, ON HIS LAST LEGS
in all .... MAINLY, OVERALL, ALTOGETHER
inclusive ...... WHOLE, INFINITE
in music .... TUTTI
in the mind .... IMAGINARY
out .... ABSOLUTE, WHOLE-HOG, DOWNRIGHT
over .... THROUGHOUT
overs .... QUALM, ANXIETY
pervading .... THOROUGH
powerful .... ALMIGHTY, OMNIPOTENT
present .... EVERYWHERE
religions, believer in .... OMNIST
right .... YES, GOOD, OKAY, AGREED, HONEST
seed .... KNOTWEED, GOOSEFOOT
seed herb .... RADIOLA
seeing .... OMNISCIENT
set .... READY, PREPPED
shook up .... STARTLED
spice .... PIMIENTO,

(MYRTLE)BERRY
"the ——— horses"
.... KING'S
the world, to Shakespeare
.... STAGE
the same .... NEVERTHELESS
the time .... ALWAYS
the way .... TO THE LIMIT
there .... SANE, NORMAL,
MENTALLY SOUND
things considered
.... BROADLY, GENERALLY
thumbs .... CLUMSY,
AWKWARD, BUMBLING
time .... UNSURPASSED
together .... JOINTLY
All Saints' Day observance
.... HALLOWEEN, HALLOWMASS
Allah .... MANITOU, THE GREAT
SPIRIT
allan .... GULL
allanite .... CERINE, ORTHITE
allay .... CALM, EASE, QUIET,
SLAKE, ASSURE, PACIFY,
ASSUAGE, GRATIFY, MOLLIFY,
SATIATE, RELIEVE
allegation .... PLEA, CLAIM,
REMARK, AVERMENT,
STATEMENT, PROFESSION
allege .... STATE, ACCUSE, AFFIRM,
ASSERT, TESTIFY
alleged electric force .... ELOD
force .... OD, ODYLE
Allegheny city .... OLEAN
allegiance .... DUTY, FEALTY,
LOYALTY, DEVOTION
allegorical .... PARABOLIC
allegory .... FABLE, PARABLE
alleluia .... CHEER, PAEAN
Allen, ——— .... IRA, FRED,
ETHAN, STEVE
allergic .... AVERSE, SENSITIVE
reaction .... COLD, RASH,
NAUSEA, SNEEZE
skin condition .... HIVES,
ECZEMA, URTICARIA
to firearms .... GUNSHY
allergy .... DISEASE, REACTION,
SENSITIVITY
common cause of .... MITE,
MOLD, POLLEN, DANDER,
CEREAL, FEATHER,
HOUSEDUST, SHELLFISH,
STRAWBERRY
medicine for .... BENADRYL
physician .... ALLERGIST
symptom of .... RASH,
VOMITING, ITCHY SWELLING
alleviate .... EASE, ALLAY,
LESSEN, LIGHTEN, MITIGATE
alleviation .... RELIEF

alley .... MIB, TAW, LANE, PATH,
ROAD, WALK, AISLE, BYPASS,
MARBLE, STREET, PASSAGE
blind .... DEAD END, CUL DE
SAC
cat .... HOMELESS
closed at one end .... DEAD
END
allheal .... PLANT, SELFHEAL,
VALERIAN
alliance .... AXIS, BLOC, UNION,
FUSION, LEAGUE, TREATY,
SODALITY
of nations .... UN, AXIS, OAS,
NATO, SEATO, BIG FIVE
of parties .... COALITION
of woman and man
.... MARRIAGE
allied .... AKIN, BOUND, YOKED,
JOINED, LINKED, UNITED,
COUPLED, KNOTTED,
MARRIED, RELATED, SIMILAR
alligator .... CAIMAN, CAYMAN,
LIZARD, LEATHER, SAURIAN,
CROCODILE
pear ..... AVOCADO, AGUACATE
allium .... LEEK, ONION, GARLIC
allocate .... GIVE, METE, ALLOT,
GRANT, ASSIGN, DETAIL,
DISTRIBUTE
allot ..... DOLE, SHARE, EARMARK
allotment .... SHARE, QUOTA,
RATION, PORTION, STIPEND,
ALIMONY, SUBSIDY
allow .... LET, GIVE, OPINE, YIELD,
BESTOW, ADMIT, EXTEND,
PERMIT, SUFFER, PROVIDE,
TOLERATE
free use .... LEND
to become known .... LEAK
allowable variance
.... TOLERANCE
allowance .... QUOTA, RATION,
WAIVER, SUPPORT, DISCOUNT,
REDUCTION, CONCESSION
depreciation .... AGIO
food .... RATION, CORODY
loss of weight .... DRAFT
slang .... KICKBACK
small .... PITTANCE
waste .... TRET, DRAFT
weight .... TARE
alloy .... METAL, AMALGAM,
MIXTURE
aluminum .... ALNICO,
DURALUMIN
black .... NIELLO
cheap jewelry .... TOMBAK,
TOMBAC(K)
copper-nickel-zinc
.... ALBATA, ELECTRUM

copper-tin .... BRONZE
copper-tin-zinc .... OROIDE
copper-zinc .... BRASS
gold-like ..... AROIDE, ORMOLU
gold-silver .... ASEM,
ELECTRUM
iron-carbon .... STEEL
lead-tin .... TERNE, PEWTER
mercury .... AMALGAM
nickel-steel .... INVAR
nonferrous .... TULA
pewter-like .... BIDRI
sulfur .... NIELLO
three-metal .... TERNARY
tin-copper-antimony
.... BABBIT, BRITANNIA
tin-copper-lead .... PEWTER
tin-zinc .... OROIDE
with aluminum ...... CALORIZE
yellow .... AICH
alloyed .... BASE, SHAM, MIXED,
TAINTED, SPURIOUS,
CHEAPENED, INSINCERE
allude .... CITE, HINT, IMPLY,
REFER, REMARK
allure .... BAIT, SWAY, TOLE,
CHARM, DECOY, SNARE,
TEMPT, ENTICE, ATTRACT
allurement .... CHARM, CONNING,
GLAMOUR, (SEX)APPEAL,
CHARISMA, SEDUCTION,
FASCINATION
slang .... SNOW JOB, SOFT-
SOAP
alluring ...... EXOTIC, APPEALING,
RAVISHING
allusion .... HINT, TOUCH,
INKLING, INNUENDO,
OVERTONE, INFERENCE
allusive .... IRONIC, SUGGESTIVE
alluvial clay .... ADOBE
deposit ..... MUD, SILT, PLACER
fan .... DELTA
matter .... GEEST
alluvion .... SILT, FLOOD
ally .... JOIN, LINK, CRONY,
COHORT, FRIEND, HELPER,
COMPEER, PARTNER
alma mater .... SCHOOL, COLLEGE
almanac .... CALENDAR,
YEARBOOK
astronomical .... EPHEMERIS
almandine .... GARNET, SPINEL
almighty .... SUPREME,
HALLOWED, OMNIPOTENT,
ALL-POWERFUL
Almighty ...... GOD, THE CREATOR
almond .... NUT, TREE, JORDAN,
BADAM, KANARI, LIGHT TAN,
AMYGDALA
emulsion .... ORGEAT

eyed .... SLANT-EYED
flavored liquor .... RATAFIA
oil .... AMARIN
shaped .... AMYGDALOID
almost .... CLOSE, NEARLY
alms .... DOLE, CHARITY
box .... ARCA
giver .... ALMONER,
PHILANTHROPIST
almshouse .... HOSPICE,
BEADHOUSE, POORHOUSE
almsman .... PAUPER, INDIGENT
almuce .... AMICE, TIPPET,
HEADDRESS
alnus .... ALDER
alod .... ESTATE, ALODIUM,
FREEHOLD
aloe .... DRUG, LILY, AGAVE,
MAGUEY
derivative .... ALOIN
aloft ...... UP, ASOAR, IN THE AIR,
UPWARD, SKYWARD,
OVERHEAD
aloha .... LOVE, GOODBYE,
WELCOME, FAREWELL,
GREETING
alone .... LONE, ONLY, SOLE,
SOLO, SINGLE, UNPAIRED, BY
ONESELF, SOLITARY
on stage .... SOLA, SOLUS
along .... ON, BESIDE, ONWARD,
LENGTHWISE
side .... ABREAST
the way .... ENROUTE
with .... AND
aloof .... COLD, APART, FRIGID,
OFFISH, DISTANT, RESERVED,
STANDOFFISH
alopecia .... ACOMIA, BALDNESS
aloud .... LOUDLY, CLEARLY,
AUDIBLY, DISTINCTLY
alow .... BELOW, UNDER
alp .... PEAK, MOUNTAIN
alpaca .... PACO, WOOL, CLOTH,
RUMINANT
like animal .... LLAMA,
VICUNA, GUANACO
alpen .... HILLY, KNOBBY,
ROLLING
alpha .... STAR, DENEB, FIRST,
START, INITIAL
rays .... BETA
Alpha and Omega .... BEGINNING
AND END
alphabet .... ABC'S, BASICS,
PRIMER, RUDIMENTS
character .... OGAM, RUNE,
LETTER
Kashmir .... SARADA
teacher .... ABECEDARIAN

alphabetical list, kind of
.... CATALOG(UE),
CONCORDANCE
Alpine .... NORDIC
animal .... IBEX, CHAMOIS
dance .... GAVOT
danger .... AVALANCHE
dress .... DIRNDL
goat .... IBEX, STEINBOK
herdsman .... SENN
house/hut .... CHALET
pass .... COL, (MONT)CENIS,
SIMPLON
plant .... EDELWEISS
primrose .... AURICULA
river .... RHONE
wind .... BISE, BORA, FOEHN
Alps .... CHAIN, TIROL, TYROL,
MOUNTAIN RANGE
highest peak ..... MONT BLANC
French .... MASSIF
mountain .... BERNINA,
JUNGFRAU, MATTERHORN,
MONT BLANC
pass .... CENIS
Spanish .... SIERRA,
CORDILLERA
already .... ERE, YET, STILL,
BEFORE, ERENOW, PRIORLY,
EARLIER, PREVIOUSLY
Alsatian .... POLICE DOG,
WHITEFRIARS
alsike .... CLOVER, FODDER
also .... AND, TOO, MORE, PLUS,
ALONG, EXTRA, BESIDES,
LIKEWISE
known as .... AKA, ALIAS
ran .... LOSER
Altair .... STAR
altar ...... BOMOS, TABLE, HESTIA,
SHRINE, ESCHARA, SCROBIS
area around .... CHANCEL
boy .... ACOLYTE, THURIFER
carpet .... PEDALE
cloth .... PALL, DOSSAL,
DOSSEL, HAPLOMA, CORPORAL,
VESPERAL
constellation .... ARA
curtain .... RIDDEL
enclosure .... BEMA
end of the church .... APSE
endowed .... CHANTRY
offering .... ALTARAGE,
EUCHARIST
part .... PISCINA, PREDELLA
piece .... DIPTYCH, TRIPTYCH
rail .... SEPTUM
screen/veil .... REREDOS,
ANTEPENDIUM
shelf .... GRADIN, RETABLE
slab/top .... MENSA

table .... CREDENCE
altazimuth of astronomer
.... ABA
alter .... FIX, TURN, VARY,
ADJUST, ADAPT, AMEND,
SHIFT, CHANGE, MODIFY,
MUTATE, REVAMP, REVISE,
CONVERT, DISTORT, PERMUTE
ego .... FRIEND, STOOGE,
ONESELF, INTIMATE, SIDEKICK,
CONFIDANT
alteration .... CHANGE, SWITCH,
REVISION
slang .... FLIP-FLOP
altercation .... SPAT, TIFF,
BICKER, FRACAS, STRIFE,
DISPUTE, QUARREL,
ARGUMENT, SQUABBLE
alternate .... DUMMY, PROXY,
OTHER, SHIFT, SECOND,
ROTATE, STAND-IN,
EXCHANGE, SUBSTITUTE
slang .... RINGER
alternating current .... AC,
ELECTRICITY
alternative .... OR, AND/OR,
CHOICE, EITHER, OPTION,
LOOPHOLE
alternator .... DYNAMO,
GENERATOR
althea .... HOLLYHOCK
Althea .... HEALER
althorn .... SAXHORN
although .... YET, WHEN, STILL,
WHILE, ALBEIT, EVEN IF,
RATHER, IN SPITE OF
altitude .... HEIGHT, STATURE,
ELEVATION
measuring device
.... OROMETER, ALTIMETER
altogether .... IN ALL, FULLY,
WHOLLY, ROUNDLY,
ENTIRELY, OUTRIGHT
the .... NUDITY, BIRTHDAY SUIT
Altona .... HAMBURG
altruism .... CHARITY, LARGESS,
GOODWILL
altruist, one kind of
.... SAMARITAN
opposite of .... EGOIST
alum .... SALT, EMETIC,
ASTRINGENT
aluminum compound
.... BAUXITE, TERMITE
ore .... BAUXITE
oxide .... RUBY, TOPAZ,
ALUMINA, CORUNDUM
alumnus .... GRAD(UATE)
alveary .... (BEE)HIVE
alveolar ...... GINGIVAL, THROATY
alveolate .... HOLEY,

POCKMARKED, HONEYCOMBED
always .... AY, E'ER, EVER,
FOREVER, STEADILY,
CONSTANTLY, INVARIABLY
poetic .... ETERNE
alyssum .... MADWORT
ama .... CUP, VESSEL
amadou .... PUNK, TINDER,
STYPTIC
amah .... AYAH, MAID, NANNY,
NURSE, WENCH, SERVANT
British .... TWEENY
French .... BONNE
amain .... GREATLY, HASTILY,
FORCIBLY, MIGHTILY
Amakusa port .... AMUTA
Amalekite king .... AGAG
amalgam .... ALLOY, BLEND,
COMBO, PASTE, MIXTURE,
COMPOUND, COMBINATION
amalgamate .... MIX, FUSE,
MERGE, UNIFY, COMBINE,
BLEND, COALESCE, SYNDICATE
amalgamating pan .... TINA
amalgamation .... MERGER,
METALLURGY
amanuensis .... WRITER,
RECORDER, SECRETARY,
SCRIBBLER, SCRIVENER
amaranth ...... FLOWER, PIGWEED,
TUMBLEWEED
amaranthine .... IMMORTAL,
UNFADING, DEATHLESS,
EVERLASTING
amaryllis .... BULB, AGAVE,
BELLADONNA, PLANT,
SHEPHERDESS
amass .... HEAP, PILE, HOARD,
STACK, STOCK, STORE,
GATHER, MUSTER, COLLECT,
COMPILE, ACCUMULATE
Amata's daughter ...... LATINIA,
LAVINIA
amateur ...... DUB, TYRO, NOVICE,
TRIFLER, NEOPHYTE,
GREENHORN, DILETTANTE
athlete's goal .... OLYMPICS
boxing championship
.... GOLDEN GLOVES
colloquial .... SIMON PURE
opposite of .... EXPERT,
PRO(FESSIONAL)
painter .... DABBLER
radio operator .... HAM
standing .... AMATEURISM
thief, sometime
.... SHOPLIFTER
amateurish .... INEPT, CLUMSY,
AWKWARD, UNSKILLED,
UNTRAINED
slang .... HALF-BAKED

Amati .... FIDDLE, NICOLO,
VIOLIN, PICCOLO
amative .... LOVING, EROTIC,
AMOROUS
amatol .... EXPLOSIVE
amaurosis .... BLINDNESS
amaze .... STUN, MARVEL,
PERPLEX, BEWILDER,
ASTONISH, SURPRISE
amazed .... AGOG, AWED,
AGHAST, PUT OUT,
MESMERIZED
slang .... FLABBERGASTED
amazement .... AWE, WONDER,
SPECTACLE
amazing event .... MIRACLE
trick .... MAGIC, SLEIGHT OF
HAND
Amazon .... ANT, TITAN, RIVER,
WOMAN, PARROT, VIRAGO,
GIANTESS, MANHANDLER
cetacean .... INIA
estuary/mouth .... PARA
fish .... LEPIDOSIREN
part of .... SOLIMOES
stone/gem .... AMAZONITE
tributary .... APA, JURUA,
JAPURA, JAVARI, JAVARY,
TAPAJOZ
valley Indian .... TAPUYAN
Amazonian .... WARLIKE,
MASCULINE
ambagious .... DEVIOUS,
INDIRECT, CIRCUITOUS
ambary .... FIBER, PLANT, NALITA
ambassador ...... AGENT, ENVOY,
EMISSARY, DIPLOMAT,
MINISTER
papal .... LEGATE, NUNCIO
amber .... RESIN, YELLOW
fish .... MEDREGAL
like .... AMBROID, AMBEROID
ambergris .... PERFUMERY,
SECRETION
ambi: comb. form .... BOTH
ambidextrous .... CRAFTY,
CUNNING, VERSATILE, TWO-
FACED, TWO-HANDED
ambience .... CIRCLE, MILIEU,
ENVIRONS, VICINITY
ambient .... ENCIRCLING,
ROUNDABOUT
ambiguous ...... VAGUE, PATCHY,
DELPHIC, JUMBLED, OBSCURE,
RAMBLING, UNCERTAIN
ambit .... SCOPE, BOUNDS,
EXTENT, LIMITS, REGION,
SPHERE, CIRCUIT
ambition .... AIM, END, GOAL,
WISH, DESIRE, MOTIVE,
PURPOSE, ASPIRATION

ambivalent .... FICKLE, IRONIC,
DUBIOUS
amble .... GAIT, PACE, TROT,
MOSEY, STROLL, WADDLE
ambling .... CRAWLING, CREEPING,
HITCHING
horse .... PADNAG
ambo .... STAND, PULPIT, LECTERN
Ambracian Gulf .... ARTA
ambrosia .... MANNA, SALAD,
NECTAR, BEEHEAD, DESSERT,
RAGWEED
ambrosial .... SWEET, TASTY,
FRAGRANT, DELICIOUS
drink .... AMRITA
ambry .... NICHE, CLOSET,
LOCKER, PANTRY, CUPBOARD
ambsace .... BAD LUCK, TWO
ACES, DOUBLE ACES
ambulance chaser, so called
.... SHYSTER, PETTIFOGGER
ambulant .... ON FOOT, WALKING
seller .... PEDDLER
ambulator .... PEDOMETER
ambush .... TRAP, BLITZ, ATTACK,
WAYLAY, ASSAULT, SURPRISE,
BUSHWHACK
ameliorate .... BETTER, UPLIFT,
IMPROVE, NURTURE, RELIEVE,
UPGRADE, MITIGATE
amen .... YES, DONE, AGREED,
VERILY, EXACTLY, SO BE IT,
APPROVAL
slang .... RIGHTO
amenable .... PLIANT, WILLING,
OBEDIENT, AGREEABLE,
RECEPTIVE
slang .... GAME
to existing conditions
.... ADAPTIVE
to reason .... BROADMINDED,
OPEN-MIND(ED)
to requests
.... ACCOMMODATING
to suggestions ..... SUBMISSIVE
amend .... ALTER, CHANGE,
MODIFY, CORRECT, IMPROVE,
REVISE, RECTIFY, REWRITE
amendment .... CLAUSE, PROVISO,
REVISION, CORRECTION
tricky .... JOKER, RIDER
amends .... PAYMENT, REDRESS,
REQUITAL, SQUARING,
ATONEMENT, INDEMNITY
amenities ...... MORES, DECORUM,
COMFORTS, NICETIES, SOCIAL
GRACES
observance of the
.... PUNCTILIO
amenity .... BLISS, NICENESS,
CIVILITY, COURTESY,

GENIALITY

ament .... CHAT, GOLEM, IDIOT,
MORON, SPIKE, CATKIN,
CATTAIL, IMBECILE,
SIMPLETON

amerce .... FINE, PUNISH,
PENALIZE

America ...... US, USA, STATESIDE,
THE STATES, THE AMERICAS,
UNITED STATES, LAND OF
LIBERTY, UNITED STATES OF
AMERICA

identified discoverer of
...... (CHRISTOPHER) COLUMBUS

national personification of
.... COLUMBIA, UNCLE SAM,
BROTHER JONATHAN

reputed discoverer of .... ERIC,
VOTAN, (AMERIGO)VESPUCCI

slang .... UNCLE SUGAR,
YANKEE-LAND

American .... YANK(EE), GRINGO,
WESTERN, AMERICANO

aborigine .... INDIAN

admiral .... KING, SIMS,
DEWEY, CARNEY, HALSEY,
NIMITZ, KINKAID, FARRAGUT

aircraft carrier .... HORNET,
AMERICA, KENNEDY,
SARATOGA, YORKTOWN,
LEXINGTON, ENTERPRISE,
THEODORE ROOSEVELT

antelope .... BLESBOK,
SASSABY

anthologist .... UNTERMEYER

archaeologist .... ANDREWS

"architect" of the Vietnam
war .... MCNAMARA

artist .... WEST, HICKS, KENT,
FLAGG, CADMUS, PEALE,
HOMER, BENTON, COPLEY,
INNESS

astronaut .... GLENN, SCOTT,
WHITE, YOUNG, BORMAN,
ALDRIN, ANDERS, CERNAN,
CONRAD, LOVELL, COLLINS,
GRISSOM, SCHIRRA, SHEPARD,
MCDIVITT, MITCHELL,
STAFFORD, ARMSTRONG,
CUNNINGHAM

author/writer ..... SHAW, ASCH,
AMES, BAUM, BUCK, MEAD,
GREY, PUZO, PYLE, POE,
ALGER, CRANE, URIS, HARTE,
HALEY, HENRY, MOORE, RILEY,
STONE, VIDAL, TWAIN, WYLIE,
ALCOTT, CAPOTE, FERBER,
HAILEY, HERSEY, HOLMES,
KRANTZ, LORING, LUDLUM,
LONDON, MAILER, RUNYON,
SCHARY, EMERSON, GARDNER,

LOWELL, O'NEILL, SAROYAN,
YERBY, SANDBURG, FAULKNER,
MICHENER, HEMINGWAY,
SPILLANE, STEINBECK,
CALDWELL, TARKINGTON,
BENCHLEY, LONGFELLOW,
BRADBURY, BURROUGHS,
DICKINSON, WILLIAMS

badger .... CARCAJOU

balladeer .... GUTHRIE

balsam .... TOLU

battle scene ..... PERSIAN GULF

battle scene, Philippines
.... BATAAN, MANILA BAY,
CORREGIDOR

battleship .... ALABAMA,
MISSOURI, WISCONSIN,
MASSACHUSETTS

bear .... MUSQUAW

beauty .... (RED)ROSE

bingo .... LOTTO

biologist .... MULLER

bird .... ROBIN, COLIN, GUAN,
TOWHEE, RHEA, GROUSE,
SPARROW, CONDOR, STARLING,
JUNCO, BOBOLINK

bishop .... SHEEN

buzzard .... VULTURE

cactus .... CEREUS, SAGUARO

capital lobbyist
.... RAINMAKER

capitalist .... ASTOR, BARUCH

cardinal .... CUSHING,
BRENNAN, SPELLMAN

caricaturist .... NAST

cartoonist .... CAPP, FISHER,
DISNEY, ARNO, NAST,
HERBLOCK, CONRAD, SANDERS,
OLIPHANT, DARCY, HESSE,
MAULDIN

chameleon .... ANOLI

choreographer .... FOKINE

coin .... CENT, PENNY, DIME,
NICKEL, EAGLE, QUARTER

columbo .... GENTIAN

commodore .... PERRY

composer .... BERLIN, IVES,
PORTER, PAINE, NEVIN, KERN,
COPLAND

Confederate soldier
.... REB(EL), BUTTERNUT

contralto
.... (MARIAN)ANDERSON

critic .... HALE, AYRES

dancer of fame
.... (MARTHA)GRAHAM

dinosaur .... BRONTOSAURUS

diplomat .... HARRIMAN,
GIBSON, BOHLEN, DULLES,
GREW, LODGE, KISSINGER

dog .... ALCO

dramatist .... HART, BARRY,
ODETS, CROUSE, WILLIAMS

driest state .... NEVADA

duck .... BUFFLEHEAD

editor .... BOK, LUCE,
MENCKEN, WALLACE, DANA,
SMITH, GREELY, DAVIS,
PARKER, MICHAELS

educator .... CONANT, FISK,
NEILSON, ELIOT, KIRK, HUME,
HUTCHINS, MANN,
WASHINGTON

elk .... WAPITI

evangelist .... GRAHAM

evergreen .... FIR, PINE

explorer .... ELLSWORTH,
BYRD, PEARY, FREMONT,
LEWIS, CLARK, CARSON

fashion designer .... STARR,
CHARLES

feminist .... CATT, PAUL,
STONE, STANTON

financier ...... ASTOR, BARUCH,
MORGAN, GOULD, LAWSON

finch .... JUNCO, SISKIN

flag .... OLD GLORY

flag maker .... ROSS

flycatcher .... PHOEBE

fowl .... WYANDOTTE

frontier scout .... HICKOK

frontiersman .... BOONE,
CARSON, CROCKETT

fur merchant .... ASTOR

game .... GOLF, BASEBALL,
FOOTBALL, POKER,
(ICE)HOCKEY, TENNIS,
BASKETBALL

general ...... LEE, GRANT, ORD,
SHERMAN, BRADLEY,
BURNSIDE, MACARTHUR,
STILLWELL, EISENHOWER, OTIS,
RENO, SCOTT, POPE, BUELL,
LEMAY, MEADE, SCHWARZKOPF

general of the army
.... PERSHING, MACARTHUR,
EISENHOWER

geologist .... DANA

girl of 1890's .... GIBSON

grapes .... NIAGARA

"Great Communicator"
.... (RONALD)REAGAN

"Great Emancipator"
.... (ABRAHAM)LINCOLN

Great White Father
.... PRESIDENT

guitarist .... GUTHRIE

hake .... LING

historian ...... BAILEY, HYMAN,
ROBINSON, SCHLESINGER

horse .... PINTO, BRONCO,
MUSTANG

horticulturist .... BURBANK
hospital ship .... MERCY, COMFORT
humorist .... COBB, NYE, NASH, ROGERS, LARDNER, ADE, TWAIN, BENCHLEY
illustrator ..... FLAGG, NEWELL, ROCKWELL
imaginary town .... PODUNK
Indian .... REE, HUPA, HOH, YUMA, TEWA, KOSO, CREE, NOZI, SERI, HOPI, UTE, PIMA, COOS, SIOUX, OTOE, CROW, POMO, MIAMI, KIOWA, APACHE, SENECA, PECOS, LENAPE, BILOXI, MAKAH, OSAGE, ARIKARA, UINTA, LUMMI, MANDAN, KANSA, SANTEE, PAWNEE, KUSAN, CADDO, SALINA, MODOC, LIPAN, MAIDU, MOQUI, TETON, CHINOOK
and African-American descent ..... SAMBO, GRIFF(E)
ax .... TOMAHAWK
baby .... PAPOOSE
beads .... WAMPUM
dwelling .... TEPEE, LODGE, WIGWAM
greeting .... NETOP
grunt .... UGH
language .... NA-DENE
peace offering .... PIPE
pipe .... CALUMET
pony .... PINTO, CAYUSE
trophy .... SCALP
woman's husband .... SQUAWMAN
insurance capital .... HARTFORD
inventor .... EDISON, HOWE, OTIS, MORSE, FULTON, WHITNEY
isthmus .... PANAMA
ivy .... WOODVINE
Japanese .... NISEI, ISSEI, KIBEI
journalist .... DANA, REID, BIGELOW, BROWN, GUNTHER
jurist .... TANEY, MARSHALL, COOLEY, PAINE, MOORE, TAFT, LANDIS, CARDOZO
jute .... MALLOW
Kennel Club .... AKC
keno .... BINGO, LOTTO
larch .... TAMARACK
lawyer .... PAINE, DARROW
leopard .... JAGUAR
lexicographer .... WEBSTER
light wood .... BALSA
lion .... PUMA, COUGAR
lizard .... ANOLE, ANOLI, BASILISK
lynx .... BOBCAT
mammal ...... OTTER, OPOSSUM
Marine .... GYRENE, LEATHERNECK
Marines' slogan .... ALWAYS FAITHFUL
Lat. .... SEMPER FIDELIS
Mexican name for .... GRINGO
monetary unit .... DOLLAR
money market .... WALL STREET
monkey .... CAPUCHIN, TITI, TEETEE, SAPAJOU
national military cemetery .... ARLINGTON
national military park .... SHILOH
naturalist .... MUIR, BAIRD, AUDUBON, SETON, ANDREWS
nature writer .... BEEBE
naval historian .... MAHAN
Navy enlisted man .... BLUEJACKET
Navy gripe session .... MAST
newspaper, oldest .... COURANT
newspaper publisher .... FIELDS, HEARST, SCRIPPS
night hawk .... PISK
nightshade .... POKEHEED, HENBANE, BELLADONNA
novelist .... FAULKNER, FERBER, STEELE, BALDWIN
nuclear physicist .... TELLER
nutmeg .... CALABASH
"Old Fox" .... (GEORGE)WASHINGTON
"Old Hickory" .... (ANDREW)JACKSON
"Old Rough and Ready" .... (ZACHARY)TAYLOR
operatic singer .... ALDA, FARRAR, STEVENS, PRICE, CALLAS
orator .... OTIS, BRYAN, HENRY
painter ...... SARGENT, BENTON, INNESS, CURRY, LUKS, RYDER, BELLOWS, HOMER, SLOAN, PETERS
painter of animals .... SETON
painter of birds ...... AUDUBON
paper money ...... GREENBACK, LONG GREEN
patriot .... REVERE, ROSS, HALE, HENRY, OTIS, ALLEN, PAINE
patron saint, humorously .... TAMMANY
philanthropist .... RIIS, FORD, CARNEGIE, BARTON, CHANNING, HEARST, ROCKEFELLER
philosopher .... DURANT
physicist .... TESLA, LAWRENCE, VAN ALLEN
pianist .... DUCHIN, CLIBURN, LEVANT
pioneer .... BOONE
pirate .... (CAPTAIN)KIDD
playwright .... SAROYAN, ODETS, MILLER, COWARD, ASCH, KAUFMAN, WILLIAMS
plover .... KILLDEER
poet .... POE, BENET, ELIOT, TATE, SANDBURG, AUDEN, NASH, FROST, LINDSAY, LANIER, GUEST, WHITTIER
poetess .... MILLAY, MOORE, STEIN, LOWELL
political scientist .... NEUSTADT, ROSSITER, MACGREGOR
portraitist .... PEALE, STUART
president .... BUSH, FORD, POLK, TAFT, ADAMS, GRANT, HAYES, NIXON, TYLER, ARTHUR, CARTER, HOOVER, MONROE, PIERCE, REAGAN, TAYLOR, TRUMAN, WILSON, CLINTON, HARDING, JACKSON, JOHNSON, KENNEDY, LINCOLN, MADISON, BUCHANAN, COOLIDGE, FILLMORE, GARFIELD, HARRISON, MCKINLEY, VAN BUREN, CLEVELAND, JEFFERSON, ROOSEVELT, EISENHOWER, WASHINGTON
president's wife .... FIRST LADY
primitive painter .... GRANDMA MOSES
professor of drama ..... BAKER
psychologist .... WATSON
publisher .... HEARST, OCHS, FIELDS, SCRIPPS, NEWHOUSE, MCCORMICK, WEIL, MILLER, HOWARD, BARR, LUCE, KNIGHT, COWLES, GANNETT
quail .... COLIN
railroad magnate .... REA, HARRIMAN
Red Cross organizer .... BARTON
reformer .... RIIS
Revolution soldier .... BUCKSKIN
river .... MISSISSIPPI, TENNESSEE, SACRAMENTO, OHIO, RAPIDAN, HUDSON, ALABAMA, COLORADO,

WABASH, MISSOURI, PEARL,
THAMES, COLUMBIA
rodent .... RABBIT, BEAVER,
SQUIRREL
sculptor ..... BORGLUM, SMITH,
CALDER, PROCTOR
shipyard .... GROTON
shrub .... CHICO, WAHOO
singer .... SINATRA, CLARK,
DURBIN, PRESLEY, PAGE,
MATHIS, JACKSON, DAVIS,
MARTIN, HOUSTON, NELSON,
ROGERS, GARLAND, TUCKER,
LANZA, CROSBY, EDDY, PRIDE,
STREISAND, KITT, BENNETT,
MANDRELL, LYNN, RICH,
RICHIE, ROSS, HORNE,
FRANCIS, BAEZ, NEWTON,
WILLIAMS
soldier .... GI, SAMMY,
YANKEE, DOGFACE, SAD SACK,
DOUGHBOY
songbird .... GREENLET
songwriter .... PORTER,
BERLIN, RODGERS
soprano .... CALLAS, PONS,
STEBER, ALDA, SILLS, MUNSEL,
STEVENS
statesman .... JAY, RUSK,
BAKER, LODGE, LOGAN,
VANCE, BARUCH, BENTON,
BLAINE, DULLES, ROGERS,
CLAY, ACHESON, KISSINGER,
DAVIS, STIMSON, STEVENSON
suffragist .... CATT
surgeon .... MAYO, PARRAN
thrush .... WAGTAIL
tree .... CALABASH, MAPLE,
OAK, REDWOOD, PINE,
SYCAMORE, ELM, ASH, FIR,
SEQUOIA, WALNUT,
BUTTONWOOD
vice-president .... BURR, BUSH,
FORD, GORE, KING, ADAMS,
AGNEW, DAWES, NIXON,
TYLER, ARTHUR, COLFAX,
CURTIS, DALLAS, GARNER,
HAMLIN, HOBART, MORTON,
QUAYLE, TRUMAN, WILSON,
BARKLEY, CALHOUN, CLINTON,
JOHNSON, MONDALE,
SHERMAN, WALLACE,
WHEELER, COOLIDGE,
FILLMORE, HUMPHREY,
MARSHALL, TOMPKINS, VAN
BUREN, FAIRBANKS,
HENDRICKS, JEFFERSON,
ROOSEVELT, STEVENSON,
ROCKEFELLER, BRECKENRIDGE
volcano .... SHASTA, SAINT
HELENS, LASSEN

weather phenomenon
.... SMOG, SMAZE, POGONIP
widgeon .... BALDPATE
wild sheep .... ARGALI,
BIGHORN
winter fog .... POGONIP
wolf .... COYOTE
woman governor, first
.... ROSS
writer in Yiddish .... ASCH
writer of fables .... ADE
writer of the national anthem
.... KEY
yew .... HEMLOCK
Americans, in Key's words
.... THE FREE
Amerind .... OTOE, REDSKIN,
CREE, INDIAN, ESKIMO
symbol .... XAT
amethyst .... VIOLET, QUARTZ,
PURPLE, CORUNDUM
amethystine .... ORCHID, LILAC,
MAGENTA, MAUVE, LAVENDER
amiable .... KIND, CORDIAL,
GENIAL, AFFABLE, LOVABLE,
GRACIOUS
amianthus .... ASBESTOS
amicable .... PEACEFUL,
FRIENDLY, HARMONIOUS
amice .... CAPE, COWL, HOOD,
ALMUCE, TIPPET
amicus curiae ...... JURAT, JUDGE,
BARRISTER, LAWYER,
OMBUDSMAN
slang .... MOUTHPIECE
amid(st) .... AMONG(ST), MIDST,
TWIXT, BETWEEN
amidine .... STARCH
Amiens river .... SOMME
amigo .... CHUM, BUDDY, FRIEND,
COMRADE
British .... MATE
French .... CAMARADE
amino acid .... PROTEIN,
PROLIN(E), PEPTIDE, LACTAM,
LYSINE, LEUCINE
amiss .... AWRY, FAULTY, ASKEW,
WRONG, ERRANT, ASTRAY,
MISPLACED
slang .... COCKEYED
amity ...... GOODWILL, HARMONY,
AFFINITY, FRIENDSHIP
Amman is capital of .... JORDAN
Ammon .... ZEUS, JUPITER
ammonia .... LOX, ETHER,
COOLANT, FERTILIZER
compound .... AMIN(E),
AMIDE, DIAMINE
in water solution
.... HARTSHORN
ammoniac .... CEMENT, GUM

RESIN, STIMULANT
ammunition .... MEANS, BULLETS,
GUNPOWDER, SHELLS,
GRENADES, POWDER AND
SHOT
box .... CANISTER
carrier .... CAISSON
depot .... ARMORY, ARSENAL,
MAGAZINE
slang .... AMMO
amnesia .... FUGUE, MEMORY-GAP
slang .... BLACKOUT
amnesty .... STAY, PARDON,
IMMUNITY, REPRIEVE,
REMISSION
amnion .... MEMBRANE
of eardrum .... TYMPANUM
amoeba .... MOLD, GERM,
FUNGUS, MICROBE,
PROTOZOON
amok .... AMUCK, KILLER,
VIOLENT, BERSERK, RABID,
FRENZIED
slang .... HOG-WILD
amole .... ROOT, SOAP, AGAVE
among .... IN, WITH, MID(ST),
AMID(ST), BETWIXT
amontillado .... SHERRY
amor .... LOVE, EROS
amoretto .... CUPID
amorous .... LOVING, EROTIC,
SPOONY, PASSIONATE
look .... OGLE, LEER
amorphous .... FORMLESS,
VAGUE, SHAPELESS
mass .... GLOB
amort .... LIFELESS, SPIRITLESS
Amos' partner .... ANDY
amount caught ...... HAUL, CATCH
lost by waste ...... DECREMENT
of boastful words
.... MOUTHFUL
of gossip .... EARFUL
of medicine .... DOSE, DOSAGE
of stake in gambling ..... MISE
offered at auction .... BID
possessed .... RATAL
produced .... OUTPUT
used .... CONSUMPTION
amour propre .... SELF-LOVE,
SELF-ESTEEM, SELF-RESPECT
amperage .... WATTAGE
ampere .... WEBER
ampersand .... AND
amphetamine .... METHEDRINE
amphibian .... FROG, TOAD,
NEWT, BATRACHIA, ANURAN,
SALAMANDER
order .... BUFO, ANURAN
tailed .... CAUDATE
tank .... ALLIGATOR

tree .... HYLA
young .... TADPOLE
amphibious carnivore ...... MINK,
SEAL, OTTER
vehicle .... DUCK, AMTRAC
amphibole .... ASBESTOS,
MINERAL, EDENITE, URALITE,
TREMOLITE
Amphion's father .... ZEUS
mother .... ANTIOPE
stone-walled city .... THEBES
wife .... NIOBE
amphioxus .... LANCELET
amphipod .... SHRIMP, SAND
FLEA, CRUSTACEAN
amphitheater ...... ARENA, BOWL,
GALLERY, GRANDSTAND
entrance .... VOMITORY
natural .... CIRQUE
amphora .... JAR, URN, VASE
ample .... FULL, MANY, MUCH,
ROOMY, ENOUGH, PLENTY,
ABUNDANT, COPIOUS,
SPACIOUS
poetic .... ENOW
amplification factor .... MU
amplify .... WIDEN, EXPAND,
ENLARGE, MAGNIFY, INCREASE
amplifying device .... LASER,
MASER
amply fleshed .... OBESE
amputate .... LOP, CUT OFF,
CHOP, PRUNE, SEVER
Amu Darya .... OXUS
amuck .... WILD, BERSERK,
FRANTIC, BARESARK
amulet .... CHARM, TALISMAN,
PERIAPT
Philippine ..... ANTING-ANTING
Amundsen, explorer ...... ROALD
Amun-Re's wife .... MUT
Amur tributary .... ARGUN,
USSURI, SUNGARI
amuse .... HUMOR, REGALE,
DIVERT, DELIGHT, BEGUILE,
ENTERTAIN
amusement .... FUN, GAME,
SPORT, DIVERSION
amusing .... FUNNY, DROLL,
RISIBLE, HUMOROUS
moment during a tragedy
.... COMIC-RELIEF
amygdala .... ALMOND, TONSIL
Amy's sister .... JO, MEG, BETH
an .... ONE, PER, EACH, ANYONE
ana .... DATA, MEMOIR, BITS,
ANECDOTES, COLLECTION
anabaena .... ALGA
anaconda .... BOA, SNAKE,
CONSTRICTOR
anadem .... GARLAND, WREATH

anadromous .... SEA-RUNNING
an(a)esthetic .... GAS, OPIATE,
DULLING, NUMBING,
SEDATIVE, ANALGESIC
drug .... ETHER, COCAINE,
PROCAINE
anagram .... REBUS, RIDDLE,
CHARADE, WORDPLAY,
LOGOGRIPH
game .... LOGOMACHY
anal .... TRIM, RECTAL, KOSHER,
PEDANTIC
disorder .... FISSURE,
HEMORRHOIDS
analgesic .... OPIATE, ANODYNE,
PAIN-KILLER
common .... ASPIRIN
narcotic .... CODEINE,
MORPHINE
analogous .... MATCHING,
SIMILAR, PARALLEL
analogy .... SIMILE, LIKENESS,
METAPHOR, COMPARISON
analysis .... TEST, STUDY, REVIEW,
WRITE-UP, DEDUCTION
analyst .... TESTER, EXAMINER
clinical .... PSYCHIATRIST
gold/ore .... ASSAYER
analyze .... ASSAY, STUDY,
DEDUCE, SIFT, DISSECT,
EXAMINE, CLASSIFY, ASSORT,
THEORIZE
grammatically .... PARSE,
CONJUGATE
anamnesis .... REMEMBRANCE
Ananias .... LIAR
wife of .... SAPPHIRA
anarchic .... LAWLESS, UNRULY
anarchist .... REBEL, RADICAL,
AGITATOR, OUTLAW,
TERRORIST, NIHILIST,
EXTREMIST
slang .... RED
anarchy .... CHAOS, TURMOIL,
VIOLENCE, DISORDER
anasarca .... EDEMA, DROPSY
anathema .... HEX, CURSE,
DECRIAL, DAMNATION
anathematize .... BAN, CUSS,
HEX, DAMN, (AC)CURSE,
BLAST, REVILE, BLASPHEME
Anatole, novelist .... FRANCE
Anatolia .... ASIA MINOR
Anatolian capital .... ANKARA
goddess .... MA
native .... HITTITE
rug .... KURDISTAN
anatomical model, of an
.... CLASTIC
model of human body
.... MANIKIN

network .... RETE
walls .... SEPTA
anatomy .... BODY, SCIENCE,
PHYSIQUE, SKELETON,
STRUCTURE
dealing with muscles
.... MYOLOGY
microscopic study of cells
.... CYTOLOGY
microspic study of tissues
.... HISTOLOGY
of animals .... ZOOTOMY
of organisms .... BIOLOGY
of regions .... TOPOLOGY
ancestor ...... ROOT, SIRE, ELDER,
FAMILY, FOREBEAR, STOCK,
FOREFATHER
Irish .... MIL, MILED
ancestral .... AVAL, AVITAL,
MATERNAL, PATERNAL,
PARENTAL
spirits .... LARES, MANES
ancestry .... KIN, FAMILY,
DESCENT, LINEAGE, KINDRED,
PEDIGREE
common .... CONSANGUINITY
Anchises' son .... (A)ENEAS
anchor .... CAT, FIX, TIE, BIND,
MOOR, REST, KEDGE, HOOK,
BERTH, FASTEN
chain .... CABLE
fluke .... BILL
heaviest of a ship ...... BOWER
lift .... CAT, WEIGH
lifting device .... CAPSTAN,
WINDLASS
man/person .... MC, EMCEE,
ENDMAN, COMMENTATOR
part .... ARM, RING, PALM,
STOCK, FLUKE, CROWN, SHANK
place of .... CATHEAD
slightly raised .... ATRIP
small .... KEDGE, KILLICK,
KILLOCK, GRAPNEL
tackle .... CAT
anchorage .... FEE, RADE,
HARBOR, MARINA, DOCKAGE,
(ROAD)STEAD, MOORAGE
anchored .... FIXED, STUCK, TIED,
HELD, RIVETED, CHAINED,
FASTENED
anchorite .... HERMIT, ABSTAINER,
RECLUSE, ASCETIC, ANCHORET
opposed to .... C(O)ENOBITE
anchovy .... SPRAT, HERRING
pear .... MANGO
sauce .... ALEC
anchusa .... ALKANET, BUGLOSS
ancient ...... ELD, AGED, OLD(EN),
ANTIQUE, ARCHAIC,
PRIMEVAL, HOARY, DISTANT

PAST

Alexandrian writer .... ORIGEN

alphabetical character

.... RUNE

Briton .... CELT, PICT

Chinese .... SERES

city .... EUS, TYRE, NICAEA,

   CORINTH, THEBES, NINEVEH

country .... ARAM, ELAM,

   GAUL, EOLIS, MEDEA

court .... EYRE, LEET

drink .... MORAT

Egyptian king .... PHARAOH,

   RAMESES

Egyptian scrolls .... PAPYRI

Greek invader .... DORIAN

language .... LATIN, GREEK,

   SANSKRIT

lyre .... ASOR

manuscript .... CODEX

musical instrument ...... ASOR,

   LUTE, REBEC, CITHARA

Persian .... MEDE

priests .... MAGI

sword .... ESTOC

tax .... CRO

temple .... NAOS

times .... YORE

warship ..... GALLEON, BIREME,

   GALLEY, LONG SHIP

weapon ...... MACE, DAG, PIKE,

   SLING, SPEAR, HALBERD,

   ARQUEBUS

wicked city .... SODOM,

   BABYLON, GOMORRAH

Ancient Mariner's victim

.... ALBATROSS

ancillary .... AID, HELPER,

   SERVANT, AUXILIARY,

   SUBORDINATE

ancon .... ELBOW, CONSOLE

and ...... TOO, PLUS, AS WELL AS,

   MOREOVER, ALSO,

   AMPERSAND

not .... NOR

others .... ET AL

so on/so forth .... USW,

   ETC(ETERA)

Andalusian .... SPANISH,

   LEGHORN, SPANIARD

port .... CADIZ

province .... JAEN

Andean .... PAMPERO

peak, 21,201 ft. .... ILLIMANI

Andersen, Christian .... HANS

Anderson, actress .... LONI

singer .... MARIAN

writer .... MAXWELL,

   SHERWOOD

Andes .... MOUNTAIN

camel-like animal ..... LLAMA,

ALPACA, VICUNA, GUANACO

deer .... PUDU

grass .... ICHU

mountain .... HUILA, MISTI,

   POTOSI, SORATA, COTOPAXI,

   HUASCARAN, ILLAMPU,

   CHIMBORAZO

peak .... ACONCAGUA

plain .... LLANO, PARAMO

plateau .... PUNA

rodent .... CHINCHILLA

ruminant ..... LLAMA, ALPACA,

   GUANACO

volcano .... MISTI, OMATE,

   CHIMBORAZO

wind .... PAMPERO

andiron .... (FIRE)DOG, HESSIAN

Andre, John, for example

.... SPY

Andress, actress .... URSULA

Andrew .... APOSTLE

Andrews, _____ ...... DANA, JULIE

androgen ...... HORMONE, STEROID

Andromache's husband

.... HECTOR

Andromeda's husband

.... PERSEUS

Andy .... HARDY, DEVINE,

   GRIFFITH, WILLIAMS

cartoon character .... GUMP

Gump's wife .... MIN

partner of .... AMOS

anecdotage .... ANA, TALES

anecdotes, expert in

.... RACONTEUR

anele .... OIL, ANOINT

anemia .... CHLOROSIS

symptom of .... CHILL,

   FATIGUE, FAINTING,

   HEADACHE, DIZZINESS

type of .... APLASTIC,

   PERNICIOUS, HEMOLYTIC

anemic .... WAN, PALE, PALLOR,

   COLORLESS, BILIOUS,

   BLOODLESS

anemone .... PLANT, POLYP,

   ANIMAL, SNOWDROP, ACTINIA,

   WINDFLOWER

anent .... INRE, ABOUT,

   REGARDING, CONCERNING

aneroid .... BAROMETER

anes .... ONCE

anesthesia .... NUMBNESS,

   UNFEELING

type of .... LOCAL, DENTAL,

   SPINAL, GENERAL

anet .... DILL(SEED)

anew .... AGAIN, AFRESH, ONCE

   MORE

do .... REPEAT, RESUME

angel .... CHERUB, PATRON, SERAF,

SPIRIT, SERAPH(IM),

   MESSENGER

fallen .... LUCIFER

gold-digger's .... SUGAR

   DADDY

loyal .... MICHAEL

of bottomless pit

.... APOLLYON

of Broadway, etc. .... SUGAR

   DADDY, FINANCIER

of death ...... AZRAEL, DANITE,

   SAMUEL

of music .... ISRAFIL

rebel .... AZAZEL, LUCIFER

Angeli, actress .... PIER

angelic .... SAINTLY, CHERUBIC

messenger .... GABRIEL

Angelica .... ARCHANGEL

angels collectively .... HIERARCHY

angelus .... BELL, PRAYER,

   VESPER, DEVOTION

anger .... IRE, IRK, FURY, RILE,

   ANNOY, WRATH, DANDER,

   ENRAGE, INCENSE

fit of .... RAGE, TIFF, PIQUE,

   CHOLER, TEMPER, TANTRUM

give vent to .... FUME, RAGE

angina .... CROUP

type of .... PECTORIS,

   VINCENT'S, ABDOMINAL

angioma .... TUMOR

Angkor relics .... RUINS, TEMPLES

temple ruins .... BAYON

Wat/Vat .... TEMPLE

angle .... BEND, FISH, PLOT,

   SLANT, POINT, TRICK, ANCON,

   CORNER, RADIAN, ASPECT,

   SCHEME, INTRIGUE

branch .... AXIL

for .... WOO, HUNT, SEEK

formed by aircraft .... YAW

in geology .... HADE

leafstalk .... AXIL

measuring device

.... GONIOMETER

off .... SWERVE

outside .... CANT

pipe .... TEE

trench .... ZIG

with no .... AGONIC

angler ...... NETTER, FISHER(MAN),

   TROLLER, SCHEMER,

   TRICKSTER

angler's basket .... CREEL

delight .... BITE, STRIKE

need .... ROD, BAIT, HOOK,

   LINE, CREEL, LICENSE

Angleterre .... LACE

Anglian kingdom .... DEIRA

Anglican anthem .... AGNUS DEI

Anglo-French battle site
.... CRECY
Anglo-Indian empire founder
.... CLIVE
kingdom .... KENT
man, rich ...... NAWAB, NABOB
nurse .... AMAH, AYAH
title of address .... BABU
troop .... RESSALA
woman, rich .... BEGUM
Anglo-Saxon .... ENGLISH
armor .... HAUBERK
assembly .... GEMOT(E)
coin .... ORA, SCEAT
consonant .... ETH, EDH
court .... GEMOT(E)
folk hero .... BEOWULF
freeman .... THANE
hunter's attendant .... GILLY,
GILLIE
king .... EDGAR
king's council .... WITAN
kingdom .... ESSEX, MERCIA
lord's attendant .... THANE,
THEGN
noble/prince .... ATHELING
slave .... ESNE
warrior .... THANE, THEGN
Angola capital .... LUANDA
port .... LOBITO, LUANDA
Angora ...... CAT, GOAT, ANKARA,
RABBIT
goat .... CHAMAL
goat fabric .... MOHAIR
angostura .... BARK, TONIC,
FLAVOR, BOLIVAR
angry .... HOT, MAD, SORE,
CROSS, FIERY, IRATE, RILED,
RAGING, WROTH, PIQUED,
STORMY, INCENSED,
INDIGNANT
creature .... AMOK, AMUCK,
BERSERK, WET HEN, SOREHEAD
expression .... SNORT
look .... GLARE, SCOWL,
GLOWER
anguillid .... EEL
anguine .... SNAKELIKE
anguish .... WOE, PAIN, DOLOR,
AGONY, DISTRESS, SORROW,
MISERY, SADNESS, PANG,
GRIEF, DESPAIR, TORMENT,
HEARTACHE
angular .... BONY, GAUNT,
CORNERED
opposite of .... AGONIC
anhydrous .... DRY, PARCHED
ani .... CUCKOO
anil .... SHRUB, INDIGO
anile .... WEAK, CRONE, INFIRM
aniline, dye/red .... MAGENTA,

FUCHSIN
anima .... SOUL, PRINCIPLE
animadversion .... CRITICISM,
NITPICKING
animal .... BEAST, BESTIAL,
BRUTE, GROSS, SENSUAL,
EROTIC, UNCOUTH, CREATURE,
SAVAGE, LUSTFUL
anatomy .... ZOOTOMY
ant-eating .... ECHIDNA,
ANTBEAR, AARDVARK,
PANGOLIN, TAMANDUA
antlered .... ELK, STAG,
CARIBOU, MOOSE, (REIN)DEER
aquatic .... SEAL, MINK,
OTTER, SEACOW, WHALE,
WALRUS
arboreal ..... AI, UNAU, KOALA,
SLOTH, TARSIER, SQUIRREL
armor .... PLATE, SHELL,
ARMATURE, CARAPACE
"armored" .... ARMADILLO
badgerlike .... RATEL
baggage carrier .... SUMPTER
body .... SOMA
bone-like covering
.... CARAPACE
born prematurely .... SLINK
breast .... THORAX, BRISKET
bristly .... HOG, BOAR,
PORCUPINE
burrowing .... MOLE, BROCK,
BADGER, MARMOT, GOPHER,
ARMADILLO, RATEL, WOMBAT,
GROUNDHOG
butting .... GOAT, SHEEP
castrated .... CAPON, OX, STAG,
STEER, GELDING, BARROW
cat family .... FELID, FELINE
clumsy .... JUMBO
coat .... FUR, HAIR, PELT,
WOOL, PELAGE
collection .... ZOO, MENAGERIE
coop .... HUTCH
dam builder .... OTTER
decay poison .... PTOMAIN(E)
dial. .... CRITTER
disease .... GID, ROT,
ANTHRAX, STAGGERS, RABIES,
GLANDERS, HEAVES,
RINDERPEST
doctor .... VET(ERINARIAN)
enclosure .... CAGE, PEN,
CORRAL
fat .... LARD, SUET, GREASE,
TALLOW
fierce .... OUTLAW
flying .... BAT, LEMUR
food .... FODDER, FORAGE
footless .... APOD
footprint .... PUG

game-killer .... VERMIN
giraffe-like .... OKAPI
handler .... TAMER, TRAINER
hibernating .... BEAR,
WOODCHUCK
hide .... FELL, PELT
homing instinct
.... ORIENTATION
hornless .... POLLARD
humped .... ZEBU, BISON,
CAMEL, DROMEDARY
imaginary .... SNARK
inferior: sl. .... PLUG
innards .... HA(R)SLET
large .... RHINO, BEHEMOTH,
ELEPHANT, PACHYDERM
lean, scrawny .... SCRAG
leopard-like .... CHEETAH
life in a region .... FAUNA
life, a study of .... ZOOLOGY
like an .... THEROID
living inside another
.... ENTEZOON
magnetism .... HYPNOTISM,
MESMERISM
male .... BUCK, BULL, JACK
marsupial .... KOALA, TAIT,
WOMBAT, KANGAROO,
(O)POSSUM, PHALANGER
microscopic .... ROTIFER
mixed breed .... MULE,
HYBRID, MONGREL
mouth opening .... RICTUS
multi-celled .... METAZOA
multi-segmented
.... CENTIPEDE
mythical ..... GRIFFIN, GRIFFON
neck hair .... MANE
"necklace" .... TORQUES
nipple .... DUG
noise .... ROAR, BARK, MEW,
GROWL, GRUNT, HOWL, SNORT,
BELLOW, HISS, OINK, WHINE,
YELP, SQUEAK, SQUEAL
of an .... ZOOID
of mixed parentage
.... HYBRID, MONGREL
one-celled .... MONAD, PROTIS,
PROTOZOAN, STENTOR,
RHIZOPOD
one-horned .... BADAK,
UNICORN, RHINO(CEROS)
pack .... SUMPTER
passage/shelter .... BURROW,
TUNNEL
pen .... STY, HUTCH, CORRAL
Peruvian .... LLAMA, ALPACA
pet .... CAT, DOG, CADE,
COSSET, POODLE
pictures painter ..... LANDSEER
plant life .... BIOS, BIOTA

pound .... PINFOLD
scent .... FOIL
sea .... ORC
sexual excitement .... RUT,
HEAT, ESTRUS
skin ..... FUR, FELL, HIDE, PELT
skin dealer .... FELLMONGER
skin disease .... MANGE
simplest form of
.... AM(O)EBA
snouted .... COATI, TAPIR
spiny .... PORCUPINE
spirits .... FRISKINESS
spot on face of .... BLAZE
spotted .... PIEBALD,
DAPPLE(D)
starch .... GLYCOGEN
stomach .... MAW, CRAW
stories, collection of
.... BESTIARY
striped .... TIGER, ZEBRA,
QUAGGA
tanned hide of .... CROP
ten-footed .... DECAPOD
thigh .... HAM
trail .... PUG, FOIL, SLOT, SPUR,
SPOOR
trainer .... LEHR (LEW)
trap .... DEADFALL
tusked .... WALRUS, WARTHOG,
ELEPHANT
uncontrollable .... OUTLAW
vital organs .... PLUCK
weasel family .... PEKAN
web-footed .... BEAVER,
DUCKBILL, PLATYPUS
with no nervous system
.... ACRITA
with pouch for young
.... KOALA, KANGA(ROO)
worship .... DEMONISM
young .... CUB, CALF, FOAL,
JOEY, BUNNY, COLT, HEIFER,
PIGLET, BULLOCK
animalcule .... ROTIFER
animals born at one time
.... FALL, LITTER
brood of young .... TEAM
carrying their young
.... MARSUPIAL
collectively .... ZOOLOGY
disease from .... ZOONOSIS
driven together .... HERD,
COFFLE
male of some ...... BULL, TOM,
BOAR, BUCK, STAG
molt of some .... EXUVIAE
painter of .... SETON, BONHEUR
rearing/culture of
.... HUSBANDRY
tied together .... COFFLE

animate .... CHEER, VIVIFY,
INSPIRE, (EN)LIVEN, QUICKEN,
ENERGIZE, STIMULATE
animated .... CARTOON,
CARICATURE
producer .... LANTZ, DISNEY
bird .... WOODPECKER
character ...... MAGOO, POPEYE
dog .... PLUTO
duck .... DONALD
person .... GRIG
animating principle .... SOUL
animation ...... PEP, LIFE, VERVE,
BRIO, ELAN, ENERGY, SPIRIT,
VITALITY, VIVACITY
anime .... COPAL, RESIN
animist .... IDEALIST
animosity .... HATE, HATRED,
FEUD, ENMITY, GRUDGE,
SPITE, RANCOR, DISLIKE,
ANIMUS, ILL WILL, HOSTILITY
animus .... MIND, GRUDGE,
PASSION, PURPOSE, SPIRIT,
VENDETTA
anion, opposite of .... CATION
anise .... ANET, FLAVOR,
DILL(SEED)
anisette .... CORDIAL, LIQUEUR
Ankara .... ANGORA
is capital of .... TURKEY,
ANATOLIA
ankh .... CRUX, CROSS, ANSATA
ankle .... CUIT, JOINT, TARSI,
TARSUS
bone ...... TALUS, ASTRAGALUS
deep .... SHALLOW
iron .... BASIL
joint protuberance
.... MALLEOLUS
pertaining to .... TARSAL,
TALARIC
anklet ...... SOCK, CHAIN, BANGLE,
FETTER
ankyloglossia .... TONGUE-TIE
anlace .... DAGGER
anlage .... PROTON
Ann, actress .... SOTHERN,
SHERIDAN
and Andy .... RAGDOLLS
anna .... COIN
¼ of .... PICE
16 of them .... RUPEE
Annabel Lee author .... POE
annalist .... RECORDER
annals .... RECORD, HISTORY,
ARCHIVES, CHRONICLES
Annamese .... MONGOL(IAN)
capital .... HUE
coin .... QUAN
measure .... GON, MAU, SAO,
TAO

Annapolis, former name
.... ANNE ARUNDEL
institution .... USNA, ACADEMY
student .... CADET,
MIDSHIPMAN
annatto .... DYE
anneal .... BAKE, FIRE, FUSE,
GLAZE, TEMPER
annealing oven .... KILN, LEER
annelid .... WORM, LEECH,
CHAETOPOD
annex .... ELL, WING, CONNECT,
ATTACH(MENT)
Annie Oakley .... PASS,
(FREE)TICKET
Annie's anxieties .... WHIMWHAM
annihilate .... END, KILL, SLAY,
ERASE, PURGE, CANCEL,
ABOLISH, ERADICATE,
DESTROY, WIPE OUT,
DEMOLISH
anniversary, 25th .... SILVER
50th .... GOLDEN
100th .... CENTENNIAL
anno _____ .... MUNDI, REGNI,
DOMINI
annotate .... EDIT, GLOSS,
REVIEW, CRITIQUE
annotation .... NOTE, RECORD,
APOSTIL, COMMENT,
FOOTNOTE, GLOSSARY,
REFERENCE
announce .... STATE, HERALD,
REPORT, AFFIRM, NOTIFY,
DECLARE, PROCLAIM
announcement .... AD, BLURB,
OBIT(UARY), NOTICE,
BULLETIN
printed .... CARD
annoy .... IRK, TRY, VEX, FASH,
GRATE, TEASE, MOLEST,
PESTER, DISTURB, (BE)DEVIL,
PROVOKE
annoyance .... PEST, NUISANCE,
TROUBLE, VEXATION,
TAILTWISTER
expression of .... BAH, OH MY,
SCOWL, GLOWER, GRIMACE
plane-ride .... BUMP,
TURBULENCE
annoyed .... RILED, PEEVED,
IRRITATED
annoyer .... PEST, HECKLER,
HARASSER
camp .... GNAT, MOSQUITO
annoyingly urgent
.... IMPORTUNATE
annual .... RECORD, YEARLY,
JOURNAL, ETESIAN,
YEARBOOK, PERIODICAL
bean .... URD

headache of a sort .... INCOME TAX
income .... RENTES
movie award .... OSCAR
plant .... OKRA
prize .... NOBEL, PULITZER
produce .... CROP
TV award .... EMMY
annually ...... YEARLY, PER YEAR, SEASONAL
annuity .... RENTE, INCOME, PENSION, SUBSIDY, TONTINE, INSURANCE
annul .... UNDO, VOID, CANCEL, NEGATE, RECALL, REPEAL, NULLIFY, RETRACT, REVOKE, RESCIND, VACATE, WAIVE, INVALIDATE
as a veto .... OVERRIDE
in law .... QUASH
annular .... ROUND, CIRCULAR, RINGLIKE
die .... DOD
annulate .... RINGED
annulet .... CIRCLET, GROMMET
in heraldry .... VAIR, VERT, VIRE, CREST, CORONET
annum .... YEAR
annunciate .... ANNOUNCE
anodyne .... BALM, DRUG, OPIATE, SOOTHER, PACIFIER, SEDATIVE
anoint .... OIL, ANELE, BLESS, ENTHRONE, ENOIL, CONSECRATE
anomalous .... ODD, KINKY, DEVIANT, IMPROPER, ABNORMAL, IRREGULAR
anomaly ...... ODDITY, DEVIATION
anon .... SOON, AGAIN, AFRESH, THENCE, THEREAT, SHORTLY, DIRECTLY, IMMEDIATELY, ANONYMOUS
anonym .... ALIAS, PSEUDONYM
anonymity .... PRIVACY, SECLUSION
anonymous .... UNKNOWN, PRIVATE, NAMELESS, INCOGNITO
anorak .... JACKET
garment like .... PARKA
another .... ELSE, NEW, EXTRA, SPARE, SECOND, OTHER, DIFFERENT, FURTHER, ADDITIONAL
calling .... ALIAS
set of clothes .... CHANGE
time .... ONCE AGAIN
ansate .... HANDLED
anschluss .... UNION
anserine .... STUPID, FOOLISH, GOOSELIKE

answer .... REPLY, RESPONSE, DEFENSE, RESPOND, REBUT(TAL), RIPOSTE, REJOIN(DER)
back .... ECHO, PROVOKE
in kind .... RETORT
insolently .... SWEAR
purpose of .... DO, SERVE, RESOLVE, SATISFY
unfavorable .... REBUFF
answerable .... LIABLE, ACCOUNTABLE, RESPONSIBLE
ant .... ANAY, EMMET, AMAZON, PISMIRE, TERMITE
bear .... AARDVARK
black .... KELEP
combining form .... MYRMECO
cow .... APHID
eater .... MANIS, ECHIDNA, AARDVARK, PANGOLIN, TAMANDUA
genus .... FORMICA
kind of .... SOLDIER
nest .... HILL, FORMICARY
thrush .... PITTA
anta ...... PIER, COLUMN, PILASTER
antacid .... ALKALI, MAGNESIA
Antaeus' father .... POSEIDON
killer .... HERCULES
mother .... GE
antagonism .... ANIMUS, ENMITY, ANTIPATHY, HOSTILITY, OPPOSITION
antagonist .... FOE, RIVAL, OPPONENT, ADVERSARY
antagonistic .... HOSTILE, OPPOSED, UNFRIENDLY
Antarctic ...... SEA, ZONE, OCEAN, CIRCLE, CONTINENT
bird .... PENGUIN
explorer .... BYRD, ROSS, AMUNDSEN
icebreaker .... ATKA
sea .... ROSS, WEDDEL
Antares .... MARS, RED STAR
antbear .... AARDVARK
ante .... PAY, PONY, PRICE, RAISE, STAKE
as prefix .... PRIOR, BEFORE
bellum .... PRE-WAR
chamber .... WAITING ROOM
natal .... PRE-BIRTH
up: sl. .... SWEETEN THE POT
antebrachium .... FOREARM
antecedence .... PRIORITY, PRECEDENCE
antecedent ...... PRIOR, ANCESTOR, PRECEDING
antecedents .... ANCESTRY
antedate .... PRECEDE, PREDATE
antediluvian .... OLD

antelope ...... GOA, BEIRA, NILGAI, SASIN, SAIGA, TAKIN, OTEROP, GAZELLE, BUBALIS, BUBALINE
African .... GNU, KOB, ASSE, KUDU, ORYX, TORA, ELAND, KONZE, ORIBI, ADDAX, BONGO, WANTO, NAGOR, IMPALA, KOODOO, DIKDIK, GEMSBOK, SASSABY, DUIKER(BOK), STEINBOK
American .... BLESBOK, SASSABY
ancient .... PYGARG
female .... DOE
goat .... SEROW, CHAMOIS
Himalayan .... CHIRU, GORAL
like .... BOVID
male .... BUCK
pygmy .... ORIBI
red .... PALLA(H), REEDBOK
sheep-like .... SAIGA
striped .... BONGO, OTEROP
tawny .... ORIBI
young .... KID
antenna .... PALP, AERIAL, FEELER, ANTENNULE
part of .... LEAD IN
anterior .... FRONT, PRIOR, EARLIER, FORWARD, PREVIOUS, PRECEDING
opposite of .... POSTERIOR
anteroom .... LOBBY
anthelion .... HALO, AUREOLE
anthem ..... SONG, MOTET, AGNUS DEI
anther .... STAMEN
anthesis .... BLOOM
anthocyanin .... PIGMENT
anthologist .... COMPILER
anthology .... ANA, POTPOURRI, COLLECTION, COLLECTANEA, COMPILATION
Anthony, ____ .... SUSAN
anthozoan .... CORAL, POLYP, ANEMONE
anthracite .... COAL
pieces/refuse .... CULM
anthrax .... BOIL, PUSTULE, CARBUNCLE
anthropoid .... APE, LAR, GIBBON, MONKEY, SIMIAN, GORILLA, MANLIKE, ORANG(UTAN), CHIMPANZEE, TROGLODYTE
anthropophagi .... CANNIBALS
anthropophagy .... CANNIBALISM
anti .... CON, FOE, CONTRA, AGAINST, HOSTILE, OPPOSED, OPPOSER
knock fuel .... TRIPTANE
knock fuel ingredient .... BROMINE

labor union contract .... YELLOW DOG

social one .... LONER

antiaircraft artillery .... ACK-ACK, POMPOM, TRIPLE-A

cannon .... BOFORS

gunfire .... FLAK, ACK-ACK

missile .... NIKE

target aiming device .... PREDICTOR

antiar .... TREE, UPAS, POISON

antibiotic .... PENICILLIN, STREPTO(MYCIN), AUREOMYCIN, TETRACYCLINE

antibody dissolving bacteria, etc. .... LYSIN(E)

antic .... DIDO, CAPER, CLOWN, COMIC, PRANK, STUNT

anticipate .... HOPE, AWAIT, EXPECT, FORESEE, PRECEDE

anticipating .... PROLEPSIS

anticlimax .... DROP, DESCENT, DECREASE

antidote .... SODA, REMEDY, SERUM, NEUTRALIZER

for acid .... ALKALI

for madness .... CHRYSOLITE

for poison .... TREACLE

Antigone's parent .... JOCASTA, OEDIPUS

sister .... ISMENE

uncle .... CREON

antihemophilic factor .... GLOBULIN

Antilles, ——— .... LESSER, GREATER

island .... CUBA, ARUBA

native .... CARIB(BEAN)

antimacassar .... TIDY

antimalaria remedy .... ATABRIN(E), ATEBRIN, QUININE

antimony ...... REGULUS, STIBIUM

source .... STIBNITE

Antiope's son .... AMPHION

antipasto ...... RELISH, APPETIZER, HORS D'OEUVRE

antipathy .... HATE, ODIUM, SPITE, ENMITY, HATRED, MALICE, DISGUST, DISLIKE, AVERSION

antiphon .... HYMN, PSALM

antipodean .... AUSTRALIAN

antipodes .... OPPOSITES

antiquate .... OUTDATE, OUTMODE

antiquated .... OLD, FOSSIL, PASSE, ARCHAIC, DEFUNCT, EXPIRED, EXTINCT, OUT OF DATE, OBSOLETE

antique .... OLD, AGED, RELIC, ANCIENT, ARTIFACT

antiques, where usually found .... MUSEUM, CURIO SHOP

antiquity .... ELD, PAST, YORE, VESTIGE, PALEOLOGY, SENIORITY

antiseptic .... EGOL, BORIC, EUSOL, EUPAD, IODIN(E), LYSOL, ARNICA, ALCOHOL, SALOL, PICROL, ARGYROL, RETINOL, TACHIOL, CATECHOL, CRESOL, CHLORINE, FORMALIN, STERILE, CARVACROL, GERMICIDE, LISTERINE, DISINFECTANT

surgery pioneer .... LISTER

antisubmarine vessel .... CORVET(TE)

antithesis .... REVERSE, CONTRAST, CONTRARY

antitoxin .... SERUM

for snake venom .... ANTIVENIN

antler .... HORN

branch .... BAY, BEZ, BROW, PRONG

furry skin .... VELVET

main shaft .... BEAM

part of .... PALM

point .... TINE, PRONG

unbranched .... SPIKE, DAG(UE)

antlered animal .... ELK, STAG, MOOSE, CARIBOU, (REIN)DEER

antlers of stag .... ATTIRE

antlion larva .... DOODLEBUG

Antony, ——— .... MARK

antra .... SINUSES

antre/antrum .... CAVE, CAVERN, CAVITY

ants, pertaining to .... FORMIC

anurous .... ACAUDAL, ACAUDATE, TAILLESS

amphibian .... FROG, TOAD

Anubis .... HERMES

Anu's husband .... ANAT

anvil .... JAW, BLOCK, INCUS, TEEST, STITHY

block .... STOCK

user .... (BLACK)SMITH

Anvil City .... NOME

anxiety .... CARE, FEAR, DREAD, WORRY, STRAIN, CONCERN, TENSION, MISGIVING

disorder .... PANIC, NEUROSIS

anxious .... EAGER, UNEASY, TENSE, QUALMY, NERVOUS, IMPATIENT

any .... AN, ALL, PART, SOME, WHICHEVER

anything .... AT ALL, AUGHT

badly matched .... CENTO

of least value .... PLACK, TRIFLE

of value .... ASSET

small .... PINHEAD

that stirs .... FILLIP

aoristic .... INDEFINITE

aorta ...... ARTERY, BLOOD VESSEL

aoudad .... ARUI, SHEEP

apace .... FAST, SPEEDY, SWIFT(LY)

Apache .... THUG, DANCE, INDIAN, GANGSTER, LANGUAGE

chief .... COCHISE, GERONIMO

ap(p)anage .... DOWRY, ADJUNCT, SUPPORT, ENDOWMENT, PERQUISITE

apart .... AWAY, ASIDE, SPLIT, ASUNDER, DETACHED, ADRIFT, DISTINCT, SEPARATE

prefix .... DIS

apartheid .... SECLUSION, SEGREGATION

apartment .... FLAT, ROOM, CONDO, SUITE, DUPLEX

at top of building .... PENTHOUSE

British .... CHAMBERS

for women .... HAREM

house, English .... MANSION

style .... HIGH-RISE

without elevator ...... WALK-UP

apatetic .... DECEIVING, IMITATIVE

apathetic .... COLD, ALOOF, DISMAL, DISTANT, RESTIVE, UNMOVED, HEEDLESS, LISTLESS, INDIFFERENT

apathy .... DESPAIR, BOREDOM, COOLNESS, ALOOFNESS, UNCONCERN, DISINTEREST

ape .... KRA, COPY, GIBBON, MONKEY, SIMIAN, GORILLA, IMITATE, PRIMATE, SIAMANG, ORANG(UTAN)

kind of .... MIME, CLOWN, MIMIC, JESTER

sound .... CHATTER

apeman .... ALALUS

of fiction .... TARZAN

Apennines people .... SABINES

aper ...... MIME, MIMIC, IMITATOR

apercu .... DIGEST, GLANCE, INSIGHT

aperient .... LAXATIVE

apéritif .... DRINK, COCKTAIL, APPETIZER

wine .... DUBONNET

aperture .... GAP, HOLE, SLOT, VENT, STOMA, OPENING, ORIFICE

apery .... MIMICRY, IMITANCY,

IMITATION

apes .... SIMIA

apetalous .... PETALLESS

apex .... TIP, TOP, ACME, CUSP,
PEAK, CREST, POINT, CLIMAX,
HEIGHT, PINIAL, SUMMIT,
VERTEX, ZENITH
covering .... EPI
of elbow .... ANCON
rounded .... RETUSE

aphasia .... ALALIA
treatment of .... SPEECH
THERAPY
type of ..... NOMINAL, GLOBAL,
RECEPTIVE, EXPRESSIVE

aphid .... LOUSE, INSECT
sucking tube .... NECTARY

aphorism .... SAW, ADAGE,
AXIOM, MAXIM, MOTTO,
VERSE, GNOME, SAYING,
DICTUM, EPIGRAM, PROVERB

aphrodisiac .... ERINGO, ERYNGO,
LOVE POTION
substance ..... HONEY, GINGER,
GINSENG

Aphrodite .... VENUS, URANIA,
GODDESS, BUTTERFLY
love of .... ARES, ADONIS
mother of .... DIONE
priestess of .... HERO
son of .... EROS, (A)ENEAS
temple site of .... PAPHOS

aphta .... THRUSH

apian .... BEELIKE

apiary .... NEST, BEEHIVE

apiculture .... BEEKEEPING

apiece .... PER, EACH

apish .... SILLY, AFFECTED,
IMITATIVE

aplomb ...... POISE, CONTROL, AIR,
NERVE, SECURITY,
ASSURANCE, CONFIDENCE,
FLAMBOYANCE
fellow of .... FOP, DUDE,
DANDY, ORATOR, COXCOMB,
BRAGGART, BLUFFER,
(PEA)COCK

apnea .... ASPHYXIA

apocalypse ...... BOOK, FORECAST,
EXPOSURE, PROPHECY,
MYSTICISM, REVELATION

apocalyptic .... GLOOMY,
OMINOUS, MENACING,
SINISTER, PROPHETIC

apocopate .... ELIDE, SHORTEN

apocope .... ELISION

apocryphal .... SPURIOUS,
COUNTERFEIT
book .... ESDRA, TOBIT

apodal .... FOOTLESS

apogee .... PEAK, CROWN, CLIMAX,

PINNACLE

Apollo ...... HELIOS, PHOEBUS, SUN
GOD, SPACECRAFT
astronaut ..... ALDRIN, ANDERS,
BORMAN, LOVELL, COLLINS
birthplace of .... DELOS
festival of .... DELIA
giant killed by .... OTUS
instrument of ...... BOW, LYRE,
LUTE
mother of .... LETO, LATONA
oracle of .... DELOS
oracle site .... DELPHI
priest of ..... ABARIS, CALCHAS
serpent slain by .... PYTHON
sister of .... DIANA, ARTEMIS
son of .... ION, IAMUS
spring sacred to ..... CASTALIA
temple site of .... DELOS
twin of .... ARTEMIS
vale .... TEMPE

Apollyon .... ANGEL, DEVIL,
SATAN, DESTROYER, EVIL
SPIRIT

apologia .... EXCUSE, APOLOGY,
EXPLANATION

apologue .... FABLE, ALLEGORY

apomixis .... APOGAMY

apoplectic with ____ ...... RAGE

apoplexy .... STROKE, SEIZURE,
PARALYSIS

aport .... NEAR, LEFT(SIDE)

apostasy .... BETRAYAL,
DESERTION

apostate .... DEFECTOR, DESERTER,
RENEGADE, RECREANT,
TURNCOAT

apostil .... FOOTNOTE,
ANNOTATION

apostle .... DISCIPLE, PREACHER,
CONVERTER, EVANGELIST,
MISSIONARY
biblical .... JOHN, JUDE, JAMES,
PAUL, JUDAS, ANDREW, PHILIP,
THOMAS, MATTHEW,
BARNABAS, MATTHIAS, SIMON
PETER, BARTHOLOMEW
of the Franks .... REMI
of the Goths .... ULFILAS
of the Indians .... ELIOT
thirteenth .... MATTHIAS

Apostles John and James
.... BOANERGES
teaching of .... DIDACHE

apostolic .... PAPAL, PONTIFICAL
See .... ROME, BISHOPRIC

apothecary .... CHEMIST,
DRUGGIST, PHARMACIST
measure .... PINT, DRAM,
MINIM, OUNCE, GALLON
store .... PHARMACY

weight .... DRAM, GRAIN,
OUNCE, POUND, SCRUPLE

apothegm .... ADAGE, AXIOM,
MAXIM, DICTUM, SAYING,
APHORISM

apotheosis .... ASCENSION,
ELEVATION, EXALTATION

apotheosize .... DEIFY, EXALT,
GLORIFY, IDEALIZE

Appalachian range ...... RAMAPO

appal(l) .... AWE, STUN, DAUNT,
SHOCK, DISMAY, ASTOUND,
HORRIFY, TERRIFY, PETRIFY,
FRIGHTEN, SICKEN, ASTONISH

apparatus .... RIG, DEVICE, TOOL,
GADGET, TACKLE, GEAR,
MACHINE, UTENSIL,
APPLIANCE, IMPLEMENT,
INSTRUMENT
air blowing .... BELLOWS
air cooling .... FAN
artificial respiration
.... PULMOTOR
beauty shop .... DRYER,
(HAIR)DRIER
binding .... BALER
blacksmith's .... FORGE
carpenter's .... SAW, DRILL,
PLANE, HAMMER, SANDER
dentist's .... DRILL
doctor's .... STETHOSCOPE
farmer's .... PLOW, BALER,
HARROW, LISTER, PICKER,
WINDROWER
for bacteria cultures
.... INCUBATOR
gardener's ...... RAKE, MOWER,
SHOVEL
hauling/hoisting .... CRANE,
WINCH, FORKLIFT, WINDLASS
machine shop .... LATHE
plumber's .... WRENCH
surgeon's ..... PROBE, SCALPEL
underwater breathing
.... SCUBA, SNORKEL,
AQUALUNG
water-drawing .... PUMP
weaver's .... LOOM

apparel ...... GARB, GEAR, DRESS,
HABIT, CLOTHES, ATTIRE,
COSTUME, GARMENT,
RAIMENT, CLOTHING

apparent .... CLEAR, PLAIN,
OVERT, PATENT, EVIDENT,
OBVIOUS, SEEMING, VISIBLE

apparently .... CLEARLY,
PLAINLY, VISIBLY, EVIDENTLY,
SEEMINGLY

apparition .... GHOST, IMAGE,
MIRAGE, VISION, WRAITH,
PHANTOM, SPECTER, EIDOLON,

SPECTER
of living person .... FETCH
appassionata .... PASSIONATE,
 IMPASSIONED
appeal ...... ASK, BEG, SUE, CALL,
 PRAY, SEEK, SUIT, PLEAD,
 CHARM, IMPLORE, PROTEST,
 PETITION, ATTRACTION
sex: sl. .... IT, OOMPH
appealing .... ALLURING,
 PLEADING, ENTICING,
 BEGGING, CATCHING,
 WINSOME, RAVISHING
appear .... ACT, COME, LOOK,
 LOOM, SEEM, ARISE, ARRIVE,
 ATTEND, EMERGE, SHOW UP
appearance .... AIR, LOOK, MIEN,
 ADVENT, ARRIVAL, SHOW,
 PRESENCE, SEMBLANCE
appease .... CALM, ALLAY,
 PACIFY, LESSEN, SOFTEN,
 SLAKE, SOOTHE, ASSUAGE,
 QUENCH, COMFORT, MOLLIFY,
 PLACATE, RELIEVE, SATISFY
appeasement, kind of .... SOP
appellation .... NAME, TITLE,
 NAMING, BAPTISM,
 DESIGNATION, CHRISTENING
append .... ADD, TAG, CLIP,
 AFFIX, ANNEX, ATTACH
appendage .... ARM, LEG, TAIL,
 LIMB, WING, JOINT, BRANCH,
 SHADOW, ADJUNCT, FIXTURE,
 ADDITION
crab .... FEELER, ANTENNA
fish .... FIN, BARBEL
leaf .... STIPULE
lobster .... PALP(US)
grain .... AWN, BEARD
threadlike .... CIRRUS
appendix .... ORGAN, RIDER,
 CODICIL, ADDENDUM,
 OUTGROWTH, POSTSCRIPT
appertain .... BELONG, RELATE
appetence .... DESIRE, THIRST,
 CRAVING, APPETITE
appetite .... YEN, ZEST, GUSTO,
 TASTE, DESIRE, SPIRIT,
 CRAVING, PASSION, STOMACH,
 APPETENCE
abnormal .... BULIMIA
for alcoholic drink
 .... DIPSOMANIA
for food .... HUNGER
for something .... TASTE,
 TOOTH
for sweets .... SWEET TOOTH
for water .... THIRST
huge .... GARGANTUAN
insatiable .... GREED,
 VORACITY

loss of .... ANOREXIA
pertaining to .... ORECTIC
appetizer .... CANAPE, TIDBIT,
 WHETTER, ANTIPASTO, HORS
 D'OEUVRE
drink ...... COCKTAIL, APERITIF,
 DUBONNET
appetizing .... TASTY, SAVORY,
 PLEASING, TEMPTING,
 DELICIOUS
applaud ...... HAIL, LAUD, CHEER,
 EXTOL, ACCLAIM, PRAISE,
 COMMEND, GIVE A HAND
applauder .... FAN, ROOTER,
 CHEERER, CLAPPER
applauders' group ...... CLAQUE,
 CHEERING SQUAD
applause .... HAND, CHEER,
 ECLAT, PRAISE, PLAUDIT,
 APPROVAL
round of .... OVATION
word of .... OLE, HEAR,
 BANZAI, BRAVO, HOORAY,
 HURRAH, MABUHAY
apple .... MAY, CRAB, LOVE,
 POME, SORB, FRUIT, GRIMES,
 GOLDEN, PIPPIN, RUSSET,
 COSTARD, WINESAP,
 GREENING, JONATHAN,
 PEARMAIN, QUEENING,
 DELICIOUS, GRAVENSTEIN
acid .... MALIC
brownish autumn .... RUSSET
butter .... JAM
center .... CORE
color .... RED, GREEN, YELLOW
cooking .... NEWTON, PIPPIN,
 GRANNY SMITH
crushed pulp .... POMACE
custard .... ANONA
disease .... STIPPEN
elongated .... CODLING
fall variety .... FAMEUSE,
 WEALTHY
fermented drink .... CIDER
for backing .... BIFFIN
fried .... ROLPENS
inferior .... CODLIN(G)
jack .... BRANDY
juice .... CIDER
kin .... POME, QUINCE, TOMATO
love .... TOMATO
of one's eye .... PET, JEWEL,
 DARLING, FAVORITE
Persian .... PEACH
pie, deep-dish .... PAN DOWDY
polisher .... TOADY,
 FLATTERER
pudding .... BROWN BETTY
red .... MCINTOSH
red winter .... BALDWIN

Russian .... ASTRACHAN
seed/stone .... PIP, PYRENE
seller .... COSTER
shaped fruit .... QUINCE
tosser: myth. .... ERIS
tree .... SORB, WILDING,
 SAPODILLA
unripe .... CODLING
variety .... NON(E)SUCH
wild .... CRAB
worm .... MOTH
apples, pertaining to ...... MALIC
applesauce .... PUREE, RELISH,
 DESSERT
colloquial .... HOKUM,
 BALONEY, NONSENSE
applethorne .... EPIGENE
appliance ...... USE, TOOL, USAGE,
 DEVICE, MACHINE, UTENSIL,
 EQUIPMENT, IMPLEMENT
electrical/household ..... IRON,
 OVEN, MIXER, RANGE,
 BLENDER, FREEZER, TOASTER,
 DISHWASHER, CAN OPENER,
 PERCOLATOR, DISPOSAL,
 REFRIGERATOR, MICROWAVE
 OVEN
applicable .... LEGAL, USABLE,
 FITTING, RELEVANT,
 SUITABLE, PERTINENT
application .... USE, FORM, OFFER,
 REMEDY, APPEAL, REQUEST,
 PROPOSAL, DILIGENCE,
 RELEVANC(E)Y
medical .... BANDAGE,
 PLASTER, COMPRESS, DRESSING
applied decoration .... OIL,
 GESSO, PAINT, APPLIQUE
science .... TECHNOLOGY
apply ...... ASK, PUT, USE, COVER,
 PLACE, DEVOTE, ASSIGN,
 BESTOW, EMPLOY, LAY ON,
 FILE FOR, REQUEST
force .... EXERT, PRESS,
 DEMAND, ENFORCE
friction ...... RUB, RASP, GRATE
justice .... BRING TO BOOK
oneself .... STRIVE
pressure .... COERCE,
 INFLUENCE
to .... VEIL, SHIELD
appoggiatura .... THANK YOU,
 GRACE NOTE
appoint ...... HIRE, NAME, ASSIGN,
 CHARGE, DETAIL, CHOOSE,
 ENGAGE, EMPLOY, PLACE,
 NOMINATE, ORDAIN,
 DESIGNATE
again .... RENAME
as agent .... DEPUTE,
 DEPUTIZE, DELEGATE

in lieu of .... PROXY
to benefice .... COLLATE
appointment .... DATE, TRYST,
DECREE, HIRING, NAMING,
MEETING, ELECTION,
INTERVIEW, ENGAGEMENT
appointments ...... GEAR, THINGS,
FURNITURE, TRAPPINGS,
BELONGINGS
apportion ...... DEAL, DOLE, GIVE,
HAND, METE, ALLOT, SHARE,
ASSIGN, PARCEL, DIVIDE,
PRORATE
apposite .... APT, FIT, PAT, RIGHT,
PROPER, GERMANE, RELEVANT
appraisal .... RATING, SURVEY,
GAUGING, PRICING, ANALYSIS,
ESTIMATE, EVALUATION
appraise .... RATE, GA(U)GE,
GRADE, JUDGE, PRICE, WEIGH,
ASSAY, ASSESS, COMPUTE,
MEASURE, (E)VALUATE
appraiser .... RATER, ASSAYER,
ASSESSOR, SURVEYOR,
ESTIMATOR
appreciable .... REAL, CONCRETE,
MATERIAL, PALPABLE,
TANGIBLE, NOTICEABLE
appreciate .... PRIZE, VALUE,
ESTEEM, NOTICE, CHERISH,
REALIZE, UNDERSTAND
fondly .... LOVE, SAVOR
highly ...... IDOLIZE, TREASURE
in value .... INCREASE
with respect .... REVERE,
VENERATE
appreciation .... THANKS,
RESPECT, COURTESY,
GRATITUDE, RECOGNITION
of value .... GAIN
apprehend .... NAB, HOLD, HENT,
CATCH, ARREST, SENSE,
GRASP, DETAIN, SEIZE,
CAPTURE, PERCEIVE
apprehension .... FEAR, DOUBT,
ALARM, ARREST, QUALM,
ANXIETY, CONCERN, CAPTURE,
PERCEPTION
apprehensive .... EDGY, ANXIOUS,
UNEASY, WORRIED, TENSE,
FEARFUL, NERVOUS, PANICKY,
PERTURBED
apprentice .... TYRO, DEVIL,
NOVICE, ROOKIE, LEARNER,
TRAINEE, BEGINNER,
NEOPHYTE, HELPER,
GREENHORN
apprenticeship .... TRAINING,
PROBATION
contract .... INDENTURE
apprise .... TELL, ADVISE, INFORM,

NOTIFY, ACQUAINT
apprised ...... AWARE, INFORMED,
COGNIZANT
approach .... COME, NEAR, ONSET,
ACCESS, ADVENT, STEP UP,
PASSAGE, OVERTURE
stealthily .... STALK
toward each other
.... CONVERGE
approbation ...... FAVOR, ASSENT,
CONSENT, BLESSING, TRIBUTE,
APPROVAL, SANCTION
appropriate .... APT, DUE, FIT,
TAKE, ADOPT, SEIZE, STEAL,
MEET, RIGHT, TIMELY,
PROPER, POCKET, GERMANE,
PREEMPT, APPOSITE,
BECOMING, SUITABLE
honestly .... PURCHASE
improperly ...... COVET, STEAL,
USURP
approval .... ASSENT, CONSENT,
SUPPORT, AGREEMENT,
SANCTION
kind of .... IMPRIMATUR
sign of .... NOD
word of .... GO, OK(AY),
SHOOT
approve .... PASS, ACCEPT,
RATIFY, CERTIFY, CONFIRM,
ENDORSE, SANCTION
approving mention
.... ACCOLADE, CITATION
approximate .... NEAR, CLOSE,
ROUGH, INEXACT, APPROACH,
PARALLEL
approximately .... ABOUT,
ALMOST, MAINLY, MOSTLY,
NEARLY, ON THE AVERAGE,
ROUGHLY, VIRTUALLY
appurtenance ...... PART, ANNEX,
ADJUNCT, ADDITION
appurtenant .... GERMANE,
ACCESSORY, PERTINENT
aprenaceous .... SANDY
apres .... AFTER
six .... SEPT
apricot .... UME, ANSU, TREE,
COLOR, FRUIT, DRUPE,
YELLOWISH-ORANGE
cordial .... PERSICO
April Dancer's colleague
.... NOEL
15 initials .... IRS
apron .... BELT, FLAP, SHIELD,
PINAFORE
child's .... BIB, BISHOP
painter's .... SMOCK
apropos .... APT, PAT, GEARED,
TIMELY, FITTING, IN PASSING,
BY THE WAY, RELEVANT,

OPPORTUNE, SUITABLE,
PERTAINING
apse .... ARCH, DOME, APSIS,
STEEPLE, PROJECTION
dome cover .... CONCHA
apt .... DEFT, PRONE, QUICK,
CLEVER, FITTING, LIKELY,
PROPER, INCLINED, RELEVANT,
SUITABLE
apteral .... WINGLESS
apteryx .... MOA, BIRD, ROA, KIWI
aptitude .... BENT, GIFT, FLAIR,
KNACK, GENIUS, ABILITY,
TALENT, FITNESS, LEANING,
KEENNESS, DEXTERITY
aptly chosen .... FELICITOUS
Apulia's capital .... BARI
aqua .... WATER, LIQUID,
SOLUTION
fortis .... NITRIC ACID
pura .... DISTILLED WATER
vitae .... BRANDY, LIQUOR,
ALCOHOL
aquamarine .... GEM, BERYL,
COLOR, PIGMENT, BLUISH-
GREEN
aquarium .... (WATER)TANK,
FISHPOND
fish .... GUPPY
large marine ..... OCEANARIUM
plant .... FANWORT
small .... FISHBOWL
aquatic .... MARINE, WATERY,
OCEANIC, WATER-DWELLING
animal .... MINK, NEWT,
OTTER, BEAVER
bird .... AUK, COOT, DUCK,
GULL, LOON, SWAN, GOOSE,
GREBE, SCAUP, PELICAN,
PENGUIN, FLAMINGO
entertainment .... AQUACADE
mammal .... MINK, SEAL,
OTTER, WHALE, DUGONG,
SEACOW, MANATEE
movie character .... FLIPPER
performer .... SEAL, DIVER,
WHALE, DOLPHIN, FLIPPER
plant .... LILY, SEAWEED
vertebrate .... FISH
aqueduct .... PIPE, CANAL,
TRENCH, CHANNEL, CONDUIT,
PASSAGE
of Sylvius .... ITER
aqueous .... WATERY
solution .... JAVEL
Aquila .... EAGLE, CONSTELLATION
star .... ALTAIR
aquiline .... BEAKED, HOOKED
ara .... ALTAR, MACAW,
CONSTELLATION
Arab .... WAIF, GAMIN, GYPSY,

ANSAR, HORSE, NOMAD,
TATAR, URCHIN, SEMITE,
BEDOUIN, SARACEN
arabesque .... BAROQUE,
ELABORATE
Arabia .... SAUDI, PENINSULA
poetic .... ARABY
Arabian abode .... DAR
antelope .... ADDAX
ape .... BABOON
beverage .... BOSA(H), BOZA,
LEBAN
bird of fable .... ROC
camel .... DROMEDARY
capital .... ADEN, SAN'A,
BAGHDAD, MUSCAT, MANAMA,
TEHRAN, RIYADH, ABU DHABI
chief .... SAYID, SHERIF
chieftain .... AMIR, EMIR, REIS,
AMEER, EMEER, SHEIK(H)
chieftain's domain
.... EMIRATE
city/town .... GAZA, JIDDA,
MECCA, AHVAZ, MUSCAT,
ARBELA, ABADAN, TEBUK,
KIRKUK, MEDINA, ARADA,
HODEIDA, DHAMAR, MAIDA,
TABRIZ, DAMMAN, HAMADAN,
AL KUWAIT, DHANK,
BAKHTARAN
cloth .... ABA
coffee .... MOCHA
coin .... TALARI
country .... IRAN, IRAQ, OMAN,
QATAR, YEMEN, SYRIA,
JORDAN, KUWAIT, BAHRAIN,
LEBANON, SAUDI ARABIA
demon/evil spirit .... AFRIT(E),
AFREET, EBLIS, GENIE, JINN(I)
dervish of story .... AGIB
desert ..... LUT, KAVIR, NEFUD,
DAHANA, MARGOW, SYRIAN
dromedary .... BELOOL,
HEJEEN
father .... ABU, ABOU
garment .... ABA, HAI(C)K
gazelle .... ARIEL
gulf ..... ADEN, OMAN, MASIRA,
PERSIAN
head cord .... AGAL
island .... DAS, YAS, ARWAD,
PERIM, MASIRA, ZIRKO,
ZUQAR, BUBIYAN, TIRAN,
KAMARAN, MASHABI, SOCOTRA
jasmine .... BELA
javelin ..... JER(R)ID, JER(R)EED
judge/magistrate .... CADI
kingdom .... SABA, SHEBA,
JORDAN
labor/peasant .... FELLAH
language .... ARABIC

letter .... BA, FA, HA, RA, TA,
YA, ZA, AYN, GAF, KAF, THA,
JIM, KHA, DAL, DAD, LAM,
MIM, NUN, SAD, SIN, ZAY,
WAW, ALIF, DHAL, SHIN,
GHAYN
measure ...... ARDEB, COVID(O)
measure, grain .... SAA,
TOMAN
mock battle .... JER(R)ID,
JER(E)ED
monarchy .... YEMEN
monetary unit .... DINAR,
RIAL, RIYAL, DIRHAM
Moslem .... WAHABI
mountain .... SABIR, SHAM,
MANAR, ANEIZA, HERMON,
TROODOS
Nights Bassorah .... BASRA
Nights spirit .... GENIE
nomad .... SLEB
oasis .... DOUMA
palm .... DOUM
peninsula .... ADEN, SINAI
potentate .... SALADIN
prince .... SHERIF
religion .... ISLAM
river ...... DEZ, KONAR, KABUL,
LURAH, KHABUR, LITANI,
HARIRUD, HELMAND,
MURGHAB, ORANTES, TIGRIS,
EUPHRATES
ruler .... EMIR, EMEER,
SHEIK(H), SULTAN
sacred territory .... HARAM
sailboat .... DHOW
Scripture .... ALCORAN
sea .... RED, DEAD
Sea river .... INDUS
seaport .... ADEN, MOCHA
sheikhdom .... KUWAIT
state .... OMAN, YEMEN
strait .... MANDEB, TIRAN
sultanate .... OMAN
sword .... SCIMITAR
system of numerals
.... ALGORISM
tambourine .... TAAR, DAIRA,
DAIRE
teacher .... ULEMA
tent village .... DOUAR
tribal chief .... SHEIK(H)
veil .... YASMAK
wagon .... ARABA
weight .... DIRHEM
wind .... SAMIEL, SIMOOM
Arabic acid .... ARABIN
arabinose .... SUGAR, PENTOSE
arable .... FERTILE, TILLABLE
araceous .... AROID
plant .... ARUM, LILY, TARO,

CABBAGE
Arachne .... SPIDER
arachnid .... MITE, TICK, ACARID,
SPIDER, SCORPION
segment .... SOMITE, TELSON
arachnoid, space below
.... CISTERNA
structure .... WEB
arado .... LAND
Arafat org. .... PLO
Aram .... SYRIA
arbalest .... CROSSBOW
Arbela .... ERBIL
arbiter .... JUDGE, EXPERT,
OVERMAN, MEDIATOR,
AUTHORITY
archaic .... DAYSMAN
baseball .... UMP(IRE)
boxing/basketball
.... REF(EREE)
fashion .... DIOR, BALMAIN,
DESIGNER, STYLIST
of taste .... GOURMET,
GOURMAND
arbitrary .... UNFAIR, ARROGANT,
CARELESS, ABSOLUTE,
DESPOTIC, WHIMSICAL,
CAPRICIOUS, HIGH-HANDED
arbitrator .... JUDGE, ARBITER,
MEDIATOR, JUSTICE,
MIDDLEMAN, OVERMAN,
MODERATOR
arbor .... BEAM, TREE, AXLE,
BOWER, SHAFT, PERGOLA,
SPINDLE, TRELLIS
vitae .... THUJA
Arboreal ...... DENDRAL, TREELIKE
amphibian .... TREETOAD
creature ..... AI, UNAU, KOALA,
SLOTH, COLUGO, TARSIER,
SQUIRREL
arbored .... TREED
arbutus .... BERRY, PLANT,
SHRUB, MAYFLOWER
arc .... BOW, ARCH, CURVE
chord .... SINE
of 90 degrees .... QUADRANT
sky .... RAINBOW
arcade .... LOGGIA, PIAZZA,
GALLERY, PORTICO,
ARCATURE
Arcadian .... RUSTIC, SIMPLE,
BUCOLIC, PASTORAL,
PEACEFUL, SHEPHERD
princess .... AUGE
Arcady .... ARCADIA
arcane .... HIDDEN, SECRET,
ESOTERIC
arcanum .... ELIXIR, REMEDY,
SECRET, MYSTERY
arch ...... ARC, SLY, BEND, DOME,

FOOT, HEEL, MAIN, CHIEF, PRIME, CLEVER, CURVE, CRAFTY, FORNIX, CUNNING, PRINCIPAL
as combining form ..... RULER
curved inside .... INTRADOS
enemy/fiend ..... DEVIL, SATAN
lower part .... IMPOST, SPRINGER
of bridge .... SPAN
of heaven .... COPE
of spears over shoulders .... YOKE
of the foot .... INSTEP
over eye .... (EYE)BROW
pointed .... OGEE, OGIVE
side of .... HAUNCH
underside .... SOFFIT
archaic .... OLD, OLDEN, ANCIENT, ANTIQUE, HISTORIC, OUTDATED, OBSOLETE
command .... HEST
archangel .... SATAN, URIEL, GABRIEL, MICHAEL, RAPHAEL, ANGELICA
archbishop .... PONTIFF, PRELATE, PRIMATE, DIOCESAN, HIERARCH
of Canterbury .... ANSELM, BECKET, CRANMER
subordinate of ..... SUFFRAGAN
archbishopric .... SEE, APOSTOLIC
arched .... COPED, CONVEX, HUMPED, CURVED, CONCAVE, VAULTED
passageway .... ARCADE
way .... CLOISTER
arch(a)eological find in 1887 .... SIDON
arch(a)eologist's concern .... RUINS, RELIC, ARTIFACT
archer .... BOWMAN, SHOOTER, CONSTELLATION
angel .... CUPID
buff .... TOXOPHILITE
of story .... ROBIN HOOD, (WILLIAM) TELL
of the sky .... SAGITTARIUS
protective band .... BRACER
target .... CLOUT, ROVER
archery, of .... SAGITTARY
arches, row of .... ARCUATION
archetype .... IDEAL, IMAGE, MODEL, EXAMPLE, PATTERN, ORIGINAL, PROTOTYPE
archfiend .... SATAN
archil .... DYE, LICHEN
archimage .... WIZARD, MAGICIAN
archipelago .... SULU, COLON, MALAY, PAUMOTO, TUAMOTU, BISMARCK

architect .... MAKER, ARTIST, BUILDER, CREATOR, PLANNER, DESIGNER
architectural .... TECTONIC
column .... PILASTER
concave molding .... CAVETTO
design .... SPANDREL
drawing .... EPURE
feature .... NAVE
ornament ..... DENTIL, CORBEIL
pier .... ANTA
type .... DORIC, IONIC, MAYAN, GOTHIC, MODERN, BAROQUE
archly .... PERTLY, SAUCILY
archon .... RULER, MAGISTRATE
Arctic .... COLD, COOL, CHILLY, POLAR, FRIGID, ICY, NORTH(ERN), OVERSHOE
base .... ETAH, THULE
bird .... AUK, ROTCH(E), DOVEKEY, JUNCO, DOVEKIE, GUILLEMOT
dog .... SAMO, SAMOYED(E), MALEMUTE
explorer ...... RAE, ERIC, KANE, PEARY
goose .... BRANT
gulf .... OB
gull ...... XEMA, BURGOMASTER
home .... IGLU, IGLOO
jacket .... PARKA, ANORAK
native .... ALEUT, ESKIMO
phenomenon .... BERG
pinniped .... SEAL
plain .... TUNDRA
seagull .... KITTIWAKE
tribesman .... LAPP
wasteland .... TUNDRA
arcuate .... ARCHED, CURVED
arcubalist .... CROSSBOWMAN
Arden, _____ .... EVE, TONI, ENOCH, ELIZABETH
ardent .... AVID, KEEN, EAGER, WARM, FERVENT, PASSIONATE
devotion .... ZEAL
partisan .... DEVOTEE, FANATIC
spirits .... GIN, LIQUOR, WHISKY
ardor .... ELAN, FIRE, HEAT, ZEAL, FERVOR, VERVE, WARMTH, PASSION
arduous .... HARD, DIFFICULT, ENERGETIC, LABORIOUS
area .... SCOPE, RANGE, FIELD, EXTENT, REGION, ZONE, DISTRICT, VICINITY
around moving body .... PERIPTER
between leaf veins .... AREOLA
measure of .... ARE, ACRE, DECARE, HECTARE, CENTIAR(E)

on bird's bill .... CERE
small .... CLOSE, AREOLA
areaway .... YARD, COURT, PASSAGE
areca .... PALM, BETEL
arena .... RING, FIELD, PIT, BOWL, RINK, LISTS, OVAL, STAGE, SPHERE, STADIUM, THEATER, BULLRING
kind of ..... COURT, (COCK)PIT, DIAMOND, GRIDIRON
arenaceous ...... SANDY, ARENOSE
arenite .... SANDSTONE
areo, as combining form .... MARS
areola .... RING, ROUND, SPACE, CIRCLE, HOLLOW
Ares .... MARS
parent of .... HERA, ZEUS
sister of .... ERIS
arete .... CREST, RIDGE, ARISTA
Arethusa .... NYMPH, ORCHID
argal .... ERGO, HENCE, SHEEP, ARGALI, TARTAR, THEREFORE
argala .... STORK, MARABOU, ADJUTANT
argali .... SHEEP, AOUDAD, BIGHORN
argent .... SILVER(Y)
Argentina's capital ...... BUENOS AIRES
Argentine armadillo ...... PELUDO
bay .... BLANCA, GRANDE
cape .... SAN DIEGO, DOS BAHIAS, SAN ANTONIO, TRES PUNTAS
city/town .... AZUL, CONCORDIA, AVELLANEDA, SALTA, BOLIVAR, ESCOBAR, CAMPANA, CORRIENTES, JUJUY, POSADAS, MENDOZA, CORDOBA, CONCEPCION, CASILDA, MAR DEL PLATA, RIO CUARTO, RIVADAVIA, TIGRE, ZARATE, BARADERO, MORON, ROSARIO, SANTIAGO, SAN JUAN, TRES ARROYOS, GODOY CRUZ
crested bird .... SERIEMA
gulf .... NUEVO, SAN JORGE, SAN MATIAS
highest point .... CERRO ACONGCAGUA
Indian .... PAMPEAN
island .... LENNOX, STATEN, TRINIDAD
lake .... VIEDMA, FAGNANO, BUENOS AIRES, ARGENTINO, MAR CHIQUITA, NAHUEL HUAPI
language .... SPANISH
monetary unit .... AUSTRAL

mountain ...... ANDES, CONICO, PISSIS, RINCON, DEL TORO, ACONGCAGUA, ZAPALERI, MERCEDARIO, TRONADOR, TUPUNGATO, CAMPANARIO
plain .... PAMPAS
port .... ROSARIO, LA PLATA
president .... PERON, MENEM, ILLIA, ONGANIA, ALFONSIN
province .... BUENOS AIRES, MISIONES, CATAMARCA, SANTIAGO DEL ESTERO, CORRIENTES, ENTRE RIOS, SALTA, FORMOSA, MENDOZA, CHACO, CORDOBA, SANTA FE, JUJUY, TUCUMAN, SAN JUAN, CHUBUT, LA PAMPA, DISTRITO FEDERAL
region ..... GRAN CHACO, PUNA DE ATACAMA, PETAGONIA, CHACO CENTRAL, CHACO AUSTRAL
river .... ATUEL, CHICO, BERMEJO, COLORADO, URUGUAY, PILCOMAYO, SALI, DULCE, DIAMANTE, GALLEGOS, FELICIANO, CHUBUT, SALADO, QUINTO, SALTO, NEUQUEN, MENDOZA, COYLE, PARANA, TERCERO, LIMAY, TEUCO, TARIJA
salt deposit .... ARIZARO
seaport .... LA PLATA
"sleeping beauty" .... (MARIA)TELLO
timber tree .... TALA
tune .... GATO
volcano .... LANIN, MAIPO, DOMUYO, PETEROA
wage earner ..... DESCAMISADO
waterfall ..... GRANDE, IGUAZU
argil .... CLAY
Argo .... SHIP, CONSTELLATION
argol .... TARTAR
Argolis native .... AGIVE
vale of .... NEMEA
Argonaut .... JASON, ACASTUS, MELEAGER
of the gold rush .... FORTY-NINER
ship .... ARGO
argosy .... SHIP, FLEET, VESSEL
argot .... CANT, LINGO, SLANG, JARGON, PATOIS, DIALECT
argue ...... JAW, DEBATE, OBJECT, REASON, CONTEND, DISCUSS, DISPUTE, WRANGLE
for argument's sake .... ARGUFY
in court .... PRAY, PLEAD, REBUT, CONTEST

price/terms .... HAGGLE, HIGGLE, BARGAIN
argument .... CASE, TOPIC, DEBATE, HASSLE, POLEMIC, DISCUSSION
about words .... LOGOMACHY
kind of .... CON, PRO, RHUBARB
lovers' .... SPAT, QUARREL
to justify .... DEFENSE, REBUTTAL
argumentation .... DIALECTICS
argumentative .... COMBATIVE, ERISTICAL, LITIGIOUS, POLEMICAL, CONTENTIOUS
Argus .... GIANT, WATCHMAN
eyed .... VIGILANT, OBSERVANT
aria .... AIR, SOLO, SONG, TUNE, MELODY, REFRAIN
brilliant flourish ..... CADENZA
like an .... ARIOSO
arias .... SOLI
Ariadne's father .... MINOS
love .... THESEUS
arid .... DRY, BARREN, JEJUNE, TORRID, STERILE, ANHYDROUS, UNFERTILE
region .... DESERT
region, U.S. .... DUST BOWL
ariel .... GAZELLE
Ariel .... SPIRIT, SATELLITE
Ariel's compeer .... SPRITE
master .... PROSPERO
Aries .... RAM, CONSTELLATION
arietta .... AIR, ARIA, SONG, MELODY
arikara .... REE
ariose .... MELODIC, SONGLIKE
arioso .... MELODIOUS
composer .... BACH
arise .... GROW, GET UP, ISSUE, STAND, WAKEN, AWAKE, ASCEND, EMANATE
arista .... AWN, BEARD, BRISTLE
aristocracy ...... ELITE, NOBILITY, OLIGARCHY
aristocrat ...... SNOB, NOBLEMAN, HIGH-BORN
Athenian/Greek ...... EUPATRID
Roman .... PATRICIAN
Russian .... BOYAR
Spanish .... GRANDEE, HIDALGO
aristocratic .... PATRICIAN
aristocrats collectively .... NOBILITY, NOBLESSE
Aristotle .... STAGIRITE
birthplace .... STAGIRA
follower .... PERIPATETIC
logic .... DEDUCTIVE, SYLLOGISM

teacher of .... PLATO
arithmetic, common .... LOGISTIC
Arizona capital .... PHOENIX
city/town .... MESA, YUMA, TEMPE, PEORIA, PRESCOTT, CHANDLER, TUCSON, NOGALES, WINSLOW, FLAGSTAFF, SCOTTSDALE, KINGMAN, CASA GRANDE
Cochise county seat .... BISBEE
county .... GILA, PIMA, APACHE, GRAHAM, LA PAZ, PINAL, MOHAVE, NAVAJO, GREENLEE, MARICOPA, YUMA, COCHISE, YAVAPAI
dam .... DAVIS, HOOVER, COOLIDGE, PAINTED ROCK
desert .... YUMA, PAINTED
highest point ...... HUMPHREYS PEAK
Indian ...... HANO, HOPI, TEWA, MOQUI, APACHE, NAVAHO, NAVAJO, YUMA, PAIUTE
lake .... MEAD, ALAMO, APACHE, CANYON, HAVASU, POWELL, SAGUARO
mountain .... ORD, ELDEN, WOODY, GRAHAM, LEMMON, TRUMBULL, FOUR PEAKS
nut .... PINON
river .... GILA, SALT, BLACK, PARIA, VERDE, WHITE, COLORADO
state bird .... WREN
state flower .... SAGUARO(CACTUS)
state nickname .... GRAND CANYON
tourist sight .... GRAND CANYON, PETRIFIED FOREST
ark .... BOAT, REFUGE
animals/birds .... PAIRS
builder .... NOE, NOAH
landing place .... (MOUNT)ARARAT
porter .... BEN
Arkansas capital .... LITTLE ROCK
city/town .... CAMDEN, MAGNOLIA, HARRISON, EL DORADO, BLYTHEVILLE, FORT SMITH, PINE BLUFF, TEXARKANA, FAYETTEVILLE, CONWAY, HORSESHOE BEND
county .... CLAY, POPE, MILLER, BOONE, ASHLEY, IZARD, CHICOT, POINSETT, BENTON, GARLAND, GREENE, YELL, LOGAN, OUACHITA, LEE, PULASKI, FAULKNER, BAXTER, MONROE, NEWTON, DREW,

PERRY, CONWAY, UNION,
CRITTENDEN, WHITE,
WASHINGTON
highest point .... MAGAZINE
MOUNTAIN
Indian .... OSAGE, CHEROKEE
lake .... BEAVER, GREESON,
NORFOLK, NIMROD, WINONA,
CONWAY, BLUE SHOALS
mountain .... MAGAZINE,
POTEAU, REEVES KNOB
river .... RED, BLACK,
BUFFALO, OUACHITA, CACHE,
SALINE, MULBERRY, SPRING,
LITTLE RED, CADDO, LITTLE
MISSOURI
state bird .... MOCKINGBIRD
state flower .... APPLE
BLOSSOM
state nickname .... WONDER,
LAND OF OPPORTUNITY
tourist sight .... CRATER OF
DIAMONDS
arles ...... ANTE, TOKEN, EARNEST,
PREPAYMENT
arm ...... LIMB, BRANCH, WEAPON,
FORTIFY, FURNISH, TENTACLE
badge .... BRASSARD
band .... BRACER
bone .... ULNA, HUMERUS
bone, pertaining to ..... ULNAR
cover .... SLEEVE
extendible .... PANTOGRAPH
hole .... SCYE
in-arm .... OXTER
joint .... ELBOW, WRIST
length of .... REACH
like .... BRACHIAL
of the sea .... BAY, FIORD,
FIRTH, FJORD, INLET
shield .... BUCKLER
armada .... FLEET
armadillo .... APAR(A), PEBA,
POYOU, TATOU
shell .... CARAPACE
6-banded .... PELUDO
3-banded .... APAR, MATACO
12-banded .... TATOUAY
Armageddon .... (LAST)BATTLE
author .... URIS
maybe .... MEGIDDO
armament ...... ARMS, ORDNANCE,
WEAPONRY, EQUIPMENT
factory .... KRUPP, SKODA
armature .... ARMOR
armchair .... FAUTEUIL
armed band .... POSSE
conflict .... WAR, BATTLE
escort .... CONVOY,
BODYGUARD
fleet .... NAVY

galley .... AESC
guard .... SENTRY, SENTINEL
Armenia's capital .... ERIVAN
mountain .... ARARAT
river .... ARAS
armet .... HELMET
armiger .... SQUIRE, ARMOR
BEARER
armistice ...... TRUCE, CEASE-FIRE
armlet .... BANGLE
armoire ...... CABINET, CUPBOARD
armor ...... MAIL, PLATE, BARD(E),
SHIELD
arm ..... BRASSARD, BRASSART,
PALLETTE
back .... CUIRASS
bearer .... SQUIRE, ARMIGER
body ...... TACE, CULET, TASSE,
LORICA, CUIRASS, SURCOAT
breast .... CUIRASS
chain .... MAIL
clamp/hook .... AGRAFFE
elbow to shoulder
.... BRASSARD
foot .... SOLLERET
hand .... GAUNTLET
head .... VISOR, BEAVER,
ARMET, BASINET, HELMET,
HAUBERK, SCONCE
horse .... BARD(E), TESTIERE
jacket .... GIPON, JUPON
joint .... GUSSET
leg .... JAMB(E), GREAVE
neck/throat .... GORGET
plate .... LAME, MASCLE
rings .... BRIGANDINE
shirt cover .... CAMISADO
shoulder .... AILETTE,
PAULDRON
snail's .... SHELL
thigh .... CUISH, TUILE, CUISSE,
TASSET
tunic .... GIPON, JUPON
turtle's .... CARAPACE
unworn .... BARESARK
armored .... MAILED, COVERED,
EQUIPPED
animal .... ARMADILLO
person of old .... KNIGHT
ship ...... MONITOR, IRONCLAD,
MERRIMAC
vehicle .... TANK
armorial .... HERALDIC
bearings/ensigns
.... HERALDRY
armory ...... ARSENAL, HERALDRY
orator's .... WORDS, CLICHES
armpit .... ALA, OXTER, AXILLA
swelling .... BUBO
arms .... WARFARE, WEAPONS,
INSIGNIA

creature with eight
.... OCTOPOD, OCTOPUS
of the night, so-called
.... DARKNESS
repository .... ARSENAL
army .... HOST, DROVE, HORDE,
COLONY, LEGION, TROOP,
THRONG, ARMED FORCES
acronym .... SNAFU
car .... JEEP
caterer/follower .... SUTLER
chaplain .... PADRE, PRIEST
engineer .... SAPPER
front of .... VAN(GUARD)
group .... UNIT, CORPS,
COMPANY, BRIGADE, PLATOON,
SQUAD(RON), REGIMENT
insignia of rank .... BAR,
LEAF, STAR, EAGLE, STRIPE
instructor ..... DRILL SERGEANT
mascot .... MULE
meal .... CHOW, MESS
mounted sentinel .... VEDETTE,
VIDETTE
of animals .... HERD, PACK
of birds .... FLOCK
of insects .... SWARM
of lions .... PRIDE
of the .... MILITARY
rank .... MAJOR, CAPTAIN,
COLONEL, GENERAL, PRIVATE,
CORPORAL, SERGEANT,
LIEUTENANT
vehicle .... JEEP, TANK,
AMTRAC, WEAPONS CARRIER
Arnaz, _____ .... DESI, LUCIE
Arndt (Felix) piece .... NOLA
arnica .... PLANT, ANTISEPTIC
Arnold (Matthew) character
.... RUSTUM, SOHRAB
aroid .... ARUM, TARO, TANIA,
ARACEOUS
aroma ...... ODOR, SAVOR, SMELL,
FLAVOR, FRAGRANCE
aromatic .... SPICY, SAVORY,
ODOROUS, PUNGENT,
FRAGRANT
bark .... ANGOSTURA,
CASCARILLA
berry .... CUBEB
beverage .... COFFEE
condiment .... SPICE
fruit .... NUTMEG
gum .... BALM, MYRRH,
ARALIA, BALSAM
herb ...... MINT, ANISE, THYME,
CARAWAY, FLEAWORT
leaf .... BAY, BUCHU, LAUREL
liquid .... BAYRUM
oil .... BALM
ointment .... NARD

plant .... MINT, NARD, SAGE, BASIL, CARUM, ANGELICA, WORMWOOD, ARTEMISIA
resin .... COPALM, COPAIBA
root .... GINSENG
seed .... DILL, ANISE, CUM(M)IN, FENNEL, GUAIAC
smoke .... FUME, INCENSE
spice .... MACE, CLOVE, NUTMEG
tree .... BALSAM, FIRPINE
weed .... TANSY
wood .... CEDAR, BASSWOOD
Arouet's nickname .... ZOZO
around ...... ABOUT, CIRCA, CLOSE TO, NEARBY, EVERYWAY
arouse ...... FAN, FIRE, SPUR, STIR, PIQUE, FOMENT, EXCITE, INCITE, ANIMATE, INFLAME
Arpachshad's brother .... LUD, ARAM, ELAM, ASHUR
father .... SHEM
grandfather .... NOAH
son .... SHELAH
arpeggio .... ROULADE
arraign .... CITE, ACCUSE, CHARGE, INDICT, IMPEACH
arrange .... FIX, SET, SORT, ADAPT, ADJUST, DESIGN, MARSHAL, PREPARE, CLASSIFY
a coiffure .... TEASE
by twos .... MATE, PAIR
for battle .... DEPLOY
for reference .... FILE
in advance .... PLAN, PREPARE, SCHEDULE
in files .... STACK
in new groupings .... REALIGN
in threes .... TERNATE
methodically .... FILE, ALPHABETIZE
the hair .... COMB, DRESS
arrangement .... FILE, PLAN, ORDER, DESIGN, LAYOUT, SETUP, AGREEMENT, SETTLEMENT, TABULATION
literary .... COMPOSITION
musical .... LIED, SONG, SONATA
arrant .... BAD, BOLD, EVIL, VILE, HEINOUS, ATROCIOUS, NOTORIOUS, OUT AND OUT, WICKED, UNMITIGATED
arras .... TAPESTRY
array ...... DRESS, ORDER, ATTIRE, FINERY, MARSHAL, DECK-OUT, TURN-OUT
arrear(s) .... BEHIND, BACKLOG, DEFICIT, SHORTFALL
arrest .... NAB, CURB, HALE, HOLD, NICK, STEM, COLLAR,

STOP, CATCH, CHECK, SEIZE
slang .... BUST, PINCH
writ .... CAPLAS
arrival, scheduled: abbr.
.... ETA
arrive .... COME, LAND, REACH, APPEAR, ATTAIN
arrivederci .... GOODBY, SO LONG, FAREWELL
arrogance .... AIRS, PRIDE, BLUSTER, BRAVADO, HAUTEUR, HUBRIS, INSOLENCE, SNOBBERY
arrogant .... COCKY, LOFTY, PROUD, HAUGHTY, CAVALIER, STUCK-UP, FLIPPANT, SNOBBISH, OVERBEARING, ON ONE'S HIGH HORSE
arrogate .... GRAB, CLAIM, USURP, ASSUME, ACQUIRE, CAPTURE, CONFISCATE
arrow .... BOLT, DART, SHAFT, POINTER, SAGITTA
ancient .... QUARREL
barb .... FLUKE
blunt .... BUTT, SHAFT
body of .... STELE
case .... QUIVER
crossbow .... BOLT
feather .... VANE
feather-fitter .... PLUMIER
feathered .... VIRE
like .... SAGITTAL
notch for bowstring ..... NOCK
poetic .... REED
poison .... INEE, UPAS, CURARE, URARI, ANTIAR(IN)
put feather on .... FLEDGE, FLETCH
user .... ARCHER, BOWMAN
arrowroot .... PIA, ARUM, CANNA, ARARAO, TAPIOCA
arrows, quiverful of .... SHEAF
Arrowsmith, Mrs. .... LEORA
arrowwood .... WAHOO, DOGWOOD, VIBURNUM
arrowworm .... SAGITTA
arroyo .... PIT, WADI, BROOK, GULLY, HONDO, RIVULET, STREAM(BED)
arse .... RUMP, BUTTOCKS
arsenal .... ARMORY, SUPPLY, STOREHOUSE
Arsene, Monsieur .... LUPIN
arsenic .... POISON
acid salt .... ARSENATE
combining form .... ARSENO
compound .... ARSENIDE
powder .... SALVARSAN
sulfide .... REALGAR
symbol .... AS

arsis .... ICTUS, UPBEAT
arsonist .... NERC, BURNER, FIREBUG, PYROMANIAC
art .... CRAFT, DANCE, DRAMA, MUSIC, SKILL, TRICK, CUNNING, ARTIFICE, SCIENCE, PAINTING
exhibition .... SALON
gallery .... TATE, FREER, SALON
Latin .... ARS
movement of 1920's .... DADA
objects .... VERTU, VIRTU
of argumentation
.... DIALECTICS
bookbinding ..... BIBLIOPEGY
carving/engraving
.... GLYPTICS
devising dances
.... CHORE(O)GRAPHY
discourse .... RHETORIC
disputation .... ERISTIC, POLEMICS
dwarfing trees/plants
.... BONSAI
horsemanship .... MANEGE
mapping ...... CHOROGRAPHY
motion pictures
.... CINEMATICS
public speaking
.... ELOCUTION
teaching .... DIDACTIC
style .... DADA, GENRE, CUBISM, MODERN, BAROQUE, FAUVISM, ARABESQUE, ART DECO, GOTHICISM, PURISM, ART NOUVEAU, IMPRESSIONISM
work .... OIL
work, formless
.... ABSTRACTION(ISM)
work, inferior .... POTBOILER
artal, singular of .... ROTL
artel .... COOPERATIVE
Artemis .... DELIA, DIANA, PHOEBE, GODDESS
birthplace .... DELOS
father .... ZEUS
mother .... LETO, LATONA
twin .... APOLLO
victim .... ORION
artemisia .... WORMWOOD
arterial obstruction .... EMBOLUS
artery .... AORTA, STREET, CHANNEL, BLOOD VESSEL
neck .... CAROTID
pulse .... ICTUS
artful .... SLY, WILY, ADROIT, CRAFTY, CUNNING, POLITIC, DECEITFUL
arthritis .... CLOT, DROP, GOUT, SWELLING, STIFFNESS,

INFLAMMATION
treatment .... ACTH, HEAT,
ANTIBIOTICS, VERATRIA,
CORTISONE, VERATRIN(E)
type .... SEPTIC, PYOGENIC,
RHEUMATOID, DEGENERATIVE
arthropod .... INSECT, ARACHNID,
MYRIAPOD, MILLEPEDE,
CRUSTACEAN
segmented part .... SOMITE,
TELSON
arthropoda .... PHYLA
Arthur. See **King Arthur**
Arthur, actress .... BEA
Arthur Conan .... DOYLE
character .... SHERLOCK
HOLMES
title .... SIR
of tennis .... ASHE
Arthurian enchantress .... VIVIAN
tales compiler .... LOOMIS,
MALORY
artichoke .... PLANT, TUBER,
CYNARA, CHOROGI,
SUNFLOWER
kin .... CARDOON
leaf stalks .... CHARD
article .... ITEM, PART, ESSAY,
PAPER, PIECE, THING, REPORT,
STORY, OBJECT, FEATURE
definite .... THE
in a document .... CLAUSE
indefinite .... A, AN
of faith/belief .... CREDO,
CREED
of personal property
.... CHATTEL
articles, miscellaneous
.... RUMMAGE
of excellence .... IMPERIALS
of virtu .... CURIO, BIBELOT
sold together .... TIE-IN
articulate .... UTTER, JOINTED,
DISTINCT, EXPLICIT, LITERATE,
ENUNCIATE, EXPRESSIVE
articulated joint .... HINGE
speech sound .... LENIS
artifice .... HOAX, RUSE, CRAFT,
FRAUD, GUILE, BLUFF, DODGE,
DEVICE, DECEIT, TRICK(ERY),
WILE, STRATAGEM
artificial ...... FAKE, MOCK, FALSE,
BOGUS, PLASTIC, SHAM,
SPURIOUS, AFFECTED,
POSTICHE, IMITATION,
SIMULATED, SYNTHETIC,
UNNATURAL
appearance .... DISGUISE
bait .... LURE, DECOY
butter .... OLEO, MARGARINE
copy of nature ...... SYNTHESIS

fly ...... DUN, NYMPH, DOCTOR,
COACHMAN
foodstuff .... ERSATZ
ivory .... IVORIDE
jewelry .... PASTE
language .... IDO, ESPERANTO
respiration apparatus
.... PULMOTOR
smile of a sort .... SIMPER
sweetener .... ASPARTAME,
CYCLAMATE, SACCHARIN
teeth .... DENTURE
waterway .... CANAL
artillery .... GUNNERY, ORDNANCE
abbreviation .... ORD
anti-aircraft .... POMPOM, ACK-
ACK, TRIPLE-A
fire angle measurement
.... MIL
man .... GUNNER, LASCAR,
CANNONER
type of ..... MOBILE, MOUNTED
wagon .... CAMION, CAISSON
artisan .... ARTIST, CRAFTSMAN,
TRADESMAN
artist .... DANCER, ETCHER,
PAINTER, PIANIST, COLORIST,
PERFORMER, MINIATURIST,
SCULPTOR, PORTRAITIST
abbreviation on painting
.... PNXT
clay .... POTTER
modern .... DALI
unconventional ..... BOHEMIAN
artistic style .... GUSTO
artist's colony .... TAOS,
GREENWICH, LATIN QUARTER
copy .... TRACING
frock .... SMOCK
medium .... OIL, CLAY,
BRONZE, CANVAS, PASTEL,
MARBLE, TEMPERA
milieu .... STUDIO, ATELIER
mixing board .... PALETTE
name on painting
.... DELINEAVIT
stand/frame .... EASEL
artless .... NAIF, FRANK, CRUDE,
CLUMSY, NAIVE, PLAIN,
SIMPLE, NATURAL, INGENUOUS
woman/girl .... INGENUE
artlessness .... NAIVETE,
INNOCENCE, SIMPLICITY
arts and ____ .... CRAFTS,
LETTERS, SCIENCES
votary .... PATRON, ESTHETE,
CONNOISSEUR
artwork .... PIECE, CREATION,
PAINTING, SCULPTURE,
COMPOSITION
great(est) .... MASTERPIECE

literary .... CLASSIC(S)
tawdry .... KITSCH
arum .... LILY, TARO, AROID,
CALLA, CALADIUM
genus .... ARALES
aruspex .... SEER, SOOTHSAYER
Aryan .... MEDE, SLAV
god .... AGNI
language .... SANSKRIT
as .... FOR, LIKE, THUS, SINCE,
QUA, WHILE, THOUGH,
BECAUSE
a rule .... GENERALLY
far as .... TO
if .... QUASI
much as .... NO LESS
said above .... DITTO
soon as .... ONCE
to .... CONCERNING
usual: music .... SOLITO
well as .... AND
written: music .... STA
As You Like It character
.... JACQUES, ROSALIND
scene .... ARDEN
Asa .... KING(OF JUDAH)
ally of .... BEN-HADAD
father of .... ABIJAH, ABIJAM
grandfather of ...... REHOBOAM
son of .... JEHOSHAPHAT
asafetida .... LASER, RESIN,
FERULA
asarum .... PLANT, GINGER
asbestos .... BOARD, SILICATE,
AMPHIBOLE
ASCAP member .... AUTHOR,
COMPOSER, PUBLISHER
ascarid .... (PIN)WORM,
HOOKWORM, ROUNDWORM
ascend ...... SOAR, CLIMB, UPRISE,
(A)RISE, CLAMBER, MOUNT,
SCALE(THE HEIGHTS)
ascendancy .... RISE, MASTERY,
SUPREMACY, DOMINATION,
PREDOMINANCE
ascent .... RISE, JUMP, RAMP,
UPLIFT, STAIRCASE, SLOPE,
UPSURGE, UPSWING,
ACCLIVITY
ascertain .... SEE, FIND, LEARN,
ENSURE, VERIFY, CERTIFY,
DISCOVER, DETERMINE,
ESTABLISH
ascertainment .... ASSURANCE,
CERTAINTY
ascetic .... MONK, YOGA, FAKIR,
ESSENE, HERMIT, STOIC,
RECLUSE, AUSTERE, EREMITE,
PURITAN, STYLITE, MONASTIC,
ANCHORET, ANCHORITE
asceticism .... FASTING, PENANCE,

AUSTERITY, (SELF)DENIAL

Asch name .... SHOLEM, SHOLOM

asci .... (SPORE)SAC

ascidian .... TUNICATE

ascot .... SCARF, (NECK)TIE

ascribe .... IMPLY, ATTACH, ASSIGN, IMPUTE, (AC)CREDIT, ATTRIBUTE

aseptic .... STERILE, SANITARY

asexual .... AGAMIC, NEUTER, SEXLESS

reproduction .... FISSION

Asgard .... ASGARTH

bridge to .... BIFROST

watchman of .... HEIMDALL

ash .... TREE, WOOD, ARTAR, EMBER, PALLOR, POWDER, RESIDUE

can .... DUSTBIN

can: sl. .... DEPTH BOMB, DEPTH CHARGE

fruit ..... KEY, MAPLE, SAMARA

gray .... CINEREOUS

holder of cremated body .... URN

mountain .... ROWAN

pertaining to .... CINERARY

solution .... LYE

tree juice .... MANNA

Ash Wednesday to Easter .... LENT

ashamed .... ABASHED, HUMBLED, CHAGRINED, MORTIFIED, EMBARRASSED

Ashanti capital .... KUMASI

ashen/ashy .... WAN, GRAY, PALE, LIVID, WHITE, PALLID

Asher's brother .... GAD

daughter .... SERAH

father .... JACOB

mother .... ZILPAH

son .... ISUI, BERIAH

ashes .... RUINS, POWDER, REMAINS

ashlar .... BEAM, PLANK, STONE

ashram .... COMMUNE, RETREAT

Ashtoreth ...... ISHTAR, ASTARTE, GODDESS

Asia Minor .... ANATOLIA

bishop .... (ST) NICHOLAS

city .... GAZA, MYRA, TROY, TYRE, ISSUS, NICAEA, SARDIS, ANTIOCH, EPHESUS, CHALCEDON

country .... CARIA, LYCIA, LYDIA, MYSIA, CILICIA, PHRYGIA, PISIDIA

district .... IONIA, TROAD

Greek city .... MILETUS

island .... SAMOS

kingdom .... PONTUS

mountain .... IDA

people .... HITTITES

province .... GALATIA, LYCAONIA

region .... EOLIS, IONIA, TROAS

river .... IRIS, CAICUS, GRANICUS

sheep .... KARAKUL, BROADTAIL

tree .... SYCAMORE

Asiatic ancient people ...... SERES

ass .... ONAGER

bean .... SOY(A)

bird .... MINA, MYNA(H), PITTA

cat ..... OUNCE, TIGER, SIAMESE

cattle .... ZEBU

civet .... ZIBET(H)

coin, Annam .... QUAN

Arabia .... QURSH

China .... LI, FEN, TAEL, TIAO, YUAN

India ..... ANNA, FELS, HOON, PICE, TARA, RUPEE

Iran ...... PUL, LARI, POUL, RIAL, DARIC, DINAR, MOHUR

Iraq .... FILS, DINAR

Laos .... AT

Malaya .... TRA(H)

Nepal .... MOHAR

Siam/Thailand .... ANNA, BAHT, TICAL

Singapore .... CENT

country .... ANNAM, BURMA, CHINA, KOREA, SIKKIM, INDIA, NEPAL, IRAN, IRAQ, VIETNAM, SYRIA, THAILAND(SIAM), LAOS, TIBET, MALAYSIA, ARABIA, CAMBODIA, PAKISTAN, SINGAPORE

country, ancient .... ELAM, ACCAD, MEDEA, EOLIA

cow .... ZO(H), ZOBO

deer ...... AXIS, SASIN, SAMBAR

desert .... GOBI

disease .... BERIBERI

fiber .... HEMP, RAMIE

finch .... SISKIN

gangster/thug .... DACOIT

gazelle ...... AHU, CORA, ARIEL

ginger/herb .... CARDAMOM, CARDAMUM

goat antelope .... SEROW

grass .... CITRONELLA

grassland .... MAIDAN

hog .... BABIRUSA

isthmus .... KRA

kingdom .... ELAM, IRAN, IRAQ, SIAM, AN(N)AM, KOREA, NEPAL

lake .... ARAL, BAIKAL

lemur .... LORIS, MACACO

medicine man .... SHAMAN

millet .... DARI

monkey .... MACAQUE

mountain .... ALTAI

native .... HUN, TAI, YUIT, MONGOL, KOREAN, CHINESE, TA(R)TAR, AN(N)AMESE, INNUIT, SIAMESE, TIBETAN

nomad .... TATAR

palm .... NIPA, ARECA, BETEL

peninsula .... KOREA, MALAY

perennial plant .... RAMIE

plague .... CHOLERA

plain .... CHOL

plant ...... HEMP, ODAL, RAMIE, SESAME, GINSENG, TAMPALA

port .... AMOY, MACAO, SAIGON, HAIPHONG, SHANGHAI

river .... ILI, AMUR, LENA, ONON, OXUS, YALU, INDUS, PEARL, MEKONG, YELLOW, YANGTZE

rodent .... CONY, PIKA, MARMOT

ruminant .... YAK, ZEBU

sardine .... LOUR

sea .... ARAL, AZOL, CHINA

sheep .... ARGALI

shrub .... TEA, TCHE, THEA

snowstorm .... BURAN

storm .... TYPHOON

tea .... CHA, PEKOE, OOLONG

trade wind .... MONSOON

tree .... ACLE, DITA, TEAK, NARRA, SIRIS, BANYAN

tribe .... LAI, TAI, AKHA, AOUL, KHAS, BUGI, KADU, KUKI, TATAR, UZBEG

weight .... TAEL, CATTY

wild hog ...... BOAR, BABIRUSA

wild sheep .... RASSE

aside .... BY, ALOOF, AWAY, APART, BESIDE

from .... EXCEPT, EXCLUDING

set .... TABLE, RESERVE

stage .... AD LIB, WHISPER

asinine ...... INANE, NUTTY, SILLY, MULISH, STUPID, FOOLISH, IDIOTIC

ask .... BEG, QUIZ, QUERY, DEMAND, INVITE, INQUIRE, SOLICIT, QUESTION

a series of questions .... INTERROGATE

for a handout .... TOUCH

for a loan: sl. .... BRACE

reverently .... PRAY

asker .... REQUESTER

askew .... AGEE, ALOP, AWRY, ASLANT, OBLIQUE

asleep .... DEAD, DOZING,

DORMANT, NAPPING, INACTIVE, SLEEPING
at the ____ .... SWITCH
Asmara is capital of .... ERITREA
asor .... LYRE
asp .... SNAKE, VIPER
on headdress .... URAEUS
asparagus tip/stalk .... SPEAR
aspect .... LOOK, MIEN, VIEW, PHASE, OUTLOOK, APPEARANCE
general .... FACIES
aspen .... POPLAR, SHAKING, QUIVERING, TREMBLING, FLUTTERING
asper .... COIN
asperity .... RIGOR, PUNGENCY, HARSHNESS, ROUGHNESS, SHARPNESS
asperse ...... SLUR, LIBEL, REVILE, VILIFY, SLANDER
aspersion .... SLUR, BAPTISM, SLANDER, INNUENDO
asphalt .... BITUMEN, UINTAITE, GILSONITE
like mineral .... ALBERTITE
asphyxia .... APNEA, ACROTISM
asphyxiate .... STRANGLE, SUFFOCATE
aspic .... MOLD, JELLY, RELISH, LAVENDER
aspirant .... CANDIDATE, CONTENDER
aspiration .... GOAL, BREATH, DESIRE, AMBITION
aspire .... HOPE, LONG, SEEK, YEARN, DESIRE, BREATHE, STRIVE(FOR)
aspirin .... TABLET
ass .... DOLT, FOOL, BURRO, DONKEY, ONAGER, SIMPLETON
female .... JENNY
hybrid .... ZEBRASS
male .... JACK
young .... FOAL
assa .... CAAMA
assagai .... SPEAR, JAVELIN
assai .... PALM, DRINK
assail .... BESET, ATTACK, SET UPON, ASSAULT, CRITICIZE
assailant .... ATTACKER, AGGRESSOR
Assamese capital .... SHILLONG
dialect .... LHOTA
Mongol .... GARO, NAGA
native .... AHOM
shrub .... TEA
silkworm .... ERI(A)
tribe .... AO, AKA, AHOM, GARO, NAGA
assassin .... THUG, BRAVO,

GUNMAN, KILLER, HITMAN, SLAYER, MURDERER
Abel's/Biblical .... CAIN
character .... DEFAMER, ROORBACH, SMEARER, SLANDERER
Garfield's .... GUITEAU
Kennedy's (John F.) .... OSWALD
Kennedy's (Robert) .... SIRHAN
Lincoln's .... BOOTH
origin of word .... HASHISM
assassinate .... KILL, SLAY, MURDER
assault .... RAID, RAPE, ONSET, ATTACK, CHARGE, OFFENSE
and battery .... BEATING
prolonged .... SIEGE
prolonged verbal .... TIRADE
assaulter .... MUGGER, RAPIST, OFFENDER
assay ...... TEST, WEIGH, ANALYZE, ANALYSIS, APPRAISE
assaying cup .... CUPEL
assemblage ...... CROWD, THRONG, COUNCIL, MEETING, CONCLAVE, GATHERING
assemble .... MEET, UNITE, COLLECT, COMPILE, CONVENE, HUDDLE, MUSTER, SHEAVE, ROUND UP, (FOR)GATHER
assembly .... BEVY, GROUP, ARRAY, RALLY, CAUCUS, GALAXY, MEETING, SESSION, HUSTINGS, AUDIENCE, GATHERING
legislative .... CONGRESS
line .... PLANT, FACTORY
of witches .... COVEN
assent .... ACCEPT, COMPLY, CONSENT, AGREE(MENT), CONCUR(RENCE)
show .... NOD
sign of .... NOD, THUMBS UP
word of .... YES, AMEN, OKAY, YES SIREE, RIGHT ON
assert .... SAY, AVER, STATE, AFFIRM, DECLARE
as a fact .... CLAIM, POSIT, ALLEGE
formally .... ALLEGATE
positively .... SWEAR
assess ...... DUN, FINE, LEVY, TAX, RATE, APPRAISE
assessment ...... FEE, TAX, RATAL, WORTH, ANALYSIS, VALUE, APPRAISAL, ESTIMATE, VALUATION
assessor .... JUDGE, RATER, APPRAISER

asset .... ESTATE, RESOURCE, PROPERTY, ADVANTAGE, POSSESSION
personal .... WIT, TACT, CHARM, BEAUTY, CHARISMA
assets and liabilities ...... ESTATE
asseverate .... AVER, STATE, ASSERT, CERTIFY, TESTIFY
assiduous .... BUSY, FEISTY, DILIGENT, ENERGETIC
assign .... ALLOT, APPOINT, ALLOCATE, RELEGATE, TRANSFER, DESIGNATE
cause/reason .... ASCRIBE, ATTRIBUTE
parts in play .... CAST
assignation .... TRYST, RENDEZVOUS
assimilate .... ABSORB, DIGEST, UNDERSTAND
facts .... LEARN
assimilation of learning .... EDUCATION
assist .... AID, HELP, ATTEND, SECOND, SUPPORT
assistance .... AID, HAND, HELP, SUCCOR, COMFORT
government .... WELFARE, SUBSIDY
in kind .... ALMS, DOLE
to disaster victims ...... RELIEF
assistant .... AIDE, DEPUTY, HELPER, ADJUTANT, AUXILIARY
first, of a sort .... RIGHT-HAND(MAN)
general's .... AIDE-DE-CAMP
in charge of a gambling table .... CROUPIER
of bishop .... VERGER, COADJUTOR
pastor .... CURATE
to an abbot .... PRIOR
assize ...... OYER, INQUEST, COURT SESSIONS
associate ...... ALLY, JOIN, CRONY, CONNECT, PARTNER, CONFRERE, COLLEAGUE
in crime .... ACCOMPLICE
with others .... HOBNOB
association .... CLUB, LINK, LEAGUE, SOCIETY, AFFINITY, FRATERNITY, ORGANIZATION
business firms' .... CARTEL
football .... SOCCER
merchants' .... HANSE
mutual aid .... ARTEL
mutual protection .... GUILD
oldest in membership .... DEAN
scholars', etc. .... ACADEMY

workers' .... UNION
assoil .... ATONE, PARDON, ABSOLVE
assonance .... PUN
assort .... MATCH, CLASSIFY, HARMONIZE
assorted .... MIX, VARIOUS, MISCELLANEOUS
assortment .... OLIO, MIXTURE, VARIETY, COLLECTION
of types .... FONTS
assuage .... CALM, ALLAY, LESSEN, PACIFY, RELIEVE, MITIGATE
assume .... FEIGN, INFER, AFFECT, PRETEND, ARROGATE, SUPPOSE, SIMULATE, UNDERTAKE
a part .... ACT, IMITATE
an attitude .... POSE
another's personality .... IMPERSONATE
as a fact .... POSIT
control .... TAKE OVER
without right .... USURP
assumed .... STAGY, FICTITIOUS
character .... ROLE
identity for disguise .... INCOGNITO
name .... ALIAS, PSEUDONYM
personality .... IMPERSONATION
assumer of other personality .... IMPOSTOR
assumption .... NOTION, PRETENSE, PRESUMPTION
assurance .... BELIEF, PLEDGE, PROMISE, CERTAINTY, GUARANTEE, CONFIDENCE
assuredly .... CERTAINLY, DECIDEDLY
assurgent ...... RISING, ASCENDING
Assyrian .... AMORITE, S(H)EMITE
capital .... NINEVEH
chief deity .... AS(S)UR, AS(S)HUR
city .... HARA, OPIS, AKKAD, ARBELA
god ..... IRA, SIN, ANAT, NABO, AS(S)UR, HADAD, ASHUR, NUSKU, NINIB, TAMMUS
goddess .... NANA, ALLATU, IS(H)TAR, SARPANIT
king .... PUL, SARGON(II)
mountain .... ZAGROS
original capital .... ASHUR
pyramid .... ZIKURAT, ZIGGURAT
queen .... SEMIRAMIS
river .... ZAB, ADHIAN
warrior .... SARGON
weight .... COLA

Astaire, ____ .... FRED, ADELE
dancing partner .... RITA
astatic ...... UNSTABLE, UNSTEADY
aster .... DAISY, OXEYE, TANSY, FLOWER, ZINNIA, TANGLEFOOT
asterisk .... MARK, SIGN, STAR
astern .... AFT, BAFT, REAR, ABAFT, BACKWARD
asteroid .... EROS, CERES, PALLAS, STARFISH, STARLIKE
asthenic .... FEEBLE
asthma medicine ...... GRINDELIA
asthmatic breath .... WHEEZE
astigmatism .... AMETROPIA
astir .... AGOG, ABOUT, AWAKE, MOVING
Astolat maid .... ELAINE
astonish .... AMAZE, ASTOUND, SURPRISE
Astor, Lady .... (NANCY)LANGHORNE
astound .... STUN, AMAZE, SHOCK, BEWILDER, CONFOUND
astraddle .... ACROSS, ASTRIDE
Astraea .... VIRGO, GODDESS
astragal(us) .... TALUS, ANKLEBONE
astrakham .... PELT, WOOL, APPLE, CLOTH, KARAKUL
astral .... ASTER, STARRY, STELLAR
astray .... LOST, AMISS, IN ERROR, OFF COURSE, WANDERING
astrict ...... BIND, LIMIT, RESTRICT
astringent .... ALUM, COTO, HARSH, STERN, CASHOO, SEVERE, TANNIN, CATECHU, STYPTIC(AL)
fruit .... SLOE
gum .... KINO
material .... CATECHU
resin .... MASTIC
root .... BISTORT
salt .... ALUM
astrolabe .... ALIDAD(E)
astrologer .... STARGAZER, ASTRONOMER
ancient ..... MAGUS, CHALDEAN
French .... NOSTRADAMUS
legendary .... MERLIN
astrological .... CHALDEAN
belief .... SIDERISM
diagram .... SCHEME
astrology, work on .... ALMAGEST
astromonk .... BONNY
astronaut .... MOONMAN, SPACEMAN
American .... GLENN, WHITE, YOUNG, SCOTT, ANDERS, BORMAN, ALDRIN, LOVELL,

CONRAD, CERNAN, GORDON, COLLINS, GRISSOM, BEAN, SHEPARD, MCDIVITT, ARMSTRONG, EISELE, CUNNINGHAM, SCHIRRA, MITCHELL, STAFFORD
Russian .... GAGARIN, KOMAROV
astronaut's perfect .... A-OK
astronautic activity .... LUNAR PROBE
vehicle .... APOLLO, GEMINI, MARINER, WESTAR, SKYLAB, SKYNET, SOYUZ, COSMOS, SPUTNIK, SURVEYOR, COMSTAR, SHINSEI, COLUMBIA, AURORA, FRIENDSHIP, OHSUMI, CHALLENGER
astronomer .... METON, BRAHE, PTOLEMY, STARGAZER
astronomical .... HUGE, LARGE, URANIC, CELESTIAL
almanac .... EPHEMERIS
arc .... AZIMUTH
cloud .... NEBULA
cycle .... SAROS
instrument .... ORRERY
intersecting points ...... NODES
measure .... APSIS, PARSEC
phenomenon .... PULSAR, QUASAR
shadow .... UMBRA, PENUMBRA
astronomy, work on .... ALMAGEST
astute .... KEEN, WILY, CLEVER, CRAFTY, CUNNING, CANNY, SHARP, SHREWD
Astyanax's parent .... HECTOR, ANDROMACHE
Asunción is capital of .... PARAGUAY
asunder .... APART, SEPARATED
Aswan .... DAM(SITE)
ancient name of .... SYENE
asylum .... HAVEN, HOME, REFUGE, RETREAT, SHELTER, ORPHANAGE, SANCTUARY
describing a kind of .... POLITICAL
inmate ...... LUNATIC, REFUGEE
asymmetric(al) .... UNEVEN, IRREGULAR
at .... BY, IN, ON, TO, NEAR
a distance .... AFAR
____ (addled) ...... SIXES AND SEVENS
all .... ANY, AUGHT
all times .... EVER, ALWAYS
an angle .... ALIST, ATILT
fault .... GUILTY
full length .... FLAT(LING)

41

hand .... HERE, NEAR(BY), PRESENT
hand: poet. .... ANEAR
home .... IN, RECEIVING
large .... FREE, LOOSE, ABROAD
last .... ENFIN, FINALLY, ULTIMATELY
no time .... NEVER
odds .... HOSTILE
once ..... STAT, PRONTO, RIGHT NOW, IMMEDIATELY
right angle to a ship's keel
.... ABEAM
sea .... LOST
that time .... THEN
the age of .... AET(AT)
the same time .... COEVAL
variance .... DIFFERENT
atabal ...... TABOR, (KETTLE)DRUM
Atahualpa .... INCA, KING
Atalanta's victor .... HIPPOMENES
ataman .... COSSACK
atap .... NIPA, PALM
Ataturk, Kemal .... MUSTAFA
Ate .... AVENGER
atelier .... STUDIO, WORKSHOP
worker .... MODEL, ARTIST, PAINTER
athanasia .... IMMORTALITY
atheist .... INFIDEL, AGNOSTIC, FREE-THINKER, NON-BELIEVER
atheling ..... PRINCE, NOBLE(MAN)
Athena .... NIKE, PALLAS, MINERVA
shield .... (A)EGIS
title of .... ALEA
Athenian .... ATTIC
aristocrat .... EUPATRID
astronomer .... METON
citadel .... ACROPOLIS
clan .... OBE
coin .... CHALCUS
courtesan .... THAIS
demagogue .... CLEON
general .... CIMON, CLEON, NICIAS, ARISTIDES, MILTIADES
judge/juryman .... DICAST
lawgiver .... SOLON
magistrate/ruler .... ARCHON
market .... AGORA
money .... OBOL
political subdivision .... PHYLE
room .... CELLA, ADYTUM
sculptor .... PHIDIAS
seaport .... PIRAEUS
statesman .... CIMON, PERICLES, ARISTIDES, ALCIBIADES
temple .... NIKE, ZEUS, PARTHENON
tribunal .... AREOPAGUS

Athens founder .... CECROPS
athirst .... AVID, EAGER, PARCHED
athlete .... BOXER, CAGER, RACER, GOLFER, JUMPER, PLAYER
sometimes called .... PRO, STAR
athlete's crown .... LAUREL
dream .... OLYMPICS, CHAMPIONSHIP
foot .... RINGWORM
jump .... BROAD
jump with pole .... VAULT
speed event ...... DASH, SPRINT
throw .... PASS, DISCUS, JAVELIN
trainer .... COACH, GYMNAST, HANDLER
athletic .... BRAWNY
contest, 5 events
.... PENTATHLON
contest, 10 events
.... DECATHLON
exercises .... CALISTHENICS, GYMNASTIC(S)
field .... OVAL, COURT, DIAMOND, STADIUM, COLISEUM
group .... CREW, FIVE, NINE, TEAM, ELEVEN
prize .... AGON, MEDAL, MONEY, TROPHY
athletics .... GAMES, SPORTS, EXERCISES, GYMNASTICS
athodyd .... RAMJET
athwart .... ACROSS, AGAINST, OBLIQUE, CROSSWISE
atilt .... TILTING, INCLINED
atingle .... AGOG, EXCITED, TINGLING
atis .... CONITE
Atlanta is capital of .... GEORGIA
atlantes .... TELAMON
Atlantic coast fish .... TAUTOG, RED DRUM
first solo flier of
.... LINDBERGH
island, famed ...... ST. HELENA
sea .... SARGASSO
tributary .... MIN(H)O, SENEGAL
atlas .... MAP, BOOK, CHART, GRAPH, FORMAT, PILLAR, VERTEBRA
Atlas' daughter .... MAIA, HYAD(E), PLEIAD, CALYPSO
name .... AGENA
wife .... PLEIONE
Atli .... HUN, KING
wife .... GUDRUN
atman .... EGO, SOUL
atmosphere ...... AIR, AURA, TONE
in some cities .... SMOG,

SMAZE
measuring instrument
.... ATMOMETER
over nation .... AIRSPACE
atmospheric condition
.... CLIMATE, WEATHER
gas .... ARGON
phenomenon .... HAIL, STORM, CYCLONE, RAINBOW, TEMPEST, TORNADO, TYPHOON, HURRICANE
pressure .... BARIC
atoll .... BIKINI, (CORAL)ISLAND
pool .... LAGOON
atom ...... JOT, ION, IOTA, MONAD, SPECK, PROTON, MOLECULE, PARTICLE
bomb target, WW II
.... NAGASAKI, HIROSHIMA
charged .... ION
negatively charged
.... ELECTRON
of specified atomic number
.... NUCLIDE
part .... ION, PROTON
smasher .... SYNCHROTON
smashing .... FISSION
type of .... ISOBAR, NORMAL, NEUTRAL, ISOTERE
with valence of two ..... DYAD
atomic .... MINUTE, ISOTERIC, MOLECULAR
particle .... NEUTRON, PROTON, ELECTRON, NEUTRINO
physicist .... BOHR, RABI, UREY, FERMI, COMPTON, MILLIKAN, SCIENTIST
submarine ..... SKATE, TRITON, NAUTILUS, SCORPION
atomize .... SPRAY, VAPORIZE, PULVERIZE
atomizer .... SPRAYER, SPRINKLER
atomy .... DWARF, PIGMY, PYGMY, SKELETON
atone .... REPAY, ASSOIL, REDEEM, EXPIATE, MAKE AMENDS, APOLOGIZE
atonement ...... AMENDS, REFUND, PENANCE, REDRESS, REDEMPTION, REPARATION
atonic sound .... SURD
atoning .... PIACULAR, EXPIATORY, APOLOGETIC
atrabilious .... CROSS, MOROSE
atramentous .... INKY
Atreus' brother .... THYESTES
father .... PELOPS
son .... MENELAUS, AGAMEMNON
atrium ...... HALL, ROOM, COURT, CAVITY, CHAMBER, ENTRANCE

atrocious .... BAD, BASE, VILE, CRUEL, BRUTAL, WICKED, HATEFUL, HEINOUS, VIOLENT
atrocity .... ABUSE, BADNESS, CRUELTY, SAVAGERY, BARBARITY, OUTRAGE, TORTURE, BRUTALITY
a physical ...... DWARF, FREAK, GNOME, MONSTER
visual .... EYESORE
atrophy .... SHRINKAGE, DEGENERATION, DETERIORATION
of horse's muscles .... SWEENY
of person's joints .... ARTHRITIS
Atropos .... FATE, WEIRD(SISTERS)
attach ...... ADD, TIE, JOIN, TACK, AFFIX, SEIZE, APPEND, CONNECT
attaché .... DIPLOMAT
kind of .... PRESS, MILITARY
attached .... FOND, DEVOTED, SEIZED, APPENDED
to branch .... SESSILE
attachment .... LOVE, SEIZURE, ADDITION, DEVOTION, AFFECTION, APPENDAGE
attack .... HIT, SIC, LUNGE, SALVO, ONSET, CHARGE, ASSAIL, POUNCE, ASSAULT, OFFENSIVE, STRIKE, VOLLEY, ONSLAUGHT
artillery .... CANNONADE
at close range .... POTSHOT
diversionary .... FEINT
fierce .... ONSLAUGHT
for quick victory .... BLITZ(KRIEG)
in words/writing .... LASH, BASTE, SQUIB, LAMPOON
kind of .... BLIND, SNEAK, VERBAL, WARLIKE, BLITZ(KRIEG), SURPRISE, TACTICAL, STRATEGIC
prolonged .... SIEGE
reputation ...... LIBEL, DEFAME, MALIGN, SLANDER
signal .... WARISON
sudden .... FORAY
swift, overwhelming .... BLITZ(KRIEG)
swift, surprise .... RAID
verbally .... BLAST, BERATE
violent, intense .... ONSLAUGHT
warning of ..... ALARM, ALERT
attacker .... RAIDER, INVADER, OFFENDER, AGGRESSOR, ASSAILANT

attain .... WIN, EARN, GAIN, REACH, ACHIEVE, SUCCEED
fame .... ARRIVE
attainment .... SKILL, SUCCESS, FRUITION, LEARNING, EDUCATION, ACHIEVEMENT
attaint .... CONDEMN, CONVICT, CORRUPT, DISGRACE, DISHONOR, ATTAINDER
attar .... OIL, PERFUME, (ROSE)EXTRACT
variation .... OTTO
attempt .... TRY, STAB, ESSAY, ATTACK, EMBARK, VENTURE, ENDEAVOR
failed .... MISS
attend .... HEAR, HEED, SERVE, ESCORT, LISTEN, BE PRESENT, ACCOMPANY
attendance .... GATE, HOUSE, TURN-OUT, PRESENCE, GATHERING
describing some .... SRO, FULL, FULL-HOUSE, STANDING ROOM
full .... PLENARY
attendant ...... SERVER, SERVANT, RETAINER, SERVITOR, CONCOMITANT
bridegroom's .... BEST MAN
fact .... CIRCUMSTANCE
hunter's .... GILLY, GILLIE, GUNBEARER
knight's .... SQUIRE
on horseback .... OUTRIDER
patient's .... NURSE
personal .... VALET
queen's .... CONSORT
attendants, group of ...... COURT, TRAIN, RETINUE, ENTOURAGE
attended by all .... PLENARY
attent .... HEEDFUL
attention .... EAR, CARE, HEED, LOOK, NOTICE, REGARD, SCRUTINY, CONSIDERATION
getter .... HEADLINE
getting sound .... PST, SST, AHEM, PSST, COUGH, HIST, YELL, WHISTLE
getting word .... HEY
holding .... GRIPPING
order of .... PRIORITY
attentive .... ALERT, MINDFUL, WATCHFUL, OBSERVANT, THOUGHTFUL
attenuate .... DILUTE, LESSEN, RAREFY, THIN OUT, WEAKEN
attest .... VOUCH, AFFIRM, DEPOSE, CERTIFY, DEMONSTRATE
as witness .... TESTIFY
in earnest .... SWEAR

attestation, formal/solemn .... OATH
sign of official .... SEAL, SIGNATURE
attic .... GARRET, (COCK)LOFT, MANSARD, ATHENIAN
bird .... NIGHTINGALE
part of .... DORMER
salt .... WIT
Attica, capital of .... ATHENS
king .... CECROPS
native .... METIC
township .... DEME
valley .... LCARIA
Attican .... ATHENIAN
Attila .... HUN, ATLI, KING, ETZEL
adjective for .... SCOURGE
attire .... RIG, GARB, ROBE, ARRAY, DRESS, FINERY, CLOTHES, RAIMENT, CLOTHING
man's complete .... SUIT
masquerader's .... COSTUME
military/police .... UNIFORM
religious/riding .... HABIT
soldier's, sometimes .... FATIGUES
stag's .... ANTLERS
winter's .... SNOW
woman's .... GOWN
Attis' love .... CYBELE
Attlee, _____ .... CLEMENT
attitude .... MOOD, MANNER, BEARING, FEELING, OPINION, POSTURE, DISPOSITION
strike an .... AIR, POSE
attract ...... DRAW, LURE, CHARM, CAPTIVATE, FASCINATE
animal/fish .... BAIT
attention/curiosity .... INTEREST
misleadingly .... SEDUCE
attraction .... CHARM, APPEAL, GRAVITY, MAGNET(ISM)
attractive .... CUTE, PRETTY, ALLURING, ENGAGING, FETCHING, PLEASING
girl, describing one ..... SEXY, PINUP, CURVACEOUS, WHISTLEBAIT
girl's body: sl. .... CHASSIS
irresistibly .... BEWITCHING
powerfully .... MAGNETIC
price to buyer .... CHEAP, BARGAIN, CUT-RATE
temptingly .... SEDUCTIVE
very .... STUNNING
attribute .... TRAIT, ASSIGN, IMPUTE, REASON, ASCRIBE, QUALITY, ACCREDIT
of an M.C. .... WIT
of good workers .... LOYALTY,

THOROUGHNESS
attribution .... BLAME, ETIOLOGY, IMPUTATION
attrition .... EROSION, FRICTION, REPENTANCE
battle of .... SIEGE, BESIEGEMENT
attune .... HARMONIZE, RECONCILE
to the times .... UPDATE, MODERNIZE
aubade .... ALBA, MATIN
counterpart .... SERENADE
auberge .... INN, HOSTEL(RY)
auburn .... TITIAN, (REDDISH)BROWN
auction .... ROUP, SALE, SELL, VENDUE
price .... BID, UPSET
auctioneer's hammer .... GAVEL, MALLET
platform .... BLOCK
word .... SOLD, GOING
audacious .... BOLD, SAUCY, DARING, BRAZEN, INSOLENT, RECKLESS
audacity .... GALL, BRASS, CHEEK, CRUST, DARING, COURAGE, BOLDNESS, TEMERITY, IMPUDENCE, INSOLENCE
audible .... ALOUD, CLEAR, HEARD, HEARABLE
audience .... HEARING, ASSEMBLY, ONLOOKERS, INTERVIEW, RECEPTION
kind of .... AUDITION
official .... DURBAR
part of, sometimes .... STANDEES
audio-visual aid ...... FILM, TAPE, SLIDE, MOCK-UP
audiphone .... HEARING AID
audition .... TEST, HEARING, TRY-OUT
auditor .... CPA, HEARER, LISTENER, ACCOUNTANT
auditorium .... HALL, THEATER
auditory .... OTIC, AURAL, AURICULAR
Audubon, John .... PAINTER, NATURALIST, ORNITHOLOGIST
Augean .... FILTHY, STABLE, CORRUPT
auger .... TOOL
groove of .... POD
relative .... AWL, BORER, DRILL, GIMLET, WIMBLE
type of .... SHIP, SCREW, LIP RING
aught .... NAUGHT, ZERO, NOTHING, ANYTHING
augment .... ADD, EKE, RAISE,

SWELL, EXPAND, EXTEND, FATTEN, ENLARGE, INCREASE
augur .... BODE, PORTEND, AUSPEX, DIVINER, PRESAGE, PROPHET, FORETELL, PROPHESY, SOOTHSAYER
augury .... OMEN, SIGN, PORTENT, PROPHECY, DIVINATION
august .... GRAND, NOBLE, EXALTED, SUBLIME, IMPOSING, MAGNIFICENT
body, so-called .... SENATE, CONGRESS, SUPREME COURT
August, first .... LAMMAS
Augustan .... ELEGANT, CLASSICAL
Age writer .... OVID
Augustinian .... FRIAR
Augustus title .... PRINCEPS
wife .... LIVIA
auk .... ALCA, MURRE, PUFFIN, ROTCH(E), DOVEKEY, DOVEKIE
family .... ALCIDINE
genus .... ALLE, URIA
small .... ROTCH(E)
aulic .... SUAVE, COURTLY, PRINCELY
Auntie of stage/movies .... MAME
aura ...... AIR, MILIEU, AMBIENCE, ENVIRONS, EMANATION, ATMOSPHERE
of splendor .... NIMBUS
aural .... OTIC, AURICULAR
aureate .... GILDED, GOLDEN, ORNATE, BRILLIANT
aureole .... HALO, GLORY, CORONA
auric .... GOLDEN
acid salt .... AURATE
auricle .... EAR, PINNA
auriculate .... EARED
auriform .... EAR-SHAPED
Auriga .... WAGONER
aurist .... OTOLOGIST
instrument .... OTOSCOPE
aurochs .... OX, URUS, BISON
Aurora .... EOS, DAWN, BOREALIS, AUSTRALIS
auroral .... EOAN, BRIGHT, RADIANT, ROSEATE
aurum .... AU, GOLD
auscultation .... LISTENING
Ausonia .... ITALY
auspex .... SEER, AUGUR, SOOTHSAYER
auspice(s) .... EGIS, OMEN, SUPPORT, APPROVAL, PROPHECY, PATRONAGE, DIVINATION
auspicious .... LUCKY, TIMELY, FAVORABLE, FORTUNATE,

PROMISING, PROPITIOUS, SUCCESSFUL
start in a theater .... FULL HOUSE, SRO SIGN
start of a speech .... APPLAUSE, LAUGHTER
austere ...... COLD, HARSH, RIGID, STERN, SEVERE, SIMPLE, ASCETIC, SPARTAN, RIGOROUS
austral .... SOUTHERN, SOUTHERLY
Australasia .... OCEANIA
Australian .... ANZAC, AUSSIE, ANTIPODEAN
aborigine .... MARA, MAORI, MYALL, BUSHMAN
aborigine weapon ...... NULLA, WO(O)MERA, BOOMERANG
acacia .... MYALL, WATTLE
anteater .... ECHIDNA
arboreal/bearlike animal .... KOALA
badger .... WOMBAT, BANDICOOT
bay .... SHARK, SMOKY, COLLIER, REPULSE, STREAKY, PORTLAND, DISCOVERY, LACEPEDE, ENCOUNTER, PORT PHILLIP
bee .... KARBI
beef-wood .... BELAR
bird .... ARA, LORY, ARARA, LOWAN, LEIPOA, EM(E)U, MALLEE, MEGAPOD, LORIKEET, PARDALOTE
boomerang .... KILEY, KYLIE
brushwood .... MALLEE
bushman .... ABO
bushranger .... HIGHWAYMAN
cake .... BROWNIE
cane .... WADDY
cape ..... HOWE, YORK, GREEN, OTWAY, WESSEL, BOWLING, MANIFOLD
capital .... CANBERRA
catlike animal .... LINSANG
cedar .... TOON(A)
chick .... SHEILA
city/town .... AYR, MOE, ALBURY, ASPLEY, ARARAT, ADELAIDE, BALLARAT, HOBART, BRIGHTON, BRISBANE, CANBERRA, CANTERBURY, GLADSTONE, DAVENPORT, CHELSEA, CONCORD, DARWIN, LIVERPOOL, MELBOURNE, PERTH, MANLY, BENDIGO, FORBES, SYDNEY, SEYMOUR, HAWTHORN, NEWCASTLE, ROMA, WARWICK, WINDSOR, ORANGE, PARKES, WAVERLEY
clover .... NARDOO

club of aborigines ..... WADDY
cockatoo .... GALAH
coin .... DUMP, SHILLING
cry/call .... COOEE, COOEY,
CODER
dasyure .... YABBI
Davis Cup player .... ROY,
HOAD, ROCHE, STOLLE,
EMERSON, NEWCOMBE
desert .... GIBSON, GREAT
SANDY, SIMPSON, TANAMI,
GREAT VICTORIA
explorer .... BASS, COOK
eucalyptus .... MALLEE
festival .... CORROBORI,
CORROBOREE
fish .... MADO, BARRAMUNDA
fish with lungs .... CERATODUS
flycatcher .... FANTAIL
gale .... BUSTER
goldfish .... FANTAIL
grass .... SPINIFEX
gulf .... CARPENTARIA,
SPENCER, VAN DIEMEN, JOSEPH
BONAPARTE
gum tree .... TUART, KAR(R)I
harrier/hawk .... KAHU
hinterland .... OUTBACK
horse .... WALER, BRUMBY,
BRUMBIE, WARRAGAL
hut .... MIMI, MIAM(IA)
island ..... MURION, TASMANIA,
MONTE BELLO, WESSEL,
CUMBERLAND, THURSDAY,
WELLESLEY
kangaroo .... WOLABA,
WOLARU, WALLABY
kingfisher .... HALCYON
lake .... AULD, DORA, CAREY,
COWAN, BLANCHE, EYRE,
FROME, DUNDAS, NASH,
MACKAY, GREGORY,
AMADEUS, CARNEGIE, NEALE,
SERPENTINE, DISAPPOINTMENT
language .... ENGLISH
laughing bird .... GIGAS,
DACELO, KOOKABURRA
lizard .... GOANNA, MOLOCH
marsupial .... KOALA, TAIT,
YABBI, WOMBAT, DASYURE,
KANGAROO, BANDICOOT,
PHALANGER
measure of capacity ..... ARNA
mining refuse .... MULLOCK
mole .... PLATYPUS
mountain .... ISA, BLUE,
MAGNET, KOSCIUSKO, BARKER,
BARTLE FRERE, ZIEL, BRUCE,
MARGARET, MORGAN,
WOODROFFE
mountain range .... GREY,

FLINDERS
native ..... ABO, MARA, MYALL,
MAORI, BUSHMAN
ostrich .... EM(E)U
oven .... UMU
parrot .... GALAH, CORELLA,
ROSELLA, COCKATOO,
COCKATEEL, PARAKEET,
BUDGERIGAR
peninsula .... EYRE
pepper .... KAVA
pigeon .... WONGA
pine .... DAMMAR
plain .... NULLARBOR
plant .... WARATAN
plateau .... KIMBERLEY
prime minister .... HOLT,
GORTON
"puritan" .... WOWSER
river ...... DALY, SWAN, ROPER,
MURRAY, DARLING, FINKE,
PAROO, FITZROY, MARGARET,
GEORGINA, COOPERS,
THOMSON, BARCOO, VICTORIA,
STURT, DIAMANTINA
salt sea .... GREGORY
sea .... CORAL, TIMOR,
ARAFURA
sea mile .... NAUT
seaport .... PERTH, DARWIN,
SYDNEY, BRISBANE
shark .... MAKO
shield .... MULGA
shrub .... CORREA
sight .... KOALA, KANGAROO
soldier .... ANZAC
spear-throwing device
.... WO(O)MERA
state .... VICTORIA, WESTERN
AUSTRALIA, NORTHERN
TERRITORY, SOUTH
AUSTRALIA, NEW SOUTH
WALES, TASMANIA,
QUEENSLAND
strait .... BASS, DUNDAS,
TORRES, CLARENCE
tennis star .... HOAD, ROY,
LAVER, STOLLE, ROCHE,
EMERSON, NEWCOMBE
territory .... PAPUA
traveler .... SWAGMAN
tree ..... BELAR, BILLA, MYALL,
PENDA, QUADANG, BOREE,
MARARA, ACACIA, TODART,
QUANDONG
tree-dwelling animal
.... KOALA
walking stick .... WADDY
wild dog .... DINGO
wild horse .... BRUMBIES
wilderness .... OUTBACK

Austria: Ger. .... OSTERREICH
Austrian amphibian .... OLM
capital .... VIENNA
chancellor .... DOLLFUSS
city/town .... GRAZ, LEOBEN,
LINZ, VIENNA, INNSBRUCK,
DORNBIRN, SALZBURG,
KLAGENFURT, STEYR,
KAPPENBERG, WIEN, WEIS,
TRAUN, ZELTWEG, WOLFSBERG
coin .... DUCAT, FLORIN,
HELLER, GROSCHEN, KRONE,
KRUE(T)ZER, GULDEN,
GUILDER
composer .... MOZART,
STRAUSS
country dance .... LANDLER
folk dance .... DREHER
grass .... MARRAM
highest point
.... GROSSGLOCKNER
hunter .... JAGER, YAGER
language .... GERMAN
lake .... BODENSEE,
CONSTANCE, NEUSIEDLER SEE
measure, dry .... MUTH
measure, liquid .... FASS
monetary unit .... CROWN,
KRONE, SCHILLING
mountain .... ALLGAU, CARNIC,
BAVARIAN, OTZTAL,
GROSSGLOCKNER, WILDSPITZE,
ZUGSPITZE
name prefix .... VON
native .... TYROLESE
pass ..... BRENNER, SEMMERING
physicist .... MACH
province .... STYRIA, TIROL,
CARINTHIA, SALZBURG,
BURGENLAND, VORARLBERG
psychiatrist ..... ADLER, FREUD
range .... HOHE, NIEDERE,
KARAWANKEN
rifleman .... JAGER, YAGER
river .... DANUBE, INN, ENNS,
DRAU, MARCH, MUR, RAAB,
DONAU, RHINE, THAYA,
TRAUN, SALZACH
ruling family .... HABSBURG
ski champ .... SAILER,
SCHRANZ
soprano .... JERITZA
violinist ..... MORINI, KREISLER
writer .... KAFKA
autarchy .... DESPOTISM
authentic ...... PURE, REAL, TRUE,
VALID, GENUINE, ORIGINAL,
VERITABLE
authenticate .... SEAL, ATTEST,
VERIFY, CONFIRM
author .... DOER, FATHER,

WRITER, CREATOR, COMPILER, FOUNDER, ORIGINATOR

concern of .... PLOT, STYLE

of America the Beautiful .... BATES

of many works .... POLYGRAPH

unknown .... ANON(YMOUS)

authoritative .... RULING, OFFICIAL, MAGISTRAL, POWERFUL, CONTROLLING

rule of law .... ORDINANCE

authority .... FORCE, POWER, LICENSE, INFLUENCE

letter of .... BREVE, BILLET

point as .... CITE, QUOTE

authorization .... BILLET, FIAT, LICENSE, MANDATE, WARRANT, SANCTION, CLEARANCE, PERMISSION

authorize ...... ALLOW, EMPOWER, ENABLE, ENTRUST, DEPUTE, ACCREDIT, DEPUTIZE, GIVE LEAVE, SANCTION, CERTIFY, PERMIT, LEGALIZE, COMMISSION, VALIDATE

authorized .... LEGAL, LEGIT(IMATE)

auto. See also **automobile** .... CAR, MOTORCAR, AUTOMOBILE

clean .... SIMONIZE

colloquial .... BUS

court .... MOTEL

explosion .... BACKFIRE

for hire .... CAB, TAXI(CAB)

obsolete .... MODEL T, REO, FLIVVER, PACKARD

old .... CRATE, JALOPY

old style .... LANDAU, VICTORIA, CABRIOLET

panel .... DASHBOARD

prefix .... MANU

racetrack .... MOTORDROME

racing champion .... CLARK, MEARS, PETTY, UNSER, BODINE, ANDRETTI, WALTRIP, ALLISON, JONES, EARNHARDT, WALLACE, FITTIPALDI

shelter .... BARN, GARAGE, CARPORT

supercharged: colloq. .... HOTROD

type .... SEDAN, COUPE, TUDOR, HARDTOP, BERLIN(E), ROADSTER, CONVERTIBLE

autobiography ...... MEMOIR, LIFE STORY

autochton ...... NATIVE, INDIGENE, ABORIGINE

autocracy .... DESPOTISM, DICTATORSHIP

autocrat .... TSAR, MOGUL, CAESAR, DESPOT, DICTATOR

automat .... RESTAURANT

automatic .... PISTOL, MECHANICAL, SELF-OPERATING, REFLEX, SPONTANEOUS

action, kind of .... TIC, REFLEX

coal stoker .... HOPPER

clothes cleaner .... LAUNDROMAT

writing .... GRAPHOSPASM, WRITER'S ITCH

automation .... ELECTRONICS, SELF-ACTION, CYBERNATION

automaton .... GOLEM, ROBOT, ANDROID

automobile. See also **auto** .... BUS, (MOTOR)CAR, WHEELS

accessory .... MUFFLER

baggage compartment .... BOOT, TRUNK

body ...... BERLIN(E), TONNEAU

canvas-topped .... CONVERTIBLE

decrepit .... CRATE, FLIVVER

fast .... CLIPPER

framework .... CHASSIS

furnishings .... TRIM

hood .... BONNET

lamp .... HEADLIGHT

like a coupe .... CABRIOLET

model .... V-EIGHT

mudguard .... FENDER

operator .... RACER, DRIVER

part .... BRAKE, BUMPER, FENDER, CLUTCH, CHASSIS, IGNITION, ALTERNATOR, RADIATOR, CARBURETOR, HOOD, GEAR, HORN, CHOKE, TAILLIGHT, GENERATOR, STARTER, SPEEDOMETER, FAN, GAUGE, HEADLIGHT, MUFFLER, EXHAUST(PIPE), OIL, COWL, DISTRIBUTOR, WINDSHIELD, TRANSMISSION

speed .... HIGH, LOW

starter .... IGNITION

two-door .... COUPE

with folding top .... CABRIOLET

automotive boo-boo .... EDSEL

autonomous .... FREE, SEPARATE, INDEPENDENT

autopsy ...... NECROPSY, INQUEST, DISSECTION, POST-MORTEM

Autry, _____ .... GENE

autumn ...... FALL, HARVEST TIME

flower .... ASTER

auxiliary .... SUB, AIDE, ALLY, HELPER, ASSISTANT, COADJUTOR, SUBSIDIARY, SUBSTITUTE

word .... VERB

avail .... USE, SERVE, PROFIT, BENEFIT, UTILIZE

available .... FREE, OPEN, HANDY, READY, USABLE, ON HAND, PRESENT, VACANT, ACCESSIBLE

money .... CASH

avalanche .... PLENTY, PLETHORA, LANDSLIDE, SNOWSLIDE, LAVISHNESS

lily .... WILDFLOWER

Avalon .... ISLE, AVILION

avant garde .... VANGUARD, FORERUNNER

avarice .... LUST, GREED, CUPIDITY, GLUTTONY

avaricious ...... GREEDY, MISERLY, COVETOUS, GRIPPLE, GRASPING, STINGY, RAVENOUS

avast .... HALT, STOP, CEASE

avaunt .... AROINT, BEGONE

ave .... HAIL, GREETING, FAREWELL, SALUTATION

avena .... OAT, GRASS

avenaceous .... OATEN

avenge .... PUNISH, REQUITE, RETORT, COUNTER, REVENGE, RETALIATE

avenger .... ATE, NEMESIS, VINDICATOR

avenging .... VINDICTIVE

spirit ...... ATE, FURY, ALECTO, MEGAERA, TISIPHONE

avenue .... LANE, PIKE, ACCESS, DRIVE, ROADWAY, ALLEY, PASS(AGE), OUTLET, PROMENADE, MEANS, THOROUGHFARE

of shops .... MALL

of trees .... ARCADE

aver .... AFFIRM, ALLEGE, ASSERT, DECLARE

average .... MEAN, USUAL, MEDIAN, NORM(AL), ORDINARY, STANDARD

averse .... LOATH, AGAINST, OPPOSED, RELUCTANT, UNWILLING

aversion .... HATE, DISLIKE, ANTIPATHY, REVULSION, REPUGNANCE

avert ...... WARD, AVOID, HINDER, DEVIATE, THWART, PREVENT, FRUSTRATE

a blow .... DUCK

a draft .... DODGE

a thrust .... PARRY
Avesta language .... ZEND
aviary ...... VOLERY, BIRD(S)CAGE
aviate .... FLY
aviator .... FLYER, PILOT, AIRMAN
free-lance .... BARNSTORMER
hazard .... BLACKOUT
signal .... CONTACT
with five kills .... ACE
aviatrix, famous
.... (AMELIA)EARHART
avid .... KEEN, EAGER, ARDENT,
GREEDY
avifauna .... ORNIS
avion .... AIRPLANE
avis indica .... APUS
aviso ...... BOAT, ADVICE, NOTICE,
INFORMATION
avital .... ANCESTRAL
avocado .... PEAR, TREE, FRUIT,
AGUACATE
Mexican .... COYO
avocation .... HOBBY, PASTIME,
SIDELINE
avocet .... COOT, STILT, STORK,
GODWIT, PLOVER
avoid .... MISS, SHUN, SHIRK,
ESCAPE, REFRAIN, SIDESTEP
a blow .... DUCK
a person .... SNUB
a plea, in law .... QUASH
commitment .... HEDGE, HEM
AND HAW
conscription .... DODGE
crowds .... SHUN, EVADE
responsibility .... SHIRK
something harmful
.... ESCHEW
voting .... ABSTAIN
work .... SHIRK, MALINGER,
GOLDBRICK
avoidable .... PREVENTABLE
avoidance .... SHUNNING,
ESCHEWAL, ANNULMENT,
ABSTINENCE
of battle .... FABIAN
of duty/tax payment
.... EVASION
of game .... DEFAULT
slang .... COP-OUT
avoirdupois .... WEIGHT,
POUNDAGE, HEAVINESS,
EMBONPOINT
1⅓ pounds .... CATTY
avouch .... AVOW, AFFIRM,
TESTIFY, GUARANTEE
avow .... AVER, ADMIT, ASSERT,
CONFESS, DECLARE, DISCLOSE,
ACKNOWLEDGE
avowal .... WORD, SHRIFT,
STATEMENT, ACCEPTANCE,

CONFESSION
avowed .... ALLEGED, CLAIMED,
PLEDGED
awa .... KAVA, MILKFISH
Scottish .... AWAY
await .... BIDE, FACE, ATTEND,
IMPEND, LOITER, HANG
AROUND, EXPECT, CONFRONT,
ANTICIPATE
awake .... KEEN, ALERT, ROUSE,
ACTIVE, KNOWING, ACTIVATE,
CONSCIOUS, UNSLEEPING
awakening .... REVIVAL
award ...... GRANT, MEDAL, PRIZE,
DECREE, REWARD, DECISION,
JUDGMENT, ADJUDGE,
SETTLEMENT
in sports .... LETTER
journalism/literature/music
.... PULITZER
kind of .... BOOBY PRIZE
movie .... OSCAR
peace/medicine/economics
.... NOBEL
TV .... EMMY
aware .... HEP, HIP, ALERT,
COGNIZANT, INFORMED,
CONSCIOUS, SENSIBLE, ON TO,
PERCEPTIVE
awash .... AFLOAT, FLOODED,
DRENCHED, FLOATING
away ...... OFF, OUT, GONE, APART,
FAR-OFF, ABSENT, ABROAD,
ELSEWHERE
from mouth .... ABORAL
from the shore .... SEAWARD
from wind .... ALEE
prefix .... AB
away, _____ (shrink) .... SHY
awe .... FEAR, DREAD, TERROR,
WONDER, RESPECT,
REVERENCE, VENERATION
aweather .... WINDWARD
opposite of .... ALEE
awesome .... GREAT, LOFTY,
EERIE, BIZARRE, FEARFUL,
DREADFUL, TERRIBLE,
APPALLING, ASTONISHING
awful .... BAD, UGLY, HORRID,
HIDEOUS, IMPOSING,
DREADFUL, TERRIBLE,
APPALLING
awfully .... VERY, EXTREMELY
awkward .... BULKY, INEPT,
CLUMSY, IGNORANT,
NESCIENT, GAUCHE,
UNWIELDY, MALADROIT
age .... ADOLESCENCE
boat .... ARK, DROGHER
person .... GAWK, LOUT,
DUFFER, GALOOT, RUSTIC,

SIMPLETON
stroke .... FOOZLE
awl .... AUGER, ELSIN, BODKIN,
GIMLET
for picking typeset .... BODKIN
shaped .... SUBULATE
type of .... PEG, SEWING
with chisel head .... BRADAWL
awn .... BARB, SETA, BEARD,
FIBER, ARISTA
awned .... ARISTATE
awning .... CANVAS, MARQUEE,
SHELTER, SUNSHADE
of bed/door .... CANOPY
Roman .... VELARIUM
AWOL .... OVER THE HILL
awry .... AGEE, ASKEW, AMISS,
AGLEY, CROOKED, OBLIQUE,
TIPSY, WRONG, DISTORTED
slang .... COCKEYED
ax(e) .... ADZ, HATCHET
bonehead .... TOMAHAWK
cut of .... KERF
head, prehistoric .... CELT
Indian/stone .... TOMAHAWK
like tool .... ADZ(E)
"the" ..... LAYOFF, DISMISSAL,
DISCHARGE
type of .... HATCHET,
HALBERT, HALBERD, POLEAX,
TOMAHAWK, BATTLE-AX
axial .... KEY, MIDDLE, ROTARY,
CENTRAL
axil .... ALA, ANGLE
axilla .... ARMPIT
axillary .... ALAR
axiom .... MAXIM, BELIEF,
PREMISE, PRINCIPLE
axis deer .... CHITAL
member .... JAPAN,
(NAZI)GERMANY,
(FASCIST)ITALY
axle .... BAR, ROD, ARBOR,
SPINDLE
bearing .... HOTBOX
ayah .... AMAH, (NURSE)MAID
ayatollah .... LEADER, TEACHER
ay(e) .... YEA, YES, EVER, YEAH,
ALAS, ALWAYS, AFFIRMATIVE
aye-aye .... LEMUR
Aymara's cousin .... INCA
ayuntamiento .... CITY HALL,
TOWN HALL
azalea .... SHRUB, FLOWER,
LAUREL
Azerbaijan's capital .... BAKU
chief city .... TABRIZ
native .... TURK
other spelling
.... AZERBAIDZHAN

47

azinuth ...... HORIZON, ALTITUDE, (COMPASS)DIRECTION
azo, as combining form .... NITROGEN
Azores city/town .... HORTA, PONTA DELGADA, LAJES DO PICO, VILA DO PORTO, ANGRADO HEROISMO
district .... HORTA, PONTA DELGADA, ANGRA DO HEROISMO

island ..... PICO, SANTA MARIA, GRACIOSA, CORVO, SAO MIGUEL, FLORES, TERCEIRA, FAIAL, SAO JORGE
port .... HORTA
volcano .... PICO
azote .... NITROGEN
azoth .... MERCURY, QUICKSILVER
azothic .... NITRIC
Aztec .... NAHUATLAN
country .... AZTLAN

emperor .... MONTEZUMA
god .... XIPE, EECATL
hero .... NATA
language .... NAHUATL
spear .... ATLATL
temple .... TEOPAN
azure .... CYANIC, (SKY)BLUE, CELESTE, CERULEAN
azygous .... ODD, SINGLE, MATELESS
azym .... BREAD

B

B .... SECOND, INFERIOR, SECONDARY
B .... GUN, SHOT
girl .... BARGIRL, BARMAID
Greek .... BETA
Hebrew .... BETH
in chemistry .... BORON
in chess .... BISHOP
letter .... BE, BEE, BETA
picture (movies): sl. .... QUICKIE
ba .... SOUL
Ba, in chemistry .... BARIUM
baa .... BLEAT
bleater .... LAMB, SHEEP
Baal .... IDOL, (SUN)GOD
Baalist .... IDOLATER
Bab .... BABUDDIN
babbitt ...... UPSTART, PHILISTINE, BUSINESSMAN
Babbitt, _____ .... ISAAC, IRVING, GEORGE
babble .... GAB, BLAB, RAVE, PRATE, GIBBER, GOSSIP, GURGLE, JABBER, MURMUR, BLABBER, CHATTER, PRATTLE
babbling .... DIZZY, GIDDY, RAMBLING, INCOHERENT
babe .... BABY, GIRL, INFANT
in the woods .... NAIVE
Babe Ruth's forte ...... HOMERUN
Babel .... TOWER, JARGON, TUMULT, CONFUSION
babirusa .... HOG
baboo .... SIR, CLERK, TITLE
baboon .... APE, CHACMA, (MAN)DRILL
babu .... SIR, TITLE
babul .... ACACIA
babushka .... SCARF, KERCHIEF
baby .... TOT, BABE, SPOIL, YOUNG, INFANT, CHILD, CODDLE, PAMPER, CHRISOM, INDULGE, SUCKLING,

OFFSPRING
ailment .... CROUP
bathtub .... BASSINET, BATHINETTE
bed .... CRIB, CRADLE
bedroom .... NURSERY
boots/shoes .... BOOTEES
breechcloth .... DIAPER
cap .... BIGGIN, BONNET
carriage .... PRAM, BUGGY, STROLLER, GO-CART, PERAMBULATOR
diaper .... TOWEL, NAPKIN
food .... PAP, FORMULA
garment/outfit .... CREEPER, LAYETTE
goose .... GOSLING
grand .... PIANO
head's soft spot .... FONTANEL(LE)
hooter .... OWLET
Indian .... PAPOOSE
Italian .... BAMBINO
jacket .... SACK, SACQUE
Kermit .... TADPOLE
pacifier .... NIPPLE, TEETHING RING
pants .... SOAKERS
powder .... TALC
premature .... PREEMIE
robe, baptismal .... CHRISOM
sitter ...... AMAH, AUNT, AYAH, NANNY, NURSE
sitter's problem .... BRAT, CRYBABY
sound .... CROW, MEWL
Spanish ..... NENA, NIÑA, NIÑO
swan .... CYGNET
talk/word .... DADA, LISP, BABBLE
teething toy .... CORAL, PACIFIER
tickle .... KOOCHY-KOO
toy .... BAUBLE

babyish .... CHILDISH
Babylonia .... SHINAR, SHINOR
founder .... SEMIRAMIS
Babylonian ...... NATIVE, WICKED
abode of dead .... ARALU
canal .... JESUF
chief god ...... ANU, BEL, HEA, ENKI
chief goddess .... IS(H)TAR
city .... AKKAD, CUNAXA
deity .... ANU, BEL, HEA, ALALU, MERODACH
division .... ELAM, NITUK, SUMER
god .... EA, ZU, ANU, BEL, UTU, ADAD, ADDU, NABU, NEBO, UTUG, DAGAN, ENLIL, MARDUK, NINIB, NANNAR, ANSHAR, RAMMAN, TAMMUZ, SIRIS, SHAMASH
goddess ...... AYA, BAU, ERUA, GULA, NANA(I), NINA, ARURU, ISHTAR
hero .... ETANA
monarch .... ALOROS
neighbor .... ELAMITE
numeral .... SAR(OS)
people .... SUMERIAN
priestess .... ENTUM
river .... TIGRIS
storm god .... ADAD
temple .... BEL, ISTAR
tower .... ZIGGURAT
weight .... MINA
baby's breath .... PLANT, MADDER, HYACINTH, GYPSOPHILA
face, sometimes .... EGGY
piggy .... TOE
bac .... VAT, CISTERN
baccarat .... (CARD)GAME, CHEMIN DE FER
baccate .... PULPY
bacchanal .... ORGY, CAROUSER

cry .... EVOE
bacchante .... M(A)ENAD,
                        CAROUSER
Bacchus .... GOD, DIONYSUS
devotee .... SATYR, TOPER,
        M(A)ENAD, BACCHANT
bachelor .... SINGLE, DIVORCÉ,
     WIDOWER, GRADUATE,
                  CELIBATE
bait .... SPINSTER
girl .... VIRGIN, OLD MAID
bachelor's button .... TANSY,
   KNAPWEED, CORNFLOWER
degree .... BACCALAUREATE
party .... STAG
Bach's composition ...... ARIOSO
back .... AID, TUB, VAT, ABET,
   FUND, HIND, REAR, SECOND,
  ENDORSE, FINANCE, SPONSOR,
  SUPPORT, REVERSE, PROMOTE
and fill .... VEER, ZIGZAG
and forth .... SEESAW,
                 ALTERNATE
at the/near the .... RETRAL
book .... ISSUE, EDITION
book's .... SPINE
call .... REVOKE, WITHDRAW
climb on .... MOUNT
country .... HINTERLAND
cramp .... CRICK
door/gate/entrance
          POSTERN, REAR ENTRY
down/out ..... YIELD, RETREAT,
                WITHDRAW
flow .... EBB, RECEDE
in zoology .... TERGUM
lying on .... SUPINE
of animal ...... RIDGE, DORSUM
of head .... POLL
of insects .... NOTUM
of neck .... NAPE, NUCHA,
           SCRAG, SCRUFF
of skull .... NION, OCCIPITAL
on one's .... HELPLESS,
               BEDRIDDEN
pain .... STITCH
part .... DERRIERE
part: comb. form .... NOTO
part of skull .... OCCIPUT
pertaining to the ...... DORSAL,
                 TERGAL
porch .... STOOP
scratcher .... TOADY
seat, carriage .... DICKEY,
                 RUMBLE
seat driver: colloq. .... WIFE
slapper .... SOFT-SOAPER
take word .... RECALL,
  RECANT, RETRACT, REPUDIATE
talk: colloq. .... LIP, SASS,
                 RETORT

the field .... BET
to back .... BEHIND, TANDEM
toward .... RETRAL
turn one's .... IGNORE
up .... SECOND, FINANCE,
       SUPPORT, SUSTAIN
wound .... STAB
backache .... LUMBAGO
backbite .... DEFAME, ATTACK,
  MALIGN, REVILE, SLANDER,
      VILIFY, TRADUCE
backbone .... PLUCK, RIDGE,
  SPINE, COURAGE, VERTEBRA,
       SPINAL COLUMN
having .... VERTEBRATE
of animal .... CHINE
of fish .... GRATE
of the land .... FARMER
backbreaker .... HERCULEAN
                  TASK
backbreaking .... HEAVY, TIRING,
    ARDUOUS, ONEROUS,
    DIFFICULT, HERCULEAN,
         STRENUOUS
backburner .... SUSPENSION,
         UNESSENTIAL
backdoor .... COVERT, SECRET,
    FURTIVE, POSTERN,
       CLANDESTINE
backdrop .... SETTING, SCENE(RY)
backed .... FAVORED, REINFORCED
backer .... ALLY, DONOR, FUNDER,
  PATRON, SPONSOR, FINANCER
stage show ..... ANGEL, SUGAR
  DADDY, FAIRY GODMOTHER
backfire .... FAIL, RECOIL,
  BOOMERANG, EXPLOSION
backgammon ...... BOARD GAME,
       TRIC(K)TRAC(K)
exposed man .... BLOT
game series .... RUBBER
background .... SETTING,
   ANCESTRY, TRAINING,
  EDUCATION, EXPERIENCE
backhanded .... SHIFTY, ABUSIVE,
  INSOLENT, INSINCERE,
        SARCASTIC
way of catching a ball
              AWKWARD
backhouse .... PRIVY
backlash .... BOUNCE, IMPACT,
  REBUFF, RECOIL, REACTION
backless .... SPINELESS
dress .... DECOLLETE
person .... COWARD, YELLOW
seat .... STOOL, OTTOMAN
backlog .... PILE-UP, RESERVE,
  FIREWOOD, ACCUMULATION
backpack .... KNAPSACK
backset .... RELAPSE
backside .... RUMP, BUTTOCKS

backslide .... FALL, TRIP, SLIP,
    LAPSE, REVERT, RELAPSE
backtrack ...... RETREAT, ABOUT-
                 FACE
backup .... ALTERNATE
backward .... SHY, SLOW,
  BASHFUL, DELAYED, REVERSE,
     REARWARD, RETARDED
backwater .... BAYOU
channel .... BILLABONG
backwoods .... PRIMITIVE
backwoodsman .... RUSTIC,
                HILLBILLY
bacon, bring home the ...... WIN,
                SUCCEED
coating .... RIND
cut .... RASHER
side of .... FLITCH, GAMMON
strip .... LARDO(O)N
bacteremia .... INFECTION
bacteria .... GERMS, MICROBE
culture .... AGAR, STAIN
destroyer/killer .... LYSIN,
   ALEXIN, BACTERICIDE
free of .... ASEPTIC
mass of .... CLUMP
organ of locomotion
            FLAGELLUM
causing food poisoning/
  diphtheria
           SALMONELLA
responsible for tetanus
           CLOSTRIDIA
rod-shaped .... BACILLI
S and comma-shaped
              VIBRIO
spherical .... COCCI
spiral-shaped .... SPIRILLA
bacteriologist's wire .... OESE
bacterium .... FUNGUS, BACILLUS
plural of .... BACTERIA
Bactria .... BALKH
bactrian .... CAMEL
bad .... ILL, BASE, EVIL, MEAN,
  UNFIT, WICKED, ROTTEN,
  HATEFUL, HEINOUS, SINFUL,
    SPOILED, INFERIOR
blood .... HATE, ENMITY,
  ANIMOSITY, RESENTMENT
boy .... IMP, RASCAL
breath .... HALITOSIS
character .... DISHONOR
check: sl. .... RUBBER
combining form .... MAL, MIS,
                 DIS
debt .... UNCOLLECTIBLE
deed .... DISSERVICE
faith .... DECEIT
for one's health ..... HARMFUL
girl/woman ..... DOXY, QUEAN,
  TRAMP, FLOOZY, WHORE,

HARLOT, FLOOZIE, TART, HUSSY, TROLLOP, STRUMPET, PROSTITUTE
guy .... VILLAIN
habit .... VICE
humor .... TIFF, TEMPER
influence .... ILL-WIND, ROTTEN EGG
language .... CURSING, SWEARING, PROFANITY
liquor: colloq. .... BOUSE
loser's reaction .... SOUR GRAPES
luck ..... CESS, JINX, AMESACE, AMBSACE, HOODOO, MISHAP, WANION, MISFORTUNE
luck man .... JONAH, JONAS
man (of the old West) .... GUNMAN, DESPERADO
mannered person .... BOOR, CLOD, GOON, LOUT, S.O.B., THUG, STINKER
mouth .... DEFAME, MALIGN, REVILE, SLANDER, CRITICIZE
move .... BALK, FALL, SLIP, ERROR, BLUNDER, MISSTEP
name .... ILL-REPUTE
news .... PROBLEM, TROUBLE
prefix .... CACO, MAL(O)
quality .... INFERIOR, DEFECTIVE
smell .... REEK, STENCH, MEPHITIS
smell of oil/fats .... RANCID
smelling .... MEPHITIC, STINKING, MALODOROUS
sport .... CRYBABY
taste .... VULGARITY, IMPROPRIETY
temper .... BILE, ANGER, SPLEEN
temper sign .... TANTRUM
tempered .... GRUFF, DORTY, SURLY, TESTY, CRUSTY, CRANKY, GRUMPY, WASPISH, SNAPPISH, PEEVISH, GRUMPISH, IRRITABLE, SPLENETIC
tempered person .... FURY, SHREW, VIRAGO, HOTHEAD
treatment .... ABUSE, TORTURE, OPPRESSION
badak .... RHINO
badge .... PIN, MARK, SIGN, EMBLEM, SYMBOL, INSIGNIA
Japanese .... MON
of braid .... CORDON
of honor .... MEDAL
of ribbon .... CORDON
on arm .... BRASSARD
on hat .... COCKADE
badger ...... NAG, ANNOY, HARRY,

HARASS, HECKLE, WORRY, TEASE, PESTER, TORMENT
animal .... HAWKER, BROCK, WOMBAT, BANDICOOT
Canadian .... CARCAJOU
European .... BROCK
game .... BLACKMAIL
genus .... MELES
honey .... RATEL
Java .... TELEDU
like animal .... PAHMI, MARMOT
Badger State .... WISCONSIN
badgered .... BESET, NEEDLED, PLAGUED
badinage .... TALK, TEASE, BANTER, CHATTER
badlands .... WASTE
Badlands mountain .... BUTTE
badly .... ILLY, POORLY, HARMFULLY, WICKEDLY
colloquial ..... MUCH, GREATLY
off .... HARD-UP
badminton .... DRINK, (COURT)GAME
cork .... SHUTTLECOCK
racket .... BATTLEDORE
Baedeker .... GUIDEBOOK
Baffin's discovery .... SEA, ISLAND
baffle .... BALK, FOIL, BLOCK, ELUDE, EVADE, STUMP, BOGGLE, PUZZLE, MUFFLE, WONDER, CONFUSE, MYSTIFY, THWART, BEWILDER, NONPLUS, CONFOUND, FRUSTRATE
baffling ...... ELUSIVE, CONFUSING, UNSCRUTABLE
device .... WALL, SCREEN
problem .... POSER, PUZZLE, DILEMMA, MYSTERY, QUANDARY
question ...... ENIGMA, PUZZLE, RIDDLE, CONUNDRUM
bag .... SAC, CYST, POKE, TRAP, CATCH, PURSE, POUCH, SEIZE, UDDER, LUGGAGE, SATCHEL, SUITCASE, CONTAINER
floating .... BALLOON
for books, papers, etc. .... BRIEFCASE
kind of .... DUFFEL, RECEPTACLE
making material .... FLAX, HEMP, JUTE, PAPER, BURLAP, SACKING
slang .... WOMAN, CAPTURE
sleeping .... SACK
toilette .... MUSETTE

with perfumed powder .... SACHET
bagasse .... MEGASS(E), (CANE)REFUSE
bagatelle .... TRIFLE
baggage .... LUGGAGE, TRUNKS, VALISES, SUITCASES
boy .... PORTER
car/wagon .... FOURGON
carrier .... HAM(M)AL, PORTER, REDCAP
slang .... GIRL, SAUCY, WOMAN
baggie .... BELLY, STOMACH
baggy .... LOOSE, PUFFED, BULGING, UNPRESSED
bagman: Eng. .... SALESMAN
bagnio .... CABANA, PRISON, BROTHEL, BATHHOUSE
Bagnold .... ENID
bagpipe .... DRONE, LOURE, MUSETTE, DOODLESACK
drone .... BOURDON
flute/part .... CHANTER
music .... PIBROCH
play/sound .... SKIRL
bagworm .... LARVA, CATERPILLAR
Bah! .... FIE, ROT, TUT, RATS, NUTS, PSHAW
Bahamas capital .... NASSAU
cay .... GUN, RUM, LONG, EXUMA, PLANA, VERDE, SAMANA, FLAMINGO
channel .... SANTAREN, TONGUE OF THE OCEAN
island .... CAT, LONG, ANDROS, ABACO, EXUMA, ACKLINS, HARBOUR, MAYAGUANA, ELEUTHERA, RAGGED, CROOKED, INAGUA, BIMINI, WATLING, NEW PROVIDENCE
major language .... ENGLISH
monetary unit .... BAHAMIAN DOLLAR
mountain .... ALVERNIA
premier .... PINDLING
Bahia .... (SAO)SALVADOR
Bahr _____, Egyptian name for the Nile .... ENNIL
Bahrain capital .... MANAMA, MANAMEH
city .... MUHURRAQ
language .... ARABIC
religion .... ISLAM
bail .... BOND, LADE, SCOOP, BUCKET, PLEDGE, FREE, RELEASE, SECURITY, PALISADES, FORTIFICATION
bond ..... SURETY, GUARANTEE, INSURANCE
one who needs ...... DETAINEE,

PRISONER
out .... JUMP, RELEASE,
PARACHUTE
Bailey, lexicographer
.... NATHANIEL
bailiff .... REEVE, MARSHAL,
SHERIFF, STEWARD,
OVERSEER, TIPSTAFF,
CONSTABLE
bailiwick .... FIELD, DOMAIN,
REGION, SPHERE, DISTRICT,
HOMEGROUND, JURISDICTION
bain-marie .... PAN
bairn ...... SON, CHILD, DAUGHTER
bait ...... DUPE, GOAD, LURE, RIDE,
DECOY, SNARE, TRAP, TEASE,
TEMPT, HECKLE,
ENTICE(MENT), BADGER,
HECTOR, SEDUCE, ATTRACT,
GUDGEON
drop .... DIP, DAP
fish .... CHUM, LURE
take .... BITE
baize ...... CLOTH, DRAPE, DOMETT
bake .... COOK, FIRE, BROIL,
ROAST, ANNEAL, HARDEN,
DRY UP
with crumbs .... ESCALOP,
SCALLOP
baked Alaska .... PIE, DESSERT
clay .... TILE
dishes, etc. .... CROCKERY
pot .... OLLA
baker bird .... HORNERO
baker's cyst .... BURSA
dozen .... THIRTEEN
equipment .... MIXER, TIMER,
BEATER, BLENDER
itch .... RASH, PSORIASIS
job .... KNEAD
kneading trough .... BRAKE
material .... FLOUR, YEAST,
LEAVEN
shovel .... PEEL
tool/utensil .... PAN, WHIP,
KNIFE, SIEVE, BOWL, SPOON,
CUTTER, TURNER, PASTRY
BAG, SPATULA, STRAINER
baking chamber ...... KILN, OAST,
OVEN
dish .... RAMEKIN, SCALLOP,
RAMEQUIN, CASSEROLE
instruction .... RECIPE
pit: Hawaiian .... IMU
soda .... SALERATUS
baksheesh .... TIP, ALMS,
GRATUITY
bal _____ .... MASQUE, TABARIN
Balaam's beast .... ASS
balalaika .... GUITAR
balance ...... EVEN, LEVEL, LIBRA,

MATCH, POISE, ADJUST,
EXCESS, OFFSET, SCALES,
SQUARE, SURPLUS,
EQUAL(IZE), REMAINDER,
SYMMETRY, STABILITY,
EQUILIBRIUM
crossbar of .... BEAM
of sales .... ATRY
sheet .... FINANCIAL
STATEMENT
state of .... EQUIPOISE
weighing .... STEELYARD
balancer .... HALTER, ACROBAT,
GYMNAST, WIRE WALKER,
TIGHTROPE WALKER
of books .... ACCOUNTANT
balancing weight .... BALLAST
balas .... SPINEL
balata gum .... CHICLE
Balboa's ocean .... PACIFIC
balcony .... LOGE, TIER, PORCH
GAZEBO, LOGGIA, GALLERY,
PORTICO, TERRACE,
MEZZANINE
bald .... BARE, BLUNT, FRANK,
GLABROUS, HAIRLESS, PLAIN,
TREELESS, UNADORNED
headed man .... PILGARLIC
baldachin ...... CANOPY, BROCADE
Balder, giant victim of ...... LOKI
parent of .... ODIN, FRIGG
slayer of .... HODER, HODUR
wife of .... NANNA
balderdash .... PALAVER,
NONSENSE, RIGMAROLE
baldness ...... ACOMIA, ALOPECIA,
CALVITIES
baldpate .... WIDGEON
cover .... WIG, TOUPEE
baldric .... BELT
Baldwin .... APPLE
cousin .... WINESAP
bale .... WOE, BAIL, BUNDLE,
SORROW, PACKAGE, DISASTER,
DEJECTION
Balearic Island .... MAJORCA,
MENORCA, MINORCA,
MALLORCA
capital .... PALMA
city/town .... INCA, ARTA,
ALAYOR, SOLLER, FELANITX,
POLLENSA, MANACOR,
CIUDADELA, ANDRAITX,
DRAGONERA
is province of .... SPAIN
language .... CATALAN
baleen .... WHALEBONE
balefire .... PYRE, BONFIRE
baleful .... BAD, EVIL, DEADLY,
HOSTILE, HURTFUL, SINISTER,
INJURIOUS

baler .... TIER, BUNDLER
Bali holy day .... NJEPI
balk .... JIB, SHY, FOIL, STOP,
ERROR, REBEL, HINDER,
THWART, BLUNDER
Balkan .... SLAV, SERB(IAN),
BULGAR(IAN), SLOVENE
state .... GREECE, ALBANIA,
BULGARIA, ROMANIA,
YUGOSLAVIA
balker, congenital .... ASS, MULE,
DONKEY
Balkh .... BACTRIA
balky .... RESTIVE, CONTRARY,
STUBBORN, OBSTINATE
ball .... SHOT, DANCE, GLOBE,
IVORY, COTILLION, BULLET,
PLANET, SPHERE, GLOBULE,
PROJECTILE
and chain: sl. .... WIFE
batted high .... FLY
game .... KENO, RUGBY,
TENNIS, BASEBALL, FOOTBALL,
CRICKET, BOWLING, LACROSSE,
SOCCER, BASKETBALL
have a: sl. .... ENJOY
hit for practice .... FUNGO
low .... LINER
metal .... BEARING
metal, athletics .... HAMMER,
SHOTPUT
of electric discharge
.... CORPOSANT
of meat/rice .... PINDA
of perfume mixture
.... POMANDER
of yarn/thread .... CLEW
on the .... ALERT, EFFICIENT
play: sl. .... COOPERATE
rolling, get the .... START
rope missile .... BOLA(S)
sign displayer .... PAWNSHOP
supporter .... TEE
swing bat at .... SWAT
throwing device .... TRAP
tiny .... GLOBULE
up .... MUDDLE, CONFUSE
used in jai alai .... PELOTA
ballad .... LAY, POEM, SONG,
CALYPSO, DERRY, CHANSON,
CHANTEY, SPIRITUAL
hero .... LOCHINVAR
monger .... POETASTER
singer .... MINSTREL,
TROUBADOUR
stanza, rhyme of .... ABCB
word .... DERRY
ballast .... STABILIZE(R)
ballerina .... DANSEUSE, TOE
DANCER

descriptive word for a
.... PRIMA, ASOLUTA
famous .... FONTEYN, RASCH,
MARKOVA, SHEARER,
ULANOVA, TALLCHIEF
finale .... TWIRL, PIROUETTE
forte .... TOE-DANCE,
PIROUETTE
garb of .... TUTU
ballet .... ADAGIO, DANCE,
BEZANT, MASQUE,
CHOREOGRAPHY
dance solo .... PAS SEUL
dancer .... BALLERINA,
DANSEUSE, CORYPHEE,
FIGURANT
dancer's buoyancy ..... BALON
director .... IMPRESARIO
famous .... SWAN LAKE
jump .... JETE, ENTRECHAT
movement .... PLIE
number .... TOE DANCE
number between acts
.... INTERMEZZO
Petipa's .... RAYMONDA
posture .... ARABESQUE
step .... PAS, GLISSADE
turn .... FOUETTE, PIROUETTE
wear .... TUTU, TIGHTS,
LEOTARD
ballista .... CATAPULT
ballistic missile launching
.... BLAST-OFF
launching place .... PAD
storage place .... SILO
warhead .... PAYLOAD
balloon .... BAG, KITE, BLIMP,
SWELL, INFLATE, DIRIGIBLE,
BALL, AEROSTAT, RUBBERBAG
altitude controller .... BALLAST
bag/covering .... ENVELOPE
ballast/mooring line
.... DRAGROPE
basket .... CAR, NACELLE
cabin .... GONDOLA
gas .... HELIUM, HYDROGEN
pilot .... AERONAUT
shape of ..... ROUND, SAUSAGE
trial .... TEST, FEELER
vine .... HEARTSEED
ballot ...... SLATE, VOICE, CHOICE,
TICKET, VOTE(S), VOTING
straw .... POLL
ballroom dance .... WALTZ,
REDOWA
balls tosser .... JUGGLER
ballyhoo .... PLUG, TALK, TOUT,
UPROAR, ADVERTISE, WRITE-
UP, HYPERBOLE, PUBLICITY,
PROPAGANDA
balm .... OIL, RESIN, SALVE,

SOOTH, ANODYNE,
FRAGRANCE, BALSAM,
UNGUENT, OINTMENT,
SEDATIVE, ANALGESIC
for divorce .... ALIMONY
for injury .... DAMAGES
kind of ..... ARNICA, MENTHOL,
GLYCERIN, LANOLIN, VASELINE
of Gilead .... FIR, OIL,
BALSAM, POPLAR, OINTMENT
Balmoral .... CAP, CASTLE,
PETTICOAT
balmy .... MILD, SOFT, CRAZY,
MOONY, GENTLE, FOOLISH,
HEALING, IDIOTIC, FRAGRANT,
SOOTHING
balneal .... BATH(ING)
baloney .... ROT, BUNK, HUMBUG,
BOLOGNA, SAUSAGE,
BUNCOMBE, NONSENSE
balsa .... RAFT, TREE, WOOD,
CORKWOOD
like wood .... BONGO
balsam .... GUM, BALM, TOLU,
MUSK, RESIN, COPAIBA,
IMPATIENS, LIQUIDAMBAR
gum resin .... BALM, STORAX
Swiss .... RIGA
tree .... TOLU
Balt .... ESTH
Baltic gulf .... RIGA
island .... DAGO, OS(S)EL,
ALSEN
port .... KIEL, RIGA, MEMEL,
REVAL, STETTIN
river .... ODER
Sea city .... LIBAU, LIEBAJA
seaport .... ROSTOCK
state .... LITHUANIA, LATVIA,
ESTONIA, FINLAND
Baltimore oriole ...... HANGBIRD,
HANGNEST, GOLDEN ROBIN
stove .... LATROBE
Balto-Slav .... LETT
Baluchistan capital .... QUETTA
city/town .... BELA, DADU,
MACH, NUSHKI, PISHIN,
MASTUNG, GANDAVA,
BARKHAN, KHUZDAR, LORALAI
grain .... JOWAR
mountain .... HALA
race .... BRAHOES
river .... BOLAN, MOOLA
ruler .... KHAN, SIRDAR
tribe .... REKI
tribesman .... MARI
balustrade .... POST, FENCE,
RAILING, BAN(N)ISTER
Balzac's father .... GORIOT
bambino: Ital. .... CHILD,
BABY(BOY)

Bambi's aunt .... ENA
bamboo ...... CANE, REED, GRASS,
SEDGE, RATTAN, TONKIN
bear .... PANDA
curtain ...... BARRIER, SECRECY
like .... REEDY
shoot pickle .... ACHAR
stalk .... REED
bamboozle .... DUPE, CHEAT,
TRICK, PUZZLE, BUFFALO,
HOCUS-POCUS
ban .... TABU, CURSE, TABOO,
FORBID, CONDEMN,
BLOCKADE, GOVERNOR,
EXCOMMUNICATION, PROHIBIT,
PROCLAMATION
Bana, daughter of .... USHA
banal .... CORNY, TRITE, STALE,
TRIVIAL, HACKNEYED
banality .... CLICHE, PLATITUDE
banana .... FEI, ENSETE, PLANTAIN
bunch/cluster .... HAND
disease .... MOSAIC
like fruit/tropical
.... PLANTAIN
of the .... MUSACEOUS
oil: sl. .... NONSENSE
Philippine .... SABA, SAGING,
LACATAN, LATUNDAN
plant .... MUSA, PESANG
bananas: sl. ...... CRAZY, WACKY,
BONKERS, EXCITED
band .... BELT, TAPE, GROUP,
COLLAR, BINDING, COMPANY,
GIRDLE, GATHER, FASCIA,
COPULA, FILAMENT, STRAP,
STRIP, STRIPE, CROWD,
FILLET, ORCHESTRA
across escutcheon .... FESS
aid .... PLASTER, DRESSING
brain .... LIGULA
deputized/sheriff's .... POSSE
head .... AGAL, CORONET
ecclesiastical .... ORPHREY
leader .... SHAW, CUGAT,
JAMES, CHORAGUS, VALLEE,
WHITEMAN
leaders .... CHORAGI
master .... CONDUCTOR
mourning .... WEED
narrow .... TAPE, STRIA(E)
of soldiers .... COHORT
of stone on wall .... CORDON
ornamental .... CORONET
priest's arm .... PHANO,
FANO(N), FANUM
together .... JOIN
wheel .... RIGGER
bandage .... GAUZE, SPICA, STUPE,
SPONGE, SWATH(E), LIGATE,
LIGATURE, POULTICE

in surgery .... FASCIA
shaped .... LIGULATE
used as compress .... DOSSIL
bandan(n)a ...... (HAND)KERCHIEF
bandeau .... (HAIR)RIBBON,
                        BRASSIERE
banderilla .... DART
banderole .... FLAG, PENNANT,
         BANNEROL, STREAMER
bandicoot .... RAT, BADGER
bandit .... ROBBER, OUTLAW,
        BRIGAND, LADRONE,
             HIGHWAYMAN
more than one .... BANDITTI
banditry .... PLUNDER,
             BRIGANDAGE
bandleader .... CHORAGUS
bandmaster .... SOUSA,
             CONDUCTOR
bandog ...... MASTIFF, WATCHDOG,
            BLOODHOUND
bandoline .... POMADE
bandore ...... PANDORA, PANDORE
bandwagon riders ...... WINNERS
bandy .... CLUB, BOWED,
   CHAFFER, GIVE-AND-TAKE,
            EXCHANGE
legs .... BOWED
some are .... LEGS
bane .... HARM, PEST, RUIN,
     CURSE, VENOM, POISON
baneful .... BAD, DEADLY,
    RUINOUS, VENOMOUS,
           PERNICIOUS
Banff National Park lake
                     LOUISE
bang .... HIT, BEAT, SLAM, CLOSE,
      STRIKE, EXPLOSION
slang .... PLEASURE,
           ENJOYMENT
up .... BRUISE, DAMAGE
Bangalore, where it is
                     MYSORE
banged-up .... A-ONE,
    EXCELLENT, WELL DONE
Bangkok is capital of ...... SIAM,
             THAILAND
Thai name of .... KRUNG THEP
bangle .... ANKLET, ARMLET,
             BRACELET
bangs .... FRINGE, HAIRDO,
             HAIRCUT
banian .... SHIRT, MERCHANT
banish .... EXILE, EXPEL, DEPORT,
   DISMISS, RELEGATE, PUNISH,
  PROSCRIBE, EXPATRIATE
banister .... BALUSTER,
   HANDRAIL, BALUSTRADE
banjo .... SAMISEN
string sound ...... TUM, TWANG
bank .... BEACH, RELY, RIDGE,

SHORE, SHOAL, VAULT,
     DEPEND, HILLSIDE,
        DEPOSITORY
clerk .... TELLER
employee .... RUNNER
kind of .... EYE, POOL, BLOOD,
     PIGGY, DOMESTIC
note .... BILL, PAPER MONEY
river .... RIPA
river, pert. to .... RIPARIAN
teller's window .... WICKET
vole .... MOUSE
bankbook .... PASSBOOK
banker .... LAMONT, GIANNINI,
     MORGAN, SHROFF,
        ROTHSCHILD
banking game .... FARO
bankroll .... WAD
colloquial .... FINANCE,
           CAPITALIZE
bankrupt .... BROKE, RUINED,
   FAILURE, DESTITUTE,
  INSOLVENT, PENNILESS
abbreviation .... BKPT
banner .... FLAG, ENSIGN,
   BLAZON, PENNON, LEADING,
   PENNANT, GONFALON,
  FOREMOST, BANDEROLE
headline .... STREAMER
bannock .... CAKE
banquet .... MEAL, FEAST, DINNER
rich, luxurious ...... LUCULLAN
banquette ...... BENCH, SIDEWALK
banshee .... SPIRIT
bant .... DIET
bantam .... FOWL, SMALL,
     MIDGET, PINT-SIZE
publication .... TABLOID,
   VESTBOOK, POCKETBOOK
banteng .... OX, TSINE
banter .... JEST, JOSH, CHAFF,
   TEASE, BADINAGE, RAILLERY,
  PERSIFLAGE, PLEASANTRY
bantling .... BRAT, YOUNGSTER
Bantu .... JAGA, KAF(F)IR
Congo .... RUA, WARUA,
            BAKALAI
language .... ILA, SUTO,
             RONGA
lion .... SIMBA
nation .... GOGO
native .... ZULU, YAKU,
   DUALA, SWAZI, BASUTO
speaking people
                  BECHUANA
tribe .... BAYA, BULE, JAGA,
  HAKU, GOMA, RAVI, RORI,
             PONDO
banzai ...... CRY, CHEER, CHARGE,
           GREETING
baobab .... TREE, FIBER

leaves, dried/powdered
                     LALO
baptism .... RITE, NAMING,
   INITIATION, PURIFICATION
for example .... SACRAMENT
of fire .... TEST, ORDEAL
baptismal basin .... FONT, LAVER,
           BAPTISTERY
cloth/robe .... CHRISOM
oil .... CHRISM
water .... LAVER
baptize .... DIP, NAME, PURIFY,
  CLEANSE, CHRISTEN, INITIATE,
            SPRINKLE
bar .... PUB, ROD, BISTRO, HINDER,
  HURDLE, OPPOSE, COUNTER,
  EXCLUDE, STRIPE, BARRIER,
    LAWYERS, TAPROOM,
  DRAMSHOP, OBSTRUCT,
   TAPHOUSE, WINESHOP
chisel-pointed .... SPUDDER
dividing .... MULLION
door .... STANG
employee ..... B-GIRL, TENDER,
             TAPSTER
for holding hair ..... BARRETTE
for mining .... GAD
habitué .... BARFLY
iron ingot .... BLOOM
legally .... ESTOP
of _____ .... SOAP, METAL,
    JUSTICE, CHOCOLATE
of justice .... COURT
of loom .... EASER
order .... CHASER, PEANUTS,
   (TROPICAL)DRINK
pin .... BROOCH
room .... SALOON, TAPROOM
sinister .... BATON
slang .... GIN MILL
soap frame .... SESS
square metal .... BILLET
supporting .... FID
used with fulcrum ...... LEVER
Bara, actress .... THEDA
barb ...... AWN, JAG, FLUE, FLUKE,
  HORSE, SPIKE, SPINE, STING,
  PIGEON, BRISTLE, SHARPNESS
of feather .... HARL, HERL
of wit .... STING
small .... BARBEL, BARBULE
Barbados fish .... GUPPY
native .... BIM, BARBADIAN
Barbara .... BUSH, EDEN, HALE,
     RUSH, WALTERS
barbarian .... HUN, GOTH(IC),
  BEAST, BRUTE, SAVAGE,
  VANDAL, PRIMITIVE
barbarism .... SOLECISM,
           IGNORANCE
barbarity .... CRUELTY,

SAVAGERY, VIOLENCE, BRUTALITY

barbarized term/word .... CORRUPTION

barbarous .... CRUEL, BRUTAL, GOTHIC, VULGAR, IGNORANT, PRIMITIVE

Barbary ape .... MAGOT

horse .... BARB

state .... ALGIERS, TUNIS, MOROCCO, TRIPOLI

barbate .... AWNED, BEARDED

barbecue .... BROIL, BURGOO, COOKOUT, ROAST, ROTISSERIE

bar .... SPIT, SKEWER

site .... PATIO, BEACH, BACKYARD

barbed .... HOOKED, CUTTING, STINGING, UNCINATE

dart .... BANDERILLA

missile .... DART, ARROW, SPEAR, HARPOON

point .... FLUE

spear .... GAFF

tool .... HOOK

wire blaster .... BANGALORE

wire obstacle .... ABAT(T)IS

barbel ...... BARB, FISH, BARBULE

fish .... WATTLE

fish with ..... MULLET, CATFISH

barber .... SHAVE(R), SNIPPER, TONSOR, HAIRCUTTER

of Seville .... FIGARO

shop chore .... SHAVE, HAIRCUT, HAIR STYLE

work .... TONSORIAL

barber's call .... NEXT

barbet .... BIRD, POODLE

barbital .... DRUG, VERONAL

barbiturate .... SEDATIVE

slang .... UPPERS, DOWNERS, UPPIES, DOWNIES

Barcarolle composer .... CHOPIN

bard .... POET, SCOP, DRUID, RUNER, MINSTREL, VERSIFIER

Bard of Avon .... SHAKESPEARE

Bard's river .... AVON

specialty .... LAY

bare .... MERE, NUDE, EMPTY, NAKED, STARK, BARREN, STRIP, EXPOSE, SIMPLE, DIVULGE, UNCLOTHED

faced .... OPEN, BRAZEN, SHAMELESS, IMPUDENT, UNCONCEALED

foot .... UNSHOD, SHOELESS

foot pilgrim, car-buyer .... SUCKER

footed .... DISCALCED

headed .... HATLESS, UNCOVERED

in mind .... EMPTY-HEADED

naked .... DENUDE

rock, standing .... SCAR

barely .... JUST, ONLY, HARDLY, MERELY, MEAGERLY, SCANTILY, SCARCELY

bargain .... (GOOD)BUY, CHEAP, BARTER, HAGGLE, TRADE, DICKER, HIGGLE, CONTRACT, NEGOTIATE

closed: colloq. .... DEAL

hunter .... SHOPPER

place .... BASEMENT

strike a .... AGREE

bargainer's delight .... BUYS, REBATE, SALE(S), CUTRATES, DISCOUNT

favorite spot .... BASEMENT

barge .... PUNT, SCOW, CASCO, WHERRY, COLLIDE, (HOUSE)BOAT, LIGHTER

heavy .... HOY

in .... CRASH, ENTER

load of coal .... KEEL

river .... GONDOLA

baric .... BAROMETER

barilla .... SALTWORT

barite .... SPAR

barium monoxide/oxide .... BARYTA

sulfate .... BARITE

bark .... BAY, TAN, YAP, RIND, SKIN, SNAP, TREE, WOOF, BARQUE, BRUISE, YELP, CORTEX, (SAIL)BOAT

aromatic .... CASCARILLA

bitter .... NIEPA, NIOTA, ANGOSTURA, CHINCHONA

buckthorn .... CASCARA

cloth/mulberry .... TAPA

drug from .... BEBEERINE

fiber .... BAST

flavoring .... SASSAFRAS

fragrant .... CANELLA

inner .... BAST, LIBER

laxative .... BEARWOOD

louse .... APHID, APHIS

medicinal ...... COTO, PEREIRA, CHINCHONA

of fear/pain .... YELP

pertaining to .... CORTICAL

remover/stripper ...... SPUDDER

shrill .... YIP, YELP

soap .... QUILLAI

spice/tonic .... CANELLA

tree .... RIND, NIEPA

yielding quinine .... CINCHONA

barkeeper/barman ...... TAPSTER, PUBLICAN, BARTENDER

barker .... TOUT, SPIELER

aide of .... SHILL

talk of .... SPIEL, PATTER

barking .... LATRANT

barley .... BERE, BIGG, GRASS, CEREAL, TSAMBA

beard .... AWN

Indian .... PAPOOSE

liquor .... WHISK(E)Y

meal cake .... BANNOCK

steeped .... MALT

water/drink .... PTISAN

barm .... YEAST

barmy: Brit. sl. .... SILLY, IDIOTIC

barn .... MEWS, SHED, STABLE, BUILDING

bar/pole .... BAIL

bird .... OWL

compartment .... BAY

cow .... BYRE

gallery .... LOFT

owl .... TYTO

part for hay/grain .... (HAY)MOW, (HAY)LOFT

barnacle .... GOOSE, CIRRIPED, SHELLFISH

of a sort .... BUR(R)

Barnacle Bill: sl. .... TAR, SAILOR

barnacles: Brit. colloq. .... EYEGLASSES

barnstorm .... CAMPAIGN

Barnum ...... PHINEAS, SHOWMAN

elephant .... JUMBO

midget .... TOM THUMB

specialty .... CIRCUS

barnyard denizen ...... COW, HEN, COCK, GOAT, TURKEY, ROOSTER

pest .... FOX, WEASEL

sound .... BAA, MOO, CROW, BLEAT, CACKLE

barometer .... ANEROID, OROMETER, STATOSCOPE

barometric .... BARIC

line .... ISOBAR

baron .... TITLE, MAGNATE, (BEEF)SIRLOIN, NOBLEMAN, CAPITALIST

heir apparent of .... MASTER

main dwelling of .... HALL

wife of .... LADY, BARONESS

Baron Munchausen .... PEARL

compiler .... RASPE

baronet's addition to name .... BART

baronial .... GRAND, SHOWY

barony, Japanese .... HAN

baroque .... ORNATE, ROCOCO

barque .... BARK, VESSEL, SAILBOAT

barracks .... ETAPE, CASERN, GARRISON

barracuda .... SPET, PICUDA, SENNET

barrage .... DAM, ATTACK, VOLLEY, BARRIER, BOMBARD, WALL, BACKSTOP, DRUMFIRE

barramunda .... CERATODUS

barranca .... GORGE, RAVINE

barrel .... KEG, VAT, BUTT, CASK, TIERCE, SPEED UP, TUBE, CYLINDER, KILDERKIN

cork/stopper .... BUNG

groove .... CROZE

house .... BAR, SALOON, TAVERN

like container .... DRUM

maker/worker .... COOPER, HOOPER

one part .... FIRKIN

part .... HOOP, STAVE

rim .... CHIMB, CHIME, CHINE

stave .... LAG

staves, set .... SHOOK

barrelful .... CASK

barren .... ARID, BARE, LEAN, BLEAK, BORING, STARK, EMPTY, EFFETE, STERILE, JEJUNE, INFERTILE, DEVOID, UNFRUITFUL

land .... USAR, DESERT, DUSTBOWL

barret .... CAP, BIRETTA

barrette .... BAR, CLASP

barricade .... BARRIER, WALL, OBSTACLE, ABAT(T)IS, FENCE, BLOCKADE, PALISADE, SCREEN, CONSTRUCT, STOCKADE, ROADBLOCK

Barrie (James) play .... MARY ROSE

barrier .... WALL, SCREEN, HINDRANCE, OBSTACLE, RAMPART, OBSTRUCTION

of logs/river .... BOOM

of stakes .... PALISADE, STOCKADE

barrio .... SUBURB

chief .... DAT(T)O

barrister .... LAWYER, ATTORNEY, COUNSELOR

headwear .... WIG

barrow .... PIG, CITY, HILL, MOUND, TRUCK, TUMULUS, HANDCART

type of .... HAND, WHEEL

Barrymore, _____ .... DREW, JOHN, ETHEL, LIONEL, MAURICE

Bart .... BARONET

barter ...... SWAP, TRADE, TRUCK, EXCHANGE

bartizan .... TURRET

Bartlett .... PEAR

Baruch, statesman ...... BERNARD

barytron ...... MESON, MESOTRON

bas bleu .... BLUE-STOCKING

basal .... BASIC, FUNDAMENTAL

basalt .... ROCK, POTTERY

source .... LAVA

basaltic rock .... TRAP, WHIN, GREENSTONE

bascule .... SEESAW

base .... BED, VILE, MEAN, LOW, ROOT, BASIS, FELON, ABJECT, MENIAL, BOTTOM, FLOOR, IMPURE, IGNOBLE, FOUNDATION, HEADQUARTERS

architectural .... SOCLE, PLINTH

attached to .... SESSILE

baseball .... BAG, SACK

coal tar .... ANILINE

hit in baseball .... SINGLE, TRIPLE, TWO-BAGGER

of bird's bill .... CERE

of column .... DADO, PLINTH, PEDESTAL

root .... RADIX

baseball abbreviation .... ERA, RBI

backstop .... CAGE

base .... SACK, PLATE

batting practice .... FUNGO

bungler in .... MUFF

catcher .... RECEIVER

catcher-pitcher combination .... BATTERY

club .... BAT

commissioner .... KUHN, FRICK, LANDIS, VINCENT, CHANDLER, GIAMATTI

curve .... HOOK

earned run average .... ERA

event .... SERIES

field/ground .... DIAMOND

field dispute .... RHUBARB

Hall of Fame name .... AARON, RUTH, COBB, GEHRIG, CAMPANELLA, OTT, SISLER, DIMAGGIO, BANKS, BERRA, YOUNG, MACK, MANTLE, ROBINSON, RICE, MAYS, DEAN, MUSIAL, PLANK, STENGEL, KOUFAX, MARICHAL, CHANDLER, CLEMENTE

hit: sl. .... CLOUT

mistake .... ERROR

pitch ..... SLIDER, CURVE, DROP BALL, SPITBALL, KNUCKLE BALL, FAST BALL

pitch aimed at batter's head .... BEANBALL

pitcher's fault .... BALK

pitcher's stand ..... BOX, SLAB, MOUND

pitcher's warm-up area .... BULLPEN

play ..... ASSIST, DOUBLE, PUT-OUT, SQUEEZE

player of fame .... RUTH, COBB, DIMAGGIO, DEAN, MANTLE, RICE, MAYS, KOUFAX, REESE, SPAHN, ROSE, AARON, ROBINSON, OTT, MARICHAL, MARIS, RYAN, MCCOVEY, JACKSON, WINFIELD, BONDS, CLARK, STEWART, VALENZUELA, HENDERSON, MIZE, PERRY, BENCH, WILLIAMS

player's miss at bat .... FAN, STRIKEOUT

player's position .... SHORTSTOP, PITCHER, CATCHER, FIRST BASE, LEFTFIELD, SECOND BASE, THIRD BASE, RIGHTFIELD, CENTERFIELD

player's shelter .... DUGOUT

Rule 8.02's concern .... SPITBALL

run(s) batted in .... RBI

seventh inning habit of fans .... STRETCH

stadium .... PARK

tactic .... BUNT

team/club .... METS, WHITESOX, CARDINALS, TWINS, SENATORS, TIGERS, PADRES, GIANTS, ORIOLES, ATHLETICS, PHILLIES, ASTROS, YANKEES, BRAVES, ANGELS, INDIANS, REDSOX, DODGERS, PIRATES, MARINERS, BLUE JAYS

team players .... NINE

term .... HOMERUN, LINE DRIVE, FLY BALL, WALK, BASE ON BALLS, BUNT, FIELDER'S CHOICE, CLEAN-UP, GROUND BALL, POP UP, LEFT STRANDED, TOP HALF, BOTTOM, INNING, TYING RUN, PINCH HIT, STOLEN BASE, BASES LOADED, DESIGNATED HITTER

VIP .... UMP(IRE), PITCHER, COMMISSIONER

baseball's Dean .... DIZZY, DAFFY

"fall classic" .... WORLD SERIES

Hank/Henry .... AARON

Mel .... OTT

"Mister Cub" .... BANKS

"Preacher" .... ROE

55

Ruth .... BABE
"Say Hey" kid .... MAYS
Sparky .... LYLE
"Stretch" .... MCCOVEY
"The Lip"
.... (LEO)DUROCHER
Yogi .... BERRA
baseborn .... BASTARD,
ILLEGITIMATE
based on 10 .... DECIMAL
baseless .... UNFOUNDED,
GROUNDLESS, UNSUPPORTED
report/rumor .... HOAX,
CANARD, IDLE TALK
basely .... IGNOBLY
bash .... PARTY, SMASH, SPREE,
STRIKE, WINGDING
Bashan King .... OG
Bashaw's title .... AGHA, AGA,
PASHAM KEMAL, PACHA
bashful .... COY, SHY, TIMID,
RETIRING, DIFFIDENT,
SHEEPISH
Bashful of fairy tale ...... DWARF
Bashkir's capital .... UFA
basic .... PRIMARY, ESSENTIAL,
ELEMENTAL, NATURAL,
FUNDAMENTAL
law .... CHARTER,
CONSTITUTION
part .... ROOT, CORNERSTONE
rule .... LAW, CANON,
PRINCIPLE
basics .... ABC(S)
basidiomycete .... RUST, SMUT,
MUSHROOM, FUNGUS,
PUFFBALL
basil .... HERB, PLANT
basilica .... PALACE, TEMPLE,
LATERAN, COURTROOM
basilisk ...... LIZARD, COCKATRICE
basin .... PAN, BOWL, DOCK, BAY,
POND, SINK, LAVER, VESSEL,
RESERVOIR
altar .... PISCINA
holy water .... FONT, ASPER,
SORIUM, STOOP, STOUP
in geology .... TALA
ornamental .... CUVETTE
basinet .... BASNET, HELMET
basis .... BASE, GROUND,
FOUNDATION, ROOT, FOOTING
of argument .... PREMISE
bask ...... HEAT, REVEL, FLOURISH,
SUN(BATHE), SWELTER,
LUXURIATE
basket .... POT, CAUL, DOSSER,
GABION, HAMPER, PANNIER,
SCUTTLE
abbreviation .... BKT
baby .... BASSINET

balloon .... CAR, NACELLE
coal/ore .... CORF, SCUTTLE
fiber .... RAFFIA
figs ..... CABAS, FRAIL, TAPNET
fish .... CREEL, WICKER
fruits/grains/vegetables
..... PUNNET, POTTLE, SCUTTLE,
CALATHUS
hop-picker's .... BIN
material .... RUSH, OSIER,
RAFFIA, WILLOW, REED,
WOOD, WICKER, BAMBOO,
RATTAN, SPLINT
official papers .... HANAFER
pack animal .... DOSSER,
PANNIER
pelotari's .... CESTA
raisins .... FRAIL
rummy .... CANASTA
sculptured .... CORBEIL
symbol of abundance
.... CALATHUS
wicker .... CORF, HANAFER,
BASSINET
basketball basket .... CAGE, HOOP
club (NBA):
Atlanta .... HAWKS
Boston .... CELTICS
Charlotte .... HORNETS
Chicago .... BULLS
Cleveland .... CAVALIERS
Dallas .... MAVERICKS
Denver .... NUGGETS
Detroit .... PISTONS
Golden State ...... WARRIORS
Houston .... ROCKETS
Indiana .... PACERS
Los Angeles .... LAKERS,
CLIPPERS
Miami .... HEAT
Milwaukee .... BUCKS
Minnesota
.... TIMBERWOLVES
New Jersey .... NETS
New York .... KNICKS,
KNICKERBOCKERS
Orlando .... MAGIC
Philadelphia ...... (SEVENTY-)
SIXERS
Phoenix .... SUNS
Portland .... TRAILBLAZERS
Sacramento .... KINGS
San Antonio .... SPURS
Seattle .... (SUPER)SONICS
Utah .... JAZZ
Washington .... BULLETS
maneuver .... PRESS, LAY-UP,
DRIBBLE, FREEZE, FAST BREAK
player .... GUARD, CAGER,
CENTER, FORWARD
player of fame .... WEST,

GALE, GREER, LUCAS, REED,
BAYLOR, BRADLEY, BARRY,
CHAMBERLAIN, JABBAR,
DEBUSSCHERE, RUSSELL,
THOMPSON, JORDAN, JOHNSON
team .... FIVE, QUINT(ET)
basking shark .... SAILFISH
basque .... BLOUSE, BODICE,
TUNIC
Basque .... IBERIAN
cap .... BERET
game .... PELOTA
land .... EUZKADI
pelota player .... PELOTARI
province .... ALVA, BISCAY,
SOULE, LABOURD, NAVARRA,
VISCAYA, GUIPUZCOA
Basra native .... IRAQI
bass .... LOW, BAST, DEEP
black .... CHUB
double .... VIOL
double-reed .... OBOE,
BASSOON
European .... BRASSE
horn .... TUBA
like fish .... SNAPPER
sea .... JEWFISH
stop of organ .... BOURDON
viol .... CONTRABASS
voice .... DRONE
wind instrument ...... HELICON
basset .... DOG, HOUND
horn .... CLARINET
bassinet .... BASKET, CRADLE,
(BABY)BED
bassoon .... OBOE, WOODWIND
basswood .... LINDEN, LIME(TREE),
WAHOO
bast .... BARK, BASS, FIBER,
RAMIE, PHLOEM
fiber .... CATENA
like .... LIBRIFORM
bastard .... SHAM, FRAUD,
BYBLOW, COUNTERFEIT,
ILLEGITIMATE, MISBEGOT(TEN)
wing of bird .... ALULA
baste .... SEW, BEAT, TACK,
ABUSE, STRIKE, THRASH,
MOISTEN
bastille .... TOWER, PRISON,
FORTRESS
bastinado .... ROD, STICK,
CUDGEL
bastion .... BULWARK, DEFENSE
Basutoland capital ...... MASERU
bat .... CLUB, STICK, CUDGEL,
CHUNK, FLYING FOX,
NOCTULE, HAMMERHEAD
an eye .... WINK, BLINK
blood-sucking .... VAMPIRE
colloquial .... BLOW, WINK,

BLINK, SPEED, SPREE, FLUTTER
flying .... KALONG
for .... DEFEND, ADVOCATE
hold on .... GRIP
like/wing-footed .... ALIPED
like fish .... GURNARD,
GURNET, (STING)RAY
manure .... GUANO
mining .... SHALE
Ping-Pong .... PADDLE
tennis .... RACKET, RACQUET
batch ...... LOT, RUN, SET, GROUP,
SERIES
bate ...... SOAK, REDUCE, DIMINISH
bateau .... BOAT
batfish .... RAY, SKATE,
(FLYING)GURNARD, DIABOLO,
STINGRAY, STINGAREE
bath .... DIP, SOAK, WASH, STEEP,
PLUNGE, ABLUTION
kind of .... MILK, SAUNA,
SHOWER, SWEDISH, TURKISH,
JACUZZI, WHIRLPOOL
therapeutic .... WET PACK
tub .... TOSH
Bath's river .... AVON
bathe .... WET, LAVE, WASH,
MOISTEN, SUFFUSE
bathhouse ...... BAGNIO, CABANA,
SAUNA
bathing, of .... BALNEAL
suit .... BIKINI
batho: as prefix .... DEPTH
batholite .... GRANITE
bathos .... ANTICLIMAX
bathroom .... HEAD, TOILET,
WATER CLOSET
fixture .... TUB, URINAL,
COMMODE
baths .... THERMAE
Bathsheba's father .... ANMIEL
husband .... DAVID, URIA(H)
mother .... SHEBA
son .... SOLOMON, NATHAN,
SHIMEA, SHOBATH
Bathurst is capital of
.... GAMBIA
batiste .... LINEN, MUSLIN,
CAMBRAI
batman .... ORDERLY, SERVANT
slang .... GOFER
baton .... ROD, STAFF, STICK,
TRUNCHEON
fairy's .... WAND
jester's .... BAUBLE
race .... RELAY
twirler .... MAJORETTE
wielder ...... SOUSA, BEECHAM,
MAGICIAN, WALTER,
BERNSTEIN, CONDUCTOR,
TOSCANINI

batrachian .... FROG, TOAD,
AMPHIBIAN
bats .... LOCO, CRAZY
batten .... FASTEN, THRIVE,
OVERFEED, WOODSTRIP
batter .... RAM, BEAT, POUND,
SMASH
cake .... PANCAKE, WAFFLE,
CRUMPET, FLAPJACK
in cricket .... BATSMAN
battered baby syndrome
.... CHILD ABUSE
battering machine .... RAM
ram of ship .... BEAK
battery .... CELL, ARRAY, ATTACK,
BEATING, ARTILLERY
compartment .... CELL
floating .... PRAM
kind of .... SOLAR, STORAGE
material .... ACID
part .... ANODE, PLATE,
CATHODE
partner of .... ASSAULT
plate .... GRID
batting, manner of .... FUNGO
order .... LINEUP
battle .... WAR, FIGHT, COMBAT,
CONTEST, CONFLICT, SIEGE,
ATTACK, HOSTILITIES
area .... RING, ARENA, FIELD,
FRONT, SECTOR, THEATER,
BEACHHEAD, NO-MAN'S-LAND
avoidance .... FABIAN
ax .... GISARME, HATCHET,
TWIBIL(L), TOMAHAWK
ax: sl. .... NAG, SHREW,
AMAZON, VIRAGO
combatant .... SOLDIER,
WARRIOR
cry .... BANZAI, REBEL-YELL,
TOM-TOM, TO HORSE,
(WAR)WHOOP
dress .... ARMOR
fatigue .... TRAUMA
formation .... ARRAY,
ECHELON, PHALANX, HERSE,
DEPLOYMENT
of politicians .... CAMPAIGN
of the _____ .... SEXES
of wits ..... BANTER, REPARTEE
of words .... DEBATE,
ARGUMENT
plane .... SPAD, FIGHTER,
SPITFIRE, ZERO, BOMBER,
SABREJET
relic .... SCAR, TROPHY
royal .... MELEE, BRAWL,
RUMBLE, FREE-FOR-ALL
scarred fighter ...... VET(ERAN)
site, 1776 .... LONG ISLAND
site, 1991 .... PERSIAN GULF

trophy of Indian .... SCALP
victim .... CASUALTY
Battle of Hastings site
.... SENLAR
battledore .... BAT, CLUB,
PADDLE, RACKET
battlement .... FORT, BASTION,
RAMPART
part of .... MERLON,
EMBRASURE, CRENEL(LE)
Battles of 1429 .... ORLEANS
battleship .... GALLEON, CRUISER,
MAN O(F) WAR, DESTROYER,
DREADNAUGHT
gun turret .... CUPOLA
slang .... BATTLE WAGON
battue .... HUNT, MASSACRE
batty .... CRAZY, INSANE,
ECCENTRIC
bauble ...... TOY, BEAD, DOODAD,
GEWGAW, GIMCRACK, TRIVIA,
TRINKET
baudekin .... BROCADE,
BALDACHIN
baudrons: Scot .... CAT
Bauhaus school founder
.... GROPIUS
Bavaria, capital of .... MUNICH
German name .... BAYERN
Bavarian city .... HOF,
BAYREUTH, NUREMBERG
river .... ISAR, EGER, MAIN,
ILLER
weight .... GRAN
bawbee .... COIN, HALF-PENNY
bawd .... MADAM, PROCURESS
bawdy .... LEWD, GROSS, COARSE,
RIBALD, OBSCENE, INDECENT
house .... BAGNIO, BROTHEL
bawl ...... CRY, SOB, HOWL, YELL,
WEEP, SHOUT, BELLOW
out/colloquial .... SCOLD,
REPROVE, REPRIMAND
bay .... ARCH, BARK, COVE, BIGHT,
INLET, ALCOVE, WING,
BAYOU, ESTUARY, HOWL,
FIORD, ULULATE
bring to .... TREE, CORNER
color .... ROAN, CHESTNUT
horse .... ROAN, BAYARD,
SORREL
keep at .... HOLD(OFF)
name of .... VOE, BAFFIN,
BISCAY, MANILA, CAMPECHE,
GALVESTON
sound ...... BARK, HOWL, PEAL,
BLARE, NEIGH
sweet .... BREWSTER
tree .... LAUREL
window .... ORIEL, PAUNCH,
MIRADOR, (POT)BELLY

Bay of Biscay city/resort
.... BIARRITZ
of Biscay river .... LOIRE
State .... MASSACHUSETTS
bayard .... HORSE, KNIGHT
Baylor eleven .... BEARS
bayou .... CREEK, INLET,
BACKWATER, EVERGLADES
bazaar ...... MART, SHOP, RIALTO,
MARKET(PLACE)
church/club .... FAIR, SALE
bbl. .... BARREL
bdl. .... BUNDLE
be .... ARE, EXIST, OCCUR,
BELONG, HAPPEN, TAKE
PLACE
a match .... COPE
a success .... CLICK
a tenant farmer .... SHARE-
CROP
at habitually .... HAUNT,
FREQUENT
cool! .... SIMMER DOWN
deficient .... WANT
elated .... TREAD ON AIR
glad .... REJOICE
jubilant .... EXULT
obligated to .... OWE
of use .... AVAIL, UTILE,
SERVICEABLE
off .... ERR
on one's guard .... BEWARE
overly fond .... DOTE, ADORE
silent, in music .... TACE(T)
still .... SSH, HUSH, QUIET,
SHUT-UP
successful .... ARRIVE
suitable .... BELONG
thrifty .... WASTE NOT, WANT
NOT
your age .... BEHAVE
beach .... SANDS, SHORE, GROUND,
STRAND, COAST(LINE)
bath house .... CABANA
bird .... SANDERLING
California .... PEBBLE,
IMPERIAL
fixture .... LIFESAVER,
UMBRELLA, LIFEGUARD,
SUNBATHER
Florida .... MIAMI, ORMOND,
POMPANO
Hawaii .... WAIKIKI
on the: colloq.
.... UNEMPLOYED
panhandler ..... BEACHCOMBER
pest .... SANDFLY
problem .... EROSION
walk .... BOARDWALK,
ESPLANADE
wave over .... COMBER

beacon .... BEAM, BUOY, GUIDE,
PHAROS, SIGNAL, SIGNAL
FIRE, LIGHTHOUSE
light .... CRESSET
on summit .... PIKE
Beaconsfield, Earl of
.... DISRAELI
bead .... DROP, BUBBLE, BALL,
PELLET, GLOBULE
draw one on .... AIM
for trimming dresses
.... BUGLE
gun muzzle's .... SIGHT
money .... PEAG, WAMPUM
beaded moisture .... DEW
beadhouse .... ALMSHOUSE
beading .... GADROON
beadle .... MESSENGER, MACE-
BEARER
of fiction .... BUMBLE
beads .... NECKLACE
Indian .... PEAG(E), WAMPUM
of perspiration .... SWEAT
prayer .... ROSARY, CHAPLET
beadsman .... BEGGAR, PRAYER
beagle .... DOG, HOUND
beak .... NEB, NIB, BILL, NOSE,
ROSTRUM
like process .... ROSTELLUM
of a pitcher .... SPOUT
ship's .... RAM, PROW
slang .... NOSE, SNOUT, JUDGE,
MAGISTRATE
trim with .... PREEN
beaked .... HOOKED, CROOKED,
AQUILINE
beaker .... CUP, GOBLET
beam .... RAY, GLOW, SHINE,
SIGNAL, SMILE, RADIATE,
DIRECT, ASHLAR, JOIST,
GLEAM, RAFTER, CROSSBAR,
SCANTLING
architectural .... TEMPLET,
TEMPLATE
monochromatic .... LASER
off the .... LOST, AMISS,
WRONG
on the .... KEEN, ALERT, RIGHT
supporting .... GIRDER
tie .... BALK
underside .... SOFFIT
beaming .... HAPPY, RADIANT,
SMILING
beamy .... BROAD, BRIGHT,
JOYOUS, MASSIVE
bean .... GOA, POD, SEED, LIMA,
SOY(A), ARBOR, PINTO,
TONKA, LEGUME
counter .... ACCOUNTANT
dish .... SUCCOTASH
flour/meal .... FARINA

fly .... MIDAS
kidney ..... HARICOT, FRIJOL(E)
like plant .... SAINFOIN
lima .... HABA
locust .... CAROB
Mexican .... FRIJOL(E)
mottled .... PINTO
oil .... CASTOR
Oriental .... MONGO, MUNGO
parasite .... BEETLE, WEEVIL
poisonous .... CALABAR
restaurant .... BEANERY
sauce .... SOY
seed .... SOY, PULSE
shaped seed, other plants
.... COFFEE
slang .... HEAD, MIND, BRAIN
soy .... SOJA
stalk/stem .... HA(U)LM
tree .... CAROB, CATALPA
used for counting .... BEANO
versatile .... SOY(A)
white .... PEA
yonka .... GUAIAC
beanie/beany .... (SKULL)CAP
beano .... BINGO
beans, don't know: sl. ...... DUMB
full of: sl. .... ALL WET
spill the: colloq. .... LET THE
CAT OUT OF THE BAG
bear .... HOLD, TOTE, WEAR,
CARRY, ENDURE, SUFFER,
SHOW, CONVEY, SUSTAIN,
ALLOW, BRUIN, STAND,
TOLERATE, TRANSPORT
black-and-white .... PANDA
brown .... URSUS
down .... PUSH, PRESS
down on .... CHARGE
honey .... KINKAJOU
in mind .... REMEMBER
like .... URSINE, URSIFORM
like animal ..... KOALA, PANDA
out .... CONFIRM, SUPPORT,
CORROBORATE
sky .... URSA
squeeze of a .... HUG
Syrian .... DUBB
that was a nymph
.... CALLISTO
variety .... BLACK, BROWN,
HONEY, POLAR, GRIZZLY
with .... ENDURE, PUT UP,
TOLERATE
witness .... ATTEST, TESTIFY
woolly .... WOOBUT,
CATERPILLAR
young .... CUB, WHELP
bearberry .... HOLLY, SHRUB
bearcat .... CIVET, PANDA
beard .... BARB, DEFY, GOATEE,

BARBEL, IMPERIAL, WHISKERS, BURNSIDES
disease of the .... SYCOSIS
grain .... AWN, ARISTA
hairlike .... CRINITE
pointed ..... GOATEE, VANDYKE
red .... BARBAROSSA
short growth .... STUBBLE
the lion .... TAME, SUBDUE
bearded .... AWNED, HAIRY, GOATEED, BARBATE, HIRSUTE, ARISTATE, WHISKERED
butter .... GOA
grass .... RYE
one .... IRIS
seal .... MAKLUK
beardless .... SHAVEN, YOUNG, CALLOW, HAIRLESS, YOUTHFUL
bearer in India .... SIRDAR
of the world: myth ...... ATLAS
bearing ...... AIR, MIEN, MANNER, RELATION, CARRIAGE, MEANING, CONDUCT, DEMEANOR, PRESENCE, CARRYING
twins .... BIPAROUS
writer's name .... ONYMOUS
bearish .... RUDE, ROUGH, CROSS, SURLY
bear's breech .... ACANTHUS
foot .... HELLEBORE
skin .... (FOR)CAP
bearwood .... CASCARA
beast .... BRUTE, ANIMAL, QUADRUPED
huge .... MONSTER, BEHEMOTH, MASTODON
like .... THEROID
of burden .... ASS, MULE, BURRO, CAMEL, YAK, LLAMA, DONKEY, ONAGER, CARABAO
of prey .... LION, TIGER, WOLVERINE
beastly .... BESTIAL, ILL-BRED, RUDE, BRUTAL, VULGAR, BRUSQUE, THEROID, HARSH, DISGUSTING
beasts, king of .... LION
beat .... MIX, CANE, RHYTHM, PULSE, PULSATE, POUND, POMMEL, CADENCE, WHIP, FLOG, FLAIL, FORGE, THROB, BATTER, ACCENT, LACE, DEFEAT, CONQUER, TEMPO, PUMMEL, TROUNCE, DRUB, THRASH, LAMBASTE
back .... REPEL, REPULSE
colloquial .... WHALE, LARRUP, SHELLACK
dead .... CHEAT, WELSHER

group member .... BEATNIK
in a race .... OUTRAN
in foil .... FOLIATE
in journalism .... SCOOP, ASSIGNMENT
into plate/thin .... MALLEATE
it! ...... SCAT, GET LOST, SHOO, SCRAM
off .... REJECT, RESIST
on the .... IN TUNE, ATEMPO, ATTUNED
police .... ROUND
repeatedly ..... FLOG, CLOBBER
slang .... LAM, PASTE, POOP OUT, TIRED, EXHAUSTED
soles of feet with stick .... BASTINADO
soundly .... DRUB, ROUT, WALLOP, OVERWHELM
to softness .... MASH
up .... MAUL, THRASH
with stick .... CLUB, DRUB, CUDGEL, BASTINADO
with whip .... FLOG, LASH
beatable .... WEAK, VINCIBLE, VULNERABLE
beaten path .... TRAIL
beatific .... JOYFUL, BLISSFUL
beatify .... BLESS, HALLOW, SANCTIFY
beating .... DEFEAT, PULSATION, PUNISHMENT
of person .... BATTERY
underbrush to flush game .... BATTUE, BATTING
Beatles, former manager of .... EPSTEIN
one of the .... LENNON, STARR, HARRISON, MCCARTNEY
beatnik .... HEPCAT, HIPSTER, BOHEMIAN
Beatrice's lover .... DANTE
beau .... LOVER, FELLOW, COURTER, SUITOR, SWEETHEART
colloquial .... BF, SPARK
geste .... GALLANTRY
ideal .... NERO
monde .... JET SET
monde's center .... SALON
plural of .... BEAUX
Beau Brummell ...... FOP, DANDY
beaucaire .... MONSIEUR
beaut .... LULU
beautician .... COIFFURIST, HAIRSTYLIST, HAIRDRESSER, MANICURIST
beautiful .... CUTE, FAIR, LOVELY, COMELY, PRETTY, STUNNING, DAINTY, ELEGANT, HANDSOME, ATTRACTIVE

eyes .... TULIPS
girl: sl. .... LULU
poetic .... BEAUTEOUS
slang ..... SHARP, PRETTY AS A PICTURE
woman .... PERI, NYMPH, CHARMER, GODDESS, HEBE, VENUS, HOURI, ENCHANTRESS
beauty, a .... ACE, LULU, DOLL, PERFECT, DAZZLER, STUNNER, KNOCKOUT
famous .... CLEOPATRA, APHRODITE, HELEN OF TROY
reigning .... BELLE
of form, etc. .... GRACE
parlor dye .... HENNA
parlor specialty .... SET, WAVE, FACIAL, MASSAGE, SHAMPOO, PERMANENT, HAIRCUT, MANICURE, MAKE-UP, DYE, PEDICURE
parlor worker .... MASSEUR, HAIRDRESSER, BEAUTICIAN, HAIRSTYLIST, MANICURIST, BARBER, PEDICURIST
shop .... SALON, PARLOR
spot .... MOLE, PATCH
beaver .... FUR, (SILK)HAT, ANIMAL
den of .... LODGE
describing one/beaverlike? .... EAGER
eager .... DOER, HUSTLER
fur hat/of armor .... CASTOR
like animal .... COYPU, NUTRIA
oily substance .... CASTOR(EUM)
skin .... PLEW
Beaver State .... OREGON
bebop .... JAZZ
because .... SINCE, OWING TO, INASMUCH
bêche-de-mer ...... TREPANG, SEA CUCUMBER
beck ...... NOD, BECKON, STREAM, SUMMON
partner of .... CALL
beckon .... CALL, LURE, ENTICE, SIGNAL, SUMMON
becloud .... DARKEN, MUDDLE, CONFUSE
become .... GROW, SUIT, BEFIT, CHANGE, TURN INTO, BEHOOVE, DEVELOP
cheese-like .... CASEFY
different .... CHANGE
dull .... BORE, PALL, HEBETATE
extinct .... DIE
forfeit .... LAPSE
less stern .... THAW, RELENT, SOFTEN

red in face ...... FLUSH, BLUSH, COLOR
shabby .... GO TO SEED
void for cause .... LAPSE
well .... HEAL
becoming .... FIT, PROPER, SEEMLY
bed .... COT, KIP, BASE, BUNK, SACK, COUCH, BOTTOM, RESTING PLACE, PALLET, STRATUM
and board .... HOME, KEEP
awning .... CANOPY
baby's .... CRIB, CRADLE
built-in .... BUNK, BERTH
canopy .... TESTER
clothes .... LINEN, SHAMS, SHEETS, RUFFLES, PILLOWS, BLANKETS
coils .... SPRINGS
covering ...... COVERLET, PUFF, QUILT, COMFORTER, TESTER, (BED)SPREAD
curtain/drapery .... VALANCE
frame .... STEAD
hanging .... HAMMOCK
kind of .... ROSES, OYSTER
maker .... CHAMBERMAID
of plants .... GARDEN
of roses: colloq. .... COMFORT, EASE, LUXURY
ore .... REEF
pest .... BEDBUG
river .... CHANNEL
size .... TWIN, FULL, KING, QUEEN, SINGLE
slang .... BAG, DOSS, SACK
small .... COT, CRIB, PALLET, BASSINET
straw .... PALLET
stream .... WADI, WADY, DONGA, ARROYO
type .... DAY, BUNK, SOFA, BERTH, HAMMOCK, TRUNDLE, ROLL-AWAY, FOLDING, HOSPITAL, WATER, FOUR-POSTER, MATRIMONIAL
bedaub .... PAINT, SMEAR, SMUDGE
bedbug .... CIMEX, CHINCH, VERMIN
bedding, hay/leaves/straw
.... LITTER
Bede, _____ .... ADAM, THE VENERABLE
bedeck .... TRIM, ADORN, EMBELLISH
bedevil .... WORRY, HARASS, PESTER, PLAGUE, TORMENT
bedew .... MOISTEN
bedfellow .... ASSOCIATE, CO-WORKER, COMPANION

bedizen .... ADORN
bedlam .... ASYLUM, UPROAR, TURMOIL, DISORDER, MADHOUSE, CONFUSION
Bedloe island .... LIBERTY
bedmate .... WIFE, SPOUSE, HUSBAND
Bedouin ...... ARAB, RIFF, NOMAD, BERBER, WANDERER
headband cord .... AGAL
home of .... SAHARA
tribe .... ABSI, AMALEKITE
bedraggled .... UNTIDY, UNKEMPT, UNCOMBED
bedrock .... BOTTOM
bedroom .... CABIN, CHAMBER, CUBICLE
caretaker .... CHAMBERMAID
eyes .... GAZE, GLOWER
bedside character .... DOCTOR, NURSE, (BABY)SITTER
manners, describing
.... BALMY, GENTLE, CHEERFUL, SOOTHING, REASSURING
bedstead ...... CHARPAI, CHARPOY, FOUR-POSTER
bedtime .... CURFEW
story: colloq. ..... YARN, FAIRY TALE, EXPLANATION
bedwarf .... BELITTLE
bee .... APIS, INSECT, SOCIAL, MEETING, GATHERING, WORKER, STINGER, HYMENOPTERA
balm ..... PLANT, (OSWEGO)TEA
bird .... FLYCATCHER
birling .... ROLEO
colony/workplace .... HIVE
eater/martin .... KINGBIRD
family .... APIDAE, APOIDEA
female .... QUEEN
girl named after .... MELISSA
glue/caulking substance
.... PROPOLIS
hive/house .... NIDUS, SKEP, APIARY
in one's bonnet .... KINK
keeper ..... APIARIAN, APIARIST
keeping .... APICULTURE
killer .... ROBBERFLY
kind of .... QUEEN, DRONE, WORKER, SEWING, BUMBLE, SPELLING, QUILTING, SHUCKING
like/of a .... APIAN
male .... DRONE
nest-building .... CARDER
nose of .... LOR(UM)
plant .... BALM, CLOVER,

SPIDERFLOWER
pollen brush of .... SCOPA
secretion .... WAX
social .... WASP, HORNET
sound ...... HUM, BUZZ, DRONE
tree .... LINDEN, BASSWOOD
wax .... CEROTIC
beebread .... AMBROSIA
beech .... NUT, TREE, WOOD, ROBLE
beechnuts .... MAST
beef .... OX, COW, BULL, MEAT, STEER, CATTLE
alternative .... VEAL
braised .... POT ROAST
cattle breed .... ANGUS, GALLOWAY, GUERNSEY, HEREFORD, HOLSTEIN
colloquial .... GRIPE, PEEVE, COMPLAIN(T)
corned/tinned .... BULLY
cut .... RIBS, CHUCK, RUMP, ROUND, BRISKET, LOIN, SHANK, KNUCKLE, SADDLE, SIRLOIN
dish .... MIROTON, PASTRAMI, MEATLOAF, STEW, CHILI-CON-CARNE
double sirloin .... BARON
dried .... JERKY, BUCCAN, CHARQUI
food for explorers
.... PEM(M)ICAN
nearest shoulder .... CLOD
roast ..... POT, ROLLED, BLADE, (PRIME)RIB, RUMP, CHUCK, LONDON BROIL
rolled .... PASTRAMI
slang .... BRAWN, MUSCLE
steak .... CLUB, CUBED, T-BONE, RIB-EYE, SIRLOIN, TENDERLOIN, PORTERHOUSE, FLANK, FILLET, MINUTE, NEW YORK, SALISBURY
stew .... GOULASH, POT-AU-FEU
tea .... BROTH
up .... FATTEN, INCREASE, STRENGTHEN
Beef State .... NEBRASKA
beefeater .... ESCORT, YEOMAN, GUARDSMAN
beefwood .... TOA
beefy ...... HEAVY, MEATY, STOUT, BRAWNY, FLESHY, MUSCULAR, CORPULENT
beehive .... SKEP, APIARY, BEEGUM, WORKPLACE
Beehive State .... UTAH
beekeeper .... APIARIAN, SKEPPER, APIARIST, SKEPPIST
beeline .... SHORTCUT

Beelzebub .... DEVIL, SATAN
beep .... CALL, HONK, PEAL, TOOT,
SOUND
beer ...... ALE, BOCK, SUDS, MALT,
KVAS(S), LAGER, STOUT,
PORTER, BITTERS, WEISS,
PILSNER, BEVERAGE
cask ..... KEG, TUN, PUNCHEON
cup/mug .... TOBY, STEIN,
SEIDEL
flavor .... HOPS, MULL
foam .... BEAD, HEAD, FROTH
glass .... SCHOONER
house .... INN, PUB, FARO,
GARDEN, PARLOR, SALOON,
TAVERN
ingredient/material .... HOPS,
MALT, MASH, MEAL, YEAST
inventor/king .... GAMBRINUS
kind of .... DARK, LIGHT,
GINGER
make .... BREW
party .... WASSAIL
plant .... HOPS, BREWERY
slang .... SUDS
sour .... KVAS(S)
spiced/sweetened .... FLIP
strong .... MUM, STINGO
sweeten and flavor .... MULL
weak .... SWIPES
beery .... TIPSY, DRUNKEN,
MAUDLIN
bees, feeding on .... APIVOROUS
genus of .... APIS
pertaining to .... APIAN
structure of wax cells made
by .... HONEYCOMB
study of .... APIOLOGY
substance produced by
.... HONEY
beet .... ROOT, CHARD, PLANT,
MANGEL
crushed .... MEGASS(E)
sugar .... SUCROSE,
SACCHAROSE
Beethoven's Archduke, e.g.
.... TRIO
birthplace .... BONN
composition .... MINUET,
MISSA SOLEMNIS
forte .... SONATA
opera .... FIDELIO
teacher .... NEEFE, HAYDN
third symphony .... EROICA
beetle .... DOR, CLUB, MELOE,
SCARAB, WEEVIL, ELATER(ID),
CURCULIO, EARWIG, MALLET,
SKIPJACK, SAWYER, SNAPPER,
WHIRLIGIG
blister .... MELOID
browed .... SULLEN,

FROWNING, SCOWLING
buzzing/click .... DOR,
ELATER, SNAPPER
dung .... COCKCHAFER
fruit-eater ...... JUNE BUG, FIG-
EATER
gaudy .... LADYBUG, LADYBIRD
grain .... CADELLE
grapevine .... THRIP
ground .... AMARA
head .... NITWIT, BLOCKHEAD
larva .... GRUB, BEEWOLF,
GRUGRU, CADELLE
like charm .... SCARAB
like insect .... EARWIG
order of .... COLEOPTERA
sacred to Egyptians
.... SCARAB
snouted .... CURCULIO
tree .... GIRDLER
wing cover .... SHARD,
ELYTRON
with club-shaped feelers
.... CLAVICORN
wood .... SAWYER
beetling .... PROJECTING,
OVERHANGING
befall .... HAP, COME, PASS,
OCCUR, BETIDE, HAPPEN
befit .... FIT, SUIT, BECOME,
BEHOOVE
befitting .... PROPER, SUITABLE,
APPROPRIATE
holiness .... SAINTLY
befog .... BLUR, CONFUSE,
OBSCURE
befool ...... DUPE, TRICK, DECEIVE
before .... ERE, AHEAD, PRIOR,
FORWARD, PREVIOUS,
FORMERLY, PRECEDING
all others .... FIRST
corn and form .... UNI
craftsy .... ARTSY
long .... ANON, SOON,
SHORTLY, PRESENTLY
mentioned .... SAME, DITTO
prefix .... PRE, ANTE
befoul .... SOIL, DIRTY
befuddle .... CONFUSE, STUPEFY
beg .... ASK, PRAY, MOOCH,
PLEAD, BESEECH, ENTREAT,
IMPLORE, REQUEST,
IMPORTUNE, PANHANDLE
off .... EXCUSE, ASK OUT,
DECLINE
the question .... EVADE
beget .... SIRE, FATHER, PRODUCE,
ENGENDER, GENERATE,
PROCREATE
beggar .... FAKIR, LAZAR, RANDY,
PAUPER, RASCAL, DERVISH,

LAZZARONE, PLEADER,
PANHANDLER, MENDICANT,
SCHNORRER
equipment of .... TINCUP
gift to .... ALMS, HANDOUT
roving .... FAKIR, GANGREL,
GABERLUNZIE
speech of .... CANT
beggarly .... MEAN, PETTY
beggars' lice .... BUR(R),
CLEAVERS
patron saint .... GILES
begging, practice of
...... MENDICITY, MENDICANCY
begin .... OPEN, ARISE, START,
COMMENCE, INITIATE, LEAD
OFF, ORIGINATE
beginner .... TIRO, TYRO, NOVICE,
ROOKIE, ACOLYTE, PUPIL,
NEOPHYTE, FRESHMAN,
GREENHORN, APPRENTICE
beginning .... GERM, ROOT,
INFANCY, ONSET, ORIGIN,
START, OPENING, GENESIS,
OUTSET, KICKOFF, INITIAL,
BIRTH, PREFACE, INCEPTION
Begone! .... SCAT, SHOO, BEAT IT,
SCRAM, AROINT, AVAUNT,
GET LOST
begrime ...... SOIL, DIRTY, SMEAR,
SMUDGE
begrudge .... ENVY, COVET,
REFUSE, GRUMBLE, OBJECT TO
beguile .... LURE, CHARM,
MISLEAD, DELUDE, DIVERT,
VAMP, AMUSE, COZEN,
DECEIVE
beguilements .... ARTS
Beguin .... BEGHARD
begum Indian .... PRINCESS
behalf .... SAKE, SIDE, BENEFIT,
STEAD, INTEREST, ADVANTAGE
behave .... ACT, BEAR, CARRY,
DEPORT, COMPORT, CONDUCT
foolishly .... FRIBBLE
behavior .... ACTION, BEARING,
CONDUCT, MANNERS,
ACTUATION
in polite society
.... ETIQUETTE
science of .... ETHOLOGY
behead .... DECOLLATE,
DECAPITATE
behemoth ...... BEAST, ELEPHANT,
HIPPO(POTAMUS)
behest .... ORDER, BIDDING,
COMMAND
behind .... LATE, ABAFT, ASTERN,
(A)REAR, DELAYED,
BACKWARD
colloquial .... BUTTOCKS

on payment of debt .... IN ARREARS

time(s) .... LATE, PASSE, TARDY, OVERDUE, OUTMODED

Behold! .... LO, SEE, VOILA

beholden ...... OBLIGED, INDEBTED

behoove .... INCUMBENT UPON

beige .... TAN, ECRU, GRAYISH

being .... LIFE, ENTITY, PERSON, CREATURE, EXISTENCE

abstract .... ENS, ENTIA

actual .... ESSE

essential .... ENS

individual .... MONAD

Beirut is capital of .... LEBANON

bejewel .... BEGEM

Bela Lugosi's pet .... BAT

belabor ...... BEAT, WHIP, POUND, ATTACK

belated .... TARDY

belay .... HOLD, STOP, SECURE

belaying cleat .... KEVEL, BOLLARD

belch .... BURP, EMIT, GUSH, VOMIT, ERUCT(ATE)

beldam .... HAG, CRONE, ALECTO, MEGAER, ERINYES

beleaguer .... BESIEGE, SURROUND

beleaguerment .... SIEGE

Belem is capital of .... PARA

belemite .... THUNDERSTONE

belfry .... BELL TOWER

dweller .... BAT

Belgian .... FLEMING, FLEMISH, WALLOON

battlesite in WWI .... YPRES

canal .... ALBERT

capital .... BRUSSELS

city/town .... AALST, ANTWERP, ARLON, ALOST, BALEN, GHENT, BERCHEM, JETTE, BRUGES, DEURNE, MONS, DOORNIK, LIEGE, SPA, LOUVAIN, TOURNAI, HUY, ROULERS, MECHELEN, NAMEN, YPRES, SERAING, BOOM, OSTEND, JEMAPPES, VORST, HOBOKEN, VILVORDE, HASSELT, ZOTTEGEM

commune .... ANS, ATH, NAMUR, VORST, JETTE, LEDE, NIEL, ROUX, SPA, TAMINES

Congo river .... UELE

currency unit .... BELGA, FRANC

dog .... SCHIPPERKE

fascist party .... REX

forest .... ARDENNES

hare/rodent .... LEPORID

highest point .... BOTRANGE

king, former .... ALBERT,

LEOPOLD, BAUDOUIN

marble .... RANCE, RANSE

mountain .... VAALSERBERG, BOTRANGE, WEISSERSTEIN

plateau .... HOHE VENN, SCHNEE EIFEL, ZITTERWALD

police .... GENDARME

port .... OSTEND

possession, former ..... CONGO

province ...... ANTWERP, LIEGE, EAST FLANDERS, NAMUR, WEST FLANDERS, HAINAUT, BRABANT, LIMBURG, LUXEMBOURG

queen .... ASTRID

reclaimed land .... POLDER

resort .... SPA, OSTEND

river .... LYS, YSER, DYLE, DEOLE, DENDER, MARK, NETHE, LESSE, SENNE, MEUSE, SAMBRE, RUPEL, OURTHE, SEMOIS, SCHELDE, VESDRE

sea .... NORTH

seaport .... OSTEND, ZEBRUGGE

statesman .... SPAAK

textile center .... GHENT

violinist .... YSAYE

watering place .... SPA

Belgrade .... BEOGRAD

is capital of .... YUGOSLAVIA

Belial .... ANGEL, SATAN

belie .... DENY, DISGUISE, DISPROVE

belief .... ISM, MIND, VIEW, TRUST, OPINION, FAITH, CREED, DOCTRINE, CREDENCE, CONVICTION

based on .... DOXIC

beyond .... INCREDIBLE

in communication through contemplation .... MYSTICISM

in genii .... DEMONISM

in ghosts .... EODOLISM

in one god .... THEISM

Mideast .... ISLAM

beliefs .... ETHOS

set of .... CREDO, CREED

believe .... RELY, COUNT, ASSUME, CREDIT, EXPECT, TRUST, CHERISH, SUPPOSE

believer .... IST, ELITIST, TRUSTER

easy .... GULLIBLE, CREDULOUS

in God .... DEIST, THEIST

in rule by superior people .... ELITIST

in spirits .... ANIMIST

of all religions .... OMNIST

believing .... CREANT

belittle .... KNOCK, DEMEAN, SLIGHT, MINIMIZE, RIDICULE,

DEPRECATE, BEDWARF, DISCREDIT, DISPARAGE, DEPRECIATE

Belize's former name .... HONDURAS

bell .... GONG, ROAR, BELLOW, CAMPANA, CARILLON

alarm .... TOCSIN

call to prayer .... ANGELUS

clapper .... TONGUE

flat .... GONG

flower .... RAMPION, CAMPANULA

jar .... CLOCHE

man ..... RINGER, (TOWN)CRIER

ring by hammer .... CHIME

ringer .... SEXTON

ringing device .... CHIME

sound ..... DONG, PEAL, KNELL, TING, TOLL, RING, CLANG, TING-A-LING

striker .... HAMMER, CLAPPER

tongue .... CLAPPER

tower ...... BELFRY, COMPANILE

town in story .... ADANO

belladonna .... MANICON, NIGHTSHADE

alkaloid/drug .... ATROPIN(E)

lily .... AMARYLLIS

bellboy .... PAGE, BELLHOP

call to .... FRONT

colloquial .... BUTTONS

belle .... BEAUTY

Belle of the West .... STARR

belles-lettres .... LITERATURE

bellhop. See **bellboy**

bellicose .... HOSTILE, WARLIKE, BELLIGERENT

belligerence .... WAR, BELLICOSITY

belligerent .... WARLIKE, BELLICOSE, PUGNACIOUS, COMBATANT, CONTENTIOUS, AGGRESSIVE, QUARRELSOME, PROTAGONIST

right of a .... ANGARY

Bellini .... PAINTER

pupil of .... TITIAN

son of ...... GENTILE, GIOVANNI

Bellini's (Vincenzo) opera .... NORMA

Bellona's brother .... MARS

bellow .... BELL, ROAR, WAIL

bellows .... BLOWER

bells, set of .... CHIME(S), CARILLON

bellwether .... SHEEP, LEADER

belly .... WAME, WOMB, BULGE, TUMMY, BAGGIE, VENTER, ABDOMEN, STOMACH

laugh .... ROAR, GUFFAW,

near/on the .... VENTRAL
protruding .... PAUNCH, BAY
    WINDOW, BREADBASKET
bellyache: colloq. .... GRIPE,
    COMPLAIN
bellyband .... CINCH, GIRTH
bellybutton .... NAVEL
bellyful .... SURFEIT
belong .... OWN, VEST IN,
    PERTAIN, APPERTAIN
belonging to certain people
    .... NATIVE, ENDEMIC,
    INDIGENOUS
belongings .... ASSETS, ESTATE,
    EFFECTS, CHATTELS,
    PROPERTY, POSSESSION(S)
beloved ...... LIEF, ANGEL, LOVER,
    DARLING, SWEETHEART
colloquial .... HONEYBUNCH
physician .... LUKE
below .... ALOW, LOWER,
    (BE)NEATH, INFERIOR,
    (UNDER)NEATH, SUBORDINATE
combining form .... HYP(O)
the belt: sl. ...... FOUL, UNFAIR
belt ...... OBI, AREA, BAND, BLOW,
    CUFF, SASH, STRAP, CESTUS,
    CORDON, ZOSTER, BALDRIC,
    GIRDLE, CIRCUIT, ZONE,
    CINCTURE, CINGULUM
case .... HOLSTER
fancy .... SASH
imaginary, heavenly
    .... ZODIAC
slang .... DECK, CLOBBER
sword .... BALDRIC
tighten .... RETRENCH,
    ECONOMIZE
Beltane .... MAYDAY
beluga .... WHALE, WHITEFISH,
    DOLPHIN, STURGEON
roe/eggs .... CAVIAR
belvedere .... GALLERY, PAVILION,
    SUMMERHOUSE
bema .... CHANCEL, PLATFORM
bemoan .... WAIL, LAMENT,
    DEPLORE
bemuse .... MUDDLE, CONFUSE,
    STUPEFY, DISTRACT
ben .... SON, PEAK, PARLOR
relative .... IBN
Ben .... HOGAN, GAZZARA
Jonson's comedy ...... EPICENE
Jonson's plague .... GOUT
bench ...... SEAT, COURT, EXEDRA,
    GALLERY, SETTEE,
    WORKTABLE
church .... PEW
in sports .... SIDELINE
judges' .... BANC

of authority .... DRIVER'S SEAT
"the" .... JUDICIARY
tool .... VISE
warmer .... JUDGE
bend .... BOW, ARCH, KINK, TURN,
    WALE, CROFT, GIVE,
    FLEX(URE), CROOK, SHAPE,
    CURVE, RELENT, YIELD,
    STOOP, SOFTEN
and bob .... NID
as of light, heat .... REFRACT
back .... REFLEX
in adoration .... KNEEL
in stream .... HOOK
in timber .... SNY
inward .... INTROVERT
knee in worship
    .... GENUFLECT
light wave .... REFRACT
sinister .... BATON
the arm .... FLEX
bender .... ORGY, SPREE, WASSAIL
bending .... BIGHT, ZIGZAG,
    FLEXION, FLECTION
bends, having two .... BIFLEX
the .... CRAMPS
bendy .... OKRA
bene .... BOON, (WILD)HOG,
    PRAYER
vale .... FAREWELL
beneath .... BELOW, UNDER,
    UNWORTHY OF
combining form .... HYP(O)
the skin .... SUBCUTANEOUS
benedict .... BACHELOR, CELIBATE
benedictine .... NUN, MONK,
    LIQUEUR
benediction ...... GRACE, BENISON,
    BLESSING, INVOCATION
benefaction .... BOON
benefactor .... PATRON,
    SYMPATHIZER
benefic ...... KINDLY, CHARITABLE
benefice, appoint to a
    .... COLLATE
first income of .... ANNAT
holder .... APPROPRIATOR
of a sort .... SINECURE
revenue .... ANNAT(E)S
temporary .... COMMENDAM
beneficial .... BENIGN, USEFUL,
    HELPFUL
beneficiary .... USEE, DONEE
benefit .... GAIN, GOOD, HELP,
    SAKE, FAVOR, AVAIL, ASSIST,
    PROFIT, ADVANTAGE
benevolent .... KIND, HUMANE,
    AMIABLE, LIBERAL, OBLIGING,
    CORDIAL, GENEROUS,
    CHARITABLE
order .... ELKS

Bengal bison .... GAUR
capital .... CALCUTTA
city .... PATNA
cotton .... ADATI
grass .... MILLET
groom .... SAICE
light .... FIREWORK
native .... KOL, BANIAN,
    BENGALI
Ben-Gurion's wife .... PAULA
benighted .... LOST
benign ...... KIND(LY), HARMLESS,
    BENEFICIAL, GRACIOUS,
    FAVORABLE
tumor/cyst .... ADENOMA
benjamin .... GUM, BENZOIN
Benjamin .... FAVORITE SON
father of .... JACOB
Franklin's musical
    instrument
    .... HARMONICA
son of .... ARD, EHI, ROSH
benne .... SESAME
bennet .... HEMLOCK, VALERIAN
Benny, comedian .... JACK
devised characteristic of
    .... STINGINESS
bent .... SET, BOUND, GRASS,
    TASTE, CROOKED, FLAIR,
    BIASED, CURVED, PROPENSITY,
    APTITUDE, INCLINED,
    DISTORTED, DESIRE, WARPED,
    TWISTED, TENDENCY,
    INCLINATION
backward .... RETRORSE
easily .... SUPPLE, PLIABLE
like a knee .... GENICULATE
Bentley's sleuth .... TRENT
benumb .... HEBETATE
benzedrine .... INHALANT,
    STIMULANT
benzene .... BENZOL, SOLVENT
Beowulf, monster slain by
    .... GRENDEL
bequeath .... WILL, ENDOW,
    LEAVE, HAND DOWN
bequest .... LEGACY, HERITAGE,
    ENDOWMENT, INHERITANCE
berate .... SCOLD, REBUKE,
    UPBRAID
Berber .... RIFF, KABYLE, HAMITE,
    MOSLEM, TUAREG
chief .... CAID
dialect .... TUAREG
hermit .... MARABOUT
tribe .... DAZA, RIFF, TEDA
tribesman .... KABYLE
berceuse .... LULLABY
bereave ...... ROB, STRIP, DEPRIVE
bereavement .... LOSS,
    DEPRIVATION

expression of .... CONDOLENCE
bereft .... LORN, LONELY,
      DEPRIVED(OF)
beret .... CAP, BIRETTA
berg .... ICE
bergamot .... PEAR, MONARDA,
      HORSEMINT
Bergen's Mortimer .... SNERD
Berger, singer .... ERNA
Bergerac's sore point ...... NOSE
Bergman, actress .... INGRID
beriberi .... DROPSY
  medicine .... THIAMIN(E)
Bering Sea river .... YUKON
Berkshire .... HOG
  county seat .... READING
  race course .... ASCOT
Berlin .... CITY, CARRIAGE
  bonnet .... EASTER
  district .... SPANDAU
  hit .... REMEMBER
  is capital of
    .... (EAST)GERMANY
  prison .... SPANDAU
  river .... SPREE
  sight (no longer) .... WALL
  songwriter .... IRVING
berm .... LEDGE, TERRACE
Bermuda capital .... HAMILTON
  arrowroot .... ARARAO
  grass .... DOOB, DOUB
  product .... ONION
  to pleasure seekers
    .... PLAYGROUND
Bern is capital of
    .... SWITZERLAND
Bernese Alps mountain
    .... WETTERHORN
bernicle .... GOOSE
berry .... BOCCA, GRAPE, BANANA,
   CURRANT, MADRONA, ACINUS,
    TOMATO, ALLSPICE
  branch .... CANE
  cigarette .... CUBEB
  combining form .... BACCI
  fragrant .... MYRTLE
  grape .... ACINUS
  like .... BACCATE
  slang .... DOLLAR
bersagliere .... RIFLEMAN,
    SHARPSHOOTER
berseem .... CLOVER
berserk .... AMOK, AMUCK,
    BARESARK
Bert .... LAHR, PARKS
berth .... BED, BUNK, POSITION,
   SLIP, PLACE, ABODE, DOCK,
    ANCHORAGE, LODGING,
    COMPARTMENT
  Pullman car .... LOWER, UPPER
bertha .... COLLAR

Bertha, Big .... CANNON
beruffled .... FURBELOWED
beryl .... EMERALD, MINERAL,
   MORGANITE, AQUAMARINE
beseech .... BEG, PRAY, HOUND,
   IMPLORE, ENTREAT, PRESS,
   PLEAD, PETITION, URGE,
    COAX, SOLICIT
beset ...... HARRY, HARASS, STUD,
   ATTACK, BESIEGE, ASSAIL,
    OBSESS, PESTER
beshow .... SABLEFISH
beshrew: arch. .... CURSE
beside .... BY, NEAR, CLOSE,
   ABREAST, ALONGSIDE
  oneself .... MAD, SORE, ANGRY
  prefix .... PAR, PARA
besides .... TOO, ALSO, ELSE,
   EXCEPT, FURTHER, MOREOVER
besiege .... PLAGUE, PESTER,
   BESET, CROWD, HARASS,
   INVEST, BELEAGUER,
   OVERWHELM, SURROUND
besieger's explosive ...... PETARD
  protective cover
    .... MANT(E)LET
besmirch ...... SOIL, DIRTY, STAIN,
   SULLY, DEFAME, TARNISH
besom .... BROOM
bespangle .... STUD, STAR,
    DECORATE
bespatter .... SOIL, SMEAR,
    SPLASH
bespeak .... SHOW, RESERVE
Bessemer process product
    .... STEEL
best .... TOPS, CHOICE, DEFEAT,
   OUTWIT, SURPASS, UTMOST,
    EXCELLENT
  colloquial .... TOPFLIGHT
  combining form .... ARISTO
  man at wedding
   ...... GROOMSMAN, PARANYMPH
  part ...... ELITE, CREAM, MEAT,
    CHOICE, FLOWER
  seller .... HIT, BIBLE
  wishes ...... CONGRATULATIONS
bestial .... VILE, BRUTAL, ANIMAL,
   BRUTISH, SAVAGE, BEASTLIKE
bestiary book author .... BORGES
bestow .... GIVE, AWARD, CONFER,
   DEVOTE, DONATE, PRESENT,
    BEQUEATH
  generously .... LAVISH
bestrew .... SCATTER
bestride .... STRADDLE
bet .... PLAY, STAKE, WAGER,
   GAMBLE, PARLAY,
    PROPOSITION
  against card dealer .... PUNT
  at dice .... FADE

  colloquial .... ENTRY,
    CANDIDATE
  fail to pay .... WELSH
  in an election ...... CANDIDATE
  in roulette .... BAS
  sure win .... IN THE BAG
  to win in horse race .... ON
    THE NOSE
  without odds .... ITOI
  you! .... CERTAINLY, YES
    INDEED
betake ...... GO, REPAIR, JOURNEY
Betancourt .... MONK, CURATE
bête noire .... LEPER, PARIAH,
   BUGBEAR, OUTCAST
  of nursery .... CROUP
betel .... SIRI, PLANT, PEPPER
  leaf .... PAN, BUYO
  nut .... SERI, CATECHU
  palm .... ARECA, PINANG
  pepper .... IKMO, ITMO
Betelgeuse .... STAR
bethel .... CHAPEL, CHURCH
betide .... OCCUR, BEFALL,
    HAPPEN
betimes .... SOON, EARLY,
   QUICKLY, PROMPTLY
betoken .... AUGUR, DENOTE,
   FORESHOW, INDICATE
beton .... CONCRETE
betray .... SELL, DECEIVE, REVEAL,
   DIVULGE, VICTIMIZE
betrayal .... PERFIDY
betrayer .... TRAITOR, SEDUCER,
    DECEIVER
  Biblical .... JUDAS(ISCARIOT)
betroth .... AFFY, ENGAGE,
   PLIGHT, AFFIANCE
betrothal .... PROMISE,
   ENGAGEMENT
betrothed person .... FIANCE,
    FIANCEE
Betsy Ross creation .... FLAG
  slang .... GAT, GUN,
    EQUALIZER
Bette .... DAVIS, MIDLER
better .... BEAT, MEND, AMEND,
   IMPROVE, OUTDO, EXCEL,
    RELIEVE, SURPASS
  half: colloq. .... WIFE
  looking .... CUTER,
    HANDSOMER
betting system .... PARLAY, PARI-
    MUTUEL
  another way: colloq. ..... ROLL
  loser's .... MARTINGAL(E)
between .... AMID, MIDDLE,
   BETWIXT, INTERMEDIATE
  bee and dee .... CEE
  come ...... BUTT IN, INTERFERE
  go- .... AGENT, MEDIUM,

MEDIATOR

in law .... MESNE

meals treat .... SODA, SNACK

Michigan and Ontario

.... ERIE

prefix .... DIA, META, INTER

the lines ...... UNSAID, HIDDEN, IMPLIED

Thomas and Edison ..... ALVA

you and me .... SECRET

betwixt and between .... MIDDLE

Bevan's nickname .... NYE

bevel .... CANT, EDGE, BEZEL, SLANT

out .... REAM

ship timber .... SNAPE

to join .... MITER, MITRE

beveled angle/surface ...... SPLAY

beverage .... ADE, ALE, TEA, BOZA, KAVA, MATE, SAKE, SOUR, WINE, COFFEE, DRINK, NOG(G), TOKAY, LEBAN, POTABLE

add liquor to .... LACE

almond-flavored .... RATAFIA

beer-lemonade .... SHANDY

brandy, sugar, spice

.... TODDY

carbonated .... POP, SODA

caffeinated .... TEA, COFFEE

Christmas .... EGGNOG

fermented .... MEAD, SAKE

from evergreen leaves

.... MATE

from leaves .... TEA

from meat extract ...... BROTH, BEEF-TEA

from molasses .... RUM

fruit(crushed) .... SMASH

hot milk .... POSSET

maker .... TEABAG

palm sap .... TODDY

sour ..... LIME-ADE, LEMONADE

vermouth, etc. .... BRONX

wine .... NEGUS, BISHOP, VERMOUTH

with anise .... KUMMEL

beverages, place for .... BAR, CELLAR(ET)

bevy .... COVEY, FLOCK

bewail .... WEEP, MOURN, GRIEVE, LAMENT, DEPLORE, COMPLAIN

beware .... SHUN, AVOID, BE ON GUARD, WATCH, LOOKOUT

bewilder .... DAZE, STUMP, PUZZLE, CONFUSE, MYSTIFY, PERPLEX

bewildering .... MAZY

bewitch .... HEX, CHARM, ENCHANT, ENTRANCE, FASCINATE

bewitchment .... SPELL

bey .... DEY, GOVERNOR

Beyoglu .... PERA

beyond .... PAST, YONDER, LATER, REMOTE, FARTHER, FURTHER, OVER, EXCEEDING

colloquial ...... GOD-FORSAKEN

combining form .... SUR, META, PARA, ULTRA

compare .... PEERLESS, MATCHLESS

reach .... UNATTAINABLE, FAR-OFF, OUT-OF-THE-WAY

Bezaleel's father: myth. ...... URI

bezant .... COIN, BALLET

bezel .... RIM, FACET, FLANGE, TEMPLATE

bhang .... HEMP

Bhutan capital(summer)

.... TASHI-CHHO

capital(winter) .... PUNAKHA

people .... BHOTIYA

pine .... KAIL

ruler .... MAHARAJA(H)

bi: prefix .... TWO, TWICE

Biafran leader .... OJUKWU

Bialystok .... BELOSTOK

biannual .... BIENNIAL, SEMI-ANNUAL

bias .... BENT, SWAY, TWIST, SLOPE, TENDENCY, PREJUDICE, DIAGONAL, INFLUENCE, PARTIALITY

biased .... UNFAIR, UNJUST, BIGOTED, PARTIAL, PARTISAN, ONE-SIDED, PREJUDICED, NARROW-MINDED

person .... BIGOT

bib .... APRON, DRINK, DICKEY, IMBIBE, NAPKIN, TIPPLE

and tucker .... CLOTHES

companion of .... TUCKER

bibb .... BIBCOCK

bibber .... DRINKER, TOPER, TIPPLER

bibcock .... BIBB, FAUCET

bibelot ...... CURIO, VERTU, VIRTU, ARTIFACT, BRIC-A-BRAC

Bible books of New Testament

.... JOHN, LUKE, MARK, MATTHEW, ACTS, CORINTHIANS, GALATIANS, EPHESIANS, PHILIPPIANS, JAMES, COLOSSIANS, TIMOTHY, TITUS, THESSALONIANS, HEBREWS, ROMANS, PHILEMON, JUDE, PETER, REVELATION

books of Old Testament

...... RUTH, EXODUS, NUMBERS, GENESIS, LEVITICUS, JUDGES,

DEUTERONOMY, KINGS, JOSHUA, SAMUEL, EZRA, ESTHER, CHRONICLES, JOB, PSALMS, PROVERBS, ISAIAH, AMOS, JEREMIAH, EZEKIEL, LAMENTATIONS, JOEL, HOSEA, DANIEL, MICAH, JONAH, OBADIAH, NAHUM, HAGGAI, MALACHI, ZECHARIAH, NEHEMIAH, ZEPHANIAH

reading .... PSALM

the .... HOLY WRIT, HOLY SCRIPTURES

translator .... ULFILA(S)

version .... DOUAI, DOUAY, HAGGADAH, KING JAMES, TORAH, TALMUD, MASORAH, HALAKAH, PESHITO, VULGATE, APOCRYPHA

biblical ...... SACRED, SCRIPTURAL, PROPHETIC, EXEGETIC, EVANGELICAL, TALMUDIC, CANONICAL, APOSTOLIC, APOCRYPHAL

ancient first-aid ..... WINE AND OIL

angel .... GABRIEL

animal .... OX, FOX, GOAT, DEER, LION, ORYX, MULE, CAMEL, HORSE, SHEEP, IBEX, DONKEY, JACKAL, BEAR, GAZELLE, LEOPARD, WILD ASS, CROCODILE

armies .... SABAOTH

ascetic order .... ESSENE

assassin .... CAIN

bird .... RAVEN, ROCK-DOVE, TURTLE-DOVE

cave .... MACHPELAH, ADULLAM

character .... ABEL, AMOS, AMNON, ABNER, AARON, EVE, CAIN, ADAM, ANNAS, NABAL, ANTIPAS, ABIGAIL, EZRA, ESAU, ENOS, JOHN, LEAH, AQUILA, ABINADAB, ELIAS, HAGAR, HEROD, DEMETRIUS, DELILAH, NOAH, MOSES, PRISCILLA, JONAH, JOSIAH, ICHABOD, LABAN, NAOMI, ELIJAH, SIMON, SALOME, PILATE, TAMAR, TOBIAH, TIMOTHY, PAUL, VARUS, BARNABAS

charioteer .... JEHU

city .... NOB, GATH, GAZA, EKRON, BABEL, HEBRON, DAN, GOLM, KABUL, RESEN, SODOM, KANAH, HAZOR, RAMAH, ACCO, TYRE, ZOAR, HELEPH, ENDOR, SARID, CHINNERETH,

BETH-SHAN, BETH-ANATH, IBLEAM, OPHRAH, GALILEE, DOTHAM, JUTBAII, MEGIDDO, GILGAL, TIRZAH, JABNEEL, MEDEBA, NAARAN, JOKMEAM, DIBON, PEREA, JERUSALEM, BETHEL, SHILOH, TAPPUAH, RAMAH, ASHDOD, ASHKELON, RABBAH, MIZPAH, JERICHO, MICHMETHATH, BEER-SHEBA, AROER, TIMNAH, CAESAREA, GOMORRAH, BETH-SHEMESH

city built by Antipas .... TIBERIAS

city of refuge .... BEZER, SHECHEM, HEBRON, KEDESH, GOLAN, RAMOTH-GILEAD

cliffs .... MOAB

coin .... PRUTAH, SHEKEL, DRACHMA, TETRADRACHMA, SESTERCE, OCTADRACHMA

cony .... HYRAX

country .... PUL, SHEBA, EDOM, GILEAD, ASSYRIA, SEIR, SEBA, CANAAN, ENON, CHALDEA

curser .... BALAAM

desert .... PARAN

expression .... SELAH

fishing village ...... BETHSAIDA

flight .... EXODUS

flower .... IRIS, TULIP, NARCISSUS, DANDELION, HYACINTH, SAFFRON CROCUS, ANEMONE, STAR OF BETHLEHEM

food .... BARLEY, MANNA, LENTIL, WALNUT, CUCUMBER

forest .... HERETH

fruit .... FIG, DATE, GRAPE, APRICOT, OLIVE, POMEGRANATE

giant .... ANAK, ENIM, GOLIATH

gift-bearer(s) .... MAGI, GASPAR, MELCHIOR, BALTHASAR

Hades .... SHEOL

herb ..... CORIANDER, CHICORY, CASTOR-BEAN, WORMWOOD, WATERCRESS

hill .... ZION, MOREH

hill country ..... JUDEA, JUDAH

hosts .... SABAOTH

hunter .... ESAU, NIMROD

island .... CAUDA

judge .... ELI, ELON, EHUD, GIDEON, JEPHTHAH, ABDON, IBZAN, SAMSON, JAIR, TOLA, OTHNIEL

king .... OG, ASA, AGAG, ABIJAM, DAVID, SOLOMON, REHOBOAM, ABIMELECH,

JEHORAM, JEHOSHAPHAT, HEROD, UZZIAH, JOTHAM, MANASSEH, HEZEKIAH, JEHOAHAZ, JEHOIAKIM, AHAZ, BAASHA, JOSIAH, ZEDEKIAH, JEHOIACHIN, AHAB, JEHU, JEROBOAM, OMRI, JEHOASH, AHAZIAH, SAUL, HOSHEA, MENAHEM, RAMSES, MELCHIZEDEK

king, assassinated .... ELAH, SHALLUM, ZECHARIAH, NADAB, JOASH, AMAZIAH, PEKAH, PEKAHIAH, AMON, JEHORAM

king who committed suicide .... ZIMRI

kingdom .... ELAM, MOAB, ISRAEL, SHEBA, JUDAH, SAMARIA

lake .... HULEH

land .... NOD, TOB, EDOM, GOSHEN

land of cedars .... LEBANON

language .... ARAMIC

lawgiver .... MOSES

Levitical city .... GEBA, BILEAM, REHOB, MISHAL, JAHAZ, ABDON, HAMMATH, GEZER, JOKNEAM, DABERATH, ALMON, GIBEON, KARTHAN, JATTIR, JUTTA, ANATHOTH, AIJALON, TAANACH, DEBIR, GIBBETHON

liar .... ANANIAS, SAPPHIRA

lion .... ARI

lyrelike instrument .... SACKBUT

mass migration .... EXODUS

measure of capacity .... HIN, OMER, EPHAH, HOMER, KAB, BATH, BUSHEL, LOG, LETHECH

measure of length ..... FINGER, SPAN, CUBIT, REED, HANDBREATH, FATHOM, FURLONG

merchant .... TUBAL

mount .... ABLA, HOR, EBAL, NAIN, PEOR, HOREB, NEBO, SIER, SINAI, TABOR, ARARAT, GILEAD, OLIVET, HERMON, GILBOA, MORIAH

name ...... ARAM, AROM, EBAL, EBED, GADDI, ONO, ANIM, REBA, ASOM, IVAH, IRA, ABIAM, AMASA, AHIRA, SERED, MAGOG, ISHMAEL, UR, HELI, MERAB, VASHTI, IRAD, ELAH, GOMER, ULAM

oldster .... ENOS

ornament .... URIM

passage used .... TEXT

password .... SHIBBOLETH

patriarch .... ADAM, ENOS, SETH, SHEM, ABRAHAM, ISAAC, JACOB, PELEG, JOB, TERAH, NOAH, JARED, REU, JOSEPH, LAMECH

people .... SEMITICS, EGYPTIANS, SUMARIANS, AKKADIANS, CANAANITES, GUTIANS, ISRAELITES, HEBREWS, AMALEKITES, BEDOUINS, AMMONITES, MOABITES, PHILISTINES, ROMANS, PHOENICIANS, ASSYRIANS, JUDAHITES, PERSIANS, BABYLONIANS, JEWS, MACEDONIANS, SELEUCIDS, PTOLEMIES, GALILEANS, HASMONEANS, PHARISEES, SAMARITANS

place .... ENON, ENDOR, SHILOH, JORDAN

place of dishonor .... GOD'S LEFT HAND

place of torment .... GEHENNA

plant .... FLAX, MYRRH, CITRON, WILLOW, COTTON, ONION, CASSIA, MYRTLE, FRANKINCENSE

plateau .... EASTERN, TRANSJORDAN

pool .... GIBEON, SILOAM

precious stone .... LIGURE, TURQUOISE, JACINTH

preposition .... UNTO

priest .... ELI, LEVI, ANNAS, AARON, JANNEUS, HYRCANUS, ARISTOBULUS

promised land .... CANAAN

pronoun .... THEE

prophet .... AMOS, EZRA, SAMUEL, HOSEA, JONAH, MICAH, MOSES, ELISHA, ELIJAH, ISAIAH, DANIEL, JOEL, EZEKIEL, JEREMIAH, HOLY MAN, ZOROASTER

prophetess .... DEBORAH

queen .... SHEBA, ESTHER, CANDACE, VASHTI, ATHALIAH

queen mother .... JEZEBEL

rich man .... DIVES

river .... NILE, JORDAN, ABANA, ARNON, TIGRIS, JABBOK, YARMUK, EUPHRATES

sacred objects .... URIM

scribe .... EZRA, BARUCH

sea .... DEAD, OF REEDS, AEGEAN, OF GALILEE

serpent .... NEHUSHTAN

sheep-owner .... NABAL

shepherd .... ABEL, AMOS

site of Calvary ..... GOLGOTHA
skeptic .... THOMAS
skipper .... NOAH
spice .... STACTE
spring ...... AIN, ESEK, MARY'S
WELL, SILOAM
spy .... CALEB
step-pyramid structure
.... ZIGGURAT
stopping place .... MARAH
symbol of danger .... VIPER,
SERPENT
fertility .... DOLPHIN
prayer .... FRANKINCENSE
suffering .... MYRRH
virtue .... GOLD
system of writing
.... CUNEIFORM
tax collector .... MATTHEW
temptress .... EVE, DELILAH
thief .... BARABBAS
timber .... ALMUG
tower .... EDAR, BABEL
town .... ENDOR, CANA,
ARBELA, NAIN, BETHEL, BETH-
AVEN, BETH-ARBEL,
BETHLEHEM, BETH-BARAH,
NAZARETH, CAPERNAUM,
GINAE, BALAH, EMMAUS,
SEBASTE, GENNESARET,
BETHANY, MAGDALA,
LEBONAH
treasure city .... PITHOM,
RAAMSES
tree ...... ACACIA, CEDAR, OAK,
ALMOND, LAUREL, CYPRESS,
TAMARISK
tribe ...... DAN, LEVI, MOABITE,
NAPHTALI, HEBREW, ISSACHAR,
ASHER, MIDIANITE, AMMONITE,
MANASSEH
valley .... BACA, NEMEA,
JORDAN, ELAH, SIDDIM,
SOREK, HINNOM, KIDRON,
JEZREEL, TYROPOEON
verb ending .... ETH
verb form .... HAST
victim .... ABEL
vineyard owner .... NABOTH
volcano ..... HORNS OF HATTIN
walled city .... MEGIDDO,
SHECHEM
wanderer .... CAIN
weed .... TARE
weight .... BEKA, MINA,
GERAH, POUND, SHEKEL,
TALENT
wicked priest .... SIMON
wild ox .... REEM
wilderness .... MAON, ZIPH,
JUDEA, PARAN

wise men .... MAGI
word .... MENE, RACA, SELAH
bibliographer's abbr. ...... OBED
bibliotheca .... LIBRARY,
CATALOG(UE)
bibulous ...... DRUNK, ABSORBENT,
ALCOHOLIC
festival .... ALE, BACCHANALIA
party .... WASSAIL
person .... SOT, TOPER,
BACCHANT, TIPPLER,
DRUNKARD
bicarbonate .... SODA, BICARB
bice .... BLUE, PIGMENT, VERDITER
bicephalous .... TWO-HEADED
bicker .... ARGUE, CAVIL,
FLUTTER, WRANGLE,
QUARREL, SQUABBLE,
GURGLE, DISPUTE
bicuspid .... TOOTH
bicycle .... BIKE, VELOCIPEDE
rider's seat .... SADDLE
two-seater .... TANDEM
bid .... ASK, OFFER, EFFORT,
TENDER, COMMAND,
INVITATION, OVERTURE
in bridge .... DECLARATION
return .... RECALL
bidarka .... CANOE
bidding ...... COMMAND, REQUEST,
SUMMONS, INVITATION,
(BE)HEST
biddy .... HEN, CHICKEN
bide .... STAY, WAIT, DWELL,
RESIDE, CONTINUE
bield .... SHELTER
bienvenue .... WELCOME
bier .... PYRE, COFFIN, HEARSE,
LITTER, FERETORY,
CATAFALQUE
bifacial .... JANUS, TWO-FACED
biff .... BOX, HIT, CUFF, STRIKE
biffin .... APPLES
bifid .... FORKED, CLEFTED
bifurcate ...... FORKED, BRANCHED
big .... HUGE, LOUD, LARGE,
SIZABLE, MASSIVE, BULKY,
NOBLE, IMPRESSIVE, POMPOUS,
ENORMOUS, WEIGHTY, MAN-
SIZE
and clumsy .... HULKING,
LUBBER(LY)
and strong ..... BURLY, HUSKY,
BRAWNY
casino .... TEN
hand .... TREMENDOUS
OVATION
house: sl. .... PRISON
pill .... BOLUS
shot: sl. .... VIP, BRASS,
BIGWIG, FATCAT

show: sl. .... THREE RING
CIRCUS
teethed .... MACRODONT
toe .... HALLUX
toe ailment .... GOUT, BURSITIS
top .... CIRCUS, TENT(ROOF)
tree .... REDWOOD, SEQUOIA
truck .... MACK
with child .... PREGNANT
Big Ben .... CLOCK
Ben's place .... TOWER,
LONDON
Bertha .... CANNON
Bertha, where cast ...... ESSEN
Dipper .... URSA MAJOR
Five member, WWI
.... JAPAN, ITALY, FRANCE
Five member, WWII
.... CHINA, FRANCE, RUSSIA
Horn .... RIVER, MOUNTAIN
Muddy .... MISSOURI
Plain .... GRAND PRAIRIE
River .... MISSISSIPPI
biggest and best portion
.... LION'S SHARE
bighead .... CONCEIT, EGOTISM
bighorn .... SHEEP, ARGALI
bight .... BAY, GULF, CORNER,
FORK, LOOP, HOLLOW, CURVE
bignonia tree .... CALABASH
bigot .... RACIST, ZEALOT
Bigtop name .... RINGLING,
BARNUM, BAILEY
bigwig: colloq. .... VIP, STAR,
FATCAT, TOPBRASS
Oriental .... AGA
Bihar's capital .... PATNA
bijou .... JEWEL, TRINKET
bikini .... ATOLL
on the beach .... SWIMSUIT
upper .... BRA
bilateral .... TWO-SIDED,
RECIPROCAL
bilbo .... RAPIER, SHACKLES
bile .... GALL, ANGER, CHOLER,
TEMPER, BITTERNESS
black .... MELANCHOLY
combining form .... CHOLE,
CHOL(O)
yellow .... CHOLER
bilestone .... GALLSTONE
bilge .... BULGE, SWELL
slang .... NONSENSE
bilingual .... DIGLOT
bilious .... BITTER, CROSS,
LIVERISH, GREEN, BAD-
TEMPERED
biliousness .... NAUSEA
bilk ...... GYP, DECEIVE, DEFRAUD,
CHEAT(ER), SWINDLE(R)
bill .... DUN, NEB, TAB, BEAK,

POSTER, STATEMENT, BELLOW, ACCOUNT, HALBERD, LIST, WILLIAM, RECKONING, ROAR, CHARGE, GREENBACK

and coo .... PET, KISS

fill the .... SUIT, QUALIFY

five-dollar .... VEE

foot the .... PAY

joker in a .... RIDER

of exchange .... DRAFT

of exchange dealer
.... CAMBIST

of fare .... MENU, CARTE

of lading .... CARGO LIST

part of .... NEB, CERE

pass through mutual aid
.... LOGROLL

stroke with .... PECK, PREEN

one-dollar .... BUCK

two-dollar .... DEUCE

ten-dollar .... TENNER, SAWBUCK

100-dollar .... C-NOTE, CENTURY

1000-dollar .... GRAND

Bill of Rights ...... MAGNA CARTA

billboard ...... POSTER, HOARDING, SIGNBOARD

billet ...... PUT UP, LODGING, POST, QUARTER(S), POSITION

doux .... LOVE LETTER

billfish .... GAR, SKIPPER, SAILFISH, SPEARFISH

billfold .... CASE, WALLET, POCKETBOOK

billhead .... LETTERHEAD

billiards .... POOL

ball .... IVORY

red ball .... CARAMBOLA

shot .... CAROM, MASSE

stick .... CUE

billing .... LISTING, DUNNING, FIGURES, INVOICE, STATEMENT

billingsgate lingo .... FOUL, VULGAR, ABUSIVE

billion .... MILLIARD

billow .... BORE, RISE, ROLL, WAVE, SWELL, EAGRE, SURGE

billy .... CAN, CLUB, STICK, KETTLE, TRUNCHEON

billycock .... HAT, DERBY

bilsted .... TREE, SWEET GUM

Bimini legend ...... FOUNTAIN OF YOUTH

bimonthly .... BIMENSAL, SEMI-MONTHLY

bin .... BOX, CONTAINER, RECEPTACLE, COMPARTMENT

fish .... KENCH

fodder .... CRATCH

for baby .... CRIB, PLAY-PEN

for ship's coal, fuel oil
.... BUNKER

storage .... HUTCH

binal .... TWOFOLD

binate .... DOUBLE

binaural .... STEREO

bind .... TIE, GIRD, HOLD, ROPE, TAPE, SECURE, ATTACH, RESTRAIN

as to a mast .... LASH UP

matrimonially .... WED, MARRY

mouth .... GAG

together .... FASTEN

together by rope .... FRAP

wound .... BANDAGE

binder .... BAND, CORD, ROPE, BALER, BANDAGE

binding .... TYING, CONFINING, BANDAGE, MANDATORY, OBLIGATORY, RESTRICTIVE

device, police ...... HANDCUFFS

document .... CONTRACT

machine .... BALER

substance .... TAR, GLUE, PASTE, ADHESIVE

bindle-stiff .... HOBO, TRAMP

bine .... HOP, STEM

Bing crooner .... CROSBY

fruit .... CHERRY

binge .... BOUT, LARK, ORGY, FLING, SPREE, TEAR, BENDER, WASSAIL, CAROUSAL, ESCAPADE

aftermath of .... HANGOVER

kind of ..... EATING, DRINKING, SHOPPING

slang .... PAINT THE TOWN RED

bingo .... KENO, BEANO, LOTTO

binocle .... TELESCOPE, OPERA GLASS, FIELD GLASS

biocatalyst .... HORMONE, VITAMIN

biographer, Ludwig .... EMIL

biographical sketch ...... PROFILE

biography .... MEMOIR, LIFE STORY, HISTORY

biological .... BIOTIC(AL)

change .... MUTATION

division .... GENERA

factor .... GENE

group .... SPECIES

reproductive cell ...... GAMETE

biology, branch of ...... GENETICS

of behavior .... ETHOLOGY

Bion .... POET

opposed to .... MORPHON

bionomics .... ECOLOGY

biped .... MAN, TWO-FOOTED

birch .... BIRK, CANE, ALDER, BETULA, HAZELNUT, WHIP,

HORNBEAM, IRONWOOD

birchbark .... BOAT, CANOE

bird .... CROW, DOVE, KIWI, MYNA, FOWL, FLYER, RAIL, SWAN, PARROT, SHRIKE

adjutant .... STORK, ARGALA, MARABOU

African .... COLY, LORY, LOURI, UMBER, TURAKOO, UMBRETTE

air route .... FLYWAY

albatross .... NELLY

American .... RHEA, JUNCO, TOWHEE

Andean .... CONDOR

apteryx .... IAO, KIWI

aquatic .... AUK, DUCK, GOOSE, GULL, LOON, SWAN, SCAUP, PELICAN, PENGUIN

Arctic .... XEMA, FULMAR, LONGSPUR

Asiatic ..... MINA, MYNA, PITA, PITTA

attack .... SWOOP, POUNCE

auk family .... DOVEKIE, ALCA, PUFFIN, ROTCH(E)

Australian .... EMU, KOEL, ARA, ARARA, COOEE, EMEW, KAHU, LEIPOA, COCKATOO, PARDALOTE

baker .... HORNERO

bastard wing .... ALULA

beach .... SANDERLING

beak ..... NEB, NIB, BILL, LORA

beak part .... MANDIBLE

beaky .... TOUCAN

bell .... MAKO

big-footed .... MEGAPOD

bill (see beak)

bittern .... HERON

black .... ANI, CROW, ROOK, RAVEN, MERL(E), GRACKLE, AMSEL, OUSEL, THRUSH

blue .... JAY, IRENA

blue-footed .... TITI

bobolink .... ORTALAN

bobwhite .... QUAIL, COLIN, PARTRIDGE

Brazilian .... TOUCAN, CARIAMA, SERIEMA

bright-colored .... HOOPOE, TOUCAN, TOURACO

bristle-billed .... BARBET

broad-billed ..... DUCK, SCAUP, SPOONBILL

brood .... NIDE, COVEY

butcher .... SHRIKE

call .... PIPE

caress .... BILL

carrion .... CROW, URUBU, VULTURE

catcher .... FOWLER
catching at night .... BATFOWL
chameleonic .... PTARMIGAN
chatterer .... JAY, COTINGA,
 (MAG)PIE, STONECHAT,
 WAXWING, WHEAT-EATER
class of .... AVES
claw-winged .... HOA(C)TZIN
cockateel .... PARROT
cockatoo .... ARARA
"collar" .... RUFF, TORQUES
colloquial .... PERSON
colored beak .... PUFFIN
cormorant .... GUANAY
corvine .... DAW, CROW,
 RAVEN
courlan .... JACAMAR,
 TINAMOU
crane .... SERIEMA,
 DEMOISELLE
craw .... MAW
crest .... COP, TUFT, HOOD,
 CALOT(TE)
crested .... BLUEJAY,
 HOA(C)TZIN, COCKATOO,
 QUE(T)ZAL
crocodile .... TROCHILUS
crop .... MAW, CRAW
crow .... CORBY, CHOUGH,
 CORBIE
crow-like .... ROOK, MAGPIE,
 CORVINE
cry .... CAW, WEEP, ROAR,
 BELLOW, SHRIEK
cuckoo .... ANI, ANO, KOEL
disease .... GAPES
diving ..... AUK, GREBE, LOOM,
 LOON, DUCKER, SMEW, PUFFIN,
 OSPREY, ALCIDINE, DIDAPPER
dodo .... GEESE
dog .... SETTER, POINTER
duck family .... SMEW,
 MERGANSER
duck-like .... COOT, GOOSE
dunlin .... STIB, SANDPIPER
eagle, sea .... ERN(E)
eagle's nest .... AERIE, EYRIE
East Indies .... SHAMA, BESRA,
 SHAHIN, REDPOOL, PEREGRINE
Egyptian sacred .... IBIS
emu-like .... CASSOWARY
European .... REED, AMSEL,
 GLEDE, TEREK, REDSTART,
 OUSEL, SEDGE, WOODCOCK
extinct .... MOA, DODO, MAMO,
 GREAT AUK, NOTORNIS,
 SOLITAIRE
eye tissue .... PECTEN
fabulous .... ROC, PHOENIX
falcon .... MERLIN, BESRA,
 SAKER, TERCEL, REDPOOL,
 PEREGRINE

fantailed .... PEACOCK
feather .... PENNA
feather-legged .... GROUSE
feather under the wing
 .... AXILLAR
feathers .... PLUMAGE
feathers near mouth
 .... VIBRISSA
feet for perching ...... ENSESSO
fighting .... AMADAVAT
finch ..... SERIN, MORO, SISKIN,
 BUNTING, CANARY, LINNET,
 TOWHEE, SPARROW, CARDINAL
finch-like .... CHEWINK,
 GROSBEAK
fish-eating .... ERN, OSPREY,
 KINGFISHER, OWL, LOON,
 GOOSANDER, AUK, GREBE,
 SKIMMER, PELICAN,
 MERGANSER, TERN, PUFFIN,
 CORMORANT, TERN, PUFFIN,
 PETREL, HERON, DARTER,
 GANNET
fish egg–eating .... DIPPER
fish hawk .... OSPREY
flightless .... AUK, MOA, KAGU,
 DODO, PENGUIN, WEKA, KIWI,
 OSTRICH, NOTORNIS,
 CASSOWARY, RHEA, EM(E)U,
 RATITE, APTERYX, TINAMOU
flock .... POD, COVEY
fluid spraying .... HOUBARA
flycatcher .... KINGBIRD,
 OSCINE, PEWEE, PHOEBE
footless: heraldry
 .... MARTLET
for food .... CAPON
forelimb .... WING
fork-tailed .... PETREL
frigate .... IWA
fruit-eating .... BARBET,
 PARROT, TROGON, TOUCAN,
 OILBIRD
fulmar .... NELLY
game bird .... QUAIL, SNIPE,
 GROUSE, TURNIX, PHEASANT
game-killer .... VERMIN
gluttonous/greedy
 .... CORMORANT
goatsucker .... GUACHARO
goldfinch .... REDCAP
goose .... GANDER
grouse .... GORCOCK,
 BLACKCOCK
guan .... ORTALIS
gull, pert. to .... LARINE
gull, sea .... MEW, TERN,
 KITTIWAKE
gull-like .... SKUA, TERN,
 JAEGER

harsh-voiced .... MACAW
Hawaiian .... IWA, IIWI, MAMO,
 OOAA, ALALA
hawk .... EYAS, KAHU, KITE,
 GOSHAWK, CARACARA
heron .... IBIS, SOCO, EGRET,
 BITTERN
hind toe .... HALLUX
homing instinct
 .... ORIENTATION
honey-eating .... IAO, TUI,
 MOHO, MANUAO
hood-like crest ..... CALOT(TE)
house .... COOP, COTE, NEST,
 NIDE, AVIARY, VOLERY
humming .... AVE, SYLPH,
 COLIBRI, TROCHILUS
hunter .... FOWLER
hunting .... HAWK, FALCON
immortalized by Poe
 .... RAVEN
Indian .... SARUS, ARGALA,
 SHAMA, JACANA, AMADAVIT
insectivorous ..... TODY, TERN,
 VIREO, HARRIER, SWALLOW,
 NIGHTJAR, JACAMAR,
 NUTHATCH, HOOPOE, BEE-
 EATER, HERON, SWIFT,
 HORNBILL, STORK, EGRET,
 ROLLER, WOODPECKER
jackdaw .... COE, DAW, KAE
jay-like .... PIET, MOTMOT
killing of .... AVACIDE
kite .... GLEDE
known for straight flight
 .... CROW
lake .... LOON
lamellirostral .... DUCK, SWAN,
 GOOSE
lapwing .... WEEP, PEWIT,
 PLOVER
laughing .... DACELO, LOON,
 GIGAS, KOOKABURRA
large .... EMU, MOA, KITE,
 GUAN, JABIRU, OSTRICH
largest species .... OSTRICH
Latin for .... AVIS
leaf-walker .... JACANA
leg outgrowth .... SPUR,
 CALCAR
leg strap .... JESS
legendary .... ROC
life .... ORNIS
like in appearance
 .... ORNITHOID
limicoline .... STILT, AVOCET
long-billed ...... IBIS, CREEPER,
 NUTHATCH
long-legged .... IBIS, AGAMI,
 HERON, BUSTARD, CRANE,
 EGRET, SERIEMA, STILT,

long-necked .... SWAN, CRANE, EGRET, HERON, FLAMINGO
loon-like .... GREBE
love-making .... BILL AND COO
lyre .... MENURA
magpie .... PIET
male ..... TOM, COCK, GANDER, ROOSTER, BANTAM, GOBBLER
marsh .... COOT, RAIL, SORA, BITTERN, STILT, GALLINULE
martin .... MARTLET
meadow .... LARK, BOBOLINK
migratory .... PLOVER, BOBOLINK, WOODCOCK, KNOT, SANDPIPER, WHIN, WHEATEATER
mina .... STARLING
monkey-faced .... OWL
morepork .... RURU
mound-building .... LEIPOA, MEGAPOD
mouth opening .... RICTUS
mythical .... ROC, PHOENIX
nail of .... CLAW
national .... EAGLE
nest-collector .... OOLOGIST
nocturnal .... OWL, GUACHARO, GOATSUCKER
noisy .... BLUEJAY
non-flying (see flightless)
non-passerine .... TODY, HOOPOE, HORNBILL, KINGFISHER
note .... PIPE, CHIRP, TWEET
ocean .... FULMAR, PETREL, MALEMUCK, ALBATROSS
of Jove .... EAGLE
of Paradise .... APUS
of peace .... DOVE
of prey .... HAWK, FALCON, ERN(E), EAGLE, BATHAWK, GLEDE, GOSHAWK, BUZZARD, KITE, KESTREL, ACCIPETER, OWL, CONDOR, ELANET, VULTURE, PEREGRINE
of Sinbad .... ROC
on a quarter .... EAGLE
one-year old .... ANNOTINE
orange-colored .... ORIOLE
order of .... RASORES
oscine .... CHAT, CROW, SHRIKE, VIREO, ORIOLE, LARK, BUNTING, TANAGER
ostrich-like ..... EM(E)U, RHEA, RATITE, TINAMOU
owl: Samoan .... LULU
owl variety .... SNOW, BARRED, GREAT-HORNED
parakeet .... BUDGIE
parrot ..... KEA, KAKAM, LORY, KAKAPOS, COCKATOO
parson .... POE, TUI
partridge .... QUAIL, SEESEE, BOBTAIL
partridge-like .... TINAMOU, TINAMIDA
passerine .... PITA, ORIOLE, SPARROW, STARLING, TANAGER
patch on throat .... GORGET
pelican-like .... SOLAN
perching .... LARK, FINCH, OSCINE, SHRIKE, BUNTING
Persian .... BULBUL
pertaining to .... AVIAN, AVINE, ORNITHIC
Peruvian .... GUANAY
petrel .... TITI, FULMAR
pewee .... PEWIT, PHOEBE
plover-like .... LAPWING, KILLDEER
protuberance .... SPUR, CALCAR
quail .... BOBWHITE, PARTRIDGE
queer: colloq. .... LOCO, IDIOT(IC), ECCENTRIC
rail .... COOT, MOHO, SORA, CRAKE, SCOTER, SULTANA, GALLINULE
rail-like .... COURLAN
rain .... PLOVER
razor-billed .... AUK, MURRE
rear young .... FLEDGE
red-backed sandpiper .... PURRE
red-eyed .... VIREO
reed .... BOBOLINK
ring-dove .... CUSHAT
robber .... DAW, SKUA, JA(E)GER
ruffed .... REEVE, GROUSE, PIGEON, PARTRIDGE, SANDPIPER
running swift .... COURSER
sacred .... IBIS
Samoan .... IAO, LULU
sandpiper .... KNOT, REEVE, DUNLIN, GREENSHANK
scaup duck .... BLACKHEAD
screamer .... CHAJA
sea .... ERN(E), GULL, SKUA, TERN, SCAUP, GANNET, MURRE(LET), PETREL, PUFFIN, JAEGER, ALBATROSS, SCOTER, CORMORANT
secretary-bird .... SAGITTARIIDAE
seed-eating .... EMU, CROW, JUNCO, NUTHATCH, FINCH, MACAW, CHICKADEE, PIGEON, SPARROW, GROSBEAK, CANARY, PARROT, OSTRICH, BUNTING, CARDINAL
sheep-killer .... KEA
shore .... RAIL, SORA, SNIPE, STILT, AVOCET, PLOVER, SANDPIPER, WILLET, PRATINCOLE
short-tailed .... BREVE, PLOVER
singing .... OSCINE
skin around eye .... ORBIT
small .... TIT, PIPIT, WREN, TODY, TITMOUSE, BIRDIE, CHICKADEE, FINCH, BLUET, COSTA, VIREO, TOMTIT, SYLPH, VERDIN, PEWEE, COLIBRI, SERIN, MANAKIN, SAPPHO
smallest species .... (BEE) HUMMINGBIRD
snake .... ANHINGA
snipe .... CURLEW, GODWIT, DOWITCHER
snipe-like .... WILLET
song .... LARK, PIPE, OUZEL, ROBIN, LINNET, BLUEBIRD, CANARY, SHAMA, BOBOLINK
sorrel .... OCA
sound .... COO, CAW, TWEET, PEEP, CHIRP, HONK, QUACK, SHRIEK, CHATTER, ROAR, WEEP, CROW, WHOOP, BELLOW, CHIRRUP, SCREECH, TIRALEE, TWITTER
South American .... GUAN, JACU, TURCO, TOUCAN, SYLPH, JACANA, TINAMOU, SERIEMA, WARRIOR, GUACHARO
space on head .... LORE
sparrow .... TOWHEE, BUNTING, PEABODY
starling .... MINA, MYNA, MINAH
stib .... DUNLIN
stitch .... IHI
stupid .... DODO, GOOSE, NODDY
swallow .... MARTLET
swallow-like .... SWIFT, MARTIN, HIRUNDINE
swan .... WHOOPER
swimming .... SWAN, DUCK, GREBE, LOON, PENGUIN, PHALAROPE, AUK, GULL, PELICAN, TERN, PETREL, MOORHEN
symbolic .... DOVE, OWL, EAGLE, STORK
tail feathers .... TRAIN, RECTRIX
tail hump .... UROPYGIUM
talking .... PARROT, MINA, MYNA(H)

thief .... DAW, ROOK, SKUA,
JA(E)GER
three-toed .... STILT, TURNIX
thrush .... THROSTLE
titmouse .... VERDIN, BLUECAP,
CHICKADEE
toe .... HALLUX
top of its head .... PILEUM
towhee .... CHEWINK, SPARROW
trill .... TIRALEE
tropical .... ANI, BARBET,
MACAW, JACANA, TROGON,
JACAMAR, TOUCAN, JABIRU
trumpeter ..... AGAMI, (BLACK)
SWAN
turkey .... TOM, GOBBLER
turkey-like .... CURASSOW
"tuxedo" .... PENGUIN
type of stork .... MARABOU,
MAGUARI
unfledged .... SQUAB
vulture .... URUBU, CONDOR
wading .... COOT, RAIL,
CURLEW, HERON, AVOCET,
EGRET, JACANA, WILLET,
CRANE, IBIS, FLAMINGO, SORA,
STORK, KILLDEER, SNIPE,
STILT, JABIRU, BOATBILL,
UMBRETTE, UMBER,
GALLINULE
wagtail .... PIPIT
warbler .... REDSTART,
TROCHILUS, BLACKPOLL,
CHICKADEE, NIGHTINGALE
water .... PELICAN, HYACINTH
water-carrier .... ALBATROSS
weaver .... TAHA, MUNIA
web-footed .... DUCK, AUK,
COOT, LOON, GOOSE
whiskered .... BULBUL
white-plumed .... EGRET,
SHRIKE
white-tailed .... ERN(E)
wing .... PINION
wing outgrowth .... CALCAR
wing part .... SPUR, ALULA,
CALCAR
wing quills .... FLAG
with changing color
.... PTARMIGAN
with irregular flight .... PEWIT,
LAPWING
with scalelike feathers
.... PENGUIN
woman .... AVIATRIX
woodpigeon .... RINGDOVE
yellow-hammer .... FINCH,
CUCKOO, FLICKER
young .... CHICK, OWLET,
EAGLET, EYAS, CYGNET,
GOSLING, NESTLING,

FLEDGLING
birds .... AVES
breeding place .... HERONRY,
ROOKERY, HATCHERY
care of .... AVICULTURE
eggs, study of .... OOLOGY
flight south .... MIGRATION
follower of ...... BIRDWATCHER
food plant .... FERN, VIOLET,
TREFOIL
habitat of .... FOREST,
WOODLAND
of a feather .... LOOK-ALIKES
of a region .... ORNIS
of singing .... OSCINE
pertaining to .... AVIAN,
AVINE, ORNITHIC
raising of .... AVICULTURE
reservation .... (GAME)
SANCTUARY
study of .... ORNITHOLOGY
bird's-eye view .... SYNOPSIS
biretta .... CAP, BARRET, BERETA,
BERRETA, BERRETTA
birk .... BIRCH
birl .... SPIN, WHIRR, REVOLVE
birling .... LOGROLLING
bee .... ROLEO
object of .... BALANCE
what lumberjacks use for
.... LOGS
birr .... FORCE, ENERGY, ONRUSH,
SPEECH
birth .... ORIGIN, DESCENT,
GENESIS, BEGINNING, BLESSED
EVENT
at no cost? .... BORN FREE
before .... PRENATAL
before full-term
.... PREMATURITY
control ...... FAMILY PLANNING
control advocate .... SANGER
control device .... PILL,
CONDOM, DIAPHRAGM,
CONTRACEPTIVE
defect .... ABNORMALITY
Jesus' .... NATIVITY
of a baby, bottom-first
.... BREECH DELIVERY
of high .... NOBLE, ROYALTY
of one's .... NATAL
of two .... BIPAROUS
pains .... LABOR
rate .... NATALITY
root .... TRILLIUM
birthmark .... MOLE, BLEMISH,
N(A)EVUS, FRECKLE,
STRAWBERRY (MARK)
birthright .... HERITAGE,
PATRIMONY, INHERITANCE
seller .... ESAU

birthstone, January ...... GARNET
February .... AMETHYST
March .... JASPER,
AQUAMARINE, BLOODSTONE
April .... DIAMOND
May .... AGATE, EMERALD
June .... PEARL, MOONSTONE
July .... ONYX, RUBY
August .... SARDONYX,
CARNELIAN
September .... SAPPHIRE
October .... OPAL
November .... TOPAZ
December .... ZIRCON,
TURQUOISE
birthwort .... ASARUM,
CLEMATITE, ARISTOLOCHIA
bis .... DI, TWICE, ENCORE, REPEAT
Biscay .... BASQUE
island .... YEU
biscuit .... BUN, RUSK, SNAP,
COOKY, SCONE, CRACKER,
COOKIE, PANAL, POPOVER,
WAFER, SIMNEL, RATAFEE,
MACAROON, ZWEIBACK
in ceramics .... BISQUE
knotted .... PRETZEL
sweetened .... RUSK
bisect .... FORK, DIVIDE
bisexual .... BIPARTITE, BISEXED
bishop .... EPARCH, PONTIFF,
PRELATE, CHESSMAN,
OVERSEER
in chess .... ALFIN
of Rome .... POPE
vestment .... DALMATIC
weed .... AMMI, GOUT
bishop's assistant .... VERGER,
COAD, COADJUTOR
cap/headdress .... MITER,
HURA, MITRE, MITERWORT
deputy .... VICAR
first year's revenue .... ANNAT
lap cloth .... GREMIAL
letter .... PASTORAL
robe .... CHIMAR, CHIMER(E)
seat ..... SEE, BEMA, CATHEDRA
see .... EPISCOPATE
skullcap .... ZUCCHETTO
staff .... CROOK, CROSIER,
CROZIER
staff bearer .... VERGER
throne .... CATHEDRA
title .... ABBA, PRIMATE
vestment .... ROCHET, COPE,
GREMIAL, SURPLICE
bishopric .... SEE, DIOCESE
bishops collectively
.... EPISCOPACY
bison .... AUROCHS, BOVINE,
BUFFALO

crossed with cattle .... CATALO
pride of .... MANE
bisque .... SOUP, BISCUIT, ICE CREAM, CERAMICS
bissextile .... LEAP YEAR
bistort .... ASTRINGENT
bistro .... BAR, CAFE, CABARET, WINESHOP, NIGHTCLUB, RESTAURANT
habitué .... BARFLY
bit .... ORT, IOTA, MOTE, WHIT, CHECK, CURB, SPECK, COIN, PIECE, MORSEL, MOMENT, SMALL, NIPPED, BLADE, GOBBET
by bit .... GRADUALLY
colloquial .... STITCH
holder .... BRACE
least .... WHIT
of comic business .... GAG
of gossip .... TIDBIT
player .... EXTRA
small .... NIP
tool .... DRILL
bitch ...... BRACH, SHREW, VIXEN, WHELP, TIGRESS, LIONESS
slang .... SCOLD, GRIPE, BOTCH, COMPLAIN, SPOIL, GRUMBLE
Bitch of Buchenwald ...... (ILSE) KOCH
bitchy .... CROSS, CRANKY
bite .... CUT, NIP, GRIP, HOLD, STING, NIBBLE, CORRODE, MOUTHFUL, SNACK, MORSEL, CHEW, PINCH, PARTAKE
bit by bit .... CHEW, GNAW, MASTICATE
colloquial .... SNACK, LUNCH
down hard .... CHAMP
impatiently .... FRET
in dentistry .... OCCLUSION
off .... CROP
one's nail .... FRET, WORRY
sharply/suddenly .... KNAP, SNAP
tentative .... NIBBLE
the bullet .... CONFRONT
the dust .... FALL, LOSE
the hand that feeds one .... BE UNGRATEFUL
with acid .... ETCH
biting ...... KEEN, SHARP, CAUSTIC, CUTTING, STINGING, NIPPY, PUNGENT, MORDACIOUS, ACRID, PIERCING, SARCASTIC
Bitolj .... MONASTIR
bits .... ANA
bitstock .... BRACE
bitt .... DECK, POST

bitter ...... ACERB, ACRID, HARSH, SEVERE, PAINFUL, TART, CUTTING, GRIEVOUS, SORE, PUNGENT, VIRULENT
apple .... COLOCYNTH
bark .... ANGOSTURA
cassava product .... TAPIOCA
combining form .... PICRO
compound .... AMARINE
cynic .... TIMON
drug/herb .... ALOE
end .... LIMIT, FINALE, UNTIL DEATH
feeling .... HATE, RANCOR, SPITE, GRUDGE, ACRIMONY
flavoring agent .... ASARUM
liquid from brine ..... BITTERN
nut .... KOLA
plant substance .... ALUM, ALOIN, LUPULIN
vetch .... ERS
bittern .... BIRD, SOCO
bitterness .... ILL WILL, HATE, REGRET, RANCOR, PUNGENCY, ACERBITY, VILE, RESENTMENT
bitters .... TONIC
bitterweed .... RAGWEED
bitumen .... PITCH, MALTHA, ASPHALT
bivalent .... DIATOMIC
bivalve .... CLAM, MUSSEL, SCALLOP, MOLLUSK, OYSTER, QUAHOG, PIDDOCK
bivouac .... CAMP, ETAPE, BARRACKS, ENCAMP(MENT)
bizarre .... ODD, LURID, QUEER, FANTASTIC, OUTRE, GROTESQUE
Bizet opera .... CARMEN
Bjorn of tennis .... BORG
blab .... GOSSIP, CHATTER, PRATTLE
blabber .... GOSSIP, BABBLE, TATTLE, TATTLER
blabbermouth .... TATTLETALE, GOSSIPMONGER
black .... JET, EBON, SABLE, WICKED, RAVEN, COLLY, JETTY, ATROUS, INKY, AFRICAN (AMERICAN), DARK(NESS)
alder .... SHRUB, WINTERBERRY
alloy .... NIELLO
and-blue .... LIVID, BRUISED
and-tan .... DOG, TERRIER, RAT TERRIER
and-white .... OPPOSITES, PRINT, WRITING, PHOTOGRAPH
art .... MAGIC, SORCERY
bass .... (GAME) FISH
beer .... DANTZIC

bile, having .... MOROSE, MELANCHOLY
bird .... DAW, CROW, MERLE, RAVEN
bread ingredient .... RYE
buck .... SASIN
chimney product .... SOOT
coal .... ATROUS
coffee .... CAFE NOIR
combining form .... ATRO, MELAN(O)
country .... MIDLANDS
cuckoo .... ANI
diamonds .... COAL
eye: colloq. .... SHAME, MOUSE, SHINER, DISHONOR
eyed nymph .... HOURI
eyed pea .... COWPEA
eyed Susan .... KETMIE, RUDBECKIA, (YELLOW) DAISY
feline .... PANTHER
fever .... KALA-AZAR
fin snapper .... SESI
flag .... JOLLY ROGER
garnet .... MELANITE
gold .... OIL
gum .... NYSSA, TUPELO, PEPPERIDGE
hair and eyes ...... BRUNET(TE)
haw .... VIBURNUM, SHEEPBERRY
hole .... DUNGEON
ink item .... ASSET
knot .... FUNGUS
lead .... GRAPHITE
letter .... UNLUCKY, UNFORTUNATE
letter type .... CAXTON
lustrous .... RAVEN
magic ...... VOODOO, SORCERY, WITCHCRAFT
make .... NIGRIFY
mark .... DISREPUTE
mineral ...... JET, COAL, IRIDE
nightshade .... MOREL
pepper .... SEASONING
race .... NEGRO
rhinoceros .... BORELE
rot/rust .... FUNGUS
saltwort .... GLAUX
sheep: colloq. .... BAD ONE, PRODIGAL
silver .... STEPHANITE
snake .... RACER
suit cards .... CLUBS, SPADES
swan .... TRUMPETER
tea .... BOHEA
tern .... DARR
tie ...... BOW, (DINNER) JACKET
very .... JETTY
vomit .... YELLOW FEVER

water .... PYROSIS
widow .... SPIDER
wood .... EBONY
Black Death .... (BUBONIC) PLAGUE
Earth area .... OREL
Forest .... SCHWARZWALD
Friar .... DOMINICAN
Hand .... CAMMORA, MAF(F)IA, BLACKMAILERS
Maria .... (POLICE) WAGON, PADDY WAGON, PATROL WAGON
Monk .... BENEDICTINE
Plague .... BUBONIC
Power leader .... BROWN, NEWTON, CARMICHAEL
Prince .... EDWARD
Rod .... USHER
Sea .... EUXINE
city .... YALTA, ODESSA
empire .... TREBIZOND
fish .... HAUSEN
inlet .... AZOV
of the .... PONTIC
peninsula .... CRIMEA
port .... ANAPA, VARNA, ODESSA
resort .... YALTA
Shirt .... NAZI, FASCIST
blackamoor .... NEGRO
blackball .... OPPOSE, REJECT, BOYCOTT
Blackbeard .... PIRATE, (EDWARD) TEACH, PRIVATEER
blackbeetle .... COCKROACH
blackberry .... BUSH, VINE, BRAMBLE
blackbird .... ANI, CROW, RAVEN, MERL(E), COWBIRD, GRACKLE, JACKDAW, THRUSH, STARLING
European .... OUSEL, OUZEL
blackboard .... SLATE
blackboy ...... PLANT, GRASS TREE
blackcap .... BIRD, CHICKADEE, RASPBERRY
blackcock .... (MALE) GROUSE
blackdamp .... GAS
blacken .... TAR, INK, SOIL, NIGRIFY, SMEAR, DARKEN, VILIFY, EXECRATE, SLANDER, JAPAN, TARNISH, DENIGRATE
blackened with soot .... COLLIED
blackface .... BOLD, MINSTREL
Blackfeet .... INDIAN
blackfellow: Austral. ...... MAORI
blackfin snapper .... SESI
blackfish .... TAUTOG, WHALE, SWART
blackguard .... CAD, VULGAR, ABUSIVE, VILLAIN,

SCOUNDREL
Blackhawk .... SAC
blackhead .... DUCK, PLUG, COMEDO, PIMPLE
blackheart .... CHERRY
blackhearted .... EVIL-MINDED, CRUEL, WICKED, MALEVOLENT
blacking .... SHOE POLISH
blackjack .... OAK, MUG, COERCE, BLUDGEON, SHANGHAI, CARD GAME, TWENTY-ONE
blackleg .... FUNGUS, RABIES, ANTHRAX
blacklist .... CENSURE, CONDEMN, DENOUNCE, OSTRACIZE
blackly ...... ANGRILY, GLOOMILY, MENACINGLY
blackmail .... BADGER, COERCE, TRIBUTE, CHANTAGE, EXTORTION
blackmailer .... CAMMORA, MAF(F)IA, VAMPIRE
blackmarket .... BOOTLEG, UNDER-THE-TABLE
blackness .... NEGRITUDE
blackout .... ECLIPSE, BROWNOUT, PASS OUT
kind of .... FAINT(ING), SWOON, AMNESIA, SYNCOPE
news .... HUSH-UP, CENSORSHIP
blackpoll .... WARBLER, REDSTART, CHICKADEE
blacksmith .... LOHAR, FARRIER
block .... ANVIL
chisel .... HARDY
furnace .... FORGE
shop .... SMITHY, STITHY
tool .... FULLER
blacksnake ...... RACER, COLUBER
blacktail .... MULEDEER
fish .... DASSY
blackthorn ...... HAW, CANE, SLOE
blacktop .... TAR, COVER, ASPHALT, PAVEMENT
blackwater fever .... MALARIA
blackwood .... BITI, EBONY
blackwort .... COMFREY
bladder ...... BAG, AIR-SAC, URINE RESERVOIR, VESICA
combining form .... VISICO
container .... STOMACH
deposit .... CALCULUS
infection .... CYSTITIS
problem .... INCONTINENCE
surgery to remove the .... CYSTECTOMY
bladdernose ...... (HOODED) SEAL
bladderworm .... HYDATID, CYSTICERCUS
blade .... OAR, LEAF, VANE, KNIFE, RUNNER, SWORD(SMAN)

grass .... SPEAR
in botany/leaf .... LAMINA
sword ..... TOLEDO, DAMASCUS
bladebone .... SCAPULA
blah: sl. .... ROT, DULL, NONSENSE
blain .... SORE, BULLA, BLISTER, PUSTULE
Blakely, _____ ...... RONEE, SUSAN
Blake's symbol .... ZOA
blame .... RAP, FAULT, ACCUSE, CENSURE, CONDEMN, REPROACH, CRITICIZE, ACCUSATION
blamed: colloq. .... DAMNED
blameless .... PURE, CLEAN, HONEST, INNOCENT, SPOTLESS
Blanc, _____ .... MEL
blanch .... PALE, SCALD, BLEACH, WHITEN, ETIOLATE
blancmange .... FLUMMERY
bland .... MILD, SOFT, GENTLE, SMOOTH, AFFABLE, SUAVE, SOOTHING, TEMPERATE
blandation .... BLARNEY, FLATTERY
blandish .... COAX, CAJOLE, FLATTER
blank .... CLEAR, EMPTY, UNWRITTEN, WHITE, BARREN, UNFILLED, (DE)VOID, MARKLESS
check of a sort .... CARTE BLANCHE
draw a .... FAIL, LOSE, ZERO, ZILCH
in baseball .... SHUTOUT
in printing .... QUAD
interval between words .... SPACE
look .... POKER FACE
look, describing one .... VACANT
sheet in book .... FLYLEAF
space .... GAP, VOID, HIATUS
blanket .... COVER, AFGHAN, SHEET, COVERLET, OVERSPREAD
approval .... CARTE BLANCHE
authority .... FULL POWER(S)
horse .... MANTA
Mexican .... SERAPE
worn as cloak .... PONCHO
blankety-blank .... DAMNED, BLASTED, CONFOUNDED, EXPLETIVE
blankminded .... IGNORANT, OBLIVIOUS, UNKNOWING
blare .... BLAZON
trumpet's .... FANFARE, TANTARA
blarney ...... COAX, FLAM, STONE,

SOFT TALK, WHEEDLE, FLATTERY

blasé ...... BORED, SATED, WEARY, SATIATED

blaspheme .... ABUSE, CURSE, REVILE, PROFANE

blasphemous .... FOUL, VILE, ABUSIVE, CURSING, IMPIOUS, IRREVERENT

blasphemy .... IMPIETY, PROFANITY, SACRILEGE

Blass or Beene .... DESIGNER

blast .... GUST, SEAR, ATTACK, BLIGHT, BLOW-UP, ERUPTION, EXPLODE, EXPLOSION

furnace .... FORGE, SMELTER

furnace part .... MANTLE, BOSH, TROMPE, TUYERE

of horn .... TOOT

off step .... COUNT DOWN

sluice .... SOW

blat .... BLAB, BLEAT, BLURT

blatant .... GAUDY, NOISY, SHOWY, COARSE, FLASHY, VULGAR, BOISTEROUS, VOCIFEROUS, LOUDMOUTHED

blather .... NONSENSE, FOOLISH TALK

blaubok .... ETAAC, ANTELOPE

blaze .... FIRE, FLAME, FLARE, FLASH, SHINE, OUTBURST

away ...... SHOOT, (RAPID) FIRE

on animal's face .... SPOT

star .... NOVA

blazer .... JACKET

blazes, go to .... HELL, BE DAMNED

blazing .... AFIRE

star .... COMET, TORCH LILY

blazon .... DISPLAY, EMBLEM, BLARE, PROCLAIM, COAT OF ARMS

bleach .... BLANCH, CHLORE, PURIFY, WHITEN, LIGHTEN, ETIOLATE, DECOLORIZE

by sunning .... INSOLATE

bleaching powder ...... CHLORIDE

vat .... KEIR, KIER

bleak ...... DIM, RAW, BARE, COLD, PALE, DREAR, STARK, DISMAL, DREARY, GLOOMY, DESOLATE, TREELESS

blear .... DIM, BLUR, MISTY, BLURRED, INDISTINCT

bleary-eyed ...... TEARY, RHEUMY, DULL-WITTED

bleat .... BAA, CRY, MAA, BLAT, WHINE

bleater .... CALF, GOAT, LAMB, SHEEP, WHINER, CRYBABY

bleb .... BULLA, BUBBLE, BLISTER,

VESICLE

bleed .... LEAK, OOZE, SUCK, FLOW, EXTORT, SUFFER, EMIT BLOOD

certain way .... LEECH

white .... IMPOVERISH

bleeder ...... LEECH, HEMOPHILIAC

bleeding .... HEMORRHAGE

gums .... GINGIVITIS

heart .... DICENTRA

stoppage of .... HEMOSTASIS

stopper .... HEMOSTAT

uncontrollable .... HEMOPHILIA

within the brain .... CEREBRAL HEMORRHAGE

bleffert .... SQUALL

blemish .... MAR, BLOT, DENT, DEFACE, MARK, FLAW, FAULT, SPECK, SMIRCH, STAIN, DEFECT, DEFORMITY, MACULATE, TARNISH

cloth .... AMPER

on an olive .... SCAB

on reputation .... DISGRACE, DISHONOR

skin .... MOLE, SCAR, NEVUS, PIMPLE, FRECKLE, NAEVUS, BIRTHMARK

blemished ...... FAULTY, MARRED, KELOIDAL

blench .... FADE, PALE, AVOID, EVADE, SHRINK, CRINGE, SHUN, FLINCH, WHITEN, SIDESTEP

blend .... MERGE, FUSE, MELD, MINGLE, MIX(TURE), HARMONIZE

colors .... FONDU

into .... MERGE, COMBINE, CONVERT

blende .... ORE, SPHALERITE

blenny .... GUNNEL, SHANNY

blended .... MERGED, MIXED, ATTUNED, COMBINED

blesbok .... NUNNI, ANTELOPE

bless .... ENDOW, FAVOR, HALLOW, BEATIFY, GLORIFY, PRAISE, SANCTIFY, CONSECRATE

against evil .... SAIN

blessed .... DIVINE, SACRED, JOYFUL, BLISSFUL, HALLOWED, HOLY, BEATIFIED, CONSECRATED

event .... BIRTH

Blessed Sacrament .... EUCHARIST

blessing .... BOON, GIFT, SAIN, GRACE, BENISON, APPROVAL, INVOCATION, BEATITUDE, BENEDICTION

at meal .... GRACE

blet .... FRUIT DECAY

blight .... NIP, FIRE, RUIN, RUST, SMUT, BLAST, DECAY, DISEASE, MILDEW, DESTROY, SEAR, TAINT, ADVERSITY, IMPAIR, FRUSTRATE

blighted .... RUINED, RUSTY, SEEDY, DAMAGED, DECREPIT, ROTTEN, SPOILED, WRECKED

blighter .... VAGABOND

blimp: colloq. .... AIRSHIP

blind .... SEEL, COVER, DARK(EN), SHADE, EYELESS, SCREEN, RECKLESS, SHUTTER, DAZZLE, OBSCURE, SIGHTLESS

a hawk .... SEEL

aid for the ...... CANE, SEEING-EYE DOG

alley .... DEADEND, IMPASSE, CUL-DE-SAC

as a _____ .... BAT

bargain .... PIG-IN-A-POKE

daters .... STRANGERS

dolphin .... SUSU

faith ...... DOTAGE, CREDULITY, GULLIBILITY

fear .... PANIC

flower girl .... NIDIA

god .... HOTH, HODER

gut .... CECUM

impulse .... ATE, NOTION

love, usually ..... INFATUATION

pig/tiger: sl. .... SPEAKEASY

shot .... HIT-OR-MISS

slang .... DRUNK

spot .... SCOTOMA

spot: colloq. .... WEAKNESS, IGNORANCE

staggers .... GID, MEGRIM, VERTIGO

system of printing for the .... BRAILLE

temporarily .... DAZZLE, ECLIPSE

to .... ASLEEP, UNAWARE, OBLIVIOUS

window .... VENETIAN

blindage .... CAMOUFLAGE, DISGUISE, SMOKE-SCREEN

blinder .... SEEL, WINKER, BLINKER

blinders .... GOGGLES, EYE-PATCH

blindfold .... SEEL, COVER, OBSCURE, MISLEAD, HOODWINK

blindly .... GROPINGLY

blindness .... CECITY, ABLEPSIA, TYPHLITIS, TYPHLOSIS

color .... MONOCHROMATISM

common cause of .... CATARACT, GLAUCOMA

day .... HEMERALOPIA
night .... NYCTALOPIA
river .... ONCHOCERCIASIS
snow .... NIPHABLEPSIA
blinds .... PERSIENNES
blindstory .... GALLERY
blindworm .... ORVET
blink .... BAT, WINK, IGNORE,
FLUTTER, NICTATE, TWINKLE
blinker .... EYE, BLINDER
blintz .... PASTRY, PANCAKE,
FLAPJACK
blip .... SIGNAL
bliss .... JOY, GAIETY, GLORY,
ECSTASY, HARMONY,
DELIGHT, RAPTURE, FELICITY
place of .... EDEN, HEAVEN,
UTOPIA, ELYSIUM, PARADISE
blissful .... HAPPY, JOYOUS,
ELYSIAN, SUBLIME
blister .... BLEB, BLAIN, BULLA,
VESICLE, VESICATE
beetle .... SPANISH FLY
causing .... VESICANT
cloth .... YAW
containing pus .... PUSTULE
on neck .... MALANDERS
blistered .... PUFFED, BULLATE
blistering agent .... VESICANT,
SPISPASTIC
reprimand .... TONGUE-
LASHING
blithe .... GAY, AIRY, GLAD,
JOVIAL, MERRY, CAREFREE,
CHEERFUL, LIGHTHEARTED
spirit, Shakespearean
.... ARIEL
blithering .... JABBERING
blitz .... ATTACK, CHARGE,
DESTROY, OVERWHELM
blitzkrieg .... RAID, WARFARE
of a sort .... COUP, COUP
D'ETAT, COUP DE MAIN
blizzard .... SNOWSTORM,
WINDSTORM
in Alaska .... PURGA
blk. .... BULK, BLACK, BLOCK
bloat .... PUFF, SWELL, TUMEFY,
AMPLIFY, INFLATE, DRUNKARD
bloated .... CURED, OBESE,
TURGID, BULGING, FLUSHED,
POMPOUS, SWOLLEN,
CORPULENT
bloater .... FISH, HERRING,
MACKEREL
blob .... BEAD, SPLASH,
DROP(LET), SPLOTCH
bloc .... BAND, BODY, RING,
GROUP, CLIQUE, TEAM,
UNION, ALLIANCE
block .... DAM, MOLD, SPRAG,

HAMPER, HINDER, IMPEDE,
OCCLUDE, OBSTACLE,
STONEWALL
butcher's .... CHOPPING BOARD
casks' .... QUOIN
for nails on wall .... NOG
go to the .... AUCTION, UP FOR
SALE
hawser .... BITT
house .... FORT
ice .... SERAC
letter .... HANDPRINTING
mechanical .... PULLEY
metal .... NUT
of metal type .... QUAD
of stamps .... PANE
of wood .... NOG, CHUMP,
DEADEYE
set against wheel .... TRIG
small .... TESSERA
up .... DAM, CLOG, CHOKE,
STEM, BLOCKADE, OBSTRUCT
wedge-shaped .... QUOIN
blockade .... ISOLATE, BOTTLE-UP,
SHUTDOWN, STOPPAGE,
ROADBLOCK
runner of a sort
.... SMUGGLER,
CONTRABANDIST
blockhead ...... ASS, CLOD, FOOL,
IDIOT, OAF, DOLT, MUTT,
DUNCE, PINHEAD, BUNGLER,
STOCK, NITWIT, NUM(B)SKULL
blocky .... PUDGY, CHUNKY,
STOCKY
bloke: sl. ...... OAF, CHAP, JOKER,
BUGGER, FELLOW, JASPER
vulgar .... MUCKER
blond(e) .... LACE, WOMAN,
TOWHEAD, FAIR-HAIRED,
FLAXEN-HAIRED
kind of .... ASH, PEROXIDE,
PLATINUM, HONEY,
STRAWBERRY
Blonde Bombshell of movies
.... HARLOW
blood .... GORE, LIFE, SERUM,
KINDRED, KINSHIP, LINEAGE,
PEDIGREE, LIFE-FLUID
accumulation in body
.... CONGESTION
and thunder .... THEATRICS,
CLOAK-AND-DAGGER
bad .... ANGER, HATRED,
ANIMOSITY, ANTAGONISM
brother .... BUDDY, FRIEND,
RELATIVE
cancer/disease .... LEUKEMIA
cell .... MONOCYTE
clot ...... GORE, CRUOR, GRUME

clot formation
.... THROMBOSIS
clotting remedy .... HISTONE
color .... RED, SANGUINE
colored .... HEMATIC
coloring matter .... CRUOR,
HEMOGLOBIN
combining form .... HEMA,
HEM(O), HAEMO, HEMAT,
SANGUI, HEMATO, HAEMATO
condition .... LITHEMIA
congestion .... HYPEREMIA
corpuscle structure
.... STROMA
coughing up/spitting
.... HEMOPTYSIS
covered/filled with ...... GORY,
HEMATOSE
emulsion .... CHYLE
escaping from its vessel
.... HEMORRHAGE
excess of .... PLETHORA
feud .... VENDETTA
flow, stoppage of .... STASIS
flowing from wound
.... GORE, CRUOR
fluid part of .... PLASMA
formation .... HEMATOSIS
having to do with
.... H(A)EMIC, H(A)EMAL
in the urine .... HEMATURIA
iron deficiency .... ANEMIA
is thicker than _____
.... WATER
kin .... GENS, RELATIVE
like .... HEMOID, HEMATOID
money .... CRO, WERGELD,
HUSH-MONEY
movement .... CIRCULATION
of gods .... ICHOR
of the .... HEMIC,
SANGUINEOUS
oxygen carrier
.... HEMOGLOBIN
particles in .... CORPUSCLES
pertaining to .... HEMATIC
poisoning .... SEPSIS,
TOXEMIA, COPR(A)EMIA,
PY(A)EMIA, SAPR(A)EMIA,
SEPTICEMIA
pressure drug ..... ADRENALIN,
HISTAMINE, EPINEPHRINE
pressure hormone .... ACTH,
RENIN
pressure instrument
.... (SPHYGMO) MANOMETER
pudding .... SAUSAGE
red .... CRIMSON, SANGUINE
red cell .... ERYTHROCYTE
red corpuscle, abnormally
large .... MACROCYTE

red corpuscle, abnormally
small .... MICROCYTE
relation ...... KIN, SIB, FAMILY,
RELATIVE
solvent .... LYSIN(E)
sport .... FOX-HUNTING,
COCKFIGHTING
stream foreign matter
.... CLOT, (AIR) BUBBLE,
EMBOLUS
study of .... HEMATOLOGY
substance in .... OPSONIN
sucking insect .... FLEA,
TABANID, LOUSE, BEDBUG,
GADFLY, HORSEFLY,
CONENOSE, MOSQUITO
sucking monster .... LAMIA
thirsty one ...... LEECH, LOMIA,
VAMPIRE
transferred to another person
.... TRANSFUSION
vessel .... VEIN, AORTA,
ARTERY, CAPILLARY
vessel, dilated .... VARIX
vessel disorder .... SCURVY
vessel obstruction
.... EMBOLISM
vessels network .... RETE
vomiting .... HEMATEMESIS
watery part of .... SERA,
SERUM
white cell .... LEUKOCYTE
with reduced corpuscles
.... AN(A)EMIA
bloodbath ...... PURGE, CARNAGE,
KILLING, MASSACRE
bloodcurdling .... DREADFUL,
TERRIBLE, FRIGHTFUL,
TERRIFYING, HORRIFYING
blooded .... PUREBRED,
PEDIGREED, THOROUGHBRED
bloodhound .... SLEUTH,
MANHUNTER, HUNTING DOG
bloodied .... GORY
bloodily ...... CRUELLY, SAVAGELY
bloodless ...... COLD, PALE, WEAK,
AN(A)EMIC
bloodletting .... BLEEDING,
LEECHING, BLOODSHED
art of .... PHLEBOTOMY,
VENESECTION
bloodline .... PEDIGREE, DESCENT,
LINEAGE, ANCESTRY
bloodroot .... POPPY, PUCCOON,
SANGUINARIA
bloodshed .... SLAUGHTER,
CARNAGE, KILLING, VIOLENCE
much .... GORY
bloodshot .... RED
bloodstone .... QUARTZ,
HEMATITE, BIRTHSTONE,

HELIOTROPE
bloodsucker .... FLEA, MITE, TICK,
DEERFLY, VAMPIRE,
EXTORTER, LEECH, PARASITE,
EXTORTIONIST
bloodthirsty .... CRUEL, WARLIKE,
PITILESS, HOMICIDAL,
MURDEROUS, SANGUINARY
bloody .... RED, GORY, BLEEDING,
CRIMSON
bloom .... BLOW, PRIME, RIPEN,
FLOWER, BLOSSOM, FLOURISH
life's .... HEYDAY
bloomer .... ERROR, BLUNDER,
MISTAKE, TROUSERS
bloomery .... FORGE, HEARTH,
FURNACE
blooming ...... FLORID, THRIVING,
BLOSSOMING, FLOWERING,
FLOURISHING
colloquial .... UTTER,
CONFOUNDED
too early .... RATH(E)
blooper .... BONER, HOWLER, BOO-
BOO, SCREW-UP
blossom .... BUD, BLOOM,
FLOWER, MELLOW, SPROUT,
FLOREATE, FLOURISH
blot .... DAB, MAR, SPOT, STAIN,
SULLY, SMUDGE, SMEAR,
EXPUNGE, DISGRACE
in printing .... MACKLE
out .... ERASE, CANCEL,
DELETE, OBSCURE, DESTROY,
WIPE OFF
blotch ...... MARK, SMEAR, STAIN,
MACULA, MOTTLE
blotchy .... SPOTTED
blotter .... RECORD, SPONGE,
ABSORBENT
usual keeper of .... POLICE
blotto: sl. .... SOT, DRUNK,
STONED, UNCONSCIOUS
blouse .... MIDDY, SHIRT, BODICE,
SMOCK, WAIST, SHIRTWAIST
front .... JABOT
Korean silk .... CHIMA
under pinafore .... GUIMPE
with tight waist .... BASQUE
blow .... BRAG, BUFF, HUFF, LASH,
SWAT, THUD, BLAST, PUFF,
BURST, SHOCK, STORM, GALE,
WALLOP, MISFORTUNE
about ...... SPREAD, CIRCULATE
colloquial .... FETE, TREAT,
SPEND
down .... TOPPLE
dull-sounding .... DUNT
for blow .... TIT FOR TAT,
RETALIATION
gently .... WAFT

horn .... TOOT
horn: colloq. ..... BRAG, BOAST
hot and cold .... WAVER,
HESITATE, FLUCTUATE,
VACILLATE
in: colloq. .... ARRIVE
off .... RANT, TALK, ERUPT,
EXPLODE
off chaff .... WINNOW
off steam .... WANTON,
CAROUSE, DEBAUCH
on the head .... NOB, CONK
on the knuckles .... RAP
one's mind: sl. .... FREAK OUT
one's nose: archaic .... SNET
one's top off: colloq.
.... RAGE, RAVE, EXPLODE
out .... SPEW, ERUPT, EXPEL
over .... COOL, PASS, DISSIPATE
resounding .... WHACK
sharp and quick .... CLIP
slang .... FLEE, LEAVE, SCRAM,
SQUANDER
stormily .... BLUSTER
the whistle .... BETRAY,
SNITCH, SQUEAL, DISCLOSE
unexpected .... BOLT,
SNEAKPUNCH
up .... ERUPT, ENLARGE,
EXPLODE, INFLATE
whistle .... TOOT, BLAST, SIREN
with club .... DRUB, CUDGEL
with fist .... POKE, PASTE
blower .... FAN, BELLOWS, WHALE,
BRAGGART, VENTILATOR
blowgun ...... SPRAYER, SUMPITAN
missile .... DART, PELLET
blowhole .... FLUE, NOSTRIL,
BREATHER
of whale .... SPIRACLE
blowing mammal .... WHALE
blown .... RANCID, BLASTED,
EXPOSED, RAVAGED,
WINDSWEPT
blowoff: sl. .... BOASTER
blowout .... FEAST, BANQUET,
TREAT, PARTY, CELEBRATION
one result of a ...... FLAT TIRE
blowpipe .... BLOWGUN
blowup: colloq. .... BLOAT,
OUTBURST, EXPLOSION
blowy .... GUSTY, WINDY,
BLUSTERY
blowzy .... FROWZY, SLOVENLY
woman .... SLUT, SLATTERN
blubber ...... CRY, WEEP, (WHALE)
FAT
piece of .... LIPPER
strip .... FLENSE
blucher .... SHOE, (HALF)BOOT
bludgeon ...... BAT, CLUB, BULLY,

COERCE, CUDGEL
blue .... SAD, ANIL, AZURE, DELFT,
LIVID, PERSE, SMALT,
COBALT, GLOOMY, CELESTE,
DEJECTED, DEPRESSED
back .... TROUT
bird .... JAY
blood .... NOBLE, ROYALTY,
NOBILITY, ARISTOCRAT
book .... DIRECTORY, SOCIAL
REGISTER
chip .... STOCK
chips: colloq. .... TOPS,
VALUABLE, EXCELLENT
collar worker .... LABORER,
UNSKILLED
combining form .... CYAN
days .... MONDAYS
deathly ...... WAN, PALE, EERIE
deep .... ULTRAMARINE
devil: sl. .... DOWNER
devils .... DUMPS, DELIRIUM
dyestuff .... ANIL, WOAD,
INDIGO
fin .... TUNA, HERRING
flag .... IRIS, FLOWER
flower .... LARKSPUR
fox .... FUR
gas .... OZONE
grass .... POA
grayish ..... BICE, TEAL, PERSE,
SLATE, AZURINE
gum .... TREE, EUCALYPTUS
in the face .... HAGGARD,
HYSTERICAL
jeans .... LEVIS, DENIMS,
DUNGAREES
language .... PROFANITY
mineral .... IOLITE
movie .... PORNOGRAPHY
or green .... EMAIL
out of the .... SURPRISE,
UNEXPECTED, UNFORESEEN
peacock .... PAON
pencil ...... CUT, EDIT, DELETE,
REVISE, CORRECT
penciled .... DELED, DELETED
peter .... SIGNAL FLAG
pigment .... BICE, SMALT
pill .... LAXATIVE
pointer shark .... MAKO
racer .... SNAKE
ribbon .... BADGE, AWARD,
FIRST (PRIZE), DECORATION
river, so called .... DANUBE
shade .... ALICE, AZURE
star .... VEGA
stem ..... GRASS, ANDROPOGON
the .... SEA, SKY, HEAVEN
wing teal .... GARGANEY
Blue Eagle of New Deal .... NRA

Grotto home .... CAPRI
Nile country .... ETHIOPIA
Bluebeard, latest .... LANDRU
wife of .... FATIMA
bluebell ...... COWSLIP, HAREBELL,
HYACINTH
bluebonnet .... CAP, LUPINE,
SCOTS(MAN)
bluebottle .... FLY, BLOWFLY,
HYACINTH, CORNFLOWER
bluecap .... TITMOUSE
bluecoat .... SOLDIER, POLICEMAN
bluegill .... SUNFISH
Bluegrass State .... KENTUCKY
bluejack .... VITRIOL
bluejacket .... MARINE, SAILOR,
SOLDIER, ENLISTED MAN
slang .... GOB, SWABBER
bluenose: colloq. .... PURITAN,
NOVA SCOTIAN
bluepoint .... OYSTER
blueprint .... MAP, SKETCH,
DIAGRAM, OUTLINE,
CYANOTYPE
blues .... MEGRIM, DOLDRUMS,
DUMPS, (FOLK)SONG,
MULLIGRUBS
bluestocking .... PEDANTIC,
SCHOLASTIC
bluestone .... VITRIOL
bluet .... PLANT, INNOCENCE
blueweed .... BUGLOSS
bluff ...... FOOL, SCARE, BLUSTER,
MISLEAD, BRUSQUE,
BRAVADO, BLUNT,
BAMBOOZLE, FOURFLUSH(ER)
in poker ...... RAISE, COUNTER-
RAISE
rounded .... MORRO
bluffer .... LIAR, IMPOSTOR,
FOURFLUSHER
bluing material .... INDIGO
bluish gray ...... PEARL, MERL(E),
BICE, SLATE, CESIUM, CAESIUS
green ..... AQUA, AQUAMARINE
red .... MALLOW
white metallic element
.... ZINC
blunder .... SLIP, ERR(OR), GAFFE,
BUNGLE, MISTAKE, STUMBLE,
FLOUNDER
in social etiquette .... FAUX
PAS, SOLECISM
stupid: sl. .... BONER
blunderbore .... OGRE
blunderbuss .... GUN
blunt .... CURT, DULL, BLUFF,
GRUFF, INERT, OBTUND,
TERSE, OBTUSE, BRUSQUE,
DOWNRIGHT, OUTSPOKEN
arrow .... BUTTSHAFT

end .... CHUMP
end of hammer .... POLL
headed bullet .... DUMDUM
refusal .... REBUFF
blur .... DIM, HAZE, BLOT, CLOUD,
STAIN, MACKLE, OBSCURE,
MACULATE
on film/photo .... FOG
blurb .... WRITE-UP, PUBLICITY,
ANNOUNCEMENT,
AD(VERTISEMENT)
blurt .... BLABBER, DIVULGE
blush .... COLOR, FLUSH, MANTLE,
REDDEN
at first .... OFFHAND, INITIALLY
cause of .... ANGER, SHAME,
EXCITEMENT, GUILT,
DISCOMFITURE,
EMBARRASSMENT
blushing .... GLOWING, COLORING,
REDDENING
bluster ...... RANT, BULLY, BLOW,
STORM, BRAVADO, RAGE,
THREATEN
blustering .... WINDY, NOISY,
SWASH, VIOLENT
blustery .... GUSTY, WINDY
blvd. .... BOULEVARD
bo: sl. .... HOBO, TRAMP,
VAGRANT
tree .... PIPAL
boa .... SCARF, SNAKE, PYTHON,
ANACONDA, CONSTRICTOR
ringed .... ABOMA
boar .... HOG, PIG, SUS, SWINE,
BARROW
flesh, picked .... BRAWN
for example .... TUSKER
tooth .... TUSK
board ...... FOOD, PLANT, GET ON,
TABLE, EMBARK, CLOSE UP,
COUNCIL, TRIBUNAL,
PLANCH(E), FACILITIES
and lodging .... KEEP
artist's .... PALETTE
for holding mortar ...... HAWK
from sugarcane residue
.... CELOTEX
game .... CHESS, DARTS,
CHECKERS, MONOPOLY,
BACKGAMMON, PA(R)CHISI
member ..... REGENT, TRUSTEE,
DIRECTOR
on bus .... EMBUS
on plane .... EMPLANE,
ENPLANE
on train .... ENTRAIN
Board, the Big: abbr. ...... NYSE
boarding house .... INN, DORM,
LODGING, PENSION,
DORMITORY

house lodger .... GUEST, EATER, ROOMER
boards, the ...... STAGE, THEATER
boardwalk .... TRAIL, PATHWAY
boarish .... SWINISH
boast .... BRAG, CROW, CLAIM, ENJOY, VAUNT, FLAUNT, ROISTER, GASCONADE
empty .... BLUFF
of .... GLOAT, MAGNIFY
boaster .... GASCON, BLOWOFF, BRAGGART, BRAGGADOCIO
of one's patriotism ...... JINGO
slang .... WINDBAG, LOUDMOUTH
boastful .... VAIN, PROUD, ARROGANT, THRASONICAL
air .... BRAVADO, SWAGGER
talk .... GAS, BRAG, HOT AIR, GASCONADE, FANFARONADE
walk .... STRUT, SWAGGER
boasting .... CROWING, BRAGGADOCIO, RODOMONTADE
boat .... GIG, TUB, RAFT, SHIP, FERRY, VESSEL, STEAMER, FREIGHTER, (WATER)CRAFT
African .... DHOW
American river .... CANOE
ancient .... BIREME, GALLEY, CORACLE, GALLEON, TRIREME
awkward .... ARK, DROGHER
basin .... MARINA
Bolivian .... BALSA
Canadian .... BATEAU
canoe-like .... PIROGUE
captain .... SKIPPER
captain of story .... AHAB, NEMO, BLIGH
Ceylon/E. Indies .... DONI, DHONI, DINGEY
Chinese .... JUNK, SAMPAN
clumsy .... ARK, TUB, HULK, HOOKER, DROGHER
dispatch .... AVISO, OOLAK
Dutch Indies .... PRAAM, HOOKER
Egyptian .... BARIS, SANDAL
English .... COBLE
Eskimo .... KYAK, KAYAK, UMIAK, OOMIAK, BIDARKEE, BIDARKA
ferry .... BAC
fishing .... DORY, COBLE, SMACK, DOGGER, CORACLE, TRAWLER
flat-bottomed .... BATEAU, DORY, KEEL, PUNT, BARGE, SCOW, SLOOP, PONTOON
for gathering shellfish .... DREDGER

freight .... SCOW, BARGE, TRAMP, WHERRY, LIGHTER
French .... CARAVELLE
front .... BOW, FORE, PROW
helm .... TILLER
Indian .... DHOW, MASOOLA
Indian river .... ALMADIA
Italian .... GONDOLA
landing .... LST
Levantine .... BUM, SAIC, XEBEC, KETCH
mail .... PACKET
Malayan .... PAHI, PRAH, PRAO, PRAU, PROA, TOUP
marker .... BUOY
Mediterranean .... SET(T)EE
merchant .... ARGOSY
narrow/light .... CANOE
Netherlands .... BILANDER
Nile river .... SANDAL
North Sea .... DOGGER
old .... HULK, HOOKER
on vessel ...... JOLLY, PINNACE
on warship .... DINGHY, LAUNCH
Philippine ...... BATEL, BANCA, CASCO
pole-propelled .... PUNT, CASCO, GONDOLA
propeller ..... OAR, POLE, SAIL, SCULL, PADDLE
race .... REGATTA
racing .... SCULL, SHELL, YACHT
raft/two-hulled .... CATAMARAN
rear end of .... AFT, STERN
river .... BARGE, CANOE, FERRY, PACKET, SAMPAN, WHERRY
row .... COBLE, SHELL, DINGHY, SKIFF, WHERRY
rudder .... WHEEL, TILLER
sail .... SKIFF, SMACK
scout .... VEDETTE, VIDETTE
shallow, small .... COCKLE
shaped .... SCAPHOID, NAVICULAR
shaped ornament .... NEF
ship's .... YAWL, PINNACE
sink deliberately ...... SCUTTLE
slow .... ARK, TRAMP, BUCKET, DROGHER
small .... COG, DORY, SKIFF, COCKLE, DINGHY, JIGGER, SHALLOP
steering part .... WHEEL, RUDDER, TILLER
tender .... HOY
three-oared .... RANDAN
tiller .... WHEEL, RUDDER

timber .... KEEL
towing .... TUG
two-masted .... DOGGER, PIRAGUA, PIROGUE
boating .... ROWING, SAILING, CRUISING
boatman .... OARSMAN, PADDLER, POLER, VOYAGEUR, GONDOLIER
on Styx .... CHARON
boats, small fleet of .... FLOTILLA
boatswain .... BOSUN
whistle .... PIPE
Boaz' son .... OBED
wife .... RUTH
bob ...... RAP, DOCK, SLED, FLOAT, CURTSY, HAIRCUT, PENDANT, REFRAIN, SHORTEN
bait .... DIB
British: sl. .... SHILLING
bobbery .... ROW, HUBBUB
bobbin .... PIN, PIRN, REEL, SPOOL
lace .... CLUNY
of weaver's shuttle .... PIRN
bobbin's holder .... CREEL, SPINDLE
bobby .... POLICEMAN
soxer: colloq. .... TEENAGER
station of a .... POINT
bobcat .... LYNX, WILDCAT
bobolink .... SORA, ORTALAN, RICEBIRD, SONGBIRD
bobsled .... TOBOGGAN
bobwhite .... COLIN, QUAIL, PARTRIDGE
bocaccio .... COD, ROCKFISH
bocca .... BERRY
Boccaccio's work .... DECAMERON
Boche ...... HUN, JERRY, GERMAN, SQUAREHEAD
bock .... BEER
bode .... OMEN, AUGUR, PORTEND, PRESAGE
bodega: Sp. .... CELLAR, WAREHOUSE
bodice .... VEST, CHOLL, WAIST, BASQUE, CORSAGE
front piece .... JABOT
posy .... CORSAGE
bodily .... SOMATIC, ENTIRE, WHOLLY, PHYSICAL
bodkin .... DAGGER, NEEDLE, HAIRPIN, STILETTO, EYELETEER
body ...... FIGURE, PERSON, SOMA, GROUP, ANATOMY, ASSEMBLAGE
animal/as a whole .... SOMA
appetite .... LUST

beautiful, adjective for
.... SEXY, SEDUCTIVE
build .... PHYSIQUE
coldness .... CHILL
combining form .... SOMA,
.... SOMAT(O)
dead .... CORSE, CORPSE,
.... CADAVER, CARCASS
duct .... MEATUS
fats .... LIPIDS, STEROLS,
.... TRIGLYCERIDES
heavenly .... SUN, MOON,
.... STAR, COMET, PLANET
injury .... TRAUMA
internal organs .... VITALS,
.... INNARDS
joint ...... KNEE, WAIST, ELBOW
judicial ...... COURT, TRIBUNAL
language ...... SHRUG, MOTION,
.... GESTURE
main .... TORSO, TRUNK
odor .... SWEAT, STENCH
odor: colloq. .... BO
odor treatment
.... DEODORANT,
.... ANTIPERSPIRANT
of advisers .... CABINET
assistants .... STAFF
horse .... BARREL
laws .... CODE
learning .... LORE
men .... ARMY, POSSE,
.... SQUAD, TROOP, PLATOON
nobility .... PEERAGE
plant .... SOMA
representatives
.... DELEGATION
retainers ..... SUITE, RETINUE,
.... ENTOURAGE
the/pertaining to the
.... SOMATIC, CORPOR(E)AL
troops .... COMPANY,
.... DIVISION, REGIMENT
vertebra .... CENTRUM
water .... BAY, SEA, COVE,
LAKE, POND, POOL, OCEAN,
BAYOU, RIVER, CHANNEL,
BROOK, CANAL, GULF,
LAGOON, STRAIT, FIORD,
STREAM, RESERVOIR
writing .... TEXT, THEME
opening .... FORAMEN
orbiting around planet
.... SATELLITE
orbiting around sun
.... PLANET
politic .... WEAL, STATE,
.... SOCIETY
servant .... VALET
shop .... GARAGE
slang .... CHASSIS

trunk of .... TORSO
weakness .... DEBILITY
body's framework ...... SKELETON
largest organ .... SKIN
bodyguard ...... ESCORT, RETINUE,
.... PROTECTOR
slang .... TORPEDO
Boeotia's capital .... THEBES
Boer dialect .... TAAL
general .... BOTHA, HERTZOG
statesman .... HERTZOG
troops .... COMMANDO
War town besieged
.... MAFEKING
Boers' victim .... MATABELE
bog .... FEN, MIRE, MOOR, MARSH,
OOZE, QUAG, SWAMP,
MORASS, MUSKEG, QUAGMIRE
berry .... CRANBERRY
orchid .... CALYPSO
peat .... MOSS
product .... PEAT
trotter .... IRISH(MAN)
bogey .... BOGY, BOGIE, MONSTER,
BUGABOO, BUGBEAR,
(HOB)GOBLIN, SPECTER
in golf .... ONE OVER PAR
bogeyman .... GHOUL, GHOST,
SCARER, PHANTOM,
HOBGOBLIN
bogged down .... STALLED
boggle .... AMAZE, BOTCH,
BUNGLE, ASTOUND, CONFUSE,
HESITATE, QUIBBLE, SCRUPLE,
EQUIVOCATE
boggy .... MIRY, MARSHY,
QUAGGY, SWAMPY
tract .... MORASS
bogie: Brit. .... CART, TRUCK
bogus .... FAKE, SHAM, SPURIOUS,
COUNTERFEIT
colloq. ...... PHONY, DOCTORED
bogy. See bogey
bohea .... (BLACK)TEA
Bohemia .... CECHY
Bohemian .... ARTY, GYPSY,
ARTIST, DILETTANTE
city .... PRAHA, PILSEN
composer .... MAHLER
dance .... POLKA, REDOWA,
TALIAN
garnet .... PYROPE
general .... ZISKA, ZIZKA
Girl .... ARLINE
hotsprings site ..... CARLSBAD,
KARLSBAD
martyr .... HUS(S)
mountain .... ERZ
patron saint .... WENCESLAUS
reformer .... HUS(S)
river .... EGER, ISER, OHRE

town .... CARLSBAD
Bohr, physicist .... NIELS
boil .... COOK, FUME, RAGE, SORE,
ANGER, CHURN, BUBBLE,
ANTHRAX, SEETHE, PUSTULE,
LUMP, FURUNCLE, CARBUNCLE
eyelid .... STY
slow .... STEW, SIMMER
boiled rice: Philippines .... KANIN
rice with meat, spiced
.... PILAF, PILAFF, PILAU
shirt: sl. .... BRAGGART,
POPINJAY
boiler .... TANK, COPPER,
FURNACE, CA(U)LDRON
coating inside of .... SCALE
covering .... LAG(GING)
safety device .... HYDROSTAT
to tend a .... STOKE
vent .... TUBE
boiling .... COOKING, BUBBLING,
SCALDING, SEETHING
over .... AFIRE, ABLAZE,
FLUSHED, STEAMING
point .... HIGH TEST
slang .... HOT UNDER THE
COLLAR
boisterous .... ROWDY, ROUGH,
TURBULENT, NOISY, STORMY,
RIOTOUS, VIOLENT,
VOCIFEROUS
fun .... JINK(S)
bola .... WEAPON
Spanish .... BALL
bolar .... CLAYEY, CLAYISH
bold ...... BRAVE, DARING, FIERCE,
FRESH, FEARLESS, INTREPID,
AUDACIOUS
and brazen .... SHAMELESS
and courageous .... HEROIC
and daring .... DEFIANT,
CHALLENGING
and free .... MOD
and resolute .... HARDY
and strong ..... LUSTY, MIGHTY
faced .... PERT, BRASSY,
SAUCY, FORWARD, IMPUDENT
front .... BLUFF
girl .... HOYDEN, TOMBOY
boldness .... CHEEK, PLUCK,
DEFIANCE, COURAGE,
TEMERITY
bole .... CLAY, STEM, TREE,
STALK, TRUNK
bolero .... VEST, DANCE
composer of .... RAVEL
boletus .... TOADSTOOL
bolide .... METEOR, FIREBALL
Bolivar .... COIN, (THE)
LIBERATOR
Bolivian boat .... BALSA

capital .... SUCRE, LA PAZ
city/town ...... SUCRE, PUNATA,
   ORURO, CAMIRI, TARIJA,
   POTOSI, COBIJA, TRINIDAD,
   VIACHA
export .... TIN
Indian .... ITE, ITEN, CHOLO,
   URO, LECA, MOJO, AYMARA
lagoon .... GAIBA, CACERES,
   COLORADA, HUATUNAS,
   MANDIORE
lake .... POOPO, COIPASA,
   ROGAGUA, TITICACA
language .... AYMARA,
   QUECHUA, SPANISH
llama .... ALPACA
money .... PESO, TOMINE,
   BOLIVIANO
mountain .... JARA, ILLAMPU,
   CHOVORECA, ANCOHUMA,
   PUPUYA, SAJAMA,
   HUANCHUPA, ZAPALERI,
   TOCORPURI
mountains .... CHARAGUA,
   BLOOMFIELD
plains .... GRAND CHACO
river ..... BENI, ABUNA, LAUCA,
   BOOPI, CLARO, BARRAS,
   BLANCO, NEGRO, PIRAY,
   GRANDE, MAMORE, RAPULO,
   MIZQUE, MADIDI, YATA,
   PARAGUAY, BERMEJO,
   MACHUPO, CANDELARIA
salt deposit .... COIPASA,
   UYUNI, EMPEXA, CHALLVIRI
seat of government .... LA PAZ
swamp ..... IZOZOG, LIVERPOOL
volcano .... OLLAGUE
weight .... LIBRA
boll .... POD, BULB, CAPSULE
weevil .... BEETLE, PICUDO
bollard .... BITT, POST, DEADHEAD
bollix: sl. ...... BUNGLE, BOTCH UP
bolo .... KNIFE, MACHETE
bologna .... SAUSAGE
slang .... BALONEY
Bolshevik .... RUSSIAN,
   COMMUNIST
leader .... LENIN, TROTSKY
secret police ...... NKVD, OGPU
bolster .... PAD, PROP, CUSHION,
   PILLOW, SUPPORT, REINFORCE
the spirit .... ELATE
bolt .... BAR, PIN, ROD, RUN,
   LOCK, PAWL, ROLL, FLASH,
   ARROW, LATCH, RIVET,
   SHAFT, COTTER, DEFECT,
   DECAMP, PINTLE, LIGHTNING
fastener .... NUT
hastily .... DASH (OFF)
pivot .... PINTLE

together .... ELOPE
turner .... SPANNER
bolter .... SIEVE, SIFTER,
   DEFECTOR, DESERTER,
   ESCAPEE, RUNAWAY
bolthead .... FLASH, ALEMBIC
bolus .... LUMP, MASS, PILL
boma .... BOA, PYTHON
bomb .... ATOM, TEAR, SHELL,
   FIREBALL, ATTACK, GRENADE,
   BLAST, MISSILE, EXPLOSIVE
aerial: sl. .... EGG,
   BREADBASKET
colloquial .... MOLOTOV
   COCKTAIL
defective .... DUD
kind of .... ATOM, ATOMIC,
   TEAR, FISSION, NEUTRON,
   HYDROGEN, INCENDIARY
pit .... CRATER
powerful .... BLOCKBUSTER
shelter .... ABRI, BUNKER,
   DUGOUT, FOXHOLE
slang .... FAIL, FLOP
small .... GRENADE
sound on way .... BUZZ,
   WHINE
underwater .... ASHCAN,
   DEPTH-CHARGE
bombard .... BLITZ, SHELL,
   ATTACK, BATTER, STRAFE
bombardment .... SIEGE, AIR
   RAID, BARRAGE, DRUMFIRE,
   CANNONADE, SHELLFIRE,
   BLITZKRIEG
bombardon .... OBOE, TUBA,
   ORGAN, BASSOON
bombast .... RANT, BOAST,
   HUMBUG, BLUSTER, FUSTIAN
bombastic .... TURGID,
   FLAMBOYANT, FLOWERY,
   OROTUND, POMPOUS, VOCAL,
   GRANDIOSE, PLETHORIC
style .... TUMID
Bombay bigwig .... RANA
city .... POONA, SURAT
native .... MARATHA,
   MAHRATTA
bomber .... AIR-RAIDER,
   DESTROYER, LIBERATOR
aircraft, British .... JAGUAR,
   HARRIER, TORNADO,
   BUCCANEER
aircraft, French .... JAGUAR
aircraft, German .... TORNADO
aircraft, Italian .... TORNADO
aircraft, U.S. .... TIGER,
   HARRIER, SKYHAWK, FALCON,
   THUNDERBOLT, STEALTH,
   STRATOFORTRESS
aircraft, U.S.S.R. .... FITTER,

   BADGER, BLINDER, FLOGGER
approach of .... RUN
crewman .... GUNNER, FLIER,
   PILOT, AVIATOR, NAVIGATOR,
   BOMBARDIER
famed .... ENOLA GAY
gunner's place in ...... TURRET
bombinate .... HUM, DRONE
bombing .... AIR ASSAULT,
   SHELLING, STRAFING
describing a kind of
   .... CARPET, PRECISION,
   TACTICAL, STRATEGIC,
   SATURATION
halt .... TRIBUTE TO PEACE
mission .... SORTIE
raid starting place
   .... SHANGRI-LA
victim ..... EVACUEE, REFUGEE,
   CIVILIAN
bombproof shelter ...... BUNKER,
   DUGOUT, CASEMATE
bombshell, sort of .... SCANDAL,
   SHOCKER, SURPRISE,
   SENSATION
bombycid .... IO, MOTH, EGGER
bombyx .... ERI(A), SILKWORM
bon ami .... FRIEND
mot .... QUIP, (APT) SAYING,
   WITTICISM
vivant ...... EPICURE, GOURMET,
   GOURMAND
bona fide .... REAL, ON-THE-
   LEVEL, RIGHTFUL, GENUINE,
   AUTHENTIC
fides .... HONESTY, GOOD
   FAITH
bonanza .... (GOLD)MINE,
   WINDFALL, PROSPERITY
Bonaparte .... LOUIS, LUCIEN,
   JEROME, NAPOLEON,
   EMPEROR, CORSICAN
bonbon .... CANDY, SUGARPLUM
bonbonniere .... CANDYBOX
bond .... TIE, VOW, JOIN, DUTY,
   LINK, UNION, SURETY,
   SHACKLE, PLEDGE, CONTRACT,
   SLAVE, COVENANT,
   AGREEMENT, GUARANTEE,
   CONNECTION
marriage .... KNOT
part of .... COUPON
bondage .... YOKE, PEONAGE,
   SUBJECTION, SERFDOM,
   SLAVERY, CAPTIVITY,
   ENSLAVEMENT, SERVITUDE
bondman ...... CARL, ESNE, SERF,
   BONDSMAN, CHURL, HELOT,
   SLAVE, VASSAL, VILLEIN,
   GUARANTOR
bone .... OS, RIB, CUBE, DICE,

FEMUR, SCAPULA, CLAVICLE, SKULL, STERNUM, VERTEBRA
ankle .... TARSUS
arched .... RIB
arm .... ULNA, HUMERUS
break .... FRACTURE
breast .... STERNUM
canals, of .... HAVERSIAN
cavity .... CYST, SINUS, ANTRUM
change to .... OSSIFY
cheek .... MALAR
colloquial .... DICE
combining form .... OSTE(O)
decay .... OSITE, CARIES
disease ...... RICKETS, RACHITIS
ear ...... ANVIL, INCUS, STAPES, HAMMER, TYMPANIC
elevation, knoblike .... TUBERCLE
face .... MAXILLA
fatty tissue .... MARROW
finger .... PHALANGE
flat .... BLADE
forelimb .... HUMERUS
formation .... OSTOSIS
growth on .... EXOTOSIS
inflammation .... OSTEITIS
joint inflammation .... ARTHRITIS
leg ...... FEMUR, TIBIA, FIBULA, PATELLA
like .... OSTEOID, OSSEOUS
malignant growth in .... CANCER
marrow, of the .... MYELOID
nasal .... VOMER
of contention, literally .... WOMAN
of sorts .... FUNNY
of sternum .... STERNAL
of thigh .... FEMUR
of wrist .... CARPUS, CARPAL(E)
opening .... FORAMEN
organic basis .... OSSEIN
pelvic .... ILIUM
pertaining to .... OSTEAL
sac between joints ...... BURSA
scraper .... XYSTER
skull ...... FRONTAL, PARIETAL, TEMPORAL, MANDIBULA
small .... OSSICLE
spine .... SACRUM, VERTEBRA
to pick .... GRUDGE
turn into .... OSSIFY
U-shaped .... HYOID
bonehead .... DOLT, FOOL, NITWIT
boneless fish/meat .... FIL(L)ET
boner .... GOOF, ERROR, BLOOPER, BLUNDER

bones .... DICE, OSSA
as in a song .... DRY
combining form .... OSTE(O)
container for .... OSSUARY
outward curving of, in legs .... BOWLEGS
boneset .... AGUEWEED
bonfire .... BLAZE, BALEFIRE
kind of .... CAMPFIRE
bongo .... DRUM, ANTELOPE
bonhomie .... AFFABLE, PLEASANT, GOOD NATURE
boniface .... HOST, LANDLORD, INNKEEPER
Bonin Island .... OGASAWARA
bonito .... FISH, TUNA, MACKEREL
bonne .... NURSEMAID, MAIDSERVANT
foi: Fr. .... HONESTY
bonnet .... CAP, HAT, HOOD, POKE, HEADDRESS
folding ...... CALASH, CALECHE
projecting rim .... BRIM
woman's .... CAPOTE
Bonnet's cousin .... TAM
bonnie/bonny ...... FINE, PRETTY, HANDSOME, BEAUTIFUL
bonnyclabber .... (CURDLED) MILK
bonus .... TIP, GIFT, BOUNTY, PREMIUM, DIVIDEND
bony .... THIN, OSSEAN, ANGULAR, OSSEOUS, SCRAGGY, OSTEAL, SCLEROUS, EMACIATED
outgrowth .... SURFER'S NODULE
part of nose .... BRIDGE
plate/scale .... SCUTE
tissue inflammation .... OSTEITIS
bonze .... MONK
boo .... HISS, HOOT, JEER
boob: sl. ...... FOOL, DUNCE, IDIOT
booboo .... SNAFU
booby .... BOOB, DOLT, DUPE, LOSER, FOOL, DUNCE, NITWIT
colloquial .... LOONY
prize scores .... LOWS
slang .... DUFFER, DUMBBELL
trap .... PITFALL
trap, lethal .... MINE
boodle .... MOB, LOOT, LOT, CABOODLE, BRIBE, CROWD
boogie-woogie .... JAZZ, ROCK-AND-ROLL
boohoo ...... CRY, SOB, WEEP(ING)
boojum .... SNARK
book .... TEXT, TOME, ENTER, LIBER, PRIMER, REGISTER, ENGAGE, RECORD, READER, ACCUSE, INDICT, VOLUME,

PUBLICATION, SCHEDULE
about saints .... PASSIONAL
announcement .... BLURB
back of .... SPINE
Bible .... SCRIPTURES
blank sheet of .... FLYLEAF
case for .... FOREL, FORRIL
circulating agency .... LIBRARY
collection .... LIBRARY, BIBLIOTHECA
collector .... BIBLIOPHILE
combining form .... BIBLIO
cover fastener .... HASP
division .... CHAPTER
end .... FINIS
ever-changing .... ATLAS
first page .... FRONTISPIECE
foreign exchange ..... CAMBIST
installment .... FASCICLE
introduction .... ISAGOGE, PREFACE, FOREWORD
jacket ad .... BLURB
large .... TOME, FOLIO, VOLUME
leaf .... PAGE
leaf turned down .... DOG-EAR
left-hand page .... VERSO
lining .... DOUBLURE
make-up ..... FORMAT, LAYOUT
marginal comment .... MARGENT
of accounts .... LEDGER, BANKBOOK, CASHBOOK, JOURNAL
charts/maps .... ATLAS
church service forms .... ORDINAL, ORDINARY
classified words .... GLOSSARY, THESAURUS, DICTIONARY
devotions .... MISSAL
feasts .... ORDO
fiction .... NOVEL
gospel .... LUKE, MARK, JOHN, MATTHEW
hours .... HORA(E)
Jewish law .... TALMUD
knowledge .... (EN)CYCLOPEDIA
listings .... DIRECTORY
loose leaves .... CAHIER
musical composition .... OPUS
nobility/nobles ...... PEERAGE
psalms .... PSALTER(Y)
public records .... LIBER
rolled script .... SCROLL
stories of same author .... OMNIBUS

synonyms/antonyms .... THESAURUS

on plants .... HERBAL

on saints' lives .... HAGIOLOGY

on strange subjects .... CURIOSA

operatic .... LIBRETTO

page size .... DUODECIMO

palm .... TARA, TALIERA

paper cover .... JACKET

part .... PAGE, COVER, INDEX, CHAPTER, FLYLEAF, JACKET, COLUMN, SECTION, TITLE, GLOSSARY, FOREWORD, PREFACE, FRONTISPIECE, TABLE OF CONTENTS

reference, familiar .... WEBSTER'S, ROGET'S, THESAURUS, DICTIONARY

sampler .... BROWSER

school .... TEXT

section .... LEAF, PAGE, INDEX, CHAPTER

shape and size .... FORMAT

shelves, set of .... STACK

size ..... DEMY, FOLIO, QUARTO

technical description of .... COLLATION

the .... BIBLE

title page .... FRONTISPIECE

unbound .... BROCHURE, PAMPHLET

bookbinding .... BIBLIOPEGY

material .... SUPER, SKIVER, VELLUM, BUCKRAM, MOROCCO

style .... GROLIER

bookie: sl. .... BET TAKER

booking .... ENGAGEMENT, RESERVATION

agent: sl. .... TEN-PERCENTER

bookish .... SCHOLARLY, ERUDITE, LEARNED, LITERARY, STODGY, PEDANTIC, STUDIOUS

bookkeeper .... ACCOUNTANT, ACTUARY, RECORDER

illegal act of .... EMBEZZLEMENT

mentor of .... AUDITOR

bookkeeping .... ACCOUNTING

book .... LEDGER, JOURNAL

column .... DEBIT, CREDIT, ASSETS, LIABILITIES, NET WORTH

item .... LOSS, INCOME, EXPENSE, PROFIT, RENTAL, CASH, BALANCE, INTEREST

booklet .... PAPERBACK, BANTAM, POCKETBOOK

unstitched .... FOLDER, BROCHURE

bookmaker .... EDITOR, COMPILER, GAMBLER, PRINTER, PUBLISHER

slang .... BOOKIE

bookmakers collectively .... RING

bookplate .... EX LIBRIS

books .... LEDGER, ACCOUNT

collection of .... LIBRARY

of public records .... LIBRI

of the Bible .... APOCRYPHA, NEW TESTAMENT, OLD TESTAMENT

bookseller .... BOOKMAN, STATIONER, BIBLIOPOLE, BOOKDEALER

catalogue of ...... BIBLIOTHECA

bookselling .... BIBLIOPOLY

bookstall .... NEWS STAND

bookstore reading .... BROWSING

bookworm .... PEDANT, SCHOLAR, BOOKLOVER

boom .... JIB, GROW, ROAR, SPAR, BOOST, RESOUND, BARRIER, SPRIT, FLOURISH, PROSPERITY

boom can .... ACE

Boomer State .... OKLAHOMA

boomerang .... KILEY, KYLIE, WEAPON

in a way .... RECOIL, REBOUND, BACKFIRE, KICKBACK, RICOCHET

boon .... GAY, BENE, FAVOR, MERRY, BENEFIT, REQUEST, BLESSING, PLEASANT

companion .... HAIL FELLOW

boondocks .... WOODLAND, HINTERLAND, WILDERNESS

Boone, —— .... PAT, DEBBY, DANIEL, RICHARD

boor ...... OAF, CLOD, LOUT, TYKE, ROWDY, CHUFF, CHURL, CLOWN, RUSTIC, PEASANT

boorish .... RUDE, ROUGH, VULGAR, AWKWARD, UNCOUTH, ILL-MANNERED

boost .... LIFT, RAISE, PUSH UP, SUPPORT, INCREASE

slang .... PLUG

booster .... ROOTER, PROMOTER

shot .... VACCINE, INJECTION

slang .... SHOPLIFTER

boot ...... KICK, STOG(E)Y, STOGIE, BROGAN, BUSKIN, DISMISS, PAC(K), GALOSH(E), RECRUIT

Eskimo .... KAMIK

kind of .... ZIPPER

named after German field marshal .... BLUCHER

part of .... VAMP

slang ...... DISMISS, DISCHARGE

to .... BESIDES, IN ADDITION

Boot of Europe, so-called .... ITALY

bootee .... CLOTH SHOE

Bootes .... HERDSMAN, PLOWMAN, CONSTELLATION

brightest star in .... ARCTURUS

bootblack .... ATTENDANT, SHOESHINER

booth .... SHED, KIOSK(O), STALL, STAND, STORE

Oriental market .... SOOK

bootlace .... LACET

tip .... AGLET

bootleg .... SMUGGLE, BLACK-MARKET

whisky maker .... MOONSHINER

bootlegger .... SMUGGLER, RACKETEER, RUMRUNNER

bootlegger's ware .... ALKY, POTEEN, WHISKY, MOONSHINE

bootless ...... LAME, VAIN, FUTILE, BARREN, USELESS, HOPELESS

bootlick .... FAWN, PANDER, FLATTER

bootlicker .... TOADY, YESMAN, SYCOPHANT

boots .... SHOES

and saddles .... BUGLE CALL

high, waterproof ...... WADERS

booty .... LOOT, PELF, SWAG, PRIZE, GAINS, SPOILS, PLUNDER

booze .... DRINK, LIQUOR, WHISKY

boozy .... DRUNK

bop .... JAZZ

slang .... HIT, BLOW, PUNCH, STRIKE

borax .... FLUX, TINCAL

Borch, Dutch painter .... TER

Bordeaux .... WINE, MEDOC, CLARET

bordel(lo) .... BROTHEL

bordelaise .... SAUCE

border .... RIM, BRIM, EDGE, MARGE, MARGIN, FRINGE, RAND, BRINK, BOUNDARY, SIDE, LIMBUS, FRONTIER

customs gate .... BARRIER

design .... GUILLOCHE

land in dispute .... MARCH

on .... ABUT

on stamps .... TRESSURE

raise and ridge .... MILL

river .... YALU, MEKONG

wall .... DADO

bordered ...... HEMMED, FLANKED, TRIMMED

by seven hills .... ROMA, ROME

borderline .... DOUBTFUL,

MARGINAL, INDEFINITE
borders, at times .... AREAS IN
DISPUTE
bore .... DRAG, HOLE, WAVE,
DRILL, WEARY, BURROW,
ANNOY, CUT, TIRE, PIERCE,
ENDURED
gun .... CHASE, GAUGE,
CALIBER, CALIBRE
mine shaft .... TREPAN
out .... REAM
river .... EAGRE
slang .... DRAG
boreal .... NORTHERN,
NORTHERLY, NORTHWIND
bored .... BLASE, FED UP
boredom .... ENNUI, TEDIUM
sign of .... YAWN
borele .... RHINO(CEROS)
borer .... AWL, AUGER, DRILL,
BEETLE, GIMLET, ANNOYER,
INSECT, TERMITE, SHIPWORM
Borges' (Jorge) forte
.... BESTIARY
(Victor) forte .... PIANO
Borgia, _____ .... CESARE,
LUCREZIA
boric acid .... ANTISEPTIC
salts .... BORATE
boring .... DULL, TEDIOUS,
STODGY, TRITE, TIRESOME
person .... PEST, NUISANCE
tool .... AWL, AUGER, DRILL,
GIMLET, JUMPER, WIMBLE
borings .... CHIPS, FLAKES
born .... NEE, INNATE, DELIVERED
dead .... STILLBORN
out of wedlock ...... BASTARD,
BASEBORN
together with ..... CONGENITAL
yesterday .... NAIVE,
INNOCENT, CHILDLIKE
being .... NASCENT
borne .... SUSTAINED, CARRIED
Borneo (South) .... KALIMANTAN
apartment .... LONGHOUSE
ape .... ORANG
burrowing animal ..... TELEDU
cape .... PUTING
hornbill .... KENYALANG
is part of .... INDONESIA
mountain .... RAYA
mountains ...... IRAN, MULLER,
SCHWANER
native .... DYAK
pepper plant .... ARA
river .... BARITO, MAHAKAM,
PEMBUANG
squirrel .... PENTAIL
town .... BUNTOK, SAMPIT,
AMUNTAI, BARABAI, MALINAU,

KETAPANG, KANDANGAN
tribe ...... IBAN, DYAK, DAYAK,
KAYAN, KENYAH, DELABIT,
MELANAUS
Borodin's prince .... IGOR
boron and one other element
.... BORIDE
borough .... BURG, TOWN
citizen .... BURGESS
borrow .... USE, COPY, TAKE,
ADOPT, FILCH, OBTAIN,
PIRATE, ACQUIRE
bort .... DIAMOND, ABRASIVE
borzoi .... DOG, WOLFHOUND
bos(s) .... COW, BEEF
bosc .... PEAR
cousin of .... ANJOU
boscage .... GROVE, THICKET,
SHRUBBERY
bosh: colloq. ...... ROT, NONSENSE
bosk. See boscage
bosky .... WOODED
bo's'n/bosun .... BOATSWAIN
bosom ...... BUST, MIDST, BREAST,
CHERISH, EMBRACE
buddy .... INTIMATE
Bosporous rowboat .... CAIQUE
boss .... KNOB, STUD, CHIEF,
LEADER, MASTER, SACHEM,
DOMINEER, FOREMAN,
EMPLOYER, SUPERVISOR,
MANAGER, HEAD(MAN)
low-profile, with no real
power .... FIGUREHEAD
on shield .... UMBO
political .... CACIQUE
bossanova .... DANCE
bossy .... ARBITRARY, STUDDED,
BITCHY, PUSHY, HIGH-
HANDED, DICTATORIAL,
DOMINEERING
Boston .... WALTZ, BEANTOWN,
CARD GAME
baseball team .... RED SOX
basketball team .... CELTICS
city near .... MALDEN,
CHELSEA, MEDFORD,
CAMBRIDGE
cultured person/snob
.... BRAHMIN
famed name .... CABOT,
FILENE, LOWELL, EMERSON
historical event, 1770
.... MASSACRE
historical event, 1773 ..... TEA
PARTY
houseplant .... FERN
is capital of
.... MASSACHUSETTS
Orchestra word .... POPS
symbol of .... CODFISH

Bostonian .... HUBBITE
bot(t) .... LARVA, MAGGOT
botanical angle .... AXIL
feat .... GRAFT
sac .... THECA
botanist .... BROWN, MENDEL
botany .... PHYTOLOGY
botch .... FAIL, FLUB, GOOF, MESS,
MUFF, BUNGLE, SPOIL, LOUSE
(UP), FUMBLE
both .... TWO, ALIKE, EQUALLY,
TOGETHER
prefix .... AMBI
bother .... ADO, AIL, FUSS,
ANNOY, WORRY, HARASS,
MOLEST, PESTER, TROUBLE
Bothnia .... ALAND
botryose .... RACEMOSE
bottle .... VIAL, CRUET, FLASK,
JUG, DECANTER, CARAFE,
CARBOY, COSTREL, FLAGON,
PHIAL, MAGNUM
containing garden
.... TERRARIUM
fancy with wicker casing/
earthenware .... DEMIJOHN
for acids/liquids .... CARBOY
for condiments .... CRUET,
CASTER
hit the .... BOOZE
indentation at bottom .... KICK
medicine .... TENREC
perfume .... FLACON
shaped vessel .... FLASK
size .... FIFTH, GALLON,
MAGNUM
stopper .... CORK
top .... CAP, CROWN
up, as emotions ...... SUPPRESS
utility/preserving liquid
temperature ..... THERMOS
vinegar .... CRUET
water/wine .... CARAFE,
DECANTER
bottleneck ...... SNAG, HINDRANCE
bottlenose .... DOLPHIN, PORPOISE
bottom .... BED, BASE, LAST,
ROOT, SHIP, LOWEST, SOURCE
colloquial .... BUTTOCKS
of ship .... KEEL
bottomless .... ABYSMAL
pit/gulf .... HELL, ABYSS,
ABADDON, UNDERWORLD
bottoms .... HOLM
boudoir .... BOWER, DRESSING
ROOM
bouffant .... FULL, PUFFED
bouffe .... COMIC OPERA
bough .... LIMB, TWIG, BRANCH
of tree .... RAMAGE
boughpot .... BOWPOT, BOUQUET,

JARDINIERE

bougie .... WAX, CANDLE

bouillabaisse .... SOUP, CHOWDER

bouillon .... CUBE, BROTH

Boulder Dam designer

.... SAVAGE

boulevard .... AVENUE, STREET,

CONCOURSE, PROMENADE

Boumedienne, Algerian

president .... HOUARI

bounce .... JUMP, LEAP, BUMP,

DASH, BOUND, EXPEL, THUMP,

SPIRIT, DISMISS, SPRING,

REBOUND

along .... SKITTER

British .... BLUSTER,

IMPUDENCE

on water surface .... DAP

slang ...... DASH, EJECT, EXPEL,

SPIRIT, DISMISS

bouncing .... BIG, BUXOM, LUSTY,

HEALTHY

bound .... JUMP, LEAP, TIED,

LIMIT, SWORN, HEADED,

OBLIGED, SADDLED WITH,

PLEDGED, DESTINED

bundle .... BALE

collection of maps ...... ATLAS

horse's .... VAULT, CURVET

boundaries, mark off

.... DEMARCATE

boundary ...... LINE, MERE, METE,

AMBIT, LIMIT, VERGE,

CONFINES, BORDER, BUTTING

combining form .... ORI

common .... CONTERMINAL,

CONTERMINOUS

outer .... PERIMETER

bounden .... FORCED, OBLIGED,

COMPELLED, INDEBTED

bounder .... CAD, BOOR,

SCOUNDREL

Bounding Main .... OCEAN,

(OPEN) SEA

boundless .... VAST, ENDLESS,

ETERNAL, COUNTLESS,

INFINITE, UNLIMITED

bounds .... AMBIT, SCOPE,

CONFINES, LIMITS

out of .... OFF LIMITS,

PROHIBITED

partner of .... LEAPS

bounteous .... AMPLE, ABUNDANT,

GENEROUS, PLENTIFUL

bounty .... TIP, BONUS, GRANT,

REWARD, PREMIUM,

ALLOWANCE, SUBSIDY,

LARGESSE, GENEROSITY

bouquet .... ODOR, POSY,

CORSAGE, AROMA, SPRAY,

SCENT, GARLAND, NOSEGAY,

PERFUME, FRAGRANCE

Bourbon .... REUNION, WHISKY,

REACTIONARY

bourg .... TOWN, VILLAGE

bourgeois .... FAIR, SMUG,

AVERAGE, ORDINARY,

PASSABLE, SHOPKEEPER,

COMMONPLACE,

MIDDLECLASS, RESPECTABLE

bourgeoisie .... CAPITALISTS,

MIDDLECLASSES

bourn(e) .... GOAL, BROOK,

DOMAIN, STREAM, OBJECTIVE

bourse .... (STOCK) EXCHANGE

bouse .... BOOZE, DRINK, HOIST,

LIQUOR, CAROUSE

bout ...... GO, GAME, TURN, FLING,

MATCH, ROUND, CONTEST

colloquial .... SETTO

of pugilists .... BOXING

boutique .... SPECIALTY SHOP(PE),

STORE, BAZAAR

boutonniere ...... POSY, BOUQUET,

BUTTONHOLE

location/zone .... LAPEL

Bovary, Mme. .... EMMA

bovid .... OX, GOAT, SHEEP,

CATTLE, ANTELOPE

bovine .... OX, COW, BULL, SLOW,

CATTLE, STOLID, PATIENT,

TAURINE

Asiatic .... YAK

Celebes .... ANOA

male .... BULL, STEER

tuberculosis .... GAPES

bow .... NOD, BEND, CURVE,

STOOP, YIELD, SUBMIT

and arrow art .... ARCHERY

decorative .... RIBBON

down to .... KOWTOW

maker .... BOWYER

of eyeglasses .... BRIDGE

of ship ..... BEAK, FORE, PROW

of woman's dress ...... BUSTLE

of wood .... YEW

Oriental .... SALAAM

ornamental/ribbon .... KNOT

out .... RETIRE

shaped .... ARCUATE

bowdlerize .... CENSOR, PURIFY,

EXPURGATE

bowed .... BENT, ARCHED,

CURVED, SURRENDERED

bowel .... COLON, INTESTINE,

DEPTH, ENTRAIL, INTERIOR

movement, abnormal

.... RUNS, DIARRHEA

movement stimulant

.... LAXATIVE, CATHARTIC

pains .... GRIPES

sounds, audible

.... BORBORYGMI

bowels .... VITALS, INNARDS,

INSIDES, VISCERA, INTESTINES

clearer .... LAXATIVE,

CATHARTIC, PURGATIVE

purge of .... CATHARSIS

slang .... GUTS

bower .... ARBOR, ALCOVE,

ANCHOR, BOUDOIR, COTTAGE,

ENCLOSURE, GROTTO,

PERGOLA, RETREAT

bowery .... FARM, LEAFY,

DISTRICT, PLANTATION

"Bowery Boys" member

.... GORCEY

bowfin .... AMIA, GANOID,

DOGFISH, MUDFISH

bowhead .... WHALE

bowie .... HUNTING KNIFE

bowl .... CUP, DISH, ROLL,

TUREEN, BASIN, VESSEL,

CRATER, ARENA, STADIUM

drinking .... MAZER, MAZARD

flower .... JARDINIERE

for pounding substance

.... MORTAR

over .... STAGGER, ASTONISH,

OVERWHELM

punch .... MONTEITH

sound .... BOO, RAH, YELL,

BOOLA, CHEERS

toilet .... CLOACA

Bowl, name of U.S. athletic

collegiate .... SUN, ROSE,

COTTON, ORANGE, FIESTA,

SUGAR, TANGERINE

bowleg .... BANDY, VARUS,

TALIPES

bowler .... DERBY, KEGLER

bowling .... TENPINS, DUCKPINS

alley .... LANE

alley track .... RUNWAY

center mark .... JACK

first-ball target .... KINGPIN

game division .... FRAME

green .... LAWN, RINK

seven/ten pins .... CORNERS

term .... BREAK, SPARE,

GUTTER-BALL, STRIKE

three splits in a row

.... GOOSE

three strikes in a row

.... TURKEY

twelve strikes in a row

.... PERFECT GAME

widest split .... GOALPOSTS

bowls .... TENPINS, NINEPINS,

SKITTLES

bowman .... ARCHER, OARSMAN

bowse .... DRINK

bowstring .... CORD, GARROTE
sound .... TWANG
bowwow .... BARK
box .... BIN, BIFF, CASE, CUFF,
    CHEST, CARTON, SPAR,
    RECEPTACLE
cash .... TILL, REGISTER
fish .... KENCH
for a dead body .... COFFIN,
    CASKET
carrying cosmetics
    .... VANITY CASE
confining birds/animals
    .... CAGE
fodder .... CRIB, MANGER
money/valuables .... KIST,
    COFFER
powdered tobacco
    .... SNUFFBOX
relics .... RELIQUARY
specimen coins ..... PIX, PYX
storing ingredients/food
    .... BIN
tea, etc. .... CADDY,
    CANISTER
funnel-shaped .... HOPPER
in .... CORNER, ENCLOSE
like sleigh .... PUNG
of explosives .... CAISSON
office receipts .... TAKE
office window .... WICKET
office window sign,
    sometimes .... SRO
score item .... HITS, RUNS,
    ERRORS
seat .... LOGE
small .... CASKET
strong .... SAFE
tool .... KIT, CHEST
voice .... LARYNX
boxcar, in dice .... CRAP, TWELVE
boxer .... DOG, PUG(ILIST),
    SLUGGER, RINGSTER,
    PRIZEFIGHTER
colloquial .... PUG, MAULER,
    BEAKBUSTER, BRUISER,
    MITTSLINGER
boxer's arm length .... REACH
combination .... ONE-TWO
    PUNCH
hands: colloq. .... MITTS
practice aide .... SPARRING
    PARTNER
savior, sometimes .... GONG
second/trainer .... HANDLER
trademark .... CAULIFLOWER
    EARS
boxing bouts collectively
    .... CARD
champion .... CLAY, BAER,
    LOUIS, CARNERA, DEMPSEY,

ALI, ORTIZ, TUNNEY, WILLARD,
    LEONARD, DOUGLAS, CORBETT,
    WALCOTT, GRIFFITH, COKES,
    HARADA, TYSON, VILLA,
    SCHMELING
decision .... TKO, KO, DRAW,
    NO-CONTEST
glove .... CESTUS
match .... GO, BOUT, SETTO,
    FISTICUFFS
of/pertaining to .... FISTIC
official .... REF(EREE)
period .... ROUND
pre-bout need .... WEIGH-IN
promoter .... (TEX) RICHARD,
    (BOB) ARUM, (DAN) DUVA,
    (DON) KING
sanctioning body .... WBC,
    IBF, WBA
science of .... FISTICUFFS
wrestling contest
    .... PANCRATIUM
boxwood .... TREE, SERON, SHRUB
boy .... LAD, YOUTH, YOUNGSTER,
    SPRIG, NIPPER, MAN-CHILD,
    TAD, GOSOON, STRIPLING
age of .... PUBERTY
assistant .... JACK
attendant .... PAGE
colloquial .... BUB, KID,
    BUSTER, SON(NY), SHAVER
friend: colloq. .... LOVER,
    BEAU, ESCORT, SWEETHEART
Scottish .... GALLAN(T)
Boy Scout assembly/gathering
    .... CAMPOREE, JAMBOREE
daily object .... GOOD TURN
founder .... BADEN-POWELL
group .... DEN, PACK, TROOP,
    PATROL
hiking gear .... HAVERSACK
motto .... BE PREPARED
new .... TENDERFOOT
popular image of .... DO-
    GOODER
boycott .... AVOID, SHUN,
    BLACKBALL
in a way .... STRIKE,
    OSTRACIZE
Boz, pseudonym .... DICKENS
BPOE .... ELKS
bra .... BRASSIERE
Brabant's princess .... ELSA
brabble .... ARGUE, CHATTER,
    QUARREL, SQUABBLE
brace .... BIT, BIND, PAIR, GIRDER,
    BRACKET, COUPLE, PROP,
    BITSTOCK, FASTENER, SPLINT,
    TIGHTEN, STIMULATE
bracelet .... BAND, CHAIN, ARMIL,
    BANGLE, ARMLET, HANDCUFF,

    WRISTLET
bracer .... DRINK, TONIC,
    REFRESHER, STIMULANT
braces .... GALLUSES
British: sl. .... SUSPENDERS
brachial .... ARMLIKE
brachyuran .... CRAB,
    CRUSTACEAN
bracing .... REFRESHING, TONIC,
    INVIGORATING
bracken .... FERN, BRAKE
bracket .... ANCON, CONSOLE,
    CORBEL, GROUP,
    CLASSIFICATION
brackish .... BRINY, SALTY,
    NAUSEOUS
bract ...... GLUME, PALEA, SPATHE
cluster .... COMA
grass .... GLUME
brad .... TACK, SPRIG, (WIRE)
    NAIL
brae: Scot. .... BANK, HILLSIDE
brag .... BOAST(ER), CROW,
    VAUNT, BRAGGART,
    GASCONADE
braggadocio .... BOASTING,
    HEROICS, BOMBAST,
    CHAUVINISM
braggart .... GASBAG, BOASTER,
    BRAGGER, GASCON,
    PRETENDER
slang .... WINDBAG,
    BLOWHARD
Bragi's parent ...... ODIN, FRIGGA
Brahma .... FOWL, CATTLE,
    CREATOR
Brahman bull .... ZEBU
rule .... SUTRA, SUTTA
title .... AYA
wiseman .... PUNDIT
Brahmin: Hindu .... PRIEST
braid .... BAND, PLAT, LACET,
    PLAIT, QUEUE, TRESS, WEAVE
decoration .... CORDON
of gold thread .... GALLOON
trimming .... RICKRACK,
    GALLOON, SOUTACHE
zigzag .... RICKRACK
braided material .... SENNIT
brain .... MIND, INTELLECT,
    MENTALITY, INTELLIGENCE,
    CONTROL CENTER
action .... COGITATION,
    CEREBRATION
and the spinal cord
    .... CENTRAL NERVOUS SYSTEM
bleeding within the
    .... HEMORRHAGE
blood clot in the
    .... HEMATOMA
canal/passage .... ITER

collection of pus in the
.... ABSCESS
colloquial .... GRAY MATTER
congenital absence of the
.... ANENCEPHALY
covering .... SKULL, MATER,
MENINGES
damage .... DEMENTIA
disease .... KURU, TUMOR,
APHASIA, ALZHEIMER'S
disorder .... MIGRAINE,
NARCOLEPSY
fever .... ENCEPHALITIS
fissure/groove .... SULCUS
fold .... GYRUS
"food" .... FISH
function .... SPEECH, EMOTION,
THOUGHT
hat .... THINKING CAP
infection within the
...... MENINGITIS, ENCEPHALITIS
lack of oxygen in the
.... HYPOXIA
layer of gray matter
.... CORTEX
linking nerve fibers
.... CORPUS CALLOSUM
lowest section of the .... STEM
membrane .... PIA MATER,
DURA MATER, ARACHNOID
nerve cells ...... GRAY MATTER
nerve fibers .... WHITE
MATTER
of the/pertaining to
.... CEREBRAL, CEREBRIC
opening .... PYLA
pan .... SKULL, CRANIUM
part .... PONS, STEM,
CEREBRUM, CEREBELLUM,
MEDULLA, MIDBRAIN,
FOREBRAIN
ridge .... HIPPOCAMPUS
structure of nerve fibers
.... FORNIS
surgery .... LOBOTOMY
tissue .... TELA
truster: sl. .... EXPERT,
ADVISER, EGGHEAD
tumor .... GLIOMA,
MENINGIOMA
water on the
.... HYDROCEPHALUS
X-ray ..... IMAGING, SCANNING,
ANGIOGRAPHY
brainchild .... IDEA, PLAN,
FANCY, CREATION
brainless .... FOOLISH, STUPID,
IDIOTIC
brains .... INTELLECT,
INTELLIGENCE
slang .... IDEAMAN, KNOWHOW,

MASTERMIND
brainstorm .... INSPIRATION,
PLAN, BRIGHT IDEA, CONCEPT,
CEREBRATION
brainwash .... ALIENATE,
MISINFORM, INDOCTRINATE
brainy .... WISE, SHARP, SMART,
INTELLIGENT, WITTY,
INTELLECTUAL
brake .... CURB, FERN, STOP,
CHECK, CLUMP, HARROW,
BRACKEN, KNEADER, RETARD,
SLOW DOWN, THICKET
for woman's tongue
.... BRANKS
part .... SHOE
Bram Stoker's thriller
.... DRACULA
bramble .... BRIER, SHRUB,
DEWBERRY, BLACKBERRY,
RASPBERRY
brambling .... FINCH
brambly .... THORNY, PRICKLY
bran .... HUSK, SKIN, GRAIN
COVERING
meal, etc. mixture .... MASH
branch .... ARM, PART, BOUGH,
LIMB, TWIG, RAMUS, SPRIG,
BROOK, DIVIDE, DIVISION,
SHOOT, OFFSHOOT, RIVULET,
RAMIFY, FURCATE, FURCATION
angle .... AXIL
in biology .... RAMUS
like .... RAMOUS
of family .... STIRPS
of learning .... ART(S), OLOGY,
SCIENCE, DISCIPLINE
off .... FORK, DIVERGE
out .... GROW, SPREAD,
DEPLOY, DISPERSE
railroad .... SPUR, SIDING
trim .... LOP
branched ...... RAMOSE, RAMOUS,
RAMIFORM
branches, bearing many
.... RAMOSE
branchine .... GILLS
branching .... ARBORESCENT
branchlet .... SPRAY
brand .... SEAR, MARK, DISGRACE,
LABEL, STAIN, STAMP,
TRADEMARK, STIGMA(TIZE)
goose .... BRANT
new .... FRESH, UNUSED
brandish .... WAVE, SHAKE,
SWING, FLAUNT, FLOURISH
brandling .... WORM, FISHBAIT
brandy .... MARC, COGNAC,
AQUA-VITAE
and soda .... PEG
cocktail .... SIDECAR,

ALEXANDER
cordial .... ROSOLIO
branks .... BIT, BRIDLE
brant .... GOOSE
brantail .... BIRD, REDSTART
brash .... RASH, HASTY, BOLD,
IMPUDENT, INSOLENT,
PYROSIS, SHOWER, FRAGMENT,
FRAGILE, BRITTLE, IMPETUOUS
Brasilia, designer of
.... NIEMEYER
is capital of .... BRAZIL
brass .... ALLOY, METAL
as imitation gold ..... ORMOLU
colloquial .... GALL,
BOLDNESS, IMPUDENCE
color .... AENEOUS
combining form .... CHALCO
hat: sl. .... BIGWIG, VIP,
GENERAL, OFFICER,
DIGNITARY, EXECUTIVE
knuckles .... BLACKJACK
like alloy .... LATTEN
mythical man of .... TALOS
plate, kind of .... CYMBAL
slang .... BUCKS, MONEY
tacks .... FACTS, DETAILS,
PARTICULARS
brassard .... BADGE, ARMBAND
brassica .... COLE, TURNIP,
CABBAGE, BROCCOLI
brassie, for example .... GOLF
CLUB
brassiere .... BRA, UPLIFT,
BANDEAU
slang .... FALSIES
brassworker .... BRAZIER
brassy .... BOLD, LOUD, SHOWY,
FORWARD, IMPUDENT,
INSOLENT
brat .... IMP, RAG, PEST, CHILD,
CLOTH, MANTLE, URCHIN,
BANTLING
brattice .... PARAPET,
BREASTWORK
brattle .... RATTLE, CLATTER,
SCAMPER
bravado .... BLUFF, BLUSTER,
BOLDNESS, COCKINESS
brave .... BOLD, DEFY, MANLY,
HEROIC, PLUCKY,
COURAGEOUS, VALIANT,
STOUT-HEARTED
front, usually .... BLUFF
Indian .... WARRIOR
bravery ...... GRIT, VALOR, NERVE,
COURAGE, HEROISM
bravo .... KILLER, ASSASSIN,
DESPERADO
Bravo! .... OLE, CHEER, WELL
DONE, APPLAUSE, VERY

GOOD, EXCELLENT
bravura .... DASH, DARING,
BRILLIANCE, TECHNIQUE
braw ...... FINE, CHIC, EXCELLENT
brawl .... ROW, FRAY, RIOT,
MELEE, FIGHT, BROIL, FREE-
FOR-ALL, FRACAS, UPROAR,
SCUFFLE
brawler .... HECTOR, HOODLUM,
HOOLIGAN
brawling .... NOISY, ROWDY
brawn .... FLESH, MUSCLE,
STRENGTH, HEADCHEESE
colloquial .... BEEF
brawny .... ROBUST, SINEWY,
STRONG, STURDY, MUSCULAR,
STRAPPING
bray .... CRUSH, LAUGH, POUND,
GRIND, GUFFAW, HEEHAW,
THRASH, SPREAD, TRITURATE
brayer, in printing .... ROLLER
braze .... SOLDER
brazen .... BOLD, HARSH,
IMPUDENT, SHAMELESS
brazier and grill .... HIBACHI
Brazilian aborigine .... ANDOA,
CARIB, AMIRANHA
armadillo ...... TATU, TATOUAY
bay .... BUZIOS, MARAJO,
SEPETIBA, GUANABARA
bird .... ARA, AGAMI, JABIRU,
SERIEMA
"Black Pearl" .... PELE
cape .... FRIO, ORANGE,
CASSIPORE
capital .... BRASILIA
capital, former .... RIO
channel .... SUL
city/town .... PARA, BELEM,
CEARA, CUIABA, CAMPINAS,
FRANCA, JUNDIAL, MANAUS,
RIO, LONDRINA, FORTALEZA,
NATAL, SAO PAULO, MARINGA,
OLINDA, RIO DE JANEIRO,
OSASCO, MARILIA, TERESINA
coin .... CENTAVO, (MIL)REI,
MOIDORE
crested bird .... SERIEMA
dam .... FURNAS, ITAIPU
dance .... SAMBA
drink .... ASSAI
estate .... PAZENDA
estuary .... PARA
fiber .... IMBE
footballer .... PELE, TOSTAO
forest .... MATTA, MATTO
heron .... SOCO
holly .... MATE
Indian ...... MURA, PURU, TUPI,
ARARA, CARIB, GUANA,
ACROA, ZAPARO, TAPUYAN

ipecac .... EVEA
island .... GRANDE, MARACA,
CARDOSO, MARAJO, BAILIQUE,
COMPRIDA, BANANAL,
CAVIANA, MEXIANA
killers .... JAGUNCOS
lagoon .... MIRIM, PATOS,
MANGUEIRA
lake .... FEIA, AIAMA,
ARARUAMA
language .... PORTUGUESE
long-legged bird ...... SERIEMA
macaw .... ARARA
measure, dry .... MOIO
measure, liquid .... PIPA
medicinal plant ...... AYAPANA
money .... CONTO, CRUZADO,
(MIL)REI, CRUZEIRO
mountain .... JAUARI, URUCUN,
LOMBARDA, PICO DA NEBLINA
nut .... PARA, CASTANA,
COQUILLA
orchid .... DICHEA
palm .... ASSAI, PIAS(S)AVA,
BABASSU, JUPATI, CARNAUBA
parrot .... ARA(RA), MACAW,
TIRBA
plant .... MANIOC, MANIHOT
port ..... BELEM, CEARA, PARA,
BAHIA, NATAL, RECIFE,
PELOTAS
president .... COLLOR DE
MELLO
quartz .... CACO
religion .... CATHOLIC
resort .... BELEM
river .... ACRE, AMAZON,
GRAJAU, ARAGUAIA, AMAPARI,
BALSAS, BRANCO, GRANDE,
ICA, FEIO, GURUPI, MADEIRA,
PARA, PARU, CLARO, IRIRI,
TEFE, JAVARI, ITAPI, IGUACO,
IVAL, JARI, JURUA, JAPURA,
MANSO, MIRANDA, MAPUERA,
RONURO, PARDO, RIBEIRA,
TURVO, PARANA, PARNAIBA,
TIBAGI, TAPAJOS, TACUTU,
VERDE, URUBU, URUGUAI
rubber port .... MANAUS
rubber tree .... ULE, HULE,
SERINGA
seaport .... RIO, BELEM,
NATAL, SANTOS
state .... ACRE, ALAGOAS,
BAHIA, CEARA, AMAZONAS,
SERGIPE, PARAIBA,
MARANHAO, GOIAS, PARANA,
SAO PAULO, PARA, PIAUI, RIO
DE JANEIRO
stork .... JABIRU
tapir .... ANTA

tea plant .... MATE
territory .... AMAPA, RORAIMA,
RONDONIA
title of respect .... DOM
tree .... APA, ANDA, MURURE,
ARAROBA, PARANAPINE
tree bark .... PEREIRA
tree powder .... ARAROBA
waterfall .... IGUAZU
weight .... ONCA, ARROBA,
LIBRA, QUINTAL
wood .... BRASIL, SATINE
Brazil's original name
.... VERACRUZ
breach .... GAP, HOLE, RIFT,
OPENING, HERNIA, RUPTURE,
BREAK, SPLIT,
BREAKTHROUGH
of etiquette .... FAUX PAS,
SOLECISM, IMPROPRIETY
of relations .... RENT, RIFT,
SCHISM
of the peace ...... RIOT, BRAWL
of trust .... BETRAYAL
bread .... AZYM, FOOD, LOAF,
RUSK, CRUST, GLUTEN, PONE,
MUFFIN, BROTCHEN
and-butter .... LIVELIHOOD,
EVERYDAY, YOUTHFUL,
COMMONPLACE
and-butter letter
.... GRACENOTE
blessed .... HOST, EULOGIA
boiled and flavored ...... CUSH,
PANADA
break .... EAT, DINE
crisp coating ...... RIND, CRUST
dough .... SPONGE
Eucharist .... HOST
from heaven .... MANNA
garnish .... SIPPET
hard .... HARDTACK
Hebrew .... AZYM
in one baking .... BATCH
ingredient .... FLOUR, YEAST,
LEAVEN
maker .... BAKER
part .... RIND, CRUMB, CRUST
roll .... BAGEL
soaked in beef broth
.... BREWIS
soaked in milk .... SOP
soaked in soup/gravy
.... SIPPET
spread .... OLEO, BUTTER, JAM,
JELLY, MARGARINE
St. John's .... CAROB
sweet, raised .... RUSK
toasted/fried .... SIPPET
unleavened .... HARDTACK
white .... MANCHET

breadbasket .... GRANARY
slang .... BELLY, STOMACH,
(AERIAL) BOMB
breadfruit .... RIMA(S)
breadth .... SCOPE, WIDTH,
EXPANSE
breadwinner: colloq. .... PAPA,
DADDY, EARNER
break .... GAP, BUST, RUIN, SNAP,
PAUSE, HIATUS, CAESURA,
CRASH, CRACK, DEMOTE,
SHATTER, FRACTURE, SMASH,
RUPTURE, DISCLOSE, SURPASS,
QUARREL
a code .... DECIPHER
a record .... SURPASS
a story .... DISCLOSE
away .... BOLT, ESCAPE,
SEPARATE
colloquial .... ESCAPE
down .... CRY, CRUSH, GIVE
WAY, ANALYZE, ITEMIZE,
DEMOLISH
from habit .... WEAN
in .... ENTER, INTRUDE,
INTERRUPT
in a beginner .... TRAIN
in a line of verse .... CAESURA
in rock strata .... FAULT
in the dike .... CREVASSE
in two .... SNAP
into parts .... DIFFRACT
into pieces ..... BURST, SMASH,
SHATTER
of day .... DAWN, MORN,
DAYBREAK
off ..... STOP, SEVER, SEPARATE
off connection .... SECEDE
one's heart .... CRUSH
out .... ERUPT, ESCAPE
popular to workers .... REST,
COFFEE
prison .... ESCAPE
religious law/moral principle
.... SIN
slang .... BOON, CHANCE,
ADVANTAGE
through .... PIERCE, PENETRATE
through eggshell .... PIP
up .... DISPERSE, SEPARATE
up marriage .... DIVORCE
breakable ...... BRITTLE, FRAGILE,
DELICATE
breakbone fever .... DENGUE
breakdown .... COLLAPSE,
BURNOUT, CRACKUP, FAILURE
breaker .... KEG, WAVE, EAGRE,
COMBER
breakers .... SURF
breakfast and lunch ...... BRUNCH
food .... CEREAL, FARINA,

OATMEAL
last .... DEJEUNER
nook .... ALCOVE
breaking of bones ...... FRACTURE
waves .... BREACH
breakneck .... FAST, WILD,
DARING, DANGEROUS
breakthrough .... BREACH,
DISCOVERY, INFILTRATION
breakup .... END, RUIN,
DISBAND(MENT), DISPERSION,
SPLIT, COLLAPSE, STOPPAGE,
DISSOLUTION, SEPARATION
breakwater .... DIKE, MOLE, PIER,
JETTY, BULWARK, SEA WALL
bream .... CHAD, PORGY,
ABRAMIS, SPAROID, SUNFISH
Japanese .... TAI
breast .... BUST, BOSOM, CHEST,
OPPOSE, PETTO
animal's .... BRISKET
disorder .... TUMOR, CANCER
inflammation .... MASTITIS
lump .... CYST
meat cut .... BRISKET
of the .... PECTORAL
plate .... CUIRASS
reconstruction
.... MAMMOPLASTY
shaped .... MASTOID
surgical removal of
.... MASTECTOMY
breastbone .... STERNUM
flat .... RATITE
of the .... STERNAL
breastfeed .... NURSE, SUCKLE
breastpin .... BROOCH
breastplate .... (A)EGIS, URIM,
PLASTRON
breastwork .... BARRIER,
REDOUBT, BRATTICE,
BARRICADE
breath .... AIR, LIFE, PUFF, ODOR,
WIND, WHIFF, BREEZE,
HALITUS, WHISPER, MOMENT,
RESPIRATION
asthmatic/whistling
.... WHEEZE
bad/odorous .... HALITOSIS
catch one's .... GASP, GULP,
PANT, PAUSE
forced noisily .... SNORT
of life .... PNEUMA
of wind .... FLATUS
out of .... WINDED
save one's .... REST, STOP,
SHUT UP
sweetener .... CACHOU, MINT,
LOZENGE
taking .... EXCITING,
THRILLING, STARTLING,

STIRRING, SURPRISING
breathe .... INHALE, EXHALE,
BLOW, MURMUR, RESPIRE
hard .... GASP, PANT, HEAVE
in .... SUCK, INHALE
noisily .... SNORE, HASSEL,
HAZZLE
one's last .... DIE, EXPIRE
out .... EXHALE, SUSPIRE
out noisily .... SNORE, SNORT
tentatively, as it were
.... SNIFF
with whistling sound
.... WHEEZE
breather .... GILL, NOSE, NARES
of fish .... GILL
of whale .... BLOWHOLE,
SPIRACLE
slang ...... REST, BREAK, PAUSE
breathing .... ALIVE, LIVING,
EXHALING, INHALING,
RESPIRATION
abnormal/rapid .... PANTING,
HYPERPNEA
device .... RESPIRATOR,
VENTILATOR
device, underwater
.... SNORKEL
difficult/painful ...... DYSPNEA,
DISPNOEA, DYSPNOEA,
DYSPNOIA
harsh .... RALE, SNORE
hole .... NOSE, NOSTRIL,
SPIRACLE
smooth .... LENE
sound .... RALE, SNORE,
STRIDOR, RHONEUS
space: colloq. .... REST, ROOM,
RESPITE
breathless .... AGOG, DEAD,
EAGER, EXCITED, AIRLESS,
GASPING, PANTING, STIFLING,
OVERCOME, (SHORT)-WINDED
bree: Scot. .... BROTH
breech .... RUMP, BEHIND,
BOTTOM, BUTTOCKS, REAR
END, DERRIERE
loading rifle .... CHASSEPOT
breechblock signature,
ballistics ...... IDENTIFICATION
breechcloth .... LOIN(CLOTH)
Polynesian .... MALO
breechclout .... G-STRING
breeches ...... TRUNKS, TROUSERS,
SLOPS, KNICKERS,
PANTALOONS
riding .... JODHPURS
Scottish .... TREWS
too big for one's .... PROUD,
ARROGANT, OVERBEARING,
SWELL-HEAD(ED)

breeching .... BRIDLE, SADDLE, HARNESS
breed .... LINE, KIND, RACE, REAR, HATCH, RAISE, CREATE, STOCK, VARIETY, MULTIPLY, STRAIN, GENERATE, ORIGINATE, CLASS, SPECIES, (RE)PRODUCE
cat .... ANGORA, PERSIAN, SIAMESE
cattle .... DEVON, GUERNSEY, HEREFORD
chicken .... BANTAM, LEGHORN, RHODE ISLAND
dog .... BOXER, BEAGLE, POODLE, (BASSET) HOUND, COLLIE, TERRIER, SPANIEL, BULLDOG, DOBERMAN PINSCHER, DALMATIAN, GERMAN SHEPHERD, CHIHUAHUA, RETRIEVER
horse .... ARABIAN, TROTTER, PONY, PALOMINO, CLYDESDALE
breeding ...... CULTURE, LINEAGE, REARING, TRAINING, ORIGIN, BACKGROUND, UPBRINGING
place .... NEST, NIDUS, ROOKERY, STUD FARM
breeze .... AIR, GENTLE WIND
colloquial .... COMMOTION, DISTURBANCE
refreshing .... CALLER
slight .... BREATH, ZEPHYR
water rippling ...... CAT'S PAW
breezing horse in a race
.... EASY WINNER
breezy .... AIRY, BRISK, LIVELY, CAREFREE
Bremen's river .... WESER
Brenner .... PASS
Breslau river .... ODER, OSAR
Breton .... CELT
breve .... WRIT, ORDER, BILLET, LETTER
brevet .... COMMISSION
breviary .... PORTAS, COMPEND
brevity .... BRIEFNESS, SHORTNESS, TERSENESS, CONCISENESS
is the soul of _____ .... WIT
of expression .... LACONISM
brew .... ALE, BEER, TEA, PLOT, CONCOCT, LAGER, PUNCH, STEEP, SCHEME, DISTILL
brewer's ferment .... LOB(B)
grain .... BARLEY
need .... MALT
tub .... KEEVE
vat .... TUN
yeast .... BARM
brewery .... DISTILLERY
refuse ..... LEES, DRAFF, DREGS

brewing, one .... GYLE
brewis ...... BREAD, (BEEF) BROTH
Brezhnev, _____ .... LEONID
Briareus, what it had many of
.... HANDS
bribe .... SOP, BAIT, LURE, BONUS, GRAFT, BOODLE, SUBORN, OVERTIP, CORRUPT
collector .... BAGMAN
money .... BOODLE, SLUSH (FUND)
slang .... FIX, PAYOLA, SQUARE, GREASE THE PALM, KICKBACK, HUSH MONEY
bribery .... GRAFT, PAY-OFF, BRIBING, CORRUPTION
bric-a-brac .... CURIO, VIRTU, BIBELOT, KNICK-KNACKS
brick ...... BAR, NOG, CLAY, TILE, ADOBE, BLOCK
burned partly .... BAT, BUR(R), CLINKER
carrier/trough for .... HOD
colloquial .... FINE FELLOW
compressed coal dust
.... BRIQUET
cracked .... CHUFF
hard .... CLINKER
making material .... PUG, MARL
masonry .... NOGGING
refuse .... SAMEL
sun dried .... ADOBE
up .... PAVE
worker .... MASON
bricklayer .... MASON
helper of .... HODMAN
tool of .... TROWEL
bricks, pile of .... HACK
brickwork .... MASONRY
bricole .... CATAPULT
bridal .... NUBILE, MARITAL, NUPTIAL, WEDDING
path .... AISLE
wreath .... SHRUB, SPIREA
Bridalveil .... WATERFALL
bride ...... WIFE, SPOUSE, FIANCEE, BETROTHED
in needle-work .... TIE, LOOP
bride's trailer .... MAID
bridesmaid .... PARANYMPH
bridewell ...... GAOL, JAIL, PRISON
bridge .... LINK, SPAN, BAILEY, CARD GAME, CAUSEWAY, PONTOON, CONNECT, RIALTO, TRESTLE, VIADUCT, CANTILEVER
bid/coup .... SLAM
boo-boo: var. .... RENEG
builder .... EADS
calls .... BIDS

card game .... AUCTION, CONTRACT
card game position
.... TRUMP, EAST, WEST, NORTH, SOUTH
contestants .... PAIRS
declaration .... BID
defeat .... SET
dental .... FALSE TEETH
expert .... GOREN
floating .... PONTOON
gaffe .... RENEGE
game series .... RUBBER
hand without trumps
.... CHICANE
holding .... TENACE
kind of .... DRAW, FOOT, BAILEY, HANGING
Midgard to Asgard
.... BIFROST
move/maneuver .... FINESSE
"no game" .... NIL
of bow instrument
.... PONTICELLO
of musical instrument
.... MAGAS
over gorge, etc. .... VIADUCT
part ...... SPAN, WALK, GIRDER, TRESTLE
pathway .... CATWALK
railroad .... TRESTLE
support .... PIER, GIRDER, TRUSS, PONTOON, ABUTMENT
term .... BID, NIL, BOOK, GOBY, PASS, RUFF, SLAM, TENACE
to Paradise .... ALSIRAT
tricks .... BOOK
type .... DRAW, TOLL, BASCULE, FLOATING, CANTILEVER, SUSPENSION
Bridges, _____ .... BEAU, JEFF, LLOYD
bridgework .... TOOTH-FOR-A-TOOTH
bridle ...... CURB, REIN, HARNESS, RESTRAIN
part .... BIT, REINS, HEADSTALL, NOSE-BAND
wise animal .... HORSE
brief .... SHORT, CURT, PITHY, TERSE, FLEETING, CONCISE, INSTRUCT, SUCCINCT, SUMMARY
biography .... VITA
case .... BAG, SATCHEL, PORTFOLIO
halt en route .... STOPOVER
in expression .... CURT, BLUNT, TERSE, LACONIC
in law .... BREVE

note .... JOT, MEMO
sleep .... NAP, DOZE, SNOOZE
summary .... GIST, FILL-IN,
               RESUME, EPITOME
telegraphic message .... FLASH
time .... FLASH, MOMENT,
               SECOND
briefed .... INFORMED,
               FAMILIARIZED
briefing .... NEWS, REPORT,
  ACCOUNT, TIDINGS, BULLETIN,
     ORDERS, INSTRUCTIONS
briefly .... IN SUM, IN SHORT,
     SHORTLY, MOMENTARILY
briefs .... UNDERSHORTS
brier .... BUSH, PIPE, HEATH,
         THORN, BRAMBLE
briery .... SPINY, THORNY,
            PRICKLY
brig ...... SHIP, PRISON, STOCKADE,
           GUARDHOUSE
brigade .... GROUP
fire, need of a .... BUCKET
brigadier general .... OFFICER,
           COMMANDER
rank below .... COLONEL
brigand .... THUG, BANDIT,
  PIRATE, LADRONE, ROBBER,
         HIGHWAYMAN
Brigham City resident
  .... UTAHAN
bright .... GAY, ROSY, LIVELY,
    BRAINY, QUICK, SHARP,
  SMART, CHEERFUL, LUMINOUS,
  LUSTROUS, ASTUTE, CANNY,
  CUNNING, CLEVER, BRILLIANT,
  RADIANT, SHINING, KEEN,
    ROSEATE, RELUCENT
and cheerful .... SUNNY
colored bird .... ORIOLE,
          TANAGER
colored fish .... OPAH,
    WRASSE, CATALINA
combining form .... HELI(O)
idea: colloq. ...... BRAINCHILD,
  BRAINSTORM, INSPIRATION
saying .... BON MOT,
         WITTICISM
star .... NOVA
youngster .... PRODIGY
youngster: sl. .... WHIZ KID
brighten .... GLADDEN, POLISH,
  FURBISH, CHEER (UP),
  (EN)LIVEN, INSPIRE, LIGHTEN
brightness .... GLOSS, LUSTER,
  SHEEN, ACUMEN, APTITUDE,
  KEENNESS, RADIANCE,
      LUMINOSITY
Bright's disease .... NEPHRITIS
brill .... TURBOT, FLATFISH
brilliance .... ECLAT, GLITTER,

RADIANCE, SPLENDOR
brilliant .... GAY, GEM, VIVID,
  BRAINY, QUICK-WITTED,
  PRISMATIC, EMINENT,
  TALENTED, MAGNIFICENT
array .... GALAXY
facet of .... CULET
gathering .... SALON,
  CONCLAVE, CONGRESS
red-yellow color
  .... GRAYSTONE
shade of blue .... PEACOCK
stroke/stratagem .... COUP
tennis stroke .... ACE
brim .... LIP, RIM, EDGE, BRINK
of bonnet .... POKE
of cap .... BILL
brimless cap .... FEZ, TAM,
  BERET, BARRET, BIRETTA
brimmer .... BUMPER
brimming .... FULL, SUFFUSED
brimstone ...... SULFUR, SULPHUR
brindled .... TABBY, BANDED
brine .... SEA, OCEAN, SOUSE,
  TEARS, SALT WATER
shrimp .... ARTEMIA
to salt residue .... BITTERN
bring .... FETCH, CARRY, CONVEY,
  TRANSFER, TRANSPORT
a good price .... COMMAND
about ...... CAUSE, ACCOMPLISH
around .... CONVINCE,
         PERSUADE
back .... RETURN, RESTORE
down .... LOWER
foot down .... VETO, STAMP
forth .... EAN, CREATE, SPAWN,
  PRODUCE, ENGENDER
forth young ..... HATCH, YEAN,
         WHELP
forward .... SHOW, PRESENT,
  CARRY OVER, INTRODUCE
home the bacon: colloq.
  .... WIN, EARN
in .... USHER, ARREST, IMPORT,
        CAPTURE
in as price .... FETCH
in forcefully .... THRUST,
  INTRUDE, INTERTRUDE
into court .... SUE, HALE,
        ARRAIGN
on/upon oneself .... INCUR
one's lunch .... BROWNBAG
out .... EDUCE, EXPOSE, ELICIT,
  REVEAL, DISPLAY, PRESENT,
  PUBLISH, INTRODUCE
ruin upon .... DAMN
to .... REVIVE
bay .... TREE, CORNER
bear .... EXERT, PRESS,
        PRESSURE

completion .... FINISH,
         FINALIZE
light ...... REVEAL, UNCOVER,
  UNEARTH, DISCLOSE
mind .... RECALL, REMIND,
  REMEMBER, RECOLLECT
naught .... RUIN, UNDO,
  DESTROY, NULLIFY
standstill .... STALL,
  STALEMATE, STATUS QUO
together .... AMASS, GATHER,
  ASSEMBLE, CONFLATE
under control .... TAME
up .... REAR, BROACH,
  PROPOSE, INTRODUCE
up the ___ .... REAR
bringer of bad luck .... JINX
bringing to central point
  .... AFFERENT
brink .... BRIM, EDGE, VERGE
brinkmanship, exponent of
  .... DULLES
briny .... SALTY
deep .... SEA, OCEAN
brio .... ZEST, ANIMATION,
         VIVACITY
brioche .... ROLL
briquet .... BRICK
brisk .... SPRY, ALERT, ACTIVE,
  BUSY, SHARP, ZIPPY, FRISKY,
  QUICK, LIVELY, SPANKING,
  BUSTLING, ENERGETIC
colloquial .... SNAPPY
in music .... ALLEGRO
brisket .... BREAST, MEAT CUT
brisling .... FISH, SPRAT, SARDINE
bristle .... HAIR, SETA, STAND,
  CHAETA, STIFFEN, STUBBLE,
      TRICHOME
combining form .... SETI
hooked .... BARB
like growth .... AWN, SETA,
  ARISTA, BARBEL, STUBBLE
pertaining to .... SETAL
ruffed animal .... BOAR
shaped .... SETIFORM
surgical .... SETON
bristles, covered with ...... HISPID
having .... SETOSE, STRIGOSE,
      SETACEOUS
tuft of .... PAPPUS
bristletail .... THYSANURAN
bristling .... IRATE, ECHINATE
bristly .... HAIRY, HISPID, SETOSE,
  HIRSUTE, HORRENT, SHAGGY,
  TUFTED, PRICKLY, ROUGH,
  SCOPATE, ACICULAR
animal .... HOG, BOAR,
      PORCUPINE
Bristol paper .... PASTEBOARD
Britain .... ALBION, ENGLAND,

BRITANNIA, GREAT BRITAIN, UNITED KINGDOM
ancients .... PICTS, SILURES
mythical king ..... BRAN, BRUT
of .... BRITANNIC
part of .... WALES, ENGLAND, SCOTLAND
B'rith, ____ .... BNAI
British .... BRITON, ENGLISH, LIMEY, SAXON, BLIGHTY
ache .... STOUND
active .... NIPPY
actor .... OLIVIER, AHERNE, ARLISS, COWARD, DONAT, EVANS, GRANGER, MARSHALL, RATHBONE
actress .... GWYN, KERR, LEIGH, GARSON, NEAGLE, ANDREWS, COLLINS, OBERON, REDGRAVE
admiral .... BEATTY, NELSON
airforce .... RAF
ale .... NOG(G)
altogether .... JOLLY
amah .... TWEENY
ambiguous .... DICEY, CHANCY
ament .... CLOT
amicus curiae ..... BARMASTER
ancient inhabitants ..... CELTS, BRYTTAS
anger .... WAX
apartment .... FLAT, CHAMBERS
apartment house ..... MANSION
archaeologist .... KENYON
architect .... ADAM, WREN, SCOTT
armor bearer .... SQUIRE, ARMIGER
army bugle call .... POST
army fur hat .... BUSBY
army staff officer: sl.
.... BRASSHAT
assurer .... UNDERWRITER
author .... MEE, MORE, DORAN, ARLEN, SHUTE, CAINE, BACON, LANDOR, ROGET, BARRIE, BELLOC, AUSTEN, WAUGH, DEFOE, MILNE, OPIE, READE, STERNE
authoress .... ELIOT, AUSTEN, BRONTE, COLLINS, CHRISTIE
baby carriage .... PRAM
baby hood/cap .... BIGGIN
bagman .... SALESMAN
bailiff .... REEVE, STEWARD
ballerina .... FONTEYN
bar .... PUB
bard, ancient .... SCOP
barge .... WHERRY
baseball-like game
.... ROUNDERS

basket .... CORF
bathe .... TUB
bay .... RYE, BUDE, LYME, MOUNTS, CARDIGAN, FALMOUTH, LIVERPOOL, MORECAMBE, BIGBURY, SWANSEA, THE WASH, TREMADOC, BARNSTAPLE
beak ...... JUDGE, MAGISTRATE, SCHOOLMASTER
beastly: colloq. .... VERY
bed .... DOSS
beer .... SWIPES
bit .... SPOT
blackbird .... THRUSH
blackleg .... SCAB, CHEAT, CROOK, GYPPER, GAMBLER, SWINDLER
blighter: sl. .... CHAP, FELLOW, RASCAL
blighty: sl. .... HOME, ENGLAND
bloke .... COVE, JOHNNY
bloody: sl. ..... VERY, CURSED, DAMNED
boat, ancient .... CORACLE
boatman .... BARGEE
bolt .... SNIB
book on the aristocracy
.... BRETT'S
borough .... BURGH, LEEDS
bottoms .... HOLM
boy .... NIPPER
boy's school ..... ETON, RUGBY
brandy soda .... PEG
bread .... MANCHET
bulrush .... CATTAIL
bunk .... DOSS
buttercup .... CROWTREE
buttocks: sl. .... BUM
canal laborer .... NAVVY
cape .... CORNWALL
capital .... LONDON
captain's boat .... GALLEY
car name .... ROVER, AUSTIN
carbine .... STEN
card game .... PATIENCE
card sharp .... BLACKLEG
carol singer .... WAIT
cascade .... LADORE
cash: sl. .... RHINO
cask .... KILDERKIN
cat-boat .... UNA
cathedral city ...... ELY, YORK, TRURO
cavalry .... YEOMANRY
certainly .... RATHER
channel ...... SOLENT, ENGLISH, BRISTOL, SPITHEAD
Channel island .... SARK, HERM, JERSEY, ALDERNEY,

GUERNSEY
Channel isle .... WIGHT
Channel, river to .... ORNE, RANCE, SEINE, SOMME
chap .... COVE
chase .... CHEVY
cheese .... STILTON
chemist .... BOYLE, FARADAY
chief, ancient ...... PENDRAGON
chinaware .... SPODE, CHELSEA, WEDGWOOD
cigarette: sl. .... GASPER
circuit court .... EYRE
city/town .... ELY, LEEDS, BARNET, BARKING, BASILDON, BRADFORD, BRISTOL, BROMLEY, HAMMERSMITH, BIRMINGHAM, DOVER, LONDON, CANTERBURY, EALING, CAMBRIDGE, COVENTRY, CAMDEN, CHESTER, HASTINGS, DURHAM, LAMBETH, GREENWICH, POOLE, LANCASTER, LIVERPOOL, HULL, PLYMOUTH, MANCHESTER, NEWHAM, OLDHAM, NOTTINGHAM, YORK, SHEFFIELD, STOCKPORT, OXFORD, TORBAY, THURROCK, WARLEY, HALIFAX, LEICESTER, WAKEFIELD, WESTMINSTER
clown .... GRIMALDI
cluster .... PLUMP
coachman .... JARVEY
coal carrier .... CORF
coal mine room .... BORD
coin .... PENCE, PENNY, GEORGE, GUINEA, FARTHING, SOVRAN, SHILLING, SOV(EREIGN)
coin, old .... ANGEL, GROAT, CAROLUS
college .... BALLIOL
college servant .... GYP
college steward ...... MANCIPLE
colonial official
.... PROCONSUL
Columbia capital .... VICTORIA
Columbia Indian .... HAIDA
comedian .... TOOLE
composer .... ARNE, ELGAR, COATES, DELIUS, BRITTEN
conductor .... BEECHAM, SARGENT, BARBIROLI
conservative party .... TORY
corner .... HERN
coronation rite .... UNCTION
country festival .... ALE
country gentleman ..... SQUIRE
county .... AVON, LONDON, BEDFORD, DORSET, ESSEX,

SHIRE, DURHAM, BUCKINGHAM, YORK, BERKSHIRE, CHESHIRE, OXFORD, SURREY, SUSSEX, DERBY, DEVON, GLOUCESTER, KENT, CORNWALL, LINCOLN, NORFOLK, SUFFOLK, SOMERSET, MIDLANDS, NOTTINGHAM, WIGHT, WILTS, CUMBRIA, TYNE-AND-WEAR, WARWICK
courage .... PECKER
court .... EYRE, LEET, SOC, HUSTINGS
cow .... RUNT
crazy .... POTTY
crook .... BLACKLEG
crow .... BRAN
crown jewel .... KOHINUR, KOHINOOR
cue ball .... MASSE
dance, ancient .... MORRIS
dandy .... TOFF, (BEAU) BRUMMEL
dealer .... MONGER
demolish .... RASE
derby hat .... BOWLER
dessert .... FLAN
diarist .... PEPYS, BURNEY, EVELYN
diplomat .... EDEN, LLOYD
divine .... INGE, DONNE
dramatist .... SHAW, MARLOWE, READE, PINERO, SITWELL, PEELE, TOBIN, SHAKESPEARE
drunk: sl. .... SCREWED
dump truck .... TIPPER
dupe .... MUGGINS
dynasty .... TUDOR, STUART
early conqueror .... HORSA, HENGIST, NORMANS
elevator .... LIFT
emblem .... ROSE
emperor of India .... PADISHAH
entry .... CLOSE
essayist .... ELLA, LAMB
estuary .... HUMBER
exam for honors .... TRIPOS
explorer .... ROSS, CABOT, SCOTT, HUDSON, LANG, BAFFIN, BURTON, RALEIGH, FROBISHER, STEELE, STANLEY
expression .... BULLY, I SAY, CHEERIO
fashion model .... TWIGGY
fell .... DOWN, HILL, MOOR
fellow .... CHAP, COVE
field marshal .... HAIG
field marshal at Arlington .... DILL

financier .... RHODES, GRESHAM
first overlord .... EGBERT
firth .... SOLWAY
fishing boat .... COBLE, HOOKER
flashlight .... TORCH
food .... TUCK
fool .... MUGGINS
foolish .... SPOON(E)Y
forest .... NEW, ARDEN, SHERWOOD
fox hunter .... PINK
franchise .... SOC
free tenant .... DRENG
freeman .... CEORL, CHURL, THANE
gambler who cheats .... BLACKLEG
gasoline .... PETROL
general .... BRADDOCK
geologist .... LYELL
giant of legend .... MAGOG
good-by .... PIPPIP
government .... WHITEHALL
grain cradle .... CADER
grove .... SPINNEY
Guiana's capital .... GEORGETOWN
gum .... DEXTRIN
gumshoe: sl. .... TEC
gun .... STEN, ENFIELD
hackney driver .... JARVEY
hamlet .... DORP
handball .... FIVES
handbook on peers .... BRETT'S
hare .... PUSS
hawker .... CHAPMAN
hayfork .... PIKEL
head .... CONK
headland .... NAZE
hedgerow .... REW
highball .... STINGER
highwayman .... TURPIN
hills .... MENDIP, CHEVIOT, CHILTERN, CLEVELAND, COTSWOLD, SOUTH DOWNS
historian .... BEDE, ACTON, GROTE, GIBBON
Honduras's new name .... BELIZE
hooligan .... SPIV
horse .... PRAD, SCREW, GARRON
horse dealer .... COPER
house-dress .... OVERALL
humorist .... STERNE
hunt .... CHEVY
hunting cry .... CHEVY, YOICKS

hunting dog .... LURCHER
hut .... NISSEN
hymnodist .... LYTE, NEALE
ID mark .... BROAD ARROW
India, founder of .... IVAN
Indian coin .... ANNA
Indian monetary unit .... ANNA, RUPEE
Indian nursemaid .... AMAH, AYAH
Indian province .... SIND, ASSAM
informer ..... SPY, NOSE, NARK
innkeeper .... PUBLICAN
island ...... ELY, HOLY, LUNDY, MERSEA, TRESCO, SHEPPEY
island in Atlantic .... ASCENSION
island in Indian Ocean .... MAURITIUS
island near Borneo .... LABUAN
islands .... SCILLY, CHANNEL
isle .... ELY, MAN, IRELAND
king .... HAL, JAMES, EDWARD, GEORGE, HAROLD
king, ancient .... A(E)THELSTAN
king, legendary .... BELI, BRAN, BRUT, ARTHUR, LUD, KNUT, CANUTE
labor strike(r) .... TURN-OUT
laborer .... NAVVY, PROLE
lake .... CONISTON
landowner ...... THANE, SQUIRE
language, ancient ...... CYMRIC
language, major ...... ENGLISH, WELSH, GAELIC
lay doggo .... HID
lecturer .... READER
legislator .... COMMONER
legislature .... PARLIAMENT
letter Z .... ZED
lexicographer .... FOWLER, GOWERS
liberal party .... WHIG
loan money .... PREST
lodgings .... DIGS
lunch .... TIFFIN
machine gun .... BREN
mail .... POST
male sheep .... TUP
malt liquor .... PORTER
manufacturing city ..... LEEDS, BIRMINGHAM
marine: sl. .... JOLLY
mark on government property .... BROAD ARROW
martyr .... ALBAN
meal .... (HIGH) TEA

measure, former .... ELL
measure, imperial liquid and
      dry ...... GILL, PECK, PINT,
    BUSHEL, GALLON, FLUID
   DRAM, FLUID OUNCE, QUART,
        MINIM, KILDERKIN
mendicant order .... FRIARS
merry-making .... RANT
mild oath .... GOR
military police .... REDCAP
military school
          .... SANDHURST
mine wagon .... CORF, ROLLEY
minister of state .... PEEL,
         PITT, WALPOLE
mint box .... PYX
miser .... SCREW
molasses .... TREACLE
money .... POUND, STERLING,
    PENCE, FARTHING, SHILLING
money advanced to enlisted
   men .... PREST
money: sl. .... RHINO
monk .... B(A)EDA
monk historian .... BEDE
mop .... MALKIN
mountain ...... AXE EDGE, PEEL
   FELL, CROSS FELL, SKIDDAW,
    BROWN WILLY, HIGH
        WILLHAYS
mountains .... PENINE,
    PRESELI, CUMBRIAN
murderer .... ARAM
national park ...... DARTMOOR,
   EXMOOR, YORKSHIRE DALES
naturalist .... SLOANE
navigator .... DRAKE
navy enlisted man
       .... BLUEJACKET
nimble .... NIPPY
noble .... DUKE, LORD, EARL,
   BARON, PRINCE, VISCOUNT
noblewoman ..... DAME, LADY,
    DUCHESS, PRINCESS
nonsense! .... HAVERS
North America .... CANADA
novelist ..... DICKENS, BRONTE,
   CAINE, CRONIN, ARTHUR,
   HUXLEY, MACHEN, RAMEE,
    READE, STERNE
nurse .... SISTER
oak .... ROBUR
oatmeal pudding .... MUSH
odd .... RUM
officer's servant .... BATMAN
orator .... BURKE, PITT,
       WILLIAM
Order .... GARTER
ore carrier .... CORF
outcry of blame .... DIRDUM
outlet .... POINT

ox .... RUNT
Pacific protectorate .... TONGA
pail .... ESHIN
pain .... STOUND
painter .... OPIE, ORPEN,
   PAYNTER, ROMNEY, TURNER,
       CONSTABLE
parish official .... OVERSEER
parliament member
       .... BURGESS
parliamentary record
       .... HANSARD
passageway ..... CLOSE, SMOOT
path .... PAD
patron saint .... ST. GEORGE
peddler .... CHAPMAN
peninsula .... LIZARD,
   PURBECK, HOLDERNESS
people, ancient .... ICENI
petty .... POTTY
philosopher .... HUME, JOAD,
   BACON, RUSSELL, SPENCER
physician .... ROSS
physicist ..... BOYLE, FARADAY
pianist .... BAUER
pickpocket .... PRIG
playwright .... SHAW, PEELE
pluck .... PECKER
pocket .... SACK
poet ...... HUGH, LANG, AUDEN,
   BLAKE, BYRON, AUSTIN,
   KEATS, DONNE, ELIOT,
 MACNEICE, MASEFIELD, GRAY,
    SITWELL, SPENCER
poet, earliest .... SCOP,
       CAEDMON
poet laureate .... DAY-LEWIS,
  AUSTIN, CIBBER, MASEFIELD
poetess .... SITWELL,
       BROWNING
Point .... DODMAN, PRAWLE,
   MANACLE, HARTLAND,
   PORTLAND, GIBRALTAR
policeman ...... BOBBY, PEELER
policeman's station ...... POINT
political party .... TORY,
 WHIG, LABOR, CONSERVATIVE
political philosopher
       .... BURKE
Pope .... ADRIAN (IV)
port ..... HULL, COWES, DOVER,
   POOLE, BRISTOL, PRESTON,
      LIVERPOOL
pot herb .... CLARY
pottery/porcelain .... SPODE
prefab shelter .... NISSEN
prep school, first-year boy
      .... SQUIT
   second-year boy ...... SQUIRT
   third-year boy .... JOLLY,
      GOOD FELLOW

prime minister ..... PEEL, PITT,
   ASQUITH, CHURCHILL, LAW,
   BALDWIN, CHAMBERLAIN,
   CANNING, ATTLEE, BALFOUR,
   EDEN, MAJOR, THATCHER,
   HOME, WILSON, MACMILLAN
prime minister called
   Ironside .... PITT
prime minister called the
   Iron Lady ...... THATCHER
prime minister with the cigar
      .... CHURCHILL
prime minister with the
   umbrella
     .... CHAMBERLAIN
prince ...... CHARLES, ANDREW,
   PHILIP, HARRY, EDWARD,
      WILLIAM
princess .... DIANA, ANNE,
   URSULA, MARGARET, SARAH,
   EUGENIE, BEATRICE
printer .... CAXTON
printing type .... RUBY
prison .... GAOL, DARTMOOR
prison: sl. .... QUAD, QUOD
property tax .... RATE
psychologist .... ELLIS
publisher .... BEAVERBROOK
pudding ..... MUSH, ROLY-POLY
pupil: sl. .... SCUM
Quaker .... PENN
queen .... ANNE, MARY,
   VICTORIA, ELIZABETH
queen, ancient .... BOADICEA
queer .... RUM
quick .... NIPPY
race course site .... ASCOT,
 NEWMARKET, EPSOM (DOWNS)
RAF fighter-bomber
   .... JAGUAR, SPITFIRE,
   BUCCANEER, HARRIER,
      TORNADO
rage .... WAX
raincoat .... WATERPROOF
range/stove .... KITCHENER
Reformation leader
       .... SEYMOUR
reformer .... SPENCE
resort .... BATH, MARGATE,
      BLACKPOOL
retail store .... WAREHOUSE
river .... ALN, AIRE, AVON,
   CAM, DART, COLNE, KENNET,
   DON, DEE, THAMES, MERSEY,
   ESK, DOVE, EDEN, HODDER,
   VER, LEA, OUSE, HUMBER,
   EXE, LUNE, TRENT, MEDWAY,
   TYNE, RIBBLE, PARRETT, URE,
   NENE, SWALE, SEVERN, USK,
   TEST, YARE, STOUR, WEY,
   TEES, TAW, TAMAR

river lowland .... HOLM,
BOTTOMS
road .... PAD
rock singer .... (MICK) JAGGER
routine .... ROTA
royal family .... TUDOR, YORK,
STUART, WINDSOR
royal guard officer .... EXON
royal house ..... TUDOR, YORK,
WINDSOR, STUART, HANOVER,
CLARENCE, HIGHGROVE,
SUNNINGHILL
royal household official
.... GROOM
royal stables .... MEWS
royal yacht .... BRITANNIA
rubbish! .... HAVERS
ruins .... STONEHENGE
ruler, early ...... OFFA, EGBERT
ruling family .... TUDOR,
YORK, WINDSOR
sailor .... LIMEY
saint .... AARON, ALBAN
salary .... SCREW
salesman .... BAGMAN
saloon-keeper .... PUBLICAN
sandhill .... DENE
scarecrow .... MALKIN
school, prep .... ETON, RUGBY,
HARROW, LUDGROVE
schoolboy servant .... FAG
schoolmaster ..... ARAM, BEAK
schoolteacher .... MASTER,
MISTRESS
scientist .... DARWIN
Scilly island .... TRESCO, ST.
MARY'S, ST. MARTIN'S, HUGH
TOWN
sea .... IRISH, NORTH
seaman .... RATING
seaport ..... GRIMSBY, RABAUL,
BOOTLE, MARGATE, DOVER,
WHITBY, BIRKENHEAD
seat in a theater .... STALL
sedan .... SALOON
sentimental .... SOPPY
serf .... ESNE, THRALL
sergeant-at-law cap .... BIGGIN
sheriff's aid .... BULLDOG
sidewalk artist .... SCREEVER
silly .... SPOON(E)Y
slaughterhouse .... KNACKER
sleep: sl. .... DOSS
smack .... HOOKER
smart .... STOUND
smock .... OVERALL
snarl .... GIRN
social event .... ASCOT
socialist .... FABIAN
soldier .... ATKINS, LIMEY,
TOMMY, REDCOAT

soldier's furlough/leave
.... BLIGHTY
solitaire .... PATIENCE
songbird .... BULBUL,
BULLFINCH
Sound .... PLYMOUTH
spa .... BATH, MARGATE
spark .... SPUNK
spot .... BIT
spy .... NARK, NOSE, ANDRE
stage .... PLATEAU
statesman .... PITT, EDEN,
BURKE, CLIVE, GREY, HOARE,
VILLIERS
steal .... PRIG
stool pigeon: sl. .... NARK
strait .... DOVER
strange .... RUM
streetcar .... TRAM
student, senior
.... PREPOS(I)TOR
subdivision .... SHIRE
surgeon .... LISTER
swell dresser .... TOFF
symbol ..... LION, (JOHN) BULL
tax .... GELD, SESS, EXCISE
taxable .... RATABLE
tea .... ELM
teacher .... MISTER CHIPS
tent .... MARQUEE
term for amusement ..... BEER
AND SKITTLES
term for good time .... BASH
thanks .... TAS
theologian .... ALCUIN
theorist .... LASKI
thicket .... SPINNEY
thief .... PRIG
tin mine .... STANNARY
title .... SIR, DUKE, EARL,
BARON, PRINCE
toast .... CHEERS
tobacco bit .... SCREW
tourist/traveler .... TRIPPER
trader .... MONGER
trout .... SEWEN, SEWIN
truck .... LORRY
tutor .... MASTER
25 pounds: sl. .... PONY
unit of measure .... STACK
university .... OXFORD,
CAMBRIDGE
university disciplinarian
.... BULLDOG
university official ...... BEADLE
university student
.... SOPHISTER
very .... JOLLY
village .... DORP, ARAWE,
BOURG
wage earner .... PROLE

waiter .... POTMAN
warrior .... CNUT
wasteland .... HEATH
waterways .... LODES
Wave .... WREN
weight .... TON, KEEL, MAST,
STONE
weight for wool .... TOD
whisky-soda .... STINGER
willow herb .... ROSEBAY
woman politician .... (LADY)
ASTOR, (MARGARET)
THATCHER
woman servant .... SLAVEY
woman, slovenly .... MALKIN
wood pigeon .... CULVER
woodland area .... WEALD
work horse .... GARRAN
World War I commander
.... HAIG
wrap .... RUG
Briton, early .... CELT, JUTE,
PICT, ANGLE, ICENI
Brittany .... ARMORICA,
BRETAGNE
brittle .... BRASH, CRISP, FRAIL,
CRACKLY, FRAGILE, VITREOUS
bones disorder
.... OSTEOPOROSIS
peanut .... CANDY
Brno name .... (JOSIP) TITO
bro. .... BROTHER
broach .... AWL, TAP, HOLE, OPEN,
SPIT, RIMER, CHISEL, LAUNCH,
REAMER, SKEWER, BRING UP,
INTRODUCE
broad .... WIDE, CLEAR, GENERAL,
LIBERAL, SPACIOUS,
EXTENSIVE, SWEEPING,
TOLERANT, WIDESPREAD
band: heraldry .... FESS
slang .... WOMAN
broadbill .... DUCK, GAPER, RAYA,
SCAUP, SPOONBILL
broadbrim: colloq. .... HAT,
FRIEND, QUAKER
broadcast .... SOW, SHOW,
PROGRAM, PUBLISH,
ANNOUNCE, STREW, SPREAD,
SCATTER, TELECAST,
TRANSMIT
broadcasting ...... ON AIR, AIRING
system/network .... ABC, ESPN,
CBS, CNN, NBC
broadcloth .... PIMA
broaden .... EXPAND, EXTEND,
WIDEN, SPREAD
broadleaf .... TOBACCO
broadminded .... LIBERAL,
RECEPTIVE, TOLERANT,
UNBIASED, UNDERSTANDING

broadside .... ABUSE, SALVO,
             ATTACK
broadsword .... BILL, CLAYMORE,
        CUTLASS, GLA(I)VE
broadtail .... SHEEP, KARAKUL,
           ASTRAKHAN
Broadway character .... ANGEL,
  HOOFER, PRESS AGENT, SUGAR
                DADDY
  event .... PLAY, SHOW
  girls, former .... FLORADORA
  impresario .... MERRICK
  Joe .... NAMATH
  (nick)name ...... COHAN, BILLY
      ROSE, FLO ZIEGFELD
  restaurateur .... SARDI
  square .... HERALD
  super hit .... MAN OF LA
               MANCHA
  venture .... PLAY, REVUE,
            MUSICAL(E)
Brobdingnagian .... GIANT,
             GIGANTIC
brocade ...... BROCHE, BAUDEKIN,
           BALDACHIN
  gold .... KINCOB
  Japanese .... NISHIKI
broccoli .... CAULIFLOWER
brochette .... SKEWER
brochure ...... BOOKLET, LEAFLET,
           PAMPHLET
brock .... BADGER
brocket .... DEER, PITA, SPITTER
brogan ...... BOOT, SHOE, BROGUE
brogue .... SHOE, ACCENT,
         PRONUNCIATION
  Scotch .... TRICK, DECEPTION
broil .... BAKE, COOK, RIOT,
      BRAWL, GRILL, BRAISE,
       ROAST, BARBECUE
broiled meat .... BARBECUE
broiler .... PAN, OVEN, CAPON,
    CHICKEN, GRIDIRON
broke: sl. ...... NEEDY, BANKRUPT,
    MONEYLESS, PENNILESS
broken .... TORN, TAMED,
      CRUSHED, SMASHED,
      VIOLATED, BUSTED,
  SPLINTERED, INTERRUPTED
  apart .... RUPTURE
  bone .... FRACTURE
  colloquial .... OUSTED,
    DEPOSED, DISMISSED
  down .... SICK, RUINED,
    CRUSHED, CHATTERED,
  DECREPIT, DESTROYED, SHAKY,
    USELESS, WRECKED
  grain husk .... BRAN
  heart .... ANGUISH, DESPAIR
  ice .... BRASH
  in .... TRAINED

mass of clouds .... RACK
off .... LOOSE, DETACHED
piece .... FRAGMENT
pieces of masonry .... RUBBLE
pieces of pottery .... SHARDS
rainbow .... WINDGALL
spike of grain .... CHOB
stone debris .... RUBBLE
tooth .... DENTAL FRACTURE
wind .... HEAVES
broker .... AGENT, DEALER,
  FACTOR, JOBBER, MIDDLEMAN
  business of .... AGIOTAGE
  order to .... BUY, SELL,
             UNLOAD
  real estate .... REALTOR
brokerage .... AGIOTAGE
  fee .... AGIO
brolly .... UMBRELLA, PARACHUTE
Brom Bones's lack .... HEAD
bromide .... SOP, CALMANT,
  SEDATIVE, TRANQUILIZER
  overuse of .... BROMISM
  side effect of .... TREMOR,
           CONFUSION
bromine .... HALOGEN
bromo .... DOSE
bronchial tube .... TRACHEA,
           WINDPIPE
bronchitis, complication of
          PLEURISY, PNEUMONIA
  form of .... ACUTE, CHRONIC
  remedy .... GRINDELIA
bronc(h)o .... PONY, HORSE,
           MUSTANG
  buster .... RIDER, TAMER,
            COWBOY
Bronte, _____ .... ANNE, EMILY,
         CHARLOTTE
  biographer .... GERIN
  brother .... BRANWELL
  family's native village
                HAWORTH
  husband of Charlotte
               NICHOLLS
  pseudonym of Anne
             ACTON BELL
  pseudonym of Charlotte
           CURRER BELL
  pseudonym of Emily .... ELLIS
               BELL
  work .... JANE EYRE,
    WUTHERING HEIGHTS
bronto as combining form
        THUNDER, HUGENESS
brontosaurus .... DINOSAUR
Bronx .... BOROUGH, COCKTAIL
  cheer ..... BOO, BOOING, HOOT,
           RASPBERRY
  cheerer's feeling .... SCORN,
  DISGUST, DERISION, RIDICULE

bronze ...... TAN, ALLOY, COPPER,
    LATTEN, AENEOUS
  coating/crust of .... PATINA
  coin/Roman .... AES
  "gold" ..... ORMOLU, VERMEIL
  green coating .... VERD,
  PATINA, ANTIQUE, VERDIGRIS
  tool .... CELT
brooch .... PIN, CLIP, OUCH,
        CAMEO, CLASP
brood .... MOPE, SULK, FLOCK,
    HATCH, HOVER, THINK,
    PONDER, LITTER, SIT(ON
  EGGS), COGITATE, FAMILY,
    REFLECT, MEDITATE
  of birds .... COVEY, CLUTCH
  chicks .... HATCH, CLUTCH
  ducks .... TEAM
  family .... CHILDREN
  fish .... SPAWN
  goats/sheep .... FLOCK
  hawks/eagles .... AERIE
  pheasants .... NIDE
  pigs .... FARROW
  over .... FRET, PINE, WORRY,
            GRIEVE
brooder .... HEN, COOP, HENNERY,
          WORRIER
  slang .... SOURPUSS
brooding hen's sound
         CLUCK, CACKLE
brook .... GILL, GHYLL, RUN,
    BEAR, RILL(ET), RUNNEL,
  RIVULET, RUNLET, CREEK,
    ENDURE, STREAM
  trout .... SALTER
Brooke .... SHIELDS
brooklime .... VERONICA
Brooklyn Dodgers' nickname
            SUPERBAS
  Institute .... PRATT
  island .... CONEY
  resident of .... BROOKLYNITE
brookweed .... PIMPERNEL
broom .... BRUSH, CLEANER,
    SHRUB, SWEEP, WHISK
  grass/material .... ZACATON
  made of twigs .... BESOM
broomcorn grain .... HIRSE
broth .... BREE, BROO, SOUP,
  GRUEL, POTAGE, CONSOMME
  cabbage/greens .... KALE
brothel .... KIP, BORDEL(LO),
    WASTE, BAGNIO,
    BAWDYHOUSE
  keeper .... BAWD, MADAM,
          PROCURESS
brother .... FRA, FRIAR, PEER,
  SIBLING, FELLOW, FRATER
  colloquial .... BUB, BROD
  Fritz's .... HANS

brotherhood .... ELKS, UNION, KINSHIP, ORDER, SODALITY, FRATERNITY, ASSOCIATION
brotherly .... FRATERNAL
brougham .... CARRIAGE, LIMOUSINE, AUTOMOBILE
brought aboard ship .... PIPED
about .... CAUSED
up .... BRED, REARED, BROACHED, INTRODUCED
up by hand .... CADE
up without reason .... LUGGED INTO
brouhaha .... ADO, STIR, HUBBUB, UPROAR, COMMOTION
brow .... CREST, BRAE, EDGE, EYEBROW, SUMMIT, FOREHEAD
browbeat .... COW, BULLY, DAUNT, HECTOR, PETRIFY, BAMBOOZLE, SCARE, TERRIFY, INTIMIDATE
brown .... DUN, TAN, BEIGE, ROAST, BISTER, RUSSET, SEPIA, SIENNA, SORREL, TAWNY, TOAST, UMBER
apple .... RUSSET
betty .... (APPLE) PUDDING
coal .... LIGNITE
dark ...... BRUNET, CHOCOLATE
kiwi .... ROA
light .... TAN, ECRU, BEIGE, KHAKI, PONGEE
paper .... KRAFT
pigment .... BISTER, BISTRE, SIENNA, UMBER
quickly .... SEAR
reddish .... RUST, AUBURN, CHESTNUT
reddish horse .... SORREL
seaweed .... KELP
shoes .... TANS, CORDOVAN
skinned people .... THAIS, MALAY(ANS), FILIPINOS, INDONS, CHAMORROS
study ..... REVERIE, DAYDREAM
thrasher .... SONGBIRD
tone .... SEPIA
yellow .... HAZEL, PABLO
Brown, actress .... VANESSA
Bess .... MUSKET
Shirt .... NAZI, HITLERITE
Browne, _____ .... SAM
browned in deep fat .... RISSOLE
brownie .... CAKE, ELF, NIS, FAIRY, GNOME, GOBLIN, DWARF, CAMERA, KOBOLD, PIXIE, GIRL SCOUT
Browning's home in Italy
.... ASOLO
poem .... PARACELSUS

brownish .... DUN
gray .... TAUPE
purple .... PUCE
red .... MAROON, RUFOUS, CORDOVAN, TERRA-COTTA
yellow .... AMBER, BUFF, TAWNY
brownout ...... DIMOUT, DIMMING
brownstone front .... STOOP, FACADE
sign .... TO LET, ROOMS
browntail .... MOTH
browse .... PRY, FEED, SCAN, GLANCE, GRAZE, NIBBLE, CANVASS, LOOK AROUND, EXPLORE
Broz, Josip .... TITO
brucine .... ALKALOID
bruin ...... JAM, BATTER, SHINER, CRUSH, CONTUSE, CONTUSION, DISCOLORATION
bruise ...... JAM, BATTER, SHINER, CRUSH, CONTUSE, CONTUSION, DISCOLORATION
application for/remedy
.... ARNICA, COLD COMPRESS
around the eye .... BLACK EYE
medical term for a
.... ECCHYMOSIS
bruiser .... BOXER, BULLY, ABUSER, BEATER, FIGHTER
bruising implement ...... PESTLE, CLUB, STICK, CUDGEL
bruit ...... TELL, CLAMOR, RUMOR, GOSSIP, REPORT, SPREAD, PUBLISH, BROADCAST
brumal .... COLD, HIEMAL, SLEETY, WINTRY, AUTUMNAL
brume .... FOG, MIST, VAPOR
brummagem: colloq. ...... FAKE, CHEAP, GAUDY
brumous .... FOGGY, MISTY
Brunei's capital .... BANDAR SERI BEGAWAN
city .... SERIA
language ..... MALAY, CHINESE, ENGLISH
monetary unit .... (BRUNEI) DOLLAR
religion ...... ISLAM, BUDDHISM
ruler .... SULTAN
Brunhild (Brunnhilde, Brynhild) .... QUEEN, VALKYRIE
brother-in-law .... SIGURD
fate of .... SLEEP
husband of .... GUNNAR, GUNTHER
mother of .... ERDA
savior of .... SIEGFRIED
sister-in-law of .... GUDRUN, GUTHRUN
Brunn .... BRNO

brunt .... FORCE, SHOCK, IMPACT, STRESS
brush .... COMB, FITCH, GRAZE, PAINT, BROSSE, POLISH, CLEAN, SWEEP, DUSTER, TOUCH, THICKET, SKIRMISH
aside .... SNUB, IGNORE, SLIGHT, SWEEP (OUT)
for sweeping .... BROOM
lightly .... SCUFF, TOUCH UP
like .... SCOPULATE
material .... ZACATON
off .... SNUB, REBUFF, DISMISS(AL), LEAVE OUT IN THE COLD
up .... NEATEN, CLEAN UP, PRACTICE, REHEARSE
brushwood .... BRAKE, COPSE, SCRUB, COPPICE, UNDERBRUSH
fence .... WEIR
brushwork .... PAINTING
brushy .... BUSHY, BRISTLY
brusque .... CURT, BLUFF, BLUNT, GRUFF, NASTY, SHORT, ABRUPT
slang .... HIGH HAT
Brussels carpet .... TOURNAI
is capital of .... BELGIUM
sprouts .... CABBAGE
brut .... DRY
brutal .... FELL, RUDE, CRUEL, FERAL, FERINE, SAVAGE, COARSE, INFERNAL, DEVILISH, RUTHLESS, COLDBLOODED
behavior .... BARBARISM
soldier .... PANDOUR
taskmaster .... LEGREE
brutalize .... MAUL, BATTER, ILL-USE, TERRORIZE
brute ...... BEAST, GROSS, ANIMAL, STUPID, INSENSATE, SCOUNDREL
"_____ **Brute?**" .... ET TU
Brynner, actor .... YUL
bryophyte ...... MOSS, LIVERWORT
bryozoan .... CORAL, HYDRA, POLYP, SEAPEN, SEA ANEMONE, POLYZOAN
Brythonic sea god .... LER
bskt. .... BASKET
bub: colloq. ...... BOY, BROTHER
bubaline .... ANTELOPES, HARTEBEESTS
bubble .... BEAD, BLOB, BOIL, FOAM, GLOBULE
air .... BLEB
archaic .... CHEAT, HUSTLE, SWINDLE
flagrantly .... PERK
maker .... GUM
over .... EXULT, OVERFLOW

up .... BOIL, SPURT
with excitement/joy ..... GUSH,
RAVE, EFFUSE
bubbler of a sort .... BROOK,
(WATER) FOUNTAIN
bubbles, full of .... BUBBLY,
HUBBLY, CHAMPAGNE
sound of .... GURGLING
bubbling .... FIZZY, SPARKLING,
EFFERVESCENT
bubbly: sl. .... CHAMPAGNE
bubonic plague carrier .... RAT,
FLEA
buccal .... MALAR
buccaneer .... GRILL, PIRATE,
CORSAIR, SEA ROBBER
ancient .... VIKING
base, one time .... HAITI
Bucephalus .... STEED,
(WAR)HORSE
Buceresti .... BUCHAREST
Bucharest is capital of
.... ROMANIA
buck .... HARE, HART, STAG, MALE
DEER, BILLY GOAT, BUNNY,
DANDY, SAWHORSE
and wing .... TAP-DANCE
antler of .... ADVANCER
black/Indian .... SASIN
colloquial .... DEFY, FIGHT,
RESIST
four-year-old .... SORE
less than a year old ..... FAWN
_____ (military rating)
.... PRIVATE, SERGEANT
off .... UNSEAT, UPROOT,
DISMOUNT
pass the .... SHUN, EVADE,
SHIRK
red .... PALLAH
slang .... GREEN, DOLLAR
(BILL)
up: colloq. .... BRACE UP,
CHEER UP, ENCOURAGE
water .... KOB
young .... PUP, CUB, KID,
COLT, (SCHOOL)BOY, LAD,
WHELP, LADDIE
Buck, novelist .... PEARL
buckaroo .... RIDER, COWBOY,
TRAINER
buckboard .... CARRIAGE
bucket .... BAIL, KEEL, PAIL,
SCOOP, VESSEL, CANNIKIN
butter/fish .... KIT
coal/mining ..... TUB, SCUTTLE
handle .... BAIL
kick the .... DIE
make of a .... OAKEN
Scottish .... STOUP
Buckeye State .... OHIO

Buckingham .... PALACE
buckish .... FOPPISH
buckle .... BOW, JOIN, KINK,
OUCH, WARP, CATCH, CLASP,
FASTEN, GRAPPLE
ancient .... FIBULA
part of .... TONGUE
under .... BEND, GIVE IN,
YIELD, SUBMIT, COLLAPSE
buckler .... ARMOR, TARGE,
(ARM)SHIELD
bucko .... BULLY
buckra, in Africa .... WHITEMAN
buckram .... RIGID, STIFF,
STARCHED
buckthorn ...... WAHOO, CASCARA
buckwheat tree ...... TITI, TEETEE
weed ...... DOCK, JUNK, JUNCO,
LOCO, TARE
bucolic .... RURAL, RUSTIC,
POETIC, AGRESTIC, ARCADIAN,
GEORGIC, GEOPONIC,
PASTORAL
sound .... BAA, LOW, MOO,
BLEAT, CROW, CACKLE
bud .... BULB, GERM, SHOOT,
SPROUT, BURGEON,
PULLULATE
dried .... CLOVE
for grafting .... (S)CION
large and compact .... HEAD
like outgrowth .... GEMMA
nip in the .... STOP, CHECK,
CURTAIL
of society .... DEB
on a flower stalk .... BULBIL
potato .... EYE
scale .... CATAPHYLL
variation .... SPORT
Bud Fisher's creation .... MUTT,
JEFF, CICERO
Budapest is capital of
.... HUNGARY
Buddha .... FO, GAUTAMA,
TEACHER
cousin of .... ANANDA
Japanese .... AMIDA, AMITA
mother of .... MAYA
tree of .... PIPAL
Buddhism, fate in .... KARMA
form of .... LAMAISM
founder of .... GAUTAMA
hatred .... DOSA
perfect blessedness
.... NIRVANA
religious language .... PALI
Buddhist angel .... DEVA
cause of infinite existence
.... NIDANA
church .... TERA, PAGODA
column/pillar .... LAT

dialect/language/tongue
.... PALI
fate .... KARMA
festival .... BON
final release (from all desires
and passion) .... NIRVANA
gateway .... TORAN
hell .... NARAKA
holy city .... LASSA, LHASA
holy man/title of respect
.... MAHATMA
literature .... SUTRA
monastery .... TERA
monk .... BO, LAMA, BONZE,
TALAPOIN
mound/monument .... STUPA
mountain .... OMEI
novice .... GOYIM
paradise .... JODO
priest .... BO, LAMA, BONZE,
MAHATMA
religious observances
.... DHARMA
saint .... AR(A)HAT
scripture .... SUTRA, SUTTA
sect, Japanese .... ZEN
shrine .... TOPE, STUPA,
DAGOBA
Siamese .... LAO
temple .... PAGODA, VIHARA
buddle .... DRAIN, TROUGH
buddy .... BOY, PAL, CRONY,
COMRADE, COMPANION
British: sl. .... CULLY
buddy .... PALLY
Buddy .... RICH, HOLLY
budge .... FUR, MOVE, ALTER,
SHIFT, POMPOUS, LAMBSKIN
budgerigar .... BUDGIE, PARAKEET
budget .... BAG, POUCH, STOCK,
ESTIMATE, SCHEDULE,
PROPOSAL, APPROPRIATION
anything .... ALLOW,
APPORTION
plan .... FORECAST,
INSTALLMENT
buds, pickled .... CAPERS
put forth .... SHOOT, SPROUT,
BURGEON
bueno: Sp. .... GOOD, VERY WELL,
SOUND, HEALTHY
Buenos Aires is capital of
.... ARGENTINA
buenos dias: Sp. ...... GOOD DAY,
GREETING, GOOD MORNING
buff .... BLOW, SHINE, POLISH,
LEATHER, SPINDLE
colloquial .... FAN, DEVOTEE,
ENTHUSIAST, AFICIONADO
in the .... NUDE, NAKED
the fingernails ...... SMOOTHEN

buffalo .... OX, ARNI, BISON, PERPLEX, CONFOUND
bird .... COWBIRD
bug .... BEETLE
Celebes .... ANOA
crossed with cattle .... CAT(T)ALO
female .... COW
hybrid .... CAT(T)ALO
Philippine .... CARABAO, TIMARAU, TIMARAW
skin ...... BUFF, HIDE, LEATHER
slang .... BULLY, BAMBOOZLE
S. African .... NIARE
wild .... ARNA
Buffalo Bill ...... (WILLIAM) CODY
buffer .... SOCK, BARRIER, BUMPER, CUSHION, ABSORBER
for the floor .... POLISHER
buffet .... BLOW, TOSS, SLAP, PUNCH, TABLE, COUNTER, CREDENZA, SIDEBOARD
meals .... SPREADS, SMORGASBORD
buffeted: poetic .... TOST
bufflehead .... DUCK, BUTTERBALL
buffo .... CLOWN, COMIC, OPERA SINGER
voice of a .... BASS
buffoon ...... FOOL, ZANY, CLOWN, DROLL, JESTER, MIME(R), PRANKSTER, (MERRY)ANDREW, PUNCH, COMEDIAN, HARLEQUIN, PUNCHINELLO
buffoonery ...... COMEDY, FROLIC, CLOWNING, DROLLERY, SLAPSTICK
bufo: Latin .... TOAD
bug .... FLY, NIT, GERM, GNAT, MITE, CIMEX, BEETLE, INSECT, CONENOSE, HOBGOBLIN
living on other insects .... ASSASSIN
river .... NAREW
slang .... TAP, WIRE, FLAW, ANGER, ANNOY, ADDICT, BOTHER, DEFECT, DEVOTEE, ENTHUSIAST, MICROPHONE
spray .... REPELLANT
with built-in light ..... FIREFLY
with sucking beak .... ASSASSIN
bugaboo .... BUGBEAR, NIGHTMARE, MUMBO-JUMBO, HEEBIE-JEEBIES, SCARECROW
African .... GOGO, BOGIE
bugbear ...... BOGY, (HOB)GOBLIN
of a kind .... OGRE, DEMON
bugger ...... CHAP, LOUSE, CREEP, STINKER, SODOMITE
buggy .... CAR, AUTO, CART, PRAM, SHAY, CHAISE, CARRIAGE, PERAMBULATOR
bughouse: sl. .... ASYLUM, MADHOUSE, NUTHOUSE
bugle ...... BEAD, HORN, CLARION, MINT PLANT, BOOTS AND SADDLES
call ...... TAPS, RALLY, SIGNAL, RETREAT, ASSEMBLY, TANTARA, TAT(T)OO, REVEILLE
carabao horn .... TAMBULI
note .... TIRALEE
signal .... TATTOO
sound .... BLARE
yellow .... IVA
bugloss .... ANCHUSA
bugs: sl. .... DIPPY, LOONY, CRAZY, NUTTY, INSANE
buhr .... WHETSTONE
build .... BODY, FORM, MAKE, REAR, ERECT, CONSTRUCT, RAISE, STATURE, PHYSIQUE
a lawn .... SOD
up: colloq. .... PLUG, PRAISE, PUBLICITY
builder .... MAKER, PRODUCER, CRAFTSMAN
kind of .... ENGINEER, ARCHITECT, STONEMASON, LANDSCAPER, STONECUTTER
knot of .... CLOVEHITCH
building .... PILE, EDIFICE, ERECTION, STRUCTURE
caretaker .... JANITOR, CONCIERGE, CUSTODIAN
crowded .... WARREN
cylindrical .... SILO
behind a big one .... BACKHOUSE
external corner of .... QUOIN
for abode ...... HOUSE, CONDO, TOWN-HOUSE, APARTMENT, CONDOMINIUM
bowling ..... LANES, ALLEYS
coed's residence (in school campus) .... DORM, DORMITORY
exhibits .... MUSEUM, ARCHIVES, PAVILION
famous dead persons .... PANTHEON
fodder .... SILO
fruit-growing .... GRAPERY
gambling .... CASINO
grains .... GRANARY, ELEVATOR
lodging/residential .... HOTEL, HOSTELRY
musical performances .... MUSIC HALL, THEATER, OPERA HOUSE, AUDITORIUM
races/games .... HIPPODROME
sociality .... CLUBHOUSE
storage of merchandise .... WAREHOUSE
worship .... CHAPEL, CHURCH, TEMPLE, CATHEDRAL, SYNAGOGUE
high-rise/tall .... TOWER, PYRAMID, SKYSCRAPER
inscription on .... EPIGRAPH
logger's .... SAWMILL
material .... ADOBE, BRICK, WOOD, STAFF, STONE, CEMENT, LUMBER, MARBLE, MORTAR, CONCRETE
projecting ornament .... GARGOYLE
projection .... BAY, APSE
roadside, for travelers .... MOTEL, MOTOR-COURT
round .... ROTUNDA
site .... LOT, STEADING
U.S. Department of Defense .... PENTAGON
wing .... BAY, ELL, ANNEX
built-in bed .... BUNK, BERTH
Bukhara product .... RUG
bulb .... BUD, LEEK, SEGO, ONION, GARLIC, HYACINTH
edible .... CAMAS(S)
glass .... AMPOULE
like root .... TUBEROSE
like stem, plant with .... CORM, TUBER, CROCUS
lily .... SEGO, CAMAS
lily, dried .... SQUILL
plant .... SEGO, TULIP
segment .... CLOVE
Bulba, ____ .... TARAS
bulbous plant .... GARLIC, TUBEROSE
bulbul .... SONGBIRD, NIGHTINGALE
Bulgarian .... SLAV, CHUVASH
cape .... EMINE, KALIAKRA
capital .... SOFIA
city ..... RUSE, VARNA, PERNIK, SHUMEN, SLIVEN, VIDIN, DOBRICH, GABROVO, YAMBOL, PLOVDIV, KHASKOVO
coin/money .... LEV, LEW, DINAR, STOTINKA
czar/tsar .... BORIS
king .... SIMEON
mountain .... RUJEN, MIDZHUR, MUSALA
mountains .... BALKAN
Moslem .... POMAK
president .... ZHIVKOV
queen .... MARGARITA
river ..... VIT, MESTA, DANUBE,

STRUMA, TIMOK, MARITSA
sea .... BLACK
seaport .... VARNA
weight .... OKA, OKE
bulge .... BAG, HUMP, LUMP,
BLOAT, FLARE, PROTRUDE,
PROJECTION, SWELL(ING)
of belly: sl. ...... BAY WINDOW
of skull .... INION
bulging .... TUMID, TOROSE,
TOROUS, BELLIED, BLOATED,
GIBBOUS, TUBEROUS
bulimia, in medicine
.... HUNGER, DIETING
bulk .... SIZE, MASS, AMOUNT,
TOTAL, VOLUME, EXPANSE,
MAJORITY, QUANTITY,
AGGREGATE
additive .... FILLER
bulkhead .... WALL, PARTITION,
EMBANKMENT
bulky .... BIG, HEFTY, LARGE,
MASSY, MASSIVE
boat .... ARK
bull .... LIE, MALE, SEAL, TORO,
STEER, TAURO, TAURUS
castrated .... BULLOCK
cry .... BELLOW
of/like a .... TAURIN(E)
of Hercules .... CRETAN
of myth .... MINATOUR
sacred: Egypt. .... APIS
shoot the: sl. .... CHAT
slang .... COP, CRAP,
MALARKEY, NONSENSE, JOHN
LAW, POLICEMAN
young .... STOT, BULLOCK
Bull, John .... ENGLAND
bulla .... BLEB, BLAIN, BLISTER,
PUSTULE, VESICLE
bullace .... PLUM, TREE
bullbat .... NIGHTHAWK
bulldog .... PUG, MASTIFF,
REVOLVER
color .... BRINDLE
soft-nosed .... DUMDUM
trait ...... COURAGE, BOLDNESS,
DARING, DEFIANCE, TENACITY
bulldogging place .... RODEO
"Bulldogs" .... ELIS
bulldoze .... RAZE, BULLY, LEVEL,
FORCE, COERCE, FLATTEN,
BROWBEAT, FRIGHTEN
bullet .... BALL, SHOT, LEAD,
SLUG, PELLET, MISSILE
charge container
.... CARTRIDGE
kind of ...... DUMDUM, TRACER
metal covering .... JACKET
size .... CALIBER
bulletin ...... REPORT, STATEMENT,

NEWS(LETTER), PUBLICATION
kind of .... MEDICAL,
WEATHER
bulletproof shield
.... MANT(E)LET
bullets, for short .... AMMO
bullfight cheer .... OLE
bullfighter .... MATADOR,
PICADOR, TOREADOR
assistant .... PICADOR
mantle .... CAPA
on foot .... TORERO
queue of .... COLETA
bullfighting dart .... BANDERILLA
participant ...... BANDERILLERO
bullfinch .... OLP, HEDGE,
REDBIRD, SONGBIRD
bullfrog's cry .... BOOM
bullhead .... FISH, CATFISH,
SCULPIN
bullheaded .... STUBBORN,
HEADSTRONG
animal, of a sort .... MULE
bullion before coinage
.... INGOT, BAR, GOLD,
BILLOT, SILVER
bullish .... OPTIMISTIC
time .... RISE
Bullitt director .... YATES
bullock .... OX, STEER, STIRK
bull's-eye .... CENTER, TARGET
circle next to .... INNER
bully .... BUCKO, PIMP, THUG,
HUFF, BRUISER, BROWBEAT,
TYRANT, HECTOR, CORNED
BEEF, BRAWLER, BULLDOZE,
BAMBOOZLE
colloquial .... FINE, GOOD,
WELL DONE
tree .... BALATA
bulrush .... TULE, PAPYRUS
British .... CATTAIL
bulwark .... WALL, SCONCE,
DEFENSE, RAMPART,
EARTHWORK, BREAKWATER,
PROTECTION
bum .... HOBO, LOAF, IDLER,
LOAFER, SPONGER, VAGRANT
a ride .... HITCH(HIKE)
ambulant .... VAGRANT
British: sl. .... BUTTOCKS
check, describing one
.... BOUNCING
____ (frame-up) .... RAP
bumble .... BLUNDER
bumblebee .... DOR
bump .... JOLT, LUMP, NODE,
STUB, JOSTLE, COLLIDE,
KNOCK, STRIKE, SWELLING
off: sl. .... KILL, MURDER
slang .... REPLACE

bumper .... TOAST, BARRIER,
BRIMMER
auto .... GUARD
crop .... LARGE, ABUNDANT
sticker .... SLOGAN
bum(p)kin .... CLOD, LOUT, RUBE,
YAHOO, YOKEL
ship's .... BOOM, SPAR
bumpkins .... CAVES
bumptious ...... PROUD, PUSHING,
ARROGANT, CONCEITED
bumpy .... JERKY, ROUGH,
JOLTING, TURBULENT
bun .... CHIGNON, KNOT, LOAF,
ROLL
bunch .... LOT, CYME, TUFT,
CROWD, GROUP, BUNDLE,
CLUSTER, COLLECTION
grass .... STIPA
of branches .... COMA
of grapes .... BOTRYOID
of sheaves ...... SHOCK, SHOOK
small .... WISP
bunchberry .... DOGWOOD
bunco: colloq. .... CHEAT, CROOK,
CON MAN, HUSTLER,
SWINDLER
buncombe .... BUNK, HUMBUG,
BOMBAST, TWADDLE,
MALARKEY
bund .... LEAGUE, CONFEDERATION
Oriental .... QUAY,
EMBANKMENT
bundle .... BALE, PACK, BUNCH,
SHEAF, GROUP, GATHER,
PACKET, PARCEL, PACKAGE
of fibers, leaves ...... FASCICLE
of hay/straw ...... WASE, TRUSS
of joy: colloq. .... BABY
of rods .... FASCES
of sheaves of grain
.... SHOCK, STOOK
of sticks/twigs .... FAGOT,
FASCINE
slang .... RICHES, WEALTH
small .... FASCICLE
bundling device .... BALER
bung .... CORK, PLUG, CLOSE,
STOPPER
slang .... BRUISE, DAMAGE
bungalow .... COTTAGE
bungle .... BOTCH, MESS (UP),
SPOIL, LOUSE (UP), FOOZLE,
FUMBLE, BLUNDER, FLOUNDER
a golf stroke .... DUB
a play .... MUFF
slang .... BOLLIX
bungling .... MALADROIT
bunion .... BURSA
bunk .... BED, COT, BERTH, SLEEP
British: sl. .... DOSS

slang .... HOKUM, HOOEY,
HUMBUG, EYEWASH,
BUNCOMBE, BOSH, TWADDLE,
NONSENSE
bunker ...... BIN, TANK, SANDTRAP
bunko. See **bunco**
bunny .... RABBIT
Playboy's .... HOSTESS
tail .... SCUT
time .... EASTER
bunt ...... TAP, BAT, SMUT, SHOVE
with horn: Brit. .... BUTT,
STRIKE
bunting .... FLAG, PENNANT, BIRD,
FINCH, ORTOLAN, ETAMINE,
STREAMER
migratory .... DICKCISSEL
Bunyan's ox .... BABE
buoy .... BOB, DAN, BEACON,
MARKER, FLOAT, MAKE FAST,
SIGNAL, SPEED-UP
for mooring boat ..... DOLPHIN
type .... CAN, BELL, SPAR,
WHISTLE
up .... BOOST, INSPIRE,
SUSTAIN, ENCOURAGE
buoyancy .... BOUNCE, GAIETY,
LEVITY, LIGHTNESS, FLOTAGE,
RESILIENCE
buoyant .... LIGHT, BOUNCY,
ELASTIC, HOPEFUL, SPRINGY
bur .... WEED, SEEDCASE
buran .... WINDSTORM
burble .... BUBBLE, GURGLE
burbot ...... CUSK, LING, MARIA
burd: obs. .... LADY
burden .... LOAD, CHARGE,
CUMBER, INCUBUS, PRESSURE,
OPPRESS, WEIGHT, WEIGH
DOWN
bearer .... AMASA, ATLAS,
PORTER
beast of .... ASS, MULE,
BURRO, CAMEL, DONKEY
of a song .... REFRAIN
of proof .... ONUS, EVIDENCE
squaw's .... PAPOOSE
burdened .... TAXED
burdensome .... HEAVY,
WEIGHTY, CUMBERSOME,
ONEROUS, OPPRESSIVE
burdock .... BURR, CLITE,
COCKLEBUR
bureau ...... DESK, CHEST, OFFICE,
DRESSER, BRANCH, SECTION,
HIGHBOY, CHIFFONIER
top cover .... SCARF
bureaucracy .... BODY POLITIC,
OFFICIALDOM, OFFICIOUSNESS
petty .... BEADLEDOM
bureaucratic failing: colloq.

.... RED TAPE
burg .... CITY, TOWN, VILLAGE
lord of .... BURGRAVE
burgeon ...... BUD, GROW, SPROUT
in a way .... TRIPLE,
MUSHROOM
burgess .... CITIZEN, FREEMAN
Burgess's invention .... GOOP
burgh .... TOWN, BOROUGH
burglar .... THIEF, ROBBER,
HOUSE-BREAKER
hazard of .... ALARM BELL
loot of .... SWAG
slang .... YEGG
burgomaster .... GULL, MAYOR
burgonet .... HELMET, MORION
burgoo .... SCUP, GRUEL,
BARBECUE, PORRIDGE
Burgundy, kingdom of .... ARLES
wine .... CHABLIS
burial .... INTERMENT, SEPULTURE,
INHUMATION
box ...... BIER, CASKET, COFFIN
clothes .... SHROUD,
CEREMENT, CERECLOTH
grave marker ...... HEADSTONE,
TABLET, TOMBSTONE
ground for the poor
.... POTTER'S FIELD
heap/mound .... BARROW,
TUMULUS
pertaining to .... FUNERAL,
FUNERARY
pile .... PYRE
place .... PIT, TOMB, CRYPT,
CATACOMB, CEMETERY,
MAUSOLEUM, SEPULCHER,
GRAVE(YARD)
procession .... CORTEGE
vault .... SEPULTURE
burin .... GRAVER
like tool .... CHISEL
burke .... MURDER, SUPPRESS,
SUFFOCATE
Burke's subject .... PEERAGE
Burkitt's tumor ...... LYMPHOMA
burl .... KNOT, VENEER
Burl, actor .... IVES
burlesque .... FARCE, COMEDY,
PARODY, CARICATURE,
VAUDEVILLE
number ...... SKIT, STRIP-TEASE
burley .... TOBACCO
burly ...... GROSS, HEAVY, HUSKY,
MUSCULAR
Burma Road's other name
.... (THE) HUMP
terminus .... LASHIO
Burmese bay .... COMBERMERE
Buddhist .... MON, PROME
cape .... NEGRAIS

capital .... RANGOON
capital, former .... AVA
channel .... COCO, HEYWOOD
chief .... BO(H)
city/town .... MANDALAY,
AKYAB, CHAUK, BASSEIN,
INSEIN, MERGUI, MOULMEIN,
PYE, HENZADA, PAKOKKU,
LASHIO, TAVOY, SITTWE,
THATON, TOUNGOO, WAKEMA
dagger .... DAH, DOW
demon .... NAT
distinguished .... U THANT
district .... PROME
division .... PEGU, RANGOON,
SAGAING, IRRAWADY,
MANDALAY
ethnic group .... MONS, CHINS,
NAGAS, KARENS, KACHINS
garment/sarong .... LONGYI
gate .... TORAN
gibbon .... LAR
girl .... MIMA
governor .... WUN, WOON
gulf .... MARTABAN
hill .... CHIN, NAGA, KACHIN
hillman/Mongol .... LAI
island ...... RAMREE, CHEDUBA,
KALEGAUK, TENASSERIM
knife .... DOW, KAH, KHAO
lake .... INLE, INDAWGYI
language .... CHIN, BURMESE,
SHAN, KAREN, KAYAH, KACHIN
measure .... DHA, BYEE, SEIT
measure, distance .... TAUN
monetary unit .... KYAT
monk .... BO
mountain .... LOILENG,
VICTORIA, HKAKABO RAZI,
KHAO LUANG
mountain range .... ARAKAN
musical instrument ...... TURR,
TORAN
native .... WA, LAI, WAS,
KADU, KUKI, PEGUAN
pagoda .... PHAYA
pass .... AMYA, CHAUKAN,
PANGSAU, THREE PAGODAS
peasant .... TAO
premier/statesman .... U NU
river .... MU, MON, MEKONG,
SALWEEN, KALADAN,
MANIPUR, ATARAN, SITTANG,
IRRAWADDY
robber .... DACOIT
shelter .... ZAYAT
shrimp .... NAPEE
spirit .... NAT
tree .... ACLE
tribe .... TAI, SHAN
weight .... VIS(S), KYAT,

RUAY, TICAL

burn .... FIRE, CHAR, BLAZE,
GLOW, SEAR, CONSUME,
SCORCH, DESTROY, OXIDIZE
a dead body to ashes
.... CREMATE
cause to .... IGNITE
degree of .... FIRST, SECOND,
THIRD
down .... RAZE
hair ends .... SINGE
incense .... CENSE
mark .... ESCHAR
mark of sun ..... TAN, SUNTAN
mark with hot iron .... BRAND
nap of cloth/slightly .... SINGE
Scottish .... STREAM
the midnight oil .... BONE,
CRAM, LUCUBRATE
the road .... RACE, BARREL,
SPEED (UP)
to stop infection
.... CAUTERIZE
treatment of ...... ANTIBIOTICS,
SKIN-GRAFTING
unsteadily .... FLICKER
up: colloq. .... FUME, IRK,
ANGER, ENRAGE, SEETHE,
IRRITATE
with hot fluid/steam
.... SCALD
with hot iron/needle
.... BRAND, CAUTERIZE
without flame .... SMO(U)LDER
burned up: sl. .... HURT, SORE,
ANGRY
burner .... ARGAND, BUNSEN,
FURNACE, FIREPLACE,
CREMATORY, INCINERATOR
burning .... AFIRE, EAGER,
BOILING, ABLAZE, AFLAME,
FERVENT, FEVERISH
bush ...... WAHOO, FRAXINELLA
coal container .... BRASIER,
BRAZIER
container for a material
.... SMUDGE POT
container for incense
.... CENSER
for gain/malicious ...... ARSON
glass .... LENS
mountain .... VOLCANO
process .... COMBUSTION
sensation .... HEAT,
CAUSALGIA
stick .... BRAND
with anger .... WILD, IRATE,
RABID, FURIOUS
with desire .... PASSIONATE
woodpile outdoors
.... BONFIRE, CAMPFIRE

vapor from .... FUME, SMOKE
burnish .... SHINE, POLISH,
FURBISH
an error/fault .... GLOSS
Burns's negatives .... NAES
sweetheart .... (HIGHLAND)
MARY
burnsides .... MUTTON CHOPS,
BEARD, WHISKERS
burnt .... ADUST
sugar .... CARAMEL
burp: sl. .... BELCH
burr .... POD, DRILL, ROUGH
EDGE, SEEDCASE
in wood .... KNAR
plant/weed .... TEASEL,
BURDOCK, THISTLE,
COCKLEBUR
Burr, _____ .... AARON, RAYMOND
burro .... ASS, DONKEY
female .... MARE
burrow .... DIG, HOLE, TUNNEL
burrowing animal .... HARE,
MOLE, BROCK, RATEL,
BADGER, GERBIL(LE), TELEDU,
WOMBAT, ARMADILLO
crustacean .... SQUILL(A)
mammal of S. Africa
.... SURICATE
mollusk .... PIDDOCK
rodent .... VOLE
tortoise .... GOPHER
Burrows of Broadway .... ABE
Burr's daughter .... THEO
burry .... PRICKLY
bursa .... SAC, POUCH
inflammation of a
.... BURSITIS
near the toe .... BUNION
operation to remove
.... BURSECTOMY
bursal .... FISCAL
bursar .... TREASURER
burse .... PURSE
Scottish .... SCHOLARSHIP
bursitis, form of .... STUDENT'S
ELBOW, CLERGYMAN'S KNEE,
HOUSEMAID'S KNEE
treatment of .... DRAINAGE,
ICEPACK, ANTIBIOTICS
burst .... BUST, REND, BULGE,
BREACH, BREAK OPEN, SPLIT,
EXPLODE, RUPTURE
forth .... ERUPT
into pieces suddenly
.... SHATTER
of anger .... HUFF
of artillery, as a salute
.... SALVO
of cheers .... OVATION, SALVO,
APPLAUSE

of energy .... RALLY, SPASM,
SPURT
of lightning .... FLASH
of thunder .... CLAP
open .... POP
open, as a seedpod
.... DEHISCE
sudden .... GUST
bursting tire .... BLOW-OUT
Burundi capital ...... BUJUMBURA
city/town ...... BURURI, GITEGA
king .... (MWAMI)
MWAMBUTSA
lake .... TANGANYIKA
language .... KIRUNDI, FRENCH,
SWAHILI
money .... FRANC, CENTIME
native .... BANTU, PYGMY,
BAHUTU, WATUSI
river .... RUZIZI
tribe .... BAHUTU, WATUTSI
bury .... SINK, INTER, INURN,
INHUME, IMMERSE, CONCEAL,
COVER, SEPULCHER
the hatchet .... RECONCILE
to hoard/hide .... CACHE
bus .... JITNEY, (MOTOR)COACH,
VEHICLE, CONVEYANCE
colloquial .... FAMILY CAR,
AUTO(MOBILE)
for excursion ..... CHARABANC,
TOURING CAR
busby .... HAT
wearer .... HUSSAR
bush .... TOD, TAIL, BRIER, HEDGE,
SHRUB, THICKET
beat around the .... HINT,
FENCE, QUIBBLE, MISLEAD
burning .... WAHOO
league .... MINORS
leaguer .... SECOND-RATER,
SECOND-STRINGER
slang .... BEARD
bushbuck .... ANTELOPE
bushed .... TIRED, SPENT,
FATIGUED, DRAINED,
EXHAUSTED
bushel, in tailoring .... ALTER,
MEND
$1/8$ of .... GALLON
$1/4$ of .... PECK
bushelman .... TAILOR
bushels, $11^{2}/_{3}$ .... HOMER
32 or 36 .... CHALDRON
bushes, stunted .... SCRUB
bushing .... LINING
bushman .... PYGMY, NEGRILLO
bushmaster .... SNAKE, VIPER
bushranger .... HIGHWAYMAN
bushwhack .... AMBUSH
bushwhacker .... RAIDER,

GUERRILLA,
(BACK)WOODSMAN,
UNDERGROUND RESISTANCE
bushy .... DENSE, HAIRY, SHAGGY,
WOODED
clump .... TOD
tail .... BRUSH
business .... TASK, WORK, TRADE,
AFFAIR, VENTURE,
COMMERCE, INDUSTRY,
OCCUPATION, ENTERPRISE,
PROFESSION
abbreviation ..... INC, LTD, CO,
CORP
agent .... BROKER, SYNDIC,
SALESMAN, COMPRADOR
association .... SYNDICATE,
PARTNERSHIP
burden .... PAYLOAD
cartel .... TRUST, ALLIANCE,
SYNDICATE
connection .... CONTACT
cycle, part of .... BOOM,
SLUMP, SETBACK, FAILURE,
PEAK, DEPRESSION,
PROSPERITY
establishment .... BANK, MART,
FIRM, STORE, COMPANY, SHOP,
MARKET, CORPORATION
event ..... BOOM, DEAL, SLUMP,
MERGER, TAKE-OVER,
GROWTH, STRIKE, RECESSION
firm .... HOUSE
location .... SITE, STAND
monopoly .... CARTEL,
CONTROL, CORNER
offshoot .... FRANCHISE
schedule .... AGENDA, PLAN,
PROGRAM
secrets, spy on .... KEEK
slump .... RECESSION, SLOW-
DOWN, DEPRESSION
solicitor ...... BIDDER, BARKER,
RUNNER
transaction .... DEAL,
BARGAIN, CONTRACT
upsurge .... BOOM, FLOURISH
businessman .... BANKER,
BROKER, MANAGER, TRADER,
MERCHANT, DEALER,
FINANCIER, EXECUTIVE
conventional .... BABBITT
Latin of .... INRE
one kind of .... ENTREPRENEUR
busk .... READY, OUTFIT, PREPARE
busker .... MINSTREL
buskin .... BOOT, DRAMA,
TRAGEDY
busline, end of .... TERMINUS
buss .... KISS
colloquial .... PECK, SMACK

slang .... SMOOCH
bust .... BOSOM, CHEST, BREAK,
BURST, BREAST
colloquial .... FLING, SPREE,
FAILURE
figure ...... STATUE, STATUETTE
form/shape .... TAILLE
in .... INTRUDE
in business .... COLLAPSE,
FOLD UP, GO BANKRUPT
slang ..... BOOBS, ARREST, HIT,
BLOW, PUNCH, DEMOTE
stock market .... CRASH
bustard .... BIRD, OTIS, TARDA
busted .... BEAT, BANKRUPT,
(FLAT) BROKE
from jail .... SPRUNG
buster of a kind .... TRUST
BREAKER
slang .... BOY
Buster's friend .... TIGE
bustle .... ADO, TO-DO, FUSS, STIR,
HASTE, HURRY, RUSTLE,
FLURRY, POTHER
colloquial .... HOOPLA
companion of .... HUSTLE
of woman's dress .... BOW,
PADDING
busy .... AT IT, ACTIVE, ENGAGED,
EMPLOYED, OCCUPIED, ASTIR,
WORKING, DILIGENT,
ENGROSSED, ASSIDUOUS
creature .... ANT, BEE, OTTER
place .... HIVE
sound .... HUM
busybody .... GOSSIP, KIBITZER,
MEDDLER, QUIDNUNC,
SNOOP(ER), EAVESDROPPER
but .... YET, EVEN, SAVE, STILL,
EXCEPT(ING), ALTHOUGH,
MERELY, UNLESS, HOWEVER
Scottish .... OUTER, OUTSIDE,
OUTER ROOM
butch .... TOMBOY
butcher ...... KILL, CUT UP, MEAT-
CUTTER, MEAT-SELLER,
BOTCH, SPOIL, SLAUGHTER
bird .... SHRIKE
hook of .... GAFF, GAMBREL
shop of .... SHAMBLES
tool of .... CLEAVER, BONER,
KNIFE, STEEL
butler .... STEWARD, MAJORDOMO,
MAITRE D'HOTEL
concern of .... WINE CELLAR,
PANTRY, SILVER(WARE)
butt .... RAM, TUP, ABUT, CASK,
PUSH, STRIKE, TARGET,
BARREL, LAUGHINGSTOCK
fish .... TURBOT, HALIBUT
in .... MEDDLE, INTRUDE,

INTERFERE, INTERVENE
of cigar(ette) .... STUB
of criticism usually
.... SCAPEGOAT
of goat .... RAM
of joke, figuratively ...... GOAT
of many jokes .... MOTHER-IN-
LAW
of tree .... STUMP
of whip .... CROP
slang .... BUTTOCKS,
CIGARET(TE)
butte .... HILL, MESA, MOUND
butter .... OIL, GHEE, CREAM,
SPREAD
and-eggs .... PLANT,
TOADFLAX
and-flour mix .... ROUX
bucket .... KIT
buffalo milk .... GHEE
color for .... ANATTO,
AN(N)ATTO
India .... GHI, GHEE
like .... OLEO, BUTTERINE,
MARGARINE, BUTYRACEOUS
lump/portion of .... PAT
making contrivance .... CHURN
roll .... BRIOCHE
substitute .... OLEO, SUINE,
BUTTERINE, MARGARINE
tree .... SHEA
tub .... KIT, CHURN, FIRKIN
up .... FLATTER
butterball .... BUFFLEHEAD
slang .... FATSO, FATTY
butterbean .... LIMA
buttercup .... CROWTOE,
GOLDILOCKS, GOLDTHREAD,
GOLDEN SEAL
buttered crumbs/crust
.... GRATIN
butterfingers .... CLUMSY,
DUFFER, FUMBLER, GOOFER,
MUFFER
butterfish .... GUNNEL
butterflies, order of
.... LEPIDOPTERA
butterfly .... IO, KIHO, SATYR,
ADMIRAL, FRENATE,
GRAYLING, MONARCH,
FRITILLARY, NYMPHALID,
SKIPPER, VANESSA, TROILUS,
VICEROY, SWALLOWTAIL
admiral .... ATALANTA
combining form .... CALIGO
fish .... PARU, BLENNY
large .... IDALIA
larva .... CATERPILLAR
lily .... SEGO
named after goddess
.... DIANA, APHRODITE

peacock .... IO
proboscis/tongue-like organ
.... LINGUA
small .... BLUE
butternut .... SOUARI
buttery .... LARDER, PANTRY,
SPENCE, STOREROOM
butting animal .... RAM, GOAT,
CARABAO
buttinsky .... INTRUDER, MEDDLER
buttocks .... ASS, BUM, ARSE,
BUTT, NATES, PRAT, BREECH,
SEAT, RUMP, BEHIND,
DERRIERE, HIPS, FUNDAMENT,
POSTERIOR
button .... KNOB, KNOP, STUD,
DISK, LOOP, EMBLEM, FASTEN
cover .... FLY, FLAP
fencing sword .... FOIL
the lips .... SHUT UP
buttonhole .... HOLD, SLIT,
DETAIN, EYELET
flower .... GARDENIA,
CARNATION
buttonholer .... BORE
buttons .... BELLBOY, (HOTEL)
PAGE
and ____ .... BOWS
Buttons, actor .... RED
buttonwood .... SYCAMORE
buttress .... PIER, PROP, STAY,
BRACE, BOLSTER, SUPPORT
butts and bounds
.... BOUNDARIES
buxom .... CURVY, JOLLY, JOVIAL,
MERRY, PLUMP, COMELY,
ENDOWED, SHAPELY,
HEALTHY
buy .... ACQUIRE, PROCURE,
SPEND, PURCHASE
at one's risk .... CAVEAT
EMPTOR
back .... REDEEM
good: colloq. .... BARGAIN,
(DIRT)CHEAP
in/into .... INVEST

off .... BRIBE
up .... CORNER, MONOPOLIZE
what one is saying, as gospel
truth .... TRUST, BELIEVE,
SWALLOW
buyer .... EMPTOR, VENDEE,
BROWSER, CONSUMER,
CUSTOMER, AGENT, SHOPPER,
PURCHASER
and seller .... DEALER, JOBBER,
TRADER, IMPORTER, RETAILER,
WHOLESALER
and seller of stolen goods
.... FENCE, BOOTLEGGER
of illegal drugs .... (DRUG)
DEALER, (DRUG) PUSHER
of office .... BARRATER
of old horses .... KNACKER
of smuggled contraband
.... BLACK-MARKETEER
buyers' strike .... BOYCOTT
buying to gain monopoly
.... COEMPTION
buzz .... HUM, DRONE, GOSSIP,
CALL, SIGNAL, WHIRR,
WHISPER
bomb: Ger. .... ROBOT
colloquial .... TELEPHONE
off! .... SCRAM
buzzard ...... TESA, HAWK, BUTEO,
OSPREY, FALCON,
COCKCHAFER, PREYER,
HARRIER, DUCKHAWK
honey .... BEEHAWK
moor .... HARPY
turkey .... VULTURE
buzzer signal .... CALL, ALARM
buzzing sound ...... HUM, DRONE
by .... AT, PER, NEAR, ASIDE,
BESIDE, BEYOND, ALONGSIDE,
PAST, THROUGH
a whisker .... BARELY
and by .... ANON, SOON,
SHORTLY
birth .... NEE, NATAL
hand .... PERSONAL

hand: prefix .... MANU
means of .... PER, THROUGH
pass .... SHUNT, DETOUR,
SWERVE, EVADE, DEVIATE,
SHIFT, AVOID, CIRCUIT
right .... DEJURE
the day .... PER DIEM
way of .... VIA, THROUGH
word of mouth .... ORAL,
PAROL, VERBAL
work .... HOBBY, SIDELINE,
AVOCATION
byblow .... BASTARD
bye .... RUN, ODD MAN,
INCIDENTAL
bye .... TATA, GOODBYE
Byelorussian city .... MOGILEV
bygone .... PAST
byname .... SURNAME, NICKNAME
byplay .... ADLIB
byre .... COWBARN
product .... MILK
Byron, name of .... NOEL,
GEORGE, GORDON
poem by .... BEPPO
Byronic .... PROUD, IRONIC,
CYNICAL, ROMANTIC
byssus .... FLAX, LINEN
bystander .... ONLOOKER,
WITNESS, SPECTATOR
bystreet .... ALLEY
byway/bypath ...... LANE, ALLEY,
SIDEROAD, SIDESTREET
byword .... ADAGE, MAXIM,
SAYING, PROVERB
Byzantine coin .... BEZANT
emperor .... ALEXIUS,
HERACLIUS
emperor's scepter ..... FERULA
empress .... ZOE
logothete, so-called
.... (WOODROW) WILSON
works of art .... ICONS
Byzantium capital .... ISTANBUL,
CONSTANTINOPLE

C

C grade in school ...... AVERAGE,
MEDIOCRE
Greek .... GAMMA
in a sequence group .... THIRD
in music .... KEYNOTE
in quality .... PASSABLE, THIRD
CLASS
letter .... CEE
mark under .... CEDILLA

Roman numeral .... HUNDRED,
100, CENTURY
symbol for .... CONSTANT
Ca, in chemistry .... CALCIUM
Caaba .... SHRINE
site .... MECCA
camma .... ASSE, FOX
cab .... TAXI, FIACRE, HACKNEY,
CALASH, HANSOM, CARRIAGE

driver .... HACK, CABBIE,
CABETTE
CAB subjects .... AIRLINES
cabal .... PLOT, JUNTA, JUNTO,
CLIQUE, INTRIGUE, FACTION,
SCHEME, CONSPIRACY
man .... PLOTTER
cabala ...... MYSTERY, OCCULTISM
cabalist .... MYSTIC

cabalistic ...... SECRET, ESOTERIC, MYSTERIOUS
caballero ...... KNIGHT, CAVALIER, GENTLEMAN, HORSEMAN
cabana ...... HUT, CABIN, BAGNIO, COTTAGE, BATHHOUSE
cabaret .... CAFE, SALOON, TAVERN, BARROOM, TAPROOM, NIGHTCLUB, COCKTAIL LOUNGE
slang .... BLIND PIG, HONKY-TONK, SPEAKEASY
cabbage ...... KAIL, KALE, SAVOY, OXHEART, COLE(WORT), KOHLRABI, VEGETABLE
broth .... KALE
fermented .... SAUERKRAUT
garden .... KALEYARD
plant like .... COLE
salad/shredded .... SLAW, COLE SLAW
tree .... PALM, YABA, PALMETTO
variety .... CAULIFLOWER
cabby .... HACK, CABBIE, CAB-DRIVER, TAXI-DRIVER
caber .... BEAM, POLE
cabin .... HUT, SHED, SHACK, CABANA, COTTAGE, LOGHOUSE
baloon/dirigible ...... GONDOLA
boy .... DECKHAND, ATTENDANT
cruiser .... SPEEDBOAT
ship's main .... SALON, SALOON, STATEROOM
ship's upper .... DECKHOUSE
Swiss .... CHALET
cabinet .... BOX, BUHL, CASE, CHEST, BUREAU, CLOSET, ALMIRAH, ARMOIRE
composition .... ADVISERS
describing one .... KITCHEN, PRESIDENTIAL
for dishes/food ..... CUPBOARD
for radio/TV .... CONSOLE
for wines .... CELLARET
government .... ADVISORY BOARD COUNCIL, MINISTRY
wood .... KOA, TEAK, CEDAR, NARRA, WALNUT, ROSEWOOD
cable .... ROPE, WIRE, CHAIN, CORD, MESSAGE, TELEGRAM
car .... ELPHER, TELFER
kind of .... JUMP(ER), IGNITION, ELECTRIC, TELEVISION, UNDERGROUND
old .... JUNK
used as brace .... STAY
cabob .... (ROAST) MEAT
holder .... SPIT, SKEWER

cabochon .... (GEM)STONE
caboodle .... ALL, LOT, GROUP
companion of .... KIT
caboose ...... CAB, COMPARTMENT
ship's .... GALLEY, KITCHEN
cabrilla .... FISH, GROUPER, REDHIND
cacao alkaloid ...... THEOBROMINE
product .... COCOA, CHOCOLATE
seed powder .... BROMA
cachalot .... SPERM-WHALE, PHYSETER
cache .... HIDE, HOARD, STORE, STASH, SCREEN, SECRETE, CONCEAL, HIDING PLACE
cachet ...... SEAL, STAMP, WAFER, CAPSULE
cachinate .... LAUGH
cacholong .... OPAL
cachou .... CATECHU, LOZENGE
cacique ...... LORD, CHIEF, PRINCE, LEADER, SACHEM, ORIOLE, TROUPIAL
cackle .... CLACK, LAUGH, CHATTER, PRATTLE
cackler .... HEN, GOOSE
cacoethes .... ITCH, MANIA
cacophonous .... AJAR, HARSH, OFF-KEY, DISCORDANT
cacophony .... DIN, BABEL, NOISE
cactus .... AGAVE, NOPAL, CHOLLA, CEREUS, MESCAL, PEYOTE, PRICKLY-PEAR, OPUNTIA, SAGUARO
fruit .... FIG, COCHAL
like plant .... SPURGE, STAPELIA, EUPHORBIA
plant .... TUNA
plant process .... SPINE
spineless .... CHAUTE
cad .... HEEL, HOOD, WORM, KNAVE, MUCKER, RASCAL, BOUNDER, SCOUNDREL
cadaver .... BODY, COR(P)SE, CARCASS, REMAINS
preserved .... MUMMY
slang .... STIFF
cadaverous .... PALE, ASHEN, WAN, GAUNT, HAGGARD, GHASTLY, GHOSTLY, SALLOW, LIVID, PALLID
caddis worm .... CADEW
caddish .... BOORISH, ILL-BRED, LOUTISH, UNCOUTH
Caddoan Indian .... REE, PAWNEE
caddy/caddie .... CARRIER, (TEA)BOX, ATTENDANT, CONTAINER
cade .... JUNIPER

cadelle .... LARVA
cadence .... BEAT, LILT, ICTUS, ACCENT, STRESS, DROOP, RHYTHM
recite in .... CHIME
cadent .... FALLING, RHYTHMICAL
cadenza .... RIFF, CADENCE
cadet .... SON, YOUTH, STUDENT
designating one .... DODO, AIR, NAVAL, PLEBE, MILITARY
mark against .... DEMERIT
military .... DRAFTEE, PRIVATE, RECRUIT
naval ...... MIDDY, MIDSHIPMAN
cadge .... BEG, BUM, HAWK, MOOCH, PEDDLE, SPONGE
cadger .... BEGGAR, HAWKER, PANHANDLER, VENDOR, PEDDLER
cadgy .... LEWD, MERRY, WILD, WANTON, EXUBERANT, LUSTFUL
cadi .... JUDGE, MAGISTRATE
Cadmean-like victory
.... PYRRHIC
Cadmus' daughter .... INO, SEMELE
parent .... AGENOR
sister .... EUROPA
wife .... HARMONIA
cadre .... CELL, GROUP, NUCLEUS, INNER CIRCLE, FRAMEWORK
caduceus .... ROD, WAND, BATON, STAFF, SCEPTER
bearer .... HERMES, MERCURY
Caen river .... ORNE
Caesar .... RULER, TYRANT, SALAD, JULIUS, EMPEROR, AUTOCRAT, DICTATOR
augur who warned
.... SPURINNA
assassin of .... BRUTUS, CASCA, CASSIUS
love of .... SERVILIA
mistress of .... EUNOE, CLEO(PATRA)
partner of Sid .... COCA
Pompey battle site
.... THAPSUS
wife of .... UXOR, POMPEIA
Caesarian "offspring"
.... CALENDAR
Caesarian/Cesarean section
.... SURGERY, OPERATION, HYSTEROTOMY
first performed in .... ROME
Caesarism .... AUTOCRACY
Caesars, one of the .... JULIUS, GAIUS, NERO, GALBA, OTHO, TITUS, CLAUDIUS, AUGUSTUS, DOMITIAN, TIBERIUS,

VESPASIAN, VITELLIUS
caesura ...... REST, BREAK, PAUSE
cafe .... BISTRO, COFFEE,
CANTEEN, SNACK BAR,
SALOON, DINER, CABARET,
COFFEE SHOP, ESTAMINET,
RESTAURANT
au _____ .... LAIT
card .... MENU
owner .... RESTAURA(N)TEUR
room .... DIVAN
society member ...... PLAYBOY
cafeteria .... AUTOMAT
caffein(e) .... STIMULANT
effect of too much
.... NAUSEA, ANXIETY,
INSOMNIA, FATIGUE,
IRRITABILITY
source ..... TEA, COLA, COCOA,
COFFEE, KOLA NUT
tea .... THEIN(E)
caftan .... ROBE
cage .... GIG, PEN, BARS, JAIL,
CONFINE, ENCLOSURE
birds', large .... AVIARY
elevator .... CAR
for trapping fish .... CREEL
hauling/hawks' .... MEW
poultry .... COOP
occupant .... PET, BIRD,
ANIMAL, TELLER, CASHIER,
CONVICT, PRISONER
cagey .... SLY, WILY, CLEVER,
CUNNING, TRICKY, SHIFTY
cahier .... REPORT, NOTEBOOK
cahoots, in .... LEAGUE, TIE-UP,
ALLIANCE, COLLUSION,
COMPLICITY, CONNIVANCE
caiman .... ALLIGATOR
Cain .... MURDERER
brother of .... ABEL, SETH
descendant of .... JUBAL
land of .... NOD
parent of .... EVE, ADAM
son of .... ENOCH
caique .... ROWBOAT, SAILBOAT
caird .... GYPSY, IDLER, TINKER,
VAGRANT
cairn ...... LANDMARK, MEMORIAL
cairngorm .... QUARTZ
Cairene .... EGYPTIAN
Cairo is capital of .... EGYPT
shopping district .... MOUSSKY
caisson ...... BOX, CHEST, WAGON,
TUMBREL, TUMBRIL
content of .... AMMO,
EXPLOSIVES, AMMUNITION
disease .... BENDS
man in a .... SANDHOG
occasional use of ...... HEARSE
caitiff .... BASE, EVIL, MEAN,

CRAVEN, POLTROON
cajeput .... LAUREL
cajole .... COAX, BEGUILE,
FLATTER, BLANDISH,
WHEEDLE
slang .... SNOW
cajolery .... PALAVER, LIP-SERVICE
slang .... SNOW JOB
cake .... CLOT, LUMP, MASS, RUSK,
CIMBAL, HARDEN, PASTRY,
GEL, CURD, SOLIDIFY,
THICKEN
barley meal .... BANNOCK
batter ...... CRUMPET, CRULLER,
FRITTER
chocolate .... BROWNIE
corn .... PONE
covering ...... ICING, FROSTING,
MERINGUE
fish/meat .... PATTY
in pipe bowl .... DOTTLE
kind of .... FRUIT, POUND,
LAYER, SPONGE, WHITE
mixture .... BATTER
porous .... SPONGE
pressed tobacco .... PLUG
rich/without flour .... TORTE
ring-shaped .... DONUT,
DOUGHNUT
rum .... BABA
seed .... WIG
small .... BUN, TART, COOKY,
ROLL, COOKIE, ECLAIR
sweet .... SIMNEL
takes the .... WINS, EXCELS,
ECLIPSES, OUTSHINES
tea .... SCONE
thin .... WAFER, JUMBLE
Spanish .... TORTILLA
India style .... POORI
tiny, griddle .... SILVER-
DOLLAR PANCAKE
topped with shredded cheese
and spices ...... STREUSEL
traditional, fruit and nut-
filled .... STOLLEN
cakes and ale, life of
.... HEDONISM
cakewalk .... DANCE, STRUT,
SWAGGER
calabash .... GOURD, SHELL
calaber .... FUR, SQUIRREL
calaboose .... GAOL, JAIL, PRISON,
STATE PEN
Calais' English neighbor
.... DOVER
calamary .... SQUID
calamine ...... LOTION, OINTMENT
calamitous .... FATAL, DEADLY,
TRAGIC, RUINOUS,
DISASTROUS

calamity .... WOE, BLOW, MISERY,
REVERSE, DISASTER, MISHAP,
HARDSHIP, CATASTROPHE
calamus .... QUILL,COMA]
PALM (TREE), RATTAN,
SWEETFLAG
calcar .... SPUR
calced .... SHOD
calcine .... BURN, OXIDIZE
calcined metal/residue .... CALX
calcium carbonate .... TUFA,
CALCITE, CALICHE
carbonate, of ..... CALCAREOUS
crust .... SINTER
gypsum .... PLASTER
oxide .... (QUICK)LIME
phosphate .... APATITE
sulphate .... HEPAR, GYPSUM,
PLASTER
calculate .... COUNT, GUESS,
APPRAISE, DEEM, FIGURE,
COMPUTE, THINK, RECKON,
SUPPOSE, ESTIMATE
calculating .... SHREWD,
CUNNING, CAUTIOUS,
DESIGNING, SCHEMING
device .... TABLE, ABACUS,
COMPUTER, CASH REGISTER,
TABULATOR, SLIDE RULE
calculation, of .... LOGISTIC
calculi, of .... LITHIC
calculus ...... ADDING, ESTIMATION
combining form .... LITHO
dental .... TARTAR
in urinary tract
.... GALLSTONE, BLADDER
STONE
Calcutta is capital of
.... BENGAL
calderite .... GARNET
caldron .... BOILER, KETTLE
Caleb's companion ...... JOSHUA
Caledonia .... SCOTLAND
calefy .... HEAT, WARM
calendar .... LOG, LIST, DIARY,
YEAR, DOCKET, ALMANAC,
JOURNAL, REGISTER,
MENOLOGY, SCHEDULE
church .... ORDO
of business .... AGENDA
type of .... JULIAN, NEW
STYLE, GREGORIAN
calender .... MANGLE, DERVISH
calenture .... FEVER
calesa .... CAB, CALASH, CALECHE,
CARRIAGE
calf .... COW, BOSS(Y), LEG,
SHANK, BOVINE, WEANER
cry .... BLAT, BLEAT
for slaughter .... FATLING
front .... SHIN

hide/skin .... KIP
leather .... ELK
like a .... VITULINE
meat .... VEAL
motherless/stray .... DOGY,
          DOGIE, MAVERICK
of the leg .... SURA
of the leg, pertaining to
    .... SURAL
skin parchment .... VELLUM
suckling .... BOB
unbranded .... MAVERICK
Caliban's master .... PROSPERO
mother .... SYCORAX
caliber .... BORE, SIZE, GAUGE,
       ABILITY, METTLE, QUALITY
calibrate .... CHECK, PROBE,
       MEASURE, GRADUATE
in advance .... PRESET
calico .... (COTTON) CLOTH,
       SPOTTED, DAPPLED,
       VARICOLORED
bass .... CRAPPIE
East Indies .... SALLOO
horse .... PONY, PINTO,
          PIEBALD
loin cloth .... LAVA-LAVA
printing .... TEER, LAPIS
printing material
    ...... LACTARENE, TRAGACANTH
California .... EL DORADO
army base .... ORD
bay .... CARMEL, MONTEREY,
    MORRO, MISSION, EMERALD,
    BODEGA, GRIZZLY, HUMBOLDT,
    HALF-MOON, SAN FRANCISCO,
       SAN DIEGO, SAN PEDRO,
    SUISUN, SANTA MONICA
bulrush .... TULE
canal ..... COACHELLA, FRIANT-
          KERN
cape .... VIZCAINO,
    MENDOCINO, SAN MARTIN
capital .... SACRAMENTO
capital, former ..... MONTEREY
channel .... GOLDEN GATE,
    SANTA CRUZ, SANTA BARBARA
city/town .... FRESNO, SAN
    JOSE, LOS ANGELES, LODI, SAN
    FRANCISCO, SAN DIEGO, SANTA
    CRUZ, CHINO, SALINAS, LONG
       BEACH, NAPA, MURRIETA,
       RIVERSIDE, VALLEJO,
       BAKERSFIELD, CARMEL,
    BARSTOW, ANAHEIM, PALM
    SPRINGS, BERKELEY, DUBLIN,
    CASTRO VALLEY, DALY,
       STOCKTON, TEMECULA,
    POMONA, ONTARIO, PASADENA,
    HOLLYWOOD, BEVERLY HILLS,
       ALTURAS, OAKLAND,

MODESTO, SAN MATEO, SAN
LEANDRO, BELMONT, BENICIA,
    CONCORD, PALO ALTO, SAN
    CLEMENTE, NEWARK, SANTA
    BARBARA, ESCONDIDO, SANTA
    MARIA, REDDING, REDWOOD,
       BURBANK, EUREKA,
    HUNTINGTON BEACH, DOWNEY,
    ORANGE, HAYWARD, VISALIA,
    MOUNTAIN VIEW, FALLBROOK,
    NEWPORT BEACH, COMPTON,
    SAN BERNARDINO, OTAY,
       YUBA, WALNUT CREEK
college .... MILLS, DELTA,
    CYPRESS, BAKERSFIELD,
    POMONA, PACIFIC-UNION,
    WHITTIER, IRVINE VALLEY,
          SADDLEBACK
county ...... ALPINE, ALAMEDA,
    BUTTE, AMADOR, BIG BEAR, EL
       DORADO, CALAVERAS,
    COLUSA, CONTRA COSTA,
    KERN, FRESNO, DEL NORTE,
    INYO, GLENN, HUMBOLDT,
    LAKE, KINGS, LOS ANGELES,
    MARIN, LASSEN, MADERA,
    MARIPOSA, MENDOCINO,
    MONO, MODOC, MERCED,
    NEVADA, NAPA, MONTEREY,
    RIVERSIDE, ORANGE, SAN
    BENITO, SACRAMENTO,
    PLACER, SAN BERNARDINO,
    PLUMES, SAN FRANCISCO, SAN
    DIEGO, SAN JOAQUIN, SAN
    MATEO, SANTA BARBARA,
    SANTA CRUZ, SANTA CLARA,
    SIERRA, SHASTA, SISKIYOU,
    SOLANO, SONOMA, SUTTER,
    YUBA, TEHAMA, STANISLAUS,
    YOLO, TULARE, TRINITY,
    VENTURA, TUOLUMNE
creek .... MILL, PINE,
    ALAMEDA, COTTONWOOD,
    WALNUT, WILLOW, SOUTH
          COW
date capital .... INDIO
desert .... MOJAVE
fish .... CABEZON, GRUNION
gold rusher .... ARGONAUT'
governor ..... BROWN, REAGAN,
          WILSON
grape picker .... BRACERO
grape pickers' strike
    .... HUELGA
gulf ..... SANTA CATALINA, THE
          FARALLONS
herb .... AMOLE
holly .... TOYON
Indian ...... YUKI, POMO, HUPA,
    YUROK, WAPPO, PAIUTE,
          PATWIN

island .... ANGEL, BROOKS,
    MARE, ALCATRAZ, CORONADO,
    SANTA ROSA, SANTA CRUZ,
    TREASURE, SAN MIGUEL,
    ANACAPA, YERBA BUENA,
    BETHEL, SAN CLEMENTE
kingfish .... OPAH, PINTADO,
          WHITING
lake ..... CLEAR, TAHOE, MEISS,
    MERCED, TULARE, PERRIS,
    FOLSOM, SHASTA, CHABOT,
    TURLOCK, CROWLEY, TULE,
    ELSINORE, SKINNER, CADIZ,
    OWENS, ARROWHEAD,
    FLORENCE, SAN ANDREAS,
    VAIL, EL MIRAGE,
    SILVERWOOD, EAGLE, HAVASU,
    PYRAMID, BRISTOL, ALMANOR,
          OROVILLE
laurel .... MYRTLE, CAJEPUT,
          CAJUPUT
mountain .... AGUANGA,
    WILSON, SHASTA, KLAMATH,
    MUIR, WHITNEY, EAGLE
    CRAGS, MARBLE, MONTARA,
    PALOMAR, INGALLS, HOFFMAN,
    HAMILTON, TAMALPAIS, SCOTT
          BAR
mountain, highest ...... MOUNT
          WHITNEY
mountains .... GRAPEVINE,
    CHOCOLATE, PROVIDENCE,
    INYO, SAN BERNARDINO,
    SISKIYOU, TEHACHAPI,
    WHIPPLE, SIERRA NEVADA
oak .... ROBLE, ENCINA
observatory .... PALOMAR
olive .... MANZANILLO
park .... YOSEMITE, GAVIOTA,
    REDWOOD, SEQUOIA, LASSEN,
          CHANNEL ISLANDS
pass .... BADGER, DONNER,
    SONORA, ALTAMONT
peak ...... HAT, LASSEN, FREEL,
    QUARTZ, FREMONT, OWENS,
    WHEELER, TELESCOPE
pioneer .... SUTTER
point .... ANO-NUEVO, DUME,
    LOPEZ, ARGUELLO, ARENA,
    BONITA, COOPER, REYES,
    BUCHON, DUXBURY, TOMALES,
          PESCADERO
point, highest .... MOUNT
          WHITNEY
range .... ARGUS, CASCADE,
    AMARGOSA, PANAMINT
ranges .... COAST
river .... EEL, MAD, NOYO,
    ALAMO, ESTRELLA, SALMON,
    CARMEL, CUYAMA, KERN,
    RUSSIAN, AMARGOSA, KINGS,

KLAMATH, FEATHER, MERCED, NAVARRO, REDWOOD, MOKULUMNE, SACRAMENTO, PIT, SALINAS, COLORADO, LOST, TRINITY, TRUCKEE, YUBA, SMITH, SAN JOAQUIN
rockfish .... RE(I)NA
sea lake .... SALTON
shrub .... SALAL, KUMQUAT, OLEANDER
state bird .... QUAIL
state flower .... (GOLDEN) POPPY
state motto .... EUREKA!, (I HAVE FOUND IT)
state nickname .... GOLDEN, GRAPE
state tree .... REDWOOD, SEQUOIA
time: abbr. .... PST
tourist site .... DISNEYLAND, SAN FRANCISCO CABLE CARS, DEATH VALLEY MONUMENT, INYO FOREST, MUIR WOODS, PINNACLES MONUMENT
university, state .... CHICO, FRESNO, FULLERTON, LONG BEACH, LOS ANGELES, SACRAMENTO, BERKELEY, SAN JOSE, SAN FRANCISCO, NORTHRIDGE, SAN DIEGO, DAVIS, POLYTECHNIC, HAYWARD, STANFORD
valley .... NAPA, DEATH, CARMEL, MORENO, FOUNTAIN, SIMI, TEMESCAL, YOSEMITE, IMPERIAL, SAN JOAQUIN, SQUAW, SAN FERNANDO, HIDDEN, PANAMINT
volcano .... LASSEN
California–U.S. Military Air Force Base .... BEALE, CASTLE, GEORGE, EDWARDS, MARCH, MATHER, NORTON, OXNARD, MCCLELLAN, TRAVIS, VANDENBERG
Army Base .... OAKLAND, FORT ORD, PRESIDIO
Army Depot .... SHARPE, SIERRA, SACRAMENTO
Marine Corps Air Station .... EL TORO
Marine Corps Base ...... CAMP PENDLETON, TWENTY-NINE PALMS
Marine Corps Recruit Depot .... SAN DIEGO
Naval Air Station .... LEMOORE, MOFFETT
Naval Weapons Center .... CHINA LAKE

Navy Yard .... MARE ISLAND
Pacific Missile Test Center .... POINT MUGU
Caligula .... BOOTIKIN
caliph .... ALI, EMIR, IMAM, OMAR, HAKIM, OMMIAD
calisthenics .... ATHLETICS, WORKOUT, EXERCISE(S), GYMNASTICS
system .... DEL SARTE
calix .... CUP, CHALICE
calk/caulk .... SEAL, BLOCK, CLOSE, PLUG UP, CHINSE, STOP
calker .... STAVER
calking/caulking material .... TAR, OAKUM, PITCH
call .... CRY, DUB, DIAL, NAME, PAGE, LABEL, SUMMON, CONVOKE, ANNOUNCE
a bluff .... DARE, FACE
a spade a spade .... TELL IT LIKE IT IS
army .... DRAFT
attention to .... SPECIFY, REFER TO
auction .... BID
baseball ...... OUT, SAFE, FOUL, STRIKE
boy .... PAGE, BELLHOP, BELLMAN
creditor's .... DUN
down .... CHIDE, SCOLD, REBUKE, UPBRAID, CRITICIZE
for .... ASK, DEMAND, SUMMON, CONVOKE
for aid .... APPEAL
for help .... SOS
for hogs .... SOOK
for repetition .... ENCORE
for silence .... HIST, HUSH, SHUSH
forth .... EVOKE, AROUSE, ELICIT, EXCITE, KINDLE
girl .... HOOKER, HOSTESS, PROSTITUTE
greeting .... AVE, HAIL
hotel lobby .... PAGE
in .... INVITE, SUMMON
in gambling .... BET, WAGER
in poker .... SEE
in question .... IMPUGN
off .... CANCEL
on .... SEE, TAP, VISIT
out .... YELL, ROUSE, SHOUT, ANNOUNCE
prayer .... ADAN, AZAN
to account .... CITE, CHARGE, ARRAIGN
to arms, medieval .... BAN
to attract attention .... HEY,

HIST, PSST
to mind .... RECALL, REMEMBER, REMINISCE
to the hounds: var. ...... YOICK
to witness .... OBTEST
together .... GATHER, COLLECT, CONVENE, CONVOKE, SUMMON, ASSEMBLE
up .... BUZZ, DIAL, RING UP, (TELE)PHONE
upon .... CHOOSE, ENJOIN, COMMAND, DESIGNATE
within .... CLOSE, NEARBY
word at flip of coin .... HEADS, TAILS
calla .... ARUM, LILY
Callas, operatic soprano .... MARIA
callboy .... PAGE, BELLHOP, BUTTONS
called .... NAMED, YCLEPT
caller .... GUEST, VISITOR
from minaret .... MUEZZIN
midnight .... CRIER
persistent .... DUTY
calligrapher .... PENMAN, COPYIST, LETTER-MAKER
calligraphy .... FINE HANDWRITING, SCRIPT, ARTISTIC PENMANSHIP
calling .... JOB, TASK, WORK, DUTY, CAREER, METIER, PURSUIT, TRADE, MISSION, VOCATION, BUSINESS, FUNCTION, POSITION, PROFESSION, OCCUPATION
Calliope .... MUSE
Callisto .... NYMPH, CONSTELLATION
callous .... HARD, TOUGH, PITILESS, HARD-BOILED, UNFEELING, THICKSKINNED
growth .... CORN
render .... NUMB, SEAR, HARDEN, LANGUID, INDIFFERENT
calloused .... BONY, HORNY, CORNEOUS
callow .... GREEN, YOUNG, IMMATURE, UNFLEDGED
bird .... FEATHERLESS
person ...... YOUTH, FLEDGLING
Calloway .... CAB
callus, horse's .... CHESTNUT
on toe .... CORN
calm .... COOL, LULL, ABATE, ALLAY, STILL, SOBER, PACIFY, PLACID, PACIFIC, PLACATE, SERENE, COMPOSED, IMPASSIVE, SEDATE, SMOOTH, SOOTHE, TRANQUIL

before the _____ .... STORM
cool and _____ .... COLLECTED
down! .... COOL IT
calmness, mental/emotional
.... ATARAXIA
calmative .... BALM, DRUG,
OPIATE, SEDATIVE
calomel ...... POWDER, CATHARTIC
caloric .... HEAT, THERMAL
calorie .... THERM(E)
counter .... DIETER, MILADY,
DIABETIC
counter's standby
.... CYCLAMATE, NUTRA-
SWEET, SACCHARIN
-free .... WATER
source of .... FAT, PROTEIN,
ALCOHOL, CARBOHYDRATE
calories, count(ing) .... DIET(ING)
measured as .... ENERGY
pertaining to .... THERMAL
calotte .... CREST, (SKULL)CAP
Calpurnia's husband
.... (JULIUS) CAESAR
caltrop .... THISTLE
calumet .... (PEACE) PIPE
user of .... INDIAN, REDSKIN
calumniate .... SLUR, LIBEL,
DEFAME, MALIGN, ASPERSE,
REVILE, SLANDER
slang .... BADMOUTH
calumnious .... ABUSIVE,
CAUSTIC, CRITICAL, LIBELOUS
calumny .... SLUR, LIBEL,
SCANDAL, SLANDER,
ASPERSION, DEFAMATION
Calvary .... ARAM, GOLGOTHA,
BURIAL PLACE, (PLACE OF A)
SKULL
Calve, soprano .... EMMA,
ROQUER
Calvinist of Toulouse ...... CALAS
Calvinist(ic) .... GENEVAN,
DOGMATIC, GENEVESE
calvities .... BALDNESS
Calydonian boar killer
.... MELEAGER
Calypso .... SONG, DANCE, LILT,
NYMPH, MUSIC, BALLAD,
CHANT(EY), FLOWER, ORCHID
island of .... OGYGIA
calypster .... ALULA
calyx leaf .... PETAL, SEPAL
part .... GALEA
cam .... CATCH, WIPER,
COG(WHEEL), TAPPET,
TRIPPER, TRIPPET
wheel projection .... LOBE
camaraderie .... COMRADESHIP,
FELLOWSHIP
camalig .... HUT, GRANARY,

WAREHOUSE
camarilla .... CABAL, CLIQUE
camasa .... LOBELIA, QUAMASH
Cambodia .... CAMBOJA,
CAMBODGE, KAMPUCHEA
capital .... PNOM PENH, PHNOM
PENH
capital, ancient .... ANGKOR
city/town ..... KAMPOT, KULEN,
KRACHEH, PAOY PET, SUONG,
LUMPHAT, SIEMPANG, PAILIN,
SAMBOR, TAKEV, VIROCHEY,
POUTHISAT
gulf .... THAILAND
island .... KAOH KONG, KAOH
RUNG, KAOH TANG
lake .... TONLE SAP
money of .... RIEL
mountains .... DANGREK
native of .... KHMER
neighbor .... LAOS, VIETNAM,
THAILAND
plain .... JONCS
premier .... NOL
river ..... MEKONG, SREPOK, LA
DRANG
ruins .... ANGKOR WAT
seaport .... KAMPOT
skirt .... SAMPORT
cambogia .... (GUM) RESIN
cambrai .... LINEN, BATISTE
cambric .... LAWN, LINEN,
COTTON, PERCALE
Cambridge U. college servant
.... GYP
exam for honors .... TRIPOS
head/fellow .... DON
student .... SIZAR, SIZER,
CANTAB, OPTIME
came about .... AROSE, BEGAN,
CAUSED, HAPPENED
down .... (A)LIT, FELL,
DROPPED, SETTLED,
DESCENDED
camel .... OONT, BELOOL, DELOUL,
HEJEEN, ARABIAN, GUANACO,
BACTRIAN, RUMINANT,
DROMEDARY
back breaker .... STRAW
driver .... SARWAN
feature .... HUMP
hair cloth/fabric .... ABA,
CAMLET, CAMLOT, CASHMERE
hair robe .... ABA
keeper .... OBIL
like animal .... LLAMA,
GUANACO
load .... FARDEL
milk, fermented .... KUMISS,
KOUMIS(S)
rawhide .... SHAGREEN

seat on ..... HOUDAH, HOWDAH
sometimes called ship of the
_____ .... DESERT
camellia .... JAPONICA
camelopard .... GIRAFFE
Camelot's lady .... ENID
sport .... TILT, JOUST,
TOURNEY
source of fame .... ARTHUR,
KNIGHTS, ROUND TABLE
Camenas .... NYMPHS
cameo .... GEM, MEDAL(LION),
EMBOSSMENT, ANAGLYPH,
PORTRAYAL
cutting tool .... SPADE
opposed to .... INTAGLIO
stone .... ONYX, SARDONYX
camera .... BOX, KODAK, LUCIDA,
CHAMBER, BROWNIE,
POLAROID
film protector .... CARTRIDGE
holder .... CASE
kind of .... CANDID, PORTRAIT,
TELEVISION
light bulb .... FLASH
opening .... APERTURE
part .... LENS, FINDER,
SHUTTER
platform .... DOLLY
portable .... KODAK
shot .... STILL
_____, sketching aid
.... OBSCURA
stand/support .... TRIPOD
tube .... ORTHICON, CATHODE
RAY
cameraman .... SHUTTERBUG,
SNAPSHOOTER,
PHOTOGRAPHER
camerlingo .... CARDINAL,
CHAMBERLAIN
Cameroon .... CAMEROUN
bight .... BIAFRA
capital .... YAOUNDE
city/town .... DOUALA, KUMBA,
GAROUA, BAMENDA, WUM,
TIKO, MAROUA
language .... FANG, DUALA,
FULANI, FRENCH, ENGLISH
money .... FRANC, CENTIME
mountain .... CAMEROON
native .... ABO
religion .... ISLAM
river .... BENUE, CROSS, DJA,
DONGA, KADEI, IVINDO, LOM,
LOGONE, MBERE, SANGA
Camille author .... DUMAS
beloved of .... ARMAND
role actress .... GARBO
camion .... DRAY, TRUCK, WAGON
camise .... SHIRT, SMOCK

camisole .... JACKET
camlet .... CLOTH, PONCHO
camomile .... MAYWEED
Camorra .... (SECRET) SOCIETY
  like group .... MAF(F)IA
  member's specialty
  .... MURDER, BLACKMAIL,
          EXTORTION, TERRORISM
camouflage .... HIDE, MASK,
  BEFOG, CONCEAL, DISGUISE,
                DECEPTION
  expert .... CAMOUFLEUR
camouflaging material .... VEIL,
        PAINT, SMOKE, LEAVES
camp ...... ETAPE, TABOR, CLIQUE,
  BIVOUAC, ENCAMP(MENT)
  barricaded by wagons
  .... LA(A)GER
  besiegers' .... LEAGUER
  follower .... DOXY, FIRE,
    DAVID, GROUND, SUTLER,
                 VIVANDIERE
  kind of .... BOOT, TRAILER,
    BOY SCOUTS, DETENTION,
    INTERNMENT, CONCENTRATION
  military .... BASE, BARRACKS
  out .... MAROON, ROUGH IT
  outdoor facility .... TENT,
                   LATRINE
  pertaining to .... CASTRAL
  political .... PARTY, FACTION
  privy/toilet .... LATRINE
campagna .... PLAIN
campaign .... PLAN, DRIVE,
  CANVASS, CRUSADE,
  BARNSTORM, ELECTIONEER
  against an idea .... JIHAD
  for .... ESPOUSE
  goal, charity .... FUND-RAISING
  goal, military .... VICTORY
  goal, political .... ELECTION
  kind of .... SMEAR, WHISTLE-
                   STOP
  matters .... ISSUES
  military .... WAR, CONFLICT,
                 HOSTILITIES
  motive .... CAUSE
  war .... TACTICS, STRATEGY
  word .... PROMISE, REELECT
campaigner .... STUMPER
  military .... SOLDIER, VETERAN
campanile ...... BELFRY, STEEPLE,
             (BELL)TOWER
campanula .... RAMPION,
                HAREBELL
Campbell, singer .... GLEN
camper's equipment .... TENT,
  POLES, STAKES, LANTERN,
             SLEEPING BAG
  kit .... DUFFEL, DUFFLE
campesino .... PEASANT

camphol .... BORNEOL
camphor ball .... MOTHBALL
  -like .... BORNEOL
  oil .... SAFROL(E)
  tree .... EVERGREEN
campo .... PLAIN, PLAZA,
        DISTRICT, FLATLAND
campstool-shaped chair
  .... CURULE
campus ...... QUAD, YARD, FIELD,
             QUADRANGLE,
          SCHOOLGROUNDS
  building .... DORM, SCHOOL,
             GYM(NASIUM)
  feature on some .... IVY
  group .... FRAT, SORORITY,
                FRATERNITY
  VIP .... DEAN, PREXY,
                   ATHLETE
can .... JUG, TIN, PAIL, MAY, BE
        ABLE, CONTAINER
  fruit .... PRESERVE
  slang .... JAIL, PRISON, FIRE,
    EXPEL, LAY OFF, DISMISS,
    JOHN, TOILET, BUTTOCKS,
                DISCHARGE
Canaan's brother .... CUSH,
             EGYPT, LIBYA
  father .... HAM
  grandfather .... NOAH
  son .... HETH, SIDON
Canaanites' ancient god
  .... MOLECH
  god of fertility .... BAAL
  goddess of fertility
  .... ASHERAH
Canada, Lower .... QUEBEC
Canada's ____ 67 .... EXPO
Canadian .... CANUCK
  airport .... GANDER
  basin .... FOXE, KANE
  bay .... FUNDY, JAMES, BAFFIN,
    HUDSON, UNGAVA, GEORGIAN
  boatman/woodsman
  .... VOYAGEUR
  canal .... WELLAND
  cape .... RAY, RACE, SABLE,
                 CHIDLEY
  capital .... OTTAWA
  channel .... FOXE, PARRY,
                MCLINTOCK
  city/town .... HULL, BANFF,
  LEVIS, CALGARY, MONTREAL,
  GUELPH, BRANDON, HAMILTON,
  MOOSE JAW, DARTMOUTH,
  EDMONTON, MEDICINE HAT,
    HALIFAX, MONCTON,
  NANAIMO, REGINA, SUDBURY,
  KINGSTON, SASKATOON,
  VANCOUVER, TORONTO,
  VICTORIA, WINDSOR, WINNIPEG

crookneck .... CUSHAW
emblem .... MAPLE
farmer .... HABITAN(T)
folk singer .... LIGHTFOOT
football scrimmage .... ROUGE
game .... LA CROSSE
game preserve .... JASPER
gannet .... MARGOT
gold field .... KLONDIKE
goose ..... BRANT(A), OUTARDE
grape .... ISABELLA
humorist .... LEACOCK
Indian ..... CREE, DENE, HAIDA,
  SIOUX, MICMAC, TAKU, TINNE,
                 SARCEE
island .... BANKS, BAFFIN,
  DEVON, BATHURST, MANSEL,
  ELLESMERE, ANTICOSTI,
  MELVILLE, NEWFOUNDLAND,
  FOGO, SABLE, VANCOUVER,
    SOMERSET, VICTORIA
islands ..... OTTAWA, BELCHER,
                MAGDALEN
lake ..... CREE, ABITIBI, MINTO,
  RAINY, ATHABASCA, GREAT
  BEAR, GREAT SLAVE, LOUISE,
  KLUANE, KOOTENAY, SWAN,
  OKANAGAN, MANITOBA,
  SELWYN, WOODS, WILLISTON,
  TESLIN, REINDEER, WINNIPEG
land measure .... ARPENT
language ..... FRENCH, ENGLISH
lynx .... PISHU, CARCAJOU
money .... DOLLAR
mountain ..... LOGAN, ROBSON,
  ALBERTA, CARLETON,
  COLUMBIA, D'UBERVILLE,
             FAIRWEATHER
mountains ...... COAST, ROCKY,
                TORNGAT
national park .... YOHO,
  FUNDY, BANFF, JASPER,
  GLACIER, PACIFIC RIM,
  NAHANNI, TERRA NOVA
official, town president
  .... REEVE
peak .... (MOUNT) LOGAN
peninsula ..... GASPE, BOOTHIA
policeman .... MOUNTIE
porcupine .... URSON
prairie province ...... ALBERTA,
  MANITOBA, SASKATCHEWAN
prime minister .... LAURIER,
  MARONEY, PEARSON, TRUDEAU
province .... ALBERTA, BRITISH
  COLUMBIA, MANITOBA, NEW
  BRUNSWICK, NEWFOUNDLAND,
  NOVA SCOTIA, ONTARIO,
  PRINCE EDWARD ISLAND,
  QUEBEC, SASKATCHEWAN,
  NORTHWEST TERRITORIES,

YUKON TERRITORY

provincial capital
.... EDMONTON, VICTORIA, WINNIPEG, FREDERICTON, ST. JOHN'S, HALIFAX, TORONTO, CHARLOTTE TOWN, QUEBEC, REGINA, WHITEHORSE, YELLOWKNIFE

resort/scenic region ..... GASPE

river .... TRENT, FINLAY, LIARD, FRASER, MACKENZIE, PELLY, PEACE, MISTASSIBI, NELSON, OTTAWA, PERIBONCA, STEWART, SAINT LAWRENCE, STIKINE, SASKATCHEWAN, PEEL, SKEENA, SLAVE, YUKON

river into Pacific .... NASS

rodent .... LEMMING

settler .... SOURDOUGH

squaw .... MAHALA

strait .... CABOT, DAVIS, NARES, HECATE

summer resort .... BANFF

territory .... YUKON

canaille .... MOB, RABBLE, RIFFRAFF

canal .... DITCH, CHANNEL, CULVERT, PASSAGE, WATERWAY, ERIE, KIEL, SUEZ, ACEQUIA, CONDUIT, PANAMA, WELLAND

bank .... BERM(E)

boat .... GONDOLA

boat tower .... MULE

ear .... SCALA, MEATUS

enclosed part .... LOCK

from mouth to anus
.... ENTERON, ALIMENTARY TRACT

in anatomy/zoology .... VAS, DUCT, TUBE

lock gate .... WICKET

Suez: colloq. .... SOO

worker .... NAVVY

zone seaport .... BALBOA

zone town ...... ANCON, GATUN

canape .... COUCH, DIVAN, APPETIZER

spread .... CAVIAR, CHEESE, SARDINE

canard ...... DUCK, HOAX, RUMOR, HUMBUG, FICTION, HEARSAY, AIRPLANE, SCUTTLEBUTT

canary .... DANCE, FINCH, ROLLER, SONGBIRD, SONGSTER

color .... YELLOW

hybrid .... MULE

kin .... SERIN

seed .... ALPIST

yellow .... MELINE

Canary .... WINE

island .... LA PALMA, LANZAROTE, TENERIF(FE), GOMERA, FUERTEVENTURA, HIERRO, GRAN CANARIA

island mount .... TEIDE, TEYDE

island seaport .... LAS PALMAS

island wine, dry, white
.... SACK

island wine, sweet
.... MADEIRA

canasta play/score .... MELD

Canaveral, Cape .... KENNEDY

Canberra is capital of
.... AUSTRALIA

cancel .... END, STOP, VOID, ANNUL, ERASE, REMIT, OFFSET, RECALL, EXPUNGE, NULLIFY, REPEAL, REVOKE, RESCIND

deletion made .... STET

in printing .... KILL, OMIT, DELE(TE)

cancellation in publishing/ printing .... EDITING, DELETION, BLUE PENCILING

mark on mail .... STAMP, CACHET, POSTMARK

of debt .... WRITE-OFF

of marriage .... SPLIT-UP, DIVORCE, ANNULMENT

cancer .... TUMOR, GROWTH, NEOPLASM, CARCINOMA, SCIRRHOUS

bone .... FIBROSARCOMA, EWING'S SARCOMA, CHONDROSARCOMA, OSTEOSARCOMA

-causing agent .... ALCOHOL, TOBACCO, SUNLIGHT

chemical element used in treatment of .... RADON, RADIUM

describing .... BENIGN, MALIGNANT

in the lymph nodes and spleen .... LYMPHOMA, HODGKIN'S DISEASE

like .... CANCROID

non-malignant .... BENIGN

of the blood .... LEUKEMIA

of the skin .... MELANOMA, CARCINOMA

producing substance
.... CARCINOGEN

surgery, bone .... AMPUTATION

surgery, breast
.... LUMPECTOMY, MASTECTOMY

surgery, colon .... COLECTOMY

treatment ..... CHEMOTHERAPY, RADIATION THERAPY

Cancer, Zodiac sign .... CRAB

candelabrum .... CANDELABRA, CANDLESTICK

candent ...... GLOWING, SPARKING, (WHITE)HOT

candescent .... LUSTROUS, SHINING, GLOWING, RADIANT

Candia .... CRETE, HERAKLEION

candid ...... OPEN, BLUNT, FRANK, DIRECT, HONEST, SIMPLE, STRAIGHT-FORWARD, TRUTHFUL, BRUSQUE, GUILELESS, UPFRONT, OUTSPOKEN, UNGUARDED

Candida author .... SHAW

candidate .... NOMINEE, ASPIRANT, APPLICANT, OFFICE-SEEKER

for graduation .... SENIOR

for knighthood .... ESQUIRE

for mending .... TEAR

kind of .... REBEL, LAME DUCK, FAVORITE, OFFICIAL, INDEPENDENT

candidates' list .... BALLOT, SLATE, TICKET

platform .... HUSTINGS

staple ...... PLEDGES, PROMISES

winning score .... MAJORITY, PLURALITY

candidiasis .... THRUSH, MONILIASIS

candied .... GLACE, GLAZED, HONEYED, SUGARED

fruit/nut .... COMFIT, SWEETMEAT

rind .... CITRON

candies, imitation of
.... CONFETTI

Candiot .... CRETAN

candle .... DIP, LIGHT, TAPER, CANDELA, RUSHLIGHT

holder .... HEARST, SCONCE, CANDELABRA, GIRANDOLE, CHANDELIER

kind of .... RUSH, CORPSE, VOTARY, BAYBERRY

lighter .... TAPER

maker/seller .... CHANDLER

material .... WAX, WICK, CARNAUBA, TALLOW, OZOCERITE

part .... WICK, SNAST

religious ..... VOTIVE, PASCHAL

slang .... GLIM

spike .... PRICKET

wax .... TAPER, BOUGIE, CARNAUBA

wick's end .... SNUFF

candlelight .... DUSK, EVENING, TWILIGHT

candlenut .... AMA
candles, storeroom of
.... CHANDLERY
candlestick ...... CRUSIE, LAMPAD,
 SCONCE, PRICKET
branched .... JESSE,
 GIRANDOLE, CANDELABRA,
 CANDELABRUM
ornamental .... LUSTRE,
 FLAMBEAU
shelf .... GRADIN(E)
candor .... HONESTY, FAIRNESS,
 FRANKNESS, SINCERITY
candy ...... KISS, BONBON, COMFIT,
 DULCIFY, CONFETTO,
 CONFECTION, SWEETEN,
 SWEETS, SWEETMEAT
chewy .... TAFFY, TOFFY,
 TOFFEE, CARAMEL, TOOTSIE
 ROLL
coating .... DRAGEE
cough drop .... LOZENGE
crisp .... BRITTLE
favorite .... TURTLE
filler .... FONDANT
flavor .... LIME, CHOCOLATE,
 LICORICE, BUTTERSCOTCH
fudge-like .... PANOCHA,
 PENUCHE
gelatinous .... JELLYBEAN
hard: sl. .... JAWBREAKER
jelly-like .... PASTE
nutty .... NOUGAT, PRALINE
on a stick .... LOLLIPOP,
 LOLLYPOP
piece .... POP, DROP, GOODY,
 WAFER
pull .... PARTY
seller .... BUCHER,
 CONFECTIONER
soft .... FUDGE,
 MARSHMALLOW
candytuft .... MUSTARD
cane ...... ROD, BEAT, FLAY, FLOG,
 STEM, WADDY, CRUTCH,
 HICKORY, RAT(T)AN,
 (WALKING) STICK
flogging .... SWISH
like a .... FERULACEOUS
metal cap .... SHOE, FERRULE
plant .... BAMBOO, RATTAN
strip .... SPLINT
sugar .... SACROSE,
 SACCHAROSE
walking .... MALACCA
canella .... SPICE, CINNAMON
Canfield (D.) play .... SOLO
cangue-like device .... PILLORY
Canicula .... DOG-STAR, SIRIUS
canicular ...... TORRID, (SIZZLING)
 HOT

canine. See also dog .... DOG,
 FOX, WOLF, JACKAL,
 EYETOOTH
disease .... MANGE, RABIES,
 DRONCIT, CORONAVIRUS,
 PARAINFLU, DISTEMPER
mongrel .... CUR, TYKE
tooth .... FANG, TUSH,
 LANIARY
canister .... BOX, CAN, CADDY,
 CARTON, CONTAINER
canker .... ROT, RUST, SORE,
 DECAY, FUNGUS, MILDEW,
 TAINT, INFECT, CORRUPT
canna .... ACHIRA
cannabin .... RESIN
cannabis .... HEMP, HASHISH
canned .... TINNED, PRESERVED
beef .... BULLY
food poisoning ...... BOTULISM
food toxin .... BOTULIN
slang ...... SACKED, DISMISSED,
 GOT THE AX, CASHIERED
Cannes .... RESORT
cannibal .... SAVAGE, MAN-EATER,
 CARNIVORE
human food of .... LONG PIG
cannikin .... CAN, CUP, PAIL,
 BUCKET
cannon .... MORTAR, HOWITZER,
 FIELDPIECE, ORDNANCE, BIG
 BERTHA, (CRACK)GUN
ball .... MISSILE, PROJECTILE
collectively .... ARTILLERY
dummy .... QUAKER
firing material .... LANIARD,
 LANYARD, LINSTOCK
fodder, so-called .... SOLDIERS
harness for men .... BRICOLE
in billiards .... CAROM
kick of .... RECOIL
mounted .... GINGAL, JINGAL
old .... ASPIC, DRAKE, FALCON,
 CULVERIN
pivot .... TRUNNION
oriental .... LANTAKA
platform .... TERREPLEIN
shot .... PROJECTILE
cannonade .... BLITZ, SALVO,
 STRAFE, BARRAGE, GUNFIRE,
 BLITZKRIEG, BOMBARDMENT
cannonball: sl. .... SWOOP, RAPID,
 POUNCE, THUNDERBOLT
cannoneer .... GUNNER,
 ARTILLERYMAN
cannonry .... BATTERY,
 ORDNANCE, ARTILLERY
cannular .... TUBULAR
canny .... WARY, ASTUTE,
 SHREWD, CLEVER, CAREFUL,
 CUNNING, WILY, SHARP,

 CAUTIOUS
canoe ...... BOAT, DUGOUT, PITPAN
African .... BONGO, ALMADIA
air chamber .... SPONSON
Arctic .... KAYAK
dugout ...... PIRAGUA, PIROGUE
Eskimo .... KAIAK, KAYAK,
 UMIAK, BIDARKA
Hawaii .... WAAPA
Malabar .... TONEE
Malay .... PAHI, PRAU, PROA,
 PRAH(O)
Maori .... WAKA
mover .... PADDLER
Philippine ..... BANCA, BANKA,
 CASCO
propeller .... POLE, PADDLE
with outrigger/sail .... PROA
canon .... LAW, CODE, RULE,
 DECREE, CRITERION
in music .... ROUND
law expert .... DECRETIST
of the Mass prayer
.... MEMENTO
canoness .... NUN, NOVICE
canonical .... PAPAL, ABBATIAL,
 DIVINE, ACCEPTED, APPROVED,
 RUBRICAL, PRESCRIBED
hour .... MATINS, PRIME,
 TERCE, TIERCE, SEXT, NONES,
 LAUDS, VESPERS, COMPLIN
law, Moslem .... SHERI
canonicals ...... ALB, COPE, HOOD,
 GOWN, ROBE, AMICE, FROCK,
 HABIT, BIRETTA, CASSOCK,
 BANDS, STOLE, FANON,
 MANIPLE, SCARF, SURPLICE,
 VESTMENTS
canonize .... DEIFY, EXALT, BLESS,
 SANCTIFY, GLORIFY, HALLOW,
 PURIFY, ENSHRINE
canonized person .... SAINT
canons, group of .... CHAPTER
canopy .... CIEL, COPE, DAIS,
 HOWDAH, TENT, COVER,
 AWNING
altar .... CIBORIUM, BALDACHIN
bed/tomb .... TESTER
boat/cart .... TILT
of heaven .... VAULT
over the earth .... SKY
support .... BAIL
canorous .... CLEAR, MUSICAL,
 PLEASING, MELODIOUS
cant ...... LEAN, TILT, TOSS, TURN,
 LINGO, ANGLE, ARGOT,
 JARGON, PATTER, PATOIS,
 SLANT, SLOPE, INCLINE,
 SWAY, SHIFT, SWERVE,
 SLANG, CAREEN, DIALECT,
 TRITE, SNIVEL, SNUFFLE

hook .... PEAV(E)Y
cantabile .... SONGLIKE
cantaloup(e) .... (MUSK)MELON
cantankerous .... CROSS,
    CRANKY, BAD-TEMPERED, ILL-
    NATURED, CONTENTIOUS,
    BELLICOSE, GRUMPY, ORNERY,
    PERVERSE
  fellow .... CURMUDGEON
  person: colloq. .... CRANK,
    GROUCH
  person: sl. .... SOREHEAD,
    SOURPUSS
cantata .... ARIA, CHORALE,
    CHORUSES, PASTORALE,
    ORATORIO, VOCAL SOLOS
  dramatic/pastoral .... MOTET,
    HYMN, SERENATA
canteen .... FLASK, BOTTLE, PX,
    SHOP, FLACON, WATERBAG,
    POST EXCHANGE,
    COMMISSARY
canter .... GAIT, LOPE, GALLOP
Canterbury, archbishop of
  .... ANSELM, CRANMER,
    DUNSTAN
  bell .... CAMPANULA
  bell variety .... CUP AND
    SAUCER
  murdered archbishop
  .... BECKET
  Tales' author .... CHAUCER
  Tales' heroine .... GRISELDA
  Tales' inn .... TABARD
cantharides .... IRRITANT,
    SPANISH FLY, STIMULANT
  singular of .... CANTHARIS
canticle .... ODE, HYMN, SONG,
    CHANT, PAEAN, PSALM,
    BRAVURA, INTROIT
Canticle of Canticles .... SONG
  OF SOLOMON, SONG OF SONGS
cantina .... DINER, CANTEEN,
    SNACK BAR, SALOON
cantle ...... PIECE, SLICE, PORTION
canto .... PASSUS, STANZA
  Archaic .... FIT
  obsolete .... SONG, BALLAD
Canton .... BILLET, CORNER,
    COUNTY, REGION, BORDURE,
    SECTION, DISTRICT,
    QUARTER(S), QUADRANS
  crepe .... SILK
  flannel .... NAP
  is capital of .... KWANGTUNG
  is former name of
  ..... GUANGZHOU, KWANGCHOW
  river .... PEARL
  river island .... MACAO,
    MACAU
cantor .... SINGER, MELODIST,

CHAZ(Z)AN, PRECENTOR
cantrip .... PRANK, TRICK,
    (MAGIC) SPELL
cantullate .... SING
cantus .... SONG, MELODY
Canuck .... CANADIAN
canvas .... DUCK, CLOTH, SAIL(S),
    TENT(S), (OIL) PAINTING
  arena .... BOXING RING
  boat .... CANOE
  cover ...... TARP, TILT, AWNING
  like fabric .... WIGAN
  shelter .... TENT
  ship's .... JIB, MIZZEN,
    SPANKER, STUDDING,
    FOREROYAL
  waterproofed ..... TARP(AULIN)
canvasback .... DUCK
  relative .... SCAUP, REDHEAD
canvass .... SEEK, DISCUSS,
    CAMPAIGN, EXAMINE, SOLICIT
  voters .... POLL, SURVEY,
    ELECTIONEER
canvasser .... POLLER
canyon .... GAP, DALE, DELL,
    VALE, CLEFT, GULCH,
    ARROYO, CREVICE, RAVINE,
    VALLEY
  entrance .... JAWS
  mouth .... ABRA
  wall .... CLIFF
canzone .... POEM, MADRIGAL
canzonet ...... LILT, CENTO, SONG,
    MATIN(S)
caoutchouc .... RUBBER,
    ELATERITE
  source ..... ULE, CEARA, LATEX
cap .... FEZ, TAM, COIF, COIL,
    BERET, TOP, COVER,
    HEADGEAR, HAT, LID, BEANIE,
    HEADPIECE, HOOD, DOME,
    SURPASS
  a-pie .... ENTIRELY,
    DOWNRIGHT, HEAD TO FOOT
  academic .... MORTARBOARD
  and bells wearer ...... (COURT)
    JESTER
  bottle .... CROWN, CAPSULE
  brim .... VISOR
  brimless .... FEZ, TAM,
    BIRETTA, CALOT(TE), PILEUS,
    BALMORAL, BERET, TARBOOSH
  child's .... BIGGIN
  children's/women's
  .... BONNET
  close/fitting .... COIF, TOQUE
  decoration .... POMPON,
    COCKADE, FEATHER
  ecclesiastical .... BERET,
    BARRET, BIRET(TA)

horseman's/with flap
  .... MONTERO
  jester's .... COCKSCOMB
  Jewish priest's .... MITER,
    MITRE
  kind of .... PERCUSSION,
    MORTARBOARD
  knitted .... THRUM
  lawyer's .... COIF
  military .... BUSBY, KEPI,
    HAVELOCK, SHAKO, PERSHING
  mushroom's .... PILEUS
  Oriental .... FEZ, CALPAC,
    KALPAK, TURBAN
  part .... BILL, BRIM, VISOR
  Scottish .... TAM, BALMORAL
  shaped .... PILEATE
  sheepskin .... CALPAC, KALPAK
  skull .... COIF, CALOT(TE),
    PILEUS
  slang .... LID
  square .... BIRETTA
  tube .... CAPSULE
  turned up front .... COCKUP
  visor .... BILL
  winter .... TUQUE
capable .... APT, ABLE, ADROIT,
    SKILLED, COMPETENT, FIT,
    EFFICIENT, QUALIFIED
  of being climbed
  .... SCALABLE
  of being felt .... TACTILE
  of being introduced from
    abroad .... IMPORTABLE
  of being repaired .... FIXABLE,
    MENDABLE
  of being turned outward
  .... REVERSIBLE
  of defense .... TENABLE
  of following advice
  .... AMENABLE
  of motion .... MOTILE
  of moving .... MOBILE
capacious .... AMPLE, ROOMY,
    SPACIOUS
capacitor .... CONDENSER
capacity .... ABILITY, CONTENT,
    VIRTUE, SIZE, VOLUME,
    FUNCTION, FACULTY, GIFT,
    APTITUDE, ABLENESS, STATUS,
    POSITION
  for feeling .... SENTIENCE
  slang .... WHAT IT TAKES
caparison .... OUTFIT,
    ADORNMENT, TRAP(PINGS),
    TROUSSEAU
  horse's .... BRIDLE, SADDLE,
    HARNESS, BLINDERS
cape .... NESS, MANTA, MANTLE,
    ORALE, POINT, TALMA,
    FORELAND, TONGUE,

HEADLAND, MANTILLA, MANTELET, PENINSULA, PROMONTORY
cotton .... MANTA
Dutch .... TAAL, AFRIKAANS
ecclesiastical ..... COPE, AMICE
fur .... ERMINE, PALATINE, PELERINE, COLLARET(TE)
hanging part .... TIPPET
hooded .... AMICE, ALMUCE, MOZ(Z)ETTA
land's .... RAS
like garment .... DOLMAN
Mexican .... SERAPE
muslin/3-cornered .... FICHU
papal .... FANON, FANUM, ORALE, PHANO
sleeveless .... INVERNESS
vestment resembling ..... COPE
women's .... SHAWL
worn for disguise .... CLOAK
Cape Cod food fish .... CERO
Verde Islands capital
.... PRAIA
Verde Islands native .... SERER
Čapek (Karel) character
.... ROBOT
play .... RUR
capelin .... SMELT
Capella ...... KID, STAR, SHE-GOAT
caper .... DIDO, JUMP, LEAP, SKIP, ANTIC, FRISK, CAVORT, GAMBOL, PRANCE, TRICK, CAPRIOLE, CURLICUE, TITTUP, OATCAKE, ROLLICK
criminal .... HEIST, RIP-OFF, ROBBERY
plant .... CAPPARIS
capillary .... VEINLET, MINUTE, SLENDER, HAIRLIKE, BLOOD VESSEL, ARTERIOLE
action .... REPULSION, ATTRACTION
tumor .... ANGIOMA
capital .... CASH, FUNDS, CHIEF, MONEY, ASSETS, RESOURCES, BACKING, PURSE STRINGS, PRINCIPAL, METROPOLIS
body .... SENATE, CONGRESS
business .... STOCK
city ..... SEAT OF GOVERNMENT
colloquial .... EXCELLENT, FIRST RATE, FIRST CLASS
is part of ____ column
.... ARCHITECTURAL
letter ..... INITIAL, UPPER-CASE, MAJUSCULE
make .... ABUSE, EXPLOIT
punishment .... HANGING, EXECUTION, DEATH PENALTY, ELECTROCUTION

ship ..... BATTLESHIP, CRUISER, DREADNAUGHT
too little .... SHOESTRING
Capital actress .... (OLYMPIA) DUKAKIS
gospel singer .... (MAHALIA) JACKSON
rock star .... (RICK) SPRINGFIELD
capitalist .... BARON, BACKER, SPONSOR, FINANCER
slang .... ANGEL
capitalize .... BACK, FUND, FINANCE
on .... CASH IN, PROFIT BY
capitate .... HEAD-SHAPED
Capitol .... STATEHOUSE
capitulary .... ORDINANCES
capitulate .... CEDE, YIELD, SUBMIT, SUCCUMB, SURRENDER
capon .... CHICKEN, ROOSTER
caporal .... TOBACCO
capote .... TOP, HOOD, COVER, BONNET, OVERCOAT, RAINCOAT
capouch .... HOOD, CAPUCHE
capra .... SHE-GOAT
Capri .... ISLE
capriccio .... WHIM, PRANK
caprice .... FANCY, FREAK, DESIRE, NOTION, VAGARY, CROTCHET, WHIM(SY), HUMORESQUE
capricious .... FANCY, FICKLE, ERRATIC, FLIGHTY, MOONISH, WAYWARD, ECCENTRIC, FANTASTIC, ROVING, HOITY-TOITY, WHIMSICAL
Capricorn .... GOAT, CONSTELLATION
capriole .... JUMP, LEAP, CAPER
capsize .... KEEL, TIP-OVER, INVERT, UPSET, OVERTURN, TOPPLE-OVER, TURN-TURTLE
capsicum .... PEPPER, CAYENNE, PAPRICA, PAPRIKA
capstan .... WHIM, WINCH, WINDLASS
bar .... LEVER
drum .... RUNDLE
top .... DRUMHEAD
capsule .... CAP, POD, PILL, AMPULE, AMPOULE, CACHET, SEAL, WAFER, CONTAINER
egg .... OVISAC
form into a .... CAPSULATE
plant .... BOLL
spore .... THECA
version .... PRECIS, SYNOPSIS
capsulize ...... ABRIDGE, SHORTEN,

CONDENSE
captain .... CHIEF, LEAD(ER), OFFICER, HEAD(MAN)
Absalom's .... AMASA
allowance of .... PRIMAGE
boat of the .... GIG
dialectic .... CAP'N
in a restaurant ...... MAITRE D, HEADWAITER
of factory/construction workers .... FOREMAN
of province/state
.... GOVERNOR
of ship, fiction .... AHAB, NEMO, BLIGH, QUEEG
rank below, in merchant ship
.... MATE
rank below, U.S. Navy
.... COMMANDER
ship's .... MASTER, SKIPPER
Captain Cook's discovery
.... SANDWICH (ISLANDS)
Hook's companion .... SMEE
Nemo's creator .... VERNE
Police .... CHIEF, COMMISSIONER
caption .... LEGEND, HEADING, HEADLINE, SUBHEAD, (SUB)TITLE
subject of .... PICTURE, EXHIBIT
captious .... TRICKY, CAVILING, CATTY, FAULT-FINDING, (HYPER)CRITICAL
captivate .... CHARM, ALLURE, ENAMOR, BEWITCH, ATTRACT, ENCHANT, ENTHRALL, FASCINATE
captive .... DETAINEE, PRISONER
bail of .... RANSOM
burden of .... YOKE
captivity .... DURESS, BONDAGE, CONFINEMENT, IMPRISONMENT
capture ...... BAG, COP, NAB, NET, TAKE, CATCH, ARREST, SNARE, ENTRAP, SEIZE, SEIZURE
slang .... COLLAR
captured object .... PRIZE
capuche. See capouch
Capuchin .... MONK, FRIAR, CLOAK, MONEY, SAPAJOU
monkey .... SAI
caput .... HEAD, DOOMED
capybara .... HOG, CAVY, RODENT
car .... AUTO, MACHINE, ROADSTER, VEHICLE, AUTOMOBILE
baggage .... FOURGON
balloon .... NACELLE
bar .... AXLE

battered .... HEAP
bubble of .... BLISTER
buslike, luxurious
.... LIMOUSINE
checkup, repair .... OVERHAUL
closed .... SEDAN
compartment .... TRUNK
decrepit .... HEAP, CRATE,
JALOPY
dome .... BLISTER
for hire .... CAB, TAXI,
TAXICAB, LIMOUSINE
hyped-up .... HOTROD, MACH
(I), RACER, MUSTANG
in a building .... LIFT, CAGE,
ELEVATOR
kind of .... COUPE, SEDAN,
USED, TOWN, MOTOR, RACER,
CLOSED, UTILITY, RAILROAD,
LUXURY, ARMORED, TOURING,
STATION WAGON,
SECONDHAND
mine .... HUTCH
old, broken-down: sl. .... DOG,
JALOPY
old-make .... REO, T-MODEL
on rails .... STREETCAR
part .... TIRE, WHEEL, BUMPER,
FENDER, MUFFLER, ENGINE,
RADIATOR, HEADLIGHT, WIPER,
IGNITION, WINDSHIELD, GAS
TANK, TURN SIGNAL
shoes .... FOUR TIRES
suspended .... TELFER, LIFT,
TROLLEY, TELPHER, ELEVATOR,
MONORAIL
tassle .... TOGGLE
touring .... PHAETON
train's last .... CABOOSE
versatile .... JEEP
with folded top
.... CONVERTIBLE
carabao ...... BUFFALO, TAMARAU,
TAMARAW
horn bugle .... TAMBULI
carabineer .... HORSEMAN,
CAVALRYMAN
carabinieri .... POLICE
caracal .... FUR, LYNX
caracara .... HAWK, FALCON
Caracas is capital of
.... VENEZUELA
carack .... GALLEON
caracole .... TURN, WHEEL
caracul .... FUR, SHEEP
carafe .... BOTTLE, DECANTER
caramel .... CANDY, BURNT
SUGAR
carangoid .... CERO, FISH,
CAVALLA, YELLOWJACK,
POMPANO, YELLOWTAIL

carapace .... LORICA, CRUST,
COVERING, SHELL, SHIELD
animal with .... CRAB, TURTLE,
TORTOISE, TERRAPIN,
ARMADILLO
material .... CHITIN
under part of .... PLASTRON
caravan ...... VAN, TOUR, WAGON,
TRAIN, PROCESSION
Arabian .... CAFILA
of a kind .... SAFARI
of horsemen/carriages
.... CAVALCADE
of vehicles .... MOTORCADE
stopping place .... OASIS,
SERAI, INN, CARAVANSARY
caravansary .... INN, KHAN,
HOSTELRY, SERAI, IMARET
caravel ...... SHIP, BEETLE, VESSEL
of history .... NINA, PINTA
caraway .... SEED, PLANT, SPICE
cooky .... SEED CAKE
carbide, tungsten ...... CARBOLOY
carbine .... STEN, RIFLE, MUSKET,
ESCOPET
firearm resembling
.... PETRONEL
carbohydrate .... SUGAR, PECTIN,
INULIN, STARCH, LEVULIN,
LICHENIN, CELLULOSE
most familiar .... SUGAR,
STARCH
most important .... STARCH
source of .... GLUCOSE,
FRUCTOSE, GALACTOSE,
LACTOSE, MALTOSE, SUCROSE,
STARCH, CELLULOSE
suffix .... OSE
type of .... DISACCHARIDES,
MONOSACCHARIDES,
POLYSACCHARIDES
carbolic acid .... PHENOL
carbon .... COAL, COKE, LEAD,
CRAYON
atom and two oxygen atoms
.... (CARBON) DIOXIDE
combine chemically with
.... CARBURET
copy: colloq. .... REPLICA,
DOUBLE, DUPLICATE,
LIKENESS, LOOK ALIKE,
FACSIMILE, (SPITTING) IMAGE
dioxide, cooled and
compressed .... DRY ICE
iron alloy .... PEARLITE
monoxide ...... POISONOUS GAS
pencil .... CHARCOAL,
GRAPHITE
precious/pure .... DIAMOND
product .... SOOT
carbonado .... HACK, MEAT,

SLASH, DIAMOND
carbonate of lime
.... STALACTITE, CALCITE,
STALAGMITE
carbonize .... CHAR
carborundum .... EMERY,
ABRASIVE
tool .... GRINDSTONE
carboy .... BOTTLE
carbuncle ...... PIMPLE, ANTHRAX,
CLUSTER OF BOILS
common site of .... NAPE,
BUTTOCKS
carburetant .... BENZENE,
GASOLINE
carcajou .... LYNX, BADGER,
COUGAR, WOLVERINE
carcass .... BODY, BONES,
SKELETON, FRAMEWORK
of a ship .... HULL
carcinoma .... CANCER,
MALIGNANT TUMOR
surgery .... MASTECTOMY
card .... ACE, PAM, JACK, LIST,
KING, TREY, CARTE, BRUSH,
QUEEN, COMB, DEUCE,
KNAVE, JOKER, CHART,
PASTEBOARD
calling .... IDENTIFICATION
cheat ...... BLACKLEG, SHARPER
colloquial .... CHARACTER
combination .... MELD,
TENACE
dealer .... TALLIER
dealer's leftovers .... STOCK,
TALON
file .... CATALOG(UE)
fortune-telling .... TAROT
French .... CARTE
game .... LOO, FARO, MONTE,
SOLITAIRE, WHIST, BACCARAT,
BEZIQUE, MUGGINS, CRIBBAGE,
SLAPJACK, PEDRO, CASINO,
HEARTS, BRIDGE, CANASTA,
POKER, FANTAN, PINOCHLE,
TWENTY-ONE, BLACKJACK,
SEVEN-UP, ECARTE, NULLO,
PATIENCE, GIN RUMMY, BRAG,
QUADRILLE
game "adviser" ..... KIBITZER
game, 18th century .... OMBER
game extra hand .... KITTY,
WIDOW
game for one .... SOLITAIRE
game for two .... ECARTE,
PIQUET, COONCAN, CONQUIAN
game holding .... HAND
game like bridge .... VINT
game like rummy
.... COONCAN, CONQUIAN
game shuffler .... DEALER

game, solitaire .... CANFIELD
game term .... BID, BYE, PASS,
   CHECK, TRUMP, FLUSH, DEAL,
                RAISE
game, 3-hand .... SKAT
game win .... GIN, SLAM, VOLE
games, authority on
   .... HOYLE
holding .... HAND, TENACE
honor .... ACE
in faro .... SODA
kind of .... PASTE, PLAYING,
   CALLING, COMPASS, POST(AL),
   GREETING, WEDDING, BUSINESS
missing .... LOOSE DEUCE
playing .... PASTEBOARD
sharp .... BLACKLEG
slang .... FLAKE, ODDBALL,
                 CRACKPOT
suit, same .... FLUSH
three-spot .... TREY
two-spot .... DEUCE
wild .... JOKER
with four spots .... QUATRE
wool .... COMB, ROVE, TEASE
cardamom ...... POD, HERB, SEED,
                 GINGER
cardboard box .... CARTON
cardialgin .... HEARTBURN
cardigan .... JACKET, SWEATER,
      WAMPUS, WAM(M)US
cardinal .... MAIN, CHIEF,
   SONGBIRD, CLERIC, PRELATE,
   RED, CLOAK, FINCH, PIVOTAL,
   PRINCIPAL, TOPMOST
American .... REDBIRD
chair of .... THRONE
is one .... PRINCE
office of .... DATARY, DATARIA
rank/position of
   .... CARDINALATE
sign of rank .... RED HAT
skullcap of .... ZUCCHETTO
title of honor .... EMINENCE
vestment .... DALMATIC
cardinals' meeting room
   .... CONCLAVE
carding machine cylinder
   .... SWIFT
cardioid .... HEART-SHAPED
cards, fortune-telling ...... TAROTS
held .... HAND
highest .... HONORS
left after dealing .... CAT,
            STOCK, TALON
player who cuts .... PONE
spots on playing .... PIPS
that are discarded by all the
   players .... CRIB
care .... HEED, CHARGE, CONCERN,
   WORRY, ANXIETY, CAUTION,

   CUSTODY, PRUDENCE,
           TUTELAGE
for .... LOVE, MIND, NURSE,
   WATCH, (AT)TEND, PROVIDE
of the aged .... MEDICARE
careen .... TIP, HEEL, LIST, SWAY,
   LEAN, TILT, LURCH, BIAS,
   SPEED, SLANT, INCLINE
career .... CALLING, PURSUIT,
   RACE, LIFEWORK, VOCATION,
   DASH, RUSH, SPEED, GALLOP,
   OCCUPATION, PROFESSION
careful .... WARY, CHARY, EXACT,
   HEEDFUL, ACCURATE,
   DISCREET, PRUDENT,
   CAUTIOUS, DAINTY, FINICAL,
   GUARDED, STUDIED,
   PAINSTAKING, METICULOUS
carefully .... GINGERLY, WITH
                CARE
careless ...... LAX, RASH, CASUAL,
   SLACK, SLOPPY, ARTLESS,
   LISTLESS, CAREFREE,
   RECKLESS, CURSORY,
   SLIPSHOD, NEGLIGENT,
   REMISS, HEEDLESS,
   NONCHALANT
caress .... PET, BILL, KISS,
   CUDDLE, DANDLE, EMBRACE,
   CODDLE, FONDLE, NUZZLE,
   NESTLE, STROKE, SNUGGLE
bear's .... HUG
bird's .... BILL, PECK
dove's .... BILL (AND COO)
Scottish .... DAUT, DAWT
slang .... NECK
caretaker .... KEEPER, CUSTODIAN
apartment .... CONCIERGE
house of .... LODGE
museum/library ...... CURATOR
of government, temporary
   .... REGENT
property .... TRUSTEE
careworn .... WEARY, ANXIOUS,
   HAGGARD, WORRIED
cargo .... LOAD, LADING, FREIGHT,
   PORTAGE, SHIPMENT
boat .... SCOW, OILER, TANKER,
   TRADER, FREIGHTER
cast overboard ship
   .... JETSAM
from wrecked ship
   .... FLOTSAM
hot .... CONTRABAND
put on .... LADE, LOAD
ship's .... BULK
space in ship .... HOLD
carhop .... WAITER, WAITRESS
Carib .... GALIBI, INDIAN
Caribbean dance .... LIMBO
island .... AVES, ARUBA,

               BONAIRE
port .... COLON, ARUBA
witchcraft .... OBEAH
caribe .... PIRAYA
caribou .... REINDEER
male .... STAG
caricature .... COPY, PARODY,
   SATIRE, BURLESQUE,
   TRAVESTY, MIMICRY,
   PRETENSE, DISTORTION
colloquial .... TAKE-OFF
means of expression
   .... CARTOON, LAMPOON,
            BURLESQUE
caricaturist .... SATIRIST,
           CARTOONIST
Berger .... OSCAR
carinate .... KEEL-SHAPED
carillon .... PEAL
cariole .... CART, CARRIAGE
cark .... ANNOY, WORRY
carl .... CHURL, BONDMAN,
            VILLEIN
carline ...... HAG, WITCH, WOMAN
Carlton's (hotel) partner
   .... RITZ
Carmelite .... (WHITE) FRIAR
Carmen composer .... BIZET
Carmichael (Hoagy) hit song
   .... STARDUST
carminative seeds ...... CARAWAY
carmine .... RED, CRIMSON
carnage .... BLOODSHED, KILLING,
   BUTCHERY, MASSACRE,
   MURDER, SHAMBLES,
   SLAUGHTER
carnal .... WILD, RAKISH, BODILY,
   SEXUAL, FLESHY, MUNDANE,
   GENTILE, SENSUAL, WORLDLY
carnation .... FLOWER, PICOTEE,
   RED, ROSY-PINK, DIANTHUS
carnauba .... PALM
product .... WAX
carnelian .... QUARTZ,
           CHALCEDONY
carnival .... FAIR, GALA,
   FESTIVAL, FETE, FESTIVITY,
   EXHIBITION, CIRCUS,
   REVELRY, MERRYMAKING
character .... SHILL, BARKER,
           GRIFTER
famous .... MARDI GRAS
feature ...... PARADE, PAGEANT,
   RIDES, CONFETTI, SIDESHOWS
gambling operator .... GRIFTER
hawker's spot .... PITCH
carnivore ...... DOG, MINK, URSUS,
   LION, WOLF, PUMA, OTTER,
   BEAR, (POLE)CAT, FOUMART,
   GENET, TIGER, LEOPARD,
   HYENA, RATEL, SERVAL,

COUGAR, OCELOT, OPPOSUM,
SEAL, LYNX, WEASEL
diet .... MEAT, FLESH
opposed to .... HERBIVORE
carnivorous insect .... MANTIS
reptile .... MONITOR, TUATARA,
ALLIGATOR, CROCODILE
carnotite ...... MINERAL, URANIUM
carob .... POD, TREE, LOCUST,
ALGAROBA
carol ...... LILT, SING, SONG, TRILL
Christmas .... NOEL
singers .... WAIT
Carol .... BURNETT, CHANNING
Caroline, diminutive of
.... CARRIE
island .... YAP, TRUK, BELAU
(PALAU), POHNPEI (PONAPE)
Carolinian .... TARHEEL
carom .... RECOIL, REBOUND,
RICOCHET
carotene .... VITAMIN A
common source of
.... CARROT, TOMATO
carotid .... ARTERY
and the basilar artery
(medical) .... CIRCLE OF
WILLIS
carousal ...... ORGY, TEAR, BINGE,
SPREE, REVELRY, WASSAIL
carouse .... DRINK, FEAST, QUAFF,
BOUSE, SPREE, REVEL, SWILL,
TIPPLE, DEBAUCH
carousel .... MERRY-GO-ROUND,
LILIOM, WHIRLIGIG
carouser .... SPONGE, REVELER
colloq. .... BARFLY, BOOZER
carp .... NAG, BLEAK, CAVIL,
LOACH, TENCH, CRITICIZE
Japanese .... KOI
kin .... MINNOW
like fish .... IDE, DACE,
GOLDFISH
minnow .... SHINER
red-eye .... RUDD
carpal tunnel syndrome
.... NUMBNESS, TINGLING,
WEAKNESS
affected part of .... HAND,
INDEX FINGER, THUMB,
MIDDLE FINGERS
Carpatho-Ukraine .... RUTHENIA
carpel .... ACHENE
carpels, united .... PISTIL
carpenter .... JOINER, WRIGHT,
CABINETMAKER,
WOODWORKER,
CONSTRUCTION WORKER
groove of .... DADO
joint of .... MITER, MORTISE
tool of ..... SAW, ADZE, BEVEL,

PLANE, CHISEL, DRILL,
HAMMER, SQUARE
with six legs .... ANT
Carpenter .... KAREN, SCOTT
carpet .... MAT, RUG, COVER,
TAPIS, COVERING, FOOTCLOTH,
FLOOR, TAPETE, FLOORING
Afghan .... HERAT
call on the ..... REBUKE, CHEW
OUT, REPRIMAND
city .... AGRA, TOURNAI
English .... WILTON
holder .... HOOK, TACK
India .... AGRA, DRUGGET
kind of .... WALL-TO-WALL,
DRUGGET, MOQUETTE,
ORIENTAL, HOOKED, WELCOME
material .... MOHAIR,
MOQUETTE, CHENILLE,
BEARSKIN, DRUGGET,
SYNTHETIC FIBER
Persian .... KALI
roll out the red .... BID
WELCOME, DO THE HONORS,
WELCOME WITH OPEN ARMS
carpetbagger .... CON-MAN, CON-
ARTIST, POLITICIAN, SLICKER,
PROMOTER, SHARPIE,
ADVENTURER
carping .... CAPTIOUS, CRITICAL
carport .... GARAGE
carpus .... WRIST
bone .... CARPAL(E)
carrack .... VESSEL, GALLEON
carrageen .... IRISH-MOSS,
SEAWEED
carreta .... CART
carriage ...... AIR, GIG, RIG, SHAY,
CARIOLE, POISE, BEARING,
CHAISE, SULKY, VOITURE,
MIEN, PORTANCE,
CONVEYANCE, CART,
CONDUCT, BEHAVIOR,
EQUIPAGE, ROCKAWAY,
WAGON, STANHOPE
attendant .... FLUNKEY,
OUTRIDER, OUTRUNNER
baby .... GO-CART, PRAM,
BUGGY, CLARENCE,
PERAMBULATOR
berlin(e) .... BAROUCHE
closed .... COUPE
dog .... DALMATIAN
driver .... HACK(MAN),
COACHMAN
driver's seat .... DICK(E)Y
folding top .... CALASH,
CALECHE, PHAETON
for hire .... HACK, FIACRE,
HANSOM, RICKSHAW

for state occasions
.... CAROCHE
four-wheeled .... CHAISE,
BERLIN(E), PHAETON,
CLARENCE, DEARBORN,
BUCKBOARD, BAROUCHE,
LANDAU, TARANTAS, VICTORIA
French .... FIACRE
hackney .... FLY
hood/top .... CAPOTE
horse-drawn .... SURREY
horseless .... CAR,
AUTO(MOBILE)
Java .... SADO
low-wheeled .... CALASH,
TARANTAS
luggage space .... RUMBLE
man-drawn .... JINRIKSHA,
RICKSHA(W)
one-horse .... SHAY, TRAP,
CHAISE, CALESIN, CARIOLE,
CARRYALL
Philippine .... CALESA,
CARETELA, CARROMATA,
CALESIN, TARTANILLA
pole .... SHAFT, THILL
Russian .... TROIKA,
TARANTAS(S)
seat .... RUMBLE
servant's seat in .... DICKEY,
RUMBLE
single-seat .... STANHOPE
two-wheeled ..... SULKY, TRAP,
CALECHE, CURRICLE,
CARETELA, CALESA, CALASH,
CHAISE, HERDIC, TILBURY
with collapsible top
...... CHAISE, CALASH, BRITSKA,
CALECHE
with liveried attendants
.... EQUIPAGE
carried .... TOTED, BORNE,
SWAYED, TRANSPORTED
a message .... CONVEYED
a motion .... ADOPTED
away .... RAPT, ENGROSSED,
OVERWHELMED
something heavy ...... LUGGED
carrier .... TOTER, BEARER,
TRANSPORTER, MESSENGER
air .... AIRPLANE
armor .... SQUIRE, ARMIGER
bad luck .... JINX
bird .... HOMING PIGEON
coal/brick/mortar .... HOD,
CORF
common .... SHIP, AIRLINER,
SUBWAY, TRAIN, STREETCAR,
TAXI, MASS-TRANSIT,
OCEANLINER
in a depot/airport ...... PORTER

in a railway station
.... REDCAP
in a port/pier .... STEVEDORE
of disease virus .... VECTOR
of God's message ..... ANGEL,
CLERIC, PREACHER
of mail .... POSTMAN
Oriental .... HAMAL
Spanish .... CARGADOR
water .... BHEESTY, BHEESTIE
carrion ...... FILTHY, DECOMPOSE,
ROTTEN, DECAYING
crow .... VULTURE
Carroll (Lewis) forte .... PARODY
heroine .... ALICE
carron oil .... LINIMENT
carrot .... (EDIBLE) ROOT,
VEGETABLE
color .... YELLOW, ORANGE-
RED
family .... PARSLEY
first cultivated in
.... AFGHANISTAN
like-plant .... PARSNIP
nutritive substance of
,,,,,,,,,,,,,,,,,,,,,,,,, CAROTENE
oil tube .... VITTA
wild .... QUEEN ANNE'S LACE
carroty .... CRECY, ORANGE, RED-
HAIRED
carrousel. See **carousel**
carry ...... LUG, WIN, BEAR, LEAD,
TOTE, SWAY, FETCH, CONVEY,
CART, SUSTAIN, TRANSMIT,
TRANSPORT, UPHOLD
across water .... FERRY
away .... RAVE, EXCITE
off .... ABDUCT, KIDNAP,
STEAL, SWIPE
on .... NAG, RANT, WAGE,
URGE, FOLLOW, PURSUE,
CONDUCT, CONTINUE
on person .... WEAR
out ...... OBEY, STAGE, EFFECT,
EXECUTE, ACCOMPLISH
out a promise .... FULFILL
over .... POSTPONE
partner of .... CASH
too far .... AMPLIFY, MAGNIFY,
OVERDO, OVERKILL
weight .... COUNT
carryall .... (TOTE) BAG, BASKET,
CARRIAGE
kind of .... BUS
carrying away .... EFFERENT
unborn child .... ENCEINTE,
PREGNANT
Carson .... KIT, JOHNNY
City is capital of ...... NEVADA
cart .... VAN, BOGY, DRAY,
LORRY, HAUL, CARRY,

CARIOLE, WAIN, WAGON,
TRUNDLE
ammunition .... CAISSON,
TUMBREL, TUMBRIL
hand .... PRAM, DOLLY
low, heavy .... DRAY
pullers .... OXEN
racing .... CHARIOT
two-wheeled .... SULKY
carte .... CARD, MENU, BILL OF
FARE, QUART(E)
blanche of a sort .... BLANK
CHECK
cartel .... POOL, COMBINE, UNION,
AGREEMENT, MONOPOLY
of a sort .... TRUST,
SYNDICATE
Carter Dickson pseudonym
.... CARR
Carthage, capital of .... CARALIS
destroyer of .... ROMANS,
SCIPIO
foe of .... CATO
founder of .... DIDO
god of .... MOLOCH
goddess .... TANIT
of .... PUNIC
queen of .... DIDO
Roman idea of ..... FAITHLESS,
TREACHEROUS
wars of .... PUNIC
Carthaginian conqueror
.... HANNIBAL
general .... HAMILCAR,
HANNIBAL, HASDRUBAL
Carthusian .... NUN, MONK,
EREMITE
order founder .... (SAINT)
BRUNO
cartilage .... TISSUE, GRISTLE
cell .... CHONDROCYTES
combining form ..... CHONDRO
dog tongue's .... LYTTA
gel-like substance
.... COLLAGEN
type of .... FIBRO, ELASTIC,
HYALINE
cartograph .... MAP, PLAT, CHART
cartographer .... MAPPER,
CHARTIST, MERCATOR
opus of .... ATLAS
cartographical half .... HEMI
cartography .... SURVEYING,
TOPOGRAPHY
cartoon .... COMICS, SKETCH,
DRAWING, COMIC STRIP
kind of .... EDITORIAL,
CARICATURE
slang .... FUNNIES
vocals .... BALLOONS
cartoonist .... DRAWER,

CRAYONIST, CARICATURIST,
NAST, CAPP, DISNEY,
SKETCHER, (PETER) ARNO,
(DAVID) LOW, KIRBY,
ADDAMS, SOGLOW, OLIPHANT,
SCHULTZ, TRUDEAU
cartoons .... COMICS, STRIPS
cartridge ...... CASE, SHOT, SHELL
box .... CARTOUCH(E)
container .... CLIP
kind of .... INK, FILM, TAPE
cartwheel .... HAT, HANDSPRING
slang .... COIN
caruncle .... COMB, GILL, WATTLE
Caruso, opera singer .... ENRICO
carvacrol .... ANTISEPTIC,
DISINFECTANT
carve .... CUT(UP), SLIT, INCISE,
CHISEL, SLICE, (EN)GRAVE,
FORM, SHAPE, SCULPT
carved .... GRAVEN, GLYPHIC,
FORMED, SHAPED, MODELED,
CHISELED, ENGRAVED,
ENCHASED, TAILORED
figure .... GLYPH, INTAGLIO
gem .... CAMEO
image .... BUST, STATUE
carver .... ARTIST, GRAVER,
SCULPTOR, SCULPTRESS,
STONECUTTER
carving .... MOLD, BRONZE,
SCULPTURE, SILHOUETTE
art .... GLYPTICS
in low relief .... ANAGLYPHY
stone .... CAMEO
tool .... CHISEL
Cary Grant ...... (ARCHIE) LEACH
casaba .... (MUSK)MELON
fruit-like .... CANTALOUPE
Casal's (Pablo) instrument
.... CELLO
cascade ...... FALL, LINN, SHOWER,
WATERFALL
cascara ...... WAHOO, BEARWOOD,
BUCKTHORN
case .... BOX, CASK, DEED, CRATE,
CAPSULE, CONTAINER, AFFAIR,
MATTER, EXAMPLE, INSTANCE,
LOOK OVER, CAUSE, EVENT,
QUESTION, SUIT, HANDBAG,
VALISE, ACTION, SHEATH,
SITUATION
armadillo's/turtle's
.... CARAPACE
auto tire .... SHOE
book .... FOREL
bullet .... CARTRIDGE
chalice linen .... BURSE
egg .... SHELL
for arnica .... BRUISE

117

for liquor bottles
.... CELLARET
fruit .... RIND
grammatical .... DATIVE,
    ABLATIVE, ACCUSATIVE,
    GENITIVE, NOMINATIVE
gun .... HOLSTER
hospital .... PATIENT
in any .... ANYHOW
in: sl. .... DIE
insect larva's .... INDUSIUM
legal .... SUIT, LITIGATION
of explosives .... PETARD
pea .... POD
portrait .... LOCKET
pupa .... COCOON
remains' .... COFFIN, CASKET
sausage .... INTESTINE
seed .... POD
ship .... HULL
slang .... LOOK OVER,
    EXAMINE
small .... ETUI, GRIP, ETWEE,
    PYXIS, CAPSULE
toiletry .... ETUI, ETWEE,
    COMPACT
trial site .... VENUE
casein preparation .... LACTARENE
synthetic fabric .... LANITAL
casemate .... ENCLOSURE
describing a .... ARMORED,
    SHELLPROOF
casement .... FRAME, WINDOW
casern .... BARRACKS
cash ...... BILLS, (READY) MONEY,
    COINS, SPECIE, CURRENCY
advance .... ARLES, IMPREST
and carry .... AS IS
box .... TILL, REGISTER
note .... VOUCHER
note of sorts .... IOU
on delivery .... COD
ready .... TILL
receipts/payments handler
.... TELLER, CASHIER
register sign .... NO SALE
cashaw .... CUSHAW, SQUASH
cashbook .... LEDGER
cashew .... MANGO, ANACARD,
    PISTACHIO
French .... (A)CAJOU
oil .... CARDOL
cashier .... PURSER, TELLER, FIRE,
    CLERK, BURSAR, DISCARD,
    DISMISS, DISCHARGE
cashmere .... WOOL, KASHMIR
cashoo .... CATECHU
Cashin, dress designer
.... BONNIE
casing .... HULL, COVER, SHELL,
    FRAME, SHEATH(ING)

casino .... CARD GAME,
    SUMMERHOUSE
cask .... KEG, TUN, VAT, BUTT,
    BARECA, BARREL, FIRKIN,
    DRUM, HOGSHEAD, PUNCHEON
bulge .... BILGE
content measurer
.... GA(U)GER
cork/stopper .... BUNG
forty-two-gallon .... TIERCE
four-gallon .... TUB
groove .... CROZE
maker .... COOPER, HOOPER
rim .... CHIMB, CHIME, CHINE
small .... RUN(D)LET
stave .... LAG
staves, set .... SHOOK
casket .... BOX, PIX, CHEST,
    COFFIN
carrier .... PALLBEARER
for sacred relics .... CIST,
    KIST, RELIQUARY
for valuables .... COFFER
Casmurro or Pedro .... DOM
Caspary (Vera) play ...... LAURA
Caspian Sea fish .... BELUGA,
    STURGEON
tributary .... KURA, URAL,
    VOLGA
casque .... HELMET
cassaba. See casaba
Cassandra .... SEERESS,
    PREDICTOR, PROPHETESS
descriptive of .... LIAR
parent of .... PRIAM, HECUBA
cassava ...... JUCA, ROOT, MANIOC,
    MANIHOT
product .... BREAD, STARCH,
    TAPIOCA
casserite .... TINSTONE
casserole .... STEW, RAGOUT,
    BAKING DISH, SERVING DISH
chicken/tuna .... TETRAZZINI
eggplant .... PARMIGIANA
cassete .... HOLDER, CARTRIDGE
cassia .... BARK, CINNAMON
cathartic drug .... SENNA
family .... LAUREL
cassimere .... CASHMERE, WOOLEN
    CLOTH
Cassini, designer .... OLEG
Cassiopeia's chair .... STARS,
    CONSTELLATION
daughter .... ANDROMEDA
husband .... CEPHEUS
cassis .... LIQUEUR
cassock .... SOUTANE, CLERIC,
    CLERGYMAN, VESTMENT
belt .... SURCINGLE
cassowary .... BIRD, RATITE
bird like .... EMU, RHEA,

    OSTRICH
descriptive of ...... FLIGHTLESS
cast .... FORM, HURL, MOLD, TOSS,
    PITCH, HEAVE, FOUND, THROW
a stone .... FLING, SLING
about .... LOOK, DEVISE,
    SEARCH
amorous glances .... OGLE
aside/away ..... VOID, DISCARD,
    ABANDON, DISREGARD
ballot .... VOTE
ballot, affirmative .... VOTE
    YES
ballot, negative .... VOTE NO
blame on .... REFLECT,
    DISCREDIT
down .... HURL, REJECT,
    DISOWN, DEPRESS
founded .... FUSIL(E)
horn .... MEW
in printing .... STEREOTYPE,
    ELECTROTYPE
iron .... HARD METAL, RIGID
medical .... PLASTER,
    POULTICE
metal .... PIG IRON
metal mass .... PIG, INGOT,
    BULLION
of characters .... TROUPE,
    DRAMATIS PERSONAE
off .... DUMP, SHED, SLOUGH,
    DISCARD, EXUVIATE
off a lover .... JILT
off by animal .... MOLT
out .... OUST, EJECT, EXPEL,
    EVICT
thing .... FLY, NET, BAIT, DICE,
    VOTE, ANCHOR, BALLOT
up/forth ..... VOMIT, THROW UP
with matrix .... MOLD
Castalia .... SPRING
castanea .... CHESTNUT
castaway .... WAIF, PARIAH,
    OUTCAST
a kind of ..... LEPER, OUTLAW,
    FUGITIVE
shipwreck's .... MAROON,
    DERELICT
caste .... GENS, RANK, CLASS,
    SOCIAL SYSTEM
castellan .... KEEPER, MASTER,
    CHATELAIN, CUSTODIAN,
    WARDEN, GOVERNOR
castellate .... ARM, ENTRENCH,
    FORTIFY
caster .... CRUET, STAND, BOTTLE,
    ROLLER, PITCHER, FISHERMAN,
    TRUCKLE, TRUNDLE
castigate .... DOCK, LASH,
    CORRECT, CHASTEN,
    CHASTISE, REBUKE, PUNISH,

CRITICIZE
Castile .... SOAP
designating part of .... NUEVA, VIEJA
province .... AVILA
river .... EBRO
casting mold .... DIE, MATRICE
place .... FOUNDRY
castle .... FORT, HOME, PALACE, BASTION, FORTRESS, MANSION, ROOK, CHESS PIECE, STRONGHOLD
attackers' explosive .... PETARD
court .... BAILEY
creek/ditch/defense ...... MOAT
entrance .... POSTERN
French .... CHATEAU
governor/warden .... CASTELLAN
in the air .... BUBBLE, DAYDREAM, ILLUSION, REVERIE, PIE IN THE SKY
keep .... DONJON
keeper .... CASTELLAN, CHATELAIN
lady of the .... CHATELAINE
open space .... WARD
tower .... KEEP, DONJON, BARRICAN
underground cell .... DUNGEON
VIP .... KING, KNIGHT
wall .... BAIL(EY)
warden .... CONSTABLE
Castles' dance .... BUNNY HOP, CASTLE WALK
castoff .... JUNK, TRASH, GARBAGE, REFUSE, REJECT, SHED, ORPHAN, DEADWOOD, DISOWNED, ABANDONED
castor .... HAT, BEAN, CRUET, BEAVER
bean protein .... RICIN
oil .... CATHARTIC, LUBRICANT, PURGATIVE
oil plant poison .... RICIN
silk .... ERI(A)
Castor .... STAR
and Pollux ..... TWINS, GEMINI, DIOSCURI
father of .... ZEUS
killer of .... IDAS
mother of .... LEDA
twin brother of .... POLLUX
castrate ...... GELD, SPAY, ALTER, UNMAN, CAPONIZE, DESEX, DISABLE, ENERVATE, EMASCULATE, STERILIZE
slang .... FIX, DEBALL
castrated .... GIBBED, IMPOTENT
animal .... STAG, NEUTER

boar .... HOG
bull .... OX
cattle .... STEER
horse .... GELDING
male cat .... GIB
man .... EUNUCH, CASTRATO
pig .... BARROW
rooster/cock .... CAPON
sheep .... WETHER
casual .... IDLE, CHANCE, RANDOM, PASSING, AIMLESS, CARELESS, OFFHAND, CURSORY, INFORMAL, INCIDENTAL, PERFUNCTORY
slang .... HAPPY-GO-LUCKY
casualty .... VICTIM, ACCIDENT, MISHAP, CALAMITY, DISASTER, DEATH, INJURY, FATALITY
casuist .... QUIBBLER
alleged .... JESUIT
of a sort .... SOPHIST
casuistic .... SPECIOUS, PLAUSIBLE, DECEPTIVE
casus .... CASE, EVENT, HAPPENING, OCCURRENCE
belli result .... WAR
cat .... FELINE, TIGER, ANGORA, LION, COUGAR, LEOPARD, PUMA, CIVET, GENET(TE), FELID, BAUDRONS, LYNX, MALKIN, MAWKIN, OCELOT, MARGAY, PANTHER, PUSS(Y)
brier .... SMILAX
burglar .... ROBBER
castrated male .... GIB
colloquial .... KITTY, PUSSY
domestic .... MANX
drinking way of .... LAP
epithet .... BAUDRONS
eyed animal .... LYNX
family .... FELI(DAE), FELINE
fastest .... CHEETAH
female .... QUEEN, TABBY, GRIMALKIN
grinning, proverbial .... CHESHIRE
like animal .... LINSANG, GENET(TE), ZIBET(H)
mice-hunting .... MOUSER
move like a .... PUSSYFOOT
musk-yielding .... CIVET
nap .... DOZE
o-nine-tails .... WHIP
of the .... FELINE
pet .... ANGORA, MALTESE, PERSIAN, SIAMESE
ring-tailed .... SERVAL
sound ...... MEW, MEOW, PURR, ROAR, MIAOW, MIAUL, CATERWAUL
spotted .... JAGUAR, OCELOT,

MARGAY, SERVAL
striped .... TIGER
young .... KITTEN
cata, as prefix ...... AWAY, DOWN, AGAINST, THROUGH, BACKWARD
catachresis, victim of .... (MRS.) MALAPROP
cataclysm ...... DELUGE, DEBACLE, DISASTER, UPHEAVAL, HAVOC, CATASTROPHE
kind of .... WAR, FLOOD, EARTHQUAKE
catacomb .... CRYPT, TOMB, VAULT, LOCULUS, CEMETERY
catafalque .... BIER
catalase .... ENZYME
catalo .... BISON, BOVINE, BUFFALO
catalogue ...... LIST, INDEX, BOOK, ROLL, RECORD, CLASSIFY, ARRANGE, REGISTER, SCHEDULE
bookseller's ...... BIBLIOTHECA
box .... CARD FILE
of goods, etc. .... STOCK, INVENTORY
of saints .... HAGIOLOGY
official .... CANON
Catalonian poet-musician .... TROUBADOR
catalyst .... URGER, INCITER, REAGENT, ACTIVATOR, PROVOKER, CAUSER, INSTIGATOR
catamaran .... BOAT, RAFT, BALSA, FLOAT
catamenia .... MENSTRUATION
catamite .... PUNK
catamount .... LYNX, PUMA, COUGAR
cataplasm .... POULTICE
catapult ...... FIRE, HURL, HURTLE, LAUNCH, BRICOLE, TAKEOFF, BALLISTA, ONAGER, TREBUCHET
kin of .... MANGONEL
projectile .... PELLET
cataract .... LINN, FALLS, DELUGE, CASCADE, DOWNPOUR, WATERFALL, EYE DISEASE
catarrh .... COLD, RHEUM
cigarette for .... CUBEB
nasal .... CORYZA
catastasis .... EXORDIUM
catastrophe ...... RUIN, ACCIDENT, CALAMITY, DISASTER, DOWNFALL, ADVERSITY, PERDITION, UPHEAVAL, MISFORTUNE
in geology .... CATACLYSM

in health .... PAROXYSM
Catawba .... WINE, GRAPE, INDIAN
catch .... NAB, GRAB, HOOK, NAIL,
    TAKE, (EN)TRAP, SEIZE,
    CAPTURE, RATCHET
at straws .... HOPE FOR THE
    BEST
breath .... GASP, PANT
fish .... HAUL, SEINE
in a bill .... JOKER, RIDER
in a ship .... TRIP
of clock .... DETENT
on ..... CLICK, FOLLOW, GET IT,
    GET THE PICTURE, REALIZE,
    UNDERSTAND
phrase .... MOTTO, SLOGAN,
    WARCRY
releaser .... PAWL, DETENT,
    TRIPPER
sight of .... ESPY, SPOT,
    DESCRY, DETECT, DISCERN
slang .... COLLAR
taken in a robbery ..... BOOTY
the eye .... GLARE, APPEAR,
    MEET THE GAZE
up .... GAIN ON, OVERHAUL,
    OVERTAKE
with the _____ .... GOODS
Catch 22 author .... HELLER
catchall .... BASKET, (RAG)BAG,
    HANDBAG, ET AL,
    ETC (ETERA)
one kind of .... ATTIC,
    CLOSET, GARAGE
catcher .... TAKER, CAPTOR,
    NABBER, ATHLETE, BASEMAN
catching .... TAKING, FETCHING,
    ALLURING, ATTRACTIVE,
    INFECTIVE, INFECTIOUS,
    VIRULENT, CONTAGIOUS
catchment, kind of ...... CISTERN,
    RESERVOIR
catchpenny .... CHEAP,
    WORTHLESS
catchpole .... TAX-GATHERER,
    CHICKEN-CHASER
catchup .... CATSUP, KETCHUP
catchword .... CUE, KEY, CLUE,
    HINT, MOTTO, PHRASE,
    SLOGAN
catchy .... FITFUL, TRICKY,
    DECEPTIVE, DECEIVING,
    ERRATIC, MISLEADING
slang .... FISHY
cate .... DAINTY, DELICACY
catechism .... GUIDE, MANUAL,
    HANDBOOK
catechize .... TEACH
catechu .... CUTCH, CASHOO,
    GAMBLER
like gum .... KINO

catechumen ...... PUPIL, STUDENT,
    CONVERT, NEOPHYTE
categorical .... DIRECT, ABSOLUTE,
    EXPLICIT, POSITIVE
categorize .... SORT, LABEL,
    TITLE, COLLATE, CLASSIFY
category .... CLASS, GRADE,
    GENRE, GROUP, ORDER,
    FAMILY, GENUS, SPECIES,
    DIVISION
catena .... SERIES, CHAIN
catenate .... LINK
cater .... SELL, SERVE, SUPPLY,
    FEED, PANDER, PURVEY,
    PROVIDE
to one's whim or mood
    .... HUMOR, INDULGE
cateran .... ROBBER
catercornered .... CROSSWISE,
    DIAGONAL(LY)
caterer .... PURVEYOR, SUPPLIER
army .... SUTLER
kind of .... PIMP, PANDERER,
    PROCURER
caterpillar .... WERI, SLUG,
    LARVA, LOOPER, CUTWORM,
    WOOBUT, WEBWORM,
    WOOLLYBEAR
disease .... WILT
hair .... SETA
Caterpillar treaded vehicle
    .... TANK, CAT, AMTRAC,
    HALF-TRACK, TRACTOR
caterwaul .... HOWL, WAIL,
    MIAUL, SCREAM, SCREECH
catface .... SCAR
catfish .... SHAL, DORAD,
    DOCMAC, BULLHEAD,
    BULLPOUT, TANDAN, SCULPIN,
    SILURID
electric .... RAAD
Catfish Row resident .... BESS,
    PORGY
catgut ...... STRING, VIOLIN, CORD,
    CATLING, WHIPCORD
catharsis ...... PURGING, RELEASE,
    CLEANSING
cathartic .... ALOE, ALOIN,
    CASSIA, PHYSIC, CALOMEL,
    GAMBOGS, EMETIC, LAXATIVE,
    EVACUANT, CASTOR OIL,
    APERIENT, PURGATIVE,
    HEALING, PURGING, REMEDIAL
drug .... SENNA
from flax .... LININ
resin .... SCAMMONY
Cathay .... CHINA
cathedra .... SEE, THRONE
cathedral .... CHURCH, DUOMO,
    TEMPLE, MINSTER, BASILICA,
    OFFICIAL, AUTHORITATIVE

city .... ELY, AMIENS,
    CHARTRES, R(H)EIMS
clergyman .... CANON
famous .... NOTRE DAME
passage .... SLYPE
presiding official .... DEAN
private land of .... CLOSE
Cather, novelist .... WILLA,
    SIBERT
Catherine, mother of 3 kings
    .... MEDICI
the Great .... TSARINA
the Great's favorite
    .... POTEMKIN
Catholic .... GENERAL, LIBERAL,
    TOLERANT, UNIVERSAL
lay society .... SODALITY
tribunal .... ROTA
tribunal member ...... AUDITOR
catholicon ...... ELIXIR, CURE-ALL,
    PANACEA
cation .... ION
catkin .... CHAT, PUSSY,
    AMENT(A), CATTAIL
tree .... BIRCH, POPLAR,
    WILLOW
catlike .... SLY, FURTIVE,
    NOISELESS, STEALTHY
animal .... LINSANG
catling .... KNIFE, CATGUT
catnap .... DOZE
catnip .... NEP
catouse .... UPROAR
cats and dogs, sometimes
    .... ENEMIES
Cats classic .... MEMORIES
cat's eye .... GEM, QUARTZ,
    CHATOYANT, CHRYSOBERYL
paw .... PAD, DUPE, KNOT,
    PAWN, TOOL, STOOGE
whisker(s) .... VIBRISSA(E)
Catt, American suffragist
    .... CARRIE
cattail .... DODD, TULE,
    (BUL)RUSH, CATKIN, RAUPO,
    REED(MACE)
cattiness .... SPITE, ENMITY,
    MEANNESS, VENDETTA
cattle .... KINE, NOWT, OXEN,
    BOVID, BOVINE, LIVESTOCK
beef .... STEER, HOLSTEIN
black .... ANGUS, KERRY,
    WELSH
boat .... TARTAN
breed .... ANGUS, DEVON,
    DEXTER, DURHAM, GALLOWAY,
    SUSSEX, BRAHMAN, HEREFORD,
    JERSEY, HOLSTEIN, LONGHORN
castrated male .... STEER
catcher .... HAYWARD
catching rope .... BOLA

crossed with bison/buffalo .... CAT(T)ALO
dairy .... JERSEY, KERRY, GUERNSEY, HEREFORD
dealer .... DROVER
dewlap .... JOWL
disease .... GID, BOTS, GARGET, NAGANA, ANTHRAX, LOCO, MEASLES, MURRAIN, LUMPY-JAW, TEXAS-FEVER, SCOURS, SHAKES, STAGGERS
dwarf .... DEVON, NIATA
dysentery .... SCOURS
enclosure .... KRAAL, RODEO, CORRAL
epidemic .... RINDERPEST
farm .... RANCH, ESTANCIA
farm manager .... RANCHER
fat .... SUET, TALLOW
feed for hire .... GIST
feed from linseed .... OIL CAKE
female that has given birth .... COW
female under 24 months of age .... HEIFER
fodder .... FARRAGO
foot of .... HOOF
frenzied run .... STAMPEDE
grazing land .... RANGE, PASTURE
group .... HERD, DROVE
hedge .... OXER
herdsman .... VAQUERO
hybrid .... CAT(T)ALO
male .... BULL
nervous ailment .... STAGGERS
parasite .... TICK
parasitic larva .... WARBLE
pen .... YARD, KRAAL, CORRAL
plague (same as epidemic)
polled .... MUL(L)EY
ranch man .... COWBOY, VAQUERO
raiser .... RANCHER, STOCKMAN
round-up .... RODEO, WRANGLE
short-horned .... DURHAM
stall .... CRIB
stealer/thief .... RUSTLER
stealing .... RUSTLING
tender .... COWHEAD, VAQUERO
tormentor .... GNAT
urine .... STALE
vertigo .... MEGRIM
cattleman ...... DROVER, HERDER, RANCHER, STOCKMAN
catty ...... MEAN, BITCHY, FELINE, PETTISH, MALICIOUS, SHREWISH, SPITEFUL
person .... VERMIN
catwalk .... BRIDGE, PATHWAY,

PLATFORM
Caucasian .... ARYAN, TATAR, IRANIAN, WHITE MAN
carpet/rug .... BAKU, KUBA
Central .... OSSET
goat .... TUR
language .... GEORGIAN, SEMITIC, CIRCASSIAN
race .... SEMITE
Caucasus inhabitant .... OSSET(IAN)
region .... OSSETIA
river .... KUBAN
wild goat .... TUR
caucho tree .... ULE
caucus .... CONFAB, MEETING
room, descriptive of a .... SMOKY, SMOKE FILLED
caudad, opposed to .... CEPHALAD
caudal appendage .... TAIL
caudillo .... LEADER, DICTATOR, COMMANDER
Caudillo, El .... FRANCO
caudle .... DRINK, GRUEL
caught .... RAPT, STUCK, SEIZED
by the police .... ARRESTED
short ...... HURRIED, SURPRISED
up in .... AMID, TANGLED
with the ____ .... GOODS
caul .... VEIL
cauld .... COLD
cauldron .... POT, VAT, BOILER, COPPER, KETTLE
caulicle .... STEM
cauliflower .... VEGETABLE
crossed with broccoli .... BROCCOFLOWER
ear ..... DEFORMITY, DEFORMED
eared one/row character .... PUG, BOXER, PUGILIST
variety .... CABBAGE, BROCCOLI
caulis .... STEM, STALK
caulk .... SEAL, BLOCK, CHINK, CHINSE, STOP UP
caulking material .... TAR, OAKUM
causal connective .... FOR, AFTER, SINCE, BECAUSE, THEREFORE
cause .... MAKE, BASE, BASIS, EFFECT, GROUND, MOTIVE, INDUCE, ORIGIN, REASON, OCCASION, MOVEMENT
bad luck .... HEX, JINK
celebre, usual .... CASE, TRIAL, SCANDAL
destruction of cells .... LYSE
for divorce .... GROUND(S)
for war .... CASUS BELLI

in law .... (LAW)SUIT
impelling .... MAINSPRING
of Archimedes' cry, "Eureka!" .... IDEA
spasm .... CONVULSE
to arch .... ROACH
to continue .... PERPETUATE
to do unwillingly .... PRESS, COERCE
to endure .... TOUGHEN
to fight .... EMBROIL
to grow .... REAR
to happen .... BRING, EFFECTUATE
to happen suddenly .... PRECIPITATE
to remember .... REMIND
wonderment .... AWE
causerie ...... CHAT, TALK, PLEAD, APERCU, DEBATE, PARLEY, DISCOURSE, DISCUSSION
causes or origins, science of .... (A)ETIOLOGY
causeuse .... SOFA, TETE-A-TETE
causeway .... ROAD, CAUSEY, HIGHWAY, PASSAGE
causing abortion .... ECBOLIC
disaster .... MALEFIC
little or no pain ..... INDOLENT
sneezing .... ERRHINE
caustic .... LIME, TART, BITING, HOSTILE, CUTTING, CORROSIVE, MORDANT, SNAPPISH, MORDACIOUS, SEVERE, SARCASTIC, SARDONIC, SHARP, STINGING, VITRIOLIC
agent ..... LYE, ACID, ERODENT
of wit .... IRONIC
soda .... SODIUM HYDROXIDE
solution .... LYE
substance, burn with .... CAUTERIZE
temper .... CROSS, TESTY, ORNERY, SNAPPISH
cauterant .... ACID, MOXA, BURNER, CAUTERY
cauterize ...... BURN, CHAR, SEAR, SCORCH, OXIDIZE
cauterizing agent .... MOXA
chemical to destroy warts .... SILVER NITRATE
caution .... BAIL, CARE, ALERT, TIP-OFF, WARN(ING), PRUDENCE, ADVICE, ADMONISH, ADMONITION
cautious .... WARE, WARY, ALERT, CHARY, CAREFUL, GUARDED, MINDFUL, PRUDENT, CIRCUMSPECT
general .... FABIUS

cavalcade ...... PARADE, PAGEANT, CARAVAN, PROCESSION
cavalier .... GAY, PROUD, ESCORT, KNIGHT, GENTLEMAN, HORSEMAN, GALLANT, ARROGANT, HAUGHTY
cavalla .... CERO, FISH, HORES, CARANGOID
cavalry .... HORSE, TROOPS, HORSEMEN, HORSE SOLDIERS, HUSSARS, DRAGOONS
attack obstacle/hazard .... CALTRAP, CALTROP
bugle call .... BOOTS AND SADDLES
command .... TO HORSE, CHARGE, DISMOUNT
commander .... HIPPARCH
flag .... CORNET
horse .... WALER, TROOPER
soldier .... LANCE(R), SPAHI
standard .... LABARUM
sword .... SABER
unit .... SQUADRON
cavalryman .... RIDER, DRAGOON, LANCER, TROOP(ER)
Algerian ..... SPAHI, CAMELEER
French .... CARABINEER, CHASSEUR, CARABINIER
German .... U(H)LAN
Hungarian/Croatian .... HUSSAR
mount of Algerian ..... CAMEL
Russian .... COSSACK
Turkish .... SPAHI, SPAHEE
weapon of .... LANCE, SABER
cavatina .... SONG, MELODY
cave .... DEN, LAIR, ANTRE, PIT, GROTTO, ANTRUM, HOLE, HOLLOW, RECESS
at a volcano's mouth .... CRATER
dweller .... BAT, BEAR, LION, TROLL, HERMIT, TROGLODYTE
dwelling .... SPEL(A)EAN
explorer .... SPELUNKER
for shelter/refuge ..... BURROW
formation .... STALACTITE, STALAGMITE
in .... SINK, STOVE, YIELD, SUBMIT, COLLAPSE
man ..... HERMIT, TROGLODYTE
man-made .... CRYPT
man's time .... STONE AGE
of a .... SPELEAN
poetic .... GROT, ANTRE
caveat ...... WRIT, NOTICE, ADVICE, CAUTION, WARNING, GUIDANCE, ADMONITION
Cavell, nurse .... EDITH
cavern .... LAIR, ANTRE, GROT(TO)

Hebrides Island ...... FINGAL'S CAVE
caves, inhabiting .... SPELEAN
researcher of .... SPELEOLOGIST
science of .... SPELEOLOGY
caviar .... ROE, RELISH
connoisseur .... GOURMET, RUSSIAN, GOURMAND
fish .... STERLET, STURGEON
material ...... ROE, (FISH) EGGS
source of .... SALMON, SHAD, STERLET, STURGEON
cavil .... CARP, BICKER, DIFFER, OBJECT, PROTEST, QUIBBLE, DISAGREE
cavities, full of .... CAVERNOUS
cavity .... PIT, CELL, HOLE, FOSSA, ANTRUM, HOLLOW, DENT, POCKET, OPENING
animal tissue .... LOCULUS
cause of dental .... PLAQUE
combining form .... C(O)ELE
crystal-lined .... GEODIC
crystal-lined rock .... VOOG, VUGG, VUGH, GEODE
dental .... CARIES, TOOTH DECAY
embryonic .... COELOM(E)
eye .... ORBIT
for excretion or secretion .... FOLLICLE
heart .... ATRIUM
honeycomb .... CELL, ALVEOLUS
in anatomy ..... BURSA, FOSSA, SINUS, ANTRUM, LACUNA, ALVEOLUS
in biology .... LACUNA
in zoology .... CLOACA, ALVEOLUS
membrane .... VESICLE
nose/nasal ...... SINUS, ATRIUM
of abdominal .... COELIAC
on the cheek or chin .... DIMPLE
outlet .... ORIFICE
plant tissue .... LOCULUS
cavort .... LEAP, ROMP, SKIP, CAPER, FROLIC, PRANCE
cavy .... PACA, RODENT, CAPYBARA, GUINEA PIG
caw sounder .... CROW, RAVEN
Cawdor castle site .... NAIRN
cay .... KEY, (CORAL) REEF, (SAND) BANK
cayene .... CANARY, PEPPER, CHILIES, CAPSICUM
cayman .... YAKI, ALLIGATOR
cayuse .... PONY
cowpoke's .... HOSS

Ceara .... FORTALEZA
cease .... END, HALT, STOP, DESIST, REFRAIN, DISCONTINUE
-fire .... TRUCE
nautical .... AVAST
prematurely .... ABORT
ceased to be .... DIED, EXPIRED
ceaseless ..... ENDLESS, INCESSANT, ETERNAL, CONTINUAL, CONTINUOUS, CONSTANT, PERENNIAL, PERSISTENT
Cechy .... BOHEMIA
Cecrops ...... KING, MAN-DRAGON
daughter of .... HERSE
cecum .... POUCH, CHAMBER
cedar .... WOOD, THUJA, DEODAR, SAVIN(E), TOONA, CONIFER, JUNIPER
Himalayan .... DEODAR
cedarbird .... WAXWING
cede .... GRANT, YIELD, ASSIGN, SURRENDER, SUBMIT, TRANSFER, HAND OVER, RELINQUISH
Cedric .... (WAR)CHIEF
ward of .... ROWENA
cedula .... PERMIT, CERTIFICATE
ceiba fibers .... KAPOK, SILK-COTTON
ceil .... LINE, COVER
ceiling ...... ROOF, COVER, CANOPY
arched .... VAULT
decorated .... PLAFOND
division .... TRAVE
hit the: colloq. .... RAGE, RAVE, ERUPT, BLUSTER
mine .... ASTEL
of sunken panels .... LACUNAR
of the universe .... SKY
picture .... MURAL
plasterwork .... PARGET(ING)
rounded .... DOME, CUPOLA
section .... PANEL
sketcher .... MICHELANGELO
Celaeno .... HARPY
celandine .... PILEWORT
celanese .... RAYON
Celebes .... SULAWESI
city .... MACASSAR
ox .... ANOA
celebrant at mass .... PRIEST
celebrate ...... FETE, HALLOW, DO HONOR TO, OBSERVE, SOLEMNIZE, KEEP, SIGNALIZE, COMMEMORATE
in song .... CAROL
celebrated .... NOTED, FAMOUS, FESTIVE, EMINENT, RENOWNED, OBSERVED, SOLEMNIZED

archaic .... NOTORIOUS
celebration .... RITE, FANFARE,
FETE, FESTIVITY, REJOICING
campus .... HOMECOMING
gala .... FIESTA
kind of .... CORONATION,
HOLIDAY, INAUGURATION
with much drinking
.... WASSAIL, CAROUSAL
celebrities' meeting place
.... SALON
celebrity .... FAME, HERO, IDOL,
VIP, LION, STAR, RENOWN,
BIG NAME, NOTABLE,
EMINENCE
treat like a .... LIONIZE
celerity .... HASTE, SPEED, HURRY,
DISPATCH, QUICKNESS,
SWIFTNESS
celery .... PLANT, SMALLAGE,
VEGETABLE
like plant .... UDO
celesta for example
.... IDIOPHONE
celeste .... BLUE, AZURE
Celeste, actress .... HOLM
celestial .... HOLY, DIVINE,
ETHEREAL, HEAVENLY,
URANIC, OLYMPIAN,
SUPERNAL
being .... ANGEL, CHERUB,
SERAPH
body .... SUN, STAR, MOON,
COMET, PLANET
circle .... HALO, COLURE
empire .... CHINA
group .... SOLAR SYSTEM
happiness ...... BLISS, ECSTASY
phenomenon .... COMET,
ECLIPSE, RAINBOW
slang .... CHINAMAN
vault .... EMPYREAN
celibacy .... CHASTITY,
SINGLENESS, BACHELORHOOD,
MISOGAMY, SPINSTERHOOD
celibate .... CHASTE, VIRGIN,
SINGLE, BACHELOR, SPINSTER,
UNMARRIED
former .... BENEDICT
one kind of .... MONK, OLD
MAID, PRIEST
cell .... EGG, GERM, OVUM, CADRE,
PROTOPLASM
cavity .... VACUOLE
center .... NUCLEUS
combining form .... CYTE,
CYTO
destruction .... CYTOLYSIS
division ...... MEIOSIS, MITOSIS,
SPIREME
fluid material ...... CYTOPLASM

formation .... CYTOGENESIS
formed by two gametes
.... ZYGOTE
framework .... STROMA
honeycomb .... ALVEOLUS
monks' .... MONASTERY
nerve .... NEURON(E)
network .... CYTOSKELETON
nucleus .... MESOPLAST
nuns' .... CONVENT
occupant .... INMATE
occurrence ...... FERTILIZATION
of animals/birds .... CAGE
of convicts .... JAIL, PRISON
regulators .... ENZYMES
small .... CELLULE, PAPILLA
stinging .... NEMATOCYST
study of the .... CYTOLOGY
vesicle .... LYSOSOME,
PEROXISOME
wall .... PARIES
wall rib .... RAPHE
with electric charge
.... BATTERY
cella .... NAOS, TEMPLE
cellar .... PANTRY, STOREROOM,
WINE-STOCK
location of .... BASEMENT
man in charge of ...... BUTLER
room .... VAULT
wine .... VAULT, BUTTERY
celled structure .... PRISON,
CONVENT, HONEYCOMB,
MONASTERY
cells, change in .... CATAPLASIA
consisting of .... LOCULAR,
CELLULAR
form into .... CELLULATE
mass of/ovum-formed mass
of .... MORULA
the gray .... BRAIN
union of .... ZYGOSIS
water-conducting
.... TRACHEID
cellular .... LOCULAR, ALVEOLATE
celluloid: colloq. .... MOVIES,
(MOVIE) FILM
cellulose fiber/fabric ...... RAYON,
CELANESE
wrapping material
.... CELLOPHANE
Celt .... GAEL, SCOT, IRISH,
WELSH, BRETON, CHISEL
Celtic .... ERSE, IRISH
chief's heir .... TANIST
dart .... COLP
god .... LER, AENGUS
island of paradise .... AVALON
judge/priest .... DRUID
king .... BELI
language .... MANX, WELSH,

BRETON, CYMRIC
lord .... TANIST
people of Wales .... CYMRIC
religious order .... DRUID
sea god .... LER
sea robber .... FOMOR
cement ...... JOIN, GROUT, MASTIC,
ADHESIVE, MALTHA, SOLDER
ingredient .... CLAY, LIME,
WATER
like substance .... GLUE,
PASTE, MUCILAGE
material .... MARL
mixture .... PUTTY, MORTAR,
SLURRY
patch with .... SLUSH
pipe joints/sealing .... LUTE
smoothing tool .... TROWEL
wall .... STUCCO
cemetery ...... GRAVEYARD, GOD'S
ACRE, BONEYARD, ACROPOLIS,
NECROPOLIS
underground .... CATACOMB(S)
cenobite .... MONK, ESSENE,
RECLUSE
dwelling .... CONVENT,
MONASTERY
opposed to .... ANCHORITE
cenotaph .... TOMB, MONUMENT
cense .... THURIFY
censer .... THURIBLE
censor .... CUT, CRITIC, KILL,
REVIEWER, STIFLE, (S)QUASH,
WATCHDOG, RED PENCIL,
FAULTFINDER
kind of .... EDITOR
tool of movie .... SCISSORS
censorious .... CRITICAL
censorship of movie scenes
.... CUTS
speech .... GAG
censure .... RAP, LASH, TASK,
BLAME, ASPERSE, IMPEACH,
DECRY, CRITICISM, CRITICIZE,
CHIDE, REPROVE, UPBRAID,
CONDEMN(ATION), OBLOQUY
census .... COUNT
literally .... HEAD COUNTING,
NOSE COUNTING
taker .... ENUMERATOR
cent .... COIN, PENNY, COPPER
five .... NICKEL
one hundred of them
.... DOLLAR
one tenth of .... MILL
per .... HUNDRED
ten of them .... DIME
twenty-five of them
.... QUARTER
centaur .... CHIRON, NESSUS,
SAGITTARY

father of .... IXION
killed by Hercules ..... NESSUS
centavo .... COIN
centenary .... CENTURY
center .... HUB, MID, CORE,
HEART, FOCUS, LOCUS,
NUCLEUS, PIVOT, MIDDLE
at, in or near .... CENTRIC
farthest from .... DISTAL
having common
.... CONCENTRIC
line .... AXIS
line of verse .... CESURA
moving from .... CENTRIFUGAL
moving toward
.... CENTRIPETAL
nearest the .... PROXIMAL
non-revolving ..... DEAD POINT
of activity .... HUB, HIVE,
FOCUS, GANGLION
of an old-fashioned party
.... QUILT
of attention .... FOCUS,
CONFLUX, FOCAL POINT
of attraction .... CYNOSURE
of command
.... HEADQUARTERS
of energy/force ..... GANGLION
of mass .... CENTROID
of operations .... THEATER
of target ...... EYE, BULL'S-EYE
toward .... ENTAD, MESIAL
wheel's .... HUB
centerpiece .... DOILY, EPERGNE
centesimal .... HUNDREDTH
unit .... GRADE
centesimo, 100 of them .... LIRA,
PESO, BALBOA
centiare, 100 of them .... ARE
centimes, five .... SOU
100 .... FRANC
centipede .... BUG, EARWIG,
INSECT, CHILOPOD, MYRIAPOD,
ARTHROPOD
legs, front pair .... FANGS
relative .... MILLEPEDE
cento .... PATCHWORK
central .... HUB, AXIAL, MAIN,
BASIC, CHIEF, FOCAL, PRIME,
MID(DLE), PRINCIPAL
and guiding .... POLAR
figure .... HERO, STAR, VIP,
ATHLETE, HEROINE
line .... AXIS
mark of target ..... BULL'S-EYE
number .... MEDIAN
part .... CORE, NUCLEUS
point(s) .... FOCUS, FOCI,
NODE, PIVOT, ESSENCE
point of an earthquake
.... EPICENTER

Central African capital
.... BANGUI
African president ...... DACKO,
BOKASSA
American bird .... JUNCO,
CACIQUE, MANAKIN,
CURASSOW
country .... BELIZE, PANAMA,
COSTA RICA, GUATEMALA,
(EL) SALVADOR, HONDURAS,
NICARAGUA
ethnic group .... BANDA,
AZANDE, MBAKA
fiber plant .... MAGUEY,
HENEQUEN
hat/plant .... JIPIJAPA
monkey .... MARMOSET
parrot ...... MACAW, AMAZON
rodent .... PACA, AGOUTI
sash .... TOBE
stinging ant .... KELEP
tortoise .... HICATEE
tree .... EBO(E), AMATE
vulture .... URUBU, ATRATA
wildcat .... EYRA, MARGAY
centralize .... MEET, FOCUS,
UNITE, CONVERGE
centrifugal force, cause of
.... INERTIA
in physiology .... EFFERENT
centripetal, in physiology
.... AFFERENT
century .... AGE, SIECLE,
HUNDRED
plant (fiber) .... ALOE, PITA,
AGAVE, MAGUEY, TEQUILA
ceorl .... CHURL, FREEMAN
cephalad, opposed to
.... CAUDAD
cephalopod .... SQUID, MOLLUSK,
OCTOPUS, CUTTLE(FISH)
Cepheus' daughter
.... ANDROMEDA
wife .... CASSIOPEIA
ceraceous .... WAXY, WAXLIKE
Ceram .... SERANG
ceramic .... CLAY, ENAMEL
mixes .... FRITS
pigment .... SMALTINE
plaque .... TILE
roofing material .... PANTILE
ceramics, of .... FICTILE
product .... TILE, BASALT,
CLOISONNE, EARTHENWARE,
CLAYWARE, CHINAWARE,
POTTERY, PORCELAIN
ceramist .... POTTER
cerate .... WAX, SALVE, OINTMENT
ceratodus .... BARRAMUNDA
ceratin product ...... CORN, HAIR,
HORN, NAIL

ceratoid/ceratose .... HORNY
Cerberus .... DOG
concern of .... HADES
descriptive of .... THREE-
HEADED
cere .... WAX, MEMBRANE
cereal .... GRAIN, GRASS
flour .... FARINA
food ...... RICE, SAMP, HOMINY,
OATMEAL
grain .... OAT, RYE, CORN,
MAIZE, WHEAT, MILLET
grass .... OAT, RYE, WHEAT,
RAGGEE, MILLET, RAG(G)I,
RAGGY
ground .... GRITS, HOMINY
husk .... BRAN
meal .... FARINA
spike .... COB, EAR
stem .... HA(U)LM, STALK
cerebral ...... MENTAL, INTERNAL,
INTELLECTUAL
palsy .... EPILEPSY, NEURALGIA
palsy, type of .... DIPLEGIA,
HEMIPLEGIA, QUADRIPLEGIA
thrombosis .... CLOT-
FORMATION
thrombosis result ...... STROKE
vitamin, so-called .... LSD
cerebrate .... THINK, PONDER,
COGITATE
cerebrum, cortex of .... MANTLE
cerecloth ...... SHROUD, CEREMENT
ceremonial ...... FORMAL, RITUAL,
SOLEMN
bow .... CURTSY, SALAAM
dance .... PAVAN(E)
drink .... TOAST
entrance/exit signal
.... SENNET
procession .... PARADE,
CORTEGE, CAVALCADE
trumpet call .... SENNET
ceremonious ...... PRIM, FORMAL,
POMPOUS, STATELY
act .... SALUTE, SALAAM
display .... BLARE, FANFARE
leave-taking .... CONGE(E)
motion .... FLOURISH
show of homage .... KOWTOW,
SALAAM
trumpet call .... TAPS
ceremony .... POMP, RITE,
FUNCTION, RITUAL,
FORMALITY, OBSERVANCE,
PUNCTILIO
hypocritical .... MUMMERY
kind of ..... PARADE, WEDDING
military .... REVIEW
official .... OATH-TAKING,
INAUGURATION

religious .... MASS, BURIAL
Ceres .... PLANET, DEMETER,
GODDESS, ASTEROID
parent of .... OPS, SATURN
cereus .... CACTUS
Cerigo Island .... KYTHERA
cerise .... RED
cerium dioxide .... CERIA
silicate .... CERITE
cero .... CAVALLA
combining form .... WAX
fish resembling ..... MACKEREL
certain .... FIXED, SOME, SURE,
TRUE, APODITIC, POSITIVE,
RELIABLE, SPECIFIED
absolutely .... COCKSURE
armrest .... SLING
birthdays .... MILESTONE
choir voice .... ALTO,
SOPRANO
count .... POLLEN
fishermen .... EELERS
friends .... FAIR WEATHER
word puzzles .... ACROSTICS
certainly .... SURELY, INDEED, OF
COURSE
archaic .... IWIS
certainty .... FACT, SURETY,
SHOO-IN, ASSURANCE,
GUARANTEE, CERTITUDE
certificate .... DOCUMENT,
RECORD, TESTIMONIAL
graduation .... DIPLOMA
insurance .... POLICY
money .... SCRIP
of transfer .... BILL OF SALE
price .... PAR VALUE
Spanish .... CEDULA
certification ...... OK, TESTIMONY,
ATTESTATION
certify .... DEPOSE, ASSURE,
STATE, ATTEST, TESTIFY,
NOTARIZE, AFFIRM, VOUCH,
VERIFY, DECLARE
certitude. See **certainty**
cerulean ...... AZURE, (SKY) BLUE
cerumen .... EARWAX
ceruse .... COSMETIC, WHITE LEAD
Cervantes, author .... MIGUEL
cervine .... DOE, DEER, ELK, STAG,
CERVID
Cesare, basso .... SIEPI
cespitose ...... MATTED, TURF-LIKE
cess .... TAX, ASSESSMENT
cessation ...... END, HALT, FINISH,
LET-UP, CEASING, STOP(PAGE),
SURCEASE
of activity, temporary
.... LULL, PAUSE, BREAK,
RESPITE
of hostilities .... PEACE

of war, temporary ...... TRUCE,
CEASEFIRE
cession .... CEDING, YIELDING
cessionary .... ASSIGNEE
cesspool ...... DUMP, SEWER, SUMP
cestode .... TAPEWORM
cestoid .... RIBBONLIKE
cestus .... BELT, GIRDLE
cesura .... PAUSE
cetacean .... INIA, SUSU, DOLPHIN,
GRAMPUS, WHALE, PORPOISE
Arctic .... NARWAL,
NARWHAL(E)
tusked .... NARWHAL
Cetus .... WHALE, CONSTELLATION
Ceylon .... SINHALA, SRI LANKA
Ceylon(ese) .... TAMIL,
CINGALESE, SIN(G)HALESE
aborigine ..... TODA, VEDDA(H)
ape .... MAHA
Buddhist temple site
.... KANDY
capital .... COLOMBO
city/town .... GALLE, KANDY,
JAFFNA, TRINCOMALEE
export .... TEA
fortress town .... GALLE
garment .... SARONG
grass .... CHENA, PATANA
hill dweller .... TODA
language .... PALI, INDIO,
TAMIL, TELUGU, KANARESE,
MALAYALAM
lotus .... NELUMBO
monkey .... MAHA, LANGUR,
TOQUE, WANDEROO
moss .... AGAR, GULAMAN
moss derivative .... ALEC
native .... TODA, TAMIL,
CINGALESE, DRAVIDIAN,
VEDDA(H), SIN(G)HALESE
palm .... TALIPOT
policeman .... PEON
rat .... BANDICOOT
seaport .... GALLE, JAFFNA
snake .... ANACONDA
strait .... PALK
tea .... PEKOE
trading vessel .... D(H)ONI
tree .... PALMYRA
water lily .... NELUMBO
CGS, part of .... CENTIMETER,
GRAM, SECOND
unit .... ERG, DYNE
cha .... TEA
chablis .... WINE
chabouk .... HORSEWHIP
chacma .... BABOON
Chad, capital of ...... N'DJAMENA
city/town .... KELO, PALA,
SARH, DOBA, BONGOR,

ABECHE, FIANGA, KOUMRA,
MOUNDOU
ethnic group .... SARA, MASSA,
KANEMBOU
lake .... CHAD, FITTRI
language ..... ARABIC, FRENCH,
BAGIRMI, MOUDANG
money .... FRANC
mountain .... EMI KOUSSI
mountains .... TIBESTI
plateau .... ENNEDI
president .... TOMBALBAYE
region .... KANEM, SUDAN,
WADAI, BAGUIRMI
river .... SARA, OUHAM, PENDE,
SHARI, LOGONE
chaeta .... SETA, SPINE, BRISTLE
chaetopod .... ANNELID
chafe .... IRK, RUB, GALL, RASP,
ANNOY, STING, ABRADE,
INFLAME, IRRITATE,
EXCORIATE
at the bit .... FRET
chafer .... BEETLE, SCARAB, ROSE-
BUG, FOOD-WARMER
chaff .... BRAN, HUSK, BANTER,
TEASING
like/mixed with .... ACEROSE
like bract .... PALEA
chaffer .... BANDY, HAGGLE,
HIGGLE, BARGAIN(ING)
chaffinch .... (SONG)BIRD
chaffy ...... ACEROSE, WORTHLESS
chafing .... GALLING
dish .... CRESSET
result of .... SORE, FROTH
chagrin .... VEXATION,
DISCOMFITURE,
MORTIFICATION
chain ...... IRON, CATENA, FETTER,
SERIES, SHACKLE, LINKWORK
ball and .... WIFE
decorative .... CHATELAINE
form into a .... CATENATE
mail .... BYRNIE, HAUBERK
mail, like .... ARMURE
mountain .... RANGE,
CORDILLERA
of logical reasoning
.... SORITES
of reasoning ..... CONSECUTION
part .... LINK
pulling .... TUG
smoker, for example
.... ADDICT
TV-radio .... NETWORK
chair .... SEAT, BENCH, PLACE,
CENTER, OFFICE, SETTEE,
ROCKER, POSITION
arrangement .... SEATING
back part .... SPLAT

backless ..... STOOL, OTTOMAN
bar connecting legs .... ROUND
board .... SLAT
bowlegged .... CURULE
cover .... TIDY
covered .... SEDAN
litter-like .... KAGO
making material .... SPLAT
of authority/state ...... THRONE
on elephant's back
.... HOUDAH, HOWDAH
on poles .... SEDAN
part .... ARM, LEG, RUNG,
SEAT, ROUND, SPLAT, BOTTOM
portable .... SEDAN, LITTER,
PALANQUIN
take the .... PRESIDE
weaver .... CANER
chairman of sorts .... MC,
EMCEE, TOASTMASTER
chaise .... SHAY, BUGGY,
CARRIAGE, SHANDRYDAN
longue .... CHAIR
chalaza .... TREAD
chalcedony .... ONYX, AGATE,
CHERT, JASPER, CAT'S-EYE,
QUARTZ, SARD(INE),
CARNELIAN, (CHRYSO)PRASE
Chaldean .... SORCERER,
ASTROLOGER
astronomical cycle ...... SAROS
city .... UR
chalet .... HUT, CABIN, COTTAGE
chalice .... AMA, CUP, CALIX,
GRAIL, GOBLET
cloth .... PALL
covering .... ASTERISKOS
flower .... DAFFODIL
veil .... AER
chalk .... TALLY, CRAYON,
CALCITE, WHITING,
LIMESTONE
composition .... SEASHELLS
linseed oil mixture ...... PUTTY
up .... SCORE
chalkstone .... TOPHUS
chalky silicate .... TALC
challenge .... DARE, DEFY, STUMP,
DEMAND, QUESTION, QUERY,
DISPUTE, EXCEPTION
as false .... IMPUGN
hurled .... DEFI, GAGE
means .... SLAP
to a duel/written .... CARTEL
challenging .... DEFIANT, BOLD,
DARING, EXCITING, BAFFLING,
BELLICOSE
Cham .... KHAN
chamber .... CAMERA,
(BED)ROOM, COUNCIL,
CAMARILLA

for dead .... VAULT
judge's .... CAMERA
of a .... CAMERAL
pot .... JORDAN
underground .... VAULT
chambered creature of poetry
.... NAUTILUS
chamberlain .... STEWARD,
TREASURER
Oriental potentate's
.... EUNUCH
chambers, legislature of two
.... BICAMERAL
chambray .... GINGHAM
chameleon .... LIZARD,
LACERT(IL)IAN
like .... FICKLE, CHANGEABLE
like creature .... AGAMA
chamfer .... BEVEL, GROOVE,
FLUTING
chamois .... AOUDAD, SHAMMY,
ANTELOPE
animal like .... GORAL,
KLIPSPRINGER
habitat .... ALPS
champ .... CHEW, MUNCH
colloquial .... CHAMPION
champagne .... WINE
bottle .... JEROBOAM
brand .... POMMERY
bucket .... ICER
capital/center .... TROYES
driest .... BRUT
for example .... FIZ(Z)
of teas, so-called
.... DARJEELING
champignon .... MUSHROOM
champion .... VICTOR, WINNER,
DEFEND(ER), ESPOUSE,
PALADIN, CHAMP, BACKER,
ADVOCATE, SUPPORTER,
SQUIRE, PROTECTOR
auto racing ...... MOSS, CLARK,
PETTY, ALLISON, UNSER,
ANDRETTI, EARNHARDT
boxer .... ALI, CLAY, LOUIS,
VILLA, HARADA, ELORDE,
DEMPSEY, GRIFFITH, TYSON,
SPINKS, FRAZIER, PATTERSON,
LEONARD, FOREMAN
golf .... HOGAN, SNEAD, JONES,
PALMER, PLAYER, KITE,
STRANGE, NICKLAUS, SANDERS,
MILLER, TREVINO, WATSON,
NORMAN, RODRIGUEZ,
BALLESTEROS, CRENSHAW
heroic .... KNIGHT, PALADIN
marathon .... BIKILA
pole vault .... SEAGREN,
BIZZARRO
soccer football .... PELE

tennis .... ASHE, HOAD, KING,
GRAF, EVERT, TILDEN, LAVER,
SELES, SANCHEZ, SABATINI,
BECKER, CONNORS,
NEWCOMBE, SAMPRAS, CASH,
EDBERG, MCENROE, AGASSI,
SANTANA, GONZALES,
COURIER, GIBSON, CHANG,
NAVRATILOVA
wrestling .... TAKTI
yacht racing .... INTREPID
1934 world heavyweight
.... BAER
1960 decathlon .... RAFER
JOHNSON
Chan expression .... AH SO
chance .... HAP, LUCK, RISK,
GAMBLE, HAZARD, RANDOM,
LOT, FATE, CASUAL,
FORTUITY, KARMA, KISMET,
POTLUCK
betting .... ODDS
big .... OPPORTUNITY
by .... ACCIDENTAL(LY)
goddess of .... TYCHE,
FORTUNA
on .... MEET, ENCOUNTER
to hit .... AT BAT
chancel .... SACRARIUM
part .... BEMA, RAILING
part surrounded by ..... ALTAR
screen .... JUBE
seats .... SEDILIA
chancellor .... JUDGE, MINISTER
chances ...... EDGE, ODDS, LAW OF
AVERAGES, ADVANTAGE
chancre ...... SORE, ULCER, LESION
chandelier .... CORONA,
ELECTROLIER, GASELIER,
CANDELABRA
describing a .... HANGING,
PENDULOUS, SUSPENDED
pendant .... LUSTER,
LAVALIERE
change ...... VARY, ADAPT, ALTER,
AMEND, MODIFY, MUTATE,
TURN, FLUX, MUTATION,
SHIFT, REVISION, DEVIATION
bad habits/conduct
.... REFORM
color .... FADE
course ..... HAUL, TACK, VEER,
SWERVE
current flow .... RECTIFY
direction .... CANT, TACK,
TURN, VEER, DEVIATE
in linguistics .... UMLAUT
in religion .... CONVERSION
into liquid .... LIQUEFY
into steel .... ACIERATE
of mind, feeling .... CAPRICE

of life .... MENOPAUSE
party .... BOLT, DEFECT
places/residence .... MOVE
policy .... TACK, DEMARCHE
secret signals .... RECODE
sentence .... COMMUTE
small .... COINS
stocks/bonds to cash
.... REDEEM
tack .... JIBE
the knot .... RETIE
to direct current .... RECTIFY
trains .... TRANSFER
wall decor .... REPANEL,
REPAPER
changeable .... FLUID, FICKLE,
ADRIFT, MOBILE, ERRATIC,
PROTEAN, MUTABLE,
VOLATILE, ROVING,
CAPRICIOUS, WHIMSICAL
person .... CHAMELEON
changeling .... OAF, DOLT, CHILD,
IDIOT, TURNCOAT, DOUBLE,
BACK-UP, STAND-IN
Changsa is capital of .... HUNAN
channel .... KILL, NECK, CHUTE,
SHOOT, COURSE, STRAIT,
DUCT, PASSAGE, RUNNEL,
MEDIUM, CONDUIT, RUNWAY
artificial .... CANAL, FLUME,
SLUICE(WAY)
between cliffs .... GAT
cutting sandbank .... SWASH
direct .... PIPELINE
entrance .... CHOPS
excess water .... SPILLWAY
fence .... WEIR
in physics .... WAVELENGTH
inland .... GAT
marker .... BUOY
narrow .... STRIA
obstruction .... WEIR
of unpredictable currents
.... EURIPUS
principal/main .... ARTERY
vertical .... GLYPH
water .... RACE(WAY)
Channel, English .... (THE)
SOLENT
island .... SARK, JERSEY,
ALDERNEY, GUERNSEY
Island official .... JURAT
swimmer, English ..... EDERLE
channeled .... ROUTED, GROOVED,
FLUTED, COURSED, FURROWED
channels .... MEDIA
5 .... SENSES
chanson .... SONG, LYRIC, BALLAD
chant .... INTONE, MELODY,
CANTICLE, SINGSONG,
INTONATION

poetic .... WARBLE
repetitive .... LITANY
chantage .... BLACKMAIL
chanterelle .... MUSHROOM
chanteuse .... SINGER
chantey .... (SAILOR)SONG
chanticleer .... COCK, ROOSTER
chantilly .... LACE
chantry .... ALTAR, CHAPEL
chaos .... MESS, JUMBLE,
DISORDER, CONFUSION
Archaic .... ABYSS, CHASM
in language .... BABEL
in printing .... PI
chaotic .... VAGUE, MUDDLED,
FORMLESS, DISORDERLY
chap ...... GUY, JAW, KIBE, BLOW,
CHEEK, SKATE, KNOCK,
BUGGER, ROUGHEN
colloquial .... BOY, MAN,
FELLOW
chapeau .... HAT, HEADGEAR
chapel .... CHURCH, TEMPLE,
VESTRY, SANCTUARY
clergyman .... CHAPLAIN
Egyptian mortuary's
.... MASTABA(H)
medieval church .... GALILEE
private .... ORATORY
sailors' .... BETHEL
small ...... CHANTRY, ORATORY
Vatican .... SISTINE
chaperon ...... DUEN(N)A, ESCORT,
MATRON, MONITOR,
ACCOMPANY
strict .... DRAGON
chapfallen .... DEPRESSED,
HUMILIATED
chaplain .... PADRE, PRIEST,
MINISTER, CLERGYMAN
prison .... ORDINARY
chaplet .... WREATH, GARLAND
poetic .... ANADEM
Chaplin .... CHARLIE
chapman .... DEALER, HAWKER,
MERCHANT, TRADER, PEDDLER
chaps .... JAW, CHEEK, CHOPS,
CHAPAREJOS
of hound .... FLEWS
chapter .... PART, LOCAL,
BRANCH, SECTION, EPISODE,
POST, VERSE, DIVISION
fraternity .... LODGE
of a .... CAPITULAR
char .... SEAR, BURN(UP),
CINDERS, TROUT, SCORCH
charabanc .... BUS
character ...... CODE, KIND, ROLE,
CLASS, TENOR, NATURE,
CIPHER, TRAIT, REPUTE
alphabet .... LETTERS

ancient alphabetical ..... RUNE,
OGHAM
assassination .... LIBEL,
SLANDER
element in .... ETHOS
giver .... TONER
ill-tempered .... VINEGAR
in .... APPROPRIATE
in a play .... ACTOR
musical ...... CLEF, NOTE, REST
odd .... CRANK, ECCENTRIC
of community .... ETHOS
police ..... CONVICT, CRIMINAL,
LAW-BREAKER, MALEFACTOR
quality of .... METTLE
representing a word
.... LOGOGRAM
set .... ALPHABET
sour .... VINEGAR
strength of .... GRISTLE
characteristic .... TRAIT,
QUALITY, DISTINCTIVE,
TYPICAL, PECULIARITY
expression .... IDIOM
marks .... INDICIA
taste .... FLAVOR
characters, drama/play
.... PERSONAE
of slums .... DEAD-END
characterize .... MARK, DEPICT,
DEFINE, DESCRIBE
charade .... PUZZLE, TRAVESTY,
RIDDLE, WORD GAME,
PANTOMIME
charcoal .... CARBON, LIGNITE,
BLACKEN, BONEBLACK
burner .... BRAZIER
burning brazier .... HIBACHI
combining form .... CARB(O)
pencil .... FUSAIN
powdered .... POUNCE
residue .... BREEZE
use of .... FILTER
chard .... BEET, LEAFSTALK
chare .... CHORE
charge .... FEE, COST, DEBIT,
ASSESS, IMPUTE, COMMAND,
DASH, INSTRUCT,
INDICT(MENT), RUSH, BLAME,
ACCUSE, BURDEN, ATTACK,
STRIKE, ATTRIBUTE, BLAST,
FILL, CARE, CUSTODY
in court .... ARRAIGN
kind of .... CAVALRY
mail .... POSTAGE
on property .... TAX, LIEN
restaurant/tavern .... TIP,
COVER, CORKAGE
road .... TOLL
school .... TUITION
solemnly .... ADJURE

to expense/loss .... DEBIT
to experience .... WRITE OFF
with crime .... INDICT
Charge of the Light _____
.... BRIGADE
charged .... TENSE, FRAUGHT
particle .... ION
water .... SODA
charger .... STEED, WARHORSE
Archaic .... PLATTER,
DESTRIER
chariot .... ESSED(E), QUADRIGA
race .... AGON
race course .... HIPPODROME
race site, ancient .... CIRCUS,
COLOSSEUM
charioteer .... WAGONER
constellation .... AURIGA
furious .... JEHU
of fiction .... BEN HUR
charisma .... AURA, GIFT, GRACE,
CHARM, APPEAL
Charisse, dancer .... CYD
charitable institution .... MISSION
charity .... ALMS, DOLE, LARGESS,
PITY, GRACE, MERCY,
BOUNTY, ALTRUISM,
KINDNESS, PHILANTHROPHY,
GENEROSITY
fair .... KERMIS, KERMESS
sale .... BAZA(A)R, RUMMAGE
charivari .... SERENADE
charlatan .... FAKER, FRAUD,
QUACK, IMPOSTOR, EMPIRIC,
PHON(E)Y, SCIOLIST,
PRETENDER
Charlemagne .... EMPEROR,
CARLO MAGNO
father of .... PEPIN (THE
SHORT)
gift to Rinaldo .... BAYARD
grandfather of .... MARTEL
knight(s) of .... PALADIN,
TWELVE, DOUZEPERS
nephew of .... ROLAND,
ORLANDO
peer .... OLIVER, ROLAND,
ORLANDO
soubriquet .... (THE) GREAT
Charles Dickens's pseudonym
.... BOZ
Charles' Wain .... AURIGA, BIG
DIPPER, URSA MAJOR
charleyhorse .... CRAMP
Charlie ...... RICH, PRIDE, BROWN
Brown expression .... RATS
charlock .... WEED, MUSTARD
charlotte .... LOTTA, LOTTY,
LOTTIE, DESSERT, PUDDING
Charlotte .... AMALIE
charm .... GRACE, SPELL,

ENAMOR, ENDEAR, ENCHANT,
HYPNOTIZE, FETISH,
FASCINATE, BEWITCH,
ATTRACT, INCANTATION
African .... OBI, JUJU, OBEAH
against evil/injury .... AMULET
bracelet disc .... BANGLE
good luck .... TALISMAN
jewel .... SCARAB
magic .... JUJU
charmer .... EXORCIST, MAGICIAN,
ENCHANTER, SORCERER
female .... SIREN
of German legend .... LORELEI
charming .... DAZZLING,
ENCHANTING, DELIGHTFUL,
WINNING, WINSOME
strangely .... ELFIN
charnel house .... TOMB,
OSSUARY
of a sort .... MORTUARY,
PANTHEON
Charon .... FERRYMAN
fee .... OBOL
river .... STYX
charpoy (charpai) .... COT,
BEDSTEAD
charqui .... BEEF
char(r) .... TROUT
chart .... MAP, PLOT, GRAPH,
LAYOUT, OUTLINE
charter ...... HIRE, GRANT, LEASE,
LET, RENT, LICENSE,
FRANCHISE
fundamental .... CONSTITUTION
package .... TOUR
Charteris (Leslie) detective
.... (THE) SAINT
forte of .... WHODUNITS
Chartres river .... EURE
chartreuse .... LIQUEUR,
YELLOWISH-GREEN
chary .... SHY, CAREFUL,
CAUTIOUS
Charybdis .... WHIRLPOOL
rock opposite/companion
.... SCYLLA
chase .... FRET, HUNT, SHAG,
DISPEL, REPEL, FOLLOW,
ENGRAVE, PURSUE, PURSUIT
after .... GET, SECURE,
RETRIEVE
continually .... HOUND
flies .... SHAG
object of .... FOX, GAME,
HARE, ESCAPEE, RAINBOW
off .... ROUT
the .... VENERY
Chase .... CHEVY
chaser .... SODA, WASH, DRINK,
CHISEL, GRAVER, HUNTER

ambulance .... SHYSTER
chasing tool ...... CHISEL, TRACER
chasm .... GAP, RIFT, ABYSS,
CLEFT, CANYON, HIATUS
in a glacier .... CREVASSE
chasseur .... HUNTER, SERVANT,
HUNTSMAN
chassis .... FRAME
slang .... BODY
chaste ...... PURE, CLEAN, SIMPLE,
DECENT, MODEST, VESTAL,
PROPER, VIRTUOUS, REFINED,
SEVERE, CELIBATE, INNOCENT
woman .... VIRGIN
chasten .... HUMBLE, PUNISH,
SUBDUE, CHASTISE
chastise .... SPANK, PUNISH,
CASTIGATE, DISCIPLINE
physically .... FLOG, WHIP
verbally .... SCOLD, BERATE
chastity .... PURITY, CELIBACY,
VIRTUE, DECENCY, VIRGINITY
vower of .... NUN, MONK,
PRIEST, VESTAL
chat .... TALK, CONVERSE,
CONVERSATION
colloquial .... CONFAB
French .... CAUSERIE
friendly .... COSE, COZE
hippie's: sl. .... RAP
of maple .... SAMARA
of plantain .... SPIKE
of willow ...... AMENT, CATKIN
slang .... BULL SESSION
chateau .... CASTLE
entrance .... PORTE
mistress of .... CHATELAINE
chatelain .... CASTELLAN
chatelaine .... PIN, ETUI, CHAIN,
CLASP, BROOCH
chatoyant .... GEM, CAT'S-EYE
chattel .... CHOSE, GOODS
Archaic .... SLAVE
chatter .... GAB, JAW, YAK, BLAB,
CLACK, PRATE, CACKLE,
BABBLE, TALK, TATTLE,
GIBBER, GOSSIP, PATTER,
BLABBER, PALAVER, PRATTLE
Aussie: colloq. .... YABBER
ceaselessly .... LALLYGAG
gossipy .... TATTLE
incoherent .... JABBER
slang .... CHIN
unintelligible .... GIBBER
chatterbox .... JAY, MAGPIE
chatterer, bird .... JAY, PIET,
MAGPIE, COTINGA, WAXWING
Chaucer pilgrim .... REEVE
poet .... GEOFFREY
songs .... CHAUNTS
title .... DAN

work .... CANTERBURY TALES
chauffer .... STOVE, HEATER
chauffeur .... DRIVER
chaussure .... BOOT, SHOE,
SLIPPER, FOOTWEAR
chauvinist .... JINGO
Chavante .... OTI
chazan .... CANTOR
cheap .... TINNY, COMMON, BASE,
MEAN, RAFFISH, PICAYUNE,
LOW, INEXPENSIVE, TWO-
PENNY
and showy .... TINHORN
but sturdy jackknife
.... BARLOW
colloquial .... BRUMMAGEN,
DIME-A-DOZEN
hotel .... RATTRAP
in Spanish .... BARATO
jewelry .... TRINKET
jewelry peddler .... DUFFER
price ...... BARGAIN, CUT-RATE,
REDUCED
race horse .... PLATER
slang .... TWO-BIT, DIRT-CHEAP
cheapest theater seats
.... GALLERY
cheapskate .... MISER, PIKER,
NIGGARD, TIGHTWAD
cheat .... FOB, FUB, GYP, BILK,
COZE, DUPE, GAFF, NICK,
MUMP, FINAGLE, FOIL, SHAM,
HUMBUG, HUSTLE, DECEIVE,
(DE)FRAUD, SWINDLE(R),
SHORT-CHANGE, WELSH(ER),
VICTIMIZE
by fraud .... FLEECE
colloquial ..... BUNCO, DIDDLE,
GOUGE, PHONY
easy to .... GULLIBLE
in schoolwork .... CRIB
slang .... CON, CLIP, MUMP,
STICK, CHISEL, FOURFLUSH
through trickery .... COZEN,
GOUGE, JUGGLE
cheated, person easily .... DUPE,
GULL, VICTIM
colloquial .... SUCKER
cheater in school .... CRIBBER
mean .... JUDAS, JACKAL
cheaters: sl. .... FALSIES,
CONTACTS, (EYE)GLASSES
chebec .... FLYCATCHER
Checchi, Signora .... DUSE
check .... CURB, REIN, DETAIN,
CONTROL, REBUFF, CHEQUE,
VERIFY, ASCERTAIN,
RESTRAIN(T), COUNTERACT
abruptly .... NIP IN THE BUD
accounts .... AUDIT
bad .... KITE, RUBBER

bleeding .... STEM, STANCH
colloquial ..... RIGHT, CORRECT
completely .... HALT, STOP
describing bad one ..... STALE,
RUBBER, BOUNCING
float a .... PREDATE
flow .... DAM, STEM, STANCH
growth/development .... NIP,
STUNT, HINDER
heads, in airplane ...... COUNT,
TALLY
in .... REPORT, REGISTER
infection by burning
.... CAUTERIZE
manuscript .... EDIT
mark .... TICK
money .... DRAFT, ORDER
out place .... COUNTER
rain .... STUB, DEFERRAL
restaurant .... TAB, CHIT
slang .... ARREST
speed .... BRAKE
unemployment .... DOLE
up .... PROBE, VERIFY,
EXPLORE
checker .... DICE, CASHIER
Archaic .... CHESSBOARD
checkerberry .... WINTERGREEN
checkered ...... VARIED, RUBBERY,
MANY-SIDED, TATTERSALL
cloth .... PLAID, TARTAN
checkers .... GAME, DRAUGHTS
checking account .... FUNDS
block .... SPRAG
checklist .... INDEX
checkmate .... STOP, CORNER,
END, ROUT, BAFFLE, DEFEAT,
STYMIE, THWART, FRUSTRATE
checkup .... PHYSICAL, SPOT-
CHECK
Cheddar .... CHEESE
cheddite .... EXPLOSIVE
cheek .... JAW, CHAP, CHOP, GENA,
JOWL, HALF-FACE, BOLDNESS,
AUDACITY, TEMERITY
bone .... MALAR
buttocks: sl. .... TUSH
by jowl ...... CLOSE, FAMILIAR,
INTIMATE
colloquial .... GALL, BRASH,
BRASS, NERVE, IMPUDENCE,
INSOLENCE, SAUCE, SAUCINESS
gangrene .... NOMA
glow of .... BLOOM
hair growth .... SIDEBURN
hollow .... DIMPLE
muscle .... BUCCINATOR
of the .... GENAL, JUGAL,
MALAR, BUCCAL
pouch .... ALFORJA
to cheek ...... CLOSE, CHUMMY

tongue in .... INSINCERE, TWO-
FACED
cheeks and mouth .... CHOPS
cheeky: colloq. .... COCKY,
SAUCY, BRASSY
cheep .... PEEP, CHIRP
cheer .... ROOT, ELATE, SHOUT,
GAIETY, COMFORT, APPLAUD,
YELL, GLADDEN, (EN)LIVEN,
MIRTH, SOLACE, ENCOURAGE
approving .... ATTABOY
bullring .... OLE
college .... RAH, HURRAH
English .... HEAR
French .... VIVE
Italian .... VIVA, BRAVO
Japanese .... BANZAI
kind of .... BRONX
Mexican .... VIVA
Nazi .... HEIL
Philippine .... MABUHAY
Spanish .... OLE
up .... CONSOLE, COMFORT,
BRIGHTEN, (EN)LIVEN
cheerer .... FAN, ROOTER
cheerful .... GAY, HAPPY, BRIGHT,
JOLLY, LIVELY, MERRY,
CHIRPY, RIANT, SUNNY,
BLITHE
cheerfully bright .... SUNNY
cheering thing .... RAY OF
SUNSHINE
cheerio: Brit. .... HELLO,
GOODBYE
cheerless .... SAD, COLD, DRAB,
GRAY, BLEAK, DISMAL,
DREARY, JOYLESS
cheers .... TOAST
cheery ...... GAY, BRIGHT, LIVELY
cheese .... CREAM, CURDS,
MYSOST
a house of .... COTTAGE
American .... BLUE, COON,
BRICK, COLBY, CREAM,
COTTAGE, CHEDDAR,
LONGHORN, MONTEREY JACK,
NEUFCHATEL, TILLAMOOK
and pastry specialists
.... DANES
and toast dish .... RAREBIT,
WELSH-RABBIT
basis of .... CASEIN
crust .... GRATIN
Danish .... BLUE, SAMSOE
dish .... FONDUE, QUICHE,
RAREBIT, SOUFFLE, RACLETTE
dry, hard .... ROMANO
drying frame .... HACK
Dutch .... EDAM, GOUDA,
COTTAGE
English .... CHEDDAR,

STILTON, CAERPHILLY
enthusiast .... MOUSE
family .... BLUE, WHEY,
DUTCH, FRESH, SWISS,
CHEDDAR, RIPENED,
PARMESAN, PROVOLONE
French .... BRIE, MUENSTER,
CAMEMBERT, ROQUEFORT,
PETIT-SUISSE, PORT DU SALUT
from curds .... GOUDA
from milk, directly
.... NATURAL
German .... LIMBURGER
goat's/ewe's milk
.... ROQUEFORT
Greek .... FETA
Italian ...... ROMANO, FONTINA,
RICOTTA, PARMESAN, BEL-
PAESE, GORGONZOLA,
PROVOLONE, MOZZARELLA
like .... CASEOUS
main type of .... NATURAL,
PASTEURIZED
making substance ..... RENNET
Norwegian .... GJETOST,
JARLSBERG
piece of .... WEDGE
Scottish .... KEBBOCK
Sovetsk, formerly .... TILSIT
Swiss ..... COTTAGE, GRUYERE,
RACLETTE, SAPSAGO,
EMMENTHALER
tang .... NIP
texture .... MILD, SHARP
white, cured in brine .... FETA
whole milk .... DUNLOP
cheesecake: sl. .... PIN-UP
cheesy .... CASEOUS
slang .... POOR, TACKY,
CRUMMY, SHABBY, INFERIOR
cheetah .... GUEPARD, LEOPARD
chef .... (CHIEF) COOK,
CULINARIAN
Chek(h)ov, writer .... ANTON
chela .... CLAW, PINC(H)ERS
India .... NOVICE, DISCIPLE
cheloid .... TUMOR
chelonian ...... TURTLE, TORTOISE
chemical catalyst .... REAGENT
change .... REACTION
combining capacity
.... VALENCE
compound ...... AMIDE, AMINE,
DIENE, CERIA, ESTER, BORIDE,
IODINE, ISOMER, KETONE,
ENOL, TOULENE, ELATERIN
compounds, describing
.... LABILE
element ...... ARGON, HALOGEN
element 43 .... MASURIUM
ink remover .... ERADICATOR

prefix .... OXA, ACETO, AMIDO,
AMINO
radical .... BUTYL, TOLYL
reaction .... CATALYSIS
reagent .... CATALYST,
CATALYSER
salt .... SAL, ESTER, BORATE,
NITRE, IODATE
substance .... AMIDE, LININ
suffix .... YL, ANE, ENE, OSE,
OLIC, YLENE
unit .... TITER, TITRE
word ending .... OL, INE, ENOL
chemin de fer .... RAILROAD,
BACCARAT
chemise ...... SLIP, SARK, CYMAR,
LINGERIE
colloquial .... SHIMMY, UNDIES
chemisette .... TUCKER
chemist ...... ANALYST, DRUGGIST,
PHARMACIST
flask of .... BOLTHEAD
pot of .... ALUDEL
chemistry, suffix in .... ENE, INE,
OLE, OSE
Chemulpo .... INCHON, JINSEN
chenille .... DOG, CORD
Chenpao to Russians
.... DAMANSKY
Cheops .... KHUFU
edifice built by .... PYRAMID
cherish .... ADORE, PRIZE, VALUE,
FOSTER, EMBOSOM, REVERE,
NURTURE, TREASURE, NURSE,
HARBOR, HOLD DEAR
companion in marriage vow
.... LOVE, OBEY
Cherokee sage .... SEQUOYAH
cheroot .... CIGAR
cherry .... DRUPE, RUDDY,
CAPULIN, MARASCA,
AMARELLE, MORELLO,
OXHEART, BLACKHEART
disease .... BLACKKNOT
like color/red .... CERISE
product .... JAM, PIE
sour .... EGRIOT
stone .... NUTLET
sweet/wild .... GEAN,
MAZZARD, BIGAROON
cherrystone .... CLAM, NUTLET,
QUAHOG
chersonese .... PENINSULA
cherub .... AMOR, ANGEL, EROTE,
LAMBKIN, SERAPH, INNOCENT
cherubic .... ANGELIC
chess castle .... ROOK
certain defeat in
.... CHECKMATE
champion .... FISHER, KARPOV,
LASKER, KASPAROV,

PETROSIAN, BOTVINNIK,
SPASSKY, CAPABLANCA
corner piece .... ROOK
defeated at .... MATED
expert .... HOYLE
opening .... CHASSE, GAMBIT
piece .... KING, PAWN, ROOK,
QUEEN, CASTLE, BISHOP,
KNIGHT
sacrifice .... GAMBIT
term .... CHECKMATE,
SELFMATE, EN PASSANT
wins .... MATES
chest .... BOX, ARCA, KIST,
BOSOM, COFFER, LOCKER,
CASE, BREAST, BUREAU,
CASKET, CABINET, THORAX
a kind of ..... TOOL, CAMPHOR,
MEDICINE, TREASURE,
COMMUNITY
animal .... BRISKET
bone .... RIB
cavity membrane ...... PLEURA
clothes .... TRUNK
combining form ..... STETH(O)
for money/valuables
.... COFFER, CASKET
for storage .... HUTCH
for supplies .... WANIGAN
human .... THORAX
located on the .... PECTORAL
of drawers .... LOWBOY,
COMMODE, CHIFFONIER,
HIGHBOY, TALLBOY
of sacred utensils .... CIST
sacred .... ARK, ARCA
Scottish .... KIST
small .... CASKET
sound .... RALE
tool .... KIT
vibration .... FREMITUS
Chesterfield .... LORD, SOFA,
TOPCOAT
Chesterfieldian .... SUAVE,
URBANE, ELEGANT
chessman .... PAWN
chestnut ...... MAST, TREE, HORSE,
OLDIE, MARRON, BUCKEYE
Chinese .... LING
colloquial .... JOKE, CLICHE
pod .... BUR
Polynesian .... RATA
preserved in syrup
.... MARRONS
tree .... CHINCAPIN,
CHINQUAPIN
water .... LING
chevalier .... NOBLE, GALLANT
Archaic .... KNIGHT
Cheviot .... OVINE, SHEEP
chevron .... BAR, STRIPE

shape .... VEE
symbol of ...... RANK, SERVICE
chevrotain .... NAPU, DEERLET
chevy .... FRET, HUNT, CHASE
chew .... GNAW, GRIND, CUD,
   CHAMP, MUNCH, MUMBLE,
   BITE, (S)CRUNCH, MASTICATE
  inability to .... AMOSESIS
  leaf to .... BETEL
  the cud .... PONDER, RUMINATE
  the fat .... CHAT, GOSSIP
  the scenery .... EMOTE
chewing gum ingredient
   .... CHICLE, MASTIC
  gum tree .... SAPODILLA
  tobacco piece .... PLUG
chewink .... FINCH, TOWHEE
chewy confection .... GUM,
   TAFFY, CARAMEL
Chiang Kai-shek .... GISSIMO
  party of ...... KUOMINTANG
  wife of .... MEI-LING
Chianti .... (RED) WINE
Chiapas, capital of ...... TUXTLA
chiaus: Turk. .... EMISSARY,
   SERGEANT
chibouk .... (TOBACCO) PIPE
chic ..... SMART, MODISH, JAUNTY,
  ELEGANT, STYLISH, SUAVE,
  NATTY, DAPPER, POLISHED
Chicago .... WINDY CITY
  airport/hub .... O'HARE
  baseball team .... WHITESOX
  basketball team .... BULLS
  business/theater area ..... LOOP
  feature .... STOCKYARDS
  football team .... BEARS
  personage .... SANDBURG
  "Wall Street" .... LA SALLE
chicalote .... POPPY
chicane .... TRICK, QUIBBLE
chicanery ...... HOAX, DECEPTION,
   TRICKERY
Chichen Itza native ...... MAYAN
chichi .... ARTY, ELEGANT
chick ...... CHILD, PEEPER, SHEILA
  pea ..... GRAM, PLANT, FODDER
chickadee .... BIRD, TOMTIT,
   TITMOUSE
chickaree .... SQUIRREL
chicken .... FOWL, BIDDY, BIRD,
   SHANGHAI
  breast (deformity), cause of
   .... RICKETS
  breed .... JAVA, ANCONA,
  BANTAM, CORNISH, HAMBURG,
  MINORCA, (WHITE) LEGHORN,
  DORKING, CAMPINE, SUMATRA,
  SULTAN, RHODE ISLAND RED,
  RHODE ISLAND WHITE,
  WYANDOTTE, PLYMOUTH ROCK

castrated .... CAPON
chaser .... SHOO, CATCHPOLE
dish/meat course
  .... GALANTINE
feed .... CORN, MEAL, GRAIN,
   BARLEY
feed: sl. .... COINS, DIMES,
  PEANUTS, PIDDLING, CHEAP,
  NEGLIGIBLE, SMALL CHANGE
female .... HEN, LAYER
five-toed .... HOUDAN
hearted/livered .... TIMID,
  GUTLESS, COWARDLY,
  YELLOW, WEAKLING
little .... ALARMIST
male .... COCK, ROOSTER
noodle scoop .... LADLE
out .... FALTER, COLD FEET
pen/cage .... COOP, RUNWAY
pen/cage material .... WIRE
pox .... VARICELLA
resting place .... PERCH,
   ROOST
slang .... PANSY, SISSY,
  COWARD, MAMA'S BOY,
  CRYBABY
small .... BANTAM
snake .... BOBA
sound .... CLUCK, CACKLE
switch .... PANIC BUTTON
young .... CHICK, FRYER,
  POULT, PEEPER, BROILER,
  PULLET
chickens, collectively
  .... POULTRY
  enclosure for .... RUNWAY
  heated shelter for
   .... BROODER
chicken's route ...... SIDE TO SIDE
chickeny TV role .... MISTER
   PEEPERS
chickweed .... ALSINE, ALSONE,
  SPURR(E)Y, STITCHWORT
chicle .... SAPOTA
  product ..... BALATA, CHEWING
   GUM
  source .... SAPODILLA
chico .... SHRUB, GREASEWOOD
chicory .... ENDIVE, SUCCORY
  use for .... COFFEE
chide .... BLAME, SCOLD, BERATE,
  LASH, REBUKE, REPROVE,
  LECTURE, UPBRAID, CRITICIZE
chider .... RATER, CRITIC
chief .... ARCH, HEAD, MAIN,
  ELDER, LEADER, CAPTAIN,
  PRIME, STELLAR, FOREMOST,
  CENTRAL, STAPLE, SUPERIOR,
  COMMANDER, PRINCIPAL
  actor .... HERO, LEAD, STAR
  barrio .... DATO, DATU,

   CABEZA
Canaan .... SISERA
character .... HERO, HEROINE
colloquial .... BOSS
commander-in .... CINC
commodity/product
  .... STAPLE
Cossack .... ATAMAN, HETMAN
excellence ..... FORTE, TALENT,
   STRONG-POINT
executive .... PRESIDENT
Indian .... BRANT, COCHISE,
  SACHEM, GERONIMO,
  POWHATAN, TECUMSEH,
  SAGAMORE, SITTING BULL
ingredient .... BASE
Italian .... DUCE
Moslem .... REIS
of foreign mission
  .... NUNCIO, AMBASSADOR
of state .... KING, RULER,
   PRESIDENT
of workmen .... FOREMAN,
   OVERSEER
official .... PREMIER, PRIME
   MINISTER
singer .... CANTOR
Spanish .... JEFE
support .... MAINSTAY
Chief Justice, U.S. ...... WARREN,
  TANEY, MARSHALL
chiefly ...... MAINLY, IN THE MAIN,
  LARGELY, MOSTLY,
  ESPECIALLY
chieftain .... LEADER
  Indian .... SACHEM
  political .... BOSS
  Scandinavian .... JARL
chield .... YOUTH
chiffon .... SILK
chigger .... FLEA, LARVA, CHIGOE
chigoe .... FLEA, LARVA, CHIGGER
Chihli .... HOPEI
Chihuahua .... (TOY) DOG
chilblain ...... PERNIO, KIBE, SORE
child .... KID, TOD, TOT, CHIT,
  BOY, BABE, BABY, INFANT,
  GIRL, SON, ISSUE, DAUGHTER,
  KIDDIE, KIDDY, PRODUCT
  abnormal .... OAF
  bad-tempered/ugly .... ELF,
   CHANGELING
  bastard .... BY-BLOW
  bear of .... TEDDY
  beggar's employer
   .... PADRONE
  bib .... DICKEY
  cap/hood of .... BIGGIN
  colloquial .... CHIT, TIKE,
  TYKE, CHICK, LAMBKIN,
   TODDLER

combining form .... PED,
                 P(A)EDO
dirty, ragged ..... RAGAMUFFIN
feet of .... PETTITOES
game of .... PEEKABOO, RED
                  ROVER
hand of .... PUD
homeless .... WAIF
impudent/unruly .... BRAT
in the old school, unlucky
      .... DUNCE
like .... NAIVE
little .... MOPPET
milk source .... WET NURSE
mischievous .... ELF, IMP,
         BRAT, URCHIN, LIMB,
              JACKANAPES
murder of .... PROLICIDE,
             INFANTICIDE
murder of one's .... FILICIDE
noble born .... CHILDE
of .... FILIAL
of illegitimate birth
      .... BASTARD, BASEBORN
of light and day, so-called
      .... EROS
of mixed blood .... MESTEE,
     MUSTEE, MESTIZO, GRIFFE,
     MULATTO, HALF-BREED, HALF-
                  CASTE
of the street .... ARAB, WAIF,
                  GAMIN
of the Sun .... INCA
pinafore .... SLIP, TIER, DICKEY
playroom .... NURSERY
pretty .... DOLL
relation to parent
      .... FILIATION
sans parents .... ORPHAN
savings bank of ..... SAVE-ALL
spoiled .... BRAT, COCKNEY
substitute .... CHANGELING
teacher/trainer ..... GOVERNESS
tiny .... PEEWEE
toy of .... PEG TOP
undershirt .... WAIST
unweaned .... SUCKLING
walk of ...... PADDLE, TODDLE,
                  WADDLE
childbearing .... NASCENCY,
             PARTURITION
primitive custom .... COUVADE
childbirth .... DELIVERY,
             PARTURITION
confinement .... LYING-IN
discharge after .... LOCHIA
pains .... LABOR, TRAVAIL,
             BIRTH THROES
childhood writings, etc.
      .... JUVENALIA
childing .... PREGNANT

childish .... ANILE, SILLY,
     ASININE, FOOLISH, PUERILE,
      SENILE, IMMATURE,
      INFANTILE, BABYISH,
     BRATTISH, JUVENILE, WEAK,
      CREDULOUS, YOUTHFUL
state due to age .... DOTAGE
talk .... BABBLE, PRATTLE
walk .... TODDLE, WADDLE
childhood disease .... MUMPS,
                MEASLES
childlike .... NAIF, NAIVE, SOFT,
     TRUSTFUL, GIRLISH, SILLY,
      TRUSTING, INNOCENT
adult .... IDIOT, MORON
speech .... LISP
children .... OFFSPRING, PROGENY
book for .... JUVENILE
colloquial .... (SMALL) FRY
of family .... BROOD, FLOCK
of heaven and earth, alleged
      .... TITANS
of Israel .... JEWS, HEBREWS
of the mist .... NIBELUNG
study of .... PEDOLOGY
without .... NONPAROUS
children's book author .... MILNE,
           OUIDA, RAMEE
book, doll in .... GOLLIWOG
disease .... MUMPS, MEASLES,
         RICKETS, RACHITIS
doctor .... PEDIATRIST,
             PEDIATRICIAN
game .... TAG, JACKSTONE
garments .... SMALLS
jacket .... PALETOT
mouth disease .... APHTHA,
                 THRUSH
patron saint .... SANTA
                 (CLAUS)
pinafore .... TIER
playroom .... NURSERY
playsuit .... ROMPERS
wasting condition
      .... MARASMUS
Chile, meaning of .... SNOW
Chilean aborigine .... INCA
archipelago .... CHONOS,
            GUAYANECO
bay ...... COOK, EYRE, DARWIN,
     INUTIL, MORENO, NASSAU,
     COPIAPO, ADVENTURE,
      INGLESA, SKYRING
cape .... HORN, CHOROS,
     DESEADO, BASCUNAN
capital .... SANTIAGO
channel .... BEAGLE,
     COCKBURN, BALLENERO,
            CONCEPCION
city/town .... ANGOL, ARICA,
     PENCO, CALAMA, BARRANCAS,

     LA SERENA, CONCEPCION,
     MAIPU, CHILLAN, IQUIQUE,
     RANCAGUA, PUENTE ALTO,
     OSORNO, ANTOFAGASTA, LOTA,
     RENCA, QUILPUE, TEMUCO,
     TALCAHUANO, VALDIVIA,
     VALPARAISO, TALCA, VINA
                 DEL MAR
coastal wind .... SURES
coin .... COLON, ESCUDO,
                CENTAVO
court dance .... CUECA
deer .... PUDU
desert .... ATACAMA
evergreen/shrub .... MAQUI
gulf .... ANCUD, ARAUCO,
       GUAFO, CORONADOS,
     TRINIDAD, ELEFANTES, PENAS,
          TRES MONTES
island .... ANGAMOS, BYRON,
     DAWSON, CHATHAM, GUAFO,
     CAMPANA, ESMERALDA, LUZ,
     LENNOX, HOSTE, GORDON,
       MOCHA, CHILOE,
     LONDONDERRY, NALCAYEC,
     MADRE DE DIOS, PIAZZI, PRAT,
     PICTON, NUEVA, TRANQUI,
     TENQUEHUEN, WOLLASTON,
          WELLINGTON
islands .... CHAUQUES,
     GRAFTON, HERMITE, WEEK,
         WOOD, PAJAROS
lagoon .... ACULEO, BLANCA
lake .... TORO, PALENA,
     BLANCO, BUENOS AIRES,
     RUPANCO, COCHRANE, RANCO,
       YELCHO, VILLARRICA
language .... SPANISH
monetary unit .... PESO,
                ESCUDO
mountain .... MACA, CONICO,
     RINCON, AGUAS CALIENTES, AP
       IWAN, CAMPANARIO,
     MELIMOYU, LADRILLERO,
     TRONADOR, MURALLON, OJOS
     DEL SALADO, ZAPALERI, TRES
            CRUCES
palm tree .... COQUITO
peninsula ...... HARDY, LACUY,
     TRES MONTES, TAITAO,
     STAINES, TUMBES, WHARTON
pianist .... ARAU
president .... ALLENDE
region .... ANTOFAGASTA,
     ATACAMA, COQUIMBO, MAULE,
       BIOBIO, LOS LAGOS,
     SANTIAGO, MAGALLANES,
     TARAPACA, VALPARAISO
river ...... ACONCAGUA, BAKER,
     BRAVO, BIOBIO, CARMEN,
     CHOAPA, CAMARONES,

GRANDE, HUASCO, IMPERIAL, LAUCA, ELQUI, LA LIGUA, LAJA, LOA, LLUTA, MAIPO, RAPEL, MAULE, PASCUA, BUENO, TOLTEN, SIMPSON
salt deposit .... ATACAMA, GRANDE, BELLA VISTA, MIRAJE, LLAMARA, SURIRE, PINTADOS
saltpeter .... NITER
seaport .... LOTA, ARICA
strait .... MAGELLAN, MAGALLANES
tree .... PELU, ULMO, ROBLE, RAULI, QUILLAI
volcano .... MAIPU, LASTARRIA, CORCOVADO, LANIN, MINCHINMAVIDA, LLAIMA, TACORA, SOCOMPA
chili con ____ .... CARNE
flavored dish .... ENCHILADA
chiliad .... THOUSAND
chill .... AGUE, COOL, ALGOR, FROST, COLD(NESS), DEPRESS, SHAKES, DISCOURAGE, SHIVERING, DISPIRIT
chilling device .... ICER, REFRIGERATOR
material .... ICE
chills and fever .... AGUE, MALARIA
chilly .... RAW, COLD, ALGID, CRISP, BLEAK, BRISK, BITING, FROSTY, WINTRY
chilopod .... CENTIPEDE
chimar .... ROBE
chimb .... RIM
chime .... RIM, BELL, PEAL, DOORBELL, HARMONY
in .... JOIN, AGREE, ACCEDE, CONCUR, JUMP AT, INTERRUPT
chimera .... FANCY, FANTASY, ILLUSION, MIRAGE, MONSTER
desert traveler's .... OASIS, WATER
sailor's .... LAND
chimerical .... FANCIFUL, NOTIONAL, FANTASTIC, UNREAL, FERTILE, IMAGINARY, VISIONARY, WHIMSICAL
chimney .... SPOUT, TEWEL, FUNNEL, (SMOKE)STACK
bird .... SWIFT, SWALLOW
carbon .... SOOT
corner .... FIRESIDE, (INGLE)NOOK
cover ..... COWL, MITER, MITRE
lining .... PARGET
of volcano .... VENT
piece .... PAREL, MANTEL
pipe .... FLUE

pot .... TALLBOY
screen .... BONNET
swallow .... SWIFT
chimpanzee .... APE, JOCKO, TROGLODYTE
relative ...... GIBBON, GORILLA, ORANGUTAN
chin flesh .... GILL
hairy growth .... BEARD, GOATEE
hollow/cleft .... DIMPLE
pertaining to .... GENIAL, MENTAL
slang ..... GAB, TALK, CHATTER
China .... SPODE, CATHAY
capital .... PEKING
made with clay .... BONE
Sea region .... ANNAM
chinaware .... CHINA, DISHES, DRESDEN, CROCKERY, PORCELAIN, STONEWARE
chincapin .... CHESTNUT
chinch .... BEDBUG
chinche .... SKUNK
chinchilla .... FUR, RODENT
relative .... VISCACHA
chine .... SILK, RIDGE, SPINE, RAVINE, BACKBONE
Chinese .... MIAO, SINO, SERIC, SINIC, ORIENTAL
A-bomb site .... LOP NOR
alimentary paste ..... WANTON, WONTON
American dish .... SUBGUM, CHOP SUEY, CHOWMEIN
ancient dominant religion .... CONFUCIANISM
arithmetical device .... ABACUS
aromatic root .... GINSENG
art/customs expert .... SINOLOGUE
artichoke .... CHOROGI
association .... TONG
autumn .... CH'IU
bamboo stick .... WHANGEE
bay .... HANGZHOU WAN
bean .... ADSUKI
boat .... JUNK, SAMPAN, TONGKANG
brand on goods .... CHOP
Buddhism .... FOISM
Buddhist monk/priest .... LAMA
bugaboo .... YELLOW PERIL
cape .... OLWAMPI
capital .... PEKING, BEIJING
capital, former .... CHUNGKING
Caucasian tribesman .... LOLO
cauterizing agent .... MOXA
channel .... BASHI

characters in Japanese .... MANA
chestnut .... LING
chicken .... GAI
city/town ...... AMOY, CANTON, KIRIN, ANSHAN, CHUNGKING, FUSHUN, CHENGDU, CHANGCHUN, HENGYANG, GUANGZHOU, TSINAN, FOOCHOW, GUIYANG, KALGAN, KUNMING, HANGCHOW, LUDA, LANZHOU, KWANGCHOW, NANJING, QIGIHAR, QINGDAO, SIAN, QUANZHOU, SHANGHAI, MUKDEN, SHENYANG, TANGSHAN, TZEPO, TIENTSIN, TSINGTAO, SUCHOW, TSINAN, YANGCHOW, ZIBO, WUHAN, ZHENGHOU
club .... TONG
coat .... MANDARIN
coin ..... LI, TAEL, TIAO, YUAN, LIANG
coin, early .... PU
coin with hole .... CASH
combining form .... SINO, CHINO
Communist leader .... MAO, PIAO, PING, CHOU, ZHAO
custom peculiar to .... SINICISM
department .... FU
dependency .... TIBET
desert .... GOBI
dialect .... CANTONESE, PEKIN(G)ESE
dialect, official ..... MANDARIN
dictator .... MAO (TSE-TUNG)
dog .... CHOW, PEKIN(G)ESE
duck eggs, preserved .... PIDAN
dynasty .... HAN, WEI, YIN, CHOU, HSIA, LIAO, MING, SUNG, T'ANG, YUAN, SHANG, MANCHU, MONGOL, TA CHING
dynasty, first .... HSIA
dynasty, last .... MANCHU
eating implement .... CHOPSTICKS
emperor .... HUANG, KUBLAI
emperor, last .... PU-YI
empress .... HOU
empress, last .... TZU-HSI
exercise .... T'AI CHI
eyes, describing .... SLIT, ALMOND
factory .... HONG
feudal state .... WEI
fiber plant .... RAMIE
fish .... TREPANG
flute .... TCHE

fruit .... LOQUAT
gambling game, cards
.... FAN-TAN
game with tiles
.... MAHJONG(G)
gateway .... PAILOU
gelatin/glue .... AGAR
god .... JOSS, SHEN
gong ...... TAM-TAM, TOM-TOM
grape .... WAMPEE
guild .... TONG
gulf .... BO HAI, TONKIN
hairdo .... PIGTAIL
Han city .... HANKOW,
        HANYANG, WUCHANG
harbor craft .... SAMPAN
herb .... GINGER, GINSENG
highest point .... MOUNT
                        EVEREST
ideograph .... KANJI
idol .... JOSS
import duties .... HAIKWAN
incense .... JOSS STICK
indigo .... ISATIS
invention .... GUNPOWDER
island .... AMOY, MATSU,
    DONGSHA, HAINAN, HUNGTOW,
    QUEMOY, YUHUAN, PINGTAN,
    MACAU, TAIWAN (FORMOSA)
islands .... TACHEN, YUSHAN,
                    PESCADORES
kingdom, old .... WEI
laborer .... COOLIE
lake .... BAGRAX, ER HAI, NAM
    CO, KHANKA, DIAN CHI, KOKO
    NOR, LOP NUR, EBINUR HU,
                    POYANG HU
language .... YI, SHAN,
    CHUANG, MONGOL, CHINESE,
    MIAO, UIGUR, KAZAKH,
    MANDARIN, TIBETAN
language/customs, study of
.... SINOLOGY
license .... CHOP
lord of lower world .... YENLO
magnolia .... YULAN
Manchu dynasty .... TA CHING
mandarin's residence
.... YAMEN
measure .... LI, CHIH, TSUN,
                        CHANG
medicinal herb .... GINSENG
metropolis .... WUHAN
mile LI
military academy
.... WHAMPOA
monetary unit ...... FEN, YUAN
money .... TAEL, SYCEE
Mongol .... MANCHU
Mongol dynasty .... YUAN

Mongol dynasty founder
.... KUBLAI
monk .... LAMA, BONZE
mountain .... LUSHAN,
    KONGUR, GONGGA, EVEREST,
    MUZTAG, MUZTAGATA,
    YUSHAN, YAGRADAGZE
Nationalist party
.... KUOMINTANG
noodles .... MEIN
notable name .... SOONG
nuclear center .... LOP NOR,
                        LANCHOW
numeral, 1 to 10 .... YIH, URH,
    SAN, SZE, WOO, LUH, TSIEH,
                    PA, KEW, SHIH
nurse/servant .... AMAH
nut .... LYCHEE, LICHI
official .... KUAN, KWAN,
                    MANDARIN
official seal .... CHOP
oil tree .... TUNG
omelet .... FOOYONG
orange .... MANDARIN
ounce .... TAEL
pagoda .... TAA
pagoda: var. .... TAAG
pear .... PYRUS
peninsula .... LIAOTUNG
peony .... MOUTAN
permit .... CHOP
philosopher .... MOTI,
    YUTANG, MENCIUS, MENG-TSE,
                    CONFUCIUS
phoenix .... FENG, HUANG
pickles .... CHOWCHOW
pine .... MATSU
plant .... MOXA, RAMIE,
                        GINSENG
poet .... LI PO
political party .... TONG,
                    KUOMINTANG
porcelain .... CELADON
port .... AMOY, CANTON,
    TSINGTAO, DAIREN, ICHANG,
    TIENTSIN, SHANGHAI
pottery .... MING
pound .... CATTY
prefix .... SINO
president .... SUN (YAT-SEN)
priest .... LAMA
principle .... TAO, YIN, YANG
province .... ANHUI, GANSU,
    HOPEI, FUJIAN, GUANGDONG,
    HUPEI, HONAN, KIANGSI,
    KIANGSU, HUNAN, LIAONING,
    KIRIN, SHANSI, SHENSI,
    SHANTUNG, CHEKIANG,
    SZECHWAN, TSINGHAI,
    YUNNAN, KWEICHOW, XIZANG,
    KWANGTUNG

provincial tax .... LIKIN
punishment .... CANGUE
puzzle .... TANGRAM
race designation .... YELLOW
rebellion of 1900 .... BOXER
religion .... ISLAM, TAOISM,
    BUDDHISM, CONFUCIANISM
river .... AMUR, PEARL, HAN
    SHUI, HAILAR HE, YELLOW,
    FEN HE, HOTAN HE, MEKONG,
    YANGTZE, SALWEEN, TUMEN,
    WEI-HE, WU JIANG, YUEN,
    YUAN, YALU, YALONG
river boat .... SAMPAN
sacred peak .... OMEI
sacred tree .... WU TUNG
salutation .... KOWTOW
satin .... PEKIN
sauce .... SOY
scripture, a .... CHING
sea cucumber .... TREPANG
season .... CH'UN, HSIA, CH'IU,
                        TUNG
secret society .... TONG
sedge .... MATI
shark fins .... YU CHI
silk .... SHA, PEKIN, PONGEE,
    SHANTUNG, TUSSA(H), TUSSER
silkworm .... SINA, TASAR
silver ingot/money ...... SYCEE
sky .... TIEN
slang .... CHINK
soapberry .... LICHEE, LITCHI
society ...... HUI, TONG, BOXER
son .... TAI
soup material .... TREPANG,
                    BIRD'S NEST
spring .... CH'UN
squash .... CASHAW, CUSHAW
stamp .... CHOP
statesman .... KOO
string money .... TIAO
summer .... HSIA
tea .... CHA, TSIA, BOHEA,
    CONGO(U), HYSON, OOLONG,
                    SOUCHONG
team work .... GUNG HO
temple .... TAA, JOSSHOUSE
trading boat .... TONGKANG
treatment by needles
.... ACUPUNCTURE
treaty port .... AMOY,
                    SHANGHAI
tree .... TUNG, GINK(GO),
            LOQUAT, WUTUNG
truth/way .... TAO
unicorn .... LIN, CHLLIN
walking stick .... WHANGEE
warehouse .... HONG
waterwheel .... NORIA
wax .... PELA

weight .... LI, FAN, HAO, TAEL,
CATTY, LIANG, PICUL
wine vessel .... TSUN
winter/wood oil .... TUNG
work together .... GUNG HO
wormwood .... MOXA
yellow .... SIL
chink .... RIMA, SLIT, CRACK,
CRANNY, CREVICE, FISSURE
filler .... GROUT
Chink: sl. .... CHINESE
chinks, full of .... RIMOSE,
RIMOUS
chinky .... RIMOUS
Chinook .... WIND, INDIAN,
SALMON
Indian .... FLATHEAD
lily/bulb .... QUAMASH
powwow .... WAWA
chinquapin .... TREE, (CHEST)NUT
chinse .... CALK, CLOSE
chintz .... CLOTH
chip .... BIT, CUT, CHOP, SCRAP,
NICK, FLAKE, PIECE, SLICE,
FRAGMENT, SPLINTER
in .... ANTE, CONTRIBUTE
of stone .... SPALL, GALLET
off the old block .... JUNIOR,
SON(NY)
on one's shoulder
.... GRUDGE, RANCOR
chipmunk ...... CHIPPY, TRACKEE,
SQUIRREL
cheek pouch .... ALFORJA
cousin of .... GOPHER
chippendale furniture leg
.... CABRIOLE
chipper .... ADZ, PERT, CHIRP,
CHISEL, LIVELY, TWITTER
colloquial .... BABBLE,
CHATTER
Chippewa ...... INDIAN, OJIBWA(Y)
chippy ...... CHIPMUNK, SPARROW,
PROSTITUTE
chips' companion .... FISH
chirk .... LIVELY, CHEERFUL
chiro, as combining form
.... HAND
chirographer .... PENMAN
chiromancer .... PALMIST
Chiron .... CENTAUR
forte of .... MEDICINE
pupil of .... ACHILLES,
HERCULES
chiropodist .... PEDICURIST
advice of .... FOOTBATH
chiropter .... BAT, ALIPED
chirp .... PEEP, CHEEP, TWEET,
TWITTER
chirper .... BIRD, CICADA,
NESTLING, FLEDGLING

chirrup .... CHIRP, TWEET
chirurgeon .... SURGEON
chisel .... CUT, PARE, TRIM, BURIN,
CARVE, GOUGE, HARDY,
BROACH, CHASER, FIRMER,
GRAVER, TOOLER, ENGRAVE,
SCULP(T)
bar .... SPUDDER
broad-faced .... DROVE
colloquial .... CHEAT, SWINDLE
in ..... ENCROACH, MUSCLE (IN)
mason's .... POMMEL
part .... TANG
polishing .... SLICK
primitive/stone .... CELT
slang .... GYP, SCREW
stonemason's .... QUARREL
chiseled profile .... ROMAN,
CLASSICAL
chiseler .... CHEAT(ER), CROOK,
GYPPER, SWINDLER
chit .... NOTE, SHOOT, SPROUT
colloquial ...... IOU, TAB, GIRL,
CHILD
of a kind .... BILL, MEMO,
VOUCHER
chitchat .... TALK, GOSSIP
chiton .... LIMPET, GARMENT,
MOLLUSK
chitter .... SHIVER, TWITTER
chive ...... ONION, SITHE, FLAVOR,
GARLIC
chiv(v)y ...... FRET, HUNT, CHASE,
HARRY
chlamys .... CLOAK, MANTLE
Chloe and others .... AUNTS
love of .... DAPHNIS
chloride .... MURIATE
chlorine .... IODINE, BROMINE,
HALOGEN
chloroform, for one
.... SOLVENT, ANESTHETIC
chlorophyll .... ETIOLIN
chock .... BLOCK, CLEAT, TRIG,
SPRAG, WEDGE
chockablock .... CROWDED
chocolate .... CANDY, DRINK
cake .... BROWNIE
candy filling .... FONDANT
flavored .... MOCHA
mixer .... MOLINET
powder .... COCOA
source/tree .... CACAO
substitute .... CAROB
choice ...... PICK, DESIRE, OPTION,
SELECTION, PREFERENCE
between two evils
.... DILEMMA
food .... DELICACY
make a .... OPT
morsel .... TIDBIT

object/role .... PLUM
of words .... DICTION
other .... ALTERNATIVE
part ...... MEAT, CREAM, ELITE,
MARROW
word .... EITHER
choices for getting there
somehow .... HOOK AND
CROOK
choir boy's collar .... ETON
leader .... CHORAGUS
leader's aide .... SUCCENTOR
of a .... CHORAL
place in church .... LOFT,
GALLERY
section .... ALTO, TENOR
vestment ..... COTTA, SURPLICE
choke .... JAM, PLUG, STIFLE,
SMOTHER, OBSTRUCT,
THROTTLE, SUFFOCATE
by squeezing throat
.... STRANGLE
by stuffing mouth .... GAG
to death .... BURKE
up .... CLOG
with iron collar ...... GARROTE
choked up: colloq.
.... SPEECHLESS
choker .... COLLAR, FUR(PIECE),
NECKTIE, NECKLACE
cholecyst .... (GALL)BLADDER
choler .... FIT, IRE, BILE, RAGE,
ANGER, WRATH
cholera bacillus .... COMMA
type of ..... MORBUS, NOSTRAS,
INFANTUM
choleric .... ANGRY, IRATE, TESTY,
IRASCIBLE, IRRITABLE
cholesterol .... LIPID
good form of .... HDL
harmful form of .... LDL
product .... GALLSTONE
cholla .... CACTUS
chololith .... GALLSTONE
Chomo-lungma .... EVEREST
chondroma .... TUMOR
choose .... OPT, CULL, PICK,
WALE, ADOPT, DECIDE,
PREFER, SELECT, EMBRACE,
DESIGNATE
for office .... ELECT
your _____ .... EXIT, WILD,
PARTNER
choosing, right of .... OPTION
choosy .... FUSSY, FINICKY,
FINICAL, FASTIDIOUS,
PARTICULAR
chop .... AXE, CUT, DICE, FELL,
HEW, JAW, LOP, HACK,
CHEEK, CLEAVE, MINCE,
STRIKE

down .... FELL, RAZE, LEVEL
in China, India .... SEAL,
PERMIT, LICENSE
off .... PRUNE
stroke, in tennis .... SLICE
up .... HACKLE
chop-chop .... AT ONCE,
PROMPTLY, QUICKLY
chophouse .... RESTAURANT
Chinese .... CUSTOMSHOUSE
specialty .... STEAK
chopine .... SHOE, PATTEN
Chopin's (Frederic) country
.... POLAND
love .... (GEORGE) SAND
work .... ETUDE
chopper .... AX(E), MOLAR
meat .... CLEAVER
slang .... HELICOPTER
chopping blows with hand
.... KARATE
surface .... BLOCK
tool .... AX(E), CLEAVER,
HATCHET
choppy .... ROUGH, JOLTING
chops .... JAWS, JOWL, PORK,
MOUTH
choral .... HYMNAL, SINGING
composition .... MOTET
music .... CANTATA, ORATORIO
chord .... CORD, STRING,
HARMONY
dissonance .... WOLF
playing of notes in
succession ...... ARPEGGIO
3-tone .... TRIAD
chordate .... VERTEBRATE
example of a .... MAN
chore .... (ODD) JOB, TASK,
CHARE, STINT, HOUSEWORK,
ASSIGNMENT
doctor's .... ROUNDS
list .... AGENDA
choreographer of note
.... ANTON, BALANCHINE
choreography .... DANCE,
DANCING, BALLET, DEPICTION,
PORTRAYAL
chorine .... STEPPER, CHORUS GIRL
chorister's garment .... CASSOCK
chorography .... MAP
choroid membrane .... TAPETUM
chortle .... SNORT, CHUCKLE
chorus .... CHOIR, UNISON
girl: colloq. .... CHORINE
leader .... CHORAGUS,
CONDUCTOR
line .... DANCERS
of a .... CHORAL, CHORIC
of song ...... BURDEN, REFRAIN
chose .... CHATTEL

Chosen .... KOREA
chosen one .... ELECTEE
Chou, Chinese bigwig .... EN LAI
chough .... CROW
chouse .... DUPE, CHEAT,
SWINDLE(R)
chow .... DOG, FOOD, MEAL
chowchow .... OLIO, MIXED,
PICKLES, ASSORTED
chowder ingredient .... CLAM
christen .... NAME, BAPTIZE
Christian .... HUMAN, DECENT,
GENTILE, BELIEVER,
CHURCHMAN
abbreviation .... XTIAN
bishop of the Goths
.... ULFILA(S)
church .... ORANT, BASILICA
church as a whole
.... CATHOLIC
church of Egypt .... COPT
church, the .... HERITAGE
love feast .... AGAPE
non .... PAGAN, PAYNIM,
HEATHEN
Oriental .... UNIAT
pulpit .... AMBO
religion founder .... JESUS
Science founder .... BAKER
Science healer
.... PRACTITIONER
theologian .... ORIGEN
traitor .... TRADITOR
Christiania, formerly .... OSLO
was capital of .... NORWAY
Christians, all .... CHURCH
Christie .... AGATHA
Christmas ...... NOEL, YULE(TIDE)
abbreviation .... XMAS
bonanza .... GIFTS
cake/fruitcake .... SIMNEL
carol .... NOEL, NOWEL
crib .... CRECHE
day .... NATIVITY
decorative item .... SEAL,
MISTLETOE
drink .... EGGNOG
favorite figure .... SANTA
(CLAUS)
gift container .... STOCKING
masked funster .... MUMMER
mock-up of Nativity
.... CRECHE
musician .... WAIT
pantomime .... GUISER,
MUMMER
season .... YULE(TIDE)
song .... NOEL, CAROL
song, Hilaire Belloc's
.... SAILOR'S CAROL
street singer .... WAIT,

CAROLER
time entertainment
.... PANTOMIME
tree .... PINE, HOLLY
vehicle .... SLED, SLEIGH
worker .... ELF
chromosome load .... GENES
chronic .... ROOTED, CONSTANT,
HABITUAL, CONFIRMED,
RECURRING, PERSISTENT
chronicle ...... ANNAL(S), DIARY,
RECORD, ACCOUNT, HISTORY
chronicler .... ANNALIST,
RECORDER, HISTORIAN
chronological .... DATED, IN
SEQUENCE
chronometer .... WATCH
chrysalis .... PUPA, COCOON
chrysanthemum ...... MUM, KIKU,
DAISY, FLOWER, POMPON,
COSTMARY, MARGUERITE
badge: Jap. .... MON
Chrysler cars of 1928–1961
.... DESOTOS
chrysolite .... OLIVINE, PERIDOT
chub .... (BLACK)BASS
chubby .... OBESE, PLUMP, STOUT,
ROTUND
one .... BUTTERBALL
chuck .... TOSS, CAST(OFF),
THROW, DISCARD
slang .... FOOD, GRUB, MEAT
chuckle .... CLUCK, LAUGH,
GIGGLE, CHORTLE, SNICKER
chucklehead .... DOLT, IDIOT
chuckleheaded .... STUPID
chuddar .... SHAWL
Chudskoe lake .... PEIPUS
chuff .... BOOR, BRICK, CHURL
chum .... PAL, BUDDY, CRONY,
FRIEND, ROOMMATE
in fishing .... BAIT
chummy .... BOSOM, FAMILIAR,
FRIENDLY, INTIMATE
chump .... BOOB, FOOL
chunk .... BAT, HUNK, LUMP,
HUNCH, PIECE, SLAB, GOBBET,
PORTION
chunky .... BURLY, HEFTY,
PORTLY, SQUAT, STOUT,
STOCKY, THICKSET,
CORPULENT
church .... SECT, CHAPEL,
MINSTER, TEMPLE, HOUSE OF
GOD, HOUSE OF WORSHIP,
DENOMINATION
altar attendant .... ACOLYTE
altar offerings .... ALTARAGE
archaic .... FANE
area .... TRANSEPT
basin .... FONT, STOUP,

LAVABO, PISCINA
bell/ringer .... SEXTON
bell tower .... BELFRY
bench/seat .... PEW, STALL
benefice .... LIVING
benefice, holding of
.... INCUMBENCY
benefit/fund-raising sale
.... BAZAAR
bishop's .... CATHEDRAL
body of .... NAVE
Buddhist .... PAGODA
building .... ECCLESIA
calendar .... ORDO
caretaker ..... SEXTON, VERGER
chancel .... BEMA
cathedral .... LATERAN,
MINSTER
chandelier .... CORONA
chapel .... CHANTRY, ORATORY
choir leader .... CHORAGUS,
CHORISTER, PRECENTOR
composition .... MOTET
contribution to .... TITHE
council/group .... SYNOD,
CONSISTORY
court .... ROTA, CLASSIS,
CONSISTORY
cup .... CHALICE
dignitary .... DEAN, POPE,
BISHOP, LEGATE, NUNCIO,
PRELATE, PRIMATE, CARDINAL
director .... CHORAGUS,
PRECENTOR
dish .... PATEN
dissenter .... SECTARY,
APOSTATE
district .... PARISH, DIOCESE
division in a .... SCHISM
doorkeeper/guard ..... OSTIARY
elder .... PRESBYTER
endowment to a
.... PATRIMONY
festival .... EASTER
finale .... AMEN
French .... EGLISE
gallery .... JUBE, LOFT
governing group .... CLASSIS
government .... HIERARCHY
grave-digger .... SEXTON
grounds .... PRECINCT
having no .... CHURCHLESS
head .... PONTIFF
Italian .... DUOMO
jurisdiction .... SEE,
BISHOPRIC, OBEDIENCE
land/property .... GLEBE
language .... LATIN
law .... CANON
lay leader .... ELDER
leader .... HIERARCH

lectern .... AMBO, ROSTRUM
living .... BENEFICE
loft .... JUBE
main part .... NAVE
members .... FOLD, FLOCK,
ECCLESIA, PARISHIONERS
monastery's .... MINSTER
morning service .... LAUD,
MATIN
Moslem .... MOSQUE
music .... HYMN, PSALM,
CANTATA
of Latter Day Saints
.... MORMON
office ...... BENEFICE, MINISTRY
office, sale of .... SIMONY
officer .... ELDER, BEADLE,
SEXTON, VERGER, ORDINARY,
PRESBYTER, SACRIST(AN)
part .... PEW, APSE, BEMA,
ALTAR, VESTRY, CHANCEL,
ORATORY, STEEPLE, SACRISTY,
TRANSEPT
place for shrines
.... FERETORY
poetic .... FANE
porch .... PARVIS, GALILEE
practice of peace ...... IRENICS
private/secret meeting
.... CONCLAVE
reader .... LECTOR
reading stand .... AMBO,
LECTERN, ROSTRUM
recess .... APSE
regular attender .... CHURCH-
GOER
revenue .... TITHE, BENEFICE
rite ..... (HIGH) MASS, BAPTISM,
BENEDICTION, COMMUNION,
MATRIMONY
Roman .... BASILICA
room for sacred vessels
.... VESTRY, SACRISTY
sale of offices, etc.
.... SIMONY, BARRATRY
sanctuary .... SACRARIUM
Scottish .... KIRK
screen .... ICONASTASIS
seamen's .... BETHEL
seat for clergy .... SEDILIA
separation from .... SCHISM
service/ceremony .... LAUD,
MASS, NONES, TE DEUM
service clothes
.... CANONICALS
service invocation
.... BENEDICTION
service reader .... LECTOR
service reading .... LECTION
singers' group .... CHOIR
tax .... TITHE

tower .... BELFRY, STEEPLE
tower top .... SPIRE
tribunal .... ROTA
vault .... CRYPT
vestibule .... NARTHEX
vestment room .... VESTRY,
SACRISTY
washbowl .... LAVABO
woman assistant
.... DEACONESS
Yiddish .... SHUL
Churchill Downs event .... RACE,
DERBY
Churchill's (W.) daughter
.... SARAH
forte .... PROSE
hobby .... BRICKLAYING
lady .... CLEMENTINE
nickname .... WINNIE
son .... RANDOLPH
son-in-law .... SOAMES
trademark .... CIGAR, VEE SIGN
churchly .... CLERICAL, PASTORAL
churchman .... CANON, ELDER,
BELIEVER, VICAR, BISHOP,
CLERGY, PASTOR, PRIEST,
CARDINAL, MINISTER,
ECCLESIASTIC
churchyard .... PARVIS, GOD'S
ACRE
churl .... OAF, BOOR, HIND, LOUT,
CARL(E), KNAVE, CEORL,
FREEMAN, PEASANT, VARLET,
YOKEL, VILLEIN
churlish .... DOUR, SURLY,
RUSTIC, SULLEN, BOORISH
churn .... BEAT, STIR, WHIP,
SHAKE, SEETHE, AGITATE
rotator .... DASHER
chute .... SHOOT, SLIDE, RAPIDS,
HOPPER, RUNWAY, ROLLWAY,
TROUGH, WATERFALL
for logs .... FLUME
chutney .... RELISH
chutzpah .... NERVE
Chuvash .... BULGARIAN
cibol .... ONION
ciborium .... CUP, PYX, CANOPY
cicada .... LOCUST
vibrating membrane of
.... TIMBAL
cicatricle .... TREAD
cicatrix .... SCAR
Cicero .... TULLY, MARCUS
target of .... CATILINE
cicerone .... GUIDE, DRAGOMAN
Cid .... LEADER
play, author of ..... CORNEILLE
name of .... RUY, (RODRIGO)
DIAZ
sword of .... COLADA

cider .... (APPLE) JUICE, PERKIN, SYTHER, VINEGAR
pear juice .... PERRY
spiced/sweetened .... FLIP
sweeten .... MULL
ci-devant .... LATE, FORMER, RECENT
cigar .... WEED, CLARO, SMOKE, CORONA, CHEROOT, CULEBRA, HAVANA, LONDRES, TOBACCO, COLORADO, BELVEDERE, PANATEL(L)A, PERFECTO
box .... HUMIDOR
butt .... STUB, SNIPE
cheap .... TOBY, STOGIE, STOG(E)Y
descriptive of a .... MADURO
end .... ETTE
Philippine .... MANILA
puff .... DRAG
self-lighting .... LOCOFOCO
Spanish .... PURO, CIGARRO
tree, e.g. .... CATALPA
cigarette, berry .... CUBEB
brand ..... KENT, CAMEL, TRUE, SALEM, DUNHILL, PALL MALL, PIEDMONT, WINSTON, MARLBORO, CHESTER(FIELD)
butt .... STUB, SNIPE
ingredient .... TOBACCO
kind of .... REGULAR, KING-SIZE, FILTER-TIP
lighter .... VESUVIAN
marijuana .... REEFER
material .... MAKINGS
non-tobacco .... CUBEB, REEFER, MARIJUANA
piece .... STICK
product .... TAR, NICOTINE
puff .... DRAG
slang .... COFFIN NAIL, FAG, BUTT, GASPER
smoke cleaner .... FILTER
smoke cooler .... MENTHOL
smoking aid .... PIPE
cigarfish .... SCAD
cilice .... HAIRCLOTH
cilium/cilia .... EYELASH(ES)
cimex .... BEDBUG
Cimmerian .... DARK, BLACK, GLOOMY
cinch .... GIRTH, FASTEN
lead-pipe .... SNAP
slang .... SURE THING
cinchona ...... BARK, TREE, QUILL
alkaloid .... QUINIDINE, QUININE
Cincinnati ball club .... REDS, REDLEGS
family .... TAFT(S)
managers .... REDHEADS

cincture .... BELT, GIRDLE, ENCLOSURE, WAISTBAND
cinder .... ASH(ES), SLAG
like lava .... SCORIA
sifter .... RIDDLE
Cinderella of Pop .... HOPKIN
cinema .... MOVIE, THEATER, MOTION PICTURE
cinerarium .... URN
cinerator .... FURNACE, CREMATORY
cingulum .... BELT, GIRDLE
cinnabar .... ORE, PIGMENT, SINOPLE, VERMILION
cinnamon .... BARK, SPICE, CANELLA
adulterant .... CASSIA
roll .... QUILL
stone .... GARNET, ESSONITE
cinquefoil .... CLOVER, FIVE-FINGER, POTENTILLA
cion .... BUD, GRAFT, SHOOT
Cipango .... JAPAN
cipher .... CODE, ZERO, DEVICE, OUGHT, NAUGHT, MONOGRAM, NONENTITY
system .... CODES
cipolin .... MARBLE
circa .... ABOUT
Circe .... TEMPTRESS, ENCHANTRESS
home of .... AEAEA
circle .... DISK, LOOP, RING, CLIQUE, CIRQUE, COTERIE, SET, GROUP, ENCIRCLE, WHIRL, ZODIAC
angle/arc .... RADIAN
describing one .... VICIOUS
flattened .... OVAL
half a .... HEMICYCLE
imaginary celestial .... COLURE
of guards .... CORDON
of light .... HALO, NIMB, CORONA
part ..... ARC, RADIUS, SECANT, SECTOR, DIAMETER, CIRCUMFERENCE
poetic .... RONDURE
quarter section .... OVOLO, QUADRANT
Circle, imaginary and parallel to equator .... ARCTIC, ANTARCTIC
circuit .... LAP, TOUR, LOOP, AMBIT, CYCLE, ORBIT, ROUND, ROUTE, CURVET, DISTRICT
court/judges' .... EYRE
in radio .... HOOKUP
of a utility system .... MAIN
track .... LAP

circuitous .... DEVIOUS, ROUNDABOUT
circuity .... ZIGZAG, INDIRECT
circular .... BILL, ROUND, BULLETIN, PAMPHLET, GLOBULAR, SPHERICAL
band .... HOOP, RING, BRACELET
course .... OVAL, RACETRACK
cross section .... TERETE
eyelet .... GROMMET
figure/line .... RING
form .... GYRE
letter, papal .... ENCYCLICAL
motion ...... EDDY, GYRE, SPIN, WHIRL, ROTATE, GYRATION
plate .... DISC, DISH, DISK
saw .... EDGER
space .... CIRQUE
step .... AMBIT
turn .... LOOP
wall of dome .... DRUM
wheel .... RUNDLE
circulate .... PASS, ISSUE, DIFFUSE, SPREAD, GET AROUND, PUBLISH, MOVE AROUND
circumference ...... AMBIT, GIRTH, PERIPHERY
circumlocution .... AMBAGE, VERBIAGE, PERIPHRASE, PERIPHRASIS
circumnavigator, first .... MAGELLAN
circumscribe .... LIMIT, CONFINE, ENCIRCLE, ENCOMPASS
circumspect .... SAFE, WARY, CAREFUL, PRUDENT, CAUTIOUS
circumspection .... PRUDENCE
circumstance .... FACT, STATE, CASE, STATUS, DETAIL, CONDITION
companion of .... POMP
circumvent .... SKIRT, ESCHEW, OUTWIT, SIDESTEP
circus .... ARENA, CIRQUE, CARNIVAL, (TENT) SHOW
animal .... BEAR, LION, SEAL, ELEPHANT
arena .... RING, HIPPODROME
colloquial .... BIG TOP
director .... RINGMASTER
horse .... GRAY
laborer .... ROUSTER, ROUSTABOUT
man .... LION TRAINER
minor attraction .... SIDE SHOW
name, bigtime .... BAILEY, BARNUM, RINGLING
net .... TRAMPOLIN(E)
perennial .... CLOWN

performer .... FLEA, SEAL,
    CLOWN, ACROBAT, AERIALIST,
    TUMBLER, UNICYCLIST,
    JUGGLER, EQUESTRIEN(NE)
  ring cover .... TANBARK
  swing .... TRAPEZE
  vehicle .... CARAVAN
cirque ...... RING, CIRCLE, CIRCUS,
    AMPHITHEATER
cirriped .... BARNACLE,
    CRUSTACEAN
cirrus .... CLOUDS, FEELERS,
    TENDRIL
  cloud .... MARE'S-TAIL
cirsoid .... VARIX, VARICOSE
cisco .... HERRING, (WHITE)FISH
cist .... TOMB, CHEST
cistern .... VAC, VAT, (RAIN) TANK
  in anatomy .... SAC, CAVITY
  natural .... RESERVOIR
cit .... CITIZEN, TOWNMAN
citadel .... FORT, TOWER, CASTLE,
    REFUGE, FORTRESS,
    ACROPOLIS, STRONGHOLD
  of justice, so-called .... COURT
  Russian .... KREMLIN
cital .... SUMMONS
citation .... NOTICE, SUMMONS,
    QUOTATION, REFERENCE
  favorable .... ACCOLADE,
    COMMENDATION
cite .... CALL, QUOTE, MENTION,
    SUMMON
  loosely .... PARAPHRASE
cithern .... CITOLE
cities, between .... INTERURBAN
citified: colloq. .... URBAN
citizen .... NATIVE, BURGESS,
    DENIZEN, FREEMAN, SUBJECT,
    CIVILIAN, NATIONAL,
    RESIDENT, INHABITANT
  army .... MILITIA
  French .... CITOYEN
  of the world ..... COSMOPOLITE
citizenry, local
  .... HOMETOWNERS
citizens, assembly of
  .... ECCLESIA
  of .... CIVIC, CIVIL
citrine .... FALSE TOPAZ
citron .... LIME, ETROG, LEMON
  fruit of, symbol of Sukkoth
  .... ESROG
citrus drink .... ADE, LIMEADE,
    LEMONADE, ORANGEADE
citrus fruit .... LIME, LEMON,
    CITRON, ORANGE, MANDARIN,
    BERGAMOT, GRAPEFRUIT
  disease .... PSOROSIS
  membrane .... RAG
  oil .... BERGAMOT

skin .... ZEST
city .... TOWN, COSMOPOLIS,
    METROPOLIS, MUNICIPALITY
  bishop's .... SEE
  business section
  .... DOWNTOWN
  cathedral .... ELY, YORK,
    R(H)EIMS, CHARTRES
  colloquial .... BURG, BURH,
    BIG TOWN
  district .... WARD
  father .... ALDERMAN,
    COUNCILOR
  fellow: sl. .... DUDE
  gangster .... PLUG-UGLY
  great .... MEGALOPOLIS
  hall .... AYUNTAMIENTO
  heavenly .... SION, ZION
  main .... METROPOLIS
  of a .... CIVIC, URBAN,
    MUNICIPAL
  of sin/wicked .... SODOM,
    BABYLON, GOMORRAH
  of the leaning tower .... PISA
  of the Rhine .... MAINZ
  of vice .... BABYLON
  official .... MAYOR,
    ALDERMAN, COUNCILOR
  on the Red River .... FARGO
  on the sea .... PORT
  Pearl of the Orient
  .... MANILA
  pertaining to .... CIVIC, URBAN
  prename .... LAS, LOS
  problem .... SMOG, CRIME,
    SLUMS, TRAFFIC, POVERTY
  square .... PARK
  state ...... VATICAN, SINGAPORE
  steel .... ESSEN
  subdivision .... WARD,
    SECTION, PRECINCT
  vice center .... TENDERLOIN
  windy .... CHICAGO
  wonder .... AGRA
City of Angels .... BANGKOK
  Bridges .... BRUGES
  Brotherly Love
  .... PHILADELPHIA
  David .... JERUSALEM
  Kings .... LIMA
  Lights .... PARIS
  Masts .... LONDON
  Pillars .... IREM
  Refuge .... BEZER, GOLAN,
    HEBRON, KEDESH, MEDINA,
    RAMOTH, SECHEM
  Saints .... MONTREAL
  Seven Hills .... ROME
  the Dead .... NECROPOLIS
  the Gods .... ASGARD
civet .... CAT, FUR, DEDES, FOSSA,

    RASSE, ZIBET, MUSANG,
    NANDINE
  like animal .... GENET(TE),
    SURICATE
  odor .... MUSK(LIKE)
  of the .... VIVERINE
civil .... LAY, CIVIC, POLITE,
    COURTLY, URBANE, SECULAR,
    CIVILIZED, TEMPORAL,
    COURTEOUS
  magistrate .... SYNDIC
  marriage performer ..... JUDGE
  wrong .... TORT
Civil War admiral .... FARRAGUT
  battlefield .... SHILOH,
    ATLANTA, ANTIETAM, BULL
    RUN, GETTYSBURG
  before the .... ANTEBELLUM
  cartoonist .... NAST
  division .... BLUE AND GRAY,
    NORTH AND SOUTH,
    CONFEDERATE AND REBEL
  general .... LEE, POPE, HOOD,
    EWELL, GRANT, MEADE,
    BRAGG, BUELL, SCOTT,
    HOOKER, FREMONT,
    MCCLELLAN, SHERMAN,
    SHERIDAN
  soldier .... REB, YANKEE
  vet .... GAR
  volunteer .... ZOUAVE
civilian .... CITIZEN, CIV(V)IES,
    RESIDENT, NONMILITARY,
    NONCOMBATANT
  clothes .... MUFTI
civilization .... CULTURE
  cradle of .... ASIA
civilize .... REFINE, RECLAIM,
    EDUCATE, CULTIVATE
clabber .... MILK, CURDLE
clack ...... BLAB, PRATE, CHATTER
clad .... ROBED, ATTIRED,
    CLOTHED, DRESSED
claim .... AVER, RIGHT, TITLE,
    ALLEGE, ASSERT, CONTEND
  legal ...... LIEN, PLEA, DEMAND
  mining .... STAKE
  on property .... LIEN
  without right .... ARROGATE
claimant, kind of .... PRETENDER
clairvoyance .... INSIGHT,
    INTUITION, DIVINATION
clairvoyant .... SEER
clam .... MYA, MOLLUSK
  hard-shell .... QUAHOG,
    QUAHAUG
  joint of .... HINGE
  killer .... WINKLE
  razor .... SOLEN
  shell .... TEST, SHUCK
  shell opening .... GAPE

soft-shell .... STEAMER
young .... LITTLENECK
clamant .... NOISY, URGENT
clambake .... OUTING, PICNIC,
                RALLY, COOKOUT
clamber .... SHIN, CLIMB, CRAWL,
             SCALE, SCRAMBLE
clammy .... DAMP, MOIST,
                   SWEATY
clamor .... DIN, RIOT, NOISE, HUE,
       GAFF, OUTCRY, UPROAR,
                 YAMMER
for .... LEVY, DEMAND,
                 REQUIRE
clamorous .... LOUD, NOISY,
    SHRILL, DINNING, VOCIFEROUS
clamp .... GRIP, VISE, FASTENER
like device .... CHUCK
clan .... GENS, SEPT, TRIBE,
      GROUP, CLIQUE, FAMILY
leader .... THANE, TANIST,
              CHIEFTAIN
of a .... GENTILE
pattern .... TARTAN
quarrel .... FEUD
symbol .... TOTEM
clandestine .... SLY, SECRET,
    HIDDEN, VEILED, FURTIVE,
    ILLICIT, UNDERCOVER,
    UNDERHAND, SURREPTITIOUS
meeting, usually .... TRYST,
             RENDEZVOUS
clang ...... TOLL, DING, PEAL, RING
clangor .... DIN, PEAL, JANGLE
clannish .... TRIBAL
clap .... BLOW, SLAM, SLAP,
          STRIKE, APPLAUD
clapboard .... SIDING
clapper, bell .... TONGUE
claptrap .... BOSH, HOKUM,
         DRIVEL, HEROICS
claque(ur) .... FAN, ROOTER,
              APPLAUDER
Clara .... BOW, BARTON
or Barbara .... SANTA
clare .... MINT
clarence .... CARRIAGE
Clarence, lawyer .... DARROW
claret .... WINE, BORDEAU
clarify .... CLEAR(UP), DEFINE,
    FILTER, PURIFY, REFINE,
    EXPLAIN, EXPOUND, SETTLE,
            ELUCIDATE
lard .... RENDER
clarinet .... REED
forerunner .... CHALUMEAU
socket .... BIRN
clarinetist, bandleader
       .... (ARTIE) SHAW
clarion .... TRUMPET
clarity ...... CLEARNESS, LUCIDITY

Clark .... ROY, DICK
claro .... CIGAR
clarry .... MINT
clash .... DIFFER, COLLIDE,
    CONFLICT, DISAGREE
clasp .... HUG, HASP, HOOK, OUCH,
    CINCH, BUCKLE, ENFOLD,
    FIBULA, TASSEL, EMBRACE,
          FASTENING
hair .... BARRETTE
ornamental .... BROOCH
class .... ILK, KIND, RATE, SORT,
    TYPE, ORDER, KIDNEY, RANK,
    SPECIES, CATEGORY
first .... A-ONE, BEST
of animal/plant .... GENUS
of ruling deities
           MONARCHY, THEARCHY
scientific .... GENUS, GENERA
slang ...... QUALITY, TOP-RATE,
          EXCELLENCE
social .... CASTE
classic ...... OLD, SIMPLE, ANTIQUE
car .... REO
classical language .... GREEK,
        LATIN, ROMAN
music ..... SONATA, CONCERTO,
         SYMPHONY
non .... MODERN, POPULAR,
         ROMANTIC
classics annotator .... SCHOLIAST
classification .... LABEL,
    GROUPING, CATEGORY
of diseases .... NOSOLOGY
science of .... TAXONOMY
classified (information)
        .... SECRET
classify .... LIST, RATE, SORT,
    TYPE, LABEL, ASSORT,
    ARRANGE, CATALOGUE
classis .... ROTA
classy .... CHIC, ELEGANT, STYLISH
clatter .... DIN, HUBBUB, HURTLE,
    RATTLE, BRATTLE
Claude .... RAINS, MONET
claudicant .... LAME, LIMPING
clavichord .... SPINET
clavicle .... COLLARBONE
clavier .... KEYBOARD
common .... PIANO
claviform .... CLAVATE, CLUB-
         SHAPED
claw .... HOOK, NAIL, TALON,
    NIPPER, POUNCE, UNGUIS,
    UNGULA, SCRATCH
having/like a .... UNGUAL
like process .... CALCAR
of crustacean .... CHELA,
         PINCER
pincer-like .... CHELIFORM
retract .... SHEATHE

claws .... UNCI
clay .... LOAM, LUTE, MARL,
    ARGIL, LOESS, KAOLIN(E),
    SAGGAR, SAGGER, FIGULINE,
    LATERITE, LITHOMARGE
baked ...... BOLE, TILE, ADOBE,
         BRICK
case .... SAGGAR, SAGGER,
         SEGGAR
chunk/lump of/disk .... BAT
clump of .... CLOD
desert .... ADOBE
earthy/ore-bearing ..... OCHER,
         OCHRE
formation .... SHALE
granite .... PETUNTSE
layer .... SLOAM
like/pertaining to .... BOLAR
mixture .... LOAM, CEMENT,
         PUDDLE
molded .... PUG
oven .... TANDOOR
paste .... PATE
pigeon .... TARGET
pigeon shoot .... SKEET
plastic .... PUG
porcelain .... PASTE, KAOLIN
potter's .... ARGIL, PASTE,
         FIGULINE
rock .... MUDSTONE
sieve .... LAUN
thinned .... SLIP
tobacco pipe .... DUDEEN
wad .... BAT
water mixture .... SLURRY
white .... PETUNTSE
clayey .... BOLAR, LUTOSE
cement .... LUTE
soil .... BOLE, LOAM, MALM,
        MARL, LOESS
claymore .... (BROAD)SWORD
clean ...... PURE, CHASTE, SINLESS,
    ABSTERGE, SPOTLESS,
         UNSOILED
and draw fowl .... DRESS
as a _____ .... WHISTLE
breast, make a .... CONFESS
by rubbing ...... SCOUR, SCRUB
clothes .... LAUNDER
copy .... LEGIBLE, READABLE
hands .... INNOCENT
of impurities .... PURGE,
         PURIFY
ship's bottom .... BREAM,
         GRAVE
slang .... SPIC AND SPAN
slate .... RASA, TABULA
up .... WASH, FINISH, SPRUCE
with abrasive .... SCOUR,
         SCRAPE
with broom .... SWEEP

with mop .... SWAB
cleaner .... SOAP, SWEEPER, MAID,
    JANITOR, CHARWOMAN
cleaning cloth .... RAG
    powder .... ARIEL, PUMICE
cleanse .... PURGE, PURIFY,
    FRESHEN, DETERGE,
    FUMIGATE, DEODORIZE,
    STERILIZE
cleansing substance ...... BORAX,
    SOAP, ARIEL, DETERGENT,
    PURGATIVE, ABSTERGENT
clear .... RID, FREE, PURE,
    HURDLE, LIQUID, LUCENT,
    SHEER, CLARIFY, EVIDENT,
    PLAIN, APPARENT, LUCULENT,
    OBVIOUS, (PEL)LUCID
    a magnetic tape .... ERASE
    a path .... MAKE WAY
    as _____ .... CRYSTAL
    conscience .... INNOCENT
    cut .... SHARP, DISTINCT,
    TRENCHANT
    day/weather ...... FAIR, SUNNY,
    CLOUDLESS, STORMLESS,
    UNCLOUDED
    of charges .... ACQUIT,
    ABSOLVE, EXONERATE
    out .... GO, LEAVE, DECAMP,
    DEPART, VACATE
    perfectly .... LUCID, LIMPID
    profit .... NET
    sky .... ETHER
    textile .... DIAPHANOUS
    the way! .... GANGWAY
    throat audibly ..... HEM, HAWK
    title .... UNENCUMBERED
    to the mind .... PLAIN,
    DISTINCT, PALPABLE
    up .... SOLVE, CLARIFY,
    EXPLAIN, STRAIGHTEN
clearance .... LEEWAY, MARGIN,
    ADJUSTMENT
    of charges .... ACQUITTAL
    of disease symptoms
    .... REMISSION
    sale .... BARGAIN, RUMMAGE
cleareyed .... AWARE, PERCEPTIVE
clearing, wood .... GLADE
cleat .... KEVEL, PITON, BATTON
    make secure around
    .... BELAY
cleavage .... GULF, RIFT, CLEFT,
    FISSION, DIVISION
cleave .... REND, RIVE, CLING,
    SEVER, SPLIT, STICK, ADHERE,
    BREAK, DIVIDE, SUNDER
cleaver .... FROE, FROW, RIVER,
    CHOPPER
    sky .... LIGHTNING
cleek .... HOOK

cleft ...... GAP, RIFT, SPLIT, CRACK,
    CREVICE, FISSURE, FORKED,
    DIVIDED, SCISSURE
    easily .... FISSILE
Clemenceau's soubriquet
    .... TIGER, TIGRE
clemency .... GRACE, MERCY,
    LENIENCY, MILDNESS
Clemens's pen name ...... MARK
    TWAIN
clement .... MILD, LENIENT,
    MERCIFUL
clench .... GRIP, CLINCH
clenched hand .... FIST
Cleopatra .... FATHER'S GLORY
Cleopatra's domain .... NILE,
    EGYPT
    killer .... ASP
    lover .... (MARK) ANTONY,
    (JULIUS) CAESAR
    maid .... IRAS
    mascara .... KOHL
    Needle .... OBELISK
    river .... NILE
    son .... CAESARION
    title .... QUEEN
clepe .... CALL, NAME
clepsydra .... (WATER) CLOCK,
    WATERGLASS
clergy .... ABBACY, MINISTRY,
    PRIESTHOOD, THE CLOTH,
    PAPACY, FIRST ESTATE
clergyman .... ABBE, CANON,
    CLERIC, CURATE, DIVINE,
    PADRE, PARSON, PASTOR,
    PRIEST, BISHOP, PRELATE,
    MINISTER, RABBI, DIOCESAN,
    CARDINAL, RECTOR, IMAM,
    VICAR, CHAPLAIN
    and author .... SHEEN
    church service vestment
    .... CANONICALS
    colloquial .... DOMINIE
    degree of .... STB
    position/garment .... FROCK,
    CASSOCK, SURPLICE
    residence of .... MANSE,
    RECTORY, PARSONAGE
    salary of .... PREBEND
    with the military .... PADRE,
    CHAPLAIN
clerical .... PASTORAL
    abbr. .... ECCL
    cap .... BIRETTA
    collar .... RABATO, REBATO
    vestment .... ALB, AMICE,
    FANON, ORALE, SURPLICE
clerisy .... INTELLECTUALS
clerk .... SCRIBE, SALESMAN,
    SECRETARY, SCRIVENER,
    TYPIST, OFFICE WORKER

Clerk's Tale heroine
    .... GRISELDA
Cleveland waterfront .... ERIE
clever .... CUTE, ADEPT, SLICK,
    SMART, ADROIT, BRIGHT,
    HABILE, CUNNING, SKILLFUL,
    TALENTED
    as a fox .... VULPINE
    remark: sl. .... MOT, CRACK,
    NIFTY
    retort .... SALLY, BON MOT,
    REPARTEE, RIPOST(E),
    WITTICISM
    stratagem .... COUP
cleverly amusing .... WITTY
    done/said .... NEAT
clew .... KEY, TIP, BALL, CLUE,
    THREAD
cliche .... TRUISM, BANALITY,
    PLATITUDE
click .... PAWL, AGREE, CATCH,
    JIBE, SNICK, PALLET, SUCCEED
    beetle .... DOR(R), ELATER
clicking sound .... TICK
client .... BUYER, PATRON,
    CUSTOMER
    without .... BRIEFLESS
clientele .... TRADE, PATRONS,
    CLIENTAGE, CUSTOMERS,
    PATRONAGE
cliff .... CRAG, SCAR, BLUFF,
    PALISADE, PRECIPICE
    debris .... TALUS
    edge .... BROW
    fissure .... CHINE
    fissure for climbing
    .... CHIMNEY
    rock pile .... TALUS
    shelf .... LEDGE
cliffs, channel between .... GAT
    line of .... PALISADES
climacteric .... CRUCIAL
    woman's .... MENOPAUSE
climate .... SKY, WEATHER
    study of .... METEOROLOGY
climax .... ACME, APOGEE,
    SUMMIT, ZENITH, PINNACLE,
    PEAK, APEX, CULMINATION
climb ...... RISE, MOUNT, ASCEND,
    SCALE, ASCENT, CLAMBER
    a rope/pole .... SHIN
    down .... DESCEND
climbers .... VINES
    social .... SNOBS, PARVENU
climbing .... RISING, SCALING
    adapted for .... SCANSORIAL
    by attachment .... SCANDENT
    iron .... SPUR, PITON, CRAMPON
    means of .... LADDER
    palm .... RATTAN
    plant process .... TENDRIL

vine .... HOP, IVY, PEA, BINE,
LIANA, LIANE, BRYONY
wall by ladder .... ESCALADE
clime .... REALM, REGION,
CLIMATE, COUNTRY
clinch .... HUG, GRIP, NAIL, CLOSE,
GRASP, RIVET, FASTEN,
GRAPPLE
argument .... SETTLE
breaker .... REFEREE
nautical .... KNOT, NOOSE,
CLENCH
slang .... EMBRACE
cling .... HOLD, GRASP, STICK,
ADHERE, COHERE
clingfish .... REMORA, TESTAR
clinic .... WARD, SEMINAR,
DISPENSARY
clink .... JAIL, RING, PRISON
clinker .... SLAG, BRICK
built .... LAPSTRAKE
clinking sound .... TINKLE
clinquant .... TINSEL(ED)
"Clinton's ditch" .... ERIE
(CANAL)
Clio .... MUSE
Clio's field .... HISTORY
sister .... ERATO
clip .... CUT, MOW, GRIP, TRIM,
SCAR, FASTEN, SHORTEN
colloquial .... HIT, PACE,
CHEAT, PUNCH, SPEED,
SWINDLE
ornamental .... BROOCH
Scottish .... COLL
slang .... GYP
clipped .... CURT, TERSE
clipper .... SHIP, AIRPLANE,
SHEARER
barber's .... SCISSORS
clippings .... SCRAPS
clique .... SET, RING, CIRCLE,
COTERIE, FACTION
advisers' .... CABAL,
CAMARILLA
cloaca .... PRIVY, SEWER
cloak .... PALL, WRAP, GREGO,
MANTUA, CONCEAL,
CHLAMYS, GARMENT,
DISGUISE
and-dagger group .... CIA,
OSS, OGPU
blanket-like .... PONCHO,
SERAPE
fur-lined .... PELISSE
hood of .... COWL
hooded .... CAMAIL, CAPOTE,
BURNOUS, BURNOOSE,
CARDINAL
over armor .... TABARD,
SURCOAT

room .... CLOSET, VESTIARY
short ..... GREGO, MANT(E)LET,
MANTILLA
Spanish .... CAPA, MANTA
used as raincoat .... PONCHO
woman's .... MANTEAU,
CARDINAL
clobber .... HIT, BEAT, MAUL,
DEFEAT
slang .... PUMMEL
cloche .... HAT, (GLASS) JAR
clock .... HOROLOGE, HOURGLASS,
TIME(PIECE)
face of .... DIAL
in .... ARRIVE, REGISTER
inhabitant .... CUCKOO
kind of .... ALARM, RADIO,
SUNDIAL, CHRONOGRAPH,
CHRONOMETER, GRANDFATHER
London's famed .... BIG BEN
maker/dealer ...... HOROLOGER,
HOROLOGIST
part .... DIAL, HAND, PAWL,
BUNDY, CHIME, CLICK,
PALLET, PENDULUM
ship-shaped .... NEF
slang .... TICKER
sound .... CHIME, TICK(TOCK)
watcher .... IDLER
water .... CLEPSYDRA
work device .... METRONOME
clocker .... TIMER
clocklike .... PRECISE, REGULAR
clockwise .... SUNWISE
clockwork .... EVENLY, PRECISELY
clod ...... DOLT, LUMP, SOIL, LOUT,
BUMPKIN, EARTH, HILLBILLY
clodhopper .... BOOR, SHOE,
PLOWMAN
clodpate/clodpoll .... DOLT, FOOL,
BLOCKHEAD
clog .... JAM, SHOE, CHOKE,
BLOCK, DANCE, SABOT,
HAMPER, HINDER, IMPEDE,
PATTEN, CHOPINE, GALOSH(E)
cloggy .... STICKY
cloisonne finish .... ENAMEL
cloister .... STOA, ABBEY, FRIARY,
PRIORY, CONVENT, RETREAT,
NUNNERY, MONASTERY
dweller .... NUN, MONK,
ABBOT, ABBESS
cloistered ...... PRIVATE, RETIRED,
ISOLATED, SECLUDED
clone .... COPY, REPLICA
original .... ORTET
close .... CAP, END, LOCK, SEAL,
FINALE, FINISH, COMPACT,
OCCLUDE, CONCLUDE,
INTIMATE, SHUT(IN), STINGY,
SULTRY

after opening .... RESEAL
British .... ENTRY, PASSAGE
building .... PADLOCK
by .... (A)NEAR, NIGH
conclusively .... CLINCH
down/up ..... FOLD, QUIT, STOP
fist .... CLENCH
fitting .... SNUG, (SKIN)TIGHT
hermetically .... SEAL
in .... ENCLOSE, ENCIRCLE,
SURROUND
in music .... CODA
mouthed .... TACITURN
mouthed one .... CLAM
of day .... EVENTIDE
poetic .... NIGH, ANEAR
tightly .... CORK, SEAL
to the wind .... LUFF
violently .... SLAM
closed at one end .... BLIND
closefisted .... CHEAP, FRUGAL,
STINGY, MISERLY, NIGGARDLY
closet ...... ROOM, AMBRY, CUDDY,
PRIVY, LOCKER, TOILET,
CUPBOARD
closing passage in music
.... CODA
word .... AMEN
closure .... END, SEAL, BLOCKADE,
CLOTURE, STOPPAGE,
BOTTLENECK, OBSTRUCTION,
BARRIER, CONCLUSION
clot .... GOUT, JELL, CRUOR,
GRUME, COAGULATE
preventing substance
.... HEPARIN
cloth .... BRAT, WOOF, GOODS,
SERGE, DENIM, FABRIC,
TEXTILE, TWILL, COTTON,
MUSLIN, TRICOT, RAYON,
FIBER, MATERIAL
a sample piece of .... SWATCH
altar .... PALL, VESPERAL
baptismal .... CHRISOM
bark .... TAPA
buff-colored .... NANKIN,
NANKEEN
calico .... DOWLAS
camel's hair ..... ABA, CAMLET
chalice .... PALL
cheap .... MUNGO
checkered ...... PLAID, TARTAN
coarsely woven .... BURLAP
corded ...... DIMITY, BENGALI
cotton ..... JEAN, DRILL, CHINO,
CRASH, CALICO, CANVAS,
DENIM, MANTA, CHINTZ,
HOLLAND, MUSLIN, MADRAS,
GINGHAM, NANKEEN, PERCALE
cover .... TILT, DRAPE
cretonne .... TOILE

crinkled .... CRAPE, CREPE
curtain .... TAPIS
damask-like .... LAMPAS
dealer .... DRAPER, MERCER,
CLOTHIER
diagonal weave .... TWILL
dressing .... GAUZE, STUPE
drying .... TOWEL
drying frame .... TENTER
edge .... SELVAGE
end part of .... FAG
equal to 2¼ inches .... NAIL
fiber .... NAP, FLAX, SILK,
LINEN, RAMIE, COTTON
figured .... BROCADE,
JACQUARD, BROCATEL(LE)
fine cotton .... PERCALINE
fine, thin .... BATISTE
finishing machine ..... BEETLE,
CALENDER
flaxen .... LINEN
flaw .... RIP, SNAG, TEAR
floor covering .... RUG
for face sweat ...... VERONICA,
SUDARIUM
for sheets, pillowcases
.... MUSLIN, PERCALE
frieze-like .... RATTEEN
gauzy .... BAREGE, ILLUSION
glazed .... CHINTZ, JACONET
glossy .... SILK, SATIN,
SATEEN, CALAMANCO,
LUSTRING, LUTESTRING
goat's hair .... ABA
gold .... CYPRUS, CYPRESS
hairy surface .... NAP
handwoven .... TAPESTRY
hanging in folds ..... DRAPERY
heavy .... MACE
hemp, unbleached .... CANVAS
jute .... GUNNY
knot .... BURL
leftover pieces (from bolt)
.... REMNANTS
lightweight .... DELAINE
linen .... DRILL, TOILE,
DOWLAS, HOLLAND
linen with striped pattern
.... SEERSUCKER
loin .... LAVA-LAVA
make of ..... WOVEN, KNITTED,
PRESSED, EMBOSSED
maker .... DRAPER, WEAVER
making spy .... KEEK
material ..... FLAX, HAIR, SILK,
SKIN, WOOL, FIBER, RAYON,
COTTON
measure ...... ELL, NAIL, YARD,
METER
measure equal to 30 yards
.... BOLT

medicated .... STUPE
metallic .... LAME
method of dyeing designs on
.... BATIK
mix-colored .... MOTLEY
mulberry bark .... TAPA
mummy .... BYSSUS
nautical .... SAIL, CANVAS
needlework on
.... EMBROIDERY
ornamental .... DOSSAL
ornamentally designed
.... LACE, DAMASK, LAMPAS
penitent's .... SACKCLOTH
plaid .... TARTAN
plush-like .... BOLIVIA
powder .... SACHET
rib .... CORD
ribbed .... CORDUROY
ridge .... RIB, WALE
selvage .... LIST
sheer .... TOILE, CHIFFON
silk .... SATIN, CHIFFON,
CREPE, TAFFETA, LUSTRING,
PONGEE, CHARMEUSE,
SARCENET, LEVANTINE
soft .... SILK, SATIN,
GOSSAMER
stiffening .... WIGAN
strip .... LIST
strips for decoration
.... BUNTING
surface .... NAP
synthetic .... NYLON, RAYON,
DACRON
table .... NAPKIN
tapestry .... TAPIS
texture .... WALE
the .... CLERGY
thin, stiff .... ORGANZA
to wrap dead person in
.... BYSSUS, SHROUD,
CEREMENT
triangular .... GORE
twilled .... JEAN, DENIM,
CHINO, PLAID, SERGE,
LEVANTINE
umbrella .... GLORIA
upholstering .... TABARET,
BROCATEL(LE)
veil .... BAREGE
velvet-like .... PANNE
wall hanging .... TAPESTRY
waste .... RAG
waterproof .... GOSSAMER
waxed .... CEREMENT
wiping .... TOWEL, NAPKIN
with decorative pictures
.... TAPESTRY
with diagonal weave .... DRILL

with raised design
.... BROCHE, BROCADE
with satin strips ...... TABARET
with uncut loops .... TERRY
wool(en)—See **woolen**
worn like a scarf .... STOLE
woven with a pebbly pattern
.... SHARKSKIN
clothe ...... DON, RIG, GARB, ROBE,
DRAPE, DRESS, ENDUE, EQUIP,
INVEST
clothed .... CLAD, ATTIRED,
DRESSED, COSTUMED,
INVESTED
clothes ...... WEAR, DRESS, ATTIRE,
RAIMENT, APPAREL,
GARMENTS, GARB,
HABILIMENT, TOGGERY
basket .... HAMPER
bride's .... TROUSSEAU, BRIDAL
OUTFIT
cheap .... SLOPS
chest .... BUREAU, DRESSER
civilian .... PLAIN, CIVVIES
closet .... VESTRY, WARDROBE,
CLOAKROOM
collection of .... OUTFIT,
ENSEMBLE, WARDROBE
colloquial .... DUDS, RAGS,
TOGS, THREADS
fancier ..... FOP, DUDE, DANDY
formal .... TUX, TAILS,
TUXEDO, EVENING GOWN
gaudy .... FRIPPERY
line .... SEAM
moth .... TINEA
ordinary .... MUFTI
party .... FINERY, GLAD RAGS
pertaining to .... VESTIARY
place for .... BUREAU, CLOSET,
DRESSER, WARDROBE
powder .... SACHET
press .... IRON, ARMOIRE
rack .... VALET
ragged .... TATTERS
set of .... SUIT, ENSEMBLE
splendid .... REGALIA
stand .... RACK, TREE
to be washed/soiled
.... LAUNDRY
work .... APRON, DENIM,
JEANS, SMOCK, COVERALL,
UNIFORM, DUNGAREES
worn .... SECOND-HAND,
HAND-ME-DOWNS
clotheshorse: colloq. .... FOP,
DUDE, DANDY, COXCOMB
famed .... (BEAU) BRUMMEL
clothespress .... ARMOIRE
clothier Strauss .... LEVI
clothing .... GARB, ATTIRE,

APPAREL, COSTUME, RAIMENT, HABILIMENT
ID .... NAMETAPE
of men's .... SARTORIAL
pin .... AGLET
store ..... CLOTHIERS, SWEATER SHOP, DRESS SHOP, TOGGERY, HABERDASHERY
store stiff .... MANNEQUIN
Clotho ...... FATE, WEIRD, SPINNER
clotting protein .... GLOBULIN
cloture ...... CLOSING, CLOSURE
cloud .... DIM, FOG, GLOOM, HAZE, SULLY, DARKEN, OBSCURE
combining form .... NEPHO
composition .... GAS, DUST, SMOKE, STEAM, WATER, VAPOR
formation .... CIRRUS, NIMBUS, CUMULUS, STRATUS
like mass .... COMA, NEBULA
nine .... JOY, BLISS, ECSTASY
of dust/smoke/gas .... MIST
photo of .... NEPHOGRAM
region .... SKY
small .... CLOUDLET
surrounding gods ...... NIMBUS
cloudburst ...... RAIN, DOWNPOUR
cloudless .... CLEAR, SUNNY, BRIGHT
clouds, fleecy .... CIRRUS
broken mass of .... (W)RACK
combining form .... NEPHO
cumulus .... WOOLPACK
in the ...... FANCIFUL, REVERIE, DAYDREAMING
study of .... NEPHOLOGY
wind-driven .... SCUD
cloudy .... DIM, HAZY, GLOOMY, MISTY, DARK, TURBID, LOWERING, FOGGY, NEBULOUS, NUBILOUS, SHADY, OVERCAST, TROUBLED
clough .... GORGE, RAVINE
clout .... HIT, RAP, BLOW, CUFF, SLAP, SWAT, KNOCK
colloquial .... PULL, POWER, IMPACT, INFLUENCE
clove ...... BUD, SPICE, CARNATION
cloven ...... CLEFT, SPLIT, DIVIDED
footed ...... DEVILISH, SATANIC, FISSIPED
hoofed .... BISULCATE
clover ...... HERB, ALSIKE, LADINO, NARDOO, BERSEEM, ALFALFA, MELILOT, TREFOIL, SHAMROCK, THREE-LEAF
family .... LEGUME
genus .... TRIFOLIUM
in ..... COMFORT, CORNUCOPIA, PROSPERITY

plant resembling .... MEDIC
yield .... HONEY
cloverland .... LEA
cloverleaf .... CROSSWAY, CROSSROAD
clown .... APER, BOOR, LOUT, MIME, ZANY, BUFFO, COMIC, JESTER, BUFFOON, COMEDIAN, HARLEQUIN, PUNCHINELLO
forte of a .... JOKES, ANTICS, PRANKS, TRICKS, ACT SILLY, (TOM)FOOLERY
garment of .... MOTLEY
of a sort: sl. .... CUTUP
Shakespearean play .... FESTE, LAVACHE
woman .... BUFFA
clownish .... RUDE, CLUMSY, BOORISH, ARTLESS, AWKWARD
cloy ...... BORE, GLUT, PALL, SATE, SATIATE, SURFEIT
cloying .... SUGARY, LUSCIOUS
club .... MAUL, STICK, CUDGEL, HIT, BEAT, STRIKE, CLIQUE, SOCIETY, BLUDGEON
aborigine's .... WADDY
armor-breaking/heavy
.... MACE
baseball .... BAT
benefit sale .... BAZAAR, RUMMAGE
billiards .... CUE, MACE
college .... SORORITY, FRAT(ERNITY)
for beating cloth .... BEETLE
for sandtraps
.... (SAND)WEDGE
golf .... IRON, WOOD, CLEEK, DRIVER, PUTTER
hockey .... BANDY
hold on .... GRIP
house figure .... PRO
local division .... CHAPTER
manager .... STEWARD
member, certain .... LIAR
metal-headed .... MACE
military service .... USO
moss .... LYCOPOD
payment .... DUES
policeman's .... BILLY, TRUNCHEON
polo .... MALLET
service .... LIONS, JAYCEES, ROTARY, KIWANIS
shaped .... CLAVATE, CLAVIFORM
social .... BRIDGE, COTERIE, SORORITY
women's ...... ZONTA, SOROSIS, SORORITY
wooden .... MAUL

clubby .... CLANNISH, SOCIABLE
clubfoot .... TALIPES
clubfooted .... TALIPED
clubman .... LION, FELLOW, JAYCEE, MEMBER, ROTARIAN, INSIDER, KIWANIAN, ASSOCIATE
clubs .... SUIT
clucking sound .... CLACK
clue ...... TIP, CLEW, HINT, GUIDE, POINTER
major .... KEY
clumber .... DOG, SPANIEL
clump .... LUMP, MASS, BUNCH, PATCH, CLUSTER, THICKET
bushy .... TOD
of bushes .... SHAW
of earth .... CLOD
of ivy, etc. .... TOD
of trees .... BOSK, TUFT, GROVE, MOTT(E)
clumps, growing in .... CEPITOSE
clumsy .... LUMPY, GAWKY, GAUCHE, OAFISH, AWKWARD, INEPT, BUMBLING, UNGAINLY, INELEGANT, MALADROIT
and stupid .... LOUTISH
boat .... ARK, BARGE, DROGHER
person .... OX, OAF, JUMBO, LUBBER, LUMMOX
player .... DUB
sometimes called .... LEFT-HANDED
thing .... JUMBO
walker .... WADDLER
worker .... BUNGLER, COBBLER, DABBLER, DABSTER
Cluny product .... LACE
clupeid .... SHAD, HERRING, SARDINE
cluster .... KNOT, TUFT, BUNCH, CLUMP, GLOME, GROUP, SORUS, GLOMERATION
arranged in .... AGMINATE
banana .... HAND
bracts .... COMA
compact .... GLOMERULE
fibers .... FASCICLE
flowers .... CYME, RACEME, PANICLE
fruits .... BUNCH
leaves .... FASCICLE
of notes: music .... TREBLE
of seven stars .... PLEIADES
of shrubs/trees .... CLUMP
of spore cases .... SORUS
clustered .... TUFTED, GLOMERATE
clusters, growing in
.... ACERVATE
clutch .... GRAB, GRIP, HOLD,

GRASP, SEIZE, SNATCH, COLLAR, SQUEEZE, EMBRACE

clutches .... GRIP, POWER, CONTROL, CUSTODY

clutter .... MESS, DEBRIS, BUSTLE, JUMBLE, LITTER, DISORDER

clyster .... ENEMA

Clytemnestra's daughter .... ELECTRA

husband .... AGAMEMNON

lover .... AEGISTHUS

mother .... LEDA

son/killer .... ORESTES

coach .... BUS, CAR, HELP, TEACH, TUTOR, TRAIN, CARRIAGE, VEHICLE, TEACHER, DIRECTOR

athletic .... TRAINER

dog .... DALMATIAN

for hire .... HACK, FIACRE, HANSOM

for state occasions .... CAROCHE

four-horse drawn .... TALLYHO

roof/top of .... IMPERIAL

coachman ...... FLY, HACK, JEHU, LURE, DRIVER

coaction .... FORCE, COERCION, COMPULSION

coagulate .... SET, CAKE, CLOT, CURD, JELL, CURDLE, CLABBER, CONGEAL, THICKEN

coagulated mass .... CLOT

substance/deposit .... CRUD

coagulating substance .... RENNET, RENNIN, STYPTIC, COAGULIN, PRECIPITIN

coagulation, blood .... CLOT, THROMBOSIS

coal ...... COKE, CARBON, LIGNITE, ANTHRACITE, BITUMINOUS

barge load of .... KEEL

bin .... BUNKER

box .... BIN, DAN, HOD

bucket/hod .... SCUTTLE

burner .... BRASIER

container of live ...... BRAZIER

deposit .... SEAM

digger/miner .... PITMAN, COLLIER

distillate .... TAR

dust .... ASH, CULM, DUFF, SMUT, SLACK

feeder .... STOKER

glowing piece of/live .... EMBER, GLEED

grade of .... WALLSEND

impurities/waste .... CULM, CLINKER

leavings .... SLACK

like substance .... JET

lump/mass .... COB

measure .... PEA, CHALDRON

mine .... PIT, COLLIERY

bed .... WINNING

carrier .... TUB, TRAM

gas ..... METHANE, FIREDAMP

roof prop .... SPRAG

shaft .... PIT, WINNING

wagon .... CORF

miner's consumption .... ANTHRACOSIS

oil ...... KEROSENE, PETROLEUM

partially burned .... CINDER

pieced .... LUMP

region .... RUHR, SAAR

screening device .... TROMMEL

ship .... COLLIER

shovel .... SCOOP

sieve .... TROMMEL

size of .... EGG, NUT, PEA, WALLSEND

stoker .... HOPPER

tar compound ...... SACCHARIN

tar derivative .... PITCH, CRESOL, BITUMEN, CREOSOTE, TOLUENE, TOLUOL(E)

tar dye .... EOSIN, ALIZARIN

truck/wagon .... CORF, TRAM

coalesce ...... MIX, BLEND, MERGE, JOIN, UNITE, COMBINE

coalescence .... UNION, MERGER

coalfish .... CUDDY, POLLACK

coalition .... UNION, FUSION, AXIS, BLOC, LEAGUE, MERGER, ENTENTE, ALLIANCE

coals, rake over the ...... ROAST, RACK, CENSURE, CRITICIZE

coarse .... BAWDY, CRASS, CRUDE, GROSS, HARSH, ROUGH, RIBALD, VULGAR, LOWBRED, OBSCENE, RUDE, UNCOUTH, UNREFINED, BROAD, INDELICATE

cloth .... JUTE, LENO, DENIM, SCRIM, BURLAP

corn meal/hominy .... GRITS, SAMP

fiber .... TOW

flour .... MEAL

lace .... MACRAME

material .... REP(P)

meal .... GROUT

coast .... BEACH, GLIDE, SLIDE, RIVAGE, SEASIDE, (SEA)SHORE, SHORELINE, WATERFRONT

line curve .... BIGHT

of the .... LITTORAL

on aircraft .... VOLPLANE

Coast Guard boat .... CUTTER

girl .... SPAR

coastal .... LITTORAL

coaster .... SLED, TOBOGGAN

glass/bottle .... MAT, DISK, TRAY

coasting vehicle .... SKI, SLED, TOBOGGAN, SURFBOARD

coat .... TOG, COVER, LAYER, JACKET, KIRTLE, GARMENT, RAGLAN, PROTECT, COVERING, ULSTER, SWALLOW-TAIL

animal ...... FUR, SKIN, WOOL

arm-pinning/madman's .... STRAITJACKET

close-fitting ...... COATEE, NEW MARKET

daytime .... CUTAWAY

double-breasted .... REEFER, MACKINAW

formal .... TAILS, CUTAWAY

fur-lined .... PELISSE

hanger .... PEG

icy .... RIME, (HOAR)FROST

kind of ...... TOP, OVER, TURN, DUSTER, TRENCH

leather .... JACK

long .... REDINGOTE

long-sleeved .... CAFTAN, KAFTAN

loose .... SACK, PALETOT

of a mammal .... FUR, HAIR, PELAGE

of alloy .... PATINA

of armor .... BRIGANDINE

of arms .... CREST, BLAZON, SHIELD, HERALDRY

of arms band .... BATON, TRESSURE

of arms edge .... BORDURE

of gold/with gold .... GILD, GILT

of icing .... GLACE

of mail .... ARMOR, BYRNIE, HAUBERK

of metal .... PLATE

of the earth .... CRUST

outer .... RIND

person in white .... DOCTOR

slang .... TOG

sleeveless .... JACK

slit .... VENT

soldier's .... TUNIC

thin .... VENEER

waterproof .... SLICKER, MACKINTOSH

with aluminum ...... CALORIZE

with brass .... BRAZE

with metal .... PLATE

with tar .... PAY

woman's .... DOLMAN, REEFER, REDINGOTE

worn as armor ..... GAMBESON

coati-like animal .... RACCOON

coating .... FILM, LAYER, COVERING, CRUSTATION
boiler's inside .... FUR
for photographic plates/ wounds .... COLLODION
fruit .... BLOOM
glossy .... GLAZE, ENAMEL
icy .... SLEET, (HOAR)FROST
metal/on copper, bronze .... PATINA, PATINE
on ceiling .... PARGET
on eyes .... GLAZE
outer .... HIDE, HUSK, RIND, SHELL
plant .... TEGUMENT
pottery .... GLAZE, ENAMEL
thin .... VENEER
wall .... PARGET
coax .... TEASE, CAJOLE, BLARNEY, WHEEDLE, BLANDISH, PERSUADE
cob .... EAR, SWAN, HORSE, (SEA)GULL
coal .... COBBLES
cobalt .... RADIUM, ISOTOPE
color .... DARK BLUE
symbol .... CO
Cobb, baseball player .... TY
cobble .... MEND, PAVE, PATCH
cobbler .... SOLER, CRISPIN, (SHOE)MENDER
block of .... LAST
form/tool of .... AWL
coble .... ROWBOAT, (FISHING)BOAT
cobra ...... NAGA, MAMBA, SNAKE, VIPER, ELAPINE
fighter .... MONGOOSE
headdress .... URAEUS
cobweb .... TRAP, GOSSAMER
describing a .... FILMY, GAUZY, FLIMSY
material .... FIBROID
Coca, comedienne ...... IMOGENE
Coca-Cola product .... TAB, FRESCA
cocaine .... DOPE, (HARD)DRUG, ALKALOID, NARCOTIC, ANESTHETIC, STIMULANT
addict .... SNOWBIRD
describing use of .... ADDICTIVE, DANGEROUS
slang .... COKE, JUNK, SNOW
source .... COCA, CUCA
Cochin-China capital .... SAIGON
cochineal .... DYE
pigment .... LAKE
silver-gray .... BLANCO
cochlear canal .... SCALA
cochleate .... SPIRAL
cock .... TAP, CROW, FAUCET, LEADER, ROOSTER
-a-hoop .... ELATED, CONCEITED
-and-bull story .... HOAX, YARN, CANARD
comb of .... CARUNCLE
fighting .... HEELER
young .... COCKEREL
cockade .... KNOT, ROSETTE
cockateel .... PARROT
cockatoo .... ARARA, PARROT
cockatrice ...... SERPENT, BASILISK
cockboat .... COG, TENDER
cockchafer .... DOR, BEETLE, BUZZARD
cockcrow .... DAWN, MORN
cocker ...... PET, CODDLE, FONDLE, PAMPER, SPANIEL
cockerel .... ROOSTER
cockeyed: sl. ...... AWRY, DRUNK, SCREWY, ABSURD, CROOKED, TWISTED, CROSS-EYED
cockfight .... SPAR
cockiness .... CONCEIT, ARROGANCE
cockle ...... BOAT, WEED, PUCKER, DARNEL, WRINKLE, SHELLFISH
cocklebur .... BURDOCK, RAGWEED
cockloft .... ATTIC, GARRET
cockney .... EGG, CHILD, DIALECT
famous .... HORNSBY
Cockney's pal .... MATEY
steed .... ORSE
cockpit .... ARENA, CABIN
occupant .... PILOT
Cockpit of Europe, so-called .... BELGIUM
cockroach .... WATERBUG
cockscomb ...... CAP, FOP, DANDY
cockspur .... (HAW)THORN
cocktail .... (MIXED)DRINK, BRONX, MARTINI, APPETIZER, SIDECAR, STINGER, MANHATTAN
fruit .... MACEDOINE
ingredient .... BITTERS
lethal .... MOLOTOV
measure .... SPLIT
mixer .... BLENDER, SHAKER, BARTENDER
room .... LOUNGE
rum .... ZOMBI(E), DAIQUIRI
tidbit .... OLIVE
with pickled onion .... GIBSON
with legs .... HORSE
cocky .... VAIN, SAUCY, FORWARD, PERT, HAUGHTY, ARROGANT, CONCEITED IMMODEST
colloquial ...... SWELL-HEADED
ones .... ROOSTERS

coco .... PALM(TREE)
cocoa .... BROMA, CHOCOLATE
bean, crushed .... NIBS
coconut .... PALM
husk fiber .... COIR
liquid .... MILK
meat, dried .... COPRA(H), COPPERAH
oil source .... COPRA
cocoon .... POD, CASE, THECA
covering .... FLOSS
fiber .... SILK
in zoology .... FOLLICLE
occupant .... PUPA
silkworm .... CLEW
Cocos Islands .... KEELING
cod ...... CUSK, LING, GADID, FISH, BURBOT, GLASHAN, BOCACCIO, WHITING
Archaic .... BAG
fishing bait .... CAP(E)LIN
kin .... HAKE
young .... SCROD
COD, part of .... ON, CASH, COLLECT, DELIVERY
coda .... FINALE
coddle .... PET, BABY, PAMPER, PARBOIL, SPOONFEED
again .... REPET
code .... LAW, CODEX, CIPHER, NORM, RULE, SALIC
breaker .... KEY
certain .... AREA
church .... CANON
emperor's .... NAPOLEON
kind of .... PENAL
message in .... CRYPTOGRAM
moral .... ETHICS
of a kind .... PASSWORD
of laws .... HAMMURABI
operator .... TELEGRAPHER
word, GI's radio .... ABLE, ECHO, OVER, BAKER, ROGER
codfish .... CUSK, LING, GADID, TORSK, BURBOT, GADOID, GLASHAN
young .... SCROD
codger .... CHURL, MISER, FELLOW, ECCENTRIC
codicil .... RIDER, APPENDIX
codling .... APPLE, SCROD
Cody, American plainsman .... (BUFFALO)BILL
coelenterate .... HYDRA, ANEMONE, ACALEPH(E), JELLYFISH
larva of .... PLANULA
coenurus .... LARVA
host of .... SHEEP
coerce .... COW, MAKE, FORCE, COMPEL, DRAGOON,

CONSTRAIN
colloquial .... BULLY,
BULLDOZE
coercion .... DURESS,
COMPULSION, AGAINST ONE'S
WILL
slang .... HEAT, PRESSURE
coercive indoctrination
.... BRAINWASHING
coetaneous .... COEVAL
Coeur d'Alene Indian
.... SALISHAN
de Lion .... RICHARD (I)
coeval .... COETANEOUS,
COINCIDENT, SYNCHRONOUS,
CONTEMPORARY
coexist ...... MESH, MATCH, AGREE,
COINCIDE, HARMONIZE
coffee .... CAFE, JAVA, MOCHA,
SHRUB, BRAZIL, MADDER,
SUMATRA, EXPRESSO,
CAPPUCCINO
alcoholic condition .... LACE
alkaloid .... CAFFEIN(E)
bean .... NIBS
blend .... MOCHA
box/can .... CANISTER
break .... RESPITE, TIME-OFF,
TAKE FIVE
brewer .... URN, SILEX
cake .... KUCHEN
cup .... DEMITASSE
cup stand .... ZARF
extract .... CAFFEIN(E)
grinder .... MILL
house .... CAFE
kind of/type .... DRIP, INSTANT
making container .... URN,
SILEX, PERCOLATOR
mixture/substitute
.... CHICORY, SUCCORY
plantation .... FINCA
pot .... URN, BIGGIN,
DRIPOLATOR, PERCOLATOR
room .... DIVAN
slang .... MUD, JAVA
tree .... CHICOT
coffer .... ARK, LOCK, CHEST,
VAULT, STRONGBOX
coffers .... CHEST, FUNDS,
TREASURY
coffin .... BIER, CASKET, LITTER,
PINE BOX, BURIAL BOX
carrier .... HEARSE, CAISSON,
PALLBEARER
cover .... PALL
nail: sl. .... CIGARETTE
stand .... BIER, CATAFALQUE
stone .... SARCOPHAGUS
cog ...... GEAR, PAWL, CHEAT, LIE,
TOOTH, WHEEL, DECEIVE,

(COCK)BOAT, SWINDLE
cogent .... VALID, STRONG,
POTENT, COMPELLING,
CONVINCING
cogitate ...... CHEW, MULL, MUSE,
THINK, PONDER, CONSIDER,
REFLECT, MEDITATE
cognac .... BRANDY
cognate .... AKIN, RELATED
cognition .... NOESIS, PERCEPTION
cognizance .... KEN, NOTICE,
INSIGHT, KNOWLEDGE,
AWARENESS
cognizant .... HEP, ON TO,
AWARE, CONSCIOUS
slang .... IN THE KNOW
cognize .... KNOW, NOTICE,
DISCERN, REALIZE, PERCEIVE
cognomen .... NICKNAME,
(SUR)NAME
cognoscente .... CONNOISSEUR
cogon .... GRASS
cogwheel .... GEAR, PINION
cohabit .... SLEEP TOGETHER
Cohan's song .... OVER THERE
coheir .... PARCENER
cohere .... CLASP, CLING, HOLD,
STICK, ADHERE
coherence .... UNITY
coherent .... STICKY, UNITED,
CONSISTENT
cohort .... ALLY, BAND,
ACCOMPLICE
one third of .... MANIPLE
cohune .... PALM
coif .... HAIRDO, SKULLCAP
coiffeur .... HAIRDRESSER
coiffure ...... HAIRDO, HAIRSTYLE,
HEADDRESS
kind of .... AFRO
pad .... RAT
quickie .... WIG, PERUKE,
TOUPEE, PERIWIG
style .... BUN, CHAR, BRAID,
CHIGNON, PIGTAIL
coign .... CORNER
coil .... CURL, LOOP, WIND, TWIST,
CIRCLE, SPIRAL, ROLL,
WHORL, CONVOLVE
cable/rope .... FAKE
in a ball .... CLEW
yarn .... SKEIN
coiled .... SPIRY, TORTILE,
HELICOID, CONVOLUTE
coiling .... WINDING
creature .... BOA, SNAKE,
PYTHON, CONSTRICTOR
coin .... MINT, MONEY, CHANGE,
DEVISE, INVENT, SPECIE
Abyssinian .... BESA, GIRSH,
TALARI

Afghanistan ...... PUL, AMANIA
Albanian .... LEK
Algerian .... CENTIME
American (U.S.) .... CENT,
DIME, EAGLE, PENNY, DOLLAR,
NICKEL, QUARTER
Anglo-Saxon ...... ORA, SCEAT
Angola .... LWEI
Annam .... QUAN
Arabian .... TALARI
Argentine .... CENTAVO
Australian .... CENT
Austrian .... DUCAT, KRONE,
GULDEN
back of .... VERSO
biblical .... BEKA, MITE,
SHEKEL, TALENT
box .... PIX, PYX
Bahamian .... CENT
Brazilian .... CENTAVO,
(MIL)REI, MOIDORE
Bulgarian .... LEV, LEW,
DINAR, STOTINKA
Burmese .... PYA
Chilean .... COLON, ESCUDO,
CENTAVO
Chinese ..... PU, FEN, TAEL, LI,
TIAO, LIANG
coating .... BLOOM
collector .... NUMISMATIST
Colombian .... CENTAVO
Costa Rican .... CENTIMO
counterfeit .... RAP, SLUG,
TOKEN
cross-figured .... KREU(T)ZER
Cuban .... CENTAVO
cut edges of .... NIG
Czech .... DUCAT, KRONE(N)
Danish .... ORA, ORE, ORAS,
CROWN, KRONE(N)
design .... INCUSE
drop .... SLOT
Dutch .... DALER, FLORIN,
GULDEN, STIVER, GUILDER
Dutch East Indies .... BONK,
DUIT
Ecuadorian .... SUCRE,
CENTAVO
edge .... NIG
Egyptian ..... PIASTER, PIASTRE
El Salvador .... CENTAVO
English .... ORA, GROAT,
PENCE, FLORIN, GUINEA,
UNITE, TESTON, CAROLUS
Ethiopian .... GIRSH, TALARI
expert .... NUMISMATIST
French .... ECU, SOU, LOUIS,
BESANT, BEZANT, AGNEL,
OBOLE, PISTOLE
front of .... OBVERSE
Gambian .... BUTUT

147

German .... MARK, KRONE, TALER, THALER
Greek .... OBOL, OBOLI, STATER, DRACHMA
Hebrew .... GERAH, SHEKEL
hole .... SLOT
Hungarian .... GARA, PENGO, FILLER
Icelandic .... AURAR, EYRIR, KRONE
imitation .... SLUG
India .... PIE, ANNA, MOHUR, RUPEE, PICE, PAISA
into money .... MINT, MONETIZE
Iranian .... RIAL, DARIC, PUL, POUL, DINAR, MOHUR, STATER, TOMAN, PAHLAVI
Iraqi .... DINAR
Irish .... RAP, PENNY
Italian ..... LIRA, LIRE, TESTER, SCUDO, SOLDO, TESTON, CENTESIMO
Japanese .... RIN, SEN
Jewish .... GERAH, SHEKEL
large .... CARTWHEEL
Latvian .... LAT, LATU
Lithuanian .... LIT, LITAI, LITAS, RUBLE
making metal .... FLAN
metal .... FLAN, PLANCHET
metallic .... SPECIE
Mexican .... PESO, CUARTO, CENTAVO
money .... MINT
Moroccan .... RIAL
Nepalese .... MOHAR
Norwegian .... ORE, CROWN, KRONE
Oman .... GAZ, GOZ, BAIZA, GHAZI
Oriental .... DINAR
Persian .... DARIC, DINAR
Peruvian .... SOL, DINERO, PESETA, CENTAVO
pewter .... TRA
plant .... MINT
Polish .... DUCAT, ZLOTY
Portuguese .... (MIL)REI
reverse side .... VERSO
ridges .... KNURL
Roman ...... AS, AES, SOLIDUS, DENARIUS, SESTERCE
Rumanian ...... LEU, LEY, BANI
Russian .... COPEC, KOPEK, RUBLE, KOPECK, CHERVONETS
Scandinavian .... KRONAR
Serbian .... DINAR
shaped .... NUMMULAR
Sicilian .... SCUDO
side .... VERSO, OBVERSE

slang .... INVENT
small value .... MITE, PICAYUNE
South American .... CONDOR
space for date, etc. .... EXERGUE
Spanish .... DURO, PESO, REAL, DOBLA, PESETA, PISTOLE
Spanish colonial .... PISTAREEN
Swedish .... ORE, KRONA, KRONER
Swiss .... BATZ, FRANC
tester .... SHROFF
Thailand .... AT, ATT, BAHT, CATTY, TICAL, TIKAL
tin .... TRA
Turkish .... LIRA, ASPER, PARA, ALTUN, MAHBUB, PIASTER, PIASTRE
Venetian .... BETSO, DUCAT
Venezuelan .... PESO
Yugoslav .... DINAR
coincide .... AGREE, CONCUR
coiner of words .... NEOLOGIST
coins .... MONEY, PENCE, SILVER
collection of/study of .... NUMISMATICS
collector of ...... NUMISMATIST
pertaining to ...... NUMISMATIC
roll of .... ROULEAU
small .... CHANGE
sound of .... JINGLE
coke .... COAL, FUEL
measure .... CHALDRON
residue .... BREEZE
slang .... COCAIN(E)
col .... GAP, PASS
colander ...... PAN, SIEVE, SIFTER, STRAINER
Colchis princess .... MEDEA
cold .... ICY, BLEAK, ALGID, GELID, RHEUM, CHILLY, MARBLY, FROSTY, CATARRH, GLACIAL
and damp .... DANK
be .... SHIVER, SHUDDER, TREMBLE
blooded ...... CRUEL, CALLOUS, PITILESS, HEARTLESS
blooded creature .... FISH
congeal by .... FREEZE
dish .... SLAW, SALAD
extremely .... GELID, FRIGID, FROZEN, FREEZING
head .... CORYZA
hearted .... SELFISH, UNKIND, RUTHLESS
leave out in the .... SNUB, ELIDE, IGNORE, ABANDON, NEGLECT, DISREGARD

prefix .... CYRO
Scottish .... CAULD
season .... WINTER
shoulder .... CUT, SNUB, REBUFF, SLIGHT, BRUSH-OFF
sore .... HERPES, LABIALIS
steel .... BLADE, SWORD
stinging .... NIP, NIPPING, CUTTING, PIERCING
tableland .... PUNA
very .... GELID, FRIGID, WINTRY, FREEZING, STONE-COLD, HYPERBOREAN
weather wear .... PARKA, ANORAK, GLOVES, EARMUFFS, EARFLAPS, THERMALS
Cold War weapon .... PROPAGANDA
coldness of body .... CHILL
cole .... KALE, RAPE, CABBAGE
Cole .... NATALIE, NAT KING
coleopter .... BEETLE, WEEVIL
coleslaw .... SALAD
Colette heroine .... GIGI
colewort .... KALE, CABBAGE, COLLARD
colic .... ILEUS
in the bile, cause of .... STONE
kind of .... INFANTILE, INTESTINAL
stone .... JADE
colima .... IRONWOOD
colin .... QUAIL, BOBWHITE
coliseum .... ARENA, STADIUM
collaborator .... LAVAL, QUISLING
what he gives enemy ..... AID, COMFORT
collage of a sort .... MOSAIC
collagen .... PROTEIN
disease .... ARTHRITIS
collapse .... FAIL, CAVE IN, SLUMP, FALL IN, FOLD UP, RUIN, DEFLATE, DOWNFALL, EXHAUSTION, BREAKDOWN
collapsible hat .... GIBUS
collar .... ETON, RUFF, GORGET, PARRAL, PARREL, CARCANET, DICKY, NECKBAND, NECKWEAR
ancient metal .... TORQUE
bird with feathered .... GROUSE, PARTRIDGE
bird's .... FLANGE
bone .... CLAVICLE
clerical .... RABATO
colloquial .... CHOKER
detachable .... TUCKER
edging .... FRAISE
English schoolboy's ..... ETON
fastener .... STUD
frilled/pleated .... RUFF

high .... FRAISE
horse's .... HARNESS
neck, describing
.... ORTHOPEDIC
ornamental .... CARCANET
projecting .... FLANGE
slang .... NAB, CATCH, ARREST,
CAPTURE
strangling .... GAROTTE,
GARROTE
turned down .... FALL,
RABATO
woman's ...... BERTHA, DICKEY
collard .... KALE
collared .... TORQUATE
collate .... ALIGN, GATHER,
COMPARE, COMPILE
collateral ...... SURETY, RELATED,
PARALLEL
collation .... TEA, MEAL,
FORMATION, PLACEMENT
colleague .... PARTNER,
ASSOCIATE, CONFRERE
collect .... REAP, AMASS, GARNER,
GATHER, COMPILE, ROUND UP,
ASSEMBLE, SCRAPE UP,
FLOCK, HUDDLE,
ACCUMULATE
grains leftovers/in bits
.... GLEAN
in church mass .... PRAYER
collectanea ...... CORPUS, MEDLEY,
MENAGERIE, ANTHOLOGY
collected .... CALM, COOL, POISED,
SERENE, COMPOSED,
AMASSED, STORED
collection ...... BEVY, HEAP, LUMP,
PACK, BUNCH, GROUP, STORE,
GALAXY, REPERTORY,
ASSEMBLAGE, COMPILATION
a complete .... SET
anecdotes .... ANA
animal fables .... BESTIARY
animals .... ZOO, HERD,
art works .... GALLERY
assorted .... MISCELLANY,
MISCELLANEA
books .... LIBRARY,
BIBLIOTHECA
Brahman maxims .... SUTRA
bridal clothes ...... TROUSSEAU
coins .... NUMISMATICS
commentaries .... GLOSSARY
documents/of writings
.... PAPERS
dried plants .... HERBARIUM
essays/opinions
.... SYMPOSIUM
explanatory notes
.... GLOSSARY
facts .... ANA, DATA

information about person
.... DOSSIER
large .... RAFF, RAFT,
MULTITUDE
laws ...... CODE, JURIS, CORPUS
literary .... ANALECTA,
ANALECTS
logs on river .... DRIVE
Norse poetry .... EDDA
of a great number of people
together .... THRONG,
MULTITUDE
of news clippings/souvenirs/
pictures .... SCRAPBOOK
operas, songs, etc.
.... REPERTOIRE
paintings/statues ..... GALLERY
piano pieces .... GRADUS
poems, etc. .... ANTHOLOGY
postage stamps ...... PHILATELY
prayers for mass .... MISSAL
precious .... TREASURE
reminiscences .... ANA,
MEMOIRS
saints' lives .... HAGIOLOGY,
LEGENDARY
sayings .... ANA
things .... CONGERIES
tools .... KIT
types .... PI(E)
collective .... GENERAL,
COMBINED, COOPERATING
bargaining result
.... CONTRACT
farm .... KOL(K)HOZ
security group .... NATO,
SEATO, UNITED NATIONS
collectively .... WHOLLY,
TOGETHER
collectivism .... SOCIALISM
collector .... BUFF, DUNNER,
EXPERT, FANCIER,
CONNOISSEUR
art/curios .... VIRTUOSO
bank .... RUNNER
birds' eggs .... OOLOGIST
book .... BIBLIOPHILE
coin .... NUMISMATIST
excise tax .... GA(U)GER
fare .... CONDUCTOR
gem .... LAPIDARY
item for a .... CURIO, RELIC,
MASTER, BIBELOT, FIRST
EDITION, FIRST ISSUE
jokes .... CERF
Munchausen's tales ..... RASPE
phonograph record
.... DISCOPHILE
plants .... HERBALIST
shell .... CONCHOLOGIST
stamps .... PHILATELIST

collector's milieu .... FLEA
MARKETS
colleen .... GIRL, LASS
college .... SCHOOL, ACADEMY,
INSTITUTE, UNIVERSITY
athletic team .... VARSITY
building .... GYM, LAB,
DORM(ITORY)
campus .... QUAD
cheer .... YELL, RAH(RAH)
cheerleader: Jap. ...... OENDAN
course: abbr. .... BOT, ENG,
ANAT, ARCH, BIOL, MED,
ECON, MATH, TRIG, ZOOL
dance .... HOP, PROM
dining hall .... REFECTORY
exams .... MIDTERMS
fellow .... DON
founded by Henry VI
.... ETON
freshman .... FROSH
get-together .... REUNION
girl .... COED
graduate(s) .... ALUMNUS,
ALUMNI
grounds .... CAMPUS,
QUAD(RANGLE)
group .... SORORITY,
FRAT(ERNITY)
half year .... SEMESTER
hall .... AULA
honor society .... ARISTA
league symbol .... IVY(LEAF)
lecturer .... PRELECTOR
living quarters .... HALL,
DORM(ITORY)
of attendance .... ALMA
MATER
office .... DEANERY
official .... DEAN, REGENT,
PROVOST, REGISTRAR
on the Thames .... ETON
optional subject ...... ELECTIVE
organization .... CLUB,
FRATERNITY, SORORITY
permit for absence ...... EXEAT
president .... PREXY
publication .... ANNUAL,
YEARBOOK
rank .... DEGREE
scholars' .... ULEMA
servant .... GYP
student .... JUNIOR, SENIOR,
FRESHMAN, SOPHOMORE
students' revelry
.... GAUDEAMUS
teacher .... PROF(ESSOR)
treasurer .... BURSAR
colleges' sports group .... NCAA,
IVY LEAGUE
collegiate .... VARSITY

149

collide .... BUMP, CLASH,
CONFLICT, CRASH, HURTLE
collie .... (SHEEP)DOG
of book .... LAD, LASSIE
of movies .... LASSIE
collier ...... SHIP, PITMAN, TENDER,
(COAL)MINER
colliery .... (COAL)MINE
tunnel .... ADIT
Collins and Mix .... TOMS
collinsia .... FIGWORT
collision .... CRASH, PILEUP,
CONFLICT, SMASHUP
colloquial ..... FENDER-BENDER
force of .... IMPACT
result .... CONCUSSION
colloidal dispersion in fluid
.... SOL
solution .... GEL
collop .... PIECE, SLICE
colloquial .... INFORMAL,
IDIOMATIC, VERNACULAR,
CHATTY, CONVERSATIONAL
affirmative .... YEP, YEAH
negative .... NARY, NOPE, NO
WAY, NOT ON YOUR LIFE
term of address .... MAC
colloquialism ...... IDIOM, SLANG,
PATOIS
Colloquies author ...... ERASMUS
colloquy .... CHAT, TALK, PARLEY,
RAPPING, CONFERENCE
collude .... CONSPIRE
colly .... SOOT, GRIME, BLACKEN
collyrium .... EYEWASH,
EYEWATER
collywobbles .... COLIC
colocynth .... VINE, APPLE, BITTER
cologne ...... TOILET WATER, ROSE
WATER, LOTION, BAY RUM
Colombia bay .... CHOCO, GUAPI,
HUMBOLDT, BUENAVENTURA
cape .... AUGUSTA, LA VELA,
LA AGUJA, CORRIENTES
capital .... BOGOTA
city/town .... CALI, PASTO,
NEIVA, CIENAGA, CARTAGENA,
ENVIGADO, BUENAVENTURA,
MANIZALES, BARRANQUILLA,
MEDELLIN, BUCARAMANGA,
TULUA, CUCUTA, MONTERIA,
IBAGUE, PALMIRA, PEREIRA,
ZARZAL, SEVILLA, SOLEDAD
coin .... REAL, CENTAVO
division .... AMAZONAS,
ATLANTICO, ANTIOQUIA,
CAUCA, BOYACA, BOLIVAR,
NARINO, CALDAS, CORDOBA,
CESAR, SUCRE, MAGDALENA
extinct language .... ARDA
falls .... ANGOSTURA, SALTO

GRANDE
gulf .... URABA, CUPICA,
TORTUGAS, TIBUGA,
MORROSQUILLO
Indian .... MIRANA
island .... FUERTE, GRANDE,
GORGONA, CUSACHON, NAIPO,
PROVIDENCIA, BARU, SANTA
CATALINA
lake .... UVA, LAGUNA,
CHAIRA, DE TOTA, MAPIRIPAN
language .... SPANISH
monetary unit .... PESO
mountain .... HUILA, TOLIMA,
CAZUELEJA
peninsula .... GUAJIRA
plains .... LLANOS
port .... LORICA, CARTAGENA
religion .... CATHOLIC
river .... AGUARICO, ARIARI,
ARAUCA, AMAZON, BITA,
CAUCA, CUSIANA, CESAR,
GUAINLA, GUAVIARE, META,
ISANA, LOSADA, MUCO, MIRA,
PUTUMAYO, PAUTO, NECHI,
SALDANA, SINU, SUAREZ,
ORINOCO, TOMO, TARAIRA,
SOGAMOSO, UPIA, YARI,
VICHADA
volcano .... PASTO, PURACE
colon .... LARGE INTESTINE
cancer .... LYMPHOMA,
CARCINOID TUMOR
examination .... COLONOSCOPY
examination instrument
.... COLONOSCOPE
layer of the ..... SEROUS COAT,
MUCOUS COAT, SUBMUCOUS
COAT
section of the .... SIGMOID,
ASCENDING, DESCENDING,
TRANSVERSE
surgical removal of
.... COLECTOMY
colonel's command .... REGIMENT
insigne .... EAGLE
navy counterpart ...... CAPTAIN
colonial newscaster .... CRIER
senate member ...... DECURION
colonist .... PIONEER, PLANTER,
SETTLER
Indian greeting to .... NETOP
colonize .... SETTLE, ESTABLISH,
POPULATE
colonizing insect .... ANT, BEE
colonnade .... GALLERY, PORTICO
colony .... PLANTATION,
SETTLEMENT
bees .... SWARM
of insects .... NEST
colophony .... ROSIN

color .... DYE, BLUSH, FLUSH,
HUE, PIGMENT, PAINT, STAIN,
TINT, RED, BICE, BLUE, SEPIA,
TINCT, GREEN, WHITE,
YELLOW, CHROMO, EBONY,
CORAL, COBALT
adding pigment .... STAINER
also called meadow lark
.... ACORN
animal .... ROAN, PINTO,
FAWN, TAUPE, DAPPLE,
TAWNY, BRINDLE
band .... FASCIA
blindness .... DALTONISM
blue ..... BICE, AZURE, COBALT,
CELESTE, CYANEAN, LAPIS-
LAZULI, CERULEAN, CYANINE,
TURQUOISE, INDIGO,
AQUAMARINE
brown .... HAZEL, ALESAN,
TAUPE, TAWNY, UMBER,
SUNTAN
brownish-red .... MAROON,
CHESTNUT, BURGANDY
brownish-yellow .... ECRU,
BUFF, AMBER
change .... BLUSH, FLUSH,
MANTLE, REDDEN
changing substance
.... ALTERANT
combining form
.... CHROMAT(O)
expert .... DYER
fixer .... MORDANT, FIXATIVE
fixer, in dyeing .... BASE
flesh ...... PINKISH, INCARNATE,
INCARNADINE
for French victory
.... MAGENTA
gradation .... TINT, TONE,
SHADE
green .... JADE, OLIVE,
MYRTLE, EMERALD, ABSINTHE,
SHAMROCK, CHARTREUSE,
VERDANT, TERRE-VERTE,
VERDET, VIRIDIAN
in music .... TIMBRE
intensity .... CHROMA
lack of .... PALLOR
lacking .... ALBINO
lightly .... TINT, TINGE
lose .... FADE, PALE
mallow .... MAUVE
neutral .... SAND, BLACK,
GRAY, GREGE, WHITE
of caution .... AMBER
of dust .... KHAKI
of pure marble .... WHITE
of ship's flag under
quarantine .... YELLOW

of telephones on highway
.... BLUE
opposite to white .... BLACK
orange .... APRICOT,
CAROTENE, MARIGOLD,
PUMPKIN, CARNELIAN,
TANGERINE, TERRA-COTTA
painter .... TITIAN
pale .... PASTEL
patch of .... FLECK
pertaining to .... CHROMATIC
pink .... MALLOW, ORCHID,
BEGONIA, CARNATION,
SALMON, PEACH-RED,
PRIMROSE, TEA ROSE
primary/prismatic .... RED,
BLUE, GREEN, INDIGO,
ORANGE, VIOLET, YELLOW
purple .... GRAPE, FUCHSIA,
LILAC, LAVENDER, AMETHYST,
PRUNE, ORCHID, VIOLET,
RAISIN, MAGENTA, PLUM,
MAUVE(INE)
quality of .... HUE, TINT,
TONE, PURITY, LIGHTNESS,
CHROMA, BRIGHTNESS
red ...... RUBY, POPPY, CLARET,
SIENA, DAMASK, CARMINE,
CRIMSON, REALGAR,
CARDINAL, SCARLET,
STRAWBERRY
reddish-brown .... OXBLOOD,
ROAN, RUSSET, CORDOVAN
reddish-yellow .... AUBURN,
TITIAN
small amount of .... TINT,
TINGE
splash .... BLOB
streak .... LACE, FLECK
white .... BONE, BLOND,
IVORY, EGGSHELL, PLATINUM,
ALABASTER
with red ocher .... RADDLE,
REDDLE
yellow .... CREAM, AMBER,
LEMON, MAIZE, CANARY,
STRAW, GOLDEN, CHAMOIS,
CHAMPAGNE, SUNFLOWER
Colorado capital .... DENVER
city/town ...... ASPEN, PUEBLO,
BOULDER, AURORA, ALAMOSA,
CRAIG, DURANGO, GREELEY,
LOVELAND, LEADVILLE,
LITTLETON, MONTROSE,
STERLING, LAKEWOOD,
CORTEZ, GRAND JUNCTION,
THORNTON, TRINIDAD,
WALSENBURG, WESTMINSTER,
LAMAR, WHEAT RIDGE,
COLORADO SPRINGS
county .... ADAMS, BOULDER,

DELTA, CHEYENNE, ARAPAHOE,
DENVER, CONEJOS, CHAFFEE,
EAGLE, ELBERT, DOUGLAS,
GRAND, FREMONT, EL PASO,
LAKE, GARFIELD, GUNNISON,
JEFFERSON, KIT CARSON,
LOGAN, LARIMER, LA PLATA,
MESA, MOFFAT, MONTEZUMA,
OTERO, MORGAN, MONTROSE,
PITKIN, PUEBLO, PROWERS, RIO
GRANDE, RIO BLANCO, ROUTT,
SUMMIT, SAGUACHE, PARK,
OURAY, SEDGWICK, WELD,
YUMA, TELLER
creek .... BEAR, BEAVER, BIG
SANDY, BIG GRIZZLY, CLAY,
CEBOLLA, CRESTONE, CROW,
DISAPPOINTMENT, HORSE,
DOUGLAS, FOUNTAIN, KIOWA,
MUDDY, LANDSMAN, OWL,
POT, PAWNEE, TROUT, TIMPAS,
TOMICHI
feature .... MESA
highest point .... MOUNT
ELBERT
Indian .... UTE, ARAPAHOE
lake .... BARR, CLAY, TWIN,
MEREDITH, GROUNDHOG,
AVERY, GRANBY, CHEESMAN,
HENRY, SAN CRISTOBAL,
ELECTRA, TRAPPERS,
SWEITZER, SWEETWATER
mountain .... BALD, ELBERT,
MESA, BAKER, ETHEL, SHEEP,
EVANS, PARKVIEW, HESPERUS,
HOLY CROSS, POLE CREEK,
YALE, HARVARD, PRINCETON,
ADAMS, ANTERO, POWELL,
SILVER, BENNETT, JUNIPER,
LINCOLN, LONE CONE, ZIRKEL,
MASSIVE, SHERMAN, SNEFFELS
mountains .... WET, ROCKY,
LARAMIE, LA GARITA, SAN
JUAN, SAN MIGUEL, SANGRE
DE CRISTO
mountain range .... GORE,
PARK, FRONT, RABBIT EARS,
SAWATCH, MEDICINE BOW
park .... ESTES, MESA VERDE,
ROCKY MOUNTAIN
pass .... VAIL, MUDDY,
MILNER, BUFFALO, CAMERON,
SCOFIELD, RABBIT EARS, LOS
PINOS, WILKERSON, KEBLER,
ROLLINGS, WILLOW CREEK
peak .... LONGS, ELBERT,
CASTLE, CONEJOS, ARAPAHOE,
PAGODA, HERMOSA, EL
DIENTE, PIKES, WETTERHORN,
WINDOM, ZENOBIA
phenomenon .... RAINBOW

Pittsburgh of .... PUEBLO
resort .... VAIL, ASPEN,
MANITOU
river ...... ELK, EAGLE, PIEDRA,
PINOS, LARAMIE, MANCOS,
SLATE, ILLINOIS, COLORADO,
RIO GRANDE, WHITE, DOLORES,
ARKANSAS, SMOKY HILL,
PURGATOIRE, TAYLOR,
CONEJOS, YAMPA, TRINCHERA
River lake .... MEAD
state bird .... LARK
state flower .... COLUMBINE
state motto .... NIL SINE
NUMINE, (NOTHING WITHOUT
GOD)
state nickname .... ROVER,
CENTENNIAL
tourist site ...... ROYAL GORGE,
BLACK CANYON, U.S. DENVER
MINT, DINOSAUR MONUMENT,
tunnel ..... GUNNISON, ALVA B.
ADAMS
coloration .... DYEING, TINTING,
STAINING
coloratura .... OPERATIC
soprano .... DIVA, PRIMA
DONNA
colored .... HUED, TINCT, SHADED
chalk .... CRAYON, PASTEL
glass .... SMALTO
highly .... PRISMAL
many .... MULTI, PRISMATIC
paper .... STREAMERS
skin .... MELANO, MELANOID
view .... BIAS, PREJUDICE
colorfast .... INDELIBLE
colorful .... VIVID, BRIGHT,
TECHNICOLOR
bird .... TODY, PARROT,
MOTMOT, ORIOLE, PEACOCK,
QUETZAL, JACAMAR,
CARDINAL, BUNTING,
KINGFISHER, TROGON,
TANAGER, TOUCAN-BARBET,
STARLING
less .... PALER
life, describing a
.... CHECKERED
spectacle .... PAGEANT(RY),
EXTRAVAGANZA
coloring agent for plants
.... CHLOROPHYLL
for crayon .... PASTEL
matter ..... DYE, MORIN, PAINT,
STAIN, ENAMEL, RUDDLE,
PIGMENT
method, fabric .... TIEDYE
colorist .... DYER
colorless .... WAN, DULL, PALE,
ASHEN, PASTY, PALLID

colloquial .... BLAH
combining form .... LEUKO
person .... ALBINO, NONENTITY
colors, artist's .... PALETTE
having three .... TRICHOIC
science of .... CHROMATICS,
    CHROMATOLOGY,
    SPECTROMETRY
the .... FLAG
colossal .... HUGE, LARGE,
    ENORMOUS, GIGANTIC
beast .... WHALE, BEHEMOTH,
    LEVIATHAN
Colossi of Memnon, actually
    .... AMUNHOTEP
colossus .... GIANT, TITAN,
    STATUE, MONSTER
sculptor of the .... CHARES
colt .... FOAL, HORSE, YOUTH,
    BOLLARD, REVOLVER
revolver: sl. .... HOG-LEG,
    PEACEMAKER
coltish .... FRISKY
Colts or Rams .... ELEVEN
columbary .... DOVECOTE
Columbia eleven .... LIONS
River catch .... SALMON
River port .... ASTORIA
columbine .... FLOWER,
    AQUILEGIA
columbite .... DIANITE
columbium .... NIOBIUM
columbo .... GENTIAN
Columbus' birthplace .... GENOA
Day month .... OCTOBER
discovery ..... AMERICA, CUBA,
    COSTA RICA
navigator of .... PINZON
ship/caravel .... NINA, PINTA,
    SANTA MARIA
starting point .... PALOS
column .... SHAFT, PILLAR,
    PILASTER
base .... PLINTH
Buddhist .... LAT
capital of a .... CHAPTER
convex swelling .... ENTASIS
designating a .... DORIC, IONIC
figure, female .... CARYATID
figure, male .... TELAMON,
    ATLANTES
foundation .... SOCLE
in architecture .... CAPITAL
of troops, ships, etc.
    .... FORMATION
ornament .... GRIFFE
part of .... BASE, SHAFT,
    CAPITAL
shaft .... SCAPE
square .... ANTA, PIER
substitute for .... ATLAS,

    ATLANTES
support of .... BASE, PLINTH,
    PEDESTAL
top of .... CAPITAL
writer's .... NEWS, ARTICLE
columnist .... WRITER, NEWSMAN,
    REPORTER, NEWS ANALYST,
    CAEN, ALSOP, PEARSON,
    WESTON, LIPPMANN,
    WINCHELL
advantage sought by a
    .... SCOOP
identification of .... BY-LINE
news source of .... GRAPEVINE
specialty of .... RUMORS
columns, row of .... COLONNADE,
    PERISTYLE
colza .... COLE(SEED), RAPESEED
coma .... TORPOR, TRANCE,
    STUPOR, CATALEPSY
having a .... COMATOSE
comate, in botany .... HAIRY,
    TUFTED
comatose .... TORPID
comb .... SCRAPE, SEARCH
horse .... CURRY
like implement .... RIPPER
like structure .... CTEN
of fowl ...... CREST, CARUNCLE
the hair .... DRESS, TEASE
wool .... CARD, TEASE
combat ...... DUEL, FIGHT, STOUR,
    BATTLE, OPPOSE, FRACAS,
    STRIFE, WARFARE, CONFLICT,
    SKIRMISH
challenge to .... CARTEL
end of mortal .... DEATH
formal, between two persons
    .... DUEL
mortal .... AMORT
operation .... MISSION
place .... LISTS
to decide issue .... DERAIGN
troops .... NAVY, MARINE,
    ARMY, AIR FORCE, CAVALRY,
    PARATROOPERS, INFANTRY
with lances .... TILT, JOUST
combatant .... G.I., FIGHTER,
    SOLDIER, WARRIOR
combative .... WARLIKE,
    MILITANT, OFFENSIVE,
    AGGRESSIVE, FORCEFUL,
    PUGNACIOUS
comber .... WAVE
combination ...... ALLOY, BLEND,
    POOL, UNION, MERGER,
    MIXTURE, ALLIANCE,
    AMALGAM, COALITION,
    FUSION, ARRANGEMENT
slang .... COMBO
combine .... FUSE, JOIN, UNITE,

    ABSORB, MERGE, COMPOUND,
    CENTRALIZE, AMALGAMATE
kind of .... COALITION,
    SYNDICATE
resources .... POOL
combined .... ALLIED, UNITED
combining form for
alike .... ISO
among .... INTER
another .... HETERO
angle .... GONIO
asunder .... DICH(O)
aviation .... AER
bad .... CAC(O), MAL
below .... INFERO
between .... INTER
bile .... CHOL(O), CHOLE
blood .... HEMA, HEM(O),
    HEMATO, SANGUI
body fluid .... SERO
both .... AMBI
brass .... CHALCO
bright .... HELI(O)
bristles .... CHAET(O)
broad .... EURY, PLAT(Y)
cartilage .... CHONDRO
cavity .... C(O)ELE
cell .... CYTE
circular .... CYCL(O)
cold .... CRY(O)
color .... CHROMAT(O)
copper .... CUPRI
corpse .... NECR(O)
curl .... CIRRI
cutter .... TOME
death .... NECR(O)
depth .... BATHO
different .... HETER(O)
digit .... DACTYL(O)
double .... DIPL(O)
drawing .... GRAPHO
dreadful .... DINO
dry .... XER(O)
dung .... COPR(O)
earth .... GEO
end .... TEL(O)
English .... ANGLO
entire .... HOLO
equal .... ISO, EQUI, PARI
external .... ECT(O)
eye defect .... OPIA
far .... TELE
fatty .... LIP(O)
feather .... PTERO
feces .... COPR(O)
feet .... PED(E), PEDI
female .... GYN(O), GYNOUS
fermentation .... ZYMO
fever .... FEBRI
fine .... LEPT(O)
finger .... DACTYL(O)

firm .... STERE(O)
fish .... PISCI
flat .... PLAT(Y)
flesh .... SARC(O)
flow .... RHEO
freezing .... CRY(O)
French .... GALLO
fruit .... CARP(O)
fungus .... MYC(O)
gall .... CHOL(O), CHOLE
gaseous .... AERI
glass .... HYALO
God .... THEO
grain .... GRANI
gyrating .... GYRO
hair .... CHAET(O)
hand .... CHIRO, CHEIRO
hatred .... MIS(O)
height .... HYPSO
hidden .... CRYPT(O)
hide .... DERMAT(O)
horn .... CERAT(O), KERATO
horse .... HIPPO
hundred .... CENTI, HECT(O)
identical .... ISO
inner .... END(O)
insect(s) .... ENTOMO
inside .... INTRA, INTRO
intestine .... ENTER(O)
iron .... FERRO
latest .... NEO, CENE
liking .... PHIL(E)
lime .... CALCI
lip .... CHIL(O)
little .... MICR(O)
liver .... HEPAT(O)
male/man/masculine
.... ANDR(O)
many .... POLY
Mars .... AREO
middle .... MESO
milky .... GALACT(O)
minute .... MICR(O)
moon .... LUNI
moving .... KINETO
much .... POLY
nitrogen .... AZO
one and a half .... SESQUI
one tenth of .... DECI
other .... HETER(O)
outside .... ECT(O)
people .... ETHN(O)
personal .... IDIO
pointed .... STYL(O)
poor .... CAC(O)
prickly .... ECHIN(O)
race .... ETHN(O)
radiant .... HELI(O)
rainbow .... IRIDO
recent .... NEO
red .... ERYTHR(O)

rib(s) .... COST(O)
ribbon .... TENE
secondary .... DEUT(O),
                          DEUTER(O)
secret .... CRYPT(O)
self .... AUTO
seven .... HEPT(A), SEPTEM
shaft .... SCAPI
sham .... PSEUD(O)
sharp .... STYL(O)
short .... BRACHY
similar .... ISO
simple/single .... HAPL(O)
skin ...... DERM(O), DERMAT(O)
sleep .... HYPN(O)
slender .... LEPT(O)
small .... MICR(O)
solid .... STERE(O)
sound .... PHONE
spiny .... ECHIN(O)
spiral .... GYRO, HELIC(O)
stalk .... SCAPI
stationary .... STAT
stomach .... GASTR(O)
stone .... LITE, LITH, LYTE
sun .... HELI(O)
swelling .... CELE
tallow .... SEBI
teeth .... DENT(I), ODONT(O)
ten .... DEC(A)
terrible .... DINO
thin .... LEPT(O)
thousand .... KILO
tissue .... HIST(O)
transparent .... HYAL(O)
tree .... DENDR(I), DENDRO,
                           DENDRON
tumor .... CELE
twin/two .... DIPL(O)
universe .... COSM(O)
water .... HYDR(O)
wave .... CYMO
wax .... CERO, SEBI
weight .... BARO
whole .... HOLO
wing .... PTERO
within .... ESO, END(O), INTRA,
                               INTRO
woman ...... GYN(E)O, GYNOUS
wood .... HYL(O)
wool .... LANI
world .... COSM(O)
worship .... LATRY
writing .... GRAPHO
yellow(ish) .... LUTEO

combo .... TRIO
combustible .... FIERY,
     BURNABLE, EXCITABLE,
          (IN)FLAMMABLE
combustion .... FIRE, FLAME,
          SPARK, BURNING

come .... REACH, APPEAR, BEFALL,
          ARRIVE, RESULT
about .... OCCUR, HAPPEN
across ..... GIVE, MEET, PAY UP
afterwards .... ENSUE
around .... VISIT, YIELD,
                          REVIVE
back .... RECUR, RETURN,
          REJOIN, RESPONSE
before .... PRECEDE, PREDATE
between .... DIVIDE,
                        INTERVENE
by .... GAIN, ACQUIRE
down .... LAND, ALIGHT,
                     DISEMBARK
forth .... EMERGE, EMERSE,
                       APPROACH
forward .... RISE, ADVANCE,
          OFFER, VOLUNTEER
in first .... WIN
in second/third .... LOSE
into .... GET, ACQUIRE,
          INHERIT, RECEIVE
into view .... LOOM, PEEP,
          PEER, BEHOLD
on! .... HURRY(UP), ON THE
                         DOUBLE
ons .... BAITS, LURES, DECOYS
ons victim .... SUCKER
out .... ARISE, APPEAR, EMERGE
out number .... SEVEN, ELEVEN
out even .... TIE, DRAW, DEAD-
                           HEAT
through a crisis ..... TURN THE
                            TIDE
to grips with .... TANGLE,
                        EMBROIL
to mind .... OCCUR, RECALL
to pass .... OCCUR, HAPPEN,
     UNDERGO, TRANSPIRE
to rest .... DECIDE, SETTLE
to terms .... AGREE, CONCUR
together .... (FOR)GATHER,
                      ASSEMBLE
up .... SOAR, ARISE, CLIMB
up to .... EQUAL, MATCH
upon ...... HAP, MEET, CHANCE,
                    STUMBLE ON
comeback .... RETORT, RETURN,
     RIPOSTE, REVIVAL, REPARTEE,
                      REJOINDER
comedian .... CARD, ZANY,
     BUFFO, COMIC, JESTER,
          FUNSTER, PIERROT
circus .... CLOWN
deadpan .... KEATON
foil of .... STOOGE,
          STRAIGHTMAN
forte .... GAGS, JOKES, WIT,
     CRACKS, HORSEPLAY,
               TOMFOOLERY

missile of .... PIE

of note .... (BOB)HOPE, FERNANDEL, (BUSTER)KEATON, (JACK)BENNY, (JERRY)LEWIS, (BERT)LAHR, (RED)SKELTON, (OLIVER)HARDY, (STAN)LAUREL, (LOU)HOLTZ, (MYRON)COHEN, (LOU)COSTELLO

comedienne .... (FANNY)BRICE, (LUCILLE)BALL, (ZAZU)PITTS, (IMOGENE)COCA, (ROSEANNE)BARR

comedo .... BLACKHEAD

comedy .... FARCE, HUMOR, PARODY, SATIRE, BURLESQUE, AMUSEMENT, HORSEPLAY, SLAPSTICK

character .... ZANY, PIERROT

muse of .... THALIA

of errors .... FIASCO

Powell, Lombard ..... MY MAN GODFREY

symbol .... SOCK

comely .... FAIR, GAINLY, PRETTY, HANDSOME, PLEASING, LOVELY, ATTRACTIVE, DECOROUS, GOOD-LOOKING

woman .... BUXOM

comestible(s) .... FOOD, EDIBLE, EATABLE, VICTUAL

comet .... BIELA'S, HALLEY'S, SWIFT'S, ALCOCK'S, HOLMES'

envelope .... COMA

head's part .... NUCLEUS

nucleus and coma .... HEAD

part .... TAIL, TRAIN

comeuppance: sl. ...... REVENGE, TIT-FOR-TAT, PUNISHMENT

comfit .... CANDY, PRALINE, CONFECTION, SWEETMEAT

comfort .... EASE, CHEER, LUXURY, SOLACE, SOOTHE, CONSOLE, PLEASURE

station .... SHELTER

comfortable .... COSE, COZY, SNUG, HOMEY, SERENE, PLEASING

chair .... ROCKER

slang .... HUNKY-DORY

comforter ...... QUILT, COVERLET, BEDSPREAD, PACIFIER

comic .... DROLL, FUNNY, AMUSING, COMICAL, COMEDIAN, HILARIOUS, HUMOROUS, LAUGHABLE

afterpiece .... EXODE

element in play .... HOKUM

famous character .... POGO

kind of .... STAND-UP

opera .... BUFFA, BUFFO,

BOUFFE

relief .... SKIT, AFTERPIECE

strip .... CARTOONS

strip brat .... HANS, FRITZ, DENNIS THE MENACE

strip character ..... LULU, JEFF, MUTT, JIGGS, NANCY, SLUGGO, MILQUETOAST, (LIL)ABNER, (ETTA)KETT

strip vocals .... BALLOON(S)

theatrical sketch .... SKIT

with wooden sword .... HARLEQUIN

comical .... ZANY, DROLL, FUNNY, CLOWNISH, FARCICAL, HUMOROUS

very .... KILLING, SIDESPLITTING

coming .... ADVENT, APPROACH

early in the day .... RATH(E)

from outside .... ALIEN, FOREIGN, ENTHETIC, EXTRANEOUS

of tide .... FLUX

out party .... DEBUT

to an end .... MORIBUND

comity .... COURTESY, POLITENESS

comma .... MARK, PAUSE

shaped organism .... VIBRIO

command .... ORDER, COMPEL, BEHEST, BID(DING), DEMAND, ORDAIN, ENJOIN, DIRECT, ENJOIN, REQUIRE, INSTRUCT, DICTATE

authoritative .... MANDATE

level of .... ECHELON

market .... CORNER, MONOPOLIZE

official .... DECREE

station .... POST

to a cat .... SCAT

to a dog ...... SIT, STAY, FETCH

to helmsman .... STEADY

to horse ...... GEE, HAW, WHOA

to huskies .... MUSH

commandeer .... SEIZE, USURP

commander .... LEADER, CAPTAIN, SKIPPER

Egyptian .... SIRDAR

in-chief, U.S. .... PRESIDENT

of 1000 men: Rom. .... CHILIARCH

of the sea .... ADMIRAL

rod/staff of .... WARDER

commanding .... EXACTING, DEMANDING, DOMINATING, INSISTENT, IMPRESSIVE

commandment .... LAW, RULE, ORDER, PRECEPT

in Judaism .... MITZVAH

Commandments, the Ten .... DECALOG(UE)

commando .... RAIDER, SABOTEUR

assignment .... MISSION

specialty ..... RAID, SABOTAGE, DEMOLITION

comme ci, comme ca ...... SO-SO

comme il faut .... PROPER, FITTING

commemorate .... OBSERVE, CELEBRATE, RECOGNIZE, REMEMBER, REMINISCE

commemorative .... MEMORIAL

piece .... MEDAL

pillar .... STELE

commence .... OPEN, BEGIN, START, LEAD OFF, LAUNCH

commencement .... OPENING, START, INCEPTION, BEGINNING

address .... VALEDICTORY

dole .... DIPLOMA

exercise .... GRADUATION

commend .... CITE, LAUD, EXALT, EXTOL, PRAISE, ACCLAIM, APPROVE, ENTRUST

commensal .... ORGANISM, BACTERIUM, INQUILINE

commensurate .... EVEN, EQUAL, ACCORDANT, PARALLEL, EQUITABLE

comment .... TALK, REMARK, DESCANT, OPINION, ANNOTATION

adverse .... CRITICISM

at bottom of page .... FOOTNOTE

derisive .... JEER

favorable .... RAVE, KUDOS, PRAISE

marginal .... MARGENT

on disapprovingly .... ANIMADVERT

wordless .... SIGH

commentary .... MEMOIR, REMARK, CRITIQUE, CRITICISM, DISCOURSE, DISCUSSION, VERSION, OBSERVATION

commentator .... CRITIC, REVIEWER, ANNOTATOR

newspaper .... EDITOR, COLUMNIST

commerce .... TRADE, BARTER, TRAFFIC, BUSINESS

commercial .... TRADING, MERCANTILE

agent .... CONSUL

paper, worthless .... KITE

rubber stamp .... RUSH

spy .... KEEK

writer .... ADMAN

comminate .... BAN, CURSE
commingle .... BLEND, MERGE,
(INTER)MIX
comminute .... MILL, CRUSH,
GRIND, PULVERIZE
comminution, product of
.... DUST, TALC, POWDER
commiserate ...... PITY, CONDOLE,
TOUCH, SOFTEN, EMPATHIZE
commiseration ...... PITY, MERCY,
EMPATHY, COMPASSION
commissary ...... STORE, DEPUTY,
CANTEEN
colloquial .... PX
commission ...... ORDER, DEPUTE,
COUNCIL, ASSIGN, EMPOWER,
APPOINT, DELEGATE,
AUTHORITY, ENGAGE,
NOMINATE, AUTHORIZE
grafter's .... KICKBACK
slang .... RAKE-OFF
commissure .... SEAM, JOINT
commit .... DO, BIND, ENGAGE,
CONSIGN, ENTRUST, PERFORM
in mind .... MEMORIZE
perjury .... LIE, FORSWEAR,
BEAR FALSE WITNESS
to paper .... RECORD
commitment .... PLEDGE,
CONCERN, PROMISE,
INVOLVEMENT
commix .... BLEND
commode .... CHEST, BUREAU,
TOILET, WASHSTAND,
CHIFFONIER
commodious .... ROOMY,
SPACIOUS
commodity ...... GOODS, WARE(S),
STAPLE, ARTICLE, PRODUCT
control of .... OLIGOPOLY
common ...... LOW, JOINT, USUAL,
COARSE, MUTUAL, PUBLIC,
SHARED, AVERAGE, GENERAL,
ILLBRED, ORDINARY,
STANDARD
abbreviation .... ETC
arithmetic .... LOGISTIC
carrier .... BUS, COACH, TRAIN,
AIRLINE
cold .... RHEUM
connector .... AND
contraction .... I'VE, ISN'T,
WE'VE, AREN'T
footing .... PAR
fund .... POOL
interest faction .... SECT
laborer: sl. .... BOHUNK
market milieu .... EUROPE
people .... FOLKS, DEMOS,
PLEBE, PLEBS, MASSES,
POPULACE, HOI-POLLOI

people, of the .... GRASS
ROOTS
run .... RUCK
saying .... SAW, ADAGE,
PROVERB
sense .... SAVVY, GUMPTION
statistic .... AVERAGE MAN
sweetener .... PLEASE
talk .... RUMOR, GOSSIP,
HEARSAY
to both sexes .... EPICENE
Common Sense author
.... PAINE
commoner .... PLEB, CITIZEN,
YEOMAN, FREEMAN,
LOWBORN, SUBJECT,
PLEBEIAN, ROTURIER
commonly accepted .... VULGATE
supposed .... PUTATIVE
commonplace .... BANAL, PROSE,
PROSY, TRITE, USUAL,
HUMDRUM, PROSAIC, TEDIOUS,
STALE, EVERYDAY,
BOURGEOIS
expression .... CLICHE,
TRUISM, BROMIDE, PLATITUDE
commotion ...... ADO, ROW, FUSS,
MUSS, STIR, TO-DO, FLURRY,
HUBBUB, POTHER, SHINDY,
TUMULT, UPROAR, TURMOIL,
UNREST, FERMENT, DISORDER,
BROUHAHA, HURLYBURLY
commove .... EXCITE
communal ...... COMMON, PUBLIC
marriage .... HETAERISM
commune .... TALK, CONFER, MIR,
CONSULT, CONVERSE, ANS,
ATH, EDE, EPE, KIBBUTZ
communicable .... CONTAGIOUS
communicate .... TALK, SPEAK,
CONVEY, IMPART, TRANSMIT
with .... WRITE, CONVERSE,
CORRESPOND
communication ...... NOTE, NEWS,
LIAISON, MESSAGE, TIDINGS,
INFORMATION
form of .... CODE, ORAL,
TALK, LETTER, SIGNAL
means of .... SIGN, WIRE,
WORD, CABLE, MEDIA, RADIO,
TELEGRAPH, TELEPHONE,
CARRIER-PIGEON
communications initials .... RCA,
ITT
link between US & USSR
.... HOTLINE
satellite .... TELSTAR
signal set .... CODE
communicative .... OUTGOING,
TALKATIVE
communion .... TALK, UNITY,

CONCORD, SHARING
cloth .... CORPORAL
cup .... AMA
plate .... PATEN
table .... CREDENCE
Communion, Holy
.... EUCHARIST, SACRAMENT
communism, exponent of
.... MARX, LENIN, STALIN,
ENGELS
Communist .... RED, LEFTIST
curtain .... IRON, BAMBOO
Party member .... COMRADE
policy body .... POLITBURO
prominent .... CHOU
spy .... BURGESS, MACLEAN,
PHILBY
youth league .... COMSOMOL
community .... BODY, TOWN,
PUBLIC, SOCIETY, DISTRICT,
PARTNERSHIP
of creatures .... COLONY
of Greek monks/hermits
.... SKETE
of peasants: Russ. .... MIR
commutator .... RHEOTROPE
commute .... TRAVEL, EXCHANGE,
INTERCHANGE
commuter .... PASSENGER
Comoro island .... MAYOTTE
Islands capital .... MORONI
neighbor of .... ALDABRA
comose .... HAIRY
compact .... CASE, MINI, NEAT,
BRIEF, DENSE, TERSE, THICK,
SOLID, CONCISE, SERRIED,
CONDENSE, AGREEMENT
among individuals/parties,
etc. .... CONTRACT,
COVENANT
between nations .... TREATY
cosmetics .... VANITY
mass .... WAD
companion .... PAL, CHUM, FERE,
ALLY, MATE, ESCORT, FRIEND,
CRONY, COMPANY, PARTNER,
ASSOCIATE
animal .... PET
at meals .... COMMENSAL
close .... BUDDY, COMRADE,
INTIMATE, BOSOM FRIEND
colloquial .... SIDEKICK
constant .... SHADOW, ALTER
EGO
of alpha .... OMEGA
back .... FORTH
beck .... CALL
bed .... BOARD
beginning .... END
betwixt .... BETWEEN
bill .... COO

black .... BLUE, WHITE
bolts .... NUTS
bread .... BUTTER
breaking .... ENTERING
cake .... ALE
cash .... CARRY
cease .... DESIST
cloak .... DAGGER
come .... GO
deaf .... DUMB
draw .... QUARTER
easy-come .... EASY-GO
ebb .... FLOW
far .... AWAY, WIDE
fair .... SQUARE
fast .... LOOSE
fire .... BRIMSTONE
fits .... STARTS
flotsam .... JETSAM
foot-loose .... FANCY-FREE
free .... EASY, CLEAR
get-up .... GO
give .... TAKE
heart .... SOUL
hook .... CROOK, LADDER,
　　　　　　LINE-AND-SINKER
hue .... CRY
huff .... PUFF
kiss .... MAKE UP
kit .... CABOODLE
kith .... KIN
life .... DEATH
live .... LET LIVE
loud .... CLEAR
man .... WIFE
might .... MAIN
mortise .... TENON
night .... DAY
nip .... TUCK
null .... VOID
on .... OFF
open .... SHUT(CASE),
　　　　　　　ABOVEBOARD
oro .... PLATA
over .... ABOVE
pick .... CHOOSE
pins .... NEEDLES
red .... WHITE AND BLUE
rock .... ROLL
snick .... SNEE
song .... DANCE
spick .... SPAN
Stars .... STRIPES
stocks .... BONDS
straight .... NARROW
stuff .... NONSENSE
thunder .... LIGHTNING
to .... FRO
Tom .... DICK AND HARRY
toss .... TURN
trial .... ERROR

tried .... TRUE
up .... DOWN, COMING
wear .... TEAR
wheel .... AXLE
wine .... DINE
wrack .... RUIN
companionable .... GENIAL,
　　AMIABLE, FRIENDLY,
　　　　COMPATIBLE
companionship .... SHARING,
　　SOCIETY, SODALITY,
　　　　FELLOWSHIP
companionway .... WALK,
　　　　　　STAIR(S)
company .... BAND, FIRM, GROUP,
　　TROOP, SOCIETY
amusing .... CAST
colloquial .... GUEST(S),
　　　　VISITOR(S)
commander .... CAPTAIN
of hunters .... SAFARI
of players .... TEAM, TROUPE
of soldiers .... TROOPS
of soldiers mounted on
　　horses .... CAVALRY
of ten soldiers .... DECURION
of travelers .... CARAVAN,
　　　　CARAVANSARY
part .... SEPARATE
comparable .... ALIKE, CLOSE,
　　PARALLEL, SIMILAR
comparative .... RELATIVE
compare .... TEST, LIKEN, RELATE,
　　CONFRONT, CONTRAST
beyond .... PEERLESS,
　　MATCHLESS, NONPAREIL
critically .... COLLATE
compared .... MATCHED
to .... THAN, AGAINST
comparison .... ANALOGY, SIMILE,
　　　　LIKENESS
example .... AVERAGE,
　　　　STANDARD
compartment ...... BOOTH, STALL,
　　　　LOCKER
desk, for filing papers
　　........................... PIGEONHOLE
grain/hay .... BAY
in aircraft .... CAPSULE
of car, describing .... GLOVE
small/sleeping .... CUBICLE
compass .... GAIN, BOUND,
　　GAMUT, RANGE, REACH,
　　SCOPE, DEFINE, EXTENT,
　　ENCIRCLE, SURROUND
beam .... TRAMMEL
cardinal point .... EAST, WEST,
　　NORTH, SOUTH
case/housing .... BINNACLE
dial .... CARD
face .... DIAL

kind of .... DRAWING,
　　GYROSIN, MAGNETIC,
　　MARINER'S, SURVEYOR'S
part .... AIRT, GIMBAL,
　　NEEDLE, HOUSING, TRAMMEL
plant .... ROSINWEED
point .... N, E, W, S, NE, NW,
　　SE, SW, ENE, ESE, NNE, NNW,
　　SSE, SSW, WNW, WSE, AIRT,
　　R(H)UMB, QUARTER
sight .... VANE
zero of .... NORTH
compassion .... PITY, RUTH,
　　GRACE, HEART, MERCY,
　　EMPATHY, TENDERNESS
compatible .... ATTUNED,
　　SUITABLE, CONGENIAL,
　　　　CONGRUOUS
compatriot .... COUNTRYMAN
compeer .... PEER, EQUAL,
　　MATCH, COMRADE
compel ...... MAKE, DRIVE, FORCE,
　　PRESS, COERCE, OBLIGE,
　　IMPOSE ON, REQUIRE,
　　　　CONSTRAIN
compelled: Arch. .... FAIN
compelling .... COGENT,
　　　　INTIMIDATING
influence .... DURESS,
　　　　PRESSURE
compend .... BREVIARY
compendium ...... DIGEST, PRECIS,
　　SUMMARY, ABSTRACT,
　　SYLLABUS, SYNOPSIS
compensation .... FEE, PAY,
　　REWARD, REDRESS,
　　　　EQUIVALENT
for loss .... DAMAGES,
　　　　INDEMNITY
for services .... WAGE,
　　SALARY, STIPEND
compete .... VIE, RIVAL, CONTEND
competence .... SKILL, ABILITY,
　　CAPACITY, PROFICIENCY
competent .... APT, FIT, ABLE,
　　CAPABLE, SKILLED, EFFICIENT
mentally .... SANE
competition .... MATCH, STRIFE,
　　CONTEST, RIVALRY, TOURNEY,
　　　　OPPOSITION
competitive .... RIVAL, VYING,
　　OPPOSING, CUTTHROAT
competitor .... ENTRY, RIVAL,
　　ENTRANT, COMPETER,
　　CORRIVAL, CONTENDER,
　　　　CONTESTANT
Compiegne river .... OISE
compilation .... SELECTION,
　　　　COLLECTION
of anecdotes .... MEMOIRS

of alphabetized words and
definitions
.... DICTIONARY
of stories, poems
.... ANTHOLOGY
compile .... EDIT, AMASS, GATHER,
SELECT, ARRANGE, COLLECT
compiler .... CERF, RILEY,
AUTHOR, GLOSSARIST,
ANTHOLOGIST,
ENCYCLOPEDIST
Arthurian tales .... MALORY
English words .... ROGET
population data .... CENSUS
TAKER
quotations .... BARTLETT
complacent .... SMUG, BLASE,
COCKY, CONTENT, PLEASED
complain ...... BEEF, CARP, CRAB,
FRET, FUSS, KICK, MOAN,
GRIPE, GROAN, WHINE,
ACCUSE, BEWAIL, GROUSE,
MURMUR, YAMMER,
GRUMBLE, PROTEST,
BELLYACHE
complainant .... ACCUSER,
CLAIMANT, LITIGANT,
PLAINTIFF
complainer, habitual ...... BITCH,
GROUCH, GROUSER
complaining .... PEEVISH,
QUERULOUS
cry .... WHINE
complaint .... KICK, PEEVE,
WHINE, CLAMOR, GROUSE,
CHARGE, AILMENT, ILLNESS,
PROTEST, SQUAWK,
GRIEVANCE
muttered .... MURMUR
part of .... GRAVAMEN
slang .... BITCHING,
BELLYACHING
complaisant ...... KINDLY, POLITE,
FLEXIBLE, OBLIGING,
AGREEABLE
complement ...... EXTRA, OFFSET,
FULFILL, NEUTRALIZE
complementary
.... SUPPLEMENTAL
complete .... END, FULL, RANK,
SOLID, UTTER, WHOLE,
CLINCH, CAP, ENTIRE, FINISH,
INTACT, TOTAL, ACHIEVE,
CONCLUDE, OUTRIGHT,
THOROUGH
attendance .... PLENARY
collection .... SET
consumption ...... EXHAUSTION
defeat .... ROUT
disorder .... CHAOS
entity .... INTEGER

growth .... MATURITY
in all respects .... PERFECT
not .... PARTIAL
set of games .... SERIES
completed .... DONE, OVER,
ENDED, FINISHED
completely .... FULLY, WHOLLY,
DOWNRIGHT, BAG AND
BAGGAGE
developed .... FULL-FLEDGED
from ____ .... A TO Z
occupied .... BUSY, RAPT,
ENGROSSED
united .... SOLIDARITY
completion .... END, FILL, CLOSE,
FINAL, FINISH, OUTCOME,
FRUITION, CONCLUSION
complex ...... KNOTTY, MIXED UP,
TANGLE, NETWORK,
INVOLVED, INTRICATE,
COMPLICATED
get .... THICKEN
kind of .... OEDIPUS,
INFERIORITY
complexion .... HUE, TINT, COLOR,
ASPECT, SKIN TEXTURE
complexity .... INTRICACY
compliant .... WEAK, DOCILE,
PASSIVE, PATIENT, OBEDIENT,
DUTIFUL, YIELDING,
TRACTABLE
complicate .... CONFUSE,
PERPLEX, INVOLVE,
COMPOUND
complicated .... KNOTTY,
COMPLEX, INVOLVED
complication .... MESS, SNAG,
NODUS, SNARL, TANGLE
compliment .... LAUD, TOAST,
PRAISE, COMMEND,
CONGRATULATE
exaggerated .... FLATTERY
kind of .... LEFT-HANDED
complimentary .... FREE, GRATIS
complot .... CONSPIRE,
CONSPIRACY
comply .... OBEY, ACCEDE,
SUBMIT, CONFORM
compo .... MORTAR, PLASTER
component .... PART, UNIT,
FACTOR, MEMBER, ELEMENT,
FEATURE
of atom .... PROTON
comport .... ACT, FIT, SUIT,
BEHAVE
comportment .... CONDUCT,
BEHAVIOR
compos mentis .... SANE
non .... MAD, CRAZY, INSANE
compose .... FRAME, WRITE,
ADJUST, CREATE, INDITE,

CONSTITUTE
differences .... RECONCILE
in printing .... TYPE
composed .... CALM, COOL, STAID,
WROTE, UNRUFFLED,
COLLECTED
composer .... INDITER, ARTIST,
HARMONIST, TUNESMITH,
BACH, BIZET, SONGWRITER,
FOOTE, HAYDN, RAVEL,
ROREM, STYNE, WEBER,
CHOPIN, MOZART, WAGNER,
DEBUSSY, PUCCINI,
BEETHOVEN, STRAVINSKY
arranger Peter .... MATZ
great .... MAESTRO
in printing shop
........., LINOTYPIST, TYPESETTER
of Aida .... VERDI
of Carmen .... BIZET
of La Boheme .... PUCCINI
of La Valse .... RAVEL
of marches .... SOUSA
of Messiah .... HANDEL
of Narcissus .... NEVIN
of poems ...... DARD, RHYMER,
VERSIFIER
of Thais .... MASSENET
of The Rosary .... NEVIN
opera .... BIZET, LEHAR, VERDI,
WAGNER, MENOTTI, DONIZETTI
composers' group .... ASCAP
composite .... MIXTURE,
COMPOUND, INTEGRAL
composition .... OPUS, ESSAY,
SETUP, THEME, CONTENTS
artistic .... PIECE
for nine instruments
.... NONET
for organ .... TOCCATA
for piano .... ETUDE, BALLADE,
TOCCATA
for practice .... ETUDE
for seven .... SEPTET(TE)
for three .... TRIO
for two .... DUET
hodgepodge musical
.... CENTO, MEDLEY
musical .... OPUS, ETUDE,
MOTET, RONDO, SUITE,
SONATA, CONCERTO,
FANTASIA, RONDEAU,
NOCTURNE, ORATORIO,
SERENADE
operatic .... SCENA
polyphonic .... FUGUE
sacred .... HYMN, MOTET,
PSALM, CANTICLE
compositor .... LINOTYPIST,
TYPESETTER
guide of .... JIGGER

compost heap part .... HUMUS

composure .... AIR, POISE, APLOMB, CALMNESS, SERENITY, CONTROL, SANG-FROID

compound .... MIX, YARD, ALLOY, MAKE UP, COMBINE, CONCOCT

carbon .... CARBIDE

of silica .... GLASS

raceme .... PANICLE

word .... CONJUGATE

words' separation of parts
.... TMESIS

comprador .... BUYER

comprehend .... SEE, KNOW, GRASP, CONCEIVE, INCLUDE, REALIZE, EMBRACE, UNDERSTAND

comprehensible .... EXOTERIC, INTELLIGIBLE

comprehension ...... GRIP, GRASP, COMMAND, MASTERY

thru intellect .... NOESIS

comprehensive .... ALL-EMBRACING

comprehensiveness .... WIDTH

compress .... PAD, WRING, DOSSIL, CROWD, REDUCE, ABRIDGE, SQUEEZE, CONTRACT

comprise ...... EMBODY, CONTAIN, INCLUDE

compromise .... TRIM, ADJUST, BARGAIN, ENDANGER, NEGOTIATE, MEDIATE, GIVE AND TAKE

compulsion .... DRAFT, FORCE, DURESS, COACTION, COERCION, PRESSURE, CONSTRAINT

compulsive .... FORCIBLE, IRRESISTIBLE

craze, obsession, etc.
.... MANIA

person, kind of ...... GAMBLER

petty thievery
.... KLEPTOMANIA

compulsory .... COERCIVE, STRINGENT, MANDATORY, COMPELLING, OBLIGATORY

military service .... LEVY, DRAFT, CONSCRIPTION

compunction .... QUALM, REMORSE, SCRUPLE, PENITENCE

compurgation .... CLEARANCE

computation .... CALCULATION

compute .... FIGURE, RECKON, CALCULATE

computer .... ADDER, MACHINE, PROCESSOR, CALCULATOR

communication device
.... MODEM

fictional .... HAL

floppy disk .... DISKETTE

fodder .... DATA, INPUT

language .... ALGOL, BASIC, COBOL, PILOT, PASCAL, SNOBOL, FORTRAN

movable pointer .... CURSOR

need .... DISK

physical part .... HARDWARE

program that instructs
.... SOFTWARE

storage device .... DRUM

system peripheral
.... TERMINAL

terminology:

billionth of a second
.... NANOSECOND

eliminate error .... DEBUG

erratic signal .... BLIP

erratic speed variation
.... FLUTTER

error .... BUG

first in, first out .... FIFO

garbage in, garbage out
.... GIGO

group of bits .... BYTE

information .... DATA, INPUT, OUTPUT, RECORD

information store
.... MEMORY

interrupt .... BREAK

list of program options
.... MENU

look for data .... SEARCH

malfunction .... CRASH

not in operation .... DOWN

one million bytes
.... MEGABYTE

output on paper .... HARD COPY

output on screen
.... DISPLAY

pattern of dots printer
.... MATRIX

run a program ...... EXECUTE

set of instructions
.... PROGRAM

systems linkage
.... INTERFACE

unwanted data ..... GARBAGE

type of .... IBM, ANALOG, DIGITAL

worker .... OPERATOR, PROGRAMMER

computerize .... AUTOMATE

computing device .... ABACUS, COMPTOMETER, SLIDE RULE

comrade ...... PAL, MATE, BUDDY, FRIEND, FRATER, PARTNER,

KAMERAD, COMPANION, TOVARISCH

comte .... COUNT

con ...... ANTI, BILK, READ, STEER, STUDY, PERUSE, AGAINST

amore .... TENDERLY, WITH LOVE

man .... SHILL, GRIFTER, STEEPER, SWINDLER

over .... SCAN

slang .... SWINDLE, HOODWINK, CONFIDENCE

vessel .... STEER

con's confines .... SLAMMER

concatenate .... LINK(ED)

concave .... ARCHED, HOLLOW

molding ..... SCOTIA, CAVETTO

conceal .... HIDE, MASK, STOW, VEIL, CLOAK, COVER, SECRETE

goods .... CACHE, HOARD, ELOI(G)N

in a way .... PALM

in law .... ELOIN

concealed .... COVERT, HIDDEN, PERDUE, CLANDESTINE

sharpshooter .... SNIPER

concealment .... DISGUISE, INCOGNITO, CAMOUFLAGE

attack from .... SNIPE, AMBUSH, AMBUSCADE

concede .... ADMIT, ALLOW, GRANT, YIELD

conceit ...... SIDE, PRIDE, NOTION, VANITY, EGO(ISM), TYMPANY, SELF-ESTEEM

colloquial .... BIGHEAD, SWELLHEAD

conceited .... COCKY, PROUD, BOASTFUL, EGO(T)ISTIC, VAIN(GLORIOUS)

colloquial .... STUCK-UP

person .... PEACOCK, EGO(T)IST

conceive .... THINK, DEVISE, CREATE, IDEATE, IMAGINE, VISUALIZE, IMPREGNATE

concenter ...... FOCUS, CONVERGE

concentrate .... AIM, FOCUS, CENTER, COLLECT, LOCALIZE

concentrated .... DENSE, CENTRAL

concentration .... ALERTNESS, DILIGENCE, ATTENTION

camp, German .... DACHAU, STALAG

concept .... IDEA, NOTION, THOUGHT

combining form .... IDEO

conceptual .... IDEAL

conception .... HENT, IDEA, IDEATION, PREGNANCY

product of .... EMBRYO,

BRAINCHILD
concern .... CARE, AFFAIR,
AFFECT, REGARD, RELATE,
WORRY, ANXIETY, DISTURB,
INTEREST, TROUBLE, LOOKOUT
of ecologist ..... ENVIRONMENT
concerned .... UNEASY, ANXIOUS,
WORRIED, UNCERTAIN
concerning .... INRE, ABOUT,
ANENT, REGARDING
concert .... ACCORD, CONCORD,
HARMONY
ceremony .... PROGRAM
hall .... ODEUM, AUDITORIUM
in .... TOGETHER
master's instrument .... VIOLIN
musical/dance performance
.... RECITAL
organizer .... IMPRESARIO
outdoor platform
.... BANDSHELL
concerted .... JOINT, COMMON,
MUTUAL, UNITED, COMBINED
concertina kin .... ACCORDION
concession .... GRANT, RIGHT,
STAND, FRANCHISE, PRIVILEGE
kind of .... SOP
conch .... SHELL
concha .... APSE
Conchobar's intended
.... DEIRDRE
concierge .... JANITOR, PORTER,
CARETAKER, DOORKEEPER
conciliar .... ADVISORY
conciliate .... CALM, ALLAY,
PACIFY, SOOTHE, APPEASE,
MOLLIFY, PLACATE,
SMOOTH(DOWN)
conciliatory .... KIND, PEACEABLE,
BENEVOLENT
offering .... SOP
theology .... IRENICS
concise ...... BRIEF, PITHY, SHORT,
TERSE, LACONIC, SUCCINCT
summary of facts .... PRECIS
conclamation .... SHOUT
conclave .... SYNOD, MEETING
conclude ...... END, CLOSE, INFER,
DEDUCE, FINISH, SETTLE,
RESOLVE, TERMINATE
a speech .... PERORATE
concluding passage in music
.... CODA, FINALE, STRETTA,
STRETTO
conclusion .... END(ING), FINIS(H),
RESULT, OUTCOME,
JUDGMENT, DECISION,
TERMINATION
in .... LASTLY
judge's .... FINDING
conclusive .... FINAL, DECISIVE

blow: sl. .... HAYMAKER,
SOCKDOLAGER, SOCKDOLOGER
point .... CLINCHER
concoct .... MIX, BREW, PLAN,
HATCH, DEVISE, COOK-UP,
COMPOUND, DREAM-UP,
TRUMP-UP
concoction, liquid .... TEA,
COFFEE, COCKTAIL
concomitant .... ANNEX,
ADDITIVE, ATTENDANT
concord .... ACCORD, UNITY,
UNISON, TREATY, ONENESS,
RAPPORT, HARMONY,
ALLIANCE
in music .... EUPHONY,
HOMOPHONY
Concord .... GRAPE
concordance .... AGREEMENT
concordant .... AGREEABLE,
ATTUNED, HARMONIOUS
concordat .... COMPACT, ENTENTE,
COVENANT, AGREEMENT
Concorde, for short .... SST
concourse .... CROWD, ARCADE,
PASSAGE, SQUARE, THRONG
concrete .... REAL, ACTUAL,
SOLID, BETON, EXACT,
SPECIFIC, DEFINITE, TANGIBLE
being .... ENS
concubinage .... HETAERISM,
HETAIRISM
concubine .... HETAERA,
MISTRESS, PARAMOUR
in harem .... ODALISK,
ODALISQUE
concupiscence .... LUST
concur .... AGREE, ACCEDE,
ASSENT, CONSENT, COINCIDE
colloquial .... JIBE
concurrence .... ACCORD, UNISON,
HARMONY, AGREEMENT
concussion .... BLOW, SHOCK,
IMPACT, SHAKING
condemn .... DAMN, DOOM,
DECRY, BLAME, CENSURE,
CONVICT, DENOUNCE
condemnation .... DECRIAL,
DOOM, DAMNATION,
CONVICTION
condemned .... DAMNED
heretic's garment
.... SANBENITO
condense .... CUT, SHORTEN,
THICKEN, ABRIDGE,
COMPRESS, COMPACT,
CONTRACT, INSPISSATE
condensed form .... CAPSULE
moisture .... DEW
condenser .... CAPACITOR
condescend .... DEIGN, STOOP

condescending ...... PATRONIZING,
HAUGHTY, HOITY-TOITY
condign .... FITTING, DESERVED,
SUITABLE
condiment .... MACE, SAUCE,
SPICE, PEPPER, RELISH,
MUSTARD, PAPRICA, PAPRIKA,
VINEGAR, SEASONING,
HORSERADISH
bottle/container .... CRUET,
CASTER
condition .... IF, FIG, CASE, RANK,
CLASS, STATE, FETTLE,
STATUS, POSTURE, STATION,
ACCUSTOM, POSITION,
STANDING, PROVISION
accompanying
.... CIRCUMSTANCE
contract .... TERM, PROVISO,
STIPULATION
of body .... HEALTH, FITNESS
of cycle/development
.... PHASE, STAGE
of decline .... DECADENCE
of great danger/trouble
.... CRISIS
of great vitality .... STHENIA
of hardship/difficulty
.... PINCH
of oblivion .... LIMBO
of payment .... TERMS
of servitude .... BONDAGE,
SLAVERY
of stupor ..... COMA, NARCOSIS
sudden, unexpected
.... EMERGENCY
conditional .... PENDING
bond .... ESCROW
freedom .... BAIL
release .... PAROLE
surrender .... CAPITULATION
conditioned .... LIMITED,
CONTINGENT
for subsequent purchase
.... PRESOLD
conditioning .... TRAINING, TUNE-
UP, ADJUSTMENT
conditions of possession
.... TENURE
condole .... LAMENT, COMFORT,
CONSOLE, COMMISERATE
condolence .... PITY, SYMPATHY
condominium .... (CO-OP)
APARTMENT
condone .... PARDON, FORGIVE,
EXCUSE, ABSOLVE, OVERLOOK
condor .... VULTURE
conduce .... LEAD, TEND,
CONTRIBUTE
conduct .... MIEN, WAGE,
BEARING, BEHAVE, DEMEAN,

HANDLE, MANAGE, BEHAVIOR, DEMEANOR, EXECUTE, TRANSACT

improperly .... MISMANAGE

in polite society .... ETIQUETTE

under guard .... CONVOY, ESCORT

conductor .... LEADER, MAESTRO, MANAGER, DIRECTOR, OPERATOR, CONVEYOR, TRANSMITTER

colloquial .... TIME BEATER

orchestra ..... BOULEZ, MEHTA, BEECHAM, ORMANDY, BERNSTEIN, TOSCANINI, BARBIROLLI

platform of .... PODIUM

stick .... BATON

tourists' ..... GUIDE, CICERONE, DRAGOMAN

woman .... QUACH

conduit .... MAIN, PIPE, CHANNEL, DRAIN, SEWER

cone .... SPIRE, BOBBIN, FUNNEL

bearing tree .... FIR, YEW, PINE, CEDAR, LARCH, ZAMIA, SPRUCE, CONIFER, CYPRESS, JUNIPER, PINASTER

seed-bearing .... STROBIL(E)

shaped ..... CONIC(AL), PINEAL, CONOID(AL), PYRAMIDAL, TURBINATE, CONIFEROUS

shaped paper container .... CORNUCOPIA

shaped pile .... COCK

shaped yarn roll .... COP

spiral .... HELIX

conepate .... SKUNK

coney .... DAMAN, HYRAX, RABBIT, RODENT

confab .... CHAT, TALK, POWWOW

confection .... SWEET, BONBON, COMFIT, CONFITURE, SWEETMEAT

almond .... NOUGAT, MARZIPAN, MARCHPANE

cold .... ICE CREAM

flavor .... VANILLA

nutty .... PRALINE

sugar .... CANDY

Turkish .... HALVAH

confederacy .... SOUTH, ALLIANCE

foe .... UNION

confederate .... ALLY, REB(EL), ACCOMPLICE

Confederate general .... LEE, BRAGG, EWELL, HAMPTON, LONGSTREET

president .... DAVIS

soldier, Civil War .... REB

confederation .... BUND

confer ...... GIVE, GRANT, AWARD, ENDOW, BESTOW, DISCUSS, CONVERSE

privately .... COLLOGUE

conference .... CONFAB, JUNTA, PARLEY, MEETING, PALAVER

church .... COUNCIL

Indian .... POWWOW

Midwest .... BIG TEN

private .... CAUCUS, HUDDLE, TETE-A-TETE

site of 1943 .... CAIRO, TEHERAN

site of 1945 .... YALTA

sitting of a .... SESSION

conferred, thing .... FAVOR, HONOR, RIGHT, TITLE, DEGREE

conferring respect .... HONORIFIC

confess .... OWN, AVOW, BARE, ADMIT, REVEAL

slang .... SING, PEACH, SQUEAL

confession .... AVOWAL, ADMISSION, REVELATION

of faith .... CREDO, CREED

Confessions author .... ROUSSEAU

confetti ...... CANDIES, PAPER BITS

confidant(e) .... FRIEND, INTIMATE

confide .... TELL, TRUST, DIVULGE, ENTRUST, BARE ONE'S MIND

confidence .... FAITH, TRUST, BELIEF, SECRET, PRIVACY, BOLDNESS, ASSURANCE

game .... BUNCO, BUNKO, SHELL GAME, SWINDLE, THIMBLERIG

game item .... CUP, SEED, NUTSHELL

man ...... CON, SHILL, GRIFTER, STEEPER, SWINDLER

show of .... BRAVADO

confident .... BOLD, SURE, SECURE, ASSURED, CERTAIN, POSITIVE

confidential .... SECRET, PRIVATE, ESOTERIC, INTIMATE

advisers' group .... CABAL, CAMARILLA

between you and me .... OFF THE RECORD

disclosure/warning .... TIP-OFF

confiding .... OPEN, NAIVE, TRUSTFUL, TRUSTING

configuration .... FORM, SHAPE, CONTOUR, OUTLINE, GROUPING

confine .... BOX, HEM, PEN, TIE, CAGE, JAIL, LIMIT, DETAIN, FETTER, IMMURE, ASTRICT, IMPRISON, RESTRICT

to a place .... LOCALIZE

confined .... BOUND, ENCLOSED, PENT-UP, SHUT-IN

in circulation .... CLOSE

confinement .... CUSTODY, CAPTIVITY, DETENTION, ENCLOSURE, RESTRAINT

cause of .... ILLNESS, CHILDBIRTH, CONVICTION

place of .... JAIL, ASYLUM, PRISON, HOSPITAL

confirm .... PROVE, ATTEST, RATIFY, VERIFY, VALIDATE, CORROBORATE, SUBSTANTIATE

confirmation .... RITE, EVIDENCE, SACRAMENT, VERIFICATION

confirmed .... TRIED, ARRANT, TESTED, VESTED, CHRONIC, HABITUAL, INVETERATE

confiscate .... TAKE, SEIZE, GRAB, ANNEX, SNATCH, USURP, ESCHEAT, COMMANDEER, APPROPRIATE

confiture .... CANDY, PRESERVE, SWEETMEAT

conflagration .... FIRE, BLAZE, COMBUSTION

conflict .... JAR, CLASH, FIGHT, STOUR, BATTLE, COMBAT, STRIFE, CONTEST, DISCORD, HOSTILITY, STRUGGLE

armed .... WAR

of characters in drama .... AGON

of interest .... BREACH, TUSSLE, CONTROVERSY

conflicting .... HOSTILE, CONTRARY, OPPOSING

confluence .... CROWD, GATHERING, CLUSTERING

conform .... ADAPT, AGREE, SHAPE UP, EXEMPLIFY

conforming to morals .... ETHICAL

conformist .... STICKLER, ASSENTER

kind of .... YESMAN

non .... HERETIC

conformity .... HABIT, CUSTOM, AGREEMENT, FORMALITY, BY THE BOOK, COMPLIANCE

confound .... ROUT, DISMAY, STUMP, PUZZLE, CONFUSE, PERPLEX, BEWILDER

confraternity ...... BROTHERHOOD

confrere .... ASSOCIATE, COLLEAGUE

confront ...... FACE, MEET, BRAVE, STAND, OPPOSE, RESIST

confuse .... ABASH, RAVEL, FLUMMOX, PUZZLE, MYSTIFY,

PERPLEX, BEWILDER,
CONFOUND, DISCONCERT,
FLABBERGAST
confused .... ASEA, LOST, MUZZY,
ADDLED, HAYWIRE
hopelessly .... OBFUSCATED
turkey .... FLUSTERED BUSTARD
confusion .... ADO, MESS, MOIL,
RIOT, MELEE, BEDLAM,
JUMBLE, CHAOS, FRACAS,
MIX-UP, MUDDLE, HAVOC,
RUCKUS, TANGLE, WELTER,
DISARRAY, DISORDER
of tongues .... BABEL
sudden .... FLURRY
confutation .... REBUTTAL
confute .... REBUT, DEFEAT,
REFUTE, DISPROVE
conge .... FAREWELL, DISMISSAL
congeal .... GEL, SET, JELL,
CURDLE, FREEZE, HARDEN,
STIFFEN, THICKEN, SOLIDIFY
congealed water (vapor) .... ICE,
SNOW
congealer, wound ...... COMFREY
congenial .... BOON, KINDRED,
FRIENDLY, PLEASING,
AGREEABLE, COMPATIBLE
congenital .... INBORN, INNATE,
CONNATE
mark .... MOLE
conger .... EEL
trap .... EELPOT
congeries .... HEAP, PILE,
COLLECTION
congest .... JAM, CLOG, PLUG,
CHOKE, BLOCK, OVERFILL,
OVERCROWD
congestion .... STOPPAGE
conglomerate .... AMASS
conglomeration .... LUMP,
MIXTURE, COHESION,
HODGEPODGE, MELTING POT
Congo ...... DYE, EEL, TEA, RIVER
capital .... BRAZZAVILLE,
KINSHASA
city/town .... EWO, OYO,
BOKO, ABALA, KELLE, NKAYI,
SEMBE, DONGOU, ZANAGA,
GAMBOMA, LOUBOMO,
KINKALA, POINTE-NOIRE
dwarf .... AKKA, ACHUAS
ethnic group .... BANTU,
BALALI, BATEKE, BAVILI,
HAMITE
language ..... BANTU, LINGALA,
SWAHILI
mountains .... CRYSTAL
peanut .... NGUBA
premier .... ADOULA,
LUMUMBA, TSHOMBE

president .... MOBUTU,
YOULOU, KASAVUBU
province .... KIVA, KWILU,
KATANGA
red .... SALT
river .... DJA, ALIMA, IVINDO,
CONGO, KADEI, OGOOUE,
NIARI, SANGHA
river tributary .... UBANGI
tribesman .... SIMBA
congou .... TEA
congratulate .... HAIL, SALUTE,
COMMEND, COMPLIMENT,
FELICITATE
congratulatory ...... GRATULANT,
COMPLIMENTARY
congregate .... GATHER, COLLECT,
ASSEMBLE
congregation .... FOLD, FLOCK,
CHURCH, PARISH, BRETHREN,
ASSEMBLY, ASSEMBLAGE
congress .... MEETING, ASSEMBLY,
CONVENTION, LEGISLATURE
Congress attendant .... PAGE
concern of ..... BILLS, BUDGET,
RESOLUTIONS
time off .... RECESS
congressman not reelected
.... LAMEDUCK
congruence .... AGREEMENT
congruity ...... FITNESS, HARMONY
congruous .... FIT(TING),
SUITABLE
conic section .... CURVE, ELLIPSE,
PARABOLA
conical .... FUNNEL-LIKE, FUNNEL-
SHAPED
roll of yarn .... COP
shelter .... TIPI, TEPEE
conifer .... FIR, YEW, PINE,
CEDAR, LARCH, SPRUCE
coniferous forest .... TAIGA
tree .... FIR, PINE, LARCH
conium .... HEMLOCK
conjecture ...... THEORY, IMAGINE,
ASSUMPTION, GUESS(WORK),
SURMISE
conjoin .... UNITE, CONNECT
conjoint .... UNITED
conjointly .... TOGETHER
conjugal .... MARITAL,
CONNUBIAL, MATRIMONIAL
conjugate .... MATED, UNITE,
COUPLE, RELATED
conjugation .... UNION, SYNGAMY
conjunction .... OR, AND, BUT,
SINCE, UNION, BLENDING,
INCLUSION, COINCIDENCE
in biology .... ZYGOSIS
conjunctivitis .... PINKEYE,
TRACHOMA

conjuration ...... MAGIC, SORCERY
conjure .... BEG, CALL UPON,
INVOKE, BESEECH, IMPLORE,
SUMMON(UP)
conjuror .... MAGE, WIZARD,
WARLOCK, MAGICIAN,
SORCERER
stick of .... ROD, WAND
words of .... HOCUS-POCUS
conk .... HIT, KNOCK
British slang ..... BLOW, HEAD,
NOSE
out .... FAIL
connate .... AKIN, INBORN,
INBRED, INNATE, GENETIC,
CONGENITAL
connect ...... FUSE, JOIN, LINK, TIE
IN, HOOK UP, COUPLE,
RELATE, ASSOCIATE
secretly .... TAP
Connecticut, capital of
.... HARTFORD
city/town .... BRIDGEPORT,
DANBURY, NEW HAVEN,
CANAAN, HAMDEN, NORWALK,
MERIDEN, GREENWICH,
PUTNAM, BRISTOL, CLINTON,
VERNON, STAMFORD,
NORWICH, MIDDLETOWN,
WATERBURY, NAUGATUCK,
TORRINGTON, TRUMBULL,
WOODBRIDGE, STRATFORD,
WILLIMANTIC
college .... TRINITY,
HARTFORD, ST. JOSEPH
county .... TOLLAND,
FAIRFIELD, HARTFORD,
WINDHAM, LITCHFIELD, NEW
HAVEN, MIDDLESEX, NEW
LONDON
island .... MASON
lake .... GLEN, BANTAM,
ROGERS, PUTNAM, ANDOVER,
TYLER, WANGUM, BETHANY,
KONOMOC, OXOBOXO,
GAILLARD, HAMMONASSET,
HIGHLAND, QUASSAPAUG,
CHAMBERLAIN, CANDLEWOOD,
SPECTACLE, TERRAMUGGUS,
WINDWING, WINCHESTER
mountain .... RED, BEAR,
CANAAN, MOHAWK, FRISSELL,
HAYSTACK, MANITOOK,
LAMENTATION
official, borough ...... WARDEN
pond .... MUDGE, PACHAUG
range .... TALCOTT
recreation site .... DINOSAUR
PARK, MARK TWAIN HOUSE,
MYSTIC AQUARIUM
river .... MAD, BYRAM, MYSTIC,

SALMON, SCANTIC, THAMES, TITICUS, NAUGATUCK, EIGHT MILE, CONNECTICUT, YANTIC, HOUSATONIC

state bird .... ROBIN

state flower .... MOUNTAIN LAUREL

state nickname .... NUTMEG, CONSTITUTION

university .... YALE

connecting body of water .... STRAIT

part .... LINK

pipe .... TEE

strip of land .... ISTHMUS

connection ...... TIE, BOND, NECK, NEXUS, UNION, CONTACT, BRIDGE, KINSHIP, RELATION

close .... LIAISON

connective .... SYNDETIC

tissue .... FASCIA, TENDON, CARTILAGE

tissue disease .... ARTHRITIS

word .... OR, AND, NOR, EITHER, NEITHER

Connelly, playwright .... MARC(US)

Connie .... MACK, FRANCIS

Mack's ballpark .... SHIBE

conning tower adjunct .... PERISCOPE

conniption .... TANTRUM

connivance .... INTRIGUE, TRICKERY, COLLUSION

connive .... PLOT, COLLUDE, CONSPIRE, COOPERATE

conniver ...... PLOTTER, FINAGLER

conniving .... SCHEMING

connoisseur ...... CRITIC, EXPERT, JUDGE, (A)ESTHETE, AUTHORITY, CO(G)NOSCENTE

art .... VIRTUOSO

fine foods/drinks ..... EPICURE, GOURMET, GO(U)RMAND

of gems .... LAPIDARY

connotation .... IMPLICATION

connote .... HINT, IMPLY, SUGGEST

connubial .... MARITAL, NUPTIAL, SPOUSAL, CONJUGAL

conquer .... DEFEAT, MASTER, QUELL, SUBDUE, SUBJUGATE, OVERCOME, OVERRIDE, OVERTHROW, SUPPRESS, VANQUISH

conquerable .... VINCIBLE

conquering .... TAMING

conqueror .... VICTOR

conquest .... VICTORY

of 1954 .... POLIO

conquistador .... CORTEZ, PIZARRO, CONQUEROR

Conrad (Joseph) character .... AXEL, LENA, SEAMAN, MARINER

(Joseph) novel .... VICTORY

Robert Falk .... ROBERT CONRAD

consanguinity .... KINSHIP, AFFINITY, RELATION

conscience, twinge of .... QUALM, REMORSE, SCRUPLE

conscientious objector .... CONCHY

conscious .... (A)WARE, AWAKE, EARNEST, MINDFUL, SENTIENT, COGNIZANT

consciousness ...... WITS, SENSES, INSIGHT, ALERTNESS, DILIGENCE

lose .... FAINT, PASS OUT, SWOON

conscript .... LEVY, DRAFT, FORCE, ENLIST, ENROLL, MUSTER, RECRUIT

conscripted person ...... DRAFTEE

consecrate .... BLESS, ANOINT, VOW, DEVOTE, HALLOW, ORDAIN, DEDICATE, SANCTIFY

consecrated .... BLEST, SACRED

bread .... SACRAMENT

Host's receptacle .... MONSTRANCE

oil .... CHRISM

consecration .... BLESSING

of the bread .... SACRING

consecutive .... ENSUING, FOLLOWING, SUCCESSIVE

consensus .... POLL, ASSENT, OPINION, AGREEMENT, COMMON BELIEF, SYMPOSIUM

consent .... AGREE, ALLOW, GRANT, YIELD, CONCUR, ACCEPT, ACCEDE, APPROVE, PERMISSION, AGREEMENT

consenting .... WILLING

consequence .... END, VALUE, FRUIT, RESULT, SEQUEL, EFFECT, PRODUCT, OUTCOME, CONCERN, IMPORTANCE

person of .... VIP, NABOB, BIGWIG, TYCOON, BIGSHOT

consequential .... MAJOR, IMPORTANT, RESULTANT

consequently .... ERGO, THUS, FINALLY, ACCORDINGLY, AS A RESULT, THEREFORE

conservation .... KEEPING, PROTECTION

conservative ...... TORY, PRUDENT, RIGHT(IST), MODERATE, STABLE, DIEHARD, STANDPAT, UNCHANGING, REACTIONARY

person .... FOG(E)Y

conservatory .... ACADEMY, MUSIC SCHOOL, GREENHOUSE

conserve ...... SAVE(UP), PRESERVE

fruit .... JAM

consider ...... DEEM, HEED, MULL, JUDGE, OPINE, STUDY, WEIGH, REFLECT, PONDER, ENTERTAIN

kindly .... FAVOR

considerable .... BIG, MUCH, LARGE, SIZABLE, WEIGHTY, GREAT DEAL, SUBSTANTIAL

colloquial .... TIDY, GOODLY, PRETTY

considerate .... KIND, THOUGHTFUL

consideration .... FEE, CARE, ESTEEM, REASON, GROUND, REGARD, MOTIVE, THOUGHT, REFLECTION

considering everything ...... ALL IN ALL

consign .... ASSIGN, COMMIT, ENTRUST, DELIVER, RELEGATE

to hell .... DAMN, CONDEMN

consist .... COMPRISE, INCLUDE

consistency .... DENSITY, HARMONY, FIRMNESS, AGREEMENT, SOLIDITY

consistent .... REGULAR, UNIFORM, ACCORDANT, COHERENT

consisting of 100 degrees .... CENTIGRADE

small spaces .... AREOLAR

consolation .... SOP, SOLACE, COMFORT, SYMPATHY

console .... ANCON, CHEER, BRACKET, CABINET, COMFORT, SUPPORT

like bracket .... CORBEL

radio/television .... FLOOR MODEL

the bereaved .... CONDOLE

consolidate .... FUSE, POOL, MERGE, UNITE, COMBINE, FEDERATE, SYNDICATE

consomme .... SOUP, BROTH

consonance .... UNITY, RHYME, CONCORD, HARMONY

consonant, aspirated .... SURD

hard .... FORTIS

unaspirated/smooth .... LENE

voiceless .... ATONIC

consonantal sound ...... SPIRANT

consort .... MATE WIFE, SPOUSE, HUSBAND, COMPEER, PARTNER, COMPANION

Queen Elizabeth's .... PHILIP

Queen Juliana's .... BERNHARD

Queen Victoria's .... ALBERT

Siva's .... DEVI
with ..... ATTEND, ACCOMPANY
consortium .... CARTEL,
COMPACT, COVENANT,
SYNDICATE
conspectus ...... DIGEST, SYNOPSIS
conspicuous .... GLARING, OVERT,
OBVIOUS, SALIENT, EMINENT,
NOTABLE, STRIKING,
PROMINENT, NOTICEABLE
consumption .... WASTE
success .... HIT, ECLAT
conspicuously .... VISIBLY,
CLEARLY, NOTABLY,
FLAGRANTLY
conspiracy .... PLOT, CABAL,
INTRIGUE, TRICKERY,
CONNIVANCE
sneaky .... SKULDUGGERY
to deceive .... CHICANERY
to defraud .... COVIN
conspirator .... TRAITOR,
SCHEMER, CATILINARIAN
conspire .... (COM)PLOT, CONCUR,
COLLUDE, CONNIVE, JOIN IN,
SCHEME, BE IN CAHOOTS
constable .... BULL, WARDEN,
BAILIFF, TROOPER, TIPSTAFF,
POLICE(MAN), PEACE OFFICER
constabulary .... SHERIFFRY,
(STATE)POLICE
constancy .... LOYALTY,
DEVOTION, EVENNESS,
FIRMNESS, STABILITY,
STEADINESS
constant ...... FAST, TRUE, LOYAL,
FIRM, STABLE, STEADY,
CHRONIC, DEVOTED,
FAITHFUL, CONTINUAL
visitor .... FREQUENTER
constantly .... DAY AFTER DAY
Constantine's birthplace
.... NISH
Constantinople .... ISTANBUL,
ISTAMBOUL
foreign quarter .... PERA,
BEYOGLU
inn .... SERAI, IMARET,
CARAVANSARY
constellate .... UNITE, CLUSTER
constellation .... GALAXY,
CLUSTER, ASTERISM,
GATHERING
altar .... ARA
archer .... SAGITTARIUS
arrow .... SAGITTA
balance .... LIBRA
bear .... URSA
bear, the Great .... URSA
MAJOR
bear, the Lesser .... URSA

MINOR
bird of paradise .... APUS
box .... PYXIS
brightest star .... COR
bull .... TAURUS
centaur .... CENTAURUS
charioteer .... AURIGA
crab .... CANCER
crane .... GRUS
cross .... CRUX
crow .... CORVUS
dog .... CANIS
dolphin .... DELPHINUS
dragon .... DRACO
eagle .... AQUILA
equatorial .... CETUS, ORION
fish .... PISCES
fish, the Flying .... VOLANS
fly .... MUSCA
foot .... RIGEL
fox .... VULPECULA
giraffe .... CAMELOPARDUS
goat .... CAPRICORN
hare .... LEPUS
harp .... LYRA
herdsman .... BOOTES
hunter .... ORION
in the Zodiac .... ARIES,
TAURUS, GEMINI, CANCER,
LEO, VIRGO, LIBRA, SCORPIO,
SAGITTARIUS, CAPRICORN(US),
AQUARIUS, PISCES
Indian .... INDUS
lady in the chair
.... CASSIOPEIA
lady, the chained
.... ANDROMEDA
lion .... LEO
lizard .... LACERTA
mast .... MALUS
monarch .... CEPHEUS
net .... RETICULUM
Northern .... LYRA, URSA,
DRACO, BOOTES, CYGNUS,
ARIES, AQUILA, AURIGA,
HYDRA, CEPHEUS, POLARIS,
SCUTUM, PERSEUS, SAGITTA,
LACERTA, PEGASUS, HERCULES,
LEO MINOR, DELPHINUS,
ANDROMEDA, CASSIOPEIA,
VULPECULA
painter .... PICTOR
peacock .... PAVO
ram .... ARIES
raven .... CORVUS
rule .... NORMA
scales .... LIBRA
scorpion .... SCORPIO,
SCORPIUS
sea serpent .... HYDRA
serpent/snake .... SERPENS

ship .... ARGO
Southern .... ARA, APUS,
CRUX, GRUS, PAVO, VELA,
CANIS, CETUS, INDUS, LEPUS,
LUPUS, ORION, MENSA, MUSCA,
NORMA, PYXIS, CARINA,
CORVUS, CAELUM, CRATER,
HYDRUS, ANTLIA, DORADO,
FORNAX, OCTANS, PICTOR,
PUPPIS, TUCANA, VOLANS,
COLUMBA, CIRCINUS, PHOENIX,
SEXTANS, SCULPTOR,
ERIDANUS, CENTAURUS,
MONOCEROS
stern .... PUPPIS
swan .... CYGNUS
table .... MENSA
toucan .... TUCANA
twins .... GEMINI
veil .... VELA
virgin .... VIRGO
water carrier .... AQUARIUS
water serpent .... HYDRUS
whale .... CETUS
winged horse .... PEGASUS
wolf .... LUPUS
woman .... VIRGO
consternation .... FEAR, PANIC,
ALARM, DISMAY, FRIGHT,
HORROR, TERROR,
AMAZEMENT
constipated .... CLOGGED,
COSTIVE
constituency .... VOTERS,
CLIENTELE, ELECTORATE
constituent .... ELECTOR,
ELEMENT, COMPONENT, PART,
VOTER, INTEGRANT
constitution .... CODE, NATURE,
MAKE-UP, CHARTER, BASIC
LAW, STATE, STRUCTURE,
COMPOSITION
addition to .... AMENDMENT
composition of .... BY-LAWS,
ARTICLES, PREAMBLE
state .... CONNECTICUT
constitutional .... BASIC, LAWFUL,
LEGAL, ORGANIC, CHARTERED,
VALID, OFFICIAL, ESSENTIAL
colloquial .... WALK, EXERCISE
constrain .... FORCE, IMPEL,
COMPEL, OBLIGE, STRESS
constraint .... DURESS, COERCION,
STRESS, PRESSURE,
COMPULSION, REPRESSION,
CONFINEMENT
constrict .... LIMIT, HAMPER,
CHOKE, CRAMP, CONTRACT,
STRANGLE, SQUEEZE,
COMPRESS

163

constriction of duct, etc.
.... STENOSIS
constrictor .... BOA, PYTHON,
CRUSHER, ANACONDA,
SPHINCTER
construct .... FORM, MAKE, REAR,
BUILD, ERECT, FRAME,
DEVISE, MODEL, COMPOSE,
ARRANGE
construction .... BUILDING,
CREATION, ERECTION,
STRUCTURE, COMPOSITION,
INTERPRETATION
battalion member ...... SEABEE
elaborate .... EDIFICE
constructive .... USEFUL,
HELPFUL, POSITIVE,
BENEFICIAL
arts .... TECTONICS
construe .... READ, INFER, PARSE,
EXPLAIN, ANALYZE, RENDER,
INTERPRET, TRANSLATE
consuetude .... USE, HABIT,
USAGE, CUSTOM, PRACTICE
consul's authority
.... EXEQUATUR
consult .... ADVISE, CONFER,
DISCUSS, REFER TO,
COMMUNE WITH
consultant, common .... DOCTOR,
EXPERT, LAWYER, ENGINEER,
TECHNICIAN
consume .... EAT, BURN, DRAIN,
DRINK, SPEND, WASTE, USE
UP, DEVOUR, EXPEND,
CORRODE, DESTROY, EXHAUST
consumed .... BATED, SPENT,
REDUCED, WASTED, DEPLETED
by fire .... CREMATED
consumer .... USER, BUYER,
EATER, VENDEE
concern .... SHORTAGES
goods .... FOOD, CLOTHING
opposed to .... PRODUCER
consumer's advocate/crusader
.... NADER
loyalty .... BRAND NAME
consummate .... END, PERFECT,
FULFILL, COMPLETE, FINISHED,
OUTRIGHT, ABSOLUTE,
THOROUGH
is what some are .... LIARS,
ARTISTS
skill .... FINESSE
consummation ...... END, RESULT,
CLIMAX, SUMMIT, OUTCOME,
REALIZATION, FULFILLMENT
consumption .... USE, WASTE,
ATROPHY, EROSION,
WASTAGE, DEPLETION,
DESTRUCTION

lung .... TABES, PHTHISIS,
TUBERCULOSIS
consumptive .... HECTIC, LUNGER,
TABETIC, PHTHISIC, DISEASED,
TUBERCULOUS
contact .... MEET, TOUCH,
TACTION, TANGENT,
ENCOUNTER, CONNECTION
closely .... OSCULATE
in physical .... CONTIGUOUS
mines .... TORPEDOES
contagion .... VIRUS, POISON,
MEASLES, VECTION,
INFECTION, TRANSFER,
SMALLPOX, EPIDEMIC
contagious .... NOXIOUS,
CATCHING, INFECTIOUS,
COMMUNICABLE
contain .... HOLD, CHECK, HOUSE,
EMBODY, ENCLOSE, RESTRAIN,
EMBRACE, INCLUDE, COMPRISE
container .... BAG, BOX, CAN,
JAR, KEG, TIN, TUN, VAT,
PAIL, CRATE, POUCH, BASKET
beer .... KEG, BARREL,
GROWLER
cardboard/pasteboard
.... CARTON
cereal .... BOWL
cigarette .... CASE
documents .... HANAPER,
BRIEFCASE
dose of medicine ..... CAPSULE
earthenware dish ...... TERRINE
earthenware pot .... PIPKIN
for burning oil .... CRESSET
for carrying drinking water
.... CANTEEN
for carrying paper money/
cards .... WALLET,
BILLFOLD
for holding traveling clothes
.... GRIPSACK
for holy oil .... AMPULLA
for liquids .... EWER, FLAGON
for liquor, flattened .... FLASK,
FLASKET
for relics .... CUSTODIAL,
RELIQUARY
for serving animal food
.... TROUGH
for serving gravy/sauce
.... GRAVY BOAT
for serving soup .... TUREEN
for table vinegar/oil/honey
.... CRUET, CRUSE
for the sacred host
.... TABERNACLE
for therapy bath ..... SITZBATH
for wine of Holy
Communion ..... CHALICE

glass .... BOTTLE, CARBOY
half-gallon .... POTTLE
info .... TARE, NET WEIGHT,
GROSS WEIGHT
material for making .... TIN,
FLAX, JUTE, GLASS, OSIER,
WOOD, STAVE, BURLAP, PAPER,
PLASTIC, ALUMINUM
metal .... COPPER
of assorted things .... ATTIC,
HANDBAG, CATCHALL
perforated .... DREDGER
perfume .... FLACON
sealed .... CAN, TIN, ENVELOPE
to keep liquids hot/cold
.... THERMOS
to spit into .... CUSPIDOR,
SPITTOON
waste .... TRASH CAN
water .... TANK, TROUGH,
CISTERN, RESERVOIR
wine .... CARAFE, DECANTER
with wicker casing
.... DEMIJOHN
wooden pail/bucket
.... CANNIKIN
containing air/wind/gases
.... PNEUMATIC
arsenic .... ARSENIOUS
carbon .... ORGANIC
copper .... CUPRIC
defects .... FAULTY
fire .... FIERY, IGNEOUS
gold .... AURIC
iron .... FERRIC
metal/ore ...... METALLIFEROUS
oil .... GREASY, SMOOTH,
SLIPPERY, UNCTUOUS
perforations .... FENESTRATE
silver .... LUNAR
sulfur .... SULFIDE
tin .... STANNIC
containment .... ENCLOSURE,
INCLUSION
contaminate .... SOIL, DIRTY,
TAINT, SPOIL, STAIN, SULLY,
BEFOUL, DEFILE, INFECT,
CORRUPT, DEPRAVE, POLLUTE
contaminator, air .... SMOG,
SMAZE
conte .... TALE, SHORT STORY
contemn .... SCORN, DESPISE
contemplate .... AIM, MUSE,
VIEW, GAZE AT, MEAN, PLAN,
BEHOLD, INTEND, PONDER,
PROPOSE, CONSIDER, REFLECT,
MEDITATE
contemplation .... INTENT(ION),
EXPECTATION
of embezzlement
...... PECULATION SPECULATION

contemporaneous .... COEVAL, CURRENT, SIMULTANEOUS
contemporary .... MODERN, MODISH, COEVAL, COETANEOUS, PRESENT-DAY, COEXISTENT
contempt .... SCORN, DISDAIN, CONTEMN, DEFIANCE
cry of .... BAH, TUT, PSHAW, FIDDLE-DE-DEE
show of .... FLEER, SNEER, JEER, SNIFF, SNORT
slang .... SLAM
contemptible .... LOW, BASE, MEAN, VILE, ABJECT, PALTRY, SCURVY, DESPISED, SCORNFUL, UNENVIED, OFFENSIVE, DESPICABLE
fellow ...... CAD, HEEL, BLOKE, SKATE, RASCAL, CULLION, SCOUNDREL
contend .... VIE, COPE, FIGHT, ARGUE, BATTLE, OPPOSE, COMPETE
with .... MEET
contender .... ENTRY, RIVAL, COMPETITOR, CONTESTANT
contendere, _____ (not contested) .... NOLO
contending parties .... SIDES, OPPONENTS, PROTAGONISTS
content .... VOLUME, MAKINGS, CAPACITY, SATISFIED
contention .... ROW, STRIFE, CONTEST, DISPUTE, ARGUMENT
in words only .... LOGOMACHY
contentious .... FISTIC, COMBATIVE, LOADED FORBEAR
contents list .... TABLE
unknown purchase ...... GRAB-BAG
contest .... AGON, FIGHT, DISPUTE, RIVALRY, TOURNEY, SKIRMISH, TOURNAMENT
armed .... WAR
boxing .... BOUT
endurance/long distance .... MARATHON
for two, armed .... DUEL
in court/in law .... LAWSUIT, LITIGATE, LITIGATION
judges .... JURY, PANEL
lures .... PRIZES
of knights .... DUEL, TILT, JOUST, TOURNEY
participant .... ENTRY, ENTRANT
second placer ...... RUNNER-UP
winner .... CHAMPION

with lances .... TILT, JOUST
contestant .... SIDE, ENTRY, RIVAL, ENTRANT, CONTENDER, PLAYER COMPETER, COMPETITOR
mercenary .... POTHUNTER
contestants as a whole .... FIELD
context .... SETTING, POSITION, BACKGROUND
contiguity ...... UNION, ABUTMENT
contiguous ...... NEXT, ADJACENT, TOUCHING
continence .... MODERATION, SOBRIETY, SELF-RESTRAINT
continent .... CHASTE, VESTAL, CELIBATE, ABSTINENT, TEMPERATE, ASIA, LANDMASS, MAINLAND, AFRICA, EUROPE, EURASIA, NORTH AMERICA, SOUTH AMERICA, AUSTRALIA, ANTARCTICA
"down under" .... AUSTRALIA
hypothetical .... LEMURIA, CASCADIA
icy .... ANTARCTICA
legendary/lost .... ATLANTIS
Continental Congress
president .... HANCOCK
contingency .... HAP, EVENT, CASUALTY, FORTUITY, PROSPECT, EMERGENCY, LIKELIHOOD, INCIDENCE, POSSIBILITY
contingent .... TEAM, GROUP, LIKELY, PENDING, BASED ON, DEPENDENT, INCIDENTAL, HINGING ON, CONDITIONAL, SUBJECT TO
continual .... CONSTANT, ENDLESS, FREQUENT, INCESSANT
change/movement .... FLUX(ION)
continually .... CONSTANTLY, FREQUENTLY, OFTEN(TIMES), REPEATEDLY, NEVER-ENDING
continuance .... ENDURANCE, EXTENSION
in time .... DURATION
continuation .... SEQUEL, ADDITION, DEFERRAL, OFFSHOOT, SEQUENCE, EXTENSION, FOLLOWING, DEFERMENT, RESUMPTION
continue ...... LAST, STAY, GO ON, KEEP-UP, CARRY-ON, STAY, ABIDE, DWELL, ENDURE, PROLONG, PERSIST, PREVAIL, PROCEED, SUSTAIN, MAINTAIN
obsolete .... DURE
tediously .... DRAG

continued story/movie
.... SERIAL
continuing ...... STEADY, LASTING, CONSTANT, PERPETUAL, DURABLE, STEADFAST
continuous .... ENDLESS, NONSTOP, CEASELESS, PERENNIAL, UNBROKEN, UNINTERRUPTED
bloom .... EVERGREEN
series .... STREAM
vexation .... HARASSMENT
contort .... WARP, TWIST, DEFORM, DISTORT, DISLOCATE
contortionist .... HOUDINI
contour .... FORM, SHAPE, FIGURE, (OUT)LINE
of head .... PROFILE
of region .... TOPOGRAPHY
contra .... OPPOSITE
contraband .... BANNED, ILLEGAL, SMUGGLED, FORBIDDEN
of a sort .... BOOTLEG
slang .... HOT GOODS
contrabandist .... SMUGGLER, (RUM)RUNNER
contrabass .... VIOL(ONE)
contraception .... STOPPER, HINDRANCE, BIRTH CONTROL
contraceptive device .... IUD, JELLY, CONDOM, THE PILL, DIAPHRAGM
slang .... RUBBER
contract .... VOW, INCUR, NARROW, PLEDGE, SHRINK, (COM)PACT, PROMISE, SHORTEN, AGREEMENT, COVENANT, DOCUMENT
a muscle .... FLEX
betrothal .... HANDFAST, ENGAGEMENT
bridge bid .... SLAM
first paragraph of .... ITEM I
illegal labor ...... YELLOW DOG
marriage .... WEDLOCK, MATRIMONY
of agency .... MANDATE
rental .... LEASE
the brow(s) .... KNIT, FROWN
the lips .... PUCKER(UP)
the skin .... WRINKLE
to marry .... TROTH
to transfer property ...... DEED
work .... INDENTURE
contracted .... CONCISE, REDUCED
contraction .... SYNCOPE, SHORTENING, COMPRESSION, ABBREVIATION
in poetry .... ELISION
of muscles .... SPASM, CRAMPS
of writing .... SHORTHAND,

STENOGRAPHY
contractor .... BUILDER
contradict .... DENY, BELIE, VETO,
REBUT, NEGATE, REFUSE,
REFUTE, GAINSAY
contradiction .... DENIAL,
NEGATION, REBUTTAL,
REFUSAL, INCONSISTENCY
in terms .... ANTILOGY
contradictory .... DENIED,
CONTRARY, NEGATIVE
contralto Nikolaidi .... ELENA
contraption .... GADGET,
CONTRIVANCE
contrary .... WRY, BALKY,
COUNTER, ADVERSE, OPPOSED,
HOSTILE, REVERSE, PERVERSE,
OPPOSITE, OBSTINATE
person .... MARY
to rules .... FOUL
contrast .... LIKEN, COMPARE
with .... DIFFER
contravene .... DEFY, OPPOSE,
VIOLATE, DISAGREE
contretemps .... MISHAP
contribute .... AID, GIVE, HELP,
TEND, SERVE, DONATE
contribution .... DOLE, GIFT,
INPUT, DONATION
form of .... CASH, KIND
small .... MITE
to the Pope .... (PETER'S)
PENCE
contributor .... DONOR, GIVER,
HELPER
newspaper .... COLUMNIST
contrite .... SORRY, PENITENT,
REGRETFUL, REPENTANT
contrition .... REMORSE,
PENITENCE
contrivance .... PLAN, DEVICE,
GADGET, GIMMICK, MACHINE,
INVENTION, CONTRAPTION
contrive .... PLAN, DEVISE,
SCHEME, FINAGLE, PLAY
TRICKS
control .... GRIP, POST, HELM,
REIN, RULE, TEST, CHECK,
DIRECT, MANAGE, COMMAND,
SUBDUE, MASTERY,
RESTRAIN(T)
center .... NUCLEUS
firm, severe .... IRON HAND
frustration .... SEETHE
kind of .... BIRTH, REMOTE
oneself .... KEEP COOL
controversial .... MOOT,
UNCERTAIN, DEBATABLE,
ERISTIC(AL), POLEMIC(AL)
area .... RUHR, SAAR, CHACO,
SABAH, KASHMIR, DAMANSKY

city .... DANZIG
theorist .... DARWIN
theory .... EVOLUTION
controversialist .... ERISTIC
controversy .... DEBATE, DISCORD,
DISPUTE, QUARREL,
ARGUMENT
controvert .... DENY, ARGUE,
DEBATE, DISCUSS, DISPUTE,
REFUTE, OPPUGN, GAINSAY
contumacious .... UNRULY,
DEFIANT, STUBBORN,
REBELLIOUS, DISOBEDIENT,
INSUBORDINATE
contumacy .... DARING, DEFIANCE
contumely .... ABUSE, INSULT,
RUDENESS, INSOLENCE
contusion .... BRUISE, INJURY,
SWELLING
conundrum ...... ENIGMA, PUZZLE,
RIDDLE, MYSTERY, QUESTION
convalesce .... RECOVER,
IMPROVE, RECUPERATE
convalescent, diet of .... SOUP,
GRUEL, LIQUIDS
convallaria .... LILY OF THE
VALLEY
convene .... SIT, CALL, MEET,
GATHER, COLLECT, CONVOKE,
SUMMON, ASSEMBLE
convenience ...... EASE, COMFORT,
UTILITY, FACILITY,
ADVANTAGE,
ACCOMMODATION
convenient .... HANDY, PROPER,
EXPEDIENT, SUITABLE
convent ...... NUNNERY, CLOISTER,
MONASTERY
cubicle .... CELL
dining hall .... REFECTORY
head .... SUPERIOR
inmate .... NUN, MONK,
CENOBITE
member, new .... NEOPHYTE
convention .... RULE, USAGE,
CAUCUS, CUSTOM, MEETING,
CONGRESS, ASSEMBLY,
PRACTICE
choice of .... NOMINEE
man .... DELEGATE
conventional .... SET, USUAL,
ACCEPTED, HABITUAL,
ORTHODOX, BOURGEOIS,
CUSTOMARY
act .... FORMALITY
measure of length .... PACE
converge .... MEET, UNITE
convergence .... FOCUS, FOCAL
POINT
conversant .... HEP, VERSED,
WELL-INFORMED, FAMILIAR

conversation .... CHAT, TALK,
COLLOQUY, DIALOGUE
between two .... DUOLOGUE
idle .... GOSSIP
on Mount Everest ..... SUMMIT
TALK
private .... TETE-A-TETE
starter .... HELLO
to settle dispute .... PARLEY
witty .... REPARTEE
conversational .... CHATTY,
SOCIABLE
comeback .... RETORT, RIPOSTE
digression .... ASIDE
event .... GABFEST
expert of a sort .... WIT
form of writing .... COLLOQUY
phrase .... I SEE, YOU KNOW
slang .... GABBY, WINDY
style, writing in ..... CAUSERIE
converse .... RAP, CHAT, TALK,
OTHER, COMMUNE, DISCUSS,
CONTRARY, OPPOSITE
conversion .... CHANGE
convert .... ADAPT, RENDER,
REMODEL, (EX)CHANGE,
PROSELYTE, TRANSFORM
fat into soap .... SAPONIFY,
SAPONIZE
into money .... REALIZE,
LIQUIDATE
new .... NOVICE, NEOPHYTE
converted .... REBORN
convertible .... MODIFIABLE,
NEGOTIABLE
into cash .... LIQUID
vehicle .... LANDAU, OPEN CAR
convertite .... MAGDALEN
convex .... BANDY, BOWED,
ROUND, CONCAVE
curve .... CAMBER
molding .... TORE, OVOLO,
TORUS, ASTRAGAL
swelling in column
.... ENTASIS
convey .... BEAR, CEDE, DEED,
BRING, CARRY, GRANT,
IMPART, INFORM, TRANSFER,
TRANSMIT, TRANSPORT
beyond jurisdiction ...... ELOIN
by deed .... REMISE
conveyance ...... BUS, CAR, CART,
CARRIER, VEHICLE, CARRIAGE,
SALE, CESSION, DISPOSAL
for dead .... HEARSE
instrument .... DEED
conveying away from center
.... EFFERENT
toward center .... AFFERENT
conveyor basket/car .... TRAM
of property .... ALIENOR

convict .... FELON, CULPRIT, CONDEMN, CRIMINAL, CAPTIVE, PRISONER
privileged .... TRUSTY
slang .... LAG, LIFER, LOSER, TERMER, JAILBIRD
conviction .... DOOM, VIEW, BELIEF, PENALTY, OPINION, SENTENCE, DAMNATION
convicts, squad of .... GANG
convince .... SELL, ASSURE, SATISFY, PERSUADE
convincing .... VALID, COGENT, CREDIBLE, PERSUASIVE
convivial ...... GAY, BOON, JOLLY, MERRY, JOVIAL, FESTIVE, SOCIABLE
drinking .... BOWL, WASSAIL
convocation .... ASSEMBLY
convoke .... CALL, GATHER, SUMMON, CONVENE, ASSEMBLE
convolute ...... COIL, ROLL, TWIRL, TWIST, CONTORT
convoy .... GUARD, ESCORT, CONDUCT, ACCOMPANY
convulse .... STIR, SHAKE, WRING, EXCITE, AGITATE
convulsion .... FIT, PAIN, QUIVER, REVOLT, TWINGE, SPASM, AGITATION, UPHEAVAL
attacks of .... ECLAMPSIA
of rage, etc. .... PAROXYSM
cony .... FUR, DUPE, PIKA, DAMAN, GANAM, HYRAX, DAS(SIE), RABBIT
coo .... CURR, MURMUR
companion of .... BILL
cooer .... DOVE, LOVER, PIGEON
cooing sound .... CURR
cook .... FIX, HEAT, MAKE, CONCOCT, PREPARE
again .... REBOIL, REHEAT
by dry heat .... BAKE
chief .... CHEF
colloquial .... DOCTOR, FALSIFY
galley of .... CUDDY
gently .... CODDLE
in cream .... SHIR(R)
in oil/fat .... FRY
in oven .... BAKE, ROAST
slang .... SPOIL
specialty of .... POTPIE, POT ROAST
up ..... PLOT, DEVISE, CONCOCT
cookbook item .... RECIPE
quantity .... CUPFUL, PINCH, TABLESPOONFUL
cooked meat shop .... DELICATESSEN

partially .... RARE
cooker ...... OVEN, BAKER, GRILL, STOVE, BROILER, TOASTER, BARBECUE, WATERLESS
cookery .... COOKING, (CULINARY) SCIENCE
cookhouse, ship's .... GALLEY
cookie maker .... AMOS, MRS. FIELD
cookies ...... BUNS, CAKES, SNAPS, MACAROON
cooking aid .... SPICE, CONDIMENT
art of .... CUISINE, CULINARY
directions/formula ...... RECIPE
glassware .... PYREX
means of ..... BAKING, FRYING, BOILING, BARBECUE, ROASTING
odor .... NIDOR
outfit .... KITCHEN
pot .... OLLA
stove .... RANGE
stove, portable .... HOTPLATE
style .... CAJUN, CUISINE
vessel .... PAN
cook's choice .... RECIPE
domain aboard ship .... CUDDY, GALLEY
cooky .... BUN, HERMIT, WAFER, JUMBLE, MACAROON, (GINGER)SNAP, LADYFINGER
cool .... FAN, CALM, ALLAY, FREEZE, QUENCH, COMPOSED
calm and _____
.... COLLECTED
color .... BLUE, GRAY, GREEN
hot liquid .... KEEL
make .... ICE, CHILL
one's heels .... WAIT
slang .... NEATO
cooled .... FRAPPE
cooler: sl. .... JAIL, CLINK
Coolidge alma mater .... AMHERST
Dam river .... GILA
singer .... RITA
coolie .... LABORER
woman .... CHANGAR
cooling off .... ON ICE
one's heels .... ARRESTED
coomb .... RAVINE
coon .... RACCOON
coop .... PEN, COTE, HUTCH
fly the .... DECAMP, ESCAPE, ABSCOND
up .... ENCAGE
cooper ...... HOOPER, CASKMAKER
Cooper, actor .... GARY, JACKIE
Mohican hero of .... UNCAS
cooperate .... HELP, COEXIST, PLAY BALL, SIDE WITH
secretly .... COLLUDE,

CONNIVE, CONSPIRE
cooperative ...... CO-OP, ALLIANCE
cooperator .... ALLY
coordinate .... ADAPT, ADJUST, ORGANIZE, HARMONIZE
system .... GRID
Coorg's capital .... MERCARA
coot .... DUCK, FOOL, AVOCET, MUDHEN, SCOTER, NOTORNIS, SHUFFLER, WATERHEN, SIMPLETON
cootie .... LOUSE
cop ...... TOP, CONE, HEAD, CREST
a plea .... CONFESS
club of .... BILLY, STICK, TRUNCHEON
out .... ALIBI, EXCUSE
slang ...... FILCH, SEIZE, STEAL, SWIPE, SNATCH, BULL, DICK, PILFER, FLATFOOT, JOHN LAW, THE FUZZ, POLICEMAN
copacetic .... FINE, GOOD, DANDY, EXCELLENT
copaiba .... TUPI, RESIN
copal .... ANIME, RESIN
copalm .... TREE, RESIN
cope .... SKY, VAULT, CANOPY, HANDLE, MANAGE, CONTEND, FACE, SURVIVE, VESTMENT
Copenhagen is capital of .... DENMARK
copier .... APER, IMITATOR
copious .... LUSH, AMPLE, WORDY, LAVISH, PROFUSE, ABUNDANT, PLENTIFUL
Copland, composer .... AARON
copper .... AES, COIN, METAL, CUPRUM, CA(U)LDRON
alchemist's .... VENUS
alloy .... AROIDE, TOMBAK, TOMBAC(K)
alloy coin .... CASH
and tin alloy .... ORMOLU
coating .... VERD, PATINA, ANTIQUE, VERDIGRIS
coin .... PENNY
color .... REDDISH BROWN
combining form .... CHALCO
gilded .... VERMEIL
nickel .... NICCOLITE
nickel, zinc alloy ...... ALBATA
ore .... CUPRITE, CHALCOCITE
skin .... INDIAN
slang .... POLICEMAN
sulphate .... VITRIOL
tin, zinc alloy .... OROIDE
zinc alloy .... PINCHBECK
copperah .... COPRA
copperhead .... SNAKE, VIPER, NORTHERNER
coppice .... COPSE, THICKET

copse .... BOSK, HOLT, SHAW,
    BUNCH, GROVE, BOSCAGE,
    COPPICE, THICKET
Coptic bishop's title .... ABBA
copula .... BAND, LINK
copulate .... JOIN, MATE, UNITE,
    COUPLE, BREED, COHABIT
copy .... APE, CLONE, MODEL,
    TRACE, ECTYPE, IMITATE,
    FAKE, RESCRIPT, DUPLICATE,
    DITTO, MIRROR, FACSIMILE
  closely .... MIMIC
  court record .... ESTREAT
  document's .... TENOR
  of original .... REPLICA
  photographic .... PRINT,
    PHOTOSTAT
  read .... EDIT, PROOFREAD
  slang .... DEAD RINGER
copycat .... APER, MIMIC,
    IMITATOR
copying machine .... XEROX,
    DUPLICATOR, MIMEOGRAPH
copyist .... ARTIST, COPIER,
    SCRIVENER, TRANSCRIBER
copyright .... PATENT
copywriter .... AUTHOR,
    COMPOSER, PUBLICIST
coquet ...... DALLY, FLIRT, TRIFLE
coquette .... VAMP, FLIRT
coquettish .... COY, FICKLE
coquina .... LIMESTONE
coquito .... PALM
cora .... GAZELLE
coracle .... BOAT, CURRACH,
    CURRAGH
coral .... POLYP, SPAWN, STONE,
    ZOOID, POLYPITE, ZOOPHYTE
  cavity .... CALICLE
  color .... RED, PINK
  formation .... REEF, ATOLL,
    SHELF, SHOAL
  group/order .... MADREPORE,
    MADREPORARIA
  lobster's .... ROE
  part .... STOLON
  reef island .... CAY, KEY,
    CAPE, HOLM, ISLE, ATOLL,
    ISLET
  shape .... MUSHROOM
  source .... POLYPS
  variety .... APOROSA
corbel .... ANCON, BRACKET,
    CONSOLE
corbeling .... SQUINCH
corbie .... CROW, RAVEN
Corcyra .... CORFU
cord .... BAND, ROPE, CABLE,
    BOND, TWINE, STRING,
    FUNICLE
  braided .... SENNIT

  cable/rope end's ...... MARLINE
  cattle catching .... BOLA
  drapery .... TORSADE
  head .... AGAL
  kind of .... SPINAL
  knob lump .... KNOT
  strangling .... GAROTTE,
    GARROTE
  tip .... TAG, A(I)GLET
  trimming .... CHENILLE
  umbilical .... FUNICULUS
cordage fiber .... COIR, FERU,
    HEMP, IMBE, JUTE, ABACA,
    AGAVE, ISTLE, SISAL, MAGUEY
  grass .... ESPARTO
corded cloth .... REP, POPLIN,
    CORDUROY
Cordelia's father .... LEAR
  sister .... REGAN
cordelle .... TASSEL
cordial .... GENIAL, HEARTY,
    KINDLY, AMIABLE, FRIENDLY,
    LIQUEUR, RATAFIA, ROSOLIO,
    ANISETTE, HIPPOCRAS,
    MARASCHINO
  apricot .... PERSICO
  less .... ICIER
cordierite .... IOLITE
cordite .... EXPLOSIVE
cordon .... BELT, CORD, RING,
    BRAID, CIRCLE, RIBBON
corduroy ...... FUSTIAN, TROUSERS
  ridge .... WALE
core .... HEART, CENTER
  bone/feather .... PITH
  corn ear .... COB
  reactor .... PILE
coreopsis .... TICKSEED
corf .... TRUCK, BASKET,
    MINEWAGON
corfu .... CORCYRA, KERKYRA
corium .... SKIN, CUTIS, DERMA,
    DERMIS
Corinthian capital's scroll
  .... VOLUTE
  volute .... HELIX
cork ...... TAP, BARK, PLUG, SEAL,
    SPILE, STOPPER, STOPPLE
  barrel's .... BUNG
  bottle/shallow .... SHIVE
  change into .... SUBERIZE
  helmet .... TOPI, TOPEE
  like .... SUBEROSE
  noise .... POP
  of a .... SUBERIC
  waxy substance
  .... SUBERIN(E)
Cork County port .... COBH
  famous feature of
  .... BLARNEY STONE
corker .... LIE, LULU, STOPPER,

    CLINCHER
corking .... EXCELLENT
corkscrew .... BOTTLE OPENER
  shape like a .... SPIRAL
corkwood .... BALSA
corm .... BULB, TUBER
  plant with .... CROCUS,
    GLADIOLUS
cormorant .... BIRD, SHAG,
    GORMAW, GREEDY, GUANAY,
    GLUTTON(OUS)
corn .... SALT, FLINT, GRAIN,
    CEREAL, KERNEL, PICKLE,
    MAIZE, GRANULE, PAPILLOMA
  and beans dish .... SUCCOTASH
  belt (per J. Luzzatto)
  .... BOURBON
  bin .... CRIB
  bread .... PONE, TORTILLA
  cake .... JOHNNY-CAKE
  color of ripe .... MAIZE
  covering .... HUSK
  crake .... RAIL, DAKER HEN
  flour .... PINOLE
  flower .... BLUENOSE
  green ear .... TUCKET
  ground .... MEAL, FLOUR,
    GRITS, HOMINY
  grower .... IOWAN
  hair .... TASSEL
  hulled .... HOMINY
  husk .... SHUCK
  imperfect .... NUBBIN
  Indian .... MAIZE
  lily .... IXIA
  liquor .... WHISK(E)Y
  meal .... MASA, SAMP, HOMINY
  meal, baked/fried
  .... HOECAKE
  meal bread/cake .... PONE,
    DODGER
  meal dish .... SCRAPPLE
  meal dough .... HUSH PUPPY
  meal mush .... ATOLE
  meal porridge .... MUSH,
    POLENTA, STIRABOUT
  meal pudding .... MUSH
  mill .... QUERN
  porridge .... SAMP
  slang .... MUSH
  small .... NUBBIN
  spike .... EAR
  stalk .... STOVER
  state .... IOWA
  stump .... STUBBLE
  toe .... BUNION, CALLUS
  variety .... FLINT
cornea bigger than normal
  .... MEGALOCORNEA
  disorder of the .... ULCER,
    KERATOCONUS,

KERATOMALACIA
inflammation .... KERATITIS
leucoma of the .... WALLEYE
opacity on .... NEBULA,
LEUCOMA
scratch .... ABRASION
shape .... DOME
smaller than normal
.... MICROCORNEA
corned .... BRINED, SALTED
beef .... BULLY
beef connoisseur .... JIGGS
beef sandwich .... REUBEN
beef's partner .... CABBAGE
cornel .... DOGWOOD
Cornelia Otis .... SKINNER
corneous .... HORNY, HORNLIKE
corner .... BEND, TRAP, TREE,
TURN, BIGHT, COIGN, CURVE,
NICHE, RECESS, REGION
angle .... CANT
chimney/fireplace
.... INGLENOOK
of building .... CANT, QUOIN
of sail .... CLEW
projecting .... COIGN(E)
support .... ARCH, LINTEL,
SQUINCH, CORBELING
the market/prices
.... MONOPOLIZE
cornered .... BENT, AT BAY,
ANGULAR, IMPERILED,
THREATENED
cornerstone .... COIGN(E), QUOIN,
FOUNDATION
of the "underground
economy" .... BLACK
MARKET
cornerwise .... DIAGONALLY
cornet .... CAVALRY FLAG
Cornhusker State .... NEBRASKA
cornice .... STRIP, MOLDING
interior window .... PELMET
projection .... DRIP, CORONA
support .... ANCON
corniculate .... HORNED
Cornish patron saint .... COLIN
town .... ST. IVES
cornu(copia) .... HORN OF PLENTY
Cornwall county seat .... BODMIN
islands .... SCILLY
corny .... BANAL, MUSHY, MUSTY,
STALE, TRITE, SENTIMENTAL
person .... CORNBALL
corolla .... LIGULE, PETALS,
PERIANTH
cuplike part .... CORONA
heraldic .... GALEA
corollary .... ADJUNCT, OFFSHOOT
a .... DEDUCTION, INFERENCE
geometrical .... PORISM

corona .... AURA, HALO, CIGAR,
CROWN, AUREOLE
Corona Australis .... WREATH
coronach .... DIRGE, THRENODY
coronal .... CROWN, DIADEM,
GARLAND
coronary .... ROUND, CIRCULAR
thrombosis .... STROKE, HEART
ATTACK
coronation .... CROWNING
coronet .... CROWN, TIARA,
ANADEM, DIADEM
corporal .... BODILY, PERSONAL
for short .... NCO
infamous .... HITLER
punishment .... FLOGGING,
WHIPPING
rank after .... SERGEANT
tobacco of .... CAPORAL
Corporal, famous/Little
.... NAPOLEON
corporate .... JOINT, COMMON,
UNITED, COMBINED,
ASSOCIATED
corporation .... MERGER,
SYNDICATE, ASSOCIATION
manager .... SYNDIC
corporeal .... SOMAL, BODILY,
SOMATIC, MATERIAL,
PHYSICAL
corps .... BRANCH, COMPANY,
SERVICE
corpse .... LICH, CARCASE
CADAVER, CARCASS
animated .... ZOMBI(E)
dissection .... NECROTOMY
embalmed .... MUMMY
platform for .... BIER
prefix .... NECR(O)
slang .... STIFF
corpsman .... MEDIC
corpulence .... OBESITY, FATNESS,
PORTLINESS
corpulent .... FAT, BULKY, GROSS,
OBESE, PURSY, STOUT,
FLESHY, PORTLY
corpus delicti .... DEAD BODY
corpuscles, lack of red
.... AN(A)EMIA
corral .... PEN, YARD, POUND,
ACQUIRE, ROUND UP,
STOCK(ADE)
correct .... CURE, EDIT, PRIM,
TRUE, AMEND, EMEND,
PROPER, REMEDY, RECTIFY,
ACCURATE
one's fault .... REFORM
correction .... REMEDY, REPAIR,
EDITION, REVISION, DISCIPLINE
correctional house
.... BRIDEWELL, REFORMATORY

correlation .... ANALOGY,
LIKENESS
correlative .... AKIN, COUPLED,
CONNECTED, RELATED,
PARALLEL
pair of .... EITHER-OR,
NEITHER-NOR
correspond .... SUIT, AGREE,
EQUAL, MATCH, TALLY,
WRITE, COINCIDE
correspondence ...... AGREEMENT,
COMMUNICATION
kind of .... BUSINESS,
OFFICIAL, PERSONAL
correspondent, kind of
.... PENPAL, FOREIGN,
STRINGER
corresponding .... IDENTICAL,
EQUIVALENT
corrida celebration .... FIESTA
cry .... OLE
personnel .... TOREROS
corridor .... AISLE, ROUTE,
GALLERY, HALL(WAY),
PASSAGEWAY
corrigenda .... ERRATA
corrigible .... DOCILE, AMENABLE,
REMEDIAL
corrival .... COMPETITOR
corroborant .... TONIC
corroborate ...... ATTEST, RATIFY,
VERIFY, CONFIRM, SUPPORT
corrode ...... ETCH, RUST, DECAY,
GNAW, ERODE, EAT INTO,
WEAR OUT, WEAR AWAY
corroded .... RUSTY, ROTTEN,
CARIOUS, CANKERED, WORN
OUT
corrosive .... ACID, CAUSTIC,
CUTTING, MORDANT,
ESCHAROTIC
corrugate .... PLEAT, FURROW,
GROOVE, WRINKLE
corrugated .... ROUGH, FLUTED,
RUGATE, CRIMPED, GROOVED,
RUGOSE, RUGOUS
corrupt ...... EVIL, SPOIL, DEBASE,
VENAL, DEFILE, INFECT,
ROTTEN, PERVERT, VITIATE
morally .... PUTRID
official .... GRAFTER
one's way ...... BRIBE, SUBORN
corruptible .... ON THE TAKE
corrupting offspring .... HEIR
POLLUTION
corruption .... GRAFT, VENALITY,
DISHONESTY
in hiring relatives
.... NEPOTISM
on the part of a ship's crew
.... BARRATRY

trace of .... TAINT
corsage .... BODICE, FLOWER,
   BOUQUET, NOSEGAY
corsair .... PIRATE, PRIVATEER,
   FREEBOOTER
ship .... XEBEC
corselet .... LORICA, CUIRASS
corset .... BODICE, GIRDLE,
   LORICA, LORLEA, SUPPORT
bone .... BUSK
stiffener .... BUSK, STAY,
   WHALEBONE
Corsican capital .... AJACCIO
famous .... NAPOLEON
seaport .... BASTIA
sheep .... MOUFLON
cortege .... TRAIN, RETINUE,
   PROCESSION
Cortes' loot .... ORO
cortex .... BARK, RIND
corundum .... RUBY, EMERY,
   TOPAZ, AMETHYST, SAPPHIRE
coruscate .... GLEAM, GLITTER,
   SPARKLE, TWINKLE
corvine bird .... CROW, ROOK,
   RAVEN
Corvus .... RAVEN
coryza .... COLD, CATARRH
sign of .... SNEEZE, SNIFFLE
cos ...... COAN, LETTUCE, ROMAINE
cosher .... PAMPER
cosi fan _____ .... TUTTI
cosmetic .... ADORNING,
   BEAUTIFYING
base for .... LANOLIN(E)
cheek/lip .... ROUGE
containing white lead,
  former .... CERUSE
eyelid/eyelash .... KOHL,
   MASCARA
hair .... HENNA
paste .... PACK
skin .... LOTION
use/decorate with .... PAINT
cosmetician **Lauder** .... ESTEE
cosmetics: sl. .... WARPAINT
cosmic .... VAST, GRANDIOSE
cycle .... EON
ray particle .... MESON
cosmography, branch of
   .... GEOLOGY, ASTRONOMY,
   GEOGRAPHY
cosmonaut .... SPACEMAN,
   ASTRONAUT, ROCKETMAN
cosmopolitan .... SUAVE, URBANE,
   REFINED, POLISHED
cosmos .... EARTH, GLOBE, ORDER,
   REALM, WORLD, HARMONY,
   THISTLE, UNIVERSE
god of the .... VARUNA
opposed to .... CHAOS

Cossack .... TATAR, RUSSIAN,
   CAVALRYMAN
chief .... ATAMAN, HETMAN
fame of the .... HORSEMANSHIP
whip .... KNOUT
cosset .... PET, LAMB, FONDLE,
   PAMPER
cost ...... PRICE, CHARGE, EXPENSE,
   PAYMENT, SACRIFICE
colloquial .... DAMAGE
exceeding contract price
   .... OVERRUN
costa .... RIB
Costa Rica bay .... SALINAS,
   CORONADA
cape .... VELAS, BLANCO,
   MATAPALO, SANTA ELENA
capital .... SAN JOSE
city/town .... LIMON, GRECIA,
   NICOYA, CARTAGO, HEREDIA,
   ESPARTA, GOLFITO, PARAISO,
   QUESADA, LIBERIA, ALAHUELA,
   PUNTARENAS, SAN RAMON,
   SANTA CRUZ, SIQUIRRES,
   TURRIALBA, SAN JOSE, SANTO
   DOMINGO
coin .... COLON
discoverer of .... COLUMBUS
gulf .... DULCE, NICOYA
highest point .... CHIRRIPO
   GRANDE
island .... CANO
language .... SPANISH
mountain .... IRAZU,
   GONGORA, CHIRRIPO GRANDE
peak .... BLANCO
peninsula .... NICOYA
port .... LIMON
president .... ARIAS, TREJOS,
   CALDERON
range .... TALAMANCA
river .... SAN JUAN
volcano .... CUILAPA
   MIRAVALLES
costard .... HEAD, APPLE
Costello .... LOU
costly ...... DEAR, PRECIOUS, HIGH-
   PRICED, EXPENSIVE
costmary .... CHRYSANTHEMUM
costrel .... FLASK, BOTTLE
costume ...... (FANCY)DRESS, GET-
   UP, OUTFIT, CLOTHING
colloquial .... RIG, TOG
jewelry ...... BAUBLE, BROOCH,
   GEWGAW, TRINKET
jewelry material .... PASTE,
   OROIDE, ORMOLU, STRASS
masquerade .... DOMINO
matching parts ...... ENSEMBLE
riding .... HABIT
silk material .... SENDAL

wear one in fun .... MUM(M)
cot .... BED, CRIB, CHARPAI,
   CHARPOY, SHELTER
poetic .... COTTAGE
cote .... SHED, SHELTER
coterie .... SET, JUNTO, CIRCLE,
   CLIQUE, CAMARILLA
cotillion .... BALL, DANCE
cotinga .... CHATTERER
Cotswold .... SHEEP
cotta .... SURPLICE
cottage .... HUT, BOWER, VILLA,
   CABIN, CABANA, CASINO,
   CHALET, HOUSE, SHACK,
   SHELTER, BUNGALOW
cheese .... SMEARCASE
cotter .... BOLT, WEDGE
pin .... FORELOCK
cotton .... CLOTH, FABRIC,
   MALLOW, THREAD
and wool cloth .... LINSEY,
   SATINET(TE)
batting fibers .... LINTERS
Bengal .... ADATI
cloth .... JEAN, MULL, PIMA,
   REP(S), REPP, CHINO, DUCKS,
   CRASH, CALICO, CHINTZ,
   KHAKI, MANTA, MADRAS,
   MUSLIN, NANKIN, OXFORD,
   CAMBRIC, ETAMINE, GALATEA,
   NANKEEN, ORGANDY,
   GRENADINE, SEERSUCKER
cloth, canvaslike .... WIGAN
cloth for curtains, etc.
   .... LAWN, SCRIM, DIMITY
cloth for handkerchiefs, etc.
   .... LAWN, BATISTE
cloth for linings .... SILESIA,
   PERCALINE
cloth for sheets .... MUSLIN,
   PERCALE
cloth, glazed .... CHINTZ,
   JACONET
cloth, glossy .... SATEEN
coarse, for shawls, capes,
  etc. .... MANTA
comb .... CARD
fiber .... LINT(ER), BATTING
fiber knot .... NEP
gauze .... LENO
gum tree .... TUPELO
hosiery/socks .... LISLES
jersey .... T-SHIRT
machine .... GIN, MULE,
   BALER, LINTER, WILLOW(ER)
measure .... LEA, HANK
medical dressing .... LINT,
   GAUZE, SPONGE
pad/piece of .... SPONGE
plug of .... TAMPON
pod .... BOLI, BOLL

printed, brightly colored
.... SARONG
roll of fiber for spinning
.... SLUB
seed cleaner .... GIN, LINTER
seed fiber .... LINTER
sheer .... VOILE
spinning wheel .... CHARK(H)A
stainer .... BUG
thin, lightweight .... NAINSOOK
thread .... LISLE
to .... GET ALONG, HIT IT OFF
tuft .... LOCK
twilled .... JEAN, CHINO,
DENIM
twisted .... ROVE
waste .... LINT, FLOCK
with fleecy nap .... FLANNEL
with glazed/water finish
.... PERCALINE
Cotton State .... ALABAMA
cottonbelt, U.S. .... SOUTH
cottonmouth .... SNAKE
cottontail .... HARE, RABBIT,
LEVERET
cottonwood ...... ALAMO, POPLAR
cottony .... DOWNY, FLUFFY
couch .... LAIR, SOFA, DIVAN,
SQUAB, CANAPE, RECLINE,
LOUNGE, PALLET, SETTEE,
OTTOMAN, DAVENPORT
hanging/swinging
.... HAMMOCK
heavily stuffed with upright
ends .... CHESTERFIELD
like chair ...... CHAISE LONGUE
poetic .... BED
to carry wounded .... LITTER
cougar ...... CAT, PUMA, PAINTER,
PANTHER, CARCAJOU,
CATAMOUNT
cough .... HACK, TUSSIS
barking .... CROUP
candy .... HOARHOUND,
HOREHOUND
drop .... TROCHE, LOZENGE,
PASTILLE
medicine .... GRINDELIA,
EXPECTORANT
medicine base .... SYRUP
of a .... TUSSAL, TUSSIVE
sound like a .... HICCUP
to attract attention .... AHEM
up .... PAY, EJECT, HAND OVER
whooping .... PERTUSSIS
coughing up blood
.... HEMOPTYSIS
pus .... VOMICA
could be Fred's or Steve's
place .... ALLEN'S TOWN
coulee ...... LAVA, GULCH, RAVINE

couloir .... GORGE, GULLY
coulter .... PLOWSHARE
council .... BOARD, JUNTA,
FORUM, CABINET, COMMITTEE
African tribe's .... INDABA
chamber ...... DIVAN, CABINET,
CAMARILLA
church .... SYNOD, CONSISTORY
jury .... PANEL
kind of .... CITY, ADVISORY,
ECUMENICAL
of deacons .... CONSISTORY
of justice .... TRIBUNAL
table .... BOARD
counsel .... REDE, ADVICE,
ADVISE, GUIDE, PROMPT,
SUGGEST
legal .... LAWYER
counselor .... GUIDE, LAWYER,
MENTOR, ADVISER
woman .... EGERIA
count .... ADD, DEEM, RATE,
SCORE, TALLY, RECKON,
FIGURE, ACCOUNT, CONSIDER,
ESTIMATE, (E)NUMERATE
calories .... DIET
down purpose ...... BLAST-OFF,
LAUNCHING
finish .... ESS
in .... INCLUDE
in law .... CHARGE
of population .... CENSUS
on .... RELY, DEPEND
out .... OMIT, FORGET,
EXCLUDE, DISREGARD
palatine .... PALSGRAVE
Count of Monte Cristo
.... DANTES
of Vienne .... DAUPHIN
countenance .... ABET, FACE,
FAVOR, ASPECT, VISAGE,
SUPPORT, SANCTION
counter .... BAR, ADDER, BUFFET,
AGAINST, COMPUTER,
CONTRARY, OPPOSITE
in cards .... MILLE
irritant .... MOXA, SALVE,
SETON, LOTION, MUSTARD,
CALAMINE, OINTMENT,
DEMULCENT
kind of .... GEIGER
sale .... RETAIL
counteract ...... OFFSET, THWART,
CHECK, FRUSTRATE,
NEUTRALIZE
counterattack .... REVENGE,
RETORT, RETALIATION
counterbalance .... EQUIPOISE
counterfeit .... FAKE, BOGUS,
SHAM, FALSE, FORGE(D),
PHON(E)Y, POSTICHE,

IMITATION, SPURIOUS
coin .... SLUG
jewelry .... BRUMMAGEM
counterfeiter .... FORGER, MINTER
counterfeiting .... FORGERY,
PAPER-CAPER
countermand .... CANCEL,
REVOKE, CALL BACK,
NULLIFY, OVERRULE
counterpane .... COVERLET
counterpart .... COPY, MATE,
TWIN, DOUBLE, REPLICA,
LIKENESS, MATCH, PARALLEL,
DUPLICATE
counterpoint .... DESCANT
of .... CONTRAPUNTAL
counterpoise .... BALANCE
countersign .... PASSWORD
countersink .... REAM
countertenor .... ALTO
counterweight .... TARE
countess's title of respect
.... LADY
counting frame .... ABAC(US)
sheep purpose .... SLEEP
ten purpose .... STALL, COOL
OFF
countless .... MYRIAD, UNTOLD,
TEEMING, NUMEROUS
countrified ...... RURAL, HODDEN,
RUSTIC, CORNFED
country .... HOME, LAND, REALM,
STATE, NATION, REGION,
TERRITORY, FATHERLAND
ancient .... PERSIA, ILLYRIA
bumpkin .... HICK, RUBE,
CHURL, YAHOO, YOKEL,
RUSTIC
dance .... HAY, REEL
dance: Brit. .... COVERLEY
fellow .... CORYDON
gallant/lad .... SWAIN
gentleman .... ESQUIRE,
COVERLEY
girl .... WENCH, PHILLIS,
PHYLLIS
house .... VILLA, CASINO,
HACIENDA
house, of a .... VILLATIC
in law .... PAIS
in the city .... RUS IN URBE
live in the .... RUSTICATE
middle region .... INLAND,
MIDLAND, INTERIOR
of fable .... EL DORADO
of the .... RURAL
officially called principality
.... MONACO, ANDORRA,
LIECHTENSTEIN
on 38th parallel .... KOREA
open, flat .... CHAMPAIGN

open, wild .... WEALD
poetical .... CLIME
pudding .... SASS
social .... BEE, BARNDANCE
ways .... PATHS
countryman .... RUSTIC, CITIZEN,
  COMPATRIOT
countryside, of the ...... BUCOLIC
twosome .... HILL AND DALE
county ...... SEAT, SHIRE, DISTRICT
law officer .... SHERIFF
coup .... PLOY, GAMBIT, TACTIC,
  STRATEGY, (MASTER)STROKE
d'____ .... ETAT
de grace .... DEATH BLOW,
  LETHAL BLOW
de grace dagger
  .... MISERICORD(E)
reporter's .... BEAT, SCOOP
couple ...... DUO, TIE, FEW, DUAD,
  DYAD, JOIN, LINK, BRACE,
  PAIR, YOKE, CONNECT, UNITE,
  SEVERAL, TWO(SOME)
coupled .... JOINED, LINKED,
  PAIRED, TEAMED, DOUBLED,
  UNITED, GEMINATED
Couples author .... UPDIKE
couplet .... DISTICH
coupling for electric fixtures
  .... HICKEY
coupon ...... TICKET, CERTIFICATE
courage .... FACE, GALL, GRIT,
  SAND, CHEEK, HEART, NERVE,
  PLUCK, SPUNK, VALOR,
  METTLE, BRAVERY, BOLDNESS
loss of .... COLDFEET
man of .... HERO, DEMIGOD
pretended .... BRAVADO
slang ..... GUTS, CRUST, MOXIE
symbol of .... TIGER, BULLDOG
woman of .... HEROINE
courageous .... BOLD, BRAVE,
  PLUCKY, HARDY, SANDY,
  DARING, GRITTY, HEROIC,
  SPUNKY, VALIANT, DASHING,
  FEARLESS, STOUT(HEARTED)
slang .... GUTSY
courier .... RUNNER, POSTMAN,
  ESTAFETTE, MESSENGER
courlan .... LIMPKIN
course .... WAY, FLOW, PATH,
  MODE, CYCLE, PASSAGE,
  PROCESS, DIRECTION
athletics .... GYMNASTICS
cross-country run
  .... LANGLAUF
kind of .... GOLF, RACE
marker .... PYLON
meal ...... DISH, SALAD, VIAND,
  ENTREE
of action .... TACK,

PROCEDURE, PROCEEDING
of motion or action
  .... ROUTE, TRACK
of official papers
  .... CHANNELS
of study .... LESSONS,
  CURRICULUM
of travel .... ROUTE, ITINERARY
court .... WOO, HALL, FLIRT,
  CAJOLE, ROMANCE, PERISTYLE
action/case .... SUIT, CAUSE,
  LAWSUIT, LITIGATION
aggressively .... RUSH
assembly .... LEVEE
castle's .... BAILEY
central/entrance .... ATRIUM
challenge .... RECUSE
church ...... ROTA, CONSISTORY
crier/messenger .... BEADLE
crier's call .... OYES, OYEZ
criminal .... ASSIZE
decree .... ARRET, EDICT
decree, to issue a ...... ORDAIN
enclosed .... PARVIS
equity .... CHANCERY
favorite .... GRACIOSO
game .... SQUASH, TENNIS,
  HANDBALL, BADMINTON,
  BASKETBALL, RACQUETBALL
hale to .... SUE
hearing .... OYER
jurisdiction .... SOKE
manorial .... LEET
martial defendant .... AWOL,
  TRAITOR, DESERTER, MUTINEER
martial in the field
  .... DRUMHEAD
minutes .... ACTA
of a/pertaining to .... AULIC
of attendants .... RETINUE,
  FOLLOWING
of justice .... BAR, BENCH,
  TRIBUNAL
of law .... FORUM
official ...... DA, JUDGE, FISCAL,
  JURIST, BAILIFF, JUSTICE,
  REFEREE, ATTORNEY
order ..... WRIT, ARRET, EDICT,
  DECREE, SUMMONS,
  MANDAMUS, SUBPOENA
order extract .... ESTREAT
panel .... JURY
proceeding .... TRIAL, HEARING
room routine .... OATH
ruling, plea for .... MOTION
session .... ASSIZE, HEARING
summons .... CITATION,
  SUBPOENA
writ .... OYER, SUMMONS,
  SUBPOENA
courted, old style .... SPARK

courteous .... CIVIL, POLITE,
  REFINED, URBANE, AMIABLE,
  AFFABLE, CORDIAL, GRACIOUS
regard .... RESPECT,
  DEFERENCE
courtesan .... THAIS, HARLOT,
  WHORE, PROSTITUTE
courtesy .... FAVOR, GRACE,
  POLISH, CHIVALRY, CIVILITY,
  COMITY, COMPLIMENT,
  POLITENESS
courtier .... PUFFER, TOUTER,
  TOADY, FLATTERER
courtly .... AULIC, SUAVE,
  REFINED, ELEGANT, POLISHED
courtship .... SUIT, PLIGHT,
  WOOING, PURSUIT
dance .... CUECA
result of, usually
  .... WEDDING, MARRIAGE
through singing ..... SERENADE
Courtship of Miles _____
  .... STANDISH
courtyard .... PATIO, ATRIUM,
  SQUARE, QUADRANGLE
sunken .... AREAWAY
cousin .... COS, COZ, KIN
busby's .... SHAKO
ferret's .... POLECAT
gnome's .... ELF
kind of .... ONCE REMOVED,
  TWICE REMOVED
pewit's .... LARK
Cousteau's challenge .... OCEAN
couteau .... DAGGER
couturier ...... STYLIST, DESIGNER,
  DRESSMAKER
fabric of .... LACE, LAME,
  SILK, SOIE, VELVET
famed .... DIOR, ADOLFO,
  CHANEL, NORELL, BALMAIN,
  CASSINI, BERGDORF,
  GIVENCHY, GERNREICH, ST.
  LAURENT, BALENCIAGA,
  MAINBOCHER
cove .... BAY, HOLE, NOOK, INLET,
  LAGOON
covenant .... BOND, PACT,
  CONTRACT, AGREEMENT,
  TESTAMENT
Coventry, goddess of .... GODIVA
cover .... LID, TOP, HIDE, COAT,
  CAP, ROOF, WHELM, CANOPY,
  ENCASE, SHEATHE,
  ENVELOP(E)
a certain hole .... DARN,
  PATCH
bottle .... CAP, CROWN
break .... EMERGE
detachable .... BINDER
face .... MASK, VEIL

for a bushing .... SLEEVE
girl .... PIN UP, MODEL
hard .... PLATE, SHELL,
                        CARAPACE
inner surface .... PAD, LINE
lap .... RUG
leg .... PUTTEE, LEGGING,
                        CHAUSSES
nipa .... THATCH
ornamental .... SHAM
pie's .... RIND, CRUST
protective .... ARMOR, HELMET,
              SHELL, CARAPACE
superficial .... VENEER
thickly .... SMOTHER
thin .... VENEER
thinly .... SKIM
top wall .... CEIL, COPING,
                       CAPSTONE
under .... HIDDEN, SECRET
up .... HIDE, INTER, CONCEAL
with asphalt .... PAVE
with cloth .... DRAPE
with feathers .... FLEDGE
with jewels .... BEGEM
with moisture .... BEDEW
with plaster .... CEIL
with trappings ...... CAPARISON
coverage, insurance .... RISK
covered .... CARPETED
colonnade .... STOA
entrance .... PORCH
garden .... HOTHOUSE
portico .... GALLERY
vehicle .... VAN
wagon .... SCHOONER,
                      CONESTOGA
walk .... MALL, STOA, ARCADE,
     GALLERY, PORTICO, CLOISTER
with blood .... GORY,
                      HEMATOSE
with bristles .... HISPID
with climbers .... IVIED
with fine feathers ...... DOWNY
with flakes .... SCURFY,
                      LEPIDOTE
with frost .... RIMY
with hair .... HISPID, PILOSE,
                      TOMENTOSE
with leaves .... FOLIOSE
covering .... GARB, SHIELD,
         TEGMEN, SHEATHE,
         OBSCURING, TEGUMENT,
              INTEGUMENT
against the sun .... SHADE,
   PARASOL, SHELTER, UMBRELLA
floor .... TILE, BOARDS,
     CARPET, TILING, LINOLEUM
for concealment .... MASK,
   VEIL, BLINDAGE, CAMOUFLAGE
gloomy .... PALL

glossy/shiny .... SHEEN
head .... CAP, HAT, HOOD,
     BERET, BONNET, HELMET
house .... ROOFING, ROOFTOP
material .... TILE, ADOBE,
   PATCH, ASPHALT, PLASTER,
     CEMENT, CONCRETE,
                   WALLPAPER
membrane of ovary
                         TUNICA
of clouds .... OVERCAST
of faults or defects
                   WHITEWASH
of reeds .... THATCH
of the skin .... CUTICLE,
                     EPIDERMIS
protective .... MAIL, ARMOR,
              SHELL, LORICA
teeth .... DENTINE
the works .... ENTIRE
thick .... CARPET
waterproof .... TARPAULIN
coverlet .... PALL, QUILT,
     BEDSPREAD, COUNTERPANE
covert .... PRIVY, ARCANE,
   HIDDEN, VEILED, SECRET,
     CLOUDED, CONCEALED
covertly .... UNDER-THE-TABLE
coverup .... WHITEWASH
covet .... ENVY, WANT, CRAVE,
                     DESIRE
covetous .... GREEDY, ENVIOUS,
                AVARICIOUS
covey .... BEVY, BROOD, FLOCK
cow .... BEEF, BOSS, VACA, BULLY,
     DAUNT, BOVINE, CRUMMY,
     CRUMMIE, FRIGHTEN,
     THREATEN, (OVER)AWE,
                INTIMIDATE
ad/famous .... ELSIE
barn .... BYRE, STABLE
breed .... ANGUS, DEVON,
     JERSEY, KERRY, DEXTER,
     GUERNSEY, HEREFORD
call/sound .... LOW, MOO
catcher .... LASSO
cud .... RUMEN
dewlap of .... LAPPET
dialectic ..... CRITTER, CRITTUR
fat .... SUET, TALLOW
fish .... TORO
genus .... BOS
gland .... UDDER
headed deity .... ISIS
hornless .... MUL(L)EY
killer .... WASP
milking .... MILCH
pilot .... PINTANO
polled .... MUL(L)EY
sea .... DUGONG, MANATEE
tuberculosis of .... GRAPE

udder inflammation
                         GARGET
unbranded .... MAVERICK
young .... CALF, STIRK, HEIFER
coward .... SISSY, CRAVEN,
   SNEAK, DASTARD, POLTROON
colloquial .... YELLOW,
                     CHICKEN
descriptive of a/streak of a
                       YELLOW
Coward (Noel) show .... BITTER-
                       SWEET
song .... NINA
cowardice .... FEAR
symbol of ..... WHITE FEATHER
cowardly ...... CRAVEN, SNEAKING,
     DASTARDLY, SPINELESS
animal .... HY(A)ENA
knight of story .... FALSTAFF
person .... CUR, SISSY, CAITIFF,
     POLTROON, MAMA'S BOY
slang .... CHICKEN, SCAREDY-
                       CAT
cowbird .... TROUPIAL
cowboy .... HERDER, COWPOKE,
     LLANERO, BUCKAROO,
     BUCKAYRO, VAQUERO,
     HORSEMAN, WRANGLER,
   RANCHER(O), BRONCOBUSTER
Australian .... RINGER,
                     STOCKMAN
bed .... BUNK
big day of .... RODEO,
                       ROUNDUP
breeches .... CHAPS
concern of .... CATTLE
friend of/slang ...... PARD(NER)
habitat .... RANCH, RANGE,
                       PAMPAS
heel device .... SPUR
jacket .... CHAQUETA
kind of .... PUNCHER
original/legendary .... PECOS
                       BILL
overalls .... LEVIS
rope .... LASSO, REATA, RIATA,
                       LARIAT
saddlebag .... ALFORJA
show .... RODEO
South American/pampas
                       GAUCHO
trousers .... CHAPS,
                 CHAPARAJOS
cowcatcher .... FENDER
cowed .... TERRIFIED
cower .... QUAIL, CRINGE,
               CROUCH, SHRINK
cowering through fear .... FUNK
Cowes, sight in .... YACHTS
cowfish .... TORO, DUGONG,
     GRAMPUS, MANATEE

cowl .... CAPE, HOOD, AMICE, CLOAK
like headdress .... COUS, ALMUCE
cowlick .... TUFT, FORELOCK
cowpox .... VACCINIA
cows .... KINE
roundup of .... WRANGLE
cowslip .... BLUEBELL, MAYFLOWER
coxa .... HIP
coxcomb .... POP, DUDE, TOFF, DANDY
coy .... SHY, TIMID, DEMURE, CHARY, MODEST, BASHFUL, RESERVED, RETIRING, DIFFIDENT
coyo .... AVOCADO
coyote .... WOLF
coypu .... NUTRIA, RODENT
coze .... CHAT, TALK
cozen .... CON, BILK, CHEAT, TRICK, DECEIVE
cozy .... SNUG, WARM, CHATTY, HOM(E)Y, COMFORTABLE
retreat .... DEN, NEST, NOOK
crab .... NAG, CARP, CRANK, GRIPE, SHELLFISH, HORSESHOE, MALACOSTRACAN
apple .... SCRAB
claw .... CHELA, NIPPER, PINC(H)ER
constellation/sign of the Zodiac .... CANCER
feeler/sense organ .... ANTENNA
front of .... METOPE
kind of .... BLUE, HERMIT, FIDDLER, DUNGENESS
king .... LIMULUS, LIMULOID
larva .... ZOEA
like a .... CANCROID
mantis .... SQUILLA
one's act .... RUIN, FRUSTRATE
Scottish .... PARTAN
shell .... TEST
upper shell of .... CARAPACE
walk of ...... SIDLE, SIDEWAYS, SIDEWISE
crabbed .... CRAMPED, SQUEEZED, IRREGULAR
handwriting .... ILLEGIBLE
crabby .... EDGY, CROSS, PEEVISH, GROUCHY, ILL-TEMPERED
crabfish .... GRAMPLE
Crabtree, actress .... LOTTA
crack ...... POP, REND, RIFT, SNAP, FLAW, BREAK, BURST, CHINK, QUIP, CLEFT, SPLIT, CREVICE
colloquial ...... SKILLED, FIRST-RATE

deep/glacier .... CREVASSE
down on .... GAG, CENSOR, ASSAULT, SILENCE
filler .... GROUT
in a bone .... FRACTURE
open, as the skin .... CHAP
seal .... CA(U)LK
shot .... MARKSMAN
slang .... TRY, JOKE, GIBE, ATTEMPT
up .... CRASH, COLLAPSE, BREAK DOWN
crackbrained .... CRAZY, NUTTY, INSANE, IDIOTIC
cracked wheat/oats ...... GROATS
cracker .... WAFER, POPPER, BISCUIT, BREAKER, SALTINE, SNAPPER
crackerjack .... ACE, WHIZ, NAILER, EXPERT, WIZARD
crackers, dish of .... PANADA
crackle .... SNAP, SPIT, CREPITATE
cracklings ...... SCRAPS, GREAVES
crackly .... CRISP
cracknel .... BISCUIT, GREAVES, CRACKLINGS
crackpot .... NUT, CRANK, LUNATIC, SCREWBALL
cracks, full of .... CHOPPY, CHAPPED
cracksman .... YEGG, BURGLAR
slang .... SAFECRACKER
cradle .... BED, CRIB, NEST, CRATE
in mining .... ROCKER
period .... INFANCY
song .... LULLABY
craft .... ART, BOAT, SHIP, CANOE, GUILE, SKILL, TRADE, TALENT, VESSEL, CUNNING, ARTIFICE, OCCUPATION
air .... AIRPLANE, DIRIGIBLE, HELICOPTER
harbor .... SCOW
union of old .... GUILD
water .... BOAT, SHIP, VESSEL
craftsman .... ARTIST, ARTISAN, ARTIFICER
chief .... MAESTRO
metal .... SMITH
crafty .... SLY, FOXY, WILY, ARTFUL, CLEVER, FELINE, SHIFTY, CUNNING, INSIDIOUS
crag .... TOR, ROCK, CLIFF, BOULDER, PRECIPICE
crake .... RAIL
cram .... JAM, BONE, PACK, TUCK, CHOKE, FORCE, STUDY, STUFF
cramp .... CROWD, SPASM, HAMPER, HINDER, CONFINE, CRIPPLE
neck .... KINK, CRICK

slang .... CHARLEY HORSE
crampfish .... TORPEDO
crampon ...... GRAPLIN, GRAPNEL
cranberry disease .... SCALD
crane ...... HERON, STORK, WADER, DERRICK, DEMOISELLE, RUBBERNECK
arm .... JIB
family .... GRUIDAE
framework .... GANTRY
genus .... GRUS
like bird .... CHUNGA, SERIEMA
lift by means of a .... HOIST
pertaining to .... GRUINE
relative .... BUSTARD
ship's .... DAVIT
sound .... CLANG
the neck ...... STRAIN, STRETCH
Crane, Ichabod, rival of .... (BROM) BONES
cranesbill .... GERANIUM
cranial nerve .... VAGUS
cranium .... SKULL
crank .... KEY, WHIM, QUIRK, TWIST, HANDLE, WINDER, CAPRICE
case reservoir .... OILPAN
colloquial ...... CRAB, GROUCH, QUEER, ODDBALL, CRACKPOT, ECCENTRIC
slang .... NUT, SCREWBALL
up .... TURN, WIND, START
cranky .... CROSS, QUEER, GROUCHY, IRRITABLE
cranny .... CHINK, CREVICE
partner of .... NOOK
crap .... DUNG, JUNK, STOOL, TRASH
in dice .... BOXCAR
out .... LOSE
slang .... HOGWASH, NONSENSE, POPPYCOCK, BULL(SHIT)
craps ...... DICE, (GAMBLING)GAME
"come out" number .... SEVEN, ELEVEN
losing number at first throw .... TWO, THREE, TWELVE
shooter .... GAMBLER
shooter's "four" .... JOE, CATER
shooter's throw .... ROLL
throw .... DIE
crape .... WEED, WEEPER
crapehanger .... PESSIMIST
crappie .... SUNFISH
crash .... FALL, BLAST, BREAK, BURST, SMASH, COLLIDE, SHATTER, COLLAPSE, COLLISION
crass ...... CRUDE, GAUDY, GROSS,

ROUGH, COARSE, STUPID, VULGAR

Cratchit's job .... CLERK

crate .... BOX, PACK, BASKET, CASE, ENCASE, HAMPER

maker .... CASER

slang .... JALOPY

crater .... PIT, HOLE, CAVITY, MOUTH, CALDERA, OPENING

lunar .... LINNE

one with .... VOLCANO

cravat .... ASCOT, SCARF, (NECK)TIE, OVERLAY

fabric .... REP

hangman's .... NOOSE

ornament .... STICKPIN

crave .... BEG, NEED, PRAY, SEEK, LONG FOR, COVET, YEARN, HANKER

craven ...... AFRAID, COWARD(LY)

person .... SISSY, CAITIFF, DASTARD, POLTROON

craving ...... YEN, MANIA, DESIRE, HUNGER, THIRST, APPETITE, APPETENCE, OBSESSION

craw .... MAW, CROP, BELLY, GULLET, GIZZARD

crawl .... LAG, INCH, DRAG, CREEP, GROVEL, SLITHER

crawler ...... BABY, WORM, SNAIL, SNAKE, REPTILE

crawling .... PACKED, DRAPED, REPENT, REPTANT, TEEMING, COWERING, CRINGING

crayfish egg .... BERRY

segment .... METAMERE

crayon .... CHALK, PENCIL, CHARCOAL

pastel .... PASTILLE

picture .... PASTEL

craze .... FAD, RAGE, FUROR, MANIA, FASHION, OBSESSION

play/exercise .... HULA-HOOP

women's style .... PANTSUIT, MINISKIRT

crazed .... DAFT, RABID, CUCKOO, INSANE, DEMENTED, MAD(DENED), DERANGED

crazy .... MAD, BUGS, DAFT, LUNY, NUTS, DOTTY, KOOKY, LOONY, POTTY, CUCKOO, INSANE, RABID, KOOKIE, CRACKED

bird .... LOON

person .... MANIAC, LUNATIC, PSYCHOPATH

slang .... LOCO, WACKY, PSYCHO, BANANAS, BONKERS

to kill .... AMOK, AMUCK, BERSERK

creak .... CHIRK, CRICK, GRATE,

SCROOP, SQUEAK

cream .... BEST, GIST, ELITE, PASTE

cleansing .... COLD CREAM, TOOTHPASTE

colored .... ECRU, BEIGE, IVORY, STRAW, OCHERY

cosmetic .... LOTION, SHAMPOO, FACE CREAM

of the crop .... PRIME, CHOICE, CHOSEN, THE BEST

ointment .... SALVE, POMADE

puff .... PASTRY

separator .... CENTRIFUGE

slang .... THRASH

creamy white ...... MILKY, IVORY

crease .... DENT, FOLD, LINE, MARK, MUSS, RUCK, RUGA, RIDGE, RIMPLE, RUMPLE, WRINKLE

creased .... RUGATE, PLEATED

create .... FORM, MAKE, DESIGN, BREED, DEVISE, INVENT, COMPOSE, PRODUCE, ORIGINATE

interest .... DRUM UP

creation .... WORK, COSMOS, GENESIS, PRODUCT, INVENTION

God's .... UNIVERSE

greatest .... MASTERPIECE

creative .... INVENTIVE

writing .... POEM, NOVEL, POETRY, FICTION

creator .... MAKER, AUTHOR, DESIGNER

of an Alice .... ALBEE

of Muppet .... HENSON

of Uncle Remus .... HARRIS

of 007 .... (IAN)FLEMING

Creator, the .... GOD

creature .... MAN, TOOL, BEAST, SLAVE, THING, ANIMAL, MORTAL, PERSON, (HUMAN)BEING

small, imaginary ..... GREMLIN

creche figure .... LAMB, MAGI, MARY, INFANT, JOSEPH, SHEPHERD

part .... CRIB, MANGER

crecopia .... MYTH

credence .... FAITH, TRUST, BELIEF, CREDIT, SURETY, MISSAL STAND

credential .... VOUCHER, AUTHORITY, REFERENCE, CERTIFICATE

credentials .... BADGE, ID CARD

military .... DOG TAG

credenza ...... BUFFET, SIDEBOARD

credibility ...... TRUTH, VERACITY

credible .... LIKELY, TRUSTY, LOGICAL, RELIABLE, PLAUSIBLE, BELIEVABLE

credit .... LOAN, HONOR, TRUST, CHARGE, REBATE, ASCRIBE, BELIEVE, ATTRIBUTE

card organization .... BANKS, DINER'S CLUB

colloquial .... TICK

financial .... BORROWING POWER

for achievement .... KUDOS

creditable ...... HONEST, ETHICAL, CREDIBLE

creditor .... DEBTEE, LENDER, MORTGAGEE, NOTE HOLDER

annoying, insistent .... DUNNER

avaricious .... USURER, LOAN SHARK

exacting .... SHYLOCK

credo .... CREED, TENET, BELIEF

credulous .... GULLIBLE

creed, one such .... NICENE

political .... ISM, DOXY

creek ...... BAY, RIA, KILL, BAYOU, BROOK, INLET, INDIAN, STREAM

creel .... BASKET

user .... ANGLER, FISHERMAN

creep .... FAWN, INCH, CRAWL, SLINK, CRINGE, SLITHER

slang .... DRIP

up on .... SNEAK

creeper .... IVY, VINE, SNAIL, SNAKE

creeping .... REPENT, REPTANT, CRAWLING

charlie, for one .... WEED

plant .... IVY, BINE, VINE, LIANA

creeps, the .... FEAR, HATE, DISGUST, AVERSION, REVULSION

creepy .... EERIE, CRAWLY

creese .... CRIS, KRIS, DAGGER

cremate .... BURN, INCINERATE

cremation .... BURNING, INCINERATION

Hindu .... SUTTEE

crematory .... FURNACE, CINERATOR

Cremona .... AMATI, VIOLIN, STRAD(IVARIUS)

river .... ADDA

violin maker .... AMATI, GUARNERI

crenate .... NOTCHED, SCALLOPED

crenel .... EMBRASURE

crenelate .... NOTCH

Creole ancestry .... FRENCH,

SPANISH
and Indian .... MESTIZO
milieu .... NEW ORLEANS
patois .... GOMBO, GUMBO
rice cake .... CALA
State .... LOUISIANA
creosol .... ANTISEPTIC
crepe suzette .... PANCAKE,
FLAPJACK
crepitate .... RATTLE, CRACKLE
crepuscle .... DUSK, TWILIGHT
crescendo ...... EXPAND, AMPLIFY,
INCREASE
in music .... FORTE, STACCATO
crescent .... CURVE, HALF-CIRCLE,
SCYTHE, SEMI-CIRCLE
moons .... MENISCI
of a .... HORN, BICORN
point of .... CUSP
shape figure .... LUNE,
LUNULA, LUNULE, MENISCUS,
HORSESHOE
shaped .... LUNE, BICORN,
LUNATE, LUNULAR, DEMILUNE,
(SEMI)LUNAR
crescive .... GROWING, INCREASING
cress .... HERB, SALAD, GARNISH
cresset .... TORCH, LANTERN
Cressida's lover .... TROILUS
crest .... CAP, TOP, ACME, APEX,
PEAK, CROWN, RIDGE,
HELMET
a kind of helmet .... TUFT
clergyman's .... CALOTTE
cock's/rooster's .... COMB,
COCKSCOMB
mountain .... ARETE
of bird/fowl .... COMB, CRISTA,
CARUNCLE
wave's .... WHITECAP
crested .... CROWNED, PILEATE,
CORONET(T)ED, CRISTATE(D)
parrot .... COCKATOO,
COCKATEEL, COCKATIEL
royalty .... KING, QUEEN,
MONARCH, SOVEREIGN
crestfallen ...... GLUM, DEJECTED,
HUMBLED, DOWNCAST,
CHAPFALLEN, DISCOURAGED
creta .... CHALK
cretaceous .... CHALKY
Cretan .... MINOAN, CANDIAN
Crete .... KRITI
born painter/sculptor .... EL
GRECO, DOMENIKOS
cape .... KRIOS, SPATHA,
SIDHEROS
capital/seaport .... CANEA,
KHANIA
city/town .... SITIA, SPILI,
VAMOS, ANOYIA, MOIRAI,

KANDANOS, KISSAMOS,
LERAPETRA, KASTELLION,
RETHIMNON, TIMBAKION
escapee .... ICARUS
former name of .... CANDIA
Greek name of .... KRETE,
IRAKLION
guard/watchman of ..... TALOS
gulf .... KHANIA, MESARA,
MERABELLOU
king .... MINOS, IDOMENEUS
King Minos' wife
.... PASIPHAE
mountain .... IDA, IDHI,
SFAKION
mythical beast/monster
.... MINOTAUR
mythical monster's killer
.... THESEUS
mythical monster's mother
.... PASIPHAE
mythical structure
.... LABYRINTH
mythical structure's builder
.... DAEDALUS
princess .... ARIADNE
cretin .... IDIOT, MORON,
SIMPLETON
cretinism .... IDIOCY, MONGOLISM,
RETARDATION
cretonne .... TOILE
crevasse .... PIT, HOLE, ABYSS,
CHASM, SPLIT, FISSURE
crevice .... CHINK, CLEFT,
CRANNY, FISSURE
crevices, full of .... CHINKY,
RIMOSE, FISSURED
crew .... MOB, BAND, GANG, HELP,
TEAM, BUNCH, CROWD,
FORCE, GROUP, STAFF,
COMPANY
member .... OAR, HAND, HIRED
HELP
member, flight .... PILOT,
NAVIGATOR, STEWARD(ESS)
of ship, full ...... COMPLEMENT
relief .... RELAY, RESERVES,
SECOND TEAM
crewel .... YARN
crib .... BED, BIN, BOX, PAD,
PONY, RACK, BOOTH,
MANGER, STALL, TROUGH,
PLAGIARIZE
baby's .... CRADLE
colloquial .... GYP, CHEAT,
FORGE, GOUGE, STEAL
content of .... FODDER
for storing grain .... SILO,
GRANARY
in writing .... PLAGIARISM
worker .... TOOLMAN

cribbage .... CARD GAME
game lost .... LURCH
score .... NOBS, PEGS
crick .... KINK, CRAMP
cricket ...... GRIG, HOOP, CICADA,
INSECT, FOOTSTOOL
bowled ball .... YORKER
club .... BAT
colloquial .... FAIR PLAY
equipment .... BAT, BALL,
WICKET
family .... GRYLLIDAE
inning unplayed .... WICKET
like insect/relative of
.... LOCUST, GRASSHOPPER
positions .... SILLY LEGS
score .... BYE
sound .... CHIRP
team .... ELEVEN
term .... (TICE)BYE
crier .... WAILER, MUEZZIN,
HUCKSTER
crime .... SIN, EVIL, GUILT,
WRONG, BREACH, MISDEED,
OFFENSE, OUTRAGE,
VIOLATION, WRONGDOING,
MALEFACTION
against king .... LESE MAJESTE
against the IRS .... INCOME
TAX EVASION
high ...... TREASON, ESPIONAGE
major .... RAPE, ARSON,
FELONY, MURDER, KIDNAPPING
minor .... MISDEMEANOR
of encroaching on rights,
patents, etc.
.... INFRACTION, INFRINGEMENT
of stealing money by fraud
.... EMBEZZLEMENT
organized .... UNDERWORLD
sophisticated .... CAPER
story question ...... WHODUNIT
syndicate .... MAFIA, COSA
NOSTRA
syndicate member
.... MAFIOSO
where committed .... VENUE
Crimea 1945 Conference site
.... YALTA
Crimean city .... YALTA,
SEVASTOPOL
lamb's fur .... CRIMMER,
KRIMMER
river .... ALMA
sea .... AZOF
seaport .... KERCH, YALTA
strait .... KERCH
criminal .... YEGG, FELON,
OUTLAW, CULPRIT, CONVICT,
SINNER, IMMORAL, GANGSTER,
EVILDOER, OFFENDER,

MISCREANT, WRONGDOER, MALEFACTOR, MALFEASANT
act .... JOB, CRIME
burning .... ARSON
charge .... RAP
colloquial .... CROOK, LOSER
conditional freedom of
.... PAROLE
conditional release of
.... PROBATION
dangerous .... DESPERADO
habitual .... ROUNDER, SCOFFLAW, RECIDIVIST
lawyer: sl. .... MOUTHPIECE
mark of a .... STIGMA
slang .... HOOD, MOBSTER
unreconstructed .... RECIDIVIST
who purposely burns
property .... ARSONIST
criminals collectively
.... FELONRY
crimp .... CURL, FOLD, WAVE, BUNCH, FLUTE, PINCH, PLEAT, PLAIT, GATHER, GOFFER, CRINKLE
crimple .... NOTCH, WRINKLE
crimson .... RED, BLOODY, MADDER, CARMINE
Crimson's rival .... YALE
cringe ...... FAWN, COWER, STOOP, CRAWL, QUAIL, WINCE, CROUCH, FLINCH, GROVEL, SHRINK
crinkle ...... FOLD, CRIMP, CREASE, CRUMPLE, WRINKLE
crinkled paper/cloth .... CREPE
crinkly .... WAVY, CORRUGATED
crinoid .... SEA LILY
crinoline .... PETTICOAT, (HOOP)SKIRT
cripple .... HURT, LAME, MAIM, DISABLE, HAMSTRING, PARALYZE
a horse .... HOCK
of Lepanto .... CERVANTES
walking aid .... CANE, CRUTCH
cripples .... (THE) HALT
patron saint of .... (ST)GILES
crisis ...... PINCH, TRIAL, CRUNCH, EMERGENCY, TURNING POINT
of disease .... SOLUTION
crisp .... CURT, WAVY, CRUMP, FIRM, BLUNT, PITHY, STIFF, BRITTLE, CRUNCHY, ANIMATED
biscuit .... SNAP, CRACKER
crisper .... CURLER
cristate(d) .... CRESTED
crisscross .... MESH, BRAID, MATTED, CROSSING, TRANSVERSE

criterion ...... NORM, RULE, TEST, CANON, GAUGE, MODEL, MEASURE, STANDARD
critic .... CARPER, EXPERT, CENSOR, SLATER, CENSURER, JUDGE, REVIEWER, FAULTFINDER
Clive .... BARNES
disapproval of a .... PAN(NING)
inferior .... CRITICASTER
literary .... REVIEWER
loud .... HOOTER
"missile" of, literally
.... EGG, TOMATO
Reed .... REX
uninhibited ..... BOOER, HISSER
work of .... CRITIQUE, REVIEW(ER)
critical .... ACUTE, RISKY, URGENT, CAPTIOUS, CRUCIAL, EXIGENT, EXACTING, DECISIVE, CENSORIOUS
analysis .... EXEGESIS
mark .... OBELUS
moment .... CRUX, CRISIS, ZERO HOUR
situation .... CLUTCH
writing .... SATIRE, LAMPOON
criticism .... NOTICE, REMARK, REPORT, REVIEW, COMMENT, DESCANT, ANALYSIS, CRITIQUE, EXEGETICS
abusive .... DIATRIBE
adverse: colloq. .... PAN
colloquial .... WRITE-UP
hostile .... FLAK, SLAM
criticize .... RAP, DAMN, FLAY, SLAM, BLAME, SLASH, SLATE, JUDGE, OPPUGN, REVIEW, CENSURE, BLAST, CONDEMN, NITPICK, REPROVE, DENOUNCE, ANIMADVERT
satirically .... ROAST
severely .... SCORE, BERATE
slang .... PAN, RAKE, BADMOUTH
critique .... REVIEW, SUMMARY, EPICRISIS, COMMENTARY
croak .... CROUP, GRUMBLE
slang .... DIE
croaker ...... CROW, FROG, RAVEN, SQUETEAGUE
croaking .... RAUCOUS
Croat .... SLAV
Croatian capital .... ZAGREB
native .... CROAT
necktie/scarf .... CRAVAT
soldier .... PANDOUR
croc .... CROCODILE
crochet .... KINK, KNIT(TING)
crock ...... JAR, POT, SMUT, SOOT,

SHARD, POTSHERD
crockery ...... JARS, POTS, DISHES, POTTERY, CERAMICS
Crockett, frontiersman
.... DAVEY, DAVID
place of heroism .... ALAMO
crocodile .... YACARE, REPTILE, SAURIAN
bird .... PLOVER, TROCHILUS
for short .... CROC
India/Malaysia .... GAVIAL, MUGGAR, MUGGER, MUGGUR
Philippine .... BUAYA
relative ..... CAIMAN, CAYMAN, ALLIGATOR
teeth picker .... TROCHILUS
Crocodile River .... LIMPOPO
crocus .... IRIS
bulb .... CORM
color .... SAFFRON
croft .... FARM
croissant .... ROLL
cromlech .... TOMB, DOLMEN, MEGALITH, MONUMENT
Cromwell (Oliver), army of
.... IRONSIDES
sobriquet .... IRONSIDES
title .... LORD PROTECTOR
victory site .... NASEBY
crone .... HAG, ANILE, WITCH, BELDAM(E), CARLINE
Cronus .... TITAN, SATURN
parent .... GAEA, URANUS
sister of .... TETHYS
son of .... ZEUS
crony .... PAL, CHUM, BUDDY, COHORT, COMPEER, CONFRERE
cronyism .... FAVORITISM
Cronyn, actor .... HUME
crook .... BEND, HOOK, CURVE
bishop's .... CROSIER
colloquial .... THIEF, CHEAT(ER), ROBBER, SWINDLER
in tree branch .... KNEE
crooked .... AGEE, AWRY, BENT, ASKEW, TIPSY, CURVED, FALSE, ZIGZAG, WINDING, DEVIOUS, TORTUOUS, DISHONEST
slang .... COCKEYED
croon .... HUM, SING
crop .... MAW, CLIP, CRAW, FRUIT, YIELD, GIZZARD, HARVEST, PRODUCT
animal feed .... FODDER
picker .... GATHERER
riding .... WHIP
up again .... RECUR
cropper .... FARMER, PEASANT, SHEARER

colloquial .... RUIN, FAILURE
croquet .... (OUTDOOR) GAME
equipment .... HOOPS, MALLET,
WOODEN BALL
handicap .... BISQUE
kind of .... ROQUE
wicket .... ARCH
croquette .... CUTLET
Crosby .... BOB, BING, GARY
crooner's soubriquet .... THE
GROANER
crosier ...... CANE, CROOK, CROSS,
SCEPTER, (PASTORAL) STAFF
cross .... EDGY, FOIL, SPAN,
SURLY, TESTY, CRANKY,
OPPOSE, THWART, PEEVISH,
LIVERISH, FRACTIOUS
as a Christian symbol
.... CRUCIFIX
bearer/carrier .... CRUCIFER
between a skirt and shorts
.... SKORT
between broccoli and
cauliflower
.... BROCCOFLOWER
between tangerine and
orange .... TANGOR
breed .... HYBRIDIZE
by wading/a river .... FORD
church .... ROOD
country highway, major
.... INTERSTATE
country runner .... HARRIER
country skiing ...... LANGLAUF
current .... RIP(TIDE)
cut .... SAWN
decoration ..... IRON, VICTORIA
each other .... INTERSECT
Egyptian .... ANKH
examination, of ...... ELENCTIC
examine .... GRILL,
INTERROGATE
eye(d) .... SQUINT,
STRABISMAL, STRABISMUS
fertilization .... XENOGAMY
grained .... CONTRARY
horizontal beam ..... TRANSOM
in heraldry/Southern .... CRUX
inscription .... INRI
mark X
off/out .... CANCEL, DELE(TE)
question .... EXAMINE
reference .... NOTATE
shaped .... CRUCIAL,
CRUCIFORM
stroke .... SERIF
up .... CONFUSE, DECEIVE
crossbar .... RUNG
crossbeam .... TRAVE, TREVE,
TRANSOM
crossbill .... FINCH

genus .... LOXIA
crossbow .... ARBALEST
missile .... BOLT, QUARREL
crossbreed .... HYBRID, MONGREL
crossed .... DEFIED, FOILED,
MARKED, OPPOSED,
THWARTED, FRUSTRATED
star .... TRAGIC, ILL-FATED
crossette .... ANCON
crosspiece ...... RUNG, SILL, SPAR,
CLEAT, LINTEL, TRANSOM
crossruff in whist .... SEESAW
crossthreads .... WOOF
crosswise .... TRANSVERSE
crossword puzzle brew ...... ALE
inventor of .... ARTHUR
WYNNE
crotchet .... HOOK, CAPRICE
half of a .... QUAVER
crotchety person .... CRANK,
GROUCH, CURMUDGEON
croton bug .... COCKROACH
crouch .... BOW, BEND, COWER,
STOOP, CRINGE
crouching position .... SQUAT
croup .... ANGINA, CATARRH,
CRUPPER
horse's .... RUMP
crouse .... BOLD, PERT, BRISK,
LIVELY
crouton .... SIPPET
crow .... CAW, BRAG, ROOK,
CRAKE, GLOAT, (JACK)DAW,
BLACKBIRD
constellation/genus
.... CORVUS
cry .... CAW
eat .... RECANT, HUMBLE
ONESELF
European, white-spotted
.... NUTCRACKER
flight route of .... DIRECT,
STRAIGHT
hooded .... GRAYBACK
Indian .... SIOUX
kin .... JAY
like a/of .... CORVINE
like bird ...... RAVEN, CHOUGH,
ORIOLE
over a victory .... BOAST,
EXULT
people .... ABSAROKE
crowbar ...... PRY, JEMMY, JIMMY,
LEVER, EXTRACTOR
crowd .... JAM, MOB, CRAM,
GANG, HOST, MASS, ROUT,
DROVE, FLOCK, HORDE,
PRESS, SERRY, SHOVE,
THRONG, CONCOURSE,
GATHERING, MULTITUDE
busy .... HIVE

close together .... HERD,
HUDDLE
colloquial .... SET, CLIQUE
every which way .... MILL
fancier .... DIP, ACTOR,
PICKPOCKET
in .... ENTER, INTRUDE
moving .... SWARM
number .... THREE
_____ (popular athletes)
.... PLEASERS
crowded .... DENSE, COMPACT,
SERRIED, TEEMING, JAM-
PACKED
crower .... BABY, COCK, BOASTER,
ROOSTER, BRAGGART
crowfoot flower .... PEONY
crown .... TOP, COIN, HEAD, PATE,
ADORN, CREST, DIADEM,
INVEST, INSTALL, WREATHE,
TREE-TOP, CORONATE,
ENTHRONE
bottle .... CAP
cock's .... COMB
Egyptian .... ATEF
for a tooth, artificial .... CAP
head's .... POLL
in botany .... CORONA
in zoology .... CREST
jewel .... TIARA
prince .... DAUPHIN,
HEIR(APPARENT)
prince, English .... CHARLES
prince, Japanese .... NARUHITO
slang .... CONK
small .... CIRCLET, CORONET
sun's .... AUREOLA, AUREOLE
victory .... PRIZE, LAUREL,
AWARD, TROPHY, GARLAND
crowning .... ULTIMATE
ceremony .... INVESTITURE
touch .... CLINCHER,
DEATHBLOW
crow's feet .... EYE WRINKLES
nest .... LOOKOUT
crowtoe .... BUTTERCUP
crucial .... SEVERE, TRYING,
URGENT, CRITICAL, DECISIVE
point .... CRUX, CRISIS
spot in game .... SET-POINT
crucible .... TEST, CRUSE, TRIAL,
ORDEAL, CALDRON, FIREPOT,
MELTING POT
crucifix .... ROOD, CROSS, SYMBOL
crucifixion, place of Jesus'
.... CALVARY
crucify .... FLOG, HANG, KILL,
WHIP, THRASH, BUTCHER,
EXECUTE, MORTIFY, TORMENT,
TORTURE
crude .... RAW, BARE, RUDE,

CRASS, GROSS, PLAIN, ROUGH,
COARSE, VULGAR, LOWBRED,
SKETCHY, UNCOUTH,
AGRESTIC, UNREFINED
bed .... DOSS
metal .... ORE
people .... YAHOOS
person .... BOOR
Scottish .... RANDY
shed .... LEAN-TO
sugar .... MELADA, PANOCHA
writing .... GRAFFITI
cruel .... MEAN, HARSH, STONY,
BRUTAL, SAVAGE, UNKIND,
BESTIAL, BRUTISH, CAUSTIC,
PITILESS, RUTHLESS, SPITEFUL,
HEARTLESS, COLDBLOODED
behavior .... BEASTLINESS
pleasure-seeker .... SADIST
ruler .... DESPOT, TYRANT
cruet ...... VIAL, CASTER, CASTOR,
AMPULLA
cruise .... ROAM, COAST, VOYAGE,
WANDER, JOURNEY
cruller .... DONUT, DOUGHNUT,
(FRIED)CAKE
crumb ...... BIT, JOT, ORT, SCRAP,
MORSEL, FRAGMENT,
PARTICLE
ore .... SPALL
crumble .... DECAY, BREAK UP,
MO(U)LDER, DISINTEGRATE
easy to .... FRIABLE
crummy .... LOW, SHABBY,
INFERIOR
crumple .... RUCK, CRUSH,
BUCKLE, WRINKLE, COLLAPSE
crunch .... CHEW, CHAMP, CRUSH,
GRIND, MUNCH
cruor .... GORE, BLOOD
crus .... SHIN, SHANK
crusade .... CAUSE, DRIVE,
MISSION, CAMPAIGN,
MOVEMENT
Moslem .... JEHAD, JIHAD
crusader ...... CATALYST, PILGRIM,
TANCRED, TEMPLAR,
REFORMER
King Richard .... LION-
HEART(ED)
crusaders' foe .... SALADIN,
SARACEN
leader .... TANCRED
objective .... REFORM(S)
port .... ACRE
crush .... JAM, BRAY, GRIND,
PRESS, QUASH, QUELL,
SHAME, SQUASH, SUBDUE,
CONQUER, SQUEEZE,
SUPPRESS, OVERCOME,
VANQUISH, OVERWHELM

colloquial .... LOVE,
INFATUATION
into fine particles
.... TRITURATE
to softness .... MASH
underfoot .... TRAMPLE
with mortar, pestle .... BRUISE
with teeth .... CHEW
crushed, as a fabric ...... ECRASE
sugarcane refuse .... BAGASSE,
MEGASS(E)
crushing defeat .... WATERLOO
Crusoe's creator .... DEFOE
crust .... LOAF, RIND, SCAB,
BREAD, SHELL, COATING
fruit-filled .... DUMPLING
metal .... PATINA
slang .... GALL, CHEEK, NERVE,
AUDACITY, INSOLENCE
crustacean .... CRAB, PRAWN,
ISOPOD, SHRIMP, LOBSTER,
COPEPOD, LIMULUS, PAGURID,
PAGURIAN, SCHIZOPOD
burrowing .... SQUILLA,
MANTIS CRAB
claw .... CHELA
covering .... SHELL
eggs .... ROE, CORAL
feeler .... ANTENNA
horny substance .... CHITIN
limb of .... PLEOPOD
parasitic .... BARNACLE,
CIRRIPED
regal .... KING CRAB
segment .... SOMITE, TELSON
skin secretion .... CHITIN
spawn .... ROE, CORAL
10-legged ..... PRAWN, SHRIMP,
DECAPOD, LOBSTER,
MACRURAN
walking and swimming
.... SHRIMP, AMPHIPOD,
SANDFLEA
crusty ...... HARSH, HUFFY, SURLY,
TESTY, BRUSQUE, HARDENED,
ILL-TEMPERED
concoction .... PIE
pieces of bread .... HEELS
spot .... SCAB
crutch .... AID, PROP, STAFF,
SUPPORT, WALKING STICK
crux .... CROSS, PUZZLE
ansata .... ANKH
cry .... BEG, SOB, PULE, WAIL,
WEEP, YELP, SHOUT, CLAMOR,
WHINE, SCREAM
animal's .... BRAY
Australian .... COOEE, COOEY
baby .... MEWL
bacchanal/of Bacchantes
.... EVOE

companion of .... HUE
for .... PLEAD, DEMAND,
ENTREAT
harsh, loud .... SQUAWK
high-pitched/shrill .... SQUALL,
SQUEAL
hunter's .... TALLYHO
like crazy/loudly .... BAWL
loud and confused
.... HULLABALOO
mournful/dismal .... YOWL
of calf/goat .... BLEAT
of cheer ..... HOORAY, HURRAH
of child .... MEWL, PULE,
WHIMPER
of disapproval .... BOO, HISS,
HOOT, CATCALL
of pain .... OUCH
of surrender, 1918
.... KAMERAD
out .... YELL, EXCLAIM,
ULULATE, VOCIFERATE
party .... SLOGAN,
WATCHWORD, SHIBBOLETH
to the hounds .... YOICKS
wolf .... FALSE ALARM
crybaby .... SOFTY, WEAKLING,
POOR LOSER, POOR SPORT
cryogen .... REFRIGERANT
cryogenics .... PHYSICS
crypt .... TOMB, VAULT
cryptic .... OCCULT, SECRET,
OBSCURE, ENIGMATIC
cryptographer's stumper
.... CODE
cryptogram .... CODE, CIPHER,
CRYPTOGRAPH
crystal .... GEM, CLEAR, GLASS,
STONE, LIMPID, HEMITROPE
a tiny embryonic
.... CRYSTALLITE
clear .... LUCID, PLAIN,
OBVIOUS
gazer ...... SEER(ESS), PALMIST,
PREDICTOR
gazing .... PALMISTRY
like a .... CRYSTALLOID
pick-up .... DETECTOR
violet .... DYE, STAINER
Crystal, singer .... GAYLE
crystalline .... SHEER, GLASSY,
PELLUCID, DIAPHANOUS,
TRANSPARENT
alcohol .... CALCIFEROL
alkaloid .... AMARINE,
ATROPINE
and granular ...... SACCHAROID
biblical .... BDELLIUM
cloth .... GOSSAMER
compound .... SERINE,
BORAZON, CATECHOL,

CELESTINE

lined stone .... GEODE

material .... GAUZE

mineral .... FELDSPAR

moisture .... DEW

resin .... CANNABIN

salt .... BORAX

substance .... UREA,

CARBAZOLE

crystallize .... SET, JELL, HARDEN,

CONDENSE, SOLIDIFY,

CONGEAL, GRANULATE,

(TAKE)FORM, TAKE SHAPE

crystallized sugar/syrup

.... CANDY

ctenophores .... NUDA

cub .... WHELP, LIONET, NOVICE,

BEGINNER, YOUNGSTER

kind of .... REPORTER

Cub Scout group .... DEN

group leader .... AKELA, DEN

CHIEF

Cuba, U.S. base in

.... GUANTANAMO

cubage .... VOLUME

Cuban .... HABANERO

archipelago .... SABANA, LOS

CANARREOS, LOS COLORADOS

bay ...... PIGS(COCHINOS), NIPE,

HONDA, MAISI, JIGUEY,

PERROS, MATANZAS,

NUEVITAS, SIGUAMEA,

BUENAVISTA, GUANTANAMO

bearded one

.... (FIDEL)CASTRO

cape .... CRUZ, PEPE, FRANCES,

LUCRECIA, CORRIENTES

capital .... HAVANA

castle .... MORRO

cay .... COCO, LARGO,

FRAGOSO, GUAJABA, SABINAL,

CANTILES

cays .... CAYAMAS, GUZMANES,

SAN FELIPE, CINCO BALAS

channel ..... INDIOS, NICHOLAS,

CABALLONES, OLD BAHAMA

chess champ ..... CAPABLANCA

cigar .... HAVANA

city/town ...... MORON, REGLA,

BAYAMO, PERICO, HOLGUIN,

NIQUERO, PALMIRA,

CAMAGUEY, CARDENAS,

MARIANAO, MATANZAS,

REMEDIOS, TRINIDAD,

RANCHUELO, GUANTANAMO,

GUANABACOA, MANZANILLO,

MANICARAGUA, SANTA CLARA,

PALMA SORIANO, PINAR DEL

RIO, SANCTI SPIRITUS,

SANTIAGO DE CUBA

dance .... R(H)UMBA,

HABANERA

dictator .... CASTRO, BATISTA

discoverer .... COLUMBUS

drum .... BONGO

food fish .... PINTADO

gulf ...... CAZONES, BATABANO,

ANA MARIA, GUACANAYABO

island .... JUVENTUD

lagoon .... LECHE

language .... SPANISH

measure .... VARA, TAREA,

MEDIDA

measure for distance

.... MILLA, KILOMETRO

measure for grains

.... FANEGA

monetary unit .... PESO

mountain .... GRAN PIEDRA,

OJO DEL TORO, PICO

TURQUINO

mountains .... SIERRA

MAESTRA, CUCHILLAS DE TOA,

SIERRA DEL CRISTAL

music .... MAMBO

palm leaf .... CHIP

passage .... WINDWARD

peninsula .... ZAPATA,

GUANAHACABIBES

premier .... CASTRO

president .... MACHADO,

DORTICOS

province .... GRANMA,

HABANA, HOLGUIN,

CAMAGUEY, MATANZAS, LAS

TUNAS, CIENFUEGOS, VILLA

CLARA, PINAR DEL RIO,

SANTIAGO DE CUBA

river .... CAUTO, SAN PEDRO,

JATIBONICO, SAGUA LA

GRANDE

rum .... BACARDI

seaport .... MATANZAS,

CIENFUEGOS, MANZANILLO

secret police .... PORRA

snake .... JUBA

tempest .... BAYAMO

tobacco .... VUELTA

weight .... KILO, LIBRA,

TONELADA

cubbyhole of a sort .... DEN

cube .... CUT, DIE, DICE, CHOP,

SOLID

shaped .... CUBICAL

cubeb .... BERRY, CIGARETTE

cubic capacity, ship's

.... TONNAGE

content .... VOLUME,

CUBATURE

decimeter .... LITER, LITRE

foot per second .... CUSEC

meter .... STERE

cubicle .... DEN, CELL, NOOK,

BEDROOM, COMPARTMENT

Cuchulain's wife .... EMER

cuckoldry .... ADULTERY,

CONCUBINAGE

cuckoo .... ANI, BIRD, GOWK,

KOEL, TOURACO

of the .... CUCULIFORM

slang .... CRAZY, SILLY,

FOOLISH

cuckoopint .... ARUM

cucullate .... COWLED, HOODED

cucumber .... PEPO, GOURD,

PICKLE, GHERKIN

cool as a .... CALM, POISED,

COMPOSED

relish .... PICKLES

cucurbit .... FLASK, GOURD-

SHAPED

cucurbitaceous herb .... GOURD,

MELON, SQUASH, CUCUMBER

cud .... BITE, CHEW, BOLUS,

MORSEL

chew the .... PONDER, RECALL,

RUMINATE

chewer's stomach ..... RUMEN,

PAUNCH

chewing animal .... COW,

DEER, GOAT, BISON, CAMEL,

LLAMA, CATTLE, BUFFALO,

CARABAO, GIRAFFE, RUMINANT

of chewing tobacco ..... PLUG,

QUID, TWIST

variant of .... QUID

cudbear .... DYE, LICHEN

cuddle .... HUG, CLASP, CARESS,

CURL UP, FONDLE, NESTLE,

EMBRACE, SNUGGLE

cuddly .... ANGELIC, LOVABLE

cuddy .... CABIN, CLOSET,

PANTRY, CUPBOARD

cudgel .... BAT, CLUB, DRUB,

STAFF, STICK, BASTINADO,

SHILLALAH, SHILLELAGH,

TRUNCHEON

one's brains .... RACK

cudgels, take up the .... DEFEND

cue .... ROD, TIP, CLUE, HINT,

TAIL, SIGNAL

actor's .... CATCHWORD

bridge of .... JIGGER

in music .... PRESA

of hair .... BRAID, QUEUE,

PIGTAIL

substitute, billiards .... MACE

cuff .... BOX, HIT, BELT, BIFF,

SLAP, CLOUT, FIGHT, STRIKE,

HANDCUFF, WRISTBAND

off the .... OFFHAND,

IMPROMPTU

Cugat, bandleader .... XAVIER

cuirass .... MAIL, ARMOR, LORLEA, LORIC(A), CORSELET, BREASTPLATE
cuisine .... COOKING, COOKERY, KITCHEN
of the .... CULINARY
cuisine, _____ .... HAUTE
cuisinier .... CHEF, COOK, KITCHENER
cul-de-sac .... BLIND ALLEY
Culbertson, card expert .... ELY
culex pipiens .... MOSQUITO
cull .... SIFT, GLEAN, REJECT, SELECT, PICK OUT
cullis .... GUTTER
cully .... DUPE, MATE, CHEAT, TRICK
British: sl. .... PAL, BUDDY
culm .... COAL, DUST, HA(U)LM
culminate .... END, COME TO A HEAD
culminating point .... CRISIS, HIGH TIDE
culmination .... ACME, CLIMAX, FINISH, FRUITION
sun's .... NOON, ZENITH
Culp, _____ (hobby) .... OVETA
culpa .... FAULT, GUILT
culpa, _____ .... MEA
culpability .... ONUS, BLAME, GUILT
culpable ...... GUILTY, TO BLAME, SINFUL, BLAMABLE, AT FAULT
culprit .... FELON, OFFENDER, CRIMINAL
cult .... FAD, ISM, SECT, VOGUE, BELIEF, WORSHIP
artistic .... DADA
naked .... NUDISM
cultivate .... FARM, GROW, TILL, WORK, NURSE, FOSTER, PURSUE, CHERISH, DEVELOP
cultivated .... TILLED, REFINED, CULTURED, HIGHBROW
land .... FARM, ARADA
plot .... GARDEN
cultivation of soil .... TILTH, CULTURE
cultivator .... TILLER
cultural studies .... ARTS
culture .... ARTS, POLISH, BREEDING, REFINEMENT, CIVILIZATION
medium .... AGAR
of people .... ETHOS
cultured person .... LADY, SCHOLAR, GENTLEMAN
culver .... DOVE, PIGEON
culvert .... DRAIN, CONDUIT, WATERWAY
opening .... INLET

cum .... WITH
cumber .... LOAD, DETER, BURDEN, HAMPER, HINDER, IMPEDE, MEDDLE, OVERLOAD
cumbersome .... CLUMSY, ONEROUS, UNWIELDY, BURDENSOME, HEAVY-LADEN
cumin .... ANISE
cummer .... GODMOTHER
cummerbund .... SASH
cumshaw .... TIP, GRATUITY
cunner .... GILTHEAD
cunning .... SLY, FOXY, WILY, GUILE, CLEVER, ARTFUL, ASTUTE, CRAFT(Y), SHIFTY
as a fox .... VULPINE
person .... KNAVE, SCHEMER, POLITICIAN
cuon .... DHOLE
cup .... BOWL, CALIX, CRATER, CHALICE, CANNIKIN
assaying .... TEST, CUPEL
ceremonial .... AMA
drinking .... MUG, CALIX, TASS, CRUSE, STEIN, STOUP, TAZZA, GOBLET, NOGGIN, RUMMER, TANKARD
druggist's/wine .... BEAKER
flower .... CALYX
gem-cutting .... DOP
holder .... ZARF, SAUCER
knight's quest .... GRAIL
like .... CALICULAR
like spoon .... LADLE
metal .... PANNIKIN
of tea: Brit. colloq. .... HOBBY, AVOCATION
shaped like a .... HOLLOW, CONCAVE
small, for coffee .... DEMITASSE
sports championship ..... DAVIS, RYDER, AMERICA'S, WIGHTMAN
to measure liquid .... JIGGER
used at the Last Supper .... (HOLY)GRAIL
cupbearer of the gods .... HEBE, GANYMEDE
cupboard .... AMBRY, CUDDY, CLOSET, LARDER, PANTRY, ARMOIRE, CABINET
Cupid .... AMOR, EROS
infant .... AMORINO, AMORETTO
mother of .... VENUS
sweetheart of .... PSYCHE
title of .... DAN
cupidity .... LUST, GREED, AVARICE

Cupid's bow, so to speak .... PUPPY LOVE
cupola .... ARCH, DOME
battleship's .... TURRET
cuprous oxide .... CHALCOCITE
cuprum .... COPPER
cur .... DOG, MUTT, TIKE, TYKE, HOUND, MONGREL
curable .... MENDABLE, MEDICABLE
curacao, orange-flavored .... COINTREAU
curare ...... URALI, URARI, POISON, OURALI, WOORALI, WOURALI
curate .... PRIEST, MINISTER, CLERGYMAN
curative ...... HEALING, REMEDIAL, SANATIVE, SANATORY, MEDICINAL, THERAPEUTIC
curator .... KEEPER, BOOKMAN, GUARDIAN
concern of .... MUSEUM, RELICS, LIBRARY, ARCHIVES
curb .... REIN, CHECK, MARKET, RETARD, SLACKEN, RESTRAIN
colloquial .... LID
for woman's tongue .... BRANKS
market item ...... BOND, STOCK
curbed .... CONTROLLED
curbing inward .... ADUNC
curbstone .... BORDER
curch .... KERCHIEF
curculio .... BEETLE
curcuma .... GINGER, TURMERIC
curd .... CASEIN
soybean .... TAHO, TOFU, TOKUA
curdle .... CLABBER, CONGEAL, LUMP, SPOIL, THICKEN, COAGULATE
curdled milk .... CLABBER
curdling material .... RENNET, RENNIN
curds with cream .... JUNKET
cure .... HEAL, TREAT, DOCTOR, REMEDY, RELIEVE, RESTORE, REGIMEN, THERAPY, PRESERVE, PHYSIC, MEDICINE, TREATMENT, PRESCRIPTION
all .... ELIXIR, NOSTRUM, PANACEA, CATHOLICON
by salting .... CORN
fish, meat, etc. .... SALT, SMOKE
foods for future use ...... DRY, DEHYDRATE, FREEZE-DRY
French .... PRIEST
fruit by cooking with sugar .... PRESERVE
hide into leather .... TAN

kind of .... REST, WATER,
    PURGATIVE, ACUPUNCTURE
vegetables with brine,
    vinegar .... PICKLE
curfew feature .... SIREN,
    WHISTLE, LIGHTS OUT
man .... TOWN CRIER
curia official, Catholic
    .... DATARY
curio(s) .... VIRTU, GEWGAW,
    ANTIQUE, BIBELOT,
    GIMCRACK, BRIC-A-BRAC,
    KNICKKNACK
collector .... VIRTUOSO
curiosa .... NOVELTIES
curious .... ODD, PRYING,
    GOSSIPY, NOS(E)Y, MEDDLING,
    MEDDLESOME, INQUISITIVE
colloquial .... SNOOP
one ...... CAT, PRY, SNOOP(ER),
    BUSYBODY, QUIDNUNC,
    PEEPING TOM
curl .... COIL, ROLL, CRIMP, WAVE,
    TRESS, TWIST, RIPPLE,
    FRIZ(ZLE)
hair .... SET, MARCEL
of long hair .... RINGLET
snugly ..... CUDDLE, ENSCONCE
the lip .... JEER, SNEER
curled .... SPIRY, CRIMPED,
    CRISPATE
curlew .... SNIPE, WHAUP, GODWIT
bird resembling .... WHIMBREL
Curlew River character
    .... FERRYMAN
curlicue .... CURL, CURVE, TWIST,
    FLOURISH
curling iron .... CRISPER
mark/target .... TEE
match .... BONSPIEL
place .... RINK
curlpaper .... PAPILLOTE
curly .... WAVY, KINKY, SPIRAL
curmudgeon ...... CRAB, GROUCH,
    GROWLER
curn .... FEW, GRAIN
curr .... COO, MURMUR
currach .... CORACLE
currant .... BERRY, GRAPE,
    SHRUB, RISSEL
genus .... RIBES
syrup .... CASSIS
currency .... CASH, COIN, MONEY,
    SPECIE, NEWNESS, FRESHNESS,
    PREVALENCE, CIRCULATION
value of .... VALUTA
current .... TIDE, FRESH, MODERN,
    COMMON, GOING(ON), IN
    VOGUE, EXISTING, STREAM,
    PREVAILING
air .... DRAFT

beneath surf .... UNDERTOW
combining form .... RHEO
expenses .... OVERHEAD
measure .... AMPS, AMPERES
opposite .... SETBACK
currently .... NOW, PRESENTLY,
    AT PRESENT
currier .... COMBER
Currier and Ives .... PRINTS
curry .... BEAT, COMB, DRUB,
    FLOG, STEW, TIDY, CLEAN,
    DRESS, GROOM
favor .... FAWN, FLATTER
ingredient .... CUMIN
curse .... BAN, BANE, DAMN,
    OATH, SWEAR, REVILE,
    ANATHEMA, DENOUNCE,
    EXECRATE, BLASPHEME,
    MARANATHA, SWEARWORD,
    IMPRECATION, MALEDICTION
Archaic ..... WANION, MALISON
colloquial .... CUSS
cursed .... EVIL, ODIOUS, WICKED,
    VICTIMIZED
colloquial .... JINXED
curser, biblical .... BALAAM
cursillo founder .... HERVAS
cursive .... FLOWING, RUNNING
cursor .... RUNNER, INDICATOR
cursory .... CASUAL, RANDOM,
    SHALLOW, TRIVIAL,
    SUPERFICIAL
look .... GLANCE, GLIMPSE
curt .... RUDE, TART, BLUFF,
    BLUNT, BRIEF, SHORT, TERSE,
    ABRUPT, BRUSQUE, CONCISE,
    SNAPPISH
dismissal .... CONGE
curtail .... CUT, CLIP, LESSEN,
    REDUCE, DEPRIVE, SHORTEN
curtain .... COVER, DRAPE,
    SCREEN, DRAPERY, VEILING
behind stage .... BACKDROP
Cold War .... IRON, BAMBOO
color/shade .... ECRU
holder .... ROD
hung in a doorway
    .... PORTIERE
material .... LENO, GAUZE,
    NINON, SCRIM, TAPIS,
    GRENADINE
of gun fire .... BARRAGE
raiser .... SKIT, PRELIMINARY
rod cover/band .... CORNICE
sash .... TIEBACK
short .... VALANCE
woman's apartment
    .... PURDAH
curtains: sl. .... END, DEATH
curtsy .... BOB, BOW, SALUTE
Archaic .... LOUT

curvature .... ARC(H)
curve .... ARC, ARCH, CURL, ESSE,
    TURN, CROOK, SINUS,
    FLEXURE, HYPERBOLA
baseball pitch/pitcher's
    .... HOOK, FASTBALL,
    SCREWBALL
double/sharp .... ESS
handwriting .... CURLICUE,
    FLOURISH
inward .... INFLECT
mark over vowel .... BREVE
of a column .... ENTASIS
of river .... BEND
path of missile
    .... TRAJECTORY
plane .... PARABOLA
S-shaped .... OGEE
to one side .... VEER, SWERVE,
    DEFLECT
curved .... BENT, ADUNC, ARCHED,
    ARCUATE, FALACTE,
    FALCIFORM
bones .... RIBS
in .... CONCAVE
molding .... OGEE
out .... CONVEX
plank, ship's .... SNY
roof .... DOME
surface of arch ..... EXTRADOS
sword .... SCIMITAR
curves, having two .... BIFLEX
curvet ...... LEAP, VAULT, FROLIC,
    GAMBOL
curving inward .... ADUNC
cushat .... (RING)DOVE,
    (WOOD)PIGEON
cushaw .... SQUASH
cushion .... MAT, PAD, SQUAB,
    ABSORB, BUFFER, PILLOW,
    SOFTEN, BOLSTER, HASSOCK
of rope, wood, at ship's side
    .... FENDER
shock .... BUMPER
Cush's father .... HAM
son .... NIMROD
cushy: sl. .... EASY
cusk .... BURBOT
relative .... COD
cusp of moon .... HORN
cuspid .... FANG, TOOTH
cuspidor .... SPITTOON
cussed ...... MEAN, NASTY, SWORE,
    BITCHY, CURSED, ORNERY
custard .... PIE
apple .... PA(W)PAW
apple's cousin .... SWEETSOP
cake .... ECLAIR
dish .... FLAN
like dish .... TIMBALE

Custer's battle site .... LITTLE BIG HORN
nemesis .... SITTING BULL
custodian .... CUSTOS, KEEPER, WARDEN, WARDER, JANITOR, JAILER, CARETAKER, CONCIERGE
museum .... CURATOR
of funds .... TREASURER
of minors .... GUARDIAN
custody .... CARE, WING, TRUST, CHARGE, KEEPING, WARDSHIP, GUARDIANSHIP
take into .... HOLD, ARREST, DETAIN
custom .... USE, WONT, HABIT, USAGE, PRAXIS, PRACTICE
built/made .... TAILORED, MADE-TO-ORDER
with force of law .... MOS, MORES
customable .... TAXABLE
customary .... RULE, USUAL, COMMON, NORMAL, WONTED, REGULAR, HABITUAL, ORDINARY
callas .... ETCETERAS
requirement .... FORMALITY
sidler .... CRAB
usage .... MODE
customer .... USER, BUYER, PATRON, CONSUMER
credit record .... PASSBOOK
present to a .... LAGN(I)APPE
customers ...... TRADE, CLIENTELE
customize .... SPECIALIZE
customs .... MORES
charge .... TAX, DUTY, IMPOST, TARIFF
collector: biblical .... MATTHEW
municipal .... OCTROI
official .... TAXMAN, ASSESSOR, SURVEYOR
station .... PORT OF ENTRY
cut ...... HEW, LOP, NIP, SAW, CLIP, SNIP, SEVER, INCISION, PRUNE(D), TRENCH, CURTAIL
across .... TRANSECT, INTERSECT
and dried .... DULL, FIXED, BORING, RIGGED, ROUTINE
apart piece by piece .... DISSECT
beef .... CHUCK
blubber .... FLENSE
close .... CLIP, CROP, SHAVE
colloquial .... SNUB, IGNORE
companion of ...... DRY, DRIED
corners .... GO DIRECT, SKIP OVER

crop .... REAP, GATHER, HARVEST
crudely .... HACKLE, HAGGLE
dead: colloq. .... SNUB, REBUFF, UPSTAGE, COLD SHOULDER
deep .... GASH
deeper, in engraving .... REENTER
down .... MOW, FELL, RAZE, SLAIN, SMASH, REDUCE
down trees .... LUMBER
edge of coin .... NIG
ends .... LOP, TRIM, SHEAR
expenses ..... SAVE, RETRENCH, ECONOMIZE
glass .... CRYSTAL
grass .... MOW
hair .... BARBER
horse's tail .... DOCK
in .... INTRUDE, INTERRUPT
in cubes .... DICE
in half .... HALVE, BISECT
in length .... ABRIDGE, SHORTEN
in thin slices .... SHAVE
into .... LANCE, INCISE
into small pieces .... DICE, HASH, MINCE
leather .... SKIVE
lengthwise .... SLIT
made by a saw/ax .... KERF
meat/roast/turkey .... CARVE
neck/off head .... BEHEAD, DECAPITATE
notch/slight .... NICK, SNICK
of meat .... CHOP, LOIN, CHINE, CHUCK, STEAK, T-BONE, SIRLOIN, SPARERIB
off ...... BOB, LOP, CLIP, DOCK, SEVER, KERF, POLL, ROACH, INTERCEPT, INTERRUPT
off piece/slice .... CANTLE
off wool .... POLL, SHEAR
out .... OMIT, ELIDE, EXCIDE, EXCEPT, EXCISE, EXSECT, EXSCIND, EXCLUDE, EXTIRPATE
out disk .... TREPAN
out unnecessary parts .... PRUNE
rind/skin .... PARE, PEEL
roughly .... HACK, HACKLE
saw-tooth edge .... PINK
short .... BOB, CLIP, CROP, POLL, STOP, BOBTAIL
slang .... SHARE
spiral grooves .... RIFLE
the mustard ..... ABLE, CAN DO
thin .... SKIVE, SLICE, SLIVER
thru water ...... PLOW, PLOUGH
to pieces .... MINCE, SHRED

to requirement .... TAILOR
to the body/skin .... WOUND
up into parts .... DIVIDE, SEPARATE
V-shaped .... NOTCH
way thru .... PLOW
with axe .... HEW, CHOP, HACK
with scissors .... SNIP
with sweeping stroke .... SLASH
cutback .... REDUCTION
on expenses ...... SAVE, SKIMP, ECONOMIZE, TIGHTEN ONE'S BELT
cutaneous .... DERMAL
cutch .... CATECHU
cute .... COY, DAINTY, SHARP, CANNY, CLEVER, PRETTY, SHREWD, CUNNING
colloquial .... SLICK
one: colloq. .... IMP
cuticle .... SKIN, EPIDERMIS
cutie .... DEARIE
cutis .... DERMA, CORIUM, DERMIS
cutlass .... CURTLE AX, (BROAD)SWORD
cutlery .... FLATWARE, TABLEWARE
item ...... FORK, KNIFE, SPOON, TEASPOON
cutlet, meat .... VEAL
veal .... SCHNITZEL
cutout pattern .... STENCIL
cutpurse .... DIP, THIEF, PICKPOCKET
cutrate .... CHEAP, BARGAIN, REDUCED, MARKED DOWN
cutter ...... BLADE, KNIFE, HEWER, SLICER, BREAKER
garment .... STITCHER, FINISHER
leaf .... ANT, WORM
of life's thread .... ATROPOS
of precious stones .... LAPIDARY
ride covering .... LAPROBE
vessel .... SLED, SLOOP, YACHT, SLEIGH
cutthroat .... THUG, ASSASSIN, STIFF, GRUELING, MURDERER
cutting .... RAW, KEEN, TART, KERF, NIPPY, SHARP, BITING, CAUSTIC, INCISIVE, STINGING, KEEN-EDGED, TRENCHANT
British .... CLIPPING
edge .... LIP
off last letter of word .... APOCOPE
off vowel .... ELISION
part of tool .... BIT, BLADE
plant .... (S)CION

remarks .... DIG, RAP, SWIPE,
INSULT, SARCASM
tool .... AX(E), ADZ(E), BUR,
SAW, BOLO, KNIFE, MOWER,
RAZOR, SCYTHE, SHEARS,
SICKLE, MACHETE, SCISSORS
tool, engraver's .... BURIN,
CHASER, CHISEL, GRAVER
tool holder .... ARBOR
tool seller .... CUTLER
tools .... CUTLERY
tooth .... INCISOR
cuttlefish .... SQUID, BELEMNITE
bone .... POUNCE
ejecting organ .... SIPHON
fluid/secretion .... INK, SEPIA
fossil .... BELEMNITE,
THUNDERSTONE
kin .... SPIRULA
cutup .... CLOWN, HUMORIST,
PRANKSTER
cutwork .... EMBROIDERY,
NEEDLEWORK
cuvette .... BASIN, TEST TUBE
Cuzco Indian .... INCA
location of .... PERU
Cy Young awardee ...... GIBSON,
MCLAIN, SEAVER
cyanic .... BLUE, AZURINE,
CERULEAN
cyanosis .... BLUENESS,
AZURENESS
cyanotype .... BLUEPRINT
Cybele .... OPS, RHEA, KYBELE,
AGDISTIS
beloved of .... ATTIS
daughter of .... JUNO, HERA
father of .... URANUS
husband of .... CRONUS,
SATURN
mother of .... GAEA
son of .... ZEUS, JUPITER
cybernation .... AUTOMATION,
ROBOT CONTROL
cybernaut .... ROBOT
Cyclades .... IOS, ZEA, KEOS,
MILO, DELOS, MELOS, NAXOS,
PAROS, TINOS
cycle .... AGE, RIDE, WHEEL,
ROUND, CIRCLE, PERIOD
of 15 years .... INDICTION
of heavenly body .... ORBIT
of the sun and moon, eclipse
.... SAROS
of years .... EON, EPOCH
vehicle .... BIKE, BICYCLE,
TRICYCLE, MOTORCYCLE
cycloid .... CIRCULAR
cyclone .... GALE, VORTEX,
TORNADO, TWISTER,
TYPHOON, HURRICANE,

WINDSTORM
cyclonic .... ANGRY, RAGING,
STORMY
cyclonite .... EXPLOSIVE
Cyclopean .... HUGE, STRONG,
MASSIVE, ENORMOUS,
GIGANTIC
Cyclops .... GIANT
characteristic of .... ONE-EYED
Odysseus' captor
.... POLYPHEMUS
cyclorama ...... EXHIBIT, PICTURE,
SCENERY, PANORAMA
cyclostome .... HAGFISH, LAMPREY
cyesis .... GESTATION, PREGNANCY
cygnet .... SWAN
Cygnus .... SWAN,
CONSTELLATION
star in .... DENEB
cylinder .... CASK, ROLL, BARREL,
COLUMN, PILLAR
covering .... LAG(GING)
for conveying air, water
.... PIPE, TRUNK
hollow .... DRUM, PIPE, TUBE
in a cylinder .... PISTON
of coins .... ROULEAU
of metal, for dams, dikes
.... GABION
of vascular tissues in plants
.... STELE
part .... END, HEAD, PISTON
printing press .... INKER,
PLATEN, ROLLER
revolving ...... WHEEL, ROLLER
spiral .... HELIX
to roll out dough ..... ROLLING
PIN
tree .... BOLE, TRUNK
water marker .... DANDY,
ROLLER
cylindrical .... TUBULAR,
COLUMNAR, TOROSE, DRUM-
SHAPED, TUBE-SHAPED
and tapered .... TERETE
cyma .... GOLA, MOLDING
cymar .... CHEMISE
cymbals .... TAL, ZEL
cyme .... PHLOX
Cymric .... WELSH, BRETON,
CELTIC
cynic .... DOUBTER, DEFEATIST,
TIMON, RAILER, PESSIMIST,
CRITIC, BELITTLER,
MISANTHROPE
look of .... COLD, LEER,
SMIRK, SNEER
of sorts ..... KNOCKER, SKEPTIC
cynical .... CAPTIOUS, CRITICAL,
DOUBTING, SARCASTIC

cynicism .... IRONY, SATIRE,
SARCASM, PESSIMISM
cynosure .... LODESTAR,
POLESTAR, NORTH STAR
Cynthia .... LUNA, MOON, DIANA,
ARTEMIS
diminutive of .... CINDY
cypress .... SILK, TREE, CLOTH,
SATIN
cyprinoid .... IDE, CHUB, CARP,
DACE, BARBEL, GOLDFISH
Cyprus cape .... GATA, GRECO,
ANDREAS, ARNAUTI
capital .... NICOSIA
city/town .... DHALI, LEFKA,
PAPHOS, KYRENIA, LARNACA,
MORPHOU, LIMASSOL,
FAMAGUSTA
language .... GREEK,
CYPRIOT(E), TURKISH
leader .... MAKARIOS
liquid measure .... CASS
monetary unit
.... (CYPRIOT)POUND
mountain .... TROODOS
native .... CYPRIAN, CYPRIOT
union with Greece ..... ENOSIS
Cyrano, creator of
.... (EDMOND)ROSTAND
shame of .... (LARGE)NOSE
Cyrenaica .... BARCA
capital .... CYRENE
Cytherea ...... VENUS, APHRODITE
cyst .... BAG, SAC, WEN, LUMP,
POUCH, VESICLE
behind the knee .... BAKER'S
infested with amoebas
.... AMEBIASIS
sebaceous .... WEN
type of skin .... DERMOID
with worm larvae
.... HYDATID
czar .... BOSS, TSAR, DESPOT,
EMPEROR, AUTOCRAT,
NICHOLAS
daughter of .... CZAREVNA,
TSAREVNA
heir of .... CZAREVITCH
wife of .... CZARINA, EMPRESS,
TSARINA, CZARITZA
Czechoslovakian .... SLAV,
SLOVAK, BOHEMIAN,
MORAVIAN, SILESIAN
brandy .... SLIVOVITZ
capital .... PRAGUE (PRAHA)
castle .... HRADCANY
city/town .... BRNO, OPAVA,
DECIN, PLZEN, TABOR,
KLADNO, KOSICE, TRNAVA,
ZVOLEN, OLOMOUC, OSTRAVA,

SUMPERK, TEPLICE CHOMUTOV, HANDLOVA, PARDUBICE, BRATISLAVA, BUDEJOVICE, GOTTWALDOV, HRADEC KRALOVE
coin .... DUCAT, KRONEN, HELLER, KORUNA
composer .... DVORAK, JANACEK, SMETANA, (RUDOLF)FRIML
dramatist .... CAPEK
folk hero .... SCHWEIK
forest .... BOHEMIAN
hero .... (JAN)HUS
historian .... PALACKY
language .... CZECH, SLOVAK
leader .... HUSAK, DUBCHEK
measure .... LAN, MIRA

measure, distance .... SAH, LATRO
monetary unit .... KORUNA
mountain .... GERLACHOVKA
mountains .... BESKIDS, JESENIKY, SUDETEN, ERZGEBIRGE, HIGH TATRA, WHITE CARPATHIANS
munition works .... SKODA
news agency .... CETEKA
passage .... JABLUNKA
patriot .... BENES, MASARYK, STEFANIK
premier .... LENART, CERNI(C)K
president .... BENES, HAVEL, MASARYK, NOVOTNY, SVOBODA, GOTTWALD
public square ...... WENCESLAS

rail center .... ZILINA
region ...... PRAHA, JIHOCESKY, BRATISLAVA, SEVEROCESKY, STREDOCESKY, ZAPADOCESKY, VYCHODOCESKY, SEVEROMORAVSKY
republic ..... CZECH SOCIALIST, SLOVAK SOCIALIST
river .... DYJE, HRON, IPEL, LABE, ODER, ODRA, OHRE, VAH, NITRA, ORAVA, HORNAD, DANUBE, MOLDAU, MORAVA, ONDAVA, SAZAVA, TORYSA, UHLAVA, VLTAVA, DUNAJEC, JIHLAVA, LUZNICE, SVITAVA, BEROUNKA
statesman .... BENES
steel works .... SKODA

D

D, Greek .... DELTA
Hebrew .... DALEDH, DALETH
in a sequence .... FOURTH
in chemistry .... DEUTERIUM
letter .... DEE, DELTA
Roman numeral ..... 500, FIVE HUNDRED
symbol for .... DENSITY
DA/D.A. ...... DISTRICT ATTORNEY
dab .... BIT, PAT, TAP, BLOT, PECK, SPOT, PAINT, STAIN, SMEAR, TOUCH, STRIKE, FLATFISH, FLOUNDER
a pitched ball .... BUNT
colloquial .... EXPERT
lightly .... BRUSH, SMOOTH
of salt .... PINCH
dabble .... DIP, WET, POTTER, TRIFLE, SPLASH, TINKER, MOISTEN, SPATTER
in .... SMATTER, TOY WITH
dabbler .... TYRO, DUFFER, AMATEUR, DABSTER, GREENHORN, DILETTANTE
dabchick .... GREBE, DIPPER, DUCKER, DIDAPPER, HELL-DIVER
dabster: colloq. .... EXPERT, DABBLER
dace .... CARP
dacha .... COTTAGE, COUNTRY-HOUSE
dachshund .... (GERMAN)DOG
characteristic ..... LONG BODY, SHORT LEGS, DROOPING EARS
dacoit .... BANDIT, ROBBER
dacron .... FIBER

dactyl, in zoology .... TOE, FINGER
dactylogram .... FINGERPRINT
dad .... FATHER
poetic .... SIRE
daddy ...... DAD, POP, PAPA, POPS, PAPPY, FATHER
kind of: sl. .... SUGAR
longlegs .... CRANE-FLY, SPIDER, SPINNER, CENTIPEDE, HARVESTMAN
dado .... DIE, BEZEL, GROOVE, RABBET, WAINSCOT
daedal .... MAZY, VARIED, RAVELED, ELABORATE, INGENIOUS, INTRICATE, MULTI-COLORED
Daedalus' son .... ICARUS
victim/nephew .... TALOS
daemon .... DEMON, DEVIL, SPIRIT, SPECTER
daffodil .... NARCISSUS
plant resembling ...... JONQUIL
Daffy, baseball player ...... DEAN
colloquial .... CRAZY, SILLY, FOOLISH, SCREWY, GOOFY, WACKY, IDIOTIC
daft .... MAD, CRAZY, SILLY, INSANE, IDIOTIC, WITLESS
slang .... LOCO, LOONY, PSYCHO, COCKEYED
dagger .... DIRK, SNEE, KNIFE, BODKIN, CREESE, WEAPON, STYLET, PIERCER
archaic .... DUDGEON
attached to gun ...... BAYONET
Burmese .... DAH

double, reference mark .... DIESIS
handle .... HAFT, HILT
look .... ANGER, HATRED
mark, in printing .... DIESIS, OBELUS, OBELISK
Malay .... CRIS(S), KRIS, CREESE
medieval .... ANLACE
of mercy .... MISERICORD(E)
old-time .... SNEE
signs in printing .... OBELI
stroke .... STAB, LUNGE, THRUST, STOCCADO
two-edged .... COUTEAU
type of .... DIRK, KRIS, SKEAN, KUTTAR, PONIARD, STILETTO, MISERICORD
wound .... STAB
daguerreotype .... COLLOTYPE, PHOTOSTAT, PHOTOGRAPH
Dahomey .... BENIN
capital .... PORTO NOVO
chief of state .... SOGLO
city/town ...... NIKKI, ABOMEY, COTONOU, LOKOSSA, PARAKOU, NATITIGOU
ethnic group .... FON, ADJA, MAHI, BARIBA, YORUBA
gulf .... GUINEA
language .... MINA, DENDI, SOMBA, BARIBA, YORUBA
monetary unit .... FRANC
mountains .... ATAKORA
native .... FON
region .... SUDAN
river ..... MONO, NIGER, OUEME

seaport .... OUIDAH
Dai Nippon .... JAPAN
Dailey, _____ .... DAN
daily .... DIURNAL, EVERYDAY,
ONCE A DAY, PER DIEM,
QUOTIDIAN
delivery .... MAIL, MILK,
NEWSPAPER
dozen .... EXERCISES,
CONSTITUTIONAL
fare .... DIET
feature article .... COLUMN
newspaper .... JOURNAL
published .... NEWSPAPER
record .... DIARY, JOURNAL
daimio .... NOBLEMAN
retainer of .... SAMURAI
dainties ...... TIDBITS, DELICACIES
dainty .... CUTE, FINE, NEAT,
NICE, RARE, SUBTLE,
DELICATE, EXQUISITE,
FASTIDIOUS
archaic .... CATE
fabric .... SILK, TAFFETA
French .... MIGNON
daiquiri .... COCKTAIL
ingredient .... RUM, LIME
Dairen .... DALNY, TALIEN
dairy .... LACTARY, LACTARIUM
cattle .... JERSEY
farm area .... MILKSHED
maid .... DEY, GOWAN
product .... MILK, CREAM,
BUTTER, CHEESE
shop .... CREAMERY
dais .... STAGE, PODIUM, ESTRADE,
ROSTRUM, TRIBUNE,
PLATFORM
daisy .... OXEYE, SHASTA, GOWAN,
MARGUERITE,
CHRYSANTHEMUM
_____ .... MAE
cutter, baseball ..... GROUNDER
English .... GOWAN
dak .... MAIL
Dakar is capital of ...... SENEGAL
natives .... SENEGALESE
Daker hen .... CORN-CRAKE
Dakota Indian .... MANDAN,
SIOUX
Dakotan .... TETON
Dalai Lama .... RULER, BUDDHIST
PRIEST
dale .... DELL, GLEN, VALE, DENE,
DINGLE, VALLEY
Dale .... EVANS, CARNEGIE
Dali, painter .... SALVADOR,
SURREALIST
art of .... SURREALISM
dalles .... RAPIDS
dalliance .... FLIRTATION

dally .... TOY, DELAY, FLIRT, IDLE,
LOITER, TRIFLE, PROLONG
Dalmatian .... DOG, SLAV
decor .... SPOTS
dog's name .... SPOT
dam .... CLOG, DIKE, PLUG,
EMBANK, BARRAGE, BARRIER,
KEEP BACK, MILLPOND
archaic .... MOTHER
builder, animal .... OTTER
designer .... SAVAGE
Egyptian/Nile .... SADD,
ASWAN
for military fortification
.... SANDBAGS
horse .... MARE
in a stream/canal
.... FLOODGATE
in the U.S. .... COULEE,
HOOVER, SHASTA, BOULDER
river .... WEIR, LEVEE
to break force of waves
.... SEAWALL
up a river .... STEM
damage .... MAR, HARM, LOSS,
HURT, ABUSE, DEFECT,
IMPAIR, BRUISE, SCATHE,
INJURE, INJURY
colloquial .... COST, EXPENSE
slang .... BUNG
suit .... TORT, TROVER
damages, claim for ...... TROVER
daman .... CONY, CONEY, HYRAX,
MAMMAL
Damansky to the Chinese
.... CHEN PAO
Damascene .... PLUM
Damascus caliph .... OMMIAD
is capital of .... SYRIA
damask .... LINEN,
(DAMASCUS)STEEL
flower .... ROSE
for hangings .... DORNICK
for vestments, etc.
.... DORNICK, DORNOCK
like cloth .... LAMPAS
dame .... LADY, MADAM, MATRON,
MISTRESS
equivalent title of .... SIR
luring .... DRAWING BROAD
slang .... GAL, GIRL, WOMAN
title of noble .... DUCHESS,
COUNTESS
dammar .... RESIN
damn .... DOOM, CURSE, VILIFY,
CONDEMN, DESTROY
damnation .... RUIN, HAVOC,
PERDITION
damned .... LOST, CURSED,
DEFAMED, ACCURSED,
CONDEMNED, CONVICTED

dialectic .... TARNAL,
TARNATION
the ...... LOST SOULS, SOULS IN
HELL
damning .... SURE, CERTAIN,
CONVINCING
beholder .... EYE-WITNESS
Damocles, word associated
with .... SWORD
damoiselle .... MISS, DAMSEL
Damon and _____ .... PYTHIAS
damp .... WET, DANK, DEWY,
MIST, HUMID, MOIST, STIFLE
and hot .... MUGGY
become .... JIG
dampen .... WET, DARKEN,
SADDEN, DEPRESS, MOISTEN,
DISCOURAGE, DISHEARTEN
the spirits .... DASH, KNOCK
DOWN
damper .... KILLJOY, WET
BLANKET
damsel .... GIRL, LASS, MAID,
MISSY, MAIDEN
fly .... DRAGONFLY
damson .... PLUM
Dan .... SIR, BUOY, MASTER
Cupid .... EROS
Dane .... JUTLANDER
dance .... HOP, BALL, ROMP,
CAPER, GALOP, BALLET,
BUNNYHOP, TRIPPING
African-American folk
.... JUBA, CAKEWALK
arranger/designer
.... CHOREOGRAPHER
attendance .... WAIT ON
Bohemian .... POLKA, REDOWA
Brazilian .... SAMBA, BOSSA-
NOVA
child on knee .... DANDLE
college/school ...... HOP, PROM
colloquial .... DRAG, SHINDIG
costume party
.... MASQUERADE
country ...... HAY, BARN, REEL,
SQUARE, LANDLER
crazed person .... TARANTIST
Cuban .... CONGA, MAMBO,
R(H)UMBA, HABANERA
English .... MORRIS
folk .... HORA, DREHER
for two .... TANGO, WALTZ,
FOXTROT
French .... BAL, GAVOT,
MINUET, GALLIARD,
RIGADOON, FARANDOLA,
QUADRILLE
frontier .... REEL
German .... ALLEMANDE
hall .... GAFF, CASINO,

CABARET, BALLROOM, NIGHTCLUB, DISCOTHEQUE

hall girl .... HOSTESS

Hawaiian .... HULA-(HULA)

Hungarian .... CZARDAS

in a boisterous way .... HORSE AROUND

in a playful manner .... FRISK, FROLIC, GAMBOL

in ragtime .... ONE-STEP

Israeli .... HORA

Italian .... COURANTE

kind of .... TAP, TOE, BELLY, FRUG, POLKA, BALLET, WALTZ, FOXTROT, SOFTSHOE

Latin-American .... CONGA, CHA-CHA

line .... CONGA

lively .... JUBA, REEL, FLING, CONGA, GALOP, CORANTO, GAVOTTE, COURANTE, FANDANGO, HORNPIPE, COTILLION, GALLOPADE, TAMBOURIN, SALTARELLO

mimetic .... HULA

modern .... FRUG, SHAG, DISCO, BOOGIE, LAMBADA, ROCK N'ROLL

music .... JAZZ, SWING, MAMBO, TANGO, VALSE, WALTZ, FOXTROT, RAGTIME, BOOGIE-WOOGIE

of death ...... DANSE MACABRE

of early 1940's ..... JITTERBUG

of 1930 .... SHAG

of 1929 .... CHARLESTON

old .... PAVIN, PAVAN(E), CAROLE

Polish .... POLKA, POLONAISE

polka like .... MAZ(O)URKA

Russian .... KAZATSKA, KAZATSKY

sailor's .... HORNPIPE

Scottish .... REEL

slang .... HOOF

slow, graceful .... ADAGIO, MINUET

South American .... TANGO, CARIOCA

Southwest .... BAILE

Spanish .... TANGO, BOLERO, MORISCO, FANDANGO, FLAMENCO

square .... DOSADOS, HOEDOWN, LANC(I)ERS

stately ..... MINUET, SARABAND

step .... PAS, SHAG, CHASSE, SHUFFLE, CURTSY, GLISSADE

triple time .... JIG

two-fourth time .... GALOP

violent .... APACHE

Virginia .... REEL

war .... PYRRHIC

watcher .... WALLFLOWER

white-tie .... FORMAL

with castanets .... BOLERO, FLAMENCO

with handclapping .... JUBA

with high kicking .... CANCAN

with wooden shoes .... CLOG

dancer .... ARTIST, HOPPER, CHORINE, PRANCER, STEPPER, RAND, ALMA, ALME(H), CASTLE, ROGERS, ZORINA, ASTAIRE

ballet .... RASCH, FONTEYN, NUREYEV, PAVLOVA, SHEARER, ULANOVA, CORYPHEE, FIGURANT, BALLERINA

burlesque .... STRIPPER, ECDYSIAST, STRIPTEASER

co-worker of .... COMET

concern of .... STEPS, RHYTHM, SLIPPERS, CHOREOGRAPHY

costume of .... TUTU, MOTLEY, TIGHTS, LEOTARD

French .... DANSEUR, DANSEUSE

jazz music .... JITTERBUG

kind of .... TAP, TOE, BELLY, LIMBO, APACHE, BALLET, FLAMENCO, STRIPTEASE

noted American .... (MARTHA) GRAHAM

noted fan .... RAND

professional/tap .... HOOFER

shoe of .... CLOG

dancing .... SALTANT, SALTATION, CHOREOGRAPHY

craze for .... TARANTISM, TARENTISM

girl, Biblical .... SALOME

girl, chorus line .... CHORINE

girl, Egyptian .... ALMA, ALME(H)

girl, employed .... TAXI DANCER

girl, feature of discotheque .... GOGO DANCER

girl, Indian .... ALME(H), BAYADEER, BAYADERE, NAUTCH GIRL

girl, Japanese .... GEISHA

horses .... LIPPIZAN(ER)

kind of .... TAP, TOE, CLOG, FRUG, FOLK, BELLY, SQUARE, POLKA, COUNTRY, BALLROOM, MONKEY, SOFTSHOE

master .... MURRAY, ASTAIRE

muse of .... TERPSICHORE

partner, professional .... GIGOLO

place also .... CASINO

position ...... CHEEK TO CHEEK

shoes .... PUMPS

dandelion ...... WEED, KOK-SAGYZ

stalk .... SCAPE

tuft .... PUFFBALL

dander .... SCALES

allergy to .... RHINITIS

colloquial .... IRE, ANGER, WRATH, TEMPER

type of human ...... DANDRUFF

dandify .... DRESS UP, SPRUCE

dandle .... PET, DANCE, CARESS, FONDLE

dandruff .... SCURF, FLAKES, FURFUR, SCALES

dandy .... FOP, BEAU, BUCK, DUDE, PRIG, TOFF, NATTY, COXCOMB

English .... MACARONI

fever .... DENGUE

roll impression .... WATER MARK

slang .... FINE, LULU, DILLY, JOHNNY, JOHNNIE, FIRST RATE, FIRST CLASS

dandyish .... BUCKISH, FOPPISH

danger ...... RISK, PERIL, HAZARD, JEOPARDY

hidden .... AMBUSH, PITFALL

in a body of water .... WHIRLPOOL

sign .... SYMPTOM

signal ...... RED, ALARM, SIREN

that attracts/tempts .... GIN, TRAP, SNARE

dangerous .... RISKY, UNSAFE, PARLOUS, CRITICAL, PERILOUS

and clever .... SHREWD

slang .... HAIRY

dangle .... HANG, LOLL

dangling .... ALOP, LOOSE

Daniel .... BOONE, DEFOE, WEBSTER

Danish .... DANE, PASTRY

astronomer .... BRAHE

cape ...... THE SKAW, SKAGENS ODDE

capital .... COPENHAGEN

channel .... LILLE BAELT, STORE BAELT

cheese .... BRIE, ELBO, TYBO, DANBO, FYNBO, MOLBO, MARIBO, MYCELLA, CAMEMBERT

chieftain .... JARL

city/town ...... VEJLE, ALBORG, LYNGBY, ODENSE, TARNBY, KOLDING, RANDERS,

GENTOFTE, HORSENSE, NAESTVED, ROSKILDE
coin .... ORA, ORE, ORAS, KRONE, RIGSDALER
composer .... NIELSEN
district .... AMT
duchy .... HOLSTEIN
"farmer prince" .... INGOLF
fjord .... ISE
historian .... SAXO
horse .... ZAIN
island .... ALS, FYN, MON, OMO, FEJO, MORS, ROMO, LAESO, SAMSO, AMAGER, SEJERO, ARNHOLT, FALSTER, LOLLAND
king .... CNUT, KNUT, CANUTE, FREDERIK, WALDEMAR
king, Shakespearean
.... HAMLET
land measure .... MORGEN
legislature/parliament
.... RIGSDAG, FOLKETING
measure, distance .... FOD, MIL, MUL, ALEN
monetary unit .... KRONE
mountain .... TRANEBJERG, YDING SKOVHOJ
native .... DANE
navigator .... BERING
noble .... JARL
novelist .... NEXO
peninsula .... JUTLAND
physicist .... BOHR, OERSTED
pianist .... BORGE
queen .... INGRID
river .... SUSAA, GELSAA, STORAA, GUDENAA
sea .... BALTIC
seaport .... AARHUS, HELSINGOR
sound .... ORESUND
strait .... FEHMARN, KATTEGAT, SKAGERRAK
toast .... SKOAL
weight .... LOD, ORT, VOG, ESER, PUND
dank .... WET, DAMP, DEWY, HUMID, MOIST, MUGGY, CLAMMY
Danny, actor .... KAYE
Danse _____ .... MACABRE
danseuse .... DANCER, CORYPHEE, FIGURANT, BALLERINA
Dante's beloved .... BEATRICE
deathplace .... RAVENNA
work ..... INFERNO, THE DIVINE COMEDY
Danube city .... ULM, LINZ
in German .... DONAU
in Hungarian .... DUNA

in Romanian .... DUNAREA
of .... DANUBIAN
river .... SAU, ULM, ISAR, SAVA, MORAVA
Danzig .... GDANSK
dap .... DAB, DIB, DIP, SKIP, BOUNCE, DIBBLE
daphne .... SHRUB, LAUREL
flower family .... MEZEREUM
Daphne .... NYMPH
Daphnis' lover .... CHLOE
dapper .... CHIC, NEAT, TRIM, NATTY, SMART, SPRUCE, DASHING
slang .... SWANK, SNAZZY
dapple .... PIED, FLECK(ED), MOTTLED, PIEBALD, SPOTTED
poetic .... FREAK
Dar es Salaam is capital of
.... TANZANIA
darb .... DART, DILLY
Darcy's forte .... PRIDE
Dardan .... TROJAN
Dardanelles .... STRAIT, HELLESPONT
dare .... TRY, DAST, DEFI, DEFY, FACE, RISK, OPPOSE, ATTEMPT, VENTURE, CHALLENGE
daredevil ...... BOLD, RASH, WILD, RECKLESS, FOOLHARDY
person .... HELLCAT, STUNTMAN, ADVENTURER
daresay ...... DEEM, INFER, THINK, RECKON, BELIEVE, CONCEIVE
Darien .... GULF, ISTHMUS
daring .... BOLD, WILD, BRAVE, HARDY, RISQUE, BRAVURA, ICARIAN, INTREPID
action .... DERRING-DO
slang .... GOING FOR BROKE
Darius scene of defeat .... ISSUS
dark ...... DIM, EBON, EVIL, INKY, BLACK, DUSKY, MIRK, MURK(Y), UNLIT, SABLE, HIDDEN, RAYLESS, CLOUDY, GLOOMY, SINISTER, TENEBROUS, TENEBREFIC
and dull ...... SOMBER, SOMBRE
area of vision .... SCOTOMA
brown .... SEPIA, BISTER, BISTRE, BRUNET(TE)
colored .... DUSKY, SOMBER, SWARTHY
complexion .... BLACK, MELANO, COLORED, SWARTHY
haired .... MELANOUS, BRUNET(TE)
horse: colloq. .... SLEEPER, LONG-SHOT, OFF-CHANCE
hue .... SWART, SOMBRE

in the .... BLIND, UNAWARE, IGNORANT
marking in marble ..... CLOUD
pigmented .... MELANOID
portending rain ..... LOWERING
red .... LAKY, WINISH
skinned .... SWARTHY, MELANOUS
skinned person ...... WOP, DAGO, NEGRO, AFRICAN, NEGRILLO, COLORED, AFRO-AMERICAN, AFRICAN-AMERICAN
wood .... EBONY, MAHOGANY
Dark Age .... BARBARISM
Continent .... AFRICA
darken .... DIM, INK, BLACKEN, (BE)CLOUD, EBONIZE, SHADOW, NEGRIFY, OBSCURE
darkey/darky ...... NEGRO, BLACK MAN
darkish .... BLACKISH
darkness .... DUSK, NIGHT, BLACKNESS, MIDNIGHT, OBSCURITY
combining form .... SCOTO
of hair/skin .... MELANISM
darling .... PET, IDOL, ANGEL, BELOVED, CHERI(E), DEAREST, MINIKIN, FAVORITE, SWEETHEART
colloquial .... DEARY, TOOTS, DEARIE
darn .... FIX, MEND, PATCH
colloquial .... DAMN, CURSE
darnel .... TARE, WEED, COCKLE
darning needle .... DRAGONFLY
dart ...... BARB, BOLT, DASH, FLIT, ARROW, SCOOT, SPEAR, SPURT, THROW, SPRING, MISSILE
darter .... SNAKEBIRD
darts, bullfighter's
.... BANDERILLA
Dartmoor .... GAOL, PRISON
Darwinian theory
.... EVOLUTION, PANGENESIS
Darwinism .... EVOLUTIONISM
dash .... DART, ELAN, ARDOR, VERVE, WRITE, SMASH, THROW, SPIRIT, SPLASH
against .... LASH
at full speed .... SPRINT
colloquial .... DAM
mark .... HYPHEN
of salt .... BIT
off .... RUSH
one's hopes .... DESTROY, SHATTER, FRUSTRATE
opposed to .... DOT
with force .... CAST, HURL

dashboard .... PANEL
for short .... DASH
dasheen .... TARO, SPROUTS
dasher .... DOLLY
of a churn .... PLUNGER
dashing .... GAY, SHOWY, FLASHY,
JAUNTY, GALLANT, SPIRITED,
GALLOPING
manner .... BRAVURA,
PANACHE, DEVIL-MAY-CARE
dastard .... CAD, CREEP, COWARD,
CRAVEN, POLTROON
dastardly ...... MEAN, COWARDLY
dasyure .... MARSUPIAL
data .... FACTS, FIGURES,
INFORMATION
computer's .... INPUT
device carried by balloon
.... RADIO-SONDE
for pupil's parents
.... PROGRESS REPORT
date .... DAY, FRUIT, TRYST,
ESCORT, TIME, PERIOD,
CALENDS, STEADY,
APPOINTMENT, RENDEZVOUS
abbreviation .... APPT
approximate .... CIRCA
for launching an attack
.... D-DAY
fruit like .... JUJUBE
go on a .... STEP OUT
plum .... KAKI, PERSIMMON
out of .... PASSE, EXPIRED,
OBSOLETE, OLD-FASHIONED
sugar .... GHOOR
tree .... PALM
up to .... FRESH, CURRENT,
MODERN, ABREAST OF,
FASHIONABLE
dated .... PAST, PASSE, DECLASSE,
OBSOLETE, OLD-FASHIONED
dateless .... STAG
dating phrase .... AS OF, AS YET,
UNTIL NOW
datum plane example .... SEA
LEVEL
datura .... JIMSON
daub ...... PAINT, SMEAR, GREASE,
SPREAD, PLASTER, SLUBBER
daughter .... HIJA, FILLE,
OFFSPRING
daughter(s) of Atlas and
Pleione .... PLEIAD(ES)
daunt .... AWE, COW, FAZE,
BULLY, SCARE, DISMAY,
INTIMIDATE
dauntless .... BRAVE, FEARLESS,
UNDAUNTED, INTREPID
davenport .... DESK, SOFA, COUCH
David, for one .... CAMP

David's (King). See **King
David**
Davidoff's subject .... CIGARS
Davis, actress .... BETTE
Davis, Jr. .... SAMMY
davit .... CRANE
Davy Jones's locker
.... SEABOTTOM
daw .... CROW
dawdle .... LAG, IDLE, LOAF,
LINGER, LOITER, PIDDLE,
POTTER, PUTTER
dawdler .... IDLER, MOPER,
GOOFOFF
dawn ...... MORN, SUNUP, AURORA,
SUNRISE, DAYBREAK
crew .... FIRST SHIFT
goddess of .... EOS
herald of .... COCK, LARK,
ROOSTER
pertaining to .... EOAN
to noon .... MORNING
to sunset .... DAYTIME
day ...... AGE, ERA, EPACT, EPOCH,
LIGHT, PERIOD
and night of equal length
.... EQUINOX
bed .... SOFA, COUCH
before .... EVE
every .... DAILY
in court .... CHANCE, HEARING,
OPPORTUNITY
just past .... YESTERDAY
Latin .... DIES
letter .... TELEGRAM
march .... ETAPE
of greatest vigor ...... HEYDAY
Roman .... IDES, NONES
scholar .... EXTERN
star .... SUN
Day, actress ...... DORIS, LARAINE
Dayan .... MOSHE
daybook .... DIARY, JOURNAL
daybreak .... DAWN, MORN,
AURORA, DAWNING, SUNRISE
daydream .... FANCY, FANTASY,
REVERY, IMAGINE, REVERIE
daydreamer .... LOTUS-EATER,
RAINBOW-CHASER
daydreaming .... AUTISM,
REVERIE, UP IN THE CLOUDS
dayfly .... MAY FLY
daylight .... DAWN, SUNLIGHT,
LIMELIGHT, PUBLICITY
slang .... EYES
dayspring .... DAWN, SUNUP,
MORNING, SUNRISE
daytime, pertaining to
.... DIURNAL
days, describing youthful
.... SALAD

gone by .... HISTORY
Dayton suburb .... KETTERING
daze .... STUN, SHOCK, DAZZLE,
STUPOR, TRANCE, STUPEFY,
CONFUSION, BEWILDER(MENT)
dazzle .... BLIND, GLARE, SHINE,
GLITTER, IMPRESS
dazzling .... BRIGHT, GLARING,
BLINDING, PRISMATIC
momentarily .... METEORIC
DC time .... EST
DDE .... IKE
D.D.S. .... DENTIST
DDT .... PESTICIDE, INSECTICIDE
de facto .... ACTUAL, IN FACT
jure .... BY RIGHT
luxe ..... ELEGANT, SUMPTUOUS
De Leon .... PONCE
Maupassant .... GUY
Mille .... CECIL
deacon ...... CLERIC, CLERGYMAN,
ADULTERATE
clergyman above .... PRIEST
deactivate .... DEMOBILIZE
dead .... GONE, (A)MORT,
DEFUNCT, EXTINCT,
DECEASED, DEPARTED,
LIFELESS, INANIMATE
animal pretending to be
.... POSSUM
beat: colloq. .... TIRED, SPENT,
DRAINED, EXHAUSTED
bodies on battlefield
.... CARNAGE
body .... LICH, CORPSE,
CORPUS, CADAVER, CARCASE,
CARCASS
body: sl. .... STIFF
calm .... DOLDRUMS
combining form .... SAPRO
duck .... GONER
end ...... IMPASSE, CUL-DE-SAC,
BLIND ALLEY
end place .... SLUM, GHETTO
flesh .... CARRION
hand .... MORTMAIN
heat .... TIE, PHOTO FINISH
house .... CHARNEL,
MORTUARY, OSSARIUM
pan .... POKERFACE
pan comedian .... KEATON
person .... DECEASED,
DECEDENT
point .... CENTER
recently .... LATE
set .... FIRM, HELL-BENT,
DETERMINED
species .... EXTINCT
stop .... STANDSTILL
tired: sl. ...... BUSHED, POOPED
to .... UNAWARE

189

to the world .... ASLEEP
when delivered ..... STILLBORN
word preceding name of
.... LATE
Dead End Kids member
.... GORCEY
Sea find .... SCROLLS
kingdom .... MOAB
river .... JORDAN
scrolls location ..... QUMRAN
deadbeat: sl. .... LEECH, LOAFER,
SPONGE(R), WELSHER,
FREELOADER
deaden .... DULL, NUMB, BENUMB,
DAMPEN, OBTUND, WEAKEN
sound .... MUTE, MUFFLE
deadener, pain .... OPIATE,
CODEINE, DEMEROL,
ANALGESIC, AN(A)ESTHETIC
deadeye .... SHARPSHOOTER
deadfall .... GIN, TRAP
deadline .... ZERO-HOUR, TIME-
LIMIT, TARGET-DATE
deadlock .... TIE, DRAW, IMPASSE,
STANDOFF, STALEMATE,
STANDSTILL
jury .... HANG, HUNG
deadly .... FATAL FERAL, LETHAL,
MORTAL, BANEFUL, HARMFUL,
VIRULENT, DANGEROUS,
MALIGNANT, INFECTIOUS
Archaic .... FELL
enemy .... NEMESIS
growth .... CANCER
plant .... IVY, UPAS, ERGOT,
HEMLOCK, BANEWORT,
LOCOWEED, WOLFSBANE,
BELLADONNA, NIGHTSHADE
poison ...... ARSENIC, CYANIDE,
NICOTINE, STRYCHNINE
sin .... ENVY, LUST, ANGER,
PRIDE, SLOTH, GLUTTONY,
COVETOUSNESS
snake .... ASP, COBRA
to both sides ..... INTERNECINE
deadpan .... MASK, BLANK,
VAGUE
deadweight .... BURDEN
deaf .... SURD, EARLESS,
HEEDLESS, UNHEARING
and _____ .... DUMB
and dumb language
...... MOTION, SIGNAL, GESTURE
and dumb person .... LIP
READER
deafen .... STUN, SOUNDPROOF
Scottish .... DEAVE
deafening .... NOISY, EAR-
SPLITTING
deafness .... IMPAIRED HEARING
at birth .... SENSORINEURAL

type of .... TOTAL, PARTIAL,
CONDUCTIVE
deal .... DOLE, GIVE, SALE, ALLOT,
TRADE, TREAT, BARTER,
BESTOW, FIR WOOD, PINE
WOOD, INFLICT, NEGOTIATE,
ADMINISTER, DISTRIBUTE
a heavy blow .... SMITE
coiloquial .... BARGAIN,
AGREEMENT
crookedly .... PALTER
frankly: colloq. .... LEVEL
give-and-take
.... (HORSE)TRADE
out .... DOLE, ISSUE
with .... COPE, HANDLE,
MANAGE
with a difficult problem
.... GRAPPLE
dealer .... BUYER, MONGER,
SELLER, TRADER, CHAPMAN,
DISTRIBUTOR
cattle .... DROVER
cloth/dry goods .... DRAPER,
MERCER, CLOTHIER
cutting tools .... CUTLER
foodstuff .... GROCER
gem .... LAPIDARY
in bonds .... (STOCK)BROKER
in house/lots .... REALTOR
in skins .... FURRIER
right of .... PONE
scrap .... RAGMAN, JUNKMAN
smuggled goods .... BLACK
MARKETEER
dealing(s) .... TRADE, COMMERCE,
RELATIONS, TRANSACTION(S)
dean .... DOYEN
ecclesiastical .... PREFECT
feminine .... DOYENNE
of a .... DECANAL
residence of .... DEANERY
Dean, baseball player .... DAFFY,
DIZZY
deanery .... DECANAL
dean's list .... ACHIEVERS
dear .... LOVE, COSTLY, BELOVED,
DARLING, PRECIOUS,
CHERISHED, EXPENSIVE
slang .... HONEY, TOOTS
dearie .... DARLING, SWEETHEART
dearness: sl. .... HIGHWAY
ROBBERY
dearth .... LACK, FAMINE,
PAUCITY, SCARCITY
death .... END, DOOM, LOSS,
MORT, DEMISE, DECEASE,
PASSING, EXPIRATION,
ETERNAL REST
by beheading ...... GUILLOTINE
by burning .... SUTTEE

by hanging, with the
.... ROPE, NOOSE
causing .... FATAL, LETHAL,
MORTAL
cup .... MUSHROOM
defying .... BOLD
herald of .... BANSHEE,
BANSHIE
march/song .... DIRGE
march scene .... BATAAN
mercy .... EUTHANASIA
near .... DYING
noise .... GASP, RATTLE
notice .... OBIT(UARY),
NECROLOGY
of .... LETHAL, MORTUARY
painless, easy .... EUTHANASIA
put to .... HANG, KILL, SLAY,
EXECUTE, ASSASSINATE
rate .... MORTALITY
rattle .... RALE
ring announcing .... TOLL,
KNELL
self-inflicted .... SUICIDE
sentence .... DAMNATION,
CONVICTION
sentence, to carry out .... GAS
CHAMBER, ELECTRIC CHAIR
slang .... CURTAINS
symbol .... SKULL
toll .... LOSS, KNELL
view of .... THANATOPSIS
deathblow .... COUP DE GRACE
deathless .... LASTING, IMMORTAL
deathlessness .... ATHANASIA,
PERPETUITY
death's-head .... SKULL
deathsman .... HANGMAN,
EXECUTIONER
deathwatch .... WAKE, VIGIL,
BEETLE
deave .... DEAFEN
deb .... BUD, DEBUTANTE
debacle .... ROUT, PANIC,
DISASTER, STAMPEDE
debar ...... DENY, FORBID, HINDER,
REFUSE, EXCLUDE
debark .... LAND, ALIGHT,
UNLOAD
debase .... LOWER, DEFILE,
DEMEAN, CORRUPT, DEGRADE,
PERVERT, PROFANE, VITIATE,
ADULTERATE
liquid .... DILUTE
metal .... ALLOY
morally .... DEBAUCH,
DEPRAVE
debasement .... IMPURITY,
CORRUPTION
debatable .... MOOT,
CONTESTABLE,

QUESTIONABLE, CONTROVERSIAL

debate .... ARGUE, FORUM, PLEAD, REASON, CANVASS, CONTEND, DISCUSS, DISPUTE, PALAVER, CAUSERIE, PHILOSOPHIZE

art of formal .... POLEMICS

ending device .... CLOTURE

pertaining to .... FORENSIC

debater .... POLEMIST, DISPUTANT, POLEMICIST

debauch .... ORGY, RUIN, DEBASE, CORRUPT, DEPRAVE

prolonged .... HELLBENDER

debauchee .... RAKE, ROUE, SATYR, LECHER, LIBERTINE

downfall of .... RIOTOUS LIVING

debauchery .... ORGY, RIOT, CAROUSAL

debenture .... BOND, VOUCHER

debilitate .... WEAKEN, SICKEN, CRIPPLE, DISABLE, ENERVATE, ENFEEBLE

debilitated .... SAPPED, RUN-DOWN

debility .... ATONY, ASTHENIA

debit .... CHARGE

debonair ...... GAY, AIRY, PERKY, SUAVE, GENIAL, JAUNTY, AFFABLE, CAREFREE

urbane fellow .... CITY SLICKER

debouch .... EXPEL, EMERGE, SURFACE

debouche .... OUTLET

debris ...... RUINS, SCREE, TRASH, LITTER, REFUSE, RUBBISH, RUBBLE, DETRITUS

tree prunings .... BRASH

debt ...... LOAN, OWING, ACCOUNT, BORROWING, LIABILITY, OBLIGATION

bad .... NONPAYMENT

evader .... DEADBEAT, DEFAULTER

gambling .... HONORARY

in theology .... SIN

overdue .... ARREAR(S)

relating to .... DEBIT

settlement .... PAYOFF

debtor .... OWER, BORROWER

debtor's note .... IOU

prison .... FLEET

debunk .... EXPOSE, REFUTE, UNMASK

Debussy, composer ...... ACHILLE CLAUDE

composition .... REVERIE

topic of .... SEA

debut .... ENTRANCE,

APPEARANCE, INTRODUCTION, PRESENTATION

debutant(e) .... BUD, DEB

ball .... COTILLION

delight of .... STAGLINE

party for .... COMING OUT

decade .... TEN, DECENNIUM

"Beat" .... THE SIXTIES

decadence .... DECAY, BLIGHT, DECLINE, DETERIORATION

decadent ...... WASTED, DECREPIT, BLASE, CRUMBLING, BROKEN DOWN

decalogue .... CODE, ETHICS

number .... TEN

part of .... COMMANDMENT

Decameron Tales author

.... BOCCACCIO

decamp .... BOLT, FLEE, ABSCOND, CLEAR OUT, RUN AWAY, VAMO(O)SE

decanal .... DEANERY

decant .... POUR, DRAIN, ELUTRIATE

decanter .... BOTTLE, CARAFE

stand .... TANTALUS

decapitate .... BEHEAD, DECOLLATE

decapitation .... EXECUTION

decapod .... CRAB, PRAWN, SQUID, SHRIMP, LOBSTER

decay .... ERODE, SPOIL, EROSION, PUTREFY, GANGRENE, DECOMPOSE

cause of tooth .... PLAQUE

dental/tooth .... CARIES

fruit .... ROT, BLET

into dust .... CRUMBLE

iron/steel .... RUST

moral .... SLOUGH, CORRUPTION

slow, crumbling .... MO(U)LDER

decayed .... PUTRID, ROTTEN, CARIOUS, CORRUPT

in botany .... DOTY

in fruit .... BLET

decaying .... WANEY, ROTTING, DECLINING

combining form .... SAPRO

dead body .... CARRION

from age .... DOTING

vegetable matter .... DUFF

decease .... DIE, DEATH, DEMISE

deceased .... DEAD, LATE, PARTED, DECEDENT, DEPARTED

deceit .... LIE, WILE, FRAUD, GUILE, COZENAGE, TRICKERY, DECEPTION, IMPOSTURE

archaic .... COVIN

deceitful .... WILY, FALSE, ARTFUL, CRAFTY, SNEAKY, TRICKY, DEVIOUS, CUNNING, DECEPTIVE, DISHONEST

colloquial .... PHONY

face .... MASK

sight .... MIRAGE, ILLUSION, HALLUCINATION

words .... LIES

deceive ...... FOB, FUB, LIE, DUPE, FOOL, COZEN, SPOOF, BETRAY, DELUDE, ENTRAP, HUSTLE, BEGUILE, MISLEAD, SWINDLE, HOODWINK

by flattery .... FLAM

slang .... CON, CLIP

deceiver .... LIAR, CHEAT, FAKER, BETRAYER, IMPOSTOR, SWINDLER

slang .... CONMAN, FOURFLUSHER

victim of: colloq. ...... SUCKER

decelerate .... SLOW DOWN

December decoration .... TINSEL, MISTLETOE

perennial .... SNOW

symbol/VIP .... SANTA (CLAUS)

28th .... CHILDERMAS

decenary .... TITHING

decency ...... DECORUM, HONESTY, GOOD TASTE, PROPRIETY

decennium .... DECADE

decent .... FAIR, KIND, RIGHT, CHASTE, MODEST, PROPER, FITTING, DECOROUS, RESPECTABLE

decentralize .... DISPERSE

deception .... LIE, HOAX, JAPE, RUSE, FRAUD, SPOOF, UNTRUTH, FLIMFLAM, TRICKERY, CHICANERY, DELUSION, FALSEHOOD, IMPOSTURE

deceptive .... SLY, FAKE, FALSE, TRICKY, DELUSIVE, ILLUSORY, AMBIGUOUS, DISGUISED, MISLEADING

front .... BLUFF

game ...... SHELL, THIMBLE-RIG

trick .... FLAM

decide .... FIX, RULE, ELECT, JUDGE, CHOOSE, SETTLE, RESOLVE, CONCLUDE, DETERMINE

issue by combat ...... DERAIGN

judicially .... ADJUDGE

decided .... SET, RULED, CLEAR CUT, SETTLED, DEFINITE

decidedly .... CERTAINLY, DEFINITELY

decider of right or wrong
.... CASUIST
deciding game to break a tie
.... PLAY-OFF
election in case of a tie
.... RUN-OFF
vote/voice .... CASTING VOTE
deciduous ...... FADING, FLITTING,
TEMPORARY, TRANSIENT
opposed to .... EVERGREEN
decimal .... TENTH, DENARY
base .... TEN
point .... DOT
point system inventor
.... STEVIN
system of counting
.... ALGORISM
decimate .... DESTROY,
MASSACRE, SLAUGHTER
decipher .... READ, DECODE,
INTERPRET, TRANSLATE
decipherable .... LEGIBLE,
READABLE
decision .... DECREE, FINDING,
RESOLVE, VERDICT,
GUMPTION, WILL, JUDGMENT,
SENTENCE
await .... PEND
basis for/good for the future
.... PRECEDENT
decisive .... FIRM, GRIM, FINAL,
FATEFUL, CONCLUSIVE
argument .... CLINCHER
point/moment .... CRUX,
CLIMAX, CRISIS, CRUCIAL,
ZERO HOUR
deck .... TRIM, COVER, FLOOR,
CLOTHE, PLATFORM
hand .... SAILOR, TRIMMER,
ROUSTABOUT
hit the .... ARISE, GET UP
lowest .... ORLOP
of cards .... PACK
on: colloq. .... READY, ON
HAND
out ..... ADORN, ARRAY, DRESS,
(BE)DIZEN, CAPARISON
Scottish .... DINK
ship's .... POOP, ORLOP
ship's, upper ...... FORECASTLE
slang .... KNOCK DOWN
the cards .... STACK
declaim .... RANT, ORATE, SPOUT,
RECITE, PERORATE
in duplicate .... RANT AND
RAVE
declaimer .... ORATOR, RANTER
declamation .... ORATION,
ORATORY, HARANGUE,
RECITATION
declaration .... AVOWAL,

ASSERTION, STATEMENT,
AFFIRMATION, PROCLAMATION
in bridge .... BID
of aims .... CHARTER,
MANIFESTO
Declaration of Independence
signer ...... WYTHE, HANCOCK
declare .... AVER, STATE, AFFIRM,
ALLEGE, ASSERT, PROFESS,
PUBLISH, PROCLAIM
guilty ...... CONDEMN, CONVICT
in cards .... MELD
innocent .... CLEAR, ACQUIT,
RELEASE, EXONERATE,
VINDICATE
legally insane .... DISABLE,
INCAPACITATE
true .... CLAIM, SWEAR
untrue .... DENY
vociferously .... THUNDER
war .... CHALLENGE
declared .... ANNOUNCED,
BROADCAST, PUBLISHED
declasse .... DATED, PASSE
decline .... DIP, EBB, WANE,
AGING, ABATE, DROOP,
SLUMP, SPURN, REFUSE,
REJECT
an offer .... REFUSE, TURN
DOWN
as in price .... SAG
period of .... DECADENCE
declivity .... SCARP, SLOPE
decoct .... DISTILL, EXTRACT
decoction .... TEA, PTISAN, TISANE
decode ...... DECIPHER, TRANSLATE
decollate .... BEHEAD, DECAPITATE
decollete .... LOW-CUT, LOW-
NECKED
decolorize .... BLEACH
decompose .... ROT, DECAY,
SPOIL, PUTREFY
decomposed .... PUTRID
decompression sickness
.... BENDS
decontaminate .... CLEAR, PURIFY
decontrol .... FREE, LIBERATE
decor .... DECORATION
decorate .... DECK, TRIM, ADORN,
DRESS, EMBELLISH
food to add color .... GARNISH
in a certain way .... ENSTAR
in a way .... ILLUMINATE
in showy way .... BEDIZEN
with jewels .... BEGEM,
ENCRUST
decorated wall .... DADO
decoration .... DECOR, AWARD,
RIBBON, GARNISH, ORNAMENT,
TRIMMING, ADORNMENT,
GARNITURE

as sign of honor .... BADGE,
MEDAL
for achievement .... TROPHY
furniture .... BUHL
hat .... COCKADE
military .... PURPLE HEART,
SERVICE MEDAL
of a page .... ILLUMINATION
on cloth/material
.... APPLIQUE, EMBROIDERY
style of .... ROCOCO
decorative .... SPANGLED,
GLITTERING, ORNAMENTAL
anklet/armlet .... BANGLE
band .... SASH
border design .... GUILLOCHE
braid .... CORDON
curve .... ESCALOP, SCALLOP
garland .... FESTOON
knot .... BOW
line in writing .... FLOURISH
plant .... HERB
ribbon .... CORDON, RIBAND
stamp .... SEAL
stroke .... TAG, FLOURISH
decorator .... TRIMMER
of a sort .... GILDER
decorous .... PRIM, PROPER,
DIGNIFIED
person .... PRIG
decorticate .... BARK, PARE, PEEL,
STRIP
decorum ...... DECENCY, DIGNITY,
PROTOCOL, ETIQUETTE,
PROPRIETY
decoupage .... ART
decoy .... BAIT, LURE, BLIND,
PLANT, ENTICE, ENTRAP
barker's .... SHILL
dog .... TOLLER
gambler's .... SHILL, CAPPER
object of .... GAME
police .... STOOLPIGEON
slang .... STOOLIE
songbird, use .... CAJOLE
decrease .... EBB, DROP, WANE,
ABATE, LOWER, TAPER,
LESSER, REDUCE, SLACKEN,
SUBSIDE, DISCOUNT, DIMINISH,
DEPRECIATE
decree .... LAW, FIAT, ARRET,
CANON, EDICT, ORDER,
(EN)ACT, DECIDE, FIRMAN,
ORDAIN, MANDATE, DECISION,
RESCRIPT
by judicial sentence
.... DECERN
by the Pope .... DECRETAL
judicial .... WRIT
Moslem ruler's .... IRADE
of outlawry .... BAN

papal .... BULL
Russian/official .... UKASE
decrees, collection of papal
.... DECRETAL
decrement .... LOSS, WASTE
opposed to .... INCREMENT
decrepit ...... OLD, WEAK, SENILE,
WORN OUT, BROKEN DOWN,
DELAPIDATED
airplane .... CRATE
automobile ..... CRATE, JALOPY
car: sl. .... DOG
decresent .... WANING
decrier ...... KNOCKER, DEPLORER
decry .... BLAME, CENSURE,
CONDEMN, DENOUNCE,
DISCREDIT, DISPARAGE
decumbent ...... PRONE, TRAILING,
PROSTRATE
opposed to .... SUPINE
decuple .... TENFOLD
decussate .... INTERSECT
dedicate .... APPLY, EXALT,
CONFER, DEVOTE, HALLOW,
ENSHRINE, INSCRIBE
dedication .... ENVOI, ENVOY,
DEVOTION, INSCRIPTION
deduce .... INFER, THINK, ASSUME,
DERIVE, RECKON, BELIEVE,
CONCLUDE
deduct .... DOCK, REMOVE,
SUBTRACT
deductible tax item
.... EXPENSES, (MORTGAGE)
INTEREST, DONATIONS
deduction .... REBATE, DISCOUNT,
REDUCTION, INFERENCE
allowed for loss of weight/
for waste .... DRAFT
kind of .... TARE
opposed to .... INDUCTION
union dues .... CHECKOFF
deed .... ACT, FEAT, GEST(E),
ACTION, EXPLOIT
in .... IN FACT, REALLY
kind of .... SALE, TRANSFER
ownership .... TITLE
deeds .... ACTA
of chivalry .... ERRANTRY
deejay's concern .... DISKS
deem .... JUDGE, OPINE, ASSESS,
REGARD, BELIEVE, CONSIDER
deep .... WISE, ABYSMAL,
ABYSSAL, LEARNED,
ABSTRUSE, PROFOUND
bow .... NOD, CURTSY,
SALAAM, OBEISANCE
crack .... CREVASSE
dish, covered .... TUREEN
dish, fruit pie .... COBBLER
dish, pudding ...... PANDOWDY

gorge .... GULLY, RAVINE
hole .... PIT
red .... CRIMSON, CARNATION
seated .... FIXED, ROOTED,
ENTRENCHED
sleep .... SOPOR, STUPOR,
LETHARGY
sound .... BOOM, RUMBLE
the .... SEA, OCEAN
valley .... CANON, CANYON
voice .... BARITONE
deep south state, U.S.
.... GEORGIA, ALABAMA,
LOUISIANA, MISSISSIPPI
deepfreeze .... REFRIGERATOR
deeply .... INLY
deepset .... CAVERNOUS
deepsix .... DISCARD
deer .... ROE, STAG, BROCKET,
MUNTJAC, MUNTJAK,
RUMINANT, WHITETAIL
American ...... MOOSE, WAPITI,
CARIBOU
Andean .... PUDU
antler .... TAG
antler branch .... POINT
antler shaft .... BEAM
antler, type .... RUSINE
Asiatic .... AHU, ROE, SAMBAR,
SAMBUR
axis .... CHITAL
barking .... KAKAR
distaff .... DOE(S)
entrails .... UMBLES
feeding place .... YARD
female .... DOE, ROE, HIND
flesh .... VENISON
foot .... HOOF
forest cover .... VERT
genus .... RUSA
hart .... STAG
hog .... AXIS, RUSA
horn .... ANTLER
hornless .... POLLARD
horn's second branch ..... BEZ
ANTLER
large .... ELK, MOOSE,
CARIBOU, REINDEER
like giraffe .... OKAPI
male .... HART, STAG,
(ROE)BUCK
maned .... RUSA, SAMBAR
moose-like .... ELK
mouse .... NAPUS
mouse-like .... CHEVROTAIN
mule .... BLACKTAIL
of a .... CERVINE
of India .... AXIS, RUSA
Persian .... MARAL
red .... HART, HIND, STAG,
ELAPHINE

secretion .... MUSK
sexual excitement .... RUT,
ESTRUS
short tail of .... SCUT
small .... ROE, NAPUS,
BROCKET, MUNTJAC,
CHEVROTAIN
spotted .... CHITAL
tail .... FLAG, SCUT
Tibet .... SHOU
track .... SLOT
three-year-old .... SOREL
two-year-old .... TEG,
BROCK(ET), PRICKET
vital organs .... NOMBLES,
NUMBLES, HUMBLE PIE
young .... FAWN, SPITTER
deerlet .... NAPU, CHEVROTAIN
deerlike .... CERVINE
deface .... MAR, MAIM, SCAR,
BLEMISH, MUTILATE,
DISFIGURE
defalcate .... EMBEZZLE
defamation .... ABUSE, LIBEL,
CALUMNY, SLANDER
defamatory .... LIBELOUS
remarks .... MUD
defame .... ABUSE, LIBEL,
MALIGN, REVILE, VILIFY,
SLANDER, TRADUCE,
CALUMNIATE
default .... BREACH, ARREARS,
FAILURE, FORFEIT
colloquial ..... WELSH, RENEGE
defaulter .... EMBEZZLER,
DEFALCATOR
defeat .... WIN, BEAT, BEST, LICK,
LOSS, UNDO, WHIP, WORST,
FOIL, SUBDUE, DESTROY,
REVERSE, TROUNCE,
OVERCOME, VANQUISH
by force .... CONQUER
by small margin .... NOSE
chess .... MATE
decisively .... DRUB, ROUT,
WALLOP, CLOBBER, TROUNCE
disorderly .... ROUT
easy to .... PUSHOVER
incumbent .... UNSEAT
overwhelming .... ROUT,
LACING, MASSACRE,
SHELLACKING
scoreless .... WHITEWASH
soundly .... DRUB, LACE,
SKUNK, WHALE
two ways .... WHIPSAW
unexpectedly .... UPSET
defeated: colloq. .... LICKED
slang .... KAPUT
defeatist, kind of .... PESSIMIST
defecate .... PURIFY, REFINE,

EXCRETE
defect .... FLAW, LACK, SPOT,
BREAK, FAULT, LACUNA,
DEMERIT, FOIBLE, FAILING,
WEAKNESS, SHORTCOMING,
IMPERFECTION
from a group/cause/country
.... BOLT, FLEE, DESERT,
RENEGE
in a cloth .... SNAG
in a plan .... KINK
in dry goods .... DAMAGE
in fabric/weave .... SCOB
in hosiery .... RUN
in machine/sl. .... BUG
in wood .... WARP
labial .... HARELIP
slight .... CRACK
superficial skin .... BLEMISH
defection .... DESERTION,
SECESSION
defective .... FAULTY, FLAWED,
MANQUE, IMPERFECT
bomb .... DUD
car .... LEMON
person .... MORON, CRIPPLE
defector .... RAT, BOLTER,
RENEGADE, TURNCOAT
defend .... FIGHT, GUARD, SHIELD,
JUSTIFY, PROTECT, GO TO BAT
FOR
slang .... STONEWALL
defendable .... TENABLE
defendant .... ACCUSED, CULPRIT,
SUSPECT, PRISONER
opposed to .... PLAINTIFF,
COMPLAINANT
place of .... DOCK
plea of .... NOLO
statement of .... PLEA
who refuses to plead
.... MUTE
defender ...... GUARD, CHAMPION,
ADVOCATE, GUARDIAN,
PROTECTOR
defense .... REFUGE, BULWARK,
PROTECTION, RESISTANCE,
FORTIFICATION, JUSTIFICATION
castle's .... MOAT
defendant's .... ALIBI
kind of .... ORAL, SELF,
LEGAL, ATTACK
line: Ger. .... LIMES
means of .... ARMOR, SHELL,
SPINE, ABATIS, HAUBERK,
WEAPON, BARRIER, MUNIMENT,
PALISADE, AIR-RAID SHELTER,
BARRICADE, SMOKESCREEN
Defense Department
monogram .... TAC
defenseless .... BARE, OPEN,

WEAK, NAKED, HELPLESS
defensible .... TENABLE,
JUSTIFIABLE
defensive .... WATCHFUL,
VIGILANT, FORTIFIED,
SHIELDING
covering ...... ARMOR, HELMET,
SHAKO, (A)EGIS, SHIELD, MAIL,
CUIRASS, BREASTPLATE
ditch .... MOAT, FOXHOLE
embankment ..... EARTHWORK,
GABIONADE
outwork .... FORTALICE
structure .... FORT, ABATIS,
CITADEL, FORTRESS, STOCKADE
wall .... FENCE, BULWARK
defer .... PEND, STAY, DELAY,
YIELD, SHELVE, SUBMIT, GIVE
IN, SUSPEND, POSTPONE
deference .... RESPECT, YIELDING,
OBEISANCE
deferment .... DELAY, RESPITE,
MORATORIUM
defi .... DARE, CARTEL,
CHALLENGE
defiance .... DARING, THREAT,
CONTEMPT, CHALLENGE,
REBELLION, RESISTANCE
defiant .... BOLD, INSOLENT,
REBELLIOUS, BELLIGERENT
confidence .... BRAVADO
one .... REB, REBEL,
CHALLENGER
sound .... YAH
deficiency .... LACK, WANT,
DEFECT, ULLAGE, DEFICIT,
POORNESS, SHORTAGE
disease .... DROPSY, SCURVY,
RICKETS, BERIBERI, PELLAGRA
in supply .... SHORTAGE
of oxygen in body .... ANOXIA
deficient .... SHORT, LACKING,
WANTING, DEFECTIVE,
INCOMPLETE, INADEQUATE
in volume .... WEAK
deficit .... LACK, SHORTAGE,
SHORTFALL
defile .... PASS, DIRTY, GORGE,
SULLY, TAINT, RAVINE,
VALLEY, BLACKEN, CORRUPT,
DEBAUCH, POLLUTE, PROFANE,
TARNISH
define .... LIMIT, EXPLAIN,
OUTLINE, DESCRIBE,
INTERPRET
definite .... EXACT, PLAIN,
CERTAIN, PRECISE, EXPLICIT,
POSITIVE
definitive .... FINAL, FIXED,
DECISIVE, CONCLUSIVE
deflate .... EMPTY, LOWER,

REDUCE, EXHAUST, HUMBLE,
COLLAPSE
deflated tire .... FLAT
deflect .... BEND, FEND, TURN,
AVERT, CURVE, SWING, TWIST,
DIVERT, SWERVE, DEVIATE
deflower .... RAVISH
Defoe, character .... CRUSOE,
FRIDAY
novelist .... DANIEL
deform .... WARP, CONTORT,
MISSHAPE, DISFIGURE
deformed ...... UGLY, DISTORTED,
MALFORMED
organism .... TERAS
person .... FREAK, CRIPPLE,
HUNCHBACK
deformity .... FLAW, DEFECT,
UGLINESS, DISTORTION,
IMPERFECTION,
DISFIGUREMENT
back .... HUMP, HUNCH
buccal .... HARELIP
foot .... VARUS, TALIPES,
CLUBFOOT
of lower limbs .... VARUS,
BOWLEGS
of mouth .... CLEFT LIP, CLEFT
PALATE
defraud .... GYP, BILK, DUPE,
NICK, CHEAT, COZEN, STICK,
FLEECE, SWINDLE
defray .... PAY, COVER COST,
FOOT THE BILL
defrost .... MELT, THAW, DEICE
deft .... APT, ADROIT, CLEVER,
SKILLFUL, DEXTEROUS
defunct ...... DEAD, PAST, EXTINCT
defuse .... CALM, PACIFY, SOOTHE,
APPEASE, PLACATE
defy .... DARE, FLOUT, OPPOSE,
RESIST, DISOBEY, CONFRONT,
CHALLENGE, FLY IN THE FACE
OF
degenerate .... DEBASED,
DEPRAVED
person .... PIMP, WHORE,
LECHER, PERVERT, TROLLOP,
SLATTERN
degeneration .... AGING,
DETERIORATION
degenerative disorder
.... DEMENTIA, BLINDNESS,
ARTHRITIS, ALZHEIMER'S
DISEASE
deglutition .... SWALLOWING
degradation .... DECLINE,
DEMOTION, DOWNGRADE,
DEBASEMENT
degrade .... ABASE, DEBASE,
DEMEAN, DEMOTE, HUMBLE,

REDUCE, DIMINISH, HUMILIATE
degraded .... SHAMED, DEMOTED,
DISGRACED, HUMILIATED
degrading .... MENIAL, INSULTING
degree .... PEG, RANK, RUNG,
STEP, LEVEL, STAGE, EXTENT
academic .... BA, BS, MD, LLD,
DOCTOR OF LAWS, BACHELOR
OF ARTS, DOCTOR OF
MEDICINE, BACHELOR OF
SCIENCE
highest/utmost .... NTH
of occurrence .... INCIDENCE
of uncertainty .... ENTH
recipient .... HONORAND
suffix .... NESS
to a .... SOMEWHAT
unspecified .... NTH
degust .... SAVOR, TASTE
dehisce .... GAPE, OPEN, BURST,
SPREAD, UNFURL
dehiscence .... CHASM, BURSTING,
SPLITTING
dehumanized .... BRUTALIZED
dehydrate .... DRY, PARCH,
DESSICATE, EVAPORATE
dehydrated .... DRIED, WITHERED,
SHRIVELED
dehydration .... DRYING, JERKING,
DESSICATION
deice ...... MELT, THAW, DEFROST,
UNFREEZE
deictic .... DEMONSTRATIVE
opposed to .... ELENCTIC
deific .... GODLY, DIVINE, GODLIKE
deiform ...... GODLIKE, CELESTIAL
deify .... ADORE, EXALT, EXTOL,
PRAISE, GLORIFY, WORSHIP,
IDEALIZE, SANCTIFY,
APOTHEOSIZE
deign .... STOOP, SUBMIT, LOSE
FACE, CONSENT, CONDESCEND
deil: Scot. .... DEVIL
Deirdre's guardian
.... CONCHOBAR
deity .... GOD, GODDESS,
GODHEAD, GODHOOD,
GODSHIP, DIVINITY,
PROVIDENCE
agricultural ..... CERES, FLORA,
POMONA, DEMETER
Buddhist .... DEVA, BUDDHA
Chinese .... HEU CHI, LEI
KUNG, CHANG FEI, LUNG
WANG
Egyptian ..... BAST, ISIS, NEPH,
PTAH, HORUS, ANUBIS
Germanic .... IDUN, ODIN,
FREY, THOR, DONAR, FRIGG,
NANNA, WODEN, WOTAN
Hindu .... AGNI, DEVI, ADITI,

BRAHMA, DAKSHA, DEVAKI,
DHARMA
Japanese .... HOTEI, INARI,
HIRUKO, IZANAGI, OMIKAMI,
AMATERASU
minor .... GODKIN, DEMIGOD
of commerce .... HERMES
of flocks .... FAUN
of forest/woodland .... PAN,
FAUN, SATYR, FAUNUS,
ZEPHYRUS
of marriage .... HERA, JUNO,
HYMEN
of music/poetry .... ERATO,
APOLLO, EUTERPRE, ORPHEUS
of water .... TRITON, NEPTUNE,
OCEANUS
secondary .... DEMIURGE
underworld/the nether world
.... LOKI, MINOS, ORCUS,
CHARON, OSIRIS
deject .... DAMP(EN), DASH,
DAUNT, SADDEN, DEPRESS
dejected .... SAD, WEARY, SULLEN,
DOWNCAST, DEPRESSED,
CRESTFALLEN,
BROKENHEARTED
dejection .... GLOOM, GRIEF,
DESPAIR, SADNESS,
MELANCHOLY
lowest point .... NADIR
dejeuner ...... LUNCH, LUNCHEON,
BREAKFAST
delate .... ACCUSE, RELATE,
ANNOUNCE, DENOUNCE
delator .... INFORMER
Delaware .... LENI, GRAPE,
LENAPE
bay .... DELAWARE, INDIAN
RIVER
Bay discoverer .... HUDSON
cape .... HENLOPEN
capital .... DOVER
city/town ...... LEWES, LAUREL,
NEWARK, SMYRNA, ELSMERE,
MILFORD, SEAFORD,
CLAUMONT, BROOKSIDE,
WILMINGTON
county .... KENT, SUSSEX, NEW
CASTLE
date of state flag: ____ 7,
1787 .... DECEMBER
Indian .... LENAPE
river .... INDIAN, LEIPSIC,
CHOPTANK, DELAWARE,
BROADKILL, MURDERKILL
River city .... TRENTON
settlers .... SWEDES
state bird .... BLUE HEN
state flower .... PEACH
BLOSSOM

state nickname .... FIRST,
DIAMOND
delay .... LAG, PEND, SLOW, FLAG,
DRAG, DALLY, DEFER(MENT),
FALTER, STALL, DETAIN,
LINGER
doing something, habitually
.... PROCRASTINATE
in getting business done
.... RED TAPE
in law .... MORA, LACHES
in law, inexcusable
.... LACHES
the advance of progress
.... HINDER, IMPEDE, RETARD
until later .... POSTPONE
delayed reaction .... DOUBLE
TAKE
delaying action .... STALL
in Congress .... FILIBUSTER
in law .... MORATORY
dele ...... ERASE, CANCEL, DELETE,
SLASH, REMOVE
delectable .... YUMMY, DELICIOUS,
PLEASING, EXQUISITE
delectation .... DELIGHT,
PLEASURE, AMUSEMENT
delegate .... AGENT, ENVOY,
DEPUTE, DEPUTY, EMPOWER,
ENTRUST, DEPUTIZE,
EMISSARY
kind of .... BACKUP,
ALTERNATE, ACCREDITED
unofficial .... OBSERVER
delegation .... BODY, MISSION,
COMMISSION, CONTINGENT
delete .... DELE, EDIT, ERASE,
OMIT, BLOT OUT, EXPUNGE,
CROSS OUT, REMOVE
deleterious .... BAD, HARMFUL,
HURTFUL, RUINOUS,
INJURIOUS, PERNICIOUS,
DETRIMENTAL
deletion .... EDITING, ERASURE,
OMISSION, BLUE-PENCILING
of word's last letter
.... APOCOPE
cancel .... STET
Delia .... ARTEMIS
deliberate .... SLOW, PONDER,
CAREFUL, KNOWING, STUDIED,
CONSIDER, UNHURRIED,
THOUGHTFUL, INTENTIONAL
discourtesy .... CUT, SNUB,
REBUFF
Delibes, composer .... LEO
ballet .... NAILA
opera .... LAKME
delicacy .... CATE, CAVIAR,
NICETY, TIDBIT, FRAILTY,
KICKSAW, FINENESS, NICENESS

195

gamey .... VENISON
of performance .... FINESSE
delicate .... NICE, FRAIL,
FINE(SPUN), DAINTY, TENDER,
FRAGILE, REFINED, TAFFETA,
TICKLISH, EXQUISITE
delicately pretty .... DAINTY,
MIGNON
delicatessen .... DELI, FOOD SHOP,
FOOD STORE
delicious .... SWEET, TASTY,
YUMMY, SAVORY, LUSCIOUS,
AMBROSIAL, APPETIZING,
PALATABLE, DELIGHTFUL
fruit .... APPLE
delict .... INJURY, OFFENSE,
MISDEMEANOR
delight .... JOY, ELATE, PLEASE,
REGALE, ENCHANT, CHARM,
RAPTURE, REJOICE, ENTRANCE,
PLEASURE
in .... SAVOR
delightful .... ALLURING,
CHARMING, PLEASING
Delilah .... HARLOT, TEMPTRESS
victim of .... SAMSON
delimit .... DEMARCATE
delineate .... DRAW, LIMN, DEPICT,
SKETCH, OUTLINE, PORTRAY,
DESCRIBE
delineation .... PLAN, SKETCH,
DRAWING, PORTRAIT
delineator .... LIMNER
delinquency ...... GUILT, MISDEED,
DEFAULT, NEGLECT,
VIOLATION
record/report: sl. .... GIG
delinquent .... GUILTY, OVERDUE,
CULPABLE, NEGLIGENT,
SINFUL, DEFAULTING,
NEGLECTFUL
a .... JUVENILE
alleged other .... PARENT
debt .... ARREARS
debtor .... DEFAULTER
likely home of .... BOYS'
TOWN, REFORMATORY
person .... SINNER, CULPRIT,
OFFENDER
deliquesce .... MELT, THAW,
LIQUEFY
delirious .... MAD, RAVING,
EXCITED, UNSTABLE
delirium .... MANIA, PANIC,
FRENZY, CONFUSION
severe .... HALLUCINATION
tremens .... JIMJAMS, JITTERS
delitescent ...... HIDDEN, LATENT,
INACTIVE
deliver .... RID, EMIT, FREE, SAVE,
CARRY, SPEAK, UTTER,

CONVEY, RESCUE, HAND
OVER, LIBERATE, TRANSFER,
DISTRIBUTE
goods for sale .... CONSIGN
prematurely .... SLINK
sermon .... PREACH
deliverance .... RESCUE, OPINION,
RELEASE, SALVATION,
REDEMPTION
deliverer .... COURIER, REDEEMER,
LIBERATOR
delivery ...... ADDRESS, TRANSFER,
UTTERANCE, CHILDBIRTH,
PARTURITION, DISTRIBUTION
boy .... JUMPER
of property, legal .... LIVERY
dell .... DALE, GLEN, VALE, SLACK,
DINGLE, RAVINE, VALLEY
denizen .... FARMER
Della, secretary .... STREET
singer .... REESE
dells .... RAPIDS
Delmar, novelist .... VINA
Delos inhabitant .... DELIAN
delouse .... SANITIZE
Delphic .... ORACULAR
priestess .... PYTHIA,
PYTHONESS
seer .... ORACLE
delphinium .... LARKSPUR
delude .... KID, DUPE, FOOL,
CHEAT, TRICK, DECEIVE,
BEGUILE, MISLEAD
deluge .... POUR, FLOOD,
CATARACT, DOWNPOUR,
INUNDATE, CATACLYSM,
INUNDATION
of blood in circulatory
system .... PLETHORA
of words .... SPATE
delul .... CAMEL, DROMEDARY
delusion .... FANCY, MIRAGE,
VISION, FALLACY, FANTASY,
ILLUSION, PARANOIA
of grandeur .... MEGALOMANIA
deluxe .... LUXURIOUS
delve .... DIG, PROBE, FATHOM,
(RE)SEARCH, INVESTIGATE
demagogue .... QUACK,
AGITATOR, MOUNTEBANK,
RABBLE-ROUSER
demand .... CRY, LEVY, NEED,
CLAIM, EXACT, ORDER,
CHARGE, REQUIRE
final .... ULTIMATUM
for identification
.... CHALLENGE
in .... SOUGHT
noisy .... CLAMOR
payment of debt .... DUN
repetition .... ENCORE

with authority .... COMMAND
demandant .... PLAINTIFF
demanding .... STRICT, ARDUOUS,
EXIGENT, EXACTING,
CLAMOROUS, DIFFICULT,
INSISTENT
demarcate .... BOUND, DEFINE,
CONFINE, DELIMIT, RESTRICT
demarcation .... LINE, LIMIT,
BORDER, BOUNDS, BOUNDARY
deme .... TOWNSHIP
demean .... ABASE, HUMBLE,
LOWER, DEGRADE
demeanor .... AIR, MIEN,
MANNER, BEARING, CONDUCT,
BEHAVIOR, CARRIAGE,
PORTANCE
having dignified .... PORTLY
dement .... DERANGE
demented ...... MAD, LOCO, LUNY,
CRAZY, LOONY, CRAZED,
INSANE, FLIGHTY, DERANGED
dementia .... INSANITY
demerit .... FAULT, MINUS,
DEFECT, (BLACK)MARK
slang .... GIG
demerol .... DRUG, SEDATIVE,
ANALGESIC
demesne .... REALM, DOMAIN,
REGION
Demeter .... CERES
demicup .... TASSE
demigod .... HERO, IDOL, DEITY
demilune .... CRESCENT
demise .... WILL, DEATH, CONVEY,
BEQUEST, DECEASE
demission .... ABDICATION,
RESIGNATION
demit .... RESIGN, ABDICATE
demitasse .... (COFFEE)CUP
demobilize .... DISARM, DISBAND,
DISMISS, DISCHARGE, MUSTER
OUT
democracy .... REPUBLIC
world's largest .... INDIA
world's smallest .... SAN
MARINO
Democrat, any .... LOCOFOCO
Democratic Party faction
.... LOCOFOCO
demode ...... PASSE, OUT-OF-DATE,
OLD-FASHIONED
demographic item .... BIRTHS,
DEATHS, MARRIAGES
demoiselle .... CRANE, DAMSEL,
DRAGONFLY
demolish ...... RASE, RAZE, LEVEL,
RUIN, SMASH, WRECK,
DESTROY
demon .... NAT, OGRE, ANITO,
DEVIL, FIEND, GHOST, GHOUL,

GNOME, D(A)EDAL, EVIL
SPIRIT
Arabian .... AFRIT, EBLIS,
GENIE, JINN(I), AFREET,
DAITYA
blood-sucking .... VAMPIRE
female .... LAMIA
Frankenstein's .... MONSTER
little .... ELF
young .... IMP
demoness .... LILITH, INCUBUS,
SUCCUBA, SUCCUBUS
demoniac(al) .... CRUEL, FRANTIC,
HELLISH, DEVILISH, FIENDISH,
DIABOLIC(AL)
demonism .... IDOLATRY,
SATANISM
demons, abode of all
.... PANDEMONIUM
demonstrable .... APODICTIC,
DEDUCIBLE
demonstrate .... SHOW, PROVE,
EVINCE, CONFIRM, EXHIBIT
demonstration ...... TEST, PROOF,
PROBATION, EXPERIMENT
demonstrative .... EVIDENT,
CONVINCING, ILLUSTRATIVE
in grammar .... D(E)ICTIC
pronoun .... THAT, THIS, THESE
demoralize .... WEAKEN,
CONFUSE, CORRUPT, DEPRESS,
DISCOURAGE, DISHEARTEN
demos .... DEME, MASSES, PEOPLE,
POPULACE
demote .... LOWER, DEGRADE,
DOWNGRADE
opposed to .... PROMOTE
slang .... BUST, BREAK
demotics .... SOCIOLOGY
Dempsey (Jack) sobriquet
.... (MANASSA) MAULER
demulcent ...... SALVE, OINTMENT,
SOOTHING
demur .... FALTER, OBJECT,
PROTEST, HESITATE, THINK
TWICE
demure .... COY, MIM, SHY, PRIM,
SOBER, MODEST, SEDATE
demurrer .... PLEA, OBJECTOR,
OBJECTION
den .... CAVE, DIVE, ROOM,
HAUNT, STUDY, HANGOUT,
RETREAT
sacred .... SANCTUM
secret .... MEW, HIDEOUT
wild animal's .... LAIR, LODGE
denarii, 12 .... SOLIDUS
denary .... DECIMAL, TENFOLD
dendritic/dendroid ...... TREELIKE
dene .... DUNE
dengue .... DANDY FEVER,

BREAKBONE FEVER
mosquito carrier of ..... AEDES
AEGYPTI
deniable .... DOUBTFUL,
SUSPICIOUS
denial ...... REFUSAL, DISAVOWAL,
REJECTION, ABSTINENCE,
REPUDIATION
in diplomacy/official
.... DEMENTI
opposed to .... COMPLIANCE,
AFFIRMATIVE
statement of ...... DENEGATION
denier .... COIN, DISOWNER,
DISCLAIMER
denigrate ...... DEFAME, ASPERSE,
VILIFY, BLACKEN
denim .... FABRIC,
(COTTON)CLOTH
use for .... (C)OVERALLS,
UNIFORMS
denizen ...... DWELLER, CIT(IZEN),
RESIDENT, OCCUPANT,
INHABITANT
Denmark. See Danish
Dennis .... DAY, HOPPER
Dennis the ____ .... MENACE
denominate .... CALL, NAME,
TITLE
denomination .... SECT, CLASS,
ORDER, STYLE, CHURCH,
NAMING, CALLING,
DESIGNATION
denominational .... SECTARY,
SECTARIAN
denote .... MARK, MEAN, EXPRESS,
SIGNIFY, SPECIFY, INDICATE
denouement .... END, EFFECT,
OUTCOME, SOLUTION
denounce .... CURSE, DECRY,
ASSAIL, ACCUSE, CHARGE,
CONDEMN, CRITICIZE,
EXCORIATE
dense .... CLOSE, GROSS, SOLID,
THICK, PACKED, STUPID,
COMPACT, POPULOUS
growth of trees .... WOODS,
FOREST, JUNGLE
dent .... MAR, DINT, HOLLOW,
DIMPLE, INDENTATION
dental device .... FLOSS
drill .... BURR
paste ..... ZIRCATE, DENTIFRICE
dentate .... NOTCHED, SERRATE,
TOOTHED
dented .... TOOTHED
denticle .... TOOTH
dentifrice .... ZIRCATE
type of .... GEL, PASTE,
POWDER
dentin(e) .... IVORY

dentist: colloq. .... TOOTH PULLER
drill of .... BURR
pincers of .... FORCEPS
tool of .... PROBE, MIRROR
dentist's aid .... LAUGHING GAS
degree .... DMD
professional helper
.... HYGIENIST
dentistry .... ODONTOLOGY
denture .... PLATE, TEETH, BRIDGE
type of .... FULL, PARTIAL,
IMMEDIATE
denude .... STRIP
denunciation .... THREAT,
CENSURE, ANATHEMA,
DIATRIBE, ACCUSATION
Denver is capital of
.... COLORADO
deny .... ABJURE, DISOWN, REFUSE,
NEGATE, REJECT, DISAVOW,
OPPOSE, GAINSAY, FORSWEAR,
PROTEST, WITHHOLD,
REPUDIATE, CONTRADICT
denying .... NEGATIVE,
DENEGATION
deodar .... CEDAR
deodorant .... MUM, PASTILLE,
FRESHENER, ANTIPERSPIRANT
drug .... BISMUTH
deontology .... ETHICS
depart ...... DIE, EXIT, LEAVE, GO
(AWAY), SET OUT, SKIP OUT
from script .... AD LIB
quickly .... VAMOOSE
secretly .... DECAMP, ABSCOND
slang ..... MOSEY, TODDLE, HIT
THE ROAD
departed .... LEFT, PAST,
(BY)GONE
the .... DEAD
department .... BUREAU, SECTION,
BUSINESS, DIVISION
store, designating a ...... FIVE-
AND-TEN
store stairway ...... ESCALATOR
departure .... EXIT, DEATH,
EGRESS, LEAVING, PARTING,
DEVIATION
from a job due to advanced
age .... RETIREMENT
from an area of danger
.... EVACUATION
mass/of Israelites from Egypt
.... EXODUS
depend .... BANK, HANG, RELY,
COUNT, HINGE
dependable .... RELIABLE,
STEADFAST, RESPONSIBLE
dependence .... RELIANCE,
ADDICTION
dependency .... COLONY,

WARDSHIP, AP(P)ANAGE, TERRITORY
dependent .... WARD, PROTEGE, SUBJECT, HANGER-ON, FOLLOWER, PARASITE, PENSIONARY, SUBORDINATE
kind of .... SATELLITE
on .... CONTINGENT
depict .... DRAW, LIMN, PAINT, RENDER, PICTURE, PORTRAY
in words .... DESCRIBE, DELINEATE
depilate .... PLUCK, SHAVE, DEHAIR
depilation .... ELECTROLYSIS
deplete .... DRAIN, ERODE, EMPTY, EXHAUST
deplorable .... SAD, RUEFUL, WOEFUL, GRIEVOUS, LAMENTABLE
deplore ...... RUE, DECRY, MOURN, BEMOAN, BEWAIL, GRIEVE, LAMENT, REGRET, REPINE
deploy .... SPREAD(OUT)
de plume, _____ .... NOM
deplume .... PLUCK
depone .... DEPOSE, TESTIFY
deponent's statement
.... AFFIDAVIT, TESTIMONY
deport ...... EXILE, EXPEL, BANISH, BEHAVE, EXPATRIATE
deportment .... MIEN, BEARING, CONDUCT, BEHAVIOR
depose .... OUST, SWEAR, AFFIRM, DISBAR, DEPONE, REMOVE, UNSEAT, TESTIFY, DETHRONE
deposit .... LEES, DREGS, PLEDGE, PAYMENT, RESIDUE, SECURITY
alluvial .... DELTA, GEEST
body .... CALCULUS
clayey .... MARL
geyser .... SINTER
glacial/water-borne
.... PLACER, MORAINE
mineral .... LODE
money .... PAY IN
on teeth .... TARTAR
sediment .... SILT
waste .... SLUDGE
wine cask ...... ARGAL, ARGOL, TARTAR
depositary ...... URN, BANK, SAFE, VAULT, TRUSTEE, DEPOSITORY
deposition .... TESTIMONY
form of .... AFFIDAVIT
depot .... STATION, ENTREPOT, WAREHOUSE, STOREHOUSE
arms .... ARMORY, ARSENAL
French .... GARE
military .... ARSENAL, MAGAZINE

deprave .... DEBASE, DEBAUCH, PERVERT
depraved ...... EVIL, VILE, PUTRID, CORRUPT, DISSOLUTE
depravity .... CORRUPTION, TURPITUDE, PERVERSION
deprecate .... BEWAIL, REGRET, DEPLORE, PROTEST, DISAPPROVE
depreciate .... FALL, LESSEN, CHEAPEN, BELITTLE, DISPARAGE
colloquial .... RUN DOWN
money officially .... DECRY
slang .... KNOCK
depredate .... ROB, PILLAGE, PLUNDER
depress ...... DENT, LOWER, UPSET, DAMPEN, DEJECT, SADDEN, DISHEARTEN
depressant .... SEDATIVE
depressed ...... SAD, BLUE, GLUM, MOODY, DEJECTED, DOWNCAST, FLATTENED, DOWN IN THE MOUTH
depressing .... BLEAK, DISMAL, DREARY, GLOOMY
periods for some workers
.... BLUE MONDAYS
depression .... DIP, DENT, HOLLOW, LOWERING, REDUCTION, ABASEMENT
between hills .... GLEN
between mountains .... COL
emotional feelings of
...... GRIEF, ANXIETY, SADNESS, DISTRESS, PESSIMISM
in economics .... RECESSION
on the cheek/chin ...... DIMPLE
small .... FOVEA
deprivation .... LOSS, DENIAL
deprive .... STRIP, DENUDE, USURP, DIVEST, TAKE(AWAY), DISPOSSESS
of ownership .... EXPROPRIATE
of power to reproduce
.... GELD, CASTRATE, STERILIZE, EMASCULATE
of sunlight .... ETIOLATE
deprived .... SHORN, (BE)REFT, CUT OFF, DENUDED
depth ...... SEA, OCEAN, LOWNESS, DEEPNESS
bomb/charge .... ASHCAN
combining form .... BATHO
of water displaced by ship
.... DRAFT
depurate .... PURIFY
deputation .... DELEGATION
depute .... SEND, APPOINT, DELEGATE, AUTHORIZE

deputies' group .... POSSE
deputy .... AGENT, ENVOY, PROXY, VICAR, (DE)LEGATE, SURROGATE, LIEUTENANT, VICE-REGENT
Der Alte .... SCHRANZ, ADENAUER
Fuehrer .... HITLER
deracinate .... UPROOT
derange .... UPSET, MESS UP, CRAZE, DEMENT, CONFUSE, DISTURB, DISTRACT
deranged .... CRAZY, INSANE
derangement .... TURMOIL, IMBALANCE
Derby .... HAT, BOWLER, HORSE RACE
English: colloq.
.... BILLYCOCK
site .... KENTUCKY, EPSOM DOWNS
winner .... ZEV, SWAPS, PONDER, ASSAULT, NEEDLES, TIM TAM, AFFIRMED, CITATION, WHIRLAWAY, KAUAI KING, BOLD FORBES, SECRETARIAT, WAR ADMIRAL, GATO DEL SOL, GENUINE RISK, TWENTY GRAND, LUCKY DEBONAIR, FOOLISH PLEASURE
winner, Triple Crown
.... ASSAULT, AFFIRMED, CITATION, WHIRLAWAY, SECRETARIAT, WAR ADMIRAL, SEATTLE SLEW
derelict .... TRAMP, WRECK, REMISS, DRIFTER, FLOTSAM, SLACKER, CASTAWAY, FORSAKEN
deride .... GIBE, JEER, MOCK, SCOFF, SCORN, RIDICULE
variant .... FLEAR
derision .... SCORN, DISDAIN, MOCKERY, CONTEMPT
derisive .... MOCKING, SCORNFUL, SARCASTIC, DISDAINFUL, CONTEMPTUOUS
cry .... BOO, HISS, HOOT, RAZZ, CATCALL
derivation .... ROOT, ORIGIN, DESCENT
word .... ETYMOLOGY
derive .... GET, DRAW, INFER, OBTAIN, (D)EDUCE, ORIGINATE
derived from oil .... OLEIC
derm, as suffix .... SKIN, COVERING
dermatoid .... SKINLIKE
dermis .... SKIN, CUTIS
dernier .... LAST, FINAL
cri .... LAST WORD, LATEST(STYLE)

derogate .... DECRY, DEFAME,
    DETRACT, DISPARAGE
derogatory .... ADVERSE,
    CRITICAL, DEFAMATORY,
    DETRACTING, HUMILIATING
    remark .... SLUR
derrick .... RIG, CRANE, DAVIT,
    HOIST, STEEVE
    part of .... JIB, BEAM, BOOM,
    SPAR, PULLEY
derriere .... REAR, BEHIND,
    BUTTOCKS
derring-do .... GEST
derringer .... GUN, PISTOL
derris extraction ...... ROTENONE
derry .... BALLAD
dervish .... FAKIR, BEGGAR,
    MENDICANT
    headgear .... TAJ
    Moslem .... SADITE
    practice .... HOWLING,
    WHIRLING
    wandering .... CALENDER
Des Moines is capital of
    .... IOWA
desalinization .... DESALT
descant .... SONG, MELODY,
    COMMENT, CRITICISM
descend .... DROP, FALL, PLUNGE,
    COME DOWN, STEP DOWN,
    PLUMMET
    upon ...... HIT, POUND, ALIGHT,
    ATTACK, STRIKE
descendant .... BREED, CHILD,
    SCION, PROGENY, INHERITOR,
    OFFSPRING
    female .... HEIRESS, DAUGHTER
    male .... SON, HEIR,
    SUCCESSOR
    of literary work .... SEQUEL
descent .... FALL, LINE, BIRTH,
    ORIGIN, DECLINE, LINEAGE,
    ANCESTRY, EXTRACTION,
    DERIVATION, SUCCESSION
    sudden, swift .... SWOOP,
    POUNCE
describe ..... DRAW, LIMN, LABEL,
    PAINT, DEFINE, DEPICT,
    RELATE, NARRATE, PICTURE
    briefly again
    .... RECAPITULATE
    exactly .... DEFINE
    grammatically .... PARSE
    graphically .... PORTRAY
    in detail .... RECOUNT, SPECIFY
description .... SKETCH,
    ACCOUNT, RELATION,
    NARRATION
    brief .... DIGEST, SUMMARY
    detailed .... PARTICULARS
descriptive .... GRAPHIC, STORIED,

    NARRATIVE
name/title .... EPITHET
poem .... EPIC
word .... LABEL
descry ...... KEN, SEE, ESPY, SPOT,
    SIGHT, DETECT
Desdemona's husband
    .... OTHELLO
    slanderer .... IAGO
desecrate .... TAINT, DEBASE,
    DEFILE, POLLUTE, PROFANE,
    VIOLATE, DISHONOR
desecration .... BLASPHEMY,
    SACRILEGE
deseret .... HONEYBEE
desert .... QUIT, LEAVE, MERIT,
    WASTE, SECEDE, ABANDON,
    FORSAKE, COLORADO,
    WILDERNESS
    Afghanistan .... DASHTE-
    MARGOW
    African .... NAMIB, LIBYAN,
    SAHARA, TENERE, ARABIAN,
    MAKTEIR, KALAHARI, GRAND
    ERG, ERG-IGUIDI, GUIR-
    HAMADA, GREAT SAND SEA
    animal .... CAMEL
    Arabian .... NEFUD, DAHANA,
    JAFURA, AR-RIMAL, BAHR-ES-
    SAFI, RUB-AL-KHALI
    Arctic .... TUNDRA
    Asiatic .... GOBI, THAR,
    SHAMO, KARA-KUM
    Australian .... GIBSON,
    SIMPSON, GREAT SANDY,
    GREAT VICTORIA
    basin floor .... PLAYA
    Chilean .... ATACAMA
    China ..... GOBI, ALXA SHAMO,
    TAKLA MAKAN
    dweller .... ARAB(IAN),
    BEDOUIN
    dwelling .... TENT
    fertile spot .... OASIS
    horse .... ARAB
    India .... GREAT INDIAN
    Iran .... LUT
    Iraq .... SYRIAN
    like .... ARID
    like condition .... XERIC
    Mongolian .... GOBI
    Pakistan .... THAR
    pertaining to .... EREMIC
    plant .... AGAVE, CACTUS,
    OCOTILLO
    plant, tree-like .... SOTOL
    pride of the .... CACTI
    Russian .... KARA-KUM,
    KYZYL-KUM
    shrub .... RETEM
    slang .... DITCH

    train .... CARAVAN,
    CARAVANSARY
    Turkestan .... KARA-KUM,
    KIZIL-KUM
    U.S. .... TULE, MOJAVE,
    PAINTED, ESCALANTE,
    COLORADO, BLACK ROCK,
    SMOKE CREEK, WHITE SANDS
    valley .... BOLSON
    wind .... SIMOOM, SIMOON,
    SIROCCO
Desert Fox .... ROMMEL
deserted .... LONELY, FORLORN,
    DESOLATE, SOLITARY,
    ABANDONED
deserter .... BOLTER, RATTER,
    RUNAWAY, APOSTATE,
    FUGITIVE, RENEGADE,
    RUNAGATE, TURNCOAT
    army .... AWOL
    describing a .... RAT
desertion .... ESCAPE, FLIGHT,
    DEFECTION, ABANDONMENT
    slang .... COP-OUT
deserts .... DUE
deserve .... EARN, MERIT,
    ENTITLED TO
deserved reward/punishment
    .... DESERT(S)
deservedly .... JUSTLY, WORTHILY
deserving .... WORTHY,
    MERITORIOUS
    punishment .... GUILTY,
    CULPABLE
desiccant .... DRIER
desiccate .... DRY
desiccated coconut meat
    .... COPRA
desideratum .... NEED
design .... AIM, IDEA, PLAN,
    STYLE, CREATE, SCHEME,
    PATTERN, PURPOSE, CONTRIVE
    having .... FIGURED
    highlight .... MOTIF
    illustrative .... DIAGRAM
    on a page .... VIGNETTE
    ornamental .... THEME, DEVICE
    rough .... SKETCH
    sinister, usually .... PLOT,
    INTRIGUE
designate .... MARK, NAME,
    ASSIGN, SELECT, APPOINT,
    ENTITLE, SPECIFY, INDICATE
    again .... RENAME
designated .... SLATED
designation .... TITLE, NAMING,
    NOMINATION, APPOINTMENT
designator .... SELECTOR
designer .... ARTIST, STYLIST,
    CREATOR, PLANNER,
    ARCHITECT

of the Wooden Horse
.... SINON
designer's forte ...... ORIGINALITY
designing .... WILY, ARTFUL,
CRAFTY, CUNNING, SCHEMING
desil .... DEIL
desinence .... SUFFIX
desirable .... IN DEMAND,
APPETIZING
part .... MEAT, CREAM
desire .... YEN, NEED, WANT,
WILL, WISH, COVET, CRAVE,
LIKING, LONGING, PENCHANT
characterized by .... ORECTIC
for sleep .... NARCOLEPSY
overwhelming .... ESTRUS
seat of .... LIVER
strong .... HUNGER
weakest .... VELLEITY
desirer .... LOVER, ASPIRANT
desirous .... AVID, FAIN, KEEN,
EAGER, HUNGRY, WISHFUL
desist .... QUIT, STOP, CEASE,
ABSTAIN, FORBEAR
desk .... POST, TABLE, PULPIT,
BUREAU, COUNTER, ROLLTOP
for prayer .... PRIE DIEU
reading .... AMBO, LECTERN
use of ..... DRAWING, READING,
WRITING
writing .... DAVENPORT,
SECRETARY, ESCRITOIRE
desman .... MUSK
desmid .... ALGA
desolate .... BLEAK, STARK,
BARREN, LONELY, (FOR)LORN,
DESERTED, FORSAKEN,
SOLITARY, MISERABLE
desolation .... RUIN, WASTE,
AGONY, GLOOM, MISERY,
SOLITUDE
despair .... WOE, BALE, MISERY,
ANGUISH, DESPOND,
DESPERATION
desperado .... THUG, BRAVO,
OUTLAW, CRIMINAL
hunters .... POSSE
desperate .... RASH, HEROIC,
FURIOUS, HOPELESS, RECKLESS
appeal .... SOS
criminal ...... BRAVO, RUFFIAN,
DESPERADO
desperation .... FUTILITY,
HOPELESSNESS, DESPONDENCY
despicable .... VILE, HATEFUL,
ODIOUS, LOW-DOWN,
OBNOXIOUS, DETESTABLE,
CONTEMPTIBLE
person .... CAD, CHEAT,
CROOK, SKUNK, COWARD,
GYPPER, COZENER, SCOUNDREL

slang .... SCALY
despise .... HATE, ABHOR, SCORN,
DETEST, CONTEMN, DISDAIN
despised .... LOWLY, UNSUNG
despite .... INSULT, MALICE,
(AL)THOUGH, IN THE FACE OF,
IN THE TEETH OF,
NOTWITHSTANDING
despiteful .... HOSTILE
despoil .... ROB, LOOT, RUIN,
RAVAGE, PILLAGE, PLUNDER
despoiled: archaic .... REFT
despond .... DESPAIR
despondency ...... BLUES, DUMPS,
DISMAY, DESPAIR, DEJECTION
despondent .... DEPRESSED
despot ...... CZAR, TSAR, TYRANT,
AUTOCRAT, DICTATOR
Persian .... SATRAP
despotic ruler .... CZAR, SHAH,
TSAR
despotism .... TYRANNY,
AUTARCHY, AUTOCRACY
despumate .... SKIM
desquamate .... PEEL(OFF)
dessert ...... ICE, FLAN, SWEET(S),
MOUSSE, SUNDAE, PARFAIT,
CONFECTION
addendum .... CREAM
fruit .... BETTY
fruit juices .... FRAPPE
fruit, gelatin .... CHARLOTTE
item .... PIE, CAKE, FRUITS,
PUDDING, ICE CREAM
kind of .... SASS
melon .... BOMBE
milk and gelatin .... BLANC-
MANGE
rum .... BABA
spongecake .... TRIFLE
sweetened cream with wine
.... SILLABUB, SYLLABUB
desserts .... DUE
destigmatize .... WHITEWASH
destination .... GOAL, ADDRESS,
JOURNEY'S END
destine .... LOOM, IMPEND,
ORDAIN
destined .... FATED, EXPECTED
destiny .... LOT, DOOM, FATE,
LUCK, STAR, FORTUNE
Oriental .... KISMET
destitute .... POOR, NEEDY,
DEVOID, HARD-UP, LACKING,
FLAT BROKE, DOWN AND OUT
colloquial .... IN THE HOLE
destitution .... NEED, PENURY,
POVERTY, INDIGENCE
destrier .... STEED, CHARGER,
WARHORSE
destroy .... BURN, RAZE, RUIN,

SACK, SLAY, CRUSH, SMASH,
WRECK, RAVAGE, SHATTER,
WIPE OUT, DEMOLISH, LAY
WASTE, STAMP OUT
by blotting out/effacing
.... OBLITERATE
by fire .... GUT
entirely .... ERADICATE,
EXTERMINATE
machinery to force
agreement .... RATTEN
slang .... TOTAL, TRASH
slowly .... ERODE, WASTE
destroyer .... RUINER, WRECKER
crop .... BLIGHT, LOCUST,
DROUGHT
historical .... ATTILA
kind of .... VANDAL,
ARSONIST, NIHILIST
military .... BATTLESHIP
of monster .... HERMES, ST.
GEORGE
of vermin ...... EXTERMINATOR
of wood .... TERMITE
destruction .... FALL, RUIN,
HAVOC, WASTE, WRACK,
WRECKAGE, PERDITION
by fire, on purpose ..... ARSON
malicious .... VANDALISM
mass .... GENOCIDE,
MASSACRE, SLAUGHTER,
DECIMATION
of life by fire/widespread
.... HOLOCAUST
of nation .... GENOCIDE
destructive .... DEADLY
insect .... MOTH, LOCUST,
TERMITE
liquid .... ACID
natural phenomenon
.... STORM, CYCLONE,
TORNADO, TYPHOON,
HURRICANE, LIGHTNING,
FLOOD, EARTHQUAKE
substance .... POISON
to metal .... RUST
destructor .... FURNACE,
INCINERATOR
desuetude .... DISUSE
desultory .... FITFUL, RANDOM,
AIMLESS, ERRATIC,
EXCURSIVE, HAPHAZARD
detach ...... LOOSE, SEVER, UNFIX,
SEPARATE, UNFASTEN
detached .... ALONE, ALOOF,
SEPARATE, INDIFFERENT
in music .... SPICCATO
detachment .... UNIT, DETAIL,
ALOOFNESS, ISOLATION
detail .... ITEM, PART, UNIT,
SPECIFY, ENUMERATE,

ASSIGN(MENT), PARTICULAR
attentive to .... METICULOUS
detailed .... ITEMIZED, SPECIFIC,
ASSIGNED, ELABORATE
account .... EXPLICATION
explanation .... EXPOSITION
list .... ROSTER, DIRECTORY,
INVENTORY, ENUMERATION
statement .... RECITAL
details, small and unimportant
.... MINUTIAE
detain ...... HOLD, DELAY, ARREST,
HINDER, CONFINE, RESTRAIN
ship in port .... INTERN
detect ...... SPY, ESPY, FIND, SPOT,
SENSE, TRACE, DESCRY,
NOTICE, DISCERN, DISCOVER,
PERCEIVE
detecting device .... BUG, RADAR,
SONAR, DOWSER FEELER,
ANTENNA, TENTACLE
detection .... ESPIAL, GLIMPSE,
DISCOVERY
radar .... INTERCEPTION
detective ...... TEC, DICK, SLEUTH,
GUMSHOE, SPOTTER,
HAWKSHAW, OPERATIVE,
POLICEMAN
Conan Doyle's .... HOLMES
describing one .... TAIL,
SHADOW, PRIVATE EYE
kind of .... UNDERCOVER,
PLAINCLOTHES
of fiction/movie .... CHAN,
MOTO, NERO, DRAKE, SAINT,
TRACY, TRENT, HOLMES,
POIROT
orchid-loving .... NERO
store .... FLOOR WALKER
story .... MAIGRET
story character .... GOON,
WARDEN, CORONER,
HOODLUM, SHERIFF,
INFORMER, HATCHETMAN,
INVESTIGATOR
detector of sorts ...... BUG, NOSE,
RADAR, SONAR, FEELER,
ANTENNA
detent .... PAWL, CATCH, CLICK
detente ...... TRUCE, COOLING OFF
of a sort ...... RAPPROCHEMENT
detention ...... DELAY, CAPTIVITY,
CONFINEMENT
deter .... BLOCK, IMPEDE,
PREVENT, OBSTRUCT,
DISCOURAGE
deterge .... CLEAN(SE)
detergent .... SOAP, ABLUENT,
SAPONIN, SOLVENT, CLEANSER
compound .... BORON
deteriorate .... ROT, DECAY,

DEBASE, PERISH, WORSEN, GO
BAD, CORRUPT, DEPRECIATE
from disuse .... RUST
determinant .... CAUSE
determinate ...... FIXED, DEFINITE,
SPECIFIC
determination .... WILL,
FIRMNESS, RESOLUTION
determine .... END, JUDGE,
DECIDE, DEFINE, SETTLE,
RESOLVE, SPECIFY, ASCERTAIN
issue by combat ...... DERAIGN
quotient .... DIVIDE
worth of .... EVALUATE,
APPRAISE
determined ...... SET, FIRM, DEAD
SET, RESOLUTE
deterrent ...... STUMBLING BLOCK
of a kind .... FEAR, DOUBT,
SHAME
war .... A-BOMB
detest ...... HATE, ABHOR, LOATHE,
DESPISE, DISLIKE, EXECRATE
detestable ...... ODIOUS, HATEFUL,
HORRID, DAMNABLE,
EXECRABLE, ABOMINABLE
person .... BOOR, LOUT,
COWARD, POLTROON
detestation ...... HATRED, DISLIKE,
LOATHING
dethrone .... OUST, DEPOSE,
UNSEAT, UNCROWN
dethronement, object of
.... KING, RULER, EMPEROR,
CHAMPION
detonate .... GO OFF, SET OFF,
FIRE, EXPLODE, FULMINATE
detonating device .... CAP, PIN,
FUSE, TRIGGER, PERCUSSION
object .... BOMB, SHELL,
SQUIB, BULLET, GRENADE,
DYNAMITE, FIRECRACKER
detour .... TURN, BYPASS, DIVERT,
DEVIATION
detract .... DECRY, BELITTLE,
BACKBITE, CRITICIZE,
DEROGATE, TAKE AWAY,
DISPARAGE, DEPRECIATE
detraction .... LAMPOON,
SCANDAL, CALUMNY,
CRITICISM
detractor .... MUDSLINGER
d'etre, _____ .... RAISON
detriment .... HARM, LOSS,
DAMAGE, INJURY, LIABILITY
detritus .... DEBRIS
Detroit of Italy .... TURIN
product .... CAR, TRUCK,
AUTOMOBILE
suburb .... ECORSE

deuce .... TWO(SPOT)
superior of/topper .... TREY
Deus .... GOD
deus ex _____ .... MACHINA
Deutschland .... GERMANY
devaluate .... LOWER, CHEAPEN,
DEPRECIATE
devastate ...... RAZE, RUIN, SACK,
CRUSH, LEVEL, RAVAGE,
DESTROY, LAY WASTE,
DEMOLISH
devastation .... RUIN, HAVOC,
WRECK, CATASTROPHE,
DESTRUCTION
devel .... BLOW
develop .... GROW, RIPEN,
EVOLVE, MATURE, UNFOLD,
ENLARGE
more fully, as with details
.... AMPLIFY, ELABORATE
plants .... CULTIVATE
start to .... GERMINATE
to make more valuable
.... IMPROVE
to make qualified .... TRAIN
development .... EVENT, CHANGE,
GROWTH, PROGRESS
building ..... HOUSING PROJECT
of fetus .... FETATION,
PREGNANCY
process of .... EVOLUTION
result of .... OUTGROWTH,
CONSEQUENCE
Devi .... MAYA, SAKTI
consort of .... SIVA
father of .... HIMAVAT
deviant .... VARIANT
deviate ...... ROAM, SHEER, STRAY,
RAMBLE, DIVERGE, MEANDER,
GO ADRIFT
from course .... YAW, VEER,
DETOUR, SWERVE, WANDER,
STRAGGLE
from main topic ...... DIGRESS,
DIVAGATE
deviating .... ABERRANT
deviation .... DETOUR, DIVERSION,
DEFLECTION
of a ship/airplane from path
.... DRIFT
sexual .... TRANSVESTISM
deviative .... INDIRECT
device .... PLAN, TOOL, DESIGN,
EMBLEM, GADGET,
MECHANISM
air moistening .... HUMIDOR
aircraft safety ...... PARACHUTE
any: colloq. .... HICK(E)Y,
DOOHICKEY
any: sl. .... DINGUS

consisting of two small
telescopes
.... BINOCULARS
deceptive/secret .... GIMMICK
fastening .... HASP
for catching criminals/fish
.... DRAGNET
for hearing sound
.... STETHOSCOPE
for holding stone in jewel
cutting .... DIAL
for raising bucket
.... WINDLASS
for secret listening .... BUG
gripping .... VISE, CLAMP
hourglass figure .... CORSET,
GIRDLE
ingenious .... GADGET
light wave amplifying
.... LASER
loosening .... EASER
measuring .... TAPE, RULE(R)
restraining .... BRAKE
sound amplifying .... MASER
thought up .... INVENTION,
CONTRIVANCE
time beating ...... METRONOME
to check vibration .... DAMPER
tone muffling .... MUTE, PEDAL
tricky .... RUSE, STRATAGEM
underwater .... SONAR
used at a bee .... QUILT FRAME
devil .... DEMON, FIEND, SATAN,
AZAZEL, BELIAL, WRETCH,
LUCIFER, MONSTER, OLD
NICK, OLD HARRY, OLD
SCRATCH
colloquial .... TORMENT
dog: sl. .... MARINE,
NAVYMAN, LEATHERNECK
little .... IMP, BRAT
may-care .... CARELESS,
RECKLESS, INSOUCIANT,
NONCHALANT, HAPPY-GO-
LUCKY
Moslem .... SHAITAN
of the .... DIABOLIC
Scottish .... MAHOUND
worship .... IDOLATRY,
SATANISM
worshiper .... DIABOLIST
devilfish .... RAY, MANTA, SKATE,
SEABAT, OCTOPUS
devilish .... CRUEL, WICKED,
HELLISH, INFERNAL,
DEMONIAC, DIABOLIC(AL)
devilkin .... IMP
devilment ...... MALICE, MISCHIEF
devil's bones .... DICE
name .... NICK, SATAN,
LUCIFER

_____ (side for argument's
sake) .... ADVOCATE
deviltry ...... DEVILRY, SATANISM,
WICKEDNESS, WITCHCRAFT
devious .... SLY, UNTRUE, SHIFTY,
TRICKY, CROOKED, ROVING,
WINDING, TORTUOUS,
CIRCUITOUS, ROUNDABOUT
devise .... GIFT, PLAN, PLOT,
COOK, WILL, INVENT,
SCHEME, CONCOCT,
BEQUEATH, CONTRIVE
devised, not .... INTESTATE
devisor .... TESTATOR
devitalize .... SAP, WEAKEN
devoid .... EMPTY, LACKING,
WITHOUT, DESTITUTE
devoir .... DUTY
devolve ...... PASS(ON), TRANSFER,
CHANGE HANDS
devote .... GIVE, LEND, APPLY,
EMPLOY, DEDICATE,
CONSECRATE
devoted .... TRUE, LOYAL,
DEVOUT, ADDICTED, FAITHFUL
devotee .... FAN, IST, BUFF,
ADDICT, VOTARY, ZEALOT,
ENTHUSIAST, FOLLOWER,
PARTISAN
avid .... FANATIC
of beauty .... (A)ESTHETE,
CONNOISSEUR
of sports, etc. ..... AFICIONADO
of the fine arts
.... DILETTANTE
devotion .... ZEAL, ARDOR, PIETY,
FEALTY, LOYALTY, FIDELITY
nine-day .... NOVENA
devotions ...... PRAYERS, WORSHIP
devour .... EAT, CONSUME,
DESTROY
greedily .... GORGE, GOBBLE,
WOLF DOWN
more .... OUTEAT
devout .... GODLY, PIOUS,
EARNEST, FERVENT,
RELIGIOUS
devoutness .... PIETY
dew .... MIST, MOISTURE
frozen ..... RIME, (HOAR)FROST
dewclaw .... DIGIT
dewlap .... JOWL, PALEA, LAPPET,
WATTLE
DEWS, part of .... DISTANT,
EARLY, WARNING, SYSTEM
dewy .... DAMP, MOIST
eyed .... AIRY, INNOCENT
dexter .... RIGHT-HAND SIDE
opposed to .... SINISTER
dexterity .... KNACK, SKILL,
ADROITNESS, CLEVERNESS

special .... CRAFT
dexterous .... DEFT, ADEPT,
HANDY, ADROIT, SKILLFUL
dextral .... RIGHT(HANDED)
dextrose .... SUGAR, GLUCOSE
dhole .... CUON
d'honneur, _____ **(duel)**
.... AFFAIRE
di, as prefix ...... TWICE, DOUBLE,
TWOFOLD
dia, as prefix .... ACROSS,
THROUGH
diabetes, form of .... BRONZE,
MELLITUS, INSIPIDUS,
GESTATIONAL
injection treatment for
.... INSULIN
oral drug to control
.... ORINASE, GLIPIZIDE
person who has ...... DIABETIC
diabetics' bread .... GLUTEN
diablerie .... SORCERY,
DEVIL(T)RY, MISCHIEF
diabolic .... WICKED, SATANIC,
DEVILISH, FIENDISH, INFERNAL
diabolism .... DEMONRY,
SORCERY, SATANISM
political .... NAZISM
diacetylmorphine .... HEROIN
diacritical mark .... TILDE,
UMLAUT, DIERESIS
diadem .... CROWN, TIARA,
HEADBAND
diagnose ...... ANALYZE, EXAMINE
diagnosis .... FINDING, PROGNOSIS
diagnostic in medicine
.... SYMPTOM, DIACRITIC
rap .... PERCUSS
diagonal .... TILTED, OBLIQUE,
ASLANT, SLANTING
line .... BIAS
line between words
.... VIRGULE
diagonally ...... CATER-CORNERED,
OBLIQUELY, CATTY-
CORNER(ED)
diagram ...... PLAN, PLOT, CHART,
GRAPH, SCHEMA, SCHEME,
SKETCH, DRAWING, OUTLINE,
BLUEPRINT
dial .... CALL, DISK, FACE, TUNE
IN, INDICATOR
compass .... CARD
miner's .... COMPASS
pointer .... HAND
dialect ...... CANT, ARGOT, IDIOM,
PATOIS, LINGO, SLANG,
JARGON, LANGUE, TONGUE,
SPEECH, DICTION, LANGUAGE,
VERNACULAR
dialects, mixture of ...... LINGUA

FRANCA
dialectician .... LOGICIAN
dialectics .... LOGIC,
ARGUMENTATION
dialogue .... LINES, SCRIPT,
CONVERSATION,
INTERLOCUTION
dialogues of Buddha ...... SUTRA
diamagnetic substance .... ZINC,
BISMUTH
diameter .... WIDTH, BREADTH,
THICKNESS
measuring device ..... CALIPER
of tube/gun .... BORE, CALIBER
diametrical .... DIRECT,
ABSOLUTE, COMPLETE,
CONTRARY, OPPOSITE
diamond .... GEM, JEWEL, STONE,
FIELD, PLAYGROUND
anniversary .... SIXTIETH
base/facet .... CULET
base, baseball .... SACK
center, ancient ..... GOLCONDA
circular, flat .... RONDEL
crystal/twin crystal .... MACLE
cup .... DOP, DODD
cut .... FACET, BRIOLETTE
cutter .... LAPIDARY
drill .... CARBONADO
feature .... BASE, HOMEPLATE
habiliment .... MITT
holder .... DOP
in baseball .... INFIELD
in the rough .... CRUDE,
UNSHAPED
industrial use .... CUTTING,
ABRASIVE, DRILLING
inferior .... BORT
native .... CARBON
official, baseball ..... UMP(IRE)
perfect .... PARAGON
plane figure .... LOZENGE
rough .... BRAIT
shape .... RHOMB(US),
PARALLELOGRAM
shaped armor plate
.... MASCLE
shaped pattern .... DIAPER
slang .... ICE, SPARKLER,
ENGAGEMENT RING
stone, describing a
.... DAZZLING, BRILLIANT,
SPARKLING, GLITTERING
synthetic .... FABULITE
Diamond of music .... NEIL
State .... DELAWARE
diamondback ...... MOTH, SNAKE,
TURTLE, RATTLER, TERRAPIN
diamonds, black .... COAL
or hearts .... RED SUIT
Diana .... DELIA, ARTEMIS

parent of ..... LATONA, JUPITER
poetic .... MOON
dianthus .... CARNATION
diapason .... (ORGAN)STOP,
TUNING FORK
diaper ...... DIDY, TOWEL, NAPKIN
diaphanous .... THIN, GAUZY,
SHEER, VAGUE, INDISTINCT,
TRANSLUCENT, TRANSPARENT
diaphoresis .... SWEAT,
PERSPIRATION
diaphragm .... MIDRIFF
device, contraceptive
.... PESSARY
pertaining to .... PHRENIC
sound .... HICCUP, HICCOUGH
diarist .... PEPYS, BURNEY,
NICOLSON, JOURNALIST
diarrhea, common cause of
...... STRESS, FOOD POISONING
form of .... ACUTE, CHRONIC
diary .... RECORD, DAYBOOK,
DIURNAL, JOURNAL, MEMOIRS,
CHRONICLE, EPHEMERIS
ship's .... LOG(BOOK)
diaskeuast .... EDITOR
diastase .... ENZYME, AMYLASE
diatomic .... BIVALENT
shell .... FRUSTULE
diatonic, opposed to
.... CHROMATIC
scale .... GAMUT
diatribe .... SCREED, TIRADE,
PHILIPPIC, DENUNCIATION
Diaz, Mexican president
.... PORFIRIO
Rodrigo .... (EL)CID
dib .... BOB, DAP, DIP
dibble .... DIB, DAP, DIP, SOW,
FISH, SCATTER
dice .... CUBE, CHOP, CUT(UP),
GAME, BONES, CUBES, IVORY,
CRAPS, IVORIES, CHECKER
cater of .... FOUR
five on .... CINQUE
game .... NOVUM, HAZARD
game losing throw .... CRAP
six in .... SICE
spot .... PIP
term .... COME, CRAPS,
ELEVEN, AMBSACE, NATURAL
three spots .... TREY
throw .... DIE, JOE, ROLL,
CATER, CHAPS, BOXCAR,
RAILROAD
throw, disallowed ..... NO DICE
throw natural .... SEVEN
trick .... COG
diced .... CUBED
dichroite .... IOLITE
dick: sl. .... DETECTIVE

dickens: colloq. .... DEUCE, DEVIL
Dickens (Charles) beadle
.... (MR.) BUMBLE
character .... PIP, TIM, DORA,
GAMP, HEEP, ROSA, FAGIN,
BUMBLE, DORRIT, PICKWICK,
(JENNY)WREN, (OLIVER)TWIST
dismal swamp of .... EDEN
hero .... CARTON
heroine .... NELL
pen name .... BOZ
pickpocket .... FAGIN
dicker .... TRADE, BARTER,
HAGGLE, BARGAIN
dickey ...... BIB, COLLAR, DONKEY,
RUMBLE, VESTEE, PINAFORE,
(BACK)SEAT, PLASTRON
dicotyledon .... EXOGEN
dictate .... BID, ORDER, ENJOIN,
COMMAND, DOMINEER
dictator .... DESPOT, TYRANT,
AUTOCRAT
propaganda of .... BIG LIE
dictatorial ...... BOSSY, DESPOTIC,
DOGMATIC, ARBITRARY,
IMPERIOUS
diction .... EXPRESSION,
ENUNCIATION
poor .... CACOLOGY
dictionary .... LEXICON,
REFERENCE, WORDBOOK,
THESAURUS, VOCABULARY
prosody .... GRADUS
small .... DICT
dictum .... MAXIM, SAY-SO,
SAYING, DECISION,
PRONOUNCEMENT
didactic .... PEDANTIC
didactics .... PEDAGOGY
didapper .... GREBE, DABCHICK
diddle .... CHEAT, JIGGLE,
SWINDLE
Diderot, Fr. philosopher
.... DENIS
dido .... ANTIC, CAPER, PRANK
Dido, love of .... AENEAS
realm of .... CARTHAGE
didy .... DIAPER
didymous .... TWIN, DOUBLE
die ...... CUBE, DADO, DICE, MOLD,
STAMP, EXPIRE, MATRIX,
PERISH, DECEASE, SUCCUMB,
PASS AWAY, SUFFOCATE
due to cold .... WINTERKILL
slang .... CROAK, KICK THE
BUCKET
Die Fledermaus maid .... ADELE
diehard ...... FANATIC, STUBBORN
dieresis .... UMLAUT
Dies Irae .... HYMN, JUDGMENT
DAY

diet .... FAST, FOOD, (DAILY)FARE, CONGRESS, COUNCIL, ASSEMBLY, VICTUALS
course of .... REGIMEN
faulty .... DISTROPHY
old style .... BANT
slang .... GRUB
successfully .... SLIM
dieter's goal .... SLIM
dietetics .... SITOLOGY
differ .... VARY, DEVIATE, EXCEPT, DISSENT, DISAGREE, TAKE ISSUE
difference .... ODDS, VARIETY, DISPUTE, QUARREL, VARIANCE, VARIATION, DISAGREEMENT
between prices bid and asked .... SPREAD
in years, ideas, beliefs .... GENERATION GAP
lunar and solar year .... EPACT
different .... ELSE, OTHER, APART, UNLIKE, VARIED, ANOTHER, DIVERSE(E), DISTINCT
combining form .... HETERO
ones .... OTHERS
differentiate .... ALTER, ISOLATE, DISTINGUISH
difficult .... HARD, TOUGH, NOT EASY, KNOTTY, TANGLED, ARDUOUS, COMPLICATED
deed .... FEAT
problem ...... POSER, DILEMMA, GORDIAN(KNOT)
to handle/treat .... STUBBORN
to hold .... SLIPPERY AS AN EEL
to please .... QUEASY, DIFFICILE, DEMANDING
to understand .... ABSTRUSE
difficulty .... SNAG, RIGOR, PLIGHT, SCRAPE, DILEMMA, PROBLEM, STRAITS, TROUBLE, HARDSHIP, QUANDARY
colloq. .... FIX, STEW, PICKLE
crucial .... CRISIS
slang .... JAM
speaking .... APHASIA
that test one's endurance .... TRIAL, TRIBULATION
trying, severe .... ORDEAL
without solution .... STALEMATE
writing .... AGRAPHIA
diffidence .... MODESTY, RESERVE, SHYNESS
diffident .... COY, SHY, TIMID, DEMURE, MODEST, BASHFUL
diffract .... SPREAD, SCATTER, DISPERSE

diffuse .... WORDY, SPREAD, RADIATE, SCATTER, PERMEATE, BROADCAST
diffusion .... SPREADING, BROADCASTING, DISSEMINATION
through a membrane .... OSMOSIS
dig .... JAB, POKE, PROD, SPUD, NUDGE, SPADE, UNEARTH, EXCAVATE
colloquial .... JEER, TAUNT
for metal .... MINE
out .... GOUGE, SCOOP, UPROOT, EXHUME, SHOVEL
slang .... SEE, ENJOY, UNDERSTAND
up .... DELVE, EXHUME, UNCOVER, DISCOVER
with snout .... ROOT, ROUT
digest .... ABSORB, APERCU, PONDER, ABSTRACT, SHORTEN, SUMMARY, SYNOPSIS, CONDENSE, ABRIDGE, SUMMARIZE, ASSIMILATE
the .... PANDECT
digestion .... ABSORPTION
good .... EUPEPSIA
impaired .... DYSPEPSIA
of .... PEPTIC
digestive enzyme .... PAPAIN, PEPSIN
digger .... HOER, MOLE, MINER, WASP, SAPPER, SPADER, SANDHOG, TRENCHER
slang .... AUSTRALIAN, NEW ZEALANDER
digging tool .... HOE, PLOW, SPUD, SPADE, SHOVEL, TROWEL, MATTOCK, PICKAX(E)
dight .... ADORN, EQUIP
digit .... TOE, CIPHER, FIGURE, HALLUX, FINGER, NUMBER, INTEGER
useless .... DEWCLAW
digital .... NUMERAL, NUMERIC, RETENTIVE
computer .... ENIAC
infection .... FELON
digitalis ...... FIGWORT, FOXGLOVE
digits .... HALLUCES
diglot .... BILINGUAL
dignified .... NOBLE, SEDATE, EXALTED, STATELY, DECOROUS
grace/richness .... ELEGANCE
dignify .... ADORN, EXALT, HONOR, ENNOBLE
dignitary .... VIP, BIGWIG, PERSONAGE

dignity .... HONOR, PRIDE, REPUTE, DECORUM, MAJESTY, EMINENCE, NOBILITY, STATELINESS
steeped in .... PRIM, STAID, DEMURE, FORMAL, AFFECTED, DECOROUS, PRIGGISH, CONCEITED
digress .... ROAM, STRAY, RAMBLE, DEVIATE, DIVAGATE
digressions of a sort ...... ASIDES, AD LIBS
dik-dik .... ANTELOPE
dike .... DAM, DITCH, LEVEE, CAUSEWAY, EMBANKMENT
break in a .... CREVASSE
protective mat .... MATTRESS
dilantin, users of ...... EPILEPTICS
dilapidated .... RATTY, RUINED, DECAYED, RUN-DOWN, CRUMBLING, BROKEN-DOWN, RAMSHACKLE
dilapidation .... RUIN, DECAY
dilate .... SWELL, WIDEN, EXPAND, DISTEND, ENLARGE, STRETCH
dilation .... EXPANSION, ENLARGEMENT
cause of eyes' .... WONDER, SURPRISE, INCREDULITY
heart's .... DIASTOLE
pupil's .... MYDRIASIS
dilatory ...... LAGGARD, DELAYING
tactic in Congress .... FILIBUSTER
dilemma ...... FIX, JAM, TROUBLE, QUANDARY, PREDICAMENT
horn of .... CHOICE, ALTERNATIVE
play's .... NODE
dilettante ...... POSEUR, AMATEUR, DABBLER, TRIFLER, (A)ESTHETE
of a sort .... BOHEMIAN, AFICIONADO
diligence .... INDUSTRY, CONSTANCY, STAGECOACH, APPLICATION, PERSEVERANCE
diligent .... BUSY, ACTIVE, CAREFUL, MINDFUL, SEDULOUS, ATTENTIVE, HARDWORKING
dill(seed) .... ANET, ANISE
dilly .... DARB
colloquial .... LULU, BEAUT, DAISY, PEACH
of the valley .... ECHO
dillydally .... WAIT, DELAY, TARRY, WAVER, LOITER, TRIFLE, HESITATE, VACILLATE
diluent .... SOLVENT
dilute .... THIN, THIN OUT, WATER,

slang .... LACE, SPIKE

diluted ...... THIN, WEAK, WASHY, WATERY

diluting substance ...... DILUENT, SOLUTION

dim .... DARK, DULL, FADE, HAZY, FAINT, VAGUE, MIRK(Y), MISTY, DARKEN, GLOOMY, MURK(Y), ECLIPSE, OBSCURE, UNCLEAR

with .... BLEAR, RHEUM

dime .... COIN, TEN CENTS

a-dozen .... CHEAP

novel detective .... (NICK)CARTER

dimension .... AREA, SIZE, SCOPE, EXTENT, HEIGHT, LENGTH, BREADTH, THICKNESS, MEASUREMENT

dimensions, of three .... CUBIC

diminish ...... EBB, WANE, TAPER, (A)BATE, LESSEN, REDUCE, SHRINK, PETER OUT, DWINDLE, DECREASE

by use .... WEAR

diminutive .... WEE, TINY, SMALL, LITTLE, PETITE, MINIKIN

animal .... RUNT

fowl .... BANTAM

helper .... ELF

suffix .... IE, KIN, LET, ULE, ETTE, LING

dimness .... HAZE, OPACITY, DARKNESS, OBSCURITY

dimple .... DENT, HOLLOW, FOSSETTE

dimsighted .... NEARSIGHTED

dimwit .... SAP, CLOD, DOLT, DUNCE, IDIOT, SIMPLETON

din ...... NOISE, OUTCRY, CLAMOR, RACKET, UPROAR

Dinah, singer .... SHORE

dinar .... COIN

dindle .... THRILL, TINGLE, VIBRATE

dine .... EAT, SUP, FEED, MESS, REGALE, SUSTAIN

diner .... EATERY, DINING CAR, RESTAURANT

ding .... RING

dingbat .... STICK, STONE

slang .... SAP(HEAD), BOOB, KLUTZ, DING-A-LING

dinghy .... SABOT, (ROW)BOAT, SHALLOP

dingle .... DALE, DELL, GLEN, VALLEY

dingus .... DEVICE, GADGET

dingy ...... DIRTY, GRIMY, DISMAL, SHABBY, DISCOLORED

dining alcove ...... NOOK, DINETTE

car .... DINER

hall .... MESS, REFECTORY

room .... GRILL, CANTEEN, DINETTE, EATERY, CAFETERIA

table .... BOARD, COUNTER

table companion .... MESSMATE

table ornament .... EPERGNE, CENTERPIECE

dink .... DECK, TRIM

dinkey .... TROLLEY, LOCOMOTIVE

dinky .... SMALL, LITTLE, PIDDLING

dinner .... SUPPER

buffet style ..... SMORGASBORD

course .... ENTREE

jacket .... TUX(EDO)

of .... PRANDIAL

treat .... POT-ROAST, PRIME-RIB

wagon .... TEACART

with toasting, etc. .... BANQUET

dinnerware .... FLATWARE, CHINAWARE, GLASSWARE, TABLEWARE, SILVERWARE

dinosaur .... SAURIAN, SAUROPOD, DIPLODOCUS, ORNITHOPOD

amphibious .... TITANOSAUR

carnivorous/flesh-eating .... MEGALOSAUR, ALLOSAUR(US)

plant-eating .... BRONTOSAUR(US)

type of .... DUCK-BILLED

dint ...... HIT, DENT, SLOG, FORCE, MARK, POWER, EXERTION

diocese .... SEE, REGION, EPARCHY, DISTRICT, BISHOPRIC

Diomedes' father .... TYDEUS

Dionne, quint, ... OLIVA, CECILE, EMELIE, YVONNE, ANNETTE

Dionysian gala .... REVEL

Dionysus' attendant ...... NYMPH, M(A)ENAD

mother .... SEMELE

son .... PRIAPUS

staff .... THYRSUS

diopter .... ALIDADE

diorama .... SIGHT, DISPLAY, EXHIBIT, LANDSCAPE

Dioscuri ...... TWINS, CASTOR AND POLLUX

dip .... BAIL, DROP, LADE, SINK, SOAK, LOWER, CANDLE, PLUNGE

a doughnut .... DUNK

bait .... DAP, DIB(BLE)

in gravy/milk .... SOP

in liquid .... DOUSE, SOUSE,

(IM)MERSE

lightly .... DAP, DIB

slang .... PICKPOCKET

the colors .... SALUTE

diplo: comb. form .... TWO, TWIN, DOUBLE

diploma .... DEGREE, CHARTER, CERTIFICATE

colloquial .... SHEEPSKIN

diplomacy .... TACT, FINESSE, SKILL, PROWESS, STRATEGY

way of .... PROTOCOL

diplomat .... ENVOY, CONSUL, EXPERT, LEGATE, MINISTER, STATESMAN, AMBASSADOR

papal .... NUNCIO

diplomatic .... SUAVE, ARTFUL, POLITIC, TACTFUL, CONSULAR

agreements/ceremonial forms/code .... PROTOCOL

change of policy .... DEMARCHE

corps .... EMBASSY, LEGATION, FOREIGN SERVICE

corps, dean of .... DOYEN

denial .... DEMENTI

dispatch container ...... POUCH

immunity .... DIPPLE

paper .... MEMORIAL

privilege .... IMMUNITY, EXEMPTION

staff member .... ATTACHE

diplopia .... DOUBLE VISION

dipody .... VERSE, SYZYGY, DIMETER

dipper ...... URSA, GREBE, LADLE, OUSEL, OUZEL, SCOOP, PIGGIN

dipsomaniac .... SOT, TOPER, BOOZER, GUZZLER, DRUNKARD, ALCOHOLIC

dipsomaniacs, society of ...... ALCOHOLICS ANONYMOUS

dipterous insect .... GNAT, HOUSEFLY, MOSQUITO

dire .... URGENT, FATEFUL, FEARFUL, DREADFUL, HORRIBLE, TERRIBLE, APPALLING, CALAMITOUS

circumstances .... STRAITS

direct .... AIM, ORDER, POINT, FRANK, MANAGE, STRAIGHT, IMMEDIATE, FIRST-HAND

a helmsman .... CONN

an orchestra .... LEAD, CONDUCT

attention to .... REFER

hit .... ON TARGET, BULL'S EYE

opposite .... ANTITHESIS

proceedings .... PRESIDE

the affairs of state .... RULE, GOVERN

the course/movement of
.... GUIDE, STEER
direction .... EAST, LINE, PATH,
WEST, NORTH, ORDER, SOUTH,
TREND, COURSE, ADDRESS,
GUIDANCE, TENDENCY,
MANAGEMENT
without fixed .... AIMLESS,
ERRATIC, MEANDERING
directions, in all .... ABOUT
directive .... ORDER, COMMAND,
INSTRUCTION(S)
directly .... SOON, FLATLY, AS
SOON AS, PROMPTLY,
INSTANTLY
colloquial .... SPANG
opposite .... DIAMETRICAL
director .... BOSS, GUIDE, LEADER,
MASTER, MANAGER,
EMPLOYER, MODERATOR,
SUPERVISOR
concern of .... SCRIPT
in music .... CONDUCTOR
of a two-wheeled cart, horse-
drawn .... CHARIOTEER
of a vessel .... HELMSMAN
of an aircraft .... FLIER, PILOT,
AVIATOR
directory .... INDEX, REGISTER
enter in .... LIST
dirge .... HYMN, MASS, SONG,
LAMENT, CORONACH,
THRENODY, EPICEDIUM
for dead .... REQUIEM
dirigible .... BLIMP, AIRSHIP,
BALLOON, ZEPPELIN
bag/covering .... ENVELOPE
cabin .... GONDOLA
gas .... HELIUM
pilot .... AERONAUT
pod .... CAB
diriment .... VOIDING, NULLIFYING
dirk ...... SNEE, DAGGER, PONIARD
dirl .... TINGLE, VIBRATE
dirndl .... SKIRT
dirt ...... MUD, DUST, MUCK, SOIL,
EARTH, FILTH, GRIME, GOSSIP
dirty .... FOUL, VILE, MURKY,
DEFILE, FILTHY, SOILED,
SORDID, OBSCENE, POLLUTE,
UNCLEAN
look .... SNEER
place .... HOVEL
writings/pictures .... SMUT,
PORNO, PORNOGRAPHY
Dis .... HADES, ORCUS, PLUTO,
UNDERWORLD
disability .... HANDICAP,
IMPAIRMENT, INCAPACITY
disable .... LAME, MAIM, UNFIT,
DAMAGE, IMPAIR, CRIPPLE,

HAMSTRING, DISQUALIFY
disadvantage .... HARM, LOSS,
DAMAGE, TROUBLE,
DRAWBACK, HANDICAP,
DETRIMENT
disadvantaged .... NEEDY,
INDIGENT
disadvantageous .... HARMFUL
disaffect .... ALIENATE, ESTRANGE
disagree .... CLASH, DIFFER,
CONTEND, CONTEST, DISPUTE
disagreeable .... CROSS, CRANKY,
UGLY, TESTY, UNSAVORY,
OFFENSIVE, UNPLEASANT
situation ...... FIX, JAM, SCOUR,
SCRAPE, PREDICAMENT
smell .... FETOR
disagreeably moist and cold
.... MUGGY, CLAMMY
moist and hot .... SULTRY,
SWELTERING
disagreement ...... ROW, DISPUTE,
QUARREL, REFUSAL,
ARGUMENT, FRICTION,
VARIANCE, DIFFERENCE
result of couple's .... SPAT,
SPLIT, DIVORCE, SEPARATION
disallow .... DENY, REFUSE,
REJECT
disappear .... GO, FADE, PASS,
FLEE, DEPART, ESCAPE,
VANISH, DISSOLVE, EVANESCE
gradually .... PETER OUT
when you stand, they .... LAPS
disappearance .... EXIT,
ABSENCE, DEPARTURE
disappoint ...... BALK, BILK, FAIL,
FOIL, JILT, LET DOWN,
DISPLEASE, DISSATISFY
disappointment .... BLOW,
CHAGRIN, LETDOWN
disapproval .... CENSURE,
DISLIKE, OBJECTION,
REJECTION
show of ...... BOO, HISS, HOOT,
SNEER, SNORT
disapprove .... DAMN, DENY,
VETO, REJECT, CONDEMN,
TURN DOWN, CRITICIZE
disarm .... CHARM, PLACATE,
DEMILITARIZE
disarming .... SOFT-SPOKEN
disarrange .... MESS(UP), MUSS,
MIX UP, RUMPLE, UNSETTLE
disarray .... UPSET, DISORDER,
CONFUSION
disarticulate .... AMPUTATE,
DISJOINT
disaster .... EVIL, CALAMITY,
TRAGEDY, MISFORTUNE,
CATASTROPHE

sudden and great .... DEBACLE
disavow .... DENY, ABJURE,
DISOWN, DISCLAIM,
REPUDIATE
disband .... DISMISS, BREAK UP,
DISPERSE, DISSOLVE, SCATTER,
DEMOBILIZE
disbar .... EXPEL, EXCLUDE
disbelief in God .... ATHEISM
disbeliever .... DOUBTER, SKEPTIC
disburse .... ALLOT, SPEND, PAY
OUT, EXPEND
disc .... DISH, PATEN, PLATE
discalced .... BAREFOOTED
discard .... RID, DROP, JUNK,
SHED, CHUCK, SCRAP, REJECT,
CAST OFF
card from hand .... THROW
discarded cargo .... JETSAM
discern .... SEE, ESPY, DETECT,
NOTICE, DISCOVER, PERCEIVE
beforehand .... FORESEE
discerning ...... ASTUTE, SHREWD,
SAPIENT, SAGACIOUS,
APPRECIATIVE
discernment .... FLAIR, KNACK,
SENSE, TASTE, ACUMEN,
APPRECIATION,
UNDERSTANDING
discharge ...... DO, EMIT, HANDLE,
FLUXION, RELEASE, RELIEVE,
REMOVE, EMISSION
a cargo .... OFF-LOAD,
UNLADE, UNLOAD
a cargo, as in a heap, mass
.... DUMP
a debt .... QUIT, RETIRE,
SETTLE, LIQUIDATE
air, gas completely
.... EXHAUST
by force .... EJECT, EXPEL
electric .... SHOCK, SPARK
from a job/position
.... CASHIER, DISMISS,
LAY OFF, DISEMPLOY, GIVE
THE AX
from a job/position: sl.
.... CAN, FIRE, SACK
from a wound, ulcer
.... SANIES
from duty/obligation .... FREE,
SPARE, EXCUSE, EXEMPT
from military service
.... MUSTER OUT
morbid .... GLEET
of blood, pus .... ISSUE
one's duties .... RENDER,
MANAGE, EXECUTE, FULFILL,
PERFORM
projectile .... FIRE, SHOOT
pus .... MATURATE, SUPPURATE

waste matter from body
.... EGEST, EXCRETE
disciple .... PUPIL, APOSTLE,
DEVOTEE, FOLLOWER,
ADHERENT
India .... CHELA
disciplinarian .... MARTINET,
STICKLER, CHASTENER
British university .... BULLDOG
stick of a .... FERULE
disciplinary mark .... DEMERIT
discipline .... DRILL, REGIMEN,
CONFORM, PRACTICE,
TRAIN(ING), CORRECT(ION),
PUNISH(MENT), GOVERN,
(SELF)CONTROL, OBEDIENCE
fellow student .... HAZE
disclaim .... DENY, REFUSE,
DISOWN, DISAVOW,
RENOUNCE, REPUDIATE
disclaimer .... DENIAL
in property rights
.... QUITCLAIM
disclose .... BARE, FIND, OPEN,
TELL, REVEAL, UNFOLD,
UNVEIL, IMPART, CONFESS,
DIVULGE, INDICATE
colloquial .... SING
slang .... SQUEAL
disclosure .... EXPOSE,
CONFESSION, REVELATION
confidential .... TIP-OFF
indirect ...... HINT, INTIMATION
to a priest .... SHRIFT
discolor .... FADE, STAIN, STREAK,
BLEMISH
discolored by bruise .... LIVID
discombobulate .... ADDLE,
UPSET, EXCITE, POTHER,
RATTLE, RUFFLE, CONFUSE,
FLUSTER, PERTURB, DISCOMFIT
discomfit ...... JAR, UPSET, ABASH,
RUFFLE, CONFUSE,
EMBARRASS, DISCONCERT
discomfort .... ACHE, PAIN,
DISTRESS, SORENESS,
ANNOYANCE, UNEASINESS
physical .... MALAISE
discommode .... BOTHER,
DISTURB, INCONVENIENCE
discompose .... UPSET, RUFFLE,
AGITATE, DISTURB, FLUSTER,
DISARRANGE, DISCONCERT
disconcert .... JAR, ABASH, FEEZE,
UPSET, RATTLE, THWART,
CONFUSE, DISTURB, PERPLEX,
F(E)AZE, EMBARRASS,
FRUSTRATE, DISCOMPOSE,
FLABBERGAST
disconnect .... SEVER, DETACH,
UNPLUG, SEPARATE,

UNCOUPLE
disconsolate .... SAD, GLOOMY,
FORLORN, MELANCHOLY
discontent .... DISSENT, SORENESS,
VEXATION, RESENTMENT
feeling of .... DYSPHORIA
discontented one .... CRAB,
GRIPER, GROUCH, WHINER,
GRUMBLER, MALCONTENT
discontinue .... HALT, QUIT, STOP,
CEASE, DESIST, DISRUPT,
PAUSE, CALL OFF, SUSPEND
discord .... DIN, ODDS, SPAT, TIFF,
CLASH, BICKER, STRIFE,
CONFLICT, FRICTION,
DISSENSION
discordant ...... AJAR, HARSH, AT
ODDS, OFF-KEY, JARRING,
TUNELESS, EMBROILED,
DISSONANT, CACOPHONOUS
ringing .... JANGLE
discotheque .... CAFE, DISCO,
NIGHTCLUB
discount .... AGIO, ALLOW,
DEDUCT, LESSEN, IGNORE,
REBATE, REDUCE, DELITTLE,
SET ASIDE, SUBTRACT,
DEDUCTION, DISREGARD
discountenance .... ABASH,
CHAGRIN, DISFAVOR, FROWN
AT, DISAPPROVE
discourage .... DAUNT, DETER,
DAMPEN, DISMAY, DEPRESS,
DISHEARTEN, DEMORALIZE
discourse .... TALK, HOMILY,
SERMON, DECLAIM, DISCUSS,
DESCANT, LECTURE, TREATISE,
CONVERSE, CONVERSATION,
DISSERTATE, DISSERTATION
art of .... RHETORIC
Ciceronian .... ORATION
combining form .... LOG(O)
long, tiresome .... SCREED
long, vehement .... TIRADE,
HARANGUE
discourteous .... RUDE, TART,
NASTY, ROUGH, BITING,
COARSE, VULGAR, BRUSQUE,
CAUSTIC, CHURLISH, ILL-
BRED, IMPOLITE
person .... CAD, BOOR, HEEL,
BRUTE, CHURL
discourtesy ...... INSULT, REBUFF,
SLIGHT, DISRESPECT, ILL-
BREEDING
discover .... ESPY, LEARN,
FIND(OUT), DESCRY, DETECT,
REVEAL, UNCOVER, UNEARTH
discoverer's cry .... OHO
discovery .... ESPIAL, FIND(ING),
DETECTION, INVENTION

of 1492 .... AMERICA
of 1521 .... PHILIPPINES
of March 13, 1781
.... URANUS
unexpected .... WINDFALL
discredit .... SLUR, DOUBT,
SHAME, IMPEACH, DISGRACE,
DISHONOR, DISPARAGE
discreditable .... DISGRACEFUL,
HUMILIATING
discredited .... BELIED, REJECTED,
SUSPECT(ED)
discreet .... SHIFTY, CAREFUL,
GUARDED, PRUDENT,
CAUTIOUS
discreetly .... WISELY,
JUDICIOUSLY
discrepancy ...... GAP, VARIANCE,
DIFFERENCE
discrepant .... INCONSISTENT
discrete ...... DISTINCT, SEPARATE,
UNRELATED
discretion .... TACT, OPTION,
CAUTION, SECRECY,
PRUDENCE, JUDGMENT
discretionary .... OPTIONAL,
ARBITRARY, INDEPENDENT
discriminate .... DEMARK, DIVIDE,
SECERN, PREJUDGE,
DEMARCATE, SEGREGATE,
DISTINGUISH, TREAT
UNEQUALLY
discriminating .... NICE, CHOOSY,
REFINED, CRITICAL,
CULTURED, SELECTIVE
discrimination .... BIAS, TASTE,
RACISM, INSIGHT, EXCLUSION,
PREJUDICE, PERCEPTION
discursive .... PROLIX,
WANDERING
discus .... DISK, QUOIT
thrower's statue
.... DISCOBOLUS
discuss .... TALK, ARGUE, DEBATE,
TREAT, ANALYZE, DISPUTE,
EXPLAIN
carefully .... DELIBERATE
formally .... DISSERTATE
in detail .... CANVASS
discussed publicly .... NOTORIOUS
discussion .... DEBATE, ANALYSIS,
DIALOGUE
group .... FORUM, PANEL,
SEMINAR
heated ...... HASSLE, RHUBARB,
SQUABBLE
kind of .... ROUND-TABLE
meeting for .... CONFERENCE
of facts .... TREATISE
secret: sl. .... HUDDLE
slang .... RAP SESSION

disdain .... SCORN, SNEER, SPURN, DESPISE, HAUTEUR, CONTEMPT

disdainful one .... PRIG, SNOB, SCORNER, SNEERER

disease .... MALADY, AILMENT, ILLNESS, DISORDER, SICKNESS, AFFECTION, COMPLAINT

affecting many organs .... WHIPPLE'S

animal .... GID, MANGE, NAGANA, SPAVIN, ANTHRAX

blood .... ANEMIA, TOXEMIA, CLOTTING, LEUKEMIA, POLYCYTHEMIA

bone .... RICKETS, RACHITIS

bone marrow .... CANCER, MYELOMA

brain virus infection .... ENCEPHALITIS

carried by aedes mosquito .... DENGUE, YELLOW FEVER

carried by anopheles mosquito .... MALARIA

carried by tsetse ...... NAGANA

carrier .... BAT, FLY, RAT, TSETSE, VECTOR, MOSQUITO

cause of .... GERM, VIRUS, MICROBE, BACILLUS, PATHOGEN

caused by fungi ...... MYCOSIS, MYCETOMA

causing/leading to .... PECCANT, MORBIFIC

childhood .... MUMPS, MEASLES, RUBELLA

chronic skin .... ROSACEA

chronic tropical .... SPRUE

combining form .... NOS(O)

consumption .... TUBERCULOSIS

contagious/infectious .... FAVUS, NAGANA, PLAGUE, MALARIA, MEASLES, PINK-EYE, SYPHILIS, GONORRHEA, PESTILENCE, TUBERCULOSIS

cranberry .... SCALD

Crohn's .... ENTERITIS

deficiency .... SCURVY, RICKETS, BERIBERI, MARASMUS, PELLAGRA, KWASHIORKOR

dust-caused .... SILICOSIS

epidemic .... PLAGUE, BUBONIC PLAGUE, PESTILENCE

ear .... MYRINGITIS

eye .... MYOPIA, CATARACT, GLAUCOMA, NIGHT BLINDNESS

fluid retention .... EDEMA

germ killer .... ANTIBODY, ANTIBIOTIC

gradual end of .... LYSIS

imaginary .... CRUD

inability to speak ...... MUTISM

indigenous .... ENDEMIC

infection of nails .... PARONYCHIA

inflammation of kidney(s) .... NEPHRITIS

inflammation of lungs .... PNEUMONIA

intestinal .... CHOLERA, MYIASIS

liver ..... CIRRHOSIS, HEPATITIS, PORPHYRIA

lungs .... EMPHYSEMA

malignant ...... FEVER, TUMOR, CANCER, PLAGUE, PESTILENCE

mental .... INSANITY, DERANGEMENT

muscles .... MYOPATHY

nervous .... TIC, CHOREA, TWITCH, EPILEPSY, PELLAGRA

of .... MORBID

acid in stomach .... PEPTIC ULCER

beard .... SYCOSIS

chills and fever .... AGUE, MALARIA

chronic skin disorder .... ACNE

cows .... COWPOX, TAPEWORM

dogs .... RABIES

fowl/poultry .... PIP, ROUP

grasses/rye .... ERGOT

hip .... COXALGIA

horses ...... LAMPAS, SPAVIN, LAMPERS, GLANDERS

joints .... GOUT, ARTHRITIS

kidney .... NEPHROPATHY

kings so-called .... HEMOPHILIA

monkeys ..... YELLOW FEVER

pigs .... BULL NOSE, TAPEWORM, BRUCELLOSIS

rabbits .... TULAREMIA

rats .... PLAGUE

sheep .... GID, ROT, ANTHRAX

wheat .... RUST

origin of/study of .... ETIOLOGY

pancreas .... DIABETES

passage into body ..... ATRIUM

plant .... SMUT

recurrence of .... RELAPSE

recurring .... CHRONIC

scratchy .... ITCH, HIVES, URTICARIA

sexually-transmitted .... SYPHILIS, GONORRHEA, "THE CLAP"

skin .... ACNE, LUPUS, TINEA, ECZEMA, TETTER, RINGWORM

"slimming" .... ANOREXIA-NERVOSA

source .... NIDUS

spreader .... CARRIER

swine .... GARGET

tropical .... YAWS, SPRUE

virus .... FLU, POX, COLD, RABIES, MEASLES, RUBELLA, VARIOLA, VIROSIS, INFLUENZA, VARICELLA

warning symptom .... PRODROME

wasting .... TABES, CONSUMPTION

diseased .... ILL, SICK(LY), MORBID, PATHIC, DISABLED, UNSOUND, CONFINED, INCURABLE

beggar .... LAZAR, LEPER

for a long period .... BEDRIDDEN

tissue due to injury .... GANGRENOUS

with impaired digestion .... DYSPEPTIC

diseases, classification of .... NOSOLOGY

deals with the nature of .... PATHOLOGY

deals with treatment and care of .... THERAPY, THERAPEUTICS

examination and analysis of .... DIAGNOSIS

disembark .... LAND, DEBUS, GET OFF, DEPLANE, DETRAIN

disembodied spirit .... SOUL

disembowel .... GUT, DRAW, EVISCERATE

disembowelment, suicide by .... HARAKIRI

disenchant .... DEFLATE, DISILLUSION, DISAPPOINT

disencumber .... RID, FREE, LIGHTEN RELIEVE, UNBURDEN

disendow .... DISINHERIT

disengage .... FREE, DETACH, RELEASE, SEPARATE, UNFASTEN

disentagle .... COMB, RAVEL, UNCURL UNKNOT, UNSNARL, ORGANIZE, EXTRICATE

in football .... UNPILE

disenthrone .... OUST, UNSEAT

disfavor .... HATE, ABHOR, DISLIKE

disfigure .... MAR, MAIM, DEFACE, DEFORM, MANGLE, UGLIFY, DISTORT, MUTILATE

disfigured ...... UGLY, DEFORMED, SCARRED, GROTESQUE
and swollen .... BLOATED
and undersized .... DWARFED
with defective legs .... BOWLEGGED, BANDY-LEGGED
with excessive scar tissue .... KELOIDAL
with inflamed skin swelling .... PIMPLY, PIMPLED
disfigurement ...... SCAR, DEFECT, BLEMISH UGLINESS
disgorge .... EJECT, EMPTY, VOMIT
disgrace ...... BLOT, ODIUM, SLUR, SHAME, TAINT, INFAMY, OBLOQUY, SCANDAL, DISHONOR, IGNOMINY
disgraced ...... CRUSHED, SHAMED, HUMILIATED
disgraceful .... INDIGN, SHOCKING, SCANDALOUS
disgruntle .... DISCONTENT, DISPLEASE, DISSATISFY
disgruntled .... CROSS
one ...... CRYBABY, SOREHEAD, SOURPUSS, AX-GRINDER, CROSSPATCH
disguise ...... MASK, VEIL, CLOAK, SCREEN, CONCEAL, MAKE-UP, CAMOUFLAGE
assumed/in .... INCOGNITO
wearer .... MUMMER
disgust .... REPEL, OFFEND, SICKEN, REPULSE, DISTASTE, NAUSEATE, REPUGNANCE
disgusted .... BORED, FED-UP, SICK AND TIRED
grunt .... UGH
disgusting .... LOUSY, ODIOUS, FULSOME, OFFENSIVE
matter .... FILTH
dish .... BOWL, PATEN, PLATE, COURSE, SAUCER, SERVER, TUREEN, PLATTER, RAMEKIN, RAMEQUIN
appetizer .... PATE, RUMAKI, CANAPES, FRESH OYSTERS, SMOKED SALMON, STUFFED MUSHROOMS
beef .... STEW, ROAST, RAGOUT, TERIYAKI, MEAT LOAF, POT ROAST, CARBONNADE, STROGANOFF, WELLINGTON, BOURGUIGNON, CHATEAUBRIAND
between courses .... ENTREE, ENTREMETS
candy .... COMPOTE, COMPOTIER
cheese .... FONDUE, QUICHE, RAREBIT, WELSH RABBIT
chicken .... KIEV, BAKED, CURRY, ROAST, POT PIE, A LA KING, FRICASSE, CACCIATORE, TETRAZZINI, CORDON BLEU, ARROZ CON POLLO
choice .... VIAND
colloquial .... FOOD, TREAT, RECIPE, SERVING
cooked on a spit .... HASLET
dessert .... PUDDING, AMBROSIA, SYLLABUB, CHEESECAKE, ZABAGLIONE, BAKED ALASKA, CREPES SUZETTE
duck/duckling .... ROAST, PEKING, SHANGHAI, A-L'ORANGE
eggs .... CREOLE, MORNAY, OMELET, QUICHE, BENEDICT
fancy .... KICKSHAW
for cookies, etc. ...... EPERGNE
for cooking .... CASSEROLE
for cooking over coal .... BRAZIER
for evaporating liquid .... CAPSULE
for serving gravy, sauce .... GRAVY BOAT
fruit .... COMPOTE, EPERGNE, COMPOTIER
highly spiced stew .... OLIO
Hungarian .... GOULASH
lamb .... STEW, CHOPS, CURRY, KABOB, ROAST
main .... ENTREE
maize and pepper ..... TAMALE
make of a ...... GLASS, METAL, CRYSTAL, PLASTIC, PORCELAIN, STONEWARE, EARTHENWARE
Mexican .... TACO, TAMALE, ENCHILADA, CHILI CON CARNE
pasta .... LASAGNA, RAVIOLI, CANNELONI, FETTUCINI, MANICOTTI, SPAGHETTI
pork ..... STEW, CHOPS, ROAST, BURRITO, HOCKS AND BEANS, BARBECUED SPARERIBS
rice .... BAKED, FRIED, PILAF(F)
seafood .... SCAMPI, SCALLOPS, SHRIMP CURRY, THERMIDOR, PAN-FRIED FISH, CLAM FRITTERS, POACHED SALMON/SOLE
served before the roast .... ENTREE
serving .... TRAY, CROCK, NAPPY, PLATTER, CASSEROLE
side .... ENTREMETS
soup .... GUMBO, POTAGE, BISQUE, GAZPACHO, SPLIT-PEA, MINESTRONE, VICHYSSOISE, CLAM CHOWDER
soup server .... TUREEN
tasty .... MORSEL
type .... CUP, JAR, BOWL, DEEP, PLATE, SAUCER, CHAFING, TWO-SECTION, WARMING, FLAT-BOTTOMED
veal .... ROAST, MARSALA, PAPRIKA, PICCATA, PARMIGIANA, STEW MILANESE
vegetable .... SALAD, AMANDINE, POLONAISE, STIR-FRIED, RATATOUILLE
dishearten ...... DAUNT, DAMPEN, DEJECT, DISCOURAGE
dishes .... WARE, CHINA
dishevel .... MUSS, RUMPLE, TOUSLE
disheveled .... BLOWZY, UNKEMPT, DISORDERLY
dishonest .... FALSE, LYING, CHEATING, DECEITFUL
card player ...... CHEAT, SHILL, SHARPER, BLACKLEG
lawyer .... SHYSTER, PETTIFOGGER
person .... LIAR, CROOK, CHEATER, STEALER, DECEIVER, SWINDLER
dishonor .... ABUSE, SHAME, INFAMY, DISGRACE, DISCREDIT, DISREPUTE, DISRESPECT
dishonorable .... BASE, SHADY, FOUL, ROTTEN, CROOKED
disillusion .... DISENCHANT
disinclined .... AVERSE, AGAINST, RELUCTANT, UNWILLING
disinfect .... FUMIGATE, STERILIZE
disinfectant ...... LYSOL, CRESOL, IODINE, CHLORINE
disingenuous .... SLY, DISHONEST, INSINCERE
disinherit .... DISOWN
disintegrate .... MELT, DECAY, WEAKEN, BREAKUP, CRUMBLE
by acid .... CORRODE
by water/wind .... ERODE
disinter .... FIND, DIG UP, EXHUME, UNEARTH
disinterested .... NUMB, UNBIASED, IMPARTIAL
disjoin .... CHANGE, SEPARATE
disjoint .... DISLOCATE, DISMEMBER
disk .... PLATE, WHEEL, CIRCLE, PATINA, ROTATOR
bright surrounding saints .... NIMBUS
for breaking soil ..... HARROW

gem-cutting .... LAP
hockey/ice hockey .... PUCK
jockey .... DEEJAY,
                       ANNOUNCER
like/shaped .... DISCAL,
                      DISCOID
metal .... PATEN
obsolete .... DISCUS
on radio/telephone .... DIAL,
                       FACE
phonograph .... RECORD
poker .... CHIP
sealing .... WAFER
small, computer .... FLOPPY
throwing device .... TRAP
to seal joints .... GASKET
dislike .... HATE, ABHOR, ENMITY,
          DISGUST, DISTASTE,
          AVERSION, ANTIPATHY
intense .... HATRED,
          DETESTATION
dislocate .... SPLAY, UPSET,
          LUXATE, DISJOINT,
          DISARRANGE
dislodge .... EJECT, EVICT, EXPEL,
          REMOVE, DISPLACE
disloyal .... FALSE, UNTRUE,
          RECREANT, FAITHLESS,
          UNFAITHFUL, INCONSTANT
person, kind of .... INGRATE,
          TRAITOR, BETRAYER,
          INFORMER, RENEGADE,
          TURNCOAT, DOUBLE-CROSSER
dismal .... BLEAK, DINGY,
          DREARY, GLOOMY,
          DEPRESSING
dismantle .... RAZE, STRIP,
          DEMOLISH
dismay ...... FEAR, ABASH, DAUNT,
          ALARM, APPAL(L), TERRIFY,
          DISCONCERT
dismember .... DISSECT, DISJOINT
dismiss .... FIRE, OUST, EXPEL,
          LAY OFF, REMOVE, RELEASE,
          DISCHARGE
an organization .... DISBAND
archaic .... DEMIT
colloquial .... BOOT, SACK,
          BRUSH OFF
from command/in disgrace
          .... CASHIER
troops .... DEMOBILIZE
dismissal ...... OUSTER, REMOVAL,
          DISCHARGE, MITTIMUS
curt/abrupt .... CONGE
notice .... PINKSLIP
dismount .... ALIGHT, GET DOWN,
          STEP DOWN
Disney, artist .... ANIMATOR,
          CARTOONIST
dog .... PLUTO

duck .... DAISY, DONALD
duckling .... HUEY, DEWEY,
          LOUIE
goldfish .... CLEO
middle name of .... ELIAS
Mortimer of .... SNERD
movie producer .... WALT
mouse .... MICKEY, MINNIE
pachyderm .... DUMBO
puppet .... PINNOCHIO
disobedient .... UNRULY, DEFIANT,
          INSUBORDINATE
disorder .... MESS, MUSS, RIOT,
          ROIL, CHAOS, HAVOC, UPSET,
          JUMBLE, LITTER, UPROAR,
          CLUTTER, CONFUSION
in .... UPSIDE DOWN
of voices/sounds .... BABEL
place of .... BEDLAM
vague: sl. .... CRUD
disorderly .... MESSY, UNRULY,
          ROWDY, UNTIDY, CHAOTIC,
          RIOTOUS, PELLMELL, SLIPSHOD
crowd .... RABBLE
flight .... ROUT, STAMPEDE
noisy fight .... MELEE
disorganize ...... UPSET, DISBAND,
          DISRUPT, DISSOLVE
disorganized .... HAYWIRE,
          DERANGED, DISORDERLY
disown .... DENY, DISAVOW,
          RENOUNCE, DISCLAIM,
          REPUDIATE, DISINHERIT,
          DISPOSSESS
disparage .... SLUR, DECRY,
          DEMEAN, LESSEN, BELITTLE,
          TRADUCE, PEJORATE,
          VILIPEND, DISCREDIT,
          DEPRECIATE
disparaging remark .... SLUR,
          SMEAR, ASPERSION
disparate ...... UNLIKE, DIFFERENT
disparity .... CONTRAST,
          CLASHING, CONFLICT,
          VARIANCE, INJUSTICE,
          DIFFERENCE
dispassionate .... CALM, COOL,
          EVEN, FAIR, LEVEL-HEADED
dispassionately .... COLDLY
dispatch .... KILL, POST,
          SEND(OFF), HASTE, ROUTE,
          SPEED, LETTER, MESSAGE,
          NEWS STORY, BULLETIN,
          QUICKNESS, PROMPTNESS
across the sea ...... SEND OVER
bearer .... COURIER,
          MESSENGER
boat/vessel .... AVISO
dispatcher .... ROUTER, SENDER
slang .... BUTCHER
dispel .... VANISH, SCATTER, BLOW

OFF, DISPERSE, DISSOLVE
dispensable .... EXCESS, INFERIOR,
          NEEDLESS
dispensary .... CLINIC,
          PHARMACY, INFIRMARY
dispensation .... FAVOR,
          EXEMPTION, MANAGEMENT,
          ALLOTMENT, DISTRIBUTION
dispense .... EXCUSE, EXEMPT,
          DEAL OUT, DISTRIBUTE
with .... FOREGO, ABSTAIN
dispenser of alms ..... ALMONER
disperse .... SPREAD, SCATTER
system .... COLLOID
dispirited .... BORED, DEJECTED
displace .... MOVE, EXILE,
          DISLODGE, SUPPLANT,
          DISCHARGE, SUPERSEDE
displaced .... HOMELESS
person .... DP, EVACUEE,
          OUTCAST, REFUGEE
displacement .... REMOVAL,
          EJECTION, MIGRATION
display .... SPORT, SHOW(OFF),
          EXPOSE, REVEAL, UNFOLD,
          UNCOVER, MANIFEST,
          EXHIBIT(ION)
brilliant .... POMP, RIOT,
          PARADE, BLAZONRY,
          SPECTACLE
case .... CABINET, COUNTER
empty .... PAGEANT(RY)
frame .... EASEL, SHELF,
          SHELVE
means of .... SHOWCASE,
          (FASHION)SHOW, SHOW-
          WINDOW
of temper .... FIT, FRENZY,
          TANTRUM, OUTBURST
ostentatiously .... WAVE,
          FLAUNT, PARADE
pretentious: colloq.
          .... SPREAD
prominent .... SPLASH
showy ...... BLAZON, FANFARE,
          SPLURGE
superficial .... VENEER
displaying amazement .... WIDE-
          EYED
displease .... VEX, MIFF, ROIL,
          ANGER, ANNOY, PIQUE,
          OFFEND, DISTURB, IRRITATE
displeasure .... IRE, ANGST
disport .... PLAY, FROLIC
disposable .... THROWAWAY
disposal .... RIDDANCE,
          DISPOSITION
of property .... CONVEYANCE
dispose .... ORDER, POSIT,
          ARRANGE, SITUATE
of .... SELL, SETTLE, GIVE

AWAY, CONSUME, LIQUIDATE
disposed .... APT, BENT, PRONE,
MINDED, TENDING, WILLING,
INCLINED
to agree .... AMENABLE
to fight .... COMBATANT,
PUGNACIOUS, BELLIGERENT
disposition .... BENT, MOOD,
MORALE, NATURE, TENDENCY,
ADJUSTMENT, ARRANGEMENT,
TEMPER(AMENT)
of mean .... ORNERY
sour .... TESTY, CRANKY,
GROUCHY, VINEGARY
dispossess .... OUST, EJECT, EVICT,
DISOWN, DIVEST, DEPRIVE,
EXPROPRIATE
disproof .... REFUTATION
disprove .... REBUT, REFUTE,
DEFEAT, CONFUTE, GAINSAY
disputable .... MOOT
at law .... LITIGIOUS
disputant .... ERISTIC
disputation .... DEBATE, POLEMIC
art of .... ERISTIC, POLEMICS
disputatious .... CONTENTIOUS,
CONTROVERSIAL
dispute ...... SPAR, ARGUE, DOUBT,
FLITE, BICKER, DEBATE,
CONTEST, DISCUSS, QUARREL,
CAUSERIE, POLEMICS,
QUESTION, ARGUMENT,
SQUABBLE
angrily ..... CLASH, ALTERCATE
beyond .... SETTLED
noisy .... FRACAS, WRANGLE
petty .... SPAT
disputer .... ARGUER, DEBATER,
OPPOSER, DISSENTER
disqualified .... UNFIT, INELIGIBLE
disqualify .... DISABLE, RULE OUT
disquiet .... FRET, UNEASE,
UNREST, ANXIETY
disquieting .... SCARY, ALARMING,
EXCITING
disquisition .... DISCOURSE
disregard .... DEFY, IGNORE,
DISOBEY, OVERRIDE,
OVERRULE
disregarding rule .... PECCANT
disrepair .... DECAY, DAMAGE,
DECLINE, INUTILITY,
IMPAIRMENT
of body tissue .... ATROPHY
disreputable .... VILE, SHADY,
HEINOUS, RAFFISH, INFAMOUS,
ODOROUS, SHAMEFUL,
UNSAVORY
shrewish woman ..... DEMIREP,
HARRIDAN
disrepute .... SHAME, TAINT,

INFAMY, DISGRACE
disrespect .... SNUB, SLIGHT,
AFFRONT, SARCASM,
CONTEMPT
disrespectful .... RUDE, IMPOLITE,
INSULTING, SARCASTIC
disrobe ...... BARE, STRIP, DIVEST,
UNDRESS
disrupt .... REND, SPLIT, UPSET,
DISTURB, BREAK APART
dissatisfied (one)
.... MALCONTENT
dissatisfy .... VEX, ANGER,
ANNOY, DISPLEASE
dissect .... CUT UP, CUT APART,
ANALYZE, DISMEMBER
dissemble .... LIE, FEIGN,
CONCEAL, PRETEND, DISGUISE,
SIMULATE
dissembler, alleged .... JESUIT
dissembling .... AESOPIC
disseminate .... SOW, STREW,
SPREAD, SCATTER, CIRCULATE,
PROPAGATE
by word of mouth
.... PREACH, BROADCAST
through the press .... PUBLISH,
PUBLICIZE
through the radio
.... BROADCAST
through TV .... TELECAST
dissension .... STRIFE, DISCORD,
QUARREL
in a way .... FLAK
dissent .... DIFFER, OBJECT,
PROTEST, DISAGREE
dissenter .... ANTI, OPPOSER,
SECTARY, OBJECTOR,
SECTARIAN, PROTESTANT,
NONCONFORMIST
dissepiment .... SEPTUM
dissert(ate) .... ARGUE, DISCUSS
dissertation .... ESSAY, PAPER,
THESIS, ARTICLE, LECTURE,
TREATISE, DISCOURSE
disserve .... HARM
disservice .... WRONG, INJURY,
INJUSTICE
dissidence .... DISCORD,
DISCONTENT
dissident .... ANTI, REBEL,
OPPOSER, CONTRARY,
RESISTER, MALCONTENT,
INTRANSIGENT
dissimilar ...... UNLIKE, UNALIKE,
DIFFERENT, DISPARATE
dissimilarity .... ODDS,
DIFFERENCE
dissimulate ...... FEIGN, PRETEND,
DISGUISE
dissipate .... FADE, SPEND, WASTE,

DISPEL, DIFFUSE, SCATTER,
SQUANDER
dissipated man ...... RAKE, ROUE,
DEBAUCHEE
dissociate .... SEPARATE,
DISENGAGE
dissociation, mental
.... PARANOIA
dissolute .... LAX, WILD, LOOSE,
RAKISH, SINFUL, VICIOUS,
LICENTIOUS, PROFLIGATE
person .... RAKE, ROUE,
ADDICT, LECHER
dissolution .... BREAKUP,
DIALYSIS, DISPERSION,
EXPIRATION, SEPARATION
combining form .... LYSIS
dissolve .... END, FADE, MELT,
THAW, VANISH, LIQUEFY
out/and wash away ..... LEACH
dissonance .... DISCORD
from violin group .... WOLF
dissonant .... ATONAL
dissuade .... DETER, REPEL,
DEHORT, RESTRAIN
opposed to .... EXHORT,
PERSUADE
distaff side ...... FEMALE, WOMAN,
WOMEN, WEAKER SEX
distal .... TERMINAL
opposed to .... PROXIMAL
distance .... REACH, FARNESS,
REMOTENESS, MEASUREMENT
around .... CIRCUMFERENCE
between ends .... SPAN
between lines/words ...... GAP,
SPACE
from equator .... LATITUDE
in behavior/manner
.... RESERVE
in radio .... DX
in the .... AFAR
runner .... MILER
shortest .... BEELINE,
STRAIGHTLINE
three-mile, nautical/statute
.... LEAGUE
traveled recorder
.... ODOGRAPH
distant .... FAR, AFAR, AWAY,
ALOOF, FAR OFF, REMOTE,
ABROAD, OVERSEAS,
RESERVED
past .... EARLY
prefix .... TEL(E)
distaste .... DISLIKE, AVERSION
distasteful .... OFFENSIVE,
UNPLEASANT
distemper .... COLOR, PAINT,
MALADY, DISEASE, DISORDER
distend .... BULGE, SWELL,

DILATE, EXPAND, INFLATE, STRETCH
distended .... TURGID
condition .... TYMPANY
distension .... BLOAT, STRAIN
distich .... COUPLET
distill .... BREW, DRIP, DECOCT, PURIFY, TRICKLE
several times .... COHOBATE
distillate .... SPIRIT
distillery .... STILL, BREWERY
mash .... SLOPS
mixing tank .... MASHTUN
waste .... POTASH
distilling apparatus .... STILL, ALEMBIC
refuse .... TAILING
vessel .... RETORT, MATRASS
distinct .... CLEAR, PLAIN, SHARP, EXPLICIT, DEFINITE, SEPARATE, DIFFERENT
part .... UNIT, FEATURE
distinction ...... HONOR, DIGNITY, ELEGANCE, EMINENCE, VARIATION, PROMINENCE
distinctive ...... PRECISE, DEFINITE, PROMINENT, DISTINGUISHING
air .... AURA, ATMOSPHERE
nature .... TRAIT, FLAVOR
taste .... SAVOR, PALATE
distinctly .... CLEARLY, VISIBLY
distinguish .... KNOW, LABEL, HONOR, SECERN, DISCERN, PICK OUT, SEPARATE, DISCRIMINATE, DIFFERENTIATE
distinguished .... FAMOUS, EMINENT, NOTABLE, RENOWNED
man .... DON
distinguishing feature ...... TRAIT, CHARACTERISTIC
moral nature .... ETHOS
distort .... WARP, TWIST, DEFORM, CONTORT, MISREPRESENT
parts of a story, etc.
.... GARBLE, MISQUOTE
distorted .... WRY, AWRY, ASKEW, CROOKED
back .... HUMPBACK, HUNCHBACK
foot .... TALIPED, CLUBFOOT(ED)
knee .... KNOCKKNEED
nose .... SNUB-NOSED
distortion .... ABERRATION
ludicrous .... TRAVESTY
of the face .... GRIMACE
distract .... AMUSE, HARASS, CONFUSE
distraction .... AMUSEMENT, DIVERSION

frenzied .... TIZZY
distraint .... POIND
distraught .... MAD, CRAZED, FRANTIC, CONFUSED, HARASSED, BEWILDERED
distress ...... PAIN, AGONY, GRIEF, GRIPE, UPSET, AFFLICT, ANGUISH, ANXIETY, STRAITS, POVERTY, TROUBLE, CALAMITY
signal/call .... SOS, MAYDAY
distribute .... DOLE, METE, ALLOT, DIVIDE, SCATTER, DISH OUT
cards .... DEAL
distributor .... DEALER, MERCHANT
district .... AREA, WARD, ZONE, REGION, SECTOR, CIRCUIT, PRECINCT, TERRITORY
distrust .... ENVY, DOUBT, SUSPECT, UMBRAGE, SUSPICION
disturb ...... ROIL, ANNOY, FEEZE, F(E)AZE, UPSET, WORRY, MOLEST, PESTER, AGITATE, PERTURB, NETTLE, INTERRUPT, DISARRANGE
disturbance .... ROW, BRAWL, HUBBUB, RUMPUS, UPROAR, DISORDER, COMMOTION
unruly .... RIOT
disunion ...... SCHISM, BREAK-UP, DISCORD, SEPARATION
disunite .... PART, DETACH, DIVIDE, SEPARATE
disuse .... WAIVE, ABSTAIN, NEGLECT, DESUETUDE
disused .... OBSOLETE
ditch .... DIKE, DYKE, CANAL, FOSS(E), GULLY, CHANNEL
a suitor .... JILT
barrier .... HAHA
castle .... MOAT
digger .... TRENCHER
filling sticks .... FASCINE
for defense .... TRENCH
road .... GUTTER
slang .... DESERT, CAST OFF, DISCARD
dither .... FLURRY, TWITTER, CONFUSION
in a .... AGOG, EXCITED
dithyramb .... ODE, HYMN, POEM, SONG, SPEECH
dittany .... MINT, FRAXINELLA
ditto ...... COPY, SAME, AGAIN, AS BEFORE, LIKEWISE
ditty .... SONG, REFRAIN
diuretic .... URETIC, URINARY
stimulant .... CANTHARIDES
diurnal .... DAILY, DIARY,

JOURNAL
opposed to .... NOCTURNAL
diva .... SINGER, PRIMA DONNA
forte of .... ARIA, OPERA
Patrice .... MUNSEL
divagate .... STRAY, DIGRESS
divan .... CAFE, SOFA, COUCH, CANAPE, LOUNGE, SETTEE, OTTOMAN
divaricate .... FORK, BRANCH
dive .... DIP, SWOOP, PLUNGE
bomber .... STUKA, AIRPLANE
colloquial .... DEN, SALOON
fancy .... SWAN, GAINER, BACKFLIP
into water .... SUBMERGE
kind of .... NOSE, POWER
slang .... HONKY-TONK
diver, a certain .... PEARLER
bird .... LOON
breathing aid of .... MASK, SCUBA
from airplane
.... PARACHUTIST, PARATROOPER
gear of .... TANK, HELMET, AQUALUNG, FLIPPERS, SPEARGUN, (PARA)CHUTE
sickness suffered by
.... BENDS
warship .... SUBMARINE
diverge .... FORK, VARY, VEER, DIFFER, SWERVE, DEVIATE, BRANCH OFF
divergent strabismus
.... WALLEYE
divergence .... VARIANCE, DEVIATION, VARIATION
divers .... SUNDRY, VARIOUS
diverse .... UNLIKE, VARIED, SEVERAL, DIFFERENT
prefix .... POLY
diversify ...... VARY, BRANCH OUT
diversion .... SPORT, CHANGE, PASTIME, AMUSEMENT, DISTRACTION
diversionary tactic .... FEINT
diversity .... VARIETY
divert .... AMUSE, DEFLECT, DISTRACT, ESTRANGE, ENTERTAIN
divertissement .... BALLET, ENTR'ACTE, DIVERSION, INTERMEZZO
divest .... BARE, STRIP, DENUDE, EXPOSE, DEPRIVE, UNCOVER
divested .... NUDE, NAKED, THREADBARE
divestment .... NUDITY
of outer skin .... ECDYSIS
divide .... PART, ALLOT, HALVE,

SHARE, SPLIT, SUNDER, ALIENATE, SEPARATE, TRANSECT, APPORTION

grammatically ..... PUNCTUATE

into feet .... SCAN

into four parts .... QUARTER

into layers .... FOLIATE

into three .... TRISECT

into two .... HALF, BISECT

voting area ..... GERRYMANDER

divided .... CLEFT, FORKED

equally .... HALVED

in parts .... PARTITE

into 100 degrees .... CENTIGRADE

into vertical stripes (in heraldry) .... PALY

dividend .... BONUS, INTEREST

dividing line .... SOLIDUS

wall .... SEPTUM, PARTITION

divination .... GUESS, AUGURY, SORCERY, PROPHECY, HYDROMANCY, NUMEROLOGY, PREDICTION

by communication with the dead .... NECROMANCY

by figures .... GEOMANCY

by lots .... SORTILEGE

by the stars .... ASTROLOGY

combining form .... MANCY

having powers of ...... MANTIC

method of .... TAROT, AXINOMANCY

pertaining to .... FATIDIC

practice of .... MANTOLOGY

divine ...... HOLY, DREAM, FANCY, GUESS, SACRED, GODLIKE, IMAGINE, HEAVENLY, SUPERNAL, CELESTIAL, DEIFIC, SPIRITUAL, CONJECTURE

bread/food .... MANNA

communication .... ORACLE

favor .... GRACE, BLESSING

intervention .... THEURGY

love .... AGAPE

presence .... SHEKINAH

punishment .... PLAGUE

spirit .... GHOST

tree .... DEVA

word .... LOGOS

work .... MIRACLE

Divine Comedy author .... DANTE

setting .... HELL, PARADISE, PURGATORY

diviner .... SEER, CONJUROR

diving aid .... AQUALUNG

apparatus .... BATHYSCAPH

bell inventor .... EADS

bird .... LOON, GREBE, DUCKER

boat .... SUBMARINE

hazard .... BENDS

divining rod .... WAND

search water with ...... DOWSE

user .... AARON

divinity .... CANDY, DEITY, NUMEN, GOD(HEAD), GODHOOD, THEOLOGY

division .... PART, UNIT, CLASS, GROUP, FISSION, SECTION, SCISSION, PARTITION, SEPARATION

book .... CHAPTER

cell .... MITOSIS

city .... WARD, ZONE, TRACT, PRECINCT

game .... SET, HALF, INNING, CHUKKER, QUARTER

in a group/religious .... SCHISM

mankind .... RACE

mark of .... OBELUS

opera .... SCENA

play .... ACT, SCENE

poem .... CANTO, VERSE, STANZA

race .... LAP, HEAT

road .... LANE

society .... CASTE

result of .... QUOTIENT

divorce .... PART, SPLIT-UP, SEPARATE

allowance .... ALIMONY

ground for .... ADULTERY, MENTAL CRUELTY, INCOMPATIBILITY

grounds for .... RENO

suit defendant .... CORRESPONDENT

suit subject .... ALIMONY, CHILD CUSTODY, SETTLEMENT

divorcee .... FEME SOLE

divorcee's alimony .... ESTOVERS

divot .... SOD, TURF

divulge ...... TELL, SPILL, REVEAL, DISCLOSE

divvy: sl. .... SHARE, PORTION

Dixie dish? .... HOMINY GRITS

hat? .... KENTUCKY DERBY

land .... (THE)SOUTH

president .... JIMMY CARTER

river .... ALABAMA

suffix used with .... CRAT

vine .... CAROLINA JASMINE

Dixieite .... ALABAMAN, SOUTHERNER

dixit, _____ .... IPSE

Dixon's partner .... MASON

dizen .... DECK

dizziness ...... VERTIGO, GIDDINESS

attack of .... FAINT

dizzy .... GIDDY, GROGGY, FLIGHTY, VERTIGINOUS

colloquial ..... SILLY, FOOLISH, MIXED-UP

of baseball fame .... DEAN

person: colloq. .... DAME

Djajapura's (Indonesia) neighbor .... SARMI

djebel .... HILL

do .... ACT, MAKE, ENACT, SERVE, CARRY OUT, PERFORM

a constable's job .... RUN-IN

a double take .... REACT, RELOOK

a fall job .... RAKE

a host's job .... GREET

a museum job .... RESTORE

a number on .... BAD-MOUTH

a pocket job .... PICK

a razing job .... BLAST

alone .... SOLO

away with .... RID, KILL, SLAY, ABOLISH

business, in a way .... BARTER

farm work .... SOW, PLOW, REAP, PLANT, HARVEST

in .... KILL, SLAY, DESTROY

it-yourself set .... KIT

handwork .... TAT

make .... EKE

newsroom work .... EDIT

one good .... BE BENEFICIAL

over .... REDECORATE

superficially .... DABBLE

the crawl .... SWIM

the Lindy .... JITTERBUG

well's leader .... NE'ER

without .... SPARE, FOREGO, ABSTAIN

dobbin .... HORSE

dobbin's lunch pail .... NOSE BAG

dobson fly .... SIALID(AN)

doby: colloq. .... ADOBE

doc. .... DOCTOR, DOCUMENT

docile .... TAME, PLIANT, WILLING, OBEDIENT, TRACTABLE, GENTLE (AS A LAMB)

dock ...... BOB, BANG, CLIP, LAND, PIER, QUAY, SLIP, BERTH, HAVEN, JETTY, WHARF, DEDUCT, HARBOR, PENALIZE

area .... MARINA

post .... BOLLARD

prisoner's ...... WITNESS STAND

worker .... LUMPER, STEVEDORE, LONGSHOREMAN

docked tail .... BOB

docket .... LABEL, AGENDA, TICKET, CALENDAR, REGISTER

docking space .... SLIP

doctor .... MEDIC, TREAT, MENDER, TAMPER, FALSIFY,

SURGEON, TEACHER,
OSTEOPATH, PHYSICIAN,
CHIROPRACTOR, MEDICINE
MAN
assistant of .... NURSE,
INTERN(E)
certain .... SHRINK
children's .... PEDIATRIST,
PEDIATRICIAN
colloquial .... DOC, VET,
MEDICO
ear .... OTOLOGIST
eye .... OCULIST
fake/herb .... QUACK
family .... GP, GENERAL
PRACTITIONER
frequent prescription of
.... REST
heart .... CARDIOLOGIST
hospital ..... INTERN, RESIDENT
inquest .... CORONER
kind of .... QUACK, WITCH,
SPECIALIST
Moslem .... HAKIM, HAKEEM
of animals .... VET(ERINARIAN)
of disorders of the mind
.... PSYCHIATRIST
of foot/hand diseases
.... PODIATRIST, CHIROPODIST
of injury to bones/joints
.... ORTHOPEDIST
of the nervous system
.... NEUROLOGIST
of women's diseases/
pregnancy
.... GYNECOLOGIST,
OBSTETRICIAN
skin .... DERMATOLOGIST
teeth .... DENTIST,
ORTHODONTIST
doctor's association .... AMA
degree .... MD
oath .... HIPPOCRATIC
rap .... PERCUSS
doctrinaire .... DOGMATIC,
VISIONARY, OPINIONATED,
DICTATORIAL
person .... BIGOT, RACIST,
DOGMATIST, CHAUVINIST
doctrinal .... CREEDAL
doctrine .... ISM, CULT, CREED,
DOGMA, TENET, BELIEF,
THEORY, PRECEPT, PRINCIPLE
mystical .... CABALA
of salvation .... LEGALISM
religious .... DOXY, CREED,
DOGMA
widespread .... GOSPEL
doctrines to be believed
.... CREDENDA
document .... DEED, PAPER,

RECORD, CONTRACT
container .... HANAPER
draft .... PROTOCOL
formal .... INSTRUMENT
handwritten by signer
.... HOLOGRAPH
legal .... WRIT
of proof .... EVIDENCE
part of .... SEAL
ribbon of .... LAPEL
written .... SCRIPT
documents, collection of
.... PAPERS
dodder .... SHAKE, TOTTER,
TREMBLE
doddering person .... DOTARD
Dodecanese island .... COS, KOS,
SIMI, KASOS, LEROS, PATMOS,
RHODES, RODHOS
dodge .... DUCK, RUSE, ELUDE,
AVOID, EVADE, PARRY,
ESCAPE, SIDESTEP
dodger .... IDLER, ELUDER,
EVADER, RASCAL, SHIRKER
equipment .... BUMPER,
FENDER
slang .... GOOF-OFF,
GOLDBRICK
Dodgers' (baseball)
"preacher" .... ROE
dodo in flying school ...... CADET
doe .... DEER
in its 2nd year .... TEG
mate of .... STAG
doer .... ACHIEVER
does gardening .... WEEDS
not understand .... SEES NOT
doff .... VAIL, STRIP, DIVEST,
REMOVE, GET RID, TAKE OFF
dog .... LAP, PET, PUG, PUP, ALAN,
HUNT, MUTT, SLUT, TYKE,
HOUND, POOCH, CANINE,
FOLLOW, PURSUE, RATTER,
YAPPER, CHENILLE
act of giving birth
.... WHELPING
African .... BASENJI
Alaskan .... MALAMUTE,
MALEMIUT, MALEMUTE
ape .... BABOON
Arctic ...... HUSKY, MALEMUTE
Australian ..... DINGO, TERRIER
Belgian/Dutch .... GRIFFIN,
GRIFFON
bird .... SETTER
breed .... CHOW, BOXER,
HUSKY, SPITZ, BEAGLE,
COLLIE, POODLE, SETTER,
BULLDOG, MALTESE, MASTIFF,
POINTER, SAMOYED, SPANIEL,
TERRIER, AIREDALE, ALSATIAN,

SHIH TZU, CHIHUAHUA,
DACHSHUND, DALMATIAN,
GREYHOUND, PEKINGESE,
RETRIEVER, SCHNAUZER,
GREAT DANE, LHASA APSO,
POMERANIAN, ROTTWEILER,
WEIMARANER, ST. BERNARD,
BASSET(HOUND), GERMAN
SHEPHERD, DOBERMAN
PINSCHER
of setter ...... IRISH, GORDON,
ENGLISH
of spaniel .... TOY, FIELD,
COCKER, SUSSEX, CLUMBER,
NORFOLK, BLENHEIM,
BRITTANY, SPRINGER
of terrier .... FOX, BULL,
SKYE, CAIRN, SILKY, WELSH,
BORDER, NORWICH,
WHEATEN, WIRE-FOX,
AIREDALE, LAKELAND,
SCOTTISH, SEALYHAM,
KERRY-BLUE, YORKSHIRE,
BEDLINGTON
Calvin Coolidge's .... ROB
ROY
Chinese breed .... CHOW,
PEKIN(G)ESE
chops .... FLEWS
coach .... DALMATIAN
collar ring .... TERRET
colloquial .... DOGGY
combining form .... CYNO
command to .... MUSH
constellation .... CANIS
cry .... HOWL
cur .... TYKE
curly-haired .... BARBET,
POODLE
days of _____ .... SUMMER
days, month of .... JULY,
AUGUST
disease .... MANGE, RABIES,
DRONCIT, DISTEMPER,
HEARTWORM, BORDETELLA
caused by tick .... LYME
Disney .... PLUTO, TRAMP
Dorothy's .... TOTO
drinking way of .... LAP
droopy-eared .... BASSET,
BEAGLE, SPANIEL, DACHSHUND
-eared .... FOLDED, TIME-
WORN, WELL-WORN, WORN-
DOWN
-eat-dog affair .... RAT RACE
Eskimo .... HUSKY
face of .... MASK
family .... CANIDAE
FDR's .... FALA
female .... SLUT, BITCH,
BRACH(ET)

fennel .... HOGWEED, MAYWEED
ferocious .... BANDOG, BULLDOG, BLOODHOUND
fictional .... RAB
footsteps, rhythm of ...... GAIT
formerly called Boarhound .... GREAT DANE
foxhound-like .... HARRIER
French breed .... PAPILLON
French/English .... BULLDOG
genus .... CANIS
George Bush's .... MILLIE
German .... POINTER, SHEPHERD
greyhound .... SALUKI
guard of the underworld/of hell .... CERBERUS
hairless breed .... INCA
hair on neck .... HACKLES
hound .... AFGHAN, BASSET, BEAGLE, GAZELLE, BRACH(ET)
house .... KENNEL
howl of .... BAY, ULULATION
Hungarian guardian .... KUVASZ
Hungarian sheep .... PULI
hunting .... BASSET, BEAGLE, SETTER, HARRIER, MASTIFF, POINTER, BRACH(ET), RETRIEVER
hybrid/of mixed breed .... CUR, MONGREL
in meteorology .... PARHELION
-in-the-manger .... GROUCH, KILLJOY
Japanese .... INU, SPANIEL
large .... MASTIFF, DALMATIAN, GREAT DANE, WEIMARANER, ST. BERNARD, DOBERMAN PINSCHER
largest breed of Japanese .... AKITA
of poodle .... STANDARD
of Schnauzer .... GIANT
of terrier .... AIREDALE
LBJ's/mongrel in White House .... YUKI
lead of .... LEASH
like animal .... JACKAL
like miniature greyhound .... WHIPPET
long-bodied .... DACHSHUND
loss of scent .... FAULT
miniature .... POODLE, PINSCHER, SCHNAUZER
mongrel .... CUR, TYKE
movie/TV .... ASTA, CLEO, NEIL, HOOCH, KELLY, PLUTO, SANDY, BENJIE, LASSIE, DREYFUS, LAD-A-DOG, RIN TIN

TIN
mythological .... CERBERUS
name of .... ACE, REX, ASTA, FALA, FIDO, SPOT, PLUTO, ROVER, SPIKE, BENJIE, LASSIE, SPOTTY, BLACKIE, BROWNIE
non-barking, yodeling .... BASENJI
Nora's .... ASTA
of India .... DHOLE
order .... CARNIVORE
Orphan Annie's .... SANDY
pack .... KENNEL
parasite .... HEARTWORM
part of foot .... PAD, PAW
pendulous upper lips of .... FLEWS
permanent ID method on .... TATTOO
pet .... LAP, POODLE, PEKINESE, CHIHUAHUA, DACHSHUND, LHASA APSO, POMERANIAN
police .... DANE, ALSATIAN, SHEPHERD
pound .... CUR, STRAY, MONGREL
pug-nosed .... PEKIN(G)ESE
rabbit/hare hunter .... HARRIER
racing .... GREYHOUND
retriever .... GOLDEN, LABRADOR
Ronald Reagan's .... REX
rounded ribcage of .... BARREL
Russian .... BORZOI, OWTCHAR, SAMOYED
saliva, result of excessive .... DROOL
Shetland .... SHEEPDOG
short-legged .... BEAGLE, DACHSHUND
show class .... OPEN, PUPPY, NOVICE, AMERICAN-BRED
Siberian ..... HUSKY, SAMOYED
slang .... MUTT, POOCH
sled .... HUSKY
small .... POM, PUG, ALCO, BEAGLE, WHIPPET, KEESHOND, POMERANIAN
smallest .... CHIHUAHUA
spaniel .... COCKER
soft hair on tail of ...... PLUME
"space" .... LAIKA
spaniel ..... COCKER, CLUMBER, SPRINGER
spotted .... DALMATIAN
swift/racing .... WHIPPET, GREYHOUND
tail of .... FLAG
tailless .... SCHIPPERKE
team leader .... OUTRUNNER

terrier .... IRISH, SILKY, SCOTTISH, SEALYHAM, SCHNAUZER, YORKSHIRE
three-headed .... CERBERUS
thumb equivalent of ..... DEW-CLAW
tongue cartilage .... LYTTA
tooth .... FANG, CUSPID, LANIARY
toy .... POM, PUG, PEKE, POODLE, SPANIEL, TERRIER, CHIHUAHUA
traditionally ladies' lap .... TOY
two-toned .... BELTON
U.S. club for registration of purebreds: abbr. ..... AKC
wagon .... DINER
Wales .... SEALYHAM
Welsh .... CORGI, COLLIE, TERRIER
who fathers litter of puppies .... SIRE
wild .... DHOLE, DINGO, JACKAL, TANATE
wire haired .... GRIFFIN, GRIFFON, POINTER, TERRIER, PINSCHER, SCHNAUZER
with foxlike head .... CORGI
with tan markings .... DOBERMAN PINSCHER
young .... PUP(PY), WHELP
Dog Star .... SIRIUS, PROCYON, CANICULA
of the .... SOTHIC
dogcart .... TRAP
dog-eared .... FOLDED, TIMEWORN
dogface: sl. .... G.I., FOOT SOLDIER, INFANTRYMAN
dogfish .... SHARK, BOWFIN
skin .... SHAGREEN
dogged .... HARRIED, HOUNDED, STUBBORN
dogger .... BOAT
doggerel .... VERSE, JINGLE
doggone! .... DAMN, DARN
doggy .... CANINE, DOGLIKE
dogie .... CALF, WAIF, STRAY, ORPHAN, MAVERICK
dogma .... ISM, CREED, TENET, BELIEF, DOCTRINE
dogmatic .... WILLFUL, OBSTINATE, DICTATORIAL
principle .... DICTA
saying .... DICTUM
dogmatics .... RELIGION, THEOLOGY
dogmatist, a .... CALVINIST
dogmatize .... PROCLAIM
dogs, collectively .... DOGGERY
slang .... FEET

dogtired .... ALL IN
dogwood .... OSIER, CORNEL,
    CORNUS, TUPELO, ASSAGAI,
    ASSEGAI
doilies .... NAPERY
doily .... MAT, NAPKIN
doings .... ACTIVITIES
doited: Scot ...... SENILE, FOOLISH
doldrums .... LULL, CALM, BLUES,
    DUMPS, TEDIUM, DEPRESSION,
    LISTLESSNESS
dole .... ALMS, METE, HANDOUT,
    PITTANCE, DISTRIBUTE
  archaic .... DOLOR, SORROW
  out .... METE, RATION
doleful .... SAD, DISMAL, JOYLESS,
    PENSIVE, UNHAPPY,
    MOURNFUL, LUGUBRIOUS
dolerite .... BASALT
doll .... TOY, CHILD, MAMMET,
    MAUMET, PUPPET, PLAYTHING,
    MARIONETTE
  kind of .... PAPER, BARBIE,
    KEWPIE, VOODOO
  rag .... MOPPET
  real .... LULU
  slang .... BABE, BABY, GIRL,
    DAME, BROAD, CHICK, CUTIE,
    DOLLY, WOMAN, SWEETHEART
  up .... BEAUTIFY, PRETTIFY,
    DRESS(UP), SPRUCE(UP)
dollar .... MONEY, CURRENCY
  bill .... SINGLE
  bill, five: sl. .... FIN, FIVER,
    FIVE-SPOT
  bill, 500: sl. ...... HALF-GRAND
  bill, one: sl. .... BUCK
  bill, 100: sl. .... C-NOTE,
    CENTURY
  bill, 1000: sl. .... GRAND
  bill, ten: sl. .... TENNER,
    SAWBUCK
  bill, twenty: sl. .... DOUBLE
    SAWBUCK
  bill, two: sl. ...... DEUCE, TWO-
    SPOT
  coin part .... CENT, DIME,
    EAGLE, NICKEL, PENNY,
    QUARTER
  coin: sl. .... CARTWHEEL
  Mexican .... PESO
  quarter: sl. .... TWO BITS
  slang .... BUCK, BERRY,
    PLUNK, SMACKER, SIMOLEON
  Spanish .... DURO
dollop .... BLOB, LUMP
dolly .... CART, TRUCK, DASHER,
    LOCOMOTIVE
  child's .... DOLL
  Indian .... TRAY
  slang .... LOTUS

  what it holds .... RIVET
Dolly Varden .... HAT, TROUT
dolman .... COAT, ROBE, WRAP,
    JACKET, MANTLE
dolmen stone .... MEGALITH
dolomite features .... ARETES
Dolomites peak .... MARMOLADA
dolor .... WOE, PANG, AGONY,
    GRIEF, SORROW, ANGUISH
dolorous .... SAD, DOLEFUL,
    FORLORN, TEARFUL,
    MOURNFUL
dolphin .... BUOY, INIA, SUSU,
    BELUGA, SEA HOG, SOOSOO,
    CETACEAN, PORPOISE
  family .... DELPHINIDAE
  frolic of .... GAMBOL
  musician saved by .... ORION
  Spanish .... DORADO
  striker .... SPAR,
    MARTINGAL(E)
  whale .... ORC
dolt .... OAF, SAP, CLOD, FOOL,
    ZANY, DUNCE, NINNY, SCHMO,
    NITWIT, HALFWIT, JACKASS,
    NUMSKULL, DUMBBELL,
    BLOCKHEAD
doltish .... STUPID, WITLESS,
    HALFWITTED
domain .... FIELD, REALM,
    DEMENE, ESTATE, REGION,
    SPHERE, DEMESNE, BAILIWICK,
    TERRITORY
  poetic .... BOURN(E)
dome .... ROOF, VAULT, CUPOLA
  apse's .... CONCHA
  building/hall with
    .... ROTUNDA
  poetic .... MANSION
  slang .... HEAD
  with cupola .... TOPE
Domenico, painter .... EL GRECO
domestic .... TAME, LOCAL,
    HOMELY, MENIAL, NATIVE,
    SLAVEY, ENCHORIC,
    INTERNAL, ENCHORIAL, HOME-
    GROWN
  animal: dia. .... CRITTER,
    CRITTUR
  animal sickness .... SURRA
  establishment .... FAMILY,
    MENAGE, DOMICILE,
    HOUSEHOLD
  fowl .... DORKING, POULTRY
  servant .... (HOUSE)MAID
  type of .... LIVE-IN, SLEEP-IN
  worker .... COOK, MAID,
    BUTLER, SERVANT, GARDENER
domesticate .... REAR, TAME,
    (HOUSE)BREAK, BREED,
    TRAIN, CORRAL, CIVILIZE

domicile .... HOME, ABODE,
    MENAGE, DWELLING,
    HOUSE(HOLD), RESIDENCE
dominance .... CONTROL,
    MASTERY, SUPREMACY
dominant .... RULING, IN
    CONTROL, PRE-EMINENT,
    PREVAILING
dominate .... RULE, REIGN,
    GOVERN, HECTOR, MASTER,
    CONTROL
dominated .... RIDDEN, UNDER
    ONE'S THUMB
domineer .... COW, BREAK,
    BULLY, OPPRESS, LORD OVER,
    OVERBEAR, TYRANNIZE
  husband .... HENPECK
Dominica capital .... ROSEAU
  city .... PORTSMOUTH
  language ..... FRENCH, ENGLISH
  monetary unit .... DOLLAR
Dominican ...... FRIAR, PREACHER
  Republic bay .... SAMANA
  cape .... BEATA
  capital ...... SANTO DOMINGO
  city/town .... AZUA, BANI,
    MOCA, NEIBA, LA VEGA,
    SANCHEZ, EL SEIBO, LA
    ROMANA, SANTIAGO
  island .... BEATA, SAONA,
    HISPANIOLA
  language .... SPANISH
  monetary unit .... PESO
  peak .... PICO DUARTE
  president .... BOSCH,
    BALAGUER
dominie .... PASTOR, CLERGYMAN,
    SCHOOLMASTER
dominion .... RULE, SWAY,
    POWER, REALM, REIGN,
    DOMAIN, EMPERY, EMPIRE,
    LORDSHIP
domino .... BONE, LUMP, TILE,
    CLOAK, (HALF)MASK
  spot .... PIP
  variant .... MUGGINS
  with four spots .... QUATRE
dominoes not dealt .... STOCK
don ...... WEAR, PUT ON, ASSUME,
    CLOTHE, INVEST
  Cambridge college ...... HEAD,
    TUTOR, FELLOW
  opposed to .... DOFF
  relative of .... TIA
  river .... DUNA
  Spanish .... NOBLEMAN,
    GENTLEMAN
Don Juan .... RAKE, PHILANDERER
  Juan, greatest
    .... (ANTOINE)DUBOIS
  Juan's mother .... INEZ

Quixote .... MAN OF LA
MANCHA
Quixote author .... CERVANTES
Quixote's horse
.... ROSINANTE
Quixote's ladylove
.... DULCINEA
dona .... LADY, MADAM
Donahue .... PHIL, TROY
Donald Duck, MD .... QUACK
DOCTOR
Donar, god of thunder .... THOR
donate .... GIVE, BESTOW,
CONFER, TENDER, PRESENT,
PROVIDE, CONTRIBUTE
colloquial .... CHIP IN
slang .... KICK IN
donation .... AID, GIFT, HELP,
GRANT, ASSISTANCE
generous .... BOUNTY
of a philanthropist
.... LARGESSE
periodic .... STIPEND
Donau river ...... DUNA, DANUBE,
DUNAREA
done for .... KAPUT, KILLED,
RUINED
with .... OVER, ENDED,
COMPLETE
with hands .... MANUAL
Donetsk .... STALINO
donjon .... KEEP, TOWER,
DUNGEON
donkey .... BURRO, CUDDY,
JENNET, ONAGER, DICK(E)Y,
(JACK)ASS
and horse offspring ..... MULE,
HINNY
animal like a .... QUAGGA
cry .... BRAY
female .... MARE
male .... JACK
man rebuked by .... BALAAM
pet name of .... MOKE
young .... COLT, FOAL
Donna .... REED, SUMMER
Donne and Bradstreet .... POETS
donnybrook .... ADO, RIOT,
BRAWL, MELEE, FRACAS,
RUCKUS, RUMPUS, FREE-FOR-
ALL
donor .... GIVER, GRANTOR,
BENEFACTOR, CONTRIBUTOR
Don't _____ that feeds you
.... BITE THE HAND
doodad .... BAUBLE, GADGET,
GEWGAW, TRINKET,
GIMCRACK
doodle .... DAWDLE, SCRAWL,
SCRIBBLE
doodlebug .... LARVA

doodlesack .... BAGPIPE
doohickey .... DEVICE, DINGUS,
DOODAD, GADGET, DINGBAT,
CONTRAPTION
doom ...... FATE, DEATH, DESTINY,
CONDEMN, DAMNATION
doomed .... GRIM, FATED, KAPUT,
DESTINED, HOPELESS
to death .... FEY
to eternal punishment
.... DAMNED
Doone, heroine .... LORNA
husband of .... RIDD
door .... ENTRY, ACCESS, PORTAL,
WICKET, BARRIER, PASSAGE
back .... POSTERN
catch .... LATCH
cover .... AWNING, CANOPY
crosspiece .... LINTEL,
TRANSOM
fastener/lock ..... HASP, LATCH
for entering .... GATE, INLET,
ENTRANCE
frame piece .... TILE
frame(work) ..... SASH, GRATE,
GRATING
grating .... GRILLE
handle .... KNOB
joint .... HINGE
knocker .... BELL, RAPPER
leading out .... EXIT, OUTLET
lower half of .... HATCH
part of ..... HASP, KNOB, JAMB,
RAIL, SILL, FRAME, LATCH,
PANEL, LINTEL, STILE,
DOORPOST
rooflike projection .... CANOPY
doorkeeper .... USHER, PORTER,
OSTIARY, CONCIERGE,
GATEKEEPER
Masonic .... TILER
doorman .... PORTER, SENTRY,
JANITOR, CONCIERGE
or maitre d' .... GREETER
doorsill .... THRESHOLD
doorway .... GATE, PORTAL,
ENTRANCE
curtain .... PORTIERE
drapery .... LAMBREQUIN
out .... EXIT
sidepost .... JAMB(E)
doozy .... EXCELLENCE
dope .... DRUG, HINT, JUNK,
OPIATE, NARCOTIC(S)
addict .... USER, FIEND, JUNKY,
ABUSER, JUNKIE, POTHEAD,
SNIFFER
out .... SOLVE, FIGURE(OUT)
seller .... PUSHER
slang .... CLOD, DUNCE,
NITWIT, STUPID

the .... INFO, LOW-DOWN,
DATA, FACTS, SCORE
doped .... SLEEPY, STONED,
DRUGGED, OUT COLD
dopester .... ANALYST,
SCRUTINEER
dopey .... DAZED, STUPID,
CONFUSED, HALF-WITTED
doppelganger .... DOUBLE,
WRAITH, REPLICA, SPECTER,
DUPLICATE
dor .... BEETLE, BUMBLEBEE
dorado .... DOLPHIN
dorbeetle .... COCKCHAFER
Dorcas .... SEWER TABITHA
dore, _____ (olive wood)
.... BRUN
Doric cornice block ...... MUTULE
droplike ornaments .... GUTTA
Dorlcote Mill site .... FLOSS
dormancy .... TORPOR, IDLENESS,
INACTION
dormant .... QUIET, STILL,
ASLEEP, LATENT, TORPID,
RESTING, INACTIVE,
QUIESCENT
dormer .... WINDOW, LUTHERN,
SKYLIGHT
area .... ATTIC
dormitory .... DORM, HALL,
QUARTERS, BOARDINGHOUSE
dormouse .... LEROT, RODENT
acquaintance leaps .... ALICE
SPRINGS
dornick .... STONE, DAMASK
dorp .... HAMLET, VILLAGE
dorsal .... BACK, TERGAL
opposed to .... VENTRAL
dorsum .... BACK, TERGUM
dorty .... SULLEN
dory .... (FISHING)BOAT
Dos Passos's trilogy .... USA
dos-a-dos .... SEAT, SOFA
dosage .... DOSE, AMOUNT
dilemma .... MEDICAMENT
PREDICAMENT
dose .... DOSAGE, MEASURE,
QUANTITY
liquid .... POTION
doss .... BED, BUNK, SLEEP,
SNOOZE
dosser .... PANNIER
dossier .... RECORD,
(PERSONAL)FILE
dossil ...... TENT, STUPE, PLEDGET,
COMPRESS
dot .... JOT, IOTA, MARK, SPOT,
WHIT, DOWRY, POINT, TITTLE,
SPECK, PERIOD, STIPPLE
dotage .... FONDNESS, SENILITY
dotard .... OCTOGENARIAN

describing a .... SENILE
dote .... DROOL, DRIVEL, SLOBBER
   on .... LIKE, ADORE, FANCY
doting .... FOND, AGING,
                     DECAYING
dotted .... PIED, DAPPLE,
   MOTTLED, SPOTTED, STIPPLED,
                   SPECKLED
   in heraldry .... SEME
dotterel ...... DUPE, GULL, PLOVER
dotty ...... CRAZY, POCKY, FEEBLE,
             SPOTTY, STUDDED
   slang .... DAFFY, DIPPY,
              GOOFY, WACKY
double .... COPY, DUAL, FOLD,
   TWIN, DUPLE, TWICE, BINATE,
   PAIRED, REPEAT, TWOFOLD,
              ALTER EGO
   aces .... AMBSACE, AMESACE
   agent .... SPY, TRAITOR,
              TURNCOAT
   apartment/house .... DUPLEX
   as a substitute in movies/
     plays .... STAND-IN,
             UNDERSTUDY
   bass .... VIOLONE
   check .... VERIFY
   chromosome .... DYAD
   cross: sl. .... DO IN, CHEAT,
   BETRAY, DECEIVE, TREACHERY
   curve .... ESS
   dagger mark .... DIESIS
   dealer .... CHEATER, DECEIVER,
             TWO-TIMER
   dealing .... DUPLICITY, FOUL
                 PLAY
   decker: colloq. ...... SANDWICH
   door part .... SWING
   duo .... TETRAD
   edged .... SHARP, BITING
   exact .... DUPLICATE
   faced .... UNTRUE, INSINCERE
   faced god .... JANUS
   faced person .... HYPOCRITE
   helix .... DNA
   meaning .... EQUIVOKE,
   AMBIGUITY, EQUIVOQUE,
            EQUIVOCACY
   minded .... DOUBTFUL,
   HESITANT, UNCERTAIN,
            UNDECIDED
   moldboard plow .... LISTER
   on the .... QUICKLY
   page spreads .... ADS
   prefix .... DI(S)
   reed instrument .... OBOE,
       SHAWN, BASSOON
   ring .... GEMEL
   ripper/runner .... SLED
   sirloin beef .... BARON
   take .... AFTERTHOUGHT

talk .... JARGON, GIBBERISH
tongued ..... TRICKY, DEVIOUS,
   CUNNING, DECEITFUL
tongued creature .... SNAKE
tooth .... MOLAR
tripod .... CAT
trouble .... RACK AND RUIN
up .... FOLD, CLENCH
vision .... DIPLOPIA
doubled .... ECHOED, FOLDED,
              REPEATED
doublet .... COUPLET, POURPOINT,
   TWEEDLEDUM AND
           TWEEDLEDEE
doubletree .... CROSSBAR
doubly .... TWICE, TWOFOLD
doubt .... FEAR, CONCERN,
   MISTRUST, SUSPICION,
   SKEPTICISM, UNCERTAINTY
   about .... WONDER
   beyond .... SURE, CERTAIN
   cause/feel .... MISGIVE
   feeling of .... SCRUPLE
   show .... WAVER, FALTER,
        TEETER, HESITATE
doubter .... THOMAS, SKEPTIC,
           MISSOURIAN
doubtful .... FISHY, MAYBE,
       UNSURE, DUBIOUS
doubting Thomas .... SKEPTIC
douce: Scot. .... PLEASANT
douceur .... TIP, BRIBE
dough .... PASTE, BATTER
   dry strip of .... NOODLE
   fermenting .... LEAVEN
   slang .... CASH, MONEY
   toughener .... GLUTEN
doughboy ...... YANK, DUMPLING,
         INFANTRYMAN
doughnut .... DONUT, CRULLER,
          FRIEDCAKE
   colloquial .... SINKER
   shape .... TORUS
   slang .... TIRE, DUNKER
doughty .... BOLD, BRAVE,
   DARING, GALLANT, VALIANT
doughy .... SOFT, PASTY
doum .... PALM
dour .... GRIM, HARD, HARSH,
   STRICT, STERN, SEVERE,
             SULLEN
Douro .... DUERO
douse .... HIT, DUCK, SOAK,
   DRENCH, EXTINGUISH
dousing .... IMMERSION
dove .... NUN, COOER, CULVER,
       CUSHAT, PIGEON
   Asian/European ..... RINGDOVE
   describing a .... WEAK,
     GENTLE, INNOCENT
   family .... COLUMBIDAE

genus .... COLUMBA
kind of .... HOMING, POUTER,
             TUMBLER
make sound of .... COO,
              MOURN
opposite of .... HAWK
shelter ...... COTE, COLUMBARY
symbol .... PEACE, HOLY
              SPIRIT
dovecote .... COLUMBARY
dovekie .... AUK, ALLE, ROTCH(E),
           GUILLEMOT
dovelike .... GENTLE, ANGELIC
Dover is capital of
               DELAWARE
dovetail .... FIT, JOINT, FASTEN
dowager .... WIDOW, MATRON,
           BELDAM(E)
dowdy .... SEEDY, TACKY,
   RAGGED, FRAYED, SHABBY,
   SHODDY, FRAZZLED,
           SLOVENLY
   woman .... FRUMP
dowel .... PIN
   like .... TENON, PINTLE
dower ...... GIFT, DOWRY, ENDOW,
   INVEST, TALENT, BEQUEST,
   ENDOWMENT, INHERITANCE
dowlas .... LINEN, CALICO
down .... FUR, ILL, FELL, HAIR,
   PILE, BELOW, FLOOR, FLUFF,
   UNDER, BENEATH, FEATHERS
   a mound like .... DUNE
   and out .... BANKRUPT,
   HELPLESS, HOPELESS
   at heels .... NEEDY, INDIGENT
   combining form .... CAT(A),
         CATH, KATA
   covered with .... PUBESCENT,
   LANUGINOSE, LANUGINOUS
   duck's .... EIDER
   east .... MAINE, NEW YORK,
        NEW ENGLAND
   facing .... PRONE, PRONATE
   feather .... PLUMULE
   in baseball .... (PUT)OUT
   in bridge .... SET
   in the mouth .... SAD,
   UNHAPPY, DEJECTED,
   (FEELING)LOW, DEPRESSED
   loose particles of .... FUZZ
   plant .... VILLUS
   source of .... EIDER
   the drain .... WASTED
   to-earth one .... REALIST
Down Under .... ANZAC,
   AUSTRALIA, NEW ZEALAND
downcast .... SAD, GLOOMY,
   BASHFUL, DEJECTED
downfall ...... DROP, RUIN, CRASH,
   DEFEAT, FAILURE, COLLAPSE,

LABEFACTION
downgrade ...... DEMOTE, REDUCE
downhearted .... SAD, DASHED,
DEJECTED, DEPRESSED,
DESPONDENT, DISCOURAGED
downhill, go .... DECLINE,
DESCEND
downier .... SOFTER
downpour .... SPATE, DELUGE,
SHOWER, TORRENT,
RAIN(STORM), CLOUDBURST
downright .... BLUNT, FRANK,
PLAIN, SHEER, STARK, DIRECT,
UTTERLY, ABSOLUTE
Downs, the .... ROADSTEAD
downtrodden .... ABUSED,
OPPRESSED
downward ...... FALLING, SINKING,
DESCENDING, PLUMMETING
downwind .... ALEE, LEEWARD
downy .... SOFT, FUZZY, NAPPY,
FLEECY, FLOSSY, FLUFFY,
VILLOUS, FEATHERY
feather .... PLUMULE
growth .... MOLD, LANUGO
mass .... FLUE
surface/fiber .... NAP
dowry .... GIFT, LEGACY, TALENT,
ENDOWMENT
of a .... DOTAL
doxology .... KADDISH
first word .... GLORIA
doxy .... ISM, CREED, DOCTRINE
slang .... HUSSY, WENCH,
MISTRESS
doyen .... DEAN, TOP DOG,
KINGPIN
doze .... SLEEP, (CAT)NAP,
DROWSE, SNOOZE
dozen .... TWELVE
baker's/long .... THIRTEEN
dozing one .... NAPPER
dozy .... DROWSY, SLEEPY
Dr. J in basketball
.... (JULIUS)ERVING
No's nemesis .... BOND
Spock, to pals .... BEN
drab ...... DUN, WAN, DULL, SLUT,
BORING, LACKLUSTER
drabbet .... LINEN
drach .... DRAM
drachma .... COIN
1/100 of a .... LEPTON
1/6 of a .... OBOL
drachmas (1700) in 1949
.... DOLLAR
Draco .... DRAGON
Draconian .... CRUEL, SEVERE
draff .... LEES, DREGS, REFUSE,
SEDIMENT
draft .... DOSE, PULL, DRAIN,

POTION, SKETCH, DRAWING,
OUTLINE, POTATION,
DRINK(ING), CONSCRIPT
a small .... TASS
animal .... OX, MULE,
CARABAO, ELEPHANT
animal and its vehicle
.... TEAM
bank .... CHECK
card burner .... DODGER,
OBJECTOR
deep .... SWIG
feudal fee to escape
.... SCUTAGE
military service .... IMPRESS
of air .... BREEZE
org. .... SSS
draftee .... ROOKIE, RECRUIT,
CONSCRIPT
drafts .... CHECKERS
draftsman .... DRAWER,
SCRIVENER
drag .... LAG, LUG, TUG, TOW,
HALE, HAUL, PULL, SWEEP,
TRAIL, DREDGE, GRAPNEL,
DRAW OUT, CONTINUE,
PROTRACT
feet .... SCUFF(LE)
slang ...... PUFF, RACE, DANCE,
INFLUENCE
dragee .... PILL, CANDY
draggletail .... SLUT, SLATTERN
dragnet .... WEB, TRAWL
dragoman ...... GUIDE, CICERONE,
INTERPRETER
dragon .... BEAST, MONSTER,
FIREDRAKE
archaic .... DRAKE, SNAKE,
SERPENT
breath of .... FIRE
deb's .... DUENNA
giant .... FAFNIR
Greek .... LADON
in astronomy .... DRACO
mythical .... BASILISK
slang .... HOTHEAD, FIRE-
EATER
slayer .... CADMUS,
(ST.)GEORGE
small .... DRAGONET
two-legged .... WIVERN
dragoon .... COERCE, HARASS,
TROOPER, CAVALRYMAN
drain .... DRIP, PIPE, DRAFT,
EMPTY, SEWER, FILTER, DRAW
OFF, DEPLETE, EXHAUST
dry .... DEHYDRATE
for washing ore .... BUDDLE
liquid from .... SAP, TAP,
SPOUT
open .... GUTTER, KENNEL

road .... CULVERT
draining hole/pit .... SUMP,
CESSPOOL
drained ...... SAPPED, WEAKENED,
EXHAUSTED
drake .... DUCK, CANNON, MAY
FLY, MALLARD
archaic .... DRAGON
Drake's adversary .... SPANISH
ARMADA
dram .... NIP, SIP, SLUG, DRAFT,
DRINK
in assaying .... CENTNER
drama .... SHOW, (STAGE)PLAY
climax .... CATASTROPHE
closing section of
.... EPILOGUE
comic scenes .... RELIEF
conflict of character ..... AGON
humorous .... COMEDY
in the sport of kings
.... TRIPLE CROWN
introduction .... PROLOGUE
Japanese .... KABUKI
main character
.... PROTAGONIST
musical .... OPERA, BALLET
opening .... PROTASIS
outdoor .... PAGEANT
pause between acts of
.... INTERMISSION
pertaining to .... THESPIAN
section .... ACT
short .... PLAYLET
staging place .... THEATER
tragic .... BUSKIN
with unhappy ending
.... TRAGEDY
wordless .... PANTOMIME
writer .... DRAMATIST,
PLAYWRIGHT
dramatic .... VIVID, EXCITING,
STRIKING
art .... THEATER
impersonator .... DISEUSE
scene/picture .... TABLEAU
dramatics .... THEATRICS,
HISTRIONICS
dramatis personae .... CAST,
CHARACTERS
dramatist .... PLAYWRIGHT
dramatize .... ENACT, SPLASH
slang .... HAM IT UP
dramshop .... BAR, SALOON
drape ...... FOLD, BAIZE, CURTAIN
draper .... CLOTHIER
drapery .... ARRAS, CLOTH,
FABRIC, CURTAIN, TEXTILE,
VALANCE
bed .... CANOPY
cloth .... MADRAS, MOREEN

cord .... TIEBACK, TORSADE
material ..... VELURE, VELOURS
shelf/door/window
.... LAMBREQUIN
drapes .... CURTAIN
drastic .... RASH, HARSH, SEVERE,
EXTREME
drat .... EXPLETIVE
draught .... SWIG, DRAFT
draughts: Brit. .... CHECKERS
Dravidian .... TELEGU, TELUGU
language .... TAMIL
draw .... TIE, TUG, HAUL, LIMN,
PULL, DRAFT, ALLURE,
DEPICT, SKETCH, ATTRACT,
RECEIVE, STALEMATE,
DISEMBOWEL
after .... TOW
as conclusion .... INFER,
ASSUME, DEDUCE, RECKON
at a cigar(ette) .... PUFF,
DRAG, INHALE
away .... DRAFT, DIVERT
back .... FLINCH, RECEDE,
RETRACT, RETREAT
back in fear .... QUAIL,
COWER, CRINGE, RECOIL
close .... NEAR, APPROACH
forth .... EDUCE, EVOKE, ELICIT
in .... WOO, LURE, ENSNARE
in dots .... STIPPLE
lots .... CAST
off .... DRAFT, SIPHON
off fluid .... TAP
off from dregs .... RACK
out ..... EDUCE, DERIVE, ELICIT,
EXTRACT, PROLONG, STRETCH,
LENGTHEN, CONTINUE,
PROTRACT
out with a ladle .... LADE
sap .... BLEED
the line .... (SET THE) LIMIT
tight ..... FRAP, TENSE, TAUTEN
to scale .... PROTRACT
drawback .... DEFECT, REBATE,
REFUND, HANDICAP,
OBSTACLE, DETERRENT,
SHORTCOMING
drawbridge .... BASCULE,
PONTLEVIS
drawer .... ARTIST, DRAFTSMAN,
DELINEATOR
for money .... TILL
handle of .... KNOB
drawers .... SHORTS
women's .... PANTIES,
PANTALET(TE)S
drawing .... PLAN, CHART,
DESIGN, SKETCH, DIAGRAM,
LOTTERY, ALLURING,
DEPICTION

architect's .... RENDU
architectural .... EPURES
carbon pencil/crayon
.... CHARCOAL
card .... BAIT, DECOY,
CELEBRITY, ENTERTAINER
charcoal .... FUSAIN
force to produce vacuum
.... SUCTION
graphic .... PORTRAYAL,
DELINEATION
humorous .... CARTOON
in dots .... STIPPLE
into the lungs, as of air
.... DRAFT
of load/vehicle .... TRACTION
on walls, etc. .... GRAFFITO
one way to make copy of
.... TRACING
paper .... ATLAS
photographic reproduction of
.... BLUEPRINT
power .... PULL, MAGNET
room .... SALA, SALON,
PARLOR
style of .... CHIAROSCURO
with crayons
.... CALCOGRAPHY
with lead-pointed instrument
.... PLUMBAGO
drawn .... WAN, EVEN, TAUT,
TIED, EQUAL, TENSE, TIRED,
WEARY, HAGGARD
out .... LONG, LENGTHY, LONG-
WINDED
dray .... VAN, CART, WAGON
drayage .... CARTAGE, FREIGHT,
HAULAGE
dread .... AWE, FEAR, ANGST,
FRIGHT, HORROR
dreaded disease .... AIDS,
CANCER, CHOLERA,
LEUKEMIA, SMALLPOX, HEART
ATTACK, TUBERCULOSIS
seizure? .... HOSTILE
TAKEOVER
dreadful .... BAD, DIRE, AWFUL,
HORRID, AWESOME, HIDEOUS,
FEARFUL, SHOCKING,
TERRIBLE
dreadfully: colloq. .... VERY,
BADLY, EXTREMELY
dreadnaught .... WARSHIP,
BATTLESHIP
dream ...... HOPE, FANCY, DESIRE,
VISION, FANTASY, IMAGINE,
DELUSION, ILLUSION
day .... REVERIE
French .... REVE
frightening .... NIGHTMARE
goal .... IDEAL

up .... IMAGINE, CONCEIVE,
CREATE, VISUALIZE
world .... UTOPIA, PARADISE
dreamer .... ROMANTICIST
impractical .... FANTAST,
VISIONARY
of dreams .... WISHFUL
THINKER
dreamily romantic
.... MOONSTRUCK, STARRY-
EYED
dreamland .... SLEEP
dreams, forecast based on
.... ONEIROMANCY
interpret .... REDE
interpretation of
.... ONEIROLOGY
interpreter .... ONEIROCRITIC
dreamy ...... RAPT, MISTY, VAGUE,
UNREAL, FANCIFUL,
ENCHANTED, IMAGINARY,
VISIONARY
from dope smoking .... KEF
person .... POET, PROPHET,
IDEALIST
dreary .... SAD, DULL, GRAY,
DISMAL, GLOOMY, LONELY,
SOMBER, TEDIOUS, CHEERLESS
Scottish .... DREE
dredge .... DRAG, SIFT, DEEPEN,
SPRINKLE
bucket .... CLAMSHELL
shovel .... SCOOP
dree .... DREARY, ENDURE,
SUFFER, TEDIOUS
dregs .... LEES, SCUM, SILT,
DRAFF, FECES, GROUT,
MAGMA, REFUSE, RESIDUE,
SEDIMENT
coffee .... GROUNDS
left in liquor glass
.... HEELTAP
of society .... RIFFRAFF
Dreiser (Theodore) character
.... STOIC, CARRIE
drench .... SOP, WET, SOAK,
DOUSE, SOUSE, SATURATE
drenched .... WET, ASOP, BATHED,
SODDEN, SOAKED, SOPPING,
STEEPED
Dresden .... CHINAWARE,
PORCELAIN
dress .... DON, RIG, TOG, DECK,
GARB, GEAR, TRIM, WEAR,
ADORN, ARRAY, FROCK,
ATTIRE, CLOTHE, APPAREL,
GARMENT, GARNISH, OUTFIT,
RAIMENT, CLOTHING,
DECORATE, EMBELLISH,
ACCOUTERMENT,
ACCOUTREMENT

a horse .... CURRY
accessory .... BAND, BELT,
　　　SASH, CESTUS, GUIMPE
by rubbing .... DUB
characteristic .... LIVERY
colloquial .... FIG, TOG(S)
cut ...... SACK, A-LINE, SHEATH
designer .... STYLIST
down .... SCOLD, BERATE,
　　　　　　　　REPRIMAND
external .... CAPE, COAT,
　　　CLOAK, SHAWL, STOLE,
　　　BURNOOSE, WRAP-AROUND
fashion designer .... DIOR,
　　　BEENE, BLASS, SARMI,
　　ADOLFO, CASHIN, CHANEL,
　　NORELL, BALMAIN, CASSINI,
　GALANOS, TIFFEAU, BERGDORF,
　　GIVENCHY, GERNREICH,
　　VALENTINO, BALENCIAGA
feathers .... PREEN
formal .... TUX, GOWN,
　　TUXEDO, CUTAWAY, FULL-
　　　　　　DRESS UNIFORM
flax .... TED
gaudily .... BEDIZEN
hat .... SHAKO, TOPPER, TOP
　　　　　　　　　　　HAT
in fine array .... DINK
judge's .... GOWN, ROBE
leather .... DUB, TAN, CURRY
man's full .... TAILS
manner of .... GUISE
material .... LAME, SILK,
　　WOOL, LINEN, PIQUE, VOILE,
　　MUSLIN, PONGEE, CHIFFON,
　　PAISLEY, SHANTUNG,
　　GEORGETTE, VELVET(EEN)
odd .... TOG
ornamental slit .... SLASH
pertaining to .... SARTORIAL
rehearsal .... WALK-THROUGH
riding .... HABIT
showily .... FIG
spangle .... SEQUIN
stone .... NIG
style, men's .... NEHRU,
　　　　　　SWALLOW-TAILED
style, women's .... SACK,
　A-LINE, CHITON, KIRTLE, MUU-
　　MUU, PALAZZO, TOPLESS,
　　PANTSUIT, CHEONGSAM,
　　CRINOLINE, MAXISKIRT,
　　MIDISKIRT, MINISKIRT
suit .... TUX(EDO)
trimming .... GIMP, RUCHE,
　　PIPING, RICKRACK, SOUTACHE
up .... PRANK, PRIMP, PRINK,
　　PRUNE, SPRUCE, DANDIFY
with beak/care .... PREEN
with tails .... CUTAWAY

dressed .... CLAD, GARBED,
　　　ARRAYED, CLOTHED
pelt .... FUR
shabbily ...... DOWDY, POK(E)Y
smartly .... CHIC, DAPPER
stylishly .... MODISH
to _____ .... KILL
to the _____ ..... NINES, TEETH
dresser .... CHEST, BUREAU,
　　　　　　　　　CUPBOARD
flashy .... SPIFF
of another person .... VALET
stylish .... FOP, DUDE, TOFF,
　　　　　　　　　　DANDY
dressing .... SAUCE, GARNISH,
　　　PLEDGET, STUFFING,
　　　　　　　DECORATION
down ...... SCOLDING, CHEWING
　　　　　　　　　　　OUT
gown .... ROBE, CAMISE,
　　DUSTER, KIMONO, CAMISOLE
medicated .... STUPE, PLASTER,
　　　　　　　　　POULTICE
room .... CLOSET
soil .... MUCK, MANURE,
　　　　　　　　　COMPOST
table .... TOILET, VANITY
wheel .... TRUER
wound .... LINT, GAUZE,
　　STUPE, DOSSIL, BANDAGE,
　　BAND-AID, COMPRESS
dressmaker ...... SEWER, SARTOR,
　　STYLIST, TAILOR, MODISTE,
　　COUTURIER(E), SEAMSTRESS
dressmaking term .... HEM,
　　FACE, GORE, PURL, BASTE,
　　GATHER, STITCH, APPLIQUE
dressy ...... CHIC, FANCY, SHOWY,
　　SMART, FORMAL, MODISH,
　　ELEGANT, STYLISH
Dreyfus' champion
　　................... (EMILE)ZOLA
dribble .... DROP, LEAK, DROOL,
　　SLAVER, SLABBER, TRICKLE
away .... WASTE, EMACIATE
in basketball .... BOUNCE
in football/soccer .... KICKS
in hockey .... TAP
driblet .... SMIDGEN, PITTANCE
dried coconut meat .... COPRA
flower bud .... CLOVE
grape .... RAISIN
grass .... HAY
orchid tuber .... SALEP
plum .... PRUNE
up .... SERE, BARREN
drier .... KILN, OAST, OVEN,
　　SERER, DRYER, BLOWER,
　　DESICCANT, DESICCATOR
natural .... SUN, FIRE
driest place in U.S. .... DEATH

　　　　　　　　　　VALLEY
drift .... GIST, PILE, FLOCK, FLOW,
　　STRAY, TENOR, TREND,
　　INTENT, ESSENCE, MEANING,
　　TENDENCY, INCLINATION
away .... FADE, SINK, DWINDLE
ice .... FLOE, SLUDGE
in mining .... HEADING
in nautical usage/off course
　　.. SAG
drifter .... HOBO, CLOUD, NOMAD,
　　TRAMP, DERELICT,
　　VAGABOND, WANDERER
drill .... AWL, BORE, QUIZ, AUGER,
　　CLOTH, TRAIN, BABOON,
　　GIMLET, PIERCE, EXERCISE,
　　PRACTICE, DISCIPLINE
dentist's .... BURR
hall .... ARMORY
team .... SQUAD
drilling equipment .... RIG
machinery support
　　............................... DERRICK
drink ...... ALE, BIB, TIFF, DRAFT,
　　ABSORB, IMBIBE, SWALLOW,
　　BEVERAGE, POTATION
a certain way .... LAP
addicted to alcoholic
　　........................... BIBULOUS
admiral's .... GROG
agave juice .... PULQUE
alcoholic .... GIN, PEG, RUM,
　　TOT, BEER, GROG, MEAD,
　　SAKE, BOOZE, BRANDY,
　　VODKA, COGNAC, LIQUOR,
　　SCOTCH, WHISKY, BOURBON,
　　SPIRITS, SWIZZLE, LIBATION
ancient .... MEAD, MORAT
appetizer .... BRACER,
　　　　　　　　COCKTAIL
aromatic .... JULEP, COFFEE
barley .... PTISAN
beer and lemonade
　　............................... SHANDY
beerlike, sour .... KVAS(S)
before bedtime ...... NIGHTCAP
before meal .... APERITIF
brandy ...... COGNAC, SIDECAR,
　　　　　　　　SANGAREE
brandy and soda .... PEG
Brazilian .... ASSAI
Christmas .... NOG
claret, soda and sugar
　　.......................... BADMINTON
cocktail .... MARTINI,
　　HIGHBALL, OLD-FASHIONED
cold .... JULEP, COBBLER
colloquial .... BOOZE,
　　　　　　　　MOONSHINE
creme de menthe and cream
　　.......................... GRASSHOPPER

crushed fruit .... SMASH
daintily .... SIP
deep .... SWILL
drug a .... HOCUS
East Indies .... NIPA, SOMA,
                       TODDY
effervescent .... FIZ(Z)
excessively .... TOPE, BOUSE
farewell .... STIRRUP CUP
fermented .... ALE, BEER, RUM,
           MEAD, SAKE, PERRY
for invalids .... CAUDLE
from apples/other fruits
                          CIDER
from fermented grain, with
         hops .... BEER
from fermented molasses
                         RUM
from fermented rice ..... SAKE
from grapes .... WINE,
     BRANDY, COGNAC, MALMSEY,
                  CHAMPAGNE
from root extracts ..... GINGER
                          ALE
fruit juice .... ADE
gin .... RICKEY
gin and lime juice ..... GIMLET
granting immortality
                         AMRITA
greedily .... GULP, SWILL,
                        GUZZLE
Greek wine .... RETSINA
habitually .... TOPE, TIPPLE
heartily/heavily .... CAROUSE
honey .... MEAD, MORAT
hot .... GROG, TODDY
hot milk .... SALOOP
iced .... SLING, COBBLER
in great gulps .... SWIG
in honor of/to one's health
                         TOAST
in large quantities ...... QUAFF,
                         SWILL
insipid/weak .... WISH-WASH
Japanese alcoholic/wine
                         SAKE
Mexican .... TEQUILA,
                  MARGARITA
mint, etc. .... JULEP, SMASH
mixed .... NOG, MAI-TAI,
     COCKTAIL, HIGHBALL, PINK
       LADY, TOM COLLINS
non-alcoholic .... MINERAL
of beverage with shaved ice
                         FRAPPE
of forgetfulness ..... NEPENTHE
of poison/medicine .... POTION
of rum .... GROG, BUMBO, TOM
                  AND JERRY
of sarsaparilla syrup .... MEAD

of spiced, sugared gruel
                         CAUDLE
of the gods .... NECTAR
old-time, fermented ..... MEAD
palm .... NIPA, TUBA
regal .... LAGER
rum and lime juice
                        DAIQUIRI
Russian .... VODKA
sassafras .... SALOOP
short .... DRAM
single .... SHOT, SLUG
slang .... SEA, LUSH, HOOCH,
                 OCEAN, SAUCE
slowly .... SIP, NURSE
sly .... NIP
small .... SIP, DRAM, TIFF,
       (S)NIP, SNORT, SNIFTER
soft .... ADE, POP, COLA
spiced .... FLIP, PUNCH, BISHOP
spiced ale .... WASSAIL
stimulant .... BRACER
stirring stick .... MUDDLER
sweet sap .... TODDY
sweetened .... FLIP, NEGUS,
     PUNCH, BISHOP, ORGEAT,
                  POSSET
syrupy, alcoholic .... CORDIAL,
                  LIQUEUR
teenage .... SODA, MALTED
to .... TOAST, SALUTE
to excess .... TOPE, SWILL,
     CAROUSE, INEBRIATE
together .... HOBNOB
vodka and orange juice
                     SCREWDRIVER
vodka and tomato juice
                    BLOODY MARY
water with syrup .... JULEP
whisky-soda .... HIGHBALL
whisky-vermouth
                     MANHATTAN
wine and honey ..... OENOMEL
wine, water and lemon juice
                     NEGUS
wine, water and spices
                     SANGAREE
drinkable .... POTABLE
drinker ...... SOT, TOPER, BIBBER,
    SOAKER, GUZZLER, CAROUSER,
    IMBIBER, REVELER, TIPPLER,
                  TOSSPOT
colloquial .... BARFLY, BOOZER
insatiable alcoholic
                     DIPSOMANIAC
slang .... LUSH, WINO, SOUSE
drinking .... TIFFIN, IMBIBING,
     LIBATION, POTATION
bout ...... BAT, SPREE, BENDER,
    WASSAIL, COMPOTATION
bowl .... JORUM, MAZER,

                     MAZARD
convivial .... BOWL, WASSAIL
cup .... MUG, TASS, TOBY,
    STEIN, BEAKER, NOGGIN,
    RUMMER, SCYPHUS, TANKARD,
                  PANNIKIN
excessive .... WASSAIL,
    POTATION, CRAPULENT,
                CRAPULOUS
fountain .... BUBBLER,
                SCUTTLEBUTT
glass .... GOBLET, RUMMER,
    TUMBLER, SCHOONER
mug, leather ..... (BLACK)JACK
party .... ORGY, WASSAIL,
                CAROUSAL
premises .... BAR, INN,
    LOUNGE, SALOON, TAVERN,
    TAPROOM, PUB, ALEHOUSE
salutation ..... TOAST, WASSAIL
spirits/liquor habitually
                   ALCOHOLISM
spree .... BINGE, BOOZE,
    BOUSE, BENDER, WASSAIL,
                CAROUSAL
toast .... SALUD, SKOAL,
    CHEERS, PROSIT, MABUHAY
drip .... DROP, LEAK, SEEP,
                  TRICKLE
coffee .... PERCOLATE
edge .... EAVE
slang .... BORE, PEST, CREEP
dripping .... ASOP, SODDEN,
           SOPPY, TRICKLING
wet .... DRENCHED
drive .... GOAD, PROD, PUSH, RIDE,
    RUSH, URGE, FEEZE, FORCE,
    IMPEL, AVENUE, CHARGE,
    ENERGY, HAMMER, CONDUCT,
    CAMPAIGN, PRESSURE
a vehicle/ship .... STEER
away .... SHOO, BANISH
back .... REPEL, REBUFF,
                REPULSE
colloquial .... HUSTLE
from cover .... FLUSH
head first .... RAM, BUTT
in offering .... FOOD,
            DRINK(S), MOVIE
in waiter .... CARHOP
into .... RAM, CRAM, POUND
into, through .... PENETRATE
nail obliquely .... TOE
off quickly: sl. .... PEEL OUT
onward/forward .... PROPEL
out .... ROUT, ROUST
out by incantation
                   EXORCISE
politician's ...... FUND-RAISING
reformer's .... CRUSADE
together by force ...... COERCE,

COMPEL
tree-lined .... AVENUE
with blows .... SLOG
with sudden force ..... THRUST
drivel .... DROOL, SLUSH, BABBLE,
SALIVA, SLAVER, MAUNDER,
SLOBBER, TWADDLE,
NONSENSE
driven obliquely .... TOED
driver .... MOTORIST, MOTORMAN,
CHAUFFEUR, STEERSMAN
aircraft .... PILOT, AVIATOR
animal ...... MAHOUT, SKINNER,
MULETEER
backseat, usual .... WIFE(Y)
camel .... SARWAN
carriage .... HACK, WHIP,
COACHMAN
coach .... JEHU, JARVEY
elephant .... MAHOUT
forklift/heavy machinery
.... OPERATOR
gear of .... CRASH HELMET
inept .... FENDER-BENDER
kind of .... PILE, TAMP,
HAMMER, MALLET, GOLF CLUB
mule .... MULETEER
of trucks for hauling loads
.... TEAMSTER
of wagons .... WAGONER,
CHARIOTEER
reckless .... JEHU, MANIAC,
SPEEDER, SCORCHER
seat of .... BOX, HELM
slave ..... MARTINET, STICKLER,
TASKMASTER
taxi .... CABBY, CABMAN
driving .... PUSHY, RIDING,
DYNAMIC, MOTORING,
COMPELLING
a .... DRIFT
ambition .... WILL, GET-UP,
RESOLVE
desire .... LUST, PASSION,
OBSESSION
jealousy .... ENVY
enthusiasm ...... ZEAL, ARDOR,
FERVOR, DEVOTION
force, human .... LIBIDO
line .... REIN
drizzle .... MIST, RAIN, SPRAY,
MIZZLE, SPRINKLE
drogher .... SAILBOAT
droghiere .... GROCER
droit .... (LEGAL)RIGHT
droll .... ODD, WAG, COMIC,
JESTER, AMUSING, BUFFOON,
COMICAL, HUMOROUS
finish .... ERY
drome, as suffix .... RUNNING,
RACECOURSE

dromedary .... CAMEL, DELUL,
MEHARI
dromon(d) .... SHIP
drone .... HUM, BUZZ, IDLER,
LOAF(ER), BAGPIPE, AIRPLANE,
(HONEY)BEE, MONOTONE
drool. See drivel
droop ...... LOP, SAG, BEND, FLAG,
LOLL, PEAK, SINK, WILT,
NUTATE, SLOUCH, WEAKEN,
DECLINE, LANGUISH
drooping .... LOPPY, NUTANT,
HANGING, SLOUCH, LANGUID
on one side .... ALOP
droopy ...... WEAK, TIRED, WEARY
drop .... FALL, GOUT, OMIT,
FLUNK, GUTTA, LOWER,
GLOBULE, DECREASE
bait .... DIB
below surface .... SINK
by/in .... VISIT
drastically, as in value
.... COLLAPSE
fish line .... DAP
gently .... DAP, DIP
heavily .... PLOP, FLUMP,
PLUMP
in the bucket .... BIT, DOLE,
MITE, PITTANCE
in trickles .... DRIP
it .... END, STOP, CEASE
of sweat .... BEAD
one .... MINIM
out .... SECEDE, ABANDON
ready to .... FAINT
sharp .... NOSE DIVE
straight down .... PLUNGE,
PLUMMET
sudden .... DIVE, CRASH,
SLUMP
the subject .... DISMISS,
FORGET(IT)
viscous substance .... BLOB
droplike ornaments .... GUTTA
dropout, for one .... QUITTER
dropper .... PIPET(TE)
droppings .... DUNG, GUANO,
MANURE
dropsical .... EDEMIC
dropsy .... (O)EDEMA, ANASARCA,
BERIBERI
drosophila .... (FRUIT)FLY
dross .... SCUM, SLAG, WASTE,
REFUSE, SCORIA, RUBBISH
drought .... ARIDITY, DRYNESS
plant .... GUAR, CACTUS,
XEROPHYTE
droughty .... DRY, ARID
drove .... HERD, CROWD, FLOCK,
HORDE
composition of .... HOGS,

SHEEP, CATTLE
drover .... CATTLE DEALER
drown .... FLOOD, DEADEN,
MUFFLE, INUNDATE,
SUBMERGE, OVERPOWER
drowning, execution by
.... NOYADE
drowse .... NAP, NOD, DOZE, SLEEP
drowsiness .... LETHARGY,
OSCITANCY
drowsy .... SLEEPY, LETHARGIC,
HEAVY-LIDDED
from using drug .... KEF
drub .... HIT, BEAT, LICK, WHIP,
KNOCK, THUMP, CUDGEL,
THRASH
drubbing .... DEFEAT, BEATING
drudge .... GRUB, MOIL, PLOD,
CHORE, GRIND, SCRUB, SLAVE,
TOIL(ER), HOUSEKEEPER
literary .... HACK
drudgery .... FAG, RUT, MOIL,
CHORE, GRIND, SWEAT,
TASKWORK
drug .... HOCUS, SALVE, OPIATE,
STUPEFY, MEDICATE,
MEDICINE, KNOCK OUT,
MORPHINE, NARCOTIC
addict .... USER, ABUSER,
JUNKIE, HOPHEAD, POTHEAD,
SNOWBIRD
addiction .... HABIT,
DEPENDENCE
anabolic/with protein-
building effect
.... STEROID
antacid .... SELTZER
bitter .... QUASSIA
causing vomit .... EMETIC
cocain(e): sl. ...... COKE, SNOW
compressed form ..... TABLOID
excessive taking of
.... OVERDOSE
eye .... MYOTIC, NEOMYCIN,
MYDRIATIC
for addicts .... METHADON(E)
for all ailments .... ELIXIR,
PANACEA
for allergy ..... ANTIHISTAMINE
for blood pressure
.... ADRENALIN
for clearing nasal passages
.... DECONGESTANT
for cough .... EXPECTORANT
for drying .... DESICCANT
for epileptic attacks
.... DILANTIN
for forgetfulness .... NEPENTHE
for pain relief .... MORPHINE
for perspiration .... BONESET
grinder .... MULLER

heroin: sl. .... JUNK, SMACK
intoxicating .... PEYOTE
laxative .... ALOE, CALOMEL,
    MAGNESIA, CASTOR OIL
LSD: sl. .... ACID
marijuana: sl. .... POT
narcotics .... OPIUM, HEROIN,
    COCAINE
orchid-based .... SALEP
plant .... ALOE, POPPY
slang .... DOPE
soothing/calming
    .... SEDATIVE, TRANQUILIZER
"speed" .... LSD,
    METHEDRINE, AMPHETAMINE
stimulant .... CAFFEINE
drugged .... HIGH, DOPED, DOPEY,
    SPACED OUT, STONED,
    SEDATED
drugget .... MAT, RUG
druggist .... CHEMIST,
    PHARMACIST
container of .... GALLIPOT
drugs, action of .... SYNERGY
drugstore .... PHARMACY,
    APOTHECARY
soap .... SAPO
drum ..... TUM, BARREL, TYMPAN,
    TAMBOUR, CYLINDER
ancient type of .... TIMBREL
beat .... DUB, RATAPLAN,
    RUB-A-DUB-DUB
beat a .... PERCUSS
call .... DIAN, TATTOO
capstan's .... RUNDLE
continuously .... TATTOO
elongated bass .... CONGA
hand .... TABOR, TIMBREL,
    TAMBOURINE
head .... TYMPANUM
jungle/Oriental .... TOMTOM
kettle .... ATABAL
like a/of a .... TYMPANIC
long .... TAMBOURIN
low continuous beating of
    .... RUFFLE
major .... BANDMASTER
major's rod .... BATON
Moorish .... ATABAL
played with hands ..... CONGA,
    BONGO
played with stick
    .... TABORIN(E)
player .... TYMPANIST
primitive ...... TAM-TAM, TOM-
    TOM
signal .... TAPS, TATTOO,
    CHAMADE
small .... TABOR, TABOUR,
    TABRET, TABORET, TABORIN(E)
sound ...... BEAT, ROLL, POUND

string across .... SNARE
with fingers .... THRUM
drumbeat .... DUB, FLAM,
    TATTOO, RATAPLAN,
    RATTATTOO, RAT-TAT-TAT,
    RUB-A-DUB-DUB
continuous .... ROLL, RUFFLE
drumfire .... BARRAGE
drumfish .... WHITING
relative of .... CROAKER
drumlin .... HILL, RIDGE
drummer .... TABORER,
    PERCUSSIONIST
famed .... (GENE)KRUPA
kind of .... SALESMAN
drumming .... BEATING,
    POUNDING, THROBBING,
    THUMPING, THRUMMING
continuous .... TATTOO
drumstick .... TYMP STICK
drunk(ard) ...... SOT, HIGH, SOAK,
    BLIND, BLOAT, BOUSY,
    BOOZY, FRIED, MALTY,
    NAPPY, RUMMY, SOUSE,
    TIGHT, TIPSY, TOPER, BARFLY,
    BLOTTO, GROGGY, LOADED,
    POTTED, STEWED, ROUNDER,
    TIPPLER, TOSSPOT, BIBULOUS,
    COCKEYED, WALLEYED,
    INEBRIATE(D), PLASTERED,
    DIPSOMANIAC, INTOXICATED
drunken .... DIZZY, GIDDY,
    SOUSED, STEWED, BACCHIC,
    SMASHED, INEBRIOUS,
    INTOXICATED
carousal .... BOUT, SPREE,
    REVELRY
carouser .... BACCHANT(E)
celebration .... JAG
party .... WASSAIL,
    BACCHANAL(IA)
spree .... SOAK, BINGE,
    BENDER
drunkenness ...... INTEMPERANCE,
    INTOXICATION
aftereffect of .... HANGOVER
drupe .... PLUM, CHERRY, APRICOT
drupelet .... TRYMA, ACINUS,
    NUTLET
drupelets, fruit of many
    .... GRAPE, RASPBERRY,
    (BLACK)BERRY, LOGANBERRY
druthers .... PERSONAL CHOICE
dry ...... ARID, SEAR, SERE, DRAIN,
    PARCHED, THIRSTY,
    WITHERED, ANHYDROUS,
    DEHYDRATE, (DE)SICCATE
as wine .... SEC, BRUT
cleaning solvent ...... BENZINE,
    NAPHTHA, GASOLINE
colloquial ...... PROHIBITIONIST

combining form .... XERO
fly .... LURE
goods dealer .... DRAPER
grass .... HAY
lake basin .... PLAYA
moderately .... SUBARID
oneself .... TOWEL
opposed to .... WET
run .... TEST, REHEARSAL
spell .... DROUGHT
story, describing .... JEJUNE
style of speaking .... DULL,
    BORING, MATTER-OF-FACT
sucked .... DRAINED, SAPLESS
throat .... HUSKY, HOARSE
to .... SUN, BLOT
tongue, sign of .... THIRST
up ..... PARCH, WIZEN, SHRINK,
    WITHER
with cloth/mop .... SWAB,
    WIPE
with heat .... SUN, BAKE,
    SCORCH, SHRIVEL, TORREFY,
    TORRIFY
dryad .... NYMPH
dryer. See drier
drying away of body tissue
    .... ATROPHY
cloth .... TOWEL
machine .... TEDDER
spread for .... TED
substance that promotes
    .... SICCATIVE
to get a concentrated product
    .... EVAPORATION
dryness .... ARIDITY, ARIDNESS
from lack of rain
    .... DROU(G)HT
from need of water .... THIRST
of mouth .... XEROSTOMIA
of skin/eyeball .... XEROSIS
DST, part of .... TIME, SAVING,
    DAYLIGHT
Du Barry's title .... MADAME,
    COMTESSE
duad .... TWO, DUAL, PAIR,
    COUPLE
dual ...... TWIN, BINARY, DUPLEX,
    DOUBLE, TWOFOLD
campaign promise .... LAW
    AND ORDER
channel audio .... STEREO
dualism, element of .... EVIL,
    GOOD, MIND, MATTER,
    PHYSICAL, SPIRITUAL
dub .... HIT, CALL, POKE, TERM,
    DUFFER, KNIGHT, THRUST,
    DRUMBEAT, (NICK)NAME
dubiety .... UNCERTAINTY
dubious .... LEERY, SHADY,
    SHAKY, VAGUE, UNSURE,

DOUBTFUL, SKEPTICAL, QUESTIONABLE
dubitation .... DOUBT
Dublin is capital of .... IRELAND
ducal .... DUKEDOM
ducat: sl. ...... (ADMISSION)TICKET
duce .... CHIEF, LEADER
   Italian .... MUSSOLINI
Duchess of Windsor
   .... (WALLIS)WARFIELD
   title of respect .... GRACE
duchy .... REGION, DUKEDOM
duck .... BIRD, DIVE, TERN, AVOID,
   CLOTH, DODGE, DOUSE,
   BUFFLEHEAD
   aquatic stifftail .... OXYURA
   Asiatic .... MANDARIN
   colloquial .... DARLING
   color on wing .... SPECULUM
   cry of .... QUACK
   dabbling .... ANAS
   decoyer .... TOLLER
   diving .... SMEW, SCAUP,
   POCHARD, REDHEAD,
   MERGANSER
   downy .... EIDER
   fabric .... LINEN, COTTON
   family .... ANATIDAE
   fish-eating .... GOOSANDER,
   MERGANSER
   foot membrane .... WEB
   genus .... ANAS, ANSER
   handsome .... WOOD
   Hawaiian .... NENE
   hawk .... FALCON, HARRIER
   hooded .... MERGUS,
   MERGANSER
   hunter's screen .... BLIND
   large .... MUSCOVY
   like .... COOT
   long-tailed .... OLDSQUAW
   lure .... DECOY
   male .... DRAKE
   merganser .... SMEW
   non-quacking .... MUSCOVY
   out .... FLEE, SPLIT
   perching .... CAIRINA
   pintail .... SMEE
   river .... TEAL, WIDGEON
   sea/marine .... COOT, EIDER,
   SCAUP, SCO(O)TER,
   MERGANSER
   shooting boat .... SKAG
   slang .... JOKER, QUEER,
   PERSON
   small .... SMEW
   torrent .... MERGANETTA-
   ARMATA
   tufted .... AYTHYA-FULIGULA
   use of man-made .... DECOY
   walk .... WADDLE

   whistling .... DENDROCYGNA
   white-faced tree
   .... DENDROCYGNA-VIDUATA
   wild ..... TEAL, DRAKE, SCAUP,
   GADWALL, MALLARD,
   WIDGEON, GOLDEN-EYE,
   SHELDRAKE, CANVASBACK
   young .... DUCKLING
duckbill .... PLATYPUS,
   MONOTREME
ducker .... GREBE, DABCHICK
duckpins .... BOWLING
ducks, brood of .... TEAM
   collectively .... WATERFOWL
duct .... VAS, FLUE, PIPE, TUBE,
   CANAL, CHANNEL, CONDUIT
   body .... MEATUS
   narrowing of .... STENOSIS
ductile .... PLIANT, ELASTIC,
   PLASTIC, PLIABLE, TENSILE,
   TRACTILE
ductless gland, of a .... ADRENAL,
   THYROID, ENDOCRINE,
   PITUITARY
   glandlike body .... THYMUS
ducts, of or having
   .... VASCULAR
dud .... FLOP, LEMON, FAILURE
duddy: Scot. .... RAGGED
dude ...... FOP, DANDY, COXCOMB
   one kind of .... TOURIST
   place of .... RANCH
   ranch's use .... RESORT
dudeen .... (TOBACCO)PIPE
Dudevant, Baronne
   .... (GEORGE)SAND
dudgeon ...... FRET, HILT, ANGER,
   PIQUE, RESENTMENT
   high .... PET
duds .... TOGS, APPAREL,
   CLOTHES, CLOTHING,
   RAIMENT, TRAPPINGS
due .... DEBT, OWED, OWING,
   RIGHT, PROPER, FITTING,
   APROPOS, PAYABLE
   one's .... DES(S)ERTS
   process .... JUSTICE
   to .... BECAUSE
duel .... FIGHT, COMBAT, CONTEST,
   RIVALRY
   challenge .... CARTEL
   mock .... TILT, JOUST
   principal of famous ..... BURR,
   HAMILTON
   victim of .... HAMILTON
dueling code/art .... DUELLO
   position .... EN GARDE
duelist .... RIVAL, KNIGHT,
   TUSSLER
duenna .... CHAPERON,
   GOVERNESS

Duero .... DOURO
dues .... FEE, TAX, CHARGE,
   ASSESSMENT
   kind of .... TOLL, UNION,
   MEMBERSHIP
duet .... DUO, PAIR, TWO(SOME)
duff .... SLACK, PUDDING
   slang .... BUTTOCKS
duffel ...... BAG, KIT, COAT, GEAR,
   OUTFIT, CLOTHING,
   EQUIPMENT
duffer .... DUB, FUMBLER,
   LUMMOX, PEDDLER
dug .... TEAT, NIPPLE
dugong .... SEACOW, COWFISH,
   MANATEE, HALICORE
   food of .... SEAWEED
dugout .... BOAT, BANCA, CANOE,
   FOXHOLE, PIRAGUA, PIROGUE,
   (BOMB)SHELTER
   French/hillside .... ABRI
   India .... DONGA
duke, of a .... DUCAL
   rank below .... MARQUIS,
   MARQUESS
   title of respect .... GRACE
   wife of .... DUCHESS
dukedom .... DUCHY
dukes: sl. .... FISTS, HANDS
dulcet .... SWEET, ARIOSE, ARIOSO,
   HONEYED, SUGARED,
   MELODIOUS, ORGAN STOP
dulcify .... APPEASE, MOLLIFY,
   SWEETEN
dulcimer .... HARP, SITAR, CITOLE,
   PSALTERY
Dulcinea .... SWEETHEART
dull .... FLAT, LOGY, FISHY,
   GROSS, HOHUM, PROSY,
   VAPID, BORING, STODGY,
   HUMDRUM, INSIPID, TEDIOUS,
   WITLESS, LISTLESS, BLAH,
   STAGNANT, LACKLUSTER
   and empty-headed ...... JEJUNE
   and slow-moving
   .... SLUGGISH, LETHARGIC
   become .... HEBETATE
   color .... DUN, DRAB, MATTE,
   TERNE
   edge/point .... BLUNT
   finish .... MAT(TE)
   grayish brown .... DUN
   grossly .... CRASS, STUPID
   make .... NUMB, BLUNT,
   DEADEN, OBTUND
   mentally .... OBTUSE, STUPID,
   VACUOUS
   period .... LULL, SLACK,
   SLUMP
   person, describing one
   .... BORE, DUNCE, DULLARD

sound .... THUD
without luster .... DIM,
    CLOUDY, OBSCURE
dullard .... OAF, DOLT, LOUT,
    BOOR, DUNCE, MORON,
    NUMSKULL, SIMPLETON
dulled .... JADED
dulse .... SEAWEED
duly .... AS DUE, JUSTLY,
    PROPERLY, FITTINGLY
Dumas character .... ATHOS,
    ARAMIS, PORTHOS, BONIFACE,
    D'ARTAGNAN
novel .... CAMILLE
dumb .... MUTE, SILENT, RETICENT
clucks .... OXEN
clucks, per J. Luzzatto
    .... OXES
colloquial .... NAIVE, STUPID,
    IGNORANT
one .... ASS
show .... APING, MIMING
show figure .... PUPPET,
    PANTOMIME, MARIONETTE
waiter .... ELEVATOR
dumb _____, old comic strip
    .... DORA
dumbbell .... IDIOT, MORON,
    NITWIT
exerciser .... WEIGHT, BARBELL
dum(b)found ...... DAZE, AMAZE,
    ASTOUND, STARTLE, ASTONISH
dumbness ...... MUTISM, APHONIA
dumdum .... BULLET
dummy .... DUPE, MUTE, TOOL,
    STRAWMAN, MANNEQUIN
cannon .... QUAKER
colloquial .... FRONT
field .... SCARECROW
in railroading .... LOCOMOTIVE
kind of ...... PROXY, STAND-IN,
    FIGUREHEAD
ventriloquist's .... SNERD
dump .... DROP, HEAP, JUNK,
    LUMP, PILE, EMPTY OUT,
    CHUCK, UNLOAD, DISCARD,
    DISCHARGE
archaic .... SONG, TUNE
slang .... DITCH
dumpling .... PIE, DOUGH
boiled .... DOUGHBOY
dumps, the .... BLUES, GLOOM,
    DOLDRUMS
dumpy .... PUDGY, SQUAT,
    MELANCHOLY
dun ...... ASK, BILL, BROWN, MAY
    FLY, ARTIFICIAL FLY, DEMAND
    PAYMENT
Duna in German .... DVINA
in Hungarian .... DANUBE
in Russian .... DON

Duncan, dancer .... ISADORA
dunce .... OAF, COOT, DOLT,
    MORON, NANNY, NUMSKULL,
    SIMPLETON
dunderhead .... DOLT, DUNCE,
    FOOL, IDIOT, DULLARD,
    NUMSKULL
dune .... DENE, HILL, RIDGE
dung .... FILTH, MANURE, ORDURE,
    DROPPING(S), EXCREMENT
beetle .... DOR, CHAFER,
    SCARAB
piece .... CHIP
dungarees .... JEANS, LEVIS,
    OVERALLS
dungeon .... PIT, CELL, JAIL,
    TOWER, DONJON, PRISON,
    OUBLIETTE
dungy .... FILTHY
dunk .... DIP, SOUSE
dunker .... SOPPER
dunlin .... SANDPIPER
dunnage .... BAGGAGE
Dunne, actress .... IRENE
dunnite .... EXPLOSIVE
duo .... DUET, PAIR
as combining form .... TWO,
    DOUBLE
plus one .... TRIO
duomo .... CATHEDRAL
dupe .... FOOL, GULL, CON(E)Y,
    CHEAT, HOCUS, TRICK,
    VICTIM, HUMBUG, MUGGINS,
    GREENHORN
kind of .... TOOL, DUMMY,
    CATSPAW
rare .... CULLY
duple .... DOUBLE, TWOFOLD
duplex .... HOUSE, DOUBLE,
    APARTMENT
duplicate .... COPY, DOUBLE,
    REPLICA, FACSIMILE
copy .... ESTREAT
duplicating machine ..... RONEO,
    (XEROX)COPIER,
    MIMEOGRAPH, MULTIGRAPH
duplication .... COPY, REPLICA,
    COUNTERPART, REPRODUCTION
duplicity ...... FRAUD, DECEPTION,
    FALSENESS, DOUBLE-DEALING
durable .... HARDY, STABLE,
    ETERNAL, LASTING,
    PERENNIAL
stage performer .... MAE
    WEST, MARLENE DIETRICH
durability .... AGE, LONGEVITY
duramen .... HEARTWOOD
durance .... IMPRISONMENT
Durante's Goodnight _____
    .... MRS. CALABASH
duration ...... TERM, TIME, PERIOD

durbar: India .... HALL,
    AUDIENCE, RECEPTION
dure .... LAST, ENDURE
duress .... COERCION,
    COMPULSION, CONSTRAINT,
    IMPRISONMENT
during .... UNTIL, PENDING,
    THROUGH
durmast .... OAK
duro: Sp. .... PESO, DOLLAR
Duroc-Jersey .... HOG
Durocher, baseball manager
    .... LEO, THE LIP
durra .... MILLET, SORGHUM
durum .... FLOUR, WHEAT
Duse, actress .... CHECCHI,
    ELEONORA
burial place .... ASOLO
dusk .... GLOOM, SUNSET,
    EVENFALL, GLOAMING,
    TWILIGHT, CREPUSCLE,
    NIGHTFALL
dusky .... DARK, TAWNY,
    DARKISH, SWART(HY)
dust .... ASH, DIRT, SOIL, SOOT,
    STOUR, EARTH, POLLEN,
    POWDER, SPRINKLE
bite the .... FALL, LOSE
British .... ASHES, RUBBISH
crumble to .... DISINTEGRATE
filter .... INHALER
lick the .... GROVEL, SUCCUMB
of flower .... POLLEN
slang .... MONEY
windblown .... STOUR
dustbin .... ASHCAN
dustbowl .... WASTELAND
duster .... RAG, COAT, WIND,
    WIPER, BROOM, BRUSH
dustheap .... DUMP, JUNKYARD
dusting powder .... TALC
dusty .... DIRTY, SANDY, SOOTY
Dutch. See also Netherlands
admiral .... RUYTER
Antilles .... ARUBA
apple, fried .... ROLPENS
astronomer .... HUYGENS
beef .... HUTSPOT
bloomer .... TULIP
botanist .... VRIES
cheese .... EDAM, GOUDA
city .... EDE
coin .... DOIT, DALER, GULDEN,
    STIVER
colonist .... BOER
colonizer .... PATROON
commune .... EDE, DOORN
cupboard .... KAS
dialect in Africa .... TAAL,
    AFRIKAANS
donkey .... EZEL

East Indies island .... JAVA, TIMOR
engraver .... LEYDEN
farm .... BOWERY
fishing boat .... HOOKER
Guiana .... SURINAM
gypsy .... BAZIGAR
Hottentot breed .... GRIQUA
housewife .... VROU(W)
humanist .... ERASMUS
measure .... AAM, KOP, ZAK, ANKER
measure, distance .... DUIM, VOET
metal .... TOMBAC
mistress in South Africa .... NOI
Mrs. .... VROUW
name for the Meuse .... MAAS
native .... BREDAN
navigator .... TASMAN
New Guinea negrito .... TAPIRO
news agency .... ANETA
painter ..... CUYP, GOGH, HALS, LELY, MEER, BORCH, STEEN, LEYDEN, REMBRANDT
philosopher .... SPINOZA
physicist .... HUYGENS, LORENTZ
river .... MAAS
scholar of the Renaissance, noted .... ERASMUS
settler's farm .... BOWERY
ship .... GALLOT, GAL(L)IOT
slang .... GERMAN
South African .... BOER
South African statesman .... KRUGER
statesman .... GROTIUS
theologian .... JANSEN, ERASMUS
title of address .... HEER, MYNHEER
town .... EDE, STAD
uncle .... OOM
vessel, flatbottomed .... FLYBOAT
village .... DOORN
weight .... ONS, LOOD
West Indies .... ANTILLES
woman .... FROU(W), VROUW
Dutchman .... MYNHEER, HOLLANDER
slang .... GERMAN
dutiful .... LOYAL, DOCILE, DUTEOUS, OBEDIENT, COMPLIANT
one .... OBEYER
duty .... JOB, TAX, DEBT, TASK, TOLL, CHORE, EXCISE

accountable .... RESPONSIBILITY
burdensome .... ONUS
imposed legally .... OBLIGATION
in the course of work .... FUNCTION
of tenant to his feudal lord .... FEALTY
on imports ..... IMPOST, TARIFF
to one's country .... ALLEGIANCE
turn of .... TRICK
duumvir .... MAGISTRATE
Dvina river ...... DUNA, DAUGAVA
Dvorak, composer .... ANTON
symphony .... NEW WORLD
dwarf ...... NANO, ATOMY, STUNT, BANTAM, MIDGET, MANAKIN, MANIKIN, OUTSHINE, HOMUNCULUS
African/Asiatic .... PIGMY, PYGMY
animal .... RUNT
antelope .... ORIBI
cattle .... DEVON, NIATA
chestnut .... CHINQUAPIN
describing a .... SHORT STATURE
kind of ...... ELF, GRIG, FREAK, GNOME, PEE WEE
like .... GNOMISH
Norse mythology .... ANDVARI
Philippine ...... AETA, NEGRITO
plant .... ALYSSUM
Scandinavian folklore .... TROLL
Scottish .... BLASTIE
shrub/tree .... BONSAI
slang .... SHRIMP
storybook .... DOC, DOPEY, HAPPY, SLEEPY, BASHFUL, TOM THUMB, THUMBELINA, LILLIPUTIAN
underground/misshapen .... GNOME
dwarfed .... STUMPY, STUNTED, DEFORMED
dwarfish deer .... CHEVROTAIN
dog .... CHIHUAHUA
horse .... PONY
dwarfism .... NANSOMA
dwarfs, any race of .... NIBELUNG
fairy tale .... DOC, DOPEY, HAPPY, GRUMPY, SLEEPY, SNEEZY, BASHFUL
king of .... ALBERICH
dwell .... LIVE, (A)BIDE, LODGE, RESIDE
on .... HARP, REPEAT
slang .... HANG OUT

dweller .... LODGER, RENTER, ROOMER, TENANT, RESIDENT, INHABITANT
on public land .... SQUATTER
prison .... INMATE
dwelling .... HOME, ABODE, HOUSE, RESIDENCE, HABITATION
bear's .... DEN, CAVE
bird's .... CAGE, NEST
fit for .... TENANTABLE
fixed place of .... DOMICILE
high .... AERIE, EYRIE
house .... TENEMENT
imposing .... MANSION
instant .... PREFAB
lion's .... DEN, LAIR
miserable .... HOVEL
mobile/on wheels ..... TRAILER
mollusk's .... SHELL
on artificial island .... CRANNOG
place, kind of .... FLAT, CONDO, APARTMENT
place to which mail is sent .... ADDRESS
royal .... PALACE
slum .... TENEMENT
unsafe .... DEATHTRAP
dwindle .... EBB, ABATE, PETER, LESSEN, SHRINK, DECREASE, DIMINISH
DX, in radio .... DISTANT, DISTANCE
dyad .... PAIR
Dyak blowgun .... SUMPITAN
knife .... PARANG
dye .... DIP, HUE, TINT, WELD, COLOR, FUCUS, STAIN, TAINT, TINGE, BRASIL, CASHOO
aniline .... FUCHSIN, MAGENTA, SAFRANINE
apparatus .... AGER
azo .... CROCEIN(E)
base .... ANILINE, FLAVONE
blue .... WOAD, PASTEL
butter coloring .... ANNATTO
class of .... AZO, VAT, XANTHENE
coal tar .... EOSIN, MAUVE
from whelks .... MUREX
gum .... KINO
hair .... HENNA
Hindu .... ALTA
indigo .... ANIL, ISATIN
ingredient .... TANNIN, ALAZARIN(E)
insect body's .... KERMES
lichen .... ARCHIL
mustard plant .... WOAD

orange .... MANDARIN
plant .... CHAY, AMIL, ANIL,
ANCHUSA, ALKANET, BUGLOSS,
PUCCOON, SUMAC(H),
BLOODROOT
purple .... MUREX, ARCHIL,
ORCHAL, ORCHIL, TURNSOLE
red .... AURIN, CERISE,
EOSIN(E), KERMES, MADDER,
ALKANET, ANCHUSA, FUCHSIN,
COCHINEAL, RHODAMINE,
SOLFERINO
reddish-brown ..... HEMAT(E)IN
source .... LICHEN, CUDBEAR,
NAPTHALENE
substance .... TANNIN
synthetic .... PHTHALEIN,
RHODAMINE
yellow .... FUSTIC
dyed in the wool .... TOTAL,
INGRAINED, STEADFAST,
CONSUMMATE
dyeing astringent .... GAMBIER

color fixer .... MORDANT
liquid/solution container
.... VAT
method .... BAT(T)IK
substance .... TANNIN,
MORDANT, NAPTHOL
dyer .... COLORER, STAINER,
COLORIST
dyestuff .... ANIL, WOAD, CASHOO,
INDIGO, CATECHU, MAGENTA
dyeweed .... WOODWAXEN
dying .... MORIBUND
on the vine .... WITHERING
star .... NOVA
dyke .... DAM, DIKE
dyna as combining form
.... POWER
dynamic ...... POTENT, FORCEFUL,
VIGOROUS, ENERGETIC
opposed to .... STATIC,
ORGANIC
dynamics .... FORCES, STATICS,
KINETICS

dynamite .... EXPLOSIVE
ingredient
.... NITROGLYCERIN(E)
inventor of .... NOBEL
kind of .... TNT
dynamo .... MAGNETO,
GENERATOR
combining form .... POWER
part .... BRUSH, STATOR,
WINDING, ARMATURE,
COMMUTATOR
dynast .... RULER
dynasty, Chinese .... MING, SUNG
dys as prefix .... BAD, ILL
dysfunctional .... IMPAIRED
dysgenic, opposed to
.... EUGENIC
dyspepsia .... INDIGESTION
medicine .... HYDRASTINE
dyspeptic ...... GLOOMY, GROUCHY
dysphoria .... ANXIETY,
DISCOMFORT, DISCONTENT
Dzhugashvili .... STALIN

E

E, Greek .... EPSILON
in a sequence .... FIFTH
in physics .... ENERGY
symbol for ..... EAST, EASTERN
each ...... AN, ALL, PER, ANY ONE,
APIECE, EVERY(ONE)
used in doctor's prescription
.... ANA
Eads (James) invention
.... DIVING BELL
eager .... AGOG, AVID, FAIN,
KEEN, AFIRE, ARDENT,
ANXIOUS, EARNEST, DESIROUS,
IMPATIENT
beaver ..... DYNAMO, HUSTLER,
GO-GETTER
to start .... CHAFING AT THE
BIT
eagerly awaiting/expecting
.... ATIP
eagerness .... ARDOR, DESIRE,
FERVOR, ALACRITY
eagle ...... BIRD, COIN, PREDATOR,
ACCIPITER
beaked .... AQUILINE
biblical .... GIER
brood .... AERIE
constellation .... AQUILA
double-crested .... HARPY
eyed .... SHARP, VIGILANT,
WATCHFUL
family .... FALCON

for one .... SCOUT
Latin .... AQUILA
like/of an .... AQUILINE
like bird .... CONDOR,
VULTURE
nest of .... AERY, AERIE, EYRIE
passenger of .... ETANA
sea .... ERN(E)
young .... EYRY, EYRIE,
EAGLET, AIGLETTE
eaglestone .... ETITE
eagre .... BORE, TIDAL WAVE
Eamon de Valera .... DEV
eanling .... KID, LAMB
ear .... LUG, HANDLE, HEARING,
ATTENTION
anvil .... INCUS
auricle .... PINNA, PAVILION
bone .... AMBOS, ANVIL,
INCUS, HAMMER, STAPES,
TEGMEN, OCCICLE, STIRRUP
canal .... SCALA
cartilage .... HELIX
cauliflower .... HEMATOMA
AURIS
cavity ..... COCHLEA, SACCULE,
UTRICLE
cosmetic surgery on outer
.... OTOPLASTY
degeneration .... DEAFNESS
discharge from infected
.... OTORRHEA

disturber .... DIN
doctor/specialist .... AURIST,
OTOLOGIST
examination .... TOMOGRAPHY,
CT SCANNING
external .... PINNA, CONCHA,
AURICLE
give/lend an .... HEED, LISTEN,
HEARKEN
gland below .... PAROTID
hammer .... MALLEUS
hollow .... CONCHA
in Latin .... AURIS
inflammation/infection
.... OTITIS
inner .... LABYRINTH
instrument .... OTOSCOPE
labyrinth .... SACCULE
like part .... LUG
lobe .... ALA, LUG, EARLAP,
LAPPET
middle .... TYMPANUM
near the ..... PAROTIC, PAROTID
noises within the .... TINNITUS
of corn .... MEALIE
of grain .... SPICA, SPIKE
opening .... FENESTRA
outer rim .... HELIX
pain .... OTALGIA
part ...... LOBE, ANVIL, CANAL,
PINNA, HAMMER,
AURICLE, COCHLEA,

STIRRUP, TYMPANUM,
VESTIBULE
pertaining to .... OTIC, AURAL,
AURIC
play it by .... AD-LIB,
IMPROVISE
prefix .... OTO
projection .... LUG, TRAGUS
science of the .... OTOLOGY
secretion .... WAX, CERUMEN
shaped .... AURIFORM
shaped mollusk .... ORMER,
ABALONE
shell .... ORMER, ABALONE,
MOLLUSK
stirrup-shaped bone
.... STAPES
turn a deaf ...... SNUB, IGNORE
wax .... CERUMEN
wheat .... SPICA
earache .... OTALGIA
eardrop .... EARRING
eardrum .... TYMPANUM
of the .... TYMPANIC
prominence .... UMBO
eared .... AURICULATE
seal .... OTARY
earful .... TIP, GOSSIP, TIRADE,
SCOLDING
slang .... INFO, NEWS, THE
LOWDOWN
Earhart, aviatrix .... AMELIA
husband of
.... (GEORGE)PUTNAM
earl .... NOBLEMAN
deputy of an .... VISCOUNT
wife of an .... COUNTESS
Earl Biggers's sleuth
.... (CHARLIE)CHAN
earlier .... PRIOR, FORMER,
PREVIOUS
earliest .... PREMIER
early ...... ANON, AHEAD, PROMPT,
BETIMES, FORWARD
bird .... FIRST COMER
bird's victim .... WORM
Christian date .... ADI
hour .... FIRST CRACK, HEAD
START
in the day/season ..... RATH(E)
Steele and Addison
periodical .... TATLER
too .... PREMATURE
earmark .... TAB, SIGN, SPOT,
DENOTE, BRAND, LABEL,
STAMP, RESERVE, SIGNIFY,
IDENTIFY
earn .... WIN, GAIN, RATE, MERIT,
DESERVE, WORK FOR
difficultly .... EKE
earnest ...... AVID, EAGER, TOKEN,

ARDENT, INTENT, PLEDGE,
FERVENT, INTENSE, SERIOUS,
SINCERE, ZEALOUS,
ASSURANCE
money .... ARLES, TOKEN,
ADVANCE, DEPOSIT, HANDSEL
request .... ENTREATY
earnings .... PAY, WAGES,
PROFITS, PAYMENT, INCOME,
SALARIES
earphone .... RECEIVER
earpiece .... FLAP
earring .... HOOP, PENDANT,
GIRANDOLE
holder .... LOBE
ears .... ANTENNA
all .... ATTENTIVE
having two .... BINAURAL
earsplitting .... LOUD, DEAFENING
earth .... DIRT, DUST, LAND,
LOAM, MOLD, SOIL, GLOBE,
TERRA, WORLD, GROUND,
PLANET, UNIVERSE
combining form .... GEO
crust .... LITHOSPHERE
deposit .... MARL, SILT
division .... ZONE
down to .... NORMAL,
REGULAR, PRACTICAL,
REALISTIC
eating of .... GEOPHAGY
goddess ..... GE, GAEA, TELLUS
greenish .... TERRE-VERTE
hypothetical figure ...... GEOID
inhabitant/of the
.... TELLURIAN
line .... EQUATOR
lump of .... CLOD
pertaining to the .... TERRENE,
GEOGRAPHICAL
pig .... AARDVARK
pigment .... UMBEL
poetic .... MARL, VALE
satellite .... ECHO, LUNA,
NOVA, ARIEL, CAMEO, MIDAS,
SOYUZ, TIROS, VENUS,
APOLLO, COSMOS, GEMINI,
SKYLAB, VOSTOK, COMSTAR,
MARINER, PIONEER, SPUTNIK,
COLUMBIA, EXPLORER,
SURVEYOR, VANGUARD,
CHALLENGER, FRIENDSHIP
shaking .... QUAKE, TREMOR
tamping implement
.... BEETLE
thickest layer of .... MANTLE
volcanic .... TRASS
white .... GYPSUM, KAOLIN,
MAGNESIA, TERRE ALBA
Eartha, singer .... KITT
earthborn .... LOW, HUMAN,

COMMON, MORTAL, VULGAR
earthbound .... MUNDANE,
TERRESTRIAL
earthdrake .... DRAGON
earthen cup .... MUG
jar .... OLLA
earthenware .... JUG, POT, CHINA,
POTTERY CERAMICS,
CROCK(ERY), PORCELAIN
cooking .... CASSEROLE
fragment .... SHARD
glazed, blue and white
.... DELFTWARE
jar .... CROCK
maker .... POTTER
making material .... PUG
pertaining to .... CERAMIC
pot .... PIPKIN
unglazed .... TERRA COTTA
water container .... GOGLET,
GURGLET
earthling .... HUMAN, MORTAL,
HUMAN BEING, MATERIALIST
earthly ...... MUNDANE, SECULAR,
WORLDLY, TERRENE,
TELLURIC, TEMPORAL,
TELLURIAN, TERRESTRIAL
not .... ETHEREAL, CELESTIAL
opposed to .... SPIRITUAL
earthnut .... POD, TUBER, FUNGUS,
PEANUT, TRUFFLE
earthquake .... QUAKE, SEISM,
SHOCK, TREMOR, TEMBLOR
combining form ...... S(E)ISMO
echo .... AFTERSHOCK
focus of .... EPICENTER
origin .... EPICENTER
over center of disturbance
.... EPIFOCAL
pertaining to .... SEISMAL,
SEISMIC
recorder .... RICHTER
slight .... MICROSEISM
starting point .... FOCUS
earthquakes, echo of
.... AFTERSHOCK
phenomena of .... SEISMISM
study of .... SEISMOLOGY
earth's treasure guardian
.... GNOME
earthshaking: colloq.
.... MEMORABLE, MOMENTOUS,
THUNDEROUS, SIGNIFICANT
earthwork .... DIKE, AGGER,
MOUND, RAMPART,
VALLATION, FORTIFICATION
earthworm .... ESS
like an .... LUMBRICOID
earthy .... GROSS, CARNAL,
CRUDE, COARSE, SIMPLE,
NATURAL, POPULAR, TERRENE,

TEMPORAL
deposit .... MARL
pigment .... OCHRE, SIENNA
earwax .... CERUMEN
earwig .... BEETLE, CENTIPEDE
ease .... REST, POISE, LUXURY,
LOOSEN, RELIEF, COMFORT,
CONTENT, LEISURE, RELIEVE,
FACILITY, PALLIATE
take one's .... RELAX
easel .... TRIPOD, CANVAS HOLDER
easement .... RELIEF, SOLACE,
COMFORT, RIGHT OF ENTRY
in law .... SERVITUDE
easily ...... IDLY, BY FAR, COZILY,
GENTLY, SIMPLY, LIGHTLY,
READILY, FACILELY,
LEISURELY, RELAXEDLY,
COMFORTABLY
affected .... SENSITIVE
angered/annoyed .... TESTY,
CRANKY, GRUMPY, FRETFUL,
IRASCIBLE, IRRITABLE
bent .... LIMBER, PLIANT,
ELASTIC, FLEXIBLE
broken .... BRITTLE, FRAGILE,
DELICATE
cheated/tricked .... GREEN,
GULLIBLE, CREDULOUS,
UNSUSPECTING
frightened .... SCARY,
NERVOUS, PANICKY
handled .... TAME, GENTLE
mixed .... MISCIBLE
offended .... TOUCHY,
SENSITIVE, THIN-SKINNED
pleased .... EASYGOING
remembered .... CATCHY, EYE-
CATCHING
set on fire .... FIERY,
FLAMMABLE, COMBUSTIBLE
tempted .... FRAIL, WEAK-
WILLED
easiness .... EASE, COMFORT,
FACILITY
colloquial .... CINCH, BREEZE
in using hands or body
.... SKILL, DEXTERITY
slang .... SNAP
easing .... RELIEF, REMEDY,
MELLOWING
east .... ASIA, LEVANT, ORIENT
East Indies .... INDONESIA
animal, small .... TARSIER
ape .... GIBBON
arboreal mammal ..... COLUGO
bark .... NIEPA
bird .... ARGUS, LORIKEET
boatman .... SERANG
calico .... SALLOO
cat-like animal .... LINSANG

cedar .... TOON, DEODAR
cereal grass .... RAG(G),
RAGEE
chief .... RAJA(H)
civet .... MUSANG
coin .... CASH
cuckoo .... KOEL
deer .... MUNTJAC
dye .... CHAY
elephant driver .... MAHOUT
fiber (plant) .... JUTE, SUNN
fish .... DORAB
fruit .... DURIAN, DURION,
MANGOSTEEN
garment .... SARONG
grass .... GLAGA, VETIVER
harvest .... RABO
hemp .... SUNN
herb .... PIA, CHAY, CHOY,
SOLA, GINGER, SESAME,
ROSELLE
honeybee .... DINGAR
island .... BALI, CERAM,
SUMATRA
lemur .... COLUGO
litter .... DOOLEE, DOOLI(E),
DOOL(E)Y
mail/mail service .... DAK
medicinal root .... ZEDOARY
mint plant .... COLEUS
monkey .... ENTELLUS
musical instrument .... BINA,
RUANA
myrtle .... CAJEPUT, CAJUPUT
oil plant .... BENNE, SESAME
palm tree .... TALIPOT
parrot .... COCKATOO
peacock-like bird .... ARGUS
perfume .... PATCHOULI
persimmon .... GA(U)B
plant .... AMIL, CHAY, JUTE,
SUNN, AMBARY, BEN(NE),
COLEUS, DERRIS, SESAME,
TURMERIC, PATCHOULI
prince .... RAJA(H)
rat .... KOK
relish .... PICALILI
root .... CHAY, CHOY
sailor .... LASCAR
sauce .... CURRY
seaweed product .... AGAR-
AGAR
shrub .... CUBEB
snake .... KUPPER
spice .... CINNAMON
squirrel .... TAGUAN
tree ..... SAJ, MEE, JACK, POON,
TEAK, TOON, ACANA, PINEY,
SIRIS, BANYAN, DEODAR,
KAMALA, CAJUPUT, CINCHONA,
SAPANWOOD, CALAMANDER,

CHAULMOOGRA
vessel .... PATAMAR
warrior .... SINGH
weight .... CATTY
wood .... ENG, TEAK, TOON,
KOKRA, LIGNALOES
Easter .... PASCH(A)
feast of .... PASCH
fruitcake .... SIMNEL
Island .... RAPANUI
lily .... CALLA
of .... PASCHAL
souvenirs .... EGGS, BUNNIES
the Sunday before .... PALM
third Sunday after
.... JUBILATE
eastern .... ASIATIC, ORIENTAL
league .... IVY
palace .... SERAI, SERAGLIO
rule .... SHAHDOM
ruler .... EMIR, SHAH, EMEER
Eastern Christian .... UNIAT(E)
European .... SLAV
Orthodox church monk
.... CALOYER
Orthodox church prayers
.... EKTENE
Eastwood, actor .... CLINT
easy .... COZY, SOFT, FACILE,
GENTLE, SIMPLE, SMOOTH,
MODERATE, EFFORTLESS,
COMFORTABLE
chair .... ROCKER
course: sl. .... PIPE
gait .... LOPE, CANTER
going .... SMOOTH SAILING
job .... SNAP, CINCH, SINECURE
mark .... DUPE, GULL, PATSY,
SUCKER, PUSHOVER
opposed to .... HARD, TENSE,
TIGHT, TOUGH
slang .... CUSHY
street .... BED OF ROSES, LAP
OF LUXURY, LIFE OF RILEY,
PROSPEROUS CIRCUMSTANCES
take it .... REST, RELAX
to convince .... NAIVE,
GULLIBLE, CREDULOUS
to "take" .... TEN
to understand .... SIMPLE,
PELLUCID
easygoing .... LAX, CASUAL,
LENIENT, RELAXED
eat .... SUP, DINE, FEED, GRUB,
FEAST, CONSUME
away ...... FRET, GNAW, ERODE,
CANKER, CORRODE
crow .... SWALLOW ONE'S
PRIDE
greedily .... GAMP, GULP,
WOLF, GORGE, DEVOUR,

GOBBLE, GUTTLE, GORMANDIZE
immoderately .... GLUT, GORGE
into .... RUST, CORRODE
one's heart out .... AGONIZE
one's word .... RECANT, RETRACT, HUMBLE ONESELF
up .... REGALE
eatable .... FOOD, EDIBLE, ESCULENT, COMESTIBLE
eater, heavy .... GLUTTON, TRENCHERMAN
eating capacity, huge .... EDACITY
disorder .... ANOREXIA NERVOSA
hall .... MESS, REFECTORY
implement .... CUTLERY, CHOPSTICK
of .... DIETARY
place .... CAFE, DINER, AUTOMAT, CHOPHOUSE, CHUCKWAGON, RESTAURANT, DINING ROOM, HOTDOG STAND
regulated .... DIET, REGIMEN
eats: colloq. .... FARE, FOOD, MEALS
slang .... CHOW, GRUB
eau .... DEVIE, WATER
de vie .... BRANDY
designating one kind .... COLOGNE, JAVELLE
eaves, trough under ...... GUTTER
eavesdrop ...... BUG, TAP, LISTEN, OVERHEAR
eavesdropper .... SPY, SNOOPER
Eban, Israeli diplomat .... ABBA
ebb .... WANE, RECEDE, REFLUX, FLOW BACK, DECLINE, SUBSIDE
and flow .... TIDE
tide .... NEAP
tide, opposed to .... FLOOD
ebbing .... REFLUX, RECEDING, REFLUENT, RECESSIVE, REFLUENCE, BACKSLIDING
Eber's father .... SHELAH
son .... PELEG, JOKTAN
Eblis .... SATAN
ebon .... DARK, BLACK
ebonite .... VULCANITE
ebonize .... BLACKEN
ebony .... INKY, WOOD, BLACK, JETTY, PITCHY
ebullience .... ELAN, EXUBERANCE
ebullient .... BOILING, EXCITED, BUBBLING, EXUBERANT
ecarte .... CARD GAME
ecce .... LO, SEE, BEHOLD
eccentric .... ODD, OFF, NUTTY, OUTRE, QUEER, CRANK(Y),

W(H)ACKY, BIZARRE, STRANGE, OFF CENTER, ABNORMAL, PECULIAR, CAPRICIOUS
person .... NUT, GEEZER, HERMIT
slang .... BATTY, KOOKY, KOOKIE, ODDBALL
somewhat .... ODDISH
wheel part .... CAM
eccentricity .... KINK, ODDITY, ABERRATION, IDIOSYNCRASY
ecchymosis .... BRUISE
Ecclesiastes, book of .... KOHELETH
ecclesiastic .... FRA, PRIEST, PRELATE, CLERGYMAN
ecclesiastical attendant .... ACOLYTE
banner .... LABARUM
benefice .... GLEBE
cape .... ORALE, MOZ(Z)ETTA
council .... SYNOD
court .... ROTA, CLASSIS
dean .... PREFECT
headdress ...... MITER, BIRETTA
hood .... AMICE
office, trading of .... BARRATRY
proceedings .... ACTA
residence .... ABBEY, MANSE, PRIORY
seat .... SEDILE
skullcap .... BIRETTA
vestment .... ALB, COPE, AMICE, ORALE, STOLE
eccrinology, subject of .... EXCRETION, SECRETION
ecdysis .... MO(U)LT
echidna .... ANTEATER, MONOTREME
echinate .... SPINY, BRISTLY, PRICKLY
animal .... HEDGEHOG, PORCUPINE
echinoderm .... TREPANG, STARFISH, SEA URCHIN
echinus .... SEA URCHIN
echo .... RING, NYMPH, OREAD, PARROT, REPEAT, RESOUND, REVERBERATE
echoing .... RESONANT, RESOUNDING
eclair .... PASTRY
eclampsia .... SEIZURE, CONVULSION
eclat .... FAME, GLORY, PRAISE, RENOWN, ACCLAIM, PLAUDIT, APPLAUSE, SPLENDOR, NOTORIETY
eclectic ...... CHOOSING, SELECTIVE

eclipse .... HIDE, CLOUD, STAIN, DARKEN, CONCEAL, OBSCURE, SURPASS, OUTSHINE, OVERSHADOW
kind of .... LUNAR, SOLAR, TOTAL, PARTIAL, STELLAR
part .... PENUMBRA
eclogue .... POEM, IDYL(L), PASTORAL
ecole .... SCHOOL
attender .... ELEVE
ecological .... ENVIRONAL, ENVIRONMENTAL
ecologist's concern .... ENVIRONMENT
word of advice .... REUSE, RECYCLE
ecology .... BIONOMICS, ECOSYSTEM, CONSERVATION
economic measure, abbr. .... GNP
nest egg .... PENSION TREASURY
policy, kind of .... AUTARKY
system .... COMMUNISM, CAPITALISM
economical ...... CHARY, FRUGAL, STINGY, SPARING, THRIFTY
economize .... SAVE, HOARD, SKIMP, SCRIMP, RETRENCH, TIGHTEN ONE'S BELT
economy .... MENAGE, THRIFT, PARSIMONY, MANAGEMENT
ecru .... TAN, BEIGE, YELLOW
ecstasy .... JOY, BLISS, DELIGHT, RAPTURE, FELICITY
ectad, opposed to .... ENTAD
ectoparasite ...... LEECH, REMORA
ectype .... COPY
ecu .... COIN, SHIELD
Ecuador bay ...... BANKS, MANTA, ISABEL
cape .... ROSA, PASADO, LA PUNTILLA, SAN FRANCISCO
capital of .... QUITO
city/town .... LOJA, MANTA, AMBATO, CUENCA, IBARRA, TULCAN, MACHALA, MILAGRO, QUEVEDO, RIOBAMBA, GUAYAQUIL, ESMERALDAS, PORTOVIEJO
gulf .... GUAYAQUIL
Indian .... CARA, ANDOA, ARDAN, KECHUA, QUECHUA
island .... PUNA, PINTA, BALTRA, PINZON, WENMAN, ESPANOLA, GENOVESA, CULPEPPER, FERNANDINA
islands .... GALAPAGOS
language .... QUECHUA, SPANISH
monetary unit .... SUCRE

mountain .... SANGAY, CAYAMBE, ANTISANA, COTOPAXI, CHIMBORAZO

province .... LOJA, NAPO, AZUAY, EL ORO, GUAYAS, CARCHI, MANABI, PASTAZA, COTOPAXI, IMBABURA, LOS RIOS, PICHINCHA, CHIMBORAZO, ESMERALDAS, TUNGURAHUA

river .... MIRA, NAPO, CHIRA, PINDO, GUAYAS, TUMBES, ZAMORA, CURARAY, PASTAZA, AGUARICO, BOBONAZA, NARANJAL, PUTUMAYO, ESMERALDAS

seaport .... MANTA, GUAYAQUIL

volcano .... ANTISANA, COTOPAXI, CHIMBORAZO

ecumenical .... GLOBAL, GENERAL, CATHOLIC, UNIVERSAL, WORLDWIDE

council site .... TRENT

eczema .... HERPES, TETTER, DERMATITIS

horse's .... MAL(L)ANDERS

edacious .... RAVENOUS, CONSUMING, DEVOURING, VORACIOUS

edacity .... GREED, VORACITY

eddo .... ROOT, TARO

eddy .... BORE, SPIN, GURGE, SURGE, SWIRL, TWIRL, WHIRL, VORTEX, BACKFLOW, WHIRLPOOL, WHIRLWIND

edema .... DROPSY, ANASARCA

edemic .... BLOATED, SWOLLEN, EDEMATOUS

Eden .... GARDEN, HEAVEN, PARADISE

resident .... EVE, ADAM

river .... PISON

edentate .... SLOTH, ECHIDNA, AARDVARK, ANTEATER, BITELESS, TEETHLESS, TOOTHLESS

edge ...... RIM, CURB, SIDE, BLADE, BRINK, LEDGE, MARGE, VERGE, BORDER, FRINGE, MARGIN

beveled .... CANT

cliff's .... BROW

colloquial .... LEVERAGE, ADVANTAGE

crater's .... LIP, MOUTH

garment's .... HEM

hat's .... BRIM

in .... ENTER, INTRUDE, ENCROACH, INFRINGE

keen .... ZEST, SHARP

move along the .... SKIRT

of a molding .... ARRIS

of a river/stream .... BANK

of fabric/paper .... SELVAGE, SELVEDGE

on .... EAGER, UNEASY, ANXIOUS, RESTLESS, IMPATIENT, IRRITABLE

roof's .... EAVE

tool .... AX, ADZ, KNIFE, RAZOR, CHISEL, NIPPER, SCYTHE, CLEAVER, SCALPEL, SHEARS, MATTOCK, SCISSORS

with loops .... PURL, PICOT

edged .... KEEN, ACUTE, SHARP, CUTTING, KNIFELIKE

object ...... AX(E), BOLO, CELT, BLADE, KNIFE, RAZOR, SABER, SWORD, COLTER, DAGGER, CUTLASS, GROOVER, HATCHET, MACHETE, TRIMMER

rough .... EROSE

edgewise .... SIDEWAYS, SIDEWISE

glance, with an .... ASKANCE

move .... SKEW, SIDLE

walker .... CRAB

edging .... FRILL, PICOT, RUCHE, FRINGE, HONING, LIMBUS, FLOUNCE, TATTING, FURBELOW, TRIMMING

edgy .... SHARP, TENSE, NERVOUS, JITTERY, IRRITABLE

slang .... UPTIGHT

edible .... FOOD, EATABLE, ESCULENT, COMESTIBLE

bulb ...... CAMAS(S), QUAMASH

fungus .... CEPE, MOREL, MUSHROOM

grain .... CEREAL

plant .... VEGETABLE

root .... YAM, BEET, TARO, CARROT, GARLIC, MANIOC, CASSAVA

seed .... PEA, BEAN, PINON, LENTIL, PEANUT

shoot .... UDO, BAMBOO

starch .... SAGO

tuber .... OCA, YAM, TARO, SALEP, POTATO

edict .... FIAT, DECREE, MANDATE, PROCLAMATION

Pope's .... BULL

sultan's .... IRADE

tsar's .... UKASE

edification .... LEARNING, TEACHING, EDUCATION

edifice .... FABRIC, BUILDING, STRUCTURE

built by ancient Egyptians .... PYRAMID

for public worship .... CHURCH, TEMPLE, TABERNACLE

large, magnificent ..... PALACE

very tall/high .... TOWER, SKYSCRAPER

edify .... TEACH, ENNOBLE, INSTRUCT

Edinburgh is capital of .... SCOTLAND

poetic .... EDINA

Edirne .... ADRIANOPLE

Edison, inventor .... THOMAS(ALVA)

edit .... ERASE, DELETE, REVISE, REDACT, ARRANGE, CORRECT, PREPARE, BLUE-PENCIL

edition .... COPY, ISSUE, NUMBER, VOLUME, PRINTING, IMPRESSION

collector's .... FIRST

early morning newspaper .... BULLDOG

in which a written work exists .... TEXT

reissue or new ..... REDACTION

six versions .... HEXAPLA

special .... EXTRA

editor .... CRITIC, REDACTOR, JOURNALIST

editorial .... ARTICLE, OPINION, COMMENT(ARY)

main .... LEADER

editorialize .... INDITE, COMPOSE, EXPOUND, EXPATIATE

Edmonton is capital of .... ALBERTA

Edna .... BEST, FERBER, MILLAY

Edna Ferber novel .... SO BIG, SARATOGA

Edo .... TOKYO

Edom .... ESAU, IDUM(A)EA

mountain .... HOR

Edson de Arantes Nacimento .... PELE, NEGRAO

educate ...... FORM, EDIFY, TEACH, TRAIN, DEVELOP, INSTRUCT, CULTIVATE, ENLIGHTEN

educated .... LEARNED, LETTERED, WELL-VERSED, CULTURED, LITERATE

education .... LEARNING, TEACHING, TRAINING, KNOWLEDGE, ATTAINMENT(S), EDIFICATION

educational .... INFORMATIVE, INSTRUCTIVE

facility .... PARK

group .... NEA

institution .... SCHOOL, ACADEMY, COLLEGE,

SEMINARY, UNIVERSITY, CONSERVATORY
materials .... BOOKS, FILMSTRIPS, RECORDINGS, MOTION PICTURES
educator .... TUTOR, MENTOR, TEACHER, PEDAGOGUE, PROFESSOR, INSTRUCTOR
Hindu .... GURU
music .... MAESTRO
educe .... EVOKE, INFER, DEDUCE, ELICIT, EVOLVE, EXTRACT, DEVELOP, DRAW FORTH
Edward Kennedy Ellington
.... DUKE
specialty .... JAZZ
Edward VII's father .... ALBERT
eek producer .... MOUSE
eel .... GRIG, CARAPO, LAMPREY, ANGUILLID
fish for/method of catching
.... SNIGGLE
fried .... SPITCHCOCK
kind of ...... MORAY, ELECTRIC
large, water .... CONGER
order .... APODES
voracious .... MORAY
young .... ELVER, SNYGGE
eeler .... FISHERMAN
eelgrass .... ZOSTERA, SEA-WRACK
eelpout .... LING, BURBOT
eelworm .... NEMA
eely .... ELUSIVE, SLIPPERY, SNAKELIKE
eerie/eery .... WEIRD, CREEPY, SPOOKY, GHASTLY, GHOSTLY, MACABRE, UNCANNY, ELDRITCH
efface .... BLUR, ODIC, ERASE, CANCEL, DELETE, EXCISE, RUB OUT, BLOT OUT, WIPE OUT, EXPUNGE, OBLITERATE
effect .... CAUSE, FRUIT, ISSUE, TENOR, RESULT, ACHIEVE, MEANING, EFFICACY, AFTERMATH, ACCOMPLISH
in .... ACTUALLY, VIRTUALLY
of an action or process
.... OUTCOME, OFFSHOOT, OUTGROWTH, CONSEQUENCE
produced, as on the mind
.... IMPRESSION
slang .... PAYOFF
effective .... ACTIVE, POTENT, CAPABLE, DYNAMIC, ADEQUATE, EFFICIENT, OPERATIVE, PRODUCTIVE, SUCCESSFUL
effectiveness .... EFFICACY
effects .... PROPERTY, BELONGINGS
effectual .... VALID, EFFECTIVE

effectuate .... ACCOMPLISH
effeminate .... SOFT, WEAK, LYDIAN, UNMANLY, FEMININE, WOMANISH
boy .... SISSY, MILKSOP
person, in a way .... FOP, DANDY
effendi .... SIR, TITLE, MASTER
effervesce .... BOIL, FIZZ, FOAM, HISS, FROTH, FERMENT, SPARKLE
effervescence .... FOAM(ING), VIVACITY, EBULLIENCE, EXUBERANCE, LIVELINESS
effervescent ...... FIZZY, BUBBLING
effete .... ARID, SPENT, WEAK, BARREN, STERILE, DEPLETED, WORN OUT, EXHAUSTED
efficacious .... EFFECTIVE
efficient .... ABLE, CAPABLE, SKILLFUL, COMPETENT, EFFECTIVE
effigy .... COPY, ICON, IMAGE, STATUE, REPLICA, LIKENESS, PORTRAIT, CARICATURE
effloresce .... BLOOM, FLOWER, BLOSSOM(OUT)
effluence .... EMANATION
effluvia .... RAIN
effluvium .... AURA, ODOR, REEK, VAPOR, FLATUS, MIASM(A)
efflux .... OUTFLOW
effluxion .... STREAM, EMANATION
effort .... TRY, NISUS, PAINS, STRAIN, ATTEMPT, CONATUS, ENDEAVOR, EXERTION
colloquial .... PUSH
effortless .... EASY, SIMPLE, NATURAL
effrontery .... GALL, GUTS, BRASS, CHEEK, AUDACITY, BRAZENRY, TEMERITY, IMPUDENCE, INSOLENCE, PRESUMPTION
effulge .... SHINE
effulgence .... GLORY, LUSTER, RADIANCE, SPLENDOR
effuse .... SPREAD
effusive .... GUSHY, GUSHING, EXUBERANT, OVERFLOWING, DEMONSTRATIVE
eft .... NEWT, LIZARD
eftsoon: archaic .... AGAIN, OFTEN, FORTHWITH
e.g., part of .... GRATIA, EXEMPLI
egad .... OATH, EXPLETIVE
Egeria .... NYMPH, ADVISER
egest .... EXCRETE, DISCHARGE
egesta .... FECES, SWEAT, PERSPIRATION
egg .... CELL, OVUM, EMBRYO

capsule ...... OVISAC, OOTHECA
case .... OVISAC
collector .... OOLOGIST
combining form .... OO, OVI
constituent .... YOLK, GLAIR, ALBUMEN
dish .... OMELET(TE)
drink .... NOG(G)
fertilized .... OOSPERM, OOSPORE
immature .... OOCYTE
insect/louse/parasite .... NIT
laying animals .... OVIPARA
laying mammal ...... ECHIDNA, ANTEATER, DUCKBILL, PLATYPUS, MONOTREME
lobster .... BERRY
mollusk's .... OOTHECA
on .... GOAD, PROD, SPUR, URGE, HOUND, INCITE
part .... YOLK, SHELL, WHITE, YELLOW, ALBUMEN
protoplasm .... ARCHIBLAST
relish .... CAVIAR(E)
shaped .... OVAL, OVATE, OVOID, OVIFORM, OBOVOID
shaped, longitudinal section
.... ELLIPTICAL, OBOVATE
slang .... PERSON
small .... OVULE
tester .... CANDLER
unfertilized .... OOSPHERE
white .... GLAIR, ALBUMEN, ALBUMIN
yolk .... VITELLUS, VITELLINE
yolk pigment .... LUTEIN
yolk substance .... LECITHIN
eggbeater .... AGITATOR
egger .... MOTH, BOMBYCID
egghead .... INTELLECTUAL
slang .... HIGHBROW
eggheads collectively .... CLERISY
egglike .... OVULAR, YOLKED
eggs ...... OVA, EXHORTS, INCITES, PROVOKES
fish .... ROE, BERRIES
for breakfast .... SARDOU, BENEDICT
nest of .... CLUTCH
to produce or deposit
.... SPAWN
eggshell color .... ECRU, IVORY, CREAMY
egis .... SHIELD, AUSPICES, PROTECTION, BREASTPLATE, SPONSORSHIP
eglantine .... SWEETBRIER
ego ...... I, SELF, ATMAN, MYSELF, CONCEIT, PERSONALITY
kind of .... ALTER
opposite of .... ID

233

egocentric .... SELF-CENTERED
egoism .... VANITY, CONCEIT,
                       INDIVIDUALISM
    opposed to .... ALTRUISM
egoist .... PRIG, NARCIST
    opposite of .... ALTRUIST
    slang .... SWELLHEAD
egotism .... PRIDE, EGOISM,
    BIGHEAD, VANITY, EGOMANIA,
    SELFISHNESS, SELF-INTEREST
egotistic(al) .... VAIN, COCKY,
          SELFISH, PRIGGISH,
    CONCEITED, NARCISSISTIC
egregious .... BAD, GROSS, UNDUE,
         EXTREME, FLAGRANT,
        OUTRIGHT, PRECIOUS
egress .... EXIT, ISSUE, OUTLET,
        WAY OUT, OUTFLOW,
             EMERGENCE
egret .... HERON, PLUME
Egypt .... MIZRAIM
Egyptian ...... ARAB, COPT, NILOT
    alloy .... ASEM
    amulet .... MENAT
    antelope .... BUBALIS
    ape: myth. .... AANI
    archaeologist .... SAAD,
                RAZEK, SALEH
    Asiatic conquerors .... HYKSOS
    asp on headdress ...... URAEUS
    astronomer .... IMHOTEP
    bay .... FOUL, ABU QIR
    boat .... FELUCCA
    bird .... IBIS, TROCHILUS
    bull: myth. .... APIS
    canal .... SUEZ
    cape .... RAS BANAS, RAS
               MUHAMMAD
    capital .... CAIRO
    capital, ancient .... SAIS,
    TANIS, AMARNA, MEMPHIS
    captain .... RAIS, REIS
    captor of Jerusalem
                       SALADIN
    city/town .... GIZA, QENA,
    SUEZ, ASWAN, ASYOT, BENHA,
       GIRGA, LUXOR, SOHAG,
    TAHTA, TANTA, RASHID,
    MALLAWI, ZAGAZIG,
    DAMANHUR, DAMIETTA, EL
    MINYA, ISMAILIA, EL FAIYOM,
    PORT SAID, ALEXANDRIA, EL
                 MANSORA
    Christian .... COPT
    cobra .... HAJE, URAEUS
    coin .... GIRSH, PIASTRE,
                 BEDIDLIK
    commander .... SIRDAR
    conquerors .... AMRU,
    LYBIANS, NUBIANS, PTOLEMY,
                NAPOLEON

cosmetic .... KOHL
cowheaded goddess
.... HATHOR
creator god .... ATUM
crocodile god .... SOBEK
cross .... ANKH, CRUX, ANSATA
dam .... ASWAN
dancing girl .... ALMA(H),
        ALME(H), GHAWAZI
dead body, preserved
.... MUMMY
desert .... LIBYAN, SAHARA,
SKETIS, ARABIAN, GREAT SAND
                     SEA
division .... MAZOR, FAIYUM,
                PATHROS
dynasty .... PEPI, SETI, UNAS,
    MENES, NECHO, AHMOSE,
    CHEOPS, DARIUS, NARMER,
       RAMSES, PTOLEMY
dynasty founder .... MENES
elf .... OUPHE
embalmed dead body
.... MUMMY
fabled monster .... SPHINX
falcon-headed god ..... HORUS,
                    MENTU
fertile land .... GOSHEN
gate .... PYLON
god .... GEB, MIN, ATEN,
    ATMU, HAPI, SETH, HORUS,
    THOTH, AMEN-RA, ANUBIS,
    KHENSU, MNEVIS, WAPUET
god bearer of the ankh
.... PTAH
god judge of the dead
.... OSIRIS
god-king .... PEPI, KHAFRE,
    RAMSES, MENKAURE,
    SENUSERT, THUTMOSE
god of creation .... PTAH
god of evil .... SET(H)
god of lower world
.... SERAPIS
god of medicine ...... IMHOTEP
god of pleasure .... BES
goddess .... DOR, MUT, NUT,
    APET, BAST, ISIS, MAAT, SATI,
    (H)ATHOR, SEKHET, SESHAT
governor .... BEY, MUDIR
gulf .... SUEZ, A'QABA, EL
                 SOLLUM
hairstyle .... SIDELOCK
hare-like animal .... HYRAX
hawk-headed god .... RA
heart .... HATI
heaven ..... AALU, AARU, LALU
high priest .... RANOFER
ibis-headed god .... THOTH
jackal-headed god .... WAPUET
khedive's domain .... DAIRA

king .... TUT, FUAD, MENES,
    CHEOPS, FAROUK, PTOLEMY
king of underworld ..... OSIRIS
king, youthful .... TUT
laborer .... FELLAH
lake .... NASSER, BIRKET
                 QARON
lakes .... BITTER
language .... ARABIC, COPTIC
lighthouse .... PHAROS
lizard .... ADDA
lord of sky .... HORUS
lute .... NABLA
magician .... IMHOTEP
measure .... ARDES
measure, distance .... PIK,
              KHET, THEB
measure, dry .... KADA,
           ARDEB, KILAH
measure, liquid .... HIN
monetary unit .... POUND
money .... MINA, TALENT,
       DRACHMA, PIASTRE
money of account .... ASPER
month .... APAP, TOTH,
       MECHIR, MESORE
monument figure
.... CARTOUCH(E)
moon god .... THOTH
mortuary chapel
.... MASTABA(H)
mountain .... SINAI, U'WEINAT,
             KATHERINA
mouse .... JERBOA
mullet .... BOURI
mummy cloth .... BYSSUS
name .... GAMAL
native ...... ARAB, COPT, NILOT,
         BERBER, NUBIAN
oasis .... SIWA, DAKHLA,
    KHARGA, FARAFRA, BAHARIYA
obsolete .... GYPSY
opium .... THEBAINE
party .... WAFD
patron of artists .... PTAH
peasant .... FELLAH
peninsula .... SINAI, PHAROS
Pharaoh .... RAM(E)SES,
          AKHENATON
phoenix .... BENU
police .... GHAFIR
port .... SAID
pound .... ROTL
premier .... SAAD
president .... NASSER
queen .... CLEOPATRA,
    NEFERTARI, NEFERTITI,
           HATSHEPSUT
queen of gods .... SATI
Rameses .... PHARAOH
rattle .... SISTRUM

reed .... PAPYRUS
relic, kind of .... MUMMY
river .... NILE
rock .... PORPHYRY
royal tomb .... PYRAMID
ruler .... KHEDIVE, PHARAOH,
　　　　　　　　MAMELUKE
sacred beetle .... SCARAB
sacred bird .... BENU, IBIS
sacred bull .... APIS
scribe .... ANI
sea .... RED, MEDITERRANEAN
seaport .... PORT SAID
serpent: myth. .... APEPI
"shepherd kings" .... HYKSOS
singing girl .... ALMA, ALME,
　　　　　　　　GHAWAZI
site of ruins .... LUXOR,
ABYDOS, AMARNA, KARNAK,
THEBES, MEMPHIS, SAKKARA,
BERENICE, PYRAMIDS
skink .... ADDA
slave-soldier .... MAMELUKE
snake .... ASP
solar deity .... SHU
solar disk/symbol .... ATEN
soul .... KA
spirit .... HAPI
statue, kind of .... SPHINX
stone .... ROSETTA
strait .... TIRAN
structure ...... PYLON, PYRAMID
sultan .... SALADIN
sun .... ATEN
sun god ..... RA, AMON, AMEN-
　　　　　　　RA, HORUS
sycamore fig tree .... DAROO
symbol of fertility .... SERAPIS
symbol of life/emblem
　........................... ANKH
tambourin .... RIKK
Tanis .... ZOAN
temple gate .... PYLON
temple site .... KARNAK
Thebes .... LUXOR
thorn .... BABUL, KIKAR
title .... PASHA, CALIPH
tomb .... MASTABA(H)
tree .... SYCAMORE
verbal shrug .... MA'ALESH
viceroy .... KHEDIVE
waterway .... SUEZ
weight .... KAT, KET, OKA,
OKE, HEML, KHAR, MINA,
OCHA, OHIA, OKIEN, KANTAR
whip .... KURBASH
wind .... KHAMSEEN,
　　　　　　　K(H)AMSIN
woman pharaoh
　........................ HATSHEPSUT

woman singer
　.................... (OM)KALTHUM
writing form .... DEMOTIC,
HIERATIC, HIEROGLYPHIC
writing material ...... PAPYRUS
Zeus .... AMMON
Egyptologist .... EADY, NIMS,
EMERY, LAUER
eider .... DOWN, (SEA)DUCK
eidolon .... ICON, IMAGE,
PHANTOM
eight ball, behind the
　........ DILEMMA, IN A FIX, IN
TROUBLE, ON THE SPOT,
PREDICAMENT
combining form .... OCT(A),
OCT(O)
group of ...... OCTAD, OCTAVE,
OCTET(TE), OCTONARY
hundred forty yards of
cotton .... HANK
multiply by .... OCTUPLE
of .... OCTONARY
of the number .... OCTAL
performers .... OCTET(TE)
series of .... OCTAD
sided figure .... OCTAGON
stringed instrument
　........................... OCTACHORD
eighteen XVIII
eightfold .... OCTUPLE
eighth day, every .... OCTAN
note .... QUAVER
part of a circle .... OCTANT
eighty .... FOURSCORE
years old .... OCTOGENARIAN
Einstein's birthplace .... ULM
theory .... RELATIVITY
Eire legislature .... DAIL
president .... HYDE
river .... SHANNON
Eisenhower, Gen. .... IKE,
DWIGHT
middle name .... DAVID
wife of .... MAMIE(DOUD)
either ...... ANY, AUGHT, ANY ONE
ejaculate .... SPEW, EJECT,
EXCLAIM, DISCHARGE
eject .... EMIT, OUST, SPEW, VOID,
ERUPT, EVICT, EXPEL, SQUIRT,
DISCARD, DISMISS, DISLODGE,
CAST OUT, DISPLACE
ejecta .... REFUSE
ejection .... EXILE, OUSTER,
RIDDANCE, EVICTION,
EXPULSION
eke .... ADD, INCREASE, LENGTHEN
out .... COPE, MAKE DO,
MANAGE, SURVIVE
el .... THE, WING, RAILWAY,
EXTENSION

El Cid .... RUY, (RODRIGO)DIAZ
Salvador, capital of .... SAN
SALVADOR
city/town .... IZALCO,
CORINTO, METAPAN,
ACAJUTLA, LA PALMA, LA
UNION, USULUTAN,
SONSONATE, SAN MIGUEL,
SAN VICENTE
gulf .... FONSECA
lake .... GUIJA
language .... SPANISH
main export .... COFFEE
monetary unit .... COLON
mountain .... SANTA ANA
port ...... CATUCO, ACAJUTLA
president .... DUARTE,
CRISTIANI
river .... LA PAZ, LEMPA
volcano .... IZALCO
weight .... CAJA, LIBRA
elaborate .... FANCY, ORNATE,
ROCOCO, REFINE, DEVELOP,
DETAILED, EXPATIATE,
INTRICATE, EMBELLISH,
PAINSTAKING
decoration .... FINERY
production .... EXTRAVAGANZA
trimming .... FURBELOW
elaborately made ...... EXQUISITE
Elam's capital .... SUSA,
SHUSHAN
elan ...... ZIP, DASH, ZEST, ARDOR,
ZING, GUSTO, VIGOR, SPIRIT,
VITALITY, VIVACITY
eland .... ANTELOPE
elanet .... HAWK, KITE
elapine .... COBRA, MAMBA
elapse .... DIE, PASS, SLIP(BY),
GLIDE(BY), EXPIRE
elastic .... SUPPLE, BUOYANT,
DUCTILE, SPRINGY, TENSILE,
FLEXIBLE, ADAPTABLE,
RESILIENT, STRETCHABLE
band/strap .... GARTER
material on whale's palate
　............. BALEEN, WHALEBONE
substance .... RUBBER
wood .... YEW
elasticity .... BUOYANCY,
DUCTILITY, RESILIENCE
muscular .... TONUS
elate ...... EXALT, EXCITE, PLEASE,
DELIGHT, ENLIVEN, GLADDEN,
GRATIFY, EXHILARATE
elated .... JOYFUL, GLEEFUL,
OVERJOYED, ON CLOUD NINE
elater .... DOR, (CLICK)BEETLE
Elatha's son .... BRES
Elba's important inhabitant
　........................... NAPOLEON

Elbe .... LABE
  city on the .... MEISSEN
  tributary .... EGER, ISER, OHRE,
                  MOLDAU
elbow ...... BEND, ANCON, ANGLE,
    CROWD, JOINT, SHOVE, JOSTLE
  bony tip of the .... FUNNY
                  BONE
  inflammation
    .... EPICONDYLITIS
  inflammation, type of
  .... TENNIS ELBOW, GOLFER'S
                  ELBOW
  jab with the .... NUDGE
  of the .... ULNAR
  part of the ...... ULNA, RADIUS,
      HUMERUS, OLECRANON
elder .... IVA, SIRE, FORMER,
    SENIOR, ANCIENT, EARLIER,
      ANCESTOR, SUPERIOR
  church .... PRESBYTER
  statesman .... ITO, GENRO,
                SAVANT
elderly .... OLD, AGED, AGING,
    ANILE, SENILE, GRAYING,
      VETERAN, WRINKLED
eldest ...... AINE, OLDEST, SENIOR,
    FIRST-BORN, FIRSTLING
  son .... PRIMOGENITURE
Eldorado's riches .... GOLD,
              DIAMONDS
eldritch ...... EERY, EERIE, WEIRD,
              GHASTLY
Eleanor, diminutive of ...... ELLA,
           NORA, NELL
  variant .... ELINOR
Eleanora, actress .... DUSE
elecampane roots .... INULA
elect ...... OPT, SEAT, VOTE, ELITE,
    CHOOSE, CHOSEN, DECIDE,
      PREFER, SELECT
election .... POLL, CHOICE,
             SELECTION
  casualty .... LAME DUCK
  district .... WARD, PRECINCT
  kind of ..... RUNOFF, GENERAL,
             PRIMARY
  landslide .... WALK-IN
  platform .... ISSUE, PLANK,
    POLICY, PROGRAM, HUSTINGS
  proceedings .... HUSTINGS
  report .... RETURNS
  tour ..... STUMP, WHISTLE STOP
electioneer ...... STUMP, CANVASS,
             CAMPAIGN
elective .... OPTIONAL, ELECTORAL,
           DISCRETIONARY
elector .... VOTER, ELISOR,
      OPTANT, SELECTOR
electorate .... ELECTORS,
         CONSTITUENTS

Electra ...... PLEIAD, SHINING ONE
  brother of .... ORESTES
  parent of .... AGAMEMNON,
         CLYTEMNESTRA
electric .... VOLTAIC, CORDLESS,
    EXCITING, MAGNETIC,
      THRILLING
  bell part .... ARMATURE
  bulb .... GLOBE
  catfish .... RAAD
  chair .... DEATH, HOT SEAT
  circuit .... LOOP
  circuit switch .... TOGGLE
  company employee
  .... READER
  current modulator .... CODER
  current regulator
  .... RHEOSTAT
  device .... RHEO, RESISTOR,
              RHEOSTAT
  engine for towing .... MULE
  eye .... PHOTOCELL
  force unit .... VOLT
  generator .... DYNAMO
  light .... BULB, GLIM, LAMP,
    NEON LAMP, FLUORESCENCE,
      INCANDESCENT LAMP
  particle .... (AN)ION, CATION
  potential .... TENSION
  power .... WATTAGE
  railway, underground
  .... METRO, SUBWAY
  ray .... TORPEDO, NUMBFISH
  unit .... OHM, REL, DYNE,
    ELOD, PERM, VOLT, WATT,
    AMP(ERE), FARAD, HENRY,
    MEGOHM, KILOWATT
  wire .... LINE, CABLE
  wires tube .... RACEWAY
electrical apparatus ...... SPARKER
  appliance .... RANGE, MIXER,
    STOVE, COOKER, FRYPAN,
    BLENDER, TOASTER,
    (FLAT)IRON, COMPACTOR,
    DISHWASHER,
    (MICROWAVE)OVEN
  atom .... ELECTRON
  circuit regulator ...... BOOSTER
  device ..... FUSE, PLUG, RELAY,
    TIMER, DYNAMO, OUTLET,
    CHARGER, RHEOSTAT,
    CAPACITOR, CONDENSER,
    TRANSFORMER
  failure .... SHORT
  force .... ELOD
  machine .... MOTOR, ENGINE,
            GENERATOR
  particle .... (AN)ION, CATION
  phenomenon .... ARC
  system .... WIRING
  terminal .... ANODE,

            ELECTRODE
  unit .... VOLT, WATT, JOULE
  unit of measurement ...... REL,
    BARAD, FARAD, FARADAY,
      HORSEPOWER
electrician ...... WIRER, WIRE MAN
electricity .... LIGHT, POWER
  generator .... EEL
  slang .... JUICE
  unit of .... MHO, OHM, AMPERE
electrified particle .... ION
electrify .... STUN, SHOCK,
    CHARGE, EXCITE, THRILL,
    STARTLE, ENERGIZE
electrode .... GRID, ANODE,
    CATHODE, THERMION,
      CONDUCTOR
electrograph .... WIRE PHOTO
electromagnet .... SOLENOID
electromotive force ...... TENSION,
    VOLT(AGE), PRESSURE
electron .... MESON
  tube .... TRIODE, IGNITRON,
    KENATRON, KLYSTRON,
    MAGNETRON, STROBOTRON
electronic "brain"
  ...... COMPUTER, CALCULATOR
  detector .... RADAR, SONAR
  device .... LASER, MASER,
             ISOTRON
  device connected to wall of
    the heart ..... PACEMAKER
  device to increase electric
    signal strength
  .... AMPLIFIER
  hearing device .... HEARING
              AID
  meter .... DUODIAL,
          VOLTMETER
  recording instrument of
    blood pressure, pulse rate,
    etc. .... POLYGRAPH, LIE
          DETECTOR
  tester .... AMMETER,
         OHMMETER
  transmitting device through
    wave frequencies
  .... RADIO
  tube .... X-RAY, DIODE, STROBE
electroplated .... ANODIZED,
         GALVANIZED
electrum .... ALLOY
eleemosynary ...... FREE, GRATIS,
    GENEROUS, CHARITABLE,
      GRATUITOUS
elegance .... EASE, LUXE, CHARM,
    GRACE, FINISH, POLISH,
    CULTURE, GOOD TASTE,
      REFINEMENT
  affected/excessive ..... PURISM,
         FROUFROU

of manners .... PANACHE
elegant .... CHIC, FINE, POSH,
NOBBY, PLUSH, DELUXE,
REFINED, ARTISTIC,
BECOMING, GRACEFUL,
SUPERB, POLISHED
affectedly .... GENTEEL,
OVERNICE, PURISTIC
in a showy way .... FLOSSY
in manners .... PROPER,
COURTLY, DIGNIFIED
elegiac .... SAD, MOURNFUL,
PLAINTIVE, THRENODIC
elegist ...... GRAY, POET, SHELLEY
elegize .... KNELL, MOURN,
LAMENT, POETICIZE
elegy .... DIRGE, NENIA, REQUIEM,
THRENODY
Shelley's .... ADONAIS
eleme .... FIG
element .... PART, STUFF, FACTOR,
COMPONENT, INGREDIENT
an .... AIR, FIRE, EARTH,
WATER
chemical .... ALKALI, ANTACID,
REAGENT, NEUTRALIZER
extracted .... DERIVATIVE
inert gas .... NEON, HELIUM
nonmetallic chemical
.... SILICON
number 5 .... BORON
number 10 .... NEON
of air .... NEON, ARGON,
HELIUM, OXYGEN, NITROGEN
of anything .... SUBSTANCE
rare-earth .... ERBIUM
similar to another ..... ISOTOPE
smallest particle of an
.... ATOM, MOLECULE
suffix .... IUM
with a valence of one
.... MONAD
with valence six .... HEXAD
with valence two .... DYAD
worthless .... SCUM
elemental .... SIMPLE, PRIMARY,
INCIPIENT, HYPOSTATIC
spirit .... DEMON, GNOME,
SYLPH
elementary .... BASIC, PRIMAL,
SIMPLE, PRIMARY, BEGINNING,
ABC'S, FUNDAMENTAL,
RUDIMENTARY
education .... RUDIMENTS,
INTRODUCTION
school ...... GRAMMAR SCHOOL
elemi .... ANIME, RESIN
elenctic .... REFUTING
opposed to .... D(E)ICTIC
elephant .... HATHI, JUMBO,
TUSKER, PACHYDERM

boy .... SABU
driver .... MAHOUT
extinct .... MAMMOTH,
MASTODON
female .... COW
frenzy of .... MUST
goad .... ANKUS
keeper .... MAHOUT
male .... BULL
maverick/outlaw .... ROGUE
nose .... SNOUT
seat on ..... HOUDAH, HOWDAH
sound .... BELLOW, TRUMPET
tooth .... TUSK
tower on .... CASTLE
trap .... KEDDAH, KHEDAH
tusk .... IVORY
white .... ALBINO
young .... CALF
elephant's ear .... TARO,
BEGONIA
elephantine .... HUGE, VAST,
BULKY, MASSIVE
eleuthera yield .... CASCARILLA
elevate .... BUOY, LIFE, EXALT,
RAISE, JACK UP, HEIGHTEN
elevated .... HIGH, LOFTY,
EMINENT, EDIFYING
railway .... EL, MONORAIL
roadway .... OVERPASS
elevating muscle .... LEVATOR
elevation .... MOUNT, HEIGHT,
UPLIFT, LIFTING, PLATEAU,
ALTITUDE, EMINENCE,
ERECTION
elevator .... HOIST, GRANARY,
WAREHOUSE
aircraft .... AIRFOIL
British .... LIFT
car .... CAGE
kind of .... DUMBWAITER
man .... OTIS
passage for .... SHAFT
pawnbroker's .... SPOUT
eleven's numerals .... ONES
eleventh hour .... CURFEW,
DEADLINE
elf .... FAY, HOB, IMP, NIX, PERI,
PIXY, PUCK, FAIRY, GNOME,
OUPHE, PIXIE, GOBLIN, SPRITE,
BROWNIE
elfdom .... WITCHERY
elfin .... FEY
shelter .... TOADSTOOL
Eli .... HIGH PRIEST
grandson of .... ICHABOD
pupil of .... SAMUEL
son of .... HOPHNI, PHINEHAS
Elia .... LAMB
elicit .... DRAW, EDUCE, EVOKE,
FETCH, EXTORT, EXTRACT

elide .... OMIT, SLUR, LEAVE OUT,
NEGLECT, SUPPRESS
eligibility .... ACCEPTANCE,
QUALIFICATION
eligible .... FIT(TED), SUITABLE,
COMPETENT, DESIRABLE,
QUALIFIED
for draft .... ONE-A
Elijah .... ELIA, ELIAS, PROPHET
diminutive .... LIGE
religious opponent of
.... JEZEBEL
successor of .... ELISHA
Elimelech's daughter-in-law
.... RUTH
son .... MAHLON
wife .... NAOMI
eliminate .... RID, DROP, OMIT,
EJECT, ERASE, EXPEL, SET
ASIDE, REMOVE, EXCLUDE,
EXCRETE, SECRETE,
ERADICATE
tension .... CLEAR THE AIR
Eliot, George .... EVANS
creation .... VERSE
hero .... BEDE, MARNER
heroine .... ROMOLA
Eliot's cruellest month .... APRIL
Elisheba's husband .... AARON
elision .... SYNCOPE, OMISSION,
CONTRACTION
victim of .... VOWEL,
SYLLABLE
elite .... PICK, CREAM, PRIME,
CHOICE, SELECT,
ARISTOCRACY
assemblage .... SALON,
GALAXY
elixir .... POTION, REMEDY,
ARCANUM, CURE-ALL,
NOSTRUM, PANACEA,
CATHOLICON
Elizabeth .... TAYLOR, ASHLEY,
MONTGOMERY
diminutive of .... LIZ, BETH,
BETTY, LISSET(T)E, LIZZIE
Elizabeth I, Queen, adviser
.... CECIL
parent .... BOLEYN,
HENRY(VIII)
tutor .... ASCHAM
Elizabeth II, Queen, daughter
of .... ANNE
daughter-in-law of ..... DIANA,
SARAH
father of .... GEORGE VI
father-in-law of .... ANDREW
granddaughter of .... ZARA,
EUGENIE, BEATRICE
grandson of .... HARRY,
PETER, WILLIAM

husband of .... PHILIP
sister of .... MARGARET
son of ...... ANDREW, EDWARD,
CHARLES
son-in-law of
.... MARK(PHILLIPS)
elk .... ALCE, LOSH, MOOSE,
SAMBAR, WAPITI
male .... BULL
of rank .... EXALTED RULER
Elkanah's son .... SAMUEL
wife .... HANNAH
ell .... WING, EXTENSION
Ella .... RAINES, FITZGERALD
Ellen's lake .... KATRINE
Ellice Islands' old name
.... LAGOON
Elliott, actor .... GOULD
ellipse .... OVAL, CURVE, OVATE
ellipsoidal .... OVAL
elliptical .... OVAL, OVATE,
OVOID, OBLONG, EGG-SHAPED
elm .... WAHOO
fruit .... SAMARA
Elman, violinist .... MISCHA
Elmo's (St.) fire ...... CORPOSANT
Elohim .... GOD
elongate .... EXTEND, PROLONG,
STRETCH, LENGTHEN
elongated .... LONG, OBLONG,
PROLATE, PROTRACTED
combining form ...... MACR(O)
elope .... DECAMP, ESCAPE, RUN
AWAY, ABSCOND
elopers, usual .... LOVERS
eloquence ...... POWER, FLUENCY,
GIFT OF GAB, ORATORY,
RHETORIC
eloquent .... FLUENT, LINGUAL,
GLIB, ARTICULATE,
EXPRESSIVE, VOLUBLE,
FLAMBOYANT, ORATORICAL
else .... IF NOT, BESIDES,
DIFFERENT, OTHER(WISE)
elsewhere .... AWAY, ALIBI
Elsie's husband .... ELMER
elsin .... AWL
elt .... PORKER
elucidate .... CLEAR, CLARIFY,
EXPLAIN, INTERPRET
elude .... FOIL, SHUN, AVOID,
DODGE, EVADE, BAFFLE,
ESCAPE
elusion ...... EVASION, AVOIDANCE
elusive .... EELY, SHIFTY, TRICKY,
EVASIVE, BAFFLING, SLIPPERY
person .... FUGITIVE
thing .... EEL
elutriate .... DECANT, PURIFY
elver .... EEL, CONGER

Elwin, anthropologist
.... VERRIER
Ely's famed building
.... CATHEDRAL
Elysian .... HAPPY, BLISSFUL
Elysium .... EDEN, HEAVEN,
PARADISE
em: colloq. .... THEM
half an .... EN
emaciated .... BONY, THIN,
DRAWN, GAUNT, SKINNY,
WASTED, HAGGARD, SCRAWNY
colloquial .... SKIN AND BONES
emaciation .... TABES, WASTE,
ATROPHY, TENUITY,
MARASMUS, THINNESS,
SLIGHTNESS
emanate .... EMIT, FLOW, (A)RISE,
EXUDE, ISSUE, EFFUSE,
EXHALE, SPRING, RADIATE,
COME FORTH
emanation(s) ...... AURAE, NITON,
EFFLUX, EMISSION, RADIANCE,
EMERGENCE, EXHALATION
flower .... AROMA, SCENT,
FRAGRANCE
invisible .... AURA, VAPOR
light .... RAY
offensive .... STINK, STENCH
subtle .... AURA, WHIFF
suffocating .... FUME
emancipate ...... FREE, MANUMIT,
SET FREE, RELEASE, LIBERATE
emancipation .... LIBERATION,
MANUMISSION
emasculate .... GELD, ALTER,
UNMAN, WEAKEN, CASTRATE,
STERILIZE, DEBILITATE
embalm ...... MUMMIFY, PRESERVE
embalmed body .... MUMMY
embalming fluid .... FORMALIN
embankment .... DAM, BANK,
BUND, DIKE, WALL, LEVEE,
STAITH
castle .... RAMPART
defensive .... BULWARK
protective mat .... MATTRESS
embar .... STOP, ARREST, CONFINE
embargo .... EXCLUSION,
RESTRAINT, PROHIBITION,
RESTRICTION
embark ...... SAIL, BEGIN, BOARD,
ENGAGE, TACKLE, UNDERTAKE
embarrass .... FAZE, ABASH,
SHAME, UPSET, HUMBLE,
FLUSTER, NONPLUS,
DISCOMFIT, HUMILIATE,
DEMORALIZE, DISCONCERT
a speaker .... GRAVEL, HECKLE
embarrassed .... QUEASY,
ABASHED, ASHAMED,

CRUSHED, SHEEPISH
embarrassing situation
.... SCRAPE
embarrassment .... PUDENCY,
INHIBITION, CONTRETEMPS
embassy ...... MISSION, LEGATION,
CONSULATE
official ..... CONSUL, ATTACHE,
AMBASSADOR
embattled .... ARMED, FORTIFIED,
AT DAGGERS DRAWN
embellish .... DECK, GILD, PINK,
ADORN, EMBOSS, POLISH,
TOUCH UP, DECORATE,
ORNAMENT, EMBROIDER
embellishment .... FILLIP,
TRAPPING, ADORNMENT
ember .... ASH, COAL, IZLE,
GLEED, SPARK, CINDER
embezzle .... STEAL, MISUSE,
PECULATE, DEFALCATE
embezzlement .... THEFT
embezzler .... CROOK, THIEF,
PECULATOR
embitter .... SOUR, ANGER,
FESTER, RANKLE, ENVENOM,
ACERBATE
emblaze .... KINDLE
emblazon .... ADORN, EXTOL,
DECORATE
emblem. See also symbol
.... SIGN, TOKEN, DEVICE,
SYMBOL, INSIGNE, INSIGNIA
authority .... MACE, BADGE,
CROWN, GAVEL, ENSIGN,
FASCES
Christianity's .... CROSS
clan .... TOTEM
French royal family
.... FLEUR-DE-LIS
hat .... COCKADE
heraldic .... CREST, SHIELD,
ESCUTCHEON
international .... RED CROSS
Ireland .... SHAMROCK
national .... FLAG
Nazi fascists' .... SWASTIKA
of dawn .... DEW
of immortality .... PHOENIX
of royalty .... CROWN, DIADEM,
PURPLE
pirates'/poison ..... SKULL AND
CROSSBONES
shield .... IMPRESA
Turkish .... CRESCENT
U.S.A. .... EAGLE
emblematic .... SYMBOLIC,
HIEROGLYPH(IC)
embodiment .... IMAGE, AVATAR,
EPITOME, RENDITION,
EXPRESSION, INCARNATION,

PERSONIFICATION
embody .... JOIN, UNITE, CONTAIN, INCLUDE, COMPRISE, ORGANIZE, INCARNATE, PERSONIFY, INCORPORATE
embolden ...... HEARTEN, INSPIRE, REASSURE, ENCOURAGE
embolism .... BLOCKAGE, OBSTRUCTION, INTERCALATION
type of .... CEREBRAL, PULMONARY
embolus .... FIBRIN
most common type of ..... AIR BUBBLE, BLOOD CLOT
embonpoint .... STOUTNESS, CORPULENCE
embosom ...... CHERISH, SHELTER
emboss ...... STUD, CHASE, RAISE, ENGRAVE, DECORATE
embossed .... CARVED, CHASED, MOLDED, SCULPTED
embossment .... IMPRINT, CONVEXITY, IMPRESSION
embowel .... EVISCERATE
embrace ...... HUG, HOLD, ADOPT, CLASP, INARM, CARESS, CUDDLE, CLUTCH, ENFOLD, ENCLASP, ENCLOSE, ESPOUSE, INCLUDE, WELCOME, ENCIRCLE, COMPRISE
affectionate .... BEARHUG
slang .... CLINCH
embracer .... ARM
embracing .... AMBIENT, ENCOMPASSING
embrasure .... CRENEL(LE)
embrocation .... OIL, LOTION, LINIMENT
embroider .... TAT, PURL, COUCH, EMBOSS, ENHANCE, DECORATE, EMBLAZON, ORNAMENT, EMBELLISH, EXAGGERATE
embroiderer .... NEEDLER
embroidery .... LACEWORK, NEEDLEWORK
design/piece of .... BREDE
frame .... TABARET, TAMBOUR, TABO(U)RET
kind of ..... GROS POINT, PETIT POINT
loop .... PICOT
stitch .... FIGURE EIGHT
style .... CREWEL
worsted yarn used in .... CREWEL
embroil .... MIX UP, MUDDLE, INVOLVE, ENTANGLE
embrown .... TAN
embrue .... WET

embryo .... BUD, CELL, GERM
developed .... FETUS
fertilized .... ZYGOTE
first stage of ..... CONCEPTION, INCIPIENCE
food for .... ENDOSPERM
membrane .... AMNION
middle layer .... MESODERM, MESOBLAST
outer cells .... EPIBLAST
emcee .... MC, NEWSCASTER, COMMENTATOR, TOASTMASTER
emend .... EDIT, AMEND, REDACT, REVISE, CORRECT, REWRITE
emerald ...... GEM, BERYL, GREEN, STONE, SMARAGD
cut .... RECTANGULAR
hiddenite .... LITHIA
Emerald Isle .... EIRE, ERIN, IRELAND
emerge .... SHOW, (A)RISE, ISSUE, COME FORTH, APPEAR
emergence .... EGRESS, SHOWING, OUTGROWTH, APPEARANCE
emergency ...... CRISIS, EXIGENCY
call .... SOS
man .... PINCH-HITTER, TROUBLE-SHOOTER
needing urgent treatment ..... BULLET WOUNDS, CARDIAC ARREST
signal .... FLARE
situation .... PINCH, CLUTCH, CRUNCH
treatment .... FIRST AID
emeritus .... RETIRED
Emerson, actress .... FAYE
essayist, poet .... RALPH WALDO
emery ...... ABRASIVE, CORUNDUM
use for .... FILING, GRINDING, POLISHING
emesis .... VOMITING
emetic ...... ALUM, ALOIN, VOMIT, IPECAC, EVACUANT, CATHARTIC, EXPECTORANT
plant .... TURPETH
emetine .... EXPECTORANT
source .... IPECAC
emigrant .... ALIEN, EMIGRE, LEAVER, SETTLER
emigrate .... MOVE AWAY, LEAVE THE HOMELAND
emigration .... EXODUS, DEPARTURE
emigre, kind of .... EVACUEE, REFUGEE
Emil, author .... LUDWIG
Emile Herzog's pen name .... MAUROIS

psychotherapist .... COUE
Zola book .... NANA
Emily .... POST, BRONTE
eminence .... NOTE, FAME, HEIGHT, REPUTE, DIGNITY
eminent .... GREAT, NOTED, FAMOUS, EXALTED, RENOWNED
emir's domain .... EMIRATE
emissary .... AGENT, ENVOY, (DE)LEGATE, MESSENGER
emission .... ISSUANCE, DISCHARGE
of urine, involuntary .... ENURESIS
emit .... ERUCT, ISSUE, UTTER, EXHALE, EMANATE, RADIATE, DISCHARGE, SEND FORTH
air .... BLOW
amplified light .... LASE
vapor .... REEK
Emma, poet .... LAZARUS
emmet .... ANT, PISMIRE
Emmy .... AWARD, STATUETTE
brother of .... OSCAR
emollient .... OIL, BALM, SALVE
emolument .... PAY, FEE(S), GAIN, WAGE(S), SALARY, STIPEND
emote .... ACT, PERFORM
emotion .... FEAR, HATE, LOVE, ANGER, PATHOS, FEELING, SENTIMENT
center .... HEART
nostalgic .... SENTIMENT(ALITY)
seat of .... LIVER, SPLEEN
self-defeating .... ENVY
strong .... FLAME, PASSION
turn of .... CAPRICE
emotional excitement .... HYSTERIA
illness .... NEUROSIS, DEPRESSION, PSYCHOSIS
injury .... SCAR
play .... MELODRAMA
state .... GRIEF, ECSTASY, MAUDLIN, PASSION
emotionless .... DEAF, NUMB, STOICAL, INSENSATE, UNFEELING
emotive .... MOVING, TOUCHING
empathy .... AFFINITY, SYMPATHY, UNDERSTANDING
emperor .... CZAR, TSAR, CAESAR, DESPOT, AUTOCRAT, PADISHAH, BUTTERFLY, IMPERATOR
decree of .... RESCRIPT
sovereignty of .... EMPERY, EMPIRE

Emperor Constantine's standard .... LABARUM

emphasis .... VALUE, ACCENT, STRESS, WEIGHT, IMPORTANCE

emphasize .... AFFIRM, STRESS, ACCENTUATE, UNDERSCORE

emphatic .... FORCIBLE, POSITIVE, STRIKING

denial .... NEVER

negative .... NOHOW

speech .... BIRR

emphatically .... WITH A CAPITAL

emphysema .... HEAVES

empire .... SWAY, REALM, DOMINION

Empire State .... NEW YORK

empiric ...... QUACK, CHARLATAN MOUNTEBANK

empirical .... BY TRIAL AND ERROR

emplace .... SET

employ .... USE, HIRE, AVAIL, PLACE, DEVOTE, ENGAGE, OCCUPY

employee .... CLERK, HELP(ER), ASSISTANT, HIRED HAND

desk plaque .... NAMEPLATE

employees .... HANDS, PERSONNEL

employer ...... BOSS, USER, HIRER, ENGAGER, MANAGER

employment .... JOB, WORK, CALLING, SERVICE, EXERCISE, OCCUPATION, PROFESSION

contract, illegal .... YELLOW-DOG

emporium .... MART, SHOP, STORE, BAZAAR, MARKET(PLACE)

employee .... FLOORWALKER

empower .... VEST, ENDOW, DEPUTE, ENABLE, PERMIT, ENTITLE, DEPUTIZE, AUTHORIZE

empress .... ZITA, QUEEN, CZARINA

emptiness .... VACUITY, BARENESS

empty .... BARE, IDLE, TEEM, VAIN, BLANK, DRAIN, FLUSH, INANE, (DE)VOID, DEPLETE, EXHAUST, LACKING, VACUOUS, WITHOUT, WORTHLESS

a place or area of people .... EVACUATE

colloquial .... HUNGRY

headed .... SILLY, STUPID, BARE IN MIND

of thought .... VACANT

talk .... FUDGE

talker .... WINDBAG

wind from sail .... SPILL

words .... BOSH

empyema .... PUS

empyreal .... SUBLIME, HEAVENLY, CELESTIAL

empyrean .... SKY, ETHER, FIRMAMENT

EMs .... RANKS, ENLISTED MEN

emu .... RATITE

emu-like bird .... OSTRICH, CASSOWARY

emulate .... APE, VIE, EQUAL, RIVAL, FOLLOW, STRIVE, COMPETE

a butterfly .... FLIT

an ibis .... WADE

Brian Boitano .... SKATE

Currier and Ives .... ETCH

Demosthenes .... ORATE

Dennis Conner .... SAIL

Einstein .... TEACH

Hamill .... SKATE

Jack Horner .... EAT, SIT

John Curry .... SKATE

Lorelei .... TEMPT

Mehta .... LEAD

Riley ...... LIVE THE GOOD LIFE

the lark .... SOAR

emulation .... COPYING, IMITATION

emulsifier .... GUM, MIXER, ARABIC, GELATIN

emunctory .... SKIN, LUNGS, KIDNEYS

en pointe .... ATIP

en route .... ON THE WAY

enable .... ENDOW, EMPOWER

enact ...... DO, MAKE, PASS, PLAY, ACT OUT, ORDER, DECREE, ORDAIN, PERFORM, PORTRAY, LEGISLATE

enactment .... LAW, EDICT, DECREE, PASSAGE, ORDINANCE, LEGISLATION

enamel .... GLAZE, PAINT, SMALTO, COATING, LACQUER, VARNISH, NAIL POLISH

enameled metalware .... TOLE

enamelware .... DISHES, LIMOGES, CERAMICS, UTENSILS, CLOISONNE, PORCELAIN

enamor .... CHARM, CAPTIVATE

encamp .... TENT, PITCH, BIVOUAC

encampment .... CAMPSITE

enceinte .... PREGNANT

enchain .... BIND, FETTER

enchant .... CHARM, PLEASE, BEWITCH, CONJURE, DELIGHT, ENTHRAL(L), FASCINATE

enchanted ...... RAPT, BEWITCHED

enchanting .... MAGIC(AL)

enchantment .... CHARM, SPELL

enchantress .... HAG, MEDEA, SIREN, WITCH, SORCERESS

in Odyssey .... CIRCE

enchiridion .... HANDBOOK

enchorial .... NATIVE, POPULAR

encina .... (LIVE)OAK

encircle .... HEM, GIRD, GIRT, RING, BESET, CORDON, ENLACE, ENGLOBE, ENVIRON, WREATHE, SURROUND, ENCOMPASS

encircling, an .... CINCTURE

enclasp .... HUG, EMBRACE

enclose .... RIM, HEM(IN), FENCE(IN), ENCASE, ENCYST, IMPOUND, CONFINE, ENVELOP

in a globe .... ENSPHERE

securely .... EMBAR

enclosed area .... RING, SEPT, YARD, CORRAL, COMPOUND, STOCKADE

part of aircraft .... NACELLE

space .... COMPOUND, CONFINES

enclosing line .... VERGE

membrane .... TUNICA

enclosure .... PEN, CASE, PALE, WALL, YARD, FENCE, COCOON, GIRDLE, WRAPPER, ENVELOPE, CARTRIDGE

birds/animals ...... CAGE, COTE

cattle .... ATAJO, KRAAL, CORRAL

dogs .... KENNEL

for a dose of medicine .... CAPSULE

for grazing .... WALK

for keeping and studying of animals .... VIVARIUM

for military prisoners .... STOCKADE

for one animal in a stable .... STALL

for small animals/small plants .... TERRARIUM

for stray animals .... POUND

in water .... CRAWL

of wagons for defense .... CORRAL

poultry .... COOP

public telephone .... BOOTH

race track .... PADDOCK

encomiast .... EULOGIST

encomium .... ELOGE, EULOGY, PRAISE, TRIBUTE, PANEGYRIC

encompass .... GIRD, RING, EXTEND, ENVELOP, ENVIRON, INCLUDE, COMPRISE, ENCIRCLE, SURROUND

encore .... BIS, OVER, AGAIN, REPEAT, OVATION, REPETITION encounter .... FIND, MEET, FIGHT, BATTLE, ENGAGE, COLLIDE, BRUSH, COME UPON, COME ACROSS, CONFRONT, SKIRMISH

encourage .... ABET, SPUR, URGE, BOOST, CHEER, EGG ON, FOSTER, INCITE, HEARTEN, INSPIRE

encroach .... USURP, INVADE, IMPINGE, INTRUDE, VIOLATE, INFRINGE, OVERSTEP, TRESPASS

encroachment .... INTRUSION

encumber .... CLOG, LOAD, BURDEN, HAMPER, HINDER, IMPEDE, SADDLE, OBSTRUCT

encumbered .... INDEBTED

encumbrance .... BURDEN, IMPEDIMENT

in law .... LIEN, CLAIM

kind of .... MORTGAGE

encyclopedic .... EXTENSIVE, COMPREHENSIVE

encyclopedist .... COMPILER, DIDEROT, D'ALEMBERT

end .... AIM, TIP, GOAL, HALT, LAST, SAKE, STOP, TAIL, CLOSE, OMEGA, FINALE, FINIS(H), OBJECT, RESULT, UPSHOT, EXPIRE, PURPOSE, TERMINATE

a pregnancy prematurely .... ABORT(ION)

combining form .... TEL(O)

in music .... FINE

man's sobriquet .... BONES

of a spar .... YARDARM

that is attained .... DESTINATION

thick .... BUTT

toward an .... TELIC

up .... LAND

with old or young .... STER

endanger .... IMPERIL, LAY OPEN, JEOPARDIZE

endangered .... CORNERED, IN PERIL, THREATENED

endearing .... LOVABLE, WINSOME

endearment .... KISS, CARESS, EMBRACE, AFFECTION

endeavor .... AIM, TRY, VIE, SEEK, ESSAY, NISUS, EFFORT, STRIVE, ATTEMPT, STRUGGLE

endemic ...... NATIVE, INDIGENOUS

ending .... FINALE, FINIS(H), CLOSURE, CLOTURE, CROWNING, ULTIMATE, EXPIRATION

comparative .... IER

for land or sea .... SCAPE

for peek or bug .... ABOO

have same .... CONTERMINAL

in chemistry .... ENE

in grammar .... DESINENCE

of a sentence .... PERIOD

with Brooklyn or Gotham .... ITES

endive .... CHICORY, ESCAROLE

endless ...... ETERN(AL), LASTING, UNDYING, INFINITE, BOUNDLESS, INCESSANT, PERPETUAL, CONTINUOUS, EVERLASTING

endmost .... LAST, FARTHEST

endocarp .... STONE

endocrine .... GLAND

designating one ...... OVARIES, THYROID, PANCREAS, PITUITARY, ADRENAL CORTEX

endocrine glands, study of .... ENDOCRINOLOGY

endogamy .... INBREEDING

opposed to .... EXOGAMY

endoparasite .... ENDAMEBA, HOOKWORM

endorse ...... BACK, SIGN, SECOND, APPROVE, SUPPORT, SANCTION, RECOMMEND

endorsement .... NOD, VISA, BACKING, APPROVAL, BLESSING

endow .... VEST, ENDUE, BESTOW, CLOTHE, ENRICH, BEQUEATH

endowment .... BOON, FUND, GIFT, GRANT, TALENT, ABILITY, BEQUEST, DONATION

for graduate student .... FELLOWSHIP

natural .... DOWER, DOWRY

endue .... COVER, DOWER, ENDOW, CLOTHE, FURNISH

endurable .... BEARABLE, TOLERABLE

endurance .... STAMINA, PATIENCE, STRENGTH, FORTITUDE

endure .... BEAR, LAST, LIVE, STAND, STAY, BROOK, HOLD(ON), PERMIT, UNDERGO, TOLERATE

enduring ...... LASTING, LIFELONG

endways .... UPRIGHT, LENGTHWISE

Endymion .... SHEPHERD

lover of .... SELENE

enema .... CLYSTER

enemy .... RIVAL, FOE(MAN), OPPONENT, ADVERSARY, ANTAGONIST, OPPOSING PARTY

alien detained .... INTERNEE

encroacher .... INVADER

kind of .... SWORN, BITTER, PUBLIC

energetic ...... KEEN, LIVE, VIVID, ACTIVE, FORCEFUL

activity .... EXERCISE, EXERTION

one/person .... DOER, DYNAMO, HUSTLER, GO-GETTER

slang .... RARING TO GO

energetically active ...... UP AND DOING

energize .... PEP UP, FORTIFY, ACTIVATE, STIMULATE

energy .... PEP, VIM, ZIP, BIRR, DASH, DRIVE, FORCE, POWER, STEAM, VIGOR

and initiative .... ENTERPRISE

crunch device .... CARPOOL

form of .... HEAT, LIGHT, SOUND, KINETIC, CHEMICAL, ELECTRICAL

luminous .... LIGHT

measure of .... ENTROPY, CALORIE(S)

potential .... ERGAL

slang .... MOXIE, SOCKO, STINGO

source of .... SUN, SOLAR

unit of .... ERG, JOULE

enervate .... SAP, DRAIN, SOFTEN, WEAKEN, UNNERVE, ENFEEBLE, PARALYZE, DEBILITATE

enfeeble .... UNMAN, WEAKEN, DISABLE, EMASCULATE

enfilade .... RAKE, BARRAGE, GUNFIRE

enfin .... AT LAST, FINALLY

enfold .... WRAP, ENLACE, EMBRACE, ENCLOSE, ENVELOP

enforce .... GOAD, LASH, URGE, COMPEL, IMPOSE, OBLIGE

enfranchise .... SET FREE, EMPOWER, LICENSE, QUALIFY, RELEASE, LIBERATE

engage .... BIND, BOOK, HIRE, MESH, EMPLOY, ENLIST, OCCUPY, PLEDGE, RETAIN, BETROTH, RESERVE, AFFIANCE

engaged .... BUSY, EMPLOYED, INVOLVED, OCCUPIED, BETROTHED

engagement .... DATE, TROTH, PROMISE, ENCOUNTER, BETROTHAL, COMMITMENT, APPOINTMENT

assurance .... AVAL

engaging .... SAPID, WINNING, WINSOME, ALLURING, CHARMING, ARRESTING engender .... BEGET, BREED, CAUSE, PRODUCE, PROMOTE, GENERATE, PROCREATE

engine .... GIN, MOGUL, MOTOR, DEVICE, MACHINE, TURBINE, APPARATUS

compressed air .... RAMJET

cylinder .... PISTON

exhaust noise .... CHUG

knock .... PING

of war .... RAM, ONAGER, CATAPULT, MANGONEL, TREBUCHET

on wheels .... LOCOMOTIVE

part .... CAM, GEAR, BOILER, PISTON, BEARING, CYLINDER, DIFFERENTIAL, TRANSMISSION

platform .... WALK

puff .... PANT

type of .... GAS, JET, FIRE, DIESEL, ROTARY

engineer ...... PLOT, PILOT, SWING, MANAGE, CONTRIVE, PRODUCE, MANEUVER, OPERATOR, EFFECTUATE, MANIPULATE

type of .... ARMY, CIVIL, NAVAL, MARINE, MINING, HIGHWAY, NUCLEAR, CHEMICAL, ELECTRICAL, MECHANICAL

engineer's aid .... OILER, STOKER

place .... CAB

engineless airplane .... GLIDER

England .... ANGLIA, ALBION, EGBERT

personified .... JOHN BULL

revenue offices .... EXCHEQUERS

English. See also British .... ANGLE, SILURES, SPIN, ANGELICAN

ale month .... OCTOBER

anthem .... MOTET

architect Christopher .... WREN

author .... LYLY, MILNE

ball game .... ROUNDERS

beefeater .... YEOMAN

chemist .... DAVY

city .... LEEDS, LONDON

coin, old .... ORA, UNITE

composer .... BAX, ARNE

country festival .... ALE

court, old .... LEET

cream .... DEVON

dramatist .... PEELE, PINERO

East India company ship .... INDIAMAN

essayist .... ELIA, BACON, PATER

explorer .... CABOT

fir pole .... UFER

freeman .... THANE

general .... CLIVE

hymnologist .... NEALE

isle .... JERSEY

judicial circuit .... ITER

letter, old .... ETH

metropolis .... LEEDS

novelist .... DEFOE, READE, YATES, BRONTE, STERNE

old money .... ORA

painter .... OPIE, MILLAIS

physicist .... CHADWICK

poet ...... POPE, BLAKE, NOYES, SASSOON

poet of 1700s .... SAVAGE

poet of 19th century ..... ASHE

portrait painter .... SIR JOSHUA REYNOLDS

queen .... ANNE, ELIZABETH

resort .... BATH

river .... EXE, AIRE, TRENT, HUMBER

statesman .... SAVILE

tar .... LIMEY

tourist site .... CASTLE

town .... EPSOM

victory, 100 Years' War .... AGINCOURT

writer of hymns .... WATTS

Englishman .... LIMEY, SAXON, SASSENACH

engram .... TRACE

engrave .... CUT, ETCH, CARVE, CHASE, HATCH, CHISEL, INCISE, STIPPLE

engraver .... CHASER, ETCHER, LAPIDARY

mark of .... REMARQUE

tool/material of .... DIE, BURIN, PLATE, PUNCH, STAMP, STYLE, CHISEL, WOODBLOCK, ETCHING POINT

engraving .... CUT, PRINT, ETCHING

by dots .... STIPPLE

by electrotyping .... CEROGRAPHY

designs on gems ...... GLYPTICS, GLYPTOGRAPHY

means of .... GRAVURE

method .... STIPPLE, MEZZOTINT

on copper or brass .... CHALCOGRAPHY

pertaining to .... GLYPTIC

process .... CEROTYPE, ELECTROTYPE

stone .... INTAGLIO

wood .... XYLOGRAPHY

engross .... ABSORB, ENGAGE, OCCUPY, CONTROL

engrossed .... RAPT, ABSORBED, THOUGHTFUL

engulf .... SWAMP, ENGORGE, ENVELOP, IMMERSE, SWALLOW, (OVER)WHELM

enhance .... ADVANCE, AUGMENT, ELEVATE, HEIGHTEN, INCREASE, INTENSIFY

Enid .... BAGNOLD

husband of: legendary .... GERAINT

enigma .... REBUS, PUZZLE, RIDDLE, SECRET, TEASER, MYSTERY, CONUNDRUM

enigmatic .... CRYPTIC, OBSCURE, BAFFLING, PUZZLING, UNCERTAIN, PERPLEXING, UNEXPLAINED

colloquial .... CLEAR AS MUD

person .... SPHINX

saying .... PARABLE

enisle .... ISOLATE, (SET)APART

enjoin ...... URGE, EXACT, ORDER, CHARGE, DIRECT, EXHORT, (FOR)BID, COUNSEL, REQUIRE

enjoy .... HOLD, LIKE, LOVE, RELISH, POSSESS

books .... READ

with great joy ...... DELIGHT IN

with others .... SHARE

enjoyed oneself greatly ...... HAD A BALL

enjoyment .... FUN, ZEST, GUSTO, DELIGHT, PLEASURE, POSSESSION

enkindle .... FIRE, HEAT, AROUSE, FOMENT, INCITE

enlarge .... GROW, SWELL, WIDEN, DILATE, EXPAND, EXTEND, AMPLIFY, BROADEN, DISTEND, MAGNIFY, INCREASE

hole/bore .... REAM

on/upon .... ELABORATE, EXPATIATE

enlarged picture: colloq. .... BLOWUP

thyroid gland .... GOITER

enlarger .... REAMER

enlighten .... EDIFY, TEACH, INFORM, CLARIFY, EDUCATE, BRIGHTEN, ILLUMINE

enlist .... ENTER, JOIN(UP), SIGN(UP), ENROLL, RECRUIT, VOLUNTEER

enlistment, compulsory .... LEVY, DRAFT, CONSCRIPTION

period .... HITCH

enliven .... CHEER, ELATE, ROUSE, ANIMATE, QUICKEN, REFRESH,

enmesh .... KNOT, SNARL, EMBROIL, (EN)TANGLE

enmity .... FEUD, HATE, ANGER, SPITE, ANIMUS, GRUDGE, HATRED, MALICE, RANCOR, DISLIKE, ILL-WILL, ANIMOSITY, ANTIPATHY, HOSTILITY

ennead .... NINE

ennoble .... EXALT, RAISE, UPLIFT, DIGNIFY, GLORIFY

ennui .... BOREDOM, LANGUOR, WEARINESS

Enoch's cousin .... ENOS(H)

father .... CAIN

grandparent .... EVE, ADAM

son .... IRAD, METHUSELAH

wife .... EDNA

enormity .... MIGHT, OUTRAGE, IMMENSITY, MAGNITUDE

enormous .... HUGE, VAST, LARGE, IMMENSE, MAMMOTH, TITANIC, COLOSSAL, GIGANTIC, GARGANTUAN

animal .... BEHEMOTH, MASTODON

number .... GOOGOL

Enos(h)'s cousin .... ENOCH

father .... SETH

grandparent .... EVE, ADAM

grandson .... MAHALEL

son .... KENAN

uncle .... ABEL, CAIN

enough .... AMPLE, EQUAL, QUITE, ADEQUATE, SUFFICIENT

archaic .... ENOW

enrage .... ANGER, FLAME, MADDEN, INCENSE, PROVOKE, INFURIATE

enrapture .... CHARM, PLEASE, BEWITCH, DELIGHT, ENCHANT, ENRAVISH, ENTRANCE, CAPTIVATE

enrich .... LARD, ADORN, ENDOW, BEAUTIFY, CULTIVATE, FERTILIZE

enrobe .... CLOTHE

enroll ...... ENTER, SERVE, ENLIST, JOIN UP, RECORD, REGISTER

enroot .... EMBED, IMPLANT

ens .... BEING, ENTITY, EXISTENCE

Ens. .... ENSIGN

ensconce .... HIDE, SETTLE, CONCEAL, SHELTER

ensemble .... SUIT

enshrine .... DEIFY, CHERISH, IMMORTALIZE

ensiform .... XIPHOID

ensign .... FLAG, BANNER, EMBLEM, GONFALON, INSIGNIA, ORIFLAMME, STANDARD-BEARER

ensilage .... ENSILE, FODDER

enslave ...... ADDICT, ENTHRAL(L), OPPRESS, DOMINATE

enslavement .... BONDAGE

ensnare .... BAG, NET, BAIT, CATCH, TRICK, ENTICE, (EN)TRAP, SEDUCE, TREPAN, SNIGGLE

ensue .... FOLLOW, HAPPEN, RESULT, SUCCEED, SUPERVENE

ensure .... SECURE, GUARANTEE

entablature, part of .... FRIEZE, CORNICE, ATLANTES, ARCHITRAVE

support .... ATLAS, COLUMN, ATLANTES

entail .... IMPLY, CALL FOR, INVOLVE, REQUIRE

entangle .... MAT, WEB, FOUL, KNOT, RAVEL, (EN)MESH, CONFUSE, EMBROIL, ENSNARE, TWIST, PERPLEX, INVEIGLE

entanglement .... KNOT, INVOLVEMENT

love affair .... TRIANGLE

entellus .... MONKEY

entente ...... TREATY, AGREEMENT

enter .... GO IN, JOIN, POST, BEGIN, COME IN, START, ENROLL, BOARD, INSERT, PIERCE, RECORD, INSCRIBE, REGISTER

clumsily .... BARGE

into conflict .... WAR, ENGAGE, AGGRESS

stealthily .... CREEP IN

enteric fever .... TYPHOID

enterprise ...... ENERGY, SCHEME, PROJECT, VENTURE, GUMPTION, BUSINESS, UNDERTAKING

colloq. .... PUSH

enterprising .... EAGER, AMBITIOUS, ENERGETIC

entertain .... FETE, HOST, AMUSE, TREAT, DIVERT, HARBOR, REGALE, CHERISH, CONSIDER, DWELL UPON

entertainer ...... COMIC, AMUSER, ARTISTE, HOST(ESS), DISEUSE, MAGICIAN, JUGGLER

Allbright .... LOLA

entertaining .... AMUSING, FESTIVE, SPORTIVE, HOSPITABLE

exhibit .... DOGSHOW

entertainment .... FETE, PASTIME, AMUSEMENT, DIVERSION, HOSPITALITY, RECREATION, SHOW BUSINESS

between acts .... RELIEF, INTERLUDE, INTERMEZZO

by swimmers/divers .... AQUACADE

dramatic .... MASQUE

for all .... GAMES

hoedown .... SQUARE DANCE

of another day .... TENT SHOW

enthrall .... CHARM, BEGUILE, DELIGHT, ENCHANT, ENSLAVE, CAPTIVATE, FASCINATE

enthralled .... RAPT, CHARMED, BEWITCHED, ENTRANCED

enthrone .... SEAT, EXALT

enthuse .... RAVE, REVEL

enthused: sl. .... GUNG-HO

enthusiasm .... ELAN, ZEAL, ARDOR, CRAZE, ECLAT, GUSTO, MANIA, VERVE, FERVOR, FRENZY, SPIRIT, ECSTASY, PASSION

enthusiast .... BUG, FAN, IST, BUFF, ADDICT, ZEALOT, DEVOTEE, FANATIC, AFICIONADO

enthusiastic .... HOT, AVID, KEEN, WARM, EAGER, RABID, ARDENT

appreciation .... GUSTO

entia .... BEINGS

entice .... WOO, BAIT, COAX, LURE, TOLE, TEMPT, CAJOLE, INDUCE, ATTRACT, INVEIGLE

enticed .... ALLURED

enticer .... DECOY, CARROT, SEDUCER, TEMPTRESS

entire .... ALL, TOTAL, WHOLE, INTACT, ABSOLUTE, COMPLETE, LIVELONG, UNDIVIDED

combining form .... HOLO

range/series .... GAMUT

"_____ , entire of itself" (Donne) .... NO MAN IS AN ISLAND

entirely .... WHOLLY, UTTERLY

for Claudius .... IN TOTO

entitle ...... DUB, FIT, CALL, NAME, QUALIFY, AUTHORIZE

entity ...... ENS, ONE, UNIT, BEING, THING, EXISTENCE

entoblast .... ENDODERM

entoil .... ENSNARE

entomb .... BURY, INTER, INURN

entourage .... ROUT, TRAIN, RETINUE, ATTENDANTS

entozoon .... HOOKWORM, PARASITE, TAPEWORM

entr'acte .... INTERVAL, INTERLUDE, INTERMISSION

entrails .... GUTS, OFFAL, BOWELS, UMBLES, INNARDS, INSIDES, VISCERA, INTESTINES
entrance .... ADIT, DOOR, GATE, CHARM, DEBUT, ACCESS, PORTAL, DELIGHT, ENCHANT, INGRESS, OPENING, ADMISSION
back .... POSTERN
court .... ATRIUM
hall .... FOYER, LOBBY, ATRIUM
intrusive .... INVASION
with evil intent .... ENTRY
entrant ...... ENTRY, COMPETITOR, CONTENDER, CONTESTANT
entrants, collectively .... FIELD
entrap .... TANGLE
entreat .... BEG, PRAY, PLEAD, OBTEST, BESEECH, IMPLORE
entreaty .... PLEA, PRAYER, SUPPLICATION
entrechat .... JUMP, LEAP
entree .... DISH, ACCESS, ADMISSION
entrench ...... SECURE, ENCROACH, INFRINGE, TRESPASS
entrepot ...... DEPOT, WAREHOUSE, STOREHOUSE
entrepeneur .... TYCOON, MAGNATE, PROMOTER, ORGANIZER
entresol .... MEZZANINE
entrust .... CHARGE, CONFIDE, CONSIGN, TURN OVER
entry .... DOOR, ACCESS, ENTRANT, RECORD, LISTING, POSTING, INGRESS, ENTRANCE
Annals .... EVENTS
illegal .... INTRUSION, TRESPASS(ING), INVASION OF PRIVACY
in ledger .... ITEM, DEBIT, CREDIT, INCOME, RENT(AL), EXPENSE, INTEREST
marginal .... NOTE
permit .... PASS, VISA, PRATIQUE
entwine .... TWIST, WEAVE, (EN)LACE
enumerate .... DETAIL, (RE)COUNT, NUMBER, TICK OFF
enumeration .... LIST, CENSUS
enumerator, kind of .... NOSE COUNTER
enunciate .... STATE, UTTER, DECLARE, ANNOUNCE, PROCLAIM, PRONOUNCE, ARTICULATE
enunciation .... DICTION
enure .... HARDEN, ACCUSTOM,

HABITUATE
enuresis .... URINATION, BED-WETTING
envelop ...... HIDE, WRAP, COVER, ENFOLD, ENCLOSE, INVEST, ENSHROUD, SURROUND
envelope .... CASE, CASING, SHROUD, WRAPPER, COVER(ING)
fetus .... CAUL
for a knife's blade
.... SHEATH(E)
silky .... COCOON
turtle's .... SHELL, CARAPACE
envenom .... MADDEN, POISON, ALIENATE, EMBITTER
enviable .... DESIRED, WINNING
envious .... JEALOUS, GREEN-EYED
person .... ENVIER
environ .... EMBRACE, ENCLOSE, ENCIRCLE, SURROUND
environment .... MILIEU, HABITAT, SETTING, AMBIENCE
slang .... HANGOUT
environmental ...... ECOLOGICAL, SURROUNDING
disease .... ANOXIA, JET-LAG, CHILBLAIN, SEASICKNESS
poison .... POLLUTANT
environs .... LOCALE, PURLIEU, SUBURBS, OUTSKIRTS, VICINITY, PERIPHERY, PRECINCTS
envisage .... EXPECT, FORESEE, PREDICT
envision .... PICTURE, VISUALIZE
envoy .... AGENT, LEGATE, DELEGATE, DIPLOMAT, EMISSARY, MESSENGER, AMBASSADOR
originally .... DEDICATION, POSTSCRIPT
papal .... NUNCIO
envy .... COVET, SPITE, DESIRE, HANKER, MALICE, ILL-WILL, (BE)GRUDGE, JEALOUSY
enzyme ...... ASE, ZYME, MUTASE, OLEASE, PEPSIN(E), RENNET, RENNIN, ZYMASE, CASEASE, EREPSIN, INULASE, MALTASE, OXIDASE, PECTASE, CATALASE, DIASTASE, INVERTASE
action of/producing
.... ZYMOLYSIS
additional component of
.... COENZYME
blood .... THROMBIN
digestive .... LIPASE, AMYLASE, PROTEASE

from bacteria
.... STREPTOKINASE
in saliva .... PTYALIN
in yeast .... LACTASE
protein-splitting .... PAPAIN
eolith .... AX
eon .... AGE, OLAM, EPOCH
eonic .... ERAL
Eos .... DAWN, AURORA, GODDESS
eosin .... DYE, NOPALIN
eparch .... BISHOP, GOVERNOR
eparchy .... DIOCESE
epaulet .... BADGE, PATCH, INSIGNIA, ORNAMENT
epee .... SWORD
ependymona .... GLIOMA
epergne .... CENTERPIECE
ephah, one tenth of .... OMER
ephemera/ephemeron
.... MAYFLY
ephemeral .... MORTAL, MOMENTARY, TRANSIENT, EVANESCENT, TRANSITORY, SHORT-LIVED
ephemeris ...... DIARY, ALMANAC, CALENDAR
Ephraim's brother .... MANASSEH
daughter .... SHEERAH
father .... JOSEPH
grandfather .... JACOB
mother .... ASENATH
son ...... EZER, ELEAD, BERIAH, REPHAH, SHUTHELAH
epic ...... SAGA, GRAND, HOMERIC, HEROIC, IMPOSING, MAJESTIC, NARRATIVE
events, series of .... EPOS
poem ..... EPOS, ILIAD, EPOPEE, (A)ENEID, BEOWULF, ODYSSEY
poetry .... EPOS, EPOPEE, EPOPOEIA
epicarp .... HUSK, RIND
epicedium .... DIRGE
epicene .... NEUTER, SEXLESS
epicenter .... FOCAL POINT
epicure .... GOURMET, GOURMAND, HEDONIST, SENSUIST, SYBARITE
of a kind .... GLUTTON
epicurean ...... APICIAN, SENSUAL, SENSUOUS, SYBARITIC, LUXURY-LOVING
epicurism .... HEDONICS, HEDONISM, GASTRONOMY
Epicurus, philosophy of
.... EPICUREANISM
epidemic .... PLAGUE, DISEASE, PESTILENCE, WIDESPREAD
among plants ..... EPIPHYTOTIC
conquered .... POLIO
most common ...... INFLUENZA

epidermal tissue .... KERATIN
epidermis .... BARK, SKIN,
 CUTICLE, SCARFSKIN,
 INTEGUMENT
epigram .... POEM, ADAGE,
 MAXIM, BON MOT, SAYING,
 MONOSTICH
epigraph .... MOTTO, QUOTATION,
 INSCRIPTION
epilepsy .... FIT, SEIZURE,
 CATALEPSY
 attack of .... GRAND MAL,
 PETIT MAL
epileptic attack, feeling before
 .... AURA
 treatment .... DILANTIN
epilogue .... POSTLUDE,
 POSTSCRIPT
Epimetheus .... TITAN
 brother .... PROMETHEUS
 wife .... PANDORA
epinephrin(e) .... HORMONE,
 ADRENALIN
epinette .... LARCH
epiphany .... (DIVINE)REVELATION
epiphyte .... MOSS, FUNGUS,
 LICHEN, ORCHID
episcopacy .... BISHOPS
episcopal minister .... PRESBYTER
 See .... CATHEDRA
episcopate .... SEE
episode .... EVENT, ACTION,
 INCIDENT, HAP(PENING),
 INSTALLMENT
episodic .... SPASMODIC,
 DIGRESSIVE, DISCURSIVE
epispastic .... VISICANT
episperm .... TESTA
epistaxis .... NOSEBLEED
epistle .... NOTE, LETTER,
 MESSAGE, BILLET(DOUX),
 MISSIVE
 wrote an .... JUDE
epitaph .... RIP, HERE LIES, HIC
 JACET, INSCRIPTION
epithem .... POULTICE
epithet .... OATH, CURSE,
 BYNAME, AGNOMEN,
 MISNOMER, SOBRIQUET
 for Alexander ...... THE GREAT
 Clemenceau .... TIGER
 Eric .... (THE)RED
 Ivan .... (THE)TERRIBLE
 Jackson .... STONEWALL
 Pitt .... IRONSIDE
 Schwarzkopf .... STORMIN'
 NORMAN
epitome ...... GIST, BRIEF, DIGEST,
 SUMMARY, ABSTRACT
epoch ...... AGE, EON, ERA, PERIOD
 Cenozoic .... EOCENE

epochal .... ERAL
epode .... AFTERSONG,
 (LYRIC)POEM
epopee .... EPOS, EPIC(POEM)
epoptic .... MYSTIC
epos .... EPIC
Epsom .... DOWNS, SALT(S)
 Downs event .... DERBY
equable .... CALM, EVEN, SERENE,
 STEADY, UNIFORM, TRANQUIL
equal .... TIE, DRAW, EVEN, SAME,
 ALIKE, MATCH, RIVAL,
 (COM)PEER, PARALLEL
 angled figure .... ISOGON
 combining form .... ISO, EQUI,
 PARI
 distribution of weight
 .... EQUIPOISE
 footing .... PAR
 make .... EQUATE
 quantity .... IDENTIC
 without .... PEERLESS,
 NONPAREIL
Equal Rights party
 .... LOCOFOCO
equalitarian of a kind
 .... DEMOCRAT
equality .... PARITY, BALANCE,
 EQUATION
 of laws/rights .... ISONOMY
 state .... WYOMING
equalizer ...... EVENER, CLINCHER,
 SOCKDOLAGER
equanimity .... POISE, REPOSE,
 CALMNESS, SERENITY,
 COMPOSURE, SANG-FROID,
 SELF-CONTROL
 colloquial .... COOL
equator crosser by ship
 .... SHELLBACK
 passes thru this country
 .... BRAZIL, ECUADOR,
 COLOMBIA
equatorial .... TORRID, SUBSOLAR,
 TROPICAL
Equatorial Guinea capital
 .... MALABO
 city/town .... BATA, LUBA,
 MBINI
 island .... BIOKO, CORISCO
 islands .... ELOBEY
 native .... BUBI, FANG
 president .... MACIAS
 territory ...... BIOKO, RIO MUNI
equestrian ...... RIDER, HORSEMAN
 order of knights .... EQUITES
equilateral figure .... RHOMB,
 TRIANGLE
equilibrist .... BALANCER, ROPE
 WALKER
equilibrium .... PARITY,

 BALANCE, COMPOSURE,
 (EQUI)POISE
 lacking .... ASTASIA
equine .... HORSE, HORSY
 cry .... NEIGH, WHINNY
 disease .... FARCY, LAMPAS,
 SPAVIN, LAMPERS, GLANDERS
 of yore .... MRED
 offspring .... FOAL
 pride of .... MANE
 sound .... SNORT
equip ...... ARM, RIG, GIRD, DIGHT,
 TRAIN, (OUT)FIT, FURNISH,
 APPOINT, PROVIDE
 for military service
 .... ACCOUTER, ACCOUTRE
equipage .... TRAIN, RETINUE,
 OUTFIT, TURN-OUT, CARRIAGE,
 FOLLOWING
equipment .... RIG, GEAR, OUTFIT,
 TACKLE, APPAREL, HARNESS,
 SUPPLIES, FURNISHINGS
equipoise .... EQUILIBRIUM,
 COUNTER-BALANCE
equisetum .... HORSETAIL
equitable ...... FAIR, JUST, HONEST,
 ETHICAL, UNBIASED
equitant .... OVERLAPPING
equitation .... MANEGE,
 HORSEMANSHIP
equity .... RIGHT, JUSTICE,
 INTEREST, FAIRNESS, JUSTNESS
Equity initials .... AEA
 member .... ACTOR, PLAYER,
 ACTRESS
equivalent .... SAME, EQUAL,
 WORTH, ANALOG(OUS),
 TANTAMOUNT
equivocal .... EVASIVE, DOUBTFUL,
 AMBIGUOUS, ENIGMATIC,
 UNCERTAIN, UNDECIDED,
 MISLEADING
equivocate ...... HAW, LIE, DODGE,
 EVADE, FENCE, HEDGE,
 PALTER, WEASEL(OUT)
equivocation .... EVASION,
 QUIBBLE, RED-HERRING
equivoke .... PUN, AMBIGUITY
era .... AGE, EON, TIME, EPOCH,
 PERIOD
 flapper .... TWENTIES
eradicate .... ANNUL, ERASE,
 ABOLISH, DESTROY, EPILATE,
 (UP)ROOT, ROOT OUT, WIPE
 OUT, EXTERMINATE
erase .... CANCEL, DELE(TE),
 EFFACE, EXPUNGE,
 OBLITERATE
 slang .... KILL, RUB OUT
erased, can't be .... INDELIBLE
eraser .... RUBBER

Erbil .... ARBELA
ere ...... BEFORE, RATHER, IN TIME,
SOONER THAN
Erebus, place after .... HADES
erect .... REAR, BUILD, EXALT, SET
UP, PITCH, RAISE, STIFF,
CREATE, UPRIGHT, ASSEMBLE,
VERTICAL, CONSTRUCT
erelong .... ANON, SOON
eremite .... HERMIT, RECLUSE
erenow .... HERETOFORE
ergo .... HENCE, THEREFORE
ergon .... ERG, WORK
ergot .... FUNGUS
of rye .... SPUR
eri .... SILKWORM
eria .... BOMBYX
Eric Blair's alma mater
.... ETON
erica .... HEATH(ER)
Erie port .... SANDUSKY
Erin .... EIRE, IERNE, IRELAND,
OLD SOD, HIBERNIA
erinaceous animal .... HEDGEHOG
Erinyes .... ALECTO, FURIES,
MEGAERA, EUMENIDES,
TISIPHONE
eristic .... DISPUTANT,
ARGUMENTATIVE,
CONTROVERSIAL
Eritrea's capital .... ASMARA
neighbor .... ETHIOPIA
seaport .... MASSAUA,
MASSAWA
ermine .... STOAT, WEASEL
fur .... MINEVER, MINIVER
ern .... (SEA)EAGLE
erode .... ABRADE, EAT INTO,
DISINTEGRATE
erodent .... CAUSTIC
Eroica composer .... LISZT
key .... E FLAT
Eros .... GOD, AMOR, CUPID
erose .... GNAWED, UNEVEN,
IRREGULAR
erosion ...... ABRASION, FRICTION,
CORROSION
erotic .... SEXY, CARNAL, SEXUAL,
AMATIVE, AMATORY,
AMOROUS, LESBIAN, PAPHIAN
slang .... X-RATED
err .... NOD, SIN, FALL, SLIP, TRIP,
STRAY, WANDER, BLUNDER,
BARK UP THE WRONG TREE
in construction .... MISMAKE
errand .... TASK, MISSION
boy .... PAGE, CADDIE,
RUNNER, BELLHOP, BUTTONS
errant .... WRONG, ROVING,
TRUANT, ITINERANT,
WANDERING

erratic .... ODD, QUEER, VAGRANT,
OFF AND ON, WAYWARD,
ABNORMAL, PECULIAR,
ECCENTRIC, IRREGULAR,
CAPRICIOUS
erring .... SINNING
Errol, actor .... FLYNN
erroneous .... FALSE, WRONG,
REFUTED, UNTRUE, MISTAKEN
error .... SIN, FALL, MISS, SLIP,
FAULT, GAFFE, LAPSUS,
MISCUE, BLUNDER, FALLACY,
FALSITY, MISTAKE, UNTRUTH,
OVERSIGHT, WRONGDOING
colloquial ..... BONER, HOWLER
companion of .... TRIAL
in etiquette .... FAUX PAS
in naming .... MISNOMER
in one's reasoning .... FLAW
mental .... LAPSE
secretary's .... TYPO
slang .... GOOF, BLOOPER
error(s) in printing ...... ERRATA,
ERRATUM, MISPRINT
ersatz .... ARTIFICIAL, SUBSTITUTE
Erse .... CELT, GAEL, GAELIC
erst .... FIRST, LONG AGO,
FORMERLY
erstwhile .... ONCE, FORMER
erubescent .... REDDISH,
BLUSHING
eruct .... BELCH
erudite .... WISE, LEARNED,
LITERATE, SCHOLARLY
person .... PUNDIT
erudition .... LORE, WISDOM,
LEARNING, SCHOLARSHIP
erupt .... EMIT, BURST, EJECT,
EXPLODE
eruption .... BLAST, BLOW-UP,
OUTBREAK, OUTBURST,
EXPLOSION
of red spots on skin ..... RASH
eryngo .... SEA HOLLY
erysipelas .... CELLULITIS
Esau .... EDOM
brother (twin) of .... JACOB
descendant of .... EDOMITE
father-in-law of .... ELON
father of .... ISAAC
grandson of .... OMAR,
GATAM, KENAZ, TEMAN,
ZEPHO, ZERAH, AMALEK,
MIZZAH, NAHATH
mother of .... REBECCA,
REBEKAH
son of .... JALAM, JEUSH,
KORAH, REUEL, ELIPHAZ
wife of .... ADAH, JUDITH,
BASEMATH, OHOLIBAMAH
escadrille .... SQUADRON

escalade .... SCALE
escalate .... EXPAND, WORSEN,
INTENSIFY
escalator ...... STAIRWAY, MOVING
STAIRCASE
escalop .... MOLLUSK
escapade .... DIDO, CAPER, JAUNT,
PRANK, SPREE, FROLIC,
ADVENTURE
escape .... LAM, FLEE, LEAK, MISS,
AVOID, ELOPE, ELUDE, BOLT,
VENT, EVADE, DEFECT,
FLIGHT, EVASION, DISAPPEAR
colloquial .... SKIP OUT
device from an airplane
.... PARACHUTE
fire .... LADDER
from prison .... JAILBREAK
means of .... LOOPHOLE
narrow .... CLOSE CALL, CLOSE
SHAVE
slang .... GETAWAY, TAKE A
POWDER
escapee ...... REFUGEE, DEFECTOR,
RUNAWAY, DESERTER,
FUGITIVE
escargot .... SNAIL
escarole .... ENDIVE
escarpment .... CLIFF, SLOPE
eschalot .... ONION, SHALLOT,
SCALLION
eschar(a) .... SCAB, BRYOZOAN
escharotic .... CAUSTIC,
CORROSIVE
eschatology subject .... DEATH,
JUDGMENT, IMMORTALITY,
RESURRECTION
escheat .... CONFISCATE
eschew .... SHUN, AVOID
food .... FAST
eschewed by monkey trio
.... EVIL
escort .... DATE, WALK, GUARD,
USHER, ATTEND, CONDUCT,
(E)SQUIRE, RETINUE,
ACCOMPANY
armed .... CONVOY
kind of .... BEAU, POLICE,
OUTRIDER, BODYGUARD
lady's .... CAVALIER,
CABALLERO
paid .... GIGOLO
woman .... DUENNA,
CHAPERONE
escritoire .... DESK, TABLE,
SECRETARY
escrow .... BOND, DEED,
CONTRACT, AGREEMENT
escudo .... COIN
1/100 of .... CENTAVO
esculent .... EDIBLE, EATABLE,

COMESTIBLE

escutcheon .... CREST, (COAT
OF)ARMS, TORSE, SHIELD
band .... FESS(E)
border .... ORLE
center .... FESSPOINT
point on .... NOMBRIL
vertical stripe .... PALLET
voided .... ORLE
Esdras .... EZRA, NEHEMIAH,
APOCRYPHA
esker (eskar) .... OS, OSAR, RIDGE
Eskimo .... ITA, YUIT, ALEUT,
HUSKY, INNUIT, ALASKAN,
ESQUIMAU
boat .... UMIAK, OOMIAC
boatman .... KAYAKER
boot .... MUKLUK
canoe .... KAYAK, BAIDAR,
OOMIAK, BIDARKA
dog .... HUSKY, MALEMUTE
garment .... PARKA, TEMIAK
Greenland .... ITA
house ...... IGLU, IGLOO, TOPEK
jacket .... ANORAK
knife .... ULU
medicine man .... ANGEKOK
memorial post .... XAT
settlement .... ETAH
transport .... SLED
esne .... SERF, SLAVE
esophagus .... GULA, GULLET,
WEASAND
infection .... THRUSH,
CANDIDIASIS
inflammation ..... ESOPHAGITIS
muscles contraction in the
.... SPASM
narrowing of the
.... STRICTURE
pain .... CARDIALGIA
rod for clearing ...... PROBANG
esoteric .... ARCANE, MYSTIC,
OCCULT, PRIVATE,
CONFIDENTIAL
doctrine .... CABALA
facts .... ESOTERICA
opposed to .... EXOTERIC
esotropia ...... SQUINT, CROSS-EYE
espalier .... LATTICE, TRELLIS,
PALISADE
España .... SPAIN
o Alemania .... PAIS
esparto .... GRASS
especial .... SPECIAL, DETAILED,
PARTICULAR, NOTEWORTHY,
EXCEPTIONAL, OUTSTANDING
especially .... MAINLY, MOSTLY,
CHIEFLY, ABOVE ALL
Esperanto .... IDO
deviser .... ZAMENHOF

espionage .... SPYING
American executed for
...... ETHEL ROSENBERG, JULIUS
ROSENBERG
esplanade .... WALK, GLACIS,
PROMENADE, ROADWAY
espousal .... WEDDING,
ADVOCACY, MARRIAGE,
BETROTHAL
espouse .... WED, AFFY, MATE,
ADOPT, MARRY, ACCEPT,
APPROVE, EMBRACE, SUPPORT,
ADVOCATE, CRUSADE FOR
esprit de corps .... ELAN,
MORALE, SPIRIT,
CAMARADERIE
espy .... SEE, SPOT, SIGHT,
BEHOLD, DESCRY, DISCERN
Esquimau .... ESKIMO
esquire .... ESCORT, NOBLEMAN,
ATTENDANT, GENTLEMAN
ess .... CURVE
essay .... TOY, TEST, PAPER,
TRACT, THEME, THESIS,
ARTICLE, ATTEMPT, TREATISE
Essay on Man poet .... POPE
essayist .... LAMB, HOLMES,
EMERSON
ess .... BEING, ESSENCE, EXISTENCE
essence .... ENS, NUB, ESSE, CORE,
GIST, LIFE, PITH, ATTAR,
BEING, HEART, ENTITY,
KERNEL, FLAVOR, NATURE,
ELEMENT, EXTRACT, PERFUME,
REALITY, SUBSTANCE
of anything .... JUICE
Essene .... MYSTIC, ASCETIC
essential .... MUST, BASAL, BASIC,
FOCAL, VITAL, NEEDFUL,
PRIMARY, INHERENT,
REQUIRED, INTRINSIC,
REQUISITE, HYPOSTATIC
element .... PART
oil .... ATTAR, ESSENCE
oil liquid .... CINEOLE
part .... CORE, PITH, MEMBER
thing .... KEY, THE BOTTOM
LINE
Essex city .... ILFORD
essonite .... GARNET
establish .... FIX, SET, ROOT,
BUILD, FOUND, CREATE,
DECIDE, FIRM UP, SETTLE,
VERIFY, CONFIRM, ENSCONCE,
ORGANIZE
by evidence .... PROVE
into law .... ENACT
securely .... EMBED, PLANT,
RIVET, ENTRENCH
established value .... PAR
establishment .... FIRM, AGENCY,

CORPORATION

domestic .... MENAGE
estafet .... COURIER
estaminet .... CAFE
estancia .... RANCH(O)
estate .... LAND, RANK, ABODE,
STATE, ASSETS, STATUS,
CAPITAL, EFFECTS, FORTUNE,
HOLDINGS, INTEREST,
PROPERTY
a freehold .... ALOD,
ALLODIUM
as in a tropical region
.... PLANTATION
country .... HACIENDA
first .... CLERGY
fourth ...... PRESS, JOURNALISM
holder .... TERMOR
in expectancy ...... REMAINDER
landed .... MANOR, DOMAIN
lands of an .... DEMESNE
overseer .... BAILIFF
pertaining to a noble's
.... DUCAL
second .... NOBILITY
Spanish-American
.... ESTANCIA
third .... BOURGEOISIE
transfer .... DEMISE
under feudal lord .... FEUD,
FIEF
esteem .... FAVOR, HONOR, PRIDE,
PRIZE, VALUE, ADMIRE,
REGARD, REVERE, RESPECT,
WORSHIP
ester .... ACETIN, IODIDE, MALATE,
OLEATE, PICRATE, STEARIN,
SILICATE, GLYCERIDE
esthesia .... SENSATE
esthete .... CONNOISSEUR
esthetic .... ARTISTIC, TASTEFUL
esthetics .... ARTS
estimable .... WORTHY,
DESERVING
estimate .... RATE, GAUGE, JUDGE,
VALUE, ASSESS, RECKON,
MEASURE, APPRAISE,
CRITIQUE, EVALUATE,
CALCULATE
in advance .... FORECAST
estimation ...... ESTEEM, REGARD,
REPORT, REPUTE, OPINION,
APPRAISAL, CRITICISM,
CALCULATION
estivate .... SUMMER
opposed to .... HIBERNATE
Estonia, capital of .... TALLINN
city/town of .... NARVA,
PARNU, PSKOV, TARTU
Estonian island .... OESEL
lake .... PEIPUS

estop .... BAR, PREVENT, OBSTRUCT
estovers .... NECESSARIES
allowed divorcee ..... ALIMONY
Estrada, actor .... ERIK
estrange .... PART, WEAN, DIVERT, ALIENATE, DISUNITE, SEPARATE, DISAFFECT
estrangement .... RIFT
estray .... WAIF
estriol .... HORMONE, THEELOL
estrone .... HORMONE, THEELIN
estrus .... HEAT, FRENZY
estuary .... ARM, BAY, RIA, LOCH, DELTA, FIORD, FJORD, FIRTH, FRITH, INLET, MOUTH
tidal wave .... BORE, EAGRE
esurient .... GREEDY, HUNGRY, VORACIOUS
et .... AND
al .... OTHERS
etagere .... WHATNOT
etamine .... CLOTH, VOILE
Etanin .... DRACONIS
etape .... ENCAMPMENT, STOREHOUSE
Etats .... UNIS
etc. ...... ET CETERA, AND OTHERS, AND SO FORTH
relative of .... ET AL
etch .... CUT, LINE, CARVE, CHISEL, ENGRAVE
etching .... STIPPLE, LITHOTINT
acid .... MORDANT
for one .... ART
Eteocles, brother of
.... POLYNICES
kingdom .... THEBES
parent of .... JOCASTA, OEDIPUS
eternal .... AGELESS, ENDLESS, CONSTANT, FOREVER, INFINITE, (A)EONIAN, TIMELESS, PERPETUAL, EVERLASTING, NEVER ENDING
Eternal City .... ROME
The .... GOD
eternally .... EVER, ALWAYS, FOREVER, EVERMORE, CONSTANTLY, TILL DEATH
eternity ...... (A)EON, OLAM, TIME, INFINITY, IMMORTALITY
etesian .... ANNUAL, PERIODIC, SEASONAL
Ethan Frome's wife .... ZEENA
of '76 .... ALLEN
Ethanim .... TISHRI
ethanol .... (ETHYL)ALCOHOL
Ethel, performer .... MERMAN, BARRYMORE
ether .... AIR, SKY, OZONE, SPACE,

HEAVENS
compound .... ESTER
use of .... SOLVENT, ANESTHETIC
ethereal .... AERY, AIRY, LIGHT, FRAGILE, DELICATE, HEAVENLY, SUPERNAL, CELESTIAL
fluid .... ICHOR
salt .... ESTER
ethical .... MORAL, RIGHT, DECENT, HONEST, VIRTUOUS
ethics ...... MORALS, MORAL CODE, STANDARDS, PRINCIPLES
Ethiopia .... ABYSSINIA
Biblical .... CUSH, KUSH
capital of .... ADDIS ABABA
Ethiopian antelope .... DIKDIK
ape .... GELADA
Black Jews .... FALASHA
capital, ancient .... MEROE
city/town .... ADWA, ZULA, ASOSA, ASSAB, AWASA, HARAR, JIMMA, SODDU, ASMARA, DESSYE, GONDAR, MAKALE, NAZRET, ASSELLE, MASSAWA, NAKAMTI, DIREDAWA
coin .... BESA, GIRSH, TALARI
cotton togs .... SHAMMA
district .... HARAR, AMHARA
fly .... ZIMB
Hamite .... AFAR, GALLA
Hamitic tribe member/
tribesman .... FALASHA
ibex .... SAOL, WALIE
king .... NEGUS, MEMNON
kingdom, former ..... AMHARA
lake .... ABAYA, CHAMO, TANA, ZWAI, ASSALE, RUDOLF, TURKANA
language .... GEEZ, ARABIC, SIDAMO, SOMALI, AMHARIC
mountain .... BALE, GONDAR, RAS DASHAN
native .... NEGRO
nomadic .... GALLA
president .... HAILE MARIAM
prince .... RAS
province .... BALE, SHOA, ARUSI, HARAR, KAFFA, TIGRE, WALLO, GONDAR, SIDAMO, ERITREA, WALLAGA
queen .... CANDACE
river .... OMO, ABAY, BARO, DAWA, WABI, AKOBO, AWASH, FAFAN, ATBARA, TAKKAZE
seaport .... MASSAUA
table-mountain .... AMBA
title .... RAS, NEGUS
walled city .... GONDAR

wolf .... KABERU
ethnarch .... GOVERNOR
ethnic .... LINEAL, RACIAL, GENETIC, HEATHEN
affiliation .... ETHNICITY
division, ancient .... TRIBE
group .... FOLK, RACE, NATIONALITY
ethologist .... LORENZ
ethos .... BELIEF, MANNER, CULTURE, IDEOLOGY
opposed to .... PATHOS
ethyl .... GASOLINE
alcohol .... ETHANOL
derivative .... ETHER
etiolate .... BLANCH, BLEACH
etiquette ...... CUSTOM, DECORUM, MANNERS, PROPRIETY
breach of .... FAUX PAS, SOLECISM
expert .... POST, BALDRIDGE
required by .... DE RIGUER
Etna .... LAMP, VOLCANO
Eton .... TOWN, SCHOOL
article of wear .... COAT, COLLAR, JACKET
rival of .... HARROW
student .... OPPIDAN
Etruscan god .... LAR(ES), TINIA, TURMS, PENATES
goddess .... UNI, TURAN, MENFRA
king .... PORSENA
Minerva .... MENFRA
Etta of comic strips .... KETT
etude .... OPUS, PIECE, STUDY
etui/etwee .... CASE
item .... NEEDLE
etymological .... LITERAL
etymon .... ROOT, RADIX
Etzel .... ATTILA
eucalyptol .... CINEOLE
eucalyptus .... YATE, MALLEE, IRONBARK
Eucharist .... RITE, HOUSEL, EULOGIA, COMMUNION, SACRAMENT
box .... PIX, PYX
bread .... HOST, WAFER
cloth .... FANON
cup for the consecrated
wafers .... CIBORIUM
cup for the wine .... CALIX, CHALICE
oblation .... HOST, WINE, BREAD, OFFERING
to dying person ..... VIATICUM
vessel .... AMA, PATEN
wafer .... HOST
wine of the .... OBLATION
eucharistic plate .... PATEN

service .... LITURGY
vestment ...... FANON, MANIPLE
Euclid .... MATHEMATICIAN
forte of .... GEOMETRY
work on geometry
.... ELEMENTS
eudaemonia .... HAPPINESS
euge .... BRAVO
eugenics, pioneer in ...... GALTON
subject of ...... RACES, BREEDS
eulogia .... EUCHARIST
eulogistic .... ELOGE, MAGNIFIC,
LAUDATORY
eulogize .... LAUD, EXTOL, PRAISE
eulogy .... ELOGE, PRAISE,
TRIBUTE, ENCOMIUM,
PANEGYRIC
Eumenides ...... FURIES, ERINYES
eunuch .... GELDING,
CHAMBERLAIN
euphemism for hell .... HECK
euphonium, like .... TUBA
euphony .... METER, MELODY
euphorbia .... SPURGE,
POINSETTIA
euphoria ...... CONTENT, ELATION,
PLEASURE, HAPPINESS,
SMUGNESS, WELL BEING
slang .... HIGH
Euphrosyne .... JOY
euphuism .... BOMBAST
Eurasian in India .... FERINGI,
FERINGHEE
range .... URAL
region, one-time .... TATARY
eureka .... AHA, SEE,
EXCLAMATION
euripus .... STRAIT, CHANNEL
Europa's father .... OGENOR
lover .... ZEUS
European ...... BALT, DANE, FINN,
LAPP, LETT, SERB, SLAV,
FRANK, GREEK, SWEDE,
BOHUNK, FRENCH, ITALIAN,
SPANIARD
alliance: abbr. .... NATO
ancient language .... NORSE
antelope .... CHAMOIS
apple tree .... SORB
aromatic herb .... FLEAWORT
ash tree juice .... MANNA
bay .... BISCAY
beetle .... DORBUG,
COCKCHAFER
bellflower .... RAMPION
bird .... HOOPOE, ROLLER,
TURNIX, REEDLING, WHIMBREL
bison .... AUROCHS
blackbird .... MERLE, OUSEL,
OUZEL
blenny .... SHANNY

"Boot" .... ITALY
brantail .... REDSTART
bunting .... ORTOLAN
buttercup .... GOLDILOCKS
butterfly .... RED ADMIRAL
canal .... KIEL
capital ..... OSLO, BERN, BOON,
ROME, PARIS, SOFIA, ATHENS,
BERLIN, LISBON, LONDON,
MADRID, MOSCOW, TIRANE,
VIENNA, WARSAW, BELFAST,
BELGRADE, BRUSSELS,
BUDAPEST, HELSINKI,
VALLETTA, THE HAGUE,
AMSTERDAM, BUCHAREST,
EDINBURGH, STOCKHOLM,
COPENHAGEN
carp .... BLEAK
catfish .... SILURID
cavalryman .... U(H)LAN,
HUSSAR
cereal grass .... MILLET
chestnut .... MARRON
chicken .... HAMBURG
coal region .... SAAR
commercial weight
.... CENTNER
country .... ITALY, MALTA,
SPAIN, FRANCE, GREECE,
NORWAY, POLAND, SWEDEN,
ALBANIA, AUSTRIA, BELGIUM,
DENMARK, ENGLAND,
FINLAND, GERMANY,
HUNGARY, ICELAND, IRELAND,
ROMANIA, PORTUGAL,
NETHERLANDS, YUGOSLAVIA
country, ancient ..... HELVETIA
crow .... CHOUGH,
NUTCRACKER
deer .... STAG, FALLOW
diving duck .... POCHARD
dog .... SETTER, BULLDOG,
GRIFFON, SPANIEL, TERRIER,
FOXHOUND, SHEPHERD,
GREYHOUND, WOLFHOUND
dormouse .... LEROT
dotterel .... PLOVER
duck .... SMEW, POCHARD,
WIDGEON
falcon .... HOBBY, MERLIN,
LANNER(ET)
finch .... SERIN, SISKIN
fish .... IDE, BOCE, RUDD,
BARBEL, PLAICE, GUDGEON
flatfish .... BRILL
fly .... FRIT
food fish .... SCAD, SAUREL
food seed .... LUPINE
gamebird .... TURNIX
garlic .... MOLY
grosbeak .... HAWFINCH

gulf .... LIONS, BOTHNIA,
FINLAND, TARANTO
hawk .... PUTTOCK
haybird .... BLACKCAP
health resort .... EMS, BADEN
herb .... BASIL, LOVAGE,
TERRAGON, ELECAMPANE
herring .... SPRAT
holly .... ACEBO
in India .... FERINGI
iris .... ORRIS
island .... ELBA, CRETE,
LESVOS, SICILY, CORSICA,
MAJORCA, BORNHOLM,
SARDINIA
islands ..... ORKNEY, CHANNEL,
FRISIAN, LOFOTEN, BALEARIC,
SHETLAND
juniper .... CADE
kite .... GLED(E)
lake .... ONEGA, GENEVA,
LADOGA, BALATON
land .... EIRE
mignonette .... WELD, WOLD
mint .... CLARE, CLAR(R)Y,
HYSSOP
mountain .... EL BRUS
mountains .... ALPS, URAL,
BALKAN, KJOLEN, CAUCASUS,
PYRENESS, CARPATHIAN
mountain goat .... IBEX
mustard herbs .... RAPES
news agency .... HAVAS
nobleman .... EARL, BARON,
COUNT
nomad .... LAPP
oak/tree .... HOLM, DURMAST
oriole .... LORIOT
pea .... LICORICE
plant .... COMFREY, LAVENDER,
LICORICE, ELECAMPANE,
ALFILARIA
plover .... DOTT(E)REL
polecat .... FITCH, FOUMART
poppy .... WINDROSE
principality .... MONACO,
ORANGE, WALACHIA
rabbit .... CONEY
range (see mountains)
ratlike animal .... HAMSTER
ray .... THORNBACK
river .... PO, BUG, DON, EBRO,
ELBE, ODER, SAVA, ARAKS,
DOURO, DRAVA, LOIRE, RHINE,
RHONE, SEINE, TIBER, VOLGA,
WESER, DANUBE, DONETS,
GARONNE, VISTULA, GUADIANA
river to Caspian Sea
.... VOLGA
river to the Rhine .... MOSEL
robin .... RUDDOCK

rodent .... DORMOUSE
rose .... EGLANTINE
rose tree .... MEDLAR
sea ..... BLACK, NORTH, WHITE,
AEGEAN, BALTIC, BARENTS,
CASPIAN, MARMARA,
ADRIATIC, TYRRHENIAN
shad .... ALOSE
shark .... TOPE
shore bird .... WHIMBREL
shrub .... MEZEREON,
OLEASTER
slang .... BOHUNK
smelt .... SPARLING
songbird .... TIT, MAVIS,
OUSEL, LINNET, THRUSH,
REDWING, THROSTLE,
WHITETHROAT
squirrel .... SUSLIK
strait .... DENMARK, BOSPORUS,
KATTEGAT, GIBRALTAR
sumac .... TEREBINTH
swallow ..... MARTIN, MARTLET
thrush .... MAVIS, OUSEL,
MISSEL, FIELDFARE
tourist quarters .... PENSIONS
volcano .... ETNA
vulture .... LAMMERGEI(E)R
water bird .... GARGANEY
wheat .... SPELT
wild duck .... WI(D)GEON,
SHELDRAKE
wild goose .... GRAYLAG,
GREYLAG
woodpigeon .... CUSHAT,
RINGDOVE
wormwood .... SANTONICA
Eustachian tube .... SALPINX
euthanasia .... MERCY-KILLING
euthenics subject .... RACES,
BREEDS
Eva .... GABOR
Marie .... SAINT
evacuant ...... EMETIC, CATHARTIC
evacuate .... EMIT, QUIT, VOID,
CLEAR, EJECT, EMPTY, EXPEL,
LEAVE, (RE)MOVE, VACATE,
ABANDON, EXCRETE,
WITHDRAW
evacuation .... DEPARTURE
evacuee ...... REFUGEE, DISPLACED
PERSON
evade .... GEE, FOIL, SHUN, AVOID,
DODGE, ELUDE, ESCAPE
direct action ..... SHADOW-BOX
payment .... BILK
the issue .... BEG THE
QUESTION
work .... SHIRK, MALINGER,
GOLDBRICK
evaginate .... EVERT

evaluate .... RATE, ASSAY, GAUGE,
PRICE, VALUE, ASSESS,
ANALYZE, APPRAISE,
ESTIMATE
evaluation .... VIEW, RATING,
OPINION, ANALYSIS,
APPRAISAL
evanesce .... FADE, VANISH,
DISAPPEAR
evanescent .... LOST, MISSING,
FLEETING, EPHEMERAL,
TRANSIENT, VANISHING
evangel .... GOSPEL
evangelical .... APOSTOLIC
Evangeline, author of
.... LONGFELLOW
home of .... ACADIA
locale .... GRAND PRE
evangelist .... JOHN, LUKE, MARK,
MATTHEW, PREACHER,
MISSIONARY, REVIVALIST
Graham .... BILLY
McPherson .... AIMEE
Mormon .... PATRIARCH
Evans, Mary Ann .... ELIOT
evaporate .... DRY, ESCAPE,
VANISH, DISTILL, EMANATE
evaporating quickly
.... VOLATILE
evasion .... SALVO, TRICK,
ELUSION, AVOIDANCE,
SUBTERFUGE, EQUIVOCATION
tax .... NONPAYMENT
evasive .... SHIFTY, TRICKY,
ELUSIVE, EQUIVOCAL
eve .... EVENING
of festival .... VIGIL
even .... FAIR, FLAT, JUST, TIED,
TRUE, EQUAL, LEVEL, PLAIN,
STILL, SMOOTH, STEADY,
UNIFORM, STRAIGHT
break .... FAIR SHAKE
chance .... TOSSUP
colloquial .... QUITS
if .... ALBEIT, THO(UGH),
ALTHOUGH
item .... KEEL
minded/tempered .... CALM,
PLACID, SERENE, EQUABLE
slang .... HUNKY
so .... AT THAT
standing .... PAR
surface .... PLANE
evener .... HALTER, BALANCER,
EQUALIZER
evenfall .... DUSK, TWILIGHT
evenhanded .... FAIR, JUST,
NEUTRAL, IMPARTIAL
evening .... DUSK, SUNDOWN,
GLOAMING, NIGHTFALL
affair .... SOIREE

deadline .... CURFEW
dress .... GOWN, TUXEDO
glory .... SUNSET
love song .... SERENADE
of .... VESPERTINE
poetic .... EEN, EVE, EVEN
prayer/service .... ANGELUS,
VESPER(S), EVENSONG
star .... MOON, VENUS, VESPER,
HESPER(US)
evensong .... VESPERS
event .... CASUS, ISSUE, AFFAIR,
RESULT, HOLIDAY, INCIDENT,
OCCASION, HAPPENING,
OCCURRENCE
causing or provoking war
.... CASUS BELLI
early Boston .... MASSACRE,
TEA PARTY
January .... WHITE SALE
of 1849 .... GOLDRUSH
of June 1953 ..... CORONATION
spurred by Sam Adams,
1773 .... BOSTON TEA
PARTY
sudden .... HAP
eventful .... NEWSY, BUSTLING,
MOMENTOUS
eventide .... DUSK, VESPER,
EVENING, TWILIGHT
eventual .... FINAL, COMING,
ULTIMATE
eventuality .... ADVENT, ARRIVAL,
PROSPECT, CONTINGENCY
eventually .... FINALLY,
ULTIMATELY, IN THE LONG
RUN, SOONER OR LATER
eventuate .... TURN, HAPPEN,
RESULT
ever .... AYE, ONCE, ALWAYS,
FOREVER, ETERNALLY,
REPEATEDLY
Everest conqueror .... (SIR
EDMUND)HILLARY,
(TENZING)NORGAY
inhabitant, alleged .... YETI,
ABOMINABLE SNOWMAN
peak .... LHOTSE
rival .... ANNAPURNA
Everett .... CHAD
everglade .... SWAMPLAND
denizen .... (ALLI)GATOR
Everglade State .... FLORIDA
evergreen .... FRESH, CONIFER,
SAVIN(E), UNFADING,
PERENNIAL, EVER-BLOOMING
bean .... CAROB
genus .... ABIES, PINUS,
CEDRUS
giant .... REDWOOD, SEQUOIA
herb .... GALAX

needles, dried ..... PINE STRAW
oak .... HOLM, ILEX
opposed to .... DECIDUOUS
poisonous .... OLEANDER
shrub .... TITI, ROSEMARY,
　OLEANDER, LEATHERWOOD
tree .... FIR, YEW, PINE,
　CEDAR, LARCH, OLIVE,
　DEODAR, SPRUCE, HEMLOCK,
　MADRONA, BALSAM-FIR
tree, nut bearing ..... CASHEW
tree bark .... CASSIA
tree fruit .... CONE
everlasting .... AGELESS,
　AGELONG, ETERN(E),
　DURABLE, CONSTANT,
　ETERNAL, ETERNITY,
　UNENDING, CEASELESS,
　PERPETUAL
Evert .... CHRIS
everted .... INSIDE OUT
every .... ALL, EACH, ENTIRE
combining form .... PANT(O)
dog has this day? .... NIGHT
　TO HOWL
everybody's unfavorite
　(Federal agency) .... IRS
everyday .... DAILY, USUAL,
　COMMON, ROUTINE, HABITUAL
everything .... ALL
slang .... THE WORKS
that .... WHATSO
everywhere .... UBIQUE, ALL
　OVER, HIGH AND LOW, ALL
　ALONG THE LINE, ALL OVER
　THE WORLD
at the same time
..... UBIQUITOUS, OMNIPRESENT
combining form .... OMNI
Eve's first son .... CAIN
husband .... ADAM
second son .... ABEL
third son .... SETH
evict .... OUST, EJECT, EXPEL, PUT
　OUT, REMOVE
evidence .... SIGN, PROOF,
　INDICATION
based on something witness
　heard .... HEARSAY
indirect .... CIRCUMSTANTIAL
indisputable ..... SMOKING GUN
evident ...... OPEN, CLEAR, PLAIN,
　PATENT, OBVIOUS, APPARENT,
　DISTINCT, MANIFEST,
　PALPABLE
evil ...... BAD, BASE, VILE, CURSE,
　WRONG, HARMFUL,
　DEPRAVITY, PECCANT,
　OFFENSIVE, DISGUSTING,
　WICKEDNESS, MALEFIC(ENT)
act .... CRIME, IMPIETY

behavior .... CORRUPTION,
　IMMORALITY
child .... IMP
colloquial .... JINX
combining form .... MAL
deed .... SIN, PECCANCY
eye .... OGLE, GLOWER,
　WHAMMY
for evil .... REVENGE,
　RETALIATION
habit .... VICE
intent .... DOLUS, MALICE
intent: law .... MALICE
　AFORETHOUGHT
looking .... GRIM, UGLY
minded ..... WICKED, NOXIOUS,
　VICIOUS, PRURIENT, SPITEFUL,
　LECHEROUS, MALICIOUS,
　SALACIOUS, BLACKHEARTED
motivation .... HATE, SPITE,
　GRUDGE, HATRED, MALICE,
　ILL-WILL, ANIMOSITY,
　ANTIPATHY
person .... BULLY, CAITIFF,
　HOODLUM, RUFFIAN, VILLAIN,
　CRIMINAL, EVILDOER,
　GANGSTER, DESPERADO,
　MISCREANT
slang .... BAD NEWS
smelling .... STINKING,
　MALODOROUS
spirit .... DEMON, FIEND,
　DAEMON, INCUBUS, SUCCUBUS,
　CACODEMON
spirit, bloodsucker
.... VAMPIRE
spirit, taken by ..... POSSESSED
spirit, woman .... HAG
spirit that feeds on flesh of
　the dead .... GHOUL
wishing .... MALIGNANT
evildoer .... SINNER, CON-MAN,
　GUN-MAN, BETRAYER,
　MURDERER, SCALAWAG,
　SWINDLER
convicted .... FELON, CRIMINAL
guilty of treason ..... TRAITOR,
　CONSPIRATOR
slang .... RAT, HOOD,
　MOBSTER, PLUG-UGLY
with snakes for hair
.... GORGON, MEDUSA
who betrayed Jesus Christ
.... JUDAS ISCARIOT
who betrayed Samson
.... DELILAH
who maliciously destroys
　property .... VANDAL
who rules oppressively
.... DESPOT, TYRANT

who turned men into swine
.... CIRCE
who willfully destroys
　property by fire
.... ARSONIST, INCENDIARY
evince .... SHOW, DISPLAY,
　EXHIBIT, SIGNIFY, INDICATE,
　MANIFEST
evincible/evincive ...... APODICTIC
eviscerate ...... GUT, DISEMBOWEL
Evita .... PERON
evitable .... AVOIDABLE
evocation ...... BIDDING, CALLING,
　SUMMONS
evoke .... CALL, DRAW, EDUCE,
　ELICIT, INVOKE, RECALL,
　REMIND, SUMMON, BRING TO
　MIND
evolution .... GROWTH, MUTATION,
　EXPANSION, DEVELOPMENT
theorist .... DARWIN, LAMARCK
theory of .... DARWINISM
theory of organic
.... LAMARCKISM
evolutionary development of
　plant or animal
.... PHYLOGENY
evolve .... EXPAND, MATURE,
　SEASON, DIG OUT, UNFOLD,
　DEVELOP, UNRAVEL, WORK
　OUT
Evreux is capital of .... EURE
ewe .... SHEEP
mate of .... RAM
-necked animal .... DOG,
　HORSE
"old" .... CRONE
udder inflammation
.... GARGET
ewer .... JUG, PITCHER
ex .... FORMER, PREVIOUS(LY)
fighter .... VET(ERAN)
＿＿＿ : from seat of authority
.... CATHEDRAL
libris .... BOOKPLATE
newscaster Newman
.... EDWIN
parte .... ONE-SIDED
post facto .... AFTER THE DEED
preposition .... WITHOUT
spouse .... DIVORCÉ(E)
TV city editor .... ASNER
exacerbate .... IRE, IRK, VEX,
　ANNOY, ENRAGE, EMBITTER,
　IRRITATE, AGGRAVATE
exact .... LEVY, TAKE, BLEED,
　CLAIM, FORCE, WRING,
　DEMAND, RIGOROUS, EXTORT,
　IMPOSE, SEVERE, STRICT,
　CORRECT, LITERAL, PRECISE,
　REQUIRE, ACCURATE

copy .... CLONE, DUPLICATE
moment .... POINT
money .... LUG
satisfaction .... AVENGE
translation .... WORD-FOR-
　　　　　　　　　　WORD
exacting ones .... PURISTS
exaction .... TAX, TOLL,
　　　　　　　　　EXTORTION
ancient .... TRIBUTE
exactitude .... ACCURACY,
　　　　　　　　　PRECISION
exactly .... TOOT, JUSTLY,
　　　　　　　　　RIGHTLY
the same words ..... VERBATIM
exaggerate .... PUFF, BOAST,
EXPAND, ENHANCE, MAGNIFY,
LAY IT ON, STRETCH,
EMBROIDER, OVERSTATE,
OVEREMPHASIZE
tendency to .... MYTHOMIA
exaggerated .... TALL, OUTRE,
STEEP, OVERDONE, EXCESSIVE,
HIGH-FLOWN, PREPOSTEROUS
comedy .... FARCE
pious feeling .... PIETISM
praise ...... PUFFERY, FLATTERY
spending .... EXTRAVAGANCE
exaggeration ...... YARN, FALSITY,
TALL TALE, DISTORTION,
OVERSTATEMENT
for effect .... HYPERBOLE
of distinguishing features
.... CARICATURE
slang .... COCK-AND-BULL
　　　　　　　　　STORY
exalt .... ELATE, EXTOL, HONOR,
RAISE, PRAISE, UPLIFT,
ELEVATE, GLORIFY
exaltation ...... ASCENT, ELATION,
RAPTURE, ELEVATION,
CONSECRATION
exalted ...... HIGH, LOFTY, NOBLE,
NOTED, TIPSY, STRONG,
EMINENT, HONORED, SUBLIME,
GLORIOUS
examination .... QUIZ, TRIAL,
INQUIRY, SCRUTINY,
TEST(ING), INSPECTION
aid .... X-RAY
colloq. .... EXAM
for uterine cancer .... PAP
　　　　　　　　　TEST
general medical ...... PHYSICAL
of dead body .... AUTOPSY,
　　　　　　　　　NECROPSY
school .... FINAL, MIDTERM
examine .... TEST, LOOK AT,
EXPLORE, INQUIRE, INSPECT
a court decision again
.... REVIEW

a job applicant ..... INTERVIEW
a person for something
concealed .... SEARCH
a witness .... QUESTION,
　　　　　　　　INTERROGATE
accounts/books .... AUDIT
by touching .... PALPATE
carefully .... SCAN
closely/in detail .... PERUSE,
　　　　　　　　SCRUTINIZE
for some specific purpose
.... REVIEW, SURVEY
judicially .... TRY
with robbery in mind
.... CASE
examiner .... EYER, CENSOR,
TESTER, INSPECTOR
books of accounts
.... AUDITOR
diagnostic .... PHYSICIAN,
　　　　　　　　RADIOLOGIST
post mortem .... CORONER
scholastic .... TEACHER,
　　　　　　　　PROFESSOR
tax .... REVENUER
example ...... CASE, COPY, MODEL,
SAMPLE, PATTERN, INSTANCE,
PARADIGM, SPECIMEN,
STANDARD, PRECEDENT,
(ARCHE)TYPE
examples, perfect .... IDEALS
set of .... PRAXIS
exasperate .... IRK, TRY, VEX,
ROIL, ANGER, ANNOY, PEEVE,
ENRAGE, NETTLE, OFFEND,
RANKLE, RUFFLE, INCENSE,
IRRITATE, INFURIATE
exasperation .... IRE, PIQUE,
ANGER, WRATH, DISGUST
excaudate .... TAILLESS
excavate .... DIG, HOE, SCOOP,
DREDGE, EXHUME, UNEARTH,
HOLLOW OUT
further .... DEEPEN
excavation .... PIT, HOLE, MINE,
SHAFT, CAVITY, HOLLOW,
QUARRY, OPENING
mining .... STOPE
excavator .... DIGGER, DREDGE(R),
　　　　　　　　SCOOP(ER)
exceed .... BEAT, PASS, EXCEL,
OUTDO, SURPASS, OUTREACH
exceedingly .... UNCO, VERY,
　　　　　　　　EXTREMELY
archaic .... AMAIN
excel .... BEST, STAR, OUTDO,
EXCEED, ECLIPSE, SURPASS,
TRANSCEND
excellence .... MERIT, VIRTU(E),
GOODNESS, PRESTIGE,
GREATNESS, SUPERIORITY

excellent ...... A-ONE, RARE, TOPS,
SUPER, PEACHY, SUPERB,
CAPITAL, RIPPING, SPLENDID,
TOPNOTCH, BRILLIANT,
OUTSTANDING
except .... BAR, BUT, OMIT, SAVE,
OBJECT, EXCLUDE
for .... ASIDE
that .... UNLESS
exception .... OMISSION,
CHALLENGE, EXCLUSION,
OBJECTION, RESERVATION
in law .... SAVING
take .... DEMUR, OBJECT,
REJECT, RESENT
exceptional .... RARE, SPECIAL,
UNUSUAL, ESPECIAL,
UNCOMMON, OUTSTANDING
excerpt .... QUOTE, SELECT,
EXTRACT, PASSAGE
excess .... EXTRA, NIMIETY,
SURFEIT, OVER(AGE),
PLETHORA, (SUR)PLUS,
REMAINDER, INTEMPERANCE
of solar over lunar year
.... EPACT
excessive .... ULTRA, UNDUE,
EXTREME, EXORBITANT,
IMMODERATE, INORDINATE,
EXTRAVAGANT
affection .... DOTAGE
combining form .... HYPER
demand .... EXACTION,
　　　　　　　　EXTORTION
formality .... RED TAPE
in belief .... RABID
joy ...... RAPTURE, EXALTATION
saliva secretion ...... PTYALISM
supply .... SPATE
vomiting .... HYPEREMESIS
zeal .... FANATICISM
excessively ...... OVERLY, UNDULY,
　　　　　　　　EXTREMELY
caustic .... ACRID
detailed report .... RED TAPE
expensive .... PROHIBITIVE
fond .... DOTING
exchange .... SWAP, BANDY,
BARTER, TRUCK, MARKET,
RIALTO, SWITCH, COMMUTE,
COMMERCE
business .... BONDS, SHARES,
STOCKS, CURRENCY
discount/fee/premium
.... AGIO
for money .... SELL
goods .... TRADE
letters .... NYSE
medium .... SYCEE
of shots .... GUNPLAY
stock .... BOURSE

visit .... GAM

exchequer .... FISC, FUNDS, FINANCES, TREASURY

excide .... CUT OUT, EXCISE, REMOVE

excise ...... TAX, DUTY, TOLL, CUT OUT, IMPOST, REMOVE, EXSCIND

tax collector .... GA(U)GER

excitable .... HOT, EDGY, FIERY, NERVOUS, HOT-HEADED

excite .... BURN, RAGE, RANT, RILE, ROIL, PIQUE, (A)ROUSE, SEETHE, STIR(UP), AGITATE, FLUSTER, PROVOKE, STARTLE, TITILLATE

excited ...... AGOG, ASTIR, HET UP, AGITATED, (A)DITHER, BOILING, BURNING, SEETHING

greatly ..... FRANTIC, FRENZIED

nervously .... FEVERISH

slang .... UPTIGHT

state .... FEY

excitement .... BUZZ, FUSS, HEAT, STIR, TO-DO, FEVER, FUROR, TIZZY, THRILL, FLUTTER, COMMOTION

pleasurable .... KICK

reducer .... SEDATIVE

exciting .... HEADY, ELECTRIC, STRIKING, THRILLING

exclaim .... SHOUT, CRY OUT, EJACULATE

exclamation .... AH, BAH, FIE, GEE, HAH, GOSH, NUTS, OH MY, POOH, PUGH, RATS, PSHAW, OUTCRY, SHUCKS, INTERJECTION

of a skeptic .... UNBELIEVABLE

of aversion/disgust .... UGH, PAH

of contempt .... BAH

of disbelief .... UMPH

of joy .... WHOOPEE

of pain .... YOW, OUCH

of praise .... HOSANNA, ADORATION

of regret .... ALAS

of sorrow .... ALACK

of success .... VOILÀ

of triumph .... EUREKA

point .... SCREAMER

to attract attention .... HEY

exclave, example of ...... PRUSSIA

exclude .... BAR, OMIT, EJECT, EXPEL, EXCEPT, REJECT, ISOLATE, BLACKLIST

by general consent .... BANISH, OSTRACIZE

from joining an organization .... BLACKBALL

from some right or privilege .... (DE)BAR

exclusion .... EXILE, BANISHMENT, QUARANTINE, SEGREGATION

exclusive .... ONLY, POSH, SOLE, CLOSED, SELECT, SINGLE

control .... MONOPOLY

of .... EX

set .... ELITE

excommunicate ...... BAN, DAMN, EXPEL, CONDEMN

excommunication .... BAN, ANATHEMA, EXCISION, CONDEMNATION

excoriate .... FLAY, CHAFE, ABRADE, DENOUNCE

excoriation .... ABUSE, ABRASION

excrement .... DUNG, FECES, MANURE, REFUSE

excrescence .... STUD, WART, APPENDAGE, OUTGROWTH

example of ..... HAIR, BUNION, FINGERNAIL

excreta .... SWEAT, URINE

excrete .... EGEST, EXUDE

excretion .... SWEAT, URINE, PERSPIRATION

excruciate .... PAIN, AGONIZE, TORMENT, TORTURE

exculpate .... CLEAR, ACQUIT, ABSOLVE, EXONERATE

excursion .... TOUR, JAUNT, JUNKET, OUTING, (SIDE)TRIP

coach .... CHARABANC

excursive .... RAMBLING, WANDERING

excusable .... VENIAL

excuse .... PLEA, ALIBI, DODGE, SALVO, ABSOLVE, APOLOGY, JUSTIFY, PRETEXT, RELEASE, OVERLOOK

for absence .... ESSOIN

partial .... EXTENUATION

excused .... IMMUNE

execrable .... HATEFUL, ABOMINABLE, DETESTABLE

execrate .... HATE, ABHOR, CURSE, DETEST, LOATHE

execute .... DO, HANG, KILL, SIGN, ENACT, FULFILL, PERFORM

unlawfully .... LYNCH

execution by burning ...... STAKE

by drowning .... NOYADE

by hanging .... SWING, HALTER, STRETCH

executioner .... HANGER, HANGMAN, HEADSMAN, DEATHSMAN

gangland's .... HITMAN, HATCHETMAN

executive .... OFFICER, OFFICIAL

privilege .... PERKS

Executive Mansion .... WHITE HOUSE

exegesis .... EXPLANATION

exemplar .... MODEL, MIRROR, EXAMPLE, PATTERN, (ARCHE)TYPE, SPECIMEN

exempt .... FREE, SPARE, EXCUSE(D), IMMUNE, RELEASE

exemption from punishment .... IMMUNITY, IMPUNITY

temporary .... GRACE

exequies .... FUNERAL, OBSEQUIES

exercise .... USE, DRILL, EXERT, TRAIN, WORRY, HARASS, LESSON, PRAXIS, PERPLEX, PROBLEM, AEROBICS, PRACTICE, EMPLOY(MENT)

exercises, athletic .... RUNNING, SWIMMING, CALISTHENICS

set of .... PRAXIS

squatting .... YOGA

trained .... MANEGE

exert .... STRAIN, STRIVE, EXERCISE, STRUGGLE

oneself to meet a challenge .... RISE TO

slang ..... BURN THE MIDNIGHT OIL

exertion .... DINT, EFFORT, ENERGY

exeunt .... EXIT

exfoliate .... PEEL, SHED, CAST OFF

exhalation .... AURA, FUME, BREATH, HALITUS, EMANATION, EXPIRATION, EVAPORATION

huge .... GIANT SIGH

exhale ...... EXPIRE, BREATHE OUT, EVAPORATE

exhaust .... FAG, TIRE, DRAIN, SPEND, USE UP, DEPLETE

exhausted .... DONE, ALL IN, EMPTY, SPENT, TIRED, EFFETE, USED UP

exhibit .... SHOW, STAGE, EXPOSE, DISPLAY, PRESENTATION

in law ...... PROOF, DOCUMENT, EVIDENCE

of difficult rides .... RODEO

exhibited .... ON VIEW

exhibiting .... SHOWING, FLAUNTING, DISPLAYING

a play of colors .... OPALESCING

exhibition .... FAIR, DISPLAY, PAGEANTRY, SPECTACLE

international .... EXPOSITION

place for historical objects .... MUSEUM

place for works of art
.... SALON, GALLERY
exhibitionist .... SHOW-OFF
exhilarate .... ELATE, PEP UP,
ANIMATE, ENLIVEN, GLADDEN,
STIMULATE
exhilaration .... ANIMATION,
LIVELINESS
exhort ...... EGG ON, PROD, URGE,
INCITE, ADMONISH
exhume .... DIG OUT, RECALL,
UNEARTH, DISINTER
exigency .... NEED, CRISIS,
DEMAND, URGENCY,
EMERGENCY
exigent .... URGENT, CRITICAL,
EXACTING, PRESSING
exiguous .... SMALL, LITTLE,
MEAGER, SCANTY
exile .... OUST, EXPEL, DEPORT,
REMOVE, RELEGATE,
BANISH(MENT), EXPATRIATE
island .... ELBA
exist .... BE, IS, ARE, (A)LIVE
existence .... ENS ESSE, LIFE,
BEING, LIVING, PRESENCE,
ACTUALITY
coming into .... NASCENT
type of .... A DOG'S LIFE
existent .... ALIVE, FACTUAL,
PRESENT
existing .... FACT, REAL, ALIVE,
EXTANT
between galaxies
.... INTERGALACTIC
exit .... ISSUE, LEAVE, EGRESS,
OUTLET, WAY OUT,
DEPART(URE)
dramatically ...... GO OUT IN A
BLAZE OF GLORY
surreptitiously .... SNEAK
exocarp .... RIND
exodus .... FLIGHT, HEGIRA,
DEPARTURE, EMIGRATION
hero .... ARI
leader .... MOSES
scene .... RED SEA
Exodus author .... URIS
exogen .... DICOTYLEDON
exogenous .... ENTHETIC
exonerate .... CLEAR, ACQUIT,
ABSOLVE, EXCULPATE
exorbitant .... DEAR, UNDUE,
EXCESSIVE, EXPENSIVE,
IMMODERATE
interest .... USURY
exorcise .... EXPEL, CAST OUT
exorcism .... EXPULSION
exordial .... INTRODUCTORY
exordium .... PROEM, PREFACE,
OPENING, OVERTURE,
BEGINNING
exoteric .... PUBLIC, POPULAR,
EXTERNAL
opposed to .... ESOTERIC
exotic .... RARE, ALIEN, VIVID,
FOREIGN, STRANGE, IMPORTED
expand .... FLAN, SWELL, DILATE,
AMPLIFY, DISTEND, ENLARGE,
INFLATE, INTUMESCE
in a way .... PAD
expanse .... SEA, AREA, OCEAN,
REACH, EXTENT, SPREAD,
BREADTH
expansion ...... GROWTH, OBESITY,
INCREASE, EXTENSION
expatiate .... RANT, DESCANT,
ENLARGE, ELABORATE
expatriate .... EXILE, BANISH,
MIGRANT
expect .... AWAIT, HOPE(FOR),
FORESEE, PREDICT, PRESUME,
ANTICIPATE
huge profits .... SEE DOLLAR
SIGNS
expectant .... ATIP, EAGER
expectantly .... WITH BATED
BREATH
expectation .... HOPE, FAITH,
BELIEF, OUTLOOK, PROSPECT
expecting ...... READY, PREGNANT
expectorant .... EMETIC,
EMETIN(E)
expectorate .... SPIT
expedience .... FITNESS
expedient .... SEEMLY, POLITIC,
FITTING, AUSPICIOUS,
CONVENIENT
expedite .... EASY, HURRY,
HASTEN, SPEED(UP),
FACILITATE
expediter: colloq. .... TICKLER
expedition .... TRIP, HASTE,
MARCH, SPEED, JOURNEY,
DISPATCH
heroic .... QUEST
hunting .... SAFARI
military .... ANABASIS
purpose .... BATTLE,
HUNT(ING), DISCOVERY,
EXPLORATION
religious .... CRUSADE
expeditious ...... EARLY, PROMPT,
SPEEDY
expel .... EMIT, OUST, EJECT,
EVICT, DRIVE OUT,
DISCHARGE
from country .... EXILE,
BANISH, DEPORT, EXPATRIATE
expellant .... EJECTOR
expend .... USE(UP), SPEND,
CONSUME, DISBURSE
expendable .... NEEDLESS,
DISPENSABLE, REPLACEABLE
expenditure .... COSTS, OUTGO,
OUTLAY, OVERHEAD
expense .... FEE, COST, CHARGE,
SACRIFICE
account: sl. .... SWINDLE
SHEET
colloquial .... DAMAGE
expensive .... DEAR, STEEP,
COSTLY, EXORBITANT
experience .... FEEL, HAVE,
UNDERGO
again in imagination
.... RELIVE
harm .... SUFFER
trying .... ORDEAL
experienced .... OLD
experiment .... TRY, TEST, TRIAL,
ATTEMPT, VENTURE
experimental .... TESTING, ON
TRIAL, TENTATIVE
plant .... PILOT
workshop .... LAB(ORATORY)
experimenter .... EMPIRICIST
expert .... ACE, PRO, DEFT, ADEPT,
SHARP, MASTER, DAB(STER),
SKILLFUL
EPA .... ECOL(OGIST)
in canon law .... DISCRETIST
in crafts/arts .... ARTISAN
in fine arts/in taste
.... CONNOISSEUR
in music .... VIRTUOSO
military .... VETERAN
on anecdotes/stories
.... RACONTEUR
on coins .... SHROFF
on figures .... CPA
on food and drinks
.... EPICURE
self-proclaimed .... MAVEN,
MAVIN
shooter .... MARKSMAN
slang .... WHIZ, WIZARD
var. .... MAVIN
expertise .... ART, KNOW-HOW,
SKIL(L)FULNESS
expertly .... ABLY, APTLY
expiate .... ATONE, REDEEM,
REPAIR, SATISFY
expiation .... AMENDS,
ATONEMENT, REPARATION
place of .... PURGATORY
expiatory .... ATONING, PIACULAR,
PURGATIVE
expiration .... END, DEATH
expire .... DIE, END, STOP, CEASE,
PERISH, RUN OUT, TERMINATE
explain .... CLEAR, SOLVE, DEFINE,
DETAIL, CLARIFY, EXPOUND,

DESCRIBE, ELUCIDATE, EXPLICATE, INTERPRET

explanation .... ANSWER, REASON, VERSION, SOLUTION, CLARIFICATION

of Biblical passage .... EXEGESIS

explanatory .... EXEGETIC(AL), CLARIFYING, GLOSSARIAL

expletive .... OATH, CURSE, EXCLAMATION

mild .... DRAT

explicable .... ACCOUNTABLE

explicate .... EXPLAIN, SPELL OUT

explicit .... CLEAR, EXACT, PLAIN, EXPRESS, PRECISE, WRITTEN, DEFINITE, SPECIFIC

explode .... POP, FIRE, BLAST, BURST, CRUMP, BLOW UP, GO OFF, DESTROY, DETONATE, DISCHARGE, DISCREDIT

exploding meteor .... BOLIS, BOLIDE

exploit .... ACT, USE, DEED, FEAT, MILK, GEST(E), ABUSE, ACTION, HEROISM, PROMOTE, UTILIZE

exploration .... QUEST

exploratory .... PRECEDING

surgery .... OPERATION

surgery on abdomen .... LAPARATOMY

surgery on chest .... THORACOTOMY

explore .... NOSE, PROBE, SEARCH, TRAVEL, EXAMINE, INVESTIGATE

explorer .... COOK, ERIC(THE RED), CABOT, LEWIS, OATES, PERRY, HUDSON, PIONEER, RALEIGH, PATHFINDER, TRAILBLAZER

first to reach the South Pole .... (ROALD)AMUNDSEN

polar .... ROSS

Venetian .... (MARCO) POLO

who conquered Mexico .... CORTES, CORTEZ

who discovered America ...... (CHRISTOPHER) COLUMBUS

who discovered Mississippi River .... DE SOTO

who discovered Philippines .... (FERDINAND) MAGELLAN

exploring admiral .... BYRD

explosion .... BLAST, BLOWUP, OUTBURST, DETONATION

explosive .... TNT, BOMB, MINE, SOUP, NITRO, AMATOL, AMYTOL, PETARD, TONITE, CORDITE, DUNNITE, LIGNOSE,

LYDDITE, CHEDDITE, DYNAMITE, ROBURITE, GUNPOWDER

charge, part of .... WARHEAD

material: prefix .... NITR

sound .... POP, BOOM, CHUG, CLAP, WHAM, DETONATION

explosives box .... CAISSON

material .... CELLULOSE

storage place .... MAGAZINE

exponent .... BACKER, SYMBOL, EXAMPLE, ADVOCATE, DEFENDER

in mathematics .... INDEX

export .... SHIP, SEND(OFF), DISPATCH, TRANSMIT

-import .... TRADE

expose .... BARE, OPEN, SHOW, REVEAL, UNMASK, UNVEIL, DISPLAY, EXHIBIT, DISCLOSE

as false ..... DEBUNK, EXPLODE

to danger .... IMPERIL

exposition .... FAIR, SHOW, EXPOSURE, EXHIBITION

expository .... EXEGETIC, EXPLANATORY

expostulate .... OBJECT, REBUKE, PROTEST, REMONSTRATE

exposure .... AIRING, AVOWAL

expound .... STATE, CLARIFY, EXPLAIN, INTERPRET, ELUCIDATE

express ...... TELL, STATE, UTTER, VOICE, EXTORT, REVEAL, SIGNIFY, EXPLICIT

a notion .... OPINE

differently .... REWORD

dissatisfaction ...... BOO, BEEF, HOOT, GRIPE, COMPLAIN

in numbers .... EVALUATE

road .... PIKE

sympathy .... CONDOLE

expression .... GRIN, LOOK, TERM, TOKEN, SAYING, WORDING, LOCUTION, INDICATION

local .... IDIOM

of agreement .... YEA

chagrin .... OOPS

contempt ...... POOH, GRUNT, SNEER, SNIFF, SNORT

disgust .... PSHAW

pain or grief .... GROAN

reproach/disapproval ..... FIE

sympathy .... CONDOLENCE

thoughts .... SPEECH

outward .... APPEARANCE

pained .... GRIMACE

underbreath .... MUTTER

villain's .... LEER

expressionless .... GLASSY

mien .... DEADPAN, POKERFACE

expressive .... ELOQUENT

action .... GESTURE

expressly .... PLAINLY, PRECISELY, DEFINITELY, ESPECIALLY, EXPLICITLY

expropriate .... DISPOSSESS

expulsion .... OUSTER, EJECTION

kind of .... DEPORTATION

expunge .... ERASE, CANCEL, DELE(TE), EFFACE, WIPE(OUT)

expurgate .... PURGE, CENSOR, PURIFY, CLEANSE, CASTRATE

exquisite .... RARE, REFINED, CHARMING, DELICATE, BEAUTIFUL, MATCHLESS, FASTIDIOUS

exsanguine .... ANEMIC

exscind .... CUT(OUT), EXCISE

exsert .... THRUST, PROTRUDE

exsiccate .... DRY, PARCH

extant .... ALIVE, EXISTING

extemporaneous .... AD LIB, OFFHAND, IMPROMPTU, IMPROVISED

extemporize .... FAKE IT, IMPROVISE

extend .... JUT, OFFER, RENEW, DEPLOY, SPREAD, PROLONG, STRETCH, CONTINUE, LENGTHEN, OUTREACH, PROTRACT

across .... SPAN

extended area .... TRACT

work leave .... SABBATICAL

extension .... SWEEP, EXPANSE, RENEWAL, ADDITION, PROJECTION

building .... ELL, WING

extent ...... AREA, SCOPE, LENGTH, MEASURE, COVERAGE, LATITUDE, MAGNITUDE

of precedence .... LEAD

utmost .... LIMIT

wide .... EXPANSE

extenuate .... LESSEN, PARDON, WEAKEN, DIMINISH, MITIGATE, PALLIATE

extenuating .... JUSTIFYING

exterior .... ECTAL, OUTER, FOREIGN, OUTSIDE, EXTERNAL, EXTRINSIC

covering .... SKIN

of an object .... SURFACE

toward the .... ECTAD

exterminate .... ABOLISH, DESTROY, ERADICATE, EXTIRPATE, ANNIHILATE

extermination .... MAYHEM, DESTRUCTION

mass .... GENOCIDE

exterminator .... NIHILIST,

DESTROYER
of vegetation .... LOCUST
external .... OUTER, EXTERIOR,
EXOTERIC, SUPERFICIAL
combining form .... ECT(O)
covering .... COAT, HIDE, PELT,
SKIN, CRUST, SHEATHE
cover of flower .... PERIANTH
world .... NONEGO
extinct .... DEAD, GONE, DEFUNCT,
OBSOLETE, EXTINGUISHED,
NON-EXISTENT
animal .... MASTODON
auto/vehicle .... EDSEL,
DESOTO
bird .... MOA, DODO, KIWI,
MAMO
elephant .... MAMMOTH
elephant-like animal
.... DINOTHERE
mammal .... GLYPTODONT
ox .... URUS
reptile .... DINOSAUR,
DINOCERAS
extinguish .... DOUSE, DOWSE,
SNUFF, PUT OUT, QUENCH,
SUBDUE, DESTROY, ECLIPSE,
SMOTHER, STAMP ON,
ERADICATE
in law .... NULLIFY
extirpate .... RAZE, UPROOT,
ABOLISH, DESTROY, EXSCIND,
ERADICATE, ANNIHILATE
extol .... LAUD, EXALT, PRAISE,
GLORIFY, COMMEND
extort .... MILK, BLEED, EXACT,
FORCE, MULCT, SCREW,
WREST, WRING, EXTRACT,
SQUEEZE
extortioner .... BLACKMAILER
extra .... ODD, OVER, SPARE,
EXCESS, SURPLUS,
ADDITIONAL
actor ...... SUPER, FIGURANT(E),
SUPERNUMERARY
asset .... PLUS
pay .... BONUS
point kicker .... TOER
extract .... DRAW, ATTAR, EDUCE,
EVOKE, WRING, DISTIL,
ELICIT, EXTORT, EXCERPT,
PULL OUT, SQUEEZE,
QUOTATION
by boiling .... DECOCT
by dissolving .... LEACH
forcibly .... EVULSE
from anything .... ESSENCE
from balsam .... TOLUENE
from plant/vegetable .... JUICE
of court record .... ESTREAT
extraction .... BIRTH, ORIGIN,

DESCENT, LINEAGE, REMOVAL
extractor, kind of .... PUMP,
CORKSCREW
extracurricular activity
.... DEBATING, ATHLETICS,
DRAMATICS
extradite .... REPATRIATE
extraneous .... ALIEN, OUTER,
EXOTIC, FOREIGN, EXTRINSIC
extraordinary .... RARE, UNCO,
GREAT, UNIQUE, NOTABLE,
UNUSUAL, UNCOMMON,
MARVELOUS, REMARKABLE,
EXCEPTIONAL
haste .... RUSH
person .... ONER
extrasensory perception ...... ESP
extravagance .... FOLLY, FRILL
extravagant .... ULTRA, BAROQUE,
PROFUSE, FANCIFUL,
PRODIGAL, WASTEFUL,
EXORBITANT
excessively .... UNREASONABLE
spending .... LAVISH
extravaganza .... REVUE,
SPECTACLE
extreme ...... LAST, FINAL, ULTRA,
ALL OUT, SEVERE, DRASTIC,
RADICAL, FARTHEST,
EXCESSIVE, IMMODERATE,
SUPERLATIVE
emotional pressure .... DURESS
hunger .... FASTING,
STARVATION
limit .... OUTRANCE
opposed to .... MEAN
unction .... SACRAMENT
unction, give .... ANELE
extremely .... UNCO, VERY,
ULTRA, HIGHLY
energetic .... BUSY AS A BEE
fertile .... RANK
fine .... SUPERB
wicked .... HEINOUS
wild .... SAVAGE, RIOTOUS
extremist .... REBEL, RADICAL,
NIHILIST
extremity ...... END, NIB, TIP, TOE,
EDGE, NEED, POLE, DYING,
POINT
extremities .... LIMBS
affliction .... GOUT
extricate .... FREE, RELEASE,
DISENGAGE
extrinsic .... ALIEN, FOREIGN,
OUTWARD, EXTERNAL,
OUTLYING, EXTRANEOUS
extrude .... EJECT, EXPEL,
PROJECT, STICK OUT
extrusive .... EJECTIVE, VOLCANIC
exuberance .... ZEST, BOUNTY,

PLENTY, GAIETY, BONANZA,
EFFUSION, ABUNDANCE
exuberant .... GAY, RANK,
GALORE, LAVISH, FERTILE,
EFFUSIVE
exudate, plant .... GUM, LAC,
RESIN
exudation .... SUDOR, SWEAT,
EMANATION, PERSPIRATION
exude .... EMIT, FLOW, LEAK,
OOZE, REEK, DRAIN, STREAM,
TRICKLE, DISCHARGE
water .... WEEP
exult .... CROW, GLOAT, GLORY,
GLORIFY, REJOICE, JUBILATE
exultant .... JUBILANT
exultation ...... ELATION, JUBILEE,
TRIUMPH
exuviae .... MOLTS, SHELLS
exuviate .... MOLT, SHED, SLOUGH,
CAST OFF
eyas .... HAWK, NESTLING
Eydie, singer .... GORME
eye .... SEE, GAZE, GLIM, LOOK,
VIEW, SIGHT, WATCH,
GLANCE, VISION, EYEBALL,
OBSERVE
abnormally small
.... MICROPHTHALMOS
aching/discomfort
.... EYESTRAIN
artificial, sometimes called
.... GLASS EYE
bean's .... HILUM
black .... MOUSE, SHINER
boldly .... OGLE, STARE
bruise under .... MOUSE,
BLACKEYE
cavity/socket .... ORBIT
central hole/opening of
.... PUPIL
coating/film .... GLAZE
colloquial .... ORB, OPTIC
colored part/membrane
.... IRIS
combining form .... OCUL(O)
congenital defect
.... ALBINISM, NYSTAGMUS
contraction of pupil
.... MYOSIS
correctional device
.... CONTACT LENS
cover .... PATCH
defect .... MYOPIA, OXYOPIA,
DIPLOPIA
dirt .... MOTE
discharge .... RHEUM
disease .... TUMOR, CATARACT,
GLAUCOMA
disorder .... SQUINT,
STRABISMUS, ASTIGMATISM,

NIGHT BLINDNESS
doctor .... OCULIST, OPHTHALMOLOGIST
drop .... TEAR
dropper .... PIPETTE
examination aid .... SNELLEN'S CHART
filler .... BEAUTY
filling .... BEAUTIFUL
-for-an-eye .... TALION, TIT FOR TAT
for detail, an .... CAREFUL, WATCHFUL
for only one ...... MONOCULAR
framer .... LASH
infection .... TRACHOMA, CONJUNCTIVITIS
inflammation .... STY, IRITIS
instrument .... ORTHOSCOPE
largest, of any living animal .... OSTRICH
lashes .... CILIA
layer .... UVEA
lazy .... AMBLYOPIA
magic .... RADAR, SONAR
main lens of .... CORNEA
of the .... OPTIC, OCULAR, VISUAL
part .... IRIS, LENS, UVEA, HUMOR, PUPIL, CORNEA, FOVEA, RETINA, SCLERA, CHOROID, OPTIC NERVE
pus .... HYPOPYON
shield .... PATCH, VISOR, BLINDER, BLINKER
simple .... OCELLUS
slang .... PEPPER, WINKER
the displays ..... WINDOW-SHOP
thing with .... STORM, NEEDLE, POTATO, TARGET, HURRICANE
wash .... EYEMO, MURINE
white of .... SCLERA
worm .... LOA
eyeball dryness .... XEROSIS
front part of outer coat .... CORNEA

main cavity of .... VITREOUS HUMOR
tough outer coat of .... SCLERA
eyebrow .... BREE
cosmetic .... MASCARA
marker .... PENCIL
eyebrows, space between .... GLABELLA
eyedrops drug .... MURINE, ESERINE
eyeful ...... STRIKING, ATTRACTIVE, SIGHT FOR SORE EYES
eyeglasses .... GLIMS, SPECS, LENSES, GOGGLES, MONOCLE, BIFOCALS, HARLEQUIN, LORGNETTE, PINCE NEZ, SPECTACLES
maker/seller of .... OPTICIAN
sidepieces .... TEMPLES
slang .... SHADES, READERS, CHEATERS
eyelash .... CILIUM, WINKER
cosmetic .... MASCARA
eyelashes .... CILIA
of .... CILIARY
eyeless .... BLIND
Eyeless in Gaza author .... HUXLEY
eyelet .... GROMMET, GRUMMET, OCELLUS, LOOPHOLE, PEEPHOLE
eyeleteer .... BODKIN, STILETTO
eyelid, corner of .... CANTHUS
cosmetic .... KOHL
drooping .... PTOSIS
inflammation .... STY, BLEPHARITIS
eyelids, of the .... PALPEBRAL
eye-opener .... SHOCKER
eyes and ears ...... SENSE ORGANS
at, make .... OGLE, FLIRT
be all .... WATCH, LOOK EAGERLY
colloquial .... SPARKLERS
cover the .... SEEL, HOODWINK,

BLINDFOLD
deep-set .... CAVERNOUS
describing some .... DOE, EVIL, GREEN, ALMOND, SHIFTY, DEEPSET, SOULFUL, SQUINT(Y)
easy on the .... PLEASANT, BEAUTIFUL, ATTRACTIVE
malalignment of the .... SQUINT, STRABISMUS
of bean .... HILA
of the .... OCULAR, VISUAL, OPTICAL
only for, have .... LOVE, WANT
poetic .... ORBS
slang .... LAMPS, DAYLIGHT
swelling .... MOUS(I)E
third .... HAW
tissue .... TARSUS
trouble .... TRACHOMA
"_____ eyes have seen . . .'' .... MINE
eyesight .... VISION
by .... OCULAR
eyesore .... UGLY
eyestalk .... STIPES
eyetooth .... FANG, CANINE, CUSPID
eyewash .... EYEMO, EXCUSE, MURINE, FLATTERY, NONSENSE, COLLYRIUM
eyewink .... HINT, SIGNAL, INSTANT
eyewitness .... OBSERVER, ONLOOKER, BYSTANDER, SPECTATOR
eyot .... AIT, ILE, ISLE(T)
eyra .... WILD CAT
eyre .... TOUR, (CIRCUIT)COURT
eyrie .... NEST, AERIE, EAGLET
Ezekiel .... PROPHET
creature in vision of .... OX, MAN, LION, EAGLE
Ezida frequenter .... NEBO
Ezra, book about .... ESDRAS

F

F grade in school .... FAILING
in a sequence/group .... SIXTH
in music .... LOUD, FORTE
in temperature .... FAHRENHEIT
is chemical symbol of .... FLUORINE
letter .... EF, EFF
letters sounding .... GH, PH
plane .... FIGHTER

f.a.s. .... FREE ALONGSIDE SHIP
fabaceous plant .... PEA
Fabian strategy .... DELAY, AVOIDANCE
Fabius, sobriquet .... CUNCTATOR, (THE)DELAYER
victim of .... HANNIBAL
fable ...... MYTH, STORY, LEGEND, FICTION, PARABLE, ALLEGORY,

APOLOG(UE), FALSEHOOD
writer .... ADE, (A)ESOP, MORALIST, PHAEDRUS
fabled .... UNREAL, MYTHICAL, LEGENDARY
being .... OGRE, DWARF, GNOME, SIREN, TITAN, TROLL, CENTAUR, MINOTAUR
bird .... ROC

fish .... MAH
fables have one .... MORAL
       LESSON
fabric .... RAG, CLOTH, ATLAS,
    TISSUE, TEXTILE, MATERIAL,
    STRUCTURE, CAMEL'S HAIR
Angora .... CAMLET, MOHAIR
any woven .... WEB
carpet .... MOQUETTE
character/quality of
  .... TEXTURE
coarse .... MAT, CRASH,
    CANVAS, DOWLAS, RATINE
corded .... REP(P), PIQUE,
              PADUASOY
cotton .... LENO, MULL,
  DENIM, MANTA, PIQUE, SCRIM,
  CALICO, DIMITY, CRETON(NE),
  MADRAS, MOREEN, MUSLIN,
  NANKIN, PENANG, NANKEEN,
              NAINSOOK
braided .... GIMP
lightweight .... ETAMINE
resembling velvet
  .... VELVETEEN
thin .... GAUZE,
             CHEESECLOTH
cravat/tie .... REP, PAISLEY
creased .... KORATRON
crinkled .... CRAPE, CREPE
curtain .... NET, SCRIM
drapery .... MOREEN
edge .... SELVAGE
fall .... WOOL
felt-like .... BAIZE
filling .... WEFT
fine woolen .... CASHMERE
floor cover .... CARPET
glazed .... CAMBRIC
glossy/lustrous .... SATIN,
               ETOILE
heavy/with raised design
  .... BROCADE
hempen .... BURLAP
jute .... BALINE
kind of .... KNIT, PRINT,
       WOOLEN, WORSTED,
  SYNTHETIC, WASH-AND-WEAR,
      PERMANENT-PRESS
knitted .... TRICOT
light wool .... ALPACA
linen .... SCRIM, DOWLAS
lining .... FLEECE, SATEEN
loose-woven .... ETAMINE
making process .... FELTING,
      WEAVING, KNITTING
merchant ..... DRAPER, MERCER
metallic .... LAME
mourning .... ALMA, CRAPE
napped .... FLEECE
net .... TULLE, MALINE

plaid .... TARTAN
printed ..... BAT(T)IK, CHALLIS,
             PERCALE
protector .... CAMPHOR
puckered .... PLISSE
resembling velvet ...... PANNE,
             TERRY
reversible .... DAMASK
rib .... WALE
ribbed .... CORD, REP(P),
      PIQUE, TWILL, TRICOT
rugs .... CHENILLE
satin .... PEKIN, ETOILE
sheer .... GAUZE, NINON,
  VOILE, BATISTE, ORGANDY,
            ORGANZA
shiny ...... SILK, SATIN, POPLIN,
      SATEEN, TAFFETA
silk .... SURAT, FAILLE,
    CHIFFON, LUSTRING,
    SARCENET, TOBINE,
  SHANTUNG, LEVANTINE,
    TAFFETA, LUTESTRING
silk, Chinese/Indian
  .... CREPE, PONGEE
silk, interwoven with gold or
  silver .... SAMITE
stiff .... WIGAN, ORGANDY
stretcher .... TENTER
striped .... DORIA, MADRAS,
  DO(O)REA, ZENANA, GALATEA,
    BAYADEER, BAYADERE
synthetic .... NYLON, RAYON,
    ACETATE, POLYESTER
threads crossing the warp in
  a .... WEFT, WOOF
threads running lengthwise
  in a .... WARP
towel .... CRASH, TERRY
twilled .... CHINO, SERGE
unwoven, made of bark
  .... TAPA
upholstery .... REP, MOREEN,
    MOHAIR, BROCATEL
veil .... LACE, TULLE
velvet ...... VELURE, VELOUR(S)
wastes .... MUNGO
watered silk/wavy patterned
  .... MOIRE
waterproof .... OILCLOTH,
         TARP(AULIN)
wax-coated .... BAT(T)IK
window shades .... HOLLAND
with fuzzy surface .... FELT
with ornamental designs
  .... LACE
woolen .... BEIGE, SERGE,
  TAMIS, ALPACA, MERINO,
  TARTAN, VICUNA, ETAMINE,
      ESTAMIN(E)

wool and cotton, napped,
  tufted .... CHINCHILLA
worsted .... SERGE, ETAMINE
woven silk .... TRICOT
woven with a pebbly pattern
  .... SHARKSKIN
fabricate .... LIE, COIN, VAMP,
  CREATE, DEVISE, INVENT,
  MAKE(UP), CONCOCT,
        CONSTRUCT
fabrication .... LIE, WEB, DECEIT,
  FIGMENT, FALSEHOOD,
      IMAGINATION
fabricator .... LIAR, MAKER,
  FIBBER, FORGER, CREATOR,
  INVENTOR, PERJURER,
       PRODUCER
forte of .... TALL TALES
fabulist .... ADE, LIAR, (A)ESOP,
  GRIMM, LA FONTAINE
fabulous .... MYTHICAL,
  LEGENDARY, IMAGINARY,
      INCREDIBLE
animal ..... CENTAUR, UNICORN
banker .... ROTHSCHILD
monster .... CHIMERA
place .... EL DORADO
serpent .... BASILISK,
      COCKATRICE
tale .... LEGEND
facade .... FACE, MASK, FRONT
main .... FRONTISPIECE
face .... MEET, BRAVE, FACET,
  PRIDE, ANSWER, FACADE,
  VISAGE, DIAL, (CON)FRONT,
  REPUTATION, COUNTENANCE
about ...... TURN TO THE RIGHT
card .... JACK, KING, QUEEN
coin's .... HEAD
colloquial .... PHIZ, BRASS,
  CHEEK, SNOOT, AUDACITY
cosmetic .... ROUGE
crease .... LINE, WRINKLE
describing some .... OVAL,
  ROUND, HEART-SHAPED
down .... LIE, PRONE, OPPOSE
expressionless .... POKER,
      DEADPAN
gem's .... FACET
guard .... MASK, VISOR,
      BEAVER
hair .... BEARD
in clubs .... BLACKJACK
obsolete .... MAZARD
of a sort .... DIAL
of rock .... BROW, CLIFF
powder .... TALCUM
slang .... MAP, MUG, PAN,
  GALL, MUSH, PUSS, CRUST,
    NERVE, KISSER
spot .... FRECKLE

the camera .... POSE
to face .... VIS-A-VIS,
TETE-A-TETE, EYEBALL-TO-
EYEBALL
value .... PAR, WORTH
with stone .... REVET
facelift(ing) .... RENOVATION
benefit? .... NO SAG
facet .... PANE, BEZEL, BEZIL,
CULET, PHASE, ASPECT,
COLLET, FLANGE
facetious .... DROLL, WITTY,
JOCOSE, COMICAL, JOCULAR
person .... WAG, JESTER,
HUMORIST
facetiousness .... WIT
facial adornment .... BEARD,
GOATEE, VANDYKE, IMPERIAL,
MUSTACHE, MUSTACHIO
expression .... GRIN, LEER,
PHIZ, POUT, SCOWL, SMILE,
SMIRK, GRIMACE
paralysis .... BELL'S PALSY
facile .... DEFT, EASY, ADROIT,
FLUENT, AFFABLE
facilitate ...... EASE, HELP, CLEAR,
SMOOTH, FURTHER, QUICKEN
facility ...... EASE, KNACK, MEANS,
SKILL, FLUENCY, DEXTERITY,
CONVENIENCE
facing .... LINER, LINING,
TOWARD, FORNENT, TRIMMING
glacier .... STOSS
inward .... INTRORSE
facsimile .... COPY, REPLICA,
LIKENESS, REPRODUCTION
fact .... FIAT, DATUM, TRUTH,
REALITY, ACTUALITY, NOT A
DREAM, CERTAINTY
of knowing .... KNOWLEDGE
state as a .... AVER, POSIT
faction .... BLOC, SECT, SIDE,
CABAL, CLASH, JUNTO,
CLIQUE, DISCORD, DISSENSION
factional .... PARTISAN
division .... SPLIT, SCHISM,
SPLINTER
factious .... DIVISIVE, PARTISAN,
SEDITIOUS, CONTENTIOUS
factitious .... FORCED, ARTIFICIAL
factor .... PART, AGENT, BASIS,
BROKER, ELEMENT,
CONDITION
biological .... GENE
factory .... MILL, PLANT,
INDUSTRIAL ESTABLISHMENT
country .... HACIENDA
factotum .... AGENT, DO-ALL,
SERVANT, HANDYMAN
facts .... DATA, DETAILS, LOW-
DOWN

slang .... THE DOPE, THE
SCORE
factual .... REAL, TRUE, ACTUAL
facultative .... OPTIONAL,
CONTINGENT
faculty .... KNACK, POWER, SENSE,
TALENT, ABILITY, APTITUDE
of apt expression ..... FELICITY
fad .... MODE, CRAZE, HOBBY,
STYLE, VOGUE, MEGRIM,
FASHION
fade ...... DIM, PALE, PEAK, WANE,
DIE(OUT), WILT, DROOP,
BLEACH, WHITEN, WITHER,
LANGUISH
from sight .... VANISH,
EVANESCE, DISAPPEAR
out .... END, DISSOLVE
faded .... DRAB, DULL, WORN,
DIMMED, WEATHERED,
DISCOLORED
fading .... DYING, EBBING,
WANING, FUGITIVE,
DWINDLING
of fame .... ECLIPSE
quickly .... EVANESCENT,
EVAPORATING
fado .... FOLKSONG
Faerie Queen .... MAB, UNA
character .... ALMA, TALUS,
AMORET, ACRASIA
Fafnir's brother .... REGIN
slayer .... SIGURD
fag .... TIRE, SLAVE, WEARY,
EXHAUST, FATIGUE, PLODDER,
WORKHORSE, DRUDGE(RY),
HOMOSEXUAL
end .... BUTT, RUCK, RUMP,
STUB, STUMP, REMNANT
slang .... CIGARETTE
fagaceous plant .... OAK, BEECH,
CHESTNUT
fagot .... SEW, FASCINE
faience ...... POTTERY, PORCELAIN
fail .... EBB, FLOP, MISS, FLUNK,
PETER OUT, FIZZLE, DEFAULT,
COLLAPSE, MISCARRY
as a motor .... CONK OUT
in duty .... SHIRK, REMISS
in health .... LANGUISH
to catch .... MUFF, FUMBLE
to follow suit .... RENIG,
RENEGE, FAINAIGUE
utterly .... GO TO THE WALL
failing .... FAULT, DEFECT, FOIBLE,
FRAILTY, WEAKNESS
failure .... DUD, LOSS, LAPSE,
(DOWN)FALL, OMISSION,
BREAKDOWN
absolute .... BOMB
colloquial .... BUST, LEMON

complete .... RUIN, CRASH,
FIASCO, WASHOUT,
BANKRUPTCY
in electric power ...... OUTAGE
slang .... BOMB, FLOP, TURKEY
to pay/to prosecute
.... DEFAULT
fain .... GLAD(LY), EAGER, READY,
WILLING, DESIROUS
faineant .... IDLE, LAZY, OTIOSE
faint ...... DIM, WAN, PALE, WEAK,
SWOON, TIMID, FEEBLE, PASS
OUT, SWOUND, UNCLEAR
fainthearted .... TIMID,
COWARDLY
fainting .... SYNCOPATION
fit .... SWOON, SYNCOPE
fair .... EVEN, JUST, COMELY,
BAZA(A)R, DECENT, KERMIS,
LOVELY, PRETTY, SERENE,
AVERAGE, CARNIVAL,
FESTIVAL, HANDSOME,
UNBIASED, BEAUTIFUL,
IMPARTIAL, EXHIBITION,
EXPOSITION
complexion .... LIGHT
game .... DUPE, CHANCE,
TARGET, VICTIM
haired .... PET, BLOND(E),
FAVORITE
place .... BOOTH, STALL,
PAVILION
play .... SQUARE DEAL
portion .... CHUNK
sex .... WOMAN, FEMALE
shake .... TOSSUP
spoken .... GLIB, BLAND,
POLITE, SMOOTH
to middling .... SO-SO,
MODERATE, PASSABLE
weather .... CLEAR, SUNNY,
SUNSHINE, CLOUDLESS
Fairbanks native .... ALASKAN
fairest ...... FLAWLESS, LOVELIEST,
FLOWERLIKE
fairly ...... DULY, FITTING, JUSTLY,
ABOVEBOARD
fairness .... EQUITY, JUSTICE,
JUSTNESS
fairy .... ELF, FAY, ELVE, PERI,
PUCK, PIXY, PIXIE, SPRITE,
HOBGOBLIN, LEPRECHAUN,
TINKERBELL
air .... SYLPH
fort/abode .... LIS(S), SHEE
king .... OBERON
lake dweller .... MORGAN(LE
FAY)
like .... ELFIN
Midsummer Night's Dream
.... COBWEB

259

queen ...... MAB, UNA, TITANIA
Slavonic .... VILA
story .... LIE, MYTH, TALE,
    FABLE, MARCHEN, ALLEGORY
tale character .... SANDMAN
tale monster .... OGRE
wood .... NYMPH
faith .... CULT, DOXY, CREED,
    DOGMA, TROTH, TRUST,
    BELIEF, LOYALTY, RELIANCE,
    RELIGION
archaic .... FAY
article of .... TENET
bad .... DECEIT, DUPLICITY,
    DISHONESTY
good .... CANDOR, SINCERITY
healer, kind of .... QUACK
matters of .... CREDENDA
of .... PIETISTIC
faithful .... FAST, TRUE, EXACT,
    TRIED, LIEGE, LOYAL,
    DEVOUT, HONEST, DEVOTED,
    CONSTANT, STA(U)NCH,
    LIFELIKE, RELIABLE
friend .... DAMON, ACHATES,
    PYTHIAS
poetic .... LEAL
servant .... SERF, HELOT,
    SLAVE, YES-MAN
faithfully .... EXACTLY, STRICTLY,
    OBEDIENTLY
faithless .... FALSE, UNTRUE,
    DISLOYAL, INCONSTANT,
    PERFIDIOUS, TRAITOROUS
faitour .... ROGUE
fake .... SHAM, BOGUS, CHEAT,
    FALSE, FRAUD, TRICK,
    PHONEY, UNREAL, SPURIOUS,
    COUNTERFEIT
attack .... FEINT
colloquial ..... FEIGN, IMITATE,
    PRETEND
jewelry: colloq.
    .... BRUMMAGEN
faker .... FRAUD, HOAXER,
    HUMBUG, IMPOSTOR,
    SWINDLER
kind of .... QUACK,
    MALINGERER
fakir .... MONK, YOGI, SWAMI,
    BEGGAR, DERVISH,
    MENDICANT
falbala .... FRILL, RUFFLE,
    FLOUNCE, FURBELOW
falcate .... CURVED, HOOKED
falchion .... SWORD
falcon .... HAWK, SAKER, CANNON,
    LUGGER, MERLIN, PEREGRINE,
    LANNER(ET), WINDHOVER,
    SPARROW-HAWK
Asian .... LAGGAR

close eyes of .... SEEL
E. Indian .... BESRA
European .... HOBBY, SAKER,
    KESTREL
eye-blinder .... HOOD, SEEL
female .... LANNER
headed deity ..... RA, MENT(U)
India .... LAGGER, SHAHIN
leg-strap .... JESS
male .... TERCEL, LANNERET
peregrine .... DUCK-HAWK
repair wing of .... IMP
small .... MERLIN, KESTREL
swoop of .... SOUSE
use of .... HUNTING
falconer .... HAWKER
falconer's decoy .... LURE
falconry .... HAWKING
falderal .... GEWGAW, TRIFLE,
    NONSENSE
fall .... DROP, PLOP, RUIN, SLIP,
    PLUNK, SLUMP, SPILL,
    AUTUMN, LITTER, PLUNGE,
    TUMBLE, DESCEND, PLUMMET,
    DECREASE
apart .... BREAK, COLLAPSE
back .... RECEDE, RELAPSE,
    RETREAT
behind .... LAG
"classic" .... WORLD SERIES
flat: sl. .... BOMB
forward .... TOPPLE
from grace/virtue .... LAPSE
guy: sl. .... DUPE, LOSER,
    PATSY, SCAPEGOAT
headlong .... PITCH
heavily .... THUD
in .... AGREE, LINE UP
in drops .... DRIP, RAIN,
    DRIB(BLE), TRICKLE
in line .... FILE
into place .... FORM, COME
    TOGETHER
mortally wounded .... BITE
    THE DUST
on evil days .... GO TO THE
    DOGS
on one's knees .... APOLOGIZE,
    KNEEL, GENUFLECT
out .... SHED, QUARREL
short/through ..... FAIL, CRASH
to .... START, LAUNCH
to pieces .... CRUMBLE,
    DISINTEGRATE
upon .... BESET
fallacious .... DECEPTIVE,
    ERRONEOUS
notion .... IDOLISM
fallacy .... ERROR, IDOLA, IDOLUM,
    MISTAKE, DECEPTION
fallal .... FINERY, FRIPPERY

fallen .... DEAD, DROPPED,
    SILENCED, DEGRADED,
    PROSTRATE
angel .... LOST SOUL,
    RECIDIVIST
fallible .... FISHY, DOUBTFUL
falling .... CADENT
_____ .... DOMINOES THEORY
out .... RIFT, QUARREL
over .... TOPPLE
sickness .... EPILEPSY
star .... METEOR
Fallopian tube .... OVIDUCT,
    SALPINX
fallout .... ATOM BLAST,
    CONTAMINATION,
    RADIOACTIVITY
effect .... AIR POLLUTION
particles .... SNOW, SLEET,
    (COSMIC)DUST
fallow .... BARREN, USELESS,
    UNTILLED
deer .... TEG, DAMA
false .... FAKE, SHAM, BOGUS,
    WRONG, FORGED, HOLLOW,
    UNTRUE, EVASIVE, MISTAKEN,
    SPURIOUS, FAITHLESS,
    UNFOUNDED, ARTIFICIAL,
    MENDACIOUS
belief .... DELUSION
entry .... RINGER
excuse .... RUSE, EVASION,
    PRETEXT, SUBTERFUGE
face .... MASK, DISGUISE
friend .... IAGO, JUDAS,
    TRAITOR, TWO-TIMER
front .... BLUFF, DUMMY
god .... BAAL, IDOL
gossip .... TALE
hair .... PERUKE, TOUPEE,
    (PERI)WIG
jewelry .... PASTE,
    BRUMMAGEN
move .... SLIP, MISSTEP
name .... ALIAS, ANONYM,
    AKA, PSEUDONYM
prefix .... PSEUDO
pretense .... AFFECTATION
reasoning .... IDOLISM
report/rumor .... HOAX,
    CANARD, HODGEPODGE,
    EXAGGERATION
seed cover .... ARILLODE
show .... MAGIC, MASQUERADE
show, make .... FEIGN
show to be .... DEBUNK,
    DISPROVE
step .... TRIP, STUMBLE
story .... YARN, FICTION,
    FUDGE, FARRAGO, TALL TALE
swearing .... PERJURY

teeth .... DENTURE
wing .... ALULA
witness .... LIAR, PERJURER
falsehood .... FIB, LIE, FLAM,
TALE, FABLE, LYING, CANARD,
FICTION, FORGERY, PERJURY,
DECEPTION, UNTRUTH,
PRETENSE, INVENTION,
FABRICATION
colloquial .... BUNK, FRONT
slang .... BLUFF,
FOURFLUSHING
falsies: colloq. .... PADS
falsify .... FIB, FAKE, (BE)LIE,
ALTER, COLOR, FORGE,
GARBLE, PAD(THE BILL),
DISTORT, MISQUOTE
Falstaff's man .... PETO
falter .... HAW, WAVER, FLINCH,
TOTTER, STAMMER, STUMBLE,
HESITATE, VACILLATE
fama .... RUMOR
fame ...... HONOR, GLORY, KUDOS,
NAME, STAR, ECLAT,
RENOWN, REPUTE, PRESTIGE,
REPUTATION
kind of .... NOTORIETY
partner of .... FORTUNE
famed .... NOTED, FAMOUS,
EMINENT, NOTABLE, REPUTED,
NOTORIOUS, CELEBRATED,
WELL-KNOWN
fly catcher .... STAN MUSIAL
Fameuse .... APPLE
familiar .... BOLD, CLOSE,
BRAZEN, COMMON, FORWARD,
VERSANT, ASSUMING,
FRIENDLY, INTIMATE,
ORDINARY
De's .... FOE, NIRO, VITO
for Ann .... NAN
lion .... LEO, MGM
Mac's .... LEOD, LAINE,
MAHON, DONALD, MILLAN,
MURRAY
Mc's .... COY, CREA, CLURE,
ENROE, CARTHY, DOWALL,
KINLEY, AULIFFE, CORMACK,
CORMICK
negative .... AREN'T
O's .... BRIEN, NEILL, TOOLE,
CONNOR
saying .... MOT, SAW, TAG,
ADAGE, MOTTO
sign .... SRO, OPEN, CLOSED,
NO VACANCY, HELP WANTED,
NO LOITERING, BEWARE OF
DOG, NO ADMITTANCE, NO
SOLICITING
Van's .... DYKE, CLEEF,
DEVERE, PATTEN

familiarity .... INTIMACY,
KNOWLEDGE, CORDIALITY
familiarize .... ACQUAINT,
ACCUSTOM
families, quarrel between
.... FEUD
family .... ILK, KIN, CLAN, LINE,
RACE, BREED, GROUP, STOCK,
TRIBE, KINDRED, KINSFOLK,
HOUSEHOLD
acting .... FONDAS
ancient .... DORIA
auto/car .... SEDAN
branch .... STEM, STIRPS
car: colloq. .... BUS
diagram .... TREE
famous .... ESTE, SOONG,
MEDICI, KENNEDY,
ROTHSCHILD, ROCKEFELLER
golfing .... SNEADS
life .... FIRESIDE
meal .... POTLUCK
name .... SURNAME,
COGNOMEN, PATRONYMIC
next door .... NEIGHBOR
of flies .... EMPIDAE
of marine worms
.... NEREIDAE
of spies .... WALKER
pertaining to .... LINEAGE,
DOMESTIC, FAMILIAL
Renaissance ...... ESTE, MEDICI
theatrical .... FOYS
tree .... PEDIGREE
famine ...... HUNGER, STARVATION
famish .... PINCH, STARVE,
EXHAUST
famous .... GRAND, NOTED,
EMINENT, NOTABLE, POPULAR,
RENOWNED, CELEBRATED,
WELL-KNOWN
anthropologist .... MEAD
Arab surgeon ..... ABUL KASIM
aunt .... MAME
ballet .... SWAN LAKE
beachhead .... ANZIO
clergyman .... PEALE
date .... D-DAY
department store maker
.... WANA
diamond .... KOH-I-NOOR
epithet in baseball .... YANKEE
CLIPPER
friend .... DAMON, ACHATES,
PYTHIAS
lake resort .... TAHOE
London Guildhall effigy
.... GOG
murderer .... ARAM, CAIN,
BOOTH, BUNDY, OSWALD
orphan .... ANNIE

postmaster .... JIM FARLEY
ship captain .... NOAH
ski resort .... VAIL, ASPEN
tower .... PISA, BABEL
trio member .... ATHOS,
ARAMIS, PORTHOS
ultimatum reply .... NUTS
unfavorably .... NOTORIOUS
Variety headline ..... HIX-NIX=
STIX-PIX
violin maker .... AMATI
Wagnerian singer ..... LAURITZ
MELCHIOR
Yankees' late Number 7
.... MANTLE
famously .... ROYALLY
famulus ...... SERVANT, ASSISTANT
fan .... BLOW, BUFF, COOL,
EXCITE, FOMENT, ROOTER,
VOTARY, ZEALOT, ADMIRER,
DEVOTEE, AFICIONADO,
ENTHUSIAST
form .... PLICATE
of leaves .... TALIPOT
oriental .... PUNKA(H)
palm .... PALMETTO
Pope's .... FLABELLUM
shaped .... FLABELLATE
slang .... ADDICT
fanatic .... NUT, BIGOT, JINGO,
RABID, ZEALOT, PARTISAN,
BELIEVER, DOGMATIST,
PHRENETIC
murderous .... AMOK, THUG,
BERSERK
fanatical .... FIERY, RABID,
RADICAL, ZEALOUS
fanaticism ...... MANIA, BIGOTRY,
ZEAL(OTRY)
fancied .... UNREAL, IMAGINED,
CONCOCTED, IMAGINARY
fear .... BOG(E)Y, BUGABOO
fancier, kind of .... GOURMET,
GOURMAND, CONNOISSEUR
fanciful .... ODD, AIRY, ANTIC,
AERIAL, QUAINT, UNREAL,
BIZARRE, ILLUSORY,
IMAGINARY, WHIMSICAL,
FANTASTIC, IMAGINATIVE
fancy .... FAD, IDEA, WEEN, WHIM,
DREAM, SHOWY, NOTION,
MEGRIM, ORNATE, VISION,
CAPRICE, DELUSION, ILLUSION
add-on .... FRILL
dive .... SWAN, GAINER,
HEADER
foolish .... CHIMERA
passing .... MOOD
slang .... FLOSSY
fancy-free .... CAREFREE,
UNCHAINED

fandango .... DANCE

fane .... CHURCH, SHRINE, TEMPLE,
SANCTUARY

fanfare .... TANTARA, FLOURISH

fanfaron .... BRAGGART

fang .... CLAW, TUSK, TALON,
CUSPID, EYETOOTH, CANINE
TOOTH

fanlight .... TRANSOM

Fannie, writer .... HURST

fanny: sl. .... BUTTOCKS

fanon ...... VANE, ORALE, MANIPLE

fantail .... PIGEON, GOLDFISH

fantasia .... MEDLEY, CAPRICE

fantast ...... DREAMER, VISIONARY

fantastic .... ODD, UNREAL,
BIZARRE, STRANGE,
FABULOUS, WONDROUS,
ECCENTRIC, GROTESQUE,
REMARKABLE, OUTLANDISH

imitation .... PARODY,
TRAVESTY

style .... OUTRE, RACOCO,
BAROQUE

fantasy .... FANCY, WHIMSY,
CAPRICE, ROMANCE, ILLUSION,
PHANTASM, (DAY)DREAM,
MAKE-BELIEVE

far .... TEL, AWAY, REMOTE,
YONDER, DISTANT,
ADVANCED, OUT OF THE WAY

above average .... SUPER

and near .... EVERYWHERE

and wide .... ABROAD

apart .... UNLIKE, DIFFERENT,
DISPARATE

arear .... TAILENDER

combining form .... TELE

cry .... LONG WAY

down/below the surface
.... DEEP

eastern .... ORIENTAL

go .... LAST LONG

left and far right
.... EXTREMES

off .... REMOTE, DISTANT

reaching .... WIDE, BROAD

farce .... MIME, SKIT, EXODE,
COMEDY, PARODY, MOCKERY,
DROLLERY, TRAVESTY,
BURLESQUE

farceur/farceuse .... WAG,
CLOWN, COMEDIAN, JOKER,
JESTER, HUMORIST

farcical .... COMIC, FUNNY,
ABSURD, LUDICROUS,
SLAPSTICK, RIDICULOUS

farcy .... GLANDERS

fardel .... PACK, BUNDLE, BURDEN

fare .... EAT, PAY, DIET, DINE,
FOOD, LUCK, MENU, GET ON,

RESULT, THRIVE, PASSAGE,
OUTCOME, PROSPER,
PASSENGER

farewell .... LAST, VALE, PARTING,
VALEDICTION, LEAVE-TAKING

appearance .... SWANSONG

drink .... STIRRUP-CUP

formal .... CONGE

party .... SEND-OFF

retirement gift .... GOLD
WATCH

word(s) ..... AVE, ADIEU, CIAO,
ADIOS, ALOHA, SO LONG,
BYEBYE, CHEERIO, GOODBYE,
SHALOM, GODSPEED,
ARRIVEDERCI, SAYONARA, AUF
WIEDERSEHEN

farfetched ...... FORCED, REMOTE,
DOUBTFUL, STRAINED,
UNLIKELY

farflung .... WIDE, BROAD,
SWEEPING

farina ...... MEAL, FLOUR, STARCH

farinaceous .... MEALY,
POWDERY, STARCHY

drink .... PTISAN

farinose .... MEALY

farm .... TILL, TORP, RANCH,
GRANGE, HACIENDA,
CULTIVATE

building/structure .... BARN,
SHED, SILO

feature .... COW, HEN, PIG,
DUCK, GOOSE, CHICKEN

grazing .... RANCH(O)

implement .... PLOW, FLAIL,
HARROW, TEDDER

kind of .... DAIRY, OYSTER

machine .... CHURN, REAPER,
SEEDER, TEDDER, PLANTER,
TRACTOR, SCARIFIER

measure .... ACRE

of a .... VILLATIC

small/worked by renter
.... CROFT

tenant .... COTTER, CROFTER

vehicle, large heavy-wheeled
.... WAIN

worker .... HIND, ORRAMAN,
PLOWMAN, CAMPESINO

yard .... BARTON

farmer .... RYOT, SOWER, TILLER,
CROPPER, GRANGER, PEASANT,
PLANTER, HABITAN(T),
HUSBANDMAN

future .... AGGIE

migrant .... OKIE

peasant .... CROFTER

farmers' weather prophet
.... ALMANAC

farmhouse, land nearest
.... INFIELD

farming .... HUSBANDRY,
AGRICULTURE

farmland .... ARABLE LAND,
ACREAGE

faro card .... SODA

form of .... MONTE

Faroes whirlwinds .... OES

farrago .... OLIO, JUMBLE,
MEDLEY, MIXTURE

Farrar, soprano ...... GERALDINE

farrier .... BLACKSMITH,
VETERINARY, VETERINARIAN

farrow .... PIG, LITTER

farseeing .... PROVIDENT

farsighted .... HYPERMETROPIC

one .... SEER, PROPHET

farsightedness .... HYPEROPIA

farther .... BEYOND, REMOTER

India .... INDO-CHINA

farthest ...... ENDMOST, ULTIMATE

back .... REAR, HINDMOST

colloquial ...... GOD-FORSAKEN

fasces carrier .... LICTOR

fascia .... STRIP, FILLET,
BAND(AGE)

fascicle .... CLUSTER

fascinate .... CHARM, ALLURE,
ATTRACT, BEWITCH,
ENCHANT, INTRIGUE,
CAPTIVATE

fascination .... CHARM, SPELL,
WONDER, OBSESSION,
ATTRACTION

fascism .... NAZISM, DESPOTISM,
FALANGISM, DICTATORSHIP

Fascist .... NAZI, FALANGIST

leader .... RAS, FRANCO,
HITLER, MUSSO(LINI)

mayor .... PODESTA

organization in Spain
.... FALANGE

theoretician .... PARETO

fash: Scot. .... VEX, ANNOY,
TROUBLE

fashion .... CUT, FAD, FORM,
KIND, MAKE, MODE, MOLD,
RAGE, SORT, CRAZE, SHAPE,
STYLE, VOGUE, DESIGN,
MANNER, METHOD

designer/VIP .... DIOR,
ADOLFO, CHANEL, NORELL,
BALMAIN, CASSINI, BERGDORF,
GIVENCHY, GERNREICH, ST.
LAURENT, VALENTINO,
BALENCIAGA, MAINBOCHER

figure .... MODEL, CUTTER,
TAILOR, MODISTE, DESIGNER

maker .... TRENDSETTER

model .... TWIGGY, CINDY

CRAWFORD, CHERYL TIEGS, NAOMI CAMPBELL, CLAUDIA SCHIFFER, CHRISTIE BRINKLEY, LINDA EVANGELISTA, PAULINA PORIZKOVA

news .... MAXI, MINI, HEMLINE, NECKLINE

past .... MINISKIRT

plate .... DUDE, DANDY, BEAU(BRUMMELL)

fashionable .... NEW, CHIC, POSH, NOBBY, RITZY, SLEEK, SMART, SWISH, TONEY, DRESSY, MODISH, ALAMODE, STYLISH

gathering .... SALON

society .... BONTON

Fashoda, Sudan town .... KODOK

fast .... DIET, FIRM, APACE, AGILE, FLEET, HASTY, QUICK, RAPID, SWIFT, PRESTO, RAKISH, SECURE, SPEEDY, STARVE, ABSTAIN, DEVOTED, EXPRESS

and loose .... ADRIFT, SHIFTY

break goal .... LAY-UP

combining form .... TACHY

driver .... JEHU

fellow .... SPRINTER

movement .... TANTIVY

plane .... SST

talk .... BLARNEY, GLIB TONGUE

time .... DAYLIGHT-SAVING

fasten .... FIX, TIE, ZIP, BIND, LASH, ROPE, CLOSE, ATTACH, TETHER, CONNECT

boat .... BERTH

firmly ...... NAIL, CHAIN, INFIX, RIVET, SECURE

in a way .... GLUE, PASTE

nautical .... BELAY, BATTEN

fastener .... BITT, CLIP, HASP, SNAP, CLAMP, CLASP, CLEAT, STRAP

slide .... ZIPPER

wire .... STAPLE

wood .... NOG, PEG, PIN

fastening ...... BOLT, LOCK, GLUE, CATCH, CLASP, LATCH, TACH(E), BUCKLE, BUTTON, HOOK(AND EYE)

fastidious .... NICE, PRIM, CHARY, FUSSY, DAINTY, QUEASY, PICKY, FINICAL, FINICKY, PRECISE, CHOOSY, REFINED, CRITICAL, TASTEFUL, PER(S)NICKETY

fastigiate .... CONELIKE

fasting .... ABSTINENCE

period .... LENT, RAMADAN, RAMAZAN

fastness .... STRONGHOLD

fat .... OILY, DUMPY, ESTER, FLAB, GROSS, LARDY, OBESE, PLUMP, PORKY, PUDGY, PUFFY, PURSY, STOUT, THICK, CHUBBY, FLESHY, PORTLY, PINGUID, CORPULENT

and squat .... FUBSY, ROLY-POLY

animal .... LARD, ADEPS, GREASE, TALLOW, ADIPOSE

beef/mutton .... SUET, TALLOW

cat: sl. .... RICH MAN, MILLIONAIRE

chance: sl. .... HOPELESS, NOTHING DOING

chew the .... GAB, CHAT

combining form ..... STEAT(O)

decomposition of .... LIPOLYSIS

hog .... LARD

in butter .... OLEO

in cow's milk .... GHEE

like .... LIPIDE, LIPOID, STEARIC, LIPAROID, UNCTUOUS, UNGUENT(OUS)

liquid part .... OLEIN

lot .... NIX, NOTHING

of .... RICH, FATTY, OLEIC, ADIP(O), ADIPIC, GREASY, TALLOWY, BLUBBERY

of the land .... WEAL, LUXURY, PLENTY

person: sl. ...... BLIMP, TUB(OF LARD), FATSO, HIPPO, HEAVYWEIGHT

refuse (from cooking) .... SLUSH

roasting meat ...... DRIPPING(S)

solid part of .... STEARIN(E)

whale .... BLUBBER

wool .... SUINT, LANOLIN

yielding tree .... SHEA

Fat Tuesday .... MARDI GRAS

Fata Morgana .... FAIRY, MIRAGE

fatal .... FEY, FERAL, VITAL, DEADLY, FUNEST, LETHAL, MORTAL, FATEFUL, RUINOUS, SERIOUS, CRITICAL

fatality .... DEATH, ACCIDENT, CASUALTY, DEADLINESS

fate .... LOT, DOOM, KISMET, DESTINY, FORTUNE, PORTION

Eighteenth Amendment's .... REPEAL

of the USS Missouri .... RECOMMISSIONED

twist of .... IRONY

unhappy .... DOOM, DAMNATION

Fate, mythological .... NONA, MORTA, NORNS, URDUR,

CLOTHO, PARCAE, DECUMA, ATROPOS, LACHESIS

fated .... FEY, DOOMED, DESTINED, ORDAINED

fateful .... DIRE, BANEFUL, OMINOUS, DECISIVE, PROPHETIC

Fates, one of the .... NONA, MORTA, NORNS, SKULD, URDUR, CLOTHO, DECUMA, PARCA(E), ATROPOS, LACHESIS

whichever one .... WEIRD

fathead ...... CLOD, DUNCE, IDIOT, STUPID

fatheaded .... DULL, DOPEY, OBTUSE, STUPID

father .... ABBA, PAPA, SIRE, BEGET, PATER, PARENT, PRIEST, CREATOR, FOUNDER, ANCESTOR, FOREBEAR, PROTECTOR

Arabic .... ABU, ABOU

brother of .... UNCLE

colloquial .... PA, DAD, POP, DADDY, PAPPY, OLDMAN

combining form .... PATRI, PATRO

dialectic .... PAW

disciples' .... ZEBEDEE

of all .... JUBAL

of American football .... CAMP

of gods .... ZEUS

of History .... HERODOTUS

of hypnotism .... MESMER

of Medicine ...... HIPPOCRATES

of the Titans .... URANUS

of the U.S. Constitution .... MADISON

of the waltz .... STRAUSS

of Waters .... MISSISSIPPI

pertaining to a .... AGNATE, PATERNAL

relative on side of .... AGNATE

superior .... ABBOT

fathered .... SIRED

fatherhood .... PATERNITY

fatherless .... ORBATE

fatherly .... PARENTAL

fathom .... DELVE, PLUMB, PROBE, SOUND

one fourth of .... QUARTER

fatigue .... FAG, BORE, JADE, TIRE, WEARY, EXHAUST, WEARINESS

clothes .... DENIM

Fatima descendant ...... SAY(Y)ID

descended from .... FATIMID, FATIMITE

father of .... MOHAMMED

husband of .... BLUEBEARD

sister of .... ANNE, JINNAH

step-brother of .... ALI
fatling ...... KID, PIG, CALF, LAMB
fats, having strong attraction for
.... LIPOPHILIC
solvent for .... ETHER
Fats's assertion of song
.... AIN'T MISBEHAVING
fatten .... FEED, NURSE, STUFF,
BATTEN, ENRICH
land .... FERTILIZE
fatty ...... OILY, GREASY, ADIPOSE,
LIPAROID, ALIPHATIC
acid .... ADIPIC, VALERIC
combining form .... LIP(O)
comedian .... ARBUCKLE
liquid .... OLEIN
organic compound .... LIPID
secretion of gland ...... SEBUM
substance from sheep's wool
.... SUINT
substance in decomposed
bodies .... ADIPOCERE
tumor .... LIPOMA
fatuity .... FOLLY, IDIOCY,
STUPIDITY, IMBECILITY
fatuous .... VAIN, INANE, INEPT,
SILLY, ASININE, FOOLISH
slang .... DUMB, SAPPY
faubourg .... SUBURB
fauces .... GULLET, THROAT
faucet .... TAP, BIBB, SPILE,
SPOUT, SPIGOT, (BIB)COCK,
PETCOCK, STOPCOCK
dance .... TAP
flow regulator .... VALVE
leak .... DRIP
fault .... FLAW, LACK, SLIP,
ERROR, LAPSE, DEFECT,
FAILING, BLEMISH, MISDEED,
MISTAKE, WEAKNESS,
IMPERFECTION
amusing .... FOIBLE
antonym of .... VIRTUE
find .... NAG, CARP, CAVIL,
KNOCK, CENSURE, LECTURE,
UPBRAID, COMPLAIN, CRITICIZE
moral .... VICE
slight/trifling ...... PECCADILLO
faultfinder ...... MOMUS, CENSOR,
CRITIC, NAG(GER), KNOCKER,
SCOLDER
faultfinding .... CARPING,
CHIDING, CAPTIOUS,
CAVILING, CRITICAL,
QUERULOUS
faultless .... IDEAL, MODEL,
CORRECT, PARAGON, PERFECT,
FLAWLESS, IMPECCABLE
faulty .... AMISS, PECCANT,
DEFECTIVE, ERRONEOUS
faun .... DEITY, SATYR

fauna's life partner .... FLORA
Fauntleroy .... ERROL, CEDRIC
mother of .... DEAREST
Faunus .... PAN
son .... ACIS
Faure, essayist .... ELIE
Faust, composer of ...... GOUNOD
poem, writer of .... GOETHE
fauteuil .... ARMCHAIR
faux pax .... SLIP, BONER, ERROR,
GAFFE, MISSTEP, FALSE STEP,
SOCIAL BLUNDER
faveolate .... CELLED, ALVEOLATE,
HONEYCOMBED
favonian .... MILD, GENTLE
favor ...... AID, BOON, HELP, LEAN,
LIKE, NOTE, BLESS, GRACE,
LEAVE, LETTER, LIKING,
PREFER, SUPPORT, COURTESY,
GOOD WILL, RESEMBLE, TAKE
AFTER
favorable .... PRO, HELPFUL,
OBLIGING, AUSPICIOUS,
PROPITIOUS, AFFIRMATIVE
in astrology .... TRINE
most .... OPTIMUM
opinion .... ESTEEM
favored .... LUCKY, BETTER,
EXEMPT, GIFTED, BLESSED,
POPULAR, FAVORITE,
PREFERABLE
in the draw .... SEEDED
favoring .... FOR, PRO, APPROVING
favorite .... PET, HERO, IDOL,
MINION, BELOVED, DARLING,
DEAREST, PREFERRED
activity .... HOBBY
activity: Brit. ...... CUP OF TEA
colloq. .... FAIR-HAIRED BOY
son .... BENJAMIN
favoritism .... BIAS, NEPOTISM
favors from public office .... PAP
fawn .... DOE, DEER, CRINGE,
BUCK, GROVEL, FLATTER
fawning .... SERVILE, TOADYING
fay .... ELF, JOIN, FAIRY, SPRITE
archaic .... FAITH
faze ...... ANNOY, DAUNT, RATTLE,
WORRY, AGITATE, DISTURB,
RUFFLE, EMBARRASS,
DISCONCERT
FBI agent .... FED, G-MAN
director, former .... HOOVER
FDR's burial place .... HYDE
PARK
letters .... NRA
Fe, in chemistry .... IRON
fealty .... DUTY, HOMAGE,
LOYALTY, DEVOTION,
FIDELITY, ALLEGIANCE
fear .... AWE, QUALM, SCARE,

WORRY, DISMAY, PHOBIA,
ANXIETY, JITTERS, MISGIVING,
APPREHENSION
excessive .... PHOBIA
frantic, unreasoning ..... PANIC
from sudden danger
.... ALARM
intensely .... DREAD
of animals .... ZOOPHOBIA
becoming insane
.... LYSSOPHOBIA
being alone .... MONOPHOBIA
being idle
.... THAASOPHOBIA
birds .... ORNITHOPHOBIA
blood .... HEMOPHOBIA
cats .... AILUROPHOBIA
children .... PEDOPHOBIA
crossing a street
.... AGYROPHOBIA
crowds .... OCHLOPHOBIA
darkness ...... NYCTOPHOBIA
death .... THANATOPHOBIA
dogs .... CYNOPHOBIA
enclosed spaces
.... CLAUSTROPHOBIA
fear .... PHOBOPHOBIA
fire .... PYROPHOBIA
flowers .... ANTHOPHOBIA
flying .... AVIOPHOBIA
food .... SITOPHOBIA
ghosts .... PHASMOPHOBIA
God .... THEOPHOBIA
gold .... AUROPHOBIA
heat .... THERMOPHOBIA
heights .... ACROPHOBIA
ice cold places
.... CRYOPHOBIA
law .... METUS
lightning .... ASTRAPHOBIA
men .... ANDROPHOBIA
mice .... MUSOPHOBIA
monsters ...... TERATOPHOBIA
new things .... NEOPHOBIA
one's own fears
.... PHOBOPHOBIA
open spaces
.... AGORAPHOBIA
pain .... ALGOPHOBIA
poison .... TOXIPHOBIA
putting on weight
.... ANOREXIA
sex .... GENOPHOBIA
snow .... CHIONOPHOBIA
speed .... TACHOPHOBIA
spiders ...... ARACHNEPHOBIA
strangers/foreigners
.... XENOPHOBIA
of the Chinese
.... SINOPHOBIA
English .... ANGLOPHOBIA

French .... GALLOPHOBIA
Germans
.... TEUTONOPHOBIA
number 13
.... TRISKAIDEKAPHOBIA
Russians .... RUSSOPHOBIA
sun .... HELIOPHOBIA
stars .... SIDEROPHOBIA
of thunder ...... BRONTOPHOBIA
travel .... HODOPHOBIA
trees .... DENDROPHOBIA
water .... HYDROPHOBIA
women .... GYNEPHOBIA
work .... ERGOPHOBIA
overwhelming/intense
.... PANIC, TERROR
slang .... HEEBIE-JEEBIES
sudden, shocking .... CHILL,
FRIGHT, SHIVERS
fearful ...... DIRE, PAVID, AFRAID,
TREPID, NERVOUS, TERRIFYING
fearless .... BOLD, BRAVE,
DARING, HEROIC, IMPAVID,
INTREPID
flyer .... ACE
slang .... GUTSY
fearlessness .... STEEL NERVES
fearsome .... SCARY, TIMID,
CHILLING, ALARMING,
TIMOROUS, DREADFUL,
FRIGHTFUL
one .... OGRE
feasible .... LIKELY, POSSIBLE,
WORKABLE, PRACTICABLE
feast .... FETE, REGALE, REPAST,
SPREAD, BANQUET, FESTIVAL
after harvest/for departing
person .... FOY
day: comb. form .... MAS
describing one ...... LUCULLAN
list .... ORDO
outdoor .... PICNIC
Feast of Lots .... PURIM
of the Nativity .... YULE
feastless day .... FERIA
feat ...... ACT, DEED, GEST, STUNT,
EXPLOIT, ACCOMPLISHMENT
feather ...... DOWN, PENNA, PINNA,
PLUME, QUILL, PLUMAGE
arrow .... FLEDGE, FLETCH
barb .... HARL, HERL
cloak .... MAMO
combining form .... PENNI
fine .... EGRET, AIGRETTE
grass .... STIPA
helmet .... PANACHE
like .... PINNATE, PLUMOSE,
PENNIFORM
neckwear .... BOA
part of .... WEB, VANE
prefix .... PTERO

quill .... BARREL, CALAMUS
resembling a .... PINNATE,
PLUMATE
shaft .... SCAPE
shed: arch. .... MEW, MOLT
small ..... PLUMULE, PLUMELET
submarine's .... WAKE
under wing .... AXILIAR
vane of .... VEXILLUM
wing .... PINION
featherbed .... MATTRESS
featherbrained .... DIZZY, GIDDY,
IDIOT, SILLY, SIMPLE,
FOOLISH, FRIVOLOUS
feathered .... PLUMY, PLUMED,
WINGED, FLEDGED, PENNATED,
PLUMOSE, PLUMAGED
featherer of arrows .... PLUMIER
featherless .... CALLOW
feathers .... DOWN, PLUMAGE
adorn with .... (IM)PLUME
bunch of .... TUFT
bird's wing .... ALULA,
COVERTS
covered with soft ...... DOWNY
for flying .... REMIGES
grow .... FLEDGE
plume of .... PANACHE
pull out the .... PLUCK,
DEPLUME
quill .... CALAMI, BARRELS,
COVERTS
smooth the .... PLUME
soft .... DOWN, EIDER
tail .... RECTRIX
trim the .... PREEN
featherweight ...... BOXER, LIGHT,
TRIVIAL, WRESTLER,
NONENTITY
feathery .... DOWNY, FLUFFY
piece .... BOA
feature .... FILM, FORM, PART,
MOTIF, TRAIT,
CHARACTERISTIC
double .... CHIN
of climber's shoes ...... CLEAT
salient .... MOTIF, HIGHLIGHT
feaze .... FAZE, FEEZE, UNRAVEL
febrile .... FEVERISH
February 2 ...... CANDLEMAS DAY
feces .... DREGS, EGESTA,
SEDIMENT, EXCREMENT
feckless .... WEAK, AIMLESS,
USELESS, CARELESS,
POINTLESS
feculence .... DREGS, FILTH
feculent .... FOUL, FILTHY
fecund .... FERTILE, FRUITFUL,
PROLIFIC, PRODUCTIVE
fecundate .... POLLENATE,
POLLINATE

fecundity .... FERTILITY
Fed .... G-MAN, T-MAN, FBI AGENT
fed up: sl. .... BORED, DISGUSTED,
SATIATED, SURFEITED, SICK
AND TIRED OF
fedayeen leader .... ARAFAT,
HABASH
federate .... UNITE
federation .... UNION, LEAGUE,
ALLIANCE
fedora .... HAT
author of play .... SARDOU
embellishment of .... BAND
fee .... TIP, AGIO, DUES, FEOD,
FIEF, TOLL, CHARGE,
GRATUITY, ASSESSMENT,
HONORARIUM
for settling accounts
.... EXCHANGE
hold in .... OWN, POSSESS
lawyer's .... RETAINER
received for work
.... EMOLUMENT
feeble .... PUNY, WEAK, FRAIL,
WASHY, FLABBY, INFIRM,
FLACCID, RICKETY, DECREPIT
minded .... DOTTY
minded person .... DOLT,
FOOL, AMENT, IDIOT, MORON,
DOTARD, HALF-WIT, IMBECILE
mindedness .... AMENTIA
feed .... EAT, FILL, GRUB, OATS,
BROWSE, COSHER, NOURISH,
PROVIDE, SUBSIST
animal .... FODDER, FORAGE
breast .... NURSE
cattle .... AGIST
colloquial .... CHOW, MEAL
fuel to .... STOKE
the kitty .... ANTE
vat .... SILO
well at other's expense
.... BATTEN
feedback .... RUMBLE, STATIC,
RESPONSE
of speaker's words
.... SIDETONE
feeder .... TRIBUTARY, SUBSIDIARY
Baltic .... ODER
Elbe .... OHRE
Moselle .... SAAR
of furnace .... STOKER
of lines .... STOOGE,
STRAIGHTMAN
Pripyat .... STYR
Rhone .... ISERE
Seine .... OISE
feeding box .... MANGER, TROUGH
feel .... BEAR, PALP, SENSE,
TOUCH, ENDURE, SUFFER,
EXPERIENCE

ability to .... (A)ESTHESIA
able to ..... PASSIBLE, SENSIBLE
about .... GROPE
absence .... MISS
achy .... AIL
compassion .... ACHE
dejected .... REPINE
for .... CARE
like .... INCLINED
out .... SOUND
pity .... YEARN
regret .... RUE, REPENT
sorry .... REGRET
feeler .... BARBEL, PALP(US),
ANTENNA, SMELLER,
TENTACLE
for public opinion .... TRIAL
BALLOON
for wind direction and
velocity .... PILOT
BALLOON
kind of .... POLL, CIRRUS
small .... ANTENNULE
feelers, having .... LONGICORN
feeling .... FIRE, HEART, EMOTION,
OPINION, AWARENESS,
SENSATION, SENTIENCE,
SENTIMENT, TOUCH(ING),
SENSITIVITY
affectionate .... LOVE,
WARMTH, TENDERNESS
capable of .... SENTIENT
impatient .... RESTIVE
of approval/agreement
.... SYMPATHY
arousal .... AGITATION,
EXCITEMENT
being emotionally affected
..... RAPT, MOVED, TOUCHED,
IMPRESSED
bitterness/resentment
.... RANCOR, ANIMOSITY
emotional warmth
.... ARDOR, FERVOR, PASSION
enjoyment/delight
.... PLEASURE
great vigor and liveliness
.... ZEST, GUSTO
ill-being .... DYSPHORIA
overpowering joy
.... ECSTASY
pity/sorrow/sympathy
.... PATHOS, COMPASSION
regret .... REMORSE,
REPENTANCE
vehemence ...... FURY, RAGE,
ANGER
weariness .... ENNUI,
LASSITUDE
wellbeing .... EUPHORIA
show .... EMOTE, REACT

strong/intense .... HEAT
sudden, violent .... SPASM
that something bad will
happen .... HUNCH,
INTUITION, FOREBODING,
PREMONITION
turn of .... WHIM, CAPRICE
feelingly .... HEARTILY,
EMOTIONALLY
feet, care of .... PODIATRY
combining form .... PED(E),
PEDI
5,280 .... A MILE
having .... PEDATE
having many ..... MULTIPED(E)
having three .... TRIPEDAL,
TRIPODAL, TRIPODIC
pertaining to the .... PEDAL,
PODAL, PEDARY
pig's .... PETTITOES
slang .... DOGS
three .... YARD
verse of two .... DIPODY
without .... APOD
feeze .... DRIVE, AGITATE,
DISTURB, DISCONCERT
feign .... ACT, FAKE, ASSUME,
INVENT, PRETEND, SIMULATE,
DISSEMBLE, FABRICATE
sickness .... MALINGER
feigned .... FICTIVE, SIMULAR
feint .... SHAM, BLIND, TRICK,
ARTIFICE, PRETENSE,
DIVERSION
in fencing .... APPEL
feis .... FEAST, FESTIVAL
feisty .... HUFFY, TESTY, CRANKY,
FRISKY, SNAPPISH, BELLICOSE
feldspar .... ALBITE, KAOLIN,
ODINITE, SILICATE, ADULARIA,
ANORTHITE, MOONSTONE,
LABRADORITE
felicitate ...... BLESS, GRATULATE,
COMPLIMENT, CONGRATULATE
felicitation .... BLESSING, BEST
WISHES, COMPLIMENTS
felicitous .... APT, HAPPY, TIMELY,
PERTINENT, APPROPRIATE
felicity .... JOY, BLISS, SONSY,
SONSIE, HAPPINESS
felid .... CAT, FELINE
feline .... SLY, LION, LYNX, PUMA,
PUSS, CATTY, OUNCE, TIGER,
CRAFTY, JAGUAR, CAT(LIKE),
CUNNING, LEOPARD, PANTHER
famous .... ELSA
fierce .... OCELOT
fell .... DROP, CRUEL, CRUSH,
TOPPLE, FLATTEN, CUT DOWN,
GUN DOWN, BRING DOWN,
KNOCK DOWN, PROSTRATE,

RUTHLESS, TERRIBLE
archaic .... DEADLY
of animal .... HIDE, PELT, SKIN
slang .... DECK
felled .... SLAIN, BROKEN,
CONQUERED
fellah: Egyptian .... LABORER,
PEASANT
feller: sl. .... FELLOW
felling .... HAG
fellow. See also **person/man**
.... EGG, CHAP, GENT, JACK,
MATE, PEER, BLOKE, EQUAL,
BUGGER, BUSTER, FRIEND,
COMPEER, CORYDON, PARTNER
archaic .... SIRRAH
big, clumsy .... LOOBY,
LUBBER
British: colloq. .... CULLY
brutish .... YAHOO, HELLION
clumsy .... OAF, LOUT, LOOBY,
MUFFER, FOOZLER,
STUMBLEBUM
colloquial .... BOY, GUY, MAN,
BEAU, PERSON, SUITOR
conceited .... FOP, DUDE,
DANDY, COXCOMB
contemptible .... CAD, SCAB,
VILLAIN, SCOUNDREL
countryman .... COMPATRIOT
faint-hearted .... SISSY,
COWARD
feeling .... KINDNESS,
SYMPATHY, COOPERATION
fine .... TRUMP, GOOD EGG
flashy .... SPORT
foolish .... SOP, FOOL, ZANY,
DUNCE, SIMPLETON
funny ..... WAG, CARD, CLOWN,
JOKER, BUFFOON
lazy .... BUM, SLOUCH
little .... BUB, LAD, SHAVER
mean .... THUG, BUCKO, BULLY
member .... BROTHER,
COMRADE, CONFRERE,
ASSOCIATE, COLLEAGUE
nicknamed Hi .... HIRAM
queer .... CODGER, GEEZER
slang .... GUY, BIRD, BOZO,
GINK, FELLER, HOMBRE
stupid .... ASS, LUG, OAF,
CLOD, GOOF, GANDER, NITWIT,
BLOCKHEAD, LOGGERHEAD
traveler .... ESCORT,
CHAPERON, COMPANION,
SYMPATHIZER
tricky .... KNAVE, ROGUE,
SCAMP, RASCAL, SHYSTER
unprincipled ...... SCAPEGRACE
wicked ..... FIEND, SCOUNDREL
worthless .... BUM, CAD,

ROGU ...CAMP, RASCAL
young .... CHAP, BLADE,
    SPARK, SPRIG, CALLAN(T)
fellowship ...... AMITY, SODALITY,
    COMPANY, SORORITY,
    ENDOWMENT, BROTHERHOOD,
    CAMARADERIE
felly .... DEADLY, CRUELLY,
    WHEEL RIM
felo-de-se .... SUICIDE
felon .... CON, BASE, WICKED,
    CONVICT, CULPRIT, VILLAIN,
    WHITLOW, CRIMINAL
felonious .... BASE, VILE, WRONG,
    SINFUL, ILLEGAL, CRIMINAL
felony .... RAPE, ARSON, CRIME,
    MURDER, OFFENSE
felt .... FABRIC, SENSED
obliged .... HAD TO,
    COMPELLED
felucca .... SHIP
felwort .... GENTIAN, MULLEIN
female .... GIRL, LADY(LIKE),
    UNMANLY, FEMININE,
    WOMAN(LY), EFFEMINATE
animal .... COW, DAM, EWE,
    ROE, SHE, SOW, JILL, MARE,
    BITCH, JENNY, VIXEN, LIONESS,
    TIGRESS
animal's teat .... DUG
buffalo .... ARNEE
camel .... NAGA
cat .... TABBY
change of life .... MENOPAUSE,
    CLIMATERIC
combining form .... GYNE
cow .... HEIFER
deer .... DOE, ROE, HIND,
    REINDEER
demon/frumpy .... HAG, LAMIA
dog .... SLUT, BITCH
donkey .... JENNET
elephant .... COW
fascinating .... SIREN
ferret .... JILL
figure, sculptured ...... ORANT,
    CARYATID
fox .... VIXEN
gonad .... OVARY
gossip .... TABBY
horse .... MARE
insect .... GYNE
kangaroo .... GIN
lobster .... HEN
mythical .... FURY
pig .... SOW, GILT
praying figure .... ORANT
prophet .... SEERESS,
    CASSANDRA
rabbit .... DOE
reproductive organ ..... OVARY

ruff .... REE, REEVE
sandpiper .... REE
servant .... MAID, WENCH
sex .... DISTAFF
sex hormone .... ESTRIOL,
    ESTRONE
sheep .... EWE
slang .... BUNNY, FEMME
slave .... DASI, ODALISK
sovereign ..... QUEEN, EMPRESS
swimmer .... MERMAID
warrior .... AMAZON
wolf .... BITCH
feme .... WIFE
sole .... WIDOW, SPINSTER
feminine ...... FEMALE, WOMANLY,
    PETTICOAT, EFFEMINATE
suffix .... ESS, INE, ETTE, TRIX,
    STRESS
femininity .... MULIEBRITY,
    WEAKER SEX
femme .... WIFE, WOMAN
fatale .... VAMP, SIREN,
    DELILAH, LORELEI, MATA HARI
femme's spouse .... MARI
femur .... THIGH(BONE)
fen .... BOG, MOOR, MARSH,
    SWAMP, MORASS
fence .... PALE, EVADE, PARRY,
    RADDLE, BARRIER, DEFENSE,
    ENCLOSE, RAIL(ING),
    PALISADE, SWORDPLAY
construction site
    .... HOARDING
crossing .... STILE
in old style .... EMPALE
material .... PALE, TITE, PICKET
of shrubs .... HEDGE
of stakes .... PALISADE
of woven work .... RADDLE,
    WATTLE
part ..... PALING, BARBED WIRE
stake .... PALE, PICKET
step .... STILE
sunken .... (H)AHA
temporary .... HURDLE,
    HOARDING
to .... SCRIME
fenced enclosure for grounds
    (surrounding a house or
    dwelling) .... CURTILAGE
holding cattle and horses
    .... CORRAL
holding sheep/cattle
    .... KRAAL
military prisoners
    .... STOCKADE
fencer .... DUELER, SWORDSMAN
cry of .... HAI, SASA, ON
    GUARD
opening position .... EN GARDE

fencing attack .... REPRISE
breastplate .... PLASTROM
dummy for .... PEL
foil .... EPEE
foil guard .... BUTTON
leap .... VOLT
mask .... HELMET
movement .... APPEL
point .... FOIL
position .... CARTE, SIXTE,
    QUARTE, QUINTE, TIERCE,
    SECONDE, SEPTIME
score .... PUNTO
stroke .... BUTT, APPEL,
    LUNGE, RIPOSTE
sword .... EPEE, FOIL, SABRE,
    RAPIER
term .... TIERCE, TOUCHE, EN
    GARDE, SECONDE
thrust .... BUTT, LUNGE,
    PUNTO, REMISE, RIPOSTE,
    REPRISE
fend .... HOLD, WARD, AVERT,
    PARRY, SHIFT, RESIST
off .... REPEL, REPULSE
off a tackler .... STIFFARM
fender .... BUMPER, MUDGUARD,
    BUFFER, SHIELD,
    COWCATCHER
damage/foible .... DENT
fenestra .... WINDOW, OPENING
fennec .... FOX
fennel .... HERB, ANISE
fenny .... BOGGY, MARSHY
feod .... FEE, FIEF
feracious .... FRUITFUL
feral .... WILD, FATAL, BRUTAL,
    DEADLY, FERINE, GLOOMY,
    SAVAGE, UNTAMED,
    FUNEREAL, TOMBLIKE
Ferber, Edna .... NOVELIST
heroine .... SELINA
novel .... SO BIG
Ferde, composer .... GROPE
fer de lance .... SNAKE, VIPER
Ferdinand .... BULL, KING, TORO,
    EMPEROR
Marcos's wife .... IMELDA
Philippines president
    .... MARCOS
Philippines discoverer
    .... MAGELLAN
V, wife of .... ISABELLA I
fere .... MATE, PEER, WIFE,
    HUSBAND, COMPANION
feretory .... BIER, SHRINE
feria .... FESTIVAL, HOLIDAYS
ferine .... WILD, FERAL, FIERCE
fermata .... HOLD, PAUSE
ferment .... BREW, FRET, RAISE,
    SOUR, YEAST, AROUSE,

(EN)ZYME, ACIDIFY, LEAVEN, SEETHE, UNREST, UPROAR, AGITATION, COMMOTION, CURDLE, EFFERVESCE, SACCHARIZE

fermented drink ...... ALE, BEER, MEAD, SAKE, WINE, KUMISS

fermentation .... FUME, SOURING, TUMULT, TURMOIL, YEASTINESS

chemistry of .... ZYMURGY

process .... ZYMOSIS

fermenting agent .... YEAST, ENZYME, LEAVEN, BACTERIA

fern .... BRACKEN, WOODSIA, MOONWORT, MULEWORT, MAIDENHAIR

coarse .... BRAKE

edible .... TARA

filaments .... RHIZOID

flowering .... OSMUND

leaf .... FROND

like plant/perennial stemmed .... ACROGEN

patches .... SORI

petiole .... STIPE

rootstock .... ROI

seed .... SPORE

spore .... SORUS

ferocious .... WILD, CRUEL, FERAL, FIERCE, SAVAGE, BEASTLY

ferocity .... CRUELTY, SAVAGERY, BRUTALITY

Ferrer, actor .... MEL, JOSE

ferret .... HARASS, SEARCH, WEASEL, UNCOVER, UNEARTH

-eyed ...... OBSERVANT, EAGLE-EYED, SHARP-SIGHTED

-eyed giant .... ARGUS

female .... JILL

-like animal .... TAYRA, MONGOOS(E)

out .... SPY, FISH, HUNT, DETECT, DIG UP

relative of .... SKUNK, POLECAT

ferric oxide, anhydrous .... HEMATITE

powder .... ROUGE

ferrotype .... TINTYPE

ferrous sulfate .... COPPERAS

ferrule .... CAP, TIP, RING, BUSHING

ferrum .... IRON

ferry .... PONT, CROSS, CONVEY, AIRDROP, AIRLIFT, SHUTTLE, TRANSPORT

ferryboat .... BAC, PONT, RAFT, SCOW, BARGE, LAUNCH, TENDER

ferryman ...... CHARON, BOATMAN

fertile .... FAT, RANK, RICH, FECUND, PINGUID, FRUITFUL, PROLIFIC, PRODUCTIVE

area .... OASIS

become .... BATTEN

land's surface .... TOPSOIL

mind .... CREATIVE, INVENTIVE, IMAGINATIVE

fertilization .... ENRICHMENT, POLLINATION, PROCREATION, IMPREGNATION

fertilize .... TILL, ENRICH, CULTURE, FRUCTIFY, FECUNDATE, CULTIVATE, POLLINATE

fertilizer .... MARL, GUANO, ALINIT, MANURE, NITRATE, COMPOST, AMMONITE

fertilizing agent .... MILT

ferule .... ROD, HERB, RULER, STICK, FERULA, SCEPTER

fervency ...... HEAT, ZEAL, ARDOR, WARMTH, FERVOR, PASSION

fervent .... HOT, ARDENT, HEATED, EARNEST, GLOWING, PASSIONATE

fervid .... HOT, FIERY, BURNING, FERVENT, INTENSE, FLAMING, FEVERISH, IMPASSIONED

fervor .... ZEAL, ZEST, ARDOR, PASSION, ENTHUSIASM

Fescennine .... VULGAR, OBSCENE

fescue .... GRASS, STICK, STRAW

festal .... GAY, GALA, JOLLY, MERRY, JOVIAL, JOYOUS

fester .... GNAW, HURT, DECAY, RIPEN, RANKLE, ABSCESS, INFECT, PUSTULE, EMBITTER, ULCERATE, SUPPURATE

festering condition .... POX, POCK, ULCER, CANKER, PIMPLE, BLISTER

festival .... ALE, FAIR, FETE, GALA, FEAST, FERIA, FIESTA, CARNIVAL, CELEBRATION, MERRYMAKING

Apollo .... DELIA

Dutch .... KERMIS

paper shower .... CONFETTI

religious .... FIESTA

festive .... GAY, GALA, MERRY, JOLLY, JOVIAL, JOYOUS

festivity .... JOY, MIRTH, PARTY, GAIETY, JOLLITY, REVELRY, MERRIMENT, REJOICING

slang .... BLOWOUT, JAMBOREE

festoon .... LEI, CHAPLET, WREATH, GARLAND, EMBELLISH

festooned .... ADORNED, SPANGLY, STUDDED, BEDECKED, FLOWERED

feta .... CHEESE

fetal .... BUDDING, EMBRYONIC

fetation .... PREGNANCY

fetch .... GET, DEAL, BRING, CARRY, CHARM, HEAVE, INFER, TRICK, YIELD, ELICIT, WRAITH, GO FOR, ATTRACT, PRODUCE, SELL FOR, RETRIEVE

fetching .... ALLURING, CATCHING, PLEASING, CHARMING, ENGAGING, APPEALING, ATTRACTIVE

fete .... FEAST, REGALE, FESTIVAL, CELEBRATE, ENTERTAIN(MENT)

feterita .... SORGHUM

fetial .... PRIESTS

fetid .... FOUL, OLID, RANK, PUTRID, RANCID, SMELLY, NOISOME, STINKING, (MAL)ODOROUS

fetiparous animal ...... WOMBAT, OPOSSUM, KANGAROO, BANDICOOT, MARSUPIAL

fetish ...... OBI, IDOL, JUJU, ANITO, CHARM, MANIA, OBEAH, TOTEM, AMULET, GRIGRI, VOODOO, TALISMAN, WEAKNESS

fetlock .... TUFT

fetor .... STINK, STENCH

fetter .... BOND, GYVE, IRON, CHECK, HAMPER, HOBBLE, HOGTIE, (EN)CHAIN, SHACKLE, MANACLE, HANDCUFF, RESTRAIN

fettle .... FORM, TRIM, ORDER, SHAPE, STATE, CONDITION

fetus .... EMBRYO

hair of .... LANUGO

malformed .... TERATISM

membrane ..... CAUL, CHORION

membrane that surrounds the .... AMNIOTIC SAC

premature birth of .... MISCARRIAGE

procedure to detect abnormalities of .... AMNIOCENTESIS

waters that surround the .... AMNIOTIC FLUID

feu .... FEE

feud .... FEE, FEOD, FIEF, GRUDGE, RANCOR, STRIFE, QUARREL, REVENGE, RIVALRY, CONFLICT, VENDETTA

feudal .... LORDLY, MAGISTRAL, MASTERFUL, SEIGNIORAL

baron .... THANE

benefice .... FEU, FIEF
estate ..... FEE, FEU, FEOD, FIEF
estate head .... LORD
jurisdiction .... SOC, SOKE
land .... FEOD, BENEFICE
lord .... THANE, SEIGNEUR
retainers .... MEINY, MEINIE
service .... AVERA
slave .... SERF
system .... MONARCHY,
ARISTOCRACY
tax .... TALLAGE, TAIL(L)AGE
tenant/underling .... COTTER,
VASSAL, SOCAGER
tenant's payment .... HERIOT
title .... EARL, BARON
feudalism .... HELOTRY, SERFDOM,
VASSALAGE
feudatory .... FIEF, LIEGE,
VASSAL, SERVILE, SUBJECT
fever ...... HEAT, CAUMA, PYREXIA,
BRUCELLOSIS, TEMPERATURE
blister .... COLD SORE
causing/pertaining to
.... PYRETIC
characterized by .... FEBRILE
chill .... AGUE, ALGOR
intermittent .... OCTAN,
QUARTAN, TERTIAN
kind of .... DANDY, DENGUE,
JUNGLE, YELLOW, MALARIA,
QUARTAN, QUINTAN, SCARLET,
TERTIAN, TROPICAL,
BREAKBONE, BLACKWATER,
YELLOWJACK
mental confusion caused by
high .... DELIRIUM
partner of .... CHILLS
recurring .... QUOTIDIAN
reducer .... PIPERINE,
FEBRIFUGE, ANTIPYRETIC
sore .... HERPES
tropical .... DENGUE,
CALENTURE
undulant .... MALTA
fevered .... HOT, HECTIC,
FLUSHED, DELIRIOUS
feverish .... FIERY, HECTIC,
BURNING, FEBRILE, PYRETIC,
FRANTIC, RESTLESS
few .... CURN, RARE, SCANT,
LITTLE, MEAGER, SCARCE
and far between .... SPARSE,
INFREQUENT
the .... MINORITY
fewer .... LESS
fewest .... LEAST
fey .... FATED, DOOMED
fez-like cap .... TURBAN,
TARBOOSH
wearer ..... SHRINER, EGYPTIAN

fi in hi-fi .... FIDELITY
fiacre .... CAB, CARRIAGE
fiance(e) .... BETROTHED
colloquial .... INTENDED
fiasco .... MESS, BOTCH, FIZZLE,
TURKEY, DEBACLE, FAILURE,
MISFIRE, WASHOUT
fiat .... EDICT, ORDER, DECREE,
COMMAND, SANCTION
fib .... (WHITE)LIE
fibber .... LIAR
fiber .... DATIL, NATURE, THREAD,
FUNICLE, QUALITY, FILAMENT
bark .... TAPA
carpet .... ISTLE
century plant ..... PITA, AGAVE
cleaning tool .... HATCHEL
coconut .... COIR
combing .... CARDING
cordage ..... HEMP, IMBE, PINA,
SUNN, ABACA, SISAL, AMBARI,
AMBARY, MAGUEY, RAFFIA,
FILASSE
East Indies plant .... RAMIE
knot .... NEP
mat/phloegm .... BAST
networks .... RETIA
palm .... TAL, ERUC
plant .... ALOE, FLAX, HEMP,
IXLE, ABACA, ISTLE, RAMIE,
SISAL, AMBARY, COTTON,
MAGUEY
roll of .... SLUB
small .... FIBRIL
strand .... YARN
synthetic .... ORLON, RAYON,
DACRON
tree .... BASS, BAST, BAOBAB
waste .... NOIL, FLOSS
wool .... PILE, STAPLE
woven fabric .... MAT(TING)
fibers, fine .... FUZZ
to clean .... SCUTCH
twist .... ROVE
fibril .... FILAMENT, ROOT HAIR
fibrin .... GLUTEN
fibrous .... ROPY
texture .... DESMOID
fibula .... PIN, BONE, CLASP,
BUCKLE
of the .... PERONEAL
fichu .... CAPE, LACE
fickle .... GIDDY, ERRATIC,
FLIGHTY, MOONISH, MOVABLE,
MUTABLE, UNFIXED,
UNSTABLE, UNSTEADY,
VOLATILE, CHANGEFUL,
WHIMSICAL, CAPRICIOUS,
CHANGEABLE, INCONSTANT
girl .... FLIRT, COQUETTE
fico .... FIG, SNAP, TRIFLE

fictile .... CERAMIC, PLASTIC
fiction .... MYTH, TALE, YARN,
FABLE, NOVEL, FANTASY,
ROMANCE, FALSEHOOD
kingdom of .... OZ
fictional .... MYTHICAL,
LEGENDARY, FABRICATED,
FICTITIOUS, MAKE-BELIEVE
animal .... BAMBI
fictitious .... BOGUS, FALSE,
PHONY, UNREAL, FEIGNED,
ASSUMED, FABULOUS,
MYTHICAL, SPURIOUS,
IMAGINARY
name .... ALIAS, JANE DOE,
JOHN DOE
story .... PIGMENT
fictive .... SHAM, FEIGNED,
FANCIFUL, IMAGINED,
IMAGINARY
fid .... BAR, PIN
fiddle .... KIT, GIGA, VIOL, FIDGET,
TRIFLE, VIOLIN
ancient .... REBEC
bow of .... ARCO
faddle .... FUSS, NONSENSE
fit as a .... HALE
fiddledeedee .... NONSENSE,
RIDICULOUS, WISHY-WASHY
fiddler .... VIOLINIST
crab .... UCA
fiddlestick .... BOW, TRIFLE
fiddlesticks! .... NONSENSE,
MALARKEY, POPPYCOCK
fiddling .... PETTY, USELESS,
TRIFLING
fide, _____ (in good faith)
.... BONA
Fidelio character .... LENORE,
FLORESTAN
fidelity .... FEALTY, LOYALTY,
ACCURACY, DEVOTION,
EXACTNESS, ALLEGIANCE,
FAITHFULNESS
fidget .... TOSS, FRET, FIDDLE,
JITTER, SQUIRM, TWITCH
fidgety .... FUSSY, UNEASY, JERKY,
ACTIVE, NERVOUS, JITTERY,
RESTIVE, RESTLESS
fie .... SHAME
fief .... FEE, FEOD, FEUD, BENEFICE
give or sell .... FEOFF
holder .... FEOFFEE
person granting .... FEOFFER,
FEOFFOR
field .... ACRE, AREA, LAND,
PLAIN, RANGE, REALM,
SPHERE, SAVANNA, CLEARING
border .... RAND
combat/house .... ARENA
cultivated .... GLEBE

enclosed .... AGER, CROFT
glacial .... FIRN, NEVE
glass .... BINOCLE,
            BINOCULAR(S)
grassy .... LEA, PASTURE
hospital .... AMBULANCE
mouse .... VOLE
of honor/conflict
.... BATTLEFIELD,
            BATTLEGROUND
of work .... LINE, CAREER,
            METIER
officer .... MAJOR, COLONEL
open .... CAMPUS
plowed .... ERD
sight ..... SNAKE IN THE GRASS
tent .... MARQUEE
unplowed strip .... RAND
used for grazing ...... PRAIRIE,
            GRASSLAND
Field of Dreams .... BASEBALL
            DIAMOND
fieldfare .... THRUSH
fiend .... IMP, DEMON, DEVIL,
            SATAN, SHAITAN, SHEITAN,
            EVILDOER
colloquial .... NUT, BUFF,
            ADDICT, (FAN)ATIC
fiendish .... CRUEL, WICKED,
            DEMONIC, HELLISH, PECCANT,
            SATANIC, VICIOUS, DEVILISH
fierce ...... WILD, LUPINE, SAVAGE,
            INTENSE, VIOLENT, FEROCIOUS
as of speech .... SCATHING,
            BELLICOSE, TRUCULENT
manner, staring in a
.... GLARING
fiery .... HOT, RED, ARDENT,
            FERVID, SULTRY, BLAZING,
            GLARING, GLOWING, IGNEOUS,
            INFLAMED, SPIRITED,
            EXCITABLE, IMPETUOUS,
            PASSIONATE, HOT-TEMPERED
fiesta .... FETE, GALA, FERIA,
            HOLIDAY, FESTIVAL,
            CELEBRATION
fife .... PIPE, FLUTE
fifth columnist .... QUISLING,
            TURNCOAT, COLLABORATOR
finger .... PINKY, PINKIE
Fifth Avenue jewelry shop
.... CARTIER
fiftieth anniversary .... JUBILEE
anniversary of a wedding
.... GOLDEN
fifty-fifty ...... EVEN, EQUAL, TOSS-
            UP, EVEN-STEVEN
percent .... HALF, MOIETY
third card .... JOKER
two cards .... PACK
fig .... A BIT, A HOOT, DRESS,

SHAPE, RETUND, TRIFLE,
            SYCONIUM, TRIFLING
basket .... CABAS
don't care a .... INDIFFERENT
dried .... CARICA
Italian .... FICO
like .... CARICOUS
marigold .... SAMH
parrot .... LORILET
producer .... BANYAN TREE
Smyrna .... ELEME, ELEMI
tree ..... UPAL, PIPAS, BANYAN,
            BOTREE
figeater .... BEETLE, JUNE BUG
fight .... ROW, FEUD, FRAY,
            BRUSH, RUN-IN, COMBAT,
            JOSTLE, AFFRAY, STRIFE,
            TUSSLE, CONTEND, QUARREL,
            WARFARE, STRUGGLE
a bright sun .... SQUINT
against .... RIVAL, OPPOSE,
            RESIST, COMPETE
between countries/factions
.... WAR, BATTLE, CONFLICT,
            HOSTILITIES
between two persons, with
            deadly weapons .... DUEL
close quarters .... HAND TO
            HAND
colloquial .... MIX-UP
desire to .... ANIMUS
fond of .... SCRAPPY
for .... VIE, STRIVE
for a cause .... SERVE,
            SUPPORT, CHAMPION
free-for-all .... RIOT, MELEE,
            RUMBLE
noisily .... BRAWL, BROIL
of a sort .... DUEL, BOXING
over .... BICKER, DISPUTE,
            WRANGLE
program .... CARD
slang .... SCRAP
with feet and fists ..... SAVATE
fighter .... PUG, BOXER, BRAVE,
            RIVAL, BATTLER, CONTENDER,
            PUGILIST, COMBATANT
for a cause .... MILITANT
frenzied .... AMOK, AMUCK,
            BARESARK
kind of .... AIRPLANE
fighting chance of a sort
.... ODDS
gal of 1942 .... WAC, WAAC,
            WAAF
man .... SOLDIER, WARRIOR,
            LEGIONARY
policy .... MILITANCY
sport .... BOXING, WRESTLING
women of the U.S. Navy
.... WAVES

Fighting Bob, sobriquet
.... EVANS
figment of the mind
.... FANTASM, FANTASY,
            PHANTASM(A)
foolish/impossible
.... CHIMERA
figuline .... CLAY, STATUE,
            POTTERY, PORCELAIN
figurant .... EXTRA,
            (BALLET)DANCER,
            SUPERNUMERARY
figuration .... ADORNING,
            FORM(ING), SHAPING,
            OUTLINE, LIMNING,
            DEPICTION, APPEARANCE
figurative .... TYPICAL, IRONICAL,
            ALLUSIVE, SYMBOLIC,
            COLLOQUIAL, ALLEGORIC(AL),
            METAPHOR(ICAL)
language ..... TROPE, IMAGERY,
            ALLEGORY
not .... LITERAL
figuratively .... IN A ·SENSE, SO TO
            SPEAK
figure .... BODY, FORM, DIGIT,
            IMAGE, SOLID, NUMBER,
            RECKON, SYMBOL, COMPUTE,
            DIAGRAM, IMAGINE, PICTURE
architectural .... TELAMON,
            CARYATID
carved .... GLYPHIC
crescent shaped .... LUNE,
            LUNULA
8-sided .... OCTAGON,
            OCTANGLE
equal-angled .... ISOGON
4-sided .... SQUARE,
            TETRAGON, RECTANGLE,
            QUADRANGLE
in a title search .... AREA
of speech .... TROPE, SIMILE,
            ZEUGMA, IMAGERY, LITOTES,
            METAPHOR, METONYMY,
            OXYMORON, HENDIADYS,
            HYPERBOLE
on .... RELY, COUNT, DEPEND
ornamental .... DEVICE
out ..... DOPE, SOLVE, DEDUCE,
            REASON, COMPUTE,
            CALCULATE, UNDERSTAND
oval .... ELLIPSE
part of human .... BUST,
            TORSO, TRUNK
skating jump .... LUTZ
10-sided .... DECAGON(AL)
3-sided/3-cornered
.... TRIANGLE
up .... ADD, SUM, TALLY,
            TOTAL, COMPUTE
used as support .... ATLAS,

TELEMON, ATLANTES,
CARYATID
figured .... PLANNED
figurehead .... DUMMY, PUPPET
figures .... DATA, ADDS UP,
STATISTICS
figurine ...... BUST, DOLL, STATUE,
CARVING, TANAGRA,
MANNEQUIN, STATUETTE
kind of .... SNOWMAN,
SCARECROW
well-known ..... EMMY, OSCAR
figwort .... MULLE(I)N, FOXGLOVE,
SNAPDRAGON
Fiji bay ...... NATEWA, SAVUSAVU
capital .... SUVA
city/town .... BA, NADI,
LAMBASA, LAUTOKA,
VATUKOULA
chestnut .... RATA
dependency .... ROTUMA
island ...... KIOA, KORO, NGAU,
MOALA, RAMBI, MATUKU,
OVALAU, TOTOYA, MBENGGA,
THITHIA, VATULELE, VITI
LEVU, VANUA LEVU
language .... HINDI, FIJIAN,
ENGLISH
mountain .... BATINI,
TOMANIIVI
point .... UNDU
tree .... BURI
filament .... BAND, CORD, HAIR,
HERL, HARL(E), LIST, TAPE,
VEIN, WIRE, CABLE, CHORD,
FIBER, FILUM, STRIP, CILIUM,
STRAND, THREAD
of a plant .... TENDRIL
spun .... YARN
filamentous .... ROPY, WIRY,
HAIRY, STRINGY
filature .... REEL
filbert .... HAZEL(NUT)
filch .... NIM, ROB, STEAL, PILFER,
PURLOIN, SHOPLIFT
slang .... SWIPE
file .... ROW, ENTER, CARLET,
FOLDER, RECORD, SUBMIT,
ARRANGE, CABINET, DOSSIER
away .... STORE
flat .... QUANNET
rough .... RASP
filet .... NET, LACE
filial .... LOVING
duty .... OBEY, HONOR
filibeg .... KILT
filibuster .... OUTTALK, TALKOUT,
HINDERER, MERCENARY,
ADVENTURER, FREEBOOTER
relative of a .... TALKATHON
filigree .... LACE, TRACERY,

ARABESQUE
filings .... REMAINS, SCRAPINGS
Filipino. See also **Philippines**
.... MORO, TAGALOG, PILIPINO
fill .... PAD, LOAD, PLUG, SATE,
STUFF, OCCUPY, SUPPLY,
PERVADE, PERMEATE
a need .... SATISFY
in .... BRIEF, INFORM,
STANDBY, SUBSTITUTE
in the blanks .... COMPLETE
the tank .... GAS
to excess .... HEAP, CONGEST
with ardor .... FIRE
with hate .... ENVENOM,
EMBITTER
with wrath .... INCENSE
fille .... GIRL, MAID, DAUGHTER,
SPINSTER
de joie .... PROSTITUTE
filled .... FULL, REPLETE
gold .... BRASS
to capacity .... SATED,
CHOCKFUL
with enthusiasm .... EAGER
filler .... SHIM, PADDING, STUFFING
seasoned .... DRESSING
shoe .... INSOLE
fillet .... BAND, BONE, FACIA,
LABEL, STRIP, LISTEL, RIBBON,
T(A)ENIA
architectural .... ORLE, ORLO
hair .... BAND, SNOOD
narrow .... ORIE, STRIA,
ANADEM
filling .... PACKING, PADDING
dentist's ...... GOLD, AMALGAM
for a tooth .... INLAY
material .... PUTTY
place .... GAS STATION,
SERVICE STATION
weaving .... WARP, WEFT,
WOOF
fillip .... TAP, SNAP, TONIC,
EXCITE, STIMULUS
fillister .... GROOVE
filly .... FOAL, MARE
colloquial .... GIRL, WOMAN
film .... BLUR, HAZE, SCUM,
MOVIE, SHOOT, COATING,
NEGATIVE, PHOTOGRAPH
award-winning ..... GONE WITH
THE WIND, THE GRAPES OF
WRATH, THE LIFE OF EMILE
ZOLA
descriptive of horror
.... KNEEKNOCKER
green .... PATINA
part .... REEL
producer Jerry .... WALD
star Edmund, early ...... LOWE

filmy ...... HAZY, GAUZY, BLURRED
cloth .... GOSSAMER
filose .... THREADLIKE,
FILAMENTOUS
fils .... SON, YOUTH
English equivalent ..... JUNIOR
filter .... OOZE, SIFT, LEACH,
SIEVE, STRAIN, COLATURE,
FILTRATE, PERCOLATE
impurities ...... PURIFY, REFINE
screen .... RESEAU
substance .... FELT, SAND,
CHARCOAL
through .... SEEP
filth .... DIRT, MUCK, SMUT, SLIME,
ORDURE, GARBAGE, SQUALOR,
IMPURITY, INDECENCY,
FECULENCE, OBSCENITY
filthy .... FOUL, LEWD, RICH, VILE,
DIRTY, MUCKY, NASTY,
SLIMY, ROTTEN, SMUTTY,
OBSCENE, SQUALID, UNCLEAN,
FECULENT
animal .... PIG
lucre ..... DIRTY MONEY, DIRTY
RICHES
smelly place .... STY,
CESSPOOL
filtrate .... FILTER, STRAIN
fin .... VEE, FIVER, PINNA,
PROPELLOR, FLIPPER, PINNULE
de _____ .... SIECLE
describing one .... CAUDAL,
DORSAL, VENTRAL
footed animal .... PINNIPED
in aeronautics .... RUDDER,
AIRFOIL
slang .... HAND
finagle .... CHEAT, RENEGE,
WANGLE, MANEUVER
final .... END, LAST, TELIC,
DERNIER, DECIDING, DECISIVE,
ULTIMATE, CONCLUSIVE
authority .... SAY-SO
CB words ...... OVER AND OUT
discharge .... QUIETUS
judgment .... DOOM
melody .... TAPS
word .... NEVER
word, frequent .... AMEN
finale .... END, CODA, SWAN SONG,
CONCLUSION
finally .... EN FIN, AT LAST, IN
TIME, IN THE END,
DEFINITELY, EVENTUALLY,
ONCE AND FOR ALL
finals to students .... BRAIN-
DRAIN
finance .... BACK, FUND,
SUBSIDIZE, CAPITALIZE,
UNDERWRITE

finances .... FUNDS, MONEY, PURSE, BUDGET, ACCOUNTS
financial ...... FISCAL, MONETARY, PECUNIARY
gain, unexpected .... WINDFALL
headache .... ARREARS
independence .... EASY STREET
venture .... FLIER
financially sound/healthy .... SOLVENT, ABOVE WATER
financier .... BANKER, TYCOON, CAPITALIST
finback .... GRASO, WHALE, RORQUAL, RAZORBACK
finch ...... SPINK, CANARY, OSCINE, SISKIN, BUNTING, REDPOLL, SPARROW, GROSBEAK, SNOWBIRD, SONGBIRD
African .... FINK, MORO
American ...... JUNCO, BURION, LINNET, TOWHEE, CHEWINK
canary-like .... SERIN
kin .... CARDINAL
like bird .... TANAGER
small/yellow .... SERIN
find .... GET, ESPY, LEARN, DECIDE, DETECT, OBTAIN, DISCOVER, PERCEIVE
fault .... BEEF, CARP, CAVIL, COMPLAIN
fault continually .... NAG
out .... LEARN, SOLVE, ASCERTAIN
finding ...... VERDICT, JUDGMENT, DISCOVERY, CONCLUSION
fine .... FAIR, KEEN, NICE, PURE, THIN, BULLY, MULCT, SHARP, AMERCE, FLIMSY, DELICATE, EXCELLENT
and _____ .... DANDY
arts .... MUSIC, DANCING, CERAMICS, PAINTING, SCULPTURE, LITERATURE
arts buff .... DILETTANTE
bearing .... BEL AIR
drawn .... SUBTLE
feather .... EGRET
fiddle .... AMATI
fixed by law .... PENALTY
for misconduct .... SCONCE
gravel .... SAND
in law .... CRO
line of letter .... SERIF
point .... NICETY
porcelain .... LIMOGES
powder .... DUST, SOOT
rain .... DRIZZLE
record of .... ESTREAT
thread .... LISLE
fineness .... PURITY, RARITY,

TENUITY, DELICACY
finery .... FRILLS, TINSEL, REGALIA, GAUD(ERY), FALDERAL, FRIPPERY, DECORATION
useless .... FALLAL
finespun .... SUBTLE, FRAGILE, DELICATE
finesse .... ART, TACT, CRAFT, SKILL, CUNNING
finest ...... BEST, PRIME, TOPMOST, MATCHLESS
part .... FLOWER
people .... CREAM, ELITE, UPPERCRUST
Fingal's Cave island ...... STAFFA
finger .... DIGIT, STEAL, TOUCH, FEEL, HANDLE, DACTYL(US)
covering/sheath .... COT, STALL
cymbals .... CASTANETS
fifth/smallest .... PINKY, PINKIE
fore .... INDEX, POINTER
game .... MORA
hole of instrument .... VENTAGE
infection/inflammation ...... FELON, AGNAIL, WHITLOW
joint .... KNUCKLE
like .... DIGITATE
little .... PINKIE
middle .... MEDIUS
nail half-moon .... LUNULE
pertaining to .... DIGITAL
ring .... HOOF
slang .... TELL ON, POINT TO, IDENTIFY, INDICATE
snap of .... FILLIP
stall .... COT
stroke .... FLIP
fingerless glove .... MITT
fingerling .... FRY, FISH, PARR, SAMLET
fingernail, care of ...... MANICURE
mark .... LUNULE
fingerprint .... DACTYLOGRAM
mark ..... ARCH, LOOP, WHORL, LUNULE
pattern .... WHIRL
fingers, membrane uniting .... WEB(BING)
finial .... EPI, TIP, APEX, PEAK, SUMMIT
finical .... FUSSY, PRUDISH, EXACTING, FASTIDIOUS, METICULOUS, PARTICULAR
finicky .... PRISSY, PRECISE, OVERNICE
finis .... END, CONCLUSION
finish .... END, STOP, CLOSE, POISE, POLISH, ACCOMPLISH,

TERMINATE, PERFECTION
colloquial .... KILL
dull/flat .... MATTE
first by small margin ...... WIN BY A NECK
line .... TAPE, WIRE
lustrous .... ENAMEL
off .... KILL, DESTROY, LIQUIDATE, ANNIHILATE
finished, for short .... THRU
finisher .... EDGER, REAMER, SOCKDOLAGER
finishing school product .... LADY
tool .... LATHE, REAMER
finite .... LIMITED
fink .... SPY, INFORMER, STRIKEBREAKER
Finland .... SUOMI
finnan haddie .... HADDOCK
Finnish .... SUOMI
bath(house) .... SAUNA
canto/poem .... RUNE
capital .... HELSINKI
city/town .... KEMI, OULU, PORI, SALO, ESPOO, KOTKA, LAHTI, NOKIA, RAUMA, TURKU, VAASA, IMATRA, KERAVA, KUOPIO, LIEKSA, JOENSUU, KARHULA, KOKKOLA, MIKKELI, TAMPERE, VARKAUS
coin .... PENNI, MARKKA
composer .... SIBELIUS
dialect .... KARELIAN
epic poem .... KALEVALA
field marshal .... MANNERHEIM
god .... JUMALA
gulf .... BOTHNIA, FINLAND
inlet .... FIORD
island .... KARLO, HAILUOTO, VALLGRUND
islands .... ALAND
lake .... ENARE, INARI, SAIMAA, KEITELE, KOITERE, JUOJARVI, ORIHVESI, PIELINEN, HAUKIVESI, KEMIJARVI, LAPPAJARVI, OULUJARVI, YLIKITKA
language .... SUOMI, FINNISH, SWEDISH
monetary unit .... MARKKA
mountain .... HALTIATUNTURI
native .... LAPP, KARELIAN, LAPLANDER
province .... HAME, KYMI, OULU, LAPPI, VAASA, KUOPIO, MIKKELI, UUSIMAA
river ..... TANA, TORNIO, IIJOKI, MUONIO, KITINEN, KALAJOKI, KEMIJOKI, OULUJOKI, SIMOJOKI, IVALOJOKI
seaport .... (ABO)TURKU

finnikin .... PIGEON
Finno-Ugric language ...... LAPP, MAGYAR, FINNISH, ESTONIAN, HUNGARIAN
Finns .... SUOMI
fiord .... INLET
fipple .... PLUG
fir .... BALSAM, EVERGREEN
board wood .... DEAL
pole .... UFER
fire .... BURN, OUST, ARDOR, BLAZE, FEVER, VERVE, ANNEAL, HURL, EXCITE, IGNITE, KINDLE, DISMISS, INSPIRE, (IN)FLAME
a gun .... SHOOT
alarm .... BELL, SIREN, WHISTLE, PYROSTAT
artillery ...... SALVO, BARRAGE
away .... START
back .... REREDOS
basket .... GRATE, CRESSET
big, destructive
.... CONFLAGRATION
catching .... IGNITION
clay .... BRICK, SAGGER
colloquial .... CAN
combining form .... IGNI, PYRO
cracker .... PETARD
damp .... METHANE
department head .... MARSHAL
feeder .... STOKER
god .... AGNI, KAMA, SIVA, VULCAN
irons .... POKER, TONGS, SHOVEL
malicious .... ARSON
of .... IGNEOUS
on a hearth .... INGLE
opal .... GIRASOL(E)
pot .... CRUCIBLE
principle of .... PHLOGISTON
produced by .... IGNEOUS
put out .... DOUSE
signal .... BEACON
starting stone .... FLINT
stir up .... STOKE
worshiper ...... PARSI, GHEBER, GHEBRE, PARSEE, PYROLATER
Fire Dance composer .... DE FALLA
firearm. See also gun .... GAT, GUN, HAGBUT, IRON, RIFLE, PISTOL, PETRONEL, REVOLVER, DERRINGER
barrel's end .... MUZZLE
charge .... LOAD
hammer .... COCK
firearms protective coating
.... COSMOLINE

fireball .... BOLIDE, METEOR
firebrand .... HOTHEAD, AGITATOR
firebug .... ARSONIST, INCENDIARY, PYROMANIAC
firecracker .... PETARD, SNAPPER, SPARKLER, NOISEMAKER
box for .... MARROON
broken .... SQUIB
fired clay .... TILE, BRICK
firedamp .... GAS, METHANE
firedog .... ANDIRON
firedrake .... DRAGON
fire-eater ...... DRAGON, HOTSPUR, SPITFIRE
firefly .... BUG, BEETLE, GLIMMER, GLOWWORM
lighting substance
.... LUCIFERIN
fireman .... VAMP, STOKER, FIREFIGHTER, SMOKECHASER
hat of .... HELMET
tool of .... LADDER
Firenze .... FLORENCE
fireplace .... GRATE, HEARTH, INGLE(NOOK), SMOKEHOLE
guard/screen .... FENDER
ledge .... HOB
log holder .... ANDIRON, FIREDOG
part .... HOB, FLUE, SPIT, SHELF, JAMB(E), MANTEL, SCREEN, CHIMNEY
tool .... POKER, TONGS
fireplug .... HYDRANT, SPRINKLER, EXTINGUISHER
firepower .... GUNFIRE
fireproof .... RESISTANT, UNBURNABLE, INCOMBUSTIBLE, NON-FLAMMABLE
fireside .... HOME, HEARTH
firewater .... RUM, WHISKY
firewood .... LOGS, BAVIN, BILLET, FAG(G)OT, BILLON, KINDLINGS
fireworks .... PETARD, RIPRAP, GERB(E), ROCKETS, SPARKLERS, ROMAN CANDLES
art of making and using
.... PYROTECHNICS
cluster .... GIRANDOLE
hissing .... SQUIB, FIZGIGS
material .... REALGAR
firing .... HURLING, IGNITION, KINDLING, DISMISSAL
from a position of trust
.... CASHIERING
line .... BATTLEGROUND, KILLING FIELD
notice .... PINK SLIP
firkin .... TUB
firm .... HARD, FINAL, FIXED,

SOLID, STIFF, STEADY, COMPANY, SETTLED, CONSTANT, DECISIVE, RESOLUTE, STEADFAST, STA(U)NCH, DETERMINED, UNFLINCHING
firmament .... SKY, ARCH, VAULT, HEAVEN
revolving .... PINWHEEL, TOURBILLION
firman .... DECREE, SANCTION
firmer .... CHISEL
firmly .... SECURELY, STRONGLY
packed .... DENSE, COMPACT
placed together .... SERRIED
set .... FIXED, PINNED, ROOTED, RIVETED, EMBEDDED
united .... SOLID
firmness .... APLOMB, SOLIDITY, STRENGTH, VITALITY
lacking .... LAX, LIMP, SOFT, LOOSE, FLABBY
of courage .... GRIT, FORTITUDE
firn .... ICE, NEVE, SNOW
first .... ALPHA, CHIEF, PRIME, INITIAL, EARLIEST, FOREMOST, ORIGINAL, PRINCIPAL
abbreviation .... ORIG.
act .... OPENER
American champion in figure skating .... TENLEY ALBRIGHT
American civil servant to lie in state in Capitol rotunda .... J. EDGAR HOOVER
animal named in the Bible
.... SERPENT
appearance .... DEBUT, MAIDEN
Archbishop of Canterbury
.... AUGUSTINE
black Justice of U.S. Supreme Court
.... THURGOOD MARSHALL
black soloist of Metropolitan Opera House .... MARIAN ANDERSON
book of the Bible .... ACTS
born ...... HEIR, EIGNE, ELDEST, OLDEST
cause .... SOURCE
circumnavigator
.... MAGELLAN
class ..... A-ONE, TOPS, DANDY, QUALITY, TOPNOTCH, TOP-DRAWER, TOP-FLIGHT
commisioner of baseball
.... LANDIS
country's flag planted at the South Pole .... NORWAY

day of ancient Roman month
.... CALENDS
day of Quakers .... SUNDAY
estate .... CLERGY
female British Prime
Minister .... MARGARET
THATCHER
female U.S. Supreme Court
Justice .... SANDRA DAY
O'CONNOR
female U.S. Surgeon General
.... NOVELLO
finger .... INDEX
game/line .... OPENER
Greek philosopher .... THALES
hydrogen bomb explosion
location .... ENIWETOK
impression .... GAMBIT,
BREAKING-IN
in rank .... PREMIER
in seniority .... OLDEST
in time .... PRIMAL
Kentuckian? .... BOONE
king of Israel .... SAUL
king of Rome .... ROMULUS
lady .... EVE
lady of radio in the 40's
.... KATE SMITH
lady's mate .... ADAM
letter .... INITIAL
man to orbit the earth
.... GAGARIN
man to walk the moon
.... ARMSTRONG
man-made satellite
.... SPUTNIK
manned suborbital rocket
.... MERCURY
martyr of Christianity
.... STEPHEN
move .... OVERTURE,
INITIATIVE
name in movie lore .... GRETA
name in spies .... MATA
name in Western fiction
.... ZANE
name of Guy de Maupassant
.... HENRI
native-born U.S. saint
.... SETON
night/performance/showing
.... OPENING, PREMIERE
nighter .... CRITIC, REVIEWER
of a clone .... ORTET
officer: nautical .... MATE
or second .... RATE
person .... ADAM
person with a palindromic
name .... EVE
place .... EDEN
Pope .... PETER

prefix .... PROTO
principles .... ABCS
prize .... AWARD, JACKPOT,
BLUE RIBBON
rate .... ACE, A-ONE, ONER,
TOPS, NOBBY, SUPER, CAPITAL,
TOPNOTCH, EXCELLENT,
TOPFLIGHT
rate: Anglo-Indian ..... PUCKA,
PUKKA
rights .... PRIORITIES
sergeant .... TOPKICK
satellite into orbit .... SPUTNIK
sight .... PRIMA FACIE
sign of the zodiac .... ARIES
space traveler .... GAGARIN
speech, describing .... MAIDEN
stage .... INCIPIENCE
State .... DELAWARE
talking picture, American
.... THE JAZZ SINGER
Thanksgiving year
.... SIXTEEN TWENTY ONE
U.S. casualty of the Cold
War .... (JOHN)BIRCH
U.S. president
.... (GEORGE)WASHINGTON
U.S. state to grant women
voting rights
.... WYOMING
U.S. vice president to
become president
.... (JOHN)ADAMS
U.S. woman in space .... RIDE
valuable issue .... EDITION
winner of the Indy 500
.... (RAY)HARROUN
winner of the World Series
.... BOSTON RED SOX
woman in space
.... (VALENTINA)TERESHKOVA
woman to fly solo across the
Atlantic .... AMELIA
EARHART
word of Ethiopia .... ADDIS
word of "Paul Revere's
Ride" .... LISTEN
year student .... FROSH,
PLEB(E), FRESHMAN
year West Pointer .... PLEBE
year's revenue of benefice
.... ANNAT

First Lady's husband
.... PRESIDENT
firsthand .... DIRECT, BRAND-NEW,
ORIGINAL
firth .... ARM, KYLE, FIORD, INLET,
ESTUARY
fisc .... TREASURY, EXCHEQUER
fiscal ...... NUMMARY, MONETARY,
FINANCIAL, PECUNIARY

officer .... BURSAR, PURSER,
PROSECUTOR
fish .... GAR, RAY, BASS, CARP,
CHUB, DACE, HAKE, LING,
OPAH, SHAD, ANGLE, PERCH,
SCROD, TRAWL, TROLL,
DARTER, SABALO, TARPON,
WRASSE, EELPOUT, LABROID,
SCULPIN, SNAPPER,
BULLHEAD, MACKEREL, PULL
OUT, STURGEON, BRAINFOOD
African .... CHARACIN
air bladder .... MAW
air swallowing .... PUFFER,
GLOBEFISH, SWELLFISH
appendage .... FIN, BARBEL,
FLIPPER
aquarium .... MOLLY,
SWORDTAIL
ascending river ...... ANADROM
Atlantic .... TAUTOG
baby .... FRY
bait .... CHUM, HOLA, LURE,
LIMPET, MINNOW, SHINER,
CAP(E)LIN, LUGWORM,
MENBRADEN
ball .... RISSOLE
barbel .... WATTLE
barracuda .... SPET
basket .... CAWL, WEEL, CREEL
batlike ..... GURNET, GURNARD,
(STING)RAY
beaked .... SAURY
beard .... BARB(EL)
beluga .... WHITEFISH
bin for salting .... KENCH
boat .... DORY, COBLE,
WHALER, TRAWLER
boneless .... FIL(L)ET
bony .... TELEOST
bright-colored .... OPAH,
MOLLY, MORAY, WRASSE,
PINTANO, COWPILOT,
DRAGONET
bucket .... KIT
burbot .... CUSK, LING,
EELPOUT
butter .... GUNNEL
butterfly .... PARU, BLENNY
capelin .... SMELT
carangoid .... CAVALLA,
POMPANO, YELLOWJACK,
YELLOWTAIL
caribe .... PIRAYA, PIRANHA
carp family .... IDE, CHUB,
DACE, ROUD, RUD(D), BLEAK,
LOACH, ROACH, TENCH,
MINNOW, REDFIN
cat .... RAAD
catch .... HAUL
char(r) .... TROUT

chopped .... CHUM
cigar .... SCAD
cleaner .... SCALER
climbing .... ANABAS
clinging ...... REMORA, TESTAR
coal .... POLLACK, POLLOCK
cod family .... CUSK, HAKE,
LING, GADID, BURBOT,
BACALAO, HADDOCK, POLLACK
combining form .... PISCI
cow .... DUGONG, GRAMPUS,
MANATEE
crab and fiddler .... UCA
creature: legendary
.... MERMAN, MERMAID
Cuban .... DIABLO
cure .... BLOAT
cusk .... BURBOT
cuttle .... SEPIA, SQUID
cyprin(o)id .... IDS, DACE,
CARP, ROUD, ORF(E), BLEAK,
BREAM, LOACH, BARBEL,
GOLDFISH
deep sea .... WEEVER
delicacy .... ROE
devil .... SKATE, MANTARAY
dish .... SHADROE,
BOUILLABAISSE
dog .... SHARK, BOWFIN
dolphin .... INIA, CETACEAN,
PORPOISE
drying frame .... HACK
East Indies .... DORAB,
GOURAMI
eating .... PISCIVOROUS
eating animal .... SEAL, OTTER
eating bird .... ERN(E),
OSPREY, PELICAN
eating fish .... ANGLER
edible .... COD, EEL, IDE, BASS,
DORY, PIKE, LOACH, TUNA,
SPRAT, TROUT, TAUTOG,
WRASSE, HADDOCK,
ARAPAIMA, BRISLING,
MACKEREL, BARRACUDA
eel .... LING, ELVER, MORAY,
CONGER, LAMPREY
eel-like .... APOD
eelpout .... BURBOT
eel-shaped .... LEPIDOSIREN
eggs .... ROE, SPAWN
eggs relish .... CAVIAR(E)
elasmobranch .... RAY,
MANTA, SHARK, SKATE,
SAWFISH, MANTA RAY
elongated .... EEL, GAR, PIKE
European .... BLEAK, BREAM,
DACE, UMBER, BARBEL,
BRASSE, PLAICE, SENNET,
WRASSE, SPRAT, TENCH,
BRISLING

eyed on head's top
.... STARGAZER
fabled .... MAH
feeler .... BARBEL
fence .... WEIR, CRAWL
fierce .... PIKE, SHARK,
BLENNY, PIRANHA, SEABASS,
PICKEREL, BARRACUDA
flat ..... DAB, RAY, BUTT, SOLE,
BRILL, FLUKE, SKATE, PLAICE,
TURBOT, HALIBUT, POMPANO,
FLOUNDER
Florida .... BONACI, TARPON
flying .... SAURY, GURNARD
food .... COD, CARP, CERO,
HAKE, LING, SCUP, SHAD,
TUNA, JUREL, MORAY, TROUT,
SMELT, BONITO, MULLET,
PLAICE, GROUPER, POLLACK,
POMPANO, SARDINE, SNAPPER
for .... SEEK, DREDGE, SEARCH,
SOLICIT
fork tailed .... JUREL,
CAVALLA, POMPANO,
CARANGOID
fresh-water .... IDE, BASS,
DACE, LOACH, TENCH,
ANABAS, DARTER, REDEYE,
CRAPPIE, ARAPAIMA, STONE-
ROLLER
frog .... ANGLER
from boat .... TROLL
full of: poetic .... FINNY
game .... CERO, TROUT,
MARLIN, SALMON, TARPON,
(BLACK)BASS, SWORDFISH
ganoid .... GAR, BOWFIN,
STURGEON
garth .... WEIR
gently .... DAP
genus .... AMIA
gig .... HOOK, SPEAR
gobioid .... GOBY
goby-like .... DRAGONET
grampus .... ORC, DOLPHIN
grasping-tailed
.... HIPPOCAMPUS
green .... PLAICE, SHANNY
grouper .... MERO, (SEA)BASS
grunting .... CROAKER,
GURNARD, PIGFISH
gurnard family ..... SEA ROBIN
haul .... MESS
Hawaiian .... AKU
hawk .... OSPREY
head of .... JOWL
herring .... CISCO, SPRAT,
TARPON, ANCHOVY, OLDWIFE,
PILCHER, SARDINE, MENHADEN,
CLUPE(O)ID, PILCHARD
herring-like .... SHAD,

ALEWIFE
herring, young .... BRIT
hide .... EELSKIN
holy .... HALIBUT
hook .... GIG, GAFF
illegally .... POACH
Japanese .... TAI, FUGU
jelly .... MEDUSA, ACALEPH
jew .... MERO, TARPON,
(SEA)BASS
jurel .... RUNNER
king .... OPAH, PINTADO,
WHITING
lacking pelvic fins .... APOD
lake .... POLLAN
land-walking .... ANABAS
largest freshwater
.... ARAPAIMA
like animal .... LANCELET
line ...... TROT, SNELL, TRAWL,
TROLL
line cork .... BOB
ling .... BURBOT
little .... SMELT, MINNOW,
SARDINE
lizard .... ULAE
loach .... SMERLIN
long-beaked .... GAR, SAURY
lure .... CHUM, SPINNER
mackerel .... TUNA, TUNNY,
BONITO, ALBACORE
mackerel-like .... CERO,
TINKER
male .... MILTER
man-eating .... SHARK
marine ...... CUSK, LING, SCUP,
BLENNY, BONITO, ROBALO,
TARPON, WRASSE, MENHADEN
maskonge .... PIKE
measure .... MEASE
meat, broiled ...... CARBONADO
migration .... RUN
milk .... SABALO
mollusk .... SQUID, OCTOPUS
mucous coating .... SLIME
mythological .... MAH
nest-building .... ACARA
net .... FLEW, FLUE, FYKE,
GILL, SEINE, TRAWL
New Zealand .... IHI
ocean bed .... WEEVER
of .... PISCINE, PISCATORY,
PISCATORIAL
organ of touch .... BARBEL
parasite .... REMORA
parrot .... LORO, LANIA
pen/enclosure .... WEIR,
CRAWL
perch family .... RUFF(E)
perch-like .... ANABAS,
DARTER, CABRILLA

pertaining to .... FINNY, PISCINE, TELEOST, PISCATORY
pickle .... ALEC
piece .... FIL(L)ET
pike .... LUCE, PICKEREL
pike-like/needle .... GAR, ROBALO, BARRACUDA
place for drying .... HACK
poor .... SIMP
porgy .... TAI, SCUP
Polynesian .... ISDA
porpoise .... INIA, DOLPHIN, CETACEAN
primitive .... COELACANTH
rainbow, of Australia
.... MAORI
ray .... MANTA, SKATE
red-eyed .... RUDD
relish .... BOTARGO
reproductive glands .... MILT
resembling .... PISCINE
river ascending .... SHAD, SALMON, ANADROM
rock .... COD, BASS, RE(I)NA, GROUPER
runner .... JUREL
Russian .... STERLET, STURGEON
salmon, young .... PARR, SAMLET
salmon-like .... SMELT
salmonoid .... TROUT, NAMAYCUSH, STEELHEAD
salt-water .... DORY, HAKE, SHAD, TUNA, CYCLOTOME
salting box .... KENCH
sardine .... SPRAT, CLUPEID, HERRING, PILCHARD
sardine-like .... CISCO, ANCHOVY, BRISLING
sauce .... ALEC, ANCHOVY
saurel .... SCAD
scabbard .... HIKU
scale .... GANOID
scaleless .... CATFISH, SCULPIN, BULLHEAD, DRAGONET
schooling .... GRUNION
sculpin family .... CABEZON, BULLHEAD
sea ..... TUNA, SAURY, SCULPIN
sergeant .... ROBALO
serpentine .... EEL
shad-like .... ALEWIFE
shark .... MAKO, TOPE, ANGELFISH
shark family .... CHIMAERA
shark's pilot .... REMORA
shell .... CLAM, CRAB, SLUG, WHELK, LIMPET, SHRIMP, ABALONE, LOBSTER, OCTOPUS, SCALLOP

shrimp-like .... KRILL
sign of zodiac .... PISCES
silver-bellied .... MACKEREL
silvery .... OPAH, SMELT, MULLET, PINTADO
skeleton .... ARETE, ARISTA
slim .... GAR
slimy .... BLENNY
small .... ID(E), FRY, DACE, SMELT, SPELT, SPRAT, DARTER, MINNOW, SAMLET, FINGERLING
smelt .... CAP(E)LIN
snouted .... GAR, SAURY, DOLPHIN, BOARFISH, PICKEREL, PORPOISE, STURGEON
South American .... CARIBE, PIRAYA, PIRANHA, ARAPAIMA
spawning movement
.... ANADROMOUS, CATADROMOUS
spear .... GIG, LEISTER
sperm .... ROE, MILT
spiny .... GOBY, SCULPIN
spiny-headed .... SEA ROBIN
spotted .... OPAH
stewed .... MATELOT(TE)
story .... YARN, EXAGGERATION
St. Peter's .... TILAPIA
sturgeon ..... BELUGA, STERLET
sucking .... REMORA, HAMMERHEAD
swimming bladder ...... SOUND
tank .... STEW, AQUARIUM, VIVARIUM
teleost .... EEL
that recently spawned
.... SHOTTEN
to .... ANGLE, TROLL
toad .... SAPO
trap .... FYKE, GILL, WEIR, CRAWL, CREEL, HATCH, SEINE, TRAWL, EELPOT, KELONG
tropical .... SARGO, ROBALO, SALEMA, SNAPPER, BARRACUDA
trout .... CHAR(R)
tub .... KIT
ugly-looking .... CATFISH
unicorn .... UNIE
upholding universe .... MAH
voracious ...... SHARK, CARIBE, CATFISH, PIRANHA
wahoo .... ONO
wall-eyed .... BLOWFISH
warm-water .... ROBALO
West Indies .... TESTAR
whale .... ORC(A), GRAMPUS, NARWHAL, CACHALOT, CETACEAN
whisker .... BARBEL

whiskered .... CATFISH
whiting ...... HAKE, MENHADEN
with a spoon .... SPIN
with lungs/gills ...... DIPNOAN, CERATODUS, BARRAMUNDA
with staring eyes .... PIKE, PERCH, ALEWIFE, POLLACK
with sucking mouth
.... REMORA, HAGFISH, LAMPREY, CYCLOSTOME
with suction disk .... GOBY
with whiplike tail ...... SKATE, (STING)RAY, STINGAREE
young .... FRY, BRIT, PARR, ELVER, ALEVIN, SAMLET, FINGERLING
fishbait .... CHUM, LUGWORM
fishbowl .... AQUARIUM
fisher ...... SEAL, PEKAN, MARTEN, WEJACK
fisherman .... EELER, ANGLER, FISHER, JACKER, WALTON, WHALER, TRAWLER, TROLLER, PISCATOR
basket .... CREEL
line of .... SNELL
fisherman's bend .... KNOT
hut .... SKEO
fishes, characteristic of
.... ICHTHYIC
fishgig .... SPEAR
fishhook .... GIG, GAFF, DRAIL
end of a .... BARB
line .... SNELL
fishing .... ANGLING, SEEKING, WHALING, PURSUING, TRAWLING, TROLLING, PISCATION
bait .... DRAKE, MAYFLY
basket .... CREEL
boat .... DORY, SMACK, DOGGER, WHALER, CORACLE, SHARPIE, TRAWLER
device .... EELPOT
event .... BITE
float .... BOB
fly .... HACKLE
fly, artificial .... NYMPH
fly trimmer .... HERL
ground/place .... POUND, FISHERY, PISCARY, PISCINA
kick .... BITE
line with hooks .... BOULTER
net .... FLUE, FYKE, GILL, FLEW, SEINE, TRAWL, TRAMMEL
pertaining to ...... PISCATORIAL
pole .... ROD, TONKIN
reel .... PIRN
right .... PISCARY
season, feast after .... FOY

smack .... DOGGER
spear .... GAFF, HARPOON
spots .... PIERS
vessel .... WHALER, TRAWLER
went .... EELED
fishline leader .... SNELL
fishmonger .... FISHWIFE, FISH
DEALER
fishnet sagging part .... BUNT
fishpond .... TANK, WEIR, PISCINA,
FARM POND
fishskin disease .... ICHTHYOSIS
fishwife .... NAG(GER), MERCHANT
fishy .... DULL, FUNNY, SHADY,
TRICKY, DUBIOUS, DOUBTFUL,
INCREDIBLE, SUSPICIOUS
fish .... RED HERRING
fissile rock .... SHALE
fission .... DECAY, SCISSION,
SPLITTING
kind of .... NUCLEAR
fissure .... RENT, RIFT, RIME,
SEAM, CHINK, CLEFT, CRACK,
SPLIT, CRANNY, CREVICE
in glacier .... CREVASSE
fissures .... RIMAE
full of .... RIMOSE, RIMOUS
fist .... HAND, NIEVE
blow .... PASTE, PUNCH
fight: sl. .... MILL
fistic .... BOXING, PUGILISTIC
fisticuffs ...... BOUT, SPAR, SETTO,
FIGHTING, PUGILISM, BOXING
(MATCH)
fists: sl. .... DUKES
fistula .... PIPE, TUBE, CAVITY
fistulous .... TUBULAR
fit .... APT, PAT, MEET, TRIG,
ATTACK, ADAPT, READY,
RIGHT, KASHER, KOSHER,
PROPER, ELIGIBLE, SUIT(ABLE)
arrow on string .... NOCK
as of disease .... SPASM,
SEIZURE, APOPLEXY,
PAROXYSM, CONVULSION
as of mind inclination
.... WHIM, FANCY, NOTION,
CAPRICE
better .... ABLER
closely, exactly .... FAY
for cultivation .... ARABLE
gamecock with spurs .... HEEL
of pique .... SNIT
of shivers .... AGUE
of temper ..... IRE, HUFF, MIFF,
RAGE, TIFF, ANGER, PIQUE,
TANTRUM, OUTBURST,
CONNIPTION
one inside another .... NEST
out .... RIG, EQUIP, CLOTHE,
FURNISH

to be _____ .... TIED
be drunk .... SORBILE
be tied .... IRATE
drink .... POTABLE
eat .... EDIBLE, KOSHER,
EATABLE, ESCULENT
live in .... HABITABLE
requirement .... TAILOR,
CONFORM
work .... ABLE
together .... MESH, DOVETAIL
fitchew .... POLECAT
fitful .... BROKEN, RESTLESS,
SPORADIC, IRREGULAR,
SPASMODIC, INTERRUPTED,
INTERMITTENT
fitly .... DULY, APTLY, TIMELY,
SUITABLY, APPROPRIATELY
fitness .... APTNESS, UTILITY,
DECORUM, PROPRIETY,
SOUNDNESS
fits and _____ .... STARTS
fitting .... APT, DUE, PAT, MEET,
RIGHT, PROPER, USEFUL,
APROPOS, DECOROUS,
SUITABLE, AUSPICIOUS
fittingly .... DULY, RIGHTLY,
CONDIGNLY, DESERVEDLY
fittings .... FIXTURES,
DECORATIONS, FURNISHINGS
Fitzgerald .... BARRY, F. SCOTT
forte .... SCAT
singer .... ELLA
Fiume .... RIJEKA
five-and-ten cent store
.... DISCOUNT STORE, BARGAIN
BASEMENT
at dice or playing card
.... CINQUE
cards in same suit, sequence
of .... QUINT
-cent coin ...... JITNEY, NICKEL
collection of .... QUINTUPLET
combining form .... PENT(A)
consisting of/fold
.... QUINTUPLE
converging arcs, design of
.... CINQUEFOIL
-day duel protagonist
.... OLIVER, ROLAND
-dollar bill .... FIN, VEE, FIVER
-dollar gold piece .... HALF
EAGLE
-event athletic contest
.... PENTATHLON
finger .... OXLIP, STARFISH,
CINQUEFOIL, POTENTILLA
Goren points .... KING AND
QUEEN
group of .... PENTAD

hundred, card game
.... RUMMY, EUCHRE
hundred fifty foot-pound per
second .... HORSEPOWER
in cards/of trumps in 7-up
.... PEDRO
-lined nonsensical poem
.... LIMERICK
lines, figure of
.... PENTAGRAM
metrical feet ...... PENTAMETER
multiple of .... QUINQUE
-percenter .... FIXER
-petaled .... STARFLOWER
-pointed star .... PENTACLE
rulers, government by
.... PENTARCHY
set of .... QUINARY,
QUINTET(TE)
sided figure .... PENTAGON
-year period .... PENTAD
LUSTRUM
Five Civilized Tribes member
.... CREEK, CHOCTAW,
CHEROKEE, SEMINOLE,
CHICKASAW
Nations member (Indian)
.... CAYUGAS, MOHAWKS,
ONEIDAS, SENECAS,
ONONDAGAS, TUSCARORAS
fiver .... FIN
fives .... HANDBALL
fix .... SET, (A)MEND, LIMIT,
PLACE, RIVET, ADJUST,
DEFINE, FASTEN, FREEZE,
REPAIR, SETTLE, ESTABLISH
a meal/dinner .... PREPARE
a tire .... RECAP
colloquial .... SPAY, SPOT,
SCRAPE, DILEMMA, CASTRATE,
PREDICAMENT
in memory .... CON,
REMEMBER
jewel in setting .... MOUNT
on .... FOCUS
shoes .... SOLE
slang .... BRIBE, HEROIN,
ILLEGAL DRUG
tea .... STEEP
the hose .... DARN
the road .... REPAVE
upon .... DECIDE
fixation .... FOCUS, MANIA,
ATTENTION, OBSESSION,
PREOCCUPATION
slang .... HANGUP
fixative .... MORDANT
fixed .... SET, FIRM, RIGID, STUCK,
FROZEN, MENDED, STEADY,
LIMITED, STABILE, RESOLUTE,
ARRANGED, IMMOVABLE,

STATIONARY
charge item .... TAX, RENT,
INTEREST
course .... ROTE
fee .... FLAT RATE
reminder .... SCAR
fixings ...... MAKINGS, TRIMMINGS,
ACCESSORIES
fixture ...... FITTING, ATTACHMENT
hanging from ceiling
.... CHANDELIER
fixtures .... FITTINGS, EQUIPMENT,
PLUMBING, FURNITURE,
APPLIANCES
fizgig .... FLIRT, FIREWORK
fizz .... HISS, DRINK, BUBBLE,
SPARKLE, CHAMPAGNE
fizzle .... FAIL, FLOP, FIASCO,
MISFIRE, COLLAPSE
fizzwater .... SODA
fizzy .... BUBBLING, SPARKLING,
EFFERVESCENT
fjeld .... PLATEAU
fjord .... INLET
passage .... GAT
flabbergast .... STUN, ABASH,
AMAZE, BOGGLE, ASTONISH,
CONFOUND, SURPRISE,
DISCONCERT
flabbergasted .... AGHAST,
DUMBFOUNDED
flabellum .... FAN
flabby .... SOFT, WEAK, FEEBLE,
PULPY, FLESHY, FLACCID
flaccid ...... LIMP, WEAK, FLABBY,
FLOPPY, RUBBERY
flacon .... FLASK
flag ...... PINE, SIGN, TIRE, DROOP,
BANNER, COLORS, PENNON,
SIGNAL, WEAKEN, PENNANT,
GONFALON, LANGUISH,
STANDARD, STREAMER,
ORIFLAMME
American .... OLD GLORY,
STARS AND STRIPES
ancient Roman troops'
.... VEXILLUM
background .... FIELD
bearer .... CORNET, GUIDON,
ANCIENT
championship .... PENNANT
cloth .... BUNTING
corner .... CANTON
deer's .... TAIL
flower/plant .... IRIS
identifying .... BURGEE
little ..... PENNANT, BANNERET,
BANNEROL, BANDEROLE
maker Ross .... BETSY
matador's .... MULETA
military .... ENSIGN, GUIDON

officer ...... ADMIRAL, CAPTAIN
over tomb .... BANDEROL(E)
pirate's .... BLACKJACK, BLACK
FLAG, JOLLY ROGER
pole .... SHAFT, STAFF
position .... FANION
rope .... HALYARD
ship's .... BURGEE
signal .... ENSIGN
signal made by a .... WAFT
swallow-tailed/triangular
.... BURGEE, PENNON
sweet .... CALAMUS
flagellant .... ALBI
flagellate ...... BEAT, FLOG, LASH,
WHIP, FLAIL, SPANK, PUMMEL,
THRASH, WALLOP
flagellum .... BELT, WHIP, SHOOT,
STRAP, THONG, RUNNER
flageolet .... PIPE, FLUTE,
RECORDER
flagging .... SLOW, FATIGUED
flagitious .... VILE, WICKED,
HEINOUS
flagon .... MUG, JUG, EWER,
FLASK, STOUP, BOTTLE,
CARAFE
flagrant .... RANK, GROSS,
GLARING, NOTORIOUS,
SHOCKING, EGREGIOUS,
OUTRAGEOUS, SCANDALOUS
flagrante delicto .... RED-HANDED
flagrantly ...... BOLDLY, UNDULY,
MEANLY, ARRANTLY,
WICKEDLY, VICIOUSLY,
CONSPICUOUSLY
flags collectively .... BUNTING
flagship, famed .... SANTA MARIA
official launch .... BARGE
flagstaff .... POLE, SHAFT, STICK
flagstone .... SLAB, BRICK
Flaherty movie film ...... MOANA
flail .... BEAT, WHIP, POUND,
PUNISH, THRESH
part .... SWINGLE, SWIP(P)LE
flair .... BENT, GIFT, SKILL,
KNACK, STYLE, VERVE,
TALENT, ABILITY, BRAVURA,
APTITUDE, TENDENCY,
DISCERNMENT
flak ...... KNOCK, SWIPE, ACK-ACK,
GUNFIRE, CRITICISM
flake .... CHIP, RACK, FLECK,
SCALE, SPALL, LAMINA,
SHAVING, FLOCCULE,
SNOWDUST, SNOWFLAKE
flakes, covered with ... LEPIDOTE
flaky .... SCALY, POWDERY,
SQUAMOSE
slang .... ODD, BATTY, DIPPY,
GOOFY, KOOKY, WACKY,

QUEER, ECCENTRIC
flam .... LIE, HOAX, CHEAT, TRICK,
HUMBUG, BLARNEY,
HOGWASH, CLAPTRAP,
DECEPTION
flambeau .... TORCH, CRESSET,
LIGHTER, CANDLESTICK
flamboyance .... DASH, PANACHE,
FLASHINESS, SHOWINESS
flamboyant .... SHOWY, FRILLY,
ORNATE, FLOWERY, POMPOUS,
BOMBASTIC, FLAUNTING,
HIGHFLOWN, (BE)DAZZLING,
GRANDIOSE, STRUTTING,
OVERELEGANT,
GRANDILOQUENT
pianist .... LIBERACE
flame .... BEAM, FIRE, ZEAL,
BLAZE, SPUNK, PASSION
long, narrow .... TONGUE
slang .... BEAU, SWEETHEART
flamen .... PRIEST
flamenco dancer .... GRECO
flamethrower .... WEAPON,
BLOWGUN, FLAME SHOOTER
flaming .... FIERY, BRIGHT,
BLAZING, EXCITED
flammable ...... FIERY, BURNABLE,
COMBUSTIBLE
flan .... TART, BLANK, METAL
Flanders battlesite .... YPRES
native .... FLEMING
river .... YSER
flanerie .... LOAFING
flaneur .... IDLER, LOAFER,
ROAMER, TRIFLER,
GADABOUT, STROLLER
flange ...... LIP, RIM, EDGE, KNOB,
COLLAR
flank .... LOIN, SIDE, SKIRT,
BORDER
combining form ..... LAPAR(O)
flannel .... LANA
flannelmouth .... CATFISH
flannels: colloq. ...... UNDERWEAR
flap .... FLY, LAP, TAB, TAG, BEAT,
FOLD, SLAP, WHIP, SWING,
LAPPET, FLUTTER, UNREST,
DISCORD, ARGUMENT
airplane ...... AILERON, AIRFOIL
of flesh .... GILL, DEWLAP,
WATTLE
vigorously .... SLAT
wings .... FLICKER
flapjack .... HOT CAKE, PANCAKE,
GRIDDLECAKE
flapper .... FIN, FLIPPER, FISHTAIL
flare .... GLOW, BLAZE, BULGE,
FLASH, FLECK, GLARE, SHINE,
TORCH, FLICKER, OUTBURST
signal .... FUSEE, FUZEE

up ...... BURST, IGNITE, KINDLE

flare-up .... BLOWUP, ERUPTION, OUTBURST, EXPLOSION

flaring .... GAUDY, LURID, GARISH, ABLAZE, AFLAME, BURNING

edge .... FLANGE

star .... NOVA

flash .... BLAZE, BURST, FLARE, GLEAM, GLINT, SPARK, MOMENT, STREAK, GLIMMER, GLITTER, SPARKLE, FLAUNT, EXHIBIT, SCINTILLATE

flood .... GULLY WASHER

in the pan .... DUD, FAILURE, MISFIRE

message .... BULLETIN, NEWS REPORT

of lightning .... BOLT, THUNDERBOLT

out .... EFFULGE

flashback .... RECALL, REVIEW, REMEMBERING, REMINISCENCE

flasher .... BEACON, STREAKER

flashing .... BLINKING, FLICKERING, GLITTERING, SHORT-TERM

flashy .... GAUDY, SHOWY, SNAZZY, SPORTY, DASHING, RAFFISH

flask .... CRUSE, CARAFE, FLACON, BOTTLE, FLAGON, MATARA, CANTEEN, AMPOULE, COSTREL, MATRASS, THERMOS, CUCURBITE

flat ...... WAN, DRAB, DULL, EVEN, LEVEL, PLANE, STALE, SUITE, VAPID, SMOOTH, SOMBER, LOW-LYING, APARTMENT, TASTELESS

and circular .... DISCUS

and even .... HORIZONTAL

bottle .... FLASK

bottom boat .... DORY, PUNT, RAFT, SCOW, BARGE, BATEAU

broke .... POOR, BUSTED, PINCHED, STRAPPED

canopy .... TESTER

colloquial .... DEFLATED

dish .... PLATTER

headed Indian .... CHINOOK

headed nail .... TACK

hill .... MESA

land .... PLAIN

nosed .... PUG, SNUB, SIMOUS

on one's back .... SUPINE

out ...... UTTERLY, EXTREMELY, ABSOLUTE(LY), AT FULL SPEED

paint finish .... PALE, LIGHT, CREAMY, MELLOW, PASTEL, PEARLY, SUBDUED

slang .... BANKRUPT, IN-THE-

HOLE, PENNILESS

stick .... FERULE

stone .... SLAB

surface .... AREA, PLAIN, PLANE, TABULAR

taste .... INSIPID

flatfoot .... PES PLANUS

slang .... COP, POLICEMAN

Flathead .... SALISH, CHINOOK

flatiron .... SADIRON

flatten .... RAZE, CRUSH, PRESS, REDUCE, SUBDUE, CONQUER, EQUALIZE, PROSTRATE, LEVEL OFF, KNOCK DOWN, SMOOTH(EN)

on impact .... SPLAT

flatter .... PET, FAWN(UPON), HUMOR, PLEASE, (OVER)PRAISE, TOADY, ADULATE, BLANDISH, COMPLIMENT, SWEET-TALK

colloquial .... BUTTER UP, SOFT SOAP

slang .... OIL, SNOW, GREASE

flatterer .... PUFFER, TOADY, ADULATOR, COURTIER, FLUNK(E)Y, TOUTER, EULOGIST, SYCOPHANT, COQUETTE, LICKSPIT(TLE)

flattery .... SUGAR, TAFFY, BLARNEY, FAWNING, PALAVER, CAJOLERY, FLUMMERY, TOADYING, ADULATION, SERVILITY, BLANDISHMENT, HONEYED WORDS

slang .... SNOW JOB

flattop: sl. .... (AIRCRAFT)CARRIER

flatulence .... GAS, VANITY

flatulent .... VAIN, WINDY, EJECTIVE, POMPOUS

flatus .... GAS, PUFF

flatware .... TABLEWARE

flatwork .... SHEETS, NAPKINS

flatworm .... PARASITE, PLATYHELMINTH

opposed to .... NEMATODE, ROUNDWORM

type of .... FLUKE, CESTODE, TAPEWORM, TREMATODE

Flaubert heroine .... EMMA

novelist .... GUSTAVE

flaunt .... WAVE, PARADE, DISPLAY, SHOW(OFF), FLUTTER, BRANDISH

flaunting .... CRUDE, GAUDY, SHOWY, FLASHY, GARISH

flautist .... FIFER, BUGLER, FLUTIST, MUSICIAN

flavescent .... YELLOWISH

flavin .... PIGMENT

flavor .... GUST, LACE, ODOR, SALT, AROMA, SAPOR, SAVOR, SMELL, SAUCE, SMACK, TASTE, TINGE, RELISH, SEASON(ING)

drinks/with spice .... MULL

keeping substance

.... ESSENCE

of .... SAPOROUS

penetrating .... TANG

spicy .... GINGER

flavored .... SAPID, SAVORY, SAPOROUS

flavorful .... SAPID, SAVORY, FULL-BODIED, FLAVOROUS

flavoring .... RELISH, ESSENCE, EXTRACT, VANILLA, SEASONER, VANILLIN, CONDIMENT, SEASONING

bulb .... ONION, GARLIC, SHALLOT

for pickles .... DILL

plant .... LEEK, MINT, ANISE, SAGE, BASIL, LAUREL, CELERY, PARSLEY, CAPSICUM

root .... GINGER, LICORICE

seed .... ANISE, POPPY, SESAME, CARAWAY, MUSTARD

spice .... CLOVE, GARLIC, NUTMEG, PEPPER, CAYENNE, OREGANO, CINNAMON, MARJORAM

flavorless .... FLAT, VAPID, INSIPID, SPICELESS, UNSAVORY, TASTELESS

flavorsome .... JUICY, SAPID, TASTY, YUMMY, SAVORY, DELICIOUS, SUCCULENT

flaw .... MAR, GUST, CRACK, KINK, ERROR, FAULT, DEFECT, SQUALL, BLEMISH, MISTAKE

flawed .... FAULTY, ERRONEOUS

entrance .... MISCUE

flawless ...... PERFECT, ACCURATE, POLISHED, SPOTLESS, FAULTLESS, UNSCATHED, UNBLEMISHED

flax .... FIBER, LINEN, BYSSUS

capsule/pod .... BOLL

clean and dress .... HACKLE, HECKLE

cloth .... STUPE, CANVAS, SACKING

comber .... CARD, HACKLE, HATCHEL

dresser .... HACKLE, HECKLE, HATCHEL

fabric .... LINEN

fiber .... TOW, SILVER

filament .... HARL

husk .... SHIVE

like .... TOWY
prepare/soak .... RET
refuse of .... TOW, HARDS,
    HURDS
remove seeds from ..... RIPPLE
seed .... LINSEED
weed .... TOADFLY
flaxen color .... GOLDEN,
    BLOND(E)
flay .... ROB, BEAT, CANE, PEEL,
    WHIP, SCOLD, SKIN(ALIVE),
    STRIP, ASSAIL, DENUDE,
    FLEECE, PILLAGE, CASTIGATE,
    CRITICIZE, EXCORIATE
flea .... CHIGOE, JIGGER, JUMPER
    REDBUG, CHIGGER
bitten ..... BLOTCHY, DECREPIT,
    SPLOTCHY, WRETCHED
in one's ear .... ADVICE,
    NOTICE, WARNING
market .... STREET MART, OPEN
    MARKET, RUMMAGE SALE
fleabag .... FLOPHOUSE
fleam .... LANCET, PHLEBOTOME
fleawort .... HERB, PLANTAIN
fleche .... SPIRE
fleck ...... JOT, IOTA, SPOT, FLAKE,
    FREAK, SPECK, TITTLE,
    SPECKLE, FLYSPECK, PARTICLE
flection ...... BEND(ING), FLEXING,
    FLEXURE, TORSION
Fledermaus character .... ADELE
fledge .... BLOOM, RIPEN, MATURE,
    FEATHER(OUT)
fledgling .... INFANT, SAPLING,
    NEOPHYTE, NESTLING,
    GREENHORN
flee .... FLY, LAM, RUN(AWAY),
    BOLT, SKIP, ELOPE, DECAMP,
    ESCAPE, DESERT, VANISH,
    ABSCOND
fleece ...... ABB, ROB, COAT, FELL,
    FLAY, HIDE, PILE, WOOL,
    CHEAT, MULCT, SHEAR,
    STEAL, TAUNT, DESPOIL,
    SWINDLE
cloth .... HODDEN
fleeced .... SHORN
fleecy .... SOFT, WOOLY
fleer ...... GIBE, JEER, LEER, MOCK,
    TWIT, FLOUT, SCOFF, SMIRK,
    SNEER, TAUNT, INSULT,
    REVILE, RUNAWAY,
    RUNAGATE
fleet .... FLY, FAST, FLIT, NAVY,
    AGILE, GROUP, RAPID, SWIFT,
    MARINE, FLOTILLA
commander's vessel
    .... FLAGSHIP
front of .... VAN
merchant .... ARGOSY

small .... FLOTILLA
Spanish .... ARMADA
unit .... SQUADRON
fleeting .... BRIEF, NIMBLE,
    EPHEMERAL, TRANSIENT,
    PASSING, FUGITIVE,
    TRANSITORY
Flemish geographer
    .... MERCATOR
mathematician .... STEVIN
painter ..... RUBENS, MEMLING,
    VAN DYCK, FRANCKEN
flense .... SKIN
flesh .... MEAT, PULP,
    (ANIMAL)TISSUE, MANKIND
and blood .... KIN, KINDRED,
    KINFOLK, RELATIVE
become .... CARNIFY
calf .... VEAL
cattle .... BEEF
deer/game animal .... VENISON
eater .... OMNIVORE,
    CARNIVORE, PREDACEAN,
    OMOPHAGIST
eating .... OMOPHAGOUS,
    PREDACEOUS, PREDACIOUS,
    CARNIVOROUS
eating, man
    .... CANNIBAL(ISTIC)
eating raw .... OMOPHAGIA
fly .... BLOWFLY
fold of .... COLLOP
of dead body .... CARRION
outgrowth ..... COMB, WATTLE,
    CARUNCLE
pertaining to .... CARNAL,
    SARCOID, SARCOUS
sheep/lamb .... MUTTON
swine/pig .... PORK
symbol of human body
    .... CLAY
fleshings .... TIGHTS
fleshly .... SEXY, BODILY, CARNAL,
    MORTAL, SEXUAL, SENSUAL,
    WORLDLY, CORPOREAL
fleshpots ...... LUXURY, BROTHEL,
    BORDELLO
fleshy .... FAT, BEEFY, MEATY,
    OBESE, PLUMP, PULPY, STOUT,
    BRAWNY, ADIPOSE,
    CORPULENT
fruit .... PEAR, PLUM, POME,
    APPLE, BERRY, DRUPE, MELON,
    BANANA, CHERRY, QUINCE,
    TOMATO, SARCOCARP
fleur-de-lis .... IRIS, LILY,
    INSIGNIA, COAT-OF-ARMS
flex .... BEND, CURL, CURVE,
    CONTRACT
one's muscles .... GET SET,
    WARM UP, GET READY

flexed .... SKEWED, DEFLECTED
flexibility .... AGILITY, PLIANCY,
    VERSATILITY, ADJUSTABILITY
flexible ..... AGILE, LITHE, DOCILE,
    LIMBER, PLIANT, SUPPLE,
    DUCTILE, ELASTIC, LISSOM(E),
    PLASTIC, TENSILE, TRACTABLE
flexile .... MOBILE, PLIANT
flexing .... FLECTION
flexor .... MUSCLE
flexuous .... PLIANT, PLIABLE,
    TWISTY, TRACTILE, BENDABLE
flexure .... FOLD, CURVE,
    BEND(ING), DEFLECTION
flibbertigibbet .... GIDDYHEAD,
    CHATTERBOX, SCATTERBRAIN
flick .... TAP, DASH, FLIP, SNAP,
    CLICK, FLECK, JIGGLE,
    FLOUNCE, FLYSPECK, STREAK,
    FLUTTER
slang .... FILM, MOVIE, MOTION
    PICTURE
Flicka creator .... OHARA
flicker .... FLAP, BLAZE, BLINK,
    WAVER, QUIVER, FLUTTER,
    WOODPECKER,
    YELLOWHAMMER
dialect .... HIGH-HOLE,
    WOODPECKER
flickering .... FITFUL, ERRATIC,
    LAMBENT, SPORADIC
flier .... PILOT, AIRMAN, AVIATOR,
    LEAFLET, WINGMAN,
    AERONAUT, CIRCULAR,
    HANDBILL
in a straight stairway ..... STEP
night .... BAT
on an eagle .... ETANA
protected .... EGRET
slang .... GAMBLE, BIRDMAN,
    SPECULATION
flight .... ESCAPE, EXODUS,
    HEGIRA, HEJIRA, FLEEING,
    SQUADRON, MIGRATION,
    VOLITATION
between floors .... STAIRS
capable of .... VOLITANT
direction of a ship or plane
    .... COURSE
disorderly .... ROUT
hasty .... SCUTTLE
headlong ...... LAM, STAMPEDE
organ .... WING
short .... HOP
sudden: slang .... LAM
sudden and secret
    .... DECAMPMENT
to get married, secret
    .... ELOPEMENT
type of .... SOLO, TEST,
    MAIDEN, NONSTOP

unit .... STAIR

flightless bird .... EMU, MOA, DODO, KIWI, RHEA, WEKA, RATITE, APTERYX, OSTRICH, PENGUIN, CASSOWARY

flighty .... BARMY, GIDDY, FICKLE, FANCIFUL, FRIVOLOUS, CAPRICIOUS, HOITY-TOITY, LIGHTHEADED, SCATTER-BRAINED

one .... BIRDBRAIN, SOCIAL BUTTERFLY

flimflam ...... LIE, HOCUS, CHEAT, TRICK, HUMBUG, RUBBISH, NONSENSE

flimsy .... POOR, THIN, WEAK, FRAIL, SHEER, FEEBLE, SLEAZY, SLIGHT, FRAGILE, TENUOUS, TRIVIAL, GOSSAMER

flinch ...... COWER, DEMUR, QUAIL, SHRINK, WINCE, BLENCH, CRINGE, RECOIL, RETRACT, RETREAT

flinder .... FRAGMENT, SPLINTER

fling .... CAST, DASH, EMIT, HURL, RUSH, TOSS, SLING, THROW, HURTLE

flint .... CORN, CHERT, SILEX, QUARTZ, SILICA

Flint's outfit .... ZOWIE

flintlock .... MUSKET

flip .... TAP, JERK, PERT, SNAP, TOSS, DRINK, SAUCY, FILLIP, FLIPPANT

in the crypt ..... TURN OVER IN THE GRAVE

slang .... GO BANANAS

talk .... SASS

flippancy .... AIRS, CHEEK, PRIDE, LEVITY, VANITY, BLUSTER

colloquial .... BRASS, SAUCE

slang .... GALL, SASS, CRUST, NERVE

flippant .... AIRY, GLIB, PERT, COCKY, SASSY, SAUCY, BRAZEN

flipped: sl. .... NUTS, NUTTY, BANANAS, BONKERS, FREAKED OUT

flipper .... FIN, PADDLE

relative .... PAW

slang .... HAND

flippered mammal .... SEAL, WALRUS

flirt .... EYE, TOY, OGLE, PLAY, DALLY, TRIFLE, COQUET(TE)

female ...... SIREN, TEMPTRESS, SEDUCTRESS

in the theater .... SOUBRETTE

male .... WOLF

slang .... VAMP

flirtation .... COYNESS, COQUETRY, INTRIGUE, DALLIANCE, HANKY-PANKY

flirtatious ...... FICKLE, ALLURING, SKITTISH, TEMPTING, COQUETTISH

flirting .... TOYING, FOOLING, DALLYING, FIDDLING, TRIFLING

flit ...... FLY, DART, GLIDE, HOVER, WANDER, FLUTTER

flittermouse .... BAT

flivver .... FAIL, CRATE, AIRPLANE, AUTO(MOBILE)

float .... BUOY, CORK, RAFT, RIDE, SELL, SWIM, WAFT, DRIFT, GLIDE, LAUNCH, PONTOON

a loan .... BORROW

fishing line .... BOB, DOBBER

floater .... ROAMER, DRIFTER, WANDERER, ROLLING STONE

floating .... AWASH, ADRIFT, NATANT, BUOYANT

debris .... FLOTAGE

ice .... BERG, FLOE, GLACIER, CLUMPERS, GROWLERS

island ingredient .... EGGS

leaf .... LILYPAD

plant .... WATERLILY

platform .... RAFT

power of .... FLOTAGE

wreckage .... FLOTSAM

flocculent .... FLAKY, FLUFFY, FLEECY, WOOLLY

flock .... BAND, PACK, BUNCH, BROOD, CROWD, GROUP, TROOP, THRONG, CONGREGATION

of bears .... SLOTH

bees .... HIVE, SWARM, COLONY

birds ...... POD, BEVY, COVEY

cats .... CLOWDER

cattle .... HERD, DROVE

dogs .... KENNEL

elks .... GANG

finches .... CHARM

foxes .... SKULK

geese/wild fowl .... SKEIN, GAGGLE

lions .... PRIDE

locusts/insects .... CLOUD, SWARM

mallards .... SUTE

partridges/quails ...... COVEY

seals .... POD

sheep .... FOLD, HERD, DROVE

whales .... GAM, POD

young animals .... LITTER

pertaining to a
.... GREGARIOUS

together .... FUSE, BUNCH UP, ASSEMBLE, CONGREGATE

floe .... GLACIER, (ICE)BERG

flog .... LAM, TAN, BEAT, CANE, GOAD, HIDE, LASH, WHIP, SWISH, PUNISH, LARRUP, THRASH, TROUNCE, SHELLACK, FLAGELLATE

flogging rod .... SWISH, SWITCH

whip .... CHAB(O)UK, KURBASH

flood .... RAIN, SPATE, SWAMP, TORRENT, INUNDATE, OVERFLOW, CLOUDBURST, INUNDATION, OUTPOURING, RAINSTORM, HIGH WATER, UNDERWATER

a great .... DELUGE, CATARACT, CATACLYSM

light .... KLIEG

the engine .... STALL

the market .... GLUT

tidal .... EAGRE

flooded condition .... SPATE, OVERSUPPLY

floodgate ...... DAM, WEIR, HATCH, SLUICE, CONTROL, SPILLWAY

floor .... DECK, DALLE, LEVEL, STORY, PUZZLE, PLANCH(E), SURFACE, PAVEMENT, PLATFORM, KNOCK DOWN

above street level
.... ENTRESOL, MEZZANINE

chateau .... ETAGE

cover .... RUG, TILE, WOOD, CARPET, MAT(TING), LINOLEUM

covering, fabric for
.... DRUGGET

raised border .... COAMING

show .... ENTERTAINMENT

walker ..... SUPERVISOR, SALES MANAGER

floorcloth .... LINOLEUM

flooring chip/slab .... DALLE, PARQUET, TERRAZZO

floorleader .... WHIP

flop .... DROP, FAIL, FALL, FLAP, LOLL, THUD

colloquial .... BUST, FAILURE

slang .... SLEEP, LAY AN EGG

flophouse .... FLEABAG

denizen .... WINO

flora .... PLANTS

and fauna .... BIOTA

floral .... GARDEN, FLOWERY, FLOWERED

arrangement .... SPRAY, WREATH, BOUQUET, GARLAND, NOSEGAY

arrangement, art of
.... IKEBANA
envelope .... PERIANTH
leaf .... BRACT, SEPAL
organs .... STAMENS
Florence .... FIRENZE, FIORENZA
Florentine friar .... SERVITE
iris .... ORRIS
name .... MEDICI
painter .... LIPPI, SARTO,
CIMABUE
florescence .... BLOOM(ING),
BLOSSOM(ING),
FLOWERING(TIME)
florid ...... ROSY, GAUDY, RUDDY,
SHOWY, FLORAL, ORNATE,
FLOWERY, TAFFETA, FANCIFUL
style ...... ROCOCO, ARABESQUE
Florida bay .... PALM, MCKAY,
TAMPA, CRYSTAL, DEADMAN,
FLORIDA, BISCAYNE,
GULLIVAN, APALACHEE,
CHEVELIER, PENSACOLA,
WACCASASSA, WHITEWATER,
HILLSBOROUGH
beach .... VERO, COCOA,
DEKLE, MIAMI, DELRAY,
VILANO, BOYNTON, DAYTONA,
FLAGLER, POMPANO,
CRESCENT, WEST PALM, FORT
MYERS, PONTE VEDRA
bird .... ANI, COURLAN,
LIMPKIN
canal .... TAMIAMI, SNAKE
CREEK
cape .... SABLE, ROMANO,
CANAVERAL, SAINT GEORGE
capital of .... TALLAHASSEE
city/town .... DADE, DANIA,
LARGO, MIAMI, OCALA, PERRY,
TAMPA, NAPLES, QUINCY,
PANAMA, ORLANDO, HIALEAH,
MARGATE, LAKELAND,
PALATKA, LEESBURG,
SARASOTA, BRADENTON,
HOLLYWOOD, MELBOURNE,
PENSACOLA, CLEARWATER,
BOCA RATON, FORT MYERS,
PLANTATION, GAINESVILLE,
JACKSONVILLE, CORAL
GABLES, DAYTONA BEACH,
FORT LAUDERDALE, SAINT
AUGUSTINE, SAINT
PETERSBURG
college .... BARRY, TAMPA,
ROLLINS
county .... BAY, LEE, CLAY,
DADE, LAKE, LEON, POLK,
DUVAL, PASCO, CITRUS,
HARDEE, MARION, MARTIN,
MONROE, NASSAU, ORANGE,

PUTNAM, SUMTER, WALTON,
ALACHUA, BREVARD,
BROWARD, COLLIER, GADSDEN,
JACKSON, MANATEE, OSCEOLA,
VOLUSIA, BRADFORD,
COLUMBIA, ESCAMBIA,
HERNANDO, OKALOOSA,
PINELLAS, SARASOTA,
SEMINOLE, SUWANNEE,
CHARLOTTE, HIGHLANDS, PALM
BEACH, SANTA ROSA, SAINT
JOHNS, SAINT LUCIE,
HILLSBOROUGH, INDIAN RIVER
creek .... PINE LOG
fish .... MERO, BONACI,
SALEMA, TETARD, PINTADO,
CABRILLA
grouper .... BONACI
harbor .... CHARLOTTE,
EVERGLADES
Indian ...... CALUSA, SEMINOLE
island ...... DOG, PINE, MARCO,
PINEY, AMELIA, ESTERO,
TALBOT, CAPTIVA, MERRITT,
SANIBEL, TREASURE,
HONEYMOON, SAINT GEORGE
islands .... HOMOSASSA, TEN
THOUSAND
key .... LONG, VACA, LARGO,
SANDS, TORCH, GRASSY,
ELLIOTT, BISCAYNE,
MATECUMBE, SUGARLOAF,
BOCA CHICA, OLD RHODES,
BOCA GRANDE
lake .... DEAD, DORR, HART,
KERR, LEVY, WEIR, YALE,
REEDY, APOPKA, BRYANT,
DEXTER, GEORGE, HARNEY,
LOWERY, MARIAN, MONROE,
ORANGE, PLACID, WIMICO,
WINDER, JACKSON, TALQUIN,
ARBUCKLE, CRESCENT,
POINSETT, ALLIGATOR
mountain .... IRON
much of .... LOWLANDS
Naval Air Station
.... MAYPORT, KEY WEST,
PENSACOLA
perchlike fish .... CABRILLA
plant .... COONTIE
recreation/historic site ...... SEA
WORLD, MARINELAND, DISNEY
WORLD, CYPRESS GARDENS,
RINGLING MUSEUMS, KENNEDY
SPACE CENTER
resort city .... MIAMI,
ORLANDO, PALM BEACH
river .... MIAMI, SHOAL,
BANANA, MYAKKA, AUCILLA,
MANATEE, S(U)WANEE,
OKLAWAHA, APALACHICOLA,

CHATTAHOOCHEE,
CHOCTAWHATCHEE
sapodilla/tree .... BUSTIC
seaport .... TAMPA, PENSACOLA
scenic road .... TAMIAMI
state bird .... MOCKINGBIRD
state flower .... ORANGE
BLOSSOM
state nickname ...... SUNSHINE,
EVERGLADE
tortoise .... GOPHER
univeristy .... HEED, NOVA,
MIAMI, TAMPA, WALDEN,
STETSON, PALM BEACH
wood oil .... TUNG
florist's specialty .... POSY,
SPRAY, WREATH, BOUQUET,
CORSAGE, NOSEGAY
floss .... SILK, FLUFF, SLEAVE
flossy .... SOFT, DOWNY, FANCY,
CLASSY, FLUFFY, LA-DI-DA,
ELEGANT
flotage .... FLOTSAM
flotation .... LAUNCHING,
UNVEILING
flotilla ...... FLEET, SHIPS, ARGOSY
Flotow opera .... MART(H)A
flotsam .... FLOTAGE, DRIFTAGE,
FLOATAGE
and jetsam .... DRIFTERS,
VAGRANTS, CASTAWAYS,
WAIFS AND STRAYS
flounce .... JERK, JUMP, TWIST,
FALTER, RUFFLE, TOTTER,
TUMBLE, FALBALA, FURBELOW
flounder .... DAB, SOLE, TOSS,
FLUKE, GROPE, FUMBLE,
PLAICE, TURBOT, WALLOP,
WALLOW, WELTER, HALIBUT,
STAGGER, FLATFISH,
STRUGGLE
flour .... MEAL, MILL, DURUM,
POWDER, BUCKWHEAT
bean/corn .... PINOLE
boiled, thick .... FLUMMERY
cereal .... FARINA
color of .... IVORY, CREAMY-
WHITE
maker/machine .... MILLER
making product ..... SEMOLINA
mixture .... ROUX, DOUGH,
PASTE
paste .... PANADA
power .... YEAST
pudding .... DUFF
sieve/sifter .... BOLTER
sprinkle with .... DUST,
DREDGE, PEPPER
flourish ...... BOOM, GROW, WAVE,
SWING, TWIRL, WIELD,
FLAUNT, THRIVE, FANFARE,

PROSPER, SUCCEED, TANTARA,
    BRANDISH
in an area .... CADENZA
in music .... ROULADE
in signature .... PARAPH
in writing .... TAG
floury .... POWDERY
flout .... JEER, MOCK, FLEER,
    SCOFF
flow .... RUN, OOZE, WELL, GLIDE,
    SPOUT, CURRENT, EMANATE
about freely .... CIRCULATE
against/along .... LAVE
and spread .... FLUSH
back .... EBB, RECEDE,
    REGORGE
combining form .... RHEO
forth .... ISSUE
in drops .... DRIBBLE
of tide .... EBB, FLUX, NEAP,
    RISE
out .... POUR, EXUDE, ISSUE,
    SPILL, STREAM
stop .... STEM, STANCH
than can .... FLUID
through .... SEEP
flower .... BEST, PICK, POSY,
    BLOOM, BLOSSOM, ORNAMENT
amaranth .... PIGWEED
annual .... ASTER
arrangement .... SPRAY,
    IKEBANA, VERTICIL
aster .... TANGLEFOOT
balsam .... IMPATIENS
bell-shaped .... HYACINTH
bending downward
    .... CERNUOUS
biennial .... FOXGLOVE
bloom .... ANTHESIS
blue .... VIOLET, LARKSPUR,
    HYDRANGEA
bract .... PALEA
bud .... KNOT, BULBIL
buds for seasoning .... CAPERS
butterfly-like
    .... MARIPOSA(LILY)
children, so-called ..... HIPPIES
Christmas .... POINSETTIA
cluster .... CYME, LILAC,
    TRUSS, UMBEL, CORYMB,
    RACEME, PANICLE, THYRSUS,
    CAPITULUM
cormus .... CROCUS,
    GLADIOLUS
cover of/covering ...... SPATHE,
    CALYPTRA
cowslip .... MARIGOLD,
    PRIMROSE
cup-shaped .... CHALICE
daisy .... OX-EYE
daisy-like .... BLACK-EYED

    SUSAN
Dutch .... TULIP
Easter .... LILY
envelope .... PERIANTH
erica .... HEATH
ericaceous .... AZALEA,
    LAUREL
extract .... AT(T)AR
fadeless .... AMARANTH,
    EVERLASTING
fall .... ASTER
field .... DAISY, GOWAN
form of .... PELORIA
fragrant .... ROSE, LILAC,
    AZALEA, JASMIN(E),
    HYACINTH, MAGNOLIA,
    JESSAMINE, HONEYSUCKLE
fringed .... GENTIAN
full-bloomed .... ANTHESIS
garden ...... ROSARY, NURSERY,
    GREENERY
genus .... ROSA, HEATH,
    LILIUM, SYRINGA, TAGETES,
    HIBISCUS
goddess .... FLORA
grower .... GARDENER,
    NURSERYMAN,
    HORTICULTURIST
growing, art of
    .... HORTICULTURE
having only one
    .... MONANTHOUS
head ...... PANICLE, CAPITULUM
heath .... AZALEA
herbaceous border
    .... VERBENA
holder .... BED, POT, VASE
honeysuckle .... ELDER,
    CLOVER
imaginary .... AMARANTH
incipient .... BUD
iris .... ORRIS, ORRICE
leaf ..... BRACT, PALEA, SEPAL,
    COROLLA
like .... ANTHOID
like animal .... ANEMONE
like ornament .... ROSETTE
lily .... SEGO, CALLA, LOTUS,
    MARIPOSA
moon .... ACHETE
musk-odored .... MOSCHATEL
night-blooming .... CEREUS
nightshade .... HENBANE,
    BELLADONNA
of .... FLORAL
of forgetfulness .... LOTUS
of varied colors .... PHLOX
orchid .... ARETHUSA,
    CYMBIDIUM, WALING-WALING
pansy .... HEARTSEASE
part ..... STEM, AMENT, BRACT,

    CALYX, OVARY, OVULE,
    PETAL, SEPAL, STYLE, ANTHER,
    CARPEL, PISTIL, POLLEN,
    SPADIX, STAMEN, STIGMA,
    COROLLA, PEDICEL
perennial .... DAHLIA,
    AMARANTH
petals .... COROLLA
pink .... TITI, ELDER,
    CARNATION, RHODORA,
    HYDRANGEA
pistil .... CARPEL
plot .... BED
pollen-bearing part
    .... STAMEN
receptacled .... TORUS,
    THALAMUS
red .... ROSE, OXALIS,
    CAMELLIA, MARIGOLD
rootstock .... TARO, ORRIS,
    ORRICE
rose of Sharon .... ALTHEA
roselike .... CAMELLIA
seed .... OVULE
seed-bearing part .... PISTIL
sex cells .... POLLEN
shaped .... FLEURON
showy ..... MARIGOLD, GOLDEN
    ASTER
small .... FLORET, FLOWERET
spike .... AMENT, SPICA,
    CATKIN, SPICULE, MIGNONETTE
spring .... TULIP, HYACINTH
stalk .... PETIOLE, PEDUNCLE
stalk bud/bulb .... BULBIL
stand .... EPERGNE, JARDINIERE
summer .... PETUNIA,
    MARIGOLD, CHRYSANTHEMUM
star .... ASTER
sun prone .... HELIOTROPE
support .... PEDUNCLE
symbol of luxury ...... ORCHID
syringa .... LILAC
the .... PICK, ELECT, ELITE
three-petaled .... ORCHID
turban-like .... TULIP
used for a corsage .... ORCHID
velvety .... PANSY
waterlily .... LOTUS
white .... TITI, ELDER, LILAC,
    CROCUS, OXALIS, GENTIAN,
    CAMELLIA, TRILLIUM,
    HYDRANGEA
wild .... THISTLE
wind .... ANEMONE
windowbox .... PETUNIA
wood sorrel .... OXALIS
yellow .... GOWAN, BENNET,
    COWSLIP, MARIGOLD
flowered vine .... CLEMATIS
flowering grass .... STIPA

herb .... HEPATICA
more than once a season
.... REMONTANT
plant .... ARUM, FERN, ROSE,
    AVENS, CANNA, YUCCA,
    ORCHID, SPIREA, LUPIN(E),
    LOBELIA, GERANIUM,
    VALERIAN, POINSETTIA
shrub .... BIXA, LILAC, SUMAC,
    AZALEA, SPIREA, MAGNOLIA,
    POINCIANA
vine .... CLEMATIS, WISTERIA
flowerless plant .... FERN,
    LICHEN, AGAMOUS, GENTIAN
flowers, bunch of .... POSY,
    BOUQUET, CORSAGE, NOSEGAY
collectively .... FLOWERAGE
in a spathe .... SPADIX
of/like .... FLORAL, FLOWERY
of Fats fame, two
.... HONEYSUCKLE ROSE
on woman's shoulder
.... CORSAGE
sculptured .... CORBEIL
flowery .... FLORID, ORNATE,
    BLOSSOMY, BOMBASTIC,
    FLAMBOYANT, HIGH-FLOWN
girl .... ROSA
flowing .... LOOSE, FLUENT,
    SMOOTH, (AF)FLUX, BILLOWY,
    CURSIVE, GRACEFUL,
    FLUXION, EMANATING
and ebbing .... TIDAL
back .... REFLUX, REFLUENT
freely .... MOBILE
locks .... TRESSES
out .... EFFLUX
together .... CONFLUX,
    CONFLUENT, CONFLUENCE
flown ...... LOOSE, FLUSHED, FLED,
    AT LARGE, FUGITIVE
flu .... INFLUENZA
drug for .... SYMMETREL,
    AMANTADINE
-like illness .... GRIPPE
symptom .... AGUE, FEVER,
    CHILLS, FATIGUE
treatment .... REST,
    ANALGESICS
variety, 1918 .... SPANISH
1957 .... ASIAN
1968 .... HONG KONG
flub ...... BOTCH, ERROR, BUNGLE,
    BLUNDER, FAILURE
slang .... BONER
fluctuant .... WAVY, VARYING,
    UNDULATING
fluctuate ...... VARY, VEER, WAVE,
    SHIFT, SWING, SEE-SAW,
    ALTERNATE, VACILLATE
fluctuating ...... FICKLE, ERRATIC,

    INCONSTANT
fluctuation .... SHIFTING,
    WAVERING, VARIATION
flue .... PIPE, FLUFF, FLUKE,
    SHAFT, FUNNEL, CHIMNEY
dust .... POTASH
fluency .... EASE, FLOW, GRACE,
    GLIBNESS, ELOQUENCE,
    SMOOTHNESS
fluent ...... GLIB, FACILE, SMOOTH,
    FLOWING, ELOQUENT,
    EXPRESSIVE
fluently .... GLIBLY, VIVIDLY
fluff .... ERR, NAP, FLUE, LINT,
    DOWN, BONER, ERROR, FLOSS
fluffy .... DOWNY, LINTY, FLOSSY,
    COTTONY, FEATHERY,
    FLOCCULENT
fluid .... GAS, SAP, SERUM, LIQUID,
    MOBILE, PLASTIC
aeriform .... GAS
body .... BILE, LYMPH
colloidal system .... SOL
life-saving .... BLOOD
matter .... FLUX
part of fruit or vegetable
.... JUICE
rock .... LAVA
stoppage .... STASIS
fluidity ...... SEROSITY, LIQUIDITY,
    SOLUBLENESS
fluke .... BARB, FLUE, HOOK,
    CLEEK, FLATFISH, FLATWORM,
    FLOUNDER, TREMATODE,
    LUCKY BREAK, STROKE OF
    LUCK
fluky .... CHANCY, UNFORESEEN
flume ...... CHUTE, GORGE, SHUTE,
    OUTLET, RAVINE, SLUICE,
    TROUGH, CHANNEL
flummery .... CUSTARD,
    OATMEAL, RUBBISH,
    FLATTERY, NONSENSE
flummox: sl. .... THWART,
    CONFUSE, PERPLEX
flump .... DROP, THUD, THUMP
flunk .... LOSE, FAIL(URE), FIASCO,
    GIVE UP, NOT PASS, RETREAT
slang .... BUST, WASHOUT
flunk(e)y .... TOADY, LACKEY,
    STOOGE, YES-MAN, FOOTMAN
flunks at Annapolis .... BILGES
fluoresce .... OPALESCE,
    LUMINESCE
fluorescent .... IRIDESCENT,
    OPALESCENT
fluorite .... JADE
fluoroscopy .... X-RAY,
    RADIOSCOPY
flurry .... ADO, GUST, STIR,
    HURRY, AGITATION,

    COMMOTION, CONFUSION
flush .... GLOW, GUSH, RUSH,
    FULL, BLUSH, ELATE, EMPTY,
    RINSE, ROUSE, START, LAVISH,
    EXCITE, REDDEN, THRILL,
    PROFUSE, EXHILARATE
with water .... WASH
flushed .... HOT, RED, AGLOW,
    RUDDY, FLORID, HECTIC,
    BLUSHING, FEVERISH
fluster .... BUSTLE, EXCITE,
    FUDDLE, DITHER, POTHER,
    CONFUSE, BLUSTER,
    UNSETTLE, EMBARRASS
flustered .... AGITATED
flute .... FIFE, PIPE, PIPING,
    GROOVE, CHANNEL
ancient .... TIBIA, HEMIOPE
bagpipe .... CHANTER
blow a .... TOOTLE
Chinese .... (T)CHE
cousin of .... PICCOLO
early form .... RECORDER
India .... MATALAN
-like instrument
.... FLAGEOLET
part of a .... KEYS, TUBE,
    FIPPLE
player .... FL(A)UTIST TOOTLER
stop .... VENTAGE
fluted .... FOLDED, GROOVED,
    SULCATE(D)
fluting .... GOFFER, GAUFFER,
    GROOVE(S)
architectural .... GADROON,
    GODROON
wavelike .... STRIGIL
flutter .... FLY, FLAP, FLIP, FLIT,
    WHIP, HOVER, SHAKE,
    BUSTLE, WAVE(R), FIDGET,
    QUIVER, FLICKER, TREMBLE,
    TWITTER, AGITATE, VIBRATE,
    PALPITATE
and shift .... RIFFLE
of eyes .... BLINK
flux .... FUSE, BORAX, PURGE,
    ROSIN, FLOW(ING), COURSE,
    MOTION, SOLDER, CURRENT,
    FLUXION, SOLVENT
and reflux .... ALTERNATION,
    UPS AND DOWNS
slang .... TROTS
fluxion ...... FLOWING, DISCHARGE,
    EXCRETION
fly .... BUG, BOLT, DART, FLAP,
    FLEE, FLIT, GNAT, SOAR,
    SCUD, WAVE, WHIR, WING,
    FLOAT, HOVER, MIDGE,
    MUSCA, AVIATE, FLUTTER,
    TACHINA, MOSQUITO
able to ..... VOLANT, VOLITANT

after game .... RAKE
agaric/amanita ..... MUSHROOM
angler's artificial
.... DOWNLOOKER
artificial .... DUN, HARL, HERL,
    ZULU, CAHILL, HACKLE
at .... ATTACK
before the wind .... SCUD
block .... PULLEY
bloodsucking .... GADFLY,
    TABANID
-by-night .... UNSURE,
    UNRELIABLE
case .... ELYTRON
catcher .... TODY, PEWIT,
    PEEWEE, PHOEBE
close to the ground
.... HEDGEHOP
experimental ...... DROSOPHILA
hit .... SWAT
in the ointment ..... OBSTACLE
insect resembling ...... CICADA
let .... THROW
nemesis .... SWATTER
of the .... MUSCID
off .... ESCAPE, RUN AWAY
sheet .... PAMPHLET
slang .... AGILE, SHARP,
    NIMBLE
small .... MITE, PUNKIE
the coop .... BREAK JAIL
to and fro .... VOLITANT
wing cover .... ELYTRON,
    ELYTRUM
flyaway .... ESCAPEE, FLIGHTY,
    STREAMING
flyblow ...... LARVA, SPOIL, TAINT
flyblown .... FILTHY, SPOILED
flycatcher .... TODY, ALDER,
    PEWIT, PE(E)WEE, PHOEBE,
    CHEBEC, FANTAIL, KINGBIRD
flyer, famous .... LINDY,
    LINDBERGH
fearless .... ACE
inky .... CROW, RAVEN
of myth .... ICARUS
stunt of .... LOOP, ROLL
flying .... ALOFT, FLIGHT,
    WINGING, AIRBORNE,
    FLITTING, HOVERING,
    SKYRIDING
act of .... VOLITATION
air matress .... PARAFOIL
airplanes, art or science of
.... AVIATION
capable of .... VOLANT,
    VOLITANT
colors .... SUCCESS, VICTORY
fish .... SAURY, GURNET,
    GURNARD
fox .... BAT, KALONG

gurnard .... GURNET
in an engineless aircraft
.... GLIDING
island, fictional .... LAPUTA
jib .... SAIL
lemur .... COLUGO
lizard's skin fold
.... PATAGIUM, PARACHUTE
machine ...... AERO, AIRCRAFT,
    AIR BALLOON, (AIR)PLANE
marsupial .... PHALANGER
saucer, for short .... UFO
signal .... ROGER
spindrift .... SCUD
squirrel's skin fold
.... PATAGIUM
start .... EDGE, ADVANTAGE
water .... SPRAY
Flying Dutchman .... SHIP,
    SAILOR
Dutchman maiden .... SENTA
Finn .... NURMI
Fortress .... BOMBER
Fortress weapon ...... TAILGUN
Flynn, actor .... ERROL
flyspeck .... DOT, SPOT
flywheel .... WHORL, WHARVE
foal .... COLT, FILLY
foam .... FIZZ, SCUM, SUD(S),
    FROTH, YEAST, BUBBLE,
    SPUME, LATHER
of .... SPUMY, SPUMOUS
poetic .... SEA
foaming .... HEADY, NAPPY
at the mouth .... MAD
foamy ...... SOAPY, SPUMY, SUDSY,
    FROTHY, LATHERY, SPUMOUS
yeast .... BARM
fob .... CHARM, CHEAT, TRICK,
    DECEIVE, PENDANT,
    (WATCH)POCKET
off .... PALM, FOIST
focal .... CHIEF, CENTRAL
point .... HUB, CYNOSURE,
    EPICENTER
focus .... HUB, CORE, HEART,
    POINT, CENTER, NUCLEUS,
    CONVERGE, SPOTLIGHT,
    CENTRALIZE, CONCENTRATE
in .... CLEAR, DISTINCT
focusing device .... LENS
fodder .... HAY, FEED, FOOD,
    OATS, GRASS, STRAW,
    FORAGE, SILAGE, ALFILARIA,
    CORNSTALK, PROVENDER,
    PROVISION
bin .... CRATCH
grain .... KAFFIR
pertaining to .... FORAGE
pit/storage place/tower
.... SILO

plant ...... GRAM, RAPE, VETCH,
    ALSIKE, CLOVER, STOVER,
    ALFALFA, BERSEEM, CHICKPEA,
    SAINFOIN
preservation .... ENSILAGE
rack .... CRATCH
straw .... STOVER
tree pod .... CAROB
trough .... MANGER
foe ...... ENEMY, RIVAL, OPPONENT,
    ADVERSARY, ANTAGONIST
Athenian's .... SPARTAN
of Richelieu .... ATHOS
of shams .... ICONOCLAST
fog .... HAZE, MIST, MURK, BRUME,
    CLOUD, VAPOR, CONFUSE
and smoke .... SMOG
fog(e)y .... DOTARD, MOSSBACK
fogeyish .... FUSTY, SENILE,
    STODGY
foggy .... DIM, MISTY, MURKY,
    CLOUDY, BRUMOUS,
    CONFUSED, NUBILOUS
foghorn .... ALARM, SIGNAL,
    SIREN(E)
foible .... FLAW, VICE, FAULT,
    WHIMSY, FAILING, FRAILTY,
    WEAKNESS
opposed to .... FORTE
foil .... BALK, EPEE, DETER, SPOIL,
    STUMP, SWORD, BAFFLE,
    THWART, FRUSTRATE,
    CIRCUMVENT
comedian's .... STOOGE,
    STRAIGHTMAN
slang ...... CRAMP ONE'S STYLE
foilsman .... FENCER
foist ...... FOB, PALM(OFF), IMPOSE
    ON
Fokine, choreographer
.... MICHEL
fold .... LAP, PLY, BEND, KNIT,
    RUCK, RUGA, WRAP, CLASP,
    CRIMP, DRAPE, FLOCK, LAYER,
    PLAIT, PLEAT, GATHER,
    EMBRACE, ENVELOP, FLEXURE,
    PLICA(TION)
animal's throat .... DEWLAP
coat .... LAPEL
mark .... CREASE
sail .... REEF
sheep .... PEN
skin .... PLICA
slang .... BUST, FAIL
stitched .... TUCK
up .... FAIL, CLOSE, GO UNDER,
    COLLAPSE
folded .... RUGATE, PLEATED,
    DOUBLED, PLICATE
edge .... HEM
part .... PLEAT, PLICA

folder .... COVER, BOOKLET, LEAFLET, PAMPHLET
folding bed .... COT
hood/bonnet .... CALASH
leaves, plant with ..... MIMOSA
money .... ONES, DOLLAR
foliage .... LEAVES, LEAFAGE, UMBRAGE, VERDURE
mass of .... SPRAY, BOUQUET
folio .... BOOK, PAGE, NUMBER
foliose .... LEAFY, VERDANT
folium .... LOOP
folk ...... KIN, KOLO, RACE, TRIBE, NATION, PEOPLE, PERSONS
dance .... HORA, DREHER, MORRIS
tale .... FICTION, MARCHEN
tale tiny hero ..... TOM THUMB
folklore .... BELIEFS, LEGENDS, SAYINGS, MYTHOLOGY
character .... OGRE, DWARF, FAIRY, GIANT, TROLL, SANDMAN
folksinger .... BAEZ, IVES
folksong .... LULLABY
folkways .... MORES
follicle .... POD, SAC, GLAND, CAVITY, COCOON, CAPSULE
follies .... REVUE
follow .... TAG, COPY, HEED, OBEY, SEEK, CHASE, ENSUE, TRACE, TRACK, TRAIL, ATTEND, COMPLY, PURSUE, RESULT, CONFORM, IMITATE, SUCCEED, ACCOMPANY
continually/relentlessly .... DOG, HOUND
in the footsteps of .... EMULATE
stealthily/secretly .... STAG, TAIL, SHADOW
suit .... MODEL AFTER
up .... PURSUE, GO AFTER
follower .... FAN, IST, ITE, BUFF, MINION, VOTARY, DEVOTEE, PURSUER, ADHERENT, BELIEVER, DISCIPLE, HENCHMAN, PARTISAN, SERVITOR, SUPPORTER
faithful .... FRIDAY, MYRMIDON
finger .... BOWL, NAIL, WAVE
fox or turkey .... TROT
kind of .... SERVANT, HANGER-ON, ATTENDANT, SATELLITE
loyal .... LIEGEMAN
of Arius .... ARIAN
of forgive .... FORGET
of Lao-tze .... TAOIST
of snick .... SNEE
of theta .... IOTA
para .... GRAPH, LEGAL,

NORMAL
followers, group of .... CULT
following .... SECT, AFTER, TRADE, TRAIN, ENSUING, PURSUIT, RETINUE, EQUIPAGE, ADHERENTS, FOLLOWERS
this .... HEREAFTER, HENCEFORTH
folly .... IDIOCY, LUNACY, FATUITY, INANITY, FRIVOLITY, SILLINESS, FOOLISHNESS
foment .... ABET, BREW, SPUR, STIR, AROUSE, EXCITE, INCITE, INSTIGATE
fond .... ARDENT, LOVING, TENDER, DEVOTED, FOOLISH, ATTACHED, ENAMORED, AFFECTIONATE
of: sl. .... STUCK ON
arguing .... DISPUTATIVE
fighting .... COMBATIVE, PUGNACIOUS
foolishly .... DOTING, SMITTEN, UXORIOUS
luxury, etc. .... EPICUREAN
Fonda .... JANE, HENRY, PETER
fondant .... CANDY
fondle .... HUG, PET, TOUCH, CARESS, COSSET, DANDLE, PAMPER, STROKE, CHERISH, EMBRACE
fondling .... MINION, DARLING, NECKING, PETTING, FAVORITE
fondness .... LOVE, ARDOR, FLAIR, TASTE, DESIRE, LIKING, REGARD, PENCHANT, AFFECTION
font .... BOWL, CASE, FACE, TYPE, BASIN, LAVER, STOOP, STOUP, ORIGIN, SPRING, SOURCE, FOUNTAIN, RESERVOIR
rite .... BAPTISM
fontal .... ORIGINAL, BAPTISMAL
fontanel(le) .... OUTLET, OPENING
food .... BITE, DIET, FARE, BOARD, TABLE, VIANDS, ALIMENT, EDIBLES, REPAST, NUTRIMENT, NUTRITION, MEAL, COMESTIBLES, NOURISHMENT
additive: abbr. .... MSG
allowance .... CORODY, RATION
and shelter .... KEEP, BOARD
animal .... FODDER, FORAGE
archaic .... DAILY BREAD
being digested .... CHYME
between meals .... SNACK
bits .... ORTS, SCRAPS
cereal .... OAT, CORN, RICE, WHEAT
chewed, solid .... BROMA
choice: arch. .... CATE

colloquial .... CHOW, EATS, GRUB, SPREAD
concentrated high-energy .... PEMMICAN
dealer .... GROCER
desire/need for .... HUNGER
diet .... FARE, REGIMEN
disk-shaped .... PATTY
drying platform .... FLAKE
fancy .... KICKSAW
fish .... COD, BASS, CERO, DACE, SHAD, TUNA, PERCH, SCROD, TROUT, SALMON, SARDINE, MACKEREL, SHEEPSHEAD
fish, Atlantic .... ALEWIFE
for beginners/infants ...... PAP, PABLUM, PABULUM
for cattle/goats .... BROWSE
from heaven .... MANNA
Hawaiian .... POI
in a hive .... BEEBREAD
in Australia: sl. .... TUCKER
liquid .... SLOP, SOUP, BROTH
list .... CARTE
look for .... SCAVENGE
Maori .... KAI
needed to sustain life ..... SUSTENANCE, SUBSISTENCE
non-flesh .... MAIGRE
of fools .... FLATTERY
of the gods .... AMRITA, AMBROSIA
place for ..... LARDER, SPENCE, SPENSE, PANTRY, CUPBOARD
place for eating .... DINER, EATERY, AUTOMAT, CANTEEN, MESS HALL, CAFE(TERIA), REFECTORY, RESTAURANT, DINING ROOM
place for eating: colloq. .... GREASY SPOON
poisoning .... BOTULISM, PTOMAIN(E)
provider/supplier ..... CATERER
rack .... FLAKE
regimen .... DIET
scrap .... ORT
served .... HELPING
serving style .... BUFFET
shavings/slices .... CHIPS
shop .... DELICATESSEN
slang .... FEED, FUEL, SLOP, JUNK FOOD
soft .... PAP, FLUMMERY
solid in medicine .... BROMA
specialist .... DIETARIAN, DIETITIAN
spoiler .... MOLD, YEAST, ENZYME, BACTERIA
stock of .... VITTLES,

VICTUALS, PROVISIONS
study of kinds and quantities
.... DIETETICS
style/manner of preparing
.... CUISINE
supplement .... MINERAL,
VITAMIN
taken after a period of
hunger .... REFECTION
thick and semi-solid, made
from milk .... YOGURT
unappetizing .... MESS
wrap .... SARAN
foods, study of .... SITOLOGY,
DIETETICS
foofaraw .... ROW, RIOT, RACKET,
UPROAR
fool .... ASS, OAF, BOOB, DOLT,
DUPE, GABY, JAPE, SIMP,
ZANY, CHUMP, DUNCE, IDIOT,
NINNY, NODDY, TRICK,
DOTARD, NOODLE, DECEIVE,
MISLEAD, MUGGINS,
SAP(HEAD), MOONCALF,
SIMPLETON
around .... TRIFLE
around with .... MEDDLE,
TAMPER
hen .... GROUSE
in a way .... SPOOF
play the .... CLOWN
professional .... JESTER
foolable .... NAIVE, GULLIBLE
foolhardy .... BOLD, RASH, BRASH,
DARING, ICARIAN, RECKLESS
person .... DAREDEVIL
foolish .... MAD, DAFT, RASH,
ZANY, CRAZY, INANE, SILLY,
ABSURD, CUCKOO, SENILE,
STUPID, UNWISE, ASININE,
LUNATIC, PUERILE, TRIVIAL,
ANSERINE, IMPRUDENT,
LUDICROUS, RIDICULOUS
action .... FOLLY,
(TOM)FOOLERY
affection .... DOTAGE
blunder .... HOWLER
fancy .... CHIMERA
from overdrinking
.... SCOTTISH
from old age .... DOITED,
SENILE
slang .... BALMY, BARMY,
DIZZY, GIDDY, GOOFY, KOOKY,
SAPPY, WACKY
talk .... BABBLE, JABBER,
CHATTER, PRATTLE,
BLAB(BER), FLAPDOODLE,
YAKKETY-YAK
undertaking .... FOLLY,
FRIVOLITY, EXTRAVAGANCE

foolishly loving .... FOND
foolishness .... FOLLY, LUNACY,
FATUITY, MISCHIEF, NONSENSE
foolproof .... TIGHT, WIELDY,
(FAIL)SAFE, RESISTANT
fool's bauble .... MAROTTE
gold .... PYRITE
paradise ...... BUBBLE, UTOPIA,
CHIMERA, DAYDREAM, FALSE
HOPE
foot .... BASE, HOOF, WALK,
TREAD, BOTTOM, UNGULA,
TROTTER, EXTREMITY
animal's .... PAD, PAW
and mouth disease
.... MURRAIN
bone of the .... TALUS,
CUBOID, CALCANEUS,
CUNEIFORM, NAVICULAR,
PHALANGES, METATARSALS
child's/woman's .... TOOTSY
colloquial .... PAY, PEG
combining form .... PED(E),
PED(I), POD(E)
deformity .... BUNION,
TALIPES, CLAWFOOT,
CLUBFOOT, FLATFOOT
disease/disorder .... CORN,
GOUT, WART, PODAGRA,
FRACTURE, ARTHRITIS,
INGROWN TOENAIL
disorders, specialist in
.... PODIATRIST
-dragging ..... DELAY, HOLDUP,
RELUCTANCE
fungal infection .... ATHLETE'S
FOOT
inability to raise the
.... FOOTDROP
lever .... PEDAL, TREADLE
metrical .... PAEON, TROCHEE
of 4 syllables .... TETRABRACH
of 3 syllables .... ANAPEST
of 2 syllables .... IAMB
on .... RUNNING, WALKING
on one's .... STANDING
pain .... TARSALGIA
part .... TOE, ARCH, HEEL,
INCH, SHIN, SOLE, ANKLE,
INSTEP
pedal .... TREADLE
pertaining to a .... PEDAL
poetic .... DACTYL, ANAPEST,
IAMB(IC), SPONDEE
prefix .... PED
race .... STEEPLECHASE
science of the .... PODOLOGY
-shaped .... PEDIFORM
soldier .... KERN(E),
INFANTRYMAN
soldier's coat .... JACK

-sole beating .... BASTINADO
sole of .... VOLAR, THENAR,
PLANTAR
sore .... CHILBLAIN
study of .... PODIATRY
swelling .... BUNION
travel gauge .... PEDOMETER
traveler .... HIKER, TRAMP,
JOGGER, RUNNER, WAYFARER,
PEDESTRIAN
with .... PEDATE
footage .... LENGTH, MEASURE,
YARDAGE, DISTANCE
football .... RUGBY, ELEVEN,
RUGGER
association .... SOCCER
bowl .... SUN, HULA, ROSE,
SUPER, COTTON, FIESTA,
ORANGE
coach .... NOLL, ALLEN,
BURNS, DITKA, REESE, SHELL,
LEVY, STAGG, WALSH, WYCHE,
FLORES, MADDEN, ROCKNE,
MORA, PARCELLS, SEIFERT,
KNOX, JOHNSON, ROBINSON
coaching greats, one of
.... HALAS, SHULA, LANDRY
colloquial .... PIGSKIN
commissioner .... BELL,
ROZELLE, TAGLIABUE
conference .... BIG TEN
"Crazy Legs" of
.... (ELROY)HIRSCH
face-off site .... LINE OF
SCRIMMAGE
field .... GRID(IRON)
five-time Super Bowl
champions of ..... FORTY-
NINERS
forefront/unit .... LINE
foul .... CLIP, HOLDING,
FACEMASK, DELAY OF GAME,
LATE HIT, PASS INTERFERENCE
"Galloping Ghost" of
.... (HAROLD RED)GRANGE
Hall of Fame name .... MIX,
BELL, CARR, FORD, HUFF,
HUNT, LANE, OTTO, OWEN
BAUGH, BERRY, BROWN,
CLARK, DAVIS, HALAS, JONES,
LILLY, LYMAN, MOORE,
MUSSO, NEALE, OLSEN, PERRY,
PIHOS, RINGO, SHELL, STARR,
BLANDA, BUTKUS, EWBANK,
GEORGE, GRAHAM, GRANGE,
HEWITT, HINKLE, HIRSCH,
MATSON, PARKER, SAYERS,
STRONG, TAYLOR, THORPE,
TITTLE, TRIPPI, TURNER,
UNITAS, WILLIS, WILSON,
ALWORTH, GIFFORD,

LUCKMAN, MCNALLY, MILLNER, SIMPSON, TUNNELL, LOMBARDI, VAN BUREN, WARFIELD, JURGENSEN, VAN BROCKLIN
kick .... PUNT, SPIRAL
most TD receptions holder, NFL history
.... (STEVE)LARGENT
national league .... NFL
official .... JUDGE, LINEMAN, REFEREE
pass .... SPIRAL
player ...... BONO, BURT, CAPP, HILL, KICK, LOTT, MOON, RICE, SIMS, ALLEN, BROWN, BYNER, CLARK, CRAIG, ELWAY, FOUTS, HALEY, KELLY, KRIEG, OKOYE, PERRY, YOUNG, DEBERG, GREEN, AIKMAN, ALZADO, BLANDA, CARTER, CSONKA, HEBERT, GANNON, HARRIS, MARINO, NAMATH, ROCKNE, RYPIEN, TAYLOR, THOMAS, TITTLE, UNITAS, WALKER, WILSON, DORSETT, EVERETT, GABRIEL, LARGENT, MCMAHON, MONTANA, RATHMAN, RIGGINS, SANDERS, SIMPSON, BRADSHAW, MICHAELS, ESIASON, PLUNKETT, STAUBACK, THEISMAN, SCHROEDER, CUNNINGHAM, TESTAVERDE
player: sl. .... GRIDDER
position .... END GUARD, CENTER, KICKER, PUNTER, SAFETY, RECEIVER, QUARTERBACK, (NOSE)TACKLE, RUNNING BACK
ref, sometimes called
.... ZEBRA
score .... SAFETY, TOUCHDOWN, FIELD GOAL
slang .... GRID
''Sunday generals''
.... QUARTERBACKS
team name, NFL:
Atlanta .... FALCONS
Buffalo .... BILLS
Carolina .... PANTHERS
Chicago .... BEARS
Cincinnati .... BENGALS
Cleveland .... BROWNS
Dallas .... COWBOYS
Denver .... BRONCOS
Detroit .... LIONS
Green Bay .... PACKERS
Houston .... OILERS
Indianapolis .... COLTS
Jacksonville .... JAGUARS

Kansas City .... CHIEFS
Los Angeles .... RAIDERS
Miami .... DOLPHINS
Minnesota .... VIKINGS
New England .... PATRIOTS
New Orleans .... SAINTS
New York .... JETS, GIANTS
Philadelphia .... EAGLES
Phoenix .... CARDINALS
Pittsburgh .... STEELERS
St. Louis .... RAMS
San Diego .... CHARGERS
San Francisco .... FORTY NINERS
Seattle .... SEAHAWKS
Tampa Bay ..... BUCCANEERS
Washington .... REDSKINS
term .... DOWN, KICK, PASS, TACKLE, PUNT, SACK, FUMBLE, HUDDLE, CUTBACK, DEFENSE, OFFENSE, OFFSIDE, PENALTY, INTERFERENCE, INTERCEPTION
footboy .... PAGE
footcloth .... RUG, CARPET
footed, large .... MEGAPOD
single .... MONOPODE
footfall .... STEP, TREAD, STRIDE
foothold .... GRIP, ACCESS, FOOTING
for example .... BEACHHEAD, LODG(E)MENT
footing .... BASIS, SUPPORT, TOEHOLD, WALKING, FOOTHOLD, POSITION
footless .... APOD(AL)
colloq. .... INEPT, CLUMSY
footlights .... KLIEG, STAGE, FLOATS, THEATER, LIMELIGHT, SPOTLIGHT
footlike .... PEDATE
organ .... PES
footloose .... FREE, ROVING, EASYGOING, WANDERING
footman .... PEON, LACKEY, FLUNK(E)Y, SERVANT
footnote .... RECORD, APOSTIL, REFERENCE, ANNOTATION, COMMENTARY
marker ...... OBELUS, ASTERISK
term .... IDEM
footpad .... THUG, BANDIT, ROBBER, BRIGAND, HOLDUPPER, HIGHWAYMAN
footprint .... PAD, CLUE, STEP, TRACK, TREAD, FOOTMARK
animal .... PUG
combining form .... ICHNO
mold .... CAST, MOULAGE
study of .... ICHNOLOGY
footrest .... STOOL, OTTOMAN
foots .... DREGS, SEDIMENT

footsie, play .... FLIRT
footslog .... DRAG, MARCH, STAMP, STOMP, TRAMP, LUMBER
footstalk .... SHANK, PEDICEL
footstep ...... CLOP, STAIR, STRIDE, FOOTFALL
dull sound of a .... PAD
sound of a heavy .... CLUMP
footstone .... TOMBSTONE, GRAVESTONE
footstool ...... CRICKET, HASSOCK, OTTOMAN
wicker .... MORA
footway .... LANE, PATH, TRAIL, SIDEWALK
ship .... CATWALK
footwear .... BOOTS, CLOGS, SHOES, SPATS, SABOTS, SKATES, PATTENS, RUBBERS, FOOTGEAR, SLIPPERS
actor's, of long ago
.... BUSKINS
preserve .... SHOETREE
slang .... CLODHOPPERS
footy .... MEAN, PETTY, PALTRY
foozle ...... FLUB, BOTCH, BUNGLE
fop .... DUDE, DANDY, JOHNNY, COXCOMB, JOHNNIE, MACARONI, POPINJAY, EXQUISITE
slang .... TRENDSETTER, CLOTHESHORSE
foppery .... CHIC, CONCEIT, DANDYISM, ELEGANCE, FRIPPERY
slang .... GLAD RAGS
foppish .... SHOWY, CHICHI, LADEDA, LADIDA, BUCKISH, CONCEITED
slang .... RITZY
for .... PRO, IN FAVOR, BECAUSE
aye .... EVER, ALWAYS
each .... PER, EVERY
example .... E.G., VIDE
fear that .... LEST
men only .... STAG
nothing .... FREE, NAUGHT
shame .... FIE
tat, _____ .... TIT
the most part .... MAINLY, LARGELY
the time being .... NONCE, PRO TEM, MEANWHILE
this reason .... HENCE, THEREFORE
what reason .... WHY
forage .... FEED, FOOD, PROG, LOOT, RAID, GRAZE, FODDER, MARAUD, RAVAGE, PASTURE, PLUNDER
crop .... MILO, SORGHUM

plant .... GUAR, ALSIKE, ALFALFA, LUCERN(E)
foramen .... PORE, MEATUS, OPENING
foray .... RAID, MELEE, ATTACK, INROAD, MARAUD, PILLAGE, PLUNDER, INVASION
forbear/forebear .... AVOID, FORGO, SPARE, ENDURE, PARENT, ABSTAIN, REFRAIN, ANCESTOR, TOLERATE
forbearance .... PITY, MERCY, LENIENCE, PATIENCE, RESTRAINT, TOLERANCE
forbearing .... KIND, LENIENT, PATIENT, ENDURING, INDULGENT, TOLERANT
forbears, of ...... AVITAL, LINEAL, PARENTAL, ANCESTRAL
Forbes, novelist .... ESTHER
forbid .... BAN, STOP, VETO, ENJOIN, IMPEDE, INHIBIT, PREVENT, PROHIBIT, INTERDICT, PROSCRIBE
forbiddance .... BAN, NO-NO, VETO, EMBARGO, STOPPAGE, HINDRANCE, INJUNCTION, INTERDICTION
forbidden .... TABU, TABOO, BANNED, ILLEGAL, OFF LIMITS, VERBOTEN, CONTRABAND
city .... LASSA, LHASA
fruit .... APPLE
forbidding .... GRIM, UGLY, STERN, ODIOUS, STRICT, DISTANT, REVOLTING, OFFENSIVE, REPELLANT, REPELLENT, DISAGREEABLE
force .... GAR, GUT, VIM, BIRR, DINT, MAKE, ODYL, BRAWN, DRIVE, IMPEL, MIGHT, POWER, SINEW, VIGOR, COERCE, COMPEL, DURESS, EFFECT, ENERGY, IMPACT, STRAIN, STRESS, IMPETUS, PRESSURE, STRENGTH, VALIDITY, VIOLENCE, CONSTRAIN
armed .... POSSE
back .... REPEL, REPULSE
by .... AMAIN
colloquial .... STEAM
down .... RAM, DETRUDE
driving .... MAINSPRING
-feed .... STUFF, FATTEN
hypothetical .... OD, OG, ELOD, ODYLE
into service ...... LEVY, DRAFT, CONSCRIPT, COMMANDEER
military .... ARMY, NAVY, MARINES, TROOPS,

OCCUPATION
of blow .... BRUNT, IMPACT
of expression/feeling .... EMPHASIS
of habit .... WONT, CUSTOM, PRACTICE
one's way in .... MUSCLE
out .... OUST, ROUT, SPEW, EJECT, EVICT, EXPEL, BANISH, EXCLUDE
rotating .... TORQUE
side of .... FLANK
to the wall .... CORNER
unit of .... DYNE
unit of 1,000 newtons .... STHENE
upon .... IMPOSE, THRUST
forced .... SULKY, HALTING, LABORED, STILTED, UNWILLING, COMPULSORY, INVOLUNTARY
feeding .... GAVAGE
journey .... FLIGHT, HEGIRA
labor .... CORVEE
forceful .... GUTSY, STOUT, VITAL, COGENT, SINEWY, STRONG, TELLING, EMPHATIC, POWERFUL, VIGOROUS, EFFECTIVE, ENERGETIC
forcefully .... FIRMLY, LOUDLY, STRONGLY, VEHEMENTLY
forceless .... WEAK, IMPOTENT
forceps .... TONGS, NIPPER, PINCERS
forces .... UNITS, TROOPS, LEGIONS, SOLDIERY, PERSONNEL, ARMED SERVICE, MILITARY SERVICE
forcible .... MIGHTY, DYNAMIC, VIOLENT, COERCIVE, FORCEFUL
ford .... WADE, CROSS, SHOAL
Ford .... EDSEL, HENRY, GERALD, HARRISON
fore ...... FRONT, PRIOR, FORWARD, ANTERIOR, PREVIOUS, FOREMOST
opposite of .... AFT, BACK, BEHIND
forearm bone .... ULNA
forearmed ...... READY, PREPARED
forebode ...... PORTEND, PREDICT, FORETELL
foreboding .... DARK, OMEN, AUGURY, OMINOUS, PORTENT, PREMONITION, PRESENTIMENT
forecast .... DIVINE, FORESEE, PORTEND, PREDICT, PRESAGE, PREVISE, PROPHESY, PROGNOSIS
forecaster .... SEER, AUGUR,

PROPHET, DOPESTER, SOOTHSAYER, WEATHERMAN
racetrack .... TOUT, TIPSTER
forefather .... ANCESTOR, PROGENITOR
forefinger .... INDEX, POINTER
forefoot .... PAW
part of .... MANUS
forefront .... FRONT, FOREMOST, FRONTAGE, VAN(GUARD)
forego .... DROP, SPARE, WAIVE, DO WITHOUT, ABSTAIN, NEGLECT, OVERLOOK
foregoing .... ABOVE, PREVIOUS, AFORESAID, PRECEDING
foregone .... PAST, FORMER, PREVIOUS
conclusion .... SURETY, SURENESS, CERTAINTY, NECESSITY
forehead .... BROW, TEMPLES, SINCIPUT
animal/bird .... FRONTLET
bone .... FRONTAL
hairy point ..... WIDOW'S PEAK
of the .... METOPIC
foreign .... ALIEN, EXOTIC, ECDEMIC, OUTSIDE, STRANGE, OVERSEAS, PEREGRINE, UNRELATED
affairs .... DIPLOMACY
article .... GERMANDER
bill period of payment .... USANCE
body .... BLEMISH, IMPURITY
exchange .... VALUTA
exchange dealer ...... CAMBIST
lands .... OUTREMER
mission .... EMBASSY, LEGATION, CONSULATE
opposed to .... DOMESTIC
origin .... EXOTIC
quarter .... PERA, ENCLAVE
service officer .... CONSUL, ATTACHE, AMBASSADOR
trade discount .... AGIO
foreigner .... ALIEN, INTRUDER, OUTSIDER, STRANGER, OUTLANDER, TRAMONTANE
in Japan .... GAIJIN
in South Africa .... UITLANDER
foreknowledge .... PRESCIENCE
foreland .... CAPE
forelimb part .... MANUS
forelock .... LINCHPIN, COTTER PIN
foreman ...... GAFFER, OVERSEER, DIRECTOR, SUPERVISOR
foremost .... FIRST, CHIEF, LEADING, PREMIER
part .... BOW, VAN, FRONT

forenoon .... MORNING
forensic .... LEGAL, JUDICIAL,
    JURIDICAL, RHETORICAL
medic .... CORONER
foreordain .... (PRE)DESTINE
forerun .... HERALD, PRECEDE,
    ANTECEDE, FORESHADOW
forerunner .... SCOUT, HERALD,
    ANCESTOR, HARBINGER,
    PRECURSOR, PROGNOSTIC,
    PREDECESSOR
foreshadow .... PRESAGE,
    ADUMBRATE, PREFIGURE
foresight ...... INSIGHT, FORECAST,
    PROSPECT, (PRE)VISION,
    SAGACITY
foresighted .... EARLY, ASTUTE,
    CAUTIOUS, CLAIRVOYANT
foreskin .... PREPUCE
forest .... GROVE, WEALD, WOODS,
    JUNGLE, COPPICE, THICKET,
    WOODLAND, HINTERLAND,
    TIMBERLAND
clearing .... GLADE
cutting right in the/green
    growth .... VERT
debris .... SLASH
decaying matter .... DUFF
deity .... PAN, FAUN, NYMPH
fire locator .... ALIDADE
floor layer .... LITTER
humus .... MOR
keeper .... RANGER
kind of .... PINERY, VIRGIN,
    PRIMEVAL
of the/pertaining to
    .... SYLVAN
open space ..... GLADE, SLASH,
    CLEARING
outlying part .... PURLIEU
ox .... ANOA
ranger's post ...... FIRE TOWER
soil .... PODZOL
trees of certain area .... SILVA
trees, the .... SYLVA
warden .... RANGER
forestall .... AVERT, THWART,
    PREVENT, STAVE OFF,
    ANTICIPATE
Forester's opera .... LORLE
forestry .... WOODCRAFT,
    CONSERVATION, SILVICULTURE
forests, coniferous .... TAIGA
foretaste .... WHET, APPETIZER
foretell .... AUGUR, PORTEND,
    PREDICT, PRESAGE,
    (FORE)BODE, FORECAST,
    PROPHESY, VATICINATE,
    PROGNOSTICATE
forethought .... PREMEDITATION
foretoken .... OMEN, SIGN,

AUGURY, PROGNOSTIC
foretold .... FORECAST, FORESEEN,
    GLIMPSED
foretooth .... INCISOR
forever .... AY(E), ALWAYS, EVER,
    ETERN(E), ETERNALLY,
    ENDLESSLY, INFINITELY, TIME
    WITHOUT END
almost .... EON
and a day: sl. .... TILL HELL
    FREEZES OVER
forewarning ...... OMEN, AUGURY,
    PORTENT, ADVANCE NOTICE
foreword .... PREFACE, PREAMBLE,
    PROLOGUE, FRONTISPIECE,
    INTRODUCTION
Forfar .... ANGUS
forfeit .... FINE, GIVE, LOSE,
    FORGO, DEFAULT, FOREGO,
    PENALTY
for pious purpose
    .... DEODAND
forfeited .... GONE, LOST, WASTED
forfeiture .... FINE, LOSS,
    PENALTY
of right for cause .... LAPSE
for(e)gather .... MEET, MERGE,
    COLLECT, ASSEMBLE,
    CONVERGE, ENCOUNTER,
    CONGREGATE
forge .... COIN, FORM, MINT,
    SHAPE, INVENT, SMITHY,
    STITHY, FALSIFY, FOUNDRY,
    FURNACE, HAMMER, IMITATE,
    BLOOMERY, FABRICATE,
    COUNTERFEIT
ahead .... (TAKE THE)LEAD
apparatus .... TROMPE
colloquial .... FUDGE
fireplace of .... HEARTH
tender .... BLACKSMITH
forged .... FAKE, PHONY,
    HATCHED, CONCOCTED,
    FICTITIOUS
forger .... FAKER, SMITH,
    COPYCAT, IMPOSTOR,
    PLAGIARIST, METALWORKER,
    COUNTERFEITER
forgery ...... MOCK, SHAM, FRAUD,
    COINAGE, MINTAGE, SWINDLE,
    IMITATION, COUNTERFEIT
slang ..... RIP-OFF, BUM CHECK
forget .... OMIT, DISMISS,
    NEGLECT, OVERLOOK
it .... DISREGARD
-me-not .... PLANT, MOUSE-
    EAR, MYOSOTIS
forgetful .... CARELESS, HEEDLESS,
    NEGLIGENT, OBLIVIOUS,
    ABSENTMINDED
one .... AMNESIAC,

PROF(ESSOR), LOTUS-EATER
forgetfulness .... LAPSE, AMNESIA,
    OBLIVION, MENTAL BLOCK
colloquial .... BLACKOUT
drug .... NEPENTHE
fruit of .... LOTUS
river of .... LETHE
forgive .... REMIT, EXCUSE,
    PARDON, ABSOLVE, CONDONE,
    PLACATE, OVERLOOK,
    CONCILIATE
a debt .... WRITE OFF
and forget .... LIVE AND LET
    LIVE
forgiven .... SPARED, EXCUSED,
    REDEEMED, ACQUITTED,
    EXONERATED
forgiveness ...... EXCUSE, PARDON,
    AMNESTY, REPRIEVE
forgiving .... KIND, HUMANE,
    MERCIFUL, PLACABLE,
    INDULGENT, CONCILIATORY
forgo. See forego
fork .... TINE, BIGHT, BOUGH,
    PRONG, TUNER, BISECT,
    DIVERGE, BRANCH(OFF),
    (BI)FURCATE, SEPARATE,
    TABLEWARE
out ...... PAY, GIVE, DOLE OUT,
    EXPEND
over: sl. .... KICK IN, PONY UP,
    COUGH UP
tuning .... TONOMETER
forked ...... BIFID, CLEFT, ZIGZAG,
    ANGULAR, FURCATE, PRONGED
organ/part .... FURCULUM
forlorn .... ALONE, BEREFT,
    DESERTED, DESOLATE,
    FORSAKEN, HOPELESS,
    WRETCHED, MISERABLE
form .... CUT, HEW, SET(UP),
    CAST, MAKE(UP), MOLD, POSE,
    TRIM, TYPE, BLANK, BUILD,
    CARVE, MODEL, SHAPE,
    CREATE, FIGURE, RITUAL,
    CONTOUR, DEVELOP, OUTLINE,
    PATTERN, CEREMONY,
    ORGANIZE, FORMALITY
a single unit .... UNITE
by fitting parts together
    .... CONSTRUCT
human .... BODY, FRAME,
    FIGURE, ANATOMY, PHYSIQUE
into a ball .... CONGLOBE,
    CONGLOBATE
into a chain .... CATENATE
into fabric .... KNIT, WEAVE
of a figure/garment
    .... SILHOUETTE
alcohol dependence
    .... DIPSOMANIA

Athena .... ALEA
bust .... TAILLE
government .... POLITY
obeisance .... BOW,
    KOWTOW, SALAAM,
    GENUFLECTION
oxygen .... OZONE
oval .... OZOID
shortened .... DIGEST,
    ABBREVIATION
square notches in molding
.... CRENELATE
take .... JELL, CRYSTALLIZE,
    MATERIALIZE
to fit requirements .... TAILOR,
    FASHION
formal .... PRIM, EXACT, STIFF,
    FRIGID, PROPER, SOCIAL,
    SOLEMN, STRICT, STUFFY,
    ORDERLY, OUTWARD,
    POMPOUS, CORRECT, PRECISE,
    STARCHY, AFFECTED,
    STYLIZED, DIGNIFIED,
    CEREMONIAL, METHODICAL,
    CEREMONIOUS, TRADITIONAL
agreement .... PACT
argument .... DEBATE
artificially .... STILTED
ceremony/practice .... RITE,
    FUNCTION
choice .... VOTE
dance .... BALL
entrance .... DEBUT
mall .... ALLEE
march .... PROCESSION
talk .... ADDRESS, LECTURE
wear .... TAILS, BLACK TIE,
    EVENING GOWN
formality .... CUSTOM, DECORUM,
    CEREMONY, PROPRIETY,
    CONVENTION
formalize .... DIGNIFY,
    CELEBRATE, SOLEMNIZE
formally .... RITUALLY,
    SOLEMNLY, IN DUE FORM
format .... FORM, PLAN, STYLE,
    DESIGN, LAYOUT, MAKEUP
formation .... ORDER, GROWTH,
    CREATION, STRUCTURE,
    FIGURATION, ARRANGEMENT,
    COMPOSITION
battle .... HERSE, PHALANX
flight/of six or more aircraft
.... SQUADRON
military .... ECHELON
panlike .... PATELLA
side of .... FLANK
formative .... PLIANT, PLASTIC,
    BENDABLE, CREATIVE,
    MORPHOTIC
formed .... BUILT, SETTLED,

COMPOSED, INCORPORATED
at base of mountain(s)
.... PIEDMONT
into a heap .... HILLED
into a rounded mass
.... CONGLOMERATE
on earth's surface .... EPIGENE
former .... EX, ONCE, PRIOR,
    WHILOM, EARLIER, QUONDAM,
    ONE-TIME, PREVIOUS,
    ERST(WHILE)
college gal .... ALUMNA
days/times .... AGO, ELD, PAST,
    YORE
emperor .... CZAR, TSAR,
    KAISER
film star Novarro .... RAMON
name of Annapolis ...... ANNE
    ARUNDEL TOWN
opposed to .... LATTER
ROK name .... RHEE
formerly .... NEE, ONCE, ERENOW,
    WHILOM, USED TO, ONE-TIME,
    SOMETIME, ERST(WHILE)
Palmer peninsula
.... ANTARCTIC
prefix .... EX
formic acid source .... ANT
formicary .... ANTHILL
formicid/formicine .... ANT
formidable ...... MEAN, ARDUOUS,
    AWESOME, FEARFUL,
    DREADFUL, MENACING,
    APPALLING, DIFFICULT,
    TREMENDOUS
formless .... ARUPA, ROUGH,
    UNCUT, VAGUE, RUGGED,
    DEFORMED, CHAOTIC,
    AMORPHOUS, SHAPELESS
void .... CHAOS, DISORDER
Formosa. See Taiwan
formula ...... PLAN, RULE, CREED,
    RECIPE, EQUATION, SOLUTION,
    PRESCRIPTION
formulate .... FRAME, DEVISE,
    ARRANGE, CONCOCT,
    ORGANIZE
fornent .... FACING, OPPOSITE
forsake .... QUIT, LEAVE, DESERT,
    VACATE, ABANDON,
    RENOUNCE
slang .... DITCH
forsaken .... LEFT, (FOR)LORN,
    DROPPED, CAST OFF,
    DESOLATE
forsooth .... INDEED, NO DOUBT
forswear .... DENY, DISOWN,
    NEGATE. REVOKE, DISAVOW,
    PERJURE
fort .... HOLD, KEEP, DONJON,
    BASTION, BULWARK, CITADEL,

FORTRESS, GARRISON,
    PRESIDIO, (ARMY)POST,
    STRONGHOLD
coastal/circular ..... MARTELLO
of fortune .... KNOX
of Moros .... COTTA
opening .... CRENEL
small .... SCONCE, FORTALICE
U.S. .... DIX, ORD, KNOX,
    SUMTER, MCHENRY,
    DONELSON, DUQUESNE
wall .... PARAPET
wooden .... BLOCKHOUSE
Fortaleza .... CEARA
forte .... LOUD, FLAIR, METIER,
    TALENT, SPECIALTY, STRONG
    POINT
opposed to .... FOIBLE
forth .... OUT(OF), ONWARD,
    FORWARD
forthcoming .... NEARING,
    IMMINENT, IMPENDING
forthright .... FRANK, CANDID,
    DIRECT, HONEST, EXPLICIT
forthwith ...... NOW, ANON, SOON,
    AT ONCE, EFTSOON,
    IMMEDIATELY
fortification .... BAIL, FORT,
    ABAT(T)IS, BASTION,
    BULWARK, OUTWORK,
    RAVELIN, REDOUBT,
    FORTRESS, PALISADE,
    EARTHWORK, STRONGHOLD
ditch/moat .... FOSS(E)
material .... GABION
outwork .... FLECHE,
    DEMILUNE, TENAIL(LE)
part of .... BAIL, PARAPET,
    RAMPART, EMBRASURE,
    BATTLEMENT, BREASTWORK
sloping embankment
.... SCARP, GLACIS
wall .... TALUS
with two parapets .... REDAN
fortified ...... ARMED, MANNED,
    BARRICADED, STRENGTHENED
hill .... MERLIN
house .... PEEL
line ...... MAGINOT, WESTWALL,
    SIEGFRIED
place .... REDAN, CASTLE,
    CITADEL, PILLBOX, FORTRESS,
    GARRISON, PRESIDIO
rampart .... BULWARK
tower .... PEEL, DONJON,
    DUNGEON
town .... BURG
fortify .... ARM, MAN, UPHOLD,
    SUSTAIN, BUTTRESS,
    BARRICADE
fortis .... SPEECH SOUND

opposed to .... LENIS
Fortissimo! to musicians
.... PLAY LOUD
fortitude ...... GRIT, GUTS, PLUCK,
SPUNK, COURAGE, STAMINA,
PATIENCE, STRENGTH,
TENACITY, ENDURANCE,
TOUGHNESS
fortnight .... FOURTEEN, TWO
WEEKS
fortnightly .... BI-MONTHLY,
PERIODICAL
fortress .... FORT, TOWER, CASTLE,
BASTION, CITADEL, BASTILLE,
FASTHOLD, FASTNESS,
SAFEHOLD, STRONGHOLD
flying .... SUPERFORT
impregnable, so-called
.... GIBRALTAR, SINGAPORE,
CORREGIDOR
mobile .... TANK
fortuitous ...... CASUAL, CHANCY,
(BY)CHANCE, ACCIDENTAL
Fortuna, Roman .... TYCHE
fortunate .... BLEST, HAPPY,
LUCKY, TIMELY, BLESSED,
FAVORED, OPPORTUNE,
FAVORABLE, AUSPICIOUS,
SUCCESSFUL
fortunately ...... HAPLY, HAPPILY,
LUCKILY, PROPITIOUSLY
fortune .... LOT, FATE, LUCK,
MONEY, STARS, CHANCE,
RICHES, WEALTH, DESTINY,
BLESSING, TREASURES,
PROSPERITY
hunter .... ADVENTURER,
TEMPORIZER
hunter's prize .... HEIR,
HEIRESS
ill .... DOOM, DAMNATION
slang .... PILE(S)
teller .... SEER, AUGUR, GYPSY,
SIBIL, SIBYL, ORACLE,
DIVINER, PALMIST, HARUSPEX,
ASTROLOGER, CRYSTAL-GAZER
teller's cards .... TAROT
telling .... GUESS, DIVINE,
FORESEE, PROPHESY,
PREDICTION, PALM-READING
forty days' fast .... LENT, CARENE
five-degree angle ...... OCTANT
inches .... ELL
niner .... MINER, ARGONAUT
rods .... FURLONG
winks .... DOZE, (CAT)NAP
winks of Spaniard ...... SIESTA
forum .... PANEL, SQUARE,
COUNCIL, ASSEMBLY,
TRIBUNAL, (LAW)COURT,
MARKET(PLACE)

wear .... TOGA
forward .... BOLD, PERT, SEND,
FLIP, AHEAD, EAGER, EARLY,
FRONT, READY, COMING,
FUTURE, PROMPT,
ADVANCE(D), DISPATCH,
TRANSMIT, INTRUSIVE
in development/maturity
.... PRECOCIOUS
in personality .... OFFICIOUS,
AGGRESSIVE
leap .... LUNGE
part .... BOW, FORE, FRONT,
ANTERIOR
tumble .... HEADER
fossa .... PIT, CAVITY, HOLLOW
fosse .... MOAT, DITCH
fossette .... DIMPLE, HOLLOW
fossil .... FOGY, ROCK, RELIC,
PINITE, MINERAL, ANTIQUATED
crinoid .... CRINITE
mollusk .... DOLITE
plants .... CALAMITE
resin .... AMBER, RETINITE
study of .... PALEOBOTANY
fossilize .... PETRIFY
foster .... REAR, SUCKLE, CHERISH,
NOURISH, NURTURE,
PROMOTE, SUPPORT,
ENCOURAGE
child .... STEPSON, FOUNDLING,
FOSTERLING, STEPDAUGHTER
Foster, songwriter ...... STEPHEN
foudroyant .... DAZZLING,
STUNNING
foul .... BAD, EVIL, DIRTY, FILTHY,
SOILED, UNFAIR, ILLEGAL,
SQUALID, UNCLEAN,
FECULENT, INDECENT,
STINKING, LOATHSOME,
UNDERHAND
as of food ...... PUTRID, STALE,
RANCID, ROTTEN
as of language .... OBSCENE,
PROFANE
at pinball .... TILT
dirt .... FILTH
place .... STY
smelling .... OLID, FETID,
ROTTEN, NOISOME
smelling fruit .... DURIAN
smelling plant .... HENBANE
up .... BUNGLE, ENTANGLE
weather .... STORMY
foulard .... SCARF, (NECK)TIE
foumart .... POLECAT
found .... BASE, CAST, AUTHOR,
FATHER, INVENT, CONCEIVE,
DISCOVER, ESTABLISH,
ORIGINATE
on earth's surface ... EPIGENE

thing .... TROVE, DISCOVERY
wanting .... SHORT, FAULTY,
LACKING, INADEQUATE
foundation .... BASE, FUND,
BASIS, BOTTOM, RIPRAP,
PREMISE, LEGACY,
BED(ROCK), ENDOWMENT
garment .... CORSET, GIRDLE,
SUPPORTER
founded .... FUSIL
abbreviation ...... EST, ESTAB
on .... FACTUAL, EVIDENTIAL
founder .... FAIL, FALL, SINK,
SLIP, CASTER, SCUTTLE,
STUMBLE, COLLAPSE,
PRODUCER, LAMINITIS,
ORGANIZER, INSTIGATOR,
ORIGINATOR, ESTABLISHER
of Bank of America
.... (AMADEO PETER)GIANNINI
Kentucky Fried Chicken
.... SANDERS
McDonald's restaurant
chain .... (RAY)KROC
Mogul empire .... BABAR
New York Evening Post
...... (ALEXANDER) HAMILTON
Oratory Fathers .... SAINT
PHILIP NERI
Rome .... ROMULUS
Stoicism .... ZENO
the Ethical Culture
Movement .... ADLER
William .... PENN
foundered ...... STUCK, GROUNDED
foundering .... FALLING, SINKING,
PLUNGING, PLUMMETING
foundling .... WAIF, EPPIE,
ORPHAN, WASTREL
place for .... CRECHE
foundry ...... SMITHY, CASTING(S),
IRONWORKS
fount ...... WELL, SOURCE, SPRING
fountain .... JET, WELL, SPRAY,
FOUNT, GEYSER, SOURCE,
SPRING, RESERVOIR
drink/specialty ...... POP, SODA
drinking .... BUBBLER
famed .... TREVI
Mt. Helicon .... HIPPOCRENE
nymph .... NAIAD, EGERIA
of wealth ..... LODE, BONANZA,
GOLD MINE
of youth chaser/seeker
.... PONCE DE LEON
of youth site .... BIMINI
poetic .... FONT
fountainhead .... ORIGIN, SOURCE
fountainpen .... STYLOGRAPH
tube .... BARREL
four .... IV, NUMBER

-bagger .... HOMER(UN)
combining form .... TETRA
dollar gold piece .... STELLA
equal-sided plane figure
.... SQUARE
-footed .... TETRAPOD,
QUADRUPED
group or set of .... TETRAD,
H-CLUB, QUATERNION
hundred, the .... ELITE
in hand item .... TEAM,
ASCOT, COACH, NECKTIE
in sets of .... QUATERNARY
-inch measure .... HAND
-legged speedster .... KELSO
letters, word of
.... TETRAGRAM
lines, poem of .... QUATRAIN
o'clock, the .... PLANT,
MARVEL-OF-PERU
pecks .... BUSHEL
persons or things, group of
.... QUARTET(TE)
petals, flower with
.... QUATREFOIL
poster .... BED(STEAD)
-sided, four-angled plane
figure .... TETRAGON,
RECTANGLE, QUADRANGLE
years, a period of
.... QUADRENNIUM
years, lasting
.... QUADRENNIAL
4-H club's concern .... HEAD,
HANDS, HEART, HEALTH
fourchette .... WISHBONE
fourflush .... BRAG, BLUFF,
DECEIVE
fourflusher ...... PHONY, HUMBUG,
BLUFFER, BRAGGART
game of a .... POKER
fourfold .... QUADRUPLE
fourgon .... CAR, VAN, WAGON,
TUMBRIL
fourpence .... COIN, GROAT
fours, on all ...... ON HANDS AND
KNEES
fourscore .... EIGHTY
foursome .... QUARTET
gathering place of .... TEE
foursquare .... FIRM, FRANK,
HONEST
14 days .... FORTNIGHT
pounds .... STONE
1492 ship .... NINA, PINTA, SANTA
MARIA
fourth .... QUARTER
canonical hour .... SEXT
class .... SHABBY, INFERIOR,
LOW GRADE
dimension .... SPACE-TIME

estate ...... MEDIA, (THE)PRESS,
JOURNALISM
of identical copies
.... QUADRUPLICATE
rate mark .... DEE
var. .... FERTH
foussa .... CIVET
fouter .... PIG
foveola .... VARIOLE
fowl ...... HEN, BIRD, COCK, DUCK,
BIDDY, GOOSE, TURKEY,
CHICKEN, ROOSTER, PHEASANT
castrated .... CAPON
comb of .... CARUNCLE
dealer .... POULTER(ER)
disease .... PIP
dish stewed in wine
.... SALMI(S)
domestic .... COCHIN,
DORKING, LEGHORN, MINORCA,
POULTRY
flesh below beak ...... WATTLE
forelimb .... WING
leg joint .... HOCK
meat, broiled ...... CARBONADO
outgrowth .... JOWL, SPUR,
WATTLE
small .... BANTAM
stuffing for .... FARCE
table .... CAPON
wattle .... JOWL
young .... POULT, BROILER,
POULARD
Fowler .... GENE
fowling piece .... GUN
fowls, domestic .... POULTRY
fox .... TOD, RE(Y)NARD
African .... ASSE, CAAMA,
FENNEC
face/head of .... MASK
female .... BITCH, VIXEN
flying .... KALONG
hunter/hunter's coat .... PINK
hunter's cry .... TALLYHO
killer .... VULPECIDE
like a .... SLY, CLEVER,
CUNNING, VULPINE,
VULPECULAR
male .... DOG
tail .... BRUSH
terrier .... WIREHAIR
terrier, RCA's .... NIPPER
young .... CUB
foxglove .... FIGWORT, DIGITALIS
foxhole ...... PIT, TUNNEL, TRENCH
foxtail .... BRUSH, GRASS
Foxx .... REDD
foxy ...... SLY, CUTE, SOUR, WILY,
CANNY, SLICK, CLEVER,
CRAFTY, SHREWD, CUNNING,
DEVIOUS, VULPINE

foy .... GIFT, FEAST, PRESENT
foyer .... HALL, LOBBY, VESTIBULE
fra .... ABBE, MONK, BROTHER
title of .... MONK, FRIAR
fracas .... BRAWL, MELEE,
RUMBLE, UPROAR, QUARREL,
DISTURBANCE
fraction .... BIT, PART, PIECE,
HALF, SCRAP, DECIMAL,
PORTION, FRAGMENT
fractious .... MEAN, CROSS,
UNRULY, TESTY, CRANKY,
ORNERY, IRRITABLE, FRETFUL,
PEEVISH
fracture .... BREAK, CRACK, SPLIT,
DAMAGE, INJURE
fragile ...... WEAK, BRASH, FRAIL,
FLIMSY, TENDER, BRITTLE,
DELICATE, FINESPUN,
BREAKABLE, FRANGIBLE
fragility ...... FRAILTY, DELICACY,
CRISPNESS
fragment .... BIT, CHIP, PART,
SNIP, PIECE, SCRAP, SHRED,
SHIVER, SIPPET, FLINDER,
SLIVER, MORCEAU, SEGMENT,
SHATTER, FRACTION
cloth .... RAG, TATTER,
REMNANT
pottery .... SHARD, SHERD
fragmentary .... BROKEN, SNIPPY,
PARTIAL, FRACTIONAL
fragrance .... ODOR, AROMA,
SCENT, INCENSE, PERFUME
of wine/brandy .... BOUQUET
fragrances: rare .... AROMATA
fragrant .... BALMY, OLENT,
MUSKY, SPICY, SWEET,
ODOROUS, PERFUMY,
AROMATIC, REDOLENT
bark .... CANELLA
flower .... ROSE, LILAC,
JASMINE
gum resin .... MYRRH
oil .... ATTAR, BALSAM
ointment .... (SPIKE)NARD
plant .... PINESAP, LAVENDER
rootstock .... ORRIS
seed ...... DILL, ANISE, ANISEED
shrub .... TIARA
wood .... CEDAR
fraidy-cat ...... COWARD, SCAREDY
CAT
frail .... WEAK, REEDY, BASKET,
FINE, THIN, WISPY FEEBLE,
FLIMSY, SLIGHT, TENDER,
FRAGILE, SLENDER, DELICATE
slang .... GIRL, WOMAN
frailty ...... FLAW, FAULT, DEFECT,
FAILING, TENUITY, DELICACY,
WEAKNESS, LIGHTNESS,

DAINTINESS
fraise .... RUFF, COLLAR
framb(o)esia .... YAWS
frame ...... FORM, SHAPE, CASING,
CREATE, DESIGN, DEVISE,
BACKING, COMPOSE, FASHION,
MOUNTING, CONSTRUCT
automobile/carriage
.... CHASSIS
bobbins' .... CREEL
body .... BUILD
building's boarding .... SIDING
cloth-stretching .... TENTER
counting .... ABACUS
display .... EASEL
drying .... RACK, HERSE,
TENTER
for embroidery
.... TABO(U)RET
for feeding animals
.... HAYRACK
for holding things .... RACK
in baseball .... INNING
of mind .... MOOD, MORALE,
SPIRIT(S), TEMPER
of ship .... HULL
openwork .... CAGE
set with spikes/spiked
.... HERSE, PORTCULLIS
soap bar .... SESS
stand .... RACK, EASEL
supporting .... TRESTLE
torch .... CRESSET
up .... RIGGING, INTRIGUE,
FALSE ACCUSATION
INCRIMINATE
framework .... SHELL, FABRIC,
FRAMING, BOUNDARY,
CONFINES
basic .... CADRE
bridge support .... TRUSS
ceiling .... BEAM, JOIST
for a fracture .... CAST
for carrying person .... LITTER
for door/window .... SILL,
LINTEL, CASEMENT
for traveling crane
.... GANTRY
of a building .... GIRDER
of animal body ..... SKELETON
of rods, sticks, etc.
.... WATTLE
on which to dry skins
.... HERSE
over oil well .... DERRICK
roof support .... TRUSS,
RAFTER
franc, 1/100 of .... CENTIME
France. See also **French**
.... GAUL, GALLIA
novelist .... ANATOLE

Southern .... MIDI
symbol of .... COCK
USA, in .... EUA
franchise .... SOC, SOKE, RIGHT,
PATENT, CHARTER, LICENSE,
SUFFRAGE, PRIVILEGE
Franciscan .... FRIAR, MINOR,
CAPUCHIN
friar .... MINORITE
mission .... ALAMO
Franck, composer .... CESAR
Franco (dictator) title .... (EL)
CAUDILLO
francolin .... TITAR, PARTRIDGE
francs, 20 .... LOUIS
frangible ...... FRAGILE, DELICATE,
BREAKABLE
frangipani .... JASMIN(E)
neckwear .... LEI
frank .... OPEN, BLUNT, PLAIN,
DIRECT, BRAZEN, CANDID,
EXEMPT, HONEST, ARTLESS,
BRUSQUE, SINCERE,
OUTSPOKEN, RIPUARIAN,
UNRESERVE
topping .... PICCALILLI
Frank crooner .... SINATRA
or Johnnie .... LOVER
Frankenstein novel authoress
.... SHELLEY
frankfurter ...... WEENY, WIENER,
HOTDOG, WEENIE, SAUSAGE
Frankfurter, jurist .... FELIX
frankincense .... OLIBANUM, GUM
RESIN
Frankish king .... CLOVIS
law .... SALIC
peasant .... LITUS
franklin .... FREEHOLDER
frankly .... OPENLY, PLAINLY,
CANDIDLY, DIRECTLY,
HONESTLY
frankness .... CANDOR, RAWNESS,
BLUNTNESS, GROSSNESS,
VULGARITY, FREEDOM,
CANDIDNESS, COARSENESS
Franks, ruler of .... PEPIN,
MARTEL
frantic ...... MAD, WILD, EXCITED,
FURIOUS, FRENETIC, FRENZIED
make .... PANIC, FRENZY,
MADDEN
person ..... MANIAC, DEMONIAC
frap .... TIGHTEN
frappe .... ICED, DRINK, DESSERT,
MILKSHAKE
frater .... FRIAR, BROTHER,
COMRADE
fraternal .... KIND, FRIENDLY,
BROTHERLY, SISTERLY
fraternity .... CLUB, SORORITY,

BROTHERHOOD,
(SECRET)SOCIETY
house .... INN, HOSTELRY,
DORMITORY
letter .... PSI
local .... CHAPTER
meeting place .... LODGE
to-do .... RUSH, INITIATION
fraternize .... JOIN, ASSOCIATE,
MINGLE WITH, COLLABORATE
frau .... WIFE, WOMAN
fraud .... HOAX, JAPE, SHAM,
BUNCO, CHEAT, CON MAN,
HUMBUG, DECEIT, SWINDLE,
ARTIFICE, DECEPTION,
FALSEHOOD, IMPOSTURE,
TRICK(ERY)
conspiracy to commit
.... COVIN
fraudulent .... FAKE, BOGUS,
PHONY, TRICKY, DEVIOUS,
GUILEFUL, DECEITFUL
fraught .... BESET, LADEN, FILLED,
LOADED, CHARGED
fraxinella .... DITTANY
fray .... RAG, RUB, WEAR, BRAWL,
FIGHT, MELEE, RAVEL,
BATTLE, FRACAS, FRAZZLE,
CONFLICT, SKIRMISH, FREE-
FOR-ALL
fraying, cord to stop
.... MARLINE, MARLING
frazzle .... VEX, FRAY, TEAR,
SHRED, ABRADE
freak .... FLECK, FLUKE, QUEER,
SPORT, WHIM, DAPPLE,
STREAK, CAPRICE, ABNORMAL,
MONSTROSITY
of nature .... HUNCHBACK,
BEARDED LADY, SIAMESE TWIN
out .... BLOW ONE'S MIND
slang .... FLAKE, ODDBALL
freckle .... BLEMISH, LENTIGO
freckled .... BLOTCHY, SPOTTED
Frederick I of Germany
.... BARBAROSSA
the Great's palace .... SANS
SOUCI
Fred's cousin .... ALF
free .... LAX, RID, EASE, LISS,
OPEN, QUIT, VOID, BROAD,
CLEAR, LIBRE, READY,
GRATIS, LOOSEN, MANUMIT,
RELEASE, UNLEASH, AT
LARGE, DETACHED, LIBERATE,
LET LOOSE, (FOOT)LOOSE,
UNHINDERED
and clear ...... OWN, UNOWING,
OUT OF DEBT
and easy .... CASUAL,
NATURAL, RELAXED,

CARELESS, FAMILIAR, INFORMAL

-for-all .... FRAY, RIOT, BRAWL, BROIL, FIGHT, MELEE, RUMPUS, RUMBLE, CONTEST, RHUBARB, COMMOTION, BATTLE ROYAL

from bacteria/infection .... ASEPTIC, STERILE

blame ..... ACQUIT, ABSOLVE, EXONERATE

bondage .... EMANCIPATE

dirt .... CLEAN, BRIGHT

discount .... NET

error .... CORRECT, ACCURATE

moisture .... DRY, DEHYDRATE

occupancy/use .... EMPTY, VACANT

restraint .... UNTIE, UNCHAIN, EMANCIPATE

sin .... PURE

suspicion .... CLEAR, ACQUIT, EXCULPATE

hand/scope .... CARTE BLANCHE

lance .... MERCENARY

of charge ..... GRATIS, FREEBIE

of dissimulation .... SINCERE

speech restraint .... GAG, CENSOR

spirit .... LIBERAL, NEUTRAL

swimming organism .... PROTOZOA

throw area in basketball .... KEYHOLE

ticket .... PASS

ticket holder .... DEADHEAD

time .... REST, RECESS, REPOSE, LEISURE

will .... VOLITION

freebie .... GIFT, COUPON

freebooter ...... PIRATE, CATERAN, BUCCANEER, PLUNDERER, FILIBUSTER

freedman ...... LAET, TIRO, THANE

freedom .... RIGHT, LIBERTY, EXEMPTION, FRANCHISE, PRIVILEGE, INDEPENDENCE

from doubt .... CERTAINTY, CERTITUDE

from punishment .... IMMUNITY, IMPUNITY

from sin .... PURITY

kind of .... LICENSE

of action .... LATITUDE

of action or emotion, unrestrained .... ABANDON

to enter .... ENTRY, ACCESS

freehanded .... OPEN, GIVING, GENEROUS, UNSELFISH

freehold .... TITLE, RIGHTS, POSSESSION

estate .... ALOD, ALLOD(IUM)

of a .... ALLODIAL

freeholder .... YEOMAN, FRANKLIN, LANDOWNER

freeloader .... BEGGAR, SPONGE(R), DEADBEAT, DEADHEAD, PARASITE

freeman .... CEORL, CHURL, THANE, BURGESS, CITIZEN, VILLEIN, FRANKLIN

Freeman, actress .... MONA

freemen's assembly .... MOOT

freespoken .... OPEN, FRANK, CANDID, OUTSPOKEN

freestone .... PLUM, PEACH

freethinker .... ATHEIST, AGNOSTIC, LIBERTINE

freeway ...... HIGHWAY, ARTERIAL, SPEEDWAY

block party .... TRAFFIC JAM

feature .... RAMP, ENTRANCE

freewheeling .... NEUTRAL, INDEPENDENT

freewill .... CHOICE, VOLITION, VOLUNTARY, VOLUNTEER

freeze .... DIE, FIX, ICE, NIP, CHILL, FROST, GELATE, HARDEN, CONGEAL, STABILIZE

freezer .... ICER, REFRIGERATOR

item .... (ICE)CUBE

freezing .... FROSTY, CHILLING, ICY-COLD, ICELIKE

freight .... LOAD, CARGO, BURDEN, LADING, SHIPMENT

boat .... SCOW, BARGE

car dumping apparatus .... TIPPLE

steamer .... WHALEBACK

surcharge .... PRIMAGE

train car .... CABOOSE

freighter .... TRAMP, TANKER, TRADER, LIGHTER, SHIPPER, (CARGO)SHIP, STEAMER

area .... HOLD

fremd .... ALIEN, FOREIGN, STRANGE

fremitus .... VIBRATION

French .... GALLIC, FRANCAIS

abbot .... ABBE

abbreviate .... ABREGER

ability .... CAPACITE

able .... HABILE

abortion .... AVORTEMENT

accede/agree .... CONSENTIR

accident .... AVARIE

according .... CONFORME

according to ...... A LA, SELON

accountant .... COMPTABLE

accurate .... PRECIS

across the board .... EN MASSE

actor .... BOYER, CHEVALIER, DELON, FERNANDEL

actress .... CARON

address .... HABILETE

adjust .... REGLER

administrative department .... INTENDANCE

admiral .... DARLAN

ado .... BRUIT, FRACAS

advance .... AVANCER

advance guard .... AVANT-GARDE

adverb .... TROP

advice .... AVIS, CONSEIL

affair of the heart .... AFFAIRE DE COEUR

affix .... APPOSER

affluent .... RICHE

afoot .... A PIED

African colony, former .... MALI

African lake .... (T)CHAD

after .... APRES

afternoon .... APRES-MIDI

again .... ENCORE

against .... CONTRE

agony .... DOULEUR

agreement .... ENTENTE-CORDIALE

airplane .... SPAD, AVION

airship .... AERONAT, AERONEF, DIRIGEABLE

alarm clock .... REVEILLE-MATIN

alcohol .... ALCOOL

ale .... BIERE

Algerian soldier .... TURCO

alien .... EMIGRE(E), ETRANGER

alive .... EN VIE, VIVANT

all .... TOUS, TOUTE

all of you .... VOUS TOUS

alley .... RUELLE

alone .... SEUL

Alp top .... PIC

alphabet .... ABECEDAIRE

Alpine sight .... ADROITE

already .... DEJA

already seen .... DEJA VU

also .... AUSSI

altar .... AUTEL

always .... TOUJOURS

amah .... BONNE

amen .... C'EST CA

amend .... CORRIGER

America .... AMERIQUE

-American .... CREOLE

amiable .... SYMPATHIQUE

amicable .... EN RAPPORT

among .... ENTRE
amount .... MONTANT
amuse .... DIVERTIR
and .... ET
angel .... ANGE
annoy .... GENER
annoyance .... ENNUI
annual income/annuity
.... RENTE
another .... AUTRE
answer .... REPONDRE
ant .... FOURMI
antique .... ANCIEN
anxiety .... SOUCI
anxious .... SOUCIEUX
any/anything .... QUELQUE
apartment .... CHAMBRE
ape .... SINGE, GUENON
appelation .... NOM
apple .... POMME
apple of the eye .... PRUNELLE
apple tree .... POMMIER
April .... AVRIL
apron .... TABLIER
aptly .... A PROPOS
architect .... ARTISAN, LE
CORBUSIER
area .... ETENDUE
arm .... BRAS
armful .... BRASSEE
armless .... SANS BRAS
arm band .... BRASSARD
arm chair .... FAUTEUIL
armpit .... AISSELE
army sharpshooter
.... TIRAILLEUR
arrow .... FLECHE
art center .... BARBIZON
art show .... SALON
artfulness .... FINESSE
article .... DA, LA, LE, DES,
UN, LES, UNS, UNE, UNES,
OBJET
artist/painter .... DORE, COROT,
DEGAS, LEGER, MANET,
MONET, DERAIN, INGRES,
RENOIR, SEURAT, CEZANNE,
CHARDIN, DAUMIER, LORRAIN,
MATISSE, POUSSIN, ROUAULT,
CHAGALL, PISSARRO
ash .... CENDRE
ashtray .... CENDRIER
aside .... DE COTE
assist .... AIDER
astrologer .... NOSTRADAMUS
astronomer .... LAGRANGE
attic .... MANSARDE
auction .... ENCHERE
audience .... AUDITOIRE
August .... AOUT
aunt .... TATA, TANTE

author .... GIDE, HUGO, LOTI,
ZOLA, CAMUS, DUMAS, RENAN,
STAEL, VERNE, AUTEUR,
FRANCE, SARTRE, COCTEAU
avail .... SERVIR
average .... MOYEN, COMMUN
avoid .... AVITER
away .... LOIN
awhile .... UN PEU
awl .... ALENE
awning .... TENTE
axe .... HACHE
baby .... BEBE, ENFANT
bachelor .... GARCON
back .... DOS, ARRIERE
backside .... DERRIERE
bacon .... LARD
bacteriologist .... PASTEUR
bad .... MALADE, MAUVAIS
badge .... PLAQUE
bag .... SAC
baker .... BOULANGER
bakery .... BOULANGERIE
bald .... CHAUVE
ball .... BAL, BALLE
ballad .... BALLADE
ballet member .... DANSEUR,
DANSEUSE
bamboozle .... TROMPER
bandy-legged .... BANCAL
bank .... BORD, BANQUE,
RIVAGE
bankrupt .... FAILLI
banner ...... FANION, BANNIERE
barber .... COIFFEUR
barefoot .... NU PIEDS
bargain .... MARCHE
bark .... TAN, ECORCE
barn .... GRANGE
barrister .... AVOCAT
base/basis .... FOND
basin .... BOL, CUVETTE
basket ...... PANIER, CORBEILLE
bath .... BAIN
bathroom .... SALLE DE BAIN
bay .... BAIE, GOLFE, SEINE,
BISCAY
be .... ETRE, AVOIR, FAIRE
beach .... UTAH, OMAHA,
PLAGE, RIVAGE
bean .... FEVE, HARICOT
beast .... BETE, COCHON
beat .... BATTRE, FRAPPER
beaten .... BATTU
beautiful .... TRES BEAU,
MAGNIFIQUE
beauty .... NINON
beauty spot .... MOUCHE
bed .... LIT, COUCHE
bedding .... LITERIE
bedspread .... COUVRELIT

bee .... ABEILLE
beef .... BOEUF
beggar .... GUEUX
behavior .... TENUE
behold .... VOILA
being .... ETRE
belfry .... CLOCHER
Belgian river .... YSER
believe .... CROIRE
belt .... CEINTURON
bench .... BANC, GRADIN
best .... LE MIEUX, LE
MEILLEUR
bet .... PARI
betray .... TRAHIR, TROMPER
between .... ENTRE
beverage .... BOISSON
beyond .... OUTRE, AU DELA,
PAR DELA
bicycle .... VELO
big .... GROS, VASTE
bigwig .... GROS BONNET
billy goat .... BOUCH
bin .... HUCHE
biologist .... CARREL
bird .... OISEAU
birth .... NAISSANCE
bitter .... ACRE, AMER
bitters .... AIGRE
black .... NOIR(E)
blackmail .... CHANTAGE
bless .... BENIR
blessed .... BENI, SACRE
blind .... AVEUGLE
blood .... SANG
blouse .... CHEMISETTE
blue .... AZUR, BLEU
"Bluebeard" .... LANDRU
boarder .... INTERNE
boarding house/school
.... PENSION(NAT)
boat .... BATEAU
bodice .... GILET, CORSAGE
bond .... RENTE
bone .... OS
book .... LIVRE, CAHIER
boredom .... ENNUI
born .... NEE
bottle case .... CANTINE
box .... BOITE
boy .... GARCON
brainstorm .... IDEE
brandy .... COGNAC
bread .... PAIN
breath .... HALEINE
brewery .... BRASSERIE
bridge .... PONT
briefcase .... SERVIETTE
broken .... CASSE
broker .... COURTIER
broth .... POTAGE

brother .... FRERE
brown .... BRUN
brush .... BROSSE
bullet .... BALLE
bunch .... BOTTE, BOUQUET
bundle .... PAQUET
busybody .... OFFICIEUX
but .... QUE, MAIS
butcher .... BOUCHER
butcher shop .... BOUCHERIE,
                       CHARCUTERIE
butterfly .... PAPILLON
cab .... FIACRE
cabbage .... CHOU, CABOCHE
cafe .... ESTAMINET
cake .... GATEAU
call .... APPEL
can .... POT, BIDON
Canadian: sl. .... CANUCK
candle .... CHANDELLE
candy .... BONBON
cape .... CORSE, HAGUE
capital .... PARIS
cap's decoration .... POMPON
car .... RENAULT
card .... CARTE
Cardinal .... MAZARIN,
                       RICHELIEU
care .... SOIN, SOUCI
carol .... CHANSON
carpet .... TAPIS
carriage .... FIACRE, VOITURE
cash .... ARGENT
castle .... CHATEAU
cater .... POURVOIR
caterpillar .... CHENILLE
cathedral city .... R(H)EIMS
cauliflower .... CHOUFLEUR
cavalryman .... CARABINIER
chain, Saint Andrew's cross
                       SAUTOIR
chair .... CHAISE
chalk .... CRAIE
challenge .... DEFI
chat .... CAUSETTE
cheap .... BON MARCHE
cheer .... CHERE, GAIETE
cheese .... BRIE, FROMAGE
chemist .... CURIE, LUSSAC,
                       PASTEUR
cherry .... CERISE
chestnut .... MARRON
chicken .... POULET, POUSSIN
chicken pox .... VARICELLE
child .... ENFANT
Christmas .... NOEL
church .... EGLISE
circle .... COTERIE
circumstance .... CAS
citizen .... CITOYEN, HABITANT
city/town ..... GEX, PAU, CAEN,

FOIX, LYON, METZ, NICE,
ORLY, SETE, ST. LO, ARLES,
ARRAS, BLOIS, BREST, CREIL,
DIJON, LILLE, MEAUX, NANCY,
NIMES, REIMS, ROUEN, TOURS,
VICHY, VILLE, AMIENS,
CALAIS, CANNES, CHOLET,
COGNAC, COLMAR, DRANCY,
EVREUX, ISTRES, RENNES,
TOULON, TROYES, VERNON,
ANTIBES, AVIGNON, BAYONNE,
BELFORS, BOURGES, DUNKIRK,
LE MANS, LIMOGES, LORIENT,
LOURDES, ORLEANS, QUIMPER,
ROUBAIX, VALENCE,
BORDEAUX, COLOMBES,
GRENOBLE, LE HAVRE,
SOISSONS, TOULOUSE,
CHANTILLY, MARSEILLE,
TOURCOING, VERSAILLES,
MONTPELLIER, SAINT TROPEZ
clean .... PROPRE
cleric .... ABBE, PRETRE
climb .... ESCALADER
cloak .... MANTEAU
cloth .... DRAP, TOILE
clothes .... VETEMENTS
cloud .... NUAGE
clown .... RUSTRE, BOUFFON,
                       PIERROT
coach for hire .... FIACRE
coastal city .... BREST
coffee .... CAFE
cognac .... MARTELL, REMY
                       MARTIN
coin .... ECU, SOU, OBOLE,
     FRANC, LIVRE, DENIER,
       TESTON, CENTIME,
           LOUIS(D'OR)
coin, old .... RIAL
cold .... FROID
colony .... TCHAD
color .... COULEUR
color-blind .... DALTONIEN
colored .... COLORE, COLORIE
colorful .... PITTORESQUE
comb .... PEIGNE
combining form .... GALLO
come .... VENIR
come back .... REVENIR
come in .... ENTREZ
comfort .... AISE
commodity tax .... OCTROI
company .... CIE, SOCIETE
composer ...... LALO, BIZET,
FAURE, RAVEL, SATIE, D'INDY,
GOUNOD, HALEVY, RAMEAU,
BERLIOZ, DEBUSSY, DE LISLE
concrete .... BETON
conqueror .... CLOVIS
contest .... LUTTE

cook .... CUISINIER(E)
cop .... FLIC
cork .... BOUCHON
corn .... BLE
cost .... PRIX
count .... COMTE
country .... PAYS
county .... DEPARTEMENT
couturier .... DIOR, BALMAIN
cow .... VACHE
coward .... LACHE, POLTRON
cream .... CREME
credit .... FOI
critic .... TAINE
crown .... ECU, SOMMET
crown prince .... DAUPHIN
crown princess ...... DAUPHINE
crude .... CRU
cruet .... BURETTE
crusader .... MONTFORT
crust .... CROUTON
cry for help .... AMOI, AU
                       SECOURS
cup .... TASSE
cupboard .... ARMOIRE
cure .... REMEDE
curse .... FLEAU, ANATHEME
curtain .... TOILE, RIDEAU
dagger .... POIGNARD
daisy .... MARGUERITE
dance .... BAL, BRAWL, GAVOT,
RONDE, APACHE, CANCAN,
COURANTE, GALLIARD,
QUADRILLE, BAL MASQUE,
                 COTILL(I)ON
daredevil .... CASSECOU
dark .... NOIR
darling/dear .... CHERI
dash .... CHOC, ELAN
daughter .... FILLE
daughter-in-law .... BELLE-
                       FILLE
day .... JOUR
dead .... MORT
dead-end .... CUL-DE-SAC
deaf .... SOURD
dean .... DOYEN
debt .... DETTE
December .... DECEMBRE
decisive moment .... CRISE
decoy .... LEURRER
decree .... ARRET
deed .... ACTE, FAIT
delightful .... CHARMANT
depart .... PARTIR
department .... AIN, VAR,
AUBE, AUDE, CHER, EURE,
GARD, GERS, JURA, OISE,
ORNE, NORD, (HAUT)RHIN,
TARN, AISNE, ALPES, CORSE,
DOUBS, DROME, ISERE, LOIRE,

MARNE, PARIS, RHONE, SEINE, SOMME, YONNE, ALLIER, ARIEGE, LANDES, LOIRET, MANCHE, SARTHE, SAVOIE, VENDEE, VIENNE, VOSGES, ARDECHE, BELFORT. CORREZE, ESSONNE, GARONNE, GIRONDE, MAYENNE, MOSELLE, ARDENNES, BAS-RHIN, CALVADOS, DORDOGNE, MORBIHAN. VAUCLUSE, YVELINES, FINISTERE
department head ...... PREFECT
depot .... GARE
desert .... MERITE, ABANDONNER
design .... DESSEIN
designer .... AUTEUR
desk .... BUREAU, PUPITRE
detained .... DETENU
detective ..... SURETE, POLICIER
devil .... DEMON, DIABLE
dew .... ROSEE
dialect .... PATOIS, LANGUE D'OC
diamond .... DIAMANT
die .... MOURIR
diet .... REGIME
diplomacy .... SAVOIR-FAIRE
dirt .... CRASSE, SALETE
disease .... MAL, MALADIE
district .... PERCHE, CONTREE
diver .... PLONGEUR
diversion .... JEU
division .... PARTAGE
dog .... CHIEN, GAILLARD
donkey .... ANE, BAUDET
door .... PORTE
down .... BAS
down with .... A BAS
dramatist ..... DUMAS, LESAGE, RACINE, COCTEAU, ETIENNE, MOLIERE, PREVOST, VOLTAIRE
draw-bridge .... PONT-LEVIS
dream .... REVE, SONGE
driver .... COCHER
dry .... SEC
duchy .... ANJOU, VALOIS, AQUITAINE
dugout .... ABRI
duke .... DUC
dungeon .... CACHOT
eagle .... AIGLE
ear .... OREILLE
early .... MATINAL
earn .... GAGNER
earth .... TERRE
east .... EST
eat .... MANGER
edict .... ARRET
eel .... ANGUILLE

egg .... OVE, OEUF, OVALE
eight .... HUIT
elder .... AINE, SUREAU
eleven .... ONZE
emblem .... LILY
emperor ..... LOUIS, NAPOLEON
emphatic word .... TRES
emporium .... ENTREPOT
empress .... EUGENIE, JOSEPHINE
enamel .... EMAIL
enamelware .... LIMOGES
encore! .... BIS
end .... FIN
end, the .... FINIS
enslave .... CAPTIVER
entertainer .... DISEUR, DISEUSE
entrance .... ENTREE
equal .... EGAL, PAREIL
equality .... EGALITE
era .... ERE
eve .... VEILLE
evening .... SOIR
ewe .... BREBIS
exclamation .... HEIN
exist .... ETRE
exit .... SORTIE
expensive .... COUTEUX
expert .... AU FAIT
explorer .... CADILLAC, LA SALLE
eye .... OEIL
eyeglass .... MONOCLE
fabric ...... DRAP, LAME, TOILE, ETOFFE
fabulist .... (LA)FONTAINE
face .... VISAGE
fact .... FAIT
fairy .... FEE
false .... FAUX
false step/error .... FAUX PAS
fan .... EVENTAIL
fascist organization .... CAGOULARD
fashion .... MODE, FACON, BON TON
fashion designer .... DIOR, CHANEL, SAINT LAURENT
fat .... GRAS, GROS
father .... PERE
father-in-law .... BEAU-PERE
fatten .... ENGRAISSER
FBI .... DST
FBI's counterpart ...... SURETE
fear .... PEUR
February .... FEVRIER
fee .... DROIT
feeble .... DABILE
feed .... PATURE, NOURRIR
feed-back .... RETRO-ACTION

feel .... SENTIR
fellow .... CONFRERE
fellow countryman .... COMPATRIOTE
fellowship/sorority/morale .... ESPRIT DE CORPS
female .... DE FEMME
fence ..... CLOTURE, PALISSADE
ferry boat .... BAC
festival .... (DE)FETE
feud .... VENDETTA
feudal tax .... TAILLE
fictitious .... FAUX
field ...... PRE, CHAMP, PRAIRIE
fiend .... DEMON
fight .... COMBATTRE
fighter .... COMBATTANT
fighter plane .... SPAD
file .... LIME, DOSSIER
finally .... ENFIN
find .... TROUVER
fine .... BON, BEAU, AMENDE
fine bearing .... BEL AIR
fine deed .... BEAU GESTE
fine literature .... BELLES LETTRES
finger .... DOIGT
fire .... FEU
fireman .... POMPIER
first .... PREMIER
first prize .... GRAND PRIX
fish .... POISSON
five .... CINQ
flag .... DRAPEAU, FAIBLIR, TRICOLOR
flavor .... SAVEUR
flax .... LIN
flight .... VOL
floor .... PARQUET
flower .... FLEUR
food .... ALIMENT
fool .... SOT, NIAIS
foot .... PIED
foot on the ground ..... PIED A TERRE
footman .... VALET DE PIED
footnote .... APOSTILLE
footstep .... PAS
for .... DE, PAR, POUR
forbidden .... INTERDIT
foreigner .... ETRANGER
forest .... BOIS
formal .... BAL
fortification .... PARADOS
fortification, part of a .... CAPONIERE
forward .... AVANCE, EN AVANT
foundation .... FOND
four .... QUATRE
"Fox, the" .... REYNARD

fragrance .... SUAVE
free .... LIBRE
friar .... FRERE, MOINE
Friday .... VENDREDI
fried potatoes .... CHIPS
friend .... AMI(E)
from .... DE(S), DEPUIS
front .... DEVANT, FACADE
froth .... BAVE
fruit .... POMME, FRUITIER
fun .... DROLERIE
fund .... FONDS, CAISSE
funeral .... FUNEBRE
gala .... FETE
gambler .... JOUEUR
gambling .... JEU(X)
game .... JEU, PARTIE
garbage .... ORDURE(S)
garden .... JARDIN
garlic .... AIL
gate .... PORTE
gauze .... LISSE
general .... KLEBER
genre painter .... WATTEAU
gentle .... DOUX
gentleman .... MONSIEUR
geologist, 17th century
.... CORDIER
geologist, 19th century
.... ELIE DE BEAUMONT
German industrial area
.... SARRE
ghost .... FANTOME, SPECTRE
gift .... CADEAU
gingerbread .... PAIN D'EPICE
girl .... FILLE
give .... DONNER
glance .... APERCU
glass .... VERRE
glassware .... VERRERIE
glove .... GANT
go .... ALLER
goal .... TERME
god .... DIEU
goddess .... DEESSE
good .... BON
goodbye .... ADIEU, AU REVOIR
goodness/goodwill ...... BONTE
goose .... OIE
gossip .... ONDIT, COMMERE
grafted shoot, in gardening
.... ENTE
grape-growing area
.... MEDOC, COGNAC,
BORDEAUX
grass .... GAZON, HERBE
gravy .... JUS
gray/grey .... GRIS
green .... VERT
grindstone .... MEULE
grocer .... EPICIER

grocery .... EPICERIE
ground .... TERRE
guard .... GARDE
guerrillas .... MAQUIS
guest .... INVITE
Guiana capital .... CAYENNE
gulf .... LIONS, AJACCIO, SAINT
MALO, SAINT FLORENT
hack .... COUPER
hair .... CHEVEU(X)
hair net .... RESILLE
hair style .... GOULUE,
CHIGNON
hairdresser .... MARCEL,
FRISEUR, COIFFEUR
half .... DEMI
half-mask .... LOUP
half-year .... SEMESTRE
hall .... SALLE
hand .... MAIN, PALME
handkerchief .... MOUCHOIR
handle .... ANSE, MANCHEE
handwriting .... ECRITURE
happiness .... BONHEUR
happy .... HEUREUX
happy trip .... BON VOYAGE
hat .... CHAPEAU
hat designer .... DACHE
head .... TETE
headache .... MAL DE TETE
health .... SANTE
health resort .... EVIAN
heart .... COEUR
heaven .... CIEL
heavenly .... CELESTE
heavenly being .... ANGE
heir to throne .... DAUPHIN
helmet .... CASQUE, HEAUME
help .... AMOI, SECOURS
here .... ICI, VOICI
hero in romance ...... AMADIS,
BAYARD
heroic verse ..... ALEXANDRINE
heyday .... BEAUX JOURS
hidden .... CACHE, PERDU,
SECRET
high .... HAUT
high society ..... HAUT MONDE
highest point ... MONT BLANC
hill .... COTEAU, COLLINE
hillock .... BUTTE
him .... LE, LUI
his .... SES, SON, LE SIEN
historian .... RENAN, TAINE,
MERIMEE
hole .... TROU
holy .... BENIT, SACRE
Holy Land .... LA TERRE
SAINTE
holy water .... EAU BENITE
honey .... MIEL

hope .... ESPOIR
horn .... CORNE
horse .... CHEVAL
horse stable .... ECURIE
hot .... CHAUD
hour .... HEUR
house .... MAISON
hungry .... AFFAME
hunter .... CHASSEUR
hunting match .... TIR
husband .... MARI
ice .... GLACE
if .... QUAND
import .... PORTEE
impressionist .... DEGAS
impressionest painter
.... MONET
in .... PAR, SUR, DANS
in the manner of .... A LA
income .... RENTE, REVENU
indication .... SIGNE
infantry man .... ZOUAVE,
CHASSEUR
infinitive .... AVOIR
ink .... ENCRE
inn .... AUBERGE
invoice .... FACTURE
iota .... RIEN
IOU .... DETTE
is .... EST
island .... RE, ILE, SEIN,
HYERES, OLERON, USHANT,
CORSICA, BELLE-ILE
island in Indian Ocean
.... REUNION
island off Newfoundland
.... MIQUELON
January .... JANVIER
join .... UNIR
joke .... BLAGUE, BON MOT
joker .... FARCEUR
journalist .... DAUDET
judge .... JUGE
judgment .... ARRET
juice .... JUS, SUC
July .... JUILLET
June .... JUIN
kill .... TUER
kind .... SORTE
king .... ROI, LOUIS, LOUIS
PHILIPPE
king's heir .... DAUPHIN
kingdom ..... ARLES, ROYAUME
kingdom, former .... NAVARRE
kiss .... BAISER
kitchen .... CUISINE
knife .... COUTEAU
know-how .... SAVOIR-FAIRE
lace .... CLUNY, DENTELLE
lady's bag .... ETUI
lagoon .... VACCARES

French

lake .... GENEVA
lamb .... AGNEAU
land .... TERRE
land measure .... ARPENT
landscape .... PAYSAGE
landscape artist .... COROT
language .... LANGUE
laugh .... RIRE
laughable .... RISIBLE
laundry .... BUANDERIE
law .... LOI, DROIT
lawyer .... AVOCAT
leather .... CUIR
leave .... CONGE
left .... GAUCHE
Legion of Honor member
.... CHEVALIER
legislature .... SENAT
leisure .... LOISIR
lemon .... CITRON
Lent .... LE CAREME
lexicographer .... LAROUSSE
liar .... MENTEUR
life/lifetime .... VIE, VIVANT
likewise .... DEMEME
liking .... GRE
lily .... LIS
line .... LIGNE
lipstick .... BATON DE ROUGE
little .... PEU, PETIT
lively wit .... ESP
lodging place .... GITE
long .... ETENDU
longest river .... LOIRE
love .... AIMER, AMOUR
love affair .... AMOURETTE,
AFFAIRE D'AMOUR
love letter .... BILLET DOUX
lover .... AMANT
loving .... AIMANT, TENDRE
luck .... BONHEUR
luxury .... LUXE
maid (servant) .... BONNE,
FILLE
mail .... POSTE
mail bag .... SAC POSTAL
make .... FAIRE
make believe .... FEINTE
man of letters: 19th century
.... GAUTIER
Manche capital .... ST. LO
mansion ...... HOTEL, CHATEAU
March .... MARS
marshal ...... NEY, FOCH, RUEL,
SAXE, MURAT, JOFFRE,
BAZAINE, MASSENA, TURENNE,
VENDOME
mask .... LOUP
master .... CHEF, MAITRE
masterpiece .... CHEF
D'OEUVRE

match .... EGAL, PAREIL
matchless .... SANS EGAL,
SANS PAREIL
matin lay .... AUBADE
May .... MAI
mayor .... MAIRE
me .... MOI
meager .... MAIGRE, PAUVRE
meal .... REPAS
measure .... PIED, METRE,
MINOT, TOISE, ARPENT, ASSISE,
PORTEE, TONNEAU
measures, old .... AUNE
meat .... VIANDE
meat dish .... SALMI
meaty .... CHARNU
mechanic .... GARAGISTE
medicine .... REMEDE,
MEDICAMENT
menu .... CARTE
menu item .... ENTRECOTE
merchant .... NEGOCIANT
merry .... GAI
midget .... NABOT
migrant/refugee .... EMIGRE
mile .... MILLE
militant .... ACTIVISTE
military ensign
.... ORIFLAMME
military group, large
.... ARMEE
milk .... LAIT
milkman .... LAITIER
mind .... ESPRIT
mink .... VISON
minstrel .... JONGLEUR
mirth .... GAIETE
misdeal .... MALDONNER
misdemeanor .... DELIT
miser .... AVARE
miss .... MANQUE,
MADEMOISELLE
model .... MANNEQUIN
monastery site .... CLUNY
Monday .... LUNDI
money ...... ARGENT, MONNAIE
money account book
.... LIVRE
moneyed .... RICHE
money market .... BOURSE
monetary unit .... FRANC
monk .... MOINE, RELIGIEUX
month .... MOIS
moon .... LUNE
morning .... MATIN
Morocco capital .... MEKNES
most/very .... TRES, LE PLUS
mother .... MERE
mother-in-law .... BELLE-MERE
mountain .... JURA, MONT,
BLANC, FOREZ, MEZENC,

VOSGES, AUVERGNE,
CEVENNES, MONTAGNE, COTE
D'OR, DORE ALPS, FAUCILLES
mountain peak .... PIC
mountain range ..... PYRENESS,
GRAIAN ALPS, COTTIAN ALPS,
MARITIME ALPS
Mrs.: abbr. .... MME
municipal official .... JURAT
museum .... MUSEE, RODIN,
CLUNY, GUIMET, LOUVRE
muslin .... MOUSSELINE
mustard .... MOUTARDE
my .... MA, MON
my dear .... MA CHERE
nail .... CLOU
naked .... DECOUVERT, AU
NATUREL
name .... NOM, RENE, HENRI,
JULIEN, PIERRE, JACQUES,
JEAN(NE), JULIETTE,
MICHEL(LE)
name of Lake Geneva
.... LEMAN
nap .... SIESTE, SOMMEIL
napkin .... SERVIETTE
national .... CITOYEN
national anthem
.... MARSEILLAISE
naturalist .... LAMARCK
naval base .... BREST
navigator .... CARTIER
near .... PRES, PROCHE
neat .... SOIGNE
neck .... COU
need .... BESOIN
needle .... AIGUILLE
negative .... PAS
nerve .... NERF, AUDACE
nest .... NID
neurologist .... CHARCOT
new .... NOUVEAU
news .... NOUVELLES
newspaper .... JOURNAL
newsreel pioneer .... PATHE
night .... NUIT
nightclub .... BOITE DE NUIT
nimble .... LESTE
nine .... NEUF
no .... NON, PAS
nobleman .... DUC, COMTE
none .... NUL, NULLE
noon .... MIDI
north .... NORD
nose .... NEZ
nothing .... RIEN, NEANT
notion .... IDEE
novelist ..... GARD, GIDE, LOTI,
LOUYS, SAGAN, VERNE,
BALZAC, FRANCE, LESAGE,
PROUST, MALRAUX, MAUROIS,

ROMAINS, STENDHAL, ROMANCIER
November .... NOVEMBRE
nursemaid .... BONNE
oath .... VOIRE DIRE
obsession .... IDEE FIXE
October .... OCTOBRE
of .... DE
office .... AGENCE, BUREAU
ogler .... LORGNEUR
oil .... HUILE
old .... ANCIEN
old-fashioned .... DEMODE
omen .... AUGURE
on .... DE, EN, SUR, DANS, DESSUS, ADROITE
on foot .... A PIED
one .... UN(E)
onion .... OIGNON
only .... SEUL
open .... OUVRIR
orchard .... VERGER
orphan .... ORPHELIN
our .... NOS, NOTRE
out .... HORS
over .... SUR
own .... AVOUER
Pacific islands .... MARQUESAS
painter .... COROT, DEGAS, LEGER, MANET, MONET, INGRES, RENOIR, SEURAT, CEZANNE, COURBET, PISSARRO
painter's surface .... MUR
pancake .... CREPE
panegyric .... ELOGE
pantomimist .... PIERROT
paper .... PAPIER
paper maker .... PAPETIER
parent .... MERE, PERE
paring knife .... TRANCHET
parliament .... SENAT
paste .... PATE
pastry .... BABA, ECLAIR, NAPOLEON, PATISSERIE
pate .... TETE, CABOCHE
patron saint .... DENIS
period of time .... TERME
pet .... FAVORI
petticoat .... COTTE, JUPON
philosopher .... TAINE, PASCAL, SARTRE, BERGSON, DIDEROT, DESCARTES
phonetician .... PASSY
physicist .... AMPERE, PERRIN
pilgrim .... PELERIN
pilgrimage town ...... LOURDES
pillow .... OREILLER
plateau ..... MORVAN, LANGRES
playing card .... DIX
playing marble .... BILLE

playwright/diplomat
.... CLAUDEL
plumcake .... BABA
plump .... DODU, GRAS
pocket .... POCHE
poem .... DIT, VERS, VILLANELLE
poet .... MAROT, RACINE, RONSARD, TROUVERE, TROUVEUR, LAMARTINE
police .... GENDARME
police official
.... COMMISSAIRE
police station
.... COMMISSARIAT
pond/pool .... MARE
Pope .... PAPE
porcelain .... SEVRES, LIMOGES
pork .... PORC
pork, pickled .... SALE
porridge .... BOUILLIE
port .... CAEN, SETE, BREST, HAVRE, ROUEN, DIEPPE
porter .... SUISSE, CONCIERGE
possessions .... ILES
possessive pronoun .... MES, MON, SES, NOUS
pout .... MOUE
premier .... HERRIOT, TARDIEU, CLEMENCEAU
preposition .... AVEC
president .... BLUM, COTY, CARNOT, POMPIDOU, (DE)GAULLE, MITTERRAND
president's residence
.... ELYSEE
pressure cooker
.... AUTOCLAVE
pretty .... JOLI(E), GENTIL
priest .... ABBE, CURE, PERE, PRETRE
prime .... ELITE, FLEUR
prime minister .... (MICHEL) ROCARD
prime minister, first woman
.... EDITH CRESSON
prime of life .... ETE, FLEUR DE L'AGE
prize .... PRIX
prize for literature
.... GONCOURT
prize winner .... GAGNANT, LAUREAT
profession .... METIER
profit .... BONI
pronoun ..... JE, TU, IL(S), CES, MES, MOI, TOI, UNE, ELLE, VOUS, VOTRE
prop .... ETAI
Protectorate now part of Vietnam .... ANNAM

Protestant .... HUGUENOT
Protestant leader ...... MORNAY
Protestant reformer
.... CALVIN
Provencal poet .... MISTRAL
province .... FOIX, ANJOU, AUNIS, BEARN, BERRY, MAINE, ALSACE, ARTOIS, MARCHE, POITOU, GASCONY, GUYENNE, PICARDY, AUVERGNE, BRITTANY, BURGUNDY, DAUPHINE, FLANDERS, LIMOUSIN, LORRAINE, LYONNAIS, NORMANDY, PROVENCE, TOURAINE, CHAMPAGNE, LANGUEDOC, NIVERNAIS, ORLEANAIS, VENAISSIN, BOURBONNAIS, FRANCHE COMTE
punishment .... PEINE
pupil/student .... ELEVE
purchase .... ACHAT
puzzle .... ENIGME
puzzle, crossword .... MOTS CROISES
quality standard .... ALOI
queen .... REINE
quick .... RAPIDE
rabbit .... LAPIN
race-course .... AUTEUIL
racetrack .... PISTE
raffle .... LOTERIE
railroad station .... GARE
rain .... PLUIE
rallying word .... LIBERTE
read .... LIRE
ready .... PRET
real .... VRAI
rebel .... JACOBIN
receipt .... RECU
recess .... NICHE, RECOIN
recipe .... RECETTE
record .... GREFFE, REGISTRE
red .... ROUGE
referee .... ARBITRE
reindeer .... RENNE
relative .... MERE, PERE, FRERE, SOEUR, TANTE
remainder .... RESTE
Republic personified
.... MARIANNE
reserve .... ENCAS
resort .... BAIN, CANNES, MENTON, ANTIBES, RIVIERA, BIARRITZ
rest .... REPOS
revenue .... RENTE
Revolution landmark
.... BASTILLE
Revolution refrain .... CAIRA

French

Revolutionary calendar,
month of .... NIVOSE
revolutionist .... MARAT,
DANTON, CARMAGNOLE
ribbon .... RUBAN, CORDON,
SAUTOIR
rifle .... CHASSEPOT
rights .... DROITES
river ..... AIN, LOT, ORB, AUBE,
CHER, EURE, GARD, GERS,
ISLE, LOIR, OISE, ORNE, SAAR,
TARN, ADOUR, AISNE, DOUBS,
DROME, INDRE, ISERE, LOIRE,
MARNE, MEUSE, RHINE,
RHONE, RISLE, SAONE, SEINE,
SOMME, YONNE, ALLIER,
CREUSE, DRONNE, VIENNE,
DURANCE, GARONNE,
HERAULT, GIRONDE, MAYENNE,
MOSELLE, VILAINE, CHARENTE,
DORDOGNE
road .... RUE
roast .... ROTI(R)
Roman Catholic .... GALLICAN
room .... SALLE
royal arms symbol ..... FLEUR-
DE-LIS
royal edict .... ARRET
royal family .... CAPET,
VALOIS
royal standard ..... ORIFLAMME
royalty .... REINE, ROYAUTE
ruling family .... VALOIS
rumor .... BRUIT, ON DIT
sad(ness) .... TRISTE(SSE)
sale .... VENTE
salt .... SEL
salt pork .... SALE
salt tax .... GABELLE
salt water .... EAU DE MER
salted .... SALEE
same .... MEME
Santa Claus .... PERE NOEL
satin fabric .... ETOILE
satirist .... RABELAIS,
VOLTAIRE
Saturday .... SAMEDI
saying .... DIT, MOT, DICTON
school .... BANDE, ECOLE
school, secondary/college
.... LYCEE
sculptor .... RODIN, HOUDON
sea .... MER, NORTH,
MEDITERRANEAN
sea nymph .... NEREIDE
seaport .... BREST, CALAIS,
TOULON, LE HAVRE,
CHERBOURG, MARSEILLE
seasoning .... SECHAGE
seaweed .... ALGUE

second set in a quadrille
.... LETE
secret intelligence .... SDECE
security .... SURETE, GARANTIE
see .... VOIR
self-esteem .... AMOUR-PROPRE
sell .... VENDRE
senior .... AINE, DOYEN
September .... SEPTEMBRE
seraph .... ANGE
servant ..... BONNE, SERVITEUR
seven .... SEPT
she .... ELLE
sheep .... MOUTON
shell .... COQUE
shelter .... ABRI, GITE,
COUVERT
shepherd .... PATRE, BERGER
shield .... ECU, ECRAN,
BOUCLIER
ship .... NAVIRE, VAISSEAU
shoe ...... SOULIER, CHAUSSURE
shoot .... TIRER
shooting gallery .... TIR
shop .... BOUTIQUE
shoplifter .... VOLEUR
short .... BREF, COURT
shout .... CRI
shrimp .... CREVETTE
shrine .... LOURDES
sick .... MALADE
sickness .... MALADIE,
NAUSEES
sight .... VUE
silk .... SOIE, SOIERIES
silk center .... LYON
sin .... PECHE
sing .... CHANTER
singer .... CHANTEUR
sir .... MONSIEUR
sister .... SOEUR
site of Roman ruins
.... ORANGE
skater .... PATINEUR
ski champ .... KILLY
skin .... PEAU
sky .... CIEL
slang .... ARGOT
sleep .... SOMMEIL
small .... FIN, PETIT
smell .... ODEUR
smile .... SOURIRE
smoke .... FUMEE
smoker .... FUMEUR
smoking room ..... ESTAMINET
snail .... ESCARGOT
snow .... NIEGE
soap .... SAVON
society .... LE MONDE
soft .... MOU
soldier .... POILU, SOLDAT,

CHASSEUR, FANTASSIN,
MILITAIRE, LEGIONNAIRE
soldier hero .... BAYARD
soldier noted for his large
nose .... CYRANO DE
BERGERAC
Somaliland capital ...... JIBUTI,
DJIBOUTI
something for something
.... QUID PRO QUO
son .... FILS
son-in-law .... GENDRE
song .... CHANSON
soprano .... PONS
soul .... AME
soup .... POTAGE
south .... SUD, (DU)MIDI
speak .... PARLER
speech ...... PAROLE, DISCOURS
spend .... PERDRE
spider .... ARAIGNEE
spinster ..... FILLE NON MARIEE
spirit .... AME, FEU, ELAN,
ARDEUR, ESPRIT
spot .... TACHE
spring .... SAUT
springtime .... MAI, AVRIL
spy .... ESPION
spy ring/spying
.... ESPIONNAGE
square .... CARRE
stage .... ETAGE, ESTRADE
stalk .... TIGE
stall, as an engine .... CALER
star .... ASTRE, ETOILE
state .... ETAT
statesman .... BRIAND,
CARNOT, MAZARIN, REYNAUD,
CLEMENCEAU
stew .... POT AU FEU
stock exchange .... BOURSE
stoneware .... GRES
stop .... HALTE
storehouse .... DEPOT, ETAPE,
MAGASIN, ENTREPOT
stork .... CIGOGNE
storm .... ORAGE
stove .... POELE
strait .... DOVER, BONIFACIO
strawberry .... FRAISE
street .... RUE
strong .... FORT, SOLIDE
studio .... ATELIER
stupid .... SOT, BETE
style .... TON, TITRE
stylist .... DIOR
subway .... METRO
Sudan .... MALI
sugar .... SUCRE
summer .... ETE, ESTIVAL
sun .... SOLEIL

Sunday .... DIMANCHE
superfluous .... DETROP
supper .... SOUPER
surnamed .... DIT
sweetbread .... RIS
sweetmeat .... DRAGEE, BON-
      BON, SUCRERIE
swimmer .... NAGEUR
sword .... EPEE
taste .... GRE
tattle .... BABIL
tawny .... FAUVE, TANNE
tea .... THE
team .... ATTELAGE
teapot .... THEIERE
tear .... LARME
ten .... DIX
thanks .... MERCI
that ...... CE, CET, CELA, CETTE
the .... LA, LE, LES
thee .... TOI
theft .... VOL
their .... LEUR(S)
them .... EUX, ELLES
then .... DONC, PUIS, ALORS
there! .... VOILA
these .... CES
they .... ILS, ELLES
thin .... MAIGRE
thine .... ATOI
thing .... ETRE, OBJET
think .... PENSER
thirst .... SOIF
thirty .... TRENTE
this .... CE, CET, CETTE
three/third .... TROIS
Thursday .... JEUDI
ticket .... BILLET
tide .... MAREE
tidy .... SOIGNE
tie .... LIER
time .... TEMPS, SAISON
tire .... PNEU
to be .... ETRE
to come in .... ENTRER
to have .... AVOIR
to me .... AMOI
to say .... DIRE
toast .... ROTIE
tobacco .... TABAC
tomato .... TOMATE
tongue .... LANGUE
too .... TROP
tooth .... DENT
town .... VILLE
tree .... ARBRE
trifle .... RIEN
trouble .... AGITER
trough .... AUGE
true .... VRAI
trust .... CONFIANCE

truth .... VERITE
Tuesday .... MARDI
tunnel .... MONT CENIS
twelve .... DOUZE
twelve o'clock midnight
 .... MINUIT
twelve peers .... DOUZEPERS
two .... DEUX
ugly .... LAID
uncle .... ONCLE
under .... SOUS
underdog .... OPPRIME
underground fighters
 .... MAQUIS
understand .... ENTENDRE
United Kingdom
 .... ROYAUME-UNI
United States .... ETATS-UNIS
untrue .... FAUX
up .... HAUT
up-to-date .... AU COURANT
upon .... SUR
upstairs .... D'EN HAUT
use .... EMPLOI
vegetable .... LEGUME
verb .... ETRE, AVOIR
verse .... ALBA, POESIE,
    RONDEL, VIRELAY
very .... BIEN, TRES
vest .... GILET
vineyard .... CRU, VIGNE
violin .... VIOLON
violinist
 .... (ZINO)FRANCESCATTI
vogue .... BON TON
voucher .... RECU
wagon .... VOITURE
waiter .... GARCON
wall .... MUR
war .... GUERRE
warehouse .... ENTREPOT
wartime capital .... VICHY
water .... EAU
water color .... AQUARELLE
watered silk .... MOIRE
wave .... ONDE
wax .... CIRE
we .... NOUS
weapon .... ARME
Wednesday .... MERCREDI
weight ..... KILO, ONCE, LIVRE,
   POIDS, TONNE, GRAMME
well .... BIEN
well-being .... BIEN-ETRE
well-groomed .... SOIGNE(E)
well-timed .... A PROPOS
west .... OUEST
whale .... BALEINE
what/which .... QUEL
wheat .... BLE
when .... QUAND

where .... OU, LA OU
white .... BLANC
who .... QUI
why .... POURQUOI
widow .... VEUVE
will .... VOULOIR
wind .... VENT
wind, cold North ..... MISTRAL
wine ..... VIN, MEDOC, PINARD,
    CHABLIS, BORDEAUX,
   BURGUNDY, HERMITAGE
wine region .... LOIRE,
    ALSACE, ARMAGNAC,
    BORDEAUX, COGNAC,
    BURGUNDY, CALVADOS,
   PROVENCE, CHAMPAGNE,
      LANGUEDOC
wing .... ALLE
winter .... HIVER
with .... AVEC
without .... SANS
witless .... SOT, SANS ESPRIT
witness .... TEMOIN
wolf .... LOUP
woman .... FEMME
wood .... BOIS
woodland .... FORET
wool .... LAINE
woolens .... LAINAGE
word .... MOT
work .... TRAVAILLER
world .... MONDE
World War I plane
 .... NIEUPORT
worldly .... MONDAIN
worldly-wise woman
 .... BLASEE
worry .... ENNUI
worship .... CULTE
wrist .... POIGNET
write .... ECRIRE
writer .... HUGO, DUMAS,
  HEINE, RENAN, STAEL, VERNE,
   FRANCE, VILLON, MAUROIS,
    PROUDHON, VOLTAIRE
writer of fables .... LA
      FONTAINE
wrong .... FAUX, ERRONE
yard .... COUR
year .... ANNEE
yearly .... ANNUEL
yellow .... JAUNE
yes .... OUI
yesterday .... HIER
you .... TU, TOI, VOUS
young .... NEUF, JEUNE
your .... TES, TON, VOTRE
youth .... JEUNESSE
Yule .... NOEL
zero .... RIEN
Frenchman .... GAUL, HUGUENOT

famous .... CHARLEMAGNE
frenzied .... MAD, RAVING,
BERSERK, ENRAGED, FRANTIC,
MADDING, FRENETIC
fighter .... AMOK, AMUCK,
BERSERK, BARESARK
frenzy .... FURY, RAGE, FUROR,
MANIA, ORGASM, MADNESS,
HYSTERICS, PANDEMONIUM
freon .... GAS, REFRIGERANT
frequent ...... OFT, OFTEN, HAUNT,
RESORT, CONSTANT,
HABITUAL, REPEATED
frequenter of a kind
.... HABITUE
frequently .... MUCH, OFTEN, A
LOT, INCESSANTLY
poetic .... OFT
frere .... FRIAR, BROTHER
fresh .... NEW, RAW, BRISK,
CLEAN, DRUNK, NOVEL, TIPSY,
RECENT
clothes .... CHANGE
colloquial .... BOLD, PERT,
SAUCY, SASSY, IMPUDENT
talk .... LIP
water alga .... DESMID
water worm .... NAID
freshen .... REFRESH, SWEETEN
freshener, skin .... LOTION
freshet .... FLOOD, SPATE,
TORRENT
freshman ...... NOVICE, BEGINNER,
NEWCOMER, GREENHORN
Annapolis/West Point
.... PLEBE
first banker of .... DAD
slang .... FROSH
fret .... NAG, VEX, FUME, FUSS,
GNAW, STEW, CHAFE, CHAMP,
WORRY, REPINE, COMPLAIN
British .... CHEVY
fretful .... GRUMPY, GROUCHY,
PEEVISH, DEJECTED,
PETULANT, REPINING,
IRRITABLE
Freud, psychiatrist .... SIGMUND
Freya's dwelling .... FOLKVANG
friable ...... CRISP, FRAIL, MEALY,
SHORT, BRITTLE, FRAGILE
friar .... FRA, MONK, ABBOT,
FRATER, LISTER, MONASTIC,
CARMELITE, BROTHER,
DOMINICAN, AUGUSTINIAN
beggar .... SERVITE
bird .... PIMLICO
head covering .... COWL,
CAPUCHE
of fiction .... TUCK
robe of .... FROCK
friar's lantern ...... IGNIS FATUUS

friary .... MONASTERY
fricative .... HISS, SPIRANT
friction .... ERASURE, SANDING,
RUB(BING), ABRASION,
DISAGREEMENT
air .... WINDAGE
match .... FUSEE
Friday, for one .... GIRL
fridge foray .... RAID
fried lightly .... SAUTE(E)D
slang .... DRUNK
friedcake .... CRULLER,
DOUGHNUT
friend .... PAL, ALLY, CHUM,
AMIGO, BUDDY, CRONY,
NETOP, COMPEER, PATRON,
INTIMATE, PLAYMATE,
SUPPORTER, SYMPATHIZER,
WELL-WISHER
boy's best ..... MAMA, MOTHER
close .... SIDEKICK
Damon's .... PYTHIAS
faithful ...... DAMON, ACHATES,
PYTHIAS
false .... IAGO
lion's .... ANDROCLES,
ANDROCLUS
man's best .... DOG
Matt Dillon's .... DOC
of the hungry .... EATERY
of Trajan and Tacitus
.... PLINY
sort of .... FAIR-WEATHER
special .... FAVORITE
friendly .... AFFABLE, AMIABLE,
KIND(LY), CORDIAL,
AMICABLE, INTIMATE,
FAMILIAR, HOSPITABLE
dwarf .... LEPRECHAUN
hint .... TIP
relations .... AMITY
sometimes .... REMINDERS
understanding .... ENTENTE
Friendly Islands .... TONGA
friendship .... AMITY, PEACE,
HARMONY, BROTHERHOOD
Friesian .... FRIESE
frieze square .... METOPE
frigate .... WARSHIP
bird .... IWA, ATAFA
hand .... SALT
Frigga's husband .... ODIN
fright .... AWE, FEAR, ALARM,
DREAD, PANIC, TERROR
frighten .... AWE, ALARM, DAUNT,
FEEZE, SCARE, STARTLE,
TERRIFY, TERRORIZE
frightened .... AFEAR, AFRAID,
SCARED, ALARMED
forest .... PETRIFIED
frightful .... HORRIBLE, SHOCKING,

UNPLEASANT
frigid .... ICY, COLD, STIFF,
FORMAL, FREEZING,
HYPERBOREAN
zone subsoil ...... PERMAFROST
frijol .... BEAN
frill .... EXTRA, JABOT, RUCHE,
RUFF(LE), FALBALA,
FURBELOW, TRIMMING,
ADORNMENT
Frimi (Rudolf) forte
.... OPERETTA
fringe ...... EDGE, LOMA, BORDER,
THRUM, MARGIN, (OUT)SKIRT
benefit ...... BONUS, VACATION,
INSURANCE
hairs, etc. .... FIMBRIA
of Jew's scarf .... ZIZITH
frippery .... FINERY
useles .... FALLAL
friseur .... HAIRDRESSER
frisk ...... CAPER, CAVORT, FROLIC,
GAMBOL, TITTUP
slang .... SEARCH, SHAKE-
DOWN
frisky .... SPRY, PEPPY, LIVELY,
PLAYFUL, KITTENISH
animal .... CAT, DOG, COLT,
GOAT, PUPPY, KITTEN
Frisson of horror .... GRUE
frith .... INLET, ESTUARY
fritter .... CAKE, DALLY, PIECE,
SHRED, WASTE, DAWDLE
away: sl. .... PISS AWAY
frivoled .... TOYED
frivolity .... JOY, GLEE, MIRTH,
LEVITY, FOOLERY, MADNESS
frivolous .... GIDDY, LIGHT,
MERRY, PETTY, SILLY,
PALTRY, FLIGHTY, TRIVIAL,
FLIPPANT, TRIFLING
frizz .... FRY, CRIMP, SIZZLE,
FRIZZLE
frizzed ...... CRISP, CURLY, KINKY,
KINKED, CRAPED, FRIZZY,
CRIMPED
fro .... AWAY, BACK(WARD)
frock .... COAT, GOWN, ROBE,
DRESS, SMOCK, TUNIC,
JERSEY, MANTLE, OVERALL,
SOUTANE
froe .... CLEAVER
frog .... RANA, TOAD, FROSH,
ANURAN, PEEPER, PADDOCK,
POLLYWOG, SALIENTIAN
farm .... RANARIA
fish .... ANGLER
genus .... RANA
larva .... TADPOLE
like .... RANINE
order .... ANURA

slang ..... JUMPER, FRENCHMAN
sound .... CROAK
young .... TADPOLE
froggery .... RANARIA
froggy .... TOADISH
frogman .... DIVER
frolic ...... FUN, GAY, PLAY, ROMP,
CAPER, FRISK, MERRY, PRANK,
SPREE, CAVORT, GAIETY,
GAMBOL, (SKY)LARK,
MERRIMENT
frolicking .... KIDDING AROUND
frolicsome .... FRISKY, PLAYFUL
from .... EX, AWAY, OUT OF
A to Z .... ALPHABET
Ash Wednesday to Easter
.... LENT
bad to ____ .... WORSE
head to foot .... CAP-A-PIE
here .... HENCE
now on .... HENCEFORTH
take .... LESSEN, SUBTRACT
that time/there .... THENCE
the original source ...... FIRST-
HAND
then till now .... SINCE
____ (thoroughly) .... STEM
TO STERN
time immemorial .... AGES
AGO, EVERSINCE
time to time .... SOMETIMES,
OCCASIONALLY
where? .... WHENCE
fromenty .... PUDDING
Frome's (Ethan) wife .... ITU,
ZEENA
frond .... LEAF
frondeur .... CRITIC
front .... VAN, BROW, FACE, FORE,
OBVERSE, FOREHEAD
boat .... BOW, PROW
hoof .... TOE
of building .... FACADE
of coin/medal .... OBVERSE
page box .... EAR
page news .... CRIME,
SCANDAL, CALAMITY,
DISASTER
page sight .... MASTHEAD
position .... FIRING LINE
slang .... DUMMY, STOOGE
frontage .... FACADE
frontal .... FORWARD, METOPIC
frontier .... BOUNDARY,
BORDERLAND, WILDERNESS
settlement .... OUTPOST
vehicle .... STAGE
frontiersman .... CODY, EARP,
BOONE, BOWIE, LOGAN,
CARSON, HICKOK
colloquial .... HILLBILLY

frontlet .... FILLET, FOREHEAD,
HEADBAND
frontispiece .... PREFACE,
PRELUDE, FOREWORD,
INTRODUCTION
fronton .... JAI ALAI
front-runner .... HARBINGER,
PRECURSOR
frosh .... FROG, FRESHMAN
hazer .... SOPH(OMORE)
frost .... ICE, NIP HOAR, RIME,
CHILL, COLDNESS
again .... RE-ICE
froster .... ICER
frosting .... ICING
equipment .... FREEZER, ICER
frosty .... ICY, RIMY, FRORE,
TENSE, HOARY, FROZEN,
AUSTERE, FREEZING,
STRAINED
froth .... FOAM, SCUM, SUDS,
CREAM, SPUME, YEAST,
LATHER
drink's .... HEAD
frothy .... FOAMY, SPUMY,
BUBBLY, TRIFLING
froufrou .... SWISH, RUSTLE
frounce .... CURL, CREASE,
WRINKLE
frow .... WIFE, WOMAN
frown .... LOUR, POUT, SCOWL,
(G)LOWER, GRIMACE,
DISAPPROVE
frowning .... GLUM, SULLEN,
MOROSE, SCOWLING
frowzy .... DIRTY, MUSTY, UNTIDY
woman .... DOWD, SLATTERN
frozen .... ICY, COLD, GELID,
GLACE, CHILLY, GLACIAL,
CONGEALED, MOTIONLESS,
PARALYZED, FROSTBITTEN
carbon dioxide .... DRY ICE
dessert .... ICE, FRAPPE, ICE
CREAM, MOUSSE, SHERBET
dew .... RIME
partly .... FRAPPE
rain ...... SLEET, SNOW(FLAKES)
vapor .... FROST
fructify .... FERTILIZE
fructose .... SUGAR, LEVULOSE
fructuous .... FRUITFUL,
PRODUCTIVE
frugal .... CHARY, CHEAP,
MEAGER, SAVING, PRUDENT,
SPARING, THRIFTY,
ECONOMIC(AL)
frugality .... ECONOMY,
PARSIMONY, THRIFT(INESS)
fruit .... CROP, SLOE, DRUPE,
BERRY, YIELD, PRODUCT,
RESULT, CONSEQUENCE

aggregate .... ETAERIO
apple-shaped .... QUINCE
basket .... POTTLE
bat .... PECA
bear .... FRUCTIFY
bearing no .... ACARPOUS
beech tree .... MAST
berry .... CURRANT,
GOOSEBERRY
berry-like .... STRAWBERRY
boat .... ORANGER
cactus .... FIG
cake .... SIMNEL
candy .... DATE
carbohydrate .... PECTIN
Chinese .... LITCHI, LOQUAT
citrus .... LIME, LEMON,
ORANGE, KUMQUAT
coating .... BLOOM
cocktail/salad ...... MACEDOINE
collective .... SYNCARP
combining form .... CARP(O)
cordial .... RATAFIA
course .... DESSERT
covering .... RIND, EPICARP,
CALYPTRA
cultivation, study of
.... POMOLOGY
date-like .... JUJUBE
dealer .... COSTER
decay .... ROT, BLET
dish ..... COMPOTE, COMPOTIER
dot(s) .... SORI, SORUS
downy bristles .... PAPPUS
dried .... PRUNE, RAISIN
drink/quaff .... ADE
dry .... ACHENE
eating .... FRUGIVOROUS
eating bat .... KALONG, FLYING
FOX, HAMMERHEAD
egg-shaped .... RAMBUTAN
elm/key/maple .... SAMARA
enzyme .... PECTASE
family ...... RUE, ROSE, GOURD,
HEATH, SAXIFRAGE,
SOAPBERRY, CUSTARD-APPLE
filled crust .... DUMPLING
fir .... CONE
flesh .... PULP
fly .... DROSOPHILA
foul-smelling .... DURIAN
fuzzy-skinned .... PEACH
genus .... MALUS, RIBES,
FRAGARIA, FORTUNELLA
gourd .... PEPO, SETON
growing, science of
..... POMOLOGY, HORTICULTURE
hard-shelled .... NUT, GOURD
hawthorne .... HAW
hybrid .... POMA
injury .... BRUISE

inner layer .... ENDOCARP
jelly ingredient .... PECTIN
juice .... MUST, STUM
juice, distilled .... BRANDY
juice, fermented .... WINE,
　　　　　　　　　　　VINEGAR
juice drink .... ADE, SHRUB,
　BRANDY, SQUASH, SHERBET,
　LEMONADE, ORANGEADE
juice squeezer .... REAMER
juicy part .... PULP
knife .... CORER, PARER
lemon-like .... CITRON
liquid .... JUICE
melon .... CASABA,
　HONEYDEW, MUSKMELON,
　　　　　　　　CANTALOUPE
multiple .... SOROSIS
oak .... ACORN
of discord .... APPLE
of forgetfulness .... LOTUS
of passionflowers
　.......................... GRANADILLA
of "virginity" .... CHERRY
oil tube .... VITTA
oily .... OLIVE
one-seeded .... NUT, AKENE
palm .... DATE, COCONUT,
　　　　　　　　　　BETEL NUT
part ..... PIT, CORE, PULP, RIND
peach-like .... NECTARINE
peel .... RIND, ZEST
picker .... OKIE, BRACERO
pie .... TART, COBBLER
pine .... CONE
plant stem .... CANE
"plum of Damascus"
　.................................. DAMSON
plum-like .... SLOE,
　　　　　　　　　PERSIMMON
preserve .... JAM, COMPOTE
prune-like .... MYROBALAN
pulp/residue ...... PAP, POMACE
pulpy .... UVA, DRUPE
refuse .... MARC
rind .... PEEL, EPICARP,
　　　EXOCARP, CALYPTRA
rosebush .... HIP
rot .... BLET
sculptured .... CORBEIL
seed .... PIP, KERNEL
seller .... COSTER(MONGER)
ship .... ORANGER, FRUITER
skin .... PEEL, RIND, EPICARP
small .... HAW, AKENE,
　　　　　　　　　　　ACHENE
sour .... LIME, LEMON
stew .... SASS, SAUCE
stone .... PIP, PIT, NUTLET,
　　　PYRENE, PUTAMEN
strained .... PUREE

sugar .... FRUCTOSE, LEVULOSE
tomato-like .... POMATO
tree planter, eccentric
　................. JOHNNY APPLESEED
trees collectively .... ORCHARD
tropical .... DATE, GUAVA,
　MANGO, BANANA, PAPAYA,
　PA(W)PAW, AVOCADO,
　COCONUT, PINEAPPLE
undeveloped .... NUBBIN
vineyard .... GRAPE
winged .... SAMARA
with acid pulp ..... TAMARIND,
　　　　　　　　　SOURGOURD
with many seeds
　....................... POMEGRANATE
with segmented pulp
　........................ MANGOSTEEN
with sweet pulp, black seeds
　.............................. SWEETSOP
fruiter .... SHIP, ORANGER
fruiterer .... COSTER
fruitful .... FECUND, FERTILE,
　PROLIFIC, FERACIOUS,
　FRUCTUOUS, PRODUCTIVE,
　　　　　　　　PROFITABLE
make .... FRUCTIFY
fruition .... OUTCOME,
　ATTAINMENT, CULMINATION,
　　　　　　REALIZATION
fruitless .... VAIN, BARREN,
　FUTILE, OTIOSE, STERILE
undertaking .... FOLLY
fruits, study of .... CARPOLOGY
fruity .... CARPIC
slang .... NUTS, NUTTY
frump .... SLOB, SLOVEN
frumpish .... SHABBY, UNTIDY
frustrate .... BALK, DASH, FOIL,
　AVERT, BAFFLE, DEFEAT,
　HINDER, IMPEDE, THWART,
　　　　　　　　　NULLIFY
frustration ...... DEFEAT, CHAGRIN
frutescent/fruticose .... SHRUBBY
fry .... FISH, FRIZZ, YOUNG,
　MINNOW, CHILDREN,
　　　　　　　　FINGERLING
lightly/quickly .... SAUTE
frying-pan .... SPIDER, SKILLET
fub .... TRICK
fubsy .... PLUMP, SQUAT, ROTUND
fuchsia red .... MAGENTA
fuchsin .... DYE, SOLFERINO
fucoid .... SEAWEED, ROCKWEED
fucus .... DYE, PAINT, SEAWEED
fuddy-duddy ...... DODO, DOTARD,
　　　　　　　　　OLD FOGY
fudge .... FAKE, CANDY, CHEAT,
　GLOSS, FALSIFY, NONSENSE
Fuego island native .... ONA
fu(e)hrer .... HITLER, LEADER

fuel .... GAS, LOG, OIL, COKE,
　FEED, FIRE, WOOD, STOKE,
　IGNITE, (CHAR)COAL,
　　　　　　　COMBUSTIBLE
brick .... BRIQUET
carrying vessel/ship .... OILER,
　　　　　TANKER, TENDER
chemical .... BUTANE
dung .... CHIP
for chafing dishes .... STERNO,
　　　　　　CANNED HEAT
liquid .... OIL, ALCOHOL,
　GAS(OLINE), PETROL(EUM)
oil .... KEROSENE
turf .... PEAT
type of .... ATOMIC, CANNEL,
　KEROSENE, PARAFFIN
fugacious .... FLEETING,
　EPHEMERAL, TRANSIENT
fugal section .... EPISODE
fugitive .... EXILE, ELOPER,
　ESCAPEE, FLEEING, REFUGEE,
　DESERTER, RUNAWAY,
　FLEETING, RUNAGATE,
　ABSCONDER, TRANSIENT
Negro slave .... MAROON
fugue .... TONAL
concluding passage
　................. STRETTA, STRETTO
fulcrum .... AXIS, PROP, PIVOT,
　　　　　　　　　BRACKET
device for holding oar
　.............. OARLOCK, ROWLOCK
filler .... OAR
for an oar .... THOLE
Fulda river .... EDER
fulfill ...... OBEY, EFFECT, REDEEM,
　GRATIFY, PERFORM, REALIZE,
　EXECUTE, SATISFY, COMPLETE,
　IMPLEMENT, ACCOMPLISH
fulfillment .... OUTCOME,
　FRUITION, COMPLETION
fulgent .... RADIANT
fuliginous .... DARK, DUSKY,
　MURKY, SMOKY, SOOTY
full .... SATED, WHOLE, ENTIRE,
　CROWDED, OROTUND,
　REPLETE, COMPLETE,
　　　　　　　　PREGNANT
and rounded .... PLUMP
apology .... AMENDE
as a skirt .... BOUFFANT(E)
attendance/meeting
　............................... PLENARY
blast .... BRUTE FORCE
blooded .... HEARTY,
　VIGOROUS, PEDIGREED,
　　　　　　THOROUGHBRED
blooded horse .... ARAB
bloom .... FLOWERING
blown .... OPEN, MATURE(D)

bodied .... VISCOUS, FLAVORSOME
dress .... TAILS, FORMAL
fig .... SUNDAY CLOTHES
flavored .... MELLOW
fledged .... MATURE
grown .... RIPE, ADULT
house: colloq. .... SRO
measure .... ABUNDANCE, AMPLITUDE
of bog products .... PEATY
of cracks .... RIMOSE
of energy .... PEPPY, SAPPY, SPIRITED
of holes .... PITTED, POCKMARKED
of life .... SPRY, LUSTY, LIVELY, BOUNCING
of: suffix .... OSE, ITOUS, ULENT
of trees .... PINY
of ups and downs
.... CHECKERED
of zeal .... AFIRE
scale .... TOTAL, GLOBAL
stop .... PERIOD, STANDSTILL
supply .... GLUT
to the edge/rim ..... BRIMMING
fullness .... PLENUM, SATIETY, SURFEIT, PLENITUDE, REPLETION
fully developed .... WELL-ROUNDED
fulmar .... NELLY, PETREL, MALDUCK, MALLEMUCK
fulminate .... BOOM, ROAR, EXPLODE, THUNDER, DETONATE
fulsome .... FOUL, COARSE, OBNOXIOUS
Fulton's (Robert) invention
.... STEAMBOAT
boat .... CLERMONT
fumarole .... HORNITO
fumble .... FLUB, MUFF, FLUFF, GROPE, BOBBLE, BUNGLE
fumbling .... CLUMSY
fume .... GAS, FRET, RAGE, RAVE, REEK, SMOKE, STEAM, VAPOR, SEETHE
fumigant .... PASTILLE, DEODORANT, DEODORIZER
fumigate .... GAS, SANITIZE, DISINFECT
fuming .... RAGING, RAVING, ENRAGED, FURIOUS
fumy .... VAPOROUS
fun ...... JEST, PLAY, JINKS, SPORT, JOLLITY, AMUSEMENT, DIVERSION, MERRIMENT

and games interval
.... PLAYTIME
-loving .... GAY
of, make ...... MOCK, RIDICULE
Funafuti .... ATOLL
funambulist .... TIGHTROPE WALKER
kind of .... ACROBAT, AERIALIST
function .... USE, DUTY, RITE, ROLE, WORK, PARTY, SERVE, OFFICE, OPERATE
trigonometry .... SINE, COSINE, TANGENT
functional .... USEFUL
functionary .... OFFICIAL
functionless ...... OTIOSE, USELESS
fund .... CACHE, KITTY, MONEY, STOCK, STORE, OUTLAY, SUPPLY, CAPITAL, COPPERS, RESOURCES
kind of .... SLUSH, TRUST
raiser .... TAGGER
fundament ...... ANUS, BUTTOCKS
fundamental .... BASAL, BASIC, VITAL, ORGANIC, CARDINAL, ORIGINAL, ELEMENTAL, ESSENTIAL, RUDIMENTARY
funeral .... BURIAL, EXEQUIES, INTERMENT, OBSEQUIES
announcement/notice
.... OBIT(UARY)
attendants .... CORTEGE, PALLBEARERS
bell .... KNELL
box .... CASKET, COFFIN
"casket team"
.... PALLBEARERS
coach/vehicle .... HEARSE
director .... MORTICIAN, UNDERTAKER
fire/pile .... PYRE
hymn .... DIRGE, EPICEDIUM
music .... DIRGE, REQUIEM
ode .... EPICEDIUM
oration .... ELOGE, EULOGY
procession .... EXEQUY, CORTEGE
pyre .... PILE, SUTTER
rite(s) .... EXEQUY, OBSEQUY, OBSEQUIES
song .... DIRGE, ELEGY, NENIA, LAMENT, REQUIEM, THRENODY
funereal ...... SAD, DARK, BLACK, FERAL, DISMAL, GLOOMY, SOLEMN, SOMBER, MOURNFUL, LUGUBRIOUS
fungi ...... SPORE, YEAST, BOLETUS
parasitic .... ERGOT
pertaining to .... AGARIC
spongy material ...... AMADOU

study of .... MYCOLOGY
tissue .... TRAMA
fungous .... SPONGY
fungus .... GERM, RUST, WART, YEAST, BLIGHT, LICHEN, RHIZOPUS, PUFFBALL, TUCKAHOE, BLACKRUST, (BLACK)KNOT
cells/sacs .... ASCI
combining form .... MYC(O)
disease .... ROT, SCAB, BRAND, ERGOT, MYCOSIS
dots .... TELIA
edible .... MOREL, TRUFFLE, EARTHNUT
foul-smelling .... STINKHORN
growth .... MOLD, ERGOT, MILDEW
growth in body .... MYCOSIS
parasitic on animal
.... EPIPHYTE
parasitic on trees .... AGARIC
plant .... MOREL, UREDO, AMANITA, MUSHROOM
poisonous .... AMANITINE, TOADSTOOL
seed .... SPORE
smut .... BUNT
spores cluster .... SORUS
thallus of .... MYCELIUM
funicle .... CORD, FIBER
funk .... FEAR, PANIC, SHIRK, COWARD, FRIGHT(EN)
funnel .... CONE, FLUE, CHANNEL, CHIMNEY, SMOKESTACK
funny .... DROLL, ABSURD, AMUSING, COMIC(AL), FARCICAL, HUMOROUS, LAUGHABLE
bone .... HUMERUS
bone site .... ELBOW
colloquial .... ODD, KILLING
line .... GAG
funnyman Foxx .... REDD
fur ...... COAT, DOWN, GRIS, HAIR, HIDE, PELT, SKIN, BUDGE, PELAGE, CARACUL, CRIMMER, KARAKUL, MINIVER, MUSKRAT
bearing animal .... FOX, LYNX, MINK, SEAL, VAIR(E), COYPU, GENET, OTTER, SABLE, BADGER, BEAVER, ERMINE, FITCH(ET), MARTEN, RABBIT, WEASEL, CALABAR, FITCHEW, POLECAT, CHINCHILLA
bearing skins collectively
.... PELTRY
cape .... PELERINE
coypu's .... NUTRIA
garment .... WRAP, PARKA, ANORAK

good .... STONEMARTEN
gray .... KRIMMER
hat .... BUSBY, CASTOR
kid pelt .... GALYAK
lamb pelt .... GALYAC
lined cloak .... PELISSE
lynx .... CARACAL
matted .... DAGLOCK
neckpiece .... BOA, STOLE,
CHOKER
pertaining to .... PELISSE
piece .... BOA, MUFF, STOLE
rabbit .... CONY, LAPIN
royal .... ERMINE
scarf .... TIPPET
seal .... SEECATCH
squirrel .... VAIR, CALABER
trader, famous .... ASTOR
type of .... FOX, MINK, SEAL,
CONEY, GENET, LAPIN, SABLE,
BEAVER, ERMINE, MARMOT,
MARTEN, NUTRIA, CARACUL,
KRIMMER, LEOPARD,
MUSKRAT, MOLESKIN,
CHINCHILLA
used for trimming, white
.... MINIVER
furbelow .... FRILL, JABOT,
RUFFLE, FALBALA, FLOUNCE
furbish .... POLISH, BURNISH,
BRIGHTEN, RENOVATE
as clothes .... DRY CLEAN
furcate .... BRANCH, FORK(ED)
furculum .... WISHBONE
furfur .... SCURF, DANDRUFF
Furies, one of the .... DIRAE,
ALECTO, ERINY(E)S,
MEGAERA, EUMENIDES,
TISIPHONE
furious .... MAD, ANGRY, WROTH,
FIERCE, RAGING, FRANTIC,
VIOLENT, FRENZIED,
STORMING
furl .... ROLL UP
furlough .... PASS, (SHORE)LEAVE,
LIBERTY
furnace .... KILN, OVEN, BLAST,
FORGE, BELLOW, CUPOLA,
SMITHY, STITHY, CRESSET,
SMELTER, BLOOMERY,
CREMATORY, CREMATORIUM
air pipe of .... TUYERE
feed/fuel the .... STOKE
for cremation
.... (IN)CINERATOR
opening .... STOKEHOLE
part .... BOSH, GRATE,
CRUCIBLE

tender .... STOKER
vent .... TUE
furnish ...... LEND, CATER, EQUIP,
YIELD, OUTFIT, RENDER,
SUPPLY, PLENISH, PROVIDE
with funds .... ENDOW
with weapons .... ARM
furnished with shoes .... SHOD
furnishings .... RIG, GEAR,
DECOR, OUTFIT, TRAPPINGS,
APPLIANCES, ACCOUTERMENTS
furniture .... GOODS, EQUIPAGE,
FIXTURES, FURNISHINGS
convertible .... SOFA BED
decoration/inlaid wood
.... BUHL
Duncan .... PHYFE
kind of .... CRADLE
lace decoration ...... MACRAME
leg, kind of .... CABRIOLE
old fashioned office
.... ROLLTOP DESK
placement .... CHEST ON
CHEST
set .... SUITE
wheel .... CASTER
wood ..... KOA, TEAK, WALNUT
furor .... FURY, RAGE, CRAZE,
MANIA, FLURRY, FRENZY,
HUBBUB, TUMULT, MADNESS,
VIOLENCE
furred .... FURRY, HAIRY, WOOLY,
SHAGGY
furrow .... RUT, PLOW, RILL(E),
SEAM, STRIA, GROOVE,
SULCUS, TRENCH, WRINKLE
for seeds .... DRILL
for planting .... WINDROW
furrowed .... SEAMED, SULCATE
furry ...... BUSHY, DOWNY, HAIRY,
NAPPY, FLEECY, FLUFFY,
LANATE, PILEOUS, UNSHORN
fellow ..... FOX, OTTER, STOAT,
BEAVER, MARTEN, WEASEL
furs collectively .... PELTRY
further .... AID, ABET, AGAIN,
ADVANCE, PROMOTE,
MOREOVER
furtherance .... PROGRESS,
PROMOTION, ADVANCEMENT
furthermore .... TOO, ALSO,
BESIDES
furtive .... SLY, WARY, COVERT,
SECRET, SHIFTY, SNEAKY,
PRIVY, TRICKY, STEALTHY,
BACKDOOR, BACKSTAIR,
CLANDESTINE
fellow .... SNEAKER

furuncle .... BOIL, ABSCESS
fury .... IRE, RAGE, ANGER,
WRATH, ERINYS, FRENZY
furze .... WHIN, GORSE, GORST
fusain .... PENCIL
fuse .... MIX, WELD, BLEND,
MERGE, UNITE, (S)MELT,
ANNEAL, MINGLE, SOLDER,
COALESCE
partly/partially .... FRIT
fused .... FUSIL
fusee .... FLARE, MATCH
fuselage .... NACELLE
fusiform .... ROUNDED
fusil .... FUSED, MUSKET
fusillade .... BURST, SALVO,
BARRAGE, DRUMFIRE
fusion .... UNION, MERGER,
ALLIANCE, COALITION
fuss .... ADO, ROW, FRET, ROUT,
STIR, TO-DO, BUSTLE, FIDGET,
BOTHER, KICKUP, POTHER,
TINKER
fusspot .... PRIG
fussy .... TENSE, PRISSY, FIDGETY,
FINICAL, FINICKY, CRITICAL,
HOITY-TOITY, PER(S)NICKETY
one .... NITPICKER
fust .... FADE, RUST, PERISH
fustian .... RANT, BOMBAST,
POMPOUS, CORDUROY,
VELVETEEN
fustic .... DYE
fustigate ...... FLAY, LASH, ROAST,
CASTIGATE
fusty ...... MOLDY, STALE, STUFFY
futile .... IDLE, VAIN, EMPTY,
INANE, OTIOSE, USELESS,
HOPELESS, FRUITLESS
futility .... DEFEAT, VANITY,
DESPAIR, FAILURE, INANITY
future .... LATER, HEREAFTER,
POSTERITY
kind of .... ROSEATE
time .... ONE DAY
futuristic .... FATED, COMING,
DESTINED, PROBABLE
futurity .... RACE, ADVENT,
EVENTUALITY
fuzz .... DOWN, LINT
slang ..... COP, THE LAW, JOHN
LAW
fuzzy .... VAGUE, BEMUSED,
BLURRED, UNCLEAR, VELVETY
dog .... RAGS
fylfot .... CROSS, SWASTIKA
Fyn Island seaport ...... ODENSE

G

G, Greek .... GAMMA
Hebrew .... GIMEL
in a sequence/group
.... SEVENTH
letter .... GEE
rating of movie .... GENERAL
AUDIENCE
slang .... GRAND, THOUSAND
string .... LOINCLOTH
Ga .... GEORGIA
gab .... TALK, CHATTER
gift of .... GLIBNESS,
ELOQUENCE
gabble .... BLAB, CACKLE, GIBBER,
JABBER, CHATTER, PRATTLE
slang .... CHIN
gabby .... TALKATIVE
gaberlunzie .... BEGGAR
gabion .... CYLINDER
gable .... DORMER, PINION,
AILERON, PEDIMENT
feature .... FINIAL
Gabon, cape .... LOPEZ
capital .... LIBREVILLE
city/town .... OYEM, BITAM,
MOANDA, MOUILA, MAKOKOU,
MOUNANA, LAMBARENE, PORT-
GENTIL
ethnic group ..... PUNU, CHIRA,
LUMBU, ADOUNA, PAHOUIN
lake .... ONANGUE
mountain .... IBOUNZI
president .... (OMAR)BONGO
river .... IVINDO, OGOOUE
Gabor, a .... EVA, MAGDA, ZSA
ZSA
Gabriel .... ARCHANGEL
what he blew .... TRUMPET
gaby .... FOOL, SIMPLETON
gad .... OATH, ROAM, ROVE,
PROWL, SPIKE, RAMBLE,
TRAIPSE, GALLIVANT
Gad, parent of .... JACOB, ZILPAH
son of .... ERI, ARELI
gadabout ...... ROAMER, FLANEUR,
PLAYBOY
gadfly .... PEST, ANNOYER,
TABANID, TORMENTOR
gadget .... DEVICE, DINGUS,
DOODAD, HICKEY, JIGGER,
JIMJAM, GIMMICK,
TECHNOLOGICAL INNOVATION
colloquial .... THINGAMAJIG,
WHATCHUMACALLIT

gadoid, a .... HAKE, CODFISH,
HADDOCK, POLLACK
gadroom .... BEADING, FLUTING
gadwall .... DUCK
Gadzooks .... OATH, EXPLETIVE
Gaea .... GE, TELLUS, GODDESS
son .... TITAN, URANUS
Gael .... CELT, SCOT
Gaelic .... ERSE, MANX, IRISH,
CELT(IC), SCOT(CH)
bard .... OSSIAN
game pole .... CABER
god .... LER, DAGDA, MIDER
poem .... DUAN
spirit .... BANSHEE
sprite .... KELPIE
warrior .... DAGDA
gaff .... HOOK, SPAR, SPUR, SPEAR,
FLEECE
rope .... VANG
slang .... HOAX, TRICK
gaffe ...... BONER, BLUNDER, FAUX
PAS
gaffer .... DODO, OLD MAN,
FOREMAN
gag ...... HOAX, JOKE, QUIP, SCOB,
CHOKE, RETCH, MUFFLE,
MUZZLE, SILENCE, WISECRACK
overworked .... WHEEZE
gage .... PLUM, PLEDGE, SECURITY,
CHALLENGE
gaggle members .... GEESE
Gahlee native .... GALILEAN
gaiety .... FUN, JOLLITY,
FESTIVITY, FRIVOLITY,
MERRIMENT
Gaillard Cut, once ...... CULEBRA
gain .... NET, WIN, EARN, REAP,
LUCRE, REACH, ATTAIN,
PROFIT, BENEFIT, REALIZE
control .... CONQUER
knowledge .... LEARN
slang .... VELVET
gainful .... LUCRATIVE
gainly .... COMELY
gainsay .... DENY, OPPOSE,
REFUTE, CONTRADICT
Gainsborough .... PORTRAIT
gait ...... LOPE, PACE, STEP, WALK,
CANTER, GALLOP, STRIDE
gaiter .... SHOE, SPAT, PUTTEE,
GAMBADE, LEGGING
gal .... GIRL
gala .... FETE, FESTAL, FIESTA,

JOVIAL, JOYOUS, FESTIVE,
FESTIVAL, MERRYMAKING
affair ...... BANQUET, BLOWOUT
galactic .... GLOBAL, LACTIC,
CELESTIAL, PLANETARY
galacto: comb. form ...... MILKY
Galahad, describing .... PURE,
NOBLE
he wrote .... ERSKINE
parent .... ELAINE, LANCELOT
quest of .... (HOLY)GRAIL
Galatea's beloved .... ACIS
lover .... PYGMALION
galaxy ...... BEVY, THRONG, MILKY
WAY, MULTITUDE,
COLLECTION
Galcha .... PAMIR(I)
gale .... GUST, SHRUB, BREEZE,
OUTBURST, WINDSTORM
Gale (Zona), novelist .... BREESE
galena .... ORE, LEAD
galenite .... ORE
Galilean .... CHRISTIAN
sea .... TIBERIAS
the .... JESUS
town .... CANA, MAGDALA,
NAZARETH
galilee .... PORCH, PORTICO
Galileo .... PHYSICIST,
ASTRONOMER
country of .... ITALY
last name of .... GALILEI
theory proven by
.... COPERNICAN
galingale .... ROOT, SEDGE
galiot .... SHIP, GALLEY
galipot .... OLEORESIN,
TURPENTINE
gall ...... VEX, BILE, FELL, ANNOY,
CHAFE, CHEEK, NERVE,
RANCOR, AUDACITY,
TEMERITY
bladder .... CHOLECYST
bladder, of the .... CYSTIC
bladder fluid .... BILE
bladder part .... CERVIX
combining form .... CHOLE,
CHOL(O)
slang .... IMPUDENCE,
INSOLENCE
gallant .... HERO, BULLY, CIVIL,
BRAVE, LOVER, NOBLE,
KNIGHT, GIGOLO, POLITE,
SQUIRE, COURTLY, CAVALIER

gallantry .... CHIVALRY
galleon .... SHIP, ARGOSY,
TRADER, CAR(R)ACK
gallery .... POY, LOFT, PORCH,
ARCADE, LOGGIA, MUSEUM,
PIAZZA, BALCONY, VERANDA,
ART-ROOM, CORRIDOR,
BELVEDERE
art .... SALON
church .... JUBE
French .... LOUVRE
Italian .... UFFIZI
London ...... TATE, GUILDHALL
gallet .... CHIP, SPALL
galley .... KITCHEN, ROWBOAT,
SAILBOAT, PROOF(SHEET)
armed .... AESC, DROMOND
bench .... BANK
Jason's .... ARGO
Mediterranean .... GAL(L)IOT
Roman .... BIREME, TRIREME,
UNIREME
ship's .... CABOOSE
slave .... DRUDGE, THRALL
word on a ...... STET, DELE(TE)
work on a .... EDIT,
PROOFREAD
Galli-Curci .... AMELITA
Gallia .... GAUL
modern .... FRANCE
Gallic .... FRENCH
chariot .... ESSED
humorist .... (JACQUES)TATI
tribe .... REMI
gallimaufry .... HASH, OLIO,
ASSORTMENT, HODGEPODGE
gallinaceous .... RASORIAL
bird .... QUAIL, TURKEY
galling .... PESKY, BITTER,
VEXING, CHAFING, ABRASIVE
gallinipper .... MOSQUITO
gallinule .... RAIL, (MUD)HEN
gallipot .... JAR
gallivant ...... GAD, ROAM, PROWL,
WANDER
galliwasp .... LIZARD
gallon, half .... POTTLE
gallons, 8 .... BUSHEL
31½ .... BARREL
galloon .... BRAID, RIBBON
gallop .... RUN, GAIT, LOPE,
AUBIN, CANTER, TANTIVY
galloping .... SWIFT, FLYING,
SPEEDY, DASHING
Galloway .... HORSE, CATTLE
gallows .... TREE, GIBBET,
YARDARM, SCAFFOLD
feature of .... NOOSE
gallstone .... CHOLOLITH
galluses ...... BRACES, SUSPENDERS
galoot .... SAP, GOOF, JERK, LOUT,

KLUTZ
galop .... DANCE
galore .... (A)PLENTY,
ABUNDANTLY, AMPLY FULL,
IN ABUNDANCE
galosh .... BOOT, (OVER)SHOE
galvanic .... EXCITING
galvanize .... SHOCK, EXCITE,
STARTLE, ENERGIZE
galvanized .... ANODIZED,
(ELECTRO)PLATED
galvanizing material .... ZINC
Galway Bay island .... ARAN
gam ...... POD, CALL, HERD, VISIT,
SCHOOL
slang .... LEG
gamb(e) .... LEG, SHANK
gambado .... LEAP, PRANK,
GAITER, LEGGING
Gambia capital .... BANJUL
city/town .... BRIKAMA,
GEORGETOWN
language .... WOLOF, FULANI,
MALINKE, MANDINGO
monetary unit .... DALASI
gambit .... PLOY, RUSE, TRICK,
OPENER, MANEUVER
gamble .... BET, RISK, STAKE,
WAGER, TOSS UP, GO OUT ON
A LIMB
Chinese style .... PLAY
FANTAN
reckless .... FLIER, FLYER
gambler .... DARER, DICER,
GAMER, BETTOR, PLAYER,
THROWER, GAMESTER
in Show Boat .... RAVENAL
kind of ..... PUNTER, PLUNGER,
TINHORN, SPECULATOR
small-time .... PIKER
gambler's accomplice ...... SHILL
capital .... STAKE
concern .... ODDS
note .... IOU
odds ...... DOUBLE OR NOTHING
run, at times .... NO LUCK
gambling center .... RENO,
CASINO, MONACO, LAS VEGAS,
LAKE TAHOE, MONTE CARLO,
LAUGHLIN, ATLANTIC CITY
disaster .... PAIR OF DICE LOST
state capital .... TRENTON,
CARSON CITY
table character .... RAKER,
BETTOR, DEALER, PLAYER,
CROUPIER, KIBITZER
gamboge .... PIGMENT, GUM RESIN
gambol .... DIDO, ROMP, CAPER,
LEAP, PLAY, FRISK, FROLIC,
CAVORT, CURVET, PRANCE
gambrel .... HOCK, ROOF

Gambrinus' invention ...... BEER
game .... FUN, PLAN, PLAY, PLOY,
MATCH, SPORT, FROLIC,
CONTEST, AMUSEMENT,
DIVERSION, RECREATION
anagrams .... LOGOMACHY
big .... BEAR, LION, HIPPO,
RHINO, TIGER, GORILLA,
ELEPHANT
board .... CHESS, DARTS,
HALMA, CHECKERS
card .... LOO, PAM, FARO,
MONTE, OMBER, POKER,
TAROT, WHIST, BRIDGE,
CASINO, RUMMY, ECARTE,
CANASTA, BLACK JACK,
TWENTY-ONE
children's ...... TAG, MARBLES,
PEEKABOO, JACKSTONE
court ..... TENNIS, BASKETBALL
crossword .... SCRABBLE
dice .... LUDO, CRAPS
divided into chukkers
.... POLO
divided into innings
.... BASEBALL
divided into quarters
.... FOOTBALL, BASKETBALL
first .... OPENER
fish ..... BASS, TROUT, MARLIN,
SALMON, TARPON, BARRACUDA
guessing ...... MORA, CHARADE
handball: Eng. .... FIVES
hockey .... SHINN(E)Y
hold scoreless in .... BLANK,
SKUNK
killer .... VERMIN
kind of ..... CARD, DICE, KENO,
GOLF, BEANO, BINGO,
CRICKET, BADMINTON
like billiards .... BAGATELLE
like handball .... JAI ALAI
lottery number .... POLICY
ninepins-like .... SKITTLES
of chance .... LOO, FARO,
KENO, BINGO, LOTTO, HAZARD,
RAFFLE, LOTTERY
of forfeits .... FILLIPEEN
of marbles .... TAW, MIGS,
MIGGLES
of skill .... POOL, CHESS,
DARTS, POKER, TENNIS,
BOWLING
oriental .... FANTAN
parlor .... LOTTO
pencil .... TICKTACKTOE
period .... SET, INNING,
CHUKKAR, CHUKKER, QUARTER
pin .... BOWLING
played on a course .... GOLF
played on horseback ..... POLO

played with tiles .... MAHJONG
point .... RUN, GOAL
preserve .... SANCTUARY
rhyming .... CRAMBO
slang .... PLUCKY, SPORTY
start of .... KICKOFF, TOSS UP
statistic .... SCORE
table net .... PINGPONG
tennis-like .... FIVES
three-handed card .... SKAT
traditional May Day
.... MORRIS DANCE
trail .... SPOOR, TRACK
trap .... GIN
gamecock .... ROOSTER
spur of .... GAFF
gamekeeper .... RANGER, WARDEN
gamete .... EGG
immature .... OOCYTE
gametes' union .... SYNGAMY,
ZYGOSIS
gamic .... SEXUAL
gamin .... TAD, BRAT, PUNK,
WAIF, URCHIN, (STREET)ARAB
gaming cube .... DICE, BONES
tile .... DOMINO
gamma .... MICROGRAM
gammon ...... HAM, FAKE, BACON,
HUMBUG, NONSENSE
gamp .... UMBRELLA
gamut ...... RANGE, SCALE, SCOPE,
EXTENT
gamy .... BOLD, GUTSY, NERVY,
GRITTY, PLUCKY
Gand .... GHENT
gander .... GOOSE, GANNET
take a .... LOOK
Gandhi .... MAHATMA, MOHANDAS
ganef .... GANOV, THIEF
gang ...... MOB, SET, BAND, CREW,
RING, GROUP, HORDE, SQUAD,
CLIQUE
fight .... RUMBLE
head of .... FOREMAN,
RINGLEADER
member .... MOBSTER
Ganges boat .... PUTELEE
city on the .... VARANASI
fish .... SOOSOO
gangland .... UNDERWORLD
gal .... MOLL
gangling .... GAWKY, LANKY,
SPINDLY
gangplank .... RAMP, CATWALK
gangrene .... ROT, DECAY,
NECROSE
gangrenous state .... NECROSIS
gangster .... MUG, THUG, YEGG,
BANDIT, GORILLA, HOODLUM,
HOOLIGAN, RACKETEER,
TOUGH(IE)

bodyguard .... TORPEDO
chief .... RINGLEADER
girl of .... MOLL
gun: sl. .... GAT, ROD, ROSCOE,
EQUALIZER
slang .... GOON, HOOD,
MOBSTER
gangue .... MATRIX
Gangway! .... OPEN UP, MAKE
WAY
gangway's handrail .... MANROPE
gannet .... GOOSE, SOLAN,
GANDER, MARGOT
ganoid .... GAR, AMIA, BOWFIN,
STURGEON
gantlet .... GLOVE
Gantry .... ELMER
Ganymede .... CUPBEARER
gaol .... JAIL, DARTMOOR,
BRIDEWELL
gap .... GULF, HOLE, BREAK,
CHASM, VOID, CLEFT, CRACK,
HIATUS, BREACH, LACUNA,
OPENING, INTERVAL
between peaks .... COL
credibility .... DISTRUST
gape .... GAWK, GAZE, OGLE,
OPEN, PEER, YAUP, YAWN,
YAWP, STARE, SPREAD,
DEHISCE
gapes, the .... RICTUS
gaping ...... AJAR, GAPPY, RICTUS,
ABYSMAL, RINGENT
gar .... SNOOK, GANOID,
STURGEON, NEEDLEFISH
garage .... MEW, CARPORT
garam masala .... CURRY
Garand .... RIFLE
Garapan Island's capital
.... SAIPAN
garb .... DRESS, GUISE, STYLE,
ATTIRE, CLOTHING
for frigid weather .... ANORAK
garbage ...... JUNK, OFFAL, SWILL,
TRASH, WASTE, REFUSE,
SCRAPS, RUBBISH
collect .... SCAVENGE
garble .... JUMBLE, MIX UP,
MUDDLE, CONFUSE, DISTORT
Garbo, actress .... GRETA
role .... CAMILLE
garcon ...... BOY, YOUTH, WAITER,
SERVANT
garden .... ARBOR, GARTH, PITCH,
ARENA, HERBARY, NURSERY,
ORCHARD, PLEASANCE
bed .... PLOT
biblical .... GETHSEMANE
decorative structure
.... TRELLIS
denizen .... FROG, TOAD

first .... EDEN
kind of .... HOTHOUSE,
TERRARIUM, GREENHOUSE
miniature .... TERRARIUM
of England .... KENT
of stone .... CEMETERY
on the Mount of Olives
.... GETHSEMANE
pest .... WEED, APHID, APHIS
plant .... ORACH(E)
rock .... ROCKERY
section .... BED, PLOT
shelter .... GAZEBO
soprano .... MARY
tool .... HOE, RAKE, DIBBLE,
TROWEL
wall/fence .... HAHA
worker .... RAKER, SPADER,
PLANTER
gardener's asset/blessing
.... GREENTHUMB
plague .... WEED, APHID,
BORER, CUTWORM
gardenia .... FLOWER, MADDER
Gardner, actress .... AVA
Erle .... STANLEY
title opener .... THE CASE
Garfield lovers' emotion
.... AILUROPHILIA
garfish .... SNOOK
Gargantua .... KING, GIANT
creator of .... RABELAIS
son .... PANTAGRUEL
gargantuan .... HUGE, VAST,
GIGANTIC, GIANTLIKE
gargle .... WASH, RINSE, LISTERINE
garibaldi .... BLOUSE
garish .... GAUDY, SHOWY
garishness .... GLARE
garland .... LEI, ANADEM, FILLET,
WREATH, CHAPLET, FESTOON
garlic .... MOLY, ALLIUM, RAMSON
part .... CLOVE
garment ...... COAT, ROBE, WRAP,
DRESS, BLOUSE, RAIMENT,
CLOTHING, VESTMENT,
HABILIMENT
corsetlike .... GIRDLE
decoration .... SPANGLE
fastener .... PATTE, AUTOMATIC
flap/fold of .... LAPPET
hooded .... PARKA, ALMUCE
knitted .... JERSEY
loose .... ROBE, TOGA, CYMAR,
BLOUSE, CAFTAN, CAMISE,
DOLMAN, KIMONO, MUUMUU
outer ..... COAT, TOGA, SMOCK,
BLAZER, CAPOTE, JACKET,
KIMONO, PALETOT, SURTOUT,
OVERCOAT, SCAPULAR
patchwork .... CENTO

rain .... PONCHO
scarflike .... TIPPET
sleeveless .... CAPE, VEST,
                                SCAPULAR
tentlike .... CHADRI
tight-fitting .... COTTE
trade spy .... KEEK
trimming .... BEADING
tunic-like ..... CHITON, TABARD
under ...... SLIP, SHIRT, TEDDY,
                                CHEMISE
worker .... SEWER
garments .... COSTUME
garner .... HOARD, STORE,
            GATHER, COLLECT, HARVEST
Garner, actor .... JAMES
garnet .... GEM, RED, PYROPE,
            TACKLE, OLIVINE, ESSONITE,
            MELANITE, ALMANDITE
garnish .... DECK, LARD, TRIM,
            ADORN, OLIVE, FLAVOR,
            RELISH, SEASON, PARSLEY,
            DECORATE, ORNAMENT,
                                EMBELLISH
garnishee .... TRUSTEE
garnishment .... LIEN,
                                DECORATION
Garrone river tributary .... LOT
garret .... ATTIC, ATELIER,
            MANSARD, (COCK)LOFT
Garrick, actor .... DAVID
garrison .... BILLET, OUTPOST,
            BARRACKS, PRESIDIO,
                (MILITARY)POST
garrote .... SCRAG, STRANGLE
garrulity .... LOQUACITY,
                                WORDINESS
garrulous .... GASSY, VOLUBLE,
            TALKATIVE, LOQUACIOUS
Garson, actress .... GREER
garter snake .... ELAP(S)
garth .... WEIR, YARD, GARDEN
gas .... BRAG, FUEL, FUME, ETHER,
            ETHYL, FREON, OZONE,
            RADON, VAPOR, BOMBAST,
            PROPANE, STIBINE, GASOLINE
balloon .... HELIUM
burner ..... BUNSEN, WELSBACH
cigarette lighter .... BUTANE
colorless .... OXAN(E),
                        ETHANE, ETHENE
combining form .... AER(O)
condense .... ABSORB
container .... TANK
engine .... PETROL
fill with ...... AERATE, INFLATE
in stomach/intestine
.... FLATUS, FLATULENCE
inert .... NEON, ARGON
marsh .... METHANE
mask part .... CANISTER

mine .... DAMP
pipe .... FLUE
plant .... BURNING BUSH
slang .... HOT AIR
station device .... PUMP
station employee .... GREASER,
                                MECHANIC
step on the .... GUN, HURRY,
                                ACCELERATE
used in a blowtorch
.... ACETYLENE
gascon .... BOASTER, LOUDMOUTH,
                                PRETENDER
gasconade .... BRAG, BOAST,
                                BLUSTER
gaseous .... AERIFORM
cloud .... NEBULA
combining form .... AERI
compound .... ETHANE
inert element .... NEON
gash ...... CUT, HACK, SLIT, SCORE,
                        SLASH, INCISE
gasket .... LINING, PADDING
gasoline .... PETROL
jellied .... NAPALM
kind of .... LEADED,
                                UNLEADED
gasp .... PANT, PUFF, CHOKE,
                                HEAVE
gastropod .... SNAIL, LIMPET,
            W(H)ELK, MOLLUSK
marine .... MUREX
gastronome .... EPICURE,
            GOURMET, GOURMAND
gastronomy .... EPICURISM
gat .... CHANNEL
gata .... SHARK
gate ...... DOOR, PORTAL, WICKET,
                                OPENING
bar .... PORTICULLIS
give the .... SACK, DISMISS,
                                DISCHARGE
horse race starting
.... BARRIER
joint/holder .... HINGE
keeper's dwelling .... LODGE
rear/back .... POSTERN
receipts: colloq. .... TAKE
revolving .... TURNSTILE
slang .... ADMISSION
tower .... BARBICAN
water .... SLUICE, PENSTOCK
gatehouse .... LODGE
gatekeeper .... PORTER
gateway .... PYLON, TORII,
                                TORAN(A)
gather .... CULL, FOLD, HERD,
            REAP, (A)MASS, INFER, PLEAT,
            HUDDLE, GARNER, MUSTER,
            PUCKER, SHEAR, SHEAVE,
            COLLECT, HARVEST,

ASSEMBLE, CONCLUDE
as oysters or logs .... TONG
fabric .... SHIRR
grain .... GLEAN
gathering .... CROWD, RALLY,
            MEET(ING), TURNOUT,
            ASSEMBLY, CONCLAVE,
                                ASSEMBLAGE
social ..... BEE, DANCE, PARTY,
            BARBECUE, CLAMBAKE
gator's kin .... CROC
gauche .... CLUMSY, AWKWARD,
                                TACTLESS
gaucho .... COWBOY, LLANERO
knife .... MACHETE
milieu .... LLANO, PAMPAS
place .... RANCHO
rope of .... REATA
weapon .... BOLA(S)
gaud .... ADORN, BAUBLE,
            TRINKET, ORNAMENT
gaudiness .... GLARE, GLITTER,
            LOUDNESS, SHOWINESS,
            FLASHINESS, GARISHNESS
gaudy ...... GAY, BRIGHT, SHOWY,
            CHEAP, FLASHY, FLORID,
            GARISH, VULGAR, TAWDRY,
                                BLATANT
ornament .... TINSEL
gauge .... RATE, SIZE, JUDGE,
            CALIBER, MEASURE, TEMPLET,
            APPRAISE, ESTIMATE,
                                EVALUATE
Gauguin's island home
.... TAHITI
wife .... METTE
Gaul .... GALLIA, FRENCHMAN
people .... REMI
gaunt .... BONY, GRIM, LANK,
            LEAN, THIN, SPARE, SICKLY,
            HAGGARD, EMACIATED
gauntlet ...... CUFF, GAGE, GLOVE
throw down the .... DEFY,
                                CHALLENGE
Gautama .... BUDDHA
gauze .... NET, HAZE, LENO, MIST,
            CREPE, SCRIM, BAREGE,
            TISSUE, BANDAGE
silk .... TIFFANY
gauzy .... FILMY, SHEER,
            DIAPHANOUS, TRANSPARENT
fabric .... LACE, TULLE
gavel .... HAMMER, MALLET
gavial .... CROCODILE
gawk .... OAF, GAPE, GAZE, STARE,
            CUCKOO, SIMPLETON
gawky .... CLUMSY, AWKWARD
one .... LOUT
gay .... JOLLY, MERRY, RIANT,
            BLITHE, BRIGHT, FESTAL,
            JOVIAL, LIVELY, FESTIVE,

HILARIOUS
—— .... PAREE
rake .... LOTHARIO
tune .... LILT
Gay-Pay-Oo .... GPU, OGPU
successor .... NKVD
gaze .... GAPE, GAWK, LEER, PEER,
GLARE, STARE
at .... EYE
intently .... PORE
gazebo .... TURRET, BALCONY
gazelle .... GOA, CORA, KUDU,
MOHR, ADDRA, ARIEL, KEVEL,
KORIN, CHIKARA, CORINNE
Sudan .... DAMA
gazette .... NEWSPAPER
GBS .... SHAW
was one .... FABIAN
Gdansk .... DANZIG
Ge .... GAEA, GAIA
gear .... CAM, COG, KIT, GARB,
DRESS, TOOLS, OUTFIT,
TACKLE, EQUIPMENT,
BAGGAGE, HARNESS,
RIG(GING), OVERDRIVE
for Eric Heiden .... RACING
SKATE
rodeo .... RIATAS
shift, for short .... STICK
transmission .... SPEED
geared .... SUITED, TAILORED
gecko .... LIZARD, TARENTE,
LACERT(IL)IAN
gee ...... GOLLY, JESUS, GO AHEAD,
TURN RIGHT, EXCLAMATION
gee .... RACEHORSE
opposed to .... HAW
geek .... NERD
geese, domestic .... EMDENS
fat .... AXUNGE
formation .... VEE
genus .... ANSER
in the air, flock of .... SKEIN
on land, flock of .... RAFT,
GAGGLE
geest .... ALLUVIUM
geetas .... STINGY
Gehenna .... HELL
Gehrig of baseball .... LOU
geisha .... DANCER, HOSTESS,
ENTERTAINER, DANCING GIRL
gel .... JELLIFY, COAGULATE
gelatin(e) .... AGAR, ASPIC, GELEE,
JELLY, GLUTIN, COLLOID
gelatinous .... VISCID, VISCOUS
geld .... CASTRATE, STERILIZE
gelding .... EUNUCH
**Gelett Burgess didn't want to
be one** .... PURPLE COW
gelid .... ICY, COLD, FROSTY,
FROZEN

gelling agent .... AGAR
gem .... JADE, ONYX, OPAL, RUBY,
SARD, AGATE, BERYL, JEWEL,
STONE, PRIZE, TOPAZ,
GARNET, LIGURE, MUFFIN,
SPINEL, EMERALD, DIAMOND,
PERIDOT, AMETHYST
artificial .... PASTE, RUTILE
believed to be unlucky
.... OPAL
biblical .... LIGURE
carved .... CAMEO
carving/engraving
.... GLYPTICS
cultured .... PEARL
cut .... BRIOLETTE
cutter/expert .... LAPIDARY
cutting device .... LAP
dealer .... BEERS, CARTIER,
LAPIDARY
facet .... BEZEL, CULET
flaw .... FEATHER
precious .... OPAL, RUBY,
PEARL, DIAMOND, EMERALD
pseudo .... SPINEL
semi-precious .... TOURMALINE
setting .... BEZEL, CHATON
slang .... ICE, SPARKLER
smart cut .... BRILLIANT
weight .... CARAT, KARAT
Gem State .... IDAHO
gemel .... HINGE
part of .... HOOK, LOOP
Gemini .... TWINS
star .... CASTOR, POLLUX
gemlike .... OPALINE
gemma .... BUD
gems dealer .... LAPIDARY
gemsbok .... ORYX, CHAMOIS,
ANTELOPE
gemstone .... IOLITE
gendarme(rie) .... POLICE(MAN)
gender .... SEX, NEUTER,
FEMININE, MASCULINE
common .... EPICENE
gene .... FACTOR
material .... DNA, RNA
Gene Autry's team ...... ANGELS
genealogical record .... TREE
genealogy .... TREE, DESCENT,
LINEAGE, HERALDRY,
PEDIGREE
general ...... RIFE, BROAD, USUAL,
COMMON, CURRENT, GENERIC,
INCLUSIVE, PANDEMIC,
UNIVERSAL, ECUMENICAL,
PREVAILING, PREVALENT,
WIDESPREAD
arrangement .... FORMAT
direction/course .... TREND
of the Armies .... PERSHING

of the Army ...... MACARTHUR,
EISENHOWER
opinion .... CONSENSUS
pardon .... AMNESTY
rule .... CANON
welfare .... COMMONWEAL
Generalissimo .... CHIANG (KAI
CHEK)
generally ...... ALWAYS, OVERALL,
BY AND LARGE, AS A RULE
generate .... MAKE, BEGET,
BREED, PRODUCE, ENGENDER,
ORIGINATE, PROCREATE,
IMPREGNATE
generation .... AGE, DESCENT,
BREEDING, LIFETIME
some of the new
.... TEENAGERS
generator .... DYNAMO
generic .... VAGUE, GENERAL,
NEBULOUS, INDEFINITE
generosity .... CHARITY,
ALTRUISM, PHILANTHROPY
generous .... AMPLE, LAVISH,
LIBERAL, GRACIOUS,
OBLIGING, UNSELFISH,
CHARITABLE, OPEN-HANDED,
OPEN-HEARTED
genesis .... BIRTH, ORIGIN,
CREATION, BEGINNING
Genesis man .... PELEG
word .... BEGAT
genetic .... GENIC, INNATE,
HEREDITARY
stuff .... DNA, RNA
genetics subject .... HEREDITY
geneva .... GIN
Geneva lake .... LEMAN
river .... RHONE
genial .... WARM, JOVIAL,
AFFABLE, AMIABLE, CORDIAL,
FRIENDLY, PLEASANT,
DEBONAIR(E)
genie .... DEMON, GNOME, JINNI,
JINNEE, SPIRIT
genius .... GIFT, PIXY, SPIRIT,
TALENT, ABILITY, BRILLIANCE
Genoa gulf seaport .... RAPALLO
Genoese city .... LIGURIA
magistrate .... DOGE
genre .... KIND, TYPE, CLASS,
STYLE, SPECIES
gens .... CLAN, TRIBE
gent .... GUY
genteel .... NICE, POLITE,
ELEGANT, REFINED, WELL-
BRED
gentian .... ROOT, FLOWER,
COLUMBO, AGUEWEED
gentile .... GOY, PAGAN, HEATHEN,
NON-JEW(ISH)

gentle .... MEEK, MILD, SOFT, TAME, AMENE, DOCILE, KINDLY, PLACID, POLITE, LENIENT, TENDER, REFINED, LAMBLIKE
breeze .... ZEPHYR
push .... NUDGE
soul/person .... LAMB
gentleman .... RYE, SIR, GENT, MILORD, SIGNOR, ESQUIRE, GALLANT, CAVALIER, COURTIER
amateur .... CORINTHIAN
attendant .... DONZEL
gentleman's man .... VALET
Gentlemen Prefer Blondes author .... (ANITA)LOOS
gentlewoman .... MILADY
gently .... SLOWLY, TENDERLY
Gentoo .... HINDU
gentry .... NOBILITY, ARISTOCRACY
genu .... KNEE
valgum .... KNOCK-KNEE
varum .... BOWLEG
genuflect .... KNEEL, CURTSY
genuine .... REAL, TRUE, LEGIT, RIGHT, VALID, HONEST, SINCERE, AUTHENTIC, SIMON PURE
genus .... KIND, SORT, BREED, CLASS, ORDER, ANALOG, GENDER, SPECIES, VARIETY
ant .... ECITON
birds .... ANSER, CORVUS
bowfin .... AMIA
campion .... SILENE
cats, big .... PANTHERA
cats, small .... FELIS
cattle/cows/ruminant .... BOS
cetaceans .... INIA
chestnuts .... CASTANEA
clams .... MYA
corncrake .... CREX
cranes .... GRUS
dogs .... CANIS
dogwood .... CORNUS
ducks .... ANAS, ANSER
eels .... CONGER
elks/moose .... ALCES
fishes .... ANABAS
fowl .... OLOR
foxes .... VULPES
frogs .... RANA, ANURA
gannet .... SULA
gastropods ...... HARPA, OLIVA, NERITA, TRITON
geese .... ANSER
ginseng .... ARALIA
goats .... CAPRIA
goose barnacles .... LEPAS

gooseberry .... RIBES
goshawks .... ASTUR, BUTEO
grapes .... VITIS
grasses ..... POA, AIRA, AVENA, STIPA, SETARIA
griffon .... GYPS
gulls .... LARI, XEMA, LARUS
herbs ..... ARUM, RUTA, INULA, ASARUM, ANEMONE, TOVARIA
herring .... ALOSA
hogs/pigs/swine .... SUS
honeybee .... APIS
housefly .... MUSCA, FANNIA
insects .... ACARUS, CICADA
lemurs .... GALAGO
lily .... ALOE
lizard .... UTA
man/primate .... HOMO
maple .... ACER
mints .... NEPETA
mollusks .... OLIVA, ANOMIA, NERITA, TEREDO
monkeys .... ATELES
mosquito .... AEDES
mussels .... UNIO
nettles .... URTICA
nuthatch .... SITTA
oats .... AVENA
olives .... OLEA
oysters .... OSTREA
palms .... ARECA
peacock .... PAVO
plants .... ARUM, LANTANA
rhubarb .... RHEUM
sea lettuce .... ULVA
shads .... ALOSA
sheep .... OVIS
shrubs .... ITEA, OLEA, RHUS, ERICA, FUCHSIA
snakes .... BOA, ELAPS, PYTHON
swans .... OLOR, CYGNUS
terns .... STERNA
thistles .... CARLINA
thrushes .... TURDUS
trees .... CELTIS, CORNUS, SAPOTA, CATALPA
turtles .... EMY
wasp .... VESPA
whales .... INIA
wrens .... NANNUS
geode .... VOOG, VUG(H), VUGG, DRUSE, CAVITY
geographer .... VAREN, PTOLEMY, MERCATOR
geography, work on
.... ALMAGEST
geologic chamber .... CAVE
geological age .... CENOZOIC, PLIOCENE
angle .... HADE

division .... EON, ERA, LIAS, LYAS
epoch .... ECCA, UINTA, EOCENE, MIOCENE, PLIOCENE, OLIGOCENE, PALEOCENE
era .... CENOZOIC, MESOZOIC, PALEOZOIC
formation ...... IONE, TERRANE, TERRAIN, TERRENE, TRIASSIC
ridge .... OSAR
suffix .... ZOIC
geology, part of ...... GEODETICS, PETROLOGY, MINEROLOGY
geomancy .... DIVINATION
geometrical body .... LUNE, PRISM
curve .... PARABOLA
figure ..... CONE, CUBE, ANGLE, PRISM, RHOMB, CIRCLE, SQUARE, ELLIPSE, POLYGON, HELICOID
line .... LOCUS, SECANT
premise .... POSTULATE
principle .... THEOREM
ratio .... PI, SINE
solid .... CONE, CUBE, LUNE, PRISM, PYRAMID
study .... CONICS
term ..... SINE, LOCUS, SECANT, VERSOR, TANGENT, THEOREM
geometry, branch of ...... CONICS
hypothesis .... THEOREM
subject of .... LINE, PLANE, POINT, SOLID
type .... PLANE, SOLID
geophagist .... CLAYEATER
geoponic .... RURAL, RUSTIC, BUCOLIC, PASTORAL
George .... RAFT, DEWEY, GOBEL, LUCAS, SCOTT, SEGAL, PATTON
Bernard .... SHAW
Cukor hit film ...... DINNER AT EIGHT
Eliot .... EVANS
Eliot, weaver of .... MARNER
Herman .... RUTH
georgette .... CREPE
Georgia, capital of ...... ATLANTA
city/town .... ROME, MACON, ALBANY, ATHENS, DALTON, PLAINS, TIFTON, AUGUSTA, GRIFFIN, AMERICUS, COLUMBUS, LA GRANGE, SAVANNAH, VALDOSTA, WAYCROSS, BRUNSWICK, BAINBRIDGE, GAINESVILLE
college .... TIFT, PAINE, BRENAU, SPELMAN
county ...... BIBB, COBB, HALL, POLK, TIFT, WARE, FLOYD,

GLYNN, HENRY, TROUP,
BARTOW, CLARKE, COWETA,
DE KALB, FULTON, GORDON,
NEWTON, THOMAS, WALKER,
BALDWIN, BULLOCH, CARROLL,
CATOOSA, CHATHAM,
CLAYTON, DOUGLAS,
HOUSTON, LAURENS,
LOWNDES, CHEROKEE,
COLQUITT, COLUMBIA,
GWINNETT, MUSKOGEE,
RICHMOND, ROCKDALE,
SPALDING, DOUGHERTY,
WHITFIELD
dam .... BARTLETTS FERRY
island .... JEKYLL, SAPELO,
WASSAW, OSSABAW,
SKIDAWAY, CUMBERLAND
lake .... BANKS, WEISS,
BURTON, CARTERS, CHATUGE,
SINCLAIR, GOAT ROCK,
BLACKSHEAR, WEST POINT,
SIDNEY LANIER
mountain .... STONE,
SPRINGER, BRASSTOWN BALD
Negro .... GULLAH
peak .... KENNESAW
recreation/historic site
.... HAY HOUSE, ROCK CITY,
TALLULAH GORGE,
APPALACHIAN TRAIL
river .... COOSA, FLINT,
OCONEE, ALAPAHA, SATILLA,
TUGALOO, ALTAMAHA,
OCMULGEE, S(U)WANEE,
SUWANNOOCHEE
seaport .... SAVANNAH
state bird .... THRASHER
state flower .... CHEROKEE
ROSE
state nickname .... PEACH,
EMPIRE STATE OF THE SOUTH
university .... EMORY, MERCER,
OGLETHORPE
Georgian seaport .... BATUM
Geraint .... KNIGHT
wife of .... ENID
geranium .... CRANESBILL
gerbil(l)e .... JERBOA
gerent .... RULER, MANAGER
geriatrics .... NOSTOLOGY
germ .... SEED, VIRUS, EMBRYO,
ORIGIN, MICROBE, BACTERIUM
cell .... GAMETE
for short .... STREP
free .... ASEPTIC
German ...... HUN, BOCHE, JERRY,
ALEMAN, ALMAIN, JUNKER,
DEUTSCHE, TEUTON(IC)
abandon .... AUFGEBEN
above .... UBER

admiral .... SPEE, RAEDER,
TIRPITZ
after .... NACH
again .... WIEDER
air .... LUFT
aircraft maker .... DORNIER
airplane .... STUKA, TAUBE
alas .... ACH
all .... ALLE(S)
also .... FERNER
and .... UND
angry .... BOSE
animal/beast .... TIER
answer .... ANTWORTEN
appreciate .... SCHATZEN
approving word .... HOCK
army .... REICHSWEHR
art songs .... LIEDER
artful .... LISTIG
article .... DAS, DER, EIN(E)
ass .... ESEL
assembly hall .... AULA
at no time .... NIE
avenue .... ALLEE
aviator .... FLIEGER
award .... ZUERKENNEN
bacteriologist .... KOCH,
LOFFLER
baggage .... GEPACK
bank .... UFER
bath .... BAD
battle .... SCHLACHT
battleship .... TIRPITZ,
BISMARCK, (GRAF)SPEE
bay .... BUCHT
beach .... STRAND
bean .... BOHNE
beard .... BART
beautiful .... SCHON
because .... WEIL
bed .... BETT
bee .... BIENE
beer .... BIER, LAGER
believe .... GLAUBEN
betray .... VERRATEN
betroth .... VERLOBEN
black .... SCHWARZ
Black Forest
.... SCHWARZWALD
Black Sea .... SCHWARZES
MEER
blanket .... WOLLDECKE
blood .... BLUT
blue .... BLAU
boar .... EBER
bomber .... STUKA
bonnet .... EASTER
book .... BUCH
boots .... HAUSKNECHT
-born architect in U.S.
.... GROPIUS

bottle .... FLASCHE
boy .... JUNGE
bread .... BROT, BROTCHEN
bride .... BRAUT
bridge .... BRUCKE
brother .... BRUDER
brussel sprouts
.... ROSENKOHL
build .... BAUEN
bullet .... KUGEL
burglar .... EINBRECHER
but .... ABER
butcher .... METZGER
buy .... KAUFEN
by .... BEI
cabbage .... KRAUT
cake .... TORTE, KUCHEN,
STOLLEN
camp .... LAGER, STALAG
canal .... KIEL
candy .... ZUCKERWERK
car .... WAGEN
carpenter .... ZIMMERMANN
cash .... GELD
cat .... KATZE
cathedral site/city .... ULM,
ESSEN, COLOGNE
cavalryman: var. .... ULAN
chancellor .... BRANDT,
ERHARD, ADENAUER,
BISMARCK
chap .... KERL, SPALT
cheese .... KASE
chicken .... KUCHLEIN
Christmas .... WEIHNACHTEN
Christmas card
.... WEIHNACHTS-KARTE
church .... KIRCHE
circle .... KREIS
clever .... KLUG
cloak .... MANTEL
clock/watch .... UHR
coal region .... RUHR, SAAR,
AACHEN
coffee .... KAFFEE
coin .... MARK, KRONE,
HELLER, GUILDER, PFENNIG,
GROSCHEN, T(H)ALER,
KREU(T)ZER
cold .... KALT
come .... KOMMEN
comic hero .... TYLL
EULENSPIEGEL
complain .... KLAGEN
composer .... ABT, BACH,
WEBER, BRAHMS, FLORIO,
WAGNER, STRAUSS
conjunction .... UND
cool .... FRECH, RUHIG
cost .... KOSTEN
cottage .... HUTTE

councilor/counsel .... RAT
count .... GRAF, ZAHLEN
countess .... GRAFIN
counterfeit .... FALSCH
county .... LANDKREIS,
                   GRAFSCHAFT
courage .... MUT
court .... HOF
cousin .... VETTER
cover .... DECKE
cow .... KUH
coward .... FEIGLING
cowboy .... KUHHIRTE
crab .... KRABBE
cradle .... WIEGE
crazy .... VERRUCKT
creator .... SCHOPFER
creature .... GESCHOPF
creature, in folklore .... NIX
credit .... GLAUBE
crime .... VERBRECHEN
criminal .... VERBRECHER
crisis .... KRISE
critic .... KRITIKER
critic/dramatist
               (GOTTHOLD)LESSING
cross .... KREUZ
crossword puzzle
              KREUZWORT RATSEL
crowd .... MENGE
crown .... KRONE
cruel .... GRAUSAM
cry of surrender/comrade
                              KAMERAD
daddy .... VATI
dagger .... DOLCH
dam .... EDER, DEICH
dance .... TANZ, COTILLION
dancer .... TANZER
darling .... LIEBLING
data .... ANGABEN
date .... DATUM
day .... TAG
dead .... TOT
deaf .... TAUB
dean .... DEKAN
dear .... LIEB
death .... TOD
debt .... SCHULD
decade .... JAHRZEHNT
December .... DEZEMBER
decorate .... ZIEREN
deed .... TAT
defeat .... SCHLAGEN
defense force ...... LANDSTURM
defenseless .... SCHUTZLOS
deity .... GOTTHEIT
delivery .... ABGABE
demon .... TEUFEL
dentist .... ZAHNARZT
desert .... WUST

dessert .... STREUSEL,
                     NACHTISCH
dictionary .... WORTERBUCH
dine .... SPEISEN
dinner .... MITTAGESSEN
direction .... RICHTUNG
disciple .... JUNGER
disease .... KRANKHEIT
dish .... SCHUSSEL
disk .... SCHEIBE
district .... BEZIRK
do .... TUN
dog .... HUND
doll .... PUPPE
donation/gift .... GABE
donkey .... ESEL
donor .... GEBER
door .... TUR
down .... FLAUM, UNTEN
dozen .... DUTZEND
draw .... ZIEHEN
drawer .... ZIEHER
dream .... TRAUM
dress .... KLEID
drink .... TRUNK, TRINKEN
drop .... TROPFEN
drum .... TROMMEL
dry .... TROCKEN
duchess .... HERZOGIN
duchy .... BADEN, HESSE, LIPPE
duck .... TAUCHEN
duke .... HERZOG
dunce .... DUMMKOPF
duplicate .... DOPPELT
dwarf .... ZWERG
dye .... FARBEN
each/every .... JEDE, JEDER,
                     JEDES
eagle .... ADLER
ear .... OHR
early .... FRUH
earth .... ERDE
earthquake .... ERDBEBEN
east .... OSTEN
Easter .... OSTERN
eat .... ESSEN
ecstasy .... RAUSCH
educate .... ERZIEHEN
eel .... AAL
egg .... EI
egg, hardboiled ..... HARTES-EI
eggplant .... AUBERGINE
egg-shaped .... EIFORMIG
eight .... ACHT
either .... EINE(R)
elder .... ALTER
election .... WAHL
embassy .... BOTSCHAFT
emblem/symbol ...... SINNBILD
emperor .... OTTO, KAISER,
                     WILHELM

empire .... REICH
envy .... NEID
epic .... EPOS
era .... ARA
error .... IRRTUM
estate .... GUT
evening .... ABEND
event .... EREIGNIS
everybody .... JEDERMANN
everything .... ALLES
evil .... UBEL
exclamation .... ACH, HOCH,
                 AUSRUF, HIMMEL
expert .... ERFAHREN
explorer .... BARTH
eye .... AUGE
eyewitness .... AUGENZEUGE
face .... GESICHT
fact .... TATSACHE
fairy .... FEE
fairytale writer .... GRIMM
faith .... GLAUBE
fame .... RUHM
famine .... HUNGERSNOT
far .... WEIT
farmer .... BAUER
fascist .... NAZI
fashion .... MODE
father .... VATER
fear .... FURCHT
feather .... FEDER
February .... FEBRUAR
fee .... HONORAR
feel .... FUHLEN
fellow .... KERL
female .... WEIB
field .... FELD
fight .... KAMPF, GEFECHT
finish .... APPRETUR
fire .... FEUER
first .... ERST
first aid .... ERSTE HILFE
five .... FUNF
flat .... EBEN, FLACH
flight .... FLUG
flirt .... KOKETTE
flower .... BLUME
fog .... NEBEL
folk dance .... ALLEMANDE,
                 VOLKSTANZ
folklore .... VOLKSKUNDE
folksong .... VOLKSLIED
follow .... FOLGEN
follower .... NACHFOLGER
follower of a German
philosopher .... HEGELIAN
food .... SPEISE
fool .... NARR
forbid .... VERBIETEN
forbidden .... VERBOTEN
forest .... WALD

forget .... VERGESSEN
fork .... GABEL
four .... VIER
fox .... FUCHS
fraud .... BETRUG
freedom/liberty .... FREIHEIT
Friday .... FREITAG
friend .... FREUND
frog .... FROSCH
from .... AUS, VON
fruit .... OBST
full .... VOLL
gambler/player .... SPIELER
game .... SPIEL
garden .... GARTEN
gardener .... GARTNER
garlic .... KNOBLAUCH
gate .... TOR
gem .... EDELSTEIN
gentleman .... HERR(EN)
germ ...... KEIM, BAZILLUS
ghost .... GEIST
ginger .... INGWER
girl .... MADCHEN
give .... GEBEN
glad .... FROH
glance/look .... BLICK
go .... GEHEN
goal/aim .... ZIEL
goat .... ZIEGE
god ..... GOTT, WODEN, WOTAN
goddess .... GOTTIN
golf .... GOLFSPIEL
good .... GUT, GUTEN
good-bye .... AUF WIEDERSEHN
government .... REICH,
        REGIERUNG, HERRSCHAFT
governor .... MARGRAVE,
                HERRSCHER
grape .... WEINTRAUBE
gray .... GRAU
green .... GRUN
grow .... WERDEN, WACHSEN
grower/planter .... PFLANZER
guard .... WACHE
guest .... GAST
gun .... GEWEHR
gypsy .... ZIGUENER
hair .... HAAR
hairy .... HAARIG
hall .... AULA, SAAL, HALLE
handle .... GRIFF
harlot .... DIRNE
harm .... SCHADEN
hat .... HUT
he .... ER, DER
head .... KOPF
headache .... KOPFWEH
health .... GESUNDHEIT
heart .... HERZ
heat .... HITZE

heaven/sky .... HIMMEL
heir .... ERBE
hero .... HELD, SIEGFRIED
heroine .... HELDIN
high .... HOCH
highway .... AUTOBAHN
historian .... RANKE, HEEREN
hit .... SCHLAG, TREFFER
hog/pig .... SCHWEIN
holiday .... FESTTAG
home .... HAUS, HEIM
honey .... HONIG
honor .... EHRE
hope .... HOFFEN
horse .... PFERD
hospital .... KRANKENHAUS
hot .... HEISS
hour .... STUNDE
housewife .... HAUSFRAU
humbug .... SCHWINDEL
humidity .... NASSE
hunt .... JAGEN
hunter .... JAGER
hypnotist .... MESMER
ice .... EIS
ill .... KRANK
income .... EINKOMMEN
indoor .... HAUSLICH
industrial town .... ESSEN
ink .... TINTE
invasion .... EINFALL
invent .... ERFINDEN
invention .... ERFINDUNG
inventor .... ERFINDER
invitation .... EINLADUNG
irate .... ZORNIG
ire .... ZORN
iron .... EISEN, PLATTEN
ironworks .... EISENHUTTE
it .... ES
itch .... JUCKEN
ivy .... EFEU
Jack .... HANS
janitor .... PFORTNER
January .... JANUAR
joke .... WITZ
joy .... FREUDE
judge .... RICHTER
juice .... SAFT
July .... JULI
jump .... SPRINGEN
June .... JUNI
kennel .... HUNDEHUTTE
key .... SCHLUSSEL
kill .... TOTEN
king .... KONIG, KAISER
king, 936-973 .... OTTO
kingdom .... HESSE, SAXONY,
        HANOVER, PRUSSIA,
                KONIGREICH
knife .... MESSER

knight .... RITTER, SPRINGER,
                TANNHAUSER
label .... ZETTEL
lace .... SPITZE
ladies .... DAMEN
lady .... DAME
lady, young .... FRAULEIN
lake .... SEE
land .... BODEN
landlady .... WIRTIN
landlord .... WIRT
language .... SPRACHE
laugh .... LACHEN
law .... RECHT
leaf .... BLATT
league .... BUND
leg .... BEIN
legend's site .... HAMELIN
legislative assembly
.... LANDTAG
lemon .... ZITRONE
lent .... FASTEN
letter .... BRIEF
lettuce .... KOPFSALAT
library .... BIBLIOTHEK
life/live .... LEBEN
lightning .... BLITZ
lion .... LOWE
lip .... LIPPE
lipstick .... LIPPENSTIFT
little .... KLEIN, WENIG
loser .... VERLIERER
love .... LIEBE
love, in tennis .... NULL
lyric .... LIED, GEDICHT
lyric poem .... LIEDER
madam/married woman
.... FRAU
magazine .... WARENLAGER
magic .... ZAUBER
magician .... ZAUBERER
mail .... POST
male .... MANN
man .... MANN, MENSCH
map .... LANDKARTE
marble .... MARMOR
March .... MARZ
master .... HERR, LEHRER,
                MEISTER
master builder
.... BAUMEISTER
master race .... HERRENVOLK
mathematician .... HESSE
May .... MAI
me .... MIR, MICH
measles .... MASERN, ROSEOLA,
        RUBELLA, RUBEOLA
measure .... KARAT, HALBER,
        KLAFTER, GALLONEN,
        SCHEFFEL, SCHOPPEN,
                KILOGRAMM

meat .... FLEISCH
medicine .... ARZNEI
menu .... SPEISEKARTE
mercenary soldier .... HESSIAN
messenger .... BOTE
middle .... MITTE
Military Intelligence
.... ABWEHR
mimic .... NACHAHMEN
mimist .... SCHARRE
miner .... BERGMANN
minnesinger ...... TANNHAUSER
minstrel .... SPIELMANN
miracle .... WUNDER
mirror .... SPIEGEL
Miss .... FRAULEIN
Mister .... HERR
Monday .... MONTAG
monetary unit .... MARK
money .... GELD
month .... MONAT
moon .... MOND
more .... MEHR
more favorable .... BESSER
morning .... MORGEN
mother .... MUTTER
mountain .... BERG
mouth .... MUND
mug .... BECHER
murder .... MORD
musician .... MUSIKER
musician, legendary .... PIED
PIPER
my .... MEIN
nail .... NAGEL
name prefix .... VON
napkin .... SERVIETTE
nation .... VOLK
naval base .... KIEL, EMDEN
near .... NAHE
neck .... HALS
necklace .... HALSBAND
necktie .... KRAWATTE
needle .... NADEL
negative/no .... NEIN, NICHT
neighbor .... NACHBAR
nephew .... NEFFE
never .... NIE, NIMMER
new .... NEU, FRISCH
newcomer .... ANKOMMLING
news .... NACHRICHT
niece .... NICHTE
night .... NACHT
nine .... NEUN
noble .... EDEL
nobleman .... EDELMANN
noise .... LARM
none .... KEINE(R)
nonsense .... UNSINN
north .... NORDEN
nose .... NASE

number .... ZAHL, NUMMER
oak .... EICHE
of .... AUF, AUS, VON
once .... EINST
one .... EIN
onion .... ZWIEBEL
only .... NUR
open .... OFFEN
operatic soprano .... LEHMANN
orange .... APFELSINE
our(s) .... UNSER
oven .... BACKOFEN
over .... UBER
overcoat .... MANTEL
overture .... VORSPIEL
owl .... EULE
ox .... OCHSE
ox, extinct .... URUS
pain .... WEH
painter .... ERNST, MALER,
GROSZ, HOLBEIN
parents .... ELTERN
parliament .... REICHSTAG
parrot .... PAPAGEI
part .... TEIL
path(way) .... PFAD
patience .... GEDULD
pay .... LOHN
pea .... ERBSE
pea soup .... ERBSENSUPPE
peace .... RUHE, FRIEDE
peacock .... PFAU
peak .... SPITZE
pear .... BIRNE
penalty .... STRAFE
pencil .... BLEISTIFT
people .... VOLK, LEUTE
perfume .... DUFT, PARFUM
pharmacist .... DROGIST
philosopher ...... KANT, HEGEL,
FICHTE, HERDER, CASSIRER
physician .... ARZT
physicist .... HERTZ
pickpocket .... TASCHENDIEB
picture/portrait .... BILD
pirate .... SEERAUBER
plant .... PFLANZE
plate .... TAFEL, PLATTE
playwright ..... SACHS, BRECHT
please .... BITTE
poem .... GEDICHT
poet ..... ARNDT, HEINE, RILKE,
SCHILLER
poison .... GIFT
police .... POLIZEI
policeman .... POLIZIST
potato .... KARTOFFEL
poverty .... ARMUT
POW camp .... STALAG
power .... KRAFT
powerful .... KRAFTIG

pray .... BETEN
prayer .... GEBET
president .... EBERT, HEUSS,
LUBKE, TALER
president, first .... EBERT
pretty .... NETT
principality .... LIPPE
printer .... GUTENBERG
problem .... AUFGABE
profit .... GEWINN
project .... ENTWURF
pronoun .... DU, ICH, SIE, UNS,
WIR
psychiatrist .... KRAEPELIN
pumpkin .... KURBIS
puzzle/riddle .... RATSEL
quarrel .... STREIT
queen .... KONIGIN
question .... FRAGE
rabbit .... KANINCHEN
radio .... RUNDFUNK
railroad .... EISENBAHN
rain .... REGEN
read .... LESEN
ready .... BEREIT
realm .... REICH
receipt .... EMPFANG
red .... ROT
Red Cross .... ROTES KREUZ
redwood .... ROTHOLZ
region .... GEBIET, GEGEND
reply .... ANTWORT
report .... BERICHT
reputation .... RUF
residence .... WOHNUNG
resort/spa .... EMS, BADEN
ribbon .... BAND
rice .... REIS
ride .... RITT
rifleman ..... YAGER, JA(E)GER,
SCHUTZE
ring .... KREIS, LAUTEN
riot .... AUFRUHR
Rip Van Winkle .... KLAUS
river .... STROM
robber .... RAUBER
robbery .... RAUB
robe .... KLEID, TALAR
rodent .... NAGETIER
roof .... DACH
rooster .... HAHN
root .... GRUND
rope .... SEIL
rubber .... GUMMI
rye bread .... ROGGENBROT
sacred place .... ABATON,
HIERON
sale .... VERKAUF
salesman .... VERKAUFER
salmon .... LACHS
salt .... SALZ

salutation .... HEIL
Saturday .... SAMSTAG
sausage .... WURST
saying .... REDE
school .... SCHULE
scientist .... MACH
sculptor .... BILDHAUER
sermon .... PREDIGT
serpent/snake .... SCHLANGE
service .... DIENST
seven .... SIEBEN
she .... SIE
ship/vessel .... SCHIFF
shoplifter .... LADENDIEB
shore .... UFER, STRAND
shout .... SCHREI
show .... ZEIGEN
silk .... SEIDE
sin .... SUNDE
since .... SEIT
siren .... LURLEI, LORELEI
sister .... SCHWESTER
six .... SECHS
slang .... DUTCH, JERRY
Slavic people .... WEND
sleep .... SCHLAF(EN)
small .... KLEIN
snare .... SCHLINGE
snow .... SCHNEE
soap .... SEIFE
society .... VEREIN
soldier .... BOCHE, HEINIE,
SOLDAT
son .... SOHN
song .... LIED, GESANG
soul .... SEELE
south .... SUDEN
sparrow .... SPERLING
speak/talk .... REDEN,
SPRECHEN
spider .... SPINNE
spirit .... GEIST
spoon .... LOFFEL
spouse .... GATTE, GATTIN
sprite .... FEE, ELFE, KOBOLD
spy .... SPION
stamp .... STANZE, STEMPEL
star .... STERN
state police .... GESTAPO
steel .... STAHL
steeple .... KIRCHTURM
stone .... STEIN
store .... VORRAT
street .... STRASSE
string .... SCHNUR
students' hall .... BURSE
submarine .... U-BOOT
sugar .... ZUCKER
sun .... SONNE
Sunday .... SONNTAG
superior/upper .... OBER

supper .... ABENDESSEN
surgeon .... CHIRURG
suspicion .... VERDACHT
swastika .... HAKENKREUZ
sweet .... LIEBSTE(R)
sword .... SABEL
table .... TAFEL, TISCH
taboo .... VERBOTEN
take .... NEHMEN
tank, armored .... PANZER
tavern .... WIRTSHAUS
teacher .... LEHRER(IN)
ten .... ZEHN
tennis .... NETZBALL
thank .... DANKEN
the .... DAS, DER, DIE
theologian .... EBER
there .... DA, DORT, DAHIN
thing .... DING, SACHE
think .... DENKEN
thirst .... DURST
three .... DREI
Thursday .... DONNERSTAG
time .... ZEIT
tip .... TRINKGELD
title, former .... KAISERIN
title of nobility .... GRAF,
PRINZ
title of respect .... HERR
to .... AN, ZU, AUF, NACH
today .... HEUTE
tooth .... ZAHN
toothache .... ZAHNWEH
tournament .... TURNIER
town .... STADT
train .... ZUG
tree .... BAUM
true .... WAHR
truth .... WAHRHEIT
Tuesday .... DIENSTAG
twenty .... ZWANZIG
twin .... ZWILLING
two .... ZWEI
understand .... VERSTEHEN
up .... OBEN
urchin .... SCHLINGEL
us .... UNS
use .... NUTZEN
valley .... TAL
very .... ECHT, SEHR
victim .... OPFER
village .... DORF
visitor .... BESUCHER
voice .... STIMME
volcano .... VULKAN
wage .... LOHN
waiter .... KELLNER
war .... KRIEG
warning .... WARNUNG
water .... WASSER
wave .... WOGE, WELLE

we .... WIR
wealth .... REICHTUM
weather .... WETTER
wedding .... HOCHZEIT
Wednesday .... MITTWOCH
week .... WOCHE
weight .... GRAMM, TONNE,
GEWICHT, KILOGRAMM
west .... WESTEN
what .... WAS, WELCHER
wheat .... WEIZEN
when .... WANN, WENN
where .... WO
whirlpool .... STRUDEL
white .... WEISS
who .... DAS, DER, WER
whole .... GANZ
why .... WARUM
widow .... WITWE
wife/woman ...... FRAU, FROW,
FRAULEIN
win .... SIEG
window .... FENSTER
wine .... HOCK, WEIN,
MOSELLE
wire .... DRAHT
wish .... WUNSCH
witch .... HEXE
with .... MIT
without .... OHNE
wood .... HOLZ
word .... WORT
work .... ARBEIT
world .... WELT
wrinkle .... WINK
write .... SCHREIBEN
WW II plane .... TAUBE
X ray .... RONTGEN
yawn .... GAHNEN
year .... JAHR
yellow .... GELB
yes .... JA
yet .... NOCH
you .... DU, SIE
young .... JUNG
your .... DEIN, EUER
youth .... JUGEND
zero .... NULL
zodiac .... TIERKREIS
germane .... AKIN, APROPOS,
RELEVANT, PERTINENT
Germanic people .... CIMBRI
tribesman .... JUTE
Germany .... REICH,
DEUTSCHLAND
bay, East .... POMERANIAN,
MECKLENBURG
bay, West .... HELGOLAND,
MECKLENBURG
cape, East .... ARKONA
capital, East .... BERLIN

capital, West .... BONN
city/town, East .... GERA,
JENA, GOTHA, HALLE, RIESA,
DESSAU, ERFURT, PANKOW,
WEIMAR, WISMAR, WOLFEN,
ZITTAU, BAUTZEN, COTTBUS,
DRESDEN, GORLITZ, LEIPZIG,
POTSDAM, ROSTOCK, STENDAL,
TREPTOW, ZWICKAU,
ARNSTADT, BERNBURG,
EISENACH, KOPENICK,
SCHWERIN, ALTENBERG,
FRANKFURT, BRANDENBURG,
LICHTENBERG
city/town, West ..... HOF, ULM,
KOLN, CELLE, EMDEN, ESSEN,
FULDA, FURTH, HAGEN,
HERNE, MAINZ, NEUSS, TRIER,
AACHEN, AMBERG, BERLIN,
BOCHUM, BREMEN, KASSEL,
LUBECK, MINDEN, MUNICH,
WITTEN, BAMBERG, BOCHOLT,
BOTTROP, COLOGNE,
HAMBURG, HAMELIN,
HANOVER, KOBLENZ,
MUNSTER, SPANDAU,
ARNSBERG, BAYREUTH,
DORTMUND, MANNHEIM,
FRANKFURT, NUREMBERG,
STUTTGART, WOLFSBURG,
DUSSELDORF, SCHONEBERG
district, East ...... GERA, SUHL,
BERLIN, ERFURT, COTTBUS,
DRESDEN, LEIPZIG, POTSDAM,
ROSTOCK, SCHWERIN,
FRANKFURT
forest, East .... SPREEWALD,
THURINGERWALD
forest, West .... BLACK,
BAVARIAN, ODENWALD,
SCHWARZWALD
island, East .... RUGEN,
USEDOM
island, West .... FOHR, SYLT,
AMRUM, JUIST, BALTRUM,
LANGEOOG, HELGOLAND
islands, West .... FRISIAN,
HALLIGEN
lake, West .... AMMERSEE,
BODENSEE, CHIEMSEE,
CONSTANCE, KONIGSSEE
mountain, East
.... FICHTELBERG
mountain, West .... FOLDBERG,
WATZMANN, ZUGSPITZE,
KAISERSTUHL, GROSSER ARBER
mountains, East .... HARZ,
RHON, ERZGEBIRGE
mountains, West .... HARZ,
RHON, HARDT
port ...... ULM, HAFEN, BREMEN

pre-1949 section of
.... RUSSIAN ZONE
range, West .... SWABIAN
JURA, BAVARIAN ALPS
region, East .... SAXONY,
ALTMARK, THURINGIA,
BRANDENBURG
region, West .... SAAR, HEGAU,
ALIGAU, BREISGAU,
SAUERLAND
river, East .... ELBE, ELDE,
ODER, HAVEL, MULDE, PEENE,
SAALE, SPREE, UCKER, WERRA,
ELSTER, NEISSE, WARNOW,
UNSTRUT
river, West .... EMS, INN, ELBE,
HASE, ISAR, LAHN, LECH,
NAAB, OKER, RUHR, SAAR,
ALLER, HUNTE, ILLER, LEINE,
LIPPE, MOSEL, RHINE, SAUER,
WESER, DANUBE, NECKAR,
TAUBER
sea .... NORTH, BALTIC
seaport .... KIEL, EMDEN,
WISMAR
state ...... LAGE, HESSE, STAAT,
BREMEN, BAVARIA, HAMBURG,
SAARLAND, RHINELAND
germicide .... ANTISEPTIC
germinate .... BEGIN, SPROUT,
PULLULATE
Gernreich, designer .... RUDI
Geronimo .... APACHE
foe of .... PALEFACE
greeting .... HOW
Gershwin, songman .... IRA,
GEORGE
Gertrude's friend Alice
.... TOKLAS
gesso .... GYPSUM, PLASTER
Gestapo chief .... HIMMLER
gestation ...... CYESIS, PREGNANCY
gest(e) .... DEED, BEARING,
EXPLOIT, ADVENTURE
gesticulate .... MIME, WAVE,
MOTION, GESTURE
gesture .... GESTE, TOKEN,
ACTION, MOTION, SIGNAL,
MOVEMENT
of contempt .... FIG, FICO
of indifference .... SHRUG
of respect .... BOW, CURTSY
get .... GAIN, OBTAIN, SECURE,
ACQUIRE
a circuit ahead in a race
.... LAP
a fitting .... TRY ON
a peek .... ESPY
a whiff of .... SNIFF
aboard .... EMBARK
about .... MOVE

across .... CONVEY, IMPART
ahead .... ADVANCE, PROSPER
along .... AGE, FARE, AGREE,
CLICK, THRIVE
along on one's own ..... FEND,
MANAGE
along peacefully .... COEXIST
around .... EVADE, SKIRT,
OUTWIT, DECEIVE
at .... GRAB, BRIBE, ARRIVE,
ACQUIRE
away .... ELUDE, DEPART,
ESCAPE
back at .... RETALIATE
back on the bus ..... REBOARD
by .... MANAGE, STRETCH,
SURVIVE
by trickery .... FINAGLE
cold feet .... CHICKEN OUT
cracking .... HURRY, STEP ON
IT
even with .... REVENGE,
RETALIATE
experience .... TASTE
going .... BEGIN, BEGONE,
HASTEN
going to .... IN FOR
hold of .... SEIZE, ACQUIRE
in .... ENTER, REACH, ARRIVE
in arrears .... DEFAULT
in touch .... ANSWER,
CONTACT
in trouble .... BE IN A CORNER,
LOSE ONE'S WAY
in uninvited .... CRASH
in with .... BEFRIEND
it .... SUFFER
it off one's chest ..... CONFESS
it over with .... END
lost .... LEAVE, DEPART, GO
FLY A KITE
married .... TIE THE KNOT
off one's feet .... SIT
on .... DON, BOARD, MOUNT
on one's nerves ..... PROVOKE,
IRRITATE
on the train! ...... ALL ABOARD
one's bearing .... ORIENT
one's dander up .... RILE
one's goat .... IRK, ANNOY,
PIQUE
oneself used to .... INURE
out .... EXIT, PRINT, EXTRACT
out of .... SHIRK
out of line .... NONCONFORM
over .... MOVE, RECOVER
rid of .... DISCARD, DISPOSE
rid of: sl. .... DITCH
set .... READY, PREPARE
stage fright .... CHOKE UP
the better of .... DEFEAT,

OUTWIT
the hang of .... FOLLOW,
REALIZE, MASTER
the message .... SEE THE
LIGHT
the point .... CATCH ON
to .... ARRIVE
to work .... DIG IN
together ..... BEE, TEA, AMASS,
ASSEMBLE, REUNION
together, of a kind .... SEANCE
up .... ARISE, AWAKE
well .... HEAL, MEND, RECOVER
getaway .... ESCAPE
getting going .... UNDER WAY
the gold watch .... RETIRING
Gettysburg general .... LEE,
MEADE
orator .... EVERETT, LINCOLN
getup .... WEAR, OUTFIT, COSTUME
geegaw .... GAUD, BAUBLE,
DOODAD, TRINKET, FALDEROL,
GIMCRACK
geyser .... (HOT)SPRING
mouth of .... CRATER
Ghana cape .... THREE POINTS
capital .... ACCRA
city/town .... HO, WA, ADA,
ODA, AXIM, BOLE, KETA,
TEMA, TUMU, BAWKU, YENDI,
BEKWAI, DUNKWA, ELMINA,
KUMASI, NSAWAM, OBUASI,
TARKWA, TAMALE, WENCHI,
BEREKUM, MAMPONG,
PRESTEA, SEKONDI, SUNYANI,
WINNEBA, CAPE COAST,
KOFORIDUA
coin .... PESEWA
gulf .... GUINEA
lake .... VOLTA
language ..... EWE, TWI, AKAN,
FANTE, HAUSA
monetary unit .... CEDI
native .... ASHANTI
"redeemer" .... NKRUMAH
region .... GOLD COAST
river ..... BLACK VOLTA, WHITE
VOLTA
ghastly .... GRIM, LURID,
GRIS(T)LY, MACABRE,
GRUESOME
gha(u)t .... PASS, RANGE
ghee .... BUTTER
Ghent river .... LYS
gherkin .... CUCUMBER
ghetto .... SLUM, JEWRY
visitor .... SLUMMER
ghost .... KER, HANT, MANES,
SPOOK, SHADOW, SPIRIT,
WRAITH, EIDOLON, PHANTOM,
SPECTRE, APPARITION

ghostly .... SPECTRAL, EERIE,
SPOOKY
milieu .... HAUNT
ghoul .... DEMON
ghoulish ..... FIENDISH, HORRIBLE,
VAMPIRIC, LOATHSOME
GI .... YANK, SAD SACK,
GOVERNMENT ISSUE
absentee .... AWOL
address .... APO
bed .... SACK
break .... LEAVE
color .... KHAKI
ex/former .... VET
hangout .... USO
ID .... DOGTAG
Joe .... DOGFACE
ration .... SPAM
rifle .... BAR, GARAND,
ARMALITE
runabout of .... JEEP
specialist .... MEDIC
Gian Carlo, composer
.... MENOTTI
giant .... BANA, ETEN, LOKI, OGRE,
YMER, ATLAS, JOTUN, JUMBO,
MIMIR, TITAN, TROLL,
BALDER, FAFNIR, GOLIATH
biblical .... ANAK
female .... GIANTESS
hundred-eyed .... ARGUS
hundred-handed ..... BRIAREUS
killer .... JACK, DAVID
living underground ..... TROLL
medieval legendary
.... GARGANTUA
mythological .... YMIR
one-eyed .... ALEC, ARGES,
CYCLOPS
-sized .... TITANIC
giantess .... GROA, NATT, NORN,
URTH, SKULD
giaour .... UNBELIEVER
gib ...... GUT, SALMON, (TOM)CAT,
GILBERT
gibbed .... CASTRATED
gibber .... JABBER, CHATTER
gibberish .... JABBER, JARGON,
CHATTER, MUMBO-JUMBO
gibbet .... GALLOWS, SCAFFOLD
adjunct .... NOOSE
gibbon .... APE, LAR, WAUWAU,
WOUWOU, PRIMATE
Gibbons, composer .... ORLANDO
concern of .... ROME
gibbous .... ROUNDED,
HUMPBACKED
gibe .... RIB, JAPE, JEER, FLEER,
SCOFF, SNEER, TAUNT, TEASE,
DERIDE, HECKLE
giblet .... GIZZARD

Gibraltar cape .... TRAFALGAR
founder of .... GEBIR
old name of .... CALPE
sight .... APE
strait port .... TANGIER
Gibson, Charles .... DANA
girl .... MODEL
tennis champ .... ALTHEA
gibus .... OPERA HAT
gid .... STAGGERS
giddiness .... VERTIGO
giddy .... DIZZY, FICKLE,
WHIRLING, HOITY-TOITY
Gide, critic .... ANDRE
gift .... ALMS, BOON, DOLE,
BOUNTY, LEGACY, TALENT,
ABILITY, BENEFIT, HANDOUT,
PRESENT, LARGESS(E),
DONATION
bearer .... SANTA
by man to bride .... DOWRY
for good luck .... HANDSEL
from the Magi .... MYRRH
giver .... DONOR
of gab/speech ...... ELOQUENCE
of money for services ..... TIP,
GRATUITY
of money, illicit .... BRIBE
recipient .... DONEE
to employee .... BONUS
gifted .... BRAINY, TALENTED
child .... PRODIGY
gig .... NAP, CHAISE, DEMERIT,
(ROW)BOAT, CARRIAGE
gigantic .... HUGE, VAST,
IMMENSE, MAMMOTH,
TITANIC, COLOSSAL,
ENORMOUS
statue .... COLOSSUS
giggle .... LAUGH, TITTER,
CHUCKLE, SNICKER
giggly sound .... TEHEE
Gigi role player .... HEPBURN
gigolo .... ESCORT
gigot ...... VEAL, MUTTON, SLEEVE
gigue .... JIG
Gil, writer .... BLAS
gila monster .... LIZARD
Gilbert and Sullivan actor
.... SAVOYARD
Island .... BERU, MAKIN,
TARAWA
gild .... GILT, ADORN, AUREATE
gill .... GIRL, GLEN, BROOK,
NOGGIN, WATTLE,
SWEETHEART
gillie .... SERVANT, ATTENDANT
gills, 4 .... PINT
gilsonite .... ASPHALT, UNTAITE
gilt .... PIG, SOW, GILD
gilthead .... SCUP, PORGY, BREAM,

321

CUNNER, SPAROID
gimcrack .... BAUBLE, DOODAD, GAUD(Y), GEWGAW, NOVELTY, TRINKET
gimlet .... WIMBLE
ingredient .... LIME
gimmick .... ANGLE, GIZMO, GADGET
gimp .... FABRIC, GUIPURE
colloquial .... VIGOR
gin .... NET, SLOE, TRAP, SNARE, RUM(MY), GENEVA
flavoring .... SLOE
liquor .... SCHNAPPS
mill .... SALOON
rummy debacle .... BLITZ
ginger .... SPICE, CURCUMA, ENLIVEN, CARDAMOM
ale-beer .... SHANDYGAFF
cookies .... SNAPS
Ginger's partner .... FRED
gingerbread .... CAKE, GAUDY, ORNATE, TAWDRY, FRIPPERY
gingerly .... CHARILY, TIMIDLY
gingersnap .... COOKY
gingham ...... CLOTH, CHAMBRAY
gingili .... SESAME
gingko/ginkgo .... ICHO, TREE, MAIDENHAIR
ginseng .... HERB, ROOT
Gioconda, La ...... OPERA, MONA LISA, PORTRAIT
painter .... DA VINCI
gip .... CHEAT, SWINDLE(R)
gipon .... TUNIC, JACKET
gipsy. (See also **gypsy**) ...... ROM
giraffe .... CAMELOPARD
feature .... LONG NECK
like animal .... OKAPI
girandole .... EARRING, PENDANT, FIREWORKS
girasol(e) .... OPAL, SUNFLOWER
gird ...... BIND, GIBE, JEER, EQUIP, ENDUE, SCOFF, STRAP, ENCLOSE, FORTIFY, ENCIRCLE
girder .... IBAR, TBAR, IBEAM, TRUSS
girdle .... BAND, BELT, SASH, GIRT(H), CORSET, ZODIAC, CEST(US), ZOSTER, CINCTURE, CUMMERBUND
stiffener .... BUSK
girdler .... BEETLER
world .... TOURIST
girl ...... SIS, TIT, CHIT, JILL, MINX, MISS, BELLE, LASS(IE), FILLE, DAMSEL, MADCAP, MAID(EN)
attacked by a ''swan''
.... LEDA
beautiful .... DOLL, STUNNER
best friend of .... DIAMONDS

bold .... SLUT, QUEAN, HOYDEN, TOMBOY
colloquial .... FILLY
contrary .... MARY
cover .... MODEL
cute .... TRICK, PIPPIN
flirtatious .... FIZGIG
haircut .... BOB, BANGS, PAGEBOY
in her early teens .... BOBBY SOXER
in uniform .... WAC, SPAR, WREN, NURSE, MAJORETTE, CHEERLEADER
introduced to society
.... DEB(UTANTE)
name meaning .... COLLEEN
beauty .... ADA
amiable .... ELMA
delight .... EDNA
happiness .... FELICITAS
holy .... OLGA
hospitable .... ZENIA
joyful .... ADA
noble .... ADELA, ETHEL
princess .... SARA
of song .... IDA, SAL, KATE, LILI, LOLA, DAISY, EADIE, FANNY, IRENE, KATIE, SALLY, RAMONA, ADELINE, MARLENE, RIO RITA
of the 1960s, young
.... TEENY-BOPPER
pert, saucy .... CHIT, MINX, SNIP, FRAIL, HUSSY
''Rain'' .... SADIE
slang .... TIT, BABE, CHICK, SKIRT, TOMATO, FLOSSIE, SPRING CHICKEN
student .... COED
very attractive ...... KNOCKOUT
young .... MOPPET
Girl Scout .... DAISY, BROWNIE
founder .... LOW
girlfriend .... STEADY, SWEETHEART
girls' group .... GSA, SORORITY
girth .... BAND, CINCH, STRAP, GIRDLE, ENCIRCLE, CIRCUMFERENCE
gisarme .... HALBERD, BATTLE-AX
gist .... NUB, CORE, CRUX, PITH, POINT, KERNEL, ESSENCE, MEANING, SUMMARY
gitano .... GYPSY
gittern .... CITHER, CITHARA
give .... PAY(OUT), GRANT, AWARD, ENDOW, YIELD, ASSIGN, CONFER, IMPART, PRESENT, HAND OVER
a bellow .... ROAR

a buzz .... RING
a cheer .... ROOT
a leg up .... AID
a legal right to .... ENTITLE
a subsequent showing
.... RERUN
a wavy appearance to
.... CRIMP
an account of .... RELATE
an instance .... CITE
and take ...... BANDY, BANTER, EXCHANGE, REPARTEE, HORSE-TRADE
away .... DONATE, BESTOW, BETRAY, EXPOSE, REVEAL
back .... RETURN, RESTORE
birth .... WHELP, FARROW, DELIVER
birth prematurely .... SLINK
ear .... HEED, LISTEN, HEARKEN
expression .... AIR, VOICE, ARTICULATE
extreme unction to: arch.
.... ANELE
forth .... EMIT, EXUDE, ISSUE, SPOUT
full consideration to ..... HEAR OUT
generously .... LAVISH
goods in return for other goods .... BARTER
in .... YIELD, CONCEDE
in law .... REMISE
it a second try together
.... REWED
medicine to .... DOSE
new courage .... REMAN
off .... EMIT
off fumes .... REEK
one the business
.... PATRONIZE
opportunity to .... ENABLE
out .... DOLE, METE
out a mephitic aura ..... STINK
party .... THROW
permission to use .... LEND
pleasure to .... GRATIFY, SATISFY
sparingly .... DOLE, STINT
the ball to (the fullback)
.... HAND-OFF
the raspberry to .... BOO
the slip .... ELUDE
title to: arch. .... INTITULE
up .... QUIT, YIELD, LET GO, WAIVE, FORSAKE, SURRENDER, CAPITULATE
up formally a high office/throne .... ABDICATE
vent to sorrow .... CRY
way .... BEND, YIELD, LET PASS

wholehearted support .... GO TO BAT FOR

with reluctance ..... BEGRUDGE

giveaway .... DOOR PRIZE, LOSS LEADER

given .... PRONE, ASSUMED

to fighting .... COMBATIVE, PUGNACIOUS

giver's recipient .... TAKER

giving lots and lots ...... RAINING

off light .... LUMINESCENT

gizzard .... GIBLET, STOMACH

glabrous .... BALD, HAIRLESS

glace ...... ICED, FROZEN, CANDIED

glacial .... ICY, COLD, FRIGID

deposit .... ASAR, OSAR, ESKAR, ESKER, PLACER, MORAINE

epoch .... ICE AGE, PLEISTOCENE

formation .... SERAC, DRUMLIN

hill .... KAME, PAHA

ice/snow .... FIRN, NEVE, SERAC

ridge .... ASAR, KAME, OSAR, ESKAR, ESKER, DRUMLIN

snowfield .... FIRN, NEVE

glaciarium feat .... AXEL

glaciate .... FREEZE

glacier .... ICECAP

facing .... STOSS

fissure .... CREVASSE

shaft .... MOULIN

glacis .... SLOPE

glad .... FAIN, HAPPY, BLITHE, PLEASED, WILLING, CHEERFUL

eye .... OGLE

rags .... FINERY, CLOTHES

tidings .... GOSPEL, EVANGEL

gladden .... ELATE

glade .... DELL, LAWN, LAUND, VALLEY, CLEARING

combining form .... NEMO

gladiator ...... LANISTA, WARRIOR

school for .... LUDI

gladiolus .... IRID, IRIS, LILY

bulb .... CORM

gladly .... FAIN, LIEF, READILY, WILLINGLY, WITH PLEASURE

glair .... ALBUMEN

glaive .... SWORD, HALBERD

glamorize .... EXALT, GLORIFY, BEAUTIFY

glamorous .... ALLURING, CHARMING, DAZZLING, GORGEOUS

glamo(u)r .... CHARM, ALLURE

colloquial .... IT, OOMPH

glance .... LEER, LOOK, OGLE, PEEK, FLASH, GLEAM, APERCU, GLIMPSE, ONCE-OVER

off .... GRAZE

sideways .... SQUINT

glancing blow .... SNICK

gland .... PINEAL, SPLEEN, CAROTID, PAROTID, THYROID, FOLLICLE, PANCREAS

milk .... MAMMA

reproductive cell .... GONAD

secretion .... BILE, GALL, URINE, SALIVA, CERUMEN, HORMONE

glanders .... FARCY

glandlike .... ADENOID

glands inflammation .... ADENITIS

glandular .... ADENOID(AL)

disease ..... GOITER, CRETINISM

tumor .... ADENOMA

glare .... LOOK, BLAZE, FROWN, STARE, GLOWER

glaring .... GARISH, FLAGRANT

Glasgow river .... CLYDE

saint .... MUNGO

glass .... LENS, CALX, PRISM, VERRE, CULLET, MIRROR, RUMMER, SMALTO, CRYSTAL, LALIQUE, TUMBLER

baking dish .... CASSEROLE

bead .... BUGLE

blowpipe .... MATRASS

bottle ..... VIAL, CRUET, PHIAL, CARBOY, CASTER, CASTOR

bowl .... AQUARIUM

brandy .... PONY, SNIFTER

bubble .... BLEB

coloring pigment .... SMALTINE, MAT(T)RASS

combining form ..... HYAL(O), VITRO

cut .... CRYSTAL

cutter .... GLAZIER

cutting tool ..... LAP, DIAMOND

drinking .... GOBLET, TUMBLER

fused .... FRIT(T)

ground .... FRIT

heat-resistant .... SILEX

jar .... BOCAL, CLOCHE

jawed one .... BOXER, PUGILIST

kind of .... LEAD, AGATE, BLOWN, PYREX, STAINED, CRYSTAL

like .... VITRIC, VITREOUS

magnifying .... LOUPE

maker .... GLAZIER

making material .... SAND, FRIT(T), POTASH, SILICA, ZAFFER, SILICON

making rod .... PONTIL

molten .... PARISON

mosaic(work) .... SMALTO, TESSERA

piece .... PANE, SLIVER

roof .... BULL'S-EYE

scraps .... CULLET

toast-drinking .... RUMMER

tube, graduated .... BURET

vessel .... JUG, VASE, VIAL

vial .... AMP(O)ULE

waste .... CULLET

window/unit .... PANE

glasses .... SPECS, GOGGLES

glassware articles .... VITRICS

cooking .... PYREX

glassy .... CLEAR, SHINY, SMOOTH, VITRIC, BRITTLE, FRAGILE, HYALINE, HYALOID, VITREOUS, POLISHED, CRYSTALLINE, TRANSPARENT

body .... TEKTITE

Glaswegian .... SCOT

glaze .... FILM, GLOSS, ENAMEL, COAT(ING), POLISH, VENEER

crack .... CRAZE

glazier .... PUTTIER

burden of .... PANE

glazing machine .... CALENDER

material .... CLAY, KAOLIN

gleam .... RAY, BEAM, GLOW, FLASH, GLINT, LUSTER, GLIMMER, GLISTEN

glean .... REAP, GATHER, COLLECT

glebe .... CLOD, LUMP, TURF, EARTH, FIELD

glede .... KITE

glee .... JOY, MIRTH, GAIETY, ELATION, MERRIMENT

gleed .... COAL, EMBER

Gleek .... TIB

gleeman .... MINSTREL

gleet .... OOZE

glen .... DALE, DELL, VALE, DINGLE, VALLEY

Glengaries .... CAPS, TAMS

Glengary man .... SCOT

Glenn .... FORD, MILLER

glib .... OILY, FACILE, FLUENT, SUAVE, SMOOTH, VOLUBLE

glide .... FLOW, SCUD, SKIP, SKIM, SLIP, COAST, FLOAT, SLIDE, SASHAY

gliding across .... LABILE

step .... GLISSADE

glim .... LAMP, LIGHT, CANDLE

glimmer .... VIEW, BLINK, GLEAM, SHINE, SIGHT, FLICKER

glimpse .... FLASH, GLINT, (SIDE)GLANCE

glint ...... FLASH, GLEAM, GLIMPSE

glioma .... TUMOR

glissade .... GLIDE, SLIDE

glisten ...... FLASH, GLEAM, SHINE, GLITTER, SPARKLE,

CORUSCATE
glitter .... FLASH, GLINT, GLISTEN, SPANGLE, SPARKLE, BRILLIANCE
glittering .... RUTILANT
glittery .... STARRY
gloaming .... DUSK, TWILIGHT
gloat .... BOAST, REVEL, CROW OVER
global .... ROUND, SPHERAL, SPHERICAL, WORLD-WIDE
globe .... ORB, BALL, CLEW, EARTH, SPHERE
thistle .... ARTICHOKE
globe-trotter .... TOURIST, (WORLD)TRAVELER
globefish .... PUFFER
globule .... BEAD, BLOB, DROP(LET)
glockenspiel, instrument like a .... MARIMBA
gloom ...... MURK, BLUES, DUMPS, DIMNESS, SADNESS, DARKNESS
gloomy .... SAD, BLUE, DARK, DOUR, GLUM, MOODY, MURKY, DISMAL, DREAR(Y), MORBID, MOROSE
glop .... GOO, SLIME
gloria .... HALO, HYMN, PAEAN
glorified ...... SAINTLY, REDEEMED
glorify ...... BLESS, EXALT, EXTOL, HONOR, PRAISE, REVERE
gloriole .... HALO
glorious .... GRAND, DIVINE, SUPERB, SPLENDID
glory .... FAME, ECLAT, EXULT, KUDOS, RENOWN, DIGNITY, REJOICE, RADIANCE, SPLENDOR
cloud of .... NIMBUS
head's .... HAIR, HALO, CROWN, TIARA, CORONA, AUREOLE
gloss .... SHEEN, SHINE, LUSTER, POLISH, VENEER, ANNOTATE
over .... FUDGE, WHITEWASH
glossary .... CLAVIS, LEXICON
glossing machine ...... CALENDER
glossolalia .... HYPNOSIS, HYSTERIA
glossy ...... SLEEK, SLICK, SHINING, LUSTROUS, SPECIOUS
fabric ..... SILK, SATIN, SATEEN
poster .... LACQUERED PLACARD
glove .... CUFF, MITT(EN), CESTUS, GA(U)NTLET
kind of .... KID, BOXING, BASEBALL
leather .... KID, MOCHA, SUEDE

glove, _____ (closely associated) .... WERE HAND AND
glow .... FLASH, FLUSH, GLEAM, WARMTH, RADIATE, RADIANCE
glower .... FROWN, GLARE, SCOWL, STARE, GRIMACE
glowerer .... BEETLEBROW
glowing .... ASHINE, CANDENT, FLUSHED, LAMBENT, LUMINOUS
coal .... EMBER
review .... RAVE
glowworm .... FIREFLY
Gluck, composer ...... CHRISTOPH
opera .... ARMIDA
soprano .... ALMA
glucose .... RUTIN, SUGAR
glucoside .... RUTIN, INDICAN, SAPONIN, SINALBIN
glue .... GOO, GUM, PASTE, CEMENT, GELATIN, MUCILAGE
gluey .... PASTY, STICKY
glum ...... SOUR, SULKY, MOROSE, GLOOMY, SULLEN, LONG-FACED
glume .... HUSK, BRACT
glut ...... FILL, CLOY, CRAM, SATE, PACK, GORGE, STUFF, SATIATE, SURFEIT
gluten .... LOAF, BREAD, FIBRIN
glutenous material .... FLOUR
glutinous .... ROPY, GLUEY, STICKY, VISCID
glutton .... HOG, PIG, EPICURE, GO(U)RMAND, CORMORANT
gluttonous ...... GREEDY, HUNGRY, PIGGISH, SWINISH, VORACIOUS
gluttony .... GREED, EDACITY, VORACITY, OVEREATING
glyceride .... ESTER
Glyn, author .... ELINOR
glyph .... CARVING
gnarl .... KNOT, KNUR, SNAG, TWIST, CONTORT
gnarled .... WIRY, ROUGH, KNOTTY, RUGGED
gnash .... BITE, GRATE, GRIND
gnat .... PEST, MIDGE, STINGER, MOSQUITO
gnaw ...... EAT, BITE, CHEW, FRET, CRUNCH, HARASS, NIBBLE, RANKLE, TORMENT
gnawed, appear .... EROSE
gneiss .... FELDSPAR
gnome .... ELF, NIS, BOGIE, DWARF, MAXIM, GOBLIN, KOBOLD, BROWNIE, GREMLIN
gnomon of sundial .... PIN, STYLE
Gnostic sect member .... MANDEAN

GNP, part of .... GROSS, PRODUCT, NATIONAL
gnu .... ANTELOPE, WILDEBEST
go ...... DIE, MOVE, WEND, LEAVE, DEPART, RETIRE, OPERATE, PROCEED
aboard ..... EMBARK, ENPLANE, ENTRAIN
ahead ..... PROCEED, CONTINUE
along ..... AGREE, ACCOMPANY, FOLLOW, COOPERATE, SWIM WITH THE STREAM
around .... SKIRT, DETOUR, CIRCULATE, CIRCUMVENT
astray/wrong .... ERR, SIN, DEVIATE, ABERRATE, MISCARRY
at high speed .... BARREL
away! ..... SCAT, SHOO, SCRAM, GET LOST
back .... RECEDE, RETURN, REVERT, RETREAT
back and forth .... SHUTTLE
back over .... RETRACE
before .... PRECEDE
between .... AGENT, MEDIATOR, MIDDLEMAN
by .... ELAPSE
down ...... FALL, SINK, LOWER, DESCEND
far and wide .... RANGE
first .... LEAD
for .... SUPPORT
for broke .... STRETCH ONE'S LUCK
forth .... SALLY
forward .... ADVANCE
in haste .... SCURRY
left .... PORT
off .... EXPLODE, DETONATE
off course .... VEER, STRAY
on hands and knees .... CREEP
over .... EXCEED, SURPASS
over the wall .... ESCAPE, BREAK JAIL
surfing .... HANG TEN
swiftly: sl. .... SCOOT
tenting .... CAMP OUT
the distance .... FINISH
to _____ (do penance) .... CANOSSA
to bed .... HIT THE HAY, HIT THE SACK
to seed .... DETERIORATE
up .... RISE, CLIMB, ASCEND
goa .... GAZELLE
Goa .... COLONY
capital of .... PANJIM
language .... KONKANI
powder .... ARAROBA
goad .... EGG, GAD, PROD, SPUR,

URGE, ANKUS, PRICK, STICK,
  STING, INCITE, NEEDLE
go-ahead .... APPROVAL
goal .... AIM, END, POST, THULE,
  INTENT, MOTIVE, OBJECT,
  TARGET
  falls short of .... MANQUE
goat .... GORAL, ANGORA, BEZOAR,
  PASANG
  antelope .... GORAL, SEROW
  castrated male .... WETHER
  constellation .... CAPRICORN
  deity .... PAN, FAUN
  female .... DOE, CAPRA,
  NANNY
  genus .... CAPRIA
  get one's .... IRK, RILE,
  ANNOY, IRRITATE
  hair of .... MOHAIR
  hair cloth .... ABA, CAMLET
  horn .... CORNUCOPIA
  leap .... CAPRIOLE
  leather .... KID, MOCHA
  like .... CAPRINE, HIRCINE
  male .... BUCK
  pertaining to .... CAPRIC
  sucker .... POTOO
  under one year old .... KID
  wild .... TUR, IBEX, KRAS,
  TAIR, TEHR, THAR
  wool .... CASHMERE
goatee .... BEARD, VANDYKE,
  IMPERIAL
goatfish .... MULLET
goatish .... CAPRINE, HIRCINE
goatman .... FAUN
goatsucker .... POTOO,
  NIGHTHAWK
gob .... TAR, LUMP, MASS, SAILOR,
  SEAMAN
gobbet .... BIT, LUMP, MASS,
  CHUNK, FRAGMENT
gobble .... EAT, SEIZE
gobbledygook ....:......... TALK
gobbler .... TOM, TURKEY
Gobbo .... LAUNCELOT
Gobi .... LAKE, SHAMO, DESERT
gobioid fish .... LOTER
goblet .... TASS, BOCAL, GLASS,
  HANAP, CHALICE
  drinking .... MAZER, MAZARD
  Eucharist .... CHALICE
goblin ...... ELF, HOB, PUCA, PUCK,
  POOK, BOGIE, GNOME,
  NIS(SE), OUPHE, KOBOLD,
  BROWNIE
  doglike .... BARHEST
goby .... FISH, MAPO
go-cart .... PRAM, STROLLER
god .... SIVA, DEITY, BRAHMA
  agriculture .... NEBO, THOR,

FAUNUS, SATURN
air .... SHU
alcoholic drinks .... SIRIS
appearance of ..... THEOPHANY
Arcadian .... PAN
avarice .... MAMMON
baboon-faced .... THOTH
beauty .... APOLLO
belief in (many)
  .... (PAN)THEISM
combining form .... THEO
commerce .... HERMES,
  MERCURY
cosmos .... VARUNA
darkness .... SIN, SETH
day .... HOR, HORUS, JANUS
dead .... YAMA, ORCUS,
  ANUBIS, OSIRIS
defender .... ANSEL
discord .... LOKE, LOKI
dog-headed .... THOTH
dreams .... MORPHEUS
earth .... BEL, GEB, DAGAN
elephant-headed ..... GANESHA
falcon-headed .... HORUS
false .... BAAL, IDOL,
  MAMMON, MOLOCH
fearing .... PIOUS, DEVOUT
fertility .... FREY, OSIRIS
fields .... PAN, FAUN
fire .... AGNI, VULCAN
flocks .... PAN
force .... SHU, PTAH
half-man, half-fish ..... DAGON
harvest .... CRONUS
heaven .... ANU, BEL
herds .... PAN
horses .... POSEIDON
household .... LARES
jackal-headed .... ANUBIS,
  WAPUET
justice .... RAMMAN
killer .... DEICIDE
lightning .... AGNI, JUPITER
like .... DEIFIC
love .... AMOR, EROS, KAMA,
  CUPID, POTHOS
lower world .... DIS, HADES,
  PLUTO, SERAPIS
marriage .... HYMEN
mirth .... COMUS
mischief .... LOKI
moon .... NANNAR
mountains .... ATLAS,
  OLYMPUS
music .... BES, APOLLO
offering to .... CORBAN
one-eyed .... ODIN
peace .... FREY, BALDER
pleasure .... BES(A)
praise to .... HOSANNA

prosperity .... FREY
rain .... INDRA, JUPITER
revelry .... COMUS, KOMOS,
  BACCHUS
river .... ALPHEUS
sea .... AEGER, DYLAN,
  NEREUS, PONTUS, TRITON,
  NEPTUNE, POSEIDON
seven-armed .... AGNI
shepherds .... PALES
sky .... ANU, NUT, TYR,
  JUPITER
sleep .... HYPNOS, SOMNUS,
  MORPHEUS
study of .... THEOLOGY
sun .... RA, SOL, BELI, FREY,
  HORUS, NINIB, AMEN-RA,
  APOLLO, HELIOS, MITHRAS,
  PHOEBUS, SHAMASH
thunder .... THOR, ZEUS,
  DONAR, JUPITER
trumpeter of the sea
  .... TRITON
two-faced .... AGNI, JANUS
underworld .... DIS, ORCUS,
  PLUTO
Vedic .... INDRA
vegetation .... ESUS, ATTIS
victory .... ODIN, ZEUS
war .... ARES, COEL, IR(R)A,
  MARS, ODIN, THOR, TYR(R),
  AS(S)UR, WODEN
waters .... NEA, FONTUS
winds .... ADDA, EURUS,
  AEOLUS, BOREAS
wing-shod .... HERMES,
  MERCURY
wisdom .... EA, NEBO, ODIN,
  SABU, GANESA
woods .... PAN, SILEN,
  SILVANUS
youth .... APOLLO
God .... CREATOR, JEHOVA,
  ALMIGHTY
  belief in one ..... MONOTHEISM
  Bless America composer
  .... BERLIN
Godden .... RUMER
goddess .... DEA, DEVI, SHRI,
  BEAUTY, LACHESIS
  agriculture .... OPS, ISIS,
  CERES, DEMETER
  air .... HERA
  arts and sciences .... CLIO,
  MUSE, ERATO, ATHENA,
  THALIA, URANIA, EUTERPE,
  CALLIOPE, MELPOMENE
  astronomy .... URANIA
  avenging .... FURY, NEMESIS
  beauty .... FREYA, VENUS
  birth .... PARCA

cat-headed .... PACHT
chase .... DIAN(A), ARTEMIS
childbirth .... UPIS, LUCINA
comedy .... THALIA
crops .... ANNONA
dawn .... EOS, US(H)AS,
AURORA
death .... DANU, HEL(A)
destiny ...... URD, NORN, URTH,
MOIRA
destruction .... ARA, KALI
discord .... ATE, ERIS
doom .... URTH, WYRD
earth .... GE, LUA, OPS, SEB,
ERDA, GAEA, GAIA, TARI,
ARURU, CERES, TERRA,
ISHTAR, SEMELE, TELLUS,
DEMETER
faith .... FIDES
fate .... NONA, NORN, PARCA
fertility .... ISIS, FAUNA,
ANNONA, ISHTAR, ASTARTE,
ASHTORETH
fields .... FAUNA, TELLUS
fire .... PELE, VESTA, HESTIA
flowers .... FLORA, NANNA,
CHLORIS
fortune .... TYCHE
fountains .... FERONIA
fruits .... POMONA
ghosts .... HECATE
giant .... NORN, URTH
grains .... CERES
harvest .... OPS, CARPO
healing .... EIR, GULA
health .... SALUS, HESTIA,
HYGEIA
heaven .... NUT
history .... CLIO, SAGA
hope .... SPES
horses .... EPONA
hunting ..... DIAN(A), VACUNA,
ARTEMIS
justice .... MAAT, THEMIS,
ASTRAEA
life .... ISIS, LACHESIS
light .... LUCINA
love .... FREYA, VENUS,
HATHOR, SELENE, ARTEMIS,
IS(H)TAR, ASTARTE,
APHRODITE, ASHTORETH
marriage ..... GE, GAEA, HERA,
JUNO
mischief .... ATE, ERIS
moon .... LUNA, DIANA,
HECATE, LUCINA, PHOEBE,
SELENE, ARTEMIS, CYNTHIA
music .... EUTERPE
nature .... CYBELE, ARTEMIS
night .... NOX, NYX, LETO
order .... HARMONIA

Pagan .... ASTARTE
peace .... EIR, PAX, IRENE,
MINERVA
plenty .... OPS
poetry .... ERATO, CALLIOPE
prosperity .... SALUS
rainbow .... IRIS
retribution .... ARA, ATE
revenge .... NEMESIS
seas .... INO, DORIS, SALACIA
seasons .... HORA, HOUR
six-armed, three-headed
.... HECATE
sky .... NUT, FRIGG
splendor .... UMA
spring .... IDUN, VENUS
strife .... ERIS
trees .... POMONA
underworld .... HEL, GAEA,
HECATE, LARUNA
vegetation .... CORA, KORE,
CERES, FLORA
vengeance .... NEMESIS
victory .... NIKE
virtue .... FIDES
volcano .... PELE
war .... ALEA, ENYO, ANATU,
ATHENA, ISHTAR, VACUNA,
BELLONA, MINERVA
waters .... ERUA
weeping .... NIOBE
welfare .... SALUS
wisdom ...... ATHENA, PALLAS,
MINERVA
womanhood .... JUNO, SATI
woods .... DIAN(A), ARTEMIS
youth .... HEBE, IDUN
goddesses of beauty/charm
.... GRACES
of destiny .... FATES
of fate .... NORNS, MOERAE
of nature .... HORAE
godfather .... SPONSOR
godforsaken .... WICKED,
FORLORN, DESOLATE
godhead .... DIVINITY
godless .... PAGAN, WICKED,
IMPIOUS, ATHEISTIC
godlike .... HOLY, DIVINE
godliness .... PIETY
godly .... PIOUS, DEVOUT
person .... SAINT
godmother .... CUMMER
godparent .... SPONSOR
godown .... WAREHOUSE
gods' abode .... MERU, ASGARD
blood .... ICHOR
cupbearer .... HEBE,
GANYMEDE
drink .... NECTAR
king of .... WODEN

messenger .... IRIS, HERMES,
MERCURY
queen of .... HERA, JUNO, SATI
race of .... VANIR
strife among ...... THEOMACHY
God's acre .... CEMETERY
chosen .... ISRAELITE(S)
godsend .... MANNA
Godwin Austen, Mount
.... DAPSANG
godwit .... SNIPE
Goebbels's (Joseph) forte
.... BIG LIE
Goethe or Bach .... JOHANN
Goethe's hero .... FAUST,
WERTHER
heroine .... MIGNON
Gog and _____ .... MAGOG
go-getter .... DOER, TIGER,
HUSTLER, ACHIEVER
goggler .... SCAD, CICHARRA
goggles .... SPECTACLES
Gogol hero .... (TARAS)BULBA
Goidelic language .... ERSE,
MANX
going .... MOVING, LEAVING,
EXPIRING, FLOWING,
OPERATING
balmy .... LOSING ONE'S
MARBLES
get .... BEGIN, START, GET
BUSY
on ..... HAPPENING, OCCURRING
on now ..... LIVE, IN PROGRESS
out .... EXIT, EXODUS,
EGRESS(ION)
strong .... BOOMING
goings-on .... ACTIONS, CONDUCT,
ACTIVITY
goiter .... STRUMA
Golconda .... MINE
gold .... ORO, CYME, GILT,
AU(RUM), RICHES, WEALTH
alchemist's .... SOL
alloy .... ASEM
bar .... INGOT
black .... OIL
braid .... ORRIS
cloth .... LAME
coat with .... GILD
coating .... GILT
coin .... LIRA, ANGEL, DARIC,
DUCAT, EAGLE, KRONE, LOUIS,
MOHUR, OBANG, TOMAN,
SCUDO, GUINEA, PISTOLE,
DOUBLOON, IMPERIAL
content .... CARAT, KARAT
deposit .... PLACER
district, African .... RAND
fineness .... CARAT, KARAT
imitation .... OROIDE, ORMOLU,

PINCHBECK
lace .... ORRIS, FILIGREE
land .... OPHIR
leaf .... FOIL
leaf, imitation .... ORMOLU
like .... AUREATE
like alloy .... ASEM, OROIDE,
ORMOLU
lump .... NUGGET
medalist Biondi .... MATT
medalist, swimming ..... SPITZ
miner .... PANHANDLER
miner, 1849 ...... FORTY-NINER
miners' camp: sl.
.... DIGGINGS
mines region .... KLONDIKE
mosaic .... ORMOLU
native .... NUGGET
pertaining to .... AURIC
rush man .... ARGONAUT
rush site .... YUKON
seeker/searcher .... MINER,
ARGONAUT, PROSPECTOR
separate gravel from ...... PAN
sheet .... FOIL, LATTEN
sometimes .... LEAF
symbol .... AU
Gold Bug author .... POE
Coast .... GHANA
Coast river .... VOLTA
Coast tribe .... AKAN
goldbrick .... LOAF, SHIRK,
MALINGER
gold-digger .... VAMP, FLIRT,
MINER, STRUMPET
"mine of" ...... SUGAR DADDY
target of .... HEIR
golden .... AURIC, GILDED,
YELLOW, AUREATE, PRECIOUS
apples, guardian of ...... IDUN,
ITHUN, HESPERID
ball, king's .... MOUND
color .... DORE
combining form ..... CHRYS(O)
king .... MIDAS
shiner .... DACE, ROACH
token .... WEDDING RING
Golden Age .... MILLENIUM
Boy author .... ODETS
Fleece keeper .... AEETES
Fleece maiden .... HELLE
Fleece searcher .... JASON,
ARGONAUT
Fleece ship .... ARGO
Treasury item ..... ODE, POEM,
SONNET
goldeneye .... BIRD, WHISTLER
goldenrod .... SOLIDAGO
goldfinger, mythological
.... MIDAS
Goldfinger hero .... BOND

goldfinch .... BIRD, REDCAP
goldfinny .... CUNNER
goldfish .... COMET, FANTAIL
Goldie .... HAWN
goldilocks .... BUTTERCUP
Goldsmith, poet .... OLIVER
golem .... ROBOT, AUTOMATON
golf aid .... CADDY, CADDIE
area around the hole
.... GREEN
area for an astronaut
.... MOON
bag item .... TEE, CLUB,
WOOD, IRONS, WEDGE,
PUTTER, CRYING TOWEL
ball material .... BALATA
ball's position .... LIE
"Bantam Ben" of .... BEN
HOGAN
championship cup ...... RYDER
club ..... WOOD, CLEEK, IRONS,
SPOON, BULGER, DRIVER,
JIGGER, MASHIE, PUTTER,
BRASSIE, NIBLICK, (MID)IRON
club part .... TOE, HOSEL
course .... GREEN, LINKS
course hazard .... POND,
WATER, BUNKER, STYMIE,
(SAND)TRAP
eagled a par-three hole in
.... ACED
feat ...... EAGLE, BIRDIE, HOLE-
IN-ONE
first to earn $100,000 in
.... ARNOLD PALMER
goof .... SLICE
hole .... CUP
holes unplayed .... BYE
instructor .... PRO
"Merry Mex" of .... LEE
TREVINO
partner, legendary ...... BOGEY
player Aaron .... TOMMY
Albus .... JIM
Alfredsson .... HELEN
Andrade .... BILLY
Andrews .... DONNA
Aoki .... ISAO
Archer .... GEORGE
Azinger .... PAUL
Baker-Finch .... IAN
Ballesteros .... SEVE
Beck .... CHIP
Bowen .... NANCY
Bradley .... PAT
Brooks .... MARK
Burton .... BRANDIE
Calcavecchia .... MARK
Casper .... BILLY
Charles .... BOB
Clements .... LENNIE

Coe-Jones .... DAWN
Colbert .... JIM
Cook .... JOHN
Couples .... FRED
Crenshaw .... BEN
Crosby .... ELAINE
Daly .... JOHN
Daniel .... BETH
Davies .... LAURA
Dent .... JIM
Descampe .... FLORENCE
Devlin .... BRUCE
Dickinson .... JUDY
Dormann .... DANA
Douglass .... DALE
Duval .... DAVID
Eichelberger .... DAVE
Elkington .... STEVE
Els .... ERNIE
Estes .... BOB
Faldo .... NICK
Faxon .... BRAD
Floyd .... RAY(MOND)
Frost .... DAVID
Funk .... FRED
Gallagher, Jr. .... JIM
Gamez .... ROBERT
Geddes .... JANE
Geiberger .... AL
Gilbert .... LARRY
Green .... TAMMIE
Hill .... MIKE
Hogan .... BEN
Irwin .... HALE
Jacklin .... TONY
Jacobsen .... PETER
Janzen .... LEE
Johnson .... CHRIS, TRISH
Jones .... BOB, ROBERT
Kean .... LAUREL
King .... BETSY
Kite .... TOM
Kobayashi .... HIROMI
Langer .... BERNHARD
Lehman .... TOM
Levi .... WAYNE
Lietzke .... BRUCE
Littler .... GENE
Lopez .... NANCY
Love III .... DAVIS
Maggert .... JEFF
Mallon .... MEG
McGann .... MICHELLE
Merten .... LAURI
Mickelson .... PHIL
Miller .... JOHNNY
Mize .... LARRY
Mochrie .... DOTTIE
Montgomerie .... COLIN
Murphy .... BOB
Nelson .... LARRY

Neumann .... LISELOTTE
Nicklaus .... JACK
Norman .... GREG
Olazabal .... JOSE MARIA
O'Meara .... MARK
Ozaki .... MASASHI
Palmer .... ARNIE, ARNOLD
Pate .... JERRY
Pavin .... COREY
Peete .... CALVIN
Perry .... KENNY
Player .... GARY
Price .... NICK
Ritzman .... ALICE
Robbins .... KELLY
Roberts .... LOREN
Rodriguez .... CHI-CHI
Sanders .... DOUG
Sauers .... GENE
Sheehan .... PATTY
Sigel .... JAY
Singh .... VIJAY
Skinner .... VAL
Snead .... SAM, JC
Stadler .... CRAIG
Steinhauer .... SHERRI
Stephenson .... JAN
Stewart .... PAYNE
Stockton .... DAVE
Strange .... CURTIS
Stricker .... STEVE
Sutton .... HAL
Thompson .... ROCKY
Trevino .... LEE
Venturi .... KEN
Wadkins .... LANNY
Waldorf .... DUFFY
Wargo .... TOM
Watson .... TOM
Woosnam .... IAN
Zarley .... KERMIT
Zembriski .... WALTER
Zoeller .... FUZZY
problem .... STYMIE
score ...... PAR, BOGEY, EAGLE,
BIRDIE
stroke .... BAFF, CHIP, FADE,
HOOK, LOFT, PUTT, DRIVE,
SLICE, SCLAFF
stroke by a duffer .... BAFF
stroke over par .... BOGEY
term .... OB, LIE, TEE, PAR,
BAFF, BONE, FADE, FORE,
HOLE, HOOK, LOFT, PUTT,
GALLERY, TRAP, BOGEY,
DIVOT, FLAG, DRIVE, EAGLE,
GREEN, STYMIE, ROUGH, SLICE,
BIRDIE, BISQUE, DORMIE,
HAZARD, DOGLEG, FAIRWAY,
CHILI DIP
tourney ..... OPEN, SKINS, PRO-

AM, MASTERS, SENIORS
tourney played for honor
.... RYDER CUP
turf .... DIVOT
VIP .... PRO
Golf, "Golden Bear" of
.... NICKLAUS
"Great White Shark" of
.... NORMAN
"King" of .... PALMER
Masters champion .... BEN
HOGAN, SAM SNEAD, TOM
WATSON, GARY PLAYER, LEE
TREVINO, TOMMY AARON,
GENE SARAZEN, ARNOLD
PALMER, CHARLES COODY,
JACK NICKLAUS
golfer .... HAAS, KITE, TEER,
AARON, COODY, FALDO,
FLOYD, GREEN, HAGEN,
HOGAN, IRWIN, DALY, JONES,
MOODY, PAVIN, SNEAD,
CASPER, LANGER, MILLER,
NELSON, NORMAN, OMEARA,
OUIMET, PALMER, PLAYER,
PRUITT, SUTTON, WATSON,
AZINGER, COUPLES, JACKLIN,
LITTLER, MANGRUM,
SANDERS, SARAZEN, STEWART,
STRANGE, TREVINO, WADKINS,
WOOSNAM, ZOELLER,
CRENSHAW, NICKLAUS,
CRAMPTON, OLAZABAL,
RODRIGUEZ, BALLESTEROS,
CALCAVECCHIA, GEIBERGER,
DIVOT DIGGER
adviser of, sometimes
.... CADDIE
attire of .... KNICKERS
cry of .... FORE
goal of .... CUP
poor .... DUBBER, HACKER
golfer's org. .... PGA, USGA
golfing glory .... EAGLES
Golgotha .... CALVARY
goliard .... JESTER, MINSTREL
Goliath .... GIANT, PHILISTINE
home of .... GATH
move of .... GIANT STEP
slayer of .... DAVID
golliwogg .... DOLL, OGRE
Golly! .... GEE, GOSH
Gomer's husband .... HOSEA
gomuti .... EJOO, PALM, SAGO
palm .... ARENG(A)
gonad .... OVARY, SPERMARY
gonagra .... GOUT
gondola .... BARGE, CABIN,
(CANAL)BOAT
man .... POLER, BOATMAN
race .... REGATTA

gondolier .... BOATMAN
song of .... BARCAROLE
work of .... POLING, ROWING
gone .... UP, AGO, OFF, OUT,
AWAY, DEAD, LOST, USED,
RUINED, CONSUMED
by .... PAST, PASSED
Gone with the Wind character
.... ASHLEY, MELANIE,
(RHETT)BUTLER,
(SCARLETT)O'HARA
goner .... DEAD DUCK
Goneril's father .... LEAR
sister .... REGAN, CORDELIA
gonfalon .... FLAG, BANNER,
ENSIGN
gong .... BELL, CYMBAL, TAMTAM,
TOCSIN
gonof/gonoph .... THIEF
gonorrhea .... CLAP
goo .... GLUE, SLUDGE
goober .... PEANUT
grease .... PEANUT BUTTER
good .... BON, MORAL, PUCKA,
SOUND, VALID, USEFUL,
GENUINE, LAUDABLE,
SUITABLE, EFFICIENT,
UNSPOILED
doing .... BENEFICENT
-for-nothing fellow .... BUM,
IDLER, ROGUE, LOAFER,
WASTREL, VAGABOND, NE'ER-
DO-WELL
health .... PEART
humored .... JOLLY
looking .... FAIR, COMELY,
PRETTY, HANDSOME
luck bringer .... MASCOT
luck present .... HANDSEL
man .... MODEL, PARAGON
natured .... AMIABLE,
PLEASANT, EASYGOING
news .... GOSPEL, EVANGEL
order .... EUTAXY
point! .... TOUCHE
references .... CLEAN SLATES
sense .... WIT, JUDGMENT
slang .... SWELL
taste, of .... ESTHETIC
time .... BALL, BASH, SPREE
turn .... FAVOR
will .... GREE
Good Book .... BIBLE
Friday song of Andalusia
.... SAETA
Shepherd .... JESUS
goodbye .... TATA, ADIEU, AU
REVOIR, SO LONG, FAREWELL
Goodbye, Columbus author
.... ROTH
goodly .... AMPLE, SIZABLE,

PLEASING, SPLENDID

goodman ...... MASTER, HUSBAND

goodness .... MERIT, WORTH, VIRTUE, BLESSING, KINDNESS

gracious! .... HEAVENS

goods .... STOCK, WARES, EFFECTS, MERCHANDISE

cast overboard .... LAGAN, LIGAN, JETSAM, LAGEND, JETTISON

deliver the ...... FULFILL, COME ACROSS

movable .... CHATTEL

on hand .... STOCK, INVENTORY

sold together .... TIE-IN

goody .... CANDY

goocy .... STICKY

goof .... DOLT, FAIL, BONER, ERR(OR), BOBBLE, BLUNDER

on diamond .... MUFF, FUMBLE

goofy .... GIDDY, SILLY, STUPID, FOOLISH

Google .... BARNEY

gook .... ORIENTAL, VIETCONG

goon .... THUG, RUFFIAN, HOOD(LUM), ROUGHNECK

goop's inventor .... BURGESS

goosander .... DUCK, MERGANSER

goose .... BRANT, IDIOT, SOLAN, GRAYLAG, BARNACLE, BERNICLE

colloquial .... DUPE, GULL

cry .... HONK, CACKLE

domestic, large .... EMDEN

eggs .... 000, ZERO(S)

foot membrane ..... WEB(BING)

footless .... GANNET

genus .... ANSER

grease .... AXUNGE

male .... GANDER

of a .... ANSERINE

pygmy .... GOSLET

sound .... HISS, CACKLE

stepper .... GERMAN

steppers march, how

.... STIFFLY

young .... GOSLING

gooseberry .... POHA, FABES

goosefoot .... BEET, SPINACH

gooseneck .... LAMP

goose-pimply .... EERIE

gopher .... RODENT, SUSLIK, TORTOISE

tortoise .... MUNGOFA

Gopher .... MINNESOTAN

State .... MINNESOTA

gorcock .... GROUSE

Gordian knot cutter

.... ALEXANDER

Gordon .... RUTH, FLASH

Gordon's killer .... MAHDI

gore .... STAB, BLOOD, CRUOR, INSET, GUSSET, PIERCE

gorge .... CLOY, CLUT, GULP, PASS, SATE, CHASM, FLUME, GULLY, KLOOF, STUFF, CANYON, CLOUGH, GULLET, RAVINE, COULOIR, BARRANCA, GORMANDIZE

gorgeous .... SUPERB, SPLENDID, BEAUTIFUL, RESPLENDENT

Gorgeous Gussie .... MORAN

gorget .... COLLAR

Gorgon .... MEDUSA, STHENO, EURYALE, JEZEBEL

Gorgons' mother .... CETO

watchers .... GRAEAE

gorilla .... APE, TROGLODYTE

slang .... GOON, GANGSTER

walk .... SHAMBLE

Gorki, novelist .... MAXIM

gormandize .... GORGE, GUTTLE

gormandizer .... FEASTER

gorse .... WHIN, FURZE, SHRUB

gory .... BLOODY

Gosh! .... GEE, GOLLY, PSHAW

goshawk .... BUTEO

Goshen race .... TROT

gospel .... DOGMA, TRUTH, EVANGEL, DOCTRINE, EVANGILE

preaching .... EVANGELISM

writer ...... JOHN, LUKE, MARK, MATTHEW

gossamer ...... FILM(Y), (COB)WEB

gossamery .... THIN, FILMY, GAUZY, DIAPHANOUS

gossip .... CAT, EME, BUZZ, TALK, RUMORS, TIDBIT, TITBIT, BLAB(BER), HEARSAY, CHITCHAT, BUSYBODY, CHATTER(ER), TATTLE(R), SCUTTLEBUTT

bit of .... ONDIT

column unit .... ITEM

malicious .... SLANDER, BACKBITING

slang .... JAW

gossoon .... BOY

Gotcha! .... AHA, OHO

Goth .... ALARIC, BARBARIAN

Gothic .... BARBAROUS

arch .... OGIVE

architecture feature ..... GABLE

bard .... RUNER

Goths' bishop .... ULFILA(S)

Gotland seaport .... VISBY

Gouda .... CHEESE

gouge .... BENT, ROUT, CHEAT, CHISEL, GROOVE, (DE)FRAUD, IMPOSTOR, SWINDLE(R)

goulash .... HASH, STEW, RAGOUT

Gounod opera .... FAUST

opera hero .... ROMEO

gourd ...... PEPO, MELON, SQUASH, PUMPKIN, CALABASH, CURCURBIT

pod's substance .... LOOFAH

rattle .... MARACA

shell .... CALABASH

gourmand .... EPICURE, GLUTTON, GOURMET

anathema to a .... DIET

gourmet .... TASTER, EPICURE, GO(U)RMAND, GASTRONOME

paradise in London ...... SOHO

gout .... GONAGRA, PODAGRA, BURSITIS, ARTHRITIS

remedy .... GUACO

govern .... RUN, RULE, REIGN, GUIDE, DIRECT, MANAGE, CONTROL, PRESIDE, MODERATE

archaic .... REGLE

badly .... MISRULE

governess .... NANNY, DUENNA

government .... RULE, STATE, POLITY, ECONOMY, REGENCY, REGIME(N), ADMINISTRATION

agent .... SPY

declaration .... MANIFESTO

fiscal problem .... BUDGET

grant ...... SUBSIDY, FRANCHISE

of a .... NATIONAL

of 2 rulers .... DIARCHY

report .... BLUE BOOK, WHITE PAPER

safety net .... WELFARE

seat .... CAPITAL

without .... ACRACY

governor .... RULER, EPARCH, VICEROY, REGULATOR

gowan .... DAISY

gown .... ROBE, DRESS, FROCK, SMOCK, MANTUA, NEGLIGEE

loose, worn in Middle Ages

.... KIRTLE

outer .... SURCOAT

goy .... GENTILE

Gozo's neighbor .... MALTA

GP .... DR., DOCTOR

org. of .... AMA

Graafian follicle .... OVISAC

grab .... HOG, TAKE, ANNEX, SEIZE, SNATCH, CAPTURE

Gracchus' brother .... GAIUS

grace ...... TACT, ADORN, CHARM, FAVOR, MERCY, BEAUTY, ATTEND, PRAYER, DECENCY, DIGNIFY, CHARISMA, COURTESY

kind of ..... RESPITE, REPRIEVE,

MORATORIUM
note .... INCIDENTAL
Grace .... KELLY
graceful .... SVELTE, LISSOME,
WILLOWY
bird .... SWAN
creature .... DEER, GAZELLE
piercing wit .... ATTIC SALT
graceless .... CLUMSY, AWKWARD,
INELEGANT
Graces, mother of .... AEGLE
one of the .... JOY, AGLAIA,
THALIA, EUPHROSYNE
gracile .... SLIM, SLENDER
gracious .... BENIGN, GENIAL,
POLITE, URBANE, MERCIFUL
grackle .... DAW, MINA, MYNA(H),
TINKLING, TROUPIAL,
BLACKBIRD
grad .... ALUM
gradate .... BLEND
gradation .... ABLAUT, DEGREE,
NUANCE
grade .... MARK, RANK, RATE,
STEP, LEVEL, DEGREE,
RATING, INCLINE
grader .... PUPIL
gradient .... SLOPE
gradin .... SEAT, STEP, SHELF
gradual .... MODERATE,
LEISURELY, PROGRESSIVE
fall .... DECLINE
reducer .... TAPERER
graduate .... GRAD, PASS,
ALUMNUS
graduated .... SCALAR
glass tube .... BURETTE
graduation ceremony
.... COMMENCEMENT
certificate .... DIPLOMA
dangler .... TASSEL
duo .... CAP AND GOWN
wear .... CLASS RING
Graeae, concern of the
.... GORGONS
describing the .... ONE-EYED
one of the .... DEINO
parent of .... PHORCUS
Graf .... COUNT
graffiti .... SCRAWLS
graft .... BUD, IMP, CLAVE,
(S)CION, INARCH,
CORRUPTION, CROSSBREED,
TRANSPLANT
Graham .... BILLY, MARTHA
grail .... AMA, CUP, CHALICE,
PLATTER
Grail, Holy .... SANGRAAL,
SANGREAL
grain .... BIT, OAT, RYE, CORN,
CURN, MEAL, RICE, SEED,

WALE, SPELT, WHEAT,
CEREAL, KERNEL, KERMES,
MILLET
basket .... SCUTTLE
beard .... AWN, ARISTA
beetle .... CADELLE
black .... URD
building .... GRANARY
chaff .... BRAN
combining form .... GRANI
cracked .... GROATS
cutter .... SCYTHE
disease .... SMUT, ERGOT
elevator .... SILO
exchange .... PIT
fungus .... ERGOT
ground .... SAMP, GRIST, GRITS
hulled .... GRITS, GROATS
husk .... BRAN, GLUME
in kernels .... CORN, MAIZE,
MEALIES
Indian .... CORN, MAIZE
loss through spillage
.... ULLAGE
measure .... MOY, SACK,
CAVAN, CHUPA, GANTA,
BUSHEL, QUARTER
mill .... MANO, QUERN
outer covering .... HUSK
pest .... CADELLE
refuse .... SCOURINGS
row, drying .... WINDROW
shelter .... HUTCH
small .... GRANULE
sorghum .... MILO, KAF(F)IR
stack .... MOW
storehouse .... SILO, GARNER,
GRANARY, ELEVATOR
stumps .... STUBBLE
grains .... SPEAR
3.17 .... CARAT
grainy .... MEALY, GRITTY,
GRANULAR
gram .... PLANT, CHICK-PEA
molecule .... MOL(E)
grama .... GRASS
gramercy .... THANKS
grammar ...... SYNTAX, WORDING,
ACCIDENCE, PHRASEOLOGY
causal connective .... FOR,
SINCE, THEREFORE
expert .... GRAMMARIAN
set of examples/exercises
.... PRAXIS
tense .... PAST, FUTURE,
PERFECT, PRESENT, PAST
PERFECT
grammarian .... PROSODIST
grammatical case .... DATIVE
construction .... SYNTAX,
SYNESIS

description/exercise ..... PARSE
divider .... PARAGRAPH
error .... SOLECISM
goof .... AINT
mark .... ASPER
term .... CASE, MODE, MOOD,
PARSE, STYLE, TENSE, GENDER,
DICTION, CONJUGATE,
PUNCTUATE
gramophone .... VICTROLA,
PHONOGRAPH
grampus .... ORC(A), WHALE,
COWFISH, SPRINGER
relative .... DOLPHIN
Granada, king of .... BOADBIL
granary .... BIN, CRIB, GOLA,
SILO, GARNER, GRANGE,
ELEVATOR, STOREHOUSE
grand ...... LARGE, LOFTY, PIANO,
AUGUST, STATELY, IMPOSING,
MAJESTIC, IMPRESSIVE
jury's word .... IGNORAMUS
mal .... FIT, EPILEPSY
slam .... VOLE, JACKPOT
theft .... LARCENY
Grand _____ .... OLE OPRY
Canal bridge .... RIALTO
Coulee designer .... SAVAGE
Lama .... DALAI LAMA
National site .... AINTREE
Old Party member
.... REPUBLICAN
Pre heroine .... EVANGELINE
grandam .... CRONE
grandchild .... OYE
Grande and others .... RIOS
or Bravo .... RIO
grandee .... PEER, NOBLEMAN
grandeur .... GLORY, DIGNITY,
MAJESTY, EMINENCE,
SPLENDOR
grandfather .... ATAVUS,
PATRIARCH
pertaining to .... AVAL,
AVITAL
grandiloquence .... BOMBAST
grandiloquent .... MAGNIFIC
grandiose .... EPIC, HOMERIC,
POMPOUS, IMPOSING,
BOMBASTIC
Grandma Moses .... ANNA
grandmother .... NANA, GRANNY,
BELDAM(E), GRANDMA
grandparents, having same
.... GERMAN
of/pertaining to .... AVAL
grandson .... NEPOTE
grandstand .... BLEACHERS
play .... STUNT
grange ...... RED, FARM, GRANARY
granger .... FARMER

granite .... ROCK, APLITE, BIOTITE, MUSCOVITE
rock resembling .... GNEISS
granny .... KNOT, GRANDMA
grant .... GIFT, GIVE, AWARD, YIELD, ASSENT, CONFER, PATENT, PERMIT, (CON)CEDE, CONSENT, (RE)MISE, APPANAGE
advance .... SECURE LOAN
by will .... DEMISE
of money .... SUBSIDY, ENDOWMENT
temporary use .... LEND
Grant, U.S. president
.... ULYSSES
granted .... EVEN SO
grantee .... RECIPIENT
Grantland .... RICE
grantor .... DONOR
granular .... SANDY, GRAINY
granulate .... CORN, COARSEN, ROUGHEN
grape .... UVA, BERRY, PINOT, TOKAY, ACINUS, MALAGA, MUSCAT, WAMPEE, CATAWBA, CONCORD, MALMSEY, NIAGARA, DELAWARE, ISABELLA, MALVASIA, MUSCADINE
acid from .... UVIC
coating .... BLOOM
disease .... ESCA, ERINOSE
dried .... PASA, RAISIN
fruit, dried .... CURRANT
jam .... UVATE
jelly .... SAPA
juice .... DIBS, MUST, SAPA, STUM
juice, unfermented .... STUM
juice deposit .... TARTAR
juice liquor .... RAKI, RAKEE
like .... UVA(L), UVIC
preserve .... UVATE
pulp .... RAPE, POMACE
refuse .... MARC, BAGASSE
seed .... ACINUS
sugar ...... GLUCOSE, MALTOSE, DEXTROSE
grapefruit ...... POMELO, PUMELO, SHADDOCK
grapes, art of growing
.... VITICULTURE
bunch .... BOB, BOTRYOID
harvester .... VINTAGER
where grown .... VINEYARD
Grapes of Wrath author
.... STEINBECK
character .... AL, JIM, JOAD, NOAH, OKIE, ROSE, CASEY, CONNIE

grapevine: colloq. ...... HEARSAY, PIPELINE, RUMOR(MILL)
graph .... CHART, DIAGRAM
graphic .... CLEAR, VIVID, LIFELIKE, PICTORIAL
art .... OFFSET, DRAWING, ETCHING, DRYPOINT, PAINTING, PHOTOGRAPHY
style .... ITALICS
graphite .... KISH, LEAD, CARBON, PLUMBAGO
graplin .... CRAMPON
grapnel .... DRAG, ANCHOR, CREEPER, GRAPLIN(E)
grapple .... GRIP, HOLD, LOCK, GRASP, CLUTCH, WRESTLE
grappler .... WRESTLER
grappling iron .... CRAMPON, GRAPLIN, GRAPNEL
grasp ...... SEE, GRAB, GRIP, HENT, HOLD, CLASP, SEIZE, CLUTCH, UNDERSTAND
grass .... OAT, POA, RIE, RYE, CORN, LAWN, NARD, REED, AVENA, BROME, GRAMA, GRAZE, SEDGE, SORGO, WHEAT, BAMBOO, BARLEY, DARNEL, FESCUE, QUITCH, REDTOP, FOXTAIL, PASTURE, VETIVER, ZACATON
Algerian .... ESPARTO
Asiatic .... MILLET
Australian .... ULLA
blade .... SPEAR
blue .... POA
brooms .... ZACATON
bunch .... TUFT
cereal .... OAT, RYE, RICE, RAG(G)I, MILLET, RAGGEE, SORGHUM
clump ...... HASSOCK, TUSSOCK
corn .... KAF(F)IR
country .... VELD(T)
covered soil ...... TURF, SWARD
cutter .... REAPER, SCYTHE, (LAWN)MOWER
dried .... HAY
for thatch .... NETI, ALANG
forage .... GAMA, SORGO, MILLET, REDTOP, SORGHUM, TEOSINTE
genus ...... POA, AVENA, STIPA, SECALE
growth, new .... FOG
hay .... TIMOTHY
husk .... GLUME
Kentucky .... POA, BLUE
killer .... DOWPON, ESTERON
kind of .... ANKEE, BERMUDA
lawn .... REDTOP
leaf .... BLADE, SPEAR

marsh .... REED, SEDGE, SPART, FESCUE
meadow .... POA, FESCUE
mesquite .... GRAMA
moor .... HEATH
ornamental .... EULALIA
paper-making .... ESPARTO
pasture .... GRAMA, FESCUE, REDTOP
pertaining to .... POACEOUS
poisonous .... DARNEL
quaking .... BRIZA
rope-making .... MUNG
rye .... DARNEL, MARCITE
scale .... PALEA
second crop .... ROWEN
sour .... SORREL
swamp .... REED, SEDGE
uncut/ungrazed .... FOG
widow .... DIVORCEE
wiry .... BENT
grasshopper .... GRIG, LOCUST, CRICKET, KATYDID
grassland .... LEA, MEAD, CAMPO, PAMPA, RANGE, SWARD, VELD(T), PASTURE, PRAIRIE, SAVANNA(H)
grassy .... TURFY
ground .... TURF
plain .... CAMPO
grate .... JAR, RUB, FRET, RASP, ANNOY, GRIDE, GRIND, ABRADE, SCRAPE, SCROOP, IRRITATE, FIREPLACE
grateful ...... OBLIGED, BEHOLDEN, THANKFUL
Grateful Dead late lead
guitarist ...... (JERRY) GARCIA
grater .... PEST, VEXER, ANNOYER, CRUSHER, GRINDER
gratification ...... EASE, COMFORT, SATISFACTION
gratify .... SATE, HUMOR, PLEASE, REWARD, INDULGE, SATISFY
gratifying .... PLEASING
gratin .... CRUST
grating .... RASPY, GRILL(E), HOARSE, LATTICE, RASPING, ANNOYING, GRID(IRON)
gratis .... FREE, GRATUITOUS
gratitude ...... THANKS, REQUITAL, APPRECIATION
gratuitous .... FREE, GRATIS
gratuity .... FEE, TIP, BOON, GIFT, PILON, CUMSHAW, PRESENT, VAIL, STIPEND, LAGN(I)APPE, PERQUISITE
graupel .... HAIL, SNOW, SLEET
gravamen .... CHARGE, COMPLAINT, GRIEVANCE
grave ...... TOMB, MOUND, SOBER,

STAID, SEDATE, SOLEMN, SOMBER, OMINOUS, SERIOUS, WEIGHTY, MAUSOLEUM, SEPULCHER

cloth .... SHROUD, CEREMENT

danger .... PERIL

digger .... SEXTON

heap of earth/stone .... MOUND, TUMULUS

marker .... STELE, BARROW, HEADSTONE

robber .... GHOUL

gravel .... SAND, HECKLE, RUBBLE, STONES, PEBBLES, CALCULUS

a boat .... BEACH, GROUND

deposit .... ESKER, GEEST

mound .... OS

ridges .... OSAR

shifter .... RIDDLE

graven ...... CARVED, SCULPTURED

image ...... ICON, IDOL, IKON

Gravenstein .... APPLE

graver .... BURIN, CARVER, CHASER, CHISEL, ETCHER, SCULPTOR

Graves' disease .... GOITER

gravestone .... SLAB, STELA, STELE, BARROW, MARKER, MEMORIAL

graveyard .... CEMETERY

gravid .... PREGNANT

gravitate .... DROP, FALL, SINK, SETTLE

gravity .... BURDEN, WEIGHT, PRESSURE, SOLEMNITY, SERIOUSNESS

gravy .... JUS, SAUCE, PROFIT

thickener .... ROUX

gray .... OLD, DULL, ASHEN, DISMAL, BLEAK, HOAR(Y), DREARY, GRIZZLE

brownish .... TAUPE

hair .... GRIZZLE

matter ...... BRAINS, THALAMUS

mole .... TAUPE

grayish .... SLATY

blue .... BICE, TEAL, LIVID, PERSE, AZURINE

brown .... DUN, TAUPE

tan .... BEIGE

graylag .... GOOSE

grayling .... FISH, TROUT, UMBER, BUTTERFLY

graze .... RUB, AGIST, BRUSH, TOUCH, BROWSE, SCRAPE, PASTURE, GLANCE(OFF), SCRATCH

with bullet .... CREASE

grazing land .... (G)RANGE, RANCH(O), PASTURE

rope .... LARIAT, TETHER

grease .... FAT, OIL, DAUB, COOM, LARD, SUET, AXUNGE, LUBRICATE

elbow .... EFFORT

monkey .... MECHANIC

refuse .... SLUSH

slang .... TIP, BRIBE, FLATTERY

greasewood .... CHICO, ORACHE

greasy ...... OILY, FATTY, PINGUID

great .... HUGE, UNCO, MAGNA, NOBLE, INTENSE, TITANIC, IMPOSING, PROFOUND, SUPER(IOR)

artist .... MASTER

artistic work .... MASTER(PIECE)

care .... PAINS

combining form .... MAGNI, MEGA(LO)

grandchild .... IER

grief .... HEARTBREAK

number .... ARMY, HOST, LOTS, HORDE, GALAXY, LEGION

omentum .... CAUL

success .... HIT

toe .... HALLUX

Great Barrier reef/island .... OTEA

Bear .... URSA

Commoner .... CLAY, PITT, BRYAN, STEVENS

Dane .... DOG

Divide .... DEATH, CRISIS

Lakes .... ERIE, HURON, ONTARIO, ST. CLAIR, MICHIGAN, SUPERIOR

Lakes boat .... MACKINAW, WHALEBACK

Lakes fish .... PIKE, CISCO, TULLIBEE, MASKALONGE

Profile .... BARRYMORE

Spirit, Indian .... MANITO

White Father .... PRESIDENT

White Way .... RIALTO, BROADWAY

greatcoat .... PALETOT

Greater Antilles island .... CUBA, JAMAICA, HISPANIOLA, PUERTO RICO

greatest .... BEST, UTMOST, VERIEST, MATCHLESS

amount .... LION'S SHARE

athlete in the world, considered .... DECATHLON WINNER

greatly .... HIGHLY, LARGELY

greaves .... ARMOR, CRACKNEL, CRACKLINGS

grebe .... LOON, GOGOL, DIPPER, DABCHICK, DIDAPPER

Grecian .... GRECO, GREEK,

HELLENIC

theater .... ODEUM

Greco-Egyptian deity .... SERAPIS

Turkish dispute, object of .... CYPRUS

Greece .... ELIS, ACHAEA, ATTICA, HELLAS

of modern .... ROMAIC

prime minister of ...... MITSOTAKIS, PAPANDREOU

to a Greek .... ELLAS

greed(iness) .... AVARICE, AVIDITY, EDACITY, CUPIDITY, GLUTTONY

greedy ...... COVETOUS, ESURIENT, GRASPING, RAVENOUS, VORACIOUS, AVARICIOUS

one .... MISER

Greek .... ATTIC, ARGIVE, CRETAN, IONIAN, ACHAEAN, AEOLIAN, HELLENE, ATHENIAN, HELLENIC

abbess .... AMMA

actor's boot .... BUSKIN

after piece .... EXODE

ancient city .... ELEA

ancient urn .... OLPE

apartment .... ANDRON

architect .... ICTINUS

assembly .... AGORA, BOULE, EKKLESIA

athlete .... MILO

athletic contest .... AGON

Aurora .... EOS

author .... ZENO, AESOP, HOMER, PLATO, TIMON, PINDAR, SAPPHO, PLUTARCH

avenging spirit ..... ATE, FURY, ERINYS

battle site .... MARATHON

bee .... MELISSA

belt .... ZOSTER

beverage .... OENOMEL

bishop .... EPARCH

boatman .... PHAON

bottle .... AMPULLA

bridesmaid .... PARANYMPH

buckle .... FIBULA

canal .... CORINTH

cape .... KRIOS, MALEA, VOUXA, SPATHA, AKRITAS, MATAPAN, KAFIREVS, SIDHEROS, TAINARON

capital .... ATHENS

Catholic .... UNIAT(E)

channel .... EURIPUS

Church, father of ...... ORIGEN

citadel .... ACROPOLIS

city/town .... ARTA, ARGOS, CANEA, DRAMA, KHIOS, LAMIA, NEMEA, POROS,

SAMOS, VOLOS, ALYION, CANDIA, KHANIA, KOZANI, LARISA, MEGARA, NAOUSA, PATRAI, PIRGOS, RODHOS, SERRAI, SPARTA, THIVAI, XANTHI, CORINTH, ELASSON, KALAMAI, KAVALLA, KERKIRA, KHALKIS, PIRAEUS, PREVEZA, SALAMIS, VERROIA, AGRINION, IRAKLION, KASTORIA, KATERINI, KOMOTINI, MITILLNI, SALONIKA, TIRNAVOS, TRIKKALA, TRIPOLIS, YIANNITSA, THESSALONIKI

city in Asia Minor .... MELETUS
city in Italy .... SYBARIS
clan .... ODE
clasp .... FIBULA
classical name .... DANAI
coin .... OBOL(I), DRACHMA, LEPTON, STATER, OBOLUS
colony .... ELEA, IONIA
column .... DORIC, IONIC
comic poet .... MENANDER
commonalty/commune .... DEME, DEMOS
concert hall .... ODEUM
contest/games .... AGON
counselor .... NESTOR
country .... ELIS, EPIRUS
courtesan ..... THAIS, HETAERA
cross design ..... SWASTIKA
cry of sorrow .... AI AI
cup .... DEPAS, SCYPHUS
dance .... PYRRHIC
dialect .... DORIC, IONIC, (A)EOLIC
dirge .... LINOS
Discordia .... ATE
district .... AONIA, ATTICA, LOCRIS, ARGOLIS, MEGARIS
earth .... GEOS
elevation .... OSSA
enchantress ..... CIRCE, MEDEA
epic poem .... ILIAD, ODYSSEY, RHAPSODY
fabulist .... AESOP
farce .... MIME
Fates, one of .... CLOTHO, ATROPO, LACHESS
feather .... PTERON
festival .... AGON, DELIA, DIONYSIA
festival, ancient .... HALOA
flask .... OLPE
garment .... CHITON, PEPLOS, CHLAMYS
geographer .... STRABO
ghost .... KER
giant .... ARGUS, CACUS,

ORION, TITAN, CYCLOPS, BRIAREUS
giant wrestler .... ANTAEUS
girdle .... ZOSTER
god .... EOS, ARES, EROS, LETO, ZEUS, CHAOS, HYMEN, APOLLO, HELIOS, ONIROS, ARTEMIS, BACCHUS
earth .... BEL
festivity .... COMUS
fire .... VULCAN
flocks .... PAN
heaven(s) .... BEL, ZEUS, URANUS
hunter .... ORION
love .... EROS
marriage .... HYMEN
medicine .... ASCLEPIUS
mockery .... MOMUS
north wind .... BOREAS
rain .... ZEUS
revelry ..... COMUS, BACCHUS
river .... ERIDANUS
sea .... NEREUS, POSEIDON
sky .... ZEUS, ARGUS
sleep .... HYPNOS, HYPNUS
sun .... APOLLO, HELIOS, PHOEBUS
supreme .... ZEUS
wealth .... PLUTUS
winds .... EURUS, AEOLUS
wine .... DIONYSUS
war .... ARES
goddess .... DEA
agriculture .... ARTEMIS, DEMETER
air .... HERA
arts .... ATHENA
beauty .... APHRODITE
chance .... TYCHE
chase .... ARTEMIS
dawn .... EOS
destruction .... ARA
discord .... ERIS
earth .... GAEA, GAIA, HECATE
fate .... MOERA
flowers .... CHLORIS
ghosts .... HECATE
goblins .... ARTEMIS
health .... HYGEIA
hearth .... HESTIA
heavens .... HERA
hunting .... ARTEMIS
justice .... THEMIS
love .... APHRODITE
marriage .... GAIA, HERA, DEMETER
memory .... MNEMOSYNE
mischief .... ATE, ERIS
moon .... HECATE, SELENE,

ARTEMIS, ASTARTE
nature .... ARTEMIS
night .... NYX, LEDA, LETO
peace .... IRENE
retribution .... ARA, ATE
seas .... INO, DORIS
sky .... INO
sorcery .... HECATE
strife .... ERIS
vegetation ...... CORA, COTYS
vengeance ..... ARA, NEMESIS
victory .... NIKE
war .... ATHENA, BELLONA
weaving .... ERGANE
wisdom .... ATHENA, PALLAS
witchcraft .... HECATE
women .... HERA
youth .... HEBE
gods, queen of .... HERA
governor .... EPARCH
guerrilla ..... EAM, EDES, ELAS, KLEPHT
guest .... XENOS
gulf .... ARTA, KHANIA, MESARA, ARGOLIS, CORINTH, LAKONIA, MESSINI, SARONIC, SALONIKA, THERMAIC, TORONAIC, KIPARISSIA
gymnasium .... XYST, PAL(A)ESTRA
hat .... PETASOS, PETASUS
headband .... MITER, TAENIA
headland .... ACTIUM
heart .... KARDIA
hedgehog .... ECHINOS
hermit .... GILES
hero .... AJAX, IDAS, JASON, THESEUS, ALCINOUS
heroine .... LYSISTRATA
historian .... PLUTARCH, HERODOTUS
holy hill .... ATHOS
hunter: myth. .... ORION
huntress .... ATALANTA
immigrant .... METIC
initiate .... EPOPT(A)
island ...... DIA, IOS, KEA, KOS, SIMI, ANAFI, CORFU, CRETE, KASOS, KHIOS, KRITI, LEROS, MILOS, NAXOS, PAROS, PAXOI, PSARA, SAMOS, SARIA, SIROS, THIRA, TILOS, TINOS, ANDROS, EVVOIA, IKARIA, ITHAKI, LESVOS, LEVKAS, LIMNOS, PATMOS, RHODES, SKIROS, THASOS, AMORGOS, KERKIRA, KIMOLOS, MIKONOS, NISIROS, SERIFOS, SKORPIOS
Islands .... OLYMPIA, CYCLADES, DODECANESE
isthmus .... CORINTH

333

Greek

jar .... AMPHORA
jump .... HALMO
king of Arcadia .... LYCAON
king of Corinth ...... SISYPHUS
king of Crete ...... IDOMENEUS
lake .... VOLVI, PRESPA
language .... KOINE
leper .... LEPRA
leprosy .... ALPHOS
letter .... MU, NU, PI, XI, CHI,
ETA, PHI, PSI, RHO, TAU, BETA,
IOTA, ZETA, ALPHA, DELTA,
GAMMA, KAPPA, OMEGA,
SIGMA, THETA, LAMBDA,
EPSILON, OMICRON, UPSILON
lighthouse .... PHARE
liqueur .... OUZO
love feast .... AGAPE
magistrate .... EPHOR,
ARCHON, DIMIURGE
mantle .... PALLA, CHLAMYS,
PALLIUM, HIMATION
marketplace .... AGORA
marriage .... GAMOS, HYMEN
Mars .... ARES
masses .... DEMOS
mathematician .... EUCLID
measure .... PIC, PIK, BEMA,
PIKI, POUS, ACAENA
mecca .... RUINS
messenger of the gods
.... HERMES
metropolitan .... EPARCH
milestone .... HERMA
militia .... PALIKAR
Modern .... ROMAIC
monks' community ..... SKETE
money .... MINA, TALENT,
DRACHMA
monster: myth. .... HARPY,
HYDRA, LAMIA, SPHINX,
TYPHON, CHIMERA
moralist .... PLUTARCH
mountain ...... IDA, IDHI, OSSA,
ATHOS, PELION, HELICON,
OLYMPUS, PARNASSUS
mountain chain .... PINDUS,
RHODOPE
Muse .... CLIO, ERATO,
THALIA, URANIA, EUTERPE,
CALLIOPE, POLYMNIA
Muses' home .... AONIA
musician .... ARION
mythical flier .... ICARUS
mythical princess ...... EUROPA
native .... SCIOT, CYPRIOT
new .... NEOS
note in music .... NETE
nymph .... HESTIA, OENONE,
ARETHUSA, NEMERTES,
M(A)ENAD, SALMACIS,

(HAMA)DRYAD
official .... EPHOR
orator .... DEMOSTHENES
overseer .... EPHOR
painter .... GRECO, ZEUXIS
parliament .... ROULE
pastoral district .... ARCADIA
pastoral poet .... BION,
THEOCRITUS
patriarch .... ARIUS
peak .... OETA
peninsula .... ACTE, AKTI,
MOREA, SITHONIA, KASSANDRA
people/masses .... DEMOS
personification of conscience
.... AIDOS
philosopher ...... ZENO, PLATO,
TIMON, THALES, DIOGENES,
ARISTOTLE
physician .... GALEN
pillar .... HERMA
pitcher .... OLPE
place for discussions
.... EXEDRA
plain .... OLYMPIA
poem .... EPIC, EPODE, ILIAD,
ODYSSEY
poet .... ARION, HOMER,
HESIOD, PINDAR, ALCAEUS,
THESPIS, ANACREON,
MENANDER
poetess .... SAPPHO
poetry .... EPOS, MELIC
political unit .... EPARCHY
populace .... DEMOS
popular dish .... MOUSSAKA
port .... AULIS
portico .... STOA, XYST
premier .... PAPAGOS
princess .... IRENE
princess: myth. .... IOLE
province .... NOME
race .... GENOS
range .... OETA
region .... CRETE, DORIS,
EPIRUS, IONIAN, THRACE,
THESSALY, MACEDONIA
resistance group .... EAM,
EDES, ELAS
river ...... ARDA, ARTA, EVROS,
NESTOS, PINIOS, VARDAR
rose .... CAMPION
sacred grove .... ALTIS
satirist .... LUCIAN
scarf .... PEPLOS, PEPLUM
scientist .... ARCHIMEDES
sculptor .... MYRON, PHIDIAS
sea .... CRETE, AEGEAN,
IONIAN, MIRTOON
seaport .... ENOS, PATRAS,
SALONIKA

senate .... BOULE
serf .... PENEST
serpent: myth. .... PYTHON
seven .... ZETA
shawl .... PEPLOS, PEPLUM
shepherd, legendary
.... ENDYMION
shield .... PELTA
shipping tycoon ...... ONASSIS,
NIARCHOS
signpost .... HERMA
skeptic .... PYRRHO
skirt, men's .... FUSTANELLA
slave .... PENEST, HETAERA
soldier ...... HOPLITE, PELTAST,
PALIKAR
song .... MELOS
soothsayer .... CALCHAS,
TIRESIAS
sophist .... GORGIAS
sorceress .... CIRCE, MEDEA
soul .... PNEUMA
speaker's dais .... BEMA
spider .... ARACHNE
spirit .... PNEUMA
star .... ASTER
statesman .... PERICLES
Stoic philosopher
.... EPICTETUS
symbol .... ORANT
talking horse .... ARION
temple part .... NAOS, CELLA
theater .... ODEON
theologian .... ARIUS
thread, legendary .... CLEW
time .... CHRONOS
titan .... CRONUS, OCEANUS
town .... SERES
township .... DEME
tragedian .... THESPIS
tribe .... PHYLE
tribe subdivision ..... PHRATRY
troop unit .... TAXIS
trumpet .... SALPINX
underground army/group
.... EAM, EDES, ELAS
"unlucky" letter .... THETA
valley .... NEMEA, TEMPE
vase .... PYXIS, PELIKE
verb tense .... AOR(IST)
village .... MARATHON
war cry .... ALALA
warrior .... AJAX, ACAMAS,
ACHILLES, DIOMEDES,
ODYSSEUS
wedding song/poem
.... HYMEN(EAL)
weight .... MINA, OBOL(US)
who sold the Trojans on a
horse .... SINON
wine .... OENOMEL

wing .... PTERON
wise man ..... NESTOR, THALES
woman .... GYNE
word .... LOGOS
wrestling school
.... PAL(A)ESTRA
green ...... NEW, RAW, BICE, JADE,
NILE, VERT, FRESH, LEAFY,
NAIVE, OLIVE, CALLOW,
RESEDA, SIMPLE, UNRIPE,
EMERALD, VERDANT,
IMMATURE
action .... PUTT
area/spot .... OASIS
bright .... EMERALD
cheese .... SAPSAGO
eyed .... ENVIOUS, JEALOUS
film on copper .... PATINA
golden .... AENEOUS
land .... ERIN
light: colloq. .... OKAY,
PERMIT, GO-AHEAD,
AUTHORIZATION
manure .... CLOVER
room .... FOYER
room occupant .... ACTOR
sand .... MARL
shade of .... PEA, BICE, JADE,
LIME, BERYL, LODEN, OLIVE
sickness .... CHLOROSIS
stamp name .... EIRE
tail .... GRANNOM
vitriol .... COPPERAS
with vegetation .... VERDANT
Green Eggs and Ham author
.... (THEODOR SEUSS)GEISEL
Gables girl .... ANNE
Hat author .... ARLEN
Mansions character ...... ABEL,
RIMA
Mountain State ...... VERMONT
greenery .... VERDURE
greenheart .... TREE, BEBEERU
greenhorn .... DUPE, TYRO,
NOVICE, ROOKIE, BEGINNER
greenhouse .... VINERY,
HOTHOUSE, SOLARIUM,
VIVARIUM
greening .... APPLE
greenish .... LODEN, VIRESCENT
blue .... BICE, TEAL, NILE,
TURQUOISE
white .... RESEDA
Greenland base/town ...... THULE
capital .... GODTHAAB
discoverer .... ERIC
feature .... ICECAP
native .... ITA
town/settlement .... ETAH
greenlet .... VIREO, SONGBIRD
greenness .... NEWNESS, VERDURE,

VERDANCY, VIRIDITY
greens .... VEGETABLES
greenshank .... SANDPIPER
greensickness .... ANEMIA,
CHLOROSIS
greenstone .... JADE, WHIN,
DIORITE
greensward .... SOD, LAWN, TURF
greet .... HAIL, MEET, ACCOST,
ADDRESS, WELCOME,
ENTERTAIN
greeting .... AVE, (ALL)HAIL,
ALOHA, SALUTE, WELCOME,
SALUTATION
card .... VALENTINE
gregarious .... SOCIAL, OUTGOING,
SOCIABLE
grego .... CLOAK
Gregory, actor .... PECK
gremlin .... GNOME, MEDDLER
grenade .... BOMB, SHELL
grenadier .... FISH, INFANTRYMAN
grenadine .... SYRUP, FABRIC,
syrup, source of
.... POMEGRANATE
Grendel .... MONSTER
slayer of .... BEOWULF
Grenoble river .... ISERE
Gretchen .... MARGARET
Gretna Green arrivals
.... ELOPERS, SWEETHEARTS
Gretzky foe .... GOALIE
grew .... SPROUTED
Grey, author .... ZANE
greyhound .... BUS, DOG, SALUKI,
WHIPPET
arena .... DOG TRACK
grid .... GRATING, ELECTRODE
slang .... FOOTBALL
griddle .... PAN, GRID, PLATE,
GRILL(ER)
cake .... SCONE, PANCAKE,
FLAPJACK
gride .... JAR, RASP, GRATE,
SCRAPE
gridiron .... GRILL(E), GRATING,
FOOTBALL FIELD
scores, briefly .... TDS
grief .... WOE, PAIN, DOLOR,
MISERY, SORROW, DESPAIR,
SADNESS, DISTRESS
Grieg .... NORSE
character .... ASE
dancer .... ANITRA
grievance .... BEEF, GRIPE, SCORE,
WRONG, GRAVAMEN,
COMPLAINT, INJUSTICE,
RESENTMENT
grieve .... CRY, RUE, MOURN,
LAMENT, REPENT, SADDEN,
DEPLORE, DISTRESS

unconsolably .... EAT ONE'S
HEART OUT
grievous .... SAD, SEVERE,
INTENSE, FLAGRANT,
LAMENTABLE
griff(e) .... SPUR, MULATTO
griffon .... DOG, GYPS
grifter .... CONMAN
assistant .... SHILL
grig .... EEL, CRICKET
grill ...... BAR, QUIZ, RACK, BROIL,
ROAST, TAVERN, HIBACHI,
GRID(IRON), QUESTION,
INTERROGATE
device .... SPIT
meat-roasting ...... BUCCANEER
grilse .... FISH, SALMON
grim .... DOUR, CRUEL, STERN,
FIERCE, GRISLY, SAVAGE,
GHASTLY, MACABRE,
RESOLUTE, RUTHLESS,
SINISTER, FORBIDDING
Grim Reaper .... DEATH
grimace .... MUG, MOUE, MOW(E),
FACE, POUT, FLEER, FROWN,
SCOWL, MOP, SNEER, SNOOT,
GLOWER
grimalkin .... CAT, WOMAN
with a grievance .... SORE CAT
grime .... DIRT, SOOT, COLLY,
SMUTCH
Grimes (Golden) .... APPLE
grimy .... FOUL, DINGY, SOOTY,
FILTHY
grin .... SMILE, SMIRK
grind .... RUB, BRAY, CHEW, FILE,
GRIT, HONE, MILL, MULL,
SAND, TASK, WHET, CRUSH,
GRATE, GRIDE, CRUNCH,
POLISH, SHARPEN, DRUDGERY,
MASTICATE, PULVERIZE,
TRITURATE
the teeth .... GNASH
grinder .... MILL, HONER, MOLAR,
TOOTH, CRUSHER
grinding device .... MILL,
METATE, MORTAR, MULLER,
MILLSTONE, WHETSTONE
substance .... SAND, EMERY,
ABRASIVE
grindstone .... HONE, MANO,
METATE
gringo .... AMERICANO
grinning .... RIDENT
grip ...... BAG, LUG, HOLD, CLAMP,
CLASP, GRASP, CLUTCH,
HANDLE, VALISE, CONTROL,
STAGEHAND
gripe .... BEEF, BITCH, PINCH,
CLUTCH, HANDLE, MUTTER,
AFFLICT, GRUMBLE,

COMPLAIN, DISTRESS

slang .... A BONE TO PICK

grip(pe) .... FLU, COLD, COLIC, INFLUENZA

gripsack .... VALISE

Griqua .... MULATTO

Griselda, like .... MEEK, PATIENT

griseous .... GRAY

grisette .... SHOPGIRL

griskin .... LOIN

grisly .... GRIM, MORBID, GHASTLY, GRUESOME, HORRIBLE, FRIGHTFUL

Grissom's first capsule

.... LIBERTY BELL

grist .... MEAL, QUANTITY

for the _____ .... MILL

gristle .... CARTILAGE

grit .... SAND, NERVE, PLUCK, GRAVEL, COURAGE, STAMINA, ENDURANCE, FORTITUDE

grith .... SECURITY, SANCTUARY

grits .... MEAL, KASHA, HOMINY

gritty .... BRAVE, SANDY, PLUCKY, SABULOUS

grivet ...... TOTA, WAAG, GUENON, MONKEY, VERVET

grizzle .... FRET, GRAY, WORRY, COMPLAIN

grizzly .... BEAR, GRAYISH

groan .... MOAN

groat .... COIN

grocer .... STOREKEEPER

groceries .... PROVISIONS

Grofe's Donkey _____

.... SERENADE

grog .... RUM, RUMBO

groggery/grogshop .... SALOON

groggy ...... DIZZY, DRUNK, TIPSY, SLEEPY

groin, of or near .... INGUINAL

swelling .... BUBO

grommet .... RING, BECKET, EYELET

Gromyko, diplomat ...... ANDREI

groom .... SICE, BRUSH, CURRY, PREEN, TRAIN, NEATEN, TIDY (UP), EQUERRY, (H)OSTLER, BENEDICT, MANSERVANT

horse .... SYCE, COISTREL

grooming process .... TOILETTE

groomsman .... BEST MAN

groove .... RUT, FLUTE, CREASE, CULLIS, FURROW, SPLINE, STRIA(E), FLUTING, SULCUS, ROUTINE

barrel .... CROZE, RIFLING

in architecture .... GLYPH

in iron .... FULLER

masonry ...... RAGGLE, RAGLET

grooved .... LIRATE, STRIATE

grope .... TAY, FEEL, HUNT, FERDE, PROBE, FUMBLE

for words .... HAW, FALTER, FLOUNDER

in the dark .... FEEL ONE'S WAY

Gropius .... GROPE

school .... BAUHAUS

grosbeak .... MORO, FINCH

gross .... RANK, RUDE, BURLY, BULKY, CRASS, CRUDE, DENSE, LARGE, THICK, TOTAL, WHOLE, COARSE, ENTIRE, VULGAR, GLARING, FLAGRANT, CORPULENT

opposed to .... NET

grot(to) .... CAVE, SHRINE

grotesque .... ODD, ABSURD, STRANGE, BAROQUE, BIZARRE, ABNORMAL, FANTASTIC

Groton product ...... SUBMARINE

grouch .... SULK, GRUMBLE(R)

Groucho .... MARX

grouchy .... CROSS, TESTY, GRUMPY, ILL-TEMPERED

ground .... SOIL, BASIS, EARTH, CAUSE, TOPIC, MOTIVE, REASON, TERRAIN, FOUNDATION

break .... DIG, START

dig in the .... GRUB

elevation .... RISE

give .... YIELD, RETREAT

hog day .... CANDLEMAS

nut .... GOBBE, PEANUT

parcel of .... SOLUM

pulverizer .... SPIDER

rising .... HURST

unplowed, solid ...... HARDPAN

up .... PULVERIZE

grounded .... ASHORE, GRATED, ABRADED, WHITTLED

grounder .... DAISY CUTTER

groundhog .... MARMOT, WOODCHUCK

groundless .... IDLE, BASELESS, UNFOUNDED, UNJUSTIFIED

groundling .... CREEPER

grounds ...... LEES, BASIS, DREGS, ESTATE, REASON, GARDENS, RESIDUE, SEDIMENT

around building .... CLOSE, COMPOUND

college .... CAMPUS

groundsel .... RAGWORT

groundwork .... BASE, BASIS, INCEPTION, FOUNDATION

group .... SET, BAND, CREW, MASS, SORT, UNIT, CLASS, COVEY, GATHER, CLUSTER, SEGMENT, ASSEMBLAGE,

COLLECTION

advisers' .... CAMARILLA, BRAINTRUST

Arafat's .... PLO

athletic .... TEAM

congressional .... BLOC

Civil War: abbr. .... GAR

discussion/gabfest .... BULL SESSION

distinctive/unique .... ORDER

established in Trygve Lie's regime .... UNESCO

grid .... ELEVEN

key .... CADRE

matched .... SET

member needing aid .... WEAK SISTER

of admirers/paid applauders

.... CLAQUE

bananas/grapes .... BUNCH

bears .... SLOTH

bees .... HIVE

birds/goats .... FLOCK

buildings .... PILE

cats .... CLOWDER

cattle/sheep .... HERD

closely related species of plants, animals

.... GENUS

dogs .... PACK, KENNEL

eight .... OCTAD, OCTAVE, OCTET(TE)

exclusive people, snobbish

.... CLIQUE

families .... CLAN

fifty: abbr. .... USA

fishes .... SHOAL, SCHOOL

five .... PENTAD, QUINTET, QUINTUPLETS

fliers .... FLIGHT

foxes .... SKULK

geese .... SKEIN, GAGGLE

girls .... BEVY

hogs/sheep .... DROVE

insects .... SWARM

lions .... PRIDE

modeled figures

.... DIORAMA

nine .... ENNEAD

nonsyllabic phonemes

.... CLUSTER

people associated for social reasons .... COTERIE

people functioning as a unit .... BODY

people inside a political party .... FACTION

people of same nationality, in one place

.... COLONY

people with same interests
.... RING, CIRCLE
performers .... CAST, TROUPE
players .... TEAM
political intriguers
.... JUNTA, JUNTO
quail .... COVEY
rooms .... SUITE
seals .... POD
seven .... HEPTAD, SEPTET
ships .... FLEET, FLOTILLA
small trees/shrubs .... COPSE
ten .... DECADE
tents .... CAMP
things of the same sort
.... BUNCH, CLUSTER
trees .... GROVE, WOODS,
FOREST, ORCHARD
twenty .... SCORE
twenty priests .... FETIAL
vehicles .... FLEET
whales .... GAM
witches .... COVEN
patriotic .... DAR, SAR
rent-paying .... TENANTRY
singing .... TRIO, CHOIR,
CHORUS, HOOTENANNY
slang .... CABOODLE
social .... TRIBE
top-flight .... ELITE
grouped .... BANDED, RANKED,
SORTED, ARRAYED,
ARRANGED, AGMINATE,
CLASSIFIED
grouper .... MERO, BONACI,
WARSAW, SEABASS
groupie .... FAN, FOLLOWER
grouse .... PINTAIL, SAGE HEN,
PHEASANT, PTARMIGAN
female .... GORHEN
male .... GORCOCK,
BLACKCOCK
slang .... CRAB, GRUMBLE,
COMPLAIN
grout .... LEES, MEAL, DREGS,
MASTIC, MORTAR, GROUNDS,
PORRIDGE, SEDIMENT
grove .... HOLT, TOPE, COPSE,
MOTTE, WOOD(S), BOSK(ET),
BOSCAGE, COPPICE, ORCHARD,
SPINNEY
near Athens .... ACADEME
pines .... PINETUM
where Aristotle taught
.... LYCEUM
grovel ...... FAWN, CRAWL, CREEP,
CRINGE, LICK THE DUST
Grover .... WHALEN
Groves, A-bomb builder
.... LESLIE
grow .... WAX, RAISE, ACCRUE,

SPROUT, THRIVE, ACCRETE,
FLOURISH, CULTIVATE
fast/rapidly .... BOOM,
MUSHROOM
tall and thin .... SPINDLE
together .... KNIT
wearisome .... BORE
grower .... FARMER
growing in couples/pairs
.... BINATE, GEMINATE
one side only .... SECUND
out/outward .... ENATE
up achievement .... AGE OF
DISCRETION
where it is not wanted
.... WEED
growl .... YAR(R), GIRN, GNAR,
HOWL, SNARL, MUTTER,
RUMBLE, GRUMBLE,
COMPLAIN(T)
archaic .... SNAR
growler .... DOG, BEAR
angry .... SNARLER
growler's content .... BEER
grown .... ADULT, MATURE
together .... ADNATE
growth .... WEN, CORN, CYST,
MOLE, SPUR, WART, POLYP,
SHOOT, WATTLE, ACCRETION,
DEVELOPMENT
abnormal body .... TUMOR
in response to force of
gravity .... GEOTROPISM
place of rapid .... HOTBED
process .... NACENCY
skin .... WEN, MOLE, WART
stunted in .... RUNTY,
SCRUBBY
grub .... DIG, LARVA, ASSART,
DRUDGE, MAGGOT, UPROOT,
RUMMAGE
axe .... MATTOCK
slang ..... EAT(S), CHOW, FEED,
FOOD
street .... MILTON
to .... SPUD, SLAVE
grubby .... DINGY, DIRTY, SHABBY
Gruber, composer .... FRANZ
grudge .... ENVY, PEEVE, PIQUE,
SPITE, STINT, ANIMUS,
MALICE, ILLWILL, WITHHOLD
grudging .... ENVIOUS,
RELUCTANT
grue .... ICE, SNOW
gruel .... ATOLE, BROTH, BURGOO,
CAUDLE, LOBLOLLY,
PORRIDGE
grueling .... ARDUOUS,
EXHAUSTING
gruesome .... GRIM, GRISLY,
MORBID, FEARFUL, GHASTLY,

HIDEOUS, MACABRE,
FEARSOME
gruff .... RUDE, BLUNT, HARSH,
ROUGH, SURLY, COARSE,
HOARSE
grugru .... PALM, LARVA
grume .... CLOT
grumble .... FRET, KICK, GRIPE,
GROWL, GROUCH, GROUSE,
MUTTER, REPINE, RUMBLE,
COMPLAIN
grumbler .... GROUCH, REPINER
grumpy .... GLUM, SURLY,
PEEVISH
Grundy, Mrs. .... PRUDE
grunion .... SILVERSIDE
grunt .... RASP, SNORT, COMPLAIN
and groaner .... WRESTLER
grunter .... HOG, PIG
former .... INDIAN
sound of .... OINK
Grus .... CRANE
Gruyere .... CHEESE
guacharo .... (OIL)BIRD
Guadalcanal town .... AOLA
guaiac .... BEAN, SEED, TONKA
Guam .... GUAHAN
American governor
.... SKINNER
bay .... AGAT, PAGO, YLIG,
BAHIA, TUMON, UMATAC,
TALOFOFO
capital .... AGANA
dialect/native .... CHAMORRO
district ..... AGAT, APRA, ASAN,
PITI, TOTO, YIGO, YONA,
TUMON, AGANA, MAITE,
DEDEDO, MERIZO, INARAJAN,
MALOJLOJ, MANGILAO,
SINAJANA, TALOFOFO,
TAMUNING, BARRIGADA,
SANTA RITA, LATTE HEIGHTS,
TUMON HEIGHTS
governor .... ADA, CALVO,
FLORES, BORDALLO,
GUERRERO, GUTIERREZ
governor who committed
suicide
.... (RICARDO)BORDALLO
harbor .... APRA
island .... COCOS, CABRAS
major language .... ENGLISH
monetary unit .... U.S. DOLLAR
mountain ..... LAMLAM, SANTA
ROSA
peninsula .... OROTE
seaport .... APRA (HARBOR)
tourist attraction .... COCOS
ISLAND, TALOFOFO FALLS
tree ..... IPIL, TANGAN-TANGAN
guama .... INGA, GUAVA

Guamanian word(s) for

Guamanian word(s) for:

above .... HULO	danger .... PILIGRO	laugh .... CHALEK
act .... AKTO	darling .... KIRIDU	law .... LAI
actor .... AKTA	date .... FECHA	lawsuit .... KAOSA
add .... SUMA	daughter .... HAGA	leader .... FAGU
advice .... PINAGAT	day .... DIA	life .... BIDA
age .... IDAT	dead .... MATAI	lightning .... LAMLAM
aid .... AYUDA	deaf .... TANGNGA	love .... GUAIYA
alien .... ESTRANGHERU	dear .... NENA	lovers .... AMANTES
all .... PURU	debt .... DIBI	magic .... ATTE
alone .... MAISA	December .... UMAYANGAN	man .... LAHI
already .... ESTA	deed .... AKSION	March .... MATSO
also .... LOKKUE	deer .... BINADU	May .... MAYU
altar .... ATTAT	devil .... DIABLO	meat .... KATNE
American .... KANU,	dream .... GUANIFI	medicine .... AMOT
AMERIKANU	eagle .... AGILA	mermaid .... SIRENA
April .... ABRIT, LUMUHU	east .... HATKATTAN	miracle .... MILAGRO
August .... AGOSTO, TENHOS	egg .... CHADA	Monday .... LUNES
aunt .... TIHA	eight .... OCHO	monkey .... MACHENG
avocado .... ALAGETA	eye .... MATA	mother .... NANA
baby .... NENI	father .... TATA	mountain .... SABANA
baby-sitter .... CHICHIGUA	February .... MAIMO	name .... NAAN
bad .... MALA	female .... PALAOAN	necktie .... KOTBATA
bake .... HOTNO	fiance .... NOBIU	nephew .... SUBRINU
baker .... PANADERU	fish .... GUIHAN	niece .... SUBRINA
bakery .... PANADERIA	fisherman .... PESKADOT	no .... AHE
ball .... BOLA	five .... SINKO	nonsense .... TONTO
balloon .... LOBU	flower .... FLORES	noodle .... UTDON
bamboo .... KARISU	forward .... SIGI	north .... NOTTE
betel nut .... MAMAON	four .... KUATRO	November .... SUMONGSONG
betel nut palm .... PUGUA	fragrant .... PAOPAO	now .... PAGO
big .... DANKOLO	free .... SAKA	October .... FAGUALO
bird .... PALUMA	free-loader .... ANKAS	of .... POT
blanket .... ONNO	Friday .... BETNES	one .... ONU
blood .... HAGA	friend .... GACHONG	only .... UNIKU
blue .... ASUT	giant .... HIGANTE	parrot .... LORU
boat .... BOTI	girl .... AKKAGA	people .... TAOTAO
book .... LEPBLO	goat .... CHIBA	plant .... TANOM
boy .... LAHI	God .... DIOS, YUUS	pray/read .... FANAITAI
bridge .... TOLLAI	gold .... ORU	pretty .... BUNITA
brother .... CHELU	good .... MAOLEK	pumpkin .... KALAMASA
burglar .... SAKKE	grape .... UBAS	race .... KARERA
butcher .... MATADERU	grass .... CHARA	rain .... UCHAN
carnival .... FERIA	greeting .... HAFA ADAI	rainbow .... ISA
cheap .... BARATU	habit .... BISIO	raisins .... PASAS
cheese .... KESU	haircut .... LAKLAK	red .... AGAGA
children .... FAMAGUON	happy .... FELIS, MAGOF	rice, cooked .... HINEKSA
chopstick .... PALITU	healthy .... BRABU	rice, uncooked .... PUGAS
circle .... SITKULU	hear .... HANGOK	ring .... ARAS
city .... SIUDAT	heir .... IRIDERU	road .... CHALAN
clock .... RELOS	here .... GAIGE	room .... KUATTO
clown .... BUREGO	holiday .... GUPOT	salt .... ASIGA
cockfight .... GAYERA,	house .... GUMA	Saturday .... SABALU
PALITADA	husband/wife .... ASAGWA	school .... ESKUELA
cockfighter .... GAYERU	ill .... MALANGU	sea .... TASI
cockpit .... RUEDA	invoice .... RISIBU	sell .... BENDE
cockroach .... KUKURACHA	jail .... KALABOSU	seller .... BIBENDE
coconut .... NIYOK	January .... ENERU	September .... LUMAMLAM
color .... KULOT	judge .... HUES	shark .... HALUU
contest .... HUEGU	July .... SEMO	sheep .... KINILU
cookie .... GUYURIA	June .... MANANAF	ship .... BAPOT
	late .... ATRASAO	shoes .... SAPATOS

signature .... FITMA
sister .... CHELU
sleep .... MAIGO
small .... HAGUI
smile .... CHICHE
smoke .... ASU
snake .... TAKPAPA
snore .... LANNAN
soap .... HABON
son .... IHU
song .... KANTA
south .... HATTAYA
souvenir .... RIKUETDO
spend .... GASTA
star .... ESTREYAS
stop .... BASTA
storm .... PAKYO
strong .... FIGO
sugar .... ASUKAT
Sunday .... DAMENGGO
surprise .... HIGEF
sweet .... MAMES
sword .... ESPADA
tall .... LOKKA
taxes .... ADUANA
teacher .... MAESTRO
thank you ...... SI YUUS MAASE
thief .... LADRON
Thursday .... HUEBES
tobacco .... CHUPA
today .... PAGO
toy .... HUGETI
true .... KLARU
Tuesday .... MATTES
umbrella .... PAYU
understand .... KOMPRENDE
vase .... FLORERU
volcano .... BOTKANU
wait .... NANGGA
waiter .... KAMARERU
walk .... LAHU
war .... GERA
warrior .... GERERU
water .... AGUA
wave .... NAPU
weather .... TIEMPO
Wednesday .... METKOLES
week .... SIMANA
well .... MAOLEK
west .... HATTICHAN
what .... HAFA
white .... APAKA
widow .... BIUDA
wind .... MANGLO
witch .... BRUHA
word .... PALABRA
work .... CHOGUE
wrong .... LACHI
year .... SAKKAN
yellow .... AMARIYU
yes .... HUNGGAN

yesterday .... NIGAP
you .... HAO, HAMYO
young .... HOBEN
your/yours .... MIYU
guanaco-like animal ...... CAMEL,
                      LLAMA
guanay .... CORMORANT
droppings .... GUANO
guano .... MANURE, TUATARA,
                 FERTILIZER
source of .... BATS, GUANAY
Guarani .... TUPI
guarantee .... BOND, VOUCH,
    ASSURE, INSURE, PLEDGE,
    SURETY, ENDORSE, PROMISE,
              WARRANT(Y)
guaranteed ...... CERTIFIED, GOOD
              AS GOLD
guarantor .... SURETY
guaranty .... SECURITY
guard .... HEDGE, WATCH,
    CONVOY, DEFEND, PATROL,
    PICKET, SHIELD, WARDER,
    OSTIARY, GARRISON,
    PROTECT(OR), PROTECTION
armed .... SENTRY, SENTINEL
Asgard's .... HEIMDALL
car's .... FENDER
post .... WATCH
ship ...... CONVOY, CORVET(TE)
Guard, _____ (Schutzstaffel)
                      ELITE
guarded ...... SAFE, WARY, LEERY,
              CAUTIOUS
guardhouse .... BRIG, HOOSEGOW
guardian .... CUSTOS, DRAGON,
    KEEPER, WARDEN, CURATOR,
    CARETAKER, TRUSTEE,
    TUTELAR, CUSTODIAN,
             PROTECTOR
concern of .... WARD
function of .... TUTELAGE
legendary .... ARGUS,
              CERBERUS
minor's .... TUTOR, CURATOR
of a sort .... WATCHDOG
spirit .... LARES, DAEMON
watchful .... ARGUS
Guatemala babushka .... TZUT
cape .... TRES PUNTAS
capital .... GUATEMALA
city/town .... OCOS, COBAN,
    IPALA, TIKAL, CHAJUL,
    GUALAN, JULAPA, PANZOS,
    SALAMA, SOLOLA, TACANA,
    ZACAPA, ANTIGUA, AMATITIAN,
             ESCUINTLA
grass .... TEOSINTE
gulf .... HONDURAS
Indian .... ITZA, MAYA
insect .... KELEP

lake .... GUIJA, IZABAL,
    ATITLAN, PETEN-ITZA
money .... QUE(T)ZAL
mountains .... MINAS
plain .... PETEN
port .... PUERTO BARRIOS
president ...... PONCE, CEREZO,
    MENDEZ, AREVALO, ESTRADA,
              SERRANO
river .... AZUL, CHIXOY,
    PASION, MOTAGUA, SARSTUN
volcano .... AGUA, FUEGO,
    TACANA, ATITLAN
guava .... ARACA
guayule .... SHRUB
gudgeon .... BAIT, DUPE, GOBY,
    GULL, TRICK, MINNOW,
              TRUNNION
Gudrun, brother of ...... GUNNAR
husband of .... ATLI, SIGURD
rival of .... BRYNHILD
guenon .... MONA, GRIVET,
    MONKEY, TALAPOIN
guerdon .... CROWN, REWARD
Guernsey .... SHIRT, CATTLE
lily .... NERINE
guerrilla .... REBEL, RAIDER,
              PARTISAN
guess .... DIVINE, THEORY,
    SURMISE, ESTIMATE,
    CONJECTURE, SUPPOSITION
guessing game .... POKER,
              CHARADE
guesswork .... SURMISE
guest .... CALLER, LODGER,
    COMPANY, VISITOR
of honor .... LION
paying .... BOARDER
guffaw .... BRAY, ROAR, HEEHAW,
    LAUGH(TER), HORSELAUGH
deep, hearty .... BELLY LAUGH
Guiana hut .... BENAB
native .... BONI
tree .... MORA
guide .... KEY, CLEW, CLUE, LEAD,
    PILOT, SCOUT, STEER
    CONDUCT, COURIER
mountain .... SHERPA
tourist's .... CICERONE,
             DRAGOMAN
guidebook .... MANUAL,
    BAEDEKER, ITINERARY
guided missile .... ICBM, IRBM
guiding .... POLAR, DIRIGENT
example .... PRECEDENT
instrument .... COMPASS
light .... BEACON, LODESTAR,
            NORTH STAR
rule .... MOTTO, PRINCIPLE
suggestion .... CUE
guidon .... FLAG, PENNANT

Guido note .... UT, ELAMI
  highest .... ELA
  lowest .... GAMUT
guild .... CRAFT, HANSE, UNION
Guild Hall statue .... GOG,
                        MAGOG
guilder .... COIN, GULDEN
guile .... WILE, CRAFT, DECEIT,
        CUNNING, TRICKERY
guileful .... SHREWD, TRICKY
guileless .... OPEN, NAIVE, FRANK,
    CANDID, HONEST, ARTLESS,
                 SINCERE
guillemot .... AUK, BIRD, COOT,
      MURR(E), DOVEKIE
  black .... TYSTIE
guillotine .... BEHEAD, MAIDEN
  wagon .... TUMBREL
guilt .... SIN, CRIME, OFFENSE,
    OUTRAGE, CULPA(BILITY)
guiltless .... CLEAR, INNOCENT,
            BLAMELESS
guilty .... NOCENT, AT FAULT,
      CRIMINAL, CULPABLE
guimpe .... BLOUSE
Guinea .... COIN
  cape .... VERGA
  capital .... CONAKRY
  city/town .... LABE, MALI,
    KANKAN, KINDIA, KOUNDARA,
            TELIMELE
  fowl .... PINTADO
  islands .... LOS
  lagoon .... NIMBA
  language .... SUSU, FRENCH,
      FULANI, MANDINGO
  money .... KORI, SYLI
  mountains .... NIMBA
  native .... SUSU, FULANI,
             MALINKE
  pig .... CAVY
  president .... TOURE
  river .... MOA, MILO, BAKOY,
        NIGER, BAFING
  weight ...... AKEY, PISO, UZAN,
             SERON
  young .... KEET
Guinevere's husband
    .... (KING)ARTHUR
  lover .... LANCELOT
guipure .... GIMP, LACE
guise .... GARB, MIEN, CLOAK,
    MANNER, BEHAVIOR,
           PRETENSE
guitar, ancient .... LUTE
  feature .... FRET
  fittings .... CAPO
  fret .... STOP
  like instrument .... ROTE,
    SITAR, CITOLE, CITTERN,

BANDORE, CITHER(N),
GITTERN, PANDORE, SAMISEN,
    UKE(LELE), BALALAIKA
  old English .... CITHER
  plucking implement
  .... PLECTRON, PLECTRUM
  ridge .... FRET
guitarist, famed .... SEGOVIA
guitarist's arpeggio .... RASGADO
guitguit .... BIRD
Guitry, playwright .... SACHA
gula .... GULLET
gulch .... ARROYO, CANYON,
    COULEE, RAVINE, VALLEY
gulden .... COIN, GUILDER
gules .... RED
gulf .... GAP, EDDY, ABYSS, BIGHT,
    CLEAVAGE, WHIRLPOOL
Gulf State ...... TEXAS, ALABAMA,
    FLORIDA, LOUISIANA
gull .... COB(B), DUPE, XEMA,
    ALLAN, CHEAT, CULLY,
    PEWEE, PEWIT, GOSLING,
    GUDGEON, KITTIWAKE
  like/of a .... LARINE
  robber .... JA(E)GER
  sea .... COB, MEW, SKUA
gullet .... MAW, CRAW, WEASAND,
          ESOPHAGUS
gullible .... NAIVE, CREDULOUS,
        UNSUSPECTING
Gulliver's Travels author
    .... (JONATHAN)SWIFT
  dwarf .... LILLIPUTIAN
  land .... LAPUTA, LILLIPUT,
         BROBDINGNAG
  people .... YAHOOS
gully .... GUT, SIKE, WADI, DONGA,
    ARROYO, RAVINE, CHANNEL,
           COULOIR
gulp .... BOLT, SWIG, SWALLOW
gum .... ASA, GLUE, KINO, CAROB,
    LATEX, MATTI, RESIN,
    BALATA, CHICLE, RUBBER,
    ADHESIVE, MUCILAGE
  arabic .... ACACIN(E)
  ball machine .... DISPENSER
  black .... TUPELO
  elastic .... RUBBER
  plant .... ULE
  resin ..... BALM, COPAL, ELEMI,
    LOBAN, MYRRH, BALSAM,
    GALBAN, CAMBOGE,
    CAMBOGIA, BDELLIUM,
    OLIBANUM, ASAFETIDA
  resin poison .... ANTIAR
  tree .... KARRI, ACACIA,
    BALATA, COPALM, TUPELO,
        EUCALYPTUS
  up .... CLOG

gumbo .... OKRA, SOUP, GOMART,
               PATOIS
gumboil .... ABSCESS, PARULIS
gummed paper .... STICKER
gummy .... STICKY, VISCID
  substance .... GUTTA
gumption .... NERVE, COURAGE
gums abscess .... GUMBOIL
  inflammation .... GINGIVITIS
  pertaining to .... ULETIC
  source .... FERULA
  the .... ULA
gumshoe .... TEC, RUBBER,
          DETECTIVE
gun .... COLT, LUGER, RIFLE,
    MAXIM, JINGAL, MAUSER,
    MORTAR, PISTOL, CARBINE,
    FIREARM, GATLING,
    REVOLVER, AUTOMATIC
  ancient .... MUSKET,
        HARQUEBUS(E)
  attachment .... SILENCER
  barrel's end .... MUZZLE
  big game .... ROER
  brush .... SWAB
  butt .... STOCK
  caliber .... BORE
  carriage ...... GALLOP, CAISSON
  carriage rope .... PROLONGE
  case .... HOLSTER
  chamber .... GOMER
  crew's shield .... TURRET,
        MANT(E)LET
  dog .... SETTER, POINTER,
        RETRIEVER
  emplacement .... PILLBOX
  girl .... MOLL
  hammer catch of .... SEAR
  muzzle plug .... TAMPION
  part .... PIN, BOLT, BORE,
    BUTT, COCK, LOCK, GOMER,
    SIGHT, STOCK, BARREL,
    BREECH, HAMMER, CHAMBER,
    TRIGGER, CYLINDER,
        MAGAZINE
  pointer .... SIGHT, DOTTER
  sight .... BEAD
  slang .... GAT, ROD, IRON,
    BETSY, PIECE, BARKER,
    ROSCOE, THROTTLE
  small .... DERRINGER
  the motor .... REV
  turret .... CUPOLA, BLISTER
gunboat .... TINCLAD
guncotton plus picric acid
  .... MELINITE
gunfire .... BURST, SALVO,
    VOLLEY, DRUMBEAT,
    SHOOTING, FUSILLADE
gung ho .... AVID, SLOGAN, WORK
        TOGETHER

gunlock catch .... SEAR
gunman .... THUG, TORPEDO,
GANGSTER
Gunnar's in-law .... SIGURD
sister .... GUDRUN, GUTHRUN
wife .... BRYNHILD
gunnel .... FISH, BLENNY,
GUNWALE
gunner .... STRAFER
gunner's platform .... BANQUETTE
seat .... TURRET
gunnery .... CANNONS, ARTILLERY
gunny .... BAG, SACK
gunpowder .... TEA, NITER
gunrunner .... SMUGGLER
guns .... WEAPONS, (FIRE)ARMS,
ORDNANCE, ARTILLERY
act of heavy .... BATTERY
gunstock .... BUTT
Gunther's wife .... BRUNHILD
gunwale .... GUNNEL
pin .... THOLE
guppy .... MINNOW
gurgle .... BICKER, BUBBLE,
BURBLE
gurglet .... GOBLET
gurgling sound producer
.... BABY, BROOK
gurnard .... GURNET, ROCHET,
BATFISH, SEA ROBIN
gurnet .... GURNARD
guru .... ADVISER, TEACHER
pupil of .... CHELA
gush .... JET, EMIT, POUR(OUT),
ISSUE, SPOUT, SPURT,
OUTFLOW
forth .... SPEW
gusher, kind of ...... GEYSER, OIL
WELL, VOLCANO
gushy .... EFFUSIVE

gusset .... GORE
gust .... BLOW, PUFF, RUSH, TANG,
BLAST, SAPOR, BREEZE,
FLURRY, RELISH, OUTBURST
gusto .... ZEST, TASTE, LIKING,
PALATE, RELISH, DELIGHT,
PLEASURE, ENJOYMENT
gusty .... WINDY, BLUSTERY
gut .... GULLY, CATGUT, DESTROY,
DEMOLISH, INTESTINE
guts .... BOWELS, INNARDS,
ENTRAILS
slang .... PLUCK, COURAGE,
FORTITUDE, DETERMINATION
gutta .... DROP, MINIM
gutter .... CURB, SLUM, DITCH,
CULLIS, KENNEL, TROUGH
guttersnipe .... ARAB, GAMIN,
URCHIN
guttural ...... DRY, GRUFF, GULAR,
HUSKY, VELAR, HOARSE,
RASPING, THROATY
guy .... CHAP, JOSH, ROPE, CHAIN,
TEASE, FELLOW
rope .... STAT, STAY, VANG
with a racket .... MOBSTER
guy's pal/date .... GAL
guzzle .... GULP, SWIG, DRINK,
SWILL
guzzler .... SOT, TOPER
gymkhana performer .... RIDER,
ATHLETE, EQUESTRIAN
gymnasium .... GYM, ARENA
gymnast .... TURNER, ACROBAT,
ATHLETE, TUMBLER
suit for .... MAILLOT
gymnastics .... TUMBLING,
ATHLETICS, EXERCISES,
ACROBATICS, CALISTHENICS
apparatus .... BUCK

equipment .... TRAMPOLINE
gymnosophist .... NUDIST
gyp .... CHEAT, CON GAME,
SERVANT, SWINDLE(R)
gypsophila .... BABY'S BREATH
gypsum .... YESO, GESSO,
SELENITE, ALABASTER
gypsy .... CALE, CALO, NOMAD,
ROAMER, ROMANY, TSIGANE,
ZINGARO
book LIL
boy/husband .... ROM
devil .... BENG
French .... BOHEMIAN
gentleman .... ROM, RYE
girl .... CHAI
horse .... GRI, GRY, GRASNI
language .... ROMANY
non .... GAJO
opera .... MANERICO
sea .... BADJAO
Spanish ...... GITANO, ZINCALO
thief .... CHOR
tongue .... CHIB
village .... GAV
wagon .... CARAVAN
winch .... CRAB
woman .... RANI, ROMI,
ZINGARA
Gypsy Rose .... LEE
gyrate .... SPIN, TURN, TWIRL,
WHIRL, ROTATE, SWIVEL,
REVOLVE
gyrating toy .... TOP
gyrator .... PILOT
gyratory .... WHIRLING
gyre .... WHIRL, VORTEX
gyrene .... MARINE, LEATHERNECK
gyro .... GYROSCOPE
part .... ROTOR, WHEEL

H

H, letter .... AITCH
-shaped .... AITCH, ZYGAL
sound .... ASPIRATE
habanera .... DANCE
habeas corpus ...... WRIT, ORDER
haberdashery .... SHIRTS,
TOGGERY
habile .... APT, ABLE, ROBE,
HANDY, CLEVER
habiliment .... DRESS, ATTIRE,
GARMENT, CLOTHING
habit .... RUT, GARB, WONT,
DRESS, USAGE, ATTIRE,
CUSTOM, COSTUME, ROUTINE,
PRACTICE

bad .... VICE
prefix .... ECO
riding .... JOSEPH, JODHPURS
habitable .... LIV(E)ABLE
habitant ...... DWELLER, RESIDENT
habitation .... HOME, LAIR,
ABODE, DWELLING
of a kind .... DEN
habitual .... USUAL, WONTED,
CHRONIC, ROUTINE,
CUSTOMARY
habitually silent .... RESERVE,
RETICENT, TACITURN
habituate .... DRILL, ENURE,
INURE, ACCUSTOM

to weather .... ACCLIMATE
habitue .... FREQUENTER
tavern .... BARFLY
hacienda .... FARM, MINE, RANCH,
ESTATE, PLANTATION
hack .... AX, CHOP, GASH, COUGH,
STALE, TRITE, DRUDGE,
MATTOCK, TAXI(CAB)
driver .... CABBIE
literary ..... DEVIL, POETASTER,
SCRIBBLER
hackbut .... HARQUEBUS
hackie .... CABBIE, TAXI DRIVER
hackle .... CUT, COMB, HAGGLE,
MANGLE, HATCHEL, FEATHERS

hackmatack ...... LARCH, JUNIPER
hackney .... FLY, FIACRE
driver .... JARVEY
hackneyed .... DRAB, BANAL,
STALE, STOCK, TRITE
expression .... CLICHE,
PLATITUDE
haddock .... COD, FISH, GADID
Hades ...... DIS, PIT, HELL, ARALU,
ORCUS, PLUTO, SHEOL,
ABADDON, AVERNUS
abyss below .... TARTARUS
guard .... CERBERUS
river .... STYX, LETHE,
ACHERON
way place to .... EREBUS
hadj .... PILGRIMAGE
haft .... BAIL, HILT, HANDLE
hag .... FURY, CRONE, DEMON,
HARPY, VIXEN, WITCH,
VIRAGO, BELDAM(E),
CARLINE, FELLING, JEZEBEL,
HARRIDAN
haggard .... WAN, HAWK, DRAWN,
GAUNT, UNRULY
Haggard novel .... SHE
singer .... MERLE
haggle .... CHOP, HACK, PRIG,
CAVIL, MANGLE, BARGAIN,
CHAFFER, QUIBBLE, WRANGLE
haha .... WALL, FENCE, LAUGH,
TEHEE
haiku .... POEM
hail .... AVE, AHOY, POUR, CHEER,
SLEET, ACCOST, SALUTE,
SHOWER, SIGNAL, ACCLAIM,
GREET(ING), RAINDROPS
Hailey novel ...... HOTEL, AIRPORT
hair .... FUR, NAP, PILE, SETA,
DOWN, SHAG, CRINE, ROACH,
TRESS, THATCH, FILAMENT
band .... FIL(L)ET
braid .... CUE, PLAIT, QUEUE,
PIGTAIL
bunch of .... WHISK
cloth .... ABA, CILICE
coat .... MELOTE
comb the .... COIF
combining form .... PILI,
PIL(O), CHAET(O), TRICHO
covered with .... HISPID,
LANATE, PILOSE, SHAGGY,
TOMENTOSE
curl of .... LOCK, RINGLET
curlylike .... CIRROSE
cut short .... CROP
disease .... MANGE, SYCOSIS,
XERASIA, TRICHOSIS
diseased state .... PLICA
do the ...... SET, COIF, MARCEL
dressing .... POMADE,

BANDOLINE
dye .... HENNA
dyer .... ANCIETTE
face .... BEARD, WHISKER,
MUSTACHE
falling out of .... PSILOSIS
false .... RAT, WIG, JANE,
PERUKE, TOUPEE
feeler .... PALP(US)
fetus .... LANUGO
fillet .... SNOOD
fine .... DOWN, FUZZ, PILE
fringe of .... TUFT
head .... TOP, CRINE
knot .... BOB, BUN, CHIGNON
lock .... TAG, CURL, TRESS
mass of .... SHOCK
matted .... SHAG, DAGLOCK
neck .... MANE, HACKLE
net .... LINT, SNOOD
nostril .... VIBRISSA
of head .... LOCK, POLL,
THATCH
ointment .... POMADE
on abdomen .... PUBES
pad .... RAT
piece .... RUG
pigment .... MELANIN
pin .... BODKIN
plant .... PILUS, VILLUS
prefix .... CRINI
-raising .... EERIE, SPOOKY
remove .... BOB, EPILATE,
TONSURE, DEPILATE
ribbon .... BANDEAU
ringlet .... CURL
roll .... BUN, RAT, PUFF,
CHIGNON
rough .... SHAG
shedding of .... ECDYSIS
short .... STUBBLE
shreds .... NOIL
stray .... WISP
substance .... KERATIN
tuft .... FLOCCUS
unruly .... COWLICK
unruly head of .... MOP
wave ..... MARCEL, PERMANENT
hairbreadth ...... CLOSE, NARROW
haircloth .... ABA, CILICE
haircut .... SHINGLE
hairdo .... BUN, BANGS, TETE,
POODLE, PAGEBOY, COIFFURE,
POMPADOUR
unbound .... TRESSES
hairdresser .... CURLER, FRISEUR,
COIFFEUR, BEAUTICIAN
at times .... TEASER
term of .... SET, COIF, RINSE,
MARCEL, SHAMPOO,
(COLD)WAVE, PERM(ANENT)

hairiness .... PILOSITY
hairless .... BALD, PELON,
GLABROUS
state .... ALOPECIA
hairlike .... TRICHOID
process .... CILIA, CILIUM
hairline point .... PEAK
hairpiece .... RUG, WIG, FALL,
PERUKE, TOUPEE
hairpin .... BODKIN
hairs, bunch of .... TUFT, PINICIL
hairsplitter .... QUIBBLER
hairy .... NAPPY, COMATE,
COMOSE, PILOSE, CRINITE,
HIRSUTE, PILEOUS, VILLOSE
Himalayan .... YETI
Hairy Ape .... YANK
Haiti .... HISPANIOLA
Haitian bandit .... CACO
bay .... BARADERES,
MANZANILLO
cape .... MOLE, IROIS
capital .... PORT-AU-PRINCE
channel .... SUD, TORTUE
city/town .... AQUIN, LIMBE,
HINCHE, JACMEL, JEREMIE,
GONAIVES, LES CAYES,
PETIONVILLE, SAINT MARC,
CAP-HAITIEN, PORT-DE-PAIX
coin .... GOURDE
department .... SUD, NORD,
QUEST, ARTIBONITE, NORD-
QUEST
evil spirit .... BAKA, BOKO
hunter (ox) .... BUCCANEER
Indian .... TAINO
island .... VACHE, GONAVE,
TORTUGA
king .... CHRISTOPHE
lake .... SAUMATRE
language ...... CREOLE, FRENCH
liberator .... DESSALINES
lord .... CACIQUE
money .... GOURDE, CENTIME
mountain .... MACAYA, LA
SELLE
passage .... WINDWARD
president .... AVRIL, ESTIME,
ARISTIDE, DUVALIER,
MAGLIORE, TROUILLOT
river .... ARTIBONITE, TROIS-
RIVIERES
seaport .... CAYES
voodoo deity .... ZOMBI(E)
voodoo priest(ess)
.... MAMALOI, PAPALOI
hake .... GADID, WHITING
kin of .... COD
hakeem/hakim .... DOCTOR
halberd .... SPEAR, GLA(I)VE,
GISARME, (BATTLE)AX,

POLEAX(E), PARTISAN
Halberstam book ...... THE BEST
AND THE BRIGHTEST
halcyon .... HAPPY, SERENE,
PEACEFUL
hale .... DRAG, HAUL, WELL,
HEARTY, ROBUST, HEALTHY
half .... DEMI, HEMI, SEMI,
MOIETY, FIFTY PERCENT
a fly .... TSE
a goof .... BOO
a sawbuck: sl. .... FIN
a Toscanini? .... SEMI-
CONDUCTOR
and half .... MILK, CREAM,
FIFTY-FIFTY
and half part .... ALE
assed .... SLIPSHOD
baked .... SOPHOMORIC,
AMATEUR(ISH)
boot .... PAC, BUSKIN
breed .... HYBRID, LADINO,
MESTEE, MUSTEE, GRIFF(E),
MESTIF(F), METIS(SE),
MESTIZO, MULATTO
farthing .... MITE
gainer .... ISANDER,
(BACK)DIVE
hearted .... LUKEWARM,
RELUCTANT, INDECISIVE
hitch .... KNOT
man, half bull ..... BUCENTAUR
man, half dragon ..... CECROPS
man, half fish .... DAGON,
MERMAN
man, half goat .... PAN,
FAUNUS
man, half horse ...... CENTAUR
mask .... LOUP, DOMINO
moon .... ARC, LUNE,
CRESCENT
note, in music .... MINIM
one's better .... WIFE,
HUSBAND
penny .... MAG
pint .... SNIP
prefix .... DEMI, HEMI, SEMI
spent before we know what
it is .... LIFE
way .... MID
wit .... DOLT, FOOL, IDIOT
witted .... SILLY, STUPID
year's income .... ANNAT
halfway .... MIDDLE, PARTIAL
home .... SECOND BASE
meet .... COMPROMISE
halibut ...... BUTT, SOLE, FLATFISH
Halicarnassus' wonder
.... MAUSOLEUM
halicore .... DUGONG, SEACOW,
MANATEE

halidom(e) .... HOLINESS
halite .... (ROCK)SALT
halitus .... AURA, VAPOR, BREATH,
EXHALATION
hall ...... DORM, SALLE, CORRIDOR,
VESTIBULE
concert .... ODEUM
hotel .... FOYER, LOBBY
Odin's/of the slain
.... VALHALLA
reception .... COURT, SALON
round .... ROTUNDA
Halley, astronomer ...... EDMUND
constellation .... APUS
discovery .... COMET
halloo .... YELL, SHOUT
hallow .... HOLY, BLESS,
SANCTIFY, CONSECRATE
hallowed .... HOLY, SACRED
place .... SHRINE
Halloween option .... TRICK,
TREAT
halluces .... DIGITS
hallucination .... ALUSIA, AUTISM,
CHIMERA, FANTASY, DELUSION
product of .... MIRAGE
hallucinogen ...... LSD, SEDATIVE,
MESCALINE, AMPHETAMINE
drug: sl. .... ACID
source .... FUNGI, PEYOTE
hallux .... (GREAT) TOE
hallway .... CORRIDOR
Halmahera .... GILOLO
halo ...... AURA, GLORY, CORONA,
GLORIA, NIMB(US), AUREOLA,
AUREOLE, GLORIOLE
halogen .... IODINE, BROMINE,
ASTATINE, CHLORINE
compound .... HALIDE
Hals, painter .... FRANS
halt .... LAME, STOP, PAUSE,
CEASE, WAVER, HOBBLE
hunter's .... TOHO
the .... CRIPPLES
to a tar .... AVAST
halter .... NOOSE, STRAP
halting place .... INN, ETAPE,
OASIS, CARAVANSARY
halve .... BISECT, DIVIDE
ham .... HOCK, MEAT, ACTOR
hog's .... GAMMON
it up .... EMOTE, OVER-ACT
last word of .... WILCO
picnic .... CALI
slang ..... AMATEUR, OVERACT,
SHOW-OFF
slice .... RASHER
Ham, parent of, Biblical
.... NOAH
son of .... CUSH
hamal .... PORTER

Hambletonian .... HORSE,
TROTTER
gait .... TROT
race site .... GOSHEN
hamburg(er) ...... PATTY, STEAK,
SANDWICH
Hamilcar's son .... HANNIBAL
Hamite ...... AFAR, GALLA, MASAI,
BERBER, LIBYAN, SOMAL(I)
Hamitic language ...... NUMIDIAN
hamlet .... MIR, BURG, DORP,
TREF, VILLAGE, THORP(E),
CLACHAN
Hamlet and others .... DANES
locale of .... ELSINGOR,
ELSINORE
Hamlet's word of contempt
.... SIRRAH
Hammarskjold .... DAG
hammer ...... BANG, BEAT, MAUL,
KEVEL, BEETLE, FULLER,
MALLET, MARTEL, OLIVER,
SLEDGE, POUND(ER),
MALLEATE
auctioneer's .... GAVEL
blow .... POUND
chairman's .... GAVEL
companion of .... TONGS
end/head of .... PEEN, POLL
firearm's .... COCK
kind of .... BALL, DROP, CLAW,
PEEN, TRIP
lead .... MADGE
lock .... HOLD
part .... CLAW, HEAD, PEEN
percussion .... PLEXOR,
PLESSOR
striking part .... TUP
hammerhead .... BAT, BIRD, FISH,
SHARK, UMBRETTE
hammock .... BED, COUCH
hamper .... CRAMP, CRATE,
MAUND, HINDER, HOBBLE,
IMPEDE, HANAPER,
ENCUMBER, TRAMMEL
Hampshire .... HANTS
Hampton Roads protagonist
.... MONITOR, MERRIMAC
hamster .... RODENT
hamstring .... LAME, MAIM,
TENDON, CRIPPLE, DISABLE
Hamsun, novelist .... KNUT
Han .... DYNASTY
cities .... WUHAN, HANKOW
hanaper .... BASKET, HAMPER
Hancock .... JOHN, SIGNER
hand .... AID, PAW, DEAL, FIST,
HELP, MANUS, CLUTCH,
CONVEY, WORKER, HOLDING,
APPLAUSE, SIGNATURE
at .... READY, NEAR(BY)

baby's .... PUD
below full house .... FLUSH
by .... MANUAL
care .... MANICURE
clapping to music .... TAL
clenched .... FIST
clock .... POINTER
combining form .... CHIRO
companion of .... GLOVE
deformity .... CLAWHAND
drum .... TOMTOM,
　　　　　　　　TAMBOURINE
first .... NEW, ORIGINAL
give a .... CLAP, APPLAUD
glass .... MIRROR
grenade .... EGG, PINEAPPLE
holder .... WRIST
jurist .... LEARNED
-me-down .... USED, READY-
　　　　MADE, SECONDHAND
measure .... SPAN
organ .... HURDY-GURDY
out .... DEAL, DOLE
over .... SHELL, DELIVER
palm of .... LOOF, VOLAR,
　　　　　　　　　　THENAR
pick .... CHOOSE, SELECT
screw .... JACK
slang .... FIN, HAM, PAW, MITT,
　　　　　　　　　　FLIPPER
sore on .... CHILBLAIN
truck .... DOLLY
upper .... EDGE, ADVANTAGE
without trumps .... CHICANE
written .... MANUSCRIPT
hand, _____ .... PAT
handbag .... ETUI, GRIP, PURSE,
　　VALISE, SATCHEL, RETIC(U)LE
handball .... FIVES, PELOTA
handbill ...... LEAF, FLIER, FLYER,
　　POSER, DODGER, NOTICE,
　　　　　　　　THROWAWAY
handbook .... TOME, MANUAL,
　　　　BAEDEKER, CATECHISM
handcar .... VELOCIPEDE
handcart .... BARROW
handclasp .... GRIP, SHAKE
handcuffs .... DARBY, FETTER,
　　MANACLE, NIPPERS, WRISTLET,
　　　　　　　　BRACELETS
Handel, birthplace of ...... HALLE
forte .... ORATORIO
opus .... NERO, LARGO,
　　　MESSIAH, BERENICE
handful .... SOME, PLENTY,
　　　　　　　　FISTFUL
of cotton .... WAD
of hay/straw .... WISP
handgun .... PISTOL
handicap .... ODDS, HINDER,
　　IMPEDE, HINDRANCE

handily .... DEFTLY, EASILY
handkerchief .... SCARF, SUDARY,
　　FOULARD, MALABAR,
　　　　　　　　VERONICA
colloquial .... WIPE(R), HANKIE
large .... MADRAS,
　　　　　　BANDAN(N)A
handle .... LUG, ANSA, ANSE,
　　BAIL, DEAL, GRIP, HAFT,
　　HEFT, HILT, WIELD, SWIPE,
　　TREAT, MANAGE, TAKE CARE
awkwardly/clumsily ...... PAW,
　　　　　　　　FUMBLE
ax .... HELVE
bar: colloq. .... MUSTACHE
boat's .... HELM, TILLER
celestial .... ANSA
cup's/pitcher's .... EAR
door .... KNOB
having .... ANSATE
roughly .... PAW, MAUL
rudder .... TILLER
slang .... NAME, MONICKER
whip's .... CROP
handmade .... MANUAL
handmaiden .... SERVANT,
　　　　　　　ATTENDANT
handout .... DOLE, GIFT,
　　　　　　　DONATION
handrail, kind of .... MANROPE
hands, clean .... INNOCENT
having two .... BIMANOUS
on hips .... AKIMBO
pertaining to .... MANUAL
warmer .... MUFF
without .... AMANOUS
handsel .... TOKEN, EARNEST,
　　　　　　　PRESENT
handshake .... GRIP
handsome .... AMPLE, BONNY,
　　SHARP, COMELY, GOOD-
　　LOOKING, IMPRESSIVE
man .... ADONIS, APOLLO
handspring .... TUMBLE
handstone .... MANO
handwriter, wall .... AGITPROP
handwriting .... SCRIPT,
　　　　　　　PENMANSHIP
on the wall ...... MENE, TEKEL,
　　GRAFFITI, UPHARSIN
pertaining to .... GRAPHIC
study of .... GRAPHOLOGY
handwritten document/will
　　................................ HOLOGRAPH
handy ...... DEFT, ADROIT, READY,
　　HABILE, DEXTEROUS,
　　　　　　CONVENIENT
man .... MOZO, JACK-OF-ALL-
　　　　　　　TRADES
song .... ST. LOUIS BLUES
hang .... LOLL, DRAPE, DROOP,

HOVER, DANGLE, (IM)PEND,
　　EXECUTE, SUSPEND
around: colloq. .... HOVER,
　　LINGER, LOITER, FREQUENT
down .... LOP, SAG, DROOP,
　　　　　　　　PERPEND
loosely/limply ...... LOP, LOLL,
　　　　　　　　DANGLE
on .... HOLD, WAIT, PERSEVERE
on, in poker .... STAY
out .... HAUNT, HOVER
slang .... STRING
hangar .... SHED, SHELTER,
　　　　　　(AIR)DROME
area .... APRON
hangbird .... ORIOLE
hangdog .... MEAN
hanger .... EXECUTIONER
on .... LEECH, TOADY, HEELER,
　　DANGLER, HABITUE, PARASITE,
　　TRENCHER, FAVOR-SEEKER
hanging .... PENDENT, PENSILE,
　　　　SESSILE, SUSPENDED
apparatus .... GIBBET,
　　　　　　　GALLOWS
crookedly .... ALOP
limply .... LANK
hangings .... WASH, ARRAS,
　　　　DRAPES, DRAPERY
hangman's noose .... HALTER
rope .... HEMP
hangnail .... WHITLOW
hangout .... DEN, HAUNT,
　　RETREAT, STAMPING GROUND
hangover feeling .... NAUSEA,
　　　　　　　HEADACHE
hank .... COIL, LOOP, SKEIN
hanker .... ITCH, LONG, PINE,
　　　　CRAVE, YEARN
hankering .... YEN, ITCH
hanky-panky .... JUGGLERY,
　　DECEPTIVE, TRICK(ER)Y
Hannibal's conqueror ... SCIPIO
father .... HAMILCAR
defeat/waterloo .... ZAMA
surname .... BARCA
victory site .... CANNAE
Hanoi's holiday .... TET
Hanover beer .... BOCK
hanse .... GUILD, LEAGUE
Hanseatic League .... HANSE
Hansen's disease .... LEPROSY
hansom .... CAB, HACK, CARRIAGE
handspring .... CARTWHEEL
hap .... LUCK, FORTUNE
haphazard .... CASUAL, RANDOM,
　　AIMLESS, HIT-OR-MISS
compound word .... HELTER-
　　　　　　　SKELTER
haphazardly .... ANYHOW
hapless ...... UNLUCKY, LUCKLESS

happen .... OCCUR, BEFALL, BETIDE, COME TO PASS, TRANSPIRE
again .... RECUR
in the end .... EVENTUATE
together .... COINCIDE
happening .... CASUS, EVENT, INCIDENT, OCCASION
before due .... RATH(E), PREMATURE
by chance .... FORTUITOUS
"happifies" .... ELATES
happiness .... BLISS, FELICITY
happy .... COSH, GLAD, LUCKY, BLITHE, JOYOUS, CONTENTED
go-lucky .... EASYGOING
medium .... AVERAGE, (GOLDEN)MEAN
times .... HALCYON DAYS
hara-kiri .... SUICIDE, SEPPUKU
harangue .... RANT, ORATE, SPIEL, EXHORT, SCREED, TIRADE, DIATRIBE
Haran's brother .... ABRAM, NAHOR, ABRAHAM
daughter .... MILCAH
father .... TERAH
son .... LOT
harass .... IRK, NAG, VEX, RIDE, ANNOY, BESET, HARRY, TEASE, BOTHER, HECKLE, MOLEST, PESTER, PLAGUE, TORMENT
harbinger .... OMEN, USHER, HERALD, FORETELL, PRECURSOR, FORERUNNER
harbor .... PIER, PORT, HAVEN, MARINA, CONCEAL, SHELTER, ANCHORAGE
and barley .... PEARLS
boat .... TUG
city .... SEAPORT
feature .... PIER, WHARF
guide .... PILOT
laborer .... STEVEDORE
pilot's concern .... TIDE
of mercy .... HOSPITAL
sound .... BELL, CHUG, TOOT, CHURN, (FOG)HORN
wall .... JETTY
hard .... DOUR, FIRM, HARSH, RIGID, SOLID, STERN, STEELY, ADAMANT, ARDUOUS, CALLOUS, DIFFICULT
bed .... PALLET
biscuit .... TACK, CRACKNEL
bitten .... TOUGH, DOGGED
boiled .... TOUGH, CALLOUS
covering .... ARMOR, SHELL
nut to crack .... POSER
prefix .... DIS

problem/puzzle .... POSER, DILEMMA
roll .... BAGEL
rubber .... EBONITE
shell .... LORICA, CARAPACE
shelled animal .... APAR
to find .... RARE
to find in the rain ...... CAB(S)
hardboard .... MASONITE
harden .... GEL, SET, ENURE, STEEL, INURE, OSSIFY, TEMPER, STIFFEN
by heat .... BAKE
hardfisted .... STINGY, MISERLY
hardhanded .... SEVERE
hardhead .... SCULPIN, MENHADEN
hardheaded .... SHREWD, STUBBORN, PRACTICAL
animal .... ASS, MULE, DONKEY
hardihood .... DARING
hardly .... BARELY, FIRMLY, RARELY, NARROWLY, SCARCELY
hardship .... RIGOR, TRIAL, STRAITS, POVERTY
hardtack .... BREAD, WAFER, TOMMY, PANTILE, SEA BISCUITS
hardware .... TOOLS, HOUSEWARES
dealer .... IRONMONGER
slang .... GUNS, WEAPONS
hardwood .... ASH, ELM, OAK, TEAK, EBONY, YAKAL, HICKORY, MAHOGANY
hardy .... BOLD, RASH, TOUGH, DARING, STURDY, DURABLE
Hardy character .... JUDE, TESS
locale .... WESSEX
hare .... CONY, PIKA, PUSS, LEPUS, MALKIN, RABBIT, RODENT, LEPORIDE, LAGOMORPH
and-hounds trail .... TORN PAPER
family .... LEPORID
genus .... LEPUS
hunting dog .... HARRIER
like .... LEPORINE
tail .... SCUT
track .... SLOT, SPOOR
young .... LEVERET
harebrained .... GIDDY, KINKY, DARING, STUPID, FOOLHARDY
harem .... SERAI, ZENANA, SERAGLIO
dweller/slave .... ODALISK, ODALISQUE
room .... ODA(H)
slang .... LOVE NEST
hari-kiri. See **hara-kiri**
haricot ...... STEW, (KIDNEY)BEAN

hark .... HEAR, HIST, LISTEN
harl .... BARB, FILAMENT(S)
harlequin .... MIME, CLOWN, COMIC, BUFFOON
Harlequin, girl of .... COLUMBINE
Harlem painter .... HALS
harlot .... RAHAB, STRUMPET
harm .... MAR, BANE, HURT, ABUSE, INJURE, DAMAGE, INJURY, MALEFIC
harmful .... ILL, NOXAL, NOCENT, BANEFUL, HURTFUL, NOISOME, NOXIOUS, INJURIOUS
gas in mine .... DAMP
very .... DEADLY
harmless ...... NAIVE, INNOCUOUS, INNOXIOUS
harmonica .... MOUTH ORGAN
harmonious .... ORDERLY, SPHERAL, IN ACCORD, CONSONANT
harmonist ...... POET, COMPOSER, MUSICIAN
harmonium .... ORGAN, MELODEON
harmonize .... AGREE, BLEND, (AT)TUNE
harmony .... TONE, TUNE, MUSIC, PEACE, UNISON, BALANCE, CONCORD, RAPPORT, SYMMETRY, AGREEMENT
harness .... RIG, GEAR, DRAFT, EQUIP, GRAITH, INSPAN
bull .... COP
course site .... GOSHEN
maker .... SADDLER
men's .... BRICOLE
part .... BIT, HAME, REIN, TRACE, BRIDLE, COLLAR, HALTER, SADDLE, BLIND(ER)
ring .... TERRET
strap/item .... TRACE, CRUPPER, MARTINGAL(E)
harnessed horses .... SPAN, TEAM
Harold, diminutive of .... HAL
harp .... KOTO, LYRE, NANGA, TRIGON
constellation .... LYRA
like instrument ...... SAMBUKE, DULCIMER, PSALTERY
slang .... IRISHMAN
Harpers Ferry event .... RAID
harpoon .... SPEAR, JAVELIN
barb .... FLUKE
missile like a .... HURLBAT
harpsichord .... SPINET, VIRGINAL
Harpy .... NAG, AELLO, EAGLE, WITCH, BUZZARD, CELAENO, MONSTER, OCYPETE
harquebus .... HAGBUT, FIREARM, HACKBUT

fork .... CROC
harridan .... HAG, NAG, FURY,
    SHREW, VIRAGO, JEZEBEL
harried .... BESET
harrier ...... DOG, HAWK, FALCON
Harriet, diminutive of
    .... HATTIE
harrow .... VEX, DRAG, BRAKE,
    LACERATE
Harrow, rival of .... ETON
harry .... RAID, BESET, TEASE,
    HARASS, PESTER, PILLAGE
Harry, Old .... DEVIL, SATAN
harsh .... GRIM, CRUDE, CRUEL,
    ROUGH, STARK, STERN,
    BITTER, COARSE, SEVERE,
    DRASTIC
and dry .... HACKING
critic .... SLATER
sharply .... ACERB
sound .... STRIDOR
taste .... ACERB, BITTER
voiced person .... STENTOR
harsher .... CRUELER
harshness .... RIGOR, ASPERITY
hart .... DEER, STAG
Harte, author .... BRET(T)
character .... AH SIN
hartebeest .... ASSE, TORA,
    CAAMA, LECAMA, ANTELOPE
kin of .... SASSABY
hartstongue .... FERN
harum-scarum ...... RASH, WILD,
    RECKLESS
haruspex .... PRIEST, SOOTHSAYER
Harvard educator .... PUSEY,
    CONANT, LOWELL
man .... CANTAB
newspaper .... CRIMSON
harvest .... CROP, REAP, YIELD
abundant .... BUMPER CROP
feast .... KIRN
festival .... LAMMAS
leftover .... STUMP, STUBBLE
harvesting machine ...... REAPER
harvestman .... DADDY-LONGLEGS
hash .... MINCE, JUMBLE, MEDLEY,
    MIX(TURE), RAMEKIN,
    MULLIGAN, HODGEPODGE
house: sl. .... JOINT, EATERY
mark: military .... STRIPE
hashish ...... B(H)ANG, CANNABIS,
    NARCOTIC, MARIJUANA
source .... HEMP
hasp .... CATCH, SKEIN
hassle ...... FRAY, BRAWL, MELEE,
    RUCKUS, SQUABBLE
Hasso, actress .... SIGNE
hassock .... MAT, CUSHION,
    TUSSOCK, FOOTSTOOL
haste .... HURRY, SPEED, URGENCY

hasten .... HIE, DASH, RUSH,
    HURRY, SPEED(UP), QUICKEN,
    ACCELERATE
hasty .... FAST, RASH, BRASH,
    QUICK, ABRUPT, URGENT,
    TEARING, CURSORY, HURRIED,
    IMPATIENT, IMPETUOUS,
    IMPULSIVE
effort .... LICK
pudding .... MUSH, SEPON
hat .... CAP, LID, TAM, FELT,
    BERET, TOQUE, BONNET,
    SCONCE, TOPPER, CAUBEEN,
    CHAPEAU, PETASOS, PETASUS,
    HEADGEAR
angel's .... HALO
beaver fur .... CASTOR
brimless .... FEZ, TOQUE
chef's .... TOQUE
collapsible .... GIBUS
crown .... POLL
cylindrical .... SHAKO
decoration .... POMPON,
    COCKADE
ecclesiastic .... BIRETTA
feature .... BRIM
felt .... FEDORA, HOMBURG
fur .... CONEY, CASTOR
holder .... BANDBOX
hunter's .... TERAI
lining leather .... SKIVER
maker .... MILLINER
making fiber .... BUNTAL,
    RAFFIA
material .... FELT, VELOUR(S)
opera .... GIBUS
part .... BAND, BRIM, LINING
pith .... TOPI, TOPEE, HELMET
rack feature .... PRONG
silk .... BEAVER
slang .... LID
small .... COIF
soldier's .... KEPI, BERET,
    BUSBY, SHAKO, HAVELOCK
straw .... PANAMA, LEGHORN
style .... HOMBURG, PORKPIE
take off .... DOFF, VAIL
tasseled .... FEZ
that crowned the West
    .... STETSON
three-cornered .... TRICORN
trimming .... ROULEAU
woman's ...... TOQUE, CLOCHE,
    TURBAN, PILLBOX
hatch .... PLAN, PLOT, DEVISE,
    CONCOCT, FISHTRAP,
    TRAPDOOR
hatchel .... TEASE
hatchery .... INCUBATOR
hatchet .... AX, TOMAHAWK
man .... GOON

stone .... MOGO
hatchway .... DOOR, SCUTTLE
hate .... ABHOR, ODIUM, SPITE,
    ENMITY, LOATHE, MALICE,
    PHOBIA, DETEST, DESPISE,
    DISLIKE, AVERSION,
    ABOMINATE
combining form .... MIS(O)
of foreigners ...... XENOPHOBIA
hateful .... ODIOUS, HEINOUS,
    HOSTILE, EXECRABLE,
    LOATHSOME, OBNOXIOUS,
    REPUGNANT, REPULSIVE,
    ABOMINABLE
person .... CAD, TOAD
Hatfield enemy .... MCCOY
hath .... CUBIT
hatred .... HATE, ODIUM, ENMITY,
    DISLIKE, ILL WILL, AVERSION,
    ANIMOSITY
combining form .... MIS(O)
of change .... MISONEISM
of debate .... MISOLOGY
of mankind ...... MISANTHROPY
of marriage .... MISOGAMY
of women .... MISOGYNY
hats, women's .... MILLINERY
hatrack .... TREE
hatter, woman .... MILLINER
Hatteras .... CAPE
hauberk .... ARMOR
haughtiness .... HAUTEUR,
    ARROGANCE
haughty .... PROUD, SNOOTY,
    STUCK-UP, ARROGANT,
    CAVALIER
haul ...... LUG, TOW, DRAG, HALE,
    DRAW, PULL, SWAG, BOOTY,
    BOUSE, CATCH, HEAVE
haulage .... CARTAGE, PORTAGE
hauling car .... VAN
haulm .... HAY, CULM, STEM,
    STALK, STRAW
haunch .... HIP, HUCKLE
bone .... ILIUM
part .... HIP, LEG, LOIN, THIGH,
    BUTTOCK
haunt ...... DEN, DIVE, LAIR, NEST,
    SPOOK, HANG-OUT, PURLIEU,
    RETREAT, FREQUENT
in mind .... OBSESS
of literary hacks .... GRUB
    STREET
hausfrau .... HOUSEWIFE
hautboy .... OBOE
haute monde .... HIGH SOCIETY
hauteur .... PRIDE, SNOBBERY,
    ARROGANCE
Havana ...... CIGAR, (LA)PARASITA
castle .... MORRO
have .... HOLD, ENJOY, POSSESS

a flat .... BLOW A TIRE
a runny nose .... SNIVEL
a session .... SIT, MEET
at .... ATTACK
at bay .... TREE
effect .... TELL
feeling .... SENTIENT
feet .... PEDATE
flavor .... SAPID, TASTY
high objectives .... ASPIRE
it made .... SUCCEED
limits .... FINITE
no worries .... CAREFREE
nothing to do with ...... AVOID
offensive smell .... OLID
on .... WEAR
one too many ...... OVERTIPPLE
relevance .... PERTAIN
ribs .... COSTATE
rough edges .... EROSE,
RAGGED
same origin .... COGNATE,
CONNATE
scruples .... DEMUR
spikes .... TINED, PRONGED
stamina .... LAST
strong desire for .... COVET,
HUNGER
the look .... SEEM
title to .... OWN
haven .... PORT, ASYLUM,
HARBOR, REFUGE, SHELTER,
SANCTUARY
animal's .... PRESERVE
ship's .... ANCHORAGE
haversack .... (CANVAS)BAG
having a dull surface ...... MATTE
a nucleus .... CORED
an incised margin .... EROSE
an old face .... LINED
difficulty ...... IN A HOLE, IN A
MESS
handles .... ANSATE
keen vision .... EAGLE-EYED
lugs/projections .... EARED
no feet .... APOD
omens of success
.... AUSPICIAL
one's marbles .... SANE
rhythm .... CADENT
the shakes .... QUIVERING
two ancestral lines of
descent .... DIPHYLETIC
two sepals or leaves
.... DIPHYLLOUS
havoc .... RUIN
haw .... SLOE, BERRY, FRUIT,
EYELID, FALTER
companion of .... HEM
inflammation .... STY
opposed to .... GEE

Hawaii .... OWYHEE, CROSSROADS
OF THE PACIFIC
author of .... MICHENER
discoverer of .... GAETANO
former status of
.... TERRITORY
garden island .... KAUAI
name in .... DOLE, INOUYE
state bird .... NENE
state flower .... HIBISCUS
state nickname .... ALOHA
valley island .... MAUI
Hawaiian .... KANAKA,
LANGUAGE, POLYNESIAN
acacia .... KOA
apple .... MAILE
association/club .... HUI
baking pit .... IMU
bathing resort .... WAIKIKI
bay .... HILO, HALAWA,
KAHANA, KIHOLO, MAMALA,
WAIMEA, WAIPIO, KANAPOU,
MAALAEA, KAWAIHAE,
NAWILIWILI
beach .... EWA, SUNSET,
WAIKIKI, KAWAILOA,
WAIMANALO, BLACK SAND
bird .... IO, OO, IIWI, KOAE,
MAMO, NENE, NOIO, OMAO,
OOAA, NUKUPUU
blueberry .... OHELO
bonito .... AKU
breech cloth .... MALO
canoe .... WAPA
cape .... KA LAE, KAWAIHOA,
KUMUKAHI
capital .... HONOLULU
channel .... KAIWI, KAUAI,
KALOHI, PAILOLO, KAULAKAHI
chant/song .... MELE
city/town .... AIEA, HILO, LAIE,
KAPAA, KIHEI, KAILUA,
MAKAHA, MOKAPU, WAIMEA,
KAHULUI, KANEOHE, LAHAINA,
WAHIAWA, WAIALUA,
WAILUKU, WAIPAHU,
MAKAKILO, HANAPEPE,
MILILANI, NANAKULI, ALA
MOANA, EWA BEACH,
MAUNAWILI, PEARL CITY
cliff/precipice .... PALI
cloak .... MAMO
cloth .... KAPA, TAPA
coffee .... KONA
county .... MAUI, KAUAI,
HAWAII, KALAWAO, HONOLULU
dance .... HULA
dancer/woman .... WAHINE
desert .... KAU
dress .... MUUMUU
drink .... KAVA

emblem .... LEHUA
falls .... WAILUA, RAINBOW
farewell/greeting .... ALOHA
feast/party .... LUAU
fern .... HEII, IWAIWA
fiber .... WAUKE
fish .... AHI, AKU, ULUA,
LANIA, PALANI
flower .... LEHUA, HIBISCUS
food .... POI, TARO
frigate bird .... IWA
fruit .... POHA
game .... HEI
garland/wreath .... LEI
god .... KANE, KUPO
goddess of fire .... PELE
goose .... NENE, NENI
grass .... HILO
harbor .... PEARL, HONOLULU
hawk .... IO
head .... KOKO, KAUIKI,
DIAMOND
herb .... NOLA
highest point ...... MAUNA KEA
hill .... PUNCHBOWL,
SUGARLOAF
honeyeater .... OO
island ...... FORD, KURE, MAUI,
OAHU, SAND, KAUAI, KAULA,
LANAI, NIHOA, HAWAII,
HIIHAU, LAYSAN, MANANA,
NECKER, MOLOKAI, MOLOKINI,
LISIANSKI
Islands, former name of
.... SANDWICH (ISLANDS)
lagoon .... KEEHI
lake .... SALT, HALALII
language .... POLYNESIAN
lava .... AA
liquor .... AWA, KAWA
lizard fish .... ULAE
loincloth .... PAU, MALO,
MARO
mountain .... KAALA,
HUALALAI, RED HILL,
TANTALUS, LANAIHALE,
MAUNA KEA, PUU KUKUI,
ROUND TOP, WAIALEALE, LUA
MAKIKA
mountain chain .... KOHALA,
KOOLAU, WAIANAE
musical instrument .... PUA,
UKE(LELE)
national park .... HALEAKALA
neckpiece .... LAI, LEI
newcomer .... MALHINI
noble .... ALII
noddy .... NOIO
nut .... LITCHI
octopus .... HEE
papercloth .... OLONA

pepper .... AVA
plant .... KALO, OLONA
plantation boss .... LUNA
porch .... LANA(I)
port .... HILO
range .... KOOLAU
raven .... ALALA
reef .... MARO
river .... WAIMEA, WAILUKU,
                   WAINIHA
royal chief .... ALII,
             KAMEHAMEHA
seaweed .... LIMU
senator .... INOUYE
shampoo .... LOMILOMI
shrub .... AKIA
singing star .... DON HO
starch .... APII
taro, fermented .... MOD
taro paste .... POI
tern .... NOIO
thrush .... (OL)OMAO
tree .... TI, KOA, AULU, OHIA,
     AALII, ALANI, LEHUA, ILIAHI
tree fern .... AMAU, PULU
valley .... MANOA
volcano ...... KILAUEA, MAUNA
         KEA, MAUNA LOA
windstorm .... KONA
wood .... KOU, MILO
yam .... HOI
hawfinch .... GROSBEAK
Hawhaw of WW II .... LORD
hawk ...... KITE, ELANITE FALCON,
    MERLIN, PEDDLE, CHEATER,
    HARRIER, CARACARA
bill of .... PAWL
blind .... SEEL
cage .... MEW
carrier .... CAD
falconry .... BATER
genus .... BUTEO, ACCIPITER
head cover .... SEEL
headed god .... RA, HORUS
leash of .... JESS, LUNE
leg's feather .... FLAG
like bird .... KITE, OSPREY
male .... TERCEL
moth .... SPHINX
nemesis of the .... HOUBARA
opponent of .... DOVE
parrot .... HIA
small ...... EYAS, KITE, ELANET
sparrow .... NISUS
stomach of .... PANNEL
swoop of .... SOUSE
young ...... EYAS, AERIE, EYRIE
hawker .... CADGER, COSTER,
    PEDLAR, CHAPMAN, PEDDLER,
    FALCONER, HUCKSTER
route of .... WALK

spot/talk of .... PITCH
Hawkeye .... IOWAN
State .... IOWA
Hawkshaw .... DICK, SLEUTH,
             DETECTIVE
hawkweed .... DINDLE
hawser frame/holder .... BITT,
           BOLLARD
iron .... CALKING
knot .... BEND
post .... BOLLARD
hawthorn .... AZAROLE,
    COCKSPUR, MAY(FLOWER)
fruit .... HAW, BERRY
Hawthorne birthplace .... SALEM
character ..... (HESTER)PRYNNE
hay ...... GRASS, CLOVER, FODDER,
    ALFALFA, TIMOTHY
bird .... BLACKCAP
box .... MANGER
bundle of .... TRUSS
fever .... ROSE COLD,
           POLLINOSIS
fever, cause of .... POLLEN
fodder .... CHAFF
for thatching .... HA(U)LM
grass .... REDTOP
hit the .... SLEEP, RETIRE
lifting tool .... PITCHFORK
pile .... COCK
second crop .... ROWEN
spread the .... TED
storage place .... LOFT
haycock .... COB, RACK, RICK
Hayden, ballerina .... MELISSA
hayloft .... MOW
hayseed .... HICK, RUBE, RUSTIC
haystack .... COB, COIL, GOAF,
    MOW, PIKE, RICK
haywire .... AMOK, CRAZY,
         DISORDERLY
Hayworth, actress .... RITA
role .... SADIE (THOMPSON)
hazard .... RISK, PERIL, STAKE,
    CHANCE, DANGER, WAGER,
    VENTURE, JEOPARDY
hazardous .... RISKY, UNSAFE,
    PERILOUS, DANGEROUS
haze .... FOG, FILM, GLIN, MIST,
    PALL, SMOG, BRUME, VAPOR
hazel .... NUT, TREE, WOOD,
    BIRCH, SHRUB
hazelnut .... FILBERT
hazy .... FOGGY, VAGUE, OBSCURE
he .... ANYONE, PERSON
carved it .... SCULPSIT
caused trouble between
   Dickens and Thackeray
    .... YATES
combining form .... MALE
had no choice .... HOBSON

has the world on his
   shoulders .... ATLAS
in chemistry .... HELIUM
is no gentleman .... CAD
Latin .... IPSE
-man, describing a
   .... MACHO, VIRILE
painted it .... PNXT, PINXIT
people .... MEN
was slain by Diana ..... ORION
who claimed to rule the
   waves .... CANUTE
wrote about man's origin
   .... DARWIN
wrote it .... SCRIPSIT
he'll never bite .... A BARKING
           DOG
he's at the pearly gates .... PETER
on first .... WHO
head .... NOB, TOP, VAN, MIND,
    PATE, POLL, TETE, FRONT,
    SKULL, CAPITA, MAZARD,
    LEAD(ER), APTITUDE
and shoulders .... BUST
and shoulders cover .... NUBIA
back part .... POLL
band .... FILLET
beer .... FROTH
cold .... CORYZA, SNIFFLES
colloquial .... PATE, WITS,
    NODDLE, SCONCE
combining form
   .... CEPHAL(O)
counting .... CENSUS,
    CAPITATION
cover .... CAP, HAT, COWL,
    HAIR, HOOD, HELMET,
    TURBAN, WIMPLE
crown of .... PATE, VERTEX
garland .... CHAPLET
hair of .... POLL
like structure .... CAPUT
monastery .... ABBOT
nautical: sl. .... TOILET
newspaper .... CAPTION
of hair .... CRINE
of nunnery .... AMMA
of the ..... CEPHALIC, PARIETAL
off .... AVERT, INTERCEPT
pain .... HEMIALGIA,
    HEMICRANIA
protective covering ..... MASK,
    HELMET, MORION
shaped like .... CAPITATE
shaved .... TONSURE
shrinker .... ANALYST
skin of .... SCALP
slang .... NOB, NUT, BEAN,
    DOME, NOGGIN
start .... LEAD
sweller .... EGO

to foot .... CAP-A-PIE
top of .... PATE, CROWN,
    VERTEX
wear .... CAP, HAT, BERET,
    BEANIE
wearing crown, describing
    .... UNEASY
wrap .... NUBIA, TURBAN,
    BURNOOSE, TARBOOSH
wreath .... LAUREL, CHAPLET
Head, _____ (Blue Ridge
range) .... CAESAR'S
headache .... MEGRIM, MIGRAINE,
    HEMIALGIA
colloquial .... WORRY,
    PROBLEM
type of .... TENSION, MIGRAINE
headband .... AGAL, FILLET,
    TAENIA
headdress .... WIG, POUF, TIAR(A),
    DIADEM, TOUPEE, TURBAN,
    COMMODE, COIFFURE
bishop's .... MITER, MITRE
capelike .... PINNER
cowl-like .... ALMUCE
nun's .... CORNET, WIMPLE
of feathers .... TOPKNOT
used by Arab .... AGAL
widow's .... BANDORE
women's .... POUF, MILLINERY,
    POMPADOUR
headgear ...... CAP, HAT, TIAR(A),
    TOQUE, HELMET, HARNESS
decorative .... CORONET
headhunter .... DAYAK
heading .... DRIFT, TITLE,
    CAPTION, GALLERY
headland .... RAS, CAPE, HOOK,
    SPIT, NESS, BLUFF,
    PROMONTORY
headless ...... ETETE, ACEPHALOUS
man of fiction
    .... (BROM)BONES
headline .... BANNER, SPLASH,
    SCREAMER, STREAMER
headliner .... LEAD, ATTRACTION,
    (SUPER)STAR
of 1898 .... MAINE
1909 .... PEARY
1914 .... WORLD WAR
1917 .... AEF, DOUGHBOY,
    ARMISTICE
1927 .... LINDBERGH
1934 .... DIONNE
1941 .... PEARL HARBOR
1945 .... A-BOMB,
    HIROSHIMA
1957 .... SPUTNIK
1959 .... CASTRO
1963 .... KENNEDY
1969 .... MAN ON MOON,

    (NEIL)ARMSTRONG
1991 .... WAR IN THE GULF
headlong .... HASTY, RASH(LY),
    PELLMELL, RECKLESS
fall .... CROPPER
flight .... LAM, STAMPEDE
headmaster .... RECTOR,
    PRINCIPAL
headpiece .... CAP, HELMET
medieval .... ARMET
headquarters .... BASE, SEATS,
    MAIN OFFICE
headrest .... PILLOW
headsman .... EXECUTIONER
headspring ...... ORIGIN, SOURCE,
    FOUNTAIN
headstone .... STELE, BARROW,
    GRAVESTONE
ancient .... DOLMEN,
    CROMLECH
headstrong .... RASH, WILLFUL,
    STUBBORN, OBSTINATE, SELF-
    WILLED
headwaiter .... CAPTAIN
headway .... GAIN, PROGRESS
of a sort .... DENT
heady .... RASH, NAPPY,
    HEADSTRONG
heal .... CURE, EASE, MEND, GET
    WELL, REMEDY, REPAIR,
    RECONCILE, RECUPERATE
healer .... DOCTOR, SHAMAN
kind of .... FAITH, QUACK,
    MEDICINE MAN
healing .... IATRIC, CURATIVE,
    REMEDIAL, MEDICINAL,
    THERAPEUTIC
substance .... BALM, DRUG,
    NOSTRUM, PANACEA, MEDICINE
health .... SALUBRITY,
    SOUNDNESS, WELL-BEING
condition .... WELFARE
drinking toast .... SALUD,
    CHEERS, PROSIT, MABUHAY
science of .... HYGIENE,
    HYGIENICS
healthful .... HYGIENIC,
    SALUTARY, WHOLESOME,
    SALABRIOUS
healthy .... HALE, WELL, PEPPY,
    SOUND, HEARTY, ROBUST,
    SALABRIOUS
looking .... TANNED
heap ...... MOW, PILE, RAFF, RAFT,
    RUCK, MOUND, (A)MASS,
    STACK, SORITE, CONGERIES
colloquial .... LOTS, GREAT
    DEAL
combustible .... PYRE
of a .... ACERVAL
of rock fragments ...... DEBRIS

piled by wind .... DRIFT
slang .... CAR
stone .... CAIRN, MOUND,
    SCREE
hear .... LEARN, LISTEN,
    HARK(EN), HEARKEN
a case again .... RETRY
ye .... OYES, OYEZ
hearer .... AUDITOR, LISTENER
hearing .... OYER, INQUEST,
    AUDIENCE, AUDITION,
    INTERVIEW
aid .... EAR(PHONE),
    AUDIPHONE
court .... TRIAL
of ..... OTIC, AURAL, ACOUSTIC,
    AUDITORY
organ .... OTOCYST
range .... EARSHOT
science of .... AUDIOLOGY
hearken .... HEAR, HEED, HIST,
    ATTEND, LIST(EN)
Hearn, writer .... LAFCADIO
hearsay .... TALK, RUMOR, GOSSIP,
    REPORT
means of spreading
    .... GRAPEVINE
hearse .... BIER
cover .... PALL
heart .... COR(E), GIST, GRIT, PITH,
    CARDIA, SPIRIT, ESSENCE
action record .... CARDIOGRAM
ailment ...... ANGINA, CARDITIS
attack .... STROKE
auricle(s) .... ATRIA, ATRIUM
beat condition .... FLUTTER,
    PALPITATION
beat regulator ..... PACEMAKER
bleeding .... DICENTRA
blood vessel .... AORTA
booster .... LVB, PACER
cavity .... ATRIUM, CAMERA,
    AURICLE
colloquial .... TICKER
contraction .... SYSTOLE
deposit .... PLAQUE,
    CHOLESTEROL
inflammation .... CARDITIS
leaf .... MEDIC
of a baboon recipient
    .... BABY FAE
of the .... CARDIAC
part .... AURICLE, VENTRICLE
point .... FESS
shaped .... CORDATE
sound .... MURMUR
stimulant .... CORDIAL,
    DIGITALIS, SPARTEIN(E)
-to-heart .... FRANK, CANDID,
    INTIMATE
trouble .... ANGINA

heartache .... WOE, GRIEF, SORROW

heartbeat .... PULSE, THROB, PULSATION

heartbroken .... FORLORN

heartburn .... ENVY, PYROSIS, JEALOUSY, CARDIALGIA

hearten .... CHEER (UP), ENCOURAGE

heartfelt .... GENUINE, SINCERE

hearth ...... HOME, LING, FIRESIDE

goddess of the .... VESTA, HESTIA

heartleaf .... MEDIC

heartless .... COLD, CRUEL, HARSH, UNKIND, CALLOUS, PITILESS, SARDONIC, MERCILESS

hearten .... CHEER(UP), GLADDEN, INSPIRE

hearts/diamonds .... (RED)SUIT

heartrending .... MOVING, PITIFUL, TOUCHING

heartsease .... PANSY, PERSICARY, WALLFLOWER

heartsick .... SAD, ANGUISHED

heartwarming .... GLAD, CHEERY, BLISSFUL, REWARDING

heartwood .... DURA(MEN)

heartworm .... NEMATODE

hearty .... HALE, WELL, LUSTY, GENIAL, ROBUST, SAILOR, STRONG, CORDIAL, VIGOROUS

heat ...... IRE, FIRE, ZEAL, ANGER, ARDOR, CALOR, CAUMA, TEPOR, FEVER, FERVOR, WARM(TH), EXCITEMENT

animal .... RUT

caused by .... THERMIC

combining form ...... THERMO, THERMY

decomposition by .... PYROLYSIS

lightning .... WILDFIRE

meas. .... BTU

oppressive .... SWELTER

pertaining to .... CALEFY, CALORIC, THERMAL, THERMIC

prostration .... SUNSTROKE

rash .... MILIARIA

resistant .... STABILE

unit .... BTU, CALORY, THERM(E), CALORIE

heated .... HOT, AFIRE, ANGRY, FIERY

to whiteness .... CANDENT

heater .... ETNA, OVEN, STOVE, BUNSEN, BURNER

portable .... CHAUFFER

heath .... BENT, MOOR, ERICA, AZALEA

heathen .... PAGAN, PAYNIM, GENTILE, INFIDEL, IRRELIGIOUS

heather .... LING, ERICA, GORSE

heating device .... ETNA, OVEN, STOVE, BOILER, BURNER, RETORT

heaume .... HELMET

heave .... CAST, GASP, HAUL, HEFT, HURL, LIFT, PANT, FLING, RAISE, SWELL

heaven .... SKY, CIEL, EDEN, GLORY, ELYSIUM, PARADISE, FIRMAMENT

arch of .... SKY

combining form .... URANO

edge of .... HORIZON

personified .... URANUS

heavenly .... HOLY, DIVINE, EDENIC, URANIC, ANGELIC, ELYSIAN, ETHEREAL, CELESTIAL

being .... ANGEL, CHERUB, SERAPH(IM)

body .... SUN, MOON, STAR, COMET, METEOR, PLANET

drink .... NECTAR

hunter .... ORION

pasta .... ANGEL HAIR

path .... ORBIT

heavens, belt of .... ZODIAC

heaves .... BROKEN WIND

get the .... RETCH

heavily .... SADLY, BLEAKLY, DENSELY, ONEROUSLY

involved .... UP TO HIS EARS

heavy .... SLOW, GRAVE, INERT, GLOOMY, LEADEN, MASSIVE, SERIOUS, TEDIOUS, WEIGHTY, PONDEROUS

blow .... ONER, HAYMAKER

duty .... TOUGH, RUGGED, STURDY

fingers .... THUMBS

handed .... CRUEL, ARBITRARY, OPPRESSIVE

load .... BURDEN

metal .... LEAD

plus .... OBESE

role .... VILLAIN

step/walk .... SLOG, TROD

weight .... TON

wire .... CABLE

with child .... PREGNANT

heavyweight ...... BOXER, BIGWIG, FIGHTER, PUGILIST

name .... ALI, TYSON

Norton .... KEN

hebdomad .... WEEK, SEVEN

hebetate .... DULL, STUPID

Hebraic law .... TORAH

Hebraism .... JUDAISM

Hebrew .... ZION, DANITE, S(H)EMITE, ISRAELITE

acrostic .... AGLA

alien resident .... GER

ancestor .... EBER

ascetic .... ESSENE, NAZARITE

bible books .... NEBIIM

bread .... AZYM

bride .... KALLAH

brotherhood .... ESSENE

bushel .... EPHA

calendar month:

first .... ABIB, NISAN

second .... ZIV, IYYAR

third .... SIVAN

fourth .... TAMMUZ

fifth .... AV

sixth .... ELUL

seventh ..... TISHRI, ETHANIM

eight ...... BUL, MARCHESVAN

ninth .... KISLEV

tenth .... TEVET, TEBETH

eleventh .... SHEBAT, SHEVAT

twelfth .... ADAR

canonical book .... TALMUD

city .... KIRJATH

coin .... GERAH, SHEKEL

day .... YOM

drum .... TOPH

ear of corn .... ABIB

father .... ABA, ABRAHAM

festival .... PURIM, SEDER

first month .... TISHRI

flute .... NEHILOTH

god .... EL, ADONAI, ELOHIM, YAHWEH, JEHOVAH

greeting .... SHALOM

healer .... ASA

herdsman .... AMOS

high priest .... ELI, EZRA

horn .... SHOFAR, SHOPHAR

hymn .... KADDISH

idols .... TERAPHIM

incantation/melody ...... ELIELI

instrument .... ASOR

judge .... ELI, ELON

juniper .... EZEL

king .... SAUL, DAVID

kingdom .... ISRAEL

language .... RABBINIC

law of Moses .... TORA(H)

lawgiver .... MOSES

letter .... PE(H), A(Y)IN, FEH, JOD, MEM, NUN, TAV, TAW, VAU, WAW, YOD(H), ALEF, BET(H), CAPH, KAPH, KOPH, RESH, S(H)IN, TET(H), ALEPH, CHET(H), GIMEL, SADHE, ZAYIN, LAMED(H), DALETH, SAMEKH

lyre .... ASOR
marriage custom
.... LEVERATE
measure .... HIN, KAB, KOR,
　　REBA, EPHA(H), (H)OMER
month, old ...... BUL, ETHANIM
my Lord .... ADONAI
name for God .... EL, ADONAI,
　　ELOHIM
name for Syria .... ARAM
order .... ESSENE
Passover month .... ABIB
perpetual lamp ...... NERTAMID
precept .... TORA(H)
priest .... LEVITE
princess .... SARAH
prophet ..... JOEL, NASI, AMOS,
　　ELIAS, HOSEA, NAHUM,
　　DANIEL, HAGGAI, ISAIAH,
　　EZRA, JONAH, MICAH, ELISHA,
　　MALACHI, JEREMIAH
prophetess .... DEBORAH
psalms of praise .... HALLEL
quarter .... GHETTO
religion .... JUDAISM,
　　HEBRAISM
sanctuary .... BAMAH
scarf .... ABNET, TALLITH
scholar ...... AMORA, HALAKIST
scripture marginal notes
.... MASORA
seer .... BALAAM
son .... BEN
teacher .... REBBE, RABBI
ten .... YOD(H)
trader .... BANIAN
tribe .... DAN, LEVITES
universe .... OLAM
weight .... OMER, GERAH,
　　SHEKEL
white .... LABAN
word .... SELAH
Hebrides island .... IONA, MULL,
　　SKYE, UIST
hecatomb .... SACRIFICE
heck! .... HELL, INTERJECTION
heckle ...... BAIT, ANNOY, TAUNT,
　　NEEDLE, HATCHEL
heckler .... BOOER, HOOTER,
　　HISSER, TEASER, TAUNTER
hectic .... FEBRILE, FEVERED,
　　FEVERISH, CONSUMPTIVE
hector .... BAIT, HUFF, BULLY,
　　TEASE, PESTER, HARASS,
　　BRAWLER, BROWBEAT
Hector, parent of .... PRIAM,
　　HECUBA
wife of .... ANDROMACHE
Hecuba's children .... PARIS,
　　HECTOR, TROILUS,
　　CASSANDRA

husband .... PRIAM
heddle .... CAAM
hedge ...... HAW, HEM, REW, ROW,
　　BOMA, BUSH, FENCE, WAVER,
　　BARRIER, HEM AND HAW,
　　TEMPORIZE, EQUIVOCATE
form a .... PLASH
pant .... PRIVET
trimmer .... PLASHER
hedgehog .... URCHIN, ECHINOS,
　　PORCUPINE
like animal .... TENREC
spine .... QUILL
hedgerow .... REW
Hedin, explorer
.... SVEN(ANDERS)
hedonist .... VOLUPTUARY
heebie-jeebies .... JITTERS,
　　NERVOUSNESS
heed .... MIND, OBEY, RECK,
　　HEAR(KEN), LISTEN, NOTICE
heedful .... ATTENT(IVE)
heedless .... DEAF, CARELESS,
　　UNMINDFUL
heehaw .... BRAY, GUFFAW,
　　LAUGH(TER)
heel ...... CAD, CALX, CANT, LEAN,
　　LIST, TILT, LOUSE, CAREEN,
　　BOUNDER
bone .... FIBULA
bone tendon .... ACHILLES
boot's .... DUCE
combining form .... TALO
down at the .... SEEDY,
　　SHABBY
over .... TILT, CAPSIZE
slang .... RAT
heeled: sl. .... RICH, ARMED,
　　MONEYED
heeler .... COCK, HANGER-ON
Heflin, actor .... VAN
heft .... PULL, HEAVE, WEIGHT,
　　INFLUENCE
hefty ...... BULKY, BURLY, HEAVY,
　　BRAWNY, WEIGHTY
Hegel, philosopher .... GEORG
hegira .... FLIGHT, JOURNEY
destination .... MEDINA
hegumen .... ABBOT
Hehe crop .... MAIZE, MILLET
Heidelberg memento .... SCAR
Heidi's peaks .... ALPS
heifer .... COW, STIRK
maid changed to .... IO
height .... TOP, ACME, SUMMIT,
　　EXTREME, STATURE,
　　ALTITUDE, PINNACLE,
　　TALLNESS, ELEVATION,
　　LOFTINESS
of play's action .... CLIMAX,
　　CATASTASIS, DENOUEMENT

prefix .... ALTI
heighten .... ENHANCE, INCREASE,
　　INTENSIFY
heinous .... ODIOUS, WICKED,
　　HATEFUL, MONSTROUS,
　　ABOMINABLE
heir .... SON, SCION, LEGATEE,
　　(IN)HERITOR
earth .... (THE)MEEK
kind of .... APPARENT
legal .... HERES
to a throne ..... CROWN PRINCE
heirloom .... KEEPSAKE,
　　SOUVENIR, HERITABLE
heist .... THEFT, HOLDUP,
　　ROBBERY, BURGLARY
slang .... CAPER
Hejaz capital .... MECCA
city .... MEDINA
Hel .... GODDESS
held .... GRIPPED, DETAINED
capable of being ..... TENABLE
in music .... TENUTO
in trust .... FIDUCIARY
Helen .... ELENA, ELAINE, AILEEN,
　　EILEEN
diminutive of .... LENA,
　　NELL(Y)
Mitchell Armstrong
.... MELBA
of Troy's abductor .... PARIS
daughter .... HERMIONE
grandson .... ION
husband .... MENELAUS
mother .... LEDA
son .... DORUS
suitor .... AJAX, PARIS
heliacal .... SOLAR
helianthus .... SUNFLOWER
helical .... TORSE, SPIRAL
helicoid .... SPIRAL
Helicon .... TUBA, MOUNTAIN
dweller .... MUSE
helicopter .... GIRO, CHOPPER,
　　WHIRLYBIRD
kin .... AUTOGIRO
part .... ROTOR
Heliopolis .... BAALBEK
Helios .... APOLLO, SUN GOD,
　　HYPERION
daughter of .... CIRCE
father of .... HYPERION
sister of .... ARTEMIS
heliotrope .... TURNSOLE,
　　(SUN)FLOWER, BLOODSTONE
helix .... SNAIL, SPIRAL, MOLLUSK
hell .... PIT, ABYSS, HADES, SHEOL,
　　ABADDON, AVERNUS,
　　GEHENNA, INFERNO,
　　TARTARUS
biblical .... TOPHET(H)

border of .... LIMBO
capital of .... PANDEMONIUM
diver .... DABCHICK
euphemism for .... HECK
in New Testament
.... GEHENNA
Sherman's .... WAR
Hellas .... GREECE
hellbender ...... SPREE, DEBAUCH,
SALAMANDER
hellbent ...... SET(ON), RESOLVED,
DETERMINED
hellcat .... SHREW, VIXEN, WITCH,
VIRAGO
Hellene .... GREEK
Hellenic Republic .... GREECE
Hellenism .... GRECISM
Hellespont .... DARDANELLES
swimmer .... LEANDER
hellhound .... FIEND, CERBERUS
hellish .... STYGIAN, FIENDISH,
INFERNAL
helm ...... STEER, WHEEL, RUDDER,
TILLER
letters .... ENE
position .... ALEE
Helmer, Mrs. .... NORA
helmet ...... HAT, ARMET, CASQUE,
HEAUME, SALLET, MORION,
SCONCE, BAS(I)NET,
BURGONET
front .... VENTAIL
light .... ARMET
opening .... VUE
part .... VISOR, BEAVER
pith .... TOPI, TOPEE
plume .... PANACHE
shaped .... GALEATE
helminth .... (TAPE)WORM
helmsman .... COX(ON), PILOT,
CONNER, TILLER, STEERSMAN
Heloise, husband of .... ABELARD
helot .... ESNE, SERF, SLAVE
Helot's home .... SPARTA
help .... AID, ABET, SERVE, ASSIST,
RELIEF, WAIT ON, REMEDY,
SERVANT, SUCCO(U)R
bring about .... LEAD TO
me signal .... SOS, MAYDAY
of any kind .... LIFT
over .... TIDE
with the dishes .... DRY
helper .... ALLY, SECOND
helpful .... USEFUL, FAVORABLE
helpless .... LOST, WEAK, FEEBLE,
CRIPPLED, IMPOTENT,
DEPENDENT, SPINELESS
rendered .... HOGTIED
helpmate .... WIFE, SPOUSE
Helsingfors .... HELSINKI
helter-skelter .... AWRY,

CHAOTIC, HAYWIRE, HURRIED,
DISORDERLY, TOPSY-TURVY
helve .... ANSE, HAFT, HANDLE
Helvetia .... SWITZERLAND
hem .... EDGE, LIST, BORDER,
MARGIN, SELVAGE, ENCIRCLE
and haw .... HEDGE, FALTER
in .... BESET, CROWD, FENCE,
CORDON(OFF), ENCLOSE
hematin .... HEME
hematite ...... IRON ORE, LIMONITE
hematoma .... TUMOR
Hemingway, author .... ERNEST
character .... BRETT, PILAR
sobriquet .... PAPA
hemiplegia .... PARALYSIS
hemipterous insect .... LICK,
APHID, BEDBUG
hemitrope .... TWIN
hemlock .... YEW, WEED, CONIUM,
POISON, VALERIAN
alkaloid .... CONIN(E)
poison .... BENNET
hemmed in .... GIRT, CAGED
hemophiliac .... BLEEDER
hemorrhage .... BLEEDING
hemorrhoid .... PILES, TUMOR
hemp .... IFE, TOW, PITA, RINE,
SUNN, ABACA, FIBER, PLANT,
RAMIE, HASHISH
cloth .... CANVAS, SACKING
fabric .... GUNNY, BURLAP
fiber .... TOW, AGAVE, SISAL
filament .... HARL
leaves .... KEF, KIEF, BHANG
narcotic ..... CHARAS, HASHISH,
MARIJUANA
refuse .... TOW, HARDS, HURDS
sisal ..... HENEQUEN, HENEQUIN
shrub .... PUA
hempen cloth .... HESSIAN
hen .... BIRD, FOWL, LAYER,
PULLET, CACKLER, CHICKEN
brooding .... SITTER
fruit .... EGG
hawk .... REDTAIL
roost .... PERCH
slang .... WOMAN
small .... BANTY
sound .... CLUCK, CACKLE,
CHUCK(LE), SQUAWK
spayed .... POULARD
henbane .... NIGHTSHADE
henbit .... MINT, PLANT
hence ...... SO, OFF, AWAY, ERGO,
THEN, THUS, THEREFORE
henchman .... LACKEY, SQUIRE,
ADHERENT, FOLLOWER,
HANGER-ON, ATTENDANT
slang .... YESMAN
henequen .... AGAVE, FIBER,

(SISAL)HEMP
Hengist's brother .... HORSA
kingdom .... KENT
henhouse .... COOP
intercom? .... SQUAWK BOX
henna .... DYE, SHRUB, ALCANA
henpeck .... NAG, HOUND,
DOMINEER
henpecked, a la ...... OBEDIENTLY
Henry Cabot .... LODGE
diminutive of ...... HAL, HANK,
HENNY
IV character .... PETO
VIII .... TUDOR
VIII's forte .... REMARRIAGE
VIII's wife .... PARR, ARAGON,
BOLEYN, CLEVES, HOWARD,
SEYMOUR
hep: sl. ...... ON TO, AWARE, WISE
TO, FAMILIAR, INFORMED
hepatic(a) .... LIVERWORT
Hepburn .... AUDREY,
KATHARINE
role .... GIGI, ONDINE
hepcat .... BEATNIK, HIPSTER,
(SWING)DANCER
cry of .... SOLID
Hephaestus .... VULCAN
heptachord .... LYRE
Hera, husband of .... ZEUS,
JUPITER
mother of .... RHEA
of Romans .... JUNO
rival of .... IO, LEDA, LETO,
EUROPA, THEMIS
son of .... ARES
Herakleion .... CANDIA
Herakles .... HERCULES
herald .... CRIER, USHER, BLAZON,
FORETELL, PROCLAIM,
ANNOUNCE(R), MESSENGER
of good news .... GABRIEL
staff of .... CADUCEUS
heraldic .... ARMORIAL
band .... FESS(E), FILLET,
TRESSURE
bearing .... ENTE, ORLE,
FESS(E), GIRON, LAVER,
PHEON, SALTIRE
cross .... PATEE, PATTE
design .... SEME
device .... CREST
dog: var. .... ALANT
fillet .... ORLE
horizontal band .... FESS
mastiff .... ALAN
shield border .... BORDURE
shield boss .... UMBO
shield stripe .... PALE
star .... ESTOILE
term .... ORLE, SEME, PATTE

triangle .... GIRON
wreath .... ORLE, TORSE
heraldry .... ENTE, ARMORY
bar .... LABEL
bastardy mark .... BATON
bear .... GRISE
bend .... COTISE
bird .... MARTLET
circle .... BEZANT, ANNULET
colter .... LAVER
creature .... LION, PARD, BISSE,
    CANNET, GRIFFON, MARTLET
crest .... MARTLET
cross .... CRUX, SALTIRE
division .... PALE, PALY
dog .... ALAN(T)
face-to-face .... AFFRONTE
grafted .... ENTE
green tincture .... VERT
headless .... ETETE
iris .... LIS
laver .... COLTER
left side .... SINISTER
line .... UNDE, UNDY, URDY,
    DEXTER
manacle .... TIRRET
orange tincture .... TENNE
position of animal .... SEJANT,
    GARDANT, PASSANT
purple .... PURPURE
red tincture .... GULES
row of squares .... COMPANY
shield .... PAVIS
shield bar .... GEMEL
shield-shaped .... PELTATE
shield's center .... FESS
shield's corner .... CANTON
sitting .... ASSIS, SEJANT
snake .... BISSE
standing .... STATANT
voided escutcheon .... ORLE
wavy .... ONDE, UNDE(E),
    NEBULE
herb ...... RUE, DILL, MOLY, RUTA,
    SAGE, WORT, YARB, BASIL,
    GRASS, SEDGE, SEDUM,
    THYME, CATNIP, YARROW,
    CARAWAY, CHERVIL,
    OREGANO, PARSLEY, PARSNIP,
    TARRAGON
Andean .... LLARETA
aromatic .... ANET, DILL, MINT,
    ANISE, BASIL, GINGER,
    FENNEL, DITTANY, GINSENG,
    BERGAMOT, ROSEMARY
aromatic root .... NONDO
aster family .... ARNICA
"bean" .... SAVORY
bean family .... PEA, LOTUS
bennet .... AVENS
bitter .... RUE, ALOE, TANSY,

    GENTIAN
bulbous .... GARLIC
cloverlike .... MEDIC, LUCERNE
coarse .... IVA, ERYNGO,
    ELECAMPANE
common mixture of
    .... BOUQUET GARNI
concoction .... TISANE
decoction .... PTISAN, TISANE
eve/yellow .... IVA
evergreen .... GALAX
flowering .... HEPATICA
forage .... SULLA
fragrant .... BALM
ginger .... ALPINIA
goose foot family .... BLITE
laxative .... SENNA
liked by felines .... CATARIA
magic .... MOLY
medicinal .... RUE, ALOE,
    SENNA, TANSY, ARNICA,
    FENNEL, BONESET
mint family ...... BALM, BASIL,
    CATNIP, HYSSOP, MARJORAM,
    PEPPERMINT, SPEARMINT
mythical .... MOLY
nightshade .... TOMATO,
    HENBANE
of grace .... RUE
parsley family .... CICELY,
    CHERVIL
perennial .... SEGO, SEDUM,
    ORPINE
phlox family .... JACOB'S
    LADDER
pink family .... CAMPION
pod .... OCRA, OKRA
remembrance .... ROSEMARY
root ...... CHAY, CHOY, NONDO,
    GINSENG
snake charm .... MUNGO
spinach-like .... ORACHE
strong-smelling .... RUE,
    RUTA, YARROW
tonic ..... BONESET, CORIANDER
tropical .... GINGER, LOOFA,
    GINSENG
use of .... FOOD, MEDICINE,
    FRAGRANCE, SEASONING
with stinging hairs .... NETTLE
woolly .... POLY
Herb Alpert's swingers
    .... TIJUANA BRASS
herbaceous borders ...... FLOWER
    BEDS
herbage .... GRASS
herbivore .... VEGETARIAN
Hercules .... ALCIDES, HERAKLES,
    STRONG MAN
captive of .... IOLE
death place of .... OETA

monster caught by
    .... ERYMANTHIAN BOAR
monster slain by .... HYDRA
parent of .... ZEUS, ALCMENE
queen slain by ...... HIPPOLYTA
tutor .... CHIRON
victim of .... NESSUS
wife of .... HEBE, DEIANIRA
woman saved by ...... HESIONE
herd .... TEND, CROWD, DROVE,
    FLOCK, CORRAL, RABBLE
animals together .... POD
of horses ..... CAVIYA, HARRAS
of whales .... GAM, POD
herdsman ...... COWBOY, DROVER,
    GAUCHO, VAQUERO,
    RANCHERO, SHEPHERD
constellation .... BOOTES
here .... NOW, HITHER, PRESENT
and ____ .... NOW, THERE
and there .... ABOUT
lies .... HIC JACET
hereafter .... FUTURE
hereditary .... INNATE, LINEAL,
    GENETIC, ANCESTRAL
factor .... GENE
right .... UDAL
ruler .... DYNAST
heredity .... GEN(E), GENETICS
theoretician on .... MENDEL
Hereford .... CATTLE
heres .... HEIR
heresy .... HERETODOXY
heretic .... ARIUS, DISSENTER
burning of .... AUTODAFE
garment of .... SANBENITO
heretofore .... ERENOW
heritable land .... ODAL
heritage .... LEGACY, BEQUEST,
    PATRIMONY, BIRTHRIGHT
heritor .... HEIR
herl .... FLY, BARB
herma ...... SIGNPOST, MILESTONE
hermaphroditic ...... EFFEMINATE
Hermes .... GOD, HERALD,
    MERCURY, MESSENGER
footwear .... TALARIA
gift to Odysseus .... MOLY
hat .... PETASOS, PETASUS
parent of .... MAIA, ZEUS
son of .... PAN
staff of .... CADUCEUS
hermetic .... MYSTIC, SEALED,
    AIRTIGHT
Hermione's brother .... DORUS
husband .... ORESTES
parent .... HELEN, MENELAUS
hermit .... LONER, SANTON,
    THRUSH, ASCETIC, EREMITE,
    RECLUSE, ANCHORET,
    ANCHORITE

crab .... PAGURID, PAGURIAN
hermitage .... WINE, RETREAT,
    CLOISTER, MONASTERY
hermitic .... SOLITARY
hernia .... BREACH, RUPTURE
   support .... TRUSS
hero .... IDOL, LION, STAR,
    DEMIGOD, PALADIN,
    CHAMPION, DEFENDER
   animal .... AKELA
   Babylonian .... ETANA
   Crusades .... TANCRED
   Faulkner .... ANSER
   follower .... INE
   legendary .... (EL)CID, AMADIS,
    PALADIN, TRISTAN, LEONIDES,
    TRISTRAM
   of an Arabian romance
    .... ANTAR
   of many ballads .... ROBIN
    HOOD
   of the Nile .... ADMIRAL
    NELSON
   to some .... SUB
   worshiper .... IDOLATER
Hero, lover of .... LEANDER
Herodias' daughter .... SALOME
   husband .... ANTIPAS
heroic .... BOLD, DARING,
    EPIC(AL), GALLANT, SPARTAN,
    VALIANT
   events .... EPOS
   narrative .... SAGA, ODYSSEY
   poem .... EPIC, EPOS, ILIAD,
    EPOPEE
   verse ...... EPOS, ALEXANDRINE
heroics .... CLAPTRAP
heroin .... HORSE, NARCOTIC
   addict .... SNOWBIRD
   slang .... SNOW, SMACK
heroine .... DARLING, FAVORITE
   C. Brontë's .... EYRE
   of Great Expectations
    .... ESTELLA
   of Il Trovatore .... LEONORA
   The Maid of Orleans .... JOAN
    OF ARC
heron .... RAIL, SOCO, CRANE,
    EGRET, GAULIN, BITTERN,
    AIGRET(TE), BOATBILL
   brood .... EDGE
   family .... ARDEIDAE
   night .... QUA, SQUAWK
   relative of .... GANNET
herpes .... SORE, ECZEMA, TETTER,
    SHINGLES
   designating one .... ZOSTER,
    SIMPLEX, LABIALIS
herpetology subject ...... REPTILE
herring .... CISCO, SPRAT,
    TARPON, ANCHOVY, BLUEFIN,

    OLDWIFE, PILCHER, SARDINE,
    MENHADEN, PILCHARD
   canned .... SARDINE
   cured .... BLOATER
   kin .... SHAD
   lake .... MELBA
   like fish .... CISCO, SPRAT,
    ALEWIFE, ANCHOVY
   measure .... CRAN
   pertaining to .... CLUPEOID
   red .... BAIT
   sauce .... ALEC
   slang .... ALEWIFE
   that recently spawned
    .... SHOTTEN
   tub .... CADE
   young .... BRIT, SMELT,
    SPARLING
Herriot, premier .... EDOUARD
Herschel's discovery .... URANUS
herse .... PORTCULLIS
Hersey novel town .... ADANO
Herzog's peak .... ANNAPURNA
   pen name .... MAUROIS
hesitant .... CHARY, TIMID,
    UNSURE, WAVERING,
    RELUCTANT, UNCERTAIN
   syllable .... ER
hesitate .... HAW, HEM, DEMUR,
    PAUSE, WAVER, FALTER,
    VACILLATE
   in speaking .... STAMMER,
    STUTTER
hesitation .... SCRUPLE,
    INDECISION, RELUCTANCE
   sound of .... ER, UM
Hesperia .... ITALY, SPAIN,
    BUTTERFLY
Hesperian .... WESTERN
Hesperides ...... AEGLE, GARDEN,
    HESTIA, NYMPHS
   treasure .... APPLES
Hesperus .... STAR, VENUS
   fate of .... WRECK
   parent .... EOS, ASTRAEUS
Hess, a Nazi .... RUDOLF
   pianist .... MYRA
Hessian .... GERMAN, MERCENARY
hest .... ORDER, BID(DING)
Hestia .... NYMPH, VESTA
   parent of .... RHEA, CRONUS
het up .... AGOG, EXCITED
hetaera .... SLAVE, THAIS,
    CONCUBINE, COURTESAN
hetero: combining form
    .... (AN)OTHER, DIFFERENT
   opposed to .... HOMO
heterodox .... HERETICAL
heterogeneous .... MOTLEY,
    VARIED, DISSIMILAR,
    MISC(ELLANEOUS)

hetman .... CHIEF, ATAMAN,
    COSSACK, COMMANDER
hew .... AX, CUT, CHOP, GASH,
    HACK
hewer .... AXE
hex .... JINX, SPELL, HOODOO,
    (BE)WITCH, SORCERER
hexad .... SESTET, SEXTET(TE)
Hexham's river .... TYNE
hexapod .... SIX-FOOTED
heyday .... MAY, PEAK, PRIME,
    YOUTH
Heyerdahl .... THOR
   craft .... RAII
Heyward novel .... PORGY
hiatus .... COL, GAP, VOID, BREAK,
    PAUSE, LACUNA, OPENING
Hiawatha's bark .... CANOE
   hideaway .... WIGWAM
hibachi .... GRILL, BRAZIER
hibernate .... SHACK, SLEEP,
    WINTER
   opposed to .... GESTIVATE
hibernating animal .... BEAR,
    LEMMING, WOODCHUCK
Hibernia .... ERIN, IRELAND
hibiscus .... TREE, PLANT, SHRUB,
    MALLOW, GUMAMELA
hic jacet ...... EPITAPH, HERE LIES,
    INSCRIPTION
hick ...... RUBE, RUSTIC, HAYSEED
hickey .... DEVICE, GADGET
hickory .... CANE, TREE, WOOD,
    PECAN, SWITCH, (WAL)NUT
   fruit .... PIGNUT
   nut .... PECAN, TRYMA
   tree .... SHAGBARK,
    SHELLBARK
   wattle .... ACACIA
Hidalgo .... NOBLEMAN
   state capital .... PACHUCA
hidden .... INNER, PERDU,
    ARCANE, COVERT, INNATE,
    LATENT, SECRET, CRYPTIC,
    OBSCURE
   attacker .... SNIPER
   fence .... HAHA
   provision .... JOKER, RIDER
hide .... BURY, FELL, FLOG, MASK,
    PELT, SKIN, STOW, VEIL,
    CLOAK, COVER, STASH,
    SCREEN, THRASH, CONCEAL,
    SECRETE, LIE-DOGGO
   and hair .... PELAGE
   behind words .... HEDGE
   calf/lamb .... KIP
   for safekeeping .... CACHE
   raw .... KIP, SHAGREEN
   softening solution .... BATE
hideaway/hideout ...... DEN, LAIR,
    RETREAT

hidebound .... INFLEXIBLE
hideous ...... GRIM, UGLY, AWFUL,
 GRUESOME, REVOLTING,
 SCABROUS, REPULSIVE,
 UNSIGHTLY
 monster ..... GORGON, MEDUSA
hiding, in .... PERDU
 place .... CACHE
hidrosis .... SWEATING,
 PERSPIRATION
hidrotic .... SUDORIFIC
hie .... RUSH, HURRY, SPEED,
 HASTEN
hiemal .... COLD, BRUMAL,
 WINTRY, HIBERNAL
hierarch .... HIGH PRIEST
hierarchy .... RANK, ORDER,
 ANGELS
hieratic .... PRIESTLY,
 SACERDOTAL
hiero: comb. form .... HOLY,
 SACRED
hieroglyph .... PICTOGRAPH
hieroglyphic .... EMBLEMATIC,
 SYMBOLICAL
hieroglyphics, pillar with
 .... OBELISK
hierophant .... HIGH PRIEST
hifi part .... TWEETER
higgle .... BARGAIN, CHAFFER
higgledy-piggledy .... JUMBLE,
 DISORDER, HELTER-SKELTER
high .... TALL, ALOFT, LOFTY,
 AERIAL, COSTLY, SHRILL,
 TOWERING
 abode .... AERIE, AYRIE
 and dry .... STRANDED
 and low .... EVERYWHERE
 and mighty .... ARROGANT,
 OVERBEARING
 and piping .... TREBLE
 brow .... CULTURED,
 CULTIVATED
 class ...... TONY, ELITE, PLUSH,
 RITZY, QUALITY, SUPERIOR
 colloquial ...... STIFF, ELATED
 combining form .... ALTI
 explosive .... TNT
 flown .... FLASHY, GARISH,
 BOMBASTIC
 flyer .... KITE
 grass .... RYE
 hat .... SNUB, SNOOTY, TOPPER,
 SNOB(BISH), STOVEPIPE
 home .... AERIE
 IQ organization/club
 .... MENSA
 jinks .... GLEE, CAPERS,
 PRANKS, REVELRY, FESTIVITY,
 MERRIMENT
 kicks, it has .... CANCAN

 note .... ELA
 note: var. .... EELA
 old time .... SPREE
 peak .... ALP
 pitch .... ALT
 pitched .... SHRILL, TREBLE
 place .... EMINENCE
 prefix .... ALTI
 prestige .... STATUS
 price .... KING'S RANSOM
 priest ...... ELI, AARON, ANNAS,
 PONTIFF
 rank .... ESTATE
 sign .... CUE, SIGNAL
 slang .... DRUNK, SOUSED,
 STINKO, STONED
 society .... BONTON, HAUTE
 MONDE
 sounding .... TENOR, SOPRANO,
 ELEVATED, SONOROUS
 spirited .... FIERY, PROUD,
 SPORTIVE
 stepper .... STRUTTER
 strung .... EDGY, TAUT, JUMPY,
 TENSE, NERVOUS, EXCITABLE,
 SENSITIVE
 tail .... RUN, RUSH, SCURRY,
 SPRINT, HOTFOOT
 time .... NONE TOO SOON
 toned .... LOFTY, MODISH,
 QUALITY, STYLISH
 up .... AERIED
 waters .... FLOOD
 wind .... GALE
High Mass celebrant
 .... DEACON
highball .... DRINK, STINGER
highborn .... BLUE-BLOODED,
 THOROUGHBRED
highboy .... CHEST, BUREAU
highbrow .... SNOB, EGGHEAD,
 ELITIST, LONGHAIR,
 INTELLECTUAL
highest .... SUMMA, SUPREME
 combining form .... ACRO
 mountain .... EVEREST
 note, in music .... ELA
 number of die .... SISE
 point .... APEX, NOON, PEAK,
 APOGEE, CLIMAX, FINIAL,
 VERTEX, ZENITH, PINNACLE
 trump card in napoleon
 .... PAM
highfalutin .... FLIGHTY,
 POMPOUS, PRETENTIOUS
highhanded .... PUSHY,
 ARBITRARY
highland lord .... THANE
 rock .... MONADNOCK
highlander .... GAEL, SCOT,
 TARTAN, PLAIDMAN

 breeches .... TREWS
 pouch .... SPORRAN
 sword of .... CLAYMORE
 weapon of .... DIRK
 wear of .... KILT
Highlands robber ...... CATERAN
highly .... VERY, GREATLY,
 LARGELY, EXTREMELY
 colored .... LURID, VIVID,
 FLORID
 compressed pad .... TIGHTWAD
 decorated .... GAUDY
 excited .... AGOG
 wrought .... D(A)EDAL
highway .... ROAD, AVENUE,
 FREEWAY, (TURN)PIKE
 Alaska-Canada .... ALCAN
 division .... LANE
 fees .... TOLLAGE
 habit .... TAILGATE
 hazard .... SKID
 men .... STATE TROOPERS
 pest .... ROADHOG
 unit .... LANE
highwayman ...... PAD, BRIGAND,
 LADRONE, HIJACKER, ROAD
 AGENT
hijack(er) .... HOLDUP(PER)
hike .... WALK, BOOST, MARCH,
 RAISE, TRAMP
hiker's bag .... KNAPSACK,
 HAVERSACK
hilarious .... GAY, MERRY
 one .... CARD
hilarity .... GLEE, MIRTH, GAIETY,
 MERRIMENT
hilding .... WRETCH
hill .... BRAE, FELL, HEAP, PILE,
 BUTTE, KOP(JE), MOUND,
 MOUNT, BARROW, CUESTA,
 DJEBEL, MONTICULE
 builder/dweller .... ANT
 flat-topped .... MESA
 fortified .... MERLIN
 glacial .... KAME, DRUMLIN
 go over the .... DIE
 isolated .... INCH, BUTTE
 long .... RIDGE
 rounded .... KNOB, MORRO,
 HUMMOCK
 sand .... DENE, DUNE
 small .... HILLOCK
 top .... CAP, TOR, BROW, KNAP,
 CREST
Hillary's conquest .... EVEREST
 Nepalese companion-climber
 .... NORGAY
 other work .... APICULTURE
hillbilly .... RUSTIC
 family member .... MAW, PAW
 food .... TATERS

hillock .... TOFT, TUMP, KNOLL, KOPJE, MOUND
hills, range of ...... RIDGE, SIERRA
hillside .... BRAE, SLOPE
  hollow .... SLACK, CORRIE
hilltop .... TOR, KNAP
Hilo handout .... LEI
hilt .... HAFT, HELVE, HANDLE
  wooden .... DUDGEON
Himalayan animal .... OUNCE, PANDA
  antelope .... GORAL, SEROW
  bearcat .... PANDA
  broadmouth .... RAYA
  capital .... GANGTOK, KATMANDU
  country .... NEPAL, SIKKIM
  forest .... BHABAR
  goat .... KYL, KRAS, TAHR, TAIR, GORAL
  grassland .... TARAI
  marmot .... PIA
  massif .... ANNAPURNA
  Mountains state .... BHUTAN
  mystery/humanoid .... YETI
  peak .... API, HUMP, NEPAL, EVEREST
  river .... INDUS
  sheep .... NAHOOR
  tea .... AUCUBA
Himalayas .... (THE) HUMP
hind ...... ROE, BACK, DEER, REAR, TAIL, RUSTIC, PEASANT, CABRILLA, POSTERIOR
  leg of animal .... HAM
hinder .... BLOCK, DELAY, DETER, EMBAR, CUMBER, HAMPER, IMPEDE, RETARD, PREVENT, OBSTRUCT
hindmost .... LAST
hindquarter .... HAUNCH
hindrance .... BAR, HITCH, OBSTACLE, IMPEDIMENT
Hindu .... SER, BABU, BANA, JAIN(A), KOLI, SIKH, TAMIL, GENTOO
  acrobat .... NAT
  age of the world .... YUGA
  ancestor .... MANU
  Anglicized .... BABU
  ascetic .... JOGI, MUNI, YATI, YOGI, FAKIR, SADHU
  bandit .... DACOIT
  banker .... SOWCAR
  barber .... NAI, NAPIT
  bear .... BHALU
  beggar .... NAGA
  betelnut .... SUPARI
  boat .... YARAHA
  brook .... NALA
  bulbul .... KALA

butter .... GHI
call to prayer .... AZAN
caste .... JAT, MAL, KORI, PASI, TELI, SUDRA, RAJPUT
caste, priestly .... BRAHMAN
cavalry .... RISALA
charitable gift .... ENAM
city .... ABAD
city, holy .... BENARES
cloth .... LUNGI, LUNGEE
congregation .... SAMAJ
cottage .... BARI
court officer .... AMALA
cremation of a widow .... SATI
cultured .... BRAHMIN
cultured person ...... BRAHMAN
cymbal .... DAL, TAL
dance drama .... RASA
dancing girl .... BAYADERE
deity .... UMA, AGNI, AKAL, DEVA, DEWA, KAMA, MANU, RAMA, SIVA, YAMA, BHAGA, VARUNA, VISHNU, KRISHNA
demon .... RAHU, ASURA
divorce law .... TALAK
drinking pot .... LOTA
dye .... ALTA
ejaculation .... OM
epic .... RAMAYAMA
epic hero .... ARJUNA
essence .... AMRITA
exchange rate .... BATTA
evil spirit .... MARA, ASURA
fair .... MELA
fate .... KARMA
festival .... HOLI, PUJA, DEWALI
flying beings .... GARUDAS
gardener .... MALI
garment .... SARI, DHOTI, SAREE
gentleman .... SRI, BABU, BABOO
giant: myth. .... BANA
gnome .... YAKSHA
god .... KA, AGNI, AKAL, DEVA, KAMA, SIVA, YAMA, BHAGA, DYAUS, INDRA, BRAHMA, VARUNA, VISHNU, GANES(H)A, TRIMURTI, JAGANNATH
goddess .... UMA, VAC(H), DEVI, KALI, MAYA, S(H)RI, SAKTI, SHREE, US(H)AS, MATRIS, LAKSHMI
gods' abode .... MERU
groom .... SYCE
guitar .... BINA, VINA, SITAR
gypsy .... KARACHEE
handkerchief .... MALABAR
hell .... NARAKA

hero ..... NALA, RAMA, ARJUNA
holy book .... VEDA, SASTRA
holy destination .... HARDWAR, VARANASI
holy man ...... FAKIR, SADH(U)
immortality .... AMRITA
incarnation .... AVATAR
kingdom .... NEPAL
kismet .... KARMA
kneeling rug .... ASAN
land grant .... ENAM, INAM, SASAN
language .... SANSKRIT
lawgiver .... MANU
leader .... GANDHI, SIRDAR
loincloth .... DHO(O)TI
lord .... SWAMI
low-caste .... MAL, KORI
magic .... MAYA
master .... MIAN, SAHIB, SWAMI, SWAMY
Maya .... DEVI, SAKTI
meal .... ATA
measure .... KOS, RYOTS
merchant .... BANIAN
monastic philosophy .... VEDANTA
money .... ANNA
month .... ASIN, JETH, KUAR, MAGH, AGHAN, CHAIT, KA(R)TIK, BAISAKH, PHA(L)GUN, SA(RA)WAN
mountain .... MERU
mountain pass .... GHAUT
mountaineer .... BHIL
musical instrument ...... VINA, SAROD, SITAR
mystic word .... OM
Nobel Prize winner .... TAGORE
noble .... RAJAH
nursemaid .... AYAH
patriarch .... PITRI
peasant .... RYOT
philosophy .... YOGA, SANKHYA, VEDANTA
pillar .... LAT
poet .... TAGORE, KALIDASA
police station .... THANA
policeman .... SEPOY
pot .... LOTA
prayer carpet/rug .... ASAN
priest .... BRAHMIN
prince .... RANA, RAJA(H), MAHARAJA
princess .... RANI, RANEE, MAHARANI
puce .... UDA
pundit .... SWAMI
queen .... RANI, RANEE
ravine .... NALA

religious creed .... JAINISM
religious observances
.... DHARMA
religious devotee .... MUND
religious sect .... SIKHISM
religious teacher .... PIR, GURU, SWAMI
rites .... ACHAR
sacred literature .... VEDA
sacred river .... GANGA, GANGES
sage ..... GAUTAMA, MAHATMA
Sanskrit school .... TOL
scarf .... SAREE
scripture ...... AGAMA, SASTRA, TANTRA
seclusion of women
.... PURDAH
sect .... JAINA
sect member .... SADH, SEIK, SIKH
serpent .... NAGA
servant .... CELA
slave .... DASIS
soldier .... SEPOY
sorceress .... USHA
soul .... ATMA(N)
sovereignty .... RAJ
spirit .... MARA
summer house .... MAHAL
supreme deity .... VARUNA
swan .... HANSA
teacher .... PIR, GURU, MULLA(H)
temple .... DEUL
temple tower .... SIKHRA
title .... MIR, RAO, SRI, NAIK, SIDI, RAJA(H), SAHIB
title of respect .... MIAN, SAHIB, SWAMI, BAHADUR
trader .... BANIAN, BANYAN
tree .... BO, DAR, PIPAL
trinity .... SIVA, VISHNU, BRAHMA, TRIMURTI
turban .... PAGRI
underworld king .... YAMA
veranda .... PYAL
water nymph .... APAS
weaver .... TANTI
weight .... SER, TAEL, TOLA, MAUND
widow .... SATI, SUTTEE
writings .... VEDA
Hinduism .... ANIMISM
cosmic principle .... KARMA
pilgrim's city .... VARANASI
Hindustan hillman .... TODA
magic .... JADU
Mogul emperor .... AKBAR
state .... PUNJAB
Hindustani .... URDU, HINDI

hinge .... AXIS, KNEE, ELBOW, JOINT, PIVOT, DEPEND
hinny ...... MULE, NEIGH, WHINNY
parent of .... DONKEY
hint .... CUE, CLUE, IMPLY, ALLUDE, INKLING, POINTER, TIP(OFF), SUGGEST, INTIMATE
hinterland .... INLAND, BACKWOODS, BOONDOCKS
hip .... COXA, ILIA, FRUIT, HAUNCH, HUCKLE
boots .... WADERS
bone .... ILIA, ILIUM, PELVIS
pains .... SCIATICA
pertaining to the .... ILIAC, SCIATIC
width of: sl. .... BEAM
hipbone .... ILIUM
part of .... PUBIS, ISCHIUM
hippocampus .... SEA HORSE
Hippocrates' birthplace .... COS
Hippocratic _____, doctors'
.... OATH
hippodrome .... ARENA, (RACING) COURSE
hippopotamus SEACOW, BEHEMOTH, PACHYDERM
hips supporter .... GIRDLE
width .... BEAM
hipster .... HEPCAT, BEATNIK
hircine .... GOATLIKE
hire .... LET, RENT, LEASE, EMPLOY, ENGAGE, CHARTER
hired applauders .... CLAQUE
assassin .... BRAVO, CUTTHROAT, HIGHBINDER
hireling .... MERCENARY
Hirondelle .... OISEAU
hirsute .... HAIRY, PILOSE, SHAGGY, BRISTLY
growth .... HAIR
Hispania .... SPAIN
ancient .... IBERIA
former part of .... PORTUGAL
Hispanic .... SPANISH
Hispaniola .... HAITI
hispid .... HAIRY, SPINY, STRIGOSE
hiss .... SISS, WOOSH, SIBILATE
hisser .... GOOSE, SNAKE, HECKLER
hissing .... FIZ(Z), FIZZY, SIBILANT
drink .... CHAMPAGNE, SODA WATER
sound ...... SSH, PSST, WHIZ(Z), FIZZLE, SIZZLE
hist .... SHUSH
histamine .... GASTRIN
historian .... ANNALIST, RECORDER, CHRONICLER
historical .... REAL, FAMOUS, FACTUAL, LEGENDARY

cars .... STANLEY STEAMERS
decade .... MAUVE
lawgiver .... MOSES
period .... ERA
records .... ANNALS, ARCHIVES, CHRONICLES, MEMORABILIA
history ...... LORE, PAST, ANNALS, RECORD, ACCOUNT, MEMOIRS, CHRONICLE, NARRATIVE
famous in .... STORIED
muse of .... CLIO
person's life .... BIOGRAPHY
histrionic .... AFFECTED, ARTIFICIAL, THEATRICAL
histrionics .... DRAMATICS
hit .... ACE, BAT, BOP, BIFF, BUMP, CUFF, SLUG, SOCK, SWAT, CLOUT, KNOCK, SMITE, SMOTE, POMMEL, STRIKE, SUCCESS
aloft/as in tennis .... LOB
baseball .... BUNT, SINGLE, HOMERUN
direct .... BULL'S-EYE
great .... SMASH
hard ...... LAM, SLOG, SLUG, SMITE
it off .... FIT IN
lightly .... TAP
of the early '30s .... GOOD NEWS
old style .... SMIT
on the head .... BOP, LAM, BEAN, CONK, BRAIN
or miss .... RANDOM, AIMLESS, HAPHAZARD
sign .... SRO
the slopes .... SKI
with a quick blow .... SWAT
hitch .... TIE, TUG, KNOT, LIMP, SNAG, FASTEN, HOBBLE, OBSTACLE, HINDRANCE
hitchhike .... BUM A RIDE, THUMB A RIDE
hitchhiker ...... RIDER, PASSENGER
quest of .... LIFT
hitchpost .... PICKET
hither .... HERE, NEARER
partner of .... YON
hitherto .... TO NOW, UNTIL NOW, HERETOFORE
Hitler's occupation .... HOUSE PAINTER
rank .... CORPORAL
third .... REICH
title .... FU(E)HRER
wife .... (EVA)BRAUN
Hitlerite .... NAZI
Hittite .... SYRIAN
hive .... SKEP, SWARM, APIARY
dweller .... BEE

hives .... URTICARIA
nettle .... UREDO
remedy for .... BENADRYL
Hizzoner .... MAYOR
HMS Pinafore character
.... BUTTERCUP
Ho! .... HALT, STOP, WHOA
hoar .... GRAY, WHITE
hoard .... HIDE, AMASS, CACHE,
STOCK, STORE, SUPPLY,
RESERVE, TREASURE
hoarder .... MISER, NIGGARD
hoarding .... FENCE, POSTER,
BILLBOARD
animal .... WOODRAT,
SQUIRREL
hoarfrost .... RAG, RIME
hoarse .... GRUFF, HUSKY, ROUPY,
RAUCOUS, THROATY,
CROAKING
hoarseness .... ROUP
hoary .... OLD, GRAY, WHITE,
FROSTY, ANCIENT
hoax .... BAM, GAFF, JOKE, SHAM,
FRAUD, HOCUS, SPOOF, TRICK,
CANARD
hob .... ELF, PEG, LOUT, PUCK,
GOBLIN, RUSTIC
hobble .... LAME, LIMP, HITCH,
FETTER, HAMPER, HINDER
hobbledehoy .... BOY, YOUTH
hobby .... FAD, WHIM, HORSE,
FALCON, PASTIME, AVOCATION
of kings .... PHILATELY
hobgoblin .... ELF, ELVE, PUCK,
BOG(E)Y, GNOME, SPRITE,
BUGBEAR
hobnail .... RUSTIC
hobnob .... MIX, MINGLE,
ASSOCIATE, PAL AROUND,
SOCIALIZE, RUB ELBOWS
hobo .... BO, BUM, TRAMP,
DRIFTER, VAGRANT,
(BINDLE)STIFF
bundle/bedding .... BINDLE
camp .... JUNGLE
city hangout .... SKIDROW
stew .... MULLIGAN
Hobson's choice .... TAKE-IT-OR-
LEAVE-IT
hock .... HAM, PAWN, ANKLE,
JOINT
again .... REPAWN
joint ailment .... SPAVIN
hockey .... SHINNY
arena .... RINK
Bobby of .... ORR
cup .... STANLEY
disk .... PUCK
division of game .... PERIOD
feint .... DEKE

field .... BANDY
goal .... CAGE
player .... GOALIE
puck maneuver .... ICING
scored a goal in .... LIGHTED
THE LAMP
star .... ORR, HULL, GRETZKY
stick .... CAMAN
hockshop .... PAWNSHOP
sign .... BALL
hocus .... HOAX, FRAUD
pocus .... MAGIC, DECEIT,
TRICK(ERY)
hod .... TROUGH, SCUTTLE
hodgepodge .... HASH, MESS,
OLIO, STEW, CENTO, MEDLEY,
FARRAGO, MELANGE,
MIXTURE, POTTAGE,
MISHMASH
hoe .... HACK, TILL
hoecake .... CORN BREAD
hoedown .... SHINDIG
hog .... PIG, GRAB, DUROC, SWINE,
PORK(ER), BABIRUSA
cholera .... ROUGET
deer .... AXIS
fat .... LARD, ADEPS
female .... SOW, GILT
food .... MAST, SLOPS
genus .... SUS
ground .... MARMOT
kind of .... ROAD
male .... BOAR
peanut .... EARTHPEA
plum .... AMRA
thigh .... HAM
vital organ .... HASLET
wild .... BENE, BOAR,
PECCARY, RAZORBACK
young ..... GILT, SHOAT, SHOTE
Hogan's Heroes setting
.... STALAG
hogback .... RIDGE
hogfish .... WRASSE, PORPOISE
hoggish .... FILTHY, GREEDY
hogshead .... CASK, BARREL
content of .... BEER
hogtie .... MANACLE, TRUSS(UP)
hogwash .... SWILL, TRASH,
BALONEY, NONSENSE
hoi polloi .... MASSES,
(THE)MAJORITY
hoist ...... CAT, JACK, LIFT, BOUSE,
HEAVE, RAISE, WINCH, PULL
UP, ELEVATOR
anchor .... WEIGH
hoisted just off bottom .... ATRIP
hoisting device .... GIN, BOOM,
CRANE, DAVIT, SLING, WINCH,
CAPSTAN, DERRICK, FORKLIFT,
WINDLASS

tackle .... CAT
hoity-toity .... FUSSY, GIDDY,
HUFFY, SNOOTY, PETULANT,
ARROGANT, CAPRICIOUS
person .... SNOB
hokeypokey .... ICECREAM,
TRICK(ERY), HOCUS-POCUS
Hokkaido, capital of .... YEZO,
SAPPORO
city .... OTARU
native .... AINU
Hoko Gunto .... PESCADORES
hokum .... BUNK, HUMBUG,
BALONEY, CLAPTRAP,
NONSENSE, APPLESAUCE
hold .... GRIP, STAY, GRASP,
CLUTCH, DETAIN, OCCUPY,
REGARD, SUSTAIN, KEEP
BACK, MAINTAIN, RESTRAIN
a session .... SIT, MEET
back .... DAM, STAY, STEM,
DETER, DETAIN, RETARD,
STIFLE, RESTRAIN
dear .... CHERISH
down .... LIMIT
due to war .... INTERN
fast .... BELAY
firmly .... RIVET
forth .... OFFER, PREACH
in custody .... DETAIN,
IMPOUND
in law .... BIND
off .... REBUFF, POSTPONE
on .... ENDURE, REMAIN,
PERSIST, CONTINUE
one's own .... COPE
out .... LAST, ENDURE, REFUSE,
RESIST
over .... DELAY, POSTPONE
scoreless .... BLANK, BLITZ
ship's .... HATCH
sway .... RULE
the deed of .... OWN
the reins .... GOVERN
up .... DELAY, ELEVATE,
STOPPAGE
your horses! .... WAIT
holder .... OWNER, PAYEE,
POSSESSOR
baby or corn .... CRIB
lease .... LESSEE, RENTER,
TENANT
shish-kebab .... SKEWER
holding .... TENURE, PROPERTY
device .... VISE, CLAMP, CLASP,
TONGS
in custody .... DETENTION
in poker .... PAIR
holdings .... BONDS, STOCKS,
ASSETS, EFFECTS, PROPERTY,
POSSESSIONS

holdout .... STRIKER, RESISTER
holdup .... HEIST, HIJACK,
STICKUP, ROBBERY
holdup man .... BANDIT, ROBBER,
BRIGAND, FOOTPAD, HIJACKER
hole .... GAP, PIT, BORE, LILL,
WELL, CAVITY, HOLLOW,
OPENING, ORIFICE, VENT(AGE),
APERTURE, EXCAVATION
ace in the .... CLINCHER
air .... SPIRACLE
cloth .... EYELET
coin .... SLOT
embankment .... GIME
enlarger tool .... REAM
gangster's .... HIDEOUT
golf course .... CUP
-in-one, golf .... ACE
of tube, etc. .... BORE
skin .... PORE
sleeve's .... SCYE
up .... DIG IN, HIDE
water .... (SWIMMING)POOL
holes, full of .... PERFORATED
holiday .... FERIA, FIESTA, RECESS,
FESTIVAL, VACATION
kind of .... ROMAN, EASTER,
WEEKEND, OFFICIAL
of a .... FERIAL
holiness .... SANCTITY
Holland. See also **Netherlands**
.... CLOTH, DUTCH
capital .... (THE)HAGUE
capital (North) .... HAARLEM
dialect ...... FRISIAN, FRANKISH
gin .... GENEVA, SCHNAP(P)S
seaport .... EDAM
sight in .... WINDMILL
village .... EDE
Hollandaise .... SAUCE
Hollandia .... KOTABARU
hollands .... GIN
holler .... YELL, SHOUT
hollow .... DENT, HOLE, COELO,
EMPTY, FALSE, FOSSA,
CAVITY, SUNKEN, CONCAVE
cheek's/chin's .... DIMPLE
circular .... CORRIE
opposed to .... SOLID
tile .... KEY
holly .... ASSI, HOLM, ILEX,
ACEBO, ERYNGO, YAUPON
hollyhock .... MALLOW,
ALTH(A)EA
Hollywood Academy people
.... AWARDERS
award .... OSCAR
columnist .... RONA,
GRAHAME, LOUELLA,
(HEDDA)HOPPER
industry .... CINEMA, MOVIE(S)

landmark .... CIRO'S
name .... BARA, DUKE, FORD,
PECK, WOOD, FONDA, GABLE,
GARBO, GRANT, KELLY, LEIGH,
NEGRI, TRACY, WAYNE,
COOPER, HARLOW, KEATON,
MARTIN, MENJOU, TAYLOR,
WELLES, DEMILLE, GARDNER,
GARLAND, HEPBURN,
STEWART, HESTON, SWANSON,
CRAWFORD, DIETRICH,
PICKFORD
street/locale ...... VINE, SUNSET
writer .... SCENARIST
holm .... AIT, OAK, HOLLY, ISLET,
BOTTOMS
oak .... ILEX
Holmes, Sherlock .... DETECTIVE
alter ego .... WATSON
creator of .... (CONAN)DOYLE
favorite word .... ELEMENTARY
holograph .... (MANU)SCRIPT,
HANDWRITTEN
Holstein .... CATTLE
holt .... HILL, COPSE, GROVE,
WOODS, COPPICE, WILLOWS
holy ...... SANTA, CHASTE, DIVINE,
SACRED, BLESSED, SAINTLY,
SINLESS, HALLOW(ED)
city ..... ROME, LHASA, MECCA,
HARDWAR, VARANASI,
JERUSALEM
communion .... EUCHARIST
cross .... ROOD
man .... FAKIR, SAINT,
MAHATMA, MARABOUT
oil .... CHRISM
person .... SAINT
picture .... ICON
place .... CHURCH, SHRINE,
TEMPLE, SANCTUM,
SANCTUARY
prefix .... HAGIO, HIERO
water sprinkling ..... ASPERGES
writings .... SCRIPTURES
Holy Father .... POPE
Grail ..... CHALICE, SANGRAAL,
SANGR(E)AL
Grail finder .... GALAHAD
Grail knight .... BORS,
AMFORTAS, PARSIPAL,
PERCIVAL
Grail knights' enemy
.... KLINGSOR
Land .... PALESTINE
Land visitor .... PALMER,
PILGRIM
Sepulcher visitor .... HADJI,
PILGRIM
Spirit ..... PNEUMA, PARACLETE

Thursday island
.... ASCENCION
War: Moslem .... JIHAD
Writ .... BIBLE
homage .... HONOR, TRIBUTE,
REVERENCE
to saints .... DULIA
hombre ...... CARD, GAME, OMBER
slang .... GUY, MAN, FELLOW
Homburg .... (FELT)HAT
home ...... ROOF, ABODE, ASYLUM,
HEARTH, REFUGE, SHELTER,
DOMICILE, DWELLING,
HOUSEHOLD, RESIDENCE
animal's .... DEN, LAIR,
HABITAT
bird's .... NEST, AERIE
for a cruise .... OCEANLINER
for poor/sick .... HOSPICE
-grown .... LOCAL, NATIVE
of Andrew Jackson .... THE
HERMITAGE
George Washington
.... MOUNT VERNON
James Madison
.... MONTPELIER
Kodak .... ROCHESTER
the .... DOMESTIC
the Braves .... ATLANTA
the Dolphins .... MIAMI
the Giants .... SAN
FRANCISCO
the surrey with the fringe
top .... OKLAHOMA
the Uzbek .... ASIA
the Wright Brothers
.... DAYTON
Thomas Jefferson
.... MONTICELLO
pastor's .... MANSE
-run king .... AARON
screen .... TV, TELLY, VIDEO,
TELEVISION
spider's .... WEB
stately .... MANOR
Home Sweet Home composer
.... PAYNE
homebody .... RECLUSE, STAY-AT-
HOME
of a kind .... TENANT
homecoming, alumni
.... REUNION
homeground .... BASE, BAILIWICK
homeless child .... ARAB, WAIF
tramp .... HOBO
homely ...... UGLY, PLAIN, SIMPLE,
HOMESPUN
homemaker .... HOUSEWIFE
homer .... KOR, HOMERUN
Homer enchantress .... CIRCE
epic of .... ILIAD, ODYSSEY

sea nymph .... CALYPSO
translator of .... CHAPMAN
Homeric .... EPIC(AL)
homerun with bases full
.... GRAND SLAM
homesick .... BLUE
homesickness .... NOSTALGIA
excessive .... NOSTOMANIA
homespun .... PLAIN, HOMELY,
SIMPLE, UNPRETENTIOUS,
DOWN-TO-EARTH
cloth .... RUSSET
homestead .... TOFT, MESSUAGE
site .... IN LOT
homesteader .... SOONER,
SETTLER
homestretch .... LAST LAP
homework .... LESSONS
homey .... COZY, FRIENDLY
homicidal .... MURDEROUS
homily .... TALK, SERMON,
LECTURE
homing faculty ...... ORIENTATION
hominy .... SAMP, GRITS
homo .... MAN, PRIMATE
combining form .... LIKE,
SAME, EQUAL
Homo sapiens .... MAN(KIND)
homogeneous .... ALIKE, SIMILAR,
IDENTICAL
homogenize .... EMULSIFY
homonym .... NAMESAKE
homopterous insect .... APHID,
CICADA
homosexual .... GAY, INVERT,
LESBIAN
homunculus .... DWARF
Hondo .... HONSHU
Honduras cape .... FALSO,
CAMARON
capital .... TEGUCIGALPA
city/town .... TELA, YORO,
DANLI, LA PAZ, MORAZAN, LA
CEIBA, CATACAMAS,
CHOLUTECA, COMAYAGUA,
JUTICALPA, OLANCHITO, EL
PARAISO, EL PROGRESO, SANTA
RITA, PUERTO CORTES
gulf .... FONSECA
hero .... LEMPIRA
Indian .... PAYA
island .... UTILA, ROATAN,
GUANAJA
lagoon .... BRUS, CARATASCA
lake .... YOJOA
language .... SPANISH
monetary unit .... LEMPIRA
mountains .... PIJA, COLON,
ESPERANZA
president .... CALLEJAS
river .... COCO, SICO, ULUA,

AGUAN, WANKS, PATUCA,
SULACO, PAULAYA, SEGOVIA,
CHOLUTECA
seaport .... TELA, LA CEIBA
hone .... STROP, YEARN,
GRIND(ER), SHARPEN,
OILSTONE, WHET(STONE)
honest .... FAIR, PURE, WHITE,
FRANK, UPRIGHT, TRUTHFUL
honesty .... HONOR, CANDOR,
PROBITY, MOONWORT,
INTEGRITY
honewort .... PARSLEY
honey .... DEAR, SWEET, DARLING
and mulberry juice .... MORAT
badger .... RATEL
bear .... KINKAJOU
bee .... APIS, DINGAR, DESERET
buzzard .... KITE, PERN
container/holder .... COMB,
CRUSE
creeper .... GUITGUIT
drink .... MEAD, MORAT
eater .... IAO, BEAR, MOHO
fermented .... MEAD
pharmacy .... MEL
plant .... FIGWORT
pollen mix .... BEEBREAD
prefix .... MELI
source .... FLOWER, NECTAR
honeybee genus .... APIS
honeycomb eater .... BEEMOTH
material .... BEESWAX
part .... CELL
honeycombed .... FAVOSE
honeydew .... MELON, NECTAR
honeyed .... SWEET, SUGARY,
CANDIED
words .... FLATTERY
honeymoon haven ...... NIAGARA
FALLS
honeysuckle .... VINE, AZALEA,
CLOVER, WOODBINE,
EGLANTINE
hong .... FACTORY, WAREHOUSE
Hong Kong bay .... REPULSE
capital .... VICTORIA
peninsula .... KOWLOON
honk .... YANG
honker .... GOOSE
honky-tonk: sl. .... DIVE,
SALOON, CABARET
Honolulu airbase .... HICKHAM
exclusive section ...... KAHALA
greeting .... ALOHA
native dance .... HULA
native dancer .... WAHINE
swimming resort ...... WAIKIKI
honor .... FAME, FETE, AWARD,
ECLAT, EXALT, GLORY,
CREDIT, ESTEEM, HOMAGE,

DIGNITY, ENNOBLE, RESPECT,
VENERATE, REVERE(NCE),
DECORATION
with insults .... ROAST
Honor Thy Father author
.... TALESE
honorable .... NOBLE, WORTHY,
UPRIGHT, REPUTABLE
mention .... CITATION
honorarium .... TIP, REWARD
honorary ...... TITULAR, EMERITUS
commission, military
.... BREVET
honors .... AWARDS, TITLES,
ACCOLADE, TRIBUTES
Honshu .... HONDO
bay .... ISE, TOYAMA
city .... KOBE, KURE, KYOTO,
HIMEJI, SENDAI, OKAYAMA,
HIROSHIMA
port .... KOBE
hooch .... BOOTLEG, WHISKEY
hood .... BIGGIN, CAMAIL
airplane's .... NACELLE
bird's .... CREST, CALOT(TE)
carriage's/cloak's ...... CAPOTE
folding ...... CALASH, CALECHE
monk's .... COWL, AMICE,
CAPOUCH, CAPUCHE
part .... CAMAIL, TIPPET
slang .... THUG, GANGSTER
tail of .... LIRIPIPE
hooded ...... COWLED, CUCULLATE
cloak .... CAPUCHIN
garment .... CAPE, PARKA,
CAPOTE
merganser .... SMEW
seal .... BLADDERNOSE
snake .... ADDER, COBRA,
PUFFING
hoodlum ...... GOON, PUNK, THUG,
ROWDY, GANGSTER,
HOOLIGAN, LARRIKIN
hoodoo .... HEX, JINX, VOODOO,
BEWITCH, BAD LUCK
hoodwink .... DUPE, SEEL, CHEAT,
DECEIVE, BLINDFOLD
hooey .... BUNK, NONSENSE
hoof .... PAW, FOOT, UNGULA
like a .... UNGUAL
on the .... ALIVE
paring tool .... BUTTERIS
shaped .... UNGULATE
slang .... DANCE
hoofbeat .... KLOP, CLIP-CLOP
hoofed .... UNGUAL, UNGULATE
hoofer .... (TAP)DANCER
Kelly .... GENE
hook .... BEND, GAFF, GORE,
CLEEK, CROOK, TACH(E),
CLEVIS, JIGGER, GRAMPON,

GRAPNEL, SWINDLE, HEADLAND
and eye .... FASTENER
and loop .... GEMEL, HINGE
colloquial .... LAND, CATCH
like .... FALCATE, UNCINAL
like mark .... CEDILLA
longshoreman's .... BALING
money .... LARI(N)
part .... BARB
shaped .... UNCINAL
hooka(h) .... PIPE, NARG(H)ILE
hooked .... GAFFED, FALCATE, ADUNC(OUS), AQUILINE, UNCINATE
person .... ADDICT
hookey player .... TRUANT
hooklike ...... FALCATE, UNCINATE
process .... UNCUS
hookup .... TIE-UP
hooligan .... SPIV, ROWDY, HOODLUM, RUFFIAN
hoop .... (EAR)RING
shaped handle .... BAIL
hooper .... SWAN, COOPER
hoopla .... BUSTLE, BALLYHOO, EXCITEMENT
hoopster .... CAGER
hoosegow ...... JAIL, POKY, CLINK, PRISON
Hoosier humorist .... ADE
novelist .... TARKINGTON
poet .... RILEY
State .... INDIANA
town .... PERU
hoot ...... BOO, CRY, SASS, SHOUT, WHOOP, ULULATE
sign of a .... SCORN
hooter .... FAN, OWL, HECKLER
Hoover .... DAM, HERBERT
blankets .... NEWSPAPERS
Dam lake .... MEAD
flag .... (EMPTY)POCKET
hop .... LEAP, VINE, CAPER, DANCE, FRISK, SPRING
airplane .... FLIGHT
kiln .... O(A)ST
o'-my-thumb .... DWARF
plant .... LUPULUS
stem .... BINE
hopbrau equipment .... STEINS
hope .... LONG, ASPIRE, DESIRE
container .... CHEST
enormously little .... FAT CHANCE
hopeful .... ASPIRANT, CONTENDER, EXPECTANT, OPTIMISTIC
Hopei .... CHIHLI
capital of .... TIENTSIN
hopeless .... VAIN, FUTILE,

DEJECTED, DESPERATE, BEYOND HOPE
position .... RATTRAP, CHECKMATE
hophead .... ADDICT
Hopi .... MOKI, MOQUI
room of .... KIVA
hopped up .... CHARGED
hopper .... FLEA, FROG, SILO, TOAD, CICADA, LOCUST, CRICKET, KANGAROO
short for a .... ROO
Hopper, columnist .... HEDDA
hops kiln .... O(A)ST
mellowed .... OLDS
powder .... LUPULIN
stem .... BINE
hora .... FOLKDANCE
Horae .... DIKE, HOURS, IRENE, EIRENE, EUNOMIA
horde .... MOB, ARMY, HOST, PACK, CROWD, DROVE, SWARM, LEGION, THRONG
hordeolum .... STY(E)
Horeb ...... MOUNTAIN, (MT.)SINAI
horehound .... MINT, JUICE
horizon .... LIMIT, SKYLINE
arc of the .... AZIMUTH
horizontal .... FLAT, FLUSH, LEVEL, PLANE
band: heraldic .... FRIEZE
position .... PRONE
hormone .... PROLON, ESTRIOL, ESTRONE, GASTRIN, INSULIN, THEELIN, ANDROGEN, ESTROGEN, SECRETIN, ADRENALIN, CORTISONE
horn .... DAG, TUBA, BUGLE, CORNU, PRONG, SIREN, CORNET, CROCKET
bell-like part .... FLARE
bird beak's .... EPITHEMA
blare .... TOOT, FANFARE, TANTARA
combining form .... CERATO
deer .... ANTLER, BALCON, CROCHE
in .... MEDDLE, INTERVENE
insect's .... ANTENNA
like .... CORNU, CORNEOUS
moon's .... CUSP
of a _____ .... DILEMMA
of plenty .... CORNUCOPIA
part of .... MUTE
pierce with .... GORE, HOOK
pout .... CATFISH, BULLHEAD
snail's .... TENTACLE
tissue .... SCUR, KERATIN
unbranched .... DAG
hornbeam .... IRONWOOD
hornbill .... TOCK, HOMARI,

TOUCAN
Hornblower of fiction .... HORATIO
Hornby (Lesley) .... TWIGGY
Horne, singer .... LENA
horneblende .... EDENITE
horned animal .... GNU, RAM, BULL, DEER, IBEX, STAG, RHINO, BUFFALO
horse .... UNICORN
problem .... DILEMMA
viper .... ASP, CERASTES
hornet .... WASP, VESPID, STINGER, YELLOW JACKET
Hornie .... SATAN
hornless .... POLLED, ACEROUS
animal .... MUL(L)EY, POLLARD
hornlike .... CORNU, CERATOID, KERATOID
hornswoggle: sl. .... HUMBUG, BAMBOOZLE
horntail .... INSECT, SAWFLY
horny .... CALLOUS, CORNEOUS
growth ..... CORN, NAIL, WART, KERATOSIS
scale .... NAIL, SCUTE, SCUTUM
skin .... CORN, CALLUS
tissue .... CERATIN
horologe .... CLOCK, WATCH, SUNDIAL, HOURGLASS
horologist .... WATCHMAKER
horoscope ...... ASPECT, FORECAST
division .... CUSP
horrendous .... HORRIBLE
horrible .... DIRE, GRIM, ALARMING, DREADFUL, GRIS(T)LY, HIDEOUS, TERRIBLE, REVOLTING
colloquial .... UGLY, SHOCKING
horrid .... FOUL, UGLY, NASTY, HATEFUL, REPULSIVE, REVOLTING
horrified ...... AGHAST, APPALLED
horrify .... SCARE, APPAL(L), SHOCK, DISMAY, FRIGHTEN
horrifying .... GRUESOME
horror .... DREAD, TERROR, AVERSION, LOATHING
hors de combat .... DISABLED
d'oeuvre .... OLIVE, CANAPE, APPETIZER
horse .... COB, ARAB, BIDET, MOUNT, STEED, BAYARD, DOBBIN, EQUINE, JENNET, PADNAG, SORREL, BOLLARD, CAVALIA
Alexander the Great's .... BUCEPHALUS
ankle .... HOCK
armor .... BARD(E)
back of .... WITHERS

back tumor .... WARBLE
backward movement
.... PASSADE
baggage .... SUMPTER
belly band .... GIRTH
blacksmith .... FARRIER
blanket ...... MANTA, HOUSING,
TRAPPING
blinder .... WINKER
body .... BARREL
box of .... STALL
breaker .... ROUGHRIDER
broken-winded .... WHISTLER
brown ..... BAY, ROAN, SORREL
buyer .... KNACKER
care for pay of .... LIVERY
caretaker .... GROOM, HOSTLER
carriage .... SHAY
castrated .... GELDING
cavalry .... WALER
chestnut .... BUCKEYE
Cisco Kid's .... DIABLO
clean coat of .... CURRY
colloquial .... BANGTAIL
color .... BAY, PIED, ROAN,
PINTO, DAPPLE, SORREL
comber .... GROOM, CURRIER
combining form .... HIPP(O),
KERAT(O)
command to .... GEE, HAW,
WHOA, GIDDAP
dancing .... LIPPIZAN
dappled .... ROAN
dark .... SLEEPER
dealer .... COPER, KNACKER
disease .... GID, BOTS, LOCO,
FARCY, VIVES, HEAVES,
LAMPAS, NAGANA, SPAVIN,
SURRA(H), DOURINE, LAMPERS,
QUITTOR, STAGGERS,
DISTEMPER, STRANGLES,
WHISTLING, MAL(L)ANDERS
dishonestly entered in race
.... RINGER
dock-tailed .... CURTAL
doctor .... VET, FARRIER
donkey offspring .... HINNY
draft .... SHIRE, SUFFOLK,
PERCHERON
eczema .... MALANDERS
exercise place .... PADDOCK
eye cover .... WINKER,
BLINDER
eyelid inflammation ...... HAW
famous ...... OMAHA, ASSAULT,
TRIGGER, CHAMPION,
CITATION, MAN O' WAR,
TRAVELLER, WHIRLAWAY, SEA
BISCUIT, BUCEPHALUS,
SECRETARIAT
female .... DAM, MARE

fictional .... BAYARD,
ROSINANTE
fetlock growth .... GRAGE
fresh .... REMOUNT
from Medusa's body
.... PEGASUS
gait of ...... LOPE, RACK, TROT,
CANTER, GALLOP, WINDING
genus .... EQUUS
golden .... PALOMINO
guide rope .... LONGE
hair .... SETON
half turn .... CARACOLE,
DEMIVOLT
halter .... HACKAMORE
handsome .... ARAB
harness-racing .... PACER
high-spirited .... STEED
hobby .... DADA
hybrid .... ZEBRULA
incisor .... NIPPER
inferior .... NAG, PLUG,
PLATER, SLEEPER
iron .... TRAIN
joint .... HOUGH, FETLOCK
keeper .... GROOM
lame a .... GRAVEL
laugh .... GUFFAW
lead .... PACER
leap .... BUCK, VAULT,
CURVET, GAMBADE, GAMBADO,
CAPRIOLE, CARACOLE
leg part .... HOCK, HOOF,
HOUGH, SHANK, GASKIN,
FETLOCK, PASTERN
longshot .... SLEEPER,
OUTSIDER
losing cause .... NAIL
magic .... BAYARD
male .... COLT, STEED,
GELDING, STALLION
man: myth. .... CENTAUR
master of the .... MARSHAL
mettle .... PRIDE
muscles atrophy .... SWEENY
nearest wheels .... POLER
nervous condition
.... STAGGERS
newborn .... FOAL
non-scratched, in a race
.... STARTER
of mixed breed .... GRADE
of the year, 1994 .... HOLY
BULL
old .... RIP, JADE, HACK, PLUG,
SKATE, PADNAG
opera .... OATER, WESTERN
ornamental covering
.... CAPARISON
pack .... DRUDGE, SUMPTER
paint .... PINTO

parasitic larva .... BOTFLY,
WARBLE
pen .... CORRAL
piebald .... PINTO, CALICO
race .... PACER, PLATER,
SWEEPS, TROTTER, YEARLING,
HANDICAP, STEEPLECHASE
race board .... TOTE
race "triple crown" winner
.... OMAHA, ASSAULT,
AFFIRMED, CITATION,
WHIRLAWAY, SIR BARTON,
COUNT FLEET, GALLANT FOX,
SECRETARIAT, WAR ADMIRAL,
SEATTLE SLEW
racing .... TURF
bet ..... FORECAST, QUINELLA
course .... HIPPODROME
fan .... TURFMAN
meet .... ASCOT, DERBY
official .... STEWARD
radish tree .... BEHEN
rawhide .... SHAGREEN
rearing of .... PESADE
relief .... RELAY
rider .... CAVALRYMAN,
EQUESTRIAN
rider's fall .... SPILL
rider's seat .... SADDLE
riding .... MOUNT, STEED,
PALFREY
river .... HIPPO
Ronald Reagan's .... LITTLE
MAN
round-up .... RODEO
rump .... CROUP, CRUPPER
runaway .... BOLTER
saddle .... MOUNT, PALFREY
shelter .... STALL, STABLE
shoer .... FARRIER
short/thick set .... COB
skin disease .... CALORIS
small .... COB, TIT, PONY,
BIDET, BRONCO, JENNET,
GALLOWAY, GENET(TE),
SHETLAND
sound ...... NIE, NEIGH, SNORT,
WHINNY
spotted .... APPALOOSA
stocky .... COB
sweat .... FOAM, LATHER
swift .... ARAB, PACER, RACER,
CLIPPER, SPANKER
tail .... CLOUD, PRELE
talking .... ARION
tamer .... ROUGHRIDER
tender .... GROOM
tooth .... TUSH, NIPPER
toy .... PONY, SHETLAND
trained .... PACER
training rope/place ..... LONGE

trappings .... HARNESS
turn of .... MANEGE,
    CARACOLE, (DEMI)VOLT
untamed .... BRONCO
war .... CHARGER, COURSER
whip .... CROP, QUIRT
wild .... TARPAN, BRUMBIE,
    BRONC(H)O, MUSTANG
winged .... PEGASUS
winless .... MAIDEN
winning gait .... ROMP
woman's .... PALFREY
worn out .... HACK, JADE,
    PLUG, YAUD, SKATE
worthless ...... NAG, RIP, JADE,
    WEED
young ...... COLT, FOAL, FILLY,
    YEARLING
horseback .... HOGBACK
on .... A CHEVAL
horsefly .... TABANID
horsehair .... SETON, SNELL
horseman .... RIDER, CABALLERO,
    EQUESTRIAN
in bullfighting .... PICADOR
horsemanship .... MANEGE,
    EQUITATION
movement in .... PIAFFER
horsemen .... CAVALRY
historical .... ROUGHRIDERS
horsemen's parade
    .... CAVALCADE
horsemint .... MONARDA
horseplay .... FUN, JINKS, PRANK,
    COMEDY
horses, ancestors of .... EOHIPPUS
art of riding .... MANEGE,
    EQUITATION
certain .... CROPEARS
collection of .... STUD, STABLE
herd of .... HARRAS, REMUDA
hold one's .... PAUSE, SLOW
    DOWN
left behind in race .... RUCK
pertaining to .... EQUINE
school for .... MANEGE
soldiers on .... CAVALRY
string of .... STABLE
horseshoe .... RINGER
gripper .... CALK
player .... TOSSER
points .... LEANERS
horseweed .... OXBALM
horsewhip .... CROP, FLOG, LASH,
    QUIRT, CHAB(O)UK
horsy crowd? .... NEIGHBORS
hortatory ...... URGING, ADVISING,
    ADVISORY
Horus .... RA, GOD, SUN
head of .... HAWK
parent of .... ISIS, OSIRIS

hosanna .... SHOUT, PRAISE,
    EXCLAMATION
hose .... TUBE, SOCKS, STOCKINGS
spout .... NOZZLE
Hosea .... OSSE
daughter of .... UNLOVED
son of .... JEZREEL
wife of .... GOMER
hosiery .... HOSE, NYLONS, SOCKS,
    ANKLETS, STOCKINGS
hospice .... INN, ASYLUM, IMARET,
    REFUGE, POORHOUSE
hospitable .... CORDIAL,
    GRACIOUS, RECEPTIVE
hospital .... SICK BAY, INFIRMARY,
    LAZARETTO
attendant .... ORDERLY
dispensary .... CLINIC
division .... WARD, CLINIC,
    PAVILION
drip IV
for foundlings .... CRECHE
for mentally sick
    ...... BUGHOUSE, BOOBY HATCH
for the poor .... SPITAL,
    LAZARET(TE)
kind of ...... ASYLUM, MENTAL,
    GENERAL, LYING-IN,
    MATERNITY, SANATORIUM
ship .... HOPE
staffer .... RESIDENT
vehicle .... AMBULANCE
host .... ARMY, BREAD, HORDE,
    LEGION, THRONG, LANDLORD,
    INNKEEPER, MULTITUDE
a toast .... REGALE
kind of .... EMCEE
receptacle .... PYX, PATEN,
    TABERNACLE
hostage .... PAWN, PLEDGE,
    SURETY
hostel(ry) .... INN, TAVERN
hostess .... ATTENDANT,
    ENTERTAINER
airline .... STEWARDESS
at times .... USHER, SEATER
famed .... HOWAR,
    (PERLE)MESTA
hostile .... ENEMY, WARLIKE,
    BELLICOSE, UNFRIENDLY
feeling .... ANIMUS, GRUDGE,
    RANCOR
hostilities .... BATTLE, COMBAT,
    WAR(FARE), CONFLICT
hostility .... SPITE, ANIMUS,
    ENMITY, HATRED, ILL-WILL,
    FRICTION, ANTAGONISM
hostler .... GROOM
hot .... ANGRY, FIERY, ARDENT,
    BITING, HEATED, HECTIC,
    SULTRY, TORRID, PEPPERY,

    THERMAL, VIOLENT,
    EXCITABLE
air .... VAPOR, HUMBUG,
    BOASTING, BOMBAST
and bothered .... UNEASY
and damp .... MUGGY
baths .... THERME
blooded .... LUSTY, ARDENT,
    INTENSE, ZEALOUS, RECKLESS,
    SPIRITED, LUSTFUL,
    PASSIONATE
cargo .... CONTRABAND
corner, so-called .... BASE,
    THIRD
fiddler .... NERO
goods .... SWAG, STOLEN,
    CONTRABAND
iron treatment .... CAUTERY
old style .... CALID
plate .... STOVE
seat .... ELECTRIC CHAIR
slang .... GOOD, FRESH,
    (BRAND)NEW, JUST OUT
spot .... DESERT
spot, of a kind .... SAUNA
spring .... GEYSER, THERME
springs, of .... THERMAL
taste .... PEPPERY
tempered ..... TESTY, IRACUND,
    PEPPERY, EXPLOSIVE
time .... SUMMER
water: colloq. .... FIX, JAM,
    PINCH, SCRAPE, TROUBLE
water hazard .... SCALD
wind .... SIROCCO
hotbed .... INCITER, TROUBLE
    SPOT
hotchpotch .... MESS, STEW,
    JUMBLE
hotdog .... WIENER
hotel .... INN, PUB, SUITE, TAVERN,
    HOSTEL(RY)
boy .... PAGE, BUTTONS
chain .... HYATT, HILTON,
    RAMADA, STATLER, SHERATON,
    HOLIDAY INN
cheap .... FLEABAG,
    FLOPHOUSE
dining room .... GRILL
foyer .... LOBBY
guest .... PATRON, TRAVELER,
    TRANSIENT
keeper .... HOST, BONIFACE
page .... BUTTONS
reception center
    .... (FRONT)DESK
resident .... GUEST, PATRON
hotfoot: colloq. .... HIE, RUN,
    RACE, HURRY, HASTEN
hothead .... FIREBRAND
hotheaded .... RASH, FIERY,

HASTY, TESTY, SPUNKY, WILLFUL, IMPETUOUS
hothouse ...... HOTBED, NURSERY, GREENERY, VIVARIUM
hotrod .... RACER, JALOPY
hotrods, race of .... DRAG
Hottentot .... NAMA, NEGRO
land .... NAMAQUA
language/tribe .... NAMA, BUSHMAN
race .... NEGROID
village .... KRAAL
Houdini, magician .... HARRY, WEISS
hound .... NAG, HUNT, CHASE, AFGHAN, HARASS, INCITE, PLAGUE, BRACHET, CERBERUS, (HUNTING)DOG
female .... BRACH
hunting .... BASSET, BEAGLE, SETTER, HARRIER, BLOODHOUND
sad-faced .... BASSET
wolf .... ALAN
hour .... MATIN
hourglass .... HOROLOGE
houri .... NYMPH
hourly .... HORAL, OFTEN, CONTINUAL, FREQUENT(LY)
house .... HOME, ROOF, LODGE, CONTAIN, COTTAGE, SHELTER, THEATER, DOMICILE, DWELLING
and lot .... PREMISE
bird's .... NEST, AERIE
correctional .... BRIDEWELL, REFORMATORY
country .... VILLA, CASINO,
extension .... PORCH, VERANDA
feature, suburban ..... PICTURE WINDOW
fortified .... PEEL
haunter .... SPOOK
ice .... IGLU, IGLOO
instant .... PREFAB
kind of ..... HASH, PENT, POOR, TOWN, DUPLEX
legislative .... DIET, CONGRESS, PARLIAMENT
log .... IZBA, CABIN
mud .... DOBE, TEMBE
organ .... PERIODICAL
pertaining to a .... DOMAL
plant .... FERN
poor man's .... HUT, HOVEL, SHACK
portable .... TENT, TEPEE, WIGWAM
ranch .... CASITA, GRANGE, HACIENDA
side covering .... SIDING,

SHINGLE
small, dingy .... HOLE
state visitor's (U.S.) .... BLAIR
stately .... PALACE, MANSION
summer .... RANCH, VILLA, CASINO, GAZEBO
houseboat .... BARGE
housebreaker .... BURGLAR
housebroken .... TAMED, TRAINED, DISCIPLINED
housefly genus .... MUSCA, FANNIA
of the .... MUSCID
household .... HOME, FAMILY, MENAGE, MAINPOST, DOMESTIC, DOMICILE
animal .... PET
food supply .... LARDER, PROVISIONS
gods .... LARES, PENATES
linen .... NAPERY
task .... CHAR(E), CHORE
housekeeping .... MENAGE
housel .... EUCHARIST
houses, buyer of old .... KNACKER
housesite .... TOFT
housewarming .... INFARE, (HOUSE)PARTY
housewife .... DAME, HUSSY, MATRON, HAUSFRAU, SEWING KIT
concern of .... DIRT, MENU, SOOT, WASH
housing .... PAD, FRAME, LODGING, SHELTER, COVERING
engine .... NACELLE
for bells .... STEEPLE
hovel .... HUT, SHED, HUTCH, SHACK, SHELTER, DWELLING
hover .... FLY, WAVER, LINGER, FLUTTER, LIBRATE, VACILLATE
how .... MANNER, METHOD
about that! .... JUST IMAGINE
come? .... WHY, WHAT FOR
de-do .... MESS
Merman sang .... BELTED
some like it .... HOT
-to book .... MANUAL
to find out .... ASK
to get to Desire .... STREETCAR
howdah .... SEAT
howdy ...... HELLO, HOW'S THINGS
however ...... BUT, YET, ANYHOW, THO(UGH), NEVERTHELESS
howitzer .... CANNON
howl .... WAIL, YOWL, BELLOW, ULULATE
lustily .... BAWL
howler .... OWL, MONKEY

colloquial .... BLUNDER
hoy .... BARGE
hoyden .... TOMBOY
hr., part of .... MIN, SEC
huaraches .... SANDALS
hub .... AXIS, NAVE, FOCUS, CENTER, MIDDLE
the .... BOSTON
Hubbard .... SQUASH
Hubbard's (Ron) dianetics .... SCIENTOLOGY
hubble .... HUMP
bubble .... PIPE, HOOKAH, HUBBUB, UPROAR
hubbly .... ROUGH, UNEVEN
hubbub .... ADO, DIN, STIR, TO-DO, NOISE, TUMULT, UPROAR, RACKET, TURMOIL, BROUHAHA
hubby .... HUSBAND
hubris .... ARROGANCE, INSOLENCE
huckle .... HIP, HAUNCH
Huckleberry Finn author .... TWAIN
vehicle of .... RAFT
huckster .... PEDLAR, HAWKER, VENDOR, PEDDLER, TRADESMAN
colloquial .... ADMAN
huddle .... CAUCUS, JUMBLE, ASSEMBLE, CONFERENCE
Hudson cliffs .... PALISADES
River city ..... TROY, YONKERS
River sight .... SINGSING
hue .... CRY, DYE, TINT, TONE, COLOR, SHADE, TINGE
and cry .... SHOUTING
area .... ANNAM
Huey P., the Kingfish ...... LONG
huff ...... MIFF, PUFF, TIFF, ANGER, BULLY, HECTOR, OFFEND, TANTRUM
and puff .... GASP
huffy .... TOUCHY, PETULANT
hug .... FIT, CLASP, CARESS, CUDDLE, ENFOLD, EMBRACE
kind of .... BEAR, BUNNY
me-tight .... VEST
huge .... LARGE, VAST, ENORM(OUS), IMMENSE, MAMMOTH, OUTSIZE, TITANIC, GIGANTIC
amount .... SCAD
exhalation .... GIANT SIGH
hugger-mugger .... SHUSH, COVERT, JUMBLE, MUFFLE, MUDDLE, SECRET, SECRECY
Hugo, novelist .... VICTOR
daughter of .... ADELE
wife of .... ADELE
Huguenot .... PROTESTANT

leader .... CONDE, ADRETS
hula hula .... DANCE
dancer .... WAHINE
hull .... POD, HUSK, CALYX,
SHELL, SHUCK
part of .... KEEL, BILGE
hullabaloo .... ADO, FLAP, TO-DO,
CLAMOR, HUBBUB, TUMULT,
UPROAR, BALLYHOO
hum .... BUZZ, SING, CROON,
DRONE, WHIR(R)
human .... BIPED, WIGHT,
MORTAL, PERSON, ADAMITE,
ANDROID, EARTHLY,
EARTHLING
body .... CORPUS, CARCASS
body model .... MANAKIN,
MANIKIN
chain .... CORDON
conflict in life .... DRAMA
flesh eater .... CANNIBAL
limb .... ARM, LEG
race .... MANKIND
race's father .... NOE, ADAM
soul .... PSYCHE
weakness .... FRAILTY
humane .... KIND, TENDER,
MERCIFUL, CIVILIZED
humanities .... (FINE)ARTS,
LANGUAGES, LITERATURE
humanity .... MERCY, PEOPLE,
MANKIND, KINDNESS,
MORTALITY
humankind .... PEOPLE
humble ...... MEEK, POOR, ABASE,
LOW(LY), DEMEAN, MODEST,
SHAME, PALTRY, DEGRADE,
CHASTISE, HUMILIATE
pie .... CROW, NOMBLES,
NUMBLES
Humboldt, city on the .... ELKO
humbug .... BOSH, DUPE, FLAM,
SHAM, CHEAT, FRAUD,
HOKUM, GAMMON, SLAVER,
IMPOSTOR
compound word ...... JIGGERY-
POKERY
humdinger ...... PIP, AONE, LULU,
ONER, DILLY, WINNER,
SNORTER, EXCELLENT
humdrum .... DRAB, DULL, SOSO,
ROUTINE, MONOTONOUS
humerus .... BONE
kind of nerve in .... RADIAL
site of .... (UPPER)ARM
humid .... WET, DAMP, DANK,
MOIST, SULTRY
humidify .... MOISTEN
humiliate .... ABASE, ABASH,
SHAME, DEMEAN, HUMBLE,
DEGRADE, MORTIFY,

DISGRACE, EMBARRASS
humiliating experience
.... BITTER PILL
humility .... MODESTY, MEEKNESS,
LOWLINESS, SUBMISSION
humming .... BRISK, ACTIVE,
BUZZING, DRONING, SINGING
sound .... DRONE, WHIR(R)
hummingbird .... AVA, BLUET,
COSTA, SYLPH, TOPAZ,
COLIBRI, RACKETTAIL
hummock .... HILL, HUMP,
KNOLL, MOUND, HILLOCK
humor .... WIT, BABY, BILE,
MOOD, WHIM, FANCY, LYMPH,
CHOLER, CODDLE, PHLEGM,
CAPRICE, GRATIFY, INDULGE
bad .... TIFF
ironic(al) .... SARCASM
out of .... CROSS, MOODY,
IRRITABLE
quaint .... DROLLERY
slang .... CORN
humoresque .... CAPRICE
humorist .... ADE, WIT, WAG,
COBB, NASH, JOKER, ROGERS,
(BOB)HOPE, FARCEUR,
BENCHLEY, RABELAIS
alleged .... WEST, BUCHWALD
humorous .... DROLL, FUNNY,
WITTY, JOCOSE, AMUSING,
COMICAL, JOCULAR
awareness .... RISIBILITY
personification .... BARLEY-
CORN
pianist .... BORGE
play .... FARCE, COMEDY
slang suffix .... EROO
verse .... LIMERICK
hump ...... ARCH, BULGE, HUNCH,
HUBBLE, HUMMOCK
of a humpback .... KYPHOS
the .... HIMALAYAS
humpback ...... WHALE, KYPHOSIS
humpbacked .... GIBBOUS
humped animal .... ZEBU,
CAMEL, DROMEDARY
Humpty Dumpty, describing
.... SQUAT
personification .... EGG
humus .... MOLD, SOIL, MULCH
Hun .... ATLI, BOCHE, ETZEL,
ATTILA, GERMAN, SAVAGE,
VANDAL
hunch .... HUMP, HUNK, LUMP,
CHUNK, PREMONITION
Hunchback of Notre Dame
author .... HUGO
character .... ESMERALDA,
QUASIMODO
hundred .... CENTUM

combining form .... CENTI,
HECTO
dollar bill: sl. .... C-NOTE
years .... CENTURY
hundredfold .... CENTUPLE
hundredth .... 100TH, CENTISMAL
abbreviation of .... PCT
hundredweight .... CENTAL,
KANTAR, CENTNER, QUINTAL
hung up .... RANG OFF
Hungarian ...... HUNKY, MAGYAR
capital .... BUDAPEST
cavalryman .... HUSSAR
city/town .... ABA, ACS, ERD,
OZD, VAC, AJKA, ARLO, BAJA,
EGER, GYOR, MAKO, PAKS,
PAPA, PECS, BEKES, GYULA,
CEGLED, SOPRON, SZEGED,
UJPEST, BUDAFOK, KISPEST,
MISKOLC, SZENTES, SZOLNOK,
DEBRECEN, KAPOSVAR,
OROSHAZA, KECSKEMET,
TATABANYA, VARPALOTA
chocolate party .... DOBOS
coin .... PENGO, FILLER
composer .... LEHAR, LISZT,
BARTOK
county .... VAS, PEST, BEKES,
FEJER, HEVES, TOLNA,
NOGRAD, SOMOGY, BARANYA,
KOMAROM, SZOLNOK,
BUDAPEST, CSONGRAD
dance .... CZARDAS
dessert .... STRUDEL
dog .... PULI
dramatist .... MOLNAR
dynasty .... ARPAD
gypsy .... TZIGANE
hero .... NAGY
king .... BELA
kingdom .... SERBIA
lake .... BALATON
language .... MAGYAR
leader .... (BELA)KUN
measure .... AKO
monetary unit .... PENGO,
FORINT, GULDEN
mountain .... KEKES
mountain range .... BUKK,
MATRA, BAKONY, MECSEK
part of .... BANAT
patriot .... KOSSUTH
people .... MAGYAR
pianist .... LISZT
plain .... GREAT ALFOLD
premier .... FOCK, KALLAI
president .... DOBI
regent .... HORTHY
river .... DUNA, EGER, MURA,
RABA, SAJO, ZALA, DRAVA,
KAPOS, KOROS, MAROS, TISZA,

DANUBE, HERNAD, BERETTYO
shepherd's food ...... GOULASH
slang .... HUNKY, HUNKIE
violinist .... AUER
wine .... TOKAY
hunger .... YEN, LUST, PINE,
 ACORIA, DESIRE, STARVE,
 CRAVING, APPETITE,
 ESURIENCE
continuous .... BULIMIA
for home .... NOSTALGIA
striker, famous .... GANDHI
hungry .... AVID, UNFED,
 STARVED, ESURIENT,
 FAMISHED
go deliberately .... FAST
hunk .... CHIP, LUMP, MASS, SLAB,
 CHUNK, HUNCH, PIECE, SLICE
hunks .... MISER, TIGHTWAD
hunky .... WELL, SQUARE,
 HUNGARIAN
hunky-dory .... OKAY, GREAT,
 SWELL
Huns, king of the .... ATLI,
 ETZEL, ATTILA
hunt .... SEEK, CHASE, CHEVY,
 HOUND, QUEST, SCOUR,
 TRACE, TRAIL, SHOOT,
 PURSUE, SEARCH
for lost scent .... CAST
goddess of the .... DIANA,
 ARTEMIS
illegally .... POACH
Hunt, actress .... MARSHA
critic, poet .... LEIGH
hunted animals .... GAME
hunter .... JAGER, ORION,
 FOWLER, NIMROD, STALKER,
 TRAPPER, CHASSEUR,
 PREDATOR
aid of .... RETRIEVER
bait of .... DECOY
cap of .... MONTERO
cry of .... TALLYHOO
kind of .... FORTUNE,
 TREASURE
prey of .... GAME
screen of .... BLIND
sea .... WHALER
Hunter, actor .... TAB
actress .... KIM
hunters, collectively .... CHASE
org. of .... NRA
hunting art .... CHASE, VENERY
bird .... FALCON
call .... CHEVY, YOICK,
 HALLOO, TANTIVY, TALLYHOO
dog .... ALAN(D), HOUND,
 BASSET, BEAGLE, SETTER,
 POINTER

dog, at times .... TREER
dog's clue .... SCENT
dogs, set of .... PACK
dog's stance .... POINT,
 DEADSET
expedition .... SAFARI
ground .... PRESERVE
hat .... TERAI, MONTERO
horn note .... MORT
hound .... BASSET
knife .... BOWIE
living by .... VENATIC
party member .... BEATER,
 GUN-BEARER
pertaining to .... VENATIC
huntress: myth. .... DIANA,
 ARTEMIS, ATALANTA
hup, sergeant's .... ONE
hupmobile .... AUTO
Hur .... BEN
ally of .... AARON
enemy .... MESSALA
hurdle ...... SLED, SNAG, BARRIER,
 OBSTACLE, SURMOUNT,
 HINDRANCE
fence on horseback ...... LARK
hurds .... TOW
hurdy-gurdy .... LIRA, ROTA,
 (BARREL)ORGAN
hurl .... TOSS, FLING, PITCH,
 SLING, THROW, HURTLE,
 LAUNCH, CATAPULT, CAST
 DOWN
hurlbat .... HARPOON, JAVELIN
hurly-burly .... FUME, BUSTLE,
 HUBBUB, TUMULT, UPROAR,
 TURMOIL, AGITATION,
 BROUHAHA
Hurok, impresario .... SOL
Huron .... LAKE, WYANDO(TE)
hurrah .... OLE, VIVA, WHEE,
 CHEER, SHOUT, APPLAUSE
hurricane ...... STORM, CYCLONE,
 TORNADO, TYPHOON
center .... EYE
hurried .... SPED, HASTY
and confused .... HELTER-
 SKELTER
in music .... AGITATO
hurry .... HIE, DASH, RUSH,
 SPEED, FLURRY, HASTE(N),
 HUSTLE, URGENCY,
 ACCELERATE
along: collog. .... SCOOT
up: inits. .... ASAP
hurrying: sl. .... BALLING THE
 JACK
Hurst, novelist .... FANNIE
hurt .... ACHE, HARM, WOUND,
 DAMAGE, INJURE, OFFEND

hurtful .... PAINFUL
hurting .... ACHY, CRUEL, BITING,
 GNAWING, STINGING
hurtle .... CAST, DASH, HURL,
 CLASH, FLING, COLLIDE
husband .... LORD, GROOM,
 SPOUSE, CONSORT, GOODMAN,
 RESERVE, CONSERVE,
 HELPMATE, HELPMEET
and wife .... COUPLE
authority of .... MANUS
bereaved .... WIDOWER
brother of .... LEVIR, IN-LAW
having one .... MONANDRY
prospective .... INTENDED
husbandman .... FARMER,
 GRANGER
husbandry .... THRIFT, ECONOMY,
 FARMING, TILLAGE,
 FRUGALITY, GEOPONICS
hush .... CALM, LULL, SOFT,
 QUIET, SHUSH, SILENCE
-hush org. .... CIA
up .... SILENCE, SUPPRESS
husk .... BRAN, HULL, CHAFF,
 GLUME, SHELL, SHUCK
rice in the .... PADDY
husky ...... DOG, ESKIMO, HOARSE,
 STURDY, ROBUST, MALEMUTE
command to a .... MUSH
hussar .... CAVALRYMAN
gear of .... LANCE(S)
jacket .... DOLMAN
hussy .... CASE, DOXY, ETUI, GIRL,
 MINX, SLUT, TART, WENCH,
 TROLLOP, SEWING KIT
hustings .... COURT, ASSEMBLY,
 PLATFORM, BOONDOCKS
hustle .... JOLT, POKE, PROD,
 PUSH, DRIVE, HURRY, SHOVE,
 HASTEN, JOSTLE
slang .... CON, SWINDLE
hustler ...... DYNAMO, GO-GETTER
slang .... SWINDLER
hut .... CABIN, HOVEL, SHACK,
 CHALET, LEANTO, MIAM(IA),
 SHANTY
kind of .... NISSEN QUONSET
hutch .... BIN, HUT, PEN, COOP,
 CHEST, TROUGH, WARREN
dweller .... DOE
Huxley, writer .... ALDOUS,
 JULIAN
huzza .... CHEER, SHOUT, HURRAH
Hwang Hai .... YELLOW SEA
hyacinth .... GEM, BIRD, BULB,
 MUSK, CAMAS, STONE,
 FLOWER, BLUEBELL
gem .... TOPAZ, ZIRCON
hyaline .... GLASSY
hyalite .... OPAL

hybrid .... MULE, MIXED, HALFBREED, CROSS(BREED)
animal .... HINNY, CATALO
citrus tree .... TANGELO
dog .... MONGREL
language .... JARGON
hybridize .... CROSS
hydatid .... CYST
Hyde .... PARK
creator of Mr. .... RSL
other self of Mr. .... JEKYLL
Hyderabad city .... GOLCONDA
ruler .... NIZAM
hydra .... POLYP, HYDROZOAN
Hydra .... SERPENT
heads and hell's rivers of .... ENNEADS
hydrangea .... SHRUB
hydrant .... FIREPLUG
attachment .... HOSE
hydranth .... ZOOID
hydrocarbon .... BUTANE, CYMENE, MELENE, OCTANE, PINENE, TOLANE, BENZENE, ETHERIN, (M)ETHANE, PROPANE, TERPENE
aromatic ...... ARENE, CARANE, CHRYSENE
coal tar .... PYRENE
compound .... IMINE
gaseous .... FLUORINE
liquid .... TOLUENE
mixture .... MALTHA
pine tar .... RETENE
radical .... AMYL, ETHYL
wax .... MONTAN

hydrocephalus victim .... WATERHEAD
hydrocortison .... CORTISOL
hydrogen .... GAS
hydroid .... POLYP
colony branch .... ZOOID
hydromedusa .... JELLYFISH
hydrometer scale .... BAUME
hydrophobia .... LYSSA, LYTTA, RABIES
hydrous .... WATERY
(magnesium) silicate .... TALC
hydrozoan .... HYDRA, POLYP, JELLYFISH, MILLEPORE
hygienic .... CLEAN, SANITARY
hyla .... TREETOAD
hymen .... SONG, MAIDENHEAD
hymenopter ...... ANT, BEE, WASP
hymn .... ODE, PAEAN, PSALM, ANTHEM, CHORALE, TE DEUM, CANTICLE, RECESSIONAL
book .... HYMNAL, GRADUAL, PSALTER
for the dead .... REQUIEM
of praise .... LAUD, ANTHEM, MAGNIFICAT
praising God .... GLORIA, ALLELUIA, ALLELUJAH
hymnoptera .... BEES
hyp .... MELANCHOLIA
hyperbole .... AUXESIS, DISTORTION, EXAGGERATION, OVERSTATEMENT
hyperbolic function .... COSH
Hyperion .... TITAN
daughter of .... EOS

parent .... GAEA, URANUS
son of .... HELIOS
hyphen .... DASH
hypnosis .... TRANCE
hypnotic .... ACETAL, LUMINAL, MESMERIC, SOPORIFIC
compound .... AMYTAL
drug .... NEMBUTAL
force .... OD, ODYL(E)
state .... TRANCE
hypnotism .... MESMERISM
founder of .... MESMER
hypnotize ...... CHARM, ENTRANCE
hypochondria ...... HYP, ANXIETY, NEUROSIS, MELANCHOLY
hypochondriac .... NEUROTIC, NOSOMANIA, VALETUDINARIAN
hypocrisy .... CANT, PRETENSE, PHARISAISM, INSINCERITY
hypocrite .... SHAM, PHARISEE, TARTUF(F)E, PRETENDER
hypothesis .... ISM, THEORY
hypothesize .... ASSUME, SUPPOSE
hypothetical .... ASSUMED
force .... OD, ELOD, ODYL, IDANT
hyrax ...... CONY, DAMAN, RABBIT
hyson .... TEA
hyssop .... MINT, THISTLE
hysteria ...... FIT, PANIC, FRENZY, ANXIETY, JITTERS, MADNESS, DELIRIUM, TARASSIS
hysterical .... WILD, FRENZIED, DELIRIOUS, EMOTIONAL

I

I .... AYE, EGO, SELF
am to blame .... MEA CULPA
beam projection .... FLANGE
believe: Lat. .... CREDO
excessive use of ..... IOTACISM
have found it! .... EUREKA
letter .... IOTA
pray thee .... PRITHEE
Remember Mama actress .... (IRENE)DUNNE
Remember Mama author .... (KATHRYN)FORBES
Iago's master .... OTHELLO
wife .... EMILIA
iamb .... FOOT
iambi .... FEET
Iasi .... JASSY
coin .... LEU
iatric .... MEDICAL, MEDICINAL

Iberia .... SPAIN, PENINSULA
author of .... MICHENER
Iberian region .... LUSITANIA
ibex ...... TUR, GOAT, KAIL, WALIE, SAKEEN
habitat .... ALPS, PYRENEES
ibid(em) .... SAME, DITTO
ibis .... HERON, JABIRU
Ibo .... NIGERIAN
Ibsen .... HENDRICK
character .... ASE, GYNT, NORA, HEDDA, ELLIDA
Icarian-like .... RASH, DARING, FOOLHARDY
Icarus's daughter .... ERIGONE
parent .... DAEDALUS
ICBM .... ATLAS, MISSILE, MINUTE MAN
ice .... FIRN, FLOE, GRUE, CHILL,

ROCKS, FREEZE, DESSERT, FROST(ING), SHERBET
breaker .... ATKA, PICK
breaking in water .... DEBACLE
coat .... RIME
cream .... BISQUE, SUNDAE
crosser .... ELIZA
field .... FLOE
flakes .... SNOW
floe .... PAN, PACK
fragments .... BRASH
hockey disc .... PUCK
mass .... BERG, FLOE, PACK, SERAC, GLACIER
of .... GLACIAL
partly melted .... SLUSH
pellets .... HAIL
pinnacle .... SERAC
rain .... HAIL, SLEET

runner .... SKI, SKATE
sheet .... GLACIER
skate's cousin .... SKI
slang .... DIAMOND(S)
iceberg .... FLOE, LETTUCE
piece from .... CALF
small .... GROWLER
iceboat .... SKIFF
icebox .... FREEZER,
REFRIGERATOR
iced .... GLACE, FRAPPE
Iceland bay .... FAXA, HUNA
cape .... HORN, GERPIR
capital .... REYKJAVIK
city/town .... NES, AKRANES,
HUSAVIK, AKUREYRI,
KEFLAVIK, KOPAVOGUR
district .... SYSSEL
epic .... EDDA
god .... LOKI, ODIN, THOR,
AESIR, WODEN, BALDER
hot spring .... GEYSIR
island .... GRIMSEY, SURTSEY
king .... ATLI
language .... NORSE,
ICELANDIC
literature .... EDDA
measure .... FET, ALEN
monetary unit .... KRONA
NATO base .... KEFLAVIK
parliament .... ALTHING
poet .... SKALD
queen .... BRUNHILD
river .... THJORSA
volcano .... ASKJA, HEKLA
Iceni, queen of .... BOADICEA
Ichabod Crane's rival ...... BROM
work .... PEDAGOGUE
ichneumon .... FLY, MONGOOSE
icing .... FROSTING
icky .... DIRTY, CRAPPY, SHITTY,
STINKY, YECCHY
icon ...... EIKON, IMAGE, PICTURE,
LIKENESS
Ictalurus punctatus ...... CATFISH
icterus .... JAUNDICE
ictus .... FIT, ARSIS, SPASM,
ACCENT, STROKE, UPBEAT,
SEIZURE
icy .... COLD, ALOOF, GELID,
FRIGID, FROSTY, GLACIAL
coat .... RIME
id. .... EGO, IDEM, SAME, IDAHO,
LIBIDO, INSTINCT
ID .... DRIVER'S LICENSE,
(IDENTIFICATION)BADGE
military .... DOG TAG
Idaho .... POTATO STATE
capital .... BOISE
city/town ..... NAMPA, JEROME,
MOSCOW, WEISER, CALDWELL,

LEWISTON, MERIDIAN,
BLACKFOOT, POCATELLO, TWIN
FALLS, IDAHO FALLS
college .... CALDWELL
county .... ADA, BOISE, LATAH,
BONNER, CANYON, CASSIA,
ELMORE, BANNOCK, BINGHAM,
MADISON, PAYETTE,
KOOTENAI, MINIDOKA,
SHOSHONE, BONNEVILLE, TWIN
FALLS
falls .... TWIN, SALMON,
AMERICAN, SHOSHONE
lake ...... MUD, BEAR, HAYDEN,
LOWELL, PRIEST, PAYETTE,
LUCKY PEAK, PEND OREILLE,
COEUR D'ALENE
main crop .... POTATOES
mountain .... POT, ALLAN,
WAUGH, MORMON, SADDLE,
CARIBOU, LOOKOUT, RAINBOW,
GREYLOCK, GOLDSTONE, TWIN
PEAKS
national park .... NEZ PERCE
pass .... LOLO, LOST TRAIL
peak .... RYAN, BORAH,
MEADE, BADGER, BANNOCK,
DIAMOND
range .... BITTERROOT
river .... RED, PACK, RAFT,
MALAD, MOYIE, SNAKE,
LOCHSA, SALMON, SELWAY
state bird .... BLUEBIRD
state flower .... SYRINGA
state motto ...... ESTO PERPETUA
state nickname .... GEM
idea .... FANCY, IMAGE, NOESIS,
NOTION, INKLING,
CONCEPT(ION), OPINION,
THOUGHT, IMPRESSION
bright .... BRAINSTORM
combining form .... IDEO
main/dominant .... MOTIF
utopian .... BUBBLE
ideal .... HERO, MODEL, PARAGON,
PERFECT, UTOPIAN,
FAULTLESS, CONCEPTUAL
state .... OCEANA, UTOPIA
idealist .... ANIMIST, DREAMER,
VISIONARY
idealize .... DEIFY, OVERRATE,
RHAPSODIZE
ideals of citizenship ...... CIVISM
ideas, sentimental .... CORN
worthless .... BILGE
ideate .... FANCY, THINK,
IMAGINE, CONCEIVE
idee fixe .... OBSESSION
idem .... (THE)SAME
identical ...... ONE, ALIKE, EQUAL,
(SELF)SAME

combining form .... EQUI
item/counterpart .... TWIN
identification, means of
.... BADGE, BRAND, CHECK,
LABEL, NOTCH, MARKER,
(DOG)TAG, DRIVER'S LICENSE
identify .... NAME, EARMARK,
DIAGNOSE, RECOGNIZE
identifying marks ...... STIGMATA
identity .... ONENESS, ONESELF,
SELF(NESS), PERSONALITY,
INDIVIDUALITY
of origin .... ISOGENY
word .... NEE
ideologist .... DREAMER,
THEORIST, VISIONARY
ideology .... ISM, DOGMA,
THEORY, DOCTRINE, PRINCIPLE
Ides, date before .... NONES
of March victim .... CAESAR
idiocy .... FOLLY, AMENTIA,
ANOESIA, FATUITY,
CRETINISM, STUPIDITY
idiom .... CANT, ARGOT, SLANG,
PHRASE, DIALECT, LANGUAGE,
LOCUTION
idiosyncrasy .... ODDITY,
PECULIARITY, INDIVIDUALISM
idiot .... OAF, AMENT, MORON,
CRETIN, NITWIT, DULLARD,
IMBECILE, SIMPLETON
idle ...... LAZE, LAZY, LOAF, VAIN,
FUTILE, LOITER, OTIANT,
OTIOSE, VACANT, USELESS,
BASELESS, INACTIVE,
POINTLESS
talk .... GAB, GAS, GOSSIP,
PATTER, CHITCHAT
idleness .... SLOTH, LAZINESS,
INDOLENCE
idler .... BUM, DRONE, LOAFER,
LOUNGER, ROUNDER,
LAZYBONES
idol .... GOD, BAAL, ICON, LION,
IMAGE, EFFIGY, EIDOLON,
CELEBRITY
Chinese .... JOSS
social .... LION
worshiper .... PAGAN
idolater .... PAGAN, ADORER
object of .... TOTEM
idolatry .... SUTTEE, ANIMISM,
DEMONISM
idolism .... SOPHISM
idolize .... ADORE, ADMIRE,
WORSHIP
Idum(a)ea .... EDOM
idyl(l) .... POEM, ECLOGUE,
PASTORAL
idyllic .... POETIC, BUCOLIC,
PASTORAL

i.e. .... ID EST, THAT IS
if .... PROVIDED, CONDITION,
    SUPPOSITION
    not .... ELSE, NISI, UNLESS
igneous .... PLUTONIC
    rock .... BOSS, BASALT,
    DIABASE
ignis fatuus ...... DELUSION, WILL-
    O'-THE-WISP
ignite .... BURN, FIRE, LIGHT,
    EXCITE, KINDLE
ignited substance .... SPARK
igniter .... FUSE, DETONATOR
ignoble .... LOW, BASE, VILE,
    MEAN, HUMBLE
ignominious ...... SHADY, SORDID,
    SHAMEFUL, DEGRADING,
    DISGRACEFUL
ignominy .... SHAME, INFAMY,
    DISGRACE
ignoramus .... DUMMY, DUNCE,
    NITWIT, KNOW-NOTHING,
    SIMPLE SIMON
ignorance .... BLINDNESS,
    INNOCENCE, STUPIDITY
ignorant ...... WITLESS, UNAWARE,
    NESCIENT, ILLITERATE,
    UNLETTERED, UNSCHOOLED
ignore .... CUT, OMIT, SNUB,
    ELIDE, NEGLECT, OVERLOOK,
    DISREGARD
Igraine's husband .... UTHER
iguana .... GOANNA, LIZARD
Il Trovatore gypsy ...... MANRICO
ileus .... COLIC
Iliad author .... HOMER
    character .... AJAX, HECTOR,
    CALCHAS, STENTOR, ACHILLES
    nephew .... MEGES
Ilion .... TROY
ilium .... HIPBONE
ilk .... KIND, SORT, BREED, CLASS,
    FAMILY, STRIPE
ill .... BAD, EVIL, SICK, QUEER,
    UNWELL, ADVERSE,
    INDISPOSED
    advised .... UNWISE
    at ease .... RESTIVE
    bred .... BOOR, LOUT, RUDE,
    IMPOLITE
    defined .... VAGUE
    disposed .... HOSTILE
    fated .... DOOMED, UNLUCKY,
    STAR-CROSSED
    favored .... UGLY
    humor .... BILE
    humored .... CROSS, SULLEN
    mannered .... RUDE, COARSE,
    CADDISH, LOW-BRED
    mannered child .... BRAT
    prefix .... MAL

temper .... PET, BILE, SPLEEN
tempered .... CROSS, SURLY,
    CRANKY, SULLEN, PEEVISH,
    WASPISH
tempered, extremely .... AS
    UGLY AS A BEAR
tempered one .... TARTAR
tempered person
    .... CURMUDGEON
treatment .... ABUSE, CRUELTY,
    MANHANDLING
will ...... HATE, SPITE, ANIMUS,
    ENMITY, GRUDGE, HATRED,
    MALICE, RANCOR, DISLIKE
illegal .... FOUL, ILLICIT,
    UNLAWFUL, CONTRABAND
    liquor .... BOOTLEG
    slang .... HOT
illegally produced chemicals
    .... DESIGNER DRUGS
illegible .... UNREADABLE
illegitimate .... BASTARD,
    ILLEGAL, MISBEGOT(TEN)
illicit .... SECRET, CLANDESTINE
Illinois capital .... SPRINGFIELD
    city/town .... ZION, ALTON,
    CAIRO, ELGIN, PEKIN, AURORA,
    DEKALB, JOLIET, MOLINE,
    NORMAL, PEORIA, QUINCY,
    SKOKIE, URBANA, CHICAGO,
    DECATUR, LANSING, LINCOLN,
    LOMBARD, WHEATON,
    DANVILLE, EVANSTON,
    KANKAKEE, ROCKFORD,
    WAUKEGAN, WHEELING,
    WILMETTE, BELVIDERE,
    CHAMPAIGN, GALESBURG,
    BELLEVILLE, DES PLAINES,
    LOUISVILLE
    college .... SHIMER
    county .... COOK, KANE, KNOX,
    LAKE, OGLE, WILL, ADAMS,
    HENRY, MACON, BUREAU,
    DUPAGE, FULTON, MARION,
    MORGAN, PEORIA, JACKSON,
    KENDALL, LA SALLE,
    MADISON, WHITESIDE,
    WINNEBAGO, WILLIAMSON,
    ROCK ISLAND
    greatest son .... LINCOLN
    historic site .... TIME MUSEUM,
    LINCOLN COURTROOM, ROCK
    ISLAND ARSENAL
    lake ..... FOX, REND, CALUMET,
    CARLYLE, MICHIGAN,
    SHELBYVILLE, CRAB ORCHARD
    river .... OHIO, PLUM, ROCK,
    SPOON, SALINE, WABASH,
    ILLINOIS, BIG MUDDY,
    MACKINAW, MACOUPIN,
    SANGAMON, KASKASKIA, BIG

    BUREAU, MISSISSIPPI
    state bird .... CARDINAL
    state flower .... NATIVE VIOLET
    state motto .... NATIONAL
    UNION
    state nickname .... PRAIRIE,
    LAND OF LINCOLN
    state tree .... OAK
    university .... DE PAUL,
    BRADLEY, ROOSEVELT,
    SANGAMON STATE
illiterate .... IGNORANT,
    UNEDUCATED, UNLETTERED
illness .... MALADY, DISEASE
    feign .... MALINGER
illume .... LIGHT
illuminate .... LIGHT(UP),
    ELUCIDATE, ENLIGHTEN
    in a certain way
    .... TORCHLIGHT
illumination .... LIGHT
    unit .... LUX
illusion .... FANCY, TULLE,
    MIRAGE, CHIMERA, FANTASY,
    DELUSION
illusionist, kind of .... MAGICIAN
illustrate .... CITE, DRAW,
    EXPLAIN, PICTURE
illustration .... GRAPH, SAMPLE,
    DIAGRAM, DRAWING,
    EXAMPLE
illustrious .... NOTED, FAMOUS,
    EMINENT, CELEBRATED
illy .... BADLY, POORLY
image .... ICON, EIKON, EFFIGY,
    STATUE, (E)IDOLON, REPLICA,
    LIKENESS
    deceptive .... CHIMERA,
    ILLUSION
    destroyer .... ICONOCLAST
    mental .... IDEA, RECEPT,
    CONCEPT(ION)
    prefix .... EIDO
imagery .... STATUES
imaginary ...... FECUND, UNREAL,
    FICTIVE, FANCIFUL, MYTHICAL
    ailment .... CRUD
    terrestrial circle ...... EQUATOR
imagination .... IDEA, MYTH,
    DREAM, FANCY, NOTION,
    VISION, INVENTION
imagine .... WEEN, FANCY, GUESS,
    CREATE, IDEATE, INVENT,
    SUPPOSE, SURMISE, CONCEIVE
imagist .... POET, DREAMER
imam .... CALIPH, PRIEST
imaret .... INN, SERAI
imbalance .... DISPARITY
imbecile .... FOOL, AMENT, ANILE,
    MORON, CRETIN, DOTARD,
    STUPID

imbecility .... IDIOCY, FATUITY

imbibe .... BIB, SIP, DRINK, ABSORB, INHALE

imbiber .... SOT, WINO, DRUNK, BARFLY, TIPPLER

imbricate .... OVERLAP

imbricated .... TILED

imbroglio ...... PLOT, CONFUSION, ENTANGLEMENT

imbrue .... WET, SOAK, STEEP

imbue .... DYE, TINCT, INFUSE, INGRAIN, INSPIRE, PERVADE, PERMEATE

imitate .... APE, COPY, ECHO, MIME, MATCH, MIMIC, FOLLOW, DUPLICATE

Niobe .... CRY

the Cheshire cat .... GRIN

imitation .... COPY, SHAM, BOGUS, PARODY, FORGERY, MIMESIS, MIMICRY, COUNTERFEIT

gem .... PASTE

ludicrous .... TRAVESTY, CARICATURE

imitative .... APISH, MIMETIC

animal .... APE, MONKEY

imitativeness .... APERY

imitator ...... APER, ECHO, MIMIC, FORGER, MONKEY, PARROT

immaculate .... PURE, CLEAN, CHASTE, SINLESS, INNOCENT, PRISTINE, SPOTLESS, UNSOILED, UNTOUCHED

immanent ...... INNATE, INHERENT

immaterial .... TRIVIAL, IRRELEVANT

immature .... RAW, GREEN, YOUNG, CALLOW, UNRIPE

immeasurable .... VAST, BOUNDLESS, LIMITLESS

immediate .... FIRST, DIRECT, PROMPT, CLOSE(ST), NEAR(EST), INSTANT, PRESENT, ADJACENT

immediately ...... NOW, AT ONCE, PROMPTLY, FORTHWITH, AS SOON AS, INSTANTLY

available .... READY

slang .... PDQ

immense .... HUGE, VAST, GREAT, ENORM(OUS), INFINITE, LIMITLESS

enjoyment .... WHALE OF A TIME

immensity .... INFINITY, VASTNESS

immerse .... DIP, DUCK, DUNK, DOUSE, ABSORB, PLUNGE, BAPTIZE, ENGROSS, SUBMERGE

in fluid .... BATHE

immersed .... RAPT, ABSORBED

immersion .... BAPTISM

immigrant .... ALIEN, SETTLER

illegal .... WETBACK

newly arrived .... GRIFFIN, NEWCOMER, GREENHORN

status .... ALIENAGE

immigrants, island of ...... ELLIS

mid-19th century ..... SCOTCH-IRISH

immobile ...... FIRM, FIXED, STILL, SESSILE, MOTIONLESS

immoderate .... UNDUE, EXCESSIVE

immodest .... BOLD, BRAZEN, FORWARD, INDECENT, IMPUDENT

immolate .... SACRIFICE

immoral .... LEWD, WANTON, WICKED, OBSCENE, INDECENT

immorality .... VICE

immortal .... DIVINE, GODLIKE, ENDURING, DEATHLESS

immovable ...... SET, FIRM, FIXED, IMPASSIVE, STATIONARY

immune ...... EXEMPT, PROTECTED

render .... INOCULATE, VACCINATE

immunity .... EXEMPTION, PROTECTION

kind of .... DIPLOMATIC

immunization .... SHOT

method .... INOCULATION

immunizing substance .... SERUM, VACCINE, ANTITOXIN

immure .... CONFINE, SHUT UP, ISOLATE, SECLUDE, IMPRISON

immutable .... FIRM, ETERNAL, CHANGELESS, UNCHANGING

imp ...... ELF, BRAT, PUCK, CHILD, DEMON, DEVIL, SPRITE

impact .... DINT, PACK, SLAM, FORCE, SHOCK, TOUCH, CONTACT, COLLISION

main .... BRUNT

impair .... MAR, HARM, SPOIL, DAMAGE, INJURE, WEAKEN, VITIATE

impairment .... INJURY

speech .... DYSPHASIA

impale .... SPIT, FENCE IN, PIERCE, TRANSFIX

impalpable .... SUBTLE

impart .... GIVE, LEND, TELL, SHARE, BESTOW, CONVEY, REVEAL, DIVULGE, DISCLOSE, COMMUNICATE

knowledge .... TEACH

impartial .... FAIR, JUST, UNBIASED, EVEN(HANDED)

impasse .... HALT, DEADLOCK, STANDOFF, STALEMATE, BLIND ALLEY

impassioned .... FIERY, ARDENT

impassive .... CALM, SERENE, STOLID, STOIC(AL), PHLEGMATIC

impasto .... PAINTING

impatience .... EAGERNESS

impatiens .... JEWELWEED, TOUCH-ME-NOT

impatient .... EAGER, ANXIOUS, RESTIVE

impeach .... ACCUSE, CHARGE, IMPUGN, INDICT, ARRAIGN, DISCREDIT

impeccable .... FLAWLESS, BLAMELESS, FAULTLESS

impecunious .... POOR, BROKE

impede .... BLOCK, DELAY, HAMPER, HINDER, RETARD, STYMIE, OBSTRUCT

legally .... ESTOP

impediment ...... HITCH, BARRIER, OBSTACLE, HINDRANCE

speech .... LISP, STAMMER, STUTTER

impedimenta .... BAGGAGE

impel .... MOVE, PUSH, URGE, DRIVE, FORCE, COMPEL, INCITE, PROPEL, ACTUATE, MOTIVATE, CONSTRAIN

impending .... IMMINENT

impenetrable .... DENSE, SOLID, IMPERVIOUS

impennate bird .... PENGUIN

imperative .... URGENT, NECESSARY, COMPELLING, COMPULSORY

imperator .... EMPEROR

imperceptible .... MINUTE, UNSEEN, INVISIBLE

imperfect .... CRUDE, FAULTY, FLAWED, CRACKED, UNSOUND

prefix .... ATELO

imperfection .... FLAW, VICE, FAULT, DEFECT, BLEMISH, FAILING, SHORTCOMING

imperial .... BEARD, REGAL, GOATEE, MAJESTIC

color .... PURPLE

decree .... RESCRIPT

domain .... EMPIRE, EMPERY

imperil .... ENDANGER, JEOPARDIZE

imperious .... URGENT, ARROGANT, MAGISTRAL

imperishable .... IMMORTAL

impersonal .... FAIR, DISTANT, REMOVED, DETACHED, OBJECTIVE

impersonate .... APE, MIMIC, EMBODY, IMITATE

impersonator .... ACTOR, IMPOSTOR
impertinence .... IMPUDENCE, INSOLENCE
impertinent .... PERT, SASSY, SAUCY, FLIP(PANT), IMPUDENT, INSOLENT, MALAPERT
one .... SNIP
talk .... LIP, SASS
impetuous .... HOT, RASH, BRASH, HASTY, TEARING, IMPULSIVE
too .... OVERRASH
impetus .... DRIVE, FORCE, IMPULSE, MOMENTUM
impi ...... ZULU, KAFFIR, WARRIOR
impiety .... SIN, APOSTASY, BLASPHEMY, PROFANITY
impinge .... ENCROACH, TRESPASS
impious .... GODLESS, PROFANE, UNCTUOUS
impish .... ELFISH, ELVISH, DEVILISH, MISCHIEVOUS
implacable .... MORTAL, PITILESS, VENGEFUL, RELENTLESS
implant .... FIX, EMBED, GRAFT, INSTILL, INCULCATE
deeply .... (EN)ROOT
implement .... TOOL, ENFORCE, DEVICE, EXECUTE, FULFILL, UTENSIL
hay spreading .... MULCHER
kitchen .... UTENSIL
pounding/crushing ..... PESTLE
threshing .... FLAIL
implicate ...... CONNECT, INCLUDE, INVOLVE, INCRIMINATE
implication .... ALLUSION, INNUENDO, OVERTONE
implicit .... TACIT, IMPLIED, ABSOLUTE, INHERENT
implied .... TACIT, IMPLICIT
implore .... BEG, PRAY, PLEAD, BESEECH, ENTREAT
imply .... HINT, ENTAIL, CONNOTE, SUGGEST, INTIMATE
impolite .... RUDE, ILL-MANNERED
impolitic .... UNWISE, TACTLESS
import ...... DRIFT, SENSE, TENOR, BRING IN, MEANING
tax .... TARIFF
important .... KEY, MAJOR, PRIME, VITAL, ESSENTIAL
celestial layer .... OZONE
document .... WILL, CONTRACT
U.S. military base ...... THULE
importance ...... VALUE, WEIGHT, ESSENCE, DISTINCTION
importune .... URGE, PRAY, PLEAD, PRESS, BESEECH, ENTREAT

importunist .... ASKER
impose .... FOB, LEVY, FOIST, FORCE, ENTAIL, PALM OFF, INFLICT
imposing .... EPIC, NOBLE, AUGUST, MAGNIFIC, GRAND(IOSE), DIGNIFIED, IMPRESSIVE
imposition .... BOTHER, NUISANCE, INTRUSION
impossible task? .... MISSION
impost .... TAX, DUTY, LEVY
impostor .... SHAM, CHEAT, FAKER, FRAUD, GOUGE, QUACK, HUMBUG, PHON(E)Y
imposture .... SHAM, FRAUD, PRETENSE, DECEPTION
impotent .... INEPT, UNABLE, STERILE, HELPLESS
impound .... POIND, SEIZE, CONFISCATE
impractical one .... DREAMER, IDEALIST
theorist .... DOCTRINAIRE
imprecation .... OATH, CURSE, EXPLETIVE
impregnable .... FIRM, INVINCIBLE
impregnate .... FILL, SOAK, INFUSE, SATURATE, FECUNDATE, FERTILIZE, POLLINATE
impresario .... PROMOTER, ENTREPRENEUR
Sol .... HUROK
impress .... DENT, LEVY, MARK, DRAFT, STAMP, AFFECT, COMPEL, (IM)PRINT
deeply .... ENGRAVE
impression .... IDEA, MARK, STAMP, EFFECT, FEELING, IMPRINT, INKLING, OPINION, PRINT(ING)
on coin .... MINTAGE
trial .... PROOF
impressionist painter .... DEGAS, MANET, MONET, RENOIR
impressive .... MOVING, AWESOME
imprest .... LENT, LOAN, (CASH)ADVANCE
imprimatur .... LICENSE, APPROVAL, SANCTION
imprint ...... ETCH, MARK, PRESS, STAMP
imprison .... CAGE, JAIL, (IM)MURE, CONFINE, INCARCERATE
improbable .... DOUBTFUL, UNLIKELY
impromptu .... OFFHAND, EXTEMPORE, IMPROVISED
improper .... AMISS, UNDUE,

WRONG, RISQUE, INDECENT, UNFIT(TING), UNSEEMLY, UNBECOMING
improperly .... UNDULY
impropriety .... MISCONDUCT, MISBEHAVIOR
improve .... AMEND, EMEND, BETTER, ADVANCE, FORWARD, REMODEL, AMELIORATE
improvisation on stage .... AD LIB, ASIDE
improvise .... VAMP, AD LIB, MAKE-DO, INVENT, CONTRIVE
improvised .... OFFHAND, IMPROMPTU
imprudent .... RASH, BRASSY, CARELESS, INDISCREET
impudence .... LIP, GALL, SASS, BRASS, CHEEK, NERVE, SAUCE, INSOLENCE
impudent ...... ARCH, BOLD, PERT, RUDE, BRASH, FRESH, SASSY, SAUCY, SNOTTY, FORWARD, MALAPERT
impugn DENY, ASPERSE, CHALLENGE, CRITICIZE
impulse .... PROD, PUSH, URGE, FORCE, SHOVE, MOTIVE, THRUST, IMPETUS
to steal .... KLEPTOMANIA
impulsive ...... RASH, IMPETUOUS, UNGUARDED, CAPRICIOUS
impunity .... EXEMPTION
impure .... BAWDY, DIRTY, MIXED, AMORAL, DEFILED, UNCLEAN, UNCHASTE
impurity .... DROSS, FILTH, LEWDNESS, OBSCENITY
impute .... CHARGE, ASCRIBE, ATTRIBUTE
in ...... AT, WITH, AMONG, AMIDST, AT HOME, INSIDE, ENCLOSE
a body/group .... EN MASSE
brown study .... RAPT, DAYDREAMING
conflict .... AT WAR
correct way .... RIGHTLY
—— (excited) .... STEW
frenzy .... AMOK
group of .... AMONG, ALTOGETHER
headlong manner .... IMPULSIVELY
heedful way .... ATTENTIVELY
hurry .... POSTHASTE
jiffy .... SOON
lethargic way .... SLEEPILY
manner of speaking .... SO TO SAY

Milquetoast manner .... TIMOROUSLY
minute .... ANON
natty way .... SNAPPILY
quandary .... UP A TREE
reversed situation .... SHOE IS ON THE OTHER FOOT
ruddy way .... REDLY
saucy way .... PERTLY
tough spot .... OUT ON A LIMB
while .... LATER
abundance .... GALORE, TEEMING
accord .... EN RAPPORT
accordance with .... ALA, PURSUANT
addition .... TOO, ALSO, MOREOVER
agreement .... UNITED
an instant .... MOMENTARILY
and out .... TIDE
any case/any way .... EVER, AT ALL, ANYHOW
arrears .... OWING
as-much-as .... SINCE
bad taste .... RANK, COARSE
better spirits .... CHEERIER
case .... LEST
cheek, ____ .... TONGUE
circulation .... ABOUT, ABROAD
close cooperation .... HAND IN GLOVE
clover .... PROSPEROUS
confusion .... AT SIXES AND SEVENS
confusion, to a GI ...... SNAFU
due manner ..... DULY, TRULY, REALLY, ACCORDINGLY
fact .... DE FACTO
favor of .... FOR, PRO
front .... AHEAD
full measure .... ENTIRELY
good time .... SOON, EARLY
high dudgeon .... IRED
high spirits .... EBULLIENT
hoc signo ____ .... VINCES
____ (in its natural place) .... SITU
like him? .... FLYNN
line .... AROW, APLUMB
love .... GAGA, INFATUATED
love with .... GONE ON
motion ...... ASTIR, UNDERWAY
name only .... NOMINAL, TITULAR
need of irrigation .... ARID
no key .... ATONAL
no manner .... NOWISE
no way .... NOHOW
on .... AWARE

one's ear, ____ .... PUT A BUG
one's element .... AT HOME
one's interest .... FOR
original position .... SITU
out .... PHASE
place of .... FOR, ELSE, LIEU, VICE, (IN)STEAD
preference to .... OVER
____ (programmed) .... A RUT
progress .... CURRENT, (ON)GOING
re .... ANENT, CONCERNING
reserve .... ON ICE
row .... ALINED, ALIGNED
seventh heaven .... THRILLED
____ (so to speak) .... A SENSE
somber style .... SADLY
status quo .... AS IS
stock .... ON HAND
succession .... ENSUITE
that case .... THEN
that respect .... THEREIN
the bag .... ON ICE
calaboose .... JAILED
capacity of .... QUA
center .... AMID
course of .... DURING
doghouse .... BAN, RIFT
dumps .... BLUE
end .... FINALLY, EVENTUALLY, ULTIMATELY
flesh .... LIVE
future .... LATER
know .... HIP
manner of a Dutch uncle .... SEVERELY
midst of .... AMONG
open .... OUTSIDE
past .... AGO
____ (popular) .... SWIM
sack .... ABED
same category .... SUCH
same community .... SYNOETIC
same place .... IBID(EM)
slightest degree ...... AT ALL
time following .... WHEREAFTER
time .... EVENTUALLY
time, musically .... ATEMPO
want .... NEEDY
with .... AMID
in, ____ (be pushy) ...... MUSCLE
(contribute) .... CHIP
Ina, actress .... CLAIRE
inability .... IMPOTENCE
inaccessible ...... ALOOF, DISTANT
inaccurate .... WRONG,

MISLEADING
inaction .... INERTIA, IDLENESS
inactive ...... IDLE, INERT, ASLEEP, LATENT, STATIC, DORMANT, PASSIVE, RETIRED
inactivity ...... LULL, DORMANCY, LOTUSLAND, STAGNATION
inadequate .... THIN, SCANTY, LACKING, NOT ENOUGH
inadvertence .... OVERSIGHT
inamorata .... MISTRESS, SWEETHEART
inane .... EMPTY, INEPT, SILLY, FATUOUS, FOOLISH, PUERILE, VACUOUS
inanimate .... DEAD, DULL, LIFELESS, SPIRITLESS
inanity .... VACUITY
inappropriate .... IMPROPER, UNBECOMING
inapt ...... UNFITTING, UNSUITABLE
inarm .... EMBRACE
inarticulate .... DUMB, MUTE, APHONIC, UNSPOKEN, VOICELESS
inasmuch .... SINCE, BECAUSE
inattention .... NEGLECT, OVERSIGHT
inattentive .... DEAF, HEEDLESS
inaugurate .... OPEN, INDUCT, INSTALL
inauspicious .... ILL, UNLUCKY, UNTIMELY, ILL-OMENED
inauthentic .... SPURIOUS
inborn .... INBRED, INNATE, NATIVE, CONNATE, NATURAL, INHERENT
incalculable .... VAST, UNTOLD
Incan .... QUECHUA(N), PERUVIAN
empire capital .... CUSCO
king .... HUASCAR, ATABALIPA, ATAHUALPA
incandescence .... GLOW
incandescent .... RED-HOT, GLOWING, WHITE-HOT
incantation .... MAGIC, SPELL, SORCERY, CHANTING
incapable .... UNABLE
incapacitate ...... LAME, DISABLE, DISQUALIFY
incarcerate .... JAIL, CONFINE, IMPRISON
incarnate .... RED, FORM, ROSY, SHAPE, EMBODY
incarnation .... EMBODIMENT
of a god .... AVATAR
of Vishnu .... RAMA
incendiary .... FIREBUG, AGITATOR, ARSONIST, PYROMANIAC
incense .... GUM, IRK, ANGER,

ENRAGE, MASTIC, STACTE, BENZOIN, PERFUME, OLIBANUM, SANDARAC
burner .... THURIBLE
incensed .... IRATE, WROTH
incentive .... SPUR, MOTIVE, IMPULSE, STIMULUS, INDUCEMENT
inception .... START, ORIGIN
incertitude .... DOUBT
incessant .... CONTINUAL
inch .... BIT, HILL, CRAWL, CREEP, ISLAND, TRIFLE
.0004 of an .... HAIR
.001 of an .... MIL
$^1/_{12}$ .... LINE
inches, eighteen .... CUBIT
forty-five .... ELL
nine .... SPAN
thirty .... PACE, STEP
twelve .... FOOT
incident .... EVENT, EPISODE
incidental ...... BYE, ODD, MINOR, CASUAL, CHANCE, PASSING
excursion .... SIDETRIP
in music .... GRACE NOTE
incinerate .... CREMATE, BURN(UP)
incinerator .... FURNACE, CREMATORY
incipient .... INITIAL
incise ...... CUT, CARVE, ENGRAVE
incision .... CUT, GASH
incisive ...... KEEN, ACUTE, SHARP, TRENCHANT
incisor .... TOOTH
incite .... GOAD, SPUR, EGG ON, EXHORT, FOMENT, INDUCE, AGITATE, INSTIGATE
inciter .... EGGER, AGITATOR, INSTIGATOR
incivility .... RUDENESS
inclement .... HARSH, SEVERE, STORMY, PITILESS
inclination .... GRADE, SLANT, SLOPE, TASTE, TREND, LEAN(ING), MINDSET
to laugh .... RISIBILITY
incline .... CANT, LEAN, SWAY, TEND, GRADE, SLANT, SLOPE
downward .... DIP
inclined ...... APT, ALIST, ASWAY, PRONE, MINDED, WILLING, OBLIQUE, DISPOSED
chute/trough .... FLUME
walk .... RAMP
include .... CONTAIN, EMBRACE, INVOLVE, COMPRISE
including everything
.... OVERALL
inclusive .... ENTIRE, GENERIC

incognito .... DISGUISE
incoherent .... RAMBLING, DISJOINTED
income .... USANCE, ANNUITY, EARNING, REVENUE
type of ..... RENTAL, ROYALTY, INTEREST, DIVIDENDS
incommode .... BOTHER, PUT OUT
incomparable .... PEERLESS, MATCHLESS
incomplete .... SHY, LACKING
incomprehensible .... GREE
inconclusive .... DOUBTFUL, UNCERTAIN
incongruous .... UNFIT
inconsequential .... TRIVIAL
inconsiderate .... TACTLESS, THOUGHTLESS
inconstant ...... FICKLE, MUTABLE, UNSTABLE, VOLATILE, CAPRICIOUS
inconvenience .... BOTHER, TROUBLE, INCOMMODE
incorporate .... MIX, MERGE, EMBODY, INCLUDE
incorporeal right .... PATENT, COPYRIGHT
incorrect .... OFF, WRONG, FAULTY, UNTRUE, IMPROPER, ERRONEOUS, INACCURATE
bite .... MALOCCLUSION
epithet/naming ...... MISNOMER
incorruptible .... HONEST, STRAIGHT
increase .... ADD, GROW, ACCRETE, AUGMENT, ENLARGE, MULTIPLY
bet on .... RAISE
money in circulation
.... REFLATE
to the highest degree
.... MAXIMIZE
incredible .... ABSURD, UNBELIEVABLE
incredulity .... DOUBT, UNBELIEF, SKEPTICISM
cry of .... WHAT, OH NO
incredulous .... SKEPTICAL
increment .... GAIN, ACCRUAL
incriminate .... CONNECT, INVOLVE, IMPLICATE
incrustation .... RIME, SCAB
incubate ...... SIT, BREED, BROOD, HATCH
incubator .... HATCHERY
incubus .... DEMON, BURDEN, SPIRIT, NIGHTMARE
inculcate .... IMBUE, IMPRESS, INSTIL(L)
incumbency .... TENURE
incumbent .... OFFICEHOLDER

incur .... RUN, ACQUIRE
incursion .... RAID, FORAY, INROAD, INVASION
incus .... ANVIL
indebted .... LIABLE, BEHOLDEN TO
indebtedness .... DEBT, OBLIGATION
certification of .... DEBENTURE
indecency .... FILTH
indecent ...... FOUL, LEWD, RACY, RANK, COARSE, RISQUE, IMMORAL, OBSCENE, OFF-COLOR, IMMODEST
indecision .... HESITATION, VACILLATION
indecisive .... WAVERING, CHANGEABLE
indecorous .... UNSEEMLY
indeed .... TRULY, REALLY, IN FACT, FORSOOTH, CERTAINLY
indefatigable ...... AVID, UNTIRING
indefensible .... UNTENABLE
indefinite .... HAZY, VAGUE, UNSURE, OBSCURE, NEBULOUS, NUBILOUS, AMBIGUOUS
amount .... ANY, SOME
article .... AN
person .... ANYBODY
pronoun .... (ANY)ONE
indelible .... LASTING
indelicate .... CRASS, CRUDE, GROSS, ROUGH, COARSE
indemnify .... PAY, REDEEM, REIMBURSE
indemnity .... SECURITY
indent .... NOTCH, IMPRESS
indentation ...... CUT, JAG, DINGE, NOTCH, MARGIN, SET IN, CRENELET
on a blade .... CHOIL
on glass bottle .... KICK
independent .... FREE
an .... LONER, MUGWUMP, LONE WOLF
island country .... MALTA, CYPRESS
indescribable .... INEFFABLE, EXTRAORDINARY
indestructible .... IMMORTAL, INDELIBLE
indeterminate .... VAGUE
in botany .... RACEMOSE
index .... LIST, MARK, SIGN, TABLE, CATALOG, POINTER, INDICATOR, FOREFINGER
sign in printing .... FIST
India(n) .... TAMIL, BHARAT, HINDUSTAN
aborigine .... BENGALI

373

acrobat .... NAT
alcoholic drink .... ARRACK
animal .... ZEBU, DHOLE
antelope .... CHIRU, SASIN,
    NILG(H)AI, NILG(H)AU
army officer .... JEMADAR
army servant .... LASCAR
artilleryman .... LASCAR
astrologer .... JOSHI
attendant .... AYAH, PEON
audience .... DURBAR
banker .... SARAF, SHROFF,
    SOUCAR
bay .... BACK
bear .... BALOO
bearer .... SIRDAR
Bihar capital .... PATNA
bird .... KOEL, RAYA, SARUS,
    SHAMA, ARGALA, JACANA,
    MARABOU, AMADAVAT
bison ..... GAUR, GAYAL, TSINE
boat .... DONGA, DUNGA
bodice .... CHOLI
bond .... ANDI
boycott .... SWADESHI
bread/cake .... CHAPATI
bride's neckwear .... TALIS
buck .... SASIN
Buddhist gateway .... TORAN
buffalo .... ARNA, ARNEE
building .... MAHAL
bulbul .... KALA
bush .... KANHER
butter .... GHEE
calico .... SAL(I)OO
camel .... CONT
canoe .... TANEE
cap .... TOPI, TOPEE
cape .... DIVI, COMORIN
capital .... (NEW)DELHI
capital, summer .... SIMLA
carpet .... AGRA
carriage .... EKKA, RATH,
    TONGA, GHARRY
cashmere .... ULWAN
caste .... JAT, MEO, SHIR,
    GADDI, MAL(I), LOHANA,
    PARIAH, SUDRA, RAJPUT
caste mark .... TILKA
caterpillar .... SUGA
cattle .... GAUR, GOUR, ZEBU,
    BRAHMA
cavalryman .... SOWAR
chamois .... SARAU
channel ..... COCO, GREAT, TEN
    DEGREE
chief .... MIR, RAJA(H), SIRDAR
church .... SAMAJ
cigarette .... BIRI
city/town .... AGRA, GAYA,
AJMER, AKOLA, DELHI, JAMMU,

PATNA, SAGAR, SALEM, SIMLA,
    SURAT, THANA, AMBALA,
    BARODA, BHILAI, BHOPAL,
    BOMBAY, DUMDUM, HOWRAH,
    IMPHAL, INDORE, JAIPUR,
    JHANSI, KANPUR, MADRAS,
    MEERUT, MYSORE, NAGPUR,
    RAIPUR, RAJKOT, ROHTAK,
    ALIGARH, ASANSOL, BELGAUM,
    BENARES, BIKANER, CALICUT,
    DHANBAD, GAUHATI,
    GWALIOR, JODHPUR, KURNOOL,
    LUCKNOW, MADURAI, PATIALA,
    VELLORE, AMRITSAR,
    BAREILLY, BHATPARA,
    CALCUTTA, DURGAPUR,
    JABALPUR, JAMNAGAR,
    LUDHIANA, SRINAGAR,
    BADODARA, VARANASI,
    WARANGAL, AHMADABAD,
    ALLAHABAD, BANGALORE,
    BHAVNAGAR, HYDERABAD,
    JULLUNDAR, KOZHIKODE,
    MORADABAD, CHANDIGARH
civet .... ZIBET(H)
clerk .... BABU, BABOO
cloth .... SALU, SURAT,
    ULWAN, SAL(L)OO
cloth strip .... PATA
coast .... MALABAR
coin .... PI(E), ANNA, FELS,
    HOON, PICE, FANAM, MOHUR,
    RUPEE
combining form .... INDO
condiment .... CURCUMA
corporal .... NAIK
cot .... CHARPOY
cow .... GAEKWAR
crocodile .... GAVIAL,
    MUGGAR, MUGGER
curtain .... PURDAH
custom .... DASTUR
dancing girl .... BAYADEER,
    BAYADERE
deer .... AXIS, CHITAL, SAMBAR
desert .... THAR, GREAT INDIAN
devil's tree .... DITA
dialect .... PUSHTU
diamond cutting center
    .... GOLCONDA
diamond, famous
    .... KOHINUR, KOHINOOR
disciple .... CHELA
district .... DIU, GOA, AGRA,
    DAMAN, MALABAR
division .... OUDH
dog .... DHOLE, KOLSUN
dormitory .... GHOTUL
drama .... NATAKA
drink .... SOMA
drug .... BHANG

dugout .... DUNGA
dust storm .... PEESASH
elephant .... HATHI
elephant driver .... MAHOUT
emperor .... ASOKA, BABER
empress of .... VICTORIA
entertainment .... TAMASHA
epic .... RAMAYANA
estate, inherited .... TALUK
Eurasian in .... SAHIB,
    FERINGI, FERINGHEE
European in .... MEMSAHIB
extra pay .... BATTA
falcon .... BAS(A)RA, SHAHEEN,
    SHASHIN
fan .... PUNKA(H)
farmer .... MEO, RYOT
festival .... DEWALI
flute .... PUNGI, MATALAN
footman .... PEON
footstool .... MORA
founder .... IVAN
fowl .... BRAHMA
fruit .... BEL
game .... PACHISI
garment/garb ..... SARI, DHOTI,
    KURTA, SAREE, BANIAN
gazelle .... CHIKARA
ghost .... BUHT
girl leader .... BELOSA
goat, wild .... TAHR
goddess .... KALI
gorge .... TANGI
gossip .... GUP
government estates ..... AMANI
granary .... GOLA, GUNJ,
    GUNGE
grant .... ENAM
greeting .... NAMASTE
groom .... SICE, SYCE
guerrilla band .... TAMIL
    TIGERS
guide .... SHIKAREE
guitar .... VINA
gulf .... KUTCH, CAMBAY,
    MANNAR
gully .... NULLAH
guru .... MAHARISHI
harem .... ZENANA
harvest .... RAB(B)I
hawk .... BADIUS, SHIKRA
headman .... PATEL,
    MOKADDAM
helmet/hat .... TOPI, TOPEE
hemp ..... KEF, KEEF, B(H)ANG,
    GANJA, RAMIE
hemp shrub ..... PUA, POOA(H)
hill .... GARO
hill dweller .... DOGRA
hills .... ABOT, MIRI, KHASI,
    MISHMI

hog deer .... AXIS, ATLAS
holy city ..... NASIK, BENARES,
                  HARDWAR
holy man .... YOGI, FAKIR,
                  SADHU
home rule .... SWARAJ
hunt(er) .... SHIKAR(I),
                  SHIKAREE
hut .... BARI
inheritance .... TALUK
instrument .... SITAR
island .... AMINI, PITTI,
    AGATTI, KADMAT, KILTAN,
    ANDAMAN, ANDROTH,
    BUTCHER, CHETLAT, KALPENI,
    MINICOY, NICOBAR, AMINDIRI,
    SALSETTE, NANCOWRY,
           ELEPHANTA
island group .... AMINDIVI,
    CANNANORE, LACCADIVE
islands near .... MALDIVES
jacket .... KOLA
Jesuit in .... PAULIST
jungle .... SHOLA
kingdom .... NEPAL
knife .... DAO
laborer .... PALLI
lace .... GOTA
lady .... BIBI, BEGUM,
            MEMSAHIB
lake .... CHILKA, COLAIR,
    PERIYAR, PULICAT, SAMBHAR
land grant .... SASAN
land grant tenant
    .... ENAMDAR
landing place .... GHAT
landowner .... ZAMINDAR
language .... URDU, HINDI,
    BIHARI, BENGALI, ASSAMESE,
    GUJARATI, SANSKRIT
leguminous plant .... GUAR
levee .... DURBAR
license .... CHOP
licorice .... ABRIN
lieutenant governor .... NAIB
litter .... DOLY, DOOLEE,
           MUNCHEEL
litter bearer .... SIRDAR
loam .... REGUR
loincloth .... LUNGI, LUNGEE
low class .... BHAT
lunch .... TIFFIN
lute .... SITAR
mahogany .... TOON
maid .... AYAH
mail .... DA(W)K
marijuana .... GANJA
market .... GUNGE, PASAR
master .... MIAN, SAHIB
master: var. .... SAHEB
matting .... TATTA

meal .... AT(T)A
measure of distance ...... GUZ,
                  KOS
Menon of .... KRISHNA
merchant .... SOUDAGUR
midwife .... DHAI
military caste .... RAJPUT
millet .... JOAR, CHENA,
        DURRA, DOURA(H)
minstrel .... BHAT
mistress .... MEMSAHIB
Mogul dynasty founder
    .... BABAR, BABER, BABUR
monetary unit ..... LAC, LAKH,
               RUPEE
money lender .... MAHAJAN
monkey .... RHESUS,
           WANDEROO
Moslem .... SWAT
mountain .... ABIL, KAMET,
    DAPSANG, NILGIRI, NANDA
    DEVI, KANCHENJUNGA
mountain chain .... GHATS,
    ZASKAR, MUSTAGH,
    HIMALAYA, KARAKORAM,
        HINDU KUSH
mountain pass .... GHA(U)T.
           SHIPKI
mulberry .... (A)AL, ACH
murder .... THUGGEE
musical instrument ...... VINA,
    RUANA, SAROD, SARON
muslin .... DOREA, GURRAH
mystic .... GURU
Naga capital .... KOHIMA
narcotic ..... BHANG, HASHHISH
national mourning .... HARTAL
native .... BENGALI
Negro .... HUBSHI
novice .... CHELA
nurse .... AMAH, AYAH
Occidental in .... GRIFFIN
official .... DEWAN, NAZIR
oil tree .... BEN
ox .... GAUR
pageant .... TAMASHA
pagoda .... CHORTEN
palanquin .... PALKEE
parliament .... LOK SABHA
part of .... DECCAN
paymaster .... BUXY
pea .... DAL
peasant .... RYOT
peninsula .... HINDUSTAN
permit .... CHOP
physicist .... BOSE, RAMAN
pigeon .... TRERON
poison .... BIKH, BISH
police station .... THANA
policeman .... PEON, SEPOY
political party .... CONGRESS,

    BHARATIYA JANATA
political protest .... HARTAL
Portuguese district .... DAMAO
powder .... ABIR
prayerlike gesture
    .... NAMASTE
president .... PRASAD, ZIA
            ULHAQ
priest .... SHAMAN
priest's garment .... DHOTI
prime minister .... NEHRU,
    (RAJIV)GANDHI,
    (INDIRA)GANDHI, SHASTRI
prince .... (MAHA)RAJA(H)
princess/queen .... RANI,
    BEGUM, RANEE, MAHARANI
property .... DHAN
protectorate .... SIKKIM
province .... PUNJAB
quilt .... RESAI
race .... JAT, TAMIL
rat .... BANDICOOT
reception (hall) .... DURBAR
region ..... CANARA, MALABAR,
           CARNATIC
religious fanatic .... THUG
religious sect .... SAMAJ
republic .... BHARAT
resort .... SIMLA
rice .... BORO
rich man .... NABOB
rifle pit .... SANGAR
river .... INDUS, JUMNA,
    CHENAB, GANGES, JHELUM,
    KAVERI, SUTLEJ, CHAMBAL,
    DAMODAR, GHAGHRA,
    HOOGHLY, NARMADA,
    GODAVARI, MAHANADI,
    TUNGABHADRA
road .... PRAYA
robber .... THUG, DACOIT
rope dancer .... NAT
rubber .... CAOUTCHOUC
rug .... DRUGGET
rule .... RAJ
ruler .... RAO, NABOB, NAWAB,
    NIZAM, RAJA(H)
sacred city .... NASIK,
    BENARES, HARDWAR
sacred lore .... VEDA
sacrificial victim .... TRAGA
sailor .... LASCAR
salute .... NAMASTE
salvation .... MOKSHA
scholar .... PANDIT, PUNDIT
screen .... TATTY, PURDAH
seal .... CHOP
seaport .... SURAT
servant .... AMAH, AYAH,
    MATY, HAM(M)AL, HAMAUL,
        SIRDAR

hero in poem .... HIAWATHA
horse .... PONY, PINTO,
   CAYUSE, PAWNEE, MUSTANG
hut ..... HOGAN, LODGE, TEPEE,
   WI(C)KIUP
Illinois .... KICKAPOO
intoxicant .... BHANG
Iowa .... SAC, SAUK
Kansas .... PANI, PAWNEE
Lake Erie .... CHIPPEWA
macaque .... RHESUS
maize .... CORN
male, married .... SANNUP
Manitoba .... CREE
matting .... TAT
medicine man .... POWWOW,
   SITTING BULL
memorial post ..... XAT, XYST,
   TOTEM
mestizo .... GRIFF(E), METIF(F),
   HALF-BREED
Michigan .... SAC, SAUK
Missouri .... MANDAN
mixed blood .... METIF(F),
   METISSE, HALF-BREED
moccasin .... PAC
money .... PIMAN, PEAG(E),
   WAMPUM, SE(A)WANT(T)
mystic symbol .... SWASTIKA
Negro .... ZAMBO
nomadic .... APACHE
North Dakota .... PAWNEE,
   CADDOAN, CHIPPEWA
Ocean arm .... RED SEA
Ocean continent ...... LEMURIA
Ocean vessel .... DHOW
palm .... TALIPOT
Panama .... CUNA
pea .... DAL
Penutian .... CHINUK, CHINOOK
pierced nose .... NEZ PERCE
pipe .... CALUMET
poet .... TAGORE
poison .... CURARE
pole .... TOTEM
pony .... TAT, PINTO, CAYUSE
porridge .... SAMP
prairie .... KAW
prayer stick .... BAHO, PAHO
priest .... POWWOW
princess .... POCAHONTAS
Pueblo .... HOPI, TANO, ZUNI
room for religious service
   .... KIVA
Salishan .... TULALIP,
   FLATHEAD
seafaring .... TLINGIT
sled dog .... HUSKY
sledge .... TRAVOIS(E)
slipper .... MOCCASIN
spirit .... MANITOU

supplanted by Incan
   .... AYMARA
tepee .... LODGE, WIGWAM
tent .... TE(E)PEE, LODGE,
   WIGWAM
tree .... MEE
trophy .... SCALP
unit of money .... PIMAN
Uto-Aztecan .... YAQUI
village .... PUEBLO
wampum .... SE(A)WAN(T)
war cry .... WHOOP
war trophy .... SCALP
warrior .... BRAVE
weapon .... TOMAHAWK
Western .... UTE, HOPI, OTO(E),
   ZUNI
whisky to an .... FIREWATER
white man to an .... PALEFACE
wife .... SQUAW
wigwam ...... LODGE, TE(E)PEE
winter festival .... POTLATCH
woman .... SQUAW
yell .... WHOOP
"yes" of .... UGH
young ...... BUCK, TENDERFOOT

Indiana capital .... INDIANAPOLIS
city/town .... GARY, PERU,
   PAOLI, SALEM, VEVAY,
   GOSHEN, KOKOMO, MARION,
   MUNCIE, SHOALS, TIPTON,
   WABASH, WARSAW, ELKHART,
   HAMMOND, LEBANON,
   SPENCER, WINAMAC,
   ANDERSON, COLUMBUS,
   RICHMOND, FORT WAYNE,
   FRANKFORT, LAFAYETTE,
   SOUTH BEND, VINCENNES,
   EVANSVILLE, GREENSBURG,
   TERRA HAUTE, BLOOMINGTON
county ..... CASS, KNOX, LAKE,
   ALLEN, BOONE, CLARK,
   FLOYD, GRANT, HENRY,
   WAYNE, DE KALB, DUBOIS,
   GIBSON, HOWARD, MARION,
   MONROE, MORGAN, PORTER,
   ELKHART, HANCOCK, JOHNSON,
   LA PORTE, MADISON,
   DELAWARE, MANILTON,
   HENDRICKS, KOSCIUSKO,
   TIPPECANOE, VANDERBURGH
creek .... WILDCAT
lake .... LEMON, MONROE,
   SHAPER, FREEMAN, WAWASEE,
   MICHIGAN, SALAMONIE,
   MAXINKUCKEE, MISSISSINEWA
native .... HOOSIER
recreation site .... SANTA
   CLAUS LAND, CLIFTY FALLS
   PARK, INDIANAPOLIS MOTOR
   SPEEDWAY

river .... EEL, FAWN, OHIO,
   WHITE, MAUMEE, PATOKA,
   WABASH, (BIG) BLUE, (LITTLE)
   ELKHART, TIPPECANOE
state bird .... CARDINAL
state flower .... PEONY
state motto .... CROSSROADS
   OF AMERICA
state nickname .... HOOSIER
state tree .... TULIP
university .... BUTLER,
   PURDUE, BALL STATE, NOTRE
   DAME
village, famed .... SANTA
   CLAUS
Indic dialect .... PALI
indicate .... SHOW, POINT, EVINCE,
   SIGNIFY, INTIMATE
indication(s) .... SIGNS, INDICIA
slight .... INKLING
indicator .... CLUE, DIAL, SIGN,
   ARROW, GAUGE, INDEX,
   POINTER, REGISTER
air pressure .... BAROMETER
airport .... WINDSOCK
wind .... VANE
indicatory statement X
   MARKS THE SPOT
indict .... ACCUSE, CHARGE,
   ARRAIGN, IMPEACH
indictment .... CHARGE
indifference .... APATHY,
   LETHARGY
indifferent .... COLD, COOL, SOSO,
   ALOOF, TEPID, LANGUID,
   DETACHED, LISTLESS,
   APATHETIC, UNCONCERNED
to hardship .... STOIC(AL)
indigence .... NEED, WANT,
   PENURY, POVERTY
indigenous .... INBORN, INNATE,
   NATIVE, EDAPHIC, ENDEMIC,
   INHERENT
indigent .... POOR, NEEDY,
   DESTITUTE
indigestion .... APEPSIA,
   DYSPEPSIA
indignant .... ANGRY, IRATE,
   WROTH
indignation .... IRE, ANGER,
   SCORN, WRATH, RESENTMENT
indignity .... INSULT, SLIGHT,
   AFFRONT, HUMILIATION
indigo .... DYE, ANIL, BLUE
bale of .... SEROON
berry .... RANDIA
blue .... INDIGOTIN
compound .... ISATIN
derivative .... INDOL(E),
   ISATIN, KETOLE

forming substance .... INDICAN
plant .... ANIL
wild .... BAPTISIA
indirect .... IMPLIED, OBLIQUE, DEVIATING, ROUNDABOUT
expression .... AMBAGE, PERIPHRASE, PERIPHRASIS
indiscreet .... UNWISE, RECKLESS, IMPRUDENT
indiscretion .... SLIP, FOLLY, PECCADILLO
indiscriminate .... SWEEPING, EXTENSIVE, WHOLESALE
indispensable .... VITAL, ESSENTIAL, NECESSARY
one .... KEYMAN
indisposed .... ILL, SICK, AVERSE, UNWILLING
indisposition .... PIP, AILMENT, MALAISE, AVERSION
indisputable .... ABSOLUTE, APOD(E)ICTIC, UNQUESTIONING
indistinct ...... DIM, HAZY, FAINT, FOGGY, VAGUE, BLURRY, UNCLEAR, OBSCURE
indite ...... PEN, WRITE, COMPOSE, INSCRIBE
individual .... ONE, SELF, SOLE, PARTY, PERSON, SINGLE, PARTICULAR
combining form .... IDIO
performance .... SOLO
individualism .... EGOISM
Indo-China, part of .... LAOS, BURMA, MALAYA, VIETNAM, CAMBODIA, THAILAND
Chinese .... LAO, TAI, SHAN
European .... ARYAN, CROAT
European language .... AVESTAN, HITTITE
indoctrinate .... BRIEF, IMBUE, TEACH, INSTILL, INSTRUCT, BRAINWASH, INCULCATE
indolence .... SLOTH, INERTIA, IDLENESS, LAZINESS
indolent ...... IDLE, LAZY, OTIOSE, SUPINE, LISTLESS, SLOTHFUL
indomitable .... INVINCIBLE, UNBEATABLE
Indonesia .... EAST INDIES
capital of .... JAKARTA
Indonesian .... ATTA, DYAK, BATTAK, LAMPONG
archipelago ...... RIAU, MALAY, LINGGA, BANGGAI, KARIMATA
bay .... BERAU, SEBUKU, GEELVINK
bird .... BULBUL, PEAFOWL
cape .... VALS, NGUNJU,

PERKAM, SELATAN, JAMBUAIR, JAMURSBA
city/town ...... AMBON, BOGOR, MEDAN, SOLOK, TEGAL, BINJAI, BLITAR, (D)JAMBI, KEDIRI, MADIUN, MALANG, MANADO, PADANG, BANDUNG, BATAVIA, CILICAP, CIREBON, SIBOLGA, BENGKULU, MAKASSAR, SEMARANG, SURABAYA, GORONTALO, PONTIANAK, SURAKARTA
gibbon .... LAR
gulf .... BONE, TOLO, TOMINI
island .... WE, BALI, BIAK, BURU, JAVA, LAUT, MUNA, NIAS, ROTI, SIAU, BABAR, KALAO, KISAR, SUMBA, WAKDE, WETAR, YAPEN, BANGKA, BORNEO, BUTUNG, FLORES, JEMAJA, KOMODO, LINGGA, LOMBOK, MADURA, MISOOL, PANTAR, RAKATA, TIDORE, WAIGEO, CELEBES, ENGGANO, KABAENA, KANGEAN, NUMFOOR, SELAYOR, SUMATRA, SULAWESI, GREAT KAI, HALMAHERA, WANGIWANGI
islands .... ARU, OBI, BATU, EWAB, SAWU, SULA, MAPIA, BANYAK, NATUNA, TALAUD, ANAMBAS, SANGIHE, MOLUCCAS, TAMBELAN, TANIMBAR
knife .... PARANG
lake .... TOBA
language ..... MALAY, BAHASA, PAPUAN, JAVANESE, MADURESE, SUDANESE
monetary unit .... RUPIAH
mountain .... RAYA, LEUSER, SEMERU, SIAMET, KERINCI, PUNCAK JAYA
mountains .... MAOKE, MULLER, BARISAN, SCHWANER
news agency .... ANTARA
ox .... BANTENG
peninsula .... DOBERAI
premier .... HATTA
president .... SUHARTO, SUKARNO
puppeteer .... (TO)DALANG
region ..... TIMOR, IRIAN JAYA, KALIMANTAN
rhino .... BADAK
river ..... MUSI, DIGUL, ROKAN, BARITO, KAPUAS, TARIKU, MAHAKAM, MAMBERAMO
sea .... JAVA, SAWU, BANDA, TIMOR, FLORES, ARATURA,

CELEBES, MOLUCCA
strait .... MULI, OMBAI, SUMBA, SUNDA, MALACCA, SIBERUT, MAKASSAR
volcano .... AGUNG, TAMBORA, KRAKATAO
xylophone .... GENDER, GAMBANG
indoors weather ...... RAINY DAY
indorse .... ATTEST, APPROVE, SUPPORT, SANCTION
indri .... LEMUR
indubitable .... SURE, CERTAIN, EVIDENT, DOUBTLESS
induce .... LEAD, URGE, CAUSE, PREVAIL, PERSUADE
love .... ENDEAR
to perjury .... SUBORN
inducement .... MOTIVE, INCENTIVE
induct .... INSTALL, INITIATE
inductance, measure of .... HENRY
induction rite .... INAUGURAL
indulge .... PET, BABY, SPOIL, HUMOR, CODDLE, PAMPER, GRATIFY, SATISFY
in happy talk .... BILL AND COO
indulgence .... FAVOR, MERCY, LENIENCY, PATIENCE
indulgent .... KIND, LENIENT, TOLERANT, EASYGOING
Indus .... CONSTELLATION
River tributary .... SUTLEJ
tribesman .... GOR
industrial .... TRADING, COMMERCIAL, MERCANTILE
activity, at times .... ACCELERATION
giant .... TYCOON, MAGNATE
spy .... KEEK
Industrial Workers of the World member ...... WOBBLY
industrialist .... BARON, TYCOON, MAGNATE, FINANCIER
of a sort .... ANT
industrious .... BUSY, ACTIVE, OPEROSE, DILIGENT, ASSIDUOUS
industry .... LABOR, TRADE, COMMERCE, MARKETING
inebriate .... SOT, TOPER, DRUNK(ARD)
inedible .... UNEATABLE
inefficient .... INEPT, UNABLE
inelastic .... RIGID, STIFF, INFLEXIBLE
inelegant .... CRUDE, CLUMSY, COARSE, AWKWARD
ineligible .... UNFIT, UNQUALIFIED

ineluctable .... DOOM, FATE, CERTAIN, DEFINITE, INEVITABLE

inept .... UNFIT, ABSURD, CLUMSY, AWKWARD, FOOLISH, PUERILE

inerrant ...... PRECISE, UNERRING, INFALLIBLE

inert .... DULL, SLOW, LATENT, SUPINE, TORPID, AT REST, NEUTRAL, INACTIVE

gas .... NEON, FREON

inertia .... LETHARGY

inescapable .... SURE, INEVITABLE

responsibility .... TAXES

inestimable .... PRICELESS

inevitable .... DUE, FATED, BINDING, CERTAIN, DESTINED

inexact .... VAGUE, WRONG, ERRONEOUS, UNSPECIFIED

inexcitable .... COOLHEADED, COLDBLOODED

inexcusable .... UNFORGIVABLE

inexhaustible .... ENDLESS

inexorable .... HARD, STERN, UNYIELDING

inexperienced .... RAW, GREEN, NAIVE

infamous .... VICIOUS, NOTORIOUS, SCANDALOUS

infanticide .... HEROD

infamy .... ODIUM, SHAME, SCANDAL, ATROCITY, DISGRACE, NOTORIETY

infancy .... BABYHOOD, MINORITY

to puberty .... CHILDHOOD

infant .... TOT, BABE, BABY, BAIRN, CHILD, CHRISOM

Cupid .... AMOR

doctor of .... PEDIATRIST

room of .... NURSERY

infanta .... PRINCESS

infante .... PRINCE

infantile .... CHILDISH

paralysis ...... POLIO(MYELITIS)

infantryman .... DOGFACE, DOUGHBOY, (FOOT)SOLDIER

mounted .... DRAGOON

infantrymen's formation
.... PHALANX

infatuate .... BESET, CHARM, ENAMOR, OBSESS

infatuated .... GAGA, FOOLISH, ENAMORED

infatuation .... RAVE, CRUSH, PASSION, FONDNESS

infect ...... IMBUE, TAINT, AFFECT, CORRUPT, CONTAMINATE

infected .... MORBID, TAINTED, DISEASED

infection .... TAINT, VIRUS, DISEASE

causing .... SEPTIC

source .... NIDUS

infectious .... CATCHING, CONTAGIOUS

infecund .... BARREN, STERILE

infer .... IMPLY, DEDUCE, GATHER, PRESUME, CONCLUDE

inference .... ILLATION, DEDUCTION, ASSUMPTION, CONCLUSION

inferior .... SAD, POOR, LOUSY, MINOR, PETTY, LOW(ER), LESS(ER), SHODDY, MEDIOCRE, SECOND-RATE, SUBORDINATE

diamond .... BORT

horse .... NAG, TIT, PLATER

lawyer .... SHYSTER, PETTIFOGGER

performer .... BUSHLEAGUER

poet .... RIMESTER, POETASTER, RHYMESTER, VERSIFIER

slang .... SECOND-STRINGER

to .... UNDER

whisky .... REDEYE

writer .... HACK

infernal .... HATEFUL, HELLISH, SATANIC, DEVILISH, FIENDISH, DIABOLICAL

machine .... BOMB

region .... AVERNUS

inferno ...... HELL, ABYSS, HADES, GEHENNA

infertile .... BARREN

infertility .... STERILITY

infest .... SWARM, OVERRUN

infidel .... PAGAN, ATHEIST, HEATHEN, SARACEN

infidelity .... ADULTERY, BETRAYAL

infield cover .... TARP

infielder .... BASEMAN, SHORTSTOP

infiltrate .... ENTER, FILTER, PENETRATE

infiltration .... SEEPAGE

infinite .... VAST, ENDLESS, ETERNAL, IMMENSE, BOUNDLESS

infinitesimal .... TINY, MINUTE

infinity .... ETERNITY

infirm .... LAME, WEAK, ANILE, FEEBLE, SENILE, DECREPIT, UNSTABLE

infirmary .... CLINIC, HOSPITAL, DISPENSARY

infirmity .... FAULT, DEFECT, FRAILTY, WEAKNESS

inflame .... FAN, FIRE, ENRAGE, EXCITE, IGNITE, KINDLE, MADDEN

with love .... ENAMOR

inflammable ...... FIERY, PICEOUS,

BURNABLE

material .... PUNK, AMADOU, TINDER, ACETONE

inflammation .... ANGINA, REDNESS, SWELLING

bone ...... OSTEITIS, ARTHRITIS

bone marrow .... MYELITIS

glandular .... ADENITIS

intestinal .... COLITIS, ENTERITIS

iris .... IRITIS, UVEITIS

respiratory passages
.... CROUP

suffix .... ITIS

throat .... CATARRH

udders of cow .... GARGET

urinary bladder .... CYSTITIS

inflate ...... PUFF, SWELL, AERATE, DILATE, EXPAND, DISTEND

inflated .... TUMID, TURGID, BLOATED, POMPOUS, SWOLLEN

condition .... TYMPANY

inflect .... BEND, TURN, CURVE, MODULATE

inflection .... TONE, CADENCE

inflexible .... SET, DOUR, FIRM, IRON, FIXED, RIGID, STERN, STIFF, STONY, ADAMANT, OBDURATE, STUBBORN, UNBENDING

inflict ...... DEAL, WREAK, IMPOSE

inflorescence ...... CYME, WHORL, RACEME, FLOWERING, BLOSSOMING

type of .... SPIKE, UMBEL, CATKIN, SPADIX

influence ...... DRAG, HEFT, HOLD, MOLD, PULL, SWAY, CLOUT, IMPEL, POWER, AFFECT, EFFECT, INDUCE, WEIGHT, PRESSURE

influential ...... POTENT, WEIGHTY, POWERFUL, EFFECTIVE, PRESTIGIOUS

influenza .... FLU, CORYZA, GRIPPE, CATARRH

influx .... INFLOW, ARRIVAL

of settlers .... IMMIGRATION

inform .... TELL, WARN, ALERT, TEACH, ADVISE, CONVEY, NOTIFY, REPORT, APPRISE, ACQUAINT,

against .... BETRAY, DELATE

slang .... RAT, SING, SQUEAL

informal .... CASUAL

party .... BARBECUE

talk .... CHAT, CAUSERIE

informant .... APPRISER, REPORTER, NEWSCASTER, STOOL PIGEON

information .... DATA, NEWS,

WORD, AVISO, FACTS, ADVICE, LEARNING, KNOWLEDGE, INTELLIGENCE
bit of .... ITEM
file .... DOSSIER
in law .... ACCUSATION
slang .... DOPE, INFO, LOW-DOWN
informative .... NEWSY, EXPLICIT, REPORTED, FACT-FULL, INSTRUCTIVE
informed ...... HEP, HIP, WISE, ON TO, AWARE, CONVERSANT, KNOWLEDGEABLE
informer .... RAT, SPY, FINK, NARK, BIRDIE, SNITCH, TIPSTER, REPORTER, SQUEALER, TATTLETALE, STOOL PIGEON
turn .... SING, PEACH, STOOL, SQUEAL, DOUBLE-CROSS
infract .... VIOLATE
infraction .... VIOLATION
infrequency .... RARENESS
infrequent .... RARE, SCARCE, SELDOM
infrequently ...... ONCE OR TWICE
infringe .... BREAK, VIOLATE, ENCROACH, TRESPASS
infringement, copyright/patent
.... PIRACY
infuriate .... RILE, ANGER, PEEVE, ENRAGE, INCITE, MADDEN
infuse .... FILL, SOAK, IMBUE, STEEP, TINGE, IMPART, INSTILL
infusion .... TEA, TINCTURE
infusoria .... PROTOZOA
ingenious ...... CLEVER, D(A)EDAL, ORIGINAL, INVENTIVE
ingenue .... ACTRESS, STARLET
ingenuity .... WIT, SKILL, CLEVERNESS
ingenuous .... OPEN, FRANK, NAIVE, NOBLE, CANDID, SIMPLE, ARTLESS, INNOCENT, GUILELESS
ingest .... EAT, SWALLOW
ingle .... BLAZE, FIRE(PLACE)
ingot .... BAR, PIG, BULLION
silver .... SYCEE
zinc .... SPELTER
ingrain .... DYE, IMBUE, INFUSE
ingrained .... DEEP-SEATED
ingratiate .... INSINUATE
ingratiating .... WINNING, CHARMING
ingredient .... CONTENT, ELEMENT, COMPONENT
ingress .... ENTRY, ACCESS, ENTRANCE

ingrown .... EMBEDDED
inhabit ...... LIVE, DWELL, PEOPLE, RESIDE, SETTLE
inhabitant .... INMATE, CIT(IZEN), DENIZEN, RESIDENT
castle's .... CASTELLAN
suffix .... ITE
inhabited .... PEOPLED
inhabiting the shore
.... LIMICOLINE
inhalant .... VICKS
inhale .... DRAW, SUCK, BREATHE, INSPIRE, RESPIRE
sharply .... SNIFF
inhere .... DWELL IN, CLEAVE, (TO) STICK
inherence .... PRESENCE, IMMANENCE
inherent .... BASIC, INBORN, INNATE, NATIVE, IMMANENT, INTRINSIC, INDIGENOUS
inherit ...... COME INTO, RECEIVE, SUCCEED
inheritance .... LEGACY, BEQUEST, HERITAGE, PATRIMONY
law .... SALIC
tax .... DEATH DUTY
unit of .... GENE
inheritor .... HEIR, DEVISEE, LEGATEE, RECIPIENT
inhibit .... BAR, CHECK, ENJOIN, FORBID, HAMPER, PROHIBIT, RESTRAIN, SUPPRESS, WITHHOLD
as appetite .... CURB
inhospitable .... HOSTILE
inhuman .... CRUEL, BRUTAL, SAVAGE, BESTIAL
inhume .... BURY, INTER
inimical ...... ADVERSE, COUNTER, HOSTILE, CONTRARY, UNFRIENDLY
inimitable .... PEERLESS, MATCHLESS
iniquitous .... EVIL, UNJUST, WICKED
iniquity .... SIN, EVIL, VICE, CRIME, INJUSTICE, WICKEDNESS
initial .... FIRST, INCEPTIVE
ornamental .... PARAPH
initials .... MONOGRAM
woven together .... CIPHER
initiate .... HAZE, OPEN, ADMIT, BEGIN, FOUND, START, INDUCT, INSTITUTE, INTRODUCE
initiative .... LEAD, ENTERPRISE
inject .... INSERT, INOCULATE
injection ...... SHOT, INOCULATION
set .... SYRETTE

injudicious .... UNWISE
injunction .... ORDER, COMMAND, MANDATE, ENJOINING
injure .... MAR, HARM, HURT, MAIM, ABUSE, SPOIL, WRONG, DAMAGE, IMPAIR, SCATHE
injurious .... TOXIC, NOISOME, HARMFUL, NOXIOUS
injury .... HARM, WOUND, DAMAGE, TRAUMA, OFFENSE
compensation for
.... DAMAGES, SOLATIUM
mark .... SCAR
injustice .... BIAS, WRONG, INJURY, INEQUITY, PREJUDICE
ink .... DAUB, SIGN, BLACKEN
fish .... CUTTLE
ingredient .... TANNIN
spreader ...... BRAYER, ROLLER
inker .... PAD, DABBER, ROLLER
inkle .... TAPE, YARN, THREAD
inkling .... HINT, IDEA, NOTION, SUSPICION, INDICATION
inky .... DARK, BLACK
inlaid work .... BUHL, MOSAIC, NIELLO, TARSIA, PARQUETRY
inland .... INTERIOR
body of water .... LAKE
sea .... ARAL, CASPIAN
inlay .... INSET, INSERT, FILLING
material .... TILE, NIELLO
inlet .... ARM, BAY, RIA, COVE, BAYOU, BIGHT, CREEK, FIORD, FIRTH, ESTUARY
shallow .... LAGOON
inmate ...... OCCUPANT, PRISONER
inmost .... DEEPEST
nature .... ESSENCE
part .... CORE, HEART
inn .... PUB, KHAN, SERAI, TAMBO, HOSTEL, IMARET, TAVERN, AUBERGE, HOSPICE, LODGING, POTHOUSE, ROADHOUSE
Canterbury Tales' .... TABARD
roadside .... MOTEL
worker ..... POTBOY, BARMAID, TAPSTER
innards .... GUTS, NUMBLES, VISCERA, ENTRAILS
innate .... INBORN, INBRED, NATIVE, NATURAL, INHERENT, CONGENITAL
inner .... BEN, ENTAL, INSIDE, INWARD, INTERNAL
bark .... BAST
circle .... CADRE
combining form .... ENTO
man .... SOUL, PALATE, STOMACH
part .... INTERIOR

wheel member
.... (ROTARY)ANN
Inner Mongolian province
...... JEHOL, CHAHAR, NINGSIA
Innisfail ...... EIRE, ERIN, IRELAND
innkeeper .... (H)OSTLER,
PADRONE, HOST(ELER),
BONIFACE, LANDLORD,
PUBLICAN
wife of .... HOSTESS
innocence .... BLUET, PURITY,
NAIVETE, SIMPLICITY
innocent .... FOOL, NAIF, PURE,
NAIVE, SIMPLE, ARTLESS,
IGNORANT, DEWEY-EYED,
GUILTLESS
bystander .... WITNESS
in the woods .... BABE
Innocents' Day ...... CHILDERMAS
innocuous .... HARMLESS
innominate bone .... ILIUM,
PUBIS, HIPBONE
innovation .... CHANGE
innovative .... NEW
Innsbruck native, e.g.
.... TYROLEAN
Innuendo .... HINT, SLUR,
ALLUSION, ASPERSION,
INSINUATION
innumerable ...... MANY, MYRIAD,
UNTOLD, COUNTLESS
Innuit's home .... IGLU, IGLOO
inoculation .... SHOT, SERUM,
VACCINE
inoculate .... INFECT, INJECT,
IMMUNIZE, VARIOLATE
Inonu, Turkish president
.... ISMET
inopportune .... ILL-TIMED,
UNTIMELY
inordinate .... UNDUE, EXCESSIVE
inordinately .... OVERLY
Ino's husband .... ATHAMAS
input, computer's .... DATA
inquest .... ASSIZE, INQUIRY,
INVESTIGATION
official .... CORONER
inquiry .... QUERY, REQUEST,
QUESTION, EXAMINATION
inquisition .... PROBE, INQUIRY,
HOLY OFFICE
inquisitive ...... NOS(E)Y, PRYING,
SNOOPY, CURIOUS
inroad .... RAID, INVASION
in's term .... TENURE
insane .... MAD, BUGS, DAFT,
BATTY, CRAZY, FOOLISH,
DEMENTED, SENSELESS
asylum .... BUGHOUSE,
MADHOUSE, NUTHOUSE
make .... DEMENT, DERANGE

person .... NUT, MADMAN,
LUNATIC, ODDBALL
slang .... LOCO, NUTTY,
PSYCHO, BONKERS
insanity .... MANIA, LUNACY,
MADNESS, DEMENTIA,
PARANOIA, PSYCHOSIS
insatiable .... VORACIOUS
inscribe .... MARK, WRITE,
ENROLL, ENGRAVE, DEDICATE
inscribed slab .... STELA
inscription ...... RUNE, GRAFFITO,
LETTERING, DEDICATION
bookplate .... EX LIBRIS
on book .... ENVOY,
COLOPHON
on coin ..... LEGEND, EXERGUE
on Unknown Soldier's tomb
.... KNOWN BUT TO GOD
tomb's .... EPITAPH
inscrutable .... ABSTRUSE,
ENIGMATIC, MYSTERIOUS
expression .... DEADPAN,
IMPASSIVE, POKERFACE
one .... SPHINX
insect .... BEE, BUG, FLY, NIT,
MITE, TICK, WASP, APHID,
THRIP, BEETLE, COCCID,
COOTIE, EARWIG, SPIDER,
ANTLION, CHALCID, MOSQUITO
adult .... IMAGO
appendage .... ENDITE
back of .... NOTUM
blood-sucking ..... FLEA, TICK,
LOUSE, MIDGE, BEDBUG,
CONENOSE
bodies, dried .... KERMES
carnival .... FLEA
colonists .... ANTS, BEES
combining form .... ENTOMO
cotton-eating .... WEEVIL
dipterous ..... GNAT, MOSQUITO
disease caused by .... DENGUE,
MALARIA, YELLOW FEVER
eating animal .... MOLE,
SHREW, DESMAN, TENREC,
TENDRAC, AARDVARK,
HEDGEHOG
egg .... NIT, OOTHECA
exudation .... LAC
eyes .... OCELLI
feeding ant .... KELEP
feeler ...... PALP(US), ANTENNA
flylike .... CICADA, CICALA
form between molts
.... INSTAR
guest of another .... INQUILINE
hard covering .... CHITIN
immature/pre-adult ...... PUPA,
LARVA
jaw .... MANDIBLE

larva .... GRUB, MAGGOT
leaping .... FLEA, LOCUST,
CRICKET, GRASSHOPPER
leg part .... TARSUS
leg segment .... COXA
lepidopterous .... MOTH,
BUTTERFLY
life stage .... EGG, PUPA,
IMAGO, LARVA, INSTAR,
MAGGOT
limb .... PROLOG
lip .... LABIUM, LABRUM
migratory .... LOCUST
molting .... ECDYSIS
nest .... NIDUS
noisy .... CICADA
order of ...... ACARID, LOCUST,
DIPTERA
part of .... COXA, HEAD, WING,
ACRON, CLAVA, NOTUM,
TARSUS, THORAX, ABDOMEN
scale .... COCCID
segment .... SOMITE, TELSON
slim-waisted .... WASP
smelly .... STINK BUG
social .... ANT, BEE
sound .... HUM, BUZZ, CHIRP,
CHIRR, DRONE, STRIDOR
stick .... EMESA
stinger of .... DART
stinging ..... BEE, GNAT, WASP,
GADFLY, HORNET
sucking .... SAPPER
sucking organ .... PROBOSCIS
trap .... WEB
tree .... KATYDID
tropical .... LANTERN FLY
wing cover .... ELYTRON
wing spot .... ISLE
winged ...... BEE, GNAT, WASP,
HORNET, MOSQUITO,
COCKROACH, GRASSHOPPER
wingless .... APTERA
with incomplete
metamorphosis
.... NYMPH
young .... NIT
insecticide .... DDT, PESTICIDE
insectivore .... MOLE, SHREW,
VIREO, DESMAN, TENREC,
HEDGEHOG
insects, kind of .... LACEWING
moving mass of .... SWARM
pertaining to .... ENTOMIC
insecure .... RISKY, UNSAFE,
UNSURE, UNSTABLE
inseminate .... IMPREGNATE
insensate .... COLD, STUPID,
FOOLISH, UNFEELING
insensibility .... COMA
insensible .... NUMB, STOIC,

IMPASSIVE, UNFEELING
insensitive .... CRASS, CALLOUS
inseparables .... CRONIES
insert .... IMMIT, INSET, PUT IN,
INGRAFT, INTROMIT,
INTRODUCE
slyly .... FOIST
insertion .... INLAY, INSET,
PENETRATION, INTRODUCTION,
AD(VERTISEMENT)
sign/mark .... CARET
inset .... INLAY, PANEL, INSERT
inside .... SECRET, WITHIN,
INDOOR(S), INTERIOR,
INTERNAL
combining form .... INTRA
out, turn .... EVERT
insidious ...... SLY, WILY, CRAFTY,
SHREWD, CUNNING,
DECEITFUL
insight .... KEY, ACUMEN,
INTUITION
insignia .... BADGE, CROWN,
EMBLEM, REGALIA, SCEPTER
corporate .... LOGO
saint's .... HALO
insignificant .... PUNY, MINOR,
PETTY, SMALL, PALTRY,
TRIVIAL, WORTHLESS
insincere .... UNTRUE, TWO-
FACED, HYPOCRITICAL
insinuate ...... HINT, FOIST, IMPLY,
SUGGEST, INTIMATE
insinuation .... HINT, INNUENDO
insipid .... DRY, DULL, FLAT,
BANAL, HOHUM, STALE,
VAPID, JEJUNE, PROSAIC,
LIFELESS, TASTELESS, WISHY-
WASHY
insist ...... URGE, PRESS, DEMAND,
MAINTAIN
insolation .... SUNSTROKE,
HEATSTROKE
insolence .... AIRS, HUBRIS,
DEFIANCE, ARROGANCE,
IMPUDENCE
insolent .... COCKY, SAUCY,
SASSY, UPPITY, HAUGHTY
insolvent .... BANKRUPT
insomnia .... VIGILANCE,
WAKEFULNESS, TROUBLE
SLEEPING
cause of .... WORRY,
DEPRESSION
insouciant .... CALM, COOL,
CAREFREE
inspan .... YOKE, HARNESS
inspect .... EYE, PRY, SCAN,
EXAMINE, SCRUTINIZE
before burglarizing .... CASE
closely .... PORE

thoroughly .... TAKE A GOOD
LOOK
inspection .... REVIEW, SURVEY,
PERUSAL, SCRUTINY
kind of ..... OCULAR, CUSTOMS
inspector .... EXAMINER,
OVERSEER, OVERLOOKER
inspiration .... IDEA, AFFLATUS,
INHALING
inspire .... SPUR, STIR, CAUSE,
IMBUE, AROUSE, EXCITE,
INHALE, UPLIFT, ANIMATE,
BREATHE, ENLIVEN,
INFLUENCE
affection .... ENDEAR
confidence .... ASSURE,
CONVINCE
inspired .... FIRED, DEMONIC
instability .... SHAKINESS,
INSECURITY, UNCERTAINTY
install .... FIX, SEAT, SET UP,
INDUCT, INVEST, ESTABLISH
installment .... PAYMENT PLAN
instance .... CASE, BEHEST,
EXAMPLE, OCCASION
of ostentatious display
.... SPLASH
instant .... WINK, TIME, HASTY,
JIFFY, QUICK, TRICE, ABRUPT,
MOMENT, SUDDEN, URGENT,
PRESSING, IMMEDIATE
instantly .... RIGHT NOW, QUICK
AS A WINK
instead .... ELSE, VICE, IN LIEU
(OF), RATHER
instigate .... EGG, ABET, SPUR,
URGE, CAUSE, FOMENT,
INCITE, INDUCE, PROMPT,
PROVOKE, INITIATE
instigation .... AROUSAL,
INSTANCE, PROVOCATION
instigator, kind of ...... PLOTTER,
AGITATOR, DEMAGOGUE,
PROVOCATEUR
instill .... IMPART, INFUSE,
INCULCATE
instinct .... BENT, GIFT, KNACK,
TALENT, IMPULSE
institute .... BEGIN, FOUND, SET
UP, START, SCHOOL,
COMMENCE, INITIATE,
ORGANIZE
institution ...... CHURCH, SCHOOL,
COLLEGE, SOCIETY,
FOUNDATION
instruct .... BRIEF, COACH, EDIFY,
TEACH, TRAIN, TUTOR, DIRECT
instruction .... ORDER, ADVICE,
LESSON, TUITION, TEACHING,
TRAINING, TUTELAGE,
TUTORSHIP

art of .... DIDACTICS
component .... STEP
editor's .... STET
to reader .... PTO
instructor .... COACH, TUTOR,
MENTOR, TEACHER,
PEDAGOGUE
instrument .... DEED, TOOL,
AGENT, MEANS, AGENCY,
DEVICE, IMPLEMENT
board .... PANEL
boring .... AUGUR, GIMLET,
JUMPER
carillon .... BELL
Casal's .... CELLO
denoting an: suffix .... TRON
in law .... DEED, CONTRACT,
DOCUMENT
measuring .... OCTANT
nautical .... SECTANT
panel, auto .... DASHBOARD
shaped like a stringed
.... LYRATE
stringed musical .... UKE,
KOTO, LUTE, LYRE, BANJO,
REBEC, VIOLA, GUITAR,
VIOLIN, CITTERN, SAMISEN,
MANDOLIN
toothed .... COMB
torture .... RACK, WHEEL,
STRAPPADO
instrumental composition
.... SONATA
introduction .... INTRADA
instrumentality .... HAND,
MEANS, AGENCY, MEDIUM,
VEHICLE
instruments .... MEDIA
for all .... TUTTI
insubordinate .... MUTINOUS,
DISOBEDIENT
insubstantial .... FLIMSY, FROTHY,
NOMINAL
insufferable .... AGONIZING,
UNBEARABLE, INTOLERABLE
insufficient .... MEAGER, SCANTY,
SKIMPY, LACKING, WANTING,
INADEQUATE
slang .... SHY OF
insular ...... DETACHED, ISOLATED,
NARROW-MINDED
insulate .... COVER, ENSILE,
DETACH, SHIELD, ISOLATE,
SET APART, SEGREGATE
insulating material .... KERITE,
BAGASSE, CELOTEX, OKONITE,
ASBESTOS
insulin discoverer .... BEST,
BANTING
disease treated with
.... DIABETES

insult .... SLAP, SLUR, OFFEND, AFFRONT, OUTRAGE, INDIGNITY
insurance agent .... UNDERWRITER
contract .... POLICY
protection .... COVERAGE
term .... RISK, POLICY, ANNUITY, TONTINE, ENDOWMENT
insure .... SECURE, GUARANTEE, SEE TO IT, UNDERWRITE
insurer ...... SURETY, GUARANTOR, UNDERWRITER
insurgence .... UPRISING, INSURRECTION
insurgent .... REBEL, RISER, MUTINEER, REVOLTER
insurrection .... REVOLT, UPRISING, REBELLION
intact .... WHOLE, COMPLETE
intaglio .... DIE, GEM, ENGRAVE
opposite of .... CAMEO
intangible ...... VAGUE, ABSTRACT
asset .... GOOD WILL, PRESTIGE
intarsia .... MOSAIC
integer ...... UNIT, WHOLE, ENTITY
odd .... GNOMEN
integral .... WHOLE, ENTIRE, COMPOSITE, ESSENTIAL
integrate .... FUSE, BLEND, UNIFY
integrity .... HONOR, VIRTUE, HONESTY, SINCERITY
integument .... ARIL, COAT, DERM, HIDE, HUSK, RIND, SKIN, SHELL, TESTA
intellect ...... MIND, BRAIN, LOGIC, SENSES, MENTALITY, INTELLIGENCE
of the .... NOETIC
intellectual ...... MENTAL, NOETIC, EGGHEAD, HIGHBROW, RATIONAL, INTELLIGENT
intellectuals, collectively .... CLERISY
intelligence .... WIT, MIND, NEWS, SENSE, ACUMEN, BRAINS, REPORT, TALENT, TIDINGS, CAPACITY, INTELLECT, KNOWLEDGE, INFORMATION
intelligent .... KEEN, SHARP, SMART, ASTUTE, BRAINY, BRIGHT, CLEVER, SENSIBLE, BRILLIANT, QUICK-WITTED
intelligentsia .... LITERATI, INTELLECTUALS
intelligible .... CLEAR, LUCID, OBVIOUS, UNDERSTANDABLE
intemperance .... EXCESS, REVELRY, CAROUSAL, DEBAUCHERY

intemperate .... WILD, RAKISH, SEVERE, VIOLENT, EXCESSIVE
intend ...... AIM, MEAN, PLAN(TO), ENDEAVOR, CONTEMPLATE
intended .... MEANT, PROPOSED
colloquial .... FIANCE(E), BETROTHED
intense .... DEEP, KEEN, ACUTE, SHARP, VIVID, ARDENT, STRONG
dislike .... HATRED
emotion .... PASSION
enthusiasm .... FANATICISM
excitement .... THRILL
rage .... FUROR
suffering ..... AGONY, ANGUISH
surprise .... SHOCK
intensify .... DEEPEN, ENHANCE, HEIGHTEN
intensity .... DEPTH, STRENGTH
intensive .... ALL-OUT
intent .... SET, EAGER, OBJECT, EARNEST, PURPOSE, SINCERE, ENGROSSED, DETERMINED
intention .... AIM, END, GOAL, PLAN, POINT, DESIRE, PURPOSE, OBJECT(IVE)
intentional .... PLANNED, WILLFUL, VOLUNTARY, DELIBERATE
inter .... BURY, INURN, ENTOMB, INHUME
companion of ..... ALIA, ALIOS
intercede .... MEDIATE, ARBITRATE, INTERPOSE, INTERVENE
intercept .... STOP, CATCH, HINDER, CUT OFF
intercessor ...... BISHOP, PLEADER, ADVOCATE, MEDIATOR, PARACLETE
interchange .... SWAP, TRADE, BARTER, EXCHANGE, ALTERNATE
intercom .... TALKBACK
interconnected ...... INTERLINKED
chain .... NETWORK
interdict .... BAN, VETO, (DE)BAR, ENJOIN, FORBID, PROHIBIT, RESTRAIN, PROSCRIBE
interest ...... WEAL, ZEAL, CLAIM, PIQUE, RIGHT, SHARE, STAKE, AFFECT, BEHALF, PROFIT, USANCE, BENEFIT, CONCERN, WELFARE
excessive .... MANIA, USURY
Dr. Rhine's .... ESP
interested .... CONCERNED, FASCINATED
interfere .... BUTT IN, MEDDLE, MOLEST, INTERPOSE,

INTERVENE
interference .... STATIC, JAMMING, HINDRANCE
interim .... INTERVAL, MEANTIME, MEANWHILE, TEMPORARY
interior .... INNER, MIDST, INLAND, INSIDE, INWARD
interject .... INSERT, INTERPOSE
interjection .... GEE, EGAD, GOSH, HECK, OUTCRY, EXPRESSION, EXCLAMATION
of surprise .... GOLLY
psalmic .... SELAH
to attract attention .... HIST
interlace .... BRAID, TWINE, WEAVE, PLEACH
interlock .... LINK, MESH
interlope(r) .... MEDDLE(R), INTRUDE(R), TRESPASS(ER)
interlude .... VERSET, EPISODE, INTERVAL, OVERTURE
intermediary .... AGENCY, MEDIUM, ARBITER, REFEREE, GO-BETWEEN, MIDDLEMAN
intermediate .... MESNE, MEDIAN, MIDDLE, HALFWAY
interment .... BURIAL
intermezzo .... INTERLUDE
interminable .... ENDLESS, LASTING, CEASELESS
intermingle .... MIX, BLEND
intermission ...... PAUSE, RECESS, ENTR'ACTE, INTERVAL, INTERLUDE
intermit .... DEFER, SUSPEND
intermittent .... FITFUL, OFF AND ON, PERIODIC, RECURRENT, SPASMODIC
intermix .... BLEND
intern .... HOLD, DETAIN, DOCTOR, CONFINE
internal .... INNER, INWARD, DOMESTIC, INTERIOR, INTRINSIC
organs .... VITALS, VISCERA
prefix .... ENTO
internally .... WITHIN
international .... GLOBAL, UNIVERSAL, WORLDWIDE
agreement ...... PACT, TREATY, ENTENTE
business combine ...... CARTEL
exhibition .... EXPOSITION
language .... RO, IDO, VOLAPUK, ESPERANTO
river .... ODER
sports .... OLYMPICS
writers' group .... PEN
International Workers Day .... MAYDAY

Internationale author
.... POTTIER
internecine .... DEADLY
interoffice note .... MEMO
interpolate .... INSERT
interpose .... INSERT, MEDDLE,
MEDIATE, INTERCEPT,
INTERRUPT, INTERVENE,
INTRODUCE
interpret .... READ, RENDER,
EXPLAIN, CONSTRUE,
TRANSLATE
dreams .... REDE
interpretation .... READING,
RENDITION, EXPLANATION,
TRANSLATION
false .... WRENCH
interpretative ...... EXPLANATORY
interpreter .... EXEGETE,
TRANSLATOR
of sacred mysteries
.... HIEROPHANT
travelers' .... DRAGOMAN
interregnum .... INTERVAL
interrogate .... ASK, QUIZ,
EXAMINE, QUESTION
interrogation mark .... EROTEME
interrogative word, usually
.... HOW, WHO, WHAT, WHEN,
WHERE, WHICH
interrogator .... PROBER,
QUERIST, INQUIRER
interrogatory, old style
.... EROTETIC
interrupt .... CUT IN, CUT OFF,
SUSPEND, BREAK INTO
interruption ...... BREAK, OUTAGE
intersect .... CUT, JOIN, MEET,
CROSS
intersecting .... CRISSCROSSING
lines .... SECANTS
interstice ...... PORE, SLIT, CHINK,
AREOLA, CREVICE
intertwine .... LACE, WEAVE,
PLEACH, TANGLE
interval ...... GAP, BREAK, HIATUS,
LACUNA, CAESURA, INTERIM,
INTERLUDE, PARENTHESIS
intervene .... MEDDLE, BUTT IN,
INTERFERE, INTERPOSE
intervening ...... MESNE, BETWEEN
intervention .... MEDIATION,
INTERFERENCE
interweave .... PLAT, BLEND,
PLAIT, RADDLE, SPLICE,
ENTWINE, (INTER)LACE
interwoven .... LACED, NETTED,
RETICULAR
intestinal .... ENTERIC
deposit .... BEZOAR
griping .... CRAMPS

not .... PARENTERAL
pains .... COLIC, CRAMPS
parasite .... ASCARIS,
PINWORM, HOOKWORM,
NEMATODE, TAPEWORM,
TRICHINA, TRICHURIS
pouch .... C(A)ECUM
intestine(s) .... GUTS, COLON,
BOWEL(S), VISCERA, ENTRAILS
combining form .... ENTERO
inflammation of .... COLITIS,
ENTERITIS
membrane .... CAUL
of the .... ALVINE, ENTERIC
part .... COLON, ILEUM,
ENTERON, DUODENUM
prefix .... COLI
process, hairlike .... VILLUS
intimate ...... HINT, NEAR, CLOSE,
CRONY, IMPLY, FRIEND,
PRIVATE, SUGGEST
wear ..... PANTY, SLIP-IN, STEP-
IN(S)
intimation .... CUE, HINT, NOTICE,
INKLING
intimidate .... COW, BULLY,
DAUNT, COERCE, (OVER)AWE,
FRIGHTEN, BAMBOOZLE
intolerable .... UNBEARABLE,
UNENDURABLE
intolerance .... BIAS, BIGOTRY
intolerant .... BIGOTED,
IMPATIENT
person .... BIGOT, ZEALOT
intone .... SING, CHANT, RECITE
intort .... COIL, CURL, TWINE,
TWIST
intoxicant .... GIN, RUM, GROG,
SOMA, LIQUOR, WHISKY
intoxicate .... ELATE, SOUSE,
EXCITE, INEBRIATE
intoxicated .... LIT, FRIED, NAPPY,
GROGGY, LOADED, POTTED,
SOUSED, STEWED, DRUNK(EN),
PLASTERED
intoxicating .... HEADY
effect .... KICK
intractable .... WILD, UNRULY,
RESTIVE, FRACTIOUS,
STUBBORN
intransigent .... STUBBORN,
IRRECONCILABLE,
UNCOMPROMISING
intrepid .... BOLD, BRAVE,
DARING, FEARLESS
intrepidity .... GUTS, NERVE,
VALOR, COURAGE
intricacy .... COMPLEXITY
intricate .... MAZY, KNOTTY,
TRICKY, DA(E)DAL, COMPLEX,
KNOTTED, INVOLUTE,

INVOLVED, COMPLICATED
knot .... GORDIAN
points/plots, etc. .... NODI
intrigue .... PLOT, AMOUR, CABAL,
AFFAIR, SCHEME, SPYING,
PERPLEX, ESPIONAGE,
CONSPIRACY
intriguer .... SCHEMER
intrinsic .... REAL, TRUE,
NATURAL, INHERENT,
INTERNAL, ESSENTIAL
intrinsically .... PER SE
introduce .... OPEN, BEGIN,
USHER, BROACH, INDUCT,
INFUSE, INSERT, IMMIT,
LAUNCH, PRESENT, INITIATE,
INSTITUTE, INTERJECT
something new ...... INNOVATE
introducer, kind of .... EMCEE,
TOASTMASTER
introduction .... PROEM, PREFACE,
PRELUDE, FOREWORD,
PRESENTATION
musical .... OVERTURE
to constitution .... PREAMBLE
to play .... PROLOGUE
to society .... DEBUT
introductory .... INITIAL,
EXORDIAL, PREFATORY
remark .... PREFACE,
FOREWORD
introit .... HYMN, PSALM
intromit .... ADMIT, ENTER, LET
IN, INSERT
intrude .... BUTT IN, INVADE,
ENCROACH, OVERSTEP,
TRESPASS
intrusive .... MEDDLESOME,
INTERFERING
intuition .... ESP, HUNCH, INSIGHT,
INSTINCT, SIXTH SENSE
intuitive .... NOUMENAL,
INSTINCTIVE
intumesce .... SWELL, BUBBLE,
EXPAND, ENLARGE
inulin .... ALANTIN
inundate .... SWAMP, FLOOD,
DELUGE, OVERFLOW,
OVERWHELM
inundation .... FLOOD, DELUGE,
SPATHE, OVERFLOW
inure .... HARDEN, TOUGHEN,
ACCUSTOM, HABITUATE
inurn .... BURY, INTER, ENTOMB
inutile .... IDLE, USELESS
invade .... RAID, ENTER, ASSAIL,
ATTACK, INTRUDE, VIOLATE,
TRESPASS
invader of Rome .... GOTH
invaders' foothold
.... BEACHHEAD

invalid .... NULL, SICK, VOID,
WEAK, INFIRM, SICKLY,
UNWELL, PATIENT, NUGATORY
invalidate .... VOID, ANNUL,
OUTLAW, NULLIFY, VITIATE
invaluable .... DEAR, COSTLY,
PRECIOUS, PRICELESS
invariable .... FIXED, STEADY,
UNIFORM, CONSTANT
invariably .... ALWAYS
invasion .... RAID, INROAD,
TRESPASS, INCURSION,
INTRUSION, INFRINGEMENT
beach of World War II
.... OMAHA
craft .... LST
invective .... ABUSE, CURSE
inveigh .... RAIL, CENSURE,
DENOUNCE
inveigle ...... COAX, LURE, TEMPT,
TRICK, CAJOLE, ENTICE,
ATTRACT, ENSNARE
invent .... CREATE, DESIGN,
DEVISE, CONCOCT, IMAGINE,
CONTRIVE, FABRICATE,
ORIGINATE
new word .... COIN,
NEOLOGIZE
invention .... DEVICE, COINAGE,
FICTION, FIGMENT, CREATION,
FALSEHOOD, INGENUITY,
BRAINCHILD, FABRICATION
kind of .... LIE
of Arthur Wynne: 1913
.... CROSSWORD PUZZLE
start of an .... IDEA
inventor .... CREATOR, DEVISER,
ARTIFICER
airplane .... WRIGHT BROTHERS
automobile .... DAIMLER
basketball .... NAISMITH
camera .... EASTMAN
computer .... BABBAGE
cordite, (co-) .... ABEL
cotton gin .... WHITNEY
crossword puzzle
.... (ARTHUR) WYNNE
cylinder lock .... YALE
dynamite .... NOBEL
dynamo .... GRAMME,
FARADAY
elevator .... OTIS
escape-lung .... MOMSEN
fountain pen .... WATERMAN
harp .... JUBAL
incandescent lamp ..... EDISON
kinetoscope .... EDISON
machine gun .... GATLING
microphone/phonograph
.... EDISON
motor .... TESLA

new words .... NEOLOGIST
postage meter ..... PITNEY AND
BOWES
Preparation H hemorrhoid
treatment .... SPERTI
protection of .... PATENT
radar .... TUVE, BREIT
radio .... MARCONI
revolver .... COLT
root beer ..... (CHARLES) HIRES
safety lamp .... DAVY
sewing machine .... HOWE
sign language .... EPEE
steam engine .... WATT
steamboat .... FITCH, FULTON
steel plow .... DEERE
tank (military) .... SWINTON
telegraph .... MORSE
telephone .... BELL
thermometer .... GALILEI
tractor .... HOLT
transistor .... BARDEEN,
BRATTAN, SHOCKLEY
typewriter .... SHOLES
Velcro .... DE MESTRAL
wireless telegraphy
.... MARCONI
inventory .... LIST, STOCK, STORE,
TALLY, CATALOG(UE)
official .... INDENTURE
Inverness .... CAPE, OVERCOAT
native .... SCOT
inverse .... OPPOSITE
inversion .... REVERSAL
invert .... REVERSE, HOMOSEXUAL
invertebrate .... SPINELESS
animal .... POLYP
covering of .... TEST, SHELL
invest .... DON, ADORN, COVER,
ENDOW, ENDUE, CLOTHE,
ORDAIN, BESIEGE, ENVELOP,
INSTALL, SURROUND,
BELEAGUER
investigate .... PROBE, SEARCH,
EXAMINE, EXPLORE,
SCRUTINIZE
for security reasons
.... SCREEN
investigation .... PROBE, HEARING,
INQUEST, ANALYSIS,
RESEARCH, SCRUTINY
investigator .... PROBER, TRACER,
EXAMINER, INQUISITOR
investiture .... VESTURE,
INDUCTION, INSTALLATION
investment .... SIEGE, CAPITAL,
COVERING, GRUBSTAKE
kind of .... BLUE CHIPS
investor .... CAPITALIST
list/securities of .... PORTFOLIO
quest of? .... BLUE CHIP

COMPANY
inveterate .... CHRONIC,
HABITUAL, OBSTINATE, DEEP-
ROOTED
invigorate .... BRACE, ANIMATE,
ENLIVEN
invigorating .... CRISP, TONIC,
BRACING
invincible .... UNDAUNTED,
INDOMITABLE,
UNCONQUERABLE
inviolable .... SACRED,
SACROSANCT
inviolate ...... SACRED, UNBROKEN
invisible .... APHAN, UNSEEN
emanation .... AURA
Invisible Man author .... WELLS
invitation .... BID, CARD
letters .... RSVP
invite .... ASK, BEG, BID, CALL,
LURE, TEMPT, SUMMON,
REQUEST
inviting ...... ENTICING, TEMPTING
invocation .... PRAYER,
INCANTATION
opening .... AGNUS DEI
invoke .... BEG, PRAY, PLEAD,
BESEECH, CONJURE, ENTREAT,
IMPLORE
involuntary .... AUTOMATIC,
ACCIDENTAL, INSTINCTIVE
action .... REFLEX
involute .... ROLLED UP
involve .... IMPLY, ENTAIL,
EMBROIL, INCLUDE, REQUIRE,
ENTANGLE, IMPLICATE,
COMPLICATE
involved .... COMPLEX, INVOLUTE,
INTRICATE, IMPLICATED
involving effort .... OPEROSE
invulnerable .... IMMUNE,
IMPERVIOUS, UNASSAILABLE
inward .... ENTAD, INTERNAL
Io, lover of .... ZEUS
rival of .... HERA
watcher of .... ARGUS
iodine antiseptic .... IODOL,
IATROL
source .... KELP
Iolanthe .... PERI
ion, negative .... ANION
positive .... CATION
Ionian gulf .... ARTA, PATRAS
island .... KAI, LAUT, CORFU,
LET(T)I, PAXOS, ZANTE,
CERIGO, ITHACA, CORCYRA
Ionic capital's volute ...... HELIX
iota ...... BIT, DAB, DOT, JOT, WEE,
DROP, HAIR, MITE, MOTE,
WHIT, FLECK, SPECK, LITTLE,
TITTLE

I.O.U. .... CHIT, NOTE
part of .... I, OWE, YOU
Iowa capital .... DES MOINES
city/town .... SAC, ADEL,
AMES, IOWA, TAMA, MASON,
ONAWA, OSAGE, SIOUX,
KEOKUK, NEWTON, ORANGE,
RED OAK, SIBLEY, TIPTON,
TOLEDO, CHARLES, CLINTON,
DECORAH, DUBUQUE,
OSCEOLA, OTTUMWA,
WAPELLO, WAVERLY,
ATLANTIC, WATERLOO,
DAVENPORT, FORT DODGE,
MUSCATINE, OSKALOOSA,
BURLINGTON, POCAHONTAS,
CEDAR RAPIDS,
MARSHALLTOWN, COUNCIL
BLUFFS
college .... COE, DORDT,
LORAS, CORNELL, WESTMAR,
VENNARD, GRINNELL,
GRACELAND
colony/co-op society
.... AMANA
county .... LEE, LINN, TAMA,
ADAIR, ADAMS, BOONE, SCOTT,
SIOUX, STORY, BENTON,
BREMER, DALLAS, HARDIN,
JASPER, MARION, CLAYTON,
FAYETTE, KOSSUTH,
PLYMOUTH, WOODBURY,
BLACK HAWK, DES MOINES
floating casino ..... PRESIDENT,
DIAMOND LADY, EMERALD
LADY
lake .... EAGLE, STORM, SPIRIT,
RATHBUN, TRUMBULL
Mississippi River town
...... DAVENPORT, BETTENDORE,
FORT MADISON
native .... HAWKEYE
recreation site .... WONDER
CAVE, CHILDREN'S MUSEUM
religious society .... AMANA
river .... BOYER, CEDAR,
SKUNK, RACCOON, MISSOURI,
THOMPSON, MISSISSIPPI
state bird .... GOLDFINCH
state flower .... CAROLINA
ROSE
state nickname .... HAWKEYE
university .... IOWA, DRAKE,
DUBUQUE
ipecac .... EVEA, MADDER
product .... EMETINE
Iphigenia's brother ...... ORESTES
sister .... ELECTRA
ipse ____ .... DIXIT
ipsissima .... VERBA
ipso ____ .... JURE, FACTO

IQ, part of .... QUOTIENT,
INTELLIGENCE
society member .... MENSA
iracund .... TESTY, CHOLERIC,
IRASCIBLE
irade .... DECREE
Iran .... PERSIA
Iranian .... KURD, TUDAH,
PERSIAN, SOGDIAN
angel .... MAH
bird .... BULBUL
cape .... KUH
capital .... TEH(E)RAN
carpet .... KALI, HAMADAN
chief .... MIR
city/town .... BAM, QOM, QUM,
REY, AHAR, AMOL, ARAK,
BAFT, EVAZ, EZNA, FASA,
YEZD, ABHAR, AHVAZ, BABOL,
KARAJ, KHVOY, RASHT, RESHT,
SAVEH, URMIA, ZABOL,
ABADAN, DIZFUL, DUZDAB,
ENZELI, GORGAN, JAHROM,
KASHAN, KAZVIN, MESHED,
MIANEH, NEYRIZ, SEMNAN,
SHIRAZ, SINNEH, TABRIZ,
ZANJAN, ZENJAN, ARDABIL,
BIRJAND, BUSHEHR, ESFAHAN,
HAMADAN, ISFAHAN,
MAHABAD, MASHHAD,
PAHLEVI, TAJRISH, ZAHEDAN,
BORUJERD, MARAGHEH,
SHAHREZA
coin .... KRAN, LARI, RIAL,
P(O)UL, DARIC, DINAR, MOHUR
coin, old .... TOMAN, STATER
communist party .... TUDEH
desert .... LUT, KAVIR
empress .... FARAH(DIBA)
evil spirit .... AHRIMAN
fairy .... PERI
gate .... DAR
gazelle .... CORA
governor .... SATRAP
gulf .... OMAN, PERSIAN
hero .... YIMA, RUSTAM
in Russia .... TA(D)JIK
island .... ARABI, FARSI,
KHARK, QESHM
lake .... TASHK, URMIA,
NAMAKSAR
language .... ARYAN, PAMIR,
AFGHAN, GALCHA, PASHTO,
PUSHTU, AVESTAN, KURDISH,
PAHLAVI, PERSIAN,
AZERBAIJANI
lower house .... MAJLIS
measure .... GAZ, GEZ, GUZ,
ZAR, ZER
monetary unit .... RIAL
moon .... MAHI

mountain .... NEZWAR, SIAH
KUH, DAMAVAND, DEMAVEND
mountain range .... ELBURZ,
ZAGROS
mystic .... SUFI
official .... KHAN
oil center .... ABADAN
poet .... OMAR
port .... ABADAN
premier ..... ZAHEDI, HOVEIDA,
RAZMARA, MOSSADEGH
province .... FARS, GILAN,
KERMAN, BUSHEHR, ISFAHAN,
KHORASAN, HORMOZGAN,
KORDESTAN, AZERBAIJAN
queen .... SORAYA
region .... MAKRAN, LARISTAN,
BALUCHSITAN
religion .... ISLAM
river .... DEZ, ARAS, SHUR,
ARAKS, KARUN, SILUP, TALAB,
BAMPUR, GORGAN, KURANG,
MEHRAN, ZILBIR, SHELAGH,
SAFID RUD
rug .... SENNA, KURDISTAN
ruins .... SUSA, BEHISTUN,
PERSEPOLIS
ruler .... SHAH, PAHLEVI
sacred cord .... KUSTI
sacred writings .... AVESTI
screen .... PARDAH, PURDAH
shah .... PAHLEVI
sir .... AZAM
tiara .... CIDARIS
tile .... KAS(H)I
trading center .... ISPAHA
Turk .... SART
water vessel .... AFTABA
water wheel .... NORIA
weight .... SER, MAUND
Iraq .... MESOPOTAMIA
capital .... BAG(H)DAD
city/town .... A'NA, FAO, HAI,
HIT, KUT, AMARA, BASRA,
DOHUK, ERBIL, HILLA, MOSUL,
ZAKHO, ARBELA, KIRKUK,
RAMADI, SAMAWA, SHATRA,
TIKRIT, SAMARRA
desert .... SYRIAN
district .... AMARA
gnostic .... MANDEAN
king .... FAISAL GHAZI
lake .... HOR SANIYA
language ..... ARABIC, KURDISH
monetary unit .... DINAR
mountain .... ANEIZA, HAJI
IBRAHIM
palace .... QASR
president .... ARIF, HUSSEIN
prime minister .... YAHYA
province .... AMARA

river ..... ZAB, ADHAIM, TIGRIS, EUPHRATES
ruins .... UR, BABYLON, NINEVEH
seaport .... BASRA, MOSQUES
irascible .... BRASH, CROSS, TESTY, IRACUND, IRRITABLE
irate .... MAD, ANGRY, WROTH, FUMING, BOILING, INCENSED
colloquial .... TEED OFF
IRBM, part of .... RANGE, MISSILE, BALLISTIC, INTERMEDIATE
ire .... FURY, RAGE, ANGER, PIQUE, CHOLER, UMBRAGE, DISPLEASURE
Ireland .... EIRE, ERIN, ERSE, IERNA, IRENA, EIRANN, HIBERNIA, IRISH FREE STATE
bay .... CLEW, INVER, SLIGO, BANTRY, DINGLE, GALWAY, ROSSES, TRALEE, DONEGAL, WEXFORD, YOUGHAL, BLACKSOD
canal .... GRAND, ROYAL
cape .... CLEAR
capital .... DUBLIN
city/town .... BRAY, CORK, ENNIS, MALIN, SLIGO, CARLOW, GALWAY, TRALEE, CLONMEL, DUNDALK, THURLES, WEXFORD, DROGHEDA, LIMERICK, TIPPERARY, WATERFORD
county ..... CORK, LEIX, MAYO, CAVAN, CLARE, KERRY, MEATH, SLIGO, CARLOW, DUBLIN, GALWAY, OFFALY, KILDARE, KILKENNY, MONAGHAN, LIMERICK, TIPPERARY
_____ Eireann of .... DAIL
emblem of .... SHAMROCK
fairy folk .... SHEE, LEPRECHAUN
island .... ARAN, OMEY, OWEY, TORY, ACHILL, DURSEY, LAMBAY, GORUMNA, SHERKIN, THE BULL, VALENTIA
mountain .... ERRIGAL, NEPHIN, KIPPURE, THE PAPS, MWEELREA, CARRANTUOHILL
patron saint .... BRIGID, PATRICK
president .... (MARY) ROBINSON
river .... DEE, LEE, MOY, DEEL(E), BANN, ERNE, FINN, INNY, NORE, SUCK, SUIR, AWBEG, BOYNE, FEALE, GLYDE, LAUNE, MAINE,

OVOCA, BARROW, BROSNA, LIFFEY, MAIGUE, SLANEY
settlers in .... OSTMEN
Spenser's .... IRENA
town in ancient .... TARA
Ireland, North bay .... RED, DUNDRUM
capital .... BELFAST
city/town .... KESH, LARNE, NEWRY, OMAGH, ARMAGH, ANTRIM, BANGOR, COMBER, LISBURN, STRABANE, COLERAINE, COOKSTOWN, CRAIGAVON, DUNGANNON, HOLLYWOOD, LONDONDERRY
district .... ARDS, DOWN, LARNE, MOYLE, ANTRIM, BELFAST, LIMAVADY
island .... RATHLIN
lake .... ERNE, NEAGH
mountain .... DIVIS, SLIEVE DONARD
mountain range .... MOURNE, SPERRIN
river .... ROE, BANN, LAGAN
Irene .... PAX
actress .... RICH, DUNNE
parent of .... ZEUS, THEMIS
irenic .... DOVISH, SERENE, PACIFIC
Irian .... PAPUA
iridescence .... LUSTER, RAINBOW, OPALESCENCE
iridescent ...... NACRY, LUSTROUS, NACREOUS, PAVONINE, OPALESCENT, RAINBOWLIKE
gem .... OPAL
iris .... EYE, IXIA, CROCUS, ORRICE, GODDESS, RAINBOW, (BLUE) FLAG, FLEUR-DE-LIS
combining form .... IRIDO
inflammation of .... IRITIS, UVEITIS
layer of .... UVEA
plant .... FLAG, ORRIS, FREESIA, TILEROOT
plural of .... IRIDES
root .... ORRIS
Irish ...... ERSE, CELTIC, MILESIAN, HIBERNIAN
accent .... BROGUE
alas .... OCHONE
alphabet .... OGUM, OG(H)AM
assembly .... DAIL
assessment .... CESS
battle cry .... ABU, SLOGAN
beauty: legendary .... EMER
buxom .... SONSIE
capital, former .... TARA
castle .... TARA
cattle .... KERRY

cheese .... KEBBOK
chisel .... CELT
church .... KIL
clan .... SEPT, SIOL
clansman .... AIRE
club/cudgel .... ALPEEN, SHILLALA, SHILLELAH
coin, fake .... RAP
colloquial .... TEMPER
composer .... BALFE
county in Connacht .... LEITRIM
dagger .... DHU, SKENE
dandy .... BUCKEEN
dialect .... OGHAM
dirge .... KEEN
doctor .... OLLAM
dissident .... FENIAN
district .... BIRR
dramatist .... SHAW, BEHAN, YEATS, O'CASEY, STEELE
emblem .... SHAMROCK
endearment term .... MACHREE
epic .... TANA
exclamation .... ARU, AROO, ARRA(H)
export .... LINEN
fairy .... SHEE, LEPRECHAUN
family .... CINEL
farmer .... SAER, COTTAR, COTTIER
fish .... POLLAN
fishing boat .... HOOKER
folklore character .... LIMER
fortification .... LIS
freebooter .... RAPPAREE
freeman .... AIRE
fuel .... PEAT
Gaelic .... ERSE
garment .... INAR, LENN
general .... SHEA
girdle .... CRISS
girl .... LASSIE, COLLEEN
god .... LER, DAGDA
god of poetry .... OGMA
handsome .... SONSY, SONSIE
hero .... FINN, RORY, FIONN, FENIAN, FERGUS
heroine .... EMER
hill .... INCH
historian .... LECKY
hockey .... HURLING
hood .... COCHULL
initials .... IRA
island group .... ARANN
jargon .... SHELTA
John .... EOIN, SEAN
king .... AED, BORU, ENNA, BRIAN
kingdom .... MUNSTER
laborers .... AIRE

lake .... LOCH
lake dwelling .... CRANNOG
lament .... KEEN, WIRRA,
                 CORONACH
landholding system
                 RUNDALE
legendary imp .... PUCA
legislature .... DAIL, EIREANN
lighthouse rock .... FASTNET
limestone .... CALP
lord .... TANIST
love .... GRA
Lowlander .... SASSENACH
luck .... CESS
lucky .... SONSY, SONSIE
moss .... CARRAG(H)EEN
mother of song ...... MACHREE
musical festival .... FEIS
musical instrument ...... CRUT,
                 TIMPAN
negative .... SORRA
novelist .... REID, SHAW,
       BEHAN, MOORE, WILDE
outlaw .... PAPIST
Papist .... TORY
partisans .... ORANGES
party .... SINN FEIN
patriot .... EMMET, PARNELL
patriotic group .... IRA
patron saint .... BRIGID,
                 PATRICK
peasant ...... KERN(E), COTTAR,
                 COTTIER
pipe (tobacco) .... DUDEEN
playwright ...... SHAW, MOORE,
                 O'CASEY
poet .... COLUM, JOYCE, WILDE,
                 YEATS
policeman .... PEELER
port .... SLIGO
potato .... YAM
pretender .... BUCKEEN
priest .... DRUID
prime minister .... LYNCH,
       LEMASS, DE VALERA
princess .... ISEULT, ISOLDE,
                 DEIRDRE
proprietor .... TANIST
province .... ULSTER,
       MUNSTER, LEINSTER,
             CONNAUGHT
rascal/scamp .... SPALPEEN
rebel .... FENIAN, FIANNA
regret .... OCH
river .... BUSH, DERG, NORE,
      SUIR, BOYNE, CAVAN, FOYLE,
          LAGAN, SHANNON
saint .... AIDAN, PATRICK
saloon .... SHEBEEN
Saxon .... SASSENACH
sea god .... LER

seaport .... COBH, CORK,
      DUBLIN, TRALEE, BELFAST,
             LIMERICK
secret organization .... IRA,
      MOLLY MAGUIRES
secret society member
             ORANGEMAN
shield .... SCIATH
shillaly .... LAH
shoe .... BROGUE
slang .... MICK
smack .... HOOKER
society .... AOH, FEINN
soldier .... KERN(E), RAPPAREE,
            GALLOGLASS
song .... RANN
sorrow .... WIRRA
spirit .... BANSHEE
sprite .... SHEE
steward .... ERENACH
sweetheart .... GRA
symbol .... DEIRDRE
tax .... CESS
tenant .... SAER
tobacco pouch ..... SPLEUCHAN
tribe .... SEPT, SIOL, CINEL
Ulster County .... DOWN
verse .... RANN
wail .... KEEN
warrior .... FENIAN
whiskey .... POT(H)EEN
white .... BAWN
woman revolutionary
             GONNE
writing, old .... OGAM
young man .... BUCKEEN
Irishman .... PAT, CELT, HARP,
      MICK, PADDY, TEAGUE,
      MILESIAN, HIBERNIAN
irk ...... VEX, GALL, TIRE, ANNOY,
      BOTHER, NETTLE, DISGUST,
            IRRITATE
irksome .... TEDIOUS, TIRESOME
iron .... PRESS, FERRUM, MANGLE,
      SMOOTH, FERRITE
alloy .... STEEL
bar .... BLOOM, JOINTER
chancellor .... BISMARK
coated .... TERNE
collar .... GARROTE
combining form ...... SIDER(O)
horse .... LOCOMOTIVE
in golf .... CLUB, MASHIE,
      DRIVER, NIBLICK
lung .... RESPIRATOR
meteorite .... SIDERITE
number one .... CLEEK
ore .... TURGITE, HEMATITE,
      LIMONITE, SIDERITE,
      TACONITE, MAGNETITE
ore area .... SAAR

out .... RECTIFY, SMOOTHEN,
            STRAIGHTEN
oxide .... RED RUST,
            MAGNETITE
oxide powder .... CROCUS
pertaining to .... FERRIC
pig .... SPIEGEL
prefix .... FERRO
ready for rolling .... LARGET
sheet .... TERNEPLATE
sulfide .... PYRITE
symbol for .... FE
ironbark .... EUCALYPTUS
ironclad ...... ARMORED, MONITOR,
      WARSHIP, MERRIMAC,
      FOOLPROOF, UNBREAKABLE
ironer .... MANGLE
ironic(al) .... SARCASTIC,
            SATIRIC(AL)
writing .... LAMPOON
irons ...... GYVE, CHAINS, FETTERS,
            SHACKLES
Ironsides .... CROMWELL
ironwood .... ACLE, TITI, COLIMA,
            HORNBEAM
ironworks .... SMELTERY
irony .... SATIRE, MOCKERY,
       SARCASM, RIDICULE
Iroquoian .... ERIE, HURON,
      MINGO, CAYUGA, MOHAWK,
      ONEIDA, SENECA, WYANDOT,
      CHEROKEE, ONONDAGA,
            TUSCARORA
irrational .... INANE, ABSURD,
      BRUTISH, W(H)ACKY,
            SENSELESS
fear .... PHOBIA
number .... SURD
Irrawaddy tributary
             CHINDWIN
irreconcilable .... CONFLICTING,
            INCOMPATIBLE
irredenta .... UNREDEEMED
irregular .... EROSE, FITFUL,
      SPOTTY, UNEVEN, ERRATIC,
      ABNORMAL, ATYPIC(AL),
      SPORADIC, VARIABLE,
      ANOMALOUS, DESULTORY,
            DISORDERLY
in shape .... BAROQUE
irregularity .... ANOMALY
irreligious .... PAGAN, UNHOLY,
      GODLESS, IMPIOUS, PROFANE,
      AGNOSTIC, ATHEISTIC
irreparable .... HOPELESS
irrepressible ...... SAUCY, ELATED,
      CHEERY, UNRULY
irreproachable .... BLAMELESS,
      FAULTLESS, ABOVEBOARD,
            IMPECCABLE
irresistible .... COMPELLING,

irresolute .... FICKLE, HESITANT
irrespective .... REGARDLESS
irreverence .... DISRESPECT
irrevocable .... FINAL, ABSOLUTE,
                      UNALTERABLE
irrigate .... FLUSH, WATER
irrigation ditch .... SLUICE,
                         ACEQUIA
irritability .... ERETHISM
irritable .... EDGY, CROSS,
     BITCHY, TESTY, CRANKY,
     GRUMPY, TOUCHY, TE(T)CHY,
     IRACUND, IRASCIBLE,
                  SPLENETIC
person .... CRANK, GROUCH,
     TARTAR, CURMUDGEON
irritant .... PEST
irritate .... IRK, VEX, GALL, ITCH,
     RASP, RILE, ANNOY, CHAFE,
     GRATE, PEEVE, PIQUE, TEASE,
     GRAVEL, NEEDLE, NETTLE,
     RANKLE, PROVOKE,
               EXASPERATE
irritation .... ITCH, PIQUE,
                  ANNOYANCE
is .... EXISTS
able .... CAN
aswarm .... TEEMS
beholden .... OWES
evicted ..... WALKS THE PLANK
green about the gills ...... AILS
in accord .... JIBES
interested .... CARES
nosy .... SNOOPS
obligated .... OWES
short .... NEEDS
too fond .... DOTES
Isaac .... PATRIARCH
father of .... ABRAM,
                 ABRAHAM
father-in-law of .... BETHUEL
(half) brother of ...... ISHMAEL
mother of .... SARAH, SARAI
son of ..... EDOM, ESAU, JACOB
wife of .... REBECCA, REBEKAH
Isadora, dancer .... DUNCAN
Isagoge .... INTRODUCTION
Isaye's pupil .... MENUHIN
Iscariot .... JUDAS, TRAITOR
ischemia .... ANEMIA
Iseult .... ISOLDE
husband of .... MARK
love of .... TRISTAN,
                TRIST(R)AM
Ishmael .... PARIAH, OUTCAST
daughter of .... MAHALATH
father of .... ABRAM,
                 ABRAHAM
(half) brother of .... ISAAC
mother of .... HAGAR

son of .... TEMA, DUMAH,
     HADAD, JETUR, KEDAR,
     MASSA, ABDEEL, MIBSAM,
     MISHMA, KEDEMAH, NAPHISH,
                NEBALOTH
Isidore, diminutive of .... IZZY
isinglass .... AGAR, MICA,
           CARLOCK, GELATIN
Isis' brother/husband .... OSIRIS
sister .... NEPHTHYS
Islam adherent .... MOSLEM,
     MUSLEM, MUSLIM
canonical law .... SHARIA
convert .... ANSAR, MURED
founder/prophet
     .... MOHAMMED
holy city .... MECCA
pilgrimage place .... CAABA
school .... MADARA
supreme deity .... ALLAH
Islamic teacher .... ALIM,
                 MULLAH
island .... AIT, ALT, CAY, ISLE
at earth's center .... MERU
between two rivers
     .... MESOPOTAMIA
British, in the South Atlantic
     .... ASCENSION
Canadian .... BANKS, DEVON,
     BAFFIN, VICTORIA, ELLESMERE,
           NEWFOUNDLAND
Caroline .... YAP, TRUK
coral .... CAY, ATOLL
empire .... JAPAN
enchanted .... BALI
famed for giant lizards
     .... KOMODO
in a lake .... HOLM
in Indian Ocean ..... REUNION
in the Aegean Sea ...... SAMOS
in the Malay Archipelago
     .... TIMOR
in the South Pacific
     .... EASTER
isolated .... INCH
King Minos's .... CRETE
largest in the Pacific ...... NEW
                  GUINEA
largest in Tuscan
     Archipelago .... ELBA
legendary .... ATLANTIS
low .... KEY
Mediterranean .... CORSICA
mythical .... NAXOS
near bigger one .... CALF
North Pacific .... WAKE
of immigrants .... ELLIS
of lepers .... MOLOKAI
of song .... BALI, CAPRI,
          HAWAII, TAHITI
off Cape Cod .... MARTHA'S

                VINEYARD
off Venezuela .... ARUBA
river .... AIT, EYOT, HOLM
small ..... AIT, CAY, KEY, ISLE,
                    ISLET
to-mainland sandbars
     .... TOMBOLOS
USSR .... SAKHALIN, NOVAYA-
                 ZEMLYA
west of New Guinea .... AROE
''Wonder Woman's''
     .... PARADISE
world's largest .... GREENLAND
world's second largest
     .... NEW GUINEA
world's third largest
     .... BORNEO
Island, Beautiful .... FORMOSA
islands, group of
     .... ARCHIPELAGO
of Langerhans secretion
     .... INSULIN
off Ecuador .... GALAPAGOS
isle .... AIT, KEY, EYOT
Apia's .... UPOLU
Isle of Man capital ...... DOUGLAS
of Man judge .... DEEMSTER
of Wight channel ...... SOLENT
of Wight town .... COWES
islet .... AIT, ALT, CAY, KEY,
                    HOLM
ism .... DOXY, DOGMA, TENET,
     BELIEF, SYSTEM, THEORY,
                DOCTRINE
isolate .... ENISLE, IMMURE,
     SECLUDE, INSULATE, SET
     APART, SEGREGATE
oneself .... HOLE UP
isolated .... (A)LONE,
               QUARANTINED
isolation .... SOLITUDE
isolationist .... LONER
Isolde .... ISEULT
love of .... TRISTAN, TRISTRAM
isomer .... MALEIC, METAMER
isometric .... CUBIC
isopod .... CRUSTACEAN
isopyre .... OPAL
Israel(i) .... SION, ZION, JACOB
a first name in .... MOSHE
airline .... ELAL
ancient capital .... SAMARIA
ancient city .... TIRZAH,
                SAMARIA
battle site .... ESDRAELON
camp .... ETHAM
cape .... CARMEL
capital .... JERUSALEM
city/town .... LOD, ACRE,
     ARAD, AFULA, EILAT, HAIFA,
     HOLON, LYDDA, RAMLA,

SAFAD, YEHUD, ZEFAT, DIMONA, HADERA, REHOBOT, TEL AVIV (JAFFA), ASHQELON, NAZARETH, BEERSHEBA
coin ..... MIL, SHEKEL, AGOROT
dance .... HORA(H)
defense line .... BARLEV
desert .... NEGEV
district .... HAIFA, CENTRAL, TEL-AVIV, NORTHERN, SOUTHERN, JERUSALEM
farm .... KIBBUTZ
first king .... SAUL
first president .... WEIZMANN
foreign minister .... EBAN
general .... DAYAN
hero .... GIDEON
high priest .... ELI
king .... AHAB, ELAH, JEHU, JORAM, OMRI, DAVID, NADAB, PEKAH, ZIMRI, BAASHA, HOSHEA, AHAZIAH, JEHOASH, JEHORAM, MENAHEM, SHALLUM, SOLOMON, JEHOASH, JEHOAHAZ, JEROBOAM, PEKAHIAH, ZECHARIAH
lake .... HULEH, TIBERIAS
language ..... ARABIC, HEBREW
legislature .... KNESSET
member of a collective farm .... KIBBUTZNIK
monetary unit .... SHEKEL
mountain ...... RAMON, TABOR, CARMEL, MEIRON
native .... SABRA
peace .... SHALOM
plain .... SHARON, JEZREEL, ESDRAELON
political party .... MAPAM
port .... ACRE, ELATH, HAIFA, JAFFA
president ..... BENZVI, SHAZAR, WEIZMANN
prime minister .... (GOLDA)MEIR, RABIN, ESHKOL, SHAMIR, BEN GURION
prophet of .... ELIAS, ELIJAH, ELISHA
region .... NEGEV, GALILEE, JUDAEA
river .... BESOR, JORDAN, QISHON, YARMUK, YARQON
seaport .... JAFFA, JOPPA
statesman .... EBAN
strip .... GAZA
Israel's border, part of .... DEAD SEA
Israelite ...... SION, ZION, DANITE, HEBREW, JEW(ISH)
judge .... ELON
king .... DAVID

land in Egypt .... GOSHEN
leader .... JOSUE, JOSHUA
paid curser .... BALAAM
strong man .... SAMSON
tribe .... JUDAH, REUBEN, SIMEON, EPHRAIM, ZEBULUN, BENJAMIN, ISSACHAR, DAN, GAD, LEVI, AS(H)ER, MANASSEH, NAPHTALI
Israelites, biblical ...... HERITAGE
issei's kin, of a sort .... KIBEI, NISEI
issue .... EMIT, EXIT, ARISE, CHILD, POINT, EMERGE, OUTLET, RESULT, UPSHOT, EDITION, DEAL OUT, OUTCOME, OUTFLOW, PROGENY, PUBLISH, QUESTION, OFFSPRING
forth .... EMANATE
minor point of .... TECHNICALITY
take .... DIFFER, DISAGREE
issuing .... COMING, EMERGING
in rays .... RADIAL
Istanbul .... STAMBOUL, BYZANTIUM, CONSTANTINOPLE
foreign quarter .... PERA, FANAR, BEYOGLU
founder .... BYSAS
inn .... SERAI, IMARET
section .... BEYOGLU, SCUTARI, USKUDAR, STAMBOUL
suburb .... GALATA
isthmus .... KRA, BALK, NECK, PANAMA, STRAIT
Corinth .... MEGARIS
Panama .... DARIEN
istle .... PITA, PITO, FIBER
ita .... NEGRITO
itacolumite .... SANDSTONE
it came after fingers .... FORK
deserts a sinking ship .... RAT
doesn't pay .... CRIME
followed the ragtime review .... HONKY TONK SHOW
has rich taste and aroma .... PORT
has 32 men .... CHESS SET
is better to be born lucky than _____ .... RICH
is legal .... LICET
is silent, in music .... TACET
is so .... AMEN
is what you make it .... LIFE
precedes rank .... NAME
reads same both ways .... PALINDROME
takes two .... TANGO
Italian .... LATIN, ROMAN, PICENE, SABINE
actress .... DUSE, LOREN,

ANGELI, MAGNANI, LOLLOBRIGIDA
adventurer .... CASANOVA
all at once .... SUBITO
anatomist .... FALOPIUS
ancient .... OSCAN, ROMAN, PICENE, SABINE
ancient city .... CAPUA, CANNAE
anew .... DE NOVO
archipelago .... TUSCAN
art period .... SEICENTO, TRECENTO
astronomer .... GALILEO
author .... DANTE, PETRARCH
baby .... BAMBINO
baked shrimp .... SCAMPI
bandit .... CACO, BRIGANTE
bathhouse .... BAGNIO
beings .... ENTES
bell .... CAMPANA
bell town .... ATRI
bonfire .... FALO
bowl .... TAZZA
bread .... PANE
breed of cattle .... MODICA, PADOLIAN
business place .... BANCA
cape .... CIRCEO, VATICANO, CARBONARA
capital .... ROMA, ROME
car .... FIAT
cathedral .... DUOMO
cathedral city .... MILAN
Celt .... SENONE
cheer .... VIVA
cheese .... GRANA, ROMANO, FONTINA, RICOTTA, BEL PAESE, PARMESAN, PROVOLONE, GORGONZOLA, MOZZARELLA
chest .... CASSO(NE)
chief .... DUCE
city/town .... ASTI, ATRI, BARI, CIRO, ELEA, ITRI, LODI, MEDA, POLA, FORIL, GENOA, LECCE, LUCCA, MASSA, MILAN, MONZA, OSTIA, PADUA, PARMA, PAVIA, PRATO, SIENA, TURIN, TERNI, UDINE, ANCONA, CASAL(E), FOGGIA, LATINA, MANTUA, MESTRE, MODENA, NAPLES, NAPOLI, NOVARA, PESARO, RAGUSA, RIMINI, SAVONA, TIVOLI, TORINO, TRENTO, VARESE, VENICE, VERONA, BERGAMO, BOLOGNA, CARRARA, CASSINO, CATANIA, FIRENZE, GORIZIA, LIVORNA, MARSALA, MESSINA, PALERMO, RAVENNA, SALERNO, TRIESTE, SAN REMO, TRAPANI, VENEZIA,

BRINDISI, CAGLIARI, FLORENCE, MOLFETTA, PIACENZA, SIRACUSA
civil government .... QUIRINAL
coin .... LIRA, LIRE, SCUDO, SOLDI, SOLDO, SEQUIN, ZECHIN, ZECCHINO, TESTON(E), CENTESIMO
coin, medieval .... TARI
comedy character .... PANTALOON, SCARAMOUCH(E)
commune .... ALBA, ASTI, IESI, ESTE, MEDA, ASOLA, TRIEA
composer .... GUIDO, LULLY, TOSTI, VERDI, MENOTTI, PUCCINI, ROSSINI, MASCAGNI, PAGANINI, SCARLATTI
condiment .... TAMARA
conductor .... MANTOVANI, TOSCANINI
country, ancient ...... LATIUM, ETRURIA
countryside .... CAMPAGNA
craftsmanship .... ARTE
cup .... TAZZA
cupid .... AMORINO, AMORETTO
customs house .... DOGANA
dance .... PAVIN, VOLTA, PAVAN(E), CALATA, SALTARELLO, TARANTELLA
dear .... CARA, CARO
department .... APULIA, EMILIA, UMBRIA, LIGURIA, LUCANIA, CALABRIA, LOMBARDY, PIEDMONT
dessert ..... SPUMONE, SPUMONI
"Detroit" .... TURIN
dialect .... LIGURIAN
dictator .... MUSSO(LINI)
dish .... PASTA, PIZZA, RISOTTO
dish, veal .... OSSO BUCO
Do Not Touch .... NON TOCCARE
dough .... PASTA
dramatist .... ALFIERI
drink .... BEVERE
dry .... SECCO
duchy .... PARMA
dynasty .... SAVOY
eight .... OTTO
enclave, Swiss .... CAMPIONE
enough .... BASTA
evening .... SERA
express train .... RAPIDO
faction .... NERI, BIANCHI
fair lady .... BELLA DONNA
family .... ASTI, ESTE, CENCI, DORIA, DONATI, MEDICI
farewell .... ADDIO
feast .... FESTA, FESTINO

festival .... RIDOTTO
field .... CAMPO
fig .... FICO
film beauty .... SOPHIA LOREN, GINA LOLLOBRIGIDA
first .... PRIMO
flower .... FIORE
fortress .... ROCA
fountain, famous .... TREVI
gallery .... UFFIZI
game .... MORA, BOCCE
gangster .... DUMINI
gentleman ..... SER, SIGNOR(E), SIGNORINO
good .... BENE
good morning .... BUON GIORNO
good-bye .... ADDIO
goose .... OCA
governor .... PODESTA
greedy .... ESOSO
Greek city .... ELEA, PESTO
Greek colony .... ELEA
guessing game .... MORA
gulf .... GAETA, GENOA, OROSEI, VENICE, SALERNO, TARANTO, TRIESTE, ORISTANO, SQUILLACE
gypsy .... ZINGABI
hair .... PELO
hamlet .... BORGO, CASAL(E)
hammer .... MARTELLO
hand .... MANO
harbor .... PORTO
harlequin .... ZANNI
harp .... ARPA
hat .... LEGHORN
hate .... ODIO
headland .... SCILLA
heir .... EREDE
helmet .... ELME
historian .... CANTU
holiday .... FESTA, FESTE
house .... CASA
hymn .... INNO
innkeeper ...... OSTE, PADRONE
island .... ELBA, CAPRI, PONZA, GIGLIO, ISCHIA, LINOSA, LIPARI, SALINA, SICILY, USTICA, ALICUDI, ASINARA, CAPRAIA, GORGONA, LEVANZO, PANAREA, PIANOSA, VULCANO, FILICUDI, SARDINIA, FAVIGNANA, GIANNUTRI, LAMPEDUSA, MARETTIMO, SAN PIETRO, STROMBOLI, MONTECRISTO, VENTOTENE, PANTELLERIA
islander .... SARD
islands .... EGADI, LIPARI, PELAGIE, PONTINE, TREMITI

judge .... PODESTA
king .... EMMANUEL, HUMBERT(O)
kiss .... BACIO
know-nothing .... NESCI
labor contractor ...... PADRONE
lady/madam .... DONNA, SIGNORA, SIGNORINA
lake .... COMO, LAGO, VICO, GARDA, ALBANO, AVERNO, BOLSENA, MAGGIORE, BRACCIANO, TRASIMENO
language .... LADIN, OSCAN, TUSCAN
leader .... RAS, DUCE, MUSSO(LINI)
little .... POCO
love .... AMORE
lover .... AMOROSO
magistrate ..... DOGE, PODESTA
man .... SIGNOR(E)
marble .... CIPOLIN, CAR(R)ARA
marshy land .... MAREMMA, PONTINE
mayor .... PODESTA
measure .... CANNA, PALMO, PUNTO, MIGLIO, BRACCIO
meat balls .... RAVIOLI
milk .... LATTE
millet ..... BUDA, MOHA, TENAI
miss .... SIGNORINA
mister .... SIGNOR
monetary unit .... LIRA
monk's title .... FRA
mother .... MADRE
mountain .... CAVO, ROSA, VISO, BLANC, CENIS, CHIANTI, MARMOLADA, GENNARGENTU, GRAN PARADISO
movie director .... (DE)SICCA
music .... TARANTELLA
musical instrument .... ARPA
musical suite .... PARTITA
musical theme .... TEMA
musical theorist .... GUIDO
muslin .... MUSSOLINO
name for Florence .... FIRENZE
name for Italy .... ITALIA
nationalist .... MAZZINI
naval base .... POLA, TARANTO, BRINDISI
night .... SERA
nine .... NOVE
noble family .... ESTE
noblewoman .... MARQUIS, CONTESSA, MARCHESA, MARCHESE, MARCHIONESS
not only .... NONCHE
novelist .... MANZONI
one .... UNO
opera .... AIDA, NORMA, TOSCA

opera house .... SCALA
opera singer .... AMATO,
GIGLI, PATTI, PINZA, CARUSO,
CORELLI, TEBALDI, ALDANESE
painter ...... RENI, LIPPI, ROSSI,
SPADA, VINCI, ANDREA,
GIOTTO, TITIAN, VASARI,
RAPHAEL
pass .... BRENNER, GREAT
SAINT BERNARD
patriot .... CAVOUR, MAZZINI,
GARIBALDI
patriotic organization
.... CARBONARI
peak .... CIMA, BERNINA,
MARMOLADA
people .... OSCAN, SARDS,
SABINES
philosopher ...... DION, BRUNO,
(BENEDETTO) CROCE
physicist .... ROSSI, VOLTA,
GALILEO, MARCONI
pie .... PIZZA
plague .... PELLAGRA
plain .... CAMPAGNA
plateau .... SILA
poet .... REDI, DANTE, TASSO,
ARIOSTO, MANZONI, LEOPARDI,
PETRARCH
police .... CARABINIERI
political party member
.... GUELF, GUELPH
porridge .... POLENTA
port ...... BARI, GENOA, MILAN,
OSTIA, TRIESTE, SORRENTO
pottery ..... FAENZA, MAJOLICA
premier .... MORO, PARRI,
RUMOR, CAVOUR, CRISPI,
ORLANDO
president .... LEONE
prima donna .... TEBALDI
province .... ASTI, BARI, COMO,
PISA, ROME, GENOA, FORIL,
LECCE, MILAN, PADUA, PAVIA,
SIENA, TURIN, UDINE, ANCONA,
FOGGIA, MANTUA, MODENA,
NAPLES, TRENTO, VENICE,
VARESE, VERONA, AVELINO,
BERGAMO, BOLOGNA, BRESCIA,
CASERTA, CATANIA, MESSINA,
PALERMO, PERUGIA, SALERNO,
TARANTO, TRIESTE, VICENZA,
CAGLIARI, FLORENCE,
ALESSANDRIA
public square .... PIAZZA
range .... CARNIC, GRAIAN,
JULIAN, ORTLES, OTZTAL,
PENNINE, MARITIME,
APENNINES
region .... APULIA, LATIUM,
MARCHE, SICILY, UMBRIA,

VENETO, ABRUZZI, LIGURIA,
TUSCANY, CALABRIA,
CAMPANIA, LOMBARDY,
PIEDMONT, SARDINIA,
TRENTINO
republic .... GENOA
resort ...... COMO, LIDO, CAPRI,
AGNONE, SAN REMO,
SORRENTO
restaurant .... PIZZERIA
river .... PO, ADDA, ARNO,
NERA, ADIGE, OGLIO, PIAVE,
SALSO, TIBER, MINCIO,
PANARO, TANARO, LIVENZA,
METAURO, OMBRONE, TREBBIA,
VOLTURNO, DORA BALTEA,
DORA RIPARIA
road .... RADA, STRADA
Romance language ...... LADIN
ruins .... POMPEII
saddle .... SELLA
sausage .... SALAMI
sculptor .... DUPRE, LEONI,
CANOVA, PISANO, CELLINI
sea .... IONIAN, ADRIATIC,
LIGURIAN, TYRRHENIAN
seacoast .... MARINA
seaport .... POLA, GENOA,
TRANI, GENOVA, NAPLES,
VENICE, PALERMO, SALERNO,
SAN REMO, TRIESTE, (LA)
SPEZIA
seashore .... RIVA
seasoning mixture
.... TAMARA
secret society .... MAFIA,
CAMORRA, CARBONARI
ship .... POLACCA
shrimp dish .... SCAMPI
sign .... SEGNO
silk .... SETA
sir .... SIGNOR(E)
sky .... CIELO
slang .... GUINEA
small .... PICCOLO
somewhat .... POCO
song .... CANZONE
soup .... MINESTRONE
spa .... ABANO, AGNONE
spider .... TARANTULA
strait .... SICILY, MESSINA,
OTRANTO, BONIFACIO
street .... VIA, CALLE, CORSO
supper .... CENA
tender .... PIA
tenor .... CARUSO, SCHIPA,
CORELLI
that .... CHE
the .... GLI
three .... TRE
time .... TEMPO

title .... CONTE, DONNA,
MARCHE, SIGNOR, MARQUIS,
CONTESSA
tobacco .... CAPORALE
today .... OGGI
tractor .... PICCOLINO
tribe .... SABINE
under .... SOTTO
valley .... SACCO
vase .... TAZZA
verse .... RANN
violin .... AMATI, CREMONA,
STRAD(IVARIUS)
violin maker .... AMATI,
GUARNERI, STRADIVARI
violinist .... TARTINI, PAGANINI
voice .... VOCE
volcano .... ETNA, VESUVIUS,
STROMBOLI
waterway .... CANALE
we .... NOI
weight .... LIBRA, ONCIA,
DENARO, SALM(A)
well .... BENE
what .... CHE
what will be, will be ...... CHE
SARA SARA
wind .... ANDAR, SOVER,
SIROC(CO)
wine .... ASTI, FALERNO
wine, white .... SOAVE
wine measure ..... ASTI, ORNA,
ORNE
winter .... INVERNO
woman's title .... MADONNA
woods .... PINETOS
woodwork .... TARSIA
you .... TU, VOI
Italic type inventor
.... MANUTIUS
Italy .... AUSONIA, HESPERIA
itch .... RIFF, URGE, CRAVE,
MANGE, PSORA, DESIRE,
SCABIES, BURN(ING),
PRURITUS, HANKER(ING)
barber's .... SYCOSIS
item .... PART, UNIT, ENTRY,
PIECE, THING, DETAIL,
ARTICLE, PARTICULAR
black ink .... CREDIT
checkroom .... HAT, COAT,
WRAP
to be weighed .... ANCHOR
itemize .... LIST
itemized list .... ROSTER
items in first-aid procedures
.... EMETICS
iterate .... ECHO, HARP, REPEAT,
RETELL
Ithunn .... IDUN
itinerant .... HOBO, TRAMP,

DRIFTER, NOMADIC, VAGRANT, TRAVELER, TRAVELING

vendor .... PEDDLER

itinerary .... ROUTE, COURSE, CIRCUIT, ROADBOOK, CHECKLIST, GUIDEBOOK

itinerate .... TRAVEL

it's been said .... UTTERANCE

how you play the game .... WIN OR LOSE

often clipped .... COUPON

often the limit .... SKY

on the barrelhead .... CASH

sometimes due .... POSTAGE

to the left of the Rive Droite .... SEINE

itself .... PER SE

itty-bitty .... TEENSY

iva .... YELLOW BUGLE

Ivanhoe author .... SCOTT

character .... BOUEF, CRONE, GURTH, ISAAC, WAMBA,

CEDRIC, ROWENA, ULRICA

weapon of .... LANCE

Ives, actor .... BURL

partner of .... CURRIER

ivied .... VINY

ivories .... DICE, KEYS, TEETH

ivorine .... WHITE

ivory .... TUSH, TUSK, DENTINE

_____ .... TOWER

animal with .... WALRUS, WARTHOG, ELEPHANT

Latin .... EBUR

like .... DENTINE

source .... TUSK, NARWHAL, ELEPHANT

synthetic .... IVORIDE

tickler .... PIANIST

time-heaters .... CASTANETS

tower .... HIDEOUT, RETREAT, HIDEAWAY

Ivory Coast capital .... YAMOUSSOUKRO

city/town .... DIVO, DALOA, BOUAKE, GAGNOA, ABIDJAN, KORHOGO, PORT-BOUET

gulf .... GUINEA

lagoon .... ABY, EBRIE

lake .... KOSSOU

president .... HOUPHOUET-BOIGNY

river .... BAGOE, COMOE, BAOULE, CAVALLY

ivy .... VINE, CLIMBER

clump .... TOD

family .... GINSENG

kind of .... POISON, GROUND

leaguers .... ELIS

of the .... HEDERAL

Iwo ____ .... JIMA

Jima mount .... SURIDACHI

ixia .... IRIS

Ixion offspring .... CENTAUR

ixtle .... PITA, ISTLE

Izmir .... SMYRNA

J

J in physics .... JOULE

letter .... JAY

ja .... YES

jab ...... DIG, BLOW, POKE, PUNCH, THRUST

jabber .... YAP, PRATE, BABBLE, GABBLE, GIBBER(ISH), CHATTER, SPUTTER

jack .... BAR, MUG, NOB, MULE, BOWER, CLOWN, HOIST, KNAVE, TORCH, DONKEY, FELLOW, OPENER, RABBIT, SAILOR, SALMON

in cribbage .... NOB

in-the-pulpit ..... ARAD, ARUM, AROID, WAKEROBIN

of-all-trades .... TINKER

of clubs .... PAM

part of .... DETENT

pudding .... FOOL, BUFFOON

rabbit .... HARE

slang .... MONEY

tree .... JACA

up .... HIKE, RAISE

Jack .... LORD, PARR, WEBB, OAKIE, BENNY, CARTER

and ____ .... JILL

Benny's stock in trade .... GAGS, VIOLIN

Horner's prize .... PIE

Ketch .... HANGMAN

Leonard's forte .... INSULT

Nasty .... SNEAK

Sprat's favorite .... LEAN

jackal .... DIEB, KOLA, THOS, CHEAT(ER), (WILD)DOG, SWINDLER, SCAVENGER

headed deity .... ANUBIS

jackanapes .... IMP, MONKEY, UPSTART

jackass .... DOLT, FOOL, DONKEY, NITWIT

and mare offspring ...... MULE

rarely one .... WISE GUY, SMART ALECK

jackdaw .... DAW

bird like .... CROW

jacket .... ETON, JUPE, RIND, SACK, SKIN, GREGO, PARKA, ANORAK, BOLERO, CASING, JERKIN, REEFER, COAT(EE), SACQUE, NORFOLK, SPENCER, WRAPPER, ROUNDABOUT

ad on book .... BLURB

Arctic .... ANORAK

armor .... ACTON, GIPON, JUPON

children's .... PALETOT

cowboy's .... CHAQUETA

dinner .... TUX(EDO)

fur .... PARKA

life-saving .... MAE WEST

mail .... HAUBERK, HABERGEON

outer ..... WAMPUS, WAM(M)US

sailor's .... PEACOAT

sleeveless/short .... VEST, BOLERO, TABARD, WAISTCOAT

sports .... WINDBREAKER

women's .... JUPE, JUPON, PALETOT, CAMISOLE

woolen .... CARDIGAN, LUMBERJACK

jackfish .... PIKE

Jackie's predecessor .... MAMIE

successor .... LADY BIRD

Jacks or better .... OPENER

jacksnipe .... SANDPIPER

Jackson, Andrew ...... ANDY, OLD HICKORY

follower of President .... JACKSONIAN

general .... STONEWALL

Jacob .... ISRAEL

burial place of .... MACHPELAH

daughter of .... DINAH

diminutive of ...... JACK, JAKE

father of .... ISAAC

father-in-law of .... LABAN

grandfather of .... ABRAHAM

grandson of .... EPHRAIM, MANASSEH

in French .... JACQUES

mother of .... REBECCA, REBEKAH

son of .... DAN, GAD, LEVI, ASHER, JUDAH, JOSEPH, REUBEN, SIMEON, ZEBULUN, BENJAMIN, ISSACHAR, NAPHTABI

twin brother of .... EDOM, ESAU

variant of .... JAMES
wife of .... LEAH, RACHEL
Jacobin .... FRIAR, PIGEON,
RADICAL, DOMINICAN
Jacob's sword .... IRIS
jaconet .... COTTON, NAINSOOK
jade .... NAG, TIT, MARE, SLUT,
TIRE, YAUD, GREEN, HUSSY,
STONE, WEARY, WOMAN,
HARASS, MURRHINE,
NEPHRITE, ROSINANTE
jaded .... BLASE
jaeger .... SKUA, ALLAN, SHOOI,
TEASER, SEABIRD
Jael's husband .... HEBER
victim .... SISERA
weapon .... TENT PEG
Jaffa .... JOPPA
home of .... ISRAEL
jag .... BUN, BARB, PINK, SNAG,
TEAR, NOTCH, SPREE
jaga .... BANTU
jager .... RIFLEMAN
jagged ...... CLEFT, EROSE, ROUGH,
RAGGED, NOTCHED, SERRATED
jaguar ...... CAR, TIGER, PANTHER
jaguarundi .... EYRA
Jahve(h) .... JEHOVAH
jai-alai .... PELOTA
cheer .... OLE
court .... FRONTON
game like .... HANDBALL
player .... PELOTARI
racquet .... CESTA
stroke .... REBOTE
jail .... PEN, CAGE, CELL, COOP,
GAOL, QUOD, LIMBO, LOCK
UP, (IM)PRISON, BRIDEWELL
official ...... WARDEN, WARDER
slang .... JUG, STIR, POK(E)Y,
COOLER, CLINK(ER), SLAMMER,
CALABOOSE
jailbird .... INMATE, CONVICT,
PRISONER, LAWBREAKER
jailer .... GAOLER, WARDEN,
PROVOST, TURNKEY
Jakarta .... BATAVIA
jakes .... PRIVY, TOILET
jalopy .... CRATE, HOTROD
jalousie .... BLIND, SHADE,
SCREEN
jam .... CRAM, BLOCK, CROWD,
SHOVE, WEDGE, SQUEEZE,
PRESERVES, CONGESTION
colloquial .... FIX, SPOT,
PINCH, PREDICAMENT
every which way
.... GRIDLOCK
like preparation .... JELLY
material .... CURRANT
Jamaican bay .... MONTEGO

bird .... TODY, GRACKLE,
TINKLING
capital .... KINGSTON
export .... RUM
grackle .... TINKLING
island .... CAYMAN
peak .... BLUE MOUNTAIN
witchcraft .... OBEAH
jamb(e) .... (SIDE)POST
James Bond's creator
.... FLEMING
direction to .... HOME
father of disciple ..... ZEBEDEE
the outlaw .... JESSE
the Second supporter
.... JACOBITE
Watson topic .... DOUBLE
HELIX
Jamshid's subjects .... PERIS
Jane, mate of .... TARZAN
singer .... FROMAN
jangle .... BICKER, QUARREL
Janis, pop singer .... JOPLIN
janitor .... SUPER, PORTER,
SEXTON, DOORMAN,
CONCIERGE
Janus, like .... TWO-FACED
Japan .... NIHON, ENAMEL,
NIPPON, CIPANGO, LACQUER,
VARNISH, ZIPANGU
foreigner in .... GAIJIN
Japanese .... NIPPONESE
a walk .... SANPO
abacus .... SORABAN
aborigine .... AINO, AINU
about .... GORO
admiral .... ITO, OKA, TOGO,
OKADA, UGAKI, NAGANO,
NOMURA, OIKAWA, SUZUKI,
TOYODA, SHIMADA,
YAMAMOTO
adviser .... GENRO
again .... MO ICHIDO
airplane .... HIKOOKI
airport .... HIKOJO, HIKOOZYOO
alien to a .... GAIJIN
all .... ZENBU
alone .... HITORIDE
always .... ITSUMO
A.M. (morning) .... GOZEN
American .... ISSEI, KIBEI,
NIS(S)EI, SANSEI
ant .... ARI
anthem .... KIMIGAYO
apple .... RINGO
apricot .... UME, ANSU
April .... SHIGATSU, YONGATSU
arm .... UDE
army reserve .... HOJU
ash/gray .... HAIIRO
assets .... ZAISAN

August .... HACHIGATSU
aunt .... OBA, OBASAN
automobile .... ZIDOOSYA
automobile manufacturer
.... HONDA, DATSUN, NISSAN,
TOYOTA, SUZUKI, MITSUBISHI
autumn/fall .... AKI
back .... USIRO, SENAKA
bad .... DAME, WARUI
badge/crest .... (KIRI)MON
bag .... KABANG
baggage .... NIMOTU
bamboo craft .... TAKESEIHIN
bamboo shoot ...... TAKENOKO
banjo .... SAMISEN
bank .... GINKO(O)
barber .... RIYOOSHI
baron .... HAN
bathroom .... HUROBA
battle cry/cheer .... BANZAI
bay .... ISE, MUTSU, OSAKA,
TOKYO, ATSUMI, SAGAMI,
TOYAMA, WAKASA, UCHIURA,
ISHIKARI, KAGOSHIMA
bean sprout .... MOYASHI
beans, all kinds .... MAME
beautician .... BIYOOSHI
beauty salon .... BIYOIN
bed .... BETTO, SINDAI
beef .... GYUUNIKU
beer .... ASAHI, BIIRU,
SAPPORO
before/front .... MAE
begin .... HAJIMERU
bell .... BERU
beriberi .... KAKKE
beside .... YOKO
big .... OKI(I)
bird .... KOTORI
birthday .... TANJOO BI
bitter .... NIGAI
black .... KURO(I)
black tea .... KOOTYA
blue .... AO(I)
board game .... GOBAN(G)
body .... KARADA
book .... HON
bookshelf .... HONDANA
bookstore .... HONYA
box .... HAKO
branch .... EDA
brazier .... HIBACHI
bread .... PAN
bream .... TAI
bride .... HANAYOME
bridegroom .... HANAMUKO
brother .... ANI, OTOOTO
brother or sister ...... KYOODAI
brown .... CHAIRO
Buddha .... AMIDA
Buddhism .... ZEN

Buddhist festival .... BON
Buddhist monastery ...... TERA
bug/worm .... MUSHI
building .... TATEMONO
bull/cow .... USI
bullet train .... SHINKANSEN
bus .... BASU
butter .... BATA
buy .... KAU, KATTE
cabbage .... KYABETSU
camellia .... JAPONICA
cape .... IRO, OMA, DAIO,
ERIMO, INUBO, KAMUI, NYUDO,
TAPPI, NOJIMA, SHIONO,
MOTSUTA, SHIRIYA
capital .... TOKIO, TOKYO,
YED(D)O
capital, former .... NARA,
KYOTO
capital, old: var. .... KIOTO
car .... KURUMA
carriage .... RICKSHA(W)
carrot .... NINJIN
caste .... SAMURAI
cat .... NEKO
cedar .... SUGI
center of city .... TOSHIN
chair .... ISU
channel .... KII
cheap .... YASUI
cheese .... CHIIZU
cheerleader .... OENDAN
cherry .... SAKURANBO
cherry blossoms .... SAKURA
Cherry Society .... SAKURAKAI
chest .... MUNE
chest of drawers .... TANSU
chestnut .... KURI
chicken .... TORI
chicken dish .... YAKATORI
child/children .... KODOMO
chinaware .... IMARI, KUTANI
chopstick .... HAS(H)I
church .... TERA
cigarette .... TABAKO
circle .... MARU
city/town .... ISE, ITO, ODA,
TSU, UBE, UJI, YAO, FUJI, GIFU,
GOBO, HINO, HOFU, KOBE,
KOFU, MITO, MOJI, NAHA,
NARA, SOKA, UEDA, YONO,
ATAMI, BEPPU, CHIBA, CHOFU,
DAITO, FUCHI, FUKUE, ITAMI,
IZUMI, IWAKI, KOCHI, OSAKA,
OTARU, SAKAI, SUITA, URAWA,
ZUSHI, AKASHI, AOMORI,
ATSUGI, HADANO, HIMEJI,
JOETSU, KADOMA, NAGOYA,
SASEBO, SENDAI, TOYAMA,
TOYOTA, YAMATO, FUKUOKA,
HITACHI, IBARAKI, KASHIWA,
MACHIDA, MORIOKA, NIIGATA,
ODAWARA, OKAYAMA,
SAPPORO, SHIMIZU, ICHIHARA,
HACHIOJI, FUKUYAMA,
ICHIKAWA, KAWASAKI,
NAGASAKI, SHIZUOKA,
WAKAYAMA, YAMAGATA,
YOKOHAMA, AMAGASAKI,
HACHINOHE, HIROSHIMA,
KAGOSHIMA, MATSUMOTO,
MATSUYAMA
clam .... ASARI
clan ...... GEN, HEI, TOKUGAWA
clap/applaud .... KASSAI
climate .... KIKOO
clock/watch .... TOKEE
clogs .... GETA
close .... SIMARU
cloth for wrapping objects
.... FUROSHIKI
cloudy .... KUMORI
clover .... HAGI
coin .... RIN, SEN, YEN,
OBAN(G), ITZEBU
cold .... SAMUI
come .... KIMASU
commoner .... HEIMIN
company boss .... SHACHOO
compete .... SERU
confection .... AME
Consulate .... RYOOZIKAN
contract .... KEIYAKU
conveyance .... KAGO
coffee .... KOOHI
cook .... RYOORI
cookie/cake .... OKASI
cool .... SUZUSHII
couch/sofa .... NAGAISU
councilor .... KARO
courage .... YUUKI
court .... DAIRI
cousin ...... ITOKO, OITOKOSAN
cover/lid .... FUTA
crash (suicide) pilot
.... KAMIKAZE
Crown Prince .... NARUHITO
cucumber .... KYURI
customer/guest .... KYAKU
cut .... KITTA
dancing girl .... GEISHA
date/plum .... UME
daughter .... MUSUME(SAN)
December .... ZYUUNIGATSU
decreased .... HETTA
deer .... SIKA
deity .... AMIDA, AMITA
delicious .... OISII
dentist .... HAISHA
department store ..... DEPAATO
diary .... NISSHI
dictionary .... ZIBIKI
difficult .... MUZUKASI
dining room .... SYOKUDOO
dish .... SUSHI, TEMPURA,
SUKIYAKI, TERIYAKI,
YAKATORI, SHABU-SHABU
divine wind .... KAMIKAZE
divorce .... RIKON
doctor .... ISHA
dog .... INU
door .... TO
drama .... NOH, KABUKI,
NOGAKU
drink .... NOMI(MASU)
drugstore .... KUSURIYA
ear .... MIMI
earthquake .... JISHIN
earthquake, 1923 .... KANTO
easy .... YASAI
eat .... TABERU
egg .... TAMAGO
eggplant .... NASU
eight .... HATI, HACHI
electric light .... DENKI
embassy .... TAISIKAN
emperor .... JIMMU, JINMU,
TENNO, MIKADO, AKIHITO,
HIROHITO, MUTSUHITO,
YOSHIHITO
emperor's reign .... MEIJI,
SHOWA, TAISHO
Empire .... EDO
Empress .... NAGAKO, MICHIKO
empty hand .... KARATE
English language .... EEGO
Englishman .... IGIRISUZIN
engraver .... HOKUSAI
Enlightened Peace era
.... MEEZI, MEIJI
ethnic group .... AINU
everyday .... MAINITI,
MAINICHI
everyone .... MINNA
expectation .... OPE
expensive .... TAKAI
eye .... ME
eyebrow .... MAYUGE
face .... KAO
family .... KAZOKU
father .... TITI, OTOOSAN
February .... NIGATSU
fighter plane .... ZERO
finger .... YUBI
fine .... KEKKO
fire .... KASAI
fish .... SAKANA
fish gill .... ERA
fishworm .... ANISAKIS
five .... GO
flag .... RISING SUN
flower/nose .... HANA

Japanese

flower arrangement .... IKEBANA
foreign language .... GAIKOKUGO
foreign ministry .... GAIMUSHO
four .... S(H)I
fork .... HOOKU
France .... HURANSU
Frenchman .... HURANSUZIN
Friday .... KINYOOBI
friend .... TOMODATI, TOMODACHI
fruit(s) .... KUDAMONO
game .... GOBAN(G)
game, ancient .... KEMARI
garlic .... NINNIKU
garment .... KIMONO
gateway .... TORII
general ..... MUTO, NOGI, TOJO, ANAMI, ARAKI, KOISO, SAKAI, UMEZU, KAWABE, TANABE, TANAKA, OKAMURA, TOMINAGA, KAWASHIMA, YAMASHITA
generalissimo .... SHOGUN
German .... DOITUZIN
German language .... DOITUGO
gift .... OMIYAGE
give .... YARU
go .... IKU, IKIMASU
goat .... YAGI
god .... KAMI, EBISU, HOTEI
goldfish .... FUNA
good .... YOROSI
good afternoon .... KONNITI-WA, KONNICHIWA
good evening ..... KONBAN-WA
good morning .... OHAYOO
good night .... OYASUMI-NASAI
goodbye .... SAYONARA
government system .... SHOGUNATE
grandchild .... MAGO
grandfather ...... SOHU, OZISAN
grandmother .... SOBU, OBAASAN
grape .... BUDOO
graveyard tombstone .... HAKA
green .... MIDORI
grill .... HIBACHI
guitar .... KOTO, SAMISEN
hand .... TE
hang .... KAKERU
Happy Birthday ..... TANJOOBI OMEDETOO
head .... ATAMA
healthy .... GENKI
Hello (on the telephone) .... MOSIMOSI
herb .... UDO

here .... KOKO
Hey there!/Say! .... ANONE
highest point .... (MOUNT) FUJI
hill/slope .... SAKA
hometown .... FURUSATO
horse .... UMA
hospital .... BYOOIN
hot .... ATSUI
house/home ...... UCHI, OTAKU
husband .... SYUZIN, GOSYUZIN
I/me .... WATASHI, WATAKUSHI
ice .... KOORI
jacket .... SEBIRO
January .... ICHIGATSU
July .... SHICHIGATSU
June .... ROKUGATSU
key .... KAGI
kind of fish .... AYU, TAI, FUGU, GOURAMI, TILAPIA
kitchen .... DAIDOKORO
knife .... NAIHU
immigrant .... ISSEI
imperial badge .... KIRIMON
important/valuable .... DAIZI
industrial family .... MITSUI, YASUDA, TOYODA, ZAIBATSU
inland sea .... SETO, NAIKAI
island .... AWA, IKI, IWO, NII, DOGO, HAHA, KUME, MUKO, SADO, TOBI, YAKU, AWAJI, IHEYA, KIKAI, YORON, CHICHI, MIYAKO, TANEGA, TARAMA, KUCHINO, NISHINO, OKINAWA, RISHIRI, ISHIGAKI
island, main .... HONSHU, KYUSHU, SHIKOKU, HOKKAIDO
island group .... IZU, GOTO, AMAMI, BONIN, DOZEN, KERAMA, RYUKYU, HABOMAI, KOSHIKI, YAEYAMA, VOLCANO
lagoon .... HACHIRO, KASUMIGA
lake .... BIWA, TOYA, TAZAWA, TOWADA, KUTCHARO, INAWASHIRO
language .... NIHONGO, NIPPONGO
lawyer .... BENGOSHI
left .... HIDARI
lightning .... INAZUMA
lily .... AURATUM
lips .... KUTIBIRU
litter .... NORIMONO
little .... SUKOSI
lobster .... ISEEBI
lord .... DAIMIO
lute .... BIWA
magazine .... ZASSI
man .... OTOKO
many/much .... TAKUSAN
map .... TIZU

March .... SANGATSU
marriage .... KEKKON
marriage ceremony .... KEKKON SHIKI
May .... GOGATSU
meaning of sayonara .... SO BE IT
measure ...... BU, MO, RI, CHO, RIN, SHO, HIRO, SHAKU
meat .... NIKU
medicine .... KUSURI
midnight .... MAYONAKA
military caste .... SAMURAI
military code .... BUSHIDO
military governor ..... SHOGUN
military police organization .... KEMPEITAI
military service .... YOBI
milk (cow's) .... GYUUNYUU
milk (mother's) .... BONYUU
mint .... HAKKA
monastery .... TERA
Monday .... GETSUYOOBI
money .... SEN, YEN, OKANE
monk .... BONZE
monopolies .... ZAIBATSU
morning .... ASA
mother .... HAHA, OKAASAN
mountain .... ASO, ZAO, HAKU, KUJU, FUJI(YAMA), NASU, ASAHI, ASAMA, IWAKI, IWATE, UNZEN, BANDAI, CHOKAI, GASSEN, HAKKEN, HODAKA, KARIBA, KOMAGA, NANTAI, ONTAKE, TESHIO, SHIRANE, DAIMANJI
mouth .... KUTI
movie .... EIGA
movie theater .... EIGAKAN
mushroom .... SHIITAKE
musical instrument ...... KOTO, SAMISEN
mystic symbol .... SWASTIKA
nail (finger, toe) .... TSUME
name .... NAMAE
national park .... ASO, AKAN, NIKKO, SAIKAI, HAKUSAN, DAISEN-OKI, BANDAI-ASAHI
naval base .... KURE, SASEBO
near .... CHIKAI
neck .... KUBI
nephew .... OI, OIGOSAN
new .... ATARASHI
news agency .... JIJI, DOMEI, KYODO
newspaper .... SINBUN, SHIMBUN, YOMIURI, MAINICHI
next door .... TONARI
niece .... MEI, MEIGOSAN
night/nighttime .... BAN, YORU

nine .... KU, KYU
no .... IIE
nobility .... SAMURAI,
                        HATAMOTO
nobleman .... KAMI, KUGE,
                   DAIMIO, DAIMYO
nobody .... DARE MO
noodle shop .... SOBAYA
noodles .... SOBA, UDON
north .... KITA
number .... BANGOO
nurse .... KANGOFU
October .... JUGATSU
office .... KAISYA, ZIMUSYO
old .... HURUI
one .... ICHI
one-way .... KATAMITI
onion .... TAMANEGI
only .... DAKE
open .... AKERU
opera .... YUZURU
orange (color) .... DAIDAIIRO
out of order .... KOSYOO
outcast/outlaw .... YETA,
                              RONIN
outer garment .... MINO,
               HAORI, KIMONO
outside .... SOTO
over there .... ASOKO
pagoda .... TAA
painter .... HIROSHIGE
painting school .... KANO,
         TOSA, SHIJO, SESSHU
palanquin .... KAGO,
                    NORIMONO
paper art .... ORIGAMI
park .... KOOEN
parliament .... DIET
paste .... AME
pay .... HARAU
peach .... MOMO
pear .... NASHI
pearl .... SHINJU
pencil .... ENPIT(S)U
peninsula ..... IZU, OGA, NOTO,
               MIURA, OSUMI
people .... NIHONGIN,
                    NIPPONGIN
persimmon .... KAKI
pine .... MATSU
pink .... MOMOIRU
"Pittsburg" .... YAWATA
plant .... UDO, AUCUBA
play .... NOH, KABUKI
play musical instrument
.... HIKIMASU
please .... DO(O)ZO, KUDASAI
plum .... KAKI, KELSEY,
                     SUMOMO
plumlike fruit .... LOQUAT
P.M. (afternoon) .... GOGO

poem .... HAIKU
point .... ESAN, SOYA, SUZU,
          MUROTO, NOSAPPU
policeman .... KEIKAN
porgy .... TAI
pork .... BUTANIKU
porter .... AKABOO
postcard .... HAGAKI
potato .... JAGAIMO
pottery ...... AWATA, SATSUMA,
                   YAKIMONO
prefecture .... MIE, GIFU,
      NARA, OITA, SAGA, AKITA,
      KYOTO, OSAKA, SHIGA,
      TOKYO, MIYAGI, NAGANO,
      TOYAMA, FUKUOKA,
      OKAYAMA, OKINAWA,
      HOKKAIDO, YAMAGUCHI
premier .... SATO, TOJO,
      IKEDA, KAIFU, KISHI, OKADA,
      INUKAI, KONOYE, TANAKA,
                  NAKASONE
pretty .... KIREI, KIREE
primitive .... AINO
prune .... SUMOMO
pumpkin .... KABOCHA
puppet emperor of .... PU-YI
puppet show .... BUNRAKU
quietly .... SOTTO
rabbit .... USAGI
radish, pickled .... TAKUWAN
radish, white .... DAIKON
rain .... AME
raincoat .... MINO
raisin .... HOSHIBUDOO
raw fish .... SASIMI, SASHIMI
read .... YOMU
red .... AKAI
religion .... BUDDHISM,
                   SHINTOISM
religious dance .... NO
resort .... NIKKO, HAKONE
rest .... YASUMU
restaurant .... RYOORIYA
rice, cooked .... GOHAN
rice, uncooked .... KOME
rice-straw floor mat
.... TATAMI
rice wine .... SAKE
rice with fish, seaweed, etc.
.... SUSHI
right .... MIGI
river ...... ARA, EDO, INA, ONO,
      FUJI, KINO, MUKO, NAKA,
      OANI, TAMA, TONE, YODO,
      AGANO, OMONO, MOGAMI,
      OBITSU, SAGAMI, TOKACHI,
      YOSHINO, KITAKAMI
robe .... KIMONO
room .... HEYA
room divider .... SHOVI

rude .... SITUREE
sake-like wine .... SHOCHU
salmon .... MASU
salesgirl .... URIKO
salt .... SIO
salty .... KARAI
same .... ONAZI
samurai warlord .... BUSHI
samurai's code .... BUSHIDO
sandals .... ZORI
sash .... OBI
Saturday .... DOYOOBI
school .... GAKKO
screen .... BYOBU, SHOVI
script .... KANA
scroll .... KAKEMONO
sculptress .... (YOKO)ONO
sea .... IYO, SUO, HARIMA,
          SAGAMI, OKHOTSK
seal, business .... HANKO
seaport .... KOBE, KURE,
      OMUTA, OTARU, SAKATA,
      TOYAMA, YAWATAH,
      NAGASAKI, YOKOHAMA
seaweed .... KAISOO
secretary .... HISHO
sect .... ZEN
see .... MIRU, MITE
self-defense forces ...... JIEITAI
self-defense system ...... JUDO,
      KARATE, JUJITSU, JUJUTSU
September .... KUGATSU
sesame seed .... GOMA
sesame oil .... GOMA-ABURA
seven .... NANA, SHICHI
ship .... HUNE, MARU
shoe .... GETA
shoot, edible .... UDO
short .... MIJIKAI
shoulder .... KATA
show .... KABUKI
shrimp .... EBI
shrine .... JINJA, JINGUU,
               OYAMA-ZUMI
sick .... BYOOKI
sightseeing .... KEMBUTSU
sister .... ANE, IMOOTO
six .... ROKU
sky .... SORA
slang .... NIP
sleep .... NERU
slow .... OSOI
small .... TISAI, CHIISAI
snake .... HEBI
snow .... YUKI
soap .... SEKKEN
social reformer .... KAGAWA
sock .... TABI, TABO
sometimes .... TOKIDOKI
son .... MUSUKO
song .... UTA

ship of .... ARGO
sorceress who helped
.... MEDEA
uncle of .... PELIAS
wife of .... MEDEA, CREUSA
jasper .... MICA, PARK, QUARTZ
jaundice .... HATE, RANCOR,
ICTERUS, PREJUDICE
cause of .... ENVY, JEALOUSY
relating to .... ICTERIC
jaundiced .... BIASED, YELLOW
eye .... JEALOUSY
jaunt .... SALLY, EXCURSION,
ESCAPADE, (SIDE)TRIP
jaunty .... GAY, AIRY, CHIC,
COCKY, PERKY, SMART,
DAPPER, MODISH, RAKISH,
SPRUCE, STYLISH, DEBONAIR
Java .... HOOD, COFFEE, ISLAND,
CHICKEN
capital of .... JAKARTA
island .... MADURA
Javanese .... SUNDANESE,
INDONESIAN
almond .... KANARI
animal .... TELEDU
bat .... KALON
carriage .... SADO
city .... KEDIRI, MALANG,
MADIUN, BANDUNG,
SEMARANG, SURABAYA
civet .... DEDES, RASSE
cotton .... KAPOK
language .... KAVI, KAWI
man .... PITHECANTHROPUS
measure .... PALEN
mountain .... AMAT
ox .... BANTENG
pepper .... CUBEB
plum .... JAMAN, LOMBOY,
JAMBOOL
port .... TEGAL
rhinoceros .... BADAK
silk .... IKAT
skunk .... TELEDU
tree .... UPAS, KAPOK,
ANTIAR(IN)
upas .... ANTIAR
village .... DESSA
volcano .... GEDE, RAUNG,
SEMERU
weight ..... AMAT, HOEN, TALI,
WANG, PICUL
javelin ...... DART, LANCE, SHAFT,
SPEAR, JER(R)ID, ASSEGAI,
HARPOON, HURLBAT,
JER(R)EED
throwing device .... AMENTA
jaw ...... MAW, CHAP, CHAT, CHOP,
JOWL, MANDIBLE
angle of .... GONION

combining form
.... GNATHOUS
cover .... GUM(S)
device with .... VISE
flesh .... GILL
lower .... CHIN, GONION,
MANDIBLE
muscle .... MASSETER
of the .... GNATHIC
slang .... TALK, SCOLD
upper .... MAXILLA
without .... AGNATHIC
jawbone .... JOWL, MAXILLA
jawbreaker .... CANDY
in boxing .... HAYMAKER
jay .... PIE, CROW, JACKSON,
CHATTERBOX
bird like a .... MOTMOT
talk .... CHATTER
Jayhawk state .... KANSAS
Jayne's man .... STEVE
jazerant .... ARMOR
jazz .... BOP, BLUES, SWING,
(BE)POP, RAG(TIME),
BOOGIEWOOGIE
composer .... (DUKE)
ELLINGTON
dance .... SHIMMY
ensemble/group .... COMBO
fan .... HEPCAT, JITTERBUG
fan jargon .... JIVE
form .... BOP
music .... SWING
singing .... SCAT
slang .... NONSENSE
style of .... DIXIELAND
time .... STOMP
Jazzman Getz .... STAN
jealous ...... ENVIOUS, JAUNDICED,
GREEN(EYED)
jeans .... LEVIS, DENIMS,
OVERALLS, TROUSERS
material .... DENIM
Jebel Musa .... MOUNTAIN OF
MOSES
believed to be .... MOUNT
SINAI
jeep .... PEEP
jeer .... BOO, GIBE, HOOT, JAPE,
JEST, JIBE, MOCK, FLOUT,
SCOFF, SNEER, TAUNT,
DERIDE, CATCALL, SARCASM
jeers .... TACKLE
Jeeves, boss of .... BERTIE
WOOSTER
creator of .... WODEHOUSE
position of .... BUTLER
Jefferson's (President) home
.... MONTICELLO
Jeffries, prize-fighter .... JIM
Jehovah .... GOD, JAH, YAHVE(H),

YAHWE(H), (THE)LORD
prophet of .... ELIAS
Jehovah's Witnesses founder
.... RUSSELL
jejune .... DRY, ARID, DULL, FLAT,
BANAL, STALE, BARREN,
INSIPID
Jekyll's (Dr.) alter ego
.... (MR.)HYDE
jell .... SET, CONGEAL, SOLIDIFY
jellied gasoline .... NAPALM
jelly .... JAM, ASPIC, SPREAD,
DESSERT, PRESERVES
animal .... GELATINE
delicacy/clear .... ASPIC
doughnut .... BISMARK
fruit .... JAM, GUAVA
like substance .... GEL,
COLLOID, GELATIN
material .... CURRANT
petroleum .... VASELINE
vegetable .... PECTIN
jellybean .... CANDY
jellyfish .... MEDUSA, ACALEPH,
AURELIA, HYDROZOAN, SEA
NETTLE
disk .... PILEUS
stinging cell ..... NEMATOCYST
jellyroll .... CAKE
jennet .... ASS, HORSE, DONKEY
Jenny, singer .... LIND, WREN
jeopardize .... RISK, IMPERIL,
ENDANGER
jeopardy .... RISK, PERIL,
DANGER, HAZARD
jerboa .... RODENT, GERBIL(LE)
jeremiad .... WOE, TALE,
LAMENT(ATION)
Jeremiah's scribe .... BARUCH
Jericho's betrayer .... RAHAB
jerk .... BOB, BEEF, FLIP, JUMP,
MEAT, PULL, SNAP, YANK,
HITCH, TWEAK, TWIST,
TWITCH, SODA MAN
jerkin .... COAT, VEST, JACKET
Jerry .... HUN, GERMAN
actor-comedian .... LEWIS
Jersey .... CLOTH, SHIRT, CATTLE,
SINGLET, SWEATER
Jerusalem .... ARIEL, SALEM,
(HOLY)CITY
artichoke .... GIRASOL(E)
captor of .... SALADIN
hill/mount .... SION, ZION
mosque .... OMAR
oak .... AMBROSE
pool .... BETHESDA
ridge .... OLIVET
spring .... SILOAM
stream .... KEDRON
theater .... KHAN

thorn tree .... RETAMA

Jespersen's language .... IDO

jess .... LEASH, STRAP

user of .... FALCON(ER)

jest .... GAG, PUN, WIT, JAPE, JEER, JIBE, JOKE, MOCK, QUIP, SALLY, BANTER, TRIFLE, BADINAGE, RAILLERY

jester .... WAG, FOOL, MIME, ZANY, CLOWN, JOKER, GAGMAN, BUFFOON, GOLIARD, COMEDIAN

cap of .... COXCOMB, COCKSCOMB

garment of .... MOTLEY

Jesuit .... CASUIST, SCHEMER

order founder .... LOYOLA

saint .... REGIS

Jesus .... LOGOS, SAVIO(U)R

agony and suffering .... PASSION

betrayer of .... JUDAS ISCARIOT

birthplace of .... BETHLEHEM

Christ, _____ .... SUPERSTAR

life's event .... MYSTERY

monogram .... IHS

of ____ .... NAZARETH

sayings of .... LOGIA

jet .... EBON(Y), GUSH, SPEW, BLACK, RAVEN, SPOUT, SPRAY, SPURT, NOZZLE, SQUIRT, STREAM, LIGNITE

boom .... SONIC

engine .... TURBO PROP

engine housing .... POD

fast .... SST

follower .... SET

plane .... SABRE

jetsam .... LAGAN, LIGAN, LAGEND, JETTISON

jettison .... JETSAM, DISCARD

jetty .... MOLE, PIER, BLACK, WHARF, STARLING

jeu .... GAME

de mots .... PUN

Jew ...... TOBIT, HEBREW, JUDEAN, SEMITE, ISRAELITE

born in Israel .... SABRA

legendary .... GOLEM

not a .... GOI, GOY(IM), GENTILE

pseudo-Christian .... MARRANO

Shakespearean .... TUBAL

jewel .... GEM, NAIF, OPAL, BIJOU, STONE, TRINKET, BRILLIANT

Biblical .... BDELLIUM

colorful .... RED CORAL

setting .... PAVE, BEZEL, MOUNT(ING)

jeweler's glass .... LOUPE

weight/unit ..... CARAT, KARAT

jewelry .... ICE, QUOIN, JEWELS, BIJOUTERIE

artificial .... PASTE, STRASS

expert .... LAPIDARY, APPRAISER, GEMOLOGIST

item .... PIN, TIARA, BROOCH, DIADEM, (EAR)RING, PENDANT, TRINKET, BRACELET, NECKLACE

making material .... GEM, TOPAZ, ORMOLU, OROIDE, TOMBAC(K), AMETHYST, CORUNDUM

set of .... PARURE

jewels, adorn with .... BEGEM

collectively .... JEWELRY

jewelweed .... CELANDINE, IMPATIENS

Jewett, writer .... SARAH

jewfish ...... BASS, MERO, TARPON

Jewish .... HEBREW, JUDAIC, JUDEAN, YIDDISH

ascetic .... ESSENE

benediction .... SHEMA

bread .... MATZOS, CHALLAH, MATZOTH

bread roll .... BAGEL

breastplate gem .... LIGURE, SARDIUS

bride .... KALLAH

calendar month ...... AB, ABIB, ADAR, ELUL, IYAR, (ZIF), NISAN, SIVAN, TEBET, KISLEV, SHEBAT, TAMMUZ, TISHRI, CHESHVAN

cantor .... CHAZ(Z)AN

Christians .... DIASPORA

cleric .... RABBI

commentaries on Scriptures .... MIDRASH

court .... SANHEDRIN

day .... YOM

Day of Atonement .... YOM KIPPUR

day of preparation ..... FRIDAY

demon .... ASMODEUS

Feast of Lots .... PURIM

festival .... PURIM, SEDER

Festival of Tabernacles .... SUCCOTH, SUKKOTH

high priest .... ELI, EZRA

holiday .... PURIM, PESACH, SUCCOS, PASSOVER, YOM KIPPUR

Holy of Holies .... ORACLE

language .... HEBREW, YIDDISH

law .... TORAH, TALMUD

liturgy's first word ..... SHEMA

marriage broker .... SCHATCHEN

measure .... SEAH

month, extra .... VEADAR

New Year .... ROSH HASHANAH, ROSH HASHONA

pancake .... LATKE

Passover .... PESACH

"penicillin" .... CHICKEN SOUP

Pentecost .... SABUOTH

people ...... SION, ZION, ISRAEL

philosophy .... CABALA

prayer book .... MAHZOR, SIDDUR

priest's girdle .... ABNET

priest's vestment .... EPHOD

quarter .... GHETTO

ram's horn .... SHOFAR

religion .... JUDAISM

religious party composed of priests .... SADDUCEES

religious party during the times of Jesus .... PHARISEES

religious service .... HALLEL

scarf .... TALLIT(H)

scholar .... RAB(BI)

school .... CHEDER, YESHIVA

scribe .... MASORITE

sect member .... PHARISEE, SADDUCEE

seminary .... YESHIVA

seventh day of week .... SABBATH

skullcap .... YAMILKE, YARMELKE, YARMULKE

slang .... YIDDISH

spices .... STACTES

teacher .... RAB(BI), SCRIBE

temple builder .... MICAH, SOLOMON

title of honor .... RAB, GAON

trumpet ..... SHOFAR, SHOPHAR

undergarment .... TALLITH

vestment .... EPHOD

weight .... OMER, GERAH

Jews' dispersion .... DIASPORA

cloak .... GABARDINE

evensong .... MINHAN

harp .... CREMBALUM

massacre .... POGROM

of the .... JUDAIC

savior .... MORDECAI

section of city .... GHETTO

Jezebel .... VIRAGO

describing .... EVIL, WICKED

husband of .... AHAB

victim of .... NABOTH

jib .... SHY, BALK, BOOM, SAIL, SPAR, SIDLE, START

jibe .... FIT, RIB, JEST, JEER, AGREE, SCOFF, TAUNT

jiffy .... TRICE, MOMENT, SECOND,

INSTANT
jig .... DANCE, GIGUE, FISHHOOK
jigger ...... CUP, FLEA, SAIL, SHOT,
TICK, CHIGOE, TACKLE
jiggle .... JERK, ROCK, TEETER
jihad .... CRUSADE, HOLY WAR
jill .... GIRL, SWEETHEART
jilt ...... DUMP, REJECT, BOOT OUT,
CAST OFF
jilted .... SENT PACKING, GIVEN
THE AIR
Jim Crow .... NEGRO
jimjams .... JITTERS
jimmy .... PRY, JACK, LEVER,
(CROW)BAR
Jimmy, pantomimist .... SAVO
tennis player .... CONNORS
jimson ...... DATURA, STINKWEED,
THORN APPLE
jingal .... CANNON, MUSKET
jingle .... CLINK, DITTY, VERSE,
TINKLE, DOGGEREL
jingo .... RADICAL, WARRIOR,
CHAUVINIST, MILITARIST
jingoism .... MILITARISM
jinks .... PRANKS, HORSEPLAY
jinn(i) .... DEMON, GENIE
jinrikisha .... RICKSHA(W)
Jinsen .... CHEMULPHO
jinx .... HEX, CURSE, HOODOO,
BAD LUCK, EVIL EYE
personification of .... JONAH
slang .... WHAMMY
jipijapa hat .... PANAMA
jitney .... BUS, NICKEL
jitter .... FIDGET, TWITCH
jitters .... NERVES, DITHERS,
HYSTERIA, NERVOUSNESS
the .... CREEPS, SHAKES,
FIDGETS, JIMJAMS, WILLIES,
(BIG)SCARE, HEEBIE-JEEBIES
jittery .... EDGY, JUMPY, ON EDGE,
SCARED, NERVOUS
jiujutsu .... JUDO
jivatma .... EGO, ATMAN
jive .... JAZZ
Joan of Arc .... PUCELLE
_____ of Orleans .... MAID
scene of triumph .... ORLEANS
job ...... DUTY, LINE, POST, STINT,
TASK, WORK, CHARE, CHORE,
CALLING, POSITION,
OCCUPATION
at Disney Studios
.... ANIMATING
choice .... PLUM
do inferior .... SCAMP
easy .... SNAP, SINECURE
opening .... VACANCY
permanence .... TENURE
Job's comforter .... BILDAD,

ELIHU, ZOPHAR
jockey ...... CHEAT, RACER, RIDER,
TRICK, MANEUVER
aid of .... CROP
famous .... AVILA, BAEZA,
SANDE, SLOAN, ARCARO,
BROOKS, DODSON, CAUTHEN,
CRUGUET, HARTACK,
MEHRTENS, TURCOTTE,
SHOEMAKER
uniform .... SILKS, COLORS
woman .... CRUMP, RUBIN,
KUSNER
jocko .... CHIMP, MONKEY
jocose .... DROLL, MERRY, WITTY,
PLAYFUL, FACETIOUS
jocular .... WITTY, JESTING,
WAGGISH, HUMOROUS,
FACETIOUS
jocund .... GAY, AIRY, GENIAL
Jodhpur .... MARWAR
jodhpurs .... BREECHES
joe .... SWEETHEART
Joel's follower .... AMOS
joey .... PAL, KANGAROO
jog .... TROT, AMBLE, SHAKE,
JIGGLE, REMIND
jogging suits .... SWEATS
John .... AGAR, DALY, DREW,
ALDEN, KEATS, LOCKE,
PAYNE, SAXON, WAYNE,
CALVIN, LENNON, GILBERT,
IRELAND, BARRYMORE
Birch society founder
.... WELCH
Brown's Body author
.... BENET
Bull .... ENGLAND,
ENGLISHMAN
Dory .... FISH
Dos _____ .... PASSOS
Dos Passos novel
.... MANHATTAN TRANSFER
father of disciple ..... ZEBEDEE
Hancock .... SIGNATURE
Irish .... IAN
_____ Jones .... PAUL
Paul's land .... POL
Silver's forte
.... SKULDUGGERY
Smith's savior
.... POCAHONTAS
the Baptist's father
.... ZECHARIAH
the Baptist's mother
.... ELIZABETH
unknown .... DOE
johnnie .... BOY, FOP, MAN,
DANDY, LOTHARIO
Johnny .... CASH, CARSON
johnny jumper .... PANSY,

VIOLET
johnnycake .... PONE, CORNBREAD
Johnson (Mrs.), hunter ...... OSA
U.S. President .... ANDREW,
LYNDON
joie de vivre .... ELAN
join ...... ADD, ABUT, LINK, MELD,
WELD, YOKE, ENTER, MERGE,
UNITE, ENROLL, FASTEN,
RABBET, SOLDER, SPLICE,
COMBINE, CONNECT, MORTISE,
COALESCE
a cause .... ENLIST
corners .... MITER, MITRE
in the chorus .... SING
in wedlock .... MARRY
the colors .... ENLIST
together .... FUSE
joiner .... ENLISTEE, FOLLOWER
joint ...... HIP, KNEE, LINK, SEAM,
ANKLE, ELBOW, NEXUS,
TENON, RABBET, TOGGLE,
JUNCTURE
arm's .... ELBOW, WRIST
carpenter's .... MITER, MITRE
cavity .... BURSA
deposit .... TOPHUS
door's .... HINGE
finger .... KNUCKLE
fluid .... SEROSITY
grass .... CULM
out of .... DISLOCATED
overlapping .... SHIPLAP
part .... TENON, TISSUE,
CARTILAGE, LIGAMENTS
partial dislocation of
.... SUBLUXATION
piping/tubing .... ELL
put out of .... LUXATE,
DISLOCATE
rheumatic pain ...... LUMBAGO,
ARTHRITIS
slang .... DIVE, REEFER,
SALOON, RESTAURANT
stem .... NODE
tighten .... STEM
type of .... HINGE, PIVOT,
ELLIPSOIDAL, BALL AND
SOCKET
jointly .... TOGETHER, HAND IN
HAND
joist .... BEAM
joke .... GAG, KID, PUN, RIB, DIDO,
HOAX, JAPE, JEST, JOSH, QUIP,
TWIT, PRANK, SALLY, SPOOF,
WAGGERY, WISECRACK,
WITTICISM
joker ...... GAG, WAG, WIT, CARD,
FLOP, CLOWN, CUTUP, JESTER,
BUFFOON, FARCEUR
in a bill, etc. .... RIDER

jollity .... FUN, MIRTH, GAIETY
jolly .... GAY, BOAT, YAWL,
MERRY, SKIFF, JOVIAL,
JOYOUS, CONVIVIAL
season .... YULE
Jolson, Al .... ASA
jolt ...... JAR, BUMP, JERK, SHAKE,
SHOCK, SURPRISE
Jonah (Jonas) .... PROPHET
to all people .... JINX, BAD
LUCK
Jonas, polio vaccine developer
.... SALK
Jonathan .... APPLE
brother of .... ABINADAB,
MALCHISHUA
father of .... SAUL
Jones, bandleader .... SPIKE
spirit of sea .... DAVY
jongleur .... MINSTREL
jonquil .... NARCISSUS
Joplin, pop singer .... JANIS
Jordan .... POT, EDOM, MOAB,
RIVER, KINGDOM
capital of .... AMMAN
city/town .... AJLUN, AQABA,
IRBID, PETRA, JARASH, ES
SALT, MADABA, NABLUS, EL
KARAK, EZ ZARKA
gulf .... AQABA
king .... HUSSEIN
language .... ARABIC
monetary unit .... DINAR
mountain .... EBAL, NEBO,
RAMM, GILEAD
peninsula .... EL LISAN
port .... AQABA
river .... ZARQA, JORDAN
ruins .... PETRA
sea .... DEAD
valley .... GHOR
Joseph .... HABIT
brother of .... BENJAMIN
Egyptian master of
.... POTIPHAR
Egyptian name of
.... ZAPENATH PANEAH
father of .... JACOB, ISRAEL
grandson of ...... EZER, ELEAD,
ASRIEL, BERIAH, MACHIR
hometown of .... ARIMATHEA
mother of .... RACHEL
of Nazareth's wife ..... MARY
wife of .... ASENATH
josh .... KID, RAG, RIB, JEST,
TEASE, BANTER
Joshua, father of .... NUN
people of .... ISRAELITES
predecessor of .... MOSES
tree .... YUCCA
Josip Broz .... TITO, DICTATOR

joss .... IDOL
house .... TEMPLE
jostle .... ELBOW, NUDGE, HUSTLE,
SHOVE, BUFFET
jot .... BIT, IOTA, MITE, MOTE,
NOTE, WHIT, MINIM, POINT,
SPECK, TITTLE, PARTICLE
jota .... DANCE
jotting .... MEMO, NOTE
Jotun(n) .... GIANT
joule, part of .... ERG
jounce .... JOLT, SHAKE
journal .... DIARY, ANNALS,
RECORD, DAYBOOK,
LOGBOOK, MAGAZINE,
REGISTER, NEWSPAPER
journalism .... PRESS, FOURTH
ESTATE
journalist .... EDITOR, SCRIBE,
DIARIST, NEWSMAN,
REPORTER, PUBLICIST,
NEWSPAPERMAN
abolitionist 1852 ..... REDPATH
budding .... CUB, COPYBOY
kind of .... LEGMAN, STRINGER
Runyon .... DAMON
journey .... TREK, TRIP, TOUR,
JUNKET, SAFARI, TRAVEL
end of .... HOMESTRETCH
extended .... ODYSSEY
for adventure .... QUEST
forced .... EXODUS, FLIGHT,
HEGIRA
man .... TRAVEL AGENT
of a .... VIATIC(AL)
of solon abroad .... JUNKET
over snow .... MUSH
part of/stage of .... LEG
stopping place ..... INN, OASIS,
SERAI, STAGE, IMARET
to shrine .... PILGRIMAGE
water .... VOYAGE, PASSAGE
journeyman .... JOBBER, WORKER
joust .... BOUT, TILT, COMBAT,
TOURNEY, TOURNAMENT
jousting arena .... LISTS
Jove .... JUPITER
jovial .... GAY, JOLLY, MERRY,
GENIAL, CORDIAL
friar .... TUCK
jowl .... CHAP, CHOP, CHEEK,
DEWLAP, WATTLE, JAW(BONE)
joy .... GLEE, BLISS, DELIGHT,
ECSTASY, ELATION, RAPTURE
ride, of a sort .... SPIN
song of .... CAROL, P(A)EAN
Joy Adamson's pet .... ELSA
joyful in triumph ...... JUBILANT
joyous .... GAY, GLAD, MERRY,
RIANT, BLITHE, FESTAL,
FESTIVE

jube .... LOFT, GALLERY
jubilee .... ANNIVERSARY
juca .... MANIOC, CASSAVA
Judah, brother of .... LEVI,
REUBEN, SIMEON, ZEBULUN,
ISSACHAR
capital of .... JERUSALEM
city of .... HEBRON, ADAR,
AMAN, ENAM, LACHISH, BEER-
SHEBA
daughter-in-law of ..... TAMAR
father of .... JACOB, ISRAEL
governor of .... GEDALIAH
king of ..... ASA, AHAZ, AMON,
JOASH, ABIJAM, JOSIAH,
JOTHAM, UZZIAH, AHAZIAH,
ZEDEKIAH, AMAZIAH,
JEHORAM, HEZEKIAH,
JEHOAHAZ, MANASSEH,
REHOBOAM, JEHOIACHIN,
JEHOSHAPHAT
mother of .... LEAH
queen of .... ATHALIAH
ruling dynasty of ..... DAVIDIC
sister of .... DINAH
son of .... ER, ONAN, PEREZ,
ZERAH, SHELAH
tree of .... REDBUD
vassal state of .... EDOM
wife of .... BATHSHUA
Judaism .... HEBRAISM
convert to .... GER
hymn of praise .... KADDISH
of/pertaining to .... JUDAIC
scriptures .... TORA(H)
Judas .... APOSTLE, BETRAYER
_____ .... ISCARIOT,
BARSABBAS, MACCABEUS
brother of .... JAMES, JESUS,
SIMON
Iscariot's death place
.... FIELD OF BLOOD
motive for betrayal
.... GREED, THIRTY PIECES
SILVER
replacement .... MATTHIAS
symbol of treachery
.... (DEADLY) KISS
Maccabeus' brother .... JOHN,
SIMON, ELEAZAR, JONATHAN
father .... MATTATHIAS
or _____, apostle of Jesus
.... THADDAEUS
tree .... REDBUD
Judea procurator .... PILATE
vale .... ELAH
judge .... TRY, DEEM, (A)EDILE,
CRITIC, UMPIRE, ARBITER,
REFEREE, DELIVERER,
ARBITRATOR
biblical .... ELI, EHUD, ELON,

JAIR, TOLA, ABDON, IBZAN, GIDEON, SAMSON, DEBORAH, OTHNIEL, SHAMGAR, JEPHTHAH
court .... TRIER
of lower world .... MINOS, AEACUS
quality/worth .... APPRAISE
judge's assistant .... ASSESSOR
bench .... BANC, TRIBUNAL
challenge .... RECUSE
chamber .... CAMERA
decision .... VERDICT, SENTENCE
lower rank .... PUISNE
order .... WRIT, SUBPOENA, INJUNCTION
robe .... GOWN
room .... CHAMBER
seat .... BANC, BENCH
symbol of authority .... MACE, GAVEL
judges, collectively .... BENCH, JUDICIARY
Rabelais' satirical term for .... FURRY LAWCATS
said of .... PUISNE
judgment .... DOOM, VIEW, ARRET, AWARD, SENSE, DECREE, RULING, FINDING, OPINION, VERDICT, DECISION, SENTENCE
against property .... IN REM
suspension of .... EPOCHE
Judgment Day ...... DOOM(SDAY)
judicial assembly .... COURT
inquiry .... INQUEST
mallet .... GAVEL
opinions .... DICTA
order .... WRIT
wear .... ROBE
writ of execution .... ELEGIT
judicious .... WISE, SOUND, POLITIC, PRUDENT
**Judith, the ____ supreme
heroine .... APOCRYPHA'S
victim of .... HOLOFERNES
judo .... JUJITSU
Judy's husband .... PUNCH
jug .... URN, EWER, TOBY, BOTTLE, FLAGON, RANTER, PITCHER, THERMOS
slang .... JAIL
jugal .... MALAR
Juggernaut .... KRISHNA
incarnation .... VISHNU
juggle .... RIG, MANIPULATE
juggler .... CHEATER, MANIPULATOR
juice .... JUS, SAP, MUST, RHOB, STUM, FLUID, LIQUID, ESSENCE

meat .... GRAVY, DRIPPING
plant/tree .... SAP, LATEX, MANNA, CHICLE
slang .... GAS, OIL, ELECTRICITY
juicy .... RACY, RICH, MOIST, TASTY, SUCCULENT
Juilliard school degree .... DMUS
specialty .... MUSIC
jujitsu/jiujutsu .... JUDO
juju .... CHARM, TABOO, FETISH
jujube .... BER, ELB, JELLY, LOZENGE
jukebox .... PHONOGRAPH
julep .... DRINK
ingredient .... MINT, SYRUP, BRANDY
Jules Verne's captain ...... NEMO
vessel .... NAUTILUS
Julia Ward .... HOWE
Juliana's (Queen) domain .... NETHERLANDS
house .... ORANGE
mother .... WILHELMINA
people .... DUTCH
spouse .... BERNHARD
julienne .... SOUP
cut .... (THIN) STRIPS
Juliet's confessor .... (FRIAR) LAURENCE
cousin .... TYBALT
family (name) .... CAPULET
love .... ROMEO
suitor .... PARIS
July 15, Roman calendar .... IDES, IDUS, IDIBUS
4th day .... INDEPENDENCE
7th day of ..... NONAS, NONES, NONIS
jumble .... MIX, HASH, MESS, COOKY, LITTER, MEDLEY, MUDDLE, CLUTTER, MISHMASH
jumbled type .... PI(E)
jumbo .... HUGE, LARGE, ELEPHANT
jump ...... BOB, HOP, BUCK, JERK, LEAP, SKIP, BOUND, START, VAULT, BOUNCE, SPRING
about .... FRISK, PRANCE
ahead, a .... ONE UP
in music .... SALTO
playful .... CAPER, FRISK, CAVORT, PRANCE
the track .... DERAIL
jumper ...... PAWL, SLED, BLOUSE, JACKET, ROMPER
accessory of .... POLE
jumping .... LEAPING, SALTANT
amphibian .... FROG, TOAD
animal .... GOAT, JERBOA, KANGAROO

dance .... JIG
insect .... FLEA, LOCUST, GRASSHOPPER
stick .... POGO
jumpy ...... EDGY, TENSE, JITTERY, NERVOUS, SKITTISH
junco .... FINCH, SNOWBIRD
junction .... UNION, MEETING, CROSSING
line .... SEAM
juncture ...... JOINT, POINT, CRISIS
June bug .... DOR, BEETLE, FIGEATER
event ..... WEDDING, MARRIAGE
14, in America ...... FLAG DAY
honorees .... DADS
promise .... I DO
6, 1944 .... D-DAY
13, Roman calendar ...... IDES
21 .... SOLSTICE
juneberry .... SHADBUSH
jungfrau .... ALPS
jungle .... WILDERNESS
fever .... MALARIA
hero .... TARZAN
Jungle Book's wolf .... AKELA
Jungles a la Kipling ...... RUKHS
junior .... CADET, PUISNE, YOUNGER
leaguer .... DEB
juniper .... CADE, EZEL, CEDAR, GORSE, RETEM, SHRUB, SAVIN(E), HACKMATAK
junk .... BOAT, SCRAP, STUFF, TRASH, DISCARD, RUBBISH
jalopy .... CRATE
part .... SAIL
junker .... GERMAN, PRUSSIAN
junket .... FEAST, PICNIC, JOURNEY, EXCURSION
junkie ...... ADDICT, (DOPE) FIEND
junkman .... SCRAPPER
Juno .... HERA, GODDESS
husband of .... JUPITER
messenger of .... IRIS
junta .... GROUP, CLIQUE, COUNCIL, ASSEMBLY
junto .... CABAL, CLIQUE
Jupiter .... JOVE, ZEUS, PLANET
consort of .... HERA, JUNO
daughter .... HEBE, MINERVA
has twelve .... MOONS
moon of .... IO, EUROPA, CALLISTO, GANYMEDE
mother of .... OPS
nurse of .... GOAT
son of .... ARCAS, CASTER, HERMES, TANTALUS, HEPHAETUS
temple .... CAPITOL
jupon .... TUNIC, JACKET

Jurassic, strata below ...... TRIAS
   system strata .... LIAS
jurisdiction .... SOC, SOKE,
   VENUE, DOMAIN, SPHERE,
   CONTROL, BAILIWICK
   bishop's .... SEE
jurisprudence .... LAW
jurist .... HAND, JUDGE, TANEY
juror .... TALESMAN, VENIREMAN
   challenge a .... RECUSE
   guard of .... BAILIFF
jurors, collectively .... PANEL
   one of the .... POLL
jury .... PANEL
   finding of .... VERDICT
   fixer .... SUBORNER
   head .... FOREMAN
   illegally influence
   .... EMBRACE
   kind of .... PETIT, GRAND
   member .... TALESMAN
   -rig .... IMPROVISE
   -rigged .... MAKESHIFT
   summons to .... VENIRE
jus .... LAW, GRAVE, JUICE
just .... FAIR, ONLY, LEGAL,
   MORAL, VALID, BARELY,
   HONEST, SIMPLY, UPRIGHT,
   EQUITABLE, IMPARTIAL,
   RIGHTEOUS
   a touch .... TRACE
   as said .... SIC
   average .... SO-SO
   beginning .... INCIPIENT
   begun .... INCHOATE
   clear of bottom .... ATRIP,
   AWEIGH
   right .... JAKE
   think! .... IMAGINE
justice .... EQUITY, FAIRNESS,
   JUSTNESS, RIGHTNESS
   colloquial .... SQUARE DEAL
   symbol .... SCALE(S)
   U.S. Supreme Court ...... JAY,
   TAFT, BLACK, CHASE, STONE,
   TANEY, WHITE, FORTAS,
   HUGHES, SCALIA, SOUTER,
   THOMAS, VINSON, WARREN,
   CARDOZO, KENNEDY, STEVENS,
   STEWART, MARSHALL,
   BLACKMUN, O'CONNOR,
   REHNQUIST
justification .... EXCUSE, REASON,
   DEFENSE

justify .... ACQUIT, EXCUSE,
   ABSOLVE, WARRANT,
   VINDICATE, RATIONALIZE
jut .... ABUT, PROJECT, OVERHANG,
   PROTRUDE, STICK OUT
jute .... FIBER, PLANT, BALINE
   chief .... HENGIST
   cloth .... GUNNY
   product .... MAT, ROPE,
   BURLAP, (GUNNY)SACK
   refuse .... TOW, HURDS
Jutland seaport .... AARHUS
Jutlander .... DANE
jutting land .... CAPE, NESS,
   HEADLAND, PROMONTORY
   rock .... TOR, CRAG
jutty .... MOLE, PIER, JETTY
Juvenal .... POET, SATIRIST
juvenile .... CHILD, IMMATURE,
   YOUTHFUL, INFANTILE,
   YOUNG(STER)
   book heroine .... OZMA
   hero .... ROLLO
   story writer .... MILNE, OUIDA,
   RAMEE, SEUSS
juxtapose .... NEIGHBOR

K, Greek .... KAPPA
   Hebrew .... KAPH
   in a sequence .... ELEVENTH
   assaying .... CARAT
   chemistry .... POTASSIUM
   chess .... KING
   electricity .... CAPACITY
   mathematics .... CONSTANT
   meteorology .... SMOKE
   nautical usage .... KNOT
kabobs .... (ROAST) MEAT
kaddish .... HYMN, PRAYER
kadi .... JUDGE, MAGISTRATE
Kaffir .... CORN, BANTU, FODDER,
   INFIDEL, SORGHUM
   language .... XOSA
   tribe .... ZULU
   war club .... KIRI
   warriors .... IMPI
kaftan .... ROBE
kago .... LITTER, PALANQUIN
kail .... COLE, KALE
Kailasa temple .... ELLORA
kailyard .... GARDEN
kaiser .... EMPEROR, WILHELM
   Biblical .... NOAH
kaka(po) .... PARROT
Kalahari .... DESERT, PLATEAU

   nomad .... BUSHMAN
kale .... BROTH, GREENS,
   CABBAGE, COLLARD,
   BORECOLE, BROCCOLI,
   COLE(WORT)
   slang .... MONEY
Kalinin .... TVER
kalinite .... ALUM
Kallikaks, the .... JUKES
kalmuck ...... ELEUT(H), MONGOL
kalong .... BAT
kalpak .... CAP
kamerad .... COMRADE
kamsin .... WIND
kanaka .... HAWAIIAN
kanari .... ALMOND
kangaroo .... ROO, JUMPER,
   WOLABA, WOLARU, WALLABY,
   WALLAROO
   court .... MOCK COURT
   describing a .... MARSUPIAL
   male .... BOOMER
   pouch .... MARSUPIUM
   rat .... POTOROO
   reddish-gray .... EURO
   young .... JOEY
Kansan .... JAYHAWKER
   famous .... EISENHOWER

Kansas, capital of .... TOPEKA
   city/town .... GOVE, HAYS,
   DODGE, PRATT, GARDEN,
   KANSAS, OAKLEY, OTTAWA,
   SALINA, SENECA, ABILENE,
   CHANUTE, EMPORIA, LIBERAL,
   RUSSELL, SHAWNEE, WICHITA,
   ARKANSAS, EL DORADO,
   LAWRENCE, CONCORDIA,
   MANHATTAN, PITTSBURG,
   GREAT BEND, LEAVENWORTH
   college .... TABOR, BETHEL,
   BETHANY, MARYMOUNT,
   MCPHERSON
   county ..... FORD, GOVE, RENO,
   ALLEN, ELLIS, GEARY, OSAGE,
   ROOKS, BARTON, BUTLER,
   COWLEY, FINNEY, HARVEY,
   SALINE, SUMNER, BOURBON,
   DOUGLAS, JOHNSON, LABETTE,
   ATCHISON, CRAWFORD,
   SEDGWICK, DICKINSON,
   MCPHERSON, WYANDOTTE,
   LEAVENWORTH
   historic site .... EISENHOWER
   CENTER, LITTLE HOUSE ON
   THE PRAIRIE
   lake .... PERRY, POMONA,

WILSON, MILFORD, TORONTO, KANAPOLIS
mountain .... SUNFLOWER
native .... JAYHAWKER
output .... WHEAT
river .... ELK, FALL, OSAGE, KANSAS, PAWNEE, SOLOMON, ARKANSAS, MISSOURI
state bird .... MEADOWLARK
state flower .... SUNFLOWER
state nickname .... JAYHAWKER, SUNFLOWER
state tree .... COTTONWOOD
university .... BAKER, OTTAWA, FRIENDS, WASHBURN
kaolin(e) .... CLAY
Kapek drama .... RUR
kapok .... CEIBA, COTTON
kaput .... FINI, LOST, RUINED, DONE FOR, DEFEATED
Karachi is its capital .... SIND
Karafuto .... SAKHALIN
karakul .... FUR, OVINE, SHEEP
Karelian .... FINN
lake .... SEG, LADOGA
Karenina, _____ .... ANNA
Karloff, actor .... BORIS
Karlovasi citizen .... SAMIAN
Karlovy Vary .... CARLSBAD
karma .... FATE, DESTINY
Karnak city .... THEBES
Kashmir, capital of .... SRINAGAR
claimant of .... INDIA, PAKISTAN
district .... LADAKH
pagoda .... CHORTEN
river .... JHELUM
wool .... CASHMERE
Katanga leader .... TSHOMBE
Katherine, diminutive of .... KAY, KATE, KIT(TY)
Katmandu is capital of .... NEPAL
native .... NEPALI
kauri .... GUM, PINE, RESIN
kava .... SHRUB, PEPPER
Kay Kyser's Kabibble .... ISH
kayak .... CANOE, UMIAK
kayo .... KNOCKOUT
Kazan, movieman .... ELIA
kea .... PARROT
favorite prey of .... SHEEP
Keats .... ODIST
Keats' concern .... URN
name by Shelley ..... ADONAIS
poem .... LAMIA
kedge .... ANCHOR
keek .... SPY, PEEP
keel ...... LIST, SHIP, TILT, BARGE, CAREEN, RUDDLE, LIGHTER
like structure .... CARINA

over ..... UPSET, CAPSIZE, TURN OVER
part .... SKEG
shaped .... CARINATE
without .... RATITE
Keeling Islands .... COCOS
keen .... WAIL, ACUTE, DIRGE, EAGER, SHARP, SMART, ASTUTE, SHREWD, SUBTLE, CUTTING, PUNGENT, INCISIVE, PERCEPTIVE
eyed animal .... CAT, LYNX
keenly perceptive .... SHARP-EYED
keenness .... EDGE, ACUITY
of mind .... ACUMEN
keep .... FORT, HAVE, SAVE, TEND, CASTLE, DETAIN, DONJON, RETAIN, CUSTODY, POSSESS, RESERVE, (WITH)HOLD, LIVELIHOOD
an eye on .... WATCH
at it .... PERSIST, PERSEVERE
company .... HOBNOB, CONSORT
from .... AVOID, DETER
from flying .... GROUND
going .... RUN ON, CONTINUE
house for oneself .... BACH
in mind .... CHERISH
in touch .... WRITE
off .... BAR
one's fingers crossed .... HOPE
out .... BAN, OMIT, (DE)BAR, EXCLUDE
score .... TALLY
secret .... SIT ON
under close observation .... TAIL
under _____ (conceal) .... ONE'S HAT
keeper .... JAILER, GUARD(IAN), CARETAKER, CUSTODIAN, PROTECTOR
concern of .... ZOO
forest .... RANGER, WARDEN
game .... WARDEN
jail .... WARDEN, TURNKEY
museum .... CURATOR
keepers, usually .... FINDERS
keeping .... CARE, CUSTODY
keepsake .... RELIC, TOKEN, MEMENTO, SOUVENIR
keeve .... TUB, VAT, KEIR
kef .... HEMP, NARCOTIC
Kefauver, senator .... ESTES
keg .... TUN, VAT, CADE, CASK, BARREL, FIRKIN
of beer .... GROWLER
open a .... UNHEAD
stopper .... BUNG

water .... BREAKER
kegler .... BOWLER
Keijo .... SEOUL
keir .... VAT
keitloa .... RHINO(CEROS)
Kelantan capital .... KOTA BHARU
kelep .... ANT
Keller, Miss .... HELEN
teacher of .... SULLIVAN
Kelly, performer .... GENE, PATSY, EMMETT
kelp .... ASH, VARIC, WRACK, SEAWEED
derivative .... IODINE
Kemal, Turkish leader .... ATATURK
Kemble, actress .... FANNY
ken .... SEE, LORE, SIGHT, DESCRY, RECOGNIZE
kench .... BIN, BOX
Kenilworth heroine .... AMY
Kennedy Space Center site .... (CAPE) CANAVERAL
kennel ...... PACK, DRAIN, SEWER, GUTTER, DOGHOUSE
sound .... YIP, BARK, HOWL, YELP
keno, game like .... BEANO, BINGO, LOTTO
Kent county seat ...... MAIDSTONE
resort/seaport .... MARGATE
Kentuckian .... LINCOLN
Kentucky capital ...... FRANKFORT
city/town .... ALBANY, BENTON, MURRAY, ASHLAND, PADUCAH, DANVILLE, FORT KNOX, RICHMOND, COVINGTON, HENDERSON, LEXINGTON, GEORGETOWN, LOUISVILLE, BOWLING GREEN, INDEPENDENCE
college .... BEREA, ASBURY, BRESCIA, BELLARMINE
county ..... BELL, BOYD, HART, KNOX, OWEN, PIKE, TODD, BOONE, CLARK, FLOYD, KNOTT, PERRY, BARREN, CARTER, GRAVES, HARDIN, HARLAN, KENTON, LAUREL, WARREN, BULLITT, DAVIESS, FAYETTE, GREENUP, HOPKINS, LETCHER, MADISON, PULASKI, WHITLEY, CAMPBELL, JEFFERSON, MCCRACKEN
Derby winner:
1948 .... CITATION
1955 .... SWAPS
1956 .... NEEDLES
1959 .... TOMY LEE
1965 .... LUCKY DEBONAIR

1973 .... SECRETARIAT
1978 .... AFFIRMED
1980 .... GENUINE RISK
1982 .... GATO DEL SOL
1983 .... SUNNY'S HALO
1984 .... SWALE
Derby winning jockey
.... ERB, YORK, AVILA,
ARCARO, CAUTHEN, VASQUEZ,
TURCOTTE, SHOEMAKER,
DELAHOUSSAYE
event .... DERBY
explorer .... BOONE, JOLIET
honorary title .... COLONEL
lake .... DEWEY, NOLIN,
BARKLEY, BUCKHORN,
FISHTRAP
mountain .... PINE, BLACK
personage .... COLONEL
pride of .... HORSES
river ..... DIX, MUD, RED, OHIO,
POND, SALT, GREEN, BARREN,
CHAPLIN, TENNESSEE,
MISSISSIPPI
state bird .... CARDINAL
state flower .... GOLDENROD
state nickname .... BLUEGRASS
tobacco .... BURLEY
tourist attraction
.... MAMMOTH CAVE, DANIEL
BOONE'S GRAVE, KENTUCKY
DERBY MUSEUM, MARY TODD
LINCOLN HOME
tree .... CHICOT
university .... LOUISVILLE,
MURRAY STATE
Kenya bay ...... WINAM, FORMOSA
capital .... NAIROBI
city/town .... LAMU, THIKA,
KISUMU, KITALE, ELDORET,
MALINDI, MOMBASA, NANYUKI
distance runner .... JIPCHO
freedom .... UHURU
gulf .... KAVIRONDO
island .... PATTA
lake .... NATRON, RUDOLF,
VICTORIA
language .... BANTU, HINDU,
KAMBA, SWAHILI
mascot .... AHMED
monetary unit .... SHILLING
mountain .... ELGON, KENYA
Olympic champ .... TEMU,
KEINO, BIWOTT
president .... (JOMO)
KENYATTA, (DANIEL)ARAP MOI
river .... DAUA, TANA, GALANA
seaport .... MOMBASA
secret society .... MAUMAU
Keos .... ZEA
kepi .... CAP

Kepler, astronomer
.... JOHANNES
keratinous .... HORNY
formation .... HAIR, NAIL
keratosis .... WART
kerchief .... CURCH, SCARF,
MADRAS, BANDAN(N)A,
BABUSHKA
kerf .... NOTCH, CUT(TING)
kermes .... DYE, OAK
kermess .... FAIR, CARNIVAL
Kern show .... SUNNY
kernel ...... PIT, CORE, GIST, PITH,
SEED, GRAIN, HEART, BARREL,
ESSENCE, NUCLEUS,
NUT(MEAT)
combining form .... CARYO,
KARYO
kerosene .... OIL
source of .... COAL,
PETROLEUM
Kerry .... CATTLE, COUNTY
blue .... TERRIER
kestrel .... FALCON, WINDHOVER
ketch .... JACK, SHIP, YAWL
Levantine .... SAIC
ketchup .... SAUCE, CATSUP
ketone .... IRONE, CARONE,
ACETONE, BUTYRONE
Kett, comic strip's .... ETTA
kettle .... BILLY, BOILER,
POT(HOLE), CA(U)LDRON
handle .... BAIL
in the South .... SIROP
part of .... SNOUT
repairer .... TINKER
stand .... TRIVET
kettledrum ...... TIMBAL, TIMPANI,
AT(T)ABAL, TIMPANO
player .... TIMPANIST
kevel .... PEG, CLEAT
key .... CAY, PIN, BOLT, CLEW,
CODE, REEF, TONE, ISLE(T),
PITCH, WEDGE, ANSWER,
CLAVIS, COTTER, ISLAND,
OPENER, SOLUTION
blade of .... WEB
emergency .... PICK
fruit .... SAMARA
notch .... WARD
part .... BIT, PIN, STEM
pertaining to .... TONAL
repairer .... LOCKSMITH
shaped .... URDE, CLECHE
sight over Ft. McHenry
.... THE ROCKETS RED GLARE
signature in music .... FLAT,
SHARP
telegraph .... TAPPER
up .... EXCITE
keyboard .... CLAVIER

instrument (musical)
.... ORGAN, PIANO, SPINET,
CELESTA, CELESTE, CLAVIER,
MELODEON, VIRGINAL
machine .... TELEX,
COMPUTER, LINO(TYPE),
TELETYPE, TYPEWRITER
shaped .... URDE
keyed up .... AGOG, EAGER,
TENSE, EXCITED
keyhole guard .... TAPPET
ridge .... WARD
keynote .... THEME, TONIC
sign .... ISON
keystone .... WEDGE, SAGITTA,
SUPPORT
characters .... COPS
prop .... PIE
Keystone State .... PENNSYLVANIA
State founder .... PENN
keyway .... SLOT
Khachaturian, composer
.... ARAM
khaki color .... DUN
khamsin .... WIND
khan .... AGA, ALI, INN, CHAM
Khartoum is capital of
.... SUDAN
Khayyam .... OMAR, POET,
TENTMAKER
birthplace .... NISHAPUR
khedive's estate .... DAIRA
Khmer .... CAMBODIAN
temple .... ANGKOR VAT
Khomeni's land .... IRAN
Khrushchev, USSR premier
.... NIKITA
Khufu .... CHEOPS
Kiang .... ONAGER
Kibbee, actor .... GUY
kibbutz .... SETTLEMENT
kibe .... CHILBLAIN
kibitz .... BUTT IN, HORN IN,
MEDDLE, COMMENT
kibitzer .... MEDDLER, ONLOOKER
kibosh .... VETO, SCRAG,
SQUELCH, NONSENSE
kick .... BOOT, GRIPE, KEVEL,
SPURN, STAMP, RECOIL,
THRILL, GRUMBLE,
COMPLAIN(T)
around .... STUDY, ANALYZE
in ...... DIE, PAY, CROAK, PONY
UP
in football .... HACK, PUNT
off .... DIE, BEGIN, START
off device .... TEE
out .... OUST, REMOVE,
DISCARD
up one's heels .... CAVORT
Kickapoo .... INDIAN

kickback .... CUT, BRIBE, PAYOLA,
   REFUND, REBATE, BACKFIRE
kickup .... ROW, FUSS
kid .... LAD, RIB, GOAT, JOKE,
   JIVE, JOSH, SUEDE, BANTER,
   DECEIVE, LEATHER, YOUNGER,
   ANTELOPE, (Y)EARLING
colloquial .... CHILD
neglected .... RAGAMUFFIN
sailor's .... TUB
slang .... FOOL, TEASE
Kidd, Captain .... PIRATE
kidnap .... SEIZE, ABDUCT,
   SNATCH, SHANGHAI, SPIRIT
   AWAY
kidney ...... SORT, GLAND, ORGAN
bean .... BON, PHASEL,
   HARICOT
combining form .... RENI,
   RENO, NEPHRO
concretion .... GRAVEL
condition .... NEPHRISM
disease .... NEPHROPATHY
duct .... URETER
of the .... RENAL, NEPHRIC
protein .... RENIN
shaped .... RENIFORM
stone .... JADE, NEPHRITE
kid's tummy .... BREADBASKET
kidskin parchment ...... VELLUM
kier .... VAT
Kierkegaard .... SOREN
Kilauea, goddess of .... PELE
kilderkin .... CASK, BARREL
Kilimanjaro peak .... KIBO
kill .... DO IN, RUIN, SLAY, PURGE,
   CANCEL, POISON, BUTCHER,
   DESTROY, DISPATCH,
   LIQUIDATE, ANNIHILATE
bill .... VETO
by drowning .... NOYADE
by hanging .... STRING UP
by mob action .... LYNCH
by stoning .... LAPIDATE
by suffocation .... BURKE
in printing .... DELE(TE)
in tennis .... SMASH
legally .... EXECUTE
time .... FOOL AROUND
unlawfully .... MURDER,
   ASSASSINATE
Killarney land .... ERIN
killer .... THUG, SLAYER,
   MURDERER, CUTTHROAT
hired .... BRAVO, HITMAN,
   ASSASSIN
of a god .... DEICIDE
political .... ASSASSIN
whale .... NAMU, ORC(A),
   DOLPHIN, GRAMPUS
killick .... ANCHOR

killing .... FATAL, DEADLY,
   CARNAGE, SLAUGHTER,
   STARVATION, ASPHYXIATION
mass .... PURGE, BATTUE,
   POGROM, CARNAGE,
   BUTCHERY, GENOCIDE,
   MASSACRE, ANNIHILATION
mercy .... EUTHANASIA
of a baby .... INFANTICIDE
of a fetus in the womb
   .... ABORTICIDE
of a king .... REGICIDE
of old men .... SENICIDE
one's mother .... MATRICIDE
one's parent .... PARRICIDE
one's relatives ..... FRATRICIDE
oneself intentionally
   .... SUICIDE
slang .... HIT, SMASH, SUCCESS
killjoy .... DAMPER, SPOILSPORT,
   WET BLANKET
Kilmer poem .... TREES
poet .... JOYCE
kiln .... O(A)ST, LEER, OVEN,
   DRIER, DRYER, STOVE,
   TILER(Y), FURNACE
type of .... SCOVE
kilograms, 100 .... CENTAL,
   CENTNER, QUINTAL
1,000 .... MILLIER
kiloliter .... STERE
kilt .... TUCK, PLEAT, SKIRT,
   FILIBEG, PHILIBEG
undergarment .... TREWS
kilter .... ORDER
kiltie .... SCOT(SMAN)
Kim .... NOVAK, O'HARA, HUNTER
friend of .... LAMA
kimono .... ROBE, DRESSING
   GOWN
sash .... OBI
kin .... SIB(S), FOLKS, FAMILY,
   SIBLINGS, RELATED,
   RELATIVE(S),
   (BLOOD)RELATION
of ave. .... RD.
of rho .... CHI
to Eureka! .... AHA
kind ...... ILK, RACE, SORT, CLASS,
   GENUS, BENIGN, GENTLE,
   SPECIES, VARIETY
in .... GOODS, PRODUCE
of .... ALMOST, SOMEWHAT
a .... ALIKE, MEDIOCRE
acid .... FOLIC
act .... RIOT
agent .... UNDERCOVER
athletic event
   .... INTERCOLLEGIATE
azole .... IMID
badge .... MERIT

bank ...... LEFT, NOTE, ROLL,
   MONEY, RIVER
bee .... DRONE, HONEY,
   QUEEN
blow .... RABBIT PUNCH,
   BELOW THE BELT
blue .... SKY, BABY, NAVY,
   POWDER
board or box .... IDIOT
board or trap .... CLAP
body .... STUDENT
book .... (TELE)PHONE
bracelet ...... CHARM, TENNIS
brush or comb .... HAIR
buffalo .... CAPE
cake .... SHORT, GRIDDLE,
   WEDDING
candy ...... CANE, LIFESAVER
case or flight .... TEST
cat .... FAT
chair .... EASY, LOUNGE,
   ELECTRIC, RECLINING
chest .... HOPE
circle .... INNER
clam .... STEAMER
club .... GLEE, GOLF
cry .... FAR
curve .... ESS
cut .... SHORT
daisy .... SHASTA
dancer .... GOGO, HULA
deck .... ORLOP
deer .... DOE, ROE, AXIS
derby .... ROLLER,
   KENTUCKY
dome .... GEODESIC
dope .... INSIDE
down .... EIDER
dream .... PIPE
driver .... PILE
energy .... SOLAR
engine .... DIESEL
father/mother .... STEP
fist .... IRON
flour or flower .... CORN
food/music .... SOUL
frost .... HOAR
garden .... BOTANICAL,
   ZOOLOGICAL
gazelle .... ARIEL
glass .... SHOT, STAINED,
   MAGNIFYING
goat .... SCAPE
goose .... SOLAN
gravure .... ROTO
gun .... RIOT, SHOT
hand or rags .... GLAD
happy .... SLAP
hydrometer ..... GRAVIMETER
introducer .... EMCEE,
   TOASTMASTER

institution .... PENAL
job .... DESK, PART-TIME
joint .... CLIP
landing .... CRASH
lark .... MUD
leave .... SICK, SHORE,
                  MATERNITY
lens .... ZOOM, CONTACT
life some lead ..... CHARMED
light .... SEARCH
lily .... CALLA, TIGER
lounge .... VIP, COCKTAIL
machine .... SLOT
man .... YES, INNER
market .... BEAR, STOCK
meal .... OAT
meat .... LEAN, CHOICE
miss .... NEAR
money ..... GREASE, EARNEST
moss .... PEAT
moth .... LUNA
music .... POP, JAZZ, ROCK,
                 CLASSICAL
nail .... HOB
numeral ..... ROMAN, ARABIC
opera .... SOAP, HORSE
orange .... NAVEL, OSAGE,
                TANGERINE
out .... INSIDE
page .... BLEED, FRONT
party .... HEN, TEA,
       SLUMBER, POLITICAL
peeve .... PET
piano or soprano ..... MEZZO
pigeon .... STOOL, HOMING
plane .... JET, MONO
plant .... EGG
plasm .... ECTO
poker .... STUD
police dog .... ALSATIAN,
       GERMAN SHEPHERD
pool or vehicle .... MOTOR
post .... GOAL
processing .... DATA
production .... INDUSTRIAL
progression .... GEOMETRIC
race .... DRAG, HORSE
race horse .... MILER
ranch .... DUDE
road .... RAIL
rocket .... RETRO
rubber .... BAND, INDIA
rule .... GAG
rumor .... IDLE
sale .... TAG, FIRE, WHITE,
GARAGE, SURPLUS, BARGAIN,
           CLEARANCE
salt .... TABLE, SAILOR
salt or wit .... ATTIC
service .... LIP
shark .... LOAN, NURSE

sheet .... TEAR, WORK
show .... GAME, TALK,
      COMEDY, ONE-MAN
shutout .... NO-HIT
sight .... HIND
skirt .... MIDI, MINI, A-LINE
soda .... POP, SAL
sole .... DOVER
space or plane .... AERO
squirrel .... TANA
sticks .... CHOP
stock .... PREFERRED, BLUE
                CHIP
stool .... TOAD
story .... SOB
suit .... PINSTRIPE
sync .... LIP
table .... POOL, STEAM
tax .... SALES, STATE,
   INCOME, PROPERTY
terrier .... CAIRN
this/that .... LIKE, SUCH
ticket .... FREE, MEAL,
     TRAFFIC, SPEEDING
tide .... LOW, HIGH, NEAP
tire .... RECAP, SPARE
triangle .... LOVE, SCALENE
type .... PICA, ELITE
wave .... TIDAL
wax .... SEALING
well .... INK, WISHING
will .... IRON, LAST
word .... NONCE
kindergarten ...... CLASS, SCHOOL
activity .... GAME, EXERCISE
pioneer .... FROEBEL
kindergartner .... LEARNER
kindle .... BURN, FIRE, LUNT,
TIND, LIGHT, ROUSE, SPUNK,
       EXCITE, IGNITE
kindled .... LIT
kindling .... PUNK, WOOD,
          AMADOU
kindly .... WARM, BENIGN,
     GENIAL, GRACIOUS
kindness .... GRACE, LENITY,
        GOOD WILL
kindred ...... SIB, TIE, AKIN, KITH,
   BLOOD, ALLIED, FAMILY,
  COGNATE, KINSHIP, RELATIVES
kine .... COWS, CATTLE
king .... REX, ROI, SIRE, RULER,
   MONARCH, PADISHAH,
      SOVEREIGN
and jack .... TENACE
Ammonite .... HANUN,
         NAHASH
beater/topper .... ACE
biblical ...... MAGUS, MAGI(PL.)
changed to mountain
              ATLAS

Cobra .... HAMADRYAD
crab .... LIMULUS, LIMULOID
do-nothing .... ROI FAINEANT
Egyptian .... PHARAOH
fairyland .... OBERON
Iranian .... SHAH
killer .... REGICIDE
maned .... LION
Midian .... EVI, HUR, REBA
morning reception of
              LEVER
of a .... REGAL, ROYAL
of Admah .... SHINAB
Amalek .... AGAG
Arcadia .... LYCAON
Argos .... DANAUS
Assyria .... PUL
Athens .... CODRUS, THESEUS
Attica .... CECROPS
Babylon .... SELEACUS,
          HAMMURABI
Bashan .... OG
beasts .... LION
Bela .... ZOAR
Belgium .... BAUDOIN,
          LEOPOLD
birds .... EAGLE
blues .... (B.B.) KING
Bohemia .... WENZEL
Britain .... LUR, LEAR,
 UTHER, ARTHUR, ARTEGAL,
         BELINUS
Bulgaria .... BORIS
Burgundy .... GUNTHER
Bythinia .... NICOMEDES
Colon .... GASPAR
Corinth .... POLYBUS
Crete .... MINOS
Crete, legendary
          IDOMENEUS
Cyprus .... PYGMALION
Damascus .... ARETUS
Denmark .... VALDEMAR,
        WALDEMAR
dwarfs .... ALBERICH
Egypt .... FUAD, FAROUK
Elam .... CHEDORLAOMER
Ellasar .... ARIOCH
elves .... ERLKING
England .... HENRY,
   EDWARD, STEPHEN,
      ETHELRED
England and Denmark
        CNUT, KNUT
England and Northern
   Ireland .... GEORGE VI
England, the Conqueror
           WILLIAM
England, the first
   Plantagenet
         HENRY II

England, the last Plantagenet .... RICHARD III
England, the Lion-Hearted .... RICHARD I
England who abdicated in 1936 .... EDWARD VIII
Ethiopia .... CEPHEUS
fairies .... OBERON
Franks .... PEPIN
Gath .... ACHISH
Gerar .... ABIMELECH
"glitz" ..... WAYNE NEWTON
Goiim .... TIDAL
Gomorrah .... BIRSHA
"golden touch" .... MIDAS
hobbies, alleged .... PHILATELY
Huns .... ATLI, ETZEL, ATTILA
Ioclus .... AESON
Iran .... XERXES
Israel (see Israel(i), king)
Israel, first .... SAUL
Israel, last .... HOSHEA
Jews .... HEROD
Judah/Judea (see Judah, king)
Judah, last .... ZEDEKIAH
Kent .... ETHELBERT
Langobards .... ALBOIN
Ligurians .... CYGNUS
Lydia .... CROESUS
Moab .... EGLON
Mycenae .... ATREUS
Myrmidons .... PELEUS
Naples .... MURAT
Norway .... OLAF, OLAV, HAAKON
Numidia .... MASINISSA
Peris .... JAMSHID
Persia .... CYRUS, DARIUS, XERXES
Phrygia ..... MIDAS, GORDIUS
Prussia .... WILHELM
"rock and roll" .... ELVIS PRESLEY
Rome .... TARQUIN
Salem .... MELCHIZEDEK
Scotland .... BRUCE
Siam .... ANANDA, MONGKUT
Siam's friend .... ANNA
Sodom .... BERA
Spain .... REY, JUAN, ALFONSO
Sparta .... LEONIDAS, MENELAUS
"swing" .... GOODMAN
Syria .... HAZAL
the blind ..... MAN WITH ONE EYE

Thebes .... CREON, LAIUS
Thessaly .... PELIAS, ADMETUS
Thrace .... TEREUS
Troy .... PRIAM
Tyre .... HIRAM
Visogoths .... ALARIC
Volsunga .... ATLI
Zeboiim .... SHEMEBER
Zulus .... CETEWAYO
sculptor .... PYGMALION
snake .... COBRA
with ass's ears .... MIDAS
with eternal thirst, hunger .... TANTALUS
King Arthur's birthplace .... TINTAGEL HEAD
Arthur's capital/court .... CAMELOT
death place .... CAMLAN
father .... UTHER
fictitious visitor ..... YANKEE
fool/jester .... DAGONET
foster brother .... KAY
knight ..... GARETH, GAWAIN, MODRED, GALAHAD, LANCELOT
knights .... ROUNDTABLE
lance .... RON(E)
magician .... MERLIN
mother ...... IGERNA, IGERNE, IGRAINE
nephew .... KAY, GARETH, GAWAIN, MO(R)DRED
place .... ASTOLAT
queen .... GUINEVERE
realm .... BRITAIN
resting place .... AVALON
seneschal .... KAY
shield name .... PRIDWIN
step-sister .... MORGAN(LE FAY)
sword .... EXCALIBUR
writer on .... PYLE
Canute's consort .... EMMA
Cole .... NAT, OLD
David's brother .... ELIAB, SHAMMAH, ABINADAB
captain/commander .... JOAB, AMASA
city .... ZION
daughter .... TAMAR
father .... JESSE
kingdom .... JUDAH, HEBRON, ISRAEL
priest .... IRA, ZADOK, ABIATHAR
rebellious son ...... ABSALOM
rebuker .... NATHAN
son .... AMNON, ABSALOM, CHILEAB, ITHREAM,

SOLOMON, ADONIJAH, SHEPHATIAH
trusted friend .... HUSHAI, JONATHAN
victim slain with sling .... GOLIATH
wife .... EGLAH, MICHAL, ABIGAIL, AHINOAM, HAGGITH, BATHSHEBA
Ferdinand .... BOMBA
Hadad's land .... EDOM
Henry VI author .... SHAKESPEARE
John's nickname .... LACKLAND
Kong .... GORILLA
Lear's daughter .... REGAN, GONERIL, CORDELIA
dog .... TRAY
Saul's ancestral tribe .... BENJAMIN
critic .... SAMUEL
daughter .... MERAB, MICHAL
deathplace .... (MOUNT) GILBOA
father .... KISH
general .... ABNER
grandfather .... NER
grandson .... MEPHIBOSETH
kingdom .... ISRAEL
servant .... ZIBA
shepherd .... DOEG
son .... ABINADAB, JONATHAN, ESHBAAL, MALCHISHUA, ISHBOSHETH
successor .... DAVID
wife/concubine .... RIZPAH
Solomon's brother .... ADONIJAH
daughter .... TAPHATH
father .... DAVID
land .... OPHIR
mines location .... ELATH, TIMNAH VALLEY
mother .... BATHSHEBA
sayings .... MAXIMS, PROVERBS
son .... MENELIK, REHOBOAM
kingcup .... MARIGOLD
kingdom .... REALM, DOMAIN, EMPIRE, MONARCHY
African .... NUBIA, NUMIDIA
ancient .... EDOM, ELAM, IDUMEA, CROATIA, MACEDONIA
Asiatic .... SIAM, KOREA, NEPAL, SIKKIM, THAILAND
Caspian .... PARTHIA
cause of loss of .... NAIL, HORSE
come ..... HEAVEN, HEREAFTER
kind of .... PLANT, ANIMAL,

VEGETABLE
kingfish .... BARB, CERO, HAKU,
OPAH, SIERRA, PINTADO,
WHITING
kingfisher .... HALCYON,
KOOKABURRA
kingfisher's kin .... MOTMOT
kingly .... NOBLE, REGAL, ROYAL,
AUGUST, LEONINE, MAJESTIC
authority/power .... DIADEM
king's chamber .... CAMARILLA
clover .... MELILOT
color .... PURPLE, ORPIMENT
evil .... SCROFULA
robe .... DALMATIC
rod .... WARDER
steward .... CHAMBERLAIN
symbol .... ORB, MOUND
symbol of authority
.... SCEPTER
King's Peak range .... UINTA
kingship ...... MAJESTY, ROYALTY
kingsman's domain: var.
.... BARONI
kink .... CURL, KNOT, WHIM,
CRICK, QUIRK, SNARL, TWIST,
BUCKLE, CROTCHET
thread .... BURL
kinkajou .... POTT(O), MAMMAL
kinky .... CURLY
kino .... GUM, ASTRINGENT
kinsfolk .... FAMILY, RELATIVES
kinship .... ENATION, AFFINITY
kinsman .... SIB, RELATIVE
kiosk ...... PAVILION, BANDSTAND,
NEWSSTAND
kip .... BED, ROOMING HOUSE
Kipling's birthplace ...... BOMBAY
character .... KIM
children's fable .... THE
JUNGLE BOOK
heroine .... MAISIE
mother .... ALICE
novel .... KIM
poem .... RECESSIONAL
Shere Khan .... TIGER
title .... SAHIB
wife .... CAROLINE
wolf .... AKELA
Kirghiz .... KAZAK(H), MONGOL
mountains .... ALAI
tent .... YURT
kirk .... CHURCH
Kirk, actor .... DOUGLAS
kirtle .... COAT, SKIRT, TUNIC
Kish's father .... NER
son .... SAUL
kismet .... FATE, DESTINY
kiss .... BUSS, PECK, CANDY,
SMACK, TOUCH, CARESS,
OSCULATE, SUGARPLUM

and _____ .... TELL
Kiss sculptor .... RODIN
Kissel and Opel .... CARS
kisser: sl. ...... FACE, LIPS, MOUTH
kissing cousins .... KIN
game .... POST OFFICE
kist .... BOX, CHEST, LOCKER
kit .... LOT, SET, TUB, GEAR,
PACK, BUCKET, OUTFIT
and _____ .... CABOODLE
kitchen .... GALLEY, COOKERY,
CUISINE, SCULLERY
chief .... CHEF
feature .... OVEN, MIXER,
RANGE, TOASTER
garden .... OLITORY
help .... SCULLION
of the .... CULINARY
police for short .... KP
ship's .... GALLEY
specialty .... AROMA
tool ...... CORER, DICER, KNIFE,
LADLE, SIEVE, GRATER,
MASHER
waste .... SLOPS
wear .... APRON
kitchener .... RANGE, STOVE
Kitchener, statesman
.... HORATIO
kitchenware .... PANS, POTS,
SKILLET, UTENSILS
kite .... BIRD, HAWK, SOAR,
GLED(E), MILAN, ROGUE,
ELANET, FALCON, SHARPER
kith and kin .... RELATIVES
kitsch .... TRASH
kittenish .... FRISKY, PLAYFUL
kittens: colloq. .... HYSTERICS
kittiwake .... ANNET, SEA GULL
kitty .... CAT, POT, ANTE, POOL,
WIDOW, STAKES
in gambling game .... POT
kiva .... ROOM, DWELLING
kiwi .... MOA, ROA, APTERYX
klaxon .... HORN
kleptomaniac .... THIEF, FILCHER,
SHOPLIFTER
Klingsor .... MAGICIAN
Klondike road .... ALCAN
kloop .... GORGE, VALLEY
knack .... ART, FLAIR, SKILL,
TRICK, TALENT, TRINKET,
APTITUDE, INSTINCT,
DEXTERITY
knap .... RAP, BITE, HILL, SNAP,
SUMMIT
knapsack ...... KIT, PACK, BINDLE,
MOCHILA, (DUFFLE)BAG,
HAVERSACK
knar .... KNOT
knarl .... NODE

knave ...... CHURL, LOREL, LOSEL,
ROGUE, SCAMP, RASCAL,
VARLET
in cribbage .... NOBS
in euchre .... BOWER
of clubs .... PAM
playing cards' .... JACK
knead .... ELT, MOLD, PRESS,
MASSAGE
kneading material .... CLAY,
DOUGH
knee .... GENU, JOINT
ailment .... GONAGRA
bend the .... GENUFLECT
bone .... DIB
inflammation .... GONITIS
joint .... HOCK, KNUCKLE
tendon .... HAMSTRING
kneecap .... ROTULA, PATELLA
kneel .... KOWTOW, GENUFLECT
kneeling desk .... PRIE DIEU
knell .... OMEN, RING, TOLL
knickerbocker(s) ...... TROUSERS,
NEWYORKER, PLUSFOURS
knickknack .... TOY, GAUD,
BAUBLE, DOODAD, GEWGAW,
NOTION, TRIFLE, NOVELTY,
TRINKET, GIMCRACK,
BRIC-A-BRAC
Knievel .... EVEL
knife .... BOLO, SHIV, SNEE, STAB,
BLADE, BOWIE, DAGGER,
MACHET(T)E
combining form .... DORI
dealer .... CUTLER
handle .... HAFT
Hindu .... KURRI
Irish .... SKEAN
kind of .... FAN, PEN, BOWIE,
TRENCH, TRIVET, CARVING
large .... COUTEAU
Malay .... PARANG
Maori .... PATU
Moro .... KRIS
sharpener .... STEEL
surgical .... CATLIN, LANCET,
SCALPEL
tosser .... JUGGLER
Turkish .... YATAGHAN
knight .... SIR, NOBLE, BAYARD,
RITTER, PALADIN, TEMPLAR,
CAVALIER, CHAMPION
arena of the .... LISTS
armor bearer of ...... ARMIGER
armorless .... BARESARK
attendant .... PAGE, SQUIRE,
DONZEL, ARMIGER
challenge .... GAGE
cloak of .... TABARD
Crusader .... TEMPLAR
ensign .... PENNON

errand of a .... QUEST
errant .... PALADIN
fratricidal .... BALIN
fight of a .... TILT, JOUST,
                    TOURNEY
groom of .... COISTREL
in chess .... HORSE
lance target .... QUINTAIN
of the road .... HOBO, TRAMP
of the Round Table .... KAY,
    BORS, BORT, BALAN, BALIN,
    GARETH, GAWAIN, GALAHAD,
    GERAINT, MO(R)DRED,
    MORGA(I)N, PELLEAS, TRISTAN,
    BEDIVERE, LANCELOT,
    PERCIVAL, TRISTRAM
page of .... VARLET
pledge .... GAGE
self-styled .... HOBO
Templar .... MASON
vocation .... CHIVALRY
weapon of .... LANCE
wife of .... DAME
knightliness .... CHIVALRY
knightly .... BRAVE, NOBLE,
            HEROIC, GALLANT
quest .... ERRANTRY
knights collectively
          .... KNIGHTHOOD
knit .... JOIN, SEAM, PURSE, UNITE,
    WEAVE, COUPLE, PUCKER,
    INTERLOCK
goods .... LISLE
knitted goods dealer ...... HOSIER
knitter .... PURLER
problem of .... SLEEVES
knitting .... BROCADE, CROCHET
machine guide .... SLEY
stitch .... PURL
knob .... HILL, KNOP, NODE, STUD,
    UMBO, KNOLL, KNURL,
    FINIAL, HANDLE, NUB(BLE)
like .... NOPAL
ornamental .... BOSS, STUD
knobbed .... NODOSE, TOROSE
knobby .... HILLY, NUBB(L)Y,
    TOROSE, STUDDED, TUBEROSE,
    TUBEROUS
knock .... HIT, PAN, RAP, TAP,
    BLOW, BUMP, POUND, SWIPE,
    STRIKE, CRITICIZE
about .... ROAM, ABUSE,
    HUSTLE, ROUGH UP
down .... DASH, FLOOR,
    DAMPEN, FLATTEN,
    DISCOURAGE
it off .... STOP
kneed .... VALGUS, WOBBLY,
    BOWLEGGED
light .... RAP, TAP
on wood .... HOPE

out .... KO, KAYO, STUN,
    CANCEL, DELETE, DEFEAT
knockabout .... YACHT
knocked down, as in equipment,
    etc. .... UNASSEMBLED
for ____ .... A LOOP
knocker .... CRITIC, NAGGER,
    RAPPER, FAULTFINDER
knockout .... STUNNER
blow ...... HAYMAKER, SUNDAY
                   PUNCH
knoll .... KNAP, TOFT, MOUND,
    HILLOCK, HUMMOCK
Knossos .... CRETE
knot .... BOW, TIE, BIND, BOND,
    KNUR, LUMP, NODE, SNAG,
    TUFT, HITCH, JOINT, NODUS,
    SNARL, FASTEN, NODULE,
    COCKADE, (EN)TANGLE,
    PROBLEM, SANDPIPER
fiber .... NEP, NOIL
hair .... BUN, NOIL, CHIGNON
kind of .... LOOP, REEF,
    GRANNY, BOWLINE, LANYARD,
    OVERHAND, CAT'S-PAW,
    TREFOIL, SHEEPSHANK,
    MAGNUS HITCH
loose .... GRANNY
nautical .... (SEA)MILE
necktie .... WINDSOR
rope .... CLINCH
running .... NOOSE
silk/wool .... NOIL
thread .... BURL
tied by King Midas
                 .... GORDIAN
tree .... GNARL
wood ...... BURL, KNAR, KNOR,
                   GNARL
yarn .... SKEIN
knots, full of .... NODOUS
knotted .... NODED, NODATED,
    TANGLED, INTRICATE
knotty .... NODOSE, NODOUS,
    PUZZLING
knotweed .... ALLSEEDS,
    PERSICARY
knout .... FLOG, WHIP
know ...... KEN, AWARE, FATHOM,
    DISCERN, UNDERSTAND
all: colloq. .... QUIDNUNC,
    WISEACRE, SMART ALECK
beforehand .... FORESEE
by observation .... PERCEIVE
come to .... LEARN, REALIZE
in a way .... KEN
in one's bones .... FEEL
it-all .... BOASTER, EGOTIST,
    WISEGUY, WISEACRE
long ago/archaic .... WOT
nothing .... AGNOSTIC,

                 IGNORANT
the ____ and outs .... INS
know-how .... SKILL, EXPERTISE
slang .... SAVVY
know-nothing .... DUNCE,
    GREENHORN, IGNORAMUS
knowing .... HEP, HIP, WISE,
    CLEVER, SCIENT, SHREWD,
    GNOSTIC, COGNIZANT,
    CONSCIOUS
knowledge ...... KEN, KITH, LORE,
    NOESIS, THEORY, WISDOM,
    AWARENESS, EXPERTISE,
    INFORMATION
branch of .... OLOGY
intuitive .... INSIGHT
lack of .... IGNORANCE
means to .... ORGANON
of .... GNOSTIC
spiritual .... GNOSIS
surface .... SCIOLISM
universal .... PANSOPHY
vague ..... INKLING, SUSPICION,
                IMPRESSION
knowledgeable .... HEP, HIP,
    WISE, SKILLED, LEARNED,
    SAPIENT, EDUCATED,
    INFORMED, WELL-READ,
    INTELLIGENT
about .... UP ON
known .... RECOGNIZED
as .... YCLEPT, YCLEPED
knuckle .... (FINGER)JOINT
down under ...... OBEY, YIELD,
    COMPLY, GIVE IN
knucklebone .... BIB, KNOB
knucklehead .... FOOL,
    THICKSKULL
knurl .... KNOB, KNOT, RIDGE
KO: sl. .... KNOCKOUT, PUT TO
                 SLEEP
koa .... ACACIA
koala .... BEAR
kobold .... GNOME, NIS(SE),
    GOBLIN, SPRITE, BROWNIE
Kodak .... CAMERA
koel .... CUCKOO
Kohinoor .... DIAMOND,
    (CROWN)JEWEL
kohl .... COSMETIC
Kohler, psychologist
               .... WOLFGANG
kohl .... COSMETIC
Kohler, psychologist
               .... WOLFGANG
kohlrabi .... CABBAGE
kok-sagyz .... DANDELION
Kok's (Adam) settlers
               .... GRIQUA
Koko's weapon .... SNEE
kola .... NUT

nut content .... CAFFEIN(E)
kolinsky .... FUR, MINK
kon-tiki .... RAFT
kook .... CUCKOO
kookaburra .... KINGFISHER
kooky ...... CRAZY, LOOPY, SILLY,
ECCENTRIC
kop .... HILL, MOUNTAIN
kopje .... HILL(OCK)
kor .... HOMER
Koran chapter .... SURO, SURA(H),
ALCORAN
interpreter .... ULEMA
memorizer .... HAFIZ
paradise bridge .... AL SIRAT
scholar .... ULEMA
supplement to the ...... SHIITE,
SUNNA(H)
teacher of .... ALFAQUI
Korea .... CHOSEN
founder of .... TANGUN
Korean, North bay .... CHUNGSAN
capital .... PYONGYANG
city/town .... IWON, HAEJU,
NAJIN, NAMPO, ONSONG,
WONSAN, HAMHUNG,
KAESONG, SINUIJI, CHONGJIN,
PANMUNJON
mountain .... SASU, TUUN,
BAKTU, KOMDOK, KWANMO,
PAEKTU, KUMGANG
river .... YALU, TUMEN,
TAEDONG
sea .... JAPAN, YELLOW
seaport .... WONSAN
South bay .... KANGHWA
capital .... KEIJO, SEOUL
city/town .... IRI, MUJU,
YOSU, CHEJU, KIMJE, MASAN,
MOKPO, PUSAN, SUWON,
TAEGU, ULSAN, WONJU,
ANDONG, CHINJU, INCHON,
KIMHAE, KOHUNG, KUNSAN,
NONSAN, POHANG, TAEJON,
YANGGU, CHECHON,
CHINHAE, CHONGJU
island .... SO, KOJE, CHEJU,
DAGELET
mountain ...... CHIRI, HALLA,

SORAK, KEBANG
river .... HAN, KUM, NAKTONG
sea .... JAPAN
seaport .... YOSU, PUSAN,
INCHON
strait .... CHEJU
coin .... WON
dynasty/kingdom .... SILLA
honorable man of justice
.... YOLSA
martial art .... TAE KWON DO
monetary unit .... WON, HWAN
president .... PARK, RHEE, ROH
TAE-WOO
religion .... BUDDHISM,
CONFUCIANISM
soldier .... ROK
statesman .... TOO SUN CHOI
stockade .... JKOJE
true faith .... AL SIRAT
weight .... KON
woman's blouse .... CHIMA
woman's skirt .... CHOGORI
Korina wood .... AFARA
koruna, 1/100 **of** .... HELLER
kosher .... FIT, CLEAN, PROPER
opposed to .... TREF
Kosygin, Russian premier
.... ALEKSEI
Kotabaru .... HOLLANDIA
Koussevitsky .... SERGE
kowtow .... BOW, HOMAGE,
SCRAPE, RESPECT,
SALUTATION
slang .... BOOTLICK
kraal .... PEN, VILLAGE
Kraft .... WRAPPING PAPER
krait .... ADDER
kraken .... MONSTER
Kreisler, violinist .... FRITZ
Kremlin .... CITADEL
Kreuger .... IVAR
Kriemhild's husband .... ETZEL,
ATTILA, SIEGFRIED
kris .... CREESE, DAGGER
Kriss Kringle .... SANTA (CLAUS)
krona .... CROWN
Kronos' wife .... RHEA
Kronstadt .... PORT, BRASOV

Kruger, Transvaal president
.... OOM PAUL
Krypton symbol .... KR
Ku Klux Klan official
.... KLEAGLE
Kublai Khan dynasty ...... YUAN
kudos ...... FAME, GLORY, CREDIT,
PRAISE, PRESTIGE
kudu .... KOODOO, ANTELOPE
Kukla's pal .... OLLIE
Kuklapolitan hostess .... FRAN
kulak .... FARMER
Kumasi is capital of .... ASHANTI
is in .... GHANA
Kung Fu-tse .... CONFUCIUS
Kuomintang .... YUAN
founder .... SUN YAT-SEN
leader .... CHIANG KAI-SHEK
Kurdistan .... RUG
Kuril(e) island .... URUP, ITURUP,
ETOROFU, KUNASHIRI,
PARAMUSHIR
Kuwait .... SHEIKDOM
capital .... AL KUWAIT
city/town .... MINA SAUD,
MINA AL AHMADI
export .... OIL
gulf .... PERSIAN
island .... BUBIYAN
language .... ARABIC
monetary unit .... DINAR
religion .... ISLAM
kvass .... BEER
Kwangchow .... CANTON
Kwangsi capital .... NANNING
Kwantung capital .... CANTON
city .... SWATOW
seaport .... DAIREN
kwashiorkor .... MALNUTRITION
Kymric .... WELSH
kyphos .... HUMP
kyphosis .... HUMPBACK
Kyser, bandleader .... KAY
Kyushu base .... SASEBO
city/town .... OITA, SAGA,
BEPPU, KURUME, NOBEOKA,
KUMAMOTO, MIYAZAKI,
NAGASAKI, KAGOSHIMA
volcano .... ASO(SAN)

L

L, Greek .... LAMBDA
in geodesy .... LONGITUDE
letter .... EL, ELL
shaped .... ELL
La Boheme character .... MIMI,
MUSETTA, RODOLPHO
composer .... (GIACOMO)

PUCCINI
La Gioconda .... MONA LISA
painter .... (LEONARDO) DA
VINCI
La Guardia, Mayor
.... FIORELLO
La in chemistry .... LANTHANUM

La Perichole composer
.... (JACQUES) OFFENBACH
La Rochefoucauld's forte
.... MAXIMS
La Salle's lieutenant ...... TONTY
La Traviata heroine
.... VIOLETTA

La Valse composer .... (MAURICE) RAVEL
laager .... CAMP
Laban's daughter .... LEAH, RACHEL
sister .... REBEKAH
son-in-law .... JACOB
labarum .... STANDARD
labdanum .... RESIN
Labe .... ELBE
labefaction .... DOWNFALL
label ...... TAB, TAG, MARK, NAME, BRAND, STAMP, TALLY, DOCKET, FILLET, LAPPET, PASTER, STICKER, DESCRIBE, CLASSIFICATION
anew .... RETAG
labellum .... LIP, PETAL
flower with .... ORCHID
labia .... LIPS
minora .... NYMPHA(E)
labial .... (ORGAN)PIPE
labiate .... LIPPED
labile .... SKIMMING, UNSTABLE
labium .... LIP, LABELLUM
labor .... MOIL, TASK, TOIL, WORK, EFFORT, STRIVE, TRAVAIL, CHILDBIRTH, PARTURITION
group .... UNION
leader .... GREEN, HOFFA, LEWIS, MEANY, REUTHER, PETRILLO
omnia ____ .... VINCIT
organization, international .... ILO
resources .... MANPOWER
-saving device ...... APPLIANCE
spy recruiter .... HOOKER
strike placard carrier .... PICKET
strikebreaker .... RAT, SCAB
throes, pains .... TRAVAIL
union .... AFL, CIO, ARTEL, ILGWU
union branch .... LOCAL
union negotiation .... COLLECTIVE BARGAINING
unionist .... NEGOTIATOR
laboratory burner .... ETNA, BUNSEN
need .... ACIDS, OLEATES, TEST TUBES
salt .... BORATE
specimen .... CELL
substance .... ACID
utensil .... RETORT
worker .... TESTER
labored .... HEAVY, FORCED, OPEROSE
breath .... GASP, PANT

laborer .... HAND, PEON, SERF, TOTY, NAVVY, PROLE, COOLIE, SEGGON, WORKER, BRACERO
day .... PEON
migratory .... OKIE
Spanish .... PEON, OBRERO, TRABAJADOR
transient .... CASUAL, FLOATER, MIGRANT, ROUSTABOUT
unskilled .... NAVVY, BOHUNK, AMATEUR
laborious .... ARDUOUS, TOILSOME, STRENUOUS
Labrador .... PENINSULA
retriever .... HUNTING DOG
tea .... LEDUM
labrum .... LIP
laburnum .... SHRUB, PEA TREE
labyrinth .... MAZE, MEANDER
builder of .... DAEDALUS
dweller .... MINOTAUR
inflammation of .... LABYRINTHITIS
site of, in human body .... EAR
labyrinthine .... DAEDAL, COMPLEX, INTRICATE
lace .... GIN, VAL, BEAT, LASH, WHIP, ADORN, BRAID, FILET, SNARE, EDGING, THRASH, GUIPURE, MACRAME, MALINES, NETTING, TATTING, FILIGREE, EMBROIDER
beer .... NEEDLE
cape .... MANTILLA
collar .... BERTHA
edging .... FRILL
frilled .... R(O)UCHE
metal tip .... TAG, A(I)GLET
opening .... EYELET
pattern .... TOILE
shoe/sandal .... LATCHET
thread .... MACRAME
three-cornered .... FICHU
trimming .... FRILL, JABOT
Lacedaemon .... SPARTA
lacerate .... CUT, RIP, REND, TEAR, WOUND, HARROW, MANGLE
lacert(il)ian .... GECKO, LIZARD
lacet .... BRAID
Lachesis .... FATE, GODDESS
companion of .... CLOTHO, ATROPOS
lachrymose .... TEARY, WEEPY, TEARFUL
lady .... NIOBE
lacing .... CORD, BRAID, BEATING, TRIMMING
lack .... NEED, WANT, DEARTH,

REQUIRE, SHORTAGE, DEFICIENCY
desire .... INAPPETENCE
of bladder control .... BED-WETTING
information ..... IGNORANCE, NESCIENCE
interest ..... ENNUI, BOREDOM
mental vigor .... CACHEXIA
oxygen .... SUFFOCATION
stress .... ATONY
vital energy .... ATONIA
lackadaisical .... BLASE, INDOLENT, LANGUID, LISTLESS, EASYGOING, NONCHALANT, SPIRITLESS
"Lackaday!" .... ALAS
lackey .... SLAVE, TOADY, FLUNK(E)Y, FOOTMAN, SERVANT, FOLLOWER, ATTENDANT
uniform of .... LIVERY
lacking .... SHY, SANS, ABSENT, (DE)VOID, IN NEED, SHORT OF, WANTING, DEFICIENT, INCOMPLETE
courage .... CRAVEN
enthusiasm .... LUKEWARM
firmness .... LIMP
grace .... CRUDE, CLUMSY, GAUCHE, AWKWARD
in symmetry .... LOPSIDED
one of "these three" .... UNCHARITABLE
refinement ...... CRUDE, GROSS, COARSE, INCONDITE
reverence .... IMPIOUS
the power .... UNABLE
lackluster .... DULL, DRAB
Laconia is capital of ...... SPARTA
people of .... SPARTAN(S)
laconic ...... BRIEF, PITHY, SHORT, TERSE, CONCISE
answer .... UGH
person .... INDIAN
lacquer .... LAC, DUCO, JAPAN, ENAMEL, VARNISH
lacquered metalware .... TOLE
lacs, 100 .... CRORE
lactary .... DAIRY
lactase .... ENZYME
lactate .... SUCKLE
lacteal/lactescent .... MILKY
lactose .... SUGAR
lactulose .... LAXATIVE
lacuna .... GAP, SPACE, HIATUS
lad .... SONNY, YOUTH, SHAVER, STRIPLING, YOUNGSTER
lad's pursuit .... LASS
ladanum .... RESIN
Ladd western .... SHANE

413

ladder .... SCALE, SCALADE
  back .... SLAT
  kind of .... STEP, FOLDING,
    GANGWAY, EXTENSION
  part .... RUNG, STEP, SPOKE,
    STAVE, RUNDLE
  used to flee a burning
    building ...... FIRE ESCAPE
lade ...... DIP, BAIL, LOAD, LADLE,
  BURDEN
ladida .... FLOSSY, FOP(PISH)
ladies' man .... SHEIK(H),
  PHILANDERER
ladies with a common
  background .... DAR
Ladin .... ROMANSH
Ladino .... DIALECT, MESTIZO
ladle .... DIP, BAIL, BOWL, SCOOP,
  SPOON, DIPPER
  pour with .... LAVE
  spout .... GEAT
ladrone .... THIEF, BANDIT,
  ROBBER
Ladrone Island(s) .... GUAM,
  MARIANAS
lady .... BIBI, DAME, MADAM,
  WIFE, FEMALE, MISTRESS
  fair .... ROWENA
  killer: sl. .... DON JUAN,
    CASANOVA
  Private Lives .... AMANDA
  silk habit .... PELISSE
Lady Churchill .... CLEMENTINE
  Godiva, he saw .... PEEPING
    TOM
  Godiva's husband .... LEOFRIC
  Hamilton .... EMMA
  of the Lake .... ELLEN, NIMUE,
    VIVIAN
ladybird .... BEETLE, VEDALIA
ladybug .... BEETLE
ladyfinger .... COOKY, COOKIE
ladyfish .... 10-POUNDERS, TEN-
  POUNDERS
ladylike .... FEMININE, WELL-BRED
lady's maid .... ABIGAIL,
  SOUBRETTE
  slipper .... ORCHID
  smock .... CRESS
Laertes' sister .... OPHELIA
  son .... ODYSSEUS
lag .... DRAG, IDLE, DALLY,
  DELAY, STAVE, TARRY, TRAIL,
  FALTER, LINGER, LOITER
lagan .... JETSAM, FLOTSAM
lager .... BEER, CAMP
Lagerlof .... SELMA
laggard .... BACKWARD, LOITERER,
  SLOWFOOT
lagn(i)appe .... PRESENT,
  GRATUITY

lagomorph .... HARE, PIKA,
  RABBIT, RODENT
lagoon .... HAFF, LAKE, POND,
  LIMAN
  islands .... ELLICE
  site of .... ATOLL
lah-de-dah one .... SNOOT
Lahr, comedian .... BERT
laic .... CIVIL, LAY(MAN),
  SECULAR, TEMPORAL
lair .... DEN, CAVE, HAUNT,
  COVERT, HANGOUT
laity .... LAYMEN, BRETHREN
Laius's son .... OEDIPUS
lake .... LOCH, MERE, POND, POOL,
  LAGOON, SALINA
  African .... CHAD, TANA,
    NYASSA, VICTORIA
  artificial .... RESERVOIR
  basin .... PLAYA
  bird .... LOON
  city .... ERIE
  fish .... POLLAN
  fourth largest in the world
    .... ARAL
  island in a .... HOLM
  largest in U.S. .... SUPERIOR
  mountain .... TARN
  of Constance .... BODENSEE
  on California-Nevada border
    .... TAHOE
  outlet .... BAYOU
  poet ..... SOUTHEY, COLERIDGE,
    WORDSWORTH
  resort .... TAHOE
  second largest in the world
    .... SUPERIOR
  spooky-sounding .... ERIE
  third largest in the world
    .... VICTORIA
  trout .... POGY
  world's highest .... TITICACA
  world's largest .... CASPIAN
    SEA
  world's lowest .... DEAD SEA
Lake Chad tributary .... SHARI
  Erie city .... LORAIN
  Erie hero .... PERRY
  Erie port .... TOLEDO
  Erie tributary .... MAUMEE
  Geneva .... LEMAN
  Great .... ERIE, HURON,
    ONTARIO, MICHIGAN, SUPERIOR
  Maggiore town .... LOCARNO
  Michigan city .... GARY,
    KENOSHA, MILWAUKEE
lakes, study of .... LIMNOLOGY
Lal Bahadur .... SHASTRI
lalique .... GLASS
lallation .... LAMBDACISM
Lalo, composer .... EDOUARD

lam .... BEAT, FLEE, FLOG,
  ESCAPE, FLIGHT, THRASH,
  VAMO(O)SE
lama .... MONK, TESHU, PRIEST
  chief .... BLAMA, DALAI
lamasery .... MONASTERY
lamb .... (Y)EAN, CHILD, SHEEP,
  COSSET, FATLING, (Y)EANLING
  breast .... CARRE
  fur .... KARAKUL
  hide .... KIP
  holy .... AGNUS
  leg of .... GIGOT
  like a .... MEEK, TIMID
  mother of .... EWE
  pet .... CADE, COSSET
  skin .... BUDGE
Lamb, Charles .... ELIA
lambast(e) ...... HIT, BEAT, SCOLD
lambda in Hebrew .... LAMED(H)
lambent .... GLOWING
lambkin .... CHILD
lamblike .... MEEK, GENTLE
lambrequin .... DRAPERY
lambskin .... BUDGE, VELLUM
lame .... HALT, MAIM, WEAK,
  HALTING, CRIPPLE(D),
  DISABLE(D), SPAVINED
lamebrain .... NIT, SAP, SIMP,
  NINNY
Lamech, daughter of .... NAAMAH
  father of .... METHUSELAH
  son of .... NOAH, JABAL,
    JUBAL, TUBAL CAIN
  wife of .... ADAH, ZILLAH
lamed(h) .... ELL, LAMBDA
lamellibranch .... CLAM, OYSTER,
  MOLLUSK
lamellirostral bird .... DUCK,
  SWAN, GOOSE
lament .... RUE, DIRGE, ELEGY,
  MOURN, (BE)MOAN, (BE)WAIL,
  GRIEVE, REGRET, (RE)PINE,
  DEPLORE, ELEGIZE
lamentation .... PLAINT, WAILING,
  WEEPING, JEREMIAD,
  MOURNING
lamenting .... TEARFUL, UNHAPPY,
  MOURNFUL, PLAINTIVE
lamia .... WITCH, VAMPIRE,
  DEMON(ESS), SORCERESS
lamina .... PLY, LEAF, FLAKE,
  LAYER, PLATE, SCALE, SHEET,
  STRATUM
laminated .... LAYERED
  material .... PLYWOOD
  rock .... SHALE
lamination .... PLY, LAYER,
  OVERLAY
lammergeier .... VULTURE
lamp .... GAS, JET, BULB, ETNA,

GLIM, TORCH, ARGAND,
GEORDIE, LANTERN, LUCERNA,
GOOSENECK, LUMINAIRE
black .... SOOT
cord/tape .... WICK
for signals .... ALDIS
fuel .... KEROSENE
holder .... CRESSET
lighter .... SPILL, TAPER
miner's .... DAVY
oil .... LAMPION, LUCIGEN
poetic .... SUN, MOON, STAR
Lamp Lady .... (FLORENCE)
NIGHTINGALE
lampblack .... SOOT, GRIME
lampoon ...... SKIT, SPOOF, SQUIB,
SATIRE, RIDICULE,
CARICATURE, PASQUINADE
lamprey .... EEL, CYCLOSTOME
lanai .... PORCH
lanate .... WOOL(L)Y
Lancashire city .... WIGAN
county seat .... LANCASTER
seaport .... LIVERPOOL,
MANCHESTER
Lancaster, actor .... BURT
lance .... CUT, DART, PIKE, SHAFT,
SPEAR, PIERCE, JAVELIN,
(SEA)FISH
barb .... FLUKE
flag of .... BANDEROL(E)
part .... REST, MORNE
Lancelot .... KNIGHT
liege of .... ARTHUR
love of .... ELAINE
mistress of .... GUINEVERE
uncle of .... BORS
lancer .... U(H)LAN, HUSSAR
lancers .... DANCE, QUADRILLE
lancet .... FLEAM, KNIFE, SCALPEL,
PHLEBOTOME
point .... NEB
Lanchester, actress .... ELSA
lancinate .... PIERCE, CRUCIFY,
LACERATE
land .... SOIL, CATCH, EARTH,
TERRA, TRACT, ALIGHT,
DEBARK, ESTATE, GROUND,
REGION, COUNTRY, TERRENE,
DISEMBARK
adjoining port .... ONSHORE
along river .... HOLM,
BOTTOMS, INTERVALE
and sea fighter .... MARINE
barren .... GALL, WASTE,
DESERT
based .... ONSHORE
biblical, rich in gold
.... OPHIR
border .... RAND
Cardiff's .... WALES

cattail .... MARSH
church .... CLOSE, GLEBE
close .... GARTH
conveyance .... DEED
cultivated ...... ARADA, ARADO,
TILTH, TILLAGE
disputed .... MARCH
division .... PLOT
east of Eden .... NOD
eroded .... PENEPLAIN
fill area .... DUMP
grant .... HOMESTEAD
grassy .... DOWN, VELDT
held in fee simple .... ALOD,
ODAL
holder .... THANE, THEGN
holdings record .... TERRIER
in general .... REAL ESTATE
irrigated to excess .... WATER-
SICK
like arable .... OPEN FIELD
Machu Picchu .... PERU
marshy .... MAREMMA
meadow .... LEA
measure .... AR(E), ACRE,
RO(O)D, HECTARE
mine .... CLAYMORE
moist area .... SWALE
of dwarfs .... LILIPUT
leprechauns .... EIRE
Lincoln .... ILLINOIS
plenty .... GOSHEN
romance .... ARDEN
shrubs, etc. .... BARRENS
sleep .... NOD
song .... ARABY
10,000 lakes ..... MINNESOTA
the massage .... SWEDEN
the shamrock .... IRELAND
on the Mekong .... LAOS
ownership, restricted .... FEE
TAIL
ownership, unrestricted
.... FEE SIMPLE
pertaining to .... AGRARIAN,
GEOPONIC
piece of .... LOT, PLAT,
PARCEL
pledged as security
.... WADSET
point of .... CAPE,
PROMONTORY
point of low .... SPIT
promised .... CANAAN
reverting to the state
.... ESCHEAT
reclaimed .... POLDER, INNINGS
rental .... FEU
strip of .... NECK
tenure .... LEASEHOLD
tenure system .... SOCAGE

title .... PATENT
triangular piece .... GORE,
DELTA
valued for taxes .... CADASTRE
west of Nod .... EDEN
wet .... MARSH, SWAMP,
MAREMMA
with heaviest rainfall
.... ASSAM
landau .... CARRIAGE,
AUTOMOBILE
landed .... ALIT, PRAEDIAL
estate .... MANOR, DOMAIN
property .... ESTATE
proprietor .... ESQUIRE
landfall .... ISLE
biblical .... ARARAT
landgrave .... COUNT
landing field/ground, aircraft
.... STRIP, RUNWAY, AIRDROME
place .... DOCK, GHAT, PIER,
QUAI, QUAY, JETTY, LEVEE,
WHARF, TARMAC, AIRPORT,
HELIPORT
place of the Ark .... ARARAT
Landis, baseball czar
.... KENESAW
landloper ...... TRAMP, VAGRANT,
SUNDOWNER
landloping .... ERRANT, ROAMING
landlord .... HOST, LAIRD, OWNER,
BONIFACE
landmark .... CAIRN, SENAL,
MONUMENT, MOUNTAIN,
MILESTONE
landowner .... LAIRD
landscape .... PAYSAGE,
SCENE(RY)
landslide .... RUNAWAY,
AVALANCHE
landsman .... SAILOR
landtag .... DIET, ASSEMBLY
lane .... PATH, ALLEY, TRACK,
COURSE, STREET
Lange, actress .... HOPE
Langtry, actress .... LILY
language ...... LIP, IDIOM, SPEECH,
TONGUE, DIALECT, DICTION,
PARLANCE
artificial .... RO, IDO,
VOLAPUK, ESPERANTO
beggars' .... ARGOT, LINGO
classical .... GREEK, LATIN
dead .... LATIN
dialect .... IDIOM, LINGO
difficulty of understanding
.... DYSPHASIA
Hebrew's sister .... ARAMAIC
hybrid .... JARGON, LINGUA
FRANCA
kind of .... SIGN, GESTURE

mixed .... PIDGIN
of .... LINGUAL, LINGUISTIC
of the soul, so-called
.... MUSIC
of the street ...... CANT, SLANG
ordinary .... PROSE, DIALECT
origin idea .... BOW-WOW
THEORY
our .... MOTHER TONGUE
pretentious .... CLAPTRAP
Romance ...... LADIN, FRENCH,
CATALAN, ITALIAN, SPANISH,
ROMANIAN, PROVENCAL,
PORTUGUESE
science of .... LINGUISTICS
thieves' .... ARGOT, FLASH
used by Egyptian natives
.... COPTIC
using click sound .... NAMA
Visogoths' .... GOTHIC
languages, he speaks/writes
several .... LINGUIST,
POLYGLOT
Languedoc's capital
.... TOULOUSE
languid .... WAN, DULL, WEAK,
SLOW, WEARY, DREAMY,
FEEBLE, DROOPING, LISTLESS
languish .... FADE, FAIL, FLAG,
DROOP, SWOON, WASTE,
PINE(AWAY)
languor .... BLUES, ENNUI,
DULLNESS, LETHARGY,
HEAVINESS, LASSITUDE,
STILLNESS
langur .... MAHA, MONKEY,
SIMPAI, WANDEROO
laniard .... CORD
laniary .... CANINE
Lanier, poet .... SIDNEY
lank(y) ...... BONY, LEAN, GAUNT,
GANGLY, SLENDER, SPINDLING
lanner(et) .... FALCON
lanose .... WOOL(L)Y
Lansbury, actress .... ANGELA
role .... MAME
lantana .... MAJORANA
lantern .... LAMP, CRESSET
feast .... BON
Lantsang .... MEKONG
lanugo .... DOWN, HAIR
lanyard .... CORD, ROPE, THONG
Lanza, singer .... MARIO
Laodicea .... LATAKIA
Laomedon's kingdom ...... TROY
son .... PRIAM
Laos .... KINGDOM
capital ...... VIENTIANE, LUANG
PRABANG
city/town ...... PAKXE, PHIAFAI,
KHAMKEUT

fortress town .... NAM BAC
king of .... VATHANA
language .... FRENCH,
LAO(TIAN)
monetary unit .... KIP
mountain .... PHOU BIA
plain .... JARS
rebels .... PATHET LAO
river .... MEKONG, SE KHONG
lap .... LICK, RACE, WRAP,
(EN)FOLD, CIRCUIT
dog .... PET, POM
of luxury .... EASY STREET
robe .... RUG
lapel .... FLAP, FOLD, REVER(S)
stiffener .... WIGAN
thing on .... BOUTONNIERE
lapidary .... ENGRAVER,
JEWEL(L)ER, GEM-CUTTER
instrument of .... ENTAL
lapidify .... PETRIFY
lapillus .... ROCK
lapin .... FUR, RABBIT
lapis .... STONE
lazuli .... AZURE-BLUE
Laplander .... LAPP
sledge of .... PULK(H)A
lapper .... CAT, DOG
lappet .... FLAP, FOLD, LOBE,
LABEL, DEWLAP, WATTLE
lapse .... FALL, ERR(OR), FAULT,
SLIP(UP), MISSTEP, PASS(AGE),
INTERVAL, OVERSIGHT
lapwing ...... BIRD, WEEP, PEWEE,
PEWIT, PLOVER, TREUTERO
lar .... SPIRIT
larboard .... APORT, PORT(SIDE)
larceny .... THEFT
kind of .... GRAND, PETTY
larch .... PINE, TREE, SPRUCE,
TAMARAC(K)
lard .... FAT, OIL, ENRICH,
GREASE, GARNISH
tub for .... FIRKIN
larder .... PANTRY, SPENCE,
BUTTERY, CUPBOARD,
PROVISIONS
Lardner, humorist .... RING
large .... BIG, HUGE, IMMENSE,
MAN-SIZE, OUTSIZE, SIZABLE
amount .... SLEW, SCADS,
OODLES
animal/person .... JUMBO
artery .... AORTA
as a sum .... TIDY
at .... FREE, LOOSE, ABROAD
bag .... CARRY-ALL
book .... TOME
bulrush .... TULE
butte .... MESA
cask .... TUN

channel .... ARTERY
exceedingly .... ENORMOUS
extra .... MAXI
extraordinarily ...... COLOSSAL,
GIGANTIC
grasshopper .... KATYDID
heap .... MOUNTAIN
heavy lifting machine
.... WHOOPING CRANE
in scope/size .... AMPLE,
SPACIOUS
kettle .... CALDRON
prefix .... MEGA, MACRO,
MAGNI
quantity .... RUCK
scale .... EXTENSIVE,
MASS(IVE)
wave .... SURGE
woody plant .... TREE
largely .... MAINLY, GREATLY,
(PRETTY) MUCH
largeness .... SIZE, SCOPE, EXTENT
largess(e) .... GIFT(S), BOUNTY,
GRATUITY
largest continent .... ASIA
inland body of water
.... CASPIAN
island .... GREENLAND
lake in the world ..... CASPIAN
SEA
lake in U.S. .... SUPERIOR
land mass .... EURASIA
ocean .... PACIFIC
of seven .... ASIA
planet .... JUPITER
lariat .... ROPE, LASSO, REATA,
RIATA
eye of .... HONDA, HONDO
loop .... NOOSE
larine bird .... GULL
lark .... PIPIT, PRANK, SPREE,
FROLIC, HURDLE, WAGTAIL,
LAVEROCK, SONGBIRD,
ADVENTURE
genus .... ALAUDA
larkspur ...... PLANT, DELPHINIUM
larrigan .... MOCCASIN
larrup .... BEAT, FLOG, WHIP,
THRASH
larva .... LOA, BOT(T), GRUB,
MAGGOT
butterfly .... CATERPILLAR
beetle's .... GRUB, WOLF,
CADELLE
botfly .... WABBLE
final stage of .... CHRYSALIS
flea's .... CHIGOE, CHIGGER
fly .... GENTLE
frog's .... TADPOLE
mite's .... JIGGER, LEPTUS
moth's .... WOLF, EGGER

non-feeding stage of ..... PUPA
of antlion .... DOODLEBUG
of horsefly .... BOT
of tapeworm .... COENURUS
of trematode .... CERCARIA
weevil's .... GRUGRU
laryngeal sound .... AHEM
larynx .... VOICE BOX
rod for clearing ...... PROBANG
lasagna .... PASTA, MACARONI
lascar .... SAILOR
lascivious .... LEWD, WANTON,
LUSTFUL, UNCHASTE
laser inventor .... TOWNEE
lash .... TIE, BIND, DASH, FLOG,
WALE, WHIP, QUIRT, SMITE,
FASTEN, REBUKE, SPLICE,
SWITCH, SCOURGE
with words .... BLISTER
lashing .... ROPE, REBUKE,
SCOLDING, WHIPPING
lass .... GIRL, MISS, MAID(EN),
SERVANT, SWEETHEART
lassie .... GIRL, COLLEEN,
SWEETHEART
Lassie of the movies ...... COLLIE
lassitude .... LANGUOR,
LETHARGY, TIREDNESS,
WEARINESS
lasso .... ROPE, NOOSE, REATA,
RIATA, LARIAT
lassoer .... ROPER
last .... END, FINAL, OMEGA,
ENDURE, NEWEST, ENDMOST,
HINDMOST, REARMOST,
ULTIMATE
act .... FINALE
but one .... PENULT(IMATE)
chance drink .... REDEYE
chance of _____ .... MONTANA
Czarina's adviser
.... RASPUTIN
mentioned of two ...... LATTER
Mohican .... UNCAS
month .... ULTIMO
of a familiar hebdomad
.... SATURDAY
of the _____ .... BIG TIME
SPENDERS
rite .... WAKE
syllable of word .... ULTIMA
three words spoken by Jesus
Christ ...... IT IS FINISHED
will and _____ .... TESTAMENT
word in a famous
palindrome .... ELBA
word of comedian
.... PUNCHLINE
word, usually .... AMEN
Last Days of Pompeii heroine
.... IONE

Judgment .... DOOMSDAY
Supper .... CENA
Supper cup .... GRAIL
lasting .... DURABLE, LIFELONG,
PERMANENT
forever .... AGE-LONG
mark .... SCAR
lastly .... ENFIN, FINALLY
Latakia ...... TOBACCO, LAODICEA
latch .... HOOK, LASKET,
FASTEN(ING), (SPRING)LOCK
latchet .... TAP, LACE(T), STRAP
late .... NEO, DEAD, SLOW, TARDY,
FORMER, BELATED, OVERDUE
arrival .... STANDEE
bloomer .... ASTER
fetal death .... STILLBIRTH
lateen .... SAIL, DHOW, VESSEL
rigged vessel .... CARAVEL
latent .... HIDDEN, DORMANT,
POTENTIAL, QUIESCENT
later .... AFTER, TARDIER
poet .... ANON
lateral .... SIDEWAYS, SIDEWISE
opposed to .... MEDIAL
laterally ...... SIDELONG, SIDEWISE
laterite .... CLAY
latest .... LAST, NEWEST,
CURRENT, PRESENT
combining form .... NEO,
CENE
thing .... FAD, CRAZE, FASHION
latex, plant's .... MILK
plural of .... LATICES
source of .... POPPY,
MILKWEED, RUBBER TREE
trees' coagulated .... GUTTA
lath .... RAIL, RAKE, SLAT, SPALE,
SPLINE, SPLINT
lathe clamp .... CHUCK
operator .... TURNER
spindle .... MANDRIL
lather .... FOAM, SCUM, SUDS,
CREAM, FROTH, SPUME,
SWEAT
latherer .... SOAPER
lathery .... SOAPY, SPUMY, SUDSY
lathing shop .... TURNERY
Latin .... ROMAN, ITALIAN,
LANGUAGE, SPANIARD
a slip of the tongue
.... LAPSUS LINGUAE
abbot .... ABBAS
above .... SUPRA
accusation of treachery
.... ETTU
actual being .... ESSE
after .... POST
after the deed .... EX POST
FACTO
aged: abbr. .... AET

alas .... VAE, (E)HEU
all .... TOTO
alone .... SOLUS
also .... ETIAM
always .... SEMPER
always faithful .... SEMPER
FIDELIS
am present .... AD SUM
America, foreigner in
.... GRINGO
American country .... PERU,
CHILE, BELIZE, BRAZIL,
GUYANA, MEXICO, PANAMA,
BAHAMAS, JAMAICA,
HONDURAS, PARAGUAY,
ARGENTINA, GUATEMALA,
NICARAGUA, COSTA RICA, EL
SALVADOR
American measure .... LINO,
MOIO, VARA
and .... ET
and others .... ET AL(II)
anger .... IRA
ankles .... TALI
Arable land .... AGER
art .... ARS
artificially maintained .... IN
VITRO
as above .... UBI SUPRA
at first sight .... PRIMA FACIE
at approximately .... CIRCA
at the age of .... AET
at the point of death .... IN
EXTREMIS
atmosphere .... AER
author's abbreviation ..... IBID
band/sash .... FASCIA
bear ..... URSA, URSUS, URSULA
before .... ANTE, PRAE
behold .... ECCE
being .... ESSE
belts .... CESTI
between .... INTER
bird .... AVIS
bird, rare .... RARA AVIS
black .... ATRA
blessed .... BEATA
blind .... CAECUM
book .... LIBER
born .... NATUS
both .... AMBI
bronze .... AES
brother .... FRATER
bug .... CIMEX
but .... SED
by itself .... PER SE
by right of office .... EX
OFFICIO
by the day .... PER DIEM
by the head .... PER CAPITA
by the year .... PER ANNUM

417

catch-all: abbr. .... ET AL
charity .... CARITAS
city .... URB(I)S
clan .... GENS
copper .... CUPRUM
countryside .... RUS
dagger man .... SICARIUS
day .... DIEM, DIES
day of wrath .... DIES IRAE
defendants .... REI
discourse .... SERMO
dog .... CANIS
duct .... VAS
dumbfounded ...... NONPLUSED
ear .... AURIS
earth/land .... TERRA
earth exhalation ...... MEPHITIS
egg .... OVA, OVUM
either .... AUT
epic .... AENEID
equal .... PAR
error .... LAPSUS
everywhere .... UBIQUE
evil .... MALA, MALUM
existing condition ...... STATUS
QUO
farewell .... VALE
fate .... NONA
field(s) .... AGER, AGRI
fillet .... FASCIA
fire .... IGNIS
first among equals ..... PRIMUS
INTER PARES
fish .... PISCES
fisherman .... PISCATOR
flag .... LABARUM
fly .... MUSCA
for .... PRO
for example .... EXEMPLI
GRATIA
for the good .... PRO BONO
for the time being .... PRO
TEMPORE
force/strength .... VIS
friend .... AMICUS
friend of the court .... AMICUS
CURIAE
from himself .... DESE
from one side only .... EX
PARTE
from the seat of authority
.... EX CATHEDRA
gentle .... LENIS
go .... ITE
God .... DEUS
God willing ..... DEO VOLENTE
goddess .... DEA
gold .... AURUM
good .... BONUM
grape .... UVA
great .... MAGNA, MAGNUS

gums .... GINGIVA
he .... ILLE, IPSE
he loves .... AMAT
he was .... ERAT
head .... CAPUT
headband .... VITTA
health .... SANITAS
heat .... CALOR
hence .... ERGO
high .... ALTA
highest .... SUMMA
himself .... IPSE
holidays .... FERIA
holy .... SANCTUS
honey .... MEL
hour .... HORA
house .... DOMUS
however .... SED
hut .... TABERNA
I love .... AMO
I know .... SCIO
in good faith .... BONA FIDE
in passing .... OBITER
in the beginning .... INITIO
in the matter of .... INRE
in what manner .... QUO
MODO
is .... EST
itself .... IPSO
knee .... GENU
ladder .... SCALA
lamb .... AGNUS
laughter .... RISUS
law .... JUS, LEX, JURA
leave of absence .... ABSIT
leisure .... OTIUM
let buyer beware .... CAVEAT
EMPTOR
letter .... LITTERA
light .... LUX, LUMEN
likewise .... SIMUL
localities .... LOCI
long .... LONGUS
magpie .... PICA
man .... VIR, HOMO
mass .... MISSA
mass, sung .... MISSA
CANTATA
masterpiece .... MAGNUM OPUS
members .... SOCII
mine .... MEUM
mint .... MONETA
month .... MENSIS
moon .... LUNA
mountain .... MONS
mouths .... ORA
name/title .... NOMEN
needle .... ACUS
net .... RETE
nine .... NONUS
nobody .... NEMO

not .... NON
not final .... NISI
note well .... NOTA BENE
now .... NONC
number .... UNUS
observe .... NOTA
of age .... AET
of anger .... IRAE
onion .... CEPA
order .... ORDO
other .... ALIA
other self .... ALTER EGO
otherwise .... ALITER
our .... NOSTER
Our Father ...... PATER NOSTER
peace .... PAX
peace-making .... PACIFUS
peacock .... PAVO
people .... POPULI
person, unacceptable/
unwelcome ...... PERSONA
NON GRATA
place(s) .... LOCI, LOCUS
pleasant .... AMOENUS
plume .... PINNACULUM
poet .... OVID
power/strength .... VIS
"Prayer and Work" .... ORA
ET LABORA
pray(ing) .... ORA(NS)
proper .... DECOROUS
proportionately ...... PRO RATA
provided that .... PROVISO
QUOD
Quarters dwellers .... ARTISTS,
STUDENTS
Quarters site .... PARIS
quickly .... CITO
ritual .... RITUS
sailor .... NAUTA
same .... IDEM
sands .... ARENAE
secretly .... SUB ROSA
see .... VIDE
shed .... TABERNA
ship .... NAVIS
sister .... SOROR
skin .... CUTIS
snow .... NIVIS
soft .... LENIS
solid ground ..... TERRA FIRMA
something in return/
something for something
.... QUID PRO QUO
son .... FILIUS
speed .... CELERITAS
star(s) .... ASTRA, STELLA
stone .... LAPIS
table .... MENSA
thank God .... DEO GRATIAS
that is .... ID EST

the Lord's Prayer .... PATER NOSTER
then .... TUNC
therefore .... ERGO
thing .... RES
this .... HIC, HOC
thread .... FILUM
throat .... GULA
throughout .... PASSIM
thus .... ITA, SIC
tile .... TEGULA
time .... TEMPUS, TEMPORA
time flies .... TEMPUS FUGIT
to a sickening degree ...... AD NAUSEAM
be evident .... PATERE
be pleasing .... COMPLACERE
close .... CLAUDERE
destroy .... PERIMERE
go astray .... ABERRARE
make .... FACERE
make worse .... PEJORARE
pour .... FUNDERE
predict .... SAGIRE
rule .... REGERE, REGNARE
run ahead ..... PRAECURRERE
toad .... BUFO
total .... SUMMA
twice .... BIS
under .... SUB
under consideration .... SUB JUDICE
unless .... NISI
vegetable .... OLER
voice .... VOX
voice of the people .... VOX POPULI
wasp .... VESPA
waste away .... TABERE
water .... AQUA
wax .... CERA
way of working .... MODUS OPERANDI
we .... NOS
weight .... PONDUS
well .... BENE
wheel .... ROTA
where .... UBI
wife .... UXOR
within .... INTRA
without .... SINE
without setting a day ..... SINE DIE
without which there is nothing .... SINE QUA NON
wolf .... LUPUS
wool .... LANA
yawn .... HIARE
year(s) .... ANNI, ANNO, ANNUS
latite .... LAVA

latitude .... SCOPE, WIDTH, EXTENT, LEEWAY, BREADTH
latitudinarian .... DEMOCRAT
Latium, ancient people of .... VOLSCI
Latona .... LETO
progeny of ..... DIANA, APOLLO
latrine .... PRIVY, TOILET
Latter-day Saint .... MORMON
lattice .... GRILLE, SCREEN, TRELLIS, ESPALIER
latticework .... PERGOLA, TRELLIS, ESPALIER
Latvian .... LETT(IC), LETTISH
capital .... RIGA
city/town .... SALDUS, JELGAVA, LIEPAJA, REZEKNE, VENTSPILS, DAUGAVPILS
coin .... LAT
gulf .... RIGA
lake .... LUBANA
monetary unit .... LAT(U)
river .... DVINA, GAUJA, VENTA
seaport .... RIGA, LIEPAJA
state, ancient .... LIVONIA, COURLAND
laud .... HYMN, EXALT, EXTOL, PRAISE, GLORIFY
publicly .... SING ONE'S PRAISES
laudable .... DESERVING, EXEMPLARY, COMMENDABLE, (PRAISE)WORTHY
laudanum .... RESIN
laudation .... EULOGY, PRAISE
laudatory .... PRAISING, EULOGISTIC
laugh .... BRAY, ROAR, FLEER, TE-HEE, CACKLE, DERIDE, GIGGLE, GUFFAW, HAW-HAW, HEEHAW, NICKER, TITTER, CHORTLE, CHUCKLE, SNICKER
able to .... RISIBLE
at .... MOCK, RIDICULE
down .... SILENCE, EMBARRASS
loudly .... ROAR
off .... SCORN, REJECT
too much .... CACHINNATE
laughable .... DROLL, FUNNY, ABSURD, AMUSING, COMICAL, RISIBLE, HUMOROUS
laughing .... RIANT, RIDENT
gas .... NITROUS OXIDE
laughingstock .... BUTT
laughs, he never .... AGELAST
laughter. See also laugh
causing .... RISIBLE
measure of .... GALES
pertaining to .... GELASTIC
sound of .... PEAL
la(u)nce .... EEL

Launcelot the clown ...... GOBBO
Launce's dog .... CRAB
launch .... HURL, BEGIN, START, SEND OFF, DISCHARGE, MOTORBOAT
Malay .... LANCA
Spanish/Portuguese .... LANCHA
launder .... WASH
laundry equipment ...... SETTUBS
frame .... AIRER
"Laura" of movie fame .... GENE TIERNEY
lauraceous tree .... LAUREL, NUTMEG, AVOCADO, CAMPHOR
laurel .... BAY, IVY, TREE, SHRUB, AZALEA, CAJEPUT
bark .... COTO
bay .... MAGNOLIA
family .... HEALTH, KALMIA
mountain .... BUSH, CALICO
woven sprigs .... LAUREATE
Laurel, actor .... STAN
laurels ...... FAME, HONOR, KUDOS
Lausanne canton .... VAUD
lava .... ASH, MAGMA, COULEE, LATITE, TAXITE, OBSIDIAN
cinder .... SCORIA
cooled .... AA
fine .... ASH
fragment .... LAPILLUS
lava .... LOINCLOTH
pieces of .... SLAG, SCORIA
lavabo .... BASIN, TOWEL, LAVATORY, WASHBOWL
lavage .... WASHING
lavalier(e) .... PENDANT
lavatory .... BASIN, LAVABO, RESTROOM, (WASH)BOWL
lave ...... DIP, FLOW, POUR, WASH, BATHE, ABSTERGE
lavender .... MINT, ASPIC, PURPLE
product .... OIL, PERFUME
laver .... FONT, BASIN, SEAWEED
lavish .... ORNATE, WANTON, LIBERAL, PROFUSE, GENEROUS, PRODIGAL, UNSPARING, UNSTINTED
law .... ACT, JUS, LEX, CODE, RULE, CANON, EDICT, STATUTE, ORDINANCE
abstract .... JUS
and order .... PEACE
and order, GIs' .... MPS
break the .... BREACH, INFRACT, VIOLATE
breaker .... FELON, SINNER, CRIMINAL, JAILBIRD
court .... BENCH, FORUM
courts of .... JUDICIARY
degree .... LLB

denying throne to women .... SALIC

expert .... JURIST

fictitious name in .... (JANE)DOE, (JOHN)DOE

imperial .... UKASE

intervening .... MESNE

kind of .... COMMON, STATUTE, (UN)WRITTEN

like for like .... TALION

municipal .... ORDINANCE

not enforced ..... DEAD LETTER

of the Middle Ages .... CURFEW

of the place .... LEX, LOCI

offenses against .... MALA

pertaining to .... JURAL, LEGAL, CANONIC, FORENSIC

points in .... LIS, RES

the .... POLICE(MAN)

unwritten .... COMMON

volume .... CODEX

Law in physics .... JOULE'S

of Moses .... TORAH, PENTATEUCH

of Moses book .... EXODUS, GENESIS, NUMBERS

lawful .... JUST, LEGAL, LICIT, VALID, LEGITIMATE

lawgiver .... MOSES, SOLON

lawless .... UNRULY, CRIMINAL, MUTINOUS, LICENTIOUS

lawlessness .... ANARCHY, LICENSE, VIOLENCE

lawmaker .... SOLON, SENATOR, LEGISLATOR

lawmaking .... LEGISLATION

lawman .... MARSHAL, OFFICER, SHERIFF, POLICEMAN

badge .... STAR

slang .... COP(PER), JOHN LAW, THE FUZZ

lawn .... GLADE, BATISTE, CAMBRIC, GRASS PLOT

pest .... MOLE

tool .... EDGER, MOWER

Lawrence of _____ .... ARABIA

laws, body of .... CODE, PANDECTS, DECALOG(UE)

describing some ..... ARCHAIC, DEAD LETTER

what some lack .... TEETH

lawsuit .... CASE, ACTION, DISPUTE, LITIGATION

expenses .... COSTS

grounds .... GIST

of a sort .... TEST CASE

party to a .... SUER, CLAIMANT, LITIGANT, DEFENDANT, LITIGATOR, PLAINTIFF

lawsuits, habitual ...... BARRATRY

prone to .... LITIGIOUS

lawyer .... LEGIST, ADVISER, COUNSEL(OR), ADVOCATE, ATTORNEY, LEGALIST, BARRISTER, SOLICITOR

cap of .... COIF

fee of .... RETAINER

inferior .... PETTIFOGGER

of fiction .... TUTT, MASON

profession of .... BAR

slang .... LIP, MOUTHPIECE

unscrupulous .... SHYSTER

woman .... PORTIA

word of .... HEREOF, WHEREFORE, HERETOFORE

lawyers' bag .... BRIEFCASE

body .... BAR

bible .... BLACKSTONE

concern .... CASE, BRIEF, TRIAL, HEARING, EVIDENCE

degree .... LLB

patron saint .... IVES

lax .... WEAK, LOOSE, SLACK, CARELESS, DISORDERLY

laxative .... ALOIN, CASSIA, PHYSIC, APERIENT, MAGNESIA, CATHARTIC, PURGATIVE

lay .... SET, LAIC, POEM, SONG, DITTY, PLACE, BALLAD, MELODY, DEPOSIT, RECLINE, SECULAR, LOUNGE LIZARD

aside .... PEND, SAVE, TABLE

away .... SAVE

by .... HOARD

down .... BET, WAGER

down arms .... SURRENDER, CAPITULATE

figure .... DUMMY, PUPPET

into .... BEAT, LASH, SCOLD

it on .... FLATTER, EXAGGERATE

off .... STOP, CEASE, DISCHARGE

open .... EXPOSE

siege .... INVEST

to rest .... BURY

up .... PILE, HOARD

waste .... RAVAGE, DEVASTATE

layer ...... PLY, COAT, FOLD, TIER, LAMINA, PATINA, VENEER, STRATUM

feathered .... HEN, BIRD

of iris .... UVEA

layered .... SCUMMY, LAMINAR, FOLIATED, TUNICATE

layette, part of .... BOOTEE

layman .... LAIC, AMATEUR

layout .... FORMAT, MAKE-UP

lazar .... LEPER, BEGGAR

Lazarus .... LEPER, BEGGAR

friend of .... JESUS

hometown of .... BETHANY

poet and essayist .... EMMA

sister of .... MARY, MARTHA

laze .... LOAF, GOOF OFF, LOUNGE

laziness .... SLOTH, INDOLENCE

lazuli, _____ .... LAPIS

lazy .... IDLE, SLOW, OTIOSE, INDOLENT, SLOTHFUL

and Hayward .... SUSANS

fellow .... DRONE, IDLER, LOAFER, DEADBEAT, NE'ER-DO-WELL

Susan .... TRAY, TURNTABLE

lazybones .... BUM, DRONE, IDLER, LOAFER

Le Gallienne, actress .... EVA

lea .... MEAD(OW), PASTURE

leach .... BLEED, EXTRACT, LIXIVIATE

lead ...... CUE, CLUE, HEAD, HINT, OPEN, GUIDE, PILOT, BULLET, DIRECT, GALENA, PROMPT, CONDUCT, PLUMBUM

a passive existence .... VEGETATE

astray ...... DECEIVE, MISGUIDE, MISDIRECT

black .... GRAPHITE, PLUMBAGO

glass .... PASTE, STRASS

in alchemy .... SATURN

in chemistry .... PB

off .... BEGIN

on .... LURE, DIRECT, ENTICE

ore of .... GALENA

oxide .... LITHARGE

pellets .... SHOT

-pipe cinch .... SNAP

poisoning .... PLUMBISM

red .... MINIUM

rope .... LONGE

shot .... PELLET

up to .... PAVE (THE WAY)

white .... CERUSE

writing tool .... PENCIL

leaden .... HEAVY, GLOOMY, SOMBER

leader .... HEAD, CHIEF, GUIDE, OVERMAN, COMMANDER, CONDUCTOR, DOWNSPOUT

Argonauts' .... JASON

chorus .... CANTOR

of the Green Mountain Boys .... ALLEN

sheep .... BELLWETHER

leadership .... GUIDANCE, HIGH COMMAND

quality, special ...... CHARISMA

leading ...... MAIN, AHEAD, CHIEF, STELLAR, FOREMOST,

PRINCIPAL, UP ON THE LINKS
actor/actress .... STAR
bid .... OPENER
leaf .... PAGE, FROND, LAMINA,
SPATHE, LAMELLA
aperture .... STOMA(TA)
attachment .... STEM, TWIG,
STIPEL, PETIOLE
beverage .... TEA
book .... PAGE, FOLIO
bud .... GEMMA
central vein .... MIDRIB
combining form ..... PHYLL(O)
cutter .... ANT, ATTA
disease .... RUST, MOSAIC
division .... PALMATE, PINNATE
drug .... HEMP, HASHISH,
MARIJUANA
floating .... PAD
flower .... BRACT, SEPAL
fodder .... RAPE
front side of .... RECTO
grass .... BLADE
lily .... PAD
metal .... FOIL
miner beetle .... HISPA
modified .... BRACT, PALEA,
CARPEL, PISTIL
part .... VEIN, BLADE, STALK,
(MID)RIB, STIPLE, PETIOLE
pores .... STOMA
rib .... VEIN, NERVURE
shape .... OVAL, LINEAR,
OBLONG, DELTOID, CUNEATE,
PELTATE
side of .... RECTO, VERSO
stalk .... PETIOLE
through book .... RIFFLE
tip .... MUCRO
tobacco .... CAVENDISH
vein .... RIB, NERVURE
leafage .... FOLIAGE
leafless plant .... CACTUS
leaflet .... PINNA, PINNULE,
HANDBILL, THROWAWAY
leafstalk .... CHARD, PETIOLE
leafy .... FOLIOSE
shelter .... BOWER
spot .... TREE-TOP
league .... BUND, ALLIANCE,
COALITION
in .... JOINT, ALLIED
merchants' .... HANSE
Leah's daughter .... DINAH
father .... LABAN
husband .... JACOB, ISRAEL
maid .... ZILPAH
sister .... RACHEL
son ...... LEVI, JUDAH, REUBEN,
SIMEON, ZEBULUN, ISSACHAR
leak .... LET, DRIP, OOZE, SEEP

leakage .... ESCAPE
leakproofing item .... GASKET
leal .... TRUE, LOYAL
lean .... BONY, CANT, LANK(Y),
LIST, SLIM, TEND, THIN, TILT,
GAUNT, SLANT, SPARE,
MEAGER, SKINNY, INCLINE,
SCRAGGY
and sinewy .... WIRY
as a ship .... ALIST
into .... CAREEN
on .... COMPEL, PRESS(URE)
pocket .... POOR,
IMPOVERISHED
sideways .... TIP, TILT, CAREEN
toward .... PREFER
Leander's love .... HERO
leaning .... BENT, OBLIQUE,
PENCHANT, INCLINATION
tower of _____ .... PISA
leanto .... HUT, SHED, SHACK
leap .... HOP, DIVE, JUMP, LOUP,
BOUND, LUNGE, SPANG,
VAULT, BOUNCE, POUNCE,
SPRING
ballet .... ENTRECHAT
over .... SKIP, CLEAR
playful .... CAPER, CAVORT,
GAMBOL
year .... BISSEXTILE
year gainer .... FEBRUARY
leaping .... SALIENT, SALTANT
amphibian .... TOAD
Lear, daughter of .... REGAN,
GONERIL, CORDELIA
dog of .... TRAY
learn ...... HEAR, KNOW, UNEARTH,
DISCOVER, ASCERTAIN
by heart .... MEMORIZE
superficially .... SMATTER
learned .... WISE, ERUDITE,
LETTERED, LITERATE
man .... SAGE, PANDIT(A),
PEDANT, PUNDIT, SAVANT,
SCHOLAR, INTELLECTUAL
people .... CLERISY, LITERATI
learning .... WISDOM, CULTURE,
ERUDITION, KNOWLEDGE
branch of .... OLOGY
shallow .... SCIOLISM
traditional .... LORE
lease .... LET, RENT, REMISE,
CHARTER, CONTRACT
grant .... DEMISE
leaseholder .... LESSEE
leash ...... CURB, JESS, REIN, ROPE,
BRACE, LONGE, THONG,
TETHER, CONTROL
hound .... LIMER
ring .... TERRET
least .... FEWEST, MINIMUM,

SMALLEST, SLIGHTEST
abrasive .... MILDEST
amount .... WHIT
costly .... LOWEST
kempt .... SEEDIEST
likely .... LAST, MINIMAL
leastwise .... ANYWAY
leather .... KID, CALF, SUEDE
armor .... GAMBESON
bag .... POUCH
band .... STROP
bookbinding .... SKIVER
bottle .... MATARA
convert into .... TAN, TAW
cutter .... SKIVER
factory .... TANNERY
fine .... VELLUM
flask .... OLPE, MATARA
glove .... KID, NAPA, MOCHA,
SUEDE, MITTEN
heel (shoe) .... RAND
jacket .... JERKIN
kind of .... ELK, KIP, CALF,
NAPA, ROAN, MOCHA, LEVANT,
OXHIDE, CHAMOIS, COWHIDE,
MOROCCO, SHAGREEN
like .... CORIACEOUS
maker .... TANNER
napped .... SUEDE
pouch .... SPORRAN
prepare .... TAN, TAW
saddle .... MOCHILA
sheepskin .... ROAN, SKIVER
shoe repair .... FOXING
soft ...... NAPA, ROAN, MOCHA,
SUEDE, CHAMOIS
softener .... DUBBIN(G)
strap .... THONG
strip .... RAND, WELT, STRAP,
THONG
thong .... BRAIL
worker .... TANNER
leatherback .... TURTLE
leatherette .... MOROCCO
leatherfish .... LIJA
leatherneck ...... GYRENE, MARINE
leave .... QUIT, EXEAT, COMMIT,
DEPART, DESERT, PERMIT,
VACATE, SET OUT, VAMOOSE,
ENTRUST, FORSAKE,
BEQUEATH, PERMISSION
a margin .... INDENT
a Pullman .... DETRAIN
behind .... ABANDON
hurriedly .... LAM, DECAMP,
SKIDDOO, HIGHTAIL
kind of .... MATERNITY,
SABBATICAL
military .... FURLOUGH
of absence .... VACATION
off .... STOP, CEASE, DESIST

out .... BAN, OMIT, ELIDE, EXCEPT, IGNORE, EXCLUDE
port .... SAIL, OUTSTAND
secretly and suddenly .... DECAMP, ABSCOND
stage .... EXIT, EXEUNT
taking .... ADIEU, CONGE, PARTING, FAREWELL
the job .... QUIT, RETIRE
leaven .... BARM, YEAST, (EN)ZYME, SOURDOUGH
leaves .... PAGES, FOLIAGE
circular arrangement of .... VERTICIL
cluster .... ROSETTE
collectively .... FOLIAGE
covered with .... FOLIOSE
fragrant .... THYME
laxative .... SENNA
seasoning .... THYME, BAY, LAUREL
vegetable .... SLAW
leaving(s) .... ORTS, CHAFF, DRAFF, DREGS, WASTE, REFUSE, RESIDUE, REMNANTS
pick up .... GLEAN
Lebanon capital .... BEIRUT
city/town .... TYRE, ALEIH, SAIDA, ZAHLE, BATRUN, HERMIL, BAALBEK, TRIPOLI
language .... ARABIC
monetary unit .... POUND
native .... LEVANTINE
president .... HELOU, (ELIAS) HRAWI
river .... LITANI
seaport .... TYRE, SAIDA, TRIPOLI
Sur of, formerly .... TYRE
Valley river .... ORONTES
lecher .... ROUE, SATYR, DEBAUCHEE
lecherous .... RANDY, LUSTFUL, SENSUAL
look .... LEER
lectern .... AMBO, STAND, PULPIT, (READING) DESK
lection .... READING
lector .... READER, LECTURER, PREACHER
lecture .... TALK, SERMON, DISCOURSE, SCOLD(ING)
hall .... LYCEUM
lecturer .... DOCENT, READER, (PRE)LECTOR
Leda's daughter .... HELEN
husband .... TYNDAREUS
lover .... SWAN, ZEUS
son .... CASTOR, POLLUX
ledge .... LODE, SILL, RIDGE, BERM(E), SHELF

altar .... RETABLE
ledger entry .... LOSS, RENT, DEBIT, CREDIT, INCOME, EXPENSE, INTEREST
lee .... SHELTER, PROTECTION
Lee, horse of R. E. .... TRAVELER
opposed to .... STOSS, WEATHER, WINDWARD
leech .... HEAL, WORM, BLEED(ER), ANNELID, PARASITE, PHYSICIAN, BLOODSUCKER
leek ...... BULB, ALLIUM, SCALLION
relation .... ONION, GARLIC, SHALLOT
leer .... EYE, MOCK, OGLE, SCOFF, SMIRK, SNEER, STARE
leery .... WARY, DUBIOUS, GUARDED, SUSPICIOUS
lees ...... DRAFF, DREGS, GROUNDS, RESIDUE, SEDIMENT
leet .... COURT
Leeward islands .... NEVIS, ANTIGUA, ST. KITTS, MONTSERRAT
leeway .... SAG, ROOM, SPACE, MARGIN, LATITUDE
left .... WENT, NEAR(SIDE), DEPARTED, LARBOARD, PORT(SIDE)
aground .... NEAPED, BEACHED, STRANDED
combining form .... L(A)EVO
hand .... LEVO, SINISTER
hand of page .... VERSO
handed .... LEFTY, CLUMSY, DUBIOUS, SOUTHPAW, INSINCERE
on the .... NIGH
on the table .... UNEATEN
political .... RADICAL
turn .... HAW
unharmed .... SPARED
leftist ...... RED, LIBERAL, RADICAL
leftover .... END, ORT, SCRAP, MORSEL, REMNANT, SURPLUS
lefty .... SOUTHPAW
leg ...... PIN, LIMB, PROP, GAMB(E), SHANK
calf, of the .... SURAL
colloquial .... GAM, PEG, PIN, STUMP
covering .... PUTTY, GAITER, PEDULE, PUTTEE, LEGGINGS
fleshy part .... CALF
fowl's .... DRUMSTICK
front of .... SHIN
from hip joint to knee .... FEMUR
from knee to ankle ...... CRUS, SHANK
hinge .... KNEE

in heraldry .... GAMB
irons .... NIPPERS
joint .... HOCK, KNEE, ANKLE
journey's .... TREK
mutton .... AVINE, GIGOT
part .... HAM, CALF, CRUS, SHIN, FEMUR, SHANK, TIBIA, CONDYLES
pertaining to .... SURAL, CRURAL
shake a .... HURRY
support .... SPLINT
thigh .... FEMUR
vein .... SAPHENA
wooden .... STUMP
legacy .... GIFT, BEQUEST, PATRIMONY, INHERITANCE
receiver of .... HEIR(ESS), LEGATEE
legal .... JURAL, LICET, LICIT, VALID, LAWFUL, LEGITIMATE
abstract .... PRECIS
action .... RES, CASE, (LAW)SUIT, REPLEVIN, LITIGATION
arrest .... CAPTION
attachment .... LIEN
charge .... FEE
claim .... LIEN, DEMAND
code .... PANDECT
contestant .... LITIGANT
defense .... ALIBI
delay .... MORA, STAY
fee .... DUE, RETAINER
hearing .... OYER, TRIAL
instrument .... DEED
minority .... NONAGE
notice .... MONITION
offense .... CRIME, DELIT, DELICT
order .... WRIT
paper .... DEED
plea .... DEMURRER
point .... RES
possession .... SIESIN, SEIZIN
profession .... BAR, LAW
record .... ACTA, ESTREAT
redress .... REMEDY
right .... DROIT
site .... VENUE
substitute .... SURROGATE
summons .... SUBPOENA
tender .... MONEY
warning .... CAVEAT
wrong .... TORT
legalism in relation ...... NOMISM
legalize .... SIGN, ENACT
legally bound .... LIABLE
competent ..... SANE, SUI JURIS
legate .... ENVOY, AMBASSADOR
Papal .... NUNCIO

legatee .... HEIR, INHERITOR
legation .... EMBASSY, MISSION
legato, opposed to .... STACCATO
legator .... TESTATOR
legend .... MYTH, SAGA, TALE,
    FABLE, MOTTO, STORY, TITLE,
    CAPTION, INSCRIPTION
legendary .... EPIC, STORIED,
    FABULOUS, FICTITIOUS
bird .... ROC, HALCYON
talespinner .... BARON
    MUNCHAUSEN
leger .... LIGHT
legerdemain ...... MAGIC, TRICKS,
    HOCUS-POCUS, SLEIGHT OF
    HAND
leges, singular of .... LEX
legging(s) .... GAITER, PUTTEE
Leghorn ...... HAT, HEN, CHICKEN,
    LIVORNO
legible .... READABLE
legion .... ARMY, HORDE,
    MULTITUDE
unit .... COHORT, MANIPLE
legionary ant .... ECITON
Legionnaires' disease
    .... PNEUMONIA
bacterium genus
    .... LEGIONELLA
legislate .... ENACT
legislative body .... DAIL, DIET,
    HOUSE, CORTES, SENATE,
    COUNCIL, ASSEMBLY,
    CONGRESS, PARLIAMENT
building .... CAPITOL
legislator .... SOLON, SENATOR,
    LAWMAKER
legislature .... HOUSE, SENATE,
    ASSEMBLY, CHAMBER,
    COUNCIL
Canada .... PARLIAMENT
Denmark .... FOLKETING
Germany .... BUNDESTAG,
    VOLKSHAMMER
Great Britain ..... PARLIAMENT
Ireland .... DAIL (EIREAN)
Israel .... KNESSET
Japan .... DIET
lameduck .... RUMP
Norway .... STORTING
Poland .... SEJM
Spain .... CORTES
Sweden .... RIKSDAG
United States .... CONGRESS
legist .... LAWYER
legit: sl. .... STAGE, THEATER
legitimate .... LEGAL, LICIT,
    VALID, LAWFUL, ALLOWED
legless amphibian .... CAECILIAN
legree .... MASTER, OVERSEER
fictional .... SIMON

legume ...... PEA, POD, SOY, BEAN,
    SEED, PLANT, PULSE, LENTIL,
    LOMENT
Lehar, composer .... FRANZ
specialty .... OPERETTA
Lehmann, soprano .... LILLI,
    LOTTE
lehua .... TREE, MYRTLE
lei .... WREATH, GARLAND
singular .... LEU
leister .... SPEAR, TRIDENT
leisure .... EASE, OTIOSE, FREE
    TIME
leisurely .... EASY, RELAXED,
    SLOW(LY), UNHURRIED
leman .... LOVER, MISTRESS
Lemberg .... LWOW, LVOV
lemming .... RAT, RODENT
destiny .... SUICIDE
kin .... VOLE
lemon .... FRUIT, CITRUS
juice squeezer .... REAMER
juice vitamin .... CITRIN
like fruit .... LIME, CITRON
peel .... RELISH
yellow ...... CITRINE, CITREOUS
lemons, of .... CITRIC
lemur .... INDRI, LORIS, POTTO,
    AYEAYE, MACACO, MONKEY,
    SIFAKA
flying .... COLUGO, GALAGO
kin of .... TARSIER
Lemuria .... CONTINENT
Lena, singer .... HORNE
tributary .... ALDAN
lenard .... LINNET
Lenape .... INDIAN
lend .... IMPART, LET OUT,
    ADVANCE
an ear .... LISTEN
words with .... AN EAR, A
    HAND
length .... EXTENT
abbreviation .... LGTH
finger to elbow .... CUBIT
having .... LINEAR
of day's march .... ETAPE
times width product ..... AREA
unit .... MIL, YARD, METER,
    MICRON
lengthen .... EKE, EXTEND,
    DISTEND, PROLONG, STRETCH,
    ELONGATE, PROTRACT
lengthening of a short syllable
    .... ECTASIS
lengthwise .... LONGWAYS
lengthy .... LONG, PROLIX, DRAWN
    OUT, EXTENDED
lenient .... MILD, GENTLE,
    AUDIENT, CLEMENT, MERCIFUL
Lenin, premier .... NIKOLAI

    (ULIANOV)
Leningrad river .... NEVA
lenis .... MILD, SOFT, SMOOTH
opposed to .... FORTIS
lenitive .... SOOTHING
lenity .... MILDNESS
leno .... WEAVE, FABRIC
lens .... MENISCUS, REFRACTOR
hand .... READER
kind of ..... CONVEX, CONCAVE
man .... PHOTOGRAPHER
of the eye .... CORNEA,
    CRYSTALLINE LENS
opacification of the eye
    .... CATARACT
plastic prosthesis ..... IMPLANT
shaped .... LENTOID
type of .... TORIC, MENISCUS
lent .... IMPREST
Lent, 4th Sunday in .... LAETARE
observance .... FASTING
revelry before .... CARNIVAL
lentigo .... FRECKLE
lentil .... PEA, SEED, PLANT,
    PULSE, LEGUME
l'envoi .... VERSE, STANZA,
    DEDICATION, POSTSCRIPT,
    INSCRIPTION
Leonard's (Jack) forte
    .... INSULT
Leonardo da _____ .... VINCI
Vinci's famous painting
    ...... MONA LISA, LA GIOCONDA
Vinci's masterpiece .... THE
    LAST SUPPER
Leoncavallo, opera by ...... ZAZA,
    PAGLIACCI
Leonidas' country .... SPARTA
scene of defeat
    .... THERMOPYLAE
leopard .... CAT, OUNCE, OCELOT,
    PANTHER
like animal .... JAGUAR
of old .... PARD
pet .... CHEETAH
young .... WHELP
leotard .... TIGHTS
leper .... LAZAR, PARIAH,
    LAZARUS, OUTCAST
colony .... LEPROSARIUM
hospital .... SPITAL
patron saint of .... GILES
lepidolite .... MICA
lepidopteron .... MOTH
lepidate .... FLAKY, SCALY,
    SCURFY
Lepontine Alps peak ...... LEONE
leporid (leporine) animal
    .... HARE, RABBIT
leprechaun .... ELF, FAIRY,
    GOBLIN

like .... ELFIN
leprosy .... LEPRA, HANSEN'S
             DISEASE
leprous .... UNCLEAN
   beggar .... LAZAR(US)
leptons, 100 .... DRACHMA
leptus .... MITE, LARVA
lepus .... HARE, CONSTELLATION
lerot .... DORMOUSE
Les Miserables author ...... HUGO
   character .... JAVERT, FANTINE,
             VALJEAN
Lesage, novelist ...... RENE, ALAIN
lesbian .... EROTIC, SAPPHO,
            HOMOSEXUAL
Lesbos .... MYTILENE
   poet .... ARION, SAPPHO,
        ALCAEUS, LESCHES
lese majeste .... TREASON
lesion .... HURT, SORE, WART,
   WOUND, DAMAGE, INJURY,
            INFECTION
Lesotho's capital .... MASERU
   city/town .... LERIBE,
            MAFETENG
   former name ..... BASUTOLAND
   language .... SESOTHO
   monetary unit .... LOTI,
            LISENTE
less .... BELOW, MINOR, MINUS,
   UNDER, FEW(ER), SMALLER
   appealing .... STALER
   colorful .... PALER
   degree/extent .... SCALED-
            DOWN
   experienced .... RAWER,
            GREENER
   feral/ferine .... TAMER
   hearty .... WEAKER
   in music .... MENO
   in quantity/value .... LOWER
   quality .... INFERIOR
   restrictive .... LOOSER
   ripe .... GREENER
   sufficient .... SHORTER
   sweet .... TARTER
   zany .... SANER
lessee .... RENTER, TENANT
lessen .... EASE, THIN, (A)BATE,
   TAPER, MINIFY, REDUCE,
   DECREASE, DIMINISH,
   MINIMIZE, MITIGATE,
          DISPARAGE
lesser .... MINOR, SMALLER
Lesser Antilles islands
   .... LEEWARD
   Bear .... URSA (MINOR)
lesson .... EXERCISE, ASSIGNMENT,
         INSTRUCTION
   from fable .... MORAL
   music .... ETUDE

lessor .... LANDLORD
let .... RENT, ALLOW, LEASE,
   ASSIGN, PERMIT, SUFFER,
          HIRE(OUT)
   fall .... DROP
   go .... FIRE, LOOSE(N),
            RELEASE
   in .... ADMIT, WELCOME,
            INTROMIT
   it go .... FORGET, IGNORE
   it stand .... STA, STET
   on .... ACT, HINT, PRETEND
   out .... EMIT, TELL, DISMISS,
       DIVULGE, RELEASE
   ____ rest, said Adam .... EVE
   sink .... VAIL
   up .... EASE, ABATE, CEASE,
   RELAX, SLACKEN, RELENT(ED)
letdown ...... BLOW, ANTICLIMAX,
      DISAPPOINTMENT
lethal .... FATAL, DEADLY
lethargic .... DULL, INERT,
   TORPID, COMATOSE, SLUGGISH
   sleep .... SOPOR
lethargy .... COMA, APATHY,
   TORPOR, STUPOR, INERTIA,
   LANGUOR, INERTNESS,
         LASSITUDE
Lethe .... RIVER, OBLIVION
Leto .... LATONA
   daughter of .... DIANA,
           ARTEMIS
   son of .... APOLLO
Lett .... BALT, LATVIAN, LIVONIAN
letter .... BREVE, EPISTLE,
   MESSAGE, MISSIVE, CREDENCE
   addition/afterthought .... (P)PS
   airmail .... AEROGRAM
   beginning a word ...... INITIAL
   bishop's .... PASTORAL
   capital, in printing ...... UPPER
            CASE
   carrier .... COURIER, MAILMAN,
           POSTMAN
   cross stroke .... SERIF
   cut off last .... APOCOPE
   large .... UNCIAL, CAPITAL,
         MAJUSCULE
   main stroke .... STEM
   of challenge .... CARTEL
   of credence .... CREDENTIAL
   official .... BULL
   opener .... SIR, MADAM,
           CENSOR
   Papal .... BULL
   representing a word
   .... LOGOGRAM
   resignation .... DEMIT
   short .... LINE, MEMO, NOTE,
         MISSIVE

small, in printing
   .... MINISCULE, LOWER CASE
   to ____ .... GARCIA
   to host .... GRACENOTE,
       BREAD-AND-BUTTER
   to the ...... EXACTLY, LITERAL,
           PRECISELY
lettered .... LEARNED, EDUCATED,
            LITERATE
letterhead detail .... TELEX,
   ADDRESS, TELEPHONE
letterpress .... TEXT
letters .... MAIL, LITERATURE
   and curves .... ESSES
   collection/delivery of
   .... MAIL, PAPERS
   Crucifixion .... INRI
   men of .... LITERATE,
   SCHOLARS, INTELLECTUALS
   slanting up .... ITALICS
   to the stars .... FAN MAIL
   woven in design
   .... MONOGRAM
lettuce .... COS, BIBB, SALAD,
   MINION, ROMAINE
   slang .... (PAPER)MONEY
letup .... LULL, PAUSE, RESPITE,
   ABATEMENT, SLACKENING
leukemia .... TUMOR, CANCER
   type of .... ACUTE, CHRONIC
Levant or Hammerstein
   .... OSCAR
Levantine .... SHIP, SILK
   garment .... GREGO, CAFTAN
   ketch ..... SAIC, XEBEC, SETTEE
   land .... ISRAEL
   port .... ACRE, ELATH
   region .... SYRIA, LEBANON,
         PALESTINE
levee .... DIKE, QUAY, DURBAR,
   RECEPTION, EMBANKMENT
level ...... AIM, EVEN, RASE, RAZE,
   EQUAL, GRADE, PLANE,
   HEIGHT, SMOOTH, LAY LOW,
   FLAT(TEN), ALTITUDE,
         DEMOLISH
   combining form .... PLANI
   headed .... RATIONAL,
         SENSIBLE
   on the .... FAIR, HONEST
leveling slip .... SHIM
lever ...... LAM, PRY, PRISE, SWIPE,
   PEAV(E)Y, SAMSON,
        (CROW)BAR
   cam-activated .... TAPPET
   foot .... PEDAL, TREADLE
leveret .... HARE
leviathan .... HUGE, WHALE,
         MONSTER
Leviathan, author of .... HOBBES
Levis .... TROUSERS, OVERALLS

Levi's father .... JACOB
mother .... LEAH
levitate .... RISE, SOAR, FLOAT
levity .... FRIVOLITY
levy .... TAX, CESS, FINE, TOLL,
DRAFT, TITHE, ASSESS,
ENLIST, IMPOSE, IMPOST,
MUSTER, COLLECT, IMPRESS
Lew Wallace hero ...... (BEN)HUR
lewd .... LUSTFUL, UNCHASTE
Lewis Carroll character
.... ALICE, SNARK,
MADHATTER
companion-explorer
.... CLARK
Gantry of Sinclair ...... ELMER
lex .... LAW
lexicographer .... ROGET,
WORDMAN, COMPILER
lexicon .... VOCABULARY
Leyte, capital of .... TACLOBAN
Lhasa holy man .... (DALAI)LAMA
is capital of .... TIBET
liability .... DEBT, DUTY,
HANDICAP, OBLIGATION
opposed to .... ASSET
liable .... APT, OPEN (TO), BOUND,
LIKELY, SUBJECT
to punishment .... PENAL
liaison .... LINK, AMOUR, GO-
BETWEEN, LINKING (UP),
LOVE AFFAIR
officer .... COORDINATOR
liana .... CIPO, SIPO, VIBURNUM
liang .... TAEL, WEIGHT
liar .... CHEAT, DENIER, FIBBER,
ANANIAS, FIBSTER, SAPPHIRA,
DISSEMBLER, PREVARICATOR
lias .... ROCK
libation .... DRINK
libel .... MUD, DEFAME, MALIGN,
CALUMNY, SLANDER,
ROORBACK
libelous .... DEFAMATORY
liber .... BOOK
liberal ...... FREE, AMPLE, LAVISH,
PROFUSE, GENEROUS,
RECEPTIVE
of others' beliefs, views
...... TOLERANT, BROADMINDED
political ...... LEFTIST, RADICAL
Liberal Arts subject ...... LOGIC,
HISTORY, RHETORIC,
LITERATURE, PHILOSOPHY
liberate .... FREE, RANSOM,
REDEEM, MANUMIT, RELEASE
liberator .... FREER
Liberian cape .... PALMAS
capital .... MONROVIA
city/town ... HARBEL, HARPER,
BUCHANAN, TUBMANBURG

coast .... KRU
ethnic group .... GIO, MANO
language .... VAI, BASSA
monetary unit .... DOLLAR
native .... VAI, TOM
president .... DOE, TUBMAN
river .... MANO, CESTOS
tribe .... KRA, KRU, GOLA,
GORA, KRAHN
"Uncle Shad" .... TUBMAN
libertine .... RAKE, ROUE,
SKEPTIC, DEBAUCHEE
liberty .... FREEDOM
abuse of .... LICENSE
Liberty Island .... BEDLOE'S
libidinous .... LEWD, LUSTFUL
libido .... SEXUAL DESIRE
librarian's bugaboo ...... ERRATA
concern .... ANA
stamp .... DATER
library .... BIBLIOTHECA
collection .... ANA
newspaper .... MORGUE
reading place .... CARREL(L)
supervisor .... CURATOR
librate .... HOVER, POISE
libretto .... BOOK, TEXT, WORDS
Libyan capital (joint) .... TRIPOLI,
BENGHAZI
city/town .... HOMS, BARCE,
DERNA, SEBHA, ZAWIA,
TOBRUK, ZLITEN, GHARIAN,
TARHUNA
desert .... SAHARA, TIBESTI
gulf .... BOMBA, SIDRA
king .... IDRIS
language ...... ARABIC, BERBER
monetary unit .... DINAR
port .... TRIPOLI
strongman .... GADAFFI
lice .... VERMIN
infested .... LOUSY
of .... PEDICULAR
license .... PATENT, PERMIT,
FREEDOM, LIBERTY,
AUTHORITY, FRANCHISE
licentious .... LEWD
licet .... LEGAL, VALID
lichee .... NUT, LITCHI
lichen .... ALGA, MOSS, ARCHIL,
FUNGUS, RATMARA, PARELLA,
EPIPHYTE, LUNGWORT
bearded .... USNEA
genus .... EVERNIA
product .... LITMUS
licit .... LEGAL, VALID, LAWFUL,
PERMITTED
lick .... LAP, BEAT, BLOW, CLIP,
WHIP, TASTE, DEFEAT,
THRASH, VANQUISH
lollipop .... SUCK

of hope .... GLEAM
of interest .... SPARK
licking .... HIDING, BEATING,
DRUBBING, WALLOPING
lickspittle .... TOADY, FLATTERER
licorice .... PEA, ABRIN
flavoring .... ANISE
seed .... GOONCH
lid .... CAP, TOP, CASE, COVER,
STOPPER
colloquial .... CURB,
RESTRAINT
lido .... BEACH, COAST, SHORE
lie .... FIB, FLAM, LIGE, REST,
TALE, SPRAWL, PERJURE,
RECLINE, STRETCH,
FABRICATE, FALSEHOOD,
PREVARICATE, MENDACITY
adjacent to .... ABUT
anchored .... MOORED
at anchor .... RIDE
big: colloq. .... WHOPPER
describing one .... WHITE
detector .... POLYGRAPH
in warmth .... BASK
Lie, U.N. Secretary General
.... TRYGVE
Liechtenstein capital ...... VADUZ
city/town .... SCHAAN, TRIESEN
king .... JOSEF II
language .... GERMAN
monetary unit .... FRANC
mountain .... GRAUSPITZ
peak .... FALKAIS
river .... RHINE
lied .... LILT, SONG, LYRIC
lief .... GLADLY, BELOVED,
WILLING(LY)
Liege ...... LORD, LOYAL, VASSAL,
SUBJECT, FAITHFUL,
SOVEREIGN
liegeman .... VASSAL
lien .... CLAIM
lierne .... RIB
lieu .... PLACE, STEAD
lieutenant .... AIDE, DEPUTY
command of .... PLATOON
slang .... LOOIE, LOOEY,
SHAVETAIL
life .... DAYS, BEING, BIOTA,
BREATH, EXISTENCE
account of one's .... MEMOIRS,
BIOGRAPHY
building block: abbr. ..... DNA
expectancy calculation, of
.... ACTUARIAL
history .... PAST
insurance .... TONTINE
Latin .... VITA, ANIMA
long .... LONGEVITY
of _____ .... RILEY

of Riley .... EASE
of the party .... CUTUP
pertaining to .... BIOTIC(AL)
plant and animal .... BIOTA
prefix .... BIO
preserver .... MAE WEST
preserver stuffing .... KAPOK
principle .... ATMAN, SPIRIT
raft .... BALSA
regional bird .... ORNIS,
                          AVIFAUNA
saving fluid .... PLASMA
size, larger than .... HEROIC
story .... BIO(GRAPHY)
without .... AMORT, AZOIC
work .... CAREER
lifeless .... ARID, DEAD, DULL,
AMORT, AZOIC, INERT, VAPID,
                         LISTLESS
lifelike .... NATURAL
lifesaver .... LIFEGUARD
lifetime .... AGE, DAYS
lift .... PERK, BOOST, EXALT,
HOIST, RAISE, STEAL, HOLD
UP, ELEVATE, UPRAISE
British .... ELEVATOR
colloquial .... PLAGIARIZE
up .... REAR
lifting implement .... TONG(S)
muscle ..... ERECTOR, LEVATOR
ligament .... TAENIA, TENDON
combining form .... DESMO
twist a .... SPRAIN
ligan .... JETSAM, FLOTSAM
ligate .... BANDAGE
ligature .... TIE, BOND, TAENIA,
                            THREAD
Ligea and Parthenope
.... SIRENS
light ...... UMA, AIRY, FAIR, GLIM,
LAMP, MILD, NEON, KLIEG,
LEGER, TAPER, ILLUME,
SLEAZY, WHERRY, (IL)LUMINE
amplifier/amplification
.... LASER
around sun .... AUREOLA
blinding .... GLARE
bright .... NEON
bulb element .... ARGON
burning .... TORCH, CRESSET
celestial .... HALO, CORONA,
                           NIMBUS
circle .... HALO, CORONA,
NIMB(US), AUREOLA, AUREOLE
contact, in billiards .... KISS
entertainment .... REVUE
flippant .... AIRY
footed .... SPRY, NIMBLE
game luring .... JACK
gas .... ETHER
giving device .... LAMP,

TORCH, LANTERN
giving substance
.... PHOSPHOR
guiding .... BEACON
Horse Harry .... LEE
line .... RAY
manufacturing, room for
.... LOFT
measure .... LUMENS
of morning, the .... AURORA
opera .... OPERETTA
period .... DAY
perfume .... ROSEWATER
pertaining to .... PHOTIC
put out .... DOUSE
reflecting .... RELUCENT
refractor .... PRISM
ring of .... CORONA
science of .... OPTICS, PHOTICS
source of .... SUN, LAMP
sudden .... FLARE
the brandy .... FLAME
touch .... PAT, TAP
type of ...... ARC, NEON, KLIEG
unit .... LUX, PYR, PHOT,
                   LUMEN, HEFNER
with glass chimney
.... HURRICANE LAMP
without .... APHOTIC
lighted: poetic .... LITTEN
viewing instrument
.... ENDOSCOPE
lighten .... EASE, FLASH, BLEACH,
WHITEN, RELIEVE, BRIGHTEN
lighter .... HOY, BOAT, KEEL,
                    SCOW, BARGE
lamp .... SPILL
than-air craft .... AEROSTAT
lightfingered person .... DIP,
                       PICKPOCKET
lightheaded .... DIZZY, GIDDY,
SILLY, FLIGHTY, FRIVOLOUS
lighthearted .... GAY, AIRY,
                  LIVELY, CAREFREE
lighthouse .... FANAL, PHARE,
                  BEACON, PHAROS
lighting fixture .... SCONCE
means of .... SPILL
lightly .... AIRILY, EASILY
lightning .... FLASH, LEVIN,
                          FIREBALL
bug .... FIREFLY
flash of .... BOLT
rod .... ARRESTER
without thunder ...... WILDFIRE
lights .... LUCES, LUNGS
out signal .... TAPS, CURFEW
lightsome ...... GAY, AIRY, PERKY,
                   BRIGHT, NIMBLE
lignaloes .... ALOES
ligneous .... WOODY, XYLOID

lignite .... JET, (CHAR)COAL
ligule .... COROLLA
ligure .... STONE, JACINTH
Ligurian Sea city .... GENOA,
LEGHORN, LIVORNO, LA
                          SPEZIA
like .... AS, AKIN, COPY, SAME,
ALIKE, ENJOY, EQUAL, RELISH,
SUCH AS, COGNATE, SIMILAR,
                     RESEMBLING
a bachelor dinner .... STAG
bug in a rug .... SNUG
fifth wheel .... USELESS
gray day .... DREAR
kepi .... VISORED
kitten .... CUTE
knight .... ARMORED
machine .... GEARED
malt drink .... ALY
pampa .... GRASSY
parabola .... ARCED
pig out of mud
.... DISGRUNTLED
pindaric .... ODIC
rosebush .... THORNY
slender candle ...... TAPERED
smart aleck .... SASSY
switch-hitter
.... AMBIDEXTROUS
triangle .... DELTAIC
turnpike .... LANED
wallflower .... MANLESS
widow .... LORN
an acrobat .... AGILE
an angry babe? .... UP IN
                           ARMS
an angry cleric? .... HOT
            UNDER THE COLLAR
an angry perfumer?
.... INCENSED
an X-rated film .... STEAMY
angry Captain Kangaroo?
.... HOPPING MAD
angry Clara Bow? ...... FIT TO
                       BE TIED
angry Ma Kettle? ..... BOILING
                         OVER
angry Mr. Burns? .... ALL
                       FIRED UP
basil or mint .... AROMATIC
bear .... URSINE
better .... PREFER
Caesar's Gallia ..... TRISECTED
Cassius' look .... LEAN
clockwork .... REGULAR
combining form ...... INE, OID,
                         HOME(O)
D.C. agencies .... FEDERAL
Don Juan's affairs
.... AMATORY

fields on the other side of
the fence .... GREENER
fine brandy .... AGED
flea market goods
.... SECOND-HAND
flotsam and jetsam .... ADRIFT
Halloween .... LURID
hotcakes, ____ .... SELLING
Humpty-Dumpty .... OVATE
Iago's purse .... TRASHY
iambic pentameter .... CADENT
many modern people
.... NEUROTIC
many of these items
.... HOMONYMIC
marl .... CLAYEY
Mary Lou .... AGILE
measles, mumps, etc.
.... VIRAL
Mercury's feet .... ALAR
Methuselah .... OLD
Milquetoast .... TIMID
new .... MINT
____ of bricks .... A TON
poetic justice .... IRONIC
quidnuncs .... NOSY
Rizzuto's cow? .... HOLY
Savalas .... BALD
sheep .... OVINE
Shelley's works .... LYRICAL
snakes .... APOD(AL)
snow or sugar ...... GRANULAR
some ale .... ON TAP
  Bach music .... FUGAL
  clothes .... SPORTY
  eggs .... BAD
  gowns .... DRAPED
  horns .... TINNY
  lagoons .... SHOALY
  leaves .... LOBED
  mortgages .... ASSUMABLE
  paths .... BEATEN
  pickles .... SOUR
  poetry .... EROTIC
  silk .... OILED
  silver .... PLATED
  soldiers .... AT WAR
  stares .... ICY
  talkers .... GLIB
  tournaments .... OPEN
  tricks .... DIRTY
  walls .... IVED
  weather .... NASTY
  Standardbreds .... GAITED
  teammates .... ALLIED
the best laugh .... LAST
  depths .... LOWERMOST
  duckling .... UGLY
  18th amendment
  .... REPEALED
  Gobi .... ARID

infantry .... ON FOOT
market, at times .... BULLISH
otary .... EARED
Pisa Tower .... ATILT
Roman Forum .... RUINED
top of Fuji .... SNOWY
worker bee .... NEUTER
Willie Winkle .... WEE
wing .... PTERIC
likelihood .... CHANCE
likely .... APT, PRONE, LIABLE,
  SEEMLY, PROBABLE
likeminded .... ONE
liken .... COMPARE
likeness ...... ICON, GUISE, IMAGE,
  EFFIGY, SIMILARITY,
  (RE)SEMBLANCE
  bad .... CARICATURE
  show .... MIRROR
likewise .... TOO, ALSO, DITTO,
  BESIDES, MOREOVER
  not .... NOR
liking ...... FANCY, GUSTO, TASTE,
  PALATE, FONDNESS,
  PENCHANT, PREFERENCE
lilac .... SHRUB, SYRINGA
Lili .... ST CYR, MARLENE
Liliom .... CAROUSEL
lilith .... DEMON, WITCH, VAMPIRE
Lilith, husband of .... ADAM
Lillie, Miss ...... PEEL, BEA(TRICE)
Lilliputian .... TINY, SMALL,
  MIDGET, DWARF(ISH)
  hallmark .... TININESS
  republic .... SAN MARINO
lilt .... SONG, SWING, RHYTHM
lily .... LIS, LYS, ALOE, ARUM,
  ARAD, IXIA, SEGO, CALLA,
  LOTUS, ONION, TULIP, YUCCA
  African .... ALOE
  arum .... CALLA
  bulb .... SQUILL
  butterfly .... SEGO, MARIPOSA
  leaf .... PAD
  Lille .... LIS
  livered .... CHICKEN,
    COWARDLY
  origin of .... BULB
  palm .... TI
  plant .... ALOE, CAMAS(S),
    CAMMAS
  relative .... ONION
  sand .... SOAPROOT
  shaped .... CRINOID
  white .... PURE
Lily, Maid of Astolat .... ELAINE
Lima, money in .... SOL
limax/limacis .... SLUG
limb .... ARM, FIN, LEG, WING,
  BOUGH, BRANCH, MEMBER
  joint .... KNEE, ELBOW

muscle .... FLEXOR, LEVATOR
limber .... SPRY, AGILE, LITHE,
  PLIANT, SUPPLE, LISSOM(E)
limbo .... JAIL, DANCE, PRISON,
  NOWHERE
Limburg(er) .... CHEESE
lime .... CALX, CATCH, FRUIT,
  CEMENT, CITRON, LINDEN
  bush .... SNARE
  combining form .... CALCI
  fruit like .... CITRON
  harden with .... CALCIFY
  powder .... CONITE, KONITE
  product .... CALCIC, APATITE
  tree ..... TEIL, LINDEN, TUPELO,
    BASS(WOOD)
limelight .... PUBLICITY,
    SPOTLIGHT
limen .... THRESHOLD
limerick man .... LEAR
limes .... BORDER, DEFENSES
limestone ...... CALP, LIAS, MALM,
  TUFA, CHALK, OOLITE,
  CALCITE, DOLOMITE, PISOLITE
limey .... BRITON, SAILOR,
    SOLDIER, ENGLISHMAN
limicoline bird .... SNIPE,
  CURLEW, PLOVER, SANDPIPER
limit ...... FIX, CURB, METE, PALE,
  SPAN, MARGIN, CONFINE,
  BOUND(ARY), RESTRICT
limitation to inheritance
  .... TAIL
limited .... SCANT, FINITE,
  NARROW, SMALL SCALE
limitless .... VAST, IMMENSE,
  INFINITE, BOUNDLESS
limits .... BOUNDS
limn .... DRAW, PAINT, DEPICT,
  SKETCH, PORTRAY, DESCRIBE,
    DELINEATE
Limoges .... PORCELAIN
limousine .... AUTO, SEDAN
limp ...... LAX, DRAG, HALT, SOFT,
  HITCH, FLABBY, FLIMSY,
  HOBBLE, WILTED, FLACCID,
    DROOPING
  went .... SAGGED
limpet .... LAMPREY, SHELLFISH
limpid .... CLEAR, PELLUCID
linage .... ALIGNMENT
linchpin .... FORELOCK
Lincoln Center offering
  .... OPERA
Lincoln's assassin .... (JOHN
    WILKES) BOOTH
  burial place .... SPRINGFIELD
  hat .... STOVEPIPE
  sobriquet .... (HONEST) ABE,
    RAILSPLITTER
  son .... ROBERT, WILLIE

wife .... (MARY) TODD
Lind, soprano .... JENNY
sobriquet .... NIGHTINGALE
Lindbergh, a .... ANNE, CHARLES
prize money, donor of
.... ORTEIG
Lindbergh's flight .... SOLO
nickname .... LUCKY LINDY
linden .... TEIL
tree .... LIME, LINN, BASSWOOD
Lindsay, poet .... VACHEL
line .... ROW, CEIL, CORD, FILE,
RANK, REIN, ROPE, WIRE,
QUEUE, ROUTE, SERIF, TRADE,
CORDON, PATTER, STRING,
VECTOR, BUSINESS
ancestral .... LINEAGE
ancient boundary ...... ULTIMA
THULE
barometric .... ISOBAR
battle .... FRONT
bottom .... NET
cut .... SLIT
cutting .... SECANT
draw the .... LIMIT
family .... TREE, BLOOD,
ANCESTRY
fine .... SERIF, STRIA
imaginary .... VECTOR
in .... AROW
in prosody .... STICH
in trigonometry .... SINE,
SECANT, TANGENT
intersecting .... SECANT,
VECTOR
nautical ...... EARING, MARLINE
of action .... DEMARCHE
cliffs .... SCARP
David Brinkley
.... GOODNIGHT CHET
Ed McMahon .... HERE'S
JOHNNY
Gordon Hathaway ...... HIHO
STEVERINO
Jackie Gleason .... HOW
SWEET IT IS
Sgt. Friday .... JUST THE
FACTS
Steve McGarret .... BOOK
'EM DANNO
pertaining to .... LINEAL,
LINEAR
reference .... AXIS
threadlike .... STRIA
through a terret .... REIN
toe the .... OBEY, CONFORM
up .... ARRAY
waiting .... QUEUE
with bricks .... REVET
with stone .... STEAN(E)
without angle .... AGONE

lineage .... BLOOD, STOCK,
FAMILY, STRAIN, DESCENT,
ANCESTRY, PEDIGREE,
GENEALOGY
lined .... RULED, STRIATE(D)
linen .... CREA, CRASH, TOILE,
FLAXEN, NAPERY, BATISTE,
HOLLAND, LINGERIE,
STATIONERY
and wool cloth .... LINSEY
bookbinding .... BUCKRAM
closet item ..... SHEET, TOWEL,
NAPKIN
cloth .... DUCK, SEERSUCKER
coarse .... DOWLAS, DRABBET
fabric .... CRASH, SCRIM,
VELOUR(S)
fiber .... FLAX
fine .... LAWN, TOILE, DAMASK,
BATISTE, CAMBRIC
measure .... CUT
plant .... FLAXEN
room .... EWERY
scraped/softened .... LINT
sheer .... LAWN, TOILE
tape .... INKLE
transparent .... LAWN, TOILE
liner .... VESSEL, STEAMER,
(STEAM)SHIP
cheapest quarters of
.... STEERAGE
lines on map .... HACHURE
on optical lens .... RETICLE
ling .... BURBOT
linger .... LAG, WAIT, DALLY,
DELAY, DWELL, HOVER,
TARRY, LOITER
lingerie ...... SLIP, LINEN, UNDIES,
UNDERWEAR
lingering luminescence
.... AFTERGLOW
lingo ...... CANT, JARGON, PATOIS,
DIALECT, LANGUAGE
slang .... JIVE
lingua .... TONGUE
linguini .... PASTA
linguist .... POLYGLOT
linguistics branch .... SYNTAX,
SEMANTICS
liniment .... ARNICA, LOTION
linin .... CATHARTIC
lining .... GASKET, BUCKRAM,
BUSHING
link ...... TIE, JOIN(T), LOOP, RING,
YOKE, CHAIN, NEXUS,
ATTACH, CONNECT, CATENATE
consaguine .... BLOOD TIE
firmly .... KNIT
train cars .... COUPLE
linked series ...... CHAIN, CATENA
Linkletter, TV man .... ART

links ..... CAT(ENA), GOLF COURSE
connect in series
.... CATENATE
feat .... HOLE-IN-ONE
former fan club of the
.... ARNIE'S ARMY
locale .... TEE
man .... CADDY, CADDIE
number .... PAR
teacher .... PRO
linn .... POOL, LINDEN, RAVINE,
CASCADE, WATERFALL
linnet .... FINCH, SONGBIRD
linotypist .... COMPOSITOR,
TYPESETTER
linseed oil, hardened
.... LINOLEUM
mixture .... MEGILP(H)
refuse .... MILKCAKE
source .... FLAX
lint ...... NAP, FLAX, FUZZ, GAUZE,
FIBER, FLUFF, LINEN
lintel .... TRANSOM, CROSSPIECE
counterpart of .... SILL
linty .... FUZZY, FLUFFY
lion .... CAT, LEO, HERO, IDOL,
SIMBA, FELINE, CELEBRITY
biblical .... ARI
communication of .... ROAR
den of .... LAIR
female .... LIONESS
feminizes .... ESS
group .... PRIDE
mountain ...... PUMA, COUGAR,
PANTHER
neck hair .... MANE
portrayer .... LAHR
pride of .... MANE, CREST
young of .... CUB, WHELP,
LIONET
Lion of God .... ARIEL
of Judah .... SELASSIE
lioness of story/movie ...... ELSA
Lionhearted, the ...... RICHARD I
lip ...... EDGE, KISS, SASS, FLANGE,
LABIAL, LABIUM, LABRUM
adornment .... LABRET, PELELE
combining form .... CHIL(O)
cup's .... BRIM
service, of sorts
...... HYPOCRISY, MALARK(E)Y,
MOUTH TO MOUTH
slang .... INSOLENCE
touch with .... OSCULATE
lipase .... ENZYME
lipoma .... TUMOR
lipped .... LABIATE
Lippi, painter .... FILIPPO
lips .... LABIA, LABRA, KISSER
combining form .... LABIO
of the .... LABIAL

lipstick .... ROUGE, POMADE
liquefied .... FUSIL(E)
liquefy .... FUSE, MELT, THAW
   opposed to .... SOLIDIFY
liqueur .... CREME, COGNAC,
   CORDIAL, CURACAO, RATAFIA,
   ABSINTH(E)
   sweet .... CREME, GENEPI,
   CURACAO, ANISETTE,
   MARASCHINO
liquid .... CLEAR, FLUID, SMOOTH,
   AQUATIC, FLOWING
   assets .... CASH
   body tissue .... LYMPH
   change into .... LIQUEFY
   fatty oil .... OLEIN
   food .... SOUP, BROTH
   hydrocarbon .... OCTANE
   in pharmacy .... AQUA
   made .... FUSIL(E)
   measure .... TUN, GILL, PINT,
   LITER, MINIM, OUNCE, QUART,
   BARREL, GALLON, HOGSHEAD
   measuring device ...... JIGGER,
   DROPPER, DOSIMETER
   opposite .... SOLID
   oxygen .... LOX
   pickling .... BRINE, SOUSE
   rock .... MAGMA
   sour .... ALEGAR
   waste .... SLOPS
liquidate .... PAY, CASH, KILL,
   SETTLE, DISPOSE (OF)
liquidity concern .... BOTTOM-
   LINE
liquor .... ALE, GIN, RUM, RYE,
   TAP, GROG, MEAD, CREME,
   DRINK, JUICE, MASTIC,
   POTTLE, WHISKY, BITTERS,
   ANISETTE, POTATION
   alcoholic .... LUSH, MESCAL
   bad .... BOUSE, BOWSE
   bitter .... ABSINTH(E)
   bootleg .... ROTGUT
   bottle .... MAGNUM
   cheap .... SLIPSLOP
   colloquial .... BOOZE
   dram of .... TOT
   drink .... DRAM, TIFF
   drugged .... MICKEY (FINN)
   follower .... CHASER
   fruit juice .... BRANDY
   glass .... SNIFTER
   leftover .... HEELTAP
   loss through leakage, etc.
   .... ULLAGE
   malt .... ALE, STOUT
   measure ...... NIP, DRAM, GILL,
   PINT, JIGGER, NOGGIN
   pick-me-up .... STIM
   sap .... NIPA

sugarcane .... TAF(F)IA
tonic .... BITTERS
lira, ¹/₂₀ of .... SOLDO
liripipe .... TIPPET
Lisbon river .... TAGUS
Lisle ...... LILLE, FABRIC, GLOVES,
   THREAD, STOCKINGS
lissom(e) .... LITHE, LIMBER,
   NIMBLE, SUPPLE, SVELTE
list .... TIP, CANT, HEEL, LEAN,
   ROLL, TILT, INDEX, SLATE,
   TABLE, CAREEN, ITEMIZE,
   CATALOG(UE), CALENDAR,
   REGISTER, TABULATE,
   INVENTORY
   actors' .... CAST
   business meeting ..... AGENDA
   candidates' ..... SLATE, TICKET
   of bonds, stocks
   .... PORTFOLIO
   of persons .... ROLL, ROSTER
   of the dead .... BEADROLL
   of things to be done
   .... AGENDA
   particulars .... ITEMS
   team players' .... LINEUP
listen .... HEAR, HEED, HIST,
   HARK(EN), HEARKEN,
   EAVESDROP
listener .... EAR, AUDITOR
   surreptitious .... BUGGER,
   EAVESDROPPER
listening .... AUDIENT
   device .... BUG, MONITOR
   post, usually .... EMBASSY
lister .... PLOW
listing .... TABLE, CATALOG,
   TABULATION
listless .... LANGUID, SPIRITLESS
listlessness .... ENNUI, APATHY
lists .... ROLLS, ARENA, TILTS
Liszt, pianist .... FRANZ
lit .... LANDED, ALIGHTED
   up .... SMILED
litany .... PRAYER
litchi .... NUT, TREE, LICHEE
literal .... REAL, EXACT, PLAIN,
   PROSAIC, TEXTUAL,
   ACCURATE, WORD-FOR-WORD
   quotation sign of .... SIC
   translation .... METAPHRASE
literally .... LITERATIM,
   PRECISELY, VIRTUALLY
literary ...... LEARNED, LETTERED,
   SCHOLARLY
   bits .... ANA, ANALECTA
   collection .... ANA,
   MISCELLANEA
   criticism .... REVIEW, CRITIQUE
   drudge .... GRUB, HACK
   extracts .... ANALECTA,

   ANALECTS
   form ...... POEM, ESSAY, VERSE
   grouping .... ODE
   hack .... GRUB
   initials .... GBS, RLS
   light .... WRITER
   patchwork .... CENTO
   quotation brief .... SNIPPET
   review .... CRITIQUE
   society .... LYCEUM
   style .... PEN, RACOCO
   work, inferior .... SCRIBBLE,
   POTBOILER
literate ...... LEARNED, CULTURED,
   LETTERED
literati .... MEN OF LETTERS
literature .... WRITINGS
lithe .... SLIM, AGILE, LIMBER,
   SUPPLE, SVELTE, LISSOM(E),
   SYLPHIC, FLEXIBLE
lithograph .... PRINT, CHROMO
lithology, subject of .... ROCKS
Lithuanian .... BALT, LETT
   capital .... VILNA, VILNIUS
   city/town .... KAUNAS,
   PLUNGE, TELSIAI, TAURAGE,
   KAPSUKAS, KLAIPEDA,
   KURSENAI, SIAULIAI
   coin .... LIT(AS), RUBLE
   president .... LANDSBERGIS
   river .... NIEMEN, VILIYA
   seaport .... MEMEL
litigant .... SUER, DEFENDANT,
   CONTESTANT, COMPLAINANT
litigate .... SUE
litigation .... LAWSUIT
litigious .... QUARRELSOME
   people .... SUERS
litotes .... MEIOSIS
litter .... BIER, FALL, MESS,
   MULCH, STREW, COFFIN,
   JUMBLE, CLUTTER, RUBBISH,
   SCATTER, OFFSPRING,
   PALANQUIN, STRETCHER
   bearer .... CAT, DOG, PIG
   last-born .... WALLYDRAG
   of pigs .... FARROW
little ...... WEE, POCO, PUNY, TINY,
   BRIEF, SMALL, YOUNG,
   MINUTE, PALTRY, TRIVIAL
   at a time, drink a .... SIP
   bird .... HUMMINGBIRD
   bit .... FIG, CRUMB, MORSEL
   bits .... SOUPCONS
   by little .... SLOWLY,
   PIECEMEAL
   combining form .... MICR(O)
   darling .... ANGEL
   Elizabeth .... BESS
   fellow .... BUB
   fib .... WHITE LIE

finger .... PINKIE
fragments .... FLINDERS
grimace .... MOUE
hours .... SEXT, TIERCE
island .... AIT
moon, old style .... LUNET
one .... SHAVER
ones: suffix .... ULI
piece of wood/stone ...... CHIP
spot/speck .... DOT, PINPOINT
Theresa .... TESSIE
umbrella .... PARASOL
Little Bear .... KOALA, URSA
MINOR
Big Horn protagonist
.... CUSTER, SITTING BULL
Boot .... KALIGULA
Boy Blue author .... FIELD
Boy Blue painter .... MONET
Caesar .... CAESARION
Corporal .... NAPOLEON
Flower, mayor .... LA
GUARDIA
Fox .... VULPECULA
Iodine cartoonist .... HATLO
Leaguer .... PEEWEE
Miss Muffet's food ..... WHEY
Orphan Annie creator
.... (JAMES WHITCOMB) RILEY
Russia .... UKRAINE
_____, Stowe character
.... EVA
Tibet .... LADAKH
littleneck .... CLAM, QUAHOG
littlest .... TINIEST
of the litter .... RUNT
littoral .... SHORE, COAST(AL)
stretch .... STRAND
litu, singular of .... LITAS
liturgical singer .... CANTOR
liturgy .... MASS, RITE, RITUAL
litus .... SERF
Litvinov, Russ, statesman
.... MAXIM
livable .... HABITABLE,
TENANTABLE
live .... ABIDE, DWELL, EXIST,
RESIDE, BREATHE, INHABIT,
SUBSIST, SURVIVE
a life of passivity
.... VEGETATE
able to .... VIABLE
alone .... BACH
coal .... EMBER
it _____ .... UP
it up .... HAVE A BALL
on bare essentials ...... ROUGH
IT
or die .... SINK OR SWIM
together .... COHABIT

under false pretenses
.... MASQUERADE
wire: colloq. .... HUSTLER, GO-
GETTER, POWERHOUSE
livelihood .... JOB, MEANS, LIVING,
(UP)KEEP, SUPPORT, (DAILY)
BREAD
liveliness .... PEP, VIVACITY
livelong .... WHOLE, ENTIRE
lively .... GAY, SPRY, AGILE,
BRISK, PE(A)RT, PERKY,
ACTIVE, ANIMATED, SPIRITED,
VIVACIOUS, SPRIGHTLY
air .... LILT
intelligence .... ESPRIT
music .... VIVO, ANIMATO
party .... BASH
liven .... CHEER (UP)
liver .... HEPAR
collection of pus in the
.... ABSCESS
diagnostic test .... BIOPSY
disease .... CIRRHOSIS
disease, sign of ...... JAUNDICE
inflammation .... HEPATITIS
is body's _____ factory
.... CHEMICAL
is supposed seat of
.... DESIRE, EMOTION
part ...... CELL, DUCT, ARTERY,
LOBULE, PORTAL VEIN,
HEPATIC VEIN
pertaining to .... HEPATIC
replacement of diseased
.... TRANSPLANT
secretion .... BILE, GALL
shape .... CONE
tumor .... HEPATOMA
livered, yellow .... COWARDLY
liverish .... CROSS, BILIOUS
liverwort .... HEPATICA,
BRYOPHYTE
genus .... RICCIA
liverwurst .... SAUSAGE
livery .... STABLE, UNIFORM
wearer of .... LACKEY,
FLUNK(E)Y, SERVANT
livestock .... COWS, CATTLE,
STEERS
bacterial infection
.... ANTHRAX
disease .... NAGANA
farm .... RANCH
round up .... WRANGLE
livid .... WAN, PALE, ASHEN,
PALLID, DISCOLORED, BLACK-
AND-BLUE
living .... ALIVE, BEING, QUICK,
EXTANT, ANIMATE, EXISTING,
LIVELIHOOD
capable of .... VIABLE

corpse .... ZOMBI(E)
matter .... PROTOPLASM
on land or in water
.... AMPHIBIAN
on river bank .... RIPARIAN
picture .... VIVANT, TABLEAU
prefix .... LIVI, VIVI
room .... SALA, PARLOR
Livonian ...... LETT, ESTH(ONIAN)
Livorno .... LEGHORN
lixivium .... LYE, LEACH
lizard ...... EFT, UTA, ADDA, GILA,
NEWT, SEPS, URAN, AGAMA,
ANOLE, ANOLI, GECKO,
GUANA, SKINK, SWIFT,
VARAN, IGUANA, MOLOCH,
MONITOR, SAURIAN, BASILISK,
CHAMELEON, LACERT(IL)AN
chameleon-like .... ANOLI
color-changing/starred
.... AGAMA, CHAMELEON
combining form .... SAURO,
SAURUS
genus .... UMA, AGAMA
like .... SAURIAN
wall/nocturnal .... GECKO
Lizette of poetry .... REESE
llama .... PACO, ALPACA, VICUNA,
RUMINANT
habitat .... ANDES
relative ...... CAMEL, GUANACO
llanero .... GAUCHO
llanero's weapon .... BOLA
llano .... PLAIN, STEPPE
LLB holder .... ATTY
lo .... SEE, ECCE, LOOK, BEHOLD
companion of .... BEHOLD
loa .... LARVA
loach .... CARP, SMERLIN
load .... FILL, LADE, ONUS,
CARGO, BURDEN, FREIGHT,
ENCUMBER, SHIPMENT
a gun .... CHARGE
transported .... HAUL
loaded .... LADEN, FRAUGHT,
WEIGHTED
carrier .... CARFUL
slang .... RICH, DRUNK,
STINKO, MONEYED, WEALTHY,
IN THE MONEY
loadstone/lodestone
.... MAGNET(ITE)
loaf .... IDLE, LOLL, BREAD,
LOITER, LOUNGE, GOLDBRICK,
TAKE IT EASY
white bread .... MANCHET
loafer .... BUM, SHOE, DRONE,
IDLER, LOUNGER
loafing .... FLANERIE
loam .... DIRT, MALM, MARL, SOIL,
EARTH, LOESS

loan .... PREST
  ask for a .... BRACE, TOUCH
  of money .... IMPREST
  note: colloq. .... IOU
  privilege .... CREDIT
  shark .... USURER, SHYLOCK
loath .... AVERSE, HOSTILE,
    RELUCTANT, UNWILLING
loathe ...... HATE, ABHOR, DETEST,
    ABOMINATE
loathsome .... FOUL, VILE,
    ABHORRENT, REPULSIVE,
    DETESTABLE
lob .... COP, LOP, LOFT
lobby ...... HALL, FOYER, LOUNGE,
    ANTEROOM, VESTIBULE
lobbyist .... RAINMAKER
lobbyists? .... THIRD HOUSES
lobe .... LAPPET
  ear .... EARLOP
  whale tail's .... FLUKE
lobelia .... CAMAS(S)
loblolly ...... PINE, BROTH, GRUEL,
    PUDDLE
lobo .... WOLF
lobster .... MACRURAN,
    CRUSTACEAN
  claw .... CHELA, NIPPER,
    PINCER
  coral .... ROE
  egg(s) .... BERRY, SPAWN
  feeler of .... ANTENNA,
    PALP(US)
  part of a .... CHELA, TELSON,
    THORAX
  protective cover .... MAIL
  spawn of .... CORAL
  trap for .... POT
local .... BRANCH, NATIVE,
    REGION, CHAPTER, TOPICAL,
    VICINAL, WAY TRAIN
  boy .... NATIVE SON
  hero .... THE TOAST OF THE
    TOWN
locale .... SITE, PLACE, SCENE,
    VENUE, LOCALITY
  for the indecisive .... FENCE
  landlubbers' .... ASHORE
  links' .... TEE
  Omsk's .... SIBERIA
locality .... AREA, SPOT, LOCUS,
    PLACE, SITUS, VENUE
  restricted to a .... ENDEMIC,
    INDIGENOUS
locate .... BASE, FIND, SPOT,
    PLACE, SETTLE, MARK OFF,
    SITUATE
locating system .... RADAR
location .... SITE, SPOT, POSITION,
    PLACE(MENT), SITUATION
  person's .... WHEREABOUTS

loch .... BAY, LAKE, POND,
    LOMOND
loci, singular of .... LOCUS
lock .... CURL, CLOSE, TRESS,
    COTTER, DETENT, FASTEN,
    SECURE, CONFINE, RINGLET
  brand .... ACE, YALE
  hair .... TAG, CURL, TRESS,
    RINGLET
  mechanism .... DETENT
  part .... BOLT, STUMP, DETENT,
    TUMBLER, CYLINDER
  stock, and barrel .... ENTIRE
  up .... JAIL
locker .... KIST, AMBRY, CHEST,
    CLOSET, COMPARTMENT
locket's content .... PICTURE
lockjaw .... TETANUS, TRISMUS
lockup .... JUG, PEN, JAIL, STIR,
    CALABOOSE
loco .... CRAZY, LOONY,
    DEMENTED
locofoco .... CIGAR, MATCH
locomotive .... DOLLY, DUMMY,
    MOGUL, DINKEY, SWITCHER,
    IRON HORSE
  coal car .... TENDER
  cowcatcher .... FENDER
  driver .... ENGINEER
  driver's place .... CAB
  sound .... CHOO, CHUFF
  stopping place ..... TANKTOWN
locus .... PLACE, POINT
locust ...... TREE, CICADA, CICALA,
    INSECT
  kin .... CRICKET
  tree .... CAROB, ACACIA
locution .... WORD, IDIOM,
    PHRASE, EXPRESSION
lode .... REEF, VEIN
  cavity .... VUG(G), VUGH
lodestar .... POLARIS, GUIDING
    STAR
lodge .... HUT, BOARD, HOUSE,
    BILLET, CHAPTER, QUARTER
  Indian .... TENT, TEPEE,
    WIGWAM
  member .... ELK, MASON
lodger .... GUEST, ROOMER
  temporary .... TRANSIENT
lodging .... ABODE, ROOST,
    QUARTERS
  house .... INN, HOTEL,
    HOSTEL(RY)
  house bed .... DOSS
loess .... LOAM
Lofgren, guitarist .... NILS
loft .... LOB, ATTIC, GARRET,
    GALLERY, MANSARD
lofty .... HIGH, GRAND, NOBLE,
    SKYEY, SUBLIME

  dwelling .... AERY, AERIE
log .... DIARY, RECORD, TIMBER
  barrier .... BOOM
  float .... RAFT, CATAMARAN
  holder .... CANT HOOK
  house/structure .... CABIN
  measure .... SCALAGE
  roller .... DECKER
  rolling contest .... ROLEO
  sling .... PARBUCKLE
  spin a .... BIRL
  splitter .... WEDGE
  splitting wedge .... FROE
  turner .... PEAV(E)Y
loganberry .... BRAMBLE
logarithm inventor .... NAPIER
  unit .... BEL
loge .... BOX, STALL
logger .... LUMBERJACK,
    WOODCUTTER
  boots of .... PACS
  sled of .... TODE, GO-DEVIL,
    TRAVOIS
loggerhead .... DUNCE, TURTLE
loggia .... ARCADE, GALLERY,
    PORTICO
logia .... MAXIMS, SAYINGS
logic .... REASONING
  deductive .... SYLLOGISM
  premise .... SUMPTION
logical .... WISE, SOUND,
    RATIONAL
  argument .... SYLLOGISM
logistic .... ARITHMETIC
logistics, concern of ...... SUPPLY,
    QUARTERS
logograph .... ANAGRAM, WORD
    PUZZLE
Logos .... WORD
logroller .... BIRLER, DECKER,
    POLITICIAN
logrolling .... BIRLING, EXCHANGE,
    LOBBYING, SWAPPING
  political booty of .... PORK
    (BARREL)
  subject .... BILL
logs floating in mass .... DRIVE
  passage down slope
    .... FLUME, SLUICE
  pile of .... ROLLWAY
Lohengrin's bride .... ELSA
  composer .... WAGNER
  father .... PARSIFAL
loin .... RACK, BEEFCUT
  combining form ...... LUMB(O)
  muscle .... PSOAS
  section .... GRISKIN
loincloth .... MALO, MARO, DHOTI,
    LUNGEE, SARONG, G-STRING,
    LAVA-LAVA
loins .... HIPS

pertaining to the ...... LUMBAR
Loire River city .... BLOIS,
            NANTES, ORLEANS
loiter .... LAG, IDLE, LOAF, DALLY,
    TARRY, DAWDLE, LINGER,
         LOUNGE, SAUNTER
loiterer .... IDLER, LAGGARD
Loki's daughter .... HEL(A)
  son .... NARE
  victim .... BALDER
  wife .... SIGYN
loll ...... LOP, HANG, LAZE, DROOP,
               LOUNGE
Lollander .... DANE
lollapaloosa .... LULU
lollipop .... CANDY, SUCKER
Lollobrigida, actress .... GINA
Lombard capital .... PAVIA
Lombardy capital .... MILAN
  city .... PAVIA
  ruler .... ALBOIN
Lombok neighbor .... BALI
loment .... LEGUME
London, ancient name of
  .... AGUSTA
  art gallery ..... TATE, SOTHEBY
  barrister .... TEMPLAR
  borough .... CHELSEA,
      LAMBETH, BATTERSEA,
    GREENWICH, WESTMINSTER
  botanical gardens .... KEW
  cleaning woman .... CHAR
  club .... KITCAT
  dessert, in .... AFTERS
  dialect/language ..... COCKNEY
  district .... SOHO, ADELPHI,
    CHELSEA, LAMBETH, MAYFAIR,
           LIMEHOUSE
  famous Guildhall effigy
  .... GOG
  fashionable section
  .... MAYFAIR, BELGRAVIA
  foreign quarter .... SOHO
  hawker .... MUN, COSTER
  hooligan .... SPIV
  horse market
  .... TATTERSALL'S
  landmark ...... TOWER, BRIDGE,
    BIG BEN, OLD VIC, MARBLE
              ARCH
  mental hospital .... BEDLAM
  native .... COCKNEY
  park .... HYDE
  people movers .... TRAMS
  policeman .... BOBBY
  prison .... NEWGATE
  river .... THAMES
  royal palace in
  .... BUCKINGHAM
  royal stables .... MEWS
  ruffian .... MOHOCK

ship of Jack .... SNARK
statue ...... GOG, EROS, MAGOG
street ...... BOND, SOHO, FLEET,
  REGENT, STRAND, DOWNING,
    LOMBARD, PALLMALL
streetcar .... TRAM
student of law .... TEMPLAR
suburb .... KEW, EALING,
            WEMBLEY
subway .... TUBE
theatre .... DRURY LANE
underwriters .... LLOYD'S
upperclass neighborhood
.... GROSVENOR SQUARE
West End .... SOHO
writer .... JACK
Londoner .... COCKNEY
lone .... SOLE, SOLO, SINGLE,
            SOLITARY
Lone Ranger's pal .... TONTO
  Star State .... TEXAS
loneliness .... MELANCHOLIA
  kind of .... NOSTALGIA
lonely .... LORN, DESOLATE,
            SOLITARY
loner, kind of .... HERMIT,
           MUGWUMP
lonesome ...... LONELY, DESOLATE
long .... LENGTHY, EXTENDED,
  FAR-GOING, EXTENSIVE
  ago .... WAY BACK, OLDEN
             TIMES
  and lean .... LANK
  before .... SOON
  distance .... (TELE)PHONE CALL
  distance contest
  .... MARATHON
  drawn .... PROLONGED
  established .... ROOTED,
         CUSTOMARY
  face .... SCOWL
  faced ..... SAD, GLUM, SERIOUS
  fish .... EEL, GAR
  for .... ACHE, PINE, CRAVE,
  YEARN, ASPIRE, HANKER
  journey .... TREK, ODYSSEY
  lasting .... DURABLE
  life .... LONGEVITY
  limbed .... LANKY, LEGGY
  live! .... VIVA, VIVE
  lived .... AGED, HARDY,
           ANCIENT
  necked animal .... GIRAFFE
  period .... EON
  range .... APOGEE
  seat .... BENCH, SETTEE
  shot ...... GAMBLE, CHANCE HIT
  shot race horse .... PLATER,
          SLEEPER
  suffering .... STOIC, PATIENT,
    TOLERANT, FORGIVING

  winded .... GABBY, WORDY,
  PROLIX, TEDIOUS, VERBOSE,
        TALKATIVE
Long Island county .... KINGS,
  NASSAU, QUEENS, SUFFOLK
  racetrack .... BELMONT
longanimity .... PATIENCE,
  ENDURANCE, WAITING GAME
longeron .... SPAR
longevity .... AGE, LIFETIME, LONG
        LIFE, SURVIVAL
longest-running Broadway
  show:
  first .... A CHORUS LINE
  second .... OH! CALCUTTA
  third .... CATS
Longfellow bell town .... ATRI
  poet .... HENRY WADSWORTH
  wife of .... FANNY
longhair .... HIGHBROW
longhand .... WRITTEN,
  HANDWRITING, SCRIPT, IN
    ONE'S OWN HAND
longhorn .... CATTLE
longing .... YEN, CRAVING,
        YEARNING
longshoreman .... DECKER,
    LUMPER, STEVEDORE
longshot hopeful .... DARK HORSE
  winner .... SLEEPER
lonicera .... HONEYSUCKLE
loo .... PAM, CARD GAME
looby .... LOUT, LUBBER
looey/looie .... LIEUTENANT
  aide of .... SARGE
loofah .... SPONGE
look .... EYE, PRY, SEE, GAPE,
  GAZE, MIEN, PEER, SEEK,
  SEEM, APPEAR, ASPECT,
  BEHOLD, GANDER, GLANCE,
         SEARCH
  after .... TEND
  alike .... RINGER
  amorous .... OGLE
  angry .... GLARE
  askance .... LEER
  at/over .... EXAMINE, INSPECT
  back .... RECALL
  _____ (be alert) .... ALIVE
  coldly upon ..... SNUB, REBUFF
  fixedly/intently .... STARE
  forward to .... EXPECT
  frowning .... LOUR, SCOWL,
        (G)LOWER
  in .... ENTER, VISIT
  into .... PROBE, EXPLORE
  into the mirror? .... MEET
    FACE TO FACE
  over quickly .... PEEK, SCAN,
        GLANCE
  over: sl. .... CASE

scornful/nasty .... SNEER
sullen .... POUT
the other way .... IGNORE,
LIVE AND LET LIVE
threatening .... LOWER
up to .... ADORE, REVERE,
IDOLIZE, RESPECT
looker-on .... WITNESS, OBSERVER,
BYSTANDER, SPECTATOR
looking glass .... MIRROR
lookout .... GUARD, SPOTTER,
WATCHER, OBSERVER
alert .... ARGUS
nautical .... CROW'S NEST
post .... WATCH TOWER
loom .... WEAVE, APPEAR, TAKE
SHAPE
bar .... EASER
frame .... BATTEN
part .... PIRN, REED, SLEY,
WARP, EASER, BATTEN,
HEDDLE, SHUTTLE, TREADLE
loon .... DOLT, LOUT, DIVER,
GREBE, (DIVING)BIRD
loony .... DAFT, CRAZY, DEMENTED
loop ..... TAG, RING, BRIDE, NOOSE,
TERRY, EYE(LET), CIRCUIT,
GROMMET
edging .... PICOT
in electricity .... CIRCUIT
in lariat .... HONDOO
on boot/garment .... TAG,
STRAP
running .... NOOSE
small .... TAGLET
looper .... WORM, LARVA
loophole .... CHINK, JOKER,
M(E)USE, ESCAPE, EYELET
Loos, writer .... ANITA
loose .... FREE, (RE)LAX, AT
LARGE, INEXACT, RELEASE,
UNBOUND
change .... CENTS, COINS
end .... TAGRAG
let .... RELEASE
sleeve .... RAGLAN
turn .... FREE, RELEASE
loosen .... EASE, UNDO, RELAX,
UNTIE, RELEASE, SLACKEN
loot .... HAUL, SWAG, BOOTY,
RIFLE, SPOILS, DESPOIL,
PILLAGE, PLUNDER,
(RAN)SACK
lop ...... CHOP, HANG, LOLL, POLL,
SNED, SNIP, TRIM, PRUNE, CUT
OFF, SNATHE
lope .... CANTER
Lopez of Hullabaloo .... TRINI
loppy .... LIMP, SAGGING,
DROOPING
lopsided .... ALOP, ALIST, ASKEW,

UNEVEN, UNEQUAL
loquacious .... GABBY, CHATTY,
GOSSIPY, VOLUBLE,
GARRULOUS, TALKATIVE
loquacity/loquaciousness
.... GARRULITY, VERBOSITY
Loran, part of .... LONG, RANGE,
NAVIGATION
lord .... EARL, PEER, RULE,
BARON, LIEGE, RULER,
ADONAI, BISHOP, MASTER,
MARQUIS, SEIGNOR,
DOMINEER, NOBLEMAN,
VISCOUNT
companion of .... MASTER
wife of .... LADY
Lord Greystoke .... TARZAN
Marmion's horse .... BEVIS
of Hosts .... GOD, JEHOVAH
the .... GOD
lord's land ...... MANOR, DEMESNE
manor .... DEMESNE
Lord's Day .... SUNDAY
Prayer, first word(s) .... OUR
FATHER, PATERNOSTER
Supper .... EUCHARIST
lordly .... NOBLE, HAUGHTY,
ARROGANT, DIGNIFIED,
OVERBEARING
lordship .... RULE, DOMINION,
SEIGNIORY
lore .... WISDOM, LEARNING,
ERUDITION, KNOWLEDGE
Lorelei .... SIREN, LURLEI
golden possession of
.... COMB
river .... RHINE
victims ...... SAILORS, MARINERS
Lorenz, ethologist .... KONRAD
Loretta Young role ...... RAMONA
lorgnette .... OPERA GLASS
lorgnon ...... MONOCLE, PINCENEZ
lorica .... SHELL, LORLEA,
CUIRASS, CARAPACE,
CORSELET
lorikeet .... LORY, PARROT
loris .... LEMUR
lorn .... BEREFT, DESOLATE,
FORSAKEN
Lorna _____ .... DOONE
Doone author ..... BLACKMORE
Doone character .... TOM,
ALAN, RIDD, LORNA
Doone rescuer .... RIDD
lorry .... TRUCK, WAGON
lory .... PARROT, LORIKEET
Lortzing's opera .... UNDINE
Los Angeles baseball team
.... DODGERS
Angeles basketball team
.... LAKERS, CLIPPERS

Angeles campus .... UCLA
Angeles football team
.... RAMS, RAIDERS
Angeles mayor .... BRADLEY
_____ (atomic energy
worksite) .... ALAMOS
Troyens .... THE TROJANS
lose .... MISS, WASTE, MISLAY,
FORFEIT, MISPLACE,
SQUANDER
ardor .... PALL
color ...... FADE, PALE, WHITEN
flavor .... PALL
footing .... SLIP, SLIDE
heart .... DESPAIR
one's head .... PANIC
purposely .... THROW
sweetness .... SOUR
traction .... SKID
weight .... DIET, SLENDERIZE
whiteness .... YELLOW
loser .... VICTIM, ALSO-RAN,
PESSIMIST
attitude of .... FED-UP
poor/bad .... CRYBABY,
SOREHEAD, SOURPUSS
to St. George .... DRAGON
to Ulysses S. Grant
.... ROBERT E. LEE
loss .... DAMAGE, DEFEAT,
PERDITION, FORFEITURE,
DEPRIVATION
at a .... BAFFLED, PUZZLED,
DISMAYED
from container .... LEAKAGE,
SPILLAGE
gambling, ultimate .... (ONE'S)
SHIRT
of ability to express thought
.... ASEMIA
appetite .... ANOREXIA
consciousness ...... SYNCOPE,
FAINTING
energy/strength
.... ASTHENIA
feeling .... NUMBNESS
hair .... ALOPECIA
hope .... DESPERATION
memory .... AMNESIA
mental power ..... DEMENTIA
reading ability .... ALEXIA
smell .... ANOSMIA
speech ...... ALALIA, APHASIA
voice .... APHONIA,
LARYNGITIS
will power .... AB(O)ULIA
writing ability .... AGRAPHIA
unexpected .... UPSET
lost ...... GONE, MISLAID, MISSING,
ENGROSSED
animal .... STRAY

animal, in law .... ESTRAY
chord's hideout .... ORGAN
chord's sound .... AMEN
often, figuratively .... SHIRT
Lost Cause hero .... LEE
Horizon author .... HILTON
Horizon site .... SHANGRI-LA
lot .... DOOM, FATE, PLOT, RAFT,
SLEW, SLUE, BUNCH, SHARE,
PARCEL, DESTINY, FORTUNE,
PORTION, CABOODLE
Lot, city of .... ZOAR
father of .... HARAN
uncle of .... NAHOR, ABRAHAM
sister of .... MILCAH
son of .... MOAB, BENAMMI
Lotario .... RAKE, SEDUCER
Loti, Pierre .... VIAUD
lotion .... COLOGNE, CALAMINE,
OINTMENT, FRESHENER
lots .... MUCH, PLENTY, REALTY
divination by .... SORTILEGE
of dog .... POMP
of something .... HEAP, PILE
Lots, feast of .... PURIM
lottery .... GAME, CHANCE,
DRAWING, TOMBOLA,
SWEEPSTAKES
kin .... KENO, BINGO, LOTTO,
RAFFLE, NUMBERS
ticket .... BLANK
winning .... TERN
lotto kin .... KENO, BINGO
lotus .... HERB, SHRUB, NELUMBO,
WATER LILY
tree .... SADR, JUJUBE
loud ...... NOISY, SHOWY, FLASHY,
SHRILL, CLAMOROUS
clamor .... OUTCRY
colloquial .... VULGAR,
DEMANDING, UNREFINED
extremely/very .... DEAFENING,
STENTORIAN, EARSPLITTING
in music .... FFF, FORTE
noise .... CLAP
speaker .... WOOFER, MONITOR,
TWEETER, AMPLIFIER
loudmouthed .... BLATANT,
BOISTEROUS
person .... STENTOR, THERSITES
lough .... LAKE
Louis of trumpet fame .... PRIMA
the ____, Benedictine Order
advocate .... PIOUS
VII's wife .... ELEANOR
XIII's minister ...... RICHELIEU
XVI's wife .... MARIE
ANTOINETTE
Louisville event .... DERBY
Louisiana bay .... DRUM, EAST,
ELOI, BOUDREAU, BARATARIA

boat .... BATEAU
capital .... BATON ROUGE
city/town .... GRETNA,
KENNER, MONROE, RUSTON,
BOSSIER, LAFAYETTE, NEW
IBERIA, ALEXANDRIA, LAKE
CHARLES, NEW ORLEANS,
SHREVEPORT
county .... PARISH
dialect .... CREOLE
farmer .... HABITAN(T)
island .... BIRD, MARSH,
TIMBALIER
lake .... MUD, IATT, GRAND,
WHITE, VERNON, VERRET,
MAUREPAS, PONTCHARTRAIN
land measure .... ARPENT
mountain .... DRISKILL
native .... CAJUN, CAIJAN,
CREOLE, ACADIAN
patois .... GUMBO, CREOLE
parish .... WINN, CADDO,
ACADIA, VERNON, BOSSIER,
ORLEANS, RAPIDES,
CALCASIEU, JEFFERSON,
LAFAYETTE, LIVINGSTON
river .... AMITE, PEARL, LITTLE,
SABINE, TENSAS, MISSISSIPPI
state bird .... (BROWN)
PELICAN
state flower .... MAGNOLIA
(GRANDIFLORA)
state nickname .... PELICAN
tobacco .... PERIQUE
university .... LOYOLA,
TULANE, XAVIER, DILLARD,
MCNEESE, GRAMBLING
lounge .... LAZE, LOAF, LOLL,
SOFA, COUCH, DIVAN, LOBBY,
LOITER, SETTEE
lounger .... IDLER, LOAFER
lounging suit .... PAJAMAS
loup .... (HALF)MASK
garou .... WEREWOLF
lour .... FROWN, LOWER, SCOWL
Lourdes miracle .... CURE
visitor .... PILGRIM
louse .... NIT, RAT, APHID, COOTIE,
INSECT, SLATER, PARASITE
plural of .... LICE
up .... BOTCH, SPOIL, BUNGLE
lousy .... MEAN, POOR, DIRTY,
· ROTTEN, WICKED, INFERIOR,
DISGUSTING
lout .... APE, HOB, OAF, BOOR,
CLOD, HICK, LOON, LOOBY,
BUMPKIN
louver .... SLAT, WINDOW,
TURRET, LANTERN, TRANSOM,
VENETIAN BLIND
lovage .... PARSLEY

love .... WOO, AMO(R), DOTE,
DESIRE, HEART, ENAMOR,
LIKING, DEVOTION, FONDNESS,
AFFECTION, SWEETHEART
according to George
Macdonald ..... THE LORD
AND THE SLAVE OF ALL
affair .... AMOUR, LIAISON,
ROMANCE, INTRIGUE
Bassanio's .... PORTIA
feast .... AGAPE
foolish .... INFATUATION
full of .... EROTIC, AMATIVE
in .... SMITTEN, ENAMORED
in tennis .... ZERO
kind of .... PUPPY
knot .... AMORET
letter: Fr. .... BILLET-DOUX
lies-bleeding .... AMARANTH
lightly .... PHILANDER
make .... WOO, COURT,
INTIMACY, BILL AND COO
note/letter .... VALENTINE
of country .... PATRIOTISM
of fine arts .... VIRTU
potion .... PHILTER
seat .... SOFA
set, in tennis .... SIX-ZERO
song ..... SERENADE, SERENATA
story .... ROMANCE
unwisely/foolishly .... DOTE
lovebird .... LOVER, PARROT
lovelier than poems .... TREES
lovelock .... CURL
lover .... BEAU, FLAME, LEMAN,
ROMEO, SPARK, SWAIN,
WOOER, ADORER, BELOVED,
PARAMOUR
boy .... WOLF, AMORIST,
LOTHARIO
silly .... SPOONER
lovers' lane frequenters
.... TRYSTERS, LOVEBIRDS
meeting .... TRYST
nemesis .... GREEN-EYED
MONSTER
loving .... FOND, ARDENT, DOTING,
EROTIC, TENDER, AMATIVE,
AMATORY, AMOROUS,
DEVOTED, AFFECTIONATE
combining form .... PHILE
couple, famous .... ROMEO
AND JULIET, SAMSON AND
DELILAH, TRISTAN AND
ISOLDE, ABELARD AND
HELOISE, ANTONY AND
CLEOPATRA
cup .... TIG, TROPHY
low .... MOO, BASE, ORRA, VILE,
WEAK, HUMBLE, MENIAL,
SCURVY, VULGAR, INFERIOR

blow .... SMEAR
brow .... PLEBEIAN
comedy .... FARCE, BURLESQUE, HORSEPLAY, SLAPSTICK
country .... BELGIUM
down: colloq. ...... DIRT, DOPE, MEAN, FACTS, DESPICABLE, INFO(RMATION)
lay .... HIDE
necked .... DECOLLETE
swinger of hymns .... CHARIOT
lowan .... LEIPOA, MALLEE
lowbred .... BASE, CRUDE, COARSE, VULGAR
lowbrow .... CRASS
Lowe, aeronaut .... THADDEUS
20,000 cubic foot balloon of .... ENTERPRISE
wife of .... LEONTINE
Lowell, astronomer .... PERCIVAL
fascination of .... MARS
observatory site of .... FLAGSTAFF
protege of .... (ROBERT) GODDARD
Lowell, poet .... AMY, ROBERT
lower .... DIP, LOUR, VAIL, ABASE, BASER, DEMIT, FROWN, SCOWL, DEBASE, DEMOTE, GLOWER, NETHER, REDUCE, DEGRADE
classman .... FRESHMAN
in rank .... JUNIOR, PUISNE
on one side .... LOPSIDED
Lower California capital .... LAPAZ, MEXICALI
World .... DIS, HELL, HADES, EARTH, SHEOL
World gods .... MANES
lowering .... CLOUDY, FROWNING, OVERCAST
lowest .... LAST, LEAST, MEANEST, LOWERMOST
animal life .... AM(O)EBA
deck .... ORLOP
form of wit .... PUN
part .... BOTTOM
point .... NADIR, BOTTOM, NETHERMOST
possible cost .... ROCK-BOTTOM PRICE
lowland .... HOLM, PLAIN
Lowlander .... SASSENACH
lowly .... MEEK, HUMBLE
lox .... OXYGEN, SALMON
loxia .... WRYNECK
loyal .... LEAL, DEVOTED, STA(U)NCH, FAITHFUL
countryman .... PATRIOT

friend .... DAMON, ACHATES
wife .... PENELOPE
loyalty .... TROTH, FEALTY, HOMAGE, FIDELITY, ALLEGIANCE
lozenge .... CANDY, RHOMB, CACHOU, JUJUBE, MASCLE, TROCHE, CATECHU, DIAMOND, COUGH DROP, PASTIL(LE), PEPPERMINT
LP .... LONG PLAY(ING)
LSD source .... ERGOT
term ..... ACID, TRIP, TURN ON, MICRODOT
Luanda is capital of .... ANGOLA
luau .... FEAST
dish .... POI
lubber .... OAF, LOOBY, SAILOR
word of .... AVAST
lube .... OIL, LUBRICANT
Lublin extermination camp .... MAIDENEK
lubricant .... OIL, DOPE, LUBE, CASTOR, GREASE, UNGUENT, VASELINE
lubricate .... OIL, GREASE, MOISTURIZE
Lucan's work .... PHARSALIA
luce .... FISH, PIKE
Luce (Clare Booth) estate .... HALENAIA
play .... THE WOMEN
lucent .... SHINING
Lucern(e) .... LAKE, MEDIC, CANTON, FODDER, ALFALFA
luces .... LIGHTS
singular of .... LUX
Lucia de Lammermoor composer .... (GAETANO) DONIZETTI
Lucian the _____ .... SKEPTIC
Luciano, Mafia chieftain .... CHARLES
sobriquet .... LUCKY (LUCIANO)
lucid .... SANE, CLEAR, BRIGHT, LIMPID, SHINING, RATIONAL
lucida .... STAR
lucidity .... SANITY, CLARITY, CLEARNESS
Lucifer .... DEVIL, MATCH, SATAN
poetic .... VENUS
lucite .... RESIN
luck .... HAP, LOT, FATE, CHANCE, FORTUNE, FORTUITY
bad .... CESS, JINX, DEUCE, HOODOO, WANION
Luck of Roaring Camp author .... HARTE
luckily .... HAPLY, TIMELY
luckless .... STAR-CROSSED

lucky .... CANNY, WITCH, FORTUNATE
number .... SEVEN
piece/thing .... CHARM, AMULET, HORSESHOE, RABBIT'S FOOT
stroke .... FLUKE
lucrative .... PAYING, GAINFUL, PROFITABLE
lucre .... GAIN, PELF, MONEY, RICHES, WEALTH
infamous connotation for .... FILTHY
Lucrezia, poisoner .... BORGIA
brother of .... JUAN, JOFRE, CESARE
father of .... RODRIGO
father's title of .... POPE ALEXANDER VI
husband of .... DUKE OF FERRARA, (GIOVANNI) SFORZA
lucule .... SUNSPOT
luculent .... CLEAR, LUCID
Lucy's TV friend .... ETHEL
ludicrous ... ABSURD, COMIC(AL), FARCICAL, RIDICULOUS
Ludwig, biographer .... EMIL
lues .... SYPHILIS
Luftwaffe bomber .... STUKA
leader .... GOERING
lug .... EAR, TOW, DRAG, HAUL, PULL, CARRY
luge .... SLED
luggage .... TAN, BAGS, TRAPS, BAGGAGE
adjunct .... STRAP
carrier .... PORTER
item .... TRUNK, VALISE, SUITCASE
lugger ...... BOAT, TOTER, FALCON, VESSEL
lugubrious .... SAD, DISMAL, DOLEFUL, MOURNFUL
lugworm .... ANNELID
Luik .... LIEGE
Luke .... EVANGELIST
lukewarm .... TEPID, INDIFFERENT
lull .... CALM, HUSH, ALLAY, QUIET, SOOTHE, RESPITE
lullaby .... (CRADLE) SONG
lulu: sl. ...... ONER, WHIZ, BEAUT, KNOCKOUT
lumbago .... BACKACHE, RHEUMATISM
lumber .... WOOD, BOARDS, RUMBLE, CLUTTER
British .... TIMBER
dressing machine .... TRIMMER
factory .... SAWMILL
marker .... KEEL
lumberjack ...... JACKET, LOGGER,

SAWYER, WOODCUTTER
blanket of .... MACKINAW
climbing iron of .... SPUR
warning cry of .... TIMBER
lumberman ...... HEWER, LOGGER,
SAWYER, GIRDLER
boot of .... PAC, LARRIGAN
hook of .... PEAV(E)Y
sled of .... TRAVOIS
tool of .... AXE, SAW, ADZE
lumen .... LUX
luminaire .... LAMP
luminal ...... HYPNOTIC, SEDATIVE
luminary .... SUN, MOON, STAR
luminous .... BRIGHT, RADIANT
lummox ...... LOON, LOUT, DUNCE,
LOOBY, LUBBER, DUMBBELL,
LUNKHEAD
lump .... WAD, WEN, BLOB, BURL,
CLOT, HUNK, KNOT, MASS,
NODE, HUNCH, DOMINO,
GOB(BET), NODULE, NUB(BIN),
NUBBLE, NUGGET, SWELLING,
COLLECTION
butter .... PAT
of earth/clay .... CLOD
round, small ..... KNOB, BOLUS
lumper ...... DOCKER, STEVEDORE
Lumumba, Congo premier
.... PATRICE
Luna .... MOON, SELENE
in alchemy .... SILVER
lunacy .... MANIA, MADNESS,
INSANITY
lunar .... PALE, ROUND, PALLID,
MOON-SHAPED
crater .... LINNE
month .... MOON
phenomenon .... ECLIPSE
spaceship .... APOLLO
super bowl .... CRATER
lunatic .... INSANE, MADMAN,
MANIAC
lunch(eon) .... BITE, MEAL,
SNACK, TIFFIN, REFLECTION
lune .... LEASH
lung air passages .... BRONCHI
air sacs .... ALVEOLI
cancer, main cause of
.... (CIGARETTE) SMOKING
disease .... TB, CANCER,
PHTHISIS, EMPHYSEMA,
SILICOSIS, BRONCHITIS,
CONSUMPTION
function .... RESPIRATION
inflammation of the
.... PNEUMONIA
location .... RIB CAGE
membrane .... PLEURA
of the .... LOBAR
prefix .... PNEU

pus-filled cavity .... VOMICA
sound .... RALE, WHEEZE
surgery .... LOBECTOMY
lunge .... FOIN, LEAP, LONGE,
THRUST, PASSADO
lungee/lungi .... LOINCLOTH
lungfish .... DIPNOAN, MUDFISH
lungs used as food .... LIGHTS
lungwort .... LICHEN
lunkhead ...... ASS, LOON, DUNCE,
LUMMOX, DUMBBELL
lunt .... MATCH, SMOKE, TORCH,
KINDLE
lunule .... HALFMOON
Lupercus .... FAUNUS
Lupescu .... MAGDA
Lupin, thief .... ARSENE
lupine .... WOLFISH, WOLFLIKE
animal .... WOLF
Lupino, actress .... IDA
Lupus .... WOLF
lurch .... LURK, ROLL, SWAY,
PITCH, CAREEN, STUMBLE
forward: naut. .... SCEND
lurcher .... DOG, POACHER
lure .... FLY, BAIT, DECOY, TEMPT,
ENTICE, INDUCE, SEDUCE,
TREPAN, ATTRACT, BEGUILE,
SPINNER, INVEIGLE
workers .... PIRATE
lurer .... SIREN, SEDUCER,
TEMPTRESS
lurid .... RED, VIVID, GARISH,
GLARING, GLOWING, SINISTER
lurk .... PROWL, SKULK, SNEAK
lurker .... CREEPER, PROWLER,
STALKER
among coral reefs ..... MORAY
Lurlei .... SIREN, LORELEI
luscious .... SWEET, TASTY,
CLOYING, DELICIOUS
lush .... JUICY, LUXURIANT
slang .... BARFLY
Lusitania, now .... PORTUGAL
lust .... DESIRE, APPETITE
luster .... NAIF, GLAZE, GLORY,
GLOSS, SHEEN, SHINE, POLISH,
REFLECT, RADIANCE
lusterless ...... WAN, DRAB, DULL,
MAT(TE)
lustful .... LEWD, RANDY, CARNAL,
SENSUAL
lustrous .... NITID, SILKY, GLOSSY,
SATINY, RADIANT, SHINING,
BRILLIANT
lusty .... HEARTY, ROBUST,
STRONG, STURDY, VIGOROUS
lute .... CLAY, SEAL, CEMENT,
INSTRUMENT
obsolete .... THEORBO
relative .... ASOR, BANJO,

GUITAR, UKELELE, MANDOLIN
Lutetia .... PARIS
Luther, theologian .... MARTIN
Lutheran .... PROTESTANT
luthern .... DORMER, WINDOW
luting .... SEAL, CEMENT
lux .... LIGHT, LUMEN
luxe .... ELEGANCE, RICHNESS
Luxemb(o)urg capital
.... LUXEMBOURG
city/town .... MAMER,
PETANGE, REMICHT,
DUDELANGET
language .... FRENCH, GERMAN
monetary unit .... FRANC
mountains .... EISLING
plateau .... ARDENNES
river .... OUR, CLERF, MOSEL,
SAUER, ALZETTE
steel center .... ESCH
Luxor's neighbor .... KARNAK
luxuriant ...... LUSH, RANK, RICH,
FERTILE, PROFUSE
luxuriate .... BASK, WALLOW
luxurious ...... POSH, RICH, TONY,
PLUSH
sedan .... LIMO(USINE)
luxury .... EASE, MILK AND
HONEY
lover ..... LUCULLUS, SYBARITE
Luzon battlesite .... BATAAN,
MANILA BAY, CORREGIDOR
bay .... BALER, DASOL, LAMON,
SUBIC, BANGUI, MANILA,
BALAYAN, PALANAN, TAYABAS
channel .... BABUYAN
city/town .... IBA, DAET,
AGOO, LIPA, NAGA, BALER,
LAOAG, PASAY, VIGAN,
APARRI, BAGUIO, BONTOC,
CAVITE, LUCENA, MAKATI,
MANILA, QUEZON, TARLAC,
ANGELES, BANGUED,
DAGUPAN, LEGAZPI, MALOLOS,
CALOOCAN, OLONGAPO,
TAGAYTAY, NAGUILIAN, LOS
BANOS, SAN FERNANDO
falls .... PAGSANJAN
gulf .... LINGAYEN
island .... VERDE, LUBANG,
ALABAT, BABUYAN, POLILLO,
CAMIGUIN, CORREGIDOR
lake .... TAAL, LAGUNA DE
BAY
mountain .... LABO, PULOG,
ARAYAT, ISAROG, PASCAN,
BANAHAO, CARBALLO,
ZAMBALES, SANTO TOMAS
mountain capital .... BAGUIO
mountain people ...... IGOROTS

mountain range .... CORDILLERA, SIERRA MADRE
native .... AETA, ILOCANO, NEGRITO, TAGALOG, BICOLANO, PAMPANGO, ZAMBALENO
peninsula .... BICOL, BONDOC
province .... ABRA, ALBAY, RIZAL, BATAAN, CAVITE, LAGUNA, QUEZON, TARLAC, BULACAN, CAGAYAN, ISABELA, LA UNION, BATANGAS, PAMPANGA, SORSOGON, ZAMBALES, ILOCOS SUR, ILOCOS NORTE, PANGASINAN, NUEVA ECIJA
river .... ABRA, CAGAYAN
volcano .... TAAL, CAGUA, MAYON, PINATUBO
walled city .... INTRAMUROS
water buffalo .... CARABAO
wild buffalo .... TAMARAU
wonder attraction .... RICE TERRACES
Lwow .... LEMBERG
LXW .... AREA
lycanthrope .... WEREWOLF
lycee .... (SECONDARY) SCHOOL

lyceum .... LECTURE HALL
Lycian city .... MYRA
king .... SARPEDON
leader .... PANDARUS
lycra .... SPANDEX
Lydia, capital of .... SARDIS
Lydian .... GENTLE, SENSUAL, EFFEMINATE, VOLUPTUOUS
king .... CROESUS
language .... ANATOLIC
lye .... BUCK, CAUSTIC, LIXIVIUM
soak in .... BATE, BUCK
source of .... (WOOD)ASHES
lying .... FALSE, DISHONEST
downward .... PRONE, ACUMBENT, PRONATED
on one's back .... SUPINE
under oath .... PERJURY
lymph .... HUMOR, SERUM
and fats .... CHYLE
gland swelling .... BUBO
vessel .... VARIX
lymphatic .... PLASMIC
lymphoid tissue back of mouth .... TONSIL
lynching, end of .... HANGING
lynx .... PISHU, BOBCAT, CARACAL, WILDCAT

fur .... CARACAL
of a .... LYNCEAN
Lyra .... HARP
lyre .... HARP, TRIGON
like instrument .... ASOR, CITHARA, SACKBUT
shaped .... LYRATE
lyrebird .... MENURA
lyric .... ALBA, LIED, MELIC, SONGLIKE
muse .... ERATO
poem ...... ODE, HYMN, ELEGY, EPODE, MELIC, RONDEL, SONNET, CANZONE, RONDEAU
poet .... ODIST, LYRIST, SAPPHO, MINSTREL
solo .... MONODY
lyrical .... ODIC
lyricist David .... HAL
noted .... HAMMERSTEIN
lyrics of opera .... LIBRETTO
Lysander's love .... HERMIA
lysin .... ANTIBODY
lysol .... ANTISEPTIC, DISINFECTANT
constituent .... SOAP, CRESOL
lytta .... WORM
Lytton heroine .... IONE

M

M .... MU, EM(MA)
ma .... MA(M)MA, MOTHER
chere .... MY DEAR
Maas .... MEUSE
mabolo .... PLUM
macabre ...... GRIM, EERIE, LURID, WEIRD, MORBID, GHASTLY, GRUESOME
part of a title .... DANSE
macaco .... LEMUR, MONKEY
macadam .... ROAD, STONES
material .... TAR, ASPHALT
Macao coin .... AVO
island .... TAIPA, COLOANE
MacArthur, general .... ARTHUR, DOUGLAS
title .... SCAP
macaque .... KRA, MONKEY, RHESUS, WANDEROO
macaroni .... DANDY, PASTA
ingredient .... DURUM, SEMOLINA
strip ...... LASAGNA, SPAGHETTI
macaroon .... COOKY, BISCUIT, RATAFIA
Macassar .... MALAYAN

macaw .... PARROT, ARA(RA), MARACAN
Macbeth bailiwick .... GLAMIS
character .... ROSS, BANQUO, DUNCAN, HECATE, MACDUFF
has three .... CRONES
maccaboy .... SNUFF
MacDonald's co-star .... (NELSON) EDDY
mace .... CLUB, MAUL, SPICE, STAFF, STICK
bearer .... BEADLE
reed .... DOD
royal .... SCEPTRE
source of .... NUTMEG
wielder .... KNIGHT
macedoine .... SALAD, MEDLEY
Macedonia capital .... SKOPJE
capital, ancient .... PELLA
city/town .... STIP, BEREA, DEBAR, BEROVO, PRILEP, TETOVO, EDHESSA
region .... PIERIA
seaport .... SALONIKA
macer .... BEADLE
macerate .... RET, SOAK, STEEP,

SOFTEN, WASTE AWAY
Mach, physicist .... ERNST
machete ...... BOLO, KNIFE, PANGA
Machiavelli .... NICCOLO
Machiavellian .... CRAFTY
machina, _____ .... DEUS EX
machinate .... PLAN, PLOT, DEVISE, SCHEME
machination .... PLOT, CABAL, DESIGN, SCHEME, ARTIFICE, INTRIGUE
machine .... TOOL, MOTOR, DEVICE, ENGINE, GADGET, MECHANISM
cloth smoothing .... MANGLE
crushing .... MILL, PRESS
cutting .... CROPPER
device .... GLAND
duplicating .... RONEO, XEROX, MIMEOGRAPH
finishing .... EDGER
flying .... GLIDER, AIRCRAFT, AIR BALLOON
grinding .... MILL
gun .... BREN, STEN, MAXIM, POM POM, GATLING

gunned .... STRAFED
gunner's post .... NEST
nap-raising .... TEASEL(LER)
ore-dressing .... VANNER
part .... CAM, COG, GEAR,
   PAWL, CRANK, ROTOR, VALVE,
      PISTON, SOLENOID
political .... PARTY
printing .... PRESS
remote-controlled,
mechanical .... ROBOT
repairer .... MECHANIC,
      TECHNICIAN
road-building .... GRADER
seed-bed preparation
.... COMPACTER
shearing .... CROPPER
stock quotation .... TICK
tool .... LATHE
weaving .... LOOM
wood-turning .... LATHE
machinist's gauge
.... MICROMETER
groove .... TSLOT
macho .... VIRILE,
      ULTRAMASCULINE
match .... DUEL
machree .... MY HEART
Mack, of baseball .... CONNIE
Mackenzie tributary ...... LIARD
mackerel ...... FISH, TUNA, SARDA,
   TUNNY, BONITO, SAUREL,
      ALBACORE
cured .... BLOATER
like fish .... CERO, SCAD,
   TUNNY, BESHOW, SIERRA,
   TINKER, CAVALLA, PINTADO,
      PLAINTAIL
net .... SPILLER
of the .... SCOMBROID
type .... ATKA
young .... SPIKE, TINKER
Mackinaw .... BOAT, COAT,
      BLANKET
trout .... NAMAYCUSH
Mackintosh .... RAINCOAT
mackle ...... BLOT, BLUR, MACULE
MacLeish, poet ...... ARCHIBALD
MacMahon, actress .... ALINE
macrocosm .... WORLD, UNIVERSE
macula .... SPOT
maculate .... SPOT, STAIN,
   BLOTCH, DEFILE, BLEMISH,
      SPECKLE
macule .... BLOT, BLUR, SLUR
mad .... SORE, ANGRY, CRAZY,
   IRATE, RABID, INSANE,
   FRANTIC, FURIOUS, FRENETIC,
   FRENZIED, SENSELESS
about .... FOND OF
Anthony _____ .... WAYNE

monk .... RASPUTIN
scientist of Cairo .... ALHAZEN
Madagascar animal ...... LEMUR,
   TEMEE, AYEAYE, TENREC
capital .... ANTANANARIVO
city/town .... TOLIARA,
   ANTALAHA, MORONDAVA
civet .... FOSSA
fiber .... RAFFIA
lemur .... AYEAYE, INDRI(S)
native .... HOVA
river .... MANGOKY
tribe .... HOVA, MALAGASY
madam .... LADY, WOMAN,
   MILADY, MISTRESS
Italian .... MADONNA
Madama Butterfly composer
.... (GIACOMO) PUCCINI
lover .... (B.F.) PINKERTON
name of .... CIO-CIO(SAN)
Madame .... MRS.
Du Barry's enemy ...... MARIE
   ANTOINETTE
Karenina .... ANNA
Spanish .... SRA, SENORA
madcap .... RASH, HOTSPUR,
   RECKLESS, IMPULSIVE
madden .... ANGER, ENRAGE,
      INCENSE
madder .... DYE, EVEA, VINE,
   PLANT, RUBIA, COFFEE,
   IPECAC, CRIMSON, GARDENIA,
      ALIZARIN(E)
made of wood .... XYLOID
reference to .... ALLUDED
to-order .... CUSTOM-BUILT
tracks .... SPED
up .... FALSE, INVENTED,
   IMAGINED, COSMETIZED,
      FABRICATED
Made in America author
.... (SAM) WALTON
Madeira .... WINE, RIVER, ISLAND
capital .... FUNCHAL
Island wind .... LESTE
wine .... TINTA
mademoiselle .... GIRL, LADY,
   MISS, WOMAN
abbreviation .... MLLE
madhouse .... BABEL, CHAOS,
   BEDLAM, ASYLUM
Madison Ave. people .... ADMEN
madman .... MANIAC, LUNATIC
madness ...... FURY, RAGE, FOLLY,
   MANIA, FRENZY, IDIOCY,
   LUNACY, RABIES, DEMENTIA
fits of .... LUNES
pertaining to .... MANIC
Madonna .... MARY
madras .... CLOTH, KERCHIEF

Madras city ...... SALEM, CALICUT
state .... COCHIN
weight .... SER, POLLAM
madre .... MOTHER
madrepore .... CORAL
formation .... REEF, ATOLL
Madrid boulevard/park/
   museum .... PRADO
madrigal .... GLEE, POEM, SONG
syllables .... FALA
Madrileno .... SPANIARD
madwort .... SHRUB, ALYSSUM
Mae West .... LIFEBELT
maelstrom .... WHIRLPOOL
maenad ...... NYMPH, BACCHANTE
maestro .... MASTER, TEACHER,
   COMPOSER, CONDUCTOR
Mafeking native .... BOER
Maffei work .... MEROPE
maf(f)ia .... BLACK HAND
chief .... CAPO
nemesis of .... FEDS, NARCO
surveyor .... CASER
Mafioso .... RACKETEER
magazine .... DEPOT, ARMORY,
   JOURNAL, WAREHOUSE,
   PERIODICAL, STORE(HOUSE)
a computer .... BYTE
a feminist .... MS
a sports .... GOLF, TENNIS
a weekly news .... TIME
classy .... SLICK
content .... AMMO,
   MUNITION(S)
inferior .... PULP
output .... ISSUE
type ..... NEWS, GIRLIE, SPORTS
VIP .... EDITOR
work .... JOURNALISM
Magdalen scholar .... DEMY
mage .... WIZARD, MAGICIAN
Magellan .... FERDINAND
discovery of: 1521
.... PHILIPPINES
ship of .... SANTIAGO,
   TRINIDAD, VICTORIA
magenta .... DYE, RED, FUCHSIN
maggot .... BOT(T), GRUB, MAWK,
   WHIM, LARVA, NOTION
Magi .... MAGUS, GASPAR,
   MELCHIOR, BALTHASAR
''guide'' .... STAR
magic .... ART, JUJU, RUNE,
   OBEAH, GRAMARY, THEURGY,
      WIZARDRY
black .... VOODOO, SORCERY,
      WITCHCRAFT
charm .... AMULET
formula .... ABRACADABRA
hammer, owner of .... THOR
horse .... BAYARD

incantation .... RUNE
lamp finder .... ALADDIN
potion .... PHILTER
practice .... CONJURE
sign .... SIGIL
spell .... CANTRIP,
CONJURATION
symbol .... WAND, PENTACLE
word .... SESAME
Magic Mountain author
.... MANN
magical .... RUNIC, HERMETIC,
MYSTICAL, ENCHANTING
conveyance .... CARPET
herb .... MOLY
piece .... CHARM, AMULET
magician .... MAGE, MAGUS,
MAGI(AN), MERLIN, SHAMAN,
WIZARD, HOUDINI, WARLOCK,
CONJURER, KLINGSOR,
SORCERER
assistants of .... FAMULI
device of .... GIMMICK
illusion of .... LEVITATION
of iron .... (ALEXANDER
GUSTAV)EIFFEL
rod of .... STAFF
skill of .... LEGERDEMAIN
talk of .... PATTER
tricks of .... HOCUS-POCUS
word of .... PRESTO
Maginot line, opposed to
.... LIMES, SIEGFRIED
magisterial .... POMPOUS,
ARBITRARY, MASTERFUL
magistral .... IMPERIOUS
magistrate .... JUDGE, JUSTICE
civil .... SYNDIC
Spanish .... JUEZ, ALCALDE
town .... REEVE
magnanimous .... GENEROUS
magnate .... BARON, MOGUL,
NABOB, BIGWIG, TYCOON
magnesia .... ANTACID, LAXATIVE
magnesium silicate .... TALC
magnet .... LOADSTONE,
LODESTONE
alloy .... ALNICO
end .... POLE
magnetic .... ELECTRIC,
MESMERIC, ATTRACTIVE
direction .... NORTH, SOUTH
flux, unit of .... WEBER,
MAXWELL
force .... OD, ODYL(E)
resistance .... RELUCTANCE
magnetism .... ALLURE, GRAVITY,
MESMERISM, ATTRACTION
magnetite .... LODESTAR,
LOADSTONE
magnetize .... SWAY, CHARM,

ATTRACT, INFLUENCE
magneto .... DYNAMO
magnific ...... POMPOUS, IMPOSING
magnificat .... HYMN, POEM, SONG
magnificence .... DASH, POMP,
GLORY, STATE, SPLASH,
GLITTER, GRANDEUR,
SPLENDOR
magnificent .... GRAND, PROUD,
SUPERB, STATELY
array .... PANOPLY
magnify .... LAUD, EXALT,
AUGMENT, ENLARGE
magnifying instrument
.... TELESCOPE, MICROSCOPE
magnitude .... BULK, SIZE,
RANGE, EXTENT
magnolia .... SHRUB, FLOWER,
SWEET BAY
Magnolia State .... MISSISSIPPI
magnum .... BOTTLE
opus ...... WORK, MASTERPIECE
magpie ...... CROW, MAG(G), PICA,
PIET
kin .... JAY
maguey .... ALOE, AGAVE, FIBER
magus .... SEER, MAGICIAN,
SORCERER
Magyar .... HUNGARIAN
maharaja's wife ...... MAHARANI,
MAHARANEE
Mahatma, famous .... GANDHI
Mahdi follower .... DERVISH
victim .... GORDON
Mahican .... MOHEGAN
mahjongg piece .... TILE
wind ...... EAST, WEST, NORTH,
SOUTH
mahogany .... TOON, TREE,
CAOBA, NARRA, BAYWOOD,
(HARD)WOOD
color .... REDDISH-BROWN
family .... MELIACEAE
of the .... MELIACEOUS
pine .... TOTARA
Mahomet .... PROPHET,
MOHAMMED
burial place of .... MEDINA
Mahren .... MORAVIA
Maia .... MAY, PLEIADE
maid .... GIRL, LASS, FILLE,
WENCH, VIRGIN, DOMESTIC
lady's .... ABIGAIL
old .... TABBY, SPINSTER
servant .... BONNE, SOUBRETTE
Maid of Astolat .... ELAINE
of Orleans .... JOAN OF ARC
maiden .... NEW, LASS, FIRST,
FRESH, NYMPH, SYLPH,
DAMSEL, VIRGIN, COLLEEN,
DAMOSEL, GUILLOTINE

appearance .... DEBUT,
INITIATION
changed to heifer .... IO
changed to spider by Athena
.... ARACHNE
in Song of Solomon
.... SHULAMITE
name .... NEE
maidenhair .... FERN, GINKO
maidenhead .... HYMEN,
VIRGINITY
maidenly .... GENTLE, MODEST,
GIRLISH, VIRGINAL
mail .... DA(U)K, DAWK, POST,
SEND, ARMOR, LETTERS
bag .... POUCH
boat .... PACKET
carrier .... POSTMAN, PONY
EXPRESS
coat of .... ARMOR, BYRNIE,
HAUBERK
examine .... CENSOR
India .... DA(W)K
mark .... STAMP, CACHET,
INDICIA
pertaining to .... POSTAL
route .... RFD
type of/unwanted .... JUNK
Mailer, author .... NORMAN
mailing charge .... POSTAGE
right .... FRANK
mailman .... POSTMAN, LETTER
CARRIER
maim .... LAME, MANGLE,
CRIPPLE, DISABLE, DISFIGURE
main .... DUCT, CHIEF, FORCE,
POWER, LEADING, FOREMOST,
PRINCIPAL
action of drama .... EPITASIS
body .... TRUNK
bounding .... SEA, OCEAN
course/dish .... ENTREE
line of motion .... AXIS
point .... NUB, CRUX, GIST
road .... PIKE
stress .... BRUNT, ACCENT
trunk .... AORTA
Main Street attractions
.... STORES
Maine admiral .... SIGSBEE
bay .... CASCO, MACHIAS
cape .... SMALL
capital .... AUGUSTA
city/town .... BATH, MILO,
PERU, YORK, ORONO, PARIS,
AUBURN, BANGOR, CAMDEN,
LISBON, MEXICO, BELFAST,
HAMPDEN, MADISON,
FREEPORT, LEWISTON,
PORTLAND, KENNEBUNKPORT
college .... BATES, COLBY,

NASSON, BOWDOIN
college town .... ORONO
county .... KNOX, YORK,
WALDO, OXFORD, HANCOCK,
LINCOLN, SOMERSET,
PENOBSCOT
game .... ELK
island .... HAUT, CROSS, GREEN
lake .... BOG, LONG, ROWE,
WEBB, EAGLE, ONAWA,
SEBAGO, SPIDER
Maritime Academy site
.... CASTINE
mountain .... ABRAHAM,
KATAHDIN
native .... DOWN-EASTER
peak .... KATAHDIN
river .... DEAD, FISH, SACO,
ELLIS, SANDY, SWIFT
state bird .... CHICKADEE
state flower .... PINE CONE
state motto .... DIRIGO, I
GUIDE, I DIRECT
state nickname ...... PINE TREE
state symbol .... PINE
trout .... OQUASSA
university site .... AUGUSTA,
MACHIAS
Mainland .... POMONA
mainly .... MOSTLY, CHIEFLY,
LARGELY
mainspring .... INCENTIVE,
MOTIVATION
maintain .... KEEP, CLAIM,
AFFIRM, ASSERT, DEFEND,
CARRY ON, (UP)HOLD,
CONTINUE, PRESERVE
maintenance .... UPKEEP,
SUPPORT, LIVELIHOOD
divorcee's .... ALIMONY
Mainz .... MAYENCE
maison de sante .... HOSPITAL,
SANITARIUM
maitre d'hotel .... BUTLER,
STEWARD, MAJOR-DOMO,
HEADWAITER
maize ...... CORN, MEALY, CEREAL,
MEALIE, YELLOW
Maja painter .... GOYA
majestic .... EPIC, GRAND, NOBLE,
REGAL, AUGUST, KINGLY,
STATELY, IMPERIAL
majesty ...... DIGNITY, GRANDEUR,
NOBILITY, SOVEREIGNTY
majolica .... POTTERY
major .... MAIN, CHIEF, OF AGE,
GREATER, SPECIALTY
domo .... BUTLER, STEWARD,
SENESCHAL
ending/chaser .... ETTE
follower .... DOMO

in .... SPECIALIZE
or minor .... URSA
premise .... SUMPTION
suit, in bridge .... HEARTS,
SPADES
Major Barbara author .... SHAW
Majorca .... ISLAND, MAJOLICA,
MALLORCA
city/port .... PALMA
sister island .... MINORCA
majority .... AGE, BULK, MOST,
PLURALITY, SENIORITY
age .... ADULTHOOD
majuscule .... UNCIAL, CAPITAL
make .... BRAND, BUILD, STYLE,
CREATE, DEVISE, FASHION
a ____ at .... STAB
boo-boo .... ERR
cast .... PLASTER
catty remark .... MEOW
chair seat .... CANE
connection .... TIE TO
deal .... COMPROMISE
dent .... IMPRESS
face .... APE, POUT
fuss .... CLAMOR
hash of .... BOTCH UP
hole in one .... ACE
hook shot .... SINK
killing ...... WIN, SCORE, HIT-
THE-JACKPOT
living .... EARN
mountain out of a molehill
.... EXAGGERATE
movement .... GESTURE
new shade .... DYE
____ of (bungle) ...... HASH
point of .... FIX, SETTLE
rustling sound .... SOUGH
scene ... GUSH, RANT, RAVE,
EMOTE
show of .... SHAM, FEIGN,
PRETEND
slip .... ERR
adherent .... PASTE
advances .... SOLICIT,
OVERTURE, PROPOSITION
airtight .... LUTE, SEAL
allowance for .... IGNORE,
DISCOUNT, OVERLOOK
amends .... ATONE
an appearance .... EMERGE
an impression .... AFFECT,
RANKLE, PENETRATE
an incised mark .... RASE
an incursion .... RAID
angry .... ROIL
as profit .... CLEAR
askew .... TILT
available, as time ..... FREE UP
believe ..... ACT, SHAM, FEIGN,

FANTASY, MIMETIC, PRETEND,
PRETENSE
beloved .... ENDEAR
black .... NEGRIFY
capital of .... EXPLOIT
certain .... ENSURE, INSURE
choice .... OPT
clear .... EXPLAIN
cloth .... WEAVE
complicated .... ENTANGLE
contact with .... ABUT
crackling sounds
.... CREPITATE
cross sign .... SAIN
crystal clear .... SPELL OUT
dainty .... PRETTIFY
do .... EKE, MANAGE
dry .... PARCH
ends meet .... ECONOMIZE
even .... TRUE
expressive gestures with
hands .... GESTICULATE
eyes at .... OGLE, FLIRT
fast .... BELAY, SECURE,
TIGHTEN
fiendish .... DIABOLIZE
flawless .... PERFECT
full again .... REFILL
fun of .... RIB, MOCK, TWIT,
DERIDE, RIDICULE
gentle .... HUMANIZE
good .... SUCCEED,
COMPENSATE
happy .... ELATE
haste .... HIE, RUSH, HURRY
hay while the sun shines
.... TAKE ADVANTAGE OF
headway .... ADVANCE,
PROGRESS
headway against .... STEM
hit .... CLICK
indistinct .... DIM, BLOT, BLUR,
SMEAR
inquiry .... ASK, QUESTION
inroads .... ADVANCE,
ENCROACH, INFRINGE
insane .... DEMENT, DERANGE
into law .... ENACT, LEGISLATE
into leather .... TAN, TAW
intricate .... COMPLICATE
iridescent .... OPALIZE
it .... ARRIVE, ACHIEVE,
SUCCEED
keen .... HONE
known .... AIR, REVEAL,
DIVULGE, DISCLOSE,
ADVERTISE, PUT ON THE MAP
lace .... TAT
less ...... DECREASE, (DI)MINISH
less distinct .... DIM
less volatile .... DEFUSE

level .... EVEN, TRUE, PLANE
light fainter .... BEDIM
light of .... DISREGARD
like ..... APE, MIMIC, EMULATE,
IMITATE
love .... PET, WOO, SPOON,
COHABIT, BILL AND COO
member .... JOIN, ENROLL
merry .... CHEER, REVEL
mistake .... ERR
money .... GAIN, PROFIT,
STRIKE-IT-RICH
more complex .... MUDDLE,
MYSTIFY, COMPLICATE
nervous ...... EXCITE, AGITATE,
RUFFLE, FLUSTER, STARTLE
night noises .... SNORE
no bones about .... STAND
FAST, STICK TO ONE'S GUNS
notch .... SERRATE
obscure .... BEDIM
one's day .... ELATE
one's mark .... SHINE
one's point .... PUTS ACROSS
one's way .... GO, COPE, WEND
oneself comfortable ...... COSE
oneself heard .... SPEAK UP
out .... ESPY, FARE, SPOT,
PROVE, DESCRY, DISCERN
out artist .... WOLF, SEDUCER
out the meaning ..... DECIPHER
over .... REDO, CHANGE,
REVAMP, CONVERT, REBUILD,
RENOVATE
peace .... MEDIATE, REUNITE,
RECONCILE
picots .... TAT
points .... SCORE
position secure .... CONFIRM,
FORTIFY, ENTRENCH
possible .... ALLOW, ENABLE,
PERMIT
prismatic .... IRIDIZE
public .... AIR, BARE,
ANNOUNCE, DISCLOSE
quiet .... MUTE, (S)HUSH,
MUFFLE
ragged .... FRAY, FRAZZLE
ready/receptive .... PRIME,
PREPARE
reparation .... ATONE
resentful .... VEX, INCENSE,
EMBITTER
road repairs .... RETAR
room .... MOVE OVER
rough .... COARSEN,
GRANULATE
safe .... SECURE
scholarly corrections
.... EMEND
selection .... OPT, PICK,

CHOOSE
sense ..... ADD UP, BE LOGICAL
sleek .... PREEN, GREASE,
LUBRICATE
smooth .... PREEN, PACIFY,
POLISH, SLICKEN
sound of boisterous laughter
.... CACHINNATE
strong .... STEEL
stupid/dull .... HEBETATE
suitable .... ADAPT
superficially attractive
.... WINDOW-DRESS
sure of .... SEE TO IT
the best of it .... ACCEPT, LIVE
WITH IT
the grade .... MANAGE,
CONTRIVE
the most of .... EXPLOIT
the scene ...... COME, JOIN, GO
TO, ARRIVE
thread .... SPIN
unfriendly .... ALIENATE,
DISAFFECT, ANTAGONIZE
unintelligible .... GARBLE,
JUMBLE
unnecessary .... EXCLUDE,
OBVIATE
up .... FORM, INVENT, LAYOUT,
COMPOSE, RECONCILE
up for .... ATONE
up ground .... GAIN ON
up one's mind .... DECIDE
up to .... REPAY, BEFRIEND
use of .... AVAIL, EMPLOY,
UTILIZE
vinegary .... SOUR
watertight .... CALK
waves .... OBJECT, PROTEST,
DISAGREE
whole .... HEAL, MEND,
COMPLEMENT
young .... REJUVENATE
maker .... DOER, SIGNER,
CREATOR, PRODUCER
of cask and tub .... COOPER
makeshift .... STOPGAP,
SUBSTITUTE
makeup .... FORM, NATURE,
COMPOSITION
delta's .... SILT
material ..... ROUGE, PANCAKE,
MASCARA, LIPSTICK,
COSMETICS, FOUNDATION
newspaper .... FORMAT,
LAYOUT
maki .... LEMUR
mako .... SHARK
mal de mer .... SEASICKNESS
Malabar monkey .... WANDEROO
Malacca .... CANE, STRAIT

malachite .... BICE, VERDITER
maladroit .... INEPT, CLUMSY,
AWKWARD
malady .... AILMENT, DISEASE,
ILLNESS, SICKNESS
Malaga .... WINE, GRAPE
Malagasy ethnic group
.... MERINA
president .... TSIRANANA
malaise .... DISCOMFORT
malanders .... ECZEMA
malapert .... BOLD, SAUCY,
IMPUDENT
Malaprop's (Mrs.) creator
.... SHERIDAN
malapropos .... IMPROPER,
UNTIMELY, INOPPORTUNE,
INAPPROPRIATE
malar .... CHEEKBONE
coloring .... FLUSH
malaria ...... MIASM(A), QUARTAN,
PALUDISM
carrier .... MOSQUITO,
ANOPHELES
characteristic/symptom
.... AGUE, FEVER, CHILLS,
RIGORS, SHAKING
drug treatment .... ATEBRIN,
QUININE, ATABRINE,
CHLOROQUINE
parasite .... PLASMODIA
malark(e)y .... HOKUM, BALONEY,
BUNCOMBE, NONSENSE, LIP
SERVICE
Malawi .... NYASALAND
capital .... LILONGWE
city/town .... DEDZA, ZOMBA,
NSANJE, KARONGA, BLANTYRE
lake .... NYASA, CHILWA
language .... YAO, BANTU,
NGONI, TONGA
money .... KWACHA
mountains .... MULANJE
president .... BANDA
river .... SHIRE
Malay ape .... LAR, MIAS
apple .... OHIA
archipelago .... INDONESIA
beverage .... TAFIA
canoe .... PRAH, PRAO, PRAU,
PROA
chief .... DATO, DATU
cloth .... BAT(T)IK
coin .... ORA, TRA(H),
TAMPANG
crane .... SARUS
dagger ...... CRIS, KRIS, CREESE
dish .... SATAY
dress .... PAREUS, SARONG
dyeing .... BAT(T)IK

English trade language .... BECHE-DE-MER
fiber .... TERAP
fruit/nut .... KANARI
gibbon .... LAR
island .... JAVA, SABAH, TIMOR, BORNEO, SUMATRA
isthmus .... KRA
jacket .... BAJU
knife .... PARANG
law .... ADAT
leather .... KULIT
"man of the woods" .... ORANGUTAN
measure .... PAU
mountain .... TAHAN
negrito .... ITA, A(E)TA
nervous disease .... LATA
palm .... ARECA, ARENG, BETEL, GEBANG, GOMUTI
Peninsula city .... KUALA LAMPUR
puppeteer .... (TO)DALANG
rattan .... SEGA
sea cucumber .... TRIPANG, TERIPANG
seaweed product .... AGAR(AGAR)
shadow play .... WAYANG
sir .... TUAN
state .... KEDAH, JOHOR(E), PERAK, MELAKA, PAHANG, PENANG, PERLIS, KELANTAN, SELANGOR, TERENGGANU
station .... STESHEN
telephone .... TALIPON
tic .... LATA
title .... TUAN
tree ..... UPAS, TERAP, DURIAN, RAMBUTAN
tribe .... ARIPAS
tribesman .... MACASSAR
ungulate .... TAPIR
verse form .... PANTUN
village .... KAMPONG
warehouse .... GODON
warrior .... KURIPAN
weapon .... PARANG
weight .... KATI, CADDY
wild ox .... BANTENG
xylophone .... GAMBANG
yam .... UBI
Malayan .... TAGALOG
Malaysia capital .... KUALA LAMPUR
city/town .... IPOH, MUAR, PEKAN, KELANG, BENTONG, KELUANG, KUANTAN, MALACCA, SEREMBAN
crocodile .... MUGGER
flower .... GUMAMELA,

HIBISCUS
flying bat .... KALONG
language ...... DAYAK, MALAY, TAMIL
master .... TUAN
monetary unit .... RINGGIT
mountain .... KINABALU
palm .... SAGO
plant .... RAFFLESIA
prime minister .... RAHMAN
river .... JOHOR, PULAI, PAHANG
seaport ..... MALACCA, GEORGE TOWN
shadow play .... WAYANG
state .... SABAH, MALAYA, SARAWAK
title for man .... TUN
title for woman ..... TOH PUAN
malcontent .... REB(EL), GRUMBLER, DISSIDENT, REBELLIOUS
Maldive Islands ...... SULTANATE
capital .... MALE
prime minister .... NASIR
sultan .... FARID DIDI
male .... HE, BOY, MANLY, MISTER, VIRILE, MASCULINE
animal ...... RAM, BOAR, BUCK, BULL, JACK, STAG
ant .... ANER
bee .... DRONE
brant/goose .... GANDER
cat .... GIB, TOM
cattle .... OX, BULL, STEER
chicken .... COCK, CAPON, ROOSTER
deer .... BUCK, HART, STAG, PRICKET, ROEBUCK
donkey .... JACKASS
duck .... DRAKE
elk/elephant .... BULL
figure of column .... TELAMON, ATLANTES
goat .... BILLYGOAT
hog/swine .... BOAR
horse .... STALLION
horse, castrated .... GELDING
human, castrated ..... EUNUCH
line of family ...... SPEAR SIDE
presumptuous: sl. ..... MASHER
servant ..... BOY, MAN, KNAVE, VALET, LACKEY
sex hormone .... ANDROGEN
sheep .... RAM, TUP, WETHER
slang .... GUY
swan .... COB
turkey .... TOM
virile .... HE-MAN
young .... BUCK
maledict .... ACCURSED

malediction .... CURSE, MALISON, SLANDER, ANATHEMA, DAMNATION
malefaction .... CRIME, GUILT
malefactor ...... FELON, CRIMINAL, EVILDOER
malefic .... EVIL, HARMFUL
malemute .... DOG, HUSKY
malevolence .... MALICE, ILL WILL
malevolent .... EVIL, FELL, VICIOUS, SPITEFUL, MALICIOUS
malfeasance .... MISCONDUCT
malformed .... MISSHAPEN
human .... HUNCHBACK
Mali capital .... BAMAKO
city/town .... GAO, SAN, KATI, KITA, KAYES, MOPTI, SEGOU, SIKASSO, TIMBUKTU
desert .... CHECH, SAHARA
ethnic group .... PEULS, MARKAS, BAMBARA, TOUAREG, MALINKES
lake .... DEBO
language ...... FULANI, SENUFU, BAMBARA
monetary unit .... FRANC
mountains .... HOMBORI
president .... (MODIBO)KEITA
region .... SUDAN
river .... BANI, NIGER, SENEGAL
malic acid salt .... MALATE
malice .... ENVY, SPITE, VENOM, GRUDGE, RANCOR, SPLEEN, ILL WILL
malicious .... CATTY, NASTY, VICIOUS, SPITEFUL, VINDICTIVE
burning .... ARSON
destruction .... SABOTAGE
malign .... ABUSE, LIBEL, DEFAME, REVILE, VILIFY, ASPERSE, SLANDER, TRADUCE
malignant .... EVIL, HARMFUL, VICIOUS, VIRULENT
opposite of .... BENIGN
skin cancer .... MELANOMA
spirit .... KER
tumor .... CANCER
Malines .... LACE, MECHLIN
malinger .... SHIRK, SKULK
malingerer .... DODGER
malison ...... CURSE, MALEDICTION
malkin .... CAT, MOP, HARE, DOWDY, SCARECROW
mall .... LANE, WALK, ALLEE, ALLEY, AVENUE, PROMENADE, SHOPPING CENTER
mallard ...... DRAKE, (WILD)DUCK
malleable .... SOFT, DUCTILE, PLIABLE, TENSILE, AMENABLE
malleate .... POUND

mallemuck ...... FULMAR, PETREL, ALBATROSS

mallet .... TUP, MAUL, GAVEL, MADGE, BEETLE, HAMMER, PESTLE

finger .... INJURY

game played with .... POLO, CROQUET

striking part of .... TUP

toe .... DEFORMITY

malleus .... HAMMER

Mallorca .... MAJORCA

area of .... MURO

mallow ...... OKRA, SIDA, ALTHEA, COTTON, HIBISCUS, (HOLLY)HOCK

malm .... LOAM, MARL, LIMESTONE

Malmo man .... SWEDE

malmsey .... WINE, GRAPE, MADEIRA, MALVOISIE

grape .... MALVASIA

Malo les _____ .... BAINS

malodorous ...... FETID, STINKING

malt .... BARLEY, LIQUOR

liquor .... ALE, BEER, STOUT, PORTER

liquor's yeast .... BARM

product .... ALE, BEER, ALEGAR, VINEGAR

strainer: var. .... STROM

sugar .... MALTOSE

Malta capital .... VALETTA

city/town .... SILEMA, VICTORIA

coin, old .... TARI

defender .... GORT

island .... GOZO, COMINO

monetary unit .... POUND

wind .... GREGALE

Maltese .... CAT, DOG, CROSS

maltha .... TAR, CEMENT, BITUMEN, OZOCERITE

maltose .... SUGAR

maltreat(ment) .... ABUSE

malvasia .... GRAPE

product .... MALMSEY

mama .... MAW, MOM, MOTHER

Mama _____ **Elliot** .... CASS

mamba .... COBRA, ELAPINE

mambo .... RIFF, DANCE

mameluke .... SLAVE

Mamie's maiden name .... DOUD

mammal .... COATI, PRIMATE, SUCKLER

antlered .... DEER

aquatic/marine .... MINK, SEAL, OTTER, WHALE, DESMAN, DUGONG, SEACOW, DOLPHIN, MANATEE, PORPOISE

"armored" .... ARMADILLO

egg-laying .... DUCKBILL, PLATYPUS

extinct .... MASTODON

flesh-eating ...... MINK, OTTER, RATEL, WEASEL

fur .... PELAGE

furry .... SEAL

hoglike .... TAPIR

lowest order .... MONOTREME

musteline ...... RATEL, MARTEN

nocturnal .... RAT, LEMUR

plant-eating ..... RHINO(CEROS)

ring-tailed .... RACCOON

snouted .... DESMAN, DOLPHIN, PORPOISE

swift .... HARE

two-handed .... BIMANE

water-loving .... OTTER

mammals, of certain

.... MUSTELINE, NOCTURNAL

mammary gland .... UDDER

inflammation .... MASTITIS

mammee ...... MAMEY, SAPODILLA

mammet ...... DOLL, IDOL, PUPPET

mammilla .... TEAT, NIPPLE

mammoth HUGE, ELEPHANT, ENORMOUS, GIGANTIC

like animal .... MASTODON

mammy .... MOTHER

man. See also **person/fellow**

.... GUY, RUN, MALE, BIPED, BRACE, STAFF, FELLER, GEEZER, HOMBRE, PERSON, FORTIFY, HUSBAND, OPERATE, PRIMATE, SERVANT, HOMO SAPIENS

ancestor of modern .... CRO-MAGNON(MAN)

and wife up to no good .... PARTNERS IN CRIME

"April Love" ...... PAT BOONE

at home .... BATTER

B.C. .... ADAM

"blushing crows" .... SPOONER

chimney .... SWEEP

country, old .... GAFFER, GAMMER

dashing, gay .... SPARK

dissolute .... ROUE

eater .... LAMIA, SHARK, CANNIBAL

elderly .... FOGY, CRONE, DOTARD

farm-implement .... DEERE

Friday .... SERVANT, FOLLOWER

from Columbus .... OHIOAN

from Punjab .... JAT

from Susa .... ELAMITE

from "U.N.C.L.E." ..... SOLO

Genesis .... ONAN

gentleman's .... VALET

gridiron .... END, CENTER, (NOSE) TACKLE, RECEIVER, LINEBACKER QUARTERBACK

handsome ..... ADONIS, APOLLO

handy .... FACTOTUM

Hang Ten .... SURFER

hideous .... OGRE

in a cast .... ACTOR

in the street .... COMMONER

in the van .... NEO

itinerant .... HOBO

kind of .... YES, STRAW

lanky .... BEANPOLE

lecherous .... SATYR

like .... ANDROID

little .... MANIKIN

-made ornament ..... ARTIFACT

mean .... CAITIFF

nautical .... TAR, SALT, SAILOR, MARINE(R)

of action .... DOER, GO-GETTER

brass .... TALOS

circa 1100, learned .... OMAR THE TENTMAKER

figures .... CPA, AUDITOR

Galilee .... JESUS

God .... RABBI, SAINT, BISHOP, HERMIT, PRIEST

learning .... PUNDIT, SAVANT

letters .... POET, SAVANT, SCHOLAR, LITTERATEUR

Nod .... CAIN

Shelah .... METHUSELAH

song Carmichael ..... HOAGY

the hour .... HERO, CHAMPION

the world .... SLICKER, GLOBETROTTER

old .... GAFFER, GEEZER, SENIOR, GRAYBEARD

on a beat .... COP, REPORTER

on the lam .... FLEER

patient .... JOB

piano .... TUNER

Prize .... NOBEL

recently married .... BENEDICT

rubber .... GOODYEAR

single .... BACHELOR

strong .... ATLAS, SAMSON

tax .... ASSESSOR

"the" .... STAN

thin .... SLAT(S), BEANPOLE

ticker-tape .... STOCKBROKER

to a .... ALL, EVERYONE

unmarried .... SINGLE, BACHELOR, CELIBATE, SPOUSELESS

vat .... DYER

"What's it all about"
.... ALFIE
wise .... SOLON, NESTOR
with "a little list" .... KOKO
without a country ..... NOLAN,
.... STATELESS
who annoys women
.... MASHER
who spilled the salt ..... JUDAS
young, gay .... SPARK
Man of a Thousand Faces
.... CHANEY
O'War, e.g. .... STEED
manacle .... FETTER, HAMPER,
SHACKLE, HANDCUFF
manage ...... RUN, GET BY, WIELD,
DIRECT, HANDLE, OPERATE,
CONTRIVE, ADMINISTER
frugally ...... NURSE, HUSBAND,
CONSERVE
to get by .... EKE
to live .... SCRAPE, SURVIVE
manageable .... RULY, TAME,
DOCILE, WIELDY, TRACTABLE
manager .... GERENT, SYNDIC,
HANDLER, STEWARD,
DIRECTOR, OPERATOR
opera .... IMPRESARIO
Managua is capital of
.... NICARAGUA
manakin .... BIRD, DWARF,
MODEL
mañana .... LATER, TOMORROW
Manassas Mauler
.... (JACK)DEMPSEY
Manasseh's brother ...... EPHRAIM
father .... JOSEPH
grandfather .... JACOB
grandson .... GILEAD
mother .... ASENATH
son .... ASRIEL, MACHIR
manatee .... DUGONG, COWFISH,
SEA COW, HALICORE,
SIRENIAN
manchet .... BREAD
Manchu .... TUNGUS, MONGOLIAN
dynasty .... TA CH'ING
dynasty, revolt against
.... TAIPING
Manchukuo .... MANCHURIA
emperor of .... PU-YI
Manchuria capital .... MUKDEN
city/town .... JEHOL, DAIREN,
TALIEN, CHENGTEN
port of .... ANTUNG, HARBIN
river .... SUNGARI
seaport of .... DAIREN
manciple .... SLAVE, STEWARD
mandamus .... WRIT, ORDER
mandarin .... COAT, DUCK,
ORANGE, BRAHMIN,

TANGERINE
Mandarin, residence of
.... YAMEN
tea .... CHA
mandate .... ORDER, BEHEST,
COMMAND, COMMISSION
mandatory .... BINDING,
COMPULSORY, OBLIGATORY
mandible .... JAW, BEAK
Mandingo .... NEGRO
mandolin strumming piece
.... PLECTRUM
mandrake .... MAY APPLE,
MANDRAGORA
mandrel .... LATHE, SPINDLE
mandrill .... APE, BABOON
manducate .... CHEW, MASTICATE
mane .... JUBA, CREST
maned .... JUBATE, LEONINE
king .... LION
manege .... HORSEMANSHIP
manes .... SOUL
Manet, famed impressionist
artist .... EDOUARD
portraitist of .... DEGAS
maneuver .... PLOY, TRICK,
JOCKEY, ARTIFICE,
STRATAGEM
manganese spar ...... RHODONITE
mange .... SCAB(IES)
cause of .... MITE
loss caused by .... HAIR
mangel .... BEET
manger .... BIN, CRIB, RACK,
STALL, CRATCH, TROUGH
mangle .... MAR, IRON, GARBLE,
HACKLE, HAGGLE, CALENDER,
LACERATE, MUTILATE,
DISFIGURE
mangler ...... IRONER, MUTILATOR
mango .... FRUIT, MUSKMELON
wild .... DIKA
mangonel kin .... CATAPULT
mangy ...... MEAN, ITCHY, SCALY,
SCABBY, SCURFY, SCURVY,
SORDID, SQUALID, SCABROUS
manhandle .... MAUL, TITLE
Manhattan, former name
.... MANAHATIN
hotel .... PLAZA, HILTON,
CHELSEA, WALDORF,
WARWICK, AMERICANA,
DELMONICO'S
in Algonquian .... HILL
ISLAND
purchaser .... (PETER)MINUIT
seller .... SEYSEYS
manhunters' group .... POSSE
mania .... RAGE, CRAZE,
DELIRIUM, DISORDER,
OBSESSION

for dancing .... TARANTISM
with mild symptoms
.... HYPOMANIA
maniac .... MADMAN, LUNATIC
maniacal .... MAD, RAVING,
FRENZIED
manifest .... LIST, OPEN, SHOW,
CLEAR, OVERT, PLAIN, PROVE,
ATTEST, EVINCE, PATENT,
REVEAL, EVIDENT, OBVIOUS,
SIGNIFY, TESTIFY WAYBILL,
APPARENT
disdain .... SNEER
manifesto .... CREDO, EDICT,
STATEMENT, DECLARATION
manifold .... COPIED, VARIED,
DIVERSE, MULTIPLE
manihot .... MANIOC, CASSAVA
manikin .... DUMMY, DWARF,
MODEL
Manila .... BAY, CITY, HEMP,
ROPE, CIGAR, PAPER
Acapulco trading ship
.... GALLEON
Bay hero .... DEWEY
Bay island .... CORREGIDOR
is capital of .... PHILIPPINES
to the Filipinos .... MAYNILA
walled city in .... INTRAMUROS
manioc ...... JUCA, YUCA, STARCH,
CASSAVA, MANIHOT
maniple .... FANO(N), ORALE
maniples, three .... COHORT
manipulate ...... RIG, USE, WIELD,
HANDLE, JUGGLE, TAMPER,
CONTROL, EXPLOIT,
MANEUVER
manipulator ...... USER, SCHEMER
Manipur capital .... IMPHAL
Manitoba capital ...... WINNEPEG
mankind .... HUMANITY
manly .... VIRILE, MASCULINE
Mann .... HORACE, THOMAS
daughter of .... ERIKA
manna .... BOON, FOOD, LERP,
GODSEND, BLESSING,
SUSTENANCE
mannequin ...... DUMMY, MODEL,
STATUE, FIGURINE
manner .... AIR, WAY, MIEN,
MODE, SORT, HABIT, METHOD,
BEARING, FASHION, BEHAVIOR
of dress .... GUISE
of running .... JOG, LOPE,
TROT, CANTER
of speaking .... DICTION
of walking ..... GAIT, WADDLE,
SWAGGER
mannerism .... POSE, QUIRK,
STYLE
mannerly .... CIVIL, POLITE,

COURTEOUS

manners .... MORES, CONDUCT, ETIQUETTE

expert .... EMILY POST

study of .... ETHOLOGY

mannish .... ANDRIC, VIRILE, MASCULINE

manor .... ESTATE, DEMESNE, MANSION

manorial court .... LEET

manpower .... WORKING FORCE

manque .... FAILED, USELESS, DEFECTIVE

manrope .... HANDRAIL

man's castle .... HOME

mansard .... ROOF, ATTIC, GARRET

manse .... PARSONAGE

manservant ...... VALET, LACKEY, YEOMAN, FLUNK(E)Y, FOOTBOY

mansion .... DOME, HOUSE, MANOR, VILLA, CASTLE

spirit .... ATUA

manslaughter .... HOMICIDE

premeditated .... MURDER

mansuetude .... TAMENESS, GENTLENESS

manta .... RAY, CAPE, SHAWL, BLANKET, DEVILFISH

manteau .... CLOAK, MANTLE

mantel ...... LEDGE, SHELF, LINTEL

band .... FRIEZE

mantelet .... CAPE, CLOAK, SCREEN, SHELTER

mantilla ...... CAPE, VEIL, CLOAK, SCARF

user .... SEÑORA, SEÑORITA

mantis, _____ .... PRAYING

crab/shrimp .... SQUILLA

mantle .... CAPE, COPE, CLOAK, COVER, FROCK

armor .... TABARD

Mantuan, the .... VIRGIL

manual .... HAND(BOOK), TEXTBOOK, GUIDEBOOK

art .... CRAFT

training .... SLOID, SLOYD

workers, all .... LABOR

manufacture ...... MAKE, INVENT, CONCOCT, PRODUCE, FABRICATE

manufacturing left-overs .... SHORTS

manumit .... FREE, LIBERATE, EMANCIPATE

manure .... DUNG, MUCK, GUANO, ORDURE, FERTILIZER

manuscript .... MS., SCREED, SCRIPT, SCROLL, (HAND)WRITTEN

copier .... SCRIBE

leaf of .... FOLIO

to be set in type .... COPY

volume .... CODEX

manx .... CAT, CELT, GAEL

many ...... LOTS, LOADS, MYRIAD, SCORES, UMPTEEN, MANIFOLD, NUMEROUS, COUNTLESS

a time .... OFT(EN)

centuries .... EON

combining form .... POLY, MYRIA

headed serpent .... HYDRA

sided .... VERSATILE

manyplies .... OMASUM

Mao Tse _____ .... TUNG

daughter of .... LI-NA, MAU-MAU

wife .... CHIANG CHING

Maori canoe .... WAKA

clan .... HAPU

club .... MARREE

food .... KAI

human flesh .... LONG PIG

parrot .... TUI

raft .... MOKI

tattoo .... MOKO

throwing stick .... BOOMERANG

village .... KAIK(A)

wages .... UTU

weapon .... PATU

wood .... RATA

map .... PLAN, PLAT, CARTE, CHART, GRAPH, ORRERY

book .... ATLAS

city .... PLAT

extra in a/feature .... INSET

giant .... ASIA

line(s) .... ISOBAR, HACHURE, ISOTHERE

maker .... MERCATOR

maker's abbreviation .... RD, ISL, RTE

maker's machine .... OROGRAPH

marker .... PUSHPIN

mini .... INSET

of lines .... CARTOGRAM

slang .... FACE

maple .... ACER, TREE, WOOD, SIRUP, SUGAR, BOX ELDER

leaf land .... CANADA

seed .... SAMARA

tree .... SYCAMORE

Maputo, once .... LOURENCO MARQUES

maquis .... GUER(R)ILLA

mar .... SCAR, SPOIL, DAMAGE, DEFACE, IMPAIR, INJURE, BLEMISH, DISFIGURE

marabou .... STORK, ARGALA

marabout .... TOMB, HERMIT, HOLY MAN

maraca .... RATTLE

marasca .... CHERRY

product .... CORDIAL

marasmus .... WASTING, MALNUTRITION

Marat (Jean), killer of .... CORDAY

marathon .... NONSTOP, (FOOT)RACE

talker .... CHATTERBOX

Marathon, victor at .... MILTIADES

maraud .... RAID, FORAY, PILLAGE, PLUNDER

marauder .... PIRATE, RAIDER

marble .... MIB, TAW, AGATE, AGGIE, ALLEY, RANCE, MIG(GLE), CALCITE, CARRARA, CIPOLIN, SHOOTER, DOLOMITE, LIMESTONE

bone disease .... OSTEOPOROSIS

colorful .... AGATE

designating a white .... PARIAN

flooring .... TERRAZO

game ..... TAW, MIGS, MIGGLES

glass .... TESSERA

imitation .... SCAGLIOLA

like/of .... MARMOREAL

players' line .... TAW

screen .... JALEE

stone like .... SODALITE

worker's tool .... BURIN

marc .... BRANDY, REFUSE

marceau .... MIME

marcel .... HAIRDRESSER

march .... FILE, HIKE, WALK, BORDER, ADVANCE, FRONTIER, PROGRESS, BORDERLAND

day's .... ETAPE

in a group .... TROOP

organized .... PARADE

style .... TRAMP, GOOSE-STEP

March date .... IDES

of Dimes advocate .... (FRANKLIN DELANO) ROOSEVELT

of Dimes fund-raising cause .... POLIO

marches, king of .... SOUSA

marchioness .... LADY, MARQUISE

Marciano, _____ .... ROCKY

Marco, traveler .... POLO

Polo's father .... NICCOLO

Polo's nationality .... VENETIAN

Polo's uncle .... MAFFEO

Marconi .... GUGLIELMO
marconigram .... RADIOGRAM
Mardi Gras .... GALA, CARNIVAL,
                       FESTIVAL
day .... TUESDAY
follower .... LENT
king .... REX
scene of .... PARIS, NEW
                        ORLEANS
mare .... SEA, JADE, HORSE
milk of .... KUMISS
nostrum .... OUR SEA,
                  MEDITERRANEAN
tail of .... CLOUD
young .... FILLY
Margaret, diminutive of
     .... MEG, PEG, MADGE, GRETA,
        MARGE, PEGGY, MAGGIE
margarin(e) .... OLEO
margarite .... PEARL
margay .... CAT, OCELOT
marge .... EDGE, BORDER
Marge Schott's boys .... REDS
margin .... LIP, EDGE, RAND,
     BRINK, LIMIT, MARGE, VERGE,
           BORDER, LEEWAY
narrow .... NECK
marginal note .... APOSTIL(LE)
notes of Old Testament
                     MASORA(H)
marguerite .... DAISY
Maria .... LING
queen of Spain .... CRISTINA
soprano .... CALLAS
Marian, contralto .... ANDERSON
Marianas Island .... GUAM,
          ROTA, PAGAN, SAIPAN,
     TINIAN, AGRIHAN, LADRONES
Marie Antoinette .... REINE
Antoinette's husband
                LOUIS XVI
Antoinette's palace
                 TRIANON
de _____, Queen Eleanor's
        daughter ..... CHAMPAGNE
Dressler role .... TILLIE
Wilson role .... IRMA
marigold .... ASTER, CAPER,
         COWSLIP, KINGCUP
marijuana .... POT, HEMP, WEED,
     GANJA(H), GRASS, HASHISH,
               NARCOTIC
cigarette .... REEFER
cigarette butt .... ROACH
cigarette holder .... ROACH
                      CLIP
form of .... HASH
smoker .... POTHEAD
marimba-like instrument
                  XYLOPHONE
marina .... DOCK, BASIN, HARBOR

marinade .... SALT, WINE, BRINE,
         PICKLE, VINEGAR
marinate .... CORN, PICKLE
marine .... FLEET, NAVAL,
     GYRENE, OCEANIC, MARITIME,
     NAUTICAL, LEATHERNECK
gastropod .... WHELK
glow .... SEAFIRE
plant .... SEAWEED
plant cast ashore .... WRACK
plant group .... BENTHOS
worm .... NEMERTEAN
mariner .... GOB, SAILOR,
        SEAMAN, JACK-TAR
colloquial .... TAR, SALT
fictional .... AHAB
victim of .... ALBATROSS
Marion, actress .... DAVIES
marionette ...... DOLL(Y), PUPPET
mariposa flower ...... LILY, TULIP
marital .... WEDDED, NUPTIAL,
                 SPOUSAL
bliss .... HONEYMOON
separation .... DIVORCE
marjoram .... HERB, MINT,
        ORIGAN, OREGANO
mark .... SCAR, SIGN, BRAND,
     GRADE, STAIN, TOKEN,
     DENOTE, MACRON, VESTIGE,
            IMPRESSION
aimed at .... TARGET,
               COCKSHY
authentication .... SEAL,
               CACHET
bad conduct .... DEMERIT
black .... STIGMA
cattle .... BRAND
critical .... OBELUS
diacritical .... BREVE, CARET,
     TILDE, ABLAUT, ACCENT,
     UMLAUT, CEDILLA
dirty ...... BLOT, SMUT, SMEAR,
        SMUDGE, SMUTCH
down .... NOTE, RECORD
footnote .... STAR, DAGGER,
       OBELISK, ASTERISK
for a Spanish n .... TILDE
for identification .... MOLE,
     BRAND, LABEL, DAGGER,
               DOGTAG
give-away .... TREAD
kind of .... DOT, DENT, LINE,
     SPOT, COMMA, STAIN, BRUISE,
     PERIOD, BLEMISH, SCRATCH
missile's .... TARGET
of bondage ...... YOKE, BRAND
of disgrace .... BRAND,
                STIGMA
of omission ...... DELE, CARET,
               ELLIPSIS
one hundredth of .... PFENIG

over consonant .... HACEK
over syllable .... BREVE
over vowel .... BREVE, TILDE,
        MACRON, UMLAUT
passing .... CEE
possessive .... APOSTROPHE
postal .... STAMP, CACHET
proofreader's ...... DELE, STET,
                 CARET
question .... QUERY
reference ...... OBELI, DAGGER,
     DIESIS, OBELUS, ASTERISK
road .... MEDIAN
skin .... MOLE, NEVUS, TATTOO
up .... HIKE, RAISE
what come to the .... TOES
with spots .... DOT, DAPPLE,
     MOTTLE, SPECKLE
Mark Antony's lover
                CLEOPATRA
Antony's wife .... OCTAVIA
VI .... TANK, TIGER
Twain .... CLEMENS
Twain's embarrassing
      affliction .... SADDLE
                   SORES
Twain's patent .... SCRAPBOOK
markdown .... DISCOUNT
marked .... OBVIOUS, DISTINCT
by inactivity .... DULL
by morbid displacement of
      parts: med. .... ECTOPIC
marker .... IOU, PEG, TAG, LABEL,
     STELE, SCORER, MONUMENT
air-race .... PYLON
boundary .... STAKER
channel .... BUOY
grave .... BARROW
slang .... IOU, PLEDGE
stone .... CAIRN, STELA
market .... MART, SELL, SHOP,
     VEND, STORE, BAZA(A)R,
     OUTLET, ADVERTISE
bid .... QUOTATION
index .... DOW
place .... SOUK, AGORA,
     FORUM, PLAZA, RIALTO,
             EMPORIUM
stock .... CURB, EXCHANGE
marksman .... SHOT, SHOOTIST,
            SHARPSHOOTER
hangout ...... RANGE, GALLERY
hidden .... SNIPER
hired .... ASSASSIN
target of .... BULL'S-EYE
marl .... MALM, EARTH, STRATUM
marlin .... GAMEFISH
colorful variety .... BLUE
kin .... SAILFISH, SPEARFISH
marlinspike .... FID
marmalade .... JAM, PRESERVE,

CONFECTION
material .... PEEL, RIND
tree .... CHICO, MAMEY,
MAMMEE, SAPOTA, SAPODILLA
Marmion hero .... LOCHINVAR
marmoreal .... MARBLELIKE
marmoset .... MICO, MONKEY,
TAMARIN
marmot .... RODENT, WHISTLER,
PRAIRIE DOG
Marner, _____ .... SILAS
Maroc .... MOROCCO
maroon .... LOAF, SLAVE, ENISLE,
STRAND, ISOLATE, CHESTNUT
Marpessa's abductor .... IDAS
Marquand's sleuth
.... (MR.)MOTO
marque .... REPRISAL
marquee .... TENT, AWNING,
CANOPY, LIGHTS, POSTER,
SHELTER
marquetry .... MOSAIC
material .... TILE, WOOD,
IVORY, PARQUET
Marquette, explorer .... PERE,
JACQUES
marquis .... DARON
Marquis, humorist .... DON
marquise .... RING, GEM CUT,
MARQUEE
marred .... UGLY
marriage .... UNION, WEDDING,
WEDLOCK, ALLIANCE,
NUPTIALS, MATRIMONY
bond .... KNOT
broker .... SCHATCHEN,
MATCHMAKER
contract .... HANDFAST
dowry .... DOT
gift .... DOWRY
god of .... HYMEN
goddess of .... HERA, FRIGG
hater of .... MISOGAMIST
kind of .... BIGAMY,
MONOGAMY, MORGANATIC,
CONVENIENCE
notice .... BAN(N)S
outside the tribe .... EXOGAMY
pertaining to .... MARITAL
second .... DIGAMY
settlement .... DOS, DOWRY
unsuitable .... MISALLIANCE
vow .... TROTH
with one of lesser status
.... MESALLIANCE
within the tribe
.... ENDOGAMY
without ceremonial rites
.... COMMON-LAW
marriageable .... NUBILE
married .... MATED, CONJUGAL

couple .... MAN AND WIFE
e.g. .... IN DOUBLE HARNESS
marron .... CHESTNUT
marrow .... PITH, ESSENCE,
MEDULLA
bone .... TISSUE
fat .... PEA
kind of bone .... RED, YELLOW
marry .... WED, WIVE, ADOPT,
HITCH, UNITE, ESPOUSE, TIE
THE KNOT
again .... REMATE
on the run .... ELOPE
Mars .... WAR, ARES, PLANET
combining form .... AREO
in alchemy .... IRON
moon of ...... DEIMOS, PHOBOS
of .... MARTIAN
sister of .... BELLONA
son of .... REMUS
Marseillaise composer
.... (DE)LISLE
marsh .... BOG, FEN, MOOR, OOZE,
QUAG, SLUE, VLEI, LERNA,
SWAMP, MORASS, MUSKEG,
SALINA, SLOUGH, WETLAND
danger spot .... QUAGMIRE
elder .... IVA, RAGWEED,
GUELDER-ROSE
fever .... AGUE, HELODES
gas .... METHANE
grass .... REED, SEDGE
hen .... COOT, RAIL
hollow .... SWALE
marigold ...... CAPER, COWSLIP
plant .... TULE, FESCUE,
BULRUSH, CATTAIL
salt .... SALINA
shrub, fragrant .... GALE
marshal .... ARRAY, GUIDE,
ARRANGE, OFFICER, SHERIFF,
ASSEMBLE
badge of .... STAR
famous ...... NEY, FOCH, GORT,
PETAIN, ROMMEL,
MONTGOMERY
Marshall Islands group/chain
.... RALIK, RATAK
island .... ARNO, KILI, MILI,
AILUK, BIKAR, WOTJE, BIKINI,
JALUIT, MAJURO, NAMORIK,
ENIWETOK, MALOELAP,
RONGELAP, KWAJALEIN
marshmallow .... CANDY,
CONFECTION
marshy .... BOGGY, FENNY,
PALUDAL, PALUDIC, PALUDINE
fertile land .... MAREMMA
hollow area .... SWALE
inlet/outlet .... BAYOU
tract .... FEN

marsupial .... TAIT, KOALA,
WOMBAT, DASYURE,
(O)POSSUM, KANGAROO,
BANDICOOT, PHALANGER
mart .... SHOP, STORE, BAZAAR,
MARKET, EMPORIUM
Marta, actress .... TOREN
Martell .... COGNAC
marten .... SABLE, MAMMAL
describing a .... MUSTELINE
fur .... BAUM
like animal .... MINK, WEASEL,
POLECAT
Martha Finley's heroine
.... ELSIE
J. Burke .... CALAMITY JANE
martial .... WARLIKE, MILITARY
martin .... BIRD, MARTLET,
SWALLOW
Martin Chuzzlewit character
.... GAMP, SAIREY
Luther King .... MLK
biography author
.... (DAVID)GARROW
biography title ...... BEARING
THE CROSS
memorable words from I
HAVE A DREAM
1964 award received by
.... NOBEL PEACE PRIZE
philosophy preached by
.... NON-VIOLENCE
martinet .... RAMROD, TYRANT,
DISCIPLINARIAN
martini .... COCKTAIL
extra/fruit .... OLIVE
ingredient ..... GIN, VERMOUTH
with a pickled onion
.... GIBSON
Martinique capital ...... FORT-DE-
FRANCE
landmark .... PELEE
music .... BEGUINE
river .... LEZARDE, LORRAINE
volcano .... (MONT) PELEE
Martinmas to X'mas
.... ADVENT
martlet .... MARTIN
marvel .... WONDER, MIRACLE,
PRODIGY
of-Peru .... FOUR-O'CLOCK
marvelous .... SPLENDID,
WONDROUS, MIRACULOUS
Marwar .... JODHPUR
Marx .... KARL, CHICO, HARPO,
ZEPPO, GROUCHO
Brothers' film .... HORSE
FEATHERS
co-worker of .... ENGELS
Marxian, a .... LENINIST
Marxism .... COMMUNISM,

SOCIALISM

Mary .... URE, ASTOR, TYLER

MOORE

Catholic queen of _____

.... SCOTS

form of: French .... MARIE

Greek .... MARIAM,

MARIAMNE

Hebrew .... MIRIAM

Italian/Spanish .... MARIA

healed of evil spirits by

Jesus .... MAGDALENE

Magdalene's home

.... MAGDALA

mother of Jesus .... MADONNA

picture of .... MADONNA

Maryland bay .... FISHING,

CHESAPEAKE

capital .... ANNAPOLIS

city/town .... ESSEX, EASTON,

ELKTON, TOWSON, DUNDALK,

ODENTON, ABERDEEN,

BETHESDA, ROSEDALE,

BALTIMORE, CAMBRIDGE,

ROCKVILLE, SALISBURY, SOUTH

GATE, CUMBERLAND, GLEN

BURNIE, HAGERSTOWN

college .... HOOD, LOYOLA,

GOUCHER, BOWIE STATE

county .... CECIL, HOWARD,

CARROLL, CHARLES, HARFORD,

ALLEGANY, WICOMICO,

BALTIMORE, FREDERICK,

MONTGOMERY, WASHINGTON

founder .... CALVERT

island .... KENT, SMITH,

POOLES, POPLAR

lake .... LIBERTY

mountain .... BACKBONE

river ..... ELK, HONGA, SEVERN,

POTOMAC, GUNPOWDER

state bird .... BALTIMORE

ORIOLE

state flower .... BLACK-EYED

SUSAN

state nickname ...... FREE, OLD

LINE

swamp .... POCOSON

symbol .... ORIOLE

tree .... OAK

U.S. Air Force Base

.... ANDREWS

U.S. Naval Academy

.... ANNAPOLIS

university .... MORGAN,

TOWSON, JOHNS HOPKINS

Mascagni, composer ...... PIETRO

opera .... IRIS

mascara .... COSMETIC

mascle .... LOZENGE

mascot .... PET

masculine .... MALE, MAN(LY),

VIRILE, MANNISH

Masefield, poet .... JOHN

work .... ODTAA

mash .... PAP, CRUSH, BATTER

masjid .... MOSK, MOSQUE

mask .... HIDE, LOUP, COVER,

VISOR, HELMET, MASQUE,

SCREEN, VIZARD, CONCEAL,

DISGUISE, PRETENSE

as of disguise .... VISOR,

FALSE FACE

half .... LOUP, DOMINO

lacy .... VEIL

wearer .... MUMMER,

MASQUER, KLANSMAN

maskalonge .... FISH, PIKE

masked .... DISGUISED

as in drama .... PORTRAY,

PERSONATE

ball .... MASQUE, MASQUERADE

masochism .... SADISM

mason .... STONECUTTER

bench .... BANKER

chisel of ..... BROACH, TOOLER

companion of .... DIXON

hammer of .... GAVEL

mortar board/holder .... HAWK

need of .... STONE

masonry .... BRICKWORK,

STONEWORK

broken pieces .... RUBBLE

leveling piece/wedge ..... SHIM

masque ...... BALL, MASK, COMUS,

MASQUERADE

masquerade ...... BALL, MUM(M),

DANCE, PARADE, DISGUISE

costume ..... DOMINO, MOTLEY

mass .... WAD, CLOT, LUMP,

MUSH, BOLUS, GOB(BET),

SQUASH, LITURGY, ASSEMBLE,

MAJORITY

book .... MISSAL

for the dead .... REQUIEM

killing .... BATTUE, POGROM,

CARNAGE, MASSACRE

media .... TV, RADIO,

NEWSPAPER(S)

meeting .... RALLY

movement .... EXODUS,

STAMPEDE, MIGRATION

of bacteria .... CLUMP

of dusts, etc. .... FOG

part of religious .... KYRIE,

GLORIA, GOSPEL, HOMILY,

SANCTUS

production .... VOLUME

Massachusetts bay ...... BOSTON,

QUINCY, BUZZARDS,

PLYMOUTH

cape .... ANN, COD, POGE

capital .... BOSTON

city/town .... AVON, AYER,

GILL, HULL, LYNN, ACTON,

ADAMS, ATHOL, DOVER,

SALEM, CANTON, DEDHAM,

GROTON, LOWELL, MALDEN,

NEWTON, REVERE, WOBURN,

AMHERST, ANDOVER,

BELMONT, CHELSEA, EVERETT,

HOLYOKE, MEDFORD,

MELROSE, METHUEN,

NORWOOD, TAUNTON,

WALTHAM, BROCKTON,

CHICOPEE, LAWRENCE,

PLYMOUTH, ARLINGTON,

BRAINTREE, CAMBRIDGE,

WORCESTER, FRAMINGHAM,

SPRINGFIELD

college .... REGIS, SMITH,

GORDON, LESLEY, BENTLEY,

EMERSON, HELLENIC, HOLY

CROSS, RADCLIFFE

college of music in Boston

.... BERKLEE

county .... DUKES, ESSEX,

BRISTOL, HAMPDEN, NORFOLK,

SUFFOLK, FRANKLIN,

PLYMOUTH, BERKSHIRE,

HAMPSHIRE, MIDDLESEX,

NANTUCKET, WORCESTER,

BARNSTABLE

famous hall .... FANEUIL

gulf .... MAINE

island .... LONG, PASQUE,

CUTTYHUNK, NANTUCKET,

CHAPPAQUIDDICK, MARTHA'S

VINEYARD

lake .... BUEL, ONOTA, MYSTIC,

SILVER, ASHMERE, WEBSTER

mountain .... TOM, TOBY,

GRACE, GREYLOCK

river ...... MILL, NORTH, SWIFT,

AGAWAM, HOOSIC, MANHAN,

MYSTIC, NASHUA, WHITMAN,

CHICOPEE, DEERFIELD,

QUINEBAUG

state bird .... CHICKADEE

state flower .... TRAILING

ARBUTUS

state nickname .... BAY, OLD

COLONY

state tree .... ELM

tourist attraction .... FRANKLIN

PARK ZOO, PAUL REVERE

HOUSE, DINOSAUR FOOTPRINTS,

NEW ENGLAND AQUARIUM

university .... TUFTS,

HARVARD, SUFFOLK

massacre ...... POGROM, CARNAGE,

SLAUGHTER

massage ...... KNEAD, RUB(DOWN),

SHAMPOO
massager .... MASSEUR, MASSEUSE
Massenet, composer .... JULES
opera by .... MANON, THAIS
masses, the .... PLEBS, PEOPLE,
HOI POLLOI, MULTITUDE
masseur ...... RUBBER, MASSAGER
Massey, performer .... ILONA,
RAYMOND
Massine, dancer .... LEONIDE
massive .... HUGE, BULKY, HEAVY,
SOLID, MASSY, MAMMOTH,
IMPOSING, PONDEROUS
mast .... POLE, SPAR, ACORNS,
BEECHNUTS, (CHEST)NUTS
iron band of .... TRUSS
platform .... LOOKOUT,
MAINTOP, CROW'S NEST
support .... BIBB
master .... BOY, DAN, DOM, MAIN,
CHIEF, SAHIB, SUBDUE,
CONTROL, EFFENDI
builder .... ARCHITECT
cruel .... LEGREE
in any art/music ..... MAESTRO
of a battle .... CONQUEROR
of a situation .... VICTOR,
WINNER
of ceremonies ..... MC, EMCEE,
COMPERE
of household .... GOODMAN
of suspense .... HITCHCOCK
of syllogism .... SOCRATES
pertaining to a .... HERILE
race ideology .... HERRENVOLK
stroke .... COUP
workman .... ARTIST,
FOREMAN, OVERSEER,
CRAFTSMAN
masterfully ...... ABLY, EXPERTLY,
SKILLFULLY
mastermind .... PLAN(NER),
DIRECTOR
masterpiece .... MAGNUM OPUS,
CHEF-D-OEUVRE
Bernini's .... ST. PETER'S
CHURCH
Leonardo da Vinci's
.... MONA LISA, THE LAST
SUPPER
marble .... TAJ MAHAL
mastery .... GRIP, SWAY, SKILL,
CONTROL, UPPER HAND
masthead .... LOOKOUT
mastic .... RESIN, CEMENT, LIQUOR
tree .... ACOMA
masticate .... CHEW, GRIND,
CRUNCH, MANDUCATE
mastication product .... CUD
mastiff .... ALAN, BULLDOG,
(WATCH)DOG

mat ...... PAD, DULL, SHAG, DOILY,
SNARL, CARPET, MATRIX,
CUSHION
leaf .... YAPA
making material .... BAST,
REED, RUSH, VETIVER
sleeping .... PETATE
Mata Hari .... SPY
Matabele .... ZULU
matador ...... TORERO, TOREADOR,
BULLFIGHTER
dart of .... BANDERILLA
garment of .... CAPE
opponent of .... BULL, TORO
passes .... FAENA
queue of .... COLETA
red cloth of .... MULETA
sweet sounds to a .... OLES
sword of .... ESTOQUE
match .... FIT, PIT, LUNT, MATE,
PAIR, SUIT, EQUAL, TALLY,
CONTEST, MARRIAGE,
PARALLEL, VESUVIAN
boxing .... BOUT, SETTO
cockfighting .... MAIN
friction .... FUSEE, FUZEE,
LUCIFER, LOCOFOCO
in dice .... MAIN
stick .... LINSTOCK
tycoon .... KREUGER
wax/wooden .... VESTA
matching pair .... SET
piece .... MATE
matchless .... SOLE, PEERLESS,
UNEQUALED, INIMITABLE
matchmaker .... SHADCHEN,
SCHATCHEN
craft of: biblical .... ARK
indefatigable ...... EROS, CUPID
matchwood .... SPLINTERS
mate .... TEA, WIFE, HOLLY,
MARRY, MATCH, COUPLE,
FELLOW, SPOUSE, CONSORT,
(SLEEPING)PARTNER
ship's .... BOATSWAIN
mated .... YOKED, WEDDED,
COUPLED
mateless .... AZYGOUS
mater .... MOTHER
dolorosa .... VIRGIN MARY
material .... DATA, METAL, VITAL,
GOODS, MATTER, CONTENT,
SENSUAL, WORSTED,
PHYSICAL, ESSENTIAL,
PERTINENT, SUBSTANCE
bat .... ASH
carton .... CARDBOARD
court .... EVIDENCE
curtain .... VOILE, BAMBOO
for hut building .... GRASS
inner surface ...... PAD, LINING

inorganic .... METAL
tablecloth .... DAMASK
materialize .... SHOW, OCCUR,
APPEAR, REALIZE
materiel .... MUNITIONS
maternal .... MOTHERLY
relationship .... ENATION
maternally related .... ENATE
maternity .... MOTHERHOOD
hospital .... LYING-IN
matgrass .... NARD, MARRAM
mathematical .... EXACT,
PRECISE, ACCURATE
arbitrary number .... RADIX
arc .... RADIAN
figure .... CONE, DIAGRAM
function .... (CO)SINE,
LOGARITHM
instrument .... VERNIER,
COMPUTER, CALCULATOR
line .... VECTOR
proposition .... THEOREM
ration .... SINE
symbol ..... DOT, DIGIT, POINT,
FACIEND, OPERAND
term .... COSII, ROOT, SURD,
(CO)SINE, FACIENT, CONSTANT
mathematician .... GAUSS,
EUCLID, NEWTON, PASCAL,
PTOLEMY, GEODETE,
DESCARTES, ARCHIMEDES
mathematics .... COMPUTATION
certain theorem in
.... BINOMIAL
subject .... ALGEBRA,
CALCULUS, GEOMETRY,
ARITHMETIC
there are two in .... EMS
Matilda of ___, Henry I's
daughter .... ANJOU
Matilda, Queen of ___
.... ENGLAND
husband of .... WILLIAM(THE
CONQUEROR)
work of .... BAYEUX TAPESTRY
matin .... AUBADE
canticle .... VENITE
of .... MORNING, DAYBREAK
matinee ...... LEVEE, SOIREE,
RECEPTION, PERFORMANCE
idol of old ..... BOYER, GABLE,
BARRYMORE, VALENTINO
Matlock's forte .... DEFENSE
matrass .... FLASK, BOLTHEAD
matriarch .... MATRON, DOWAGER
of "Dallas" .... ELLIE
matriculate .... ENTER, ENROL(L),
REGISTER
matriculation fee .... TUITION
matrimonial .... MARITAL,
NUPTIAL, CONJUGAL

matrimony .... MARRIAGE
matrix .... DIE, MAT, CAST,
WOMB, MODEL, MO(U)LD,
GANG(UE), PATTERN
matron .... DAME, WIFE, WIDOW
matronly ...... SEDATE, DIGNIFIED
matted .... CESPITOSE
matter .... STUFF, CONTENT,
ELEMENT, SUBSTANCE
arcane .... SECRET
business .... AFFAIR, INTEREST,
COMMERCE
classification of .... ANIMAL,
MINERAL, ORGANIC,
VEGETABLE
in law .... RES
of course .... ROUTINE
of fact .... CASUAL, LITERAL,
PROSAIC, PRACTICAL
of law .... CASE
of opinion .... MOOT,
DEBATABLE
printed .... CALENDAR,
CIRCULAR, NEWSPAPER
written .... DRAFT, LETTER,
MANUSCRIPT
Matterhorn .... MOUNTAIN, MONT
CERVIN
matters of faith .... CREDENDA
Matthew .... APOSTLE,
EVANGELIST
alternate name of .... LEVI
hometown of ...... CAPERNAUM
job of .... TAX COLLECTOR
symbol of .... WINGED MAN
mattock .... HACK, PICK(AX),
TWIBIL(L)
mattress .... FUTON, PALLET,
PAILLASE
case/cover .... TICK, BEDDING
stuffing material .... CEIBA,
FLOCK, KAPOK
maturation .... AGING, MEIOSIS
mature .... AGE, ADULT, RIPEN,
EVOLVE, FULL-GROWN,
DEVELOP(ED)
note .... DUE, PAYABLE
Mau Mau land .... KENYA
maud .... RUG, WRAP, PLAID,
SHAWL
wearer of .... SHEPHERD
maudlin .... MUSHY, SOBBY,
TEARY, WEEPY, TEARFUL,
SENTIMENTAL
sentiment .... MUSH
Maugham heroine .... SADIE
(THOMPSON)
play .... RAIN
Maui volcano .... HALEAKALA
maul .... CLUB, MACE, BEETLE,
BRUISE, HAMMER, MALLET,

MANGLE, CLOBBER
mauler .... BOXER, WRESTLER
Maumee River city ...... TOLEDO
maumet .... DOLL, IDOL, PUPPET
Mauna Loa crater .... KILAUEA
volcano .... KEA, LOA
maund .... BASKET, HAMPER
Mauriac, novelist ...... FRANCOIS
Maurois, novelist .... ANDRE,
HERZOG
work on George Sand
.... LELIA
work on Shelley .... ARIEL
Mauritania bay .... ARGUIN,
LEVRIER
cape .... BLANC, MIRIK
capital .... NOUAKCHOTT
city/town .... ALEG, ATAR,
BOGUE, KAEDI, KIFFA, ROSSO,
ZOUIRAT
desert .... IGUIDI, SAHARA
ethnic group .... MOOR,
NEGRO, BERBER
island .... TIDRA
language .... WOLOF, ARABIC
money .... KHOMS, OUGIYA
president .... DADDAH
river .... SENEGAL
Mauritius capital .... PORT LOUIS
islands .... MASCARENE
monetary unit .... RUPEE
Mauser .... RIFLE, PISTOL
mausoleum .... TOMB, GRAVE,
VAULT, SHRINE, SEPULCHER
Buddhist .... TOPE, STUPA
Egyptian .... MASTABA,
PYRAMID
India .... TAJ MAHAL
pertaining to/of
.... MAUSOLEAN
mauve .... DYE, MALLOW, PURPLE,
PIGMENT
maverick ...... CALF, WAIF, DOGIE,
LONER, REBEL
Texas rancher .... SAM
mavis .... BIRD, THRUSH
maw .... CRAW, CROP, GULLET,
THROAT, ABDOMEN, STOMACH
mawkish .... SOUPY, MAUDLIN,
BATHETIC, NAUSEOUS,
SPOON(E)Y, SICKENING,
SENTIMENTAL
max., opposite of .... MIN
Max, the boxer .... BAER
maxilla .... JAW BONE, UPPER JAW
disorder .... SINUSITIS
segment of .... STIPES
maxim .... SAW, REDE, ADAGE,
AXIOM, GNOME, MORAL,
MOTTO, TENET, BYWORD,
SAYING, TRUISM, SLOGAN,

FORMULA, PRECEPT, PROVERB,
APHORISM, PRINCIPLE
Maxim, inventor .... HUDSON,
HIRAM STEVENS
invention of .... EXPLOSIVES,
(MACHINE)GUN
maxims, collection of ...... SUTRA
religious leader's .... LOGIA
maximum .... MOST, UTMOST,
HIGHEST, SUPREME
penalty .... EXECUTION, THE
CHAIR
Maxwell .... ELSA, WEBER
Anderson play
.... SATURDAY'S CHILDREN
may .... CAN, PRIME, HEYDAY,
MAIDEN, SPRINGTIME
apple .... MANDRAKE
fly .... DUN, DRAKE
May Day .... BELTANE
Day celebration, subject of
.... ARMED FORCES
Day folk dance .... MORRIS
fifteen .... IDES
first .... BELTANE
tree .... HAWTHORN
VIPs .... MOTHERS
Maya .... DEVI, SAKTI, INDIAN
consort of .... SIVA
Mayan .... INDIAN
city .... UXMAL
maybe .... MAYHAP, PERHAPS,
POSSIBLY, PERCHANCE
Mayday .... SOS, SIGNAL, M'AIDEZ
Mayence .... MAINZ
mayflower .... ARBUTUS,
ANEMONE, COWSLIP,
HAWTHORN, MARIGOLD
Mayflower passengers
.... PILGRIMS
mayhem .... MAIMING, CRIPPLING,
MUTILATION
mayor .... BURGOMASTER
domain of .... CITY, TOWN
term of office of
.... MAYORALTY
title: sl. .... HIZZONER
Mayotte capital .... DZAOUDZI
Mays' one-time job .... GIANT
mazard ...... FACE, HEAD, MAZER,
SKULL
Mazarin, statesman .... JULES
maze ...... DAZE, ADDLE, STUPEFY,
JUNGLE, NETWORK,
LABYRINTH
exit aid .... CLEW
mazer .... CUP, BOWL, GOBLET
mazurka .... DANCE, POLKA
mazzard .... CHERRY
MC .... EMCEE, TOASTMASTER
asset of .... WIT

McAuliffe's historic reply:
  12/23/44 .... NUTS
McCambridge, actress
  .... MERCEDES
McCoy, the real .... GENUINE
McCrea, the actor .... JOEL
McDonald's franchise chain
  creator .... RAY KROC
McGuffey's volume ...... READER
McIntosh .... (RED) APPLE
McLaglen's role .... INFORMER
McMahon, Carson's
  announcer .... ED
  drawn-out word of ..... HERE'S
McPherson, evangelist .... AIMEE
MD .... DOC(TOR), PHYSICIAN
M.D. Zaharias .... BABE
me .... EGO, (ONE)SELF
  _____ and I .... MYSELF
  thinker .... EGOIST
mead .... LEA, HYDROMEL
meadow .... LEA, PASTURE,
  GRASSLAND
  barley .... RIE
  bird .... LARK, BOBOLINK
  grass .... POA, FESCUE
  mouse .... VOLE
  poetic .... MEAD
  rue .... CROWFOOT
Meadowlands event .... TROT
meadowlike .... GRASSY
meager .... BARE, LEAN, POOR,
  THIN, GAUNT, SPARE, LENTEN,
  SCANT(Y), SLIGHT, SPARSE,
  SPARING, MARGINAL
meal .... BRAN, CHOW, CORN,
  FARE, FEED, FOOD, MASH,
  FLOUR, GRIST, LUNCH, SNACK,
  FARINA, PINOLE, REPAST,
  SPREAD, SUPPER, COLLATION,
  REFECTION
  boiled in milk .... MUSH
  coarse .... SAMP, GRITS,
  GROUT, GROATS, HOMINY
  corn .... SAMP, HOMINY
  end's serving .... DESSERT
  family .... POTLUCK
  field .... K-RATION
  main course .... ENTREE
  noon .... LUNCH(EON)
  oat/wheat .... GROATS
  table .... BOARD
mealies .... CORN, MAIZE
meals .... EATS, BOARD
  complete .... TABLES D'HOTE
mealy .... PALE, SPOTTY,
  POWDERY, FARINOSE
mealymouth .... HYPOCRITE
mealymouthed .... OILY,
  EVASIVE, UNCTUOUS,
  INSINCERE

mean .... LOW, BASE, EVIL,
  CATTY, CRUEL, IMPLY, INFER,
  NASTY, PETTY, SNIDE,
  DENOTE, HUMBLE, INTEND,
  MEDIUM, PALTRY, SORDID,
  STINGY, TYPIFY, AVERAGE,
  CAITIFF, IGNOBLE, LOW-
  DOWN, MISERLY, PITIFUL,
  SIGNIFY, VICIOUS, INFERIOR,
  TWO-PENNY
  abode .... HOVEL
  person .... CAITIFF
meander .... ROAM, ROVE, STRAY,
  RAMBLE, WANDER
meandering .... FLOWING,
  WINDING, LABYRINTHINE
meanie .... OGRE, BULLY, GORILLA
meaning .... AIM, GIST, SENSE,
  IMPORT, INTENT, PURPOSE,
  PURPORT, SIGNIFICANCE
  ambiguous in .... CRYPTIC
meaningful .... PITHY, LITERAL,
  ARTICULATE, EXPRESS(IVE)
meaningless .... IDLE, FUTILE,
  AIMLESS, SENSELESS
means .... WAY, DINT, TOOL,
  AGENCY, ASSETS, AVENUE,
  METHOD, RICHES, WEALTH,
  RESOURCES
  by all .... CERTAINLY, OF
  COURSE
  by any .... SOMEHOW
  of entry .... DOOR, GATE,
  PORTAL, INGRESS
  of escape .... LOOPHOLE
  of living .... LIVELIHOOD
  of propulsion .... OARS
  of surmounting .... STILE
meant .... VOLUNTARY,
  INTENTIONAL
meantime .... WHILST, INTERIM
measles .... ROSEOLA, RUBELLA,
  RUBEOLA
  characteristic .... RED RASH
  symptom .... COUGH, FEVER,
  SORE EYES
measly .... PUNY, PETTY, SCANTY,
  TWO-BIT, MISERLY
measure .... LAW, BILL, FOOT,
  INCH, METE, POLE, SPAN,
  STEP, YARD, INDEX, GAUGE,
  LITER, AMOUNT, BUSHEL,
  EXTENT, CRITERION
  cloth .... ELL
  combining form .... METRO
  depth .... FATHOM
  distance ...... MILE, KILOMETER
  dry .... CORD, PECK, ROTL,
  BARREL, BASKET, BUSHEL
  for oil .... KULA
  grain .... PECK, BUSHEL

  land .... AR(E), ACRE, MORGEN,
  HECTARE
  length .... ELL, ROD, FOOT,
  MILE, STEP, YARD, CUBIT,
  METER
  liquid .... TUN, DRAM, GILL,
  PINT, LITER, OUNCE, QUART,
  GALLON, TIERCE
  medicine .... DOSE
  nautical .... KNOT
  of .... MENSURAL
  astronomical distance
  .... PARSEC, SECPAR
  capacity .... TUN, CASK,
  GILL, PECK, PINT, LITER,
  QUART, STERE, BARREL,
  BUSHEL, GALLON
  earth .... GEODESY
  length, ancient .... ELL,
  CUBIT
  length: naut. .... CABLE
  stone .... PERCH
  wood .... CORD
  work .... ERGON
  paper .... REAM, QUIRE
  poetry .... SCAN
  speed .... KNOT
  type .... EM, EN
  up to .... EQUAL
  weight .... GRAM, KILO,
  CARAT, GRAIN, OUNCE,
  POUND, METAGE
  wine .... BUTT
  yard .... VERGE
measured .... TIMED, GAUGED
  medicine .... DOSE, DOSAGE
measurement .... METERAGE,
  DIMENSION(S), MENSURATION
  content/weight .... METAGE
measurer .... METER, GAUGER
  lung capacity ...... SPIROMETER
measuring instrument .... METER,
  GA(U)GE, STADIA, SEXTANT,
  TRANSIT, CAL(L)IPER
  standard .... YARDSTICK
  stick .... ROD, RULE
  worm .... LARVA, LOOPER
meat .... BEEF, FOOD, PITH, PORK,
  VEAL, FLESH, STEAK, TRIPE,
  KERNEL, MUTTON, ESSENCE,
  VENISON, SUBSTANCE
  and vegetable dish .... HASH,
  OLLA, RAGOUT, CASSEROLE
  carving board .... TRENCHER
  cooking method .... FRYING,
  BOILING, STEWING, BRAISING,
  BROILING, GRILLING,
  ROASTING, ROTISSERIE
  covering/coating .... GLAZE
  cured .... HAM
  cut ...... HAM, RIB, CHOP, LOIN,

RUMP, CARVE, CHUCK, FLANK, STEAK, FIL(L)ET, BRISKET, ICEBONE
dish .... LOAF, STEW, CURRY, RAVIOLI, RISSOLE, HAMBURGER, STROGANOFF, WELLINGTON, BOURGUIGNON, YANKEE POT ROAST
dried .... JERK(Y), BILTONG, CHARQUI, PEM(M)ICAN
dried coconut .... COPRA
eater .... CARNIVORE
hard, salted .... JUNK
jelly .... ASPIC
juice .... GRAVY
kind/grade of .... PRIME, CHOICE, SELECT
leg .... CUTLET
paste .... PATE, PEM(M)ICAN
pie .... PATE, PASTY, RISSOLE
piece ..... COLP, CUBE, CHUNK, STRIP, COLLOP, FIL(L)ET
preserved, pickled .... CORNED BEEF, SALMAGUNDI
rib .... CUTLET
roast .... BAR, CABOBS, KEBABS, KABOBS, FRICANDO
roasting device .... SPIT, GRILL, BROACH, SKEWER, BUCCANEER
roll .... RISSOLE, ROULADE
sauce, type of .... MINT, RAISIN, AU JUS, BARBECUE, MUSHROOM, BEARNAISE, CRANBERRY, BORDELAISE
seller ...... BUTCHER, KNACKER
shop .... SHAMBLES, ROTISSERIE, DELI(CATESSEN)
skewered .... CABOB, KABOB, KEBAB
smoked .... HAM, BACON
spiced ...... SALAMI, BOLOGNA, SAUSAGE
spread .... PATE
stew .... OLLA, RAGOUT, GOULASH, HARICOT, MILANESE, FRICASSEE
strips .... BILTONG
stuffed .... SAUSAGE
tenderizer .... PAPAIN
tenderizing, mechanical
.... GRINDING
you cannot identify
.... MYSTERY(MEAT)
meatball .... PINDA, RISSOLE
meatman .... BUTCHER
meatus .... DUCT, CANAL, PASSAGE(WAY)
meaty .... HEFTY, PITHY, STOUT, FLESHY

Mecca black stone location
.... KIBLAH
chief magistrate .... SHERIF
pilgrimage .... HADJ
pilgrim's dress .... IHRAM
shrine .... CAABA, KAABA
son of .... MAHOMET, MOHAMMED
to Medina journey
.... HEGIRA, HEJIRA
Meccawee, e.g. .... ASIAN
mechanic .... RESETTER, REPAIRMAN
military .... ARTIFICER
wear of .... COVERALLS
mechanical .... POWERED, AUTOMATIC, INVOLUNTARY, SPONTANEOUS
bar .... LEVER
contrivance .... DEVICE, GADGET
game .... PINBALL
man .... ROBOT, AUTOMATON
method/routine .... ROTE
mechanically repetitious
.... SINGSONG
mechanics .... DYNAMICS, WORKINGS
Mechlin .... LACE, MALINES
medal ...... AWARD, BADGE, PRIZE
back of .... VERSO
face of .... OBVERSE
present .... DECORATE
space .... EXERGUE
Medal of Honor, only woman
awardee .... MARY WALKER
symbol of _____ ...... HEROISM
medallion .... CAMEO
medals collector .... NUMISMATIST
of .... NUMISMATIC
meddle ...... PRY, MELL, BUTT IN, TAMPER, INTRUDE, INTERFERE, INTERLOPE, INTERVENE
meddler .... GREMLIN, BUSYBODY, KIBITZER
meddlesome .... CURIOUS, OFFICIOUS, INTERFERING
man .... PAUL PRY
Medea .... SORCERESS
consort of .... JASON
father of .... AEETES
victim of ...... CREON, CREUSA, GLAUCE
Medean king .... CAMBYSES
Medes' language .... AVESTAN
media, part of mass ...... PRESS, RADIO, TELEVISION
medial .... MIDDLE, AVERAGE, MIDDLING, MEDIOCRE
median .... MEAN, MESAL, MIDST, MESNE, CENTER, MESIAL,

MIDDLE, AVERAGE, MIDMOST
priests .... MAGI
mediate .... ARBITRATE, INTERCEDE, RECONCILE, CONCILIATE
mediation .... PARLEY, ARBITRATION
mediator ...... ARBITER, REFEREE, GO-BETWEEN, INTERCESSOR
medic .... DOC, HEALER, ALFALFA, SURGEON, CORPMAN, THERAPIST
medic's sorting process
.... TRIAGE
medicable .... CURABLE, CURATIVE
medical .... IATRIC, CLINICAL, CURATIVE
abbreviation DX, meaning of
.... DIAGNOSIS
abbreviation PX, meaning of
.... PROGNOSIS
assistant .... INTERN(E)
beam .... X-RAY
combining form .... IATRO
examiner .... CORONER
group .... AMA
instrument .... PROBE, FORCEPS, SCALPEL, SYRINGE, CATHETER, STETHOSCOPE, THERMOMETER
patient .... CASE
profession symbol
.... CADUCEUS
student .... MEDIC(O), INTERN(E)
suffix .... OMA, EMIA, ITIS
tool, obsolete .... LEECH
treatment .... THERAPY
treatment: comb. form
.... IATRY
medicate ...... CURE, HEAL, TREAT
medicated candy .... LOZENGE, SUCRETS, COUGH DROP
cloth .... STUPE
liquid .... LOTION
medication .... DRUG, REGIMEN, THERAPY, TREATMENT
Medici, ruler of Florence
.... LORENZO
brother of .... GIULIANO
grandfather of .... COSIMO
father of .... PIERO
rival family of .... PAZZI, ALBIZZI
sobriquet of .... THE MAGNIFICENT
medicinal .... LATRIC, HEALING
bark .... COTO, PEREIRA, CINCHONA, VIBURNUM
cigarette .... CUBEB

fluid .... SERUM
herb ..... ALOE, SENNA, ARNICA
lozenge .... TROCHE
root ...... ARTAR, JALAP, ORRIS,
GINSENG
shrub .... ALEM
medicine .... CURE, DRUG,
REMEDY
branch of .... SURGERY,
NEUROLOGY, GYNECOLOGY,
OBSTETRICS, PEDIATRICS,
PSYCHIATRY, DERMATOLOGY
chest .... CABINET
cure-all .... ELIXIR, PANACEA
dropper .... PIPETTE
giver .... DOSER
liquid .... DROPS
man .... QUACK, SHAMAN,
ANGEKOK, MAGICIAN,
MUMBOJUMBO,
(WITCH)DOCTOR
man, Sioux ...... SITTING BULL
measure .... DOSE, DOSAGE
mock .... PLACEBO
obsolete .... LEECHCRAFT
patent/quack .... NOSTRUM
pertaining to .... IATRIC
vomit .... EMETIC
Medicine Lodge ——— of 1867
.... TREATY
medieval catapult .... ONAGER,
MANGONEL, TREBUCHET
coat .... GAMBESON
collar .... RABATO
emperor .... OTTO,
CHARLEMAGNE, JUSTINIAN I,
FREDERICK II
empire .... AZTEC, PERSIA,
ARMENIA, TREBIZOND,
CAROLINGIAN
empire held together with
string .... INCA
empress .... THEODORA
feudal vassal .... VAVASOR
folk hero, a ..... HSUAN-TSANG
galley .... AESC, BIREME,
GALIOT
helmet .... ARMET
judicial council .... CURIA
knight .... PENNON
land under the lord's control
.... DEMESNE
latitude-measuring device
.... KAMAL
man-eating race .... TAFUR
musical instrument ...... LUTE,
LYRE, ROT(T)E, REBEC(K)
musician .... MINSTREL,
TROUBADOUR
plague ...... THE BLACK DEATH
ruler .... KING ALFRED, KING

HAROLD, GENGHIS KHAN
servant .... SEWER
shield .... ECU, PAVIS
sport .... TILT, TOURNEY,
JOUST(ING), TOURNAMENTS,
CHARIOT-RACING
stable boss .... AVENER
sultan of Egypt .... SALADIN
Teutonic estate .... ODAL
tool .... AX, KNIFE
town .... BOURG
trading vessel ..... NEF, KNORR
tribe .... MONGOL
war engine .... BOAR,
TREBUCHET
warrior .... TAFUR, VIKING
warship .... DROMON
weapon .... MACE, SPEAR,
SWORD, HARPOON, LONGBOW
wind instrument ..... SACKBUT
mediocre .... SO-SO, AVERAGE,
INFERIOR, MIDDLING,
ORDINARY
meditate ...... MULL, MUSE, PORE,
PONDER, REFLECT
moodily .... BROOD
meditative .... MUSING, PENSIVE
Mediterranean .... INLAND
bush .... CAPER
city .... ORAN
country .... MALTA, TUNISIA
fish .... OMBER
galley ...... BIREME, GAL(L)IOT,
TRIREME
grass .... DISS
gulf .... TUNIS, TARANTO
island .... ELBA, GOZO, LIDO,
RODI, CAPRI, CRETE, MALTA,
SICILY, CORSICA, SARDINIA
pirate .... XEBEC
plant .... ANISE, MANDRAKE,
TURNSOLE
principality .... MONACO
regions .... LEVANT
resort .... LIDO, NICE, MENTON,
RIVIERA
river to the .... EBRO, NILE,
RHONE
seaport .... TETUAN, TOULON,
TRIPOLI, PORT SAID
ship .... SAIC, SETEE, XEBEC,
LATEEN, TARTAN, ZEBEC(K),
FELUCCA, POLACRE
ship master .... PADRONE
shrub .... TAMARISK,
LAURUSTINE
trading ship .... PADRONE
tributary .... TIBER, TEVERE,
ORONTES
volcanic island .... LIPARI
warship .... BIREME, TRIREME

wind .... SOLANO, MISTRAL,
PTESIAN, SIROCCO, LEVANTER
medium .... TOOL, AGENT,
MEAN(S), AGENCY, CENTER,
MIDDLE, AVERAGE, VEHICLE
advertising .... PRESS, RADIO,
MAGAZINE, NEWSPAPER,
BILLBOARDS, SKYWRITING,
TELEVISION, DIRECT MAIL
artist's ...... OIL, CLAY, STONE,
MUSIC, PIANO, BRONZE,
CANVAS, VIOLIN, PAINTING
exchange .... MONEY,
CURRENCY
in music .... MEZZO
response of a .... ORACLE
session with a .... SEANCE
spiritualistic .... PSYCHIC
medley .... OLIO, CENTO, JUMBLE,
FARRAGO, MELANGE,
MIXTURE, VARIETY, FANTASIA,
POSTICHE, MACEDOINE,
POTPOURRI, HODGEPODGE
of skits .... REVUE
race .... RELAY
medrick .... TERN
medulla .... PITH, MARROW
Medusa .... GORGON, JELLYFISH
hair of .... SNAKE(S)
sister of ..... STHENO, EURYALE
slayer of .... PERSEUS
medusan .... JELLYFISH
meed .... REWARD, RECOMPENSE
meek .... LOWLY, HUMBLE,
PATIENT
meekness .... LOWNESS
meerschaum ...... PIPE, SEAFOAM
meet .... SIT, FACE, GREET,
MATCH, OPPOSE, CONVENE,
FIT(TING), WELCOME,
ASSEMBLE, CONFRONT,
RENDEZVOUS
a poker bet .... SEE
companion of .... PROPER
halfway .... COMPROMISE, GIVE
AND TAKE, SPLIT THE
DIFFERENCE
the day .... ARISE
the eye .... APPEAR, EMERGE
with fortitude .... BREAST
meeting .... BEE, DATE, RALLY,
SYNOD, CAUCUS, HUDDLE,
SESSION, ASSEMBLY,
CONGRESS
atmosphere of a .... TENOR
full attendance .... PLENARY
lovers'/secret .... TRYST
necessity .... AGENDA
of minds .... AGREEMENT
place of "Big Three"
.... YALTA, POTSDAM,

point .... JUNCTION CASABLANCA

room .... CAMARILLA

to discuss particular topics
.... SYMPOSIUM

to elect Pope .... CONCLAVE

mega .... MILLION

megalomania .... DELUSION

megapod .... MALEO, LEIPOA

megalith .... STONE, MENHIR

megaphone .... AMPLIFIER,
LOUDSPEAKER

megrim(s) .... WHIM, VERTIGO,
HEADACHE, MIGRAINE

Mehitabel .... CAT

Mehta, conductor .... ZUBIN

Meiji emperor .... MUTSUHITO

Mein Kampf author ..... HITLER

meiosis .... LITOTES

Meir, Israeli prime minister
.... GOLDA

Mekong .... LANTSANG

Mel .... HONEY

actor .... FERRER, GIBSON

baseballer .... OTT

singer .... TORME

melancholia .... HYP, GLOOM,
DEPRESSION

melancholic spell .... HUMP

melancholy .... BLUE, DREAR,
GLOOMY, HIPPED, SOMBER,
PENSIVE, SAD(NESS),
DEJECTED

fit of .... HYP(S), HUMP,
HYPOCHONDRIA

Melanesian islands .... FIJI,
SOLOMON, ADMIRALTY

native .... FIJIAN

melange .... OLIO, MIXTURE,
HODGEPODGE

melanin .... PIGMENT

melanite .... GARNET

melanoma .... TUMOR

Melba, soprano .... NELLIE

Melchior, tenor .... LAURITZ

meld .... FUSE, BLEND, MERGE,
UNITE

Meleager .... ARGONAUT

father of .... OENEUS

mother of .... ALTHEA

melee .... RIOT, BRAWL, MIX-UP,
(AF)FRAY, HASSLE, RUCKUS,
RUMBLE, SCUFFLE, SKIRMISH,
TURMOIL, FREE-FOR-ALL

melic .... LYRIC

melicocca .... GENIP

Melissa, singer ...... MANCHESTER

mellow .... SOFT, RIPE(N), LOAMY,
TIPSY, MATURE

melodeon .... ORGAN, ACCORDION

melodic .... ARIOSE, ARIOSO,

embellishment .... CADENZA, LYRICAL
GRACE NOTE

melodious .... ARIOSE, ARIOSO,
DULCET, LILTING, MUSICAL,
ORPHEAN, CANOROUS

melodrama .... SHOCKER,
THRILLER

melodramatic .... HISTRIONIC

melody .... AIR, LAY, ARIA, SONG,
TUNE, STRAIN, ARIETTA,
CAVATINA

meloid .... BEETLE

melon .... PEPO, GOURD,
CAS(S)ABA, HONEYDEW,
CANTALOUP(E)

dessert .... BOMB

pear .... PEPINO

slang .... PROFITS

Melpomene .... MUSE

melt .... FUSE, THAW, SOFTEN,
LIQUEFY, DISSOLVE

into mold .... FOUND

ore .... SMELT

melted .... FUSIL(E)

melting pot .... AMERICA,
CRUCIBLE

Melville .... HERMAN

character .... AHAB, BUDD,
WHALE, MOBY DICK

novel ..... OMOO, TYPEE, MOBY
DICK

protagonist .... AHAB

member .... ARM, LEG, LIMB,
PART, ORGAN, AFFILIATE

academy .... FELLOW

Aesir .... TYR, LOKI, ODIN

club .... ELK, LION, JAYCEE,
ROTARIAN

fraternity .... BROTHER

of a law firm .... ASSOCIATE

of an old English sect
.... SHAKER

of the ''woodpile'' .... BAT

sorority .... SISTER

membership .... BODY, SEAT,
MEMBERS, INCLUSION,
AFFILIATION

fee .... DUES

grass roots .... RANK AND FILE

membrane .... PIA, WEB, TELA,
VELUM, TISSUE, VELAMEN,
COVERING, PELLICLE

abdominal cavity
.... PERITONEUM

animal eye .... TAPETUM

bird's beak .... CERE

brain .... MENINGES

combining form .... HYMEN(O)

ear .... EARDRUM

ear: descriptive ...... TYMPANIC

embryo's sac .... AMNION

enclosing .... CAUL

eye .... IRIS, UVEA, CORNEA

eyeball .... SCLERA

fetus .... CAUL, CHORION

nictitating .... HAW

uniting toes .... WEB(BING)

web-like .... TELA

Memel River city .... TILSIT

memento .... PRIZE, RELIC,
TOKEN, TROPHY, KEEPSAKE,
SOUVENIR, REMEMBRANCE

album .... SCRAPBOOK

Memnon, killer of ...... ACHILLES

memo .... CHIT, NOTE

memoir .... BIOGRAPHY,
MONOGRAPH, REMINISCENCE

memorabilia .... ANA

memorable .... NOTABLE,
SPECIAL, STRIKING

period .... ERA, EPOCH

memoranda .... ITEMS

memorandum .... CHIT, NOTE,
BRIEF, RECORD, MINUTES

pad .... TICKLER

memorial .... TOMB, CAIRN,
SHRINE, STATUE, TROPHY,
MONUMENT

ancient .... DOLMEN,
CROMLECH

of a sort .... PETITION

post .... XAT, XYST, TOTEM,
COLUMN, PILLAR

memory .... ROTE, RETENTION,
RECOLLECTION

book .... ALBUM, DIARY,
MEMOIR

loss of .... AMNESIA

of .... MNESIC, MNEMONIC

Memphis god .... PTAH

high priest .... RANOFER

river .... NILE

ruler .... PHARAOH

men in blue .... UMP(IRES)

of letters .... LITERATI

menace .... BULLY, DANGER,
THREAT(EN)

menacing .... DIRE, ALARMING,
MINATORY, MINACIOUS

menad .... NYMPH, BACCHANTE

menage .... DOMICILE,
HOUSEHOLD, HUSBANDRY,
HOUSEKEEPING

menagerie .... ZOO

mend .... FIX, DARN, PATCH,
COBBLE, REPAIR, CORRECT,
IMPROVE

a seam .... RESEW

in tailoring .... BUSHEL

mendacious .... FALSE, LYING

mendacity .... LIE, FALSEHOOD

Mendel, botanist .... GREGOR

forte of .... GENETICS,

     HEREDITY

Mendelssohn .... FELIX

mender ...... REPAIRER, RESTORER

pots/pans .... TINKER

shoe .... COBBLER

socks/tear .... DARNER

mendicant ...... BEGGAR, PAUPER,

     BEGGING

kind of .... FRIAR

Menelaus' brother

     .... AGAMEMNON

daughter .... HERMIONE

father .... ATREUS

wife .... HELEN

menhaden .... FISH, POGY,

HERRING, OLDWIFE, WHITING,

     GREENTAIL

menhir .... MEGALITH

menial .... VARLET, SERVANT,

     SERVILE, DOMESTIC

meninges .... MEMBRANES

inflammation .... MENINGITIS

innermost .... PIA MATER

middle layer .... ARACHNOID

     MATER

outermost layer .... DURA

     MATER

tumor .... MENINGIOMA

meniscus .... DISK, LENS,

     CARTILAGE

plural of .... MENISCI

shape .... CRESCENT

site of .... JAW JOINT, KNEE

     JOINT, WRIST JOINT

Menlo Park initials .... TAE

invention of Edison at

     .... PHONOGRAPH,

     INCANDESCENT BULB

inventor/man

     .... (THOMAS)EDISON

inventor's sobriquet

     .... WIZARD OF MENLO PARK

Mennonite .... AMISH

founder .... MENNO

menopause .... CLIMACTERIC

symptoms .... HOT FLASHES

Menotti .... GIAN-CARLO

heroine .... AMELIA

men's affair/party .... STAG,

     SMOKER

organization .... YMCA

mensal .... MONTHLY

mental .... NOETIC, PHRENIC

attic .... MIND

bias .... WARP

communication .... TELEPATHY

condition .... LUNACY,

     MADNESS, DEMENTIA

deficiency .... IDIOCY,

AMENTIA, MONGOLISM

discipline .... YOGA

disorder .... NEUROSIS,

     PARANOIA, DISTEMPER

disposition .... HUMOR

drug .... METRAZOL

hospital .... BEDLAM,

BUGHOUSE, MADHOUSE,

     NUTHOUSE

illnesses, category of

     .... NEUROSES, PSYCHOSES

patient .... LUNATIC,

BEDLAMITE, PSYCHO(PATH)

perception .... KEN

picture .... FANCY, IMAGE,

VISTA, RECEPT, VISION,

     CONCEPT, FANTASM

position .... VIEWPOINT

reservation .... SALVO

state .... MOOD, MORALE,

     DISPOSITION

telepathy .... MIND READING

telepathy: abbr. .... ESP

view .... OUTLOOK

mentality .... MIND, ATTITUDE

mentally alert .... ACUTE

deficient person .... IDIOT,

MORON, IMBECILE

ill .... PARANOID, DISTURBED,

     PSYCHOTIC

retarded .... HALF-WITTED

sound .... SANE, LUCID,

     COMPETENT

wandering .... DELIRIOUS

mention .... CITE, NAME, ALLUDE,

SPECIFY, REFER(ENCE)

mentor .... COACH, ADVISER,

     TEACHER

of Luke Skywalker ...... YODA

menu .... CARTE, BILL(OF FARE)

item .... ENTREE

Menuet .... DANSE

Menuhin, violinist .... YEHUDI

teacher of .... ENESCO

Mephisto(pheles), debtor of

     .... FAUST(US)

mephitic .... NOXIOUS, POISONOUS

mephitis .... DAMP, MIASMA,

     STENCH

mercantile .... COMMERCIAL

paper .... CHECK, DRAFT

Mercator .... MAPMAKER,

GEOGRAPHER, CARTOGRAPHER

work .... ATLAS

mercenary .... VENAL, GREEDY,

SORDID, HIRELING,

     POTHUNTER

soldier .... HESSIAN, SWISSER

mercer .... DRAPER

mercery .... TEXTILES

merchandise .... GOODS, WARE(S)

merchant .... COSTER, DEALER,

TRADER, RETAILER

fleet captain ...... COMMODORE

ship .... ARGOSY, TRADER

ship, India-England

     .... INDIAMAN

U.S. fur .... ASTOR

Merchant of Venice character

     .... GOBBO, TUBAL, PORTIA,

ANTONIO, JESSICA, NERISSA,

SALERIO, SHYLOCK, SOLANIO,

     BASSANIO

merchantman .... SHIP

merchants, guild of .... HANSE

merci .... THANKS

merciful .... HUMANE, LENIENT

be .... SPARE

merciless .... GRIM, CRUEL

Mercouri, actress .... MELINA

mercurial .... FICKLE, VOLATILE

mercuric chloride .... CALOMEL

sulfide .... CINNABAR,

     VERMILION

mercury .... QUICKSILVER

in chemistry .... HG

ore .... CINNABAR

Mercury .... AZOTH, HERMES,

     MESSENGER

cap of .... PETASUS

shoes of .... TALARIA

staff of .... CADUCEUS

mercy .... GRACE, LENITY,

CHARITY, CLEMENCY,

HUMANITY, COMPASSION

grant .... SPARE

in military usage .... QUARTER

killing .... EUTHANASIA

mere .... LAKE, ONLY, POND,

MARSH, SHEER, SIMPLE,

     BOUNDARY

nonsense .... FALDERAL

nothing .... FIDDLESTICK

merely .... JUST, ONLY, SIMPLY

merganser .... DUCK, SMEE,

SMEW, HARLE, GOOSANDER

merge .... FUSE, MELD, BLEND,

UNITE, ABSORB

merger .... FUSION, COMBINE,

     AMALGAMATION

Merida is capital of

     .... YUCATAN

meridian .... NOON, ZENITH

merino .... WOOL, YARN, SHEEP

merit .... EARN, VALUE, WORTH,

DESERT, VIRTUE, DESERVE

anew .... RE-EARN

Merkel, actress .... UNA

merl(e) .... BLACKBIRD

Merle, actress .... OBERON

merlin .... FALCON, PIGEON HAWK

Merlin .... SEER, MAGICIAN

forte of .... MAGIC
mistress of .... VIVIAN
Merovingian king .... CLOVIS
Merrimac(k) .... (UNION)FRIGATE,
    IRONCLAD WARSHIP
adversary of .... MONITOR
rechristened name of
    .... VIRGINIA
merriment .... GLEE, FROLIC,
    GAIETY
merry .... GAY, JOLLY, FESTAL,
    JOCOSE, FESTIVE, MIRTHFUL
go-round .... WHIRL,
    TURNABOUT, CAR(R)OUSEL,
    WHIRLIGIG
maker .... REVEL(L)ER
making time .... CARNIVAL,
    FESTIVAL
monarch .... COLE
Merry Andrew .... MIME, CLOWN,
    JESTER, BUFFOON
Widow composer .... LEHAR
mesa .... BUTTE, PLATEAU,
    TABLELAND
Mesabi output .... ORE
Range locale .... MINNESOTA
mescal .... AGAVE, CACTUS,
    LIQUOR, PEYOTE
mesh .... WEB, ENGAGE, TISSUE,
    NETTING, NET(WORK),
    ENTANGLE, INTERLOCK,
    SCREENING
meshed .... GEARED, SHRINE
fabric .... NET, LACE
Meshed is in _____ .... IRAN
mesmeric .... HYPNOTIC,
    MAGNETIC
force .... OD
mesmerist .... HYPNOTIST
mesne .... MIDDLE, INTERMEDIATE
Mesopotamia .... IRAK, IRAQ
boat .... GUFA
city ..... URFA, EDESSA, NIPPUR
region .... SUMER
wind .... SHAMAL
mesquit(e) .... ALGARROBA
mess .... CHOW, FOOD, HASH,
    MEAL, MUSS, BOTCH, SNAFU,
    JUMBLE, MUDDLE, PUTTER
up .... ERR, SLIP
message .... WORD, REPORT,
    DISPATCH
Messala, enemy of .... (BEN)HUR
messenger .... PAGE, HERALD,
    COURIER, HARBINGER
messer-upper .... LITTERBUG
Messiah .... JESUS, CHRIST,
    SAVIOR, DELIVERER
composer .... HANDEL
Messina rock .... SCYLLA
Messrs. ...... MISTERS, MESSIEURS

messuage ...... TOFT, HOMESTEAD
messy .... DIRTY, SLOPPY, UNTIDY,
    DISORDERLY
Mesta, _____ .... PERLE
mestizo .... CHOLO, METIS, LADINO
metabolism .... BASAL,
    METASTASIS
process .... ANABOLISM,
    CATABOLISM
metal ...... TIN, IRON, LEAD, ZINC,
    ALUMINUM, CASTIRON
alloy .... BRASS, STEEL,
    BRONZE, MONEL(L), NIELLO,
    SOLDER
assaying vessel .... TEST,
    CUPEL
band .... COLLET
bar .... FID, INGOT, OFFSET
barracks .... QUONSETS
block .... DIE
casting(s) .... PIG, INGOT,
    FOUNDRY
coat with .... PLATE, TERNE
coating .... RUST, PATINA
comb .... CARD
covering of an airplane
    .... SKIN
cutting tool .... HACKSAW
disk .... MEDAL, PATEN,
    SEQUIN, MEDALLION
dross .... SLAG
fastener .... TNUT, RIVET,
    U-BOLT
filings .... LEMEL
for coinage .... FLAN,
    PLANCHET
hard .... COBALT
hard-tipped end .... TAG
heavy .... LEAD
japanned .... TOLE
lightest .... LITHIUM
line of type .... SLUG
lining .... BUSH(ING)
marker .... DIE, STAMP, SWAGE
mixture .... ALLOY
patching .... SOLDER
peg/pin .... BOLT, SPILL,
    GUDGEON
piece .... SHIM
plate .... PATEN, PATIN(A)
plate, cut .... TREPAN
refine .... SMELT
refuse .... SCUM, SLAG, DROSS,
    SCORIA
ring .... BEE, GROMMET
rod .... BOLT
rod, thin .... WIRE
shaper ..... DIE, LATHE, STAMP,
    SWAGE
shavings .... WOOL
sheet cutter .... SHEAR

sheet of .... FOIL, LAMINA,
    LATTEN, TAGGERS
suit .... MAIL, ARMOR,
    HAUBERK
thread .... LAME, WIRE
used for trays .... TOLE
waste ...... CALX, SLAG, SPRUE,
    CALCES
welding .... SOLDER
worker .... SMITH, WELDER
works .... SMITHY, FOUNDRY
Metalious novelist .... GRACE
work .... PEYTON PLACE
metallic oxidation .... RUST
rock .... ORE
sulfide .... PYRITE
wire .... LAME
metalware, enameled .... TOLE
metalworker .... WELDER,
    RIVETER, (TIN)SMITH
metamorphose .... TRANSFORM
Metamorphoses author ...... OVID
character .... THISBE
metamorphosis ...... METASTASIS
metaphor .... TROPE, SIMILE,
    ANALOGY, COMPARISON
incorrect use of/mixed
    .... CATACHRESIS
metaphorical .... FIGURATIVE,
    ALLEGORICAL
metaphrase .... TRANSLATE
metaphysical .... SUBTLE,
    ABSTRACT, ABSTRUSE,
    ESOTERIC
poet .... DONNE, COWLEY
metastasis .... METABOLISM
metathesis .... INTERCHANGE
metazoan stage .... BLASTULA
mete .... DOLE, GIVE, ALLOT,
    LIMIT, MEASURE, BOUNDARY,
    APPORTION
meteor .... HAIL, STAR, FIREBALL,
    FALLING STAR, SHOOTING
    STAR
exploding/fiery .... BOLIS,
    BOLIDE
train of .... TAIL
visible during August
    .... PERSEIDS
visible during November
    .... LEONIDS
meteoric .... FLEET, SWIFT,
    BLAZING, DAZZLING,
    FLASHING
shower ...... LEONIDS, PERSEIDS
meteorite .... TEKTITE, AEROLITE,
    SIDERITE
meteorological line .... ISOBAR
prefix .... STRATO
meteorologist's concern
    .... CLIMATE, WEATHER

instrument .... ACTINOMETER
meter .... RHYTHM, CADENCE
  cubic .... STERE
  face of .... DIAL
  millionth part .... MICRON,
    MIKRON
meters, 25.293 square .... POLE
  100 square .... AR(E)
  1000 square .... DECARE
  10,000 square .... HECTARE
methane .... PARAFFIN
metheglin .... MEAD, LIQUOR
  material .... HONEY
method ...... WAY, MODE, MODUS,
  MANNER, SYST(EM), PROCESS,
  PROCEDURE, TECHNIQUE
methodical .... FORMAL,
  ORDERLY, SYSTEMATIC
Methodism founder ...... WESLEY
Methodist Church, of the
  .... WESLEYAN
  preacher .... ROUNDER
Methuselah's fame .... AGE
  father .... ENOCH
  grandson .... NOAH
meticulous .... FUSSY, FINICAL,
  PRECISE, EXACTING,
  PARTICULAR
metier .... FORTE, TRADE,
  VOCATION, SPECIALTY
metif(f) ...... MESTEE, HALFBREED
metis .... MULATTO
metopic .... FRONTAL
metric measure .... AR(E), GRAM,
  KILO, LITER, METER, STERE,
  DECIARE, HECTARE
  ton .... MILLIER
metrical accent/beat .... ICTUS
  composition ..... POEM, VERSE,
  POETRY
  foot .... DACTYL, IAMB(US),
  ANAPEST, PYRRHIC, TROCHEE,
  TRIBRACH, CHORIAMB(US)
  time unit .... MORA
metrician .... POET
metrify .... VERSIFY
metro .... SUBWAY
metropolis .... SEE, CITY, SEAT,
  CAPITAL
metropolitan .... URBAN, EPARCH,
  OPPIDAN, (ARCH)BISHOP
Metropolitan Opera man
  .... BING
Mets' home .... SHEA
mettle .... ARDOR, PLUCK, SPUNK,
  SPIRIT, COURAGE
mettlesome .... BRAVE, SPUNKY
Metz's river .... MOSELLE
Meuse .... MAAS, LESSE
  River city .... SEDAN
mew .... DEN, BARN, CAGE, MOLT,

SHED, GARAGE, STABLE,
  (SEA)GULL
mewl ...... MEOW, MIAOW, WHINE,
  WHIMPER
Mexican .... NAHUATL
  agave .... PULQUE
  American to a .... GRINGO,
  YANQUI
  ancient .... MAYAN
  bandit ..... BANDIDO, LADRONE
  basket grass .... ISTLE
  battlesite .... BUENAVISTA
  bay .... LA PAZ, CHAMELA,
  BALLENAS, BANDERAS,
  CAMPECHE
  bean .... FRIJOL(E)
  bean beetle .... LADYBUG
  beverage .... OCTLI, MESCAL,
  PULQUE, TEQUILA
  beverage seed .... CHIA
  bird .... VERDIN, TINAMOU
  blanket .... SERAPE
  bread/cake .... TORTILLA
  cab .... ARANA
  cape .... FALSO, LOBOS,
  CATOCHE
  capital .... MEXICO CITY
  cat .... EYRA, MARGAY
  Christmas pot for children
  .... PIÑATA
  city/town .... LERDO, MANTE,
  CANCUN, CELAYA, COLIMA,
  JALAPA, JUAREZ, LAREDO,
  MADERO, MERIDA, OAXACA,
  CORDOBA, MORELIA,
  OBREGON, ORIZABA, PACHUCA,
  TAMPICO, TIJUANA, TORREON,
  ACAPULCO, CAMPECHE,
  CULIACAN, ENSENADA,
  MAZATLAN, VICTORIA,
  ZARAGOZA, MONTERREY,
  GUADALAJARA
  coin .... PESO, CENTAVO
  coin, small old .... TLACO
  conqueror
  .... (HERNAN)CORTES
  corn mush .... AMOLE
  dance .... BAILE, RASPA
  dish .... CHILI, TACOS,
  TAMALE, ENCHILADA
  district .... TEQUILA
  dog .... CHIHUAHUA
  dollar .... PESO
  emperor .... MONTEZUMA,
  MAXIMILIAN
  farm worker .... PEON
  fiber plant .... PITA, DATIL,
  ISTLE, IXTLE, SISAL
  gopher .... TUZA
  grass .... OTATE, TUCAN,

ZACATON, TEOSINTE
  grinding stone .... METATE
  gulf ...... MEXICO, CALIFORNIA,
  TEHUANTEPEC
  handyman .... MOZO
  hill .... CERRO
  hut .... JACAL
  Indian .... PIMA, SERI, TECA,
  ZUNI, WABI, ALAIS, AZTEC,
  LIPAN, MAYAN, OLMEC,
  OPATA, OTOMI, SERIA, YAQUI,
  APACHE, TOLTEC
  Indian craft .... OJOS
  island .... PEREZ, CARMEN,
  CEDROS, CLARION, SOCORRO,
  TIBURON, MONSERRATE
  laborer .... PEON, BRACERO
  lagoon .... MADRE, TERMINOS
  lake .... GUZMAN, BACALAR,
  CHAPALA
  liquor .... MESCAL, PULQUE,
  TEQUILA
  man .... HOMBRE
  manor .... CASA
  mat .... PETATE
  measure .... VARA, CARGA,
  LABOR, LEGUA, LINEA, SITIO,
  FANEGA, PULGADA
  migrant .... WETBACK
  monetary unit .... PESO
  mountain .... ORIZABA,
  CITLALTEPETL
  mountain range .... BURRO,
  SIERRA MADRE
  mullet .... BOBO, LISITA
  muralist .... OROZCO, RIVERA
  musical instrument .... CLARIN
  muzhik .... PEON
  native .... AZTEC, MAYA(N)
  noble .... HIDALGO
  onyx .... TECALI
  peasant .... PEON
  peninsula .... YUCATAN
  persimmon .... CHAPOTE
  plant .... CHIA, AGAVE, AMOLE,
  DATIL, JALAP, SOTOL, CACTUS,
  MESCAL, PULQUE
  policeman .... RURALES
  president .... DIAZ, ORDAZ,
  ALEMAN, CALLES, HUERTA,
  JUAREZ, MATEOS, CAMACHO,
  OBREGON, ZEDILLO,
  CARDENAS, PORTILLO
  pyramid .... TEOCALLI
  race .... MAYA, AZTEC, TOLTEC
  reed .... OTATE
  resin tree .... DRAGO
  resort .... TAOS, CANCUN
  revolutionary .... PANCHO
  VILLA
  river ..... TULA, BABIA, HONDO,

NAZAS, RAMOS, VERDE, YAQUI, ATOYAC, BALSAS, BLANCO, COYUCA, FUERTE, GRANDE, PANUCO, SONORA, URIQUE, CONCHOS, SABINAS, RIO BRAVO, COLORADO
robber .... BANDIDO
rodent .... TUCAN
scarf .... TAPALO
seaport .... TAMPICO, ACAPULCO, MATAMOROS
shawl .... SERAPE
"spitfire" .... (LUPE)VELEZ
state .... MEXICO, OAXACA, PUEBLA, SONORA, CHIAPAS, DURANGO, HIDALGO, JALISCO, SINALOA, TABASCO, YUCATAN, COAHUILA, GUERRERO, VERACRUZ, CHIHUAHUA, MICHOACAN, NUEVO LEON, ZACATECAS, GUANAJUATO
state capital .... LA PAZ, TEPIC, COLIMA, JALAPA, OAXACA, PUEBLA, TOLUCA, DURANGO, MORELIA, CULIACAN, MEXICALI, SALTILLO, VICTORIA, CUERNAVACA, HERMOSILLO, GUADALAJARA
sugar ..... PANOCHA, PANOCHE, PENUCHE
tea .... APASOTE
temple .... TEOCALLI
tennis star .... OSUNA
thong .... ROMAL
timber tree .... EBANO
tree .... ULE, ABETO, DRAGO, RETAMA, GUAYULE, MESQUIT(E), AHUEHUETE
volcano .... ORIZABA, PARICUTIN
weight .... ONZA, LIBRA, ARROBA, QUINTAL
wood .... LINOLOA
Mexico City district
.... TACUBAYA
empress of .... CARLO(T)TA
watercourse in .... RIO
Meyerbeer ...... JAKOB, GIACOMO
opera by .... L'AFRICAINE
mezzanine .... ENTRESOL
mezzo .... MEDIUM, MIDWAY, HALFWAY, MODERATE, SOMEWHAT
Marilyn .... HORNE
MGM trademark .... THE LION'S ROAR
mho, reciprocal of .... OHM
miasma .... METHANE
disease .... MALARIA
mib .... MARBLE
mica .... TALC, BIOTITE, MINERAL,

NACRITE, SILICATE, ISINGLASS, MUSCOVITE
Micah .... PROPHET
Micawber, Dickens' .... WILKINS
mice .... VERMIN
of .... MURINE
Michael .... (ARCH)ANGEL
Michaelmas daisy .... ASTER
Michelangelo's birthplace
.... CAPRESE
trio, one of a .... PIETA
Michel's follower .... ANGELO
Michener .... JAMES
novel .... HAWAII, IBERIA
Michigan bay .... GREEN, HURON, MISERY, AU-TRAIN
capital .... LANSING
city/town .... HART, HOLT, NOVI, TROY, YALE, FLINT, IONIA, MASON, GARDEN, MONROE, TAYLOR, WARREN, DETROIT, JACKSON, LINCOLN, LIVONIA, MIDLAND, PONTIAC, PORTAGE, ROMULUS, SAGINAW, TRENTON, WYOMING, ANN ARBOR, DEARBORN, FERNDALE, MUSKEGON, KALAMAZOO, MARQUETTE
college .... ALMA, HOPE, MERCY, JORDAN, AQUINAS, FERRIS STATE, CONCORDIA, JOHN WESLEY
county .... BAY, CASS, KENT, LAKE, BARRY, CLARE, DELTA, EATON, IONIA, IOSCO, WAYNE, INGHAM, MACOMB, MONROE, OTTAWA, ALLEGAN, BERRIEN, CALHOUN, GENESEE, LENAWEE, MIDLAND, OAKLAND, SAGINAW, TUSCOLA, WEXFORD, ISABELLA
island .... SUGAR, GARDEN, MANITOU, POVERTY, DRUMMOND
lake .... ELK, GUN, BURT, ERIE, GLEN, CEDAR, PERCH, TAWAS, BEAVER, OTSEGO, PLATTE, MICHIGAN, PARADISE, SUPERIOR
lake city .... MUSKEGON, MILWAUKEE
lake port .... RACINE
mountain .... CURWOOD
river .... CASS, DEAD, FORD, FLINT, PAINT, RIFLE, PIGEON, RABBIT, PRAIRIE, SAGINAW
state bird .... ROBIN
state flower .... APPLE BLOSSOM
state nickname .... WOLVERINE
tourist site ..... DOW GARDENS,

PIONEER VILLAGE
university .... ANDREWS, DETROIT, DEARBORN, WAYNE STATE, MICHIGAN STATE
Mick, Rolling Stones'
.... JAGGER
Mickey .... FINN, MOUSE, ROONEY
Mickey's friend .... MINNIE
micra, singular of .... MICRON
microbe .... GERM, VIRUS, PATHOGEN, BACTERIUM
microcosm .... MAN, WORLD, SMALL WORLD, UNIVERSE
Micronesia island .... MOEN, TRUK, NAURU, KOSRAE, PONAPE, POHNPEI
microorganism(s) .... AM(O)EBA, BACTERIA, PROTOZOA
microphone .... MIKE
microscope glass plate .... SLIDE
microscopic .... MINUTE
Midas' touch product ...... GOLD
midday .... NOON
middle .... HUB, CORE, MESNE, MIDST, WAIST, CENTER, MEDIAL, MEDIAN, MESIAL, CENTRAL
class ..... COMMON, ORDINARY, BOURGEOISE
combining form .... MEDI(O)
ear .... DRUM, TYMPANUM
in law .... MESNE
kingdom .... CHINA
name in mysteries ...... CONAN
name of:
Alexander Bell, inventor
.... GRAHAM
Alvah Roebuck, Sears'
partner .... CURTIS
Amadeo Giannini, owner
of Bank of America
.... PETER
Anne Royall, first woman
editor .... NEWPORT
Dwight Eisenhower
.... DAVID
Edgar Poe, poet .... ALLAN
Francis Key, The Star-
Spangled Banner
writer .... SCOTT
Franklin Roosevelt
.... DELANO
George Bush .... HERBERT WALKER
Gerald Ford .... RUDOLPH
Harriet Stowe, author
.... BEECHER
Henry Beecher, preacher-
abolitionist .... WARD

Henry Longfellow, poet .... WADSWORTH
Howard Hughes, billionaire .... ROBARD
James Carter .... EARL
James Garfield .... ABRAM
James Polk .... KNOX
John Adams .... QUINCY
John Astor, fur trader .... JACOB
John Booth, assassin .... WILKES
John Coolidge .... CALVIN
John Kellogg, cereal company founder .... HARVEY
John Kennedy .... FITZGERALD
Lyndon Johnson ...... BAINES
Ralph Emerson, poet .... WALDO
Richard Nixon ..... MILHOUS
Richard Sears of mail-order business .... WARREN
Ronald Reagan ...... WILSON
Thomas Edison, inventor .... ALVA
Thomas Jackson, nicknamed "Stonewall" .... JONATHAN
Ulysses Grant .... SIMPSON
Walt Disney .... ELIAS
William Hearst, newspaper tycoon .... RANDOLPH
William Taft .... HOWARD
of the roader .... NEUTRAL
part .... CORE, DEEP
toward the .... MESAD
Middle Ages empire .... INCA, MALI, ASIAN, AZTEC, CHIMU, ROMAN, MONGOL, ANGEVIN, BYZANTINE
of the .... MEDIEVAL
middlebreaker .... LISTER
middleman ...... AGENT, BROKER, RETAILER, GO-BETWEEN
middling .... PORK, SOSO, MEDIUM, AVERAGE, MEDIOCRE, ORDINARY
middy .... BLOUSE, MIDSHIPMAN
Midgard .... EARTH
to Asgard .... BIFROST
midge .... FLY, GNAT, DWARF, BANTAM, MIDGET, PUNKIE
midget .... DWARF, PYGMY, MINIATURE
slang .... SHRIMP
Midianite king .... EVI, HUR, REBA
midland .... INTERIOR

dialects .... MERCIAN
mid-May or mid-July .... IDES
midmost .... CENTER, MIDDLE
midnight .... WITCHING HOUR
assembly of witches .... SABBAT
sun, land of .... NORWAY
midriff .... DIAPHRAGM
midshipman .... MIDDY, PLEBE, REEFER
Midsummer Night's Dream
character ...... PUCK, HERMIA, OBERON, THISBE, TITANIA
tinker .... SNOUT
midterm event .... EXAM(S)
midway .... HALFWAY
features .... SIDESHOWS
Midway Islands discoverer .... BROOKS
midweek .... WEDNESDAY
midwifery .... TOCOLOGY, OBSTETRICS
mien .... AIR, LOOK, ASPECT, MANNER, BEARING, APPEARANCE
miff .... HUFF, TIFF, ANNOY, OFFEND
miggle .... TAW, MIBS, MIGS, MARBLE
might ...... FORCE, POWER, VIGOR, ENERGY, POTENCY, STRENGTH
and _____ .... MAIN
mightily .... AMAIN
mighty .... VERY, GREAT, POTENT, STRONG, POWERFUL, PUISSANT
batsman .... MAYS, RUTH, AARON, CASEY
implement .... PEN
mite .... ATOM
symbol .... OAK
mignon .... DAINTY, PRETTY, DELICATE
mignonette .... WELD, WOLD, PLANT, RESEDA
migraine .... MEGRIM, HEADACHE
type of .... COMMON, CLASSICAL
migrant .... ROVER, TREKKER
farm worker .... OKIE
slang .... WETBACK
migrate .... MOVE, TREK
migration .... TREK, EXODUS
migratory .... ROVING, NOMADIC, PEREGRINE, WANDERING
bird .... TERN, KUTSARA, WI(D)GEON, SHOVELER
creature ..... LOCUST, LEMMING
worker ...... HOBO, JOAD, OKIE, PEON, ARKIE, BRACERO, WETBACK
Mikado .... OPERA, EMPEROR

character ..... KOKO, YUM YUM
court of .... DAIRI, DAIRO
mike .... LOAF, MICROPHONE
man .... EMCEE
Mike's friend .... PAT
Mikhaelovitch ally .... CROAT
milady's concern .... DIET, FIGURE, HAIRDO, WEIGHT, WAISTLINE
Milan operahouse .... (LA)SCALA
mild .... SOFT, WEAK, BALMY, BLAND, GENTLE, PLACID, LENIENT, MODERATE, TEMPERATE
drink .... CHASER
oath .... GEE, DRAT, EGAD, GOSH
smoke .... CLARO
mildew ...... MOLD, RUST, BLIGHT, FUNGUS
mile, nautical .... KNOT
$^{1}/_{8}$ of .... FURLONG
$^{1}/_{3}$ of LI
Miled, son of .... EBER
Milesian .... IRISH
milestone .... EVENT, HERMA, STELE, PILLAR, LANDMARK, PROGRESS
milfoil .... PLANT, YARROW
miliaria ...... HEAT RASH, PRICKLY HEAT
milieu .... CLIMATE, ENVIRON, AMBIENCE
militant .... WARLIKE, ACTIVIST, FIGHTING, COMBATANT, COMBATIVE
militarist .... JINGO
military .... ARMY, MARTIAL, SOLDIERLY, ARMED FORCES
abode .... CAMP
academy site .... WEST POINT
acronym .... AWOL
address .... APO, FPO
assistant .... AIDE
banner .... STANDARD
blockade .... SIEGE
cap .... KEPI, BUSBY, SHAKO, HAVELOCK, PERSHING
ceremony .... REVIEW
coat .... TUNIC
decoration .... DSC, BATTLE STAR, MEDAL OF HONOR
depot .... ARMORY, ARSENAL, MAGAZINE
engineer .... PIONEER, PONTONIER
equipment .... HARDWARE
exercises .... WAR GAMES
felony .... AWOL
force .... MILITIA, AIR POWER
formation .... PHALANX

greeting .... SALUTE
group ..... UNIT, NAVY, CORPS,
DIVISION
guardhouse .... BRIG
landing point ...... BEACHHEAD
meal .... MESS, K-RATION
messenger .... ESTAFET
movement .... MARCH,
MANEUVER, DEPLOYMENT
music .... TAPS
officer .... BRASSHAT
operations .... WARFARE
police .... MP, REDCAP
post ..... BASE, FORT, STATION,
GARRISON, PRESIDIO
prisoner .... POW
rank, temporary .... BREVET
roll .... MUSTER
salute .... SALVO
school site .... ANNAPOLIS,
WEST POINT
signal for parley/retreat
.... CHAMADE
station .... GARRISON
store .... PX, CANTEEN,
(POST)EXCHANGE
storehouse .... DEPOT, ETAPE,
ARMORY, ARSENAL, MAGAZINE
student .... CADET, PLEBE
supplies .... MUNITIONS
truck .... AMTRAC, CAMION,
CARRIER
unit .... CADRE, SQUAD,
COMPANY, PLATOON
weapons .... ORDNANCE
militate .... OPERATE, FUNCTION
militia .... RESERVES, SOLDIERY,
(CITIZEN)ARMY
member .... RESERVIST
milk .... LAC, SUCK, BLEED,
EXTRACT, LACTOSE,
EMULSION
animal's .... K(O)UMISS
beverage .... SHAKE
coagulated part .... CURD
coagulating enzyme
.... RENNIN
combining form .... LACT(O)
constituent .... CASEIN
curd .... CASEIN
curdler .... RENNET, RENNIN
farm .... DAIRY, LACTARY
fermented .... K(O)UMISS
food from .... YOG(H)URT
from .... LACTIC
giving .... MILCH
gland .... MAMMA
kind of .... SKIM, FRESH,
CONDENSED, EVAPORATED
like .... LACTEOUS
not giving .... YELD

of magnesia .... LAXATIVE
part of .... CURD, WHEY,
SERUM, CASEIN, PLASMA,
LECITHIN
pertaining to .... LACTIC,
LACTARY, LACTEAL
product, cultured ...... YOGURT
protein .... CASEIN
secrete .... LACTATE
separator .... CENTRIFUGE
shake .... FRAPPE
sickness .... SHAKES
sour .... CURD, CLABBER
source .... COW, GOAT,
COCONUT, COCOANUT
store .... DAIRY
teeth .... FIRST TEETH
with .... AU LAIT
milker's seat .... STOOL
milkfish .... AWA, SABALO,
TARPON
milkless .... YELD
milksop .... SISSY, MOLLYCODDLE
milkweed .... SOMA, SPURGE,
ANGLEPOD, STAPELIA
juice .... LATEX
milkwort .... SENEGA
milky .... LACTEAL, LACTEOUS
liquid .... LATEX
Milky Way .... GALAXY
area .... COALSACK
of the .... GALACTIC
shape .... SPIRAL
mill .... FACTORY, GRIND(ER)
dam .... WEIR
hand .... MANO, QUERN
owner's fee .... MULTURE
Millay, Edna _____ .... ST.
VINCENT
millenium .... GOLDEN AGE
millepore .... CORAL
miller .... MOTH
fee of .... MULTURE
who dances .... ANN
Miller's salesman .... LOMAN
millet ...... DURRA, GRAIN, GRASS,
HIRSE, PEARL, DOURA(H)
sorghum-like .... MILO
milliard .... BILLION
milliner .... HATTER
millinery .... HATS, HEADDRESSES
worker .... FACER
milling charge .... TOLL,
MULTURE, THIRLAGE
refuse .... TAILING
millimeter, ¹/₁,₀₀₀ of a
.... MICRON, MIKRON
million electron volts .... MEV
hardest to earn .... FIRST
times: comb. form .... MEGA

ton explosive force
.... MEGATON
millions of years .... EON
millipede .... MYRIAPOD,
WIREWORM, ARTHROPOD
it has plenty of .... LEGS
millpond .... DAM, DIKE
Mills bomb .... GRENADE
millstone .... BUHR, BURDEN
part .... INK, RYND
Milne character .... PIM
readers .... CHILDREN
Milo .... MELOS, SORGHUM
milord .... NOBLEMAN
Milquetoast .... CASPAR
creator of .... WEBSTER
milt .... ROE, SPLEEN
mime ...... APERY, CLOWN, MIMIC,
JESTER, BUFFOON, IMITATE
mimeograph .... STENCIL,
DUPLICATE
mimesis .... IMITATION
mimetic .... APISH, IMITATIVE
mimic .... APE(Y), COPY, MIME,
MOCK, IMITATE, IMITATIVE,
SIMULATE(D)
female .... MIMA
mimicking .... APERY
mimicry ...... MIMESIS, IMITATION
mimosa .... HERB, SHRUB,
ACACIA, SOAPBARK
descriptive word for
.... SHRINKING
mina .... STARLING
minaret .... TOWER
caller from a .... MUEZZIN
place of .... MOSQUE
mince .... CHOP, DICE, HASH
minced meat .... RISSOLE
oath .... GAD, GEE, DRAT,
EGAD, HECK
mincing bite .... NIBBLE
mind .... CARE, HEED, MOOD,
NOUS, OBEY, TEND, BELIEF,
PSYCHE, REASON, OPINION,
MENTALITY, LOOK AFTER
bear in .... REMEMBER
-boggling ...... BREATH-TAKING
call to .... RECALL, RECOLLECT
drug .... LSD, SEDATIVE,
MESCALINE, AMPHETAMINE
of the .... MENTAL, PHRENIC
part of the .... ID, EGO,
SUPEREGO
to-mind communication
.... TELEPATHY
Mindanao bay .... MAYO,
BUTUAN, ILIGAN, ILLANA,
LANUZA, LIANGA, PUJADA,
MACAJALAR
city .... DAVAO, BUTUAN,

ILIGAN, OROQUIETA, ZAMBOANGA, CAGAYAN DE ORO

gulf .... MORO, DAVAO

inhabitant .... MOSLEM, MUSLIM

lake .... LANAO, MAINIT

province .... DAVAO, LANAO, AGUSAN, SURIGAO, BUKIDNON, COTABATO, ZAMBOANGA

river .... AGUSAN, PULANGI

volcano .... APO, RAGANG

mindful .... ALERT, AWARE, CAREFUL, CAUTIOUS

mindless .... DUMB, HEEDLESS

followers .... SHEEP

one .... IDIOT

mine .... DIG, PIT, SOURCE, TUNNEL, EXCAVATE, EXPLOSIVE

arch .... OVERCAST

car .... TRAM, HUTCH

ceiling .... ASTEL

channel .... TAILRACE

claim .... STAKE

entrance/access .... ADIT

excavation .... STOPE

gas .... DAMP, MEPHITIS

kind of .... COAL, GOLD, NICKEL, SILVER, DIAMOND

layer .... SAPPER

partition .... SOLLAR

passage .... STULM, WINZE

pit/pool .... SUMP, STOPE, ARROYO

prop .... NOG, SPRAG, STULL

refuse/waste .... ATTLE, MULLOCK, TAILING

remover .... SWEEPER

rich .... BONANZA

shaft .... WINZE, ARROYO, DOWNCAST

sieve .... JIG(GER)

step .... LOB

thrower .... MORTAR

timber .... STULL

truck .... CORF, HUTCH

tunnel .... ADIT, STOPE

vein .... LODE

wall .... ASTEL

winch .... WHIM

Mineo, _____ .... SAL

miner .... PITMAN, SAPPER, COLLIER, DRILLER, EXCAVATOR, GOLDDIGGER

disease of .... SILICOSIS

safety lamp of .... DAVY

mineral .... ORE, TALC, SPALT, TOPAZ, TRONA, BARITE, GYPSUM, PINITE, PYRITE, QUARTZ, SPINEL, APATITE,

CALCITE, DIAMOND, EPIDOTE, LEUCITE, URALITE, SERPENTINE

black .... COAL, GRAPHITE

black crystalline .... SPINEL(LE)

blue .... IOLITE, LAZULITE

concretion .... CALCULUS

crystalline .... MICA, SPAR, FELDSPAR

deposit .... BED, LODE, VEIN, PLACER, SINTER

essential to health .... IRON, ZINC, SODIUM, CALCIUM, MAGNESIUM, POTASSIUM, PHOSPOROUS

glassy .... SILICA

hardest .... DIAMOND

in quartz .... SILICA

jelly .... VASELINE, PETROLEUM

luster of .... SCHILLER

lustrous .... SPAR, RUTILE

mixture .... MAGMA

oil .... KEROSENE

radioactive .... CARNOTITE

salt .... ALUM

softest/soapy .... TALC

spot in a .... MACLE

spring .... SPA

water .... VICHY, SELTZER

wax .... OZOCERITE

worthless .... GANGUE

miners' group .... MFD, UMW

Minerva .... ATHENA, AZALEA, GODDESS

shield of .... (A)EGIS

minestrone .... SOUP, TUREEN

minesweeper .... TRAWLER, PARAVANE

Ming .... PORCELAIN

mingle .... MIX, JOIN, MELL, BLEND, ASSOCIATE

as vapor .... COALESCE

mini .... MINIMAL, MINISCULE, VERY SHORT, VERY SMALL

swallow .... SIP

miniature .... MODEL, SMALL, PORTRAIT, DIMINUTIVE

aquarium .... BOWL, TANK

garden .... TERRARIUM

tree .... BONSAI

minify .... REDUCE

opposed to .... MAGNIFY

minikin .... DOLL, PEEWEE, DARLING, SNIPPET

minim .... DASH, DROP, TINIEST, SMALLEST

in music .... HALF NOTE

minimal .... LEAST

minimize .... LESSEN

minimum .... LEAST, LOWEST,

SMALLEST

as a .... NO LESS

mining bar/chisel .... GAD

basket .... CORF

bed of ore .... REEF

claim .... STAKE

kind of .... PLACER

nail .... SPAD

trough .... HUTCH

minion .... TYPE, FAVORITE, FOLLOWER, MISTRESS

of the law .... POLICEMAN

minister .... CATER, SERVE, CURATE, (AT)TEND, PASTOR, VIZIER, CLERGYMAN

assistant of .... DEACON

home of .... MANSE, RECTORY, PARSONAGE

title of .... REVEREND

ministry .... CLERGY, PULPIT

admit to the .... ORDAIN

miniver .... FUR, ERMINE

mink .... FUR, MAMMAL

kin of .... OTTER, SKUNK

Minnehaha's love .... HIAWATHA

minnesinger .... MINSTREL

Minnesota bay .... MUSKEG

capital .... ST. PAUL

city/town ... ADA, ELY, MORA, ANOKA, AUSTIN, BLAINE, DULUTH, WADENA, WILMAR, WINONA, FRIDLEY, HIBBING, HOPKINS, MANKATO, RED WING, BRAINERD, FAIRMONT, MOORHEAD, ROCHESTER, TWIN LAKES, ALEXANDRIA, COON RAPIDS, MINNETONKA, MINNEAPOLIS

county ...... CASS, CLAY, LAKE, LYON, POLK, RICE, ANOKA, MOWER, CARVER, DAKOTA, ITASCA, RAMSEY, WINONA, WRIGHT, GOODHUE, OLMSTEAD, STEARNS, FREEBORN, HENNEPIN, KANDIYOHI, OTTER TAIL, SAINT LOUIS

lake .... MUD, RED, CASS, DEER, GULL, LONG, NETT, RENO, RICE, EMILY, HERON, LEECH, RAINY, TROUT, WOODS, ITASCA, SUPERIOR

mountain .... EAGLE

native .... GOPHER

river .... MUD, RUM, COBB, CROW, HILL, LEAF, PIKE, ROCK, ROOT, CEDAR, MAPLE, SAUK, RAPID, SHELL, SNAKE, ZUMBRO, PELICAN, MUSTINKA, PARTRIDGE, WHITEFACE, MISSISSIPPI

state bird .... LOON
state flower .... SHOWY LADY
SLIPPER
state nickname .... GOPHER,
NORTH STAR
tourist site ...... BELL MUSEUM,
ZOOLOGICAL GARDEN
university .... HAMLINE,
MANKATO STATE, MOORHEAD
STATE
minnow .... MINNY, SHINER,
GUDGEON, MOONFISH
minor .... PETTY, YOUTH,
LESS(ER), INFERIOR, UNDER-
AGE
details .... MINUTIAE
in law .... PETIT, PUPIL
offense .... MISDEMEANOR
suit .... CLUBS, DIAMONDS
Minorca .... ISLAND, CHICKEN
sister island .... MAJORCA
minoress .... CLARE
Minorite ...... FRIAR, FRANCISCAN
minority .... NONAGE, PUPILAGE
group's persecution
.... POGROM
Minos' co-judge .... AEACUS
daughter .... ARIADNE
kingdom .... CRETE
monster .... MINOTAUR
parent .... ZEUS, EUROPA
structure .... LABYRINTH
wife .... PASIPHAE
Minotaur's dwelling
.... LABYRINTH
killer .... THESEUS
minster ...... CHURCH, CATHEDRAL
minstrel .... BARD, RIMER, SKALD,
MUSICIAN, TROUBADOUR,
(MINNE)SINGER
musical instrument ...... HARP,
LUTE
show end man .... BONES
wandering .... GLEEMAN,
GOLIARD, JONGLEUR
mint .... COIN, HERB, SAGE, BASIL,
CANDY, CLARY, PLANT,
STAMP, THYME, CATNIP,
HYSSOP, INVENT, SAVORY,
DITTANY, MONARDA,
OREGANO, MARJORAM,
FABRICATE
charge .... BRASSAGE
drink .... JULEP
genus .... MENTHA
product .... COIN(S), SPECIE
mintage .... COINAGE
minuet .... DANCE
Minuit's bargain
.... MANHATTAN
minus .... LESS, WITHOUT,

NEGATIVE
minuscule .... DROP, TINY, SMALL,
MINUTE
minute .... WEE, NOTE, TINY,
PETTY, SMALL, MOMENT,
INSTANT, MINUSCULE
combining form .... MICRO
distinction .... NICETY
organism .... GERM, AM(O)EBA,
MICROBE
orifice .... PORE, STOMA
quantity .... MITE
minutiae .... TRIVIA, DETAILS
minutes .... ACTA, RECORD
15 .... QUARTER
minx .... GIRL, JADE, TART,
HUSSY, MALAPERT
play the .... FLIRT
miracle .... MARVEL, WONDER
bread/food .... MANNA
scene of .... CANA, LOURDES
worker .... THAUMATURGE
miraculous .... MARVELOUS,
WONDERFUL, SUPERNATURAL
mirage .... VISION, DELUSION,
ILLUSION
in Arabia .... SERAB
mire ...... BOG, MUD, MUCK, OOZE,
EMBOG, SLUSH
Miriam's brother .... AARON,
MOSES
mirror .... CRYSTAL,
REFLECT(OR),
(LOOKING)GLASS
tinfoil of .... TAIN
mirth ...... GLEE, GAIETY, JOLLITY,
HILARITY, MERRIMENT
provoker .... SCREAM
miry .... OOZY, BOGGY, MUDDY
misadventure .... MISHAP, BAD
LUCK, ACCIDENT
misalliance .... MISMATCH
misanthrope .... (MAN)HATER
of sorts .... CYNIC, LONER
misbegotten .... BASTARD
misbehavior .... MISCONDUCT
miscalculate .... ERR, GOOF,
MISJUDGE
miscarriage .... ABORTION
miscarry .... FAIL, ABORT
miscellanea .... ANA, MISCELLANY
miscellaneous .... MIXED, VARIED,
SUNDRY, ASSORTED
miscellany .... ANA, OLIO,
MEDLEY, MELANGE, MIXTURE,
POTPOURRI, ODDS AND ENDS
mischief .... HOB, DIDO, HARM,
PRANK, TRICK, INJURY,
TROUBLE, DEVILTRY
maker .... IMP, ERIS, LOKI,
PEST, PUCK, DEVIL, SCAMP,

PLOTTER, INTRIGUER,
PRANKSTER
mischievous .... PESKY, IMPISH,
NAUGHTY, PUCKISH, ROGUISH,
DEVILISH, PRANKISH
misconduct .... IMPROPRIETY
miscreant .... INFIDEL, HERETIC,
VILLAIN, CRIMINAL
miscue .... ERROR, MISTAKE
misdeed .... SIN, CRIME, FAULT
misdemeanor .... CRIME, DELICT,
OFFENSE, INFRACTION,
MISCONDUCT
misdoing .... ERRING
mise .... PACT, AGREEMENT
miser .... HUNKS, WRETCH,
HOARDER, NIGGARD,
TIGHTWAD, SKINFLINT
of fiction .... MARNER,
SCROOGE
miserable .... MEAN, ABJECT,
PALTRY, FORLORN, PITIABLE,
WRETCHED
misericord .... DAGGER
miserly .... TIGHT, GREEDY,
SORDID, STINGY, CRIPPLE,
NIGGARDLY, PENURIOUS
person .... NIGGARD,
TIGHTWAD, SKINFLINT
misery .... WOE, PAIN, AGONY,
DOLOR, GRIEF, DISTRESS
misfire .... FAIL, FIZZLE
misfortune .... WOE, MISHAP,
CALAMITY, ADVERSITY
misgiving .... FEAR, DOUBT,
QUALM, SCRUPLE,
PREMONITION
misguided .... MISLED
mishandle ...... ABUSE, MALTREAT
mishap ...... BAD LUCK, ACCIDENT
on Broadway .... FLOP
mishmash .... MESS, OLIO,
JUMBLE, FARRAGO, MELANGE,
HODGEPODGE
Mishnah .... TALMUD, TEACHINGS
section .... ABOT
misinform .... MISLEAD,
MISDIRECT
misjudge .... ERR, MISDEEM
mislay .... LOSE, MISPLACE
misle .... MIST, MIZZLE, DRIZZLE
mislead .... DELUDE, DECEIVE
misleading appearance
.... FACADE
clue .... RED HERRING
mismanage .... BOTCH, BUNGLE
mismatch .... MISFIT,
MISALLIANCE
misogynist .... WOMAN-HATER
misplace .... LOSE, MISLAY,
DERANGE

misrepresent .... (BE)LIE, COLOR, GARBLE, DISTORT
miss .... GIRL, LADY, LOSE, NEED, OMIT, SKIP, WANT, AVOID, ESCAPE, MISLAY, OVERLOOK
a catch .... MUFF
archaic .... SPINSTER
contrary .... MARI
intentionally .... BALK
the bus .... FAIL
Miss America, first: 1921
.... MARGARET GORMAN
America pageant emcee
.... BERT PARKS
Bagnold .... ENID
Barrett, Hollywood's
.... RONA
_____ : Bleak House
character .... FLITE
Bryant .... ANITA
Cantrell .... LANA
Cilento .... DIANE
Claire .... INA
Davis .... BETTE
Diller .... PHYLLIS
Dinsmore .... ELSIE
D'Urberville .... TESS
Gam .... RITA
Garson .... GREER
Hagen .... UTA
Haver .... JUNE
Hayworth .... RITA
Horne .... LENA
Kett .... ETTA
Le Gallienne .... EVA
Lollobrigida .... GINA
Loren .... SOPHIA
Lupino .... IDA
Miles .... VERA
Moreno .... RITA
Munson .... ONA
O'Grady .... ROSIE
Oyl .... OLIVE
Piggy's cry .... MOI
Reese .... DELLA
St. John .... JILL
Street .... DELLA
Taylor .... ELIZABETH
Verdugo .... ELENA
West .... MAE
Woodhouse .... EMMA
Missa Solemnis composer
.... BEETHOVEN
missal .... PRAYERBOOK
missel .... THRUSH
misshape ...... DEFORM, CONTORT, DISTORT
missile .... BOLT, DART, MIRV, ARROW, LANCE, SHAFT, SHELL, SPEAR, BULLET, ROCKET, GRENADE,

PROJECTILE, TRAJECTILE
acronym .... ABM, ASM, SAM, SSM, ICBM, IRBM, XAAM
anti-missile .... PATRIOT
anti-ship .... EXOCET
detecting device .... RADAR
guided .... SAM, IRBM, NIKE, SCUD, TALOS, ROCKET
launching .... BLAST OFF
part of .... WARHEAD
pit/housing .... SILO
tip of .... WARNOSE
type .... BALLISTIC
whaler's .... HARPOON
missing .... LOST, ABSENT, LACKING, OMITTED
link? .... APEMAN
mission .... TASK, ERRAND, CALLING, EMBASSY
to remember .... ALAMO
missionary .... APOSTLE, EVANGELIST
Mississippi capital .... JACKSON
city/town .... PEARL, YAZOO, BILOXI, LAUREL, TUPELO, GRENADA, NATCHEZ, COLUMBUS, GULFPORT, MERIDIAN, VICKSBURG, PASCAGOULA, HATTIESBURG
college .... BELHAVEN, MILLSAPS
county .... LEE, CLAY, PIKE, ADAMS, HINDS, JONES, LAMAR, YAZOO, ALCORN, DE SOTO, MONROE, RANKIN, WARREN, COAHOMA, FORREST, JACKSON, LEFLORE, LINCOLN, LOWNDES, MADISON, LAFAYETTE, SUNFLOWER
explorer ...... JOLIET, HENNEPIN
Indian .... TIOU, BILOXI
island .... CAT, HORN
lake .... ENID, SARDIS, TCHULA, PICKWICK
mountain .... WOODALL
river .... LEAF, WOLF, AMITE, PEARL, SKUNA, YAZOO, STRONG, NOXUBEE, MISSISSIPPI, YOCKANOOKANY
state bird .... MOCKINGBIRD
state flower .... MAGNOLIA
state nickname .... BAYOU, MAGNOLIA
steamboater .... RIVERMAN
tourist site .... GOVERNOR'S MANSION, OLD CAPITOL MUSEUM
university ...... JACKSON STATE
U.S. Air Force Base
.... KESSLER, COLUMBUS

U.S. Naval Air Station
.... MERIDIAN
Mississippian, any .... TADPOLE
missive .... LETTER, MESSAGE
Missouri capital .... JEFFERSON CITY
caverns .... MERAMEC
city/town .... AVA, LAMAR, MACON, MILAN, FULTON, JOPLIN, KANSAS, WARSAW, CLINTON, MEMPHIS, RAYTOWN, SEDALIA, CARTHAGE, HANNIBAL, CRESTWOOD, GLADSTONE, FLORISSANT, SAINT LOUIS, SPRINGFIELD, INDEPENDENCE
college .... AVILA, DRURY, LOGAN, TARKIO, COLUMBIA, ROCKHURST, FONTBONNE, MARYVILLE
county .... RAY, CASS, CLAY, COLE, DADE, HOLT, IRON, KNOX, LINN, PIKE, POLK, ADAIR, BOONE, SCOTT, TEXAS, BUTLER, GREENE, JASPER, MARION, MILLER, NEWTON, PETTIS, PHELPS, PLATTE, DUNKLIN, JACKSON
guerrilla .... JAWHAWKER
lake .... OZARKS, NORFOLK, TANEYCOMO, WAPPAPELLO
mountain .... TAUM SAUK
notable .... TRUMAN, PERSHING
plateau .... OZARK
river .... KAW, SAC, GRAND, OSAGE, PLATTE, MERAMEC, MISSOURI, MISSISSIPPI
state bird .... BLUEBIRD
state flower .... HAWTHORN
state nickname .... SHOW ME
state tree .... DOGWOOD
tourist attraction
.... RIVERBOATS, WORLDS OF FUN, BOTANICAL GARDEN, MARK TWAIN MUSEUM
tributary .... PLATTE
university .... LINCOLN, ST. LOUIS, WASHINGTON
U.S. Air Force Base
.... WHITEMAN, RICHARDS GEBAUR
misspelling .... CACOGRAPHY
misspend ...... WASTE, SQUANDER
misstep .... SLIP, TRIP, ERROR, FAUX PAS
missy: colloq. .... GIRL
mist .... FOG, HAZE, SMOG, BRUME, GAUZE, MISLE, VAPOR, SEREIN
rain like .... DRIZZLE
mistake .... SLIP, TRIP, BONER,

ERROR, FAULT, LAPSE, MISCUE, BLUNDER, OMISSION, SOLECISM
in conduct .... FAUX PAS
in printing .... ERRATUM
mistaken .... WRONG, ERRONEOUS, INCORRECT
mister .... SIR, HERR, SENOR, SIGNOR, MONSIEUR
mistle thrush .... MAVIS
mistral .... WIND
Mistral, poet .... FREDERIC
mistreat .... ABUSE
mistress ...... MRS., MOLL, LEMAN, MADAM, MINION, MISSIS, MISSUS, PARAMOUR, INAMORATA
mistrial, one cause of
.... TECHNICALITY
mistrust .... DOUBT, SUSPICION
misty .... BRUMOUS, NEBULOUS
rain .... SEREIN, MIZZLE
misunderstanding .... ODDS, QUARREL, DISPARITY, IMBROGLIO
misuse .... ABUSE, WASTE, MISTREAT
of words .... MALAPROPISM
Mitchell (Helen) singer
.... MELBA, NELLIE
mite .... MOTE, TICK, ATOMY, ACARID, ACARUS, SPIDER
larva .... CHIGOE, JIGGER, LEPTUS, CHIGGER
miter .... TIARA, HEADBAND, BISHOPRIC, HEADDRESS
mitigate .... EASE, ALLAY, LESSEN, SOFTEN, TEMPER, ASSUAGE, MODERATE, EXTENUATE
mitosis, stage of .... ANAPHASE
mitt .... PAW, GLOVE
slang .... HAND
mitten .... GLOVE
mitzvah .... PRECEPT, BLESSING, COMMANDMENT
mix .... FUSE, STIR, ADDLE, BLEND, MERGE, JUMBLE, MINGLE, INFUSE, COMBINE, COALESCE
archaic .... MELL
dough .... KNEAD
up ...... FIGHT, SNAFU, GARBLE, TANGLE, EMBROIL, COMPOUND
with .... ASSOCIATE, (INTER)MINGLE
mixed, capable of being
.... MISCIBLE
language .... JARGON, PIDGIN
type .... PI
variety .... HYBRID, CROSS-BRED

mixer, drink ...... SODA, SHAKER, BARTENDER
mixing implement .... AGITATOR
mixture ...... HASH, OLIO, BLEND, AMALGAM, FARRAGO, MELANGE, COMPOUND, (MISH)MASH, POTPOURRI, HODGEPODGE
flour, milk, etc. .... BATTER
musical .... MEDLEY
Mizar .... ALCOR
Mize, ballplayer .... BIG JAWN
mizzen .... SAIL
mizzle .... RAIN, DRIZZLE
Mme. Bovary .... EMMA
Chian Kai-shek, nee
.... SOONG
mnemonic routine .... ROTE
subject .... MEMORY
Mnemosyne's daughter(s)
.... MUSE(S)
concern .... MEMORY
moa .... RATITE
relative .... KIWI, APTERYX
Moab .... KINGDOM
father of .... LOT
giant .... EMIM, ZUZIM
king .... MESHA
mountain .... NEBO
Moabite stone, name on
.... AMRI
moan .... (BE)WAIL, LAMENT, BELLYACHE
moat .... DITCH, FOSS(E)
structure surrounded by
.... CASTLE
mob ...... GANG, CROWD, BOODLE, RABBLE, THRONG, CANAILLE, HOI POLLOI, RIFFRAFF
scene .... RIOT
mobile .... FREE, LOOSE, MOVABLE, FLEXIBLE
hospital .... AMBULANCE
mobilize .... MUSTER, ORGANIZE
mobster .... GOON, PUNK, GANGSTER, RACKETEER
girl .... MOLL
Moby Dick .... PELEG, WHALE
author of .... MELVILLE
foe/hunter of .... AHAB
moccasin .... PAC, SNAKE, FLOWER, LOAFER, SLIPPER, LARRIGAN
mocha .... COFFEE, LEATHER
mochila .... KNAPSACK
mock ...... APE, DEFY, FAKE, GIBE, JAPE, JEER, JEST, JIBE, TWIT, FLEER, FLOUT, MIMIC, SCOFF, SNEER, TAUNT, DERIDE, IMITATE, RIDICULE
attack .... FEINT

orange .... SHRUB, SERINGA, SYRINGA
sea battle .... NAUMACHY
sun .... PARHELION
up ...... COPY, DUMMY, MODEL, REPLICA
mocker .... MIME, MIMIC, DERIDER
mockery ...... JOKE, SHAM, FARCE, DERISION, TRAVESTY, BURLESQUE
mod .... TRENDY
modal .... CONDITIONAL
mode .... FAD, WAY, STYLE, VOGUE, METHOD, FASHION
model .... COPY, POSE, TYPE, DESIGN, MOCK-UP, SIT(TER), EXAMPLE, MANIKIN, PATTERN, EXEMPLAR, PARADIGM, STANDARD
artist's .... NUDE
of a planned building
.... MAQUETTE
of perfection .... IDEAL, PARAGON
original .... ARCHETYPE, PROTOTYPE
small .... MINIATURE
Model T .... TIN LIZZIE
moderate .... DRY, MILD, (A)BATE, SOBER, TEMPER, ABSTAIN, LENIENT, PRESIDE, MITIGATE, RESTRAIN
in music .... MEZZO
in politics .... MIDDLE-OF-THE-ROAD
moderation .... SOBRIETY, TEMPERANCE, SELF-CONTROL
modern ...... NEO, NEW, LATE(ST), RECENT, UP-TO-DATE
city sight .... SKYSCRAPER, TRAFFIC JAM
person .... NEOTERIC
Modernismo's Ruben .... DARIO
modernist .... NEO
modernize .... RETOOL, UPDATE, RENOVATE
modest .... COY, SHY, LOWLY, TIMID, DECENT, DEMURE, FRUGAL, HUMBLE, SIMPLE, BASHFUL, RESERVED
modicum .... BIT, DAB
modifier ...... ADVERB, ADJECTIVE
modify .... VARY, ALTER, AMEND, LIMIT, CHANGE, QUALIFY
modish .... CHIC, SMART, DRESSY, STYLISH, FASHIONABLE
modiste .... COUTURIER, DRESSMAKER
modulate .... ADAPT, ADJUST, ATTUNE, (IN)TONE
modulation .... CADENCE

module .... UNIT
modus operandi ...... PROCEDURE
   vivendi .... COMPROMISE
Moffo, singer .... ANNA
mogul .... RULER, AUTOCRAT,
                      LOCOMOTIVE
   slang .... VIP, BIGWIG
Mogul ...... NABOB, MONGOL(IAN)
   emperor .... AKBAR, BABAR,
     BABER, BABUR, JEHAN,
                  HUMAYUN
   ruler .... NAWAB
mohair .... FABRIC, MOREEN
   source of .... ANGORA
Mohammed .... MAHOMET,
       MAHOUND, PROPHET
   birthplace of .... MECCA
   burial place of .... MEDINA
   daughter of .... FATIMA
   descendant of .... SEID, SAYID,
                  SHERIF
   flight of .... HEGIRA, HEJIRA
   follower of .... ISLAM,
        MOSLEM, MUSLIM
   opus .... KORAN
   religion founded by
   .... ISLAM, MOSLEM
   sister of .... JINNAH
   son-in-law .... ALI
   successor of .... CALIF,
        CALIPH, K(H)ALIF
   wife of ...... AISHA, AYESHA(H)
Mohammedan .... ISLAMIC,
                 ISLAMITE
   angel .... AZRAIL
   beggar/ascetic .... FAKIR
   bible .... KORAN, ALCORAN
   bier .... TABUT
   blacksmith .... LOHAR
   call to prayer ..... ADAN, AZAN
   canonical law .... SHARIA
   cup .... LOTAH
   demon .... JENNI(E)
   devil .... EBLIS, SHAITAN,
                 SHEITAN
   fasting period .... ASHURA,
               RAMADAN
   festival .... BAIRAM
   god .... ALLAH
   hermit/monk .... SANTON
   holy war .... JEHAD, JIHAD
   infidel .... KAFIR
   inn .... IMARET, CARAVANSARY
   judge/magistrate .... CADI
   law .... SUNNA(H)
   leader .... IMAM, MAHDI
   Malay .... MORO
   messiah .... MAHDI
   month .... RABIA, RAJAB,
     SAFAR, JUMADA, SHABAN,
               RAMADAN

mystic .... SUFI, SUNNITE
mysticism .... SUFISM
noble ...... AMIR, EMIR, AMEER,
          EMEER, SHERIF
nymph .... HOURI
orthodox .... SUNNITE
prayer hour .... AZAN
priest .... IMAM
prince's title .... NAWAB
principle .... IJMA
religion .... ISLAM
ruler .... AMIR, AMEER,
        CALIPH, SULTAN
ruler's decree .... IRADE
saint .... PIR
salutation .... SALAAM
scholars .... ULEMA
sect member ...... SUFI, SHIAH,
      SHIITE, SUNNITE
shrine .... KAABA
slave .... MAMELUKE
teacher .... MOLLAH, MULLA(H)
title .... AGA, AMIR, EMIR,
   EMEER, NAWAB, CALIPH,
               SAY(Y)ID
unbeliever .... KAF(F)IR
uncle .... ABBAS
veil .... YASHMAC, YASHMAK
woman's clothing .... ISAR
Mohave .... YUMA(N)
Mohawk .... RIVER, INDIAN
   chief .... BRANT, HIAWATHA
   city on the .... UTICA
mohur, ¹⁄₁₅ of .... RUPEE
moiety .... CLAN, HALF, PART,
        SHARE, PORTION
moil .... DRUDGE(RY), COMMOTION
   and ___ .... TOIL
moire .... SILK, TABBY, FABRIC,
              TAFFETA
moist .... WET, DAMP, DANK,
     DEWY, HUMID, RORIC
   to the touch .... CLAMMY
moisten .... WET, SOAK, WASH,
   (BE)DEW, WATER, DAMPEN,
        SPONGE, SPLASH
   and rub with oil
   .... EMBROCATE
   as flax .... RET
moisture .... WETNESS, DAMPNESS
   combining form ...... HYGR(O)
   condensed .... DEW, FOG, MIST
moke .... NAG, DOLT, IDIOT,
                 DONKEY
molar .... TOOTH, CHOPPER,
               GRINDER
molasses .... SYRUP, TREACLE
   beverage .... RUM, TAFIA,
                 ARRACK
   candy .... TAFFY, TOFFEE
   source .... SORGO

molave .... TREE, WOOD, VITEX
mold .... CAST, COPY, FORM,
   MUST, DECAY, KNEAD, SHAPE,
   FUNGUS, MATRIX, MILDEW,
              MOULAGE
   core .... NOWEL
   opening for molten metal
   .... GIT, GEAT, SPRUE
   product .... CASTING
Moldavia, capital of .... KISHINEV
   town .... JASSY
molder .... DIE, DECAY, STAMP
molding .... CYMA, CONGE,
   BORDER, EDGING, FILLET,
      REGLET, TRINGLE
   building's .... CORNICE
   concave .... COVE, COVING,
                 SCOTIA
   convex .... OVOLO, TORUS,
     REEDING, BAGUET(TE)
   curved .... NEBULE
   edge .... ARRIS
   egg-shaped .... OVOLO
   material .... ORMOLU
   ogee .... TALON
   rounded .... REED, TORUS
   S-shaped .... OGEE
   square .... LISTEL
   wall .... CORNICE
moldy .... HOAR, FUSTY, MUCID,
          MUSTY, STALE
mole .... NOSE, PIER, QUAY, STAR,
   JUTTY, TAUPE, N(A)EVUS,
   HARBOR, MAMMAL, FRECKLE,
     LENTIGO, PLATYPUS
   animal resembling
   .... DESMAN
molecular film .... MONOLAYER
   makeup .... ATOMS
molecule .... PARTICLE
   component ..... ATOM, (AN)ION
   genetic .... DNA
molehill .... TRIFLE, ANTHILL
molest .... VEX, HARM, ABUSE,
   ANNOY, HARASS, INJURE,
   PESTER, DISTURB, TROUBLE
Moliere character ...... ALCESTE,
             TARTUF(FE)
Moll Flanders author .... DEFOE
mollifier, baby's .... THUMB,
   SUCKER, RATTLE(R), PACIFIER
mollify ...... CALM, TAME, PACIFY,
   SOFTEN, SOOTHE, APPEASE,
              PLACATE
moll's friend .... GOON,
   MOBSTER, GANGSTER
mollusca .... SLUG
mollusk ...... CLAM, SLUG, HELIX,
   MUREX, SNAIL, SQUID,
   WHELK, CHITON, COCKLE,
   LIMPET, MUSSEL, OYSTER,

TRITON, ABALONE, OCTOPUS, SCALLOP, NAUTILUS, RETEPORE

beaked .... SQUID, OCTOPUS, CUTTLEFISH

bivalve .... CLAM, CHAMA, MUSSEL, PIDDOCK

borer .... TEREDO, SHIPWORM

cephalopod .... NAUTILUS

egg(s) of .... OOTHECA

genus .... MUREX, OLIVA

gills .... CERATA

product .... PEARL

shell .... CONCH, COWRY, COWRIE

spiral-shaped .... SNAIL

study of .... CONCHOLOGY

sucking organ .... PROBOSCIS

teeth .... RADULA

tentacled ...... SQUID, OCTOPUS

two-gilled .... SPIRULA

molly .... FISH

where seen usually .... AQUARIUM

mollycoddle .... PET, SPOIL, PAMPER, MILKSOP

Molnar, dramatist .... FERENC

work .... LILIOM

Moloch .... GOD, LIZARD

sacrificial site .... TOPHET

Molotov .... PERM

cocktail .... BOMB, GRENADE

molt ...... MEW, SHED, CAST(OFF), EXUVIA(T)E, SLOUGH(OFF)

molten .... FUSED, MELTED, LIQUEFIED

discharge .... LAVA

rock .... LAVA, MAGMA

waste .... SCUM, DROSS, SPRUE, SCORIA

Molucca island .... BANDA, CERAM, GILOLO, SERANG, TERNATE

moly .... GARLIC

mom .... MOTHER

title of .... MRS

moment .... SEC, TICK, JIFF(Y), FLASH, POINT, TRICE, INSTANT, IMPORT(ANCE)

of truth .... CRISIS

momentarily ...... SOON, SHORTLY

momentous .... HISTORIC, SOLEMN, NOTABLE

momentum .... FORCE, SPEED, THRUST, IMPETUS

Mona Lisa .... PORTRAIT, (LA)GIOCONDA

painter .... DA VINCI

smile of .... CRYPTIC, ENIGMATIC

Monaco's first Grimaldi .... LANFRANCO THE SPITEFUL

First Lady (deceased) .... PRINCESS GRACE

former ruling enclave .... GENOESE

language .... FRENCH

monarch .... RANIER

monetary unit .... FRANC

playground ...... MONTE CARLO

prince .... ALBERT

princess .... GRACE, CAROLINE, STEPHANIE

Princess Caroline's child .... ANDREA, PIERRE, CHARLOTTE

Princess Caroline's husband .... JUNOT, CASIRAGHI

ruling family .... GRIMALDI

monad .... ATOM, UNIT, ELEMENT, MICROCOSM

monarch .... REX, REY, ROI, CZAR, KING, SHAH, TSAR, RULER, KAISER, EMPEROR, BUTTERFLY, POTENTATE, SOVEREIGN

golden ball of .... MOUND

monarchist .... ROYALIST

monarchy, type of ...... CZARISM, LIMITED, TYRANNY, DESPOTISM, DICTATORSHIP, ABSOLUTISM

monarda .... BERGAMOT

monastery .... ABBEY, LAURA, FRIARY, PRIORY, CONVENT, HOSPICE, NUNNERY, CLOISTER, LAMASERY, HERMITAGE

church of .... MINSTER

dining hall .... FRATER

head of .... ABBOT, PRIOR, MANDRA, HEGUMEN

island .... IONA

resident .... MONK, CENOBITE

room .... CELL, LAVABO

monastic .... MONK, OBLATE, ASCETIC, MONACHAL

brother .... FRA

haircut .... TONSURE

monasticism .... MONKHOOD, FRIARHOOD

monde .... WORLD, SOCIETY

Monegasque land .... MONACO

Monet, painter .... CLAUDE

monetary ...... FISCAL, FINANCIAL, PECUNIARY

craving .... YEN

money ...... CASH, FUND(S), GOLD, BILLS, COIN(S), COWRY, LUCRE, SILVER, SPENSE, TENDER, CAPITAL, CURRENCY, BANKNOTES, FINANCIAL

CONSIDERATIONS

advance .... ARLES, EARNEST, IMPREST

assessed .... SCOT

at interest .... LOAN

bead .... PEAG(E), WAMPUN

box .... ARCA, KIST, TILL

bribe .... FUND, SOAP, SLUSH, GREASE

certificate .... BOND, SCRIP, TENDER

changer ...... SHROFF, CAMBIST

coin .... MINT

coined .... SPECIE

counterfeit .... SLUG

"dirty" .... FILTHY LUCRE

drawer for .... TILL

earnest .... ARLES, TOKEN, ADVANCE

exchange fee .... AGIO

fishhook .... LARI(N)

for political purposes ..... LUG

from public office .... PAP

handler .... TELLER, CASHIER

hoard .... DEPOSITORY

in reserve .... NEST EGG

in the bank .... ASSET

legalize as .... MONETIZE

lender .... USURER, SHYLOCK

make .... ENRICH, PROFIT

-making .... LUCRATIVE, PROFITABLE

market .... BOURSE

of account .... ORA

on hand .... CASH

player .... PRO

political patronage .... PAP

premium .... AGIO

ready .... CASH, FUND

receiver .... PAYEE

roll of .... WAD, ROULEAU

slang .... TIN, DUST, GELT, JACK, KALE, ROLL, BREAD, BEANS, BUCKS, CHIPS, DOUGH, MOOLA, SUGAR, BOODLE, BUNDLE, MAZUMA, SHEKEL, TENNER, WAMPUN, CABBAGE, LETTUCE, SCRATCH

small amount .... PITTANCE

stone .... FEI

substitute .... SCRIP, COUPON

temporary paper .... SCRIP

token .... ARLES, ADVANCE, EARNEST

tray .... TILL

voucher .... CHIT

moneybags .... 1000000AIRE, ZILLIONAIRE

moneyed .... RICH, OPULENT WEALTHY, AFFLUENT, WELL-TO-DO

slang .... LOADED
monger .... DEALER, TRADER
Mongol .... MOGUL, BURIAT,
 ELEUT(H), ESKIMO, INDIAN,
 TA(R)TAR, ASIATIC
 conqueror .... TAMERLANE,
  TIMURLENK, GENGHIS(KHAN)
 emperor .... KUBLAI KHAN
Mongolian .... KALMYK, TUNGUS,
  KALMUCK
 capital ..... URGA, ULAN BATOR
 conqueror .... KUBLAI,
  GENGHIS(KHAN)
 desert .... GOBI, SHAMO
 dynasty .... YUAN
 lake .... NOR
 monetary unit .... TUGRIK
 monk .... LAMA
 priest .... LAMA, SHAMAN
 river .... TES
 tent .... YURT
 tribesman .... BURYAT
 weight .... LAN
mongolism .... IDIOCY, DOWN'S
  SYNDROME
Mongoloid .... LAI, LAPP, SHAN,
 TURK, DURBAN, SHAR(R)A
mongoos(e) .... URVA,
  ICHNEUMON
 prey of .... RAT, COBRA,
  SNAKE
mongrel .... CUR, DOG, MUTT,
 TYKE, MIXED, STRAY, HYBRID
 relative .... SURICATE
mongst .... MIDST
moni(c)ker .... (NICK)NAME
monition .... NOTICE, CAUTION,
  SUMMONS, WARNING
monitor .... CHECK, WATCH,
 CENSOR, LIZARD, WARSHIP,
 IRONCLAD, REMINDER,
  SUPERVISE
 builder of the .... ERICSSON
 foe of the .... MERRIMAC(K)
 lizard .... URAN
 skeptics' nickname of the
  .... ERICSSON'S FOLLY
monk .... FRA, ABBE, BEDE, LAMA,
 BONZE, FRIAR, PRIOR,
 SANTON, VOTARY, BROTHER,
 CALOYER, EREMITE, RECLUSE,
 CENOBITE, CAPUCHIN,
 TALAPOIN, CARMELITE
 Buddhist .... BONZE, AR(A)HAT
 cloak of .... COWL
 ever silent .... TRAPPIST
 habit .... FROCK
 head .... ABBOT
 head cover .... COWL, HOOD,
 AMICE, CAPOUCH, CAPUCHE
 hermit .... ANCHORET

room of .... CELL
 settlement .... SCETE
monkey .... APE, RAM, SAI, FOOL,
 MONA, TOTA, ZATI, JOCKO,
 MIMIC, HOWLER, LANGUR,
 NISNAS, RHESUS, SIMIAN,
 TRIFLE, VERVET, MACAQUE,
 PRIMATE, TAMARIN, TARSIER,
 CAPUCHIN, MARMOSET,
 TALAPOIN, WANDEROO
 arboreal ...... SIME, TITI, TOTO,
 POTTO, GRIVET, TARSIER
 astronaut .... BONNY
 bearded .... ENTELLUS
 bonnet .... SATI, TOQUE
 bread .... TREE, FRUIT, BAOBAB
 business .... MISCHIEF, HURDY-
 GURDY, FOOLISHNESS
 capuchin .... SAI, SAPAJOU
 crab-eating .... KRA
 flower .... FIGWORT
 green .... GRIVET, GUENON,
  VERVET
 howling .... MONO, ARABA,
  STENTOR
 nocturnal cousin of ... LEMUR
 proboscis .... NOSEAPE
 puzzle .... TREE, PINON
 red .... PATAS
 sacred .... RHESUS
 space traveler .... BONNY,
  ASTROMONK
 spider .... QUATA, ATELES
 squirrel .... SAMIRI
 suit .... JACKET, UNIFORM
 tailless .... APE
 wrench part .... JAW
monkeyshine .... DIDO, JOKE,
 PRANK, MISCHIEF
monkish .... MONASTIC
 title .... DOM
monkshood .... ATIS, ATEES,
 ACONITE, WOLFSBANE
monocle .... LORGNON, EYEGLASS
monogram .... CIPHER, INITIALS
monograph .... ESSAY, PAPER,
 MEMOIR, THESIS, TREATISE
monolith ...... COLUMN, DOLMEN,
 MENHIR, PILLAR, OBELISK
 inscribed .... STELE
monologue .... SOLILOQUY
monologuist .... ENTERTAINER,
  SOLILOQUIST
monomania .... CRAZE,
  OBSESSION
monopolize .... CORNER, ENGROSS
monopoly .... POOL, TRUST,
 CARTEL, CORNERING,
  SYNDICATE
 grant .... PATENT
 maneuver .... COEMPTION

monosaccharide .... OSE, SUGAR,
 GLUCOSE, PENTOSE
monoski .... SLED
monosodium glutamate .... MSG,
  AJINOMOTO
monotone .... DRONE
monotonous .... DRAB, FLAT,
 DREARY, HUMDRUM, TEDIOUS,
  SINGSONG
 routine .... RUT
 talk .... DRONE
monotony .... TEDIUM
Monroe _____ .... DOCTRINE
 actress .... MARILYN
 poet .... HARRIET
mons _____ .... PUBIS, VENERIS
Mon's language .... PEGU
monsieur .... MR, SIR, MISTER,
  (GENTLE)MAN
monsoon .... (TRADE)WIND
 weather .... RAINS, RAINY
monster .... GILA, BOGIE, DEMON,
 FREAK, GIANT, CENTAUR,
 UNICORN, CERBERUS,
 TERATISM, MONSTROSITY
 combining form ..... TERAT(O)
 fabulous ..... HARPY, CHIMERA,
 BASILISK, MINOTAUR,
  COCKATRICE
 fairy tale .... OGRE
 female .... HARPY, GORGON,
 MEDUSA, SCYLLA, CHIMERA,
  CHARYBDIS
 fire-breathing .... DRAGON,
  CHIMERA
 half man-half bull
  .... MINOTAUR
 half woman-half bird
  .... HARPY
 half woman-half serpent
  .... LAMIA
 hundred-eyed .... ARGUS
 killed by Hercules .... GERYON
 many-headed .... HYDRA
 mythical ...... HARPY, DRAGON,
 SPHINX, CENTAUR, CHIMERA,
 GRIFFIN, GRYPHON, MINOTAUR,
 CHARYBDIS, HIPPOGRIFF
 resembling a .... TERATOID
 sea .... WHALE, KRAKEN
 slain by Beowulf .... GRENDEL
 winged .... GERYON
 with lion's body and
  woman's head .... SPHINX
 with snakes for hair
  .... GORGON, MEDUSA
monstrosity .... FREAK, MONSTER,
  TERATISM
monstrous .... HUGE, HIDEOUS,
 ENORMOUS, FIENDISH,
 HORRIBLE, TERATOID,

ATROCIOUS
Mont Cervin .... MATTERHORN
montage .... ASSEMBLAGE
Montague Barstow .... ORCZY
   scion of .... ROMEO
Montana capital .... HELENA
   city/town .... BAKER, BUTTE,
    MALTA, DILLON, SIDNEY,
    WIBAUX, BOULDER, WINNETT,
    BILLINGS, MISSOULA,
    KALISPELL, GREAT FALLS,
    LIVINGSTON
   college .... CARROLL
   county ...... HILL, LAKE, PARK,
    BLAINE, CARTER, CUSTER,
    CASCADE, LINCOLN, RAVALLI,
    FLATHEAD, GALLATIN,
    MISSOULA, YELLOWSTONE
   Indian .... CREE, CROW
   lake .... BIG, SWAN, ENNIS,
    ASHLEY, HELENA, HOLTER,
    BIGHORN, FLATHEAD,
    MEDICINE, EARTHQUAKE
   motto ..... ORO Y PLATA, GOLD
    AND SILVER
   mountain .... ALLEN, SHEEP,
    SPHINX, GRANITE, JACKSON,
    STIMSON, HURRICANE
   mountain range .... CABINET,
    PURCELL
   national park .... GLACIER,
    YELLOWSTONE
   river .... SUN, MILK, RUBY,
    TETON, JUDITH, MARIAS,
    POPLAR, POWDER, BIGHORN,
    MADISON, MISSOURI, LITTLE
    HORN
   state bird .... MEADOWLARK
   state flower .... BITTERROOT
   state nickname ...... BONANZA,
    MOUNTAIN, TREASURE
   U.S. Air Force Base
   .... MALMSTROM
Monte Carlo location
   .... MONACO
Monte Cristo author ...... DUMAS
   castle .... D'IF
   hero .... DANTES
Montenegro capital, former
   .... CETINJE
   city/town .... KOTOR, NIKSIC,
    KOLASIN, TITOGRAD
   lake .... SCUTARI
   mountain .... BOBOTOV KUK
   port .... BAR, ULCINJ
montero .... CAP
Montez, dancer .... LOLA
Montezuma's conqueror
   .... CORTES
   revenge .... CHOLERA,
    DIARRHEA

Montgomery is capital of
   .... ALABAMA
month after Ab/Av .... ELUL
   Black History .... FEBRUARY
   Eliot's "cruellest" ...... APRIL
   excess of calendar over lunar
   .... EPACT
   first day .... KALENDS,
    CALEND(I)S
   last .... ULT(IMO)
   of proposed calendar
   .... NIVOSE
   shower .... APRIL
   the present, for short ..... INST
monthly .... MENSAL, MENSES,
   MENSTRUAL, PERIODICAL
Montreal fair .... EXPO
monument .... CAIRN, STELE,
   DOLMEN, MENHIR, PILLAR,
   STATUE, CENOTAPH,
   (CROM)LECH, MEMORIAL
   inscription .... EPIGRAPH
   upright .... STELE
monumental .... COLOSSAL
moo .... LOW
   juice .... MILK
mooch .... BEG, LOAF, CADGE,
   SKULK, SNEAK, STEAL,
   BORROW, LOITER, PILFER,
   SPONGE
   slang .... BUM
mood .... HUMOR, MORALE,
   TEMPER, SPIRIT(S),
   DISPOSITION
moody .... GLUM, TESTY,
   GLOOMY, SULLEN, PEEVISH,
   VARIABLE, DEPRESSED
Moog feat .... SAVE
moola ...... KALE, DOUGH, MONEY
moon .... ORB, LUNI, MONTH,
   LUMINARY, SATELLITE
   age of new, Jan. 1st
   .... EPACT
   apogee/perigree .... APSIS
   between half and full
   .... GIBBOUS
   crater .... TYCHO, COLOMBO
   dark area on .... MARE
   first on .... ARMSTRONG
   flower .... ACHETE
   goddess .... LUNA, HECATE,
    HEKATE, PHOEBE, SELENE,
    CYNTHIA, ARTEMIS, ASTARTE
   goddess, virgin .... DIANA
   half .... DEMILUNE
   horn .... CUSP
   inhabitant .... LUNARIAN
   mountain .... PYRENESS
   of delight .... HONEY
   of Saturn .... TITAN
   of song .... PAPER

   of the .... LUNAR, SELENIC
   orbit closest to .... PERILUNE
   orbiter .... ROOSA, YOUNG,
    APOLLO, BORMAN, GORDON,
    LOVELL, WORDEN, COLLINS
   personified .... LUNA
   phase .... GIBBOUS
   point .... APOGEE, PERIGREE
   sea .... RAINS, CRISES, NECTAR,
    SERENITY
   shadow .... UMBRA
   shaped ..... LUNATE, CRESCENT
   trench/valley .... RILL(E)
   vehicle .... LEM, ROVER
   walker .... DUKE, IRWIN,
    SCOTT, ALDRIN, CERNAN,
    CONRAD, SHEPARD, SHIMITT,
    ARMSTRONG
   watcher .... ASTROLOGER
mooncalf .... FOOL, IDIOT,
   IMBECILE
moonling, fictional .... SQUAPS
moonshine .... WHISKY, BOOTLEG,
   FUSTIAN, HOME BREW,
   NONSENSE
   apparatus .... STILL
   slang .... BOOZE, HUMBUG,
    HOGWASH
moonshiner .... BOOTLEGGER
   worry of .... RAID
moonstone ...... OPAL, ADULARIA,
   FELDSPAR
moonstruck .... DAFT, CRAZED,
   LUNATIC
moonwort .... FERN, LUNARIA
moor .... FEN, BENT, BRAE, DOCK,
   FELL, HEATH, LANDE,
   ANCHOR, FASTEN, MOSLEM,
   SECURE, MORISCO
   fowl .... GROUSE, GORCOCK
   grass .... NARD
   grouse .... GORHEN
   hen .... GROUSE, GALLINULE
Moore, actress .... DEMI
mooring .... WHARF
   buoy/spar .... DOLPHIN
   fee .... WHARFAGE
   place ...... DOCK, PORT, BERTH,
    MARINA
Moorish .... MORESQUE,
   MORISCAN
   cloak .... BURNOUS
   coin .... MARAVEDI
   drum/tabor .... AT(T)ABAL
   fabric .... TIRAZ
   garment .... JUPON
   king of Granada ...... BOABDIL
   palace/fortress .... ALCAZAR,
    ALHAMBRA
   sailboat .... SAPIT
moose .... ELK, DEER, ALCES

feeding place .... YARD
kin .... CARIBOU, REINDEER
male .... BULL
pouch .... BEL
territory .... MAINE
moot .... SUSPECT, ASSEMBLY,
    CONTESTED, DEBATABLE
mop .... RUB, SWAB, WASH, WIPE,
    MALKIN, MAUKIN, GRIMACE
mope .... FRET, MOON, POUT,
    SULK, BROOD
moppet .... TAD, DOLL, GIRL,
    CHILD, (SMALL)FRY
Moqui .... HOPI
moraine .... ESKER
moral ...... JUST, MAXIM, DECENT,
    LESSON, ETHICAL, UPRIGHT,
    VIRTUOUS, RIGHTEOUS
allegorical story with
    .... FABLE, APOLOGUE
decay .... ROT, CORRUPTION
distinction ...... RIGHT, WRONG
fault .... VICE
lapse .... SIN
law .... DECALOG(UE)
obligation .... DUTY
philosophy/principle
    .... ETHICS
poem .... DIT
slip .... LAPSE
talk .... HOMILY, SERMON
teachings .... PRECEPTS
weakness .... FRAILTY
morale ...... MOOD, CHEER, FAITH,
    NERVE, SPIRIT, TEMPER,
    COURAGE
morality .... ETHICS, VIRTUE,
    ETHICALITY
talk .... HOMILY, SERMON
moralized tale .... EXEMPLUM
morally corrupt .... VENAL,
    ROTTEN
instructive .... DIDACTIC
weak .... FRAIL
morals, pertaining to ...... ETHICS
supervisor .... CENSOR
morass ...... BOG, FEN, MARSH,
    SLACK, SWAMP, QUAGMIRE
moratorium .... GRACE
Moravia .... MAHREN
capital .... BRNO
moray .... EEL, ELGIN, CONGER
morbid .... GLOOMY, GRISLY,
    DISEASED, GRUESOME
morbilli .... MEASLES
morceau .... BIT, MORSEL,
    FRAGMENT
mordant .... ACID, ACRID, BITING,
    CUTTING, EROSIVE, SARCASTIC
more .... ELSE, PLUS, ADDED,
    AGAIN, BESIDE(S), FURTHER,

ADDITIONAL
accurate/agreeable .... NICER
acute .... KEENER, SMARTER
aloof .... ICIER
ancient .... OLDER
attractive .... CUTER
bashful .... SHIER
Bohemian .... ARTIER
comely .... PRETTIER
comfortable .... EASIER
compendious .... TERSER
crafty .... SLYER
cry for .... ENCORE
delicate .... FINER, AIRIER,
    DAINTIER
distressed .... NEEDIER
docile .... TAMER
domineering .... BOSSIER
eccentric .... ODDER
efficient .... ABLER
elegant .... FINER
energetic .... SPRIER
frequent .... OFTENER
frugal .... SPARER
gentle .... MILDER
gentle creature of mythology
    .... UNICORN
grating .... RASPIER
greedy .... THIRSTIER
hideous .... UGLIER
in music .... PIU
ineffectual .... LAMER
inexplicable .... EERIER
infrequent/unusual ...... RARER
laid-back .... MELLOWER
lawnlike .... GRASSIER
likely to be plucked ..... RIPER
malicious .... CATTIER
melodious .... AIRIER
normal .... SANER
or less .... ABOUT, SOMEWHAT,
    APPROXIMATE(LY)
orderly .... NEATER
peevish .... CRABBIER
perspicacious .... SAGER
pleasing .... NICER
positive .... SURER
precious .... DEARER
precipitous .... STEEPER
prevalent .... RIFER
primitive .... RUDER
rational/reasonable ...... SANER
restless .... ANTSIER
savory .... TASTIER
secret .... INNER
secure .... SAFER
shoddy .... SEEDIER
spherical .... ROUNDER
stylish: slang .... CLASSIER
tender .... SORER
than a few .... MANY

than eager .... AGOG
than enough .... AMPLE,
    PLENTY, OVERDOSE
than one/once .... SEVERAL,
    MULTIPLE
than unpleasant .... RUDE
unctuous .... OILIER
unfeeling .... STERNER
unusual .... ODDER
vulgar .... RAWER
wary .... LEERIER
willing .... READIER
moreen .... TABBY, FABRIC
morel .... MUSHROOM,
    NIGHTSHADE
morello .... CHERRY
moreover .... AND, TOO, ALSO,
    ELSE, BESIDES, LIKEWISE,
    FURTHER(MORE)
morepork .... RURU
mores .... CULTURE, CUSTOMS,
    FOLKWAYS
Moresque .... MOORISH
Morgan ...... TROTTER, STALLION,
    BUCCANEER
actress .... FAIRCHILD
Morgana, ___ .... FATA
morganite .... BERYL
Morgiana's master .... ALI BABA
morgue .... LIBRARY, MORTUARY,
    DEADHOUSE
Moriarty's foe .... HOLMES
moribund .... DYING
moringa .... BEN
morion .... HELMET, QUARTZ
Morisco .... MOOR
Mormon .... DANITE
Church founder .... SMITH
leader, U.S.
    .... (BRIGHAM)YOUNG
not a .... GENTILE
priest .... ELDER
sacred instrument .... URIM
morning .... A.M., EOS, DAWN,
    MATIN, AURORA, MORROW,
    DAYBREAK
-after retribution
    .... HANGOVER
canticle .... VENITE
delivery .... MAIL, MILK,
    (NEWS)PAPER
early .... SMALL HOURS
glory .... IPOMEA, SUNRISE
music .... MATIN, AUBADE
nuisance .... ALARM
of .... MATIN(AL)
poetic .... MORN
prayer .... MATINS
reception .... LEVEE
song .... ALBA, MATIN,
    AUBADE, MATTINS

star .... VENUS, SATURN,
PHOSPHOR
Moro cannon .... LANTAKA
chief .... DATO, DATU
Italian premier .... ALDO
priest .... PANDITA
sailboat .... VINTA
tribesman: var. .... ILANO
Moroccan .... MOOR, RIFF,
BERBER
wife .... SHERIFA
Morocco ...... KINGDOM, LEATHER
cape .... SIM, JUBY, RHIR
capital .... RABAT
city/town ...... FEZ, SAFI, SALE,
TAZA, NADOR, OUJDA, AGADIR,
FEDALA, MEKNES, SETTAT,
KENITRA, LARACHE, TANGIER,
MARRAKECH, CASABLANCA
coin .... RIAL
district .... RIFF
French name .... MAROC
hat .... FEZ
hilly region .... ERRIF
international zone .... TANGIER
king .... HASSAN
language ...... ARABIC, FRENCH
monetary unit .... DIRHAM
mountain .... JEBEL MUSA,
JEBEL TOUBKAL
mountains .... BANI, ATLAS,
SARHRO
native ..... MOOR, RIFF, BERBER
prime minister .... (AZEDDINE)
LARAKI
region .... RIF, TAFILET
river .... SEBOU, MOULOUYA
ruler .... HASSAN, SULTAN
seaport .... CEUTA, RABAT,
AGADIR, TETUAN, MOGADOR,
TANGIER, CASABLANCA
soldier .... ASKAR
moron ...... AMENT, IDIOT, NITWIT,
IMBECILE, SIMPLETON
morose .... SAD, BLUE, DOUR,
GLUM, MOODY, MOPEY,
SULKY, SURLY, GLOOMY,
SULLEN
Morpheus, god of _____
.... DREAMS
father of .... HYPNOS
morphine drug .... METHADONE
refined .... HEROIN
morro .... BLUFF, HILL(OCK)
morrow ...... MORNING, NEXT DAY
Morse code symbol .... DASH
code word .... DIT
invention .... TELEGRAPH
recourse .... SOS
morsel .... BIT(E), ORT, DISH,
CRUMB, PIECE, SCRAP, TIDBIT,

MORCEAU
mort .... DEAD, DEATH
mortal .... FATAL, HUMAN,
DEADLY, LETHAL, PERSON,
IMPLACABLE
remains .... DUST, CORPSE,
CADAVER
mortality .... DEATH(RATE)
mortar .... BOWL, COMPO,
CANNON, CEMENT, PLASTER
and _____ .... PESTLE
crush in a .... BRAY
for filling .... GROUT
mixer/beater .... RAB
patch with .... SLUSH
tray .... HOD
mortarboard .... CAP, HAWK
part .... TASSEL
mortgage ...... DEED, LIEN, LOAN,
PLEDGE, WADSET
mortgagee .... LIENOR
mortician .... UNDERTAKER
mortification .... SHAME,
CHAGRIN, GANGRENE,
VEXATION
mortify .... ABASH, SHAME,
EMBARRASS, HUMILIATE
Mortimer, the dummy
.... SNERD
mortise .... JOIN, FASTEN
counterpart of a .... TENON
mortuary .... MORGUE, CHARNEL,
CREMATORY, CINERARIUM
carriage/vehicle .... HEARSE
mosaic .... INLAY, COLLAGE
gold .... ORMOLU
law .... TORA(H)
material .... TILE, SMALTO,
TESSERA
work .... INTARSIA, TESSERAE
Moscow .... MOSKVA
chief rabbi .... LEVIN
citadel .... KREMLIN
square .... PUSHKIN
turndown .... NYET
Moselle .... WINE
city on .... METZ, TRIER,
TREVES
tributary .... SAAR
Moses .... LEADER, LAWGIVER
brother of .... AARON
father of .... AMRAM
father-in-law of .... JETHRO
mount/death place of
.... NEBO
saw Canaan there .... NEBO,
PISGAH
sister of .... MIRIAM
spy/scout of .... CALEB, NAHBI,
JOSHUA
successor of .... JOSUE,

JOSHUA
wife of .... ZIPPORAH
mosey: sl. .... MOVE, AMBLE,
STROLL, SHUFFLE
Moslem. See also Muslim
.... BERBER, MUSLIM, PATHAN,
PAYNIM, ISLAM(IC), SARACEN,
MUSSULMAN, MOHAMMEDAN
angel .... ISRAFIL
beggar .... FAKIR, DERVISH
brass .... AGAS
bridge to paradise .... ALSIRAT
caliph .... OMMIAD
call to prayer ..... ADAN, AZAN
cap .... FEZ, TARBOOSH
chief .... REIS
Christian to a .... GIAOUR
chronicle .... SARSILA, TARSILA
coin .... DINAR
college .... ULEMA
converts .... ANSAR
devil/Satan .... EBLIS
doctor .... HAKIM, HAKEEM
drinking cup .... LOTAH
Egyptian .... FULA(H)
fasting period .... RAMADAN,
RAMAZAN
festival .... BAIRAM
garment .... IZAR, JUBBAH
governor .... HAKIM
head .... RAIS, REIS
headgear .... FEZ, TAJ,
TARBUSH, TARBOOSH
hermit .... SANTON, MARABOUT
hero .... GHAZI
holy book .... KORAN
holy city ...... MECCA, MEDINA,
KAIROUAN
holy man .... IMAM,
MARABOUT
holy war .... JEHAD, JIHAD
idol .... MAUMET
interpreter of religious laws
..... MUFTI, MOLLAH, MULLA(H)
judge .... CADI, CAZI, KADI,
KAZI, HAKIM
lady .... BEGUM
language .... URDU
law .... SUNNA(H)
lawyer .... MUFTI
leader .... AGA, IMA(U)M,
CALIPH
marketplace .... SOUK
marriage .... MUTA
measure .... ARDEB
mendicant ..... FAKIR, DERVISH
messiah .... MAHDI
minister .... VIZI(E)R
monk .... SANTON
month .... RABIA, RAJAB,
SAFAR, JUMADA, SHABAN,

RAMADAN, RAMAZAN
mosque .... MASJID, MUSJID
mystic .... SUNI
noble .... EMIR, AMEER,
EMEER, SHERIF
nomad .... KURD
non .... RAIA, GIAOU, RAYAH,
KAF(F)IR
nymph .... HOURI
official .... HAJIB
people .... PATHAN
pilgrim .... HA(D)JI, IHRAM
pilgrimage .... HADJ
pilgrim's costume .... IHRAM
place for prayer .... MOSQUE
prayer .... SALAT
prayer caller .... MUEZZIN
prayer's direction ...... KAABA,
KIBLAH
priest .... IMA(U)M
prince .... AMIR, EMIR, AMEER,
EMEER, NAWAB
princess .... BEGUM
principle .... IJMA
prophet .... MAHDI
religion .... ISLAM
religious brotherhood
.... SENUS(S)I
religious duty .... HADJ
rosary .... TASBIH
ruler .... CALIF, HAKIM,
CALIPH, SULTAN
sacred book .... KORAN
saint .... PIR, SANTON
scholar(s) .... ULEM(A)
school .... MADRASA
sect adherent .... BAHAI
sect member .... SUFI,
WAHABI, SUNNITE, WAHABEE
shrine .... CAABA, KAABA,
MESHED
slave .... MAMELUKE
spirit ...... JIN(N), GENIE, GENII,
JINN(I), JINNEE
sword .... SCIMITAR,
(Y)ATAGHAN
teacher .... ALIM, MOLLAH,
MULLA(H)
temple .... MOSQUE
title .... AGA, HADJI, HAFIZ,
MAHDI, MOLLA, MULLA(H),
SHERIF
title of respect .... AG(H)A,
SYED, NAWAB, SA(I)YID
tomb .... TABUT
tribe .... BASHKIR
tunic .... JAMA(H)
Turkestan .... SALAR
Turko-Tartar .... BASHKIR
viceroy .... NABOB, NAWAB
weight .... ROTL

Moslems collectively .... ISLAM
mosque .... MOSK, MASJID,
MUSJID, TEMPLE
tower .... JAMI, MINARET
mosquito .... CULICID, SKEETER,
STEGOMYIA
bite injection .... ALLERGEN
carried disease .... DENGUE,
MALARIA
dangerous .... AEDES, CULEX,
ANOPHELES
genus/species .... AEDES,
CULEX
hawk .... DRAGONFLY
larva .... W(R)IGGLER
yellow fever .... STEGOMYIA
moss .... LICHEN, EPIPHYTE,
BRYOPHYTE, CARRAGEEN
filaments .... RHIZOID
shade of green .... BLUE
mossbunker .... POGY, MENHADEN
mosstrooper .... RAIDER,
MARAUDER
most .... GREATEST
aged .... OLDEST
ancient .... HOARIEST
appropriate .... APTEST
ashen .... PALEST
barren .... DRIEST
base .... MEANEST
calamitous .... DIREST
cerulean .... BLUEST
cherished/precious
.... DEAREST
costly ..... DEAREST, PRICELESS
desirable .... BEST
dictatorial .... BOSSIEST
difficult to find .... RAREST
dignified .... STATELIEST
disagreeable .... MEAN AS CAN
BE
distinctive ..... FINEST, RAREST
doubtful .... IFFIEST
elegant .... FINEST
eligible bachelor .... CATCH
enraged .... SOREST
extensive .... WIDEST
famous of the Black Hills
.... MOUNT RUSHMORE
fascinating game .... CHESS
fit/healthy .... HALEST
haunting .... EERIEST
indigent .... POOREST
important .... ARCH
insignificant .... LEAST
ironic .... WRIEST
joyful .... MERRIEST
like a leopard .... SPOTTIEST
likely .... PROBABLY,
DOUBTLESS
obscure .... VAGUEST

orderly .... NEATEST
peculiar .... ODDEST
populous city in Western
Hemisphere
.... MEXICO(CITY)
populous country .... CHINA
rational .... SANEST
robust .... HARDIEST
savage .... WILDEST
sensible .... SANEST
sordid .... BASEST
spare .... LEANEST
unpleasant/unsatisfactory
.... WORST
vague .... PALEST
valuable possession ...... LIFE
vile .... DIRTIEST
weighty .... GRAVEST
mostly ...... CHIEFLY, PRINCIPALLY
mot .... REPARTEE, WITTICISM
mote .... SPECK
motel .... INN
motet .... SONG, ANTHEM
moth .... IO, LUNA, EGGER, GYPSY,
MILLER, AGLOOSA, ARRINDA,
BOMBYCID, CECROPIA,
FORESTER
clothes .... TINEA
destroying apples
.... CODLIN(G)
kin .... BUTTERFLY
larva .... LOOPER
night-flying .... NOCTUID
proboscis .... LINGUA
repellent .... CAMPHOR
wing spot .... FENESTRA
mother .... MATER, MATRON,
PARENT
colloquial ..... MAMA, MOM(S),
MAMMA, MAMMY, MOMMY,
MOMSY
combining form/prefix
.... MATRI
country .... HOMELAND
famous .... MARY
-in-law, biblical .... NAOMI
killing of one's .... MATRICIDE
kind of .... DEN
Little Lord Fauntleroy's
.... DEAREST
of a four-legged animal
.... DAM
of gods .... RHEA, CYBELE
of Gracchi .... CORNELIA
of Hippothous .... ALOPE
of pearl .... NACRE
of quintets .... ZAHRA
of several children
.... MULTIPARA
superior .... ABBESS
tongue .... VERNACULAR

who rules .... MATRIARCH
wit .... COMMON SENSE
Mother Cary's chicken
.... PETREL
Earth .... GAEA
Goose creator .... PERRAULT
Hubbard .... CRONE
Hubbard's quest .... BONE
———, Nobel laureate
.... TERESA
of Cities .... KIEV
of God .... VIRGIN MARY
motherhood .... MATERNITY
motherly .... MATERNAL
motif .... IDEA, THEME, TOPIC,
CONCEPT, FEATURE, SUBJECT
motion .... FLUX, SIGNAL,
GESTURE, MOVEMENT,
PROPOSAL
downward .... DESCENT
in .... MOVING, TRANSIT,
TRAVELING
neurotic .... TIC
pertaining to .... KINETIC
picture .... FILM, MOVIE,
CINEMA, FLICKER
picture first prints ..... RUSHES
producing .... MOTILE
rolling/swelling .... SURGE
motionless .... FIXED, INERT,
STILL
motivate .... IMPEL, INCITE,
INDUCE, PROMPT, INSPIRE
motivation .... CAUSE, IMPETUS,
INFLUENCE, MAINSPRING
motive .... GOAD, SPUR, CAUSE,
DESIGN, GROUND, REASON,
PURPOSE, KEYSTONE,
INCENTIVE, INTENTION,
ENTICEMENT, INDUCEMENT
power .... STEAM
motley .... COLORFUL,
VARICOLORED,
KALEIDOSCOPIC
motor .... ENGINE, TURBINE
speed .... RPM
speed up .... REV, RACE
vehicle frame .... CHASSIS
motorbike .... MOPED
motorcycle .... SCOOTER
extra .... SIDECAR
Motown .... DETROIT
mistake .... EDSEL
squad .... LIONS
mott(e) .... GROVE
mottle .... SPOT, BLOTCH, DAPPLE,
STREAK
mottled .... PIED, PINTO, DAPPLED,
PIEBALD, SPOTTED
gray .... GRISEOUS
motto .... SAW, ADAGE, GNOME,

MAXIM, DEVICE, SAYING,
SLOGAN, PRECEPT,
CATCHWORD
in a book .... EPIGRAPH
in a ring .... POSY
moue .... POUT, GRIMACE
mouflon .... SHEEP
mould .... FORM, KNEAD, MATRIX,
FASHION
moulin .... SHAFT
mound .... DUNE, HEAP, HILL,
HUMP, PILE, TELL, TERP,
AGGER, ESKER, GLOBE,
KNOLL, RAISE, BARROW,
HILLOCK, HUMMOCK
domelike .... STUPA
formed by wind .... DOWN
golfer's .... TEE
Goose .... GOSSAGE
of burrowing animal
.... MOLEHILL
of sand/gravel .... ESKAR,
ESKER, RIDGE
mount .... FIX, SET, HILL, POST,
RISE, CLIMB, HORSE, PLACE,
ASCEND, MOUNTAIN
Balaam's .... ASS
by ladder .... SCALE,
ESCALADE
Mount Hood's range
.... CASCADES
of Olives .... OLIVET
Rushmore location .... SOUTH
DAKOTA
portrait carved on
.... LINCOLN, JEFFERSON,
WASHINGTON,
(THEODORE)ROOSEVELT
sculptor
.... (GUTZON)BORGLUM
mountain .... KOP, HEAP, PILE,
BUTTE, MOUND, MOUNT,
BARROW, ELEVATION
antelope .... KLIPSPRINGER
Apollo's .... PARNASSUS
ash .... SORB, ROWAN
base .... PIEDMONT
biblical .... NEBO, ZION,
HOREB, SINAI, ARARAT
cat .... PUMA, COUGAR
chain .... RANGE, SIERRA
climber .... ALPINIST
climber's aid .... PITON,
CRAMPON
climber's slide .... GLISSADE
climber's staff
.... ALPENSTOCK
combining form .... ORO,
OREOS
crest .... SPUR, ARETE
feature ...... TOR, SPUR, ARETE,

CRATER, SNOWCAP
formation .... OROGENY
goat .... IBEX, TAHR, GORAL
gorge/gully .... COULOIR
group .... RANGE
high .... ALP
highest .... EVEREST
lake .... TARN
legendary .... MERU
lion .... PUMA, COUGAR,
PAINTER, PANTHER
main mass .... MASSIF
nymph .... OREAD
of China, sacred .... OMEI
of the Muses .... PARNASSUS
pass .... COL, GAP, GHAT,
DEFILE
peak .... BEN, CIMA, CONE,
HORN
pool .... TARN
range .... ANDES, SIERRA,
CORDILLERA
ridge .... ARETE, SIERRA,
SAWBACK
road peril ...... HAIRPIN CURVE
road's bend .... LOOP
rocky .... TETON
rubble .... SCREE
sheep ...... BIGHORN, MOUFLON
sickness .... PUNA, VETA
slope .... VERSANT
small .... MONTICULE
spur .... ARETE
stem for .... OREO
sunrise .... ALPENGLOW
top .... PEAK
top cover .... ICECAP,
SNOWCAP
trail marker .... KARN
valley .... GLEN
way .... TUNNEL
Mountain State .... MONTANA
mountaineer .... SHERPA,
CLIMBER, ALPINIST, HILLBILLY
mountainous .... LOFTY, CRAGGY,
RUGGED
mountains between France and
Switzerland .... JURA
formation of .... OROGENY
study of .... OROLOGY,
OROGRAPHY
mountebank .... QUACK, EMPIRIC,
CHARLATAN
mounted .... ASTRIDE
policeman .... MARSHAL,
CONSTABLE
rider ...... JOCKEY, EQUESTRIAN
sentinel .... VEDETTE
traveler ...... RIDER, HORSEMAN
Mountie .... POLICE, TROOPER
outfit of .... RCMP

mourn .... RUE, (BE)WAIL, GRIEVE, LAMENT
in sympathy .... CONDOLE
mourner .... LAMENTER
hired .... MUTE, WEEPER
mournful .... SAD, DREARY, GLOOMY, GRIEVOUS
piece .... DIRGE
mourning band .... CRAPE, CREPE, WEEDS
clothes .... WEEDS, SABLES, BOMBASINE, SACKCLOTH
silk .... ALMA
song .... DIRGE
mouse .... RODENT, BLACKEYE
bird .... COLY
deer .... NAPUS, CHEVROTAIN
genus .... MUS
he's not one .... MAN
like animal .... VOLE, SHREW
meadow/field .... VOLE
relative .... JERBOA, GERBIL(LE)
mouser .... OWL
mousseline .... MUSLIN
mousy .... DRAB, QUIET, TIMID
mouth .... OS, LIPS, INLET, STOMA, DECLAIM, OPENING, ORIFICE, ENTRANCE
and lower cheeks .... CHOPS
away from .... ABORAL
by word of ..... ORAL, VERBAL
combining form .... ORI, STOMA, STOM(E)
disease .... APHTHA
disorder .... ULCER, CANDIDIASIS
gag .... MUZZLE
gaping .... RICTUS
Latin .... OS, ORIS
of the .... ORAL, BUCCAL, OSCULAR, STOMATIC
off .... SASS
organ ..... (BAG)PIPE, OCARINA, HARMONICA
part .... GUMS, LIPS, TEETH, PALATE, TONGUE
pertaining to .... BUCCAL
river .... DELTA, FRITH, ESTUARY
roof .... PALATE
slang .... MUG, YAP, PUSS, TRAP, KISSER
strap .... MUZZLE
thru the .... ORAL
to pharynx passage .... FAUCES
toward the .... ORAD
ulcerous condition .... NOMA
volcano .... CRATER
wash .... GARGLE, LISTERINE

-watering .... TEMPTING, APPETIZING
mouthed, loud ...... STENTOR(IAN)
open- .... AGAPE
mouthful .... BITE, GOBBET
small .... MORSEL
mouthlike .... MANDIBULAR
entrance .... OSTIUM
mouthpiece .... REED, BOCAL, NOZZLE, SPOKESMAN
slang .... LAWYER
mouths .... ORA
mouthy .... GASSY, WINDY, BOMBASTIC
mouton .... FUR
movable .... MOBILE, PORTABLE
defense structure .... BASTIL(LE)
mountain .... OSSA
part of tabletop .... LEAF
shelter in siege .... CAT
support .... TRESTLE
move .... ACT, STIR, BUDGE, (A)ROUSE, IMPEL, SHIFT, TOUCH, AFFECT, PROMPT, PROPOSE
able to .... MOTILE
ahead steadily .... BORE
aimlessly .... MAUNDER
along .... PROD, MOSEY, SASHAY
at a certain marching cadence .... DOUBLE-TIME
back .... RECEDE, REGRESS, RETREAT
back and forth .... DIDDLE, SEESAW, SHUTTLE
camera .... PAN
carefully .... EASE
clumsily .... BARGE, LUMBER
confusedly .... MILL
crabwise .... SIDLE
easily .... SLIDE
furtively .... LURK, PROWL, SKULK, SLINK, SNEAK
gently .... LAP
heavily .... LUMP, LUMBER
in a smooth motion .... UNDULATE
in a stream .... FLOW
in and out .... WEAVE
in opposition .... RETROACT
it! .... STEP ON IT, ON THE DOUBLE
merrily .... DANCE
on .... RESETTLE
on wheels .... ROLL
shakily .... DODDER
sidewise ...... JIB, EDGE, SKEW, SLUE, SIDLE
slowly .... INCH, WORM,

CRAWL, CREEP
smoothly .... SLIDE
swiftly .... DART, FLIT, SCUD, SPEED
to a new job .... RELOCATE
toward .... GRAVITATE
unfair .... FOUL
unsteadily: var. .... WABBLE
up .... RISE
wary .... FEELER
without power .... GLIDE
movement .... ACTION, MOTION, CRUSADE, GESTURE, ACTIVITY
ballet .... ENTRECHAT
deceptive .... FEINT
in music ...... TEMPO, RHYTHM
in prosody .... CADENCE
of goods .... FREIGHT
of organism .... TAXIS
of the sea .... TIDE
mover, slow .... SNAIL, TURTLE
movie .... CINEMA, PHOTOPLAY, MOTION PICTURE
award .... OSCAR
camera platform .... DOLLY
cartoon producer ...... BAKSHI, DISNEY
combining form .... CINE
director's command .... CUT, ACTION
fade-out .... THE END
fare .... COMEDY, CARTOON, MUSICAL, MYSTERY, WESTERN, MELODRAMA
film, 1000 ft. .... REEL
full length .... FEATURE
immortal star .... VALENTINO
last word of a .... END
low budget .... QUICKIE
ma and pa .... KETTLES
operator/theater owner .... EXHIBITOR
part .... LEAD, ROLE, HEAVY, INGENUE
projector .... BIOSCOPE
role, minor .... CAMEO
role, small .... BIT, EXTRA
script .... SCENARIO
short ...... CARTOON, NEWSREEL
shot .... CLINCH, CLOSE-UP
studio worker .... GRIP, STAGEHAND
theater, oldtime .... NICKELODEON
with sound .... TALKIE
moving .... MOTILE, AMBULANT, ELOQUENT, PATHETIC, POIGNANT, STIRRING, TOUCHING, AFFECTING, IMPRESSIVE
combining form .... KINETO

staircase .... ESCALATOR
vehicle .... VAN
mow .... CLIP, DESS, MATH, REAP,
CUT DOWN, DESTROY,
GRIMACE, (HAY)LOFT,
HAYSTACK
Mowgli, friend of .... BALU,
BEAR, AKELA, BALOO
tiger of .... SHERE KHAN
mowing implement ...... MOWER,
REAPER, SCYTHE, SICKLE
Mowrer, Edgar _____ .... ANSEL
moxa .... PLANT, CAUTERY
moxie .... NERVE
Mozambique bay .... DELAGOA
cape .... DELGADO
capital .... MAPUTO
city/town .... BEIRA, LUMBO,
LURIO, MABOTE, MANDIE,
MUCOJO, CHIBUTO, MACHAZE,
MUALAMA
island .... ANGOCHE
lake .... NYASA, CHILWA
language .... MAKUA, SHONA,
THONGA
monetary unit .... METICAL
mountain .... BINGA
native .... YAO, BANTU
port .... BEIRA
river ..... SAVE, LURIO, MAZOE,
SHIRE, ROVUMA, LIMPOPO,
LUGENDA, ZAMBEZI, OLIFANTS
Mozart .... WOLFGANG
opera .... FIGARO, SERAGLIO,
MAGIC FLUTE, DON GIOVANNI,
COSI FAN TUTTI
Mozart's city .... SALZBURG
mozetta .... CAPE
wearer of .... POPE
Mr. "Blackwell" .... (RICHARD
SYLVAN)SELZER
Borgnine .... ERNEST
Brinkley, for short .... DAVE
Brubeck .... DAVE
Cassini .... OLEG
Catastrophe, sobriquet
.... TRIPP
Chaney .... LON
Connery .... SEAN
Cupid .... DAN
Duck .... DONALD
Europe, sobriquet .... MONNET
Foxx .... REDD
Greer, of track fame .... ROSIE
Hirt .... AL
Hodges .... GIL
Houston .... SAM
Marner .... SILAS
O'Casey .... SEAN
Onassis .... ARI
Preminger .... OTTO

Preston .... CHARLES
Previn .... ANDRE
Roberts on Broadway creator
.... (HENRY)FONDA
Sevareid .... ERIC
Sinatra .... FRANK
Slaughter .... ENOS
Sparks .... NED
T's group .... A-TEAM
"Tambourine Man" group
.... BYRDS
Ulyanov .... LENIN
Vidal .... GORE
Ziegfeld, to friends .... FLO
Mrs. .... MADAM(E), MISTRESS
Bogart .... (LAUREN)BACALL
Chaplain .... OONA
Copperfield .... DORA
Grundy .... PRUDE, SNOOPER
Hoover .... LOU
"Machine Gun Kelly"
.... KATHRYN SHANNON
Montagu Barstow .... ORCZY
Sairey .... GAMP
Tanqueray's creator
.... PINERO
Walter Findlay .... MAUDE
Ms. .... MRS, MISS, MIZZ,
MANUSCRIPT
Adams .... EDIE
Adoree .... RENEE
Claire .... INA
Lee .... PEGGY
LeShan .... EDA
Lillie, to friends .... BEA
Ono .... YOKO
Robson .... FLORA
MS .... MULTIPLE SCLEROSIS
much ...... LOT(S), MANY, AMPLE,
SLEWS, PLENTY, COPIOUS,
PROFUSE
combining form .... ERI
in music .... MOLTO
traveled .... BEATEN
mucid .... MOLDY, MUSTY
mucilage ...... GUM, GLUE, PASTE,
ARABIN, ADHESIVE
muck .... DIRT, MIRE, FILTH,
MANURE
mucker .... CAD
muckworm .... MISER
mucous: comb. form .... MYX(O)
membrane disease ..... LUPUS
fold .... PLICA
inflammation .... CATARRH
secretion .... MUCIN
watery discharge ..... RHEUM
mud .... MIRE, MUCK, OOZE, SILT,
LIBEL, SALSE, SLIME, SLUSH,
PELOID, SLUDGE, SLANDER
bath .... WALLOW

dauber .... WASP
hen .... COOT, RAIL,
GALLINULE
viscous .... SLIME
mudcap .... ADOBE
mudder or bangtail .... RACER
muddle ...... MESS, ADDLE, SNAFU,
BUNGLE, FIASCO, JUMBLE,
MIX UP, CONFUSE, FLUSTER
muddled .... DAZED, DIZZY,
GIDDY, WOOZY, STUPID
muddlehead .... ADDLEPATE
muddy .... DINGY, ROILY,
DAGGLE, SLOPPY, SLUDGY,
TURBID
mudfish .... BOWFIN, DIPNOAN
mudguard .... FENDER
mudhole .... WALLOW, LOBLOLLY
mudslinger .... MUCKRAKER
lawsuit .... LIBEL
mudworm .... IPO
muezzin .... CRIER
call of .... AZAN
place of .... MINARET
muff .... BOTCH, FUMBLE,
BUNGLE(R)
muffin ...... BUN, COB, GEM, ROLL,
BREAD, POPOVER
muffle .... MUTE, OVEN, WRAP,
DEADEN, STIFLE
muffler .... SCARF, NECKWEAR,
SILENCER
mufti .... ULEMA
slang .... CIV(V)IES
mug .... CUP, TOBY, MUNGO,
STEIN, NOGGIN, SEIDEL,
TANKARD
leather .... JACK
man-shaped .... TOBY
material .... PEWTER
slang .... FACE, KISSER,
ATTACK, HOLD UP, ASSAULT
mugger .... GOA, ACTOR, ROBBER,
HOODLUM, CROC(ODILE)
nemesis of .... COP
muggins .... DUPE, FOOL, DOMINO,
CARD GAME
muggy .... DANK, HUMID, STICKY,
SULTRY
mugwump .... REPUBLICAN
Muhammad Ali
.... (CASSIUS)CLAY
Muhammadan deity ...... ALLAH
Mukden is capital of
.... MANCHURIA
mulatto .... METIS, CREOLE,
GRIFF(E), GRIQUA
mulberry ...... AAL, TREE, FUSTIC,
MURREY, SYCAMINE
bark .... TAPA
tree genus .... MORUS,

CECROPIA
mulct .... BILK, FINE, AMERCE,
DEFRAUD, PENALIZE
mule .... HINNY, HYBRID, SLIPPER,
PIGHEAD, TRACTOR,
SHAVETAIL
cry .... BRAY
driver .... SKINNER
female .... MARE
of songdom .... SAL
on the Erie Canal .... SAL
pack .... BURRO, SUMPTER
parent .... MARE, DONKEY
young .... FOAL
muliebrity .... WOMANHOOD
mulish .... STUBBORN, OBSTINATE,
PIGHEADED
mull ...... THINK, FLAVOR, MUSLIN,
PONDER, REFLECT, SWEETEN,
COGITATE, CONSIDER
in a way .... DEBATE
mulla(h) .... TEACHER
mullc(i)n .... PLANT, FIGWORT,
FOXGLOVE
muller .... PESTLE, GRINDER
mullet .... LIZA, (GOAT)FISH
mulley .... POLLED COW
mulligan .... HASH, STEW
connoisseur .... HOBO
mulligatawny, for one ...... SOUP
mulligrubs .... COLIC
multifarious ...... MANY, VARIED,
DIVERSE, MANIFOLD
multiped(e) arthropod
.... CENTIPEDE
multiple .... MANIFOLD,
NUMEROUS
multiplicand .... FACIEND
multiplication ...... PROCREATION
result .... PRODUCT
multiply itself .... SQUARE
multitude .... ARMY, HOST,
CROWD, HORDE, SWARM,
GALAXY, LEGION, MYRIAD,
SCORES, THRONG
colloquial .... PILES, RAFTS,
SCADS
multitudinous ...... MANY, LARGE,
CROWDED, MANIFOLD,
NUMEROUS
mum .... ALE, BEER, MOTHER,
SILENT, DEODORANT,
CHRYSANTHEMUM
is the _____ .... WORD
mumble .... CHEW, MUMP,
MURMUR, MUTTER
mumbojumbo .... IDOL, SPELL,
FETISH, GIBBERISH, MEDICINE
MAN
mummer .... ACTOR, GUISER,
MASKER, PARADER,

PANTOMIMIST
mummify .... DRY, SHRIVEL,
PRESERVE
mummy .... CORPSE
cloth .... BYSSUS
mump .... MUMBLE, MUTTER
slang .... BEG, CHEAT
mumps .... PAROTITIS
munch .... BITE, CHEW, CHAMP,
CRUNCH, NIBBLE
Munchausen specialty .... YARNS
tales collector .... RASPE
title of .... BARON
Munchen .... MUNICH
mundane ...... CARNAL, EARTHLY,
WORLDLY, TEMPORAL
mundungo .... TOBACCO
Mundy work .... OM
Munich .... MUNCHEN
municipal .... URBAN
building .... CITY HALL,
COURTHOUSE
council member
.... ALDERMAN
tax .... OCTROI
municipality .... CITY, TOWN,
PUEBLO
munificent ...... LAVISH, PROFUSE,
GENEROUS
munitions .... ARMS
manufacturer .... KRUPP,
SKODA
storehouse .... ARSENAL
Munro, H. H. .... SAKI
Munsel, singer .... PATRICE
Munster seaport .... CORK
mural ...... PAINTING, WALL-LIKE
or state .... INTRA
painter .... (DIEGO)RIVERA
Murat .... JOACHIM
murder .... KILL, SLAY, BUMP
OFF, HOMICIDE
by drowning .... NOYADE
by suffocation .... BURKE
king's .... REGICIDE
victim, first .... ABEL
murdered .... SLAIN
murderer .... KILLER, BUTCHER,
ASSASSIN, MANSLAYER
biblical .... CAIN
murderous frenzy .... AMOK,
BERSERK
murex .... WHELK
murid .... RAT, DISCIPLE
murine .... MICE, RATS, RODENT
murk .... DIM, DUSK, HAZE,
GLOOM, DARK(NESS)
murky .... VAGUE, CLOUDY,
OBSCURE
murmur .... HUM, CURR, PURL,
MUMBLE, MUTTER, WHISPER

cat's .... PURR
dove's .... COO
fondly .... COO
wind's .... SOUGH
murmuring sound .... SUSSURUS
murphy ...... BED, TATER, POTATO
murre .... AUK, GUILLEMOT
murrey .... MULBERRY
musaceous plant .... BANANA
musca .... FLY
Muscat .... WINE, GRAPE
and _____ .... OMAN
lover .... WINO
natives .... OMANI
muscatel .... WINE
muscle .... BRAWN, SINEW, BICEPS,
TENSOR, TISSUE, LEVATOR,
TRICEPS
arm .... BICEPS, DELTOID
attachment .... TENDON
bending .... FLEXOR
builder .... STEROID
buttocks .... GLUTEUS
combining form .... MY(O)
contraction .... TIC, SPASM,
CRAMPS
infection .... GANGRENE
injury .... TEAR, SPRAIN
jaw .... MASSETER
like .... MYOID
loin .... PSOAS
movement .... CONTRACTION
of .... SARCOUS
pain .... MYALGIA
part of .... HEAD, CELLS,
FIBERS, T(A)ENIA, MYOFIBRIL
protein .... ACTIN
spasm(s) .... CRICK, CLONOS,
CRAMP(S)
tension .... TONUS
type .... SMOOTH, CARDIAC,
SKELETAL
muscles .... BRAWN, THEWS
science of .... MYOLOGY
wasting of .... DYSTROPHY
Muscovite .... MICA, GRANITE,
RUSSIAN, SERICITE
Muscovy .... DUCK, RUSSIAN
duck .... PATO
muscular .... BURLY, THEWY,
BRAWNY, TOROSE
contraction .... TIC, CRAMP
contraction, childbearing
.... LABOR
disorder .... MYASTHENIA
elasticity .... TONUS
impotence .... ATAXIA
tissue tumor .... MYOMA
muscularity .... BRAWN,
BEEF(INESS)
muse .... MULL, PIERIS, PONDER,

(DAY)DREAM, MEDITATE, MEDITATION

Muse, astronomy .... URANIA
chief .... CALLIOPE
comedy .... THALIA
dance .... TERPSICHORE
eloquence .... CALLIOPE
history .... CLIO
love .... ERATO
memory .... MNEME
music .... EUTERPE
poetry .... ERATO, THALIA, EUTERPE, CALLIOPE
sacred song .... POLYMNIA, POLYHYMNIA
tragedy .... MELPOMENE

Muses' domain .... AONIA, PARNASSUS
fountain .... HIPPOCRENE
home .... HELICON
mountain .... HELICON, PARNASSUS
of the .... PIERIAN
one of the .... CLIO, ERATO, THALIA, URANIA, EUTERPE, CALLIOPE, PIERIDES, POLYMNIA, MELPOMENE
place of worship .... PIERIA
spring of the .... CASTALIA

musette .... OBOE, BAGPIPE

museum .... GALLERY
custodian .... CURATOR

mush .... GOO, PAP, SAMP, ATOLE, JOURNEY, POTTAGE, PORRIDGE
slang .... CORN

mushroom .... MOREL, MORIL, AGARIC, FUNGUS, AMANITA, TOADSTOOL, DEATH CUP, CHAMPIGNON
alkaloid .... MUSCARIN(E)
cap .... PILEUS
cap's part .... LAMELLA
covering .... VOLVA
immature .... BUTTON
umbrella .... MITRA
underground .... TRUFFLE

mushy .... SOFT, PAPPY, SENTIMENTAL

Musial .... STAN, THE MAN

music .... AIR, LAY, TUNE, MELODY, HARMONY, HARMONICS
adapter .... ARRANGER
aftersong .... EPODE
as is .... STA
canto .... PASSUS
change in .... MUTA
clef .... TREBLE
composition .... FUGUE, RONDO, RONDEAU
concluding .... CODA

country/folk .... BALLAD, BLUEGRASS
cradlesong/nursery .... LULLABY
drama set to .... OPERA
first part .... PRIMO
for a movie .... SCORE
for nine .... NONET
grace note .... SANGLOT
hall .... GAFF, ODEA, ODEON, ODEUM, THEATER
high in .... ALT
high part .... TREBLE
interval in .... OCTAVE, TRITONE
lead in .... PRESA
leap in .... SALTO
lively .... GALOP, GIACOSO
lumberman's? ..... LOGARITHM
major in .... DUR
major scale .... GAMUT
mark in .... SLUR, SEGNO
measured beat .... MOTO, PULSE, TEMPO
melodious .... ARIOSO
military .... MARCH
modern .... BOP
modern type .... RAP
mournful .... DIRGE
mute .... SORDINO
night .... NOCTURNE, SERENADE
played on bells .... CHIMB, CHIMES, CARILLON
portamento .... GLIDE
rate of speed .... LENTO, TEMPO, ALLEGRO, ANDANTE
sacred .... CHORAL(E)
sentimental .... CORN, SCHMALTZ
sign .... PRESA, SEGNO
silent: direction .... TACET
slow in .... LARGO, LENTO, TARDO, ANDANTE
slow movement .... ADAGIO
soft in .... DOLCE, PIANO
solo .... ETUDE
solo, opposed to .... TUTTI
source .... TAPEDECK
stately .... LARGO, MINUET
sustained .... TENUTO
swing .... JIVE
symbol .... REST
syncopated .... RAG(TIME)
teacher .... MAESTRO
tempo .... LENTO, PRESTO, ALLEGRO, ANDANTE
theme .... MOTIF, MOTIVE
throughout .... SEMPRE
timing device ..... METRONOME

together in .... ADUE
twice in .... BIS
unaccented/upbeat .... ARSIS
whole note .... SEMIBREVE

musical .... MELIC, LYRIC(AL), CANOROUS, MELODIOUS
accompaniment .... OB(B)LIGATO
Aquarian .... HAIR
beginning .... INTRO
bells .... CHIMES, CARILLON
character ..... KEY, CLEF, REST, SHARP
chord .... TRIAD, CATGUT
comedy .... REVUE, PARODY
composition ..... OPUS, FUGUE, MOTET, OPERA, PIECE, RONDO, SUITE, ARIOSO, MINUET, SONATA, CANTATA, CONCERTO, NOCTURNE, ORATORIO, SERENADE, SERENATA, SYMPHONY
direction .... PPP, STA, POCO, SOLI, LARGO, MOLTO, PRESA, TACET
disability .... AMUSIA
Domino .... FATS
drama .... OPERA
ending/closing .... CODA
entertainer .... MINSTREL
excerpt .... MORCEAU
exercise .... ETUDE
family .... TRAPPS
flourish .... CADENZA, FANFARE
group .... BAND, DUET, TRIO, CHOIR, COMBO, OCTET, CHORUS, MAZURKA, QUARTET, GLEE CLUB
half step .... SEMITONE
horn, comic .... BAZOOKA
interval .... REST, OCTAVE, TRITONE
instruction ..... LARGO, LENTO, FORTISSIMO, PIANISSIMO
instrument .... LUTE, LYRE, OBOE, REED, FLUTE, PIANO, ROTTE, SITAR, CORNET, GUITAR, SPINET, VIOL(IN), BASSOON, CITHERN, OCARINA, CALLIOPE, CLARINET, MANDOLIN, SAXOPHONE
brasswind .... BUGLE, CORNET, TRUMPET, TROMBONE
fingerboard .... VINA
fipple flute .... FLAGEOLET
guitar-like ...... LUTE, BANJO, GITTERN, UKULELE, MANDOLIN
harp-like .... SAMBUKE

inventor .... JUBAL
keyboard ..... ORGAN, PIANO,
SPINET, CELESTA, CLAVIER,
CALLIOPE
lute, obsolete .... THEORBO
lyre-like .... CITHARA
muffler .... MUTE
organ-like .... CALLIOPE
player ..... FLUTIST, HARPIST,
PIANIST(E), GUITARIST,
TRUMPETER, VIOLINIST
range of .... DIAPASON
string .... CHORD, CATGUT
stringed .... ASOR, LUTE,
LYRE, ROTE, VINA, VIOL,
BANJO, REBEC, VIOLA,
CITOLE, GUITAR, VIOLIN,
ZITHER, BANDORE,
CITHER(N), CLAVIER,
SAMBUKE, SAMISEN,
UKULELE, DULCIMER,
MANDOLIN
tone changer .... PEDAL
toy .... KAZOO
violin-like ...... VIOL, CELLO,
VIOLA, REBEC(K)
wind .... REED, TUBA, FLUTE,
ORGAN, OCARINA, CLARINET,
FLAGEOLET, SAXOPHONE
instruments, collectively
.... BRASS, TRAPS, WINDS,
STRINGS, PERCUSSION
introduction .... OVERTURE
key .... B FLAT, E FLAT
keys .... CLEFS
lines .... STEM, STAFF
medley .... OLIO, CENTO,
PASTICHE, PASTICCIO
movement .... SCHERZO
notation ..... REST, TABLATURE
org. .... ASCAP
ornament .... ROULADE
part .... CODA
passage .... PRESTO, BRAVURA,
CADENZA, MORCEAU
performance .... REVUE,
CONCERT, RECITAL
phrase .... LEITMOTIF
pipe .... OAT, OBOE, REED,
FLUTE, CLARINET, FLAGEOLET
play .... OPERETTA
range .... GAMUT
river .... DANUBE
scale .... SOLFA
short interlude .... VERSET
show that fails .... TURKEY
sign .... DOT, CLEF, ISON,
REST, PRESA, SEGNO, SHARP
signature .... THEME
sound .... TONE, CHIME

sounds, science of
.... HARMONICS
study .... ETUDE
suite .... PARTITA
syllable .... DO, RE, MI, FA,
SOL, LA, TI
symbol .... CLEF, SHARP
transition .... SEGUE
trill .... TREMOLO, VIBRATO
work .... OPUS, RHAPSODY
musicale .... CONCERT, SYMPHONY
musically together .... ADUE
musician .... FIFER, JUBAL,
BUGLER, HARPER, OBOIST,
CELLIST, DRUMMER, FIDDLER,
FLUTIST, HARPIST, ORPHEUS,
PIANIST, ARRANGER,
COMPOSER, ORGANIST,
HARMONIST, VIOLINIST
Hamelin .... PIPER
musicians' patron .... CECILIA
musing .... REVERIE, MEDITATION,
REFLECTION
musk cat .... CIVET
product .... PERFUME
smell .... MOSCHATE
muskeg .... BOG, MARSH
muskellunge .... PIKE
musket .... GUN, DRAGON,
GINGAL(L), JINGAL, CULVERIN
musketeer of fiction ...... ATHOS,
ARAMIS, PORTHOS,
D'ARTAGNAN
muskmelon ...... MANGO, ATIMON,
CASABA, CANTALOUPE
muskrat kin .... VOLE
Muslim. See also Moslem
.... SENUSI, MUSSULMAN
ascetic ...... WHIRLING DERVISH
branch .... SHIAH
cap .... TAJ, KOPIA
chronicle .... TARSILA
court .... AGAMA
faith .... ISLAM
fasting month .... RAMADAN
group .... ULAMA
maid .... HOURI
prayers, part of .... RAKA
queen in India .... BEGUM
religious person .... IMAM,
HADJI, HATIB, PAKIL
sacred city .... MECCA
muslin ...... MULL, ADATI, MOSAL,
SHELA, BATISTE, NAINSOOK,
TARLETAN
bag .... TILLOT
gauze .... TIFFANY
striped .... DORIA
very fine .... ORGANDY
muss .... ROW, MESS, CREASE,

MUDDLE, RUMPLE, TANGLE,
TOUSLE, DISHEVEL, DISORDER
mussel .... UNIO, MOLLUSK
product .... PEARL
Mussolini .... BENITO
nickname .... MUSSO
son-in-law .... CIANO
title of .... (IL)DUCE
Mussulman .... MOSLEM,
SARACEN
must .... ALBA, MAUN, MOLD,
SAPA, STUM, WINE, BOUND,
JUICE, OUGHT, MILDEW,
SHOULD
elephant's .... FRENZY
mustache ...... BEARD, WHISKERS,
HANDLE BAR
Mustafa Kemal ____
.... ATATURK
mustang .... PONY, HORSE,
BRONCO
mustard .... WEED, WOAD, CRESS,
RADISH, TURNIP, CHARLOCK,
CONDIMENT, SEASONING
application .... POULTICE
counterpart of .... CRESS
gas .... YPERITE, VESICANT
plaster .... SINAPISM
pod .... SILIQUE
mustee .... MESTIZO, OCTOROON
musteline animal .... MINK,
OTTER, RATEL, MARTEN,
WEASEL, POLECAT,
WOLVERINE
muster .... CALL, LEVY, LIST,
POLL, ROLL, GATHER,
SUMMON, COLLECT,
ASSEMBLE, MOBILIZE
in .... ENLIST
out .... DISBAND
musty .... DULL, HOAR, RANK,
FETID, FUSTY, MOLDY, MUCID,
STALE, TRITE, RANCID
mutable .... FICKLE, VOLATILE
mutate .... VARY, CHANGE
mutation .... CHANGE,
EVOLUTION, SALTATION
in linguistics .... UMLAUT
mute .... MUM, DUMB, SURD,
DUMMY, DEADEN, MUFFLE,
SILENT, VOICELESS
become .... CLAM UP
consonant .... LENE
for trumpet .... SOURDINE
mutilate .... MAR, MAIM, DAMAGE,
DEFACE, DEFORM, MANGLE,
CRIPPLE, DISFIGURE
mutineer .... REBEL
mutiny .... RISE, REVOLT,

UPRISING, REBELLION
Mutsuhito's realm .... JAPAN
reign .... MEIJI
son .... HIROHITO
mutt .... CUR, DOG, POOCH,
MONGREL
mutter .... GROWL, MUMBLE,
MURMUR, GRUMBLE,
COMPLAIN
mutton .... SHEEP, (RED)MEAT
bird .... OII
chop .... CABOBS
chops .... WHISKERS,
BURNSIDES, SIDEBURNS
cut .... SADDLE
fish .... SAMA, EELPOUT
leg of .... GIGOT
neck .... SCRAG
soup .... SCOTCH BROTH
stew .... HARICOT
muttonhead .... DOLT, DUNCE
mutual .... JOINT, COMMON,
COMBINED, RECIPROCAL
muzhik .... PEASANT
muzzle .... GAG, NOSE, SNOUT,
SILENCE
loader .... RAMROD
muzzy .... DAZED, DRUNK,
SOUSED, MUDDLED
my faith .... MA FOI
fault .... MEA CULPA
heart, literally .... MACHREE
"kingdom for a ____"
.... HORSE
"my dear Watson, ____"
.... ELEMENTARY
My Fair Lady author .... SHAW,
LOWEW
Gal ____ .... SAL
Sweetness .... NAOMI
Myanmar neighbor .... LAOS
myna(h) .... BIRD
kin of .... STARLING
Mynheer .... SIR, DUTCHMAN
myopic .... NEARSIGHTED,
SHORTSIGHTED
Myra Breckinridge personified
.... (RAQUEL)WELCH

pianist .... HESS
myriad ..... TEEMING, COUNTLESS,
MULTITUDE, TEN THOUSAND
myriapod .... CENTIPEDE,
MILLIPEDE
segment .... SOMITE, TELSON
myrmicid .... ANT
Myrmidon .... ADHERENT,
FOLLOWER
Myrna, actress .... LOY
myrrh .... CICELY
myrtle .... SHRUB, GUAVA,
CAJEPUT, CAJUPUT,
PERIWINKLE
berry .... ALLSPICE
Mysore capital .... BANGALORE
mysterious .... RUNIC, WEIRD,
ARCANE, OCCULT, SECRET,
CRYPTIC, MYSTIC(AL),
ESOTERIC, ENIGMATIC
object .... UFO
mystery .... RUNE, PUZZLE,
RIDDLE, ENIGMA, SECRET,
ARCANUM, SECRECY
solve one .... UNRAVEL
story ..... MAIGRET, WHODUNIT
writer's award .... EDGAR
mystic .... YOGA, YOGI, ESSENE,
EPOPT(IC), HIDDEN, OCCULT,
SUFIST, CABALIST, ESOTERIC
art .... MAGIC, CABALA,
VOODOO, ALCHEMY, SORCERY,
ASTROLOGY
cry .... OM, EVOE
number .... SEVEN
practice .... YOGA
writing .... RUNE
mystical ...... OCCULT, ENIGMATIC
biblical word .... SELAH
British chronicle .... BRUT
doctrine .... CAB(B)ALA,
KABALA
interpretation .... ANAGOGE
mystify .... HOAX, BAFFLE,
PUZZLE, PERPLEX, BEWILDER,
CONFOUND, OBFUSCATE
mystique .... AURA, MAGIC,
CHARISMA

myth ...... FABLE, STORY, LEGEND
mythical ...... UNREAL, FABULOUS,
FICTIONAL, IMAGINARY,
LEGENDARY
animal .... GRIFFIN, GRIFFON,
GRYPHON
antelope .... YALE
beast .... DRAGON
being .... CENTAUR
bird .... ROC
character .... MOTHER GOOSE
ferryman .... CHARON
flyer .... ICARUS
giant ...... YMER, YMIR, JOTUN,
FAFNIR, CYCLOPS
hero .... EGIL(E)
horse/steed .... PEGASUS,
UNICORN
hunter .... ORION
island/continent ...... ATLANTIS
king .... ATLI, OLAF, MIDAS
lance .... RON
land .... LEMURIA
maiden .... IO, DANAE
man of brass .... TALOS
monster ...... DRAGON, SPHINX,
CHIMERA, GRIFFIN, MINOTAUR
mountain .... OSSA, HELICON,
PARNASSUS
musician .... ORPHEUS
river .... STYX
serpent .... APEPI, MIDGARD
sisters .... GORGONS
symbol of purity ..... UNICORN
trio .... FATES, GORGONS
watchdog .... GARM, CERBERUS
wolf .... FENRIR
woman .... IDUN
mythicize .... ALLEGORIZE
mythmaker .... FABULIST
mythologist .... MULLER
mythology ...... LEGEND, MYTHOS,
FOLKLORE
mythomania ...... LYING, FIBBERY
mythomaniac .... LIAR, ANANIAS,
MUNCHAUSEN
Mytilene .... LESBOS
myxoma .... TUMOR

N

N, Greek .... NU
Hebrew .... NUN
in physics .... NEUTRON
letter .... EN
'n' calls, ____ .... PUTS
N.B. .... NOTA BENE
Na .... SODIUM

nab .... BAG, GRAB, SNAG, CATCH,
SEIZE, ARREST, COLLAR,
CORNER, SNATCH, CAPTURE
Nabal's wife .... ABIGAIL
nabob .... DIVES, NAWAB
Nabokov, author .... VLADIMIR
heroine .... IDA

nacelle .... CAR, BASKET,
FUSELAGE
NaCl .... SALT
nacre .... SHELLFISH, MOTHER-OF-
PEARL
nacreous .... LUSTROUS
Nader .... RALPH

nadir .... DEPTHS, LOW POINT
opposite of .... ZENITH
nag .... TIT, PONY, RIDE, URGE,
ANNOY, HORSE, SCOLD,
SHREW, TEASE, BADGER,
HECTOR, PESTER, PLAGUE,
VIRAGO, HENPECK,
TERMAGANT
slang .... HOSS
naga .... COBRA, SNAKE
nagana disease carrier
.... TSETSE
nagger .... SHREW, GRIPER,
VIRAGO, TERMAGANT
Nagoya bay .... ISE
Naha is capital of ...... OKINAWA
nahoor ...... SNA, SHEEP, BHARAL
Nahor's brother .... ABRAM,
HARAN, ABRAHAM
concubine .... REUMAH
son .... UZ, BUZ, HAZO,
GAHAM, TERAH, CHESED,
KEMUEL, BETHUEL, JIDLAPH,
PILDASH
wife .... MILCAH
naiad .... NYMPH, OREAD
naid .... WORM
nail .... FIX, PIN, BRAD, CLAW,
SPAD, TACK, CATCH, SPIKE,
SPRIG, TACH(E), FASTEN,
SECURE, TENTER
board .... EMERY
finishing/thin .... BRAD
half-moon shape in the
.... LUNULA
having .... UNGUAL
part of the .... BED, PLATE,
LUNULA, CUTICLE
polish .... CUTEX, ENAMEL
puller .... CLAW
shoemaker's .... SPARABLE
short .... TACK
short, thick .... STUB
slang .... CIGARETTE
slantingly .... TOE
substance .... KERATIN
3-inch .... TENPENNY
unit of weight .... KEG
wooden .... PEG
nailhead .... STUD
nainsook .... COTTON, MUSLIN
naive .... NAIF, GREEN, SIMPLE,
ARTLESS, INNOCENT,
CHILDLIKE, GUILELESS,
INGENUOUS
girl .... INGENUE
one .... BABE
naivete .... INNOCENCE
naked .... BARE, NUDE, PLAIN,
STARK, UNCLAD, EXPOSED
in law .... INVALID

namaycush .... TOGUE, TROUT
namby-pamby ...... SILLY, VAPID,
INSIPID, WISHY-WASHY
person .... PHILIPS
name .... DUB, CITE, FAME, TERM,
LABEL, (EN)TITLE, APPOINT,
EPITHET, MENTION,
COGNOMEN, IDENTIFY,
MONICKER, NOMINATE,
DESIGNATE, REPUTATION
aristocratic .... PATRICK
assumed .... ALIAS, INCOG,
PSEUDONYM, SOBRIQUET
bad .... CACONYM
characteristic .... EPITHET,
SOBRIQUET
claimed by Naomi .... MARA
derivation of .... EPONYM
divine .... AMBROSE
dropper .... SNOB
fake .... ALIAS
false .... ANONYM
heavenly .... CELESTE
lively .... VIVIAN
meaning beauty .... ADA
bee .... DEBORAH
bitter .... MARA
breath .... ABEL
bright .... BERTA
champion .... NEAL
comfort .... NOAH
daughter .... INGA
ewe .... RACHEL
flaxen-haired .... LINUS
girl .... COLLEEN
God's protector .... ANSEL
great fame .... ELMER
healer .... ASA
high .... ELI
holy .... OLGA
life/life-giving .... EVA
little .... ETTA
merry .... HILARY
moon goddess .... DELIA
mortal man .... ENOS
noble .... PATRICK
peace .... IRENE
pleasure .... EDNA
princess .... SARA
rose .... RHODA
sad .... DOLORES
serving .... OBED
spring born .... VERNA
"the harvester" .... TESS
twins .... THOMAS
wild cow/weary .... LEAH
of A-bomb dropped in
Hiroshima .... LITTLE
BOY
A-bomb dropped in
Nagasaki ...... FAT MAN

eight popes .... URBAN
Jesse James' wife and
mother .... ZERELDA
Oz canine .... TOTO
thing, etc. .... NOUN
on a green stamp .... EIRE
on envelope .... ADDRESSEE
plate .... FACIA
shaggy dog's .... RAGS
slang .... HANDLE, MONI(C)KER
substitute .... DINGUS
to remember .... MAINE
named .... CITED, YCLEPT,
YCLEPED, APPOINTED,
IDENTIFIED
nameless .... UNKNOWN,
ANONYMOUS
person .... ANONYM
namely .... VIZ, TO WIT, SILICET
names list .... BEADROLL
namesake .... EPONYM, HOMONYM
La Douce .... IRMA
of Chinese leader .... MAO
nana .... AMAH, NANNY, NURSE
Nancy .... NARCISSUS
nankin .... BUFF, COTTON
nanny .... (DRY)NURSE
vehicle of .... PRAM, BUGGY,
STROLLER
Naomi .... MARA
daughter-in-law .... RUTH
naos .... CELLA, TEMPLE
nap ...... DOZE, PILE, SHAG, SLEEP,
SIESTA, SNOOZE, FORTY
WINKS
Brit. .... KIP
raising device ...... GIG, CARD,
TEASEL, TEAZEL
shearer .... CROPPER
napalm inventor .... FIESER
nape .... PALL, NUCHA, NUQUE,
SCRAG, SCRUFF
napery .... DAMASK, LINENS,
DOILIES, NAPKINS
napkin .... BIB, DOILY, DIAPER,
NAPERY, SERVIETTE
Naples .... NAPOLI
beggar .... LAZZARONE
island .... CAPRI
king of .... MURAT
lake near .... AVERNUS
native of .... NEOPOLITAN
Napoleon ..... CARD, COIN, GAME,
PASTRY
birthplace of .... AJACCIO
brother of ..... JEROME, LUCIEN
conqueror of .... KUTUZOV,
WELLINGTON
downfall of .... WATERLOO
game like .... PAM
general .... RAPP, KLEBER

isle identified with .... ELBA, HELENA, CORSICA

marshal of .... NEY, MURAT

scene of defeat .... WATERLOO

scene of victory .... JENA, LODI, WAGRAM, MARENGO, AUSTERLITZ

sister of .... ELISA, CAROLINE

wife of .... JOSEPHINE

Napoleonic marshal .... NEY, MURAT

victory site: 1796 .... LODI

Napoli .... NAPLES

napped, as fabrics .... FRIEZED

nappy .... ALE, DOWNY, HAIRY, WOOLLY, FOAMING

narcissism .... SELF-LOVE

narcissus .... NANCY, FLOWER, JONQUIL, DAFFODIL

Narcissus .... EGOIST

composer .... NEVIN

love of .... SELF

nymph who loved .... ECHO

narcosis .... SLEEP, STUPOR

narcotic .... DOPE, DRUG, JUNK, OPIUM, HEROIN, OPIATE, ANODYNE, COCAINE, CODEINE, HASHISH, MORPHINE, SEDATIVE

beechnut .... FAGINE

cigarette .... KEF, REEFER, MARIJUANA

dreamy tranquility .... KEF

drug, inject .... MAINLINE

plant ..... CUCA, HEMP, K(H)AT, BHANG, DUTRA, POPPY, MANDRAKE, MARIJUANA

slang .... POT, ACID, COKE, JUNK, SNOW

under influence of .... HIGH, DOPEY, STONED

user .... DOPER, FIEND, ADDICT, JUNKIE, SMOKER, POTHEAD, SNOWBIRD

nard .... SALVE, OINTMENT

nares .... NOSTRILS

narghile .... PIPE, HOOKA(H)

narial .... RHINAL

narine .... NASAL

nark .... SPY, AGENT, INFORMER

Narragansett vegetable dish .... SUCCOTASH

narrate .... TELL, RECITE, RELATE, REPORT, RECOUNT

narrative .... SAGA, TALE, CONTE, STORY, ACCOUNT, NOVELLA, RECITAL

poem .... LAY, EPIC, EPOS, ILIAD, BEOWULF, ODYSSEY

narrator .... RELATOR

narrow ...... CLOSE, LIMIT, TAPER, ANGUST, STRAIT(EN)

combining form .... STENO

escape .... CLOSE CALL

gash .... SLIT

minded .... PETTY, BIASED, BIGOTED, PEDANTIC

opening .... SLOT

pew .... SLIP

point of land .... SPIT

street .... LANE, ALLEY

narrowed .... STENOSED

narrowing of a passage .... STENOSIS

narrows .... SOUND, STRAIT

narwhal .... WHALE, CETACEAN

nary .... NO, NOT ANY

NASA effort .... MOONSHOT

nasal .... NARINE, RHINAL

catarrh .... CORYZA

cavity .... NARE

intonation .... TWANG

mucous .... SNOT, SNIVEL

passage .... NARES, NOSTRIL

nascency .... BIRTH, ORIGIN, GENESIS, BEGINNING, FORMATION

Nash, humorist .... OGDEN

Nasser .... GAMAL(ABDEL)

nasty .... FOUL, MEAN, FILTHY, OBSCENE, ILL-TEMPERED

type .... DASTARD

Nat and Natalie .... COLE

natal .... INNATE, NATIVE

day .... BIRTHDAY

natant ...... FLOATING, SWIMMING

natatorium .... POOL

Nathan, George _____ ...... JEAN

nation .... STATE, PEOPLE, COUNTRY

massacre of .... GENOCIDE

"of shopkeepers" .... ENGLAND

Nation, temperance leader .... CARRY

national .... CITIZEN, FEDERAL

character .... ETHOS

hymn .... ANTHEM

National Guard .... MILITIA

nations, alliance of .... AXIS

native .... SON, NATAL, INBORN, ENDEMIC, NATURAL, INHERENT, ABORIGINE, INDIGENOUS

ability .... GIFT, TALENT, APTITUDE

agent .... COMPRADOR

animal/plant .... INDIGENE

chief .... DATU, CACIQUE

inhabitant .... DENIZEN

policeman .... SEPOY

ruler .... NIZAM

salt .... HALITE

suffix .... ITE

Native American. See **Indian/ Native American**

nativity .... BIRTH

NATO .... ALLIANCE

natty .... CHIC, TRIM, SHARP, SMART, SPRUCE

natural .... REAL, WILD, PLAIN, INBORN, INNATE, NORMAL, SIMPLE, UNPOSED

ability .... GIFT, FLAIR, KNACK, GENIUS, TALENT, APTITUDE

abode .... HABITAT

endowment .... TALENT

flier .... BIRD

inclination .... PROPENSITY

pigment .... OCHRE

naturalist .... MUIR, BEEBE, DARWIN, ANDREWS, ANIMIST, AUDUBON, BURBANK, BIOLOGIST, COMSTOCK, ECOLOGIST

prefix .... ECO

naturalize ...... ADOPT, CONVERT, AFFILIATE

naturally .... OF COURSE

nature .... KIND, SORT, TYPE, ESSENCE, CREATION, CHARACTER

group .... EPA

nature's soil builder .... EARTHWORM

naught .... NIL, ZERO, NOTHING

bring to .... UNDO, VOID, CANCEL, NULLIFY

naughty .... IMPISH, OBSCENE, WAYWARD, MISCHIEVOUS

-naughty .... NO-NO

nausea .... PALL, QUALM, WAMBLE, DISGUST, AVERSION

affected with .... QUEASY

nauseate .... REVOLT, SICKEN

Nausicaa's discovery .... ODYSSEUS

father .... ALCINOUS

nautical .... NAVAL, MARINE, OCEANIC, MARITIME

call .... AHOY

chain .... TYE

command/cry .... ALEE, AVAST

cry: var. .... OHOY

dick .... DEADEYE

fly .... BURGEE

Halt! .... AVAST

mile .... KNOT

rope .... HAWSER, NETTLE, MARLINE, RATLINE

term .... AYE, ALEE, ATRY, ABAFT, ABEAM, AFORE, ASTERN, AWEATHER, PORTSIDE

time: abbr. .... GST
nautilus .... MOLLUSK, ARGONAUT
Nautilus, commander of
.... NEMO
Navaho .... INDIAN
hut .... HOGAN
naval .... MARINE, MARITIME,
NAUTICAL
academy .... ANNAPOLIS
cadet ...... MIDDY, MIDSHIPMAN
commander .... ADMIRAL,
CAPTAIN, SKIPPER
detection method .... SONAR
force .... FLEET, ARMADA
hero .... DEWEY, NELSON,
FARRAGUT
officer .... MATE, ENSIGN,
YEOMAN
pass of a sort .... NAVICERT
title .... ADMIRAL, COMMODORE
unit .... FLOTILLA
unit list/roll .... MUSTER
vessel .... UBOAT, TENDER,
CRUISER, FLATTOP, WARSHIP,
CORVETTE, DESTROYER
Naval Reserve woman .... WAVE
nave .... HUB
navel .... UMBILICUS
of Sicily .... ENNA
point .... NOMBRIL
navigate .... SAIL, STEER, AVIATE,
CRUISE
navigation detecting systems
.... LORAN, SONAR, SHORAN
device .... RACON
hazard .... REEF
navigator .... COOK, ERIC, NAVVY,
BAFFIN, BERING, TASMAN,
MAGELLAN
Navigators Island .... SAMOA
navvy .... LABORER
navy .... FLEET, WARSHIPS, SEA
FORCE
bed .... SACK
color .... BLUE
engineer .... SEABEE
group ...... ARMADA, FLOTILLA,
SQUADRON, TASKFORCE
man .... CPO, MATE, SEABEE
mascot of .... GOAT
pharmacist .... CORPSMAN
ration .... HARDTACK
recruit .... BOOT
scout boat .... VEDETTE
nawab .... NABOB, TITLE
nay .... NO, VOTE, DENIAL
naysayer .... DENIER
Nazarene .... JESUS
Nazarite, he was one
.... SAMSON
Nazi .... FASCIST, HITLERITE

airforce .... LUFTWAFFE
collaborator .... LAVAL,
QUISLING
concentration camp
.... BELSEN, DACHAU
defector .... HESS
district .... GAU
district leader .... GAULEITER
emblem .... FYLFOT, SWASTIKA
greeting .... HEIL
ideology .... HERRENVOLK
leader .... LEY, HESS, HITLER,
FUEHRER, GOERING, HIMMLER,
GOEBBELS
organization, U.S. .... BUND
salute .... HEIL HITLER
state police .... GESTAPO
Nazimova, actress .... ALLA
NB, part of .... NOTA, BENE
NBA all time record holder:
for assists .... EARVIN
"MAGIC" JOHNSON, JOHN
STOCKTON
for points ...... KAREEM ABDUL
JABBAR
for rebounds .... WILT
CHAMBERLAIN
NCO .... SARGE, CORPORAL,
SERGEANT
Ne ____ ultra (acme) ...... PLUS
neap .... TIDE
near .... NIGH, ABOUT, CLOSE,
APPROACH, FRIENDLY,
INTIMATE
solution .... HOT
the ankle .... TARSAL
where the action is
.... RINGSIDE
Near East country .... EGYPT,
SYRIA, ISRAEL, JORDAN,
TURKEY, LEBANON
nearby .... CLOSE, HANDY,
AROUND, BESIDE, A STONE'S
THROW AWAY
poetically .... ANIGH
nearest .... NEXT, NIGHEST,
IMMEDIATE
nearly .... ALL BUT, ALMOST, NOT
QUITE
nearsighted .... MYOPIC
person .... MYOPE
nearsightedness .... MYOPIA
neat ...... CHIC, PURE, TIDY, TRIG,
TRIM, CLEAN, NATTY, SLEEK,
ADROIT, SOIGNE, SPIFFY,
SPRUCE
neb .... TIP, BEAK, BILL, NOSE,
SNOUT
Nebraska capital .... LINCOLN
city/town .... ORD, ALMA,
YORK, BLAIR, OMAHA, PONCA,

SIDNEY, CHADRON, FREMONT,
KEARNEY, BEATRICE,
COLUMBUS, HASTINGS, WEST
POINT, SCOTTSBLUFF
college ..... DOANE, BELLEVUE,
HASTINGS
county ..... BOYD, CASS, CLAY,
GAGE, HALL, HOLT, KNOX,
OTOE, POLK, YORK, ADAMS,
DODGE, SARPY, DAKOTA,
DAWSON, PLATTE, SEWARD,
DOUGLAS
dam .... KINGSLEY
Indian .... OTOE, KIOWA,
PONCA, OMAHA, PAWNEE
lake .... DADS, MOON, SWAN,
ALICE, SWANSON, CRESCENT
river ..... LOUP, CEDAR, SNAKE,
WHITE, DISMAL, NEMAHA,
PLATTE, COLAMUS, ELKHORN,
MISSOURI
state bird .... MEADOWLARK
state flower .... GOLDENROD
state nickname
.... CORNHUSKER
tourist attraction .... BOYS
TOWN, PIONEER VILLAGE
U.S. Air Force Base
.... OFFUT
university .... WESLEYAN
nebulous .... HAZY, MISTY,
VAGUE, CLOUDY, OBSCURE,
UNCLEAR, INDEFINITE
necessaries .... ESTOVERS
necessarily .... PERFORCE,
INEVITABLY
necessary .... MUST, VITAL,
URGENT, NEEDFUL, PRESSING,
REQUIRED, ESSENTIAL,
REQUISITE
necessitate ...... COMPEL, ENTAIL,
OBLIGE, REQUIRE
necessity ...... FATE, NEED, WANT,
DEMAND, URGENCY,
COMPULSION
neck .... PET, KISS, SCRAG, SPOON,
CARESS, CERVIX, GULLET,
STRAIT, CHANNEL
and shoulder covering
.... SHAWL, TUCKER
animal with long ...... GIRAFFE
armor .... GORGET
artery .... CAROTID
back of .... NAPE, NUCHA,
CERVIX, SCRUFF
covering .... MANE, RUFF
cramp .... CRICK
ligament .... PAXWAX
of beef .... CLOD
of land .... SPIT, ISTHMUS
of the ..... JUGULAR, CERVICAL

pain .... CRICK
part of horse .... WITHERS
piece .... BOA, TIE, FICHU,
SCARF, STOLE, COLLAR,
CRAVAT
scarf .... ASCOT, TIPPET
slang .... SMOOCH
neckerchief .... SCARF
necklace .... BEAD, STRAND,
STRING, TORQUE, CHAPLET,
RIVIERE, CARCANET
appendage .... LOCKET,
PENDANT, LAVALIER
colloquial .... CHOKER
ornament .... LAVALIER(E)
neckline, low .... DECOLLETE
shape .... VEE
necktie .... BOW, ASCOT, SCARF,
CHOKER, CRAVAT
ornament .... STICKPIN
party .... HANGING
neckwear .... RUFF, COLLAR,
MUFFLER
necrology .... OBIT(UARY)
necromancer .... DIVINER,
SORCERER
necromancy .... SORCERY,
(BLACK)MAGIC
necropolis .... CEMETERY,
GRAVEYARD
necropsy .... AUTOPSY, POST
MORTEM
nectar .... DRINK, BEVERAGE,
HONEY(DEW)
of the gods .... AMBROSIA
product .... HONEY
nectarine .... PEACH
nee .... BORN
need .... LACK, WANT, DESIRE,
EXIGENCY, REQUISITE
needle .... GOAD, PROD, PRICK,
TEASE, BODKIN, HECKLE,
POINTER, PROVOKE,
INDICATOR
bug .... NEPA
case .... ETUI, ETWEE
combining form .... ACU
crystal like .... ACICULA
etching .... STYLE
hole .... EYE
pushing disk .... PALM
shaped ...... ACUATE, ACERATE,
ACEROSE, ACIFORM, SPICULE
needlefish .... GAR, PIPEFISH
needlewoman .... SEAMSTRESS,
SEMPSTRESS
needlework .... SEWING,
KNITTING, EMBROIDERY
beginner's .... SAMPLER
loop .... BRIDE
needy .... POOR, INDIGENT,

DESTITUTE, PENNILESS
ne'er-do-well .... DRIFTER,
WASTREL
nefarious .... EVIL, WICKED,
VICIOUS
Nefertiti's husband .... PHARAOH
negate .... VOID, ANNUL, BELIE,
CANCEL, NULLIFY,
COUNTERACT
negation .... DENIAL, NULLITY
act of .... VETO
polite .... NO SIR
negative .... NO, MINUS
conjunction .... NOT
connective .... NOR, NEITHER
emphatic .... NEVER
ion .... ANION
opposite of .... POSITIVE,
AFFIRMATIVE
outcome .... NIL
particle .... ION
photo .... FILM
prefix .... NON
slangy .... NAW, NIX, NOPE, NO
DICE, NO SOAP
terminal .... CATHODE
vote .... NAY, NYET
neglect .... MISS, OMIT, SKIP,
SHIRK, FORGET, IGNORE,
OMISSION, OVERLOOK,
OVERSIGHT
neglected .... ABANDONED
neglectful .... LAX, SLACK,
REMISS, DERELICT
negligee .... (NIGHT)GOWN,
PEIGNOR
negligent .... LAX, REMISS,
CARELESS, DERELICT,
DELINQUENT
negligible .... SLIGHT, TRIVIAL,
TRIFLING
amount .... PEANUTS
negotiable .... WORKABLE
negotiate .... DEAL, TREAT,
HANDLE, PARLEY, ARRANGE,
BARGAIN, DISCUSS, TRANSACT
Negri of films .... POLA
Negrillo .... BUSHMAN
negus, Ethiopia's
.... (HAILE)SELASSIE
Nehru .... JAWAHARLAL
neigh .... (W)HINNY, (S)NICKER
neighborhood ...... AREA, VENUE,
REGION, PURLIEU, LOCALITY,
VICINAGE, VICINITY,
COMMUNITY
neighboring .... NEXT, NEARBY,
ADJACENT, ADJOINING
neighbor's gathering .... BEE
neither, companion of .... NOR
moral or immoral .... AMORAL

right or left .... MIDDLE OF
THE ROAD
Nejd, capital of .... RIYADH
robe .... ABA
Nejdi .... ARAB
Nellie, journalist .... BLY
Nelson, Admiral .... HORATIO
victory scene ...... TRAFALGAR
"Nelson's blood" .... RUM, GROG
nelumbo .... LOTUS
nemathelminth .... (HOOK)WORM
nematode .... ASCARID, PINWORM,
(HOOK)WORM, ROUNDWORM
nembutal .... HYPNOTIC, SEDATIVE
nemesis .... BANE, CURSE,
PLAGUE, AVENGER, GODDESS
Nitti's .... NESS
neon .... LIGHT
neophyte .... TYRO, NOVICE,
AMATEUR, CONVERT,
TRAINEE, BEGINNER
Neopolitan secret society
.... CAMORRA
neoteric .... NEW, MODERN,
RECENT
Nepal capital .... KAT(H)MANDU
city/town .... JUMLA,
MUSTANG, PYUTHAN,
SALLYAN, LALITPUR,
BHAKTAPUR
coin .... MOHAR
inhabitant .... KHA, MAGAR,
NEWAR, GURKHA, GURUNG
king .... PRITHWI, BIRENDRA,
MAHENDRA
language .... THARU, NEPALI,
BHUTIA, NEWARI
monetary unit .... RUPEE
Mongoloid .... LAI, RAIS
mountain .... LHOTSE,
EVEREST, ANNAPURNA
mountaineers .... SHERPAS
neighbor .... CHINA, INDIA,
TIBET
panda .... WAH
peak .... API
people .... GURKHA
premier .... KOIRALA
river .... BHERI
sect .... ACHAR(A)
warrior .... GURKHA, RAJPUT
wild goat .... TAHR
Nephele, daughter of ...... HELLE
nephrite .... JADE
nephritic .... RENAL
nepotism .... FAVORITISM
beneficiary of .... RELATIVE
subject of .... EMPLOYMENT
nepotists, first .... PRELATES
beneficiaries .... NEPHEWS
Neptune .... LER, PLANET,

discoverer of .... GALLE
scepter of .... TRIDENT
son of .... TRITON
nerd .... DRIP
nereid .... THETIS, (SEA)NYMPH,
AMPHITRITE
Nereus' daughter .... NEREID,
THETIS
wife .... DORIS
Nero .... DESPOT, EMPEROR
band leader .... PETER
mother of .... AGRIPPINA
start of his reign LIV
teacher of .... SENECA
wife of ..... OCTAVIA, POPPAEA
Wolfe's creator .... STOUT
neroli .... OIL
nerve .... GRIT, PLUCK, SINEW,
TENDON, COURAGE,
BOLDNESS, TEMERITY
cell .... NEURON(E)
cell branch .... DENDRON
cell process .... AXON,
NEURITE, DENDRITE
colloquial .... FACE, GALL,
GUTS, BRASS, CHEEK, CRUST,
AUDACITY
combining form .... NEUR(O)
fiber, sheath of .... MYELIN
fibers, bundle of .... TRACT,
PEDUNCLE
inflammation .... NEURITIS
injury .... NEURAPRAXIA
layer .... ALVEUS
network .... RETE, RETIA
of a .... NEURAL
pain .... NEURALGIA
passage for .... HILUM
sensory .... AFFERENT,
EFFERENT
substance .... ALBA
tonic .... NERVINE, SEDATIVE
(w)racking .... TRYING,
JARRING
nerves ...... FIT, JITTERS, HYSTERIA
network of .... PLEXUS
pertaining to .... NEURO,
NEURAL, NERVINE
nervous .... EDGY, TENSE,
FEARFUL, JITTERY, SKITTISH,
TIMOROUS
condition .... NEURALGIA
disease .... NEURITIS,
TARANTISM
disorder .... TIC, CHOREA,
NEUROSIS, PARALYSIS
feeling .... JIMJAMS, JITTERS
seizure .... PANIC, FRENZY,
ANEURIA, JITTERS, EPILEPSY
state .... TIZZY

strain .... TENSION
twitch .... TIC
nervy .... BOLD, BRASH, GUTSY
nescient .... AGNOSTIC, IGNORANT,
INNOCENT
ness .... CAPE, HEADLAND
Nessus .... CENTAUR
slayer of .... HERCULES
nest .... DEN, NIDE, HAUNT, NIDUS,
RESORT, RETREAT
ant's ..... ANTHILL, FORMICARY
bird of prey's/eagle's
...... AERY, EYRY, AERIE, EYRIE
build a .... NIDIFY
egg .... MONEY, SAVINGS
mare's .... HOAX
of eggs .... CLUTCH
on a cliff .... EYRIE
nested boxes .... INRO
nestle .... CUDDLE, NUZZLE,
SETTLE, SHELTER, SNUGGLE
nestling .... EYAS, OWLET, POULT,
SQUAB, EAGLET
noise of .... CHIRP
Nestor .... SAGE, WISE MAN,
COUNSELOR
relative of .... SOLOMON
net ...... GIN, GAIN, MESH, CLEAR,
FILET, TULLE, (EN)TRAP,
SAGENE, BALANCE,
(EN)SNARE, RETICLE, LEFT-
OVER
fishing .... SEINE, TRAWL,
TRAMMEL
like a .... RETIFORM
making of .... RETIARY
ornamental .... FRET
silk .... MALINE(S)
trapping .... TOIL
nether ...... DOWN, LOWER, UNDER
world .... HELL, HADES
world deity .... DIS, CORA,
KORE, LOKI, MINOS, ORCUS,
CHARON
Netherlands. See also **Dutch**
.... HOLLAND
anatomist .... RAU
Antilles capital
.... WILLEMSTAD
Antilles island .... SABA,
ARUBA, BONAIRE, CURACAO
bay .... DOLLARD
canal .... ORANGE, WILLEMS
capital .... AMSTERDAM, THE
HAGUE
cheese market .... EDAM
city/town .... EDE, BREDA,
DELFT, EMMEN, GOUDA,
VENLO, ZEIST, ARNHEM,
LEIDEN, ZWOLLE, HAARLEM,
TILBURG, UTRECHT, ZAANDAM,

FLUSHING, NIJMEGEN,
APELDOORN, DORDRECHT,
EINDHOVEN, GRONINGEN,
HILVERSUM, ROTTERDAM
coin .... RYDER, GULDEN,
GUILDER
colonist .... BOER
commune .... EDE, EPE
cupboard .... KAS
duchy .... BRABANT
fair/carnival .... KERMIS,
KERMESS
island .... TEXEI GOEREE,
GRIEND, MARKEN, VOORNE,
AMELAND
lake .... IJSSELMEER,
SLOTERMEER
language .... DUTCH
measure ...... ROEDE, MORGEN,
STREEP
monetary unit .... GUILDER
mountain .... VAALSERBERG
premier .... (DE)JONG,
ZIJLSTRA
province .... DRENTHE,
LIMBURG, UTRECHT, ZEELAND,
FLEVOLAND, FRIESLAND,
GRONINGEN, GELDERLAND
queen of .... JULIANA,
WILHELMINA
queen's consort .... BERNHARD
river .... LEK, EEMS, MAAS,
MARK, ROER, WAAL, HUNSE,
IJSSEL, MEUSE, REGGE, RHINE,
VECHT, DOMMEL
ruling family .... NASSAU
seaport .... ROTTERDAM
tulip center .... HAARLEM
weight .... ONS, WIGT(JE)
youth gangs .... PROVOS
nethermost .... LOWEST
nettle .... BUG, VEX, WEED,
ANNOY, STING, RUFFLE,
IRRITATE
Latin .... URTICA
plant .... RAMEE, RAMIE
rash .... HIVES, UREDO,
URTICARIA
sting .... URTICATE
network .... WEB, LACE, MAZE,
MESH, RETE, RETIA, HOOKUP,
PLEXUS, TISSUE, LATTICE,
NETTING, TRELLIS
neuralgic pain .... HEMIALGIA
neurasthenia .... NEUROSIS,
MELANCHOLIA
neuron, part of .... AXON,
DENDRITE
type of .... MOTO, INTER,
SENSORY

POSEIDON

neurons' contact point
.... SYNAPSE
neurotic .... NEURAL, PSYCHIC
disorder .... ANXIETY,
DEPRESSION
neuter .... GENDER, ASEXUAL
verbal nown .... GERUND
neutral .... ALOOF, MUGWUMP,
INDIFFERENT, NONPARTISAN
ground .... FENCE
neutralize .... ANNUL, CANCEL,
NEGATE, OFFSET, NULLIFY,
COUNTERACT
magnetic field .... DEGAUSS
Nevada capital ...... CARSON CITY
city/town .... ELY, ELKO,
RENO, SPARKS, LAS VEGAS,
LOVELOCK, BOULDER CITY,
HENDERSON, SUNRISE MANOR,
PARADISE VALLEY
county .... NYE, ELKO, LYON,
CLARK, WASHOE, DOUGLAS,
ESMERALDA, CARSON CITY
dam .... DAVIS, HOOVER
desert ..... TULE, BLACK ROCK,
SMOKE CREEK
desert event .... A-TEST
Indian .... PAIUTE
lake ...... MEAD, RUBY, TAHOE,
CARSON, MOHAVE, MASSACRE
mountain .... BIG, LONE,
CEDAR, TABLE, BERLIN,
POTOSI, TIMBER
mountain range .... BUTTE,
MUDDY, SNAKE, MORMON,
VIRGIN
peak .... PIPER, VIRGIN,
BOUNDARY
river ..... KINGS, QUINN, REESE,
WHITE, OWYHEE, TRUCKEE
state bird .... BLUEBIRD
state flower .... SAGEBRUSH
state nickname .... SILVER,
SAGEBRUSH
state tree .... PINON
tourist attraction .... RENO,
TAHOE, LAS VEGAS, HOOVER
DAM
U.S. Air Force Base
.... NELLIS
valley .... SPRING, CRESCENT,
BIG SMOKY, LITTLE SMOKY
neve .... ICE, FIRN, SNOW
never ...... NOT EVER, AT NO TIME
ending .... ETERNAL
mind! .... SKIP IT
say die .... GO FOR BROKE
nevertheless ..... BUT, YET, STILL,
ANYHOW, ANYWAY, HOWEVER
Nevin's song .... ROSARY,
NARCISSUS

nevus .... MOLE, FRECKLE,
LENTIGO, BIRTHMARK
main type of .... VASCULAR,
MELANOCYTIC
new .... RAW, CENE, LATE, FRESH,
GREEN, NOVEL, YOUNG,
MODERN, RECENT, UNUSED,
CURRENT, FOREIGN, STRANGE,
NEO(TERIC)
deal .... RETRADE
combining form .... NEO
New Britain city .... RABAUL
Caledonia capital ..... NOUMEA
Deal agency .... NRA, TVA
Deal president .... FDR,
ROOSEVELT
England boat .... SHARPIE
England state .... MAINE,
VERMONT, CONNECTICUT,
RHODE ISLAND,
MASSACHUSETTS, NEW
HAMPSHIRE
Englander .... YANK(EE),
DOWN EASTER
Guinea .... PAPUA
bay .... MILNE
brain disease .... KURU
capital .... PORT MORESBY
city/town .... LAE, WEWAK,
GOROKA, MADANG
gulf .... HUON
hog .... BENE
island .... ARU, LONG,
KARKAR, MISIMA, ROSSEL,
TAGULA, WOODLARK
lodge .... YEU
monetary unit .... KINA
native .... ASMAT, KARON,
PAPUAN
pole .... BIS
port .... LAE, DARU
river .... FLY, RAMU, SEPIK
strait .... TORRES, DAMPIER
Hampshire
capital .... CONCORD
city/town .... DERRY, DOVER,
KEENE, SALEM, BERLIN,
DURHAM, EXETER, HUDSON,
NASHUA, PELHAM, TILTON,
AMHERST, HAMPTON,
LACONIA, ROCHESTER,
MANCHESTER, PORTSMOUTH,
LONDONDERRY
county .... COOS, BELKNAP,
GRAFTON, MERRIMACK,
STRAFFORD
dam .... MOORE, WILDER,
EVERETT
island .... WHITE
lake .... BOW, CONWAY,
MASCOMA, OSSIPEE,

SUNAPEE, NUBANUSIT
mountain .... TOM, BLUE,
BOND, CUBE, LONG, RICE,
ADAMS, CABOT, CANNON,
SANDWICH, WHITEFACE
river .... MAD, COLD, GALE,
PINE, SACO, BAKER, ELLIS,
SUGAR
state bird ...... PURPLE FINCH
state college .... KEENE,
PLYMOUTH
state flower .... PURPLE
LILAC
state nickname ...... GRANITE
U.S. Air Force Base
.... PEASE
Haven blue .... YALE
Hebrides
capital .... VILA
island .... TANA
Jersey bay .... NEWARK,
RARITAN, BARNEGAT,
DELAWARE
cape .... MAY
capital .... TRENTON
city/town .... LODI, WALL,
BRICK, UNION, CAMDEN,
EDISON, HAZLET, JERSEY,
LINDEN, LEONIA, NEWARK,
NUTLEY, ORANGE, RAHWAY,
BAYONNE, HOBOKEN,
PARAMUS, PASSAIC,
TEANECK, WYCKOFF,
GARFIELD, ATLANTIC,
PATERSON, ELIZABETH,
LAKEHURST, HACKENSACK,
MONTCLAIR, LIVINGSTON,
RUTHERFORD
college .... CALDWELL,
FELICIAN, DON BOSCO
colonizer .... PATROON
county .... ESSEX, OCEAN,
SALEM, UNION, BERGEN,
CAMDEN, HUDSON, MERCER,
MORRIS, SUSSEX, PASSAIC,
ATLANTIC, SOMERSET,
CUMBERLAND
island .... LONG BEACH
lake .... BUDD, ECHO, UNION,
MOHAWK, OWASSA, TAPPAN,
CULVERS, POMPTON,
WAWAYANDA
mountain .... HIGH POINT
resort .... LONG BRANCH
river .... TOMS, SALEM,
HUDSON, OSWEGO, RAMAPO,
SADDLE, MULLICA, PASSAIC,
PEQUEST, RARITAN,
COHANSEY, DELAWARE,
NAVESINK, TUCKAHOE
state bird .... GOLDFINCH

state college ..... MONTCLAIR
state flower .... BOGBICE
VIOLET
state nickname ...... GARDEN
tourist site .... LIBERTY
VILLAGE, WATERLOO
VILLAGE, ATLANTIC CITY
BOARDWALK
university .... DREW,
PRINCETON
Mexico
artists' colony .... TAOS
canyon ..... CHACO, CHIVATO
capital .... SANTA FE
caverns .... CARLSBAD
city/town .... TAOS, ZUNI,
HOBBS, RATON, CLOVIS,
SILVER, ROSWELL, SOCORRO,
CARLSBAD, LAS CRUCES,
FARMINGTON, ALAMOGORDO,
ALBUQUERQUE
colonizer .... ONATE
county .... LEA, EDDY, TAOS,
CURRY, OTERO, CHAVES,
DONA ANA, SAN JUAN,
SANDOVAL, VALENCIA, LOS
ALAMOS, BERNALILLO
Indian .... SIA, UTE, PIRO,
TANO, TEWA, ZUNI, APACHE,
NAVAHO, NAVAJO, PUEBLO,
MESCALERO
Indian pueblo .... ACOMA
lake .... SALT, SUMNER,
BOULDER, CONCHAS, RED
BLUFF
mountain .... BLACK,
GROUSE, TAYLOR, WHEELER
resort .... TAOS
river ..... GILA, ZUNI, CHACO,
PECOS, ANIMAS, PUERCO,
CIMARRON, RIO GRANDE
state bird .... ROADRUNNER
state flower .... YUCCA
state nickname
.... SUNSHINE, LAND OF
ENCHANTMENT
state tree .... PINON
university .... HIGHLANDS
Orleans
festival .... MARDI GRAS
institution .... TULANE
music .... RAGTIME
native .... CREOLE
nickname of .... CRESCENT
CITY
pro .... SAINT
South Wales capital
.... SYDNEY
Testament book .... ACTS,
JOHN, JUDE, LUKE, JAMES,
MARK, PETER, TITUS, ROMANS,

MATTHEW, TIMOTHY,
EPHESIANS, REVELATION
gospel .... JOHN, LUKE,
MARK, MATTHEW
hell .... GEHENNA
in Syriac .... PESHITO
language of .... GREEK,
KOINE
longest book in the ..... LUKE
measure of capacity
.... COR, POT, BATH, SEAH,
QUART, BUSHEL
measure of length ..... MILE,
CUBIT, FATHOM, FURLONG
middle book in the
.... THESSALONIANS
oldest complete copy of
the .... CODEX SINAITICUS
shortest book in the .... JOHN
weight .... MINA, LIBRA,
TALENT
Year's Day sight .... FLOATS
York
bay ..... PECONIC, GARDINERS
capital .... ALBANY
city/town .... ROME, TROY,
OLEAN, UTICA, AUBURN,
CARMEL, ELMIRA, ITHACA,
NASSAU, ONEIDA, OSWEGO,
BUFFALO, YONKERS, DEER
PARK, LOCKPORT, OSSINING,
SYRACUSE, JAMESTOWN,
NEW YORK, OCEANSIDE,
ROCHESTER, BINGHAMTON,
GLENS FALLS, HICKSVILLE,
MOUNT VERNON, NEW
ROCHELLE, WHITE PLAINS
college .... BARD, IONA,
VASSAR, DOWLING,
LADYCLIFF, MARYMOUNT
college town .... ITHACA
colonizer .... PATROON
county .... ERIE, BRONX,
ESSEX, KINGS, TIOGA,
YATES, ALBANY, GREENE,
MONROE, NASSAU, ONEIDA,
ORANGE, OSWEGO, QUEENS,
ULSTER, NEW YORK,
STEUBEN, SUFFOLK,
ONONDAGA, SARATOGA,
WESTCHESTER
creek .... CONEWANGO
division .... BORO(UGH)
falls .... NIAGARA
fictitious name .... JUKES
Indian .... ERIE, CAYUGA,
ONEIDA, SENECA
Institute .... PRATT
Institute of Technology
.... ROCHESTER
island .... LONG, PLUM,

ELLIS, GRAND, STONY,
GALLOO, STATEN, FISHERS,
SHELTER, VALCOUR,
GARDINERS, GRENADIER,
MANHATTAN
islands .... THOUSAND
lake .... ERIE, LILA, BRANT,
TITUS, CAYUGA, ONEIDA,
KEUKA, PLACID, SENECA,
SILVER, TUPPER, HEMLOCK,
ONTARIO, SARANAC,
SARATOGA, CHAMPLAIN,
BONAPARTE
Military Academy/post
.... WEST POINT
motto .... EXCELSIOR, EVER
UPWARD
mountain ..... MARCY, SLIDE,
HUNTER, HAYSTACK,
SKYLIGHT, WHITEFISH
mountains .... CATSKILL,
ADIRONDACK
newspaper .... TIMES
newspaper founder
.... GREELEY
old name .... NEW ORANGE
planetarium .... HAYDEN
repertory company ...... APA
reservoir .... KENSICO
resort .... LAKE PLACID
river .... DEER, BLACK,
GRASS, MOOSE, BEAVER,
HUDSON, MOHAWK, OSWEGO,
SALMON, SENECA, GENESEE,
NIAGARA, SARANAC,
CHENANGO, COHOCTON,
DELAWARE, UNADILLA,
WALLKILL
state bird .... BLUEBIRD
state flower .... ROSE
state nickname .... EMPIRE
state penitentiary .... SING
SING
team .... JETS, METS, GIANTS,
KNICKS, YANKEES
time zone .... EST
tourist attraction ...... BRONX
ZOO, WALL STREET, TIMES
SQUARE, NIAGARA FALLS,
STATUE OF LIBERTY, EMPIRE
STATE BUILDING
university .... ADELPHI,
CORNELL, FORDHAM,
HOFSTRA, COLUMBIA,
ROCHESTER, ROCKEFELLER
village .... NYACK,
GREENWICH
New York City borough
.... BRONX, QUEENS,
BROOKLYN, STATEN ISLAND,
MANHATTAN

modernism showplace of .... MOMA, MUSEUM OF MODERN ART
nickname .... THE BIG APPLE
political machine .... TAMMANY
prison .... TOMBS
section .... HARLEM
street .... BOWERY
subway .... BMT, IND, IRT
New Yorker .... GOTHAMITE, MANHATTANITE, KNICKERBOCKER
cartoonist .... STEIG
New Zealand aborigine .... MAORI
author .... MARSH
bay .... BREAM, HAWKE, CLOUDY, GOLDEN, TASMAN
bird ..... MOA, TUI, KIWI, MIRO, PEHO, RURU, WEKA, LOWAN, APTERYX, MOREPORK, NOTORNIS
cape .... BRETT, EGMONT, REINGA, FAREWELL, KIDNAPPERS
capital .... WELLINGTON
caterpillar .... WERI, AWETO
cattail .... RAUPO
city/town ..... NAPIER, NELSON, DUNEDIN, ROTORUA, AUCKLAND, HASTINGS, TAKAPUNA, TAURANGA, WANGANUI, WHANGAREL
corn .... KANGA
demon .... TAIPO
discoverer .... TASMAN
explorer .... COOK
extinct bird .... MOA
firth .... THAMES
fish .... IHI, HIKU
gorge .... OTIRA
gulf .... HAURAKI
harbor .... OTAGO, KAIPARA, MANUKAU
hen .... WEKAS
island .... PITT, RUAPUKE, STEWART, WAIHEKE
islands .... CHATHAM, MERCURY
lake .... TAUPO, PUKAKI, TEKAPO, WANAKA, ROTORUA, WAKATIPU
language ...... MAORI, ENGLISH
locust .... WETA
mollusk .... PIPI
monetary unit .... DOLLAR
morepork .... PEHO, RURU
mountain .... UNA, COOK, OWEN, EGMONT, TASMAN, WHITCOMBE

mountain climber .... HILLARY
mulberry .... AUTE
native .... M(A)ORI
owl .... RURU
palm .... NIKAU
parrot .... KEA, KAKA, KAKAPO
peninsula .... BANKS, MAHIA, OTAGO, COROMANDEL
pigeon .... KUKU
pine ...... RIMU, KAURI, KAURY
plant .... KARO
prime minister .... KIRK, BOLGER, COATES, WHITLAM
raft .... MOKI
river .... HUTT, WAIPA, BULLER, CLUTHA, RAKAIA, WAIRAU, WAIKATO
sandalwood .... MAIRE
seaport .... AUCKLAND, WELLINGTON
shark .... MAKO
shrub .... KARO, TUTU, RAMARAMA
smelt .... INANGA
soldier .... ANZAC
strait .... COOK, FOVEAAUX
tree .... AKE, AUTE, GOAI, KOPI, MIRO, PUKA, PELU, RATA, TORU, WHAU, HINO(U), HINAU, MAIRE, NAPAU, TARATA, TATARA, TOTARA, KAIKAKA
tribe .... RINGATU
vine .... AKA
volcano .... RUAPEHU
wages .... UTU
war club .... MERI
weapon .... PATU
wild hog .... BENE
wineberry .... MAKO
wood hen .... WEKA
newborn .... INFANT, NEONATE, YEANLING
Newcastle product .... COAL
river .... TYNE
newcomer .... ROOKIE, STRANGER, GREENHORN, TENDERFOOT
flock .... KID, LAMB
in January .... YEAR
newel .... POST
Newfoundland airport .... GANDER
bay ...... HARE, BONNE, SHOAL, CANADA, ESPOIR, SAGLEK, HOLYROOD, BONAVISTA
cape .... RAY, PINE, RACE, BAULD, CHIDLEY, ANGUILLE, TERRITOK
capital .... ST. JOHN'S
city/town .... GANDER, WABANA, KILBRIDE,

LABRADOR, CARBONEAR, GRAND FALLS, MOUNT PEARL, CORNER BROOK
cod-fisher .... BANKER
falls .... CHURCHILL
fishing grounds .... BANKS
floating ice .... GROWLER
Indian .... MICMAC
island .... RED, BELL, FOGO, GLOVER, GROAIS
lake ...... DYKE, LONG, GRAND, MEALY, GANDER, VICTORIA
mountain .... CIRQUE, THORESBY, GROS MORNE
mountains .... TORNGAT, KAUMAJET
national park ..... TERRA NOVA
peninsula .... AVALON
river .... EAGLE, GOOSE, ALEXIS, BRANCH, PINWARE, SALMONIER
sea .... LABRADOR
seal hunter .... SWILER
strait .... CABOT, BELLE ISLE
tea .... SWITCHEL
newfangled .... BRAND-NEW
newly .... AFRESH
newlywed .... BRIDE(GROOM), BENEDICT, HONEYMOONER
serenade to .... SHIVAREE
newness .... NOVELTY
news ...... WORD, ADVICE, REPORT, TIDINGS, INFORMATION
agency .... AP, INS, UPI, JIJI, TASS, ANETA, DOMEI, HAVAS, KYODO, CETEKA, REUTERS, WIRE SERVICE
aid .... NOSE
beat .... SCOOP
bit .... ITEM
commentator .... KALB, DOWNS, SHAW, BROKAW, DUNPHY, KOPPEL, RATHER, HUNTLEY, BRINKLEY, CRONKITE, JENNINGS, LAWRENCE
flash/brief .... ITEM
item .... OBIT, REPORT
last minute ..... BREAK, FLASH, FUDGE
medium .... RADIO, RUMOR, GOSSIP, BULLETIN, GRAPEVINE
report .... FLASH, BULLETIN
source .... PIPELINE
summary .... WRAP-UP
newsboy's territory .... ROUTE
wheels .... BIKE
newscast .... TELECAST, BROADCAST
newsletter .... BULLETIN, CIRCULAR

newsman .... ANCHOR, SCRIBE, REPORTER, JOURNALIST
newsmonger .... GOSSIP, TATTLER
newspaper .... DAILY, SHEET, WEEKLY, GAZETTE, JOURNAL, TABLOID
bit .... ITEM, FILLER
columnist .... CAEN, ALSOP, RESTON, WINCHELL
extra leaf .... INSERT
facing pages .... SPREAD
feature .... ESSAY, SCOOP, COLUMN, COMICS, ARTICLE, SPORTS, HEADLINE, EDITORIAL, ROTO(GRAVURE), CROSSWORD PUZZLE
headline .... BANNER, STREAMER
item .... FILLER
issue .... EXTRA, EDITION, STARFINAL
makeup ...... FORMAT, LAYOUT
name, for short .... TRIB
notice .... OBIT
official ..... EDITOR, REDACTOR
page insert .... FUDGE
paid circulation .... SUBSCRIPTION
section ..... ROTO, SUPPLEMENT
slang .... RAG
VIP .... EDITOR
work .... JOURNALISM
Newspaper Days author
.... MENCKEN
newspaperman ...... CUB, SCRIBE, PRESSMAN, REPORTER, COLUMNIST, INKSLINGER, JOURNALIST
archaic .... GAZETTEER
feat of .... BEAT, SCOOP
report of .... COPY, STORY, DISPATCH
reporting from a distant place .... CORRESPONDENT
source of .... CONTACT, INFORMER, PIPELINE
territory of .... BEAT
newspapers and networks
.... MEDIA
in general .... PRESS
newsprint .... PAPER
roll of .... WEB
newsstand .... KIOSK
newt .... EFT, SWIFT, TRITON, SALAMANDER
Newton, mathematician
.... ISAAC
next .... THEN, AFTER, LATER, BESIDE, ENSUING, NEAREST
best thing to a strike
.... SPARE

door resident .... NEIGHBOR
in musical directions .... POI
to last .... PENULT(IMATE)
year's alumni .... SENIORS
nexus ...... TIE, LINK, CONNECTION
Ney, Marshal .... MICHEL
Nez Perce .... INDIAN
Niagara .... FALLS
falls .... HORSESHOE
greatest drawing card of
.... BLONDIN ROPEWALK
or a range .... CASCADE
nib .... END, BEAK, BILL, POINT, PRONG
nibble .... BIT, EAT, NIP, BITE, CHEW, GNAW, KNAP, PECK, SNACK, BROWSE, MORSEL
Nibelung .... DWARFS
guard .... FAFNIR
leader .... ALBERICH
Nibelungenlied king .... ETZEL
knight .... HILDEBRAND
niblick .... IRON, (GOLF)CLUB
Nicaragua bay .... SALINAS
capital .... MANAGUA
cays .... KING, TYRA, PEARL
city/town .... LEON, RIVAS, ESTELL, MASAYA, GRANADA, JINOTEPE, CHINANDEGA
coin .... CENTAVO, CORDOBA
gulf .... FONSECA
island .... OMETEPE, ZAPATERA, GREAT CORN, LITTLE CORN
lake .... MANAGUA
language .... SPANISH
measure ...... SUERTE, ESTAJAL
monetary unit .... CORDOBA
mountain .... MOCOTON
mountains .... HUAPI
point .... GORDA, MONKEY
president .... ORTEGA, SAMOZA, CHAMORRO
river ...... COCO, TUMA, WAWA, GRANDE, WASPUK, SAN JUAN, KUKALAYA, ESCONDIDO
nice .... FINE, NEAT, DAINTY, PRETTY, PROPER, FINICAL, REFINED, DELICATE, PLEASING
discernment .... ACUMEN, INSIGHT
figure .... SVELTE, LISSOM(E)
guy .... TRUMP
Nelly .... PRIG, PRUDE
nicely .... KINDLY, ROYALLY
nicety .... AMENITY, DELICACY, SUBTLETY
niche .... APSE, NOOK, SLOT, AMBRY, ALCOVE, CORNER, RECESS, TABERNACLE
nick .... CUT, JAG, CHIP, DENT, CHEAT, GOUGE, NOTCH,

SCORE, TALLY, ARREST
Nick, actor .... ADAMS, NOLTE
Charles's dog .... ASTA
Old .... DEVIL, SATAN
the detective .... CARTER
nickel .... COIN, FIVE CENTS
alloy .... INVAR
like metal .... MONEL
slang .... JITNEY
nickname .... AGNAME, AGNOMEN, COGNOMEN, MONI(C)KER, DIMINUTIVE, SO(U)BRIQUET
Amelia Earhart's .... LADY LINDY
Attila the Hun's
.... FLAGELLUM DEI
Belle Starr's .... BANDIT QUEEN
Casal's .... ROSIE
Charles Lindbergh's
.... LUCKY LINDY
city of witches .... SALEM
feminine/masculine .... LOU
for Detroit .... MOTOWN
General Arnold's .... HAP
General Schwarzkopf's
.... STORMIN' NORMAN
Joan of Arc's .... MAID OF ORLEANS
Joan of Arc of the Confederacy .... BELLE BOYD
Martha Jane Canary's
.... CALAMITY JANE
Martin's .... DINO
Mrs. Lyndon B. Johnson's
.... LADY BIRD
Mrs. James Madison
.... DOLLEY
Mrs. Rutherford B. Hayes
.... LEMONADE LUCY
of Edward Teach
.... BLACKBEARD
of the Beatles .... THE FAB FOUR
of U.S. President
Eisenhower, Dwight ..... IKE
Garfield, James .... THE PREACHER
Harrison, Benjamin
.... LITTLE BEN
Jackson, Andrew .... OLD HICKORY
Jefferson, Thomas ..... LONG TOM
Lincoln, Abraham .... OLD ABE
Roosevelt, Franklin ..... NEW DEALER

Roosevelt, Theodore .... TEDDY BEAR, ROUGH RIDER
Taylor, Zachary .... OLD ROUGH-AND-READY
Washington, George .... OLD FOX
Wilson, Woodrow .... WOODY
Thomas J. Jackson's .... STONEWALL JACKSON
Wizard of Menlo Park .... EDISON
Nicosia is capital of ...... CYPRUS
nicotine .... TAR
acid .... NIACIN
nictate/nictitate ...... WINK, BLINK
nide/nidus .... NEST
Niemen .... MEMEL, NEMAN
river .... RUSS
Nietzsche .... FRIEDRICH
nieve .... FIST, HAND
nifty .... SMART, STYLISH
Niger capital .... NIAMEY
city/town .... GAYA, TERA, AGADES, ILLELA, TAHOUA, ZINDER
desert .... SAHARA, TENERE
lake .... CHAD
language ...... HAUSA, DJERMA, FULANI, SONGHAI
monetary unit .... FRANC
mountain .... BANGUEZANE
people .... IJO, PEUL, HAUSA, TOUAREG
president .... DIORI
river mouth .... NUN
Nigerian capital .... LAGOS
city/town .... ABA, ADO, EDE, IFE, IWO, OYO, KANO, BENIN, ENUGU, ZARIA, IBADAN, ILESHA, ILORIN, ISEYIN, KADUNA, CALABAR, KATSINA, ONITSHA, OSHOGBO, ABEOKUTA, OGBOMOSHO
gulf .... GUINEA
island .... FOGE
king of Asaba .... (JOSEPH)EDOZIEN
lake .... CHAD
language .... EDO, IBO, TIV, HAUSA, FULANI, KANURI, YORUBA
monetary unit .... NAIRA
mountain .... DIMLANG
native .... ARO, EDO, IBO, BENI(N), HAUS(S)A
region .... SUDAN
river ...... OSSE, BENUE, CROSS, DONGA, KEBBI, NIGER, KADUNA, SOKOTO

seaport .... BONNY, LAGOS
state .... IMO, OYO, KANO, OGUN, ONDO, BENUE, BORNO, KUARA, LAGOS, NIGER, BAUCHI, BENDEL, KADUNA, RIVERS, SOKOTO, ANAMBRA, GONGOLA
tribal chief .... OBA
tribe .... ARO, EDO, IBO, BINI, EBOE, EKOI, BENIN, HAUSA, FULANI, YORUBA
niggard .... CHURL, MISER, STINGY, SKINFLINT
niggardly .... FEW, MEAGER, SCANTY, MISERLY, STINGILY
night .... EVENING, DARK(NESS), EVENTIDE
attack .... CAMISADO
bash .... SOIREE
before .... EVE
clothes .... NIGHTY, NIGHTIE, PAJAMAS
club .... BOITE, BISTRO, CABARET, ROADHOUSE
combining form .... NOCT(I)
flyer .... BAT, OWL, MOTH, FIREFLY
letter .... TELEGRAM
lights .... NEONS
noise-maker .... ALLEYCAT
nuisance .... SNORER
of the .... NOCTURNAL
nightcap .... DRINK
nightfall .... DUSK
occurring at .... ACRONICAL, ACRONYCAL
nighthawk .... BULLBAT, GOATSUCKER
nightingale ...... BULBUL, THRUSH, PHILOMEL, SONGBIRD
note of .... JUG
so-called .... (JENNY)LIND
nightjar .... BIRD, POTOO, GOATSUCKER
nightmare .... DREAM, INCUBUS
demon .... MARA
kicker's .... BLOCKED
nightrider .... TERRORIST, VIGILANTE
nightshade .... MOREL, MORIL, PLANT, DATURA, HENBANE, PETUNIA, SOLANUM, MANDRAKE, BELLADONNA
nightstick .... CLUB, BILLY, TRUNCHEON
user .... COP, POLICE(MAN)
nightwalk .... PROWL, TIPPYTOE
nightwalker .... THIEF, NOCTAMBULIST
nihil .... NOTHING
nihilist .... CYNIC, PESSIMIST

Nihon .... JAPAN
Nike .... ATHENA, VICTORIA
nil .... NULL, ZILCH, NOTHING
Nile .... HAPI, NILUS
bird .... IBIS
boat .... BARIS, DAHABEAH
catfish .... BAGRE
city ...... SAIS, ASWAN, MEROE, TANIS, TANTA, THEBES, KHARTOUM, OMDURMAN
dam .... ASWAN
feature .... DELTA
feeder of Blue .... (LAKE)TANA
feeder of White .... (LAKE)VICTORIA
goddess .... ISIS
has one .... DELTA
island .... RODA
native .... NILOT
negro .... JUR, SUK
of the .... NILOTIC
plant .... PAPYRUS
queen .... CLEO(PATRA)
reeds/weeds .... SUDD
sailboat .... CANGIA
ship's captain .... RAIS, REIS
source of .... T(S)ANA, BLUE NILE, WHITE NILE
town .... LUXOR, ROSETTA
village on the .... KARNAK
Nilgiri .... TEA, BADAGA
nim .... STEAL
nimble .... YAR, DEFT, SPRY, AGILE, ALERT, LIGHT, QUICK, ADROIT, LIVELY, VOLANT, LISSOM(E)
nimbus ...... AURA, HALO, CLOUD, GLORIA, AUREOLA
nimiety .... EXCESS, PLEONASM
Nimitz, admiral .... CHESTER
Nimrod .... HUNTER
city of .... ACCAD
parent of .... CUSH
nincompoop .... DOLT, FOOL, IDIOT, NITWIT, SOFTHEAD, SIMPLETON
nine: comb. form .... ENNE
days' devotion .... NOVENA
group of .... ENNEAD
"ladies" .... MUSES
number .... ENNEA
part opus .... NONET
sided plane .... NONAGON, ENNEAGON
team of .... BASEBALL
ninefold .... NENARY
ninepins .... GAME, SKITTLE
ninesome .... NONET
nineteen XIX
nineteenth hole: colloq. .... BAR,

CLUBHOUSE, LOCKER ROOM
Nineveh founder .... NINUS
ninny .... ASS, DOLT, FOOL,
DUNCE, IDIOT, SIMPLETON
ninnyhammer .... ASS
ninth day before ides .... NONES
Ninus .... NINEVEH
Niobe, brother of .... PELOPS
fate of .... STONE
father of .... TANTALUS
husband of .... AMPHION
Niobean .... WEEPY, WEEPING
nip .... CUT, SIP, BITE, DRAM,
PECK, DRINK, PINCH, SEVER,
BLIGHT, SHORTEN
and tuck .... CLOSE, NECK AND
NECK
in the bud .... CHECK
slang .... CATCH, STEAL,
JAPANESE
nipa .... PALM, AT(T)AP
liquor .... TUBA
nipper .... CLAW, PLIERS,
FORCEPS, PINCERS, TWEEZERS
nippers .... HANDCUFFS, LEG
IRONS
Nipper's co. .... RCA
nipping .... SHARP, BITING
nipple .... DUG, PAP, TIT, TEAT,
PAPILLA, MAMMILLA
abnormal .... INVERTED
baby's toy .... PACIFIER
benign swelling of the
.... PAPILLOMA
disorder .... CYST, CANCER,
MASTITIS
inflammation .... THELITIS
shaped like a .... MASTOID
Nippon .... JAPAN
nippy ...... SHARP, BITING, NIMBLE
nirvana .... BLISS, HEAVEN,
OBLIVION
nis .... KOBOLD
Nishapur's famous son
.... OMAR(KHAYYAM)
nisi .... UNLESS
Nissen hut .... PREFAB
nit .... EGG, LOUSE, INSECT
niter .... SALT, NITRATE,
SALTPETER
nitid .... SHINY
niton .... RADON
nitpick .... CAVIL, QUIBBLE
nitpicker .... FAULT-FINDER
nitrate .... SALT, ESTER, NITER,
SALTPETER, FERTILIZER
drugs .... VASODILATOR
nitric .... AZOTIC
acid .... AQUA FORTIS
nitrogen .... AZOTE, NONMETAL
atmospheric .... GAS

containing .... AZO(TIC)
describing atmospheric
.... ODORLESS, COLORLESS
nitroglycerin(e) .... TNT,
CORDITE, MELINITE,
GLONOIN(E)
nitrous oxide ...... LAUGHING GAS
nitty-gritty .... BRASS TACKS
nitwit ...... FOOL, BOOB(Y), IDIOT,
MORON, DIMWIT, JACKASS,
LAMEBRAIN
Niven, actor .... DAVID
niveous .... SNOWY, SNOWLIKE
nix(ie) .... FAIRY, KELPIE, NEGATE,
REFUSE, SPRITE
slang .... NO, NAY, NOPE, NO
SIREE, NOT AT ALL
Nixon "bete noir" .... TAPES
Nizam .... NABOB
domain .... HYDERABAD
Njorth .... VANIR
child of .... FREY(A), FREYJA
no .... NAY, NOT-SO, NOWISE,
NEGATIVE
doubt .... CERTAINLY
gentleman he ...... CAD, BOOR,
LOUT, BRUTE
he-man .... SISSY
longer ahead .... OVERTAKEN
longer existing .... DEAD,
EXTINCT
longer recumbent .... RISEN
more ...... DEFUNCT, OBSOLETE
more! .... ENOUGH
more room .... FULL
more than .... MERE, ONLY
-no .... DONT
_____ (nothing doing)
.... WAY, DICE
one .... NONE, NOBODY
rod sparer .... SWITCHER
sailor he .... LANDLUBBER
seats available sign .... SRO
slang .... FAT CHANCE, IN A
PIG'S EYE
slangy .... NIX, NAW, NOPE
-sweat state .... EASE
vote .... NAY
Noah, boat of .... ARK
father of .... LAMECH
grandson of .... ARAM
landing place of .... ARARAT
pertaining to .... NOETIC
son of .... HAM, SHEM,
JAPHETH
nob .... HEAD, JACK
nobby .... CHIC, STYLISH, FIRST-
RATE
Nobel, industrialist .... ALFRED
invention of .... DYNAMITE
laureate .... UREY

Prize decliner .... SARTRE,
PASTERNAK
Prize winner:
chemistry .... HAHN, UREY,
ADLER, CURIE, BAEYER,
SANGER, WERNER, PAULING,
SEABORG
literature .... MANN, SHAW,
CAMUS, ELIOT, SACHS,
JENSEN, SARTRE, BRODSKY,
FAULKNER, GORDIMER,
CHURCHILL, PASTERNAK,
STEINBECK
medicine .... KOCH, GOLGI,
KREBS, LYNEN, MINOT,
BURNET, ECCLES, RICHET
peace ...... ORR, KING, MOTT,
LANGE, BUNCHE, DUNANT,
WILSON, GORBACHEV,
SCHWEITZER
physics .... BOHR, RABI,
TAMM, YANG, BRAUN,
CURIE, DALEN, FERMI,
RAMAN
nobility .... PEERS, PEERAGE,
ROYALTY, GRANDEUR,
NOBLESSE, BLUE BLOOD,
ARISTOCRACY
rank below .... GENTRY
noble .... PEER, GRAND, LOFTY,
KINGLY, GALLANT, STATELY,
SUBLIME, MAJESTIC,
PATRICIAN
birth .... EUGENY, HIGHBORN
obsolete .... ATHEL
nobleman ...... DUKE, EARL, JARL,
LORD, PEER, BARON, COUNT,
THANE, KNIGHT, MILORD,
PRINCE, GRANDEE, HIDALGO,
MARQUIS, MAGNIFICO
noblewoman ...... LADY, MILADY,
DUCHESS, PEERESS, CONTESSA,
COUNTESS, MARCHESA,
MARCHIONESS
nobody .... NONE, NO ONE,
NONENTITY
nocent .... GUILTY, HURTFUL
nock .... NOTCH
noctambulist .... SLEEPWALKER
nocturnal .... NIGHT(LY)
bird .... OWL, KAKAPO
creature .... BAT, COON,
LEMUR, RATEL, TAPIR,
JACKAL, WEASEL, (O)POSSUM,
RAC(C)OON, TARSIER
sawyer .... SNORER
nocturne .... SERENADE
nod .... BOW, BECK, DOZE,
DROWSE, NUTATE
auction .... BID
Nod, land of .... SLEEP

nodding .... NUTANT
noddle .... GULL, HEAD, PATE
noddy .... FOOL, SIMPLETON
node .... KNOB, KNOT, FOCUS,
       GNARL, JOINT, DILEMMA,
              SWELLING
  abnormal .... NODULE
nodular .... LUMPY, KNOTTY,
       NODOSE, GNARLED, STUDDED
nodule .... KNOT, LUMP, JOINT
  tone's .... GEODE
noel .... CAROL, CHRISTMAS
Noel Coward's song .... NINA
noesis .... PERCEPTION
noetic .... SCHOLAR
nog .... ALE, PIN, BRICK
noggin .... CUP, MUG, GILL, HEAD,
                     PATE
noise .... DIN, FLAP, BRUIT,
       SOUND, CLAMOR, HUBBUB,
       RACKET, (UP)ROAR, STRIDOR
  activity .... ADO
  of revelers .... RIOT
  resounding .... BAM
  surf .... ROTE
noiseless .... QUIET, STILL, SILENT,
                     CATLIKE
noisome .... FETID, HARMFUL,
              NOXIOUS, STINKING
noisy .... LOUD, BLATANT,
       CLAMANT, CLAMOROUS,
              CACOPHONOUS
  bird .... JAY, (MAG)PIE
  merry-making .... REVELRY,
                     CAROUSAL
  revelry .... JAMBOREE
nom de plume. See also pen
  name .... PEN NAME,
                     PSEUDONYM
nomad .... GYPSY, ROVER, TRAMP,
       ROAMER, WANDERER,
              ITINERANT
  desert ...... ARAB, KURD, SLEB,
       BEDOUIN, BUSHMAN
  Northern .... LAPP
nomadic .... ITINERANT,
              WANDERING
nominal .... SMALL, TOKEN,
              SLIGHT, TITULAR
  value .... PAR
nominate .... CALL, NAME,
       APPOINT, DESIGNATE
nomination .... NAMING,
              APPOINTMENT
nominee .... CANDIDATE,
              APPOINTEE
non-accidental injury .... CHILD
                     ABUSE
  believer .... PAGAN, ATHEIST,
       INFIDEL, AGNOSTIC
  Christian .... PAGAN, PAYNIM

clergy .... LAITY
  member .... MAVERICK,
              OUTSIDER
  payer, proverbially ...... CRIME
  paying activity .... CRIME
  paying one .... DEADBEAT
  professional .... LAY, LAIC,
              AMATEUR
  union place .... OPEN SHOP
  workers .... LILIES
nonage .... MINORITY
nonce .... MEANTIME, MEANWHILE
noncom .... CPL, NCO, SARGE,
              SERGEANT
nonchalant .... COOL, CASUAL,
       INSOUCIANT, INDIFFERENT
nonconformist .... REB(EL),
       HERETIC, SECTARY,
       MAVERICK, RECUSANT,
       DISSIDENT, DISSENTER
nondescript .... ODD, PLAIN,
       COMMON, ORDINARY
none .... NARY, NO ONE, NOT ANY,
              NOTHING
nonentity .... CIPHER, NOBODY,
       STRAWMAN, UNPERSON
nonesuch .... ONER, APPLE,
       RARITY, PARAGON, NONPAREIL
nonmetallic element ...... BORON,
       IODINE, SILICON, ASTATINE,
              FLUORINE
nonpareil .... SUPREME, UNEQUAL,
       NON(E)SUCH, MATCHLESS,
       PEERLESS, UNRIVALED
nonpartisan .... NEUTRAL,
              INDEPENDENT
nonplus .... STUMP, BAFFLE,
       PUZZLE, CONFUSE, MYSTIFY,
       PERPLEX, SQUELCH
nonprofit organization
       .... FOUNDATION
nonsense .... BAH, BLAH, BOSH,
       BULL, BUNK, TOSH, BILGE,
       FOLLY, FUDGE, HOKUM,
       HOOEY, PRATE, TRASH,
       DRIVEL, SLAVER, BALONEY,
       BLATHER, RUBBISH, TWADDLE,
       FALDEROL, FLIMFLAM,
       FOLDEROL, MALARK(E)Y,
       (TOMMY)ROT, TRUMPERY,
       ABSURDITY, POPPYCOCK,
       SILLINESS, RIG(A)MAROLE
  deceitful .... GAMMON
  high-sounding .... FUSTIAN
  singing .... SCAT
nonsensical .... INANE, SILLY,
       ABSURD, FOOLISH,
              RIDICULOUS
  creature .... GOOF, GOOP, NOIO,
       SMOO, SNARK
nonspiritual .... MATERIAL

nonstick pan spray .... PAM
nonstop .... MARATHON,
              CONTINUOUS
noodle .... FOOL, HEAD, PASTA,
       FARFEL, FERFEL
  dish .... CHOW MEIN
nook .... DEN, NICHE, (AL)COVE,
       CORNER, RECESS, RETREAT
  and ____ .... CORNER,
              CRANNY
noon .... MIDDAY, MERIDIAN
  rest .... SIESTA
noose .... LOOP, TRAP, HALTER,
       (EN)SNARE
  trap .... SPRINGE
nope .... NO, NIX
  opposite of .... YEP
Nordic .... ARYAN, CAUCASIAN,
       TEUTON(IC)
Norfolk .... JACKET
Norge .... NORWAY
noria .... (WATER)WHEEL
norm .... RULE, MODEL, AVERAGE,
       PATTERN, STANDARD,
              CRITERION
Norma .... RAE
  actress .... SHEARER
normal .... PAR, MEAN, USUAL,
       AVERAGE, NATURAL,
       REGULAR, TYPICAL, ORDINARY
  breathing .... EUPN(O)EA
Norman .... LEAR, MAILER
  crusader .... TANCRED
  Vincent ____ .... PEALE
Normand, actress .... MABEL
Normandy capital .... ROUEN
  conqueror of .... ROLLO
  department .... EURE, ORNE,
              MANCHE
  duke of .... HROLF, ROLLO
  liqueur .... BENEDICTINE
Norn .... URTH, SKULD, GODDESS,
       VERTHANDI
Norse .... LANGUAGE,
       SCANDINAVIAN
  Adam .... ASKR
  chieftain .... JARL, ROLLO
  deity .... EIR, ODIN, THOR
  destiny .... NORN
  dwarf .... ANDVARI
  earth: myth .... MIDGARD
  epic .... EDDA
  explorer .... ERIC, ERICSSON
  galley .... AESC
  giant .... ATLI, EGIL, WATE,
       YMER, (H)YMIR, MIMIR,
       TROLL, FAFNIR, JOTUN(N)
  giantess .... GROA, NORN
  goat .... HEIDRUN
  god ...... LOK, TYR, ULL, FREY,
       LOKI, ODIN, THOR, VALI,

AEGER, AEGIR, AESIR, BRAGI, DONAR, HODER, HODUR, VANIR, BALDER, HOENIR, FORSETI, HEIMDALL
goddess .... EIR, SIF, HEL(A), IDUN, NORN, RANA, URTH, WYRD, FREYA, FRIGG(A), ITHUN(N), MOIRA, SKULD, VERTHANDI
gods, king of .... ODIN, WODEN
hall of heroes .... VALHALLA
hero .... OLAF, EGIL(L)
home of gods .... ASGARD
king .... ATLI, OLAF
land holding .... ODAL
letter/lore .... RUNE
minstrel .... SCALD
name .... LARS
navigator .... ERIC
Nibelung dwarf ...... ALBERICH
patron saint .... OLAF
plateau .... FJELD
poet .... SCALD, SKALD
poetry .... EDDA, RUNE(S)
race of gods .... VANIR
rainbow bridge .... BIFROST
river .... KLAR
saga/heroic work .... EDDA
underworld .... HEL
viking .... ROLLO
watchdog .... GARM
watchman of Asgard
.... HEIMDALL
wolf .... FENRIR
woman, first .... EMBLA
Norseman .... VIKING
of the .... RUNIC
North African bread wafer
.... ABRET
city .... ALGIERS
garment .... HAIK
garment, shirtlike .... TOB
region .... SUDAN
seaport .... ORAN
sheep .... AOUDAD
wind .... LESTE
North Atlantic alliance: abbr.
.... NATO
fish .... LING, BURBOT, CAP(E)LIN, MACKEREL
North Borneo .... SABAH
North Carolina bay .... ONSLOW, RALEIGH
cape .... FEAR, LOOKOUT, HATTERAS
capital .... RALEIGH
city/town .... BOONE, DURHAM, CONCORD, HICKORY, GASTONIA, ASHEVILLE, CHARLOTTE, HIGH POINT,

SALISBURY, BURLINGTON, GREENSBORO, WILMINGTON
college .... ELON, BENNETT, CAMPBELL, GUILFORD, JOHN WESLEY, LIVINGSTONE, GARDNER-WEBB, LENOIR-RHYNE
county .... LEE, ASHE, CLAY, DARE, HOKE, HYDE, NASH, PITT, POLK, MOORE, ROWAN, SURRY, UNION, DURHAM, ONSLOW, ORANGE, CATAWBA, FORSYTH, ROBESON, WATAUGA, BUNCOMBE, DAVIDSON, RANDOLPH
island .... ASHE, BODIE, OCRACOKE
lake .... LONG, PUNGO, THORPE, CATFISH, WACCAMAW, ALLIGATOR
mountain .... GUYOT, MITCHELL
native .... TARHEEL
resort town .... TRYON
river .... DAN, HAW, TAR, NEUSE, ROCKY, TRENT, CHOWAN, PEE DEE
state bird .... CARDINAL
state flower .... DOGWOOD
state nickname .... TARHEEL, OLD NORTH
tourist attraction .... OLD SALEM, TRYON PALACE, ZOOLOGICAL PARK
university ...... DUKE, CENTRAL
North Dakota capital
.... BISMARCK
city/town .... FARGO, MINOT, MANDAN, JAMESTOWN, WILLISTON, GRAND FORKS
college .... MARY
county .... CASS, DUNN, WARD, STARK, WALSH, BARNES, MCLEAN, MORTON, RAMSEY, PEMBINA, BURLEIGH
lake .... FAN, VAN, ETTA, TURTLE, DARLING
mining town .... ZAP
mountain .... WHITE BUTTE
river .... ELM, GREEN, HEART, FOREST, TONGUE
state bird .... MEADOWLARK
state flower ...... WILD PRAIRIE ROSE
state nickname .... SIOUX, FLICKERTAIL
tourist attraction ..... FRONTIER VILLAGE
tree .... BLACK HILLS SPRUCE
North Pole discoverer .... PEARY
North Sea feeder .... YSER

port .... KIEL, EMDEN, BERGEN, BREMEN
serpent .... KRAKEN
tributary .... TAY, ELBE, MAAS, TEES, TYNE, YSER, MEUSE, RHINE, WESER, THAMES, SCHELDE
water .... KATTEGAT
North Star .... POLARIS, LODESTAR
northern .... BOREAL
constellation .... BOOTES
diver .... LOON
sea bird .... SKUA, JAEGER, PUFFIN
Northern Bear .... RUSSIA
Cross .... CYGNUS
Rhodesia .... ZAMBIA
Spy .... (WINTER)APPLE
Northerner .... YANKEE, COPPERHEAD
Northampton landmark .... MT. TOM
Northman .... THULE, NORMAN, NORSE(MAN)
Northumberland river ...... ALN, TYNE
Norway. See also **Norse; Norwegian** .... NORGE
betrayer of .... QUISLING
in Norway .... NORGE
Norwegian. See also **Norse**
.... NORSE(MAN)
bay ..... FROHAVET, LOPPHAVET
cape .... LINDESNES
capital .... OSLO
city/town .... MO, BODO, MOSS, HAMAR, MOLDE, SKIEN, BERGEN, LARVIK, NARVIK, TROMSO, ALESUND, DRAMMEN, HARSTAD, SANDNES, LYSAKERT, TONSBERG, HAUGESUND, PORSGRUNN, SARPSBORG, STAVANGER, TRONDHEIM
coin .... ORA, ORE, KRONA
composer .... GRIEG, OLSEN
county .... OSLO, TROMS, OPPLAND, AKERSHUS, BUSKERUD, FINNMARK, NORDLAND, ROGALAND, TELEMARK
dramatist .... IBSEN
explorer .... NANSEN, AMUNDSEN
fish .... LING, BURBOT
fjord .... RANA, FOLDA
goblin .... NIS(SE), KOBOLD
inlet .... FIORD, FJORD
island .... LEKA, VEGA, DONNA, HITRA, HOPEN, SENJA, SMOLA,

ALSTEN, ANDOYA, LANGOY, SOROYA, VAEROY, VANNOY, KVALOYA
island off .... ANDO
islands .... VIKNA, LOFOTEN, SVALBARD
king ..... OLAF, OLAV, HAAKON
lake .... VAGAVATN, FEMUNDSJO, TYRIFJORD
language .... SAMISK, RIKSMAAL, LANDSMAAL
measure .... FOT, MAL, ALEN, MORGEN, SKIEPPE
monetary unit .... KRONE
mountain .... SULITJELMA, GLITTERTINDEN
mountains .... KJOLEN
native .... LAPP, LAPLANDER
noble .... JARL
novelist .... NOJER, HAMSUN
parliament .... LAGT(H)ING, STORT(H)ING
peninsula .... LISTA
poetry .... EDDA
port .... HAMMERFEST
region .... LAPLAND
river ...... OTRA, TANA, LAGEN, RAUMA, TOKKE, NAMSEN, BARDUELV, PASVIKELV
saint .... OLAF
sea monster .... KRAKEN
seaport .... BERGEN, STAVANGER, TRONDHEIM, HAMMERFEST
sight .... FIORD
soprano .... FLAGSTAD
statesman .... LIE
territorial subdivision .... AMT
The People's King
.... FOLKEKONGEN
toast .... SKOAL
traitor .... QUISLING
weight .... LOD, MARK, PUND
writer .... IBSEN, NOJER
warship .... WASA
nose .... NEB, PRY, BEAK, CONK, SCENT, SMELL, SNIFF, SNOOP, SNOUT, SPOUT, MUZZLE, NOZZLE, PROBOSCIS
ailment ..... CORYZA, CATARRH
allergy .... HAY FEVER
bone .... VOMER
combining form .... NASI, RHIN(O)
counting .... POLL, CENSUS
describing one ..... PUG, SNUB, ROMAN, SHARP, SIMOUS, TILTED, AQUILINE
discharge .... RHEUM
dive .... PLUNGE
elephant's .... TRUNK

inflammation .... RHINITIS
Latin .... NASUS
long .... SNOUT, PROBOSCIS
obstruction .... POLYP
of the .... NASAL, NARIAL, RHINAL
opening .... NARE, NARIS, NOSTRIL
person with famous
.... DURANTE, CYRANO(BERGERAC)
point on .... ALARE
reshaping .... RHINOPLASTY
slang ..... SPY, SNOOT, NOZZLE, INFORMER, SCHNOZZLE
nosebag contents .... OATS
nosebleed .... EPISTAXIS
nosegay .... POSY, BOUQUET, CORSAGE
nos(e)y .... PRYING, SNOOPY, CURIOUS, MEDDLESOME, INQUISITIVE
animal .... TAPIR
one .... SPIER, SNOOPER
person .... PEEPING TOM, EAVESDROPPER
Nosey Parker .... MEDDLER
nosferatu .... (THE)UNDEAD
nosh .... EAT, NIBBLE
nostalgia .... PATHOS, REGRET, LONGING, NOSTOMANIA, HOMESICKNESS
noster, _____ .... PATER
nostology .... GERIATRICS
subject of .... OLD AGE
nostomania .... NOSTALGIA, HOMESICKNESS
Nostradamus .... SEER, ASTROLOGER
nostril .... NARE
hairs .... VIBRISSA
of the .... NARIAL, NARINE
nostrum .... REMEDY, PANACEA
not .... NEGATIVE, NOTHINGNESS
a person/a (living) soul .... NO ONE
a quarternary .... TRIAD
a whit .... NONE
absent .... HERE
absolutely .... NO WAY
absolved .... UNVINDICATED
adequate .... SCANTY
allowed apostles .... FOOD, MONEY
an easy catch .... EEL
any/one .... NARY, NONE
appropriate .... INAPT, INEPT, UNFIT, IMPROPER
as common .... RARER
as dotty .... SANER
as lovely as a tree .... A POEM

as many .... FEWER
as tight .... LOOSER
at all .... NOWISE
at home .... OUT, AWAY, ABROAD
aweather .... ALEE
barefoot .... SHOD
belligerent .... IRENIC
cautious .... RASH, RECKLESS
completed .... UNDONE
complex .... EASY, SIMPLE
compulsory .... ELECTIVE, OPTIONAL
conforming .... IRREGULAR
copy .... ORIGINAL
divided .... WHOLE, UNITED
ecclesiastic .... LAIC
even .... EROSE
even once/even sometimes
.... NEVER
feral .... TAME
final: law .... NISI
fitting .... UNAPT
fixed .... UNRESTORED
flat .... HILLED
for .... AGAINST
for bargain hunters .... DEAR
forbidden .... ALLOWED
fresh .... STALE
friendly .... ICY
gained .... LOST
gross .... NET
guaranteed .... RISKY
harsh .... LENIENT
hep .... SQUARE
here .... THERE
hollow .... SOLID
identified .... UNKNOWN
idle .... BUSY, IN USE
illuminated .... UNLIT
in a whisper .... ALOUD
in any way .... NEVER
in cipher .... UNCODED
in house .... OUTSIDE
in jail anyway .... LOOSE, AT LARGE
indisputably .... ARGUABLY
jerky .... EVEN
just a note .... LONG LETTER
kindled .... UNLIT
knowing which way to turn
.... UNSURE
level or flat .... UNEVEN
live .... TAPED
long .... BRIEF
make sense .... TALK IN RIDDLES
many .... FEW
mature .... GREEN
mounted .... UNSET
moving .... INERT, STILL,

STATIC
nearly settled .... UP IN THE AIR
_____ (no way) .... AT ALL
now .... LATER
of this world ..... SUPERLUNAR
on your life! ..... NOPE, NO SIR
one or the other .... NEITHER
pawned .... UNGAGED
permanent .... PROTEM
planned ..... CASUAL, RANDOM, HAPHAZARD
poetry .... PROSE
precise .... INEXACT
prefix of .... DIS, MIS, NON
pronounced .... ELIDED, UNSPOKEN
pungent .... UNSPICY
ready .... ILL-PREPARED
refined .... COARSE, VULGAR
seldom .... OFT
severe .... MILD
showing any wear .... GOOD AS NEW
skillful .... UNAPT
so hot .... TEPID
so shaky .... STEADIER
_____ (so-so) .... SO HOT
speaking .... MUM, MUTE
straight .... ALOP
the Occident .... ORIENT
the original color .... DYED
the real reason .... PRETEXT
to weather: naut. .... ALEE
too many .... SOME
up and about .... ABED
up to standard ..... IRREGULAR
us .... THEM, OTHERS
violent .... GENTLE
warranted .... UNCALLED FOR
well-reasoned: colloq.
.... HALF-BAKED
with it, they're ..... OUTSIDERS
working .... IDLE, ON THE BLINK, OUT OF ORDER
written, as a will
.... NUNCUPATIVE
yet mature .... YOUTHFUL
youthful .... PASSE
nota bene .... NOTE WELL
notable .... VIP, UNCO, FAMOUS, SIGNAL, EMINENT, STRIKING
act .... DEED, FEAT, GEST(E), EXPLOIT, HEROISM
one .... STANDOUT
personage .... VIP, HERO, LION, STAR, CELEBRITY
notarize .... ATTEST, CERTIFY
notary .... SCRIVENER
notation .... NOTE, ENTRY, COMMENT

notch .... GAP, JAG, PEG, MARK, NICK, SCORE, TALLY, DEGREE, (IN)DENT, RECORD
edged .... SERRATE
key .... WARD
made by ax/saw .... KERF
notched .... EROSE, CRENATE, DENTATE, SERRATE
bar .... RATCH
part .... JOG
wheel .... RATCHET
note .... FAME, HEED, MARK, TONE, BILLET, LETTER, REMARK, MISSIVE, OBSERVE, EMINENCE
an eighth .... QUAVER
explanatory .... POSTIL
Guido's .... GAMUT
half .... MINIM
highest .... ELA
marginal .... (A)POSTIL
musical .... THESIS
part of .... STEM
promissory .... IOU
short .... CHIT, LINE, MEMO
stem of .... TAIL
well .... NOTA BENE
notebook .... CAHIER
noted .... FAMOUS, EMINENT, RENOWNED
noteworthy .... EMINENT, NOTABLE, SPECIAL, EXCEPTIONAL
nothing .... NIL, NONE, ZERO, BLANK, NIHIL, NAUGHT, NOUGHT
but .... ONLY, MERELY
doing! .... NO, NO DICE, NO SOAP
else than .... MERE
for .... FREE, GRATIS
in tennis .... LOVE
more or less .... MERE
slang .... NAPOO, ZILCH
to be worried about .... NOT REAL BAD
notice .... AD, SEE, HEED, SIGN, ADVICE, DETECT, REGARD, REVIEW, BILLING, DISCERN, OBSERVE, WARNING, PERCEIVE
for display in a public place
.... POSTER, PLACARD
of payment due .... PROMPT
official .... BULLETIN, MONITION
to desist .... CAVEAT
noticeable ...... EVIDENT, VISIBLE, CONSPICUOUS
notification .... AVISO, ADVICE
sort of .... THREAT
notify .... TELL, WARN, BRIEF,

ADVISE, INFORM, APPRISE, ACQUAINT
notion .... IDEA, VIEW, WHIM, CURIO, FANCY, BELIEF, DESIRE, CAPRICE, INKLING, OPINION, THOUGHT
commonplace .... BROMIDE
counter item .... THREAD, SHOELACE, SAFETY PIN
fallacious .... IDOLISM
foolish .... MOONSHINE
notions .... ARTICLES
notoriety .... FAME, ECLAT, REPUTE, BLATANCY, PUBLICITY
notorious .... ARRANT, FLAGRANT, INFAMOUS, TALK OF THE TOWN
notornis relative ...... COOT, RAIL
Notre Dame .... OUR LADY, CATHEDRAL
bench .... PEW
coach .... ARA, ROCKNE
notwithstanding .... THO, YET, EVEN, STILL, MAUGRE, DESPITE, HOWEVER, (AL)THOUGH
nougat .... CANDY, CONFECTION
nought .... ZERO, CIPHER, NOTHING, USELESS
bring to .... VOID, NULLIFY
nomenal .... INTUITIVE
noun .... SUBSTANTIVE
form .... CASE
kind of ...... APTOTE, TRIPTOTE
modifier .... ADJECTIVE
of common gender
.... EPICENE
suffix ...... AST, ENT, ERY, FER, ICS, IER, ISE, IST, ITE, ULA, ULE, ENCE, ITIS, TUDE, ATION
verbal .... GERUND
nourish .... FEED, FOSTER, NURTURE, SUPPORT, SUSTAIN
nourishing .... ALIBLE, NUTRIENT, ALIMENTAL, ALIMENTARY, NUTRITIOUS
nourishment .... FOOD, ALIMENT, PABULUM, NUTRIMENT, NUTRITION, SUSTENANCE
baby's .... PAP, MILK
nous .... MIND, REASON, INTELLECT
nouveau or theater .... ART
riche .... PARVENU, UPSTART, NEWLY RICH
nova .... STAR
Nova Scotia(n) .... ACADIA(N), BLUENOSE
basin .... MINAS, ANNAPOLIS
bay .... ASPY, CLAM, MIRA,

493

FUNDY, SCOTS, SHOAL, VERTE,
FORCHU, JORDAN, MAHONE,
GABARUS, ADVOCATE,
CHIGNECTO
cape ..... JOHN, ARGOS, CANSO,
CLIFF, PERCE, SABLE, SMOKY,
SPLIT, BRETON, GEORGE,
LINZEE, MORIEN, DAUPHIN
capital .... HALIFAX
city/town .... DIGBY, TRURO,
PICTOU, SYDNEY, AMHERST,
WINDSOR, YARMOUTH,
DARTMOUTH, LIVERPOOL
county .... DIGBY, HANTS,
KINGS, PICTOU, QUEENS,
HALIFAX, COLCHESTER
harbor .... COLE, MABOU,
CODDLE, HALIFAX
island .... MUD, OAK, BRIER,
CROSS, GOOSE, HAUTE, SOBER,
ANDREW, BARREN, MADAME,
TUSKET, CARIBOU, LISCOMB,
CHETICAMP, CAPE BRETON
lake .... OCEAN, FISHER,
GEORGE, JORDAN, MOLEGA,
TUPPER, BRAS D'OR,
GASPEREAU, ROSSIGNOL, LOCH
LOMOND
mountain .... NUTTBY,
DALHOUSIE
river .... AVON, GOLD, MIRA,
OHIO, MERSEY, SALMON,
TUSKET, BADDECK, CARLETON,
KENNETCOOK
seaport .... TRURO
strait .... CANSO
village .... GRAND PRE
Novarro, actor .... RAMON
movie role .... BEN HUR
novel .... NEW, BOOK, EPIC, RARE,
FRESH, PROSE, STORY,
ROMANCE, SIMENON,
STRANGE, UNUSUAL
by Bronte .... JANE EYRE
Edna Ferber .... SO BIG
Felix Salten .... BAMBI
Fielding .... AMELIA
H. Rider Haggard .... SHE
Helen Hunt Jackson
.... RAMONA
Hugo .... LES MISERABLES
James Clavell .... SHOGUN
Jane Austen .... EMMA
Nabokov .... ADA
Uris .... TOPAZ
Isaac Singer's last .... SCUM
novelist Anatole .... FRANCE
aptly named .... READE
Bernard .... MALAMUD
Dunn .... OLAV
Eugene .... SUE

Felix .... SALTEN
Ferber .... EDNA
Hobson .... LAURA
Hunter .... EVAN
Michael .... ARLEN
Nevil .... SHUTE
Norman .... MAILER
romance .... (VICTORIA)HOLT
Stephen .... CRANE
Willa .... CATHER
novella .... NARRATIVE
Novello .... IVOR
novelty .... FAD, CHANGE,
NEWNESS, TRINKET,
GIMCRACK, BRIC-A-BRAC
November 11 .... MARTINMAS
event .... VETERANS' DAY
13, Roman date .... IDES
novena .... NINE, DEVOTIONS
novice .... CUB, TIRO, TYRO,
ACOLYTE, AMATEUR,
BEGINNER, NEOPHYTE,
GREENHORN, APPRENTICE,
TENDERFOOT
novitiate .... NOVICE, TRAINEE,
NEOPHYTE
novocaine .... ANESTHETIC
Novotna .... JARMILA
tennis star .... JANA
now .... TODAY, AT ONCE,
IMMEDIATELY
nowadays .... PRESENTLY, AT
PRESENT
noway .... NOWISE, NOT AT ALL
nowhere place .... LIMBO
nowt .... OXEN, CATTLE
Nox .... NYX, GODDESS
brother of .... EREBUS
husband of .... CHAOS
is goddess of .... NIGHT
noxious .... EVIL, NOCENT,
BANEFUL, HARMFUL, MIASMIC,
NOISOME, MEPHITIC,
PERNICIOUS
air/effluvium .... MIASMA,
MALARIA
vapor .... FUME, REEK
Noyes, poet .... ALFRED
nozzle .... JET, NOSE, ROSE,
SNOUT, SPOUT
furnace .... TUYERE
thing with .... HOSE, PIPE,
TEAPOT, BELLOWS
nuance .... SHADE, VARIATION
nub ...... CORE, GIST, KNOB, LUMP,
PITH, SNAG
nubbin ...... CORN, LUMP, BUTTON
nubble .... KNOB, KNOT, LUMP
nubby .... STUDDED
nubia .... WRAP
Nubian .... NEGRO(ID)

harp .... NANGA
nubile .... RIPE, ADULT, OF AGE,
MATURE, MARRIAGEABLE
nubilous .... FOGGY, MISTY,
CLOUDY, OBSCURE, VAPOROUS
nucha .... NAPE, SCRUFF
nuclear device .... REACTOR
division in germ cells
.... MEIOSIS
missile .... ICBM, MIRV,
A-BOMB, H-BOMB
scientist .... BRAUN
nucleic acid: abbr. .... DNA
nucleus .... CORE, HEART, CENTER,
KERNEL
atom's .... PROTON,
DEUT(E)RON
cell .... MESOPLAST
military unit's .... CADRE
nude ...... BARE, NAKED, UNCLAD,
EXPOSED, UNCLOTHED
nudge .... JOG, POKE, PROD, PUSH,
ELBOW, JOSTLE
nudist .... ADAMITE,
GYMNOSOPHIST,
CLOTHESTROPHOBIAC
Nuevo Leon capital
.... MONTERREY
nugatory .... FUTILE, INVALID,
USELESS, HELPLESS
nugget .... HUNK, LUMP, SLUG
nuisance .... BANE, BORE,
BOTHER, PLAGUE, TROUBLE,
ANNOYANCE
colloquial .... PEST, TERROR
insect .... GNAT
null .... NIL, VOID, INVALID
nullah .... GORGE, GULLY, RAVINE,
WATERCOURSE
nullify .... VETO, VOID, UNDO,
ANNUL, ABJURE, CANCEL,
NEGATE, REPEAL, REVOKE,
RESCIND, RETRACT,
ABROGATE, OVERRIDE,
INVALIDATE
nulliparous .... BARREN
nullipore .... SEAWEED
numb .... DAZED, TORPID,
DEADEN(ED), DRUGGED,
SHOCKED, UNFEELING,
INSENSIBLE, NARCOTIZED
number .... COUNT, TALLY,
CIPHER, FIGURE, SYMBOL,
ENUMERATE
added .... ADDEND
after due .... TRE
astronomic .... GOOGOL
before sette .... SEI
biggest/greatest .... MOST
countless ...... HORDE, SWARM,
MYRIAD

dividing evenly .... ALIQUOT
8 iron .... NIBLICK
5 iron .... MASHY, MASHIE
in Brooklyn .... TREE
indefinite .... SEVERAL
irrational .... SURD
large .... MANY, RAFF, RAFT,
SLEW, LEGION, MULTITUDE
leaves of book .... FOLIATE
less than ten .... DIGIT
lonely .... ONE
lost .... TOLL, CASUALTY
magazine .... ISSUE
of a crowd .... THREE
of deadly sins .... SEVEN
of Sinbad's voyages
.... SEVEN
of tails on a cat .... NINE
of winks in a short nap
.... FORTY
page .... FOLIO
part of .... FRACTION
whole .... INTEGER
numbers .... BOOK, QUANTITY
game .... KENO, LOTTO,
LOTTERY
racket .... POLICY GAME
specialist .... BOOKIE
numbfish .... TORPEDO,
(ELECTRIC)RAY
numbles .... INNARDS
numen .:.......... SPIRIT, DIVINITY
numerate .... READ, TELL, COUNT,
TALLY, NUMBER
numerical ending .... ETH
numerous .... MANY, THICK,
MYRIAD, PLENTY, MANIFOLD
combining form .... MYRIA
Numidian crane ...... DEMOISELLE
king .... MASINISSA
town .... ZAMA
numismatist .... COLLECTOR
concern of ..... COINS, MEDALS
numskull .... DOLT, DUNCE,
MORON, NITWIT, MEATHEAD,
BLOCKHEAD, DUNDERHEAD
nun .... SMEW, CLARE, MONASA,
PIGEON, SISTER, VESTAL,
VIRGIN, VOTARY, TITMOUSE,
CARMELITE
abode of .... CONVENT,
MONASTERY
dress of .... HABIT
head covering .... WIMPLE
moth .... TUSSOCK
throat cover .... BARB
nunbird .... MONASE
nuncio ...... LEGATE, AMBASSADOR
nuncupative .... ORAL, VERBAL,
UNWRITTEN
nunnery .... ABBEY, PRIORY,

CONVENT, CLOISTER
head of a .... ABBESS,
PRIORESS, SUPERIOR
nuns, of .... MONASTIC
nuptial(s) .... BRIDAL, SPOUSAL,
WEDDING, HYMENEAL,
MARRIAGE, CONNUBIAL
agreement .... I DO
participant .... BESTMAN,
SPONSOR, BRIDESMAID,
RINGBEARER
principal .... BRIDE(GROOM)
yes/pledge .... I DO
nuque .... NAPE, SCRUFF
Nuremberg war crimes
defendant ...... HESS, KEITEL,
GOERING, RIBBENTROP
nurse .... AMAH, AYAH, CARE,
NANA, TEND, NANNY, SERVE,
FOSTER, SUCKLE(R),
ATTENDANT
head covering of .... WIMPLE
instrument of
.... THERMOMETER
part-time .... SITTER
nursery ...... ASYLUM, HOTHOUSE,
PLAYROOM, GREENHOUSE
bete noire .... CROUP
furniture .... CRIB, PLAYPEN,
BASSINET, ROCKING CHAIR
public/day .... CRECHE
rhyme character .... GILES,
SPRAT
rhyme eloper .... SPOON
rhyme home .... SHOE
rhyme Miss .... MUFFET
rhyme opening words
.... PAT-A-CAKE
song .... LULLABY
VIP .... BABY
word .... DADA, MAMA, TATA
worker .... (BABY)SITTER
nurture .... FEED, FOOD, REAR,
BREED, TRAIN, FOSTER,
CHERISH, NOURISH, SUSTAIN
nut .... COCO, KOLA, PARA, PILI,
SEED, ACORN, BEECH, BETEL,
PECAN, PINON, TRYMA,
ALMOND, BRAZIL, CASHEW,
LICHEE, LI(T)CHI, HICKORY
combining form .... NUCI,
CARYO, KARYO
confection .... NOUGAT,
PRALINE, MARZIPAN
covering .... HUSK, SHELL
kidney-shaped .... CASHEW,
KASHEW
meat .... KERNEL
off one's .... CRAZY, INSANE
slang .... HEAD, KOOK, CRANK,
FOOLISH, ECCENTRIC

three-sided .... BRAZIL
tonic/used in beverages
.... KOLA
turner .... WRENCH, SPANNER
nutant .... NODDING, DROOPING
nutcracker .... BIRD, CROW,
PECKER
nuthatch .... CREEPER, TITMOUSE,
NUTCRACKER
genus .... SITTA
nutlet .... PIT, STONE, PYRENE
nutmeg ...... MACE, SPICE, KERNEL
nutria .... FUR, COYPU, RODENT
animal like .... BEAVER
nutriment .... FOOD, ALIMENT,
NUTRIENT
nutrition, of .... TROPHIC
study of .... DIETETICS
nutritionist .... DIETICIAN,
DIETITIAN
nutritive .... ALIBLE
nuts .... FOOL, GAGA, BATTY,
CRAZY, QUEER, ENTHUSIASTIC
about .... FOND OF
collectively .... MAST
counterparts of .... BOLTS
pertaining to .... NUCAL
nutshell .... DIGEST, CAPSULE,
OUTLINE, SYNOPSIS
nutty ...... CRAZY, MEATY, QUEER,
GAGA, CUCKOO, BONKERS,
FOOLISH, HAYWIRE, OFF
ONE'S ROCKER
nux vomica .... SEED, PLANT
product .... STRYCHNIN(E)
nuzzle .... RUB, NOSE, PUSH,
CUDDLE, NESTLE, SNUGGLE
Nyasaland .... MALAWI
capital .... LILONGWE
president .... BANDA
nylon .... HOSE, FIBER, THREAD,
BRISTLE
flow of .... RUN, SNAG
thread weight of .... DENIER
nylons .... HOSE, SHEERS,
HOSIERY, STOCKINGS
nymph ...... PUPA, AEGLE, HOURI,
LARVA, SYLPH, WOMAN,
DAPHNE, EGERIA, HESTIA,
MAENAD, MAIDEN, OENONE,
ONDINE, SYRINX, OCEANID,
SALMACIS
changed into bear
.... CALLISTO
changed into laurel tree
.... DAPHNE
changed into a rock ..... ECHO
changed into a stream
.... ARETHUSA
fountain .... NAIAD

guards .... HESPERIDES
mountain .... OREAD
pursuer of .... SATYR
river .... NAIS, NAIAD
sea .... SIREN, NEREID,
       NEMERTES
tree .... (HAMA)DRYAD
water .... APAS
nymphet .... LOLITA
nymphs, father of 50 .... NEREUS
fountain .... CAMENAE
nyssa .... TUPELO
Nyx .... NOX
daughter of .... ERIS
is goddess of .... NIGHT

O

O .... ZERO, CIPHER, EXCLAMATION
Greek .... OMEGA, OMICRON
in chemistry .... OXYGEN
in pharmacy .... PINT
in physics .... OHM
O gosh! .... O GEE
oaf .... BOOR, DOLT, GAWK, LOUT,
  RUBE, DUNCE, RUSTIC,
  DEADHEAD, DULLHEAD
variant of .... OUPHE
Oahu city .... HONOLULU
oak .... HOLM, ILEX, TREE, WOOD,
  ALDER, EMORY, ROBLE,
  ROBUR, CERRIS, DURMAS,
        ENCINA
bark .... TAN, CRUT, EMORY
British slang .... DOOR
evergreen .... ILEX, ENCINA
fruit .... MAST, ACORN,
        CAMATA
genus .... QUERCUS
moss .... EVERNIA
starter .... ACORN
thicket of evergreen
.... CHAPARRAL
Oak Ridge work .... NUCLEAR
Oakley, rifle expert .... ANNIE
slang .... PASS
oakum .... FIBER
seal with .... CA(U)LK
oar ...... BLADE, ROW(ER), SCULL,
  SPOON, SWEEP, PADDLE,
        PROPEL
blade .... PALM, WASH
fulcrum/lock .... THOLE
part of .... LOOM, PEEL
shaped .... REMIPED
oarlock support .... POPPET
oars, row of .... BANK
oarsman .... ROWER, STROKE,
        SCULLER
oasis .... WADI, WADY, DOUMA,
        SPRING
fruit .... DATES
sight .... DATE PALM
oast .... KILN, OVEN
oat .... REED, GRASS, CEREAL
burner .... NAG
genus .... AVENA
rental .... AVENAGE

oatcake .... CAPER
oater .... HORSE OPERA
locale .... SALOON
Oates, Popish Plot's .... TITUS
oath .... VOW, CURSE, PLEDGE,
  PLIGHT, EXPLETIVE,
       PROFANITY
breaking of .... PERJURY
mild .... DRAT, EGAD, GOSH,
      HECK, ZOUNDS
take .... SWEAR, PROMISE
taker .... JURANT
testify under .... DEPOSE
oatmeal .... PORRIDGE
cake .... PONE, SCONE
porridge .... BURGOO,
       STIRABOUT
oats .... FEED, AVENA
hulled, cracked .... GROATS
Oaxaca is in .... MEXICO
Ob river is in .... SIBERIA
Obadiah .... ABDIAS, PROPHET
obdurate .... FIRM, DOGGED,
  MULISH, ADAMANT,
  STUBBORN, OBSTINATE,
  BULLHEADED, INFLEXIBLE
obeah .... CHARM, MAGIC, FETISH,
  TALISMAN, WITCHCRAFT
obedience .... DEFERENCE,
  COMPLIANCE, SUBMISSION
obedient .... LOYAL, DOCILE,
  DUTIFUL, AMENABLE,
  COMPLIANT, HENPECKED,
       TRACTABLE
obeisance .... BOW, CONGE(E),
  CURTSY, HOMAGE, KOWTOW,
  SALAAM, DEFERENCE
obelisk .... PYLON, SHAFT,
  NEEDLE, OBELUS, PILLAR,
       MONOLITH
obelus .... MARK, DAGGER,
       OBELISK
Oberammergau is in
.... BAVARIA
religious play .... PASSION
Oberon .... KING, FAIRY
actress .... MERLE
domain of .... FAIRYLAND
wife of .... TITANIA
obese .... FAT, PLUMP, PUDGY,

  PUFFY, PURSY, STOUT,
  FLESHY, PORTLY, ROTUND,
  ADIPOSE, BLUBBERY,
  LIPAROUS, CORPULENT
obesity .... FATNESS, LIPOSIS,
       ADIPOSIS
medical syndrome
.... PICKWICKIAN
obey .... HEED, MIND, COMPLY,
  FOLLOW, SUBMIT, FULFILL,
      CARRY OUT
obfuscate ...... DARKEN, CONFUSE,
  OBSCURE, STUPEFY, BEWILDER
obi .... SASH, CHARM, MAGIC,
  OBEAH, FETISH, TALISMAN
obiter dictum .... ASIDE,
  REMARK, COMMENT
obit(uary) .... MEMORIAL,
  NECROLOGY, (DEATH)NOTICE
words .... IN MEMORIAM
object ...... AIM, END, GOAL, ITEM,
  KICK, MIND, DEMUR, THING,
  INTENT, OPPOSE, RESIST,
  TARGET, DISSENT, PROTEST,
  PURPOSE, REMONSTRATE
art .... CURIO, BIBELOT
of infatuation .... IDOL
of manipulation .... PUPPET,
       MARIONETTE
of pursuit ...... GAME, QUARRY
objecting fan .... BOOER
objection .... KICK, CAVIL,
  BARRIER, PROTEST, QUARREL,
  DEMURRER, OPPOSITION
objectionable .... CULPABLE,
  OFFENSIVE, UNDESIRABLE
gray .... TATTLETALE
objective .... AIM, GOAL, REAL,
  ACTUAL, TARGET, PURPOSE,
  DETACHED, UNBIASED
objector .... REBEL, OPPOSER,
  DISSENTER, DISSIDENT
objet d'art .... VASE, VIRTU,
       FIGURINE
collector .... VIRTUOSO
objurgate .... CHIDE, BERATE,
  REBUKE, REPROVE, UPBRAID
oblate .... NUN, MONK, ASCETIC
oblation ...... OFFERING, SACRIFICE
obligate .... OWE, BIND

obligated .... BEHOLDEN, INDEBTED
obligation ...... DUE, BOND, DEBT, DUTY, ONUS, BURDEN, PROMISE
abbr. .... IOU
evade an .... WELSH
obligatory .... BINDING, BOUNDEN
oblige .... FORCE, ASSIST, COMPEL, PLEASE, GRATIFY, CONSTRAIN
obliging .... HELPFUL, ACCOMMODATING
oblique .... AWRY, CANT, SKEW, ASLANT, EVASIVE, INCLINED, INDIRECT
glance .... SQUINT
line .... BIAS
obliquely .... ASKANCE, SIDEWAYS, SIDEWISE
obliterate .... RAZE, ERASE, DEFACE, EFFACE, BLOT OUT, DESTROY, EXPUNGE, SPONGE OUT
obliteration .... ERASURE, ERASEMENT
oblivion .... LETHE, PARDON, FORGETFULNESS
drug of .... NEPENTHE
place of .... LIMBO
river of .... LETHE
oblivious .... HEEDLESS, FORGETFUL
oblong .... ELONGATED
obloquy .... INFAMY, CENSURE
obnoxious .... GROSS, ODIOUS, HATEFUL, OFFENSIVE, REPULSIVE, TASTELESS, UNPLEASANT
one .... PILL, CREEP
oboe .... REED, WIND, WOOD, SHAWN, BASSOON, HAUTBOY, BOMBARDON
oboli, six .... DRACHMA
obol(us) .... COIN
Obote, Uganda president
.... APOLO
Obregon, Mex. president
.... ALVARO
obscene .... RAW, FOUL, LEWD, DIRTY, GROSS, COARSE, FILTHY, SMUTTY, NAUGHTY, INDECENT, REPULSIVE
language .... BAWDRY, RIBALDRY
pictures/writings
.... PORNO(GRAPHY)
obscure .... DIM, DARK, DUSKY, FOG(GY), MURKY, VAGUE, GLOOMY, HIDDEN, CRYPTIC, ECLIPSE, SHADOWY, NUBILOUS, OBFUSCATE

by smearing .... BLUR
obscurity .... ANONYMITY
obsequies .... EXEQUY
obsequious .... ABJECT, FAWNING, SERVILE
observance .... RITE, RULE, CUSTOM, PRACTICE
for a dead .... WAKE
of formalities .... PUNCTILIO
of official precedence
.... PROTOCOL
observant .... ALERT, VIGILANT, WATCHFUL, ATTENTIVE
observation .... ESPIAL, NOTICE, REMARK, COMMENT, ASSERTION
car feature .... BLISTER
irrelevant .... POINTLESS REMARK
to little star .... TWINKLE TWINKLE
work .... SURVEY, RECONNAISSANCE
observatory, California
.... PALOMAR
concern of an .... MOON, STARS, PLANETS, WEATHER
observe .... EYE, SEE, NOTE, OBEY, ABIDE, NOTICE, REMARK, DISCERN, CELEBRATE
secretly .... SPY, STALK
Yom Kippur .... FAST
observer .... LOOKOUT, WATCHER, EYEWITNESS
forward .... SCOUT
obsess .... BESET, HAUNT, HARASS, PREOCCUPY
obsessed .... HIPPED, RIDDEN
stubbornly .... HELLBENT
obsession .... FIXE, IDEE, FIXATION, (MONO)MANIA
obsidian .... LAVA, ROCK, PERLITE, TEKTITE
obsolescence .... DISUSE
obsolete ...... OLD, DATED, PASSE, ARCHAIC, DISUSED, EXTINCT, OUTMODED, OUT OF DATE, DISCARDED, OLD-FASHIONED
auto .... PEERLESS
seat .... SEDE
obstacle .... BAR, SNAG, CRIMP, HITCH, HURDLE, BARRIER, HINDRANCE, IMPEDIMENT
course .... GANTLET
unexpected .... SNAG
obstinate .... DOUR, DOGGED, MULISH, ORNERY, WILLFUL, CONTRARY, RESOLUTE, STUBBORN, PIGHEADED, UNBENDING, BULLHEADED, HARD(HEADED)

obstreperous .... NOISY, UNRULY, RIOTOUS, BOISTEROUS, VOCIFEROUS
obstruct .... BAR, DAM, CLOG, BLOCK, CHECK, CHOKE, HINDER, IMPEDE, RETARD, STOP UP, BARRICADE
obstruction .... BARRIER, OBSTACLE, HINDRANCE
obstructionist's trick
.... FILIBUSTER
obtain .... GET, WIN, EARN, GAIN, DERIVE, SECURE, ACQUIRE, PREVAIL, PROCURE
fresh energy .... REVIVE
obtainable .... AVAILABLE, ATTAINABLE
obtrude .... EJECT, MEDDLE, INTRUDE
obtund .... DULL, BLUNT, DEADEN
obtuse .... DULL, BLUNT, DENSE
opposite of .... ACUTE
obverse .... FRONT, COUNTERPART
opposite of .... VERSO, REVERSE
obviate .... PREVENT
obvious .... PLAIN, PATENT, EVIDENT, PALPABLE, UNSUBTLE, OPEN AND SHUT
not .... SUBTLE, SUBTILE
oca .... OXALIS
ocarina .... SWEET POTATO
O'Casey, dramatist .... SEAN
occasion .... TIME, CAUSE, EVENT, NONCE, HAPPENING
occasional .... RARE, CASUAL, SPORADIC, IRREGULAR, INCIDENTAL
occasionally .... RARELY, SOMETIMES, NOW AND THEN
occident .... WEST
opposite of .... ORIENT
occidental .... PONENT, WESTERN, HESPERIAN
occipital protuberances .... INIA
occlude ...... SHUT, BLOCK, CLOSE, ABSORB
occlusion .... SHUTDOWN
occult .... HIDDEN, MYSTIC, ORPHIC, SECRET, CRYPTIC, ESOTERIC, MYSTERIOUS
art .... MAGIC, ALCHEMY, ASTROLOGY
knowledge .... GRAMARY(E)
philosophy .... CABALA
occultism .... MAGIC, KABALA, CAB(B)ALA
occupancy .... TERM, TENANCY
occupant .... INMATE, TENANT, HABITANT
occupation .... WORK, TRADE,

METIER, TENURE, CALL(ING),
PURSUIT, PROFESSION
occupied .... BUSY, ENGROSSED
occupy .... USE, FILL, EMPLOY,
ENGAGE, INVEST, LIVE IN,
POSSESS
attention .... ENGROSS
occur .... PASS, EXIST, LIGHT,
BEFALL, BETIDE, HAPPEN
again .... RECUR, REPEAT
at the same time .... COINCIDE
irregularly .... SPORADIC
once a year .... ANNUAL(LY)
occurrence .... CASE, EVENT,
EPISODE, INCIDENT,
OCCASION, HAPPENING
degree of .... INCIDENCE
occurring at intervals
.... SEASONALLY
every 8th day .... OCTAN
5th day .... QUINTAN
4th day .... QUARTAN
3rd day .... TERTIAN
two years .... BIENNIAL
together .... SIMULTANEOUS
ocean .... SEA, DEEP, MAIN, BRINE,
ARCTIC, INDIAN, EXPANSE,
PACIFIC, ATLANTIC,
ANTARCTIC
current .... UNDERTOW
denizen, inflatable .... PUFF
FISH
depression .... DEEP
greyhound .... LINER,
STEAMSHIP
largest and deepest
.... PACIFIC
route .... LANE
Oceania island .... MELANESIA,
POLYNESIA, MICRONESIA
oceanic .... VAST, PELAGIC
oceanid .... NYMPH
Oceanus .... GOD, TITAN
ocellus .... SPOT, EYE(LET)
ocelot .... CAT
cat-like .... MARGAY
ocher .... SIL, CLAY, YELLOW,
PIGMENT
red .... TIVER, RADDLE,
REDDLE, RUBRIC
ochre .... ALMAGRA
Ochs, publisher .... ADOLPH
folksinger .... PHIL
octan .... FEVER
octave .... UTAS, EIGHT
Octavia's husband ...... ANTONY
octet(te) .... EIGHT
October 15 .... IDES
Revolution leader .... LENIN,
TROTSKY
octogenarian .... DOTARD

age of .... EIGHTIES
octopus .... SQUID, POULPE,
MOLLUSK, OCTOPOD,
DEVILFISH
arm of .... TENTACLE
octoroon .... METIS, MESTEE,
MUSTEE
octroi .... TAX
octuple .... EIGHTFOLD
ocular .... LENS, VISUAL,
OPTIC(AL), EYESIGHT
oculist's concern .... EYE
Ocypete .... HARPY
od, manifestation of
.... HYPNOTISM, MAGNETISM
odalisque ...... SLAVE, CONCUBINE
place of .... ADA, IDA, ODA
odd .... RUM, DROLL, EXTRA,
QUEER, QUAINT, AZYGOUS,
STRANGE, PECULIAR,
SINGULAR, ANOMALOUS,
ECCENTRIC
job .... CHAR(E), CHORE
job man .... JACK
mannerism/trait .... QUIRK
slang .... BATTY, SCREWY
oddity .... FREAK, QUIRK,
VAGARY, QUEERNESS
odds .... CHANCES, ADVANTAGE
and ends .... JOBLOT, SCRAPS,
REMNANTS, RUMMAGE,
ETCETERAS
ode .... HYMN, POEM
division of .... STROPHE
odeon .... HALL, THEATRE
Oder, city on the .... BRESLAU,
STETTIN
tributary .... WARTHE
odeum .... HALL
odiferous .... AREEK
Odin .... GOD, WODEN, WOTAN
concern of .... WAR, DEAD
horse of .... SLEIPNER
maiden of .... VALKYR(IE)
parent of .... BOR
son of .... TIU, TYR, THOR,
VALI, BALDER
victim of .... YMIR
wife of .... FRIA, JORD,
FRIGG(A)
wolf of .... GERE, GERI
odious .... HATEFUL, HEINOUS,
OFFENSIVE, REPUGNANT,
REPULSIVE, DETESTABLE,
DISGUSTING
odium .... HATE, HATRED,
INFAMY, DISGRACE,
APPROBIUM
odometer .... TAXIMETER
odontoid .... TOOTHLIKE
odontology .... DENTISTRY

subject of .... TEETH
odor .... FUME, NOSE, AROMA,
SCENT, SMELL, TRAIL,
BOUQUET, FRAGRANCE
disagreeable .... STINK,
F(O)ETOR, STENCH
musty .... FUNK
pleasant .... INCENSE,
PERFUME, FRAGRANCE
odorless .... AOSMIC
odorous ...... FETID, OLENT, SPICY,
PUNGENT, AROMATIC,
FRAGRANT, REDOLENT,
OLFACTORY
Odysseus .... KING, ULYSSES
captor of .... POLYPHEMUS
father of .... LAERTES
monstrous beings
encountered by
.... LAESTRYGON OGRES
nephew of .... MEGES
protection against Circe
.... MOLY
realm of .... ITHACA
to Cyclops .... NOMAN
wife of .... PENELOPE
odyssey .... QUEST, VOYAGE,
JOURNEY, WANDERING,
PILGRIMAGE
Odyssey .... POEM
author of .... HOMER
beggar of .... IRUS
enchantress in .... CIRCE
nymph .... CALYPSO
queen in .... PENELOPE
Oedipus daughter ...... ANTIGONE
father .... LAIUS
mother .... JOCASTA
son .... ETEOCLES, POLYNICES
wife of .... JOCASTA
oenologist's concern .... YEAR
need .... YEAST
oenology, subject of .... WINES
Oenone .... NYMPH
husband of .... PARIS
rival of .... HELEN
of .... BY, FROM, HAVE, WITH,
ABOUT
a biological partition
.... SEPTAL
a great poet .... KEATSIAN
a killing: comb. form
.... CIDAL
a metallic element
.... EUROPIC
a reign .... REGIME, REGNAL
a target spot .... FOCAL
a time period .... ERAL
a verse .... ODIC
an age/epoch .... ERAL
any kind .... SO EVER

Attica .... IONIC
course: sl. .... NATCH
distinction .... NOTABLE
each .... PER
flight .... AERO
grandparents .... AVAL
greater size .... LONGER
inferior quality .... BUM
Lamb's writings .... ELIAN
lunar stages .... PHASIC
melody/pitch .... TONAL
mysterious meaning .... RUNIC
no _____ .... USE, MOMENT,
ACCOUNT
old age .... GERIATRICS
poetic feet .... ANAPAESTIC
roses, _____ .... ATTAR
seers .... VATIC
sight .... OPTIC
sound mind .... SANE
substance .... MEATY
summer .... ESTIVAL
the cheekbone .... MALAR
the dawn .... EOAN
the kidneys .... RENAL
the mind .... PSYCH
the source of origin
.... PARENTAL
the tail .... CAUDAL
the world .... MUNDANE
this planet .... EARTHLY
thread .... FILAR
Of _____ and the River ...... TIME
Mice and Men author
.... STEINBECK
Mice and Men character
.... LENNIE
off .... AGEE, AWAY, GONE,
WRONG, ABSENT, IN ERROR
-base, slightly .... LOONY
-color .... RACY, DIRTY,
RISQUE, OBSCENE
-key .... FLAT
nautical .... SEAWARD
one's rocker .... LOCO
the beaten path .... AMISS
the mark/track .... AMISS
the regimen .... EX-DIET
-the-streets signal ..... CURFEW
-white .... ECRU
off, _____ (get along) ...... HIT IT
(go away) .... BUZZ
(irate) .... TEED
offal .... WASTE, REFUSE,
GARBAGE
offbeat ...... ODD, KOOKY, WACKY,
WEIRD, UNUSUAL
Offenbach, composer
.... JACQUES
offend .... VEX, HARM, HUFF,
HURT, MIFF, ANGER, PIQUE,

UPSET, WRONG, INSULT,
SLIGHT, AFFRONT, MORTIFY,
OUTRAGE, DISPLEASE
offender .... CULPRIT
offense .... SIN, CRIME, FELONY,
OUTRAGE, UMBRAGE,
RESENTMENT
against law .... MALA
in law .... DELICT
offensive .... UGLY, ATTACK,
ODIOUS, FULSOME, NOISOME,
UNSAVORY, REPULSIVE
for quick victory
.... BLITZ(KRIEG)
to morals .... OBSCENE,
IMPROPER, INDECENT
offer .... BID, EXTEND, TENDER,
PRESENT, PROFFER, PROPOSE,
PROPOSAL, SUGGEST(ION)
final .... ULTIMATUM
in sacrifice .... IMMOLATE
introductory .... OVERTURE
of one's free will
.... VOLUNTEER
offering .... GIFT, TRIBUTE,
DONATION, OBLATION,
SACRIFICE, CONTRIBUTION
at a wedding ..... RING-FINGER
to God .... CORBAN
widow's .... MITE
offhand .... CURT, ABRUPT,
CASUAL, INFORMAL,
SLAPDASH, EXTEMPORE,
IMPROMPTU
office .... JOB, DUTY, POST, RANK,
ROLE, SERVICE, FUNCTION,
POSITION
bigwig .... BOSS
boss .... MANAGER
holder .... IN, INCUMBENT
of the Dead: Eccles .... DIRGE
remove from .... OUST,
DEPOSE, RECALL
wall sign .... THINK
worker, for short .... STENO
officer .... DIRECTOR, CONSTABLE,
POLICEMAN, PRESIDENT
abbey .... ABBOT
abbreviation .... LT, ADM, COL,
GEN, MAJ, NCO, CAPT, LIEUT
assistant to an .... AIDE,
DEPUTY
church .... ELDER, BISHOP,
DEACON, PRIEST, SEXTON,
MINISTER, PRESBYTER
court .... BAILIFF
Customs .... EXAMINER
IRS .... AGENT, COLLECTOR
kind of ...... TRUANT, FINANCE,
WARRANT
medical .... CORONER

military ...... MAJOR, ADMIRAL,
CAPTAIN, COLONEL, GENERAL,
LIEUTENANT
national chief law
.... ATTORNEY GENERAL
police .... CHIEF, INSPECTOR
school .... DEAN, PRINCIPAL,
REGISTRAR
officer's insignia .... BAR, EAGLE,
INSIGNE
official .... FORMAL, OFFICER,
DIGNITARY, AUTHORIZED,
BUREAUCRAT
approval .... IMPRIMATUR
course .... CHANNEL(S)
decree .... EDICT, IRADE,
UKASE, RESCRIPT
denial .... DEMENTI
elected .... POLITICIAN
family, President's
.... CABINET
list .... CANON
paper container .... POUCH,
HAMPER, HANAPER
proceedings .... ACTA
residence, U.S. President's
.... WHITE HOUSE
routine .... RED TAPE
seal .... SIGNET
self-important .... BASHAW,
PANJANDRUM
snafu .... RED TAPE
statement .... BULLETIN,
COMMUNIQUE
officialdom .... BUREAUCRACY
officiate .... DIRECT, PRESIDE
officious .... BOSSY, PUSHY,
PUSHING, PRAGMATIC,
GRATUITOUS, MEDDLESOME
offish .... ALOOF
offset .... SPUR, BRANCH,
BALANCE, (OFF)SHOOT,
COMPENSATE, NEUTRALIZE
offshoot ...... STEM, ISSUE, SCION,
BRANCH
offshore .... SEAWARD
O'Flaherty, author .... LIAM
offspring .... ISSUE, PRODUCT,
PROGENY, CHILD(REN)
in womb .... FETUS
oft .... OFTEN
often .... FREQUENTLY, AGAIN AND
AGAIN
plastered .... PARIS
Ogasawara island .... BONIN
Ogden .... NASH
ogee .... MOLDING
molding .... TALON
ogle ...... EYE, GAZE, LEER, LOOK,
STARE, GLAD EYE, OEILLADE
ogler .... EYER, STARER

Ogpu .... GAYPAY-OO
  predecessor of .... CHEKA
ogre .... BOGY, BEAST, DEMON,
  FIEND, GIANT, BUGABOO,
  MONSTER, BLUNDERBORE
Oh, what a girl .... SUSIE
O'Hara's manse .... TARA
Ohio bay .... MAUMEE, SANDUSKY
  capital .... COLUMBUS
  city/town .... KENT, LIMA,
  TROY, AKRON, BEREA, PARMA,
  XENIA, CANTON, DAYTON,
  ELYRIA, LORAIN, MARION,
  NEWARK, TIFFIN, TOLEDO,
  WARREN, FINDLAY, WOOSTER,
  HAMILTON, CLEVELAND,
  CINCINNATI, SPRINGFIELD
  college .... DYKE, HIRAM,
  WALSH, KENYON, MALONE,
  EDGECLIFF, NOTRE DAME,
  HEIDELBERG
  college town .... WOOSTER
  county .... ERIE, WOOD, ALLEN,
  CLARK, LUCAS, STARK,
  WAYNE, ATHENS, BUTLER,
  GREENE, LORAIN, MARION,
  MEDINA, SCIOTO, SUMMIT,
  WARREN, BELMONT, PORTAGE,
  CUYAHOGA, TRUMBULL
  lake ...... ERIE, DOVER, BERLIN,
  DILLON, INDIAN, BUCKEYE,
  LORAMIE, DELAWARE,
  PIEDMONT
  native .... BUCKEYE
  oil corporation, one time
  .... ESSO
  river .... MAD, OHIO, BLACK,
  GRAND, HURON, MIAMI,
  ROCKY, SCIOTO, TIFFIN,
  WABASH
  river city .... BELLAIRE
  state bird .... CARDINAL
  state flower .... SCARLET
  CARNATION
  state nickname .... BUCKEYE
  tourist attraction .... SEA
  WORLD, TAFT MUSEUM,
  CINCINNATI ZOO
  university .... KENT, TIFFIN,
  TOLEDO, XAVIER, CAPITAL,
  DENISON, FRANKLIN,
  WESLEYAN
Ohm, physicist .... GEORG
oikologist .... HOUSEKEEPER
oil .... LUBE, TUNG, BENNE, BRIBE,
  IRONE, ACEITE, ANOINT,
  SAFROL(E), PAINTING,
  LUBRICATE, LUBRICANT
  antiseptic .... CARVACROL
  aromatic ...... ATTAR, BALSAM,
  LAVENDER

baptismal .... CHRISM
bottle .... CRUET, CRUSE,
  CASTOR, AMPULLA
burner .... LAMP, CRAMMER,
  CRESSET
butter .... GHEE
colloquial .... FLATTER(Y)
combining form .... OLEO
consecrated .... CHRISM
container .... DRUM, CRUSE
countries, for short .... OPEC
country .... IRAQ, IRAN,
  KUWAIT, SAUDI ARABIA
driller .... WILDCATTER
essential .... ESSENCE
flower .... ATTAR, NEROLI
fragrant .... NARD, ATTAR
fruit rind .... BERGAMOT
lubricating .... LUBE
of/obtained from .... OLEIC
painting .... CANVAS
painting board .... PANEL
perfume-making .... BEN,
  ATTAR, BERGAMOT
plant .... RAMTIL, PATCHOULI
refining waste .... SLUDGE
rub with .... ANOINT
seed .... TIL, POON, RAPE,
  BEN(NE), RAMTIL, SESAME
ship .... TANKER
skin .... SEBUM
solvent .... ACETONE
source ..... COD, OLIVE, SHALE,
  PEANUT, BLUBBER
tree .... EBO(E), TUNG
well .... GASSER, GUSHER
well adjunct .... RIG
oilbird .... GUACHARO
oiler .... SHIP, TANKER
oilstone .... HONE
oily .... FATTY, SLEEK, SLICK,
  SOAPY, GREASY, SMOOTH,
  PINGUID, SLIPPERY,
  UNCTUOUS, SEBACEOUS
hydrocarbon in petroleum
  .... CETANE
ointment .... BALM, NARD, SALVE,
  POMADE, CALAMINE,
  VASELINE
base for .... LANOLIN(E)
Oise tributary .... AISNE
Ojibway .... INDIAN, CHIPPEWA
OK .... GO, ROGER, CORRECT, ALL
  RIGHT, APPROVAL
Oka city .... OREL
okapi relative .... GIRAFFE
Okie is from .... OKLAHOMA
Okinawa capital .... NAHA
Oklahoma capital .... OKLAHOMA
  CITY
city/town ...... ADA, JAY, ENID,

  ALTUS, MOORE, PONCA,
  TULSA, YUKON, DUNCAN,
  EDMOND, LAWTON, NORMAN,
  ARDMORE, BETHANY,
  CATOOSA, GUTHRIE, SHAWNEE,
  WAGONER, MUSKOGEE,
  CHICKASHA
college .... CHRISTIAN
county .... KAY, BRYAN,
  CADDO, CREEK, GRADY,
  OSAGE, PAYNE, TULSA,
  CARTER, JACKSON, CANADIAN,
  CHEROKEE, COMANCHE,
  SEMINOLE
cowboy hero .... CURLY
falls .... TURNER
fish hatchery site
  .... MEDICINE PARK
hiding place of outlaws, once
  .... DEVIL'S DEN
Indian ...... SAC, SAUK, CREEK,
  KIOWA, PONCA, APACHE,
  PAWNEE, ARAPAHO,
  CHEROKEE, COMANCHE
Indian Cheyenne chief
  .... BLACK KETTLE
Indian Comanche chief
  .... QUANAH PARKER
lake .... KAW, HUGO, EUCHA,
  HULAH, CANTON, TEXOMA,
  WISTER, KEYSTONE,
  LAWTONKA
largest fishing lake ..... ELMER
  THOMAS
migratory worker .... OKIE
mountain .... OZARK, SCOTT,
  PICHOT, BLACK MESA
mountains .... QUARTZ,
  WICHITA
national park .... PLATT
native .... OKIE, SOONER
part of .... PANHANDLE
refuge for crows .... FORT
  COBB
river .... RED, BLUE, CANEY,
  POTEAU, WASHITA, CIMARRON,
  ILLINOIS
state bird .... FLYCATCHER
state flower .... MISTLETOE
state nickname .... SOONER
state park ..... LITTLE SAHARA,
  RED ROCK CANYON
tourist attraction ...... COWBOY
  HALL OF FAME, WILL ROGERS
  MEMORIAL
university .... CAMERON,
  PHILLIPS, ORAL ROBERTS,
  PANHANDLE STATE
okra .... POD, SOUP, BENDY,
  GUMBO, PLANT, MALLOW
old ...... AGED, AULD, GRAY, WISE,

WORN, YORE, DATED, PASSE, STALE, SENILE, ANCIENT, ANTIQUE, ARCHAIC
age .... SENILITY
campaigner .... VET, WARHORSE
car .... REO
car's noise .... RATTLE
chaise longue .... DAYBED
"chap" preceder .... I SAY
country .... MOTHERLAND, NATIVE LAND
enough .... OF AGE
exclamation .... FIE
fashion .... COCKTAIL
fashioned .... DATED, FUSTY, PASSE, DEMODE, SQUARE
growing .... AGING, SENESCENT
hand .... PRO, EXPERT, STAGER, VET(ERAN)
hat .... RATED, STALE
heater .... ETNA
lady: sl. .... WIFE, MOTHER
landowner .... LORD
maid .... SPINSTER
man .... DODO, FATHER, GAFFER, GEEZER, HUSBAND
movies .... SILENTS
novel price .... DIME
one .... CRONE
pen .... QUILL
pies .... SPOILED ROTTEN
refrain .... FALA
salt .... SAILOR
saying .... SAW
structure .... RUNE
things, done over
.... RETREADS
time auto .... MERCER
time flour container
.... BARREL
time zither .... ASOR
very .... HOARY
wheeze .... ADAGE
woman/witch .... HAG, GAMMER
Old Dominion .... VIRGINIA
English letters .... EDHS
Faithful .... GEYSER
Faithful's activity
.... SPURTING
Faithful's locale
.... YELLOWSTONE PARK
Glory .... FLAG, STARS AND STRIPES
Harry .... DEVIL, SATAN
Hickory .... (ANDREW) JACKSON
Nick .... SATAN
_____: NY historic shrine
.... FORT NIAGARA

Saxon poem .... HELIAND
Scratch .... DEVIL, SATAN
Sod .... ERIN
Testament aboriginal giant
.... ANAK
addenda .... APOCRYPHA
book .... JOB, NEH, AMOS, EZRA, JOEL, RUTH, KINGS, HOSEA, JONAH, MICAH, NAHUM, DANIEL, ESTHER, EXODUS, HAGGAI, ISAIAH, JOSHUA, JUDGES, PSALMS, SAMUEL, EZEKIEL, GENESIS, MALACHI, NUMBERS, OBADIAH, JEREMIAH, NEHEMIAH, PROVERBS, LEVITICUS, CHRONICLES, DEUTERONOMY, LAMENTATIONS, ECCLESIASTES
first five books of the
.... PENTATEUCH
Greek translation of the
.... SEPTUAGINT
in Syriac .... PESHITO, PESHITTA
language .... HEBREW
longest book in the
.... PSALMS
marginal notes
.... MASORA(H)
measure of capacity .... HIN, KAB, LOG, BATH, OMER, EPHAH, HOMER, LETHECH
measure of length ..... SPAN, CUBIT, FINGER, HANDBREATH
middle book .... PROVERBS
Origen's .... HEXAPLA
scribe .... EZRA
shortest book in the
.... OBADIAH
weight .... BEKA, MINA, GERAH, SHEKEL, TALENT
wisdom book of the .... JOB, PROVERBS, ECCLESIASTES
writer .... ELOHIST
"Tin Lizzie" .... CRATE
West schoolteacher ..... MARM
World falcons .... SAKERS
lizard .... SEPS, AGAMA
rulers .... ROMANS
sedge .... GALINGALE
swan .... WHOOPER
olden .... ANCIENT
older .... SENIOR
people, discrimination
against .... AGEISM
people, discriminator against
.... AGEIST
oldest continent .... AUSTRALIA
member .... DEAN

person in the Bible
.... METHUSELAH
son .... HEIR, SCION
street in L.A. .... OLVERA
U.S. national park
.... YELLOWSTONE
oldfangled .... PASSE, OLD-HAT
oldtimer .... VET(ERAN)
oldwife .... MENHADEN, TRIGGERFISH
Ole, Norwegian composer
.... OLSEN
oleaceous tree .... ASH, LILAC, OLIVE, FORSYTHIA
oleaginous .... OILY, GREASY
oleander .... SHRUB, ROSEBAY
oleate .... SALT, ESTER
olefine .... ALKENE
olent .... FRAGRANT
oleo .... SPREAD, MARGARINE
oleoresin .... TOLU, ANIME, ELEMI, BALSAM
olfactory organ .... NOSE
stimulant .... ODOR
olibanum .... INCENSE
olio .... MESS, OLLA, STEW, MEDLEY, MELANGE, HODGEPODGE, MISCELLANY, SALMAGUNDI
olive .... TREE, RELISH, WREATH, OLEA(STER)
branch offering .... PEACE
genus .... OLEA
pimiento-stuffed .... PIMOLA
refuse .... BAGASSE
wild .... OLEASTER
Oliver .... NORTH, TWIST
composer .... BART
Twist author .... DICKENS
Twist character .... ROSE, TOBY, FAGIN, NANCY, SALLY, SIKES, BUMBLE, DODGER
Oliver's request .... MORE
Olivia's clown .... FESTE
olivine .... GARNET, PERIDOT
olla .... JAR, JUG, POT, STEW
ollapodrida .... HASH, OLIO, STEW, MEDLEY, ASSORTMENT
Ollie's friend .... FRAN
oloroso .... SHERRY
Olympian .... GOD, EROS, ATHLETE, EXALTED, GODLIKE, MAJESTIC, CELESTIAL
chief .... ZEUS
cupbearer .... GANYMEDE
queen .... HERA
reckless .... ATE
Olympic giant .... TITAN
gofer .... HEBE
name .... ATHENA

Olympic games site: first .... ELIS
1912 .... STOCKHOLM
1928 .... AMSTERDAM
1956 .... MELBOURNE
1992 .... BARCELONA
Olympics ...... ATHLETIC CONTEST
Number 1 award .... GOLD MEDAL
Number 2 award .... SILVER MEDAL
Number 3 award .... BRONZE MEDAL
Olympus .... SKY, MOUNT, HEAVEN
mountain .... OSSA, PELION
Oman bay .... SAUQIRA
cape .... HADD, JIBSH
capital .... MASQAT, MUSCAT
city/town .... MATRAH, SALALA
gulf .... MASIRAN
language .... ARABIC
money .... RIAL
sultan .... TAIMUR
Omar, actor .... SHARIF
general .... BRADLEY
Khayyam's birthplace .... NISHAPUR
country .... IRAN
work .... RUBAIYAT
omasum .... MANYPLIES
omber ...... HOMBRE, CARD GAME
omber, trump in .... MANILLA
omega .... END
antithesis of .... ALPHA
omelet(te) .... EGG DISH
omen .... SIGN, AUGUR(Y), AUSPICE, PORTENT, PRESAGE, PRECURSOR
death's .... KNELL
omentum .... CAUL
omers, ten .... EPHA
Omicron (variable star) .... CETI
ominous .... GRAVE, BODEFUL, FATEFUL, MENACING, SINISTER, PORTENTOUS
omission .... CUT, EVASION, NEGLECT, OVERSIGHT
sign of .... CARET
syllable .... APOCOPE
vowel .... ELISION
word .... ELLIPSIS
omit .... DROP, MISS, SKIP, DELETE, EXCEPT, EXCLUDE, NEGLECT, LEAVE OUT, PRETERMIT
a syllable .... ELIDE
omnia vincit _____ .... AMOR
omnibus .... BUS, COACH, READER, COLLECTION, ALL-EMBRACING

omnipotent .... ALMIGHTY
omnipresent .... IMMANENT, UBIQUITOUS
omnivorous animal .... SWINE
Omphale's domain .... LYDIA
servant .... HERCULES
Omri's son .... AHAB
on .... AT, ATOP, UPON, ABOUT, ABOVE, ONWARD, FORWARD
a bunt .... SACRIFICE
a grand scale ..... WORLDWIDE
a miscue .... ERROR
a par with .... EVEN, BESIDE
a ship's left side .... APORT
a ship's right side ...... ABEAM
a voyage .... ASEA
_____ (active) .... THE GO
and on .... ALWAYS, (FOR)EVER
call .... READY
dit .... RUMOR, GOSSIP
edge .... TENSE, KEYED UP
every side .... ABOUT
guard .... ALERT
horseback .... ASTRIDE
land .... ASHORE
one's toes .... ALERT, ALIVE
one's uppers .... POOR
pins and needles .... EAGER, TENSE, NERVOUS
tap .... NEXT
the _____ (at odds) .... OUTS
ball .... ALERT, SHARP
blue/briny/coral .... ASEA
crest .... ATOP
face of document .... EX FACIE
go .... BUSY
heights .... ATOP
_____ (honest) .... LEVEL
house .... FREEBIE
house, in a way .... RENT-FREE
left: comb. form .... LEVO
line .... AT STAKE
main .... ASEA
make .... SOCIAL-CLIMBING
mend .... IMPROVING
move .... ASTIR
other hand .... AGAIN
road .... AWAY
rocks .... ICED, AGROUND, FAILED, BUSTED, RUINED, WRECKED
sheltered side .... ALEE
side .... MORE
spot .... TREED, CORNERED
up and up .... LEGIT
warpath .... IRATE
way .... OFF, BOUND, EN ROUTE, PREGNANT, IN

TRANSIT
this earth .... HERE
time .... SHARP, PROMPT, PUNCTUALLY
to .... HEP, AWARE
two occasions .... TWICE
_____ (very busy) .... GO
windward side .... LEE, AWEATHER
your way! .... GIT, SCAT, SCRAM
on, _____ **(gather facts)** .... READ UP
on the donkey, _____ .... PIN A TAIL
onager .... ASS, DONKEY, CATAPULT
Onassis, (A) nickname of .... ARI, DADDY-O
yacht of .... CHRISTINA
once .... ANES, WHILOM, ONE TIME, QUONDAM, FORMER(LY), ERST(WHILE)
all at .... SUDDENLY
around Sol .... YEAR
around (the track) .... LAP
called .... NEE
called Ptolemais .... ACRE
more .... AGAIN, AFRESH, ENCORE
once-over ...... GLANCE, SCRUTINY
oncoming .... IMPENDING, APPROACHING
one .... ACE, EACH, SAME, UNIT, SINGLE, UNITED, UNDIVIDED
against .... ANTI
and only .... SOLE
and the other .... BOTH
-armed bandit: sl. .... SLOT MACHINE
base hit .... SINGLE
behind another .... TANDEM
billionth .... NANO
bottled up .... GENIE
bringing a case .... SUER
-celled creature ...... STENTOR, AM(O)EBA, PROTOZOA, INFUSORIA
combining form .... UNI, MONO
eighth of dollar .... BIT
Eve had three .... FACES
-eyed .... MONOCULAR
-eyed giant .... CYCLOPS
-footed .... UNIPED
fourth of an anna .... PICE
headed for defeat .... GONER
hopelessly behind the times .... DODO
-horned animal .... RHINO, UNICORN

-horned fish .... UNIE
horse .... PETTY
horse town .... PODUNK
horse vehicle .... SHAY
hundred: comb. form
.... HECTO
hundred kopecks .... RUBLE
hundred percent .... WHOLE,
ENTIRE
hundred thousand in India
.... LAC
hundred years .... CENTURY,
CENTENARY
in line .... STANDER
kind of horse .... IRON,
WOODEN, ARABIAN
kind of pen .... POISON
kind of steer .... BUM
-legged .... UNIPOD
liner .... GAG
more .... ANOTHER
more than septi- .... OCTA
more time .... AGAIN
next to the last .... PENULT
of a cold weather pair
.... EARMUFF
a famous five .... QUINT
a friendly pair .... DAMON,
PYTHIAS
a trio .... TOM, DICK, HARRY,
CALM, COOL, COLLECTED,
ATHOS, ARAMIS, PORTHOS
Columbus' ships .... NIÑA,
PINTA, SANTA MARIA
eighteen .... HOLE
nine .... MUSE
of the Bowls .... SUN, HULA,
ROSE, GATOR, FIESTA, SUPER,
ORANGE
Carolines .... YAP, MOEN,
TRUK, BELAU, PALAU,
ULITHI, PELELIU
Cartrights .... BEN, HOSS,
LITTLE JOE
elite ..... SOCIAL REGISTERITE
Great Lakes ...... LAKE ERIE,
LAKE HURON, LAKE
ONTARIO, LAKE MICHIGAN,
LAKE SUPERIOR
towels .... HIS, HERS
Trimurti .... SIVA, VISHNU,
BRAHMA
of two .... EITHER
on the payroll .... EARNER
or another .... ANY
out on bond .... BAILEE
pound sterling .... QUID
recently hatched ..... NESTLING
result of thinking .... PLAN
sending an overseas message
.... CABLER

sergeant's .... HUP
showing promise .... COMER
sided .... ROUT, BIASED,
PARTIAL, EX PARTE,
UNILATERAL
spot .... ACE
square meter .... CENT(I)ARE
tenth are .... DECIARE
tenth of annual income
.... TITHE
thing .... UNIT
thousand .... MIL
time .... EARLIER
-time St. Petersburg residents
.... TSARS
-track mind .... MONOMANIA
type of photograph .... X-RAY,
GLOSSY
way of breaking glass
.... SHOOTING PANES
-way sign .... ARROW
way to go for dinner
.... DUTCH
way to ride .... ASTRIDE
way to stand .... PAT
who: suffix .... STER
acquires .... ASSUMER
catches sight of
.... DESCRIER
dodges .... EVADER
enjoys .... SAVORER
entertains .... HOST
goes in haste .... HIER
incites .... URGER
is being quizzed ..... TESTEE
is being tutored .... TUTEE
is quoted .... CITEE
makes a statement
.... RESOLUTIONER
practices witchcraft
.... SORCERER, SORCERESS
transfers property
.... ALIENOR
walks in water .... WADER
watches .... SPIER
worships only one god
.... MONOLATER
with a bright future
.... COMER
with a foreign accent
.... XENOEPIST
with a taxing job
.... ASSESSOR
with dependents
.... BREADWINNER
within the playing field
.... ONSIDER
one's betrothed .... FIANCE(E)
dialect .... IDIOLECT
own: comb. form .... IDIO

personal mannerism
.... IDIOSYNCRASY
public .... AUDIENCE,
FOLLOWING
strong point .... FORTE
Oneida .... INDIAN, IROQUOIS
O'Neill, playwright ...... EUGENE
character .... ANNA, NINA,
ORIN
daughter .... OONA
field of .... DRAMA
son-in-law
.... (CHARLIE)CHAPLIN
oneness .... UNITY, IDENTITY,
SAMENESS
oner .... LULU, LONER
onerous .... DIFFICULT,
BURDENSOME, OPPRESSIVE
ones here .... THESE
onion .... BULB, CEPA, LEEK,
CIBOL, ALLIUM, SHALLOT,
ESCHALOT, SCALLION
plant .... CHIVE
sea .... SQUILL
onions, prepared with
.... LYONNAISE
onionskin .... PAPER
onlooker .... BYSTANDER,
WITNESS, SPECTATOR
only .... BUT, LONE, MERE(LY),
SIMPLY, SINGLY, SOLE(LY)
onomatopoeia .... ECHOISM
onomatopoeic .... ECHOIC,
IMITATIVE
Onondaga .... LAKE, INDIAN,
IROQUOIS
onrush .... BIRR, DASH, FLOW,
STAMPEDE
onset .... START, ATTACK,
ASSAULT, APPROACH,
OUTBREAK, BEGINNING
onslaught .... RUSH, DRIVE,
ONSET, ATTACK, CHARGE,
THRUST, ASSAULT, OFFENSIVE
Ontario .... LAKE, PROVINCE
bay .... SOUTH, GEORGIAN
canal .... WELLAND
cape .... HURD, CROKER
capital .... TORONTO
city/town .... BARRIE, LONDON,
SUDBURY, TRENTON, WINDSOR,
BRAMPTON, HAMILTON,
KINGSTON, WATERLOO,
BRANTFORD, CAMBRIDGE,
ETOBICOKE, KITCHENER,
BURLINGTON, SCARBOROUGH
island .... PARRY, BARRIE,
AMHERST, WALPOLE,
COCKBURN, CHRISTIAN,
FLOWERPOT
lake .... DORE, ERIE, RICE,

SEUL, HURON, RAINY, WOODS, RIDEAU, SIMCOE, NIPIGON, PANACHE, SUPERIOR, NIPISSING, SAINT CLAIR

mountain .... OGIDAKI

river .... DON, GRAND, HUMBER, OTTAWA, SEVERN, ABITIBI, NIAGARA, MISSINAIBI

onto .... HEP, AWARE, WISE TO, COGNIZANT, CONVERSANT

onus .... DUTY, LOAD, TASK, BURDEN, CHARGE, OBLIGATION

onward .... AHEAD, FORTH, ADVANCING

onyx .... GEM, AGATE, NICOLO

007 .... JAMES BOND

antagonist of (in a '64 film) .... GOLDFINGER

creator .... IAN FLEMING

portrayer ..... MOORE, DALTON, BROSNAN, CONNERY, LAZENBY

oocyte .... EGG, GAMETE

oodles .... HEAP, LOTS, MANY, RAFTS, SCADS, SLEWS

oolite .... LIMESTONE

oology subject ...... (BIRD'S)EGGS

oolong .... TEA

Oom Paul .... KRUGER

oomiak .... CANOE, KAYAK

oomph .... VIGOR, SEX APPEAL

oorial .... SHA

oosperm .... ZYGOTE

ootheca .... OVISAC, EGG CASE

ooze .... BOG, MUD, DRIP, FLOW, LEAK, MIRE, SEEP, EXUDE, GLEET, MARSH, SLIME, SWEAT, FILTER, SLUDGE, EXUDATE, PERMEATE, SEDIMENT

oozy .... MIRY, SOFT, SLIMY, SLUDGY, SLOUGHY

opacate .... DIM

opah .... SOKO, (MOON)FISH

opal .... GEM, PITCH, RESIN, SILICA, HYALITE, ISOPYRE, CACHOLONG

fire .... GIRASOL(E), GIROSOL

opalescent .... IRIDESCENT

opaline .... GLASS

opaque ...... DARK, DULL, OBTUSE, OBSCURE

OPEC .... CARTEL

open .... BARE, FREE, UNDO, CLEAR, FRANK, OVERT, START, CANDID, EXPOSE(D), PUBLIC, UNFOLD, UNLOCK, UNSEAL(ED), LIBERAL, DISCLOSE, GENEROUS

air ..... ALFRESCO, OUTDOOR(S)

and shut .... CLEAR, SIMPLE,

EVIDENT, OBVIOUS

car .... PHAETON

country .... VELDT

-eyed ...... AWARE, WATCHFUL, OBSERVANT

-handed ...... GIVING, LIBERAL, GENEROUS

-hearted .... FRANK, CANDID, GENIAL, CORDIAL

in a way .... UNBOLT

-minded .... AMENABLE, RECEPTIVE

-mouthed .... AGOG, AGAPE

partly .... AJAR

sea .... MAIN

sesame .... PASSWORD

the bottle .... UNCAP

to attack .... VULNERABLE

to view .... OVERT

up .... UNDO

widely .... GAPE

opener .... KEY, CLAVIS

opening .... GAP, GATE, HOLE, PORE, SLIT, SLOT, MOUTH, CHANCE, ORIFICE, VACANCY, APERTURE, LOOPHOLE

in chess .... GAMBIT

small .... PORE, CRANNY, FORAMEN, ORIFICE, OSTIOLE

openings, in zoology
.... STOMATA

opera .... AIDA, FAUST, MANON, NORMA, THAIS, TOSCA, CARMEN, ERNANI, MIKADO, RIENZI, SALOME, FIDELIO, LA BOHEME

box .... LOGE

by Gershwin .... PORGY AND BESS

Gounod .... ROMEO ET JULIETTE

Handel .... NERO, SERSE

Humperdinck .... HANSEL AND GRETEL

Massenet .... THAIS

Puccini .... TOSCA, TURANDOT, LA BOHEME, MADAMA BUTTERFLY

Rossini .... WILLIAM TELL, THE BARBER OF SEVILLE

Salieri .... A TAR

Smetana ...... THE BARTERED BRIDE

Strauss .... SALOME

Verdi .... ERNANI, RIGOLETTO

Von Weber .... OBERON

Wagner .... LOHENGRIN, GOTTERDAMMERUNG, TRISTAN UND ISOLDE

comic .... BUFFO, BOUFFE

company director/manager
.... IMPRESARIO

composer .... BIZET, VERDI, HANDEL, GOUNOD, MOZART, WAGNER, MENOTTI, PUCCINI, ROSSINI, SMETANA, STRAUSS, MASSENET, HUMPERDINCK

describing an .... SOAP, COMIC, HORSE, LIGHT, BALLET

glass .... LORGNETTE

hat .... GIBUS, TOPPER

heroine ...... AIDA, ELSA, MIMI, LUCIA, SENTA, GRETEL, ISOLDE, PAMINA, ARIADNE, CIO CIO SAN

highlight .... ARIA

horse .... OATER

house .... MET, (LA)SCALA

singer .... ALDA, PONS, EAMES, HORNE, MELBA, PINZA, PRICE, CALLAS, GARDEN, PETERS, STEBER, TUCKER, CABALLE, CORELLI, DOMINGO, NILSSON, STEVENS, TEBALDI, CHALIAPIN

solo .... ARIA, CAVATINA

star .... DIVA, PRIMA DONNA

text of .... LIBRETTO

operate .... ACT, RUN, USE, TEND, WORK, MANAGE, CONDUCT

against .... MILITATE

on .... TREAT, INFLUENCE

operatic character .... BUFFO

impresario, 1843–89 ..... ROSA

prince .... IGOR

slave .... AIDA

solo .... ARIA

operation .... ACTION, PROCESS, PROJECT

operative .... SPY, AGENT, WORKING, DETECTIVE, EFFECTIVE

operator .... AGENT, HANDLER

operculum .... LID, FLAP

operetta composer .... FRIML, LEHAR, STRAUS, HERBERT, ROMBERG, STRAUSS, OFFENBACH

Herbert's .... NAUGHTY MARIETTA

Lehar's .... THE MERRY WIDOW

Offenbach's .... LA PERICHOLE

Romberg's .... THE STUDENT PRINCE

singer .... MOFFO, SILLS, FRANCHI

Straus' .... THE CHOCOLATE SOLDIER

Strauss' .... DIE FLEDERMAUS

operose ...... ARDUOUS, ONEROUS, DIFFICULT, LABORIOUS

Ophelia's love .... HAMLET

parent .... POLONIUS
ophidian .... ASP, COBRA, SNAKE,
REPTILE, SERPENT
Ophir's wealth .... GOLD
ophthalmologist .... OCULIST
ophthalmology, subject of
.... EYE, SIGHT, VISION
opiate .... SEDATIVE, ANALGESIC
opine .... THINK, BELIEVE,
SUPPOSE
opinion .... IDEA, VIEW, TENET,
ADVICE, BELIEF, NOTION,
THEORY, THOUGHT, VERDICT,
JUDGMENT, SENTIMENT,
CONVICTION, IMPRESSION,
PERSUASION
barometer .... GALLUP POLL
general .... CONSENSUS
having opposite .... POLES
APART
man .... POLLSTER, POLL-
TAKER
opposing .... HERESY
united in .... AGREEING,
CONSENTIENT
opinionated .... BIASED, BIGOTED,
DOGMATIC
speaker .... DOGMATIZER
opium .... DRUG, NARCOTIC
addict .... USER, DOPER,
JUNKY, JUNKIE, NOSCAPINE,
(DOPE)FIEND
alkaloid ...... CODEA, CODEINE,
MORPHINE, PAPAVARINE
seed .... MAW
seller .... PUSHER
source .... POPPY
tincture of .... LA(U)DANUM
traffic center .... TACHILEK
opossum .... QUICA, YAPO(C)K,
MARSUPIAL
place of young .... POUCH
play .... DEAD, FEIGN
oppidan .... URBAN
opponent ...... FOE, ANTI, ENEMY,
ADVERSARY, ANTAGONIST
of change .... DIEHARD
opportune .... APT, TIMELY,
APROPOS, FORTUITOUS, WELL-
TIMED, PROPITIOUS,
SEASONABLE
opportunist .... EXPLOITER, TIME-
SERVER
opportunity .... CHANCE,
OPENING, OCCASION
oppose .... DARE, DEFY, DENY,
FACE, FOIL, CROSS, REPEL,
HINDER, OBJECT, REPUGN,
RESIST, COUNTER(ACT),
PROTEST, DISAGREE,
WITHSTAND

opposed .... ANTI, AVERSE,
AGAINST, CONTRARY
opposing .... RIVAL
opposite ...... FORNENT, REVERSE,
VIS-A-VIS, ANTIPODE,
CONTRAST, CONTRARY,
ANTITHESIS, ANTITHETIC
Adam's .... LAST MAN
belief .... HERESY
directly ..... HEAD-ON, INVERSE
exact .... ANTIPODE
extremity .... POLE
number .... COUNTERPART
of what's expected ..... IRONIC
prefix .... ANTI
opposition .... FOE, RIVAL,
DEFIANCE, ANTIPATHY,
HOSTILITY, RESISTANCE,
COMPETITION
abrupt show of ...... WALKOUT
act of .... STRIKE, BOYCOTT
in .... CON, ANTI, AGAINST
party .... MINORITY
oppress .... CRUSH, GRIPE,
BURDEN, MISTREAT,
PERSECUTE, TYRANNIZE
oppressive ...... CRUEL, ONEROUS,
TYRANNICAL
anything .... INCUBUS
oppressor .... BULLY, TYRANT
opprobrious .... ABUSIVE,
MALICIOUS, DEROGATORY
opprobrium .... ODIUM, SCORN,
SHAME, INFAMY, DISGRACE
oppugn .... OPPOSE, DISPUTE,
CRITICIZE, CONTROVERT
Opryland's Wagoner .... PORTER
Ops .... RHEA, GODDESS
concern of .... HARVEST
daughter of .... CERES
husband of .... SATURN
opt .... CHOOSE, DECIDE, SELECT
optic .... EYE
branch of .... CATOPTRICS
optical .... OCULAR, VISUAL
aid .... LENSES, GLASSES,
LORGNON, MONOCLE,
PINCENEZ, LORGNETTE,
BINOCULARS
glass .... LENS, SPECS,
CONTACT
illusion .... MIRAGE
instrument .... VIEWER,
ALIDADE, PERISCOPE,
TELESCOPE, MICROSCOPE
instrument lines .... RETICLE
optician .... OPTOMETRIST
Optics author .... NEWTON
optimism .... HOPE, TRUST,
ENTHUSIASM
optimistic .... ROSY, UPBEAT,

HOPEFUL, ROSEATE,
SANGUINE, CONFIDENT,
EXPECTANT
optimum .... BEST, PRIME, CHOICE
option ...... VOTE, RIGHT, CHOICE,
PREFERENCE, ALTERNATIVE
optional .... ELECTIVE
opulent .... RICH, WEALTHY,
ABUNDANT
opuntia .... TUNA, CACTUS
opus .... WORK, OPERA,
SYMPHONY, COMPOSITION
plural of .... OPERA
oquassa .... TROUT
or .... GOLD, YELLOW,
CONJUNCTION
ora .... COIN, MOUTHS
orach(e) .... SPINACH, GOOSEFOOT
oracle .... SEER, AUGUR, DELOS,
PROPHET, HOLY OF HOLIES
giver .... FAUNUS
seat .... DODONA
site of .... DELPHI
woman .... SYBIL, SIBYL
oracular .... VATIC, ORPHIC,
PROPHETIC, SYBILLINE
oral .... VOCAL, SPOKEN, VERBAL,
STOMATIC, UNWRITTEN
pledge .... WORD, PAROLE
orale .... FANON
orally .... PAROL, VIVA VOCE
Oran is in .... ALGERIA
orange .... CITRUS, TANGELO,
MANDARIN, TANGERINE
flower oil .... NEROLI
genus .... CITRUS
inedible .... OSAGE
juice squeezer .... REAMER
mock .... SYRINGA
of an .... CITRIC
peel .... ZEST
pekoe .... TEA
preserve .... MARMALADE
red chalcedony .... SARD
seed .... PIP
skin .... RIND
variety/type .... NAVEL,
MICHAEL, VALENCIA
yellow ...... CROCUS, LUTEOUS,
SAFFRON
Orange River tributary
.... VAAL
orangewood .... HEDGE
orangutan .... APE, MIAS
habitat ...... BORNEO, SUMATRA
orate .... MOUTH, DECLAIM,
PERORATE, SPEECHIFY
oration .... SPEECH, ADDRESS,
DISCOURSE
orator ...... OTIS, BRYAN, CICERO,
RHETOR, SPEAKER

in law .... PLAINTIFF,
PETITIONER
oratorio lyrics .... LIBRETTO
part of .... ARIA, DUET, TRIO,
CAVATINA
oratory .... CHAPEL, CHANTRY,
ELOQUENCE
fathers, founder of .... NERI
master of .... RHETOR
orb ...... EYE, SUN, MOON, GLOBE,
SPHERE
orbit .... PATH, REALM, SCOPE,
TRACK, CIRCUIT, EYE SOCKET
heavenly body's .... CYCLE
perigee of .... NADIR
orbital point .... APSE, APSIS,
APOGEE, PERIGEE
orc .... WHALE, GRAMPUS
kind of .... DOLPHIN
orchard .... GROVE, GARDEN
orchal .... LICHEN
orchestra .... BAND, PARQUET,
SYMPHONY
circle .... PARTERRE
conductor/leader .... MACE,
SHAW, BOULT, CUGAT, GOULD,
JAMES, LEWIS, MEHTA, SANTI,
DUCHIN, PREVIN, VALLEE,
FIEDLER, ORMANDY, FERRARIS,
GERHARDT, WILLIAMS,
LEINSDORF, STOKOWSKI,
HAMMERSTEIN
platform .... BANDSTAND
section .... BRASS, REEDS,
TRAPS, WINDS, STRINGS,
PERCUSSION
space for .... PIT
theater's .... GROUND FLOOR
orchestral exclamation point
.... CYMBAL
orchestrate .... ARRANGE
orchid .... SATYR, DICHEA,
FLOWER, POGONIA, EPIPHYTE,
BUTTERFLY, PUTTYROOT
as food .... SALEP
climbing .... VANILLA
genus .... DISA, ORCHIS
third petal of .... LIP
tuber .... SALEP
orchil .... DYE, LICHEN
Orcus .... DIS, HADES, PLUTO
ordain .... ENACT, FROCK, ORDER,
DECREE, INVEST, APPOINT,
PRESCRIBE
ordeal .... TEST, CROSS, TRIAL,
CRUCIBLE, HARDSHIP,
TRIBULATION
order ...... BID, HEST, KIND, SORT,
CLASS, LODGE, DEMAND,
DIRECT(ION), METHOD, SERIES,
SYSTEM, COMMAND,

MANDATE, CATEGORY,
PRESCRIBE, COMMISSION,
INSTRUCT(ION)
back .... REMAND
good .... EUTAXY
marching .... FALL IN
of animals .... INI
to cease .... RESTRAINER
Order of the Garter
.... KNIGHTHOOD
ordered, old style .... BADE
orderly .... AIDE, NEAT, TIDY,
TRIM, SPRUCE, REGULAR,
ATTENDANT, METHODICAL,
SYSTEMATIC
arrangement .... PLAN
ordinal .... NUMBER
number .... FIRST, SECOND,
THIRD, FOURTH, FIFTH
suffix .... (E)TH
ordinance .... LAW, EDICT,
STATUTE, REGULATION
ordinary .... SO-SO, USUAL,
COMMON, MEDIAL, MEDIUM,
NORMAL, TAVERN, AVERAGE,
MILL-RUN, REGULAR,
ROUTINE, CHAPLAIN,
MEDIOCRE, MIDDLING,
CUSTOMARY
ordnance .... GUNS, ARMOR,
CANNON, WEAPONRY,
ARTILLERY
ordure .... DUNG, FILTH, MANURE
ore .... MINERAL
analyze .... ASSAY
bearing rock layer .... LEDGE
bed of .... REEF
crushing machine .... STAMP
deposit .... LODE, POCKET
digger .... MINER
extract/refine .... SMELT
iron .... OCHER, OCHRE
layer .... SEAM, STOPE
lead .... GALENA
refiner .... SMELTER
screening sieve ...... TROMMEL
shovel for washing .... VAN
smelting product .... SPEISS
truck/wagon .... CORF
vein .... LODE, STREAK
washing container .... PAN
washing device .... DOLLY
worthless .... MATTE
oread .... NAIAD, NYMPH
oregano .... MINT, PLANT,
MARJORAM
Oregon bay .... TILLAMOOK,
WINCHESTER
beach ...... NYE, GOLD, AGATE,
SECCHI, CRESCENT
cape .... ARAGO, BLANCO,

FALCON, MEARES, LOOKOUT,
PERPETUA, SEBASTIAN
capital .... SALEM
city/town .... BEND, ALOHA,
ALBANY, DALLAS, EUGENE,
KEIZER, TIGARD, KIWANDA,
ASHLAND, ASTORIA, GRESHAM,
LEBANON, LINCOLN, MEDFORD,
NEWPORT, ALTAMONT,
PORTLAND, ROSEBURG,
WOODBURN, BEAVERTON,
CORVALLIS, HILLSBORO,
GRANTS PASS
college .... REED
county ..... COOS, LAKE, LANE,
LINN, POLK, BAKER, CURRY,
GRANT, UNION, WASCO,
BENTON, MARION, DOUGLAS,
KLAMATH, YAMHILL,
CLACKAMAS, JOSEPHINE
dam .... OXBOW, MCNARY,
OWYHEE, THE DALLES,
BONNEVILLE, HELLS CANYON
falls .... MUNSON, PUNCHBOWL,
STEAMBOAT
Indian .... COOS, KUSAN,
MODOC, YANAN, CAYUSE,
CHINOOK, NEZ PERCE
island .... WIZARD
lake .... HART, LAVA, LOST,
ABERT, ASPEN, DAVIS, GUANO,
WALDO, ALVORD, CRATER,
CULTUS, DORENA, EWAUNA,
HARNEY, SILVER, SPARKS,
SUMMER, TUMTUM, DETROIT,
DIAMOND, PAULINA,
WALLOWA, FOURMILE,
UMATILLA
mountain .... HART, HOOD,
STEENS, THIELSEN,
MCLOUGHLIN
mountain, twin-peaked
.... SADDLE
mountain range .... BLUE,
OWYHEE, PUEBLO, CASCADE,
KLAMATH, WALLOWA,
SISKIYOU
Myrtle Grove site
.... MILLICOMA
National forest .... SIUSLAW
National memorial to Lewis
and Clark .... FORT
CLATSOP
National park .... CRATER
LAKE
National wildlife refuge
.... MALHEUR
river .... COOS, HOOD, ALSEA,
BURNT, ROGUE, SMITH, SNAKE,
SYCAN, WHITE, CHETCO,
UMPQUA, NEHALEM, SPRAGUE,

MALHEUR, COLUMBIA, ILLINOIS, CALAPOOIA, DESCHUTES, WALLA-WALLA, WILLAMETTE
seaport .... ASTORIA
state bird .... MEADOWLARK
state flower .... (OREGON)GRAPE
state nickname .... BEAVER, SUNSET
state park .... ECOLA, SMITH ROCKS, SILVER CREEK
state university .... EUGENE, CORVALLIS
Trail users .... PIONEERS, SETTLERS
underwater marine science center site .... YAQUINA BAY
village, once upon a time .... BAY OCEAN
volcano that exploded and collapsed .... MOUNT MAZAMA

Orestes, parent of .... AGAMEMNON
sister of .... ELECTRA
wife of .... HERMIONE
orfe .... IDE
org. .... ASSN, SYST
ecological .... EPA, STE
for doctors .... AMA
for sharp students .... NHS
for teachers .... NEA
organ .... MEANS, VEHICLE, BOMBARDON, HARMONIUM, INSTRUMENT, PERIODICAL
atrophied .... VESTIGE
barrel .... HURDY-GURDY
connecting tissue .... PONS
device .... PIPE, REED, STOP, TREMOLO
falling of .... PTOSIS, PROLAPSE
grinder's assistant .... MONKEY
keyboard .... CLAVIER, MELODEON, ACCORDION, HARMONIUM
loft .... GALLERY
matrix of .... STROMA
mouth .... HARMONICA
of flight .... WING
of speech .... TONGUE
outgrowth .... APPENDIX
part .... PIPE, REED, STOP, PALLET, CONSOLE
pipe .... FLUE, REED, LABIAL, MONTRE
pipe plug .... TAMPION
place in church .... LOFT,

GALLERY
point/tip .... MUCRO
seed-bearing .... PISTIL
stop .... SEXT, TUBA, DOLCE, FLUTE, GAMBE, VIOLA, DULCET, MONTRE, OCTAVE, BASSOON, BOURDON, CELESTA, MELODIA, TREMOLO, VIOLONE, BOMBARDE, DIAPASON, DULCIANA
touch .... BARBEL, PALP(US)
transplantation pioneer .... BARNARD, DEBAKEY
vital .... EYE, LUNG, HEART, LIVER, KIDNEY
voice .... LARYNX
organic .... INBORN, INHERENT
body .... ZOOID
compound .... ENOL, AMINE
law .... CHARTER, CONSTITUTION
substance of .... MEDULLA
organism .... MONAD, MONAS, PLANT, ANIMAL
animal .... ZOOID
ductless .... SPLEEN
life cycle of .... ONTOGENY
living on another .... PARASITE
mode of formation .... MORPHOSIS
one-celled .... AM(O)EBA, PARAMECIUM
reaction to stimulus ..... TAXIS
requiring no air .... ANAEROBE
sea .... NEKTON
with parasite .... HOST
organist .... BACH, BIGGS
organization .... CLUB, CADRE, SETUP, UNION, OUTFIT, COMPANY, STRUCTURE
organize .... FORM, SET UP, ARRANGE, ESTABLISH, SYSTEMATIZE
organized movement ...... DRIVE, CRUSADE, CAMPAIGN
orgeat .... SIRUP
orgy .... BASH, BINGE, SPREE, REVELRY, CAROUSAL
oribi .... ANTELOPE
oriel .... NOOK, ALCOVE, (BAY)WINDOW
part .... PANE
orient .... ASIA, ADAPT, PEARL, ADJUST, (FAR)EAST
Oriental .... ASIAN, ASIATIC, EASTERN, CHINESE, JAPANESE
banker .... SHROFF
beverage .... CHA, TEA
bow .... SALAAM
cloth .... CAMLET
coin ..... RIN, SEN, ANNA, PICE,

TAEL, DINAR
decree .... FIRMAN
destiny .... KISMET
drink .... SAKE, TUBA, ARRACK
dwelling .... DAR
gate .... TORII
greeting .... SALAAM
inn ...... KHAN, SERAI, IMARET, CARAVANSARY
laborer .... COOLIE, SACADA
litter .... KAGO, DOOLEE, PALANQUIN
market .... SOOK, SOUK
martial art ...... JUDO, KARATE, JUJITSU, TAI CHI
money-changer .... SHROFF
name .... ALI, OMAR
nurse ...., AMA(H), AYAH, EYAH
opposite of .... WESTERN, OCCIDENTAL
palanquin .... DOOLEE
porter .... HAMAL, HAMAUL
potentate .... AGA
prince .... EMIR, AMEER
prison .... BAGNIO
punishment .... BASTINADO
rice dish .... PILAU, PILAF(F)
rug .... USHAK
ruler .... KHAN, SHAH, NAWAB, RAJAH, SULTAN
salute .... KOWTOW, SALAAM
sash .... OBI
seed .... SESAME
ship .... GRAB
sword .... SCIMITAR
taxi .... RICKSHA
title .... BABA, RAJAH
trousers ..... AJAMAS, PYJAMAS
weight .... ROTL, TAEL, CATTY, PICUL
wind .... MONSOON
orientate .... ADJUST, FAMILIARIZE
orientation of sorts .... BRIEFING
orifice .... HOLE, PORE, VENT, MOUTH, STOMA, OUTLET, OPENING, OSTIOLE, SPIRACLE
Origen, for one ...... THEOLOGIAN
origin .... GERM, ROOT, SEED, BIRTH, CAUSE, FATHER, SOURCE, GENESIS, LINEAGE, BEGINNING, PARENT(AGE)
of the .... GENETIC
original .... NEW, FIRST, FRESH, NOVEL, NATIVE, INITIAL, EARLIEST, PRISTINE, AUTHENTIC
name of Camp David .... SHANGRI-LA
native .... ABORIGINE
settler .... PIONEER
sin .... DISOBEDIENCE

sin site .... EDEN
sinner .... EVE, ADAM
Yellow Rose of Texas
.... EMILY MORGAN
words .... TEXT
originally .... ERST, INITIALLY
the ninth hour .... NOON
originate .... (A)RISE, BEGIN,
FOUND, START, CREATE,
DERIVE, INVENT
originator ...... AUTHOR, FATHER,
CREATOR, INVENTOR
Orinoco River tributary
.... ARO, APURE
oriole .... BIRD, PIROL, LORIOT,
FIREBIRD, HANGBIRD,
HANGNEST, TROUPIAL,
GOLDENROBIN
genus .... ICTERUS
kin of .... STARLING
Orion .... HUNTER, ALGEBAR
lover/killer of .... DIANA
star .... RIGEL, BETELGEUSE
orison(s) .... PRAYER
Orkney county seat
.... KIRKWALL
fishing waters .... HAAF
inlet .... VOE
island .... POMONA
islands channel .... SCAPA
FLOW
Orlando .... ROLAND
servant of .... ADAM
Orleans heroine .... JOAN OF ARC
orlon .... FIBER, FABRIC
orlop .... DECK
ormer .... (EAR)SHELL
ormolu ...... ALLOY, GOLD MOSAIC
ornament .... ADORN(MENT),
DECOR(ATE), EMBOSS,
SPANGLE, BEAUTIFY,
DECORATION
by engraving .... CHASE
cheap .... GAUD, BAUBLE,
GEWGAW, TRINKET
dangling .... MOBILE
drop-like .... GUTTA
metal .... ETCH, CHASE,
EMBOSS, ENGRAVE
metal collar .... TORQUE
showy .... GAUD, BAUBLE,
GEWGAW, BIJOU(TERIE)
silverware .... CHASE
ornamental .... ARTY, FANCY,
ARTISTIC, DECORATIVE
accessories .... TRAPPINGS
article .... TRINKET, GIMCRACK,
KNICKKNACK
band/belt .... SASH
border .... DADO
button/knob .... STUD

clasp .... CHATELAINE
cloth headband .... DIADEM
collar ...... TORQUE, CARCANET
design .... LACE
dish .... EPERGNE
feathers .... PLUME
garden area .... PARTERRE
lacework of gold and silver
wire .... FILIGREE
lacing .... PICOT
metal foil .... TINSEL
needlework .... EMBROIDERY
network .... FRET
pin .... AGLET, BROOCH
plasterwork .... PARGET
shrub .... HENNA
tuft of cords .... TASSEL
tuft of silk .... POMPON
vessel .... VASE
work .... TRACERY
ornate .... FANCY, SHOWY,
FLORID, PURPLE, AUREATE,
BAROQUE, ELEGANT,
ARABESQUE, ELABORATE
plastering .... CEIL
ornery .... MEAN, TESTY, MULISH,
STUBBORN, OBSTINATE,
QUARRELSOME
person .... CURMUDGEON
ornis .... BIRDS, AVIFAUNA
ornithologist .... AUDUBON
ornithology subject of .... BIRDS
oro .... GOLD
de _____ .... PLATA
oroide .... ALLOY
orology subject .... MOUNTAINS
orotund .... ROUND, SHOWY,
POMPOUS, RESONANT,
BOMBASTIC
orphan .... WAIF
Jane's family .... EYRES,
EYRIA
orphanage .... ASYLUM
Orpheus, for one .... MUSICIAN
instrument of .... LYRE
wife of .... EURYDICE
orphic .... MYSTIC, OCCULT,
ORACULAR
orpiment .... PIGMENT
orpin(e) .... STONECROP
orra .... ODD, EXTRA
orrery .... PLANETARIUM
orris/orrice .... IRIS, PLANT
Orsino's (duke) wife ...... VIOLA
Orson, actor .... WELLES
daughter of .... REBECCA,
BEATRICE
wife of .... RITA, PAOLA,
VIRGINIA
ort ...... CRUMB, SCRAP, REMNANT,
FRAGMENT, LEFTOVER

of a sort .... CRUST
orthodox .... PROPER,
CONVENTIONAL
Orthodox, Eastern Church
diocese .... EPARCHY
orthographer .... SPELLER
orthopedist's concern .... BONES
orthopteron .... INSECT, CRICKET,
COCKROACH
ortolan .... SORA, BUNTING,
BOBOLINK
Orwell's Farm .... ANIMAL
oryx .... GEMSBOK, ANTELOPE
os .... BONE, ESKER, MOUTH,
OPENING
Osage .... SIOUX, INDIAN
Osaka Bay port .... KOBE
location of .... HONSHU
Oscar .... AWARD, STATUETTE
film: 1928 .... WINGS
1932 .... GRAND HOTEL
1933 .... CAVALCADE
1943 .... CASABLANCA
1968 .... OLIVER
1970 .... PATTON
1976 .... ROCKY
1977 .... ANNIE HALL
1984 .... AMADEUS
1986 .... PLATOON
1993 .... PHILADELPHIA
1994 .... FORREST GUMP
kin of .... EMMY, TONY
1952 winner .... HUMPHREY
BOGART
1960 winner .... ELIZABETH
TAYLOR
1991 winner ..... JODIE FOSTER
1993 winner .... TOM HANKS
1994 winner .... TOM HANKS
Osceola's tribe .... SEMINOLE
oscillate ...... WAG, SWAY, WAVE,
SWING, LIBRATE, VIBRATE
oscillating .... PENDULAR
device .... ELECTRIC FAN
oscillation transformer
.... JIGGER
oscine .... CHAT, CROW, LARK,
FINCH, SHRIKE, BUNTING,
TANAGER
oscitancy .... APATHY, STUPOR,
DROWSINESS
oscitate .... GAPE, YAWN
osculate .... BUSS, KISS, SMACK,
TOUCH
osculation .... KISS(ING), CONTACT
osier .... ROD, WAND, SALLOW,
WILLOW, DOGWOOD
twig .... WITHE
Osiris' brother .... SET, SETH
crown .... ATEF
domain .... AMENTI

emblem .... APIS
father .... GEB, KEB, SEB
mother .... NUT
sister .... ISIS
son .... HORUS, ANUBIS
wife .... ISIS
Oslo .... CHRISTIANIA
Osman sobriquet .... CONQUEROR
empire founded by
.... OTTOMAN
Osmanli .... TURK, OTTOMAN
osmosis, e.g. .... DIFFUSION
osmund .... FERN
osprey .... HAWK, OSSIFRAGE
O.S.S.'s successor .... CIA
Ossa's companion .... PELION
osseous .... BONY, OSTEAL
ossicle .... BONELET, (EAR)BONE
ossifrage .... HAWK, OSPREY,
LAMMERGEIER
Ossining institution .... SING
SING
ossuary .... URN, VAULT
content of .... BONES
ostensible .... SEEMING, APPARENT
ostentation .... POMP, GLOOD,
PARADE, DISPLAY, SPLURGE,
SHOWINESS, EXHIBITION
ostentatious .... ARTY, GAUDY,
SHOWY, POMPOUS,
PRETENTIOUS
display: colloq. .... RITZ
show .... POMP, PARADE
osteo: comb. form .... BONE(S)
osteoid .... BONE-LIKE
osteoma .... TUMOR
Osterreich .... AUSTRIA
ostiary .... GUARD
ostiole .... PORE, STOMA, OPENING,
ORIFICE
ostler .... STABLEMAN
ostracism ...... EXILE, EXCLUSION,
REJECTION
ostracize .... BAR, EXILE, BANISH,
REJECT, EXCLUDE, SHUT OUT
ostrich ...... RHEA, NANDU, RATITE
bird like .... EM(E)U,
CASSOWARY
kin of .... TINAMOU
Oswego .... TEA
tea .... BEE BALM, MONARDA
Otaheite .... TAHITI
otalgia .... EARACHE
otary .... SEAL
like an .... EARED
Ot(h)ello .... MOOR, OPERA,
TRAGEDY
author .... SHAKESPEARE
opera composer .... VERDI
tormentor of .... IAGO
wife of .... DESDEMONA

other .... ELSE, ALTERNATE,
DIFFERENT, ADDITIONAL
comb. form .... ALLO,
HETER(O)
"____, other rooms":
Capote .... VOICES
than .... APART FROM
others, and .... ET AL, REST
otherwise .... THAN, (OR)ELSE
otic .... AURAL, AUDITORY
otiose .... IDLE, VAIN, FUTILE,
STERILE, USELESS, INDOLENT
Otis (Cornelia) .... SKINNER
otitis externa .... SWIMMER'S EAR
otological subject .... EAR
otologist .... AURIST
concern of .... EAR(ACHE)
Ott .... MASTER, MEL(VIN)
Ottawa .... INDIAN, ALGONQUIN
Ottawan chief .... PONTIAC
otter .... FUR, MAMMAL,
PARAVANE, BROADTAIL
genus .... LUTRA
relative of .... MINK, SKUNK,
WEASEL
Otto .... GRAHAM, PREMINGER
ottoman ...... POUF, SILK, COUCH,
DIVAN, (FOOT)STOOL
Ottoman .... TURK, OTHMAN
court/government .... PORTE
emperor .... SELIM
Empire founder .... OSMAN
non-Moslem .... RAIA
official .... PASHA
standard .... ALEM
sultan .... MURAD, SULEIMAN
oubliette .... PRISON, DUNGEON
ouch .... CLASP, BROOCH, BUCKLE
ought ...... ZERO, AT ALL, CIPHER,
NAUGHT
oui .... YES
ouija equipment .... BOARD,
PLANCHETTE
ounce .... ONS, WEIGHT,
(SNOW)LEOPARD
ouph(e) .... ELF, GOBLIN
our pilots .... USAF
times .... TWENTIETH CENTURY
Our Lady .... MARY, NOTRE DAME
"Miss Brooks" .... EVE
ARDEN
oust .... EJECT, EVICT, EXPEL,
BOUNCE, DEPOSE, REMOVE,
FORCE OUT
ouster .... EVICTOR, EVICTION,
DISMISSAL
out .... AWAY, BEGONE, NOT IN,
OUTSIDE, WITHOUT, EXTERNAL
-and-out .... RANK, GROSS,
SHEER, UTTER, ARRANT,
ABSOLUTE, COMPLETE,

CONFIRMED, DOWNRIGHT
in ____ (stranded) .... LEFT
FIELD
in the open .... OVERT
of .... FROM, BEYOND
bounds .... OFF-LIMITS
date .... DEMODE
gear .... CRANKY
harmony .... AJAR
line .... ASKEW
order ...... BROKEN, HAYWIRE
place .... INAPT, INEPT,
MISLAID, UNSEEMLY
practice .... RUSTY, STIFF
reach .... UNTOUCHABLE
sight .... PERDU(E),
CONCEALED
sort(s) .... MOODY, GRUMPY,
CAUSTIC, INDISPOSED
the blue .... ABRUPTLY,
SUDDENLY
the ordinary .... RARE,
UNIQUE, UNUSUAL,
DIFFERENT
the way .... REMOTE,
SECLUDED
the wind .... ALEE
town play opening
.... PREVIEW
on a limb .... IN A JAM
slang .... ALIBI, EXCUSE
way .... EXIT, EGRESS
out, ____ (betray one's cause)
.... SELL
(serve) .... DISH
outage .... BREAK, INTERVAL,
INTERRUPTION
outbreak .... RASH, RIOT,
ERUPTION, OCCURRENCE
outbuilding .... BARN, SHED,
GARAGE
outburst .... GUST, STORM,
TIRADE, FLAREUP, TANTRUM,
ERUPTION
uncontrolled .... HYSTERIA
outcast .... EXILE, PARIAH,
WRETCH, OUTLAW, DERELICT
Biblical .... HAGAR,
ISHMAEL(ITE)
of a sort .... LEPER
outclass .... BEST, EXCEL, SURPASS
outcome ...... END, ISSUE, EFFECT,
RESULT, UPSHOT, AFTERMATH
outcropping .... BASSET
outcry .... SHOUT, CLAMOR,
DIRDUM, UPROAR, PROTEST,
OBJECTION
outdated .... PASSE
outdo .... CAP, TOP, BEAT, EXCEL,
EXCEED, SURPASS
outdoor .... ABROAD, OPEN-AIR,

ALFRESCO

bench .... EXEDRA

party .... FETE, PICNIC,
BARBECUE

stairs .... PERRON

theatre .... DRIVE-IN

time .... SUMMER

outer .... ECTAL, EXTERIOR,
EXTERNAL

covering .... COAT, HUSK,
RIND, SKIN, WRAP, CRUST,
SHELL, TESTA, COCOON

edge .... LIP, RIM, PERIMETER

garment .... ROBE, WRAP,
DOLMAN, JACKET, KIMONO,
PALETOT, SURTOUT,
(OVER)COAT

layer of cells .... ECTODERM

space explorer
.... ASTRONAUT, COSMONAUT

space visitor .... ET

outfit ...... RIG, GARB, GEAR, SUIT,
UNIT, GETUP, TURN-OUT,
CAPARISON

bride's .... TROUSSEAU

matching .... ENSEMBLE

to .... ACCOUTER

outflank .... OUTWIT, THWART

outflow .... EFFLUX, ESCAPE

outgo .... EXPENDITURE

or income .... RENT

outgoing .... SOCIABLE,
GREGARIOUS

outgrowth .... RESULT, OFFSHOOT

outhouse .... PRIVY

outing .... TRIP, AIRING, PICNIC,
CLAMBAKE, EXCURSION

outlander ...... ALIEN, STRANGER,
FOREIGNER

outlandish .... ALIEN, ABSURD,
BIZARRE, STRANGE, PECULIAR,
FANTASTIC, GROTESQUE

outlast .... OUTLIVE, OUTWEAR,
SURVIVE

outlaw .... BAN, BANDIT, BRIGAND,
CRIMINAL, FUGITIVE,
DESPERADO, PROSCRIBE,
HIGHWAYMAN

outlay .... COST, FUND

outlet .... EXIT, VENT, AGENCY,
MARKET, PASSAGE

outline .... DRAW, SCHEMA,
SKETCH, PROFILE, SUMMARY,
ADUMBRATE, DELINEATE

sharply .... LIMN

outlive .... SURVIVE

outlook .... VISTA, PROSPECT,
VIEW(POINT), EXPECTATION

outlying .... REMOTE, OFF-CENTER

district .... SUBURB, PURLIEU

outmoded .... PASSE, DESUETE,

HORSE AND BUGGY

outpost guard .... PICKET, SENTRY

of an empire .... COLONY

outpouring .... SPATE, TORRENT

output .... YIELD, HARVEST,
PRODUCT(ION)

outrage .... INSULT, OFFEND,
OFFENSE, SCANDAL, ATROCITY

outrageous .... DAMNED, HEINOUS,
DAMNABLE, FLAGRANT,
SHOCKING, ATROCIOUS,
MONSTROUS

wickedness .... VILLAINY

outre .... BIZARRE, ECCENTRIC

outrigger ...... PRAO, PRAU, PROA,
CANOE

outright .... TOTAL, WHOLE, AT
ONCE, OPENLY, COMPLETE

outset .... START, BEGINNING,
INCEPTION

outshine .... EXCEL, ECLIPSE

outside: prefix .... ECTO

outsider .... ALIEN, STRANGER,
NON-MEMBER

outsize .... HUGE, LARGE

outskirts ...... SUBURBS, ENVIRONS

outsmart .... OUTWIT

outspoken .... LOUD, OPEN,
BLUNT, BRASH, FRANK,
CANDID, ARTICULATE

outstand .... SAIL, ENDURE

outstanding .... DUE, OWING,
UNPAID, NOTABLE, STELLAR,
(E)SPECIAL, PROMINENT,
UNSETTLED, EXCEPTIONAL

example: sl. .... BEAUT

person .... ONER

outstretched .... PRONE,
EXTENDED

outstrip .... BEST, EXCEL, OUTDO,
OUTRUN, SURPASS

outward .... ECTAD, OUTER,
VISIBLE, EXTERIOR, EXTERNAL

outwit .... FOIL, EUCHRE,
OUTSMART, OVERCOME,
FRUSTRATE

ouzel .... THRUSH, BLACKBIRD

water .... PIET

ova .... EGGS

oval .... EGG-SHAPED,
ELLIPSOIDAL, ELLIPTIC(AL)

figure .... ELLIPSE

-Office related
.... PRESIDENTIAL

ovary .... GONAD

inflammation .... OOPHORITIS

malignant growth ..... CANCER

production .... OVUM,
HORMONE

wall .... EPICARP, ENDOCARP,
PERICARP

ovate .... EGG-SHAPED

ovation .... PLAUDIT, APPLAUSE

oven ...... KILN, LEER, LEHR, OAST,
MUFFLE, FURNACE

part of .... RACK, BROILER

portable .... BAKER

quick-cooking .... MICROWAVE

var. .... OST

over .... ATOP, DONE, UPON,
ABOVE, AGAIN, ENDED,
ACROSS, BEYOND, SURPLUS,
FINISHED, MORE THAN

a ____ .... BARREL

and above .... EXTRA, IN
EXCESS OF

and over .... OFTEN

combining form .... SUR,
HYPER, SUPER, SUPRA

expose film .... SOLARIZE

one's head .... DEEP, TOUGH

the hill: colloq. .... AWOL

there: poetic .... YON(DER)

over, ____ **(capsize)** .... KEEL

Over There songwriter
.... COHAN

overabundance .... PLETHORA

overact .... EMOTE, HAM(FAT)

overacting .... HISTRIONIC

overage .... EXTRA, EXCESS,
SURPLUS

overall .... BLANKET, ALTOGETHER

overalls ...... FROCK, JEANS, LEVIS,
SMOCK, DUNGAREES

overawe .... COW, DAUNT,
SUBDUE, BUFFALO, IMPRESS

overbearing .... BOSSY, PROUD,
LORDLY, ARROGANT,
CAVALIER, IMPERIOUS,
DOMINEERING

overcast .... SEW, DARK, CLOUDY,
GLOOMY, LOWERING

overcharge .... CHEAT, GOUGE,
HOLD UP, FLEECE

for tickets .... SCALP

slang .... SOAK

overcoat .... BENNY, CAPOTE,
RAGLAN, ULSTER, PALETOT,
SURTOUT, INVERNESS

double-breasted
.... REDINGOTE

overcome .... WIN, BEAT, BEST,
DEFEAT, MASTER, SUBDUE,
CONQUER, SURMOUNT,
OVERWHELM

difficulties .... COPE

overconcern with oneself
.... EGOMANIA

overconfident .... COCKSURE

overcrowd .... CONGEST

overdo .... EXHAUST, EXAGGERATE

overdresser .... DUDE

overdue .... LATE, TARDY, BELATED
instalment .... ARREAR
overeat .... GORMANDIZE
overfed .... GROSS
overflow .... FLOOD, SPATE, SPILL, DELUGE, RUN OVER
overflowing .... INUNDANT
overhang .... JUT, BEETLE, LAPPET, PROJECT
overhaul .... REDO, GAIN ON, REPAIR, OVERTAKE
overhead .... ABOVE, ALOFT, COSTS, UPKEEP
conveyor's car .... TRAM
item .... RENT, WAGES
overheat .... PARBOIL
overheated .... FEBRILE
overindulge .... GLUT, SATE
overindulgence .... ORGY, EXCESS
overjoy .... ELATE, DELIGHT
overlaid .... APPLIQUED
overlap .... IMBRICATE, EXTEND(OVER)
overlapping .... EQUITANT
overlay .... CEIL, PAVE
overlook .... MISS, IGNORE, CONDONE, NEGLECT, PRETERMIT, SUPERVISE
overlord .... BAN, LIEGE
overly .... TOO MUCH
overman .... ARBITER, REFEREE
overnice .... FINICAL, FINICKY, PRECISE
overpass .... SPAN, BRIDGE, EXCEED
overpower .... BEAT, MASTER, SUBDUE, CONQUER
overproud ...... LOFTY, TOO VAIN
override .... NULLIFY
overrule .... VETO, ANNUL, CANCEL, RESCIND, SET ASIDE, COUNTERMAND
overrun .... SWARM, INFEST, INVADE
overseas .... ABROAD, FOREIGN
oversee .... STEER, WATCH, DIRECT, MANAGE, SURVEY, SUPERVISE, SUPERINTEND
overseer .... BOSS, LEGREE, REEVE, BAILIFF, MANAGER, SUPERVISOR, TASKMASTER
overshadow .... DIM, ECLIPSE, OBSCURE, DOMINATE
overshoe .... BOOT, ARCTIC, PATTEN, ZIPPER, GALOSH(E), RUBBERS
overshoes, rubber .... GUMS
oversight .... ERROR, LAPSE, SLIP(UP), MISTAKE, OMISSION
oversize .... HUGE, LARGE

overstate .... EXAGGERATE
overstrung .... TAUT, TENSE, JITTERY
oversupply .... SATE
overt .... OPEN, PUBLIC
overtake .... CATCH UP, PASS(BY), OVERHAUL
overtax .... STRAIN
overthrow .... DOWN, RUIN, UPSET, DEPOSE, TOPPLE, UNSEAT, CONQUER, OVERCOME
overtone .... HINT, IMPLICATION
overtrained .... STALE
overture .... BID, OFFER, PRELUDE, PROPOSAL
overturn .... UPEND, UPSET, CAPSIZE, TIP OVER
overweening .... ARROGANT
overweight .... HIPPY, OBESE
overwhelm .... CRUSH, DEFEAT, SWAMP, DELUGE
overwhelming .... DAMNING, COMPELLING, OVERPOWERING
defeat .... SHUTOUT, NO-CONTEST
desire .... ESTRUS
emotion .... PASSION
terror .... PANIC
overworked .... STALE
overwrought .... ORNATE, FRANTIC, NERVOUS, FATIGUED
Ovid .... NASO
wife of .... UXOR
work of .... AMORES, METAMORPHOSES
oviform .... OVATE, OVOID
ovine .... SHEEP(LIKE)
ovisac .... OOTHECA
ovoid .... OVATE, OVIFORM
ovolo .... THUMB, MOLDING
ovule .... EGG, SEED, EMBRYO
center of .... NUCELLUS
covering .... PRIMINE
ovum .... EGG
content .... YOLK
owing .... DUE, INDEBT, UNPAID, BEHOLDEN
monies .... ARREARS
owl .... BUBO, MOMO, RURU, UTUM, KAKAPO
barn .... MADGE
leg feathers .... FLAG
-like .... STRIGINE
like an .... WISE
shipmate of .... PUSSY
sound .... HOOT, WHOOP
young .... OWLET
Owl and Pussycat author
.... LEAR
owlish appearance .... SOLEMN

own .... HAVE, HOLD, ADMIT, CONFESS, POSSESS, RECOGNIZE
owner .... LANDLORD, POSSESSOR, PROPRIETOR, TITLEHOLDER
ownership ...... TITLE, POSSESSION
yield .... CEDE, QUITCLAIM
ox .... YAK, BEEF, ANOA, GAUR, REEM, BISON, GAYAL, STEER, BOVINE, BANTENG, BUFFALO, BULL(OCK)
command to .... GEE, HAW
disease .... GRAPE
extinct .... URUS, AUROCHS
eyed goddess .... HERA
hornless .... POLLARD
joint .... HOUGH
like .... BOVINE
like animal .... ZEBU
meat, dried .... BILTONG
stomach .... TRIPE
strap .... REIM, RIEM
tuberculosis .... GRAPE
young .... STIRK
oxalis .... OCA
oxen .... KINE, NOWT
stall .... CRIB
oxeye .... DAISY, PLANT, DUNLIN
oxford .... SHOE, BROGAN, COTTON
Oxford bell .... GREAT TOM
college .... BALLIOL
fellow .... DON
grad .... AUNT
movement leader .... KEBLE, BUCHMAN
officer .... BEADLE, BEDEL(L)
scholar .... DON, DEMY
Thames at .... ISIS
University Day ...... ENCAENIA
University fine .... SCONCE
University student
.... OXONIAN
oxheart .... CHERRY, CABBAGE
oxide .... CALX
cobalt .... ZAFFER
lead .... LITHARGE, MASSICOT
oxidize .... RUST, CALCINE
oxlip ...... PLANT, PRIMROSE, FIVE-FINGER
oxpecker .... STARLING
oxter .... ARMPIT
oxtongue .... PLANT, BUGLOSS
oxygen .... OZONE
compound .... OXIDE
lack .... ANOXIA
liquid .... LOX
oyes .... HEAR(YE), ATTENTION
oyster .... BAY, BIVALVE, MOLLUSK, SCALLOP, BLUEPOINT
bed .... LAYER
bed material .... CULCH,

CULTCH
fish .... TAUTOG
gatherer .... TONGMAN
joint .... HINGE
killing snail .... DRILL
order .... RAW
plant ...... SALSIFY, LUNGWORT
product .... NACRE, PEARL
shell .... TEST, SHUCK
spawn .... SPAT, CULTCH
species .... MOLLUSCA

young .... SPAT
Oz books illustrator .... NEILL
creator of .... BAUM
Ozarks' animal .... DEER,
BOBCAT, RABBIT, CRITTER,
OPOSSUM, RACCOON,
SQUIRREL
bird .... OWL, QUAIL,
(BLUE)HERON, WOODPECKER,
WILD TURKEY,
WHIPPOORWILL

fish ..... TROUT, BLUEGILL, RED
BASS
most famous fighting fish
.... SMALLMOUTH BASS
river .... CURRENT, JACKS FORK
wildflower .... IPECAC,
PRIMROSE, HORSEMINT,
GOAT'S RUE, PEPPERMINT,
BEGGAR-TICKS, BLAZING STAR
ozocerite .... WAX, MALTHA
ozone .... AIR, OXYGEN, BLUE GAS

P

P .... PI, PEE, PEH, RHO
38 .... (WAR)PLANE, LIGHTNING
pa .... NOTE, DADDY, FATHER
pabulum .... FOOD, CEREAL,
PABLUM, SUSTENANCE
pac .... BOOT, LARRIGAN
paca ...... CAVY, AGOUTI, RODENT
pace .... GAIT, RATE, STEP, WALK,
SPEED, TEMPO, STRIDE
kind of .... RUN, LOPE, TROT,
AMBLE, SPRINT
setter .... LEADER
Pacelli, Eugenio .... POPE, PIUS
XII
pachyderm .... ELEPHANT,
RHINO(CEROS),
HIPPO(POTAMUS)
trap .... KEDDAH, KHEDAH
Pacific ...... CALM, OCEAN, IRENIC,
PEACEFUL, TRANQUIL
Antarctic arm of the ..... ROSS
SEA
archipelago .... SULU,
BISMARCK
battlesite .... GUAM, SAIPAN,
WAKE ISLAND
coast evergreen .... MADRONA,
REDWOOD, SEQUOIA
coast peak .... LASSEN
discoverer .... BALBOA
island .... YAP, GUAM, MOEN,
ROTA, TRUK, WAKE, BELAU,
EFATE, MANUS, PAGAN,
PALAU, TANNA, UPOLU,
AMBRYM, KOSRAE, MAJURO,
MIDWAY, MOOREA, SAIPAN,
TAHITI, TINIAN, PELELIU,
POHNPEI, TUTUILA,
ADMIRALTY, VITI LEVU,
BABELTHUAP, NEW GUINEA,
VANUA LEVU, NEW BRITAIN,
NEW CALEDONIA
island group .... COOK, FIJI,
LINE, BONIN, SAMOA,

AUSTRAL, GILBERT, LOYALTY,
SOLOMON, VOLCANO,
CAROLINE, HAWAIIAN,
MARIANAS, MARSHALL,
SENYAVIN, MARQUESAS,
MICRONESIA
pact .... SEATO
shrub .... SALAL
pacifier .... SOP, NIPPLE,
APPEASER, (TEETHING)RING
pacifist: colloq. .... DOVE
pacify .... ALLAY, SOOTHE,
APPEASE, MOLLIFY, PLACATE,
CONCILIATE
pack .... WAD, CRAM, GANG,
LOAD, MASS, STOW, TAMP,
CROWD, GROUP, PRESS,
TRUSS, BUNDLE, (EM)BALE,
FARDEL, COLLECTION
animal ..... ASS, MULE, BURRO,
CAMEL, LLAMA, DONKEY,
SUMPTER
animal basket .... DOSSER,
PANNIER
animal cover .... MANTA
dishonestly .... DEACON
down .... TAMP
girth .... CINCH
led by Sinatra and Martin
.... RAT
mule .... SUMPTER
of _____ .... LIES
of cards .... DECK
of dogs .... KENNEL, CANAILLE
of pups .... LITTER
rat .... HOARDER
package .... BOX, BALE, CASE,
WRAP, BUNDLE, CARTON,
CEROON, PARCEL
packer .... CASER, CANNER
packet .... BOAT, DECK, ROLL,
BUNDLE, PARCEL
boat .... PAQUEBOAT
packing .... BUFFER, FILLER,

CANNING, STUFFING
box .... CRATE
house .... CANNERY
packman .... PEDDLER
packsack .... KYACK
packsaddle .... APAREJO
pact .... MISE, TREATY, COMPACT,
COVENANT, AGREEMENT
Atlantic .... NATO
pad .... MAT, ROAD, WALK, STUFF,
BUFFER, PILLOW, SADDLE,
TABLET, CUSHION, ENLARGE,
FOOT(PRINT), HIGHWAYMAN
expense account .... INFLATE
gauze .... SPONGE
hippie's .... BED, COMMUNE
ink .... DABBER
medicated cloth .... COMPRESS
of hay .... WASE
portable .... TENT
powder .... PUFF, SACHET
silk .... VELURE
slang .... BED, FLAT, JOINT,
CONDO, APARTMENT
padded cell inmate .... MADMAN,
PRISONER
item .... DASHBOARD
padding .... WAD, DOWN, FELT,
EXTRA, KAPOK, STRAW,
COTTON, CUSHION, ADDITIONS
paddle .... BAT, OAR, ROW,
SCULL, SPANK, SPOON,
PROPEL
pingpong .... BAT, RACKET
paddlefish .... GANOID, SPOONBILL
paddock ...... FROG, PARK, TOAD,
FIELD, ENCLOSURE
parent .... MARE
paddy .... RICE(FIELD)
wagon .... BLACK MARIA
Paddy .... IRISH(MAN)
paddywack .... RAGE, BEATING
Paderewski ...... IGNACE, PIANIST
padina .... ALGAE

padishah .... KING, SULTAN, EMPEROR
padlock .... CLOSE
padnag .... HORSE
padre .... FATHER, PRIEST, CHAPLAIN
padrone .... MASTER, PATRON, INNKEEPER
Padua, Katherina of ...... SHREW
paean .... HYMN, SONG
paella .... STEWS
pagan .... ETHNIC, PAYNIM, GENTILE, HEATHEN, INFIDEL, IDOLATOR, NON-MOSLEM
god .... ODIN
pagan's forte .... IDOL
Paganini, violinist .... NICOLO
page .... CALL, LEAF, FOLIO, RECORD, SUMMON, BELL-BOY, (FOOT)BOY, SERVANT, ATTENDANT
boy .... BUTTONS
left hand .... VERSO
ledger .... FOLIO
lines on .... LINAGE
number .... FOLIO
ornamental design .... VIGNETTE
person served by .... NOBLE, KNIGHT, SENATOR
place of employment .... HOTEL, CONGRESS
right hand .... RECTO
size .... OCTAVO
slang .... BUTTONS
title .... RUBRIC
Page, singer .... PATTI
pageant .... POMP, SHOW, PARADE, SPECTACLE, EXHIBITION
pageantry .... SHOW, DISPLAY, SPLENDOR, SPECTACLE
pages .... RECORD
of history .... ANNALS, CHRONICLES
set of 24 .... QUIRE
Paget, actress .... DEBRA
Pagliacci character .... BEPPO, CANIO, NEDDA, TONIO, SILVIO
word .... RIDI
Pago Pago is in .... SAMOA, TUTUILA
pagoda .... TAA, TEMPLE
pagurian .... CRAB
pah .... TUT, POOH
paid .... HIRED, BRIBED, SETTLED, RETAINED, DISBURSED
athlete .... PRO
witness .... PERJURER
pail .... SKEEL, STOUP, BUCKET, PIGGIN, CANNIKIN
paillasse .... MATTRESS

paillette .... SPANGLE
pain ...... AIL, ACHE, HURT, PANG, AGONY, THROE, TWINGE, ANXIETY, PENALTY, DISTRESS, OFFEND
abdominal ..... COLIC, TUMMY-ACHE
common description of .... ACHING, BURNING, GNAWING, GRIPPING, THROBBING
emotional .... PANG
in the neck .... CRICK
in the side .... STITCH
minor .... FLEABITE
muscle .... CRAMP
non-drug treatment of ..... ICE PACK, MASSAGE, POULTICE, ACUPUNCTURE
of jealousy .... HEARTACHE, HEARTBURN
sharp .... ACHE, TWINGE
undergo ...... SUFFER, AGONIZE
painful ...... ACHY, SORE, BITTER, WOEFUL, HURTING, IRKSOME
urination .... DYSURIA
painkiller .... TONIC, OPIATE, ANODYNE, CODEINE, DEMEROL, NARCOTIC, SEDATIVE, ANALGESIC, PAREGORIC, ANESTHESIA
painless .... NUMB, UNFELT, ANESTHETIC
puller .... DENTIST
pains, great .... CARE, EFFORT
partner of .... ACHES
painstaking .... CAREFUL, DILIGENT, ELABORATE
paint .... LIMN, ADORN, COLOR, ROUGE, STAIN, DEPICT, ENAMEL, PIGMENT, PORTRAY, STIPPLE, VARNISH, LIPSTICK
badly .... DAUB
drier .... JAPAN
face .... FARD, ROUGE, COSMETIC
factory employee .... TONER
finishing oil .... TUNG
first coat of .... BASE, PRIMING
grinder .... MULLER
in dots .... STIPPLE
ingredient .... TUNG, BARITE
laid on thickly .... IMPASTO
layer .... COAT
remover .... ACETONE
spreader .... SPATULA
wall .... PARGET
painter .... DALI, GOYA, MIRO, DEGAS, HOMER, MANET, MONET, COROT, ARTIST, COUGAR, LIMNER, RUBENS,

TITIAN, CEZANNE, PANTHER, PICASSO, VAN GOGH, STIPPLER, REMBRANDT
Chagall .... MARC
designating one .... SUNDAY
Dutch genre .... STEEN
early Venetian .... BELLINI
eccentric .... DALI
Guido .... RENI
handrest of .... MAULSTICK
impressionist .... MANET
limp-watch .... DALI
mediocre .... DAUBER
medium of .... GESSO
of American Indians .... CATLIN
animals .... BONHEUR, LANDSEER
Fish Magic .... KLEE
Little Boy Blue .... MONET
Mona Lisa .... DA VINCI
Olympia .... MANET
presidents .... STUART
Street Scene .... SOYER
The Last Supper .... DA VINCI
oil of .... MEGILP
who illustrated Dante's works .... DORE
painting .... OIL, CANVAS, IMPASTO, PORTRAIT, SEASCAPE, LANDSCAPE
board .... PALLET, PALETTE
cult .... DADA(ISM)
form of expression .... OP ART
genre .... CUBISTIC, ABSTRACT, ORIENTAL
material .... DYE, ROUGE, CANVAS, PIGMENT, COSMETIC
medium .... OIL, PASTE, WATER COLOR
on a board .... PANEL
on ceiling .... MURAL
plaster .... SECCO, FRESCO
plasterlike surface for .... GESSO
religious .... ICON
small .... MINIATURE
stand .... EASEL
style .... GENRE, SESSHU, CLASSIC, DADAIST, ABSTRACT
technique ...... SECCO, FRESCO, IMPASTO, TEMPERA
tool .... BRUSH, ROLLER, SPRAY GUN
wall .... MURAL
water color .... AQUARELLE
paintings, collection of .... GALLERY
pair ...... DUO, TWO, DUAD, DUET, DYAD, MATE, SPAN, TEAM,

YOKE, BRACE, COUPLE
dos-a-dos ...... ACES BACK-TO-
BACK
harnessed .... YOKE
one of a .... MATE, MATCH
paired .... GEMEL, MATED,
JUGATE, TEAMED, COUPLED,
MATCHED
paisley .... SHAWL
Paiute .... INDIAN
pajamas .... TROUSERS
Pakistan cape .... RAS MUARI
capital .... ISLAMABAD
city/town .... BANNU, KASUR,
KOHAT, CHAGAI, JHELUM,
LAHORE, MARDAN, MULTAN,
QUETTA, SUKHUR, KARACHI,
LARKANA, SAHIWAL, SIALKOT,
LYALLPUR, PESHAWAR,
HYDERABAD, RAWALPINDI
coin .... ANNA, PICE
disputed land .... KASHMIR
language .... URDU, HINDI,
PUSHTU, SINDHI, BALUCHI,
BENGALI, PUNJABI
monetary unit .... RUPEE
mountain .... TIRICH MIR
mountain range .... HINDU
KUSH
native .... SIKH, PATHAN,
BENGALI
port .... KARACHI
president .... AYUB, MIRZA,
JINNAH
province .... SIND, PUNJAB,
BALUCHISTAN
region .... SWAT
river .... RAVI, ZHOB, INDUS,
KONAR, TALAB, CHENAB,
JHELUM, SUTLEJ
sea .... ARABIAN
spiritual guide of .... PIR
Pakistani .... SIKH, PATHAN
U.N. president .... SHAHI
pal .... CHUM, BUDDY, CULLY,
HOBNOB
Joey author .... O'HARA
palace .... COURT, CHATEAU,
MANSION, EL PARDO,
VATICAN, SERAGLIO,
TUILERIES, BUCKINGHAM,
MALACAÑANG
of a .... PALATIAL, PALATINE
resident .... KING, QUEEN,
BISHOP, PRINCE(SS), EMPEROR,
PRESIDENT
paladin .... PEER, KNIGHT,
CHAMPION
paladins, Charlemagne's 12
.... DOUZEPERS
palanquin .... JAUN, KAGO,

DOOLEE, LITTER
bearer .... SIRDAR, HAMA(U)L
palatable .... SAPID, TASTY,
SAVORY, AGREEABLE,
FLAVORFUL, TOOTHSOME
palate ...... TASTE, UVULA, LIKING
covering .... VELUM
palatial .... STATELY
Palatinate .... PFALZ
palatine .... CAPE, ROYAL
Palau Islands ...... BELAU, PELEW
palaver ...... CHAT, TALK, PARLEY,
CHATTER, FLATTER(Y),
CONFERENCE
pale .... DIM, WAN, ASHEN, FAINT,
FENCE, LIVID, STAKE,
BLANCH, FEEBLE, PALLID,
PICKET, SALLOW, ORDINARY,
WHITE(FACED)
tan .... ECRU
yellow .... FLAXEN
palea .... FOLD, BRACT, SCALE,
DEWLAP
paleface .... AMERICAN,
WHITE(MAN)
paleness .... PALLOR
Paleolithic Age division
.... CHELLEAN
paleontologist Hutchinson
.... HOWARD
paler than citrine .... GREEN
Palermo is in ____ .... SICILY
Palestine .... CANAAN, ISRAEL,
HOLY LAND
animal .... DAMAN
capital .... JERUSALEM
city/town .... ACRE, CANA,
GAZA, HAIFA, SILOH, HEBRON,
MEGIDDO, SAMARIA,
CAPERNAUM
coin .... MIL
district .... DECAPOLIS
division .... GILEAD, PERAEA,
GALILEE
guerrilla .... FEDAYEEN
guerrilla leader .... ARAFAT
guerrilla outfit .... EL FATAH
kingdom .... SAMARIA
mountain .... EBAL, NEBO,
CARMEL, GILEAD
plain .... SHARON
port ...... ACRE, HAIFA, JAFFA
tiger cub .... ASHBAL
tribesman .... ADANITE
village .... BETHEL
palestra .... SCHOOL, GYMNASIUM
trainee .... WRESTLER
paletot .... JACKET, OVERCOAT,
GREATCOAT
palette .... BOARD, COLORS
knife .... SPATULA

palfrey .... (SADDLE)HORSE
palimpsest .... TABLET,
PARCHMENT
palindrome .... ANAGRAM,
ACROSTIC, WORDPLAY
a ladylike .... MADAM
for father .... DAD, ABBA
for mother .... MOM
for sheep, female .... EWE
palindromic before .... ERE
name .... ANA, AVA, EVE, BOB,
NAN, TUT, OTTO
pop quartet .... ABBA
time .... NOON
word .... BIB, BOB, DAD, DID,
EKE, ERE, EWE, EYE, GAG,
KAYAK, GIG, MOM, MUM, NUN,
PAP, PUP, TIT, TAT, ABBA,
MADAM
paling .... FENCING
palisade .... BAIL, FENCE,
ESPALIER
composition of .... STAKES
pall .... BORE, CLOY, SATE,
CLOAK, WEARY, DISGUST,
SATIATE
Palladium of Rome .... ANCILE
Pallas .... ATHENA, ASTEROID
statue .... PALLADIUM
pallbearer .... MOURNER
pallet .... BED, PATE, PAWL,
CLICK, PALETTE, MATTRESS,
PLATFORM
palliate .... EASE, SALVE, EXCUSE,
SOOTHE, TEMPER, RELIEVE,
MITIGATE, ALLEVIATE,
EXTENUATE
palliative .... OPIATE, REMEDY,
BROMIDE, SEDATIVE
treatment .... THERAPY
pallid .... WAN, PALE, FAINT,
WHITE, SALLOW
pallor .... WANNESS, PALENESS
palm .... ENG, COCO, D(O)UM,
JARA, NIPA, SAGO, TREE,
ASSAI, NIKAU, PRIZE, COHUNE,
GOMUTI, GRIGRI, COQUITO,
TALIPOT, TRIUMPH, VICTORY
Asiatic .... NIPA, BETEL,
CALAMI, PALMYRA
betel .... ARECA, BONGA
Brazilian .... ASSAI, JUPATI,
BABASSU, CARNAUBA
cabbage .... PALMETTO
climbing .... RATTAN
drink .... NIPA, TUBA, ASSAI,
TODDY
fiber .... DOH, BURI, DATIL,
GOMUTI, RAFFIA
fruit .... DATE, DOUM, SASA,
COCONUT

grease the .... BRIBE, CORRUPT
leaf ..... OLA, PAN, ATAP, NIPA, FROND
leaf fan .... PUNKA(H), TALIPOT
leaf mat .... YAPA, PETATE
leaf's symbol .... TRIUMPH, VICTORY
leaves, plaited .... SENNIT
like plant .... CYCAD, ZAMIA
liquor .... BINO, NIPA, TODDY
Madagascar .... RAFFIA
Malayan .... ARENG, GOMUTI
muscle .... LUMBRICALIS
nipa .... AT(T)AP
nut .... COCO
of the hand .... VOLAR, THENAR
off .... FOB, FOIST, IMPOSE
pest .... GRUGRU
pith product .... SAGO
plant resembling .... CYCAD
raised part of .... MOUNT
reader .... PALMIST, CHIROMANCER
sap liquor .... NIPA, TODDY
showy fan .... TALIPOT
shrub like .... ZAMIA
starch .... SAGO
stem .... CANE, CAUDEX, RAT(T)AN
stroke on the .... PANDY
sugar .... JAGGERY
tree .... DATE, DOUM, SAGO, ARENG, ROYAL, TODDY, GRIGRI, RAFFIA, CALAMUS, PALMYRA, TALIPOT, PALMETTO
tree bud .... CABBAGE
wax .... CARNAUBA
wine .... TUBA, TAREE, TODDY, GOMUTI
Palma capital .... SANTA CRUZ
palmate .... WEB-FOOTED
palmer .... PILGRIM
need of .... DRIVER
palmetto .... SABAL, SERENOA
palmist .... FORTUNE-TELLER
interests of .... LINES
palmistry .... CHIROMANCY
Palmyra .... TADMOR
leaf .... TAL, OLA(Y)
leaf fan .... PUNKA(H)
queen of .... ZENOBIA
palomino .... HORSE, EQUINE
palp(us) .... FEELER, ANTENNA
palpable .... CLEAR, PLAIN, EVIDENT, OBVIOUS, MANIFEST, TANGIBLE
palpate .... FEEL
palpitate .... BEAT, THROB, QUIVER, FLUTTER, PULSATE,

TREMBLE, VIBRATE
palpitation .... BEATING, SALTATION, THROB(BING)
cause of heart .... ARRHYTHMIA
palsied .... SHAKING
palsy .... PARALYZE, PARALYSIS
kind of .... ERB'S, BELL'S, CEREBRAL
palter .... LIE, TRIFLE, QUIBBLE
paltry ...... MEAN, PETTY, SMALL, MEAGER, TRIVIAL, PICAYUNE, TRIFLING, WORTHLESS
paludal .... BOGGY, MARSHY, SWAMPY
paludism .... MALARIA
pam .... GAME, JACK
game like .... NAPOLEON
Pamir .... GALCHA
pampas .... PLAIN
country of .... ARGENTINA
native .... GAUCHO
weapon .... BOLAS
pamper .... PET, GLUT, HUMOR, SPOIL, COSHER, COSSET, FONDLE, GRATIFY, INDULGE, (MOLLY)CODDLE
pampero .... WIND
pamphlet .... TRACT, MANUAL, BROCHURE, FLYSHEET, TREATISE
of poems .... CHAPBOOK
unstitched .... FOLDER
Pamplona animal .... TORO
pan .... POT, DISH, KETTLE, ROTATE, GRIDDLE, (ICE)FLOE, SKILLET
oil .... SUMP
out .... SUCCEED
perforated .... COLANDER
slang .... RIB, FACE, ROAST, CRITICIZE
small .... PATELLA, PANNIKIN
warming .... CALEFACTORY
Pan .... GOD, FAUNUS
concern of .... FLOCKS, SHEPHERDS
panacea .... CURE, ELIXIR, REMEDY, CURE-ALL, NOSTRUM, MEDICINE, CATHOLICON
panache .... PLUME, VERVE, APLOMB, ECLAT, ELEGANCE, FLAMBOYANCE
Panama .... HAT, GULF, CANAL, DARIEN, ISTHMUS
archipelago .... PERLAS
bay .... PARITA
boxing champ .... DURAN
Canal locks .... GATUN, MIRAFLORES

cape .... PUNTA BURICA
capital .... PANAMA
city/town .... NATA, SONA, ANTON, COLON, DAVID, GATUN, TOCUMEN, PENONOME, SANTIAGO, AGUADULCE, LA CHORRERA
coin/explorer .... BALBOA
gulf .... PANAMA, MONTIJO, SAN BLAS, CHIRIQUI, MOSQUITOS
hat material .... JIPIJAPA
island ..... REY, COIBA, COLON, CEBACO, PARIDA, TABOGA, JICARON
island group .... SECAS, LADRONES, CONTRERAS
lagoon .... CHIRIQUI
lake .... GATUN
monetary unit .... BALBOA
mountain .... PANDO, BREWSTER, SANTIAGO
mountain range .... DARIEN, SAN BLAS, TABASARA
peninsula .... AZUERO, VALIENTE
port .... COLON
president .... ROBLES
river .... CHEPO, CHAGRES, CHUCUNAQUE
tree .... COPA, CATIVO
Panamanian jockey .... ICAZA
leader .... NORIEGA
panatella .... CIGAR
Panay city .... ILOILO
native/negrito .... ATI
pancake .... FRITTER, FLAPJACK
flaming French .... CREPE SUZETTE
mix .... BATTER
turner .... SPATULA
Pancake Tuesday .... MARDI GRAS
pancreas .... GLAND, SWEETBREAD
disorder .... CANCER, DIABETES
enzyme produced by ..... LIPASE, AMYLASE, TRYPSIN
inflammation .... PANCREATITIS
injury .... TRAUMA
part of .... DUCT, HEAD, TAIL
secretion .... INSULIN, GLUCAGON
panda .... WAH, BEARCAT
anamial resembling the .... RACCOON
pandanus ...... TREE, SCREW PINE
pandects .... LEGAL CODE
pandemic .... GENERAL, PREVALENT, WIDESPREAD
pandemonium .... DIN, HELL,

CHAOS, NOISE, BEDLAM, DISORDER, CONFUSION

pander .... PIMP, CATER, PROCURER

Pandora .... BANDORE

pandowdy .... PUDDING, APPLE PIE

pane .... QUARREL, ROUNDEL

panegyric .... ELOGE, EULOGY, PRAISE, TRIBUTE, ENCOMIUM, LAUDATION

panegyrist .... EULOGIST, ENCOMIAST

panel ...... JURY, JURORS, SADDLE, VENIRE

sunken .... COFFER

panelist .... CERF, JUROR

panes, frame for .... SASH

panfry .... SAUTE

pang .... ACHE, PAIN, AGONY, DOLOR, THROE, TWINGE

Pangloss' pupil .... CANDIDE

pangolin .... MANIS, ANTEATER

pangs of childbirth ...... THROES

panhandle .... BEG

panhandler .... BEGGAR

panic .... FEAR, ALARM, GRASS, SCARE, BUTTON, FRIGHT, MILLET, TERROR

result of .... STAMPEDE, HYSTERICS

slang .... DELIGHT

panicky .... EDGY, FUNKY

panicle .... RACEME, CLUSTER

panoply .... ARRAY, REGALIA

panorama .... VIEW, SCENE, VISTA

Panpipe .... SYRINX

pansy .... PENSE, VIOLA, HEARTSEASE

slang .... QUEER

pant .... GASP, HUFF, PUFF, HEAVE, THROB, PULSATE

Pantagruel .... GIANT

companion/friend of .... PANURGE

father of .... GARGANTUA

grandmother of .... GARGAMELLE

mother of .... BADEBEC

pantalets .... DRAWERS

pantaloons .... TROUSERS

Pantelleria .... COSYRA

pantheon .... TOMB, TEMPLE

member .... GOD

panther .... PARD, PUMA, COUGAR, JAGUAR, LEOPARD, PAINTER

panties .... DRAWERS, UNDERPANTS

panting .... PUFFY, GASPING, HYPERPNEA

pantomime .... SAVO, MIMIST

game .... CHARADE

pantry .... AMBRY, EWERY, CLOSET, LARDER, SPENCE, SPENSE, BUTTERY, CUPBOARD

pants .... JEANS, LEVIS, SLACKS, DRAWERS, TROUSERS

baby's .... SOAKERS

pantywaist ...... SISSY, WEAKLING

Panza squire .... SANCHO

panzer .... ARMORED

pap .... MASH, PULP, TEAT, NIPPLE

papa ...... PA, PAW, POP, DAD(DY), FATHER

Papa .... ERNEST

Papa's Lady Ashley .... BRETT

papal. See also **Pope**

.... APOSTOLIC

ambassador .... LEGATE, NUNCIO

book of decrees .... DECRETALE

cape/veil .... FANO(N), FANUM, ORALE, FANNEL, MOZ(Z)ETTA

chamberlain ...... CAMERLINGO

court .... SEE, CURIA

decree .... BULL, DECRETAL, RESCRIPT

envoy, special .... ABLEGATE

letter .... TOME, BREVE, BULL(A), ENCYCLICAL

order .... RESCRIPT

palace .... VATICAN

seal .... BULI(A)

skullcap .... ZUCCHETTO

papaveraceous plant ...... POPPY

papaverine .... VASODILATOR

papaw .... PAPAYA

papaya .... PA(W)PAW

enzyme .... PAPAIN

Papeete's location .... TAHITI

paper .... DAILY, ESSAY, SHEET, TRACT, PAPIER, THESIS, JOURNAL, WRAPPER, WRITING, TREATISE, MONOGRAPH

ancient .... PAPYRUS

candy holder .... CORNET

cutter ..... SLITTER, GUILLOTINE

damaged .... CASSE, RETREE

fastener .... CLIP, STAPLER

filler .... KAOLIN(E)

gummed .... PASTER

holder .... FOLDER

kind of ..... TAR, BOND, CREPE, LINEN, MANILA, TISSUE, PAPYRUS, FOOLSCAP

legal size pad .... FOOLSCAP

making material .... PULP, ESPARTO, CELLULOSE

manufacturer's technique .... PLATEGLAZING

match .... SPILL

measure .... REAM, QUIRE, BUNDLE

money ...... BILL, NOTE, SCRIP, LETTUCE

nautilus .... MOLLUSK

official .... DOCUMENT

roll of .... BOLT

scrap of, sometimes .... TREATY

seller .... NEWSBOY, STATIONER

shell .... MARRON

size .... CAP, DEMY, POST, POTT, ATLAS, CROWN, FOLIO, ROYAL, FOOLSCAP, IMPERIAL

small town .... WEEKLY

spoiled .... SALLE, CASS(I)E, RETREE

sugar holder .... CORNET

untrimmed edge .... DECKLE

used for newspapers .... NEWSPRINT

waterproofing substance .... PARAFFIN

white .... REPORT

wrapping .... KRAFT

writing .... FOOLSCAP, STATIONERY

yellow .... MANILLA

papers .... WRITINGS, CREDENTIALS

papilla .... NIPPLE

papilloma .... CORN, WART, TUMOR

papillon .... SPANIEL

papillote .... CURLPAPER

pappy ...... PAPA, DADDY, MUSHY

paprika .... PIMIENTO, CONDIMENT

vitamin .... CITRIN

Papua .... IRIAN

papule .... ACNE, PIMPLE, BLISTER

papyrus .... SEDGE, BULRUSH

par .... EQUAL, LEVEL, NORMAL, AVERAGE, STANDARD

avion .... (BY)AIR MAIL

one over, in golf .... BOGEY

one under, in golf ...... BIRDIE

two under, in golf ...... EAGLE

Para, capital of .... BELEM

parable .... FABLE, STORY, ALLEGORY, APOLOGUE

parabolic .... ALLEGORICAL

Paracelsus' remedy .... AZOTH

parachute .... PARAFOIL

gear .... HARNESS

jumper .... STUNTMAN, PARAMEDIC, PARATROOPER

release device .... RIP CORD

shape of .... UMBRELLA

paraclete .... PLEADER, ADVOCATE, HOLY SPIRIT

parade .... MARCH, STRUT, FLAUNT, DISPLAY, SHOW(OFF), CAVALCADE, PROMENADE
church .... PROCESSION
feature .... FLOAT
march .... GOOSESTEP
military .... REVIEW
of cars .... MOTORCADE
official .... MARSHAL
prefix .... CADE
parader .... MODEL, MUMMER
paradigm ...... MODEL, EXAMPLE, PATTERN
Paradise .... EDEN, HEAVEN, UTOPIA, ELYSIUM
Arthurian .... AVALON
imaginary .... SHANGRILA
Lost character ...., EVE, ADAM, (ITH)URIEL
paraffin .... WAX
parafoil .... PARACHUTE
paragon .... IDEAL, MODEL, PATTERN, NON(E)SUCH
paragonite .... MICA
paragraph .... ITEM, NOTE, CLAUSE
Paraguay capital .... ASUNCION
city/town .... LUQUE, PILAR, LAMBARE, CONCEPCION, VILLARRICA, SAN LORENZO, ENCARNACION
department .... CHACO, GUAIRA, ITAPUA, AMAMBAY, CAAZAPA, BOQUERON, MISIONES
explorer of .... CABOT
falls .... IGUAZU
lagoon .... VERA
language .... GUARANI, SPANISH
measure ..... PIE, LINO, LEGUA, CORDEL, CUADRA
monetary unit .... GUARANI
mountain .... CHOVORECA
plains .... GRAN CHACO
river .... APA, NEGRO, VERDE, ACARAY, MONDAY, TIMANE, CONFUSO, PILCOMAYO, ALTO PARANA
tea .... MATE, YERBA
territory .... CHACO
wood .... QUEBRACHO
parakeet .... BUDGIE, PARROT, BUDGERIGAR
parallel .... EQUAL, MATCH, COUNTERPART
parallelogram .... DIAMOND, RHOMB(US), RHOMBOID, RECTANGLE
remains of a .... GNOMON
paralysis .... PALSY, PTOSIS,

STROKE, PARESIS, HEMIPLEGIA
combining form .... PLEGY, PLEGIA
infantile .... POLIO
paralyze .... NUMB, PALSY, SHOCK
Paramaribo is capital of
.... SURINAM
paramo .... PLAIN
paramount ...... CHIEF, SUPREME, DOMINANT, FOREMOST
paramour .... LEMAN, LOVER, MINION, MISTRESS, INAMORATA, SWEETHEART
paranymph .... BEST MAN, BRIDESMAID
parapet .... WALL, RAILING, BRATTICE
opening .... EMBRASURE
part .... MERLON
paraphernalia .... GEAR, OUTFIT, EQUIPMENT, TRAPPINGS, BELONGINGS
paraphrase .... RESTATE, REWORD(ING)
paraplegic .... CRIPPLE, PARALYTIC
paraquet .... PARROT
parasite .... FLEA, LEECH, TOADY, MOOCHER, SPONGE(R), HANGER-ON, TRENCHER, SYCOPHANT
blood .... TRYP
feeder of .... HOST
fish .... REMORA
intestinal .... HELMINTH, TAPEWORM
living inside plant/animal .... ENTEZOON, ENTOPHYTE
outside body .... EPIZOON
plant ..... BINE, APHID, LICHEN, MISTLETOE
root .... PINESAP
parasite's find .... HOST, MEAL TICKET
parasitic insect ...... FLEA, GNAT, LICE, MITE, APHID, LOUSE, ACARID, CHIGOE, CHIGGER, MOSQUITO
plant .... DODDER, ORCHID
worm .... FLUKE, LEECH, NEMATODE, TRICHINA, TREMATODE
parasol .... SUNSHADE, UMBRELLA
ant .... ATTA
paratrooper's cry .... GERONIMO
paravane .... OTTER
parboil .... SCALD, OVERHEAT
Parcae .... FATES
parcel .... LOT, PLAT, BUNCH, BUNDLE, PACK(ET), PACKAGE, (AP)PORTION

out .... METE, ALLOT
parch .... DRY, HEAT, TORREFY, TORRIFY, DESICCATE
parched .... DRY, ARID, ADUST, THIRSTY, ANHYDROUS
parchment .... FOREL, VELLUM, DIPLOMA, KIDSKIN, PAPYRUS, SHEEPSKIN
inscribed .... PALIMPSEST
roll .... PELL, SCROLL
pard .... PANTHER, PARTNER, COMPANION
pardon .... REMIT, SPARE, ASSOIL, EXCUSE, ABSOLVE, CONDONE, FORGIVE, OVERLOOK, INDULGENCE
archaic .... ASSOIL
general .... AMNESTY
pardonable .... VENIAL, EXCUSABLE
pare .... CUT, PEEL, SKIN, TRIM, SHAVE, SKIVE, REDUCE, WHITTLE
paregoric .... SEDATIVE
parent .... DAM, SIRE, MATER, PATER, FATHER, MOTHER, SOURCE, ANCESTOR
parentage .... BIRTH, ORIGIN, ANCESTRY, PATERNITY
parenthesis .... EPISODE, INTERLUDE
parenthetical remark ...... ASIDE
paresis .... PARALYSIS
paretic .... PARALYTIC
pareu .... SKIRT
parfait .... DESSERT
parhelic circle's halo
.... SUNDOG
parhelion .... SUNDOG, (MOCK)SUN
pari ____ (side by side)
.... PASSU
pariah .... EXILE, LEPER, WRETCH, OUTCAST
paries .... WALL
parietal .... SOMATIC
Paris .... PAREE, LUTETIA
airport near .... ORLY
ancient royal palace
.... LOUVRE
artists' quarter
.... MONTMARTRE
beloved of .... HELEN
brother of .... HECTOR, TROILUS
cathedral .... NOTRE DAME
chief of police .... PREFECT
church of Sainte-Genevieve
.... PANTHEON
district in .... AUTEUIL
express train .... RAPIDE

famous avenue .... CHAMPS
ELYSEES
famous iron structure
.... EIFFEL TOWER
father of .... PRIAM
Gothic architecture ..... NOTRE
DAME
green .... POISON
mother of .... HECUBA
museum .... CLUNY, LOUVRE
native .... PARISIAN
palace .... TUILERIES
patron saint .... GENEVIEVE
police department .... LA
SURETE
police inspector, fictional
.... MAIGRET
police station
.... COMMISSARIAT
rival of .... ROMEO
river .... SEINE
section .... MONTMARTRE
sister of .... CASSANDRA
stock exchange .... BOURSE
suburb .... ISSY, VITRY,
CLICHY, DRANCY, SEVRES,
NEUILLY, MONTREUIL
subway .... METRO
thug .... APACHE
tube .... METRO
university .... SORBONNE
victim of .... ACHILLES
war caused by .... TROJAN
weapon of .... ARROW
wife of .... OENONE
woman kidnapped by
.... HELEN
parish .... CONGREGATION
head of .... PARSON, PASTOR,
RECTOR
official .... OVERSEER
Parisienne .... FEMME
parity .... PAR, EQUALITY
park .... SQUARE, DEPOSIT,
STADIUM
fence/wall .... HAHA
parka .... SHIRT, ANORAK, JACKET
parker's watchdog
.... METERMAID
Parkinson's disease .... PALSY
characteristic of ...... TREMOR,
WEAKNESS, STIFFNESS,
TREMBLING
drug for .... L-DOPA,
LEVODOPA
patient's deficiency
.... DOPAMINE
parlance .... IDIOM, SPEECH,
LANGUAGE
parlay ...... BET, WAGER, EXPLOIT
parley .... TALK, TREAT,

POWWOW, PALAVER,
CONVERSE, NEGOTIATE,
CONFER(ENCE), DISCUSSION
signal .... CHAMADE
parliament .... DIET, SEJM,
LEGISLATURE
figure .... LORD
report .... CAHIER, HANSARD
parliamentary move
.... CLOSURE, CLOTURE
parlor .... BEN, DEN, SALA, SHOP,
SALO(O)N, LIVING-ROOM
instrument .... PIANO
kind of ...... BEAUTY, FUNERAL
Parnassus dweller .... MUSE
spring .... CASTALIA
parochial .... LOCAL, NARROW,
INSULAR, LIMITED,
EXCLUSIVE, PROVINCIAL
parodist .... APER, IMITATOR
parody .... SKIT, COMEDY, SATIRE,
BURLESQUE, CARICATURE
parol(e) .... ORAL, PROMISE,
(PASS)WORD
paronomasia .... PUN
parotitis .... MUMPS
paroxysm .... FIT, SPASM,
ATTACK, SEIZURE, OUTBURST,
CONVULSION
parquet .... FLOORING,
ORCHESTRA
circle .... PARTERRE
parr .... SALMON
parrot ...... KEA, ECHO(ER), JAKO,
KAKA, LORO, LORY, VASA,
ARA(RA), BUGIE, MACAW,
POLLY, AMAZON, KAKAPO,
REPEAT, IMITATE, COCKATOO,
LORIKEET, PARAKEET,
POPINJAY
cry of .... SQUAWK
Dr. Doolittle's ...... POLYNESIA
fever .... PSITTACOSIS
fish ..... LORO, LANIA, COTORO,
SCARID, SHANNY
hawk .... HIA
like .... ARINE
parry .... FEND, VOID, WARD,
EVADE, FENCE, DEFLECT
fencing .... SEPTIME
parse .... ANALYZE
Parsee .... ZOROASTRIAN
priest .... MOBED
sacred writings .... AVESTA
parsees, e.g. .... SECT
Parsi ''baptismal'' rite
.... NAVJOT
fried rice .... PULLAO
language .... GUJARATI
platform for dead bodies
.... TOWER OF SILENCE

undershirt .... SUDRA
Parsifal composer .... WAGNER
magician .... KLINGSOR
person healed by
.... AMFORTAS
priest .... MOBED
son of .... LOHENGRIN
woman in .... KUNDRY
parsimonious ...... CLOSE, TIGHT,
SHABBY, STINGY, MISERLY,
PIDDLING, NIGGARDLY
parsley .... DILL, CICELY, LOVAGE,
GARNISH, POTHERB, SANICLE
parsnip .... PLANT
parson .... PASTOR, MINISTER,
SKYPILOT, CLERGYMAN
assistant of .... CURATE
bird .... POE, TUI, KOKO
concern of a .... PARISH
parsonage .... MANSE, RECTORY
part .... DUTY, ROLE, LEAVE,
PIECE, SHARE, SEVER, DIVIDE,
PARCEL, PORTION, SECTION,
SEGMENT, SEPARATE
eagle-part lion .... GRIFFIN
main .... KEYSTONE
of a book .... COVER, CHAPTER
a chopper .... ROTOR
a document .... CLAUSE,
ARTICLE
a garment .... YOKE
A.M. .... ANTE, MERIDIEM
a maison .... SALLE
a seafood platter .... CRAB,
SHRIMP, SCALLOP,
FISHCAKES
a shoe .... SOLE, TONGUE
a sound system
.... COMPONENT
a worm's body .... SOMITE
a yard .... FOOT
an axel .... LINCHPIN
an impeller .... ROTOR
BLADE
an ounce .... DRAM
chromosome .... GENE
C.O.D. .... ON, CASH,
DELIVERY
Israel and Jordan
.... PALESTINE
P.M. .... POST, MERIDIEM
Q.E.D. .... ERAT, QUOD,
DEMONSTRANDUM
Q.I.D. .... IN, DIE, QUATER
some street scenes
.... GASLAMP
speech .... (AD)VERB,
(PRO)NOUN, ADJECTIVE
the ear .... ANVIL, CANAL,
PINNA, HAMMER, COCHLEA,
EARDRUM, STIRRUP,

VESTIBULE, EUSTACHIAN TUBE
the eye .... IRIS, PUPIL, CORNEA, RETINA, SCLERA, SOCKET
the ionosphere .... E-REGION, D-REGION, F-REGION
the scheme .... IN ON
the street scene .... ALLEYCAT
TLC .... CARE, LOVING, TENDER
payment .... DEPOSIT, INSTALMENT
proportional .... QUOTA
remaining .... REMNANT
song .... GLEE, MADRIGAL
stage .... ROLE
that separates .... SEPTUM, DIVIDER
partake ...... EAT, SHARE, RECEIVE
parted .... SPLIT, DIVIDED
Parthenon .... TEMPLE
designer .... ICTINUS
sculptor of .... PHIDIAS
site .... ATHENS, ACROPOLIS
Parthenope .... SIREN
intended victim of .... ULYSSES
partial .... BIASED, ONE-SIDED, PREJUDICED
partiality .... BIAS, LIKING, FONDNESS, PREJUDICE
participant .... PLAYER, ENTRANT, PARTAKER
in a beauty pageant .... CONTESTANT
in a confidence game .... SHILL, SWINDLER
in a fight with deadly weapon .... DUELIST, DUELLER
in a quarrel .... FEUDIST
participate .... SHARE, SIT IN, ENTER INTO, PARTAKE, COOPERATE
particle ...... BIT, JOT, IOTA, MITE, MOTE, WHIT, FLECK, SHRED, SPECK, TITTLE, GRANULE, SCINTILLA
accelerator .... BETATRON, CYCLOTRON
atom .... PROTON, NEUTRON
beam .... DEATH RAY
glowing .... SPARK(LE)
in space .... COSMIC DUST
particular .... ITEM, FUSSY, DETAIL(ED), EXACT(ING), FINICAL, PRECISE, SPECIAL, DISTINCT, SPECIFIC, FASTIDIOUS

moment .... JUNCTURE
particularize .... DETAIL, ITEMIZE, SPECIFY
parties, fast round of .... WHIRL
parting .... FAREWELL
partisan .... MAQUI, ZEALOT, DEVOTEE, FANATIC, ADHERENT, FOLLOWER, FACTIONAL, GUERRILLA
combining form .... CRAT
partita .... SUITE
partition .... WALL, SCREEN, SEPTUM, DIVIDE(R), DIVISION, (AP)PORTION
partlet .... HEN, RUFF, BIDDY, COLLAR
partly .... SOMEWHAT
open .... AJAR
prefix .... SEMI
partner ...... SHARER, CO-OWNER, TEAMMATE, ASSOCIATE
bill's .... COO
Chase's (coffee) ..... SANBORN
cry's .... HUE
in crime .... ACCOMPLICE
itsy's .... BITSY
marriage .... MATE, SPOUSE
of bounds .... LEAPS
rod's .... REEL
slang .... PARD
partnership .... CAHOOTS, ALLIANCE
partridge ...... BIRD, KYAH, YUTU, QUAIL, TITAR, GROUSE, SEESEE, TINAMOU, PHEASANT, FRANCOLIN
call .... JUCK
parturition .... LABOR, BIRTHING, DELIVERY, CHILDBIRTH
party .... TEA, BASH, GROUP, CLIQUE, PERSON, SOCIAL, SOIREE, FACTION, SHINDIG, GATHERING, MERRIMENT
afternoon .... TEA
beach .... CLAMBAKE
boisterous, noisy .... JAMBOREE
dance .... BALL
declaration .... MANIFESTO
didoes .... HIGHJINKS
disciplinarian .... WHIP
drinking .... WASSAIL, CAROUSAL
festive .... GALA
for bride-to-be .... SHOWER
giver .... MESTA, HOST(ESS)
goer .... GUEST
kind of .... HEN, TEA, STAG, BRIDAL, PAJAMA, SOCIAL, SHOWER, SEND-OFF, CAROUSAL, DESPEDIDA,

POLITICAL
member .... JOINER
organization .... FACTION, MACHINE
pooper .... FLAT-TIRE
slang .... BLOWOUT
stags .... SINGLES
wild .... ORGY
with speeches, formal .... BANQUET
withdraw from .... BOLT
parvenu .... UPSTART, SNOB(BISH), PRETENDER, (SOCIAL)CLIMBER
parvis .... COURT, PORTICO, COLONNADE
pas .... STEP, DANCE
de Calais .... DOVER
Pascal, Fr. mathematician .... BLAISE
Pasch .... EASTER, PASSOVER
paschal lamb .... JESUS
pasha .... DEY, DOWLAH
Pasiphae's husband .... MINOS
island .... CRETE
son .... MINOTAUR
son, killer of .... THESEUS
pasquinade .... SQUIB, SATIRE, LAMPOON
pass .... END, GAP, ABRA, GHAT, GO BY, GORGE, OCCUR, ELAPSE, KHYBEE, STRAIT, ADVANCE, BRENNER, PROCEED, NACIVERT
away .... DIE, (E)LAPSE
between peaks .... COL
come to .... OCCUR, HAPPEN, TRANSPIRE
downward .... SWOOP
football .... LATERAL
for .... IMPERSONATE
holder .... DEADHEAD
in/through .... REEVE
in sports .... BYE
judgment .... RULE
let it .... ALLOW, TOLERATE
lightly .... FLIT, FLUTTER
matador's .... FAENA
mountain .... COL, GHAT, DEFILE
off .... FOB, PALM, FOIST
on .... RELAY
out .... FAINT, SWOON
over .... OMIT, SKIM, SKIP, ELIDE, IGNORE, TRANSIT
over lightly .... SCAN
pretty .... FIX, JAM
slang .... ANNIE OAKLEY
tongue over .... LAP, LICK
up .... LET GO, REJECT
passable .... FAIR, SOSO, TOLERABLE, ACCEPTABLE

519

passado .... LUNGE, THRUST

passage .... WAY, PATH, ROAD, VENT, AISLE(S), TRAVEL, VOYAGE, OPENING, CORRIDOR, CROSSING, TRANSIT(ION)

between cliffs .... GAT, DEFILE

between house and garage .... BREEZEWAY

between train cars .... VESTIBULE

body .... MEATUS

closed at one end .... IMPASSE, DEAD-END, BLIND-ALLEY

covered .... SLYPE, ARCADE

in(to) .... ENTRY, ENTRANCE

mine .... ADIT

mouth to anus .... ENTERO

organ .... LUMEN

out .... EXIT

performed by all .... TUTTI

sloping .... RAMP

smoke .... STACK, FUNNEL, CHIMNEY

passageway .... DUCT, HALL, RAMP, AISLE, ALLEY, CANAL, SLYPE, ARCADE, CATWALK, CHANNEL, CORRIDOR, GANGPLANK

covered .... ARCADE

underground .... SAP, TUBE, BURROW, SUBWAY, TUNNEL

passe .... PAST, DATED, OBSOLETE, OLD-HAT, OUT-OF-DATE, OUTMODED

barber treatment .... SINGE

passed .... ADOPTED, CARRIED, APPROVED, QUALIFIED

passenger .... FARE, RIDER, COMMUTER, TRAVELER

boat on a regular schedule .... PACKET

kind of .... CHANCE, TENDER, STEERAGE, STOW-AWAY

passerine .... SPARROW

passing .... DEATH, CASUAL, CURSORY, FLEETING, MOMENTARY, TRANSIENT

fancy .... FAD, WHIM

over .... LABILE

passion .... FIRE, FURY, HEAT, LOVE, LUST, RAGE, ZEAL, ANGER, ARDOR, FLAME, DESIRE, FERVOR, EMOTION, FEELING

for big things .... MEGALOMANIA

fruit .... MAYPOP, GRANADILLA

passionate .... ARDENT, TORRID, AMOROUS, EMOTIVE, FERVENT, INTENSE, IRASCIBLE

passionflower .... MAYPOP

passive .... INERT, QUIET, PATHIC, DORMANT, PATIENT, INACTIVE

resistance exponent .... GANDHI

Passover .... PASCH(AL), SEDER, PESACH

bread .... MATZOS, MATZOTH

feast, according to Matthew, Mark and Luke .... THE LAST SUPPER

festival: var. .... PESAH

Hebrew word for ...... PESACH

meal .... SEDAR

month .... NISAN

of the .... PASCHAL

sacrificial animal .... LAMB

passport .... SAFE-CONDUCT

endorsement .... VISA, VISE

password .... PAROLE, SIBBOLETH, OPEN SESAME, COUNTERSIGN

past ...... EX, AGO, WAS, YORE, OF OLD, SINCE, BEHIND, BEYOND, BYGONE, GONE BY, HAS-BEEN, PRETERITE

middle age .... ELDERLY

of yore .... AGONE

recovery .... GONER

pasta dish .... LASAGNA, RAVIOLI, CANNELONI

ingredient .... DOUGH, SEMOLINA, DURUM WHEAT

long ..... LINGUINE, SPAGHETTI, FETTUCCINE

manufacturer, first in U.S. .... (ANTOINE)ZEREGA

sauce for .... MEAT, PESTO, CHEESE, MARINARA

short .... ZITI, MACARONI, MANICOTTI, CAPPELLETTI

paste .... HIT, PAP, BLOW, GLUE, MASH, DOUGH, PUNCH, STICK, BINDER, FASTEN, ADHESIVE, MUCILAGE

clay .... PATE

food .... POI, PEM(M)ICAN

jewelry .... STRASS

slang .... SLUG, WALLOP

pasteboard .... FAKE, PHONY, TICKET, BRISTOL, (PLAYING)CARD

container .... CARTON

pastel .... DYE, PALE, WOAD, TINT(ED), LIGHT, CRAYON, DRAWING, DELICATE, PASTILLE

Pasternak heroine .... LARA

Pasteur treatment, object of .... RABIES

pasteurize .... STERILIZE

pasticcio .... CENTO, MEDLEY, PASTICHE, POTPOURRI

pastiche .... MEDLEY, POTPOURRI, HODGEPODGE

pastille .... CACHOU, TABLET, LOZENGE

pastime .... PLAY, HOBBY, SPORT, AMUSEMENT, DIVERSION, RECREATION

St. Andrew's .... GOLF

pastor .... PARSON, PRIEST, DOMINIE, MINISTER, SHEPHERD, CLERGYMAN

pastoral .... RURAL, RUSTIC, BUCOLIC, CROSIER, IDYLLIC, ARCADIAN

god .... PAN, FAUNUS

melody .... MUSETTE

pipe .... OAT, REED

place .... ARCADIA

sound .... LOW, MOO, BLEAT, CANTATA

staff .... PEDA, CROSIER

pastrami .... BEEF

pastry .... PIE, CAKE, FLAN, TORTE, ECLAIR, STRUDEL, TART(LET)

cook/chef .... ICER, BAKER

fried .... TIMBALE

shell ...... PUFF, CRUST, ECLAIR

tool ...... BRUSH, WHEEL, BLENDER, SCRAPER, ROLLING PIN

type of .... PUFF, FLAKY, PLAIN

pasture .... LEA, GRASS, GRAZE

for pay .... AGIST

grass .... GRAMA, REDTOP, SACATON

land .... LEA, LLANO, RANCH, RANGE, ESTANCIA

pasty .... DOUGHY, (MEAT)PIE

substance for cloth filler .... SIZE

pat .... APT, DAB, RAP, TAP, TOUCH, CARESS, STRIKE, STROKE, TIMELY, FITTING, OPPORTUNE

Patagonia is in .... CHILE, ARGENTINA

Patagonian .... INDIAN, TEHUELCHE

rodent .... CAVY, MARA

patch .... DARN, PLOT, SPOT, VAMP, PIECE, SCRAP, COBBLE, REPAIR, REMNANT

up .... MEND, REVAMP, SETTLE, TINKER, RECONCILE

Patch, famous trotter .... DAN

patchouli .... MINT, PLANT

patchwork .... VAMP, CENTO, QUILT, JUMBLE, MOSAIC

pate .... HEAD, PASTE, NODDLE
de foie _____ .... GRAS
patella .... PAN, ROTULA,
KNEECAP, KNEEPAN
paten .... ARCA, DISC, HOST,
PLATE, PATIN(A)
patent .... OPEN, PLAIN, TITLE,
EVIDENT, LICENSE, OBVIOUS,
MANIFEST
basis .... IDEA
patentee, usually .... INVENTOR
pater .... FATHER, OLD MAN
companion of .... NOSTER,
FAMILIA
paternal .... FATHERLY
paternity .... ORIGIN, PARENTAGE,
FATHERHOOD
paternoster ...... PRAYER, ROSARY
path .... WAY, LANE, ROAD,
WALK, ORBIT, ROUTE, TRACK,
TRAIL, COURSE, FOOTWAY
finder .... SCOUT, PIONEER,
TRAILBLAZER
heavenly .... ORBIT
like some .... BEATEN
winding .... AMDAGE
Pathan .... MOSLEM, PAKISTANI
Pathet _____, **Communist**
group .... LAO
pathetic .... SAD, MOVING, TEARY,
PITIFUL, TOUCHING
pathogen .... GERM, VIRUS,
MICROBE
pathological .... MORBID
subject .... DISEASE
pathos .... POIGNANCY,
SENTIMENT, SUFFERING
false .... BATHOS
opposite of .... ETHOS
patience .... LENIENCY, STOICISM,
ENDURANCE, SOLITAIRE
patient .... CASE, STEADY,
INVALID, TOLERANT,
FORBEARING
man .... JOB, STOIC
patina .... FILM, VERD, CRUST,
PATEN, PLATE, ANTIQUE,
COATING, VERDIGRIS
patio .... TERRACE, VERANDA,
COURT(YARD)
patisserie .... BAKERY, PASTRY
SHOP
patois .... GUMBO, SLANG, SPEECH,
DIALECT, LANGUAGE
patriarch .... ELDER, PATER,
BISHOP, FATHER, LEADER
biblical, antediluvian
.... NOAH, SETH, LAMECH,
METHUSELAH
biblical, postdiluvian
.... ISAAC, JACOB, ABRAHAM

patrician .... NOBLE,
ARISTOCRAT(IC)
patrimony ...... ESTATE, HERITAGE
patriot, kind of .... JINGO,
CHAUVINIST, NATIONALIST
of '76 .... PAINE
target of a .... SCUD
patriotism, fanatical
.... JINGOISM, CHAUVINISM
patrol .... SCOUT, RECONNOITER
wagon .... BLACK MARIA
patrolman .... (BEAT)COP,
POLICEMAN
patron .... SAINT, BACKER,
PADRONE, SPONSOR,
CUSTOMER, PROTECTOR,
BENEFACTOR
animals' .... PAN, FAUNUS
art .... MASCENAS
Broadway .... ANGEL
largesse of a .... PENSION
literature .... MAECENAS
mariners' .... ELMO
music .... CECILIA
sailors' .... ELMO, NICHOLAS
saint of Cornish parishes
.... COLIN
saint of Ireland .... PATRICK
saint of Russia ...... NICHOLAS
saint of shoemakers
.... CRISPIN
youth's .... NICHOLAS
patronage .... FAVOR, (A)EGIS,
SUPPORT, AUSPICES,
CLIENTELE, SPONSORSHIP
solicitor .... RUNNER
patronize .... ENDORSE, SPONSOR,
SUPPORT
patronizing .... HOITY-TOITY
patrons, collectively
.... CLIENTELE
Patrons of Husbandry
association .... GRANGE
patsy .... SAP, FALLGUY,
SCAPEGOAT
patten .... CLOG, SANDAL,
CHOPINE, OVERSHOE
patter .... CANT, TALK, TAPS,
BICKER, JABBER, JARGON,
CHATTER
pattern .... MOLD, IDEAL, MODEL,
DESIGN, FORMAT, DIAGRAM,
PARADIGM, TEMPLATE
of flow movement ..... TREND,
RHYTHM
of human behavior
.... CULTURE
Patti, singer .... ADELINA
patty .... PIE, CAKE
paucity .... DEARTH, FEWNESS,
SCARCITY

Paul, actor .... MUNI, NEWMAN
Bunyan .... LUMBERJACK
Bunyan's ox .... BABE
companion of .... TITUS
pry .... SNOOP(ER)
Reubens, performer .... PEE
WEE HERMAN
singer .... ANKA, ROBESON,
MCCARTNEY
paunch .... RUMEN, ABDOMEN,
STOMACH, (POT)BELLY, BAY
WINDOW
paunchy .... FAT, BLOATED,
POTBELLIED
pauper .... BEGGAR
paupers' place .... POORHOUSE
pause .... LULL, REST, STOP,
BREAK, LET UP, RESPITE,
HESITATE
in music .... FERMETA
in prosody .... C(A)ESURA
indicator/sign .... COMMA
momentary .... LAPSE
vocalized .... ER
pave .... TAR, COAT, COVER,
COBBLE, ASPHALT, OVERLAY
pavement .... ROAD, CEMENT,
CONCRETE, FLAGGING,
(SIDE)WALK
pounder .... BEAT COP,
PATROLMAN
walker .... PEDESTRIAN
paver .... PAVIOR
mallet of .... TUP
of a sort .... PIONEER
pavid .... TIMID, AFRAID, FEARFUL
pavilion .... TENT, KIOSK,
GALLERY, MARQUEE,
BELVEDERE, SUMMERHOUSE
paving material .... TAR, SETT,
SLAB, TILE, BRICKS, CEMENT,
ASPHALT, MACADAM,
FLAGSTONE
Pavlova, ballet dancer .... ANNA
pavo .... PEACOCK
pavonine .... IRIDESCENT
paw .... PUD, FOOT, GAUM, HAND,
MAUL, PAPA, TOUCH, FATHER,
HANDLE, OLD MAN
pawl .... BOLT, CLICK, DETENT,
PALLET, RATCHET, TRIPPER
pawn .... DUPE, GAGE, HOCK,
TOOL, SPOUT, STAKE, WAGER,
PLEDGE, HOSTAGE, CHESSMAN
queened .... FERS
receipt .... TICKET
slang .... HOCK
superior of .... PIECE
pawnbroker ...... (MONEY)LENDER
shop of .... SPOUT
slang .... UNCLE

Pawnee .... CHAUI, INDIAN
pawnshop: sl. .... SPOUT
pawpaw .... PAPAYA, CLASPED
                              HANDS
pax .... PEACE, GODDESS
pay ...... FEE, QUIT, WAGE, CLEAR,
           REMIT, DEFRAY, SALARY,
           SETTLE, STIPEND, LIQUIDATE
as-you-go taxer .... RUML
attention .... CARE, HEED,
                            LISTEN
back .... REIMBURSE
boost .... RAISE
for .... FOOT(THE BILL)
for injury .... DAMAGES
for loss .... INDEMNIFY
heed .... MIND
homage/respect .... HONOR
load .... CARGO
one's share .... ANTE
off .... RECKONING
something additional to
                           PERQUISITE
up .... ANTE, PONY, KICK IN,
                        COME ACROSS
payable .... DUE
paying guest .... BOARDER
paymaster .... PURSER, CASHIER
payment, advance .... ANTES,
                     HERIOT, HANDSEL
back .... REBATE
behind in .... ARREAR(S)
call for .... DUN
forced .... LEVY, EXACTION
plan .... LAYAWAY
to atone for killing
     .... WER(E)GILD, BLOOD MONEY
token .... ARLES, HANDSEL
paynim .... PAGAN, MOSLEM,
                            HEATHEN
payola .... BRIBE
PB in chemistry .... LEAD,
                          PLUMBUM
PBX .... SWITCHBOARD
P.D.Q. .... ASAP
part of .... PRETTY, DAMN,
                            QUICK
pea .... PEASE, SENNA, LEGUME,
                          LICORICE
covering .... POD
heath .... CARMELE
pod .... PEASECOD
pod, removal of ..... SHELLING
relative .... REDBUD, BLACK
                           LOCUST
seed .... PULSE
soup .... FOG
stalk/stem .... HA(U)LM
tree .... AGATI, LABURNUM
peabody bird .... SPARROW
peabrain .... NITWIT

relative .... IDIOT
peace .... CALM, AMITY, GRITH,
          QUIET, SHALOM, CONCORD,
          HARMONY, SERENITY
agreement .... TREATY
branch of .... OLIVE
keep the .... POLICE
offering .... GIFT, SACRIFICE
officer ...... MARSHAL, SHERIFF,
         CONSTABLE, POLICEMAN
pipe .... CALUMET
symbol of .... DOVE
Peace Prize winner .... ORR,
      KING, MOTT, ROOT, LANGE,
      BUNCHE, DUNANT, WILSON,
                       GORBACHEV
peaceable .... IRENIC, HENOTIC
peaceful .... CALM, IRENIC(AL),
        SERENE, HALCYON, PACIFIC
period .... CALM, TRUCE,
                        CEASE-FIRE
person .... PACIFICO
peacemaker .... SOOTHER,
         MEDIATOR, PACIFIER,
                      ARBITRATOR
slang .... COLT
peach .... PAVY, TREE, FRUIT,
         BRANDY, VICTORINE
fuzzless .... NECTARINE
kind of ...... CLING, FREESTONE
peel .... EPICARP, EXOCARP
slang .... RAT, SING, BEAUT,
      BETRAY, SNITCH, SQUEAL
state .... GEORGIA
stone .... PIT, NUTLET,
                       PUTAMEN
peachy .... FUZZY
peacoat .... JACKET
peacock .... MAO, BIRD, PAON,
          PAVO, PEAFOWL
bird resembling .... ARGUS
butterfly .... IO
feather's spot .... OCELLUS
female .... PEAHEN
fish .... WRASSE
genus .... PAVO
like a .... VAIN
neck feathers .... HACKLE,
                       PLUMAGE
of a .... PAVONINE
ore .... BORNITE
symbol of the .... VANITY
walk .... STRUT
peacockish .... PROUD
peag(e) .... WAMPUM
peak .... ALP, TOP, TOR, CRAG,
      FADE, PEEP, CREST, CROWN,
      DROOP, PITON, HEIGHT,
         SUMMIT, MAXIMUM
of rock .... AIGUILLE
volcano's .... CONE

peaked .... TOPPED, POINTED
peal .... CLAP, RING, TOLL, CHIME,
              (RE)SOUND, CARILLON
peanut .... MANI, GOOBER
pear .... BOSC, POME, TREE,
          ANJOU, FRUIT, NOPAL,
          SECKEL, BARTLETT,
          JARGONEL(LE)
family .... ROSE
juice drink .... PERRY
prickly .... TUNA, NOPAL,
          CACTUS, OPUNTIA
prince's .... BERGAMOT
seed .... PYRENE
shaped ..... PEG-TOP, PYRIFORM
shaped fruit .... FIG,
          AVOCADO, SHADDOCK
winter .... BOSC
pearl .... GEM, BEAD, PURL,
          OLIVET, MARGARITE
biblical .... BDELLIUM
high quality .... ORIENT
imitation .... OLIVET
mother of .... NACRE
producer .... NACRE, OYSTER,
                       MOLLUSK
quality of a .... LUSTER
Pearl .... MINNIE
Buck heroine .... OLAN
Harbor is in .... OAHU
Mosque city .... AGRA
novelist .... BUCK
River .... CHU-KIANG
singer .... BAILEY
site perfidiously bombed:
     1941 .... HARBOR
pearlweed .... SAGINA
pearly ...... LUSTROUS, NACREOUS
pearmain .... APPLE
Pearson, Canadian premier
                            LESTER
peart .... PERT, CLEVER, LIVELY
Peary's discovery .... NORTH
                            POLE
peas and beans .... LEGUMES
variety .... SNOW, CHICK,
                     SUGAR(SNAP)
peasant ...... TAO, BOOR, CARL(E),
         HIND, PEON, RYOT, SERF,
         CEORL, CHURL, COTTAR,
         FARMER, FELLAH, KASAMA,
         MUZHIK, RUSTIC, TILLER,
         LABORER, VILLEIN,
         CAMPESINO
farmer .... CROFTER
peasants' revolt .... JACQUERIE
pease .... PEAS
peat .... FUEL, TURF
bog .... MOSS
land .... TURBARY
moss .... SPHAGNUM

spade .... SLADE
peav(e)y .... CANTHOOK
pebble .... SCREE, STONE, NUGGET,
QUARTZ
pecan ...... NUT, NOGAL, HICKORY
peccadillo .... SIN, FAULT
peccant .... SINFUL, SINNING
peccary .... BOAR, JAVALI
peck .... DAB, NAG, NIP, TAP,
BITE, KISS, PICK, NIBBLE
e.g. .... DRY MEASURE
¼ of .... QUARTERN
pecker .... PICK
pecks, 4 .... BUSHEL
peculate .... EMBEZZLE
peculiar .... ODD, QUEER,
SCREWY, UNIQUE, SPECIAL,
STRANGE, UNUSUAL,
SINGULAR
to locality .... ENDEMIC
peculiarity .... TRAIT, ODDITY,
ANOMALY
pecuniary .... MONETARY,
FINANCIAL
affairs .... FINANCES
pedagogical .... ACADEMIC,
SCHOLASTIC
pedagogue .... TUTOR, TEACHER
pedagogy .... TEACHING,
DIDACTICS
pedal ...... TREADLE, (FOOT)LEVER
decade .... TOES
digit .... TOE
pedant .... TUTOR, SCHOLAR,
TEACHER, EDUCATOR
pedantic .... BOOKISH, ACADEMIC,
DIDACTIC
pedate .... FOOTED, FOOTLIKE
peddle .... HAWK, SELL, VEND
peddler .... COSTER, DUFFER,
HAWKER, PEDLAR, PUSHER,
VENDOR, CHAPMAN,
PACKMAN, HUCKSTER
confederate of .... SHILL
vehicle of .... PUSHCART
pederasty .... SODOMY
boy used in .... CATAMITE
pedestal .... BASE, SUPPORT
part of .... DADO, SOCLE,
PLINTH
put on a ..... IDOLIZE, WORSHIP
pedestrian .... DULL, WALKER,
STROLLER, PROSAIC, WALKING
pediatrist's concern .... INFANTS
pedicel .... RAY, STEM, STALK,
PEDUNCLE
without .... SESSILE
pedicular .... LOUSY
pediculosis .... LOUSE
INFESTATION
problem .... LICE

pedicure, subject of
.... TOENAILS
pedidigitally misaligned
.... PIGEON-TOED
pedigree .... DESCENT, LINEAGE,
ANCESTRY, GENEALOGY
pedro ...... SEVEN UP, CARD GAME
peduncle .... STEM, SCAPE, STALK,
STIPE(S), PEDICEL, PEDICLE,
PETIOLE
without .... SESSILE
Pee Dee .... RIVER, YADKIN
Pee Wee of baseball .... REESE
peek .... LOOK, PEEP, PEER,
GLANCE
peel ...... BARE, FLAY, PARE, RIND,
SHED, SKIN, TRIM, STRIP,
TOWER, EPICARP, UNDRESS
for flavoring .... ZEST
skin off .... EXCORIATE
peen, tool with .... HAMMER
peep .... PRY, SPY, KEEK, LOOK,
PEEK, PEER, PULE, CHEEP,
CHIRP, GLIMPSE
military slang .... JEEP
show .... RAREE
peeper ...... EYE, PRY, TOM, FROG,
CHICK, SNOOP(ER), NESTLING
peephole .... EYELET, KEYHOLE
Peeping Tom .... PEEKER,
VOYEUR
saw her .... GODIVA
peer .... DUKE, EARL, LOOK, LORD,
PEEP, BARON, EQUAL, NOBLE,
SQUINT, MARQUIS, PALADIN,
VISCOUNT, ARISTOCRAT
domain of .... EARLDOM
Peer Gynt author .... IBSEN
character .... ASE, ANITRA
composer .... GRIEG
peerage .... NOBILITY
Peerce, operatic singer ...... JAN
peeress .... LADY, DUCHESS,
BARONESS, MARQUISE
peerless .... MATCHLESS,
NONPAREIL, UNRIVALED
peetweet .... SANDPIPER
peeve .... IRK, PIQUE, GRUDGE,
NETTLE, IRRITATE,
ANNOY(ANCE)
peevish .... PET, SOUR, CROSS,
MOODY, TESTY, TE(T)CHY,
CRANKY, GRUMPY, TOUCHY,
FRETFUL, PETULANT,
IRRITABLE, SPLENETIC
peewee ...... RUNT, CHILD, DWARF,
LAPWING, SMALL FRY
peg .... HOB, NOG, PIN, BOLT,
PLUG, STEP, DOWEL, KEVEL,
SPILL, STAKE, THOLE, SPIGOT,
TRE(E)NAIL

and rings game .... QUOITS
colloquial .... LEG, FOOT,
TOOTH
golf .... TEE
joining timbers ...... TRUNNEL,
TRE(E)NAIL
mountaineer's .... PITON
pega .... REMORA
Pegasus .... HORSE, STEED
part of .... STAR
Peggy .... MARGARET
pegs, set of .... SPILIKIN
Pegu capital .... RANGOON
ironwood .... ACLE
peignor .... ROBE, NEGLIGEE
Peiping .... PEKING
pejorative .... DISPARAGING
pekan .... WEASEL, WEJACK
pekin .... SILK, SATIN
Peking .... PEIPING
Pekingese .... DOG
pekoe .... TEA
pelage .... FUR, HAIR
pelagic .... MARINE, OCEANIC
Pele, football star .... EDSON,
NEGRAO
Peleg's father .... EBER
son .... REU
pelerine .... CAPE
Peleus, son of .... ACHILLES
wife of .... THETIS
Pelew .... PALAU
pelf .... BOOTY, WEALTH
Pelias' nephew .... JASON
son .... ACASTUS
Pelides .... ACHILLES
Pelion, companion of .... OSSA
pelisse .... COAT, CLOAK
pelite .... SHALE
pellagra treatment .... NIACIN
pellet .... BALL, SHOT, BULLET,
PEBBLE, MISSILE
of medicine .... PILL, PILULE,
TABLET, CAPSULE
pellmell .... JUMBLED, HEADLONG,
DISORDER(LY), HELTER-
SKELTER
pellucid .... CLEAR, SHEER, LIMPID
peloid .... MUD
Pelop's father .... TANTALUS
son .... ATREUS, THYESTES
Peloponnesus city .... MESSENE
country .... LACONIA
promontory .... MATAPAN
seaport .... PATRAS
pelota .... JAI ALAI
basket .... CESTA
court .... FRONTON
player .... PELOTARI
pelt .... FUR, BEAT, CAST, FELL,
HIDE, SKIN, POUND, STONE,

PEPPER, BOMBARD
pelter .... STONER
peltry .... FURS, SKINS
pelvic .... ILIAC, PUBIC
bones .... ILIA, SACRA
pemmican .... MEAT
pen ...... COOP, COTE, JAIL, YARD,
STIR, HUTCH, KRAAL, QUILL,
WRITE(R), CORRAL, INDITE,
PRISON, BALLPOINT,
ENCLOSURE
name (see also **pseudonym**)
.... NOM DE PLUME
pig .... STY
point .... NEB, NIB, STUB
up .... CONFINE
variant .... CRAAL
penal .... PUNITIVE
penalize .... FINE, PUNISH
penalty .... FINE, FORFEIT,
HANDICAP, PUNISHMENT
penance .... FASTING,
ATONEMENT, PUNISHMENT
penates .... LARES
pence .... COPPERS
penchant ...... YEN, FLAIR, TASTE,
DESIRE, LIKING, LEANING,
FONDNESS, INCLINATION
pencil .... STYLUS
lead .... GRAPHITE
well-used .... STUB
pend .... HANG
pendant .... FOB, LOCKET, TASSEL,
EARRING, GIRANDOLE,
LAVALIER(E)
pendent .... HANGING, PENSILE,
SUSPENDED
pending .... UNTIL, DURING,
DEPENDENT, UNDECIDED
pendulous ...... LOOSE, HANGING,
PENSILE, SWINGING
pendulum, device with inverted
.... METRONOME
weight .... BOB
Penelope .... WEAVER
father of .... ICARIUS
husband of .... ULYSSES,
ODYSSEUS
son of .... TELEMACHUS
penetrable .... PERVIOUS
penetralia .... SECRETS
penetrate .... BORE, GORE, ENTER,
IMBUE, REACH, INVADE,
PIERCE, PERMEATE,
PERFORATE
penetrating .... DEEP, KEEN,
ACUTE, SHARP, ASTUTE,
PUNGENT, INCISIVE
penetration .... INSIGHT,
INVASION, INTRUSION
open to .... PERMEABLE

penetron .... MESON
pengo replacement .... FORINT
penguin .... AUK, BIRD, JOHNNY
breeding place .... ROOKERY
describing a .... IMPENNATE
peninsula .... KOLA, NECK, GASPE,
MALAY, SINAI, BONDOC,
IBERIA, ISTRIA, KOWLOON,
LABRADOR, KAMCHATKA,
CHERSONESE, PROJECTION
penitence ...... REGRET, REMORSE,
CONTRITION, REPENTANCE
penitent .... SORRY, CONTRITE,
REPENTANT, REMORSEFUL
wear of .... SACKCLOTH,
SANBENITO
Penitentes .... CULT,
BROTHERHOOD
aim of .... PENANCE,
ATONEMENT
practice .... SELF-
FLAGELLATION
sacred holiday .... GOOD
FRIDAY
two-wheeled vehicle of
.... DEATH CART
penitential period .... LENT
penitentiary .... PRISON
penman .... AUTHOR, SCRIBE,
WRITER, CHIROGRAPHER
penmanship .... SCRIPT,
HANDWRITING, CHIROGRAPHY
Penn, actor .... SEAN
William .... QUAKER
penna .... FEATHER
pennant .... FLAG, BANNER,
BURGEE, ENSIGN, PENNON,
STREAMER
pennies .... PENCE
penniless .... POOR, NEEDY,
BANKRUPT, INDIGENT,
(FLAT)BROKE
Pennine Alps peak .... ROSA
pennon ...... FLAG, WING, ENSIGN,
PINION, PENNANT
Pennsylvania capital
.... HARRISBURG
city/town .... ONO, ERIE, YORK,
EASTON, SHARON, ALTOONA,
BRISTOL, CHESTER, HANOVER,
HERSHEY, INDIANA, LEBANON,
READING, SUNBURY, SWATARA,
BRADFORD, HAZLETON,
KINGSTON, SCRANTON,
ALLENTOWN, BETHLEHEM,
HAVERFORD, LANCASTER,
LEVITTOWN, NEW CASTLE,
PITTSBURGH, UPPER DARBY,
SPRINGFIELD, WILKES-BARRE,
PHILADELPHIA
college .... YORK, CARLOW,

WILSON, CHEYNEY, WESLEYAN,
HAVERFORD, GETTYSBURG,
POINT PARK, SETON HILL,
HOLY FAMILY, SWARTHMORE,
GWYNEDD-MERCY
county .... ELK, ERIE, ETNA,
KANE, KNOX, TROY, YORK,
BERKS, BLAIR, BUCKS,
BUTLER, LEHIGH, MERCER,
PLAINS, CAMBRIA, DAUPHIN,
FAYETTE, LEBANON, LUZERNE,
DELAWARE, LAWRENCE,
LYCOMING, ALLEGHENY,
LANCASTER
"Dutch" .... GERMAN
SETTLERS
founder .... (WILLIAM)PENN
Institute of Music ...... CURTIS
insurrection, cause of
.... WHISKY
island .... LITTLE TINICUM
lake .... ERIE, ARTHUR,
GLENDALE, WALLENPAUPACK
line .... READING RAILROAD
mountain .... BLUE, DAVIS,
NORTH, SOUTH, ARARAT, BLUE
KNOB, TUSCARORA
mountain range .... POCONO,
ALLEGHENY, APPALACHIAN
newspaper .... PACKET,
GAZETTE
port .... ERIE
river .... OHIO, TIOGA, BEAVER,
LEHIGH, CLARION, JUNIATA,
DELAWARE, ALLEGHENY,
CONEMAUGH
sect .... AMISH
state bird .... GROUSE
state flower .... MOUNTAIN
LAUREL
State House .... INDEPENDENCE
HALL
State House bell ...... LIBERTY
BELL
state nickname ...... KEYSTONE
state park .... PYMATUNING,
PRESQUE ISLE
state tree .... HEMLOCK
university .... DREXEL, LEHIGH,
TEMPLE, LINCOLN, BUCKNELL,
DUQUESNE, VILLANOVA,
PITTSBURGH, CARNEGIE-
MELLON
penny ...... COIN, GROAT, COPPER,
SALTEE, (RED)CENT
a-liner .... (HACK)WRITER,
SCRIBBLER
candy .... LICORICE
pincher .... TIGHTWAD
wise .... FRUGAL, THRIFTY
Penologist Lewis E. .... LAWES

penpoint .... NEB, NIB, STUB
Penrod's pal .... SAM
pensile .... HANGING, PENDENT
pension .... ANNUITY, STIPEND,
         SUBSIDY
pensionary ...... PUPPET, HIRELING
pensive .... SAD, MEDITATIVE
penstock .... SLUICE, TROUGH
pent(up) ...... PENNED, GUARDED,
    CONFINED, SUPPRESSED
pentacle .... STAR, SYMBOL,
        PENTAGRAM
pentad .... FIVE, QUINTET
pentagram .... PENTACLE
Pentateuch .... TORA(H)
 lesson read from .... PARASHAH
Pentecost .... WHITSUNDAY,
      ASCENSION DAY
penthouse .... AERIE, LEANTO,
        APARTMENT
pentose .... SUGAR, ARABINOSE
penurious .... POOR, STINGY,
         MISERLY
 one .... MISER
penury ...... POVERTY, INDIGENCE
peon .... SERF, LABORER
peony .... MOUTAN
 flower .... PIP
people .... FOLK, RACE, DEMOS,
    LAITY, NATION, PUBLIC,
  MANKIND, MORTALS, NATIVES,
   CITIZENS, HUMANITY,
        POPULATE
 angry .... FUMERS
 biased .... OPINIONISTS
 characteristics of .... ETHOS
 common .... PLEBE, MASSES,
    HOI POLOI, POPULACE
 full of .... POPULOUS
 in a legation .... DIPLOMATIC
         CORPS
 in second childhood
  .... DOTARDS
 insignificant .... NOBODIES,
       SMALL FRY
 mass killing of .... NOYADE,
    POGROM, GENOCIDE,
       HOLOCAUST
 of all the .... PANDEMIC
 of great interest ...... USURERS,
  SHYLOCKS, LOAN SHARKS
 of high social standing
   .... GENTRY
 on the move .... GOERS
 prehistoric .... PELASGI(AN)
 primitive .... SAVAGES
 violent .... TARTARS
 worthless .... RIFFRAFF
 young .... TEENS
pep .... VIM, DASH, ZEST, ZING,
 SNAP, VERVE, VIGOR, ENERGY

drug .... ELAVIL, TRIAVIL
pill .... DMT, LSD, STP
talk .... HYPE
peplos .... SCARF, SHAWL, PEPLUM
peplum .... SKIRT, PEPLOS
pepo .... GOURD, MELON, SQUASH,
        PUMPKIN
pepoaza .... WHISTLING BIRD
 habitat .... ARGENTINA
pepper .... ARA, BEAT, KAVA,
 PELT, BETEL, SPICE, RIDDLE,
 SEASON, STRAFE, CAYENNE,
 CHILI(ES), CAPSICUM,
 PIM(I)ENTO, SPRINKLE,
        CONDIMENT
 and-salt .... GRAY, MOTTLED,
        SPOTTED
 berry .... CUBEB
 beverage .... KAVA
 fruit .... CHILI, PAPRIKA
 grinder .... MILL
 hottest .... CAYENNE
 mild, sweet .... PIMENTO
 mildest variety of .... WHITE
 picker .... PIPER
 plant .... KAVA, BETEL,
        PAPRIKA
 pod .... CHILI
 pot .... STEW
 sauce .... TABASCO
 shrike .... VIREO(NINAE)
 shrub ...... CAVA, KAVA, KAWA
 slang .... VIM, ZIP
 variety .... BELL, BLACK, CHILI,
    WHITE, JALAPENO
pepperidge .... TUPELO
peppermint .... OIL, CANDY,
    PLANT, LOZENGE
 camphor/oil product
  .... MENTHOL
peppery .... HOT, FIERY, SHARP,
  SPICY, TESTY, SPUNKY,
  PUNGENT, IRRITABLE
peppy .... BRISK, SPIRITED
pepsin .... ENZYME
Pepys, Samuel .... DIARIST
Pequod .... WHALER, WHALEBOAT
 captain of .... AHAB
 quest of .... WHALE, MOBY
         DICK
per ...... BY, VIA, EACH, THROUGH
 annum .... ANNUALLY
 diem .... DAILY
 hundred .... PER CENT
 pro. .... BY PROXY
 se .... BY ITSELF
Pera .... BEYOGLU
peradventure .... MAYBE,
   PERHAPS, POSSIBLY
perambulate .... WALK, STROLL
perambulator ...... PRAM, BUGGY

percale .... COTTON
perceive .... SEE, HEAR, KNOW,
 NOTE, GRASP, SENSE, NOTICE,
   DISCERN, OBSERVE
percentage .... FEE, PORTION
perceptible ...... TACTILE, VISIBLE,
  PALPABLE, SENSIBLE,
       TANGIBLE
perception .... EAR, GRASP,
 NOESIS, INSIGHT, COGNITION
 false .... HALLUCINATION
perceptive .... KEEN, ACUTE,
    AWARE, KNOWING
perch .... SIT, FISH, REST, SEAT,
 ROOST, RUFF(E), ALIGHT,
 SAUGER, SETTLE, PERCOID
 chance-taker's .... LIMB
 fish like ..... ANADAS, DARTER,
       CABRILLA
 high .... AERY, AERIE
perchance ...... MAYBE, MAYHAP,
   PERHAPS, POSSIBLY
percheron .... HORSE, TROTTER
 repast of .... OATS
percoid .... FISH, PERCH
percolate ...... BREW, DRIP, OOZE,
 PERK, SEEP, DRAIN, LEACH,
 FILTER, TRICKLE, PERMEATE
percolator .... BREWER,
      COFFEEPOT
percuss .... RAP
percussion .... SHOCK, IMPACT
 cap .... PRIMER
 hammer ...... PLEXOR, PLESSOR
 instrument .... BELL, DRUM,
 PIANO, TRAPS, MARACA,
       CYMBALS
 section .... TRAPS
Percy, Sir Henry .... HOTSPUR
perdition .... PIT, FALL, HELL,
 LOSS, RUIN, DAMNATION
perdu(e) .... HIDDEN, CONCEALED
perdurable .... PERPETUAL
perdure .... LAST
pere .... FATHER, SENIOR
peregrinate .... TRAVEL, JOURNEY
peregrinator .... PILGRIM,
       TRAVELER
peregrine .... ALIEN, FALCON,
  FOREIGN, MIGRATORY
 falcon .... T(I)ERCEL
 falcon relative .... MILVAGO,
      CARACARA
peremptory ...... FINAL, BINDING,
 ABSOLUTE, DECISIVE,
 DOGMATIC, ARBITRARY,
       IMPERIOUS
perennial .... LASTING, PERPETUAL
 plant ...... DAHLIA, EVERGREEN
 Presidential hopeful
  .... STASSEN

perfect .... PURE, EXACT, IDEAL, MODEL, SOUND, UTTER, REFINE, PRECISE, ACCURATE, FLAWLESS, FAULTLESS, CONSUMMATE
blessedness .... NIRVANA
diamond .... PARAGON
shot .... ACE
perfection .... EXCELLENCE
model of .... PARAGON, PRECISION, MASTERPIECE
standard of .... IDEAL
perfectionist .... STICKLER
perfectly .... FULLY
perfecto .... CIGAR
perfidious ...... SHIFTY, FAITHLESS
perfidy .... BETRAYAL, TREACHERY
perforate .... BORE, DRILL, PINK(Y), PUNCH, PIERCE, PINKIE, RIDDLE, PUNCTURE
perforated .... FENESTRATE
utensil .... SIEVE, COLANDER, STRAINER
perforator .... PUNCHEON
perforation .... HOLE, PUNCH
perforce .... NECESSARILY
perform ...... DO, (EN)ACT, PLAY, WORK, EFFECT, RENDER, EXECUTE, FULFILL
in unison .... ACT AS ONE
with restraint .... UNDERACT
performance ...... SHOW, ACTION, RENDITION, EXHIBITION
balance-beam .... GYMNASTICS
between acts .... INTERLUDE
by king's comedians
.... JESTING
in person .... LIVE
kind of .... MIMING, REPEAT
musical ..... CONCERT, RECITAL
thrilling .... STUNTS
performer .... DOER, ACTOR, PLAYER, ARTIST(E), TROUPER, PRETENDER, ENTERTAINER
actuated by wires ...... PUPPET, MARIONETTE
aquatic .... SEAL, DOLPHIN
kind of .... MAGICIAN, MUSICIAN
stock of .... REPERTORY, REPERTOIRE
performers, group of ...... CAST, TROUPE
perfume .... AROMA, A(T)TAR, SCENT, BOUQUET, ESSENCE, (IN)CENSE, FRAGRANCE
bag/pad .... SATCHET
base .... MUSK, ATTAR
box/case .... POMANDER
flask .... FLACON
making substance .... MUSK,

ATTAR, IRONE, MYRRH, ORRIS, IONONE, ORRICE, SAFROL(E), BERGAMOT, AMBERGRIS, VERDIGRIS
oil .... BEN, ATTAR, NEROLI, CITRONELLA
perfumed .... SCENTED, FRAGRANT, SWEET(SMELLING)
perfumer .... ATOMIZER
perfunctory .... CARELESS, SUPERFICIAL
Pergamum physician ...... GALEN
pergola .... ARBOR, ARCADE, GAZEBO
perhaps .... HAPLY, MAYBE, MAYHAP, POSSIBLY, PERCHANCE
peri .... ELF, FAIRY
cousin .... NISSE
meaning of: as prefix
.... AROUND
Periander's wife .... MELISSA
perianth .... CALYX, PETAL
periapt .... AMULET
pericarp .... SEEDCASE
Pericles' mistress .... ASPASIA
peridot ...... OLIVINE, CHRYSOLITE
peril ...... RISK, DANGER, HAZARD, MENACE, JEOPARDY
perimeter .... BORDER, BOUNDARY
perinatologist ...... OBSTETRICIAN
period ...... AGE, DOT, ERA, STOP, TERM, CYCLE, EPACT, POINT, SPELL, STAGE, DURATION, (LIFE)TIME, SENTENCE
academic .... SEMESTER
break .... RECESS
brief .... SEC, SNAP, SPELL, MOMENT, SNATCH
dormant .... HIBERNATION
dull/slow .... SLACK
economic .... SLUMP, RECESSION
endless .... ETERNITY
extension .... GRACE
fast(ing) .... LENT
geological .... JURA(SSIC), ERIAN, UINTA, EOCENE, MIOCENE, SILURIAN
holding/occupancy ...... TERM, TENURE
inactive .... LULL, REST, RESPITE, DORMANCY, VEGETATION
leisure .... HOLIDAY, VACATION
of authorized delay
.... MORATORIUM
decline .... SUNSET
existence .... LIFE
grief .... MOURNING

maturation, hopefully
.... TEENS
100 years .... CENTURY
peace and prosperity
.... MILLENNIUM
rest .... SABBATH
satellites .... SPACE AGE
seclusion .... RETREAT
sunlight .... DAYTIME
ten years .... DECADE
time .... AGE, DAY, ERA, (A)EON, HOUR, WEEK, YEAR, EPOCH, MONTH, DECADE, MINUTE, SECOND, CENTURY
twenty years .... SCORE
unemployment .... LAYOFF
vigil .... WAKE
year .... SEASON
quiet .... CALM, LULL
short .... SNAP, SPELL
significant .... ERA
temporary .... INTERIM
trial .... PROBATION
two-week .... FORTNIGHT
unbroken .... STRETCH
woman's .... MENSES
periodic .... ETESIAN, REGULAR, SEASONAL, RECURRENT
periodical .... WEEKLY, GAZETTE, JOURNAL, MONTHLY, MAG(AZINE)
employee .... REPORTER
periodontal disease
.... GINGIVITIS
peripatetic .... WALKER, ITINERANT, PEDESTRIAN
peripheral .... OUTER, DISTAL, EXTERNAL
periphery .... RIM, AMBIT, ENVIRONS, PERIMETER
periphrasis .... AMBAGE
periphrastic .... VERBOSE
perique .... TOBACCO
periscope trail ....WAKE, FEATHER
perish .... DIE, END, EXPIRE
perissodactyl ungulate .... TAPIR
peristyle ...... COURT, COLONNADE
peritoneum .... MEMBRANE
fold .... OMENTUM
periwig .... PERUKE
periwinkle .... SHELL, SNAIL, MUSSEL, MYRTLE
perjure .... LIE
perjury, induce to commit
.... SUBORN
perk .... LIFT, RAISE, BUBBLE
perky .... GAY, SAUCY, JAUNTY, SPIRITED
Perle, society hostess ...... MESTA
perlite .... ROCK, OBSIDIAN
permanence .... FIXITY

permanent .... FIXED, LASTING, STABLE, INDELIBLE, PERPETUAL
calling .... CAREER
permeable .... PERVIOUS
permeate .... OOZE, IMBUE, DIFFUSE, PERVADE, PENETRATE
permissible .... ALLOWABLE
permission .... GRACE, LEAVE, CONSENT, LICENSE, FURLOUGH
authorized .... SANCTION
to enter .... ENTREE
permissive .... LENIENT, ALLOWING, INDULGENT
permit ...... LET, FIAT, PASS, VISA, ALLOW, GRANT, LEAVE, CEDULA, LICENSE, WARRANT, SANCTION, AUTHORIZE
reluctantly .... BEAR, BROOK, ENDURE, SUFFER, TOLERATE
to leave .... EXCUSE
permitted .... LEGAL, LICIT, LAWFUL
permutation .... CHANGE
permute ...... ALTER, REARRANGE
Pernambuco .... RECIFE
pernicious .... EVIL, FATAL, DEADLY, WICKED, BANEFUL, HARMFUL, NOISOME, NOXIOUS, VICIOUS
per(s)nickety .... FUSSY, FASTIDIOUS
Peron's lady .... EVA, EVITA, ISABEL
slogan .... CUMPLE
perorate ...... ORATE, HARANGUE, SPEECHIFY
peroration .... EPILOGUE
perpend .... PONDER
perpendicular .... SINE, ERECT, PLUMB, UPRIGHT, VERTICAL, STRAIGHT UP
perpetrate .... DO(TO), COMMIT
perpetual .... ENDLESS, ETERNAL, LASTING, CONSTANT, INFINITE, INCESSANT, PERMANENT
perpetually .... ALWAYS, (FOR)EVER
perpetuate .... PRESERVE, ETERNALIZE
perpetuity .... ETERNITY, INFINITY
perplex .... ELUDE, STUMP, BAFFLE, PUZZLE, CONFUSE, FLUMMOX, MYSTIFY, NONPLUS, INTRIGUE
perplexed .... IN A DILEMMA
perquisite .... TIP, BONUS, REWARD, APPANAGE, GRATUITY
slang .... PERK

perron .... STAIRCASE
Perry, lawyer of fiction .... MASON
singer .... COMO
perse .... BLUE
persecute .... ABUSE, ANNOY, HOUND, HARASS, OPPRESS, MALTREAT
persecution .... DOGGING, TORMENT, TORTURE
complex .... PARANOIA
of minority group .... POGROM
victim of .... JEW, MARTYR
persecutor .... PLAGUER, OPPRESSOR, TORMENTOR
Perseid .... METEOR
Persephone .... CORA, PROSERPINA
husband/abductor of .... HADES, PLUTO
parent of .... ZEUS, DEMETER
Perseus, daughter of ...... PERSEIS
mother of .... DANAE
victim of .... MEDUSA
wife of .... ANDROMEDA
perseverance .... PATIENCE, TENACITY
slang .... GUT
perseverant ones .... STAYERS
persevere .... KEEP ON, PERSIST, STICK TO IT
Pershing's command .... AEF
Persia .... IRAN
conqueror of .... CYRUS
Persian .... MEDE, ELAMITE, PAHLAVI, IRANI(AN), PARTHIAN
ally .... MEDE
almond .... BADAM
angel .... MAH
apartment .... ZENANA
bird .... BULBUL
blinds .... PERSIENNES
capital ..... ESFAHAN, ISFAHAN, PERSEPOLIS
carpet/rug .... KALI, SENNA, HAMADAN
city .... ERBIL, ARBELA, TABRIZ, TEH(E)RAN
coin .... PUL, ASAR, POUL, DARIC, DINAR, TOMAN, STATER, ASHRAFI, PAHLAVI
dance .... SARABAND
deity, supreme .... ORMAZD
dynasty ...... SELJUK, SASSANID
elf .... PERI
emigree .... PARSI, PARSEE
empire founder .... CYRUS
evil spirit .... AHRIMAN
fairy .... ELF, PERI
father .... BABA

fire worshipper .... PARSI
Gate of Faith .... BAB
god of light .... MITHRA(S)
governor .... SATRAP
Gulf region .... CHALDEA
Gulf sight .... OILER
gypsy .... SISECH
hemp .... KANAB
hook money .... LARI
inn .... SARAI, SERAI
javelin .... JERID
judge .... CADI
king .... CYRUS, DARIUS, CAMBYSES, (ARTA)XERXES
king of peris .... JAMSHID
language .... ZEND, PASHTO, AVESTAN, KURDISH, PAHLAVI
lynx .... CARACAL
measure .... PARASANG
monk .... DERVISH
mystic .... SUFI
native .... LUR, MEDE
nightingale .... BULBUL
official .... HAMAN
pal .... MEDE
people .... MEDES, ELAMITES
perfume .... ATAR
pixie .... PERI
poet .... SADI, HAFIZ, FIRD(A)USI, OMAR(KHAYYAM)
potentate .... SHAH
pottery .... GOMBROON
priestly caste .... MAGI
prince .... SATRAP
prophet .... MANI, MANES
pungent .... TEZ
refugee .... PARSI, PARSEE
religion .... BABISM, MITHRAISM
rice dish .... PILAU, PILAW
ruler .... SHAH, DARIUS, SULTAN, XERXES
sect .... BABI(SM)
screen/veil .... PARDAH
servant .... BACHA
spinel .... BALAS
sprite .... PERI
symbol .... SWASTIKA
teacher .... MULLA(H)
tiger .... SHER
title .... BAB, AZAM, KHAN, SHAH, MIR(ZA)
water wheel .... NORIA
weight .... SER, ABBAS
writings .... (ZEND)AVESTA
persicary .... KNOTWEED
persiennes ...... BLINDS, SHUTTERS
persiflage .... BANTER, BADINAGE, RAILLERY
persimmon(s) .... FRUIT
family .... EBONY

kind of .... ORIENTAL,
AMERICAN, JAPANESE,
DATE-PLUM
Oriental/Japanese .... KAKI
shape of .... EGG, ROUND
persist ...... PLOD, ENDURE, INSIST,
KEEP ON, CONTINUE,
PERSEVERE
persistence .... TENACITY
persistent .... DOGGED,
STUBBORN, CONTINUED,
TENACIOUS
assault/attack .... SIEGE
is .... LEAVES NO STONE
UNTURNED
person ...... EGG, MAN, ONE, SELF,
BEING, CHILD, WIGHT,
WOMAN, FELLOW, INDIVIDUAL
abject .... WORM, WRETCH
actively modern ...... SWINGER
African American–Native
American .... GRIFF(E)
an idle ...... SCOBBER LOTCHER
Anglo–Native American
.... WALLA(H)
angry/disgruntled
.... SOREHEAD
annoying .... CUSS, PEST,
HUNKS
argumentative .... POLEMIST
ark .... NOAH, SHEM
at least 100 years old
.... CENTENARIAN
authorized to practice
profession .... LICENTIATE
awkward ..... DUFFER, FOOZLE,
GALOOT
bad luck .... JONAH, JONAS,
HOODOO
beastly .... YAHOO
between ages of 60 and 70
.... SEXAGENARIAN
between ages of 80 and 90
.... OCTOGENARIAN
boastful .... GASCON
boorish .... GOOP, LOUT
burdensome/useless
.... DEADWOOD
callow .... CALF
clumsy .... DUB, OAF, HULK,
LOON, SLOB, SWAB, CHUMP,
JUMBO, LUBBER, LUMMOX,
CHUKKER
coarse .... MUG, BOOR, LOUT,
OGRE, RUBE, MUCKER, SAVAGE
colorless .... ALBINO
common .... PLEBEIAN
complaining .... CRAB, CRANK,
GROUCH, GROUSE, WHINER,
CRYBABY
contemptible .... CAD, CUR,

RAT, SNOT, TOAD, WORM,
LOUSE, SKUNK, SWINE,
BUGGER, INSECT, ROTTER,
STINKER, SCOUNDREL
cowardly .... CUR, SISSY,
CAITIFF, POLTROON
cunning .... FOX, WEASEL
dangerous .... DESPERADO
dark-skinned .... NEGRO
deceitful .... KNAVE
defeated in a contest
.... ALSO-RAN
demented .... NUT, LOCO,
LOONY, MORON, CRACKPOT
destructive ...... HUN, VANDAL,
ARSONIST
diabolical ..... FIEND, HELLION,
MEPHISTO
disorderly .... LARRIKIN
dissolute .... RIP, RAKE
drunken .... LUSH, STIFF,
HELLBENDER
dull .... BORE, JERK, LUMP,
MOKE, DUNCE, FOOZLE,
LURDAN(E), DULLARD,
PLODDER
easily cheated ..... DUPE, GULL
easily seduced .... PUSHOVER
eccentric .... NUT, JERK, KOOK,
CRANK
eminent .... VIP, NOTABLE,
LUMINARY
energetic .... DYNAMO,
HUSTLER, LIVEWIRE
engaged to be married
.... FIANCE(E)
entertaining .... SCREAM
evil .... THUG, DEMON, YAHOO,
CAITIFF, HOODLUM, HOOLIGAN,
MISCREANT
excessively formal .... PRIG,
PRUDE, STIFF
extraordinary .... ONER,
PRODIGY
famous .... NOTABLE,
CELEBRITY
feeble-minded .... AMENT,
IDIOT, MORON
fiendish .... HELLKITE
fine/nice .... BRICK, TRUMP
fleeing from justice
.... FUGITIVE
fond of fighting ..... HOTHEAD,
SCRAPPER
foolish .... FOP, JAY, COOT,
GOOF, BOOB(Y), BUFFOON
foppish .... LADIDA
formal .... STICKLER,
CONFORMIST
frenzied .... AMOK, AMUCK,
BERSERK(ER)

fuzzy .... FUDDY-DUDDY,
HOITY-TOITY
gifted .... WHIZ, GENIUS,
TALENT, WIZARD
greedy .... HOG, PIG, KITE,
HARPY, VULTURE
guilty of a crime .... FELON,
LAWBREAKER
gullible .... BABE, DUPE,
SUCKER
handsome .... ADONIS, LOOKER
head of .... COSTARD
high in society .... NOB
high-born .... NOBLE
high-ranking .... MAGNIFICO
holy .... MAHATMA
hotheaded .... HOTSPUR
humorous ...... WAG, CLOWN,
JESTER, WISECRACKER
ill-humored .... GROUCH,
SOREHEAD
ill-mannered ...... BOOR, CRAB,
GOOP, LOUT, YAHOO
important .... VIP, NIBS,
MOGUL, BASHAW, BIGWIG,
MAGNATE, (BIG)WHEEL,
DIGNITARY, MAGNIFICO
impractical .... DREAMER,
FANTAST, IDEALIST, VISIONARY
impudent .... HUSSY, UPSTART,
MALAPERT
impulsive .... MADCAP
inquisitive .... SNOOP, MOUSER,
BUSYBODY
insane .... LUNATIC,
PSYCHO(PATH)
insignificant ..... SNIP, SHRIMP,
SQUIRT, NONENTITY
intellectual .... NOETIC,
PUNDIT, SAVANT, EGGHEAD,
SCHOLAR
irresponsible
.... FLIBBERTIGIBBET
lazy .... POKE, DRONE, IDLER,
LOAFER, LURDAN(E)
learned .... SAGE, ORACLE,
PUNDIT, SAVANT, SCHOLAR,
SOPHIST
lively .... GRIG
living by his wits .... SPIV
living in town .... OPPIDAN
loud-voiced .... STENTOR,
THERSITES
lovable .... DOLL
maladjusted .... MISFIT
matchless/unique .... ONER
mean ..... CAD, LOUSE, CAITIFF
meddling .... BUTTINSKY
mentally deficient .... IDIOT,
MORON, IMBECILE, SIMPLETON
mischievous .... SCAMP,

HELLION
miserly .... CHURL, NIGGARD,
TIGHTWAD, SKINFLINT
mix-blooded .... METIS,
CREOLE, GRIFF(E), LADINO,
MESTEE, METIF(F), MUSTEE,
MESTIZO, MULATTO, HALF-
CASTE
modern .... NEOTERIC
much-admired .... PIP(PIN)
mythical .... SANDMAN
naive .... BABE, GREENHORN
name of .... HANDLE,
MONICKER
nameless .... ANONYM
nearsighted .... MYOPE
noble born .... CHILDE
obnoxious .... CAD, FINK,
SNOB, HUNKS
obstinate .... ASS, MULE
odd .... QUEER, ECCENTRIC
of great courage .... LION
of great energy .... DEMON
of prominence .... NABOB
of recognized excellence
.... CRACKERJACK
of unbalanced mind
.... MATTOID
old-fashioned .... FOG(E)Y,
FOSSIL, MOSSBACK
optimistic .... POLLYANNA
out of place .... ESTRAY
overnice .... PRIG
overweight .... FATSO
pale-looking .... WHEYFACE
panel .... JUROR
partly paralyzed .... PARETIC
pedantic .... PRIG
pleasure-loving .... SPORT
pledged .... HOSTAGE,
BETROTHED
poor .... BEGGAR, PAUPER
popular ..... HERO, LION, STAR,
CELEBRITY
powerful .... GIANT, MOGUL,
TITAN, PARAMOUNT,
POTENTATE
pretending to knowledge
.... SCIOLIST
prominent: sl. .... WHEEL
promising .... COMER
prone to argue .... POLEMIC,
POLEMIST
prying .... SPY, GOSSIP,
MOUSER, SNOOPER, BUSYBODY,
DETECTIVE
pugnacious .... BANTAM,
SCRAPPER
punctilious .... PRIG
puritanical .... BLUENOSE
quarrelsome .... SCRAPPER

queer ...... NUT, DUCK, CRANK,
GOOSE, CODGER, ODDBALL,
CHARACTER
quick-tempered .... HOTSPUR
rebellious .... DISSIDENT,
MALCONTENT
reckless .... MADCAP,
HOTSPUR, PLUNGER,
DAREDEVIL
resembling another .... RINGER
rich/wealthy .... NABOB, FAT
CAT, CROESUS, MONEYBAGS,
PLUTOCRAT, CAPITALIST
rough .... MUG, LARRIKIN
saucy .... MALAPERT
savage .... HUN, BRUTE,
VANDAL, BARBARIAN
second .... YOU
self-centered .... EGOIST,
EGOTIST, EGOMANIAC
self-important .... NIBS,
BASHAW
servile .... TOADY, MINION,
FLUNK(E)Y, SPANIEL
short, fat .... SQUAB,
DUMPLING
silly .... GOOF, GOOP, KOOK,
GOOSE, PINHEAD, TOMFOOL
simple, country .... BUMPKIN
slow-moving ..... POKE, SNAIL,
DAWDLER, LAGGARD
sly .... FOX, SNEAK, WEASEL,
SHYSTER
small/undersized .... BUB,
RUNT, AGATE, DWARF, PYGMY,
BANTAM, INSECT, MIDGE(T),
SHRIMP, SQUIRT, SNIP(PET),
HALFPINT, PIPSQUEAK,
LILLIPUTIAN
stateless .... REFUGEE
stingy .... HUNKS, MISER,
NIGGARD, SKINFLINT
stubborn .... ASS, MULE
stupid .... NIT, OAF, SAP, DOLT,
DOPE, GABY, LOON, MOKE,
MUTT, SLOB, NINNY, BOOB(Y),
SCHMO, DIMWIT, DUFFER,
LUMMOX, ZOMBI(E), CHUKKER,
DULLARD, JACKASS, PINHEAD,
DUMBBELL, LUNKHEAD,
NUMSKULL, SOFTHEAD,
LAMEBRAIN, SIMPLETON,
DUNDERHEAD, MUTTONHEAD
stylish .... FOP, DUDE, SWELL
surly .... HUNKS
sweet-faced .... CHERUB
sworn legally .... JURAT
syphilitic .... LUETIC
talkative ..... GABBER, MAGPIE,
(POPIN)JAY, CHATTERBOX
tall, lean: colloq.

.... BEANPOLE, LONGLEGS
terrible-tempered ...... TARTAR
third .... HE, IT, SHE, THEY
timid ..... LAMB, MOUSE, SISSY
tireless .... DYNAMO
tiresome .... PILL
tongue of .... CLAPPER
tricky .... FOX, SHYSTER,
SLICKER
tuberculous .... LUNGER,
CONSUMPTIVE
ugly .... GOON, HOOD, OGRE,
FRIGHT, GALOOT, ZOMBI(E),
GORILLA, GOLLIWOG,
SOURPUSS
under patronage .... WARD,
PROTEGE
ungrateful .... INGRATE
unhappy .... WRETCH
unprincipled .... ROGUE,
SCAMP, SCALAWAG,
SCAPEGRACE
unreasonable .... MISOLOGIST
unsophisticated, country
.... HICK, YOKEL, RUSTIC,
HAYSEED
untidy .... SLOB
unwanted .... LEPER, PARIAH,
OUTCAST, PERSONA NON
GRATA
used as tool .... PAWN,
DUMMY, FRONT, PUPPET,
STOOGE, SCAPEGOAT
utterly foolish .... IDIOT
vain ...... PEACOCK, NARCISSIST
very funny .... RIOT
violent, lawless .... RUFFIAN,
ROUGHNECK, TERRORIST
vulgar .... CAD, BOOR, LOUT,
MUCKER
waist measure of .... GIRTH
weak .... WIMP, NAMBY-PAMBY
white .... CAUCASIAN
who acts as prostitute's
agent .... PIMP, PROCURER
who avoids obligation
.... SLACKER
who betrays .... RAT, TRAITOR,
SQUEALER
who browbeats .... THUG,
BULLY, CUTTHROAT
who defrauds .... SWINDLER
who has great skill
.... DEMON, GENIUS
who makes kids sleepy
.... SANDMAN
who never laughs
.... AGELAST, DEADPAN,
POKERFACE
who sells on installment
.... TALLYMAN

529

wicked .... FIEND, MONSTER, VILLAIN, SCOUNDREL

wise .... GURU, SAGE, SEER, SOLON, SAVANT, MAHATMA

with free ticket .... DEADHEAD, DEADBEAT

with unsatiable thirst .... TANTALUS

with the same name as another .... NAMESAKE

withered, thin .... MUMMY

without melanin pigment .... ALBINO

wonderfully dull .... COLOSSAL BORE

working off a debt .... PEON

worthless .... BUM, LOSEL, CADGER, VAGRANT, RAKE, WASTREL

young .... CALF, SLIP, LAMBKIN, WHIFFET, TEENAGER

persona non grata, designating a .... UNWANTED, UNDESIRABLE, UNACCEPTABLE

personable ...... COMELY, GENIAL, CHARMING, HANDSOME

personage .... NIBS, BIGWIG, NOTABLE, DIGNITARY, MAGNIFICO

personal .... OWN, PRIVATE, CORPORAL, INTIMATE, INDIVIDUAL

appearance .... MIEN, BEARING, PRESENCE

aura ..... CHARISMA, MYSTIQUE

belongings .... TRAPS

characteristic .... TRAIT

charm .... CHARISMA

combining form .... IDIO

effects .... DUNNAGE

well-being .... COMFORT, WELFARE, CONVENIENCE

personality .... EGO, SELF, PRESENCE, CHARACTER

test .... RORSCHACH

personate .... PORTRAY, REPRESENT

personator .... IMPOSTOR

personified .... INCARNATE

personify .... EMBODY, TYPIFY, SYMBOLIZE

personnel .... CREW, STAFF, WORKERS, EMPLOYE(E)s

concern .... ABSENTEEISM

perspective .... ANGLE, VISTA, ASPECT, OUTLOOK, STANDPOINT, (POINT OF)VIEW

perspicacious .... KEEN, ACUTE, SHREWD

perspicacity .... ACUMEN, INSIGHT

perspicuous .... CLEAR, LUCID, LIMPID

perspiration ...... SUDOR, SWEAT, EGESTA, HIDROSIS

stimulator .... BONESET

perspire .... EGEST, SWEAT

profusely .... SWELTER

persuade .... COAX, URGE, INDUCE, WORK ON, CONVINCE, PREVAIL ON

by giving reasons .... ARGUE

persuasible .... DOCILE, AMENABLE

persuasion .... PLEA, BELIEF, CONVICTION, INSISTENCE

art of .... SOFT SELL

persuasive .... COGENT, CONVINCING

pert ...... ARCH, BOLD, FLIP(PANT), BRASH, SASSY, SAUCY, FORWARD, IMPUDENT

girl .... CHIT, MINX

language .... SASS

pertain .... REFER, BELONG, RELATE

pertaining .... APROPOS, RELATIVE, INVOLVING, REFERRING

to a certain pope .... SISTINE

to a nonmetallic element .... SELENIC

to 4th century Franks .... SALIC

Perth river .... TAY

pertinacious .... FIRM, STUBBORN

pertinence .... BEARING, RELEVANCE

pertinent .... APT, GERMANE, RELEVANT

perturb .... ALARM, UPSET, RUFFLE, AGITATE, DISTURB, DISTRESS

perturbation .... FEEZE

pertussis ...... (WHOOPING)COUGH

Peru, capital of .... LIMA

conqueror of .... PIZARRO

peruke .... HAIR, PERI(WIG)

peruse .... CON, READ, SCAN, STUDY, EXAMINE, SCRUTINIZE

Peruvian .... INCA(N), LIMAN

animal .... LLAMA, ALPACA, VICUNA

austerity program .... FUJISHOCK

bark/tree .... CINCHONA

bay .... PAITA, PISCO, SECHURA

beef .... CHARQUI

bird .... YUTU, TINAMOU

cape .... BLANCO

carrot .... APIO

city/town ...... ICA, ILO, JAEN, PUNO, CUSCO, PISCO, PIURA, TACNA, CALLAO, TALARA, TUMBES, SULLANA, AREQUIPA, AYACUCHO, PUCALLPA, TRUJILLO

coin .... SOL, LIBRA, DINERO, PESETA

current .... EL NINO

dance .... CUECA

department .... ICA, LIMA, PUNO, JUNIN, PIURA, TACNA, ANCASH

falcon .... ALETO

first ambassador to the Soviet Union .... DE CUELLAR

fox .... ATOC

goddess .... MAMA

hill .... LOMA, MEDANO

Indian ...... ANDE, CANO, INCA, PANA, COLLA, AYMARA, CHANCA, CHUNCHO, QUECHUA

inn .... TAMBO

island .... CHINCHA, SAN GALLAN, INDEPENDENCIA

king .... INCA, ATABALIPA, ATAHUALPA

lake .... JUNIN, TITICACA

language .... AYMARA, QUECHUA, SPANISH

monetary unit .... SOL

mountain .... EL MISTI, COROPUNA, HUASCARAN, SALCANTAY

mountain range .... ANDES

peninsula .... PARACAS

plant .... OCA, TOLA

plateau .... TABLAZO

port .... CALLAO

president .... BELAUNDE, FUJIMORI

recording device .... QUIPU

river .... ENE, ICA, MANU, MAYO, NAPO, SAMA, ACARI, CASMA, JURUA, NANAY, PURUS, RIMAC, SANTA, TIGRE, VITOR, GRANDE, MORONA, PAMPAS, PERENE, PICHIS, TUMBES, YAGUAS, YAVARI, MANTARO, MARANON, UCAYALI, APURIMAC

singer .... SUMAC

tanager .... YENI

tobacco .... SANA

volcano .... MISTI, OMATE

wind .... PUNA, SURES

pervade .... FILL, IMBUE, DIFFUSE, PERMEATE

pervasive .... SUFFUSIVE

quality .... ODOR

perverse .... WRY, WICKED, CONTRARY, UNTOWARD, DIFFICULT

attitude .... CONTRARINESS
pervert .... WARP, TWIST, DEBASE, GARBLE, MISUSE, CORRUPT, DISTORT, MISLEAD, VITIATE
pervious .... PERMEABLE
Pesach .... PASSOVER
Pescadores .... HOKO GUNTO
pesky .... IRKSOME, ANNOYING, MISCHIEVOUS
peso .... DURO
$^1/_{100}$ of ..... CENTAVO, CENTIMO
pessimist .... CYNIC, KILLJOY, WORRIER
opposite of .... OPTIMIST
slang .... CRAPEHANGER
pessimistic .... GLOOMY, CYNICAL, NEGATIVE, DEFEATIST
pest .... IMP, BANE, BORE, PLAGUE, VERMIN, NUISANCE
colloquial .... TERROR
in a pool .... SPATTERER
problem .... TROUBLER
pester .... DUN, NAG, VEX, ANNOY, HARRY, TEASE, BADGER, BOTHER, HARASS, HECTOR
pesticide .... DDT, BUG BOMB
controversial .... ALAR
pestiferous .... NOXIOUS
pestilence ...... PLAGUE, MURRAIN, SCOURGE, EPIDEMIC
pestle .... BRAY, BEETLE, MULLER, POUNDER
companion of .... MORTAR
pet .... SULK, CODDLE, COSSET, DANDLE, FONDLE, DARLING, FAVORITE
lamb .... CADE, COSSET
name .... NICKNAME, SOBRIQUET
of the wicked witch
.... BLACK CAT
Petain, Marshall .... HENRI
petal .... LEAF, LABELLUM
base .... UNGUIS
protuberance .... CALCAR
petals, arrangement of
.... WHORL, ROSETTE
without .... APETALOUS
petard .... FIRECRACKER
petasus .... CUPALO, (WINGED)HAT
petcock .... VALVE, FAUCET
Pete of baseball fame ...... ROSE
peter .... WANE, DWINDLE
out .... END, EXPIRE, PERISH, COLLAPSE
Peter, actor .... FALK, FONDA, LORRE, O'TOOLE, USTINOV
Bull's subject .... TEDDIES, TEDDYBEAR
Falk role .... COLUMBO

Pan's author .... BARRIE
captain .... HOOK
dog .... NANA
loss .... SHADOW
opponents .... PIRATES
pal .... WENDY
pirate .... SMEE
the Great's wife ...... EUDOXIA
Peter's tribute to Pope
.... PENCE
petiole .... STIPE, PEDUNCLE, (LEAF)STALK
petit .... PETTY
mal .... EPILEPSY
petite .... TINY, SMALL, DIMINUTIVE
petition .... ASK, SUE, PLEA, SUIT, APPLY, APPEAL, PRAY(ER), IMPLORE, REQUEST, SOLICIT, ENTREATY
petitioner, in law .... ORATOR
petits fours .... CAKES
Petrarch's lady .... LAURA
petrel ...... TITI, FULMAR, STINKER, MALLEMUCK
describing one .... STORMY
Leach's storm
.... OCEANODROMA
relative .... FULMAR, PUFFIN
resembling diving .... AUK
white-faced storm
.... PELAGODROMA
Wilson's storm .... OCEANITES
petrified ...... FROZEN, APPALLED, TERRIFIED
goddess .... NIOBE
substance .... COAL, FOSSIL
Petrified Forest site .... ARIZONA
petrify .... STUN, SHOCK, HARDEN, DEADEN, CALCIFY, STUPEFY, PARALYZE, FOSSILIZE
Petrograd .... LENINGRAD
petrol .... GAS(OLINE)
petrolatum .... VASELINE
petroleum jelly .... PARAFFIN, VASELINE, PETROLATUM
product .... COKE, PITCH, BUTANE, OILTAR, BENZENE, BITUMEN, NAPHTHA, PROPENE, CYMOGENE, GASOLINE, KEROSENE, LIGROIN(E), PARAFFIN
solvent .... OCTANE
tanker .... OILER
Petrosian, chess champ
.... TIGRAN
Petrova, actress .... OLGA
petticoat .... GIRL, WOMAN, BALMORAL, CAMISOLE, (HALF)SLIP, (UNDER)SKIRT
material .... CRINOLINE

pettifogger .... SHYSTER
petting .... CARESSING
pettish .... CROSS, FRETFUL, PEEVISH
pettitoes .... FEET, TOES
petty .... MEAN, MINOR, SMALL, PALTRY, TRIVIAL, FIDDLING, PICAYUNE, TRIFLING
fault .... PECCADILLO
officer .... MATE, BOSUN, YEOMAN
Petula, singer .... CLARK
petulance .... PEEVISHNESS, PETTISHNESS
petulant .... CROSS, SHORT, TESTY, FRETFUL, PEEVISH, WASPISH, IRRITABLE, HOITY-TOITY
petunia .... NIGHTSHADE
pew .... SLIP, STALL, BENCHES
end carving .... POPPYHEAD
pewee .... PEWIT, PHOEBE, FLYCATCHER
pewit ...... GULL, PEWEE, PHOEBE, LAPWING
pewter .... TRIFLE
peyote .... CACTUS, MESCAL
product .... MESCALINE
Peyton Place author
.... METALIOUS
pfennig, $^1/_2$ of .... HELLER
100 .... MARK
pH is measure of .... ACIDITY, ALKALINITY
result of high .... ALKALOSIS
result of low .... ACIDOSIS
7 of body fluids
.... NEUTRALITY
Phaedra's husband ...... THESEUS
parent .... MINOS
Phaedrus' forte .... FABLES
phagocyte .... CELL
"free" .... MONOCYTE, GRANULOCYTE
locale .... BLOOD, LUNGS, SPLEEN, ALVEOLI
phalanger .... ARIEL, TAPOA
phantasm .... GHOST, VAPOR, EIDOLON, SPECTER
phantasmal .... EERIE
phantom .... GHOST, SPIRIT, (E)IDOLON, SPECTER, ILLUSION, APPARITION
Pharaoh .... SETI, CHEOPS, RAM(E)SES
residence .... MEMPHIS
pharmacist .... DRUGGIST
obsolete term .... APOTHECARY
pharmacology subject .... DRUGS
pharmacy .... DRUGSTORE
pharos ...... BEACON, LIGHTHOUSE

builder .... SOSTRATOS
pharynx .... TUBE, THROAT,
PASSAGE
inflammation .... PHARYNGITIS,
SORE THROAT
part of .... OROPHARYNX,
NASOPHARYNX,
LARYNGOPHARYNX
phase .... FORM, PART, SIDE,
ANGLE, FACET, STAGE, STATE,
ASPECT
Ph.D. applicant .... TESTEE
pheasant .... CHIR, MONAL,
POULT, GROUSE, LEIPOA,
RING-NECK, TRAGOPAN
brood .... NYE, NID(E)
Elliot's .... SYRMATICUS
family .... NUMIDIDAE,
PHASIANIDAE
genus .... PAVO, PHASIANUS,
ARGUS(IANUS)
nest .... NIDE
relative .... QUAIL, FRANCOLIN,
PARTRIDGE
Swinhol's .... LOPHURA
phenazopyridine ...... PAINKILLER
phenobarbital .... LUMINOL,
SEDATIVE
effect .... DIZZINESS,
DROWSINESS
phenomenon .... EVENT,
HAPPENING
phial .... VIAL, BOTTLE
philabeg .... KILT
philanderer: sl. .... WOLF,
PLAYBOY, CASANOVA
philanthropic .... GENEROUS,
ALTRUISTIC, CHARITABLE
philatelist's delight .... STAMP
Philip II's kingdom .... MACEDON
naval fleet .... ARMADA
son .... ALEXANDER(THE
GREAT)
wife .... OLYMPIAS, CLEOPATRA
Philip IV's enemies
.... TEMPLARS
philippic .... SCREED, TIRADE,
ORATION, DIATRIBE,
HARANGUE, INVECTIVE
Philippine(s) abbot ...... MONGHE
abode .... TAHANAN
aborigine .... ATA, ATI, ITA,
AETA, NEGRITO
abyss .... BANGIN
accident .... SAKUNA
ace .... ALAS
act .... GAWA
activity/affair .... GAWAIN
actor/actress .... BITUIN,
ARTISTA
adage .... KAWIKAAN

advantage .... BENTAHA
advice .... PAYO
afternoon .... HAPON
age .... TANDA, GULANG
aid .... ABULOY, TULONG
all .... LAHAT
alligator .... BUWAYA
ally .... ALYADO
almond .... PILI
alum .... TAWAS
American base (erstwhile)
.... CLARK, SUBIC, CAVITE,
OLONGAPO, SANGLEY POINT
amulet .... ANTING-ANTING
anchovy .... DILIS
anger .... GALIT
animal .... HAYOP, CARABAO,
TAMARAW, TARSIER
answer .... SAGOT
ant .... LANGGAM
antidote .... LUNAS
ape .... BAKULAW, ORANG-
UTAN
apostle .... ALAGAD
apple .... MANSANAS
archipelago .... SULU
ash .... ABO
aunt .... ALE, TIYA
baby .... BATA, SANGGOL
badge .... TSAPA
bag .... SUPOT
bakery .... PANADERYA
bamboo dance .... TINIKLING
barge .... CASCO, KASKO
barracks .... KUARTEL
bat .... PANIKI
battlesite, WW II .... BATAAN,
CORREGIDOR
bay .... BALER, HONDA,
ORMOC, SUBIC, ILIGAN,
BALAYAN, TAYABAS
bear .... OSO
bell .... KAMPANA
bet .... TAYA, PUSTA
binoculars .... LARGABISTA
bird .... IBON, KULASISI
birthmark .... BALAT
blanket .... KUMOT
boat .... BATEL, BANGKA
book .... AKLAT, LIBRO
boss .... AMO
boy .... TOTOY
bread .... TINAPAY
breadfruit .... RIMA
brook .... BATIS
broom .... WALIS
brother/sister .... KAPATID
bucket .... TIMBA
buffalo .... CARABAO,
KALABAW, TAMARAW,
TIMARAU

bullet .... BALA
cabbage .... REPOLYO
cage .... HAWLA
can .... LATA
cannon .... LANTAKA
canoe .... BANCA
cape .... MAYO, LAMON,
ENGAÑO, ILLANA, LIANGA,
PUJADA, BOLINAO
capital .... MANILA, QUEZON
CITY
cat .... PUSA
Catholic cardinal .... SIN,
SANTOS
chair .... SILYA, UPUAN
channel ...... BASHI, MAQUEDA,
BALINTANG, JINTOTOLO
charcoal .... ULING
cheer .... MABUHAY
chicken .... MANOK
chief .... HEPE
child .... ANAK, BATA
Chinese invader .... LIMAHONG
church ..... IGLESIA, SIMBAHAN
cinema .... PELIKULA
circle .... BILOG
citizen ...... TAGALOG, PILIPINO
city/town .... IBA, BOAC, CEBU,
JOLO, LIPA, NAGA, DAVAO,
LAOAG, VIGAN, APARRI,
BAGUIO, BONTOC, BUTUAN,
CAVITE, ILAGAN, ILIGAN,
ILOILO, LUCENA, MAKATI,
TARLAC, ANGELES, BACOLOD,
BALANGA, BANGUED,
CALAMBA, DAGUPAN, LEGAZPI,
MALOLOS, BATANGAS,
CALBAYOG, COTABATO,
LINGAYEN, OLONGAPO,
TACLOBAN, ZAMBOANGA,
CABANATUAN, TAGBILARAN,
NAGUILIAN, SAN FERNANDO
civet .... MUSANG
clam .... TULYA
client .... SUKI
clock/watch .... RELOS
cloud .... ULAP
clown .... BUBO
cobbler .... SAPATERO
cockfight .... SABONG
coconut .... NIOG
kind of .... MACAPUNO
meat .... COPRA
toddy .... TUBA
young .... BUKO
coin .... PESO, BARYA, PESETA,
SALAPI, CENTAVO, CENTIMO
condiment/spice .... REKADO
Congress .... KAPULUNGAN
contest .... TIMPALAK
contribution .... AMBAG

convict .... BILANGGO
cop .... PULIS
cork .... TAPON
corn .... MAIS
cotton .... BULAK
cough .... UBO
country .... BAYAN
court .... HUSGADO
cousin .... PINSAN
cow .... BAKA
coward .... DUWAG
cross .... KRUS
crow .... UWAK
dagger .... DAGA, PUNYAL,
                        BALISONG
dart .... PANA
day .... ARAW
dead .... PATAY
deaf .... BINGI
debt .... UTANG
decision .... PASIYA
decoy .... PAIN
decree .... BATAS
deer .... USA
depot .... BODEGA
devil ...... DIABLO, DIMONYO
dew .... HAMOG
dialect .... WIKA, BICOL,
     IBANAG, ILONGO, ILOCANO,
     VISAYA, TAGAL(OG),
     PAMPANGO, PANGASINAN,
     WARAY-WARAY
diaper .... LAMPIN
discoverer of .... MAGELLAN
dissident .... HUK
dog .... ASO
door .... PINTO
dove .... KALAPATI
drama .... DULA
dress .... DAMIT
drink .... ALAK, BASI, TUBA,
     VINO, CERVEZA, LUMBANOG
drum .... TAMBOL
duck .... BIBI, ITIK, PATO
dwarf .... AETA, UNANO,
                       NEGRITO
eagle .... AGILA
ear .... TAINGA
earth .... LUPA, MUNDO
east .... SILANGAN
eel .... IGAT
egg .... ITLOG
eggplant .... TALONG
ego .... AKO, SARILI
election .... HALALAN
error/mistake .... MALI
evening .... GABI
eye .... MATA
fabric .... PINA, JUSI, TELA,
                       RAMIE
fad .... USO, MODA

fairy .... DIWATA
falls .... PAGSANJAN
famous .... BANTUG
fan .... ABANIKO
farewell .... PAALAM
farm .... BUKID
farmer .... KASAMA,
                   MAGSASAKA
fat .... TABA
father ...... AMA, PAPA, PADRE,
                       TATAY
fear .... TAKOT
fee/rent .... UPA
fence .... BAKOD
fern .... PAKO
fetish .... ANITO
fever .... LAGNAT
fiber .... HEMP, JUSI, PINA,
     ABACA, BUNTAL, MAGUEY
fish .... ISDA, DALAG, BACOCO,
     BANGUS, TILAPIA, TULINGAN,
               GALONGGONG
dried .... TUYO
sauce .... PATIS
smoked .... TINAPA
flag .... BANDERA, WATAWAT
flood .... BAHA
floor .... SAHIG, PALAPAG
flour .... ARINA
flower .... BULAKLAK
follower .... KAMPON
food .... PAGKAIN
staple ..... CORN, RICE, BIGAS
fool .... ULOL
foot .... PAA, PIYE
forefather .... NINUNO
forest .... GUBAT
fork .... TENEDOR
fort .... KUTA, COTTA
free .... LIBRE, MALAYA
freedom .... KALAYAAN
fruit .... BUNGA, PRUTAS
fruit tree .... CHICO, DUHAT,
     GUAVA, DURIAN, LANGKA,
   MANGGA, SANTOL, LANZONES,
     SAMPALOK, TAMARIND
funeral .... LIBING
gag/joke .... BIRO
garbage .... BASURA
garlic .... BAWANG
gift .... REGALO
ginger .... LUYA
God .... DI(Y)OS
gold .... GINTO
goon .... MATON
grapes .... UBAS
grapefruit .... SUHA
grass .... DAMO, COGON,
       SAKATE, TALAHIB
guard .... BANTAY
guava .... BAYABAS

guess .... HULA
guest/visitor .... BISITA
gulf .... MORO, DAVAO, LEYTE,
     RAGAY, LAGONOY, LINGAYEN
hammock .... DUYAN
hand .... KAMAY
hardwood .... IPIL, NARRA,
             YAKAL, MOLAVE
hat .... GORA, SOMBRERO
hawk .... LAWIN
head .... ULO
heart .... PUSO
heaven .... GLORIA
heir .... EREDERO
hell .... IMPI(Y)ERNO
hemp .... ABACA, ABAKA
hero .... BIDA, BAYANI
hero, national .... RIZAL,
     MABINI, BONIFACIO,
   AGUINALDO, LAPU-LAPU, ABAD
                   SANTOS
highest peak .... MOUNT APO
hobgoblin .... DWENDE
horse .... KABAYO
-drawn vehicle ...... CALESA,
     CARRETELA, CARROMATA
hot springs .... ASIN, LOS
                   BANOS
house .... BAHAY
hunchback .... KUBA
ice .... YELO
income .... KITA
island .... CEBU, CUYO, BOHOL,
     CORON, LEYTE, LUZON,
     PANAY, SAMAR, CULION,
   MACTAN, NEGROS, BABUYAN,
   BASILAN, MASBATE, MINDORO,
     PALAWAN, ROMBLON,
     MINDANAO, TAWI-TAWI,
              CORREGIDOR
island group .... BATAN,
   SIBUTU, TURTLE, CAMOTES,
     LAPARAN, SAMALES,
              CALAMIAN
jackfruit .... LANGKA
jail .... KARSEL
jar .... BANGA
jewelry .... ALAHAS
jockey .... HINETE
juror .... HURADO
kettle .... KALDERO
key .... SUSI
kiss .... HALIK
kitchen .... KUSINA
knee .... TUHOD
knife .... BOLO, ITAK,
                 KUTSILYO
lake .... TAAL, LANAO,
     LAGUNA DE BAY
lamb .... KORDERO
language .... ENGLISH,

Philippine(s)

TAGALOG, PILIPINO

lantern .... PAROL
law .... BATAS
lawyer .... ABOGADO
leech .... LINTA
lemon .... CALAMANSI
Lent .... KUWARESMA
leper colony .... TALA, CULION
library .... AKLATAN
light .... ILAW
lime .... DAYAP
lip .... LABI
liver .... ATAY
luck .... SUWERTE
lungs .... BAGA
mahogany .... NARRA,
KAMAGONG
maid .... ALILA, DALAGA
mail .... KOREO
box .... BUSON
carrier .... KARTERO
man/male .... LALAKI
mate/spouse .... ASAWA
mayor .... ALKALDE
measure .... CAVAN, CHUPA,
GANTA, SALOP
meat .... KARNE
dried, salted .... TAPA
medicine .... GAMOT
mendicant .... PULUBE
mental institution
.... MANDALUYONG
mermaid .... SIRENA
midwife .... HILOT
miracle ...... HIMALA, MILAGRO
mirror .... SALAMIN
monetary unit .... PESO
money .... KUWARTA
monkey .... UNGGOY
moon .... BUWAN
morning .... UMAGA
Moro boat .... LIPA, VINTA,
KUMPIT
chief .... DATO, DATU
Moslem .... MORO, MUSLIM,
MARANAW
mosquito .... LAMOK
moss .... LUMOT
mother .... INA, NANAY
mountain .... APO, PULOG,
HALCON, BANAHAW,
CANLAON, ARAYAT,
ZAMBALES, CABALASAN,
MALINDANG, SANTO TOMAS,
SIERRA MADRE, DIWATA,
CORDILLERA
mouse .... DAGA
municipality/town ..... BAYAN,
PUEBLO, MUNISIPYO
mystery/puzzle .... HIWAGA
myth .... ALAMAT

namesake .... TUKAYO
nation .... BANSA
national park .... LUNETA,
MOUNT APO
native .... MORO, IGOROT,
DUMAGAT, TAGALOG
naval base ...... SUBIC, CAVITE,
OLONGAPO
negrito .... ATA, ITA, AETA
news .... BALITA
newspaper .... DIARYO
no .... HINDI
none/nothing .... WALA
north .... NORTE, HILAGA
number ...... BILANG, NUMERO
one .... ISA
two .... DALAWA
three .... TATLO
four .... APAT
five .... LIMA
six .... ANIM
seven .... PITO
eight .... WALO
nine .... SIYAM
ten .... SAMPU
nut .... PILI
oil .... ACIETE, LANGIS
omelet .... TORTA
omen .... BABALA
orange .... KAHEL
oven .... HURNO
overseer .... KATIWALA
ox .... TORO
oyster .... TALABA
pail .... TIMBA
palace .... MALACANANG
palm .... PALAD
palm tree .... NIPA, ANAHAW
parent .... MAGULANG
parrot .... LORO
partridge .... PUGO
passenger .... SAKAY
peacock .... PABOREAL
peanut .... MANI
pear .... PERAS
peasant .... KASAMA
pencil .... LAPIS
person .... TAO
plum .... DUHAT
poem .... TULA
poison .... LASON
Pope .... PAPA
port .... CEBU, MANILA
president ...... ROXAS, AQUINO,
GARCIA, LAUREL, MARCOS,
RAMOS, OSMENA, QUIRINO,
MACAPAGAL, QUEZON,
MAGSAYSAY
prison .... MUNTINGLUPA
province .... ABRA, CEBU,
SULU, ALBAY, BOHOL, CAPIZ,

DAVAO, LANAO, LEYTE, RIZAL,
SAMAR, AGUSAN, BATAAN,
CAVITE, ILOILO, LAGUNA,
NEGROS, QUEZON, TARLAC,
BULACAN, CAGAYAN, ISABELA,
LA UNION, MASBATE,
MINDORO, PALAWAN,
ROMBLON, SURIGAO,
BATANGAS, COTABATO,
MOUNTAIN, PAMPANGA,
ILOCOS SUR, PANGASINAN,
ILOCOS NORTE
public transportation ...... BUS,
JITNEY, JEEPNEY
pugilist .... ELORDE
race driver .... MARCELO
rain .... ULAN
raincoat .... KAPOTE
raisin .... PASAS
rattan .... YANTOK
rebel .... HUK, KATIPUNAN,
INSURRECTO
resort .... TAGAYTAY
rice .... BIGAS, PALAY
variety .... MACAN, WAGWAG
ring .... SINGSING
river .... AGNO, ILOG, CHICO,
PASIG, AGUSAN, APARRI,
CAGAYAN, PULANGI,
MINDANAO
sailboat .... BATEL, PARAW,
VINTA
salt .... ASIN
sapodilla .... CHICO
sash .... BIGKIS
sausage .... LONGGANISA
scavenger .... BASURERO
Scriptures .... BIBLIA
sea ...... SULU, BOHOL, DAGAT,
SAMAR, CAMOTES, CELEBES,
SIBUYAN, VISAYAN
seaman .... MARINERO
servant .... ALILA, UTUSAN
shadow .... ANINO
sharecropper .... KASAMA
sheep .... TUPA, KARNERO
ship .... BAPOR, BARKO
shoes .... SAPATOS
shovel .... PALA
shrimp .... HIPON
silk .... SEDA
silver .... PILAK
sin .... SALA
sir .... GINOO
skirt .... SAYA, PALDA
sky .... LANGIT
slave/serf ..... ALIPIN, BUSABOS
snafu .... GULO
snail .... SUSO
snake .... AHAS
snob .... HAMBOG

soap .... SABON
society .... LIPUNAN
song .... AWIT, KANTA
soup .... CALDO, SABAW,
                                    SOPAS
south .... SUR, TIMOG
souvenir .... ALAALA
soy sauce .... TOYO
specter .... MULTO, IMPAKTO
spider .... GAGAMBA
spinach .... TALINUM
spleen .... LAPAY
sponsor .... NINANG, NINONG,
                    MADRINA, PADRINO
spy .... TIKTIK
squid .... PUSIT
stateroom .... KAMAROTE
statesman .... RECTO, OSMENA,
                    QUEZON, ROMULO
stew .... NILAGA
stone .... BATO
story .... KUWENTO
strait .... LUZON, TANON,
                    TABLAS, MINDORO
street .... KALYE
suet .... SEBO
sugar .... ASUKAL
suitcase .... MALETA
sultanate .... SULU
summer capital .... BAGUIO
sun .... ARAW
sweet potato .... CAMOTE
sword .... SABLE
table .... MESA
tail .... BUNTOT
tailor .... SASTRE
taro .... GABI
tea .... CHA, TSA(A)
teacher .... MAESTRA,
                                 MAESTRO
tear(drop) .... LUHA
tempest .... UNOS
termite .... ANAY
thatch .... ATIP, NIPA, COGON
theater .... DULAAN
thief .... TULISAN
thimble .... DEDAL
thread .... SINULID
tick .... PULGAS
tiff .... AWAY, LABAN
tomato .... KAMATIS
tongs .... SIPIT
tongue .... DILA
tooth .... NGIPIN
tree .... DAO, IPIL, ABETO,
             LIGAS, YAKAL, ACACIA,
        LANETE, MOLAVE, SAMPALOK
tribe .... ATI, LIPI
tribesman .... BADJAO, IGOROT,
    TAUSUG, KALINGA, MARANAW,
         NEGRITO, TINGGIAN

tripe .... GOTO
trousers .... PANTALON
turnip .... SINGKAMAS
turtle .... PAGONG
twins .... KAMBAL
typhoon .... BAGYO
uncle .... TIYO, AMAIN
vagrant .... LAGALAG
vegetable .... GULAY
village .... BARYO, NAYON,
                                   SITIO
vinegar .... SUKA
volcano .... APO, TAAL,
   MAYON, CANLAON, PINATUBO,
                         HIBOK-HIBOK
walkout .... WELGA
wall .... PADER
"walled city"
.... INTRAMUROS
water .... TUBIG
  buffalo .... CARABAO
  chestnut .... APULID
  melon .... PAKWAN
  well .... BALON
weapon .... BOLO, KRIS,
   ARMAS, SANDATA, KAMPILAN
weasel .... MUSANG
weed .... DAMO
week day: Sunday
.... LINGGO, DOMINGO
  Monday .... LUNES
  Tuesday .... MARTES
  Wednesday
   .... MI(Y)ERKOLES
  Thursday .... HUWEBES
  Friday .... BI(Y)ERNES
  Saturday .... SABADO
weight .... KILO, FARDO,
   PICUL, QUINTAL, TONELADA
west .... KANLURAN
wheel .... GULONG
whip .... LATIKO
widow .... BIYUDA
wig .... PELUKA
wind .... HANGIN
wish .... NAIS
witch .... BRUHA
witness .... TESTIGO
wolf .... LOBO
woman/female .... BABAE
word .... SALITA
work .... TRABAHO
worm .... BULATE
yam .... UBI, GABI, TUGI
year .... TAON
yes .... OO, OHO, OPO
youth .... KABATAAN
zone .... POOK
philistine .... BABBIT
Philistine city .... GATH, GAYA,
                                    GAZA

giant .... GOLIATH
Philo, dick .... VANCE
philology .... LINGUISTICS
philomel .... NIGHTINGALE
Philomela, sister of ...... PROCNE
philosopher .... HUME, KANT,
      SAGE, ZENO, CYNIC, HEGEL,
      LOCKE, PLATO, SKEPTIC,
                                 SPINAGE
   great .... PLATO, THALES,
         ARISTOTLE, LEUCIPPUS,
         DEMOCRITUS, EMPEDOCLES
   "laughing" .... DEMOCRITUS
   scientist .... THALES
   stone of .... ELIXIR
philosophy ...... EGOISM, MONISM
   abstract beings, in ..... ENTIA
philter .... CHARM, POTION
phlebotome .... FLEAM, LANCET
phlegm is one .... HUMOR
phlegmatic .... COOL, DULL,
         SLUGGISH, IMPASSIVE
phloem .... BARK, BAST, TISSUE
phlogistic .... INFLAMMATORY
phlogosis .... ERYSIPELAS
phobia .... FEAR, AGORA, HATRED
phocid .... SEAL
Phoebe ...... MOON, DIANA, PEWEE,
      PEWIT, SELENE, ARTEMIS,
                              GODDESS
Phoebus .... SOL, SUN, APOLLO
Phoenician capital .... TYRE,
                                  SIDON
   god .... BAAL, DAGON,
                              MOLOCH
   goddess .... ASTARTE
   princess .... EUROPA
Phoenix .... BENU
phone and zip .... CODES
   call .... BUZZ, RING
   cubicle .... BOOTH
   emergency .... HOTLINE
   system .... INTERCOM
   system, part of
   .... TRUNKLINES
phonetic .... ORAL, VOCAL,
                                 SPOKEN
   elision .... SLUR
phonetics, smooth .... LENE
phonics .... ACOUSTICS
phonograph .... VICTROLA,
                         GRAMAPHONE
   needle .... STYLE, STYLUS
   record .... DISC, PLATTER,
                            LONG-PLAY
   record mold .... MASTER
   with coin slot .... JUKE BOX
phony .... FAKE, SHAM, FLASE,
   POSEUR, IMPOSTOR, SPURIOUS,
                             CHARLATAN
phosphate .... APATITE

535

photo ...... MUG, PIX, SHOT, SNAP, PIC(TURE)
finish .... STAT, DEAD HEAT
finishes .... GRAPHS, SYNTHESIS
light .... STROBE
solution .... HYPO, REDUCER
photocopy .... STAT
photograph .... FILM, SHOT, SNAP, PRINT, STILL, PICTURE
book .... ALBUM
enlarge a .... BLOW UP
photographer .... CAMERIST, SHUTTERBUG, SNAPSHOOTER
Adams .... ANSEL
fixing agent .... HYPO
Morath .... INGE
place of .... DARKROOM
test print of .... PROOF
word of .... SMILE, CHEESE
photographic camera .... CANON, KODAK, LEICA, REFLEX, BROWNIE, GRAFLEX, MINOLTA, OLYMPUS, POLAROID
equipment .... LENS, TIMER, CAMERA, FINDER, TRIPOD, SHUTTER, ENLARGER, FLASHGUN, FLASHBULB
prints, certain .... ROTOGRAPHS
result .... PICTURE, SNAPSHOT
solution .... HYPO, FIXER, TONER, REDUCER, DEVELOPER
photographs pieced together .... MOSAIC, MONTAGE
photography ...... ARTS, PICTURE-TAKING
word .... FOCAL
photoplay .... MOVIE, MOTION PICTURE
phrase .... CLAUSE, LOCUTION, EXPRESSION
applying to a celebrity ...... IN THE NEWS
dictator's .... IN RE
figuratively ..... SO TO SAY, AS IT WERE, IN A SENSE, SO TO SPEAK
in law .... IN REM
in liturgy .... PARSE
in song .... REFRAIN
listener's .... I SEE
meaning "about" ...... OR SO, MORE OR LESS
meaning "concerning" .... IN RE
on many dietary foods ...... FAT FREE, LESS SALT, ALL NATURAL, NO CHOLESTEROL
phraseology .... DICTION, WORDING, EXPRESSION
phratry .... CLAN, PHYLE

phrenetic .... WILD, INSANE, EXCITED, FANATIC, FRENZIED
phrenic .... MENTAL, NOETIC
phrenitis .... DELIRIUM
Phrygian king .... MIDAS
lunar god .... MEN
slave .... AESOP
phthisis .... CONSUMPTION, TUBERCULOSIS
phylactery .... CHARM, REMINDER
phyletic .... RACIAL, TRIBAL
Phyllis/Phillis .... SWEETHEART
phylloid .... LEAFLIKE
physic .... APERIENT, LAXATIVE, CATHARTIC, PURGATIVE
physical .... SOMAL, BODILY, NATURAL, SOMATIC, MATERIAL, ANATOMICAL
dimension ..... WIDTH, HEIGHT, LENGTH
direction .... UP AND DOWN, BACK AND FORTH, LEFT AND RIGHT
discomfort .... DYSPHORIA
examination .... CHECKUP
science .... GEOLOGY, PHYSICS, ASTRONOMY, CHEMISTRY
therapy, kind of ..... MASSAGE, EXERCISE, HEAT TREATMENT
vigor .... ENERGY, VITALITY
physician ...... MD, MAYO, GALEN, DOC(TOR), LISTER, MEDIC(O), MESMER, SURGEON
former .... LEECH
second century AD .... GALEN
symbol .... CADUCEUS
physicist ...... OHM, HAHN, MACH, RABI, BOYLE, CURIE, FERMI, AMPERE, EINSTEIN
physics, branch of .... OPTICS, STATICS, DYNAMICS, KINETICS, ACOUSTICS, MECHANICS
Nobelist .... RABI, CURIE, BRAUN, FERMI, RAMAN
preceder .... NNE
physiognomy .... FACE
phytology .... BOTANY
pi ...... MIX UP, JUMBLE, MIXTURE
follower .... RHO
piacular .... SINFUL, WICKED, ATONING, EXPIATORY
pianist .... ANDA, HESS, ITURBI, LEVANT, CLIBURN, LIBERACE
Claudio from Chile .... ARRAU
kind of .... CONCERT
White House .... NIXON, TRUMAN
piano .... SOFT(LY), SPINET
favorite .... NOLA
forerunner .... CLAVICHORD

grand .... BABY, PARLOR, CONCERT
in music .... SOFT
key .... IVORY
keyboard .... CLAVIER
skill in playing the .... PIANISM
small, upright .... PIANETTE
pianolike instrument .... SPINET, CELESTA, CLAVICHORD
piaster, 1/120 of .... ASPER
piazza .... PORCH, ARCADE, SQUARE, GALLERY, PORTICO, VERANDA(H)
pibroch instrument ...... BAGPIPE
pica .... TYPE
picador's prey .... BULL, TORO
picaresque .... ROGUISH
character .... VAGABOND
picaroon .... ROGUE, THIEF, PIRATE, ADVENTURER
Picasso, painter .... PABLO
picayune .... CHEAP, PETTY, PALTRY, TRIVIAL, TRIFLING
Piccadilly Circus figure .... EROS
piccolo .... FLUTE
pick .... BEST, CULL, ELITE, GLEAN, PLUCK, CHOOSE, NIBBLE, PECKER, SELECT, CHOICE(ST), MANDREL, MATTOCK
at .... NAG, FINGER
-me-up .... TONIC
on .... ANNOY, TEASE
over .... CULL
the .... ELITE
up .... LEARN, IMPROVE
up the pieces .... RECOVER
pickax .... GURLET, MATTOCK
Pickens of films .... SLIM
pickerel .... PIKE
amphibian .... GREEN FROG
weed .... HERB
picket .... PALE, POST, FENCE, GUARD, STAKE, PATROL, TETHER, STRIKER
station of a .... OUTPOST
pickiness .... CHOOSINESS
pickings .... SCRAPS, SPOILS
pickle ...... FIX, JAM, ALEC, CORN, DILL, MESS, ACHAR, BRINE, SOUSE, GHERKIN, MARINADE
pickled ...... TREATED, PRESERVED
food/meat .... SOUSE
pepper picker .... PETER
slang .... DRUNK, INTOXICATED
pickles .... RELISH
pickling solution .... BRINE, SOUSE, MARINADE
picklock .... THIEF, BURGLAR
pickpocket .... DIP, PRIG,

CUTPURSE
trainer .... FAGIN
working place of ..... CROWDS
picky .... CHOOSY, PARTICULAR
picnic ...... EAT, JUNKET, OUTING,
COOKOUT, CLAMBAKE
area .... GROVE
author of .... INGE
game .... HORSESHOES,
VOLLEYBALL
visitor .... ANT
picot .... PURL
picotee .... CARNATION
pictograph .... (HIERO)GLYPH
pictorial .... VIVID, GRAPHIC,
ILLUSTRATED
picture ...... IMAGE, PHOTO, PRINT,
SLIDE, STILL, SCENE(RY),
DEPICT, SKETCH, DRAWING,
IMAGINE, REFLECT, TABLEAU,
LIKENESS, PAINTING
composite .... MONTAGE
frame .... EASEL
girl .... PIN-UP, CHEESECAKE
in words .... DESCRIBE,
DELINEATE
life .... STILL
moving .... FILM, MOVIE,
CINEMA
of many images ..... MONTAGE
of the Last Supper .... CENA
person's .... PORTRAIT
pertaining to a .... ICONIC
poorly painted .... DAUB
puzzle .... REBUS
section .... ROTO
show .... MOVIE, CINEMA
tube .... KINESCOPE
wall .... MURAL
picturesque .... VIVID, QUAINT,
SCENIC, GRAPHIC, IDYLLIC,
STRIKING
piddle .... DABBLE, TRIFLE,
URINATE
piddling .... PETTY, USELESS
pidgin .... JARGON, CHINOOK
pie .... PATE, TART, PASTY, PATTY,
JUMBLE, PASTRY, COBBLER,
DUMPLING
baker .... OVEN
covering .... CRUST, MERINGUE
cracker .... GRAHAM
cut, shape of .... WEDGE
deer's vitals .... HUMBLE
eyed .... DRUNK
faced .... MOONFACED
filling .... APPLE, PECAN,
PEACH, RAISIN, CHERRY,
MINCEMEAT
piebald .... PIED, HORSE, PINTO,
CALICO, DAPPLED

piece ...... BIT, CHIP, HUNK, PART,
CHUNK, SCRAP, SLICE,
CANTLE, COLLOP, MORSEL,
SLIVER, PORTION, FRAGMENT,
SPLINTER
burlesque .... SKIT
de resistance .... ENTREE,
MAIN EVENT
of cake .... A CINCH
candy .... DROP
eight .... REAL
evidence .... CLUE
marble .... SLAB
news .... ITEM
one's mind .... SCOLDING
soap .... CAKE
the rock .... SLAB
turf .... SOD, DIVOT
wood .... PANEL, SPLAT
together .... PATCH
worker .... JOBBER
piecemeal .... GRADUALLY,
PARTIALLY, BIT BY BIT,
SEPARATELY
piecen .... SPLICE
pieces, go to .... COLLAPSE
pied .... MOTTLED, PIEBALD,
SPOTTED, VARIEGATED
-a-terre .... LODGING,
FOOTHOLD
Pied Piper .... MAGICIAN
Piper's river .... WESER
Piper's town .... HAMELIN
Piedmont .... PIEMONTE
city .... OSTI, TRINO, TURIN
native of .... PIEDMONTESE
ruling family .... SAVOY,
SAVOIE
village .... MARENGO
pieplant .... RHUBARB
pier .... ANTA, DOCK, MOLE,
QUAY, SLIP, JETTY, JUTTY,
WHARF, LANDING, PILASTER
architectural .... ANTA
glass .... MIRROR
landing .... DOCK, JETTY
rectangular .... ANTA
space .... SLIP
support .... PILES, COLUMNS
pierce .... BORE, GORE, STAB,
CHILL, DRILL, LANCE, GRIDE,
GOUGE, PRICK, PUNCH, SPEAR,
THIRL, WOUND, IMPALE,
THRUST, PUNCTURE,
PENETRATE
piercing .... KEEN, ACUTE, SHARP,
BITING, SHRILL, CUTTING,
CHILLING, INCISIVE
pieridine .... BUTTERFLY
Pierre .... PETER, PIETRO
piers, space between .... SLIP

piet .... OUSEL, OUZEL, MAGPIE
pietist .... DEVOTEE
piety .... FAITH, BELIEF,
DEVOTION, HOLINESS
exaggerated .... PIETISM
piffle .... GAS, ROT, WIND, HOKUM,
HOGWASH, TWADDLE
pig .... HOG, SOW, PORK(ER),
DUROC, SHOTE, SWINE,
GRUNTER, JACOBIN
animal like .... PECCARY
castrated .... BARROW
disease .... BULLNOSE
80 to 189 lbs. weight
.... SHOAT
famous ...... ARNOLD, BIG RED,
LOUISA, WILBUR, SALOMEY,
NAPOLEON, PORKY PIG, MISS
PIGGY
feature .... SNOUT
feet of .... TROTTERS
female .... SOW, GILT
female that has given birth
.... FARROWED
51 to 79 lbs. weight
.... FEEDER
for slaughter .... FATLING
intestines .... CHITTERLINGS
iron .... INGOT
like a .... PIGGISH
litter .... FARROW
little .... PIGGY, PIGLET
male .... BOAR
nursing .... PIGLET
190 to 240 lbs. weight
.... MARKET
out .... OVEREAT
pen/paddock .... STY
slang .... SLOB, GLUTTON
vital organs .... HA(R)SLET
wild .... BOAR
young .... ELT, GILT, GRICE,
SHOAT, SHOTE, PIGLET,
WEANER
pig's eye, in a .... NEVER
pigboat .... SUBMARINE
pigeon .... NUN, BARB, DOVE,
RUFF, PIPER, CULVER, PIDGIN,
POUTER, TURBIT, FANTAIL,
TUMBLER
——— .... TOED
call .... COO
carrier .... HOMING
crested .... TRUMPETER
hawk .... MERLIN
house .... (DOVE)COTE,
COLUMBARY
ID tag .... LEGBAND
neck feathers .... HACKLE
pea .... DAL
slang .... DUPE, PUSHOVER

tumbler .... ROLLER
walk like .... TOE IN
wood .... CUSHAT, RINGDOVE
young .... PIPER, SQUAB
pigeonhole .... SHELVE,
    CUBBYHOLE
pigfish .... GRUNTER
piggery .... STY
piggin .... PAIL, PIPKIN
piggish .... FILTHY
piggyback .... PICKABACK
pigheaded .... STUBBORN,
    OBSTINATE
piglet .... GILT
pigment .... DYE, BICE, COLOR,
    SMALT, STAIN, UMBER,
    ZAFFER, ZAFFRE, ETIOLIN,
    GAMBOGE, STAINER,
    CINNABAR, ORPIMENT
absence of .... ALBINISM,
    ALPHOSIS, LEUCODERMA
black .... MELANIN
blood's .... HEMACHROME
bluish green .... VIRIDIAN
brown .... SEPIA, UMBER,
    BISTER, BISTRE, SIENNA
calico printing .... CANARIN
coal tar ...... MAUVE, MADDER,
    ANILIN(E), ALIZARIN
cuttlefish .... SEPIA
grayish-blue/green .... BICE
red .... CARMINE, CINNABAR,
    VERMILION
reddish brown .... SIENNA
skin tissue .... MELANIN
soot .... BISTER, BISTRE,
    LAMPBLACK
without .... ALBINO
yellow .... OCHER, OCHRE,
    ETIOLIN, FLAVIN(E), RETINENE,
    QUERCETIN
pigmentation .... DISCOLORATION
comb. form .... CHROMAT(O)
dark .... MELANISM
pigmy. See **pygmy**
pignus .... PAWN, PLEDGE,
    CONTRACT
pigpen .... STY
sound .... OINK, GRUNT(LE),
    SQUEAL
pigs' feet .... PETTITOES
litter .... TEAM, FARROW
pigskin .... SADDLE, FOOTBALL
pounce .... TACKLE
pigsticker .... POCKETKNIFE
pigtail .... CUE, BRAID, PLAIT,
    QUEUE, COLETA, TOBACCO
pigweed .... AMARANTH
pika .... CONY, HARE, LAGOMORPH
pike .... FISH, GATE, PICK,
    LUCE(T), PIERCE, MOUNTAIN,

PICKEREL, SPONTOON, TOLL
    ROAD, SPEARHEAD
collection .... TOLL
full-grown .... LUCE
like fish .... GAR, ROBALO,
    ARAPAIMA
perch .... SAUGER
piked .... PEAKED, POINTED
piker: sl. .... MISER, TIGHTWAD,
    CHEAPSKATE
pilaster ...... ANTA, PIER, ALETTE,
    COLUMN
groove .... STRIA
top of .... CAPITAL
Pilate .... PONTIUS
realm of .... JUDEA
pilau/pilaw .... PILAF(F)
pilchard .... FUMADO, HERRING,
    PILCHER, SARDINE
pilcher .... SCABBARD
pile ...... NAP, HEAP, LOAD, MASS,
    RICK, HOARD, SPILE, STACK,
    EDIFICE, BUILDING,
    CONGERIES, STRUCTURE
driver .... RAM, TUP, MAUL,
    OLIVER
fabric .... NAP
hay .... MOW, RICK, STACK
on .... RUN UP
slang .... MONEY, FORTUNE
up .... AMASS
pileous .... HAIRY
piles .... HEMORRHOIDS
pileus .... (SKULL)CAP
pilewort .... CELANDINE
pilfer .... COP, ROB, FILCH, MICHE,
    MOOCH, STEAL, SWIPE,
    THIEVE, SHOPLIFT
pilferage .... THEFT
pilferer .... THIEF
pilgrim .... ALDEN, IHRAM,
    PALMER, DEVOTEE, PIONEER,
    WANDERER, WAYFARER,
    SOJOURNER
badge of .... SCALLOP
bottle of .... COSTREL
destination of .... ROME,
    MECCA, SHRINE, JERUSALEM
Fathers .... SETTLERS
garment of .... IHRAM
leaders ..... JOHN SMITH, MILES
    STANDISH
protector .... TEMPLAR,
    CRUSADER
pilgrimage .... HADJ
pilgrims, Indian friend of
    ...... MASSASOIT, WAMPANOAG
settlement .... PLYMOUTH
ship of .... MAYFLOWER
traveling together
    .... CARAVAN

Pilgrim's Progress author
    .... BUNYAN
pill .... BOLUS, DRAGEE, PELLET,
    PILULE, TABLET, CAPSULE
kind of: sl. .... UPPER,
    DOWNER
like a .... PILULAR
slang .... BORE, GOOFBALL
vet's/big .... BOLUS
pillage .... LOOT, SACK, FORAY,
    HARRY, RIFLE, SPOIL, STRIP,
    MARAUD, RAPINE, RAVAGE,
    PLUNDER
pillar ...... LAT, PIER, POST, STELE,
    COLUMN, OBELISK, SUPPORT,
    MAINSTAY, MONUMENT
combining form .... STYL
of _____ .... FIRE, SMOKE,
    STELAR, STRENGTH
of Hercules .... GIBRALTAR,
    JEBEL MUSA
projecting ring .... CINCTURE
sitter .... STYLITE
support .... PEDESTAL
tapering .... OBELISK
top inhabitant .... STYLITE
top of .... IMPOST
with figure .... TELAMON,
    ATLANTES, CARYATID
writing on .... GRAFFITO
pillbox .... HAT
pillory .... YOKE, CANGUE,
    GIBBET, STOCKS
pillow .... PAD, BOLSTER,
    CUSHION, HEADREST
covering .... SLIP, TICK
covers .... SHAM
fight .... ROMP
slip .... CASE
stuffing .... CEIBA, KAPOK,
    COTTON, FEATHERS
pilose .... HAIRY, HIRSUTE
pilot .... LEAD, FLYER, GUIDE,
    AVIATOR, CONDUCT,
    HELMSMAN, STEER(SMAN)
biscuit .... CRACKER,
    HARDTACK
cow .... PINTANO
fish .... REMORA
lifesaver for .... CHUTE,
    PARAFOIL
milieu of .... SKY
place of .... COCKPIT
stove .... SWITCH
student .... CADET
test flight .... SOLO
wear of .... WINGS
pilotless plane .... DRONE, GLIDER
piloua .... HAIRY
Pilsudski, president .... JOSEF
pilule .... PILL

pilum .... SPEAR
Pima .... COTTON, INDIAN
pimento .... (ALL)SPICE
   spread .... CHEESE
pimiento .... PEPPER, RELISH,
                  PAPRIKA
pimola .... OLIVE
pimp ...... PANDER(ER), PROCURER
   occupation of .... PIMPERY
pimpernel .... PRIMROSE
pimple .... BOIL, POCK, WHEAL,
     WHELK, PAPULE, BLEMISH,
       PUSTULE, CARBUNCLE
   scar .... POCK
pin .... FID, NOG, PEG, ACUS,
     BOLT, COAG, LILL, NAIL,
    TACK, BADGE, DOWEL, RIVET,
     BODKIN, BROOCH, COTTER,
    FASTEN, TOGGLE, TRIFLE,
              FASTENER
   buckle's .... TONGUE
   colloquial .... LEG
   cotter .... KEY
   down .... BIND, HOLD, NAIL
   firing .... TIGE
   flatheaded .... TACK
   gunwale/oar .... THOLE
   in bowling .... CLUB
   meat-cooking .... SPIT,
         BROACH, SKEWER
   metal .... RIVET
   money .... ALLOWANCE
   pivot .... PINTLE
   -up .... CHEESECAKE
pina .... PINEAPPLE
pinaceous tree .... FIR, PINE,
                 CEDAR
pinafore .... SLIP, TIER, APRON,
        DICKEY, SAVE-ALL
   initials for .... HMS
pinball worry .... TILT
pince-nez .... LORGNON,
            EYEGLASSES
pincer ...... CLAW, CHELA, TONGS,
    NIPPER, PLIERS, FORCEPS,
     GRIPPER, TWEEZER
   movement, in a way .... SIEGE
pinch ...... NIP, BITE, HURT, RAID,
    CRAMP, FILCH, GRIPE, PUGIL,
     STEAL, ARREST, STRESS,
     SQUEEZE, DISTRESS
   and twist .... TWEAK
   hit .... SUBSTITUTE
   in a .... HARDSHIP
   of something .... BIT, DASH
pincher .... TWEAKER
pindaric .... ODE, EPODE
pine .... LONG, MOPE, CEDAR,
     CRAVE, KAURI, KAURY,
    OCOTE, PINON, WASTE,
   YEARN, CONIFER, LANGUISH,

    LOBLOLLY, PONDEROSA
   board/wood .... DEAL
   cone .... STROBILE
   disease .... RUST, BLISTER
   fruit .... CONE
   leaves .... NEEDLES
   nut/seed .... PINON
   Pacific .... HALA
   product/ooze .... RESIN,
                 GALIPOT
   resin .... DAMMER
   siskin .... FINCH
   tar extract .... RETENE
   tree, kind of .... CHIR
   wild .... PINASTER
Pine Tree State .... MAINE
pineapple .... PINA, ANANA
   plantation .... PINERY
   slang .... BOMB,
        (HAND)GRENADE
   topknot .... COMA
pinfold .... POUND
ping pong .... TABLE TENNIS
   racket .... BAT, PADDLE
pinguid .... FAT, OILY, GREASY,
       FERTILE, UNCTUOUS
pinion .... WING, PENNON,
    FEATHER, SHACKLE,
         COGWHEEL
pink .... SHIP, STAB, PRICK,
    RADICAL, FOXHUNTER
   become .... PINKEN
   color/shade ...... ROSY, CORAL,
      DAMASK, SALMON
   lady .... COCKTAIL
   turn .... BLUSH
Pinkerton .... DETECTIVE,
         PRIVATE EYE
pinkie .... SHIP, FINGER
pinkish red skin blemish
         STORK BITE, SALMON
              PATCHES
Pinkster .... WHITSUNTIDE
   flower .... AZALEA
pinna .... EAR, FIN, WING,
    AURICLE, FEATHER, LEAFLET
pinnace .... BOAT
pinnacle .... ACME, PEAK, CROWN,
        SPIRE, SUMMIT
   of ice .... SERAC
pinnae .... FINS
pinner .... HEADDRESS
pinniped ...... SEAL, WALRUS, SEA
                 LION
   feet of .... FLIPPERS
pinnule .... LEAFLET
pinny .... PINAFORE
pinochle .... (CARD)GAME
   action .... MELD
   deck, card not in .... TREY,
    DEUCE, CINQUE, QUATRE

   game like .... BEZIQUE
   lowest cards .... NINES
   score .... DIX
   term .... DIX, MELD, KITTY
pinole .... FLOUR
pinon .... NUT, PINE
pinpoint .... DOT, LOCATE
pins and needles .... PARESTHESIA
   or pence .... TEN
pinscher .... DOG, DOBERMAN
pint, 1/4 .... NOGGIN, QUARTERN
1/2 .... SPLIT
pintado .... CERO, SIERRA,
               KINGFISH
pintail .... DUCK, SMEE, GROUSE
pintano .... FISH, COWPILOT
pintle .... PIN, BOLT
pinto .... PONY, MOTTLED,
        PIEBALD, SPOTTED
pinweeds .... LECHEA
pinwheel, noisy action of
                WHIRRING
pinworm .... ASCARID, ASCARIS
Pinza, operatic singer .... EZIO
Pinzon's caravel .... PINTA
pioneer .... PAVER, PLANTER,
             SETTLER
   farm implement .... DEERE
pious .... GODLY, DEVOUT,
    SACRED, SAINTLY, RELIGIOUS
   feeling .... PIETISM
   person .... PIETIST
pip .... HIT, PEEP, ROUP, SEED,
           SPOT, CHIRP
pipa .... TOAD
pipal .... (BO)TREE, FIG TREE
pipe .... FLUE, HUB(B), TUBE,
    BRIAR, BRIER, CHALAM,
    DUDEEN, CALUMET, WHISTLE
   air .... VENTIDUCT
   bending tool .... HICKEY
   bowl leaving .... DOTTEL,
               DOTTLE
   collar of .... FLANGE
   curve of .... OFFSET
   down .... SHUT UP
   fitting .... TEE
   Irish .... DUDEEN
   joint .... ELL
   joint ring .... GASKET
   line .... SOURCE, CONTACT
   musical .... OAT, FIFE, FLUTE
   nozzled .... HOSE
   oriental .... REED, HOOKAH,
            NARG(H)ILE
   part .... BOWL, STEM
   peace .... CALUMET
   player .... FLUTIST
   principal .... MAIN
   run-off .... DRAIN
   shape .... BULLDOG, FULL-BENT

shaped .... TUBULAR
shepherd's .... OAT, REED,
                      LARIGOT
small .... TUBULE, PIPETTE
smoke .... TEWEL, HOOKAH,
              CALUMET, NARGILE
smoker, at times .... TAMPER
steam .... RISER
tobacco .... CHIBOUK
tobacco bag .... POUCH
up .... SAY, SPEAK
pipefish .... GAR
pipelike .... TUBATE
piper .... TRILLER
actress .... LAURIE
piping ...... FOLD, REEDY, SHRILL,
    HISSING, SIZZLING, TRIMMING
bird .... PLOVER
hot .... BOILING
joint .... ELL
pipit .... (TIT)LARK
pipkin .... POT, PIGGIN
pippin .... SEED, APPLE
pipsqueak .... SNIP
pipy .... SHRILL
piquancy .... NIP, ZEST
piquant .... RACY, SALTY, SHARP,
    SPICY, BITING, PUNGENT,
                STINGING
pique .... VEX, PEEVE, STING,
    EXCITE, FABRIC, NETTLE,
    OFFEND, OFFENSE, PROVOKE,
           RESENTMENT
piqued .... IRATE
piracy .... ROBBERY
literary .... PLAGIARY,
             PLAGIARISM
piragua .... BOAT, CANOE,
             PIROGUE
Pirandello .... LUIGI
piranha .... FISH, CARIBE, PIRAYA
pirate .... XEBEC, SEA-RAT,
    CORSAIR, SEAWOLF,
    (SEA)ROVER, MARAUDER,
    PICAROON, PRIVATEER,
          FREEBOOTER
arm .... CUTLASS
famed .... KIDD, DRAKE,
    MORGAN, ROGERS, CORNISH,
          BLACKBEARD
flag .... (JOLLY)ROGER
literary .... PLAGIARIST
ship .... FRIGATE, PICAROON,
    PRIVATEER, BRIGANTINE
state .... TUNISIA
pirn .... SPOOL, BOBBIN
pirogue .... CANOE, PIRAGUA
Pisa feature .... TOWER
river .... ARNO
Pisan .... ITALIAN
piscatorial abode ...... AQUARIUM

Pisces .... FISH(ES)
piscine egg .... ROE
lore name .... WALTON
Pisgah's biblical climber
    .... MOSES
summit .... NEBO
pishu .... LYNX
pismire .... ANT, EMMET
pisolite .... LIMESTONE
piss .... URINE, URINATE
Pissarro, Fr. painter
    .... CAMILLE
pistachio .... NUT, CASHEW
pistil, part of ...... OVARY, STIPE,
    STYLE, CARPEL, STIGMA
pistol .... DAG(G), LUGER,
    MAUSER, ZIP GUN, FIREARM,
    HANDGUN, (SIDE)ARM,
    REPEATER, REVOLVER,
    AUTOMATIC, DERRINGER
case .... HOLSTER
chamber .... MAGAZINE
slang .... GAT, ROD, HEATER,
    EQUALIZER, PEACEMAKER
pistole .... COIN
piston .... VALVE, PLUNGER
pit .... GAP, HOLE, HELL, SCAR,
    SEED, TRAP, WELL, ABYSS,
    ARENA, FOVEA, GRAVE,
    SNARE, STONE, ARROYO,
    CAVITY, CRATER, POTHOLE,
        POCK(MARK)
bottomless ...... ABYSS, CHASM
for draining or storing
    liquids .... SUMP
in anatomy .... FOSSA
mine .... SUMP
peach/plum .... PUTAMEN,
             ENDOCARP
theater .... PARQUET
pita .... AGAVE, FIBER, BROCKET
pitch .... KEY, SHY, TAR, CANT,
    CAST, HURL, REEL, ROLL,
    SWAY, TOSS, ERECT, FLING,
    LURCH, RESIN, SET UP,
    THROW, ENCAMP, PLUNGE,
    ASPHALT(UM), BITUMEN
a complete game .... GO THE
             ROUTE
black .... PICEOUS
in .... CONTRIBUTE
in golf .... CHIP, LOFT
indicator .... CLEF
musical .... DIAPASON
salesman's .... LINE, PLUG,
         SPIEL, PATTER
uncompleted .... BALK
pitchblende ingredient
    .... URANIUM
pitcher .... JUG, EWER, OLLA,
    TOBY, CARAFE, HURLER,

    TOSSER, THROWER
and catcher .... BATTERY
aspiration of .... NO HIT
crime of .... BALK
goal of .... OUTS
Gooden .... DWIGHT
Hershiser .... OREL
Koufax .... SANDY
leaf .... ASCIDIUM
left-handed .... SOUTHPAW
Marichal .... JUAN
Perry .... GAYLORD
pitch of .... CURVE, TWIRL,
    SLIDER, SPITTER, BEANBALL,
    KNUCKLER, SPITBALL,
        KNUCKLE BALL
plant ...... EVE'S CUP, FLYTRAP
plate of the .... BOX, SLAB,
            MOUND
preparatory motion of
    .... WINDUP
relief .... FIREMAN
Ryan .... NOLAN
Seavers .... TOM
stat. .... ERA
Welch .... BOB
pitching niblick ...... IRON, GOLF
            CLUB
pitchman .... HAWKER
pitchy .... DARK, BLACK
piteous .... PITIFUL, PATHETIC
pitfall .... GIN, SNAG, TRAP, SNARE
pith ...... CORE, GIST, MEAT, PULP,
    MARROW, MEDULLA,
        SUBSTANCE
Pithecan-thropine .... APEMAN
Pithecanthropus erectus
    .... JAVA MAN
pithecoid .... SIMIAN
pithless .... WEAK
pithy .... TERSE, CONCISE,
    LACONIC, POINTED, FORCEFUL
pitiable .... MEAN, PALTRY,
          DEPLORABLE
pitiful .... MEAN, PITEOUS,
    PATHETIC, WRETCHED
pitiless .... CRUEL, RUTHLESS
pitman .... MINER
pittance .... BIT, ALMS, DOLE,
    STIPEND, ALLOWANCE
pitted .... STONED, FOVEATE
pitter-patter .... PITAPAT,
        DRUMBEAT
Pittsburgh rooter .... PIRATE FAN
pituitary hormone .... PROLACTIN
secretion .... MUCUS,
        HORMONE
pity .... MERCY, SYMPATHY,
        COMPASSION
pivot .... SLUE, TURN, HINGE,
    WHEEL, PINTLE, STATOR,

SWIVEL
on one's _____ .... HEEL
pivotal .... CRUCIAL, CARDINAL
pixilated .... DRUNK, LOOPY,
BEMUSED, BEDEVILED,
POSSESSED
pixy .... ELF, IMP, FAIRY, SPRITE
pixyish .... ELFIN, IMPISH
Pizzaro's conquest .... PERU
pizzicato .... PLUCKED
placard .... BILL, SIGN, POSTER
placate .... PACIFY, SOOTHE,
APPEASE, MOLLIFY
colloquial .... BUTTER UP
placatory .... CONCILIATORY
place .... PUT, SET, LIEU, RANK,
ROOM, SITE, SPOT, LOCUS,
POINT, SPACE, STEAD,
LOCALE, REGION, APPOINT,
LOCATION, POSITION,
PREMISES, STANDING
accurately .... TRUE
apart .... ENISLE, ISOLATE,
SEGREGATE
between .... INTERPOSE
Blue Ribbon .... FIRST
busy .... HIVE
camping .... ETAPE, BIVOUAC
city's .... PLAZA, SQUARE
dancing ..... CASINO, CABARET,
BALLROOM
down under .... CELLAR,
BASEMENT
drafty .... BARN
first .... EDEN
for a coin .... SLOT
a dance .... BARN
a hero .... DELI
a padlock .... HASP
a pigskin .... GRID
aging .... VAT
bargains .... FLEA MARKET
bric-a-brac .... ETAGERE
clinging things .... VINERY
coal .... BIN
eggs .... NEST
eleves .... ECOLE
exes .... RENO
fans .... ARENA, STADIUM
outerwear .... CLOAKROOM
races .... OVAL
relics .... SEPULCHER
rubbish .... DUMP
tankers: abbr. .... SPT
trees .... ARBOR
"trois" .... MENAGE
white water .... RAPIDS
for: suffix .... ORIA
gambling .... CASINO
hiding .... DEN, MEW, LAIR,
CACHE, HANGOUT, HIDEOUT

ideal .... UTOPIA
in a wall .... NICHE
an envelope .... ENCLOSE
office .... INSTALL
proximity/next to .... APPOSE
inside .... INSERT
like Camp David ..... RETREAT
mat .... DOILY
meeting .... TRYST,
RENDEZVOUS
of .... LIEU, STEAD
abode .... HOME, HOUSE,
DWELLING, RESIDENCE
accused in court .... DOCK
agony .... GOLGOTHA
confusion/noise
.... MADHOUSE
honor .... PEDESTAL,
HEADTABLE
oblivion .... LIMBO
offering .... PARATORIUM
penitence .... CANOSSA
rapid growth .... HOTBED
refreshment .... OASIS
religious seclusion
.... ABBEY, PRIORY,
CONVENT, CLOISTER,
NUNNERY, MONASTERY
reputed fabulous wealth
.... ELDORADO
safety .... HAVEN, ASYLUM,
(ASYLA-PL.), HARBOR,
REFUGE, SANCTUARY
torment .... GEHENNA
trial .... VENUE
worship .... ALTAR
out of .... ILL-TIMED
pea .... POD
resting .... PARK BENCH
rough .... SEAM
secret/secluded ..... DEN, MEW,
NOOK, HIDEOUT, RETREAT
set in .... POSIT, SITUATE
side by side .... COLLOCATE
snugly .... ENSCONCE
stopping .... HOSTEL
storage ..... CRIB, SILO, CACHE,
DEPOT, CELLAR, CLOSET,
WAREHOUSE
take .... OCCUR, HAPPEN,
TRANSPIRE
that has had its day .... TUNIS,
TRIPOLI
to caulk .... SEAM
lie, bad ...... WITNESS STAND
remember .... ALAMO
see stars .... PLANETARIUM
stand on .... POU STO
trading .... MART, MARKET,
EXCHANGE
under water .... IMMERSE,

SUBMERGE
where an artist starves
.... ATTIC
beer is served ...... TAPROOM
bones meet .... JOINT
placid ...... CALM, QUIET, SERENE,
PEACEFUL, TRANQUIL,
IMPASSIVE
placket .... POCKET
plagiarism .... CRIB, PIRACY
plagiarist .... THIEF
plagiarize ...... CRIB, LIFT, STEAL,
PIRATE
plagiarized phrase
.... PEACOCK'S FEATHER
plague ...... VEX, ANNOY, HARRY,
TEASE, HARASS, HECTOR,
PEST(ER), WANION, MURRAIN,
SCOURGE, TORMENT,
CALAMITY, NUISANCE
plagued .... BESET
plagues, one of the .... LOCUST
plaice .... SOLE, (FLAT)FISH,
FLOUNDER
plaid .... MAUD, TARTAN
plaidman .... TARTAN,
HIGHLANDER
plain .... BARE, FLAT, MERE,
OPEN, CAMPO, CLEAR, LEVEL,
LLANO, HOMELY, PATENT,
SIMPLE, EVIDENT, OBVIOUS,
CAMPAGNA, PALPABLE
barren, high .... PARAMO
dweller .... GAUCHO, LLANERO,
LOWLANDER
grassy .... CAMPO, LLANO,
VELD(T), PRAIRIE, SAVANNA(H)
high ..... MESA, WOLD, WEALD,
PARAMO
hill on a .... BUTTE
ingenuous .... GUILELESS
one .... JANE
spoken .... BLUNT, FRANK,
CANDID
treeless .... WOLD, VELD(T),
PAMPAS, PARAMO, STEPPE,
TUNDRA, SAVANNA(H)
vast arid .... STEPPE
Plains, _____ .... DES
Indian .... KIOWA, PAWNEE
plainsman .... WESTERNER
plaint ...... GRIPE, LAMENT(ATION)
plaintiff .... SUER, USEE, ORATOR,
SUITOR, ACCUSER, LITIGANT,
DEMANDANT, COMPLAINANT
answer of .... REPLICATION
list of wrongs .... LIBEL
withdrawal of case
.... NONSUIT
plaintive .... SAD, FRETFUL,

WISTFUL, MOURNFUL
plait ...... PLY, PLAT, PLEX, BRAID,
PLEAT, QUEUE, TRESS,
PLEACH, WIMPLE, PIGTAIL
plaited .... BRAIDED, PLICATE
gass/leaves .... SENNIT
trimming .... RUCHE
plan ...... AIM, MAP, PLAT, DRAFT,
ETTLE, DESIGN, INTEND,
SCHEMA, SCHEME, SKETCH,
OUTLINE, PROJECT
artful .... MACHINATION
for a proposed journey
.... ITINERARY
for deceiving enemy in war
.... STRATAGEM
of action .... IDEA, DEVICE
secretly to commit a crime
.... PLOT, CONNIVE, CONSPIRE
spoiler .... MARPLOT
townsite .... PLAT
planch(e) .... BOARD, FLOOR
plancher .... PALLET
plane .... EVEN, FLAT, GLIDE,
GRADE, LEVEL, SMOOTH,
AIRFOIL, SURFACE
controversial .... SST
curve .... ELLIPSE
inclined .... RAMP
instruments on
.... ALTIMETERS
lane .... RUNWAY
smoothing .... TROWEL
swift .... SST
10-sided .... DECAGON
tree .... CHINAR, PLATAN
war .... MIG, SPAD, ZERO,
STUKA, NAPIER, SABREJET,
SPITFIRE, SUPERFORT
planet ...... MARS, EARTH, PLUTO,
VENUS, PALLAS, SATURN,
URANUS, JUPITER, MERCURY,
NEPTUNE
fastest .... MERCURY
largest .... JUPITER
minor .... ASTEROID
Mork's .... ORK
most brilliant .... VENUS
movement of .... LIBATION
red-colored .... MARS
ringed .... SATURN
satellite .... MOON, RHEA,
DIONE, MIMAS, DEIMOS,
HESTIA, NEREID, PHOBAS,
UMBRIEL
secondary .... MOON
shadow of .... (PEN)UMBRA
smallest .... MERCURY
planetoid .... ASTEROID
planetarium .... ORRERY
plank .... DECK, BOARD, SLATE,

POLICY, FLOORING, PRINCIPLE
curve of .... SNY
or way .... GANG
planks above keel .... DEADWOOD
planoblast .... JELLYFISH
plant. See also **shrub** .... SOW,
HERB, MILL, TREE, WORT,
AROID, BUGLE, ORACH,
SHRUB, STOCK, CLOVER,
HYSSOP, FACTORY, FREESIA,
PLANTAIN
a tap .... BUG
aconite .... MONKSWOOD,
WOLFSBANE
agave .... PITA
air ..... MOSS, LICHEN, ORCHID,
EPIPHYTE
Alpine .... BISTORT, EDELWEISS
amaranth .... COCKSCOMB
amaryllis .... CRINUM,
EUCHARIS
and animal life .....BIOS, BIOTA
appendage .... STIPEL, STIPULE,
TENDRIL
arum family ..... JACK-IN-THE-
PULPIT
Asiatic .... RAMIE
axis ..... STEM, STALK, CAUDEX
banana .... ABACA, CANNA,
PLANTAIN
base .... CAUDEX, CAULIS
beetle .... SCARAB, ROSEBUG,
(COCK)CHAFER
biblical .... TARE, HYSSOP
bitter .... RUE
blue-flowered .... BLUET,
LUPINE
body .... THALLUS
branch .... TWIG, SPRAY, SPRIG
breathing pore .... STOMA
broom .... SPART
bud .... (S)CION
bug .... CHINCH
bulb .... SEGO, GARLIC,
SQUILL, JONQUIL, ATAMASCO,
NARCISSUS
bursting .... PUFFBALL
cabbage-like .... KALE
cactus .... CEREUS, MESCAL,
SAGUARO
capsule .... POD
carbohydrate ..... PENTOSAN(E)
carrot family ...... DILL, ANISE,
CONIUM, CUM(M)IN, ERINGO,
ERYNGO, CHERVIL, COWBANE,
HEMLOCK, CORIANDER
celery family .... CARROT
century .... ALOE, AGAVE,
MAGUEY
chili .... CAPSICUM

classification .... LINNEAN
climbing .... YAM, VINE,
LIANA, LIANE, RATTAN,
RUNNER, SCAMMONY
clinging part of .... TENDRIL
cloverlike ..... MEDIC, MELILOT
composite family .... ASTER,
DAISY, COSMOS, DAHLIA,
YARROW, MILFOIL, COREOPSIS,
DANDELION, SUNFLOWER
covering .... PEAT, TUNIC,
ARMATURE
creeping ...... PYXIE, IPOMOEA,
GROUNDLING, PERIWINKLE
crow family .... COLUMBINE,
HELLEBORE
crowfoot family .... HEPATICA,
MOUSETAIL
cruciferous .... CRESS,
MUSTARD
cutting .... SLIP
cycad family .... COONTIE
cyperaceous .... SEDGE
daisylike .... OXEYE
decay .... ROT, NECROSIS
delicate .... FERN, MOSS
disease ..... BLET, BUNT, CURL,
ESCA, GALL, RUST, SCAB,
SMUT, WILT, BRAND, ERGOT,
SCALD, BLIGHT, CANKER,
MILDEW, MOSAIC, YELLOW,
ERINOSE, ICTERUS,
(BLACK)ROT, CLUBROOT,
NECROSIS, PSOROSIS
dry climate .... CACTUS,
XEROPHYTE
dwarf .... ALYSSUM
dye .... ANIL
eating animal .... HERBIVORE
eating aquatic mammal
.... DUGONG, MANATEE
emetic .... IPECAC
environment .... HABITAT
experimental garden
.... NURSERY
exudation .... GUM, LAC,
COPAL, RESIN
feature .... STOLON
fiber .... FLAX, HEMP, JUSI,
PITA, SUNN, ABACA, AGAVE,
ISTLE, RAMIE, SISAL, MAGUEY
figwort .... COLLINSIA
firmly .... EMBED
floating .... LOTUS, WATER
LILY
flowering .... ROSE, CALLA,
ORCHID, RHODORA, ACANTHUS
flowerless .... FERN, LICHEN,
LYCOPOD
fluid .... SAP, MILK, LATEX
fodder .... VETCH, LENTIL,

forage .... GUAR

form, habitat .... ECAD

fossil .... CALAMITE,
 HORSETAIL

foundation .... TAPROOT

fragrant .... ANISE, BASIL,
 THYME, HYSSOP, ANGELICA,
 CAMOMILE, MARJORAM,
 TARRAGON, (SPEAR)MINT

fungus .... ERGOT

garden .... ORACH(E)

gentian .... CENTAURY

genus .... ARUM, AGAVE,
 ERINGO

geranium .... ALFILARIA

ginger family .... CURCUMA,
 TURMERIC

goosefoot .... BEET, SPINACH

gourd .... CANTALOUPE,
 (MUSK)MELON

gout medicine .... GUACO

grass .... AVENA

grasslike .... RUSH

growing from inside
 ENDOGEN

growing in solutions, science
 of .... HYDROPHONICS

growing within another
 .... ENDOPHYTE, ENTOPHYTE

growth on a .... GALL

gumbo .... OKRA

hair .... VILLUS

hairlike growth .... BRISTLE,
 PRICKLE, TRICHOME

hairy-leafed .... ANCHUSA

heath .... ERICA, AZALEA,
 LAUREL

hemp .... CANNABIS

herbaceous .... LOBELIA,
 PLANTAIN

honeysuckle family ..... ELDER

insect/louse ...... APHID, APHIS,
 SCALE

insect-catching .... FLYTRAP

insect-eating .... CARNIVORE

iris family .... IXIA, ORRIS,
 CROCUS

juice .... SAP, MILK

kind of .... ANNUAL

kingdom part .... PHYLUM

leaf, poisonous .... JABORANDI

leguminous .... PEA, GUAR,
 DERRIS, LENTIL

lice genus .... APHIS

life .... FLORA, VEGETATION

lilaceous .... LEEK, SEGO,
 ONION, TULIP

lily family .... ALOE, LEEK,
 LOTUS, ONION, YUCCA,
 ALLIUM, CAMAS(S), GARLIC,

NERINE, SQUILL, ASPHODEL,
 HELLEBORE, SABADILLA

madder .... CHAY, BLUET,
 COFFEE, IPECAC, CINCHONA,
 GARDENIA, HOUSTONIA

male .... MAS

mallow family .... HIBISCUS,
 HOLLYHOCK, CHECKERBLOOM

marsh .... CATTAIL

material spread around
 .... MULCH

matter, decaying .... PEAT

meadow .... INNOCENCE

medicinal .... RUE, ALOE,
 HERB, SENNA, TANSY, URENA,
 ARNICA, IPECAC, SIMPLE,
 SPURGE, BONESET, GENTIAN,
 LOBELIA, PENNY ROYAL

menthaceous .... OREGANO

milkweed family .... STAPELIA

milkwort family .... SENEGA

milky liquid .... LATEX

mint family .... SAGE, BASIL,
 BUGLE, CLARY, THYME,
 BETONY, CATNIP, COLEUS,
 HENBIT, HYSSOP, SALVIA,
 DITTANY, MONARDA,
 OREGANO, BERGAMOT,
 LAVENDER, MARJORAM,
 ROSEMARY, GERMANDER,
 PATCHOULI, FRAXINELLA

moor .... HEATHER

mosslike .... LICHEN,
 LIVERWORT, TILLANDSIA

mulberry .... CONTRAYERVA

mushroom-like .... PUFFBALL

mustard .... COLE, KALE, RAPE,
 WOAD, CRESS, STOCK, RADISH,
 ALYSSUM, CABBAGE,
 MADWORT, CHARLOCK,
 CRUCIFER

narcotic .... HEMP, POPPY,
 HASHISH, MARIJUANA

nettle family .... HEMP,
 PELLITORY

nightshade family .... POTATO,
 PETUNIA, SOLANUM, TOBACCO

non-flowering .... FERN

not native .... EXOTIC

noxious .... WEED, TARE

odorous .... BUGBANE

oil .... RAPE, BENNE, RAMTIL

one-celled .... PROTIST

onion family .... CHIVE

onion-like .... CEPA

ornamental .... CLARY,
 BEGONIA

palmlike .... CYCAD

parasite .... APHID, BLIGHT,
 LICHEN

parasitic ..... DODDER, ORCHID,

MISTLETOE

parsley family .... CICELY,
 SANICLE

pea family .... DHAL, GRAM,
 SENNA, VETCH, INDIGO,
 LEGUME, LUPINE, ALFALFA,
 LENTIGO, LICORICE,
 LOCOWEED, COCKSHEAD

pepper .... KAVA, BETEL,
 CAYENNE, CAPSICUM

perennial .... IRIS, OXLIP,
 SEDUM, THYME, CROCUS,
 DAHLIA, DOGBANE,
 COLUMBINE

pest .... CHINCH

phlox family .... JACOB'S
 LADDER

pink .... CAMPO, CAMPION,
 DIANTHUS, CARNATION

pith .... PULP

pithy .... SOLA

poisonous ..... LOCO, ACONITE,
 HEMLOCK, HENBANE,
 WOLFSBANE

poppy family ..... BLOODROOT,
 CELANDINE, CHICALOTE

pore .... STOMA, LENTICEL

potato family .... DATURA

potherb .... ORACHE

prickly .... BRIER, CACTUS,
 NETTLE, TEASEL, BRAMBLE,
 THISTLE

primrose family .... OXLIP,
 COWSLIP, FUCHSIA,
 CYCLAMEN, MARIGOLD

ragweed .... BURDOCK,
 COCKLEBUR

ramie .... RHEA

receptacle .... TORUS

red-sapped .... BLOODROOT

reedlike, sweet-smelling
 .... CALAMUS

rheumatism medicine
 .... GUACO

rock .... MOSS, LICHEN,
 STONECROP, LITHOPHYTE

Rocky Mountain .... PINON

root .... EDDO, RADIX

edible ..... MANIOC, CASSAVA

fragrant .... ORRIS

ointment .... NARD

purgative .... JALAP

rose family .... AVENS,
 BENNET, BURNET, DROPWORT,
 SHADBUSH, CINQUEFOIL, FIVE-
 FINGER, POTENTILLA

rudimentary .... EMBRYO

rue family .... LIME, LEMON,
 ORANGE

runner .... STOLON

rushlike .... SEDGE

sacred .... RAGTREE
salad .... ENDIVE, CHICORY,
(WATER)CRESS
salty soil .... HALOPHYTE
saxifrage .... MITERWORT
scale .... PALEA, SQUAMA
sea .... ENALID
sea animal resembling
.... SPONGE
sea-bottom .... BENTHOS
secretion .... GUM, RESIN
sedge .... PAPYRUS
seed .... HERB
seed case .... POD
seed yielding oil .... BENNE,
SESAME
seedless .... FERN
sensitive .... MIMOSA
sesame .... TIL, TEEL
shoot .... LAYER, (S)CION,
SPRIG
shoots .... ASPARAGUS
single-seeded .... PSORALEA
slang ..... TRAP, DECOY, TRICK,
SWINDLE
smelly .... RUE, TANSY,
YARROW, BUGBANE, BURDOCK,
FIGWORT, HENBANE, MILFOIL,
MULLE(I)N, RAFFLESIA,
STINKWEED
soap .... AMOLE
spiny .... CACTUS
sprout .... SPIRE
stalk .... STEM, SPIRE,
HA(U)LM, CAULIS
stand .... JARDINIERE
starch .... CORN, TARO,
MANIOC, POTATO, CASSAVA
stem .... AXIS, BINE, CORM,
HA(U)LM, CAUDEX, CAULIS
stem joint .... NODE
stem spongy center .... PITH,
MEDULLA
stinging .... NETTLE
stunted .... SCRAG
stunter .... HERBICIDE
suckers .... APHID
sun-turning .... HELIOTROPE
swamp ..... COWSLIP, DIONAEA,
MARIGOLD
swelling on .... BLEB
syrup-yielding .... SORGHUM
tendril .... CIRRUS
thistlelike .... ARTICHOKE
thorny .... ROSE, BRIAR, BRIER,
BRAMBLE, WAIT-A-BIT
threadlike part .... TENDRIL
tissue .... XYLEM
tissue cavity .... LOCULUS
trained to grow flat
.... ESPALIER

trifoliate .... SHAMROCK
tropical ..... UDO, PALM, TARO,
CYCAD, BANANA, CLEOME,
PAPAYA, RAMTIL, CASSAVA,
LANTANA, QUASSIA,
MANGROVE, PLANTAIN
trumpet .... BIGNONIA
tumor .... GALL
twining .... IPOMOEA
underwater .... BENTHOS,
HORNWORT
used in religious ceremonies
.... HYSSOP
vegetable .... CELERY,
TOMATO, ARTICHOKE,
CAULIFLOWER
verbena family .... VERVAIN
violet family .... PANSY
water ...... ALGA(E), FANWORT,
PAPYRUS, SEAWEED,
HYDROPHYTE
with aromatic seeds
.... ANISE, CUMIN
bulblike root .... TUBEROSE
edible root .... SKIRRET
edible stalk .... CARDOON
fragrant root .... ORRIS
fragrant seed .... ANISE
fruit .... BEARER
heart-shaped flowers
.... DICENTRA
no seeds .... FERN
perennial stem ..... ACROGEN
pungent pods ...... CAPSICUM
sun-turning flowers
.... TURNSOLE, HELIOTROPE
trumpet-shaped flower
.... SEGO, BIGNONIA
underground buds
.... GEOPHYTE
woody .... BUSH
woody tissue .... XYLEM
yielding fruit .... BEARER
yielding hashish .... CANNABIS
young .... SAPLING
yuccalike .... SOTOL
Plantae's counterpart
.... ANIWALIA
plantain .... WEED, RIBWORT,
FLEAWORT
fruit .... BANANA
spike .... CHAT
plantation ...... BOWERY, COLONY,
ESTATE, HACIENDA
boss of yore .... MASSA
cacti .... NOPALRIE
coffee .... FINCA
fictional .... TARA
kind of .... COFFEE, COTTON,
RUBBER, SUGAR CANE
Scarlett O'Hara's .... TARA

planter .... SOWER, SEEDER,
PIONEER, COLONIST
planting tool .... DIBBLE, SEEDER
plantlike animal .... CORAL,
SPONGE, ZOOPHYTE
plants, book on .... HERBAL
collector of .... HERBALIST
of .... VEGETAL
scourge of .... BLIGHT,
LOCUSTS
stand for .... JARDINIERE
study of .... PHYTOLOGY
where sold .... NURSERY
plantsman .... FLORIST
plaque .... BADGE, BROOCH,
TABLET
relative of a .... MEDAL
plash .... POOL, PUDDLE
plasma .... WHEY, QUARTZ,
PROTOPLASM
plaster .... DAUB, COMPO, COVER,
GROUT, SMEAR, PARGET,
STUCCO, OVERLAY
bandage .... SPICA
cement .... PUTTY
cover with .... CEIL
first coat .... RENDER
for broken limb .... CAST
mustard .... SINAPISM
of ____ .... PARIS
of Paris .... YESO, GESSO,
GYPSUM, STUCCO, HYDRATE
smoothing tool .... TROWEL
wall .... STUCCO
plastered: sl. .... DRUNK
plasterwork .... PARGET,
SCAGLIOLA
plastic .... VINYL, FICTILE,
PLIABLE, STYRENE, FLEXIBLE,
NEOPRENE
art .... CERAMICS, MODELING,
SCULPTURE
clay .... PUG
material .... LIGNIN, LUCITE,
MORTAR, FORMICA
synthetic .... BUNA, NYLON,
LUCITE, FORMICA, BAKELITE
wrap .... SARAN
plastid .... CELL
plastron .... DICKEY,
BREASTPLATE, SHIRT FRONT
plat .... MAP, PLAN, BRAID,
CHART, PLAIT
Plata river city ...... MONTEVIDEO
plate ...... COAT, DISC, DISH, DISK,
PATIN(A), SCUTE, SHARD,
LAMINA, LAMELLA, OVERLAY,
PLATTER
armor .... TASSE
baseball .... (HOME)BASE
battery .... GRID

bony/horny .... SCUTE, SCUTUM
dental .... BRIDGEWORK, FALSE TEETH
Eucharist .... PATEN
hot .... STOVE
hurler's .... DISCUS
metal .... LAME
metal cooking .... GRIDDLE
metallic .... PATEN
ship-shaped .... NEF
with brass .... BRAZE
with zinc .... GALVANIZE
plateau ...... MESA, PUNA, KAROO, DEGREE, ALTIPLANO, TABLELAND
top cover .... ICECAP
plated .... COATED, ARMORED
platelet .... SCUTUM
platelike organ .... LAMELLA
platen .... ROLLER
plater .... NAG, HORSE
platform .... BEMA, ARENA, DOLLY, STAGE, STOOP, SOLLAR, BALCONY, ESTRADE, GALLERY
ancient .... SOLEA
article .... PLANK
car .... FLATCAR
election .... HUSTINGS
engineroom .... CATWALK
floating .... RAFT
food-drying .... FLAKE
for execution .... SCAFFOLD
fort's gun .... BARBETTE
kind of .... SKID, ALTAR, HUSTINGS, POLITICAL
on wheels .... TRUCK
painter's .... SCAFFOLD
politician's .... STUMP, HUSTINGS
portable .... PALLET
principle .... PLANK
raised .... DAIS, STAND, PODIUM, PULPIT, TRIBUNE
revolving .... TURNTABLE
ship's .... DECK, MAINTOP, CROW'S NEST
speaker's .... ROSTRUM, TRIBUNE
streetcar .... VESTIBULE
platina .... PLATINUM
platinum .... ORE, PLATINA
-blonde actress .... HARLOW
symbol .... PT
platitude .... MAXIM, CLICHE, TRUISM, BROMIDE
platitudinous .... DULL, STALE, TRITE
platoon leader .... LIEUTENANT
unit .... SQUAD

Platoon director .... STONE
Plato's dialogue .... ION
school .... ACADEME
work .... CRITO, PHAEDO, APOLOGY, REPUBLIC, DIALOGUES, SYMPOSIUM
platter .... DISC, DISH, TRAY, PLATE, RECORD, SALVER, (HOME)BASE, TRENCHER
platyhelminth .... FLUKE, FLATWORM, PLANARIAN, TREMATODE
platypus .... DUCKBILL
plaudit .... PRAISE, ACCLAIM, OVATION, APPLAUSE
plausible ...... CREDIBLE, SPECIOUS
play ...... ACT, FUN, TOY, BET(ON), GAME, IDLE, LARK, DALLY, FRISK, SPORT, FROLIC, GAMBLE, GAMBOL, TRIFLE, COMPETE, PERFORM, RECREATE, (MELO)DRAMA
a part .... PERSONATE
a role .... EMOTE
actors in a .... CAST, PERSONAE
amateurs' .... DRAMATICS
around .... GAD
at love .... DALLY, FLIRT
award-winning .... STATE OF THE UNION, DEATH OF A SALESMAN, THE SKIN OF OUR TEETH, THE TIME OF YOUR LIFE
backer of .... ANGEL
between acts .... INTERLUDE
bridge .... FINESSE
by ear .... AD LIB, IMPROVISE
dilemma in a .... NODE, NODUS
direction .... ENTER, ACTION
down .... MINIMIZE
famous morality
.... EVERYMAN
fast and loose .... DALLY, TRIFLE
first performance
.... PREMIERE
for one actor ..... MONOLOGUE
for stakes .... GAMBLE
grandstand .... STUNT
heroine .... PREMIERE
host .... TREAT
introduction .... PROLOGUE
joke on .... RAG
on words .... PUN, QUIBBLE
orchestral reeds .... BLOW SAXOPHONES
part in a .... BIT, ROLE
part of a .... ACT, ACT I, ACT II, ACT IV, ACT III, SCENE

possum .... DEAD, FEIGN, PRETEND
silent .... PANTOMINE
successful .... HIT
the beau .... GALLIVANT
the game ..... FIT IN, CONFORM
the lead .... STAR
the violin .... FIDDLE
tricks on .... JAPE
truant .... MICHE
unsuccessful .... BOMB, TURKEY
up .... ADVERTISE
up to .... BUTTER, SOFT-SOAP
with fire .... DARE, RISK, GAMBLE
wrong card .... RENIG
playa .... BASIN, BEACH, SHORE
playboy .... GADABOUT, SENSUALIST, MAN-ABOUT-TOWN
Playboy bunny .... HOSTESS
Club founder .... HEFNER
player .... ACTOR, MUMMER, ACTRESS, GAMBLER, THESPIAN, COMPETITOR, CONTESTANT
at dealer's right .... PONE
baseball .... BATTER, BASEMAN, CATCHER, PITCHER, SHORTSTOP, INFIELDER, OUTFIELDER
basketball .... GUARD, CENTER, FORWARD
contest .... VIER, DUELIST, ENTRANT
football .... END, CENTER, TACKLE, FULLBACK, HALFBACK, QUARTERBACK
fraudulently substituted in a competition .... RINGER
incompetent .... DUB, PALOOKA
links .... GOLFER
match .... RIVAL
music .... SINGER, DRUMMER, FLUTIST, PIANIST, MINSTREL, INSTRUMENTALIST
performing arts ...... ARTIST(E)
piano .... NICKELODEON
sports .... JOCK, BOXER, ATHLETE, PUGILIST, PRIZEFIGHTER
unwilling to sign contract
.... HOLDOUT
who cuts the cards .... PONE
with lowest score .... BOOBY
players' position .... LINEUP
playful .... MERRY, FRISKY, JOCOSE, PRANKISH, SKITTISH, SPORTIVE, KITTENISH

playground .... OVAL, PARK, ARENA, FIELD, SANDLOT
  baseball .... DIAMOND
  basketball/tennis .... COURT
  billiard .... PARLOR, POOL HALL
  boxing .... RING, CANVAS
  football .... GRIDIRON
  golf .... LINKS, COURSE
  item .... SLIDE, SWING
  skating .... RINK
playing card(s) extra .... JOKER
  shuffle .... RIFFLE
  spot .... PIP
  suit .... CLUBS, HEARTS, SPADES, DIAMONDS
playing field .... OVAL, PARK, ARENA, DIAMOND, GRIDIRON
playlet .... SKIT, SKETCH
playroom .... NURSERY
plays collectively .... DRAMA
  performed by amateurs .... DRAMATICS
plaything .... TOY, PAWN, BAUBLE, TRIFLE, TRINKET
playwright .... DRAMATIST
  ploy of .... ASIDE
  Williams .... EMLYN
plaza .... MART, MARKET, SQUARE
plea .... APPEAL, EXCUSE, PRAYER, REQUEST, ENTREATY, PETITION, ALLEGATION
  bargain .... NEGOTIATE
  for dismissal .... DEMURRER
pleach .... PLAIT, (INTER)LACE, INTERTWINE
plead ...... BEG, SUE, PRAY, URGE, ARGUE, STATE, ALLEGE, APPEAL, ENTREAT, IMPLORE
  in law .... SHOW
  in protest .... REMONSTRATE
pleader .... ADVOCATE, PARACLETE
pleading, act of .... SUIT
pleasant .... GAY, NICE, MERRY, GENIAL, AFFABLE, AMIABLE, FRIENDLY, AGREEABLE, ENJOYABLE
  and cheerful .... ALL SMILES
  existence .... LIFE OF EASE
  place .... SUNNY SIDE OF THE STREET
  weather .... SUNNY
Pleasant Island .... NAURU
pleasantries .... AMENITIES, CIVILITIES
pleasantry .... WIT, JOKE, BANTER
please ...... SUIT, ELATE, DELIGHT, GLADDEN, GRATIFY, INDULGE, PRITHEE, SATISFY
pleased .... GLAD, HAPPY,

THRILLED, CONTENTED
pleasing .... NICE, ROSEATE, PLEASANT, AGREEABLE
pleasure .... JOY, WILL, WISH, BLISS, GRACE, CHOICE, LIKING, RELISH, COMFORT, DELIGHT, ECSTASY, ENJOYMENT
  boat .... BARGE, YACHT, CRUISER
  carriage .... SURREY
  craft harbor .... MARINA
  ground .... RESORT, PLEASANCE
  pursuit of .... HEDONISM
  seeker .... PLAYBOY, HEDONIST, PLAYGIRL, SYBARITE
  slang .... KICKS
  trip .... JUNKET, OUTING
  voyage .... CRUISE
pleat .... FOLD, PLAIT, SHIRR, CREASE, GATHER, RUFFLE, PLICATE
pleated .... PLICATE
pleating .... GOFFER, GAUFFER
plebe .... FROSH, FRESHMAN
plebeian .... COARSE, COMMON, VULGAR, ILL-BRED
plebiscite .... REFERENDUM
plebs .... MASSES
plectron .... PLECTRUM
plectrum .... PICK, QUILL, PLECTRON
pledge .... VOW, BOND, GAGE, HEST, OATH, PAWN, WORD, SWEAR, TOAST, TOKEN, ENGAGE, PAROLE, PIGNUS, PLIGHT, DEPOSIT, EARNEST, HOSTAGE, PROMISE, SPONSION
  slang .... HOCK
pledged .... BOUND, SWORN
pledget .... WAD, SWAB, DOSSIL, DRESSING
pledgor .... PAWNER
Pleiades, eldest of the ...... MAIA
  one of the ...... MAIA, MEROPE, ALCYONE, CELAENO, ELECTRA, STEROPE, TAYGETA
  parent of .... ATLAS, PLEIONE
Pleione's daughter .... MAIA, PLEIAD, STEROPE, TAYGETA
  husband .... ATLAS
plenary .... FULL, ABSOLUTE, COMPLETE
plenipotentiary .... FULL, ENVOY, PLENARY, AMBASSADOR
plenitude .... FULLNESS
plenteous .... COPIOUS, ABUNDANT
plentiful .... FULL, RIFE, AMPLE, COPIOUS, REPLETE,

ABUNDANT, BOUNTIFUL
plenty .... ENOW, AMPLE, ENOUGH, WEALTH, OPULENCE
plenum .... FULL(NESS)
  opposite of .... VACUUM
pleon .... TELSON
pleonasm .... NIMIETY, TAUTOLOGY, VERBOSITY, REDUNDANCY
pleonastic .... REDUNDANT
plessor .... HAMMER, PLEXOR
plethora .... EXCESS
plexor .... PLESSOR
plexus .... RETE, RETIA, NETWORK
pliable .... PLIANT, PLASTIC, SUPPLE, FLEXIBLE, MALLEABLE
plice .... FOLD
pliers .... CLAMP, PINC(H)ERS
plight .... ENGAGE, PLEDGE, BETROTH, DILEMMA, TROUBLE, CONDITION, SITUATION
plinth .... BASE, ORLO, BLOCK, SOCLE
PLO leader ...... (YASSER)ARAFAT
plod ...... SLOG, STEP, TOIL, WALK, DRUDGE, TRUDGE, PERSIST
plop .... DROP, PLUMP
plot .... LOT, MAP, DRAW, PLAN, PLAT, CABAL, CHART, FIELD, PATCH, SCHEME, DIAGRAM, OUTLINE, CONSPITE, INTRIGUE, MACHINATE, CONSPIRACY
  of story/play .... NODE, SCENARIO
plottage .... AREA
plotter .... CABAL, SCHEMER, INTRIGANT(E), INTRIGUER, MACHINATOR
plotters group .... CABAL
plough .... PLOW
ploughshare .... CO(U)LTER
plover .... PEWIT, STILT, LAPWING, DOTT(E)REL, KILLDEER, SURFBIRD, SANDPIPER
  bird like .... TURNIX
  kin of ...... BUSTARD, COURSER
plow .... DIG, ROVE, TILL, TURN, BREAK, LIST(ER), FURROW, PLOUGH
  blade .... SHARE, CO(U)LTER
  land .... ARABLE
  part .... SOLE, SHARE, SLADE, CLEVIS, SHE(A)TH
  pullers .... OXEN
  through .... WADE
plowed land .... ERD, ARADO, FURROW
plowman .... RUSTIC, TILLER
  shoe of .... CLODHOPPER

plowshare part ...... MOLDBOARD
ploy .... RUSE, MANEUVER,
 STRATEGY, STRATAGEM
business .... MERGER
pluck ...... TUG, GRIT, GUTS, PICK,
 NERVE, SPUNK, STRUM,
 AVULSE, TWANG, VALOR,
 SPIRIT, TWEEZE, COURAGE,
 DEPLUME, PULL(OUT),
 STAMINA, SWINDLE,
 FORTITUDE
slang .... FLEECE
plucky .... GAME, BRAVE, SPUNKY
plug .... NAG, TAP, WAD, BUNG,
 CORK, PLOD, QUID, SLOG,
 DOWEL, SHOOT, SPILE,
 DOSSIL, PLATER, SPIGOT, STOP
 UP, PLUNGER, STOPPER,
 PUBLICIZE, ADVERTISEMENT
absorbent .... TAMPON
colloquial .... LINE, PITCH
for wound .... DOSSIL, TAMPON
gun .... TAMPION, TOMPION
in radio/TV .... COMMERCIAL
of dirt .... COMEDO
slang .... BLURB, PROMO,
 COMMEND
tobacco .... PERIQUE
ugly .... GOON, HOOD, THUG,
 ROWDY, TOUGH, TERROR,
 RUFFIAN, GANGSTER
wind instrument .... FIPPLE
with a spigot .... SPILE
plugger, kind of .... BARKER,
 PRESS AGENT
plum .... GAGE, KAKI, SLOE,
 DRUPE, FRUIT, PRIZE, RAISIN,
 TROPHY, FREESTONE
brandy .... SLIVOVITZ
cake .... BABA, PUDDING
color .... PURPLE, VIOLET,
 LAVENDER
common .... GRAVY TRAIN
disease .... BLACKKNOT,
 BLACKRUST
family .... ROSE
fleshy part of .... MESOCARP
fruit like .... LOQUAT,
 PERSIMMON
Java .... LOMBOY
pit of .... PUTAMEN, ENDOCARP
powdery coating .... BLOOM
small .... DAMSON,
 DAMASCENE
stone .... NUTLET
variety .... GREENGAGE
wild .... SLOE, BULLACE
plumage .... DOWN, PLUME,
 FEATHERS
plumb ...... ERECT, PROBE, SOUND,
 FATHOM, VERTICAL

bob .... PLUMMET
colloquial .... WHOLLY,
 UTTERLY, ENTIRELY,
 DOWNRIGHT
plumbago .... LEAD, GRAPHITE
plumbeous .... LEADEN
plumber .... (GAS)FITTER,
 PIPEFITTER
concern of .... AIRTRAP
helper of .... PLUNGER
tool of .... SNAKE, WRENCH
plumbing device .... ELL, PIPING,
 TUBING
plumbum .... LEAD
plume ...... DOWN, CREST, EGRET,
 QUILL, AIGRET, FEATHER,
 MARABOU, PLUMAGE
helmet .... PANACHE
heron's .... AIGRET(TE)
plummet .... DROP, FALL, PLUMB,
 PLUNGE
plumose .... FEATHERED
plump .... FAT, PLOP, BUXOM,
 FUBSY, PLUNK, PUDGY,
 ROUND, STOUT, CHUBBY,
 BLUNT(LY), ROTUND
and short .... ROLY-POLY
plumule .... BUD, FEATHER,
 PLUMELET
plunder .... ROB, LOOT, PREY,
 PROG, SWAG, BOOTY, FORAY,
 HARRY, RIFLE, STEAL, STRIP,
 FORAGE, MARAUD, RAPINE,
 RAVAGE, (DE)SPOIL, PILLAGE,
 (RAN)SACK
archaic .... REAVE
search for .... RAVEN, RAVIN
plunderer .... LOOTER, RAPPAREE,
 FREEBOOTER
plunge .... DIP, DIVE, DROP, FALL,
 SWIM, FLING, LUNGE
headlong .... PITCH
into a liquid .... DUNK, DOUSE,
 SOUSE, IMMERSE
plunger .... DIVER, DASHER,
 PISTON, GAMBLER
plunk .... BLOW, PLUCK, PLUMP,
 STRUM
slang .... DOLLAR
sound .... THUD, TWANG
plural marriage ...... POLYGAMY,
 POLYANDRY
plurality .... MAJORITY
plus .... AND, ADDED, EXTRA
fours .... KNICKERS
value .... ASSET
plush .... POSH, SWANKY,
 LUXURIOUS
cloth like .... BOLIVIA
fabric .... SILK, WOOL
Plutarch's forte ...... BIOGRAPHY

Pluto ...... DIS, DOG, GOD, HADES,
 ORCUS, PLANET
domain of .... HELL, HADES,
 SHEOL, INFERNO, LOWER
 WORLD
wife of .... PERSEPHONE,
 PROSERPINE
plutocrat .... NABOB, CROESUS
plutonic .... IGNEOUS
pluvial .... RAINY, SOPPY
ply .... FOLD, URGE, WORK, EXERT,
 LAYER, TWIST, HANDLE,
 THICKNESS, LAMINATION
plywood layer .... VENEER
Plymouth Colony governor
 .... CARVER, WINSLOW,
 BRADFORD
Rock figure .... PILGRIM
 FATHER
Rock locale
 .... MASSACHUSETTS
pneuma .... SOUL, SPIRIT, HOLY
 SPIRIT
pneumatic .... AERY, AIRY,
 AERIAL
pneumatics .... AERODYNAMICS
pneumogastric nerve ...... VAGUS
Po, city on the .... TURIN, TORINO
river .... PADUS, ERIDANUS
tributary .... ADDA, TESSIN,
 TICINO, TREBBIA
valley tribesman .... LOMBARD
poach .... MIX, BOIL, COOK, FILCH,
 SHIRR, STEAL, PILFER,
 TRAMPLE, TRESPASS
eggs .... CODDLE
poacher .... THIEF, FILCHER,
 LURCHER
dog of .... LURCHER
poachy .... SOGGY, SODDEN
Pocahontas' adapted Christian
 name .... REBECCA
father .... POWHATAN
half sister .... MATACHANNA
husband .... (JOHN)ROLFE
sister .... CLEOPATRA
son .... THOMAS(ROLFE)
pochard .... DUCK, SMEE
kin of ..... REDHEAD, WIDGEON
pochette .... KIT
pock .... PIT, SCAR, PIMPLE,
 PUSTULE
pocket .... BAG, BIN, FOB, HIDE,
 POKE, SACK, TAKE, POUCH,
 CAVITY, PLACKET
billiards .... POOL
bread .... PITA
contents .... KEYS, COINS
fuzz .... LINT
money .... CASH
shape of .... U-CUT

size .... SMALL
pocketbook ...... PURSE, WALLET,
       BILLFOLD
pockmark .... PIT, SCAR
poco .... LITTLE
pod .... GAM, ARIL, BOLL, HULL,
 HUSK, BENDY, FLOCK, POUCH,
  SHELL, SHUCK, CHIL(L)I,
 ACHENE, COCOON, GROOVE,
 LEGUME, SCHOOL, CAPSULE,
  CYPSELA, SEEDCASE
edible .... OCRA, OKRA
fodder .... CAROB
gastric stimulant .... CAPSICUM
like fruit bearers .... CAROB,
       CATALPA
mustard plant .... SILIQUE
tree .... LOCUST
podagra .... GOUT
podesta .... JUDGE, MAYOR,
      GOVERNOR
podium .... DAIS, PLATFORM
Poe, ——— Allan .... EDGAR
bird .... RAVEN
character .... PYM
foster father of .... ALLAN
girl in poem/heroine
  ... LENORE, ANNABEL(LEE)
gold bug .... SCARAB
work of .... RAVEN,
      TAMERLANE
poem ...... LAI, ODE, RUNE, VERSE,
 BALLAD(E), RONDEL, SESTINA,
  VIRELAY, PALINODE
by Frost .... FIRE AND ICE
Homer .... ILIAD, ODYSSEY
Kilmer .... TREES
Poe .... THE RAVEN
concluding stanza ..... ENVOY,
      (L)ENVOI
dirgelike .... REQUIEM
division .... FIT, CANTO,
    FYTTE, STANZA
epic .... EPOS, EPODE, ILIAD,
  EPOPEE, ODYSSEY
for singing .... LAY
four-line .... QUATRAIN
14-line .... SONNET
handed down orally ...... EPOS
heroic .... EPIC, EPOS
Icelandic .... EDDA
introduction to a
  .... PROLOGUE
love .... MADRIGAL
lyric ..... ODE, EPODE, RONDEL,
 CANZONE, RONDEAU,
    MADRIGAL
mourning .... MONODY
mystical .... RUNE
narrative .... LAY, EPIC,
  IDYL(L), ILIAD, ODYSSEY

nonsense .... LIMERICK
of lament .... ELEGY
of praise .... MAGNIFICAT
of rural life .... GEORGIC
one-line .... MONOSTICH
oral .... EPOS
part of .... CANTO, PASSUS,
  STANZA, STROPHE
pastoral ..... IDYL(L), BUCOLIC,
  ECLOGUE, GEORGIC
play's .... EPILOGUE,
      PROLOGUE
popular .... ILIAD, TREES,
  ODYSSEY, THE RAVEN
postscript .... (L)ENVOI,
      (L)ENVOY
sacred .... PSALM
said at play's end
  .... EPILOGUE
satirical/witty .... IAMBIC,
      EPIGRAM
set to music .... ORATORIO
short .... VIRELAY,
 TELESTIC(H), VILLANELLE
with six six-line stanzas
  .... SESTINA
poems collection .... GARLAND,
    ANTHOLOGY
poet .... BARD, ODIST, LYRIST,
 RHYMER, ELEGIST, METRIST,
 MINSTREL, TROUBADOUR,
    MINNESINGER
Civil Elegies .... LEE
inferior .... RIMER, RHYMER,
 RHYMESTER, POETASTER,
 SONNETEER, VERSIFIER
inspiration of .... MUSE
of a .... HOMERIC
old English .... SCOP
singer .... BARD, MINSTREL
unknown .... ANON
Poet and Peasant composer
  .... (VON)SUPPE
poetaster .... POETLING, VERSIFIER
activity of .... RIMING
poetess .... LOWELL, MILLAY,
 PARKER, SAPPHO, SEXTON,
    TEASDALE
poetic dusk .... EVE
foot .... DACTYL, IAMB(US),
 SPONDEE, TROCHEE, CHORIAMB
inspiration .... PEGASUS
measure .... METER
pronoun .... THEE, THOU,
      THINE
pugilist .... ALI
retraction .... PALINODE
trio .... NOD
verb .... DOST, HAST, HATH
poetry .... POESY, BALLADRY
ancient reciter of .... BARD

epic .... EPOPEE
incomplete line of
  .... HEMISTICH
line of .... STICH
muse of .... ERATO, THALIA,
     CALLIOPE
of .... LYRIC, MELIC, HEROIC
short excerpt .... MORCEAU
poets, collectively .... PARNASSUS
pogonia .... ORCHID
pogonip .... FOG
Pogo's friend .... OWL
pogrom .... CARNAGE, KILLING,
  MASSACRE, SLAUGHTER
pogy .... FISH, MENHADEN
poi source .... TARO
poignancy .... PATHOS
poignant ...... KEEN, TART, SHARP,
 BITING, MOVING, PAINFUL,
 PIQUANT, PIERCING, TOUCHING
poignard .... DAGGER
poilu .... SOLDIER
poind .... SEIZE, IMPOUND,
     DISTRAINT
point .... AIM, DOT, END, JOT, NIB,
 PIN, TIP, CAPE, CUSP, PEAK,
 SPOT, ISSUE, PRICK, PRONG,
 PUNTO, SPECK, OBJECT,
     PERIOD
antler's .... SNAG
beside the .... UNRELATED,
    IRRELEVANT
barbed .... FLUE
blank .... BLUNT, PLAIN,
 DIRECT, STRAIGHT
central .... CRUX, FOCUS
compass .... AIRT(H), RHUMB
culmination .... SOLSTICE
deep under the ocean floor
  .... MOHO
earthquake's starting
  .... FOCUS
ending in a .... MUCRONATE
essential .... CRUX
farthest ...... APOGEE, SOLSTICE
having ..... ACUATE, HEBETATE
highest .... ACME, APEX, PEAK,
 CLIMAX, SUMMIT, ZENITH
in/to the .... APT, PERTINENT
in game .... SCORE
in law .... RES
joint .... JUNCTURE
land .... CAPE, NESS, SPIT,
    PROMONTORY
lowest .... ZERO, NADIR
magnet .... POLE
make a .... SCORE
meeting .... FOCUS
of a curve .... ACNODE
concentration .... NODE
debate .... ISSUE

difference .... LIMEN
land .... MORRO
law: sl. .... BUTTON
time ..... INSTANT, JUNCTURE
view .... ANGLE, SLANT,
BELIEF, OPINION
on the skull .... INION
orbital .... APSIS, APOGEE
out .... SIGNIFY, INDICATE
pen .... NEB, NIB, TIP
spear .... GAD, PIKE
starting .... POST
turning .... HINGE, PIVOT
won .... GOAL, SCORE
won by a single stroke
.... ACE
pointed ...... KEEN, PIKED, SHARP,
TERSE, ACUATE, BARBED,
PEAKED, CONICAL, TAPERED,
INCISIVE, TAPERING
arch ...... OGEE, OGIVE, GOTHIC
dull .... ACUATE, HEBETATE
end .... CUSP
missile .... BOLT, DART,
LANCE, SPEAR, HARPOON
stick .... GOAD
weapon ...... STYLET, STILETTO
pointer .... DIAL, HAND, SIGN,
VANE, WAND, AIMER, ARROW,
INDEX, (GUN)DOG, SETTER,
INDICATOR, RETRIEVER,
HUNTING DOG
colloquial ..... TIP, CLUE, HINT,
GUIDE, DIRECT
dial's .... STYLE
printer's .... FIST
sundial .... GNOMON
teacher's .... FESCUE
pointing out .... INDICANT
pointless .... DULL, BLUNT, INANE,
SILLY, USELESS, FECKLESS,
SENSELESS, MEANINGLESS
poise ...... CALM, HOVER, APLOMB,
BALANCE, BEARING, DIGNITY,
LIBRATE, SUSPEND, CARRIAGE,
PRESENCE, COMPOSURE,
STABILITY
poised .... (COCK)SURE
poison .... BANE, DRUG, GALL,
KILL, TAINT, TOXIN, VENOM,
DATURA, ARSENIC, CORRUPT,
TOXICANT, TOXICITY
antidote .... TREACLE,
THERIACA, MITHRIDATE
archaic .... VIRUS
arrow .... INEE, UPAS, CURARE,
(C)URARI, OURARI
castor bean .... RICIN
caused by .... TOXIC
deadly ...... ARSENIC, CYANIDE,
STRYCHNIN(E)

food .... BOTULIN
gas .... MUSTARD, LEWISITE
hemlock .... BENNET,
CONIN(E), CONIUM
ivy .... SUMAC
ivy aftermath .... ITCH, RASH
label for .... SKULL AND
CROSSBONES
remedy for .... TREACLE
snake .... VENOM, VIRUS
weed .... LOCO, CONIUM,
HEMLOCK
poisoned .... SEPTIC, PECCANT
poisoner, alleged .... BORGIA
poisoning .... KILLING, BOTULISM,
TOXICATION
blood .... TOXEMIA
poisonous .... DEADLY, NOCUOUS,
NOXIOUS, MEPHITIC,
TOXIC(ANT), VENOMOUS,
VIPERINE, VIRULENT
air .... MIASMA, MALARIA
alkaloid .... CONINE,
TROPIN(E), NICOTINE,
STRYCHNINE
bark .... UPAS, SASSY
compound .... TOXIN(E),
PHENOL, CYANIDE
element ..... ARSENO, ARSENIC,
MERCURY
fungus/mushroom
.... AMANITA
liquor .... ROTGUT
lizard .... GILA
oil .... TUNG
plant .... UPAS, ERGOT,
CONIUM, DATURA, ACONITE,
HEMLOCK, HENBANE,
FOXGLOVE, LARKSPUR,
MANDRAKE, MAY APPLE, NUX
VOMICA, BELLADONNA,
NIGHTSHADE
protein .... RICIN(E)
resin .... CANNABIN
seed .... CALABAR
shrub .... OLEANDER
snake ..... ASP, ADDER, COBRA,
KRAIT, VIPER, BUSHMASTER,
COPPERHEAD, FER-DE-LANCE
spider .... TARANTULA
substance ..... OPIUM, COCAINE
tint .... RED DYE
vine .... IVY, BITTERSWEET
weed .... LOCO, HEMLOCK
poitrel .... ARMOR
pokal .... GOBLET
poke .... BAG, DUB, HIT, JAB, JOG,
PRY, GOAD, PROD, PUSH,
PUNCH, BONNET, MEDDLE,
POCKET, THRUST, DAWDLE(R),
INTRUDE

around .... ROOT
with elbow .... NUDGE
poker .... ROD, STOKER, CARD
GAME
aces and eights in .... DEAD
MAN'S HAND
bet .... RAISE
chips .... STACK
counter .... DIB, CHIP
deal .... DRAW, STUD
faced comedian .... KEATON
game like .... BRAG
hand .... PAIR, TRIO, STRAIGHT,
FULL HOUSE, (ROYAL)FLUSH
holding .... ACE HIGH
kind of .... LIARS
move .... FOLD, RAISE
player .... FOURFLUSHER
stake .... POT, ANTE, KITTY
term .... ANTE, FOLD, HOLD,
RAISE, KICKER, PIGEON,
BOBTAIL
to call in .... SEE
variety of .... DRAW, STUD
pokerface .... DEADPAN
pokeweed .... POCAN, INKBERRY
pok(e)y .... DULL, SLOW, STIR,
DOWDY, STUFFY
slang .... JAIL, SLAMMER
Pola .... PULA
movie actress .... NEGRI
Poland .... POLSKA, POLONIA,
SARMATIA
capital of .... WARSAW
dictator .... GOMULKA
Mrs. in .... PANI
native of .... POLE, SLAV,
POLACK
polar .... ICY, COLD, FRIGID,
EXTREME, ENDMOST,
MAGNETIC, OPPOSITE
cover .... ICECAP
Polaris .... POLESTAR, NORTH
STAR
polarize .... SPLIT, OPPOSE
pole .... HUB, ROD, AXIS, BEAM,
MAST, POST, PUNT, SLAV,
CABER, PIVOT, SHAFT, STAFF,
STICK, STILT, THILL
battery .... ANODE, CATHODE
boat .... QUANT
carriage .... SHAFT
curtain/fishing .... ROD
fir .... UFER
forked .... NEAP
in Gaelic game .... CABER
memorial .... XAT
metal cap .... SHOE
positive .... ANODE
propelled watercraft ..... PUNT,
CASCO, GONDOLA

symbolic .... TOTEM
to pole .... AXIAL
tribal .... TOTEM
vertical .... MAST
wagon/vehicle .... SHAFT,
                       THILL
with decoy bird .... STOOL
with footrest .... STILT
wooden .... TREE
poleax(e) ...... HALBERD, HALBERT
polecat .... SKUNK, MUSANG,
    FITCHEW, FITCH(ET),
    FOUMART, STINKER,
    CARNIVORE
animal like .... FERRET,
    WEASEL, ZORIL(A)
polehorse .... POLER
poleman ...... LOGGER, SURVEYOR
polemic .... MOOT, ARGUER,
    ARGUMENT, DEBATABLE,
    CONTROVERSIAL
polemics .... DEBATE, DISPUTE
polenta .... PORRIDGE
poler .... HORSE, OARSMAN,
    GONDOLIER
poles apart .... OPPOSITE
walking .... STILTS
polestar .... GUIDE, MAGNET,
    POLARIS, NORTH STAR
poley .... HORNLESS
police .... PATROL, PROTECT,
    (SAFE)GUARD, CARABINIERI,
    CONSTABULARY
action .... RAID, ARREST
concern .... RIOT, CRIME,
    THEFT, MURDER, BURGLARY
inspector, fictional
    .... MAIGRET
line .... CORDON
military .... MP, REDCAP
perusal .... LINEUP
procedure .... DRAGNET
record book .... BLOTTER
record, letters in .... AKA
state .... TROOPER
test ...... PARAFFIN, POLYGRAPH
vehicle .... WAGON, BLACK
    MARIA
policeman .... BOBBY, MINION,
    REDCAP, MARSHAL, OFFICER,
    SHERIFF, TROOPER, ZAPTIAH,
    BLUECOAT, GENDARME,
    CONSTABLE, DETECTIVE
a native .... PEON
baton/club of .... MACE,
    BILLY, STICK, TRUNCHEON
mounted .... TROOPER
of lowest rank .... PATROLMAN
slang ..... PIG, COP(PER), BULL,
    DICK, PEELER, JOHN LAW, THE
    FUZZ, FLATFOOT

policewoman .... MATRON
policy .... PLAN, CONDUCT,
    WISDOM, PLATFORM,
    STRATEGY, PRINCIPLE(S),
    MANAGEMENT
insurance .... CONTRACT
polio .... INFANTILE PARALYSIS
research, noted name in
    .... SABIN
treatment method .... KENNY
vaccine man .... SALK
vaccine, type of .... IPV, OPV
polish .... RUB, WAX, BUFF, SAND,
    GLAZE, GLOSS, GRACE, POISE,
    SCOUR, SCRUB, SHEEN, SHINE,
    SLEEK, FINISH, LUSTER,
    LUSTRE, REFINE, VENEER,
    BURNISH, FURBISH, PERFECT,
    BRIGHTEN, LEVIGATE
by friction .... RUB, BURNISH
by hammering .... PLANISH
friend of .... SPIT
up .... EDIT, IMPROVE
Polish bay .... POMERANIAN
carriage .... BRITSKA
city/town .... ELK, KOLO,
    LODZ, NYSA, PISZ, ZARY,
    BREST, BRZEG, BYTOM,
    CHELM, OPOLE, RADOM,
    TORUN, TYCHY, CRACOW,
    DANZIG, ELBING, ELBLAG,
    GDANSK, GDYNIA, KALISZ,
    KIELCE, KOSLIN, KRAKOW,
    LUBLIN, OPPELN, POZNAN,
    RYBNIK, TARNOW, BRESLAU,
    CHORZOW, LEGNICA, STETTIN,
    WROCLAW, GLEIWITZ,
    KATOWICE, SZCZECIN,
    LANDSBERG, WALDENBURG
coin .... DUCAT, GROSZ,
    MARKA
commander .... BOR, HETMA,
    ANDERS
dance .... MAZURKA,
    POLONAISE
dictator .... GOMULKA,
    PILSUDSKI
diet member .... MAGNATE
dress .... POLONAISE
gulf .... DANZIG, GDANSK
island .... UZNAM, WOLIN
king .... CONTI, SOBIESKI
lake .... MAMRY, SNIARDWY
legislator .... MAGNATE
marshy region .... PRIPET
measure ..... CAL, MILA, LINJA,
    MORG(A), SAZEN, STOPA,
    KORZEC, KUARTA
monetary unit .... ZLOTY
mountain .... RYSY
mountain range .... BESKIDS,

    SUDETEN, HIGH TATRA
music .... MAZURKA,
    POLONAISE
parliament .... SEJM
peninsula .... HEL
physicist .... CURIE
pianist .... CHOPIN,
    PADEREWSKI, RUBINSTEIN
port .... DANZIG, GDANSK,
    GDYNIA
premier .... SIKORSKI,
    PILSUDSKI, PADEREWSKI
president .... PILSUDSKI,
    (LECH)WALESA
province .... LODZ, OPOLE,
    CRACOW, GDANSK, KIELCE,
    LUBLIN, POZNAN, WARSAW,
    BIELSKO, WROCLAW
region .... WARMIA, MASURIA
river .... BUG, SAN, BRDA,
    GWDA, LYNA, ODER, WKRA,
    NAREW, NOTEC, SERET,
    WARTA, NEISSE, PILICA,
    PRIPET, PROSNA, WIEPRZ,
    BRYNICA, DUNAJEC, VISTULA
sea .... BALTIC
seaport .... DANZIG, GDANSK
slang .... POLACK
soldier .... UHLAN
soup .... ZUPA
title of address .... PANI
weight ..... LUT, FUNT, UNCYA,
    KAMIAN, SKRUPUL
polished .... SLEEK, SUAVE,
    GLOSSY, POLITE, URBANE,
    ELEGANT, REFINED, CULTURED
polishing material .... WAX,
    BUFF, EMERY, RABAT,
    CROCUS, LUSTER, PUMICE,
    RUBIGO, ABRASIVE
polite .... CIVIL, URBANE,
    CORRECT, GENTEEL, REFINED,
    GRACIOUS, MANNERLY,
    POLISHED, WELL-BRED,
    COURTEOUS
act .... CIVILITY
society .... BON TON
politic ...... WARY, WISE, CRAFTY,
    SHREWD, PRUDENT, TACTFUL,
    DISCREET, EXPEDIENT,
    DIPLOMATIC
political .... CIVIC, CIVIL,
    OFFICIAL, BUREAUCRATIC,
    GOVERNMENTAL
casualty .... LAMEDUCK
division .... HUNDRED
faction/group .... BLOC, RUMP,
    JUNTA
favor .... PLUM
gathering .... CAUCUS,
    POWWOW

henchman ...... (WARD)HEELER
line-up .... SLATE
organization ..... PARTY, STATE
patronage .... PAP,
     PORK(BARREL)
policy .... PARTYLINE
radical .... JACOBIN
rostrum .... STUMP
science .... CIVICS, POLITICS,
     GOVERNMENT
spoils ..... MELON, PATRONAGE
system .... REGIME
weight .... CLOUT
politician ...... HEELER, DIPLOMAT,
    POLITICO, STRATEGIST
not reelected .... LAMEDUCK
politics of a .... LEFT, RIGHT,
    CENTER, LIBERAL,
     CONSERVATIVE
unattached .... MAVERICK,
     INDEPENDENT
politicians' stock in trade
     HANDSHAKES
polity .... STATE
polka-like dance .... REDOWA,
     MAZURKA
poll .... CUT, TOP, CLIP, CROP,
   HEAD, PATE, VOTE, COUNT,
   JUROR, SKULL, BALLOT,
   SURVEY, REGISTER,
   TABULATE, CANVASS(ING)
taker .... ROPER, GALLUP,
     HARRIS
pollack .... SEY, GADID, COALFISH
relative .... COD, HADDOCK
pollard .... OX, DEER, GOAT,
     SHEEP
polled .... MUL(L)EY, HORNLESS,
     CANVASSED
pollen .... DUST, FLOUR, POWDER,
     MICROSPORES
bearing organ .... STAMEN
brush .... SCOPA
grains, body of ..... POLLINIUM
sac .... ANTHER
pollex ...... BIG TOE, DIGIT, THUMB
pollinate .... FERTILIZE
pollinator .... BEE
polling place .... BOOTH
pollinosis .... HAYFEVER
polliwog .... TADPOLE
pollock .... CODFISH
pollster .... ROPER, GALLUP,
   HARRIS, POLL TAKER
pollute .... SOIL, DIRTY, SULLY,
   TAINT, BEFOUL, DEFILE,
     CONTAMINATE
polluted .... IMPURE, UNCLEAN,
     CORRUPTED
Pollux and Castor .... ANAX,
   TWINS, GEMINI, DIOSCURI

father of .... ZEUS
mother of .... LEDA
twin brother of .... CASTOR
Pollyanna, for example
     OPTIMIST
pollywog .... FROG, TADPOLE
polo play period .... CHUKKAR,
     CHUKKER
player .... POLOIST
requirement .... HORSE,
   MALLET, WOODEN BALL
stick .... MALLET
team .... FOUR
Polo, Venetian traveler .... MARCO
Polonius' daughter .... OPHELIA
servant .... REYNALDO
son .... LAERTES
Polska .... POLAND
poltergeist .... GHOST, SPIRIT
poltroon .... CAD, COWARD,
   CRAVEN, CAITIFF, DASTARD
polyanthus ...... OXLIP, PRIMROSE,
     NARCISSUS
polygamy .... HAREM
polyglot .... LINGUIST
polygon .... ISAGON, HEXAGON,
   NONAGON, TETRAGON
kind of .... ISOSCELES
     TRIANGLE
polygraph .... LIE DETECTOR
they swear by the .... POLICE
Polynesian ...... MAORI, KANAKA,
   SAMOAN, NUKUORO,
   HAWAIIAN, TAHITIAN
apparel .... GRASS SKIRT
apple .... HEVI
baking pit .... UMU
beverage .... KAVA, KAWA
chestnut .... RATA
cloth .... TAPA
dress .... MALO
god .... ATUA, PELE, TANE
herb .... PIA
hero .... MAUI
human body (cannibals'
   food) .... LONG PIG
island .... FIJI, SAMOA, TONGA,
   HAWAII, TAHITI, TOKELAU,
   PITCAIRN, MARQUESAS
kingdom .... TONGA
language .... TONGAN
loincloth .... PARAE
louse .... KUTU
mound .... AHU
mulberry bark .... TAPA
oven .... UMU
sky .... LANGI
spirit .... ATUA
supernatural force .... MANA
tree .... IPIL
wages .... UTU

yam .... UBE, UBI
polyp .... CORAL, HYDRA, SEA
   PEN, HYDROZOAN, SEA
     ANEMONE
colony .... CORAL
like a .... HYDROID
Polyphemus ...... MOTH, CYCLOPS
captive .... ULYSSES, ODYSSEUS
polypody .... FERN
Polyxena's father .... PRIAM
mother .... HECUBA
slain bridegroom .... ACHILLES
polyzoan ...... HYDRA, POLYP, SEA
   PEN, BRYOZOAN, SEA
     ANEMONE
Pom's pal .... PEKE
pomace .... (FRUIT)PULP
pomaceous fruit .... POME,
   APPLE, HAWTHORN
pomade .... POMATUM, COSMETIC,
   OINTMENT, BANDOLINE
pomatum .... POMADE
pome .... PEAR, APPLE, QUINCE
disease .... BROWN ROT
like fruit .... AZAROLE
pomegranate .... BERRY
flower .... BALUSTER
syrup .... GRENADINE
pomelo .... SUHA, SHADDOCK,
     GRAPEFRUIT
Pomeranian .... SPITZ DOG
pommel ...... BEAT, KNOB, STRIKE
pomp .... SHOW, GLITTER,
   FLOURISH, DISPLAY,
   GRANDEUR, SPLENDOR,
     PAGEANTRY
empty .... PAGEANT
Pomp and Circumstance
 composer .... ELGAR
pompadour .... HAIRDO, POISSON
base/pad .... RAT
Pompadour, paramour of
 Marquise de .... LOUIS XV
pompano .... SAUREL, ALEWIFE,
     CARANGOID
Pompey's scene of defeat
     THAPSUS
pompom .... CANNON, MACHINE
     GUN
fire .... FLAK, ACK-ACK
pompon ...... DAHLIA, ORNAMENT,
   (CHRYSANTHE)MUM
pomposity .... WIND
pompous .... VAIN, TUMID,
   TURGID, OROTUND, STATELY,
   MAGNIFIC, BOMBASTIC,
   GRANDIOSE, HIGHFALUTIN
slang .... GASSY
speech .... BOMBAST
walk .... STRUT, SWAGGER
Ponca .... SIOUX, SIOUAN

Ponce de Leon's discovery
.... FLORIDA
quest ..... FOUNTAIN OF YOUTH
Ponchielli opera .... (LA)
GIOCONDA
poncho .... CLOAK, RAINCOAT
pond .... LAKE, MERE, POOL,
TARN, LAGOON, LAGUNE,
SALINA, WATER HOLE
kind of .... FISH, MILL, STEW
plumed dweller .... EGRET
ponder .... MULL, MUSE, PORE,
THINK, WEIGH, PERPEND,
REFLECT, CONSIDER,
MEDITATE, RUMINATE
ponderer .... MUSER
ponderosa .... PINE
ponderous .... BULKY, HEAVY,
MASSIVE, WEIGHTY, DULL
AND LABORED, HUGE AND
AWKWARD
ponds, study of ...... LIMNOLOGY
pone .... LOAF, BREAD
poniard .... DAGGER
Pons, operatic singer .... LILY
pontiff .... POPE, BISHOP,
PONTIFEX, HIGH PRIEST
pontifical .... PAPAL, EPISCOPAL
pontil .... PUNTY, POINT
Pontius, Roman governor
.... PILATE
pontlevis .... DRAWBRIDGE
pontoon .... RAFT, BARGE, FLOAT,
BRIDGE, CAISSON
pony .... NAG, CRIB, HORSE,
PINTO, BRONCO, CAYUSE,
SHELTY, SHELTIE
tail .... HAIRDO
up .... PAY, ANTE
pooch .... DOG
poodle .... DOG, BARBET
pooh .... TIRE, EXHAUST,
EXCLAMATION
pooh .... DISMISS, DISREGARD
Pooh's creator .... MILNE
friend .... ROO
pool ...... POT, CARR, LINN, MERE,
POND, PLASH, PUDDLE,
MONOPOLY, BILLIARDS,
WATER HOLE
artificial .... TANK
ball .... RINGER
bettors' .... POT, KITTY
business firms' .... TRUST,
MONOPOLY
member .... STENO, TYPIST
mine .... SUMP
mountain .... TARN
pouch .... POCKET
rod .... CUE
shallow .... PLASH, PUDDLE

triangle .... RACK
waterfall .... LINN
poon .... DILO, TREE, DOMBA,
TELUGU
poop out .... TIRE, WEAKEN
pooped .... SPENT, EXHAUSTED
slang .... BEAT, BUSHED
poor .... LEAN, NEEDY, PALTRY,
SHABBY, INDIGENT, INFERIOR,
DESTITUTE, PENNILESS
person .... PAUPER
player .... DUB, HAM
slang .... LOUSY
sport .... SOREHEAD
poorhouse .... HOSPICE
poorly ILL
born .... LOWBRED
done literary work
.... INCONDITE
lit .... DIM
pop ...... BANG, SHOT, SLAP, SNAP,
SODA, BURST, CRACK, SHOOT,
SMACK, FATHER, EXPLODE
art .... FUNK
conductor .... WHITEMAN
singer .... ANKA, JOPLIN,
MADONNA
the question .... PROPOSE
Pope. See also Papal .... LEO,
JOHN, PAUL, PIUS, URBAN,
VICAR, ADRIAN, PONTIFF,
PRIMATE
cape of .... MOZ(Z)ETTA
cathedral of the ...... LATERAN
collar of the .... ORALE
crown of the .... TIARA
decree of the .... BULL,
DECRETAL, RESCRIPT
envoy .... (AB)LEGATE
first .... PETER
headdress of .... MITER, MITRE
meeting to elect
.... CONCLAVE
of Video .... SULLIVAN
palace of .... VATICAN
pertaining to the .... PAPAL
see of the .... ROME
tenure of the .... PAPACY
the .... PAPA
title of .... HOLINESS, HOLY
FATHER
vestment of .... FANO(N),
FANUM
Pope's (Alexander) love
.... GONNE
popes collectively .... PAPACY
Popeye, rival of .... BRUTO
sweetheart of ..... OLIVE (OYL)
the _____ .... SAILOR (MAN)
popinjay .... FOP, PARROT,
WOODPECKER

poplar .... ABELE, ALAMO, ASPEN,
LIARD, COTTONWOOD
balsam .... TACMAHACK
glucoside from .... SALICIN
spike .... AMENT, CATKIN
white .... ABELE
poplin .... FABRIC
popover .... MUFFIN
Poppaea, Nero's wife .... SABINA
popping the eyes .... OGLING
poppy .... OPIUM, PAPAVER,
CELANDINE, CHICALOTE,
BLOODROOT, SANGUINARIA
genus .... PAPAVER
juice extract .... OPIUM
prickly .... CHICALOTE
sap .... LATEX
seed .... MAW
poppycock ...... ROT, BOSH, BULL,
BUNK, CRAP, BALONEY,
HOGWASH, MALARKEY,
NONSENSE
populace .... DEMOS, PLEBS,
MASSES, PEOPLE
popular .... COMMON, FAMOUS,
ADMIRED, CURRENT, DEMOTIC,
VULGATE, ACCEPTED,
EXOTERIC, ENCHORIAL,
PREVALENT, WELL-LIKED,
PREVAILING
beauty .... BELLE
no more .... HAS-BEEN
opinion .... CONSENSUS
parlance .... SLANG
social figure .... LION, STAR,
CELEBRITY
success .... HIT
popularity .... FAME
populate .... PEOPLE, INHABIT
population .... PEOPLE,
DWELLERS, POPULACE,
CITIZENRY, INHABITANTS
count .... CENSUS
populous .... CROWDED
Poquelin, Fr. writer .... MOLIERE
porbeagle .... SHARK
porcelain .... MING, CHINA,
SPODE, SEVRES, CELADON,
FAIENCE, LIMOGES, FIGULINE,
EARTHENWARE
art of making .... CERAMICS
clay .... PATE, CHINA,
KAOLIN(E)
fine .... MING, CHINA
of/relating to .... CERAMIC
worker .... POTTER
porch ...... STOA, LAN(A)I, STOOP,
PARVIS, PIAZZA, BALCONY,
GALILEE, GALLERY, PORTICO,
VERANDA(H)
church .... GALILEE

seat .... GLIDER
porcine animal .... HOG, PIG
  disease .... BULLNOSE
porcupine .... HEDGEHOG
  anteater .... ECHIDNA
  Canadian .... URSON
  spine .... QUILL
pore .... CON, READ, STUDY,
  PERUSE, PONDER, CHANNEL,
  FORAMEN, OPENING, OSTIOLE,
  MEDITATE
  breathing .... STOMA
  plant .... STOMA, LENTICEL
pores, block the .... OPPILATE
  having .... PORIFEROUS
porgy .... TAI, SCUP, BREAM,
  PARGO, (PIN)FISH, SPAROID
poriferan .... SPONGE
pork .... HOG, PIG, LARDO(O)N
  chops on the hoof .... HOG
  cut .... HAM, CHOP, LOIN,
  BACON, ROAST, SHANK,
  SPARERIBS
  loin .... GRISKIN
  pie .... HAT
  sausage .... BOLOGNA
  shoulder .... CALA
porker ...... ELT, HOG, PIG, SWINE
porkfish .... SISI
porky .... FAT
pornographic .... LEWD, DIRTY,
  SMUTTY, OBSCENE,
  SALACIOUS
  slang .... BLUE
porous .... LEAKY, LEACHY
porpoise .... INIA, SEA HOG,
  DOLPHIN, HOGFISH, CETACEAN
porridge .... MUSH, SAMP, ATOLE,
  BROSE, GROUT, GRUEL,
  BURGOO, OATMEAL, POLENTA,
  POTTAGE, STIRABOUT
  bowl .... PORRINGER
  oat husks .... SOWENS
Porsena, king .... LARS
  Tarquin's .... AVENGER
port .... WINE, HAVEN, HARBOR,
  GATE(WAY), LARBOARD,
  ANCHORAGE
  ancient .... TYRE
  facilities .... WHARFAGE
portable .... MOVABLE
  bridge .... BAILEY, PONTOON
  chair .... SEDAN
  float .... PONTOON
  hut .... QUONSET
  kitchen cart .... CHUCK
  WAGON
  lamp .... LANTERN
  light .... TORCH
  linens .... HANKIES
  oven .... BAKER

sanctuary .... TABERNACLE
serving stand .... DUMB
  WAITER
shelter .... TENT
stove .... CHAUFFER
portal .... GATE, DOOR(WAY),
  ENTRY, POSTERN, ENTRANCE
portamento .... GLIDE
portance ...... BEARING, CONDUCT,
  CARRIAGE
portas .... BREVIARY
portcullis .... BAR, GRATE, HERSE,
  GRATING
portend .... MEAN, WARN, AUGUR,
  PRESAGE, SIGNIFY,
  (FORE)BODE, FORESHADOW
portent .... OMEN, SIGN, MARVEL,
  WONDER, PRODIGY, WARNING
portentous .... AMAZING,
  OMINOUS, SINISTER
porter ...... ALE, BEER, HAMA(U)L,
  REDCAP, CARRIER, DOORMAN,
  JANITOR, CONCIERGE,
  GATEKEEPER
  brew like .... STOUT
  musical .... ROSALIE
Porter, songwriter .... COLE
porterhouse .... BEEF, STEAK,
  T-BONE
portfolio .... OFFICE, HOLDINGS,
  BRIEFCASE, SECURITIES,
  ATTACHE CASE
porthole .... PEEPHOLE,
  EMBRASURE
Portia .... LAWYER
  maid of .... NERISSA
portico .... STOA, PORCH, ARCADE,
  LOGGIA, PARVIS, PIAZZA,
  PROSTYLE, COLONNADE,
  VERANDA(H)
portion ...... BIT, DUE, LOT, FATE,
  PART, SHARE, DIVIDE,
  DESTINY, ALLOTMENT
  book .... CHAPTER, SECTION
  marriage .... DOWER, DOWRY
  meal .... HELPING, SERVING
  of food .... MORSEL
  out .... DEAL, DOLE, METE
  slang .... DIVVY
  slight .... WISP
  tiny .... MINIM, MODICUM
portly .... FAT, BULKY, OBESE,
  STOUT, FLESHY, STATELY,
  IMPOSING
portmanteau .... TRUNK, VALISE,
  SUITCASE
Porto Rico. See **Puerto Rico**
portrait .... EFFIGY, SKETCH,
  PICTURE
  on U.S. currency:
  $1 .... WASHINGTON

  $2 .... JEFFERSON
  $5 .... LINCOLN
  $10 .... HAMILTON
  $20 .... JACKSON
  $50 .... GRANT
  $100 .... FRANKLIN
  self .... PAINTING
portray .... LIMN, ENACT, DEPICT,
  PICTURE, DESCRIBE,
  REHEARSE, DELINEATE,
  PERSONATE, REPRESENT
  verbally .... DESCRIBE
portrayer .... ACTOR, PLAYER,
  DEPICTER, PERFORMER
  of Cohan: 1942 .... CAGNEY
portside .... LEFT
Portugal .... LUSITANIA
  capital of .... LISBON
Portuguese bay .... SETUBAL
  cape ...... ROCA, ESPICHEL, SAO
  VINCENT
  city/town .... FARO, MIRA,
  OVAR, ALGES, BELEM, BRAGA,
  EVORA, LAGOS, PORTO, VISEU,
  ALMADA, AVEIRO, LISBON,
  OPORTO, QUELUZ, SINTRA,
  AMADORA, BENFICA, COIMBRA,
  COVILHA, ESTORIL, FUNCHAL,
  MONTIJO, OLIVAIS, SETUBAL,
  BARREIRO, CAPARICA,
  ODIVELAS, SANTAREM,
  CARNAXIDE, MOSCAVIDE
  coin ...... REI, DOBRA, ESCUDO,
  CENTAVO, CRUSADO, MOIDORE,
  JOHANNES
  colony/territory .... MACAO,
  MACAU, TIMOR, ANGOLA, SAO
  TOME, CAPE VERDE,
  MOZAMBIQUE
  colony, former .... GOA
  dictator .... SALAZAR
  district .... BEJA, FARO,
  BRAGA, EVORA, PORTO, VISEU,
  AVEIRO, GUARDA, LEIRIA,
  LISBON, OPORTO, SETUBAL,
  SANTAREM, VILA REAL
  folk song .... FADO
  former colony in SE Africa
  .... MOZAMBIQUE
  gentleman .... SENHOR
  governess .... AIA
  Guinea capital .... BISSAU
  India district .... DAMAO
  Indian ..... FERINGI, FERINGHEE
  island .... PORTO SANTO
  islands ...... AZORES, MADEIRA,
  DESERTAS, TERCIERA
  lady .... DONA
  legislature .... CORTES
  measure ..... PE, VARA, BRACA,
  LEGOA, MILHA, COVADO

molasses .... MELACO
monetary unit .... ESCUDO
mountain .... MONSANTO,
    MALHAO DA ESTRELA
mountain ranges .... SERRAS
mountains ..... OSSA, ESTRELA,
    MONCHIQUE
navigator .... DIAZ, (DA)
    GAMA, MAGELLAN
nobleman .... GRANDEE
novelist .... ECA DE QUEIROZ
poet .... CAMOE(N)S
port .... LISBON, SETUBAL
premier .... SALAZAR,
    CAETANO
river .... LIMA, MIRA, SADO,
    TEJO, DUORO, MINHO, TAGUS,
    TAMEGA, MONDEGO,
    XARRAMA, GUADIANA
sail .... LATEEN
saint .... SAO
seaport .... LISBON, OPORTO
ship .... CARVEL, CARAVEL(LE)
Timor capital .... DILI
title ..... DOM, DONNA, SENHOR
weight .... GRAO, ONCA,
    LIBRA, ARROBA, QUILATE,
    QUINTAL
West Africa .... ANGOLA
wine .... PORTO, MADEIRA
yard .... VARA
pose .... SIT, QUIZ, PUZZLE,
    INQUIRE, POSTURE, PROPOSE,
    ATTITUDE, PRETENSE,
    PROPOUND, MANNERISM
as .... (EN)ACT, PRETEND
Poseidon .... GOD, NEPTUNE
attendant of .... PROTEUS
brother of .... ZEUS
father of .... CRONUS
mother of .... RHEA
realm of .... SEA
scepter .... TRIDENT
sister of .... HERA, HESTIA,
    DEMETER
son of .... TRITON
wife of .... AMPHITRITE
Posen .... POZNAN
poser .... FACER, MODEL, ENIGMA,
    POSEUR, RIDDLE, SITTER,
    TEASER, PROBLEM, IMPOSTOR
posh .... CHIC, RITZY, ELEGANT,
    LUXURIOUS
Posidonius' contemporary
    .... GEMINUS
invention .... (RHODES)
    CALCULATOR
posit .... PUT, PLACE, ASSERT,
    ASSUME, SET (FORTH),
    SITUATE, POSTULATE
position .... LAY, LIE, JOB, SET,

RANK, ROLE, SITE, SPOT,
    SITUS, STAND, OFFICE,
    STANCE, STATUS, STATION,
    ATTITUDE, LOCATION,
    POST(URE), PLACE(MENT),
    SITUATION, (VIEW)POINT
a difficult .... FIX
anchor .... ATRIP
change .... MOVE
jockey for .... MANEUVER
of a part, abnormal
    .... ECTOPIA
of abused pinball machine
    .... ATILT
of authority .... IN THE
    SADDLE
of the arms, in ballet
    .... ENBAS
secure .... FOOTING, FOOTHOLD
positive .... FIRM, PLUS, SURE,
    UTTER, CERTAIN, DECIDED,
    EXPRESS, GENUINE, PRECISE,
    ABSOLUTE, DEFINITE,
    EMPHATIC, SPECIFIC, OUT-
    AND-OUT
answer .... AYE, YEA, YES
electrode/pole .... ANODE
sign .... PLUS
terminal of a battery
    .... CATHODE
positively .... QUITE, TRULY,
    REALLY, EXACTLY
charged electrode .... ANODE
positivism .... COMTISM,
    ASSURANCE, CERTAINTY,
    DOGMATISM
originator .... COMTE
posse .... BAND, DETAIL,
    SEARCHERS
possess .... OWN, HAVE, HOLD,
    ENJOY, OCCUPY, DOMINATE
possessed .... MAD, CRAZED,
    CHARMED, BEWITCHED
possession(s) ...... ASSET, ESTATE,
    WEALTH, PROPERTY,
    OWNERSHIP
in actual: law .... MANUAL,
    SEISIN
possessive .... GREEDY, SELFISH
possessor .... OWNER, HOLDER
posset .... DRINK, BEVERAGE
possible .... LATENT, FEASIBLE,
    PROBABLE, POTENTIAL
possibly .... MAYBE, LIKELY,
    PERHAPS
possum .... COON
play .... FEIGN, PRETEND
post .... JOB, DA(W)K, MAIL, POLE,
    STOB, STUD, ENTER, PLACE,
    STAKE, ASSIGN, INFORM,
    MARKER, PILLAR, BOLLARD,

PUBLISH, STATION, GARRISON,
    POSITION
box device .... US MAIL
boy .... COURIER
chaise .... COACH, CARRIAGE
doorway .... JAMB(E)
exchange .... PX, STORE,
    CANTEEN
memorial .... XAT
mortem .... AUTOPSY,
    INQUEST, NECROPSY
mortem conductor
    .... CORONER, AUTOPSIST
office bank .... GIRO
staircase .... NEWEL
window frame .... JAMB(E)
wooden framework
    .... PUNCHEON
postage stamp country .... SAN
    MARINO
sticker .... STAMP
postal stamp .... CACHET
system .... MAIL
poster .... PLACARD, STICKER,
    BILL(BOARD)
posterior ..... HIND, REAR, LATER,
    DORSAL, RETRAL, BUTTOCK
opposed to .... PRIOR,
    ANTERIOR
posterity .... FUTURE, SEQUEL
postern .... BACKDOOR,
    (BACK)GATE, ENTRANCE
postfree mail .... FRANK
posthaste .... SWIFTLY
posthumous .... AFTERDEATH
postiche ...... WIG, FALSE, TOUPEE,
    PRETENSE, ARTIFICIAL
postmark .... CACHET, IMPRINT
substitute .... INDICIA
postmeridian .... PM, AFTERNOON
"post office" delivery .... KISS
postpone .... WAIT, DEFER,
    DELAY, TABLE, SHELVE, PUT
    OFF, ADJOURN, SUSPEND, PUT
    ON ICE
postponement .... STAY, STOP,
    RAIN CHECK
postponing, in law
    .... MORATORY
postrider .... COURIER
postscript .... ADDITION,
    AFTERTHOUGHT
of poem ..... LENVOY, LIENVOI
postulant .... CANDIDATE,
    PETITIONER
postulate .... AXIOM, CLAIM,
    POSIT, ASSUME, THESIS,
    PREMISE, PRESUME, THEORIZE
posture .... MOOD, POSE, STANCE,
    BEARING, ATTITUDE,
    CARRIAGE, POSITION

posy .... SPRAY, FLOWER,
 BOUQUET, CORSAGE, NOSEGAY
pot ...... PAN, OLLA, POOL, CROCK,
 KITTY, SHOOT, ALUDEL,
 KETTLE, SKILLET
au-feu .... (BEEF) STEW
coffee .... URN
earthenware .... CROCK, PIPKIN
go to .... ROT, GO BAD,
 DECLINE, FALL OFF,
 DETERIORATE
handle .... BAIL
herb .... CLARY
holder .... COSY, MITT
kind of ...... FLOWER, LOBSTER
marigold .... CALENDULA
mender .... TINKER
ornamental .... JARDINIERE
slang .... MARIJUANA
small .... CRUSE, PIPKIN
stand .... TRIVET
tea .... SAMOVAR
user .... ADDICT, HIPPIE
user's feeling .... HIGH
water .... LOTA(H)
potable .... DRINKABLE
potage .... SOUP, BROTH
potash and saltpeter .... NITRES
source .... SUINT
potassium .... ALUM
bitartrate .... TARTAR
carbonate .... POTASH
chloride .... MURIATE, SYLVITE
nitrate .... NITER, SALTPETER
potation .... DRAFT, DRINK,
 LAGER, LIQUOR
potato .... OCA, SPUD, IDAHO,
 TATER, TUBER
bud .... EYE
bug .... BEETLE
disease .... CURL, BLIGHT
flour/meal .... FARINA
fried .... CHIP
scraper .... PARER
skin .... JACKET
slang .... MURPHY
starch .... FARINA
sweet ...... OCA, YAM, BATATA,
 CAMOTE
potatoes with fried onions
 .... LYONNAISE
potbellied .... BLOATED,
 PAUNCHY, PAUNCHED
potbelly .... PAUNCH, BAY
 WINDOW
potboiler .... LITERARY HACK
poteen/potheen .... WHISK(E)Y
potency .... VIS, POWER, VIGOR,
 STRENGTH
potent .... STRONG, VIRILE,
 (CAP)ABLE, EFFECTIVE

potable .... BOILERMAKER
potentate .... KING, RULER,
 PRINCE, MONARCH,
 (MAJA)RAJAH, SOVEREIGN
potential ...... LATENT, CAPACITY,
 POSSIBLE, PROMISING
difference .... TENSION
energy .... ERGAL
mutiny .... UNREST
potentilla ...... ROSE, CINQUEFOIL,
 FIVE-FINGER
pothead ...... ADDICT, MARIJUANA
 SMOKER
pother .... ADO, FUSS, STIR,
 WORRY, BUSTLE, UPROAR
potherb .... CLARY, CHIVES,
 PARSLEY
pothole ...... PIT, CAVE, MUDHOLE
potholer .... SPELUNKER
pothook .... SCRAWL
user .... STENO
pothouse .... INN, TAVERN,
 ALEHOUSE
potiche .... JAR, VASE
potion .... DOSE, DRAFT, DRINK,
 LIBATION, NEPENTHE
love .... PHILTER, PHILTRE
mesmeric .... OPIATE,
 MANDRAGORA
sleep-inducer .... NARCOTIC
potlatch .... GIFT, FEAST,
 FESTIVAL
potman .... WAITER
potoo .... NIGHTJAR, GOATSUCKER
potpie .... STEW, MEAT-PIE
potpourri .... OLIO, STEW,
 MEDLEY, MIXTURE,
 ANTHOLOGY, HODGEPODGE,
 SALMAGUNDI
scented .... SACHET,
 POMANDER
Potsdam conference member
 ...... ATTLEE, STALIN, TRUMAN
potsherd .... CROCK, SHARD
potshot .... SNIPE
potsy .... HOPSCOTCH
need .... PEBBLE
pottage .... SOUP, STEW, BROSE,
 PORRIDGE, HODGEPODGE
potted .... DRUNK, SMASHED
potter .... DOODLE, PIDDLE,
 CERAMIST
potter's clay .... PATE, ARGIL,
 SAGGER, SEGGAR
field .... CEMETERY,
 GRAVEYARD
field of Judas .... ACELDAMA
ore .... GALENA
tool .... PALLET
wheel .... LATHE
pottery .... BASALT, FAIENCE,

 CERAMICS, DELFT(WARE),
 FIGULINE, GOMBROON,
 MAJOLICA, (EARTHEN)WARE
art of making .... CERAMICS
before glazing .... BISCUIT
clay .... PATE, ARGIL, KAOLIN
enameled, glazed
 .... MAJOLICA
finest type of .... PORCELAIN
fragment .... CROCK, SHARD,
 SHERD
glaze on .... REFLET
glazed .... DELFT(WARE)
glazing material .... GALENA
making device .... SAGGER
of/relating to .... CERAMIC,
 FICTILE
speckled .... GRANITEWARE
unglazed, black .... BASALT
white .... GOMBROON
pottle .... BASKET, TANKARD
potto .... LEMUR, KINKAJOU
potty .... JOIN, BATTY, FLAKY,
 KOOKY, NUTTY, PETTY,
 TOILET, TRIVIAL
plan .... CRACKBRAINED
 SCHEME
pouch .... BAG, POD, SAC, BURSA,
 CECUM, PURSE, POCKET,
 SPORRAN, SPLEUCHAN
intestinal .... C(A)ECUM
like a .... SACCATE,
 MARSUPIAL
pouched animal ...... KANGAROO
pouchy .... BAGGY
pouf .... OTTOMAN, HEADDRESS
poulard ...... HEN, FRYER, PULLET
poule .... PROSTITUTE
poult .... PULLET, CHICKEN
poultice ...... PLASTER, DRESSING,
 CATAPLASM, APPLICATION
poultry .... DUCKS, FOWLS, GEESE,
 TURKEYS, CHICKENS
breeding place .... HENNERY
disease .... PIP, POX, ROUP,
 GAPES
man .... POULTER(ER)
pen .... COOP, HUTCH
shelter .... HENNERY,
 HENHOUSE
shelter, heated .... BROODER
pounce ..... CLAW, SWOOP, TALON
pound .... HIT, PEN, SOV, BEAT,
 BLOW, BRAY, QUID, TAMP,
 THUD, CRUSH, LIBRA, THROB,
 THUMP, CORRAL, KENNEL,
 MALLEATE, ENCLOSURE,
 PULVERIZE
dog .... MONGREL
down .... TAMP
dweller .... STRAY

-foolish .... WASTEFUL
fraction .... OUNCE
out .... FLATTEN
put in a .... IMPOUND,
IMPRISON
sterling, one .... QUID,
SOVEREIGN
Pound, educator .... ROSCOE
poet .... EZRA (LOOMIS)
pounder .... WAVE, CANNON,
TAMPER
of the pavement ...... JOBLESS,
JOB-SEEKER
pounding implement .... GAVEL,
HAMMER, MALLET, PESTLE
pounds, 100 .... CENTAL,
CENTNER
2,000 .... NET TON, SHORT TON
2,240 .... LONG TON
pour .... FLOW, GUSH, RAIN,
TEEM, SERVE, SPOUT, SWARM,
DECANT, EFFUSE, SQUIRT
forth .... EMIT, GUSH, WELL
metal into mold .... CAST,
FOUND
out swiftly .... SWOOSH
pourboire .... TIP, GRATUITY
pouring hole .... SPRUE
on water in baptism
.... AFFUSION
pourpoint .... JUPON, TUNIC,
DOUBLET
pout .... MOPE, MOUE, SULK,
(CAT)FISH, GRIMACE
pouter .... PIGEON
pouting spell .... MAD
poverty .... LACK, NEED, WANT,
DEARTH, PENURY, PAUCITY,
SCARCITY, INDIGENCE
stricken .... POOR, BROKE,
NEEDY, HARD-UP, BANKRUPT,
DESTITUTE, PENNILESS
pow .... HEAD, POLL
powder .... DUST, MEAL, TALC,
CRUSH, PICRA, POUNCE,
SPRINKLE, PULVERIZE
burn to/by heat .... CALCINE
clothes scenting .... SACHET
crush/pound into .... BRAY,
GRIND
dried fly .... CANTHARIDES
explosive .... TETRYL, CORDITE
flower .... POLLEN
grind into fine .... LEVIGATE,
TRITURATE
insect .... PYRETHRUM
kind of .... GUN, BATH, FACE
perfumed .... SACHET
polishing .... ROUGE
room ...... LOUNGE, LAVATORY
skin .... TALC(UM)

stain removing .... PUMICE
powdered tobacco .... SNUFF
powdery .... DUSTY, MEALY,
CRUMBLY, FRIABLE
power .... VIS, DINT, SWAY,
DYNAS, FORCE, MIGHT,
VIGOR, ENERGY, ABILITY,
CONTROL, POTENCY,
CAPACITY, STRENGTH,
AUTHORITY, PUISSANCE
colloquial ..... STEAM, MUSCLE
failure .... OUTAGE
kind of .... SOLAR, STEAM,
ATOMIC, MOTIVE, ELECTRIC
loom inventor
.... CARTWRIGHT
of attorney .... AUTHORIZATION
of divination: abbr. .... ESP
producer .... DYNAMO
source of .... SUN, FUEL
symbol of .... FASCES
theoretical .... OD(YL)
to affect others ..... INFLUENCE
to survive .... VITALITY
unit .... VOLT, WATT
will .... SELF-CONTROL
world .... USA, RUSSIA,
AMERICA, ENGLAND
powerful .... POTENT, STRONG,
DYNAMIC, (AL)MIGHTY,
ELECTRIC, PUISSANT
beam .... LASER
powerless .... WEAK, IMPOTENT
Powers of Hollywood ...... MALA
Powhatan's daughter
.... POCAHONTAS
powwow .... GATHERING,
CONFERENCE, MEDICINE MAN
place .... TEPEE
political .... CONVENTION
Zuluans' .... INDABA
pox .... ACNE, PUSTULE,
SMALLPOX, SYPHILIS
practicable .... UTILE, USABLE,
USEFUL, FEASIBLE, OPERABLE,
POSSIBLE, EXPEDIENT
practical .... SOUND, UTILE,
USEFUL, LOGICAL, RATIONAL,
SENSIBLE, WORKABLE,
PRAGMATIC, REALISTIC
joke .... HOAX, JAPE, PRANK,
TRICK
joker .... PRANKSTER
person .... REALIST
practically ...... ALMOST, NEARLY
practice .... DO, USE, DRILL,
HABIT, USAGE, CUSTOM,
MANNER, METHOD, PRAXIS,
PERFORM, WORKOUT,
EXERCISE, REHEARSE
common .... USAGE

composition .... ETUDE
dishonest .... RACKET
established .... USAGE,
CUSTOM, PRAXIS
firearms with blanks ...... DRY
RUN
game .... WORKOUT
one-upmanship .... PUT ON
AIRS
performance .... REHEARSE
religious .... CULT
systematic .... EXERCISE
practiced .... DEFT, SKILLED,
TRAINED, SEASONED
practicing economy .... AUSTERE,
THRIFTY
practitioner ...... DOER, WORKER,
OPERATOR, PERFORMER
Christian science ...... HEALER
medical .... DOCTOR,
SURGEON, PHYSICIAN
pragmatic .... ACTIVE, DOGMATIC,
OFFICIOUS, PRACTICAL
Prague .... PRAHA
castle .... HRADCANY
river .... VLTAVA
square .... WENCESLAS
prairie ...... MESA, LLANO, PLAIN,
MEADOW, PAMPA(S),
PLATEAU, SAVANNA,
GRASSLAND
dog .... MARMOT
grove .... MOTT(E)
hen .... GROUSE
province .... ALBERTA,
MANITOBA
soil .... GUMBO
squirrel .... GOPHER
vehicle .... SCHOONER
wolf .... COYOTE
Prairie State .... NEBRASKA
praise .... LAUD, TOUT, BLESS,
ELOGE, EXALT, EXTOL,
GRACE, KUDOS, EULOGY,
GLORIA, HOMAGE, ACCLAIM,
APPLAUD, COMMEND,
GLORIFY, TRIBUTE,
ENCOMIUM, EULOGIZE,
PANEGYRIC
excessive .... IDOLIZING
expression of .... PLAUDIT,
APPLAUSE
extravagantly .... HONOR,
GLORIFY
insincerely/too much
.... FLATTER
phrase of .... WELL DONE
sign of .... ACCOLADE
song of .... HYMN, CAROL,
PAEAN
undue .... PUFF

praiseworthy .... LAUDABLE, DESERVING, EXEMPLARY
praline .... CANDY, CONFECTION
pram .... BUGGY, STROLLER, PERAMBULATOR
pusher ...... AMAH, NURSEMAID
prance .... CAPER, DANCE, STRUT, CAVORT, SWAGGER
prandial meal .... DINNER, SUPPER
prank .... DIDO, HOAX, JAPE, JEST, JOKE, LARK, ANTIC, CAPER, TRICK, FROLIC, CANTRIP, CAPRICE, DRESS UP, GAMBADO, ESCAPADE, MISCHIEF
reckless .... ESCAPADE
with lighted match .... HOTFOOT
pranks .... (HIGH)JINKS
full of .... PRANKISH
prankster .... JOKER, BUFFOON
prase .... QUARTZ, CHALCEDONY
prat: sl. .... BUTTOCKS
prate .... GAB, YAP, BLAB, BABBLE, TATTLE, CHATTER, PRATTLE
prattle .... BLAB, PRATE, BABBLE, JABBER, MURMUR, CHATTER
Pravda founder .... LENIN
prawn .... SCAMP, MACRURAN, CRUSTACEAN
praxis .... CUSTOM, PRACTICE
pray .... ASK, BEG, ORA, PLEAD, APPEAL, BESEECH, ENTREAT, IMPLORE
prayer .... AVE, BENE, PLEA, SUIT, GRACE, LITANY, NOVENA, ORISON, REQUEST, ENTREATY, PETITION, ROGATION
bead .... ROSARY
bones .... KNEES
book .... ORDO, HOURS, MISSAL, PRIMER, PORTAS(S), BREVIARY
desk .... PRIEDIEU
ending .... AMEN
evening .... VESPER
for another .... BEADSMAN, INTERCESSION
hour .... MATIN, VESPER
hour, Moslem .... AZAN
in gibberish .... GLOSSOLIA
last of the day .... COMPLIN(E)
meal .... GRACE
morning .... MATIN
nine-day .... NOVENA
of supplication ...... SUFFRAGE
offer a .... WORSHIP
protect by .... SAIN
rug .... ASAN

shawl .... TALLITH
short .... GRACE
wheel user .... LAMA, BUDDHIST
prayerful .... DEVOUT
prayers, endowment for .... CHANTRY
praying figure .... ORANT
Indians .... NATICKS
pre .... BEFORE, PRIOR TO
feast period .... EVE
war .... ANTEBELLUM
wedding surprise ...... SHOWER
preach .... EXHORT, LECTURE, ADVOCATE, SERMONIZE, EVANGELIZE
preacher .... PASTOR, HOMILIST, MINISTER, CLERGYMAN, PREDICANT, PULPITEER, EVANGELIST
circuit .... ROUNDER
pronouncement ...... MAN AND WIFE
talk of .... HOMILY, SERMON
traveling .... EVANGEL(IST), MISSIONARY
preachers collectively .... PULPIT
preaching .... SERMON, PREDICANT
Preakness winner: 1942 .... ALSAB
winning horse .... AFFIRMED, CITATION, WHIRLAWAY, COUNT FLEET, SECRETARIAT
winning jockey .... ARCARO, CAUTHEN, LONGDEN, TURCOTTE
precarious .... RISKY, UNSAFE, CRITICAL, INSECURE, UNCERTAIN
state .... TOUCH-AND-GO
precaution .... CARE, WARNING
precede .... HEAD, FOREGO, FORERUN
in time .... ANTEDATE
the fall .... PRIDE
precedence .... LEAD, PRIORITY
precedent .... PRIOR, FORMER, EXAMPLE
preceder .... PRECURSOR, FORERUNNER
of bravo .... ABLE
craftsy .... ARTSY
daisy .... UPSA, UPSY
geste .... BEAU
poly .... ROLY
puzzle .... JIGSAW
valorem .... AD
preceding ...... BEFORE, PREVIOUS, FOREGOING
all others .... FIRST, PIONEER,

FOREMOST
precentor .... CANTOR
precept ...... CODE, RULE, CANON, MAXIM, ORDER, DICTUM, APHORISM, DOCTRINE
Brahmanism .... SUTRA
in law .... WRIT, WARRANT
preceptor .... TUTOR, TEACHER
precepts, collection of .... SUTRA
precinct(s) .... AREA, WARD, DISTRICT, ENVIRONS, NEIGHBORHOOD
precious .... DEAR, RARE, ARRANT, COSTLY, WORTHY, BELOVED, VALUABLE
colloquial .... VERY, UTTER
stone .... GEM, JADE, ONYX, OPAL, RUBY, SARD, BERYL, JEWEL, TOPAZ, GARNET, DIAMOND, EMERALD, CABOCHON, SAPPHIRE, BRILLIANT
stone cutter .... LAPIDARY
precipice ...... CRAG, DROP, SCAR, BLUFF, CLIFF
precipitate .... FALL, RASH, CAUSE, HASTY, HEADY, ABRUPT, FOMENT, HASTEN, SUDDEN, HURRIED, BRING ON, CONDENSE, HEADLONG, IMPETUOUS, IMPULSIVE
precipitation .... DEW, HAIL, MIST, RAIN, RUSH, SNOW, HASTE, SLEET
prognosticator .... WEATHER MAN
precipitator .... REAGENT, CATALYST, CATALYZER
precipitous .... RASH, HASTY, SHEER, STEEP
rock .... CRAG, SCAR, BLUFF, CLIFF
precis .... DIGEST, RESUME, SUMMARY, ABSTRACT, SYNOPSIS
precise .... PRIM, EXACT, FORMAL, PRISSY, CORRECT, ACCURATE, DEFINITE, EXPLICIT, SPECIFIC, PARTICULAR
pace .... GOOSE-STEP
precisely .... EXACTLY
precision .... ACCURACY
preclude ...... BAR, CHECK, ESTOP, HINDER, INHIBIT, PREVENT, SHUT OUT
precocious .... ADVANCED
child .... PRODIGY
precognitive one .... SEER
precollege exam .... SAT
precook .... PARBOIL
precursor .... OMEN, HERALD,

HARBINGER, FORERUNNER
predator .... USURER, VAMPIRE,
BLACKMAILER, BLOODSUCKER
predatory .... PREYING,
RAVAGING, RAVENOUS,
PREDACIOUS
bird .... OWL, EAGLE, HAWK,
VULTURE
fish .... SHARK
mammal .... WOLF,
WOLVERINE
worm .... LEECH
predecessor .... ANCESTOR,
PRECURSOR
predestinate .... FOREDOOM
predestination .... FATE, DESTINY,
ELECTION
predicament ...... FIX, JAM, MESS,
PASS, SPOT, CORNER, CRISIS,
PICKLE, PLIGHT, SCRAPE,
DILEMMA, RATTRAP,
QUANDARY
with no way out .... IMPASSE
predicant .... PREACHER
predicate .... BASE, ASSERT
predict .... AUGUR, PORTEND,
(FORE)BODE, FORECAST,
FORETELL, PROPHESY
prediction .... FORECAST,
PROPHECY
predictor .... PALMIST, SEER(ESS),
SORCERER, FORECASTER,
PROPHET(ESS), WEATHERMAN
predilection .... BIAS, TASTE,
LIKING, LEANING, FONDNESS,
PREJUDICE, PARTIALITY,
PREFERENCE
predisposed .... PRONE, READY,
BIASED, PARTIAL, WILLING,
INCLINED, PREPARED
predominant .... RULING,
REGNANT
preeminent .... NOTABLE,
RENOWNED
preempt .... COOPT, SEIZE, USURP,
OCCUPY, APPROPRIATE
preen ...... GROOM, PRIMP, PRINK,
DOLL UP, DRESS UP
prefab(ricated) .... NISSEN,
QUONSET(HUT), READY-BUILT
preface ...... OPEN, BEGIN, PROEM,
START, PRELUDE, FOREWORD,
PREAMBLE, PROLOGUE,
FRONTISPIECE, INTRODUCTION
prefatory note .... FOREWORD
prefect .... DEAN
prefer .... FAVOR, CHOOSE,
SELECT, PRESENT
preferably .... RATHER
preference .... PICK, CHOICE,
LIKING

prefix .... BEFORE
a place for .... ORY
about .... PERI
across .... TRANS
after .... META, POST
against .... ANTI, CONTRA
air .... ATMO
all .... OMNI
archaic .... PALES
aside from .... PARA
backward .... RETRO
bad .... MAL
before .... PRE, ANTE
between .... META, INTER
bigness .... MEGALO
black .... MELA
blood .... HEMO
both .... AMBI, AMPH
cast .... TELE
cold .... CYRO
decay .... SAPRO
distant .... TEL(E)
eight .... OCTA, OCT(O)
entire .... HOLO
equal .... ISO
external .... ECTO
false .... PSEUDO
far .... TEL(E)
farm .... AGRO
father .... PATRI
fire .... PYR(O)
fix .... TRANS
foreign .... XENO
front .... ANTERO
gaseous .... AER
glade/green .... EVER
gold .... AURI
half .... DEMI, HEMI, SEMI
hap .... MIS
inner .... ENTO
insect .... ENTOMO
intermediate .... MED
intestine .... COLI
kidney .... RENI
lateral .... UNI
many .... MULT(I)
mind .... PHREN
mountain .... ORO, OREO
nautics .... AERO
nine .... ENNEA
nomer .... MIS
nose .... NAS
not .... DIS, MIS, NON
numerical .... TRI, PENTA
numerical: var. .... DEK
outer .... EXO, ECT(O)
outside .... ECT
over .... SUPRA
partial .... DEMI
physician .... IATRO
plane .... AERO

pod .... TRI
rainbow .... IRID
recent .... CAENO
root .... RHIZO
scient .... OMNI
scope .... TELE, STETHO
single .... MONO
size .... DEMI
sphere .... ATMO, HEMI
syllable .... MONO
thought .... IDEO
thrice .... TER
through .... DIA
tooth .... DENTI
totally .... HOL
touch .... TAC
town .... TRE
under .... SUB
upon .... EPI
upward .... ANO
usage .... NOMO
where .... UBI
width .... LATI
wind .... ANEMO
with .... SYN
with cure and center .... EPI
within .... ENDO, INTRA, INTRO
wrong .... MIS
pregnable .... VULNERABLE
pregnancy ...... CYESIS, FETATION,
GESTATION
complication
.... MISCARRIAGE,
PREMATURITY
discomfort .... NAUSEA,
MORNING SICKNESS
false .... PSEUDOCYESIS
outside uterus .... ECTOPIC
pregnant .... GRAVID, FERTILE,
CHILDING, ENCEINTE,
ABOUNDING, EXPECTING
prehistoric .... ARCHAIC,
PRIMITIVE
chisel .... CELT
combining form .... PALE(O)
human .... CAVEMAN
upright stone .... MENHIR
prejudge .... ASSUME, PRESUME
prejudice .... BIAS, HARM, COLOR,
IMPERIL, OPINION, ENDANGER,
PARTIALITY
prejudiced .... BIASED, PARTIAL
prejudicial .... HARMFUL,
DAMAGING, INJURIOUS
prekindled .... PRELIT
prelate .... BISHOP, PRIMATE,
CARDINAL
prelect .... LECTURE
preliminary .... PREFATORY
meeting .... CAUCUS
race .... HEAT

statement .... PREFACE, FOREWORD, PREAMBLE
work .... PREPARATION
prelude .... PROEM, OPENING, PREFACE, PROLOGUE, OVERTURE
of fugue .... TOCCATA
premature ...... EARLY, FORWARD, UNTIMELY, INCOMPLETE
aging .... PROGERIA
as in action .... RASH
baby .... PREEMIE
development .... PRECOCITY
premeditate .... PLAN, PLOT, SCHEME
premeditated .... PREPENSE, DELIBERATE
killing .... MURDER
premier .... CHIEF, FIRST, FOREMOST
premiere .... OPENING
Preminger, movie director .... OTTO
premise .... BASIS, PREFACE, PROPOSITION
premises, series of .... SORITES
premium .... FEE, AGIO, GIFT, BONUS, PRIZE, BOUNTY, REWARD
premonition .... HUNCH, FOREBODING
Prentiss, actress .... PAULA
preoccupation .... FIXATION, OBSESSION
with sex .... EROT(IC)ISM
preoccupied .... LOST, RAPT, ABSTRACTED, ABSENT-MINDED
preoccupy .... ABSORB, OBSESS, ENGROSS
preparation .... FORESIGHT, READINESS
concrete .... FOUNDATION
prepare .... SET, ADAPT, GIRD(UP), EQUIP, PRIME, READY, TRAIN, FIT(OUT), DISPOSE, ARRANGE, ACCUSTOM
copy .... EDIT, REDACT
by special treatment .... CURE, PROCESS
for a play .... REHEARSE
action .... GIRD UP, LIMBER UP, UNLIMBER
an exam .... BONE UP
conflict .... ARM
roasting .... LARD
the try-pot .... FLENSE
war .... DEPLOY, MOBILIZE
meat .... DRESS
the ground .... CULTIVATE
to solder .... START A BLOWTORCH

prepared .... YARE, READY, COACHED, GROOMED
as skins .... TAWED
for war ..... ARMED, ON ALERT
medicine .... PRESCRIPTION
to take on fares .... BOARDABLE
prepense .... AFORETHOUGHT
preponderant .... DOMINANT
preposition .... AT, BY, IN, ON, TO, BUT, FOR, OUT, FROM, INTO, ONTO, UNTO, UPON, WITH, AFTER
prepossessing .... WINNING, PLEASING, ATTRACTIVE
prepossession .... BIAS
preposterous .... ABSURD, FOOLISH, SENSELESS, RIDICULOUS
prerequisite .... MUST
prerogative ...... RIGHT, PRIVILEGE
king's .... REGALIA
presage .... BODE, OMEN, SIGN, AUGUR(Y), PORTEND, PORTENT, WARNING, FORETELL, FORESHADOW
presbyter .... ELDER, PRIEST, PRESTER, MINISTER
prescience .... FORESIGHT
prescind .... ISOLATE, SEGREGATE
prescribe .... LIMIT, ORDER, ASSIGN, DIRECT, ORDAIN, OUTLAW, DICTATE, SET(DOWN)
prescribed .... THETIC
share .... STINT
prescript .... RULE, ORDER
prescription .... RECIPE, FORMULA
physician's .... INSTRUCTION
presence .... GHOST, SPIRIT, COMPANY, APPEARANCE, ATTENDANCE
of mind .... WIT
present .... BOON, GIFT, HERE, SHOW, NONCE, SERVE, AT HAND, BESTOW, TENDER, DISPLAY, DONATION, INTRODUCE
at .... NOW, TODAY
at birth .... CONGENITAL
charges against .... PREFER
good luck .... HANDSEL
time .... NONCE
to departing person .... FOY
with .... FURNISH
presentable .... PASSABLE
presentation .... GIFT, SHOW, DEBUT, DISPLAY, EXHIBIT, OFFERING, PERFORMANCE, INTRODUCTION
presentiment .... HUNCH,

FOREBODING, PREMONITION
presently ...... NOW, ANON, SOON, SHORTLY, NOWADAYS
preservative ...... BRINE, NITRATE, VINEGAR
preserve .... CAN, DRY, JAM, CORN, CURE, KEEP, SALT, SASS, SAVE, JELLY, SMOKE, PICKLE, RETAIN, MAINTAIN, CONFITURE, MARMALADE, PERPETUATE
by drying .... DESSICATE, DEHYDRATE
game .... SANCTUARY
with salt .... CORN
with wax .... CERE
preserved dead body .... MUMMY
preshrink cloth .... SANFORIZE
preside .... DIRECT, MANAGE, CONDUCT, MODERATE
at rural hops .... CALL BARN DANCES
at tea .... POUR
over .... CHAIR
president, college .... PREXY
yacht club .... COMMODORE
presidential disapproval .... VETO
monogram ..... DDE, FDR, GRF, HST, JEC, JFK, LBJ, RMN, RWR, GHWB
nickname ...... ABE, CAL, BILL, IKE, RON, ANDY, JACK, JERRY, TEDDY, RONNIE
pet's name:
Bush .... FRED, MILLIE, RANGER
Coolidge .... TIGER, ROB ROY, BOUNDER, REBECCA
DDE .... TELEK, CAACIE
FDR .... FALA
Harrison .... SUKEY
Hayes .... DUKE, HECTOR, NELLIE
Hoover .... KING TUT
Jackson .... POLL
Jefferson .... DICK
JFK .... WOLF, CHARLIE, CLIPPER, SHANNON
LBJ .... HER, HIM, YUKI, BLANCO
Nixon .... CHECKERS, KING TIMAHOE
Reagan .... REX, LUCKY
Washington .... TIPLER, SWEETLIPS, MADAME MOOSE
Wilson ..... OLD IKE, PUFFINS
reception .... LEVEE
presiding officer .... SPEAKER, CHAIRMAN, MODERATOR, PRINCIPAL
officer's vote .... CASTING

presidio .... FORT, GARRISON
press ...... BEG, HUG, CRAM, IRON,
    PUSH, URGE, CROWD, CRUSH,
    DRIVE, FORCE, WEDGE,
    WRING, COMPEL, SMOOTH,
    SQUASH, SQUEEZE, NEWS
    MEDIA, JOURNALISM
a request .... DEMAND
agency (see **news agency**)
agent .... PUBLICIST,
    JOURNALIST
agentry .... BALLYHOO,
    PUBLICITY, PROPAGANDA
dough .... KNEAD
down .... TAMP
equipment .... LINOTYPE
for payment .... DUN
one's suit .... WOO
person .... PRINTER, REPORTER,
    COMPOSITOR, PROOFREADER
presser .... IRONER, MANGLE
pressing .... URGENT, EXIGENT,
    CRITICAL
iron .... GOOSE
need .... IRON
piece .... SADIRON
pressure .... FORCE, DURESS,
    STRAIN, STRESS, DEMANDS,
    URGENCY, INFLUENCE
gauge .... MANOMETER
group .... BLOC, LOBBY
measuring device .... GAUGE
prefix .... BARO
system .... HIGH
unit .... BARAD, BARIE
prest .... LOAN
prester .... PRIEST, PRESBYTER
prestidigitator .... MAGICIAN
prestige ...... FAME, NOTE, KUDOS,
    RENOWN, REPUTE,
    REPUTATION
presto .... QUICKLY
person who says .... MAGICIAN
Preston's milieu .... YUKON
presume ...... DARE, IMPLY, INFER,
    ASSUME, SUPPOSE, VENTURE
presumption .... GUESS,
    AUDACITY, TEMERITY,
    INFERENCE
presumptive .... LIKELY,
    PROBABLE, SUPPOSED,
    ASSUMPTIVE
presumptuous ...... BOLD, BRASH,
    FORWARD, ARROGANT,
    INSOLENT
presuppose .... PREJUDGE
pretend .... ACT, FAKE, SHAM,
    CLAIM, FEIGN, LET ON,
    ALLEGE, PROFESS, SIMULATE,
    DISSEMBLE, FANTASIZE,
    MASQUERADE, (PUT ON AN)

    ACT, PLAY A PART
pretended .... FALSE
courage .... BLUFF, BRAVADO
pretender .... SHAM, SNOB,
    FAKER, FRAUD, USURPER,
    ASPIRANT, CLAIMANT,
    IMPOSTOR, IMPERSONATOR
to knowledge .... QUACK,
    SCIOLIST, CHARLATAN
pretending .... MAKE BELIEVE
pretense .... ACT, AIR, RUSE,
    SHAM, SHOW, CLAIM, FEINT,
    GUISE, EXCUSE, PRETEXT
of virtue .... HYPOCRISY
transparent .... CHARADE
pretension .... AIR, BLUFF, CLAIM,
    PRETEXT, ALLEGATION
pretentious ...... ARTY, POMPOUS,
    ASSUMING, BOASTFUL
art .... KITSCH
preterition .... OMISSION
pretermit .... OMIT, NEGLECT,
    OVERLOOK
pretext ...... PLEA, FRONT, COVER-
    UP, EXCUSE, PRETENSE
for war .... CASUS BELLI
pretty .... FAIR, NICE, BONNY,
    BONNIE, COMELY, LOVELY
and delicately formed
    .... DAINTY, MIGNON
girl .... CUTEY
woman .... PERI
pretzel .... BISCUIT
Preussen .... PRUSSIA
prevail .... WIN, RULE, EXIST,
    SUCCEED, TRIUMPH,
    DOMINATE
on .... INDUCE, PERSUADE
prevalent .... RIFE, COMMON,
    CURRENT, GENERAL,
    RAMPANT, REGNANT,
    PANDEMIC, PREVAILING,
    WIDESPREAD
prevaricate .... LIE, PALTER,
    QUIBBLE, EQUIVOCATE
prevarication .... LIE, FALSEHOOD
prevaricator .... LIAR
prevent .... BALK, STOP, AVERT,
    BLOCK, CHECK, DETER,
    HINDER, IMPEDE, THWART,
    OBVIATE, WARD OFF,
    PRECLUDE, FORESTALL,
    FRUSTRATE
legally .... ESTOP
prevention .... STOPPAGE,
    RESTRAINT
legal .... ESTOPPEL
preventive court order
    .... INJUNCTION
medicine .... ANTIBIOTIC
preview .... TRY OUT, TRAILER

sneak .... SHOWING
Previn of music .... ANDRE
previous .... PRIOR, FORMER,
    PRECEDING, ANTECEDENT
previously .... AFORE
mentioned .... AFORESAID
previse .... WARN, FORESEE,
    FORECAST
prexy .... PRESIDENT
prey .... ROB, GAME, VICTIM,
    QUARRY, PILLAGE, PLUNDER
bird of .... OWL, HAWK,
    EAGLE, VULTURE
high sea .... PRIZE
insect of .... (PRAYING)
    MANTIS
of cats .... MICE, BIRDS
on .... EAT, DUPE, KILL,
    VICTIMIZE
search for .... HUNT, RAVEN,
    RAVIN
Priam's daughter .... CREUSA,
    CASSANDRA
domain .... TROY
father .... LAOMEDON
son .... PARIS, HECTOR,
    TROILUS
son-in-law .... AENEAS
son who caused the Trojan
    War .... PARIS
wife .... HECUBA
price .... FEE, COST, RATE, QUOTE,
    VALUE, WORTH, AMOUNT,
    CHARGE
cutting event .... SALE
go up in .... BULL
kind of .... FIXED, ASKING
list .... CATALOG(UE)
of ride .... FARE
slang .... ANTE, DAMAGE
priceless .... PRECIOUS
pricey .... EXPENSIVE
prick .... DOT, GOAD, PINK, PROD,
    SPUR QUALM, STING, WOUND,
    PIERCE, TINGLE, PUNCTURE
pricket .... BUCK, DEER,
    CANDLESTICK
prickle .... BARB, BUR(R), SETA,
    BRIAR, SPINE, STING, THORN,
    TINGLE, ACULEUS, TRICHOME
prickly .... BURRY, SPINY,
    BARBED, BRIERY, THORNY,
    ECHINATE, SMARTING,
    STINGING, TINGLING
bush .... ROSE, BRIAR, BRIER
heat .... RASH, LICHEN,
    MILIARIA
pear .... TUNA, NOPAL,
    CACTUS, OPUNTIA
seed coat .... BUR(R)
shrub .... BRAMBLE,

DEWBERRY, RASPBERRY
weed .... NETTLE
pride ...... AIRS, VANITY, CONCEIT,
RESERVE, ARROGANCE,
VAINGLORY, SELF-ESTEEM
according to Alexander Pope
.... NEVER FAILING VICE OF
FOOLS
disdainful .... HAUTEUR
lion's .... MANE, LITTER
member .... LION
ruffled .... PIQUE
priest .... FRA, CURE, CURATE,
FLAMEN, SHAMAN, CASSOCK,
PRESTER, MINISTER,
CLERGYMAN, PRESBYTER
armband .... FANON
army .... PADRE, CHAPLAIN
assistant of .... ACOLYTE,
SACRISTAN
authorized to hear
confessions
.... CONFESSOR
Buddhist .... LAMA
gift to a .... MORTUARY
high .... ELI, AARON, PONTIFF
house of a .... PRESBYTERY
Indian ...... SHAMAN, MEDICINE
MAN
Jewish .... RABBI(N)
neckpiece of .... AMICE
newly ordained ..... NEOPHYTE
office of .... CURACY,
MINISTRY
salaried .... VICAR
shaven head of .... TONSURE
skullcap .... ZUCCHETTO
title of respect .... FATHER,
REVEREND
vestment .... ALB, COPE,
ORALE, SURPLICE
priestess of Aphrodite ...... HERO
of Apollo .... PYTHIA
priestly .... AARONIC, HIERATIC,
SACERDOTAL
priests group of 20 .... FETIAL
prig .... PRUDE, THIEF, PEDANT,
PICKPOCKET, STUFFED-SHIRT
prill and cinnabar .... ORES
prim ...... NICE, DEMURE, FORMAL,
MODEST, PRISSY, PROPER,
PRUDISH, PRIGGISH
prima _____ .... FACIE,
BALLERINA
donna .... ALDA, DIVA, PONS,
MELBA, CALLAS, STEBER,
TEBALDI
primal .... FIRST, ORIGINAL
primary ...... MAIN, FIRST, CHIEF,
ORIGINAL, ULTIMATE,
PRINCIPAL

primate ...... APE, LEMUR, ORANG,
BABOON, BONOBO, GIBBON,
MONKEY, GORILLA, SIAMANG,
(ARCH)BISHOP
prime .... MAY, A-ONE, PICK,
CREAM, CHOICE, FINEST,
PREPARE, FIRST(RATE)
in music .... UNISON
minister .... PREMIER
mover .... LEADER
of life .... HEYDAY
primer .... READER, HORNBOOK,
(TEXT)BOOK
primitive .... OLD, WILD, BASIC,
CRUDE, ROUGH, ANCIENT,
BARBARIC, ABORIGINAL
combining form .... PALE(O)
fish .... COELACANTH
tribesman's ornament
.... LABRET
primogenitor .... ANCESTOR
primordial .... ORIGINAL
primp ...... GROOM, PREEN, PRINK,
PRUNE
primrose .... OXLIP, SPINK,
COWSLIP, FAIRYCUP
genus .... PRIMULA
prince .... RAS, KING, RAIA,
RULER, MONARCH, PRINCIPE
consort's wife .... QUEEN,
EMPRESS
ecclesiastical .... CARDINAL
Ethiopian .... RAS
in India .... RANA,
(MAHA)RAJAH
look-alike of .... PAUPER
Monaco's reigning
.... RAINIER
Moslem .... IMAM, NAWAB
of Broadway .... HAL
opera .... IGOR
the church .... CARDINAL
Wales .... CHARLES
royal, of England .... CHARLES
Prince Albert's (of England)
wife .... (QUEEN) VICTORIA
Charming's wife, fairy tale
.... CINDERELLA
Norodom, Cambodian
.... SIHANOUK
of Darkness .... SATAN
of Peace .... MESSIAH, JESUS
(CHRIST)
princeling .... SATRAP
princely .... NOBLE, REGAL,
ROYAL, LAVISH, LIBERAL,
GENEROUS
princess .... RANI, RANEE,
INFANTA, MAHARANI
disguised as a bull
.... EUROPA

loved by Zeus .... EUROPA
marble .... SODALITE
mythical .... INO
swift-footed .... ATALANTA
Princess Ida character .... GAMA
Princetonian .... COED
principal ...... ARCH, MAIN, CHIEF,
MAJOR, PREMIER, PRIMARY
actor .... LEAD, STAR
crop .... STAPLE
principality .... PRINCEDOM
principle .... LAW, CODE, RULE,
IDEAL, MAXIM, TENET,
THEORY, PRECEPT, DOCTRINE,
THEOREM, POSTULATE
first .... RUDIMENTS
main .... KEYSTONE
Principles of citizenship
.... CIVISM
of Scientific Management
author: 1911 ..... TAYLOR
princox .... FOP, COXCOMB
prink .... PREEN, PRIMP, PRUNE,
DECK OUT, DRESS UP
print .... COPY, STAMP, IMPOSE,
RUN OFF, ETCHING, PICTURE,
PUBLISH, IMPRESS(ION)
blurred/double .... MACKLE
direction .... STET
in red letters .... RUBRICATE
printed books, early
.... INCUNABULA
printer .... PRESSMAN, STONEMAN,
PUBLISHER, COMPOSITOR,
TYPESETTER
of first books in English
.... (WILLIAM) CAXTON
printer's aid .... GUIDE, INKER,
GRIPPER
apprentice/helper .... DEVIL
direction .... STET, RESET,
DELE(TE)
ink pad .... DABBER
ink spreader .... BRAYER
lock .... QUOIN
mark ..... DASH, CARET, TILDE,
DAGGER, DIESIS, ASTERISK
marking equipment ..... BEVEL
measure .... EM, EN, PICA
metal block for spacing
.... QUAD
metal mold .... MATRIX
metal roller .... PLATEN
pawl .... RATCHET(WHEEL)
proof .... GALLEY
roller .... BRAY
shop spirit .... RALPH
sign for special attention
.... FIST
star .... ASTERISK
printing .... ISSUE, EDITION

art/business of .... PRESS
assortment of type, one size
    and style .... FONT
capital letter in
    .... MAJUSCULE, UPPER CASE
error(s) ..... ERRATUM, ERRATA
establishment .... PRESS
form .... DIE, MAT, MOLD
method .... LITHOGRAPHY
modern method of ...... LASER
part of a letter .... FACE
plate .... STEREO(TYPE)
press, part of ..... BED, BEVEL,
    FRAME, GUIDE, INKER, QUOIN,
    BRAYER, PLATEN, REGLET,
    ROUNCE, FRISKET, GRIPPER
press, type of .... HAND,
    GALLEY, GRAVURE
process .... OFFSET, STENCIL,
    STEREOTYPY, LITHOGRAPHY,
    ROTOGRAVURE
second .... REISSUE
slanted type .... ITALICS
small letter in ...... MINISCULE,
    LOWER CASE, MINUSCULE
system for the blind
    .... BRAILLE
term .... STET, DELE(TE),
    RESET, STONE, CENTER, EM
    DASH, EN DASH, INDENT,
    INSERT, CLOSE UP, LIGATURE,
    LOGOTYPE
trial impression .... PROOF
type ...... PICA, ITALIC, SCRIPT,
    BOLDFACE, LIGHTFACE
part of .... BODY, FEET,
    NICK, STEM, BEARD, SERIF,
    GROOVE
-setting machine
    .... LINOTYPE
size ...... PICA, ELITE, MINION
style .... DORIC, ROMAN,
    GOTHIC, OLD ENGLISH
prior .... ELDER, FORMER,
    EARLIER, PREVIOUS
superior to a .... ABBOT
to .... BEFORE
priority .... PRECEDENCE
priory .... ABBEY, NUNNERY,
    MONASTERY
Priscilla's husband .... ALDEN
suitor .... (MILES) STANDISH
prism .... NICOL
prison .... PEN, CAGE, COOP,
    GAOL, JAIL, QUAD, QUOD,
    LIMBO, BRIDEWELL,
    BASTIL(L)E, PENITENTIARY
camp .... GULAG
cell .... HOLE
chaplain .... ORDINARY
colloquial/slang ..... CAN, JUG,

PEN, STIR, CLINK, POKEY,
    COOLER, LOCKUP, SLAMMER,
    BIG HOUSE, HOOSEGOW,
    CALABOZO, CALABOOSE
cubicle .... CELL
division .... WARD
employee .... GUARD, JAILER,
    WARDER, TURNKEY
federal .... ALCATRAZ, SING
    SING
for stray animals .... POUND
grounds .... BARRED YARD
guard: sl. .... SCREW
head of a .... WARDEN
in California .... SAN QUENTIN
Devonshire .... DARTMOOR
island of pelicans
    .... ALCATRAZ
Kansas .... LEAVENWORTH
London .... NEWGATE
New York .... SING SING
Paris .... BASTILLE
occupant .... FELON, INMATE,
    CONVICT, CRIMINAL
priest .... CHAPLAIN, ORDINARY
sentence .... RAP, STRETCH,
    PUNISHMENT
ship's .... BRIG, HULK
spy .... MOUTON
term .... RAP
underground .... DUNGEON
prisoner .... FELON, INMATE,
    TERMER, CAPTIVE, CONVICT,
    JAILBIRD
at bar .... CULPRIT
bond of .... BAIL, PAROLE
guard of .... BAILIFF
kind of .... LIFER, RAPIST,
    MURDERER
privileged .... TRUSTY
redeem a .... RANSOM
shackles of .... BILBO
prissy ...... PRIM, FUSSY, PRECISE,
    OVERNICE, EFFEMINATE
pristine .... NEW, PURE, FIRST,
    FRESH, PRIME, ORIGINAL,
    UNSPOILED
prithee ...... PLEASE, I PRAY THEE
privacy ...... SECRECY, ISOLATION,
    SECLUSION
private .... INNER, SECRET,
    INTIMATE, PERSONAL,
    SECLUDED, CONFIDENTIAL
apartment .... MAHAL
army .... PFC
entrance .... POSTERN
eye ...... TEC, DICK, DETECTIVE
eye task .... TAIL
information .... TIP
remarks .... ASIDES, AD LIBS
road .... DRIVEWAY

room .... DEN, MEW, LAIR,
    CLOSET
teacher .... COACH, TUTOR
wrong .... TORT
privateer .... KIDD, DRAKE,
    PIRATE, CORSAIR, FREEBOOT,
    SEA ROVER, BUCCANEER
privateering .... PIRACY
privation .... NEED, WANT,
    POVERTY
privilege .... FAVOR, RIGHT,
    OPTION, LICENSE
corporation's .... FRANCHISE
exclusive .... PATENT,
    COPYRIGHT
king's .... REGALITY
people's .... FREEDOM,
    LIBERTY
privileged .... EXEMPT(ED)
privileges, equality of
    .... ISONOMY
privy ...... JAKES, STOOL, CLOACA,
    HIDDEN, SECRET, LATRINE,
    PRIVATE, OUTHOUSE
council .... CAMARILLA
ones .... EPOPTS
to (the secret) .... IN ON,
    AWARE OF, INFORMED
prize .... PRY, AWARD, BOOTY,
    LEVER, STAKE, VALUE,
    ESTEEM, REWARD, TROPHY,
    CHERISH, TREASURE
award since 1917
    .... PULITZER
donor .... NOBEL, PULITZER
fighter ...... BOXER, PUG(ILIST),
    SLUGGER, RINGSTER,
    BEAKBUSTER
fighter's wear .... SILKS
fighting program .... CARD
kind of .... BOOBY
money .... PURSE
of a sort .... BRASS RING
winner .... CHAMPION,
    MEDALIST
pro .... FOR, EXPERT,
    PROFESSIONAL
bono _____ .... PUBLICO
tempore .... TEMPORARY
proa .... PRAU, CANOE
probability .... ODDS, CHANCE,
    LIKELIHOOD
probable .... LIKELY, ODDS-ON,
    POSSIBLE
probandi, _____ .... ONUS
probate court's concern
    .... WILLS, ESTATES
judge .... SURROGATE
probation .... TRIAL, TEST(ING)
probationer .... ROOKIE
probe .... DELVE, SEARCH,

EXPLORE
surgical .... STYLET
probity .... VIRTUE, DECENCY,
HONESTY, INTEGRITY
problem ...... CRUX, KNOT, TASK,
ISSUE, POSER, QUERY,
ENIGMA, PUZZLE, RIDDLE,
DILEMMA, TICKLER,
QUESTION, DIFFICULTY
airport .... NO SHOW
of scarcity ..... BLACK MARKET
problematic .... MOOT
proboscidian .... ELEPHANT,
MASTODON
proboscis .... (BANANA) NOSE,
SNOUT, TRUNK
butterfly's/moth's ...... LINGUA
insect .... HAUSTELLUM
procedure .... WAY, METHOD,
POLICY
proceed ...... GO ON, MOVE, ISSUE,
MARCH, ADVANCE, CONTINUE
at great speed .... HIGHBALL
laboriously .... WADE
without power .... COAST
proceedings .... ACTA, ACTS,
STEPS, MEASURES,
TRANSACTIONS
last part of .... TAG
legal .... LAWSUIT
proceeds ...... GAIN, ISSUE, YIELD,
INCOME, PROFIT, EARNINGS,
RECEIPTS
process .... COURSE, METHOD,
CONDUCT, PRACTICE,
TUBERCLE, APPENDAGE,
OUTGROWTH
fish .... BARBEL
in law .... SUIT, WRIT, (LEGAL)
ACTION, PROSECUTE
of decline .... DECADENCE
of knowing .... NOESIS,
COGNITION
server .... SHERIFF
steel-making .... BESSEMER
procession .... FILE, TRAIN,
PARADE, CORTEGE, RETINUE,
SEQUENCE, CAVALCADE
of cars .... MOTORCADE
official .... MARSHAL
staff .... VERGE
staff bearer .... VERGER
processional .... HYMN
prochein, in law .... NEAREST
proclaim .... CRY, SING, EXTOL,
STATE, HERALD, PRAISE,
DECLARE, ENOUNCE,
TRUMPET, ANNOUNCE,
BROADCAST
proclamation .... FIAT, EDICT,
BAN(N)S, UKASE, NOTICE,

BULLETIN, MANIFESTO
proclivity .... LEANING,
TENDENCY, INCLINATION
Procne's husband .... TEREUS
parent .... PANDION
sister .... PHILOMELA
transformation .... SWALLOW
procrastinate ...... DEFER, DELAY,
LINGER, NEGLECT, POSTPONE,
DILLY-DALLY
procreate .... BEGET, BREED,
PRODUCE
proctor .... AGENT
procumbent .... PRONE
procurator ...... PILATE, PROCTOR
procure .... BUY, GET, OBTAIN,
SECURE, ACQUIRE
procurer .... PIMP, PANDER
prod .... EGG(ON), DIG, JAB,
GOAD, POKE, URGE, DRIVE,
IMPEL, ROUSE, PUNCH, INCITE,
PIERCE, THRUST
prodder .... NEEDLER
elephant .... MAHOUT
prodigal .... LAVISH, WASTER,
SPENDER, PROFUSE, WASTREL,
WASTEFUL, ABUNDANT,
SPENDTHRIFT
one .... SON
prodigious .... HUGE, VAST,
AMAZING, IMMENSE,
ENORMOUS
prodigy .... MARVEL, WIZARD,
WONDER, MIRACLE, MONSTER
prodrome .... SYMPTOM
produce ...... BEAR, MAKE, BEGET,
BREED, CAUSE, FETCH,
HATCH, ISSUE, RAISE, YIELD,
CREATE, ENGENDER,
GENERATE
a musical .... COMPOSE
cloth .... WEAVE
colloquial .... FRUITS,
VEGETABLES
from raw materials
.... MANUFACTURE
proof .... SHOW
produced on earth's surface
.... EPIGENE
producer's favorite letters
.... SRO
producing abundantly
.... FRUITFUL, FERACIOUS
vinegar .... ACETIC
product ...... CROP, FRUIT, YIELD,
RESULT, OUTCOME, CREATION,
OFFSPRING, OUTGROWTH
for combustion .... SMOKE
of dexterity .... FEAT
of imagination .... FIGMENT
of wood distillation ...... PINE-

TAR
production .... OUTPUT
excess .... OVERRUN
sleeper's .... ZEES
productive .... RICH, FECUND,
FERTILE, CREATIVE, FRUITFUL,
PREGNANT, PROLIFIC,
THRIVING, FRUCTUOUS
source .... FONT, MINE
proem .... PREFACE, PRELUDE,
INTRODUCTION
prof. .... PROFESSOR
profanation .... SACRILEGE
profane ...... FOUL, VILE, DEBASE,
DEFILE, VULGAR, VIOLATE,
IMPIOUS, BLASPHEME,
DESECRATE
profanity ...... CURSING, CUSSING,
SWEARING
profess .... AVOW, CLAIM, AFFIRM,
ALLEGE, PURPORT
professed .... AVOWED,
PRETENDED
profession .... LINE, TRADE,
AVOWAL, CAREER, METIER,
CALLING, PURSUIT, VOCATION
"the oldest"
.... PROSTITUTION
professional .... PRO, EXPERT,
SKILLED
non .... LAY, LAIC, AMATEUR
professor .... DON, DOCENT,
TEACHER
assistant .... READER
proffer ...... GIVE, OFFER, EXTEND,
SUBMIT, TENDER, PRESENT
proficient .... APT, ABLE, DEFT,
ADEPT, EXPERT, SKILLED
profile .... BIO-DATA, SKETCH,
CONTOUR, OUTLINE, SIDE
VIEW, SILHOUETTE
profit .... BOOT, GAIN, AVAIL,
BENEFIT, IMPROVE, EARNINGS,
CASH IN ON, ADVANTAGE
addition .... EER
clear .... NET, VELVET
easy .... GRAVY
kind of extra .... PERQUISITE
sudden, great .... KILLING
profitable .... PAYING, GAINFUL,
FRUITFUL, LUCRATIVE
thing, in high finance
.... PLUM
profiteer .... LEECH, SCALPER
profits .... RETURNS, PROCEEDS
for distribution .... MELON
from lands, etc. .... ISSUE
profligate .... WASTEFUL,
DISSOLUTE
person .... ROUE, SPENDER
profound .... DEEP, ABYSS,

HEAVY, INTENSE
profundity .... DEPTH
profuse .... LUSH, LAVISH,
GENEROUS, PRODIGAL,
PLENTIFUL
profusion .... EXCESS,
ABUNDANCE
prog .... FORAGE, PLUNDER
progenitor .... PARENT, ANCESTOR
progeny ...... SEED, BREED, ISSUE,
SCION, CHILDREN, OFFSPRING
prognosis .... ASSESSMENT,
FORECAST(ING), INFORMED
GUESS
prognosticate .... AUGUR,
PREDICT, FORETELL,
PROPHESY
prognosticator .... SEER, DIVINER,
PROPHET, PREDICTOR,
FORECASTER
program .... CARD, PLAN, DRAFT,
AGENDA, OUTLINE, PLAYBILL,
SYLLABUS, PROSPECTUS
progress .... GAIN, COURSE,
STRIDE, ADVANCE,
IMPROVE(MENT)
in work .... HEADWAY
level .... GRADE
planned .... TELESIS
slowly .... CRAWL
progressing by tens .... DECIMAL
progressive loss of hearing
.... PRESBYCUSIS
Progressive of 1912
.... BULLMOOSE
prohibit .... BAN, DENY, TABU,
VETO, (DE)BAR, TABOO,
DISBAR, ENJOIN, FORBID,
HINDER, EXCLUDE, INHIBIT,
PREVENT, DISALLOW
prohibited .... TABU, BANNED,
ILLEGAL, TABOO(ED),
CONTRABAND
prohibition .... BAN, DONT, NO-
NO, TABU, TABOO, EMBARGO
opponents/foes .... WETS
trade .... EMBARGO
prohibitionist .... DRY
prohibitive .... RESTRICTIVE
price .... DEAR, COSTLY,
GOUGING
project .... JUT, HURL, IDEA,
PLAN, PITCH, THROW, DEVISE,
INTEND, SCHEME, PURPOSE,
ENDEAVOR, PROPOSAL,
PROTRUDE
projectile .... BALL, BOMB, SHELL,
BULLET, PELLET, ROCKET,
JAVELIN MISSILE
part of .... WARHEAD, WAR
NOSE

path of .... TRAJECTORY
projecting corner .... COIGN(E)
edge .... BRIM, EAVE
knob .... BOSS
part .... JOG, SOCLE
point .... NEB
rim .... FLANGE
projection .... EAR, FIN, JAG, JOB,
NOB, LOBE, SPUR, BULGE,
LEDGE, SHELF, SOCLE, TORUS,
EXTENSION
on horse collar .... HAME
projector .... VIEWER,
CINEMATOGRAPH
early motion-picture
.... VITASCOPE
old-fashioned term for
.... MAGIC LANTERN
room .... BOOTH
Prokofiev ballet: 1935
.... ROMEO AND JULIET
prolapse .... PTOSIS,
DISPLACEMENT
structure subject to .... DISK,
EYELID
prolegomenon .... FOREWORD
proletarian .... WORKER,
LABORER
proletariat .... WORKING CLASS
proliferate .... SPREAD, MULTIPLY
prolific .... FECUND, FERTILE,
FRUITFUL, INVENTIVE,
PRODUCTIVE
prolix .... WORDY, LENGTHY,
VERBOSE, DISCURSIVE, LONG-
WINDED
prolocutor .... CHAIRMAN,
SPOKESMAN, MOUTHPIECE
prologue reciter .... CHORUS
prolong .... HOLD, NURSE,
EXTEND, STRETCH, CONTINUE,
LENGTHEN, PROTRACT
prolonged dry weather
.... DROUGHT
oppression .... PERSECUTION
shortage of food .... FAMINE
suffering .... AGONY
torment .... HARASSMENT
prom .... HOP, BALL, DANCE
organizers .... JUNIORS
queen's date .... ESCORT
promenade .... BALL, MALL,
WALK, DANCE, MARCH,
PASEO, AVENUE, OUTING,
PARADE, STROLL, GALLERY,
ESPLANADE
along a coast .... FRONT
leisurely ..... STROLL, SAUNTER
ship's .... DECK
tree-lined .... ALAMEDA,
BOULEVARD

Prometheus' boon to man
.... FIRE
brother .... ATLAS
chastiser .... ZEUS
prominence .... EMINENCE,
EMPHASIS, PRESTIGE
between eyebrows
.... GLABELLA
give .... HIGHLIGHT, SPOTLIGHT
prominent .... CONVEX, MARKED,
RAISED, EMINENT, JUTTING,
NOTABLE, SALIENT,
IMPORTANT, NOTICEABLE,
PROTRUDING, CONSPICUOUS
promiscuous .... LAX, LOOSE,
MIXED, CASUAL, CONFUSED
woman .... COCOTTE
promise .... VOW, OATH, WORD,
TROTH, ASSURE, AVOWAL,
ENGAGE, PAROLE, PLEDGE,
SPONSION, GUARANTEE
broke a .... RENEGED
formal .... SPONSION
in marriage .... BETROTH
manufacturer's
...... WARRANT(Y), GUARANTEE
solemn .... VOW, OATH
to tell the truth .... SWEAR
Promised Land .... SION, ZION,
CANAAN
for immigrants .... AMERICA
promises, not always kept
.... PRE-ELECTION
promising ...... ROSY, BRIGHT, UP
AND COMING
one .... COMER
promissory note .... IOU
signer .... MAKER
promontory ...... TOR, CAPE, NESS,
SKAW, SPIT, HEADLAND
promote .... AID, BOOST, RAISE,
FOSTER, ADVANCE, DIGNIFY,
ELEVATE, FURTHER, SUPPORT
vigorously .... BOOM
promoter .... FLACK, LOBBYIST,
IMPRESARIO, PRESS AGENT
promotion .... PUBLICITY,
ADVANCEMENT
advertising .... BUILDUP,
CAMPAIGN
sales .... MARKETING
prompt .... CUE, EGG, LEAD,
MOVE, URGE, YARE, EARLY,
QUICK, READY, RATH(E),
INCITE, INDUCE, PUNCTUAL
prompter .... CUER, TICKLER
promptly .... SOON, AT ONCE,
PRONTO
promulgate .... ISSUE, PUBLISH,
ADVOCATE, ANNOUNCE
prone .... APT, FLAT, LIKELY,

SUPINE, DISPOSED, INCLINED, PROSTRATE, RECUMBENT

proneness to anger .... BILE

pronephros .... KIDNEY

prong .... NIB, TIP, FANG, STAB, TINE, POINT, PIERCE

pronged thing .... FORK, HORN, RAKE, SPEAR, TOOTH, ANTLER, TRIDENT

pronounce .... SAY, JUDGE, SPEAK, UTTER, DECLARE, ARTICULATE

distinctly .... ENUNCIATE

imperfectly .... LAMBDACISM

indistinctly .... SLUR

pronounced .... GLARING, OBVIOUS, DISTINCT

by using the tongue .... LINGUAL

pronouncement .... ORDER, DECREE, RULING, JUDGMENT, SENTENCE

pronto .... AT ONCE, QUICKLY, (RIGHT) NOW, INSTANTLY

pronunciamento ...... MANIFESTO

pronunciation .... UTTERANCE

aid .... BREVE

childlike .... LISP

nasal way of .... TWANG

of r like l .... LALLATION

pause .... HIATUS

poor .... CACOLOGY

prolonging the vowels .... DRAWL

rough .... BURR

standard .... ORTHOEPY

study of .... PHONOLOGY

unit of .... SYLLABLE

proof .... COPY, TEST, BASIS, TRIAL, REASON, SAMPLE, EXHIBIT, DOCUMENT, EVIDENCE

burden of .... ONUS

kind of .... IRONCLAD

math .... QED

printing .... GALLEY

proofreader's mark ...... BF, LC, LD, LF, SP, TR, WF, ROM, CAPS, DELE, ITAL, STET, CARET

prop ...... GIB, BACK, BASE, STAY, BLOCK, BRACE, SHORE, STAFF, TRUSS, CRUTCH, HOLD UP, PILLAR, UPHOLD, SUPPORT, SUSTAIN, BUTTRESS

briefing .... GRAPH

"Hansel and Gretel" .... OVEN

one-legged .... UNIPOD

propaganda .... BALLYHOO, PUBLICITY

propagate .... BREED, RAISE, SPREAD, PRODUCE, PUBLISH, GENERATE, INCREASE, MULTIPLY

propagator .... SOWER

propel .... OAR, PUSH, DRIVE, FORCE, IMPEL, SHOVE, SLING

a bayou boat .... POLE

with a pole .... PUNT

propeller .... BLADE, ROTOR, SCREW, DRIVER

driving force of .... THRUST

part of .... BLADE

propensity .... BENT, FLAIR, TALENT, APTITUDE, PENCHANT, TENDENCY, INCLINATION

proper .... FAIR, JUST, MEET, PRIM, RIGHT, DECENT, SEEMLY, APROPOS, CORRECT, FIT(TING), DECOROUS, SUITABLE, BEFITTING

code of precedence .... PROTOCOL

order .... EUTAXY

slang .... KOSHER

properly .... DULY

property .... ASSETS, ESTATE, REALTY, WEALTH, CHATTEL, HOLDINGS, ATTRIBUTE, OWNERSHIP, POSSESSION

absolute .... AL(L)OD

act to regain .... REPLEVIN

captured at sea .... PRIZE

claim to/charge .... LIEN

delivery of .... LIVERY

endowed .... PATRIMONY

ill-gotten .... PELF, BOOTY, LUCRE

illegal detention of .... DETINUE

landed .... ESTATE

law .... BONA

legally held ...... SEISIN, SEIZIN

lock .... LIEN

movie-making .... PROP

personal .... CHOSE, CHATTEL

reverted .... ESCHEAT

stationary .... PRAEDIAL

taken by conqueror .... SPOILS

transfer document ..... BILL OF SALE

transferee .... ALIENEE

transferor .... ALIENOR

willed to someone .... LEGACY

prophecy .... AUGURY, FORECAST, PREDICTION

by lots .... SORTILEGE

prophesy .... AUGUR, DIVINE, PORTEND, PREDICT, PRESAGE, FORECAST, FORETELL

prophet .... AMOS, JOEL, JOHN, SEER, HOSEA, JONAH, DANIEL, ELIJAH, ISAIAH, ORACLE, DIVINER, EZEKIEL, MICAIAH, JEREMIAH, PREDICTOR

anointed by Elijah ..... ELISHA

first biblical .... ABRAHAM

great .... MOSES

Moslem .... MOHAMMED

non-Israelite .... BALAAM

of disaster .... ALARMIST

prophetess .... ANNA, SIBYL, DEBORAH, SEERESS, PYTHONESS

discredited .... CASSANDRA

prophetic ...... MANTIC, FATEFUL, FATIDIC, ORACULAR, PYTHONIC, VATIC(AL), SYBILLINE, VATICINAL

prophets, book of the .... NEBI'IM

garb of the .... HAIR-SHIRT

prophylactic .... CONDOM, PROTECTIVE

propinquity .... KINSHIP, AFFINITY, NEARNESS, VICINITY, PROXIMITY

propitiate .... ATONE, PACIFY, APPEASE, MEDIATE

propitious .... TIMELY, GRACIOUS, FAVORABLE, OPPORTUNE, AUSPICIOUS

proponent .... BACKER, ADVOCATE, CHAMPION, PROPOSER, STALWART

of self-realization .... ENERGIST

proportion .... PART, RATE, QUOTA, RATIO, SHARE, EXTENT, BALANCE, SYMMETRY, DIMENSION

proposal .... BID, PLAN, OFFER, MOTION, TENDER, REQUEST, OVERTURE, SUGGESTION

legislative .... BILL

tentative .... FEELER

propose .... MOVE

for office .... NOMINATE

proposed international language .... IDO, ESPERANTO

proposer .... MOVER

proposition .... PLAN, OFFER, THEORY, PREMISE, PROJECT, THEOREM, PROPOSAL, (HYPO)THESIS

secondary .... LEMMA

self-evident .... AXIOM

propound .... POSE, STATE, PROPOSE, SET FORTH

proprietor .... LORD, OWNER, MANAGER, TITLEHOLDER

propriety .... APTNESS, DECORUM,

FITNESS
propulsion .... PUSH, FLING,
EJECTION
prorogue .... ADJOURN
prosaic ...... DULL, PLAIN, SOBER,
LITERAL, UNPOETIC
proscribe .... BAN, EXILE, BANISH,
FORBID, OUTLAW, CONDEMN,
INTERDICT
prosecute ...... SUE, URGE, PRESS,
CHARGE, INDICT, PURSUE,
ARRAIGN, CARRY ON, FOLLOW
UP
prosecuting attorney .... DA,
FISCAL
proselyte .... CONVERT
Proserpina .... CORA, PERSEPHONE
husband of .... PLUTO
mother of .... CERES
proseuchae .... ORATORIES
prosit .... TOAST
prosody .... METRICS, SCANSION
verse .... STICH
prospect ...... HOPE, VIEW, SCENE,
SIGHT, VISTA, SEARCH,
OUTLOOK, PROMISE
A-one .... COMER
prospective ...... COMING, FUTURE,
LIKELY, EXPECTED, IMMINENT
prospector .... MINER
advance to .... GRUBSTAKE
colloquial .... SOURDOUGH,
FORTY-NINER
companion of .... MULE
helper of .... BURRO
quest of .... LODE
transportation of
.... PACKHORSE
prospectus .... CATALOG,
PROGRAM, BROCHURE
prosper .... GROW, BATTEN,
FATTEN, THRIVE, BURGEON,
SUCCEED, FLOURISH,
MULTIPLY
prosperity .... BOOM, BONANZA
archaic .... WEAL
slang .... FAT CITY
Prospero's slave .... CALIBAN
sprite .... ARIEL
prosperous .... FAT, RICH, PALMY,
WEALTHY, WELL-OFF,
AFFLUENT, WELL-TO-DO,
THRIVING
prostitute ...... DRAB, SLUT, TART,
TRAMP, TRULL, WHORE,
CHIPPY, HARLOT, TROLLOP,
FILLE DE JOIE
biblical .... GOMER, RAHAB,
MARY MAGDALENE
kind of .... COURTESAN
prostitution .... HARLOTRY,

STREETWALKING, WHITE
SLAVERY
house of .... BROTHEL,
BORDELLO
prostrate .... FLAT, ABASE,
PRONE, FALLEN, LAY LOW,
SUPINE, LAID LOW, SUPINATE,
POWERLESS, RECUMBENT
prosy ...... DULL, JEJUNE, PROSAIC,
COMMON(PLACE)
protagonist .... HERO, STAR,
RIVAL, LEADER, HEROINE,
EXPONENT, CONTENDER
protean .... MULTIFORM
protect .... SAVE, POLICE, SCREEN,
SECURE, SHIELD, SHELTER,
(DE)FEND, PRESERVE,
(SAFE)GUARD
from heat .... INSULATE
protection .... AID, CUSTODY,
(A)EGIS, DEFENSE,
PASS(PORT), SECURITY,
TUTELAGE
against loss .... INSURANCE
means of .... MOAT, ARMOR,
PAINT, QUILL, SPINE, HELMET,
CAMOUFLAGE
palatial .... MOAT
racket .... EXTORTION
protective band, fencing
.... BRACER
coloration .... DISGUISE
cover .... FOIL, ARMOR, CRATE,
SHELL, HELMET, SCREEN,
SHIELD, CAMOUFLAGE
protector .... KEEPER, PATRON,
REGENT, DEFENDER,
GUARDIAN
of auto .... GARAGE
of the President .... SECRET
SERVICE
protectorate .... CONDOMINIUM,
TRUST TERRITORY,
TRUSTEESHIP
protege(e) .... WARD, PUPIL,
CHARGE
proteid(e) .... AMINE, PROTEIN
protein .... AMINE, CASEIN,
ENZYME, FIBRIN, RICIN(E),
ALBUMIN, HISTONE,
ALEURONE, GLOBULIN,
PROTEID(E)
building acid .... AMINO
component of hemoglobin
.... GLOBIN
egg yolk .... LECITHIN,
VITELLIN
enzyme that digests
.... PROTEASE
in muscles ..... ACTIN, MYOSIN
in tissue/bone .... MUCIN,

COLLAGEN
insoluble ...... FIBRIN, KERATIN
milk .... CASEIN
soluble .... PEPTONE
type of .... LIPID, MUCIN,
ALBUMIN, EDESTIN, ELASTIN,
FIBROIN, KERATIN, PEPTIDE,
SALMINE, LECITHIN, VITELLIN
white albuminoid ...... FIBROIN
proteose .... ALBUMOSE, ELASTOSE
protest .... ASSERT, OUTCRY,
REFUSE, SQUAWK, DISSENT,
COMPLAIN, (COM)PLAINT,
OBJECT(ION)
Protestant .... BAPTIST,
ANGLICAN, LUTHERAN,
OBJECTOR, DISSENTER,
METHODIST, NON-CATHOLIC
Anglo-Saxon .... WASP
non-conformist .... SECTARY
protocol .... CUSTOMS,
PROCEDURES
proton .... ANLAGE
accelerator .... COSMOTRON
provide with a .... PROTONATE
protoplasm .... PLASMA, COLLOID
composing nucleus of a cell
.... NUCLEOPLASM
granule in .... MICROSOME
of a cell .... CYTOPLASM
unit of .... PLASTID
prototype ...... DIE, MOLD, IDEAL,
MODEL, EXAMPLE, PATTERN,
EXEMPLAR, ORIGINAL,
STANDARD
protozoan .... MONAD, AM(O)EBA,
SPORE, EUGLENA, PROTIST
organ of locomotion
.... FLAGELLUM
protract .... DRAG, DEFER, DELAY,
EXTEND, PROLONG, STRETCH,
LENGTHEN
protrude .... BULGE, EXSERT,
JUT(OUT), PROJECT
protrusion of organ ...... HERNIA
of the eyeball .... PROPTOSIS
protuberance ...... EAR, JAG, JUT,
NUB, HUMP, KNOB, LOBE,
LUMP, NODE, SNAG, UMBO,
BULGE, INION, VENTER,
SWELLING
camel's back .... HUMP
protuberant .... CONVEX, TOROSE,
TOROUS, BULGING
proud .... VAIN, BYRONIC,
HAUGHTY, ARROGANT,
BOASTFUL, SPIRITED,
SUPERIOR, OVERBEARING
as a _____ .... PEACOCK
Proust, F., novelist ...... MARCEL
prove .... SHOW, TEST, CHECK,

TRY(OUT), VERIFY, CONFIRM, DEMONSTRATE
false .... BELIE, DEBUNK, REFUTE
successful .... PAN OUT
provenance .... ORIGIN, DERIVATION
Provençal love song .... ALBA
poet .... MISTRAL
provender ...... HAY, CORN, FEED, FOOD, OATS, GRAIN, FODDER, PROVISIONS
proverb ...... SAW, ADAGE, AXIOM, MAXIM, BY-WORD, SAYING, PARABLE, PRECEPT, APHORISM
proverbial blushers .... BRIDES
provide .... CATER, AFFORD, PURVEY, SUPPLY, FURNISH, STIPULATE
a crew .... MAN
food .... CATER
for .... SUPPORT
for oneself .... FEATHER ONE'S NEST
services .... RENDER
with a top .... ENCAP
with means .... ENABLE
with what is needed .... EQUIP, OUTFIT, ACCOUTER
provided .... IF, THOUGH
Providence .... LORD, HEAVEN, PRUDENCE, GOD(ALMIGHTY)
provident ...... FRUGAL, PRUDENT, THRIFTY, CAUTIOUS
providential .... LUCKY, FORTUNATE, AUSPICIOUS, HEAVEN-SENT
provider .... DONOR, ENDUER, BREADWINNER
province .... REGION, SPHERE, DISTRICT, TERRITORY
ruler of .... ETHNARCH, GOVERNOR
provincial .... LOCAL, RUSTIC, INSULAR, NARROW(-MINDED)
speech .... IDIOM, PATOIS, DIALECT
proving directly .... D(E)ICTIC
ground .... LAB(ORATORY)
provision ...... FARE, FEED, FOOD, CATES, LARDER, PROVISO, EATABLES, PLANNING, VICTUALS, CONDITION, GROCERIES, STIPULATION
search for .... FORAGE
storage for .... CELLAR
provisional .... IFFY, INTERIM, TEMPORARY, TENTATIVE
provisioner ...... GROCER, SUTLER, CATERER, PURVEYOR
proviso .... CLAUSE, CONDITION(S),

REQUIREMENT, STIPULATION
provisory .... SUBJECT, CONDITIONAL
provocation .... AFFRONT, VEXATION, INCITEMENT
with little .... AT THE DROP OF A HAT
provocative .... RACY, PIQUANT, EXCITING, INVITING, SEDUCTIVE, TANTALIZING
provoke .... IRE, VEX, BAIT, GOAD, RILE, STIR, ANGER, ANNOY, PIQUE, AROUSE, EXCITE, INCITE, NEEDLE, NETTLE, IRRITATE
provost .... JAILER
officer .... MARSHAL
prow .... BOW, BEAK, NOSE, FRONT
prowess .... SKILL, VALOR, ABILITY, COURAGE, HEROISM
prowl .... LURK, ROAM, ROVE, SKULK, SLINK, SNEAK
proximal .... NEXT, NEAREST
opposed to .... DISTAL
to the fingernail .... KNUCKLE
to the hip joint .... KNEE
proximity .... NEARNESS
proxy .... AGENT, DEPUTY, SUBSTITUTE
prude .... PRIG
prudence .... CARE, TACT, DISCRETION, CAUTION, FORESIGHT
prudent .... WISE, CHARY, CAREFUL, HEEDFUL, CAUTIOUS, DISCREET, SENSIBLE
prudery-personified .... GRUNDY
prudish .... DEMURE, PRISSY
prune .... CUT, LOP, CLIP, PARE, PLUM, SNIP, TRIM, SHEAR, REMOVE
prunella .... TEXTILE
prurient .... LEWD, LUSTFUL
prurigo .... RASH
pruritus .... ITCHING
Prussian ...... GERMAN, JUNKER
cavalryman .... U(H)LAN
city .... EMDEN, ESSEN, AACHEN
district .... STADE
land measure .... MORGEN
legislature .... LANDTAG
province .... SAXONY
resort .... EMS
river .... RUHR
seaport .... KIEL, EMDEN, STETTIN
prussiate .... CYANIDE
pry ...... LOOK, NOSE, PEEK, PEER,

SEEK, FORCE, JIMMY, LEVER, PRIZE, RAISE, CROWBAR, INSPECT, SNOOP(ER)
pryer .... BUSYBODY
prying .... NOSY, CURIOUS, INQUISITIVE
person .... SPY, SNOOP, GOSSIP, PEEPER, MEDDLER, PEEPING TOM
PS .... POSTSCRIPT
psalm .... HYMN, LAUD, SONG, MOTET, PAEAN, ANTHEM, CANTATA, CANTATE, CHORALE, INTROIT, CANTICLE
word .... SELAH
psalter .... PSALMBOOK
psalterium .... OMASUM, MANYPLIES
psaltery .... DULCIMER
plucker .... PLECTRUM
psammite .... SANDSTONE
pseudo .... FAKE, MOCK, SHAM, BOGUS, FALSE, PHONY, SPURIOUS, COUNTERFEIT
intellectual .... PUNDIT, SCIOLIST, CHARLATAN
pseudodementia ...... DEPRESSION
pseudogout .... ARTHRITIS
pseudologist .... LIAR
forte of .... LIES
pseudonym ...... ALIAS, ANONYM, BYNAME, PEN NAME, NICKNAME, INCOGNITO, SOBRIQUET, NOM DE PLUME
Arouet .... VOLTAIRE
Athorton .... LIN
Austen .... DAPSANG
Bronte .... (CURRER) BELL
Clemens .... (MARK) TWAIN
Dickens .... BOZ
Dodgson .... (LEWIS) CARROLL
Dudevant ...... (GEORGE) SAND
Evans, Mary Ann .... (GEORGE) ELIOT
Gardner, E.S. .... FAIR
Geisel, Theodor Seuss .... DR. SEUSS, THEO LESIEG
Goodman .... ADAM SMITH
Herzog ...... (ANDRE) MAUROIS
Josip Broz .... TITO
Lamb .... ELIA
Millay .... (NANCY) BOYD
Moir .... DELTA
Mrs. Humphrey .... RITA
Munro .... SAKI
Poquelin .... MOLIERE
Porter .... (O) HENRY
Pyeshkov, Aleksei .... (MAXIM) GORKI
Rabelais, Francois .... (ALCOFRIBAS) NASIER

Ramee, M. L. .... OUIDA
Rosegger .... PK
Stein .... (ALICE) TOKLAS
Thibault .... (ANATOLE)
.... FRANCE
Ulyanov, Vladimir
.... (NICOLAI) LENIN
Viaud, L. M. ..... (PIERRE) LOTI
Wright .... (S.S.) VAN DINE
pshaw .... TUT, POOH
Psiloriti, Mount .... IDA
location of .... CRETE
psilosis .... SPRUE
psittacosis .... INFLUENZA
spreader .... PARROT, PIGEON
psoas .... LOIN, MUSCLE
disorder .... ABSCESS
location .... FEMUR, PELVIS
psora .... SCABIES
psoriasis .... ECZEMA, DERMATITIS
type of ..... DISCOID, GUTTATE,
PUSTULAR
psychasthenia .... NEUROSIS
psyche .... MIND, SOUL, SPIRIT
Psyche, love of ...... EROS, CUPID
psyched up .... PRIMED
psychedelic experience ...... LSD
psyches, part of .... IDS, EGOS
psychiatrist .... ADLER, FREUD,
MESMER, ANALYST, ALIENIST
concern of .... EGO
slang .... HEADSHRINKER
psychic ...... MENTAL, PREDICTOR,
SPIRITUAL
disorder .... NEUROSIS
energy .... LIBIDO
person .... MEDIUM
power: abbr. .... ESP
psycho .... NEUROTIC
psychological .... MENTAL
jargon, trite
.... PSYCHOBABBLE
psychologist .... BINET, REICH,
PAVLOV, PIAGET, WATSON
psychology, branch of
.... HEDONICS
psychopath .... MADMAN
psychopathic .... LOCO, SCHIZY
psychosis .... INSANITY
psychotic .... CRAZY, LUNATIC,
PARANOID
Pt, in chemistry .... PLATINUM
ptarmigan .... RIPA, GROUSE
pteric .... ALAR
pteridophyte .... FERN, MOSS
pteris rootstock .... ROI
pterodactyl .... PTEROSAUR
pteropod .... CLIONE, MOLLUSK
pterygoid .... WINGLIKE
ptisan .... TEA, DRINK, TISANE,
DECOCTION

Ptolemais, formerly .... ACRE
ptomaine, liquid .... CHOLINE
ptosis .... PROLAPSE
ptyalin .... ENZYME
pub .... BAR, INN, HOTEL, SALOON,
TAVERN
missile .... DART
potion ...... ALE, BEER, PORTER
worker ..... BARMAID, TAPSTER
puberty .... MATURITY, NUBILITY,
ADOLESCENCE
of .... HEBETIC
pubescence .... DOWN
public .... FREE, OPEN, CIVIC,
KNOWN, OVERT, COMMON,
PEOPLE, GENERAL, POPULAR,
COMMUNAL, COMMUNITY
announcer .... CRIER
assistance .... WELFARE
auction .... VENDUE
baths .... THERMAE
disclosure .... EXPOSE
enemy .... CRIMINAL,
GANGSTER, RACKETEER
funds, steal .... PECULATE
good .... COMMONWEAL
house .... BAR, INN, HOTEL,
TAVERN
indignation .... FUROR
land .... AGER
life .... CAREER
notice .... AD, BULLETIN,
PUBLICITY, SPOTLIGHT
opinion .... CONSENSUS
opinion-taker .... ROPER,
GALLUP, HARRIS
outcries: sl. .... STINKS
press ...... THE FOURTH ESTATE
prosecutor .... DA, FISCAL
recreation spot .... PARK
square .... FORUM, PLAZA,
PIAZZA
supervisor of accounts
.... COMPTROLLER
transportation .... BUS,
TAXI(CAB), STREETCAR
utility .... GAS, POWER,
WATER, TELEPHONE,
ELECTRICITY, MAIL DELIVERY
walk .... ESPLANADE
welcome, enthusiastic
.... OVATION
worship, science of
.... LITURGIES
publican .... TAXER, TAXMAN,
INNKEEPER, BARKEEP(ER)
publication .... BOOK, ORGAN,
ARTICLE, GAZETTE, JOURNAL,
TABLOID, BULLETIN,
MAGAZINE, NEWS(PAPER),
PERIODICAL

examiner .... CENSOR
publicist .... AUTHOR, WRITER,
COLUMNIST, JOURNALIST,
(PRESS)AGENT
publicity .... NOTICE, RECLAME,
EXPOSURE, LIMELIGHT,
NOTORIETY
exaggerated .... PUFFERY
ploy .... PRESS RELEASE
society .... MEDIA WORLD
publicize .... AIR, PLUG, VOICE,
REPORT, ADVERTISE,
CIRCULATE
publish .... AIR, EDIT, ISSUE,
NOISE, PRINT, BLAZON,
HERALD, PUT OUT, RELEASE,
ANNOUNCE, PROCLAIM
publisher .... OCHS, VALK,
MCKAY, FIELDS, HEARST,
PUTNAM, MERRIAM,
NEWHOUSE, SULZBERGER
publisher's announcement
.... BLURB
trademark .... COLOPHON
Puccini, composer ...... GIACOMO
heroine ...... MIMI, TOSCA, CIO-
CIO SAN
opera .... MANON, TOSCA,
LESCAUT, LA BOHEME,
TURANDOT, MADAMA
BUTTERFLY
puccoon .... DYE, BLOODROOT
puce .... PURPLE
puck .... ELF, IMP, DISK, SPRITE,
(HOB)GOBLIN
pucka ...... GOOD, REAL, GENUINE
pucker .... FOLD, KNIT, POUT,
RUCK, TUCK, PURSE, SHIRR,
COCKLE, CREASE, CRINKLE,
WRINKLE
puckered .... BULLATE,
CORRUGATED
puckerel .... IMP
puckish .... ELFIN, IMPISH,
DEVILISH, MISCHIEVOUS
pudding .... DUFF, MUSH,
BURGOO, JUNKET, SPONGE,
CUSTARD, DESSERT, SAUSAGE,
PORRIDGE, ROLY-POLY
baked apple .... BROWN BETTY
in England .... TRIFLE
Indian .... CORNMEAL
ingredient .... MILK, SAGO,
SUET, FLOUR, FRUIT, TAPIOCA,
VANILLA, MOLASSES,
SEMOLINA
kind of .... PLUM, RICE,
CARROT, CHARLOTTE,
CHOCOLATE, YORKSHIRE
sailor's/seaman's .... DUFF
puddle .... POOL, SLOP, SUMP,

MUDDY, SLUSH, WALLOW, PLASH(ET), LOBLOLLY

puddling tool .... RABBLE

pudency .... MODESTY

pudendum .... VULVA

pudgy ...... FAT, DUMPY, CHUBBY, STOCKY, ROLY-POLY

Pueblo .... TOWN, INDIAN, VILLAGE

council room .... KIVA

Indian .... HOPI, PIRO, TANO, ZUNI, MOQUI

Indian dwelling .... KIVA

puerile .... SILLY, YOUNG, FOOLISH, TRIVIAL, CHILDISH, IMMATURE, INFANTILE

passion .... PUPPY LOVE

Puerto Rico bay .... HONDA, JOBOS, SUCIA, ANASCO, RINCON, BOQUERON, MAYAGUEZ, AGUADILLA, GUAYANILLA

beverage .... MABI

cape .... ROJO

capital .... SAN JUAN

city/town .... CAYEY, COAMO, LARES, PONCE, YAUCO, CAGUAS, CATANO, DORADO, MANATI, ARECIBO, BAYAMON, FAJARDO, GUAYAMA, HUMACAO, ISABELA, CAROLINA, MAYAGUEZ, VEGA ALTA, VEGA BAJA, LEVITTOWN, RIO GRANDE

conqueror .... MILES

discoverer of .... COLUMBUS

district .... PONCE, ARECIBO, BAYAMON, GUAYAMA, HUMACAO, SAN JUAN, MAYAGUEZ, AGUADILLA

governor ..... MUNOZ, ROMERO, ALBERTO, SANCHEZ, MAYAGUEZ, HERNANDEZ

island .... CULEBRA, VIEQUES

lake .... GUAYO, YAUCO, CARITE, GUANICA, CARRALZO, GUAYABAL, PATILLAS, CAONILLAS

language .... ENGLISH, SPANISH

measure .... CUERDA

monetary unit .... DOLLAR

mountain .... EL TORO, PIRATA, EL YUNQUE, GUILARTE

mountains ..... CAYEY, JAICOA, LUQUILLO

passage .... MONA, VIEQUES

porkfish .... SISI

river .... BAUTA, CAMUY, COAMO, LOIZA, NIGUA, PLATA, ANASCO, MANATI, YAQUEZ, TANAMA, ARECIBO, FAJARDO,

GUAYANES, JACAGUAS, CANOVANAS, CULEBRINAS

sea .... CARIBBEAN

seaport .... ARECIBO

puff .... PAD, BLOW, BRAG, FLAM, GASP, PANT, WAFF, WHIFF, BREATH, PRAISE, INFLATE, SWELL(ING)

adder .... SNAKE

at a cigarette .... DRAG

ball .... FUNGUS

bird .... BARBET, MONASA

headdress .... POUF

of wind .... GUST, FLATUS

out .... BOUFFANT

small .... WHIFFET

up .... BLOW, BLOAT, ELATE, SWELL, INFLATE

puffed .... BAGGY

puffer .... (GLOBE)FISH

puffin .... BIRD

kin of .... AUK

puffing .... BREATHLESS

puffy .... FAT, OBESE, BLOATED, PANTING, SWOLLEN

pug .... CLAY, BOXER, TRACK, TRAIL, (BULL)DOG, PAW(MARK), PUGILIST, FOOTPRINT

Puget Sound seaport
.... TACOMA

pugging .... CLAY, MORTAR, SAWDUST

puggree .... SCARF

pugh .... BAH, PAH, PISH, EXCLAMATION

pugilism ...... BOXING, FISTICUFFS

pugilist .... PUG, BOXER, FIGHTER, RINGSTER, BEAKBUSTER

aide, in practice ..... SPARRER, SPARRING PARTNER

arena .... RING

assistant of .... SECOND, HANDLER

encounter .... MILL

pants .... TRUNKS

pugnacious .... BELLICOSE, COMBATIVE, BELLIGERENT, QUARRELSOME

man .... BRUISER

puisne .... JUDGE, JUNIOR

puissant .... MIGHTY, STRONG

puke ...... SPIT, VOMIT, THROW UP

pukka .... REAL, GENUINE

pulchritude ...... CHARM, GRACE, BEAUTY

pulchritudinous .... BEAUTIFUL

one .... PIN-UP, VENUS

pule .... WHINE, WHIMPER

pulex .... FLEA

Pulitzer Prize author, 1984
.... GEISEL

author Tuchman's book
.... THE GUNS OF AUGUST

cartoonist, 1955 .... (DAN) FITZPATRICK

novelist, 1958 .... AGEE

poet .... (ROBERT) FROST

winning play .... HEIDI CHRONICLES, DRIVING MISS DAISY

work category .... MUSIC, JOURNALISM, LITERATURE

Pulj, former name of ...... POLA

pull .... DO, LUG, TOW, TUG, DRAG, DRAW, HAUL, JERK, MOVE, SWAY, PLUCK, GRAVITY, PERFORM, (RE)STRAIN

a fast one .... OUTWIT, OUTSMART

an oar .... CREW

apart .... PAN, RIP, REND, TEAR, SEPARATE, CRITICIZE

back ...... RETREAT, WITHDRAW

down .... RAZE, HUMBLE, REDUCE, DOWSE, DESTROY

for .... BACK, ROOT, CHEER

forcibly .... YANK, WRENCH

off .... DO, EFFECT, MANAGE, SUCCEED, ACCOMPLISH

one's leg .... FLATTER

one's punches .... HESITATE

out .... UPROOT, ABANDON

out by the root .... STUB

slang .... POWER, INFLUENCE

teeth .... EXTRACT

through .... RECOVER, SURVIVE

toward .... ATTRACT, MAGNETIZE

up .... HIKE, REIN, STOP

up stake .... LEAVE, DEPART

pullet .... HEN, POULARD

pulley .... WHEEL, ROLLER, SHEAVE, TACKLE, TRUCKLE

pullman .... BERTH, SLEEPER

pullover .... SHIRT, SWEATER

pullulate ...... BUD, TEEM, BREED, SWARM, GERMINATE

pulmonary disease ...... PHTHISIS

pulp .... PAP, CURD, MASH, MASS, MUSH, PITH, CHYME, PASTE

apple/fruit .... POMACE

grape .... RAPE

in mining .... SLIME

product .... PAPER

slang .... MAGAZINE

pulper ...... MASHER, MACERATOR

pulpit .... BEMA, DESK, ROSTRUM, MINISTRY, PLATFORM

early Christian .... UMBO

preachings .... SERMONS,
HOMILIES
pulpiteer .... PREACHER
pulpy .... PAPPY, PASTY, PITHY,
FLESHY
fruit .... FIG, UVA, DRUPE,
GRAPE, MANGO, PEACH,
CASABA, PAPAYA, AVOCADO,
CANTALOUPE, POMEGRANATE
pulque .... AGAVE, MESCAL
pulsate ...... BEAT, DRUM, THROB,
THRILL, QUIVER, VIBRATE,
PALPITATE
pulsation .... PULSE, BEAT(ING),
HEARTBEAT, THROB(BING),
VIBRATION
pulse .... SEED, ARSIS, THROB,
THUMP, SPHYGMUS,
(HEART)BEAT
beat absence .... ACROTISM
combining form ..... SPHYGMO
instrument for measuring
.... SPHYGMOMETER
kind of .... ECHO, TRIGGER
of the .... SPHYGMIC
plant .... PEA, (SOY)BEAN,
VETCH, LENTIL
split .... DAL
pulverize ...... BRAY, MILL, MULL,
CRUSH, GRIND, POUND,
POWDER, ATOMIZE, CRUMBLE,
LEVIGATE, TRITURATE
pulverized material .... DUST,
POWDER
pulverizing device .... SPIDER
pulverulent .... DUSTY, POWDERY
puma .... CAT, FUR, COUGAR,
PANTHER, CATAMOUNT,
(MOUNTAIN) LION
pumice ...... ROCK, STONE, POLISH
source of .... LAVA
pummel .... BEAT, DRUB, PELT,
BASTE, POUND, BATTER,
THRASH, WALLOP, BELABOR
pump .... QUIZ, SHOE, GRILL,
DRAW (OUT), INFLATE,
INJECTOR, QUESTION,
INTERROGATE
handle .... SWIPE
iron .... EXERCISE, WEIGHT-
LIFT
kind of ...... RAM, LIFT, CHAIN,
FORCE, SUCTION, PRESSURE
part .... RAM, VALVE, PISTON
plunger of .... RAM
pumpernickel .... BROT, BREAD
pumpkin .... PEPO, FRUIT, GOURD,
MELON, SQUASH
"eater" .... PETER
pumpkinseed .... (SUN)FISH
pun .... JOKE, QUIP, GROANER,

QUIBBLE, EQUIVOKE,
WORDPLAY, PARONOMASIA
slang .... WISECRACK
puna .... PLATEAU
punch .... ADE, AWL, BOP, BOX,
GAD, HIT, JAB, BLOW, POKE,
PROD, DRINK, DOUSE, FORCE,
STAMP, BUFFET, PIERCE,
PUPPET, STRIKE, PUNCTURE,
PERFORATE
bowl .... MONTEITH
drunk .... DAZED, DIZZY,
PUNCHY
drunk boxer .... STUMBLE BUM
engraver's .... MATTOIR
in .... TIME IN, CLOCK IN
slang .... PASTE
weak .... TIFF
Punch and ____ .... JUDY
and Judy character .... PUPPET
and Judy dog .... TOBY
wife of .... JUDY
puncheon .... AWL, DIE, CASK,
POST, TIMBER, PERFORATOR
punchinello .... CLOWN, BUFFOON
punchpoked ...... KNITTED SOCKS
punctate .... DOTTED, SPOTTED
punctation .... DOT
punctilio .... NICETY
punctilious .... PRIM, EXACT,
FUSSY, FORMAL, SEVERE,
STRICT, PRECISE, SCRUPULOUS
person .... PRIG, PRUDE
punctual .... EARLY, ON TIME,
PROMPT, TIMELY, TO THE
MINUTE
punctually .... IN GOOD TIME
punctuate .... MARK, POINT,
INTERRUPT
punctuation mark .... DOT,
COLA, COMMA, HYPHEN,
PERIOD, BRACKETS,
(SEMI)COLON, APOSTROPHE,
PARENTHESES, QUESTION
MARK, EXCLAMATION MARK
puncture .... JAB, HOLE, PRICK,
PUNCH, PIERCE, DEFLATE,
OPENING, PERFORATE
pundit .... SAGE, SAVANT,
SCHOLAR, AUTHORITY
slang .... WISE GUY
pung .... SLED, SLEIGH, TOBOGGAN
pungent .... TEZ, KEEN, RACY,
TART, ACERB, ACRID, SALTY,
SHARP, SPICY, TANGY, ZESTY,
BITING, STRONG, CAUSTIC,
GINGERY, PEPPERY, PIQUANT
bulb ..... LEEK, ONION, GARLIC,
SHALLOT, SCALLION
seasoning ..... CURRY, GINGER,
PEPPER, CAYENNE, MUSTARD

Punic citizen ...... CARTHAGINIAN
War battlesite .... ZAMA
belligerent .... ROME,
CARTHAGE
general .... SCIPIO
victor .... ROME
punish .... CANE, DOCK, FINE,
FLOG, FRAP, LASH, WHIP,
SPANK, STRAP, WREAK,
AVENGE, BEAT UP, CHASTEN,
CORRECT, CHASTISE,
PENALIZE, CASTIGATE,
DISCIPLINE
by depriving right to practice
profession .... EXPEL,
DISBAR
imposing fine .... AMERCE
lowering rank .... DEMOTE
retaliation .... REQUITE
cruelly ...... CRUCIFY, TORTURE
errant priest .... UNFROCK
severely .... SLATE
to correct .... CHASTEN,
CHASTISE
punished: sl. .... GOT IT, WORKED
OVER
punishing .... KILLING, CRUSHING,
GRUELING
punishment ...... RAP, FINE, EXILE,
TALION, FORFEIT, PENALTY,
REQUITAL, BASTINADO
capital ..... DEATH, EXECUTION,
GAS CHAMBER, ELECTRIC
CHAIR
convicted person's
.... JUDGMENT, SENTENCE
divine .... PLAGUE
eye for an eye .... TALION
endless .... DAMNATION
instrument of ...... ROD, RACK,
STICK, FERULE, STOCKS,
GARROTE, PILLORY
of .... PENAL, PUNITIVE
retaliatory .... REVENGE,
REPRISAL
unlawful .... LYNCHING
voluntary .... PENANCE
punitive .... PENAL, PUNITORY,
INFLICTIVE
Punjab, capital (India)
.... CHANDIGARH
capital (Pakistan) ...... LAHORE
city/town ..... SIMLA, AMBALA,
PATIALA, SIALKOT, AMRITSAR,
JULLUNDAR
native .... JAT, SIKH
warrior .... SIKH
punk .... AMADOU, TINDER,
TOUCHWOOD
slang .... BUM, MUG,
HOOD(LUM), (SNOTNOSE) KID

punka(h) .... FAN
punkie .... FLY, GNAT, MIDGE
punster .... WAG, WIT, COMIC,
JOKER
punt .... BET, QUANT, SCULL,
WAGER, GAMBLE, PROPEL,
(PLACE)KICK
punter .... BETTOR, KICKER
punty .... POINTIL
puny .... TINY, WEAK, FRAIL,
SMALL, SLIGHT, STUNTED
one .... RUNT
pup ...... CUB, DOG, SEAL, POOCH,
PUPPY, WHELP
pupa .... NYMPH, CHRYSALIS
covering of .... THECA,
COCOON
pupil .... TYRO, WARD, GRADER,
LEARNER, STUDENT, TRAINEE,
DISCIPLE
constrict the .... NARROW
constrictor .... PILOCARPINE
contraction of .... MYOSIS
dilatation of .... MYDRIASIS
dilate the .... WIDEN
dilator .... ATROPINE
organ with .... EYE
pupilage .... NONAGE
puppet .... DOLL, DUPE, PAWN,
TOOL, DUMMY, FIGURE,
MAMMET, MAUMET, VASSAL,
MANIKIN, HIRELING,
MARIONETTE, PENSIONARY
maker .... SARG
Mortimer .... SNERD
show .... GALANTY
show character .... JUDY,
PUNCH(INELLO)
show dog .... TOBY
puppeteer .... SARG
Lewis .... SHARI
puppy .... CUB, DOG, FOP, TAD,
WHELP, UPSTART
purblind .... MOLE-EYED
purchasable .... VENAL,
AVAILABLE
purchase .... BUY, ORDER,
ACQUIRE, PROCURE
or sale of office .... BARRATRY
purchaser ...... EMPTOR, VENDOR,
SHOPPER, CONSUMER
purdah .... VEIL, SCREEN,
ZENANA, CURTAIN
pure .... MERE, NEAT, CLEAN,
CLEAR, FRESH, SHEER, UTTER,
CHASTE, SIMPLE, VIRGIN,
GENUINE, PERFECT, SAINTLY,
ABSOLUTE, VIRTUOUS,
UNDEFILED
air .... OZONE
gold .... TWENTY FOUR CARATS

silver, almost .... STERLING
puree .... SOUP, GUMBO
purfle .... PURL, BORDER,
TRIMMING
purgation .... CATHARSIS
purgative .... JALAP, EMETIC,
PHYSIC, CALOMEL, APERIENT,
LAXATIVE, CASTOR OIL,
CATHARTIC, CLEANSING
bitter .... ALOIN
rectal .... ENEMA
purgatory .... HELL, LIMBO,
EREBUS
purge ...... RID, FLUX, KILL, SOIL,
WASH, ATONE, FLUSH, PHYSIC,
PURIFY, CLEANSE, ABSTERGE,
EXORCISE
purification .... CATHARSIS,
REFINEMENT
by holy water .... BAPTISM
purified .... CLEAR, REFINED,
DISTILLED
capable of being ...... FINABLE
purifier .... REFINERY
purify ...... WASH, CLEAN, CLEAR,
PURGE, FILTER, REFINE,
STRAIN, CLARIFY, CLEANSE,
DISTIL(L), DEPURATE,
SANCTIFY, SUBLIMATE
by distillation .... RECTIFY
by holy water .... BAPTIZE
Puritan .... BLUENOSE,
ROUNDHEAD
nickname .... CANTER
of a sort .... WOWSER
puritanical ...... STRICT, AUSTERE,
STRAITLACED
purity .... HONESTY, CHASTITY,
SANCTITY, CLEANNESS,
INNOCENCE, WHITENESS
purl .... RIB, EDDY, LOOP, REEL,
PEARL, SWIRL, TRILL, WHIRL,
FRINGE, GURGLE, MURMUR,
RIPPLE
purlieu .... HAUNT, LOCALE,
MILIEU, HANGOUT
purlieus .... BOUNDS, LIMITS,
CONFINES, ENVIRONS,
OUTSKIRTS
purloin .... ROB, FILCH, STEAL,
PILFER
purple .... MAUVE, REGAL, ROYAL,
ORNATE, AMETHYST,
IMPERIAL, LAVENDER,
AMARANTHINE
brown .... PUCE
medic .... ALFALFA
red .... CARMINE, CRIMSON,
FUCHSIA
shade .... PLUM, GRAPE, LILAC,
MAUVE, MODENA, ORCHID,

VIOLET, AMARANTH
Purple Heart ...... MEDAL, ORDER,
DECORATION
Rain star .... PRINCE
purplish red .... WINE, CLARET,
MURREY, MAGENTA,
MULBERRY
purport .... AVOW, CLAIM, SENSE,
TENOR, ALLEGE, IMPORT,
INTEND, OBJECT, MEANING,
PROFESS, INTENTION
purpose .... AIM, END, USE, GOAL,
PLAN, SAKE, VIEW, POINT,
DESIGN, INTENT(ION)
purposeful/purposive ...... TELIC,
DECIDED, WILLFUL, DECISIVE,
RESOLUTE
purr .... HUM, SING, SMILE
purse .... KNIT, BURSE, POUCH,
PRIZE, PUCKER, WALLET,
HANDBAG, SPORRAN,
WRINKLE, BILLFOLD,
FINANCES, MONEY(BAG),
RETICULE
purser .... BURSAR, CASHIER
purslane .... WEED
pursuant .... ACCORDING,
FOLLOWING
pursue .... DOG, HUNT, SEEK,
CHASE, COURT, HOUND,
TRAIL, FOLLOW, CARRY ON,
CONTINUE, GO AFTER, RUN
AFTER
a tort .... SUE
foxes .... HUNT
hares .... SNARE
pursuer .... HOUND, HUNTER,
PROSECUTOR
pursuit .... CHASE, QUEST,
CAREER, VENTURE,
ENDEAVOR, OCCUPATION
pursy .... FAT, OBESE, PUDGY,
PUCKERED
purulence .... PUS
purulent .... PYIC
purvey ...... GIVE, CATER, SUPPLY,
DELIVER, FURNISH, PROVIDE,
PROVISION
purveyor .... DONOR, SUTLER,
CATERER, PROVIDER
of the past .... ICEMAN
purview .... VISION, INSIGHT,
SCOPE (OF VISION)
pus .... MATTER, SANIES,
PURULENCE, SUPPURATION
accumulation .... EMPYEMA
cause formation of .... FESTER
collection in tissue
.... ABSCESS
filled cavity .... VOMICA
form .... FESTER, MATURATE,

SUPPURATE
formation of .... PYOSIS
forming organism
.... PNEUMOCOCCI,
STREPTOCOCCI
in the urine .... PYURIA
of .... PYIC, PYOID
substance .... PYIN
push .... URGE, ELBOW, FORCE,
IMPEL, NUDGE, PINCH, SHOVE,
CLIQUE, HUSTLE, JOSTLE,
PROPEL, THRUST, PRESS(URE)
along .... PLOD
colloquial ...... DRIVE, EFFORT,
ENTERPRISE
firmly .... RAM
forward .... MOVE, ADVANCE
in .... ENTER
off .... LEAVE, DEPART
on .... PROCEED, CONTINUE
with nose .... NUZZLE
pushcart operator ...... VENDER,
VENDOR, PEDDLER
pusher .... SHOVER, PEDDLER,
RACKETEER
commodity of .... LSD, POT,
DOPE, HEROIN, COCAINE,
NARCOTIC, MARIJUANA
pushing .... ARROGANT,
BUMPTIOUS, CONCEITED
pushover .... DUPE, SETUP,
SUCKER
pushy .... FORCEFUL, INSOLENT,
AGGRESSIVE
pusillanimous .... COWARDLY,
IRRESOLUTE
puss ...... CAT, FACE, GIRL, HARE,
MOUTH
pussy .... CAT, CATKIN
pussycat .... DOLL, TABBY, KITTEN
pussyfoot .... GUMSHOE
pustule .... BLAIN, BUBBLE,
FESTER, PIMPLE, BLISTER
caused by insect bite
.... WHEAL, WHELK
content .... PUS
eyelash .... STYE
on face and back .... ACNE
on neck .... MALANDERS
scar .... POCK
put .... FIX, LAY, SET, PUSH,
APPLY, DRIVE, IMPEL, PLACE,
PLANT, STATE, WAGER,
IMPOSE, EXPRESS
a blanket on .... COVER
a crew again .... REMAN
a watch on .... TIME
aside .... DAFF, DISCARD
aside: sl. .... STOW
at rest .... ALLAY
away .... KILL, STOW, STORE,

CONSUME
back .... REPOSIT, RESTORE
back in the microwave
.... REHEAT, REWARM
back on the payroll
.... REHIRE
by .... STASH
down .... ABASE, CRUSH,
PLUMP, DEMEAN, HUMBLE
down in writing .... INDITE,
RECORD
effort/forth .... EXERT,
PROPOSE
faith in .... TRUST(ED)
film in camera .... LOAD
forth a perplexing problem
.... POSE(D)
forward ..... PRESENT, PROPOSE
in .... ENTER, FOIST, INSERT,
INSTALL, INTROMIT
in a cask .... BARRELED
in a new voice .... REDUB
in irons .... FETTER, MANACLE,
SHACKLE
in jeopardy .... ENDANGER
in office .... ELECT
in the wrong pigeonhole
.... MISASSIGN
in writing .... RECORD, SET
DOWN
into a cipher .... ENCODE
into use anew .... RECYCLE
it there .... SHAKE
off .... DOFF, AVOID, DEFER,
DELAY, DODGE, EVADE, STALL,
DIVERT, POSTPONE
off position .... LUXATE
on .... DON, APPLY, COVER,
CLOTHE, SPREAD
on a ship .... LADE
on guard/notice .... WARN,
ALERT
on the block .... SELL,
AUCTION
on the Exchange .... LIST
one's foot down .... INSIST,
REFUSE, REJECT
out .... EMIT, OUST, EGEST,
DOUSE, EVICT, EXPEL,
QUENCH, DISMISS, PUBLISH,
INCOMMODE
out of office .... UNSEAT
right .... AMEND
side by side .... JUXTAPOSE
the kibosh on .... NIXED
to flight .... FEEZE, CHASED,
ROUT(ED)
to rights .... EMEND
to test .... ASSAYED
to work .... HARNESS

together .... MERGE, CREATE,
COMBINE, COMPILE, ASSEMBLE
together again .... RE-FORM
under restraint .... ARREST
up .... ANTE, POST, SHOW,
BUILD, ERECT, LODGE
up with .... BEAR, ABIDE(D),
ENDURE(D), TOLERATE(D)
upon .... BESET, IMPOSE,
INTRUDE
with force .... CAST, HURL,
FLING, THROW
putamen .... PIT, STONE
putative ...... ALLEGED, REPUTED,
PRESUMED, SUPPOSED
putdown .... INSULT
Put-in-Bay hero .... PERRY
Putnam, Revolutionary general
.... ISRAEL
put-on .... AIRS, HOAX, SHAM,
STAGE
putrefaction .... DECAY,
ROT(TING)
putrefy .... ROT, DECAY,
DECOMPOSE
putrescent .... ROTTING,
DECAYING
putrid ...... FOUL, RANK, ROTTEN,
CORRUPT, DECAYED, STINKING
putsch .... UPRISING, REBELLION
puttee .... PUTTY, GAITER,
LEGGING
putter .... CLUB, IDLE, LOAF,
DABBLE, DAWDLE, NIGGLE,
TINKER
puttier .... GLAZIER
putting area .... GREEN
putty .... CEMENT
knife .... SPATULA
puttyroot .... ORCHID
Putumayo river .... ICA
puzzle ...... POSER, REBUS, STUMP,
BAFFLE, ENIGMA, KITTLE,
RIDDLE, CONFUSE, DILEMMA,
MYSTIFY, NONPLUS, PERPLEX,
BEWILDER, QUESTION,
CONUNDRUM, DUM(B)FOUND
certain word ...... ACROSTIC
inexplicable .... MYSTERY
like crossword .... SCRABBLE
picture .... JIGSAW
using anagrams
.... LOGOGRIPH
using clues .... CROSSWORD
word .... LOGOGRAPH
puzzled .... STUCK, STUMPED
puzzler .... CRUX, POSER
puzzler's problem, often
.... ERASURE
wish .... LEARN A WORD

(OR TWO)

puzzling .... ODD, BAFFLING, KNOTTING, ENIGMATIC

mystery .... ENIGMA

problem .... POSER

thing .... CRUX

PX .... COMMISSARY, POST EXCHANGE

pygarg .... ADDAX

Pygmalion's creator .... SHAW

statue/love .... GALATEA

pygmy .... RUNT, ATOMY, DWARF, MINIM, PIGMY, MIDGET, MANIKIN, HOMUNCULUS

antelope .... ORIBI

Pyle, _____ .... GOMER

newspaperman .... ERNIE

pylon ...... POST, TOWER, MARKER, GATEWAY, PYRAMID

Pylos king .... NESTOR

pyralidid .... MOTH

pyramid .... CONE, HEAP, PILE, STACK

builder of largest .... KHUFU, CHEOPS

builders .... EGYPTIANS

dweller .... UNAS, DJOSER

pharaoh entombed in .... KHUFU, KHAFRE, MENKAURE

site of .... EL GIZA

terraced .... ZIKURAT, ZIGGURAT

truncated .... PYLON

Pyramid of the Sun site .... TENOCHTITLIN

Step, builder of .... IMHOTEP

Pyramus' lover: myth .... THISBE

pyre .... PILE, BONFIRE

pyrene .... PIT, STONE, NUTLET

Pyrenees goat .... IBEX

highest point .... ANETO, ANETHOU

mammal .... DESMAN

republic .... ANDORRA

pyretic .... FEVERISH

pyrexia .... FEVER

pyriform .... PEAR-SHAPED

pyrite .... FOOL'S GOLD

pyrogenic .... IGNEOUS

pyromaniac .... FIREBUG, ARSONIST, INCENDIARY

pyrope .... GARNET

pyrosis .... BRASH, HEARTBURN

pyrotechnics .... FIREWORKS

pyrrhic .... WAR DANCE

like victory .... CADMEAN

victory site .... ASCULUM

Pyrrhonism .... SKEPTICISM

Pythagoras birthplace .... SAMOS

forte .... MATHEMATICS

Pythia .... ORACLE, PRIESTESS

city of the .... DELPHI

house of the .... APOLLO'S TEMPLE

original .... VIRGIN

purifying rite of the ..... BATH

skeptic .... DAPHNITAS

Pythias' friend .... DAMON

python .... BOA, SNAKE, SERPENT, ANACONDA

deity .... ZOMBI(E)

Python, killer of .... APOLLO

shrine guarded by .... GE'S, GAEA'S

pythoness .... PRIESTESS, PROPHETESS, SOOTHSAYER

pythonic .... ORACULAR, PROPHETIC

pyx .... BOX, CIBORIUM

pyxis .... BOX, CASE, VASE

Q, Greek .... KAPPA

in chess .... QUEEN

Qatar's cape .... RAKAN

capital .... DOHA

city/town .... DUKHAN, UMM SAI'D

gulf .... PERSIAN

language .... ARABIC

monetary unit .... RIYAL

QED, part of .... QUOD, ERAT, DEMONSTRANDUM

quack .... CRY, FAKER, CROCUS, IMPOSTOR, SCIOLIST, WISEACRE, CHARLATAN, DEMAGOGUE, EMPIRIC(IST), MOUNTEBANK

crier .... DUCK

doctor's aide .... TOADY, TOADEATER

medicine ...... HERB, NOSTRUM

method of a .... QUACKERY

quad .... JAIL, QUOD, PRISON

quadragesima .... LENT

quadragenarian .... FORTYISH

quadragesimal .... FORTY, LENTEN

quadrangle .... CAMPUS, SQUARE, TETRAGON, (COURT)YARD

quadrant .... ARC, FOURTH, ALTIMETER

graduated edge of .... LIMB

quadrate .... AGREE, SQUARE, CONFORM, QUARTER, RECTANGLE, RECTANGULAR

quadrel .... TILE

quadriga .... CHARIOT

quadrille .... LANC(I)ERS, (SQUARE)DANCE

card .... MATADOR

second highest trump .... MANILLA

quadriplegia .... PARALYSIS

quadrivium, part of ...... MUSIC, GEOMETRY, ASTRONOMY

quadroon ...... HYBRID, MULATTO

quadrumane .... APE, BABOON, MONKEY, PRIMATE

quadruped .... ASS, CAMEL, HIPPO, RHINO, TAPIR, ZEBRA, DONKEY, MAMMAL, GIRAFFE, FOUR-FOOTED

quadruple .... FOURFOLD

quaff .... ALE, NOG, GULP, DRINK, SWILL, SWALLOW

fall/rustic .... CIDER

holiday .... NOG

quagga-like animal .... ZEBRA, DONKEY

quaggy .... MIRY, SOFT, BOGGY, FLABBY

quag(mire) .... BOG, FEN, MIRE, MORASS, DILEMMA, QUICKSAND

quahaug/quahog .... CLAM

young .... LITTLENECK

quail .... BIRD, WILT, COLIN, COWER, WINCE, CRINGE, FLINCH, RECOIL, BOBWHITE, PARTRIDGE

flock .... BEVY, COVEY

quaint .... ODD, ANTIQUE, CURIOUS, STRANGE, UNUSUAL, FANCIFUL, SINGULAR, OLD-FASHIONED

humor .... DROLLERY

quake .... SHAKE, WAVER, QUIVER, SHIVER, TREMOR, SHUDDER, TEMBLOR, TREMBLE, EARTHQUAKE

Quaker .... FRIEND

colonist .... PENN

gray .... ACIER

in a grove .... ASPEN

ladies .... BLUETS

midweek of a ..... WEDNESDAY
pronoun of .... THEE
quaking tree ...... ASPEN, POPLAR
quaky .... SHAKY
qualification ...... SKILL, ABILITY,
PROVISO, CONDITION,
EXPERIENCE
qualified .... FIT, ABLE, CAPABLE,
LIMITED, COMPETENT
qualifier .... MODIFIER
qualify .... FIT, PASS, LIMIT,
ENTITLE, DESCRIBE, RESTRICT
qualifying word .... ADVERB,
ADJECTIVE
quality .... AURA, KIND, TONE,
GRADE, TRAIT, NATURE,
STATUS, CALIBER, FEATURE,
PROPERTY, ATTRIBUTE,
CHARACTER(ISTIC)
admirable .... GRIT
bad/poor .... BUM, PUNK,
LOUSY, INFERIOR
colloquial .... CLASS
distinctive/pervasive ..... AURA
distinguishing .... TRAIT
of being fleeting
.... TRANSIENCE
of high .... TONY, PLUSH
of sound .... TONE, TIMBRE
special .... (DE)LUXE
qualm .... PANG, DOUBT, NAUSEA,
REGRET, TWINGE, REMORSE,
SCRUPLE, MISGIVING,
UNEASINESS, COMPUNCTION
qualmish .... QUEER, QUEASY,
NAUSEOUS
quamash .... LILY, CAMAS(S)
quandary ...... PLIGHT, DILEMMA,
NONPLUS, STRAIT(S),
PREDICAMENT
Quandary Peak site
.... COLORADO
quant .... POLE, PUNT, PROPEL
quantify .... COUNT, MEASURE
quantity .... LOT, SUM, BULK,
DOSE, MASS, AUGHT, BATCH,
GRIST, AMOUNT, NUMBER,
PORTION
abundant .... SPATE
fixed .... UNIT
indefinite .... ANY, MANY,
SOME, HANDFUL, SEVERAL
large .... LOTS, RAFF, RAFT,
SLEW, BUSHEL
small .... BIT, DAB, DASH,
LICK, WHIT, SCRUPLE,
SMIDGEN, SCANTLING
Quantrill's men .... RAIDERS
quantum ...... AMOUNT, PORTION,
QUANTITY, MAGNETON,
PARTICLE

of heat energy .... PHOTON
of sound energy .... PHONON
quarantine ...... DETAIN, ISOLATE,
CORDON OFF, ISOLATION
building/ship .... LAZARETTO
signal .... YELLOW JACK
quarrel .... JAR, ROW, FEUD, FUSS,
MIFF, SPAT, TIFF, BRAWL,
BROIL, BRUSH, CLASH, FIGHT,
FLITE, RUN-IN, SCRAP,
(AF)FRAY, BICKER, FRACAS,
STRIFE, BRABBLE, DISPUTE,
RUCTION, WRANGLE,
CONFLICT, SQUABBLE,
ALTERCATION
quarreling ...... AT LOGGERHEADS
quarrelsome .... HOSTILE,
SCRAPPY, BELLICOSE,
COMBATIVE, LITIGIOUS,
PUGNACIOUS, BELLIGERENT
quarry .... PIT, GAME, MINE,
PREY, CATCH, DIG UP,
TARGET, VICTIM, EXCAVATE
output .... GRAVEL
quarrying tool .... TRAPAN,
TREPAN
quarryman .... STONECUTTER
quart(e) .... CARTE
quarter .... SPAN, LODGE, MERCY,
BILLET, CANTON, FOURTH,
LODGING, TWO BITS, DISTRICT
eagles .... OLD GOLD
note .... CROTCHET
of a circle .... QUADRANT
phase .... DIPHASE
round .... OVOLO
quartern .... GILL
quarters .... ABODE, ROOMS,
BILLET, BARRACKS, LODGINGS
slang .... DIGGINGS
quartet .... FOUR(SOME)
quarts, 4 .... GALLON
quartz .... CACO, ONYX, AGATE,
CHERT, FLINT, PRASE, SILEX,
TOPAZ, JASPER, MORION,
PLASMA, SILICA, CAT'S EYE,
CITRINE, CRYSTAL, RUBASSE,
SARD(INE), SINOPLE,
AMETHYST, SARDONYX,
CAIRNGORM, CARNELIAN,
AVENTURINE, CHALCEDONY,
CHRYSOPRASE
quartzite .... SANDSTONE
quash .... VOID, ANNUL, QUELL,
SQUELCH, SET ASIDE,
SUPPRESS
in law .... ABATE
quasi .... AS IF, SEEMINGLY
quass .... KVASS
quaternion .... TETRAD
quatrain .... POEM, STANZA

quaver .... SHAKE, TRILL,
TREMBLE, TREMOLO
quavery .... TREMULOUS
quay .... PIER, LEVEE, WHARF,
LANDING
quean .... JADE, MINX, SLUT,
HUSSY, PROSTITUTE
queasy .... QUALMISH,
NAUSEATED, FASTIDIOUS
Quebec acre .... ARPENT
bay .... HUDSON, CHALEUR
cape .... GASPE
capital .... QUEBEC
city/town .... HULL, LAVAL,
GRANBY, VERDUN, LA SALLE,
BROSSARD, GATINEAU,
JOLIETTE, MONTREAL,
JONQUIERE
dam .... MERCIER
gulf .... SAINT LAWRENCE
island .... ALMA, VERTE,
COUDRES, LIEVRES, ORLEANS
lake .... BROME, MINTO,
ALLARD, AYLMER, KIAMIKA,
BROMPTON, MEGANTIC,
CHAMPLAIN, TREMBLANT
mountain .... JACQUES-CARTIER
peninsula ...... GASPE, UNGAVA
river .... BELL, NORD, YORK,
DITTON, GEORGE, LIEVRE,
MATANE, MOISIE, OTTAWA,
FEUILLES, SAGUENAY
Quechuan .... INCA(N), INDIAN,
PERUVIAN
queen ...... REINA, RULER, REGINA
ace combination .... TENACE
beheaded .... ANTOINETTE
"City of the South"
.... SYDNEY
English .... ANNE, BESS,
VICTORIA, ELIZABETH
fairy .... MAB, UNA, TITANIA
Greek gods' .... HERA
it .... DOMINEER
legendary .... DIDO
Moslem .... BEGUM
nicknamed "The Catholic"
.... ISABELLA
of Aquitaine .... ELEANOR
daughter of .... MARIE
husband of .... HENRY II,
LOUIS VII
son of .... JOHN, RICHARD
of Calydon .... ALTHEA
of Crete .... PASIPHAE
husband of .... MINOS
offspring .... MINOTAUR
of gods ...... HERA, JUNO, SATI
of Ithaca .... PENELOPE
of Iceland ..... BRUN(N)HILD(E)
of Lydia .... OMPHALE

of Palmyra .... ZENOBIA
of scat .... ELLA
of spades in solo .... BASTA
of Spain, deposed
.... ISABELLA
of the Antilles .... CUBA
of the jungle .... SHEENA
of the Nile .... CLEO(PATRA)
of the nymphs .... MAB
of Thebes .... JOCASTA
Olympian .... HERA
Roman gods' .... JUNO
Sheba .... BALKIS
widowed .... DOWAGER
Queen Anne's lace
.... (WILD)CARROT
Charlotte Island Indian
.... HAIDA
Mab author .... SHELLEY
queening .... APPLE
queenly .... NOBLE, REGAL,
ROYAL, REGINAL, MAJESTIC
Queens .... BOROUGH
Queensland's bay .... ALBATROSS
capital .... BRISBANE
city/town .... CAIRNS, IPSWICH,
BUNDABERG, GLADSTONE,
REDCLIFFE, TOOWOOMBA,
TOWNSVILLE, ROCKHAMPTON
island .... BANKS
mountain .... BARTLE FRERE
river .... ARCHER, BALONNE
Queenstown .... COBH
queer .... ODD, RUM, FUNNY,
GIDDY, WEIRD, CRANKY,
BIZARRE, ERRATIC, STRANGE,
SINGULAR, ECCENTRIC
bird .... NUT, CRANK
notion .... KINK
person .... NUT, KOOK,
SCREWBALL
slang .... SHADY, SPOIL,
HOMOSEXUAL, COUNTERFEIT
quell .... END, ALLAY, CRUSH,
QUASH, QUIET, SUBDUE,
SUPPRESS
quelque chose .... TRIFLE
quench .... COOL, SATE, DOUSE,
SLAKE, PUT OUT, SATISFY,
EXTINGUISH
quercetin .... DYE, FLAVIN(E)
quercitron .... DYE, OAK
quercus genus .... OAKS
querist .... ASKER
quern .... MILL, GRINDER
querulous ...... FRETFUL, PEEVISH,
WHINING, PETULANT
query ...... ASK, DOUBT, INQUIRY,
QUESTION
quest .... AIM, GOAL, HUNT,
PROBE, DESIRE, SEARCH,

PURSUIT, SEEK(ING)
question .... ASK, POSE, QUIZ,
DOUBT, GRILL, ISSUE, POINT,
QUERY, DISPUTE, INQUIRY,
PROBLEM, CHALLENGE,
INTERROGATE
and answer teaching
.... CATECHESIS
baffling .... POSER, DILEMMA
of ownership .... WHOSE
questionable .... MOOT, FISHY,
SHADY, DUBIOUS, SUSPECT,
DOUBTFUL, DEBATABLE,
UNCERTAIN, SUSPICIOUS
questioning .... CURIOUS,
PROBING, ROGATORY
questionnaire ...... POLL, SURVEY
quetzal .... BIRD, TROGON
queue .... CUE, FILE, LINE, BRAID,
PLAIT, TRESS, (PIG)TAIL
torero's .... COLETA
**Quezon, first Philippine
president** .... MANUEL
wife of .... AURORA
quibble .... PUN, CARP, QUIP,
CAVIL, EVADE, PALTER,
EVASION, SHUFFLE
quick ...... APT, FAST, YARE, SPRY,
AGILE, ALERT, ALIVE, BRIEF,
BRISK, FLEET, HASTY, RAPID,
READY, SWIFT, PROMPT,
SNAPPY, VOLANT, PREGNANT
answer .... RIPOSTE
assets .... CASH
bread .... MUFFIN, BISCUIT
drink .... SNORT
in learning .... APT
look .... GLANCE, EYEBEAM,
ONCEOVER
response to helm .... YARE
sharp blow .... SLAP
tempered .... FIERY, SPUNKY,
IRACUND, HOT(HEADED),
IRASCIBLE
witted .... KEEN, ALERT,
SHARP, SMART, WITTY,
BRAINY, NIMBLE
witticism .... SALLY
quicken ...... STIR, HURRY, SPEED,
(A)ROUSE, HASTEN, REVIVE,
VIVIFY, ANIMATE, REFRESH,
ENERGIZE, ACCELERATE
quickie .... DRINK, MOVIE,
B-PICTURE
quickly .... ANON, FAST, SOON,
AMAIN, APACE, PRESTO,
PRONTO
in music .... SUBITO
slang .... PDQ
quicksand .... BOG, MIRE,

MORASS, SLOUGH, SYRT(IS),
PITFALL, (DEATH)TRAP
quickset .... SLIP, HEDGE,
CUTTING
quicksilver .... AZOTH, MERCURY,
VOLATILE, MERCURIAL
quid .... CUD, PLUG, POUND,
SOVEREIGN
pro quo .... TIT-FOR-TAT,
SUBSTITUTE
quiddle .... FUSS
quidnunc .... SNOOP, GOSSIP,
BUSYBODY
Quien _____? (Who knows?)
.... SABE
quiescent .... QUIET, STILL,
LATENT, DORMANT, INACTIVE
quiet .... MIM, MUM, CALM,
ALLAY, STILL, GENTLE,
HUSH(ED), PACIFY, SERENE,
SILENT, SILENCE, PEACEFUL,
STILLNESS
interval .... LULL
quietism, teacher of .... MOLINOS
quietude .... REST, ORDER, PEACE,
SILENCE, CALMNESS,
STILLNESS
quietus ...... RELEASE, ACQUITTAL,
DEATH(BLOW), DISCHARGE
quill .... PEN, REMEX, SPINE,
BARREL, PINION, CALAMUS,
FEATHER, PLECTRUM
driver .... WRITER
feathers ...... CALAMI, REMIGES
pig .... PORCUPINE
quillai .... SOAPBARK
quilt .... DUVET, CADDOW, STITCH,
BEDCOVER, BEDSPREAD,
COMFORT(ER), PATCHWORK
stuffing .... DUVETYN(E),
EIDERDOWN
quilting party .... BEE
Quimby, ... HARRIET
occupation .... AVIATRIX
quince .... BEL, POME
quinia .... QUININ(E)
quinine, illness remedied by
.... MALARIA
source .... CINCHONA
water .... TONIC
quinnat salmon .... CHINOOK
quinsy .... TONSILLITIS
quintessence .... PITH, CREAM,
ELIXIR
quintuple .... FIVEFOLD
Quintuplet Altar site .... LA
VENTA
quintuplets .... DIONNE, FISHER
quip .... MOT, GIBE, JEST, JOKE,
SALLY, SNEER, RETORT,

QUIBBLE, (WISE)CRACK, WITTICISM
quipper Mort .... SAHL
quippish .... WITTY, SARCASTIC
quipus .... KNOTS
keepers of the ...... CAMAYOCS
system .... TALLYING
system, users of .... INCAS
quire .... PAPER
20 .... REAM
var. .... CHOIR
quirk .... JIBE, KINK, TURN, HABIT,
SHIFT, TRICK, TWIST, ODDITY,
STROKE, MANNERISM,
PECULIARITY
quirky .... FLAKY, KINKY,
DEVIANT, TWISTED
quisling .... TRAITOR,
COLLABORATOR
fifth columnist .... VIDKUN
quit .... RID, FREE, STOP, CEASE,
CLEAR, LEAVE, REPAY,
DESIST, GIVE UP, RESIGN,
RETIRE, ABANDON,
DISCHARGE, RELINQUISH
quitch .... WEED, GRASS
quitclaim .... RELEASE,
QUITTANCE
document .... DEED
quite .... ALL, VERY, TRULY,
ENOUGH, REALLY, WHOLLY,
UTTERLY, ENTIRELY,
SOMEWHAT

Quito is capital of ...... ECUADOR
quits .... EVEN
quittance .... FREEDOM, PAYMENT,
RECEIPT, REPRISAL
quitter .... LOSER, COWARD,
AVOIDER, SHIRKER, WELSHER
quiver .... QUAKE, SHAKE, THRILL,
TREMOR, FLUTTER, SHUDDER,
TREMBLE, VIBRATE
content of .... ARROWS
quivering .... PALPITANT,
FLUTTERING
tree .... ASPEN, POPLAR
Quixote's giant .... WINDMILL
horse .... ROSINANTE
love .... DULCINEA
squire .... SANCHO (PANZA)
title .... DON
quixotic .... ABSURD, FOOLISH,
UTOPIAN, ROMANTIC,
VISIONARY, WHIMSICAL,
CHIVALROUS
quiz .... ASK, HOAX, JOKE, PROBE,
TEASE, BANTER, QUESTION,
EXAM(INATION)
kid .... PRODIGY
master .... MC, HOST, EMCEE
show .... JEOPARDY, FAMILY
FEUD, PRESS YOUR LUCK
quizzical .... ODD, QUEER,
COMICAL
quod .... JAIL, PRISON
quoddy .... SAILBOAT

quodlibet .... DEBATE, MEDLEY
quoin .... (B)LOCK, WEDGE,
CORNER, KEYSTONE
var. .... COIN
quoit .... DISCUS, RINGER
quoits pin .... HOB, PEG
player ...... QUOITER, THROWER
target .... HOB, PEG, TEE
quomodo .... WAY, MEANS,
MANNER
quondam .... ONCE, FORMER,
WHILOM, ONETIME,
ERSTWHILE
quonset hut .... PREFAB,
BUILDING
British kind .... NISSEN
quorum .... PLENUM, MAJORITY
quota .... SHARE, PORTION,
ALLOTMENT
quotation .... CITAL, PRICE,
EXCERPT, EXTRACT, CITATION,
REPETITION
ending speech/story .... TAG
opening chapter ..... EPIGRAPH
reader .... SPECULATOR,
STOCKBROKER
quote .... CITE, REFER, ADDUCE,
RECITE, REPEAT, ABSTRACT
quoth .... SAID, SPOKE
quotha .... INDEED
quotidian .... DAILY
quotient .... RATIO, RESULT,
FRACTION

R

R, Greek .... RHO
Hebrew .... RESH
in chemistry .... RADICAL
in chess .... ROOK
in mathematics .... RATIO,
RADIUS
pronunciation like L
.... LALLATION
Ra .... SUN GOD
crown of .... ATEN
in chemistry .... RADIUM
symbol of .... SUNDISK
wife of .... MUT
raad .... CATFISH
Rabat is capital of .... MOROCCO
rabato .... RUFF, COLLAR
Rabbat Ammon .... AMMAN
rabbet .... JOINT, REBATE
rabbi .... AMORA, MASTER,
TEACHER
seminary .... YESHIVA
teachings .... MISHNA(H)

rabbinical .... CHURCHLY,
PASTORAL
early group .... AMORA
rabbit ...... CONY, HARE, ANGORA,
RODENT, LEPORID,
LAGOMORPH, COTTONTAIL
baby .... KID
breeding place .... WARREN
ears .... ANTENNA
family .... LEPORID
female .... DOE
fever .... TULAR(A)EMIA
foot .... CHARM, TALISMAN
fur .... CON(E)Y, LAPIN
fur hat .... CASTOR
hunting dog .... HARRIER
hybrid .... LEPORIDE
like rodent .... MARMOT
male .... BUCK
pen .... HUTCH
pet name .... BUNNY
rock .... HYRAX

tail of .... SCUT
variety .... LOP
young .... BUNNY
rabbitry .... HUTCH, WARREN
rabble .... MOB, SCUM, CROWD,
RAGTAG, TRASH,
DOGGERY, CANAILLE,
(RIFF)RAFF
rouser .... RIOTER, INCITER,
AGITATOR, DEMAGOGUE
the .... MASSES, POPULACE, HOI
POLLOI
Rabelais, Fr. satirist
.... FRANCOIS
Rabelaisian .... EARTHY
voracity .... GARGANTUAN
APPETITE
rabid .... RAGING, FURIOUS,
VIOLENT, ZEALOUS,
FANATICAL
rabies .... LYSSA, MADNESS,
HYDROPHOBIA

RCA trademark .... NIPPER
raccoon .... TREEBEAR
  tropical cousin of .... COATI,
                    PANDA
race .... CLAN, FOLK, RUSH,
        SPEED, TRIBE, FAMILY,
        PEOPLE, STIRPS, CHANNEL,
      COMPETE, CONTEST, LINEAGE,
        MANKIND, PEDIGREE
  black .... NEGROID
  channel .... FLUME
  contestant .... ENTRY,
        ATHLETE, ENTRANT
  division .... HEAT, NEGROID,
    CAUCASIAN, MONGOLOID
  downhill .... SLALOM
  easily won .... RUNAWAY
  engine .... REV
  hotrods' .... DRAG
  kind of .... RAT, DERBY,
    HORSE, SWEEPS, REGATTA,
    MARATHON, STOCK-CAR,
    TROT(TING), SWEEPSTAKE(S)
  of dwarfs .... NIBELUNG
  official .... TIMER
  open to anyone ..... FREE-FOR-
                   ALL
  pertaining to .... ETHNIC
  prelims .... HEATS
  short .... DASH, SPRINT
  start of .... BREAKAWAY
  sulky .... TROT
  track .... OVAL, PATH, TURF,
      CINDER, HIPPODROME
  track tout: Brit. .... SPIV
  water .... ARROYO
  white .... CAUCASIAN
  yellow .... MONGOLOID
racecourse/racetrack ...... OVAL,
  TURF, ARENA, TRACK, CIRCUS,
          HIPPODROME
  character .... TOUT, TIPSTER,
          DOPESTER
  circuit .... LAP
  combining form .... DROME
  cover .... TANBARK
  fence .... RAIL
  marker .... LANE, PYLON
  name/site of .... ASCOT,
    EPSOM, HIALEAH, JAMAICA,
      PIMLICO, SARATOGA
  official .... TIMER, STARTER
  performers .... HORSES
  section .... BEND, STRETCH
racehorse .... TROTTER
  disability .... SPAVIN,
    GLANDERS, STRINGHALT
  enclosure/exercise area
  .... PADDOCK
  inferior .... PLATER, SLEEPER
  kind of .... MUDDER, PLATER

  winless .... MAIDEN
raceme .... CLUSTER, PANICLE
racer .... MILER, HOTROD,
    RUNNER, SPRINTER,
    TRACKMAN, (BLACK)SNAKE
  course of .... LANE
raceway .... CHANNEL
Rachel's father .... LABAN
  husband .... JACOB, ISRAEL
  maid .... BILHAH
  sister .... LEAH
  son .... JOSEPH, BENJAMIN
rachis .... STEM, SPINE, BACKBONE
rachitis .... RICKETS
Rachmaninoff, composer/
  pianist .... SERGEI
  title of .... MAESTRO
racial .... FAMILY, TRIBAL,
            ANCESTRAL
  division, of .... ETHNIC
  origin .... ETHNOGENY
Racine (Jean), Fr. poet
  .... BAPTISTE
  masterpiece .... PHEDRE
racing colors .... SILKS
  course .... CAREER,
          HIPPODROME
  program .... CARD, FORM
  sailboat .... MOTH
  scull .... WHERRY
racism .... BIGOTRY, PREJUDICE
  slang .... JIM CROW
racist .... BIGOT, HATER
rack .... GIN, FRAME, STAND,
  CLOUDS, STRESS, ANGUISH,
  TENSION, TORMENT, TORTURE,
  DISTRESS, UPHEAVAL,
         WRECKAGE
  corn .... CRIB
  display .... EASEL
  fodder .... CRIB, HACK,
          CRATCH
  food .... FLAKE
  for storing boxes .... RICK
  for storing hay/grain ..... BAY,
          BIN
  hat .... TREE
  horse's .... GAIT, PACE
  lay on the .... AGONIZE
  partner of .... RUIN
racket .... BAT, DIN, BABEL,
  NOISE, HUBBUB, PADDLE,
  RUMPUS, UPROAR, CAROUSE,
  REVEL(RY), SNOWSHOE
  hold on .... GRIP
  -shaped footwear
  .... SNOWSHOE
  slang .... LINE, BUSINESS,
         PROFESSION
  string .... CATGUT
racketeer .... HOODLUM, MOBSTER

rackets .... SQUASH, TENNIS
raconteur .... NARRATOR
  forte of ...... STORIES, STORIER,
    STORYTELLER, ANECDOTES
racy .... FRESH, SMART, SPICY,
  LIVELY, RISQUE, PIQUANT,
  PUNGENT, ZESTFUL, SPIRITED
Radames' love .... AIDA
radar device, for short .... TFR
  display .... SCAN
  image .... BLIP
  like device .... SONAR
  part of word .... RADIO,
    DETECTING, RANGING
  screen .... SCOPE
  screen flash .... BLIP
  sound .... BEEP, RACON
  system .... SHORAN
  transmitter .... BEACON
Radcliffe's sister .... VASSAR
raddle .... KNIT, OCHER, STICK,
         INTERWEAVE
Radek, Soviet writer .... KARL
Radha's consort .... KRISHNA
radian .... ARC
radiance .... GLORY, LIGHT,
  LUSTER, SPLENDOR,
  BRIGHTNESS, BRILLIANCE,
        REFULGENCE
radiant .... AGLOW, BRIGHT,
  BEAMING, GLOWING, SHINING,
  GLORIOUS, SPARKLING
  combining form .... HELI(O)
  energy .... RADIATION
  look .... BEAM
radiate .... BEAM, CAST, EMIT,
  SHINE, DIVERGE, TRANSMIT
radiation .... EMISSION, DIFFUSION
  measure .... ROENTGEN
radiator .... HEATER
  additive .... COOLANT
radical ...... BASIC, JINGO, REBEL,
  ULTRA, DRASTIC, EXTREME,
  JACOBIN, LEFTIST, FIREBRAND
  colloquial .... RED, PINK
  sign .... SQUARE ROOT
  slang .... COMMIE
  with valence of two ..... DYAD
radicle .... RADIX, ROOT(LET)
radio .... WIRELESS
  active shower .... FALLOUT
  ad .... COMMERCIAL
  aerial .... ANTENNA
  broadcasting outfit .... VOA
  cabinet .... CONSOLE
  control, kind of .... REMOTE
  converting device .... BALUN
  dash in .... DAH
  detector .... RADAR
  dial .... TUNER
  father of .... MARCONI

frequency band .... CHANNEL
gear .... AERIAL, ANTENNA
interference .... STATIC
news, brief .... FLASH
newscaster .... SWING,
   MURROW, CRONKITE, HEATTER
operator, amateur .... HAM
performer .... TALENT,
   NEWSCASTER
performer: sl. .... DEEJAY
person .... DISC JOCKEY
receiver .... SET, CRYSTAL,
   TRANSISTOR
reception disturbance
   .... STATIC, STRAYS
signal .... BEEP
signal for aviators .... BEAM
signoff .... ROGER
station ID .... CALL LETTERS
term .... ROGER
transmitting antenna
   .... RADIATOR
true inventor of
   .... STUBBLEFIELD
tube .... GRID
TV, et al .... MEDIA
radio's Cronkite .... WALTER
Dallas .... STELLA
Murrow .... EDWARD
radioactive matter .... NITON,
   RADON, NOBELIUM,
   CARNOTITE
particles .... GEIGERS
radioactivity, measure of
   .... CURIE
radiolocator .... RADAR
radiotelephony term ...... ROGER,
   TEN-FOUR
radium F .... POLONIUM
discoverer .... CURIE
disease treated with
   .... CANCER
emanation .... NITON, RADON
source of .... URANITE,
   PITCHBLENDE
radius .... RAY, RANGE, SCOPE,
   SPOKE, EXTENT
radix .... BASE, ROOT, ETYMON,
   RADICLE
radon .... NITON
RAF, part of .... ROYAL, AIR,
   FORCE
raff .... TRASH, RABBLE
companion .... RIFF
raffish ...... LOW, CHEAP, FLASHY,
   TAWDRY, VULGAR,
   DISREPUTABLE
raffle .... LOTTO, LOTTERY
ticket .... BLANK
raft .... BALSA, BARGE, FLOAT,
   CATAMARAN

colloquial .... LOT,
   MULTITUDE, COLLECTION
component of .... LOGS,
   BOARDS, BARRELS
log .... CATAMARAN
rafter .... BEAM, SPAR, TIMBER
rag .... SCRAP, SCOLD, SHRED,
   SLATE, TATTER, REMNANT,
   CASTOFFS
baby .... DOLL
chew the ..... CHAT, CONVERSE
slang .... KID, RIB, BRAT, JOSH,
   MOCK, TEASE
ragamuffin .... WAIF,
   TATTERDEMALION
ragamuffinly .... RAGGED,
   SLOVENLY
rage .... FAD, IRE, BOIL, FUME,
   FURY, RAVE, ANGER, CRAZE,
   FUROR, STORM, VOGUE,
   WRATH, FRENZY, SPREAD,
   BLUSTER, FASHION, RAMPAGE
ragged .... HARSH, ROUGH,
   FRAYED, JAGGED, SHABBY,
   SHAGGY, UNEVEN, UNKEMPT,
   TATTERED
child, poor .... RAGAMUFFIN
plant .... ROBIN
raggee .... RAGI, GRASS
ragger .... TEASER
Raggedy doll .... ANDY, ANNE
raging .... RAMPANT, VIOLENT,
   RAMPAGING
raglan .... TOPCOAT, OVERCOAT
ragman/ragpicker ...... JUNKMAN
ragout .... HASH, STEW, SALMI,
   TUCKET, GOULASH, HARICOT
rags .... CLOTHES
Rags to Riches author
   .... ALGER
ragtag .... RABBLE
ragtime .... JAZZ
ragweed .... IVA, AMBROSIA,
   COCKLEBUR
ragwort .... TANSY, JACOBY,
   GROUNDSEL
rah .... CHEER, HURRAH
opposite of .... HISS
raid ...... FORAY, ONSET, ATTACK,
   FORAGE, INROAD, INVADE,
   MARAUD, SORTIE, ASSAULT,
   INVASION, INCURSION
slang .... PINCH
raider .... UBOAT, RANGER,
   COMMANDO
rail .... BAR, BIRD, COOT, RANT,
   SORA, WEKA, CHIDE, CRAKE,
   FENCE, HERON, SCOFF, SCOLD,
   MUDHEN, ORTOLAN,
   COMPLAIN
bird like .... COURLAN

collar of .... FLANGE
kin of .... NOTORNIS
railer .... REVILER
railing .... FENCE, BALUSTRADE
bridge .... PARAPET
raillery .... BANTER, SATIRE,
   BADINAGE, RIDICULE,
   PERSIFLAGE
slang .... KIDDING
railroad ...... RAILWAY, TRAMLINE
baggage car .... VAN
bridge .... TRESTLE
car .... COACH, DINER,
   SMOKER, CABOOSE, PULLMAN,
   SLEEPER
car compartment .... DUPLEX
center .... YARD
colloquial ..... RUSH, EXPEDITE
crossing .... GATE
elevated .... EL, MONORAIL
engine .... LOCOMOTIVE
engine serviceman
   .... HOSTLER
flare .... FUSEE, FUZEE
freight car .... GONDOLA
handcar .... VELOCIPEDE
industrial .... TAPLINE
line end .... TERMINUS
side track .... SPUR
siding .... TURN-OUT
signal .... HIGHBALL,
   SEMAPHORE
single track .... MONORAIL
slang .... FRAME
sleeping car .... WAGON-LIT
station .... DEPOT
stop for locomotives .... TANK
   TOWN
supply car .... TENDER
switch device .... FROG, SHUNT
tie .... SLEEPER
track section .... GANTLET
trunkline .... MAIN
underground .... METRO,
   SUBWAY
workers' vehicle .... HANDCAR
raiment .... DRESS, ATTIRE,
   APPAREL, CLOTHING
of the early wilds .... TIGER
   SKIN
rain .... FALL, HYET, BESTOW,
   FLURRY, LAVISH, SEREIN,
   SHOWER, (OUT)POUR,
   DOWNPOUR
briefly .... SPIT
combining form .... HYETO
forest .... SELVA
fine mist .... MIZZLE, SEREIN,
   DRIZZLE
formed by .... PLUVIAL
frozen/icy .... HAIL, SNOW,

SLEET

gauge .... UDOMETER

heavy .... TORRENT

mist .... SCUD

or shine ..... COME WHAT MAY

sudden .... BRASH, SPATE,

CLOUDBURST

sunset .... SEREIN

tree .... SAMAN, ZAMIA

Rain girl .... SADIE

setting .... SAMOA

rainbird .... CUCKOO,

WOODPECKER

rainbow .... ARC(H), IRIS,

METEOR, SPECTRUM

bridge .... BIFROST

combining form .... IRIDO

fish .... GUPPY

horse .... APPALOOSA

like colors, having ..... IRISED,

PAVONINE, IRIDESCENT

trout .... STEELHEAD

raincheck .... STUB, TICKET

raincoat .... PONCHO, SLICKER,

MACKINTOSH, TRENCH COAT

raindrops, frozen .... HAIL

Rainer, actress .... LUISE

Maria, Ger. poet .... RILKE

rainfall .... SHOWER, WETNESS,

PRECIPITATION

heavy .... DELUGE

place of heaviest .... ASSAM

Rainier (Mount) site

.... TACOMA

Rainier's domain, Prince

.... MONACO

rainless .... ARID

rainmaker: sl. .... LOBBYIST

rainproof canvas ...... TARPAULIN

rainy .... WET, SOPPY, SLOPPY,

PLUVIAL, SHOWERY, PLUVIOUS

season .... MONSOON

raise .... EAN, HIKE, REAR, STIR,

BOOST, BREED, BUILD, ERECT,

EXALT, HOIST, AROUSE,

INCITE, MUSTER, PULL UP,

(UP)LIFT, COLLECT, ELEVATE,

NURTURE

a check .... KITE

goose pimples .... SCARE

in relief .... EMBOSS

in value .... ENDEAR

nap .... TEASE(L)

rents exorbitantly .... RACK

to third power .... CUBE

raised .... EMBOSSED

again .... RE-ELEVATED

road .... CAUSEWAY

raisin .... GRAPE, SULTANA

in pudding .... PLUM

raisins drink .... CORDIAL,

ROSOLIO

raison .... D'ETAT, D'ETRE

raj .... RULE

rajah's wife .... RANI, RANEE

Rajasthan's capital .... JAIPUR

rake .... COMB, ROUE, SCOUR,

SLANT, GATHER, LECHER,

SCRAPE, SEARCH, COLLECT,

RANSACK, LOTHARIO,

DEBAUCHEE, LIBERTINE

off: sl. .... BRIBE, PAYOFF,

REBATE, KICKBACK,

COMMISSION

with gunfire .... STRAFE,

ENFILADE

rakish .... JAUNTY, DASHING,

DISSOLUTE

man .... RAKEHELL

rale .... RATTLE, RHONCHUS

ralline bird .... RAIL

rally .... MOCK, ROUSE, TEASE,

BANTER, MUSTER, REVIVE,

COLLECT, MARSHAL,

MEET(ING), RESURGE,

ASSEMBLY, GATHERING

ram ...... TUP, DUMP, BUTT, CRAM,

PUMP, TAMP, DRIVE, PRESS,

POUND, SHEEP, STUFF,

BATTER, THRUST

constellation .... ARIES

headed god .... AMMON

horn .... SHOFAR, SHOPHAR

kind of .... (BELL)WETHER

ship's .... BEAK

Rama .... KRISHNA

Ramachandra's wife .... SITA

Ramadan/Ramazan .... FASTING

ramage .... BOUGH

Ramayana character .... SITA,

HANUMAN

ramble .... GAD, ROAM, ROVE,

STRAY, STROLL, WANDER,

MAUNDER, MEANDER,

SAUNTER

rambler .... ROSE, NOMAD,

ROVER, TRAMP, TRUANT

Rambouillet ...... (MERINO) SHEEP

rambunctious ...... WILD, ROWDY,

UNRULY, BOISTEROUS,

DISORDERLY, PUGNACIOUS

one .... TEARER

ramekin/ramequin .... DISH,

HASH

Rameses/Ramses ...... MONARCH,

PHARAOH

domain .... EGYPT

ramie .... HEMP, FIBER

ramification .... SPUR, BRANCH,

RESULT, IN AND OUT,

OFFSHOOT

ramify .... DIVIDE, SPREAD

ramjet .... ENGINE, ATHODYD

rammer .... BEAK, RAMROD

ramose .... BRANCHED

ramp .... RAGE, REAR, RUSH,

TEAR, PITCH, SLANT, SLOPE,

STAND, STORM, RUNWAY,

INCLINE, PASSAGE, ROADWAY

rampage .... RAGE, FRACAS,

FRENZY, TANTRUM,

OUTBREAK, COMMOTION

rampaging person .... AMOK,

BERSERK, JURAMENTADO

rampant .... LUSH, RIFE,

EPIDEMIC, WIDESPREAD

rampart .... WALL, REDAN,

BULWARK, PARAPET, RAVELIN,

VALLATION, EMBANKMENT

rampion .... CAMPANULA,

BELLFLOWER

ramrod .... POKER, RAMMER

ramshackle ...... SHAKY, RICKETY,

RUN-DOWN

ramson .... ROOT, GARLIC

ramtil .... SESAME

ramus .... BRANCH

ran, also .... LOST, COMPETED

tan .... SPREE

rana .... FROG, RAJA, PRINCE

rance .... MARBLE

ranch .... FARM, GRAZE,

(G)RANGE, ESTANCIA,

HACIENDA, PLANTATION

event .... RODEO, ROUNDUP

hand .... COWBOY, COWPOKE

tyro .... DUDE

rancher ...... COWBOY, STOCKMAN

rancho .... HUT, RANCH

rancid ...... RANK, STALE, PUTRID,

SMELLY, SPOILED, STINKING

rancor ...... GALL, SPITE, ENMITY,

HATRED, MALICE, ILL WILL

rand ...... EDGE, BORDER, MARGIN

random .... CASUAL, CHANCE,

AIMLESS, DESULTORY,

HAPHAZARD, HIT-OR-MISS

archer .... CUPID

randy .... BAWDY, CRUDE,

BEGGAR, COARSE, VULGAR,

LUSTFUL

woman .... SHREW

range .... ROW, RANK, ROAM,

SPAN, GAMUT, REACH, SCALE,

SCOPE, STOVE, SWEEP, TRAIN,

EXTENT, SERIES, CALIBER,

COMPASS, LATITUDE,

GRASSLAND

auditory .... EARSHOT

finder ...... STADIA, TELEMETER

mountain .... CHAIN, SIERRA

of emotion .... GAMUT

of hills .... RIDGE

of vision .... SCAN, SCOPE,
EYESHOT, EYESIGHT
over .... SCOUR
Rocky Mountains ...... TETON,
UINTA
sighting for .... ZERO
ranger .... WARDEN, SOLDIER,
FORESTER
before 1972 .... SENATOR
concern of a .... FOREST
Rangoon is capital of .... BURMA
measure .... DHA
measure, distance .... TAUN
weight .... CATTY
rangy .... LANKY, SPARE
rani/ranee .... QUEEN
garb of .... SARI
husband of .... RAJA(H)
ranine .... FROGLIKE
rank ...... ROW, LINE, LUSH, TIER,
CASTE, GRADE, GROSS,
RANGE, REEKY, UTTER,
ARRANT, COARSE, RANCID,
STATUS, FERTILE, EMINENCE,
FLAGRANT, INDECENT,
POSITION, STANDING
above viscount .... EARL
and file .... RUCK, SOLDIERS,
FOLLOWERS
having .... GENETIC
of lower .... JUNIOR, PUISNE
pulling .... BOSSY
rankle .... RILE, ROIL, FESTER
ranks .... ARMY
ransack .... LOOT, RAKE, RIFLE,
SEARCH, PILLAGE, RUMMAGE
ransom .... REDEEM, RESCUE,
BLOODMONEY
person held for .... HOSTAGE
rant ...... NAG, RAGE, RAIL, RAVE,
BOAST, SCOLD, TIRADE,
BLUSTER, BOMBAST, DECLAIM,
HARANGUE
ranunculaceous plant .... PEONY,
ANEMONE, LARKSPUR
ranunculus .... CROWFOOT,
BUTTERCUP
rap .... BOP, BOX, TAP, BLOW,
CUFF, KNAP, SWAT, BLAME,
CLOUT, KNOCK, (TH)WACK,
SENTENCE, PUNISHMENT
colloquial .... CHAT, CONVERSE
gently and firmly ..... PERCUSS
rapacious .... GREEDY,
RAVENOUS, PREDATORY,
VORACIOUS, AVARICIOUS
bird .... SHRIKE, VULTURE
fish .... PIRANHA
rapacity .... GREED, VORACITY
rape .... COLE, PULP, SEIZE,
FODDER, RAVISH, SEDUCE,

ASSAULT, CABBAGE, PLUNDER,
VIOLATE
rapeseed .... COLZA
mass of crushed ..... OIL CAKE
rapid .... FAST, FLEET, HASTY,
QUICK, SWIFT, SPEEDY
combining form .... TACHY
fire ...... STACCATO, FUSILLADE
in a stream .... RIPPLE
rapidity .... SPEED, VELOCITY
rapidly .... AMAIN, APACE
rapids ...... CHUTE, DELLS, DALLES
rapier .... EPEE, TUCK, BILBO,
SWORD
rapine .... RAVIN, PILLAGE,
PLUNDER
rapparee .... ROBBER, VAGABOND,
PLUNDERER
rappee .... SNUFF
rapper .... DOOR KNOCKER
rapping .... TATTOO
rapport ...... ACCORD, HARMONY,
AFFINITY, AGREEMENT,
RELATION(SHIP)
heightened .... VIBES
rapscallion .... ROGUE, RASCAL
rapt .... INTENT, CHARMED,
ABSORBED, ENGROSSED,
ENTRANCED
raptorial bird .... OWL, HAWK,
EAGLE, FALCON, VULTURE
rapture ...... JOY, BLISS, DELIGHT,
ECSTASY, TRANSPORT
rapturous .... ECSTATIC
Rapunzel's specialty .... TRESSES
Raquel Welch's pet name
.... BIRDLEGS
soubriquet .... SEX QUEEN
rara avis .... BIRD, ONER, RARITY
rare ...... ODD, RAW, THIN, SCANT,
SCARCE, UNIQUE, TENUOUS,
UNUSUAL, UNCOMMON,
UNDERDONE
find .... ONE OF A KIND
rarebit .... RABBIT
raree .... (PEEP)SHOW
rarefy .... REFINE, THIN(OUT),
ATTENUATE
rarely .... SELDOM
rareripe fruit .... PEACH
rarity .... ONER, TENUITY,
SCARCITY, THINNESS
rascal .... CAD, IMP, YAP, KNAVE,
ROGUE, SCAMP, VARLET,
VILLAIN, SCALAWAG,
SPALPEEN, SCOUNDREL,
SCAPEGRACE
rascally .... BASE, MEAN, VILE,
DISHONEST
rase .... RUIN, LEVEL, DESTROY
rash .... WILD, HASTY, HEADY,

DARING, WANTON, MEASLES,
ROSEOLA, ERUPTION,
RECKLESS, EXANTHEMA,
FOOLHARDY
person .... BRAVO, HOTSPUR,
PLUNGER
rasher .... HAM, BACON
rashness .... FOLLY, TEMERITY
Rasmussen, Arctic explorer
.... KNUD
rasorial .... GALLINACEOUS
bird .... HEN, CHICKEN
rasp .... RUB, FILE, CHAFE, GRATE,
ABRADE, SCRAPE, IRRITATE
raspberry .... SASS, FRUIT,
SHRUB, ACINUS
Raspe's character
.... MUNCHAUSEN
Rasputin, Russian monk
.... GRIGORI
raspy .... HUSKY, ROUGH, HOARSE,
GRATING, ABRASIVE,
IRRITABLE
rasse .... CIVET
rassle .... WRESTLE
rat .... VOLE, GNAWER, RODENT,
VERMIN, APOSTATE
catcher .... MOUSER
colloquial .... SKUNK
domesticated .... GUINEA PIG
family .... MURIDAE
genus .... MUS
hair .... PAD
i.e. .... DESERTER
kind of .... MOLE
poison .... RATSBANE
race .... SCURRY, SCRAMBLE,
STRUGGLE
rodent resembling ..... MOUSE,
HAMSTER
slang .... LIAR, SNEAK,
SQUEAL, TRAITOR, DESERTER,
INFORMER, STOOL(PIGEON)
"Rat Pack" associate .... DAVIS,
MARTIN
leader .... SINATRA
ratable .... TAXABLE
ratal .... ASSESSMENT
ratafia .... COOKY, CORDIAL,
LIQUEUR, MACAROON
rataplan .... DRUMBEAT
ratchet .... PAWL, WHEEL, BOBBIN,
DETENT, SPINDLE, SPROCKET
rate .... CHIDE, CLASS, JUDGE,
MERIT, PRICE, RATIO, SCOLD,
VALUE, WORTH, DEGREE,
ESTEEM, DESERVE, PERCENT,
APPRAISE, PROPORTION
at any .... ANYWAY
exchange .... AGIO
military .... GRADE

of mass to volume
.... DENSITY
rated .... TAXED, RANKED,
VALUED
ratel-like animal .... BADGER
Rathbone, actor .... BASIL
rathe .... EAGER, EARLY, QUICK,
PROMPT
rather .... SOONER, SOMEWHAT,
CERTAINLY, PREFERABLY
than .... ERE
Ratibor river .... ODER
ratification .... APPROVAL,
SANCTION, AFFIRMATION
ratify ...... OK, OKAY, PASS, SEAL,
APPROVE, ENDORSE, CONFIRM,
SANCTION
rating .... MARK, RANK, CLASS,
GRADE, SCORE, REPRIMAND
ratio .... RATE, QUOTIENT,
PERCENTAGE, PROPORTION
phrase .... IS TO
ratiocinate .... REASON
ration .... METE, LIMIT, SHARE,
DOLE OUT, RESTRICT,
ALLOT(MENT), ALLOWANCE
rational .... SANE, LUCID, SOUND,
LOGICAL, SENSIBLE,
REASONABLE, CLEARHEADED
rationale .... BASIS, REASON,
THEORY, COMMON SENSE,
EXPLANATION
rationalize .... EXPLAIN
rations .... FOOD
bag .... HAVERSACK
ratite .... MOA, EM(E)U, RHEA,
OSTRICH, CASSOWARY
ratoon .... SHOOT, SPROUT
rats, of .... MURINE
rattail .... GRENADIER
rattan .... CANE, PALM, REED,
SEGA, BAMBOO
ratter .... DOG, STINKER,
BETRAYER, DESERTER,
QUISLING, SNITCHER
rattle .... JAR, RALE, CLACK,
UPSET, BABBLE, MARACA,
UPROAR, CHATTER, CLAPPER,
CRACKLE, FLUSTER, SISTRUM,
CREPITATE, DISCONCERT,
NOISE(MAKER)
rattlebrain ...... ASS, FOOL, IDIOT,
RATTLEPATE
rattlebrained .... SILLY,
FRIVOLOUS, TALKATIVE
rattlesnake .... VIPER, CASCABEL,
MASSASAUGA, SIDEWINDER
plantain .... ORCHID
without rattle ..... COPPERHEAD
rattletrap .... MOUTH, JALOPY
rattling .... CREPITANT

rattrap .... CAT, FIX, JAM,
PREDICAMENT
ratwa .... MUNTJAC
raucous .... HARSH, HOARSE,
GRATING
Raul's brother .... FIDEL
ravage .... RUIN, SACK, HAVOC,
DESPOIL, PILLAGE, PLUNDER,
DEVASTATE
rave .... RAGE, RANT, ROAR, TEAR,
STORM
ravel .... FRAY, UNDO, SLEAVE,
INVOLVE, UNTWIST,
ENTANGLE, SEPARATE,
UNTANGLE
stocking's .... RUN
Ravel, composer .... MAURICE
opera .... BOLERO, LA VALSE
ravelin .... REDAN, OUTWORK,
FORTIFICATION
raveling .... LINT
raven .... CROW, PREY, CORBIE,
DEVOUR, PLUNDER,
BLACK(BIRD)
Barnaby Rudge's .... GRIP
constellation .... CORVUS
cry of .... CAW
like a/of a .... CORVINE
quote of .... NEVERMORE
ravenous .... GREEDY, HUNGRY,
LUPINE, RAPACIOUS,
VORACIOUS, GLUTTONOUS
ravin ...... PREY, RAPINE, PLUNDER
ravine .... GAP, DELL, GILL, GULF,
LINN, OMB(E), WADI, WADY,
CHINE, COOMB, FLUME,
GORGE, GULCH, GULLY,
NOTCH, CANYON, CLOUGH,
COULEE, NULLAH, BARRANCA
raving .... EXCITED, NOTABLE,
FRENZIED, DELIRIOUS
ravish .... RAPE, CHARM, SEDUCE,
DELIGHT, ENCHANT, VIOLATE,
ENTHRALL, ENRAPTURE
ravishment .... ECSTASY, RAPTURE
raw .... SORE, BAWDY, BLEAK,
CRUDE, HARSH, UNCOOKED,
UNTESTED
cotton .... LINT
deal .... WRONG, INJUSTICE
in the .... NUDE, NAKED
material .... STOCK, STUFF,
STAPLE
recruit .... ROOKIE
slang .... UNFAIR
rawboned .... BONY, LEAN,
GAUNT
Rawalpindi is capital of
.... PAKISTAN
native of .... PAKISTANI
rawhide .... WHIP, PARFLECHE,

LEATHERETTE
kind of .... SHAGREEN
whip ..... LASH, KNOUT, QUIRT,
STRAP, THONG
ray .... BEAM, BETA, ALPHA,
GAMMA, GLEAM, LASER,
MANTA, PETAL, SKATE,
TRACE, STRIPE, SAWFISH,
STINGAREE, THORNBACK
eagle .... OBISPO
flower .... FLORET
from a satellite
.... MOONBEAM
huge .... MANTA
kind of .... BETA, GAMMA,
LASER
like part .... RADIUS
Ray, actor .... ALDO
rayah .... RAIA, NON-MOSLEM
Rayburn, Speaker .... SAM
rayless .... DARK, GLOOMY
Raymond or Ilona .... MASSEY
Raymonda ballet composer
.... PETIPA
rayon ...... FIBER, FABRIC, JERSEY,
ACETATE, TEXTILE, VISCOSE
cellulose acetate .... CELANESE
corded/ribbed .... REPP,
REP(S), OTTOMAN
making material
.... CELLULOSE
sheer .... VOILE
twilled .... SERGE
with knotty surface
.... RATINE
raze .... ERASE, LEVEL, SHAVE,
SCRAPE, DESTROY, DEMOLISH
razee .... SHIP
razer .... DESTROYER
razor .... SHAVE(R)
billed bird .... ALCA
clam .... SOLEN
seller .... CUTLER
sharpen(er) .... HONE, STROP
razorback .... HOG, FINBACK,
(RORQUAL) WHALE
razz .... JEER, SASS, TEASE,
DERIDE, HECKLE, RIDICULE
razzle-dazzle .... CONFUSE,
BEWILDER, CONFUSION
Rb, in chemistry .... RUBIDIUM
RCA founder .... (DAVID)
SARNOFF
part of .... RADIO, AMERICA,
CORPORATION
re .... ABOUT, ANENT, REGARDING,
CONCERNING
echoing .... REBOANT
Re in chemistry .... RHENIUM
rea .... TURMERIC
reach .... GAIN, PASS, SPAN,

GRASP, RANGE, TOUCH, ARRIVE, ATTAIN, EXTEND, FATHOM, LENGTH, ACHIEVE, STRETCH
a conclusion .... DECIDE
reachable .... OBTAINABLE
reachless .... LOFTY, UNATTAINABLE
react .... ANSWER, RESPOND, REDOUND
reacting easily/readily .... RESPONSIVE
reaction .... REPLY, IMPACT, REFLEX, RESPONSE, TROPISM
angry .... RISE
challenging .... DEFIANCE
disapproving .... PROTEST
drowsy .... YAWN
of disgust .... REPULSION
of refusal .... REBUFF, REJECTION
reverberating .... ECHO
to stimuli .... TROPISM
reactionary .... TORY, RIGHT(IST), CONSERVATIVE
read .... CON, PORE, STUDY, TEACH, PERUSE, CONSTRUE, DECIPHER, FORETELL, REGISTER, INTERPRET, RENOUNCE, UNDERSTAND
all about it! .... NEWS
aloud .... RECITE
closely .... PORE(D)
cursorily .... SKIM
inability to .... ALEXIA
letter by letter .... SPELT
metrically .... SCAN
numbers .... NUMERATE
out of .... EXPEL, DISMISS
readable .... LEGIBLE
reader ...... BOOK, CRITIC, PRIMER, PERUSER, RECITER, LECTURER
meter .... RECORDER
scripture .... LECTOR
readily .... EASILY, QUICKLY, PROMPTLY, WILLINGLY
readiness .... EASE, ALACRITY
reading .... LECTION, PERUSAL, RECORD(ING)
desk/stand .... AMBO, LECTERN, PRIE-DIEU
disability .... DYSLEXIA
of Scriptures .... LECTION
reads alike forward or backward .... PALINDROME
ready .... APT, SET, FAIN, KEEN, OPEN, RIPE, WARE, YARE, ALERT, HANDY, QUICK, SHARP, LIKELY, MATURE, POISED, PRIMED, PROMPT, WILLING, INCLINED,

PREPARE(D), AVAILABLE
artillery .... UNLIMBER
at the bar .... ON TAP
for action .... ARMED
for bed .... SLEEPY
made .... STOCK, INSTANT
money .... CASH
to eat .... DONE
to swing .... AT BAT
Reagan, familiarly ...... RONNIE
real .... COIN, SURE, TRUE, PUCKA, PUKKA, ACTUAL, CERTAIN, FACTUAL, GENUINE, CONCRETE, AUTHENTIC, SIMON PURE
estate .... LAND, LOTS, REALTY
estate broker .... REALTOR
estate bugaboo .... TERMITES
plural of .... REIS
thing, the .... MCCOY
tidy .... APPLE-PIE ORDER
realgar ...... MINERAL, SANDARAC
realism .... VERITY
opposite of .... IDEALISM
realistic .... GRAPHIC, PRACTICAL, DOWN-TO-EARTH
opposite of .... VISIONARY
reality .... FACT, TRUTH, VERITY
realize .... NET, GAIN, KNOW, ATTAIN, OBTAIN, ACHIEVE, IMAGINE, UNDERSTAND
really ...... QUITE, TRULY, INDEED, SURELY, ACTUALLY, ABSOLUTELY
realm .... CLIME, DOMAIN, EMPIRE, REGION, SPHERE, DEMESNE, KINGDOM, BAILIWICK
realty .... PROPERTY
bargain of New World .... MANHATTAN ISLAND
ream .... ENLARGE
reamer .... BORER, BROACH, ENLARGER
reams .... LOTS
reanimate .... REVIVE
reap .... MOW, GAIN, GATHER, COLLECT, HARVEST
reaper .... MOWER
Reaper, Grim .... DEATH
reaping tool ...... SICKLE, SCYTHE, TWIBIL(L)
reappearance .... RERUN
rear ...... AFT, END, GROW, RAMP, RISE, BREED, BUILD, ERECT, NURSE, RAISE, (BE)HIND, SUCKLE, ARRIERE, REVERSE, BACK(PART), BACKSIDE
colloquial .... FANNY
horse's .... PESADE
young bird .... FLEDGE
reared by hand .... CADE

rearmost .... LAST
rearrange .... PERMUTE
reason .... WHY, NOUS, ARGUE, BASIS, CAUSE, LOGOS, GROUND, MOTIVE, SANITY, DISCUSS, JUSTIFY, EXPLANATION, RATIOCINATE
against .... OPPUGN
deprive of .... DEMENT
for being .... END, RAISON D'ETRE
for ill-will .... GRUDGE
with .... RIGHTLY
reasonable ...... FAIR, JUST, SANE, SOUND, LOGICAL, RATIONAL, SENSIBLE
reasoning, correct ...... LOGIC(AL)
false .... IDOLISM, SOPHISM
faulty .... SYLLOGISM, PARALOGISM
subtle, difficult .... METAPHYSICS
reata .... LASSO, NOOSE, LARIAT
reave ...... ROB, REND, TEAR, SEIZE
rebaptize .... RENAME
rebate .... RABBET, RAKE-OFF, DISCOUNT, KICKBACK, DEDUCTION
partial .... REFUND
rebec(k) .... FIDDLE, VIOLIN
Rebecca, diminutive of .... REBA, BECKY
Rebekah's brother .... LABAN
father .... BETHUEL
husband .... ISAAC
niece .... LEAH, RACHEL
son .... ESAU, JACOB
rebel .... DEFY, DEFIER, RELUCT, RESIST, RISE (UP), OPPOSE(R), MUTINEER, RECUSANT, REVOLT(ER), DISOBEY(ER), DISSENTER, DISSIDENT, INSURGENT, INSURRECTO, MALCONTENT
angel .... BELIAL
rebellion .... MUTINY, REVOLT, SEDITION, UPRISING, INSURGENCE, REVOLUTION, INSURRECTION
minor .... PUTSCH
rebellious .... BOLD, DARING, UNRULY, DEFIANT, LAWLESS
rebelliously .... IN DEFIANCE OF
rebirth .... REVIVAL, UPSURGE, REDEMPTION, RENAISSANCE
rebound .... DAP, CAROM, RECOIL, RESILE, RICOCHET, BOUNCE (BACK)
rebuff .... CUT, SLAP, SNUB, CHECK, REPEL, SPURN, REFUSE, REJECT, REPULSE

slang .... COLD-SHOULDER
rebuild .... RESTORE
rebuke ...... SLAP, CHIDE, BERATE,
DERIDE, CENSURE, REPROVE,
UPBRAID, REPREHEND,
REPRIMAND
obsolete .... REPRESS,
INCREPATE
old style .... SNEAP
rebus for example .... PUZZLE
rebut .... OPPOSE, REFUSE,
DISPROVE, CONTRADICT
rebuttal .... RETORT, REJOINDER
brat's .... SASS
colloquial .... CLINCHER
recalcitrant .... REBEL, MULISH,
UNRULY, DEFIANT, RENITENT,
STUBBORN, RESISTANT
recall .... ANNUL, CANCEL,
REPEAL, REVIVE, REVOKE,
RETRACT, REMEMBER,
WITHDRAW, RECOLLECT
recant .... ABJURE, DISAVOW,
RETRACT, RENOUNCE,
WITHDRAW
recantation .... DENIAL
recap .... GIST, RETREAD
recapitulate .... SUM UP, REPEAT,
RESTATE, SUMMARIZE
recapitulation .... REPRISE,
SUMMARY
recast .... REMOLD, REMODEL
recede .... EBB, WANE, DRAW
BACK, FALL BACK
receipt .... RECIPE, QUITTANCE,
ACKNOWLEDGMENT
receipts .... TAKE, INCOME,
PROCEEDS
receivable .... DUE
receive .... GET, HOLD, TAKE,
ADMIT, ABSORB, ACCEPT,
ACQUIRE
for work done .... EARN
information from ..... DEBRIEF
received, in radio .... ROGER
receiver .... PAYEE, ACCEPTER,
COLLECTOR, RECIPIENT,
TREASURER, BENEFICIARY
in baseball .... CATCHER
inheritance .... HEIR
insurance .... BENEFICIARY
stolen goods .... FENCE
trust property .... BAILEE,
TRUSTEE
receiving .... RECEPTION
callers .... IN, AT HOME
recent .... NEW, LATE, FRESH,
MODERN, NEOTERIC
arrival .... NEWCOMER
combining form .... NEO
recently .... ANEW, LATELY, OF

LATE, LATTERLY
receptacle .... BIN, BOX, CAN,
CASE, BASIN, CHEST, BASKET,
VESSEL, CONTAINER
flower .... VASE, TORUS
holy water .... FONT, STOUP
of a sort .... HOD
reception .... LEVEE, PARTY, AT
HOME, DURBAR, SOIREE,
WELCOME, ADMITTANCE
receptionist .... GREETER
receptive .... AMENABLE,
RESPONSIVE, OPEN(-MINDED)
receptor .... EAR, EYE, NOSE
recess .... NOOK, REST, BREAK,
NICHE, PAUSE, HOLLOW,
INTERIM, VACATION
recession ...... DECLINE, SETBACK,
RECEDING
business .... SLUMP,
SLOWDOWN
economic .... DEPRESSION,
UNEMPLOYMENT
recessional .... HYMN
recessionary ill .... LAYOFF
recherche .... RARE
Recife is capital of
.... PERNAMBUCO
recipe .... METHOD, REMEDY,
FORMULA, RECEIPT,
DIRECTIONS, PRESCRIPTION
recipient .... DONEE, PAYEE,
TAKER, ACCEPTER, ENDORSER,
RECEIVER
reciprocal .... MUTUAL
ohm .... MHO
reciprocate .... RETURN,
EXCHANGE, INTERCHANGE
recital .... STORY, ACCOUNT,
CONCERT, MUSICALE,
NARRATION, REHEARSAL
recitation .... STORY, READING,
RECITAL, NARRATIVE
recite .... RELATE, REPEAT,
NARRATE
item by item .... DETAIL
loudly .... DECLAIM, REHEARSE
main points briefly
.... SUMMARIZE,
RECAP(ITULATE)
mechanically .... PATTER
monotonously .... CHANT,
DRONE
reciter of literary works
.... READER
reck .... HEED
reckless .... RASH, WILD, DARING,
WANTON, CARELESS,
HEEDLESS, AUDACIOUS
courage .... DERRING-DO
person ..... MADCAP, HOTSPUR,

PLUNGER, DAREDEVIL
reckon .... COUNT, GUESS, JUDGE,
OPINE, THINK, COMPUTE,
SUPPOSE, CONSIDER, FIGURE
(UP), CALCULATE
long ago .... ARET
reckoning .... TAB, COUNT,
GUESS, TALLY, CALCULATION
reclaim .... REDEEM, REFORM,
RECOVER, RESTORE
reclaimed land .... POLDER
reclame .... PUBLICITY
recline ...... LAY, LIE, REST, LEAN
(ON), REPOSE
reclining .... RECUMBENT
recluse .... MONK, LONER, HERMIT,
ASCETIC, EREMITE, SOLITARY,
ANCHORESS, ANCHORITE,
SOLITAIRE, TROGLODYTE
recognition .... NOTICE,
GREETING, ADMISSION,
AWARENESS, COGNIZANCE
recognizance .... BOND, BADGE,
TOKEN, PLEDGE, OBLIGATION
recognize .... OWN, KNOW, ADMIT,
GREET, ACCEPT, SALUTE,
IDENTIFY, PERCEIVE
recoil .... KICK, COWER, QUAIL,
BOUNCE, CRINGE, RESILE,
SHRINK, REDOUND, RETREAT,
DRAW BACK, REACTION
recollect ...... RECALL, REMEMBER
recollection .... MEMORY,
ANAMNESIS, REMEMBRANCE,
REMINISCENCE
recolor .... DYE
recommend .... TOUT, URGE,
ADVISE, COMMIT, COUNSEL,
ENTRUST, SUGGEST
recommendation .... PLUG,
BOOST
recompense ...... REPAY, REWARD,
COMPENSATE
reconcile .... ATONE, ADJUST,
MAKE UP, SQUARE,
SYNCRETIZE
differences .... SETTLE,
COMPOSE, HARMONIZE
recondite .... DEEP, SECRET,
OBSCURE, ABSTRUSE,
PROFOUND
recondition .... OVERHAUL
reconnaissance .... SURVEY,
OBSERVATION
reconnoiter .... CASE, SCOUT,
SURVEY, EXPLORE
reconstruction .... PLASTIC
SURGERY
record .... TAB, ACTA, DISC, DISK,
FILE, HIGH, NOTE, POST, TAPE,
ANNAL, ENTER, ENTRY,

ENROLL, NOTATE, SET DOWN
Captain's/ship .... LOG
copy of .... ESTREAT
formal .... MINUTES,
    DOCUMENT, REGISTER
historical .... ANNALS
of arrests/crime .... BLOTTER
of past events .... HISTORY
of travel .... ITINERARY
off the .... PRIVILEGED
personal .... DIARY, DOSSIER
police .... BLOTTER
recorded proceedings ...... ACTA
recorder .... CLERK, FLUTE,
    STENO, TAPER, NOTARY,
    HISTORIAN, REGISTRAR,
    SECRETARY
recording device .... TAPE,
    DATER, METER, TIMER
of chess moves ...... NOTATION
records, place for public
    .... ARCHIVES
recount .... RECITE, RELATE,
    (RE)TELL, NARRATE
recoup .... REGAIN, RECOVER, WIN
    BACK, REIMBURSE
recourse .... REFUGE, RESORT
way of .... SUIT
recover .... RALLY, RECOUP,
    REGAIN, RECLAIM, RETRIEVE,
    RECUPERATE
from illness .... GET WELL,
    CONVALESCE
one's spirit .... RALLY, PERK
    (UP)
quickly .... BOUNCE BACK
recreant ...... CRAVEN, APOSTATE,
    COWARD(LY), DISLOYAL,
    TRAITOR(OUS)
recreate, as a movie .... REMAKE
recreation .... PLAY, SPORT,
    PASTIME, AMUSEMENT,
    DIVERSION
area .... PARK, BEACH
recrement .... DROSS, WASTE,
    REFUSE
recrimination
    .... COUNTERCHARGE
recruit .... MUSTER, NOVICE,
    ROOKIE, DRAFT(EE),
    ENLIST(EE), ENROLL(EE),
    CONSCRIPT
conditioning site .... BOOT
    CAMP
raw .... TENDERFOOT
rectangle/rectangular
    .... QUADRATE
rectifier .... ADJUSTER
tube .... DIODE
rectify .... AMEND, ADJUST,
    PURIFY, REFINE, REMEDY,

CORRECT
rectitude .... HONESTY, INTEGRITY
recto, opposed to .... VERSO
rector .... PASTOR, PREFECT,
    MINISTER
assistant of .... CURATE
dwelling of .... MANSE
recumbent .... LYING, PRONE,
    LEANING, RESTING
recuperate .... RECOVER
recuperation .... RECOVERY
recur .... REPEAT, RETURN,
    REVERT, COME BACK
recurrence .... RETURN,
    REPETITION
recurrent seizures ...... EPILEPSY
recurring period .... CYCLE
women's .... MENSES
recuse .... REJECT, CHALLENGE
red .... RUBY, COLOR, CORAL,
    CERISE, CHERRY, GARNET,
    CRIMSON, RADICAL, RUBIOUS,
    SCARLET, COMMUNIST
admiral .... BUTTERFLY
alert ...... VIGILANCE, WARNING
    SIGNAL
and blue color .... PURPLE
apple .... DELICIOUS
berry .... HAW
bird ...... TANAGER, CARDINAL,
    BULLFINCH
blood cell .... ERYTHROCYTE
blood cell content
    .... HEMOGLOBIN
breasted bream .... SUNFISH
bright .... CERISE, SCARLET,
    CARDINAL
brilliant .... SCARLET
carpet ...... (GRAND) WELCOME
cedar .... JUNIPER, SAVIN(E)
cent .... PENNY
corundum .... RUBY
country .... CHINA
deep .... RUBY, GARNET,
    CARNATION
deer .... STAG(GARD),
    STAGGART
dye ..... EOSIN, HENNA, AURINE
eye .... CONJUNCTIVITIS
eyed fish .... CARP, RUDD
faced .... FLUSHED
flag signal .... DANGER
fuchsia .... MAGENTA,
    PURPLISH
haired .... CARROTY
hat .... BIRETTA
hat wearer .... CARDINAL
herring .... PLOY, RUSE,
    TACTIC
hind .... CABRILLA
hue .... PINK, ROSE, BLOOD,

SCARLET
in heraldry .... GULES
in the .... LOSING, INDEBTED
ink indicator .... LOSS, DEFICIT
inscribed in .... RUBRIC
item .... DEBT
lattice .... INN, TAVERN
lead .... MINIUM
letter .... MEMORABLE
letter day .... HOLIDAY
light signal ..... STOP, DANGER
man .... (AMERICAN) INDIAN
meat .... BEEF, LAMB, PORK,
    MUTTON
mineral .... GARNET, RUTILE
mud .... CLAY
ocher .... RADDLE, REDDLE,
    RUBRIC, RUDDLE
osier .... DOGWOOD
pepper .... CAYENNE
pigment .... CHICA, ROSET,
    CAROTENE
planet .... MARS
purplish .... CARMINE,
    FUCHSIA, MAGENTA,
    AMARANTH
shade .... CLARET, TOMATO,
    CARNATION, STRAWBERRY
squirrel .... CHICKAREE
star .... MARS, ANTARES
stone .... RUBY, SARD
striped apple .... NORTHERN
    SPY
suit .... HEARTS, DIAMONDS
wine .... CLARET
yellow .... ORANGE, TITIAN
Red Book author .... MAO
Cross' concern ..... CALAMITY,
    DISASTER
Cross fund raiser ...... TAGGER
Desert .... NEFUD, NEFUF
Polled .... CATTLE
River .... SONGKOI
River city .... FARGO
Sea city .... JEDDA, JIDDA
Sea kingdom .... YEMEN
Sea peninsula .... ARABIA
Sea seaport .... MOCHA
Sea ship .... DHOW
Square figure .... LENIN
Square landmark ..... KREMLIN
redact .... EDIT, REVISE
redactor .... EDITOR
redbreast .... KNOT, BREAM,
    ROBIN, SANDPIPER
redbug .... FLEA, CHIGGER
redcap .... TOTER, PORTER,
    CARRIER, GOLDFINCH
redd .... TIDY-UP
redden ...... BLUSH, COLOR, FLUSH
reddish ...... PUCE, RUST, RUFOUS,

RUFESCENT
aromatic wood .... CEDAR
brown ..... BAY, ROAN, HAZEL,
AUBURN, MADDER, RUSSET,
SORREL, BURGUNDY,
CHESTNUT, CORDOVAN,
MAHOGANY, CHOCOLATE
brown wood .... MAPLE
fish .... MULLET
wood .... FIR
yellow .... AMBER, SANDY,
ORANGE, TITIAN, LUTEOUS,
TANGERINE
rede .... PLAN, TALE, STORY,
ADVISE, SCHEME, COUNSEL
redecorate .... READORN
redeem .... ATONE, RANSOM,
RESCUE, DELIVER, FULFILL,
RECOVER
Redeemer .... GOEL, SAVIOR,
JESUS CHRIST
redemption .... SALVATION
Redemptorist founder
.... LIGUORI
redeye .... RUDD, VIREO
redfin .... CARP, FISH
redhead ...... DUCK, CARROT TOP,
WOODPECKER
kin of ..... POCHARD, WIDGEON
redhot ...... NEW, FRESH, VIOLENT,
SCALDING, SIZZLING,
SPIRITED, INCANDESCENT
redingote .... OVERCOAT
redneck .... LOWBROW
redness, excessive .... ERYTHRISM
of skin .... RUBEFACTION
redo .... REVAMP
redolence .... ODOR, SCENT
redolent .... SCENTED, FRAGRANT,
SMELLING
redouble ...... (RE)ECHO, REFOLD,
REPEAT, INCREASE
redoubt .... BREASTWORK,
STRONGHOLD
redoubtable .... DREAD,
FEARSOME
redound .... REACT, RECOIL
redowa-like dance .... POLKA,
WALTZ
redpoll .... FINCH
redress .... REMEDY, CORRECT
redskin .... INDIAN
trophy of .... SCALP
redstart .... BIRD, WARBLER,
BRANTAIL
redtop .... GRASS
reduce .... CUT, DIET, PARE, SLIM,
THIN, ALLAY, LOWER, QUELL,
SLASH, DELETE, LESSEN,
SHRINK, SUBDUE, CONQUER,
CURTAIL, DECREASE, DIMINISH

expenses .... PARE
in rank .... DEMOTE
in value .... CHEAPEN,
DEPRECIATE
one's dignity .... DEGRADE,
HUMILIATE
one's weight .... SLENDERIZE
reduction .... CUTBACK
in biology .... MEIOSIS
redundance/redundancy
.... NIMIETY, SURFEIT,
SURPLUS, PLEONASM,
TAUTOLOGY
redundant .... WORDY,
EXCESS(IVE), PLEONASTIC,
REPETITIOUS, SUPERFLUOUS
reduplicate, in botany
.... VALVATE
redware .... SEAWEED
redwing .... THRUSH, SONGBIRD
redwood .... SEQUOIA
ree .... ARIKARA
reecho .... RESOUND
reechoing .... REBOANT
reed .... OAT, GRASS, STALK,
STRAW, RATTAN
bird .... BOBOLINK
buck .... BOHOR, NAGOR,
ANTELOPE
in architecture .... MOLDING
instrument with .... OBOE,
ORGAN, BASSOON, CLARINET,
SAXOPHONE
like .... FERULACEOUS
loom/weaver's .... SLEY
mace .... CATTAIL
poetic .... ARROW
Reed, surgeon/bacteriologist
.... WALTER
reeding .... GADROON, MOLDING
reedy .... SLIM, THIN, PIPING,
FRAGILE, SLENDER
reef .... KEY, BANK, LEDGE, RIDGE,
SHELF, SHOAL, SANDBAR
coral .... CAY, KEY
mining .... LODE, VEIN
reefer ...... COAT, MIDDY, JACKET,
MUFFLER, MIDSHIPMAN,
(MARIJUANA) CIGARETTE
prototype of .... JOINT
reek .... FUME, EXUDE, SMOKE,
STINK, VAPOR, STENCH
reel .... SPIN, SWAY, WIND, DANCE,
LURCH, SPOOL, SWIFT, SWING,
WHEEL, WHIRL, WINCE,
BOBBIN, TEETER, TOTTER,
WAMBLE, STAGGER, FALL
BACK
to hold skeins of silk
.... SWIFT
reeling appearance .... SWIM

of cocoon silk .... FILATURE
reem .... UNICORN
Reese, baseball player .... PEEWEE
Tears author .... LIZETTE
reeve ...... SLIP, PASS IN, THREAD,
BAILIFF, STEWARD, OVERSEER,
SANDPIPER
refection .... MEAL, LUNCH,
REPAST
refectory .... FRATER,
MESS(HALL), DINING HALL
refer .... POINT, ADVERT, ALLUDE,
ASSIGN, DIRECT, SUBMIT,
ASCRIBE, CONSULT
to .... CITE, VIDE
referee .... JUDGE, UMPIRE,
ARBITER, OVERMAN,
MODERATOR
for short .... REF, UMP
reference ...... REGARD, BEARING,
CONCERN, MENTION, RESPECT,
ALLUSION, PERTINENCE
book .... ATLAS, MANUAL,
ALMANAC, DIRECTORY,
DICTIONARY, ENCYCLOPEDIA
expertise .... CREDENTIAL(S)
mark ...... FIST, STAR, DAGGER,
DIESIS, OBELUS, ASTERISK,
PUNCTUATION
personal character
.... TESTIMONIAL
to a law .... CITATION
referendum .... PLEBESCITE
refine .... POLISH, PURIFY,
CLARIFY, CLEANSE, EDUCATE,
IMPROVE, PERFECT,
SUBLIMATE
by distillation .... RECTIFY
metal .... SMELT
refined .... GENTEEL, CULTURED
refinement .... POLISH, CULTURE,
DELICACY, ELEGANCE,
GENTILITY
refiner .... SIEVE, TRIER, FILTER
refinery .... SMELTERY,
DISTILLERY
refining vessel .... CUPEL
refinish the floor .... SAND
reflect ...... MUSE, THINK, MIRROR,
PONDER, CONSIDER
exactly .... MIRROR, DUPLICATE
reflection .... IMAGE, BLAME,
MUSING, REFLEX, SHADOW,
LIKENESS, ASPERSION,
DISCREDIT
of a sound .... ECHO
reflective .... PENSIVE, WISTFUL
reflet .... LUSTER
reflex .... INSTINCT
refluent .... EBBING, REFLUX
reform .... BETTER, CHANGE,

reformatory .... PRISON, MAGDALENE

reformed .... TURNED OVER A NEW LEAF

reformer .... CRUSADER, MORALIST

CONVERT, CORRECT

Bohemian .... HUSS

Protestant .... CALVIN

religious .... LUTHER

social .... (JACOB) RIIS

refract .... BEND, DEFLECT

refractory ...... UNRULY, RESTIVE, STUBBORN, FRACTIOUS, OBSTINATE

refrain ...... CURB, MUSIC, VERSE, WHEEL, BURDEN, CHORUS, DESIST, PHRASE, ABSTAIN, FORBEAR, HOLD BACK, REPETEND

of a song .... BURDEN, CHORUS

short .... BOB

syllable .... TRA

refresh .... AIR, FAN, COOL, RENEW, REVIVE, ENLIVEN

with food/drink .... REFECT

refresher .... REMINDER

refreshing .... BALMY, BRISK, CRISPY, BRACING

drink .... LEMONADE

refreshment .... FOOD, DRINK, SNACK, REPAST, REFECTION

refrigerant .... ICE, FREON, ETHANE, CRYOGEN

refrigerate .... COOL, CHILL, FREEZE

refrigerator .... ICEBOX, FREEZER, FRIGIDAIRE

for short .... REEFER

gas .... FREON

kind of .... WALK-IN

Refrigerator, football player nicknamed .... PERRY

reft .... ROBBED

refuge .... HAVEN, ASYLUM, HARBOR, CITADEL, HOSPICE, RETREAT, SHELTER, SANCTUARY

refugee .... EMIGRE, ESCAPEE, EVACUEE, FUGITIVE

organization .... IRO

refulgent .... GLOWING, RADIANT, SHINING

refund .... REBATE, REIMBURSE, REPAY(MENT)

refurbish .... RENOVATE

refusal ...... NAY, DENIAL, OPTION, REJECTION

phrase .... NO WAY, NO DICE, NO SOAP

word .... NO, NAY, NEVER

refuse .... BALK, DENY, NILL, SCUM, OFFAL, SPURN, TRASH, WASTE, EJECTA, NAYSAY, REBUFF, REJECT, DECLINE, RUBBISH

brewery .... DRAFF, DREGS

cane .... BAGASSE

collectors .... ASHMEN

consent to .... VETO

grape .... MARC

metal .... SCUM, DROSS

nourishment .... FAST

table .... ORT, SCRAPS

to acknowledge .... DENY

to move .... STAY PUT

to talk: sl. .... CLAM UP

wine .... LEES

refusing to plead in court .... MUTE

refutation .... DISPROOF

refute .... REBUT, DISPUTE, DISPROVE

regain .... RECOUP, RECOVER

consciousness .... COME TO

regal .... ROYAL, KINGLY, QUEENLY, STATELY, MAJESTIC

regale .... FEAST, TREAT, ENTERTAIN

regalia .... TIARA, FINERY, EMBLEMS, INSIGNIA, DECORATIONS

king's .... CROWN, SCEPTER

Regan's father .... LEAR

sister .... GONERIL, CORDELIA

regard .... EYE, DEEM, GAZE, LOOK, NOTE, ESTEEM, CONCERN, OBSERVE, RESPECT, CONSIDER, REFERENCE

closely .... SCRUTINIZE

with terror .... DREAD

regarding .... IN RE, ABOUT, CONCERNING

regardless .... ANYHOW, CARELESS, HEEDLESS, NEGLIGENT

of circumstances ...... RAIN OR SHINE

regards .... EYES, ESTEEM, AFFECTION

regatta .... BOAT RACE

boat ..... SCULL, SHELL, YACHT

sights .... CATBOATS

Venetian .... GONDOLA RACE

regenerate .... RENEW

regent .... DEPUTY, INTERREX

of the sun .... URIEL

regentship .... REGENCY

Reggae relative .... SKA

regicide's victim .... KING

regime .... RULE, REIGN, GOVERNMENT

regimen .... DIET, COURSE, METHOD, SYSTEM

regiment commander .... COLONEL

part of .... BATTALION

regimental flag .... PENNON

Regin, son of .... SIGURD, SIEGFRIED

regina .... QUEEN(LY)

Regina, monastery .... LAUDIS

region .... AREA, ZONE, CLIME, PLACE, REALM, SPACE, DOMAIN, SPHERE, SECTION, VICINITY, TERRITORY

of shifting sands .... REG

regional .... LOCAL, SECTIONAL, TERRITORIAL

register ...... LIST, ENROL, ENTER, METER, (EN)ROLL, RECORD, ROSTER, EXPRESS, CALENDAR

death .... NECROLOGY

regma .... MAPLE, SCHIZOCARP

regnant .... RULING, REIGNING, PREVALENT

regorge .... VOMIT

regress .... RETURN

regret .... RUE, MOURN, GRIEVE, REPENT, REPINE, DEPLORE, REMORSE, PENITENCE

regretful .... SORRY, CONTRITE

sounding garment .... SARI

regular .... EVEN, USUAL, NORMAL, PROPER, STABLE, STEADY, ORDERLY, UNIFORM, CONSTANT, HABITUAL, CUSTOMARY

method .... HABIT, PRACTICE

patronage .... CUSTOM

recurrence of beat .... RHYTHM

regulate .... FIX, RULE, ADJUST, DIRECT, MANAGE, CONTROL

regulation .... LAW, RULE, ORDER

regulator ...... VALVE, GOVERNOR

temperature .... CRYOSTAT

regurgitate .... SPEW, VOMIT

rehabilitate .... RESTORE, RECONDITION

rehash .... REVIEW, RECOUNT

rehearsal ...... RECITAL, PRACTICE, PROLUSION

kind of .... DRESS, DRYRUN

rehearse .... DRILL, TRAIN, RECITE, PRACTICE

quickly .... RUN OVER

Rehoboam's father .... SOLOMON

taskmaster .... ADORAM

Reich .... GERMANY

reign .... RULE, SWAY, GOVERN, REGIME, COMMAND, PREVAIL

of a family .... DYNASTY

reigning .... REGNANT
reimburse .... REPAY, REFUND,
PAY BACK
rein .... CHECK, LEASH, CONTROL,
RESTRAIN
draw .... STOP
reincarnation .... REBIRTH
reindeer .... CARIBOU
man/herder .... LAPP
reine's husband .... ROI
Reiner .... ROB, CARL
reinforce .... SUPPORT,
STRENGTHEN
reinstate .... REVEST, RESTORE,
REINSTALL
reiterate ...... HARP, REPEAT, SAY
AGAIN
reject .... EJECT, REPEL, SPURN,
VOMIT, ABJURE, REBUFF,
REFUSE, DECLINE, DISCARD
a lover abruptly .... JILT
bill .... VETO
slang .... BRUSH OFF
rejoice .... ENJOY, EXULT, GLORY,
REVEL, DELIGHT, GLADDEN
rejoin .... REPLY, ANSWER,
RESPOND, REUNITE
rejoinder .... REPLY, RETORT,
RESPONSE
rejuvenate .... RENEW, REFRESH
relapse .... FALL BACK, SLIP
BACK, BACKSLIDE
relate .... TELL, REPORT, CONNECT,
NARRATE, PERTAIN, RECOUNT
related .... AKIN, TOLD, ALLIED,
COGNATE, GERMANE,
CONNECTED
by blood .... SIB, KIN(DRED)
on father's side .... AGNATE,
AGNATIC
on mother's side .... ENATE,
ENATIVE
relating to backbones .... SPINAL
relation .... TIE, LINK, FAMILY,
ACCOUNT, KINFOLK, KINSMAN,
KIN(SHIP), RECITAL
relationship .... KINSHIP,
AFFINITY, COGNATION,
RELEVANCE, CONNECTION
sympathetic .... RAPPORT
relative .... SIB, COGNATE,
KIN(FOLK), KINSMAN,
RELEVANT, PERTINENT
by marriage .... AFFINE
for short .... SIS, BROD
of a grimace .... LEER
of a kickback .... SHAKEDOWN
of a sort .... IN-LAW
of OSS .... CIA
relatives, employment of
.... NEPOTISM

relator .... NARRATOR,
COMPLAINANT
relax .... EASE, REST, ABATE,
LOOSEN, RELENT, SOFTEN,
UNBEND, SLACKEN, EASY
DOES IT
relaxation .... REPOSE,
AMUSEMENT, DIVERSION,
RECREATION
relaxer .... OPIATE
relay .... AGENT, SHIFT, FORWARD,
REMOUNT, TRANSMIT
release .... FREE, UNDO, CLEAR,
LET GO, UNTIE, EXEMPT,
LOOSEN, RELIEF, RELIEVE,
LIBERATE, DISCHARGE,
QUITCLAIM
air .... DEFLATE
claim .... REMISE, WAIVER
conditionally .... PAROLE
from sin .... CLEANSE
hold .... DROP
mass of ice .... CALVE
relegate .... EXILE, ASSIGN,
BANISH, COMMIT, CONSIGN
relent ...... THAW, YIELD, SOFTEN,
SUBMIT
relentless .... GRIM, HARSH,
PITILESS
relevant .... APT, APROPOS,
FITTING, GERMANE, RELATED,
APPOSITE, PERTINENT,
APPLICABLE
reliability .... SOUNDNESS
reliable .... SOLID, TRIED, TESTED,
TRUSTY, DEPENDABLE,
TRUSTWORTHY
reliance .... FAITH, TRUST,
CREDENCE, DEPENDENCE
relic ...... CURIO, TOKEN, ANTIQUE,
MEMENTO, SOUVENIR
sacred .... HALIDOM
relics .... RUINS
relict .... WIDOW, WIDOWED,
SURVIVOR
relief .... AID, EASING, REMEDY,
SOLACE, SUCCOR, COMFORT,
RELEASE, RELIEVO, EASEMENT
emotional drug
.... TRANQUILIZER
from difficulty .... OASIS
medicinal .... PAINKILLER
provider .... RED CROSS
relieve .... RID, CURE, EASE, FREE,
HELP, ALLAY, SOFTEN,
SOOTHE, COMFORT, LIGHTEN,
PALLIATE, ALLEVIATE
by talking .... ABREACT
thirst .... SLAKE, QUENCH
relievo .... RELIEF
religieuse .... NUN, SISTER

religieux .... MONK, PIOUS,
OBLATE
religion .... CREED, FAITH, BELIEF,
DOCTRINE
religionist .... DEIST, FANATIC
religious .... TRUE, GODLY, PIOUS,
DIVINE, DEVOUT, STRICT,
FAITHFUL, ORTHODOX,
CANONICAL, SECTARIAN,
GODFEARING, SCRUPULOUS,
EVANGELICAL
beggar .... FAKIR, SERVITE
belief .... CREED
belief, antagonistic .... HERESY
blessing said over the wine
.... KIDDUSH
brotherhood .... ORDER,
SODALITY
candidate .... POSTULANT
day of atonement, Jewish
.... YOM KIPPUR
denomination .... ISLAM,
JUDAISM, BUDDHISM,
HINDUISM, CATHOLICISM,
UNITARIANISM,
PROTESTANTISM
devotee .... FAKIR, ZEALOT
devotion .... NOVENA
dietary regulation, Judaism
.... KASHRUT(H)
emotion .... THEOPATHY
exclamation .... HOSANNA,
ALLELUIA
expedition .... CRUSADE
group chief .... HIERARCH
holy day .... SABBATH,
HANNUKAH, PASSOVER,
ASCENSION
journey .... PILGRIMAGE
lay society .... SODALITY
leader .... POPE, PONTIFF,
SHEPHERD
leader's saying .... LOGIA
lore .... HIEROLOGY
man .... LAMA, MONK, SAINT,
PRIEST, SHAMAN
military order member
.... TEMPLAR
mysticism .... QUIETISM
observance .... FAST, LENT
offering .... OBLATION,
SACRIFICE
order .... JESUIT, MARIST,
TEMPLAR, URSULINE,
DOMINICAN, FRANCISCAN
period .... LENT, EASTER,
HANNUKAH
person .... OBLATE, THEIST,
DEVOTEE, PIETIST, BELIEVER,
EVANGELIST
rebel .... HERETIC

recluse .... EREMITE
reformer .... HUSS, KNOX,
LUTHER
rites, of .... SACRAL
ritual .... CULT
school head .... RECTOR
sect .... DENOMINATION
springtime holy day
.... PASSOVER
statue .... PIETA
vigil .... WATCH
war .... CRUSADE
worship, system of .... CULT
relinquish .... CEDE, DROP, LET
GO, WAIVE, YIELD, FOR(E)GO,
RESIGN, ABANDON, RELEASE,
PART WITH, RENOUNCE,
SURRENDER
slang .... DITCH
reliquary .... ARCA, CASKET,
SHRINE, SEPULCHER
relish .... ZEST, ACHAR, ENJOY,
GUSTO, SAPOR, SAUCE,
SAVOR, SPICE, TASTE,
FLAVOR, LIKING, RADISH,
CHUTNEE, CHUTNEY, PICKLES,
PLEASURE, CONDIMENT
fish egg .... CAVIAR(E)
meat juice .... ASPIC
the scene .... FEAST ONE'S
EYES
relucent .... BRIGHT
reluct .... REVOLT
reluctant .... LO(A)TH, AVERSE,
HESITANT, UNWILLING
rely .... BANK ON, LEAN, TRUST,
RECKON, COUNT (ON),
DEPEND (ON)
relying on experience
.... EMPIRICAL
remain .... LAST, STAY, ABIDE,
ENDURE
balanced .... LIBRATE
close .... CLING
firm .... STAND (PAT)
in a fixed position .... STAY
PUT
undecided .... PEND, HANG
FIRE
remainder .... REST, EXCESS,
BALANCE, REMNANT, RESIDUE,
LEAVINGS, LEFT-OVER,
RESIDUAL, RESIDUUM
bolt of cloth .... REMNANT
cigarette .... BUTT
drunken binge ...... HANGOVER
of destruction .... DEBRIS
of partially burned wood
.... CINDER
of thorough burning .... ASH
pencil .... STUB

tree .... STUMP
remains ...... LEES, DREGS, RUINS,
TRACES, CADAVER, REMNANT,
SEDIMENT, VESTIGES
person's .... CORPSE
worthless .... CARCASS
remand .... RECALL, RETURN,
SEND BACK
remark .... NOTE, WORD, NOTICE,
EXPRESS, MENTION, OBSERVE,
REMARQUE, COMMENT(ARY)
clever .... NIFTY, SALLY, BON
MOT, (WISE)CRACK, WITTICISM
correct: sl. .... MOUTHFUL
cutting ...... DIG, NIP, SARCASM
indirect, derogatory
.... INNUENDO
mocking .... JEST
nasty/pointed .... BARB
unfavorable .... BRICKBAT
remarkable .... UNCO, SIGNAL,
NOTABLE, UNUSUAL,
STRIKING, EXTRAORDINARY
remarkably bad ...... EGREGIOUS
Remarque, Ger. novelist
.... (ERICH) MARIA
Rembrandt, Dutch painter
.... VAN RIN, VAN RIJN
work .... TITUS, THE
ASCENSION
remedy .... CURE, HEAL, HELP,
TREAT, RECIPE, RELIEF,
REPAIR, CORRECT, REDRESS,
ANTIDOTE
any .... TREACLE
bacteria-fighting
.... ANTIBIOTIC, PENICILLIN,
TETRACYCLINE
cure-all .... ELIXIR, PANACEA
in coinage .... TOLERANCE
medicinal .... DRUG, POTION,
SIMPLES
preventive .... ANTITOXIN
quack .... NOSTRUM
secret .... ELIXIR, ARCANUM
soothing .... BALM, SALVE,
BALSAM, LOTION, UNGUENT,
LINIMENT, DEMULCENT
to counteract poison
.... ANTIDOTE
remember ...... RECALL, REMIND,
OBSERVE, RECOLLECT,
REMINISCE
remembrance .... TOKEN,
MEMORY, MEMENTO,
KEEPSAKE, SOUVENIR
remex .... FEATHER, OARSMAN
remiges .... FEATHERS
remind .... PROMPT
reminder .... MEMO, MEMENTO,
TICKLER, SOUVENIR

reminiscence .... MEMORY
reminiscent .... SUGGESTIVE
remiss .... LAX, SLACK, DERELICT,
NEGLIGENT, NEGLECTFUL
remission .... PARDON, RESPITE,
ABATEMENT, SUSPENSION
remit .... PAY, SEND, CANCEL,
PARDON, FORGIVE, SLACKEN
remnant .... RAG, DREG, SCRAP,
TRACE, (TAG) END, LEAVING,
ODDMENT, RESIDUE,
FRAGMENT, LEFT-OVER,
REMAINDER
remodel ...... RECAST, MODERNIZE
remo(u)lade .... SAUCE
remonstrance .... PROTEST,
COMPLAINT, OBJECTION
remonstrate ...... PLEAD, OBJECT,
PROTEST
remora .... PEGA, SUCKFISH
favorite host of .... SHARK
remorse .... PITY, GRIEF, REGRET,
QUALMS, PENITENCE,
COMPASSION, COMPUNCTION,
SELF-REPROACH
remorseful .... SORRY, ASHAMED,
CONTRITE, FEEL BADLY
remorseless .... CRUEL, CALLOUS,
PITILESS, MERCILESS,
UNTOUCHED
remote .... ALIEN, ALOOF, FAR
(OFF), SLIGHT, DISTANT,
SECLUDED, ULTERIOR
remount .... HORSE, RELAY
removable .... PORTABLE,
DETACHABLE
removal .... OUSTER, DISMISSAL,
ELIMINATION
as by killing ...... LIQUIDATION
of decayed tooth ..... PULLING,
EXTRACTION
diseased tissue ...... ERASION
rank, rights ..... DIVESTMENT
something undesirable
.... RIDDANCE
unwanted hair
.... ELECTROLYSIS
waste products from blood
.... DIALYSIS
surgical .... ABLATION
remove .... DELE, DOFF, KILL,
OUST, EJECT, EXPEL, DELETE,
DEPOSE, EXCISE, DISMISS,
TAKE OFF, DISPLACE,
ELIMINATE
as graffiti .... ERASE
as one's hat .... DOFF
bark .... DECORTICATE
by popular vote .... RECALL
clothes .... STRIP, UNDRESS

clothes from suitcase
.... UNPACK
feathers .... PLUCK
from grave .... DISINTER
from office/the throne
.... OUST, DEPOSE
grease .... DEFAT
grit .... DESAND
hair .... SHAVE
ice .... DEFROST
impurities ...... SMELT, FILTER,
REFINE, DISTILL, RECTIFY
in law .... ELOIN, ELOIGN
juice .... REAM, SQUEEZE
marks .... ERASE
scum .... SCOUR
stopple .... UNCORK
to a distance; law .... ELOIN
to another place .... TRANSFER
tumor .... EXCISE
waste from body ..... EXCRETE
water .... DEHYDRATE
removed .... APART, DISTANT
remunerate .... PAY, REWARD,
REIMBURSE, RECOMPENSE
remuneration .... PAY, WAGES,
INCOME, SALARY,
EMOLUMENT, COMPENSATION
remunerative .... PAYING,
GAINFUL, LUCRATIVE,
REWARDING
Remus' brother .... ROMULUS
parent .... MARS, RHEA
Renaissance .... REBIRTH,
REVIVAL
archetypal man .... DA VINCI
artist .... RAPHAEL
humanist .... ERASMUS
masterpiece .... MONA LISA,
THE LAST SUPPER
sword .... ESTOC
renal .... NEPHRIC, NEPHRITIC
Renard .... FOX
renascence .... REBIRTH,
RENEWAL, REVIVAL
rend .... CUT, RIP, PULL, RIVE,
TEAR, REAVE, SPLIT, CLEAVE
render .... DO, PAY, PUT, GIVE,
ACT (OUT), DEPICT, RECITE,
SUBMIT, DELIVER, FURNISH,
PERFORM, PRESENT,
CONSTRUE, HAND OVER,
TRANSLATE
a musical .... PERFORM
fluid .... FUSE, LIQUEFY
unclear .... BEFOG
rendezvous .... DATE, TRYST,
MEET(ING), APPOINTMENT
rocket .... AGENA
rendition .... VIEW, VERSION,
PERFORMANCE, TRANSLATION

renegade .... RAT, TRAITOR,
APOSTATE, DEFECTOR,
DESERTER, TURNCOAT
renege .... WELSH, BACK OUT,
DISAVOW, FINAGLE
renew .... REPEAT, RESUME,
REVIVE, REFRESH, RESTORE,
CONTINUE, RENOVATE,
REGENERATE
Reni, Ital. painter .... GUIDO
rennet .... RENNIN
Reno is in .... NEVADA
rival of .... LAS VEGAS, (LAKE)
TAHOE
Renoir, painter .... PIERRE
renounce .... DENY, ABJURE,
DISOWN, GIVE UP, RECANT,
REJECT, ABANDON, ABDICATE,
FORSWEAR, RELINQUISH
throne .... ABDICATE
renovate .... REDO, RENEW,
REPAIR, REVIVE, FRESHEN,
FURBISH
renown .... FAME, ECLAT, GLORY,
REPUTE, REPUTATION,
DISTINCTION
person of .... CELEBRITY
renowned .... FAMOUS
bridge master .... GOREN
rensselaerite .... TALC
rent .... GAP, LET, RIP, HIRE,
HOLE, SLIT, TEAR, RENTAL,
LEASE, SCHISM, PAYMENT
again .... RELET
asunder .... RIVEN
rente .... ANNUITY, REVENUE
renunciation .... WAIVER,
CESSATION, ABDICATION
reopen .... RESUME
reorganization .... REVAMP,
SHAKE-UP
rep .... FABRIC
repair .... GO, FIX, (A)MEND,
BETAKE, REMEDY, RESTORE
a coat .... RELINE
a green .... RESOD
a hole tear .... DARN
a threaded hole .... RETAP
loose paper .... REPASTE
shop .... GARAGE
repairman .... FIXER, MENDER,
COBBLER, MECHANIC,
TECHNICIAN
reparable .... MENDABLE
reparation .... AMENDS, REDRESS,
REPAIRS, ATONEMENT,
INDEMNITY
reparative .... MENDING
repartee .... MOT, QUIP, SALLY,
BANTER, RETORT, RIPOSTE,
DIALOGUE, REJOINDER

engage in .... FENCE
skilled in .... WITTY, CLEVER
repast ...... MEAL, SNACK, SPREAD,
REFECTION
repatriate .... RETURN, SEND
BACK
repay .... REFUND, REWARD,
REIMBURSE, RECOMPENSE
repeal .... ANNUL, CANCEL,
RECALL, REVOKE, ABOLISH,
NULLIFY, RE-SOUND,
ABROGATE
repeat .... BIS, ECHO, REDO,
RECUR, PARROT, RECITE,
(RE)ITERATE
gossip, secrets .... RETAIL
performance .... ENCORE
tiresomely .... HARP
repeatedly .... ANEW, OFT(EN),
AGAIN, FREQUENTLY
repeater .... ECHO, CLOCK, RIFLE,
WATCH, PARROT, PISTOL
repeating rifle inventor
.... MAUSER
repel ...... SPURN, REFUSE, REJECT,
RESIST, REPULSE
danger .... DEFEND
repellent .... REPULSIVE,
RESISTANT, WATERPROOF
repent ...... RUE, GRIEVE, REGRET,
CRAWLING, CREEPING,
APOLOGIZE
repentance .... REGRET, REMORSE,
ATTRITION, PENITENCE,
CONTRITION
repercussion .... ECHO, EFFECT,
IMPACT, RECOIL, RESULT,
REBOUND, REACTION
repertoire .... ACTS, STOCK,
ROUTINES
repertory .... STOCK, COLLECTION,
STORE(HOUSE)
repetend .... REFRAIN
repetition .... COPY, HARPING,
RECITATION, RECURRENCE,
DUPLICATION
in music .... REPRISE
mechanical .... ROTE
of a movie scene ...... RETAKE
performance .... ENCORE,
REPLAY
same sound, uninterrupted
.... MONOTONE
TV show .... RERUN
repine .... FRET, MOPE, GRIEVE,
COMPLAIN
replace .... RETURN, RESTORE,
SUCCEED, SUPPLANT
a performer .... SUBSTITUTE
a starter .... RELIEVE
replenish .... REFILL, RESTOCK

replevin .... BOND, PLEDGE, TROVER

replete .... FULL, STUFFED

repletion .... GLUT, SATIETY, FULLNESS

replica ...... COPY, CLONE, IMAGE, DOUBLE, DUPLICATE, FACSIMILE, REPRODUCTION

replicate .... FOLD, REPEAT

replication .... ECHO, FOLD, REPLY, ANSWER, COPY(ING), PARROT(ING), DUPLICATION

reply .... ANSWER, RETORT, RETURN, RESPOND, COMEBACK, RESPONSE, REJOIN(DER)

to a knock .... ENTER

repondez s'il vous plait .... RSVP

report .... SAY, NEWS, TALK, TELL, BLAST, BRUIT, NOISE, RUMOR, STATE, CAHIER, GOSSIP, ACCOUNT, HANSARD, HEARSAY, BULLETIN, DENOUNCE, BROADCAST

card entry .... MARK, GRADE

on policy and procedure .... CAHIER

slanderous .... SCANDAL

reportable infectious disease ...... AIDS, MALARIA, MEASLES, RUBELLA, SYPHILIS, GONORRHEA, DIPTHERIA, HEPATITIS, CHICKENPOX, TUBERCULOSIS

reporter .... CRIER, SCRIBE, NEWSMAN, COLUMNIST, NEWSHOUND, JOURNALIST

concern of .... BEAT, DATA, FACTS, SCOOP, ACCURACY, CONTACTS, DEADLINE

delight of .... BY-LINE

material of .... STORY

paper of .... FLIMSY

routine of .... LEGWORK

repose ...... LAY, LIE, CALM, REST, PEACE, RELAX, SLEEP, RECLINE, RESPITE, BREATHER

archaic .... RELY, ENTRUST

repository ...... BOX, SAFE, CHEST, VAULT, CLOSET, MUSEUM, CONFIDANT, SEPULCHER, WAREHOUSE

reprehend .... BLAME, REBUKE, CENSURE, REPROVE

reprehensible .... CENSURABLE, BLAMEWORTHY

represent .... ENACT, DENOTE, EMBODY, DEPICT, TYPIFY, EXHIBIT, PICTURE, PORTRAY, DESCRIBE, PERSONATE, DELINEATE, SYMBOLIZE,

VISUALIZE, SUBSTITUTE

facts, information .... OUTLINE, ILLUSTRATE

graphically .... PLOT

representation ...... ICON, IMAGE, MIMESIS, ALLEGORY, LIKENESS, RENDITION, ALLEGATION

of heavenly bodies .... ORRERY

ridiculous .... TRAVESTY

representative .... AGENT, ENVOY, PROXY, SOLON, DEPUTY, TYPICAL, DELEGATE, AMBASSADOR, LEGISLATOR, DESCRIPTIVE

repress ...... CURB, CRUSH, QUELL, SIT ON, STIFLE, SUBDUE, SMOTHER, HOLD BACK, RESTRAIN

reprieve .... STAY, DELAY, GRACE, RESPITE, SUSPENSION, POSTPONEMENT

reprimand .... BAWL, SCOLD, RATING, REBUKE, CENSURE, REPROVE, ADMONISH

reprint .... REISSUE, REVISION

reprisal ...... REVENGE, REQUITAL, QUITTANCE, RETORSION, RETORTION, VENGEANCE, RETALIATION

obs. .... MARQUE

reprise .... ENCORE, REPEAT, SUMMARY, REPETITION

reproach .... TWIT, BLAME, CHIDE, REBUKE, CENSURE, REPROVE, UPBRAID

reproachful word .... FIE

reprobate .... RAKE, ROUE, ROGUE, SINNER, VICIOUS, DEPRAVED, SCOUNDREL

reproduce .... BREED, REFLECT, MULTIPLY, PROCREATE

reproduction .... COPY, FACSIMILE, DUPLICATION

reproductive .... FECUND, CREATIVE

agent/unit .... SPORE

cell .... GONAD, GAMETE

organ .... OVARY, TESTIS

reproof .... RATING, REBUKE, REPROACH, SCOLDING

reprove ...... RATE, CHIDE, SCOLD, REBUKE, CENSURE, UPBRAID, ADMONISH

reptant .... REPENT, CRAWLING, CREEPING

reptile .... SNAKE, LIZARD, TURTLE, SAURIAN, SERPENT, OPHIDIAN, ALLIGATOR, CROCODILE, LACERT(IL)IAN

carnivorous .... TUATARA

edible .... TERRAPIN

endangered ..... GREEN TURTLE

extinct .... PTEROSAUR

eye tissue .... PECTEN

footless .... APOD, SNAKE

fossil .... STEGOSAURUS

movement of .... CRAWL, CREEP, SLITHER

mythical .... SALAMANDER

Nile .... CROC

scale .... SCUTUM, PLATELET

reptiles, study of .... HERPETOLOGY

republic .... COUNTRY, DEMOCRACY

not quite one .... BANANA

of letters .... LITERATI

Republic author .... PLATO

Republican .... WHIG

mascot .... ELEPHANT

Mr., soubriquet .... TAFT

Party .... GOP

recalcitrant .... MUGWUMP

repudiate .... DENY, DISOWN, RECANT, REJECT, DISAVOW

repugnance .... HATE, DISGUST, DISLIKE, AVERSION, DISTASTE

repugnant .... HATEFUL, OFFENSIVE, REPULSIVE

repulse ...... SNUB, REPEL, SPURN, REBUFF, REFUSE, REJECT, DRIVE BACK

repulsion ...... DISLIKE, AVERSION, DISTASTE, REJECTION, ABHORRENCE

repulsive .... UGLY, COARSE, ODIOUS, MAWKISH, LOATHSOME, OFFENSIVE, REVOLTING, DISGUSTING

reputable .... NOTABLE, ESTEEMED, CREDIBLE, RESPECTABLE

reputation .... FAME, NAME, RENOWN, REPUTE, PRESTIGE, CHARACTER, DISTINCTION

repute .... ODOR, ESTEEM, REGARD, GOODWILL

reputed .... KNOWN, PUTATIVE, SUPPOSED

request ...... ASK, BEG, SUE, PRAY, SUIT, APPLY, PLEA(D), APPEAL, ENLIST, BESEECH, IMPLORE, ENTREAT(Y), INSTANCE, PETITION

requiem ...... HYMN, MASS, DIRGE

requiescat in _____ .... PACE

require ...... NEED, FORCE, ORDER, COMPEL, DEMAND, ENTAIL, OBLIGE, INVOLVE

requirement .... NEED, WANT,

NECESSITY, REQUISITE

unjust .... IMPOSITION

requisite .... NEED, REQUIRED, ESSENTIAL

requite .... ATONE, (RE)PAY, RETALIATE, COMPENSATE

reredos .... SCREEN, PARTITION

reroute .... DETOUR

rerun .... REPEAT, REPLAY, RESHOW

rescind .... ANNUL, CANCEL, RECALL, REPEAL, ABOLISH, ABROGATE

rescript .... COPY, ORDER, DECREE

rescue .... SAVE, RANSOM, REDEEM, RECLAIM, RECOVER, SALVATION, DELIVER(ANCE)

research .... STUDY, EXPLORATION

center .... LAB(ORATORY)

reseau .... NETWORK

resect .... EXCISE

reseda .... MIGNONETTE

resemblance .... LIKENESS, SIMILARITY

resent .... ENRAGE, OFFEND, RANKLE, INCENSE

resentful .... SORE

resentment .... HATE, HUFF, ANGER, PIQUE, DUDGEON, OFFENSE, UMBRAGE, BAD BLOOD, ANIMOSITY, INDIGNATION

reservation, in law .... SALVO, SAYING

without .... OUTRIGHT

reserve .... KEEP, CASH, STOCK, STORE, RETAIN, BACKLOG, DIGNITY, EARMARK, SILENCE, SET ASIDE, RETICENCE

space .... BOOK

reserved ...... SHY, ALOOF, QUIET, STAID, DISTANT, INDRAWN, RETICENT, RETIRING, TACITURN

reserves, armed forces
.... MILITIA

reservoir .... SUMP, STORE, SOURCE, SUPPLY, CISTERN

overflow of .... SPILTH

reset gem .... REMOUNT

resettle .... MOVE

reside .... LIVE, ABIDE, DWELL, LODGE

residence .... HOME, ABODE, DOMICILE, DWELLING

king's .... CASTLE, PALACE

minister's .... MANSE, RECTORY, PARSONAGE

papal .... VATICAN

place of .... ADDRESS

restricted .... HAREM

rural .... BOWER

slang .... DIGS

stately .... VILLA, PALACE, MANSION

resident ...... DENIZEN, INHERENT, (IN)HABITANT

aquarium .... TETRA

doctor .... INTERN(E)

residential blind alley .... CUL-DE-SAC

street .... TERRACE

residual .... EXTRA, SURPLUS, REMAINDER

residue .... ASH, DREG, LEES, REST, SILT, BITTERN, REMNANT, LEAVINGS, LEFT-OVER, REMANENT, SEDIMENT, SIFTINGS, REMAINDER

resign ...... QUIT, DEMIT, VACATE, ABDICATE, STEP DOWN, RELINQUISH

resignation .... PATIENCE, DEMISSION, SURRENDER, ABDICATION, SUBMISSION

resile .... REBOUND

resiliency .... BUOYANCY, ELASTICITY

resilient .... SUPPLE, DUCTILE, BUOYANT, ELASTIC, PLIABLE, TENSILE, FLEXIBLE

resin .... GUM, TUPI, ALKYD, AMBER, ANIME, COPAL, KAURI, PITCH, ROSIN, SARAN, COPALM, MASTIC, COPAIBA, ASAFETIDA, ELATERITE, LA(B)DANUM, SHELLAC(K)

aromatic .... COPAIBA

asphaltic .... BITUMEN

cathartic .... SCAMMONY

fossil .... AMBER, RETINITE

fragrant .... ELEMI, MYRRH, FRANKINCENSE

gum .... COPAL, MYRRH, MASTIC, GAMBOGE, AMMONIAC, EDELLIUM, RESINOID

hemp .... CHARAS, HASHISH

incense .... MYRRH, SANDARAC

perfume-making ...... BENZOIN

pine .... DAMMAR, DAMMER

poisonous .... CANNABIN

solvent for .... ETHER

sweet-smelling .... MYRRH

synthetic .... LUCITE, CATALIN, BAKELITE, SILICONE

thermoplastic .... SARAN

tropical .... COPAL

used as paint drier ...... JAPAN

used to give glossy surface
.... VARNISH

used to rub on thread
.... WAX

varnish .... ANIME, COPAL, DAMMAR, DAMMER

resinous juice .... LABDANUM

powder, hops .... LUPULIN

secretion .... LAC

resist .... BUCK, DEFY, FACE, FEND, FIGHT, OPPOSE, REPUGN, CONFRONT, WITHSTAND

resistance .... REFUSAL, DEFIANCE, FRICTION, OPPOSITION

fighter ..... EDES, ELAS, MAQUI, ACTIVIST, PARTISAN, GUERRILLA

labor union .... STRIKE, WALKOUT

passive .... DISOBEDIENCE, INSUBORDINATION

purchaser .... BOYCOTT

to authority .... MUTINY

resister .... REBEL, HOLDOUT, STRIKER

resolute ...... FIRM, GRIM, STEADY, DECISIVE, RESOLVED, DETERMINED

resolve .... END, DECIDE, ANALYZE, DETERMINE

resonance .... ECHO, RINGING, SYNTONY, SONORITY, VIBRANCY, VIBRATION

resonant ...... OROTUND, VIBRANT, SONOROUS, REECHOING, RESOUNDING

resort .... SPA, HAUNT, RECOURSE, RESOURCE

city .... ASPEN, MIAMI, HONOLULU

Riviera .... CANNES

resound .... BOOM, PEAL, RING, CLANG, EXTOL, (RE)ECHO, VIBRATE, REVERBERATE

resource(s) .... CASH, MEANS, ASSETS, RESORT, WEALTH, CAPITAL, EXPEDIENT

resourceful .... CUNNING, INGENIOUS, VERSATILE, QUICK-WITTED

respect .... HONOR, ESTEEM, HOMAGE, REGARD, REVERE, DEFERENCE

respectable .... DECENT

respectful .... OBEISANT, REVERENT

Respighi, composer
.... OTTORINO

respiration .... EUPN(O)EA, DYSPN(O)EA, BREATHING

combining form .... SPIRO

stimulant .... METRAZOL

respirator .... INHALER, GAS MASK, IRON LUNG, VENTILATOR
respiratory arrest .... ANOXIA
arrest consequence ..... COMA, BRAIN DAMAGE
disease .... ASTHMA, EMPHYSEMA, PNEUMONIA, BRONCHITIS
disease of horses ...... HEAVES
failure .... HYPOXIA
organ .... LUNG
rattle .... RALE
system, part of .... LUNG, ALVEOLI, TRACHEA, BRONCHUS, BRONCHIOLE
tract infection .... COLD, CROUP, SINUSITIS, LARYNGITIS
respire .... EXHALE, INHALE, BREATHE
respite ...... LULL, DELAY, GRACE, PAUSE, REPRIEVE
from conflict .... TRUCE
resplendent ...... GRAND, SHINING, DAZZLING, GORGEOUS, SPLENDID, BRILLIANT
respond .... REACT, REPLY, ANSWER, RETURN
response .... REPLY, ANSWER, REACTION
evokers .... STIMULI
responsibility .... DUTY, ONUS, LIABILITY, OBLIGATION
responsible .... LIABLE, RELIABLE, DEPENDABLE, ACCOUNTABLE
responsive .... RECEPTIVE, SENSITIVE
rest ...... EASE, SEAT, STOP, SLEEP, OTHERS, REPOSE, BALANCE, RECLINE, SUPPORT, REMAINDER
colloquial .... BREAK, PAUSE, BREATHER
eternal .... DEATH
in prosody .... C(A)ESURA
midday .... SIESTA
restaurant .... DINER, GRILL, BISTRO, EATERY, AUTOMAT, CABARET, CANTEEN, CAFE(TERIA)
bench .... BANQUETTE
compartment .... BOOTH
vehicle .... BUS
restauranteur Toots .... SHOR
restful .... QUIET, PEACEFUL, TRANQUIL
resting .... ABED, DORMANT
place of great men .... VALHALLA
restive .... EDGY, BALKY, UNEASY, UNRULY, FRETFUL, NERVOUS,

RESTLESS, IMPATIENT
restless .... ITCHY, UNEASY, AGITATO, FRETFUL, RESTIVE, AGITATED, PERTURBED
seeker after fun .... GADABOUT
restock .... REPLENISH
restoration .... RENEWAL, REVIVAL, RENOVATION, REINSTATEMENT
restorative .... ANODYNE, CURATIVE, REMEDIAL
restore .... CURE, RENEW, REPAIR, RETURN, PUT BACK, REBUILD, RETROCEDE
energy .... REFRESH
to a good condition .... RENOVATE
to health .... HEAL, RECUPERATE
restrain .... CURB, HOLD, STAY, STEM, CHECK, DETER, BRIDLE, HINDER, CONTAIN, INHIBIT, HOLD BACK, SUPPRESS
freedom of expression .... SHACKLE
one's activity .... HOGTIE, MANACLE, HANDCUFF
restrainer .... LEASH, MUZZLE, TRAMMEL
restraint .... CURB, REIN, CONTROL, RESERVE, DISCIPLINE
kind of .... DETERRENT
of free speech .... GAG
restrict .... LIMIT, IMPEDE, CONFINE
restrictive .... LIMITING, EXCLUSIVE, HINDERING, RESTRAINING
over-garment .... STRAIT-JACKET
restroom .... LAVATORY, POWDER ROOM, (WATER)CLOSET
slang .... JOHN
result .... ENSUE, FRUIT, ISSUE, ANSWER, EFFECT, UPSHOT, OUTCOME, EVENTUATE
of extreme starvation .... CACHEXIA
old age .... SENILITY
thrift .... RICHES
worry .... LINES
resume .... RENEW, PRECIS, REOPEN, REPRISE, SUMMARY, ABSTRACT, CONTINUE, CURRICULUM VITAE
resurge .... RALLY, REVIVE
resurrect .... REVIVE, RESTORE
resurrection .... REVIVAL
he experienced .... JESUS, LAZARUS

resuscitate .... REVIVE
resuscitation .... ANABIOSIS
ret .... DAMP, SOAK, STEEP, MACERATE
retable .... SHELF
retail ...... SELL, VEND, PEDDLE
business .... STAND
retailer .... CLERK, DEALER, VENDOR, PEDDLER, MERCHANT
retain .... OWN, HAVE, HOLD, KEEP, SAVE, RESERVE
retainer .... FEE, ADHERENT, FOLLOWER, ATTENDANT, DEPENDENT
retainers, body of .... RETINUE
retaining wall .... REVETMENT, EMBANKMENT
material ..... PILING, SANDBAGS
retake .... REFILM, RECAPTURE
retaliate .... AVENGE, REQUITE
retaliation ...... TALION, REVENGE, REPRISAL, RETORSION, RETORTION
in kind .... TIT-FOR-TAT, BLOW-FOR-BLOW, AN-EYE-FOR-AN-EYE
retard ...... SLOW, DELAY, HINDER, IMPEDE
retch .... GAG, KECK, VOMIT
rete .... PLEXUS, NETWORK
obs. var. .... RIET
retem .... JUNIPER
retention .... MEMORY
retentive .... TENACIOUS
retepore .... MOLLUSK
rethink .... REVIEW
retiarius .... GLADIATOR
retiary/reticular .... NETLIKE
reticence .... RESERVE
reticent .... SILENT, RESERVED, TACITURN
reticule ...... RETICLE, (HAND)BAG
reticulum .... NETWORK
retina, disease of the .... RETINOPATHY
inflammation .... RETINITIS
tear .... SPLIT
tumor/cancer .... RETINOBLASTOMA
retinue .... CREW, ROUT, MEINY, SUITE, TRAIN, ESCORT, MEINIE, CORTEGE, ENTOURAGE, RETAINERS
retire .... QUIT, REST, LEAVE, SLEEP, REMOVE, RESIGN, RETREAT, WITHDRAW
retired .... ABED, ASLEEP, EMERITUS, SECLUDED, TURNED IN
retiree .... GOLDENAGER

retirement association: abbr.
.... AARP
retiring .... SHY, MODEST,
BASHFUL, RESERVED
retort .... QUIP, REPLY, SALLY,
ALEMBIC, RIPOSTE, SQUELCH,
REJOIN(DER), WITTICISM
retortion .... REPRISAL
retouch .... FIX
retract .... UNSAY, ABJURE,
RECALL, RECANT, RENEGE,
REVOKE, DISAVOW,
WITHDRAW
a statement .... EAT ONE'S
WORDS
retraction .... PALINODE
retral .... POSTERIOR
retread .... RECAP
retreat .... LAIR, NEST, ARBOR,
STUDY, ASYLUM, ESCAPE,
REFUGE, RETIRE, HIDEOUT,
PULLOUT, SANCTUM, SHELTER,
BACK DOWN, WITHDRAW,
KATABASIS
cozy .... DEN, NOOK, ALCOVE
disorderly .... ROUT, FLIGHT
kind of .... CONVENT,
NUNNERY, HERMITAGE,
MONASTERY
shaded .... BOWER
signal .... CHAMADE
retrench .... LESSEN, REDUCE,
CURTAIL, CUT DOWN,
DECREASE, ECONOMIZE
retrenchment .... RAMPART
retribution .... AMENDS, REWARD,
NEMESIS, REQUITAL,
RESTITUTION
retributive justice .... NEMESIS
retrieve .... FETCH, MAKE UP,
REGAIN, REVIVE, RECLAIM,
RECOVER, RESTORE, SET
RIGHT
fly balls .... SHAG
retriever ...... (GUN)DOG, SETTER,
POINTER
retroactive .... BACK(WARD)
retrocede .... RESTORE
retrograde .... DECLINE, INVERSE,
RELAPSE, REVERSE
retrogress ...... REVERT, DECLINE,
BACKSLIDE, DEGENERATE
retrospect .... REVIEW
return ...... RECUR, REPLY, YIELD,
GO BACK, REPORT, REVERT,
REELECT, REPLACE, REQUITE,
RESPOND, RESTORE, COME
BACK, RESPONSE
as in performance ..... REPEAT
as in ticket .... ROUND-TRIP
in kind .... RECIPROCATE

of the Jews to Palestine: 538
B.C. .... RESTORATION
to soundness ...... HEAL, MEND
returns .... YIELD, PROFIT,
REVENUE
Reuben sandwich meat
.... CORNED BEEF
Reuben's brother .... LEVI,
JUDAH, SIMEON
father .... JACOB
grandfather ...... ISAAC, LABAN
mother .... LEAH
reunion .... GET-TOGETHER
kind of .... CLASS, FAMILY
with Brahma .... NIRVANA
Reunion capital .... ST. DENIS
city/town .... LE PORT, ST.
PIERRE
mountain .... PITON DES
NEIGES
Reu's son .... SERUG
rev .... RACE, SPEED, ACCELERATE
Reval .... TALLINN
revamp .... REDO, CHANGE,
REVISE, SHAKE UP,
RENOVATE, REORGANIZE
reveal .... BARE, SHOW, TELL,
EXPOSE, DISPLAY, DIVULGE,
EXHIBIT, DISCLOSE, MANIFEST
unknowingly .... BETRAY
revealing .... SEE-THROUGH
reveille .... ROUSE, SIGNAL,
AWAKENING, (WAKE-UP) CALL
revel ...... ROMP, ENJOY, GAMBOL,
CAROUSE, DELIGHT, ROISTER,
CAROUSAL
revelation .... ORACLE,
DISCLOSURE
revelations .... APOCALYPSE
revel(l)er .... CORYBANT,
MERRYMAKER
exclamation of a .... WHOOPEE
revelry .... ORGY, RIOT, SPREE,
FESTIVITY, SATURNALIA
revenant .... GHOST, EIDOLON
revenge .... AVENGE, TALION,
RETALIATE, VENGEANCE
revenue .... NET, INCOME, PROFIT,
EARNINGS, RECEIPTS
bishop's .... ANNAT
revenuers' target .... STILL
reverberate .... RECOIL,
(RE)ECHO, REBOUND,
REFLECT, RESOUND
revere .... ADORE, HONOR,
ADMIRE, RESPECT, WORSHIP,
VENERATE
reverence .... AWE, BOW, CURTSY,
HOMAGE, WORSHIP,
ADORATION, VENERATION
gesture of .... OBEISANCE

lacking .... IMPIOUS
reverie .... FANCY, MUSING,
NOTION, FANTASY,
(DAY)DREAM
revers .... LAPEL
reversal .... UPSET, SETBACK,
ABOUT-FACE, ANNULMENT,
TURNABOUT, VOLTE-FACE
combining form .... ALLO
reverse ...... BACK, UNDO, ANNUL,
EVERT, INVERT, REVOKE,
CONTRARY, OPPOSITE
a situation .... TURN THE
TABLES
reversion .... RETURN
of property .... ESCHEAT
to primitive type .... ATAVISM,
THROWBACK
revert .... RECUR, RETURN,
REGRESS
revest .... REINSTATE
review .... REVUE, NOTICE,
PARADE, REPORT, SURVEY,
ACCOUNT, INSPECT, CRITIQUE,
CRITICISM, CRITICIZE,
EPICRISIS
adverse .... PAN
briefly .... RECAP
enthusiastic .... RAVE
for an exam hurriedly
.... CRAM
four-star .... RAVE
of marching troops
.... PARADE
one's thoughts .... RETHINK
reviewer .... CRITIC
revile ...... ABUSE, SCOLD, DERIDE,
MALIGN, VILIFY, ASPERSE,
BELITTLE, VILIPEND
revise .... EDIT, ALTER, AMEND,
REHASH, CORRECT, REWRITE
revival .... REBIRTH, RENEWAL
revivalist .... EVANGELIST
revive .... RALLY, COME TO, PERK
UP, RESURGE, RESUSCITATE
memory .... JOG, RECALL,
REMIND, REFRESH
revocation .... REPEAL,
ANNULMENT, NULLIFICATION
revoke .... ADEEM, ANNUL, RENIG,
ABJURE, CANCEL, RECALL,
RECANT, RENEGE, REPEAL,
DISAVOW, RESCIND
revolt .... (A)RISE, MUTINY,
DISGUST, SEDITION, UPRISING,
REBEL(LION)
revolting .... HORRID, LOATHSOME,
OFFENSIVE, REPULSIVE
revolution .... GYRE, TURN,
CYCLE, ROTATION, COUP
(D'ETAT), REBELLION

593

fighter .... MINUTEMAN
general of the .... ASHE,
    GATES, ARNOLD, GREENE,
    LINCOLN, SULLIVAN
statesman of the .... OTIS
revolutionary .... REBEL,
    RADICAL, INSURGENT
Allen .... ETHAN
revolutionist .... REB(EL),
    ANARCH(IST)
revolve .... ROLL, SPIN, TURN,
    ORBIT, CIRCLE, GYRATE,
    ROTATE
revolver .... GAT, ROD, COLT,
    PISTOL, BULLDOG, HANDGUN,
    REPEATER, AUTOMATIC
part .... COCK, LOCK, SEAR,
    TRIGGER, CYLINDER
revolving part .... ROTOR
revue .... SHOW, REVIEW, FOLLIES,
    VAUDEVILLE
revulsion ...... DISGUST, AVERSION
reward .... FEE, PAY, TIP, AWARD,
    BONUS, PRIZE, ENRICH,
    RETURN, GUERDON, PREMIUM
of a sort .... SOP, WAGES,
    SALARY
slang .... PAYOFF
reword .... EDIT
rewrite .... REVISE
rewriting .... RESCRIPT
rex .... KING
Rex Stout's Wolfe .... NERO
Reynard .... FOX
Rey's consort .... REINA
RH factor .... RHESUS
rhabdomancy .... DOWSING,
    DIVINATION
rhapsodic .... LYRIC
rhapsodical .... ECSTATIC
Rhapsody in Blue composer
    .... (GEORGE) GERSHWIN
rhea .... EMU, OPS, NANDU,
    CYBELE, OSTRICH
Rhea, husband of .... CRONUS
parent of .... GAEA, URANUS
progeny of .... HERA, ZEUS,
    HADES, HESTIA, DEMETER,
    POSEIDON
rheotrope .... COMMUTATOR
rhesus .... MONKEY, MACAQUE
rhetor .... ORATOR
rhetoric .... ORATORY
rhetorical .... FORENSIC
device .... ANAPHORA
figure .... LITOTES
rheum .... COLD, CATARRH,
    RHINITIS
rheumatic pain .... LUMBAGO
person .... ACHER

rheumatism of back/loins
    .... LUMBAGO, BACKACHE
of joints ...... GOUT, ARTHRITIS
remedy .... MOTRIN, ASPIRIN,
    THERAPY
rhinal .... NASAL
Rhine .... RIJN, RHEIN, RIVER
branch .... WAAL
city on the .... KOLN, MAINZ,
    WORMS, MAYENCE, MANNHEIM
siren .... LURLEI, LORELEI
tributary .... MAIN
wine .... HOCK, MOSELLE
rhinitis, allergic .... HAY FEVER
viral .... (COMMON) COLD,
    SINUSITIS
rhino(ceros) .... CASH, ABADA,
    MONEY, BORELE
feature .... HORN
for one .... PACHYDERM
one-horned .... BADAK
two-horned .... KEITLOA
rhinology subject .... NOSE
rhinoplasty .... NOSE JOB
object .... NOSE
rhizoid .... ROOTLIKE
rhizome .... STEM, TUBER,
    STOLON, ROOTSTALK,
    ROOT(STOCK)
rhizopod .... TESTACEAN
protozoan .... AMOEBA
rhizopus .... FUNGUS
Rhode Island bay
    .... NARRAGANSETT
capital .... PROVIDENCE
city/town .... BRISTOL,
    NEWPORT, WARWICK,
    COVENTRY, CRANSTON,
    TIVERTON, WESTERLY,
    PAWTUCKET, BARRINGTON,
    WOONSOCKET
college .... BRYANT,
    PROVIDENCE, ROGER WILLIAMS
county .... KENT, BRISTOL,
    NEWPORT, PROVIDENCE
founder .... (ROGER) WILLIAMS
island .... BLOCK, PRUDENCE,
    CONANICUT
naval base .... NEWPORT
point .... SANDY, NOYES
rebel: 1842 .... DORR
red .... HEN, CHICKEN
river .... SAKONNET,
    PAWCATUCK
state flower .... VIOLET
state nickname .... OCEAN,
    LITTLE RHODY
tourist attraction .... TENNIS
    HALL OF FAME
tree .... MAPLE
university .... BROWN

Rhodes .... RODI
ancient wonder ...... COLOSSUS
Rhodesia, new name of
    .... ZIMBABWE
Northern .... ZAMBIA
port .... BEIRA
premier .... SMITH
tribe .... ILAS
rhododendron .... LAUREL,
    ROSEBAY
kin of .... AZALEA
rhodolite .... GARNET
rhomb(us) .... LOZENGE,
    PARALLELOGRAM
rhombencephalon .... HINDBRAIN
part .... PONS, CEREBELLUM
rhonchus .... RALE, SNORE,
    RATTLE
Rhone tributary .... ISERE,
    SAONE
rhubarb .... SCRAP, SET-TO,
    HASSLE, ARGUMENT,
    PIEPLANT, DISCUSSION
rhyme .... POESY, VERSE,
    CRAMBO, CONCORD,
    HARMONY
and reason .... SENSE
inferior .... DOGGEREL
scheme .... ABABA
rhymer/rhymester
    .... POET(ASTER), VERSIFIER
rhyming .... CRAMBO
rhythm .... BEAT, LILT, TIME,
    METER, METRE, SWING,
    TEMPO, CADENCE, MEASURE
in verse .... METER
meter .... IONIC
method .... CONTRACEPTION
rhythmic .... PULSATING
flow .... CADENCE
rise and fall .... HEAVE
rhythmical accent .... ICTUS
ria .... INLET
rial .... COIN
rialto .... MART, BRIDGE, MARKET
riant .... GAY, BLITHE, SMILING,
    CHEERFUL, LAUGHING
riata .... LARIAT
rib .... BONE, VEIN, COSTA, RIDGE
Adam's .... EVE, WIFE
colloquial .... KID, TWIT,
    TEASE
cut, meat .... SPARERIB
disorder .... FRACTURE
in architecture .... LIERNE
leaf .... NERVURE
of a .... COSTAL
slang .... ROAST
ribald .... LOW, COARSE, VULGAR,
    PROFANE
ribaldry .... JAPERY

riband .... RIBBON
ribbed .... KIDDED, RIDGED,
　　　　　　　TEASED, COSTATE
as cloth .... WALED
ribbon .... BAND, BADGE, STRIP,
　　　　　　　DECORATION
award .... CORDON
cutting, for example
　........................... CEREMONY
decorative .... RIBAND
document's .... LABEL
elastic .... GARTER
hair .... BANDEAU
knot .... COCKADE
like part .... T(A)ENIA
of cotton, etc. .... FERRET
paper .... TICKER TAPE
seal .... LABEL
trimming .... GALLOON
worsted .... CADDIS
woven .... BRAID
Ribbon, Blue .... FIRST PRIZE
ribbons .... SHREDS, TATTERS,
　　　　　　　STREAMERS
ribwort .... PLANTAIN
Ricardo, actor .... MONTALBAN
rice .... GRAIN, GRASS, SEEDS,
　　　　　　　PADDY, CEREAL
alcoholic drink .... BASI,
　　　　　　　SAKE, ARRACK
boiled with meat .... PILAU,
　　　　　　　　　PILAF(F)
cooked with gravy
　.................................. RISOTTO
dessert .... PUDDING
dish, spicy ...... CURRY, PILAU,
　　　　　　　　　PILAF(F)
field .... PADDY
husk .... BRAN
in the husk .... PADDY
nutritive substance .... STARCH
playwright .... ELMER
type of .... WILD, BROWN,
　　SWEET, WHITE, PARBOILED
riceball .... PINDA
ricebird ...... SPARROW, BOBOLINK
rich .... VIVID, FERTILE, OPULENT,
　　WEALTHY, AFFLUENT,
　　VALUABLE, WELL-TO-DO,
　　ABOUNDING, LUXURIANT,
　　LUXURIOUS, PLENTIFUL
oil country .... KUWAIT
person .... DIVES, MIDAS,
　　NABOB, TYCOON, CROESUS,
　　FINANCIER, MONEYBAG(S),
　　PLUTO(CRAT), CAPITALIST
slang .... LOADED
source .... LODE, MINE
streak .... LODE
the .... MONEYED
Richard I of England ..... LION-

HEARTED, COEUR DE LION
brother of .... JOHN
father of .... HENRY II
mother of .... ELEANOR
Richard, unknown .... ROE
riches .... PELF, LUCRE, MONEY,
　　ASSETS, WEALTH, FORTUNE,
　　OPULENCE, PROPERTY
antipode of .... RAGS
deified .... MAMMON
richest part .... FAT, CREAM
richly .... AMPLY, FULLY
mellow .... GOLDEN
richness .... LUXE, MEANS,
　　AFFLUENCE, PROSPERITY
Richter scale's concern
　....................... EARTHQUAKES
Richthofen's forte .... DOGFIGHT
ricin .... PROTEIN
rick .... PILE, STACK
Rickenbacker, American ace
　.................................... EDDIE
rickets .... RACHITIS
feature .... BOWLEGS,
　　DEFORMITY
is deficiency of
　................................ VITAMIN D
rickety ...... WEAK, FRAIL, SHAKY,
　　FEEBLE, RACHITIC
rickey .... DRINK
ingredient .... GIN
Rickover, Adm. .... HYMAN
rickrack .... BRAID, TRIMMING
ricksha(w) .... JINRIKISHA
ricochet .... SKIP, BOUNCE,
　　CAR(R)OM, DEFLECT,
　　REBOUND
rictus .... GAPING, RINGENT
rid .... FREE, SHED, CLEAR,
　　RELIEVE, DISENCUMBER
of defect .... REAM
of false ideas .... DISABUSE
riddance .... RELEASE, SEVERANCE
ridden .... OBSESSED
riddle ...... POSER, SIEVE, ENIGMA,
　　PEPPER, PUZZLE, MYSTERY,
　　PROBLEM, CONUNDRUM,
　　PERFORATE
bandleader .... NELSON
picture .... REBUS
Ridd's heroine .... LORNA
　　(DOONE)
ride .... BAIT, ANNOY, DRIVE,
　　MOUNT, TEASE, HARASS,
　　TRAVEL
at full speed .... GALLOP
pay for .... FARE, PASSAGE
take for a .... KILL, DECEIVE
to hounds .... HUNT
rider .... FARE, JOKER, CLAUSE,
　　JOCKEY, CODICIL, ADDITION,

PASSENGER, EQUESTRIAN
for free .... DEADHEAD
1775 .... (PAUL) REVERE
ridge .... BACK, RAND, RUGA,
　　WALE, ARETE, CHINE, CREST,
　　ESKAR, RANGE, ARISTA,
　　CUESTA
between furrows .... LIST
between peaks .... SADDLE
glacial .... OSAR, ESKER,
　　DRUMLIN
having a .... RIDGY
like part .... KEEL, CARINA
of earth .... HOGBACK,
　　HORSEBACK
sand .... DENE, DUNE
sandy .... LANDE
saw-toothed .... SIERRA
ridgepole .... ROOFTREE
ridicule .... JEER, JEST, MOCK,
　　TWIT, ROAST, SCOFF, SCOUT,
　　TAUNT, DERIDE
expose to .... PILLORY
playfully .... KID
satirical .... LAMPOON
ridiculous .... INANE, ABSURD,
　　FOOLISH, DERISIVE,
　　GROTESQUE, LUDICROUS,
　　SARCASTIC
laugh .... SNICKER
look .... LEER
rite .... MUMMERY
riding boot .... JEMMY
breeches .... JODHPURS
costume .... HABIT
horse .... MOUNT, PALFREY,
　　ROADSTER
master .... TEACHER
place .... TRACK
school/academy .... MANEGE
whip .... CROP, QUIRT
Rienzi composer .... WAGNER
Ries, composer .... FERDINAND
rife .... CURRENT, PROFUSE,
　　TEEMING, PREVALENT,
　　PREVAILING, WIDESPREAD
Riff .... BERBER
riffle .... REEF, SHOAL, SHUFFLE
riffraff .... MOB, SCUM, TRASH,
　　RABBLE, DOGGERY, CANAILLE
rifle ...... GUN, ROB, PIECE, STEAL,
　　GARAND, MAUSER, CARBINE,
　　FIREARM, PILLAGE, PLUNDER,
　　RANSACK, REPEATER,
　　CHASSEPOT
automatic ..... BAR, BROWNING
bullet .... MINIE (BALL)
chamber .... MAGAZINE
light .... CARBINE
pin .... TIGE
position .... READY

rifleman .... YAGER, JA(E)GER
rating of .... EXPERT,
    MARKSMAN, SHARPSHOOTER
rifler .... ROBBER
rift .... GAP, FLAW, BREAK, CLEFT,
    CRACK, SPLIT, BREACH,
    CREVICE, FISSURE, DISUNITY,
    SEPARATION
rig .... CART, GEAR, DRESS,
    ATTIRE, CLOTHE, FIT (OUT),
    OUTFIT, TACKLE, COSTUME,
    CARRIAGE, EQUIP(MENT),
    MANIPULATE
Riga gulf island .... OESEL
native .... LATVIAN
rigatoni .... PASTA
Rigel .... STAR
rigger .... SCAFFOLD
rigging ...... GEAR, TACK, ROPING,
    TACKLE, EQUIPMENT
part .... SPAR, MASTS, ROPES,
    SAILS, YARDS, CHAINS,
    SHROUDS
type of .... LIFT, BRACE,
    SHROUD, BOWLINE, HALYARD,
    (BOOM)VANG, BACKROPES
Rigg's disease .... PYORRHEA
right ...... SOUND, TITLE, NORMAL,
    CURRENT, DEXTRAL, FITTING,
    LICENSE, REDRESS, STRAIGHT,
    SUITABLE, VIRTUOUS,
    PREROGATIVE
a wrong .... REDRESS
and wrong decider
    .... CASUIST
angle gauge .... TRYSQUARE
by .... PROPERLY
combining form .... RECT(I)
exclusive .... PATENT
hand side .... DEXTER
hand page .... RECTO
hand side of ship or airplane
    .... STARBOARD
hereditary .... UDAL
in politics .... RIGHTIST,
    CONSERVATIVE
in politics: extreme ...... TORY
king's .... REGALITY
legal .... DROIT, TITLE
now .... AT ONCE, PRONTO,
    IMMEDIATELY
of expression .... VOICE
of holding .... TENURE
of way .... EASEMENT
on the .... OFF(SIDE)
slang .... ROGER
special .... CHARTER,
    FRANCHISE
to choose .... OPTION
to decide .... SAY-SO
to enter .... ENTREE, INGRESS

to mail free .... FRANK
to ownership .... TITLE
triangle ratio .... SINE
turn .... GEE
word .... MOTJUSTE
righteous .... JUST, MORAL,
    VIRTUOUS
rightfully .... DULY
righto .... YES, CERTAINLY
rights, equality of .... ISONOMY
relating to .... JURAL
rigid ...... SET, FIRM, TAUT, STIFF,
    SEVERE, STRICT, AUSTERE,
    RIGOROUS
rigmarole .... BLATHER,
    NONSENSE
Rigoletto author .... VERDI
rigor .... HARDNESS, HARDSHIP,
    RIGIDITY, SEVERITY,
    STIFFNESS
companion of .... MORTIS
rigorous .... HARSH, RIGID, STERN,
    STIFF, SEVERE, STRICT,
    PRECISE, DIFFICULT
Rigsdag, part of .... FOLKETING,
    LANDSTING
Riis, social reformer ...... JACOB
Rijeka .... FIUME
Rijn .... RHINE
rile .... IRK, VEX, ROIL, ANGER,
    IRRITATE
Riley, coach .... PAT
of Knots Landing .... LARRY
Rilke, Ger. poet .... RAINER
rill ...... BROOK, FURROW, STREAM,
    TRENCH, VALLEY, RIVULET
rim .... LIP, BRIM, EDGE, BRINK,
    VERGE, BORDER, MARGIN
cap's projecting .... VISOR
cask's .... CHIME, CHINE
rail/pipe's .... FLANGE
roof's .... EAVE
wheel .... FELLY, FELLOE
rime .... RHYME, (HOAR)FROST
rimer .... MINSTREL
rimple .... CREASE, WRINKLE
rimy .... FROSTY
Rinaldo's magic horse
    .... BAYARD, BAJARDO
rind .... BARK, PEEL, SKIN, CRUST,
    CORTEX, COATING, EPICARP,
    EXOCARP
candied .... CITRON
ring .... RIM, SET, DING, GYRE,
    TOLL, ARENA, KNELL, CALL
    (UP), CIRQUE, CLIQUE,
    SIGNAL, ANNULET, RESOUND,
    (EN)CIRCLE
again .... RETOLL
around the collar
    .... NECKLINE

around the sun/moon
    .... HALO
bell .... PEAL, TOLL, CHIME,
    KNELL
decision .... TKO, DRAW
gem .... CAMEO
give a ...... CALL, (TELE)PHONE
harness .... TERRET
jeweled .... MARQUISE
master .... PUG, BOXER
metal .... BEE
mounting style .... TIFFANY
neck .... PHEASANT
of fiction .... LARDNER
guards .... CORDON
leaves .... INVOLUCEL,
    INVOLUCRE
light .... HALO
neck feathers .... RUFF,
    TORQUES
rope .... GROMMET
rubber .... GASKET
virtue .... HALO
out .... PEAL
result .... TKO, DRAW,
    KNOCKOUT
shaped .... ANNULAR
shaped cake .... DOUGHNUT
single gem of .... SOLITAIRE
stone setting .... COLLET
tailed animal .... COON
up .... CALL, DIAL,
    (TELE)PHONE
wedding .... BAND
ringdove .... CUSHAT
ringent .... GAPING, RICTUS
ringer .... QUOIT, POSEUR,
    HORSESHOE, LOOK-ALIKE
ringing, persistent ...... CLANGOR
sound in ear .... TINNITUS
ringleader .... TROUBLE-MAKER
ringlet .... CURL, LOCK, TRESS
ringmaster .... MC, EMCEE,
    DIRECTOR
ringworm .... TINEA, SERPIGO
rinse .... LAVE, WASH
rinsings .... DREGS
rio .... RIVER
Rio _____ .... MUNI, BRAVO,
    NEGRO, GRANDE
de _____ .... ORO, JANEIRO
Grande, city on .... LAREDO
Grande national park ...... BIG
    BEND
Grande tributary .... PECOS
Mister in .... SENHOR
Muni city .... BATA
seaport .... MATAMOROS
riot ...... HIT, ROW, ORGY, BRAWL,
    EMEUTE, FRACAS, HUBBUB,
    UPROAR, DISORDER

rioter .... BRAWLER, RABBLEROUSER
riotous .... WILD, NOISY, WANTON, DISSOLUTE, LUXURIANT, TURBULENT
rip .... CUT, REND, RIVE, TEAR, SPLIT, SEVERE
colloquial .... NAG, HORSE
into .... ATTACK
roaring .... NOISY, BOISTEROUS
Rip van Winkle author
.... IRVING
riparian .... RIVERINE
glitter .... SPARKLE ON THE WATERS
recess .... INLET
ripe ...... ADULT, READY, MATURE, MELLOW, DEVELOPED
ripen ...... AGE, MATURE, TEMPER
ripening agent .... AGER
early .... RATH(E), RARERIPE
ripoff .... SWINDLE
riposte .... MOT, RETORT, RETURN, THRUST
ripping .... FINE, SPLENDID, EXCELLENT
ripple .... LAP, PURL, RAPID, BABBLE, GURGLE, SPLASH, WAVE(LET), UNDULATION
riptide .... UNDERTOW
Ripuarian .... FRANK
ris de veau .... SWEETBREAD
rise .... HILL, LOOM, SOAR, GET UP, OCCUR, REBEL, SLOPE, STAND, ASCEND, APPEAR, ASCENT, REVOLT
again .... RESURGE
and fall .... WELTER, FLUCTUATE
and float in the air
.... LEVITATE
from the dead ...... RESURRECT
high .... SOAR
in the ground .... LIFT
of the tide .... FLOOD
with success .... PROSPER
Rise, soprano .... STEVENS
risibility .... MIRTH
risible .... FUNNY, AMUSING, LAUGHABLE, LUDICROUS
rising .... BOIL, MONTANT, ANABATIC, MOUNTING
risk .... SINK, PERIL, CHANCE, GAMBLE, HAZARD, JEOPARDY, (EN)DANGER
risky .... CHANCY
risque .... RACY, SEXY, DARING, OFF-COLOR, SCABROUS
rhyme .... LIMERICK
rissole .... MEATBALL
rite .... LITURGY, CEREMONY,

(HOLY) ORDERS
meaningless .... MUMBO-JUMBO
public worship .... LITURGY
washing .... LAVABO
ritual ...... FORMAL, LITURGIC(AL)
beads .... ROSARY
ceremony .... BAPTISM, MATRIMONY, CONFIRMATION
container .... CENSER, THURIBLE
greeting .... PAX
supper .... SEDER
symbol .... CROSS, CRUCIFIX
Ritz, Swiss hotelman ...... CESAR
ritzy .... POSH, TONY, PLUSH, SWANK, SWELL, CLASSY, ELEGANT, LUXURIOUS
auto .... LIMO
rivage .... BANK, COAST, SHORE
rival .... FOE, VIE, EQUAL, MATCH, COMPETE, EMULATE, OPPONENT, COMPETITOR, CONTESTANT
Las Vegas' .... RENO, TAHOE
rivalry .... EMULATION, COMPETITION
rive .... REND, TEAR, SPLIT, CLEAVE
riven .... RENT, TORN, SPLIT
river .... STREAM, WATERWAY, WATERCOURSE
Avignon's .... RHONE
bank .... RIPA, LEVEE
bank, of a .... RIPARIAN
barge .... GONDOLA
barrier .... BOOM, WEIR, BARRAGE
"beautiful" .... OHIO
bed .... CHANNEL
bed, dry .... WADI
bend .... OXBOW
Bern's .... AAR(E)
blindness ..... ONCHOCERCIASIS
blue, poetically .... DANUBE
boat .... BARGE, FERRY, PACKET, SAMPAN
bottom .... BED
branch .... ARM
Caen's .... ORNE
channel .... FAIRWAY
Chauny's .... OISE
cross a .... FERRY
crossed by Caesar
.... RUBICON
curve in .... BEN, BIGHT
dam .... WEIR
deep, still spot of .... POOL
deposit .... LOESS
duck .... TEAL, SHOVEL(L)ER
edge/embankment .... BANK,

DIKE, LEVEE
elbow .... BEND
falls .... SAULTS
famous .... AVON, NILE, AMAZON, DANUBE, RUBICON
Firenze's/Florence's ..... ARNO
Flanders .... YSER
flowing into Lake Rudolf
.... OMO
Frankfurt's .... ODER
Giza's .... NILE
horse .... HIPPO(POTAMUS)
in a Burns poem .... AFTON
in Central India .... PURNA
in the broads .... YARE
in the Hades .... LETHE
in Zaire .... UELE, CONGO
inlet .... BAYOU, SLOUGH
island/isle .... AIT, HOLM
land near ..... HOLM, BOTTOMS
landing .... GHAT, LEVEE
large .... NILE, AMAZON, YELLOW, YANGTZE, MISSOURI, MISSISSIPPI
longest .... NILE
Mexico .... RIO GRANDE
mouth .... BOCA, DELTA, ESTUARY, EMBOUCHURE
nymph .... NAIS, NAIAD
of song .... OHIO, AFTON, VOLGA, DANUBE, SWANEE
of wailing .... COCYTUS
or monster .... GILA
outlet .... BAYOU
Parisian .... SEINE
Pultusk's .... NAREV
rapid .... SAULT
Rheine's .... EMS
sacred .... ALPH, GANGES
sell down the .... BETRAY, DECEIVE
siren .... LORELEI
soil .... DELTA
source .... HEAD
South American .... NEGRO, PURUS, JAPURA, MADEIRA, ORINOCO, URUGUAY, PARAGUAY, PILCOMAYO
Stratford's .... AVON
through Belgium .... YSER
to the Baltic .... ODER
Caspian .... URAL
Congo .... UELE
Elbe .... EGER, ISER
Euphrates .... MURAT
Mediterranean .... NILE
North Sea .... YSER
Rhine .... (THE) RUHR
Seine .... OISE
Yellow Sea .... YALU

tributary of the James
.... COW PASTURE (RIVER)
underworld .... STYX
U.S.A. ...... RED, OHIO, PECOS,
SNAKE, TEXAS, BRAZOS,
ARKANSAS, COLORADO,
COLUMBIA, MISSOURI,
MISSISSIPPI
U.S.S.R. .... DON, OKA, KAMA,
LENA, URAL, VOLGA, ANGARA,
KOLYMA, DNIEPER, PECHORA
valley .... DALE, STRATH
wade across .... FORD
widened part .... LAKE
winding of .... ESS
Yuma's .... GILA
River, Big .... MISSISSIPPI
Big Muddy .... MISSOURI
Rivera, Mex. painter ...... DIEGO
forte .... MURAL
riverine .... RIPARIAN
rivet ...... BOLT, FASTEN, HAMMER
holder .... DOLLY
washer of .... BURR
riveter, female .... ROSIE
Riviera beach .... PLAGE
port .... CANNES
resort .... NICE, CANNES
rivulet .... RILL, BROOK, ARROYO,
RUNNEL, STREAM, RUN(D)LET
rix-dollar .... DALER
Riyadh is capital of the .... NEJD
Rizal, Filipino patriot ...... JOSE
Rizpah's husband .... SAUL
RMN, to friends .... DICK
Rn, in chemistry .... RADON
R.N. .... ROYAL NAVY,
REGISTERED NURSE
roach ...... CARP, INSECT, SUNFISH,
COCKROACH
movie producer .... HAL
road .... ITER, PATH, TRACK,
TRAIL, COURSE, (HIGH)WAY,
MACADAM, CAUSEWAY
agent .... HIGHWAYMAN
along embankment .... STAITH
Canada to Key West .... USI
character .... HOG, HOBO,
TRAMP, JOGGER, (HITCH)HIKER
charge .... TOLL
contractor .... PAVER
curve .... ESS
descriptive of a ...... UNPAVED
fast .... SPEEDWAY
feature .... JOG
for locomotive .... RAILWAY
ledge/shoulder .... BERM(E)
map abbreviation .... RTE
of a .... VIATIC(AL)
on the .... ON TOUR,
TRAVELING

pavement .... TELFORD
private .... DRIVEWAY
runner .... BIRD, COCK,
CUCKOO, JOGGER
sign .... ESS, MILEPOST,
MILESTONE
surface .... TAR, ASPHALT,
MACADAM
toll .... (TURN)PIKE
treatment, winter .... GRIT
worker ...... NAVVY, CAMINERO
roadbed fill .... GRAVEL
roadblock .... BLOCKADE
border .... CHECKPOINT
roadhouse .... INN, TAVERN,
NIGHTCLUB
roads scholar .... HOBO
roadside sign .... GAS, EATS,
MOTEL, DETOUR, LODGING,
REST AREA, SPEED LIMIT
weed .... DOG, FENNEL
roadster .... HORSE, RUNABOUT,
TWO-SEATER
feature .... RUMBLE SEAT
roadway, sloping .... RAMP
roam .... GAD, ROVE, RANGE,
STRAY, RAMBLE, STROLL,
WANDER, MEANDER
roan ...... BAY, HORSE, SHEEPSKIN
color ..... CHESTNUT, REDDISH-
BROWN
Roanoke bell .... COWSLIP
tributary .... DAN
roar ...... DIN, BAWL, BELL, BOOM,
HOWL, ROLL, GROWL, NOISE,
SHOUT, STORM, BELLOW,
RUMBLE, THUNDER,
LAUGHTER
roaring .... BRISK, NOISY,
BOOMING
Roaring Twenties dance
.... CHARLESTON
roast .... BAKE, HEAT, BROIL,
BROWN, PARCH, PICNIC,
BARBECUE, CRITICIZE
meat .... CABOBS, KABOBS
slang .... TEASE, RIDICULE
turner .... JACK
roaster .... PIG(LET), BROILER,
CHICKEN
roasting device/tool .... PAN,
OVEN, SPIT, GRILL, GRIDIRON,
BUCCANEER
rob ...... CLIP, FLAY, LOOT, REAVE,
RIFLE, STEAL, PLUNDER,
PURLOIN
a house .... BURGLARIZE
a truck .... HIJACK
slang .... MUG
—— to pay Paul .... PETER
Rob Roy author .... SCOTT

robalo .... FISH, SNOOK, PICKEREL
roband .... ROPE
robbed .... REFT, DEPRIVED,
PILFERED, PURLOINED
robber ...... YEGG, THIEF, BANDIT,
DACOIT, RIFLER, BANDIDO,
BRIGAND, CATERAN,
(FOOT)PAD, LADRONE,
RAPPAREE, SPOLIATOR
bank ...... YEGG, SAFECRACKER
bird .... DAW, SKUA, SHOOI,
JA(E)GER
cattle .... RUSTLER
den of .... LAIR, HIDEOUT
fond of crowds .... DIP,
PICKPOCKET
highway .... BANDIT, HIJACKER
house .... BURGLAR
kind of .... BANK, HOUSE,
TRAIN
sea .... PIRATE, CORSAIR,
PRIVATEER
slang .... MUGGER
robbery .... THEFT, HOLD-UP,
PIRACY, DACOITY, STICKUP
literary .... PLAGIARISM
Robbia, Ital. sculptor ...... LUCA
DELLA, ANDRE DELLA
robe ...... TOGA, WRAP, VESTMENT,
(DRESSING) GOWN
at-home/long-sleeved
.... CAFTAN, KAFTAN
bishop's ...... CHIMAR, CHIMER
long .... TALAR
loose/woman's .... SIMAR,
KIMONO
monk's .... FROCK
of office .... TOGA
plural ...... APPAREL, CLOTHES,
COSTUME
robed .... VESTED
Robert, actor .... YOUNG,
TAYLOR, REDFORD
American muralist .... REID
"Robert E. Lee" .... MISSISSIPPI
RIVERBOAT
robin .... THRUSH, RUDDOCK,
REDBREAST
Robin Goodfellow ...... ELF, PUCK,
FAIRY, SPRITE, HOBGOBLIN
Hood .... OUTLAW, DO-GOODER
Hood's companion
.... (FRIAR) TUCK, WILL
(SCARLET)
Forest .... SHERWOOD
sweetheart .... (MAID)
MARIAN
weapon .... LONGBOW
Robinson, baseball coach
.... FRANK
Crusoe's man .... FRIDAY

model .... SELKIRK
of baseball hall of fame
.... FRANK, BROOKS, JACKIE
Ray .... SUGAR
roble .... OAK, TREE, BEECH
roborant .... TONIC
robot .... GOLEM, PUPPET,
AUTOMATON
robots, play about .... RUR
robust ...... HALE, HARDY, HUSKY,
LUSTY, ROUGH, SOUND,
STOUT, WALLY, STURDY,
HEALTHY, MUSCULAR,
VIGOROUS
roc .... BIRD, SIMURG
passenger .... SIN(D)BAD
rocambole .... LEEK, ONION
rochet .... FROCK, SURPLICE,
VESTMENT
rock .... CRAG, SWAY, CANDY,
SHAKE, STONE, SWING,
GNEISS, JIGGLE, TEETER,
TOTTER, DOLOMITE,
GANISTER, PSEPHITE
above a plain .... MONODOCK
basaltic .... WHIN(STONE)
bass .... SUNFISH
black .... BASALT
boring tool .... TRAPAN,
TREPAN
bottom .... LOWEST
carving .... PETROGLYPH
cavity .... VUG(G), VUGH,
GEODE
combining form .... SAXI,
LITH(O), PETR(O)
colorful, glassy ...... FELDSPAR
conglomerate ..... GRAYWACKE
containing gem, fossil, etc.
.... MATRIC
crushed .... BALLAST
crystal .... QUARTZ
decomposed .... SAPROLITE
dug out .... FOSSIL
easily split .... SCHIST
ejected by volcano
.... LAPILLUS
eroded .... BOSS
face .... PRECIPICE
fine-grained ..... SHALE, SLATE
finely broken .... SAND
fluid .... LAVA
formation .... SIAL, TERRANE
formation at Colorado
Springs .... GARDEN OF
THE GODS
formed by geyser ...... SINTER
fragment(s) ..... BRASH, SPALL,
DETRITUS
fragmental .... PSEPHITE
garden .... ROCKERY

granitelike .... GNEISS
green .... OPHITE, VERD
ANTIQUE
growths on ...... TRIPE, LICHEN
hard .... GRANITE
igneous .... TRAP, BASALT,
DIORITE, GRANITE, PICRITE,
SYENITE, PORPHYRY,
PEGMATITE, PHONOLITE,
PERIDOT(ITE)
in another rock ...... XENOLITE
isolated .... SCAR
jagged .... CRAG
like/of .... PETROUS
like fish roe .... OOLITE
mass .... HORST
metamorphic .... GNEISS
mica and quartz .... GREIN
molten .... MAGMA
mottled .... OPHITE
oil .... NAP(H)THA, PETROLEUM
pinnacle .... TOR, NEEDLE
plant .... MOSS
porous .... TUFA, TUFF,
TOPH(E)
projecting .... SCAR, LEDGE
rabbit .... HYRAX
ribbed .... FIRM, RIGID
road-making .... TRAP, BASALT
rose product ...... LA(B)DANUM
salt .... HALITE
salt money .... EMOL
sediments .... ELUVIA
sedimentary .... PELITE,
MUDSTONE
siliceous .... GANISTER
steep .... CLIFF
stratified .... SHALE
system .... TRIAS
volcanic .... LAVA, WACK,
BASALT, LATITE, PERLITE
weed .... FUCUS, SEA OAK
rockaway .... CARRIAGE
Rockefeller, John _____
.... DAVISON
one other .... EDSEL, NELSON
rocker .... CHAIR, SKATE, CRADLE
off one's: sl. .... CRAZY
rockery .... GARDEN
rocket ...... SOAR, AGENA, ASROC,
MISSILE, PROJECTILE
bomb .... TORPEDO
firing platform .... LAUNCHING
PAD
French-built .... ARIANE
fuel .... LOX, HYDRAZINE
gun/launcher .... BAZOOKA
load .... WARHEAD
part of .... CAPSULE,
(NOSE)CONE, JET ENGINE
propellant .... FUEL

to get astronaut back
.... RETRO
upper stage for a .... AGENA
rockfish .... BASS, RE(I)NA,
GROUPER, BOCACCIO,
YELLOWTAIL
rockfoil .... SAXIFRAGE
Rockies' range .... TETON, UINTA
Rockne, football coach
.... KNUTE
rocks at foot of cliff .... TALUS
bluish .... LIAS
living on .... SAXATILE,
SAXICOLINE
of the oldest .... ARCHEAN
on the ...... RUINED, BANKRUPT
pile of .... TALUS, DEBRIS
slang .... GEM, ICE, MONEY,
DIAMOND(S)
study of .... LITHOLOGY,
PETROLOGY
rockweed .... FUCUS, FUCOID
rocky .... HARD, WEAK, DIZZY,
SHAKY, STONY, CRAGGY,
RUGGED, UNSTEADY
cliff .... SCAR
hill/crag .... TOR
outcrop .... CRAG
pinnacle/ridge ...... TOR, SCAR,
ARETE
Rocky Mountain feature
.... CONTINENTAL DIVIDE
Mountain mammal .... ELK,
BADGER, COYOTE, MARMOT,
RED FOX, CHIPMUNK, MULE
DEER, SQUIRREL, BLACK BEAR,
GRIZZLY BEAR
Mountain sheep ...... BIGHORN
Mountain wind .... CHINOOK
Mountains .... ROCKIES
rococo .... FLORID, ORNATE,
BAROQUE, ARABESQUE
rod ...... BAR, POLE, TWIG, WAND,
PERCH, SHAFT, SHOOT, STAFF,
STICK, VERGE, HEATER,
TOGGLE, WATTLE, SCEPTER
biblical use ...... RACE, STOCK,
OFFSHOOT
billiards .... CUE
birds' .... PERCH
cap .... FERULE
connecting .... PITMAN
divination .... DOWSING,
RHABDOMANCY
emblematic .... CADUCEUS
king's/royal .... WARDER,
SCEPTER
mate of .... REEL
of authority ...... MACE, GAVEL
shaped .... BACILLAR,
VIRG(UL)ATE

slang .... GAT, GUN, PISTOL, REVOLVER
steadying .... GUY
twirling .... BATON
used for flogging/whipping .... CANE, SWITCH
walking .... CANE, STICK
Rod, actor .... STEIGER
tennis great .... LAVER
rodent .... RAT, CAVY, HARE, PIKA, CON(E)Y, MOUSE, BEAVER, RABBIT, GNAWING, LEPORID, SQUIRREL
albino .... WHITE MOUSE
aquatic ..... BEAVER, MUSKRAT
Belgian .... LEPORIDE
burrowing ...... VOLE, GOPHER, MARMOT, SUSLIK, CHIPMUNK, GERBIL(LE), VISCACHA
eight-toothed .... OCTODON
European .... CON(E)Y
fur .... BEAVER, RABBIT
genus .... MURIS, CASTOR
largest extant .... CAPYBARA
leaping .... JERBOA
nocturnal .... PACA
Patsy winner .... BEN
pet .... HAMSTER
poison .... RODENTICIDE
rapid .... SNOWSHOE RABBIT
short-eared .... AGOUTI
squirrel-like .... GOPHER, SUSLIK, CHIPMUNK, DORMOUSE
suicidal .... LEMMING
tailless/spotted .... PACA
that collects small particles .... PACKRAT
water .... COYPU, NUTRIA, MUSKRAT
Western .... PACKRAT
rodents' disease .... TULAR(A)EMIA
enemy .... RATTER
of .... MURINE
rodeo .... ROUNDUP
competitor .... COWBOY
skill .... LASSOING
Rodi .... RHODES
Rodin, Fr. sculptor .... AUGUSTE
work .... THINKER
rodomontade .... BOAST(ING), BRAG(GING)
Rodrigo Diaz de Bivar ...... (EL) CID
rods, 40 .... FURLONG
roe ...... OVA, DEER, MILT, CORAL, SPAWN, (FISH)EGGS
roebuck .... DEER
Roentgen's discovery ...... X-RAY
rogation .... PRAYER
rogatory .... QUESTIONING

roger .... OK, OVER, RIGHT, RECEIVED
Rogers .... ROY, CARL, WILL, KENNY, GINGER
religious freedom fighter .... JOHN
followers of ...... ROGERENES
Rogers' prop .... LASSO
Rogers St. John, ____ .... ADELA
rogue .... IMP, KITE, CHEAT, SCAMP, BEGGAR, RASCAL, PICAROON, SCOUNDREL, SCAPEGRACE
animal .... ELEPHANT
wandering .... TRAMP, VAGABOND
rogues, of .... PICARESQUE
gallery item .... MUG, ALIAS
roguish .... ARCH, PRANKISH, FUN-LOVING
Rohrer, humor hobbyist .... DICK
roil .... IRK, VEX, RILE, ANNOY, MUDDY, AGITATE, IRRITATE, DISPLEASE
roily ...... ANGRY, MUDDY, TURBID
roi's heir .... DAUPHIN
realm .... FRANCE
wife .... REINE
roister .... BULLY, REVEL, FROLIC, BLUSTER, SWAGGER
Roland's magic possession .... HORN, OLIVANT
role ...... JOB, DUTY, PART, OFFICE, PERSON, FUNCTION, CHARACTER
bit/without speech ...... WALK-ON
lead .... STAR
minor .... EXTRA
minor, well-defined .... CAMEO
movie .... HERO, LEAD, HEAVY, HEROINE, VILLAIN
roll .... BUN, CAKE, LIST, PEAL, PUSH, TOLL, WRAP, CHIRR, LURCH, SCONE, TRILL, ELAPSE, ENFOLD, MUFFIN, ROSTER, SCROLL, SLIP BY, BISCUIT, BRIOCHE, TRUNDLE, DRUMBEAT, REGISTER, CATALOG(UE)
about .... WALLOW, WELTER
along .... TRUNDLE
around .... ROTATE, REVOLVE
back .... REDUCE, REPULSE
call response .... HERE, PRESENT
from side to side, speedily .... CAREEN

hard .... BAGEL
of bills .... WAD
bread .... MANCHET
cloth .... BOLT
coins .... ROULEAU
paper .... WEB, BOLT
something, like ribbons, etc. .... ROULEAU
out .... SPREAD, FLATTEN
over ..... REINVEST, REFINANCE
parchment .... SCROLL
slang .... WAD, ROB, MONEY
the eyes .... GOGGLE
up .... FURL
up one's sleeves .... DIG IN
Rolland, Fr. novelist .... ROMAIN
rollback .... CUTBACK, REDUCTION
rolled backward .... REVOLUTE
roller .... WAVE, SKATE, WHEEL, WINCE, BRAYER, CANARY, PIGEON, RUNDLE, CYLINDER
coaster .... SWITCHBACK
of hardened steel .... MILL
on a typewriter .... PLATEN
printing .... BRAYER
rollick .... ROMP, CAPER, FRISK, GAMBOL
rollicking ...... LIVELY, CAREFREE
rolling fields, having ...... ACRED
prevent from .... TRIG
sound .... RUMBLE
stock .... LOCOMOTIVES
sudden .... LURCH
Rolling Stones member ...... WATTS, WYMAN, JAGGER
Rollo .... VIKING
rolltop .... DESK
rollway .... CHUTE
roly-poly .... DUMPY, PODGY, PUDGY, TUBBY, CHUBBY, PUDDING
person .... FATSO
rom .... GYPSY
romaine .... COS, LETTUCE
Romains, Fr. novelist ...... JULES
Roman .... LATIN, QUIRIS, ITALIAN, QUIRITES
actor's boot .... BUSKIN
administrator .... PATRICIAN
agreement .... PACTA
ancient, black marble .... NERO ANTICO
apostle .... NERI
assembly ..... FORUM, COMITIA
awning .... VELARIUM
basilica .... LATERAN
bathhouses .... THERMAE
bishop .... POPE
bottle .... AMPULLA
boxer's strap .... CESTUS

boxing-wrestling contest .... PANCRATIUM
bronze .... AES
buckle .... FIBULA
building for musical
  performances ..... ODEUM
camps .... CASTRA
cap .... PILEUS
candle .... FIREWORK, FIRECRACKER
Catholic .... LATIN, PAPIST, ROMANIST
Catholic Church .... ROME, LATERAN
Catholic Church supreme
  head .... POPE
Catholic festival ...... LAMMAS
Catholic French ..... GALLICAN
censor .... CATO
census taker .... CENSOR
chariot .... ESSED
circus arena .... HIPPODROME
circus fighter .... GLADIATOR
citizens .... EQUITES
civil law digest .... PANDECT
civilian .... QUIRITE
clan .... GENS
clasp .... FIBULA
cloak .... SAGUM, ABOLLA, PALADUMENTA
coin .... AES, ASSES, SEMIS, AUREUS, BEZANT, DINDER, TRIENS, SOLIDUS, DENARIUS, SESTERCE
cold bath .... FRIGIDARIUM
cool room .... TEPIDARIUM
commander .... CENTURION
commoner .... PLEBEIAN
conspirator .... CASCA
corselet .... LORICA, LORLEA
court(s) .... ATRIUM, ATRIA
cuirass .... LORICA, LORLEA
date .... IDES, NONES
deity .... LAR
dictator .... SULLA
diviner .... AUSPEX
emperor .... NERO, OTHO, OTTO, CARUS, GALBA, NERVA, TITUS, CAESAR, PROBUS, TRAJAN, HADRIAN, AUGUSTUS, CALIGULA, CLAUDIUS, JUSTINIAN, VESPASIAN, THEODOSIUS, CONSTANTINE
emperor's bodyguard .... PRETORIAN
  decree .... RESCRIPT
  standard .... LABARUM
Empire founder .... AUGUSTUS
Empire part .... GAUL, HISPANIA, BYZANTIUM
empress .... POPPAEA,

                       THEODORA
entrance court/hall .... ATRIUM
epigrammatist .... MARTIAL
estate .... LATIFUNDIUM
fable writer .... PHAEDRUS
farce .... MIME
farewell .... ADDIO
fates .... PARCAE
festival .... OPALIA, LUPERCAL(IA), SATURNALIA
fiddler .... NERO
foot soldiers .... VELITES
fountain, famed .... TREVI
frontier fortification ..... LIMES
galley .... BIREME, TRIREME
games .... LUDI
games official .... (A)EDILE
garment .... TOGA, STOLA, STOLE, TUNIC
general .... SULLA, TITUS, DRUSUS, MARIUS, SCIPIO, AGRIPPA, CASSIUS, AGRICOLA, LUCULLUS, BELASARIUS
general, defeated Attila .... AETIUS
girdle .... CESTUS
girl traitor .... TARPEIA
gladiator .... RETIARIUS
god, agriculture .... PICUS, SATURN
chief .... JOVE, JUPITER
festivity .... COMUS
fire .... VULCAN
gates .... JANUS
Hades .... DIS, ORCUS, PLUTO
herds .... PAN
household ..... LAR, PENATES
lightning .... JUPITER
love .... AMOR, CUPID
lower world .... ORCUS, SERAPIS
night .... SOMNUS
pastoral .... FAUNUS, LUPERCUS
patron .... MERCURY
rain .... JUPITER PLUVIUS
sea .... NEPTUNE
season .... VERTUMNUS
sleep .... SOMNUS, MORPHEUS
sun .... SOL
tutelary .... LAR
underworld ...... DIS, ORCUS, PLUTO
war .... ARES, MARS, QUIRINUS
wind: east .... EURUS
  north .... BOREAS
  south .... NOTUS
  west .... ZEPHYR
wine .... BACCHUS
woods .... SYLVANUS

goddess .... DEA
agriculture .... OPS, CERES
beauty .... VENUS
birth .... PARCA, LUCINA, MATUTA
crops .... ANNONA
crossroads .... TRIVIA
dawn .... AURORA, MATUTA
earth .... TERRA, TELLUS
faith .... FIDES
fates .... PARCAE
fertility .... OPS, CERES, FAUNA, DEMETER
fields .... TERRA, TELLUS
fire .... VESTA
flowers .... FLORA
fountain .... FERONIA
fruits .... POMONA
harvest .... OPS
health .... SALUS
hearth .... VESTA
herds .... PALES
hope .... SPES
horses .... EPONA
hunting ...... DIANA, VACUNA
light .... LUCINA
love .... VENUS
marriage .... JUNO
moon .... LUNA, ARTEMIS, CYNTHIA
nether world .... CORA, PROSERPINA
night .... NOX
peace .... PAX
plenty .... OPS
sea .... MARE
summer .... AESTAS
vegetation .... CERES
virtue .... FIDES
war .... BELLONA, MINERVA
wisdom .... MINERVA
governor ...... LEGATE, PILATE, PROCONSUL
guard .... LICTOR
guardian spirits .... LARES, PENATES
Hades/hell .... AVERNUS
half boot .... CALIGA
hall .... OECUS, ATRIUM
harvest festival .... OPALIA
headband .... VITTA
helmet .... GALEA
highway .... VIA, ITER
hill .... (SEE **Rome**)
historian .... LIVY, NEPOS, TACITUS, SUETONIUS
holiday .... FERIA
hot bath .... CALDARIUM
hot room .... LACONICUM
household gods .... LARES, PENATES

jar .... AMPHORA
judge .... (A)EDILE,
　　　　　　　　　QU(A)ESTOR
lady .... DONNA
law .... LEX
lawmaker .... SENATOR
legion commander
.... TRIBUNE
leisure center .... BATH,
　　　　　　　　　AQUAE SULIS
list .... ALBE
lower world .... HADES, ORCUS
magistrate ..... EDILE, CENSOR,
CONSUL, DUUMVIR, PR(A)ETOR,
　　　　PREFECT, TRIBUNE
magistrate's symbol
.... FASCES
maiden traitor .... TARPEIA
marble .... CIPOLIN
masses .... PLEBS
matron's garment .... STOLE
meal .... CENA, GENA
measure .... URNA, CLIMA,
　　　　　　　CULEUS, DOLIUM
military unit .... COHORT,
　　　　　　　　　　　LEGION
monster: myth. .... LAMIA,
　　　　　　　　　　　TYPHON
month's first day .... CALENDS
name .... NOMEN
naturalist .... PLINY
noble .... PATRICIAN
nose .... NASUS
nothing .... NIHIL
nymph: myth. .... EGERIA,
　　　　　　　　　M(A)ENAD
officer for 10 men
.... DECURION
official .... EDILE, SATRAP,
　　　　　　　　　　　PREFECT
official with the fasces
.... LICTOR
Optimus Princeps ...... TRAJAN
orator .... CATO, CAESAR,
　　　　　　　　　　　CICERO
palace .... LATERAN
patriot .... RIENZI
patron of literature
.... MAECENAS
people .... SABINES
philosopher .... SENECA
physician, 1st century AD
.... CELSUS
physician, 2nd century
.... GALEN
physician's tool ...... FORCEPS,
SCALPEL, (SURGICAL) SCISSORS
pin .... ACUS
plain .... CAMPAGNA
playwright .... TERRENCE
poet ...... OVID, CINNA, LUCAN,

VERGIL, VIRGIL, JUVENAL,
　　　　　　　　LUCRETIUS
poet banished by Augustus
.... OVID
pontiff .... CAESAR
port .... OSTIA
portrait, wax .... IMAGO
pound .... LIBRA
priest .... AUGUR, AUSPEX,
　　　　　　　　　　FLAMEN
procession .... TRIUMPH
province .... DACIA, MOESIA,
NUMIDIA, PISIDIA, PANNONIA
public land .... AGER
racing course ..... HIPPODROME
revolt, leader of
.... SPARTACUS
river .... LETHE, TIBER
road .... VIA, ITER
road, famous .... APPIAN
robe .... TOGA, STOLA, STOLE
room(s) .... ATRIUM, ATRIA
royal standard .... LABARUM
secret cult .... BACCHUS
senator .... CATO, CICERO,
　　　　　　　　　　PUBLIUS
Senate house .... CURIA
serf .... COLONA, COLONUS
shield(s) .... EGIS, SCUTA,
　　　　SCUTUM, CLIPEUS
soldier ..... VELITE, LEGIONARY
soldier's covering
.... TESTUDO
soothsayer .... HARUSPEX
spirits .... LARES, MANES,
　　　　　　　　　　LEMURES
standard .... LABARUM
stern .... CATO
street .... CORSO
tablet .... TESSERA
taxman .... PUBLICAN
temple .... NAOS, CELLA
theater awning ...... VELARIUM
theater's stage
.... PROSCENIUM
ticket/token .... TESSERA
tragedian .... SENECA
traitor's cliff .... TARPEIAN
treasurer .... QU(A)ESTOR
triumvir .... LEPIDUS
two-wheeled cart .... BIROTA
tyrant .... NERO
urn .... CAPANNA
vase .... PYXIS
vestment .... ROBE, TOGA
war trumpet .... TUBA
warrior .... GLADIATOR
way .... VIA
weapon .... SPEAR, SWORD,
　　　　　　　　　GLADIUS
weight .... AS, BES, LIBRA,

UNCIA, DUELLA, SCRUPLE,
　　　　　　　　SEXTULA
writer .... LIVY, PLINY, VARRO,
PLAUTUS, TERENCE, VEGETIUS
writing tablet .... DIPTYCH
romance .... WOO, COURT, NOVEL,
FICTION, (LOVE) AFFAIR
icon .... FABIO
Romance language .... LADIN,
FRENCH, CATALAN, ITALIAN,
SPANISH, ROMANIAN,
PROVENCAL
Romancero gitano poet
.... LORCA
Romania, etc. of yore ...... DACIA
president .... (ION) ILIESCU
prime minister .... (PETRE)
　　　　　　　　　　　ROMAN
Romanian. See Rumanian
Romanov, Russ. czar
.... MIKHAIL
Romansh .... LADIN
romantic .... DREAMY, POETIC,
BYRONIC, FABULOUS,
FANCIFUL, QUIXOTIC,
FANTASTIC, VISIONARY,
PICTURESQUE, SENTIMENTAL
Romany .... GYPSY
Rome .... ROMA, ETERNAL CITY
amphitheater .... COLOSSEUM
Beauty .... APPLE
conqueror of .... ALARIC
dominant building of ancient
.... (THE) FORUM
first emperor of .... AUGUSTUS
founder of .... ROMULUS
fountain of .... TREVI
grandeur of .... EMPIRE
is capital of .... ITALY
nemesis of .... NERO
"pest" of .... PAPPAGALLO
port .... OSTIA
rebel against .... SPARTACUS
river .... TIBER
saviors of, in 390 BC
.... GEESE
second king of .... NUMA
POMPILIUS
Seven Hills, one of
.... CAELIAN, VIMINAL,
AVENTINE, PALATINE,
QUIRINAL, ESQUILINE,
CAPITOLINE
unlucky, in ancient XIII
Romeo .... LOVER
and Juliet .... TRUE LOVERS
author .... SHAKESPEARE
character ..... ABRAM, PARIS,
TYBALT, CAPULET, ESCALUS,
LAWRENCE, MERCUTIO,
MONTAGUE

enemy of .... TYBALT
father of .... MONTAGUE
kinsman of .... MERCUTIO
love of .... JULIET, ROSALINE
rival of .... PARIS
to Juliet .... SWEETHEART
Rommel, Ger. marshal
.... ERWIN
romp .... PLAY, CAPER, FRISK,
CAVORT, FROLIC, GAMBOL,
ROLLICK
rompers .... JUMPERS
Romulus .... QUIRINUS
brother of .... REMUS
conqueror of .... ODOACER
parent of .... MARS, RHEA
savior of .... (SHE) WOLF
Ronald, actor .... COLMAN,
REAGAN
U.S. president .... REAGAN
rondeau .... POEM, RONDO,
RO(U)NDEL
rondure .... CIRCLE, SPHERE
ronin .... OUTLAW, OUTCAST
rood .... CROSS, CRUCIFIX
roof .... DOME, CUPOLA, LEAN-TO,
CEILING, GAMBREL, MANSARD,
SHELTER, COVERING,
(HOUSE)TOP
arched .... VAULT
architectural style ...... GABLE,
CUPOLA, GAMBREL, MANSARD
coach's .... IMPERIAL
covering .... TILE, SLATE,
THATCH, SHINGLE
drain .... GUTTER
edge/overhang .... EAVE
feature .... EAVES
figuratively .... HOME, HOUSE
finial: arch. .... EPI
glass for admitting light
.... BULL'S-EYE
lantern .... LOUVER
of straw, palm leaves, etc.
.... THATCH
opening .... LUNET(TE),
SCUTTLE, SKYLIGHT
raise the .... COMPLAIN
raised border .... COAMING
rounded .... DOME, CUPOLA
sloped .... SHED, LEANTO
support .... SPRAG, TRUSS,
RAFTER, PURLIN(E)
timber .... RIDGEPOLE
top indicator .... VANE
trough .... GUTTER
two-sloped on two sides
.... GAMBREL
two-sloped on four sides
.... MANSARD
type of .... DOME, TILE, SLATE,

SHINGLE, THATCHED,
PENTHOUSE
window .... DORMER,
SKYLIGHT
woven work .... WATTLE
"Roof of the World" .... PAMIR,
TIBET
roofer .... SLATER
roofing material .... TILE, THATCH
slate .... RAG
slate trimmer .... ZAX
tile .... SLATE, PANTILE
roofless .... HOMELESS,
HYPETHRAL
rooflike covering .... CANOPY
rooftree .... HOME, SHELTER,
RIDGEPOLE
rook .... CROW, CHEAT, CASTLE,
SWINDLE(R)
cry of .... CAW
rookery .... SLUM, TENEMENT
inhabitant .... CROW, SEAL,
PENGUIN
rookie .... NOVICE, RECRUIT,
BEGINNER, NEWCOMER,
GREENHORN
room .... CELL, HALL, SALA,
CUDDY, LODGE, SALLE,
SPACE, STUDY, CLOSET,
LEEWAY, QUARTER, ROTUNDA
band, ornamental .... FRIEZE
beneath roof .... LOFT, ATTIC
conversation .... LOCUTORY
dressing .... BOUDOIR
for dance lessons .... STUDIO
harem .... ADA, ODA
hot bath .... CALDARIUM
inner .... BEN
Maison .... SALLE
perfumer .... INCENSE
private .... DEN, STUDY,
CLOSET, SANCTUM
Pueblo Indian .... KIVA
wine .... CELLAR
woman's sitting ...... BOUDOIR
roomer .... LODGER, BOARDER
rooming house .... KIP
housekeeper .... LANDLORD
rooms .... LODGINGS, QUARTERS
roomy .... AIRY, AMPLE, SPACIOUS
dress style .... TENT
roorback .... LIE, LIBEL, CANARD,
MUDSLINGING
roose .... PRAISE
Roosevelt, president .... FDR,
TEDDY, THEODORE, FRANKLIN
(DELANO)
Roosevelt's (F.D.) charity
.... MARCH OF DIMES
cottage in Warm Springs
.... LITTLE WHITE HOUSE

mother .... SARA
pet's name ..... FALA, BIG BOY
wife .... (ANNA) ELEANOR
roost .... SIT, BERTH, PERCH,
NEST(LE), SETTLE
rooster .... COCK, BANTAM,
CHANTICLEER
castrated .... CAPON
comb of .... CARUNCLE
cry of .... CROW
fattened .... CAPON
feathers of .... HACKLE
leg outgrowth .... SPUR
mate of .... HEN
young .... COCKEREL
root .... BASE, CORE, PLUG,
CAUSE, CHEER, RADIX,
ORIGIN, SOURCE, RHIZOME
aromatic ..... ORRICE, GINSENG
combining form .... RHIZ(O)
diuretic .... PAREIRA
dried .... RHATANY
dye .... CHAY, CHOY
edible .... YAM, EDDO, TARO,
MANIOC, POTATO, RADISH,
CASSAVA, PARSNIP,
GIRASOL(E)
emetic .... MANDRAKE
expectorant .... SENEGA
flavoring .... SARSAPARILLA
fleshy .... TUBER
for ..... HAIL, CHEER, ACCLAIM,
APPLAUD
for planting .... SLIP
fragrant .... ORRIS
garlic .... RAMSON(S)
growth .... TUBERCLE
hair .... FIBRIL, TRICHOME
medicinal .... GINSENG,
RHATANY
narcotic .... MANDRAKE
of the .... RADICAL
out: obs. .... ARACE
part of .... RADICLE
perfume making .... ORRIS,
ORRICE
purgative .... JALAP
relish/used for salads
.... RADISH
salad .... RAMPION, RAMSON(S)
seasoning .... TURMERIC
shoot .... SUCKER, TILLER
small .... RADICEL
stock .... GINGER
substance .... ZEDOARY
tip tissue .... MERISTEM
word .... ETYMON, RADICAL
Root, U.S. statesman ...... ELIHU
rooter .... FAN
rooting out .... EVULSION
rootlet .... RADICEL

rootlike .... RHIZOID
rootstalk .... GINGER, RHIZOME
rootstock .... PIP, ORIGIN, SOURCE,
.... RHIZOME
rope .... TIE, BIND, CORD, LINE,
.... CABLE, LASSO, TWIST,
.... FASTEN, MARLIN, STRAND
anchor .... CLEAT
and pulley block .... TACKLE
cattle catcher's .... BOLA
cord tied to .... MARLINE
cowboy's .... LASSO, RIATA,
.... LARIAT
dancer/walker
.... FUNAMBULIST
dancer's .... POY
fiber .... BAST, COIR, HEMP,
.... JUTE, ABACA, ISTLE, IXTLE,
.... SISAL, GOMUTI, MAGUEY
flag .... LANYARD
for cable's end .... MARLINE,
.... MARLING
for hanging ..... HEMP, NOOSE,
.... HALTER
for hoisting yards: naut.
.... TYE
for Tarzan .... LIANA
frayed end of .... FAG END
gaff to deck .... VANG
guiding .... GUY, LONGE,
.... LUNGE, DRAGLINE
guy .... VANG
horse trainer's .... LONGE
in .... LURE, ENTICE
knotted at end .... COLT
lead .... LONGE
loop .... LAP, FRAP, BIGHT
mooring .... PAINTER
old .... JUNK
part .... END, FIBER
pulling .... TUG
ship's .... GUY, TYE, STAY,
.... VANG, EARING, SHROUD,
.... LANYARD, PAINTER, RATLINE
steadying .... GUY, VANG
tether .... LARIAT
thin .... CORD, WIRE, STRING
thread a .... REEVE
towing .... CORDELLE
wire .... CABLE
roped .... LASSOED, TETHERED
Roper, Elmo .... POLLSTER
ropy .... GLUTINOUS
roque .... CROQUET
Roquefort .... CHEESE
rorqual .... WHALE, FINBACK,
.... RAZORBACK
Rosa, _____ (1929 song) .... NINA
odorata, descendant of
.... TEAROSE
rosaceous .... ROSY

plant .... PLUM, AGRIMONY,
.... STRAWBERRY
rosary .... BEADS, GARDEN,
.... CHAPLET, GARLAND
prayer .... AVE, HAIL MARY,
.... OUR FATHER, GLORIA PATRI,
.... PATER NOSTER
subject .... MYSTERY
Roscoe .... GAT
rose .... RHODA, DAMASK,
.... FLOWER, NOZZLE, PERFUME,
.... RAMBLER, ROSETTE
aborigine boxing champ
.... LIONEL
apple .... POMAROSA
bush .... SHADBLOW,
.... SASKATOON
extract .... ATTAR
garden .... ROSARY
hermosa .... PINK PEARL
mallow .... HIBISCUS,
.... HOLLYHOCK
moss .... PORTULACA
noble .... RYAL
plant .... AVENS
petal oil/perfume .... ATTAR
rash .... MEASLES, RUBELLA,
.... ROSEOLA
red spinel .... BALAS RUBY
straggling/climbing
.... RAMBLER
time .... JUNE, SPRING
tree .... RHODODENDRON
under the .... SECRETLY, SUB
.... ROSA
wild .... BRIER, EGLANTINE
Rose Bowl players .... USC, UCLA
of Sharon .... ALTHEA
roseate .... ROSY, BRIGHT,
.... PROMISING
rosebay .... OLEANDER,
.... RHODODENDRON
rosebush .... SHRUB
feature .... BUD, THORN
fruit .... HIP
roseola .... RASH, MEASLES,
.... RUBELLA
Rose's love .... ABIE
rosette .... COCKADE
Rosie the _____ .... RIVETER
rosin .... FLUX, RESIN, ROZET
Rosinante .... JADE, HORSE
master of .... QUIXOTE
rosolio .... CORDIAL
Ross, flag-maker .... BETSY
U.S. woman governor
.... NELLIE
Rossetti, poet .... DANTE,
.... CHRISTINA
Rosshalde author .... HESSE

Rossini, composer
.... GIOACCHINO
hero of .... TELL
last opera of .... WILLIAM
.... TELL
work ...... OT(H)ELLO, WILLIAM
.... TELL, THE BARBER OF SEVILLE
Rossiya .... RUSSIA
roster .... LIST, ROTA, COUNT,
.... TALLY, RECORD, REGISTER,
.... ROLL CALL
rostrum .... BEAK, DAIS, STAGE,
.... PODIUM, PULPIT, LECTERN,
.... TRIBUNE, PLATFORM
rosy .... PINK(Y), RUDDY, BRIGHT,
.... BLUSHING, ROSACEOUS
fingered goddess ...... AURORA
rot .... RET, DECAY, SPOIL, WASTE,
.... PUTREFY, DECOMPOSE
slang .... BOSH, BALONEY,
.... RUBBISH, NONSENSE
rota .... LIST, COURT, ROUND,
.... WHEEL, AGENDA, ROSTER,
.... CLASSIS, ROUTINE
member .... AUDITOR
Rotarian, female .... ANN
rotate .... PAN, ROLL, SPIN, TURN,
.... TWIRL, WHEEL, WHIRL,
.... GYRATE, SWIVEL, REVOLVE
unevenly .... WOBBLE
rotating device .... CAM, AXIS,
.... AXLE, REEL, ROTOR, DASHER,
.... SPINDLE
firework .... GIRANDOLE
ride .... CAROUSEL, MERRY-GO-
.... ROUND
toy .... TOP, WHIRLIGIG
water .... WHIRLPOOL
wing craft .... GIRO
rotation ...... TURNING, GYRATION,
.... REVOLUTION
wind-operated .... WINDMILL
rotch(e) .... AUK, DOVEKEY,
.... DOVEKIE, GUILLEMOT
rote .... ROUTINE, PRACTICE
by .... MEMORY
rotenone source .... DERRIS
rotgut .... WHISKY
rotifer .... ANIMALCULE
rotisserie .... GRILL
pin .... SKEWER
rotl .... WEIGHT
plural of .... ARTAL
rotor .... STATOR
rotten .... BAD, FOUL, RANK,
.... ADDLE, FETID, NASTY,
.... PUTRID, CORRUPT, DECAYED,
.... SPOILED, TAINTED,
.... DISGUSTING
rottenstone .... TRIPOLI
rotund .... FAT, PLUMP, OBESE,

ROUND, STOUT, SONOROUS
roturier .... COMMONER
roue .... RAKE, RAKEHELL,
DEBAUCHEE, LIBERTINE
rouge .... PAINT, BLUSH-ON,
MAKEUP, COSMETICS
Rouge, _____ .... BATON, MOULIN
rough .... RUDE, CRUDE, HARSH,
COARSE, HUBBLY, JAGGED,
RAGGED, RUGGED, SHAGGY,
STORMY, UNEVEN, RIOTOUS,
SCRAGGY, VIOLENT, AGRESTIC
and disorderly .... LARRIKIN
and tumble .... HAYWIRE,
SLOVENLY, DISORDERLY,
TOPSY-TURVY, HELTER-
SKELTER
and tumble fight .... BRAWL,
MELEE
as in ride ..... BUMPY, JOLTING
boisterous activity
.... HORSEPLAY
cloth .... SHAG, DENIM, TERRY,
DUFFEL, DUFFLE
combining form .... TRACHY
edged .... FROSE
facial growth .... WHISKER
handler .... PAWER
in manner/speech .... BLUNT,
GRUFF, HARSH
make .... FRAY, FRET, RASP,
GRATE
outline .... DRAFT
skin .... SHAGREEN
sounding ...... RASPY, HOARSE,
RAUCOUS
water .... SEA
with small knobs
.... BLOTCHY, SCABROUS
roughage .... FIBER
roughen .... CHAP, FRAY, FRET,
RASP, RUFFLE
roughly .... ABOUT
roughneck .... BOOR, GOON,
HOOD, THUG, BULLY, ROWDY
roughness .... RIGOR, ASPERITY,
SEVERITY
roughshod, go .... TRAMPLE
rouleau .... ROLL
roulette color .... RED, BLACK
man .... CROUPIER
term .... BAS, NOIR, PASSE,
ROUGE, MANQUE
round ...... AMBIT, CYCLE, ORBED,
SALVO, COURSE, ANNULAR,
GLOBOID, CIRCULAR,
GLOBULAR, SPHERICAL
and plump .... CHUBBY
and round .... BY TURNS
clam .... QUAHOG
dance .... POLKA

figure .... ORB
filing desk .... RENT TABLE
make .... CIRCINATE
of applause .... PLAUDIT
of consecutive games
.... SERIES
of duty .... BEAT, TOUR
of play .... LAP, INNING
protuberance ..... KNOB, UMBO
shield, small .... TARGET
this is sometimes .... ROBIN
trip .... EXCURSION
tripper .... HOMER
up .... CORRAL, GATHER,
RUSTLE, COLLECT
watchman's .... TOUR
Round Table, central image of
.... ROSE
king .... ARTHUR
king's sword .... EXCALIBUR
knight .... KAY, BORS, BORT,
BALAN, BALIN, GARETH,
GAWAIN, GALAHAD, GERAINT,
MO(R)DRED, MORGA(I)N,
PELLEAS, TRISTAN, BEDIVERE,
LANCELOT, PARSIFAL,
PERCIVAL, TRISTRAM
roundabout .... JACKET, DEVIOUS,
INDIRECT, AMBAGIOUS,
CIRCUITOUS
expression .... AMBAGE,
PERIPHRASIS
way .... AMBAGE, DETOUR
rounded ...... ROTUND, FUSIFORM,
RINGSHAPE
and bulging .... GIBBOUS
edge .... NOSING
projection/protrusion
.... KNOB, LOBE
rounder ...... GUARD, DRUNKARD,
SENTINEL, WATCHMAN,
POLICEMAN
Roundhead .... PURITAN
roundly .... FULLY, SEVERELY
roundup ...... RODEO, GATHERING
roundworm .... ASCARID,
NEMATODE, PARASITE,
STRONGYL(E), LUMBRICALIS
disease .... ASCARIASIS,
FILARIASIS, TRICHINOSIS
roupy .... HUSKY, HOARSE
rouse .... HAUL, ROUST, WAKE(N),
EXCITE, INCITE, STIR (UP),
REVEILLE
rousing .... BRISK, BRACING,
STIRRING
Rousseau work/hero .... EMILE
roust ...... ROUT, STIR (UP), DRIVE
(OUT)
roustabout .... LUMPER, LABORER,
DECK HAND, STEVEDORE

rout .... MOB, RUCK, PANIC,
ROUST, DEFEAT, FLIGHT,
RABBLE, DEBACLE, STAMPEDE
in a way .... SKUNK
route .... RUN, WAY, PATH, ROAD,
TRACK, COURSE, FORWARD,
PASSAGE, ITINERARY
circuitous .... DETOUR
for excess water .... SPILLWAY
shortest .... BEELINE
to oblivion for defeated
candidates? .... SALT
RIVER
traveling .... ITINERARY
routine .... ROTA, HABIT, ROT(T)E,
SYSTEM, HUMDRUM,
REGULAR, PRACTICE,
CUSTOMARY
dull .... RUT
monotonous .... GRIND
task .... CHARGE, CHORE
rove .... GAD, ROAM, RANGE,
RAMBLE, WANDER, MEANDER,
STRAGGLE
in search of plunder
.... FORAGE, MARAUD
rover ...... HOBO, NOMAD, PIRATE,
TARGET, VAGRANT,
WANDERER
roving .... CURSORY, RESTLESS,
WANDERING
band .... GANG
for adventure .... ERRANT
row .... OAR, FILE, LINE, TIER,
BRAWL, MELEE, NOISE, SCULL,
CLAMOR, KICK-UP, PADDLE,
RUCKUS, RUMPUS, SHINDY,
DISPUTE, QUARREL, SQUABBLE
form in a .... ALIGN, ALINE
of cut grass .... SWATH
of planted seeds .... DRILL
rowan .... ASH
rowboat ...... GIG, BANCA, CANOE,
COBLE, SKIFF, CAIQUE,
WHERRY, GONDOLA
racing .... GIG, SCULL, SHELL
warship's .... GALLEY
rowdy .... THUG, BULLY,
HOOD(LUM), LARRIKIN, PLUG-
UGLY, ROUGH(NECK)
one .... YAHOO
young .... HOOLIGAN
Rowe's (Nicholas) play ...... THE
FAIR PENITENT
rake .... LOTHARIO
rowed .... OARED
rowel .... SPUR, PRICK, WHEEL
rowen .... HAY, GRASS,
AFTERMATH
rower .... OAR(SMAN), GONDOLIER
seat of .... THWART

rowing contest .... REGATTA
rowlock .... THOLE, POPPET
Roxas, Philippine president
.... MANUEL
Roy Crane's captain .... EASY
Rogers' horse .... TRIGGER
royal ...... NOBLE, REGAL, AUGUST,
KINGLY, REGIUS, IMPERIAL,
MAJESTIC, PRINCELY
authority .... SCEPTER,
SCEPTRE
color .... PURPLE
council, Oriental .... DIVAN
court official
.... CHAMBERLAIN
crown .... TIARA, DIADEM,
CORONET
domain/realm .... EMPIRE,
CZARDOM, KINGDOM,
SULTANATE
flush, part of .... ACE, TEN,
JACK, KING, QUEEN
fur .... ERMINE
house .... YORK, TUDOR,
STUART, WINDSOR, HAPSBURG,
PLANTAGENET
initials .... HRH
palace .... COURT
residence .... PALACE,
BALMORAL, BUCKINGHAM
seat .... THRONE
staff .... ROD, SCEPTER
symbol ..... ORB, SEAL, SIGNET
title .... REY, ROY, DUKE,
EARL, EMIR, KING, SIRE, TSAR,
QUEEN, RAJAH, PRINCE,
SULTAN, CZAR(INA), DAUPHIN,
DUCHESS, EMPEROR, EMPRESS,
ESQUIRE, INFANTA,
BARON(ESS), COUNT(ESS),
MARQUESS, MARQUIS(E),
PRINCESS, VISCOUNT
treasury .... FISC
royalist .... TORY, CAVALIER,
MONARCHIST, IMPERIALIST
royalty .... NOBILITY, BLUE
BLOOD, ARISTOCRACY,
SOVEREIGNTY
payment .... DIVIDEND
RSVP, part of .... REPONDEZ,
S'IL, VOUS, PLAIT
rub .... BUFF, RASP, SAND, CHAFE,
GRATE, GRIND, SCOUR,
ABRADE, POLISH, MASSAGE
a-dub .... DRUMBEAT
against .... CHAFE
dry .... WIPE
off .... ABRADE
out ...... KILL, ERASE, MURDER,
SCRAPE, EXPUNGE
the wrong way .... RILE,

ANNOY, IRRITATE, DISPLEASE
to brightness .... POLISH,
FURBISH
with a file .... RASP
with nose .... NUZZLE
with oil/liniment
.... EMBROCATE
Rubaiyat author .... OMAR
(KHAYYAM)
rhyming .... ABBA
rubasse .... QUARTZ
rubber .... GUM, BUNA, PARA,
ERASER, EBONITE, GUAYULE,
MASSEUR, MASSEUSE,
MASSAGIST, CAOUTCHOUC
band .... ELASTIC
boot .... WADER
cement .... ADHESIVE
filler in .... KAOLIN(E)
game .... TIEBREAKER
game, first .... LEG
gas bubbles in liquid
.... FOAM
hard .... EBONITE, VULCANITE
necking vehicle .... STAGE
overshoe .... GUMSHOE
plant .... ULE, CAUCHO,
GUAYULE, MILKWEED
plant family .... MULBERRY
ring .... GASKET
roller .... SQUEEGEE
sap .... LATEX
sheeting .... PLIOFILM
shoe .... GALOSH(E),
GOLOSH(E)
slang .... CONDOM
stamp .... DATER, RATIFY,
APPROVE
stamp inker .... PAD
substance like .... GUTTA-
PERCHA
synthetic .... BUNA, BUTYLE,
CARIFLEX, NEOPRENE
synthetic material .... THIOKOL
synthetic polymer
.... SILICONE, ELASTOMER
thing made of .... BALL,
BAND, SHOE, TIRE, ERASER,
GASKET, SQUEEGEE
thread wound with cotton
.... LASTEX
tree ...... ULE, HEVEA, SERINGA
type of .... CEARA, INDIA,
CAUCHO, EBONITE, NITRILE,
KOROSEAL, VULCANITE
Rubber City .... AKRON
rubberneck .... GAWK, CRANE,
GAZE(R), SIGHTSEER
rubbers .... GUMSHOE, OVERSHOE,
GALOSHES, SNEAKERS
rubbery .... TOUGH, ELASTIC

rubbing ...... FRICTION, STROKING
liquid .... ALCOHOL
tool .... FILE
rubbish .... DUST, JUNK, RAFF,
DROSS, OFFAL, TRASH, TRIPE,
TRUCK, WASTE, DEBRIS,
LITTER, REFUSE, NONSENSE,
(TOMMY)ROT, TRUMPERY
collect .... SCAVENGE
mine .... STENT
pile .... DUMP
slang .... ROT
rubble ...... RUINS, SCREE, TRASH,
DEBRIS, LITTER, SHARDS
rubdown .... MASSAGE
rube .... HICK, YOKEL, RUSTIC
rubefacient ...... SALVE, PLASTER
rubella .... RASH, MEASLES,
RUBEOLA, ROSEOLA
rubellite .... TOURMALINE
rubeola .... MEASLES, RUBELLA
rubiaceous plant .... COFFEE,
IPECAC, CINCHONA, GARDENIA
Rubicon, he crossed the
.... CAESAR
rubicund .... ROSY, RUDDY,
FLORID, RED(DISH)
Rubinstein opera .... DEMONIO
pianist .... ANTON, ARTUR
rubious .... RED
ruble, 1/100 of a .... KOPE(C)K
rubric .... TITLE, HEADING,
RED(DISH)
ruby .... GEM, RED, STONE,
SARDIUS, CORUNDUM
spinel .... BALAS
ruche .... FRILL, TRIMMING
ruck .... FOLD, HEAP, SLEW,
STACK, CREASE, PUCKER,
WRINKLE
ruckus .... ROW, FRAY, BRAWL,
MELEE, HASSLE, RUMPUS,
UPROAR
ruction .... UPROAR, QUARREL
rudbeckia .... CONEFLOWER
rudd ...... CARP, FISH, VIREO, RED-
EYE
rudder .... HELM
guide with .... STEER
handle .... WHEEL, TILLER
ruddle .... KEEL
ruddock .... ROBIN
ruddy .... ROSY, FLORID,
FLUSH(ED), RED(DISH),
RUBICUND, SANGUINE
rude .... CRUDE, GROSS, GRUFF,
HARSH, ROUGH, SAUCY,
COARSE, RUGGED, BOORISH,
UNCIVIL, UNCOUTH, IMPOLITE,
INSOLENT
dwelling .... HUT, HOVEL

rudimentary .... INCHOATE, EMBRYONIC, VESTIGIAL, ELEMENTARY, ABECEDARIAN

rudiment(s) .... ABC, GERM, ROOT, FIRST, BASICS, EMBRYO, VESTIGE, ELEMENT(S), BEGINNING(S)

rue .... HERB, MOURN, BEMOAN, BEWAIL, GRIEVE, LAMENT, REGRET, REPENT, DEPLORE

plant .... LIME, LEMON, ORANGE

rueful .... SORRY, WOEFUL, ASHAMED, DOLEFUL, PITEOUS, PENITENT

ruff ...... COLLAR, FRAISE, PIGEON, SANDPIPER

female .... REE(VE)

in card game .... TRUMPING IN

turned down .... FALL

ruff(e) .... FISH, PERCH

ruffed .... UPSET, PIQUED, ABRISTLE

grouse .... PHEASANT, PARTRIDGE

ruffian .... GOON, THUG, BRAVO, BULLY, ROWDY, HOODLUM, TOUGH(IE), HOOLIGAN, PLUG-UGLY, HIGHBINDER

ruffle .... VEX, RILE, FRILL, PLEAT, SHIRR, GATHER, RIPPLE, AGITATE, DERANGE, DISTURB, FLOUNCE, SHUFFLE, WRINKLE, FURBELOW, IRRITATE

rufous .... RUSTY, REDDISH

rug .... MAT, MAUD, CARPET, RUNNER, TOUPEE, WILTON, DRUGGET, COVERING, FOOTCLOTH

ruga ...... FOLD, CREASE, WRINKLE

rugate .... FOLDED, CREASED

rugby .... FOOTBALL

football .... RUGGER

formation .... SCRUM(MAGE)

play .... TRY

rival .... ETON

rugged .... RUDE, HARD(Y), HARSH, HILLY, ROUGH, STERN, CRAGGY, ROBUST, SEVERE, STORMY, STURDY, UNEVEN

rugger .... RUGBY

score .... TRY

rugose/rugous .... RIDGED, CORRUGATED

ruin .... BANE, RAZE, UNDO, CHAOS, HAVOC, SPOIL, DIDDLE, DESTROY, LOUSE UP, DOWNFALL, WRECK(AGE), PERDITION

irretrievably .... COOK ONE'S GOOSE

ruined: sl. .... KAPUT

ruinous .... TRAGIC, HARMFUL

ruins .... RELIC, DEBRIS, REMAINS

in .... RUN-DOWN

rule .... FIX, LAW, CODE, LINE, NORM, SWAY, AXIOM, HABIT, MAXIM, ORDER, REIGN, CUSTOM, DECIDE, GOVERN, SETTLE, SYSTEM, PRECEPT, REGIME(N), DECISION, STANDARD, CRITERION, PRESCRIPT, ADJUDICATE, REGULATION

as a .... USUALLY

book .... HOYLE, MANUAL

for rapid calculations .... SLIDE RULE

of conduct .... PRECEPT

of thumb basis ...... PRACTICE, EXPERIENCE

out .... OMIT, FORBID, EXCLUDE

ruler .... CZAR, EMIR, KING, TSAR, EMEER, QUEEN, RAJAH, FERULE, GERENT, PRINCE, REGENT, EMPEROR, MONARCH, GOVERNOR, POTENTATE

absolute .... SHAH, DESPOT, SHOGUN, TYRANT

amuser of a .... CLOWN, JESTER

ancient Egypt .... PHARAOH

Arab .... SHEIK(H)

cruel .... DESPOT

Ethiopian .... NEGUS

15th century Florentine .... LORENZO DEMEDICI

hereditary .... DYNAST

Indian .... SACHEM, CHIEF(TAIN)

length of a .... FOOT

Tatar .... KHAN

Tunisian .... BEY

who dusted his body with gold .... ELDORADO

wife of .... RANI, QUEEN, RANEE, REINA, CZARINA, EMPRESS, TSARINA

rules of conduct .... CODE

one kind of .... GROUND

Rules of Order author .... ROBERT

ruling ...... LINE, ORDER, DECREE, DECISION, REIGNING, GOVERNING, PREVALENT

party .... MAJORITY

rum .... LIQUOR, ROM(ANY), TAF(F)IA, BACARDI

dessert .... BABA

low grade .... TAF(F)IA

slang .... BAD, ODD, POOR, QUEER, STRANGE

source .... MOLASSES, SUGAR CANE

Rumania .... ROMANIA

once .... DACIA

Rumanian .... MAGYAR

capital .... BUCHAREST

city/town .... ARAD, BRAD, DEVA, IASI, BACAU, BUZAU, LUGOJ, ROMAN, SIBIU, TURDA, ZALAU, BRAILA, BRASOV, GALATI, MEDIAS, ORADEA, RESITA, TECUCI, TULCEA, PITESTI, FOCSANI, CRAIOVA, SLATINA, SUCEAVA, PLOIESTI, SATU MARE, CONSTANTA, TIMISOARA

coin .... BAN, LEI, LEU, LEY, BANI

composer .... ENESCO

district .... DOBRUJA

dramatist .... IONESCO

folk dance .... HORA

king .... CAROL, (MIHAI) MICHAEL

monetary unit .... LEU

mountain .... PELEAGA, PIETROSUL, MOLDOVEANUL

mountain range .... CARPATHIAN

native .... MAGYAR, MOLDAVIAN

part of .... WALACHIA

premier .... MAURER, ANTONESCU, CEAUSESCU

river .... JIU, OLT, PRUT, ARGES, BUZAU, JIJIA, MURES, SIRET, SOMES, TIMIS, BIRLAD, DANUBE

sea .... BLACK

rumba .... DANCE

exponent .... CUBAN, CUGAT

rumble .... BOOM, PEAL, ROAR, ROLL, BRAWL, GROWL, MELEE, FRACAS, LUMBER, FREE-FOR-ALL

seat .... DICKEY

rumbling .... THUNDER

rumdinger .... ONER

rumen .... CUD, GULLET, PAUNCH, STOMACH

of the .... RUMINAL

ruminant ...... PENSIVE, WISTFUL, CUD-CHEWING, MEDITATIVE

animal .... GNU, ROE, YAK, DEER, GOAT, IBEX, KUDU, ORYX, ZEBU, ADDAX, BISON, BONGO, CAMEL, ELAND, LLAMA, MOOSE, OKAPI, IMPALA, NILGAI, WAPITI,

BLESBOK, BUFFALO, GAZELLE, GIRAFFE, MUNTJAC, ANTELOPE, REEDBUCK

chew of .... CUD

stomach chamber ...... RUMEN, (AB)OMASUM, RETICULUM

ruminate .... CHEW, MUSE, PONDER, REFLECT, COGITATE, CONSIDER, MEDITATE

rummage .... COMB, GRUB, SEARCH, RANSACK, ODDS-AND-ENDS

sale .... BAZAAR

rummer .... CUP, GLASS

rummy .... GIN, ODD, QUEER, STRANGE, CARD GAME

bonus, sometimes
.... ROODLES

game like .... COONCAN

slang .... SOT, TOPER, DRUNK(ARD)

strategy .... KNOCK

rumor .... BUZZ, TALK, BRUIT, NOISE, ONDIT, GOSSIP, REPORT, HEARSAY, GRAPEVINE

monger .... TATTLER, BUSYBODY

personified .... FAMA

rump .... ARSE, HIPS, CROUP, BREECH, FAG END, BUTT END, BUTTOCKS

Rumpelstiltskin .... DWARF

rumple ...... FOLD, MUSS, CREASE, TOUSLE, CRUMPLE, WRINKLE, DISHEVEL

rumpus .... ROW, STIR, POTHER, RACKET, RUCKUS, SHINDY, UPROAR, RUCTION, COMMOTION, DISTURBANCE

room .... GAMEROOM, PLAYROOM

rumrunner .... SMUGGLER, BOOTLEGGER

run .... ACT, HIE, PLY, FLOW, LEAK, LOPE, RACE, RILL, SCUD, TRIP, TROT, WORK, YARD, CREEP, INCUR, RAVEL, ROUTE, SCORE, SPEED, ELAPSE, EXTEND, HASTEN, SPREAD, TRAVEL, COMPETE, OPERATE, PUBLISH

about .... GAD

across .... MEET, ENCOUNTER

after .... CHASE, PURSUE

at full speed .... SPRINT

away .... BOLT, FLEE, ELOPE, DECAMP, ABSCOND

baseball .... HOME

colloquial .... STREAK

counter to .... BELIE

cricket .... BYE

down ..... OUTLINE, SUMMARY, NARRATIVE

in ...... BUST, ARREST, COLLAR, INSERT, INCLUDE

in haste ...... SCURRY, SCUTTLE

in the long .... EVENTUALLY, ULTIMATELY

in unbroken order
.... SEQUENCE

of-the-mill ...... SO-SO, USUAL, COMMON, AVERAGE, ORDINARY

off .... PRINT

off, in a way .... ELOPE

off the tracks .... DERAIL

off with .... STEAL, ABDUCT, KIDNAP, SNATCH

out .... LAPSE

over .... SPILL, TRAVERSE

playfully .... SCAMPER

producer .... SNAG

swiftly .... DART

through .... REEVE, PIERCE, THRUST, PASS INTO

runabout .... ROADSTER

runagate .... RAT, DRIFTER, DESERTER, FUGITIVE, VAGABOND

runaround, (the) .... DELAYS, EVASION, EXCUSES, AVOIDANCE, PASSING-THE-BUCK

runaway .... FLEER, ELOPER, ESCAPEE, FUGITIVE

military .... AWOL, DESERTER

school .... TRUANT

slave .... MAROON

traitorous .... DEFECTOR

runcible spoon .... FORK

runcinate .... SAWTOOTHED

rundle .... RUNG

rundlet .... CASK, BARREL

rundown .... SEEDY, RICKETY, RAMSHACKLE

rune .... POEM, SONG, VERSE

rung .... STEP, SPOKE, STAVE, RUNDLE, CROSSBAR

runic alphabet .... FUTHARK

run-in .... TIFF, FIGHT, SCRAP, HASSLE, RHUBARB

runnel .... BROOK, RUNLET, CHANNEL, RIVULET

runner .... SKI, SKEE, AGENT, BLADE, RACER, SKATE, COURIER, SMUGGLER, SPRINTER, CONTENDER, ERRAND BOY, MESSENGER, (RACE)HORSE

botanical ...... SHOOT, STOLON, FLAGELLUM, SARMENTUM

Budd Schulberg's ...... SAMMY

corridor/floor .... MAT, RUG

foundry .... GATE, SPRUE

machine .... OPERATOR

table .... SCARF

-up .... SECOND

way of .... LANE

running .... EASY, LINEAR, MOVING, CURRENT, CURSIVE, FLOWING, MELTING, PASSING, CLIMBING, CREEPING, CONTINUOUS

knot .... NOOSE

nicely .... SPINNING LIKE A TOP

start .... EDGE

runt .... CHIT, DWARF, PYGMY, BANTAM

runway ...... PATH, RAMP, APRON, CHUTE, TRACK, CHANNEL, TROUGH, (AIR)STRIP

rupee, newly minted .... SICCA

weight of .... TOLA

rupees, 15 .... MOHUR

100,000 .... LAC

rupture ...... RIFT, BREAK, BURST, SPLIT, BREACH, HERNIA

support .... TRUSS

Rur characters .... ROBOTS

rural .... RUSTIC, BUCOLIC, AGRESTIC, ARCADIAN, GEOPONIC, PASTORAL

abode .... BOWER, VILLA, HACIENDA

building .... BARN

life, of .... PASTORAL

musical composition
.... CANTATA, PASTORALE

one .... HICK, RUBE, YOKEL

opposed to .... URBAN

poem ..... ECLOGUE, PASTORAL

power initials .... REA

sound .... BAA, LOW, MOO, CROW, BLEAT

ruse .... DODGE, TRICK, GAMBIT, ARTIFICE, DECEPTION, STRATAGEM

rush .... HIE, RUN, DASH, RACE, DRIVE, HASTE, HURRY, PRESS, SCOOT, SPATE, SPEED, SURGE, HUSTLE, TORRENT, HIGHTAIL, ONSLAUGHT, SCRIMMAGE

an order .... EXPEDITE

furiously .... RAMP

grass .... CANE, REED, BAMBOO

headlong .... DIVE, PLUNGE, PRECIPITATE

hour .... GRIDLOCK

hour, usually .... NOON, FIVE (PM), NINE (AM)

line member (football)
.... GUARD, CENTER, TACKLE

mass movement, panicked .... STAMPEDE
of air/wind ...... GUST, FLURRY
emotion .... THRILL, EXCITEMENT
sudden, strong rain .... FLASH FLOOD
water .... WASH, FLUSH, SWASH, SPLASH
words .... SPATE, TORRENT
plant .... BULRUSH, JONQUIL
strong onward .... BIRR, SURGE, ONRUSH
the opposing football passer .... BLITZ
travel period .... PEAK (SEASON)
upon .... CHARGE
violently .... RAMP(AGE)
with a .... QUICKLY
rushlight .... CANDLE
rusk .... CAKE, BREAD, BISCUIT, ZWIEBACK
Russ .... RUSSIAN
Russell, Miss .... GAIL, JANE, CONNIE, LILLIAN, ROSALIND
philosopher .... BERTRAND
russet .... APPLE, CLOTH, HOMELY, SIMPLE, (REDDISH-)BROWN, YELLOWISH-BROWN
Russia .... ROSSIYA, RUTHENIA, THE NORTHERN BEAR
former capital of .... PETROGRAD
former name of ..... MUSCOVY
founder of .... IVAN
Russian .... MUSCOVITE
administrative body .... ZEMSTVO
airline .... AEROFLOT
alcoholic drink .... KVASS, VODKA
America, capital of ...... SITKA
anarchist .... KROPOTKIN
antelope .... SAIGA
aristocrat .... BOYAR(D)
assembly .... RADA
astronaut .... LAIKA, TITOV, KOMAROV, POPOVICH, (YURI) GAGARIN
author/novelist .... GOGOL, GORKI, GORKY, TOLSTOI, TOLSTOY, (ALEKSANDR) SOLZHENITSYN
bag .... CYMKA
ballet dancer .... MASSINE, NUREYEV, (ANNA) PAVLOVA
bay .... OLENEK, GIZHIGA, PENZHINA
beer: var. .... QUAS
cape .... GOVENA, DEZHNEV,

LOPATKA, NAVARIN, OZERNOY, CHELYUSKIN
capital .... MOSCOW
carriage .... TROIKA, DROS(H)KY, TARANTAS(S)
cart .... TELEGA
cathedral .... SOBOR
cereal .... EMMER
chalet .... DACHA
chess champion .... TAL, SMYSLOV, SPASSKY, ALEKHINE, BOTVINNIK, PETROSIAN
choreographer .... MASSINE
citadel .... KREMLIN
city/town .... UFA, BAKU, INTA, KIEV, LUGA, LVOV, MERV, OMSK, OREL, PERM, SUMY, TULA, BIYSK, BREST, CHITA, GOMEL, KAZAN, KIROV, KIZEL, KURSK, MINSK, NAVOI, PENZA, SEROV, TARTU, TOMSK, VILNA, ERIVAN, FRUNZE, GRODNO, KALUGA, KARSHI, KOVROV, KURGAN, ODESSA, RYAZAN, TAMBOV, URALSK, ACHINSK, ANGARSK, DARNAUL, BUKHARA, DONETSK, FERGANA, IRKUTSK, IVANOVO, KALININ, KHARKOV, KHERSON, LIPETSK, SARATOV, TALLINN, TBILISI, USTINOV, VOLOGDA, ZHDANOV, ANDROPOV, BELGOROD, CHIMKENT, DUSHANBE, TASHKENT, VLADIMIR, ARCHANGEL, ASTRAKHAN, CHERNIGOV, KARAGANDA, LENINAKAN, LENINGRAD, SAMARKAND, VOLGOGRAD, SEVASTOPOL, VLADIVOSTOK
coin ..... ALTIN, COPEC, RUBLE, KOPE(C)K, POLTINA, IMPERIAL, CHERVONETS
collective farm .... KOLKHOZ
comedian .... RAIKIN
community .... MIR
composer .... GLIERE, BORODIN, PROKOFIEV, STRAVINSKY, T(S)CHAIKOVSKY
cooperative .... ARTEL
Cossack .... TATAR
council .... DUMA, SOVIET
country estate .... DACHA
county .... OKRUG, OBLAST
dancer .... PAVLOVA, DANILOVA
dandelion .... KOK-SAGYZ
desert .... KARA-KUM, KYZL-KUM
diet .... DUMA
dramatist .... GOGOL

drink .... KVAS(S), QUASS, VODKA
dwelling/hut .... ISBA
edict .... UKASE
elite .... COSSACK
empress ... CZARINA, TSARINA
exile's place .... SIBERIA
farmer .... KULAK
fur .... CARACUL, KARAKUL
"Great" .... CATHERINE
great salt lake .... ELTON
greeting .... BEAR HUG
guitar .... BALALAIKA
guild .... ARTEL
gulf .... OB, RIGA, ANADYR, FINLAND, SAKHALIN, SHELEKHOV
hemp .... RINE, KONOPEL
holy city .... KIEV
holy picture .... ICON, IKON
hood .... BASHLYK
horse team .... TROIKA
horseman .... COSSACK
ibex .... TEK
imperial order .... UKASE
inland sea .... ARAL, AZOV
island .... AYON, URUP, BELYY, WIESE, BERING, PIONER, ETOROFU, HIIUMAA, WRANGEL, KOLGUYEV, SAAREMAA, SAKHALIN, BOLSHEVIK, PARAMUSHIR, GRAHAM BELL
island group .... KURIL, SHANTAR, NOVOYA ZEMLYA, KOMANDORSKIYE, SERGEYA KIROVA
James Bond .... ZAKHOV
lake .... ARAL, NEVA, ELTON, ILMEN, ONEGA, ALAKAL, BAYKAL, BELOYE, KHANKA, LADOGA, PEIPUS, TAYMYR, TENGIZ, IMANDRA, BALKHASH, ISSYK-KUL
language .... RUSS, TATAR, UEBEK, KAZAKH, KIRGIZ, SLAVIC, YIDDISH
leather .... YUFT, JUPTI
Little .... UKRAINIAN
log hut .... ISBA, ISPA
mammal .... DESMAN
marshal .... ZHUKOV, KUTUZOV
measure .... FUT, LOF, DUIM, FASS, VERST, ARSHIN, CHARKA, PALETZ, SAGENE, ARCHINE, BOTCHKA, VERCHOK
mister .... GOSPODIN
monarchy founder .... RURIK
monetary unit .... RUBLE
"mother of cities" .... KIEV
mountain .... ALAI, URAL, NARODNAYA

mountains ..... ALTAY, SAYAN, URALS, BAYKAL, ULUTAU, CAUCASUS
museum .... HERMITAGE
musical instrument .... BALALAIKA
name for Russia ...... ROSSIYA
negative/no .... NYET
news agency .... TASS, NOVOSTI
nurse .... BABA
oboe .... SZOPELKA
oil center .... BAKU
operatic singer ...... CHALIAPIN
painter .... CHAGALL
parliament .... D(O)UMA
peak ..... POBEDA, COMMUNISM
peasant .... KULAK, MUZHIK, MUZJIK
peasant cap .... ASKA
peasants' district .... VOLOST
peninsula .... GYDA, KOLA, KONI, KANIN, YAMAL, CRIMEA, TAYMYR, CHUKCHI, RYBACHIY
physiologist .... PAVLOV
pianist .... RACHMANN
plain .... STEPPE, TUNDRA
plane .... MIG, ILYUSHIN
poet .... PUSHKIN
port ...... ODESSA, SEVASTOPOL
pound .... POOD
praenomen .... IGOR
premier ...... STALIN, KOSYGIN, ANDROPOV, BREZHNEV, BULGANIN, MALENKOV, CHERNENKO, GORBACHEV, KHRUSHCHEV
president .... YELTSIN, SHVERNIK, GORBACHEV
prison .... ETAPE
range .... OLOY, GYDAN, URALS, ANADYR, KOLYMA, KORYAK, CHERSKIY
region .... MARI, SIBERIA
resort .... SOCHI, YALTA, ODESSA
revolutionary leader .... LENIN, KERENSKY, (LEON) TROTSKY
river .... OB, DON, ILI, OKA, PUR, TAZ, TYM, UDA, UFA, AMGA, AMUR, EMBA, KUMA, KURA, LENA, MAYA, NEVA, URAL, VAKH, YANA, ZEYA, ALDAN, AMGUN, ATREK, CHUNA, DVINA, ISHIM, KHETA, KOTUY, MEZEN, NADYM, ONEGA, TOBOL, TYUNG, VITIM, VOLGA, ANABAR, ANGARA, CHULYM, CHUNYA, DONETS, IRTYSH, KOLYMA, MARKHA, MURGAB, OLEKMA, OMOLON, TAYMYR, USSURI, VILYUY, DNIEPER, PECHORA, PYASINA, YENISEY
ruler .... CZAR, TSAR
ruling family .... ROMANOV, ROMANOFF
saint .... OLGA
scarf .... BABUSHKA
sea .... ARAL, AZOV, KARA, BLACK, WHITE, BALTIC, BERING, LAPTEV, BARENTS, CASPIAN, OKHOTSK, SIBERIAN
seaport .... PETSAMO, PECHANGA, LENINGRAD
secret service .... KGB, MVD, NKVD, OGPU, CHEKA, GAY-PAY-OO
soup .... BORSCH
Soviet, rural .... VOLOST
spacecraft .... LUNA, LUNIK, SOYUZ, COSMOS, VOSTOK, YANTAR, SPUTNIK
squadron .... ESKADRA
strait .... LONG, TATAR, BERING, SANNIKOVA
stockade .... ETAPE
teapot/urn .... SAMOVAR
trade union .... ARTEL
vehicle .... TROIKA
villa .... DACHA
village .... MIR
violinist .... ELMAN, ZIMBALIST
wagon .... TELEGA
water barrier ...... ROGUN DAM
weight .... LOT, PUD, DOLA, FUNT, POOD, KAMIAN
wheat .... EMMER
whip .... KNOUT
windstorm .... BURAN
wolfhound .... ALAN, BORZOI
yes .... DA
youth organization .... KOMSOMOL

Russo-Japanese warship .... MIKASA

rust .... ERODE, OXIDE, AERUGO, FUNGUS, CORRODE, OXIDIZE, VERDIGRIS
colored .... RUFOUS
fungus .... AECIA
life cycle of .... TELIAL
on bronze .... PATINA
plant .... FERRUGO
sorus .... TELIUM
rusted .... ATE
rustic .... HOB, CLOD, HICK, HIND, RUBE, RUDE, CHURL, RURAL, YOKEL, ARTLESS, AWKWARD, BUCOLIC, BOOR(ISH), BUM(P)KIN, HAYSEED, ARCADIAN, GEOPONIC
lover/gallant .... SWAIN
musical instrument ...... OBOE, PIPE, REED, BASOON
peasant .... AGRESTIAN
pipe .... CORN, REED
quaff .... CIDER
rusticate .... COUNTRIFY
rustle .... STEAL, SWISH, CRINKLE, SUSURRATE
cattle .... ROUND UP
of silk skirt .... FROUFROU
up .... FORAGE, COLLECT
rustler .... ROBBER, (CATTLE) THIEF
object of .... CATTLE
rustling .... FROUFROU, SWISHING, SUSURRANT
sound .... SOUGH, SWISH, MURMUR, SUSURROUS
Rustum's son .... SOHRAB
rusty ...... STIFF, RUSTED, SHABBY, TIMEWORN, OUT-OF-PRACTICE
rut .... HEAT, RUCK, HABIT, TRACK, FURROW, GROOVE, ROUTINE, (BEATEN) PATH
rutabaga .... SWEDE, TURNIP
rutaceous plant .... RUE, LIME, LEMON, ORANGE
ruth .... PITY, GRIEF, SORROW
Ruth, baseball player .... BABE, GEORGE (HERMAN)
husband of .... BOAZ
mother-in-law of .... NAOMI
sister of .... EILEEN
son of .... OBED
Ruthenia .... RUSSIA
Ruthenian .... UKRAINIAN
ruthless .... CRUEL, GRUELING, PITILESS, MERCILESS
rutilate .... GLOW, GLEAM, GLITTER
rutty ...... HOT, IN HEAT, BURNING
Ruy Diaz de Bivar ...... (EL) CID
Rwanda capital .... KIGALI
city/town ..... BUTARE, GISENYI
lake .... KIVU
language .... SWAHILI
monetary unit .... FRANC
mountain .... KARISIMBI
neighbor .... BURUNDI
people .... HUTU
president .... KAYIBANDA
river .... RUZIZI
Rx .... RECIPE, REMEDY
is symbol for .... PRESCRIPTION
writer ..... GP, MEDIC, DOCTOR, PHYSICIAN

rye .... RIE, GRASS, GYPSY, CEREAL, WHISKY, GENTLEMAN
disease .... ERGOT, BLACKRUST

grass .... DARNEL
grass genus .... LOLIUM
gypsy .... ROMANO

liquor .... WHISK(E)Y
ryot .... PEASANT
Ryukyu island .... OKINAWA

S

S-curve .... ESS, OGEE
Greek .... SIGMA
Hebrew .... SIN
letter .... ESS
mark .... POTHOOK
shaped .... ESS, OGEE, SIGMATE, SIGMOID
shaped seat .... VIS-A-VIS, TETE-A-TETE
shaped worm .... ESS
sound .... HISS
Sa, in chemistry ...... SAMARIUM
Saar(land) capital
.... SAARBRUCKEN
Saarinen, architect .... EERO
Saba .... SHEBA
sabadilla alkaloid .... VERATRIA, VERATRIN(E)
Sabah .... NORTH BORNEO
bay .... LABUK
capital .... JESSELTON, KOTA KINABALU
city/town .... LAMAG, PAPAR, RAMAU, TAWAU, WESTON
mountain/peak .... KINABALU
seaport .... JESSELTON
Sabaist's object of worship
.... STARS
sabalo .... MILKFISH
Sabatini affair .... DUEL
novelist .... RAFAEL
sabbat .... MEETING
Sabbath ...... SUNDAY, SATURDAY
Sabbatical privilege .... REST, LEAVE, VACATION
saber .... SWORD, CUTLASS, SCIMITAR, YATAG(H)AN
sable ...... FUR, CAPE, FELT, PELT, BLACK, SKUNK, SOBOL, LEMMING, DARK(ENED), MUSTELINE
animal like .... MARTEN, WEASEL
fur .... ZIBEL(L)INE
imitation .... KOLINSKY
sablefish .... BESHOW
sabot ...... CLOG, DINGHY, PATTEN, (WOODEN)SHOE
sabotage .... RUIN, SPOIL, DESTROY, DISABLE, UNDERMINE, VANDALISM, SUBVERSION

perpetrator .... SABOTEUR
Sabrina river .... SEVERN
sabulous .... SANDY, GRITTY
sac ...... BAG, BLEB, CYST, ASCUS, BURSA, POUCH, INDIAN, POCKET, VENTER, VESICLE
air .... BLADDER
bubblelike/cavity-like
.... BLISTER
kangaroo .... MARSUPIUM
like a .... SACCULAR
-like organ .... STOMACH
organ(ism) .... THECA
pus-filled .... BOIL
seed .... POD, CASE, SILIQUE
small .... SACCULE
spore .... ASCUS
SAC, part of .... STRATEGIC, AIR, COMMAND
sacaton .... HAY, GRASS
saccate .... POUCHLIKE
saccharin .... SWEETENER
saccharine .... SWEET, SIRUPY, SUGARY, HONEYED
saccharize .... FERMENT
saccharose .... SUGAR, SUCROSE
saccule .... SAC, BOSS
sacerdotal .... HIERATIC, PRIESTLY
sachem .... CHIEF, SAGAMORE
sachet .... BAG, PAD, POWDER
Sachs, Ger. playwright .... HANS
trade of .... COBBLER
Sachsen .... SAXONY
sack .... BAG, BED, BASE, BUNK, LOOT, POKE, WINE, GUNNY, POUCH, JACKET, RAVAGE, SACQUE, PILLAGE, PLUNDER
hit the .... SLEEP, RETIRE
kind of .... SAD
making cloth .... OSNABURG
slang .... FIRE, DISCHARGE, DISMISS(AL)
sackbutlike instrument
.... LYRE, TROMBONE
sackcloth and _____ .... ASHES
symbol of .... REMORSE, MOURNING, PENITENCE
sacking .... JUTE, BURLAP, LOOTING
sacque .... SACK, JACKET
sacrament .... MASS, RITE, BAPTISM, PENANCE,

(HOLY)COMMUNION, EUCHARIST, MATRIMONY, CONFIRMATION
sacrarium ...... SHRINE, CHANCEL, SANCTUARY
sacred .... HOLY, PIOUS, SAINT, DIVINE, BLESSED, HALLOWED, INVIOLATE, VENERATED, INVIOLABLE, SACROSANCT, SANCTIFIED, CONSECRATED
beetle .... SCARAB
bird .... IBIS
book/tome ...... BIBLE, KORAN, ALCORAN
bull .... APIS, HAPI
chest .... ARCA, CIST
city .... MECCA, MEDINA, BENARES, LOURDES, JERUSALEM
combining form .... HIERO, HAGI(O)
container .... AMA, PYX, CIST
cord .... KUSTI
cow .... IDOL, UNTOUCHABLE
fig tree .... PIPAL
food .... MANNA
fountain .... HIPPOCRENE
hymn .... PSALM
image .... ICON, IKON, PIETA
language .... PALI, HEBREW, ARAMAIC
literature .... VEDA
make .... BLESS, HALLOW, SANCTIFY, CONSECRATE
melody .... CHORALE
music .... MOTET
object .... RELIC
ode .... HYMN
opposed to .... PROFANE, SECULAR
picture .... ICON
place .... CHURCH, SHRINE, TEMPLE, SANCTUM, SYNAGOGUE
plant .... RAGTREE
poem .... HYMN, PSALM
prohibition .... TABU, TABOO
relic .... HALIDOM
scriptures .... BIBLE, KORAN, ALCORAN
shield .... ANCILE
song .... MOTET, PSALM

things, traffic in .... SIMONY
tree .... PIPAL, BO(TREE)
wine vessel .... AMA
word .... OM, LOGOS
writer .... HAGIOGRAPHER
writing .... TORAH, AVESTA,
    GOSPEL, TALMUD,
    HAGGADA(H), MASORA(H),
    SCRIPTURE

Sacred College member
.... CARDINAL
sacredness .... SANCTITY
sacrifice .... COST, LOSS, GIVE UP,
    OBLATION, OFFERING
burning place of .... PILE
by killing .... IMMOLATE
god demanding .... MOLECH,
    MOLOCH
human .... SUTTEE
object of .... HOMAGE,
    ATONEMENT, EXPIATION,
    APPEASEMENT
place of .... ALTAR
play, in baseball .... FLY,
    BUNT
sacrificial animal .... LAMB
block/place/table .... ALTAR
fire .... IGNI
lamb, of a sort ...... FALL GUY
offering .... LAMB, HIERA,
    IMMOLATION
rite .... LIBATION
sacrilege .... SIN, INFAMY,
    IMPIETY, BLASPHEMY,
    PROFANITY
sacrilegious .... IMPIOUS,
    PROFANE, IRREVERENT
condition .... SCANDAL,
    DESECRATION
sacrilegist .... RENEGADE,
    BLASPHEMER
sacrist(an) .... SEXTON
sacristy .... VESTRY
sacrosanct .... HOLY, DIVINE,
    SACRED, HALLOWED,
    INVIOLABLE
slang .... LILY-WHITE
sacrum .... SPINAL BONE
of the .... SACRAL
pain in the .... SACRALGIA
sad .... BAD, GLUM, DISMAL,
    DOLENT, GLOOMY, TRISTE,
    DOLEFUL, UNHAPPY,
    DEJECTED, DOLOROUS,
    MELANCHOLY
colloquial .... BLUE, DOWN
sack .... BOLO
sack at dockside .... DEPORTEE
shack .... HOVEL
saddle .... PAD, HUMP, LOAD,
    SEAT, PANEL, HARNESS

attachment .... HOLSTER
bag .... ALFORJA
band .... GIRTH
blanket .... TILPAH
block .... ANESTHESIA
bow/front part .... POMMEL
cloth .... MANTA, PANEL
colloquial .... PIGSKIN
cover for .... MOCHILA
footrest .... STIRRUP
gaiter/legging .... GAMBADO
girth .... CINCH
gun case .... HOLSTER
horse .... NAG, HACK, REMUDA,
    PALFREY
lining .... PANEL
pack .... APAREJO
pad .... CORONA
part .... PAD, CINCH, GIRTH,
    CANTLE, LATIGO, POMMEL,
    STIRRUP
rear part .... CANTLE
seat behind .... PILLION
slang .... RIG
stirrup .... GAMBADO
strap .... CINCH, GIRTH
upon .... LOAD, ENCUMBER
with charges .... BLAME,
    ACCUSE
Sadducee, opposite of
.... PHARISEE
Sadduceeism .... SKEPTICISM
sadhe .... TSADI
sadiron .... FLATIRON
sadism .... ABUSE,
    MALTREATMENT
is derived from name
of ____ ..... MARQUIS DE
    SADE
sadistic .... CRUEL, BRUTAL,
    FIENDISH
activity .... BEATING,
    BONDAGE, WHIPPING
sadness ...... WOE, DOLOR, GRIEF,
    MISERY, PATHOS, SORROW,
    ANGUISH, DESPAIR
expression of .... ALAS
slang .... BLUES, DUMPS
safari .... TREK, CARAVAN,
    JOURNEY, EXPEDITION
safe .... CHEST, ON ICE, VAULT,
    COFFER, SECURE, UNHURT,
    UNHARMED, PROTECTED,
    STRONGBOX
and ____ .... SOUND
conduct .... PASS, CONVOY,
    ESCORT, PASSPORT
cracker .... YEGG(MAN)
safeblower ...... YEGG, PETERMAN
safeguard .... COVER, GUARD,
    WATCH, CONVOY, DEFEND,

    SHIELD, DEFENSE, PROTECT
safekeeping .... CARE, (A)EGIS,
    CUSTODY, STORAGE,
    TUTELAGE, PROTECTION
of public lands
.... RESERVATION-
    PRESERVATION
safely .... WITHOUT RISK
safety .... SURETY, SECURITY
device .... ARMOR, CATCH,
    VALVE, BUFFER, BUMPER,
    FENDER, SCREEN, SHIELD
device, airplane
.... PARACHUTE
device, sea .... MAE WEST,
    LIFE PRESERVER
lamp .... DAVY
place of .... HOME, HAVEN,
    ASYLUM, HARBOR, REFUGE,
    HOSPICE, SHELTER,
    SANCTUARY
zone .... ISLAND
saffron .... CROCUS, YELLOW
family .... IRIS
use of .... DYE, COLORING,
    SEASONING
safrol(e) .... OIL
sag ...... HANG, SINK, WARP, WILT,
    CURVE, DROOP, SLUMP,
    BUCKLE, SLOUCH, WEAKEN,
    DECLINE
nautical .... DRIFT, LEEWAY,
    LEEWARD
saga ...... EDDA, EPIC, TALE, ILIAD,
    LEGEND
sagacious .... ASTUTE, SHREWD,
    SAPIENT, DISCERNING,
    PERCEPTIVE, WISE(AS AN
    OWL)
sagacity .... WIT, ACUMEN,
    WISDOM
sagamore .... SACHEM
Sagan, modern scholar .... CARL
sage ...... HERB, MINT, SEER, WISE,
    SOLON, NESTOR, SAPIENT,
    SCHOLAR
scarlet .... SALVIA
hen .... GROUSE
of Emporia .... WHITE
Sagebrush State .... NEVADA
sagger .... (FIRE)CLAY
Sagitta .... ARROW, KEYSTONE,
    CONSTELLATION
sagittary .... CENTAUR
sago .... PALM, GOMUTI, STARCH
saguaro .... CACTUS
Sahara ...... DESERT, WASTELAND
fertile area .... FEZZAN
like the .... ARID
section .... ERG
wind .... LESTE

sahib .... SIR, MASTER
saiga .... ANTELOPE
Saigon Chinese district
.... CHOLON
new name of .... HO CHI MINH
sail ...... LUG, KITE, FLOAT, GLIDE,
CANVAS, CRUISE, JIGGER,
LATEEN, VOYAGE, SPANKER,
NAVIGATE
around the world
.... CIRCUMNAVIGATE
bellying part of .... BUNT
billowing .... SPINNAKER
close to the wind .... LUFF,
POINT
corner/attachment .... CLEW
edge of .... LUFF
fastener .... CLEW
for a sloop .... JIB
fore-and-aft .... MIZ(Z)EN,
SPANKER
free edge of .... LEECH
furl .... REEF
haul up .... TRICE
hoist .... CLUE UP
ice .... SCOOTER
into .... SCOLD, BERATE,
ASSAIL
kind of ...... JIB, MAIN, ROYAL,
LATEEN, SPANKER, TOPMAST,
FOREROYAL, TOPGALLANT
loop .... CRINGLE
near the wind .... LUFF
out to sea .... OUTSTAND
part of ..... BUNT, CLEW, FOOT,
HEAD, LUFF, MAST, REEF,
YARD, LEECH, EARING,
CRINGLE, BOLTROPE
poetic .... SHEET
reduce size of .... REEF
ring .... CRINGLE
rope .... TYE, HALYARD
specified distance .... LOG
square .... LUG
support .... MAST
tackle .... HALYARD
tapering cloth .... GORE
triangular .... JIB, LATEEN
tuck .... REEF
sailboat ...... BARK, DHOW, YAWL,
KETCH, SKIFF, SLOOP, SMACK,
VINTA, YACHT, BARQUE,
CAIQUE, KUMPIT, SAILER,
VESSEL, CRUISER, SCHOONER
sailed at Newport ...... YACHTED
sailer, 1492 .... PINTA, NINA,
SANTA MARIA
sailfish .... (BASKING) SHARK
kin of .... MARLIN
sailing, oblique .... LOXODROMICS
race .... REGATTA

raft .... BALSA, CATAMARAN
vessel .... YAWL, KETCH,
SLOOP, FRIGATE, GALLEON,
SCHOONER
sailor .... GOB, HAT, TAR, JACK,
SALT, LASCAR, SEAMAN,
MARINER, NAVYMAN,
SHIPMAN, DECK HAND,
SEAFARER
bed of .... HAMMOCK
clumsy .... LUBBER
contentious .... SEA LAWYER
drink of .... GROG
experienced .... SEADOG,
SHELLBACK
jersey .... FROCK
kidnap .... SHANGHAI
new, inexperienced
.... LUBBER, LANDSMAN
prospective .... MIDDY
sailor's bad luck .... JONAH,
JONAS
biscuit .... TACK
brew .... RUM
call .... AHOY
choice .... PORGY, PIGFISH
church .... BETHEL
cord .... LANIARD, LANYARD
dish .... SCOUSE
handicraft .... SCRIMSHAW
hat .... SOU(TH)WESTER
hello .... AHOY
jumper .... BLOUSE
leave .... FURLOUGH
mess tub .... KID
patron saint .... ELMO
patroness .... EULALIA
quarters .... FOCSLE,
FORECASTLE
rebellion .... MUTINY
social call .... GAM
sword .... CUTLAS(S)
underwear .... SKIVY
(work)song .... CHANTEY,
SHANT(E)Y
"yes" .... AYE-AYE
sain .... BLESS, CROSS
saint. See also patron ...... HOLY,
SAN(TA), SACRED, BLESSED,
CANONIZE
celebrated on January 21st
.... AGNES
colloquial .... ANGEL
declare person a .... CANONIZE
early .... AUGUSTINE
first native-born American
.... SETON
homage to a .... DULIA
memorial of .... RELIC
sacred image of .... ICON,
(E)IKON

tomb of .... SHRINE
topper .... HALO
worshiper .... HAGIOLATER
Saint Andrew's Cross .... SATIRE,
SALTIER
Anthony's fire ..... ERYSIPELAS
Bernard .... DOG
Bernard monk's concern
.... TRAVELER, WAYFARER
Elmo's fire .... CORPOSANT
Joan character .... DAUPHIN
John's bread .... CAROB,
ALGAROBA
John's evil .... EPILEPSY
Laurent, fashion stylist
.... YVES
Patrick's Day celebrant
.... IRISH
Peter Gonzalez .... ELMO
Vitus' dance .... CHOREA
saintly .... PIOUS
saints, author of lives of
.... HAGIOGRAPHER
catalogue/list of .... CANON,
DIPTYCH, HAGIOLOGY
register .... MENOLOGY
rule by .... HAGIARCHY,
THEOCRACY, HAGIOCRACY
worship of .... HAGIOLATRY
Saint's day .... FIESTA
sake .... END, GOOD, WINE, CAUSE,
BEHALF, MOTIVE, REGARD,
ACCOUNT, BENEFIT, PURPOSE
source .... RICE
saker .... FALCON
Sakhalin .... KARAFUTO
Saki .... MUNRO
Sakti .... MAYA
sal volatile .... HARTSHORN
salaam .... BOW, GREETING,
OBEISANCE
salable .... VENDIBLE,
MARKETABLE
salacious .... LEWD, BAWDY,
RIBALD, LUSTFUL, OBSCENE
salad .... GREENS, (COLD)DISH,
(COLE)SLAW
days .... TEENS, YOUTH
dressing .... RANCH, ITALIAN,
REMO(U)LADE, MAYONNAISE,
BLUE CHEESE, VINAIGRETTE,
THOUSAND ISLAND
fruit .... AMBROSIA,
MACEDOINE
green .... UDO, CRESS(E),
ENDIVE, DANDELION
herb ...... DILL, CRESS, ENDIVE,
FENNEL, PARSLEY
kind of .... CHEF, CAESAR,
POTATO, TOSSED, WALDORF,
FOUR-BEAN

leaves ..... SPINACH, ESCAROLE, WATERCRESS, (ROMAINE)LETTUCE
molded .... ASPIC, JELLO
vegetable .... BEET, CELERY, RADISH, TOMATO, CABBAGE, CHICORY, SUCCORY, CUCUMBER, MUSHROOM, SCALLION, ASPARAGUS, BELL PEPPER
Saladin's foes .... CRUSADERS
salamander .... EFT, NEWT, POKER, AXOLTL, LIZARD, REPTILE, MUD PUPPY, WATER DOG, HELLBENDER
obsolete .... EVET
Salambria .... PENEUS
salami .... SAUSAGE
salary .... FEE, PAY, HIRE, SCREW, WAGE(S), STIPEND, EMOLUMENT, COMPENSATION
additional to .... BONUS, PERK, PERQUISITE
increase .... RAISE
limit .... CAP
payment other than .... FRINGE BENEFIT
sale ...... DEAL, BARTER, MARKET, BARGAIN, SELLING, VENDITION
incentive .... REBATE
kind of ..... CASH, FIRE, YARD, WHITE, GARAGE, AUCTION, RUMMAGE, CLEARANCE, INVENTORY
public .... VENDUE, AUCTION
proviso/term .... AS IS
Salem witchcraft trial judge
.... SEWALL
salep .... TUBER
drink from .... SALOOP
source of .... ORCHID
saleratus .... BAKING SODA
sales caveat .... AS IS
promotion .... FREE SAMPLE, ADVERTISING
talk .... LINE, PITCH, SPIEL, PATTER
salesman .... CLERK, SELLER, DRUMMER
kind of .... PEDDLER, TRAVELING, AUCTIONEER, DOOR-TO-DOOR
salicaceous tree .... POPLAR, WILLOW
salicin .... GLUCOSIDE
saliferous .... SALTY, SALINE
salient .... LEAPING, NOTABLE, CAPERING, STRIKING, PROMINENT
points .... GIST
salientian .... FROG, TOAD

salina .... LAKE, POND, (SALT)MARSH, SALT PITS
saline .... SALTY, MARINAL
drop .... TEAR
solution .... BRINE
Salisbury steak ...... HAMBURGER
Salish .... INDIAN, FLATHEAD
saliva .... SPUTUM, SPIT(TLE)
content .... UREA, MUCIN, SALTS, SODIUM, ALBUMIN, AMYLASE, CHLORIDE
enzyme .... AMYLASE, PTYALIN
excessive secretion of
.... PTYALISM
insufficient secretion of
.... DRY MOUTH
resembling .... SIALOID
running from mouth
.... DROOL, DRIVEL, SLAVER
wet/smear with .... SLOBBER
salix .... ITEA, OSIER, WILLOW
Salk, vaccine developer
.... JONAS
salle .... HALL, ROOM
sallet .... HELMET
sallow .... WAN, PALE, MUDDY, OSIER, PASTY, PALLID, SICKLY, WILLOW, YELLOW
sally .... JEST, JOKE, QUIP, RAID, TRIP, FORAY, JAUNT, ISSUE, BANTER, RETORT, SORTIE, RIPOSTE, REPARTEE, OUTBURST, EXCURSION, WIT(TICISM)
forth .... RUSH OUT
Sally, actress .... FIELD
Lunn .... TEACAKE
with the fan .... RAND
salmacis .... NYMPH
salmagundi .... OLIO, JUMBLE, MEDLEY, MIXTURE, POTPOURRI, HODGEPODGE
salmi .... STEW
salmon .... COHO, JACK, MORT, HADDO, HOLIA, SPROD, ALEVIN, GRILSE, CHINOOK, CHINUCK, QUINNAT, SOCKEYE
color .... PINK
dog .... CHUM, KETA
eggs .... ROE
eggs relish .... CAVIAR(E)
female .... RAUN, BAGGIT
gristle .... GIB
hook .... GIB, KIP
humpback .... HADDO, HOLIA
male .... COCK, KIPPER
net .... MAUD
one year old .... BLUECAP
red .... SOCKEYE
running up river
.... ANADROMOUS

salted .... LOX
trout .... HARDHEAD, NAMAYCUSH, STEELHEAD
variety ..... RED, PINK, PACIFIC, ATLANTIC
young .... PARR, SMOLT, GRILSE, SAMLET
salmonella .... BACTERIA
disease caused by .... TYPHOID FEVER, FOOD POISONING
salmonoid .... TROUT, NAMAYCUSH, STEELHEAD
Salome's mother .... HERODIAS
stepfather .... HEROD
salon .... HALL, SHOP, LEVEE, STUDIO, ATELIER, GALLERY, BALLROOM, SHOWROOM, DRAWING ROOM, (BEAUTY)PARLOR
service .... SET, PERM, TRIM
Salonika .... THERMA
saloon ...... BAR, PUB, DIVE, HALL, SEDAN, BISTRO, TAVERN, CANTINA, GINMILL, TAPROOM, DRAMSHOP, GROGGERY, GROGSHOP, HONKY-TONK, BARRELHOUSE
keeper .... PUBLICAN
slang .... OASIS
saloop .... DRINK
Salop .... SHROPSHIRE
salpa .... TUNICATE
salt .... SAL, TAR, WIT, NACL, BRINE, HUMOR, SOUSE, PICKLE, SAILOR, SEASON, PICRATE, SALINIZE
away ...... BANK, SAVE, STORE, INVEST
acid .... OLEATE
alkaline .... BORAX
bed .... VAT
bottle .... CRUET, CASTER, CASTOR, SHAKER
chemical .... ESTER
crystalline .... NITER, NITRE
deposit .... LICK
factory .... SALTERN
lake .... SINK
malic acid .... MALATE
marsh/pond .... SALINA
meat .... SALAMI
organic .... ESTER
person who makes or sells
.... SALTER
pertaining to .... SALINE
pork .... SOWBELLY
preserve with .... CORN
resembling .... HALOID
rheum .... ECZEMA
rock .... HALITE
soluble .... SALAR

spring .... LICK, SALINA
tax .... GABELLE
tree .... ATLE, TAMARISK
water .... BRINE
saltant .... DANCING, JUMPING,
           LEAPING
saltation ...... BEATING, DANCING,
     LEAP(ING), MUTATION,
         PALPITATION
salted .... CORNED
saltpeter .... NITER, NITRE
salts, _____ .... EPSOM
saltworks .... SALINA, SALTERN
saltwort .... KALI, BARILLA
salty .... RACY, BRINY, SHARP,
      WITTY, CORNED, SALINE,
       PIQUANT, PUNGENT
salubrious .... SALUTARY,
          HEALTHFUL
Salus .... HYGEIA
  concern of .... HEALTH,
         PROSPERITY
salutary .... TONIC, HEALTHY,
     HEALING, HEALTHFUL,
    WHOLESOME, BENEFICIAL,
       SALUBRIOUS
salutation .... AVE, BOW, HAIL,
     ALOHA, CURTSY, SALAAM,
     WELCOME, GREETING,
         RESPECTS
salute .... BOW, TIP, HAIL, KISS,
    GREET, CURTSY, WELCOME
  flag .... DIP (COLORS)
  gun/military .... SALVO
salvage .... SAVE, REDEEM,
    RESCUE, RECLAIM, RETRIEVE
salvation .... RESCUE,
    REDEMPTION, DELIVERANCE
Salvation Army founder
           BOOTH
salve ...... OIL, BALM, HAIL, NARD,
    ANOINT, LOTION, POMADE,
    REMEDY, SOOTHE, ASSUAGE,
     PLASTER, UNGUENT,
    OINTMENT, DEMULCENT,
         EMOLLIENT
  sacramental .... CHRISM
salver .... TRAY, WAITER
salvia .... SAGE
salvo .... BURST, EXCUSE, SALUTE,
    VOLLEY, EVASION, FANFARE,
    GUNFIRE, HEDGING, STRAFING,
    BROADSIDE, FUSILLADE
  in law .... RESERVATION
Samantha, actress .... EGGAR
samara .... CHAT, KEY FRUIT
  tree bearing .... ASH, ELM,
          MAPLE
Samaritan magician ...... MAGUS
sambar .... DEER, MAHA, RUSA

sambuke-like instrument
          HARP
same .... IBID, IDEM, ALIKE,
     DITTO, EQUAL, SIMILAR,
        IDENTICAL
  combining form .... ISO,
          HOMO
  in value .... EQUIVALENT
  sound, without variation
       MONOTONOUS
Samedi .... SATURDAY
samiel .... SIMOOM
samisen-like instrument
          BANJO
samite .... LAME
samlet .... PARR, SALMON
Sammy Cahn creation .... LYRIC
Samoa .... NAVIGATORS
Samoa, American bay
         MASSACRE
  cape .... TAPUTAPU
  capital .... PAGO PAGO
  island .... TUTUILA
Samoa, Western bay .... SAFATA,
         PALAULI
  cape .... MULINU'U
  capital .... APIA
  city/town .... ASAU,
    SALA'ILUA, SATUPAITEA
  island .... UPOLU, SAVAI'I
  monetary unit .... TALA
  mountain .... VAEA, SILISILI,
         VAAIFETU
  seaport .... APIA
  strait .... APOLIMA
Samoan .... POLYNESIAN
  bird .... IAO
  cloth .... TAPA
  clothes .... PAREUS
  costume .... PULETASI
  council .... FONO
  loincloth .... LAVA-LAVA
  maiden .... TAUPO
  mollusk .... ASI
  owl .... LULU
  waistcloth .... LAVA-LAVA
  warrior .... TOA
samovar .... URN, TEAPOT
samp .... GRITS, HOMINY,
    (CORN)MEAL, PORRIDGE
sampan .... BOAT
samphire .... GLASSWORT
sample .... TEST, TASTE, TRIAL,
    EXAMPLE, PATTERN, SPECIMEN
  cloth .... SWATCH
sampler .... TESTER, NEEDLEWORK
  item .... MOTTO
Samson and Delilah composer
       SAINT SAENS
Samson in Hebrew .... SHIMSHON
Samson's deathplace .... GAZA

  father .... MANOAH
  mistress .... DELILAH
  mother .... ZORAH
  tribe .... DAN
  vulnerable part .... HAIR
  weapon .... JAWBONE
Samuel .... PROPHET
Samuel's birthplace .... RAMAH
  father .... ELKANAH
  mother .... HANNAH
  son .... ABIA
  teacher .... ELI
samurai .... RONIN, WARRIOR
San .... SAINT
  Antonio shrine .... ALAMO
  _____ fault .... ANDREAS
  Francisco .... FRISCO
  Francisco's _____ Tower
          COIT
  _____ of Hearst fame
         SIMEON
  Marino mount .... TITANO
  Marino rulers .... REGENTS
sana in corpore sano, _____
          MENS
sanatory .... CURATIVE
sanbenito wearer .... HERETIC,
         PENITENT
Sancho Panza's master
       (DON)QUIXOTE
sanctify .... BLESS, HALLOW,
    PURIFY, BEATIFY, GLORIFY,
        CONSECRATE
sanctimonious .... DEVOUT,
    PRUDISH, HYPOCRITICAL
  colloquial .... GOODY-GOODY
sanction .... OK, LAW, AMEN,
     FIAT, ALLOW, DECREE,
    PERMIT, RATIFY, APPROVE,
    CONFIRM, ENDORSE, PENALTY,
     SUPPORT, APPROVAL,
       IMPRIMATUR
  given by an Oriental ruler
         FIRMAN
sanctioned .... LEGAL
sanctity .... PURITY, HOLINESS,
         GODLINESS
sanctuary .... BEMA, FANE,
    HAVEN, ASYLUM, CHURCH,
    REFUGE, TEMPLE, CHANCEL,
     SHELTER, HALIDOM(E)
  animal/bird .... RESERVATION
  portable .... TABERNACLE
sanctum .... DEN, STUDY,
    ADYTUM, OFFICE, RETREAT
sand .... GRIT, BEACH, GRAIN,
    SPECK, DESERT, POLISH,
    SILICA, SMOOTH, ABRASIVE,
        GRANULES
  bank .... CAY, DUNE, SHOAL
  bar .... REEF, SPIT, SHELF,

SHOAL
dab .... FLATFISH
deposit .... ESKER
dollar .... SEA URCHIN
eel .... LA(U)NCE
flea .... CHIGOE, CHIGGER
hill .... DENE, DUNE
lily .... SOAPROOT
lot game .... BASEBALL
living in .... ARENICOLOUS
mist .... BAI
mound .... DENE, DUNE
particles .... GRIT, SILT
ridge ...... DUNE, OSAR, ESKAR,
ESKER
slang ..... GRIT, PLUCK, SPUNK,
COURAGE
snake .... ERYX
trotter .... CAMEL
viper .... HOGNOSE
Sand, George .... DUPIN,
DUDEVANT
sandal .... THONG, LOAFER,
SLIPPER, HUARACHE,
(OVER)SHOE
fastener .... LACET, LATCHET
wooden .... PATTEN
sandals, winged .... TALARIA
sandalwood ...... ALGUM, ALMUG,
SANTAL, INCENSE, LABURNUM
Sandalwood Island .... SUMBA,
SOEMBA
sandarac .... ARAR, RESIN,
ALERSE, INCENSE, REALGAR
sandbank .... CAY, DUNE, SPIT
channel .... GAT
Sandburg, poet .... CARL
sander ...... POLISHER, SMOOTHER
sandglass .... HOURGLASS
what it tells .... TIME
sandhog .... DIGGER
sandpaper .... ABRASIVE
sandpiper .... REE, BIRD, RUFF,
STILT, STINT, TEREK, DUNLIN,
CURLEW, RED KNOT,
TATTLER, JACKSNIPE,
GREENSHANK, YELLOWLEGS
African .... RUFF
American .... PEEP
Arctic .... PECTORAL
beach .... SANDERLING
European .... STINT
female .... REEVE
gathering place of male
.... LEK
genus .... TRINGA, CALIDRIS,
VANELLUS
long-beaked ..... SNIPE, TEREK,
CURLEW, GODWIT, WOODCOCK
means of feeding ..... PROBING
relative .... SNIPE, PLOVER

short-beaked .... STINT,
DOWITCHER
spotted .... PEETWEET
sands .... BEACH, MOMENTS
sandstone .... PAAR, BEREA,
ARKOSE, PSAMMITE,
ITACOLUMITE
formed from granite
.... ARKOSE
sandstorm .... SAMIEL, SIMOOM
sandwich .... INSERT, PUT
BETWEEN
bread .... BUN, RYE,
CROISSANT, PUMPERNICKEL
cookie .... OREO
Dagwood .... HERO, HOAGIE
filling .... EGG, HAM, TUNA,
BACON, BURGER, CHEESE,
SALAMI, WIENER, BOLOGNA
garnish .... ONION, LEMON,
PICKLE, TOMATO
kind of ...... HOT, CLUB, COLD,
POOR BOY, OPEN(-FACE)
underwater .... SUBMARINE
Sandwich Islands .... HAWAII
sandy .... GRITTY, ARENOSE,
SABULOUS, SHIFTING,
ARENACEOUS
color .... GINGER
mound .... DOWN
soil .... LOAM, LOESS
waste(land) .... DESERT
sane .... WISE, LUCID, SOBER,
SOUND, NORMAL, RATIONAL,
SENSIBLE, REASONABLE
colloquial .... ALL HERE
sanforize .... PRESHRINK
sang-froid .... CALM, COOL, POISE,
APLOMB, COMPOSURE,
INSOUCIANCE
Sangraal .... (HOLY)GRAIL
sanguinaria .... PLANT, POPPY,
BLOODROOT
sanguinary .... GORY, BLOODY,
SAVAGE, BLOODTHIRSTY
sanguine .... RUDDY, HOPEFUL,
CHEERFUL, CONFIDENT,
OPTIMISTIC
color .... RED, RUDDY,
MURREY, CRIMSON
person .... OPTIMIST
Sanhedrin .... COURT, COUNCIL
sanicle .... PARSLEY
sanies .... PUS, DISCHARGE
sanitarium .... RESORT, RETREAT,
HOSPITAL, SANATORIUM
building .... PAVILION
sanitary .... CLEAN, HYGIENIC
protection .... NAPKIN,
TAMPON
sanity .... REASON, SENSES,

SOBRIETY
sannup ...... INDIAN, ALGONQUIAN
sans .... WITHOUT
culotte .... RADICAL,
REVOLUTIONARY
doute .... SURE, CERTAINLY,
DOUBTLESS
ethical standards ...... AMORAL
pareil .... PEERLESS
souci .... GAY, CASTLE,
CAREFREE
Sans Souci site .... POTSDAM
Sanskrit .... INDIC, VEDIC
dialect .... PALI
epic .... RAMAYAMA
god .... VAYU, INDRA
god's elephant .... AIRAVATA
word meaning "kinsmen"
.... ARYAN
Santa .... HOLY, SAINT
_____ .... FE, CLAUS, ANITA,
BARBARA
_____, Antonio Lopez de,
Mexican leader against
the Alamo .... ANNA
Claus .... NICK, KRISS KRINGLE
Claus' illustrator
.... (THOMAS) NAST
Claus' sled runner
.... REINDEER
Claus' vehicle .... SLED,
SLEIGH
Claus' way .... CHIMNEY
Claus who first arrived in
America: 17th century
.... (SAINT)NICHOLAS
_____, Columbus' flagship:
1492 .... MARIA
Fe _____ .... TRAIL
Severa .... PYRGI
stand-in of .... POP, PAPA,
DAD(DY)
Santiago de Cuba .... ORIENTE
santon .... MONK, HERMIT
santonica .... WORMSEED,
WORMWOOD
Santorini, former name of
.... THERA
Sao Salvador .... BAHIA
sap ...... DIG, DRAIN, FLUID, JUICE,
VIGOR, SPIRIT, TRENCH,
WEAKEN, EXHAUST,
UNDERMINE
drain .... TAP, SPILE, SPOUT
flow of .... LACTESCENCE
poisonous .... UPAS
slang .... BOOB, DUPE, FOOL
the foundations of
.... DESTROY
tree .... MILK, UPAS, LATEX,
BALATA, RUBBER

sapajou .... GRISON, MONKEY, CAPUCHIN

saphead .... BOOB, DOLT, DUPE, FOOL, DINGBAT, DING-A-LING

sapid .... TASTY, SAVORY, FLAVORY, TASTEFUL

sapience .... WISDOM, SAGACITY

sapient .... SAGE, WISE, KNOWING, LEARNED, DISCERNING

sapindaceous plant .... SOAPBERRY

sapless .... DRY, INSIPID

sapling .... YOUTH, SPROUT, SEEDLING, YOUNGSTER

sapodilla .... PLUM, ACANA, CHICO, MAMEY, MAMMEE, SAPOTA, MARMALADE

saponaceous .... SOAPY

saponin .... GLUCOSIDE

sapor .... TANG, SAVOR, TASTE, FLAVOR, RELISH

saporous .... TASTY, SAVORY

sapota .... MARMALADE, SAPODILLA

sapped .... SPENT, DISABLED

sapper .... DIGGER, TRENCHER

Sapphira's husband .... ANANIAS

weakness .... LYING

sapphire ...... GEM, BLUE, STONE, CORUNDUM

sapphirine .... SPINEL

Sappho's home .... LESBOS

work .... POETRY

sappy .... JUICY

slang ..... INANE, INEPT, SILLY, FATUOUS, FOOLISH

saprophyte .... FUNGUS, PARASITE

sapsago .... CHEESE

sapsucker .... WOODPECKER

sapwood .... ALBURNUM

saraband .... DANCE

Saracen .... ARAB, MOOR, MOSLEM

foe of .... CRUSADER

holy man .... IMAM

leader .... SALADIN

Sarah .... MILES, BERNHARDT

diminutive of ...... SAL, SADIE, SALLY

handmaid of/slave of .... HAGAR

husband of .... ABRAHAM

son of .... ISAAC

saran .... RESIN

Saratoga general .... GATES

Sarawak's rajah .... BROOKE

sarcasm .... GIBE, JEER, IRONY, SCORN, SATIRE, CONTEMPT, CYNICISM

sarcastic .... ACID, CAUSTIC, CYNICAL, MORDANT, IRONIC(AL), SARDONIC, SCORNFUL, SATIRIC(AL), VITRIOLIC

sarcoma .... TUMOR, CANCER

bones .... OSTEO(SARCOMA), CHONDRO(SARCOMA)

skin .... KAPOSI'S

sarcophagus .... TOMB, COFFIN

sard .... CHALCEDONY

sardine .... LOUR, HERRING, PILCHARD

fish like .... BRISLING

_____ like .... PACKED

local .... CAN

relative .... KIPPER

Sardinian cape .... TESTA, TEULADA, CARBONARA, SPARTIVENTO

capital .... CAGLIARI

city/town .... BOSA, BITTI, NUORO, SORSO, ARBOREA, SASSARI, CARBONIA, IGLESIAS

coin .... CARLINE

duchy .... SAVOIE

gulf .... OROSEI, ASINARA, CAGLIARI, ORISTANO

language .... CATALAN

mountain .... GENNARGENTU

neighbor island .... CORSICA

province ...... NUORO, SASSARI, CAGLIARI

river .... MANNU, TIRSO, COGHINAS

ruling family .... SAVOY

seaport .... BOSA

sheep .... MOUF(F)LON

strait .... BONIFACIO

sardius .... RUBY, SARD

sardonic .... CAUSTIC, TWISTED, DERISIVE, IRONIC(AL), SARCASTIC, SATIRIC(AL)

sardonyx product .... CAMEO

Sarg, U.S. puppeteer ...... TONY

sargasso .... SEAWEED, (GULF)WEED

sark .... SHIRT, CHEMISE

sarmentose plant .... STRAWBERRY

sarong .... PAREUS, LOINCLOTH, WAISTCLOTH

Sarpedon's father .... ZEUS

killer .... PATROCLUS

mother .... EUROPA

sarsaparilla .... MEAD, SMILAX, GINSENG, BEVERAGE

sartor .... TAILOR

sash ...... OBI, BAND, BELT, TOBE, SCARF, GIRDLE, RIBBON, WAISTBAND, CUMMERBUND

door/window .... FRAME, CASING

pane holder .... SPRIG

sashay .... GAD, GLIDE

sasin .... BUCK, ANTELOPE

Saskatchewan capital .... REGINA

city/town .... MELFORT, TISDALE, WEYBURN, YORKTON, HUMBOLDT, ROSETOWN, MOOSE JAW, SASKATOON, PRINCE ALBERT

hills .... CYPRESS, PORCUPINE

lake .... CREE, DORE, TOBIN, MONTREAL, REINDEER, OLD WIVES, ATHABASCA

lakes .... QUILL, WHITESWAN

mountain .... MOOSE

river .... SWAN, MAKWA, MOSSY, TORCH, CARROT, GEIKIE, OLDMAN, POPLAR, MUDJATIK, SASKERAM, CHURCHILL, ASSINIBOIA

saskatoon .... SHADBLOW, (SHAD)BUSH, JUNEBERRY

Sasquatch .... BIG FOOT

sass ...... LIP, SAUCE, (BACK)TALK, RUDENESS, VEGETABLES

sassaby .... ANTELOPE

sassafras drink .... SALOOP, ROOT BEER

oil .... SAFROL(E)

Sassenach .... SAXON, LOWLANDER, ENGLISHMAN

Sassoon, poet .... SIEGFRIED

sassy .... RUDE, TREE, SAUCY, IMPUDENT

one .... SNIP

Satan .... DEIL, EVIL, DEMON, DEVIL, EBLIS, BELIAL, HORNIE, ABADDON, LUCIFER, OLD NICK, SHAITAN, APOLLYON, MEPHISTO, OLD HARRY, ARCHFIEND, BEELZEBUB

co-rebel of .... AZAZEL

satanic .... WICKED, DEVILISH, INFERNAL, DIABOLICAL

satchel .... ETUI, ETWEE, SCRIP, VALISE, (HAND)BAG, GRIP(SACK)

sate .... FILL, GLUT, GRATIFY, SATIATE, SATISFY, SURFEIT

sated .... BLASE

satellite .... MOON, PLANET, FOLLOWER, DEPENDENT

artificial .... ECHO, LUNA, NOVA, LUNIK, SOYUZ, APOLLO, GEMINI, HELIOS, OHSUMI, VOSTOK, MERCURY, PIONEER, SPUTNIK, EXPLORER, CHALLENGER

path of .... ORBIT

shadow of .... UMBRA

unmanned .... IRAS
satiate .... CLOY, FILL, GLUT,
JADE, SATE, SLAKE, GRATIFY,
SATISFY, SURFEIT
satin, adjective for .... SOFT,
GLOSSY, SMOOTH
fabric .... SILK, NYLON,
RAYON, CYPRUS, CYPRESS
fabric smooth like ..... PANNE,
PONGEE, VELVET
flower .... LUNARIA
imitation .... SATEEN,
SATINET(TE)
satiny .... SILKY, LUSTROUS
satire ...... WIT, IRONY, LAMPOON,
MOCKERY, SARCASM,
RIDICULE, PASQUINADE
satirical .... WRY, CAUSTIC,
CUTTING, IRONIC(AL),
SARCASTIC
work .... SKIT, PARODY,
LAMPOON, BURLESQUE,
CARICATURE
satirist .... JUVENAL
satirize .... LAMPOON, RIDICULE
in verse .... BERIME
satisfaction .... CONTENT,
PAYMENT, PLEASURE,
ATONEMENT, REPARATION
for a killing .... CRO
for injuries .... GREE,
DAMAGES
satisfactory .... GOOD, JAKE,
AMPLE, ADEQUATE
satisfied .... HAPPY
satisfy .... PAY, MEET, SOLVE,
ANSWER, PLEASE, APPEASE,
FULFILL, GRATIFY, PLACATE,
MEASURE UP
every whim .... CATER
satisfying .... HUNKY, REWARDING
satrap .... RULER, TYRANT,
GOVERNOR
saturate .... SOP, FILL, SOAK,
IMBUE, STEEP, DRENCH,
SEETHE
saturated state ...... WET, SOGGY,
SOAKED, SODDEN
Saturday night special ...... GUN,
PIECE, REVOLVER, AUTOMATIC
Saturn .... CRONUS, PLANET
ancient god and ruler of
.... REPHAN
in alchemy .... LEAD
largest satellite .... TITAN
moon of .... DIONE
orbiters of .... RINGS
wife of .... OPS
saturnalia .... ORGY, REVELRY,
CARNIVAL, FESTIVAL
saturniid .... MOTH

saturnine .... GLUM, GRAVE,
GLOOMY, MOROSE, TACITURN
satyr .... FAUN, DEITY, LECHER,
SILENUS, BUTTERFLY
deity resembling a
.... SILENUS
Satyr, god attended by
.... BACCHUS
staff of .... THYRSUS
Sau .... SAVA
sauce .... DIP, SOY, CHILI, CURRY,
GRAVY, FLAVOR, MORNAY,
RELISH, SEASON, SOUBISE,
VELOUTE, DRESSING,
MATELOTE, WORCESTER
and liqueurs .... CREMES
bean .... SOJA, SOY(A)
colloquial .... IMPUDENCE,
INSOLENCE
dessert .... MINT, MELBA,
CARAMEL, HOT FUDGE,
CHOCOLATE, BUTTERSCOTCH
fish .... ALEC
flavoring material .... EGGS,
MINT, WINE, LEMON, ONION,
CAPERS, CHEESE
kind of ..... WHITE, BARBECUE,
BECHAMEL, MUSHROOM,
BEARNAISE, BORDELAISE,
HOLLANDAISE
made with eggs and cheese
.... MORNAY
made with onion puree
.... SOUBISE
pepper .... TABASCO
slang .... LIQUOR
spicy .... REMO(U)LADE
thickener .... ROUX
tomato .... CATSUP, KETCHUP
white .... VELOUTE
saucepan .... POT, POSNET,
CASSEROLE
saucer .... DISH, DISK, DISCUS
flying .... UFO
object likened to .... EYE
saucy .... ARCH, BOLD, CHIC,
PERT, RUDE, BRASH, COCKY,
PERKY, SASSY, SMART,
FLIP(PANT), IMPUDENT,
INSOLENT, IMPERTINENT
girl .... CHIT, MINX, MALAPERT
slang .... FRESH, BRASSY,
CHEEKY
talk .... LIP
Saudi Arabian cape .... ABU-
MAD, BARIDA, HATIBA, AL
ASWAD, MISHAAB, SAFANIYA
capital .... RIYADH
city/town .... ABHA, HAIL,
TAIF, HOFUF, JIDDA, JIZAN,
MECCA, QIZAN, TEBUK,

DAMMAM, MEDINA, NAJRAN,
BURAIDA, MUBARRAZ
coin .... QURSH, QURUSH
desert .... DAHANA, JAFURA,
AR RIMAL, NEFUD(DAHI),
BAHR ES SAFI, RUB AL KHALI
district .... MIDIAN
gulf .... AQABA, PERSIAN
inhabitant .... BEDOUIN
island .... TIRAN, FARASAN,
MASHABI, SHAIBARA
language .... ARABIC
monetary unit .... RIYAL
mountain .... SUBH, SALMA,
ANEIZA, ARAFAT
plateau .... ARMA, SUMMAN
port .... JIDDA
principality .... ASIR
province .... HE(D)JAZ
range .... TUWAIQ, HADHB
DAWASIR
region .... TIHAMA
religion .... ISLAM
religious center .... MECCA,
MEDINA
river, dry .... ARAR, RIMA,
BISHA, RANYA, SIRHAN,
DAWASIR
ruler .... KING, FEISAL,
(IBN)SAUD
sea .... RED
state .... NEJD
strait .... TIRAN
sauger .... PERCH
Sauk .... SAC
Saul. See **King Saul**
Sault Ste. Marie canals .... SOO
sauna .... BATH(HOUSE)
saunter ...... GAIT, WALK, AMBLE,
MOSEY, LOITER, STROLL
across street .... JAYWALK
saurel .... SCAD, SKATE
saurian .... LIZARD, REPTILE,
DINOSAUR, ALLIGATOR,
CROCODILE
sauropod .... DINOSAUR
saury .... SKIPPER, LIZARDFISH
sausage ...... PIG, WEENY, SALAMI,
WEENIE, WEINER, BOLOGNA,
PUDDING, SAVELOY,
(LIVER)WURST, FRANKFURTER
cover .... INTESTINE
shaped .... ALLANTOID
saute .... FRY
sauterne .... WINE, YQUEM
savage .... HUN, FELL, WILD,
ANGRY, CRUEL, FERAL,
BRUTAL, FERINE, FIERCE,
RUGGED, BESTIAL, UNTAMED,
TERRIBLE, BARBARIAN,
BARBAROUS, FEROCIOUS

beast .... BRUTE
state .... FERITY
Savage Island .... NIUE
savagery .... WILDNESS,
BARBARISM, BARBARITY,
BRUTALITY
savanna(h) .... PLAIN, GRASSLAND
plain like ..... LLANO, PAMPAS,
STEPPE
savant .... SAGE, EXPERT, PANDIT,
PUNDIT, SCHOLAR
save ...... BUT, KEEP, HOARD, LAY
BY, SPARE, STORE, EXCEPT,
REDEEM, RESCUE, BARRING,
SALVAGE, PRESERVE,
ECONOMIZE
all .... OVERALLS, PINAFORE
saveloy .... SAUSAGE
savin(e) .... CEDAR, JUNIPER
saving .... EXCEPT, FRUGAL,
REDEEMING
clause .... SALVO, LOOPHOLE
in law .... EXCEPTION
savings .... FUNDS, ACCOUNT,
NEST EGG, RESERVE(S)
and loan association
.... BANK, (MONEY)LENDER
bank .... SAVE-ALL
investments .... BONDS,
LEGALS, PORTFOLIO
savior .... RESCUER, REDEEMER,
LIBERATOR, JESUS(CHRIST)
financial .... PATRON,
BENEFACTOR
savoir-faire .... TACT, POISE,
DIPLOMACY
Savonarola, Ital. reformer
.... GIROLAMO
savor .... AROMA, ENJOY, EAT UP,
SAPOR, SMELL, TASTE, TINGE,
FLAVOR, RELISH, SEASON,
DELIGHT IN, SMACK (THE
LIPS)
savorless .... FLAT
savory .... MINT, SALTY, SAPID,
SIPID, TASTY, YUMMY,
DAINTY, PIQUANT, DELICIOUS,
FLAVORFUL, PALATABLE,
TOOTHSOME, APPETIZING
smell .... AROMA
savoy .... CABBAGE
Savoyard show(man) ...... RAREE
savvy ...... CRAFT, SENSE, WISDOM,
KNOW-HOW,
UNDERSTAND(ING)
slang .... SMARTS
saw ...... CUT, RASP, REDE, ADAGE,
GRATE, MAXIM, MOTTO,
SAYING, PROVERB
blade .... WEB
cut of .... KERF

kind of .... RIP, BUCK, HACK,
HAND, EDGER, CIRCULAR
notch .... KERF
sawfish's .... SERRA
surgical ..... TREPAN, TREPHINE
toothed .... SERRATE
sawbones: sl. .... SURGEON
sawbuck: sl. .... TEN(SPOT)
sawdust .... COOM, SCOBS
sawfish .... RAY
snout .... SERRA
sawfly .... HORNTAIL
sawhorse .... BUCK, TRESTLE
sawing frame .... HORSE
sawtooth .... SERRA
ridge .... SIERRA
sawtoothed .... RUNCINATE
sawyer ...... BEETLE, WOODCUTTER
Sax Rohmer character
.... DOCTOR FUMANCHU
Saxe ___ .... COBURG
Coburg and Gotha
.... WINDSOR
saxhorn .... TUBA
saxifrage .... SESELI, ROCKFOIL
Saxon .... ENGLISH, SASSENACH
Saxony .... YARN, SACHSEN
capital of .... DRESDEN
city .... ERFURT
say .... AVER, TELL, MOUTH,
SPEAK, STATE, UTTER,
AFFIRM, ALLEGE, DICTUM,
RECITE, REPORT, DECLARE,
MENTION
again .... REPEAT, RESTATE
"cheese" .... SMILE
further .... ADD
it's so .... AVER, AVOW
over .... ITERATE
repetitiously ..... HARP, CHANT
something meaningful
.... TALK SENSE
"There, there" ...... COMFORT
under oath .... VOW, SWEAR,
DEPOSE, TESTIFY
what you ___ .... MEAN
sayid .... SAID, FATIMID
saying .... MOT, SAW, ADAGE,
AXIOM, GNOME, MAXIM,
MOTTO, DICTUM, EPIGRAM,
PROVERB, APHORISM
common .... BYWORD
wise .... GNOME, MAXIM
sayings attributed to
Jesus(Christ) .... LOGIA
Sb in chemistry .... STIBIUM,
ANTIMONY
scab .... SORE, CRUST, MANGE,
ESCHAR, BLACKLEG,
SCOUNDREL
slang .... FINK

scabbard .... CASE, PILCHER,
SHEATH(E)
plate .... CHAPE
what it sheathes .... BOLO,
SWORD, DAGGER, BAYONET,
SCIMITAR
scabby .... LOW, BASE, MEAN,
MANGY, SCALY, SCURVY
scabies ...... ITCH, MANGE, PSORA,
PSORIASIS, INFESTATION
treatment .... LINDANE
scabrous .... FLAKY, MANGY,
SCALY, RISQUE, SCABBY, OFF-
COLOR, SALACIOUS
scad .... SKATE, SAUREL
scads .... GOBS, LOTS, TONS,
OODLES, PLENTY
scaffold .... STAGE, GIBBET,
RIGGER, GALLOWS, PLATFORM
scaffolding timber .... PUTLOG
scalawag .... SCAMP, RASCAL
scald .... BOIL, BURN, HEAT, SEAR,
SCORCH, SEETHE
scale .... GO UP, CLIMB, FLAKE,
GAMUT, PLATE, RATIO,
WEIGH, DEGREE, ESCHAR,
LAMINA, CLAMBER, LAMELLA,
ESCALADE, GRADUATION
animal/plant .... SQUAMA
chaffy .... PALEA
charges .... TARIFF
horny .... SCUTUM
insect's secretion .... LAC
measuring .... VERNIER
model .... MOCK-UP
musical .... GAMUT
pointer .... TONGUE
skin off .... BLANCH
weighing .... STEELYARD
scales .... BALANCE
covered with .... LEPIDOTE,
SQUAMATE, SQUAMOSE,
SQUAMOUS
kind of .... BEAM, SPRING,
COUNTER, TORSION, PLATFORM
the .... LIBRA
scaling ladder .... SCALOSE
of wall .... ESCALADE
scall .... SCURF
scallion .... LEEK, ONION,
SHALLOT
scallop .... PINK, QUIN, BADGE,
CRENA, NOTCH, WHELK,
MUSSEL, MOLLUSK,
CRENULATE, PERIWINKLE,
CRENEL(L)ATE, CRENULATION
scalloped ...... CRENATE, NOTCHED
scalp .... EPICRANIUM
colloquial .... ROB, FLAY,
PEEL, SKIN, CHEAT, GOUGE,
STRIP, DEFEAT, FLEECE,

OVERCHARGE
disease .... FAVUS, SCALL
disorder .... LICE, DANDRUFF
infant's crusty patch on
.... CRADLE CAP
muscle .... EPICRANIUS
preparation .... TONIC
to an Indian .... TROPHY
tumor .... WEN
scalpel .... KNIFE, LANCET,
BISTOURY
scalper .... INDIAN, PROFITEER,
SPECULATOR
scaly .... LOW, BASE, MEAN,
FLAKY, MANGY, SCABBY,
SCURFY, LEPROSE, SCABROUS,
SQUAMATE, SQUARROSE
bark .... PSOROSIS
coating .... SCURF
combining form ...... LEPID(O)
Scamander .... MENDERES
scammony .... RESIN
scamp .... ROGUE, RASCAL,
SCALAWAG, SPALPEEN,
SCOUNDREL, SCAPEGRACE
scamper .... RUN, DASH, RACE,
SCUD, SKIP, SCOOT, SCURRY,
BRATTLE
scampi .... PRAWN
scan ...... STUDY, SWEEP, GLANCE,
RECITE, ANALYZE, SCRUTINIZE
type of .... CAT
scandal .... SHAME, GOSSIP,
INFAMY, SLANDER, OUTRAGE,
DISGRACE
scandalize .... SHOCK, APPALL,
DEFAME, INSULT, MALIGN,
OFFEND, OUTRAGE
scandalmonger .... GOSSIP(ER),
BACKBITER, TALEBEARER
scandalous .... LIBELOUS,
SHAMEFUL, SHOCKING,
OFFENSIVE
scandent plant .... VINE
Scandinavian .... DANE, FINN,
LAPP, SWEDE, NORDIC,
NORSE(MAN), NORTHMAN,
SQUAREHEAD
chieftain .... JARL, RURIK
coin .... ORE, KRONA, KRONE
collection of myths ...... EDDA
country .... NORWAY, SWEDEN,
DENMARK, ICELAND
equivalent of Lawrence
.... LARS
explorer .... ERIC
folklore being .... TROLL
giantess .... URTH, WYRD
goblin .... NIS
god .... LOKI, THOR, ALFADIR
goddess .... HEL

heaven: myth. .... ASGARD,
ASGARTH
legend .... EDDA, SAGA
legislature .... T(H)ING
measure .... ALN, FOT, REF,
TUM, ALEN, FAMN, LINJE
monster .... KRAKEN
musician .... SKALD
name .... ERIC, NILS, OLAF,
SVEN
nation .... GEATAS
navigator .... ERIC
pirate/sea rover .... VIKING
plateau .... FJELD
poem .... EDDA, RUNE
poet .... SKALD
race of gods: myth. ..... AESIR
settler .... VARANGIAN
territorial division .... AMT
war deity .... TYR
weight .... LOD, ORT, MARK,
PUND, STEN, UNTZ, NYLAST,
LISPUND
scant .... FEW, SHORT, STINT,
MEAGER, SLIGHT, SPARSE,
EXIGUOUS, INADEQUATE
scantling .... BEAM, STUD, TIMBER
scanty .... SHORT, SMALL,
MEAGER, SCARCE, SPARSE,
SPARING
scape .... STALK
bearing .... SCAPOSE
scapegoat .... BUTT, TOOL, PATSY,
VICTIM, FALL GUY, WHIPPING
BOY
scapegrace .... ROUE, ROGUE,
SCAMP, RASCAL
scaphoid .... BOAT-SHAPED
scapolite .... SILICATE, WERNERITE
scar ...... PIT, CRAG, FLAW, MARK,
POCK, CLIFF, NAVEL,
BLEMISH, CICATRIX,
CICATRICE
scarab .... CHARM, BEETLE
scaramouche .... RASCAL,
BRAGGART, POLTROON
Scaramouche author
.... SABATINI
scarce .... FEW, DEAR, RARE,
SCANTY, UNCOMMON
in rainy weather .... CAB, TAXI
scarcely .... BARELY, HARDLY
scarcity .... LACK, DEARTH,
RARITY, PAUCITY, SHORTAGE
scare .... FEAR, ALARM, PANIC,
STARTLE, FRIGHT(EN)
off .... STOP, DAUNT
slang .... SPOOK
suddenly .... STARTLE
up .... PRODUCE
scarebabe of a sort .... OGRE

scarecrow ...... MALKIN, MAUKIN,
MAWKIN, BUGABOO,
MONSTER, STRAWMAN,
JACKSTRAW
stuffing .... STRAW
with grotesque features
.... GARGOYLE
scared .... AFRAID, TERRIFIED
scaredy-cat .... SISSY, COWARD
scarehead .... BANNER, HEADLINE,
STREAMER
scaremonger .... ALARMIST,
TERRORIST
scarf .... HOOD, SASH, VEIL,
ASCOT, TAPALO, TIPPET,
FOULARD, MUFFLER, NECKTIE,
MANTILLA, (NEC)KERCHIEF
clerical .... STOLE, TIPPET
cloth .... LUNGI, LUNGEE
fluffy/long .... BOA
head .... BABUSHKA
pope's .... ORALE
shoulder .... SASH, STOLE
sun helmet .... PUGGRY,
PUG(G)REE
woman's .... BOA, STOLE,
PEPLOS, MANTILLA
Scarface .... (AL)CAPONE
scarfskin ...... CUTICLE, EPIDERMIS
scarlatina .... FEVER
scarlet .... RED
bird .... TANAGER
cloak .... CARDINAL
fever .... SCARLATINA
woman: sl. .... HOOKER
Scarlett O'Hara's home
.... TARA
scarp .... SLOPE, DECLIVITY
Scarpia's nemesis .... TOSCA
scarum, _____ .... HARUM
scary creature .... OGRE
scat .... GIT, TAX, SCRAM
scathe ...... HARM, HURT, SCORCH,
LAMBASTE
scathing .... SEARING
scatter .... SOW, SHED, STUD,
STREW, DISPEL, LITTER,
DISPERSE, SPRINKLE,
DISSIPATE
by blowing .... WINNOW
for lost scent .... CAST
grass .... TED
scatterbrained ...... DAFT, DAFFY,
DIZZY, GIDDY, FLIGHTY,
FRIVOLOUS
scattered ...... STREWN, STUDDED,
SPORADIC
scattergood .... WASTREL,
PRODIGAL, SPENDTHRIFT
scattering of Jews ...... DIASPORA
scaup .... DUCK, REDHEAD,

GRAYBACK, SHUFFLER, CANVASBACK

scavenge .... PICK, HUNT, RANSACK, SCROUNGE

scavenger .... HYENA

cry of .... CAW

fish .... WRASSE

scenario .... TEXT, SCRIPT, OUTLINE, LIBRETTO

scend .... TOSS, HEAVE, PITCH, BILLOW

scene .... SITE, VIEW, VISTA, LOCALE, SETTING, TABLEAU, TANTRUM, OUTBURST, SPECTACLE

scenery .... VIEW, VISTA, DIORAMA, PICTURE, PANORAMA, LANDSCAPE

chewer: sl. .... HAM

mover .... PROP(MAN)

natural .... LANDSCAPE

sceneshifter .... GRIP

scenic .... STAGY, DRAMATIC, PICTURESQUE

peninsula .... GASPE

representation .... DIORAMA

view .... SCAPE, VISTA, PANORAMA

scent .... CLUE, NOSE, ODOR, AROMA, SMELL, TRACK, TRAIL, DETECT, PERFUME, FRAGRANCE

animal's .... FOIL

bag .... SACHET

kitchen .... AROMA, NIDOR

left by animal .... DRAG, SPOOR

of wine .... BOUQUET

subtle .... AURA

scented .... OLENT

water ...... BAY RUM, COLOGNE

scepter .... ROD, MACE, WAND, BATON, STAFF, FERULA, WARDER, TRIDENT

Schacht, Ger. financier .... HJALMAR

Scharre, mimist .... ROLF

schedule .... BOOK, LIST, PLAN, TIME, SLATE, AGENDA, DOCKET, RECORD, CALENDAR, REGISTER, CATALOGUE, INVENTORY, TIME-TABLE

Scheherazade's life-saver .... TALES

Scheldt .... ESCAUT

schema .... PLAN, DIAGRAM, OUTLINE

schematic .... ANALYTICAL

scheme .... PLAN, PLOT, CABAL, DESIGN, DEVICE, METHOD, SYSTEM, OUTLINE, PROJECT,

PURPOSE, INTRIGUE

fraudulent .... SCAM

utopian .... BUBBLE

scheming .... CRAFTY, TRICKY, CUNNING, DECEITFUL

Schick, pediatrician .... BELA

Schicklgruber's son .... (ADOLF)HITLER

schipperke .... DOG

schism .... RENT, RIFT, SECT, SPLIT, DISSENT, FACTION, DIVISION, CONCISION, SECESSION, SEPARATION

schist .... ROCK, SLATE

schistosome .... FLUKE

schizocarp .... MAPLE, REGMA

schizoid person .... LONER

schizophrenia .... SPLIT PERSONALITY

drug treatment .... CHLORPROMAZINE

schizophrenic syndrome .... CATATONIA

Schlesien .... SILESIA

Schleswig-Holstein capital .... KIEL

canal .... NORD-OSTSEE

schnapps .... GIN

schnauzer .... DOG, TERRIER, PINSCHER

Schneider, actress .... ROMY

schnozzle .... NOSE

Schnozzola .... DURANTE

scholar .... SAGE, CLERK, PUPIL, MASTER, PANDIT, PUNDIT, SAVANT, LEARNER, STUDENT, CLASSICIST

assistant/attendant .... FAMULUS

half .... DILETTANTE

inferior .... PEDANT

literary .... HARMONIST

Moslem .... ULEM

overstudying .... BOOKWORM

scholarly ...... ERUDITE, LEARNED, STUDIOUS

paper .... THESIS

people .... LITERATI

scholars' association .... ACADEMY

scholarship .... AWARD, BURSE, BURSARY, SUBSIDY, LEARNING, PEDANTRY, ERUDITION, PHILOLOGY, FELLOWSHIP

scholastic ...... BOOKISH, ERUDITE, ACADEMIC, DOGMATIC, PEDANT(IC), STUDIOUS, LETTERED, CURRICULAR, PROFESSORIAL

scholiast .... ANNOTATOR

school .... SECT, ECOLE, LEARN, LYCEE, TEACH, TRAIN, LYCEUM, ACADEME, ACADEMY, COLLEGE, EDUCATE, INSTITUTE, UNIVERSITY

assignment .... LESSON

athlete .... LETTERMAN

athlete: sl. .... HOTSHOT

banner .... PENNANT

book .... TEXT, PRIMER, READER

boy .... LAD, PUPIL

boy, new .... SCUM

charge for instruction .... TUITION

children's .... NURSERY, KINDERGARTEN

courses offered, collectively .... CURRICULUM

eastern .... YALE, VASSAR, CORNELL, HARVARD, MARYMOUNT, RADCLIFFE

for training horses .... MANEGE

girl .... COED

graduation ceremony .... COMMENCEMENT

grounds .... CAMPUS, QUADRANGLE

group .... PTA

headmaster .... RECTOR, PRINCIPAL

honor society .... ARISTA

kind of .... HIGH, MUSIC, NIGHT, PUBLIC, COLLEGE, DANCING, PRIVATE, MILITARY, SUMMER, SEMINARY, FINISHING, ELEMENTARY, VOCATIONAL, PREP(ARATORY)

of bees .... SWARM, COLONY

birds .... FLOCK

fish .... SHOAL

locusts .... CLOUD

seals .... POD

thought .... ISM, LOGIC, THEORY

whales .... GAM, POD

official .... DEAN, PROVOST, PRINCIPAL, SUPERINTENDENT

official in charge of records .... REGISTRAR

partisan .... POLEMIST

quitter: sl. .... DROPOUT

riding .... MANEGE

student, high/college .... JUNIOR, SENIOR, FRESHMAN, SOPHOMORE

studies leading to a degree .... COURSE

supervisor .... PROCTOR

teacher .... MASTER,
PROFESSOR, INSTRUCTOR
teaching staff .... FACULTY
term .... SEMESTER
term, of a .... TRIMESTRIAL
that one attended .... ALMA
MATER
treasurer .... BURSAR
young women's, private
.... SEMINARY
schooled .... (WELL-)VERSED
schooling .... LEARNING,
EDUCATION
schoolmaster .... PEDANT,
DOMINIE, PROCTOR, SNAPPER,
TEACHER, PEDAGOGUE,
INSTRUCTOR
rod of .... FERULE
schooner ...... SHIP, SAILS, WAGON
three-masted .... TERN
schorl .... T(O)URMALINE
schottish, dance like ...... POLKA
Schranz, Austrian skier
.... KARL
Schubert, composer .... FRANZ
classic .... AVE MARIA
Schumann, composer .... ROBERT
well-known song ...... WARUM
Schumann-Heink, singer
.... ERNESTINE
Schwarzenegger .... ARNOLD
film .... THE TERMINATOR, THE
RUNNING MAN, KINDERGARTEN
COP
wife of .... MARIA (SHRIVER)
Schweiz .... SWITZERLAND
sciatic area .... HIP
science .... ART, OLOGY, SKILL,
STUDY, TECHNICS,
KNOWLEDGE
applied .... TECHNOLOGY
attempting to explain the
brain .... CYBERNETICS
combining form .... TECHNO
electrical .... MAGNETICS,
ENGINEERING
fiction writer .... VERNE,
ASIMOV
natural .... PHYSICS
of boxing .... FISTICUFFS
causes .... ETIOLOGY
crop production
.... AGRONOMY
deciphering documents
.... DIPLOMATICS
earthquakes ..... SEISMOLOGY
fruit cultivation
.... POMOLOGY
government .... POLITICS
heard sound .... ACOUSTIC(S)

human behavior
.... PSYCHOLOGY
law-making .... NOMOLOGY
life history of cells
.... CYTOLOGY
medicine .... IATROLOGY
motion .... DYNAMICS,
KINETICS, KINEMATICS
mountains .... OROLOGY
musical sounds
.... HARMONICS
origins .... ETIOLOGY
plants .... BOTANY
public worship
.... LITURGICS
soils .... AGROLOGY
versification .... PROSODY
vital statistics
.... DEMOGRAPHY
words .... SEMANTICS
on freezing points
.... CRYOSCOPY
on races .... EUGENICS,
EUTHENICS
system of principles .... LOGIC
scientific .... EXACT, SOUND,
ACCURATE
quack .... EMPIRIC
research animal ...... HAMSTER
routine .... TEST
study of trees
.... DENDROLOGY
sub .... SEA LAB
scientist .... EXPERT, SAVANT,
STARGAZER, SPECIALIST
ancient, "most brilliant"
.... ARCHIMEDES
of bathysphere fame
.... BEEBE
of Cairo, "mad" .... ALHAZEN
Sci-fi .... SCIENCE-FICTION
award .... HUGO
type .... ANDROID
scilicet .... TO WIT, NAMELY
scimitar ...... SAX, SABER, SWORD,
RAPIER
scincoid .... SKINK
scintilla .... BIT, IOTA, WHIT,
SPARK, TRACE, PARTICLE
scintillate .... FLASH, SHINE,
GLISTEN, GLITTER, SPARKLE,
TWINKLE
sciolist .... QUACK, PEDANT,
AMATEUR, CHARLATAN
scion .... BUD, SON, HEIR, SLIP,
TWIG, GRAFT, SHOOT, SPRIG,
SPROUT, OFFSPRING,
DESCENDANT
Scipio, Roman general
.... AFRICANUS
victim of .... CARTHAGE,

HANNIBAL
scirrhus .... TUMOR, CANCER
scission .... FISSION, DIVISION
scissorbill .... SKIMMER
scissors .... CUTTER, CLIPPER
kind of .... SURGICAL
-like instrument .... NIPPER,
SHEARS
scissortail .... FLYCATCHER
sciurine animal .... MARMOT,
RODENT, SQUIRREL
sclera, inflammation of the
.... SCLERITIS
location of the .... EYE
softening of the
.... SCLEROMALACIA
sclerite .... SPICULE
scoff .... GIBE, GIRD, JEER, JIBE,
MOCK, RAIL, TWIT, FLEER,
FLOUT, SCORN, SNEER,
TAUNT, DERIDE, DISDAIN,
LAUGH(AT), RIDICULE
scofflaw .... CROOK, FELON
scold .... JAW, NAG, FLAY, RAIL,
CHIDE, FLITE, (BE)RATE,
DERIDE, REBUKE, REVILE,
REPROVE, UPBRAID,
LAMBASTE
severely .... BLISTER
scolder .... BITCH, CARPER,
MAGPIE, NAG(GER), BERATER
scolding .... EARFUL, TONGUE-
LASHING
lengthy .... LECTURE
scombroid .... MACKEREL
sconce .... HUT, FORT, HEAD,
SHED, SKULL, BRAINS,
HELMET, SCREEN, BRACKET,
BULWARK, FORTIFY, PROTECT,
SHELTER
scone .... BISCUIT, (TEA)CAKE
scoop .... BEAT, ROUT, GOUGE,
LADLE, SPOON, DIPPER,
DIG(OUT), DREDGE, SHOVEL,
TROWEL
slang .... EXCLUSIVE
scoot .... GO, HIE, RUN, DART,
DASH, EXIT, DECAMP, SCURRY
scooter .... SAILBOAT, MOTORBOAT
scop .... BARD, POET
scope .... AREA, AMBIT, FIELD,
RANGE, SPACE, SWEEP,
EXTENT, SPHERE, LATITUDE
limited .... LOCAL
of an act or bill ...... PURVIEW
of authority .... POWER
Scopes' counsel
.... (CLARENCE)DARROW
prosecutor .... BRYAN
trial reason .... EVOLUTION
trial venue .... DAYTON

scopolamine .... NARCOTIC
effect .... DROWSINESS
scopulate .... BRUSHLIKE
scorch .... BURN, CHAR, SEAR,
SERE, PARCH, SCALD, SINGE,
TOAST, SCATHE, WITHER,
BLISTER, SHRIVEL, CRITICIZE
scorcher .... HOT DAY, SPEEDER
score .... TAB, DEBT, MARK,
CHALK, NOTCH, TALLY,
GRUDGE, RATING, REASON,
RECORD, TWENTY, ACCOUNT,
SCRATCH
scoreless .... NO GOAL
hold .... BLANK
scoria .... AA, LAVA, SLAG, DROSS
scorn .... MOCK, SCOFF, SPURN,
CONTEMN, DESPISE, DISDAIN,
CONTEMPT, DERISION
scorpine .... HOGFISH
scorpion .... WHIP, SCOURGE,
ARACHNID, VINEGARROON
claw .... CHELA
fish .... LAPON
number of legs .... EIGHT
pain caused by .... STING
poison reservoir of .... TAIL
Scorpio's brightest star
.... ANTARES
Scot .... TAX, GAEL, LEVY, KILTIE,
SCOTCHMAN
Scotch .... CUT, MAIM, BLOCK,
CRUSH, NOTCH, SCORE,
WEDGE, HINDER, STIFLE,
STINGY, WHISKY
companion, sometimes
.... SODA, WATER
for one .... BROTH
sheepdog .... SHELTIE
scoter .... COOT, DUCK, EIDER
Scotia .... MOLDING, SCOTLAND
Scotland .... SCOTIA
ancient tongue of ...... GAELIC
capital of .... EDINBURGH
capital's poetic name
.... EDINA
largest lake of .... LOCH
LOMOND
legendary beast of
.... LOCHNESS
Roman name of
.... CALEDONIA
scotoma .... BLIND SPOT
Scot's nickname .... MAC
Scotsman .... SANDY, BLUECAP
Scott, black .... DRED
hero: 1812 war and Mexican
war .... WINFIELD
novel .... IVANHOE
poem .... MARMION
Scottish .... CALEDONIAN

absent .... AWA
accuse .... DELATE
ache .... WARK, STOUND
active .... YAULD
ago .... SYNE
alas .... OCHONE
alder tree .... ARN
alderman .... BAILIE
ale/beer .... YILL, NAPPY
alley .... WYND
assembly signal .... SLOGAN
attempt .... ETTLE
attendant .... GILLY, GILLIE
awl .... ELSEN
awry .... AGL(E)Y
bagpipe music .... PIBROCH,
CORONACH
bailiff .... REEVE
bank .... BRAE
barren .... YELD
barter .... TROKE
bay ...... LUCE, BROAD, ENARD,
DUNNET, LAGGAN, WIGTOWN,
GRUINARD, SINCLAIR'S
beef cut .... SEY
beg .... SORN
beggar .... RANDY
belly .... WAME
biscuit .... SCONE
blastie .... DWARF
blaze .... INGLE
blow .... BLAW, DEVEL
bold .... CROUSE
boor .... TYKE
bound .... STEND
boundary .... MEAR
box/chest .... KIST
boy .... LOON
brandy .... ATHOLE
breeches .... TREWS
broadsword .... CLAYMORE
brook .... SIKE
broth .... BREE, BROO
brow of hill .... SNAB
bucket .... STOOP, STOUP
burden .... BIRN
burn .... STREAM
bushel .... FOU
buxom .... SONSIE
cake .... SCONE, BANNOCK
canal ...... CALEDONIAN, FORTH
AND CLYDE
cap/hat .... BALMORAL,
GLENGARRY,
TAM(-O-SHANTER)
cape .... WRATH, RUDH RE
cascade .... LINN
cat .... MALKIN
catch .... KEP
cattle .... NOWT
channel .... NORTH, SCAPA

FLOW
charm .... CANTRIP
cheese .... KEBBOK
chemise .... SARK
child .... WEAN, BAIRN
church .... KIRK
churl .... CARLE
city/town .... AYR, PERTH,
TROON, DUNDEE, IRVINE,
AIRDRIE, FALKIRK, GLASGOW,
PAISLEY, RENFREW, ABERDEEN,
DUMFRIES, GREENOCK,
HAMILTON, LARKHALL,
STIRLING, DUMBARTON,
EDINBURGH, INVERNESS,
KIRKCALDY, SALTCOATS,
LIVINGSTON
clan chief .... THANE
cleanser .... SAIP
clothe .... CLEAD
codfish .... GLASHAN
coin ..... DEMY, LION, BAUBEE,
BAWBEE
comb .... KAME
congress .... MOD
corner .... NEUK
corpse .... LICH
countrified .... HODDEN
county .... AYR, BUTE, FIFE,
ANGUS, PERTH, NAIRN,
MORAY, BANFF, ARGYLL,
LANARK, ORKNEY, BERWICK,
KINROSS, PEEBLES, RENFREW,
SELKIRK, ZETLAND, ABERDEEN,
INVERNESS, MIDLOTHIAN
court officer .... MACER
cow .... RUNT, CRUMMIE
crab .... PARTAN
cravat .... OVERLAY
craw .... CRAG
crowd .... MEINY, MEINIE
cry of blame .... DIRDUM
cuckoo .... GOWK
cuddy .... FOOL, DONKEY
cup .... TASS
curlew .... WHAUP
cut .... SNEG
dagger .... SKEAN
dairymaid .... DEY
daisy .... GOWAN
darling .... DAUTIE
deception .... BROGUE
dell .... SLACK
devil .... DEIL, MOHOUND
dining room .... SPENCE
dirge .... CORONACH
dish .... HAGGIS
dismal .... OORIE
disordered .... UNRID
district ...... MAR, PARK, APPIN,
ATHOL, COWAL, LEWIS,

LORNE, SLEAT, ARGYLL, ASSYNT, BUCHAN, HARRIS, MORVEN, ARDGOUR, BRAEMAR, CARRICK, GARIOCH, MOIDART, RANNOCH, BADENOCH, GALLOWAY, KNAPDALE, LOCHABER
do .... DAE
dog .... SEALYHAM
dolt .... GOWK, GOMERAL
donkey .... CUDDY
dramatist .... BARRIE
dwarf .... BLASTIE
ear .... LUG
earnest money .... ARLES
earth .... YIRD
else .... ENSE
empty .... TOOM
endure .... DREE
exchange .... NIFFER
explorer .... RAE
extent .... STENT
extra .... ORRA
eyes .... EEN
factor .... BAILIFF, STEWARD
fair .... TRYST
faithful .... LEAL
fall of rain .... ON-DING
falls .... SHIN
farm worker .... HIND, ORRAMAN
farmer .... COTTAR, COTTER, CROFTER
fellow .... WAT, CARL(E), CALLAN(T)
festivity .... KIRN
few .... WHEEN
fine/first-rate .... WALLY
fireplace .... INGLE
firth .... TAY, CLYDE, KYLE, FORTH, LORNE, MORAY, SOLWAY, DORNOCH, CROMARTY, PENTLAND
fold .... WIMPLE
fool .... GOMERAL
fox .... TOD
friend .... EME
game .... SHINTY
garment .... SARK
girl .... QUEAN, CUMMER, LASSIE
glimmer .... STIME
go .... GAE, GANG
goblet .... TASS
godmother .... CUMMER
goldsmith .... GED
good .... GUDE
good-for-nothing .... ORRA
gooseberry .... THAPRES
guillotine .... MAIDEN
gulf .... BISM

gypsy .... CAIRD
hag .... CARLINE
haggle .... PRIG
hamlet .... CLACHAN
handsome .... SONSY, SONSIE
hare .... MALKIN, MAUKIN
hawk .... ALLAN
head .... POW
headwear .... TAM
heath .... MUIR
heir .... TEIND
hellside hollow .... CORRIE
Highlander .... CELT, GAEL
hill .... DOD(D), INCH
hill(side) .... BRAE
hills .... OCHIL, LENNOX, SIDLAW, CHEVIOT, CUILLIN, MOORFOOT
historian .... HUME
hoe .... PADLE
holiday .... VACANCE
hut .... BOTHY
inlet .... GIO
inventor .... WATT
island .... HOY, RUM, BUTE, EDAY, EIGG, HOLY, IONA, JURA, MUCK, MULL, RONA, SEIL, SOAY, ULVA, UNST, WYRE, YELL, ARRAN, BARRA, CANNA, FOULA, GIGHA, ISLAY, LUING, SANDA, SCARP, SHONA, SWONA, TIREE, BURRAY, FETLAR, PABBAY, PLADDA, RAASAY, ROUSAY, STROMA, BERNERA, ERISKAY, GOMETRA, LISMORE, INCH(CAPE), MAINLAND, INCHKEITH
islands ..... ORKNEY, FLANNAN, HEBRIDES, SHETLAND
jackdaw .... KAE
jade .... YAUD
jail/prison .... TOLBOOTH
keen .... GLEG
kilt .... FILIBEG
kindle .... LUNT, TIND
kindred .... SIB
king .... BRUCE
kiss .... PREE
knowledge .... KENNING
laborer .... HIND
lake .... AWE, EIL, LIN, TAY, LOCH, EARN, NESS, SHIN, GARRY, LEVEN, LOCHY, LOYAL, MAREE, SHIEL, ARKAIG, ERICHT, LOMOND, QUOICH, KATRINE, RANNOCH
lake dwelling .... CRANNOG
land, flat .... LINKS
land tax .... CESS
landholder ...... LAIRD, THANE, THEGN

language .... ERSE, GAELIC, LALLAN(S)
lark .... LAVEROCK
legally excessive .... ENORM
light .... LICHT
list of candidates .... LEET
little .... SMA
lively .... CROUSE
locker .... KIST
long ago .... LANG SYNE
lord .... THANE
love .... LOE
lowland .... CARSE
lowlander .... SASSENACH
Lowlands .... LALLAN
lucky .... SONSIE
magic spell .... CANTRIP
magistrate .... BAILIE, PROVOST
marauder ...... CATERAN, MOSS TROOPER
mare .... MEER, YAUD
market .... TRYST
match .... LUNT
mathematician .... NEPER, NAPIER
Mayday .... BELTANE
measure .... CRAN, LIPPY, FIRLOT, CHALDER
miscellaneous .... ORRA
mist .... URE, DROW
money .... SILLER
more .... MAIR
mortgage .... WADSET
mountain .... BEN LUI, MORVEN, ASKIVAL, BATTOCK, BEN AVON, BEN MORE, BEN MHOR, CARN BAN, CLISHAM, MERRICK, BEN ALDER, BEN NEVIS, CARN EIGE, GOAT FELL, PEEL FELL, BEN LAWERS, LOCHNAGAR, BEN MACDHUI
mountains .... GRAMPIAN, CAIRNGORM, MONADHLIATH
much .... MICKLE, MUCKLE
mud .... GLAR
municipal official .... BAILIE
musical instrument .... BAGPIPE
must .... MAUN
myself .... MASEL
national emblem .... THISTLE
native .... CELT, GAEL, CALEDONIAN
neck .... CRAG
negative .... NAE, DINNA
New Year's eve .... HOGMANAY
nimble .... YAULD
no .... NAE
oatmeal dish .... BROSE

odd .... ORRA
once .... ANES
one .... AIN, ANE, YIN
otherwise .... ENSE
outcry of blame .... DIRDUM
own .... AIN, ANE
ox .... NOWT, RUNT
oxter .... ARMPIT
pail .... STOUP, COGGIE
pain .... WARK, STANG,
STOUND
parlor .... BEN
pay for a killing .... CRO
peak .... NEVIS
peasant/tenant .... COTTAR,
COTTER, CROFTER
peep .... KEEK
peninsula .... RHINNS,
KINTYRE, MACHERS, ROSS OF
MULL
people driven from Great
Britain .... PICT
pert .... CROUSE
philosopher .... HUME, CAIRD
physicist .... BAIRD
pig .... GRICE
pipe .... CUTTY
pirate/privateer .... KIDD
plaid .... MAUD, TARTAN
pleasant .... DOUCE
pocket .... POUCH
poet ..... HOGG, BURNS, EDINA,
DUNBAR
pole .... CABER
poll .... POW, HEAD
pool .... CARR, LINN
porridge .... BROSE, SOWENS
port .... OBAN
pottage .... BROSE
pouch .... SPORRAN,
SPLEUCHAN
praise .... ROOSE
prank .... CANTRIP
precipitation .... SNA
prefix to names .... MAC
presently .... NOO
pronunciation .... BURR
pudding .... SAUSAGE
puzzle .... KITTLE
rafter .... SILE
ragged .... DUDDY, DUDDIE
reef .... SKERRY
region .... FIFE, ORKNEY,
BORDERS, CENTRAL, LOTHIAN,
TAYSIDE, GRAMPIAN,
SHETLAND
relish .... GUST
require .... NEID
resort .... OBAN
river ...... AYR, DEE, DON, ESK,
TAY, AVON, DOON, EARN,

EDEN, ISLA, LYON, NITH, OICH,
SPEY, TYNE, ANNAN, ARDLE,
CLYDE, FORTH, GLASS, NAIRN,
NAVER, ORCHY, OYKEL,
SPEAN, TEITH, TWEED, YTHAN,
ALMOND, BEAULY, CARRON,
TEVIOT, THURSO, YARROW,
DEVERON, FINDHORN,
MORISTON, STINCHAR
river land .... CARSE
rivulet .... RINDLE
robber .... CATERAN
robbery .... REIF
rock .... SKERRY
rock projection .... SNAB
rope .... WANTY
rosin .... ROZET
rowboat .... COBLE
rug .... MAUD
Satan .... DEIL, HORNIE
scholarship .... BURSE
schoolmaster .... DOMINIE
scold .... THREAP
scone .... FARL(E)
scratch .... RIT
sea .... HEBRIDES
seaport .... AYR, DUNDEE,
ABERDEEN, GREENOCK
seize .... VANG
seldom .... SINDLE
self .... SEL
servant .... GILLY, GILLIE
sharp .... GLEG, SNELLY
shawl .... MAUD
shelter .... BIELD
shirt .... SARK
silver .... SILLER
simpleton .... GOWK
since .... SYNE
sister .... TITTY, TITTIE
skirt .... KILT
small/wee .... SMA
smart .... STOUND
smoke .... LUNT
snow .... SNA
snowfall .... ON-DING
soldier .... KERN(E)
spell .... CANTRIP
spirit .... BANSHEE
sponge .... SORN
squall .... BLEFFERT
stomach .... KYTE
stream .... BURN
stretch out .... STENT
student scholar .... BURSAR
stumble .... STOT
suffer .... DREE
supple .... WANDLE
sweetheart .... JO(E)
sword .... SKEAN, CLAYMORE
tap .... TUCK

tartan pattern ...... SETT, PLAID
taste .... GUST, PREE
tatter .... TAVER
tea cake .... SCONE
tedious .... DREE
tern .... TARRET
terrier .... SKYE, CAIRN,
SEALYHAM
theologian .... DUNS
thicket .... RONE
throat .... CRAG
thumb .... THOOM
tickle .... KITTLE
tinker .... CAIRD
toad .... TADE
tobacco pouch ..... SPLEUCHAN
toes .... TAES
topper .... TAM
torch .... LUNT
tower .... PEEL
town .... BUR(G)H
toy .... WALLY
trade .... TROKE
tribal payment .... CRO
trick .... BROGUE
trousers .... TREWS
true .... LEAL
turnip .... NEEP
tuyere .... TEW
twang .... TIRL
uncanny .... UNCO
uncle .... EAM, (Y)EME
underwear .... TREWS
urge .... ERT
vagabond .... WAFF
vagrant .... CAIRD
valley ...... SLACK, TROSSACHS,
STRATH(MORE)
vex .... FASH
vigor .... VIR
village .... REW
violet .... BLAVER
vulgar .... RANDY
walk .... GO
water spirit ..... KELPY, KELPIE
waterfall .... LYN, LIN(N)
wear under kilts .... TREWS
weeds .... WRACK
weighing machine ...... TRONE
weight ..... BOLL, DROP, TRONE
whether .... GIN
whirlpool .... WEEL
whiskey .... ATHOL(E),
MOUNTAIN DEW, USQUEBAUGH
witch .... CARLINE
woman .... RANDY, CUMMER,
CARLINE
woman, unmarried ..... QUEAN
womb .... WAME
world .... WARL
worse .... WAUR

worthless .... WAUF
wrap .... MAUD
wrestle .... WARS(T)LE
yawn .... GANT
yell .... GOWL
scoundrel .... CAD, BASE, SCAB,
KNAVE, ROGUE, SCAMP,
BEGGAR, RASCAL, VARLET,
VILLAIN, DECEIVER,
REPROBATE
scour .... RUB, RAKE, SAND,
FLUSH, PURGE, SCRUB, SKIRR,
ABRADE, POLISH, SCRAPE,
SEARCH, CLEANSE, FURBISH,
LOOK OVER
scourer .... CATHARTIC
scourge .... BANE, BELT, FLAY,
FLOG, LASH, WHIP, CURSE,
SLASH, STRAP, PLAGUE,
PUNISH, TORMENT, SCORPION,
AFFLICTION
of clothing .... MOTH
of God .... ATTILA
of serge .... LINT
scouring rush .... HORSETAIL
scout ...... GUY, SPY, SCOFF, SPIER,
FELLOW, REJECT, SPOTTER,
DO-GOODER, OBSERVER,
RIDICULE, FORERUNNER,
TENDERFOOT, RECONNOITER
boat .... VEDETTE
group .... DEN, PACK, TROOP,
PATROL
scow .... BARGE, LIGHTER,
FLATBOAT
puller .... TOWBOAT,
TUG(BOAT)
scowl .... LOUR, MOUE, FROWN,
(G)LOWER, GRIMACE
scrabble .... PAW, DOODLE,
SCRAPE, SCRAWL
scrag ...... HANG, NECK, GARROTE,
THROTTLE
scraggly .... JAGGED, RAGGED,
UNKEMPT
scram ...... GIT, LAM, SCAT, SHOO,
BEAT IT, VAMO(O)SE, GET
LOST
scramble .... TEAR, CLIMB, MIX
UP, SWARM, JUMBLE, TUSSLE,
CLAMBER, RAT RACE,
SCUFFLE, STRUGGLE
in football .... RUN,
MANEUVER
scrambled .... PIED, GARBLED
scrannel ...... LEAN, THIN, SLIGHT,
SQUEAKY, SHRIVELED
scrap .... BIT, END, ORT, FIGHT,
PIECE, SHRED, MORSEL,
TATTER, DISCARD, JUNK(RAG),
ODDMENT, QUARREL,

ARGUMENT, FRACTION,
FRAGMENT, LEFTOVER
glass .... CULLET
hunt for .... SCAVENGE
of paper only, sometimes
.... PACT, TREATY
scrapbook .... ALBUM
scrape ...... FIX, RUB, RAKE, RASP,
BRUSH, GRATE, GRAZE, GRIDE,
GRIND, SCOUR, SCUFF, SHAVE,
ABRADE, PLIGHT, SCRATCH,
PREDICAMENT
along .... MANAGE, SURVIVE
bottom .... SCOUR, DREDGE
ground in golf .... SCLAFF
leaves off the grass ...... RAKE
together .... GATHER,
ASSEMBLE
scraped linen .... LINT
metal .... FILING
scraper, strings .... FIDDLER,
GUITARIST
water .... SQUEEGEE
scraping .... SHAVING
act of .... RASURE
scrapman .... JUNKMAN
scrapper .... BATTLER, FIGHTER
scrappy .... GAME, PATCHY,
SPOTTY, SKETCHY,
PUGNACIOUS
scraps ...... MEMENTOS, CLIPPINGS,
SOUVENIRS
literary .... ANA
scratch .... RUB, GASH, RAKE,
RASP, CHAFE, ERASE, GRATE,
DEFACE, REJECT, SCRAPE,
SCRAWL, LACERATE, SCRIBBLE
Scratch, Old .... DEVIL
scratching ground for food
.... RASORIAL
scratchy .... ITCHY
scrawl .... DOODLE, SCRIBBLE
scrawny .... BONY, LEAN, PUNY,
THIN, SCRAGGY
unkempt creature .... SCRAG
screak .... SCREECH
scream .... CRY, WAIL, YELL,
SHRIEK, SQUALL, SCREECH,
CATERWAUL
comics style .... EEK
screamer .... HEADLINE
black-necked .... CHAVARIA
crested .... TORQUATA
horned .... ANHIMA CORNUTA
scree ...... STONE, TALUS, PEBBLE,
RUBBLE
screech .... CRY, SCREAM, SHRIEK
screechy .... SHRILL
screed .... EDGING, SPEECH,
TIRADE, HARANGUE
screen .... HIDE, MASK, SIFT, VEIL,

BLIND, PAVIS, SHADE, GRILLE,
MOVIES, SCONCE, SHIELD,
SHROUD, CURTAIN, NETTING,
SECLUDE
altar/chancel .... REREDOS
bar .... MULLION
bulletproof .... MANT(E)LET
canvas .... PAVESADE
chimney .... BONNET
for concealment/protection
.... BLINDAGE
making material .... VETIVER
mesh .... SIEVE
wall .... PARTITION
wind .... PARAVENT
screening .... TESTING
screw .... JACK, TURN, MISER,
TWIST, SALARY, TIGHTEN,
PROP(ELLER)
part .... THREAD
pine tree .... PANDANUS
relative .... NAIL
slang .... JAILER
thread .... HELIX
threader .... CHASER
up .... FOUL UP, BOTCH UP
screwball .... PITCH
slang .... NUT
screwy .... ODD, CRAZY,
PECULIAR, ECCENTRIC
scribble .... DASH(OFF), WRITE,
DOODLE, SCRAWL
scribbler .... HACK
scribe .... CLERK, AUTHOR,
WRITER, PENMAN, SCRIVENER,
SECRETARY, AMANUENSIS
biblical .... BARUCH
scrimmage .... FIGHT, MELEE,
AFFRAY, TUSSLE
scrimp .... SKIMP, STINT, SCANTY,
ECONOMIZE
scrip .... BAG, LIST, WALLET,
SATCHEL, WRITING,
CERTIFICATE
script .... RONDE, SERTA,
DIALOGUE, LIBRETTO,
SCENARIO, PENMANSHIP,
HANDWRITING
scriptural ...... SACRED, BIBLICAL,
APOSTOLIC
analysis .... EXEGESIS
interpreter .... EXEGETE
scripture(s) .... BOOK, BIBLE,
ITALA, KORAN, SUTRA,
TORAH, ALCORAN
interpretation of ..... ANAGOGE
passage .... TEXT
reader .... LECTOR
scrivener .... NOTARY, SCRIBE,
COPYIST, AMANUENSIS
scrivener's palsy .... WRITER'S

CRAMP

scrobiculate .... PITTED

scrod .... CODFISH

scrofula .... STRUMA, KING'S EVIL

scroll ...... LIST, ROLL, MEMORIAL,
SCHEDULE

of Ionic capitals .... VOLUTE

shaped .... TURBINATE

tablet like .... CARTOUCH(E)

scromboid fish .... CERO

Scrooge .... EBEN, MISER

before reforming .... MEANIE

word .... BAH

scrouge .... CROWD, PRESS,
SQUEEZE

scrounge .... EKE, PILFER, SPONGE

scrub .... MOP, RUB, MEAN, POOR,
SWAB, BRUSH, SCOUR, SMALL

scrubber .... CHARWOMAN

scrubbing implement .... MOP

scruff .... NAPE, NUBIA, NUQUE

scrunch .... CHEW, CRUSH,
CRUMPLE

scruple .... DOUBT, QUALM,
MISGIVING

scrupulous .... EXACT, MORAL,
HONEST, CAREFUL, CORRECT,
FINICAL, PRECISE, UPRIGHT,
RELIGIOUS, METICULOUS,
PUNCTILIOUS

scrutinize .... CON, EYE, SEE,
SCAN, VIEW, PROBE, PERUSE,
EXAMINE, INSPECT

scrutiny .... SCAN, REVIEW,
SURVEY, PERUSAL,
INSPECTION

of financial records ..... AUDIT

Scuba enthusiast .... DIVER

fishing .... SPEARING

gear .... MASK, TANK,
SNORKLE

scud .... RUN, SKIM, GLIDE

Scud destroyer .... PATRIOT

scuff .... BRUSH, SCRAPE, SHUFFLE,
SLIPPER

mark .... SCAR

scuffle .... FRAY, BRAWL, FIGHT,
MELEE, FRACAS, STRIFE,
TUSSLE, SHUFFLE, STRUGGLE

scull .... OAR, ROW, SHELL,
PADDLE, PROPEL, WHERRY,
(RACING)BOAT

sculler .... OARER, BOATMAN,
OARSMAN

scullery, content of .... PANS,
POTS, DISHES, UTENSILS

equipment .... DISHWASHER

scullion .... WRETCH, SERVANT

sculpin .... BULLHEAD,
HARDHEAD, ROCKFISH, SEA
RAVEN

sculptor .... ARTIST, CARVER,
MOLDER, MODELER,
STATUARY, STONECUTTER

abstract .... CALDER

famous:

American
.... (GUTZON)BORGLUM,
(ALEXANDER)CALDER,
(DANIEL CHESTER) FRENCH

American (born in Ireland)
.... SAINT-GAUDENS

American (born in
Lithuania)
.... (JACQUES)LIPCHITZ

American (born in
Sweden)
.... (CARL)MILLES

Athenian .... PRAXITELES

British .... (HENRY)MOORE,
(JACOB)EPSTEIN

Florentine
.... (LORENZO)GHIBERTI,
(LUCA)DELLA ROBBIA

French .... (JEAN)ARP,
(AUGUSTE)RODIN,
(ARISTIDE)MAILLOL

Greek ...... SKIPAS, BRYAXIS,
LEOCARES, PH(E)IDIAS,
TIMOTHEOS

Italian .... DONATELLO,
MICHELANGELO,
(NICOLA)PISANO,
(BENVENUTO)CELLINI

Romanian ..... (CONSTANTIN)
BRANCUSI

Spanish .... (PABLO) PICASSO

Swiss .... (ALBERTO)
GIACOMETTI

framework of .... ARMATURE

of Mount Rushmore
.... BORGLUM

The Colossus of Rhodes
.... CHARES

The Statue of Zeus
.... PH(E)IDIAS

The Temple of Artemis
.... KING CROESUS

The Thinker .... RODIN

tool of .... BURIN, POINT,
PUNCH, TORCH, CHISEL,
GRAVER, ROCKER, STYLE(T),
CALIPER, SPATULA

woman .... SCULPTRESS

work of .... BUST, TORSO,
STABILE, STATUARY,
STATUE(TTE)

sculpture .... CARVING,
(PLASTIC)ARTS,
STONECUTTING

earliest .... STONE AGE
VENUSES

famous .... PIETA, PARTHENON,
THE PHAROS, MOUNT
RUSHMORE, STATUE OF
LIBERTY, GREAT WALL OF
CHINA, THE PYRAMIDS (OF
GIZA)

head to chest .... BUST

medium ..... GEM, WAX, CLAY,
WOOD, SHELL, STONE,
BRONZE, MARBLE, PLASTICINE,
TERRA COTTA

on gems .... GLYPTICS

on wood .... XYLOGRAPHY

piety personified in .... ORANT

style of .... GROTESQUE

sculptured ...... CARVED, CARVEN,
GRAVEN, MOLDED, GLYPHIC,
CHISELED

animal/person .... STATUE

design on a gem
.... GLYPTOGRAPH

gem/shell .... CAMEO

in low relief .... ANAGLYPH

oval ornament
.... MEDAL(LION)

work in metal .... TOREUTIC

scum .... SKIM, ALGAE, DROSS,
SPUME, REFUSE, PELLICLE

of society .... RIFF-RAFF

rid of .... SKIM, DESPUMATE

scup .... FISH, BREAM, PORGY,
BURGOO, SPAROID

kin of .... GRUNT, SNAPPER

scupper .... DRAIN

scuppernong .... WINE, GRAPE,
MUSCADINE

scurf .... SCALL, FURFUR,
DANDRUFF

scurfy .... FLAKY, MANGY,
SCABBY, LEPROSE, LEPIDOTE

scurrilous ...... COARSE, VULGAR,
ABUSIVE, OFFENSIVE, FOUL-
MOUTHED, THERSITICAL

scurry .... RUN, DART, DASH,
RACE, SCOOT, HASTEN,
SCAMPER, HIGHTAIL

scurvy .... LOW, MEAN, VILE,
NASTY, DISEASE

caused by deficiency of
_____ .... VITAMIN C

scut .... TAIL

work, describing ...... MENIAL,
ROUTINE, TEDIOUS

scutage .... TAX

Scutari .... LAKE, SHKODER,
USKUDAR

scutellate .... ROUND

scutter .... BUSTLE

scuttle ...... HOD, RUN, FLEE, PAIL,
SINK, SCOOP, BASKET,
BUCKET, ESCAPE, SCURRY,

DESTROY, SCAMPER,
        HATCHWAY
scuttlebutt .... RUMOR, GOSSIP,
        HEARSAY
scutum .... SHIELD, PLATELET
    plural of .... SCUTA
Scylla .... ROCK
    and Charybdis
        personification
        .... MONSTERS
    whirlpool opposite
        .... CHARYBDIS
scye .... ARMHOLE
scyphozoan .... JELLYFISH
scythe bearer .... DEATH
    cut, one stroke .... SWATH
    handle .... NIB, SNEAD,
        SNATH(E)
    sharpener .... STRICKLE
    sweep of .... SWATH
sea .... DEEP, MAIN, MARE, WAVE,
        OCEAN, SWELL, BILLOW
    anemone .... POLYP, ACTINIA
    animal, fishlike .... LANCELET,
        AMPHIOXUS
    arm .... BAY, GULF, LAKE,
        FIORD, FIRTH, FRITH, LOUGH,
        ESTUARY
    bass .... JEWFISH
    bat .... DEVILFISH
    beast .... MOBY DICK
    bird .... MEW, ERN(E), GULL,
        SHAG, SKUA, TERN, EIDER,
        NODDY, SCAUP, SOLAN,
        FULMAR, GANNET, PETREL,
        PUFFIN, SCOTER, KASTREL,
        ALBATROSS, CORMORANT
    biscuit/bread .... HARDTACK
    born goddess .... APHRODITE
    borne .... AFLOAT
    bottom .... BED, FLOOR
    calf .... SEAL
    coast .... SHORE, STRAND,
        LITTORAL
    cock ..... PEG, VALVE, STOPPER
    cow .... DUGONG, WALRUS,
        MANATEE, SIRENIAN,
        HIPPOPOTAMUS
    creature, legendary
        .... MERMAN, MERMAID
    cucumber .... TREPANG,
        HOLOTHURIAN
    devil .... RAY, SHARK,
        OCTOPUS, ANGELFISH
    disaster aid device ...... SOFAR
    dog .... GOB, TAR, SEAL,
        SAILOR, MARINER
    duck ...... COOT, EIDER, SCAUP,
        SCO(O)TER
    eagle .... ERN(E), TERN,
        OSPREY

ear .... ABALONE
east of the Caspian ...... ARAL
elephant .... SEAL
fan .... CORAL
farer .... MAORI, SAILOR,
        MARINER, FISHERMAN
foam .... SPUME, MEERSCHAUM
fox .... SHARK
god .... LER, AEGIR, NEREUS,
        TRITON, NEPTUNE, PROTEUS,
        POSEIDON
grave .... LOCKER
greeting .... AHOY
gull .... MEW, COB(B),
        KITTIWAKE
heavy .... RACE
hog .... PORPOISE
holly .... ERINGO, ERYNGO
horse .... WALRUS,
        HIPPOCAMPUS
inhabitant: myth. .... MERMAN,
        MERMAID
inland .... ARAL
inlet .... RIA, FIORD, FJORD
jettison, temporary ..... LAGAN
lands beyond the
        .... OUTREMER
lawyer .... SAILOR
lettuce .... ULUA, LAVER
lily .... CRINOID
lion .... SEAL
marker .... DAN, BUOY
mew .... GULL
mile .... KNOT, NAUT
monster .... KRAKEN,
        LEVIATHAN
near the/on the ...... MARITIME
needle .... GAR(FISH)
nettle .... MEDUSA, ACALEPH,
        JELLYFISH
nymph .... NAIAD, SIREN,
        NEREID, THETIS, CALYPSO
of the .... NAVAL, MARINE,
        PELAGIC, MARITIME,
        NAUTICAL, THALASSIC
onion .... SQUILL(A)
pen .... POLYP
personified .... NEPTUNE
poetic .... FOAM
prefix .... MARI
put to .... SAIL
raven .... SCULPIN
robber .... PIRATE, CORSAIR,
        PICAROON, BUCCANEER,
        PRIVATEER
robin .... GURNARD
rock .... SKERRY
route .... LANE
rover .... PIRATE, SAILOR,
        JASON, SEAMAN, VIKING,
        MARINER, ARGONAUT

serpent .... ELAPS, OARFISH
shell .... MOLLUSK
shell, Pacific .... NETTED CONE
shell with curved edge
        .... SCALLOP
slug .... TREPANG
snail .... W(H)ELK
soldier .... MARINE, SAILOR
spot at .... ISLE(T)
spray .... SPINDRIFT
squirt ..... ASCIDIAN, TUNICATE
surface movement ...... LIPPER
swallow .... TERN, PETREL
swooper .... GULL
tangle .... SEAWEED
trip .... CRUISE
unicorn .... NARWHAL
urchin ...... ECHINUS, ECHINOID
wall .... JETTY, BREAKWATER
water .... BRINE
with many islands
        .... ARCHIPELAGO
wolf .... PIRATE, BLENNY
Seabee's concern .... HARBOR,
        AIRFIELD
seaboard .... COAST
seaflower .... POLYP, ANEMONE
seafood delicacy .... ORMER
seal .... DIE, BULLA, CLOSE, SIGIL,
        STAMP, CACHET, FASTEN,
        RATIFY, SECURE, SIGNET,
        INITIAL, PINNIPED,
        BLADDERNOSE
    bottle/tube .... CAPSULE
    Christmas .... STAMP
    cut skin of .... FLENSE
    eared .... OTARY, SEA LION
    fur .... URSAL, SEECATCH
    hooded .... BLADDERNOSE
    hunter .... SWILER
    kind of .... EARED, WAFER
    large .... SEA LION
    letter .... CACHET
    male .... SEECATCH
    off .... TRAP
    point .... SIAMESE CAT
    Pope's .... BULL
    rawhide .... SHAGREEN
    skin .... FUR, PELT
    sound of .... BARK
    tusked .... WALRUS
    with lead .... PLUMB
    young .... PUP, CALF, HARP
sealed completely ...... HERMETIC
sealer .... PUTTY, SWILER,
        CA(U)LKER
sealing agent .... LUTE
    material .... GLUE, TAPE,
        PASTE, MUCILAGE,
        WAX(WAFER)
    wax ingredient .... LAC

seals, breeding place of
.... ROOKERY
flock of .... POD
pertaining to .... PHOCINE
sealskin .... SCULP
seam .... LINE, PURL, SCAR, JOINT,
LAYER, RIDGE, FURROW,
SUTURE, WRINKLE, JUNCTURE
fill up .... CALK
filling material .... TAR,
OAKUM
tapered .... DART
seamaid .... NYMPH, SIREN(A),
MERMAID
seaman .... GOB, TAR, SALT,
JACKY, RATING, SAILOR,
MARINER, SEAFARER
rating of .... ABLE
seamark .... DAN, BUOY, BEACON,
PHAROS, LIGHTHOUSE
seamen's chapel .... BETHEL
seamstress .... SEWER, TAILOR,
STITCHER, SEMPTRESS
seamy .... SHADY, SORDID
seance .... COUNCIL, MEETING,
SESSION, SITTING,
SPIRITUALISM
noise .... RAP
participant .... MEDIUM,
SPIRITUALIST
recording device .... OUIJA
seaplane .... AEROBOAT, FLYING
BOAT
stabilizer .... SPONSON
sear .... BURN, SERE, BRAND,
BROWN, DRY(UP), PARCH,
SINGE, BRAISE, HARDEN,
SCATHE, SCORCH, WITHER
search .... HUNT, SEEK, TEST,
DELVE, GROPE, PROBE, QUEST,
FERRET, FORAGE, EXPLORE,
LOOK FOR, RANSACK,
RUMMAGE
deeply .... DREDGE
diligently .... SCOUR
for food .... FORAGE
for Holy Grail .... QUEST
for mineral .... PROSPECT
for talent .... SCOUT
party of a sort .... POSSE
person's person .... FRISK
steadily .... MOUSE
thoroughly .... COMB
with divining rod .... DOWSE
with "out" .... FERRET
searching .... KEEN, SHARP,
PENETRATING
Seas predecessor .... SEVEN
seashore .... BEACH, COAST,
STRAND, WATERFRONT
of the .... LITTORAL

seasickness ...... NAUSEA, MAL DE
MER, MOTION SICKNESS
seaside strip .... BOARDWALK
structure .... WHARF
season .... AGE, CORN, CURE,
FALL, SALT, TIME, IMBUE,
INURE, SPICE, SPELL, FLAVOR,
HARDEN, PERIOD, SPRING,
SUMMER, TEMPER, WINTER
in .... AVAILABLE
dry .... SUMMER
rainy .... MONSOON
yield of .... VINTAGE
seasonable .... TIMELY, SUITABLE,
OPPORTUNE
seasonal .... PERIODIC
employees .... SANTAS
observation .... VERNAL
EQUINOX, AUTUMNAL EQUINOX
phenomenon .... SUMMER
SOLSTICE, WINTER SOLSTICE,
DAYLIGHT LESSENS
symbol .... SNOW, HOLLY,
PUMPKIN, SWALLOW
time ..... FALL, LENT, AUTUMN,
EASTER, SPRING, SUMMER,
WINTER, CHRISTMAS
seasoned .... TRIED, MATURE,
MELLOW, SOFTENED,
TEMPERED
seasoning .... SAGE, SALT, HERBS,
ONION, GARLIC, SPICES,
MUSTARD, CONDIMENT
leaf .... BAY, LAUREL
pod .... CHILI
seasons .... HORAE
four .... YEAR
seat .... SITE, SOFA, BENCH, CHAIR,
PERCH, STOOL, CENTER,
CHAISE, GRADIN, SEDILE,
SETTEE, INSTALL, OTTOMAN,
VIS-A-VIS
bishop's ...... SEE, METROPOLIS
chair's .... BOTTOM
coach .... DICKY
colloquial .... RUMP,
BUTTOCKS
for a judge .... BANC
high .... ROOST
mobile .... WHEELCHAIR
of a sort .... SADDLE
of early Irish kings ...... TARA
of government .... CAPITAL
of judgment .... TRIBUNAL
of power .... THRONE
on camel/elephant
.... HOUDAH, HOWDAH
royal .... THRONE
seating area, at times ...... AISLE
SEATO .... TREATY
seats, church .... PEW, SEDILIA

seawall .... JETTY, BREAKWATER
se(a)wan .... WAMPUM
seaward .... OFF
away from the wind
.... LEEWARD
toward the wind
.... WINDWARD
seaweed .... AGAR, ALGA(E), KELP,
FUCUS, LAVER, VAREC, MOSS,
FUCOID, LICHEN, TANGLE,
REDWARE, GULFWEED,
SARGOSSO, SEA LETTUCE,
NULLIPORE, SARGASSUM
edible ..... AGAR, LIMU, DULSE,
LAVER, TANGLE,
CARRAG(H)EEN
extract/product
.... AGAR(AGAR)
genus .... ALARIA
leaflike part .... FROND
red .... FUCUS
red-purplish
.... CARRAG(H)EEN
soda ash .... BARILLA
washed ashore .... WRACK,
SEAWARD
with fluted ribbonlike blades
.... LAMINARIA
seaworm .... SAO, LURG
seaworthy .... BOLD, SNUG,
STURDY, STA(U)NCH,
WATERTIGHT
sebaceous .... OILY, FATTY
glands secretion .... SEBUM
glands disorder
.... SEBORRHEA
matter .... FAT, TALLOW
sec .... DRY, BRUT, INSTANT
secant .... CROSSED, CROSSING,
DIAGONAL, INTERSECTING
secede .... BOLT, SEPARATE,
WITHDRAW
secern .... SECRETE, SEPARATE,
DISTINGUISH
secessionist .... BOLTER,
APOSTATE, SEPARATIST
Seckel .... PEAR
seclude .... IMMURE, RETIRE,
SCREEN, CONFINE, ISOLATE
secluded .... REMOTE, PRIVATE,
SHUT OFF, HERMITIC,
ISOLATED, SEQUESTERED
religious place .... CONVENT,
CLOISTER
safe, quiet place ...... RETREAT
spot .... DEN, NOOK
valley .... GLEN
seclusion .... PRIVACY, SOLITUDE,
(H)ERMITISM, ISOLATION,
QUARANTINE
second .... ABET, AID(E), JIFFY,

TRICE, BACK(ER), MOMENT, INSTANT, STAND-IN, ASSISTANT
as of time to wink .... TWINKLING
best .... RUNNER-UP
brightest star .... BETA
childhood .... DOTAGE, SENILITY
estate .... NOBILITY
growth crop .... ROWEN
-guess .... ANTICIPATE
lieutenant: sl. .... SHAVETAIL
look .... REVIEW, RECHECK
mentioned .... LATTER
nature .... HABIT, CUSTOM
of two .... LATTER
person .... YOU
placer ..... ALSO-RAN, RUNNER-UP
-rate .... LESSER, INFERIOR, MEDIOCRE
self .... ALTER EGO
sight .... INTUITION
smallest sovereign state .... MONACO
story man .... BURGLAR
string .... RELIEF, RESERVE, SUB(STITUTE), BENCH-WARMER
team .... SCRUB
thought ...... CHANGE OF MIND, MISGIVING
to first, sometimes .... DOUBLE-PLAY
to none .... FIRST, UNIQUE, PEERLESS, MATCHLESS
secondary .... BYE, MINOR, INFERIOR, RESULTANT
disease .... METASTASIS
secondhand .... OLD, USED, WORN, HEARSAY, INDIRECT
dealer ..... RAGMAN, JUNKMAN, SCRAPMAN
secque .... SHOE
secrecy .... PRIVACY, COVERTNESS, CONFIDENTIALITY
fraudulent .... DECEPTION
of identity .... INCOGNITO
of withholding name .... ANONYMITY
secret ...... INNER, PRIVY, ARCANE, COVERT, HIDDEN, OCCULT, ARCANUM, CRYPTIC, MYSTERY, VEILED, PRIVATE, UNDERHAND
action .... PROWL, STEALTH, STALKING
adviser's group .... CAMARILLA
agent .... SPY, OPERATIVE
agent's work .... ESPIONAGE

colloquial .... HUSH-HUSH
date .... TRYST
device/plan .... STRATAGEM, SUBTERFUGE
discussion .... HUDDLE
file on a person .... DOSSIER
government information/ reports, designation of .... CLASSIFIED
identity .... INCOGNITO
meaning, having a .... RUNIC
meeting .... CONCLAVE
most .... TOP, INMOST, RESTRICTED
murder, e.g. ..... DARK HIDDEN ACT
place .... HIDEOUT, RETREAT, SANCTUM
remedy .... ELIXIR
service .... INTELLIGENCE
society .... BUND, PORO, TONG, MAF(F)IA, CAMORRA, BLACKHAND, KU KLUX KLAN (KKK)
watch ...... SPYING, ESPIONAGE, SURVEILLANCE
writing .... CODE
secretary .... DESK, CLERK, STENO, AMANUENSIS, ESCRITOIRE
abbreviation .... SECY
bird .... SERPENTARIUS
bird's prey .... SNAKES, INSECTS, RODENTS
Ollie's document-shredding .... (FAWN) HALL
public .... SCRIBE
secrete .... HIDE, MASK, CACHE, STASH, SECERN, CONCEAL
secretion .... SAP, BILE, LATEX, MUCUS, SUDOR, SWEAT, SALIVA, CHALONE, EXUDATION
cells/glands .... MUCUS, SEBUM, ENZYMES, HORMONES
liver .... BILE
secretive ...... SLY, DARK, SHIFTY, EVASIVE, FURTIVE, RETICENT, STEALTHY, CLOSE (-MOUTHED)
secretly ...... SLYLY, SUBROSA, ON THE SLY, UNDERHAND
secrets .... PENETRALIA, SKELETONS IN THE CLOSET
sect .... CULT, PARTY, SCHOOL, FACTION, FOLLOWING, DENOMINATION
early Christian .... DOCETAE
sectarian .... BIGOTED, APOSTATE, PARTISAN, FACTIONAL
sectary .... DISSENTER, NON-

CONFORMIST
section .... LEG, PART, GROUP, PORTION, SEGMENT, DIVISION
book .... INDEX, CHAPTER, GLOSSARY
city .... ZONE
of a country .... REGION
secular .... LAY, LAIC(AL), EARTHLY, MUNDANE, WORLDLY, TEMPORAL
secund .... UNILATERAL
secundine .... AFTERBIRTH
secure .... GET, FIRM, HOLD, MOOR, NAIL, SAFE, SNUG, SURE, BELAY, GUARD, ANCHOR, FAST(EN), INSURE, STABLE, ACQUIRE
a door again .... REBOLT
a sail .... TRICE
place .... FORT, VAULT, FASTNESS, SANCTUARY, STRONGHOLD
tightly .... TRUSS
security ...... BOND, GAGE, GRITH, PLEDGE, SAFETY, SURETY, WARRANTY, GUARANTEE, SAFEGUARD, PROTECTION
against loss .... INSURANCE
for payment .... BOND, LIEN, COLLATERAL
interest .... LIEN
money, binding .... DEPOSIT, EARNEST
object .... TOY, BLANKET
on property .... TITLE DEED
sedan .... CHAIR, (CLOSED)CAR, LIMOUSINE, AUTOMOBILE
sedate .... CALM, GRAVE, QUIET, SOBER, STAID, DEMURE, SERENE, SERIOUS, COMPOSED
sedation .... CALMNESS
sedative .... DRUG, OPIATE, AMYTAL, ANODYNE, BROMIDE, CALMANT, CODEIN(E), DEMEROL, LUMINAL, BARBITAL, HYPNOTIC, NARCOTIC, URETHAN(E), PAINKILLER
sedentary ...... PASSIVE, INACTIVE
Seder, event commemorated by .... EXODUS
sedge .... REEDS
clump .... TUSSOCK
sediment .... LEES, OOZE, SILT, DRAFF, DREGS, FOOTS, GROUT, MAGMA, SLUDGE, RESIDUE
sedimentary .... RESIDUAL
deposit layer .... VARVE
sedition .... TREASON, INSURGENCE

seduce .... LURE, TEMPT, BETRAY,
ENAMOR, ENTICE, DEBAUCH,
MISLEAD, PERSUADE
seducer .... VAMP, SIREN, LECHER,
ENTICER, CASANOVA,
LOTHARIO, DON JUAN,
PHILANDERER
seductive .... WINNING, ALLURING,
CHARMING, BEGUILING
sedulous .... BUSY, DILIGENT,
ASSIDUOUS, INDUSTRIOUS
sedum .... STONECROP
see ...... ESPY, MEET, NOTE, VIEW,
VISIT, BEHOLD, DESCRY,
DISCERN, OBSERVE, WITNESS,
PERCEIVE, COMPREHEND
bishop's .... DIOCESE,
METROPOLIS
head of a .... BISHOP
slow to .... PURBLIND
socially .... DATE
See! .... LO AND BEHOLD
seed .... SOW, BEAN, CORN, GERM,
CAUSE, GRAIN, OVULE,
SPERM, ORIGIN, PIP(PIN)
again .... REGROW
aromatic .... TONKA,
CUM(M)IN, GUAIAC, ANISE(ED)
bearing organ .... PISTIL
bud .... PLUMULE
case .... POD, BUR(R), CYPSELA
coat .... ARIL, BRAN, HULL,
HUSK, TESTA, TEG(U)MEN
combining form .... SPERM,
SPERMAT(O)
container ...... PIT, POD, STONE
cover, false .... ARILLODE
edible .... PEA, BEAN, CORN,
GRAIN, PINON, PULSE, LENTIL,
SOYBEAN, PISTACHIO
flavoring .... ANISE, CUM(M)IN,
CARAWAY
food .... PEA, SOY, BEAN,
LEGUME, LENTIL, SESAME,
COQUITO
hole-making tool .... DIBBLE
immature .... OVULE
integument/covering ..... ARIL,
BRAN, HUSK
leaf .... COTYLEDON
lense-shaped .... LENTIGO
like .... SEMINAL
oil-yielding .... TILL, BENNE,
SESAME, GINGELI, GINGILI,
CHAULMOOGRA
one-celled .... CARPEL
oyster .... SPAT
pear/orange .... PIP
plant .... HERB, EXOGEN
plant dust .... POLLEN
pod .... CYPSELA

poisonous .... NUX VOMICA
prematurely produce ..... BOLT
remove .... GIN, RIPPLE
remover .... GIN, RIPPLER
rudimentary .... OVULE
scar(s) .... HILUM, HILA
spice ..... NUTMEG, CARDAMON
stalk .... FUNICULUS
strong-smelling ..... CARAWAY
vessel .... BUR, POD, SILICLE,
CAPSULE, PERICARP
wings .... ALAE
seeded .... SOWN
seedless .... AGAMOUS
plant .... FERN
seedling .... SAPLING
seeds: comb. form .... CARPO
row of planted .... DRILL
study of .... CARPOLOGY
seed(s)man .... SOWER
seedy .... TACKY, SHABBY,
RUNDOWN, RAMSHACKLE
seeing .... SIGHT, VISION
eye dog .... GUIDE
seek .... TRY, HUNT, PURSUE,
ATTEMPT, EXPLORE, REQUEST,
ENDEAVOR, SEARCH(FOR)
information .... INQUIRE
pleadingly/earnestly
.... SOLICIT
to accomplish a goal
.... ASPIRE
seel .... BLIND, HOODWINK, STITCH
UP
seeled bird .... HAWK, FALCON
seely .... POOR, FRAIL, TRIFLING
seem .... LOOK, APPEAR,
RESEMBLE
seeming .... SHOW, QUASI,
EVIDENT, OUTWARD,
APPARENT, OSTENSIBLE
seemingly .... QUASI
endless .... VAST
true .... PLAUSIBLE
seemliness .... DECENCY,
DECORUM, PROPRIETY
seemly ...... FAIR, MEET, COMELY,
DECENT, PROPER, FITTING,
BECOMING, DECOROUS,
SUITABLE
seen, can be .... VISIBLE,
DISCERNIBLE, MATERIALIZE,
PERCEPTIBLE
seep .... DRIP, LEAK, OOZE,
EXUDE, TRICKLE, PERMEATE,
PERCOLATE
seer .... ORACLE, PROPHET,
ARUSPEX, SOOTHSAYER
stock in trade of .... OMENS
woman .... SIBYL, SEERESS,
CASSANDRA, PROPHETESS

seersucker .... LINEN, FABRIC
characteristic of ..... CRINKLED
seesaw .... WAG, FLAP, TILT,
WAVER, TESTER, BASCULE,
CROSSRUFF, VACILLATE,
TEETER (-TOTTER)
seethe .... BOIL, SOAK, STEW,
STEEP, BUBBLE, SIMMER,
AGITATE, FERMENT
seething .... ABOIL, ANGRY,
FUMING, EBULLIENT
segment .... PART, SLICE, BRANCH,
MEMBER, SECTOR, PORTION,
SECTION, DIVISION
of crustacean .... TELSON
sego .... LILY, PLANT
segregate .... SEVER, DIVIDE,
EXCLUDE, ISOLATE, SECLUDE,
SET APART, SEPARATE
segregation, racial
.... APARTHEID,
DISCRIMINATION
seidel .... MUG
seigneur .... LORD, NOBLE
Seine .... NET, RIVER
city on the ... ROUEN, TROYES
tributary .... EURE, OISE,
MARNE
Seinfeld character .... ELAINE
seism .... EARTHQUAKE
seismograph subject .... QUAKE,
TREMOR, TEMBLOR
seize .... NAB, GRAB, LASH, TAKE,
GRASP, ARREST, ATTACK,
CLUTCH, COLLAR, CAPTURE,
CONFISCATE
first .... PREEMPT
for debt .... GARNISH,
DISTRAIN
for official use
.... COMMANDEER
in law .... LEVY
power, etc. .... USURP
property as security
.... SEQUESTER
seizure ...... FIT, ATTACK, STROKE,
CAPTURE, CONVULSION,
CONFISCATION
recurrent .... EPILEPSY
type of .... PARTIAL, GRAND
MAL, PETIT MAL
selachian .... RAY, SHARK,
DOGFISH
Selassie, Emperor .... HAILE
country of .... ETHIOPIA
sobriquet of .... LION OF
JUDAH
seldom .... RARELY
select .... OPT, CULL, WALE,
ELECT, CHOOSE, PICK(ED),
PREFER

by elimination .... SCREEN
group .... ELITE, EXCLUSIVE
selectee .... DRAFTEE, RECRUIT,
INDUCTEE
selection .... CHOICE, OPTION,
PREFERENCE
of one out of two
possibilities
.... ALTERNATIVE
selective service .... DRAFT
Selene ...... LUNA, MOON, HECATE,
ARTEMIS
love of .... ENDYMION
selenite .... GYPSUM
self .... I, EGO, BEING,
PERSONA(LITY)
addressed item ...... ENVELOPE
assertive person .... WISE GUY,
SMART ALEC(K)
assurance ...... POISE, APLOMB,
CONFIDENCE
centered .... SELFISH,
EGOCENTRIC
combining form ...,....... AUTO
conceit .... PRIDE, EGOISM,
VANITY, EGOTISM
conceited person .... EGOIST,
EGOTIST
confidence .... PANACHE
confident .... COCKY, PROUD,
POISED, ASSURED, (COCK)SURE
conscious .... COY, SHY,
TIMID, DEMURE, AWKWARD
contained .... INDEPENDENT
control, power of .... WILL
cremation .... SUTTEE
defense art ..... JUDO, KARATE,
JUJITSU, JUJUTSU
denial .... SACRIFICE
denying .... MONASTIC
destruction .... SUICIDE,
IMMOLATION
determination ...... FREE WILL,
AUTOMATION
esteem .... PRIDE, EGOISM,
VANITY
evident .... AXIOMATIC
explanatory .... CLEAR,
OBVIOUS
fertilization .... ORTHOGAMY
governing .... AUTONOMOUS
government .... HOME RULE
immolation .... SUICIDE
importance .... VANITY,
POMPOSITY
important ...... VAIN, POMPOUS,
ARROGANT, BUMBLING,
BUMPTIOUS, OVERPROUD
important person .... NIBS,
EGOIST, EGOTIST
love .... NARC(ISS)ISM

possessed .... CALM, COOL,
COMPOSED
possession .... APLOMB
propelled .... AUTOMOTIVE
protection .... DEFENSE
reliant .... DEPENDABLE
reproach .... REMORSE,
REPENTANCE
restraint .... MODERATION,
TEMPERANCE
righteous .... SMUG
sacrificing .... DEDICATED,
UNSELFISH
salesman .... EGOTIST
satisfied .... SMUG,
COMPLACENT
service .... PUMP YOUR GAS,
FIX YOUR OWN PLATE
serving .... GREEDY, SELFISH
winding .... AUTOMATIC
selfheal .... SANICLE
selfish .... MEAN, VENAL,
WORLDLY, SELF-CENTERED
one .... EGOIST
sell .... DEAL, DUPE, HAWK, VEND,
OFFER, TRADE, BARTER,
MARKET, PEDDLE, AUCTION,
DISPOSE OF
for ..... BRING, FETCH, REALIZE
out .... BETRAY
short .... BELITTLE,
DOWNGRADE
tickets illegally .... SCALP
seller .... COSTER, DEALER,
VENDOR, PEDDLER,
MERCHANT, RETAILER
on installment ...... TALLYMAN
sellout .... HIT, SMASH,
CLEARANCE
sign .... SRO
Selm .... LAGERLOF
selvage .... HEM, LIST, BORDER
semantics, concern of
.... MEANING
semasiology .... SEMANTICS
semblance .... COPY, GUISE,
IMAGE, ASPECT, LIKENESS,
PRETENSE
seme .... DOTTED
Semele's father .... CADMUS
son .... DIONYSUS
semester .... TERM, HALF-YEAR
seminar .... SYMPOSIUM,
DISCUSSION
Seminole chief .... OSCEOLA
semiology, subject of ...... SIGNS,
SYMPTOMS
Semiramis' husband .... NINUS
kingdom .... BABYLON
semisolid substance .... GELATIN
Semite .... JEW, ARAB, HEBREW,

BABYLONIAN, PHOENICIAN
god .... STERAPH
Semitic language .... PUNIC,
ARABIC, HEBREW, ARAMAIC,
AMHARIC
people .... CHALDEAN,
BABYLONIAN
tribe .... AMMON
vampire .... LILITH
semolina .... MEAL
"Semper Fidelis" .... ALWAYS
FAITHFUL
composer .... SOUSA
is U.S. Marine Corps' ____
.... MOTTO
Semple McPherson, ____
.... AIMEE
sempstress ...... SEWER, STITCHER,
SEAMSTRESS
sen, 1/10 of a .... RIN
senate .... ASSEMBLY,
LEGISLATURE
gofer .... PAGE
house .... CURIA
senator .... SOLON, LAWMAKER,
LEGISLATOR
send .... DRIVE, REMIT, FORWARD,
DISPATCH, TRANSMIT
abroad .... EXPORT
another message .... REWIRE
as signals .... EMIT
back .... REMIT, RETURN,
REMAND, REPATRIATE
flying .... ROUT
for .... SUMMON
forth .... EMIT
out .... ISSUE, DESPATCH,
DISPATCH
packing .... OUST, DRIVE,
DISMISS
up supplications ...... PRAY TO
send-off .... FAREWELL
Seneca .... CAYUGA, INDIAN,
IROQUOIAN
senega .... MILKWORT
Senegal cape .... VERDE
capital .... DAKAR
city/town .... KOLDA, LOUGA,
M'BOUR, THIES, KAOLACK,
DIOURBEL, SAINT-LOUIS,
ZIGUINCHOR
ethnic group .... PEUL, WOLOF,
SERERE
language .... MENDE, WOLOF,
FRENCH, FULANI, MANDINGO
monetary unit .... FRANC
president .... SENGHOR
region .... FERIO
river .... FALEME, GAMBIA,
SENEGAL, CASAMANCE
senescent .... AGING

seneschal ...... KAY, MAJOR-DOMO
senhor .... MR., SIR, (GENTLE)MAN
senile .... AGED, DOITED, ELDERLY
senility .... DOTAGE, OLD AGE
senior .... OLDER, ELDER,
SUPERIOR
citizen .... RETIREE, OLD-TIMER
class publication ..... ANNUAL,
YEARBOOK
member of group .... DEAN,
DOYEN
seniority .... RANK, PRIORITY,
PRECEDENCE
senna ...... PEA, PLANT, LAXATIVE
family .... LEGUME
source of .... CASSIA
sennet .... FLOURISH
sennight .... WEEK
señor ...... MR., SIR, (GENTLE)MAN
señora .... MRS., LADY, MADAM
señorita .... LADY, MISS
sensate ...... ESTHESIA, CONSCIOUS
sensation .... HIT, FEELING,
EXCITEMENT, IMPRESSION,
PERCEPTION
abnormal ..... PAIN, NUMBNESS
of touch .... THRILL
pins and needles .... TINGLING
that does not involve thought
.... SENTIENCE
sensational ...... LURID, EXCITING,
SHOCKING, STARTLING,
THRILLING
sensationalism .... PUFFERY,
BALLYHOO, MELODRAMATICS
sense .... SIGHT, SMELL, TASTE,
TOUCH, INTUIT, VISION,
FEEL(ING), HEARING,
MEANING, PERCEIVE,
SAPIENCE, FEEL IN ONE'S
BONES
of hearing disorder
.... DEAFNESS, TINNITUS
of sight .... OPTIC
of smell .... OLFACTION
of smell disturbance
.... ANOSMIA
of taste .... GUSTATION
organ .... EAR, EYE, NOSE,
FEELER, PALP(US), ANTENNA,
RECEPTOR, TASTE BUD
sixth .... ESP, INTUITION
sound .... LOGIC
senseless ...... MAD, INANE, INEPT,
SILLY, ABSURD, STUPID,
WANTON, UNWISE, FATUOUS,
FOOLISH, IRRATIONAL,
UNCONSCIOUS
senses, one of the .... SIGHT,
SMELL, TASTE, TOUCH,
VISION, HEARING, INTUITION

the five .... SENSORIUM
sensible .... KEEN, SANE, WISE,
ACUTE, ALERT, AWARE, VIVID,
PASSIBLE, RATIONAL,
REASONABLE, LEVEL-HEADED
sensitive .... RAW, SORE, ALERT,
AWARE, TENSE, PLIANT,
TENDER, TE(T)CHY, TOUCHY,
SENTIENT, CONSCIOUS
extremely .... TICKLISH
favorably .... RECEPTIVE
plant .... MIMOSA
sensitivity .... ERETHISM
to dust or pollen ..... ALLERGY
to strong light
.... PHOTOPHOBIA
sensual .... LEWD, CARNAL,
LYDIAN, LUSTFUL, SYBARITIC
sensualist .... SYBARITE,
LIBERTINE
sensuous .... EMOTIONAL,
EPICURIAN, VOLUPTUOUS
sentence .... DOOM, OPINION,
DECISION, JUDGMENT,
STATEMENT, EXPRESSION
break down .... PARSE
mark .... COLON, COMMA,
PERIOD
part ...... NOUN, VERB, PHRASE,
SUBJECT, PREDICATE
reading same backward
.... PALINDROME
slang .... RAP
structure .... SYNTAX
sententious .... CURT, PITHY,
LACONIC, POINTED,
MORALISTIC
sentient .... ALIVE, FEELING,
CONSCIOUS
sentiment .... BELIEF, EMOTION,
FEELING, OPINION, PASSION,
ATTITUDE, FONDNESS
sentimental .... GUSHY, MUSHY,
SOPPY, SPOONY, MAUDLIN,
MAWKISH, ROMANTIC,
EMOTIONAL, NAMBY-PAMBY
sentimentalism .... SCHMALTZ
sentimentality, kind of
.... BEERY, NOSTALGIA
slang .... CORN, MUSH
sentinel .... GUARD, PICKET,
SENTRY, WATCH(DOG)
mounted .... LOOKOUT,
VEDETTE, VIDETTE
sentry .... GUARD, WATCH,
BIVOUAC, SENTINEL
box .... BOOTH
challenge of .... WHO GOES
THERE
challenge of French .... QUI
VA LA

order of .... HALT
Seoul .... KEIJO
sepal .... LEAF, CALYX
separate ...... PART, SORT, SEVER,
SPLIT, DETACH, DIVIDE,
SECEDE, SECERN, ISOLATE,
SEVERAL, ALIENATE,
DISCRETE, DISTINCT,
DISUNITE, INSULATE, SET
APART, SEGREGATE
checks .... DUTCH TREAT
coarse from fine particles
.... SIFT
forcibly .... REND, SUNDER,
WRENCH
from military service
.... DISCHARGE
in botany .... SOLUTE
into filaments .... SLEAVE
into parts .... DISMEMBER
metal from ore .... EXTRACT
threads .... RAVEL
useless undesirables ..... WEED
OUT
separately .... APART
separation .... SCHISM, BREAK(
UP), DIVORCE, PARTING,
SPLIT-UP, AVULSION,
ISOLATION, SECESSION
center .... RENO
from employment
.... SEVERANCE
in chemistry .... DIALYSIS
separatist .... DISSENTER, NON-
CONFORMIST
separator .... WALL, SEPTUM,
BARRIER
of two continents ...... BERING
STRAIT
Sephardic dialect .... LADINO
Sephardim .... JEWS
sepia .... DUN, PIGMENT,
BROWNISH, CUTTLEFISH,
(REDDISH-)BROWN
sepiolite .... MEERSCHAUM
seppuku .... SUICIDE, HARAKIRI
seps .... SKINK, SNAKE
sept .... CLAN, TRIBE
septal defect .... HOLE IN THE
HEART
type of .... ATRIAL,
VENTRICULAR
September 13, Roman
calendar .... IDES
septic .... POISONED, INFECTIVE
tank .... CESSPOOL
septicemia .... SEPSIS, BLOOD
POISONING
consequence of .... SEPTIC
SHOCK
septime .... PARRY

633

septum .... WALL, PARTITION
  nasal .... CARTILAGE
septuple .... SEVENFOLD
sepulcher .... BURY, TOMB,
          CRYPT, GRAVE, VAULT,
          RELIQUARY, SEPULTURE
sepulchral ...... DISMAL, GLOOMY,
          FUNEREAL, TOMBLIKE
sepulture .... BURIAL, SHRINE,
          INTERMENT, MAUSOLEUM
  pharaohs' .... PYRAMIDS
sequel .... EFFECT, UPSHOT,
          OUTCOME, AFTERMATH,
          CONTINUATION
sequence .... RUN, ORDER,
          SEQUEL, SERIES, SUCCESSION
sequester .... SEIZE, ENISLE,
          CONFINE, ISOLATE, SECLUDE,
          SEPARATE, SET APART,
          SEGREGATE, CONFISCATE
sequestered .... RETIRED,
          ISOLATED, SECLUDED,
          CLOISTERED
sequin ...... SPANGLE, ZECCHIN(O)
sequoia .... REDWOOD
seraglio .... HAREM, SERAI,
          PALACE, ZENANA
  segment .... ODA
serai .... INN, KHAN, IMARET,
          SERAGLIO, CARAVANSARY
Serang .... CERAM
serape .... SHAWL, BLANKET
seraph .... ANGEL, CHERUB
seraphic .... ANGELIC
Serapis' temple .... SERAPEUM
  site of .... ALEXANDRIA
Serb .... SLAV
Serbian former capital .... NIS
  guerrilla .... CHETNIK
  language .... BALKAN
  measure .... RIF
sere ...... DRY, DRIED, WITHER(ED)
serein .... RAIN
serenade .... WOO, COURT,
          NOCTURNE, SERENATA,
          ENTERTAIN
  mock .... SHIVAREE,
          CHARIVARI
  the moon .... BAY
serendipity .... GOOD LUCK
serene ...... CALM, QUIET, PLACID,
          EQUABLE, COMPOSED,
          TRANQUIL, IMPASSIVE
serenity .... PEACE, REPOSE,
          CALMNESS
serf .... ESNE, HELOT, LITUS,
          SLAVE, THRALL, BONDMAN,
          VILLEIN
  female .... NEIF
  liberate a .... MANUMIT
serfdom ...... BONDAGE, HELOTRY,

          SLAVERY
sergeant .... NCO, SARGE,
          NONCOM, TOPKICK
  at-law's cap .... BIGGIN
  fish .... COBIA, ROBALO
  slang .... GUNNY
serial .... EPISODIC
seric .... SILKEN
sericeous .... DOWNY, SILKY
series .... RUN, SET, CYCLE,
          STRING, SEQUENCE,
          SUCCESSION
  of columns .... COLONNADE
  of links .... CHAIN
  of six .... HEXAD
  of stairs .... FLIGHT
  of steps .... SCALE
  of trouble .... GA(U)NTLET
serin .... FINCH
serious ...... GRIM, GRAVE, SOBER,
          SEDATE, SOLEMN, SOMBER,
          EARNEST, LIFE AND DEATH,
          ALARMING, CRITICAL
  reserved .... STAID
sermon .... HOMILY, SPEECH,
          LECTURE, DISCOURSE
sermonize .... PREACH
sermons, study of
          .... HOMILETICS
serous .... WATERY
  membrane .... PERITONEUM
serow .... JAGIA, ANTELOPE
serpent .... ASP, BOA, SEPS,
          (A)BOMA, ELAPS, SATAN,
          SNAKE, VIPER, DRAGON,
          BASILISK, OPHIDIAN,
          COCKATRICE
  fabulous and deadly
          .... COCKATRICE
  harmless .... GARTER SNAKE
  like a .... OPHIDIAN
  monster .... ELOPS, HYDRA,
          LAMIA
  nine-headed .... HYDRA
  slain by Apollo .... PYTHON
  symbol of royalty .... ASP
  worship .... OPHISM,
          OPHIOLATRY
  worshiping group, of a
          .... OPHITIC
Serpent Mound site .... OHIO
serpentine .... WILY, COILED,
          OPHITE, CUNNING, SINUOUS,
          WINDING, OPHIDIAN,
          SLITHERY, VENOMOUS,
          REPTILIAN
Serpico author .... MAAS
serpigo .... RINGWORM
serranoid fish .... REDHIND,
          CABRILLA
serrated .... JAGGED, SCALLOPED,

          SAW-TOOTHED
serried .... DENSE, PACKED,
          COMPACT
serum .... WHEY, ANTITOXIN
serval .... WILDCAT
servant .... HIND, MAID, GILLY,
          SLAVE, (BAT)MAN, GILLIE,
          HELP(ER), MENIAL, DOMESTIC,
          SERVITOR, ANCILLARY,
          ATTENDANT
  airplane/ship ...... ATTENDANT,
          STEWARD(ESS)
  all-around .... FACTOTUM
  boy .... PAGE, GARCON,
          GROOM, GOSSOON
  college .... GYP
  devoted .... FRIDAY
  female .... MAID, WENCH,
          SLAVEY, HANDMAID(EN)
  feudal .... SERF, BONDMAN,
          SERGEANT
  head .... BUTLER, STEWARD,
          MAJORDOMO
  hospital .... ORDERLY
  hotel .... BELLBOY, BELLMAN
  house of .... LODGE, QUARTERS
  household .... COOK,
          FOOTMAN, CHARWOMAN,
          LAUNDRESS
  kitchen .... SCULLION
  lady's .... MAID, ABIGAIL
  liveried .... FLUNKY, LACKEY
  male .... PAGE, GROOM,
          BUTLER, LACKEY, SQUIRE,
          HENCHMAN
  office .... ERRAND BOY,
          MESSENGER, ERRAND GIRL
  personal ..... VALET, EQUERRY,
          HANDMAID(EN)
  royal .... EQUERRY, LADY-IN-
          WAITING
  seat in carriage .... RUMBLE
  stable .... GROOM, HOSTLER
  uniformed .... CHASSEUR
serve .... AID, AVAIL, (AT)TEND,
          ASSIST, SUPPLY, DELIVER,
          FURTHER, SATISFY, SUFFICE
  flawless .... ACE
  food .... CATER, WAIT ON
  leftovers .... REHEAT
server .... TRAY, SALVER, WAITER,
          WAITRESS, ATTENDANT
  alcoholic drinks
          .... BARTENDER
  counter .... SODA JERK
  drive-in restaurant .... CARHOP
service .... AID, USE, HELP, MASS,
          WORK, UTILITY, FUNCTION,
          RITE, VIGIL, SERVITUDE,
          EMPLOYMENT

attendants, accompanying
.... CORTEGE, RETINUE
charge .... TIP, GRATUITY
club .... LIONS, JAYCEE,
ROTARY, KIWANIS
club, military .... USO
military .... DUTY
stripe, military .... HASH
MARK
tree .... SORB, SHADBUSH
serviceable .... HANDY, UTILE,
USABLE, USEFUL, HELPFUL,
EXPEDIENT, CONVENIENT
serviceman .... SOLDIER,
REPAIRMAN, TECHNICIAN,
TROUBLE-SHOOTER
services, one of the .... ARMY,
NAVY, AIR FORCE, COAST
GUARD, MARINE CORPS,
NATIONAL GUARD
serviette .... NAPKIN
servile .... BASE, MEAN, TAME,
ABJECT, MENIAL, PLIANT,
FAWNING, SLAVISH, CRINGING
one .... YESMAN
serving .... HELPING, PORTION
boy .... KNAVE
girl .... MAID
man .... POTMAN
stand .... DUMB WAITER
to delay .... DETERRENT
servite .... MENDICANT
servitor .... SERVANT, ADHERENT,
FOLLOWER, ATTENDANT
servitude .... YOKE, BONDAGE,
PEONAGE, SERFDOM,
SLAVERY, SUBJECTION
symbol of .... YOKE
sesame .... TIL, TEEL, BENNE,
SEMSEM, GINGILI
grass .... GAMA
oil .... BENI, GINGILI
seed .... GENGELI, GINGILI,
GINGELLY
sess .... TAX
sessile .... IMMOBILE
session .... TERM, PERIOD,
HEARING, MEETING, SITTING,
ASSEMBLY
diamond practice .... PEPPER
GAME
discontinue ..... ADJOURN, SINE
DIE, PROROGUE
spirited .... SEANCE
sestet .... SEXTET(TE)
set .... FIX, KIT, LAY, PUT, JELL,
POST, SEAT, WANE, BATCH,
EMBED, GROUP, MOUNT,
PLANT, CLIQUE, HARDEN,
RECORD, ARRANGE, COTERIE,
SCENERY, REGULATE,

RESOLUTE, ESTABLISH,
PRESCRIBE, COLLECTION
a course .... NAVIGATE(D)
afire .... IGNITE
afloat .... LAUNCH
against .... PIT
all .... READY, PREPARED
apart .... ISOLATE, RESERVE,
SEPARATE, SEGREGATE
as the sun .... SINK, DECLINE
aside .... PEND, ANNUL, DEFER,
QUASH, SPARE, REJECT,
DISCARD, EARMARK
back .... PULL, RECESS,
RETARD
down .... LAY, PUT, RECORD
down as a fact .... POSIT
firmly .... INFIX
forth .... START, STATE, THETIC
free .... CLEAR, ACQUIT,
DELIVER, RELEASE, UNLOOSE,
LIBERATE, EXTRICATE
in competition ..... PIT, MATCH
in motion .... AROUSE, EXCITE,
STIR UP, ACTIVATE
in operation .... START,
LAUNCH
in type .... COMPOSE
into a groove .... DADO
of clothes .... SUIT, OUTFIT,
COSTUME
nine .... ENNEAD
players .... TEAM
rules .... CODE
steps .... STILE
three .... TERNION
tools .... KIT
off .... EXPLODE, DETONATE
on .... SIC ON, INCITE
on end .... UPEND
on fire .... IGNITE, KINDLE
on horse .... MOUNT
out .... GO, PLAN, BEGIN,
LEAVE, DEFINE, DEPART
playing cards ...... DECK, PACK
right .... ALIGN, AMEND,
ADJUST, REPAIR, CORRECT
sail .... CAST OFF
since the 40's .... TV
straight .... ALIGN, UNBEND,
RECTIFY
system .... ROTE
tables .... BUS
thickly .... STUD
up .... ERECT, FOUND, PITCH,
ESTABLISH
up in advance ..... PRO FORMA
upon .... SIC, AMBUSH, ATTACK
value on .... PRICE, APPRAISE
seta .... CHAETA, BRISTLE
setback ...... EDDY, DELAY, UPSET,

HOLDUP, RELAPSE, REVERSE,
REVERSAL
Seth's brother .... ABEL, CAIN
father .... ADAM
mother .... EVE
son .... ENOS(H)
Seti I .... PHARAOH
son and successor of
.... RAMSES II
setoff .... OFFSET
setose .... BRISTLY
settee .... SEAT, SOFA, BENCH,
LOUNGE
setter .... (GUN)DOG, RETRIEVER
setting .... ARENA, MOUNT, SCENE,
LOCALE, MILIEU, SCENERY,
BACKGROUND
jewels' .... PAVE
of As You Like It ...... ARDEN
scheme .... DECOR, MOTIF
used on stage .... SCENERY
settle .... END, FIX, PAY, SAG, SET,
SIT, NEST, REST, SEAT, SINK,
BENCH, CLEAR, COUCH,
ALIGHT, DECIDE, ENCAMP,
RESIDE, APPEASE, ARRANGE,
CLARIFY, RESOLVE, COLONIZE,
CONCLUDE, LIQUIDATE
argument .... CLINCH
down .... ABATE, DESCEND,
SUBSIDE
for the night .... BED DOWN
in cozily .... NEST
on land illegally .... SQUAT
snugly .... ENSCONCE
settled .... LIT ON, SQUARE
in law .... VESTED
settlement ...... AWARD, COLONY,
OUTPOST, PAYMENT, VILLAGE,
JUDGMENT, AGREEMENT,
PLANTATION
settler .... BOOMER, SOONER,
PIONEER, COLONIST,
HOMESTEADER
land .... HOMESTEAD
settlers led by Kok .... GRIQUA
settlings ...... LEES, DRAFF, DREGS,
SEDIMENT
set-to .... BOUT, BRAWL, FIGHT,
HASSLE, CONTEST, QUARREL
setup .... PLAN, LAYOUT, MAKEUP
Sevastopol is in .... CRIMEA
seven .... VII, SEPT, HEPTAD
against Thebes, one of
.... TYDEUS
combining form .... HEPT(A)
companion of .... ELEVEN
days .... HEBDOMAD
deadly sins, one of the
.... ENVY, LUST, ANGER, PRIDE,
SLOTH, GLUTTONY,

COVETOUSNESS
-foot dunkers .... CAGERS
group of .... HEPTAD
of eleven, on offense ..... LINE
of number .... SEPTIMAL,
SEPTENARY
on the first cast ...... NATURAL
series of .... HEPTAD
-year period .... TEENS
Seven Dwarfs, one of .... DOC,
DOPEY, HAPPY, GRUMPY,
SLEEPY, SNEEZY, BASHFUL
Hills of Rome, one of the
.... CAELIAN, VIMINAL,
AVENTINE, PALATINE,
QUIRINAL, ESQUILINE,
CAPITOLINE
Wonders of the World, one
of .... PHAROS, COLOSSUS,
PYRAMIDS, MAUSOLEUM,
STATUE OF ZEUS
sevenfold .... SEPTUPLE
seventeen XVII
-year locust .... CICADA
17th century opener .... MDCI
seventh son .... SEER
sever .... CUT, PART, CLEAVE,
DIVIDE, SUNDER, DISJOIN,
BREAK(OFF), SEPARATE
several .... FEW, SUNDRY,
DIVERS(E), VARIOUS,
DISTINCT, SEPARATE
severe .... DOUR, HARD, ACUTE,
HARSH, RIGID, STERN, TOUGH,
STRICT, DRASTIC, SERIOUS,
RIGOROUS
not .... BENIGN, LENIENT
Severn river .... USK
severity .... RIGOR, FEROCITY,
AUSTERITY, HARSHNESS
sew .... FELL, MEND, SEAM, TACK,
BASTE, QUILT, STITCH,
SUTURE
lightly .... BASTE
together .... ENSEAM
up .... CLOSE, MONOPOLIZE
up the market .... ENJOY A
MONOPOLY
sewage .... OFFAL, WASTE, REFUSE,
RUBBISH, DRAINAGE
disposal .... SANITATION
hole .... CESSPOOL
sewan .... SHELL
Seward's "folly" .... JUNEAU
(ALASKA)
sewer .... PIPE, DRAIN, GUTTER,
KENNEL, CLOACA, PASSAGE,
STITCHER, SEAMSTRESS
entrance .... MANHOLE
sewing .... NEEDLEWORK
case .... ETUI, ETWEE

kit .... HUSSY, HOUSEWIFE
machine inventor .... HOWE
part .... LOOPER
technique .... CROSS-STITCH
sex .... GENDER
appeal .... CHARM, OOMPH
glands .... GONADS
glands, female .... OVARIES
glands, male .... TESTES
hormone .... STEROID
of a .... MALE, FEMALE,
FEMININE, MASCULINE
sexes, common to both
.... EPICENE
sexism .... BIAS, BIGOTRY,
INEQUITY, PREJUDICE
sexless .... FRIGID, NEUTER,
IMPOTENT
sext .... HOUR
sextant .... QUADRANT, ALTIMETER
sextet .... HEXAD
sexton .... BEADLE, VERGER,
SACRIST(AN), BELLRINGER,
GRAVEDIGGER
sextuple .... SIXFOLD
sexual .... GAMIC, CARNAL,
SENSUAL
attraction to either sex
.... BISEXUALITY
attraction toward the
opposite sex
.... HETEROSEXUALITY
attraction toward the same
sex .... HOMOSEXUALITY
continence .... CHASTITY
desire, of .... EROTIC
excitement .... RUT, HEAT,
(O)ESTRUS
inclination/urge .... LIBIDO
pervert .... DEVIATE
sexually cold .... FRIGID
ineffective .... STERILE
transmitted disease .... AIDS,
HERPES, SYPHILIS, GONORRHEA
unable .... IMPOTENT
sexy .... HOT, EROTIC, STEAMY,
WANTON, AMOROUS
picture .... PINUP
movie, describing a
.... X-RATED
Seychelles, capital of
.... VICTORIA
city/town .... CASCADE, ANSE
ROYALET
island .... MAHE, NORTH,
ASTOVE, FRIGATE, LA DIGUE,
PRASLIN
Sforza, Ital. statesman
.... CARLO
Sgts. and Cpls. .... NCOS
shabby ...... MEAN, WORN, DINGY,

DOWDY, MANGY, RATTY,
SEEDY, SORRY, TACKY,
CRUMMY, RAGGED,
RUNDOWN, UNKEMPT,
THREADBARE, DISGRACEFUL
color .... CHEESY
woman .... DOWD, SLOVEN,
SLATTERN
shack .... HUT, SHED, CABIN,
HOVEL, SHANTY
figure .... HAM
shackle .... BOND, CURB, GYVE,
BILBO, CHAIN, IRON(S),
FETTER, HAMPER, HOBBLE,
PINION, LEG-IRON, MANACLE,
TRAMMEL, HANDCUFF,
RESTRAIN
shad .... ALLIS, ALOSA, ALOSE,
ALEWIFE
fish like .... MENHADEN
running upriver
.... ANADROMOUS
shadbush ...... ROSE, JUNEBERRY,
SASKATOON, SERVICE(BERRY)
shaddock .... POMELO
family .... RUE
shade .... HUE, TINT, TONE,
COLOR, TOUCH, TRACE,
UMBER, UMBRA, BLIND(S),
SCREEN, SHADOW
bamboo ...... SCREEN, CURTAIN
blue .... SKY, ALICE, AZURE
canvas .... AWNING, CANOPY
cap's .... VISOR
fabric .... VEIL
for the eyes .... VISOR,
GOGGLES, SPECTACLES
for windshield .... VISOR
green .... AQUA, BICE, JADE,
EMERALD
lines .... HATCH
of color, pale .... PASTEL
of difference/meaning
.... NUANCE
orange ...... MADDER, PUMPKIN
pink .... ROSE, ORCHID,
SALMON
purple .... GRAPE, LILAC,
ORCHID, VIOLET, FUCHSIA,
AMETHYST
red .... WINE, OCHER,
CRIMSON, CARDINAL
tree .... ELM, LIN, ACACIA,
POPLAR, MAGNOLIA
used in church processions
.... BALDACHIN, BALDAQUIN
yellow .... AMBER, LEMON,
GOLDEN
shaded .... SHELTERED
walk .... MALL, ARBOR,
ALAMEDA, CLOISTER

Shades, the .... HADES
shadow .... DOG, SPY, OMEN,
TAIL, CLOUD, GHOST, GLOOM,
SHADE, TRACE, TRAIL,
UMBER, UMBRA, FOLLOW,
OUTLINE, VESTIGE,
REFLECTION, SILHOUETTE
astronomer's .... UMBRA
fighting .... SCIAMACHY
man without .... ASCIAN
Shadow, The
.... (LAMONT)CRANSTON
shadowbox .... SPAR
shadowy appearance
.... UMBRAGE
Shadrach's fellow-captive
.... MESHACH, ABEDNEGO
shady .... DARK, UMBRAL,
DUBIOUS, DOUBTFUL,
SINISTER, DISHONEST, ILLICIT
retreat .... NOOK, ARBOR,
KIOSK
SHAEF commander .... (IKE)
EISENHOWER
theater .... ETO, EUROPE
shaft .... BEAM, BOLT, FLUE, POLE,
ARBOR, ARROW, SHANK,
SPEAR, SPIRE, THILL, ARROYO,
COLUMN, HANDLE, CONDUIT,
JAVELIN, MISSILE, OBELISK,
SPINDLE, FLAGPOLE
bearing .... HOTBOX
building .... WELL
column's .... FUST, SCAPE,
TRUNK, VERGE
connecting .... AXLE
feather's .... SCAPE
give someone the ...... CHEAT,
TRICK
handle .... HELVE
mine .... PIT
part of .... BOSS, GUDGEON,
JOURNAL, TRUNNION
shag .... NAP, PILE, TOBACCO,
CORMORANT
shagbark ...... WALNUT, HICKORY
shaggy .... BUSHY, FUZZY, HAIRY,
NAPPY, WOOLY, HIRSUTE,
UNKEMPT, SCRUBBY,
THRUMMY
shagreen .... RAWHIDE,
(SHARK)SKIN
Shah Jahan's masterpiece .... TAJ
MAHAL
of Iran .... PAHLEVI
shaitan ...... DEVIL, FIEND, SATAN
shake .... JAR, RID, JOLT, LOSE,
ROCK, SWAY, WAVE, QUAKE,
MOMENT, QUIVER, SHIVER,
THRILL, TREMOR, WOBBLE,
SUCCUSS, TREMBLE, UNNERVE,

VIBRATE, CONVULSE
down .... EXTORT, SEARCH,
PRY LOOSE
due to cold .... SHIVER
due to fear, horror
.... SHUDDER
____ (hurry) .... A LEG
in a menacing way
.... BRANDISH, FLOURISH
up .... CHANGE, RATTLE,
REVAMP, AGITATE
shakedown: sl. .... BLACKMAIL,
EXTORTION
shaken .... RATTLED, STARTLED
Shakespeare .... THE BARD,
WILLIAM
enough of .... ENOW
form used by .... BLANK
VERSE
wife of ...... ANNE(HATHAWAY)
Shakespearean actor .... BURTON,
GIELGUD, OLIVIER,
BARRYMORE, WILLIAMSON
Athenian .... TIMON
character .... IAGO, KATE,
LEAR, CASCA, DIANA, PARIS,
REGAN, ROMEO, BRUTUS,
CICERO, CLITUS, HAMLET,
HELENA, JULIET, LUCIUS,
OBERON, OSWALD, PORTIA,
TYBALT, BERTRAM, CASSIUS,
HORATIO, OCTAVIA, OPHELIA,
ORLANDO, OTHELLO, SHYLOCK,
SOLINUS, TITANIA, BENVOLIO,
CORDELIA, FALSTAFF,
MERCUTIO
clown .... FESTE, GOBBY,
COSTARD
Danish Prince .... HAMLET
elf .... PUCK
forest .... ARDEN, SHERWOOD
king .... LEAR, HAMLET
play .... HAMLET, MACBETH,
OTHELLO, KING LEAR,
PERICLES, CYMBELINE, THE
TEMPEST, JULIUS CAESAR, AS
YOU LIKE IT, ROMEO AND
JULIET, MERCHANT OF VENICE,
TAMING OF THE SHREW,
ANTONY AND CLEOPATRA
river .... AVON
seven .... AGES
shrew .... KATE
songwriter .... ARNE
theatre .... GLOBE
villain .... IAGO
witch .... CYCORAX
shaking .... ASPEN, PALSIED
shako decoration .... POMPON
Shakti .... DEVI, POWER
shaky ...... WEAK, DOTTY, LOOSE,

QUAKY, ROCKY, CRANKY,
FLIMSY, UNSURE, WOBBLY,
JITTERY, RICKETY, UNSOUND,
UNSTEADY
shale .... ROCK, PELITE
product .... TARE
shall .... MUST
shallop .... BOAT, DINGHY
shallot .... BULB, ONION,
ESCHALOT, SCALLION
kin .... LEEK
shallow .... DULL, SHOAL, SIMPLE,
SUPERFICIAL
container .... TRAY
cut .... SCRATCH
lake .... LAGOON, LAGUNE
sham .... FAKE, HOAX, BOGUS,
FALSE, FEIGN, HUMBUG,
PHON(E)Y, BASTARD,
PRETENSE, IMITATION,
ARTIFICIAL, COUNTERFEIT
fight .... SCIAMACHY
knife .... SNEE
ridiculous .... FARCE
shaman .... PRIEST, MEDICINE
MAN
Shamash .... SUN GOD
shamble .... GAIT, WALK,
LUMBER, SHUFFLE
shambles .... MESS, CHAOS,
ABATTOIR, DISORDER,
SLAUGHTERHOUSE
shame ...... FIE, ABASH, MORTIFY,
BLACKEYE, DISGRACE,
DISHONOR, HUMILIATE
shamefaced .... SHY, BASHFUL,
BLUSHING
shameful .... BASE, MEAN,
ARRANT, IGNOBLE, INDECENT,
SHOCKING, OFFENSIVE,
SCANDALOUS
shameless .... BRAZEN
shammy .... CHAMOIS
Shamo .... GOBI
shampoo .... SOAP, WASH,
MASSAGE, LOMILOMI
shamrock .... CLOVER
country .... EIRE, ERIN,
IRELAND
describing .... GREENEST
Shan .... T(H)AI
shandrydan .... CART, CHAISE
Shandy's creator .... STERNE
Shanghai .... KIDNAP, CHICKEN,
SEAPORT
Shangri-la ...... UTOPIA, PARADISE
shank .... LEG, CRUS, SHIN,
GAMB(E), SHAFT
in botany .... FOOTSTALK
shanny .... BLENNY
Shantung .... TUSSA(H)

capital of .... TSINAN
city .... CHEFOO
shanty .... HUT, SHED, HOVEL,
　　　　　　　　　　HUTCH, SHACK
shantytown .... SLUM
shape .... CAST, FORM, GUISE,
　　　MODEL, MO(U)LD, STATE,
　　　FIGURE, CONTOUR, PATTERN,
　　　　　　　　　　CONDITION
abalone .... EAR
bust's .... TAILLE
for a dunce cap .... CONE
illusory .... PHANTOM
jinxed? .... HEXAGON
like a teapot .... OBLATE
tondo .... ROUND
shaped .... SET, CAST, MADE,
　　　FORMED, MOLDED, DEVISED
roughly, as stone
　　　.............................. SCABBLED
shapeless .... VAGUE, AMORPHOUS
shapely ...... NEAT, LITHE, SVELTE,
　　　　　　　　　　CURVACEOUS
shaping machine .... EDGER,
　　　　　　　　　　　　　LATHE
shard .... PIECE, PLATE, SHELL,
　　　　FRAGMENT, POTSHERD
share .... BIT, CUT, LOT, METE,
　　　PART, ALLOT, QUOTA, STAKE,
　　　MOIETY, RATION, DOLE OUT,
　　　PARTAKE, (AP)PORTION
in common .... JOINT, MUTUAL
slang .... DIVVY
shark .... GATA, MAKO, TOPE,
　　　CHEAT, DOGFISH, MAN-EATER,
　　　SWINDLER, THRESHER,
　　　ANGELFISH, PORBEAGLE,
　　　HAMMERHEAD, SHOVELHEAD
eating fish .... PEGA
genus .... LAMNA, SPHYRNA
loan .... USURER
nurse .... GATA
of northern seas
　　　............................ PORBEAGLE
rider/sucker .... REMORA
skin .... SHAGREEN
slang .... EXPERT
voracious .... MAN-EATER
young .... PUPPY
sharp .... GLEG, KEEN, ACERB,
　　　ACUTE, CLEAR, EDGED, NIPPY,
　　　SMART, SPINY, CLEVER,
　　　CUSPED, PEAKED, SEVERE,
　　　ACIFORM, CUTTING, NIPPING,
　　　POINTED, PUNGENT, DISTINCT,
　　　HANDSOME, INCISIVE,
　　　PIERCING, TRENCHANT,
　　　VITRIOLIC
as a tack .... HEP, HIP, IN-THE-
　　　　　　　　　　KNOW
at the end .... ACUATE

blade .... RAZOR
colloquial .... ADEPT, EXPERT
combining form .... ACET(O)
cornered .... ANGULAR
cry .... YELP
edged .... KEEN
end .... POINT
eyed one .... LYNX, EAGLE
horn .... ANTLER
in phonetics .... VOICELESS
metal device on a gamecock
　　　...................................... SPUR
pain .... STING
point on a leaf .... MUCRO
rejoinder .... REPARTEE
reply .... RETORT
ridge .... ARETE
spot .... RAZOR'S EDGE
taste .... TANG, TART
tooth .... FANG, TUSH, TUSK,
　　　　　　CANINE, CUSPID
toothed wheel .... RATCHET
turn .... ZIG
witted .... KEEN
sharpen ...... EDGE, HONE, WHET,
　　　GRIND, STROP, ACUATE
sharpening device .... HONE,
　　　STEEL, STONE, STRAP, STROP,
　　　GRINDER, ABRASIVE,
　　　WHETSTONE, GRINDSTONE
sharper .... GYP, KITE, CROOK,
　　　SHARK, CHEAT(ER), CON-MAN,
　　　　　　　　　　SWINDLER
sharpness .... BARB, EDGE,
　　　ACUITY, ACERBITY,
　　　PUNGENCY, ALERTNESS
of temper .... ASPERITY
Shasta .... DAISY, VOLCANO
sharpshooter .... SNIPER,
　　　MARKSMAN, RIFLEMAN,
　　　(CRACK)SHOT, TIRAILLEUR
shatter ...... DASH, BREAK, BURST,
　　　CRASH, SMASH, WRECK,
　　　SHIVER, DESTROY
shave ...... CUT, CROP, PARE, SKIM,
　　　TRIM, GRAZE, PLANE, SHEAR,
　　　SKIVE, SCRAPE, WHITTLE
the jowls .... BARBER CHOPS
shaveling .... MONK, PRIEST
shaven .... TONSURED
shaver .... BOY, LAD, RAZOR,
　　　YOUTH, YOUNGSTER
shavetail .... MULE, LIEUTENANT
Shavian forte .... WIT
shaving ...... CHIP, FLAKE, PARING,
　　　　　　　　　　SAWDUST
shaw .... COPSE, THICKET
shawl .... CAPE, MAUD, WRAP,
　　　MANTA, SCARF, STOLE,
　　　MANTLE, PEPLOS, SERAPE,
　　　MUFFLER, PAISLEY, TALLITH,

CASHMERE, MANTILLA
shepherd's .... MAUD
woolen .... CASHMERE
shawn .... OBOE
Shawnee .... INDIAN
bread .... PONE, JOHNNYCAKE
chief .... TECUMSEH,
　　　　　　　　　　TECUMTHA
shay .... BUGGY, CHAISE,
　　　CARRIAGE, STANHOPE
puller of song .... HOSS
"Shazam!" .... PRESTO
she .... HER, FEMALE, FEMININE
carved it .... SCULPSIT
-demon .... LAMIA
died .... OBIT
escaped with "Declaration
　　of Independence"
　　................... DOLLEY MADISON
let down her hair
　　............................. RAPUNZEL
opened a box of evils
　　............................... PANDORA
painted it .... PNXT, PINXIT
pulled a switch on a witch
　　................................... GRETEL
raised Cain with an apple
　　... ERIS
reads and writes in her sleep
　　...................... LADY MACBETH
speaks .... LOQUITUR
was born free .... ELSA
wrote it .... SCRIPSIT
sheaf .... BALE, BATCH, BUNCH,
　　　　　BUNDLE, PACKET
of arrows .... QUIVER
of twigs .... FAGOT
shear .... CUT, LOP, MOW, CLIP,
　　　CROP, POLL, SNIP, TRIM,
　　　SHAVE, STRIP, FLEECE
Shearer, _____ .... MOIRA, NORMA
shearing machine .... MOWER,
　　　　　　　　　　CROPPER
tool .... CLIPPER(S), SCISSORS
sheatfish .... CATFISH
sheath .... COT, DRESS, OCREA,
　　　STALL, THECA, CASING,
　　　(EN)CASE, FASCIA, SLEEVE,
　　　SPATHE, CAPSULE, SCABBARD
metalplate on .... CHAPE
sheathe .... COVER, ENCLOSE,
　　　　　　　　　　RETRACT
sheathed ...... OCREATE, THECATE
sheaves of grain .... SHOCK,
　　　　　　　　　　STOCK
Sheba .... SABA
people .... SAB(A)EAN
queen of .... BALKIS
shebang .... THING, AFFAIR,
　　　MATTER, BUSINESS,
　　　CONTRIVANCE

shed .... COTE, EMIT, MOLT,
SHACK, LEAN-TO, SCONCE,
SHANTY, CAST(OFF), DROP
OFF, DIFFUSE, DISCARD, FALL
OUT, RADIATE, SHELTER
aircraft ..... HANGAR, AIRDOCK,
AIRDROME
animal .... HOVEL, HUTCH
chicken/sheep .... COTE
for storing grain .... CRIB
guard .... SENTRY BOX
livestock .... STALL
newsstand .... KIOSK
skin/feathers .... MEW, PEEL,
MO(U)LT, SLOUGH OFF
temporary .... BOOTH
train .... DEPOT
shedding leaves annually
.... DECIDUOUS
Sheean, writer .... VINCENT
sheen .... GLOW, GLEAM, GLOSS,
SHINE, LUSTER, LUSTRE,
POLISH
Sheen, Bishop .... FULTON
Sheena's domain .... JUNGLE
sheep ...... SHA, TEG, ARUI, URIAL,
MERINO, OORIAL, NAHOOR,
BLEATER, CARACUL, CHEVIOT,
KARAKUL, BROADTAIL,
LEICESTER
brain ailment .... GID
breed .... MERINO, OXFORD,
PANAMA, ROMNEY, CHEVIOT,
KARAKUL, LINCOLN, TARGHEE,
LEICESTER
caretaker .... SHEPHERD
castrated .... WETHER
cry of .... BAA, MAA, BLAT,
BLEAT
descriptive of .... MEEK, TIMID
disease .... COE, GID, ROT,
LOCO, SHAKES, STURDY,
ANTHRAX, SCRAPIE, STAGGERS,
RINDERPEST
dog .... COLLIE, SHELTY,
SHELTIE, SHEPHERD
enclosure/pen .... FOLD,
KRAAL
fat .... SUET, TALLOW
female/mama .... EWE
flesh/meat .... LAMB, VEAL,
MUTTON
flock .... FOLD, DRYBAND
flock leader .... BELLWETHER
foot of .... TROTTER
fur .... MOUTON, CARACUL,
KARAKUL
genus .... BOS, OVIS
grease .... SUINT
group of .... FOLD, FLOCK
head .... JEMMY

infectious disease of
.... RINDERPEST
intestinal disorder ...... BRAXY
killing bird .... KEA
like/pertaining to .... OVINE
like animal .... SAIGA
male .... RAM, TUP, WETHER
mountain .... IBEX
mutton .... SUFFOLK
neck growth of .... POKE
parasite ..... FLUKE, COENURUS
sexual excitement .... RUT,
HEAT, ESTRUS
shelter .... COTE, FOLD
stomach trouble .... BRAXY
tender .... SHEPHERD
tick .... KED
unshorn .... HOG
walk .... SLAITH
white .... WILTSHIRE
white-faced .... CORRIEDALE
wild .... SHA, SNA, ARUI,
UDAD, RASSE, URIAL, ARGALI,
AOUDAD, NAHOOR, OORIAL,
MOUF(F)LON
wool .... FLEECE
wool secretion .... YOLK
young .... HOG, TEG, LAMB,
(Y)EANLING
sheepfold .... PEN, REE, COTE,
KRAAL
sheepish .... COY
sheeplike .... MEEK, OVINE, TIMID,
DOCILE
sheepshank .... KNOT
sheepshead .... SPAR(O)ID
sheepskin .... ROAN, SKIVER,
DIPLOMA, PARCHMENT
cap .... KALPAK, CALPAC(K)
dealer .... FELLMONGER
disease .... SCAB, MANGE
sheepwalk .... SLAITH, PASTURE
sheer .... MERE, PURE, THIN,
TURN, VEER, STARK, STEEP,
UTTER, SIMPLE, SWERVE,
DEVIATE, ABSOLUTE,
DIAPHANOUS
delight ..... ECSTASY, RAPTURE
joy .... GLEE
legs .... SHEARS
sheet .... LEAF, PAGE, SAIL,
LAYER, LINEN, BEDDING,
EXPANSE, NEWSPAPER
bend .... KNOT
blurred .... MACKLE
metal(piece) .... LATH, LEAF,
PLATE
metal cutter .... SNIP
of lava .... COULEE
of matted cotton .... BATT
sheeting material .... LINEN,

SATIN, PERCALE
shekel .... MONEY
3000 .... TALENT
sheldrake ...... DUCK, MERGANSER
shelf .... REEF, BERM(E), LEDGE,
MANTEL, BEDROCK,
GRADIN(E), RETABLE,
SANDBAR
drapery .... VALANCE,
LAMBREQUIN
shell ...... POD, CASE, HULL, HUSK,
BIELD, CONCH, COVER,
SHARD, SHUCK, STRIP,
LORICA, STRAFE, TUNICA,
BOMBARD, MISSILE, MOLLUSK,
CARAPACE, CARTRIDGE,
INTEGUMENT, RACING BOAT
abalone .... ORMER
artillery .... OBUS, SHRAPNEL
bean .... FAVA, LIMA
boat .... HULL
cone-shaped .... LIMPET,
PERIWINKLE
corn .... HUSK
crab, clam, etc. .... TEST
defective .... DUD
dish, baking .... SCALLOP
ear .... ORMER, ABALONE
enclosed in a .... OBTECTED
explosive .... BOMB, GRENADE,
SHRAPNEL
fragments .... SHRAPNEL
fruit .... PEEL, RIND
game .... THIMBLERIG
hole .... CRATER
hurling device .... MORTAR
invertebrate's .... TEST
kernel .... NUT
kind of .... EGG, NUT, SEA,
COCKLE
many-chambered
.... NAUTILUS
mollusk's .... CONCH
money .... COWRY, PEAG(E),
COWRIE, SE(A)WAN, WAMPUM
of .... TESTACEOUS
of the burrito .... TORTILLA
1/20 of .... GERAH
out .... PAY, GIVE, FORK OUT
oysters .... SHUCK
pastry .... TART
seed .... HUSK, TEST(A)
shock .... AMNESIA, COMBAT
FATIGUE
slow-moving .... SNAIL,
WHELK
spiral .... CONCH, SNAIL,
WHELK, NAUTILUS
structures resembling a
.... CONCHA
tip of .... WARNOSE

trumpet .... CONCH
turtle/tortoise .... CARAPACE,
　　　　　　　　　　PLASTRON
used for cameo .... CONCH
shellac(k) ...... BEAT, DRUB, FLOG,
　　WHIP, RESIN, LAC(QUER),
　　　　　　　　　　VARNISH
shellacking .... BEATING,
　　CREAMING, WHIPPING,
　　　　　　　　CLOBBERING
shellback .... SAILOR
shellbark ...... WALNUT, HICKORY,
　　　　　　　　　SHAGBARK
Shelley, poet .... ARIEL, PERCY
elegy by .... ADONAIS
shellfish .... CLAM, CRAB, NACRE,
　　COCKLE, OYSTER, SHRIMP,
　　ABALONE, LOBSTER,
　　MOLLUSK, SCALLOP,
　　BARNACLE, MOSSBACK
spawn .... SPAT
trap .... CREEL
shelter .... ROOF, SHED, BIELD,
　　HAVEN, CABANA, COVER(T),
　　NESTLE, REFUGE, SHIELD,
　　RETREAT, (EN)SCONCE
aircraft .... HANGAR,
　　　　　　　　　AIRDROME
airraid .... ABRI, DUGOUT
auto .... GARAGE, CARPORT
canvas/collapsible .... TENT
cattle .... KRAAL, CORRAL
decorative .... PAVILION
dove's .... COTE
hillside .... ABRI
movable .... MANT(E)LET
overhanging .... AWNING,
　　　　　　　　　CANOPY
portable .... TENT
rain .... UMBRELLA
refugee's .... ASYLUM,
　　　　　　　　SANCTUARY
ship's .... HARBOR
small .... COT(E), CABANA
soldier's .... FOXHOLE,
　　　　　　　　(PUP)TENT
sheltered area/side .... LEE
shelty .... PONY, (SHEEP)DOG
shelve .... DEFER, RETIRE, LAY
　　　　　ASIDE, POSTPONE
Shem's descendants
　　.......................... S(H)EMITES
father .... NOAH
son .... LUD, ARAM, ELAM,
　　　　　　　　AS(S)HUR
shenanigan(s) .... PRANK, FROLIC,
　　MISCHIEF, NONSENSE,
　　　　　　　　TRICK(ERY)
Shensi, capital of .... SIAN
sheol .... HELL, HADES,
　　　　　　　UNDERWORLD

shepherd .... LEAD, TEND,
　　HERDER, PASTOR, CORYDON,
　　DAPHNIS, ENDYMION,
　　MINISTER, SHEEP DOG,
　　　　　　　LEADING MAN
concern of .... SHEEP
dog .... COLLIE
kings .... HYKSOS
pie of .... MASHED POTATOES
pipe .... OAT, REED
plaid .... MAUD
staff of .... KENT, PEDA,
　　　　　　　　　CROOK
shepherdess .... AMARYLLIS
shepherds, god of .... PAN,
　　　　　　　　　FAUNUS
pertaining to .... BUCOLIC,
　　　　　　　　PASTORAL
sherbet .... DRINK, SORBET,
　　DESSERT, BEVERAGE,
　　　　　　　ICE(CREAM)
Sheridan, Union general
　　.................................. PHILIP
sherif .... EMIR
ancestor of .... FATIMA,
　　　　　　　MOHAMMED
sheriff .... REEVE, MARSHAL,
　　　　　　　　VISCOUNT
aid of .... YEOMAN, BAILIFF,
　　BULLDOG, CATCHPOLL
armed group of .... POSSE
badge of .... STAR
deputy .... BAILIFF
Sheriff Pusser's story
　　.................... WALKING TALL
Sherlock Holmes, creator of
　　.................................. DOYLE
man of .... WATSON
sherry .... WINE, JEREZ, OLOROSO,
　　　　　　　AMONTILLADO
Sherwood Forest hero .... ROBIN
　　　　　　　　　HOOD
Shetland .... PONY, WOOL
fishing grounds .... HAAF
island .... MAINLAND
island tax .... SCAT(T)
pony .... SHELTY, SHELTIE
sheep dog .... COLLIE, SHELTY,
　　　　　　　　SHELTIE
shibboleth .... SLOGAN,
　　PASSWORD, TEST WORD
shield .... ECU, (A)EGIS, ARMOR,
　　COVER, MULGA, PAVIS,
　　SCUTA, TARGE, DEFEND,
　　SCREEN, SCUTUM, BUCKLER,
　　PROTECT, MANT(E)LET,
　　　　　　　ESCUTCHEON
arm/hand .... BUCKLER
Athena's/Zeus' ...... (A)EGIS
band across .... FESS
bar, heraldic .... GEMEL

bearer .... SQUIRE, ARMIGER
border .... ORLE
boss/knob of .... UMBO
bulletproof .... MANT(E)LET
center point .... FESS
of shields .... TESTUDO
rawhide .... PARFLECHE
Roman .... TESTUDO
shaped ..... PELTATE, SCUTATE,
　　CLYPEATE, CLYPEIFORM
spike of .... UMBO
strap .... ENARME
shift .... MOVE, VARY, VEER,
　　SHUNT, TRICK, CHANGE,
　　SWITCH, CHEMISE, DEVIATE,
　　TRANSFER, ASSIGNMENT
descriptive of a work
　　........................... GRAVEYARD
direction .... HAUL, DIVERT
for oneself .... FREE-LANCE
from side to side .... JIBE
shiftless .... LAZY
shifty .... ALERT, TRICKY,
　　CUNNING, EVASIVE, FURTIVE
Shiite .... SHIAH, MOSLEM
opposed to .... SUNNITE
shikar .... HUNT(ING)
shikari .... GUIDE, HUNTER
shill .... DECOY, PLANT,
　　　　　　　ACCOMPLICE
confederate of a ...... BARKER,
　　　　　　　　GAMBLER
shillelagh .... CLUB, CUDGEL
shilling: sl. .... BOB
shillings, 21 .... GUINEA
shilly-shally .... HEDGE, TARRY,
　　WAVER, DAWDLE, HESITATE,
　　FLUCTUATE, VACILLATE,
　　　　　　　(DILLY)DALLY
shimmer .... FLASH, GLINT,
　　GLIMMER, TWINKLE
shimmy .... DANCE, WOBBLE,
　　　　　　　　CHEMISE
shin .... LEG, SHANK, CLIMB(UP)
Shinar .... SUMER, BABYLONIA
shinbone .... TIBIA
shindig .... GALA, DANCE, PARTY,
　　SPREE, AFFAIR
shindy .... ROW, RIOT, BRAWL,
　　HUBBUB, RACKET,
　　　　　　　COMMOTION
shine .... WAX, GLOW, EXCEL,
　　GLEAM, GLOSS, LIGHT,
　　LUSTER, POLISH, FLICKER,
　　GLITTER, RADIATE, TWINKLE
shiner .... MINNOW
slang .... MOUSE, BLACKEYE
shingle .... BOB, CLIP, SHIM,
　　FACIA, SLAT(E), GRAVEL,
　　SIDING, SIGN(BOARD)
man with .... DOCTOR,

LAWYER
use of .... ROOF, SIGN
shingles .... ZONA,
HERPES(ZOSTER)
drug treatment ..... ACYCLOVIR
shining ...... LUCID, NITID, SUNNY,
BRIGHT, GLOSSY, LUCENT,
EMINENT, RADIANT,
LUMINOUS, LUSTROUS
example .... HERO
"star of the Carribean"
.... PUERTO RICO
shinleaf .... WINTERGREEN
shinny ...... CLUB, STICK, HOCKEY
shinplaster .... SCRIP, POULTICE
Shinto .... SINTU
deity .... KAMI
temple .... SHA
temple gate .... TORII
text .... KOJIKI, NAHONGI
ship .... BARK, BOAT, BRIG, DHOW,
HULK, SAIL, SCOW, SEND,
LINER, PINKY, YACHT,
EMBARK, HOOKER, PINKIE,
TARTAN, VESSEL, WHERRY,
CARRACK, CLIPPER,
DROMON(D), GALLEON,
(AIR)CRAFT, BILANDER
abandoned .... DERELICT
accommodation .... CABIN,
PASSAGE
accommodation, no frills
.... STEERAGE
afterpart of .... QUARTER
anchor rope .... HAWSER
anchorage .... MARINA,
ROAD(STEAD)
ancient .... BIREME
balance of .... TRIM
ballast .... LASTAGE,
KENTLEDGE
beak .... ROSTRUM
big, unwieldy .... HULK
biscuit .... (HARD)TACK
boat on .... GIG, YAWL, JOLLY,
DINGHY, LAUNCH, PINNACE
body of .... HULK, HULL
boom .... BUMPKIN
bottom .... KEEL
bow flag .... JACK
breadth .... BEAM
cabin .... CUDDY
canal .... GOTA, KIEL, SUEZ,
ALBERT, PANAMA
canvas .... SAIL
capacity .... TONNAGE
captain .... MASTER, SKIPPER
captive .... PRIZE
cargo .... FREIGHTER
cargo/passenger, from port to
port .... COASTER

carpenter .... CHIPS
chains .... TYES
change course of .... TACK
channel .... GAT
clean bottom of .... BREAM
clean hull of .... GRAVE
cleaning tool .... HOG
clock .... NEF
clumsy .... ARK, TUB,
DROGHER
coal .... COLLIER
coal bin .... BUNKER
crane .... DAVIT
crew-member .... HAND,
MATE, OILER, STOKER,
YEOMAN
crosspiece .... BEAM
device for raising sunken
.... CAMEL, CAISSON
dimension .... ABEAM
direct a .... NAVIGATE
drain hole .... SCUPPER
entrance of .... GANGWAY
equipped with sails .... SAILER
fender .... SKID
fictional .... CAINE
fishing .... TRAWLER
flag ..... JACK, BURGEE, ENSIGN
flat-bottomed .... KEEL
fleet .... ARGOSY
for transporting oil ..... OILER,
TANKER
forward part .... BOW, PROW,
STEM
framework ..... HULL, CARCASS
fraud .... BARRATRY
fuel tank of .... BUNKER
galley .... CUDDY, CABOOSE,
KITCHEN
gun platform .... SPONSON
heave of .... SCEND
hold .... BULK
hospital .... SICK BAY
hunting .... RAIDER, SEALER,
WHALER, WHALEBOAT
jail/prison .... BRIG, HULK
Jason's .... ARGO
ladder .... RATLINE
land from .... DEBARK
lateen-sailed .... TARTAN
left-side ...... PORT, LARBOARD
line on side .... PLIMSOLL
list .... MANIFEST
load .... BULK, CARGO,
FREIGHT
logbook .... JOURNAL
lookout point of .... CROW'S
NEST
lowest deck .... ORLOP
made smaller .... RAZEE
master .... CAPTAIN, SKIPPER

master's declaration
.... PROTEST
merchant .... ARGOSY,
TRADER, CARRACK, GALLEON,
GAL(L)IOT
metal plating .... STRAKE
mooring place/slip ...... DOCK,
BERTH, MARINA, ANCHORAGE
mythical/legendary .... ARGO
not sea-going .... HULK
of 1492 .... NINA, PINTA,
SANTA MARIA
of the desert .... CAMEL
officer .... BOS'N, MATE,
MASTER, PURSER, CAPTAIN,
SKIPPER, BOATSWAIN
opening .... HATCH(WAY)
part of ...... BOW, BEAM, BRIG,
HULL, KEEL, MAST, PROW,
HAWSE, SALON, STERN,
WHEEL, BUNKER, GALLEY,
RUDDER, SCUPPER,
(POOP)DECK, STEERAGE,
PROMENADE
passage .... GAT, STEERAGE
passenger, clandestine
.... STOWAWAY
path of .... LANE
peg .... KEVEL
permit .... PRATIQUE
personnel .... CREW,
COMPLEMENT
petty officer .... BOS'N,
BOSUN, BOATSWAIN
pirate .... CORSAIR, FRIGATE,
PRIVATEER
planking .... STRAKE
platform .... DECK, SPONSON
poetic .... BARK, KEEL
pole .... MAST
position finder .... LORAN
provisioner .... CHANDLER
prow's front .... CUTWATER
pull .... KEDGE
pursuit .... CHASER
rear of .... AFT
record .... LOG
rib .... FUTTOCK
rigging .... GEAR, TACKLE
rope .... TYE
sailing .... TARTAN, CLIPPER,
GALLEON, SCHOONER
sails .... KITES
scout .... PINNACE
side opening .... PORTHOLE
side scaffold .... FLAKE
sidewise motion of .... ROLL
single-masted .... TARTAN
sink a .... SCUTTLE
skipper .... MASTER, CAPTAIN
slow .... TUB, BUCKET

small .... LUGGER, TARTAN,
GALLIOT
small, armed .... CUTTER
smoke pipe .... STACK,
FUNNEL
space for provisions
.... LAZARETTO
speed measuring device
.... LOG
square-masted .... BRIG
square-rigged .... CLIPPER
steer a .... CONN, NAVIGATE
stern section .... POOP,
BUTTOCKS
supplier .... CHANDLER
supply .... TENDER, COLLIER,
TRANSPORT
table railing .... FIDDLE
tender .... PINNACE, COCKBOAT
tax on .... TONNAGE
the .... SHE
timber .... SNY, BITT, CARLING,
FUTTOCK, KEELSON, STEMSON
torpedoed May 1915
.... LUSITANIA
track .... WAKE
trading ..... ARGOSY, GALLEON,
GAL(L)IOT
troop .... TRANSPORT
two-masted .... BRIG, GRAB
water in the hold .... BILGE
waterline .... PLIMSOLL
wheel .... HELM
whistle .... HORN, BLAST
windlass .... CAPSTAN
''window'' .... PORTHOLE
with two or more masts
.... SCHOONER
wrecked .... WRACK
shipbuilding peg .... TRUNNEL,
TRE(E)NAIL
shipjack .... SHAD
shipment .... LOAD, CARGO,
LADING, FREIGHT
shipping hazard .... FOG, REEF,
STORM, ICEBERG, TYPHOON
list .... MANIFEST
news .... SAILINGS
ships, collectively .... CRAFT
group of ...... FLEET, FLOTILLA
shipshape ...... NEAT, SNUG, TIDY,
TRIM, TIGHT, TIPTOP,
ORDERLY
shipworm .... BORER, TEREDO
shipwreck goods .... JETSAM,
FLOTSAM
shipwrecked .... SUNK, WRACK,
GROUNDED, MAROONED
person .... CASTAWAY
shire .... COUNTY
shirk .... FUNK, SHUN, AVOID,

DODGE, EVADE, SKULK,
NEGLECT, MALINGER
slang .... GOLDBRICK
shirker .... DODGER, EVADER,
TRUANT, SLACKER,
GOLDBRICK(ER)
shirr .... GATHER
shirt .... SARK, PARKA, CAMISE,
JERSEY, SKIVVY, CHEMISE,
GUERNSEY
broadcloth .... PIMA
closefitting, worn by seamen
.... GUERNSEY
collar stiffener .... STAY
front ...... DICK(E)Y, PLASTRON
front ornament .... STUD,
BUTTON
loose, long-sleeved .... CAMISE
sleeve .... PLAIN, SIMPLE,
HOMESPUN
sleeve button .... CUFFLINK
shittah .... ACACIA
shiv .... KNIFE
shivaree .... SERENADE,
CHARIVARI
shive .... CORK, FRAGMENT,
SPLINTER
shiver ...... BREAK, BURST, QUAKE,
SHAKE, QUIVER, CHITTER,
SHATTER, SHUDDER, TREMBLE,
FRAGMENT, SPLINTER
shivery .... COLD, CHILLY,
BRITTLE, CHILLING
Shkoder .... SCUTARI
shoal .... BANK, HOST, MASS,
REEF, SPIT, CROWD, HORDE,
RIFFLE, SCHOOL, (SAND)BAR,
SHALLOW
shoat .... SHOTE, PIG(LET)
shock .... JAR, BLOW, JOLT, STUN,
BRUNT, SHAKE, APPAL(L),
IMPACT, STROKE, TRAUMA,
DISGUST, HORRIFY, STARTLE,
PARALYZE, SURPRISE,
CONCUSSION
absorber .... CUSHION,
SNUBBER
dog .... POODLE
electric .... SPARK, CHARGE,
ELECTRIFY
emotional .... TRAUMA
gather into a .... STOOK
main .... BRUNT
of grain sheaves .... SHOOK
sudden, brief .... START
tactics .... BLITZKRIEG
therapy drug .... INSULIN,
METRAZOL
to action .... ENERGIZE,
GALVANIZE
shocked .... AGHAST

shocking .... GHASTLY,
OUTRAGEOUS, SCANDALOUS
shod .... SHOED, BOOTED, CALCED
shoddy .... JUNK, SHAM, CHEAP,
SEEDY, SHABBY
shoe .... BOOT, CLOG, PUMP,
BROGAN, BROGUE, GAITER,
LOAFER, OXFORD, STEP-IN,
STOG(E)Y, GALOSH(E),
CLODHOPPER
armor .... SOLLERET
canvas .... SNEAKER,
ESPADRILLE
cloglike .... PATTEN
designer ...... VIVIER, PERUGIA,
FERRAGAMO
fastener .... LATCHET
flap .... TONGUE
form/model .... LAST
front .... VAMP
heavy .... SABOT, GALOSH(E)
high, thick-soled .... BUSKIN
house .... MULE, SLIPPER
implement .... HORN
insertion .... TREE
lace tag .... AGLET
leather .... SUEDE, FOXING
low .... PUMP, SANDAL,
SLIPPER
material ..... KID, CORK, BARK,
METAL, STRAW, SUEDE,
RAFFIA, RUBBER, EELSKIN,
LEATHER, SNAKESKIN,
CROCODILE SKIN
mender .... COBBLER
moccasin-like .... PAC
ornament .... BUCKLE
oxford .... BROGAN
part .... FLAP, HEEL, LACE,
LAST, RAND, SOLE, VAMP,
WELT, THONG, UPPER, EYELET,
(IN)SOLE, INSTEP, TASSEL,
TOECAP, TONGUE
plate .... CALK, TRAMP,
CLAMPER, CRAMPON, CREEPER
repair .... COBBLE
security .... LACING
sheepskin .... PAC
sole addition .... HOBNAIL
sole part .... SHANK
specialist .... SOLER
spike .... CLIMBER
sport .... LOAFER
style .... PUMP, LACED, WEDGE,
SANDAL, BLUCHER, CHOPINE,
PLATFORM, SLING(BACK),
(CHUKKA)BOOT, ORIENTAL
MULE
tennis/sports .... GUMSHOE,
SNEAKER
uppers material .... CLOTH,

FOXING, LASTING, PRUNELLA
walking .... BALMORAL
wing-tipped .... BROGUE
woman's .... PUMP, STEP-IN,
CHOPINE
wooden .... CLOG, GETA,
SABOT, PATTEN
wooden-soled .... CLOG,
SABOT
shoebill .... HERON, STORK
shoelace tip .... TAG, AGLET
shoeless .... UNSHOD
shoemaker .... SNOB, SOLER,
SOUTER, COBBLER,
CORDWAINER
awl of .... ELSEN
block of .... LAST
need of .... WELT
patron saint of .... CRISPIN
shoes .... PUMPS, FOOTGEAR,
FOOTWEAR
brown .... TANS
for vehicle .... BRAKE LINING
golf .... CREEPERS
open-heeled .... STEP-INS
patent-leather .... SHINERS
rubber .... GUMS, SNEAKERS
work .... BOOTS, BROGANS
shoestring .... LACE(T)
shofar/shophar .... (RAM'S) HORN
shogun .... TYCOON, GOVERNOR
Sholem, author .... ASCH
shoo ...... GIT, SCAT, SCRAM, BEAT
IT, BEGONE, GET OUT, GET
LOST, DRIVE(AWAY)
shooi .... JAEGER
shoo-in ...... CINCH, (SURE)WINNER
shook .... UPSET, SHAKEN
shoot .... BUD, HIT, ROD, CAST,
CHIT, DART, EMIT, FILM, FIRE,
GROW, HURL, KILL, TEAR,
TWIG, SPRIG, THROW, WHISK,
PROPEL, SPROUT, TWINGE,
BURGEON, EXPLODE, PROJECT,
DETONATE, FLAGELLUM
a bullet into .... PLUG
a disk .... DISCUS
a marble .... TAW
down ...... KILL, SLAY, RIDDLE,
GUN DOWN
firearm .... FIRE
forth .... BURGEON
from cover ..... SNIPE, AMBUSH
game for food .... POT
grafting .... (S)CION
lichen .... FROND
long, flexible .... VIMEN
plant .... BUD, BINE, SLIP,
(S)CION, SPEAR, VIMEN,
RUNNER, STOLON, TENDRIL,
THALLUS

root/stem .... TILLER,
RAT(T)OON
scene again .... RETAKE
seaweed .... FROND
strawberry .... RUNNER
threadlike .... FLAGELLUM
up .... GROW, SPROUT
young, tender .... TENDRIL
shoot-out .... GUNFIGHT
shooter .... TAW, ALLEY, MARBLE
arrow .... AMOR
bow and arrow .... ARCHER,
BOWMAN
expert .... MARKSMAN
infantry .... RIFLEMAN
shooting .... FIRING, GUNFIRE,
KILLING
iron GAT, GUN, ROD, RIFLE,
PISTOL, CARBINE, FIREARM,
REPEATER, REVOLVER,
DERRINGER
match .... TIR, DUEL, SKEET
pain .... SPASM, TWINGE,
TWITCH
star .... BOLIDE, LEONID,
FIREBALL, METEOR(OID)
shoots .... BROWSE
shop .... MART, MILL, STORE,
BAZAAR, MARKET, PARLOR,
FACTORY, BOUTIQUE,
EMPORIUM
girl .... GRISETTE
nameplate of .... FACIA
shoplifter .... THIEF, BOOSTER,
STEALER
shopman/shopkeeper .... CLERK,
DEALER, MERCHANT,
RETAILER
shopping .... BUY(ING), EMPTION,
PURCHASE
aid .... CART, BASKET
center .... MALL, PLAZA,
MARKET(PLACE)
shoptalk .... SLANG, JARGON
shoran .... RADAR
part of .... SHORT, RANGE,
NAVIGATION
shore .... SAND, BANK, PROP,
BEACH, RIVAGE, SEASIDE,
COAST(LINE), WATERSIDE
along .... LITTORAL
bird .... RAIL, RUFF, SNIPE,
STILT, AVOCET, CURLEW,
PLOVER, DOTT(E)REL,
DOWITCHER, SANDPIPER
dinner attire .... BIBS
dinner item .... ROE
feature .... SAND
of the ..... COASTAL, LITTORAL
poetic .... STRAND
short ...... LOW, SHY, CURT, BRIEF,

BREVI, SCANT, ABRUPT,
CONCISE, FRIABLE, LACKING
air/aria .... ARIETTA
and fat .... PODGY, PUDGY,
SQUAT, TUBBY
and not so sweet .... CURT
and plumply round
.... ROLYPOLY
and stout .... SQUAB
and thick ..... PODGY, CHUNKY
branch .... SNAG
bristly haircut .... CREW
cake .... BISCUIT
combining form .... BRACHY
comedy .... SKIT, SKETCH
dowel .... PEG
drink .... DRAM, SNORT,
QUICKIE
fibers removed in combing
.... NOILS
for .... IN BRIEF
for a physical .... EXAM
for Augustus .... GUS
for Henry .... HANK
for throat infection ...... STREP
ln .... BRIEFLY
in loan money ...... STRINGENT
jacket .... ETON, BOLERO,
REEFER
laughs .... HOS
-lived ...... FLEETING, FLITTING,
DECIDUOUS, EPHEMERAL,
TRANSIENT, TRANSITORY
-lived Arab confederation
.... UAR
musical passage ..... MORCEAU
-necked duck .... TEAL
of .... LACKING, WANTING
order .... TOAST, OMELET
overcoat .... REEFER
poem .... LAY, RONDEL
projecting part .... STUB
race .... DASH, SPRINT
reminder .... MEMO
rest .... NAP, SIESTA
ride .... SPIN
_____ (scant consideration)
.... SHRIFT
seller .... BEAR
shrift .... ABRUPT, REBUFF
skirt .... MINI
slang .... SHY
snort .... SHOT
sock .... ANKLET
song ..... ODE, DITTY, ARIETTA,
ARIETTE
sound .... SNAP
spoken .... CURT, BRIEF,
TERSE, LACONIC
stature .... DWARFISM
story .... CONTE

story: var. .... NOVELA
supply, in .... SCARCE
swim .... DIP
tail .... SCUT
-tempered .... TESTY
term .... TEMPORARY
time .... TRICE
visit .... CALL
wave .... PERM
-winded .... PUFFY, PURSY
window drapery ..... VALANCE
shortage .... LACK, NEED, DEFICIT,
                  DEFICIENCY
shortchange .... CON, GYP, CHEAT
shortcoming ...... FAULT, DEFECT,
    FAILING, WEAKNESS, WEAK
                  POINT
shorten .... BOB, CUT, LOP, CHOP,
    CLIP, CROP, DOCK, ELIDE,
    PRUNE, REEVE, DIGEST,
    REDUCE, ABRIDGE, CURTAIL,
    CONDENSE, ABBREVIATE
mast/bowsprit .... REEF
shortened .... CUT, CONCISE,
        CURTATE, ABSTRACT
shortening .... FAT, OIL, LARD,
             OLEO, SUET
shortest route to anywhere
    .... BEELINE
shortfall .... LACK, DEFICIT
shorthand .... GREGG, PITMAN,
    STENOTYPE, STENOGRAPHY
character .... POT, HOOK
girl .... STENO
sign .... PHONOGRAM
shortly .... ANON, SOON, RUDELY,
              ABRUPTLY
shorts .... BRIEFS, TROUSERS,
            LEFT-OVERS
shortsighted .... MYOPY, MYOPIC,
          NEARSIGHTED
person .... MYOPE
shorty .... RUNT
Shoshonean Indian .... UTE,
    HOPI, OTOE, P(A)IUTE,
          COMANCHE
Shostakovich, composer
    .... DMITRI
shot ...... TRY, BALL, DOSE, DRINK,
    GUESS, RANGE, SCOPE, SHELL,
    BULLET, PELLET, FLECKED,
    LANGREL, LANGRAGE,
          MARKSMAN
and shell .... AMMO,
        AMMUNITION
give it a .... GO, TRY, FLING
of booze .... SLUG, JIGGER
of liquid into the body
    .... INJECTION
that hits target .... CLOUT
shote .... SHOAT, PIG(LET)

shotgun sport .... SKEET
shoulder .... BEAR, PUSH, CARRY,
    EPAUL, ASSUME, JOSTLE,
    SCAPULA, SUPPORT
armor .... PAULDRON
belt .... BALDRIC
blade .... SCAPULA
blade part .... ACROMION
bone .... HUMERUS
combining form .... OMO
muscle .... DELTOID
of the .... ALAR, SCAPULAR
ornament .... EPAULET(TE)
pack .... KNAPSACK
protection for .... PAULDRON
road's .... BERM(E)
wrap .... SCARF, SHAWL, STOLE
shoulders, covering for .... NUBIA
draw up .... SHRUG
fur piece .... PALATINE
of the .... HUMERAL
squared .... ERECT
shout .... CRY, CALL, ROAR, YELL,
    YOHO, CHEER, WHOOP,
    HOLLER, SCREAM
down .... SILENCE
of derision .... HOOT
of greeting .... HULLO
of joy/approval .... OLE, HEAR,
    VIVA, BRAVO, HUZZA, HURRAH
shove ...... JAR, JOG, BUNT, CRAM,
    PUSH, ELBOW, FORCE, NUDGE,
    HUSTLE, JOSTLE, THRUST
off .... LEAVE, DEPART, BEAT
    IT, HIT THE ROAD
shovel .... DIP, VAN, LADLE,
    SCOOP, SPADE, DIG(GER),
          TROWEL
baker's .... PEEL
shovelhead .... SHARK, STURGEON
show .... PLAY, FLASH, GUIDE,
    PROVE, SIGHT, APPEAR,
    ESCORT, EVINCE, EXPOSE,
    PARADE, DISPLAY, EXHIBIT,
    PAGEANT, MANIFEST,
        PRETENSE
amusement .... GRIN, TEHEE
anger .... FUME
bill .... PLACARD
biz assn. .... ASCAP
biz award .... OBIE, EMMY,
          OSCAR
biz report, famed .... STIX-
    NIX-HIX-PIX
contrition .... RUE
empty .... FARCE
excessive fondness .... DOTE
fatigue .... NOD
gumption .... DARE
hit .... SMASH
hypocritical .... MUMMERY

in .... USHER
in a way .... COME IN THIRD
in law .... PLEAD, ALLEGE
indecision .... WAVER, FALTER,
          VACILLATE
likeness .... MIRROR
mercy .... SPARE
of embarrassment ..... SQUIRM
off .... SWANK, FLAUNT,
          PARADE
opener .... ACT ONE
partiality .... SIDE
peep .... RAREE
pleasure .... SMILE
restraint .... PLAY IT COOL
scorn .... SNEER
stage .... REVUE, FOLLIES
street .... RAREE
up ...... COME, APPEAR, ARRIVE
vain .... POMP
water .... AQUACADE
shower .... BATH, HAIL, POUR,
    PARTY, SLEET, SPRAY, PEPPER,
    FALLOUT, SCATTER,
    RAIN(FALL), SPRINKLE
fall in a .... CASCADE
fine, mistlike .... DRIZZLE
kind of .... BABY, BRIDAL
of meteors .... LEONID,
          ANDROMID
sudden .... BRASH
sudden heavy rain .... SPATE
showing .... DISPLAY
good taste .... DECOROUS
sorrow .... PENITENT
showman, famous .... ROSE,
    BARNUM, CARROLL, RINGLING,
        ZIEGFELD
showmanship .... STYLE,
        FANFARE
show-off .... HOTSHOT
showpiece .... SAMPLE, EXAMPLE,
        EXHIBIT
showroom model .... DEMO
showy .... ARTY, LOUD, GAUDY,
    FLASHY, FLORID, GARISH,
    ORNATE, SWANKY, TAWDRY,
    DASHING, COLORFUL,
    FLAUNTING, FLAMBOYANT,
        OSTENTATIOUS
display .... BLAZON, SPLURGE
display in dress ...... FRIPPERY
display of daring .... DASH,
        BRAVURA
gaieties .... GAUDS
pretense .... TINSEL
show .... PAGEANT(RY),
    SPECTACLE, EXTRAVAGANZA
style .... FLAIR
thing, worthless .... TRUMPERY
shrapnel .... SHELL, FRAGMENT

shred .... BIT, DAG, RAG, RIP, SNIP, TEAR, WISP, GRATE, SCRAP, SPECK, STRIP, TRACE, TATTER, FRAZZLE, MAMMOCK, VESTIGE, FRAGMENT
shredded cabbage .... SLAW
shrew .... ERD, HAG, NAG, HARPY, SCOLD, VIXEN, VIRAGO, BELDAM(E), FISHWIFE, TERMAGANT
domineering .... HENPECKER
like .... SORICINE
mouse .... HYRAX
name of Shakespeare's .... KATE
sister of Shakespeare's .... BIANCA
shrewd .... SLY, FOXY, KEEN, WILY, ACUTE, CAGEY, CANNY, SHARP, SMART, ARTFUL, ASTUTE, CLEVER, CUNNING, PRUDENT, SAGACIOUS
person .... FOX, CUTIE, SMOOTHIE
shrewdness .... ACUMEN
shrewish .... DITCHY, CRANKY, NAGGING, IRASCIBLE, TERMAGANT
shriek .... CRY, YELL, SCREAM, SQUEAL, SCREECH
shrieve .... SHERIFF
shrift .... ABSOLUTION
shrike .... BIRD, OSCINE, WOODCHAT
shrill .... PIPY, NASAL, SHARP, STRIDENT, HIGH-PITCHED
sound/voice ..... REEDY, SKIRL, PIPING, SCREAM, SHRIEK, SQUEAL, TREBLE
shrimp .... RUNT, MACRURAN, CRUSTACEAN
appendage .... UROPOD
covering .... MAIL
kin .... GRIBBLE
like crustacean .... PRAWN
shrine .... TOMB, ALTAR, DAGOBA, GROTTO, TEMPLE, MARTYRY, TABERNACLE
for relics .... FERETORY, RELIQUARY
visitor .... PILGRIM
Shrine bowl team .... EAST, WEST
shrink .... COWER, WINCE, WIZEN, CRINGE, FLINCH, RECOIL, REDUCE, SHRIVEL, CONTRACT
from .... FUNK, RECOIL
shrinkage .... LOSS
shrinkee .... ANALYSAND
shrinker, head ...... PSYCHIATRIST
shrinking .... SHY, TIMID

one .... CRINGER
violet .... MOUSE
shrive .... ABSOLVE
shrivel .... CURL, SEAR, WIZEN, SHRINK, WITHER, MUMMIFY, WRINKLE
shroff .... BANKER, MONEYCHANGER
Shropshire .... SALOP
river .... SEVERN
shroud .... PALL, VEIL, CLOAK, COVER, SHEET, SCREEN, CEREMENT
Shrove Tuesday ...... MARDI GRAS
Shroyer role .... ENOS
shrub .... BUSH, ALDER, ELDER, GORSE, LILAC, PLANT, SALAL, SENNA, SUMAC, ALTHEA, LAUREL, SMILAX, SPIREA, BRAMBLE, RHODORA, TREELET, MAGNOLIA, OLEASTER, MISTLETOE, CASCARILLA
aromatic .... MINT, BERGAMOT, LAVENDER, ROSEMARY
bean family .... BROOM, RETEM
berry .... HOLLY, COFFEE, CURRANT
birch family .... HAZEL
bushy .... TOD, CADE, SAVIN
climbing .... LIANA, CLEMATIS, AMPELOPSIS
dwarfed .... BONSAI
ericaceous .... SHEEP-LAUREL
evergreen ..... YEW, ILEX, TITI, ERICA, FURZE, HEATH, SALAL, SAVIN, TOYON, LAUREL, MYRTLE, JASMINE, JUNIPER, CAMELLIA, OLEANDER, OLEASTER, LAURUSTINE
fence .... HEDGE(ROW)
fiber source .... HEMP, JUTE, SISAL
flowering .... ITEA, LILAC, AZALEA, JASMINE, SYRINGA, GARDENIA, HIBISCUS, MAGNOLIA, OLEANDER, MOCK ORANGE
genus .... EVEA, ITEA, OLEA, RHUS, ERICA, SPIREA, LANTANA, SYRINGA
grape family .... AMPELOPSIS
grown flat .... ESPALIER
heath family .... KALMIA
holly family .... ILEX
honeysuckle .... WEIGELA, VIBURNUM
legume family .... INDIGO
madder family .... COFFEE
mallow family ..... ALTH(A)EA,

HIBISCUS, HOLLYHOCK
mint family .... ROSEMARY
olive ..... OLEA, LILAC, PRIVET, JASMIN(E)
Pacific Coast .... SALAL
pea family ...... LOTOS, LOTUS, CASSIA, MIMOSA, LABURNUM, MESQUIT(E), WISTERIA
pepper family .... KAVA, CUBEB
poisonous .... SUMAC(H), OLEANDER
prickly .... CAPER, CHICO, BRAMBLE
rose family .... SPIR(A)EA, HARDHACK
rubber source .... GUAYULE
spiny .... CHICO, FURZE, GORSE
spurge family ..... CASCARILLA
stunted .... SCRUB, BONSAI
tea family .... CAMELLIA
tropical .... INGA, HENNA, ABELIA, JASMIN(E), LANTANA, HIBISCUS, JESSAMINE
shrubbery .... TOD, BRIER, GARDEN, BOSCAGE, COPPICE
shrubby .... FRUTICOSE, FRUTESCENT
shrubs, clump of .... SCRUB
collectively .... SHRUBBERY
shrug .... GESTURE
one's shoulders .... DISLIKE, DISAPPROVE
shuck .... POD, HUSK, SHELL
shudder .... QUAKE, SHAKE, QUIVER, SHIVER, TREMOR, TREMBLE
shuffle .... MIX, DRAG, EVADE, SCUFF, SHIFT, TRICK, FIDGET, JUMBLE, RIFFLE, SWITCH, DECEIVE, SHAMBLE
shuffler .... COOT, DUCK
Shufu .... KASHGAR
Shumagin islander .... ALEUT
shun .... AVOID, DODGE, ELUDE, EVADE, IGNORE
shunt ...... SHIFT, DIVERT, SWITCH, TURN OFF, SIDETRACK
shush .... HIST, HUSH, QUIET, SILENCE
Shushan .... SUSA
shut .... BAR, FOLD, CLOSE, SECURED
in .... PENT(UP), CONFINE, INVALID
out .... BAN, BLANKED, EXCLUDE, OSTRACIZE
up ..... MEW, CLOSET, IMMURE, IMPRISON
with force .... SLAM
shutdown .... END, CLOSURE,

STOPPAGE

shuteye .... SLEEP

shutout .... (TOTAL)DEFEAT

shutter .... SHADE, SLIDE,
BLIND(S), GRILLE, LOUVER,
PERSIENNES

shutterbug .... PHOTOGRAPHER

shuttle .... SWING, SEESAW,
TEETER

bobbin/spool .... PIRN

thread .... WEFT

shuttlecock .... BIRD

shy .... COY, JIB, MIM, BALK,
WARY, CHARY, SHORT, START,
TIMID, DEMURE, MODEST,
RECOIL, BASHFUL, LACKING,
RESERVED, RETIRING,
TIMOROUS, VERECUND,
DIFFIDENT

and cautious .... TIMID

and fearful .... TIMOROUS

and mistrustful .... SUSPICIOUS

and modest .... DEMURE

off .... DUCK, DODGE

Shylock .... USURER,
MONEYLENDER

daughter of .... JESSICA

money of .... DUCATS

shylocking .... USURY

shyster .... PETTIFOGGER

sialid .... INSECT, DOBSONFLY

Siam .... THAILAND

siamang .... GIBBON

Siamese. See also **Thailand**

capital .... AYUDHYA,
BANGKOK, THONBURI

coin .... ATT, BAHT, TICAL

dynasty .... CHAKRI

isthmus .... KRA

king ...... MAHIDOL, MONGKUT,
ADULYADEJ, PRACHATIPOK,
CHULALONGKORN

kingdom capital
.... CHIENGMAI

measure ...... KUP, SOK, NGAN,
NIOU, SISTI

monetary unit .... BAHT, TICAL

premier .... THANARAT

queen .... SIRIKIT

river .... MENAM, CHAUPAYA

tongue .... LAO, TAI

tribe .... MEO

twins, one of ..... ENG, CHANG

weight .... PAI, KLAM, KLOM,
TICAL

Sian is capital of .... SHENSI

sib .... SISTER, BROTHER,
KIN(SMAN), RELATIVE

Sibelius, composer .... JEAN

work ..... FINLANDIA, SWAN OF
TUONELA

Siberian .... VOGUL, SAMOYED(E)

antelope .... SAIGA

city .... OMSK, TOMSK

dog .... SAMOYED(E)

forests .... TAIGA

fur .... CALABAR, CALABER

ibex .... TEK

leopard .... OUNCE

mountains .... ALTAI

native .... YUIT, TATAR,
YAKUT, KIRGIZ

peninsula .... TAIMIR,
KAMCHATKA

plain .... STEPPE

region .... OMSK, TA(R)TARY

river .... OB, AMUR, LENA,
TOBOL, IRTISH, KOLIMA,
YENISEI

sheep .... ARGALI

squirrel .... CALABAR,
CALABER, MINIVER

tent .... YURT

warehouse .... ETAPE

wasteland .... STEPPE

wild cat .... MANUL

windstorm .... BURAN

sibilance/sibilate .... HISS

sibling .... KIN, SIS(TER), BROTHER

sibyl .... WITCH, ORACLE, SEERESS,
SORCERESS, FORTUNETELLER

sibylline .... ORACULAR

sign .... OMEN

sic .... SO, SUCH, THUS, ATTACK,
INCITE, JUST SO, RIGHTLY

sicca .... SEAL

siccative .... DRIER, DRYING

Sicilian .... SICANIAN, TRINACRIAN

cape .... PASSERO

capital .... PALERMO

city/town .... ENNA, GELA,
NOTO, MODICA, RAGUSA,
CATANIA, MARSALA,
MAZZARO, TRAPANI,
CORLEONE, SYRACUSE,
VITTORIA, AGRIGENTO

code of silence .... OMERTA

evergreen .... MAQUIS

gulf .... CASTELLAMMARE

hero .... ENTELLUS

inhabitant, legendary
.... CYCLOPS

king .... RENE

landmark .... ETNA

resort .... ENNA

river .... SALSO, BELICE,
SIMETO

seaport .... MARSALA,
MESSINA, MILAZZO, PALERMO

secret society .... MAFIA

shotgun .... LUPARA

sizzler .... ETNA

strait .... SICILY, MESSINA

volcano .... (A)ETNA

whirlpool .... CHARYBDIS

wine .... MARSALA

sick .... ILL, AILING, ATTACK,
UNWELL, UNSOUND,
NAUSEOUS, NAUSEATED,
SURFEITED, INDISPOSED

and tired .... FED UP

of .... BORED

person .... INVALID, PATIENT

sickbed, of a .... CLINICAL

sicken .... AIL, AFFLICT, NAUSEATE

sickening .... GROSS, NASTY,
DISGUSTING

sickle .... HOOK, SIVE, SCYTHE,
BUSHWHACKER

shaped .... FALCATE

sickly .... WAN, PALE, FAINT,
AILING, LANGUID

sickness .... MALADY, NAUSEA,
AILMENT, DISEASE, ILLNESS,
COMPLAINT

Sid .... CAESAR

Caesar's dog .... CONUS

Caesar's partner ...... IMOGENE
COCA

Caesar's wife .... FLORENCE

Siddhartha .... BUDDHA

side .... EDGE, PART, VIEW, FACET,
FLANK, ASPECT, BORDER,
FACTION, SURFACE, POSITION

arm(s) .... SWORD, DAGGER,
PISTOL, BAYONET, REVOLVER

by one's .... NEAR, CLOSE

by side .... BESIDE, ABREAST,
ALONGSIDE, COLLATERAL

dish .... SLAW, SOUP, SALAD,
ENTREE, TRIMMING,
ENTREMETS

effect .... REACTION

hill .... SLOPE

interest .... HOBBY, AVOCATION

meat .... BACON

of a .... LATERAL

pain .... STITCH

person's .... LEFT, RIGHT

portion .... RASHER

road .... BYWAY

trip .... SALLY, EXCURSION

view .... PROFILE

with .... AGREE, ALINE

sideboard .... CABINET, CREDENZA

sideburns .... WHISKERS, MUTTON
CHOPS

sidecar .... COCKTAIL

sidekick ...... PAL, CHUM, BUDDY,
FRIEND, PARTNER, ALTER EGO

of Red Ryder .... LITTLE
BEAVER

sideline .... BENCH, BY-WORK

sidelong look .... GLANCE, SQUINT
sidereal .... STARRY, STELLAR
siderite .... IRON(ORE), METEORITE
sidero, as combining form
.... IRON, STAR
sides, _____ (everywhere) .... ON
ALL
unequal .... SCALENE
sideslip .... SKID
sidesplitter ...... JOKE, LAUGHTER
sidesplitting .... FUNNY, HEARTY,
CONVULSIVE
sidestep .... SHUN, AVOID, DODGE,
EVADE, CIRCUMVENT
sidetrack .... TURN, AVERT,
DETER, SHUNT, DIVERT,
SIDING, SWITCH
sidewalk .... FOOTPATH,
PAVEMENT, BANQUETTE
entrepreneur .... ARTIST,
BEGGAR, HAWKER, VENDOR,
NEWSBOY, PEDDLER
sideways, move .... EDGE, SKID,
SIDLE
walker .... CRAB
sidewinder .... CROTALUS,
RATTLESNAKE
sidewise .... ASKANCE, LATERAL
move .... SKEW, SIDLE
siding .... SPUR, SHINGLE,
PANELING, CLAPBOARD
sidle .... JIB, EDGE, SKEW, FLANK,
SLITHER
Sidon's name now .... SAIDA
siecle .... AGE, ERA, PERIOD,
CENTURY
siege ...... BLOCKADE, CORDONING,
INVESTMENT
lay .... BESET, INVEST, SUBJECT
TO
siegers' shelter .... CAT, MANTLET
Siegfried .... SIGURD
follower .... NIBELUNG
Line .... LIMES, WESTWALL
sword of .... BALMUNG
wife of .... KRIEMHILD
sienna .... PIGMENT
color .... REDDISH-BROWN
Sierra .... LEONE, MADRE, RANGE,
NEVADA, PINTADO, KINGFISH
fish resembling .... MACKEREL
Leone capital .... FREETOWN
mountain .... DANA
Nevada fog .... POGONIP
Nevada lake .... TAHOE
Nevada peak .... WHITNEY,
MULHACEN
siesta .... NAP, REST, SNOOZE
sieur .... SIR
sieve ...... LAWN, LAUNE, BOLTER,
FILTER, RIDDLE, SCREEN,

SIFTER, CRIBBLE, TROMMEL,
COLANDER, STRAINER
coal, ore .... TROMMEL
like a .... ETHMOID
sift .... BOLT, SORT, WEIGH,
FILTER, SCREEN, WINNOW,
SEPARATE
dialect .... REE
sifter .... SIEVE, BOLTER,
COLANDER, STRAINER
siftings .... DREGS, RESIDUE
sigh ...... SOB, LONG, MOAN, SOUF,
SOUGH, YEARN, MURMUR,
SUSPIRE
sight .... AIM, EYE, ESPY, LOOK,
VIEW, SCENE, VISTA, VISION,
DISPLAY, GLIMPSE, PICTURE,
SPECTACLE
by .... VISUAL(LY)
colloquial ...... UGLY, EYESORE
come into .... LOOM, APPEAR
gun .... BEAD
of .... OCULAR, VISUAL
sightless .... BLIND
sightly .... COMELY
sightsee .... TOUR
sightseer .... TOURIST, VISITING
FIREMAN
sightseeing .... RUBBERNECKING
sigil .... SEAL, SIGNET
sigmoid .... ESS, SIGMATE
sign .... INK, MARK, NEON, OMEN,
BADGE, INDEX, TOKEN,
TRACE, EMBLEM, SYMBOL,
EARMARK, GESTURE, INDICIA,
PORTENT, VESTIGE, SYMPTOM,
EVIDENCE, INDICATION
affirmative .... NOD
arithmetical .... PLUS, MINUS
away .... CONVEY
Blue Eagle .... NRA
display ..... PLACARD, SHINGLE
handicapped person's
.... WHEELCHAIR
homage .... BOW, KNEEL,
CURTSY, SALAAM,
GENUFLECTION
in magic .... SIGIL
in music .... BAR, SLUR,
NEUM(E), PRESA, SEGNO,
STAFF, (TREBLE)CLEF
language .... AMESLAN
language science
.... SEMIOLOGY
of a hit .... SRO
a skunk .... ODOR
assent .... NOD
disapproval .... SHRUG
pleasure .... GRIN, SMILE
possession .... APOSTROPHE
sorrow .... RED EYES

omission .... CARET
road/street .... STOP, ARROW,
FLARE, YIELD
up .... HIRE, JOIN, EMPLOY,
ENGAGE, ENLIST, ENROL(L)
signal .... CUE, BUZZ, FLAG, SIGN,
WARN, ALARM, ARROW,
TOKEN, WIGWAG, NOTABLE,
STRIKING
actor's .... CUE
assembly .... REVEILLE
bell .... GONG
board .... SHINGLE
danger .... SIREN, SYMPTOM,
RED FLAG, RED LIGHT
entrance/exit .... SENNET
eye .... WINK
flag .... ABLE, JACK, WAIF,
ENSIGN
for parley .... CHAMADE,
WHITE FLAG
Indian .... SMOKE
light .... FLARE, BEACON
lights out .... TAPS
of quarantine .... YELLOW
FLAG, YELLOW JACK
railroad .... FUSEE
retirement .... TAPS, CURFEW
retreat .... CHAMADE
seance .... TAP
set .... CODE, LORAN
stage .... CUE, SENNET
to attract attention .... PST
tone, short high-pitched
.... PIP
warning .... WINK, ALARM,
ALERT, SIREN, CAUTION, RED
LIGHT
signaling apparatus ...... BEACON,
HOWLER, BLINKER, FOGHORN,
SEMAPHORE
system of .... SEMAPHORE
trumpet ..... SHOFAR, SHOPHAR
signatory .... CO-MAKER, (CO-
)SIGNER
signature .... HAND, SEAL,
AUTOGRAPH
faked .... FORGERY
flourish .... PARAPH, SCROLL
historic .... RELEE
in radio/musical .... THEME
of a sort .... THUMBMARK,
CRISS-CROSS
slang ..... FIST, JOHN HANCOCK
signboard .... SHINGLE
signet .... SEAL, SIGIL
significance ...... VALUE, WEIGHT,
MOMENT, MEANING,
IMPORT(ANCE)
significant .... TELLING,
EVENTFUL, IMPORTANT,

MOMENTOUS, MEANINGFUL
signify .... BODE, MEAN, SHOW, IMPLY, DENOTE, INDICATE
Signoret, actress .... SIMONE
signpost .... CLUE, GUIDE, HERMA
signs, of .... SEMIOTIC
Sigurd .... SIEGFRIED
father of .... REGIN
victim of .... FAFNIR
Sikh religion founder .... NANAK
Sikkim capital .... GANGTOK
inhabitants .... NEPALESE
king .... CHOGYAL
queen .... GYALMO
woman's dress .... KHO
Sikorsky, airplane builder
.... IGOR
silage .... FODDER
Silas Marner author .... ELIOT
ward of .... EPPIE
silence .... GAG, LULL, OYEZ, PEACE, APHONY, MUFFLE, (S)HUSH, (W)HIST, STIFLE, REPRESS, MUTE(NESS), THROTTLE, STILLNESS, QUIET(UDE)
slang .... SHUT UP
silencer ...... GAG, MUTE, HUSHER, MUZZLE, MUFFLER
judge's .... GAVEL
silent ...... MUM, MUTE(D), QUIET, STILL, TACIT, WHIST, INACTIVE, NOISELESS, SOUNDLESS
actor .... MIMER
habitually .... TACITURN
it is .... TACET
killer .... HYPERTENSION
one .... CLAM
Silenus .... DEITY, SATYR
foster son of .... BACCHUS, DIONYSUS
Silesia .... LINEN, SLASK
silex .... FLINT, QUARTZ, SILICA
silhouette ...... SHADOW, OUTLINE, PORTRAIT
silica .... MICA, SAND, SILEX, QUARTZ, MINERAL
deposit .... SINTER
silicate ...... MICA, ESTER, CERITE, EPIDOTE, TREMOLITE
silique .... POD
silk ...... TULLE, FABRIC, ALAMODE
and cotton cloth ..... EOLIENNE
and wool cloth .... BARATHEA, EOLIENNE
cloth, damask-like .... LAMPAS
cloth for ribbons, etc.
.... SARCENET
cloth, striped .... TABARET
coarse .... TUSSA(H), TUSSAR,

TUSSER
cocoon .... BAVE
color of raw .... ECRU
corded .... REPP, REP(S), FAILLE, OTTOMAN, PADUASOY
cotton (tree) .... CEIBA, KAPOK
crinkled cloth of .... CREPE
fabric .... GROS, CAFFA, MOIRE, PEKIN, QIANA, SATIN, SURAH, VOILE, BAREGE, MADRAS, PONGEE, SENDAL, SAMITE, VELVET, TAFFETA, VELOUR(S), SHANTUNG, CHARMEUSE, MESSALINE
fiber .... FLOSS
filament .... BRIN
fine, thin .... SARCENET, SARSENET
finely woven ...... LANSDOWNE
floss .... SLEAVE
for mourning .... ALMAS
glossy .... SATIN, TAFFETA, LUSTRING, LUTESTRING
hat .... TILE, TOPPER
heavy .... GROS
hit the .... PARACHUTE
knitted .... JERSEY
like .... SERICEOUS
lining material ...... SARCENET, SARSENET
lustrous .... PANNE
net .... MALINE(S)
netting .... TULLE
patterned .... MOIRE
prefix meaning .... SERIC
producing moth
.... AILANTHUS
raw .... GREGE, MARABOU
ribbed .... REPP, REP(S), FAILLE
ribbonlike .... GIMP
screen print .... SERIGRAPH
sheer ...... VOILE, CHIFFON
shreds .... NOIL
source of .... ERIA, COCOON, AILANTHUS
-stocking .... WHIG, ELITE, ELEGANT, WEALTHY
synthetic .... NYLON, ORLON, RAYON, DACRON
taffeta with stripes ..... TABBY
thread .... TRAM, FLOSS, SLEAVE
thread, twisted .... TRAM, FLOSS
thread, very fine quality
.... ORGANZINE
threadmaker .... THROWSTER
tree .... SIRIS, MIMOSA
twilled .... ALMA, SERGE, SURAH
twisted .... ROVE

veil .... TULLE
waste .... KNUB, NOIL, FLOSS, FRISON
watered .... MOIRE, TABBY, MOREEN
weight .... PARI
with metal threads .... LAME
with raised design
.... BROCADE
Silkeborg Museum site
.... JUTLAND
silken .... SOFT, SERIC, GLOSSY, SMOOTH, ELEGANT
silkworm .... ERI(A), BOMBYX, TUSSA(H), TUSSER, TUSSORE
cocoon covering .... FLOSS
covering .... COCOON
disease .... UJI
food/leaves .... MULBERRY, AILANTHUS
moth .... BOMBYCID, CECROPIA
raising .... SERICULTURE
silky .... SOFT, SLEEK, SATINY, SMOOTH, LUSTROUS, SERICEOUS
furred animal .... TAMARIN, MARMOSET, CHINCHILLA
sill .... FRAME, LEDGE, SHELF
counterpart .... LINTEL
projection .... DRIP
sillabub ...... DESSERT, BEVERAGE
siller .... MONEY
sillier .... INANER
silliness .... INANITY
Sills, singer .... BEVERLY
silly .... DAFT, ANILE, DAFFY, INANE, KOOKY, SAPPY, ABSURD, KOOKIE, ASININE, FATUOUS, FOOLISH, PUERILE, IMBECILE, SLAP-HAPPY
language .... BOMBAST
one .... GOOSE
smile .... SIMPER
silo .... BIN, PIT, CRIB, TOWER
silt ...... WASH, LOESS, ALLUVIUM, SEDIMENT
silurid .... CATFISH
silva .... WOODS
silver .... COIN, MONEY, SYCEE, SILLER, ARGENT(UM)
abbreviation .... STER
alloy .... ALBATA, BILLON
containing .... LUNAR, ARGENTOL
dollar: sl. .... CARTWHEEL
fluoride .... TACHIOL
fox fur .... PLATINA
gilded .... VERMEIL
in alchemy .... LUNA
ingot .... SYCEE, BULLION
lacework .... FILIGREE

like/of .... ARGENTINE
oxidizer .... TARNISHER
screen .... CINEMA, MOVIES
sulfide .... ARGENTITE
symbol .... AG
telluride .... HESSITE
-tongued .... ELOQUENT
-tongued person .... ORATOR
unminted ...... SYCEE, BULLION
wire work .... FILIGREE
Silver Age writer .... JUVENAL,
            MARTIAL, TACITUS
State .... NEVADA
silverfish .... SARGO, TARPON
Silverheels' role .... TONTO
silverside(s) .... MINNOW, TINKER,
                 GRUNION
silverware decoration
.... GADROON
silverweed .... TANSY
silvery .... ARGENT(INE)
silviculture .... FORESTRY
simar .... ROBE, JACKET
Simenon, author .... GEORGES
detective .... MAIGRET
novel .... MAIGRET
simian .... APE, MONKEY
astronaut .... BONNY,
                ASTROMONK
similar ...... AKIN, NEAR, (A)LIKE,
     CLOSE, AGNATE, SUCH(AS),
                ANALOGOUS
combining form .... HOMEO
similarity .... ANALOGY,
         LIKENESS, SAMENESS
similarly .... LIKEWISE
simile .... METAPHOR
similitude .... IMAGE, DOUBLE,
         LIKENESS, FACSIMILE
simmer .... COOK, FUME, STEW,
      BROOD, SEETHE, (PAR)BOIL
down .... COOL, SUBSIDE
simnel .... BISCUIT, FRUITCAKE
simoleon .... DOLLAR
Simon .... PETER, APOSTLE
pure .... REAL, AMATEUR,
                 GENUINE
the overseer .... LEGREE
Simon's acquaintance .... PIEMAN
sporty slob .... OSCAR
simoom/simoon .... WIND,
                SAMIEL, TEBBAD
simp .... DOLT, SIMPLETON
simper .... SMILE, SMIRK
simple .... BARE, EASY, MERE,
     SNAP, CLEAR, GREEN, LOWLY,
      NAIVE, PLAIN, COMMON,
     HOMELY, SINGLE, ARTLESS,
                 NATURAL
in law .... ABSOLUTE
machine .... AXLE, LEVER,

SCREW, WHEEL, PULLEY
minded .... STUPID, FOOLISH
organism ..... MONAD, AMOEBA
simpleton .... DAW, OAF, SAP,
      COOT, DOLT, DOPE, FOOL,
     GABY, GAUP, GAWK, GOWK,
     ZANY, BOOBY, DUNCE, GOOSE,
      MORON, NINNY, NODDY,
     DIMWIT, DOODLE, GANDER,
     NITWIT, GOMERAL, IMBECILE,
      SOFTHEAD, NINCOMPOOP
Simplon ____ .... PASS
simply ...... JUST, ONLY, MERELY,
         PURELY, SOLELY
simulacrum .... SHAM, IMAGE,
                 TRAVESTY
simular .... FEIGNED
simulate .... ACT, APE, FAKE,
     SHAM, FEIGN, MIMIC, AFFECT,
      ASSUME, IMITATE, PRETEND
simulation .... FEINT, FEIGNING,
                 PRETENSE
simultaneous .... COINCIDENT
simurgh .... ROC
sin .... ERR, ENVY, EVIL, VICE,
      FAULT, GREED, GUILT, SLOTH,
     OFFENSE, INIQUITY, TRESPASS,
                TRANSGRESS
against a person, place or
thing .... SACRILEGE
capable of .... PECCABLE
petty .... PECCADILLO
repentance for .... REMORSE,
     ATTRITION, PENITENCE,
                CONTRITION
Sinai .... HOREB, MOUNT
sinalbin .... GLUCOSIDE
Sinaloa capital .... CULIACAN
sinapism .... PLASTER
Sinatra, former Mrs. .... AVA,
                 MIA
since .... AGO, SITH, HENCE,
     BEFORE NOW, INASMUCH AS
sincere .... OPEN, FRANK, CANDID,
      HEARTY, HONEST, EARNEST,
      GENUINE, FAITHFUL,
                HEARTFELT
sincerely .... WITH ALL MY HEART
sinciput .... FOREHEAD
Sinclair, novelist .... MAY, LEWIS,
         UPTON, CATHERINE
character .... CASS, BABBITT,
                 DOREMUS
Sind, capital of .... KARACHI
Sin(d)bad the ____ ...... SAILOR
number of voyages taken by
.... SEVEN
supposed birthplace of
.... SOHAR
transport of .... ROC
sine .... WITHOUT

prole .... CHILDLESS
qua ____ .... NON
sinecure .... SNAP, CINCH
sinew(s) .... FORCE, THEWS,
     MUSCLE, TENDON, STRENGTH
sinewy .... WIRY, TOUGH,
     BRAWNY, ROBUST, STRONG,
                MUSCULAR
sinful .... EVIL, WICKED,
     IMMORAL, PECCANT
sing .... HUM, BUZZ, CAROL,
     CHANT, WARBLE, WHISTLE
cheerfully .... LILT
in certain way .... HUM,
         CROON, YODEL
in full rolling voice .... TROLL
praises to .... LAUD, EXTOL,
                 GLORIFY
slang .... SQUEAL, CONFESS,
         BLOW THE WHISTLE
the opening phrase of a
canticle .... INTONE
Singapore founder .... RAFFLES
garment .... SARI, KEBAYA,
     SAMFOO, CHEONGSAM
nickname of .... LION CITY
old name .... TEMASEK
president .... YUSOF
prime minister .... LEE
soup .... SOTO
singe .... BURN, SEAR, SCORCH
singer .... BIRD, POET, CANTOR,
     CAROLER, WARBLER,
     YODELER, MINSTREL,
     VOCALIST, CHORIST(ER)
Arnold .... EDDY
Bennett .... TONY
Brewer .... TERESA
Brooks .... GARTH
Campbell .... GLEN
Cash .... JOHNNY
choir .... ALTO, SOLOIST
Como .... PERRY
Donkey Serenade .... NANETTE
                 FABRAY
female .... DIVA, COLE, LIND,
     JONES, PRICE, SILLS, SMITH,
     SOPRANO, STEVENS,
     CHANTEUSE, MADONNA,
     CHANTRESS, STREISAND,
     CANTATRICE, COLORATURA
Iglesias .... JULIO
Jones .... TOM, GEORGE
male .... COMO, JONES, LANZA,
     NEWTON, ROGERS, JACKSON,
     PRESLEY, SINATRA, BARITONE,
     CAMPBELL, IGLESIAS,
                 MINSTREL
Manilow .... BARRY
Mathis .... JOHNNY
Moffo .... ANNA

Nabors .... JIM
Nelson .... WILLIE
Newton .... WAYNE
of a chantey .... SEAMAN
of Israel .... DAVID
opera ..... ALDA, PONS, GLUCK,
    HORNE, MELBA, PATTI, PINZA,
    SILLS, CALLAS, CARUSO,
    TAUBER, TIBBET, TUCKER,
    DOMINGO, NILSSON, STEVENS,
    TEBALDI, TRAUBEL
Orbison .... RAY
Parton .... DOLLY
pop .... ANKA
Presley .... ELVIS
Price .... LEONTYNE
Pride .... CHARLEY
Richie .... LIONEL
Rogers .... KENNY
Robbins .... MARTY
Sinatra .... FRANK, NANCY
stock of .... REPERTORY,
    REPERTOIRE
Streisand .... BARBRA
sweet .... LARK
Twitty .... CONWAY
wandering .... BUSKER,
    MINSTREL
Whittaker .... ROGER
Williams .... ANDY, HANK
singers' aid .... MIKE
group .... CHOIR, CHORUS,
    TROUPE, ENSEMBLE
singing voice .... ALTO, BASSO,
    TENOR, SOPRANO, BARITONE,
    FALSETTO, COLORATURA
single ...... ACE, ONE, SOLE, SOLO,
    UNAL, (A)LONE, UNWED,
    SOLITARY, UNMARRIED,
    INDIVIDUAL
combining form .... UNI,
    MONO, HAPLO
family dwelling, descriptive
    of .... DETACHED
file .... TANDEM
foot .... RACK
footed .... MONOPODE
handed .... UNAIDED
in baseball .... BASE HIT
in biology .... UNIVALENT
in telegraphy .... SIMPLEX
instance/time .... ONCE
man .... BACHELOR
-minded .... ONE-TRACK
out ...... PICK, CHOOSE, SELECT
period in office ..... ONE TERM
point .... ACE
rack railway .... MONORAIL
service charge .... ONE FEE
sticker .... SLOOP, SAILBOAT
thing .... UNIT

unit .... MONAD
singlet .... JERSEY, UNDERSHIRT
singly .... SOLO, ALONE, UNAIDED,
    ONE BY ONE
singsong recitation .... CHIME
singular .... ODD, RARE, SOLE,
    QUEER, UNIQUE, CURIOUS,
    STRANGE, UNUSUAL,
    PECULIAR, INDIVIDUAL
opposed to .... PLURAL
sinigrin .... GLUCOSIDE
sinister .... BAD, EVIL, GRIM,
    LEFT, WICKED, BALEFUL,
    HARMFUL, OMINOUS,
    INJURIOUS, PORTENTOUS
opposed to .... DEXTER
sink .... DIP, EBB, SAG, BOWL,
    FALL, WANE, BASIN, DROOP,
    DROWN, LAPSE, LOWER,
    SEWER, SLUMP, DEEPEN,
    RECEDE, SETTLE, DECLINE,
    DESCEND, IMMERSE, SUBSIDE,
    SUBMERGE
capital in a venture .... RISK,
    GAMBLE, PLUNGE
hole .... CESSPOOL
in .... PENETRATE
ship deliberately ...... SCUTTLE
-side convenience .... TOWEL
    RACK
sinker .... DONUT, DOUGHNUT
Sinkiang capital .... URUMCHI
sinking in the mud .... MIRING
sinless .... INNOCENT
Sinn _____, Irish society .... FEIN
sinople .... CINNABAR
sinuate .... WAVY, SINUOUS
sinuous .... WAVY, CURVED,
    DEVIOUS, WINDING, SLITHERY,
    SERPENTINE
sinus .... BEND, ANTRA, CURVE,
    TRACT, ANTRUM, CAVITY
    _____ (dark moon plain)
    .... RORIS
kind of .... FRONTAL,
    ETHMOIDAL, MAXILLARY,
    SPHENOIDAL
sinuses .... AIR SPACES
drainage organ of .... NOSE
inflammation .... SINUSITIS
location of .... NOSE,
    FOREHEAD, CHEEKBONE
Sioux .... CROW, IOWA, OTO(E),
    OSAGE, PONCA, TETON,
    DAKOTA, MANDAN, CATAWBA,
    TUTELOS
chief .... SITTING BULL
sip .... NIP, SUCK, TIFF, DRINK,
    TASTE, IMBIBE, SAMPLING
siphon .... DRAW, STRAW,
    EXTRACT

sipid .... SAVORY
sipper .... STRAW
sippet .... TOAST, CROUTON,
    FRAGMENT
sipping tube .... STRAW
sir .... MR, SRI, TUAN, BWANA,
    SAHIB, SENOR, MISTER,
    EFFENDI, SEIGNOR,
    (MON)SIEUR
sire .... BEGET, PROCREATE,
    (FORE)FATHER
siren .... VAMP, CIRCE, NYMPH,
    WITCH, CHARMER,
    (FOG)HORN, LORELEI,
    WHISTLE, PARTHENOPE,
    ENCHANTRESS
like a .... SEDUCTIVE
Rhine .... LURLEI, LORELEI
sirenian .... DUGONG, SEA COW,
    MANATEE
Sirius .... DOG STAR, CANICULA
of .... SOTHIC
sirloin beef .... BARON
sirocco .... WIND
Madeira island .... LESTE
sirup. See **syrup**
sisal .... HEMP, AGAVE, FIBER,
    HENEQUIN
Sisera's enemy .... BARAK
murderer .... JAEL
soldiers .... CANAANITES
siskin .... FINCH, TARIN
sissy .... MILKSOP, WEAKLING,
    MAMA'S BOY, PANTYWAIST
like a .... EFFIMINATE
slang .... CHICKEN
sister .... NUN, SIB, NANCE,
    NURSE, SOROR, TITTY,
    WOMAN, TITTIE
fictional .... CARRIE
headdress of a .... CORNET
sisterhood .... SODALITY,
    SORORITY
Sistine Chapel feature
    .... FRESCOES
Madonna painter ..... RAPHAEL
sistrum .... RATTLE
sit .... POSE, BROOD, PERCH,
    ROOST
down to meet .... CONVENE
in .... ATTEND
in on .... LISTEN
on ..... PERCH, STIFLE, REPRESS
tight .... WAIT
Sita's husband .... RAMA
site .... SEAT, ARENA, SCENE,
    STEAD, LOCALE, LOCATION
for a drum .... EAR
for a lot of bucks .... RODEO
of abortive Cuban invasion
    .... BAY OF PIGS

Apollo oracle .... DELOS
Disneyland .... TOKYO, ANAHEIM
Disney World ...... ORLANDO
famous California
    aquarium
    .... MONTEREY
famous Florida aquarium
    .... MARINELAND
rods and cones .... RETINA
sitology .... DIETETICS
Sitsang .... TIBET
sitter .... NURSE, BROODER
sitting .... SEATED, MEETING, SESSION
of the court .... SESSION
room .... SALA, PARLOR, BOUDOIR
spiritual .... SEANCE
Sitting Bull's antagonist
    .... CUSTER
sobriquet .... MEDICINE MAN
son .... CROWFOOT
situate .... PUT, SET, PLACE, POSIT, LOCATE
situation .... PLACE, STATE, LOCATION, POSITION
advantageous .... CAT-BIRD SEAT
difficult .... FIX, JAM, PINCH, PLIGHT, STRAIT, DISTRESS, HARDSHIP
entrapping .... NET, WEB
situs .... LOCATION, POSITION
Sitwell, poet .... EDITH, OSBERT
Siva's wife .... DEVI, MAYA, S(H)AKTI
six .... HEXAD, SESTET
combining form .... HEXA
footed .... HEXAPOD
group of ...... HEXAD, SENARY, SESTET, SEXTET(TE), SEXTUPLET
in dice game .... SICE, SISE
line stanza .... SESTET
of .... SENARY
pointed figure .... STAR
prefix .... HEXA
shooter .... REVOLVER
-sided figure .... HEXAGON
-sided solid .... CUBE
years, lasting .... SEXENNIAL
16-½ feet .... ROD, POLE, PERCH
sixth day, occurring every
    .... SEXTAN
sense .... INTUITION
sense for short .... ESP
60's musical .... HAIR
sixty grains .... DRAM
sizable .... BIG, HUGE, VAST, AMPLE, GREAT, HEFTY,

LARGE, BULKY, PORTLY, IMMENSE, MASSIVE, SUBSTANTIAL
size .... AREA, BULK, EXTENT, DEGREE, VOLUME, CAPACITY, MAGNITUDE
exceeding the usual
    .... ENORMOUS, GIGANTIC
of a bullet .... CALIBER
book page .... OCTAVO
great .... TITANIC
hole .... BORE
measurements
    .... DIMENSION
paper .... DEMY, ROYAL, FOOLSCAP
of type .... AGATE
prefix .... DEMI
up .... EYE
sizy .... VISCOUS, GLUTINOUS
sizzle ...... FRY, BURN, HISS, SEAR, FRIZZ(LE), SPUTTER
sizzling .... ANGRY, (RED)HOT
skate .... RAY, CHAP, GLIDE, ROCKER
blade .... RUNNER
slang .... NAG, HORSE
skater's leap .... AXEL
skating arena .... RINK
sign .... REDBALL
skean .... SWORD, DAGGER
skedaddle ...... RUN, BLOW, BOLT, FLEE, DECAMP
skee .... SKI
skeg .... FIN
skein .... RAP, HANK, MESH
of yarn .... HASP
skeletal .... LEAN, THIN, SKINNY
disease ...... RICKETS, RACHITIS
skeleton .... ATOMY, BONES, DRAFT, CARCASS, OUTLINE, FRAME(WORK)
additional small bones in the
    .... SESAMOIDS
bone, appendicular ...... ULNA, FEMUR, TIBIA, FIBULA, RADIUS, HUMERUS, PATELLA, SCAPULA, CLAVICLE, PHALANGE, (META)CARPAL, (META)TARSAL
bone, axial .... RIB, SPINE, SKULL, COCCYX, SACRUM, STERNUM, MANDIBLE, VERTEBRA(E)
connective tissue ..... TENDON, LIGAMENT
copy in printing .... DUMMY
force .... CADRE
hiding place of .... CLOSET
in the closet ..... PAST, SECRET
key .... MASTER(KEY)

limb girdle of the ...... PELVIS, SHOULDER
main part of the .... AXIAL, APPENDICULAR
sea animal .... CORAL
skellum .... SCAMP, RASCAL
skelp .... SMACK
skelter .... RUSH
Skelton, comedian .... RED
skep .... BASKET, HAMPER, BEEHIVE
skeptic .... CYNIC, LUCIAN, PYRRHO, DOUBTER, AGNOSTIC
Biblical .... THOMAS
skeptical .... WAVY, LEERY, DUBIOUS, PYRRHONIC
skepticism .... DOUBT, MISTRUST, UNBELIEF, AGNOSTICISM
skerry .... REEF
sketch .... MAP, SKIT, CHART, DRAFT, DESIGN, DRAW(ING), OUTLINE, PLAYLET, AFTERPIECE
aimlessly .... DOODLE
exaggerated .... CARICATURE
out .... DELINEATE
sketchy .... ROUGH, UNEVEN
skete member .... MONK, HERMIT
skew .... SIDLE, TWIST, SQUINT, SWERVE, DISTORT, OBLIQUE
on a .... SLANTWISE
skewer .... PIN, SPIT, TRUSS, BROACH, PIERCE, SKIVER, BROCHETTE
ski .... RUNNER, SNOWSHOE
lift .... T-BAR
mecca .... ASPEN
move .... RUADE
resort, famed .... ASPEN
run .... JUMP, SCHUSS, SLALOM, DOWNHILL
trail .... PISTE
skid ...... SLUE, SPIN, TRIG, BRAKE, SLIDE, (SIDE)SLIP
skiddoo .... LEAVE, DEPART
skid row character .... HOBO, BEGGAR, VAGRANT, DERELICT
skier's garment .... PARKA
hazard .... WINDBURN
transport .... T-BAR
skiff .... CAIQUE, ROWBOAT
skiing fan .... SNOWBIRD
race .... SLALOM
skill .... ART, GIFT, CRAFT, ADROIT, TALENT, FINESSE, KNOW-HOW, PROWESS, DEXTERITY, EXPERTISE, PROFICIENCY
combining form .... TECHNO
manual .... HANDICRAFT
skilled .... DEFT, WISE, ADEPT,

SHARP, ASTUTE, EXPERT, GIFTED, MASTER, VERSED, EDUCATED, SURE-FOOTED

skillet .... SPIDER, (FRYING)PAN

skillful .... APT, ABLE, DEFT, ADEPT, CLEVER, HANDY, ADROIT, EXPERT, DEXT(E)ROUS, ACCOMPLISHED

one .... PRO

workmanship .... D(A)EDAL

skim .... FLIT, SCAN, SCUD, SCUM, CREAM, GLIDE, BROWSE, GLANCE, COAT(ING)

skimmer .... SCISSORBILL

skimp .... SAVE, PINCH, SCAMP, SCANT, STINT, SCRIMP, ECONOMIZE

skimpy .... MEAGER, SCANTY, STINGY, NIGGARDLY

skin .... BARK, COAT, CUTIS, DERM(A), SHELL, STRIP, LAMINA, PLATING, COVERING, (EPI)DERMIS

abscess .... FURUNCLE

allergy .... ECZEMA, URTICARIA, DERMATITIS

analysis .... BIOPSY

animal .... FUR, KID, FELL, HIDE, PELT, SUEDE, PELLAGE

benign tumor .... CYST, KERATOSIS, PAPILLOMA

blemish .... MOLE, WART, NEVUS, FRECKLE

bulge .... INION

cast off .... SLOUGH

colloquial .... CHEAT, DEFRAUD, SWINDLE

coloration .... CYANOSIS

combining form .... DERMA, DERM(O), DERMAT(O)

condition/disorder .... RASH, HIVES, UREDO, ALLERGY, BLISTER, LENTIGO, URTICARIA

container .... KENCH

covering .... FUR, HAIR

cut away .... PARE, PEEL

dark .... MELANIC

decoration/design ...... TATTOO

-deep ..... CURSORY, SHALLOW, EPIDERMAL, SUPERFICIAL

deer antler's .... VELVET

discoloration .... BRUISE

disease ..... ACNE, ITCH, YAWS, FAVUS, HIVES, LUPUS, MANGE, PINTA, PSORA, SCALL, SCURF, TINEA, TUMOR, ULCER, ARAKIS, CANCER, ECZEMA, HERPES, LICHEN, TETTER, LEPROSY, PURPURA, PRURIGO, SCABIES, SERPIGO, IMPETIGO, MILIARIA, RINGWORM,

VITILIGO, PSORIASIS, ERYSIPELAS

disease drug .... RETIN-A, NEOMYCIN, ANTIBIOTIC

disease, oil for .... CAJUPUT

diver's aid .... SCUBA

diving device .... AQUALUNG

drying frame .... HERSE

dryness .... XEROSIS

duct dirt .... COMEDO

elevation .... WALE, WELT, WHEAL, PAPULE, PIMPLE, BLISTER, PUSTULE

eruption .... EXANTHEMA

flaw .... WRINKLE

flick .... PORNO

fold .... PLICA

fruit .... PEEL, RIND, ZEST

hemangioma .... BIRTHMARK

horny growth .... CORN, KERATOSIS

infection .... RINGWORM, ATHLETE'S FOOT

inflammation .... BOIL, PAPULE, PIMPLE, PUSTULE, SHINGLES, CARBUNCLE

injury ...... BRUISE, CONTUSION

irritating rash .... PRICKLY HEAT

layer .... CUTIS, CORIUM, DERM(A), (EPI)DERMIS

like ...... DERMOID, DERMATOID

lotion .... CALAMINE

nodule .... MILIUM

of the/pertaining to .... DERMAL, DERMIC, CUTANEOUS

oil .... SEBUM

opening .... PORE

outer layer .... CUTICLE, EPICARP, EPIDERMIS

peel off .... EXCORIATE

person with abnormal white .... ALBINO

pigment .... MELANIN

redness ..... RUBOR, ERYTHEMA

scales .... SCURF

scar ...... BRAND, VACCINATION

shed .... MOLT

shed by snake .... SLOUGH

shedding .... ECDYSIS

sheep's/goat's ..... PARCHMENT

ship's .... ARMOR, PLATE, SHELL

slang .... BLEED, SCREW, FLEECE

sore .... GALL

specialist ...... DERMATOLOGIST

spot .... N(A)EVUS

strip the .... FLAY, PEEL

swelling .... BLEB

tough .... BARK, RIND

treat .... TAN, TAW

tree .... BARK, RIND

true .... DERMIS

tumor .... WEN, CYST

untanned .... KIP, SHAGREEN

whip mark .... WALE, WELT, WHEAL, STRIPE

skinflint .... MISER, HOARDER, NIGGARD, TIGHTWAD

skink .... ADDA, SEPS, LIZARD

like/of the .... SCINCOID

skinless .... APELLOUS

skinner ...... MULETEER, STRIPPER, SWINDLER, (MULE)DRIVER

Skinner, actress/writer .... CORNELIA (OTIS)

skinny .... LANK, LEAN, SLIM, THIN, SCRAGGY, SLENDER, SKELETAL, EMACIATED

skip .... DAP, HOP, JUMP, LEAP, OMIT, CAPER, DECAMP, SPRING, ABSCOND, SKITTER, PASS OVER, RICOCHET

skipjack .... FISH, BEETLE, ELATER

skipper .... RAS, RAIS, PILOT, SAURY, MASTER, CAPTAIN, BUTTERFLY

Biblical .... NOAH

fictional sub .... NEMO

skirmish ...... SPAR, TILT, BRUSH, CLASH, MELEE, FIGHT, (AF)FRAY, BATTLE

skirr .... GLIDE, SCOUR

skirt ...... EDGE, BORDER, DIRNDL, FRINGE, KIRTLE, CHOGORI, PANNIER, PURLIEU, PETTICOAT

armor .... TASSE

ballet dancer's .... TUTU

expander .... HOOP

feature .... GORE

he wears one .... SCOT

men's .... KILT

slang .... GIRL, WOMAN

slit .... PLACKET

swish of silk .... FROUFROU

triangular part .... GORE

waist .... PEPLUM

skit .... GIBE, PARODY, SATIRE, SKETCH, LAMPOON, PLAY(LET), SLAPSTICK

skitter ...... RUN, SKIP, SCAMPER

skittish ...... COY, JUMPY, FICKLE, LIVELY, JITTERY, NERVOUS, PLAYFUL

skittle(s) .... PIN, BOWL, NINEPINS

skive .... PARE, SHAVE, SLICE

skivvy .... UNDIES, UNDERWEAR, UNDERSHIRT

skoal .... TOAST

skua .... JAEGER, (SEA)GULL

skulduggery .... TRICKERY
skulk .... HIDE, LURK, MICHE,
   PROWL, SHIRK, SLINK, SNEAK,
   MALINGER
skull .... HEAD, MAZARD, SCONCE,
   CRANIUM
and ＿＿ (death symbol)
   .... CROSSBONES
back part .... OCCIPUT
bone .... ZYGOMA, MAXILLA,
   SPHENOID, PARIETAL (BONE),
   OCCIPITAL (BONE)
bulge .... INION
cavity .... FOSSA, SINUS
domed part .... CALVARIA,
   CALVARIUM
first cervical vertebra of
   .... ATLAS
holes in the .... FORAMENS
injury .... FRACTURE
of the .... INIAL, CRANIAL,
   CEPHALIC
part of ..... BREGMA, CRANIUM,
   BRAINPAN, CALVARIA
protuberance .... INION
second cervical vertebra of
   .... AXIS
study of the ...... CRANIOLOGY
surgical saw for .... TREPAN,
   TREPHINE
skullcap .... COIF, BEANIE,
   IVETTA, PILEUS, CALOT(TE)
Jewish .... YARMULKE
Roman Catholic
   .... ZUCCHETTO
skunk .... CHINCHE, POLECAT,
   STINKER, CONEPATE, MEPHITIS
animal resembling
   .... TELEDU, ZORIL(A)
colloquial ...... SCAMP, RASCAL
kin of .... MINK, OTTER
slang .... BLANK, SHUT OUT
spray of .... MUSK
sky .... COPE, VAULT, CLIMATE,
   HEAVEN(S), OLYMPUS,
   EMPYREAN, FIRMAMENT
altar .... ARA
bear .... URSA
blue .... AZURE, CERULEAN
curved vault of .... WELKIN
highest point .... ZENITH
of the .... CELESTIAL
pilot .... PADRE, AVIATOR,
   CHAPLAIN, CLERGYMAN
prefix .... SCIO
rare phenomenon .... LUNAR
   ECLIPSE
sight .... SUN, MOON, STAR,
   CLOUD, PLANE
strange sight .... UFO
skylark .... FROLIC, HORSE

   AROUND
genus .... ALAUDA
skylight .... DORMER
skyline .... HORIZON
sight .... SPIRE
skyrocket .... JET, SOAR, ZOOM,
   POP UP
skyways .... AIR LANES
slab .... TILE, CHUNK, DALLE,
   PIECE, SLICE, STELE,
   TABLE(T), VISCID
atop column .... ABACUS
slack ...... LAX, DUFF, DULL, IDLE,
   LAZE, LULL, SLOW, WEAK,
   LOOSE, MORASS, REMISS,
   RELAXED, CARELESS,
   SLUGGISH
time for newspapers .... SILLY
   SEASON
slacken .... ABATE, LET UP,
   RELAX, EASE(UP), LESSEN,
   LOOSEN, RETARD, DWINDLE,
   SLOW DOWN
slacker ...... SPIV, IDLER, EVADER,
   LOAFER, TRUANT, QUITTER,
   SHIRKER
slacks .... PANTS, TROUSERS
slag .... LAVA, DROSS, CINDER,
   SCORIA
slake ...... SATE, ALLAY, QUENCH,
   HYDRATE, SATISFY
slalom .... SKI
slam .... HIT, PAN, BANG, BASH,
   SHUT, SWAT, VOLE, CLOSE,
   POUND, BATTER
-dunker .... CAGER
slammer .... JAIL, CLINK
slander .... MUD, LIBEL, SMEAR,
   DEFAME, MALIGN, REVILE,
   ASPERSE, CALUMNY,
   TRADUCE, CALUMNIATE,
   MALEDICTION
slanderous story ...... ROORBACK
slang .... CANT, ARGOT, LINGO,
   JARGON, PATOIS, DIALECT,
   SHOPTALK
suffix .... EROO
slant .... BIAS, CANT, COCK, HEEL,
   KEEL, RAKE, SKEW, TILT,
   ANGLE, SLOPE, GLANCE,
   INCLINE, OPINION
a nail .... TOE
combining form .... CLINO
line .... SOLIDUS
slanted .... ATILT
edge .... BEVEL
slanting .... ASKEW, ATILT,
   ASLOPE, OBLIQUE
type .... ITALIC
slap .... HIT, RAP, BIFF, BLOW,
   CUFF, SPAT, SWAT, SMACK,

   SPANK, WHACK, INSULT,
   REBUFF, THWACK
-happy .... GIDDY, SILLY,
   GROGGY, FOOLISH
slapdash .... OFFHAND, HIT OR
   MISS
slapjack .... PANCAKE
slapstick .... COMEDY, HORSEPLAY
slash ...... CUT, JAG, GASH, HACK,
   LASH, SLIT, SEVER, SCOURGE
prices .... LOWER, MARK DOWN
Slask .... SILESIA
slat ...... BEAT, FLAP, LATH, STRIP,
   SPLINE, STRIKE
barrel .... STAVE
movable .... LOUVER
slate .... BOOK, LIST, ROCK, ROOF,
   TILE, ABUSE, BRICK, SCOLD,
   BALLOT, ENROLL, TABLET,
   TICKET
ax/trimmer .... SAX, ZAX
excavation site .... QUARRY
roofing .... RAG
slater .... WOOD LOUSE
tool of .... STAKE
slatted box .... CRATE
slattern ...... DRAB, SLUT, SLOVEN,
   TROLLOP
slaughter ...... MURDER, POGROM,
   CARNAGE, KILLING,
   BUTCHER(Y), HECATOMB,
   MASSACRE
slaughterhouse .... ABATTOIR,
   BUTCHERY, SHAMBLES
waste .... TANKAGE
Slav .... POLE, SORB, WEND,
   CROAT, CZECH, SLOVAK,
   RUSSIAN, SERB(IAN),
   SLOVENE, BULGAR(IAN)
slave .... PEON, SERF, TOIL, HELOT,
   DRUDGE, THRALL, VASSAL,
   SERVANT, BOND(S)MAN
Biblical .... HAGAR
block .... CATASTA
driver .... TASKMASTER
educated .... HETAERA
female ..... HETAERA, HETAIRA,
   ODALISK, ODALISQUE
feudal .... ESNE
liberate .... MANUMIT
mark of .... BRAND, STIGMA
Moslem .... MAMELUKE
runaway .... MAROON
Scott .... DRED
ship .... SLAVER
soldier .... MAMELUKE
temple .... HIERODULE
to a habit .... ADDICT
slaver .... DROOL, DRIVEL,
   HUMBUG, TRADER, SLOBBER,
   NONSENSE

slavery .... CHAINS, BONDAGE, HELOTRY, SERFDOM, DRUDGERY, SERVITUDE, THRAL(L)DOM
free from .... MANUMIT, EMANCIPATE
to drugs, vice .... ADDICTION
slaves, dealer in .... MANGO
tied together .... COFFLE
slavish .... MENIAL, SERVILE
slaw .... SALAD
slay .... DO IN, KILL, MURDER, DESTROY, ASSASSINATE
slayer .... KILLER, ASSASSIN
of Castor .... IDAS
of Goliath .... DAVID
sleave .... FLOSS, TANGLE, THREAD
sleazy .... CHEAP, FLIMSY, SHABBY, TAWDRY
sled .... LUGE, PUNG, TODE, CUTTER, JUMPER, HURDLE, SLEDGE, SLEIGH, BOBSLED, GO-DEVIL, TOBOGGAN, TRAVOIS(E), DOUBLE-RIPPER
dog .... HUSKY
dog, command to .... MUSH
logging .... TODE
slider .... RUNNER
sledge ...... DRAG, SLED, HAMMER, SLEIGH, TRAVOIS(E)
sleek .... CHIC, OILY, SLICK, SUAVE, GLOSSY, POLISH, SMOOTH, UNCTUOUS
sleep .... NOD, BUNK, DOSS, REST, DROWSE, REPOSE, SHUTEYE, SLUMBER
cessation of breathing during .... (SLEEP)APNEA
combining form .... HYPNO
deep .... COMA, SOPOR, STUPOR
disturber .... PEE(PEE), WEE-WEE
drugged .... NARCOSIS
god of .... HYPNOS, HYPNUS, SOMNUS
inability to .... INSOMNIA
inducing drug .... OPIATE, NARCOTIC, SEDATIVE
last .... DEATH
lightly .... NAP, DOZE
midday .... SIESTA
restlessly .... TOSS
short .... DOZE, WINK, (CAT)NAP, SIESTA, SNATCH, SNOOZE
type of .... REM, NREM
unnatural .... COMA, SOPOR, STUPOR, TRANCE, LETHARGY
winter .... HIBERNATION
sleeper .... TIE, BEAM, TRAIN,

AMTRAK, PULLMAN, RACE HORSE
long .... RIP, SLUGABED
sleeper's production? .... ZEES
sleepiness .... SOMNOLENCE
sleeping bag .... SACK
car business .... PULLMAN
car part .... BERTH
compartment .... CUBICLE
dress .... PJ, NIGHTIE, PAJAMAS, NIGHTGOWN
pill .... SECONAL, VERONAL, BARBITAL, GOOF BALL
place .... BED, COT, PAD, BUNK, DOSS, FLOP, BERTH, COUCH, CUBICLE, LODGING
schedule, disruption of .... JET LAG
sickness carrier .... TSETSE
sickness cause .... TRYPANOSOME
sickness remedy ..... SURAMIN
sleepless one .... INSOMNIAC
sleeplike state .... COMA, TRANCE
sleepwalker .... SOMNAMBULIST
sleepy .... DOZY, DROWSY, LANGUID, OSCITANT, LETHARGIC, SOMNOLENT
Sleepy Hollow Crane .... ICHABOD
sleet .... ICE, HAIL, RAIN, GRAUPEL
sleety .... ICY, BRUMAL, WINTRY
sleeve .... GIGOT, ARM(LET), BUSHING
bar on .... CHEVRON
end of .... CUFF
hole .... SCYE, SKYE
kind of .... DOLMAN, LANTERN, LEG-OF-MUTTON
sleeveless garment .... ABA, CAPE, VEST, CLOAK, MANTLE
sleigh ...... SLED, CUTTER, SLEDGE
boxlike .... PUNG
puller .... REINDEER
rider .... SANTA
slider .... RUNNER
sleight .... FEINT, SKILL, TRICK(ERY), CHICANERY
of hand .... PASS, MAGIC, HOCUS-POCUS, ILLUSIONISM, LEGERDEMAIN
of hand artist .... JUGGLER, SHARPER, MAGICIAN
slender .... LANK, LEAN, SLIM, THIN, FRAIL, LITHE, SVELT, WISPY, FEEBLE, LISSOM, MEAGER, SKINNY, SLIGHT, GRACILE, TENUOUS, WILLOWY
and graceful .... LITHE, SVELT(E)
finial .... EPI

in phonetics .... CLOSE
waisted .... WASPISH
sleuth .... TEC, HAWKSHAW, DETECTIVE, OPERATIVE, PRIVATE EYE
fictional .... CHAN, MOTO, NERO, TRENT, HOLMES, HERCULE
slang .... DICK
slew .... LOT(S), SLUE, WAD(S), RAFTS, SPATE, SWAMP, SLOUGH
Slezsko .... SILESIA
slice ...... CUT, CHIP, GASH, HUNK, SLAB, CHUNK, LAYER, PIECE, SHAVE, SKIVE, SLASH, CANTLE, COLLOP, PORTION, SPATULA
a roast/a turkey .... CARVE
of bacon/ham .... RASHER
of meat, small .... COLLOP
of thrice .... ONCE
thick .... SLAB
slicer's cry .... FORE
slick .... OILY, SHINY, SLEEK, SMART, SUAVE, CLEVER, GLOSSY, SMOOTH, SLIPPERY, UNCTUOUS
colloquial .... SLY
slang .... MAGAZINE
slicker .... PONCHO, OILCOAT, (RAIN)COAT
colloquial .... SHARPER, SWINDLER
slide .... SKID, SLIP, SLUE, CHUTE, COAST, GLIDE, PLATE, LAWINE, AVALANCHE
by a mountain climber .... GLISSADE
by force of gravity ..... COAST
fastener .... ZIPPER
photograph .... TRANSPARENCY
rule .... SLAPSTICK
slight .... CUT, GO-BY, SLIM, SNUB, THIN, FAINT, FRAIL, SCANT, WISPY, IGNORE, MEAGER, AFFRONT, FRAGILE, NEGLECT, TENUOUS
cast .... TINGE
trace .... WHIFF
slightest .... LEAST
amount .... GRAIN
slightly .... SOMEWHAT
slim .... THIN, SCANT, SPARE, MEAGER, SLIGHT, SVELTE, GRACILE, SLENDER
slime .... MUD, MIRE, MUCK, OOZE, FILTH, SLUDGE, SEDIMENT
combining form .... MYX(O)
slimsy .... FLIMSY, SLIGHT,

SLENDER

slimy .... EELY, VISCID, VISCOUS

fish .... EEL, LAMPREY

matter ...... GOB, OOZE, GLEET,

SLUDGE

sling .... CAST, HANG, HURL,

DRINK, FLING, PITCH, SHOOT

barrel/log .... PARBUCKLE

slingshot .... CATAPULT

killer with .... DAVID

slink .... LURK, CREEP, SKULK,

SNEAK, STEAL, SLITHER

slinky .... FELINE, SHIFTY,

SNEAKY, FURTIVE, SINUOUS,

STEALTHY

slip .... SKID, TRIP, BONER,

ERR(OR), FAULT, GAFFE,

LAPSE, LEASH, REEVE, SCION,

SLIDE, LAPSUS, TUMBLE,

CUTTING, MISTAKE,

PETTICOAT

away .... ELOPE, ELAPSE

back .... RELAPSE

knot .... NOOSE

loose, short .... CHEMISE

on garment .... SWEATER

out of place .... PROLAPSE

stream .... RACE, WASH

up .... ERROR, BOOBOO,

OVERSIGHT

slipcase, book .... FOREL

slipover .... SWEATER

slipper .... MULE, SCUFF, STEP-IN,

PANTOF(F)LE

flat-heeled .... MARY JANE

lounging .... MULE

strap .... SANDAL

slippery .... SLY, EELY, SLICK,

SLIMY, GREASY, SHIFTY,

ELUSIVE, EVASIVE

customer .... EEL, DEBTOR

slipshod .... SLOPPY, CARELESS,

SLOVENLY, WISHY-WASHY

slipstream .... (PROP)WASH

slit ...... CUT, GASH, SLASH, SLICE,

SPLIT

slither .... SLIP, CRAWL, CREEP,

GLIDE, SLIDE

sliver .... CHIP, FIBER, SHARD,

SLICE, FRAGMENT, SPLINTER

slob .... PIG, SLATTERN

slobber .... DROOL, DRIVEL,

SLAVER

sloe .... GIN, HAW, PLUM,

BLACKTHORN

slog .... PLOD, SLUG, TOIL

slogan .... MAXIM, MOTTO,

BYWORD, PASSWORD,

(BATTLE)CRY, CATCHWORD,

SHIBBOLETH

sloop .... DANDY, CUTTER,

SAILBOAT

of war .... FRIGATE

vessel like a .... HOY

slop .... MUD, MUCK, SNOW,

SLIME, SLOSH, SLUSH, SWILL,

WASTE, REFUSE, GARBAGE

over .... GUSH, SPILL

slang .... CHOW

slope .... BANK, BRAE, CANT,

RAMP, RISE, TILT, GRADE,

SLANT, SPLAY, TALUS,

INCLINE, GRADIENT,

DECLIVITY

combining form .... CLINO

gradual .... GLACIS

of a mountain .... VERSANT

steep .... SCARP

sloped .... DEVELLED

sloping angle/surface ...... BEVEL,

SPLAY

edge .... BEZEL, BISEL

runway .... RAMP

sloppy .... MESSY, MUDDY,

UNTIDY, CARELESS, SLIPSHOD

slops .... SMOCK, BREECHES,

TROUSERS, COVERALLS

slosh .... SLOP, WADE, SPILL,

SPLASH

slot .... TRACK, TRAIL, GROOVE,

KEYWAY

machine .... ONE-ARMED

BANDIT

machine coin .... SLUG

machine windfall ..... JACKPOT

sloth .... BEAR, MAMMAL, INERTIA,

EDENTATE, IDLENESS,

LAZINESS, SLOWNESS,

INDOLENCE

three-toed .... AI

two-toed .... UNAU

slothful .... LAZY

slouch .... SAG, HULK, SLUMP,

DROOP(ING)

slough ...... SHED, MARSH, SWAMP,

MORASS, CAST OFF, DISCARD

Slovakian city .... KOSICE

sloven .... SLOB

slovenly .... LAX, DOWDY, TACKY,

FROWZY, SLOPPY, UNTIDY,

UNKEMPT, SLIPSHOD

Slovensko .... SLOVAKIA

slow .... DULL, SLACK, TARDY,

RETARD, GRADUAL, LANGUID,

SLUGGISH

as _____ .... MOLASSES

boat's destination .... CHINA

down .... EASE

footed creature .... SLUG,

UNAU, LORIS, SLOTH, SNAIL,

TURTLE, TORTOISE

in music .... LARGO, LENTO,

TARDO, ANDANTE

leak .... DRIP

learner .... DUNCE

mover .... SNAIL

moving-person .... IDLER,

LAGGARD

progress/tempo .... SNAIL'S

PACE

train .... LOCAL

up .... BRAKE, DELAY

walk .... STROLL, TRUDGE

witted .... DULL, DENSE

witted person ..... DOLT, DOPE,

DUMMY, DUNCE, DIMWIT

slowly .... LEISURELY

slowpoke .... IDLER, SLOTH,

SNAIL, LAGGARD, LOITERER,

SLUGGARD

slubber .... DAUB, BOTCH, SMEAR,

STAIN

sludge .... MUD, MIRE, FLOE,

OOZE, SLAG, FILTH, SLEET,

SLUSH, SEWAGE, (DRIFT)ICE,

SEDIMENT

slue .... LOT(S), SLEW, PIVOT,

SLOUGH

slug .... HIT, BELT, BASH, BLOW,

SWAT, SMASH, SNAIL, TOKEN,

BULLET, PELLET, MOLLUSK,

TREPANG, GASTROPOD

genus .... LIMAX

sluggard .... LAZY, DRONE,

IDLE(R), SNAIL, LOAFER

object lesson of .... ANT

slugger .... PUG(ILIST),

PRIZEFIGHTER

sluggish .... DULL, LAZY, LOGY,

SLOW, INERT, LEADEN,

TORPID, LANGUID, STAGNANT,

LETHARGIC, TARDIGRADE

condition .... TORPOR

creek .... BAYOU

slugs, of/like .... LIMACINE

sluice ...... SOW, FLUME, TROUGH,

CHANNEL, PENSTOCK,

(FLOOD)GATE

slum .... GHETTO

kid .... GUTTERSNIPE

slumber .... NAP, DOZE, SLEEP,

REPOSE

sound .... SNORE

slump .... SAG, DROP, FALL, SINK,

WANE, DROOP, SPRAWL,

DECLINE

business .... RECESSION

slur .... BLUR, ELIDE, SMEAR,

STAIN, SULLY, SLIGHT,

SMIRCH, ASPERSE, DISCREDIT,

DISPARAGE

slush .... MUD, MIRE, SLOP,

PATCH, DRIVEL

fund's use .... BRIBE(RY)

slut ...... DOG, DOXY, DRAB, JADE, SLOB, BITCH, QUEAN, TROLLOP, SLATTERN, PROSTITUTE

sly .... FOXY, WILY, CAGEY, ARTFUL, CRAFTY, TRICKY, CUNNING, FURTIVE, INSIDIOUS

look .... LEER

on the .... COVERTLY, SECRETLY

one .... FOX

very .... AS CUNNING AS A FOX

Slye, pathologist .... MAUD

smack .... HIT, BLOW, BUSS, KISS, SLAP, TANG, GUSTO, SAVOR, SLOOP, SMITE, TASTE, TRACE, WHACK, FLAVOR, STRIKE, THWACK, (SAIL)BOAT

slang .... HEROIN

smacking .... ALIVE, BRISK, LIVELY, SPANKING

small .... LIL, LOW, WEE, MEAN, PUNY, TINY, DINKY, PETTY, SHORT, TEENY, BANTAM, LITTLE, MINUTE, PALTRY, PETIT(E), TRIVIAL, MINIATURE, MINUSCULE

allowance .... PITTANCE

amount ...... DAB, DOIT, DRAM, GRAM, IOTA, MITE, GRAIN, MINIM, PINCH, MORSEL, MODICUM, FRACTION

and active .... DAPPER

and trim .... PETITE

animal .... RUNT

anything .... PINHEAD

armadillo .... PEBA

arms .... RIFLES, PISTOLS, CARBINES, REVOLVERS

bag .... SATCHEL

barracuda .... SPET

bite .... NIP

blisters .... CHICKENPOX

body of land .... ISLE

body of water .... POND

bottle .... VIAL, PHIAL

boy .... TAD

bright object .... SPANGLE

brook .... RILL

bunch .... WISP

burg .... DORP

cactus .... MESCAL

canyon .... CANADA

car .... COMPACT

case .... ETUI

cask .... KEG

cavity atop a volcano

.... CRATERLET

cavity in the body

.... FOLLICLE

change .... COIN(S), PETTY CASH

chest .... COFFRET

children .... TADS

cloud .... CLOUDLET

cobra .... ASP

combining form .... LEPTO, MICR(O), STENO

contribution .... MITE

cottage .... BUNGALOW

craft threat .... GALE

cube .... DICE

cucumber .... GHERKIN

cyst .... WEN

dam .... WEIR

demon .... IMP

distance .... HAIR

donkey .... BURRO

drink .... SNORT

drop .... GLOB

drum .... BONGO, SNARE

egg .... OVULE

error .... SLIP

fastener .... THUMBTACK

featured role .... CAMEO

finch .... SERIN

fish .... FRY, ID(E), DACE, SMELT, MINNOW, SARDINE, FINGERLING

flag .... FANION, PENNANT

flock .... COVEY

fly .... GNAT

fry .... TAD, KIDS, CHILDREN, YOUNGSTERS

generator .... MAGNETO

glass .... VIAL, JIGGER

handbill .... FLYER, DODGER

heater .... ETNA

hen .... BANTY

hill .... KNOLL

hollow .... AREOLA

horse .... PONY, BIDET, SHETLAND

house of yore .... COT

in law .... PETIT

in worth .... POOR

immature mushroom

.... BUTTON

island .... AIT, CAY

lake .... POND

lemur .... ANGWANTIBO

letter(s) .... MINUSCULE

lie .... FIB

lump .... NODULE

mammal .... COON, HARE

margin .... HAIR

marsh bird .... RAIL

mass .... WAD

minded .... MEAN, PETTY

monkey .... TITI

mound .... TEE

nail .... BRAD, FOUR PENNY

napkin .... DOILY

opening .... PORE, STOMA

parakeet .... LORIKEET

part .... BIT, DETAIL, FRACTION

particle .... ATOM

passerine bird .... VIREO

pastry shell .... TIMBALE

perforated glass object

.... BEAD

person .... RUNT, DWARF, MIDGE, PYGMY, BANTAM, SHRIMP

pest .... IMP, GNAT

piano .... SPINET

pie .... TART

piece .... CHIP, SNIP(PET)

plateau .... MESA

point .... DOT

porch .... STOOP

portion .... NIP, MODICUM

quantity .... BIT, IOTA, SPOT

ring .... ANNULET

sailboat .... YAWL

salmon .... GRILSE

sculpture .... CAMEO

shield .... ECU

shops .... ARCADE

shot .... COG

something extremely

.... MINIM

space .... AREOLA

spot .... DOT

stream .... BAYOU, RUNLET, RIVULET

suitcase .... GRIP

table .... STAND

talk .... CHITCHAT

telescope .... SPYGLASS

thing to pick .... NIT

time .... MINOR, PETTY

tool .... AWL, BIT

tower .... TURRET

town .... BURGH, VILLAGE

town paper .... WEEKLY

truck .... PICKUP

unspecified number

.... BAKER'S DOZEN

very .... WEE

violin .... KIT

yard, old style .... GARTH

smallage .... CELERY, PARSLEY

smallest .... LEAST, MINIM, TINIEST

amount .... LEAST

bird .... HUMMINGBIRD

carnivore .... WEASEL

finger .... PINKIE

liquid measure .... MINIMUM

of all mammals .... SHREW

of the Dionne quintuplets
.... MARIE
offspring .... RUNT
particle of an element
.... ATOM, MOLECULE
planet .... MERCURY
rabbit .... PYGMY
sovereign state .... VATICAN
CITY
smallpox .... VARIOLA, VARICELLA
disease of .... ZYMOTIC
mark .... POCK
resembling .... VARIOLOID
smalt .... BICE, BLUE, GLASS,
PIGMENT
smalto .... ENAMEL
smaragd .... EMERALD
smart .... APT, CHIC, KEEN, NEAT,
PERT, TRIM, BRISK, NIFTY,
QUICK, SHARP, SLICK, STING,
WITTY, CLEVER, DAPPER,
SHREWD, SPRUCE, SUFFER,
SWANKY, DASHING, STYLISH
aleck .... QUACK, WISE GUY
alecky ...... SAUCY, FLIP(PANT)
as a _____ .... WHIP
blow .... RAP
elegance .... CHIC
guy .... SLICK
set .... ELITE, LITERATI
slang .... SPIFFY
smartly dressed .... NATTY
phrased .... NEAT
smash .... HIT, DASH, ROUT,
BREAK, CRUSH, WRECK,
DEFEAT, STRIKE, SHATTER
sign .... SRO
smashup .... RUIN, CRASH,
WRECK, ACCIDENT, DISASTER,
COLLISION
smaze .... SOOT
relative of .... SMOG
smear .... DAB, DAUB, SOIL, SPOT,
DEFAME, GREASE, MALIGN,
SMUDGE, SLANDER, SLUBBER
smearcase .... CHEESE
smee .... POCHARD
smell ...... NOSE, ODO(U)R, SCENT,
SENSE, SNIFF, WHIFF, DETECT,
FLAVOR, INHALE
fats' .... RANCID
goatlike .... HIRCINE
loss of .... ANOSMIA
of the sense of .... OLFACTORY
offensive .... FOUL, OLID,
ODOR, RANK, REEK, FETOR,
STINK, STENCH
organ of .... NOSE, OLFACTORY
NERVE
perception, abnormal
.... DYSOSMIA

pleasant/savory .... AROMA
stale .... FUSTY, MUSTY
smeller .... NOSE, FEELER,
ANTENNA
smelling .... REDOLENT
salts ...... AMMONIA, INHALANT
smelly: var. .... REEKIE
smelt .... FISH, FUSE, MELT,
REFINE, CAP(E)LIN, SPARLING
fish like .... TROUT
smelter .... BLAST, FORGE,
FURNACE
smelting by-product .... SLAG,
DROSS, SPEISS
waste .... TUTTY
Smetana, composer .... BEDRICH
opera .... DANCE OF THE
COMEDIANS
smew .... DUCK, SCOTER,
MERGANSER
smidgen .... BIT, IOTA, MITE
smilax .... VINE, SARSAPARILLA
smile .... BEAM, GRIN, LAUGH,
SMIRK, SNEER, SIMPER,
GRIMACE
broadly .... GRIN
certain .... TOOTHY
Mona Lisa .... CRYPTIC,
ENIGMATIC
scornful .... SNEER
self-satisfied .... SMIRK
silly .... SIMPER
smiling .... RIANT, RIDENT
smirch ...... BLOT, DIRTY, SMEAR,
STAIN, SULLY, SMUDGE,
SMUT(CH), TARNISH,
DISCOLOR
smirk .... GRIN, LEER, SMILE,
SIMPER, GRIMACE
smite .... HIT, CUFF, AFFECT,
DEFEAT, ENAMOR, PUMMEL,
STRIKE, AFFLICT, DISTRESS
smith .... FORGE, TINKER,
VULCAN, METALWORKER
block of .... ANVIL
furnace of .... FORGE
invisible .... WAYLAND
Smith, confederate general
.... KIRBY
smithereens .... BITS, PIECES,
FRAGMENTS
smithsonite .... CALAMINE
smithy .... FORGE, STITHY,
BLACKSMITH
smitten .... TAKEN, ENAMORED,
STRICKEN, AFFLICTED
smock .... APRON, FROCK, CAMISE,
CHEMISE
smog .... MIST, SMAZE
ingredient .... SOOT, SMOKE
smoke .... CURE, FLOC, FUME,

LUNT, MIST, PUFF, REEF,
SMOG, VAPOR, INHALE,
CIGARET, POLLUTE,
CIGAR(ETTE)
a pipe .... WHIFF
and mist .... SMOG, SMAZE
country boy's .... CORNSILK
fragrant .... INCENSE
go up in .... EVAPORATE
meat .... REEST
out .... FLUSH, FORCE OUT
pipe .... STACK, FUNNEL
screen .... CAMOUFLAGE
tree .... YELLOWWOOD
smokeless power .... FILITE,
CORDITE
smoker .... STAG, PARTY
smokestack .... FLUE, FUNNEL,
CHIMNEY
worker .... STEEPLEJACK
smooking pipe .... BRIAR,
HOOKAH, CALUMET,
NARGHILE
room .... DIVAN
smoky .... HAZY
quartz .... CAIRNGORM
smolder .... BURN, FUME
Smollett, novelist .... TOBIAS
smolt .... SALMON
smooch .... KISS, SMUTCH
old style .... SPOON
smooth .... CALM, EVEN, IRON,
OILY, SAND, SOFT, BLAND,
GRIND, SLEEK, SUAVE,
REFINE, SERENE, SLICK,
SOOTHE, URBANE, VELVETY,
GLABROUS, POLISH(ED)
and lustrous .... SILKY
and white .... ALABASTER
combining form .... LIO
consonant .... LENE
feathers/with beak .... PREEN
in mechanics .... FRICTIONLESS
in music .... LEGATO
in performance .... DOLCE
in phonetics .... LENE
over .... GLOSS
pated .... BALD
talker .... CHARMER
tongued/talking .... GLIB,
OILY, SUAVE
with an abrasive .... SAND
smoother .... PLANE, BUFFER,
MANGLE
smoothing rock .... PUMICE
smorgasbord .... BUFFET
treat .... EELS, CANAPE,
DESSERT, KICKSHAW
smother .... CHOKE, DEADEN,
STIFLE, WELTER, REPRESS,
SUFFOCATE

smudge .... BLOT, BLUR, DIRT,
SLUR, SOIL, SOOT, SPOT,
GRIME, SMEAR, SMOKE,
STAIN, SMUTCH
smug .... NEAT, TRIM, SLEEK,
CONCEITED, COMPLACENT
one .... PRIG
smuggle .... RUN, SNEAK IN,
BOOTLEG
smuggled goods .... CONTRABAND
whisk(e)y .... MOONSHINE
smuggler .... GUNRUNNER,
(RUM)RUNNER, BOOTLEGGER
ship of .... RUNNER
smugness .... VANITY, CONCEIT
smut ...... ROT, BUNT, DIRT, SOOT,
CROCK, FILTH, FUNGUS,
MILDEW, OBSCENITY
smutch .... DIRT, SMUT, SOOT,
GRIME, SMUDGE
Smuts, S. African statesman
.... JAN
smutty .... OBSCENE, INDECENT
Smyrna .... IZMIR
fig .... ELEME
snack .... EAT, BITE, LUNCH,
CANAPE, REPAST, TIFFIN
bar .... CAFETERIA
snaffle .... BIT, CURB
snafu .... CHAOS, MIX-UP,
BOOBOO, FOUL-UP, MUDDLE,
SCREW-UP
snag .... TEAR, HITCH, TOOTH,
OBSTACLE, FLY-IN-THE-
OINTMENT
snail ...... HELIX, WHELK, NERITA,
MOLLUSK, ESCARGOT,
SLUG(GARD), GASTROPOD
genus .... NERITA, OLEACINA
oyster-killer .... DRILL
shell .... CARACOLE,
PERIWINKLE
snails, of/like .... LIMACINE
snake .... ASP, LORA, (A)BOMA,
COBRA, VIPER, PYTHON,
REPTILE, SERPENT, OPHIDIAN
big .... BOA, PYTHON,
ANACONDA, PUFF ADDER, FER-
DE-LANCE, CONSTRICTOR
bite remedy .... GUACO,
CEDRON
black .... KRAIT, RACER
burrowing .... GOPHER
castoff of .... SLOUGH
charmer's flute .... PUNGI
charmer's tool .... MUSIC
combining form .... OPHI(O)
common .... ADDER
coral .... HARLEQUIN
crusher .... PYTHON,
ANACONDA, BOA

(CONSTRICTOR)
deity .... ZOMBI(E)
doctor ...., DRAGONFLY
eyes .... CRAPS, AMBSACE
fish like .... EEL, LAMPREY,
OARFISH, LIZARD FISH
genus .... NAJA, ELAPS,
ELAPHE, NATRIX, PYTHON,
HETERODON, COLUBER,
BUNGARUS, PITUOPHIS,
DENDRASPIS
haired woman .... GORGON,
MEDUSA
harmless .... MILK, RACER,
GARTER, HOGNOSE
hooded .... COBRA
horned .... RATTLER,
CERASTES, SAND VIPER
in the grass ..... RAT, DOUBLE-
CROSSER
killer .... SECRETARY BIRD
kind of .... RAT, BULL, MILK,
PINE, CORAL, WATER, RACER,
HOODED, HORNED
king ...... COBRA, HAMADRYAD
like .... APODAL, ANGUINE,
SINUOUS, COLUBRINE
movement .... SLITHER
non-poisonous .... BULL,
GARTER, PYTHON
pit .... BEDLAM, JUNGLE,
MADHOUSE
poison .... VENOM, VIRUS
poisonous .... ASP, SEPS,
COBRA, KRAIT, MAMBA, VIPER,
CERASTES, MOCCASIN, PUFF
ADDER, COPPERHEAD, FER-DE-
LANCE, COTTONMOUTH
root .... STEVIA, SANICLE
sand .... SIDEWINDER
sea .... KERRIL
skin(s) .... EXUVIA(E)
skin shedding .... ECDYSIS
slain by Apollo .... PYTHON
small .... ASP, ADDER, GARTER,
HOGNOSE, SIDEWINDER
space on head of .... LORE
teeth .... FANGS
tempter of Eve .... SERPENT
tree .... MAMBA
type of .... BOA, ADDER,
RACER, VIPER, PYTHON,
RATTLER, CONSTRICTOR
(warning) sound of .... HISS,
RATTLE
water .... MOCCASIN,
COTTONMOUTH
snakebird .... DARTER, PLOTUS,
WRYNECK
snakehead .... FIGWORT
snakemouth .... ORCHID

snakes, study of ...... OPHIOLOGY
snakestone .... AMMONITE
snaky .... ANGUINE, WINDING,
SERPENTINE
snap .... NIP, PEP, POP, BARK,
BITE, CLAP, CLIP, DASH, EASY,
KNAP, BREAK, COOKY,
CRACK, FLICK, SNARL, SPELL,
WAFER, FILLIP, SIMPLE,
SNATCH, FASTENER, SINECURE
a coin in the air .... FLIP
colloquial .... CINCH
of fingers .... FILLIP
snapdragon .... FIGWORT
snapper .... SESI, BEETLE,
TAMURE, TURTLE
kin of .... SCUP
snappish ...... EDGY, RUDE, TART,
CROSS, TESTY, SNARLY,
UNCIVIL, IRRITABLE
snappy ...... BRISK, CROSS, QUICK,
SHARP, SMART, STYLISH
answer .... RETORT
make it .... HURRY
snare .... GIN, WEB, MESH, BENET,
CATCH, NOOSE, (EN)TRAP,
(DRAG)NET, PIT(FALL),
RATTRAP, SPRINGE
snared .... BAGGED
snark .... BOOJUM
snarl .... GIRN, KNOT, GNAR(L),
GROWL, GRUMBLE,
(EN)TANGLE
snatch ...... BIT, GET, NAB, GRAB,
JERK, TAKE, GRASP, PLUCK,
SEIZE, SPELL, SWIPE, WREST,
KIDNAP(PING)
sneak ...... LURK, MOOCH, SKULK,
SLINK, STEAL
sneakers .... GUMSHOES,
(CANVAS)SHOES
sneaking .... FURTIVE, COWARDLY
snee .... DIRK
sneer .... MOCK, FLEER, SCOFF,
SCORN, SMILE
sneering ...... DERISIVE, SCORNFUL
sneeze ...... SNUFF, STERNUTATION
at .... BRUSH OFF, DISREGARD
sound .... ACHOO
sneezewort .... YARROW
sneezing, cause of .... COLD,
ALLERGY, HAY FEVER
snell .... GUT, KEEN, ACUTE,
HARSH, QUICK, SMART,
LEADER, SEVERE
Snerd, dummy .... MORTIMER
snick .... CUT, NICK, CLICK,
NOTCH
and _____ .... SNEE
snicker .... LAUGH, NEIGH, TEHEE,
GIGGLE, TITTER

snickersnee .... KNIFE
snide .... SLY, BASE, MEAN,
    NASTY, ORNERY, CYNICAL,
    MALICIOUS, SARCASTIC
sniff .... NOSE, SCENT, SMELL,
    SNORT, DETECT, INHALE,
    BREATHE
sniffles .... (HEAD)COLD
sniffy .... SCORNFUL, DISDAINFUL
snifter .... NIP, SIP, SHOT, DRINK,
    GOBLET
snigger .... LAUGH, GIGGLE,
    CHUCKLE, SNICKER
sniggle ...... HOOK, NOOSE, SNARE
snip .... BIT, CUT, CLIP, PIECE,
    SHEAR, SHRIMP
snipe .... BIRD, CIGAR, GODWIT,
    WOODCOCK
sniper .... AMBUSHER
snippet .... TAG, CHIP, SCRAP,
    DOLLOP, FRAGMENT
snippy .... CURT, GRUFF, BRUSQUE
snit .... PIQUE, TIZZY, DITHER
snitch .... TELL, PEACH, STEAL,
    SWIPE, PILFER, SQUEAL,
    INFORM(ER)
snivel .... CRY, FRET, WEEP, SNIFF,
    WHINE, SNUFFLE, WHIMPER,
    COMPLAIN
snob .... PRIG, PRUDE, TOADY,
    HIGH-HAT, PARVENU, UPSTART
snobbery .... HAUTEUR, PRIGGERY
snobbish .... PROUD, RITZY,
    SELECT, SNOOTY, SNOTTY,
    UPPISH, UPPITY, HIGH-HAT,
    STUCK-UP, PRIGGISH
snood ...... SNELL, FILLET, RIBBON,
    (HAIR)NET
snook .... ROBALO
snoop .... PRY, LURK, PROWL,
    SKULK, SPIER, NOSE AROUND
snooper .... PRY, MEDDLER,
    BUSYBODY
electronic .... BUG
snoopy one .... PRIER
snoot .... FACE, NOSE, SNUB,
    GRIMACE
snooty .... ALOOF, PROUD,
    HAUGHTY, SNOBBISH
one .... SNOB
snooze .... NAP, DOZE, SLEEP,
    CATNAP, DROWSE
snore .... RALE, SNIFF, WHEEZE,
    RHONCUS, STERTOR
snorer .... SAWER
loud .... GRAMPUS
snort .... NIP, DRINK, LAUGH,
    SNIFF, SNUFF
snorter .... HUMDINGER
snot .... MUCUS, PHLEGM
snotty .... MUCOID, HAUGHTY,

    IMPUDENT, OFFENSIVE
snout ...... NEB, BEAK, BILL, JAWS,
    NOSE, SERRA, MUZZLE,
    NOZZLE, ROSTRUM
dig with .... ROOT, ROUT
elephant's .... TRUNK
push/rub with .... NUZZLE
tapir's .... PROBOSCIS
snouted creature .... HOG, PIG,
    TAPIR, DESMAN, ECHIDNA,
    ANTEATER, AARDVARK,
    ELEPHANT
snow .... SNA, FIRN, HAIL, PASH,
    DRIFT, SLEET
become heaped with .... DRIFT
briefly .... SPIT
bunting .... FINCH
field .... NEVE
granular .... FIRN, NEVE
growing under .... NIVAL
gust of .... FLURRY
house .... HOLE, IGLOO,
    IG(D)LU
job .... SONG-AND-DANCE
leopard .... OUNCE
of .... NIVAL
on a glacier .... NEVE
partly melted .... SLUSH
pellets .... HAIL
runner/glider .... SKI, SKEE,
    (BOB)SLED, TOBOGGAN
slang .... HEROIN, COCAINE
slide, mass .... AVALANCHE
small feathery piece of
    .... FLAKE
travel through .... MUSH
vehicle .... SLED, SLEDGE,
    SLEIGH, SNOWMOBILE
watery .... SLOP, SLUSH
Snow White's friends
    .... DWARFS
snowbird .... FINCH, JUNCO,
    LERWA, ADDICT
snowbird's need .... DOPE, DRUG,
    HEROIN, COCAINE
snowdrift .... NEVE
snowdrop .... ANEMONE
snowfall .... HAIL, SLEET
snowflake .... FINCH, BUNTING
snowlike .... NIVEOUS
snowshoe .... PAC, SKI, RACKET
snowstorm .... BLIZZARD
snowy .... WHITE, BRUMAL,
    WINTRY, NIVEOUS, SPOTLESS
weather need .... MITTEN,
    EARMUFF, MUFFLER,
    OVERSHOES
snub .... CUT, CURB, STOP, CHECK,
    SCORN, IGNORE, REBUFF,
    SLIGHT, AFFRONT, HIGH-HAT,
    SET DOWN, UPSTAGE,

    TURNED-UP
nose(d) .... PUG
snubber .... PRIG, SNOB
snuff .... ODOR, PINCH, SCENT,
    SMELL, SNIFF, SNORT, INHALE,
    POWDER, PUT OUT, RAPPEE,
    TOBACCO, MACCOBOY
out .... DOUSE, EXTINGUISH
perfumed .... MACCABOY,
    MACCOBOY
snuffle ...... SMELL, SNIFF, SNORT,
    TWANG, SNIVEL
snug .... COSY, COZY, NEAT, SAFE,
    TAUT, TRIM, WARM, SECURE,
    FRIENDLY, COMFORTABLE
as a bug ____ .... IN A RUG
retreat .... DEN, NEST
spot .... CUDDYHOLE
snuggle .... CUDDLE, NESTLE,
    NUZZLE
so .... SIC, ERGO, THEN, THUS,
    TRUE, VERY, HENCE,
    LIKEWISE, THEREFORE
and so .... SOMEONE,
    SOMEBODY
be it .... AMEN
long! .... TATA, GOOD-BY
on, and .... ETCETERA
or .... NEARLY, ROUGHLY
-so .... AVERAGE, ORDINARY,
    PASSABLE
that .... PROVIDED
what! .... NO MATTER, ALL
    THE SAME
So Big author .... FERBER
Big heroine .... SELINA
Red the ____ .... ROSE
soak .... RET, SOG, SOP, WET,
    IMBUE, SOUSE, STEEP,
    DRENCH, SODDEN, IMMERSE,
    SATURATE
as fiber/flax .... RET
colloquial .... DRINK
customer .... BLEED, GOUGE,
    OVERCHARGE
in brine/vinegar .... MARINATE
in liquid .... STEEP, SOUSE
slang .... BOX, HIT, PAWN,
    TIPPLER, DRUNKARD
to soften .... RET, STEEP,
    MACERATE
up .... (AB)SORB, SPONGE
with blood .... IMBRUE
soaked .... SOGGY, SODDEN,
    SOPPING
soaker .... SOT, DELUGE, GUZZLER,
    TIPPLER, RAINSTORM
soaking medium .... BATH
pit .... FURNACE
soap ...... SAPO, LATHER, CASTILE,
    CLEAN(S)ER, DETERGENT

acid of .... OLEIC
bar frame .... SESS
convert into .... SAPONIFY
cresol mixture .... LYSOL
foam .... SUDS, BUBBLES
ingredient .... LYE
kind of .... BAR, BATH, LIQUID,
     POWDER, LAUNDRY
material ...... POTASH, TALLOW
no .... NOTHING DOING
oil .... CITRONELLA
olive oil .... CASTILE
opera .... SOAPER, MELODRAMA
opera sphere .... DAYTIME
plant .... AMOLE
segment .... EPISODE
slang .... (BRIBE)MONEY
substitute ...... AMOLE, QUILIAI
vine .... GOGO
soapbark .... MIMOSA, QUILIAI
glucoside .... SAPONIN(E)
soapberry .... LICHEE, LITCHI,
     RAMBUTAN
soapbox character .... QUACK,
     ORATOR, RANTER, AGITATOR,
     DEMAGOGUE
race .... DERBY
soapstone .... TALC, STEATITE
soapsuds .... FOAM, LATHER,
     BUBBLES
soapy .... OILY, FOAMY, SUAVE,
     UNCTUOUS, SAPONACEOUS
water .... SUDS
soar .... FLY, RISE, SAIL, GLIDE,
     TOWER
in a way .... FLY OFF THE
     HANDLE
soaring .... HIGH, LOFTY,
     MOUNTING, TOWERING
sob ...... CRY, BAWL, MOAN, SIGH,
     WEEP
story .... TEAR-JERKER
sober .... CALM, SANE, GRAVE,
     PLAIN, QUIET, SOUND, STAID,
     FRUGAL, SEDATE, SOLEMN,
     SOMBER, SERIOUS, MODERATE,
     TEMPERATE
sobriety .... GRAVITY, FRUGALITY,
     MODERATION, TEMPERANCE
sobriquet .... ALIAS, AGNAME,
     BYNAME, PET-NAME,
     COGNOMEN, NICKNAME
of the Supreme Court
     (former) .... THE NINE
     OLD MEN
soccer .... FOOTBALL
player, famed .... PELE,
     CHARLTON
Soche .... YARKAND
sociable .... NICE, CHATTY,
     FOLKSY, JOVIAL, SOCIAL,

     AFFABLE, FRIENDLY,
     OUTGOING, HOSPITABLE,
     NEIGHBORLY
colloquial .... CLUBBY
social .... BEE, CIVIC, PARTY,
     PUBLIC, COMMUNAL,
     CONVIVIAL, GATHERING
affair .... TEA, SOIREE,
     SHINDIG, MUSICALE
appointment .... DATE
asset .... TACT, GRACE,
     DIPLOMACY
call .... GAM
class .... CASTE
climber .... SNOB, UPSTART,
     ADVENTURER, TUFTHUNTER,
     NAME-DROPPER
contract theorist .... HOBBS,
     LOCKE, ROUSSEAU
disease in short .... VD
error ...... FAUX PAS, SOLECISM
event .... BALL, DANCE, DEBUT,
     MARDIGRAS
event of 1773 .... BOSTON TEA
     PARTY
evil .... PROSTITUTION
finesse .... TACT
gathering .... BALL, LEVEE,
     PARTY, SOIREE, REUNION,
     RECEPTION
gathering, costumed
     .... MASQUERADE
gathering for men .... STAG,
     SMOKER
gathering for women ...... HEN
     PARTY
grace .... ETIQUETTE
grace, lacking .... GAUCHEE
group .... CLAN, CLUB, CLIQUE,
     CIRCLE, COTERIE
hierarchy .... CASTE
insect .... ANT, BEE, WASP,
     VESPID, TERMITE
order .... REGIME
outcast .... LEPER, PARIAH
outdoors gathering .... BBQ,
     FRY, BARBECUE
person .... JOINER
reformer, American ..... MOTT
rules of conduct .... DECORUM
science .... SOCIOLOGY
security .... INSURANCE
service .... WELFARE
standing .... STATION
system .... CASTE, REGIME
unit .... FAMILY
virtue .... TACT
visit .... GAM, CALL
wasp .... VESPID
Social Contract author
     .... ROUSSEAU

Register .... BLUEBOOK
socialist .... MARX, ENGELS,
     FOURIER
socialite .... JET-SETTER,
     TRENDSETTER, CLOTHESHORSE
potential .... DEB(UTANTE)
socialize .... VISIT, HOBNOB,
     MINGLE, FRATERNIZE
in restaurant .... TABLE-HOP
society .... BODY, CLUB, GUILD,
     ORDER, VEREIN, COMPANY,
     COMMUNITY, ASSOCIATION
bigwig .... NOB
bow .... DEBUT
bud ..... (SUB)DEB, DEBUTANTE
combining form .... SOCIO
doings .... SOCIALS
entrance into .... DEBUT
fashionable .... BONTON
for animals .... SPCA
of the learned .... ACADEMY
page figure ..... DEB, SWINGER,
     SOCIALITE
with government .... POLITY
Society Islands' capital
     .... PAPEETE
Islands, one of the .... TAHAA,
     MOOREA, TAHITI, BORA-BORA
of Friends .... QUAKERS
of Friends founder .... FOX
of Jesus founder ..... IGNATIUS
     (OF LOYOLA)
socials .... GALAS, PARTIES
sociology .... DEMOTICS
sock .... BOP, BOX, HIT, BLOW,
     HOSE, SHOE, ANKLET,
     COMEDY, WALLOP, STOCKING
sockdolager .... ONER, FINISHER
socket .... CUP, PAN, HOLE,
     MORTISE
bit .... POD
roof beam .... OPA
sockeye .... (RED)SALMON
socko .... HIT, SMASH
socks .... SOX, HOSE, ARGYLE,
     BOOTEES
Socrate composer .... SATIE
Socrates' disciple .... PLATO
wife .... XANTHIPPE
sod .... DIRT, PEAT, SOIL, TURF,
     EARTH, GLEBE, SWARD
clod .... DIVOT
soda .... SELTZER, BEVERAGE,
     (CARBONATED)DRINK
——— .... POP, JERK, FOUNTAIN
adjunct .... STRAW
ash .... ALKALI, BARILLA
ash source .... SEAWEED
baking .... SALERATUS, SODIUM
     BICARBONATE
caustic .... LYE, SODIUM

HYDROXIDE
fountain .... COUNTER
fountain order .... MALT,
           SHAKE, SUNDAE
jerk .... COUNTERMAN
water .... FIZZ
sodality .... FELLOWSHIP
sodden .... SOGGY, STEEP,
    POACHY, SOAKED, DRUNKEN
sodium and aluminum
           .... NATROLITE
benzoate use .... ANTISEPTIC,
           PRESERVATIVE
bicarbonate ...... BAKING SODA
borate .... BORAX
bromide use .... SEDATIVE
carbonate .... TRONA, NATRON,
    SAL SODA, SODA(ASH)
chloride .... SALT
chloride works .... SALTERN
combining form .... NATRO
hydroxide .... LYE, CAUSTIC
                    SODA
nitrate .... NITER, CALICHE,
    SALTPETER, SALTPETRE
oxide .... SODA
thiosulfate .... HYPO
Sodom forsaker .... LOT
inhabitant .... SODOMITE
instrument of God's
    punishment on ...... FIRE,
           BRIMSTONE
neighbor of .... GOMORRAH
sodomite .... BUGGER
sodomy .... BUGGERY
form of .... PEDERASTY,
           BESTIALITY
sofa .... COUCH, DIVAN, SQUAB,
    DAYBED, SETTEE, SETTLE,
    VIS-A-VIS, DAVENPORT,
          CHESTERFIELD
backless .... LOUNGE
boxy, overstuffed ..... LAWSON
covering .... TIDY
small .... SETTEE, LOVE-SEAT
soft ...... LOW, EASY, HUSH, MILD,
    WEAK, BLAND, PAPPY, SILKY,
    GENTLE, MELLOW, PLIANT,
    SMOOTH, TENDER, SUBDUED,
    VELVETY, TEMPERATE
and limp .... FLABBY
and sweet .... DOLCE
breeze .... AURA
-cover .... PAPERBACK
drink .... ADE, POP, COKE,
    MEAD, SODA, PEPSI, COCA-
        COLA, GATORADE
fabric ..... SILK, PANNE, SATIN,
    VELVET, CASHMERE
feathers .... DOWN, EIDER
food .... PAP, SOUP

goods ..... CLOTHING, TEXTILES
hair .... VILLUS
ice .... LOLLY
in music .... PIANO
in phonetics .... SIBILANT
in the head .... STUPID,
           FOOLISH
job .... SNAP, SINECURE
mass .... PULP
metal .... TIN, LEAD
mineral .... TALC
palate .... UVULA, VELUM
pedal .... EASE, MUTE,
    MODERATE, PLAY DOWN, TONE
           DOWN
roll .... BUN
rustling sound .... WHISPER
saddle .... PANEL
shoe .... PAC, DANCE
shoulder .... BERM(E)
-soap .... SNOW, URGE,
    CAJOLE, BLARNEY, FLATTER
sound .... HUM, BUZZ, SIGH,
           MURMUR
sound of leaves .... RUSTLE
spoken .... QUIET, SUAVE,
    GENTLE, SMOOTH
spot ..... FONTANEL, WEAKNESS
tissue .... BREI
toned organ stop .... DOLCE
touch .... TAP, EASY MARK,
          PUSHOVER
soften .... EASE, MELT, RELAX,
    YIELD, LOOSEN, RELENT,
    TEMPER, MOLLIFY, MITIGATE
by soaking .... RET, STEEP,
          MACERATE
softening .... LENITIVE
of the brain .... DEMENTIA
softhead .... SIMPLETON
softie .... SISSY, WEAKLING
softly .... LOW, MUTED, PIANO,
          FAINTLY
softness .... LAXITY, LOWNESS,
    PLIANCY, LENIENCY,
    WEAKNESS, MELLOWNESS
Sogdian .... IRANIAN
soggy .... WET, DOUGHY, POACHY,
    SOAKED, SODDEN
Soho feature .... RESTAURANTS
optimism .... OPE
radial .... TYRE
soigne .... CHIC, NEAT, TIDY,
    MODISH, STYLISH
soil ...... SOD, CLAY, DAUB, LAND,
    LOAM, MARL, DIRT(Y),
    EARTH, GLEBE, GUMBO,
    LOESS, PURGE, STAIN, SULLY,
    BLOTCH, DEFILE, GROUND,
    SMIRCH, SMUDGE, (BE)SMEAR,
        COUNTRY

good .... LOAM
hard layer of .... PAN
hole-making tool .... DIBBLE
in combination .... AGRO
infertile .... PODZOL
organic part of .... HUMUS
poetic .... GLEBE
restorer .... VETCH
science .... PEDOLOGY
unfruitful .... BARREN
wind-deposited .... LOESS
soja .... SAUCE, SOY(BEAN)
sojourn .... REST, STAY, VISIT,
          LODGE, TARRY
sojourner ...... LODGER, BOARDER,
          PILGRIM
Sojourner .... TRUTH
sol .... COIN, GOLD, NOTE
Sol .... SUN(GOD)
impresario .... HUROK
sola .... ALONE
solace ...... CALM, ALLAY, CHEER,
    RELIEF, SOOTHE, ASSUAGE,
    COMFORT, CONSOLE
solan goose .... GANNET
solanaceous family
           .... NIGHTSHADE
plant .... POTATO, TOMATO,
    PETUNIA, TOBACCO
solano .... WIND
solanum .... NIGHTSHADE
family .... TREES, VINES,
          SHRUBS
solar .... HELIACAL
companion .... PLEXUS
deity .... SOL, LLEU, HELIOS
disk .... ATEN
disk: var. .... ATON
furnace site .... ODEILLO
phenomenon .... CORONA,
          ECLIPSE
spot/streak .... FACULA
system model .... ORRERY
system, part of .... SUN, MARS,
    EARTH, PLUTO, VENUS,
    SATURN, URANUS, JUPITER,
    MERCURY, NEPTUNE
solarium .... PORCH, PARLOR,
          SUNROOM
solder .... BOND, FUSE, JOIN,
    MEND, WELD, BORAX, BRAZE,
    PATCH, ROSIN, UNITE, CEMENT
soldering tool .... GUN, IRON
soldier .... POILU, FIGHTER,
    TERMITE, WARRIOR,
    COMMANDO, MAN-AT-ARMS
artillery .... GUNNER,
    CANNONEER, BOMBARDIER
bag of .... DUFFEL, DUFFLE,
    MUSETTE, KNAPSACK,
    HAVERSACK

brutal .... PANDOUR
call to quarters .... TATTOO
cap of .... BERET, SHAKO
cavalry .... UHLAN, SPAHI,
HUSSAR, TROOPER
civies of .... MUFTI
employed to lay mines
.... SAPPER
fellow .... BUDDY
fighting on horseback or on
foot .... DRAGOON
food of .... CHOW, MESS,
K-RATION
foot .... INFANTRY
forced into military service
.... DRAFTEE, SELECTEE,
CONSCRIPT
freebooting .... RAPPAREE
from Down Under ..... ANZAC
headgear .... CAP, BERET,
SHAKO, HELMET
hired to serve in foreign
army .... MERCENARY
involved in a series of
military operations
.... CAMPAIGNER
infantry .... RIFLEMAN,
GRENADIER, MUSKETEER
killed .... CASUALTY
kind of .... FOOT, LANCE(R),
CAVALRY, INFANTRY,
LEGIONARY, MERCENARY
mercenary .... HESSIAN,
SWISSER, SWITZER
mounted ..... SPAHI, CAVALRY,
TROOPER
not on active duty
.... RESERVE, RESERVIST
of fortune .... ADVENTURER
old .... VET(ERAN)
pack of .... KIT
recently enlisted ...... RECRUIT,
ENLISTEE
shelter of .... BUNKER,
FOXHOLE
slang ...... DOGFACE, SADSACK,
DOUGHBOY
subject to call .... RESERVE,
RESERVIST
the President as
.... COMMANDER-IN-CHIEF
trainee .... CADET, DRAFTEE
volunteer .... ZOUAVE,
GUERRILLA
who served in the armed
forces .... VET(ERAN)
who shoots from hidden
position .... SNIPER
with musket .... DRAGO(O)N,
MUSKETEER

wounded in battle
.... CASUALTY
soldierly .... ERECT, MARTIAL
soldiers, body of .... ARRAY
collectively .... TROOPS,
MILITIA, MILITARY, RESERVES,
ARMED FORCES
rebellion of .... MUTINY
Soldiers Three author
.... KIPLING
sole .... ONE, ONLY, MERE,
(A)LONE, PLAICE, SINGLE,
UNIQUE, HALIBUT, (FLAT)FISH,
SOLITARY
foot's .... VOLA, PLANTAR
of the foot's .... VOLAR
plow's .... SLADE
solecism ...... SLIP, ERROR, LAPSE,
BLUNDER, MISTAKE,
BARBARISM, IMPROPRIETY
Soleil, _____ (Louis XIV)
.... LEROI
solely ...... ONLY, ALONE, MERELY,
EXCLUSIVELY
solemn .... GRAVE, SOBER,
FORMAL, SACRED, SOMBER,
SERIOUS, REVERENT,
DIGNIFIED
wonder .... AWE
looking .... OWLISH
word .... VOW, OATH, TROTH,
PAROL(E), PLEDGE
solemnity .... WEIGHT, DIGNITY,
GRAVITY, SOBRIETY,
FORMALITY
solemnize .... OBSERVE, PERFORM,
CELEBRATE
solfatara emission .... GAS,
VAPOR
solferino .... DYE, FUCHSIN
solicit .... ASK, BEG, BID, SEEK,
APPLY, ENTREAT, PETITION
business .... CALL ON
CUSTOMERS
customers .... TOUT, INVITE,
CANVASS
solicitation .... ENTREATY,
PETITION, PERSUASION
soliciting .... PANDERING,
PROSTITUTION
solicitor ...... LAWYER, PETITIONER
solicitous .... EAGER, ANXIOUS,
CAREFUL, CONCERNED
solicitude .... CARE, WORRY,
ANXIETY, CONCERN
solid .... FIRM, HARD, REAL,
DENSE, MASSY, RIGID, SOUND,
THICK, WHOLE, STABLE,
COMPACT, GENUINE, MASSIVE,
RELIABLE
blow .... WHAM

ground .... TERRA FIRMA
six-sided .... CUBE
solidago .... GOLDENROD
solidarity .... UNION, UNITY
solidified lava .... COULEE
solidify .... GEL, SET, CAKE, JELL,
HARDEN, COMBINE, CONGEAL
solidity .... DENSITY, FIRMNESS,
SOLVENCY, STABILITY
solidus .... BEZANT, VIRGULE,
DIAGONAL, SLANT(LINE)
soliloquist .... MONOLOGIST
soliloquy .... MONOLOGUE
solipsism, core of .... SELF
solitaire .... GEM, HERMIT,
RECLUSE, CANFIELD, CARD
GAME, PATIENCE, DIAMOND
RING
solitary .... ONE, ONLY, SOLE,
SOLO, ALONE, APART,
HERMIT, LONE(LY), REMOTE,
SINGLE, HERMITIC, ISOLATED,
CONFINEMENT
solitude ...... PRIVACY, ISOLATION,
SECLUSION, LONELINESS
sollar .... GALLERY, BRATTICE
solleret .... SHOE
solo .... ONE, ARIA, ALONE,
SINGLE, UNAIDED, SURAKARTA
Solomon .... KING, SAGE, WISE
MAN
island .... BUKA, MALAITA,
CHOISEUL, GUADALCANAL,
BOUGAINVILLE
Islands' capital .... HONIARA
Islands' city/town .... AUKI,
KIETA, SOHANO
of rhyme .... GRUNDY
seaport .... LAE
Solomon's brother .... AMNON,
ABSALOM, ADONIJAH
chariot cities, one of
.... GEZER, HAZOR, TAMAR,
BAALATH, MEGGIDO
famous structure .... TEMPLE
father .... DAVID
kingdom .... ISRAEL
land .... OPHIR
mines location .... TIMNAH
VALLEY
mother .... BATHSHEBA
sayings .... MAXIMS, PROVERBS
seal .... STAR OF DAVID
son .... MENELIK, REHOBOAM
supplier of architects,
masons and skilled
builders ..... (KING)HIRAM
solon .... SAGE, SENATOR,
WISEMAN, LAWGIVER,
LAWMAKER, LEGISLATOR
soluble salt .... SALAR

solus .... ALONE
solution .... KEY, OUT, CLUE,
BREAK, ANSWER, SEPARATION,
EXPLANATION
in pharmacy .... AQUA
part of .... SOLUTE, SOLVENT
photographer's .... REAGENT
strength of .... TITER, TITRE
solve .... CLEAR UP, EXPLAIN,
UNRAVEL, WORK OUT
a message .... DECODE,
DECIPHER
a problem .... IRON OUT,
RESOLVE
solvent .... SOUND, WATER,
HEXONE, ACETONE, DILUENT,
DISSOLVER, MENSTRUUM
abuse .... GLUE SNIFFING,
INHALING FUMES
abuse effect .... COMA, HIGH,
STUPOR
financially .... MONEYED
wood tar .... FURAN(E)
Solway Firth tributary .... EDEN
soma .... BODY, TRUNK
related to the ...., SOMATIC
type of .... ECTOMORPH,
ENDOMORPH, MESOMORPH
Somalia bay .... NEGRO
cape .... ASER, SURA, HAFUN
capital .... MOGADISHU
city/town .... BRAVA, BURAO,
MARKA, MERKA, AFMADU,
ZEILA, BORAMA, GIOHAR,
JAMAMA, BERBERA, CORIOLE,
ERIGABO, HARGEYSA,
CHISIMAYU
coin .... BESA
gulf .... ADEN
language ...... ARABIC, SOMALI
measure .... CABA
money ...... SOMALO, SHILLING
mountain .... SURUD AD
plateau .... HAUD
premier .... EGAL
president .... (SIAD) BARRE
province ..... BAY, BARI, GEDO,
MUDUG, SANAAG, TOGDHEER,
MOGADISCIO
region .... GUBAN, NOGAL
river .... GIUBA
Somaliland antelope .... BEIRA
_____ Guiba .... OLTRE
somatic .... BODILY, PARIETAL,
PHYSICAL, CORPOREAL
somatization disorder
.... HYSTERIA
somatoform disorder
.... HYPOCHONDRIASIS
somber .... SAD, DARK, DULL,
GRAVE, DISMAL, GLOOMY,

SOLEMN
sombrero .... HAT
some .... ANY, A FEW, ABOUT,
CERTAIN, VARIOUS
are black, some are green
.... TEAS
are fine .... ARTS
are golden .... OLDIES
are green .... BERETS
are liberal .... ARTS
are purple .... PASSAGES
are spilled .... BEANS
are tight .... ENDS
are wild .... OATS
band leaders .... CAKE
WALKERS
bears .... GRISLY
books .... DOGEARED
carriers .... MAILMEN
controls .... DUALS, REMOTES
eateries .... TEAROOMS
economic downers ...... STOCK
MARKET TIPS
future fliers .... EGGS
get this kind of deal
.... ROTTEN
haymakers .... LEFTS
kind of nut .... FADDIST
legislatures .... DIETS
MDs .... GPS
other time .... MANANA
putti .... CUPIDS
reviews .... RAVES
saws .... RIPPERS
time .... LATER, ONE DAY
somersault ...... TOPPLE, TUMBLE,
CAPSIZE, TWISTER, FLIP(FLOP),
SOMERSET
something .... PART, MATTER,
ANYTHING
done for effect .... EYEWASH
easy .... PIE
else .... OTHER, ANOTHER
for thought .... FOOD
imagined .... FIGMENT
kept .... RETENT
monstrous .... FREAK, PRODIGY
notable/outstanding ..... DAISY
often copped .... PLEA
stated .... PAROL
that links .... COPULA
to bend .... EAR
carry .... ONUS
do with notes ...... COMPARE
pump .... IRON
purfle .... BORDER
set .... PACE
stand on .... LEG, FOOTING
sometime .... ONCE, FORMER,
ERST(WHILE)
in the future .... ONE DAY

sometimes .... NOW AND THEN,
OCCASIONALLY
bald .... PATE
Blue .... NUN(S)
found in the fire .... FAT
gold .... LEAF, LEAVES
it is bitter .... END
of woe .... TALE
raves, too .... RANTS
somewhat ...... KIND OF, NEARLY,
PARTLY, RATHER
ill .... POORLY
suffix .... ISH
somewhere .... SOMEPLACE
somite .... TELSON, SEGMENT,
MATAMERE
somnambulist ...... SLEEPWALKER
somniferous .... SOPORIFIC
somnolence .... LETHARGY,
DROWSINESS, SLEEPINESS
somnolent ...... DOZING, DROWSY,
SLEEPY, LETHARGIC
son .... HEIR, SCION, JUNIOR,
PROGENY, INHERITOR,
OFFSPRING
favorite .... BENJAMIN
in law .... GENER
kind of .... GOD, STEP, IN-LAW,
PRODIGAL
of: prefix .... MAC, FITZ
of a .... FILIAL
prodigal ...... WASTREL, GOOD-
FOR-NOTHING
rey's .... INFANTE
roi's .... DAUPHIN
younger .... CADET
sonance .... TUNE, SOUND
sonant .... VOICED, SOUNDING
opposed to .... SURD,
VOICELESS
sonata, part of .... CODA, RONDO,
SCHERZO, MOVEMENT
short .... SONATINA
sonderclass .... YACHT
song .... AIR, LAY, ARIA, GLEE,
LILT, POEM, RUNE, SOLO,
CAROL, CHANT, DITTY, LYRIC,
VERSE, BALLAD, LIED(ER),
MELODY, POETRY, CANZONE,
CHANSON, CANTICLE
accompaniment .... VAMP
after .... EPODE
-and-dance performer
.... DISEUSE
baby's .... LULLABY
Christmas .... NOEL, CAROL
contrapuntal .... FUGUE,
MOTET, MADRIGAL
dirgelike .... REQUIEM
evening .... SERENA, VESPERS
flourish .... CADENZA

gay .... LILT
Goodnight girl of .... IRENE
handy .... ST. LOUIS BLUES
identification .... THEME,
    SIGNATURE
improvisation .... VAMP
joyful .... P(A)EAN
kind of .... POP, FOLK, SOUL,
    BLUES, P(A)EAN, TORCH,
    COUNTRY, SPIRITUAL
last words .... TAG
like .... ARIOSE, CANOROUS,
    CANTABILE
lively .... CANZONET
love .... AUBADE, SERENA,
    SERENADE
merry .... GLEE, LILT
minstrel's .... LAY, BALLAD
monotonous .... CHANT
morning .... MATIN
mystical .... RUNE
of .... MELIC
  gondoliers .... BARCAROLE
  joy .... CAROL
  lamentation .... DIRGE,
    THRENODE, THRENODY
  praise .... HYMN, LAUD,
    PAEAN, (H)ALLELUIA,
    MANIFICAT, HALLELUJAH
  sailors .... CHANTEY
  the 30's, popular
    .... COCKTAILS FOR TWO
  triumph .... PAEAN
  WW II .... MADELON
offered for a .... DIRT-CHEAP
operatic .... ARIA
part .... MADRIGAL
part of opera .... CAVATINA
poetic .... RUNE
prefix .... MELO
radio program .... THEME,
    SIGNATURE
refrain .... FALLA, BURDEN,
    CHORUS
religious .... ORATORIO
romantic, old .... RAMONA
sacred .... HYMN, MOTET,
    PSALM, ANTHEM
sad .... BLUES, DIRGE
section .... FIT
sentimental .... BALLAD
set of verses of .... STAVE
sheikdom of .... ARABY
short .... ODE, DITTY, ARIETTA,
    CANZONET, CAVATINA
syllable .... TRA
thrush .... MAVIE, MAVIS
with a refrain ..... ROUNDELAY
words of .... LYRIC
writer .... LYRICIST
Song of Solomon ...... CANTICLES

of Songs .... SONG OF
  SOLOMON, CANTICLE OF
  CANTICLES
songbird .... LARK, WREN, MAVIS,
  PIPIT, VIREO, BULBUL,
  CANARY, LINNET, ORIOLE,
  SINGER, THRUSH, VEERIE,
  BUNTING, REDWING,
  ROBIN(ET), SPARROW,
  TANAGER, WARBLER,
  BOBOLINK, CARDINAL,
  REDSTART, THRASHER,
  WHINCHAT, GOLDFINCH,
  NIGHTINGALE
  mewing .... CATBIRD
  of the .... TURDINE
  vocal organ .... SYRINX
songfest .... CONCERT
songlike .... LYRIC, MELIC,
  ARIOSE, CANOROUS,
  CANTABILE
songs, a collection of
  .... MINSTRELSY
  anthology of .... GARLAND
  composer of .... SONGSMITH
  made up of various
  .... MEDLEY
  medley of .... FANTASIA,
    POTPOURRI
songster .... CANTOR, SINGER,
  WARBLER
  of melodies .... MELODIST
songstress ...... SINGER, WARBLER,
  VOCALIST, CHANTRESS
  Bryant .... ANITA
  Clark .... PETULA
  Cline .... PATSY
  Clooney .... ROSEMARY
  Cole .... NATALIE
  Day .... DORIS
  Durbin .... DEANNA
  Farrell .... EILEEN
  Flack .... ROBERTA
  Froman .... JANE
  Gayle .... CRYSTAL
  Horne .... MARILYN
  Houston .... WHITNEY
  Jones .... SHIRLEY
  Judd .... NAOMI, WYNONA
  Lynn .... LORETTA
  Mandrell .... BARBARA
  McEntire .... REBA
  Murray .... ANNE
  of popular ballads
  .... CHANTEUSE
  Page .... PATTI
  Reddy .... HELEN
  Ronstadt .... LINDA
  Ross .... DIANA
  Sills .... BEVERLY
  Smith .... KATE

  Steber .... ELEANOR
  Warwick .... DIONNE
  West .... DOTTIE
  Wynette .... TAMMY
  Yuru .... TIMI
Sonja of the ice .... HENIE
sonnet's last six lines .... SESTET
Sonora, capital of
  .... HERMOSILLO
  Indian .... YAQUI
sonority .... RESONANCE
sonorous ...... ROTUND, MAJESTIC,
  RESONANT, HIGH-FLOWN
sonsy .... BUXOM, LUCKY,
  HANDSOME
soon .... ANON, ENOW, EARLY,
  BETIME, PRONTO, ERELONG,
  QUICKLY, READILY, SHORTLY,
  PROMPTLY, BEFORE LONG
  afterward .... THEN
sooner .... RATHER, EARLIER,
  OKLAHOMAN, HOMESTEADER
  than .... ERE
soosoo .... DOLPHIN
soot .... COOM, GRIT, SMUT,
  COLLY, CROCK, GRIME,
  SMAZE, SMOKE, CARBON,
  LAMPBLACK
  full of .... FULIGINOUS
  holder .... FLUE
  pigment .... BISTER, BISTRE
sooth .... FACT, REAL, TRUTH,
  SMOOTH
soothe .... EASE, LULL, ALLAY,
  SALVE, (BE)CALM, PACIFY,
  APPEASE, ASSUAGE, COMFORT,
  MOLLIFY, PLACATE, RELIEVE
soother ...... ANODYNE, SOLACER,
  CONSOLER, TRANQUILIZER
soothing .... BALMY, EASING,
  CALMING, LENITIVE
soothsay .... PREDICT, FORETELL
soothsayer .... SEER, AUGUR,
  MANTIS, ORACLE, DIVINER,
  PROPHET, (H)ARUSPEX,
  TIRESIAS
  blind .... TIRESIAS
  brew of a .... HELLBROTH
soothsaying .... AUGURY
sooty .... DARK, BLACK, DUSKY
  matter .... DUST, SMUT
sop .... DIP, WET, OOZE, SOAK,
  BRIBE, STEEP, MORSEL,
  PACIFIER, INDUCEMENT
Sophia Scicolone .... LOREN
sophism .... FALLACY, IDOLISM
sophist .... CASUIST
sophisticate .... CORRUPT,
  FALSIFY, SLICKER,
  ADULTERATE, COSMOPOLITAN,
  MAN OF THE WORLD

sophisticated ...... HEP, HIP, CHIC,
BLASE, SUBTLE, COMPLEX,
REFINED, WORLDLY,
ADVANCED, INTELLECTUAL
sophistication ...... WORLDLINESS
sophistry ...... FALLACY, IDOLISM,
ABSURDITY, CHICANERY
sophomore .... HAZER
sophomoric ...... INANE, CALLOW
sopor .... STUPOR, LETHARGY
soporific .... DULL, SLOW, OPIATE,
NARCOSE, SOMNIFIC,
SULFONAL
sopping .... WET, SOAKED,
DRENCHED
soppy ...... WET, RAINY, MAUDLIN,
MAWKISH, SENTIMENTAL
soprano .... PONS, AMARA,
HORNE, MOFFO, PATTI, VOICE,
CALLAS, FARRAR, SINGER,
TREBLE, FARRELL, NILSSON,
ALBANESE
Sopwith plane .... TABLOID
sora .... BIRD, RAIL, CRAKE,
ORTOLAN
Sorata .... ILLAMPU
Sorb .... SLAV, APPLE
descendants .... WENDS
Sorbonne, the .... PARISU
sorcerer .... HEX, MAGUS,
WIZARD, WARLOCK,
CHALDEAN, CONJURER,
MAGICIAN
attendant .... FAMULUS
sorceress .... CIRCE, LAMIA,
MEDEA, SYBIL, WITCH
sorcery .... OBE(AH), HOODOO,
VOODOO, ALCHEMY,
THEURGY, WIZARDRY,
DIABLERIE, DIABOLISM,
SORTILEGE, (BLACK)MAGIC,
WITCHCRAFT, CONJURATION
sordid .... BASE, MEAN, DIRTY,
GROSS, FILTHY, IGNOBLE,
SQUALID, WRETCHED
sordino .... MUTE
sordor .... DREGS
sore .... DIRE, ANGRY, ACHING,
FESTER, LESION, TENDER,
TOUCHY, PAINFUL, PUSTULE,
RESENTFUL, DISGRUNTLED
dressing .... GAUZE, PATCH
inflamed .... BLAIN
mustard application on
.... POULTICE
open .... ULCER, WOUND
throat, kind of .... STREP
ulcer-like .... CANCER
sorehead .... CRANK, LOSER,
GRIPER, GROUCH,
MALCONTENT

sorghum .... MILO, GRASS, SYRUP,
FODDER, KAF(F)IR, FETERITA
grain .... DURRA, SORGO,
DOURA(H), MILLET, KAOLIANG
millet-like .... MILO
soricine animal .... SHREW
sorority .... SODALITY,
FELLOWSHIP, SISTERHOOD
sorosis .... FRUIT, MULBERRY
sorrel .... HORSE, REDDISH-BROWN
wood .... OCA
sorrow .... WOE, DOLOR, GRIEF,
ANGUISH, SADNESS, DISTRESS
sorrowful expression .... ALAS,
WOE IS ME, ALACK(ADAY)
sinner .... PENITENT
sorry .... SAD, MEAN, POOR,
DISMAL, PALTRY, RUEFUL,
CONTRITE, INFERIOR,
PENITENT, WRETCHED,
MISERABLE, REGRETFUL,
REMORSEFUL
sort .... ILK, KIND, SIFT, TYPE,
CLASS, GRADE, GROUP,
MATCH, NATURE, VARIETY,
CLASSIFY
of .... SOMEWHAT
of appeal .... SNOB
sortie .... RAID, FORAY, SALLY,
ATTACK, MISSION
sortilege .... SORCERY, PROPHECY,
DIVINATION
sorts, out of .... ILL, CROSS,
INDISPOSED
SOS .... HELP WANTED
sotol, plant like .... YUCCA
sot .... BLOAT, RUMMY, SOUSE,
TOPER, TIPPLER, DRUNKARD
soubise .... SAUCE
soubrette .... MAID, FLIRT,
ACTRESS, COQUETTE
soucar .... BANKER
souchong .... TEA
souffle .... PUFFY, MOUSSE,
MERINGUE, SPOONBREAD
sough ...... MOAN, SIGH, MURMUR,
RUSTLE
soul .... AME, EGO, ELAN, MIND,
ANIMA, ATMAN, BEING,
ESPRIT, PNEUMA, SPIRIT,
ESSENCE, EMBODIMENT,
INDIVIDUAL
dead person's .... MANES
dwelling place .... (THE)BODY,
TABERNACLE
lost ...... THE DAMNED, FALLEN
ANGEL
mate .... LOVER
personified .... PSYCHE
seller .... FAUST
singer ...... (ARETHA)FRANKLIN

timid .... LAMB
soulful .... EMOTIONAL
soulless .... HEARTLESS
sound .... FIT, GOOD, HALE, HONK,
PURL, SAFE, SANE, SEEM,
SONO, TONE, TRIG, WELL,
AUDIO, INLET, NOISE, PLUMB,
SOLID, VALID, APPEAR,
FATHOM, SECURE, STABLE,
STRAIT, HEALTHY, PERFECT,
STRIDOR, RELIABLE
a bubbling .... HUBBLE-
BUBBLE
a horn .... BEEP, TOOT
after-dinner .... BURP
amplifier .... RESONATOR
auto horn .... BEEP, HONK
bagpipe .... SKIRL
banging door .... SLAM
Banshee .... WAIL
barnyard .... BAA, BRAY
beating with a loud
.... PLANGENT
bee's/insect .... HUM, DRONE
bell-like .... TING
bell's ...... PEAL, TOLL, CHIME,
CLANG, JINGLE, TINKLE, DING-
(DONG)
bird .... PEEP, CHIRP, TWEET,
TWITTER
black sheep .... BAA-BAA
bomb .... WHINE
branch of physics dealing in
.... ACOUSTICS
breathing .... RALE, STRIDOR
breathy .... PANT
bullet .... ZIP, PING, PHUT
butterfingers' .... OOPS
buzzing .... WHIR(R)
by reflection of sound waves
.... ECHO
oats'/household .... PURR,
MEOW, MEWL, MIAOW
Christmas .... TINKLE
chuckling/gleeful .... CHORTLE
clock .... CHIME
combining form ...... AUDI(O),
PHON(O)
comic strip .... BAM
continued clanging
.... CLANGOR
cooing .... CURR
deep .... BOOM, RUMBLE,
CAVERNOUS
depth .... PLUMB
discordant .... DIN, JANGLE
disturbing motor .... PING
donkey's .... BRAY, HEEHAW
dove's .... COO, CURR
drum .... RATATAT, RATYTAT
dull .... THUD

effect .... ECHO
elephant's ..... ROAR, TRUMPET
escaping steam .... HISS
explosive .... POP
faster than .... SUPERSONIC
feline fight .... CATERWAUL
for quiet .... SSH
from a corner .... AMEN
from a steamwinder ..... TICK
from cold .... CHATTER
from spirits .... HIC
gentle flute .... TOOTLE
grating .... JAR, SCROOP
grimalkin .... MEOW
guttural .... GRATE, GRUNT
harsh .... JAR, RASP, GRIDE,
JANGLE
heard .... ACOUSTIC
hesitation .... ER
hissing ...... ZIP, FIZ(Z), SWISH,
FIZZLE, SIZZLE
hog's .... GRUNT
in harmony .... CHIME
in mind .... SANE
kennel .... YAP, YELP
large bell's .... DONG
light .... SWISH
loud, brassy .... BLARE
loud, prolonged .... PEAL
loud enough to be heard
.... AUDIBLE
loud in .... SONOROUS
low buzzing .... HUM
lung .... RALE
making crackling
.... CREPITATING
may be heard, distance
.... EARSHOT
menacing ..... GR-R-R, GROWL,
SNARL
metallic .... TING, CLANG,
monotonous buzzing
.... DRONE
mournful .... SOB, KNELL
murmuring .... COO, HUM,
CURR, SOUGH
mystery .... SCREAM
nocturnal .... SNORE
of .... SONIC, TONAL, PHONIC,
SONANT
a quiet motor .... PURR
activity .... HUM
bells, ringing
.... TINTINNABULATION
contentment .... PURR
delight .... SQUEAL
disapproval .... BOO, HISS,
HOOT, CATCALL
footsteps ..... CLUMP, TRAMP
goose .... HISS
gunfire/laughter .... PEAL

heart, abnormal .... MURMUR
heavy guns .... BOOM
indignation .... SNORT
merriment .... HA-HA
pain ..... MOAN, OUCH, YELL,
GROAN, SHRIEK
silence, meaning ... NO
surprise .... AH, OHO, GASP
thunder .... CLAP
time .... TICK
violence .... WHAM
warning .... HISS, ALARM,
SIREN, RATTLE, TOCSIN
whale .... MEW, CLICK,
SQUEAL, CHIRRUP
yearning .... SIGH
off .... ORATE, SPEAK
ominous .... KNELL
opposite of .... SILENCE
out .... PROBE, FEEL OUT
out the public .... POLL
paddock .... NEIGH
painful .... OW, OUCH
pastoral .... BAA
pertaining to .... SONIC
pertaining to speech
.... PHONETIC
plosive .... SPUTTER
-proofing material .... PUG
repetitive .... TICTAC, TOM-
TOM, DRUMBEAT, TICKTACK,
TICKTOCK, RAT-TAT-TAT
resonant .... TONE
reverberating .... ROLL
ringing .... TANG
rolling .... RUMBLE
rooster's .... CROW
rustling .... SWOOSH
sabot's .... CLOP
science of .... ACOUSTIC(S)
scolding .... TSK(TSK)
sharp .... SPANG
short, sharp .... CLACK
shrill ..... ZING, SKIRL, SQUEAK
signaling .... BEEP
slapping .... SPLAT
sleeper's .... ZEEZ, SNORE
slight .... CLICK
snake .... HISS, RATTLE
sob .... BLUB
soft, rubbing .... SWISH
stadium .... ROAR
storm .... ROAR, BLUSTER
sty .... OINK, GRUNT
surf .... ROTE
swelterer's .... PHEW
thin, sharp .... SQUEAK,
SQUEAL
thinking .... LOGIC
throat-clearing .... AHEM
thunder .... BOOM, CLAP, PEAL,

ROLL, (G)RUMBLE
trumpet .... BLARE
undignified .... WHINE
unit of measurement
.... MACH, DECIBEL
usually in triplicate .... RAH
veldt .... ROAR
voiceless .... CEDILLA
warbling .... CHIRM
warning: poet. .... ALARUM
wave, bend .... REFRACT
wave reflection phenomenon
.... ECHO
wavy .... ROTES
whiplash .... WHISH
whirring ...... BIRR, BURR, ZIZZ
whispering/rustling
.... SUSURRUS
wind .... PUFF, WAFT, WHIFFLE,
WHISTLE
Sound, _____ .... PUGET
soundless .... MUTE, STILL,
SILENT, ASONANT
soundly .... FULLY, TOTALLY,
COMPLETELY, THOROUGHLY
soundness .... SOLVENCY,
VALIDITY, STABILITY
soundproof .... QUIET,
NOISEPROOF
make .... PUG, DEADEN,
INSULATE
sounds in ear, ringing
.... TINNITUS
soup ...... BROTH, GUMBO, BISQUE,
BORSCHT, CHOWDER,
POT(T)AGE, BOUILLON,
CONSOMME, JULIENNE
accompaniments
.... CRACKERS, SALTINES,
BREAD STICKS
base for .... STOCK
bread .... CROUTON, MELBA
TOAST
clear .... CONSOMME
clear, Scotch style .... BROO
cold .... GAZPACHO,
VICHYSSOISE
dish .... TUREEN
flavor ..... DILL, CHIVE, CURRY,
ONION, CHEESE
flavored with curry
.... MULLIGATAWNY
garnish .... EGG, CHEESE,
ALMONDS, PARSLEY, BACON
BITS
in the .... IN TROUBLE
ingredient .... BEAN, BEEF,
CLAM, LENTIL, NOODLE,
MACARONI, VEGETABLE
kind of .... POTATO, CHOWDER,
NAVY BEAN, (SPLIT-)PEA,

BLACK BEAN, MINESTRONE, FRENCH ONION
meat .... BISQUE, BURGOO
plant .... LEEK
pods .... OKRA
potato .... VICHYSSOISE
slang .... OVERCAST, NITROGLYCERIN
spoon .... LADLE
thick .... GUMBO, PUREE, BISQUE, CHOWDER, POTTAGE
thickener .... EGG, FLOUR, CORNSTARCH
thickening mixture ...... ROUX, RIVELS
thin .... BROTH
to _____ .... NUTS
to nuts .... MEAL, MENU
vegetable ...... GUMBO, BISQUE, BURGOO, MINESTRONE
yegg's: sl. .... NITRO
soupçon .... TASTE, TRACE, SUSPICION
souped-up cars .... RACERS
sour .... RANK, TART, ACRID, CROSS, ACIDIC, BITTER, RANCID, ACERB(IC), ACETOSE, ACETOUS, ACID(ULOUS)
ale .... ALEGAR, VINEGAR
disposition, of .... CROSS, TESTY, CRANKY, MOROSE, SULLEN, PEEVISH, LIVERISH
gourd .... BAOBAB
grass .... SORREL
gum .... NYSSA, TUPELO
milk drink .... LEBAN
source ...... ROOT, CAUSE, ORIGIN, SPRING, FOUNT(AIN), HEADSPRING
of genius/inspiration .... MUSE
guidance .... ORACLE
iodine .... KELP
nuclear energy .... FISSION
spirits .... POTSTILLS
sourdine .... MUTE
sourdough ...... LEAVEN, SETTLER, PROSPECTOR
sourdough's town .... NOME
sourpuss .... CRAB, PRUNE, GROUCH, BROODER
Sousa, composer .... JOHN PHILIP
employment of
.... (MARINE)BANDLEADER
sobriquet of .... (THE)MARCH KING
work of .... WASHINGTON POST MARCH, STARS AND STRIPES FOREVER
sousaphone .... HORN
souse .... SOAK, BRINE, STEEP, SWOOP, PICKLE, PLUNGE,

DRUNKARD, INTOXICATE
soused ...... DRUNK, TIPSY, STINKO
soutache .... BRAID, TRIMMING
soutane .... TUNIC, CASSOCK
South Africa, foreigner in
.... UITLANDER
South African .... BOER, AFRIKANER
animal ..... QUAGGA, SURICATE
antelope .... GNU, SASSABY, BUSHBACK
archbishop .... TUTU
assembly .... RAAD
aunt .... TANTA
bay .... FALSE, TABLE, WALVIS, SAINT HELENA
beverage .... MATE
camp .... LAAGER
cape .... AGULHAS, GOOD HOPE
capital .... CAPE TOWN, PRETORIA
city/town .... DURBAN, SOWETO, WELKOM, BRAKPAN, SPRINGS, BOKSBURG, GERMISTON, KIMBERLEY, JOHANNESBURG
coin .... CENT, POND, RAND, FLORIN, DAALDER
district .... RAND
Dutch .... BOER, TAAL
farmer .... BOER, WERF
field marshal .... SMUTS
fox .... ASSE
golfer ..... PLAYER, SEWGOLUM
grassland .... VELD(T)
hill .... KOP
island .... ROBBEN
issue .... APARTHEID
javelin .... ASSAGAI
lake .... SAINT LUCIA
language .... ZULU, SESOTHO, AFRIKAANS
legislature .... RAAD
monetary unit .... RAND
monkey .... VERVET
mountain .... TABLE, SNEEUWKOP
mulatto .... GRIQUA
native .... ZULU, BANTU, KAFFIR
plain .... VELD(T)
plateau ...... (GREAT)KAR(R)OO
polecat .... MUSANG
policeman .... ZARP
president .... DONGES, DE KLERK, MANDELA
prime minister .... SMUTS, HERTZOG, VORSTER, VERWOERD
province .... CAPE, NATAL, TRANSVAAL

racial policy .... APARTHEID
republic .... VENDA, CISKEI, TRANSKEI
river .... BOT, SAK, KLIP, SAND, VAAL, GROOTE, MOLOPO, ORANGE, LIMPOPO, PALMIET, HARTBEES, OLIFANTS, CROCODILE, ZONDEREND
road .... KLIP
settler .... BOER
spear .... ASSAGAI
swamp .... VLEI
tableland .... KAR(R)OO
thong .... RIEM
town .... STAD
tribal council .... INDABA
valley .... VAAL, KLOOP
village .... KRAAL
weapon .... KNOBKERPIE
workmen .... VOLK
South American animal
.... LLAMA, TAPIR, TAYRA, ALPACA, VICUNA
alligator ..... CAIMAN, CAYMAN
arid ground .... ESPINAL
armadillo .... POYOU, MATACO, TATOUAY
bean .... TONKA
bird .... GUAN, JACU, RHEA, AGAMI, TOPAZ, TURCO, JACANA, ARACARI, MANAKIN, SERIEMA, TINAM(O)U, CURASSOW, GUACHARO, HOA(C)TZIN, SCREAMER
butternut .... SOUARI
city/town .... LIMA, LA PAZ, BOGOTA, MEDELLIN, SAO PAULO, MONTEVIDEO, BUENOS AIRES, RIO DE JANEIRO
coin .... CONTO, CONDOR, ESCUDO, (MIL)REIS
crocodile .... YACARE
dance .... SAMBA, TANGO, CHA-CHA, BEGUINE, CARIOCA
deer .... GEMUL
desolate region .... PUNA
duck .... PATO
fish .... PIRANHA, ARAPAIMA, CHARACIN
guinea pig .... PACA
hare .... TAPETI
hat .... JIPIJAPA
hawk .... CARACARA
herdsman .... LLANERO
hog .... TAPIR
hummingbird .... WARRIOR
Indian .... ONA, INCA, CARIB, MAYAN, GUARANI, TEHUELCHE, PATAGONIAN
Indian, pertaining to
.... PEBAN

knife .... MACHETE
laborer .... PEON, BRACERO
lake .... MERIN, MIRIM,
    VIEDMA, TITICACA,
    MARACAIBO
lapwing .... TREUTERO
liberator .... SUCRE
lizard .... TEJU
mammal .... GRISON,
    KINKAJOU, PACARANA
marmoset .... TAMARIN
missile weapon .... BOLA
monkey .... TITI, ACARI,
    ARABA, TETEE, SAPAJOU,
    CAPUCHIN, MARMOSET
mountain .... HUILA, TOLIMA,
    RORAIMA, BANDEIRA,
    ACONCAGUA, CHIMBORAZO,
    HUASCARAN
nightbird .... GUACHARO
opossum ..... QUICA, YAPO(C)K
ostrich .... RHEA
palm .... ITA, GRUGRU
parrot .... MACAW, AMAZON(A)
plain .... CAMPO, LLANO,
    PAMPA(S), PARAMO
plant .... GUACO, COPAIBA,
    PAREIRA, RHATANY, JIPIJAPA,
    JABORANDI
raccoon .... COATI
reptile .... ABOMA
river .... PARA, META, PLATA,
    JURUA, NEGRO, PURUS,
    AMAZON, ARAUCA, CHUBUT,
    CUYUNI, GRANDE, IGUACU,
    JAPURA, MORONI, PARANA,
    DESEADO, GUAPORE, MADEIRA,
    ORINOCO, OYAPOCK,
    URUGUAY, PARAGUAI,
    PUTUMAYO
rock .... TALPATATE
rodent .... PIG, PACA, COYPU,
    RATEL, TAPIR, AGOUTI,
    AGOUTY, GUINEA, NUTRIA,
    TAPETI, CAPYBARA
ruminant .... LLAMA
seed .... TONKA, GUAIAC
snake .... BOA, ABOMA,
    BUSHMASTER
tanager .... YENI, LINDO
tea leaf .... MATE
tick .... CARAPATO
tortoise/turtle .... MATAMATA
toucan .... ARACARI
tree .... MORA, TOLU, BALSA,
    CAROB, CEBIL, BEBEERU
trumpeter .... AGAMI
tuber .... OCA
ungulate .... TAPIR
weapon .... BOLAS
wild cat .... EYRA, MARGAY

wind .... PAMPERO
wood sorrel .... OCA
South Carolina Air Force base
    .... SHAW, DONALDSON,
    CHARLESTON, MYRTLE BEACH
bay .... BULLS, WINYAH
cape .... ROMAIN
capital .... COLUMBIA
city/town .... CAYCE, CONWAY,
    EASLEY, LADSON, SUMTER,
    LAURENS, PICKENS, ANDERSON,
    FLORENCE, ROCK HILL,
    CHARLESTON, GREENVILLE,
    ORANGEBURG, SPARTANBURG
county ...... LEE, YORK, AIKEN,
    HORRY, UNION, DILLON,
    JASPER, ANDERSON, BEAUFORT,
    BERKELEY, FLORENCE,
    RICHLAND, LEXINGTON,
    CHARLESTON
dam .... SANTEE, HARTWELL,
    BUZZARD ROOST
island .... BULL, CAPE, CAPERS,
    FRIPP, JAMES, JOHNS, DEWEES,
    EDISTO, KIAWAH, MORRIS,
    MURPHY, WADMALAW, HILTON
    HEAD, PRITCHARDS
lake .... WYLIE, KEOWEE,
    MARION, MORRIS, MURRAY,
    WATEREE, HARTWELL,
    MOULTRIE, ROBINSON
Marine Air Station
    .... BEAUFORT
mountain .... SASSAFRAS
mountain range .... BLUE
    RIDGE
river .... NEW, BUSH, BLACK,
    BROAD, REEDY, SANDY,
    TYGER, WANDO, ASHLEY,
    COOPER, COOSAW, EDISTO,
    ENOREE, LUMBER, PEE DEE,
    SALUDA, SANTEE, SENECA,
    ASHEPOO, CATAWBA,
    LYNCHES, PACOLET, TUGALOO,
    WATEREE, WACCAMAW
state bird .... WREN
state flower .... JASMINE,
    JESSAMINE
state nickname ...... PALMETTO
South Dakota Air Force base
    .... ELLSWORTH
capital .... PIERRE
city/town .... HURON, SALEM,
    SELBY, CANTON, WINNER,
    BRITTON, IPSWICH, MADISON,
    YANKTON, ABERDEEN,
    DEADWOOD, MITCHELL,
    BROOKINGS, WATERTOWN,
    RAPID CITY, SIOUX FALLS,
    VERMILLION
county .... DAY, LAKE, BROWN,

    BUTTE, GRANT, MEADE,
    UNION, HUGHES, TURNER,
    DAVISON, LINCOLN, SHANNON,
    LAWRENCE, WALWORTH,
    CODINGTON, MINNEHAHA,
    PENNINGTON
creek .... ELK, CAIN, NASTY,
    WOUNDED KNEE
dam .... OAHE, BIG BEND
lake .... DRY, MUD, RED, LONG,
    OAHE, REID, SWAN, ANDES,
    BRANT, BYRON, PIYAS, WHITE,
    HERMAN, PLATTE, SHARPE,
    SPIRIT, WAUBAY, BUFFALO,
    KAMPESKA, POINSETT, LEWIS
    AND CLARK
mountains .... BLACK HILLS
river .... BAD, ELM, GRAND,
    JAMES, MAPLE, WHITE, BIG
    SIOUX, KEYA PAHA, MISSOURI,
    MINNESOTA
state bird .... PHEASANT
state flower
    .... PASQUEFLOWER
state nickname .... COYOTE
tourist site .... MOUNT
    RUSHMORE
South Pacific craft .... PROA
garment .... PAREU
island .... FIJI, SAMOA, TONGA,
    TAHITI
star .... PINZA
South Pole explorer
    .... AMUNDSEN
South Sea canoe .... PROA, PRAU
garment .... SARONG
island ...... ARU, BALI, SAMOA,
    TAHITI
island drink .... KAVA(KAVA)
loincloth .... LAVA-LAVA
native .... KANAKA, SAMOAN,
    BALINESE, TAHITIAN,
    POLYNESIAN
novel .... OMOO
shrub .... KAVA(KAVA)
staple .... TARO
South wind .... NOTUS, AUSTER
southerly .... AUSTRAL
southern .... AUSTRAL
beauty .... BELLE
Southern Cross .... CRUX
France .... MIDI
States .... DIXIE
southpaw .... LEFTY, SINISTRAL,
    LEFT-HANDED, LEFT-HANDER
souvenir .... FAVOR, RELIC,
    SCRAP, MEMENTO, KEEPSAKE
sou'westers .... STORMHATS
sovereign ...... KING, LORD, QUID,
    CHIEF, LIEGE, POUND, ROYAL,
    RULER, PRINCE, SOVRAN,

EMPEROR, MONARCH,
SUPREME, POTENTATE

dignity .... MAJESTY

female .... LADY, QUEEN,
EMPRESS, TSARINA

of a .... REGNAL

power .... SWAY

sovereignty .... RULE, EMPERY,
THRONE, ROYALTY, SCEPTRE,
DOMINION

Soviet. See also **Russian**

.... COUNCIL

administrative body

.... PRESIDIUM

caucasian .... KURD

government .... KREMLIN

gulf .... RIGA, ANADYR,
SAKHALIN

island .... AYON, BELYY,
WIESE, PIONER, WRANGEL,
PARAMUSHIR

lake .... ONEGA, BAYKAL,
BELOYE, LADOGA, TAYMYR,
PEIPUS, TENGIZ, IMANDRA

money .... RUBLE, KOPECK

mountains .... URAL, ALTAY,
SAYAN, ULUTAU

news agency .... TASS

newspaper .... PRAVDA

peninsula .... KOLA, YAMAL,
CRIMEA

poet .... YEVTUSHENKO

president .... KALININ,
MIKOYAN, PODGORNY,
GORBACHEV

range .... OLOY, URAL, VILYUY

republic .... UZBEK, KAZAKH,
KIRGIZ, LATVIA, RUSSIA,
ARMENIA, ESTONIA, GEORGIA,
TADZHIK, TURKMEN, UKRAINE,
MOLDAVIA, LITHUANIA,
AZERBAIDZHAN

river .... OB, CHU, DON, ILI,
OKA, PUR, TAZ, TYM, UDA,
AMGA, AMUR, EMBA, KUMA,
KURA, LENA, MAYA, URAL,
VAKH, YANA, ZEYA, ALDAN,
ATREK, CHUNA, ISHIM, KHETA,
MEZEN, NADYM, TOBOL,
VITIM, VOLGA, DONETS,
IRTYSH, MURGAB, TAYMYR

Russia .... USSR

sea .... ARAL, AZOV, KARA,
WHITE, LAPTEV, CASPIAN,
OKHOTSK

Union founder .... LENIN

workers' collective/group

.... ARTEL

sovran .... SOVEREIGN

sow .... HOG, PIG, SEED, PLANT,
STREW, SWINE, SLUICE,

SCATTER, BROADCAST,
PROPAGATE, DISSEMINATE

bug .... ISOPOD, SLATER, WOOD
LOUSE

young .... GILT

sowens .... PORRIDGE

sox .... SOCKS

soy(a) .... BEAN, SOJA, SAUCE

soybean cake .... TAHURE

enzyme .... URASE

product .... OIL, MISO, SUFU,
TAHO, NAT(T)O, TAUSI, TOKUA

sauce .... SOY, SOJA, TOYO

spa .... BATH, RESORT, SPRING,
BALNEUM

space .... GAP, AREA, ROOM,
RANGE, EXTENT, SPHERE,
SPREAD, EXPANSE

agcy. .... NASA

beacon .... QUASAR, PULSAR

between .... DISTANCE

between bird's eye and bill

.... LORE

between vocal cords

.... GLOTTIS

blank .... GAP, LACUNA

critter .... ALIEN

dog .... STREIKA

empty .... HOLE, VOID, BLANK,
CAVITY, HOLLOW, VACUUM

filled with matter ..... PLENUM

filler .... SHIM

for freedom of action

.... LEEWAY, ELBOW ROOM

for goods .... STORAGE

in biology .... LACUNA

in from margin .... INDENT

monkey .... ENOS, ASTROMONK

of time .... SPAN, INTERVAL

on a written sheet, blank

.... MARGIN

overhead .... HEADWAY,
HEADROOM

pertaining to .... AMPLE,
ROOMY, SPATIAL, SPACIOUS

science .... ASTRONAUTICS

ship blister .... MODULE

suit .... G-SUIT

travel .... FLIGHT

traveler .... SPACEMAN,
ASTRONAUT, COSMONAUT

triangular .... SPANDREL

unlimited .... INFINITY

vehicle .... SOYUZ, APOLLO,
COSMOS, GEMINI, SKYLAB,
VOSTOK, FREEDOM, MARINER,
SPUTNIK, COLUMBIA,
EXPLORER, SATELLITE,
CHALLENGER

void .... VACUUM

Space Age initials .... NASA

launcher .... SPUTNIK

spacecraft .... ROCKET, SATELLITE

capsule .... SPECS

first .... SPUTNIK

instrumented .... PROBE

into the earth, insertion of

.... REENTRY

landing on water of

.... SPLASHDOWN

launch site .... CAPE KENNEDY,
CAPE CANAVERAL

launch site, Soviet Union

.... COSMODROME

launching of a ...... BLAST-OFF

on the moon, first ..... APOLLO

part .... MODULE, CAPSULE

path taken by .... ORBIT

point nearest to earth in orbit
of .... PERIGEE

point nearest to moon in
orbit of .... PERILUNE

schedule of operations just
before launching

.... COUNTDOWN

small rocket on a large

.... RETRO

to Venus .... MARINER

unit .... LEM

spacer .... BAR

spacious .... VAST, AMPLE, LARGE,
ROOMY, SPATIAL, INFINITE,
SWEEPING

spade .... DIG, SAM, SCOOP

tool like .... SPUD, SHOVEL

spadefoot .... TOAD

spades .... SUIT

spaghetti .... PASTA, NOODLES

associate .... MEATBALLS

food like .... MACARONI

ingredient .... DURUM

spahi/spahee .... CAVALRYMAN

Spain .... ESPANA, IBERIA,
HESPERIA

capital of .... MADRID

district of .... GALICIA,
GRANADA, ASTURIAS,
NAVARRE, ANDALUSIA

kingdom of .... LEON,
ARAGON, CASTILE

Olympic site in

.... BARCELONA

Spalato .... SPLIT

spale .... LATH

spall .... CHIP, FLAKE, SPLIT,
GALLET

spalpeen .... SCAMP, RASCAL

span .... ARCH, PAIR, TEAM, YOKE,
CROSS, REACH, BRIDGE,
EXTENT, PERIOD, MEASURE,
STRETCH, WINGSPAN,
WINGSPREAD

in inches .... NINE
of man's life .... LIFETIME
spang .... ABRUPTLY, DIRECTLY
spangle ...... BEAD, STUD, SEQUIN,
GLITTER, TRINKET, SPARKLER,
PAILLETTE
Spaniard .... SENOR, IBERIAN,
CASTILIAN
16th century
.... CONQUISTADOR
spaniel .... DOG, COCKER,
CLUMBER, PAPILLON,
SPRINGER
kind of .... TOY, WATER
Spanish .... ESPANOL, LANGUAGE,
CASTILIAN
abbot .... ABAD
above .... ARRIBA
absent .... AUSENTE
according to .... SEGUN
ache/pain .... DOLOR
add .... SUMAR
address .... DIRECCION
after .... DESPUES
afternoon .... TARDE
again .... OTRA VEZ
against .... CONTRA
aid .... AYUDA
airplane .... AVION
airport .... AEROPUERTO
alarm clock ..... DESPERTADOR
all .... TODA, TODO
all at once .... PRONTO
all right .... BIEN
almond .... JORDAN
almost .... CASI
alone .... SOLA, SOLO
also .... TAMBIEN
always .... SIEMPRE
American country .... MEXICO
mestizo .... LADINO
plain .... LLANO
town .... PUEBLO
war soldier ..... ROUGHRIDER
amiable .... SIMPATICO
and .... Y
another/other ...... OTRA, OTRO
answer .... RESPONDE
ant .... HORMIGA
any .... CUALQUIER
apple .... MANZANA
April .... ABRIL
apron .... DELANTAL
arm .... BRAZO
armada .... FLOTA
art .... ARTE
article .... EL, LA, LAS, EN, UN,
LOS, UNA
as .... COMO
asphalt .... BREA
August .... AGOSTO

aunt .... TIA
author of Don Quixote
.... CERVANTES
avenue .... AVENIDA
baby .... BEBE, NINA, NINO
back .... ESPALDA
bad .... MALO
bag .... BOLSA
baker .... PANADERO
bakery .... PANADERIA
ball .... PELOTA
balloon .... GLOBO
banana .... PLATANO
bank .... BANCO
barrel .... TONEL
basket .... CESTA, CESTO
bath .... BANO, BANARSE
bay .... BISCAY, ALCUDIA
bayonet .... YUCCA
beach .... PLAYA
beak .... PICO
bean .... HABA, FRIJOL
bear .... OSO
beautiful .... BELLA, BELLO,
HERMOSA, HERMOSO
because .... PORQUE
bed .... CAMA
bee .... ABEJA
beer .... CERVEZA
before .... ANTES
behave .... PORTARSE
believe .... CREER
bell .... CAMPANA
berry, dried .... PASA
best .... MUY BUENO
bet .... PONER, PARAR
better .... MEJOR
between .... ENTRE
bib .... BABERO
big .... GRANDE
bird .... AVE, PAJARO
birth .... NACIMIENTO
birthday .... CUMPLEANOS
bishop .... OBISPO
black .... NEGRA, NEGRO
blackboard .... PIZARRA
blanket .... MANTA, COBIJA,
PONCHO, SERAPE
blind .... CIEGA, CIEGO
blond .... RUBIA, RUBIO
blood .... SANGRE
blow .... GOLPE
blue .... AZUL
boat .... BARCO, VAPOR,
LANCHA
body .... CUERPO
bonnet .... GORRA
book .... LIBRO
boot .... BOTA
booth .... TIENDA, CASILLA
born .... MACIDA, MACIDO

boss .... AMO
botanist .... MONARDES
box .... CAJA
boy .... NINO, CHICO
branch .... RAMA
bread .... PAN
break .... ROMPER
breakfast .... DESAYUNO
-bred sheep .... MERINO
breech .... BRAGA
bridge .... PUENTE
broom .... ESCOBA
brother .... HERMANO
brown/red .... CAFE, PARDO
brush .... CEPILLO
buffoon/clown .... COMICO,
GRACIOSO
building .... EDIFICIO
bull .... TORO
bullfight/race .... CORRIDA
bullfighter .... MATADOR
bullfighter's cloak .... CAPA
burglar/thief .... LADRON
but .... PERO
butcher .... CARNICERO
butter .... MANTEQUILLA
button .... BOTON
cabbage .... COL, REPOLLO
cake .... TORTA
candy/sweet .... DULCE
cape .... NAO, GATA, CREUS,
MAYOR, PALOS, PENAS,
TORTOSA, FORMENTOR,
TRAFALGAR, FINISTERRE
capital .... MADRID
car .... COCHE
card .... TARJETA
card game .... MONTE, OMBER,
OMBRE
carnation .... CLAVEL
castle .... TORRE, ALCAZAR,
ALHAMBRA, CASTILLO
cat .... GATO
cathedral city .... AVILA,
SEVILLE
cellar .... BODEGA
cellist .... CASALS
center .... CENTRO
certain .... SEGURO
chair .... SILLA
chalk .... TIZA
change .... CAMBIO
cheap .... BARATO
cheer .... OLE, BRAVO
cheese .... QUESO
chest .... PECHO
chicken .... POLLO
chickpea .... GARBANZO
chop/cutlet .... CHULETA
church .... IGLESIA
cigar .... PURO

city/town .... TOL, ADRA, ARTA, ASPE, BAZA, ELDA, LEON, LUGO, REUS, TORO, VIGO, ALCOY, AVILA, CADIZ, ELCHE, GIJON, JEREZ, LORCA, OLIVA, PALMA, YECLA, AVILES, BILBAO, BURGOS, CIUDAD, CUENCA, GERONA, HUELVA, LERIDA, MALAGA, MURCIA, ORENSE, OVIEDO, TOLEDO, ZAMORA, ALMERIA, CORDOBA, GRANADA, LEGANES, SEGOVIA, SEVILLE, TARRASA, VITORIA, ALBACETE, ALICANTE, BADALONA, GUERNICA, LA CORUNA, PAMPLONA, SABADELL, VALENCIA, ZARAGOZA, BARCELONA, CARTAGENA, SALAMANCA, SARAGOSSA

clean .... LIMPIA, LIMPIO

clear .... CLARA, CLARO

clever .... LISTA, LISTO

cloak .... CAPA

clock/watch .... RELOJ

closed/shut .... CERRADO

cloth/dress .... VESTIDOS

clothing .... ROPA

cloud .... NUBE

club(house) .... CASINO

coal .... CARBON

coat .... ABRIGO

coffee .... CAFE

coffeepot .... CAFETERIA

coin ...... DURO, REAL, PESETA, CENTAVO, CENTIMO, PISTOLE, MARAVEDI

coin, obsolete .... DOUBLOON

coin, old .... DOBLA, PISTOLE

cold .... FRIA, FRIO

cold (illness) .... CATARRO

collar/neck .... CUELLO

colony in Africa .... IFNI

comb .... PEINE

composer .... FALLA

conqueror .... CORTEZ, PIZARRO, CONQUISTADOR

cookie .... GALLETA

cord/rope .... CUERDA

corn .... MAIZ

corner .... ESQUINA

cot .... CATRE

cotton .... ALGODON

cough .... TOS

council .... JUNTA

country/nation .... PAIS

countryman .... PAISANO

court .... CORTE, JUZGADO

courtyard .... PATIO

cousin .... PRIMA, PRIMO

cow .... VACA

cowboy .... GAUCHO, VAQUERO

cradle .... CUNA

cucumber .... PEPINO

cultivated/plowed land .... ARADO

cup .... TAZA

Cupid .... AMORINO, AMORETTO

dance .... JOTA, BAILE, DANZA, PAVIN, TANGO, VALSE, BOLERO, CANARY, PAVAN(E), CARIOCA, CACHUCHA, CHACONNE, FANDANGO, FLAMENCO, GUARACHA, SARABAND(E)

date .... FECHA

daughter .... HIJA

daughter-in-law .... NUERA

Davis Cupper .... ARILLA, GIMENO, GISBERT, SANCHEZ, SANTANA

day .... DIA

dear (beloved) .... QUERIDA, QUERIDO

dear (expensive) .... CARO

December .... DICIEMBRE

desert .... DESIERTO

desire .... GANA

dessert .... POSTRE

dialect .... CATALAN, ASTURIAN, ARAGONESE, CASTILIAN, ANDALUSIAN

dictator .... FRANCO

dictionary .... DICCIONARIO

difficult .... DIFICIL

dining-room .... COMEDOR

dinner/meal .... CENA, COMIDA

dish .... OLLA, PLATO, PAELLA, BACALAO

doctor .... MEDICO

dock .... MUELLE

dog .... PERRO

doll .... MUNECA

donkey .... ASNO, BURRO

door .... PUERTA

doorbell .... TIMBRE

doubloon .... ONZA

dramatist .... TELLEZ

dress suit .... TRAJE

dressing gown .... BATA

driver .... CHOFER

drink .... VINO

drop .... GOTA

dry .... SECO

drugstore .... FARMACIA

drum .... TAMBOR

duck .... PATO

each/every .... CADA

ear .... OREJA

early .... TEMPRANO

earn .... GANAR

earth/land .... TIERRA

east .... ESTE

easy .... FACIL

egg .... HUEVO

eight .... OCHO

eighth .... OCTAVO

end .... FIN

England .... INGLATERRA

enough .... BASTANTE

envelope .... SOBRE

equal .... PAR, IGUAL

error .... FALTA

estuary .... RIA

evening .... NOCHE

event .... CASO

everything .... TODO

evidence .... PRUEBA

evil .... MALIGNO

ex-queen .... ENA

execution .... GARROTE

exhibit .... MOSTRAR

expense .... GASTO

explorer .... ONATE, BALBOA, CORTES, DESOTO, CORONADO, MAGELLAN, MENENDEZ

eye .... OJO

eyebrow .... CEJA

eyeglasses .... GAFAS, ANTEOJOS

eyesight .... VISTA

face .... CARA

factory .... FABRICA

fair .... FERIA, JUSTA, JUSTO

fairy .... HADA

fan .... AFICIONADO, VENTILADOR

far .... LEJOS

farm .... FINCA, GRANJA, RANCHO, HACIENDA

fascist .... FALANGIST

fast/quick ..... PRONTO, RAPIDO

fat .... GORDA, GORDO

father .... PADRE

fear .... MIEDO

feast .... FIESTA

February .... FEBRERO

fellow .... ENTE, COMPADRE

fellow, young .... CHICO

fiance(e) .... NOVIA, NOVIO

field .... CAMPO

fight .... LUCHA

film .... PELICULA

fine arts .... BELLAS ARTES

finger .... DEDO

fire .... FUEGO

fireman .... BOMBERO

fireplace .... FOGON

first .... PRIMERA, PRIMERO

fish .... PEZ, PESCADO

fish tank .... ACUARIO

fisherman .... PESCADOR

five .... CINCO
flag .... BANDERA
flask/bottle .... FRASCO
fleet .... FLOTA, ARMADA
flesh/meat .... CARNE
flight .... VUELO
flower .... FLOR
floor .... PISO, SUELO
flour .... HARINA
fly .... MOSCA
foot .... PIE
for .... POR, PARA
forehead .... FRENTE
forest .... MONTE, BASQUE
fork .... TENEDOR
fortress official .... ALCAIDE
four .... CUATRO
fourth .... CUARTO
France .... FRANCIA
freedom .... LIBERTAD
Friday .... VIERNES
fried .... FRITO
friend .... AMIGO
frog .... RANA
from .... DE
fox .... ZORRO
game .... JUEGO, PELOTA, JAI
ALAI
garden .... JARDIN
gay/happy .... ALEGRE
general .... ALVA
gentleman .... DON, SENOR,
CABALLERO
German .... ALEMAN
giant .... GIGANTE
gift .... REGALO
girl .... NINA, CHICA
glad .... FELIZ
glass .... VASO, CRISTAL
glove .... GUANTE
goat .... CABRA, CHIVO
goblet .... COPA
God .... DIOS
god of love .... AMADIS
gold .... ORO
good .... BUENA, BUENO
good afternoon .... BUENAS
TARDES
goodbye/so long/farewell
.... ADIOS, HASTA LA VISTA
good gracious! ...... CARAMBA
good luck .... BUENA SUERTE
good morning .... BUENOS
DIAS
good night .... BUENAS
NOCHES
goose .... GANSO
gossip .... CHISME
governess .... AYA, DUENNA
granddaughter .... NIETA
grandfather .... ABUELO

grandmother .... ABUELA
grandson .... NIETO
grape .... UVA, MALAGA
grapefruit .... POMELO
grass .... YERBA, HIERBA,
ESPARTO
grasshopper .... CHAPULIN
gray .... GRIS
great .... GRAN(DE)
great! .... MAGNIFICO
green .... VERDE
greeting .... HOLA
grocer .... TENDERO
grocery .... TIENDA
guest .... INVITADO,
CONVIDADO
guide .... GUIA
guitarist .... SEGOVIA
gulf .... CADIZ, ROSAS, SAN
JORGE, VALENCIA
gun .... FUSIL
gypsy .... GITANO
dance .... FLAMENCO
lingo .... CALO
habit .... MANANA, SIESTA
hair .... PELO, CABELLO
half .... MEDIO, MITAD
half-breed .... LADINO
hall .... SALA
ham .... JAMON
hamlet .... ALDEA
hammer .... MARTILLO
hand .... MANO
hand of clock ...... MANECILLA
handkerchief .... PANUELO
handsome .... GUAPO
harbor/port ..... ASILO, PUERTO
hard .... DURO, FIRME
harm .... MAL
hat .... SOMBRERO
he .... EL
head .... CABEZA
headdress .... MANTILLA
health .... SALUD
heart .... CORAZON
heat .... CALOR
heavy .... PESADO
Hebrew dialect .... LADINO
hello .... HOLA, QUE TAL
help! .... SOCORRO
her .... LA, LE, SU, SUS
herdsman .... PASTORES
here .... AQUI
hero .... (EL)CID, AMADIS
high .... ALTA, ALTO
high society .... ALTA
SOCIEDAD
highest peak .... PICO DE
TEIDE
highway .... CARRETERA
hill .... ALCOR

him .... LE, LO
his .... SU, SUS
hole .... AGUJERO
holiday .... DIA DE FIESTA
home/house .... CASA
horse .... GENET, JENNET,
CABALLO
horseman .... JINETE,
CAVAL(I)ERO
hot/warm .... CALIENTE
hour/time .... LA HORA
how much .... CUANTO
hunger .... HAMBRE
hunter .... CAZADOR
hunter's cap .... MONTERO
hurray! .... OLE, BRAVO
husband .... ESPOSO
I .... YO
immediately .... ENSEGUIDA
in/into .... EN
inn .... FONDA, MESON, VENTA,
POSADO
ink .... TINTA
inkwell .... TINTERO
Inquisition prey .... HERETIC
introduce .... PRESENTA
invite .... CONVIDA
iron .... HIERRO
is ...... EL ES, UNO ES, ELLA ES
island .... ISLA, IBIZA
GOMERA, HIERRO, ALBORAN,
CABRERA, LA PALMA,
MAJORCA, MENORCA
islands .... CANARY, BALEARIC,
COLUMBRETES
it .... LA, LO
its .... SU
jacket .... SACO, CHAQUETA
jail/prison .... CALABOZO
janitor .... PORTERO
January .... ENERO
jar .... OLLA, JARRO, TARRO,
TINAJA
jeopardy .... PELIGRO
jewel ...... JOYA, JUGO, ALHAJA
job .... PUESTO, TRABAJO
joke .... BROMA
joker .... BROMISTA
journey .... VIAJE
joy .... ALEGRIA
Juan Carlos .... EL REY
judge .... JUEZ
July .... JULIO
jump .... SALTA, SALTO
June .... JUNIO
jungle .... SELVA
jury .... JURADO
kettle .... OLLA, CALDERA
kettledrum .... TIMPANO
key .... LLAVE
killer .... MATADOR

kind .... CLASE, AMABLE
king ...... REY, JUAN, ALFONSO, MILESIAN
kingdom .... LEON, ARAGON, CASTILE, NAVARRE
kiss .... BESO
kitchen .... COCINA
kite .... PAPALOTE
kitten .... GATITO
knapsack .... MOCHILA
knee .... RODILLA
knife .... CUCHILLO
knight .... CABALLERO
know .... SABER
lady .... DONA, SENORA, SENORITA
lagoon .... MAR MENOR
lake .... LAGO
lamb .... CORDERO
lame .... COJO
lamp .... LAMPARA
landlady .... DUENA, CASERA
landmark ...., ALHAMBRA, ESCORIAL
language/tongue ...... LENGUA, CATALAN, CASTILIAN
lantern .... FAROLA
lapel .... SOLAPA
large .... GRANDE
lasso .... LAZAR, REATO, RIATA
last/latest .... ULTIMO
late .... TARDE
later .... LUEGO, MAS TARDE
laugh .... REI(R)
laughter .... RISA
lawyer .... ABOGADO
lazy .... PEREZOSO
lead .... GUIAR
leader .... JEFE
leaf .... HOJA
leather .... CUERO
left .... IZQUIERDA
leftover .... SOBRAS
leg .... PIERNA
legislature .... CORTES
Lent .... CUARESMA
less/least .... MENOS
lesson .... LECCION
letter .... CARTA, LETRA
lettuce .... LECHUGA
library .... BIBLIOTECA
lie .... MENTIRA
life .... VIDA
light ...... LUZ, CLARO, LIGERO, CLARIDAD
lighthouse .... FARO
lightning .... RELAMPAGO
lily .... LIRIO
linen .... CREA, HILO
lip .... LABIO
little/small ..... POCO, PEQUENO

long .... LARGO
love .... AMOR, CARINO
lover .... AMADOR
low .... BAJA, BAJO
luck .... SUERTE
luggage .... EQUIPAJE
lung .... PULMON
machine .... MAQUINA
mackerel .... SIERRA
mad/crazy .... LOCA, LOCO, FURIOSO
Madrid boulevard .... PRADO
magazine/review ...... REVISTA
magician .... MAGO
maid .... DONCELLA, MUCHACHA, SIRVIENTA
mailbox .... BUZON
mailman .... CARTERO
Main .... CARRIBEAN
man .... HOMBRE
manager .... GERENTE
mantle .... CAPA
many .... MUCHAS, MUCHOS
marble .... CANICA, MARMOL
March .... MARZO
market .... MERCADO
marriage .... MATRIMONIO
marriage ceremony ...... BODA
married .... CASADO
marry .... CASAR
match .... FOSFORO
matchless .... SIN PAR
mate .... PAREJA
matter .... CASO
Matthew .... MATEO
May .... MAYO
maybe .... QUIZAS
mayor .... ALCALDE
me/my .... MI
meadow .... PRADO
meal .... COMIDA
measure ..... PIE, VARA, LINEA, MILLA, CANTARA, PULGADA, KILOMETRO, CENTIMETRO
measurement .... MEDIDA
melody .... AIRE, COPIA
member .... SOCIO, MIEMBRO
merchant .... MERCADER
merchantship .... GALLEON
mercy .... GRACIA, PIEDAD
mermaid .... SIRENA
merry-go-round .... TIOVIVO
midnight .... MEDIANOCHE
mile .... MILLA
milk .... LECHE
mine .... MIO, MINA
mirror .... ESPEJO
mischief .... MAL, DANO
misfortune .... DESGRACIA
Mister/Mr. .... SENOR
model .... TIPO, PARANGON

mole .... TOPO
Monday .... LUNES
monetary unit .... PESETA
money .... PLATA, DINERO, MONEDA
monkey .... MONO
month .... MES
moon .... LUNA
Moorish .... MORO
Moorish capital ...... CORDOBA
more .... MAS
morning .... MANANA
Morocco .... MARRUECOS
Morocco seaport .... TETUAN
Moss .... MOHO, TILLANDSIA
most .... MUY
moth .... POLILLA
mother .... MAMA, MADRE, MAMACITA
mother-in-law .... SUEGRA
mountain .... MONTE, MONTANA, PERDIDO, ALMANZOR, MULHACEN, PENALARA, BALAITOUS, PENA VIEJA, MONTSERRAT
mountain pass ,,,,,,,,,,,, ABRA
mountain range .... GUDAR, CUENCA, GREDOS, MORENA, ALCARAZ, DEMANDA, MONCAYO, PYRENESS, CANTABRIAN
mountains ...... GATA, TOLEDO, SIERRA NEVADA
mouse .... RATON
mouth .... BOCA
movies .... CINE
mower .... SEGADORA
much .... MUCHO
mud .... LODO
muffler .... BUFANDA
muralist .... SERT
museum .... MUSEO, PRADO
music .... MUSICA, MELODIA
musician .... MUSICO
mustard .... MOSTAZA
mute .... MUDO
mutineer .... REBELDE
muzzle .... BOZAL
my .... MI, MIO, MIS
myself .... YO MISMO
nail (finger) .... UNA
nail (metal) .... CLAVO
name .... NOMBRE
namesake .... TOCAYO
napkin .... SERVILLETA
narrow ..... ESCASO, ESTRECHO
naught .... CERO, NADA
naughty .... PICARA, PICARO
near/close .... CERCA, JUNTO
neat .... LIMPIO
necktie .... CORBATA

needle .... AGUJA
needy .... POBRE
neighbor .... VECINA, VECINO
neither .... NI
nephew .... SOBRINO
nest .... NIDO
never .... NUNCA
new .... NUEVA, NUEVO
newcomer .... NOVATO
news .... NOVEDAD
newspaper .... DIARIO,
                     PERIODICO
next/nearest .... DESPUES,
        PROXIMA, PROXIMO
nice .... AGRADABLE,
                 SIMPATICO
nickname .... MOTE, APODO
niece .... SOBRINA
night .... NOCHE
nightmare .... PESADILLA
nine .... NUEVE
ninth .... NOVENO
no admittance ..... NO ENTRAR
   longer .... YA NO
   one .... NADIE
   smoking .... PROHIBIDO
                     FUMAR
nobleman .... DON, CONDE,
   DUQUE, GRANDEE, HIDALGO,
               CABALLERO
nobody .... NADIE
none/nothing .... NADA
noise .... RUIDO
noon .... MEDIODIA
north .... NORTE
nose .... NARIZ
notebook .... CUADERNO
novelist .... BAROJA, IBANEZ,
              CERVANTES
November .... NOVIEMBRE
now .... AHORA
number .... NUMERO
nun .... MONJA
nurse .... ENFERMERA
nymph .... NINFA, ZAGALA
oar .... REMO
object .... COSA
obscene .... VERDE, GROSERO
October .... OCTUBRE
octopus .... PULPO
odor/smell .... OLOR
of .... DE
oil .... GRASA, ACEITE, CRISMA,
               PETROLEO
old .... VIEJA, VIEJO
omelet .... TORTILLA
on .... EN, ENCIMA DE
once again .... UNA VEZ MAS
one .... UNA, UNO
onion .... CEBOLLA
only .... SOLA, SOLO, UNICA,

       UNICO, SOLAMENTE
open .... ABIERTA, ABIERTO
or .... O
orange .... NARANJA
order .... MANDA(R)
other .... OTRA, OTRO
our .... NUESTRA(S),
              NUESTRO(S)
outside .... AFUERA
over there .... ALLA
owl .... BUHO
own .... PROPIA, PROPIO
ox .... BUEY
oyster .... OSTRA
pack .... FARDO, PAQUETE
   back .... MOCHILA
   of cards .... BARAJA
   saddle .... ALBARDA
package .... BULTO, FARDO,
               PAQUETE
page .... PAGINA
pail ..... CUBO, BALDE, CUBETA
painter ..... DALI, GOYA, MIRO,
   SERT, PINTOR, MURILLO,
   PICASSO, VELASQUEZ
pair .... PAR(EJA)
palace ...... PALACIO, ESCORIAL
palm .... PALMA, PALMERA
pant .... PALPITAR, RESUELLO
pants .... PANTALON(ES)
paper .... PAPEL
paprika .... PIMIENTO
parade .... FASTO, PARADA,
       DESFILE, REVISTA
paradise .... PARAISO
pardon me .... PERDON(E)
park .... PARQUE
parrot .... LORO
party .... FIESTA
pass .... PASA(R)
past .... PASADO
paste .... PEGA
path .... SENDA, VEREDA
pawn in game .... PEON
pay .... PAGA(R)
payer .... PAGADOR
peace .... PAZ, SOSIEGO
peach .... DURAZNO
peacock .... PAVOREAL
peak .... ANETO, ESTATS,
   MULHACEN, PICO DE TEIDE
peanut .... MANI, CACAHUETE
pear .... PERA
pearl .... PERLA
peas .... CHICHAROS,
              GUISANTES
pebble .... GUIJA
pedestal .... BASA
pen .... PLUMA
pen, ballpoint ...... BOLIGRAFO
penal colony .... PRESIDIO

penalty .... MULTA
pencil .... LAPIZ
peninsula .... IBERIA
people .... GENTE
pianist .... ITURBE
picture .... RETRATO
pie .... PASTEL
piece .... PEDAZO
pig .... PUERCO, COCHINO
piggy-bank .... ALCANCIA
pillow .... ALMOHADA
pin .... BROCHE
pin, straight .... ALFILER
pineapple .... PINA
pitch .... BREA, BITUN
place .... LUGAR
plague .... PESTE
plain .... LLANO
plantation .... ARBOLEDA,
               HACIENDA
play .... JUEGO, JUGAR
please .... POR FAVOR
pocket/purse .... BOLSA
poem .... ODA
poet .... BARDO
point .... PUNTO
poison .... VENENO
police .... RURALE, POLICIA,
              GENDARME
pool .... ALBERCA
poor .... POBRE
Pope .... PAPA
porridge .... ATOLE, GACHAS
port .... CADIZ, PALOS,
       MALAGA, PUERTO
post office .... CORREO
pot .... OLIA, OLLA
potato .... PATATA
prefix .... HISPANO
pretty .... LINDO, BONITA,
               BONITO
price .... VALOR, PRECIO
priest .... CURA, PADRE,
            SACERDOTE
prince .... PRINCIPE
princess .... INFANTA,
              PRINCESA
prize .... PREMIO
profile .... CORTE, SILUETA
promenade .... PASEO
prompt .... PRONTO
property .... BIENES
province .... JAEN, LEON,
   ALAVA, CADIZ, BURGOS,
   CUENCA, GERONA, HUELVA,
   MADRID, MALAGA, MURCIA,
   ORENSE, OVIEDO, TERUEL,
   TOLEDO, ZAMORA, BADAJOZ,
   CACERES, CORDOBA,
   GRANADA, SEVILLA, VIZCAYA,
   ALICANTE, BALEARES, LA

CORUNA, VALENCIA, ZARAGOZA, BARCELONA, LAS PALMAS, SALAMANCA, SANTANDER, PONTEVEDRA, VALLADOLID
pump .... BOMBA
pumpkin .... CALABAZA
pupil .... NINA, ALUMNA, ALUMNO
puppy .... PERRITO
pure .... CASTO, VIRGEN
purple ...... MORADA, MORADO, VIOLETA
purse .... CARTERA
puzzle .... ENIGMA, EMBARAZO
quantity .... CANTIDAD
quarrel .... PLEITO, DISPUTA
quarter .... CUARTO
queen .... ELENA, REINA
queer .... RARO
question .... PREGUNTA
quickly .... PRONTO, RAPIDO
quiet ...... CALLADA, CALLADO, TRANQUILA
quilt .... SOBRECAMA
rabbi .... RABINO, MAIMONIDES
rabbit .... CONEJO
Railroad .... FERROCARRIL
rain .... LLUVIA
rainbow .... ARCO IRIS
raisin .... PASA
read .... LEER
reader .... LECTOR
ready .... LISTA, LISTO
record .... DISCO
red .... ROJA, ROJO
Red Cross .... CRUZ ROJA
region .... ARAGON, CASTILE, ASTURIAS, LA MANCHA, VALENCIA, ANDALUSIA, CATALONIA, COSTA BRAVA, ESTREMADURA
relative .... PARIENTE
relief .... SOCORRO
rest .... DESCANSO
return .... VUELTA
rib .... COSTILLA
ribbon .... CINTA
rice .... ARROZ
rich .... RICA, RICO
right .... JUSTO, DERECHA, DERECHO
ring .... ANILLO, SORTIJA
riot .... MOTIN, ALBOROTO
river .... RIO, SIL, TER, EBRO, ESLA, MINO, TAJO, ULLA, CINCA, DOURO, DUERO, GENIL, JALON, JUCAR, NAVIA, SEGRE, TAGUS, TINTO, TURIA, ERESMA, JARAMA, ORBIGO, SEGURA, BARBATE, HENARES,

GUADIANA, ALMANZORA, LLOBREGAT, GUADALIMAR, GUADARRAMA, MANZANARES
river, longest/to the Mediterranean .... EBRO
road .... VIA, CAMINO
roast beef .... CARNE ASADA
robber .... LADRON
robe .... TOGA, MANTO
roof .... TECHO
room .... SALA, CUARTO
rooster .... GALLO
round ..... REDONDA, REDONDO
row .... FILA
rubber .... GOMA, HULE, CAUCHO
rug .... ALFOMBRA
ruler .... REGLA, FRANCO
ruling house .... BOURBON
sack .... SACO, COSTAL
sad .... TRISTE
safe and sound .... SANO Y SALVO
Sahara .... RIO DE ORO
sailing vessel .... CARVEL, GALLEON, CARAVEL(LE)
sale .... VENTA
saltwort .... BARILLA
sand .... ARENA
Saturday .... SABADO
school .... ESCUELA
scissors .... TIJERAS
sea .... MAR
seaport .... ADRA, VIGO, CADIZ, PALOS, BILBAO, MALAGA, ALMERIA, ALGECIRAS
seaport in Africa .... CEUTA
season/station .... ESTACION
second .... SEGUNDA, SEGUNDO
September .... SEPTIEMBRE
seven .... SIETE
several .... VARIAS, VARIOS
shadow .... SOMBRA
shawl .... MANTA, SERAPE, MANTILLA
she .... ELLA
she-bear .... OSA
sheep .... OVEJA, MERINO
sheepfold .... REDIL
sheepskin .... ZALEA
sheet .... HOJA, PLIEGO, SABANA
shell .... CONCHA
shepherd .... PASTORES
sherry .... JEREZ
ship .... BARCO, BUQUE
shirt .... CAMISA
shirtwaist .... BLUSA
shoe .... BOTIN, ZAPATO
shoot .... TIRA
shop .... TALLER, TIENDA

short .... CORTO
shoulder .... HOMBRO
shovel .... PALA
shower .... REGADERA
shrimp .... CAMARON
shrine .... URNA, TEMPLO
shy .... HURANO, TIMIDO
sick .... MALO, ENFERMO
sickle .... HOZ
side .... LADO
sidewalk .... ACERA
sign(al) .... SENA, SENAL
signature .... FIRMA
silk .... SEDA
silly .... BOBO, TONTO
silver .... PLATA
sing .... CANTA
sister .... HERMANA
sitting room .... (ANTE)SALA
six .... SEIS
size .... TAMANO
skate .... PATIN
skin .... PIEL, CASCARA
skipper .... PATRON, CAPITAN
skirt .... FALDA
sky .... CIELO
skyscraper .... RASCACIELOS
sled .... TRINEO
sleep .... SUENO
slowly .... DESPACIO
smoke .... FUMAR
snack .... MERIENDA
snake .... CULEBRA
snow .... NIEVE
soap .... JABON
soil .... TIERRA
soldier .... SOLDADO
some .... ALGUN
somebody .... ALGUIEN
something .... ALGO
sometimes .... ALGUNAS VECES
son .... HIJO
song .... CANTO, CANCION
sorrow .... DOLOR
soup .... SOPA, CALDO, GAZPACHO
sour .... ACIDO, AGRIO
south .... SUD, SUR
souvenir .... RECUERDO
spider .... ARANA
spoon .... CUCHARA
sport .... DEPORTE
spot/stain .... MANCHA
spring .... PRIMAVERA
square .... CUADRADO
stairs/staircase .... ESCALERA
stamp .... SELLO
star .... ESTRELLA
state .... ESTADO
statesman .... AZANA
steel .... ACERO

step .... ESCALON
stick .... PALO
stock farm .... RANCHO
stockings .... MEDIAS
stomach .... ESTOMAGO
stone .... PIEDRA
stopover .... PARADA
stopper .... TAPON
store .... TIENDA, ALMACEN
storeroom/warehouse
.... BODEGA
storm .... TORMENTA
story .... CUENTO
stove .... ESTUFA
strange .... RARO, EXTRANO
strawberry .... FRESA
street .... CALLE
streetcar .... TRANVIA
strong .... FUERTE
student .... ESTUDIANTE
subway .... METRO
suddenly .... DE REPENTE
sugar .... AZUCAR
suit .... TRAJE
suitcase .... MALETA
summer .... VERANO
sun .... SOL
Sunday .... DOMINGO
sweet .... DULCE
swing .... COLUMPIO
switch .... ENCHUFE
sword .... ESPADA, TOLEDO
table .... MESA
tablecloth .... MANTEL
tail .... COLA, RABO
tailor .... SASTRE
tall .... ALTO, GRANDE
tape recorder .... GRABADOR
taste .... GUSTO
tea .... TE
teakettle .... TETERA
teacher .... MAESTRA,
                             MAESTRO
team .... EQUIPO
tear .... LAGRIMA
ten .... DIEZ
tennis star .... ARILLA,
   GIMENO, GISBERT, SANCHEZ,
                             SANTANA
test .... EXAMEN
thank you/thanks ..... GRACIAS
that .... ESO
the .... EL, LA, LAS, LOS
their .... SU, SUS
them .... LAS, LOS
then .... ENTONCES
there .... ALLI
these .... ESTAS, ESTOS
they .... ELLAS, ELLOS
thick .... GRUESO
thimble .... DEDAL

thin .... FLACO
thing .... COSA
third .... TERCERO
thirst .... SED, ANSIA
this .... ESTA, ESTE
those .... ESAS
three .... TRES
throat .... GARGANTA
thunder .... TRUENO
Thursday .... JUEVES
ticket .... BILLETE
tiger .... TIGRE
time .... VEZ, HORA, TIEMPO
tin can .... LATA
tip .... PROPINA
tired .... CANSADO
title .... DON, DONA, CONDE,
       DUQUE, SENOR, SENORA,
                             TITULO
to add .... SUMAR
aid .... AYUDAR
answer/reply ..... RESPONDER
arrange/fix .... ARREGLAR
arrest .... ARRESTAR
arrive .... LLEGAR
ask .... PEDIR, PREGUNTAR
attend .... ASISTIR
be .... SER, ESTAR
be born .... NACER
begin .... EMPEZAR
believe .... CREER
borrow .... PRESTAR
burn .... QUEMAR
buy .... COMPRAR
call .... LLAMAR
carry .... CARGAR
clean .... LIMPIAR
climb .... SUBIR, TREPAR
come .... VENIR
come into .... ENTRAR
cook .... COCINAR
count/to tell .... CONTAR
cry .... LLORAR
cut .... CORTAR
dance .... BAILAR
deceive .... ENGANAR
do/to make .... HACER
drink .... BEBER, TOMAR
drive .... MANEJAR
feel .... SENTIR
finish .... TERMINAR
fly .... VOLAR
follow .... SEGUIR
forget .... OLVIDAR
go down .... BAJAR
go out .... SALIR
grow .... CRECER
have .... TENER
keep .... GUARDAR
kill .... MATAR
know .... CONOCER

leap .... SALTAR
look .... MIRAR
lose .... PERDER
love .... AMAR, QUERER
open .... ABRIR
pay .... PAGAR
play .... JUGAR
play a musical instrument
.... TOCAR
put .... PONER
raise .... LEVANTAR
rest .... DESCANSAR
run .... CORRER
save .... SALVAR
say .... DECIR
shout/to scream ...... GRITAR
see .... VER
sell .... VENDER
send .... ENVIAR
sing .... CANTAR
sit down .... SENTARSE
sleep .... DORMIR
smile .... SONREIR
stay .... QUEDARSE
take .... LLEVAR
take a bath .... BANARSE
talk/to speak .... HABLAR
think .... PENSAR
travel .... VIAJAR
try .... TRATAR DE
turn off .... APAGAR, CERRAR
understand .... ENTENDER
wait .... ESPERAR
wash .... LAVAR
work .... TRABAJAR
write .... ESCRIBIR
today .... HOY
toe .... DEDO
tomorrow .... MANANA
tooth .... DIENTE
top .... TROMPO
towel .... TOALLA
tower .... TORRE
toy .... JUGUETE
tree .... ARBOL
truck .... CAMION
true .... VERDAD
Tuesday .... MARTES
turkey .... PAVO
turtle .... TORTUGA
twice .... DOS VECES
two .... DOS
ugly .... FEO
umbrella .... PARAGUAS
uncle .... TIO
until .... HASTA
valley .... HOYA
versifier .... POETA
very .... MUY
vessel .... GALLEON
waiter .... MOZO

waitress .... MOZA
walking cane .... BASTON
wall .... MURO, PARED
wallet .... CARTERA
want .... QUIERO
war .... GUERRA
warm .... CALLENTE
watchman .... SERENO
watchtower .... MIRADOR
watchword .... LEMA
water .... AGUA
waterfall .... CASCADA,
                                     CATARATA
watermelon .... SANDIA
wave .... OLA, ONDA
wax .... CERA
we .... NOSOTROS
weak .... DEBIL, FLOJO
weapon .... ARMA, BOLA
weather .... TIEMPO
web .... TELA
wedding .... BODA
Wednesday .... MIERCOLES
wee .... CHIQUITO
week .... SEMANA
weight .... PESA, PESO, CARGA,
      MARCO, ARROBA, TONELADA,
                            KILO(GRAMO)
weighty .... GRAVE
welcome .... BIENVENIDA,
                               BIENVENIDO
well .... BIEN
West .... OESTE
wet .... HUMEDA, HUMEDO,
                     MOJADA, MOJADO
whale .... BALLENA
what .... QUE, COMO
   is the matter? ..... QUE PASA
   will be, will be .... QUE
                               SERA SERA
wheat .... TRIGO
wheel .... RUEDA
when .... CUANDO
where .... DONDE
which .... CUAL(ES)
whim .... CAPRICHO
whip .... LATIGO
whistle .... SILBA(TO)
white .... PURO, BLANCA,
                                    BLANCO
who .... QUIEN
who knows .... QUIEN SABE
whole .... ENTERO
why .... POR QUE
wide .... ANCHA, ANCHO
widow(er) .... VIUDA, VIUDO
wife .... MUJER, ESPOSA
wig .... PELUCA
wild .... FEROZ, SALVAJE
win .... GANAR, VENCER
wind .... VIENTO

windy .... VENTOSO
window .... VENTANA
wine .... VINO, TINTO,
                       MALAGA, SHERRY
wine-making center ..... JEREZ
wing .... ALA
winner .... GANADOR
winter .... INVIERNO
wire .... ALAMBRE
wisdom .... SABIDURIA
wise .... SABIA, SABIO
wish .... DESEO, RUEGO
witch .... BRUJA
with .... CON
without .... SIN
witness .... TESTIGO
wolf .... LOBO
woman .... MUJER, HEMBRA,
                                     SENORA
wonderful ..... DIVINA, DIVINO,
                              PEREGRINO
wood .... MADERA
woodland .... MONTE, SELVA
wool .... LANA
word .... PALABRA
work .... OBRA, TRABAJO
workman .... OBRERO
world .... MUNDO
worm .... GUSANO
worship .... CULTO
wrinkle .... ARRUGA
writer .... AUTOR, IBANEZ,
                     ALARCON, ESCRITOR
year .... ANO
yellow .... AMARILLO
yes .... SI
yesterday .... AYER
you .... TU, USTED, USTEDES
you're welcome ..... DE NADA,
                                  POR NADA
young .... JOVEN
your .... SU, TU, SUS, TUS
youth .... JUVENTUD
youthful .... JOVEN, JUVENIL
zealot .... FANATICO
zero .... CERO
zest .... GUSTO
zoo .... ZOOLOGICO
spank .... CUFF, SLAP, SMACK,
                       PADDLE, WALLOP
spanker .... SAIL, DRIVER
spanking .... BRISK, QUICK,
                        RAPID, THRASHING
spanner .... WRENCH
spar .... ROD, BEAM, BOOM, GAFF,
      MAST, POLE, YARD, ARGUE,
      SPRIT, BARITE, BICKER,
      RAFTER, DISPUTE, WRANGLE,
      LONGERON, (SHADOW)BOX
   branch of service .... USCG,
                             COAST GUARD

   for stowing .... STEEVE
   lower a .... REEF
   part of .... SEMPER, PARATUS
spare .... BONY, LEAN, SAVE,
      THIN, EXTRA, LANKY,
      EXEMPT, FOREGO, MEAGER,
      SCANT(Y), RESERVE
   time .... LEISURE
   tire: sl. .... POTBELLY
sparge .... SPLASH, SPRINKLE
sparing .... FRUGAL, MEAGER,
                       SCANTY, THRIFTY
spark ...... ARC, JOT, WOO, BEAU,
      IOTA, COURT, FLASH, LOVER,
      SWAIN, TRACE, KINDLE,
      ACTIVATE, PARTICLE,
                                 SCINTILLA
   gives off .... IGNESCENT
   plug of a sort .... CATALYST
   stream .... ARC
sparked .... ARCED
sparkle .... GLOW, FLASH, GLEAM,
      GLINT, GLISTEN, GLITTER,
      TWINKLE, VIVACITY,
      CORUSCATE, BRILLIANCE,
                              EFFERVESCE
sparkler .... EYE, DIAMOND,
                 FIREWORK, BRILLIANT
sparkling .... FIZZY, BUBBLY,
      LIVELY, GLITTERING
   water .... FIZZ, SODA WATER
Sparks .... NED
Sparky, baseballer .... LYLE
sparling .... SMELT, HERRING
spar(o)id .... GAR, TAI, SCUP,
      PORGY, GILTHEAD,
      (SEA)BREAM, SHEEPSHEAD
sparrow .... FINCH, CHIPPY,
      RICEBIRD, PASSERINE,
      WEAVERBIRD
   hawk .... KESTREL
   hedge .... DUNNOCK
   house .... PASSER
sparry .... SPATHIC, FOLIATED,
                                 SPATHOSE
sparrowgrass .... ASPARAGUS
sparse .... FEW, THIN, MEAGER,
                       SCANTY, SCARCE
   opposite of .... DENSE,
                                   CROWDED
Sparta .... LACEDAEMON
Spartan .... BRAVE, HARDY,
      FRUGAL, HEROIC, SEVERE,
      SIMPLE, STOIC(AL), WARLIKE
   admiral .... LYSANDER
   bondman .... HELOT
   king .... LEONIDAS, AGESILAUS,
      CLEOMENES, TYNDAREUS
   lawgiver .... LYCURGUS
   magistrate .... EPHOR
   queen .... LEDA

677

serf/slave .... HELOT
spasm ...... FIT, TIC, KINK, SPELL,
THROE, CHOREA, CONVULSION
caused by calcium deficiency
.... TETANY
diaphragm .... HICCUP
facial .... TIC
muscle .... CRAMP, CRICK
nervous system .... CHOREA,
MYOCLONUS
of distress .... PANG
of pain .... SHOOT
twitch .... TIC
spasmodic .... JERKY, FITFUL,
SPORADIC, INTERMITTENT
spasms, series of .... CLONUS
Spassky, chess champ .... BORIS
spastic paralysis, cause of
.... STROKE
spat .... ROW, SLAP, TIFF, GAITER,
OYSTER, DISPUTE, QUARREL
spate .... FLOOD, STORM, DELUGE,
FRESHET, DOWNPOUR,
INUNDATION, OUTPOURING
spathe .... GLUME
enclosure .... SPADIX
spathic .... SPARRY
spatial .... DIMENSIONAL
spatiate .... RAMBLE
spatter ...... SOIL, SPRAY, DEFAME,
SPLASH, SCATTER, SPRINKLE
spatterdash .... LEGGING
spatterdock .... LILY
spatula .... SLICE, BLUNGER
shaped like a ...... SPATULATE,
SPOONLIKE
spavined .... LAME
spawn .... OVA, ROE, EGGS, SPAT,
BEGET, BREED, SPORE
obs. dial. .... RAUN
spay .... CASTRATE, STERILIZE
spayed hen .... FOULARD
S.P.C.A. concern .... STRAY
speak .... SAY, TALK, TELL,
ORATE, UTTER, ADDRESS,
DELIVER, CONVERSE,
DISCOURSE
angrily .... SNARL
at length .... LECTURE,
EXPATIATE
evasively .... HEDGE, STALL
from the bench .... RULE
from memory .... RECITE
imperfectly .... LISP,
STAMMER, STUTTER
in dramatic way ...... DECLAIM
in silly way .... DROOL,
SLOBBER
inability to .... ALALIA
incoherently .... GIBBER
irreverently .... BLASPHEME

lengthily .... PERORATE
loudly .... EXCLAIM
noisily .... RANT, RAVE,
BLUSTER
of .... MENTION
off the cuff/without
preparation .... AD LIB,
IMPROVISE
one's thoughts .... EXPRESS
sharply .... SNAP, SNARL
slowly .... DRAWL
softly .... MURMUR, WHISPER
unable to .... DUMB, MUTE
under the breath ...... MUTTER
speakeasy .... BLINDPIG, BLIND
TIGER
speaker .... SAYER, ORATOR,
TALKER, UTTERER
baseball's .... TRIS
bete noire of .... HECKLER
loud .... STENTOR
place of/spot of .... DAIS,
PODIUM, ROSTRUM
speaking in a blase manner
.... SOUNDING BORED
in a certain way .... ALISP
many tongues .... POLYGLOT
style .... DELIVERY, PARLANCE,
PERSIFLAGE
spear .... DART, GAFF, PIKE, STAB,
BLADE, LANCE, SHAFT,
SHOOT, PIERCE, ASSAGAI,
HARPOON, JAVELIN
barbed .... GAFF
body of a .... SHAFT
fish .... GIG, GAFF, LEISTER
Neptune's .... TRIDENT
of grass .... BLADE
point .... PIKE
shaped .... HASTATE
three-pronged .... LEISTER,
TRIDENT
thrower .... WOMERA
spearfish .... MARLIN
spearhead .... VAN, LEAD,
VANGUARD
spearwort .... CROWFOOT
special .... UNIQUE, UNLIKE,
CERTAIN, UNUSUAL, DISTINCT,
PECULIAR, SPECIFIC,
EXCLUSIVE, PARTICULAR
ability .... TALENT
knowledge .... LORE
talent .... FORTE
specialist, aquatint .... ETCHER
foot diseases .... PODIATRIST
glasses .... OPTICIAN
in crime .... SAFECRACKER
specialize .... LIMIT, CONFINE,
SPECIFY, RESTRICT
in a subject .... MAJOR IN

specialized .... TECHNICAL
specialty .... AREA, LINE, FIELD,
FORTE, METIER
fountain ..... SUNDAE, BANANA
SPLIT
of parrots and doctors
.... HOUSE CALL
of some sharks .... USURY
shop .... FLORIST, JEWELER,
CLOTHIER, MILLINER,
BOOKSTORE, STATIONER,
HABERDASHERY
specie .... COIN
factory .... MINT
species .... KIND, SORT, CLASS,
VARIETY, CATEGORY
grouping(s) .... GENUS,
GENERA
specific .... EXACT, PRECISE,
SPECIAL, CONCRETE, DEFINITE,
EXPLICIT
gravity scale .... BAUME
specify ...... NAME, ORDER, STATE,
DEFINE, DETAIL, IDENTIFY,
STIPULATE
specimen .... MODEL, SAMPLE,
TASTE(R), EXAMPLE
of body fluids .... BLOOD
of waste products ...... STOOL,
URINE
specious .... GILDED, SEEMING,
APPARENT, PLAUSIBLE
reasoning .... IDOLISM,
SOPHISM, SYLLOGISM
speck .... BIT, JOT, IOTA, MARK,
MITE, MOTE, SPOT, FLECK,
STAIN, BLEMISH, PARTICLE
speckle .... DOT, SPOT, FLECK,
DAPPLE, MOTTLE, MACULATE
specs .... EYEGLASSES
spectacle .... SHOW, VIEW, SCENE,
SIGHT, PARADE, DISPLAY,
PAGEANT, EXHIBITION
spectacles .... SPECS, LENSES,
GOGGLES, EYEGLASSES,
SUNGLASSES
opera .... LORGNON,
LORGNETTE
part .... ARM, RIM, LENS
spectacular .... AMAZING,
GLARING, STRIKING, BREATH-
TAKING
musical show
.... EXTRAVAGANZA
parade .... PAGEANT
spectator ...... VIEWER, WATCHER,
BEHOLDER, LOOKER(-ON),
OBSERVER, ONLOOKER
devoted .... FAN, BUFF,
AFICIONADO
frequent .... HABITUE

mere .... BYSTANDER
seatless .... STANDEE
specter .... AURA, BOGEY, GHOST,
    SPOOK, SHADOW, SPIRIT,
    VISION, WRAITH, FANTASM,
    PHANTOM, PHANTASM(A),
    APPARITION
spectral .... EERY, SPOOKY,
    GHOSTLY, PHANTOM,
    WRAITHY
spectrum .... RAINBOW
colors, one of the .... RED,
    BLUE, GREEN, INDIGO,
    ORANGE, VIOLET, YELLOW
speculate .... GUESS, THINK,
    GAMBLE, PONDER, REFLECT,
    THEORIZE, CONSIDER,
    MEDITATE, CONJECTURE
speculation, reckless .... FLIER,
    FLYER
speculative .... IFFY, RISKY,
    CHANCY, THEORETICAL
art .... THEORETICS
business scheme ..... WILDCAT
idea .... THEORY
speculator .... GAMBLER,
    GUESSER, PLUNGER, THEORIST,
    THINKER
inexperienced .... LAMB
kind of .... SCALPER,
    ADVENTURER
welshing .... LAME DUCK
speculum .... DEVICE, MIRROR
shape of .... FUNNEL,
    SHOEHORN
type of .... METAL, PLASTIC
speech .... LIP, LINE, TALK,
    SERMON, TONGUE, BLARNEY,
    DIALECT, OENOMEL, ORATION,
    WHISPER, EPILOGUE,
    PARLANCE, DISCOURSE,
    SOLILOQUY, UTTERANCE,
    EXPRESSION, DECLAMATION
abusive .... TIRADE, DIATRIBE
art .... ORATORY, RHETORIC
at beginning of special
    occasion ..... INVOCATION
brevity of .... LACONISM
combining form .... LOG(O)
defect .... LISP, STAMMER,
    STUTTER
delirious .... RAVING
disorder .... ALALIA, ALEXIA,
    APHASIA, DYSPHASIA,
    DYSPHONIA, DYSARTHRIA,
    IMPEDIMENT
disorder: comb. form .... DYS,
    LALIA
disorder treatment
    .... THERAPY, PATHOLOGY
ecstatic .... RHAPSODY

emphatic .... BIRR
exalted to trivial .... BATHOS
farewell .... VALEDICTORY
figure of .... TROPE, SIMILE,
    LITOTES, METAPHOR
formal ...... ADDRESS, ORATION
graduation .... VALEDICTORY
human .... LANGUAGE
incoherent .... JARGON,
    GIBBERISH
ill-tempered .... VINEGAR
last words .... TAG
loss of .... MUTISM, APHASIA,
    APHONIA
loud, wild .... RANT
manner of .... SLUR, DRAWL
Marc Antony's .... ELOGE
narrative part ...... CATASTASIS
noisy, blustering .... TIRADE,
    HARANGUE
of praise .... PANEGYRIC
opening part .... EXORDIUM
organ .... LARYNX, TONGUE,
    VOICE BOX, VOCAL CORDS
ornamental ending .... TAG
part of .... (AD)VERB,
    (PRO)NOUN, ADJECTIVE
pattern of words
    .... PHRASEOLOGY
plain in .... OUTSPOKEN,
    POINT-BLANK
pompous .... BOMBAST
regional style .... BURR,
    TWANG, ACCENT, BROGUE
slang .... JIVE, SPIEL
sound .... LENIS, FORTIS,
    SONANT, CADENCE,
    ALLOPHONE, PHONE(ME)
sounds, ability to produce
    .... ARTICULATION
sounds, system of
    .... PHONETICS, PHONOLOGY
style of .... EUPHUISM,
    LOCUTION
surplusage .... PADDING
tiresome .... SCREED
voiceless sound .... SURD
wild .... RANT
speechify .... ORATE
speechless .... DUMB, MUTE,
    SURD, SILENT, APHASIC,
    APHONIC, VOICELESS,
    TONGUE-TIED
speed .... FLY, HIE, REV, ZIP,
    RACE, RATE, RUSH, TEAR,
    HASTE(N), VELOCITY
drug .... METHEDRINE,
    AMPHETAMINE
full .... AMAIN
measuring device
    .... TACHOMETER,

SPEEDOMETER
of sound .... MACH, SONIC
setter .... PACER
unit, proposed .... VELO
up .... HURRY, HASTEN,
    ACCELERATE
writing .... SHORTHAND
speed(st)er .... RACER
speedily .... AMAIN, APACE, BY
    EXPRESS, POSTHASTE
speedway .... TRACK, RACECOURSE
speedwell .... PLANT, VERONICA
speedy ...... FAST, AMAIN, APACE,
    QUICK, RAPID, SWIFT,
    PROMPT, EXPRESS
spelean .... CAVE-LIKE
speleology, subject of .... CAVES
spell .... FIT, HEX, MEAN, TIME,
    TERM, TURN, CHARM, MAGIC,
    PERIOD, STREAK, TRANCE,
    SIGNIFY, SORCERY
of activity .... SPURT, SPRINT
out .... READ, INTERPRET
spellbind .... HOLD, CHARM,
    ENCHANT, ENTRANCE,
    FASCINATE
spellbinder .... ORATOR
Spellbound Concert composer
    .... ROZSA
director .... HITCHCOCK
star .... PECK, BERGMAN
spelldown .... BEE
spelling ____ .... BEE
incorrect .... CACOGRAPHY
spelt .... WHEAT
spelter .... ZINC, INGOTS
spelunker's interest .... CAVE
spence .... LARDER, PANTRY
spencer .... JACKET, TRYSAIL
spend .... USE, LOSE, PASS,
    EXPEND, PAY OUT, CONSUME,
    EXHAUST, WEAR OUT,
    DISBURSE
lavishly .... DISPEND, SLATHER,
    SQUANDER
more than one has
    .... OVERDRAW
the night .... SHACK UP
the summer .... ESTIVATE
time for a special purpose
    .... DEVOTE, DEDICATE
uselessly .... WASTE
spendthrift .... WASTER,
    ROUNDER, SPENDER,
    WASTREL, PRODIGAL,
    WASTEFUL, SQUANDERER,
    SCATTERGOOD
Spengler, philosopher
    .... OSWALD
Spenser, poet .... EDMUND
spent .... WORN, ALL IN, TIRED,

WEARY, FAGGED, DRAINED, USED UP, CONSUMED, BURNED OUT, EXHAUSTED

and sterile .... EFFETE, IMPOTENT

sperm .... GERM, SEED, SEMEN, WHALE, SPERMATOZOON

fish .... MILT

flower .... POLLEN

whale .... CACHALOT

spermary .... GONAD, TESTIS

spermatozoid .... GAMETE

spermophile .... GOPHER, SUSLIK, CHIPMUNK

spew ...... EMIT, GUSH, SPIT, SPUE, EJECT, EXPEL, RETCH, VOMIT, THROW UP

Speyer .... SPIRES

sphacelate .... MORTIFY

sphagnous .... PEATY

sphagnum .... (PEAT)MOSS

sphene .... TITANITE

sphere .... ORB, SKY, BALL, STAR, FIELD, GLOBE, ORBIT, RANGE, REALM, DOMAIN, PLANET, RONDURE, PROVINCE

celestial .... ORB

of action .... ARENA

spherical .... CUBIC, OVOID, ROUND, GLOBATE, GLOBOID, GLOBOSE, GLOBOUS, GLOBULAR

spheroid, example of a .... BALL, EARTH

spherule .... GLOBULE

sphery .... STARLIKE, CELESTIAL

sphincter .... CONSTRICTOR

sphinx .... MONSTER, (HAWK)MOTH

body of .... LION

head of ...... MAN, RAM, HAWK

query of .... RIDDLE

site of .... GIZA, GIZEH, THEBES

sphinxlike .... PUZZLING, ENIGMATIC

sphragistics' subject .... SEALS

sphygmus .... PULSE

spica .... STAR, SPIKE

spice .... MACE, MINT, AROMA, CHILE, CLOVE, CURRY, CHIL(L)I, FLAVOR, GINGER, NUTMEG, PEPPER, SEASON, STACTE, CANELLA, CINNAMON, TURMERIC, SASSAFRAS

anise-like flavor .... BASIL, FENNEL, TARRAGON

"bean herb" .... SAVORY

berries .... ALLSPICE

bud .... CAPER, CLOVE,

SAFFRON

heat with/flavor with .... MULL

kingly .... BASIL

leaf .... BAY, MINT, SAGE, BASIL, THYME, BORAGE, BURNET, CHIVES, SAVORY, CHERVIL, OREGANO, PARSLEY, ANGELICA, MARJORAM, ROSEMARY, TARRAGON

legendary .... ROSEMARY

lemony flavor ...... CORIANDER

licorice flavor .... ANISE

mint family .... SPEARMINT, PEPPERMINT

of life .... VARIETY

onion family .... CHIVES

parsley family .... CHERVIL

powder .... CHILI, CURRY, PAPRIKA

root .... GINGER, TURMERIC, SASSAFRAS

seed .... DILL, MACE, ANISE, CUMIN, POPPY, CELERY, FENNEL, SESAME, CARAWAY, MUSTARD, CARDAMOM, CORIANDER

slightly bitter flavor ...... DILL, CUMIN, CELERY, TURMERIC

sticks .... CINNAMON

sweet marjoram's cousin .... OREGANO

up .... LIVEN

used as a tonic .... CANELLA

used in incense preparation .... STACTE

whole pods .... CHILI, CARDAMOM

whole nail-shaped buds .... CLOVES

"wild marjoram" .... OREGANO

wisdom .... SAGE

Spice Island(s) .... TERNATE, MOLUCCAS

spiceberry .... WINTERGREEN

spiced .... SEASONED

ale .... WASSAIL

dish .... OLLA, SALMI, TAMALE, CHILI(BEANS), CHILI CON CARNE

meat .... SAUSAGE, BRATWURST

sausage .... SALAMI, KIELBASA, PEPPERONI

spick and span ...... NEAT, TRIM, CLEAN, FRESH

spiculate .... NEEDLELIKE

spicule .... SPIKE, ACTINE, SCLERITE

spicy .... RACY, JUICY, SALTY, RISQUE, GINGERY, PIQUANT, PUNGENT, AROMATIC,

FRAGRANT

joke, describing a .... OFF-COLOR

sensation .... HEAT

taste .... TANG

spider .... MITE, TRIVET, SKILLET, ARACHNID, ARTHROPOD, (FRYING)PAN

class .... ARACHNIDA

crab .... MAIA, MAJA, THORNBACK

dangerous type of .... RECLUSE, FUNNEL WEB, BLACK WIDOW

fear of .... ARACHNOPHOBIA

girl turned into .... ARACHNE

habitat .... SHEDS, HOUSES, CREVICES, WOODPILES

job of ..... WEAVING, SPINNING

largest .... TARANTULA

like .... ARACHNOID

monkey .... QUATA, ATELES

nest of .... NIDUS

poison .... VENOM

poison antidote ..... ANTIVENIN

poison injectors of ...... FANGS

poisonous .... TARANTULA, FUNNEL WEB, BLACK WIDOW, BROWN RECLUSE

trap of .... WEB

spiegel .... MIRROR, PIG IRON

spiel .... LINE, SPEECH, (SALES)TALK, SALES PITCH

spiffy .... CHIC, NEAT, NIFTY, SMART, CLASSY, SPRUCE

spigot ...... PEG, TAP, PLUG, SPILE, VALVE, FAUCET

spike .... GAD, BROB, FOIL, GOAD, NAIL, PROD, RIVET, SPINE, ANTLER, IMPALE, PIERCE, SKEWER, THWART, MACKEREL

broken grain .... CHOB

cereal .... EAR

fork's .... TINE, PRONG

heels .... STILETTO

lavender .... MINT

like .... SPINATE

mountain climber's ...... PITON

of flowers ...... AMENT, SPADIX

of plantain .... CHAT

shield's .... UMBO

slang .... LACE WITH

soles' .... CLEAT

spikelet .... SPINULE

spikenard .... GINSENG, OINTMENT

spile .... TAP, PLUG, SPOUT, STAKE, SPIGOT

spill .... PEG, PIN, ROD, FALL, PLUG, SLOP, SPILE, TUMBLE, OVERFLOW, OVERTURN, SPLINTER the beans: sl. .... SING, TELL, SQUEAL, CONFESS, DIVULGE, DISCLOSE

Spillane's hero .... HAMMER

spin ...... BIRL, EDDY, REEL, RIDE, TURN, SWIRL, TWIRL, WEAVE, WHIRL, GYRATE, ROTATE, DRAW OUT, REVOLVE

a _____ .... WEB, DISK, TALE, YARN, BATON, TOY, WHEEL

spina bifida, type of
.... OCCULTA, MYELOCELE, MENINGOCELE

spinaceous plant .... SPINACH

spinach .... GREENS, ORACH(E), TALINUM, GOOSEFOOT

like .... SANDY

spinal .... RACHIDIAN

anesthesia method
.... EPIDURAL

column ...... SPINE, R(H)ACHIS, BACKBONE

column, having
.... VERTEBRATE

cord .... MYELON

cord cut .... PITH

cord inflammation
.... MYELITIS, RACHITIS

cord membrane .... EPENDYMA

cord sheath .... MATER, MYELIN(E)

cord tumor .... GLIOMA

curvature ..... KYPHOSCOLIOSIS

injury result .... PARALYSIS

marrow .... NUCHA

nerves, group of ..... LUMBAR, SACRAL, CERVICAL, THORACIC

nerves network .... PLEXUS

surgical procedure ..... FUSION

tap .... LUMBAR PUNCTURE

spindle .... PIN, ROD, AXIS, AXLE, BUFF, STEM, ARBOR, SHAFT, SPIKE, STALK, STICK, DISTAFF, MANDREL, TRIBLET, HYDROMETER

flywheel .... WHARVE

shaped like .... FUSIFORM

weaver's .... QUILL

spindling .... BONY, LEAN, GAUNT, LANKY, GANGLY, GANGLING

spindrift .... FOAM, SCUD, FROTH, SPUME, (SEA)SPRAY

spine .... RAY, CHINE, QUILL, SPIKE, THORN, CHAETA, NEEDLE, RACHIS, PRICKLE, BACKBONE

curvature, backward
.... KYPHOSIS

inward .... LORDOSIS

to one side .... SCOLIOSIS

cylindrical bones of the
.... VERTEBRAE

inflammation .... RACHITIS

section ...... COCCYX, LUMBAR, SACRUM, CERVICAL, THORACIC

spinel .... BALAS, STONE, SAPPHIRINE

gem .... RUBY

spineless .... LIMP, WEAK, BONELESS, INVERTEBRATE

slang .... CHICKEN, GUTLESS

spines, covered with .... HISPID

spinet .... ORGAN, PIANO, VIRGINAL, HARPSICHORD

spinnaker .... SAIL

spinner .... TOP, LURE, SPIDER, WEAVER, SILKWORM

of life's thread .... CLOTHO

spinney .... GROVE, THICKET

spinning apparatus .... BOBBIN, COILER

machine .... MULE, WHEEL, JENNY, THROTTLE

mule inventor .... CROMPTON

platform .... TURNTABLE

toy .... TOP, FRISBEE

wheel .... CHARK(H)A

wheel part .... DISTAFF, TREADLE

spinster .... FILLE, MAIDEN, SINGLE, VIRGIN, SPINNER, (OLD)MAID, FEMME SOLE

spiny .... HISPID, THORNY, PRICKLY, SPINOSE, ACICULAR, ACANTHOID

spiracle .... AIR HOLE, OPENING, BLOWHOLE

spiraea .... HARDHACK, MEADOWSWEET

spiral .... HELIX, HELICAL, WINDING

combining form .... HELICO

curl .... RINGLET

downward .... TAILSPIN

like a .... SPIROID

motion .... GYRE

of wire .... COIL

scroll .... VOLUTE

shaped .... HELICOID, TURBINATE

shaped device ..... CORKSCREW

shell whorl .... VOLUTE

spiraled .... VOLUTE, SCROLLED

spiraling .... SKYROCKETING

spirant .... FRICATIVE

spire .... APEX, PEAK, CROWN, SHAFT, STALK, FLECHE, SPROUT, STEEPLE

mountain .... ARETE, PINNACLE

ornament .... FINIAL

shaped like a needle
.... AIGUILLE

topper .... EPI

tower .... PAGODA, MINARET

spirit .... PEP, VIM, DASH, ELAN, GALL, LIFE, MIND, MOOD, SOUL, WILL, ARDOR, BOGEY, BOGIE, DEMON, GHOST, HEART, SPUNK, VERVE, VIGOR, ENERGY, METTLE, MORALE, COURAGE, ESSENCE, PIZ(Z)AZZ, VITALITY, VIVACITY

cane .... RUM

chief evil .... SATAN

good .... DEVA, ANGEL

guiding .... ANGEL

heralding death ...... BANSHEE, BANSHIE

in a jar .... GENIE

living in fire ..... SALAMANDER

mischievous .... GOBLIN, ERLKING, GREMLIN

of chivalry .... ERRANTRY

of evil .... AHRIMAN

of good .... ORMAZD

of the sea .... DAVY JONES

presiding .... NUMEN

the .... GOD, HOLY GHOST

spirited .... BOLD, RACY, BRISK, FIERY, PERKY, ARDENT, BLITHE, LIVELY, SPUNKY, ANIMATED, VIGOROUS, ENERGETIC

self-assurance .... ELAN

spiritless ...... COLD, DEAD, DULL, LIFELESS, LISTLESS, DEPRESSED, LACKADAISICAL

spirits .... MOOD, HUMOR, LIQUOR, TEMPER, ALCOHOL, ETHANOL, LIQUEURS, DISPOSITION

alcoholic strength of
.... PROOF

believer .... ANIMIST

night-walking .... LEMURES

of hartshorn .... AMMONIA

of the dead .... MANES

of wine .... ALCOHOL

out of .... SAD

spiritual .... PIOUS, SACRED, FOLK SONG, SUPERNATURAL

being .... ENS, ANGEL

charge .... CURE

guide .... FATHER, PRIEST, CONFESSOR

knowledge .... GNOSIS

mother .... AMMA

opposite of .... CORPOREAL

sitting .... SEANCE

spiritualism .... OCCULTISM

third party in .... MEDIUM

681

well-known champion of
.... DOYLE
spiritualist's equipment
.... OUIJA
spirituous drink .... WINE
spiritus frumenti .... WHISKY
spirochete .... TREPONEMA
disease .... YAWS
spirogyra .... ALGA
spirt .... GUSH, SPURT
spirula .... MOLLUSK
kin of .... SQUID, CUTTLEFISH
spiry .... COILED, CURLED
spit .... EMIT, HISS, RAIN, SNOW,
STAB, SHOAL, BROACH,
IMPALE, PIERCE, SALIVA,
SKEWER, DRIZZLE, SANDBANK,
EXPECTORATE
spital .... HOSTEL, SHELTER,
HOSPITAL
spitball .... WAD, CURVE, SINKER,
SLIDER
spitchcock .... EEL
spite .... VENOM, GRUDGE,
HATRED, MALICE, RANCOR,
SPLEEN, ILL WILL
spiteful ...... MEAN, CATTY, SNIDE,
HOSTILE, VENOMOUS,
VIPERINE, VIPEROUS,
MALICIOUS, SPLENETIC,
VINDICTIVE
woman .... CAT
spitefulness ...... ANGER, CHOLER,
SPLEEN, CATTINESS
spitfire .... HELLCAT, HOTHEAD
Mexican .... (LUPE)VELEZ
spitter .... DEER, BROCK, PITCHER,
SPITBALL
spitting image .... LIKENESS,
DEAD RINGER
spittle .... SALIVA
insect .... FROGHOPPER
spittoon .... CUSPIDOR
spitz dog .... POMERANIAN
spiv .... IDLER
splanchnic .... VISCERAL
splash .... LAP, DASH, DAUB,
PLOP, SLOP, SPILL, SWASH,
SPARGE, SPATTER, SPLOTCH,
SPLATTER, SPRINKLE
the fingers .... DABBLE
splashboard .... MUDGUARD
splashdown .... REENTRY
splashy .... SHOWY
splat .... LATH, SLAT
splatter .... DAB, SPLASH,
SPATTER, SPRINKLE
splay ...... AWRY, BEVEL, CLUMSY,
EXPAND, EXTEND, AWKWARD,
OBLIQUE, DISLOCATE,
SPREAD(ING)

spleen .... MILT, WHIM, ENNUI,
SPITE, MALICE, BOREDOM,
CAPRICE, MELANCHOLY
production .... ANTIBODIES,
PHAGOCYTES, LYMPHOCYTES
site .... ABDOMEN
surgery .... LIENECTOMY,
SPLENECTOMY
splendid .... FINE, GRAND,
SUPERB, RADIANT, GLORIOUS,
GORGEOUS, LUSTROUS,
EXCELLENT, GRANDIOSE,
MAGNIFICENT
slang .... RIPPING
splendor .... POMP, ECLAT,
GLORY, LUSTER, GLITTER,
RADIANCE, GRANDEUR,
BRILLIANCE
splenetic .... PEEVISH, SPITEFUL,
IRRITABLE
splice .... WED, JOIN(T), MARRY,
UNITE
splint .... CAST, LATH, SLAT,
BRACE, SUPPORT
use of .... FIRST AID
splinter ...... CHIP, SHARD, SHIVE,
SPILL, SPLIT, SHIVER, SLIVER,
FLINDER, FRAGMENT
splinters .... MATCHWOOD
split ...... CHAP, REND, RIFT, RIVE,
BREAK, BURST, CLEFT,
BREACH, CLEAVE, DIVIDE,
SCHISM, SLIVER, SPALATO,
DISUNITE, SEPARATE(D)
a marriage legally
.... DIVORCE
asunder .... REND
capable of being .... FISSILE
colloquial .... SHARE
hairs .... QUIBBLE, STRAIN AT
A GNAT
into thirds .... TRISECT
open .... BREAK, DEHISCE
personality, of .... MULTIPLE
pulse .... DAL
rattan .... CANE
slang .... LEAVE, PEACH,
DEPART, SQUEAL
the difference .... COMPROMISE
with violence .... REND
splitsville .... RENO
splitting .... ACHING, SEVERE
apart .... FISSION
splotch .... BLOB, BLOT, SPOT,
STAIN, SPLASH
splurge .... SPLASH, SHOW OFF,
OSTENTATION
spode .... CHINAWARE, PORCELAIN
Spohr, composer .... LOUIS
opera by .... JESSONDA
spoil .... MAR, ROB, ROT, LOOT,

MESS, RUIN, SACK, DECAY, GO
BAD, HUMOR, SEIZE, TAINT,
DAMAGE, IMPAIR, FERMENT,
LOUSE UP, PILLAGE, PLUNDER,
VITIATE, (OVER)INDULGE
liable to .... PERISHABLE
spoiled .... WASTED, PAMPERED
_____ .... ROTTEN
child .... BRAT
spoiler .... BANE
spoils .... LOOT, BOOTY, PRIZE,
TROPHY
spoilsport .... KILLJOY, MARPLOT,
SOURPUSS, WET BLANKET
spoke .... BAR, PIN, RUNG,
RUNDEL
spoken .... ORAL, VOCAL, VERBAL,
UTTERED
clearly .... ARTICULATED
merely .... LIP
spokes .... RADII
spokeshave .... PLANE
spokesman/spokesperson
.... AGENT, PROXY, VOICE,
MOUTHPIECE
spoliate .... ROB, DESPOIL,
PLUNDER
sponge .... BUM, MOP, SOP, BLOT,
SOAK, SWAB, ASCON, CADGE,
LEECH, MOOCH, ABSORB,
BLOTTER, PUDDING, PARASITE,
TRENCHER, PORIFERAN
cake .... JELLYROLL
gourd .... LOOF(A), LOOFAH
opening .... OSCULUM
pertaining to .... PORIFEROUS
slang .... MOOCHER, DEAD
BEAT, FREELOADER
spicule .... OXEA, TOXA,
ACTINE
substitute .... LUFFA, LOOFAH
throw in the .... YIELD, GIVE
UP, SUBMIT, CONCEDE,
SURRENDER
sponger .... DRUNK, LEECH,
CADGER, MOOCHER, HANGER-
ON, PARASITE
spongy .... POROUS, ELASTIC,
ABSORBENT
sponsor .... ANGEL, BACKER,
PATRON, SURETY, GODFATHER
beneficiary of .... PROTEGE
slang .... ANGEL
sponsorship .... (A)EGIS, AUSPICES
spontaneous .... AUTOMATIC,
IMPULSIVE
spontoon .... PIKE, HALBERD
spoof .... FOOL, JOKE, HOAX,
TRICK, BANTER, PARODY,
SATIRE, DECEIVE, LAMPOON,
HOODWINK, BAMBOOZLE

spook .... GHOST, SPECTER, FRIGHTEN

spooky .... EERIE, WEIRD, GHOSTLY, HAUNTED, SPECTRAL

spool .... COP, PIRN, REEL, BOBBIN, SPINDLE

out .... UNREEL

weaver's shuttle .... PIRN

spoon .... DIP, PET, LIFT, KISS, NECK, SCOOP, CARESS, CUTLERY

large .... LADLE

like implement .... OAR, SPADE, PADDLE, SPATULA

out .... DOLE, METE

shaped .... CONCAVE, SPATULATE

spoonbill .... AIAIA, AJAJA, PADDLEFISH

spoonfed .... CODDLED, PAMPERED

spooning .... SMOOCHING

spoony .... SILLY, AMOROUS, FOOLISH, MAWKISH, KISSABLE, LOVESICK, SENTIMENTAL

spoor .... TRACK, TRAIL

Sporades island .... SAMOS

sporadic .... RARE, FITFUL, SCARCE, ERRATIC, IRREGULAR, DESULTORY, OCCASIONAL

sporangium .... SPORE CASE

spore .... GERM, SEED, ZYGOTE

capsule .... URN

case .... ASCI, SORI, ASCUS, THECA, SPORANGIUM

cluster(s) .... SORUS, SORI

producer .... FERN, MOSS

sac .... ASCUS, THECA

small .... SPORULE

sporran .... PURSE, POUCH

sport .... FUN, GAME, JEST, FREAK, FROLIC, MUTANT, TRIFLE, DISPLAY, JESTING, PASTIME, ATHLETICS, DIVERSION, MERRIMENT, RECREATION

for short .... REC

group .... TEAM, COUPLE, TWOSOME

slang .... JOCK, SPENDER

sporting .... FAIR, GAMING, ATHLETIC, GAMBLING

chance .... BEST BET

events, certain .... ROUND-ROBIN

house .... HALL, ALLEY, CASINO

sportive .... FRISKY, FESTIVE, PLAYFUL, TRICKSY, WAGGISH

sports attendance .... GATE

devotee/fan .... ROOTER

"English" .... SPIN

event .... BOUT, HUNT, RACE, MEET, MATCH, CONTEST

meet .... GYMKHANA, OLYMPICS

nickname: Crazy Legs .... ELROY HIRSCH

Galloping Ghost .... RED GRANGE

Magic ...... EARVIN JOHNSON

Nasty .... ELIE NASTASE

Say Hey Kid .... WILLIE MAYS

Super Mex ..... LEE TREVINO

The Golden Bear .... JACK NICKLAUS

The Great White Shark .... GREG NORMAN

The King .... ARNOLD PALMER

The Stilt .... WILT CHAMBERLAIN

Yankee Clipper .... JOE DIMAGGIO

of kings .... HORSE RACING

of skill .... CHESS

official .... JUDGE, TIMER, UMP(IRE), REFEREE, COMMISSIONER

permit for a series of games .... SEASON TICKET

shirt .... TEE, JERSEY

shoe .... LOAFER, SNEAKER

site .... GYM, GRID, OVAL, POOL, RING, RINK, ARENA, COURT, FIELD, GREEN, LINKS, TRACK, COURSE, DIAMOND, STADIUM, COLISEUM, HIPPODROME

team .... CREW, FIVE, NINE, SQUAD, ELEVEN, STRING, FOURSOME

team, in charge of ..... COACH, MANAGER, TRAINER

type of/game .... POLO, CATCH, CHESS, RUGBY, TRACK, BOXING, DISCUS, SOCCER, TENNIS, BOWLING, HUNTING, BASEBALL, FOOTBALL, PING-PONG, SOFTBALL, (ICE)HOCKEY, BASKETBALL, VOLLEYBALL

sportscast .... ANNOUNCE, BROADCAST, GO ON THE AIR

sportscaster .... HILL, GOWDY, HEARN, GUMBEL, HODGES, MADDEN, SCULLY, COSSELL, GIFFORD, DIERDORF, BRADSHAW, MICHAELS, MUSBURGER

sportsmanship .... FAIRNESS

sporty .... SHOWY, CASUAL,

DRESSY, FLASHY, SNAZZY

spot .... BIT, SEE, DAUB, FLAW, MARK, SITE, FLECK, PLACE, SMEAR, STAIN, BLOTCH, DAPPLE, SMUT(CH), BLEMISH, SPECKLE, (FLY)SPECK, MACULA(TE)

colloquial .... JAM, PINCH, TROUBLE

domino .... PIP

hot .... OVEN

in diamond .... CARBON

in mineral .... MACLE

in the ocean .... ISLET

of color .... BLOB

on animal's face .... BLAZE

on lunar halo ..... PARASELENE

on solar halo .... PARHELION

playing card .... PIP

skin .... MOLE, SCAR, MACULA, STIGMA, BIRTHMARK

small .... DOT, FLECK, PRICK, (PIN)POINT

sun .... FRECKLE

spotless .... PURE, CLEAN, CHASTE, HONEST, INNOCENT, IMMACULATE, SPIC AND SPAN

reputation, of .... ABOVEBOARD

spotlight .... FOCUS, BEACON, EMPHASIZE, LIMELIGHT

spotted .... EYED, PIED, DAPPLE(D), MOTTLED, PIEBALD, MACULATE

animal .... CAVY, PACA, HYENA, CHITAL, DAPPLE, OCELOT, CHEETAH, (LEO)PARD

dog .... DALMATIAN

fever .... TICK, TYPHUS

with drops .... GUTTATE

spotter ...... LOOKOUT, DETECTIVE

spotty .... DOTTED, PATCHY, UNEVEN, IRREGULAR

spousal .... NUPTIAL

spouse .... MATE, WIFE, CONSORT, HUSBAND, PARTNER

spout .... JET, GUSH, SNOUT, SPILE, NOZZLE, STREAM, ELEVATOR

slang .... PAWN(SHOP)

steam .... JET, GEYSER

water .... GARGOYLE

whale's .... BLOWHOLE

spraddle .... SPAN

sprag .... TRIG, BLOCK, CHOCK, WEDGE

sprain .... TWIST, WRICK, WRENCH, TEARING

most common spot of .... ANKLE

sprat .... BRIT, HERRING, BRISLING

Sprat's diet no-no .... FAT
   predilection .... LEAN
sprawl .... LIE, LOLL, CRAWL,
   LOUNGE, SPREAD
spray .... MIST, TWIG, SPRIG,
   SPUME, LIPPER, PEPPER,
   SHOWER, BOUQUET,
   ATOMIZE(R), NEBULIZE,
   SPRINKLE
   products .... AEROSOLS
   with bullets .... RIDDLE
   with medicated liquid
   .... NEBULIZE
spread .... FAN, JAM, OLEO,
   BRUIT, COVER, JELLY, SPLAY,
   STREW, BUTTER, EXTEND,
   UNFOLD, UNFURL, EXHIBIT,
   OVERLAY, SCATTER, STRETCH,
   DISPERSE, PROPAGATE
   abroad .... RADIATE,
   DISSEMINATE
   apart .... SPLAY, EXPAND
   by scattering .... STREW
   colloquial .... MEAL, FEAST,
   BANQUET, DISPLAY
   eagle .... SPRAWL
   false rumors .... ASPERSE
   for drying .... TED
   from person to person
   .... CIRCULATE
   grass/hay .... TED
   here and there .... STREW,
   SCATTER
   linen .... COVERLET,
   BEDSPREAD
   newspaper .... LAYOUT
   out .... FAN, FLARE, DEPLOY,
   EFFUSE, DIFFUSE
   out awkwardly .... SPRAWL
   out freely .... POUR
   perfume .... CENSE
   rapidly .... MUSHROOM
   rumors .... HAWK, BRUIT
   thick .... SLATHER
   thin .... BRAY
   through .... PERMEATE
   troops .... DEPLOY
spreading .... PATULOUS
   from the center .... RADIAL
   implement .... TEDDER,
   MULCHER, SPATULA
spree .... BOUT, LARK, ORGY,
   TEAR, FLING, SPELL, FROLIC,
   REVELRY, WASSAIL,
   CAROUSAL, (HELL)BENDER
   drunken .... WASSAIL,
   CAROUSAL, BACCHANAL(IA)
   kind of .... SHOPPING
   slang .... BAT, JAG, TOOT,
   BINGE, BUST(ER)
sprig .... BRAD, TWIG, SHOOT,

SPRAY, BRANCH, FELLOW,
   STRIPLING
sprightly .... GAY, TID, AIRY,
   PERT, AGILE, BRISK, SAUCY,
   SMART, BLITHE, JAUNTY,
   LIVELY, CHIPPER, ANIMATED
spring .... BEND, BOLT, JUMP,
   LEAP, STEM, WELL, (A)RISE,
   VAULT, BOUNCE, DART(LE),
   ORIGIN, SEASON, SOURCE,
   EMANATE, REBOUND,
   FOUNT(AIN)
   Apollo's .... CASTALIA
   artificial .... FOUNTAIN
   back .... BOUNCE, RECOIL,
   RESILE, REBOUND
   biblical .... AIN
   bloomer/flower .... PANSY,
   TULIP, CROCUS
   chicken .... FRYER, BROILER
   deposit .... TUFA, TRONA,
   TRAVERTIN
   festival .... MAYDAY
   fever .... BLAHS
   guard .... MIMIR
   herald .... ROBIN
   holiday .... EASTER
   like/of .... FONTAL, VERNAL
   lizard .... SALAMANDER
   mineral .... SPA
   month .... MAY, APRIL, MARCH
   phenomenon .... THAW
   poet's .... CASTALIA
   poetic .... FONT
   sign of .... BUDS, SWALLOW
   slang ..... BAIL, FREE, RELEASE
   small .... GEYSER
   tide .... FLOOD
   water .... LYMPH, SELTZER
springboard .... BATULE
springbok .... GAZELLE, SPRINGER
springe .... TRAP, SNARE
springer .... IMPOST, GRAMPUS,
   SPANIEL
springhead .... SOURCE
springing back .... ELASTIC,
   RESILIENT
springs .... SPA, BATHS, THERMAE
springtime .... MAY
springy .... PLIANT, ELASTIC,
   FLEXIBLE
sprinkle .... DEG, SOW, WET,
   DUST, RAIN, SPRAY, STREW,
   DREDGE, SHOWER, SPLASH,
   DRIZZLE, SCATTER
   as holy water .... SPARGE
   water to purify .... BAPTIZE
   with flour .... DREDGE
   with sieve .... SIFT
sprinkling .... ASPERSION
   in heraldry .... SEME

   with holy water ..... ASPERGES
sprint .... RUN, DASH, RACE,
   RUSH, SPEED
sprinter .... DASHER, RUNNER,
   TRACKMAN, SPEEDSTER
sprit .... BOOM, SPAR
sprite .... ELF, FAY, HOB, NIX,
   PIXY, ARIEL, FAIRY, GHOST,
   GNOME, PIXIE, SPIRIT,
   BROWNIE
   helpful .... KOBOLD
   mischievous .... IMP, PUCK,
   GOBLIN, KOBOLD
   prankish .... ELF
   water .... NIS, NIX, UNDINE
spritelike .... ELFIN
sprout .... BUD, CHIT, GROW,
   (S)CION, SHOOT, BURGEON,
   SAPLING, GERMINATE,
   PULLULATE
   root/stem .... TILLER,
   RAT(T)OON
spruce .... CHIC, NEAT, TIDY,
   TRIM, NATTY, PICEA, SMART
   fruit .... CONE
   slang .... DAPPER, JAUNTY,
   SPIFFY, SHIPSHAPE
   tree .... FIR, PINE, CEDAR,
   LARCH, CONIFER, EPINETTE
   up .... FRESHEN, TITIVATE
sprue .... PSILOSIS
   form of ...... CELIAC, TROPICAL
   organ affected by
   .... INTESTINE
spry .... AGILE, ALERT, BRISK,
   QUICK, ACTIVE, LIVELY,
   NIMBLE
spud .... TATER, POTATO
   tool like .... SPADE, CHISEL
spue .... SPEW
spumante, _____ .... ASTI
spume .... FOAM, SCUM, FROTH
spun .... WOVE(N)
   sugar .... COTTON CANDY
spunk .... GRIT, PUNK, PLUCK,
   SPARK, AMADOU, KINDLE,
   METTLE, SPIRIT, TINDER,
   COURAGE
spunky .... GAME, BRAVE,
   PLUCKY, SPIRITED
spur .... GOAD, URGE, BRACE,
   ERGOT, HURRY, PRICK, RIDGE,
   STRUT, CALCAR, GRIFFE,
   INCITE, SIDING, STIMULUS
   adjunct/wheel .... ROWEL
   gamecock's .... GAFF
   mountain .... ARETE
spurge .... MILKWEED, EUPHORBIA
spurious .... TIN, FAKE, SHAM,
   BOGUS, FALSE, PSEUD,
   FORGED, PHON(E)Y, BASTARD,

ARTIFICIAL, COUNTERFEIT
spurn .... KICK, FLOUT, REPEL,
SCORN, REFUSE, REJECT,
DECLINE
spurr(e)y .... (CHICK)WEED
spurt .... JET, DART, GUSH, BURST,
SPOUT, SPRAY, SQUIRT,
STREAM
of energy .... LICK
Sputnik .... SATELLITE
proprietor .... USSR, RUSSIA
sputter .... SPEW, SPIT, BLURT,
EJECT, BABBLE, FIZZLE,
JABBER, SPLUTTER
sputum .... SALIVA, SPIT(TLE)
spy .... PRY, SEE, FINK, KEEK,
NOSE, ANDRE, FUCHS, SCOUT,
WATCH, ARNOLD, CAVELL,
CICERO, GEISLER, STEIBER,
DISCERN, INFORMER,
(MATA)HARI, SPOTTER,
PERCEIVE, RINTELEN,
OPERATIVE, ROSENBERG,
PRIVATE EYE, (SECRET)AGENT,
UNDERCOVER MAN
Andre .... JOHN
Arnold .... BENEDICT
Arnold's wife .... PEGGY
glass .... BINOCULARS
in one's midst .... MOLE,
INSIDE MAN
lure of .... SECRETS
numerals .... OOVII
obsolete .... ESPIAL
slang .... FINK, MOLE, TAIL,
STOOLIE
who thwarts enemy
espionage
.... COUNTERSPY, DOUBLE
AGENT
woman .... MATA HARI,
(EDITH)CAVELL
work of a .... BUGGING,
STAKEOUT, SHADOWING,
OBSERVATION, WIRETAP(PING)
spying .... PRYING, SNOOPING,
WATCHING, ESPIONAGE,
INTELLIGENCE, SURVEILLANCE
work, of .... CLOAK AND
DAGGER
Spyri's heroine .... HEIDE
squab .... SOFA, COUCH, PIPER,
PIGEON, CUSHION
squabble .... ROW, MUSS, SPAT,
BICKER, HASSLE, DISPUTE,
QUARREL, WRANGLE,
COMMOTION
squad .... BAND, CREW, TEAM,
UNIT, PATROL
car adjunct .... SIREN
leader .... SERGEANT

squadron, navy .... FLEET,
ARMADA
of airplanes .... ESCADRILLE
squads, two or more
.... PLATOON
squalid ...... FOUL, DINGY, DIRTY,
MANGY, FILTHY, SORDID,
UNCLEAN, WRETCHED,
UNSIGHTLY
squall .... CRY, BAWL, BLOW,
FLAW, GALE, GUST, WAIL,
WAUL, WAWL, SCREAM,
TROUBLE, TURMOIL,
(WIND)STORM
squally .... GUSTY, STORMY
squalor ...... DIRT, FILTH, MISERY
squama(e) .... SCALE(S)
squamate/squamous .... SCALY
cell carcinoma .... TUMOR,
SKIN CANCER
squander .... LOSE, WASTE,
LAVISH, CONSUME, EXHAUST,
(DI)SPEND, MISSPEND,
DISSIPATE
slang .... BLOW, PISS AWAY
square .... FIT, FAIR, PARK,
AGREE, BLOCK, COURT,
FORUM, LEVEL, PLAZA,
TALLY, EVEN(UP), HONEST,
PIAZZA, SETTLE, CUBICAL,
BALANCE(D), QUADRATE,
TETRAGON, RECONCILE
all .... EVEN
college campus
.... QUADRANGLE
column .... PILASTER
dance .... REEL, HOEDOWN,
LANC(I)ERS, QUADRILLE
dance, four couples in a
.... (SQUARE) SET
dance need .... CALLER
feet .... AREA
nearly .... RECTANGLE
off .... CLASH, DISAGREE
one, back to .... IMPASSE,
DEADLOCK
person .... FOGY, MISFIT,
FUDDY-DUDDY
-rigged feature ..... YARD ARM
root of nine .... THREE
shooter .... FAIR DEALER
slang .... BRIBE, HUNKY,
WHITE, STRAIGHT, OLD-
FASHIONED
small .... QUADRILLE
the score .... TIE
up .... REPAY
squared circle .... ARENA,
(PRIZE)RING
quantities that are
.... QUADRATIC

squarehead ...... BOCHE, GERMAN,
SCANDINAVIAN
squaring circle ...... CYCLOTOMY,
CYCLOMETRY
squarrose .... SCALY
squash .... MASH, PEPO, CRUSH,
GOURD, PRESS, QUELL, SPORT,
SQUISH, FLATTEN, SILENCE,
SQUEEZE, SQUELCH
crookneck .... CASHAW,
CUSHAW
family .... GOURD
genus .... CURCUBITA
summer .... ZUCCHINI
winter .... HUBBARD,
BUTTERNUT
squashy .... MUSHY, PULPY
squat ...... DUMPY, FUBSY, PUDGY,
TUBBY, CROUCH
and pudgy .... ROLY-POLY
fat and .... FUBSY, PLUMP
on public land .... SETTLE
squatter .... CATCHER, SETTLER
squatter's domain
.... HOMEPLATE
squaw .... WOMAN, MAHALA
Indian .... WIFE
squawbush .... SUMAC
squawk .... CRY, CALL, KICK,
GRIPE, HERON, GROUSE,
OBJECT, SCREAM, GRUMBLE,
PROTEST, COMPLAIN
squeak .... CRY, PEEP, CHEEP,
CREAK, SQUEAL
squeal .... CRY, BLAB, SING, YELL,
YELP, PEACH, RAT ON,
INFORM, SHRIEK, TELL ON,
CONFESS, DIVULGE
squealer .... THIRD EAR, STOOL
PIGEON
of a sort .... CANARY
squeamish .... PICKY, DAINTY,
QUEASY, FINICAL, NERVOUS,
NAUSEOUS, QUALMISH,
SKITTISH, FASTIDIOUS
person .... PRUDE
squeezable container .... TUBE
squeeze .... EKE, HUG, JAM, NIP,
CRAM, CRUSH, WRING, EXACT,
EXTORT, SQUASH, EXTRACT,
(COM)PRESS
chin .... CHUCK
payment by threat
.... BLACKMAIL
squeezer, elongated .... BOA
juice .... REAMER
squelch .... CRUSH, SIT ON,
KIBOSH, MUFFLE, (S)QUASH,
STIFLE, SUBDUE, SILENCE,
SUPPRESS
squeteague .... CROAKER,

GRUNT(ER)
squib ...... LAMPOON, DETONATOR, PASQUINADE, FIRECRACKER
squid .... MOLLUSK, CALAMARY, CUTTLEFISH
arm of .... TENTACLE
relative .... SPIRULA
shell of .... PEN
squilgee .... SQUEEGEE
squill .... LILY, SEA ONION
squilla .... CRAB, PRAWN, MANTIS, SHRIMP, CRUSTACEAN, STOMATOPOD
squinch .... LINTEL, CORBELING
squint .... PEEK, PEER, SKEW, GLANCE, STRABISMUS
convergent .... CROSS-EYE
divergent .... WALLEYE
sideways .... SKEW
squire .... BEAU, DONZEL, ESCORT, ARMIGER, GALLANT, HENCHMAN, ATTEND(ANT), GENTLEMAN, ARMOR-BEARER
squirm .... TWIST, WIGGLE, WRITHE, WRIGGLE
squirrel .... XERUS, MARMOT, RODENT, STORER, HOARDER, TAMARIN, CHIPMUNK, CHICKAREE, PHALANGER, WOODCHUCK, SPERMOPHILE
away .... CACHE
burrowing .... GOPHER, MARMOT
flying .... ASSAPAN, PHALANGER
flying aid .... PATAGIUM
fodder .... ACORN
fur .... VAIR, SUSLIK
ground .... SISEL, GOPHER, SUSLIK
like rodent .... DORMOUSE
monkey .... TAMARIN
nest .... DRAY, DREY
parasite of .... WABBLE
red .... CHICKAREE
shrew .... TANA
skin fold .... PATAGIUM, PARACHUTE
stash of .... NUTS, ACORN
squirt .... JET, HOSE, SHOOT, SPIRT, SPRAY, STREAM
colloquial .... IMP, RUNT
gun .... WATER PISTOL
sri .... MISTER
Sri Lanka. See also **Ceylon**
former name of .... CEYLON
monetary unit .... RUPEE
SRO, part of .... STANDING, ROOM, ONLY
charge .... STANDAGE
patron? .... SEATLESS

sign .... SOLDOUT
SS Nazi .... BLACK SHIRTS
hcad .... IIIMMLER
St. See also **Saint** .... SAINT, STREET
Anthony's cross .... TAU
Anthony's fire ..... ERYSIPELAS
Catherine's commune .... SIENA
Elmo's fire .... CORPOSANT
Francis' birthplace ...... ASSISI
John's bread .... CAROB
Lawrence river discoverer .... (JACQUES)CARTIER
Lawrence river feature .... 1000 ISLANDS
Valentine's way ..... HEART TO HEART
stab ...... GORE, HURT, PINK, SPIT, PUNCH, STICK, WOUND, PIERCE, THRUST
colloquial .... TRY, ATTEMPT
stabile .... STATIONARY
opposite of .... LABILE
stabilize(r) .... BALLAST
stable .... BARN, FAST, FIRM, MEWS, FIXED, LODGE, SECURE, STEADY, CONSTANT, ENDURING, STEADFAST
compartment .... STALL
field .... PADDOCK
member .... BOXER, FIGHTER, RACEHORSE
part .... HAYMOW, HAYLOFT
sound .... NEIGH, SNORT, (W)HINNY
stableman ...... GROOM, CURRIER, (H)OSTLER
stables, royal .... MEWS
staccato, opposed to .... LEGATO
stack ...... FIX, MOW, HEAP, LOAD, PILE, RICK, RUCK, MOUND, BUNDLE, ARRANGE, CHIMNEY
as of fuel .... RUCK
as of papers .... SHEAF
base of .... STADDLE
blow one's ..... FLARE UP, FLY INTO A RAGE, HIT THE CEILING
of grain .... MOW
of hay/straw .... RICK
of iron/steel .... FA(G)GOT
steamship/factory .... FLUE, CHIMNEY, SMOKESTACK
the cards .... CHEAT
stacked .... CURVACEOUS, VOLUPTUOUS
deck .... SETUP
stacte .... SPICE
staddle .... BASE, FRAME, CRUTCH, SUPPORT
stadia .... ROD, TRANSIT,

RANGEFINDER
stadium .... BOWL, PARK, ARENA, FIELD, COLISEUM
passageway .... RAMP
plural of .... STADIA
receipts .... GATE
section .... TIER
shape .... OVAL
staff ...... MAN, ROD, CANE, CLUB, POLE, WAND, ANKUS, BATON, STAVE, STICK, VERGE, CUDGEL, OFFICE, RETINUE, TRUNCHEON
again .... REMAN
bearer .... VERGER
bishop's .... ROD, CROOK, CROSIER
flag .... FLAGPOLE
for leading an elephant .... ANKUS
household .... DOMESTIC
in music .... STAVE
member .... AIDE
metal cap .... SHOE
mountain climber's .... ALPENSTOCK
of an aircraft .... CREW
of attendants .... RETINUE
office ...... FORCE, MANPOWER, PERSONNEL
officer, in short .... ADC
officer's .... CADRE
plural of .... STAVES
shepherd's .... CROOK
symbol .... CLEF
symbol of authority .... MACE, WARDER
symbol of sovereignty .... SCEPTER
teaching .... FACULTY
winged .... CADUCEUS
Stafford, singer .... JO
stag ...... HART, WAPITI, POLLARD, (RED)DEER
horn's tine .... BROCKET
mate of .... HIND
party .... SMOKER
stage .... DAIS, DOCK, SHOW, STEP, DRAMA, PHASE, DEGREE, PRESENT, PRODUCE, THEATER, PLATFORM, SCAFFOLD, FOOTLIGHTS, (THE)BOARDS
act on .... EMOTE, PERFORM
advanced .... WORSE
ancient Greek/Roman .... PROSCENIUM
assignment .... PART, ROLE
assistant .... PROMPTER
curtain .... BACKDROP
direction .... EXIT, ASIDE, ENTER, MANET, EXEUNT,

SENNET
extra .... SUPE(R)
for public speaking
.... ROSTRUM, PLATFORM
fright .... BUCK FEVER
front .... PIT, APRON,
ORCHESTRA
group: abbr. .... ANTA
in lunar cycle .... PHASE
kind of .... REVOLVING
lighting .... FLOATS,
SPOTLIGHT, FOOTLIGHTS
name .... PSEUDONYM
of change .... PHASE
disease/illness .... PHASE,
DEGREE, PERIOD
life .... ESTATE
psychosexual development
.... ANAL
overact on .... HAM, MUG
part of ..... PIT, APRON, WINGS,
BOARDS, PODIUM, COULISSE,
PROSCENIUM
piece .... SKIT, SKETCH,
RECITAL, VARIETY
play .... DRAMA, COMEDY,
MUSICAL
elaborate .... OPERA,
OPERETTA, EXTRAVAGANZA
first showing of a
.... PREMIERE
held in the afternoon
.... MATINEE
part in .... LEAD, ROLE,
STAR, HEAVY, VILLAIN
part in, minor .... EXTRA,
WALK-ON
pause .... INTERMEZZO,
INTERMISSION
performance between acts
of .... INTERLUDE
players .... CAST
profession .... ACTING,
DRAMATICS, HISTRIONICS
prop .... (BACK)DROP,
FOOTLIGHTS, CURTAIN(RISER)
setting ...... DECOR, SCENE(RY)
show .... REVUE, MUSICAL,
BURLESQUE, VAUDEVILLE
side scene .... COULISSE
slang .... LEGIT
trumpet call .... SENNET
vehicle ..... DRAMA, PLAY(LET)
whisper .... SIGH, AD LIB,
ASIDE
stagecoach .... CONCORD
travel by .... STAGING
stagehand .... GRIP, CALLBOY,
PROMPTER, TECHNICIAN
stager .... OLD HAND, VETERAN
Stagg, Amos _____ .... ALONZO

stagger ...... REEL, SWAY, LURCH,
WAVER, FALTER, TOTTER,
WAMBLE, STARTLE,
FLOUNDER, ALTERNATE,
OVERWHELM, VACILLATE
staggered arrangement
.... ZIGZAG
staggering .... AMBLING,
SHOCKING, STUNNING,
SURPRISING, ASTONISHING
stagger(s) .... GID, MEGRIM(S)
cause of .... COENURUS
staghorn _____ .... CORAL
Stagirite .... ARISTOTLE
stagnant ...... DULL, FOUL, INERT,
STALE, TORPID, DORMANT,
SLUGGISH, STANDING
stagnate .... VEGETATE
stagnation .... STASIS
stagy ...... AFFECTED, THEATRICAL
staid .... FIXED, SOBER, SEDATE,
STEADY, SETTLED
stain .... DYE, BLOT, SOIL, SPOT,
TINT, BRAND, SMEAR, SPOIL,
SULLY, TAINT, TINGE,
BLOTCH, IMB(R)UE, SMUDGE,
STIGMA, BLEMISH, CORRUPT,
SPLOTCH, TARNISH,
DISHONOR, MACULA(TE)
escutcheon .... BLOT
remover .... LEMON, PUMICE
stainer for microscope
.... SAFRANIN(E)
staining .... DYEING
art of .... MARBLING
method .... PAP(ANICOLAOU)
stair .... STEP, STILE
edge .... NOSER
face .... RISER
lights .... FOOTS
post .... NEWEL
slope .... INCLINE
staircase .... PERRON, STAIRS
bend .... RAMP
guard .... HANDRAIL
landing .... HALFPACE
part ...... POST, RISER, RUNDLE,
RAILING, BALUSTRADE
post .... NEWEL, BALUSTER
railing .... BALUSTRADE
spiral .... CARACOLE
step .... WINDER
stairs pillar .... NEWEL
plane .... RAMP
set of .... FLIGHT
shaft .... WELL
stairway, horizontal surface of a
step .... TREAD
mechanical .... ESCALATOR
outside building .... FIRE
ESCAPE

step .... FLIER
vertical piece between steps
.... RISER
stake .... BET, PEG, POT, ANTE,
PALE, PILE, POST, RISK,
CLAIM, HITCH, SHARE, SPILE,
GAMBLE, IMPONE, PICKET,
TETHER, FINANCE, INTEREST
fence .... PALE, WEIR, PICKET
for foundation .... SPILE
for swordplay practice .... PEL
out ..... TAIL, WATCH, OBSERVE
played for .... MAIN
wooden .... PEG, TREE
stakeout ...... BUG, SURVEILLANCE
stakes .... BETS, KITTY, PRIZE,
WAGERS
driver .... MAUL
fence of .... PALISADE
stalactite site .... CAVE
stalag inmate .... POW, PRISONER
stale .... DRAB, DULL, FLAT, HACK,
HOAR, BANAL, FUSTY, MUSTY,
PASSE, TRITE, VAPID, RANCID,
INSIPID, NOT FRESH,
STAGNANT, HACKNEYED,
TASTELESS
slang .... CORNY
stalemate .... JAM, TIE, DRAW,
CHECK, STALL, IMPASSE,
DEADLOCK, STAND-OFF
Stalin's daughter .... (SVETLANA)
ALLILUYEVA
now a.k.a. .... LANA PETERS
Stalinabad .... DUSHANBE
Stalingrad .... VOLGOGRAD
Stalinism .... COMMUNISM
Stalino, former .... DONETSK
stalk .... CULM, LURK, STEM,
HAULM, PROWL, SCAPE, STIPE,
STRUT, CAULIS, PRANCE,
STOVER, PEDICEL, PETIOLE,
STRIPE(S), FILAMENT,
PEDUNCLE
eyed crustacean .... CRAB,
PRAWN, SHRIMP, LOBSTER,
CRAYFISH
flower .... PEDUNCLE
grass .... CULM, HA(U)LM,
STRAW
having a .... PETIOLATE
leaf .... PETIOLE
like structure .... PEDICEL,
PEDICLE
stalking horse .... BLIND, DECOY,
PRETEXT, SMOKE-SCREEN
stall .... COT, CRIB, LOGE, SEAT,
BOOTH, DELAY, HEDGE,
KIOSK, NICHE, STAND,
ALCOVE, MANGER, PUT OFF,
STABLE, CHAMBER,

TEMPORIZE, COMPARTMENT
covering .... TILT
shop's front .... BULK
stallion .... STEED, MORGAN,
STUD(HORSE), ENTIRE(HORSE)
Stallone's nickname .... SLY
stalwart .... FIRM, HUSKY,
ROBUST, STRONG, LOYALIST,
TIRELESS, DAUNTLESS,
SUPPORTER
Stamboul .... ISTANBUL
stamen .... STALK, ANTHER,
FILAMENT, POLLEN SAC
stamina ...... GRIT, PLUCK, VIGOR,
BACKBONE, HARDNESS,
STRENGTH, VITALITY,
ENDURANCE, TOUGHNESS
staminate .... MALE
stammer .... HALT, PAUSE,
FALTER, STUTTER, HESITATE,
HEM (AND HAW)
stamp .... DIE, MARK, SIGN, TAMP,
BRAND, SIGIL, CACHET,
IMPRESS, IMPRINT
Chinese .... CHOP
mail .... POSTAGE
official/ornamental .... SEAL
on coin .... MINTAGE
out .... CRUSH, CANCEL,
SCOTCH, ELIMINATE,
ANNIHILATE
stampede ...... RUN, ROUT, PANIC,
CHARGE, FLIGHT, ONRUSH,
RAMPAGE
stamper .... DATER
stamping device .... DATER,
PUNCHEON
ground .... TURF, HAUNT,
RESORT, FOOTING, HANGOUT
stamps, substitute for
.... INDICIA
Stan, the Man .... MUSIAL
stance .... POSE, POST, BEARING,
POSTURE, CARRIAGE, POSITION
stanch .... STEM, STOP, CHECK,
QUELL, QUENCH, SUPPRESS
stanchion .... POST, BRACE,
PILLAR
stand .... BEAR, BIER, FACE, HALT,
LAST, RACK, STAY, VIEW,
ABIDE, BOOTH, STALL,
CASTER, ENDURE, REMAIN,
RESIST, OPINION, STATION,
UNDERGO, ATTITUDE,
POSITION, TANTALUS,
TOLERATE
against .... OPPOSE
apart .... VARY, DIFFER
artist's/painter's .... EASEL
behind ...... BACK UP, SUPPORT
by ...... BACK, AWAIT, DEFEND,

MAINTAIN
conductor's .... PODIUM
fast .... RESIST
for .... MEAN, REPRESENT
for election .... RUN
in .... PROXY, SUBSTITUTE
in the way .... FOIL, BLOCK,
THWART, OBSTRUCT
high .... TOWER
kind of ...... LAST, NEWS, ONE-
NIGHT
on hind legs .... RAMP, REAR
orator's .... SOAPBOX
ornamental .... TABORET,
PEDESTAL
out .... GLARE, PROJECT,
DISSENTER
priest's .... PULPIT
sacrificial .... ALTAR
stockstill .... FREEZE
three-legged .... TEAPOY,
TRIPOD, TRIVET
two-legged .... BIPOD
standard .... FLAG, NORM,
CANON, GRADE, MODEL,
NORIA, BANNER, COLORS,
EMBLEM, ENSIGN, NORMAL,
CLASSIC, EXAMPLE, REGULAR,
TYPICAL, UNIFORM,
GONFALON, CRITERION,
YARDSTICK
battle .... ORIFLAME
bearer .... CHIEF, ENSIGN,
LEADER, CHAMPION,
CANDIDATE
of a .... VEXILLARY
of excellence/of perfection
.... IDEAL
pasha's .... HORSETAIL
standby .... STAPLE, MAINSTAY,
ALTERNATE
at airport .... PASSENGER
standee, bus/subway
.... STRAPHANGER
standing .... RANK, ERECT,
RATING, STATUS, UPRIGHT,
POSITION, PRESTIGE,
STAGNANT, REPUTATION
order .... SOP
out .... GLARING, SALIENT
room area .... AISLES
room charge .... STANDAGE
with feet on ground
.... STATENT
Standish, colonist .... MILES
standoff .... TIE, DRAW
standoffish ...... ALOOF, DISTANT,
RESERVED, WITHDRAWN
standout .... ONER
standpat(ter) .... TORY, DIEHARD,
CONSERVATIVE

standpoint .... ANGLE, ASPECT,
VIEWPOINT
standstill .... HALT, IMPASSE,
DEADLOCK, (DEAD)STOP,
CESSATION
stang .... PAIN
stanhope .... SHAY, CARRIAGE
Stanley _____ (early auto)
.... STEAMER
stannite .... ORE
stannum .... TIN
Stanovoi mountain ...... ANADYR,
KOLYMA, YABLONOI
Stan's pal .... OLLIE
stanza ...... ENVOI, STAVE, VERSE,
(L)ENVOY, DISTICH,
STROP(H)E
eight-line .... OCTAVE,
TRIOLET, OCTONARY
four-line .... QUATRAIN,
TETRASTICH
seven-line .... HEPTASTICH
six-line .... SESTET, SEXTAIN,
HEXASTICH
stapelia .... MILKWEED
stapes .... STIRRUP
location .... MIDDLE EAR
staple .... SALT, CHIEF, FIBER,
FLOUR, SUGAR, POPULAR,
REGULAR, COMMODITY,
PRINCIPAL
food .... CORN, RICE, POTATO
star ...... ACE, SUN, NOVA, EXCEL,
PLANET, LEADING, ASTERISK
apple .... CAIMITO
binary .... ALGOL, ALBIREO,
ANTARES
blue .... VEGA
brightest .... COR, LUCIDA,
SIRIUS
cluster .... GALAXY, ASTERISM,
MILKY WAY
combining form .... ASTRO,
SIDER(O)
Cygnus .... DENEB
evening .... VENUS, VESPER,
HESPER(US)
fallen .... ALGA, HAS-BEEN
five-pointed .... PENTACLE,
PENTAGRAM
grazer .... BOVINE
group .... DIPPER, MILKY WAY,
CONSTELLATION
in an opera ...... PRIMA DONNA
in Cetus .... MIRA
in Perseus, fixed .... ALGOL
in Serpens .... ALYA
like a/of a .... ASTRAL,
STELLAR
Lyra .... VEGA
Mars .... ANTARES

morning .... VENUS, PHOSPHOR

neutron .... PULSAR

new .... NOVA

Orion .... RIGEL

path of .... ORBIT

pertaining to a .... SIDEREAL, CELESTIAL

poetic .... LAMP

pulsating ..... CEPHEID, PULSAR

red .... RUSSIA, ANTARES

rising .... COMER

Scorpio .... ANTARES

shaped .... ASTROSE, ASTEROID, STELLATE, ASTERIATED

shell .... FLARE

shooting .... METEOR

show-biz ...... ACTOR, ACTRESS

six-pointed .... HEXAGRAM

small .... STARLET

spangled, in heraldry

.... SEME

sports .... ACE, CHAMPION

temperamental .... PRIMA DONNA

thistle .... WEED, CALTRAP, CALTROP

with long luminous tail

.... COMET

yellow .... CAPELIA

Star Chamber .... COURT, TRIBUNAL

of David .... HEXAGRAM

Spangled Banner, The, writer

.... FRANCIS SCOTT KEY

____: The New Generation

.... TREK

Trek creator .... (GENE) RODDENBERRY

Trek's milieu .... SPACE

starch .... SAGO, MANIOC, AMYL(UM), AMIDINE, AMYLOSE, CASSAVA, TAPIOCA, GLYCOGEN, ARROWROOT, CARBOHYDRATE

food .... FARINA

grain nucleus .... HILUM

grain part .... GRANULOSE

like .... AMYLOID

pudding .... SAGO

source .... ARUM, SAGO, TARO, CANNA, MANIOC, CASSAVA, COONTIE, CURCUMA

to sugar, enzyme that changes .... AMYLASE

starchy .... RIGID, STIFF, FORMAL, AMYLACEOUS

food/substance .... AMYLOID

plant .... AROID

root/tuber .... YAM, TARO, (SWEET)POTATO

stare .... GAPE, GAWK, GAZE, OGLE, GLARE, GOGGLE

down .... OUTFACE

open-mouthed .... GAPE

stupidly .... GAWK

starfish .... SEA STAR, FIVE-FINGER, ASTEROID(EAN)

arm/limb .... RAY

relative .... COMATULID

starflower .... PRIMROSE

stargazer .... ASTROLOGER, ASTRONOMER

staring .... AGAPE

stark .... BLEAK, RIGID, SHEER, STIFF, BARREN, UTTER(LY), DESOLATE, DOWNRIGHT

naked ..... BARE, NUDE, IN THE RAW

raving-mad .... WILD, MANIAC, FURIOUS

starlet .... ACTRESS, INGENUE

starling .... MINO, REDWING, OXPECKER, (BLACK)BIRD

kin of .... MYNA(H), ORIOLE

starnose .... MOLE

Starr, bandit queen .... BELLE

husband of Belle .... SAM

of comic strips .... BRENDA

of football fame .... BART

starry .... SHINY, ASTRAL, STELLAR, SIDEREAL, GLITTERING

stars .... FATE, DESTINY, FORTUNE

dotted with .... SEME

group of .... CONSTELLATION

in Ursa Major, group of

.... BIG DIPPER

large group of .... GALAXY, MILKY WAY

of the .... ASTRAL, STELLAR, SIDEREAL, CELESTIAL

visible winter nights, group of .... ORION, PLEIADES

worshiper of .... SABAIST

Stars and Stripes Forever

composer .... (JOHN PHILIP)SOUSA

start .... JIB, SHY, EDGE, JERK, BIRTH, LEAD, OPEN, BEGIN, CRACK, ROUSE, ONSET, SET IN, SHOCK, LAUNCH, COMMENCE, INCEPTION

a set .... SERVE

anew .... REOPEN

card game .... DEAL

of a refrain .... TRA

of a tale .... ONCE

to take off .... UNZIP

START concerns, informally

.... NUKES

starting point .... GATE, SCRATCH

startle .... ALARM, AMAZE, SCARE, SHOCK, EXCITE, AFFRIGHT, FRIGHTEN, SURPRISE, GALVANIZE

starvation .... FASTING

widespread .... FAMINE

starve .... DIET, DENY, FAST, PINE, FAMISH, HUNGER, SCRIMP

starved .... HUNGRY, FAMISHED

starwort .... ALGA, ASTER

stash .... HIDE, CACHE, HOARD, CONCEAL, SECRETE

cash .... IRA

state .... SAY, AVER, AVOW, ETAT, FORM, MODE, MOOD, POSIT, UTTER, NATION, PLIGHT, POLITY, STATUS, COUNTRY, DECLARE, EXPRESS, NARRATE, SPECIFY, CONDITION, SITUATION, TERRITORY

admitted to the Union in the 20th century .... ALASKA, HAWAII, ARIZONA, OKLAHOMA, NEW MEXICO

attorney .... DA

council .... SENATE

dependent .... SATELLITE

dial. .... GAUP

dominant .... SUPERPOWER

medium's .... TRANCE

of affairs .... CASE, DOINGS, CONCERNS

agitation .... SNIT

balance .... EQUIPOISE

being fat .... ADIPOSITY

body and mind .... FETTLE

continuing .... ABIDANCE

equilibrium .... STASIS

excitement .... FERMENT

mind .... MOOD, MORALE, SPIRITS, DISPOSITION

suspended animation

.... ANABIOSIS

over and over .... REITERATE

police .... TROOPER

positively .... AVER, ASSERT

proposed by the Mormons: 1849 .... DESERET

treasury .... FISC

troops .... MILITIA

under oath .... SWEAR, DEPOSE

with confidence .... ASSURE

without proof .... CLAIM, ALLEGE

State, Aloha .... HAWAII

Badger .... WISCONSIN

Bay .... MASSACHUSETTS

Beaver .... OREGON

Beehive .... UTAH

Blue Hen .... DELAWARE

Bluegrass .... KENTUCKY

Buckeye .... OHIO
Centennial .... COLORADO
Constitution ..... CONNECTICUT
Cornhusker .... NEBRASKA
Cotton .... ALABAMA
Coyote .... SOUTH DAKOTA
Creole .... LOUISIANA
Department endorsement
.... VISA
El Dorado .... CALIFORNIA
Empire .... NEW YORK
Equality .... WYOMING
Evergreen .... WASHINGTON
Fair author .... STONG
First .... DELAWARE
Free .... MARYLAND
Garden .... NEW JERSEY
Gem .... IDAHO
Golden .... CALIFORNIA
Gopher .... MINNESOTA
Grand Canyon .... ARIZONA
Granite .... NEW HAMPSHIRE
Green Mountain .... VERMONT
Hawkeye .... IOWA
Hoosier .... INDIANA
Keystone .... PENNSYLVANIA
Land of Enchantment .... NEW
MEXICO
Little Rhody .... RHODE
ISLAND
Lone Star .... TEXAS
Magnolia .... MISSISSIPPI
Mountain .... WEST VIRGINIA
Nutmeg .... CONNECTICUT
Old Colony
.... MASSACHUSETTS
Old Dominion .... VIRGINIA
Old Line .... MARYLAND
Palmetto ..... SOUTH CAROLINA
Peach .... GEORGIA
Pelican .... LOUISIANA
Pine Tree .... MAINE
Prairie .... ILLINOIS
Show Me .... MISSOURI
Silver .... NEVADA
Sioux .... NORTH DAKOTA
Sooner .... OKLAHOMA
Sunflower .... KANSAS
Sunshine .... FLORIDA
Tar Heel ..... NORTH CAROLINA
The Last Frontier ..... ALASKA
Treasure .... MONTANA
Volunteer .... TENNESSEE
Wolverine .... MICHIGAN
statehood .... NATIONALITY
statehouse .... CAPITOL
stately .... GRAND, LOFTY, NOBLE,
REGAL, ROYAL, AUGUST,
FORMAL, COURTLY, IMPOSING,
MAJESTIC, DIGNIFIED,
GRANDIOSE, MAGNIFICENT

house .... DOME, VILLA,
PALACE, CHATEAU, MANSION
music .... LARGO
statement .... BILL, WORD, PRECIS,
REMARK, REPORT, THESIS,
ACCOUNT, ADDRESS,
BULLETIN, ASSERTION,
TESTIMONY, DECLARATION
absurd, self-contradictory
.... PARADOX
authoritative .... DICTUM
brief, casual .... REMARK,
COMMENT
defamatory .... LIBEL
ex-employer's ...... REFERENCE
false, malicious .... CANARD
formal .... CITATION,
AFFIDAVIT, COMMUNIQUE,
DEPOSITION, DECLARATION
in belief .... CREDO, CREED
lying witness' .... PERJURY
of account, final .... AUDIT
of facts .... CASE
of principles, systematic
.... THEORY
positive .... ASSERTION
preliminary .... PREFACE
sanctimonious .... CANT
unsupported/without proof
.... SAY-SO, ALLEGATION
stater .... COIN
stateroom .... CABIN
statesman ...... SOLON, DIPLOMAT,
POLITICIAN
archaic .... STATIST
in Japan .... GENRO
retired ..... ELDER(STATESMAN)
static ...... FIXED, INERT, PASSIVE,
FEEDBACK, INACTIVE,
STATIONARY, ATMOSPHERICS
on radio reception
.... STRAY(S)
opposed to .... DYNAMIC,
KINETIC
result on TV set .... SNOW
station .... POST, RANK, DEPOT,
PLACE, ASSIGN, STATUS,
LOCATION, POSITION,
TERMINAL, TERMINUS,
STOP(PING) PLACE
wagon .... AUTO(MOBILE)
stationary .... FIXED, AT REST,
ROOTED, STATIC, STABILE,
CONSTANT, IMMOBILE
combining form .... STAT
stationer .... PUBLISHER,
BOOKSELLER, SHOPKEEPER
stationery .... LINEN, PAPETERIE
item .... PEN, CARD, PAPER,
PENCIL, ENVELOPE
statistician ...... FIGURER, STATIST

insurance .... ACTUARY
statistics .... DATA
statoscope .... BAROMETER
statuary ...... STATUES, SCULPTOR
piece of .... BUST, TORSO
statue .... IMAGE, EFFIGY,
CARVING, ACROLITH,
FIGULINE, FIGURINE,
SCULPTURE
Aphrodite bestowed life on
this .... GALATEA
base of ...... PLINTH, PEDESTAL
gigantic .... COLOSSUS
goddess of victory .... NIKE
ledgelike foundation
.... SOCLE
London .... GOG, MAGOG
mold .... (PLASTER)CAST
of _____ .... ZEUS, LIBERTY
Galatea sculptor
.... PYGMALION
Mary .... MADONNA
Sun god Helios
.... COLOSSUS OF RHODES
Sun god Helios sculptor
.... CHARES
Zeus sculptor .... PHEIDIAS
Zeus site .... OLYMPIA
religious .... PIETA
with arms raised in prayer
.... ORANTE
Statue of Liberty poetess
.... LAZARUS
sculptor .... BARTHOLDI
statuesque .... TALL, STATELY,
GRACEFUL
dimness .... MONUMENTAL
STUPIDITY
woman .... JUNO
statuette .... FIGURINE
award .... EMMY, OSCAR
stature .... RANK, HEIGHT,
IMPORTANCE
status .... AGE, RANK, STATE,
POSITION, STANDING,
CONDITION
asthmaticus
.... ASTHMA(ATTACK)
epilepticus .... SEIZURE,
EPILEPSY
seeker .... SOCIAL CLIMBER
symbol .... MINK, POOL,
YACHT, DIAMONDS, ROLLS
ROYCE
symbol of retiree?
.... ROCKING CHAIR
statute .... ACT, LAW, RULE, EDICT
part of .... TITLE, ARTICLE
staunch .... FIRM, TRUE, LOYAL,
SOLID, SOUND, STABLE,
STEADY, FAITHFUL, RELIABLE,

WATERTIGHT supporter .... LOYALIST

stave ...... BAR, LAG, RUNG, SLAT, STAP, STAFF, STICK, PIERCE, STANZA, VERSES, PUNCTURE

off .... FEND, WARD, AVERT, STALL, HOLD OFF, DELAY, PREVENT

staves, bundle of .... SHOOK

hold .... HOOP

stavesacre .... LARKSPUR

stay .... GUY, HALT, KEEP, LAST, LIVE, PROP, STOP, TACK, WAIT, (A)BIDE, BRACE, CEASE, CHECK, DEFER, DELAY, DWELL, STICK, TARRY, ENDURE, LINGER, REMAIN, RESIDE, SUPPORT, SUSPEND

continue to .... LINGER

longer .... TARRY

out of mischief .... BEHAVE, TOE THE LINE

to the end .... SIT OUT

staying .... ARRESTING

power ... STAMINA, STRENGTH, ENDURANCE

staylace .... A(I)GLET

stays .... CORSET

Ste. See also **Saint** ...... SAINT(E)

stead .... LIEU, SITE, PLACE, SERVICE

steadfast .... FIRM, FIXED, STABLE, CONSTANT, RESOLUTE

steady .... CALM, EVEN, FIRM, FIXED, STAID, SECURE, STABLE, EQUABLE, REGULAR, UNIFORM, CONSTANT, HABITUAL

colloquial .... BEAU, BOY FRIEND, SWEETHEART

opposite of .... JERKY, ADRIFT, FICKLE, ROVING, ASTATIC, ERRATIC, RESTLESS

steak .... CLUB, FLANK, T-BONE, NEW YORK, SIRLOIN, FILET MIGNON, PORTERHOUSE

steal .... DIP, NIM, ROB, CRIB, HOOK, LOOT, PALM, PRIG, SACK, FILCH, MOOCH, PINCH, POACH, BURGLE, FORAGE, PILFER, SNITCH, THIEVE, PURLOIN, ABSTRACT

cattle, etc. .... RUSTLE

colloquial .... CRIB, BARGAIN

ideas, writings .... CRIB, PIRATE, PLAGIARIZE

slang .... LIFT, HEIST, SWIPE, SNITCH

trust money .... EMBEZZLE, PECULATE

stealer .... CROOK, THIEF, ROBBER,

BURGLAR, FILCHER, SHOPLIFTER

compulsive .... KLEPTOMANIAC

literary .... PIRATE, PLAGIARIST, PLAGIARIZER

tricky ...... CONMAN, SWINDLER

who loves crowds .... DIP, PICKPOCKET

stealthy ...... SLY, FELINE, SECRET, SNEAKY, CUNNING, FURTIVE, CLANDESTINE, SURREPTITIOUS

steam .... GAS, BOIL, COOK, FUME, CLEAN, VAPOR

above earth's surface .... FOG, MIST

boiler safety device .... HYDROSTAT

burn with .... SCALD

colloquial ...... FORCE, POWER, ENERGY

engine .... LOCOMOTIVE

give off .... REEK

steamboat stateroom ...... TEXAS

steamer ...... SHIP, LINER, BOILER, LAUNCH, RIVERBOAT, STEAMBOAT, WHALEBACK

Steamer, Stanley .... AUTOMOBILE

steaming .... BOILING, EXCITED, SEETHING

hot, descriptive of .... PIPING

under high pressure .... AUTOCLAVING

vapor from decomposing matter .... MIASMA, MEPHITIS

steamroll(er) .... RAZE, BULLY, CRUSH, LEVEL, OVERRIDE, OVERWHELM, BULLDOZE(R)

steamship .... LINER, GREYHOUND

abbreviation .... SS

family, noted .... DOLLARS

part of ..... BOW, KEEL, DAVIT, BRIDGE, ENGINE, GUNNEL, RUDDER, BOLLARD, FANTAIL, FUTTOCK, SCUPPER, TRANSOM, LARBOARD, POOPDECK, PORTHOLE, GANGPLANK, PROPELLER, STARBOARD, STOKEHOLD, STEAM PIPE

smokestack of .... FUNNEL

steamy ...... HOT, SEXY, LUSTFUL, PASSIONATE

stearin .... SUET, TALLOW

steatite .... TALC, SOAPSTONE

steed .... MOUNT, CHARGER, PRANCER, STALLION, (STUD)HORSE

steel ...... INURE, METAL, HARDEN, TEMPER, FORTIFY, TOUGHEN

alloy .... INVAR

beam/bar .... HBAR, IBAR, IBEAM, IRAIL, GIRDER

change to .... ACIERATE

covering .... ARMOR

kind of ...... DAMASK, TOLEDO, TEMPERED

making plant .... (RE)FINERY

making process .... DUPLEX, CEMENTATION

oneself for action .... GIRD

poetic .... SWORD, DAGGER

shape .... H-BAR, I-BAR, T-BAR, I-BEAM

with inlaid gold .... DAMASK

steelhead ...... TROUT, SALMONOID

steelyard .... SCALE, BALANCE

Steen, painter .... JAN

steenbok .... ANTELOPE

steep ...... RET, SOP, SOAK, HILLY, IMBUE, LOFTY, SHEER, ABRUPT, IMMERSE, MACERATE, SATURATE, EXCESSIVE, PRECIPITOUS

colloquial .... EXPENSIVE

slope .... CHUTE, SCARP

steeple .... TOWER, BELFRY, FLECHE, MINARET

kind of .... CAMPANILE

part of ..... EPI, SPIRE, BELFRY, FINIAL

steeplebush .... HARDHACK

steeplechase .... HORSERACE

steer .... GUIDE, PILOT, DIRECT, MANAGE, CONTROL

cattle .... YAK, BEEF, COWS, OX(EN), STOT, STIRK, BOVINE, BULL(OCK)

clear of .... SNUB, AVOID

ship .... CONN

slang .... TIP(OFF)

zigzag course .... PLY, YAW

steering gear ...... HELM, WHEEL, RUDDER, TILLER

steersman .... PILOT, WHEELER, HELMSMAN, COX(SWAIN), NAVIGATOR

steeve .... SPAR, STOW, DERRICK

stegomyia .... MOSQUITO

stegosaurus .... DINOSAUR

stein .... (BEER)MUG

Stein, writer .... GERTRUDE

song town ...... ORONO(MAINE)

Steinbeck, author .... JOHN

character .... OKIE

work .... THE GRAPES OF WRATH

steinbok .... ANTELOPE

stele .... LAT, PILLAR, MONUMENT, HEADSTONE

stella .... STAR

stellar .... CHIEF, ASTRAL,

LEADING, RADIANT, STARRING

stellate .... STARRY

stem ...... AXIS, BINE, REIN, STOP, TUBE, ARISE, CHECK, STALK, ARREST, SPRING, PEDICEL, PETIOLE, PEDUNCLE

angle .... AXIL

climbing .... BINE

covering .... OCREA

cylinder .... STELE

fleshy .... TUBER

for grafting .... SLIP

fore part of a ship's

.... CUTWATER

hollow .... CANE

joint .... NODE

leaf's .... FOOTSTALK

main .... TRUNK

of arrow/of spear .... SHAFT

palm .... CAUDEX

plant .... AXIS, CAULIS

raceme's .... R(H)ACHIS

rootlike .... RHIZOME

rudimentary .... CAULICLE

ship's .... BOW, PROW

shoot .... TILLER

trailing .... RUNNER

twining .... BINE

underground ..... CORM, TUBER

stench .... REEK, STINK, F(O)ETOR, MIASMA, (MAL)ODOR, MEPHITIS, (ROTTEN)SMELL

Stendhal hero .... SOREL

Stengel, baseball's .... CASEY

steno, combining form .... THIN, SMALL, NARROW

stenosis .... NARROWING, STRICTURE

form of .... AORTIC, PYLORIC

stenography .... SHORTHAND

Stentor .... HERALD

stentorian .... LOUD

step .... GAIT, PACE, RANK, RUNG, WALK, STAGE, STAIR, TREAD, ACTION, GRADIN, STRIDE, FOOTBALL, FOOTPRINT

as in course of action

.... MEASURES

by step .... GRADUALLY

dance .... PAS, CHASSE, ELECTRIC SLIDE

down .... REDUCE, RESIGN, ABDICATE

fence .... STILE

forward .... VOLUNTEER

giant .... STRIDE

in .... ENTER, MEDIATE, INTERVENE

in a rustic dance ..... DOUBLE-TROUBLE

ins ...... SLIPPERS, UNDERPANTS

ladder .... RUNG

lightly .... TRIP

mincingly .... SASHAY

on heavily ..... PLOD, TRAMPLE

on it ...... HIE, HURRY, HASTEN

on the gas .... REV

part of a .... RISER

projecting part .... NOSING

softly .... PAD, TIPTOE

substitute .... RAMP

to success .... RUNG

up ..... INCREASE, ACCELERATE

stepmother, of/like a

.... NOVERCAL

steppe .... PLAIN, WASTELAND

plain like a .... LLANO, PAMPAS, SAVANNA(H)

stepper .... DANCER

steps, outdoor .... STILE, PERRON

sterculiaceous tree .... KOLA, CACAO

stere .... CUBIC METER

stereo .... HI-FI, BINAURAL

stereotype .... LINOTYPE

printing plate .... CLICHE

stereotyped .... ALIKE, TRITE, COMMON, FAMILIAR, HACKNEYED

sterile .... BARREN, EFFETE, MULISH, OTIOSE, ASEPTIC, GERM-FREE, INFERTILE, UNFRUITFUL

in botany .... ACARPOUS

sterility .... INFERTILITY

sterilization, female

.... LAPAROTOMY, HYSTERECTOMY

male .... VASECTOMY

means of .... BOILING, STEAMING, AUTOCLAVING

sterilize .... GELD, SPAY, CASTRATE, SANITIZE, EMASCULATE

sterlet .... STURGEON

sterling .... PURE, PENNY, SILVER, GENUINE, EXCELLENT, UNALLOYED

stern ...... AFT, DOUR, FIRM, GRIM, HARD, REAR, HARSH, SEVERE, STRICT, AUSTERE, RIGOROUS, FORBIDDING

opposite of .... BOW, PROW, STEM

section of a ship .... COUNTER, POOP(DECK)

toward the .... AFT, REAR, ABAFT

wheeler .... STEAMBOAT

sternum .... BREASTBONE

attachment ...... RIB, CLAVICLE

joint in the .... SYMPHYSIS

part of .... BODY, MANUBRIUM, XIPHOID PROCESS

site .... CHEST

sternutation .... SNEEZE, SNEEZING

sternutatory .... ERRHINE

substance .... SNUFF

steroid drug .... NANDROLONE, STANOZOLOL, OXANDROLONE

drug abuser .... ATHLETE

possible effect of .... ACNE, EDEMA, IMPOTENCE, INFERTILITY

protein-building .... ANABOLIC

stertor .... SNORE

stet .... LET IT STAND

Stettin river .... ODER

stevedore .... LADER, NAVVY, DOCKER, LUMPER, STOWER, DOCKMAN, (UN)LOADER, LONGSHOREMAN

Stevens-Johnson syndrome

...... RASH, HIVES, URTICARIA, ERYTHEMA MULTIFORME

singer .... RISE

Steven's modifier .... EVEN

Stevenson, statesman ...... ADLAI

stew ...... BOIL, DISH, HASH, OLIO, OLLA, CURRY, BURGOO, POTPIE, RAGOUT, SIMMER, GOULASH, HARICOT, POTTAGE, POTPOURRI, HODGEPODGE

colloquial .... FRET, FUME, SNIT, SWEAT, WORRY, DITHER, AGITATION

dish ...... GOULASH, MULLIGAN, BRUNSWICK, FRICASSEE, HOTCHPOTCH, BOURGUIGNON

flavor .... CHIVE, CURRY, ONION, CHERVIL, BAY LEAF

highly seasoned .... RAGOUT, HARICOT

highly spiced .... OLIO, OLLA

hobo's .... MULLIGAN

Hungarian .... GOULASH

in one's own _____ ...... JUICE

meat .... BEEF, LAMB, PORK, VEAL

pan ...... SKILLET, DUTCH OVEN

sailor's .... LOBSCOU(R)SE

slang .... TANK

steward .... REEVE, BUTLER, FACTOR, BAILIFF, MANAGER, TRUSTEE, MAJOR DOMO, SENESCHAL, MAITRE D'HOTEL

college/monastery

.... MANCIPLE

stewardess .... HOSTESS, ATTENDANT

stewardship .... MANAGEMENT

stewed fruit .... FOOL

slang .... DRUNK, PISSED, SOUSED, TANKED
stibium .... ANTIMONY
stich .... LINE, VERSE
stick ...... BAT, ROD, CANE, CLUB, GLUE, POKE, POLE, STAB, WAND, ABIDE, BATON, CLING, PASTE, PRICK, STAFF, ADHERE, CLEAVE, COHERE, CUDGEL, FERULE, IMPALE, PADDLE, PIERCE, THRUST, PUNCTURE
around .... STAY, LINGER
celery .... STALK
colloquial .... PUT, SET, STUMP, BAFFLE, PUZZLE
conductor's/cheerleader's .... BATON
fairy's .... WAND
for leveling grain .... STRICKLE
in-the-mud .... FOGY, IDLER
insect .... EMESA, PHASMID
jab with a .... POKE
jumping .... POGO
match .... LINSTOCK
measuring .... YARD, METER, RULER
metal cap .... FERRULE
out .... JUT, EXTRUDE, PROJECT, PROTRUDE
pointer .... FESCUE
policeman's .... BILLY, TRUNCHEON
primitive/caveman's ...... CLUB
propelling .... POLE
revertible .... BOOMERANG
sharp-pointed .... GOAD
slang .... CHEAT, DEFRAUD, CIGARETTE, OVERCHARGE
steering .... OAR
stirring ..... PADDLE, MUDDLER
throwing .... DINGBAT, BOOMERANG
to one's guns ...... NEVER SAY DIE
together ..... FUSE, JOIN, CLING
up .... ROB
up for .... DEFEND
stick-to-itiveness .... NOSE TO THE GRINDSTONE
sticker ...... BARB, BUR(R), DECAL, KNIFE, LABEL, THORN, PUZZLE
stickler .... MARTINET, QUIBBLER, PERFECTIONIST, DISCIPLINARIAN
of a sort .... PURIST
stickpin's place .... LAPEL, CRAVAT, NECKTIE
sticks, bundle of .... FAGOT
golf ..... CLUBS, IRONS, WOODS
the ...... COUNTRY, BOONDOCKS

sticktight (fruit) .... (COCKLE)BUR
stickum ...... GLUE, GUNK, PASTE, CEMENT, MUCILAGE
stickup .... HEIST, HOLDUP, ROBBERY
sticky .... GLUEY, GOOEY, GUMMY, HUMID, MUGGY, PASTY, TACKY, SWEATY, VISCID, TREACLY, VISCOUS, ADHESIVE, GLUTINOUS
sleuth .... GUMSHOE
substance .... GOO, GUM, GLUE, PASTE, MOLASSES
stiff ...... FIRM, HARD, HIGH, TAUT, WIRY, HARSH, RIGID, TENSE, TIGHT, FORMAL, SEVERE, WOODEN, STILTED
neck .... WRYNECK, TORTICOLLIS
neck cause .... SPASM, WHIPLASH
necked .... PROUD, STUBBORN, DIFFICULT, OBSTINATE
slang .... HOBO, CORPSE
stiffen .... GIRD, PRIM, STEEL, HARDEN, TAUTEN, BRACE(UP), TOUGHEN
the punch .... LACE
stiffened .... STARCHY
stiffening material .... STAY
stiffly .... WOODENLY, AWKWARDLY
stiffness .... RIGOR, PRIMNESS
stifle ...... CHECK, CHOKE, SCOTCH, PUT DOWN, REPRESS, SILENCE, SMOTHER, SUPPRESS, SUFFOCATE
stigma .... BLOT, MARK, PORE, SCAR, BRAND, STAIN, BLEMISH, (EYE)SPOT
stigmatize .... MARK, SLUR, BRAND, DEFILE, VILIFY
stile .... STEP(S)
stiletto .... DIRK, DAGGER, STYLET
still ...... YET, CALM, EVEN, INERT, PHOTO, QUIET, WHIST, HUSHED, PLACID, SERENE, SILENT, WITHAL, ALEMBIC, DISTILLERY, MOTIONLESS, STATIONARY, NEVERTHELESS
existing .... EXTANT
stillbirth ...... LATE FETAL DEATH
stillborn .... DEAD, ABORTIVE, LIFELESS
Stillenacht composer .... GRUBER
stillness .... HUSH, PEACE, SILENCE, QUIETUDE
Still's disease .... JUVENILE ARTHRITIS
stilt .... BIRD, POST, PLOVER,

(BEAN)POLE, SANDPIPER
stilted .... PRIM, RIGID, STIFF, STUFFY, POMPOUS, PEDANTIC, BOMBASTIC
stiltlike toy .... POGO STICK
stilton .... CHEESE
Stilwell's nickname .... VINEGAR JOE
stimulant .... TONIC, BRACER, COFFEE, EXCITANT
drug .... CAFFEINE, DOXAPRAM, AMPHETAMINE
stimulate .... FAN, SPUR, STIR, URGE, WHET, ELATE, (A)ROUSE, AWAKEN, EXCITE, INCITE, ANIMATE
by electric shock .... GALVANIZE
colloquial .... PEP UP
slang .... REV UP
stimulating .... ROUSING, REFRESHING
stimulus .... BASE, GOAD, SPUR, BASIS, DRIVE, STING, FILLIP, MOTIVE, IMPULSE, CATALYST, ENERGIZER, INCENTIVE, INCITEMENT, INDUCEMENT
tantalizing, deceptive .... CARROT
sting .... BITE, GOAD, PAIN, SMART, WOUND, NETTLE, TINGLE, PRICK(LE), STIMULUS, URTICATE
in zoology .... ACULEUS
ray .... BATFISH, STINGAREE
relief .... CALAMINE
slang .... DUPE, CHEAT, GOUGE
stinger ..... BEE, GNAT, WASP, CORAL, GADFLY, HORNET, ANEMONE, SCORPION, STINGRAY, JELLYFISH
plant .... RAMIE, NETTLE
stinging .... NIPPY, CAUSTIC, SCATHING, SMARTING, TINGLING
ant .... KELEP
creature .... ANT, BEE, RAY, WASP, GADFLY, HORNET, SCORPION, JELLYFISH
hairs, plant with .... RAMIE, NETTLE
sensation .... TINGLE, URTICATION
taste .... PUNGENT
stingo ...... ALE, VIM, BEER, ZEST, ENERGY
stingy .... NEAR, CLOSE, TIGHT, MEAGER, SCANTY, SKIMPY, MISERLY, NIGGARDLY, PENURIOUS
stink .... ODOR, REEK, FETOR,

SMELL, STENCH
stinker .... SKUNK, STOAT,
PETREL, POLECAT
stinking/stinky ...... FOUL, RANK,
FETID, FUSTY, GASSY, GOATY,
MUSTY, STALE, PUTRID,
RANCID, SMELLY, MIASMIC,
NOISOME, MEPHITIC,
MALODOROUS, BAD-SMELLING
smut .... BUNT
stinko .... BLOTTO
stint ...... JOB, BOUT, DUTY, TASK,
TURN, CHORE, SHIFT,
RESTRICT, SANDPIPER,
ASSIGNMENT, LIMIT(ATION)
stipe .... STEM, STALK, PETIOLE
stipel .... STIPULE
stipend ...... FEE, WAGE, SALARY,
PENSION, PREBEND,
ALLOWANCE
stipes ...... (EYE)STALK, PEDUNCLE
stipple .... DOT, DAPPLE, MOTTLE,
SPECKLE
stipulate ...... DEMAND, ARRANGE,
PROVIDE, REQUIRE, SPECIFY
stipulation ...... CLAUSE, PROVISO,
AGREEMENT, CONDITION,
PROVISION
stir .... ADO, FUSS, ROIL, TO-DO,
CHURN, ROUST, SHAKE,
(A)ROUSE, (A)WAKEN, EXCITE,
INCITE, TUMULT, AGITATE,
INFLAME, PROVOKE,
MOVE(MENT)
slang .... JAIL, PRISON
slightly .... BUDGE
up .... RILE, ROIL, AROUSE,
FOMENT
stirabout .... PORRIDGE
stirk .... HEIFER, BULLOCK
stirps .... RACE, STOCK, FAMILY
stirring .... BUSY, ACTIVE,
MOVING, ROUSING
stirrup ...... GAMBADO, FOOTREST
bone .... STAPES
cup .... DRINK, TOAST
stitch .... HEM, ACHE, DARN,
MEND, PAIN, SEAM, TACK,
BASTE, CRICK, QUILT,
SEW(UP), FASTEN, SUTURE
bird .... IHI
colloquial .... BIT
line .... SEAM
stitching material .... GUT, CORD,
WIRE, STAPLE, THREAD
stitchwort .... CHICKWEED
stithy ...... ANVIL, FORGE, SMITHY
stoa .... WALK, PORTICO
stoat .... ERMINE
like animal .... MINK, OTTER,
MARTEN, WEASEL

stoccado .... STAB, THRUST
stock .... BUTT, FUND, RACE,
BREED, GOODS, STORE, TRITE,
TRUNK, STIRPS, SUPPLY,
CAPITAL, LINEAGE, PLENISH,
PROVIDE, RHIZOME,
ANCESTRY, ORDINARY,
INVENTORY, REPERTORY,
REPERTOIRE
exchange .... BOURSE
dealer .... BEAR, BULL,
BROKER, JOBBER
member(ship) .... SEAT,
TRADER
speculator .... LAMEDUCK
telegraph device ..... TICKER
trick .... WASH SALE
farm .... STUD, RANCH(O)
high-priced .... BLUE CHIP
in .... ON HAND, AVAILABLE
in trade .... LINE, STAPLE
keep in .... CARRY
laughing .... BUTT, GOAT
kind of .... CAPITAL,
FLOATING, TREASURY,
PREFERRED
market .... CURB, BOURSE,
EXCHANGE
market event .... CRASH, PANIC
market figures .... BEARS
market gamble .... FLYER
market maneuver .... RAID
of inferior .... LOWBRED
of special skills
.... REPERTORY, REPERTOIRE
purebred .... PEDIGREE
replace .... REPLENISH
still .... MOTIONLESS
''strip'' .... WALL STREET
take .... COUNT, APPRAISE,
INVENTORY
stockade .... PEN, BOMA, FORT,
ETAPE, CORRAL, BARRIER,
COMPOUND, BARRICADE,
ENCLOSURE
stockbroker .... AGENT
concern of .... BONDS, STOCKS
stockfish .... COD, HADDOCK
stocking ...... HOSE, SOCK, NYLON
stockish .... DULL, STUPID
stockman .... RANCHER
stockpile .... AMASS, CACHE,
HOARD, STORE, SUPPLY,
RESERVE, SURPLUS,
RESERVOIR
stockroom .... STORAGE,
STOREHOUSE
stocky .... DUMPY, PLUMP, SQUAT,
STOUT, CHUNKY, STUBBY,
STURDY, STUBBED, THICKSET
stodgy ...... DULL, BULKY, SHORT,

STOCKY, STOLID, TEDIOUS
stogie .... BOOT, SHOE, CIGAR,
CORONA
stoic .... ASCETIC, PATIENT,
SPARTAN, IMPASSIVE,
UNFEELING
Stoic, first .... ZENO
philosopher .... SENECA,
EPICTETUS
stoke ...... FEED, FIRE, FUEL, POKE,
STIR, TEND
stoker .... POKER, TEASER,
FIREMAN
Stoker, Count Dracula's
creator .... BRAM
Stokowski, conductor
.... LEOPOLD
stola .... PALLA
stole .... BOA, CAPE, SCARF,
ROBBED
stolen goods buyer .... FENCE
money, riches .... FILTHY
LUCRE
property .... LOOT, PELF, SWAG
stolid ...... CALM, DULL, WOODEN,
SLUGGISH, LETHARGIC,
IMPASSIVE, PHLEGMATIC
stolon .... RUNNER, RHIZOME
stoma ...... PORE, MOUTH, ORIFICE
stomach .... SAC, BEAR, CRAW,
CROP, BELLY, DESIRE,
ENDURE, ABDOMEN, CRAVING,
APPETITE, TOLERATE
abscess .... PEPTIC ULCER,
GASTRIC ULCER
animal's .... MAW, CRAW,
OMASUM, PAUNCH
colloquial ..... BELLY, TUMMY,
GIZZARD, CORPORATION
combining form .... GASTRO
disease .... TUMOR, ULCER,
CANCER
disorder .... BRASH, NAUSEA,
PYROSIS, HEARTBURN
enzyme .... PEPSIN
gas .... FLATUS, FLATULENCE
inflammation .... GASTRITIS
opening .... PYLORUS
opening, surgically produced
.... GASTROSTOMY
part .... ANTRUM, FUNDUS,
LINING, MUSCLE, PYLORIC
SPHINCTER
passage tube to the
.... ESOPHAGUS
pertaining to .... GASTRIC
protruding .... BAYWINDOW
removal, partial/whole
.... GASTRECTOMY
ruminants' .... MAW, TRIPE,
OMASUM, PAUNCH,

PSALTERIUM
secretion .... GASTRIN,
GASTRIC JUICE
slang .... BREADBASKET
stony concretion
.... GASTROLITH
upset .... DYSPEPSIA,
INDIGESTION
wall movement
.... PERISTALSIS
washing out of .... LAVAGE
stomachache .... COLIC, GRIPE(S),
BELLYACHE, TUMMYACHE,
COLLYWOBBLES
reliever ..... ANTACID, ASPIRIN,
MAGNESIA
stomatic .... ORAL
stomatopod .... SQUILLA,
CRUSTACEAN
stomp .... CLUMP, STAMP,
TRAMPLE
stone .... GEM, PIT, PELT, ROCK,
JEWEL, LAPIS, MARBLE,
PEBBLE, PYRENE, DORNICK,
GRANITE
azure-blue .... LAPIS LAZULI
bright green, transparent
.... EMERALD
broke .... PENNILESS, DOWN
AND OUT
cameo .... ONYX
carver .... GRAVER
carved in relief .... CAMEO
cavity, crystal-lined .... GEODE
change into .... PETRIFY
chip .... SPALL, GALLET
chisel .... CELT
clay .... SHALE
clear, deep-red .... RUBY
combining form .... LITE,
LYTE, LITH(O), PETR(O)
crop .... ORPIN, SEDUM
cubic measure for .... PERCH
dark-green .... OLIVINE
dark-green with red spots
.... BLOODSTONE
deep-blue, transparent
.... SAPPHIRE
dress .... NIG, TRIM, SCABBLE
dressing tool .... ADZ(E),
HACKHAMMER
drupe .... NUTLET
engraved on .... LAPIDARY
engraving .... INTAGLIO
excavation site .... QUARRY
fire-starting .... FLINT
flake .... SPALL
flintlike .... HORNSTONE
for pavement
.... COBBLE(STONE)
for throwing .... DINGBAT,

DORNICK
fragments .... BRASH, DEBRIS
fruit .... PIP, PIT, PYRENE,
PUTAMEN
fruit with .... PLUM, APPLE,
DRUPE, OLIVE, PEACH,
CHERRY, APRICOT
green or white .... JADE
greenish-blue .... TURQUOISE
grinding .... MANO
hammer .... MASH
hard .... FLINT, ADAMANT
headed ax .... TOMAHAWK
heap .... CARN(E), SCREE,
CAIRN(E)
hearted .... CRUEL
huge .... MENHIR, BOULDER,
MEGALITH
hurling apparatus .... ONAGER,
CATAPULT, MANGONEL,
TREBUCHET
implement .... MANO, EOLITH
in chemistry .... LAPIS
jar .... CROCK
kidney/gallbladder
.... CALCULUS
kissable .... BLARNEY
lifting device .... LEWIS(SON)
like .... LITHOID(AL)
marker/pillar .... STELE
marker of a grave
.... HEADSTONE
masses .... SARSENS
monument .... CAIRN, STELE,
DOLMEN, MENHIR, CROMLECH
monument with inscription
.... TOMBSTONE
nodule .... GEODE
of a structure, uppermost
.... CAPSTONE
of an arch, central
.... KEYSTONE
of great brilliance
.... DIAMOND
oil .... PETROLEUM
ornamental .... JADE,
SODALITE, TIGER'S EYE
parsley .... HONEWORT
particles .... GRIT
paving .... FLAG, SETT, SLAB,
MACADAM
pertaining to .... LITHIC
pestle .... MULLER
philosopher's .... CARMOT
piece(s) .... SPALL, GALLET,
RUBBLE
pile .... TALUS
precious .... GEM, OPAL, RUBY,
PEARL, DIAMOND, EMERALD,
SAPPHIRE
prefix .... LITHO

red .... RUBY, GARNET, SPINEL,
CARNELIAN
roller .... CARP, DACE, TOTER
roller, eternal .... SISYPHUS
semi-precious .... JADE, ONYX,
AGATE, BERYL, CORAL, TOPAZ,
GARNET, JASPER, SPINEL,
ZIRCON, OLIVINE, PERIDOT,
AMETHYST, SARDONYX,
TURQUOISE, AQUAMARINE,
BLOODSTONE, CHALCEDONY,
CHRYSOLITE, TOURMALINE,
ALEXANDRITE, CHRYSOPRASE,
LAPIS LAZULI
sharpening .... HONE, WHET,
OILSTONE
slab ..... STELA, STELE, TABLET
small .... PEBBLE
spark-producing .... FLINT
square hewn .... ASHLAR,
ASHLER
tablet .... STELE
throwing device .... ONAGER,
CATAPULT, MANGONEL,
SLING(SHOT)
to death .... LAPIDATE
tool .... NEOLITH, PALEOLITH
trim .... NIG, DRESS
turn to .... PETRIFY, LAPIDIFY
unbreakable .... ADAMANT
upright prehistoric .... MENHIR
used in optical equipment
.... TOURMALINE
used to better one's position
.... STEPPING(STONE)
variety of jade .... JADEITE,
NEPHRITE
wall .... FENCE, BRICKWALL
wall-facing .... ASHLAR,
ASHLER
with brilliant play of colors
.... GIRASOL(E), FIRE OPAL
woman turned to .... NIOBE
worker .... MASON
Stone Age human ...... CAVEMAN
Age period .... EOLITHIC,
NEOLITHIC
Age tools .... (N)EOLITH
author .... IRVING
author-director of "JFK"
.... OLIVER
Chief Justice .... HARLAN
site of Blarney .... CORK
(IRELAND)
stonechat .... BIRD, THRUSH
stonecrop .... PLANT, SEDUM,
ORPIN(E)
stonecutter ...... MASON, CARVER,
ENGRAVER, LAPIDARY,
LAPIDARIST
chisel of .... DROVE

695

disease of .... SILICOSIS,
PNEUMOCONIOSIS
stoned ...... HIGH, DRUNK, ZONKED
Stonehenge, for one ...... CIRCLE
stones, cast .... ATTACK,
CONDEMN, CRITICIZE
heap of .... CAIRN, SCREE,
TALUS
roadbuilding .... MACADAM
stonewall .... FOIL, EVADE,
THWART, FRUSTRATE
Stonewall, general ...... JACKSON
stoneware .... GRES, CERAMIC,
POTTERY, CLAYWARE,
EARTHENWARE
stonework ...... MASONRY, BRICK-
LAYING
stonily .... COLDLY, HARSHLY
stony .... HARD, ROCKY, ROUGH,
CALLOUS, PETROUS,
PETROSAL, PITILESS
deposit in body ..... CALCULUS
stood .... AROSE, UPROSE
stooge .... DUPE, FOIL, PAWN,
TOOL, DUMMY, LACKEY,
HECKLER, UNDERLING
Stooges, one of the Three
.... MOE, LARRY, CURLY
stook .... SHOCK
stool .... SEAT, PRIVY, STUMP,
FOOTREST, PRIE-DIEU,
TABO(U)RET
foot .... CRICKET, HASSOCK,
OTTOMAN
pigeon .... SPY, LURE, MARK,
DECOY, PEACHER, BETRAYER,
INFORMER
stoolie, e.g. .... RAT
stoop .... BEND, LOUT, DEIGN,
PORCH, STOUP, SWOOP,
CROUCH, SUBMIT,
VERANDA(H), CONDESCEND
greeting .... WELCOME
stop .... END, CLOG, HALT, WHOA,
BELAY, BLOKE, BRAKE,
CEASE, CHECK, CLOSE, LET
UP, DEFEAT, DESIST, PULL UP,
TERMINATE, BLOW THE
WHISTLE
course of .... INTERCEPT
flow of blood or tears
...... QUELL, STANCH, STAUNCH
football carrier .... TACKLE
hole .... COVER, PLUG UP
legally .... ESTOP
nautical .... AVAST
overnight .... LAY OVER
progress of .... IMPEDE,
STYMIE
resisting .... YIELD,
SURRENDER, CAPITULATE

short .... BALK
spread of .... ARREST
talking .... DRY UP, SHUT UP
temporarily .... REST, PAUSE
to, put a .... NIP IN THE BUD
stopcock .... VALVE, FAUCET
stopgap .... EXPEDIENT,
MAKESHIFT, SUBSTITUTE
stoppage .... GAP, BREAK,
EMBARGO, DISRUPTION,
DISCONTINUANCE
legal .... ESTOPPEL
of a death penalty,
temporary .... REPRIEVE
activity, authorized
.... MORATORIUM
body fluid .... STASIS
breath .... CHOKING,
STRANGULATION
debate .... CLOSURE,
CLOTURE
execution .... STAY
hostilities .... TRUCE,
RESPITE, ARMISTICE
movement/traffic
.... BOTTLENECK
progress .... BARRIER,
OBSTACLE
right/privilege
.... DEBARMENT
operation .... SHUTDOWN
phonetic .... OCCLUSION
stopped diapason .... MELODIA
stopper/stopple .... TAP, BUNG,
CORK, PLUG, CAULK, COVER,
SHIVE, TAMPON, TAMPION,
TOMPION
stopwatch .... TIMER
storage .... STORING, SAFE-
KEEPING, WAREHOUSING
computer .... MEMORY
device .... BATTERY
fee/charge .... CELLARAGE,
DEMURRAGE
for small savings .... PIGGY
BANK
kind of .... DRY, COLD
place .... LOFT, CACHE,
HUTCH, VAULT, LOCKER,
STOREROOM
below ground level
.... CELLAR, BASEMENT
below the roof .... ATTIC,
GARRET
place for:
bus/train .... DEPOT
clothes .... CHEST, CLOSET,
DRAWER
dishes .... CUPBOARD
fodder .... CRIB
food .... BIN

food, ingredient, utensils
.... LARDER, PANTRY
funds, public/private
.... TREASURY
grain .... SILO, GRANARY
historical objects
.... MUSEUM
long-range ballistic missile
.... SILO
merchandise .... WAREHOUSE
personal valuables .... SAFE-
DEPOSIT BOX
public records
.... ARCHIVE(S)
streetcars/trucks/taxicabs
.... BARN
wine/liquor .... CELLAR,
BUTTERY
temporary .... DUMP
underground .... PIT, SILO
water .... TANK, CISTERN,
RESERVOIR
storax .... BALSAM, STYRENE,
GUMRESIN
store .... FUND, HOLD, SAVE,
SHOP, AMASS, CACHE, HOARD,
STOCK, GARNER, OUTLET,
SUPPLY, DEPOSIT, PUT(AWAY),
RESERVE, BOUTIQUE,
LAY(ASIDE), STOW(AWAY),
WAREHOUSE
ammo .... MAG
army .... PX, CANTEEN,
COMMISSARY, POST EXCHANGE
away .... STASH
fodder/in a silo .... ENSILE
helper .... CLERK, CHECKER
kind of .... BOOK, DRUG,
BAZAAR, GROCERY,
SPECIALTY, FIVE-AND-TEN,
HEALTH FOODS, SPORTING
GOODS
manager .... FLOOR-WALKER
small articles .... NOTIONS
stiff .... MANNEQUIN
storehouse .... BARN, DEPOT,
GRANARY, REPERTORY,
DEPOSITARY, DEPOSITORY
public .... ETAPE
weapons .... ARMORY,
ARSENAL, MAGAZINE
storekeeper .... GROCER,
MERCHANT
storeroom .... VAULT, CELLAR,
CLOSET, PANTRY, BUTTERY
storied ...... FAMOUS, LEGENDARY
stork .... AYAYA, JABIRU,
MARABOU, ADJUTANT
delivery of .... BABY
kin of .... IBIS, HERON,
HAMMERHEAD

stork's bill .... GERANIUM
storm .... BLOW, FUME, RACE,
 RAGE, RANT, STOUR, ASSAIL,
 ATTACK, ASSAULT, BLUSTER,
 TEMPEST, RIPSNORTER
accompaniment .... HAIL,
 RAIN, SNOW, WIND, FLOOD,
 SLEET, THUNDER, LIGHTNING
center .... EYE
certain kind .... NOR'EASTER,
 NOR'WESTER, SOU'EASTER,
 SOU'WESTER
cloud formation
 .... WATERSPOUT
cyclonic .... TYPHOON,
 BLIZZARD, HURRICANE
with rotating winds
 .... CYCLONE, TORNADO
Storm Country girl .... TESS
stormed about .... RAMPAGED
storming .... IRATE
stormy ...... FOUL, WILD, RAGING,
 FURIOUS, VIOLENT,
 INCLEMENT, TURBULENT,
 TEMPESTUOUS
Storting .... PARLIAMENT
 sits in .... OSLO
story .... REDE, TALE, TIER,
 FABLE, FLOOR, LEVEL,
 RUMOR, GOSSIP, REPORT,
 ACCOUNT, MARCHEN,
 NARRATION, NARRATIVE
animal .... FABLE
bedtime .... YARN
colloquial .... FIB
complication in a .... NODE,
 NODUS
correspondent's ...... DISPATCH
exaggerated .... YARN
exclusive .... BEAT, SCOOP
false .... HOAX, FABLE,
 CANARD
heroic .... SAGA
imagined .... FICTION
long .... NOVEL
newspaper ...... ITEM, ARTICLE,
 PRESS RELEASE
of past events .... HISTORY
of person's life .... BIOGRAPHY
of person's life written by
 oneself
 .... AUTOBIOGRAPHY
of some personal happening
 .... ANECDOTE
part of .... PASSUS
romantic .... GEST(E)
short .... CONTE, PARABLE
tell a .... SPIN
traditional ...... MYTH, LEGEND
with moral lesson ...... FABLE,
 PARABLE, ALLEGORY

storyteller ...... AUTHOR, RECITER,
 RACONTEUR, ALLEGORIST,
 MUNCHAUSEN, SCHEHERAZADE
colloquial .... LIAR, FIBBER
stoss, opposite of .... ALEE
stound .... ACHE, PAIN, SMART
stoup .... FONT, PAIL, BUCKET,
 TANKARD
stour .... STORM, COMBAT,
 TURMOIL
stout .... ALE, FAT, BEER, BOCK,
 BOLD, BURLY, BRAVE, HUSKY,
 OBESE, BRAWNY, PORTER,
 PORTLY, ROBUST, STOCKY,
 STURDY, THICKSET,
 CORPULENT
Stout hero .... NERO(WOLFE)
novelist .... REX
stouthearted .... BOLD, BRAVE,
 DAUNTLESS
stove .... ETNA, OVEN, RANGE,
 COOKER, HEATER, FURNACE,
 CHAUFFER, HOT PLATE,
 KITCHENER
stovepipe .... FLUE, SILK(HAT)
stover .... FODDER, CORNSTALKS
stow .... CAN, CRAM, LADE, PACK,
 CHUCK, STASH, STORE,
 CONCEAL
away .... STASH, STORE,
 SECRETE
away again .... RESTASH
cargo .... STEEVE
it away .... EAT
stowage .... LADING, PACKING,
 STORAGE, TANKAGE
stowaway .... DEADBEAT, FREE
 RIDER
of a sort ..... SQUATTER, GATE-
 CRASHER
Stowe, author .... HARRIET
 (BEECHER)
book of .... UNCLE TOM'S
 CABIN
brother of .... EDWARD, HENRY
 (WARD)
character .... ELIZA, TOPSY,
 LITTLE EVA, (UNCLE)TOM,
 SIMON LEGREE
nickname of .... HATTIE
strabismic .... CROSS-EYED
strabismus .... SQUINT, WALLEYE,
 CROSS-EYE
"Strad" .... VIOLIN
straddle .... BYPASS, BESTRIDE
colloquial .... HEDGE
Stradivarius .... VIOLIN
strafe .... RAKE, ATTACK, PEPPER,
 RIDDLE, BOMBARD, CHASTISE
straggle ...... DRAG, ROVE, STRAY,
 TRAIL, DAWDLE, RAMBLE,

SPRAWL, WANDER, MEANDER
straggler .... ROVER, STRAY,
 ROAMER, DRIFTER, RAMBLER,
 GADABOUT, WANDERER
straggling ...... ERRANT, SHIFTING
straight .... EVEN, FAIR, NEAT,
 PURE, TRUE, ERECT, FRANK,
 DIRECT, HONEST, UNBENT,
 ALIGNED, UNMIXED,
 (UP)RIGHT
as an _____ .... ARROW
away .... DIRECT, AT ONCE,
 POINT-BLANK
combining form .... RECT(I)
edge .... LINER, RULER
face .... DEAD-PAN, LONG
 FACE, POKER FACE
faced .... GRIM, GRAVE, SOBER,
 SEDATE, EARNEST, SERIOUS,
 IMPASSIVE
jacket .... CAMISOLE,
 RESTRAINT, RESTRAINER
liner .... BEE, RULER
man .... FOIL, STOOGE
man's companion
 .... COMEDIAN
out .... CLEAR, DIRECT,
 EXPLICIT, OUTRIGHT
passage .... ENFILADE
route .... BEELINE
row .... RANK
up .... VERTICAL
straighten .... ALIGN, UNBEND,
 RECTIFY, UNRAVEL
as hair .... UNCURL
as rope strands .... UNLAY
variant .... ALINE
straightforward .... OPEN, BLUNT,
 FRANK, CANDID, DIRECT,
 HONEST, SINCERE,
 FORTHRIGHT
strain .... LINE, PULL, RACE, SIFT,
 BREED, EXERT, HEAVE, PRESS,
 STOCK, TRACE, EFFORT,
 FILTER, REFINE, STREAK,
 STRIVE, DESCENT, LINEAGE,
 STRETCH, TENSION, FILTRATE
commonly affected by
 .... ATHLETE(S)
of muscle fibers ...... TEARING
strained .... TAUT, TENSE,
 UPTIGHT, UNFRIENDLY
strainer .... SIEVE, STRUM, TAMIS,
 FILTER, SIFTER, COLANDER,
 PERCOLATOR, CHEESECLOTH
strains .... AIR, TUNE
strait ...... NECK, TIGHT, CHANNEL,
 EURIPUS, ISTHMUS,
 NARROW(S), PASSAGE,
 WATERWAY

between Alaska and USSR
.... BERING
between Corsica and
   Sardinia .... BONIFACIO
between Spain and Morocco
.... GIBRALTAR
between Sumatra and
   Malaysia .... MALACCA
in Argentina .... MAGELLAN
Australia .... BASS
British Columbia
.... HECATE, JUAN DE FUCA
China .... TAIWAN
Indonesia .... BANGKA
Iran .... HORMUZ
Ireland .... DAVIS, HUDSON
Italy .... SICILY, OTRANTO,
               MESSINA
Michigan .... MACKINAC
Newfoundland .... MCLELAN,
             BELLE ISLE
Northwest Territories
..... HAZEN, NARES, BARROW,
           BALLANTYNE
Nova Scotia .... CANSO
Papua New Guinea
.... TORRES, VITIAZ,
   DAMPIER, BOUGAINVILLE
Philippines .... LUZON,
   TANON, TABLAS, BASILAN,
     MINDORO, SURIGAO
Saudi Arabia .... TIRAN
Solomon Islands
.... MANNING
Sri Lanka .... PALK
Tasmania .... BANKS
Turkey .... BOSPORUS
USSR .... TATAR, LA
   PEROUSE, SANNIKOVA
Virgin Islands .... THE
           NARROWS
Washington .... HARO,
          GEORGIA
jacket .... HOGTIE, RESTRAINER
laced .... DOUR, PRIM, STAID,
   STRICT, FORMAL, PROPER,
   STRICT, STUFFY, PRUDISH,
         PRIGGISH
seaport on a .... KERCH
straiten .... LIMIT, HAMPER,
   ENCLOSE, CONTRACT,
        DISTRESS
straits .... PLIGHT, POVERTY,
   DISTRESS, HARDSHIP,
       DIFFICULTY
financial .... BIND, PINCH,
   CLUTCH, CRISIS, CRUNCH,
    EMBARRASSMENT
Straits of Messina rock
.... SCYLLA

Settlement, part of
.... LUBUAN, PENANG,
   MALACCA, SINGAPORE
weight .... CHEE, CATTY
strand .... ROPE, BEACH, FIBER,
   SHORE, GROUND, MAROON,
   STRING, THREAD, NECKLACE
stranded .... PENNILESS, HIGH
         AND DRY
strange ...... FEY, ODD, OFF, RARE,
   UNCO, ALIEN, EERIE, FREMD,
   NOVEL, OUTRE, QUEER,
   EXOTIC, QUAINT, FOREIGN,
   UNCANNY, UNKNOWN,
   UNUSUAL, PECULIAR,
   SINGULAR, ECCENTRIC
mysteriously .... WEIRD,
        UNEARTHLY
very .... BIZARRE, OUTLANDISH
strangely beautiful .... EXOTIC
stranger .... ALIEN, GUEST,
   ODDER, EMIGRE, NOVICE,
   NEWCOMER, OUTSIDER,
   FOREIGNER, OUTLANDER,
      TRAMONTANE
combining form .... XENO
strangle .... KILL, CHOKE, SCRAG,
   STIFLE, GARROTE, REPRESS,
   SMOTHER, SQUEEZE,
   JUGULATE, SUPPRESS,
   THROTTLE, CONSTRICT,
      SUFFOCATE
hold .... DEATH GRIP
strangler .... THUG, BRAVO,
      GARROTER
strangulate .... CHOKE, GARROTE,
   SQUEEZE, THROTTLE
strangulation .... STRICTURE,
    CONSTRICTION
means of .... HANDS,
      LIGATURE
strangury .... URINATION
cause of .... CYSTITIS,
     PROSTATITIS
strap .... TAB, TIE, BAND, BELT,
   LASH, REIN, ROPE, TAPE,
   LEASH, THONG, THRASH,
     FASTEN(ER)
falcon's .... JESS
for leading animal .... HALTER
shaped ...... LORATE, LIGULATE
shoulder .... HALTER
waist, hips .... GIRDLE
straphanger .... STANDEE,
      COMMUTER
strapped .... NEEDY, FLAT-BROKE
strapping .... HARDY, ROBUST,
   STEELY, FLOGGING, WHIPPING,
     WELL-BUILT
Strasberg or Sontag ...... SUSAN
strass .... PASTE, (LEAD)GLASS

stratagem ...... PLOY, RUSE, WILE,
   FEINT, GUILE, TRICK, DEVICE,
   DESIGN, GAMBIT, SCHEME,
   TACTIC, TRAPAN, TREPAN,
   ARTIFICE, CHICANERY,
   MANEUVER, DECEPTION
strategic position .... VANTAGE
strategy .... PLAN, SCHEME,
   GIMMICK, TACTICS, ARTIFICE,
   MANEUVER, (WAR)CRAFT
Stratford's river .... AVON
stratified .... TIERED, LAYERED,
      LAMINATED
stratum ...... BED, LAYER, LEVEL,
      LAMELLA
horizontal, in geology
.... TABLE
of mineral .... STREAK
soft, crumbly .... MARL
Straus, composer .... OSCAR,
      OSKAR
work .... THE CHOCOLATE
      SOLDIER
Strauss, composer .... JOHANN
sobriquet ..... THE WALTZ KING
wife of .... JETTY
work of .... INDIGO, SALOME,
   DIE FLEDERMAUS, THE BLUE
      DANUBE
Stravinsky, composer .... IGOR
work .... AGON, FIREBIRD,
   OEDIPUS REX, PERSEPHONE,
   PULCINELLA, THE RITE OF
      SPRING
straw .... CULM, REED, STEM,
   TUBE, STALK, FODDER, TRIFLE
bale of .... TRUSS
bed .... PALLET
boss .... ASSISTANT
bunch of .... WISP, TRUSS,
      WHISK
coat .... MINO
colored .... BLOND, FLAXEN
cover around plant ..... MULCH
fine-cut/for fodder .... CHAFF
for pointing .... FESCUE
hat .... PANAMA, SAILOR
in the wind .... OMEN, SIGN,
      PORTENT
like .... STRAMINEOUS
man ...... DUMMY, JACKSTRAW,
   NONENTITY, SCARECROW
plaited .... SENNIT
spread .... MULCH
stack .... MOW, RICK
thatching .... HA(U)LM
unsplit for hats .... YEDDA
vote .... POLL
vote man ...... ROPER, GALLUP,
   HARRIS, POLLSTER
vote objective ...... CONSENSUS

worm .... CADDIS
strawberry bush .... WAHOO
like fruit .... ETAERIO
nevus .... BIRTHMARK
stray .... ERR, LOST, ROAM, ROVE,
RAMBLE, WANDER, DEVIATE,
DIGRESS, MEANDER,
STRAGGLE
animal .... WAIF, MAVERICK
animal's place .... POUND,
PINFOLD
strays .... STATIC
streak .... RUN, BAND, TEAR,
VEIN, FREAK, HURRY, LAYER,
SMEAR, SPELL, STRIA, TRAIT,
MOTTLE, STRAIN, STRIPE
streaked ...... LINEATE, BRINDLED,
STRIATED, STRIGOSE
streaker .... HARE, GREYHOUND
heavenly .... COMET,
LIGHTNING
streaks, full of .... LIN(E)Y,
STRIPY
streaky .... TABBY, UNEVEN,
VARYING
stream .... RUN, BECK, FLOW,
GUSH, RILL, RUSH, BROOK,
CREEK, RIVER, ARROYO,
BOURN(E), OUTLET,
POUR(OUT), RUNNEL,
CURRENT, TORRENT
bed .... RUNWAY, CHANNEL
fence .... WEIR
limestone deposit .... TUFA
little/small .... BECK, RILL,
BAYOU, BROOK, CREEK
of lava .... COULEE
of light .... RAY, BEAM
overflow .... FRESHET
rocky obstruction .... RIFFLE
sound .... PURL, MURMUR
source .... FOUNTAIN-HEAD
swift, violent .... TORRENT
streamer .... FLAG, BANNER,
BURGEE, BUNTING, PENNANT,
HEADLINE, SCAREHEAD
streamlet ...... BECK, RILL, CREEK,
RUNNER, RIVULET,
BROOK(LET)
streamlined .... FAST, TRIM,
SPEEDY, UP-TO-DATE,
EFFICIENT, SIMPLIFIED
Streep, actress .... MERYL
street .... RUE, VIA, WAY, LANE,
ROAD, CALLE, DRIVE,
AVENUE, CAUSEWAY,
BOULEVARD
Arab .... WAIF, GAMIN,
URCHIN, MUDLARK
designating a ..... EASY, MAIN,
ONE-WAY, DEAD-END

ditch .... GUTTER
fight .... (AF)FRAY, RUMBLE
hydrant .... FIREPLUG
market .... CURB
musician ...... ORGAN-GRINDER
musician's employer
.... PADRONE
musician's organ ...... HURDY-
GURDY
narrow .... ALLEY
of flophouses in NYC
.... (THE)BOWERY
of shops .... BAZ(A)AR
of theatrical world in NYC
.... BROADWAY
open at both ends
.... THOROUGHFARE
principal: sl. .... MAIN DRAG,
MAIN STEM
private .... DRIVEWAY
public .... FREEWAY, HIGHWAY,
TURNPIKE, TOLL ROAD,
EXPRESSWAY
short .... COURT
show .... RAREE
sign ..... STOP, YIELD, DETOUR,
ONE-WAY, NO-U-TURN,
SCHOOL ZONE
sound of old .... CLOP
stray .... DOG, ARAB, WAIF,
GAMIN, URCHIN
urchin .... ARAB, WAIF, GAMIN,
MUDLARK, GUTTERSNIPE
W. C. Handy's .... BEALE
with houses both sides
.... ROW
streetcar .... TRAM(CAR),
TROLL(E)Y
cowcatcher .... FENDER
driver .... MOTORMAN
streetwalker .... ARAB, GAMIN,
WHORE, HARLOT, HOOKER,
PEDESTRIAN, PROSTITUTE
strength .... FORCE, MIGHT,
POWER, VIGOR, ENERGY,
FOISON, POTENCY, INFLUENCE,
MAIN(FORCE)
degree of .... INTENSITY
having manly .... VIRILE
mental/physical .... ABILITY,
VITALITY
muscular .... BRAWN, SINEW,
THEWS
of endurance .... STAMINA
of the body .... PHYSIQUE
regain .... RALLY
slang .... GRIT
to resist .... TOUGHNESS
strengthen .... GIRD, PROP,
BRACE, REMAN, STEEL,
HARDEN, FORTIFY, TOUGHEN,

ENERGIZE
as spirits .... LIFT, ENLIVEN
as thread .... MERCERIZE
by adding alcohol ..... NEEDLE
slang .... PEP UP
with more troops
.... REINFORCE
strengthener .... ROBORANT
strenuous ...... ACTIVE, ARDUOUS,
VIGOROUS, EXHAUSTING
strep throat .... SORE THROAT
streptomycin discoverer
.... WAKSMAN
stress .... ACCENT, STRAIN,
TENSION, URGENCY,
EMPHASIS, PRESSURE,
EMPHASIZE
in music .... ARSIS, ACCENT
metrical .... ICTUS
result of continued ..... ULCER
symptom of .... ANXIETY,
DEPRESSION
stretch ...... SPAN, FORCE, RANGE,
REACH, SWEEP, TRACT,
EXPAND, EXTEND, SPREAD,
STRAIN, TAUTEN, EXPANSE
a point .... MAGNIFY,
EXAGGERATE
mark(s) .... STRIA(E)
of water .... RIFFLE
out .... EXPAND, SPRAWL,
LENGTHEN
stretched one's neck .... CRANED
out .... PROLATE, ELONGATED
stretcher .... FRAME, LITTER,
TENTER, CARRIER, CROSSPIECE
sophisticated .... TROLLEY BED
stretching muscle .... TENSOR
strew .... SPREAD, SCATTER,
DISPERSE, SPRINKLE
stria ...... RIDGE, FILLET, GROOVE,
STREAK, STRIPE, STRETCH-
MARK
common site of .... THIGH,
ABDOMEN
striated .... LINY
stricken .... ILL, HURT, BESET,
STRUCK, AFFLICTED
strict .... RIGID, STERN, PRECISE,
ACCURATE, EXACT(ING),
RIGOROUS, STRINGENT,
METICULOUS, PUNCTILIOUS
adherence to law
.... LEGALISM, BY THE BOOK
disciplinarian .... SPARTAN,
MARTINET, STICKLER
stricture .... BLAME, CENSURE,
STENOSIS, CRITICISM
stride .... GAIT, LOPE, PACE, STEP,
MARCH, STRADDLE
cowhand's .... SIDLE

strident .... LOUD, HARSH, SHRILL, GRATING, RAUCOUS

sound .... STRIDOR

strides .... PROGRESS, ADVANCEMENT

stridulate .... CHIRR

strife .... FEUD, CONTEST, DISCORD, DISPUTE, QUARREL, RIVALRY, WAR(FARE), CONFLICT, STRUGGLE, CONTENTION

strigil .... FLUTING

strigose .... HISPID

strike .... DAB, HIT, BEAT, BITE, BLOW, BUMP, FIND, HOOK, LASH, OCCUR, SMITE, THUMP, TOUCH, ATTACK, IGNITE, IMPRESS, WALKOUT, HAUL DOWN

a bargain .... AGREE

back .... REACT, RETALIATE

caller .... UMP

demonstrator, etc. ...... PICKET

dumb .... AMAZE, ASTOUND, CONFOUND, FLABBERGAST

feature .... LOCKOUT

gently .... PAT, TAP

it rich .... SUCCEED, HIT THE JACKPOT

kind of .... SIT-IN, HUNGER, SIT-DOWN, WILDCAT, SYMPATHY, SLOW-DOWN

lightly .... DAB, BUMP

of a sort .... BOYCOTT

off .... ERASE, DELETE, EXPUNGE

out .... FAN, FAIL, DELE, CANCEL, DELETE, EXPUNGE

the Gold's prize .... ROSES

violently .... RIP, BASH

violently against each other .... CRASH, COLLIDE

weapon .... PICKET

with closed fist .... PUNCH

with open palm .... SLAP

with the foot .... KICK, SPURN, TRAMPLE

strikebreaker .... RAT, FINK, GOON, SCAB, BLACKLEG

strikebreakers' leader .... NOBLE

striker .... BAT, HAMMER, MALLET, CLAPPER, HARPOONER

of a sort .... HOLDOUT

striking .... VIVID, ATTRACTIVE, IMPRESSIVE, REMARKABLE

string .... ROW, SET, CORD, HANG, LACE, LINE, ROPE, CHAIN, THREAD, CATGUT, SERIES, THREAD

along .... DUPE, FOOL, HOAX,

JOSH, DECEIVE

in horse racing .... STABLE

of beads ..... ROSARY, STRAND, CHAPLET, NECKLACE

out ...... DRAW, PULL, STRETCH

quartet member .... VIOLA, VIOLONCELLO

section mezzo .... VIOLA

tipped end .... TAG, A(I)GLET

up .... HANG, SCRAG

stringed instrument .... HARP, KOTO, LUTE, LYRE, BANJO, CELLO, REBEC, VIOL(A), CITOLE, GUITAR, ZITHER, CITHARA, CITHER(N), CITTERN, PANDORA, SAMISEN, UKE(LELE), DULCIMER, MANDOLIN, PSALTERY, CLAVICHORD

instrument player ...... LUTIST, CELLIST, BANJOIST, LUTANIST, LUTENIST, STRUMMER, GUITARIST

instrument ridge .... NUT

toy .... TOP, KITE, YOYO

stringency .... RARITY, SCARCITY, SEVERITY

stringent .... STERN, TIGHT, SEVERE, STRICT, EXACTING, DEMANDING

strings attached: colloq. .... TERM(S), PROVISO, CONDITION

stringy .... LONG, ROPY, WIRY, FIBROUS, THREADY, VISCOUS

strip ...... TAB, BARE, LATH, PEEL, TAPE, SPOIL, SWATH, BATTEN, DENUDE, DIVEST, FASCIA, FLENSE, DISROBE, UNDRESS, DISARRAY, DISMANTLE

from tree trunk .... FLITCH

in a way .... DEPRIVE, DISPOSSESS

landing .... RUNWAY

metal/wood .... LIST, SLAT

of land .... NECK

of leaves .... DEFOLIATE

of silk, velvet, etc. .... RIBBON

skin .... FLAY, EXCORIATE

slang .... SKIN

wool from sheep .... FLEECE

stripe .... BAR, BAND, BELT, KIND, LINE, MARK, SORT, TYPE, FILLET, STREAK, CHEVRON

colored .... STRIA

of color .... LIST

on skin .... WALE, WELT, WHEAL, STRETCH-MARK

on the sleeve, as of military or police uniform .... CHEVRON

service: sl. .... HASH MARK

striped .... STRIPY, ZONATE(D), STREAKED, STRIATE(D)

animal .... BONGO, ZEBRA

cloth .... MADRAS

lengthwise .... VITTATE

squirrel .... CHIPMUNK

stripling .... BOY, KID, LAD, SPRIG, YOUTH, SHAVER

stripped .... NEEDY, DENUDED, FLEECED, SHORN(OF), DEPRIVED, DIVESTED

stripteaser .... STRIPPER, ECDYSIAST, (SALLY)RAND

covering for .... FAN, G-STRING

strive ...... TRY, VIE, COPE, EXERT, FIGHT, LABOR, STRAIN, CONTEND, ENDEAVOR, STRUGGLE

ambitiously .... SEEK, ASPIRE

strobil(e) .... CONE

stroke .... FIT, PET, PAT, BEAT, BLOW, BOLT, MARK, SHOT, ICTUS, THROB, CARESS, FONDLE, STRIPE, SEIZURE, APOPLEXY, CONVULSION

brilliant ...... ACE, COUP, FEAT, EXPLOIT

cutting .... CHOP, SLICE

finishing .... COUP DE GRACE

indirect/oblique .... BRICOLE

lucky .... COUP, FLUKE

of luck .... WINDFALL

on hand's palm .... PANDY

tender .... CARESS

with a whip ...... WELT, STRIPE

stroll .... WALK, RAMBLE, WANDER, SAUNTER, PROMENADE

stroller .... ROVER, ROAMER, WALKER, DRIFTER, VAGRANT, CARRIAGE

occupant .... TOT, BABY

Stromboli ...... ISLAND, VOLCANO

strong .... HALE, FIRM, BURLY, HARDY, HUSKY, LUSTY, STOUT, TOUGH, ROBUST, SINEWY, STURDY, VIRILE, HEALTHY, INTENSE, VIOLENT, ATHLETIC, FORCEFUL, POWERFUL, PUISSANT, VIGOROUS

arm .... BULLY, COERCE, INTIMIDATE

arm man ..... GOON, BOUNCER, GANGSTER

articulation .... FORTIS

as an ox .... HUSKY

attachment .... ADHESION

current .... RIPTIDE, UNDERTOW

desire .... HUNGER, THIRST
drink .... LIQUOR, SPIRITS
feeling .... FIRE, HATRED,
　　　　　　　　PASSION
giant .... ANTAEUS, GOLIATH
man .... ATLAS, TITAN,
　SAMSON, DICTATOR, HERCULES
man: colloq. .... HE-MAN
masculine woman .... AMAZON
muscled ..... THEWY, BRAWNY,
　　　　　　　　HERCULEAN
odor .... REEK
passion .... FLAME
point .... FORTE, TALENT
scented .... OLID
smelling ...... ACRID, PIQUANT,
　　　　　　　　PUNGENT
yearning .... ACHE
strongbox .... SAFE, CHEST,
　　　　VAULT, COFFER
slang .... PETE
stronghold .... KEEP, AERIE,
　CASTLE, REFUGE, BULWARK,
　CITADEL, REDOUBT, FASTNESS,
　　　　　　FORT(RESS)
strongroom .... VAULT
strongyl(e) .... ROUNDWORM
strontium sulfite .... CELESTITE
strop .... STRAP, SHARPEN
strophe .... STANZA
strophulus .... MILIARIA
struck .... SMIT, SMOKE,
　　　　　　SHUTDOWN
paydirt .... MINED
structural .... TECTONIC
beam .... GIRDER
order .... TEXTURE
structure .... MAKEUP, ANATOMY,
　　　EDIFICE, BUILDING
basic .... CADRE
containing Buddha relics
　................................ DAGOBA
defensive .... FORT
enclosed .... CAGE
strudel .... PASTRY
struggle .... TRY, TOIL, FIGHT,
　LABOR, BATTLE, SQUIRM,
　STRAIN, STRIFE, STRIVE,
　TUSSLE, WRITHE, CONTEST,
　WRESTLE, CONFLICT,
　　　　　　EXERTION
strum .... TIRL, PLUCK, THRUM,
　　　　　　　　FINGER
struma .... GOITER, SCROFULA
strummer ...... LUTIST, GUITARIST
strumpet .... HARLOT
strut .... GAIT, SPUR, BRACE,
　STALK, SASHAY, SWAGGER
struthious bird .... EMU, RHEA,
　　　　OSTRICH, SPARROW
struts .... CABANE, SUPPORT

strutter .... PEACOCK
strychnine source .... NUX
　　　　　　　　VOMICA
tropical plant .... STRYCHNOS
stub .... END, BUTT, STUMP,
　UPROOT, RECEIPT, STUBBLE
stubble .... BEARD, STALKS,
　STUMPS, BRISTLES, REMNANTS
stubborn .... TOUGH, DOGGED,
　MULISH, ORNERY, DIEHARD,
　FROWARD, WILLFUL,
　OBDURATE, OBSTINATE,
　　　　　　HARDHEADED
animal ..... ASS, MULE, BURRO,
　　　　　　　　DONKEY
hair tuft .... COWLICK
individual .... PIGHEAD,
　　　　　　　　STICKLER
ones .... MISSOURI MULES
stubbornly disagreeable
　............................. CONTRARY
disobedient .... UNYIELDING
refusing to go on .... BALKY
stubbornness .... HARDNESS,
　TENACITY, WILLPOWER,
　PERSISTENCE, PERTINACITY
stubby .... STOCKY, BRISTLY
stuckup .... VAIN, ALOOF, MIRED,
　PROUD, SNOOTY, UPPISH,
　UPPITY, HAUGHTY,
　ARROGANT, SNOBBISH, HIGH-
　　　　　　　　NOSED
stud .... DOT, PIN, PEG, BOSS,
　ADORN, BUTTON, SUPPORT,
　NAILHEAD, PROJECTION
horse .... BREEDER, STALLION
shoe .... HOBNAIL
studded .... SPANGLY, TEEMING,
　SPANGLED, BEJEWELED
student .... COED, PUPIL,
　LEARNER, SCHOLAR, TRAINEE,
　DISCIPLE, COLLEGIAN,
　SCHOOLBOY, SCHOOLGIRL
Annapolis .... MIDSHIPMAN
bane of .... TEST
class exercise of
　............................ RECITATION
failing .... FLUNKEE
first year .... PLEBE, FRESHMAN
former .... DROPOUT
fourth year .... SENIOR
group .... CLASS, SEMINAR
high school: sl. .... TEENER
in charge .... MONITOR
initiate .... HAZE
international law .... PUBLICIST
military school .... CADET
of words .... LEXICOLOGIST
population .... ENROLLMENT
second year .... SOPHOMORE
third year .... JUNIOR

university .... COED,
　　　　　　VARSITARIAN
West Point .... CADET
wise .... SCHOLAR, THINKER
students' bugaboo .... EXAM
job schedule .... PART-TIME
scrimmage .... RUSH
second chance .... RETEST
studied .... ADVISED, CAREFUL,
　MEDITATED, DELIBERATE(D)
studies .... LEARNING, EDUCATION,
　　　　　　SCHOOLING
studio .... SALON, ATELIER,
　　　　　　WORKSHOP
studious .... BOOKISH, DILIGENT
study .... CON, DEN, READ, ROOM,
　ESSAY, ETUDE, WEIGH,
　PERUSE, PONDER, EXAMINE,
　CONSIDER, MEMORIZE,
　PORE(OVER), RESEARCH,
　　　　　　SCRUTINIZE
assignment .... LESSON
by candlelight ..... LUCUBRATE
colloquial .... DIG, GRIND
frequently/repeatedly
　..................... DRILL, PRACTICE
group .... CLASS, SEMINAR
hard .... BONE, CRAM
intensely .... FOCUS,
　　　　　　CONCENTRATE
layout of .... CASE
musical .... ETUDE
of cells .... CYTOLOGY
creative processes
　............................. SYNECTICS
drugs and effects
　.................. PHARMACOLOGY
tissues .... HISTOLOGY
values .... EXIOLOGY
the Bible .... ISAGOGICS
over again .... REVIEW
private .... DEN, SANCTUM
product of .... ESSAY, THESIS
superficially .... SMATTER
up ..... BONE, CRAM, BRUSH UP
with .... TRAIN
stuff .... JAM, PAD, WAD, CRAM,
　FILL, JUNK, PACK, PLUG,
　SATE, THINGS, ESSENCE,
　OVEREAT, SATIATE,
　MATERIAL, SUBSTANCE
oneself: sl. .... PIG OUT
slang .... WHAT IT TAKES
the stomach .... GORGE,
　　　　　　OVEREAT
stuffed .... FULL, BLOCKED,
　CRAMMED, REPLETE
stuffing .... WAD, KAPOK, COTTON,
　FILLING, CONTENTS, DRESSING
stuffy .... DULL, PRIM, CLOSE,
　MUSTY, STIFF, AIRLESS,

STRAIT-LACED
nose .... CONGESTION
Stuka .... (DIVE)BOMBER
stulm .... ADIT
stum .... MUST, GRAPE-JUICE
stumble .... ERR, SLIP, TRIP,
HOBBLE, BLUNDER, FLOUNDER
upon .... FIND, DISCOVER
stumblebum .... MUFFER,
BUTTERFINGERS
stumbling block .... SNAG,
HURDLE, DRAWBACK,
OBSTACLE, HINDRANCE
stump ...... END, LOP, BUTT, FOIL,
STUB, TREAD, BAFFLE, PULPIT,
PUZZLE, NONPLUS, PERPLEX,
REMNANT, STUBBLE, TRAMPLE
colloquial .... ELECTIONEER
stumper ...... PUZZLE, CANDIDATE,
CAMPAIGNER
stumps: sl. .... LEGS
stumpy .... STUBBY, SQUATTY
stun .... DAZE, FLOOR, SHOCK,
BENUMB, DEADEN, ASTOUND,
STARTLE, STUPEFY
stunning .... NIFTY, CUTESY,
LOVELY, CUTESIE, DAZZLING,
STRIKING, ATTRACTIVE,
REMARKABLE, DEVASTATING
stunt .... FEAT, CHECK, DWARF,
TRICK, RETARD
flying tour .... BARNSTORM
stunted tree .... SCRAG, SCRUB,
BONSAI
stuntman .... ACROBAT,
DAREDEVIL
or substitute .... STAND-IN
stupa .... MOUND, TOWER, SHRINE
stupe .... COMPRESS
stupefacient .... NARCOTIC
stupefy .... DAZE, DOPE, PALL,
STUN, AMAZE, BESOT,
DEADEN, ASTOUND, ASTONISH,
BEWILDER, NARCOTIZE,
OBFUSCATE
stupendous .... VAST, IMMENSE,
COLOSSAL, ENORMOUS,
OVERWHELMING
stupid .... DULL, DUMB, BANAL,
CRASS, DENSE, DOPEY, INANE,
INEPT, SILLY, ABSURD,
ASININE, FOOLISH, TEDIOUS,
TOMFOOL, TIRESOME,
INSIPIENT
blunder .... BONER
from overdrinking .... SOTTISH
person .... ASS, CLOD, COOT,
DOLT, LOON, DUMMY, DUNCE,
GOOSE, IDIOT, LOOBY, MORON,
NINNY, NITWIT, FATHEAD,
DUMBBELL, BLOCKHEAD,

LAMEBRAIN, NINCOMPOOP
stupor .... COMA, DAZE, SOPOR,
APATHY, TORPOR, TRANCE,
LETHARGY, NARCOSIS,
OSCITANCY
combining form .... NARCO
in a .... DOPEY
"Stupor Mundi" .... WORLD'S
WONDER
to his followers .... FREDERICK
II
sturdy .... GID, FIRM, HARDY,
HUSKY, STOUT, ROBUST,
STRONG, DURABLE, STAGGERS
sturgeon .... BELUGA, GANOID,
HAUSEN, STERLET,
SHOVELHEAD
eggs .... ROE
eggs relish .... CAVIAR(E)
Sturm und ____ .... DRANG
stutter .... FALTER, STAMMER,
HESITATE
Stutz competitor .... REO
sty .... HAW, PEN, BOIL, SHED,
STYE, HOVEL, PIGPEN, PIGSTY
Stygian .... DARK, GLOOMY,
HELLISH, INFERNAL
style .... FAD, TON, WAY, CALL,
CHIC, FORM, MAKE, MODE,
NAME, RAGE, BRAND, GENRE,
HABIT, VOGUE, DESIGN,
MANNER, METHOD, NEEDLE,
STYLUS, ENTITLE, FASHION,
POINTER, VARIETY,
TECHNIQUE
architectural .... ROMAN,
GOTHIC, ROCOCO, BAROQUE,
SPANISH, BYZANTINE,
ROMANESQUE, RENAISSANCE
artistic .... GUSTO
bombastic .... TUMID
decorative .... ART DECO
dress .... COSTUME
furniture .... EMPIRE, RUSTIC,
ARCADIAN, FRENCH-
PROVINCIAL
genderless .... UNISEX
literary .... ATTIC, ROCOCO,
CICERONIAN, SURREALISM
of abstract painting .... OP
ART
out of .... DATED, PASSE
painting .... GENRE, CUBISM,
DADAISM, FAUVISM, ABSTRACT
type .... DORIC, IONIC, ROMAN,
FUTURA, GOTHIC, ITALIC,
SCRIPT, CURSIVE, GROTESQUE
styled .... NAMED, CALLED,
YCLEPT
stylet .... PROBE, DAGGER,
LANCET, STILETTO

surgical .... PROBE, TROCAR
stylish .... CHIC, TONY, NOBBY,
NIFTY, SMART, DRESSY,
JAUNTY, MODISH, TRENDY, A
LA MODE, ELEGANT, VOGUISH,
FASHIONABLE
dresser .... FOP, DUDE, TOFF,
DANDY, SPARK, SWELL,
SOCIALITE, (BEAU)BRUMMEL,
TRENDSETTER, CLOTHESHORSE
ostentatiously .... SWANK(Y)
stylist ...... DESIGNER, MANNERIST
stylite .... ASCETIC
stylized flower .... LIS
stylograph .... PEN
stylus .... PEN, NEEDLE, SCRIBER
stymie/stymy .... BALK, FOIL,
BLOCK, BAFFLE, HINDER,
IMPEDE, THWART, OBSTRUCT
colloquial .... FLOOR
styptic .... ALUM, AMADOU,
ASTRINGENT
action of .... STYPSIS
substance .... ALUM
Styx .... LETHE, RIVER
ferryman of .... CHARON
suave .... OILY, AULIC, BLAND,
SOAPY, POLITE, SMOOTH,
URBANE, COURTLY,
GRACIOUS, POLISHED,
COURTEOUS
sub .... BELOW, UNDER,
SUBMARINE, SUBSTITUTE
rosa ..... COVERTLY, SECRETLY,
PRIVATELY
subaltern .... AIDE, JUNIOR,
UNDERLING, SUBORDINATE
subalternate .... SUCCESSIVE
subaqueous .... UNDERWATER
subatomic ...... MINUTE, INVISIBLE
subclavian steal syndrome
.... DIZZINESS, DOUBLE VISION
subconscious ...... ID, SUBLIMINAL
mind .... ANIMA, PSYCHE
psychic energy .... LIBIDO
subcontinent .... INDIA, NEW
GUINEA
subcontract .... SUBLET,
SUBLEASE
subdivide ...... DISSECT, SPLIT UP,
TRANSECT, PARCEL OUT
subdue ...... CALM, TAME, QUELL,
SOBER, MASTER, SOFTEN,
CONQUER, CONTROL, REPRESS,
HOLD BACK, OVERCOME,
RESTRAIN, VANQUISH,
OVERPOWER, SUBJUGATE
by reverence .... OVERAWE
subdued .... DOWNED
subereous ...... CORKY, CORKLIKE
subgum dish .... CHOW MEIN

subject .... NOUN, TEXT, BASIS, SLAVE, THEMA, THEME, TOPIC, MOTIVE, SERVANT, OCCASION, SUBJUGATE, SUBSTANCE

all courses, collectively, in a particular

.... CURRICULUM

change to another

.... METASTASIS

main .... MOTIF

Markham's .... HOER

matter .... CASE, GIST, ISSUE, TOPIC

of a famed 1897 editorial

.... SANTA

a musical composition

.... THEME

a nation/state .... CITIZEN

a sentence

.... NOUN(PHRASE)

an Aesop fable

.... SOURGRAPES

an essay, lecture, sermon, etc. .... THEME

to an action/ radiation

.... EXPOSE

another's control

.... TRIBUTARY

defects .... FAULTY

depression .... SAD, GLUM, MOODY, SULLEN

difficult circumstances

.... REDUCE

discussion .... MOOT, DEBATABLE

dispute .... QUESTIONABLE

horseplay .... HAZE

obligation .... MORTGAGE

possibility of something unpleasant .... LIABLE

reversal .... INVERTIBLE

severe questioning .... GRILL

something uncertain

.... CONTINGENT

taxation .... DUTIABLE, ASSESSABLE

third degree .... SWEAT

under the feudal system

.... LIEGE, VASSAL

subjection .... YOKE, THRALL

subjective ...... IN-GOING, SELFISH, INTERNAL, PERSONAL

subjoin ...... ADD, ANNEX, APPEND

subjugate .... TAME, SUBDUE, CONQUER, ENSLAVE, VANQUISH, OVERTHROW

subjugation .... BONDAGE, CONQUEST

subleased .... RELET

sublimate .... PURIFY, REFINE

sublime .... HIGH, GRAND, LOFTY, NOBLE, DIVINE, EXALTED, STATELY, GLORIOUS, MAJESTIC

submachine gun ...... THOMPSON

submarine .... TUB, U-BOAT, U-BOOT, SUBMERSIBLE, TORPEDO-BOAT

chaser .... CORVET(TE)

colloquial .... SUB

device against .... PARAVANE

"eye" of .... PERISCOPE

locator .... SONAR

nuclear .... GATO

slang .... PIGBOAT

submaxilla .... JAW(BONE)

submerge/submerse .... DIP, DIVE, HIDE, SINK, SOAK, DROWN, SWAMP, WHELM, DELUGE, DRENCH, ENGULF, PLUNGE, IMMERSE, INUNDATE

submerged continent

.... ATLANTIS

submersible .... U-BOAT, U-BOOT, SUBMARINE

submission .... CESSION, PATIENCE, OBEDIENCE, SURRENDER, COMPLIANCE, RESIGNATION

act of/sign of .... BOW, VAIL, KNEEL, CURTSY, KOWTOW, SALAAM

submissive .... MEEK, TAME, LOWLY, DOCILE, DUTIFUL, PASSIVE, OBEDIENT, YIELDING, PROSTRATE

submit .... BOW, BEND, CEDE, OBEY, REFER, STATE, STOOP, YIELD, ACCEDE, COMPLY, GIVE IN, RESIGN, PROPOSE, RETREAT, SUCCUMB, SURRENDER

subordinate .... AIDE, LOWER, UNDER, INFERIOR, ASSISTANT, DEPENDENT, SECONDARY

an unquestioning

.... MYRMIDON

suborn .... BRIBE, CORRUPT, PERJURE

subpoena .... WRIT, ORDER, SUMMONS, CITATION

subrogate .... SUBSTITUTE

subscribe .... AID, ABET, BACK, SIGN, AGREE, PLEDGE, CONSENT, ENDORSE, SUPPORT

subscription .... DONATION, ENDORSEMENT

subsequent ...... LATER, ENSUING, FOLLOWING

to .... AFTER, BEYOND

subsequently .... ANON, LATER,

AFTERWARDS, THEREAFTER

subservience .... SERVILITY

subservient ...... ABJECT, SERVILE, OBEISANT

subside .... EBB, FALL, SINK, WANE, ABATE, LOWER, LESSEN, SETTLE

subsidiary .... BRANCH, ANCILLARY, AUXILIARY, SECONDARY, SUCCURSAL, TRIBUTARY, PENSIONARY

subsidize .... AID, BACK, FINANCE, SPONSOR, UNDERWRITE

subsidy .... AID, GRANT, BACKING, FUNDING, PENSION, SUPPORT, SUBVENTION

subsist ...... BE, FARE, FEED, LIVE, ABIDE, EXIST, CONTINUE

subsistence ...... BEING, (UP)KEEP, EXISTENCE, PROVISION, LIVELIHOOD

substance ...... BODY, GIST, MEAT, PITH, STUFF, ENTITY, MATTER, WEALTH, ESSENCE, MEANING, PURPORT, REALITY, MATERIAL

drying .... DESSICANT

recording tape .... MYLAR

resinous .... LAC

sticky .... GOO

substances, one of the four "natural" .... AIR, FIRE, EARTH, WATER

substandard .... POOR, BELOW PAR, INFERIOR

substantial .... REAL, AMPLE, SOLID, SOUND, MASSIVE

substantially .... BASICALLY, ESSENTIALLY

substantiate .... PROVE, EMBODY, VERIFY, BEAR OUT, CONFIRM

substantiation .... PROOF, EVIDENCE

substantive .... NOUN, BASIC, SOLID, ACTUAL, CONCRETE

substitute .... VICE, PROXY, DEPUTY, FILL-IN, REPLACE, STAND-IN, EXCHANGE, SUPPLANT, ALTERNATE, SUBROGATE

closely resembling another

.... RINGER

empowered .... PROXY

food .... ERSATZ

for .... PINCHHIT

for a name .... DINGUS

for actor/actress

.... UNDERSTUDY

for the real thing ...... DUMMY

give up for a .... EXCHANGE

person for father or mother

.... SURROGATE

pitcher .... RELIEF
slang .... PATSY, DOUBLE
standing by as a ...... BACK-UP
temporary .... STOPGAP,
    MAKESHIFT
substitution .... METONYMY,
    REPLACEMENT
of obligation .... NOVATION
subterfuge .... RUSE, BLIND,
    TRICK, DEVICE, EVASION,
    PRETEXT, ARTIFICE, PRETENSE,
    DECEPTION
subterranean .... HIDDEN,
    NETHER, SECRET, INFERNAL,
    UNDERGROUND
subtile .... KEEN, RARE, THIN,
    DAINTY, SUBTLE, TENUOUS
subtitle .... SUBHEAD(ING)
subtle .... SLY, DEFT, KEEN, NICE,
    RARE, THIN, WILY, ACUTE,
    DAINTY, ARTFUL, CLEVER,
    CRAFTY, CUNNING, DEVIOUS,
    FRAGILE, REFINED, SUBTILE,
    DELICATE, FINESPUN,
    (SUPER)FINE
emanation .... AURA,
    ATMOSPHERE
variation .... SHADE, NUANCE
subtlety .... ART, CRAFT, GUILE,
    ACUMEN, NICETY, FINESSE,
    QUILLET, DELICACY
subtract .... DEDUCT, LESSEN,
    REMOVE, DETRACT, TAKE
    AWAY
suburb(s) .... BURG, TOWN,
    BARRIO, VILLAGE, ENVIRONS,
    FAUBOURG, PURLIEU(S),
    OUTSKIRTS
suburban residence .... VILLA
society .... VILLADOM
sward .... LAWN
subvention .... AID, GRANT,
    RELIEF, SUBSIDY
subversion .... MUTINY,
    REBELLION
subversive .... RED, REBEL,
    RADICAL, MUTINEER,
    REVOLTER, DISSIDENT
subvert .... RUIN, REVOLT, UP-
    END, DEFEAT, CORRUPT,
    OVERTHROW, UNDERMINE
subway .... TUBE, METRO,
    TUNNEL, RAILWAY,
    UNDERGROUND
entrance .... COVER, KIOSK,
    TURNSTILE
fare .... TOKEN
rider, sometimes ..... STANDEE
stairway .... ESCALATOR
succeed ...... WIN, ENSUE, ARRIVE,
    FOLLOW, THRIVE, ACHIEVE,

ADVANCE, INHERIT, PREVAIL,
PROSPER, REPLACE, FLOURISH,
SUPPLANT, SUPERSEDE,
    ACCOMPLISH
colloquial .... CLICK
succeeding .... NEXT,
    SEQUENT(IAL)
success .... TRIUMPH, VICTORY,
    CONQUEST, PROSPERITY,
    BREAKTHROUGH
colloquial .... (SMASH)HIT
easy .... PICNIC, RUNAWAY
great .... BEST SELLER
overwhelming ...... LANDSLIDE
sign of .... RANK, RICHES,
    WEALTH
sure .... WINNER, NATURAL
successful .... ON TOP, DOMINANT,
    UNBEATEN, EFFECTIVE,
    FORTUNATE, OUT IN FRONT,
    PROSPEROUS, VICTORIOUS
person .... HERO, COMER,
    NABOB, VICTOR, WINNER,
    CHAMP(ION), CONQUEROR
successfully reach one's ends
    .... ARRIVE, ACHIEVE,
    COMPASS, ACCOMPLISH
succession ...... SERIES, SEQUENCE
of rulers .... DYNASTY,
    HERITAGE
successive .... LINEAL,
    CONSECUTIVE
successively .... SERIALLY
successor .... HERES, HEIR(ESS),
    FOLLOWER, (IN)HERITOR,
    REPLACEMENT
Babist's .... BAHAI
to Caligula .... CLAUDIUS
Claudius .... NERO
David .... SOLOMON
Genghis Khan .... KUBLAI
    KHAN, UGUDAI KHAN
Julius Caesar .... AUGUSTUS,
    OCTAVIAN
Philip II .... ALEXANDER
    (THE GREAT)
Queen Hatshepsut
    .... THUTMOSE III
Saul .... DAVID
Solomon .... REHOBOAM
succinct .... BRIEF, CRISP, MEATY,
    PITHY, SHORT, TERSE,
    CONCISE, LACONIC
succor .... AID, HELP, SERVE,
    RELIEF, COMFORT,
    ASSIST(ANCE)
succory .... CHICORY
succubus .... INCUBUS,
    DEMON(ESS), CACODEMON
succulent .... JUICY, MOIST, TASTY
plant .... ALOE

succumb .... DIE, FALL, YIELD,
    EXPIRE, GIVE IN, SUBMIT,
    SURRENDER
succursal .... AUXILIARY,
    SUBSIDIARY
succus .... JUICE
succuss .... SHAKE(UP)
such .... SIC, LIKE
suck ...... SIP, DRAW, LURE, PULL,
    BLEED, DRAIN, ABSORB,
    GUZZLE, INHALE, EXTRACT
sucker .... BABY, DUPE, GULL,
    PIPE, LEECH, PATSY, SHOOT,
    SPROUT, LOLLIPOP, PUSHOVER
suck(er)fish .... REMORA
suckers, having/producing
    .... SURCULOSE
suckle ...... REAR, NURSE, FOSTER,
    LACTATE, NOURISH, NURTURE,
    BREAST-FEED
suckler .... CHILD, NURSE,
    MAMMAL, SUCKLING
suckling .... BABY, NEONATE,
    TODDLER, NURSLING,
    WEANLING
sucrose ...... SUGAR, SACCHAROSE
suction ...... SUCKING, SIPHONAGE
device .... REED, LEECH,
    STRAW
Sudan cape .... KASAR, ABU DARA
capital .... KHARTOUM
chief of state .... AZHARI
city/town .... WAU, KODOK,
    KOSTI, NYALA, ATBARA,
    RUMBEK, DAMAZIN, EL OBEID,
    GEDAREF, KASSALA, MALAKAL,
    OMDURMAN
desert .... LIBYAN, NUBIAN,
    SAHARA
lake .... NUBIA
language .... BEJA, NUER,
    DINKA, ARABIC, NUBIAN
monetary unit .... POUND
mountain .... KINYETI, JEBEL
    ODA, JEBEL MARRA
prime minister .... SADIG,
    KHALIL, MAHGOUB
province .... DARFUR,
    KHARTOUM, KORDOFAN
region .... DAR HAMID, EL
    GEZIRA
river .... JUR, SUE, ADDA, NILE,
    AKOBO, PIBOR, SETIT, ATBARA,
    BARAKA, DINDER
swamp .... SUDD
Sudanese .... FULAH, MOSSI,
    NILOT, HAUSSA
antelope .... OTEROP
inhabitant .... NILOTE
medicine man .... MUMBO
    JUMBO

natives, of the .... NILOTIC
sultanate .... WADAI
Sudanic language .... TOSHI,
   YORUBA, MANDINGO
sudarium/sudary ...... VERONICA,
   HANDKERCHIEF
sudden ...... RASH, HASTY, QUICK,
   ABRUPT, PRECIPITATE
attack .... SORTIE
change/twist .... QUIRK
feeling of longing .... PANG
outpouring .... SPATE
spell of activity .... SPASM
thrust .... LUNGE
sudor .... SWEAT, PERSPIRATION
sudorific .... CLAMMY, SWEATY,
   HIDROTIC, PERSPIRY
sud(s) .... BEER, FOAM, FROTH,
   SPUME, LATHER, BUBBLES
sudsy .... FOAMY, SOAPY, BUBBLY,
   FROTHY
in a way .... ALEY
sue .... WOO, COURT, PLEAD,
   APPEAL, SOLICIT, LITIGATE,
   PETITION, BRING SUIT,
   PROSECUTE
suede .... LEATHER
source .... KID, CALF
suer .... SUITOR, LITIGANT,
   PLAINTIFF
suet .... FAT, TALLOW
Suez Canal builder ...... LESSEPS
suffer ...... AIL, LET, ACHE, BEAR,
   DREE, ALLOW, ENDURE,
   PERMIT, SUSTAIN, UNDERGO,
   TOLERATE, EXPERIENCE
punishment .... FACE THE
   MUSIC
sufferable .... BEARABLE
sufferance .... PATIENCE,
   ENDURANCE, TOLERATION
sufferer .... PREY, MARTYR,
   VICTIM, PATIENT, INVALID
suffering .... PAIN, DOLOR,
   THROES, DISTRESS
as of hopelessness
   .... DESPAIR
as of pressure .... STRESS
as through great loss
   .... SHOCK
intense .... GRIEF, SORROW
martyr's .... PASSION
suffice ...... DO, SATE, SERVE, GET
   BY, SATISFY
sufficiency .... FULLNESS,
   ABUNDANCE, PROFUSION,
   REPLETION
colloquial .... LOTS, OODLES
excessive .... GLUT, FLOOD,
   SURFEIT
kind of .... QUORUM,

AFFLUENCE
slang .... SCADS
sufficient .... ENOW, AMPLE,
   ENOUGH, PLENTY, ADEQUATE
barely .... MINIMAL
suffix .... ENDING, POSTFIX,
   SUBINDEX, DESINENCE
action .... URE, ANCE, XION
adjective .... ENT, IAL, ISH,
   IST, OUS, IBLE, PATHIC
alcohol .... OL
aphid .... IDAE
believer .... IST, ARIAN
boy .... ISH
capable of .... ILE
carbohydrate .... OSE
changing one .... TROPE
chemical .... ANE, ENE, IUM,
   OLE, ENOL, ITOL, OLIC
common .... ENT, INE, ING,
   ION
comparative .... IER, IOR
condition .... ATE, ILE, ISE,
   ANCE, EMIA, SION, STER
denoting agent .... STER
depend .... ENT
diminutive .... ULE, CULE,
   ETTE
disease .... PATHIC
enzyme .... ASE
fear .... PHOBIA
female/feminine .... ESS, ELLA,
   ETTE, GYNY
follower .... IST, ITE
good .... NESS
having to do with a
   .... SUFFIXAL
icy/cold .... CRYO
indicating quality .... ISE
inflammation .... ITIS
inhabitant/native .... ITE
intensifying: sl. .... AROO
killer .... CIDE
lacking .... LESS
like .... OID
lover .... PHILE
make .... ISE
meaning cavity .... COELE
enlargement .... MEGALY
government .... ARCHY
like .... ISH
recent .... CENE
mineral(ogical) .... ITE, LITE
noun .... EE, TUDE, ATION,
   ILITY, OSITY
number .... TEEN
occupational .... ARIAN
oil .... OLE
one connected with .... AST
one who .... IST, STER
ordinal .... ETH

pain .... ALGIA
plural .... IES
resembling .... PHANE
science .... OLOGY
skin .... DERM
snake .... OPHIS
state of being .... TUDE
stone .... LITH, LITHIC
sugar .... OSE
superlative .... EST
transfer .... ENCE
tumor .... OMA
used with para .... NOIA
used with song or prank
   .... STER
verb .... IRE, ISE, ESCE
voice .... PHONIA
way .... ODE
with ecto or proto ...... PLASM
worship .... LATRY
zoological .... ATA, ACEA
suffocate .... CHOKE, STIFLE,
   SMOTHER, OBSTRUCT,
   STRANGLE, SUPPRESS,
   ASPHYXIATE
suffocating .... AIRLESS, STIFLING
suffocation .... CHOKING,
   STRANGULATION
first aid .... CPR, ARTIFICIAL
   RESPIRATION
medical term for
   .... ASPHYXIA
result of untreated ...... DEATH
temporary .... APNEA
suffragan ...... BISHOP, AUXILIARY
suffrage ...... VOTING, FRANCHISE,
   (RIGHT TO)VOTE
woman supporter of
   .... LIBBER, FEMINIST,
   SUFFRAGIST, SUFFRAGETTE
suffragist Lucy _____ ...... STONE
U.S. .... CATT
suffuse .... WASH, BATHE, COLOR,
   IMBUE, TINGE, PERVADE,
   OVERSPREAD
suffusion .... GLOW, TINT, BLUSH,
   FLUSH, DIFFUSION
Sufi disciple .... MURID
wandering dervish
   .... CALENDER
sugar .... OSE, HEXOSE, GLUCOSE,
   LACTOSE, MALTOSE,
   MANNOSE, DEXTROSE,
   FLATTERY, FRUCTOSE,
   ARABINOSE, MUSCOVADO,
   SWEETEN(ER), SACCHAROSE
alcohol .... SORBITOL
apple .... SWEETSOP
beets .... SUCROSE
beets refuse .... BAGASSE
burnt .... CARAMEL

candy .... TAFFY, BONBON, NOUGAT, CARAMEL, DIVINITY, LOLLIPOP
cane .... SUCROSE
cane, crushed .... MEGASS(E)
cane cutting tool .... MACHETE
cane disease .... ILIAU
cane refuse .... TRASH, BAGASSE
cane sprout .... RATOON
can waste juice .... VINEGAR
coating .... ICING, FROSTING
combining form
.... SACCHAR(O)
company personnel
.... REFINERS
convert into .... SACCHARIZE
crude .... GUR
crystalline .... GLUCOSE, LACTOSE, MALTOSE, FRUCTOSE
crystalline, white
.... TREHALOSE
cube .... LUMP
daddy .... BOYFRIEND, SANTA CLAUS
flavoring .... CARAMEL
form of/type of .... RAW, BROWN, WHITE, POWDERED, GRANULATED, CONFECTIONERS'
foundation for candy
.... FONDANT
fruit .... KETOSE, FRUCTOSE, LEVULOSE
mass of hard refined .... LOAF
measure .... CUP, SPOON
mill/factory .... REFINERY, SUGARWORKS
mushroom .... TREHALOSE
of lead .... ACETATE
of milk .... LACTOSE
orchard .... PLANTATION
palm sap .... JAGGERY
pentose .... RIBOSE
raw .... CASSONADE, MUSCOVADO
simple .... OSE
slang .... MONEY, MOOLAH
solution .... SIRUP, SYRUP
source of .... BEET, CANE, MAPLE
sprinkler .... DUSTER
substitute .... ASPARTAME, SACCHARIN
syrup ..... TREACLE, MOLASSES
tree .... MAPLE
without .... DRY, SEC, SUGARLESS, UNSWEETENED
yeast .... TREHALOSE
sugared/sugary .... SWEET, SYRUPY, CANDIED, HONEYED

pastry .... DONUT, COOKIE, DOUGHNUT
sugarplum .... KISS, BONBON, COMFIT
suggest ...... HINT, IMPLY, ADVISE, SUBMIT, CONNOTE, PROPOSE, INTIMATE, INSINUATE
suggestion .... HINT, TRACE, ADVICE, INKLING, PROPOSAL, INDICATION
open to .... LIBERAL, AMENABLE, PERVIOUS, BROADMINDED
subtle .... INSINUATION
suggestive .... INDICATIVE
of something improper
.... RISQUE, OFF-COLOR
suggests separate bedrooms
.... SNORE
sui ____ .... JURIS, GENERIS
generis .... RARE, UNIQUE
juris .... SANE, COMPETENT
suicidal .... DEADLY, DESOLATE, MURDEROUS, DESPONDENT
charge .... BANZAI, WAR CRY
dive, bomber's ...... KAMIKAZE
suicide .... SEPPUKU, HARAKARI, HARAKIRI, SELF-RUIN, SELF-MURDER
commit .... BLOW OUT ONE'S BRAINS
describing an attempted
.... NON-FATAL
Hindu widow's .... SUTTEE
in law .... FELO-DE-SE
sacrificial .... IMMOLATION
suint .... GREASE
derivative .... POTASH
Suisse .... SWITZERLAND
suit .... SET, ADAPT, AGREE, (BE)FIT, GROUP, APPEAL, OUTFIT, PLEASE, WOOING, SATISFY, PETITION
beneficiary .... USEE
bring .... SUE
court .... CASE, ACTION
fabric for a .... SUITING
maker .... SARTOR
of armor .... PANOPLY
of mail .... ARMOR
part of a .... COAT, VEST, PANTS, TROUSERS
playing card .... CLUBS, HEARTS, SPADES, DIAMONDS
tarot card .... CUPS, WANDS, SWORDS, PENTACLES
to a ____ .... TEE
type of .... ZOOT
suitable .... APT, MEET, RIGHT, FIT(TED), PROPER, APROPOS, FITTING, BECOMING,

EXPEDIENT, COMPATIBLE, APPROPRIATE
for .... ELIGIBLE
for the block .... SALABLE
too exactly .... PAT
suitability .... FITNESS, PROPRIETY
suitably .... MEETLY, TIMELY
suitcase .... BAG, GRIP, VALISE, LUGGAGE
suite .... SET, FLAT, GROUP, STAFF, TRAIN, ESCORT, RETINUE
suited .... FITTED, APPROPRIATE
for tilling .... ARABLE
suiting .... SERGE
suitor .... BEAU, SUER, WOOER, FELLOW, ADMIRER, PETITIONER
song of .... SERENADE
Sulawesi .... CELEBES
sulcate .... FLUTED, GROOVED, FURROWED
sulcus .... FURROW, GROOVE
Suleiman soubriquet
.... MAGNIFICENT
sulfate .... ALUM, COPPERAS
sulfide mixture .... MATTE
sulfonal .... SOPORIFIC
sulfur .... BRIMSTONE
alloy .... NIELLO
combining form .... THI(O)
sulfuric acid .... VITRIOL
sulk ...... PET, MOPE, POUT, GRIPE, GROUCH, GRUMBLE
sulky .... GIG, GLUM, MOROSE, SULLEN, CARRIAGE
puller .... HORSE
sullage .... SILT, SEWAGE
sullen .... DOUR, DULL, GLUM, GRIM, SOUR, DORTY, MOODY, SULKY, SURLY, CRUSTY, MOROSE, BALEFUL, CRABBED
Sullivan, ____ .... ED, BARRY
Sullivan's collaborator
.... GILBERT
forte .... COMIC OPERA
sully .... BLOT, SOIL, SMEAR, STAIN, TAINT, DEFILE, BLEMISH, TARNISH, BESMIRCH
sulphate barium .... BARYTE
calcium .... GYPSUM
double .... ALUM
sulphide arsenic .... ORPIMENT
lead .... GALENA
zinc .... BLENDE
sulphur .... BUTTERFLY
alloy .... NIELLO
bottom .... WHALE
color .... LEMON
sulphuric acid .... VITRIOL
sulphurous .... ANGRY, FIERY, HEATED, HELLISH, PROFANE,

INFERNAL, PASSIONATE

sultan .... EMIR, IMAM, KHAN, MURAD, RULER, SELIM, CALIPH, CHICKEN, SALADIN, PADISHAH, SULEIMAN

chamberlain of .... EUNUCH

decree of .... IRADE

palace .... SERAI

wives' apartment .... HAREM

Sultan of Swat .... BABE(RUTH)

specialty of ...... GRAND-SLAM, FOUR-BAGGER

sultana .... GRAPE, RAISIN

sultanate .... OMAN, KUWAIT, MUSCAT, KINGDOM

sultry .... HOT, SEXY, CLOSE, FIERY, HUMID, MUGGY, STUFFY, TORRID, GLOWING, SENSUAL, STIFLING, TROPICAL, PASSIONATE, SWELTERING, VOLUPTUOUS

Sulu capital .... JOLO

Moslem .... MORO

sum .... ADD, GIST, TOTAL, AMOUNT, SUMMARY, QUANTITY, AGGREGATE, SUBSTANCE

and substance .... EPITOME

of money .... POT, BANK, LUMP-SUM

subtracted .... DEDUCTION

up .... RECAP, SUMMATE, SUMMARIZE

up a speech .... PERORATE

sumac .... RHUS, TEREBINTH, POISON IVY

family .... CASHEW

genus .... RHUS

Sumatra burrowing animal
.... TELEDU

cape .... PUTING

city/town .... MEDAN, (D)JAMBI, LANGSA, PADANG, PALEMBANG

deerlike animal .... NAPU, CHEVROTAIN

gibbon .... SIAMANG

gutta .... SIAK

island near .... BATU, NIAS, BANYAK

lake .... TOBA

mountain ...... DEMPO, LEUSER, KERINCI

mountain range .... BARISAN

native .... BAT(T)AK, MALAYAN

primate .... ORANG

river .... HARI, MUSI, ROKAN

shrew/squirrel .... TANA

volcano .... SARIK, MERAPI

wild cat .... BALU

Sumbara volcano ...... TAMBORA

Sumerian god .... ABU

sumless .... VAST, COUNTLESS, INCALCULABLE

summarily ...... CURTLY, SWIFTLY

summarize .... SUM UP, RECOUNT, RESTATE

briefly/concisely
.... RECAP(ITULATE)

summary .... GIST, BRIEF, SHORT, DIGEST, PRECIS, RESUME, CONCISE, EPITOME, RUN-DOWN, ABSTRACT, SYNOPSIS, ABRIDGMENT, COMPEND(IUM)

of main points .... SYLLABUS

summer ailment ...... HEAT-RASH, PRICKLY HEAT

beverage .... ADE

headliner .... HEATWAVE

house .... KIOSK, MAHAL, ALCOVE, CASINO, GAZEBO, COTTAGE, PAVILION, BELVEDERE

insect .... FLY, GNAT

pertaining to/of
.... (A)ESTIVAL

place for furs .... STORAGE

porch hazard .... ROLLERSKATE

problem .... HEATWAVE

refresher .... LEMONADE, ORANGEADE

resort state .... MAINE

squash .... ZUCCHINI

suit fabric .... PALM BEACH

theater .... STOCK

time .... DST

triangle stars, one of the
.... VEGA, DENEB, ALTAIR

summery .... SUNNY, TOASTY, AESTIVAL, SUNSHINY

summit .... TOP, ACME, APEX, KNAP, PEAK, CLIMAX, ZENITH, PINNACLE, ULTIMATE

summon .... BID, CALL, CITE, EVOKE, ROUSE, SERVE, ARRAIGN, CONVENE, SEND FOR, SUBPOENA

back .... RECALL

up .... ELICIT, PROMPT

summons ...... CALL, WRIT, CITAL, NOTICE, BIDDING, WARRANT, MONITION, SUBPOENA, EVOCATION, CONVOCATION

carrier .... PROCESS SERVER

summonses/serenades ...... LOVE CALLS

sump ...... PIT, WELL, (CESS)POOL, SEPTIC TANK

mine .... TUNNEL

oil .... RESERVOIR

sumpter .... PACKHORSE

animal ...... OX, MULE, CAMEL, HORSE

horse .... BIDET

mule .... HINNY, JENNET

sumptuous .... RICH, GRAND, COSTLY, LAVISH, DE LUXE, IMPOSING, SPLENDID

sun .... DRY, SOL, TAN, (DAY)STAR, LUMINARY

baked .... DRIED, PARCHED

bittern .... HELIAS

bow .... IRIS, RAINBOW

burn .... TAN

clock .... SUNDIAL

combining form .... HELI(O)

cured .... DRIED

darkening of the .... ECLIPSE

deck .... PORCH, TERRACE

disk .... ATEN

dried brick .... DOBIE, (A)DOBE

for drying .... INSOLATE

god .... RA, SHU, SOL, TUM, AMON, ATEN, HORUS, TITAN, APOLLO, HELIOS, MURDUK, VARUNA, MITHRA(S), PHOEBUS, SHAMASH, HYPERION

greatest distance from
.... APSIS

halo of .... CORONA

helmet .... TOPI, TOPEE

helmet scarf .... PUGGRY, PUGGREE

in the morning .... RISER

mirror .... HELIOSTAT

mock .... PARHELION

moon differential .... EPACT

orbit/path .... ECLIPTIC

overexposure to the
.... SUNBURN

personification of .... TITAN

pertaining to the/of the
.... SOLAR, HELIACAL

poetic .... LAMP, PHOEBUS

point farthest from
.... APHELION

radiation .... INSOLATION

shadow .... UMBRA

shield .... VISOR, PARASOL

shield, window .... AWNING (VENETIAN)BLIND

spot .... FACULA, MACULA, FRECKLE

spurge .... TURNSOLE

streak .... FACULA

vitamin, so-called .... (COD) LIVER OIL

worship .... HELIOLATRY

worshipers .... NUDES, NUDISTS

Sun, Chinese president
.... YAT-SEN

The Rising, author ..... (JOHN) TOLAND

Yat-Sen's party
.... KUOMINTANG
sunbath, in a way .... FRY
sunbeam .... RAY
sunburn .... TAN
sunblock .... SUNSCREEN
ingredient .... PABA
sunburnt .... ADUST
sunburst-like jewelry
.... BROOCH
Sunda island .... BALI, JAVA,
FLORES, LOMBOK, SUMATRA
sundae .... PARFAIT, ICE CREAM
Sunday ...... HOLIDAY, HOLY DAY,
FIRST DAY, LORD'S DAY,
(CHRISTIAN)SABBATH
best .... FINERY, CLOTHES
evangelist .... BILLY (GRAHAM)
holy .... PALM, EASTER
school .... CHURCH
treat .... PICNIC, JOYRIDE
sunder .... PART, REND, RIVE,
TEAR, BREAK, SEVER, SPLIT,
CLEAVE, DIVIDE, SEPARATE
sundial .... CLOCK, HOROLOGE
gnomon .... STYLE
pointer .... GNOMON
sundog .... PARHELION
sundown .... SUNSET, TWILIGHT
sundowner .... DRINK, TRAMP,
DRIFTER
sundries .... NOTIONS, KNICK-
KNACKS, ODDS AND ENDS
sundry .... DIVERS, VARIOUS,
MISCELLANEOUS
sunfish ...... MOLA, OPAH, BREAM,
ROACH, CICHLID, CRAPPIE,
CROPPIE, BLUEGILL
genus .... MOLA
relative .... CARP, PERCH
sunflower .... GIRASOL(E),
MARIGOLD, TURNSOLE,
HELIANTHUS, HELIOTROPE
family .... COMPOSITE
Sunflower State .... KANSAS
sunk .... IN DAVY JONES'S LOCKER
sunken .... HOLLOW
fence .... HAHA
place .... SAG
sunket .... DAINTY, TIDBIT
Sunkian capital .... HARBIN
sunless .... DARK, SHADY
sunn .... HEMP, FIBER
sunny .... GAY, WARM, PALMY,
BRIGHT, CHEERY, CHEERFUL
sunrise .... DAWN, SUNUP,
AURORA, DAYBREAK
sunroom .... PORCH, SOLARIUM
sunset .... DUSK, SUNDOWN,
TWILIGHT, NIGHTFALL
occurring at .... ACRONICAL

sunshade .... VISOR, AWNING,
PARASOL, UMBRELLA,
SUNSCREEN
slang .... SUNGLASS(ES)
sunshine .... WARMTH,
(DAY)LIGHT, HAPPINESS, FAIR
WEATHER
bit of .... RAY
days .... ROSY ERA
Sunshine State .... FLORIDA, NEW
MEXICO, SOUTH DAKOTA
sunshiny .... ROSY, HAPPY,
BRIGHT, CHEERFUL
sunspot .... FACULA, MACULA
dark part .... UMBRA
sunstroke .... ICTUS, HELIOSIS,
HEATSTROKE, INSOLATION
suntan color ...... BROWN, KHAKI
sunwise .... CLOCKWISE
Suomi .... FINLAND
sup .... EAT, SIP, DINE, DRINK
super .... ACTOR, EXTRA,
SUPERIOR, EXCELLENT
ego .... CONSCIENCE, (ETHICAL)
SELF
patriot ..... JINGO, NATIONALIST
superabundance .... EXCESS,
PLEONASM, PLETHORA,
SUPERFLUX, OVERSUPPLY,
BUMPER CROP
superabundant .... RANK, RIFE,
LAVISH, REPLETE, TEEMING,
SWARMING, PLETHORIC
superannuate .... RETIRE,
(OUT)DATE, ANTIQUATE,
FOSSILIZE, OBSOLESCE
superannuated ...... AGED, ANILE,
ANTIQUE, RETIRED, OBSOLETE,
OUTDATED
superb .... FINE, RICH, FANCY,
ELEGANT, STATELY,
GORGEOUS, SPLENDID,
EXCELLENT, EXQUISITE,
GRAND(IOSE)
supercilious .... PROUD, SNIFFY,
SNOBBY, SNOOTY, SNOTTY,
HAUGHTY, ARROGANT,
CAVALIER, SCORNFUL,
SNOBBISH
person .... SNOB
superficial ...... LIP, GLIB, HASTY,
INANE, CASUAL, FLIMSY,
SLIGHT, SQUARE, CURSORY,
OUTWARD, PASSING,
SHALLOW, SKETCHY,
SURFACE, TRIVIAL, EXTERNAL,
SKIN-DEEP
blood vessel .... CAPILLARY
knowledge .... NOTION
polish .... VENEER
wound .... GASH, NICK,

SCRATCH
superficially .... SLAPDASH
superfine .... FANCY, DE LUXE,
SUBTLE, SUPERB, DELICATE,
GLORIOUS, OVERNICE,
EXQUISITE
superfluity .... REDUNDANCE
superfluous .... DE TROP, OTIOSE,
SURPLUS, NEEDLESS,
OVERMUCH, EXCESSIVE,
REDUNDANT
Superfort .... BOMBER,
B-TWENTY-NINE
superhighway .... FREEWAY,
AUTOBAHN, SPEEDWAY,
TURNPIKE, AUTOROUTE
superhuman ...... GODLY, DIVINE,
GODLIKE, SUBLIME
superimpose .... COVER, OVERLAY
superimposed .... OBSCURED
superintend .... DIRECT, MANAGE,
CONTROL, OVERSEE,
SUPERVISE, ADMINISTER
superintendent .... BOSS,
FOREMAN, MANAGER,
OVERSEER, SURVEYOR,
CONTROLLER
colloquial .... STRAW BOSS
police .... CHIEF, INSPECTOR,
COMMISSIONER
school .... PRINCIPAL
superior .... BOSS, ABOVE, MAJOR,
ULTRA, UPPER, BETTER,
HIGHER, UTMOST, GREAT(ER),
TOPNOTCH, EXCELLENT,
FIRST-RATE
slang .... TOPS
superiority .... EDGE, POWER,
SUPREMACY
superiors .... CHIEFS, BETTERS,
LEADERS, MASTERS
superlative .... ACME, ULTRA,
EXTREME, SUPREME,
EXCEEDING, EXCESSIVE
absolute .... ELATIVE
ending/suffix .... EST
Superman's city .... METROPOLIS
Lois .... LANE
other identity .... (CLARK)
KENT
portrayer .... (DEAN) CAIN,
(CHRISTOPHER) REEVE
supernal .... DIVINE, ETHEREAL,
HEAVENLY, CELESTIAL
supernatural ...... MAGIC, DIVINE,
OCCULT, ABNORMAL,
UNEARTHLY, MIRACULOUS
being ...... ELF, DEMON, FAIRY,
GHOST, PIXIE, GENIUS, GOBLIN,
SPIRIT, SPRITE, PHANTOM,
SPECTER

force .... MANA
happening .... MIRACLE
supernumerary .... ACTOR,
EXTRA, WALK-ON, STAND-IN,
FIGURANT(E)
superpower, a .... USA, USSR,
AMERICA, SOVIET UNION
economic .... JAPAN
superscribe ...... WRITE, ADDRESS
supersede .... REPLACE, SUCCEED,
DISPLACE, SUPPLANT
superseded .... OBSOLETE
supersensitive .... SORE,
OVERTENDER, THIN-SKINNED
reaction .... ALLERGY
supersonic noise .... BOOM
transport .... SST
superstar .... HERO, STANDOUT
superstition .... FEAR, BELIEF,
PHOBIA, (FOLK)LORE,
TRADITION
superstitious .... CREDULOUS
unlucky number ..... THIRTEEN
supervene .... ENSUE, HAPPEN,
EMANATE
supervise .... BOSS, DIRECT,
GOVERN, MANAGE, OVERSEE
supervision .... SURVEILLANCE
supervisor .... HEADMAN,
MANAGER, DIRECTOR,
OVERSEER
college .... PROCTOR,
PRINCIPAL
corporation .... SYNDIC
government .... MAGISTRATE
morals .... CENSOR
prison .... WARDEN
town/district .... REEVE
very exacting .... TASKMASTER
wildlife .... RANGER, GAME-
WARDEN
supination, opposed to
.... PRONATION
supine .... TORPID, PASSIVE,
INACTIVE, LISTLESS,
SLUGGISH, PROSTRATE,
RECUMBENT
opposite of .... PRONE
supper .... MEAL, FEAST, DINNER,
REPAST, REFECTION
club .... NITERY, NIGHTCLUB
supplant .... OUST, REPLACE,
SUCCEED, DISPLACE,
SUPERSEDE
supple .... SOFT, LITHE, LIMBER,
LISSOM(E), PLIABLE, SERVILE,
FLEXIBLE, YIELDING,
(COM)PLIANT
supplement .... EKE, ADJUNCT,
ADD(ITION), APPENDIX

supplemental material
...... INDEX, TABLE, ADDENDA,
GLOSSARY, ADDENDUM,
APPENDIX
supplementary .... ADDED,
EXTRA, SECOND, ADDITIONAL
rail .... EASER
story .... SEQUEL
suppliant/supplicant .... BEGGAR,
SUITOR, PLEADER, PETITIONER,
WORSHIP(P)ER
supplicate .... BEG, PRAY, PLEAD,
APPEAL, OBTEST, BESEECH,
ENTREAT, REQUEST, PETITION
supplication ...... BID, PLEA, SUIT,
APPEAL, ORISON, PRAYER,
REQUEST, ENTREATY,
PETITION, ROGATION,
DEVOTIONS
supplier .... PROVIDER, PURVEYOR
food .... GROCER, CATERER
ship .... CHANDLER
supplies .... STOCK, ISSUES,
STORES, PROVENDER,
PROVISIONS
office .... STATIONERY
supply .... FEED, GIVE, EQUIP,
STOCK, STORE, AFFORD,
FURNISH, PROVIDE
food .... CATER, PURVEY,
PROVISION
for consumption .... FEED
hidden .... HOARD
ship .... OILER, TENDER,
VICTUAL(L)ER
weapons .... ARM
workers .... MAN
support .... AID, ABET, BEAR,
STAY, BRACE, CARRY, SHORE,
TRUSS, BACK(UP), HOLD(UP),
SECOND, UPHOLD, (UP)KEEP,
BOLSTER, SUSTAIN, BUTTRESS,
MAINTAIN, SHOULDER,
UNDERPIN
chief .... KEYSTONE, MAINSTAY
idea/cause .... ESPOUSE,
SPONSOR
in a way ..... SIDE WITH, STICK
UP FOR
kind of .... LEG, PEG, BASE,
LIMB, POST, PROP, MORAL,
TABLE, PILLAR, TRIPOD,
UNIPOD, PEDESTAL, FINANCIAL
main .... PILLAR, BACKBONE
oar .... THOLEPIN
rim .... SPOKE
roof .... BEAM, RAFTER
supporter .... FAN, ALLY, DONOR,
GIVER, BACKER, BEARER,
PATRON, ROOTER, SECOND,
ABETTOR, CARRIER,

ADHERENT, ADVOCATE,
FOLLOWER, PARTISAN
athletic .... JOCKSTRAP
figure .... CORSET, GIRDLE
financial .... ANGEL, FUNDER,
PATRON, SPONSOR
of some big wheels ...... AXLE
zealous .... BOOSTER,
DEVOTEE, ENTHUSIAST
supporting framework .... EASEL,
TRELLIS, TRESTLE, SKELETON
member .... LEG, MAST,
STRUT, BRACER, GUY(LINE),
PILASTER
role .... HEAVY, VILLAIN,
SOUBRETTE
supportive .... CHEERING,
REASSURING, SUSTAINING
suppose ...... DEEM, TROW, WEEN,
FANCY, GUESS, OPINE, THINK,
ASSUME, DIVINE, GATHER,
RECKON, BELIEVE, IMAGINE,
PRESUME, SURMISE, THEORIZE,
CONJECTURE
supposed .... GIVEN, IMPLIED,
REPUTED, INFERRED,
PUTATIVE
supposition .... IF, HUNCH,
BELIEF, NOTION, THEORY,
INKLING, SURMISE, THEOREM,
GUESS(WORK), HYPOTHESIS
suppository .... PESSARY
shape .... CONE, BULLET,
CYLINDER
suppress .... BAN, HIDE, STOP,
CHECK, CRUSH, QUASH,
QUELL, CENSOR, SUBDUE,
CONCEAL, REPRESS, SILENCE,
THROTTLE
suppression .... LOCKING-IN,
BOTTLING-UP
of emotion .... INHIBITION
of memories .... REPRESSION
suppurate .... FESTER, RANKLE,
PUTREFY, MATURATE
suppuration .... PUS, PYOSIS
supra .... ABOVE
suprarenal .... ADRENAL
gland .... CORTEX, MEDULLA
glands location .... KIDNEYS
glands secretion
.... HORMONES
supremacy .... MASTERY
supreme ...... LAST, CHIEF, FINAL,
PRIME, UTMOST, HIGHEST,
FOREMOST, GREATEST,
DOMINANT, ULTIMATE,
PARAMOUNT
power .... IMPERIUM
Supreme Being .... GOD

Court nickname (former) .... NINE OLD MEN
supremo .... COMMANDER, GENERALISSIMO
Surakarta .... SOLO
Surat river .... TAPTI
surcease .... END, STOP, LET UP, DESIST
surcingle .... GIRDLE
surcoat ...... CLOAK, GIPON, JUPON
surd .... RADICAL, VOICELESS, IRRATIONAL
sure .... SAFE, TRUE, SECURE, STABLE, CERTAIN, POSITIVE, UNERRING, CONFIDENT, CONVINCED, INFALLIBLE
grip .... CINCH
success .... WINNER
thing .... CINCH, (LEAD)PIPE, CERT, IN THE BAG, TRUMP CARD
surely ...... YES, INDEED, REALLY, CLEARLY, OF COURSE, CERTAINLY, ABSOLUTELY, DEFINITELY
surety .... BAIL, BOND, PLEDGE, SAFETY, HOSTAGE, SPONSOR, GUARANTY, SECURITY, ASSURANCE, GUARANTEE, GUARANTOR
surf .... WAVES, SWELL(S), ROLLERS, BREAKERS, WHITECAPS
duck .... SCOTER
noise .... ROTE, THUNDER
part .... CAP, FOAM, CREST
surface .... AREA, OUTER, OUTSIDE, EXTERIOR, EXTERNAL, SUPERFICIAL
antique .... PATINA
curve .... CAMBER
flat .... PLANE
front/main .... OBVERSE
gem's .... FACET
in aeronautics .... AIRFOIL
lower .... FLOOR
rise to the ..... EMERGE, FLOAT UP
slanting/sloping .... CANT, RAMP
thing with smooth .... EGG, FACE, GLASS
transit .... LAND, WATER
surfacing .... PAVING, ARISING, EMERGING, FLOORING, PAVEMENT
material .... ASPHALT, MACADAM
surfactant .... WETTING-AGENT
kind of ..... SOAP, DETERGENT, EMULSIFIER

surfbird .... PLOVER
surfcaster .... FISHERMAN
surfeit .... CLOY, GLUT, JADE, PALL, SATE, GORGE, EXCESS, SATIATE, SATIETY, PLETHORA
surfeited .... BLASE, FED-UP, SATED, REPLETE, STUFFED
surge .... GUSH, GUST, RISE, RUSH, TIDE, WAVE, HEAVE, SWELL, SWIRL, BILLOW, SEETHE, UNDULATION
surgeon .... PHYSICIAN, SPECIALIST
colloquial .... DOCTOR, MEDIC(O)
extractor of .... FORCEPS
hammer of .... PLESSOR
head and neck .... OTOLARYNGOLOGIST
knife of ..... LANCET, SCALPEL, BISTOURY
of a kind .... AMPUTATOR, UROLOGIST
probe of .... STYLET
saw of .... TREPAN, TREPHINE
slang .... SAWBONES
starter .... NEURO
surgery ...... EXCISION, OPERATION
abdominal .... LAPAROTOMY
abortion .... HYSTEROTOMY
blood clot removal .... THROMBECTOMY
body contour .... LIPECTOMY
bone .... OSTEOTOMY, AMPUTATION
breast removal .... MASTECTOMY
breast reshaping .... MAMMOPLASTY
childbirth .... CESAREAN SECTION
chin .... MENTOPLASTY
cosmetic .... FACELIFT, HAIR-TRANSPLANT
eyelid .... BLEPHAROPLASTY
gall bladder removal .... CHOLECYSTECTOMY
goiter removal .... THYROIDECTOMY
heart .... OPEN-HEART, BALLOON-ANGIOPLASTY
heart valve .... VALVULOPLASTY
kidney removal .... NEPHRECTOMY
kind of .... MAJOR, MINOR
lip defect .... CHILOPLASTY
male sterilization .... VASECTOMY
nose .... RHINOPLASTY
outer ear .... OTOPLASTY
perform .... OPERATE

skull .... CRANIOTOMY
specialty division .... ORAL, NEURO, PLASTIC, COSMETIC, GYNECOLOGY, OBSTETRICS, ORTHOPEDICS, OPHTHALMOLOGY
starter .... MICRO, NEURO
suffix meaning reshaping by .... PLASTY
technique, plastic .... IMPLANT, BONE GRAFT, SKIN GRAFT
testis removal .... ORCHIECTOMY
to correct infertility .... TUBOPLASTY
to improve appearance .... COSMETIC
to repair eardrum .... TYMPANOPLASTY
to replace a diseased organ .... TRANSPLANT
uterus removal .... HYSTERECTOMY
voice box ..... LARYNGECTOMY
windpipe ...... TRACHEOSTOMY
surgical appliance .... BRACES, CRUTCH, SPLINT, COLOSTOMY BAG
compress ..... STUPE, ICE PACK
cut .... INCISION
electronic device .... PACEMAKER
incision, closing of .... STAPLING, SUTURING
instrument ...... FLEAM, PROBE, LANCE(T), NEEDLE, STYLET, TREPAN, TROCAR, LEVATOR, SCALPEL, SYRINGE, BISTOURY, OTOSCOPE, SPECULUM, TREPHINE, OSTEOTOME
instrument to hold incision open .... RETRACTOR
knife .... FLEAM, LANCET, SCALPEL, BISTOURY, PHLEBOTOME
operation .... RESECT, EXCISION, PROCEDURE
operation, brain .... LOBOTOMY
operation: comb. form .... TOMY
operation, common .... BIOPSY, COLECTOMY, MASTECTOMY, APPENDECTOMY, HERNIA REPAIR
operation to relieve pressure in muscles .... FASCIOTOMY
pad .... SWAB, SPONGE

painkiller .... ANESTHESIA
pincers/extractor ...... FORCEPS
removal of diseased tissue or
    body part .... ABLATION
stitch .... SETON, SUTURE,
    STAPLING
thread .... WIRE, CATGUT,
    LIGATURE
wound plug .... TAMPON
Suribachi, site of .... IWO JIMA
suricate, kin of .... CIVET,
    MONGOOSE
Surinam capital .... PARAMARIBO
city/town .... ALBINA,
    MOENGO, DOMBURG, TOTNESS,
    CALCUTTA, LELYDORP
district .... PARA, CORONIE,
    NICKERIE, PARAMARIBO
governor of .... VRIES
lake .... BLOMMESTEIN
language .... DUTCH, HINDI
monetary unit .... GUILDER
mountain .... JULIANATOP
mountain range .... LELY,
    KAYSER, ORANGE,
    WILHELMINA
prime minister .... PENGEL
river .... LITANI, COTTICA,
    COEROENI, NICKERIE,
    SURINAME, SARAMACCA
toad .... PIPA
tree .... BALATA
surly .... RUDE, CROSS, GRUFF,
    SULKY, CRUSTY, GRUMPY,
    MOROSE, SULLEN, BOORISH,
    UNCIVIL, ARROGANT,
    CHURLISH
surmise ...... GUESS, INFER, OPINE,
    IMAGINE, PRESUME, SUPPOSE,
    SUSPECT, CONJECTURE
surmount ...... CAP, TOP, CROWN,
    SCALE, EXCEED, HURDLE,
    MASTER, CONQUER, SURPASS,
    OVERCOME
surmounting .... ATOP
surname .... AGNOMEN,
    COGNOMEN, FAMILY NAME,
    PATRONYMIC
surpass .... CAP, TOP, BEST,
    EXCEL, OUTDO, BETTER,
    EXCEED, ECLIPSE, OUTCLASS,
    OUTSHINE, OUTSTRIP,
    TRANSCEND
in marketing .... OUTSELL
surpassing .... PEERLESS,
    EXCELLENT, MATCHLESS,
    UNMATCHED, CONSUMMATE
surplice .... GOWN, COTTA
vestment like .... ROCHET
surplus ...... GLUT, EXTRA, SPARE,
    EXCESS, BALANCE, RESERVE,

OVER(AGE), RESIDUE,
    REMAINDER, OVERSUPPLY
value .... PROFIT
surprise .... AWE, DAZE, JOLT,
    STUN, TURN, AMAZE, SHOCK,
    DAZZLE, WONDER, ASTOUND,
    STARTLE, ASTONISH,
    DUMBFOUND, EYE-OPENER,
    FLABBERGAST,
    CATCH(NAPPING)
attack .... RAID
surprised .... UNWARNED,
    UNSUSPECTING
surpriser's cry .... AHA
surprising .... SUDDEN,
    UNEXPECTED, UNFORESEEN,
    THUNDERCLAP
**Surratt, first woman hanged in
U.S.** .... MARY
surrealist painter .... DALI
surrender ...... CEDE, YIELD, GIVE
    UP, REMISE, RESIGN, SUBMIT,
    CESSION, SUBMISSION
a citizenship .... RENOUNCE
a throne .... RELINQUISH
conditionally .... CAPITULATE
sign of .... HANDS UP, WHITE
    FLAG
surreptitious .... SLY, COVERT,
    SECRET, SNEAKY, BOOTLEG,
    FURITVE, STEALTHY,
    DECEITFUL, UNDERCOVER,
    CLANDESTINE
surrey .... CARRIAGE
Surrey village .... KEW
surrogate .... JUDGE, DEPUTY,
    STAND-IN, SUBSTITUTE
concern of .... WILLS
surround .... LAP, GIRT, RING,
    INVEST, WRAP, BESET,
    HEM(IN), CORRAL, ENFOLD,
    GIRD(LE), BESIEGE, EMBRACE,
    ENCLOSE, ENVELOP, ENVIRON,
    (EN)CIRCLE, BELEAGUER,
    ENCOMPASS
surrounded (by) .... AMID
surrounding .... MIDST, MILIEU,
    AMBIENT, SETTING,
    ENVIRONMENT,
    CIRCUMSTANCE
surtax .... DUTY, LEVY
surtout .... (OVER)COAT
surveillance ...... WATCH, PATROL,
    SCRUTINY, VIGILANCE,
    OBSERVATION
slang .... STAKEOUT
survey ...... POLL, VIEW, LOOK AT,
    EXAMINE, INSPECT, CANVASS,
    MEASURE, APPRAISE
surveying instrument ...... LEVEL,
    ALIDADE, CALIPER, TRANSIT,

STADIA(ROD), VERNIER,
    TACHYMETER, THEODOLITE
method .... STADIA, DIALING
personnel .... RODMEN
surveyor's assistant .... RODMAN,
    LINEMAN
map .... PLAT
transit .... STADIA
survive .... ABIDE, ENDURE,
    REMAIN, (OUT)LAST,
    (OUT)LIVE, WEATHER
surviving .... LEFT, REMANENT
survivor .... ORPHAN, RELICT,
    WIDOW(ER)
Susa, location of .... ELAM, IRAN
Susan, diminutive of .... SUE,
    SUZY, SUSIE
susceptibilities .... EMOTIONS,
    FEELINGS, PASSIONS,
    SENTIMENTS
susceptible .... SOFT, LIABLE,
    OPEN TO, ALLERGIC,
    RECEPTIVE, SENSITIVE,
    RESPONSIVE
to attack .... VULNERABLE
to mistake .... FALLIBLE
suslik .... SISEL, GOPHER,
    SQUIRREL, SPERMOPHILE
suspect .... INFER, ACCUSED,
    IMAGINE, PRESUME, SUPPOSE,
    SURMISE, DISTRUST,
    MISTRUST, PRISONER,
    QUESTIONABLE
suspect's defense .... ALIBI
suspecting .... SHY, WARY, LEERY,
    SKEPTICAL
suspend ...... HALT, HANG, HOLD,
    STOP, DEBAR, DEFER,
    DANGLE, RECESS, ADJOURN,
    EXCLUDE, POSTPONE,
    INTERRUPT
suspended .... HUNG, UNUSED,
    HANGING, PENDANT, PENDENT,
    PENDING, PENSILE
suspenders .... BRACERS,
    GARTERS, HANGERS,
    GALLUSES
suspense .... PAUSE, STRAIN,
    ANXIETY, TENSION,
    ABEYANCE, INACTION
suspenseful .... AGAPE, TENSE,
    ANXIOUS, ALL AGOG,
    APPREHENSIVE
suspension .... DELAY, PAUSE,
    ABEYANCE, PENDENCY,
    STOPPAGE, CESSATION,
    POSTPONEMENT
of court sentence
    .... PROBATION
of hostilities .... TRUCE,
    ARMISTICE

of proceedings .... RECESS, ADJOURNMENT
suspicion .... FEAR, HINT, DOUBT, HUNCH, SHADE, TRACE, ANXIETY, INKLING, MISTRUST, MISGIVING
emotional .... JEALOUSY
suspicious .... LEERY, DUBIOUS, ENVIOUS, FEARFUL, JEALOUS, DOUBTFUL, PARANOID, WATCHFUL, CONCERNED, SKEPTICAL
one .... ALARMIST, PARANOIAC, PESSIMIST
suspiration .... SIGH
Susskind, TV man .... DAVID
sustain .... BUOY, ASSIST, ENDURE, RATIFY, SUFFER, UPHOLD, CONFIRM, NOURISH, PROLONG, SUPPORT, MAINTAIN
sustenance .... FOOD, BREAD, UPKEEP, ALIMENT, SUPPORT, NUTRITION, PROVISION, SUBSISTENCE
susu .... DOLPHIN
domain .... INDUS, GANGES
susurrant .... RUSTLING, MURMURING, MUTTERING, WHISPERING
susurration/susurrus .... DRONE, JABBER, MUMBLE, MURMUR, MUTTER, RUSTLE, WHISPER
sutler .... MERCHANT, TRADESMAN, VICTUAL(L)ER
customer of .... SOLDIER
sutor .... BOOTER, SOUTER, COBBLER
sutra .... TEXT, VERSE, DISTICH
suttee .... SUICIDE, SACRIFICE, SELF-CREMATION, (SELF)IMMOLATION
suture .... SEW, SEAM, RAPHE, JOINT, STITCH, CLOSURE, JUNCTION
relating to a .... SUTURAL
suzerain .... LORD, LIEGE, RULER, SOVEREIGN
svelte .... SLIM, LITHE, SLINKY, GIRLISH, LISSOM(E), SLENDER, WILLOWY, WASP-WAISTED
Svengali .... HYPNOTIST, MESMERIST, HYPNOTIZER
Sverige .... SWEDEN
neighbor of .... NORGE
swab ...... DAB, MOP, DAUB, WIPE, Q-TIP, BRUSH, SCRUB, MALKIN, SPONGE, CLEANSE
swabbie .... GOB
swaddle .... BIND, TAPE, WRAP, CLOTHE, SWATHE, BANDAGE
swaddling clothes .... DUDS, BANDS

swag .... CANT, LIST, REEL, ROCK, SWAY, LURCH, DANGLE, FESTOON
slang ..... HAUL, LOOT, BOOTY, SPOILS, PLUNDER
swage .... DIE, STAMP
swagger .... BLUFF, BOAST, BULLY, STALK, STRUT, PRANCE, RUFFLE, BLUSTER, FLOUNCE, ROISTER
garment .... (SPORTS)COAT
swaggerer .... BRAVO, BUCKO, BULLY, PEACOCK, SWASHER, STRUTTER, SWASHBUCKLER
swaggering .... SWASH(ING), BOISTEROUS
Swahili .... BANTU
cheer word .... HARAMBEE
swain .... BEAU, LOVER, YOUTH, FELLOW, SUITOR, (E)SQUIRE, GALLANT, CAVALIER, BOYFRIEND
swallow .... BEAR, BIRD, BOLT, GULP, TERN, QUAFF, ABSORB, ACCEPT, DEVOUR, ENDURE, ENGULF, INGEST, TAKE IN, CONSUME, ENVELOP, RETRACT
bird like a ..... SWIFT, MARTIN, NIGHTJAR, STARLING
genus ...... HIRUNDO, PHEDINA, RIPARIA, PETROCHELIDON
greedily .... GORGE, DEVOUR
like .... HIRUNDINE
well known species of .... PURPLE MARTIN
swallowing difficulty .... DYSPHAGIA
swallowtail .... COAT, BUTTERFLY
swallowwort .... CELANDINE
family .... MILKWEED
swami ...... LORD, FAKIR, EXPERT, MASTER, PUNDIT, TEACHER
swamp .... BOG, FEN, MOOR, SINK, SOAK, FLOOD, MARSH, DELUGE, DRENCH, MORASS, IMMERSE, SLOUGH, WETLAND, INUNDATE, (QUAG)MIRE, OVERWHELM
air .... MIASMA, MALARIA
bird .... ROBIN, TOWHEE, REDWING, SPARROW
fever .... MALARIA
flower .... AZALEA, HONEYSUCKLE
forest site .... FLORIDA, GEORGIA
plant .... SOLA, COWSLIP, MAGNOLIA, MARIGOLD
trees .... MANGROVE
vapor ..... MIASM(A), MEPHETIS

Swamp Fox soubriquet .... MARION
swamped .... FLOODED, WHELMED, GROUNDED, SNOWED UNDER
swampland .... EVERGLADES
swamps .... SLEW, WETLAND, EVERGLADES, OVERSUPPLY
denizen of .... ALLIGATOR
swampy .... BOGGY, FENNY, MOIST, MARSHY, PALUDAL
area .... SLASH
region .... FLORIDA, GEORGIA
swan .... ANSA, BIRD, BARD, POET, SWEAR, WHOOPER, COSCOROBA, TRUMPETER, WATERFOWL
black-necked .... MELANOCORYPHUS
constellation .... CYGNUS
family .... ANATIDAE
female .... PEN
goose .... CYGNOIDES
largest .... CYGNUS OLOR
like a .... PURE, GRACEFUL
lover .... LEDA
male .... COB
mute .... CYGNUS OLOR
relative .... DUCK, GOOSE
song .... VALEDICTORY
sub-family .... ANSERINAE
trumpeter .... BUCCINATOR
whistling .... COLUMBIANUS
young .... CYGNET
Swan Lake role .... ODILE
swanky ...... POSH, FANCY, PLUSH, SHOWY, SMART, STYLISH
slang .... RITZY
swap .... TRADE, BARTER, EXCHANGE
swaraj .... HOME RULE
sward .... SOD, LAWN, TURF
swarm .... HIVE, HOST, NEST, TEEM, CROWD, GROUP, HORDE, COLONY, THRONG, CLUSTER, MIGRATE, OVERRUN, ASSEMBLE, MULTITUDE
cell .... ZOOSPORE
of birds .... FLOCK
of locusts .... CLOUD
off .... LEAVE, MIGRATE
up a tree .... SHIN
with .... INFEST, PLAGUE
swarmer .... ANT, BEE, INSECT, LOCUST
swarming .... TEEMING
swart(hy) .... DUN, DUSKY, DARK(-COMPLEXIONED)
swash ...... DASH, STRUT, PRANCE, SPLASH, SWAGGER
swashbuckling .... DARING

swastika .... FYLFOT, GAMMADION

swat .... HIT, RAP, BLOW, CLIP, SLAP, SLUG, CLOUT, WHACK

Swat, King of .... (BABE) RUTH

SWAT, part of .... SPECIAL, WEAPONS, ATTACK, TEAM

swatch .... SAMPLE, SPECIMEN

swath .... TIER, QUEUE, STRIP, TRACK, STRING, (WIND)ROW

swathe .... BIND, CLOTHE, BANDAGE, ENVELOP, SWADDLE, WRAP(PING)

sway .... BIAS, REEL, ROCK, RULE, VEER, WARP, LURCH, POWER, SWING, DANGLE, DIRECT, CONTROL, DOMINION, FLOUNDER, FLUCTUATE, OSCILLATE

swayback .... SAG, CURVATURE

sweal .... BURN, MELT(AWAY), WASTE(AWAY)

swear ...... (A)VOW, CUSS, CURSE, AFFIRM, DEPONE, DEPOSE, PLEDGE, PROMISE, BLASPHEME

by .... BET ON, TRUST

falsely .... PERJURE

in court ...... TESTIFY, WITNESS

off .... GIVE UP, ABANDON, RENOUNCE

to .... VOUCH, ATTEST, CERTIFY

word .... VOW, CUSS, OATH, CURSE, EXPLETIVE, BLASPHEMY, PROFANITY

words .... I DO

swearing .... JURANT, OATH-TAKING

sweat .... WET, BEAD, DRIP, HEAT, OOZE, SEEP, EXUDE, SUDOR, EGESTA, LATHER, EXCRETE, FERMENT, SWELTER, EXERCISE, OVERWORK, PERSPIRE, TRANSUDE, PERSPIRATION

causing .... HIDROTIC

colloquial .... STEW

drenched with .... CLAMMY, SWEATY, WILTED, SWELTER

it out .... STICK IT OUT, AWAIT(ANXIOUSLY)

no .... NO EFFORT, NO PROBLEM, NO TROUBLE

shirt .... JERSEY

sweater .... JERSEY, SLIP-ON, CARDIGAN, GUERNSEY, KNITWEAR, PULLOVER, SUDORIFIC

sweating .... SLAVING, TOILING

sweaty .... PERSPIRY, TOILSOME, LABORIOUS

Sweden .... SVERIGE

bay .... HANOBUKTEN

canal .... GOTA

capital .... STOCKHOLM

city/town .... LUND, ORSA, TABY, UMEA, BODEN, BORAS, ESLOV, FALUN, GAVLE, LULEA, MALMO, VAXJO, VISBY, YSTAD, AVESTA, OREBRO, LIDINGO, UPPSALA, BORLANGE, GOTEBORG, HALMSTAD, HUDDINGE, VASTERAS, JONKOPING, LINKOPING, OSTERSUND, SUNDSVAIL, NORRKOPING, HELSINGBORG

county .... KALMAR, OREBRO, HALLAND, UPPSALA, ALVSBORG, GOTEBORG, MALMOHUS, VARMLAND, JONKOPING, KRONOBERG, STOCKHOLM

gulf .... BOTHNIA

island .... FARO, ORNO, GRASO, OLAND, GOTLAND

lake .... ASNEN, BOLMEN, SILJAN, SOMMEN, VANERN, MALAREN, UDDJAUR, VATTERN, STORSJON, HJALMAREN

mountain .... SULITELMA, KEBNEKAISE

mountain range .... K(J)OLEN

peninsula .... HORNSLANDET

region .... LAPLAND

river .... GOTA, UME(ALV), KLAR(ALV), LJUSNAN, LULE(ALV), PITE(ALV), DALALVEN, KALIX(ALV), TORNE(ALV), MUONIO(ALV)

sea .... BALTIC

seaport .... MALMO, VISBY, KALMAR, GOTEBORG, HELSINGBORG

sound .... ORESUND, KALMARSUND

strait .... KATTEGAT, SKAGERRAK

Swedish .... LANGUAGE

balloonist, North Pole casualty .... ANDREE

clover .... ALSIKE

coin ..... ORE, CROWN, KRONA, KRONE(R), KRONOR

district .... LA(E)N

dwelling/hut .... CHALET

explorer .... HEDIN

farm .... TORP

hero .... WASA

import .... SAAB

island resident .... OLANDER, GOTLANDER

king .... ERIC, GUSTAV, BERNADOTTE

manual training .... SLOYD

measure, area .... MORGEN

measure, distance/length .... ALN, FOT, REF, FAMN

measure, liquid .... AM(AR), KAPP

monetary unit .... KRONA

native .... LAPP, SWEDE

"nightingale" .... (JENNY)LIND

Nobel Prize winner .... LAGERLOF

noble's title .... GRAF

novelist .... LAGERLOF

painter .... ZORN

parliament .... RIKSDAG

prime minister ...... ERLANDER

prime minister murdered 1985 .... PALME

rug .... RYA

ruler of Kiev .... OLEG

singer .... YODLER, YODEL(L)ER

soprano .... LIND, NILSSON

thimble .... FINGERBORG

turnip .... RUTABAGA

weight .... ASS, ORT, PUND, STEN, UNTZ, NYLAST

sweeny .... ATROPHY

sweep .... OAR, BLOW, DRAG, DUST, PUSH, RAKE, SKIM, SCAN, BROOM, BRUSH, CLEAN, CLEAR, GLIDE, IMPEL, RANGE, TRAIL, STRETCH

away .... REMOVE

out .... CLEAN, EJECT, UNCLOG, VACUUM

sweeper .... WHITEWING

sweeping .... BROAD, TOTAL, RADICAL, EXTENSIVE, WIDE(-RANGING)

blow .... SWIPE

movement .... SWOOP

sweepstakes .... DRAW, RAFFLE, LOTTERY, (HORSE)RACE

sweet ...... LUSH, CANDY, DULCET, SIRUPY, SUGARY, CANDIED, LUSCIOUS, HONEY(ED), PLEASANT, SUGAR-COATED

and soft .... DOLCE

anise .... FENNEL, FINOCCHIO

bay .... MAGNOLIA

chervil .... ANISE

cicely .... MYRRH, PARSLEY

clover .... MELILOT

drink .... PUNCH, NECTAR

flag .... SEDGE, CALAMUS

gum .... BALSAM, COPALM, BILSTED, LIQUIDAMBAR

liqueur .... CREME, CORDIAL, RATAFIA

natured .... DOUCE, GENTLE

nothings .... BLARNEY,
FLATTERY, FLUMMERY

pepper ...... PAPRIKA, PIMIENTO

potato .... YAM, BATATA,
CAMOTE, OCARINA

sap source .... GOMUTI

smelling .... OLENT, ODOROUS,
FRAGRANT

sound .... MUSIC, MELODY

sounding .... DULCET,
MELODIC, MUSICAL,
MELODIOUS

stream .... AFTON

talk .... URGE, CAJOLE, SOFT-
SOAP

tempered .... GENIAL,
AFFABLE, AMIABLE, CORDIAL

Sweet, actress .... BLANCHE

sweetbread .... RUSK, THYMUS,
PANCREAS

sweetbriar ...... ROSE, EGLANTINE

sweeten .... CANDY, GLAZE,
FRESHEN, DULCIFY,
SUGARCOAT

and spice .... MULL

the pot .... RAISE

sweetened drink ...... FLIP, JULEP

sweetener .... SUGAR, SYRUP,
REWARD, GLUCOSE, SUCARYL,
SUCROSE, ASPARTAME,
CYCLAMATE, INCENTIVE,
SACCHARIN

sweetening .... HONEY, SIRUP,
SUGAR, SYRUP, MOLASSES,
STIMULUS

sweetheart ...... JO(E), GIRL, JILL,
LOVE, AMOUR, DEAR(Y),
LEMAN, LOVER, POPSY,
LASS(IE), SUITOR, BELOVED,
LADYLOVE, TRUELOVE,
VALENTINE

colloquial .... BEAU, SWAIN,
DARLING, BOY FRIEND, GIRL
FRIEND

idealized .... DULCINEA

in pastoral poetry ..... PHILLIS,
PHYLLIS

slang .... GAL, FLAME,
FELLOW, STEADY,
HONEY(BUNCH), SWEETIE(PIE),
LOLLAPALOOSA

sweetly .... BONHOMOUSLY

sweetmeat(s) .... CAKE, MINT,
CANDY, TAFFY, BONBON,
COMFIT, DRAGEE, JUJUBE,
NOUGAT, TOFFEE, CARAMEL,
LICORICE, PRESERVE,
CONFECTION

sweetness .... HONEY, SUGAR,
NECTAR

sweetsop .... ATES, ATTA

swell .... GROW, HUFF, RISE, SNOB,
WAVE, BLOAT, BULGE, HEAVE,
SURGE, BILLOW, DILATE,
EXPAND, PUFF(UP), TUMEFY,
DISTEND, INFLATE, INTUMESCE

box .... ORGAN

colloquial .... FOP, CHIC,
NATTY, NOBBY, DAPPER,
STYLISH, EXCELLENT

dresser .... FOP, DUDE, TOFF,
DANDY, SPARK, BRUMMEL

in the ground .... LIFT

sea .... SURF

slang .... COOL, DANDY,
GREAT, GROOVY

the pot .... RAISE

with water .... BLOAT

swelled .... TUMID, TURGID,
SWOLLEN

swellfish .... PUFFER

swellhead .... EGOTIST,
BRAGGART, NARCISSIST

swellheaded .... COCKY, STUCK
UP, PUFFED UP, BOASTFUL,
CONCEITED

swelling .... BLEB, BUMP, LUMP,
NODE, PUFF, BULGE, EDEMA,
TORUS, TUMOR, GOITER,
GROWTH, TUMESCENT,
TURGESCENCE

armpit/groin .... BUBO

combining form .... C(O)ELE

foot .... CHILBLAIN

harmony .... DIAPASON

pertaining to a .... NODAL

wave .... ROLLER

swelter ...... HEAT, ROAST, SWEAT,
SCORCH, PERSPIRE

sweltering .... HOT, HEATED,
SULTRY, TORRID, SIZZLING

swerve .... SKEW, VEER, DODGE,
SHEER, SHIFT, STRAY,
CAREEN, DEFLECT, DEVIATE,
DIVERGE

away .... SHY

swift .... BIRD, FAST, ALERT,
FLEET, QUICK, RAPID,
PROMPT, SPEEDY

combining form .... TACHY

footed animal .... DEER,
GAZELLE

footed maiden ...... ATALANTA

footed reptile .... IGUANA,
LIZARD

ride .... TANTIVY

runner of myth ..... ATALANTA

rush .... WHOOSH

Swift, satirist .... JONATHAN

swiften .... HASTEN

swiftly .... APACE

swiftness .... HASTE, SPEED,
VELOCITY

Swift's ''flying island''
.... LAPUTA

hero .... GULLIVER

imaginary island ...... LILLIPUT

name for himself .... CADENUS

pen name .... DRAPIER

swig .... GULP, DRINK, SWILL,
GUZZLE

swiler .... SEALER

swill .... GULP, MESS, SOAK,
DRINK, FILTH, OFFAL, QUAFF,
SLOP(S), SLOSH, WASTE,
GARBAGE, (HOG)WASH,
SWALLOW, OUT-RINSE

swim .... DIP, KICK, REEL, BATHE,
CRAWL, FLOAT, STEEP,
SWOON, WHIRL, PADDLE,
STROKE, (FEEL)DIZZY

in the nude .... SKINNY-DIP

of things, in the .... FLOW,
STREAM, CURRENT

with the stream .... GO WITH
THE TIDE

swimmer .... FISH, NAIAD,
MERMAN, MERMAID, NATATOR

swimmer's ear .... OTITIS-
EXTERNA

swimming .... CTENE, NATANT,
AQUATICS

act of ..... BATHING, NATATION

bird .... DUCK, LOON, SWAN

of the head .... VERTIGO

pool .... TANK, WATERHOLE,
NATATORIUM

stroke/style .... CRAWL,
PADDLE, FLOATING,
BUTTERFLY, BACKSTROKE,
SIDESTROKE, BREASTSTROKE

suit .... BIKINI, MAILLOT

swimmingly ...... EASILY, SIMPLY,
LIGHTLY, SUCCESSFULLY

swimmy .... DIZZY, GIDDY,
BLURRED

Swinburne, poet ...... ALGERNON

swindle .... CON, GIP, GYP, ROB,
BILK, CLIP, GULL, HOAX,
ROOK, SKIN, BUNCO, BUNKO,
CHEAT, COZEN, FUDGE,
GOUGE, TRICK, WELSH,
DIDDLE, FLEECE, (DE)FRAUD,
VICTIMIZE, HORNSWOGGLE

sheet: sl. .... EXPENSE
ACCOUNT

slang .... GYP, SCAM

swindler .... HAWK, CHEAT,
(C)ROOK, FAKER, GOUGE,
SHARK, THIEF, BILKER,
CONMAN, FORGER, GYPPER,
JACKAL, TREPAN, COZENER,

SHARPER, SKIN(NER), BLACKLEG, TRICKSTER
swindling scheme .... PLANT
swine .... HOG, PIG, PORCINE
breed .... DUROC, CHESTER, CHESHIRE, LANDRACE, TAMWORTH, BERKSHIRE, HAMPSHIRE, YORKSHIRE
characteristic of ...... PORCINE, SWINISH
colloquial .... SLOB, SLUT, SLOVEN, SLATTERN
disease .... GARGET, ROUGET
disease, infectious .... POX, PLAGUE
feeding of .... PANNAGE
female .... SOW
fever .... CHOLERA
flesh .... PORK
flu .... INFLUENZA
genus .... SUS
litter of .... FARROW
male .... BOAR
tender ..... HOGHERD, PIGHERD, SWINEHERD
wild .... PECCARY
young .... PIGLET, PORKER
swinelike .... PORCINE
swing .... FLAP, HANG, LILT, REEL, SWAY, TURN, WAVE, LURCH, CAREEN, RHYTHM, SWITCH, (WIG)WAG, STRETCH, BRANDISH, OSCILLATE
and miss .... STRIKE
around ...... SLUE, SPIN, PIVOT, SWIVEL
at .... FLAIL, SWIPE, THRUST
fan .... HEPCAT
in full .... ABSOLUTE, CAREFREE, UNCHAINED, UNRESTRAINED
music .... JAZZ, JIVE
the deal .... PUT OVER, PUT THROUGH
vote .... NEUTRAL
swinge .... BEAT, FLOG, LASH, WHIP
swinger .... JET-SETTER
swinging .... PENDULOUS
swingle .... SWIP(P)LE
swingman Goodman ...... BENNY
swingy .... JAZZY
swinish .... DIRTY, COARSE, FILTHY, GREEDY, HOGGISH, PIGGISH
swink .... TOIL, LABOR, SLAVE, DRUDGE, OVERWORK
swipe .... HIT, BLOW, GLOM, LIFT, CRACK, FILCH, LEVER, SMACK, STEAL, WHACK, PILFER, SNATCH, STRIKE,

THWACK
swipes .... BEER
swip(p)le .... FLAIL, SWINGLE
swirl .... CURL, EDDY, PURL, STIR, GURGE, SURGE, TWIRL, TWIST, WHIRL, WHORL
swirling ...... TURNING, GYRATION, ROTATION
aircraft .... HELICOPTER
hub .... PROPELLER
mass of water .... VORTEX, WHIRLPOOL
movement .... EDDY, TWIST, WHIRL
object .... WINDMILL
part of motor .... ROTOR
toy .... TOP, WHIRLIGIG
windstorm .... TORNADO
swirly .... KNOTTY, GNARLED, KNOTTED, TANGLED, TWISTED
swish .... CANE, FLOG, WHIP, SLOSH, RUSTLE, SPLASH, WHOOSH
swishy: sl. .... EFFEMINATE
Swiss architect .... (LE)CORBUSIER
army .... LANDWEHR
cake .... JELLYROLL
castle .... CHILLON
chard .... BEET
cheese .... GRUYERE, SAPSAGO, RACLETTE, EMMENTHALER
coin ...... BATZ, FRANC, RAPPE, CENTIME
cottage .... CHALET
district .... CANTON
Family Robinson author .... WYSS
federal council .... BUNDESRAT
herdsman .... SENN
highest Alp .... BLANC
Italian enclave .... CAMPIONE
Italian-speaking canton .... TICINO
language .... FRENCH, GERMAN, ITALIAN, ROMANS(C)H
largest city .... ZURICH
man of story .... TELL
mathematician .... EULER
measure ...... POT, AUNE, FUSS, IMMI, MUID, PIED, SAUM, ZOLL, POUCE, SCHUH, STAAB, TOISE, PERCHE, SETIER, KLAFTER
mercenary soldier .... SWISSER, SWITZER
money .... FRANC
mountaineer's horn .... ALP(EN)HORN
national flower ..... EDELWEISS
native .... BRISON, VAUDOIS

Nobel Prize winner, medicine .... KOCHER
painter .... KLEE
patroit .... ZWINGLI
plant .... EDELWEISS
political division ...... CANTON
president .... BONVIN
Protestant .... HELVETIC
psychologist .... JUNG
resort .... YVERDON, INTERLAKEN
Rhine port .... BASEL, BASLE
scientist .... HALLER
shepherd .... SENN
sled .... LUGE
song .... YODEL
state .... CANTON
state council .... STANDERAT
union .... SONDERBUND
wind .... BISE
Swisser .... SWITZER
switch .... ROD, CANE, LASH, TURN, TWIG, WHIP, BIRCH, SHIFT, SHUNT, SPRAY, SPRIG, STICK, DIVERT, RAT(T)AN, TOGGLE, DEFLECT, HICKORY, (EX)CHANGE, TRANSFER, TRANSPOSE
blade knife .... SHIV
position .... ON, OFF, LOW, MED, HIGH
switchback ...... ROLLER COASTER
switchboard feature .... PLUG, PANEL
switchman .... SHUNTER
Switzerland .... SUISSE, HELVETIA
canton .... URI, ZUG, BERN, JURA, VAUD, AARGAU, GENEVA, GLARUS, LUZERN, SCHWYZ, TICINO, VALAIS, ZURICH, GRISONS, LUCERNE, SOLEURE, THURGAU, FRIBOURG, BASELLAND, NEUCHATEL, SOLOTHURN, BASELSTADT
capital of .... BERN(E)
city/town .... EGG, WIL, ZUG, ARTH, BIEL, CHUR, ELGG, NYON, THUN, VISP, WALD, WORB, ZOUZ, AARAU, ARBON, BADEN, BASEL, DAVOS, EMMEN, KONIZ, LANCY, PULLY, USTER, VEVEY, GENEVA, HORGEN, LUGANO, LUZERN, MORGES, RENENS, RIEHEN, WOHLEN, ZURICH, CAROUGE, HERISAU, LIESTAL, LOCARNO, LUCERNE, SOLEURE, YVERDON, BURGDORF, FRIBOURG, GRENCHEN, LAUSANNE, MONTREUX,

DUBENDORF, NEUCHATEL, RORSCHACH, WINTERTHUR
lake .... SIHL, AGERI, BODEN, LEMAN, MORAT, UNTER, ZUGER, BIELER, GENEVA, LUGANO, SARNEN, THUNER, ZELLER, ZURICH, GREIFEN, LUCERNE, SEMPACH, BRIENZER, MAGGIORE, CONSTANCE
mountain .... DOM, NAPF, RIGI, ROSA, TODI, JORAT, LEONE, VELAN, VORAB, DOLENT, HORNLI, LA DOLE, OCHSEN, RISOUX, SANTIS, TAMARO, TITLIS, MUTTLER, PILATUS, ROTHORN, BALMHORN, CLARIDEN, GENEROSO, HOCHWANG, JUNGFRAU, NAAFKOPF, NOIRMONT, OFENHORN, ROSSTOCK, BREITHORN, CHASSERON, GLARNISCH, KAISEREGG, MARMONTANA, MATTERHORN
mountain pass .... OFEN, FURKA, FLUELA, GREINA, PRAGEL, SUSTEN, BERNINA, GRIMSEL, OBERALP, SIMPLON, SPLUGEN, SEPTIMER
mountains .... JURA, LINDEN, BUCHEGG, RHATIKON, SILVRETTA, GLARUS ALPS
peak .... ERR, AULT, BUIN, KESCH, TERRI, LINARD, TENDRE, VADRET, BERNINA, UMBRAIL, SESVENNA
range .... PENNINE ALPS, RHAETIAN ALPS, LEPONTINE ALPS
region .... UNTERWALDEN, BERNESE-OBERLAND
river ...... AA, INN, AARE, BIRS, ORBE, SEEZ, THUR, TOSS, VISP, BROYE, DOUBS, LINTH, MOESA, MUOTA, REUSS, RHINE, RHONE, SAANE, SIMME, BORGNE, DRANCE, LAMMAT, MAGGIA, SARINE, TAMINO, TICINO, PLESSUR, EMMENTAL, LANDQUART, HINTERRHEIN
tunnel .... SIMPLON, LOTSCHBERG, SAINT GOTTHARD
valley .... DAVOS, ENGADINE
swivel .... TURN, VEER, PIVOT, SWING, ROTATE
swivet .... DITHER, FRENZY
in a .... AGOG
swizzle .... STIR
stick .... STIRRER
swollen .... BLOWN, PUFFY, TUMID,

BOLLEN, EDEMIC, TOROSE, TOROUS, TURGID, BLOATED, BULGING, TURGENT, ENLARGED, VARICOSE, DISTENDED
swoon .... SYNCOPE, FAINT(ING)
swoop .... FLY, DIVE, CLUTCH, PLUNGE, POUNCE, SNATCH, DESCEND, DESCENT, SWEEP UP, CARRY OFF
sword ...... BLADE, ESTOC, SABER, SKEAN, GLA(I)VE, RAPIER, ATAGHAN, CUTLAS(S), FALCHION, SCIMITAR
archaic .... TUCK, BILBO, GLAIVE
belt .... BALDRIC
blade, weaker part of
.... FOIBLE
bullfighter's .... ESTOQUE
cavalry .... SABER, SABRE
curved .... SABER, CUTLASS, SCIMITAR
fencing .... EPEE, FOIL
fine-tempered .... TOLEDO
grass .... SEDGE
handle .... HAFT, HILT
Highlander's .... CLAYMORE
hilt's knob .... POMMEL
legendary .... BALMUNG, EXCALIBUR
lily .... GLADIOLUS
poetic .... STEEL
pointless/duelling .... EPEE
put to the .... KILL, SLAUGHTER
shaped .... ENSATE, XIPHOID, ENSIFORM, GLADIATE
short .... ESTOC, SKEAN
Siegfried's .... BALMUNG
St. George's .... ASCALON
strongest part of .... FORTE
thin .... TUCK, RAPIER
swordfish .... AUS, DORADO
saw of .... SERRA
swordplay .... FENCING
swords, cross .... DUEL, FIGHT
swordsman .... BLADE, FENCER
sworn .... BOUND, PLEDGED, ATTESTED, PROMISED, CERTIFIED
statement .... AFFIDAVIT, TESTIMONY, DEPOSITION
word .... VOW, OATH
swound .... FAINT, SWOON
sybarite ...... EPICURE, HEDONIST, SENSUALIST, VOLUPTUARY
sybarite's delight .... EASE, LUXURY
sycamine .... MULBERRY
sycamore .... BUTTONWOOD

syce .... GROOM, ATTENDANT
sycee .... SILVER
syconium .... FIG
sycophant .... TOADY, FAWNER, YES-MAN, FLUNK(E)Y, SPANIEL, HANGER-ON, PARASITE, FLATTERER, TOADEATER, BOOTLICKER, COOKIE PUSHER
sycophantic .... PARASITIC(AL)
sycosis victim .... BEARD
vulgaris .... BARBERS' ITCH
Syene .... ASWAN
syllabic .... SONANT
syllable, accented/unaccented
.... TONIC, THESIS
contraction of a
.... SYNALEPHA
last .... ULTIMA
metrical stress on .... ICTUS
musical .... LA, TRA
omission of last ...... APOCOPE
short .... MORA
shortening of a .... SYSTOL
syllables, contraction of
.... SYNERESIS
syllabus ...... OUTLINE, PROGRAM, SUMMARY, ABSTRACT, SYNOPSIS
syllogism ...... LOGIC, REASONING
major or minor in .... PREMISE
master of .... SOCRATES
middle term of .... MEAN
syllogisms, elliptical series of
.... SORITES
sylph ...... FAIRY, GNOME, UNDINE
sylphlike .... SLIM, THIN, GRACILE, SLENDER, WILLOWY, GRACEFUL
sylvan .... RURAL, WOODY, WOODED, BUCOLIC
area .... WOODS, FOREST
diety .... PAN, SATYR, FAUN(US)
sight .... LEA
symbol. See also **emblem**
.... MARK, SIGN, TOKEN, TOTEM, EMBLEM
American .... EAGLE, UNCLE SAM
bad luck .... OPAL
British .... LION, JOHN BULL
Indian .... TOTEM POLE
Libra's .... SCALES
of achievement .... MEDAL, RIBBON, TROPHY, DIPLOMA
attenuation .... SLAT
authority .... ROD, MACE, BADGE, CROWN, GLOBE, STAFF, SWORD, ENSIGN,

FASCES, SCEPTER
benevolence .... SANTA
CLAUS
birth .... STORK
bondage .... YOKE
comedy .... SOCK
death .... CROSS BONES
excellence .... ACADEMY
AWARD
family authority, once
.... PANTS
fortune/success .... RAINBOW
grief .... RUE
hardness .... NAIL
immortality .... PH(O)ENIX
Michael Arlen heroine
.... GREEN HAT
mourning .... CREPE,
CYPRESS
Ms. Nightingale .... LAMP
office .... VERGE
peace .... DOVE
"plain speaking" ..... SPADE
purity .... LILY
rank .... BADGE
remoteness ,,,,,,,, TIMBUKTU
renewal ..... SNAKE, SERPENT
rigidity .... STEEL
royal power .... ORB,
SCEPTER
saintliness .... HALO
servitude .... YOKE
sovereignty .... MOUND,
URAEUS
strength .... ATLAS, SINEW
sun .... ATEN
swiftness .... BLUE STREAK
sword of Damocles
.... MENACE, THREAT
universe .... MANDALA
victory .... PALM, LAUREL
war .... ARES, MARS
wisdom .... OWL
phallic .... LINGA(M)
physician's .... CADUCEUS
picture used as a
.... PICTOGRAM, PICTOGRAPH
Pope's .... PALLIUM
registered .... TRADEMARK
remembrance .... ROSEMARY
shorthand .... LOGOGRAM
single speech sound
.... PHONOGRAM
status .... MINK, YACHT
suburban status .... POOL
symbolic .... ICONIC, TYPICAL,
EMBLEMATIC, FIGURATIVE
light .... HALO
representation ...... ICONOLOGY
symbolize .... MEAN, IMPLY,

FIGURE, TYPIFY, BETOKEN,
EXPRESS, SIGNIFY, STAND FOR
symmetric(al) ...... EVEN, EQUAL,
ORDERLY, REGULAR, SPHERAL,
BALANCED, PARALLEL
symmetry ...... ORDER, BALANCE,
HARMONY, EURYTHMY,
CONGRUITY, PROPORTION,
UNIFORMITY
many-sided .... MULTILATERAL
of similarity ..... PARALLELISM
three-sided .... TRILATERAL
sympathetic .... KIND, TENDER,
MERCIFUL, AGREEABLE,
CONDOLENT, CONGENIAL,
COMFORTING, COMPASSIONATE
response .... ECHO
sympathize .... CONDOLE, FEEL
FOR, UNDERSTAND,
COMMISERATE
sympathizer .... WELL-WISHER
sympathy .... PITY, RUTH,
ACCORD, CONCORD, EMPATHY,
HARMONY, KINSHIP, RAPPORT,
AFFINITY, GOODWILL,
RESPONSE, COMPASSION
expression of .... CLEMENCY,
CONDOLENCE
symphonic jazz leader
.... WHITEMAN
movement ..... LARGO, FINALE,
STRETTO
symphonize .... HARMONIZE
symphony .... CONCERT,
CONCORD, HARMONY,
SINFONIA
division of .... MOVEMENT
form .... SONATA
intended for Napoleon
.... EROICA
orchestra, particular
.... PHILHARMONIC
orchestra, philharmonic
.... VIENNA, NEW YORK
third section of ...... SCHERZO
symposium .... FEAST, FORUM,
BANQUET, MEETING,
COLLOQUY, GATHERING,
CONFERENCE
kind of .... CONSENSUS
like a .... SYMPOSIAC
purpose .... DISCUSSION
symptom ...... HINT, MARK, SIGN,
TOKEN, WARNING, INDICATION
of illness .... PAIN, FEVER,
PRODROME, TEMPERATURE
of pregnancy, usually
.... MORNING SICKNESS
symptoms appearing together
.... SYNDROME

branch of medicine dealing
with .... SEM(E)IOLOGY
pertaining to ...... SEM(E)IOTIC,
SYMPTOMATIC
synagogue .... SHUL, TEMPLE,
TABERNACLE, CONGREGATION
figure .... RABBI
official .... HAZZAN, PARNAS
singer .... CANTOR, CHAZZAN
synchronize .... JIBE, MESH,
AGREE, MATCH, CONCUR,
COEXIST, COINCIDE,
HARMONIZE, COORDINATE,
CORRESPOND
synchronous .... COEVAL,
COINCIDENT, SIMULTANEOUS
syncopation .... JAZZ, BLUES,
RAGTIME
syncope .... SWOON, ELISION,
FAINTING
syncretize .... COMBINE,
RECONCILE
syncrisis .... CONTRAST
syndic .... JUDGE, MANAGER,
MAGISTRATE
syndicate .... POOL, TRUST,
CARTEL, COMBINE, COUNCIL,
MONOPOLY, CONSORTIUM,
ASSOCIATION
syndrome .... SIGNS, SYMPTOMS
syne .... AGO, SINCE
synergistic .... COACTING,
COACTIVE, CONCURRENT
synergy .... CONCERT,
COINCIDENCE
synod .... COUNCIL, MEETING,
ASSEMBLY, CONCLAVE
synonymous .... SIMILAR,
ANALOGOUS
synopsis ...... GIST, BRIEF, DIGEST,
PRECIS, REVIEW, SUMMARY,
ABSTRACT
synoptic gospel .... LUKE, MARK,
MATTHEW
syntax .... STRUCTURE
synthesis .... BLEND, UNION,
FUSION, MERGER
synthesized by means of light
.... PHOTOSYNTHESIS
synthetic .... SHAM, ERSATZ, MAN-
MADE, IMITATION, ARTIFICIAL
fabric .... NYLON, ORLON,
RAYON, DACRON, ACETATE
organic compound .... PLASTIC
rubber .... BUNA, NEOPRENE
silk .... NYLON, RAYON
syntony .... RESONANCE
syphilis .... POX, LUES
lesion .... CHANCRE
remedy .... SALVARSAN

slang .... CUPID'S ITCH
stage .... LATENT, PRIMARY,
TERTIARY, SECONDARY
test for .... HAHN
syphilitic .... POCKY, LUETIC
Syria .... ARAM
Syriac script .... SERTA
Syrian .... ALAWITE, HITTITE,
DAMASCENE, LEVANTINE
antelope .... ADDAX
bear .... DUBB
capital .... ANTIOCH,
DAMASCUS
city/town .... AZAZ, DERA,
DUMA, HAMA, HOMS, EL BAB,
HALEB, HARIM, IDLIB, JEBLE,
RAQQA, ALEPPO, MEMBIJ,
SAFITA, TADMUR, TARTUS,
BANIYAS, LATAKIA, MEYADIN,
ZEBDANI, EL HASEKE, EL
RASHID, SELEMIYA
goddess .... ASHTORETH
head of state .... AL-ATASSI
island .... RUAD, ARWAD
king .... ANTIOCHUS
measure ...... MAKUK, GARAVA
mountain .... HERMON
political party .... BAATH
premier .... ZAEYEN
president .... (HAFEZ)ASSAD
province .... DEIR, DERA,
HAMA, HOMS, IDLIB, ALEPPO,
HASEKE, RASHID, TARTUS,
LATAKIA, DAMASCUS
religious follower .... DRUSE
river .... KHABUR, EL FURAT,
ORONTES, EUPHRATES
ruins .... A'MRIT, TADMOR,
PALMYRA
ruler .... ATASSI
seaport .... TRIPOLI
sect member .... SUNNI, SHIITE
storm god .... HADAD
tribe .... AMALEK, SARACEN
tribesman .... DRUSE, SARACEN
weight .... COLA, MINA
syringa .... LILAC, MOCK ORANGE
syringe .... NEEDLE, SPRAYER,
INJECTOR
kind of .... ENEMA, DOUCHE,
HYPODERMIC
syrinx .... PANPIPE
syrphus fly .... GNAT
syrtis .... QUICKSAND
syrup .... SIRUP, ORGEAT,
EXTRACT, GLUCOSE,
SORGHUM, TREACLE,
MOLASSES, SWEETENER
cane molasses:
first extraction .... LIGHT
third extraction
.... BLACKSTRAP
kind of .... CORN, KARO,
MAPLE
source .... SORGO
type of .... THIN, FUDGE
syrupy .... SWEET, SACCHARINE
system .... ISM, WAY, PLAN,
ORDER, METHOD, SCHEME,
ROUTINE, PROCEDURE,
ARRANGEMENT

betting .... PARIMUTUEL
for classifying blood groups
.... ABO, RH FACTORS
for sharing ideas
.... INTERCOM
for the entire ..... SYSTEMWIDE
of government/rule
.... REGIME
magnitude .... SOLAR
priorities .... TRIAGE
weights .... TROY
worship .... CULT
orderly .... COSMOS
part of the digestive
.... LIVER, MOUTH, STOMACH,
PANCREAS, ESOPHAGUS,
INTESTINES, GALLBLADDER
political/social ...... REGIME(N)
signals .... CODE
voting .... BALLOT
systematic .... ORDERLY,
REGULAR, ORGANIZED,
METHODICAL, REGIMENTAL
arrangement .... SCHEMA
systematics .... TAXONOMY
systematize ...... PLAN, ARRANGE,
ORGANIZE, STANDARDIZE
systole .... PULSE, CONTRACTION
syzygy .... DIPODY
Szczecin .... STETTIN
location .... POLAND
Szechwan .... SICHUAN
capital .... CHENGDU, CHENGTU
lyricist .... LIPO
szopelka .... OBOE

T

T-bone .... PORTERHOUSE
Greek .... TAU
Hebrew .... TAU, TAV, TAW,
TETH
letter .... TEE
shaped cross .... TAU
Ta in chemistry .... TANTALUM
taa .... PAGODA
Taal .... AFRIKAANS
tab .... LUG, TAG, BILL, CHIT,
FLAP, LOOP, CHECK, LABEL,
STRIP, CHARGE, TICKET,
ACCOUNT
colloquial .... CHOOSE,
RECORD, SELECT, RECKONING
in aeronautics .... AIRFOIL
shoe .... STRAP, LATCHET
slang .... FINGER
Tab, actor .... HUNTER

tabanid ...... GADFLY, (HORSE)FLY
tabard ...... CAPE, CLOAK, JACKET,
MANTLE
tabaret .... CLOTH, TABBY, FABRIC
Tabasco .... (HOT)SAUCE
capital of .... VILLAHERMOSA
tabby .... SILK, MOIRE, FELINE,
MOREEN, TAFFETA, BRINDLED,
BUSYBODY, GOSSIP(ER),
(PUSSY)CAT, SPINSTER,
GRIMALKIN
taberna .... HUT, SHED, TAVERN
tabernacle .... SHUL, TENT, HILET,
NICHE, MOSQUE, PAGODA,
SHRINE, TEMPLE, SANCTUARY,
SYNAGOGUE
tabes .... ATROPHY, MARASMUS,
PHTHISIS, EMACIATION,
CONSUMPTION, TUBERCULOSIS
dorsalis .... SYPHILIS
tabescent .... WASTING,
WITHERING
tabetic .... TABID, CONSUMPTIVE
Tabitha .... DORCAS
table .... DESK, DIET, FARE, FOOD,
MENU, PEND, SLAB, BOARD,
CHART, DEFER, FREEZE,
SHELVE, COUNTER, LIST(ING),
POSTPONE, TABULATION,
COMPILATION
centerpiece .... EPERGNE
cloth .... TAPIS, RUNNER,
SPREAD
communion .... ALTAR,
CREDENCE
companion .... MESSMATE
cover .... BAIZE, SCARF,
SPREAD

decoration .... DOILY, EPERGNE, PLACEMAT
decorative cloth .... RUNNER
d'hote .... MEAL
formal setting item .... CANDELABRUM
game .... POOL, CARDS, MAHJONG, PINGPONG, BILLIARDS
in architecture .... PANEL, CORNICE, MOLDING
insert .... LEAF
linen .... DAMASK, NAPERY, NAPKIN
napkin .... SERVIETTE
of contents .... INDEX
of the .... MENSAL
on wheels .... TEA WAGON
opposite of .... ACT ON
scrap .... ORT
server .... WAITER, WAITRESS
subject with Junior .... SPINACH
tennis .... PINGPONG
three-legged .... TRIVET
time .... SCHEDULE
-top hand cleaner .... FINGER BOWL
top's section .... LEAF
tray .... LAZY SUSAN
with drawers .... DESK
writing .... SECRETARY, ESCRITOIRE
tableau .... SET, ARRAY, SCENE, DIORAMA, PICTURE
tableland .... MESA, PUNA, KAR(R)OO, PLATEAU
tablet .... PAD, PILL, SLAB, FACIA, SLATE, STELE, STONE, BOOKLET, TESSERA, MEMORIAL
blank/erased .... TABULA RASA
medicinal .... PILL, WAFER, TROCHE, LOZENGE, TABLOID, PASTILLE, COUGH DROP
ornamental .... PLAQUE
religious .... PAX
reused .... PALIMPSEST
scroll-like .... CARTOUCH(E)
writing .... PAD, SLATE, TRIPTYCH
tableware item .... DISH, FORK, KNIFE, PLATE, SPOON
tabloid .... PILL, TROCHE, NEWSPAPER
taboo/tabu ...... BAN, DON'T, NO-NO, DEBAR, BAR(OUT), EXCLUDE, PROHIBIT, VERBOTEN, FORBID(DEN), PROHIBITION
opposite of .... NOA

tabor .... DRUM, SNARE, AT(T)ABAL, TIMBREL, TABOURET
small .... TABRET
taboret .... STAND, STOOL
Tabriz native .... IRANI(AN)
tabula .... TABLE(T)
____ (clean slate) .... RASA
tabular .... FLAT
tabulate ...... LIST, CHART, TALLY, FIGURE
TAC, part of ...... TACTICAL, AIR, COMMAND
tacamahac .... GUM, RESIN, POPLAR
tache .... HOOK, BUCKLE
tachina .... FLY
tachometer meas. .... RPM
tacit .... MUTE, STILL, SILENT, UNSAID, IMPLIED, IMPLICIT, WORDLESS, UNSPOKEN, SOUNDLESS, UNUTTERED, UNEXPRESSED
for a certain time, in music .... TACET
taciturn ...... CURT, MUTE, SHORT, STILL, TERSE, SILENT, LACONIC, RESERVED, RETICENT, SATURNINE, TIGHT-LIPPED, CLOSE(-MOUTHED)
one .... CLAM, INDIAN
opposite of .... GLIB, GUSHY, CHATTY, GOSSIPY, GARRULOUS, TALKATIVE, LOQUACIOUS
tack .... ADD, PIN, SEW, YAW, BRAD, JIBE, NAIL, PATH, VEER, BASTE, ROUTE, ATTACH, COURSE, FASTEN, STITCH, ZIGZAG
kind of .... THUMB, CARPET
machine ..... DRIVER, HAMMER
on .... APPEND
room item ...... SPUR, SADDLE, STIRRUP
slang .... FARE, FOOD
tackle ...... RIG, TRY, GEAR, LUFF, GRASP, SEIZE, ADDRESS, ATTEMPT, APPARATUS, EQUIPMENT, UNDERTAKE
for lifting weights ..... PULLEY
hoisting .... CAT, GARNET
in football .... STOP, THROW, GRAPPLE WITH
kind of .... FISHING
ship's .... LUFF, JEERS
small .... JIGGER
tacky ...... CHEAP, DOWDY, SEEDY, SHABBY, SHODDY, SLEAZY, STICKY, TAWDRY, ADHESIVE
Tacoma mount .... RAINIER

tact ...... GRACE, POISE, CONCERN, FINESSE, DELICACY, DIPLOMACY, SAVOIR-FAIRE
tactical .... STRATEGIC
unit .... BRIGADE
tactics .... PLOY, METHOD, POLICY, SYSTEM, DEVICES, PROCESS, STRATEGY, MANEUVERS, STRATAGEM
warfare .... AERIAL, MANEUVER, GUERRILLA, BLITZKRIEG
tactics, ____ .... SHOCK, AERIAL, GUERRILLA
tactile .... TACTUAL, PALPABLE, TANGIBLE, TOUCHABLE
taction .... TOUCH, CONTACT
tactless RUDE, BLUNT, DIRECT, GAUCHE, CALLOUS, IMPOLITE, THOUGHTLESS
act .... FAUX PAS, GAUCHERIE
tad .... TOT, CHIT, CHILD, PEEWEE, URCHIN, YOUNGSTER
of salt .... PINCH
Tadmor .... PALMYRA
tadpole .... LARVA, POLLIWOG, POLLYWOG
Tadzhik's capital .... STALINABAD
taels, 16 .... CATTY
taenia .... FILLET, HEADBAND, TAPEWORM
taffarel .... (TAFF)RAIL
taffeta ...... SILK, GAUDY, TABBY, DAINTY, FLORID, SAMITE
characteristic .... GLOSSY
taffy .... CANDY, TOFFEE
colloquial .... BLARNEY, FLATTERY
Taffy .... WELSHMAN
tafia .... RUM
Taft, sculptor .... LORADO
U.S. president .... WILLIAM (HOWARD)
tag ...... TAB, LOCK, STUB, LABEL, TALLY, A(I)GLET, APPEND, FOLLOW, TAIL(END)
end .... STUB, SCRAP, STUMP, REMNANT
game chaser .... IT
line .... CATCHWORD, CATCH-PHRASE
rag .... SHRED, RABBLE, TATTER
Tagalog. See also **Philippines** .... MALAYAN, FILIPINO, LANGUAGE
Tagore's forte .... POETRY
Tagus .... TAJO, TEJO, RIVER
city on the .... TOLEDO
taha .... BAYA, WEAVER(BIRD)

black-headed ..... CUCULLATUS
genus .... PLOCEUS
habitat .... AFRICA, ETHIOPIA
Tahiti, capital of .... PAPEETE
former name .... OTAHEITE
lake .... VAIHIRIA
mountain .... OROHENA
neighbor island .... MOOREA
point .... TATAA, VENUS
port .... PHAETON
seaport .... PAPEETE
town .... FAAA, PAPARA,
MAHAENA, PAPENOO
Tahitian .... POLYNESIAN
canoe .... PAHI
god .... ORO, TAAROA
people .... POLYNESIAN
Tai .... THAI, SIAMESE
taiga .... FORESTS
Taihoku .... TAIPEH
tail .... CUE, END, TAG, TIP, BUNT,
BUSH, CODA, HIND, REAR,
SCUT, CAUDA, QUEUE,
FOLLOW, RETINUE,
APPENDAGE
bone .... COCCYX
breath on one's ...... TAILGATE
bushy .... BRUSH
coin's .... VERSO
colloquial .... STALK, TRAIL,
FOLLOW
combining form .... URO
deer's/hare's/rabbit's .... SCUT
docked .... BOB
end .... TAG, TIP, REAR
end of a ship, metal
.... RUDDER
ender .... LAST, FINAL
feathers .... TRAIN
hair .... BRAID, PIGTAIL
having a .... URA, CAUDATE
hood .... LIRIPIPE
like a/pertaining to a
.... CAUDAL
off .... FLEE
plane .... STABILIZER
short, erect .... SCUT
slang .... SHADOW(ER),
DETECTIVE, PRIVATE EYE
solid part .... DOCK
turn .... FLEE, RETREAT
word with .... BOB, CAT, HIGH,
COTTON
tailing .... SURVEILLANCE
tailings .... WASTE, REFUSE,
SCRAPS, REJECTS, RESIDUE
tailless .... ACAUDAL, ANUROUS,
ACAUDATE
amphibian .... FROG, TOAD,
BATRACHIA
monkey .... APE

tailor .... (OUT)FIT, DRAPER,
SARTOR, SNYDER, FASHION,
CLOTHIER, DESIGN(ER),
BUSHELMAN, COSTUMIER
concern of .... FIT, STYLE
of Coventry ...... PEEPING TOM
pattern of .... DELINEATOR
pressing iron of .... GOOSE
vent of .... SLIT
woman .... SEAMSTRESS
work of .... SARTORIAL,
TAILORING
tailors, of .... SARTORIAL
tails .... FORMAL, FULL DRESS
slang .... FISH AND SOUP
tailspin .... NOSE DIVE
tailwind welcomer .... SHIP,
AIRCRAFT
tain .... (TIN)FOIL, TIN PLATE
taint .... DYE, HUE, FLAW, COLOR,
SPOIL, STAIN, SULLY, TINGE,
DEFILE, POISON, STIGMA,
CORRUPT, POLLUTE, TARNISH,
INFECT(ION), CONTAMINATE
Taisho emperor .... YOSHIHITO
Taiwan .... FORMOSA
cape .... OLWAMPI
capital .... TAIPEH, TAIPEI
city/town .... ILAN, SUAO,
CHIAI, SINCHU, TAINAN,
TAOYUAN, CHANGHUA,
TAICHUNG, PINGTUNG,
CHUNGHSING
deer .... SIKA
government ...... KUOMINTANG
island .... HUNGTOW
islands .... PENGHU,
PESCADORES
legislature .... YUAN
mountain .... YU SHAN
port ..... KEELUNG, KAOHSIUNG
premier .... YEN
president .... CHIANG
strait port .... AMOY, XIAMEN
tea .... OOLONG
taj .... CAP, CROWN, DIADEM
Taj Mahal .... MAUSOLEUM
builder .... (SHAH) JAHAN
site of .... AGRA
take .... BUY, EAT, GET, USE, WIN,
RENT, ADOPT, CHARM, DRINK,
FETCH, GRASP, LEASE,
ABSORB, ACCEPT, ASSUME,
OBTAIN, OCCUPY, ACQUIRE,
PRESUME, RECEIVE
a breather .... REST, PAUSE
a crack at .... SNIPE
a dip .... BATHE
a liking to .... COTTON
a powder .... LEAVE, SCRAM
a risk .... DARE, GAMBLE

a stroll .... GO FOR A WALK
aback .... STARTLE, SURPRISE
_____ (accept a challenge)
.... A DARE
action .... PROCEED
advantage of .... ABUSE,
IMPOSE, EXPLOIT
advice .... HEED, MIND
apart .... RUIN, UNDO
as one's own .... ADOPT
away .... DEDUCT, REMOVE,
SUBTRACT
back .... DENY, RECANT,
RETURN, RECOVER, RETRACT
by force .... GRAB, REAVE,
SEIZE, USURP, WREST, KIDNAP,
SNATCH, CAPTURE
by storm .... RAID, SEIZE,
ATTACK
care .... BEWARE
care of .... TEND, SEE TO,
NURSE, SERVE, WATCH
chances .... RISK, GAMBLE,
PLAY WITH FIRE
cover .... HIDE
_____ (criticize) .... APART
dishonestly ..... STEAL, PILFER,
(SHOP)LIFT
down .... NOTE, LOWER,
WRITE, RECORD, HUMILIATE
edge off ..... DEADEN, OBTUND
effect .... INURE
exception ...... DEMUR, DIFFER,
DISAGREE
first .... PREEMPT
five .... REST, PAUSE, RELAX
for granted .... ASSUME,
EXPECT, IGNORE, NEGLECT,
PRESUME
heart .... REVIVE, CHEER UP
heed ..... MIND, RECK, BEWARE
in .... SEE, GAIN, ADMIT,
CHEAT, ACCEPT, DECEIVE,
INCLUDE, RECEIVE
in again .... RESORB
in livestock for feeding: obs.
.... AGIST
into custody .... ARREST,
IMPOUND
it easy .... LAZE, REST, LET UP,
GO SLOW
it on the lam .... FLEE, ESCAPE
_____ (loll) .... IT EASY
notice .... SEE, HEED, LOOK,
NOTE, OBSERVE
off .... FLY, DOFF, FLEE, BEGIN,
LEAVE, START, DEDUCT,
DEPART, DETACH, REMOVE
offense/umbrage .... HUFF,
BRIDLE, RESENT
on .... HIRE, ADOPT, ASSUME,

EMPLOY, OPPOSE
on an obligation .... CO-SIGN
on cargo .... LADE
one's dust .... TAILGATE
one's way: poet. .... WEND
out .... ELIDE, DELE(TE),
ESCORT, REMOVE, EXPUNGE,
EXTRACT, ABSTRACT
out a policy .... INSURE
out again .... REDATE
over .... HAVE, ASSUME
over, unduly ...... SEIZE, USURP
part .... JOIN, PARTICIPATE
place .... OCCUR, HAPPEN,
SUPERVENE
potshot at .... SNIPE
precedence over ..... OUTRANK
shape .... FORM, LOOM
side with .... GO TO BAT FOR
slang ..... GATE, CHEAT, TRICK,
PROFIT, RECEIPTS
steps .... ACT
testimony from .... HEAR
the blame .... CONFESS
cake .... WIN
character of
.... IMPERSONATE
helm .... STEER
law into one's hands
.... COMMIT A CRIME
loss .... WRITE OFF
pits out .... DESTONE
roll .... COUNT NOSES
starch out of .... TAME
time ..... LOAF, DELAY, LINGER
to ____ .... TASK
court .... SUE
one's heels .... FLEE
task .... PUNISH
the bath .... TUB
the soapbox .... ORATE
turns .... ALTERNATE
unfair share .... HOG
up .... PURSUE, TACKLE,
DISCUSS
up a dare .... VIE, DEFY,
FIGHT, CONTEND
up again .... RENEW, RESUME
up as one's own .... ADOPT
voluntarily .... ADOPT
with a grain of salt
.... DOUBT, DISTRUST,
DISREGARD
without permission ..... STEAL
taken aback .... STARTLED,
SURPRISED, DUMBFOUNDED
unawares .... UNPREPARED
with ..... CHARMED, IMPRESSED
taking .... WINNING, FETCHING,
ACCEPTING, RECEIVING,
RECEPTION, INFECTIOUS

money by intimidation
.... BLACKMAIL, EXTORTION
turns .... ROTATIVE
takings .... PROFITS, RECEIPTS,
WINNINGS
talapoin .... MONK, GUENON,
MONKEY
talaria, location of .... ANKLES
of Hermes .... WINGS,
SANDALS
talc .... POWDER, AGALITE,
STEATITE, SOAPSTONE
talcum .... TALC, POWDER
tale .... REDE, YARN, FABLE,
RUMOR, STORY, GOSSIP,
LEGEND, REPORT, FICTION,
MARCHEN, FALSEHOOD,
NARRATIVE
adventure ...... CONTE, GEST(E)
bearer .... BUSYBODY,
GOSSIP(ER), SCANDALMONGER
epic .... SAGA, ILIAD, AENEID
kind of .... TELL
medieval .... LAI
of lamentation/woe
.... JEREMIAD
tall .... YARN, FISH STORY
Tale of Two Cities heroine
.... LUCIE
talent .... ART, GIFT, FLAIR,
KNACK, POWER, SKILL,
GENIUS, METIER, ABILITY,
FACULTY, APTITUDE,
ENDOWMENT
founder .... SCOUT
natural .... DOWER, DOWRY
talented .... ABLE, SHARP,
CLEVER, GIFTED, ENDOWED,
ARTISTIC
tales ...... WRIT, JUROR(S), VENIRE
tales, ____ .... TWICE-TOLD
talesman .... JUROR
taleteller .... NARRATOR
Talien(wan) .... DALNY, DAIREN
taliera .... TARA
talion ...... REVENGE, PUNISHMENT
taliped .... CLUBFOOTED
talipes .... CLUBFOOT
talipot .... PALM
kind of .... BURI
talisman .... OBI, CHARM, OBEAH,
AMULET, FETISH, GRIGRI
beetle .... SCARAB
talk ...... SAY, BLAB, BLAT, CHAT,
CHIN, SPEAK, UTTER, SPEECH,
YABBER, CONSULT, DECLAIM,
DISCUSS, LECTURE, PALAVER,
CONVERSE, CONFER(ENCE),
CONVERSATION
abusive .... JAW
back .... LIP, SASS, RETORT,

PROVOKE, RIPOSTE,
COMEBACK, REJOINDER
big .... BRAG, BOAST,
MAGNIFY, EXAGGERATE
boastful .... GAS, BRAG,
CRACK, BLUSTER, GASCONADE
chatty .... GAB, GOSSIP
childishly .... DROOL, SLOBBER
colloquial .... RAP
down .... OUTLAST, SILENCE
effusively .... GUSH
empty .... GAS, BULL, CANT,
FUDGE, HUMBUG, PATTER,
CHATTER, HOGWASH,
BUNCOMBE, CLAPTRAP,
MOONSHINE
evil .... CURSE, MALEDICTION
excited .... RANT, RAVE
flippant .... BANTER,
PERSIFLAGE
foolish ..... GAB, BULL, DROOL,
PRATE, BABBLE, DRIVEL,
TATTLE, BLAB(BER), BLATHER,
CHATTER, PRATTLE, TWADDLE,
TWATTLE, FAPDOODLE,
MOONSHINE, POPPYCOCK
fresh .... LIP
friendly ..... CHAT, COSE, COZE
from pulpit .... HOMILY,
SERMON
glib .... PATTER, PALAVER
hearsay .... RUMOR, GOSSIP
idle .... GAS
impudent .... LIP, SASS
incoherent(ly) .... JABBER,
MAUNDER, GIBBER(ISH)
informal .... CAUSERIE,
(CHIT)CHAT
insincere .... BUNCOMBE
insincerely .... PALTER
light .... CHAFF, BANTER,
RAILLERY, PERSIFLAGE
like an ass .... BRAY
made for effect .... BUNCOMBE
meaningless .... CANT,
PATTER, PIFFLE, MALARK(E)Y
melodramatic .... HEROICS
moral/solemn .... HOMILY,
SERMON
noisily .... YAP, RANT, YAUP,
YAWP
noisy .... YAP, BLAT, RANT,
JANGLE
nonsense .... DROOL
nonsensical .... JABBER, PIFFLE
offensive .... JAW
out of .... DISSUADE,
PERSUADE, UNCONVINCE
over .... RERAP, DISCUSS
peevishly .... CARP

persistently on something
.... HARP
pert .... LIP
pointless .... TWADDLE,
SLIPSLOP
pompous .... BOMBAST,
FUSTIAN
quiet(ly) .... MURMUR,
WHISPER
rapid .... PATTER, CHATTER
sales .... SPIEL, PATTER
senseless .... BALDERDASH
sentimental .... SLUSH
show format .... PANEL
silly ...... BULL, DROOL, PRATE,
CACKLE, FLUMMERY
small .... GOSSIP, PATTER,
CHITCHAT
stupid .... DROOL
to .... ADDRESS, BESPEAK
to oneself .... MONOLOGIZE,
SOLILOQUIZE
vernacular .... CANT, LINGO,
JARGON
while crying .... BLUBBER
with .... CHIN
with another .... CONVERSE,
DIALOGUE, CONVERSATION
talkative .... GLIB, GABBY, GASSY,
WINDY, CHATTY, FLUENT,
MOUTHY, VOLUBLE,
GARRULOUS, LOQUACIOUS
bird .... MAGPIE, (BLUE)JAY
person .... JAY, GABBER,
GASBAG, MAGPIE, WINDBAG,
CHATTERBOX
talked about .... FAMOUS,
NOTORIOUS, WELL-KNOWN
slang .... SPIELED
talker .... SAYER, SPEAKER,
PARLEYER, CONVERSER
incessant .... GASBAG, MAGPIE,
WINDBAG, CHATTERBOX
talking dummy .... SNERD
fond of .... GABBY, WINDY,
GOSSIPY, GARRULOUS, LONG-
WINDED, LOQUACIOUS
picture .... TALKIE
to .... REBUKE, SCOLDING
tall ...... BIG, HIGH, HUGE, LARGE,
LOFTY, TAUNT, HIGHFLOWN,
LONG(LEGGED),
EXAGGERATED
and lean .... LANKY, LATHY,
GANGLY
chest .... HIGHBOY
drink with nutmeg
.... SANGAREE
order .... CHORE,
BACKBREAKER
story .... FIB

tale .... YARN
thin person .... STRINGBEAN
tallboy .... CHEST
Tallchief, ballerina .... MARIA
tallest animal .... GIRAFFE
tallier ...... SCORER, SCOREKEEPER
Tallinn .... REVAL, REVEL
tallith ...... COVER, SCARF, SHAWL,
MANTLE
tallow .... FAT, OIL, SEBO, SUET,
SEBUM, STEAT, GREASE,
STEARIN
product .... SOAP, CANDLE
tree .... CERA, ROKA
yielder .... SUET
tallowy .... LARDY, OLEIC,
UNCTUOUS
tally .... TAB, TAG, JIBE, SUIT,
TALE, AGREE, CHECK, COUNT,
LABEL, MATCH, NOTCH,
SCORE, RECORD, SQUARE,
ACCOUNT, CHALK UP,
REGISTER, CORRESPOND
tallyho .... CRY, COACH
crier .... HUNTER
pullers .... HORSES
Talmud, part of .... GEMARA,
HAGGADA, HALAKHA,
MISHNA(H)
version .... JERUSALEM,
BABYLONIAN
Talmudic .... GEMARIC, MISHNAIC,
RABBINIC
anecdote/parable
.... HAGGADA(H)
talon .... CLAW, FANG, HEEL,
NAIL, OGEE, SPUR, STOCK,
CLUTCH, HALLUX, POUNCE,
ZIPPER
taloned .... DENTATE
Talos .... MISSILE, WATCHMAN
killer of .... DAEDALUS
make of .... BRASS
talus .... SCREE, SLOPE,
ANKLE(BONE), ASTRAGALUS,
ANKLE-JOINT, HUCKLEBONE
part of .... ANKLE, TIBIA,
FIBULA
tam-o-shanter .... CAP, BERET
tam .... GONG
tamandu(a) .... ANTEATER
tamarack .... TREE, LARCH
tamarau ...... BUFFALO, CARABAO
tamarin .... MARMOSET
tamarind, Philippine
.... SAMPALOC
taste of .... ACERB
tamarisk salt tree .... ATLE(E)
tamasha .... SHOW, SPECTACLE
tambour .... DRUM, FRAME,
TABORET, EMBROIDERY

tambourine .... DRUM, RIKK,
TAAR, DAIRA, DAIRE, TABOR,
TIMBREL
Tamburlaine the Great author
...... (CHRISTOPHER) MARLOWE
tame ...... COW, DRY, BUST, DEAD,
DULL, MEEK, MILD, ACCOY,
BREAK, DAUNT, QUIET,
DOCILE, FEEBLE, GENTLE,
SOFTEN, SUBDUE, INSIPID,
SERVILE, DOMESTICATE
tamed .... BROKEN, GENTLE,
CRUSHED, CHASTENED
tameless .... WILD, FIERCE
tameness .... DOCILITY,
MEEKNESS, GENTLENESS,
MANSUETUDE
tamer .... BREAKER, TRAINER
wild horse .... COWBOY,
BRONC(H)OBUSTER
Tamerlane .... TIMUR-I-LENK
birthplace of ...... SAMARKAND
descendant of .... BABER
tomb of .... GUR AMIR
Tamil .... DRAVIDIAN
Taming of the Shrew author
.... SHAKESPEARE
Tamiroff, actor .... AKIM
Tammany Hall .... POLITICAL
MACHINE
Society official .... BOSS,
SACHEM, CACIQUE
tamp .... JAM, RAM, CRAM, DENT,
PACK, POUND, PUNCH, STAMP,
THUMP, (DE)PRESS
tamper .... PLOT, ALTER, BRIBE,
TAINT, CHANGE, DOCTOR,
MEDDLE, MONKEY, SEDUCE,
TINKER, CORRUPT, FALSIFY,
POUNDER
Tampico man .... SENOR
tampion .... PLUG, STOPPER
tampon .... PLUG, SPONGE,
PACKING, PADDING
tan .... DUN, TAW, BARK, BEAT,
BUFF, BURN, CURE, ECRU,
FLOG, HIDE, WHIP, BEIGE,
TAWNY, BRONZE, TANNIN,
THRASH, (EM)BROWN,
LEATHER
believe it or not! .... LUGGAGE
Tana .... LAKE
site .... ETHIOPIA
tanager .... REDBIRD, SONGBIRD
blue-gray .... THRAUPIS
family .... EMBERIZIDAE
paradise .... TANGARA
relative .... BUNTING, SPARROW
swallow .... TERSINA
Western .... PIRANGA
tanbark .... NAPA, ROSS

tandem .... BICYCLE, CARRIAGE
tandoor(i) .... (CLAY)OVEN
tandour .... HEATER
Tandy's husband .... CRONYN
Taney, U.S. chief justice
.... ROGER
tang .... NIP, BITE, GUST, ODOR,
ZEST, SAVOR, TASTE, TOUCH,
TRACE, FLAVOR, SHARPNESS
on chisel/knife .... POINT,
PRONG
ringing sound .... TWANG
Tanganyika merged with
Zanzibar .... TANZANIA
mountain .... KILIMANJARO
town .... UJIJI
tangent ...... ADJACENT, TOUCHING
tangerine .... ORANGE, MANDARIN
crossed with grapefruit/
pomelo .... TANGELO
tangible .... REAL, SOLID,
TACTILE, CONCRETE,
DEFINITE, MATERIAL,
PALPABLE, SENSIBLE,
TOUCHABLE, PERCEPTIBLE,
SUBSTANTIAL
tangle .... MAT, KNOT, TRAP,
CATCH, MIX(UP), SNARE,
SNARL, WEAVE, ENMESH,
JUMBLE, MUDDLE, SLEAVE,
EMBROIL, INVOLVE, PERPLEX,
SEAWEED, COMPLICATE,
INTERTWINE
foot .... WHISKEY
footed .... STUMBLING
legs: sl. .... BEER, LIQUOR
toad .... BUTTERCUP
tangled .... MESHED, COMPLEX,
BALLED UP, INTRICATE
mass .... MAT, SHAG, RAVEL
structure .... MAZE, LABYRINTH
tangy .... RACY, NIPPY, ZESTY,
SNAPPY, PIQUANT
Tanis .... ZOAN
tanist .... HEIR
tank ...... VAT, POND, POOL, STEW,
CISTERN, VEHICLE,
CONTAINER, RESERVOIR
destroyer .... BAZOOKA,
HALFTRACK
farming .... HYDROPONICS
fish .... AQUARIUM
gunner's place .... TURRET
hot water .... BOILER
military .... DD, MARK,
SHERMAN, DUPLEX DRIVE
oil .... BUNKER
rainwater .... CISTERN,
RESERVOIR
slang .... JAIL
top .... (UNDER)SHIRT

tankard .... CUP, MUG, STOUP,
POTTLE
tanker .... SHIP, OILER, BUNKER
tanned hide .... CROP, LEATHER
tannic acid .... TANNIN
source .... OAK, TEA, SUMAC,
MANGROVE
tanning bark .... KOA, ALDER
material .... KINO, FURAN,
CASHOO, SUMAC(H), CATECHU,
GAMBIER, CATECHIN,
QUEBRACHO
powdered leaves .... SUMAC(H)
tansy .... WEED
poisonous .... RAGWORT,
FELONWEED
tantalize .... VEX, BALK, TEASE,
TEMPT, EXCITE, HARASS,
PLAGUE, SEDUCE, BEWITCH,
TITILLATE
tantalizing .... ALLURING,
INVITING, TICKLING,
DESIRABLE, PROVOKING
Tantalus' daughter .... NIOBE
father .... ZEUS
kingdom .... PHRYGIA
punishment .... HUNGER,
THIRST
river of doom .... TARTARUS
son .... PELOPS
tantamount .... COEQUAL,
EQUIVALENT
tantara .... BLAST, FANFARE,
FLOURISH
tantivy .... CRY, FAST, RUSH,
SWIFT, GALLOP, HEADLONG
tantrum .... FIT, HUFF, RAGE,
RAVE, FRENZY, OUTBURST,
CONNIPTION
activity .... CRY, BITE, KICK,
SPIT, YELL, SCREAM
thrower .... CHILD, RAVER,
TODDLER
Tanzania cape .... KANZI
capital .... DAR ES SALAAM
city/town .... LINDI, MBEYA,
MOSHI, TANGA, ARUSHA,
BUKOBA, DODOMA, IRINGA,
MUSOMA, MWANZA, SONGEA,
TABORA, SINGIDA, ZANZIBAR
falls .... KALAMBO
island .... JUANI, MAFIA,
PEMBA, ZANZIBAR
lake .... EYASI, NYASA,
RUKWA, NATRON, MANYARA,
VICTORIA, TANGANYIKA
monetary unit .... SHILLING
mountain ...... MERU, RUNGWE,
KILIMANJARO
national park .... RUAHA,
MIKUMI, SERENGETI

part of .... ZANZIBAR,
TANGANYIKA
president .... NYERE
region .... MARA, LINDI,
MBEYA, PEMBA, PWANI,
RUKWA, TANGA, ARUSHA,
DODOMA, IRINGA, KAGERA,
KIGOMA, MWANZA, TABORA,
MOROGORO, ZANZIBAR,
SHINYANGA, DAR ES SALAAM,
KILIMANJARO
river .... WAMI, RUAHA,
NJOMBE, ROVUMA, RUFIJI,
RUNGWA, PANGANI, WEMBERE,
MBEMKURU, KILOMBERO
seaport .... ZANZIBAR
tap .... BAR, PAT, RAP, TIT, BUNG,
COCK, CORK, FLIP, OPEN,
PLUG, DRAFT, KNOCK, SPILE,
TOUCH, VALVE, BROACH,
DECANT, FAUCET, LIQUOR,
OUTLET, SPIGOT, STRIKE,
STOPPER
chin .... CHUCK
dance .... SOFT SHOE
dancer .... HOOFER, ASTAIRE
for an office/position
.... APPOINT, NOMINATE
tapa cloth source ...... MULBERRY
wearer .... POLYNESIAN
tape .... BAND, BIND, DEMO, STRIP,
RIBBON, BANDAGE
braided .... INKLE
kind of .... SCOTCH, TICKER,
MASKING, MEASURE,
ADHESIVE, FRICTION,
MAGNETIC, CELLOPHANE,
ELECTRICAL
record .... COPY
taper .... WANE, WICK, LIGHT,
CANDLE, LESSEN, NARROW,
SLACKEN, DECREASE,
DIMINISH
tapered .... CONOID, TERETE
tapering object ...... CONE, SHIM,
SPIRE, PYRAMID, VOLCANO
to a point .... SUBULATE
tapestry .... RUG, ARRAS, TAPIS,
DOSSAL, DOSSEL, DOSSER,
MOSAIC, GOBELIN, WEAVING
tapeworm .... T(A)ENIA, CESTODE,
CESTOID, PARASITE
disease .... HYDATID,
CYSTICERCOSIS
disease of cattle and hogs
.... MEASLES
disease of sheep .... STAGGERS
drug .... T(A)ENIACIDE,
T(A)ENIAFUGE, NICLOSAMIDE
habitat .... LIVER, LUNGS,
INTESTINES

head of .... SCOLEX
infestation .... T(A)ENIASIS
larva ..... MEASLES, COENURUS,
CYSTICERCUS
larva formation .... CYSTS
shape .... RIBBON
sucker .... HOOK, OSCULUM
type of .... BEEF, FISH, PORK,
DWARF
taphouse .... INN, TAVERN,
BAR(ROOM)
tapioca base/source .... MANIOC,
CAS(S)AVA, MANIHOT
tapir .... DANTA, MAMMAL,
UNGULATE
animal resembling ....HOG, PIG
pride of a .... SNOUT
relative .... HORSE,
RHINOCEROS
tapis .... TAPESTRY
tapper .... TELEGRAPHER
tappet .... ARM, CAM
tapping sound .... DRUM, TICK
tappings .... SAP
taproom .... BAR, SALOON
taps instrument .... DRUM, BUGLE
series of .... PATTER
tapster .... BARMAID, BARTENDER
Tapuyan .... GES, INDIAN,
LANGUAGE
tar .... GOB, GOO, BREA, SALT,
SOIL, PITCH, RESIN, SMEAR,
STAIN, DEFAME, MALTHA,
SAILOR, SEAMAN, SLUDGE,
ASPHALT, BITUMEN, BLACKEN,
MARINER, ALKITRAN,
ALCHITRAN
and _____ .... FEATHER
and feather ..... GRILL, PUNISH,
TORTURE
taramasalata .... APPETIZER
ingredient .... BREAD, POTATO,
FISH ROE
tarantas(s) .... CARRIAGE
tarantula .... SPIDER
tarboosh .... CAP, FEZ
tardy .... LATE, SLOW, SLACK,
BELATED, DELAYED,
OVERDUE, DILATORY,
SLUGGISH, BEHIND TIME
opposed to .... PROMPT
tare .... SEED, WEED, VETCH,
DISCOUNT, ALLOWANCE,
DEDUCTION
allowance additional to
.... TRET
noxious .... DARNEL
Tarentum .... TARANTO
targe .... SHIELD, BUCKLER
target ...... AIM, END, BUTT, GOAL,
MARK, QUARRY, OBJECT(IVE)

center of .... EYE, BLANK
circle .... INNER
circular central mark of a
.... BULL'S-EYE
date .... DEADLINE
easy .... SITTING DUCK
finder .... RADAR, SONAR
get on .... ZERO
in a game .... PIN
knight's .... QUINTAIN
mound behind .... BUTT
of a Patriot .... SCUD
of blame .... SCAPEGOAT
of ridicule .... BUTT,
LAUGHINGSTOCK
of white cloth .... CLOUT
practice place .... RANGE
range .... BUTTS
shooting gallery .... DUCK
shooting post ..... MANT(E)LET
towed .... DROGUE
Tarheel .... CAROLINIAN
State .... NORTH CAROLINA
tariff ...... TAX, COST, DUTY, LIST,
IMPOST, CUSTOMS
Tarkington, novelist ...... BOOTH
tarlatan .... MUSLIN
tarmac .... (AIRPORT)RUNWAY
tarn .... LAKE, LOCH, POND
location .... MOUNTAIN
'tarnal .... ETERNAL
tarnation .... DAMNED,
DAMNATION
tarnish .... DIM, DULL, SOIL, SPOT,
STAIN, SULLY, TAINT,
SMUDGE, BLEMISH,
(BE)SMIRCH
as reputation .... DEFAME,
DEFILE, MALIGN
as silverware .... DISCOLOR
taro .... TUBER, ELEPHANT EAR
dish .... POI
fermented in pit .... MOD
root .... ED(D)O, GABI, KALO
sprouts .... DASHEEN
tarot .... CARD
tarpaulin .... TARP, CANVAS,
OILCLOTH
raincoat ...... PONCHO, SLICKER
shelter .... TENT
tarpon .... SABALO, GAMEFISH,
MILKFISH, SILVERFISH
Tarquin's avenger ...... PORSENA
tar(r)adiddle .... FIB
tarring and feathering
.... PUNISHMENT
person subjected to .... CON-
MAN, WIFE-BEATER
person subjected to: 18th
century .... TAX
COLLECTOR

tarry .... IDLE, STAY, WAIT,
(A)BIDE, DELAY, DAWDLE,
LINGER, LOITER, REMAIN,
PERSIST, SOJOURN,
(DILLY)DALLY
tarsal bone .... CALCANEUS
tarsier's habitat .... INDONESIA,
PHILIPPINES
relative .... LEMUR
tarsus .... BONE, HOCK, ANKLE
combining form .... TARSO
tart .... FLAN, KEEN, SOUR, SHARP,
PASTRY, ACERBIC, CUTTING,
(FRUIT)PIE, ACID(ULOUS)
slang .... HUSSY, TRAMP,
HARLOT, WANTON, STRUMPET
tartan .... SHIP, CHECK, PLAID,
FREIGHTER, HIGHLANDER
pattern: var. .... SETT
trousers .... TREWS
wrap-around ..... KILT, FILIBEG
tartar, containing .... TARTAROUS
emetic .... MORDANT,
EXPECTORANT
teeth .... CALCULUS
Tartar .... TURK, TATAR, MONGOL
of/pertaining to a
.... TARTARIAN
wine cask .... ARGAL, ARGOL
Tartarus .... HELL, HADES
of/pertaining to ...... INFERNAL
Tartuf(f)e .... COMEDY,
HYPOCRITE
author .... MOLIERE
Tarzan .... JUNGLE HERO
cloth .... LOIN
friends of .... APES
mate of .... JANE
portrayer of .... CRABBE,
(RON)ELY
rope for .... LIANA
stories author ..... BURROUGHS
task .... JOB, TAX, DUTY, ONUS,
WORK, LABOR, STINT,
BURDEN, CHARGE, LESSON,
ASSIGNMENT
force .... COMMANDO
menial .... DRUDGERY
routine .... CHORE
take to .... SCOLD, REBUKE
tedious .... GRIND
taskmaster .... LEGREE,
MARTINET, OVERSEER, SLAVE-
DRIVER
Tasman, Dutch navigator
.... ABEL
discovery ...... TASMANIA, NEW
ZEALAND
Tasmanian bay .... FIRES, STORM,
MARION, OYSTER, ELLIOTT,
NORFOLK, PHOQUES,

ANDERSON

cape ..... GRIM, RAOUL, SOUTH,
BARREN, PILLAR, SORELL,
WICKHAM, PORTLAND,
NATURALISTE

capital .... HOBART

city/town .... BURNIE,
WYNYARD, KINGSTON,
DEVONPORT, GLENORCHY,
LAUNCESTON

devil .... DASYURE

discoverer .... TASMAN

gulf ...... BATHURST, CIRCULAR

harbor .... MACQUARIE

island ...... DEAL, KING, SWAN,
BABEL, MARIA, HUNTER,
CLARKE, HUMMOCK, ROBBINS,
FLINDERS, SCHOUTEN, EAST
SISTER, WEST SISTER, NORTH
BRUNY, SOUTH BRUNY,
VANSITTART

island group .... KENT,
HOGAN, CURTIS, FURNEAUX

lake .... ECHO, GREAT,
ARTHUR, GORDON, SORELL,
CRESCENT, SAINT CLAIR, KING
WILLIAM

mountain .... ANNE, OSSA,
HARTZ, LYELL, MUNRO,
CRADLE, PICTON, RAMSEY,
STANLEY, BARN BLUFF,
LEGGES TOR, STRZELECKI,
FRENCHMAN'S CAP

ocean .... INDIAN

peninsula .... TASMAN,
FORESTIER, FREYCINET

phalanger .... TAPOA

pine .... HUON

range .... LOFTY, ARTHUR,
DENISON, D'AGUILAR,
FRANKLAND

river .... DEE, HUON, KING,
LAKE, NIVE, OUSE, CLYDE,
DAVEY, FORTH, LEVEN,
TAMAR, ARTHUR, GORDON,
MERSEY, PEDDER, PIEMAN,
SAVAGE, DERWENT, FLORENCE,
FRANKLIN, NORTH ESK,
MACQUARIE

sea .... TASMAN

strait .... BASS, BANKS

tiger/wolf .... THYLACINE

wolf: native name .... YABBI

tass .... CUP, DRAFT, GOBLET

tassel .... TUFT, TERCEL, ZIZITH,
CORNSILK

taste .... BIT, TRY, BENT, TANG,
ZEST, GUSTO, SAVOR, TINGE,
SNACK, TRACE, DEGUST,
FLAVOR, LIKING, PALATE,
SAPO(U)R, TIDBIT, SOUPCON,

PENCHANT, EXPERIENCE,
PREFERENCE

daintily .... SIP

delicacy of .... NICETY,
POLISH, REFINEMENT

distinctive .... TANG, SMACK,
FLAVOR

for artistic objects .... VIRTU

for some specific food
.... APPETITE

for something .... TOOTH

have a pleasing .... SAPID,
RELISH, SAVORY

having .... SAPOROUS

kind of .... SOUR, SALTY,
SHARP, SWEET, BITTER, SPICY,
PEPPERY, PUNGENT

offensive .... RANK

organ of .... TONGUE

quality of being delicate in
.... DELICACY, SOFTNESS

showing refined .... DAINTY,
FASTIDIOUS

stylish .... DASH, FLAIR,
ELEGANCE

try the .... SAMPLE

tasteful ...... KEEN, SAPID, TASTY,
DAINTY, SAVORY, ELEGANT,
REFINED, CULTURED,
DELICATE, PARTICULAR,
DISCRIMINATING

luxury .... ELEGANCE

tasteless ...... DULL, FLAT, BLAND,
STALE, VAPID, INSIPID

taster .... SIPPER, SAMPLER,
SAVORER

kind of .... JUDGE, CRITIC,
GOURMET

tasty .... SAPID, SAVORY, STRONG,
PUNGENT, FLAVORED,
GUSTABLE, LUSCIOUS,
DELICIOUS, FLAVORFUL,
PALATABLE, SAPORIFIC,
TOOTHSOME

and delicious .... AMBROSIAL

colloquial .... YUMMY

dish .... MORSEL

food, small portion of
.... ANTIPASTO, APPETIZER,
HORS D'OEUVRE(S)

Tatar .... TURK, TARTAR,
MONGOL(IAN)

capital .... KAZAN

drink .... KUMISS, KOUMIS(S)

ruler .... CHAM

Strait feeder .... AMUR

tater .... POTATO

tatouay .... ARMADILLO

tatter ...... DAG, RAG, TAG, PIECE,
SCRAP, SHRED, FRAGMENT

tattered .... DUDDY, DUDDIE,

RAGGED, SHABBY, MANGLED

tatterdemalion ...... RAGAMUFFIN

tattersall .... CHECKERED

tatters .... RAGS, RIBBONS,
FRAGMENTS, ODDS AND ENDS

tatting .... LACE

tattle .... BLAB, TALK, PEACH,
PRATE, GOSSIP, JABBER,
INFORM, SNITCH, CHAT(TER),
DIVULGE, PRATTLE, DISCLOSE

tattler .... GOSSIP, TELL-TALE,
INFORMER, SANDPIPER,
CHATTERBOX

tattoo .... DOT, MARK, PINK,
PRICK, SALVO, SIGNAL,
SUMMON, VOLLEY, DRUBBING,
PUNCTURE

tau .... TAV, TEE

cross .... ANKH, CRUX

taunt .... GIBE, JAPE, JEER, JEST,
MOCK, TWIT, CHAFF, FLOUT,
SCOFF, DERIDE, NEEDLE,
REVILE, PROVOKE, REPROACH,
RIDICULE

as a ship's mast .... HIGH,
TALL

slang .... POOH-POOH

taupe .... GRAY, BROWNISH-GRAY,
GRAYISH-BROWN

taurine .... BOVINE, BULLISH

animal .... BULL

tauromachy ...... BULLFIGHT(ING)

Taurus .... BULL, CONSTELLATION

cluster .... HYAD(E)S

taut .... EDGY, FIRM, NEAT, SNUG,
TIDY, TRIM, STIFF, TENSE,
TIGHT, NERVOUS, STRAINED,
SHIPSHAPE, STRETCHED

tautog .... CHUB, MOLL,
BLACKFISH

tautology .... PLEONASM,
VERBOSITY, REDUNDANCE,
REPETITION

tav .... TAU, TEE

tavern .... BAR, INN, PUB, CAFE,
KHAN, BISTRO, HOSTEL,
SALOON, TAPROOM,
ALEHOUSE, ORDINARY,
POTHOUSE, ROADHOUSE

character .... SOT, TOPER,
BARFLY

keeper .... PROPRIETOR

server .... POTBOY, BARMAID,
BARTENDER

taw .... MIB, LINE, AGATE, ALLEY,
MARBLE

tawdry .... CHEAP, GAUDY,
SHOWY, FLASHY, GARISH,
SLEAZY, VULGAR, RAFFISH,
GINGERBREAD

tawny .... TAN, DUSKY, SWART,

FULVOUS, RUBIATE,
BROWNISH-YELLOW

tax ...... CESS, DUTY, LEVY, RATE,
SCOT, SESS, TOLL, SCAT(T),
TITHE, ASSESS, BURDEN,
CHARGE, EXCISE, IMPOST,
STRAIN
agency .... IRS
allowance .... DEDUCTIBLE
church .... TITHE
collector .... TAXER, OCTROI,
CATCHPOLE, CATCHPOLL
evader's nemesis .... TMAN
export/import .... TARIFF
extra .... SURTAX
feudal .... TALLAGE, TRIBUTE
forms .... RETURNS
man .... AGENT, ASSESSOR,
PUBLICAN
municipal .... OCTROI
official .... CUSTOMS,
ASSESSOR, REVENUER,
COLLECTOR
on imports according to
value .... AD VALOREM
on ship .... TONNAGE
ploy .... IRA
privilege .... TOLL
protection .... TRIBUTE
schedule .... TARIFF
stratagem .... DODGING,
EVASION
substitute .... SCUTAGE
type of .... SALES, INCOME,
CUSTOMS, ROAD USE,
PROPERTY
voluntary .... TITHE
taxable .... DUTIABLE,
RAT(E)ABLE, CHARGEABLE
taxation .... ASSESSMENT,
IMPOSITION
taxeme .... ORDER, ARRANGEMENT
taxi .... CAB, HACK, FIACRE,
JITNEY, DROSHKY
adjunct .... METER
driver .... HACK, CABMAN,
CABETTE
driver: colloq. .... CABBY,
CABBIE, HACKIE
rider .... FARE
three-wheeled .... PEDICAB
two-wheeled .... HANSOM,
RICKSHAW, (JIN)RIKISHA
taxicab .... HACK
parking space .... STAND
taximeter for one .... ODOGRAPH,
ODOMETER
taxonomy subject
.... SYSTEMATICS,
CLASSIFICATION
Taygeta .... STAR, PLEIAD

Taylor, actor .... ROD, ROBERT
actress .... LIZ, ELIZABETH
Caldwell play .... MELISSA
comedian .... RIP
comedienne .... RENEE
composer, critic .... DEEMS
poet, writer .... BAYARD
U.S. president .... ZACHARY
Tay-Sachs disease .... IDIOCY
symptom .... DEAFNESS,
DEMENTIA, SEIZURES,
BLINDNESS, PARALYSIS
tazza .... CUP, BOWL, VASE
TB .... TUBERCULOSIS
Tchaikovsky ballet: 1890 .... THE
SLEEPING BEAUTY
opus .... PATHETIQUE
Te Deum .... HYMN
Kanawa's talent .... VOICE
tea .... CHA(A), MATE, TCHA, TSIA,
LEDUM, PARTY, PEKOE,
SNACK, YERBA, OSWEGO,
PTISAN, CAMBRIC, LAPSANG,
PARAGUAY, COLLATION,
GATHERING, RECEPTION
add liquor to .... LACE
alkaloid .... CAFFEIN(E)
beverage like .... BEEF(TEA),
CAMOMILE
biscuit .... COOKY,
SHORTBREAD
bitter principle .... THEINE
black .... BOHEA, OOPAK,
PEKOE, OOLONG, CONGO(U),
SOUCHONG
bowl .... CHAWAN
box/container .... CADDY,
CANISTER
brand .... LIPTON, NESTEA,
SALADA, TETLEY, BIGELOW
caffeine .... THEINE
cake .... SCONE
decoction .... TISANE
drink .... CAMBRIC
family .... THEACEAE
family shrub .... BAY,
CAMELLIA, LOBLOLLY
for two .... DUET
from meat .... BROTH,
BEEF(TEA), BOUILLON
garden .... PLANTATION
green .... HYSON
medicinal .... YERBA BUENA
party: sl. .... BRAWL
plant .... THEA
pot .... URN, KETTLE,
SAMOVAR
rolled .... CHA
serve .... POUR
slang .... MARIJUANA
substitute .... YAUPON

table .... TEAPOY
waterboiler for ...... POT, URN,
KETTLE, SAMOVAR
with mint flavor .... OSWEGO
with smoky flavor
.... LAPSANG
Tea and _____ .... SYMPATHY
teaberry .... WINTERGREEN
teach .... FORM, REAR, BREED,
COACH, DRILL, EDIFY, INURE,
TRAIN, TUTOR, INFUSE,
PREACH, SCHOOL, DEVELOP,
EDUCATE, EXPOUND,
NURTURE, PREPARE, INSTRUCT
Teach, Edward .... PIRATE,
PRIVATEER, BLACKBEARD
teacher .... DON, GURU, COACH,
GUIDE, RABBI, TUTOR,
MASTER, MENTOR, READER,
MULLA(H), PUNDIT, ADVISER,
TRAINER, DIRECTOR,
EDUCATOR, EXPONENT,
LECTURER, PREACHER,
PEDAGOG(UE), PRECEPTOR,
PROFESSOR, INSTRUCTOR
bird .... VIREO, WARBLER
favorite of .... PET
gift to .... APPLE
goal of .... TENURE
job security .... TENURE
movie .... (MR.) CHIPS
narrow-minded .... PEDANT
of music, great .... MAESTRO
of the deaf .... ORALIST
old style name for
.... SCHOOLMARM
pointer of .... FESCUE
project of .... EXAM
unattached .... DOCENT
teacher's group .... NEA
teaching ...... TUITION, GUIDANCE,
TRAINING, TUTELAGE,
DIRECTION, SCHOOLING,
TUTORSHIP, INSTRUCTION
science of .... PEDAGOGY,
DIDACTICS
teachings ...... PRECEPT, DOCTRINE
teak .... TECA, TEGA, TREE, WOOD
family .... VERBENA
teakettle spout .... NOZZLE
teal .... BLUE, DUCK
team. See also **baseball;**
football; basketball
.... CREW, PAIR, GROUP,
JOIN(UP), SIDE(WITH)
athletic .... SQUAD
baseball .... NINE
basketball .... FIVE, QUINTET
cricket .... ELEVEN
diamond .... NINE
football .... ELEVEN

manager .... COACH
of ducks/pigs .... BROOD
of two animals .... SPAN,
　　　　　　　　　　　　　 YOKE
pet .... MASCOT
play .... COOPERATION
rowing .... CREW
second placer ...... RUNNER-UP
teacher .... TRAINER
valuable player .... MVP,
　　　　　　　　　　 SUPERSTAR
winning .... CHAMPION
working .... CREW, GANG
teamster .... CARTER, DRIVER,
　　　　　　 CARRIER, TRUCKER,
　　　　　　　　　 TRUCKMAN
teapot .... KETTLE, SAMOVAR
cover .... COS(E)Y
tear .... GAP, JAG, RIP, DASH,
　　　　 PART, RACE, RAZE, REND,
　　　　 RENT, RIVE, BREAK, BURST,
　　　　 REAVE, SPEED, SHRED, SPLIT,
　　　　 REMOVE, TATTER, DISRUPT,
　　　　 RAMPAGE, LACERATE,
　　　　 SEPARATE, LANCINATE
apart .... RIP, OPEN
down .... RAZE, WRECK,
　　　　 BULLDOZE, DEMOLISH,
　　　　　　　　 DISMANTLE
from violently .... WREST,
　　　　　　 WRING, WRENCH
gas .... LAC(H)RIMATOR,
　　　　　　 LACHRYMATOR
gas grenade secretion
　..................................... SMOKE
into ...... RIP, ATTACK, TACKLE
jerker .... NOSTALGIA, SOB
　　　　 STORY, SOAP(OPERA)
jerking .... SAD, NOSTALGIC,
　　　　　　 SENTIMENTAL
limb from limb
　.......................... DISMEMBER
loose .... FREE, UPROOT,
　　　　　　　　　 DISLODGE
out .... REMOVE, EXTRACT
skin .... CRACK, WOUND,
　　　　　　　　　 FISSURE
slang .... BINGE, SPREE,
　　　　 BENDER, CAROUSAL
to pieces .... SHRED, SMASH,
　　　　　　　　　 SHATTER
teardrop diamond cut
　.......................... BRIOLETTE
tearful ...... SAD, TEARY, CRYING,
　　　　 RUEFUL, TRISTE, ELEGIAC,
　　　　 UNHAPPY, WEEPING,
　　　　 MOURNFUL, LAMENTING,
　　　　 SORROWFUL, LAC(H)RYMOSE
mother .... NIOBE
person .... MOURNER,
　　　　　　 LAMENTER

tale .... JEREMIAH
tearing .... RUSHING, VIOLENT,
　　　　　　　 RECKLESS
apart .... DIVULSION,
　　　　　　 SEPARATION
for .... LANIARY
tearless .... DRY-EYED,
　　　　　　 UNEMOTIONAL
tears .... LACHRYMA, SECRETION
characteristic of .... SALTY
combining form .... DACRY(O)
condition, deficiency of
　.............................. DRY EYE
condition, excessive shedding
　of .... WATERING EYE
excessive secretion of
　......................... LACRIMATION
inclined to shed many
　......................... LACHRYMOSE
of .... LACHRIMAL,
　　　　　　 LACHRYMAL
producer .... LACRIMAL
　　　　　　　 GLANDS
teary lady .... NIOBE
Teasdale, poetess .... SARA
tease .... BEG, IRK, KID, RAG, RIB,
　　　 VEX, CARD, COMB, MOCK,
　　　 RAZZ, RIDE, TWIT, ANNOY,
　　　 CHAFF, TAUNT, BOTHER,
　　　 EXCITE, HARASS, HECTOR,
　　　 PESTER, NEEDLE(R),
　　　 IMPORTUNE, TANTALIZE,
　　　　　　 TITILLATE
teasel .... BURR, HERB, FLOWER,
　　　　　　 BONESET
teaser .... JOKER, POSER, COME-
　　　 ON, KIDDER, NEEDLER,
　　　 PUZZLE(R), TEMPTER, LEG-
　　　　　　 PULLER
teasing, critical but playful
　................................... ROAST
good-natured .... CHAFF,
　　　　　　　 BANTER
humiliating .... HAZE,
　　　　　　 RIDICULE
teat .... DUG, PAP, TIT, UDDER,
　　　 NIPPLE, MAMMILLA
Tebaldi, Met star .... RENATA
technetium .... MASURIUM
technical .... SKILLED, SCIENTIFIC,
　　　　　　 SPECIALIZED
technicality ...... DETAIL, NUANCE,
　　　 RUBRIC, LOOPHOLE,
　　　 MINUTIAE, FORMALITY
technician .... EXPERT
technique .... ART, STYLE,
　　 METHOD, SYSTEM, PROCEDURE
technology .... CRAFT, SKILL,
　　　 TECHNICS, AUTOMATION
colloquial .... KNOW-HOW
subject .... SCIENCE,

　　　 MECHANICS, ENGINEERING
techy. See **tetchy**
tectonics .... STRUCTURE,
　　　　　 ARCHITECTURE
ted .... SPREAD, SCATTER
Teddy .... BEAR
Roosevelt word .... BULLY
tedious .... DRY, DULL, PROSY,
　　　 BORING, DREARY, HUMDRUM,
　　　 IRKSOME, TIRESOME,
　　　 WEARISOME, MONOTONOUS
tedium .... ENNUI, BOREDOM,
　　　　　　 MONOTONY
tee .... TAU, MOUND
hee .... HA-HA, GIGGLE, HEE-
　　　 HAW, TITTER, SNICKER
off .... BEGIN, DRIVE, START
shaped thing ...... ANKH, CRUX
to green .... HOLE
teel .... SESAME(OIL)
teem .... BEAR, POUR, EMPTY,
　　　 SWARM, ABOUND, PRODUCE,
　　　　　　 MULTIPLY
teeming .... RAINING, REPLETE,
　　　 ABUNDANT, CHOCKFUL, JAM-
　　　 PACKED, PLENTIFUL
teen's term of approval ..... FAR
　　　　　　 OUT
teenage trouble .... ACNE
teenager .... YOUTH, ADOLESCENT,
　　　　　　 BOBBYSOXER
favorite record of ..... TOP TEN
teeny .... WEE, TINY
bopper .... TEENER, TEENAGER,
　　　 YOUNGSTER, BOBBYSOXER
weeny .... PEEWEE
teepee ...... HUT, LODGE, WIGWAM,
　　　　　　 WICKIUP
teeter .... REEL, ROCK, SWAY,
　　　 WAVER, SEESAW, TOTTER,
　　　 WOBBLE, TREMBLE, HESITATE,
　　　　　　 VACILLATE
teeth. See also **tooth** .... MOLARS,
　　　 CANINES, CUSPIDS, INCISORS
appearance of new
　........................... ERUPTION
arrangement .... DENTITION
artificial .... PLATE, DENTURE
chisel-shaped .... INCISORS
cleaning substance
　.............................. DENTIFRICE
clenching/grinding of the
　.............................. BRUXISM
click of .... CHATTER
coating .... ENAMEL
colloquial .... GRINDERS
combining form .... DENT(I),
　　　　　　 ODONT(O)
decay .... CARIES
deciduous ...... MILK, PRIMARY
deposit .... TARTAR

doctor .... DENTIST
extraction .... EXODONTIA
eye .... UPPER CANINES
hard tissue surrounding pulp
   of .... IVORY, DENTIN(E)
having ..... DENTATE, TOOTHED
having large .... MACRODONT
having small .... MICRODONT
last to erupt .... WISDOM,
       THIRD MOLARS
long pointed .... FANGS,
      TUSKS, TUSHES
of/for the .... DENTAL
premolar .... BICUSPIDS
roots covering ...... CEMENTUM
rough sticky coating on
  .... PLAQUE
science dealing with
  .... DENTISTRY, ODONTOLOGY
sets of .... PRIMARY,
      PERMANENT
shaped .... DENTOID,
      DENTIFORM
sharp .... FANGS
shock absorber of
  .... PERIODONTAL LIGAMENT
slang .... IVORIES
small .... DENTICLES
sockets .... ALVEOLI
sound .... GNASH, CHATTER
tearing .... LANIARY
use of .... CHEWING,
      MASTICATION
without .... EDENTATE
teething .... ERUPTION
process .... DENTITION
toy .... RING
teethridge .... ALVEOLUS
teetotal .... ALL, ENTIRE,
      COMPLETE
teetotaler .... DRY, NAZARITE,
    ABSTAINER, NON-DRINKER
beverage of .... ADAM'S ALE
teetotalism .... ABSTINENCE,
      TEMPERANCE
teetotum .... TOP
tegmen ...... COATING, COVERING,
      TEGUMENT
Tegucigalpa is capital of
  .... HONDURAS
tegula .... TILE, ALULA
tegular .... TILE-LIKE
tegument ...... ARIL, SKIN, SHELL,
    COCOON, TEGMEN, CAPSULE
Tehuelche .... PATAGONIAN
teil .... LINDEN
Tejo .... TAGUS
Tel Aviv greeting .... SHALOM
tela ...... WEB, TISSUE, MEMBRANE
telar .... WEBLIKE
Telamon .... ATLAS, BEARER,

    COLUMN, ATLANTES
son of .... AJAX
telecast .... TELEVISE
telegram .... WIRE, TELEX,
      MESSAGE
slower .... DAYLETTER,
      NIGHTLETTER
word .... STOP
telegraph .... CABLE, SIGNAL
code .... MORSE
jungle .... TOM-TOM
kind of .... GRAPEVINE
lever .... KEY, TAPPER
signal .... DOT, DASH
wire support .... PYLON
telegraphic dash .... DAH
device for quotations
  .... TICKER
Telemachus' father ...... ULYSSES,
      ODYSSEUS
mother .... PENELOPE
telemeter .... RANGE-FINDER
teleost fish .... EEL
telepathic .... PSYCHIC
telepathy, mental .... MIND
      READING
telephone .... BUZZ, CALL, PHONE,
      RING(UP)
book .... DIRECTORY
book classified section
  .... YELLOW PAGES
diaphragm .... TYMPANUM
emergency number .... NINE-
      ONE-ONE
exchange .... CENTRAL,
      SWITCHBOARD
inventor .... BELL
main line .... TRUNK
on freeways for emergency
  .... CALL BOX
operator .... CENTRAL,
      TELEPHONIST
part .... CORD, DIAL, RINGER,
    CRADLE, RECEIVER,
    MOUTHPIECE
shared by a number of
  people .... PARTY LINE
structure for a public
  .... BOOTH
type of .... DIAL, WALL,
  RADIO, UNLISTED, WIRELESS,
  EXTENSION, PUSH-BUTTON
wire .... LINE
telescope .... TUBE, ABRIDGE,
  BINOCLE, SHORTEN,
  CONDENSE, (SPY)GLASS,
  REFRACTOR, FIELD GLASS,
  BINOCULARS
attached to another .... FINDER
measuring device
  .... MICROMETER

opening .... APERTURE
part .... LENS, MIRROR,
      EYEPIECE
telescopic .... FARSEEING
telestic(h) .... POEM, ACROSTIC
telethon moderator .... STAR,
    CELEBRITY, POLITICIAN
purpose of .... FUND-RAISING
televiewer .... VIDEO-GAZER
television/TV .... SET, TELLY,
    VIDEO, TELESCREEN
ad .... COMMERCIAL
adjunct ...... AERIAL, ANTENNA
annoyance .... SNOW
award .... EMMY
Bart of .... SIMPSON
blurb .... AD
broadcast .... TELECAST
cabinet .... CONSOLE
camera move .... PAN
camera plate .... MOSAIC
camera platform .... DOLLY
caveman .... FLINTSTONE
classic, Mary Martin
  .... PETER PAN
commercial cat .... MORRIS
cop .... STONE, KELLER,
  COLUMBO, WILLIAMS,
  (PETER)GUNN, MCGARRETT
deletion .... BLEEP
doctor, early .... WELBY,
      KILDARE
dragon .... OLLIE
educational channel .... PBS,
      DISCOVERY
emcee .... COMPERE
Endora of .... AGNES
excellent interviewer
  .... (LARRY)KING,
  (BARBARA)WALTERS
extra terrestrial of .... ALF
fare ...... GAME, MOVIE, SOAPS,
    SPORTS, SERIALS
fare, monotonous .... RERUN
game show host .... CLARK,
  PERRY, SAJAK, WHITE,
  BARKER, COOMBS, DAWSON,
  TREBEK, EUBANKS, WOOLERY,
  DAVIDSON, TOMARKEN,
  MARTINDALE
hook-up .... CABLE
horse .... MISTER ED
host, avuncular early
  .... MILTIE
host, former .... PAAR,
      CARSON
interference .... SNOW
inventor of
  .... (VLADIMIR)ZWORYKIN
Jeannie of .... EDEN
lawyer .... BEN MATLOCK,

letter turner ..... VANNA WHITE
lines on tube .... RASTER
"Love Connection" star
.... (CHUCK) WOOLERY
"magic" .... (TECHNI)COLOR
movie channel .... HBO,
CINEMAX, SHOWTIME
name .... LUCY, RHODA,
IMOGENE
network .... ABC, CBS, NBC,
CNN, PBS, USA, ESPN
no-no .... CIGARETTE
AD(VERTISEMENT)
pickup tube .... ORTHICON
plug .... COMMERCIAL
priest, old-time .... SHEEN
"Private Eye" .... CANON,
JONES, HAMMER, ROCKFORD
radar air navigation
.... TELERAN
receiver .... SET
role for Burt Reynolds
.... DAN AUGUST
room .... DEN, FAMILY
series, popular .... MASH,
DALLAS, DYNASTY, IRONSIDE,
FALCON CREST, HAWAII
FIVE-O, KNOTS LANDING,
MURDER SHE WROTE
"shopping" channel ...... QVC
show .... GAME, LIVE, NEWS,
QUIZ, MOVIE, PANEL, RERUN,
SPORTS, PAGEANT, GIVEAWAY,
DOCUDRAMA, DOCUMENTARY
sound .... AUDIO
specialty .... SOAP OPERA
Spock portrayer .... NIMOY
spoiler .... SNOW
spoof .... SOAP
stand .... ROLLAWAY
street for tots .... SESAME
talk show host .... HALL,
KING, LENO, JONES, CARSON,
POVICH, RIVERA, RIVERS,
DONAHUE, RAPHAEL, WINFREY,
WOOLERY, WILLIAMS
talk show pair ...... REGIS AND
KATHIE LEE
technique .... VIDEOTAPE
time .... SLOT
time buyer .... SPONSOR
topper, old-time ..... ANTENNA
tube .... KINESCOPE,
ICONOSCOPE
visual element .... VIDEO
waitress .... ALICE
weathercasters .... STORM
TEAM
weatherman .... NANCE,
SCOTT, PEREZ, MCKUEN,

COLEMAN
witch ..... ENDORA, SAMANTHA
witch portrayer
.... MOOREHEAD, MONTGOMERY
tell .... SAY, DEEM, MEAN, ORDER,
SPEAK, STATE, IMPART,
INFORM, UTTER, NUMBER,
RECITE, RECKON, RELATE,
REPEAT, REPORT, REVEAL,
DECLARE, DIVULGE, EXPRESS,
MENTION, NARRATE,
(RE)COUNT, ACQUAINT
a story .... SPIN A YARN
all .... BLAB
apart .... DISCERN, DISTINGUISH
as by appearance
.... RECOGNIZE
in detail .... RELATE, NARRATE,
RECOUNT
it like it is ...... CALL A SPADE
A SPADE
it to ____ .... SWEENEY
it to the ____ .... JUDGE,
MARINES
off .... RATE, CHIDE, SCOLD,
REBUKE, LECTURE, CHASTISE
on ...... BLAB, PEACH, BETRAY,
INFORM, SQUEAL, TATTLE
privately .... CONFIDE, WHISPER
publicly .... PUBLISH,
ANNOUNCE, PROCLAIM
slang .... RAT, SING, SNITCH
the truth .... CONFESS,
DISCLOSE
teller .... CLERK, CASHIER,
INFORMER, NARRATOR,
REPORTER, ANNOUNCER,
MONEY-COUNTER
place of .... CAGE
slang ..... RAT, FINK, SNITCHER
window of .... WICKET
telling .... COGENT, FORCEFUL,
STRIKING, EFFECTIVE
tales on someone .... RATTING
Tell's canton .... URI
telltale .... HINT, TATTLER,
INDICATOR, REVEALING
tellurian .... EARTHLY,
EARTHMAN, TERRESTRIAL
telluride .... HESSITE
Tellus' domain .... EARTH
telson .... SOMITE, SEGMENT
Telugu .... DRAVIDIAN
temblor .... TREMOR,
(EARTH)QUAKE
temerarious ...... RASH, RECKLESS
temerity .... GALL, BRASS, CHEEK,
NERVE, DARING, AUDACITY,
BOLDNESS, RASHNESS,
EFFRONTERY
temper .... PET, MOOD, TONE,

HUMOR, (AN)NEAL, NATURE,
SOFTEN, SPIRIT, QUALITY,
TANTRUM, MODERATE,
CHARACTER, COMPOSURE,
DISPOSITION
bad ...... BILE, CHOLER, SPLEEN
colloquial ..... ANGER, DANDER
kind of .... ILL, IRISH
of ugly .... ORNERY
tantrum .... FIT, CONNIPTION
violent .... FURY, RAGE
tempera painting .... SECCO
temperament ...... MOOD, ETHOS,
GAMUT, NATURE, DISPOSITION
condition of .... BILIOUS,
CHOLERIC, SANGUINE,
IRRITABLE, PHLEGMATIC,
MELANCHOLIC
temperamental .... MOODY,
TESTY, INNATE, EXCITABLE,
IRRITABLE, SENSITIVE, HIGH-
STRUNG
temperance .... SOBRIETY,
ABSTINENCE, CONTINENCE,
MODERATION,
(SELF)RESTRAINT
temperate .... COOL, MILD,
SOBER, ASCETIC, CAUTIOUS,
MODERATE, CONTINENT,
ABSTEMIOUS
temperature .... HEAT, FEVER,
HOTNESS, COLDNESS
measuring instrument
.... CRYOMETER,
THERMOMETER
regulator .... CRYOSTAT,
THERMOSTAT
tempered ...... MELLOWED, HEAT-
TREATED
tempest .... GALE, STORM,
SQUALL, TUMULT, TURMOIL,
BLIZZARD, OUTBURST,
HURRICANE
tempestuous .... WILD, GUSTY,
WINDY, RAGING, STORMY,
FURIOUS, VIOLENT,
TURBULENT
Templar ...... KNIGHT, CRUSADER,
BARRISTER
Templar, ____ .... SIMON
portrayer .... MOORE
temple ...... FANE, NAOS, CHAPEL,
CHURCH, MOSQUE, PAGODA,
RATH(A), CATHEDRAL,
SANCTUARY, TABERNACLE
ancient .... NAOS
Aztec .... TEOPAN
chamber .... NAOS, CELLA
Chinese .... PAGODA, JOSS
HOUSE
for all gods .... PANTHEON

for private prayer
.... ORATORY
gateway .... TORII
girl ..... BAYADEER, BAYADERE
Jewish .... SYNAGOGUE
Jupiter's .... CAPITOL
secret/innermost parts
.... PENETRALIA
shrine ...... ADYTUM, SANCTUM
Temple's (Shirley) first spouse
.... AGAR
Templeton, _____ .... ALEC
tempo .... BEAT, PACE, RATE,
TIME, SPEED, RHYTHM
temporal .... CIVIL, CARNAL,
EARTHLY, MUNDANE,
SECULAR, WORLDLY,
POLITICAL, TEMPORARY,
TRANSIENT, TRANSITORY
temporary .... BRIEF, ACTING,
INTERIM, STOPGAP, FLEETING,
SEASONAL, MAKESHIFT,
TENTATIVE, PROVISIONAL
amnesia .... FUGUE
bridge .... PONTOON,
GANGPLANK
property holder: law
.... BAILEE
quiet .... LULL
refuge .... ASYLUM
relief .... RESPITE
sale .... RENTAL
stopping of activity
.... MORATORIUM
warfare cessation, mutual
.... TRUCE, CEASE-FIRE
temporize .... DELAY, HEDGE,
STALL, PROCRASTINATE
tempt .... BAIT, COAX, LURE,
APPEAL, CAJOLE, ENTICE,
INCITE, INDUCE, SEDUCE,
ATTRACT, PROVOKE
temptation ...... BAIT, SEDUCTION,
ENTICEMENT
tempter .... DEVIL, SATAN,
TEASER, CHARMER, SERPENT
tempting .... ALLURING,
SEDUCTIVE, TOOTHSOME,
ATTRACTIVE, APPETIZING
temptress ...... EVE, VAMP, FLIRT,
CIRCE, SIREN, DELILAH,
LORELEI, ENCHANTRESS
ten .... IO, DECAD(E)
ares .... DECARE
cents .... DIME
combining form .... DEC(A),
DECI, DEKA
cubic meters .... DECASTERE
decibels .... BEL
dollar bill .... SAWBUCK
dollar gold piece .... EAGLE

gallon hat .... SOMBRERO
group of .... DECADE
legged .... DECAPOD
legged crustacean .... CRAB,
PRAWN, SHRIMP, LOBSTER,
MACRURAN
men, company of .... DECURIA
men, officer in charge of
.... DECURION
per center .... AGENT
pfennig coin .... GROSCHEN
plane surfaced figure
.... DECAHEDRON
rins .... SEN
Roman numeral for X
sided .... DECAGONAL
sided and ten angled figure
.... DECAGON
slang .... TENNER
square meters .... DECIARE
thousand .... MYRIAD
times as large .... DECUPLE,
TENFOLD
to one .... ODDS
year period .... DECADE,
DECEN(N)ARY, DECENNIAL,
DECENNIUM
Ten Commandments
.... DECALOG(UE)
10%er .... AGT
tenable .... VIABLE, CREDIBLE,
PLAUSIBLE
tenace .... KING-JACK, QUEENLACE
tenacious .... BOLD, TOUGH,
CLINGY, DOGGED, STICKY,
ADHESIVE, COHESIVE,
CONSTANT, RESOLUTE,
STUBBORN, OBSTINATE,
RETENTIVE, PERSISTENT
animal .... BULLDOG
follower .... TAIL, SHADOW
tenacity ...... HOLDING, PATIENCE,
STRENGTH, CONSTANCY,
OBSTINACY, RESISTANCE,
PERSISTENCE
tenancy .... OCCUPANCY
tenant .... INMATE, LESSEE,
RENTER, VASSAL, VILLEIN,
OCCUPANT, OCCUPIER,
RESIDENT, INHABITANT
tench .... CARP
tend .... BEND, KEEP, LEAN, MIND,
BE APT, GUARD, SERVE,
WATCH, MANAGE, WAIT ON,
CARE FOR, INCLINE, OPERATE,
MINISTER
toward .... PREFER
tendency ...... BENT, BIAS, MOOD,
TONE, TURN, DRIFT, TENOR,
TREND, APTNESS, LEANING,
PENCHANT, LIKELIHOOD,

PROPENSITY, DISPOSITION,
INCLINATION
tender .... BID, BOAT, KIND, SOFT,
SORE, FRAIL, LIGHT, OFFER,
YOUNG, FEEBLE, GENTLE,
LOVING, FRAGILE, PAINFUL,
PRESENT, PROFFER, PROPOSE,
DELICATE, SENSITIVE,
(SUPPLY)SHIP
feeling .... FONDNESS,
SENTIMENT
loving care .... CONCERN,
SUPPORT
ship's ..... PINNACE, COCKBOAT
sort of .... SORER
spot .... SORE POINT
yacht .... DINGHY
tenderfoot .... NOVICE, ROOKIE,
RECRUIT, BEGINNER, BOY
SCOUT, NEWCOMER
tenderhearted ...... SOFT, KINDLY,
HUMANE, LOVING, AMOROUS,
COMPASSIONATE
tenderizing sauce ...... MARINADE
tenderloin .... MEAT, STEAK, RED-
LIGHT DISTRICT
tenderness .... PAIN, LENITY,
SENSITIVITY
of mood .... LANGUOR
tending ...... APT, PRONE, LIABLE,
LEANING(TO),
CONDUCTIVE(TO)
tendon .... CORD, THEW, SINEW,
LEADER, MUSCLE, TISSUE,
LIGAMENT
combining form .... TENO
composition of a .... FIBERS,
PROTEIN, COLLAGEN
disorder ...... RUPTURE, TENNIS
ELBOW, TRIGGER FINGER
division of .... TENOTOMY
heel .... ACHILLES
inflammation .... TENDINITIS
knee .... HAMSTRING
nodule .... SESAMOID
of/like a .... TENDINOUS
operation .... TENDOLYSIS
shape .... CYLINDRICAL
sheets of fibers in a
.... APONEUROSES
tendrac .... TENREC
tendril .... BINE, CURL, CIRRUS,
BRANCH, STIPULE
having .... CAPREOLATE
resembling a ..... TENDRILLAR,
TENDRILOUS
tendron .... BUD, SHOOT
tenebrific .... OBSCURING
tenebrous .... DIM, SAD, DARK,
DUSKY, MURKY, GLOOMY
tenement .... FLAT, SLUM, ABODE,

BUILDING, DWELLING, (APARTMENT)HOUSE
district/house .... ROOKERY
Tenerife mountain .... TEYDE
tenet .... ISM, CREDO, CREED, DOGMA, MAXIM, BELIEF, OPINION, DOCTRINE, PRINCIPLE
tenfold .... DENARY, DECUPLE
Tennessee Air Force base .... SEWART
capital .... NASHVILLE
city/town .... ALAMO, BRISTOL, JACKSON, JOHNSON, MEMPHIS, CLEVELAND, KINGSPORT, OAK RIDGE, KNOXVILLE, COOKEVILLE, CHATTANOOGA, CLARKSVILLE
college .... LEE, LANE, BELMONT, LAMBUTH, SCARRITT, MARYVILLE
county .... DYER, KNOX, MAURY, OBION, ROANE, BLOUNT, CARTER, COFFEE, GIBSON, GREENE, MCMINN, SHELBY, SUMNER, TIPTON, WARREN, WILSON, BRADLEY, HAWKINS, WEAKLEY, SULLIVAN
dam .... NORRIS, CHEROKEE, GREAT FALLS
federal agency .... TVA
Indian .... CHICKASAW
lake .... BOONE, NORRIS, DOUGLAS, WATAUGA, CHEROKEE, KENTUCKY, PICKWICK, REELFOOT, TIMS FORD, WATTS BAR, MELTON HILL, OLD HICKORY
mountain .... GUYOT, CHILHOWEE, CLINGMANS DOME
mountain inhabitant .... MELUNGEON
mountain range .... BALD, IRON, STONE, UNAKA, UNICOI, GREAT SMOKY, APPALACHIAN
national park .... SHILOH
national military park .... FORT DONELSON
native .... TENNESSEAN
Naval Air Station .... MEMPHIS
plateau .... CUMBERLAND
playwright .... WILLIAMS
river .... ELK, RED, DUCK, OBED, WOLF, EMORY, GREEN, OBION, OCOEE, CLINCH, POWELL, STONES, BUFFALO, COLLINS, HARPETH, HATCHIE, HOLSTON, TELLICO, BIG SANDY, FORKED DEER, FRENCH BROAD, MISSISSIPPI
state bird .... MOCKINGBIRD

state flower .... IRIS
state nickname .... VOLUNTEER
tourist attraction ...... DOLLYWOOD, GRACELAND, THE HERMITAGE, GRAND OLE OPRY
university .... FISK, UNION, VANDERBILT, LINCOLN MEMORIAL
tennis .... RACKETS
career most singles title holder .... CONNORS
champ ...... ASHE, BETZ, BORG, CASH, GRAF, HOAD, KING, NOAH, BUDGE, BUENO, CHANG, COURT, EVERT, KODES, LAVER, LENDL, PERRY, RIGGS, SELES, SMITH, WADE, STICH, WILLS, AGASSI, AUSTIN, BECKER, EDBERG, FORGET, GIBSON, GIMENO, KRAMER, MARBLE, STOLLE, TILDEN, CONNORS, COURIER, LACOSTE, MCENROE, SANCHEZ, SANTANA, TRABERT, WHEATON, SHRIVER, CAPRIATI, GONZALES, ROSEWALL, SABATINI, GERULAITAS, NAVRATILOVA, SAMPRAS, SANCHEZ-VICARIO
competition ...... TOURNAMENT
competition, four-player .... DOUBLES
competition, two-player .... SINGLES
court surface .... CLAY, GRASS
equipment .... BAT, NET, PADDLE, RACKET, RACQUET
first ball .... SERVICE
ground .... COURT
handicap .... BISQUE
"Little Mo" of .... (MAUREEN)CONNOLY
love in .... ZERO
modified .... SQUASH, HANDBALL
player, Agassi .... ANDRE
Ashe .... ARTHUR
Austin .... TRACY
Becker .... BORIS
Borg .... BJORN
Bruguera .... SERGI
Capriati .... JENNIFER
Casals .... ROSIE
Cash .... PAT
Chang .... MICHAEL
Coetzer .... AMANDA
Connors .... JIMMY
Courier .... JIM
Court .... MARGARET
Date .... KIMIKO
Davenport .... LINDSAY

Drysdale .... CLIFF
Edberg .... STEFAN
Enqvist .... THOMAS
Evert .... CHRIS
Fendick .... PATTY
Fernandez .... GIGI, MARY-JOE
Ferreira .... WAYNE
Fleming .... PETER
Forget .... GUY
Frazier .... AMY
Garrison .... ZINA
Gerulaitis .... VITAS
Gibson .... ALTHEA
Gilbert .... BRADLEY
Graf .... STEFFI
Haarhuis .... PAUL
Huber .... ANKE
Ivanisevic .... GORAN
King .... BILLIE JEAN
Korda .... PETR
Krajicek .... RICHARD
Krickstein .... AARON
Kriek .... JOHAN
Larsson .... MAGNUS
Laver .... ROD
Lendl .... IVAN
Maleeva .... MAGDALENA
Martin .... TODD
Martinez .... CONCHITA
Mayotte .... TIM
McEnroe ..... JOHN, PATRICK
McNeil .... LORI
Muster .... THOMAS
Nagelsen .... BETSY
Navratilova .... MARTINA
Newcombe .... JOHN
Noah .... YANNICK
Novotna .... JANA
Palmer .... JARED
Perry .... FRED
Pierce .... MARY
Pugh .... JIM
Raymond .... LISA
Reneberg .... RICHEY
Riggs .... BOBBY
Rostagno .... DERRICK
Sabatini .... GABRIELA
Sampras .... PETE
Sanchez .... EMILIO
Sanchez-Vicario .... ARANTXA
Schultz .... BRENDA
Seles .... MONICA
Shriver .... PAM
Stich .... MICHAEL
Stolle .... FRED, SANDON
Tanner .... ROSCOE
Vilas .... GUILLERMO
Washington .... MALIVAI
Wheaton .... DAVID

Wilander .... MATS
Woodforde .... MARK
Zvereva .... NATASHA
player, forward .... NETMAN
player's nemesis .... NET
racket string .... CATGUT
replay .... LET
score .... LOVE, DEUCE, FORTY,
THIRTY, FIFTEEN
score of 40 each .... DEUCE
scoring system .... VASS
series of games .... SET
shoes .... SNEAKERS
stroke .... ACE, BAT, CUT, LOB,
CHOP, DRIVE, SLICE, SMASH,
VOLLEY, SERVICE, BACKHAND,
FOREHAND
table .... PINGPONG
term .... ACE, BYE, LET, SET,
LOVE, BREAK, DEUCE, FAULT,
LINER, MATCH, DOUBLES,
LOVE SET, SINGLES, BASELINE,
(AD)VANTAGE, TIE BREAKER,
SERVICE(LINE)
uncounted service .... LET
world championship cup
.... DAVIS
Tennyson, poet .... ALFRED
heroine .... ENID, ISOLT,
ELAINE(THE FAIR)
heroine's home .... ASTOLAT
tenon, companion of
.... MORTISE
tenor .... GIST, MOOD, TONE,
DRIFT, SENSE, COURSE,
IMPORT, MANNER, NATURE,
SINGER, MEANING, PURPORT,
TENDENCY, VOCALIST
counter .... ALTO
great .... CARUSO, MELCHIOR
kind of .... FALSETTO
violin .... ALTO, VIOLA
tenpins .... BOWLS, BOWLING
tenpounder .... TARPON,
LADYFISH
tenrec .... TENDRAC
food of .... INSECTS
habitat .... MADAGASCAR
tense .... FLEX, TAUT, DRAWN,
RIGID, STIFF, UNEASY,
ANXIOUS, EXCITED, NERVOUS,
(UP)TIGHT, FRENETIC,
STRAINED
change .... ABLAUT
opposite of .... LAX, LOOSE,
SLACK, PLIANT, RELAXED,
EASY-GOING
verb .... PAST, FUTURE,
PRESENT
very .... ELECTRIC, EXCITING,
ELECTRIFYING

tensile .... DUCTILE, FLEXILE,
PLASTIC, PLIABLE, FLEXIBLE,
STRETCHABLE
strength .... ELASTICITY,
RESISTANCE
tensimeter .... MANOMETER
tension .... STRAIN, STRESS,
ANXIETY, PRESSURE
tent ...... YURT, CANVAS, ENCAMP,
SHELTER, TABERNACLE
arena enclosed in a
.... CIRCUS
circus .... BIG TOP
cone-shaped .... TEPEE
dweller .... ARAB, KEDAR,
NOMAD, INDIAN, BEDOUIN,
SCENITE
felt .... YURT
flap .... FLY
Indian .... LODGE, TE(E)PEE,
WIGWAM
kind of .... PUP, OXYGEN,
UMBRELLA
large .... PAVILION
of animal skins .... TUPIK
of Meeting .... TABERNACLE
show .... CIRCUS, MARQUEE,
MARQUISE
show man .... CARNIE, CARNEY
surgical .... PLUG, DOSSIL
tentacle .... PALP, GRASP, POWER,
FEELER, ANTENNA
feature .... SUCKER
tentacles, creature with
.... SQUID, OCTOPUS,
CEPHALOPOD, CUTTLE(FISH)
tentative .... TRIAL, INTERIM,
MAKESHIFT, TEMPORARY,
CONDITIONAL, PROVISIONAL
tenterhook .... NAIL
tenterhooks, on .... TENSE,
ANXIOUS
tenth .... DIME, TITHE, DENARY
muse .... SAPPHO
part, a .... TITHE
revolutionary year
.... MESSIDOR
wave .... DECUMAN
wedding anniversary gift
.... TIN
tenths, pertaining to
.... DECIMAL
tentmaker .... OMAR
Aquila's wife .... PRISCILLA
tenuity .... RARITY, FINENESS,
THINNESS, FAINTNESS
tenuous ...... RARE, THIN, FLIMSY,
SLIGHT, SLENDER, RAREFIED
tenure .... TERM, HOLDING,
DURATION
land .... SOCAGE

of office .... INCUMBENCY
teocalli .... TEMPLE
teosinte .... GRASS
tepee ...... TENT, LODGE, WIGWAM
tepid .... MILD, (LUKE)WARM
tequila .... AGAVE, DRINK,
LIQUOR, MESCAL, PULQUE
drinker .... MEXICAN(O)
Terah's son ...... ABRAM, HARAN,
NAHOR
teraphim .... IDOLS
teratism .... FETUS, FREAK,
MONSTROSITY
teratoid .... MONSTER,
MONSTROUS
tercel .... HAWK, PEREGRINE
tercet .... TRIPLET
terebinth ...... TEIL, TREE, SUMAC,
LINDEN
yield .... TURPENTINE
teredo .... BORER, MOLLUSK,
SHIPWORM
tergal .... BACK, DORSAL
tergiversate .... LIE, DUCK,
EVADE, DODGE, HEDGE,
PARRY, SIDESTEP,
APOSTATIZE, EQUIVOCATE,
PREVARICATE
tergiversation .... EVASION,
APOSTASY, SUBTERFUGE
tergum .... BACK
term .... CALL, NAME, TIME,
WORD, LIMIT, BOUND(ARY),
DURATION, SEMESTER,
EXPRESSION
bookbinding .... QUIRE
geometric .... SECANT
mod .... AGOGO
of address for a young boy
.... SONNY
of endearment .... BABY,
TOOTS, HON(EY), DEARIE
of imprisonment: sl.
.... STRETCH
of office .... TENURE
paper .... THESIS
school .... SEMESTER
termagant .... SHREW, VIXEN,
HELLCAT
termer .... PRISONER
terminal .... END, LAST, DEPOT,
FINAL, CLOSING, STATION,
TERMINUS, EXTREMITY
negative .... CATHODE
positive .... ANODE
terminate .... END, HALT, STOP,
ABATE, CEASE, CLOSE,
EXPIRE, COMPLETE, CONCLUDE
at point of contact .... ABUT
prematurely .... ABORT
termination .... END(ING),

EXPIRY, FINISH, RESULT, CONCLUSION, EXPIRATION
in grammar .... DESINENCE
of pregnancy .... ABORTION
of right .... LAPSE
word .... SUFFIX
terminology .... WORDING, NOMENCLATURE
terminus ...... END, GOAL, DEPOT, LIMIT, MARKER, STATION, BOUNDARY, EXTREMITY
termite .... ANAY, WHITE ANT
terms .... AGREEMENT, CONDITIONS, PROVISIONS, STIPULATIONS
come to .... AGREE
make .... TREAT, NEGOTIATE
tern .... NODDY, (SEA)BIRD, SEA SWALLOW, (LOTTERY)PRIZE
Arctic .... PARADISAEA
common .... HIRUNDO
genus .... ANOUS, STERNA
Inca .... LAROSTERNA
largest .... CASPIA
Little .... ALBITRONS
relative .... GULL
roseate .... DOUGALLII
ternary .... TRIO, THIRD, TRIAD, TRIPLE, THREE(FOLD)
terpene alcohol .... LINALOOL
derivative .... CAMPHOR
isomeric .... LIMONENE
Terpsichore .... MUSE
concern of .... DANCE, DANCING
terra .... SOIL, EARTH
alba .... GYPSUM, KAOLIN, MAGNESIA
cotta .... CLAY
firma .... SOLID GROUND
incognita .... UNEXPLORED LAND, UNEXPLORED REGION
sigil lata .... SEALED EARTH
Terra Nova ...... NEWFOUNDLAND
terrace .... BERM(E), LEVEL, PATIO, PLANE, PORCH, BALCONY, GALLERY, PLATEAU, PORTICO
staircase .... PERRON
terrain .... FIELD, GROUND, SPHERE
terramycin .... ANTIBIOTIC
terrapin .... EMYD, TURTLE, CHELONIAN
type of .... DIAMONDBACK
terrazo .... FLOORING
material ...... CEMENT, MARBLE
terrene .... LAND, EARTH(Y), MUNDANE, WORLDLY, TERRITORY
terrestrial ...... GAEAL, EARTHLY,

MUNDANE, WORLDLY, SECULAR, TEMPORAL
planet .... MARS, EARTH, VENUS, MERCURY
terret .... LOOP, RING
terrible .... BAD, DIRE, AWFUL, HORRID, SEVERE, AWESOME, FEARFUL, HIDEOUS, INTENSE, ALARMING, DREADFUL, HORRIBLE, SHOCKING, APPALLING, FRIGHTFUL
colloquial .... EXCESSIVE, UNPLEASANT
one/tsar .... IVAN
terribly: colloq. .... VERY, EXTREMELY, EXCEEDINGLY
terrier ...... AIREDALE, WIREHAIR, SCHNAUZER, (HUNTING)DOG
kind of .... FOX, RAT, SKYE, CAIRN, IRISH, SILKY, WELSH, LAKELAND, SEALYHAM, SCOTTISH, KERRY BLUE, YORKSHIRE, BEDLINGTON, AUSTRALIAN, (BOSTON)BULL
terrific .... GREAT, EXCELLENT, FABULOUS, WONDERFUL
terrified .... AGHAST, STUNNED, PETRIFIED
terrify ...... COW, ALARM, DAUNT, SCARE, SHOCK, APPAL(L), DISMAY, FREEZE, STUPEFY, FRIGHTEN, TERRORIZE, INTIMIDATE
terrifying .... SCARY, HORRID, GRIS(T)LY, CHILLING, DREADFUL
terrigenous .... EARTHBORN
terrine .... STEW
territorial .... AREAL, ZONAL, REGIONAL
division .... AMT, SHIRE, CANTON, COUNTY
territory .... REALM, STATE, DOMAIN, REGION, TERRENE, DISTRICT, PROVINCE, POSSESSION
disputed ..... SABAH, CHENPAO, KASHMIR, DAMANSKY
terror .... FEAR, DREAD, PANIC, FRIGHT, HORROR
colloquial ..... PEST, NUISANCE
terrorism ...... THREAT, ANARCHY, TYRANNY, SABOTAGE, VIOLENCE
terrorist .... GOON, OGRE, BOMBER, ALARMIST, ASSASSIN, VIGILANTE, NIGHTRIDER
1836 .... SEPTEMBRIST
terrorize .... COW, BULLY, SCARE, BROWBEAT, FRIGHTEN,

THREATEN
terse .... CURT, BRIEF, CRISP, PITHY, SHORT, COMPACT, CONCISE, LACONIC, SUCCINCT
tertiary .... THIRD
tessellate ...... TILE, INFIX, INLAY, CHECKER
tesselation .... MOSAIC
tessera .... TILE
test .... FEEL, ASSAY, CHECK, PROVE, TRIAL, TRY(OUT), EXAMINE, WORKOUT, EXPERIMENT
by which something is judged .... STANDARD, CRITERION
colloquial ..... EXAM, MIDTERM
clam's/crab's .... SHELL
device .... WIND TUNNEL
diagnostic .... BIOPSY
flight .... TRIAL RUN
general, medical ..... PHYSICAL
kind of .... ORAL, MEDICAL, WRITTEN
knowledge, oral or written .... QUIZ
match .... CONTEST
of patience .... TRIAL
operation .... SHAKEDOWN
ore .... ASSAY
paper .... LITMUS
print .... PROOF
quality of ...... ESSAY, SAMPLE
severe .... ORDEAL, STRAIN, CRUCIBLE, TRIBULATION
vessel .... CUPEL, CRUCIBLE
testa .... SHELL, INTEGUMENT
testacean .... RHIZOPOD
testament .... WILL, COVENANT
testator .... LEGATOR
beneficiary of .... HEIR(ESS), (IN)HERITOR
tester .... CIEL, CANOPY, SIPPER, ASSAYER, EXAMINER
testifier .... WITNESS, DEPONENT
statement of .... AFFIDAVIT, DEPOSITION
testify ...... AVOW, STATE, SWEAR, AFFIRM, DEPONE, DEPOSE, DECLARE, WITNESS, MANIFEST
testimonial .... GALA, TRIBUTE, EVIDENCE, REFERENCE, COMPLIMENT, CERTIFICATE
testimony ...... PROOF, EVIDENCE, ATTESTATION, DECLARATION
testing place ...... LAB(ORATORY)
testis .... GONAD
teston .... COIN
testudinate .... TURTLE, TORTOISE
testudo .... SCREEN, SHIELD, SHELTER

testy .... CROSS, ORNERY, TOUCHY, PEEVISH, PEPPERY, WASPISH, HOTHEADED, IRASCIBLE, IRRITABLE

tetanus .... LOCKJAW, TRISMUS, INFECTION

tetany .... SPASMS

tetched .... LOCO, WITLESS, DEMENTED

tetchy .... TOUCHY, PEEVISH, PRICKLY, IRRITABLE, SENSITIVE

tete-a-tete ...... CHAT, SEAT, FACE TO FACE, HEAD TO HEAD, CONVERSATION

tether .... TIE, ROPE, LEASH, LONGE, STAKE, FASTEN, LARIAT, PICKET

Tethys .... TITANESS
father of .... URANUS
husband of .... OCEANUS

tetracaine .... ANESTHETIC

tetrad .... FOUR

tetragon .... SQUARE, QUADRANGLE

Tetragrammaton .... ADONAI, ELOHIM, YAHWEH, JEHOVAH

tetrarch .... HEROD

tetter .... ECZEMA, HERPES, LICHEN

Teucrian .... TROJAN

Teutoburger ⸻ **in Germany** .... WALD

Teuton(ic) .... DUTCH, NORDIC, ENGLISH, GERMAN(IC)
Fate .... NORN
god .... TYR, ULL, ODIN, THOR, AESIR, WODEN, BALDER
goddess .... MERTHUS
hero .... OFFA
metal collar .... TORQUE

Teutonism .... GERMANISM

Tevere .... TIBER

tew .... TOIL

tewel .... BORE, PIPE, FUNNEL, TUYERE

Texas Air Force Base ...... DYESS, KELLY, REESE, CARSWELL, LACKLAND, LAUGHLIN, SHEPPARD, BERGSTROM, ELLINGTON, GOODFELLOW
battlesite town .... RESACA
bay .... WEST, BAFFIN, COPANO, TRINITY, GALVESTON, MATAGORDA, SAN ANTONIO
capital .... AUSTIN
city/town .... WACO, BRYAN, PLANO, TYLER, DALLAS, DENTON, EL PASO, IRVING, LAREDO, ODESSA, TEMPLE, ABILENE, DENISON, GARLAND, HOUSTON, KILLEEN, LUBBOCK, MCALLEN, MIDLAND, AMARILLO, BEAUMONT, LONGVIEW, PASADENA, VICTORIA, ARLINGTON, FORT WORTH, GALVESTON, SAN ANGELO, SAN ANTONIO, WICHITA FALLS, CORPUS CHRISTI
college ...... BISHOP, MCMURRY
county .... BEE, BELL, CASS, CLAY, COKE, HILL, HUNT, WEBB, BEXAR, BOWIE, DELTA, ECTOR, ELLIS, GREGG, AUSTIN, BRAZOS, COLLIN, DALLAS, DENTON, EL PASO, HARRIS, ORANGE, POTTER, TAYLOR, CAMERON, CORYELL, GRAYSON, HIDALGO, LUBBOCK, MIDLAND, TRAVIS, TARRANT, ANGELINA, BRAZORIA, MCLENNAN, VICTORIA, DEAF SMITH, GALVESTON, JEFFERSON
dam .... DENISON
fever victim .... CATTLE
Indian tribe .... CADDO(AN)
island .... PADRE, MUSTANG, GALVESTON, MATAGORDA
lagoon .... MADRE
lake .... KEMP, CADDO, CEDAR, LAVON, TOYAH, WORTH, MEDINA, TEXOMA, TRAVIS, HOUSTON, STAMFORD, ARLINGTON, GRAPEVINE, LIVINGSTON, CORPUS CHRISTI
leaguer .... HIT, FLY BALL
mission .... ALAMO
mountain .... LOCKE, ELEPHANT, CATHEDRAL, LIVERMORE, CERRO ALTO, SAN ANTONIO
mountain range .... DAVIS, GLASS, HUECO, VIEJA, APACHE, CHISOS, DIABLO, FINLAY, CHINATI, QUITMAN, DELAWARE, SANTIAGO, GUADALUPE
mounted state police .... RANGER
national park .... BIG BEND
native .... TEXAN
Naval Air Station ...... CHASE, KINGSVILLE, CORPUS CHRISTI
peak .... EAGLE, EMORY, CHINATI, SANTIAGO, GUADALUPE
peninsula .... BOLIVAR, MATAGORDA
plant .... LOCO
plateau .... EDWARDS, STOCKTON

ranger John Reed's secret identity .... THE LONE RANGER
river .... RED, FRIO, LEON, LLANO, PEASE, PECOS, WHITE, BRAZOS, DEVILS, MEDINA, NECHES, NUECES, SABINE, ELM FORK, NAVIDAD, SAN SABA, SULPHUR, TRINITY, WASHITA, WICHITA, COLORADO, LAMPASAS, NAVASOTA, GUADALUPE, RIO GRANDE, PEDERNALES
seaport .... GALVESTON
shrine .... ALAMO
shrub .... GUAYULE
state bird .... MOCKINGBIRD
state flower .... BLUEBONNET
state motto .... FRIENDSHIP
state nickname ..... LONE STAR
state tree .... PECAN
strip of land .... PANHANDLE
university .... A AND M, LAMAR, BAYLOR, DALLAS, EASTERN, CHRISTIAN, ST. THOMAS
winter wind .... NORTHER

text .... BOOK, THEME, TOPIC, VERSE, MATTER, SUBJECT, VERSION, WORDING, LETTERPRESS

textile .... RAG, FLAG, WOOL, CLOTH, LINEN, WOVEN, COTTON, FABRIC, DRAPERY, MATERIAL
dealer .... MERCER, CLOTHIER
goods .... LINENS, NAPERY, MERCERY, KNITWEAR, SPORTSWEAR
machine regulating device .... EVENER
making apparatus .... LOOM, WEAVER, SHUTTLE
pattern, broken-check .... HOUND'S TOOTH
printing material .... CATECHIN
shop .... MERCERY
worker .... DYER, WEAVER, INTERLACER

textual .... LITERAL

texture .... WEB, FEEL, WALE, WEFT, WOOF, GRAIN, WEAVE, STUFF, FABRIC, FINISH, TISSUE, STRUCTURE, COMPOSITION
kind of .... FINE, ROUGH, COARSE, RIBBED, SMOOTH, TOOTHED, TWILLED

TFR, part of .... TERRAIN, RADAR, FOLLOWING

T.G.I.F., part of .... THANK,

GOD, IT'S, FRIDAY

Thackeray character ...... BECKY SHARP

Thailand .... SIAM, SHAN

air base .... KORAT

canal .... KLONG

cape .... LAEM PHO, LAEM TALUMPHUK

capital .... BANGKOK

city/town .... LAE, NAN, TAK, YALA, TRANG, HAT YAI, HUA HIN, KHORAT, BURIRAM, KALASIN, LAMPANG, PATTANI, SINGORA, RAT BURI, CHON BURI, SARA BURI, THON BURI, AYUTTHAYA, CHIANG MAI, UDON THANI

coin .... ANNA, BAHT, TICAL, SATANG

gulf .... SIAM

island .... KUT, TAO, CHANG, LANTA, SAMUI, PHUKET

islands .... THALU

king .... ANANDA, BHUMIBOL, NARESUAN

language .... LAO, SHAN, THAI, KHMER, MALAY

lake .... NONG LAHAN

measure .... KWIEN, TANAN

monetary unit .... BAHT

mountain .... KAO PRAWA, (KHAO)LUANG, DOI PIA FAI, DOI INTHANON

mountains .... DANGREK, DONGRAK

native ..... LAO, THAI, SIAMESE

palace .... OHITRA LADA

pass .... AMYA, THREE PAGODAS

premier .... THANARAT, KITTIKACHORN

queen .... SIRIKIT

range .... BILAUKTAUNG

religion .... BUDDHISM

resort .... HUA HIN, PATTAYA

river ..... CHI, MUN, NAN, PING, TAPI, WANG, PASAK, MEKONG, MAE NAM, PAKCHAN, THA CHIN, MAE KLONG, CHAO PHRAYA

state guesthouse .... BOROMABIMAN

strait .... SAMUI

temple .... WAT

throne room .... CHAKRI

twin city of Bangkok .... THON BURI

weight .... PAI, BAHT, HAPH, KATI, KLAM, CATTY, FUANG, PICUL, TICAL, SALUNG, SOMPAY

Thais .... OPERA, COURTESAN

composer .... MASSENET

thalamus .... TORUS

thalassic .... MARINE

Thalia .... GRACE, (COMIC)MUSE

sister of .... CLIO, ERATO, URANIA, EUTERPE, CALLIOPE, MELPOMENE, POLYHYMNIA, TERPSICHORE

sphere of .... BLOOM, COMEDY, POETRY

thallophyte .... ALGA(E), FUNGUS, LICHEN, BACTERIA

Thames landmark .... ETON, BRIDGE

than .... AS, OR, NOR, TILL, BESIDE, OR ELSE, ASIDE FROM

Thanatos personified ...... DEATH

thane .... THEGN, FREEMAN

latter-day equivalent of .... BARON, KNIGHT

thankful .... BEHOLDEN, GRATEFUL

thankless .... UNGRATEFUL

person .... INGRATE

thanks .... GRACE, GRAMERCY, GRATITUDE, APPRECIATION

deserving of .... THANKWORTHY

thanksgiving ...... GRACE, PAEAN, PRAISE, PRAYER, THANK(S)-OFFERING

Thanksgiving day .... THURSDAY

fruit .... CRANBERRY

main course at the first .... FOUR WILD TURKEYS

pie .... MINCED, PUMPKIN

tuber .... YAM

vehicle .... SNOWPLOW

VIP .... COOK

Thant, U .... SITHU

nationality .... BURMESE

Thapsus, victor at .... CAESAR

that .... WHO, WHEN, WHOM, WHICH, YON(DER)

identical one .... ITSELF

is (to say) .... ID, I.E., EST, VIZ, IN OTHER WORDS

man .... HE

place .... THERE

so .... BECAUSE

woman .... SHE

"that rocks the cradle, ____" .... THE HAND

thatch .... HAIR, PALM, ROOF(ING), COVER(ING)

thatched beach shelter .... RAMADA

Thatcher, English prime minister .... MARGARET

thatching material .... NIPA,

COGON, GRASS, HA(U)LM, STRAW, RUSHES

thaumatology subject .... MIRACLE(S)

thaumaturge's working .... MIRACLE

thaumaturgy .... MAGIC

thaw .... EASE, MELT, RELENT, SOFTEN, UNBEND, LIQUEFY, DISSOLVE

subject of a .... ICE, BERG, SNOW, RESERVE

the affluent vote .... SILK STOCKING DISTRICTS

Babe .... RUTH

"Bandit Queen" .... BELLE STARR

bears .... TRIO

"Beautiful Whistler" .... ALICE SHAW

bench .... COURT

best offense .... DEFENSE

Big Board .... NYSE

Big Dipper .... CHARLES'S WAIN

"Bird Man of Alcatraz" .... (ROBERT)STROUD

"Blessed One" .... BUDDHA

Book .... BIBLE

"bottom of the sea" .... DAVY JONES'S LOCKER

bounding main .... OCEAN

busy bee .... HONEYMAKER

"Catholic" .... ISABELLA

Crooner .... BING(CROSBY)

Crossroads of the Pacific .... HAWAII

day of surprise attack on Pearl Harbor ..... DAY OF INFAMY

____ Decade: 1890's .... MAUVE

Draft: abbr. .... SSS

____ Eagle .... LONE

Edge author .... FRANCIS

1890's .... MAUVE DECADE

Elder and the Younger: ancient Romans .... CATOS

Enchanted Isle .... ERIN

____ (end) .... PITS

____ (English channel) .... SOLENT

"Enlightened One" .... BUDDHA

external world .... NATURE

Father of the Waltz .... STRAUSS

"few, the proud, the ____" .... MARINES

First State .... DELAWARE

Flintstones' pet .... DINO
Gloomy Dean .... INGE
golden shiner .... WINDFISH
Grateful _____ .... DEAD
Great Commoner and son
.... PITTS
"greatest": boxing .... ALI
heavens .... ETHER
in crowd .... THE HAVES
"Killer Whale" .... NAMU,
ORCA
king .... LE ROI
latest .... CURRENT, NEW
MODEL
law's appendage .... LONG
ARM
least bit .... FICO
Little Corporal ..... NAPOLEON
Little Paris of the Balkans
.... BUCHAREST
Lone Eagle's monogram
.... CAL
Lord .... REDEEMER
Lord _____ me up .... TAKETH
Louvre is here .... PARIS
"_____ made me do it!"
.... DEVIL
"march king" .... SOUSA
master chemistry lab
.... LIVER
Messiah, e.g. .... ORATORIO
mother of all living .... EVE
mother of civil rights
movement .... ROSA
PARKS
musical Count .... BASIE
"Northern Bear" ...... RUSSIA
one that got away .... ESCAPEE
ones at hand .... THESE
"Original Private Eye"
.... (ALLAN)PINKERTON
Ould Sod .... EIRE, IRELAND
"peanut" president
.... CARTER
period after midnight ..... WEE
HOURS, SMALL HOURS
preponderance .... MOST
"red" explorer .... ERIC
Rhine of America .... HUDSON
rite thing to say .... I DO
rocks near Gibraltar
.... ROCAS
same .... ONE, IDEM, DITTO
"Scorpion's" eye
.... ANTARES
Scouts: abbr. .... BSA
seducer .... LOTHARIO
"Seeress of Washington"
.... JEAN DIXON
ship of the desert .... CAMEL
"Spruce Goose" designer

.... (HOWARD)HUGHES
"Steel King" .... CARNEGIE
Ten Commandments
.... TORAH, DECALOG(UE)
"tentmaker" .... OMAR
_____ the limit .... SKY'S
_____, the merrier .... MORE
Thin Man's pooch .... ASTA
365th day .... YEAR-END
Tight Little Isle ...... ENGLAND
top grossing film studio in
the 40's .... DISNEY
trachea .... WINDPIPE
two .... BOTH
_____ (walking papers)
.... SACK
"Waltz King"
.... (JOHANN)STRAUSS
"Witch of Wall Street"
.... (HETTY)GREEN
whole enchilada .... ALL
Word .... LOGOS
works .... SOUP TO NUTS
world over .... UNDER THE SUN
yuppies .... INS
The Bells interpreter .... POE
_____ Brothers Show
.... SMOTHERS
_____ Carson Show
.... JOHNNY
_____ Clooney Show
.... ROSEMARY
Dance of Life author
.... ELLIS
_____ DeLuise Show ..... DOM
Fair Penitent author ..... ROWE
Golden Lotus setting
.... CHINA
Good _____ .... EARTH
Grass Harp author .... CAPOTE
Green Hat author .... ARLEN
Gulag Archipelago author
.... SOLZHENITSYN
Jungle Book author
.... KIPLING
Kiss sculptor .... RODIN
Lodger author .... LOUNDES
_____: Nolte film .... DEEP
_____: Philip Barry play
.... ANIMAL KINGDOM
Prince author .... (NICCOLO)
MACHIAVELLI
Raven author .... POE
"Saga of an American
Family" is subtitle
of _____ .... ROOTS
Snake Charmer painter
.... O'HUSSO
Sons of Katie _____
.... ELDER
Source author .... MICHENER

Source character .... ELIAV,
CULLINANE, DR. VERED BAR-EL
Star Spangled Banner writer
.... (FRANCIS SCOTT)KEY
Unmade Bed author
.... SAGAN
Untouchables' Eliot ...... NESS
_____ Year Itch .... SEVEN
Thea's daughter ...... EOS, SELENE
husband .... HYPERION
son .... HELIOS
theaceous tree .... TEA
thearchic .... SUPREME,
SOVEREIGN
thearchy .... THEOCRACY
theater .... ARENA, DRAMA,
STAGE, BOARDS, STUDIO,
PLAYHOUSE, MOVIEHOUSE,
OPERA(HOUSE)
audience .... GOER, HOUSE,
ATTENDER, SPECTATOR
award .... TONY
awning .... MARQUEE
box/compartment .... LOGE
call .... CURTAIN
central stage .... ARENA, FIELD
OF ACTION
cheap .... GAFF
cheapest seat .... GALLERY
club .... LAMBS
crew .... CAST
curtain .... DROP, TEASER
district .... SOHO, RIALTO,
BROADWAY
drop .... SCRIM
entrance hall .... FOYER,
LOBBY
famous .... PALACE
figure in the .... THESPIAN,
DRAMATURGE
fixture .... PROP, MARQUEE,
CALLBOARD
goer .... FAN, BUFF, PATRON,
SPECTATOR, AFICIONADO
goer on free ticket
.... DEADHEAD
ground floor/area .... PIT,
PARQUET, ORCHESTRA
group .... ANTA
light .... SPOT
of combat/war .... FRONT
LINE, BATTLEFIELD, KILLING
FIELD
of sports .... ARENA,
DIAMOND, STADIUM
of war, 1945 .... ETO
part below balcony
.... PARTERRE
presentation .... FILM, PLAY,
DRAMA, MOVIE, OPERA,
REVUE, BALLET, CONCERT,

LECTURE, MUSICAL, VARIETY
program .... (PLAY)BILL
seat .... LOGE, STALL,
BALCONY, GALLERY,
ORCHESTRA
sign .... SRO, EXIT
slang .... GAFF, LEGIT,
SHOWBIZ
stage scenery .... COULISSE
street .... BROADWAY
the .... STAGE, BOARDS,
PLAYLAND, FOOTLIGHTS
theatrical .... SHOWY, STAGY,
VIVID, SCENIC, POMPOUS,
AFFECTED, DRAMATIC,
HISTRIONIC
company .... STOCK
curtain .... DROP
employee .... CALLBOY,
PROMPTER, STAGEHAND
exciting event .... SHOW-
STOPPER
extra .... SUPER
financier ...... ANGEL, BACKER,
PATRON
group ...... ANTA, CAST, CREW,
TROUPE
itinerary .... ROAD, TOUR, TRIP
lights .... FOOTS, FLOATS,
MARQUEE, LIMELIGHT,
SPOTLIGHT, FLOODLIGHT
nickname .... FLO, BILLY
producer .... ROSE, COHAN,
ZIEGFELD
production ...... PLAY, DRAMA,
REVUE, BALLET, PAGEANT,
EXTRAVAGANZA
profession .... STAGE
role .... LEAD, STAR, HEAVY,
INGENUE, VILLAIN
show .... PLAY, DRAMA,
OPERA, REVUE, BALLET,
CONCERT, VARIETY, MUSICAL,
BURLESQUE, PANTOMIME,
VAUDEVILLE
sketch .... SKIT
Theban blind soothsayer
.... TIRESIAS
deities .... CABIRI
general .... PELOPIDAS
god .... AMUN-RE
goddess .... MUT
king .... CREON, LAIUS
poet .... PINDAR
queen .... JOCASTA
town .... LUXOR
Thebes, founder of ...... CADMUS
is ancient capital of .... EGYPT
one of seven against
.... TYDEUS
site of .... KARNAK

(talking) statue of ...... VOCAL
MEMNON
theca .... SAC, CASE, COCOON,
CAPSULE
content .... PUPA, SPORE
thecate .... SHEATHED
Theda, actress .... BARA
theelin .... ESTRONE, HORMONE
theelol .... ESTRIOL, HORMONE
theft .... LARCENY, ROBBERY,
BURGLARY, STEALING,
THIEVERY
describing one .... GRAND,
PETTY, QUALIFIED,
EMBEZZLEMENT
literary .... PLAGIARISM
theine .... CAFFEINE
source .... TEA
theism .... PIETY
Thelma of filmdom .... RITTER
variation of .... SELMA
them .... THEY
thematic .... TOPICAL, PERIODIC
theme .... TEXT, ESSAY, TOPIC,
THESIS, SUBJECT, (LEIT)MOTIF
heading .... LEMMA
in a design/art, etc. ..... MOTIF
in music .... TEMA
in radio/song .... SIGNATURE
Themis .... GODDESS, TITANESS
concern of .... LAW, JUSTICE
father of .... URANUS
mother of .... GAEA
what she holds .... SCALE
then .... NEXT, SOON, AGAIN,
ALORS, HENCE, THEREFORE,
AFTERWARDS
thenar .... PALM, SOLE
thence .... THUSLY, HEREAFTER,
THEREFROM
thenceforth .... THEREAFTER,
CONSEQUENTLY
theodolite .... TRANSIT
user of a .... SURVEYOR
theologian .... BEDE, CALVIN,
DIVINE, LUTHER, ORIGEN,
AQUINAS
theological .... DIVINE,
CANONICAL, RELIGIOUS
list .... SEVEN DEADLY SINS
virtues, one of the .... HOPE,
FAITH, CHARITY
theology .... CREED, DOGMA,
BELIEF, DOCTRINE
theopany .... REVELATION,
APOCALYPSE
theorbo .... LUTE
theorem .... PREMISE, PREPOSITION
expression of a ..... FORMULA,
EQUATION
theoretical .... ABSTRACT,

ACADEMIC, PLATONIC,
SPECULATIVE, HYPOTHETICAL
force .... OD(YLE), ODYL(E)
opposed to .... APPLIED,
PRACTICAL
theorize .... GUESS, SPECULATE
theory ...... ISM, LAW, IDEA, PLAN,
GUESS, DOCTRINE, PRINCIPLE,
CONJECTURE, (HYPO)THESIS,
SUPPOSITION
Darwin's .... EVOLUTION
Einstein's .... RELATIVITY
Malthusian .... POPULATION
Newton's .... GRAVITY
suffix .... ISM
therapeutic .... HEALING,
CURATIVE
agent .... REMEDY
draught .... DOSAGE
therapy .... CURE, REMEDY,
TREATMENT
for cancer .... RADIATION
for mental, emotional
disorder .... PSYCHOTHERAPY
there .... AT, THEN, TOWARD,
YON(DER), THITHER
thereabouts .... CLOSE, NEAR(BY)
thereafter .... NEXT, LATER,
SINCE, SUBSEQUENTLY
thereby .... UPON, THROUGH
therefor ...... FOR THAT, FOR THIS
therefore .... SO, ERGO, THEN,
HENCE, ACCORDINGLY,
CONSEQUENTLY
therefrom ...... THENCE, THEREOF
thereto .... ALSO, BESIDES,
MOREOVER
theriac(a) .... TREACLE,
ANTIDOTE, MOLASSES
therianthropic being ...... HARPY,
THOTH, SPHINX, TRITON,
CENTAUR, MERMAID
therm .... CALORIE
Therma .... SALONIKA
thermae ...... BATHS, BATHHOUSES
thermal .... HOT, WARM
underwear: sl. .... LONG JOHNS
unit ..... BTU, THERM, CALORIE
thermion, negative .... ELECTRON
positive .... ION
thermometer .... GLASS,
MERCURY, HEAT DETECTOR
type of .... CELSIUS, DIGITAL,
REAUMUR, CLINICAL,
CRYOMETER, CENTIGRADE,
FAHRENHEIT
thermoplastic .... SARAN
Thermopylae protagonist(s)
.... XERXES, LEONIDAS,
PERSIANS, SPARTANS
thermos .... JUG, FLASK

theroid .... BEASTLIKE
Thersites' slayer .... ACHILLES
   target of abuse .... ULYSSES,
                      ODYSSEUS
thersitical .... LOUD, ABUSIVE,
          REVILING, SCURRILOUS
thesaurus .... LEXICON,
      TREASURY, DICTIONARY,
    STOREHOUSE, ENCYCLOPEDIA
   compiler .... ROGET
these days .... TIMES
Theseus' father .... AEGEUS
   friend .... PIRITHOUS
   mother .... AETHRA
   victim .... MINOTAUR
   wife .... PHAEDRA
thesis ...... ESSAY, TOPIC, THEORY,
       ARGUMENT, TREATISE,
    MONOGRAPH, POSTULATE,
    STATEMENT, COMPOSITION,
   PREPOSITION, DISSERTATION
Thespian .... ACTOR, PLAYER,
     ACTRESS, PERFORMER,
            TRAGEDIAN
   quest of .... LEAD,
     (RECOGNITION)AWARD
   whisper .... ASIDE
Thespis' forte .... TRAGEDY
Thessalian city .... LARISSA
   mountain .... OSSA, PELION
   river .... SALAMBRIA
   tribe .... MYRMIDON
   valley .... TEMPE
   warrior .... MYRMIDON
thetic .... PRESCRIBED
Thetis .... NEREID
   husband of .... PELEUS
   son of .... ACHILLES
theurgist .... MAGICIAN
theurgy .... MAGIC
thews .... SINEWS, MUSCLES
thewy .... MUSCULAR
they .... THEM, PEOPLE, THINGS,
        ANIMALS, PERSONS
   once were checkered
               CABS, TAXIS
   revere ratings .... TV
               NETWORKS
   ring twice .... POSTMEN
   rode with Jesse James
            YOUNGER BROTHERS
   speak for themselves
                 FACTS
   used to be carried by four
                 SEDANS
   used to clang .... TROLLEYS
thiamine .... VITAMIN B(COMPLEX)
   deficiency disease
                 BERIBERI
   source .... BRAN, FISH, NUTS,
    PORK, BEANS, PASTA, CEREAL,

            WHEAT GERM
thick .... FAT, DULL, WIDE,
    BROAD, CRASS, DENSE,
   GROSS, HEAVY, SOLID, STOUT,
   STUPID, TURBID, COMPACT,
     MASSIVE, LUXURIANT
   as thieves .... CLOSE
   colloquial .... FRIENDLY,
              INTIMATE
   consistency .... CREAMY
   end .... BUTT
   lay it on .... EXAGGERATE
   lipped .... LABROSE
   liqueur .... CREAM
   skin .... SHELL
   skinned .... HARD, NUMB,
     CALLOUS, SHAMELESS
   slang .... GOOKY
   slice .... SLAB
   sound of voice .... HOARSE,
     THROATY, GUTTURAL
   soup .... PUREE
   sticky consistency, having
                VISCOUS
   sticky fluid .... GRUME
   with .... TEEMING,
           (JAM)PACKED
thicken .... CURDLE, DEEPEN,
    CONGEAL, CONDENSE,
   SOLIDIFY, COAGULATE,
          INSPISSATE
thicket .... TOD, BOSK, BUSH,
   RONE, SHAW, BRAKE, COPSE,
   GROVE, BOSCAGE, COPPICE,
    SPINNEY, CHAPARRAL,
        (UNDER)BRUSH
thickhaired .... TRESSY
thickhead .... FOOL, DUNCE, IDIOT
thickheaded .... DENSE, STUPID,
   FOOLISH, WITLESS, HEBETATE
thickly populated ...... CROWDED,
             POPULOUS
thickness .... PLY, LAYER,
            STRATUM
thickset .... BEEFY, STOUT,
   CHUBBY, CHUNKY, PORTLY,
   STOCKY, SQUATTY, HEAVYSET
thief .... CROOK, GANEF, GANOF,
   GONOF, GONOV, GONOPH,
   FILCHER, LURCHER, POACHER,
    STEALER, LARCENER,
   PICAROON, PILFERER,
   LARCENIST, PURLOINER
   building/house .... BURGLAR,
      HOUSEBREAKER
   buyer of his loot .... FENCE
   cattle .... RUSTLER
   compulsive
           KLEPTO(MANIAC)
   discards of a .... WAIF
   fraudulent .... EMBEZZLER

high seas .... PIRATE,
   PICAROON, BUCCANEER
literary .... LIFTER, PIRATE,
   USURPER, PLAGIARIST
petty .... FILCHER, PILFERER
slang .... DIP, PRIG, YEGG
store .... SHOPLIFTER
trainer .... FAGIN
tricky ...... CONMAN, SWINDLER
violent .... ROBBER
wallet .... PICKPOCKET
thieve .... ROB, FILCH, STEAL,
   PILFER, RUSTLE, DEFRAUD,
    SWINDLE, SHOPLIFT
   slang .... SWIPE, SNATCH
thievery .... FRAUD, THEFT,
   PLUNDER, ROBBERY, SWINDLE
thieves' language .... CANT,
   ARGOT, SLANG, JARGON
thievish .... SLY
thig .... BEG, CADGE, BORROW
thigh, and buttock .... HAM
   animal's .... HAM
   armor plate .... TUILLE
   back of .... HAM
   bone .... FEMUR
   combining form .... MER(O)
   muscle .... SARTORIUS
   of the .... FEMORAL
   pains .... SCIATICA
   part .... FLANK
   upper .... HIP
thill .... POLE, SHAFT
thimble .... THUMBSTALL
thimbleful .... SIP
thimblerig .... SHELL GAME, CON,
   GYP, GULL, CHEAT,
        (DE)FRAUD
   bettor .... SUCKER
thimblerigger .... CHEAT,
         SWINDLER
thimbleweed .... ANEMONE,
   RUDBECKIA, CONEFLOWER
thin ...... FINE, LEAN, RARE, SLIM,
   WEAK, LANKY, LIN(E)Y,
   REEDY, SCANT, SHEER, SPARE,
   DILUTE, FLIMSY, MEAGER,
   NARROW, SLIGHT, SPARSE,
   SUBTLE, SLENDER, TENUOUS,
    DELICATE, HAIRLINE
   and bony .... GAUNT,
          EMACIATED
   as air .... RARE
   as an excuse ..... LAME, POOR,
     FLIMSY, SHALLOW
   become .... SHRINK,
         ATTENUATE
   cake .... WAFER
   coating .... FILM, VENEER
   combining form .... STENO
   glue .... SIZE

layer .... FILM, LAMINA, VENEER
line/stripe .... HAIRLINE
man .... SLATS
man's nickname .... SLIM, LANKY, SLATS
nail .... BRAD
narrow strip .... SLAT
paper .... TISSUE
skinned .... DELICATE, SENSITIVE
stratum .... SEAM
soup .... BROTH, CONSOMME
tall person: colloq.
.... BEANPOLE
tuft .... WISP
Thin Man's dog .... ASTA
thine .... YOUR(S)
thing .... ACT, DEED, ITEM, BEING, ISSUE, AFFAIR, DETAIL, DEVICE, ENTITY, MATTER, OBJECT, ARTICLE, CONCERN, BUSINESS
chosen .... CHOICE, OPTION, PREFERENCE
decisively forceful
.... SOCKDOLOGER
dimpled .... GOLF BALL
easy to do .... SNAP, CINCH
emitted .... EMANATION
excreted .... SWEAT, URINE, WASTE
feared by elephants?
.... MOUSE
hard to handle .... HOT POTATO
imaginary .... MYTH, IDEAL
in law .... RES
ineffectual .... DUD
insubstantial .... STRAW
of same class .... CONGENER
of small value .... STIVE, TRIFLE
of value .... ASSET
out of place .... ESTRAY
slang .... BAG, CUP OF TEA
sometimes spared .... ROD
thought of .... IDEA, PLAN, BRAINCHILD
to lend .... EAR
worthless .... CHIP, JUNK, LEES, SCUM, WEED, CHAFF, DREGS, FROTH, TRASH, WASTE, REFUSE
thingamabob/thingumabob
.... DEVICE, GADGET, THINGAMAJIG
thingamajig/thingumajig
...... GIZMO, DEVICE, DOODAD, GADGET, DOOHICKEY, CONTRIVANCE

things .... PERSONAL EFFECTS
authentic .... REALIA
one thousand .... CHILIAD
that should meet .... ENDS
to be done .... CHORE, AGENDA
to be sold .... WARES
think .... DEEM, MUSE, TROW, WEEN, BROOD, DREAM, FANCY, JUDGE, OPINE, WEIGH, IDEATE, REASON, RECKON, IMAGINE, REFLECT, CEREBRATE, STIR GREY MATTER, USE THE OLD NOODLE
about intently
.... CONTEMPLATE
ahead ...., PLAN
back .... RECALL, REMEMBER, RECOLLECT
deeply ...... PONDER, MEDITATE
in a morbid way .... BROOD, WORRY
nothing of it .... DISREGARD
of .... REGARD, CONSIDER, REMEMBER
over .... MULL, PONDER, DELIBERATE
seriously .... COGITATE, MEDITATE
slang .... KICK AROUND
tank product .... IDEA, INVENTION
things out .... PLAN, STUDY, RATIONALIZE
twice .... HESITATE
up .... CREATE, IDEATE, INVENT, CONCEIVE
thinker .... PHILOSOPHER, INTELLECTUAL
Thinker sculptor .... RODIN
thinness .... RARITY, TENUITY
thinnest .... RAREST
discernible layer .... LAMINA
thiol .... MERCAPTAN
thiosulfate .... HYPO
Thira .... SANTORINI
third .... TERNARY, TIERCE(L), TERTIARY
day, every .... TERTIAN
degree .... GRILLING
degree user .... POLICE, PROBER, INTERROGATOR, INVESTIGATOR
estate .... COMMONS, BOURGEOISIE
in music .... TIERCE
largest island, world's
.... BORNEO
man mentioned in the Bible
.... ABEL

man, the .... REF(EREE)
power .... CUBE
rate .... POOR, COMMON, SHABBY, INFERIOR
son of Adam .... SETH
string .... SUB(STITUTE)
widow's .... DOWER
Third International
.... COMINTERN
Reich .... GERMAN EMPIRE
Worlder .... ASIAN, AFRICAN
Thirkell, writer .... ANGELA
thirl .... PIERCE, THRILL
thirst .... DESIRE, CRAVING, DRYNESS, PARCHEDNESS
abnormal, excessive
.... POLYDIPSIA
quencher .... POP, LIQUID
relieve .... SLAKE
stimulant .... SALT
thirsty .... DRY, ARID, FERVID, PARCHED, PRURIENT
boon to the .... OASIS
cat or dog .... LAPPER
Thirsty's wife .... IRMA
thirteen .... XIII, LONG DOZEN, BAKER'S DOZEN
witches .... COVEN
"30" on copy .... END
39.37 inches .... METER
thirty-two are a mouthful
.... TEETH
this and no more .... ONLY
has class .... SCHOOLROOM
minute .... NOW, AT ONCE, PRONTO
world .... HERE
Thisbe's love .... PYRAMUS
thistle ...... BURR, ASTER, ARNICA, COSMOS, HYSSOP
like plant .... CARDOON, ARTICHOKE
plant .... SAFFLOWER
thistledown .... PAPPUS
thither ...... YON, THERE, FARTHER
thole .... PIN, OARLOCK
purpose of .... FULCRUM
Thomas, ___ .... DANNY, MARLO
archaeologist .... CYRUS
clockmaker .... SETH
Fr. composer .... AMBROISE
opera by .... MIGNON
thong .... RIEM, KNOUT, LEASH, STRAP, WHIP(LASH)
strangling .... GAROTTE, GARROTE
Thor .... SISECH
father of .... ODIN
noise of .... THUNDER
sphere of .... WAR

739

weapon of
.... (MAGIC)HAMMER
wife of .... SIF
thorax .... CHEST
insect's .... TRUNK
thorn .... ETH, STOB, TREE, BRIAR,
BRIER, SPINA, SPINE, TORUN,
NETTLE, BRAMBLE, PRICKLE
apple .... HAW, METEL,
DATURA
thornback ...... RAY, SPIDER-CRAB
Thorne Smith's novel .... TOPPER
Topper .... COSMO
thorny .... SPINY, BRAMBLY,
PRICKLY, SPINATE, SPINOSE
pig .... PORCUPINE
plant .... BRIAR, BRIER
thorough .... DEEP, EXACT,
CAREFUL, ABSOLUTE,
COMPLETE, SWEEPING, OUT-
AND-OUT
thoroughbred .... NOBLE,
HIGHBORN, PUREBRED,
PEDIGREED, BLUEBLOOD(ED),
ARISTOCRATIC
thoroughfare .... ROAD, AVENUE,
STREET, HIGHWAY,
BOULEVARD, TURNPIKE,
CONCOURSE, (PASSAGE)WAY
thoroughgoing .... ARRANT,
PRECISE, COMPLETE
thoroughly ...... FULLY, WHOLLY,
SOUNDLY
thoroughwort .... PLANT,
BONESET
thorp(e) .... DORP, HAMLET,
VILLAGE
Thorstein's (Ericsson) brother
.... LEIF
father .... ERIC THE RED
wife .... GUDRID
Thorvald's grandson .... LEIF,
THORSTEIN
hometown .... JAEDEREN
place of death .... ICELAND
son .... EIRIK, ERIC THE RED
those at the helm ...... STEERSMEN
in office .... INS
who are extremely loyal
.... DIEHARDS
boast loudly .... GASCONS,
BLOW-HARDS
comprehend .... GRASPERS
corroborate
.... (EYE)WITNESSES
exaggerate .... FIBBERS
flirt .... COQUETTES
Thoth's head .... IBIS, BABOON
sphere .... MAGIC, SPEECH,
WISDOM
thou .... YOU, THOUSAND

though ...... YET, STILL, EVEN(IF),
HOWEVER, NEVERTHELESS,
NOTWITHSTANDING
thought .... HEED, IDEA, LOGIC,
STUDY, WEIGH, BELIEF,
NOTION, CONCEPT, INTELLECT,
IMAGINATION
combining form .... IDEO
deep, continued
.... MEDITATION
disorder .... SCHIZOPHRENIA
distorted .... DELUSION
formulated .... IDEA,
JUDGMENT, SOLUTION
out .... CONSIDERED
representation of ...... SPEECH,
WRITING, BEHAVIOR
seat of .... BRAIN
transference of .... TELEPATHY
thoughtful .... KIND, HEEDFUL,
PENSIVE, TACTFUL,
CONSIDERATE
thoughtless .... RASH, SLACK,
REMISS, STUPID, RECKLESS
act .... FOLLY
thousand .... FIFTY SCORE
dollars: sl. .... THOU, YARD,
GRAND
prefix .... MILLI
years .... CHILIAD, MILLENNIUM
thousandth .... MILLESIMAL
anniversary .... MILLENARY
of an inch .... MIL
Thracian king .... TEREUS
slave .... SPARTACUS
soldier .... MYRMIDON
thrall ...... ESNE, SERF, BONDMAN,
(EN)SLAVE, SLAVERY,
SUBJECTION
thralldom .... BONDAGE,
SLAVERY, CAPTIVITY,
SERVITUDE, DOMINATION
thrash .... LAM, TAN, BEAT, CANE,
DRUB, FLOG, HIDE, LACE,
LASH, LICK, ROUT, WHIP,
FLAIL, POUND, WHALE,
DEFEAT, LARRUP, STRIKE,
WALLOP, BELABOR, CONQUER,
TROUNCE, LAMBAST(E)
out .... ARGUE, DISCUSS
over .... ANALYZE
thrasher .... (SONG)BIRD
genus .... TOXOSTOMA
relative .... MOCKINGBIRD
thrashing .... FLAGELLATION
thrasonical .... BOASTFUL
thread .... DUD, CORD, YARN,
FIBER, FILUM, INKLE, LINEN,
LISLE, STRAND, STRING,
FILAMENT
a needle .... REEVE

appendage like .... CIRRUS
ball of .... CLEW
bits of .... LINT
combining form .... NEMAT(O)
cotton .... LISLE
cutters, screws .... TAP
discharge .... SETON
end .... THRUM
fine .... FILM
holder .... SPOOL, BOBBIN,
SHUTTLE
knot .... BURL
like .... FILAR, FILOSE, FIBROID
like part ..... FILUM, FILAMENT
linen .... INKLE
loosely twisted .... FLOSS
lump .... BURL, KNOT
material .... FLAX, SILK, YARN,
LINEN, NYLON, COTTON
metal .... LAME, WIRE
producer .... SPIDER,
SILKWORM
pulled .... SNAG
quantity .... SKEIN
rubber .... LASTEX
separate .... SLEAVE
silk .... TRAM
skein of .... COIL, HASP
spun by a spider ...... COBWEB
surgical .... SETON, CATGUT,
LIGATURE
tangled .... RAVEL(L)ING
thick .... STRING
use of .... SEWING, SUTURE,
WEAVING
used in labyrinth .... CLEW
weight to measure fineness
of .... DENIER
threadbare .... SEEDY, TRITE,
WEARY, FRAYED, RAGGED,
SCANTY, SHABBY,
WORN(OUT), TATTERED
joke, describing a .... STALE
threadlike outgrowth .... HAIR
threadworm .... FILARIA,
PINWORM, NEMATODE
thready .... ROPY, WIRY, FIBROUS,
STRINGY
threap ...... ARGUE, CHIDE, SCOLD,
REBUKE
threat .... DANGER, MENACE,
NOTICE, PROMISE, WARNING
empty .... BLUFF, BLUSTER
getting money by
.... BLACKMAIL, EXTORTION
threaten .... COW, BULLY,
HARASS, HECTOR, MENACE,
BLUDGEON, BROWBEAT,
TERRORIZE, INTIMIDATE
threatening .... DARK, AWFUL,
BLACK, SULLEN, LOOMING,

OMINOUS, WARNING, IMMINENT, MENACING, MINATORY, SINISTER, MINACIOUS

three ...... TER, TREY, TRIO, TRIAD

an association of ...... TROIKA, TRIUMVIR(ATE)

angled .... TRIGONOUS

banded armadillo .... APAR

base hit .... TRIPLE, THREE-BAGGER

biblical symbolic meaning of .... TOTALITY

card's .... TREY

cut into .... TRISECT

cornered .... TRIGONAL, TRIGONOUS, TRIANGULAR

days, man in whale's belly for .... JONAH

decker .... TRIREME, SANDWICH

dimensional .... CUBIC, STEREO

feet .... YARD

group of .... TRIO, TRIAD, TRINE, TRINARY, TRINITY, TRIPLE(T), TRIPLEX, TRIPLICATE

hand card game .... SKAT

horned .... TRICORN

in dice/domino .... TREY, DEUCE-ACE

in one .... TRIUNE, TRINITY

in sequence, same suit .... TIERCE

languages, using .... TRILINGUAL

leafed .... TERNATE, TRIFOLIATE

leafed clover .... TREFOIL, SHAMROCK

legged seat .... STOOL

legged stand .... EASEL, TEAPOY, TRIPOD

legged table .... TRIVET

lines, group of .... TERCET

lobes/parts, divided into .... TRIFID

lobbed .... TRILOBATE

metrical feet, verse of .... TRIPODY

month period .... QUARTER, TRIMESTER

mountain peaks island .... TRINIDAD

pairs of leaflets, having .... TRIJUGATE

parts, having .... TRINAL, TRIFORM

parts of completeness, one of .... END, MIDDLE, BEGINNING

performers .... TRIO

pointed .... TRICUSPID

prefix .... TER, TRI

pronged .... TRIDENT, TRIDENTATE

pronged spear .... LEISTER, TRIDENT

related plays, set of .... TRILOGY

rhyming lines, group of .... TERCET

ribbed .... TRICOSTATE

set of .... TRIAD, TERNION

shakes .... SECS

sided figure .... TRIGON, TRIANGLE

significance of the number .... COMPLETENESS

song for .... TRIO

times .... THRICE, TREBLE, TRIPLE

toed sloth .... AI

trios .... NINE

wheeled vehicle .... TRICYCLE, MOTORCYCLE

years, happening every .... TRIENNIAL

years, period of .... TRIENNIUM

three blind mice .... MCEMCEMCE

300, in Rome CCC

Three Wise Men, gift of .... GOLD, MYRRH, FRANKINCENSE

one of the .... GASPAR, MELCHIOR, BALTHASAR

threefold .... TER(N), TRINE, THRICE, TREBEL, TRINAL, TRIPLE, TRIPLEX, TRIPARTITE

threepenny .... PALTRY

threes, arranged in .... TERNATE

threescore .... SIXTY

threesome .... TRIO

threnody .... SONG, DIRGE, REQUIEM, CORONACH

thresh .... FLOG, POUND, WINNOW, THRASH, BEAT(OUT)

out .... ARGUE, DISCUSS

over .... DWELL ON

thresher .... FLAIL, SHARK

shark .... SEAFOX

threshing implement ...... FLAIL, COMBINE

threshold .... EVE, LIMEN, OUTSET, GATEWAY, (DOOR)SILL, ENTRANCE

of consciousness .... LIMEN

threw ...... CAST, FLUNG, HURLED, TOSSED, PITCHED

thrice .... VERY, GREATLY, THREEFOLD

combining form .... TER

thrift .... WORK, LABOR, VIGOR,

GROWTH, SAVING, ECONOMY, FRUGALITY

thrifty .... CANNY, CHARY, FRUGAL, SAVING, STINGY, CAREFUL, SPARING, THRIVING, PROVIDENT, ECONOMICAL

opposite of .... LAVISH, WASTEFUL

person .... MISER, HOARDER, NIGGARD, SKINFLINT, PENNY PINCHER

thrill .... STIR, FLUSH, THIRL, THROB, EXCITE, QUIVER, TINGLE, TREMOR, TREMBLE, VIBRATE, ELECTRIFY, SENSATION, EXHILARATE

thrilled .... PLEASED

thriller .... CHILLER, SHOCKER, SUSPENSE, WHODUNIT

thrilling ...... ELECTRIC, EXCITING

thrips .... WOODWORM

thrive .... WAX, GROW, ADDLE, BLOOM, BATTEN, FATTEN, FLOWER, PROSPER, SUCCEED, FLOURISH

thriving .... SITTING PRETTY

throat .... MAW, CRAG, NECK, GORGE, FAUCES, GULLET, PHARYNX, WEASAND, THROTTLE, WINDPIPE

armor .... GORGET

clearing .... HEM, HAWK

condition .... GOITER

cut competitor's .... UNDERSELL

cut the .... JUGULATE

disease .... CROUP, ANGINA, CANCER, GARGET, THRUSH

inflammation ..... PHARYNGITIS

lozenge .... PASTIL(E)

middle section of .... OROPHARYNX

of the .... (JU)GULAR, GUTTURAL

part .... LARYNX, PHARYNX, TRACHEA, ESOPHAGUS, VOICE BOX

skin, animal .... DEWLAP, WATTLE

sore .... PHARYNGITIS

sound .... CROAK

troublesome growths .... TONSILS

uppermost part of .... NASOPHARYNX

wrapper .... MUFFLER

throaty .... HOARSE, GUTTURAL

throb .... ACHE, BEAT, PAIN, PUMP, POUND, PULSE, THUMP, PULSATE, VIBRATE, PALPITATE, PULSATION

throbber .... HEART
throbbing .... ACHY, ACHING,
BEATING, PITAPAT, PULSING,
STACCATO, PALPITANT,
SALTATION
throe(s) ...... PANG, RACK, AGONY,
CRAMP, QUALM, SPASM,
SCRUPLE
childbirth .... LABOR PAINS
thrombocyte .... PLATELET
reduction in the number of
.... THROMBOCYTOPENIA
thrombosis .... COAGULATION,
BLOOD-CLOTTING
thrombus .... FIBRIN, BLOOD CLOT
combining form ..... THROMBO
formation in veins
.... THROMBOPHLEBITIS
fragment .... EMBOLUS
removal of a
.... THROMBECTOMY
throne .... CHAIR, RULER,
SCEPTER, ROYAL SEAT,
SOVEREIGN(TY)
bishop's .... CATHEDRA
covering .... CANOPY
seat of a .... DAIS, TRANSOM
sitter .... CZAR, KING, POPE,
TSAR, QUEEN, RULER,
EMPEROR, CARDINAL
throng .... MOB, ARMY, HOST,
CROWD, HORDE, PRESS,
SWARM, CONCOURSE,
MULTITUDE
throstle .... (SONG)THRUSH
throttle ...... GAG, CHOKE, CLOSE,
SCRAG, VALVE, STIFLE,
SILENCE, STRANGLE,
SUPPRESS, SUFFOCATE
engine .... GUN
hold .... STRANGLEHOLD
through ...... BY, PER, VIA, DONE,
OVER, WITH, AMONG, DURING,
FINISH, BY WAY OF
and through .... FULLY,
ENTIRELY, COMPLETELY
force .... BY DINT OF
throughout .... EVERYWHERE
throw .... CAST, DASH, HURL,
SHED, TOSS, FLING, HEAVE,
PITCH, SLING, UPSET
a monkey wrench into
.... SABOTAGE
a party .... HOST
about .... STREW, SCATTER
at .... PROJECT
at a mark .... COCKSHY
away .... WASTE, DISCARD,
SQUANDER
back .... RETURN, REVERT
back light .... REFLECT

dice .... CAST, MAIN, ROLL
football opponent .... STOP,
TACKLE
in .... INSERT, SUPPLEMENT
in with .... JOIN
into confusion ...... BEWILDER,
CONFOUND, EMBARRASS,
DEMORALIZE, DISCONCERT
lava .... ERUPT
obstacles at .... HAMPER,
HINDER, IMPEDE, OBSTRUCT
of ball .... PITCH, DELIVERY
off .... SHED, UNSEAT, SHAKE
OFF
out .... OUST, EJECT, EXPEL,
BOUNCE, REJECT, DISCARD
over .... JILT, ABANDON
overboard .... JETTISON
snake eyes .... LOSE
so as to make it roll .... BOWL
stones at .... LAPIDATE
the book at criminal
.... MAXIMUM PENALTY
the towel .... QUIT, YIELD
together .... MIX, ASSEMBLE,
IMPROVISE
up .... PUKE, SPEW, EJECT,
RETCH, VOMIT, REJECT,
REGORGE
with a short, quick motion
.... CHUCK
throwaway .... LEAFLET,
HANDBILL
throwback .... ATAVISM, RELAPSE,
SETBACK, REVERSION
thrower .... BOWLER, HEAVER,
HURLER, TOSSER, PITCHER,
SLINGER
discus .... DISCOBOLUS
kind of .... JAVELIN,
SHOTPUTTER
thrown .... CAST, FLUNG, OUSTED,
PITCHED, DEPORTED,
UNSEATED
thrum .... DRUM, TIRL, STRUM,
FRINGE
thrummy .... SHAGGY
thrush ...... MAVIS, OUZEL, PITTA,
ROBIN, VEERY, MISTLE,
REDWING, BLUEBIRD,
(SONG)BIRD, THROSTLE,
STONECHAT, NIGHTINGALE
blackbird .... MERULA
disease .... APHTHA,
CANDIDIASIS
family .... TURDIDAE
genus .... BABAX, TURDUS,
TURDOIDES
genus, bluebird .... SIALIA
genus, ground- ..... ZOOTHERA

genus, laughing-
.... GARRULAX
long distance migrant
.... WHINCHAT, NIGHTINGALE
mistle .... VISCIVORUS
of the .... TURDINE
relative .... BLACKCAP,
FERNBIRD, FLYCATCHER,
WHITETHROAT
rock .... SAXATILIS
slang .... WARBLER
song .... PHILOMELOS
water .... WAGTAIL
with one leg .... BLACKBIRD
wood .... MUSTELINA
thrust ...... DIG, JAB, RAM, BLOW,
POKE, PUSH, STAB, TILT,
DRIVE, FORCE, LUNGE, SHOVE,
ATTACK, COMPEL, DARTLE,
EXSERT, PIERCE
answer of .... PARRY
aside .... PUSH, SHOVE,
BRUSH(OFF)
away ..... DETRUDE, CHASE OFF
back .... REPEL, REBUFF
down .... DEPRESS, DETRUDE
in .... ENTER, INTRUDE
in fencing ...... FOIN, PASSADO
out .... EJECT, EXSERT,
EXTEND, STRETCH
out lips .... POUT
thruster .... RAM, CUDGEL,
FENCER, LUNGER, PLUNGER,
SWATTER
thruway .... AISLE
Thsombe, Congo premier
.... MOISE
thud .... BLOW, CLOP, CLUMP,
THUMP
thug ...... TOUGH, DACOIT, KILLER,
HOOD(LUM), RUFFIAN,
ASSASSIN, HOOLIGAN,
CUTTHROAT, STRANGLER
slang .... GOON, YEGG,
MUGGER, GORILLA
thuja .... PINE, CEDAR,
ARBORVITAE
Thule, part of .... NORWAY,
ICELAND
thumb .... DIGIT, FINGER, POLLEX
a ride .... HITCHHIKE
fleshy bulge of .... THENAR
in architecture .... OVOLO
index .... TAB
one's nose at .... FLOUT,
SCOFF, SNEER, DISDAIN
protector .... STALL, THIMBLE
through .... SCAN, BROWSE
thumbnail .... BRIEF, SMALL
thumbs, all .... CLUMSY
down ...... NO DICE, REJECTION

up .... NOD, OKS, YES, AFFIRMATIVE
thumbstall .... THIMBLE
thump .... BEAT, THUD, POUND, THROB, CUDGEL, POMMEL, THRASH
thumper .... JUMBO, WHALE, WHOPPER
thumping: colloq. .... HUGE, LARGE, WHOPPING, WALLOPING
thunder .... BOOM, PEAL, ROAR, NOISE, FULMINATE
and lightning .... STORM
at the beach .... SURF
forth .... FULMINATE
god .... THOR, DONAR
sound .... CLAP, PEAL, ROAR, ROLL, CRASH, MUTTER, RUMBLE
thigh thinner ..... LIPOSUCTION
thunderbolt .... LIGHTNING
thunderer .... ZEUS, JUPITER
thunderfish .... RAAD, LOACH
thundering .... AROAR, BOOMING, GROWLING, TONITRUANT
thunderous .... LOUD, DEAFENING
thunderstone .... BELEMITE, CUTTLEFISH
thunderstruck .... AGHAST, SPELLBOUND
Thurber, humorist .... JAMES
hero .... MITTY
thurible .... CENSER
thurifer .... ACOLYTE, ALTAR BOY
thurify .... CENSE
Thuringian capital .... ERFURT
castle .... WARTBURG
city ..... JENA, GOTHA, WEIMAR
forest .... THURINGER WALD
Thurman, actress .... UMA
thus .... SO, SIC, ERGO, HENCE, THEREFORE, CONSEQUENTLY
far .... YET
thwack ...... SLAP, SMACK, WHACK
thwart .... BALK, FOIL, BLOCK, SPITE, BAFFLE, DEFEAT, HINDER, HOGTIE, OBLIQUE, OBSTRUCT, FRUSTRATE
thy .... YOUR
Thyestes' brother .... ATREUS
father .... PELOPS
grandfather .... TANTALUS
son .... AEGISTHUS
thyme .... HERB, MINT
thymus .... GLAND
animal's .... SWEETBREAD
part .... FAT, LOBE, EPITHELIUM, LYMPHOCYTE
site .... CHEST, THORAX
tumor .... THYMOMA

thyroid gland disease ...... CANCER, GOITER, GOITRE, CRETINISM
hormone .... THYROXINE, CALCITONIN
inflammation ...... THYROIDITIS
location .... NECK
scanning method .... ULTRASOUND, RADIONUCLIDE
surgical removal of .... THYROIDECTOMY
thysanuran .... BRISTLETAIL
Ti, in chemistry .... TITANIUM
tiara .... CROWN, DIADEM, CORONET, HEADDRESS
pope's .... TRIPLE CROWN
wearer .... POPE, QUEEN, DUCHESS, EMPRESS, PEERESS, PRINCESS
Tiber .... TEVERE
Tiberias Sea .... GALILEE
Tibet .... XIZANG, SITSANG
capital of .... LHASA
lake .... NAMCO, SILINGCO, NGANGZECO, TANGRA YUMCO
mountain .... NANSHAN
mountain pass ..... LEKH, LIPU, MANA, NITI
mountain range .... GANGDISE, HIMALAYA
river .... INDUS, SUTLEJ, SALWEEN
Tibetan antelope .... GOA, SUS, CHIRU
chief lama .... DALAI, PANCHEN
coin .... TANGA
deer .... SHOU
dog .... TERRIER
gazelle .... GOA
general .... CHANG
goat wool .... CASHMERE
high priest .... BLAMA
monastery .... LAMASERY
monk .... LAMA
ox .... YAK
oxlike animal .... ZEBU
priest .... LAMA
religion .... LAMAISM
wild sheep .... SHA, BHARAL, NAHOOR
zoo animal .... PANDA
tibia .... FLUTE, CNEMIS, SHIN(BONE)
common disorder of .... FRACTURE
location of .... LEG
Tibur .... TIVOLI
tic .... SPASM, TWITCH, CONTRACTION

douloureux ...... (TRIGEMINAL) NEURALGIA
organ commonly affected by .... ARM, FACE, SHOULDER
typical ..... JERKING, BLINKING, SHRUGGING, TWITCHING
tic-tac-toe .... GAME
number of squares in .... NINE
win .... OOO, XXX
tical's replacement .... BAHT
Ticino .... TESSIN
tick .... BUG, DOT, BEAT, MITE, CLICK, ACARID, INSECT, JIGGER, MOMENT, ARACHNID, PARASITE, (CHECK)MARK, PILLOW CASE
British .... TRUST, CREDIT
broad category of .... HARD, SOFT
colloquial .... TICKING
disease spread by .... LYME, Q FEVER, TULAREMIA
food .... BLOOD
host of ...... DOG, MAN, SHEEP, CATTLE
of the clock .... SECOND
off .... CHECK, COUNT, ENUMERATE
ticked off .... MAD, IRATE, PISSED, INCENSED
ticker .... TAPPER
slang .... CLOCK, HEART, WATCH, TIMEPIECE
tape figures .... QUOTATIONS
tape man .... STOCKBROKER
ticket .... TAG, LIST, PASS, LABEL, DOCKET, NOTICE, RECORD, LICENSE
baggage .... TAG, CHECK
candidates' ..... SLATE, BALLOT
free .... PASS, ANNIE OAKLEY
losing-lottery .... BLANK
of leave .... PAROLE
part .... STUB
slang .... DUCAT, DOCKET, PASTEBOARD
speculator, theater .... SCALPER
stub .... RAINCHECK
to go ashore, sailor's .... LIBERTY
traffic .... SUMMONS
tickle .... STIR, AMUSE, EXCITE, PLEASE, TINGLE, DELIGHT, GRATIFY, OVERJOY, TITILLATE
tickler .... POSER, PUZZLE, REMINDER
ticklish .... RISKY, FICKLE, TOUCHY, CRITICAL, DELICATE, SENSITIVE
tickseed .... DAISY, COREOPSIS

tid plus two .... BITS
tidal flow .... EBB, NEAP
   wave .... BORE, EAGRE,
         TSUNAMI
tidbit .... CATE, OLIVE, CANAPE,
   BONBON, GOSSIP, MORSEL,
         KICKSHAW
   for a pangolin .... ANT,
         TERMITE
tiddly .... DIZZY, TIPSY
tide .... FLOW, CURRENT
   designation of a ...... EBB, RIP,
      NEAP, FLOOD, SPRING
   over .... LAST, ENDURE
tidings ...... NEWS, WORD, ADVICE,
   GOSPEL, REPORT, EVANGEL,
        INFORMATION
tidy ...... NEAT, PRIM, TAUT, TRIG,
   TRIM, LARGE, NIFTY, SPRUCE,
      ORDERLY, SHIPSHAPE,
   STRAIGHTEN, CONSIDERABLE
tie ...... BEAM, BIND, BOND, EVEN,
   JOIN, KNOT, LASH, LINK,
   ASCOT, EQUAL, HITCH,
   TACH(E), TRUSS, UNION,
   ATTACH, CRAVAT, FASTEN,
   TETHER, LIGATURE, RELATION,
   STANDOFF, STALEMATE
   beam .... BALK
   between individuals of a
     group .... NEXUS
   boat/ship .... MOOR, ANCHOR
   connecting .... LIGAMENT
   contest .... DRAW, STANDOFF
   down .... HOLD, CONFINE,
         RESTRAIN
   down securely .... LASH
   fabric .... REP
   game to break .... RUBBER
   in .... JOIN, CONNECT
   in a race .... DEAD HEAT
   kind of .... BOW, ASCOT,
        FOUR-IN-HAND
   situation .... DEADLOCK,
        STALEMATE
   up .... HALT, STOP, SNARL,
   DELAY, HINDER, LIAISON,
   BLOCKADE, CONNECTION
   up, traffic .... JAM
tieback .... SASH
tied .... WED, EVEN, RELATED
   feet and hands .... HOGTIED
   one up .... BOUND, KNOTTED
   up .... BUSY
Tientsin river .... HAI
tier ...... ROW, BANK, DECK, RANK,
   FLOOR, LAYER, LEVEL, STAGE,
      STORY, PINAFORE
   of bare benches
        .... BLEACHERS
   theater seats .... BOX, LOGE,

      BALCONY, GALLERY
tierce .... CASK, HOUR, THIRD
Tierra del Fuego Indian .... ONA
ties .... OXFORDS
   support .... ROADBED
Tietze's syndrome .... CHEST
         PAIN
tiff .... FIT, ROW, HUFF, MIFF,
   SPAT, PUNCH, LIQUOR,
   TEMPER, BICKER, QUARREL,
   TANTRUM, WRANGLE,
   ARGUMENT, SQUABBLE
tiffany .... SILK, GAUZE, MUSLIN
tiffin .... TEA, LUNCH, SNACK
tig .... TAP, DALLY, TOUCH,
        MEDDLE
tiger .... PUMA, COUGAR, JAGUAR,
   LEOPARD, SABERTOOTH
   cat ..... LYNX, CHATI, MARGAY,
   OCELOT, SERVAL, PANTHER
   female .... TIGRESS
   of Malaya, so-called
       .... YAMASHITA
   of the sea .... BARRACUDA
   Persian .... SHER, SHIR
   young .... CUB, WHELP
tigerish .... CRUEL, FIERCE,
   VALIANT, FEROCIOUS,
   BELLIGERENT, BLOODTHIRSTY
tight .... SNUG, TAUT, CLOSE,
   TENSE, SCARCE, SEVERE,
   COMPACT, HERMETIC
   colloquial .... STINGY,
   MISERLY, SOUNDLY
   in .... FAMILIAR, INTIMATE
   manner, in a .... SECURE
   place .... FIX, JAM, SPOT
   slang .... DRUNK, TIPSY,
   LOADED, INEBRIATED
   spot .... PINCH, SCRAPE
tighten ...... FRAP, CLAMP, SCREW,
   TAUTEN, SQUEEZE, STRAITEN
tightfisted .... CHEAP, STINGY,
   FRUGAL, MISERLY, PENNY-
        PINCHING
tightlipped .... MUM, SILENT,
   TACITURN, SECRETIVE
tightness .... TENACITY,
        PARSIMONY
tightrope walker .... ACROBAT,
   AERIALIST, EQUILIBRIST,
       FUNAMBULIST
tightwad .... HUNKS, MISER,
   PIKER, NIGGARD, SCROOGE,
   SKINFLINT, CHEAPSKATE,
      PENNY-PINCHER
"Tijuana Brass" boss
      .... ALPERT
til .... SESAME
tilbury .... COACH, CARRIAGE
tile .... BRICK, DALLE, SLATE,

   QUARRY, TEGULA, CERAMIC,
     PANTILE, TESSERA
   arranged in a mosaic pattern
      .... TESSELLATED
   game .... DOMINO, MAHJONG
   like/of .... TEGULAR
   making art .... CERAMICS
   material .... CLAY, STONE,
   KAOLIN, RUBBER, ARGILLI,
   PLASTIC, CONCRETE, PETUNTSE
   mosaic .... TESSERA
   roofing .... SLATE, PANTILE
   square-shaped/diamond-
     shaped .... QUARRY
   structure .... TILING
   use .... ROOFING, COVERING,
         FLOORING
tiler .... DOORKEEPER
till .... FARM, PLOW, UNTO, UP TO,
   UNTIL, CULTIVATE,
   CASH(REGISTER)
   land .... SUBDUE
tilled land .... FARM, ARADA,
      TILTH, TILLAGE
tiller ...... HELM, SHOOT, FARMER,
   GRANGER, PEASANT,
   PLOWMAN, CULTIVATOR,
      HUSBANDMAN
Tillie the _____ .... TOILER
Tillis, _____ .... MEL
tilt .... TIP, HEEL, LIST, JOUST,
   SLANT, SLOPE, AWNING,
   CANOPY, DEBATE, SEESAW,
   DISPUTE, INCLINE, TOURNEY,
      TOURNAMENT
   and pour .... DECANT
tilted .... ACOCK
tilth .... FARM, ARADA, TILLAGE
tilting arena .... LISTS
   target .... QUINTAIN
   tournament .... CAR(R)OUSEL
timarau .... BUFFALO
timbal .... KETTLEDRUM
timber .... LOG, BEAM, BITT,
   STUD, WOOD, TREES, LUMBER
   above keel .... DEADWOOD
   arched .... CAMBER
   borer .... GRIBBLE
   crack .... ANEMOSIS
   deciduous .... HARDWOOD
   down bend .... SNY
   dressed .... PUNCHEON
   foundation .... SPILE
   grooved .... COULISSE
   heartwood .... DURAMEN
   hewn piece .... BALK
   hitch .... KNOT
   joining peg .... TRUNNEL,
        TRE(E)NAIL
   natural split in .... SHAKE
   nautical .... BITT

prop .... STULL
roof .... RAFTER
rot .... CONK, DODDER
sawn .... LUMBER
small .... SCANTLING
soak .... RET
standing .... STUMPAGE
state .... OREGON
support .... CORBEL
tree .... YEW
upward bend in .... SNY
wolf .... LOBO
timberland .... FOREST,
WOODLAND
Timberlane, Judge .... CASS
timbre .... RING, TONE, SOUND
timbrel ...... TABOR, TAMBOURINE
Timbuktu .... TOMBOUCTOU
location .... MALI
slang .... BOONDOCKS,
(THE)STICKS, (THE)TULLIES
time .... AGE, EON, ERA, DATE,
SPAN, CLOCK, EPOCH, SPELL,
MOMENT, PERIOD, INSTANT,
DURATION, INTERVAL,
OCCASION
A.D., part of .... ANNO,
DOMINI
all the .... ALWAYS
at no .... NEVER
at the same .... MEANTIME,
MEANWHILE
B.C., part of .... BEFORE,
CHRIST
bearish .... DROP
beating device
.... METRONOME
between .... INTERIM,
INTERVAL
comb. form .... CHRON(O)
Coronation .... MAY DAY
differential .... EPACT
extension .... GRACE
for an egg hunt .... EASTER
(SUN)DAY
for pistols .... SUNRISE
free .... BREAK, LEISURE
honored .... TRADITIONAL
in history .... ERA
in music .... BEAT, TEMPO,
VOLTA
incalculable .... EON
indefinite period of ...... SPELL
indicating device .... CLOCK,
WATCH, SUNDIAL, CLEPSYDRA,
HOURGLASS
limit .... DEADLINE
of day .... MORNING,
(AFTER)NOON
greatest vigor .... HEYDAY
imprisonment .... TERM

judgment .... DOOMSDAY
life .... TEENS, DOTAGE,
NONAGE, PUBERTY
rejoicing .... JUBILEE
the year .... SEASON
want .... FAMINE
yearly event .... BIRTHDAY,
NATAL DAY, ANNIVERSARY
youth and inexperience
.... SALAD DAYS
out .... REST, BREAK, RECESS,
RESPITE
pass the .... WHILE AWAY
period .... DAY, WEEK, YEAR,
HOUR, MONTH, SECOND
pertaining to .... FAST, LATE,
SLOW, EARLY, HORAL,
AORISTIC, PERIODIC
poetic .... EVENTIDE
prosperous .... BOOM, HEYDAY
science of .... HOROLOGY
span .... HOUR
spend .... WHILE
teller .... SUNDIAL
waster .... IDLER, LOAFER,
SLACKER, LINGERER, LOITERER
without end .... ETERNITY
timeless .... ENDLESS, ETERNAL,
IMMORTAL, LEGENDARY,
PERPETUAL, EVERLASTING
timely .... SOON, EARLY, RIGHT,
PROMPT, EXPEDIENT,
OPPORTUNE, AUSPICIOUS,
SEASONABLE
caravel .... NINA, PINTA, SANTA
MARIA
king .... FERDINAND
queen .... ISABELLA
observance .... HOLIDAY,
COLUMBUS DAY, VETERANS
DAY, THANKSGIVING DAY
painting of 1912
.... SEPTEMBER MORN
reminder .... TAX TIME,
SCHOOL DAYS AGAIN
treat .... LONG WEEKEND
visitors .... DWARFS AND
GNOMES, GHOSTS AND
SHADES, GOBLINS AND ELVES
timepiece .... CLOCK, WATCH,
HOROLOGE, TIMEKEEPER
art of making .... HOROLOGY
kind of .... SUNDIAL,
HOURGLASS
timer .... STOPWATCH
timeserver ...... TOADY, TRIMMER,
OPPORTUNIST
timetable .... SKED, SCHEDULE
timeworn .... OLD, AGED,
SHABBY, RAGGED(Y), OUT-OF-
DATE

timid .... SHY, WEAK, PAVID,
AFRAID, BASHFUL, CHICKEN,
COWARDLY, HESITANT,
RESERVED, RETIRING,
SHEEPISH, TIMOROUS
timidity, symbol of .... MOUSE
timing .... PACE, PACING,
CLOCKING
device .... METRONOME,
STOPWATCH
timon .... HELM, TILLER,
MISANTHROPE
Timon of Athens author
.... SHAKESPEARE
Timor Archipelago part
.... SUMBA, FLORES, SUMBAWA
capital .... DILI, KUPANG
city/town .... SOE, AUBA,
BAUKAU, ATAMBUA
coin .... AVO
timorous ...... SHY, PAVID, TIMID,
TREPID, BASHFUL, FEARFUL
Timoshenko, Soviet Marshal
.... SEMYON
timothy .... HAY, GRASS
Timothy, actor .... BOTTOMS
timpani .... KETTLEDRUMS
tin ...... CAN, STANNUM, PRESERVE
alloy .... BRONZE, PEWTER
and lead alloy .... TERNE
box .... TRUMMEL
coated sheet metal .... TAGGER
describing thing made of
.... CHEAP
fish .... TORPEDO
foil .... TAIN
hat .... HELMET
(metal) sheet .... LATTEN
mine .... STANNARY
of .... STANNOUS
plate .... FOIL, TAIN
pyrite .... STANNITE
slang .... MONEY
smeltery .... STANNARY
strips .... TINSEL
symbol for .... SN
threads, decorative ..... TINSEL
Tin Lizzie .... CRATE, MODEL T
FORD
Pan Alley character
.... COMPOSER, PROMOTER
Pan Alley females .... GALS
Pan Alley group .... ASCAP
tinamou family .... TINAMIDAE
genus .... NOTHOPROCTA
-like bird .... QUAIL,
PARTRIDGE
relative .... RHEA
tincal .... BORAX
tinct .... COLOR, TINGED, TINT(ED)
tincture .... DASH, TINT, VERT,

COLOR, SHADE, TINGE, TOUCH, TRACE, ELIXIR, SOUPCON, VESTIGE

tind .... KINDLE

tinder .... PUNK, AMADOU

tinderbox, like a .... POWDER KEG

tine ...... BIT, FORK, TYND, PRONG, SPIKE, ANTLER

tinea .... (FUNGAL)INFECTION

corporis .... RINGWORM

cruris .... JOCK ITCH

fungi causing .... DERMATOPHYTES

pedis .... ATHLETE'S FOOT

tinge .... DYE, DASH, TINT, COLOR, SHADE, STAIN, TAINT, TOUCH, TRACE, FLAVOR

tinged .... TINCT

tingle .... NIP, DIRL, STING, THIRL, DINDLE, THRILL, PRICKLE

tingling feeling ...... PARESTHESIA

sensation, describing a .... PINS AND NEEDLES

tinhorn .... CHEAP, PIKER, SHOWY, GAMBLER, TWO-BIT, SMALL-TIME

tiniest .... MINIM

tinker .... FUSS, BOTCH, CAIRD, PATCH, MEND(ER), PUTTER, REPAIR, TAMPER, BUNGLER, MACKEREL, SILVERSIDES

colloquial .... DOCTOR

jargon of .... SHELTA

Shakespearean .... SNOUT

slang .... MR. FIXIT

target of .... EVERS

to chance connector .... EVERS

Tinker Bell, for one .... FAIRY

tinkering ...... TOYING, DABBLING, PIDDLING

tinkle .... CLINK, JINGLE, URINATE

tinkling .... GRACKLE

tinned .... CANNED, PRESERVED

tinnitus (noise) .... BUZZING, HISSING, RINGING, WHISTLING

tin(s)man .... (TIN)SMITH

tinsel .... GAUDY, SHOWY, BAUBLES, GLITTER, SPANGLE

tinseled .... CLINQUANT

tinstone .... CASSITERITE

tint .... DYE, HUE, CAST, TONE, COLOR, SHADE, STAIN, TINGE

Tintagel Head's famous son .... ARTHUR

tinted .... TINCT

tinter .... DYER

tintinnabula .... BELLS

tintinnabulate .... RING

tinware .... PANS, POTS

tiny .... WEE, SMALL, TEENY,

ATOMIC, LITTLE, MINUTE, PETITE, MINUSCULE, DIMINUTIVE

being/creature .... RUNT, ATOMY, DWARF

bit .... IOTA, MORSEL

copy/model .... MINIATURE

extremely .... MICROSCOPIC

gold particles .... DUST

letter .... MINUSCULE

margin .... HAIR

opening .... PORE

person/thing .... DIMINUTIVE

portion .... MINIM

slang .... HALFPINT

speck .... MOTE

Tiny, singer .... TIM

tip .... END, FEE, NEB, TAP, TOP, APEX, CANT, CLUE, GIFT, HEEL, HINT, LIST, TILT, VAIL, SLANT, STEER, UPSET, ADVICE, GREASE, REWARD, TOPPLE, CUMSHAW, POINT(ER), GRATUITY

as of a hill or mountain .... PEAK, CREST, SUMMIT

off .... HINT, INFORM, WARN(ING)

one's hat .... DOFF

over .... UPEND, UPSET, TOPPLE, CAPSIZE, OVERTURN

pen's .... CAP, NEB, NIB

tipped .... CAPPED, CRESTED

rod .... CUE

"Tipper" .... MRS. AL GORE

tippet .... AMICE, SCARF, ALMUCE, CAMAIL, LIRIPIPE

tipping .... ALIST

hats .... DOFFING

tipple .... BIB, DRAM, DRINK, GUZZLE, IMBIBE, LIQUOR

tippler .... SOT, DRUNK, TOPER, BARFLY, BIBBER, SOAKER

tippler's haunt .... PUB, BAR(ROOM), TAPROOM, ALEHOUSE

tippy .... SHAKY

tips seller .... TOUT

tipstaff .... BAILIFF, CONSTABLE

tipster .... TOUT(ER), ADVISER, DOPESTER

tipsy .... AWRY, DRUNK, GROGGY, LOADED, CROOKED, INTOXICATED

slang .... HIGH, TIGHT

tiptoe .... LURK, CREEP, SNEAK

tiptop .... FIT, A-ONE, BEST, SHIPSHAPE

tirade ...... RANT, SPATE, SCREED, SPEECH, DIATRIBE, HARANGUE, JEREMIAD,

PHILIPPIC

tirailleur .... MARKSMAN, SHARPSHOOTER

tire ...... FAG, BORE, CLOY, DO IN, JADE, PNEU, SHOE, WEARY, EXHAUST, WHITEWALL

burst .... BLOWOUT

casing .... SHOE

filled with compressed air .... PNEUMATIC

iron .... STRAKE

kind of ...... RADIAL, TUBELESS

out .... FAG, EXHAUST

part of .... RIM, SHOE, TUBE, FELLY, TREAD, CASING

puncturer .... CALTRAP, CALTROP

tread mold .... MOULAGE

with low air pressure .... BALLOON

tired .... WEAK, JADED, WEARY, WORN-OUT, BREATHLESS

easily .... FATIGABLE

feeling .... ENNUI, FATIGUE, LANGUOR, WEARINESS

looking .... WAN, DRAWN, HAGGARD

of .... BORED

very ...... BEAT, ALL IN, SPENT, BUSHED, POOPED

tiredness, cause of .... OVERWORK

tireless .... INDEFATIGABLE

Tiresias .... SOOTHSAYER

tiresome .... DRY, DRAB, DULL, BORING, DREARY, HUMDRUM, IRKSOME, TEDIOUS, MONOTONOUS

person .... BORE, DRIP, NUISANCE

tiring .... TRYING, ANNOYING, DRAINING, GRUELING, STRAINING, STRESSFUL, WEARISOME

tirl .... STRUM, THRUM, QUIVER, THRILL, TREMOR

tisane .... TEA, PTISAN, DECOCTION

Tisiphone .... FURY

tissue .... WEB, BAST, MESH, TELA, CLOTH, FLESH, GAUZE, PAPER, PHLOEM, GRISTLE, NET(WORK)

animal .... GRISTLE, CARTILAGE

area of dead .... INFARCT

breaking down of organic .... HISTOLYSIS

cavity ...... LOCULUS, VACUOLE

cell in connecting .... HISTIOCYTE

change in .... CATAPLASIA

combining form .... HIST(O)

connecting ..... PONS, STROMA, TENDON, LIGAMENT
contracting .... MUSCLE
cutting instrument .... MICROTOME
decay .... CARIES, GANGRENE
development process .... HISTOGENESIS
divider .... SEPTUM, SEPTA (PL.)
elastic .... TENDON, CARTILAGE
fluid content ...... ION, WASTE, NUTRIENT
hardening .... SCLEROMA, SCLERIASIS
healed .... SCAR
horny: comb. form .... KERATO
inflammation .... CELLULITIS
like .... HISTOID
matching for transplant .... TYPING
nerve .... ALBA
orange/grapefruit .... PITH
plant .... BAST, LIGNIN, PHLOEM
sagging .... FLAB
skin .... EPITHELIUM
study of .... HISTOLOGY, HISTOPATHOLOGY
under epidermis .... HYPODERMA
wood .... LIGNIN, PHELLODERM, PHELLOGEN, CORK-CAMBIUM
tit .... NAG, TAP, BIRD, BLOW, GIRL, JADE, TEAT, HORSE, BREAST, NIPPLE
kapok .... ANTHOSCOPUS
long-tailed .... AEGITHALOS
penduline .... REMIZIDAE
Titan .... ZEUS, ATLAS, COEUS, CREUS, GIANT, CRONUS, HELIOS, IAPETUS, OCEANUS, COLOSSUS, HYPERION, PHAETHON, EPIMETHEUS, PROMETHEUS
father .... URANUS
female ...... LETO, MAIA, RHEA, DIONE, THEIA, AMAZON, PHOEBE, TETHYS, GIANTESS, EURYNOME, TITANESS
in lexicography .... ROGET, WEBSTER
in wrestling .... ANTAEUS
mother .... GE, GAEA, GAIA
noted for great strength .... SAMSON, HERCULES
place of consignment .... TARTARUS
Titania .... FAIRY-QUEEN
husband of .... OBERON

titanic .... HUGE, GIGANTIC
titanium dioxide .... RUTILE
titanite .... SPHENE, MINERAL
Titans' war with Olympians .... TITANOMACHY
tithe .... TAX, CESS, LEVY, TENTH, CHARGE, DONATION
tithing .... DECENARY
Tithonus' brother .... PRIAM
father .... LAOMEDON
love .... EOS
transformation .... GRASSHOPPER
titi .... TREE, MONKEY, IRONWOOD
titian .... AUBURN
titillate .... AMUSE, EXCITE, TICKLE, STIMULATE, TANTALIZE
titivate .... DRESS(UP), SPRUCE(UP)
titlark .... PIPIT
title .... NAME, CLAIM, RIGHT, LEGEND, PARENT, CAPTION, HEADING, PEERAGE, APPELLATION, DESIGNATION, CHAMPIONSHIP
colloquial .... HANDLE
degree .... MASTER, BACHELOR, EMERITUS, DOCTORATE
descriptive .... EPITHET, SURNAME, COGNOMEN
ecclesiastical ..... DOM, PADRE, RABBI, FATHER, SISTER, BROTHER, CARDINAL, HOLINESS, HIS GRACE, REVEREND, MONSIGNOR, MOTHER SUPERIOR
holder .... OWNER, TITLIST, CHAMPION, PROPRIETOR
inaccurate .... MISNOMER
of a noble .... RAS, DAME, DUKE, EARL, LADY, LORD, MILADY, DUCHESS, MARQUISE, BARON(ESS), COUNT(ESS), MARCHIONESS, VISCOUNT(ESS)
of a parliament's chief executive .... PRIME MINISTER
of a ruler .... EMIR, EMEER, CALIPH, PRINCE, SULTAN, (PADI)SHAH
of respect .... AGA, BEY, SIR, MILADY, MADAM(E), MONSIEUR
of Roman Catholic Church dignitary .... MONSIGNOR, (ARCH)BISHOP
of Roman Catholic Church head .... PAPA, POPE
of royalty .... KING, BEGUM, QUEEN, PRINCE, EMPEROR, EMPRESS, PRINCESS,

MAHARANI, MAHARAJA(H), MAHARANEE
of Shiite leader .... AYATOLLAH
of the highest executive officer .... PRESIDENT
of UK's highest state officer .... LORD CHANCELLOR
ownership .... DEED, CERTIFICATE
pages .... ODDMENTS
sports .... TITLIST, CHAMPION(SHIP)
subordinate .... SUBHEAD
to property .... DEED, MUNIMENT
transfer .... CEDE
titled person .... NOBLE, PEER(ESS)
titmouse .... MAG, NUN, TIT, VERDIN, BLUECAP, CHICKADEE
family .... PARIDAE
genus .... PARUS
relative .... NUTHATCH
Tito, Marshal .... (JOSIP)BROZ
country of .... YUGOSLAVIA
position held by .... PRESIDENT, PRIME MINISTER
resistance followers .... PARTISANS
titter .... GIGGLE, TEE-HEE, SNICKER, LAUGH(TER)
tittie .... SISTER
tittle .... DOT, JOT, IOTA, WHIT, SPECK, PARTICLE
tattle .... GOSSIP, JABBER, CHATTER, CHITCHAT
tittup .... CAPER, FRISK, FROLIC, PRANCE
titular .... NOMINAL, HONORIFIC
Titus' father .... VESPASIAN
Tiu .... TYR
Tivoli .... TIBUR
neighbor .... ROME
tizzy .... FUSS, SNIT, SWEAT, DITHER, SWIVET, FLUSTER, FOOFARAW, CONFUSION
Tlingit .... TONGA, INDIAN
Tman .... AGENT
tmesis .... DIACOPE
TNT .... TROTYL, DYNAMITE, EXPLOSIVE
part of .... NITRO
to .... AT, ON, UPON, WITH, UNTIL, TOWARD, AS FAR AS, THITHER
a degree .... SOMEWHAT
a point in time .... UNTIL
a T .... EXACTLY
adapt to new conditions .... ACCLIMATE
and fro .... UP AND DOWN,

monetary unit .... FRANC
mountain .... AGOU
president .... EYADEMA,
                          OLYMPIO
river .... OTI, MONO
tribe .... EWE, MINA
Togoland plus Gold Coast
                                   GHANA
toil ...... MOIL, SLOG, TASK, WORK,
       LABOR, SLAVE, DRUDGE,
       EFFORT, STRIVE, TRAVAIL
toile .... CLOTH, LINEN, CRETONNE
toilet .... COMMODE, LATRINE,
                        LAVATORY
case .... ETUI, ETWEE, MUSETTE
outdoor .... JAKES, PRIVY
slang .... CAN, HEAD, JOHN
water ...... BAYRUM, COLOGNE,
                    LAVENDER
toiletry item .... SOAP, LOTION,
   CREAM, POWDER, COLOGNE,
               COSMETICS
toils .... GIN, NET, WEB, MESH,
             TRAP, SNARES
toilsome .... ARDUOUS,
   LABORIOUS, STRENUOUS
Tojo, Japan premier ...... HIDEKI
tokay .... WINE, GRAPE
token .... SIGN, SLUG, INDEX,
   EMBLEM, PLEDGE, SYMBOL,
   KEEPSAKE, INDICATION
currency .... SCRIP
of servitude .... YOKE
payment ..... ARLES, ADVANCE,
                  EARNEST
tokens .... INDICIA
Tokyo .... EDO, YEDO
center .... SHIMBASI
coin .... SEN
Fifth Avenue of .... GINZA
fork .... CHOPSTICK
formerly .... EDO, YEDO
is capital of _____ .... JAPAN
Shogun's .... EDO
tole .... ALLURE, ENTICE
Toledo .... BLADE, SWORD
tolerable .... SO-SO, BEARABLE,
   PASSABLE, ENDURABLE
tolerably .... FAIRLY,
             MODERATELY
tolerance .... MARGIN,
   ALLOWANCE, LENIENCY,
             ENDURANCE
tolerate .... BEAR, ALLOW, BROOK,
   STAND, ENDURE, PERMIT,
                SUFFER
Tolkien badlands .... MORDOR
tree creature .... ENT
toll .... FEE, TAX, RING, KNELL,
     CHARGE, EXACTION
collector .... PUBLICAN

road .... (TURN)PIKE
tol(l)booth .... PEN, JAIL, LOCKUP,
                    PRISON
toller .... DOG, BELL RINGER
Toller, German poet ...... ERNST
Tolstoy, Russian novelist
                    LEO, LEV
Toltec .... NAHUATL(AN)
Tom .... TURKEY, MALE-CAT
Bosley role .... FATHER
                  DOWLING
Dick and Harry ...... ANYONE,
                EVERYONE
the General .... THUMB
Thumb .... DWARF, MIDGET
Thumb's bride .... LAVINIA
              (WARREN)
tom tom .... DRUM
tomahawk .... HATCHET,
             (BATTLE)AX
tomalley .... LIVER
tomato .... GIRL, BERRY, FRUIT,
    WOMAN, LOVE-APPLE
blend of potato and
                    POMATO
eaten whole .... CHERRY
juice jelly/salad .... ASPIC
sauce .... CATSUP, KETCHUP
variety .... TAXI, PEACH,
   ZEBRA, RED-ROMA, LEMON-
   BOY, BEEFSTEAK, EARLY GIRL,
   (RED)CHERRY, GREEN GRAPE,
   RED CURRANT, MARVEL-STRIPE
tomb .... CIST, CRYPT, GRAVE,
   VAULT, BURIAL, DOLMEN,
   OSSUARY, CROMLECH,
   MASTABA(H), SEPULCHER,
          SARCOPHAGUS
commemorative .... CENOTAPH
cover .... PALL
empty .... CENOTAPH,
             MONUMENT
famous Indian ..... TAJ MAHAL
flag .... BANDEROL(E)
for absent dead ..... CENOTAPH
heroes' .... PANTHEON
imposing .... MAUSOLEUM
inscription on .... EPITAPH, HIC
   JACET, HERE LIES, IN
            MEMORIAM
mummy's .... MASTABA(H)
prehistoric/rock .... CIST
room .... CRYPT
royal .... PYRAMID
saint's .... SHRINE
stone over .... LEDGER,
  MENHIR, MEGALITH, MONOLITH
towerlike .... STUPA
underground .... PIT,
            CATACOMB(S)
tomblike .... GRIM, BLEAK,

DISMAL, DOLEFUL, FUNEREAL,
           SEPULCHRAL
tomboy .... ROMP, HOIDEN,
             HOYDEN
tomboyish .... MANNISH, ROMPISH
tombstone .... CAIRN, STELA,
   STELE, MARKER, TABLET
marshal .... (WYATT) EARP
tomcat .... GIB
tomcod or pollock ...... GAD(O)ID
tome .... BOOK, VOLUME
tomentose .... FLEECY, MATTED
tomfool .... ZANY, CLOWN, SILLY,
   STUPID, BUFFOON, FOOLISH
tomfoolery .... BANTER,
   NONSENSE, SILLINESS,
           BUFFOONERY
Tomlin, _____ .... LILY
Tommy, Brit. soldier .... ATKINS
tommyrot .... BOSH, RUBBISH,
           NONSENSE
tomography .... X-RAY
tomorrow .... MANANA
tomtit .... BIRD, WREN,
           CHICKADEE
ton .... STYLE, VOGUE, FASHION
unit of measure:
  1,000 kg. .... METRIC
  2,000 lbs. .... SHORT
  2,240 lbs. .... LONG
tonal .... TONIC, PHONIC
tonality .... TONE, MELODY,
          HARMONICS
tondo .... PAINTING
tone .... HUE, KEY, TINT, TUNE,
   PITCH, SHADE, SOUND, STYLE,
      ACCENT, QUALITY
arm .... PICKUP
certain kind of .... DIAL
color .... TIMBRE
combination .... CHORD
down .... MUTE, SOFTEN
lack of .... ATONY
quality of .... TONALITY
reiteration .... TREMOLO
shade of .... NUANCE
toneless .... ATONY
Tong member .... CHINESE
Tonga capital .... NUKUALOFA
city/town ...... NEIAFU, PANGAI
coin .... SENITI
king .... TUPOU
language .... TONGAN, ENGLISH
monetary unit .... PAANGA
tongs .... CLAMP, PLIERS, FORCEPS,
     NIPPERS, PINCERS
tongue .... TAB, FLAP, IDIOM,
   ORGAN, GLOSSA, LINGUA,
  SPEECH, DIALECT, LANGUAGE
bell's .... CLAPPER
bone of .... HYOID

buckle's .... PIN
coating .... FUR(RING)
combining form ..... GLOSS(O)
curbing device .... BRANKS
disorder .... TUMOR, ULCER,
CANCER, FISSURE
elevation on .... PAPILLA
examining instrument
.... DEPRESSOR
fold under the .... FRENUM,
FRENULUM
in cheek .... INSINCERE
inflammation .... GLOSSITIS
lashing ...... JAWING, REPROOF,
(BE)RATING, SCOLDING,
REPRIMAND
of the .... GLOSSAL, LINGUAL
"of vanity" .... EGO
part of .... BLADE, NODULE,
PAPILLA(E), EPIGLOTTIS
sensory organs of the
.... TASTE BUDS
-shaped .... LANGUET(TE),
LINGULATE
shoe's .... TAB
thickened patches on
.... LEUKOPLAKIA
-tied .... MUM, SHY, SILENT,
WORDLESS, DUMB(STRUCK),
SPEECHLESS
use of .... TASTE, SPEECH,
INGESTION, SWALLOWING,
MASTICATION, ARTICULATION
wagon's .... NEAP, POLE
tongueless .... MUM, DUMB, MUTE
tonguelike .... GLOSSAL, LINGUAL
organ .... LINGUA, PROBOSCIS
tongue-tie .... ANKYLOGLOSSIA
tonic ...... BRACER, ELIXIR, FILLIP,
PICKUP, REMEDY, BRACING,
BEVERAGE, MEDICINE,
ROBORANT, INVIGORATING
bark .... CANELLA
content .... VITAMIN, MINERAL,
HERBAL EXTRACT
effect, medically ..... PLACEBO
in medicine .... IRON
tonka bean .... GUAIAC
flavor .... COUMARIN
Tonkin .... BAMBOO
city .... HANOI
tonneau, later .... CHASSIS
tons and tons .... SCADS
tonsil .... AMYGDALA
abscess on the .... QUINSY
inflammation .... TONSILLITIS
instrument for .... FORCEPS,
GUILLOTINE
neighbor .... TONGUE,
ADENOID

surgical removal of
.... TONSILLECTOMY
tonsorial artist .... BARBER
tenet? .... BARBARISM
tonsured person .... MONK,
PRIEST
tontine .... ANNUITY
tonus .... TONICITY
tony .... CLASSY, STYLISH,
LUXURIOUS
Tony, actor .... CURTIS, RANDALL
too .... ALSO, VERY, AS WELL,
OVER(LY), BESIDES, LIKEWISE,
EXTREMELY, ADDITIONALLY
large ..... OUTSIZE, MONSTROUS
many/much .... DE TROP
much .... EXCESSIVE
much, in music .... TANTO
old .... OVERAGE
soon .... EARLY, UNTIMELY,
PREMATURE
tool ...... MEANS, DEVICE, GADGET,
STOOGE, MACHINE, UTENSIL,
APPARATUS, IMPLEMENT,
INSTRUMENT, INTERMEDIARY
adz-shaped .... MATTOCK
binding .... STAPLER, STAPLE
GUN
bookbinding .... GOUGE
boring .... AWL, AUGER, DRILL,
GIMLET, JUMPER, TREPAN
carpenter's .... SAW, BEVEL,
DRILL, LEVEL, PLANE,
HAMMER, NAILSET
case .... KIT
cleaving: var. .... FROE
cobbler's .... AWL
cutting .... SAW, ADZ(E), BOLO,
BLADE, KNIFE, CUTTER,
SCYTHE, SHEARS, SICKLE,
MACHETE, SCISSORS
digging ..... SHOVEL, MATTOCK
docking .... ANCHOR, BOAT-
HOOK
engraver's .... BURIN
fastening .... RIVETER,
STAPLER
finishing .... PLANER
garden ...... HOE, RAKE, SPADE,
SHOVEL, TROWEL,
BUSHWHACKER
grinding .... FILE
handle .... HAFT, HELVE
hoisting .... JACK, PULLEY
holding .... HAWK, VISE
hole-enlarging .... REAMER
hole-making .... BODKIN,
DIBBLE
knifelike .... SPATULA
lifting .... CRANE

lifting and tossing
.... PITCHFORK
lumberman's .... PEAVEY
mason's .... CHISEL, CUTTER
measuring .... CALIPER(S)
metal worker's .... SWAGE
mining .... CRADLE
molding .... DIE
person as a .... DUPE, PAWN,
DUMMY, PATSY, PUPPET,
STOOGE, CAT'S-PAW
pincers .... PLIERS, FORCEPS,
TWEEZER(S)
pipe-bending .... HICKEY
polishing ..... BUFFER, SANDER
pruning .... SHEARS, BILLHOOK
prying .... LEVER, CROWBAR
reaper's .... FLAIL
rotary .... REAMER
sculptor's .... CARVER, CHISEL,
MOLDER, WHITTLE
set .... KIT
shaping .... DIE, LATHE
sharpening .... HONE, STEEL,
STROP, GRINDER, WHETSTONE,
(GRIND)STONE
shaving .... (SAFETY)RAZOR
smoothing .... BUFFER
soil-breaking .... PICK
spike-toothed .... HARROW
surgical ...... LANCET, SCALPEL
surveyor's .... Y-LEVEL,
TRANSIT
toothed .... SAW,
RATCHET(WHEEL)
trimming .... SHEARS,
SCISSORS
turning .... WRENCH,
SCREWDRIVER
with serrated jaws ...... PLIERS
toolmaker .... MACHINIST
toon .... TREE, WOOD
family .... MAHOGANY
toot .... HORN, WHISTLE
sound .... HONK, BLAST,
WHISTLE
tooth .... PEG, TUSH, TUSK, IVORY,
MOLAR, TASTE, CUSPID,
CHOPPER, INCISOR, APPETITE
and ____ .... NAIL
and nail .... FIERCELY
back .... WISDOM(TOOTH)
boar's .... TUSK
broken .... SNAG
canine .... FANG, CUSPID,
LANIARY
combining form .... DENT(I),
ODONT(O)
covering .... ENAMEL
crooked .... SNAG
crust .... CEMENT

decay .... CARIES
deposit .... CRUST, TOPHUS
doctor .... DENTIST,
    ORTHODONTIST
dog's .... FANG
elephant .... TUSK
filler .... CEMENT
filling .... INLAY
for a tooth .... TALION
gear .... COG
growth on .... EXOSTOSIS
hollow in .... CAVITY
horse canine .... TUSH
like .... DENTOID, ODONTOID
long, projecting .... TUSK
long, sharp .... FANG
molar .... GRINDER
of the .... DENTAL
part .... PULP, CROWN,
    CEMENT, ENAMEL, DENTIN(E)
prefix .... DENTI
pre-molar .... BICUSPID
puller .... DENTIST
root tissue layer
    .... CEMENTUM
shaped .... DENTOID,
    DENTIFORM
small .... DENTIL, DENTICLE
snake's .... FANG
socket .... ALVEOLUS
substance .... PULP
upper canine .... EYETOOTH
use of ..... BITE, CHEW, GNAW,
    GRIND, PIERCE
walrus .... TUSK
wheel .... COG, GEAR
toothache .... ODONTALGIA
toothed .... DENTED, DENTATE,
    SERRATED
    wheel .... GEAR, RATCHET,
    SPROCKET
toothlike part .... COG, TINE,
    PRONG
    projection .... JAG, DENTIL,
    DENTICLE, DENT(ATION)
toothless .... EDENTATE
toothpaste .... ZIRCATE,
    DENTIFRICE
toothsome .... TASTY, DAINTY,
    SAVORY, LUSCIOUS,
    PALATABLE, APPETIZING
toothy look .... GRIN
    tool .... HARROW
    wheel .... RATCHET
tootle .... WHISTLE
toots: slang .... DEAR, DARLING
tootsy .... FOOT
top .... COP, LID, TOY, ACME,
    APEX, HEAD, LEAD, PICK,
    ROOF, COVER, ELITE, EXCEL,
    OUTDO, ZENITH, HIGHEST,

SURPASS, DOMINATE,
    PINNACLE
____ (A-One) .... DRAWER
altar .... MENSA
ballerina .... PRIMA
banana .... STAR
blow one's .... ERUPT
bottle .... CAP, CROWN
brass .... OFFICER, OFFICIAL(S),
    MANAGEMENT
carriage's .... CAPOTE
cover .... CAP, LID
dog .... ACE, BOSS, HEAD
drawer .... A-ONE, TOPS, FIRST-
    RATE
flight ...... BEST, A-ONE, FIRST-
    RATE
gallant .... ACME
grade .... BEST, CHOICE
hat .... GIBUS
hill .... COP, BROW
hole .... FIRST-RATE
kick: sl. .... SERGEANT
mast support .... FID
of head .... CROWN
of mountain ...... PEAK, CREST,
    SUMMIT
of the front page
    .... HEADLINE
of wave .... FOAM, CREST
off a room .... CEIL
priority ..... URGENT, URGENCY
quality .... SUPERIOR, FIRST-
    RATE
row on a form .... LINE-A
secret .... CLASSIFIED
shaped .... TURBINATE
spun with the fingers
    .... TEETOTUM
the next guy .... ONE-UP
topaz .... GEM, QUARTZ,
    HUMMINGBIRD
Topaz, author of .... URIS
topazolite .... GARNET
topcoat ...... RAGLAN, OVERCOAT,
    CHESTERFIELD
tope .... DRINK, SHARK, SHRINE
topee/topi ...... CAP, HAT, HELMET
toper .... SOT, SOAK, WINO,
    RUMMY, SOUSE, BIBBER,
    TOSSPOT, DRUNK(ARD)
topgallant .... MAST
tophat .... GIBUS
toph(e) .... TUFA, TUFF
Tophet(h) .... HELL
topic .... ITEM, TEXT, THEME,
    THESIS, HEAD(ING), SUBJECT
topical .... LOCAL
topkick .... SARGE, SERGEANT
topknot .... TUFT, HEADDRESS
topnotch ...... A-ONE, BEST, ONER,

TOPS, EXCELLENT, FIRST-RATE
toponym .... NAME
topper .... HAT, COAT, BERET,
    STETSON
    beer glass .... FOAM, SUDS
topping ...... CRUST, ICING, LAYER
topple .... FAIL, FALL, TRIP,
    LEVEL, DEFEAT, TOTTER,
    TUMBLE, COLLAPSE,
    OVERTURN
tops .... A-ONE, BEST, SUPER
topsail .... RAFFE
topside .... DECK
topsoil .... LOAM, LAYER
Topsy's friend .... EVA
topsy-turvy .... CHAOTIC,
    CONFUSED, INVERTED,
    DISORDERLY, UPSIDE-DOWN
toque .... CAP, HAT, BONNET
tor .... CRAG, HILL, KNOLL
    relative of .... ALP
Torah .... TETEL, PENTATEUCH
torch .... BURN, LINK, LUNT,
    IGNITE, CRESSET, FLAMBEAU,
    (FLASH)LIGHT
    bearer ...... LINKBOY, LINKMAN
    for lure .... JACK
    material .... TOW, PITCH,
    TAPER, CANDLE, TALLOW
    song .... BALLAD
tore .... RACED, TORUS
toreador .... BULLFIGHTER
    assistant of .... PICADOR
torero .... MATADOR, BULLFIGHTER
    queue of .... COLETA
torii .... GATEWAY
Torino .... TURIN
Torme, singer .... MEL
torment .... VEX, BAIT, PAIN,
    RACK, AGONY, ANNOY,
    HARRY, TEASE, BADGER,
    HARASS, PLAGUE, ANGUISH,
    HAGRIDE, TORTURE, AGITATE,
    DISTRESS, SUFFERING
    archaic .... HASE
tormentor .... NAG, PEST, BULLY,
    TEASER, HARRIER, HECKLER
torn .... REFT, RENT, RIVEN,
    DAMAGED, SEVERED,
    TATTERED
tornado .... CYCLONE, TWISTER,
    TYPHOON, HURRICANE,
    WHIRLWIND, WIND(STORM)
toro .... BULL, COWFISH,
    TRUNKFISH
torose .... BULGING, KNOBBED,
    SWOLLEN, CYLINDRICAL
torpedo .... NUMBFISH,
    CRAMPFISH, PROJECTILE,
    (ELECTRIC)RAY
    boat .... WARSHIP

colloquial .... EGG, ATTACK,
DESTROY, SABOTAGE
part of .... FIN, RUDDER,
TRIGGER, WARHEAD,
EXPLOSIVE, PROPELLER
slang .... FISH, GUNMAN,
ASSASSIN, GANGSTER,
BODYGUARD
type of .... HOMING, ROCKET,
BANGALORE
torpid .... DULL, NUMB, INERT,
STILL, SLEEPY, STUPID,
DORMANT, LISTLESS,
SLUGGISH, STAGNANT,
LETHARGIC
torpor .... APATHY, STUPOR,
INERTIA, LANGUOR,
LETHARGY
torquate .... COLLARED
torque .... CHAIN, TWIST, COLLAR,
STRESS, TORSION, NECKLACE
torques .... RUFF
torrefy .... DRY, PARCH
torrent ...... RUSH, FLOOD, RIVER,
SPATE, SPURT, SURGE,
DELUGE, RAPID(S), CASCADE,
DOWNPOUR
torrential ...... COPIOUS, ERUPTIVE
torrid .... HOT, ARID, ARDENT,
STEAMY, SULTRY, BURNING,
PARCHED, SIZZLING,
TROPICAL, SCORCHING,
PASSIONATE
torsion .... STRESS, PRESSURE,
TWISTING, CONTORTION
torsk .... CUSK, BURBOT, CODFISH
torso .... TRUNK
tort .... WRONG, DAMAGE, INJURY,
MISDEED, OFFENSE,
MISDEMEANOR
torte .... CAKE, PASTRY
torticollis .... WRYNECK, STIFF
NECK
tortile .... COILED, TWISTED
tortilla .... BREAD, CORNCAKE,
CORNMEAL, FLAT(STONE)
tortoise .... EMYD, TURTLE,
HICATEE, TESTUDO,
GALAPAGO, TERRAPIN,
CHELONIAN
burrowing/land .... GOPHER
of .... CHELONIAN,
TESTUDINAL, TESTUDINATE
shell .... CARAPACE,
BUTTERFLY
Tortue .... TORTUGA
tortuous .... SPIRAL, CROOKED,
DEVIOUS, SINUOUS, WINDING
torture .... PAIN, RACK, AGONY,
TWIST, PUNISH, ANGUISH,
CRUELTY, DISTORT, TORMENT,

MARTYR(DOM), THIRD-DEGREE
for information .... SWEAT
instrument of .... RACK,
WHEEL, STRAPPADO
method of .... WATERCURE,
KEELHAUL(ING), TAR-AND-
FEATHERING
torus .... TORE, MOLDING,
SWELLING, THALAMUS,
ELEVATION
Tory .... RIGHTIST, REACTIONARY,
CONSERVATIVE
Toscana .... TUSCANY
Toscanini, conductor .... ARTURO
Tosca's love .... MARIO
toss .... LOB, PEG, CAST, FLIP,
HURL, JERK, ROLL, SNAP,
STIR, SWAY, FLING, PITCH,
THROW, BUFFET, TUMBLE,
AGITATE
about .... BANDY, FLOUNDER
and turn .... STAY AWAKE
out .... CHUCK, EJECT, DISCARD
side to side .... CAREEN
tossing expert .... JUGGLER
tosspot .... SOT, SOAK, SOUSE,
TOPER, DRINKER, DRUNK(ARD)
tossup .... STANDOFF
tot .... TAD, ADD UP, CHILD,
COUNT, DRINK, TOTAL,
TODDLER
total .... ADD, SUM, GROSS, UTTER,
WHOLE, AMOUNT, ENTIRE,
ABSOLUTE, COMPLETE,
OUTRIGHT, AGGREGATE
loss .... BOMB, FLOP
slang .... WRECK
tonal effect .... TUTTI
wipeout .... MASSACRE
totalitarian ruler ...... DICTATOR
totality .... ALL, ENTIRETY
totalizator .... TOTE-BOARD, PARI-
MUTUEL
tote .... ADD, HAUL, LOAD, CARRY,
COUNT, TOTALIZER
board word .... WIN, SHOW,
PLACE
totem .... PHYLE, EMBLEM,
MOIETY
pole .... XAT
toter .... LUGGER, CARRIER
totipalmate bird .... DUCK,
GOOSE, PELICAN, CORMORANT
tot's "little piggy" .... TOE
-totsy, _____ .... HOTSY
totter .... REEL, ROCK, SHAKE,
WAVER, DODDER, FALTER,
TODDLE, STAGGER
toucan .... TOCO, ARACARI
family .... RAMPHASTIDAE
food .... FRUITS

genus .... ANDIGENA,
RAMPHASTOS, PTEROGLOSSUS
mountain .... ANDIGENA
small green .... TOUCANET
toucanet genus .... SELENIDERA
touch .... HIT, LAP, PAT, RAP, RUB,
TAP, ABUT, FEEL, LICK, LOAN,
TINT, TINGE, TRACE, ADJOIN,
AFFECT, FINGER, STROKE,
CONTACT, MENTION
and go .... HASTY, RISKY,
CASUAL, GAMBLE, TOSS-UP,
UNSURE, UNCERTAIN
at .... STOP
bottom .... GO-TO-POT
caused by .... TACTUAL
closely .... OSCULATE
clumsily .... PAW
doctor's .... PALPATE
examine by .... FEEL
excite by .... TICKLE
for medical diagnosis
.... PALPATE
ground with forehead
.... KOWTOW
having sense of .... TACTILE
light, passing .... BRUSH
lightly .... KISS, GRAZE
lovingly .... CARESS, FONDLE
-me-not .... IMPATIENS,
JEWELWEED
means of/organ of .... PAW,
TOE, HAND, PALM, FEELER,
FINGER, PALPUS, TONGUE,
ANTENNA, VIBRISSA
microscopic structures of
.... RECEPTORS
of .... TANG, HAPTIC, TACTIC,
TACTILE
off .... FIRE, START, IGNITE
perceptible by .... TACTILE
prefix .... TAC
soft: sl. .... DUPE, GULL,
SUCKER, PUSHOVER
stimulating .... MASSAGE
system for the blind
.... BRAILLE
system worker .... STENO,
TYPER, TYPIST
the emotions .... MOVE,
AFFECT
up .... FIX, REFINE, FRESHEN,
IMPROVE
upon .... CITE, MENTION
with the hand ...... RUB, PALM,
CLASP, KNEAD, HANDLE,
STROKE, MASSAGE
touchable ...... TACTILE, TANGIBLE
touchdown .... GOAL, SCORE,
LANDING
touched .... MOVED, HUMBLED,

AFFECTED, DEMENTED, SOFTENED
touching .... MOVING, TENDER, PITIFUL, TACTION, TANGENT, PATHETIC, POIGNANT
touchstone ...... TEST, STANDARD, CRITERION
touchwood .... PUNK, AMADOU, TINDER
touchy .... SORE, HUFFY, RISKY, CRITICAL, DELICATE, TICKLISH, IRRITABLE, SENSITIVE, PRECARIOUS
king .... MIDAS
tough .... FIRM, WIRY, HARDY, ROUGH, STIFF, SEVERE, STICKY, STRONG, VISCOUS, COHESIVE, HARDENED, GLUTINOUS, HARDBOILED
colloquial .... DIFFICULT
guy .... GOON, THUG, BULLY, BUTCH, RUFFIAN
it out .... NEVER SAY DIE
job .... BACKBREAKER
luck .... BAD BREAK
minded .... WISE, DOGGED, WILLFUL
situation .... FIX, PINCH, PICKLE
street .... HOODLUM, HOOLIGAN
toughen .... STEEL, ANNEAL, TEMPER, STIFFEN
Toulouse, painter .... LAUTREC
toupee .... WIG, PERUKE, HAIRPIECE
slang .... RUG
tour ...... EYRE, TREK, TRIP, TURN, JAUNT, ROUND, SHIFT, JUNKET, TRAVEL, CIRCUIT, JOURNEY
de force .... FEAT
touraco kin .... CUCKOO
tourbillion .... FIREWORK, WHIRLWIND
tourist .... TREKKER, TRIPPER, VOYAGER, TRAVELER, SIGHTSEER
court .... MOTEL
guide of .... CICERONE, DRAGOMAN
mecca ..... LINCOLN MEMORIAL
stopping place .... INN, HOTEL, MOTEL, HOSTELRY
travel schedule ...... ITINERARY
tourmaline .... GEM(STONE)
black variety .... SCHORL
red variety .... RUBELLITE
tournament .... JOUST, MATCH, CONTEST, TOURNEY, COMPETITION
draw .... BYE

fighting area .... LIST
kind of .... PRO, OPEN, AMATEUR, CAR(R)OUSEL
knights' .... TILT, JOUST
tourney .... TILT, JOUST, TOURNAMENT
tourniquet .... PAD, BINDER, GARROT, BANDAGE, COMPRESS
tousle .... MUSS, RUFFLE, RUMPLE, TANGLE, DISHEVEL
tousled .... UNTIDY, SNARLED, UNKEMPT, MESSED-UP
tout .... SPY, PUFF, PRAISE, TIP(STER), DOPESTER, PITCHMAN, BALLYHOO(ER), SOLICITOR
subject of .... WAGER
tovarisch .... COMRADE
tow .... LUG, TUG, DRAG, DRAW, HALE, HAUL, PULL, FIBER, HARDS
and pitch torch .... LINK
-away zone .... NO PARKING
rope .... HAWSER, CORDELE, TOWLINE
towage .... FEE
toward .... NEAR, ABOUT, DOCILE, FACING, FORWARD, DIRECT(LY)
center .... ENTAD, INNER
exterior .... ECTAD
mouth .... ORAD
the rear .... AFT
the stern .... ABAFT
towardly .... WILLINGLY
towboat .... MULE, TUG(BOAT)
towel .... DRY, SWAB, WIPE(R), DIAPER, NAPKIN, ABSORBENT
church service .... LAVABO
fabric .... TERRY(CLOTH)
kind of ...... BATH, DISH, FACE, HAND, BEACH, PAPER
small .... SERVIETTE, TOWELETTE
tower .... LOOM, REAR, RISE, SILO, SOAR, SPIRE, CASTLE, PILLAR, PULLER, TURRET, DRAGGER, BASTIL(L)E, TOURELLE, ZIGGURAT, SKYSCRAPER
a kind of .... IVORY
above .... EXCEL, EXCEED, TRANSCEND
ancient .... BABEL, ZIGGURAT
bell .... BELFRY, CAMPANILE
Biblical .... BABEL, DAVID'S
canal boat's .... MULE
castle .... DONJON, BARBICAN
church .... STEEPLE
famed .... PISA, BABEL, EIFFEL, LONDON
feature .... SPIRAL STAIRCASE

fodder .... SILO
fortified .... PEEL, DONJON, CITADEL, DUNGEON, FORTRESS, STRONGHOLD
fortress, four- .... HERODIUM
gate .... BARBICAN
guide of ships .... LIGHTHOUSE
marker .... PYLON
mosque .... MINARET
observation ...... WATCHTOWER
of Babel .... MADHOUSE
of confusion .... BABEL
of strength .... ROCK
pointed .... SPIRE
portable .... TURRET, BASTIL(L)E
pyramidal .... PAGODA
signal .... BEACON
small .... TURRET, MIRADOR
tapering .... SPIRE, STEEPLE
towering .... LOFTY, HIGH(-UP), EMINENT
Towers, The Pool of
.... HEZEKIAH'S POOL
towhead .... BLOND
towhee .... FINCH, CHEWINK
kin .... BUNTING, SPARROW
town .... CITY, WICK, BURG(H), HAMLET, PUEBLO, BOROUGH, VILLAGE
———— .... CRIER
fortified/walled .... BURG, BURH
imaginary .... PODUNK
in Tamil Nadu, historic
.... ARCOT
league .... HANSEATIC
magistrate .... REEVE
map .... PLAT
near castle .... BOURG
of WWI fame
.... ARMENTIERES
on the Po .... CREMONA
prefix .... TRE
section .... WARD
square .... CAMPO, PLAZA
street .... MAINDRAG
"Too Tough to Die"
.... TOMBSTONE
township .... DEME, MUNICIPALITY
townsman .... CIT(IZEN), OPPIDAN, RESIDENT
toxic .... VENOMOUS, POISONOUS
toxicant .... POISON(OUS)
toxin .... VENOM, POISON
bacterial .... EXOTOXIN, ENDOTOXIN, ENTEROTOXIN
canned food .... BOTULIN
toxocariasis .... INFESTATION
toxophilite .... ARCHER
toxoplasmosis .... INFECTION

753

toy .... DOLL, PLAY, DALLY, FLIRT, BAUBLE, FIDDLE, PUPPET, TRIFLE, TRINKET, TEETOTUM, PLAYTHING
bear .... TEDDY
"brought to life" .... VELVETEEN RABBIT
dog .... PEKE, POODLE, TERRIER, CHIHUAHUA
musical instrument .... KAZOO
stilt-like .... POGO-STICK
stringed .... TOP, YOYO, DIABOLO
tra la la .... REFRAIN
trace .... COPY, DRAW, HINT, MARK, SIGN, SLOT, TANG, SCENT, SHADE, TINGE, TOUCH, TRACK, TRAIL, DETECT, ENGRAM, FOLLOW, VESTIGE, DELINEATE
trachea ...... WEASAND, WINDPIPE
trachoma .... CONJUNCTIVITIS
track .... RUT, WAY, PATH, ROUTE, TRACE, TRAIL, COURSE, FOLLOW, RUNWAY, CIRCUIT, VESTIGE
back .... RETRACE
circuit .... LAP
down .... HUNT, SEARCH
event .... FLAT RACE
game .... PUG, SPOOR
horse racing .... TURF, HIPPODROME
man .... TOUT, RUNNER, ATHLETE
mark .... RUT, SLOT, SPUR, SPOOR, FOOTPRINT
racing .... CINDERS, SPEEDWAY, CINDER PATH
run .... MILE
ship's .... WAKE
speedster .... KELSO
tipster .... TOUT
tracker .... TAIL, HOUND, HUNTER, DETECTIVE
tracks connection .... TIE
train .... RAILS
tract .... AREA, EXTENT, STEPPE, ENTERON, LEAFLET, STRETCH, PAMPHLET, TREATISE
tractable .... EASY, TAME, DOCILE, PLASTIC, WILLING, OBEDIENT, YIELDING, COMPLIANT, MALLEABLE, FLEXI(B)LE, (COM)PLIANT
tractate .... TREATISE
tractile .... DUCTILE, TENSILE
traction .... GRIP, DRAWING, PULLING, FOOTHOLD
tractor .... MULE, AIRPLANE, BULLDOZER

and trailer .... SEMI
for short .... CAT
type of .... FARM, LAWN, PLOW, TRUCK, GRADER, TRAILER
trademark for a .... CATERPILLAR
Tracy, _____ .... DICK, SPENCER
trade .... DEAL, SELL, SWAP, WORK, CRAFT, BARTER, METIER, BUSINESS, COMMERCE, EXCHANGE, CLIENTELE, CUSTOMERS, LIVELIHOOD, OCCUPATION
agreement .... CARTEL
association .... CARTEL, SYNDICATE
exclusive control .... MONOPOLY
of .... MERCANTILE
questionable .... TRAFFIC
route ...... AIR LANE, SEA LANE
union member .... UNIONIST, CARDHOLDER
union strategy .... RATTEN
unlawful .... CONTRABAND
variant .... SWOP
wind .... MONSOON
trademark .... LOGO, BRAND, LABEL, SYMBOL
publisher's .... COLOPHON
R with a circle around it .... REGISTERED
trader .... SHIP, MONGER, MERCHANT
of illegal commodity .... TRAFFICKER
ploy of .... HARD BARGAIN
unauthorized .... INTERLOPER
tradesman ...... DEALER, ARTISAN, HUCKSTER, SHOPKEEPER, STOREKEEPER
trading .... BUSINESS, COMMERCE, SWAPPING, COMMERCIAL, MERCHANDISING
center .... PIT, FAIR, MALL, MART, RIALTO, EMPORIUM, EXCHANGE, (FLEA)MARKET
directly to consumers .... RETAIL
grains .... PIT
in large quantities .... WHOLESALE
place, stocks .... EXCHANGE
post currency .... WAMPUM
settlement .... FACTORY
ship .... CRAY
stamp .... PREMIUM
tradition .... USAGE, BELIEF, CUSTOM, CULTURE, (FOLK)LORE, PRACTICE

traditional .... ROOTED, CUSTOMARY, LEGENDARY, ESTABLISHED, CONVENTIONAL
knowledge .... LORE
tales .... FOLKLORE
traduce .... SLUR, DEFAME, MALIGN, REVILE, VILIFY, ASPERSE, SLANDER, CALUMNIATE
traffic .... TRADE, BARTER, BUSINESS, COMMERCE, DEALINGS, TRANSPORTATION
circle .... ROTARY
crush .... JAM
direction ...... UTURN, DETOUR, ONE-WAY
jam .... GRIDLOCK
light ...... RED, AMBER, GREEN, BLINKER
stopper .... LIGHT, SIREN
summons .... TICKET
violator .... MOTORIST, JAYWALKER, SPEED(ST)ER
trafficker .... DEALER, TRADER, MERCHANT
kind of .... PUSHER
tragacanth .... GUM
tragedian .... ACTOR, THESPIAN, SHAKESPEARE
tragedy .... PLAY, DRAMA, CALAMITY, DISASTER, CATASTROPHE
tragic ...... SAD, FATAL, PATHETIC, CALAMITOUS, DISASTROUS, (MELO)DRAMATIC
tragopan .... PHEASANT
trail .... LAG, DRAG, DRAW, HEEL, HUNT, PATH, HOUND, TRACK, TRAIPSE, VESTIGE
along .... TAG, FOLLOW
animal .... PUG, FOIL, SLOT, SCENT, SPOOR
behind .... LAG, CRAWL, STRAGGLE
marker .... BLAZE
of scent .... DRAG
of wild animal .... SPOOR
secretly .... TAIL, SHADOW
slowly .... DAWDLE
through mud .... DAGGLE
trailblazer .... PIONEER, PATHFINDER
trailer .... VAN, CART, TAIL, WAGON, TRACER, TRACKER
arbutus .... MAYFLOWER
branch .... RUNNER, STOLON, RHIZOME
trailing .... AREAR, DECUMBENT
train .... AIM, CHAIN, DRILL, SUITE, TEACH, SERIES, RETINUE, INSTRUCT,

JERKWATER, PROCESSION

desert .... CARAVAN

designating a .... FLIER,
LOCAL, EXPRESS, FREIGHT,
LIMITED, SPECIAL, COMMUTER

for position .... GROOM

of attendants .... SUITE,
CORTEGE, RETINUE,
ENTOURAGE

overhead .... EL, MONORAIL

rider with free ticket
.... DEADHEAD

track .... RAIL

trained canine dog ...... GERMAN
POLICE DOG

trainee .... PUPIL, NOVICE,
BEGINNER, NOVITIATE,
APPRENTICE

trainer .... COACH, GYMNAST,
HANDLER, TEACHER,
INSTRUCTOR

trainmen's car .... CABOOSE

traipse .... GAD, TRAIL, TRAMP,
WANDER

trait .... CUSTOM, FEATURE,
QUALITY, CHARACTERISTIC

traitor .... RAT, JUDAS, APOSTATE,
BETRAYER, DESERTER,
INFORMER, ISCARIOT,
RECREANT, RENEGADE,
TURNCOAT, FIFTH COLUMNIST

American ..... HISS, CHAMBERS

Austrian .... REDL

Czechoslovakian
.... GOTTWALD

Finnish .... KUSHNEN

French .... LAVAL, PETAIN,
ESTERHAZY

Hungarian .... RAKOSI

Norwegian .... QUISLING

Romanian .... PAUKER

traject .... CAST, THROW

trajectory .... ARC, CURVE,
PARABOLA

tram ...... CAR, WAGON, TROLLEY,
STREETCAR

cargo .... ORE, COAL

coal mine .... TUB

trammel .... CHAIN, FETTER,
HAMPER, CONFINE, MANACLE,
POTHOOK, SHACKLE,
RESTRAIN

tramontane .... ALIEN, STRANGER,
FOREIGNER

tramp .... BUM, HIKE, HOBO,
HOOF, PLOD, TART, YEGG,
CLUMP, RAMBLE, TRUDGE,
VAGRANT, VAGABOND

identification mark
.... MONI(C)KER

offering to .... HANDOUT

trample .... CRUSH, STOMP, TREAD

trampolin(e) .... NET

user .... ACROBAT, TUMBLER

Tramp's girlfriend .... LADY

trance .... COMA, DAZE, SPELL,
STUPOR, HYPNOSIS

tranquil ...... CALM, QUIET, STILL,
PLACID, SERENE, COMPOSED,
PEACEFUL

tranquility .... REST, PEACE,
POISE, CALMNESS, SERENITY

of the mind .... ATARAXY,
ATARAXIA

of the spirit .... QUIETISM

Tranquility Base site ...... MOON

tranquilize(r) .... CALM, QUIET,
OPIATE, PACIFY, SEDATE,
SOOTHE, APPEASE, ATARAXIC,
SEDATIVE, DEPRESSANT

drug .... VALIUM

for hypertension
.... RESERPINE

transact .... DEAL, TREAT,
CONDUCT, PERFORM,
NEGOTIATE

transaction .... ACT, DEAL, DEED,
SALE, AFFAIR, BUSINESS

binding .... COMPACT,
COVENANT

favorable to buyer
.... BARGAIN

formal .... CONTRACT

garage/lawn .... RESALE

law enactment .... PASSAGE

transcend .... EXCEL, OUTDO,
EXCEED, SURPASS, OVERPASS,
OVERSTEP

transcendental .... ECLIPSING

transcribe .... COPY, WRITE,
RECORD

transcriber .... CLERK, COPIER,
COPYIST, STENO(GRAPHER)

transcript(ion) .... COPY,
RECORDING, REPRODUCTION

transect .... (SUB)DIVIDE

transeunt, opposed to
.... IMMANENT

transfer .... CEDE, DEED, GIVE,
PASS, SEND, DECAL, GRANT,
ASSIGN, CONFER, CONVEY,
REMOVE

blood .... TRANSFUSE

by will ..... LEGACY, BEQUEST,
BEQUEATH

from one position to another
.... SHIFT

of court suit .... REMOVER

of disease .... CONTAGION

of property to an
organization
.... MORTMAIN

of sovereignty .... DEMISE,
SUCCESSION

property .... DEED, GRANT,
CONVEY

residence .... MOVE

sticker .... DECAL

transference .... SWITCH

of heat .... CONVECTION

transfigure ...... EXALT, GLORIFY,
TRANSFORM

transfix .... PIN, NAIL, STAB,
FASTEN, IMPALE, PIERCE,
IMMOBILIZE

transform .... ALTER, CHANGE,
CONVERT, TRANSMUTE,
TRANSFIGURE,
METAMORPHOSE

transformation .... CHANGE,
SWITCH, ALTERATION,
METASTASIS, TRANSITION,
METAMORPHOSIS

transformer .... CONVERTER

type of .... STEP-UP, STEP-
DOWN

transfuse .... POUR, IMBUE,
INFUSE, INJECT, INSERT,
INSTILL

transgress .... ERR, SIN, INFRACT,
VIOLATE, INFRINGE,
OVERSTEP, TRESPASS,
CONTRAVENE

transgression .... SIN, SLIP,
CRIME, FAULT, LAPSE,
MISDEED, OFFENSE, TRESPASS,
VIOLATION

transgressor .... SINNER, CULPRIT,
OFFENDER, DELINQUENT

transient .... MORTAL, ELUSIVE,
PASSING, FLEETING, FLITTING,
EPHEMERAL, FUGACIOUS,
MOMENTARY, TEMPORARY,
EVANESCENT

ball of gas .... BUBBLE

be .... VANISH, EVAPORATE

burst of energy .... SPURT

laborer ...... DRIFTER, FLOATER

lodger .... PASSERBY,
SOJOURNER

runaway .... FUGITIVE

transit .... RAPID, CHANGE,
PASSAGE, CONVEYANCE,
THEODOLITE

transition ...... FALL, RISE, SHIFT,
CHANGE, PASSAGE, PASSING,
TRANSFER, SWITCH-OVER

transitional .... CONVERTIBLE

transitive .... VERBAL, TRANSEUNT

transitory .... BRIEF, MUTABLE,
FLEETING, TEMPORARY,
TRANSIENT, CHANGEABLE

translate .... CHANGE, DECODE,

RENDER, CONSTRUE, TRANSFER, INTERPRET

a coded message ..... DECODE, DECIPHER

literally .... METAPHRASE

translation .... VERSION, RENDITION, PARAPHRASE, INTERPRETATION

of foreign writing .... CRIB, PONY

translations of the Scriptures in Aramaic .... TARGUMS

translator .... EXEGETE, INTERPRETER

translucent .... CLEAR, LUCID, FROSTY, PELLUCID, DIAPHANOUS, TRANSPARENT

transmit .... BEAM, MAIL, POST, SEND, WIRE, CARRY, CONVEY, IMPART, FORWARD, BROADCAST

in a way .... RADIO

transmogrify .... ALTER

transmute .... CONVERT

transom .... SLAT, TRAVE, LINTEL, LOUVER, TRESTLE, CROSSPIECE

transparent .... OPEN, THIN, CLEAR, GAUZY, SHEER, CANDID, FLIMSY, GLASSY, LIMPID, LIQUID, HYALINE, HYALOID, OBVIOUS, GOSSAMER, (PEL)LUCID, DIAPHANOUS, TRANSLUCENT

combining form ...... HYAL(O)

not .... OPAQUE

transpire .... PASS, OCCUR, SWEAT, EXHALE, HAPPEN, UNFOLD, LEAK OUT, TAKE PLACE

transplant .... GRAFT, REPLANT, RELOCATE, RESETTLE, TRANSFER

of a kind .... ALIEN

transport ..... CART, MOVE, TOTE, CARRY, BANISH, CONVEY, CARRIER, ECSTASY, EMOTION, AIRPLANE, ENTRANCE, TRANSFER, (EN)RAPTURE, (TROOP)SHIP

transportation .... WHEELS, PASSAGE, MOVEMENT, TRANSFER, CONVEYANCE, DEPORTATION

Arctic .... REINDEER

charge .... FARE

route .... LINE, AIRLANE

service/system ...... BUS, TAXI, TRAM, FERRY, TRAIN, SUBWAY, AIRLINE, RAILWAY, STREETCAR

transported .... RAPT, CARRIED, ENTRANCED, DELIVERED

transporter .... MOVER

transporting, act of .... CARTAGE, PORTAGE, DELIVERY

transpose .... INVERT, REVERSE, EXCHANGE, INTERCHANGE

transposition .... METATHESIS

transude .... DRIP, OOZE, SEEP, EXUDE, SWEAT, SECRETE

Transvaal capital .... PRETORIA

city .... BENONI

gold region .... RAND

transverse .... OBLIQUE, CROSS(ING), CROSSWISE

Transylvania city .... CLUJ

trap .... GIN, NET, FOOL, LURE, NAIL, TOIL, WHIN, CATCH, SNARE, ENMESH, TREPAN, LUGGAGE, PIT(FALL), CARRIAGE, CAPARISON

fish .... GIN, WEIR

game .... GIN

kind of .... WEB, DECOY, AMBUSH, DEADFALL

lobster .... POT

slang .... MOUTH

trapan .... TRAP, TRICK

trapdoor .... DROP, HATCH

trapeze .... BAR

locale .... GYM, CIRCUS

performer .... ACROBAT, GYMNAST, AERIALIST

trapper .... HUNTER, SNARER, TREPAN

trappings .... DUDS, FRILLS, OUTFIT, REGALIA, TRICKERY, CAPARISON, ADORNMENTS

Trappist .... MONK

trait .... AUSTERITY

writer .... MERTON

traps, orchestra .... BELLS, DRUMS, CYMBALS

trapshooting .... SKEET

target .... (CLAY)PIGEON

trash .... LAM, JUNK, OFFAL, SCRAP, TRIPE, WASTE, COLLAR, DEBRIS, LITTER, REFUSE, GARBAGE, RUBBISH, NONSENSE, (RIFF)RAFF, RESTRAIN(T)

gaudy .... KITSCH

receptacle .... ASHCAN, (DUST)BIN

slang .... TRIPE

trashy .... CHEAP, JUNKY, SHABBY, SHODDY, WORTHLESS

trattoria .... EATERY

trauma .... SHOCK, WOUND, INJURY

travail .... PAIN, TASK, TOIL, WORK, AGONY, LABOR, ANGUISH, TORMENT, DRUDGERY

trave .... CROSSBEAM

travel .... GO, PAD, HIKE, MOVE, RIDE, TOUR, TRIP, WEND, DRIVE, JOURNEY, TRAFFIC

back and forth .... COMMUTE

business .... RENT-A-CAR

by car .... DRIVE, MOTOR

by ox wagon .... TREK

class of .... COACH, ECONOMY, BUSINESS, STEERAGE, FIRST(CLASS)

extended .... ODYSSEY

for pleasure .... SIGHTSEE(ING)

from place to place .... DRIFT, CRUISE, MIGRATE

in circle .... ORBIT

of .... VIATIC

on foot .... JOG, PAD, HIKE, WALK, TRAMP

on foot over snow .... MUSH

swiftly .... JET

to holy place ...... PILGRIMAGE

what it does .... BROADENS, EDUCATES

widely .... SAIL THE SEVEN SEAS

traveler .... RIDER, ROVER, VIATOR, TOURIST, TREKKER, TRIPPER, MOTORIST, VOYAGE(U)R

aid of ...... COURIER, CICERONE

from place to place .... CRUISER, DRIFTER, EMIGRANT, ITINERANT

fun-seeking .... GADABOUT

guidebook for .... BAEDEKER

kind of .... HOBO, GYPSY, NOMAD, TRAMP, PILGRIM, SALESMAN, VAGABOND

on foot .... PEDESTRIAN

refuge of .... OASIS, HOSPICE

stopping place of .... INN, HOTEL, MOTEL, SERAI, HOSPICE, ROADHOUSE

who asks for ride .... HITCHHIKER

who reneges .... NO-SHOW

travelers, company of .... CARAVAN

travelers' diarrhea .... TOKYO TROTS, MONTEZUMA'S REVENGE

hunting expedition ..... SAFARI

traveling .... GADDING, FOOTLOOSE

bag .... VALISE, HOLDALL, GRIP(SACK), BRIEFCASE

companion .... ESCORT,
COURIER, CHAPERON
group .... TROUPE
show .... CIRCUS
yen for .... WANDERLUST
traverse .... DENY, PIVOT, RANGE,
COURSE, OPPOSE, PATROL,
SURVEY, SWIVEL, EXAMINE,
OBSTRUCT, CROSS(PIECE)
traversely .... ACROSS
travertine .... LIMESTONE
travesty .... FARCE, FIASCO,
PARODY, SATIRE, LAMPOON,
MOCKERY, BURLESQUE,
CARICATURE
travois .... SLEDGE
trawl .... FISH, HAUL, SEINE,
(DRAG)NET
trawler .... BOAT
trawling .... FISHING
tray .... TILL, SALVER, SERVER,
COASTER, PLATTER
agriculture .... HYDROPONICS
dish .... SALVER, WAITER
for types .... GALLEY
liquids .... CAPSULE
wooden .... TRENCHER
treacherous ...... SHIFTY, SNEAKY,
TRICKY, CUNNING, DEVIOUS,
FURTIVE, DISLOYAL, TWO-
FACED, DECEITFUL,
FAITHLESS, PERFIDIOUS
greedy person .... BARRACUDA
person .... CROOK, BASTARD,
TRAITOR, BETRAYER,
RENEGADE, TURNCOAT
treachery .... DECEIT, FALSITY,
PERFIDY, TREASON, BETRAYAL
treacle .... REMEDY, ANTIDOTE,
MOLASSES
treacly .... STICKY
tread .... PAD, PACE, STEP, WALK,
CRUSH, STAMP, CHALAZA,
TRAMP(LE), FOOTPRINT,
CICATRICLE
sound .... CRUNCH
treadle .... LEVER, PEDAL
treadmill .... WHEEL
treason ...... BETRAYAL, SEDITION,
TREACHERY
kind of .... LESE MAJESTE
treasure .... HOARD, PRIZE, STORE,
TROVE, VALUE, ESTEEM,
RICHES, WEALTH, CHERISH,
REMEMBER, APPRECIATE
container .... CHEST
isle of fiction .... MONTE
CRISTO
Treasure Island author
.... STEVENSON
Island character ...... BEN, JIM,

PEW
State .... MONTANA
treasurer .... BANKER, BURSAR,
PURSER, PAYMASTER
treasury .... BOX, BANK, FISC,
SAFE, CHEST, PURSE, VAULT,
COFFER(S), BURSARY,
EXCHEQUER, THESAURUS,
DEPOSITORY, POCKETBOOK
agent .... TMAN
treat ...... USE, CURE, DEAL, DOSE,
HEAL, ATTEND, HANDLE,
PARLEY, PAY FOR, REGALE,
BARGAIN, DELIGHT, DISCUSS,
ENTERTAIN, NEGOTIATE, FOOT
THE BILL
a broken bone .... RESET
a wound .... DRESS
as a celebrity .... LIONIZE
badly .... MOCK, ABUSE,
SCORN, ILL-USE, INSULT
disdainfully .... UPSTAGE
flour .... AGENIZE
handsomely .... REGALE
hides again .... RETAN
insolently .... HUFF, ABUSE,
BLUSTER, SWAGGER,
PATRONIZE
lightly .... FIDDLE, PALTER,
BELITTLE, DOWNPLAY
shabbily .... STEP ON
tenderly .... PET, SPOIL,
CODDLE, DOTE ON, PAMPER,
INDULGE
with .... BARGAIN, MEDIATE
with contempt .... CONTEMN
with warm application
.... FOMENT
wrongfully .... HARM
treatise .... ESSAY, PAPER, TRACT,
THESIS, (TEXT)BOOK,
DISCOURSE, MONOGRAPH,
COMPOSITION, DISSERTATION
opening part .... EXORDIUM
prelude/introduction
.... ISAGOGE
treatment ...... USE, CARE, STUDY,
USAGE, REMEDY, ANALYSIS,
APPROACH, HANDLING,
MANAGEMENT
before doctor's arrival
.... FIRST AID
by physical means
.... THERAPY
harsh .... ABUSE
hormone for short stature
.... SOMATREM
kind of .... DRUG, BED REST,
SURGERY, THERAPY
sprain .... ARNICA
water .... TORTURE

treaty .... MISE, (COM)PACT,
PACTION, CONTRACT,
DOCUMENT, COVENANT,
PROTOCOL, AGREEMENT,
CONCORDAT, NEGOTIATION
acronym .... NATO, SALT,
SEATO
kind of .... PEACE, LEAGUE,
CONCORD, ENTENTE, ALLIANCE
Trebizond ...... EMPIRE, SEAPORT,
TRABZON
treble .... SHRILL, TRIPLE,
SOPRANO, THREEFOLD
trebuchet's kin .... CATAPULT
missile .... STONE
tree .... BUSH, POLE, POST, WOOD,
ARBOR, PLANT, SHRUB,
STAKE, CORNER, TIMBER,
GALLOWS, HATRACK
American larch .... TAMARACK
American olive
.... DEVILWOOD
aromatic .... BALSAM,
BAYBERRY, EUCALYPTUS,
CANDLEBERRY
Asiatic, tall .... ACLE
Asiatic, with fan-shaped
leaves .... GINGKO,
GINKGO
Australian eucalyptus
.... IRONBARK
balsam .... TOLU
bark .... CORTEX
bark remover .... SPUDDER
beech .... ROBLE, CHESTNUT,
CHINQUAPIN
betelnut .... ARECA
biblical .... FIG, OLIVE
birch family .... ALDER,
HAZEL, HORNBEAM
bombacaceous .... BALSA
bombax family .... SILKCOTTON
boxwood .... SERON
branch(es) .... TWIG, SPRAY,
SPRIG, RAMAGE
Brazilian .... SERINGA
buckwheat .... TITI
bully .... BALATA
butter .... SHEA
California .... REDWOOD,
SEQUOIA
cashew family .... PISTACHIO
caucho .... ULE
Central American ...... AMATE
Chinese evergreen ...... LITCHI
citrus .... LIME, LEMON,
ORANGE
climber, Himalayan .... PANDA
climbing .... HOP
-climbing bird
.... WOODPECKER

coffee .... CHICOT
combining form ..... DENDR(I),
                       DENDR(O)
cone-bearing/coniferous
.... FIR, YEW, PINE, CEDAR,
            SPRUCE, SEQUOIA
cottonwood .... ALAMO,
                     POPLAR
covering .... BARK
crook .... KNEE
custard apple .... SOURSOP,
                  SWEETSOP
cutting .... LOP(PING)
cypress family .... JUNIPER
decay .... NECROSIS
desert .... DATE PALM
disease .... KNOT, MOSAIC
dogwood ..... TUPELO, ASSAGAI
driller .... WOODPECKER
dwarf(ing)/stunting .... BONSAI
-dwelling creature
.... OPOSSUM
East Indian .... TEAK, BANIAN,
         BANYAN, NUTMEG
ebony family .... KAKI,
                 PERSIMMON
European .... SERVICE TREE,
           SERVICEBERRY
evergreen .... BAY, FIR, YEW,
    PINE, TITI, CAROB, OLIVE,
    THUJA, SPRUCE, REDWOOD,
    SEQUOIA, EUCALYPTUS
excrescence .... OAKAPPLE
exudation .... GUM, SAP, MILK,
  COPAL, LATEX, RESIN, ROSIN,
                    BALATA
family .... LINEAGE,
    ANCESTRY, PEDIGREE
fiber ..... BASS, BAST, BAOBAB,
                     RAFFIA
flowering .... TITI, MAPLE,
      LOCUST, CATALPA,
    HAWTHORN, MAGNOLIA
fragrant .... HENNA, LINDEN
fragrant wood ...... BASSWOOD
fraxinus .... ASH
frog .... HYLA, TOAD, PEEPER
fruit .... FIG, DATE, PEAR,
   PLUM, APPLE, GUAVA, MANGO,
   PAPAW, PEACH, CHERRY,
   LITCHI, ORANGE, PAPAYA,
   APRICOT, AVOCADO, COCONUT,
   NECTARINE, PERSIMMON,
   TANGERINE, POMEGRANATE
fustic .... MORA
gamboge family .... CALABA
genus .... ACER, ALNUS,
   CARYA, HEVEA, KHAYA,
   LARIX, MORUS, PICEA, PINUS,
   SALIX, TAXUS, TILIA, ULMUS,
   CASSIA, CEDRUS, CORNUS,

LAURUS, CATALPA, JUGLANS,
   QUERCUS, AESCULUS,
   CASTANEA, FRAXINUS,
   SAMBUCUS, BOSWELLIA,
   CRATAEGUS, DIOSPYROS,
   SWIETENIA, EUCALYPTUS,
                 FORTUNELLA
giant .... REDWOOD, SEQUOIA
gingko .... ICHO
graceful .... ELM
group .... GROVE, ORCHARD
grown flat .... ESPALIER
gum .... BUMBO, ICICA,
   XYLAN, ACACIA, BALATA,
   CHICLE, RUBBER, SAPOTA,
  TUPELO, WALNUT, SAPODILLA,
   SATINWOOD, EUCALYPTUS,
               PEPPERIDGE
gum resin .... ANTRA,
          FRANKINCENSE
hardwood ...... ASH, ELM, OAK,
   IPIL, TEAK, BEECH, BIRCH,
   PLANE, TULIP, MOLAVE,
  WALNUT, WILLOW, DOGWOOD,
   BASSWOOD, LIGNUMVITAE
head of/top .... CROWN
heart-shape leafed
.... CATALPA
heath family .... MADRONO
hive .... BEEGUM
holly family .... ILEX
horse-chestnut family
.... BUCKEYE
honeysuckle family ..... ELDER
icy coating of .... SLEET
iron .... ACLE
ironwood .... HOP, TITI,
               HORNBEAM
Javanese .... UPAS
juice ...... SAP, MANNA, CHICLE
kapok .... CEIBA
knot .... BURL
laurel family .... CASSIA,
   CINNAMON, SASSAFRAS
lawn .... ELM
legume family .... ACACIA,
   CASSIA, LOCUST, LOGWOOD,
   LABURNUM, ROSEWOOD
leguminous .... MIMOSA,
               TAMARIND
lemon/lime .... CITRUS
lightwood .... BALSA
like a .... PINY, ARBOREAL,
   DENDROID, DECIDUOUS,
   DENDRITIC, ARBORESQUE
linden family ...... LIME, LINN,
        TEIL, BASSWOOD
lily family .... DRACAENA
locust .... ACACIA
lotus .... SADR
madder family .... BANCAL

magnolia .... TULIP, CHAMPAC,
   CHAMPAK, CUCUMBER,
               WHITEWOOD
mark on .... BLAZE
marmalade .... CHICO, MAMEY,
       MAMMEE, SAPODILLA
Mediterranean .... CAROB
mimosa family .... ACACIA
moss .... USNEA
mulberry family .... UPAS,
   FUSTIC, SYCAMORE,
             BREADFRUIT
myrtle family .... CLOVE,
   LEHUA, CAJEPUT, CAJUPUT
nut .... PECAN, ALMOND,
   CASHEW, WALNUT, HICKORY,
   CHESTNUT, HAZELNUT,
   PISTACHIO, CHINQUAPIN
oak .... ROBLE, ENCINA
of a .... CEDARN, CITROUS,
   ARBOREAL, ARBOREOUS
of heaven .... AILANTHUS
of life .... ARBORVITAE
of life site .... EDEN
of the Lord .... ACACIA,
   ALMOND, LAUREL, CYPRESS,
   HOLM OAK, TAMARISK, CEDAR
              OF LEBANON
oil .... BEN
olive .... OLEA
olive family .... ASH
orange .... OSAGE
ornamental .... HOLLY
palm .... ARECA, RAFFIA,
   CALAMUS, COCONUT, TALIPOT
palm-like .... ZAMIA
pea family .... CASSIA,
   MIMOSA, DIVI-DIVI, LABURNUM
pear .... NOPAL
Philippine .... DAO, IPIL,
   DUHAT, MANGO, NARRA,
   YAKAL, ACACIA, PAPAYA,
   MOLAVE, SANTOL, SAMPALOC
pine .... CEDAR, LARCH, PINON,
   THUJA, SPRUCE, CYPRESS,
   HEMLOCK, JUNIPER
plum .... DAMSON
poisonous .... UPAS, SASSY,
   HEMLOCK, LABURNUM, NUX
               VOMICA
pomegranate .... BLAUSTINE
poplar .... ASPEN,
            COTTONWOOD
powder .... ARAROBA
product .... GUM, NUT, OIL,
   CONE, FRUIT, LUMBER,
        RUBBER, TIMBER
protuberance .... KNOT
pulse family .... LOCUST
rain .... SAMAN, ZAMIA
remnant .... STUB, STUMP

resin .... FIR, PINE, BALSAM
rose family .... PEAR, PEACH,
    LOQUAT, MEDLAR, QUINCE,
    HAWTHORN, JUNEBERRY
rue family .... LEMON, CITRON,
    KUMQUAT, SATINWOOD
rubber .... ULE, SERINGA
salicaceae family ...... POPLAR,
    WILLOW
salt .... ATLE
sandarac .... ARAR
sapodilla family .... BUSTIC
screw pine .... PANDANUS
shade .... ASH, ELM, LINN,
    LINDEN, WALNUT, SYCAMORE
shaped .... DENDROID,
    DENDRIFORM
shoots .... TWIGS, BROWSE
shrew .... TANA
silk .... SIRIS
silk-cotton .... CEIBA
smoke .... SUMAC
soapberry .... LITCHI
softwood .... FIR, PINE, CEDAR,
    SPRUCE, HEMLOCK, REDWOOD
sorrel .... TITI
specialist .... ARBORIST
spiny .... LOCUST
stock .... STEM, TRUNK
stump ..... RUNT, SNAG, STOOL
stunted .... SCRAG, SCRUB
sumac .... TEREBINTH
swamps .... TAMARACK
sweet-smelling/used for
    incense .... SANDALWOOD,
    FRANKINCENSE
toad .... PEEPER
toad genus .... HYLA
treatment of diseased
    .... SURGERY
"trembling" .... ASPEN
trimmings .... BRASH
tropical ...... ULE, ATTA, PALM,
    ARECA, CACAO, LEHUA,
    MANGO, PAPAYA, COCONUT,
    LOGWOOD, DATE PALM,
    MANGROVE, CINCHONA,
    TAMARISK, LANCEWOOD,
    BREADFRUIT
trunk .... BOLE
trunk, growth on .... LICHEN
trunk protuberance .... KNAR
trunk ring .... GIRDLE
trunk strip .... FLITCH
trunk wood .... DURAMEN
tulip .... POPLAR
verbena family .... TEAK
walnut family .... PECAN,
    HICKORY
wide-spreading .... CEDAR,
    WALNUT, JUNIPER

with apple-like fruit
    .... MEDLAR
buoyant wood .... BALSA
dark hard wood ...... EBONY,
    MAHOGANY
drooping branches
    .... WEEPING-WILLOW
elastic wood .... YEW
orange wood .... OSAGE
pliant branches .... WITCH-
    HAZEL
plum-like fruit .... LOQUAT
striped wood .... ARAROBA
winged fruit .... ASH, ELM,
    MAPLE, SAMARA
young ...... SAPLING, SEEDLING
treeless plain ...... WOLD, LLANO,
    PAMPAS, STEPPE, TUNDRA,
    SAVANNA
treelike .... ARBOREAL,
    BRANCHED, DENDRITIC
in form .... DENDROID
plant .... BANANA
vegetable .... BROCCOLI
treenail .... PEG, PIN, SPIKE,
    TRUNNEL
trees ...... WOODS, FOREST, TIMBER
book on .... SILVA, SYLVA
clump of .... BOSK, TUFT,
    GROVE, SCRUB
grove of pine .... PINETUM
of .... ARBOROUS
of a region .... SILVA
pertaining to .... ARBOREAL
place where sold .... NURSERY
study of .... DENDROLOGY
stunted .... SCRUB
treatise on .... SILVA
Trees poet .... KILMER
trefoil .... CLOVER, SHAMROCK,
    TRIFOLIUM
trehalose .... SUGAR
source ...... YEAST, MUSHROOM
trek .... HIKE, WALK, TRAMP,
    TRAVEL, TRUDGE, JOURNEY,
    MIGRATION
trellis .... ARBOR, BOWER,
    LATTICE, ESPALIER
part .... LATH
trelliswork .... PERGOLA,
    NETWORK, LATTICEWORK
trematode .... FLUKE, FLATWORM
larva .... CERCARIA
tremble .... QUAKE, SHAKE,
    QUIVER, SHIVER, TOTTER,
    WOBBLE, PULSATE, SHUDDER,
    VIBRATE, VACILLATE
trembling .... PALPITANT
tremendous .... HUGE, GREAT,
    COLOSSAL, ENORMOUS,
    GIGANTIC, EXTRAORDINARY

tremolite .... AMPHIBOLE
tremolo .... CRACK, TRILL,
    QUAVER, TWITTER, VIBRATO
tremor .... QUAKE, SHIVER,
    THRILL, SHAKING, TREMBLING,
    VIBRATION, TREPIDATION
tremulous .... ASPEN, SHAKY,
    TIMID, FEARFUL, QUAVERY,
    UNSTEADY, QUIVERING,
    TREMBLING, TREMULANT
trenail. See treenail
trench .... CUT, SAP, LEAT, DITCH,
    FOSSE, DUGOUT, FURROW
embankment .... PARADOS
knife .... BAYONET
moon .... RILL(E)
strengthener .... FASCINE
trenchant ,... KEEN, CRISP, SHARP,
    BITING, CUTTING, CLEAR-CUT,
    FORCEFUL, INCISIVE,
    ENERGETIC, PENETRATING
trencher .... BOARD, DIGGER,
    SAPPER, PLATTER
trencherman .... EATER,
    GLUTTON, SPONGER, HANGER-
    ON, PARASITE
trend .... FLOW, DRIFT, TENOR,
    VOGUE, COURSE, STREAM,
    FASHION, TENDENCY,
    DIRECTION
bearish .... SAG
trendy one .... HIPSTER
trepan .... AUGER, TREPHINE,
    TRICK(STER)
trepang .... ECHINODERM, SEA
    CUCUMBER
trephine .... SAW, TREPAN
trepidation .... FEAR, ALARM,
    DREAD, DISMAY, TREMOR,
    QUAKING, AGITATION,
    TREMBLING
treponema .... SPIROCHETE
trespass ...... SIN, POACH, INROAD,
    INVADE, OFFEND, INTRUDE,
    OFFENSE, ENCROACH,
    INFRINGE, TRANSGRESS
trespasser .... INVADER, POACHER,
    INTRUDER, (GATE)CRASHER
tres _____ .... BIEN, CHIC
tress .... CURL, HAIR, LOCK,
    BRAID, PLAIT, QUEUE,
    STRAND, PIGTAIL, RINGLET
trestle .... (SAW)HORSE
Treves .... TRIER
trews .... TROUSERS
trey, thing with .... DIE, CARD,
    DICE, DOMINO
triad ...... TRINE, TRIUNE, TRINITY
trial .... TEST, CROSS, ESSAY,
    TRY(OUT), ATTEMPT,
    HEARING, INQUEST,

PROBATION, AFFLICTION, EXPERIMENT
ancient method of .... ORDEAL
and _____ .... ERROR
balloon .... KITE, FEELER
by _____ .... FIRE, JURY, COMBAT
decisive .... ACID TEST
panel .... JURY
performance .... PROLUSION, REHEARSAL
scene of .... COURT
severe .... ORDEAL, CRUCIBLE
site .... VENUE
trials and _____
.... TRIBULATIONS
triangle .... TRIO, TRIAD, TRIGON, SCALENE, TRIQUETRA
for example .... IDIOPHONE
kind of .... LOVE, ETERNAL, ISOSCELES
love .... ADULTERY, INFIDELITY
part .... BASE, SIDE, HYPOTENUSE
side of .... LEG
word for a love .... ETERNAL
triangular .... DELTOID, TRIGONAL, TRIGONOUS, TRIQUETROUS, THREE-CORNERED
aircraft structure .... DELTA WING
blower .... FAN
brace .... GUSSET
deposit of sand/soil .... DELTA
flag .... PENNON, BUNTING, PENNANT
insert in seam .... GUSSET
muscle of a shoulder
.... DELTOID
piece in a sail .... GORE
piece of land .... GORE
sail .... JIB, LATEEN, SPINNAKER
sides, structure with
.... PYRAMID
triarchy .... TRIUMVIRATE
tribal sign .... TOTEM
tribe .... CLAN, FOLK, GENE, RACE, SECT, GROUP, FAMILY, NATION, PEOPLE
Boadicea's .... ICENI
leader .... CHIEFTAIN, PATRIARCH
wandering .... HORDE
tribulation .... WOE, CARE, TRIAL, MISERY, SORROW, TROUBLE, DISTRESS, AFFLICTION
tribunal .... BAR, ROTA, SEAT, BENCH, BOARD, COURT, FORUM

mock .... KANGAROO COURT
tribune .... DAIS, PULPIT, ROSTRUM, PLATFORM, MAGISTRATE
tributary .... RIVER, SOURCE, STREAM, SUBJECT, SUBSIDIARY
creek .... BAYOU
of the Rhone .... ISERE
to the Elbe .... EGER, ISER
tribute .... TAX, GIFT, HOMAGE, PRAISE, OVATION, PAYMENT, OFFERING, COMPLIMENT
to a dead person ..... EULOGY, EPITAPH
to a victor .... ENCOMIUM
trice ...... TIE, MOMENT, SEC(OND), INSTANT, TWINKLE, TWINKLING
tricentennial ...... TERCENTENARY
triceps ..... THREE HEADS, TRIPLE-HEADED
muscle site .... (UPPER)ARM
triceratops .... DINOSAUR
trichoid .... HAIRLIKE
trichome .... BRISTLE, PRICKLE, ROOT HAIR
trichord .... LYRE
trick .... CON, FOB, FUB, GAG, DIDO, DUPE, FOOL, GAFF, GULL, HOAX, JAPE, JEST, JOKE, RUSE, SCAM, WILE, CHEAT, CRAFT, DODGE, FRAUD, KNACK, PRANK, SHIFT, STUNT, ENTRAP, TREPAN, DECEIVE, ARTIFICE, (FLIM)FLAM, HOODWINK, ILLUSION, CHICANE(RY), DECEPTION, STRATAGEM, SUBTERFUGE
device .... GIMMICK
easy to .... GULLIBLE
person easy to .... DUPE, GOOF, GULL, CULLY
trickery ...... ART, CRAFT, FRAUD, DECEIT, JAPERY, DODGERY, SLEIGHT, ARTIFICE, JUGGLING, CHICANE(RY), DECEPTION, HOCUS-POCUS
kind of .... SWINDLE
trickle .... FEW, DRIP, DROP, FLOW, LEAK, OOZE, SEEP, DRIBBLE
tricks, win all .... CAPOT
trickster ...... FOX, CHEAT, JOKER, TREPAN, JUGGLER, SHYSTER, CONJURER, MAGICIAN, SWINDLER, PRANKSTER, ILLUSIONIST
tricksy .... SMART, CLEVER, CUNNING, PLAYFUL,

MISCHIEVOUS
tricktrack .... BACKGAMMON
tricky .... SLY, WILY, SMART, ARTFUL, CATCHY, CLEVER, CRAFTY, SHIFTY, SNEAKY, CUNNING, FURTIVE, DECEITFUL, DECEPTIVE, INTRICATE
and sly .... DEEP
condition .... CATCH
tricolor .... FLAG
tricorn .... HAT
tricresyl phosphate: abbr.
.... TCP
tricycle .... IRON HORSE, VELOCIPEDE
trident .... SPEAR, LEISTER
bearer ..... NEPTUNE, POSEIDON
warrior with .... RETIARUS
tridentate .... TRIFID
Tridentum .... TRENT
tried .... PROVED, PROVEN, TESTED, SAMPLED
and true .... RELIABLE, DEPENDABLE, TRUSTWORTHY
trierarch's command
.... GALLEY, TRIREME
trifle .... BIT, DAB, PIN, SOU, TOY, DOIT, FICO, FOOL, MOTE, PLAY, DALLY, FLIRT, TRACE, DIDDLE, FRIVOL, GEWGAW, LITTLE, MONKEY, MORSEL, PALTER, PEWTER, DESSERT, TRINKET, FALDERAL, FALDEROL, GIMCRACK, KICKSHAW, BAGATELLE
trifler .... IDLER, DALLIER, PIDDLER, PUTTERER
trifles .... TRIVIA
trifling ...... MERE, PETTY, SMALL, FLIMSY, PALTRY, SLIGHT, TRIVIAL, PIDDLING, FRIVOLOUS
amount .... FIG, PEANUTS
objection .... CAVIL, QUIBBLE
sum .... GROAT
with danger .... PLAYING WITH FIRE
trifoliate .... TERNATE, THREE-LEAFED
plant .... CLOVER, TREFOIL, SHAMROCK, TRILLIUM, TRIFOLIUM
trifolium .... CLOVER, TREFOIL, SHAMROCK
trig .... FIT, CHIC, NEAT, PRIM, PROP, TIDY, TRIM, WELL, CHOKE, SMART, SOUND, WEDGE, SPRUCE
trigeminal .... TRIFACIAL
trigger .... FIRE, TRIP, SPARK,

KINDLE, LAUNCH, INITIATE

-happy .... JUMPY

triggerfish .... OLDWIFE

trigo .... WHEAT

trigon .... HARP, LYRE, TRINE, TRIANGLE

trigonal .... TRIANGULAR

trigonometric function .... (CO)SINE, SECANT

line .... SECANT, TANGENT

term .... COSEC

trigonous .... TRIANGULAR, THREE-CORNERED

trilateral .... THREE-SIDED

trill .... ROLL, SING, QUAVER, WARBLE, MORDENT, TIRALEE, TREMOLO, VIBRATO, VIBRATION

trilogy writer .... ASCH, GALSWORTHY

trim .... CUT, LOP, CLIP, DECK, DOCK, NEAT, PARE, TAUT, TIDY, TRIG, ADORN, CHEAT, CHIDE, DRESS, NATTY, NIFTY, PRUNE, SCOLD, ADJUST, DAPPER, DEFEAT, FETTLE, ORDERLY, DECORATE

and simple .... TAILOR-MADE

beard/hair .... CLIP, BARBER

coin .... NIG

feathers .... PREEN

in curves .... ESCALOP, SCALLOP

lumber .... DRESS

rosebush .... PRUNE

shrubbery/wool .... SHEAR

trimmer .... TOADY, ADJUSTER, TIMESERVER, OPPORTUNIST

trimming .... GIMP, EXTRA, RUCHE, EDGING, GUIPURE, ORNAMENT, DECORATION

braid/ribbon .... GALLOON

coat of arms .... BORDURE

colloquial .... DEFEAT, BEATING, CHEATING

food .... PARSLEY, GARNISH(EE)

for dresses ..... RUCHE, PIPING, RUFFLE, FLOUNCE, RICKRACK

of lace .... FRILL, GUIPURE

showy .... FURBELOW

tool .... ZAX, SHEARS, CLIP(PER), SCISSORS

window drapes .... VALANCE

zigzag .... RICKRACK

Trimurti .... TRINITY

Trinacrian .... SICILIAN

trinal .... TRIPLE, THREEFOLD

trinary ...... TERNARY, THREEFOLD

trine ...... TRIAD, TRIGON, TRIPLE, TRINITY, FAVORABLE,

THREEFOLD

Trinidad & Tobago bay .... ERIN, COCOS, GUAPO, MARACAS

capital .... PORT OF SPAIN

city/town .... TOCO, ARIMA, COUVA, LA BREA, SIPARIA, TUNAPUNA, CHAGUANAS, MARABELLA, SAN FERNANDO

dance .... CALYPSO

fish .... GUPPY

island .... CHACACHACARE

lake .... PITCH

language .... HINDI, ENGLISH

monetary unit .... DOLLAR

mountain .... ARIPO, EL TUCUCHE

music .... CALYPSO

native .... TRINIDADIAN

passage .... BOCA GRANDE

point .... GALERA, ICACOS, GALEOTA

river .... ORTOIRE

strait .... DRAGON'S MOUTH

Trinidad's partner ...... TODAGO

Trinity College scholar .... SIZAR, SIZER

of Hindu gods .... TRIMURTI

trinitrotoluene ...... TNT, TROTYL, DYNAMITE, EXPLOSIVE

trinket .... TOY, GAUD, BIJOU, BAUBLE, GEWGAW, TRIFLE, JEWELRY, GIMCRACK, KICKSHAW, ORNAMENT, KNICKNACK, PLAYTHING

seller .... FAKER

trio .... THREE(SOME)

alphabetic .... ABC, LMN

cards .... TIERCE

classical .... THE THREE B'S

mythical .... FATES, FURIES, GRACES

of fiction .... MUSKETEERS

of sizes .... SML

one of a .... TOM, DICK, HARRY, HOPE, FAITH, CHARITY, CALM, COOL, COLLECTED, ATHOS, ARAMIS, PORTHOS, CLOTHO, ATROPOS, LACHESIS

trioxide of arsenic .... RATSBANE

trip .... HALT, SKIP, SLIP, TILT, CAPER, ERR(OR), JAUNT, OUTING, TUMBLE, VOYAGE, BLUNDER, JOURNEY, STUMBLE, OBSTRUCT, EXCURSION

slang .... HALLUCINATIONS

the light fantastic .... DANCE

tripartite .... THREEFOLD

tripe .... TRASH, RUBBISH

triple .... TRIAD, TRINE, TREBLE, TRINAL, TERNARY, THREEFOLD, TRIPLICATE

alliance .... AXIS, DREIBUND

crown .... TIARA

crown winner .... OMAHA, ASSAULT, AFFIRMED, CITATION, SEATTLE SLEW, SECRETARIAT

for draft .... SSS

for motorists .... AAA

for school .... RRR

from Minnesota .... HHH

time .... TRIPLEX

triplet .... TRISTICH

in music .... TERCET

tripod .... CAT, STAND, SPIDER, TRIPOS, TRIVET

part .... LEG

Tripoli .... ROCK, ABRASIVE, ROTTENSTONE

badmen, former .... PIRATES

ruler .... DEY, PASHA

where it is .... LIBYA, LEBANON

tripos .... TRIPOD

tripper ...... CAM, PAWL, DETENT, TOURER, TREKKER, TOURIST, TRAVELER, WAYFARER

slang .... DOPER, ADDICT

trippet .... CAM

triptych .... TABLET

triquetrous .... TRIHEDRAL, TRIANGULAR

trireme .... GALLEY

commander .... TRIERARCH

propellant .... OAR

Tris, baseball player .... SPEAKER

trisaccharide .... TRIOSE

trismus .... LOCKJAW, TETANUS

is symptom of ____ .... MUMPS, QUINSY

triste .... SAD, BLEAK, GLOOMY

tristesse .... SADNESS

tristful .... SAD, RUEFUL, WOEFUL, MOURNFUL, SORROWFUL

tristich .... TRIPLET

Tristram's beloved .... ISEULT, ISOLDE

trite .... OLD, DULL, BANAL, CORNY, MUSTY, PASSE, STALE, STOCK, JEJUNE, ORDINARY, SHOPWORN, HACK(NEYED), COMMONPLACE

expression ...... CORN, CLICHE, BANALITY, PLATITUDE

opposite of .... FRESH, ORIGINAL

triton .... EFT, NEWT, SNAIL, SALAMANDER

Triton .... (SEA)GOD
  father of .... POSEIDON
  lower extremity of .... TAIL
  mother of .... AMPHITRITE
  trumpet of .... CONCH
triturate ...... RUB, BRAY, CRUSH,
               GRIND, PULVERIZE
triumph ...... JOY, WIN, CONQUER,
    PREVAIL, REJOICE, SUCCEED,
      SUCCESS, VICTORY,
    CONQUEST, CELEBRATE,
          EXULT(ATION)
triumphant .... FLUSHED,
      EXULTANT, JUBILANT,
    SUCCESSFUL, VICTORIOUS
triumvirate .... TRIARCHY
  member of a .... TRIUMVIR
  member of the first
  ..... CAESAR, POMPEY, CRASSUS
triune .... TRIAD, TRINITY
trivet .... SPIDER, TRIPOD
trivia .... TRIFLES, MINUTIAE
trivial ...... MEAN, BANAL, PETTY,
    SMALL, FLIMSY, LITTLE,
    PALTRY, SLIGHT, ONE-HORSE,
    PICAYUNE, PIDDLING,
          TRIFLING
  objection .... CAVIL
trivium, part of .... LOGIC,
    MUSIC, GRAMMAR,
    GEOMETRY, RHETORIC,
    ASTRONOMY, ARITHMETIC
troche .... ROTULA, LOZENGE,
    PASTIL(LE), COUGH-DROP
trochee .... TROCHAIC
  and iamb .... CHORIAMB
trochilus .... SCOTIA, WARBLER,
          HUMMINGBIRD
trochlear nerve
  .... CRANIAL(NERVE)
  damage result .... DOUBLE
          VISION
  location .... BRAIN
troglodyte .... APE, HERMIT,
    SAVAGE, CAVEMAN, GORILLA,
    RECLUSE, BARBARIAN,
          CHIMPANZEE
trogon .... BIRD, QUE(T)ZAL
  family .... TROGONIDAE
  genus ..... NARINA, HARPACTES,
    APALODERMA, EUPTILOTIS,
        PHAROMACHRUS
  habitat .... FORESTS
troika ...... VEHICLE, TRIUMVIRATE
Troilus' brother .... PARIS,
          HECTOR
  father .... PRIAM
  killer .... ACHILLES
  love .... CRESSIDA
  mother .... HECUBA
  sister .... CASSANDRA

Trojan .... ILIAN, TEUCRIAN,
          DARDAN(IAN)
  commander .... ANTENOR
  country .... TROY, ILIUM
  epic .... ILIAD
  epic poet .... HOMER
  hero .... (A)ENEAS
  horse builder .... EPE(I)US
  king .... PRIAM
  peace offering
  .... (WOODEN)HORSE
  prince .... PARIS, HECTOR,
          TROILUS
War allies .... DARDANOI
  cause .... HELEN(OF TROY)
  hero .... AJAX, MEMNON
  protagonist .... PARIS,
    AGENOR, (A)ENEAS,
    DARDAN, HECTOR, ACHILLES
  warriors .... MYRMIDON(E)S
troll .... IMP, WAG, FISH, ROLL,
    SING, SPIN, CHANT, DWARF,
    GIANT, GNOME, WHIRL, REVOLVE
trolley ...... CART, TRAM, PULLEY,
          CARRIAGE
  car .... DINKEY, STREETCAR
  hand .... WHEELBARROW
  line .... ROUTE
trollop ...... SLUT, HUSSY, WHORE,
    HARLOT, SLATTERN
  slang .... HOOKER
trombone .... HORN, SAMBUKE
  forerunner of .... SACKBUT
  mouthpiece .... BOCAL
  part .... SLIDE
trommel .... SIEVE, SCREEN
trona .... NATRON
Trondheim .... NIDAROS
  type .... NORSE
trone .... SCALE
troop ...... GO, BAND, UNIT, WALK,
    FLOCK, GROUP, MARCH,
    PARTY, NUMBER, COMPANY
  barracks .... CASERN(E)
  disposition .... DEPLOYMENT
  formation .... HERSE, ECHELON
  member .... SOLDIER, BOY
    SCOUT, GIRL SCOUT
  quarters .... BILLET, CASERN,
    BARRACKS, CANTON(MENT)
  theatrical .... TROUPE
trooper .... MOUNTIE, POLICEMAN,
          CAVALRYMAN
troops .... ARMY, FORCES
troops' halting place .... ETAPE
  quarters .... BILLET, CANTON,
          BARRACKS
  screen .... BLINDAGE
  spread .... DEPLOY
  station .... POST, GARRISON

  temporary encampment
  .... BIVOUAC
  turning movement ...... WHEEL
troopship .... TRANSPORT
trop .... TOO, TOO MANY, TOO
          MUCH
trope .... METAPHOR
trophy ...... PALM, AWARD, PRIZE,
    LAUREL, PLAQUE, SPOILS,
    MEMENTO, MEMORIAL,
        (LOVING)CUP
  athletic contest .... MEDAL
  Indian .... SCALP
  matador's .... EARS
  trapping .... SKIN
  war .... ARMS, FLAG, BANNER
tropic .... SOLAR, CIRCLE
  circle ..... CANCER, CAPRICORN
tropical .... HOT, WARM, FIERY,
    SULTRY, TORRID,
    EQUATORIAL, FIGURATIVE
  affliction .... HEAT STROKE,
        MALNUTRITION
  animal .... TAPIR, ANTBEAR,
    CARABAO, ECHIDNA,
    ANTEATER, TAMANDUA,
        RHINOCEROS
  bird .... COLY, RHEA, CRANE,
    MACAW, BARBET, MOTMOT,
    TOUCAN, TROGON, HOATZIN,
    JACAMAR, OSTRICH, QUETZAL,
    TINAMOU, COCKATOO,
        FLAMINGO
  disease .... AGUE, BUBO,
    YAWS, SPRUE, DENGUE,
    CHOLERA, MALARIA, MEASLES,
    BERIBERI, PSILOSIS, AMEBIASIS,
    DIPTHERIA, FRAMB(O)ESIA,
        TUBERCULOSIS
  evergreen .... PALM, CASHEW
  fever .... YELLOW, TYPHOID,
        CALENTURE
  fish .... OPAH, COBIA, GUPPY,
    SNOOK, WAHOO, PUFFER,
    GROUPER, SNAPPER
  flower .... EVERLASTING
  fruit .... DATE, GUAVA,
    MANGO, BANANA, PAPAYA,
    PA(W)PAW, POMELO,
    COCONUT, TAMARIND,
        PINEAPPLE
  grass .... BAMBOO
  herb .... LOOFAH
  infectious disease .... DENGUE,
    DIPTHERIA, TUBERCULOSIS
  lizard .... SKINK, SCINCOID
  snake .... FER-DE-LANCE
  tree .... ULE, ATTA, PALM,
    BALSA, CACAO, LEHUA,
    MANGO, CASHEW, CASSIA,
    COLIMA, ACACIA, PAPAYA,

SAPOTA, COCONUT, LOGWOOD, MANGROVE, CINCHONA, TAMARIND, LANCEWOOD, BREADFRUIT

trot .... JOG, RUN, GAIT, LOPE, AMBLE, HURRY, CANTER, HASTEN

troth .... VOW, FAITH, PLEDGE, PLIGHT, PROMISE

Trotsky, Russian revolutionist .... LEON

trotter .... PACER, MORGAN

trotyl .... TNT

troubadour .... BARD, LAUREATE, MINSTREL, MUSICIAN, BALLADEER, (LYRIC)POET, MINNESINGER, (STREET)SINGER

forte of .... POEMS, SONGS, SINGING, RECITING

song .... BALLAD, SERENADE

theme of ...... LOVE, CHIVALRY

traveling/wandering .... JONGLEUR

trouble .... ADO, AIL, ILL, IRK, VEX, WOE, CARE, FASH, ANNOY, PAINS, WORRY, BOTHER, EFFORT, HARASS, OBSESS, PESTER, AFFLICT, AILMENT, DISTURB, DISORDER, INCOMMODE

cause .... RAISE CAIN

troublemaker .... IMP, ERIS, PEST, RIOTER, ROUSER, HELLION, INCITER, AGITATOR, PROVOKER, PROVOCATEUR

troubleshooter .... FIXER

troublesome .... HARD, TRYING, ANNOYING, DIFFICULT

situation .... SCRAPE

trough .... BIN, HOD, BOSH, CHUTE, DITCH, DRAIN, HUTCH, SHOOT, FURROW, GUTTER, MANGER, RUNWAY, SLUICE, VALLEY

brining .... SALTER

fodder .... CRIB

for cooling hot metal .... BOSH

for logs .... FLUME

for washing ore .... BUDDLE, LAUNDER

mining .... HUTCH, BUDDLE, LAUNDER

water wheel .... PENSTOCK

trounce .... BEAT, FLOG, HIDE, LASH, WHIP, DEFEAT, PUNISH, THRASH, DESTROY

troupe .... BAND, GROUP, TROOP

trouper .... ACTOR, PLAYER, SINGER, ACTRESS, PERFORMER

troupial .... ORIOLE, COWBIRD, CACIQUE, GRACKLE

trousers .... JEANS, PANTS, SLOPS, SLACKS, PAJAMAS, PEGTOPS

below the knees .... BREECHES

bottom fold .... CUFF

close-fitting, denim ...... LEVIS

cotton .... CHINO(S), DUCKS

leather .... CHAPS, CHAPARAJOS

tight-fitting .... PANTALOON

trousseau .... BUNDLE, BRIDE'S OUTFIT

item .... GOWN, VEIL, LINGERIE

trout .... CHAR(R), DOLLY, VARDEN, OQUASSA, BLUEBACK, NAMAYCUSH, SALMONOID, STEELHEAD

family .... SALMON

fish like .... SMELT

flap .... FLY

sea .... KIPPER

trowel ...... DARBY, FLOAT, PLANE

Troy .... ILION, ILIUM, WEIGHT

defender of: var. .... ENEAS

environs of ancient ..... TROAS

founder of .... ILUS, LAOMEDON

tale of .... ILIAD

truant .... ERRANT, SHIRKER, SLACKER, TRIVANT, VAGRANT, ABSENTEE, DESERTER

play .... MICHE

truce .... LULL, DELAY, PEACE, RESPITE, ARMISTICE, CEASEFIRE

signal .... WHITE FLAG

Trucial Coast region ...... OMAN

truck .... VAN, BOGY, CART, DRAY, BOGIE, LORRY, BARROW, BARTER, WAGON, CAMION, RUBBISH, TROLLEY, TRUNDLE, VEHICLE, WHEELER, DEALINGS, EXCHANGE

area .... CAB

army .... HALF-TRACK

artillery .... CAMION, WEAPONS-CARRIER

dump .... TILLER

factory .... DOLLY

farm product ..... VEGETABLES

low-temperature .... REEFER

part .... SEMI

rail .... LORRY

small .... PICKUP

-stop sight ...... CAFE, TRAILER

Truckee city .... RENO

truckle .... TOADY, YIELD, CASTER, CRINGE, KOWTOW, SUBMIT, TRUNDLE

truculent .... MEAN, RUDE, CRUEL, HARSH, DEADLY, FIERCE, SAVAGE, BESTIAL, SCATHING, BELLIGERENT

trudge .... PLOD, SLOG, WALK, ANKLE, MARCH, TRAMP, TRAIPSE

true .... REAL, SURE, ALINE, EXACT, ACTUAL, LAWFUL, CERTAIN, CORRECT, GENUINE, SINCERE, ACCURATE, RIGHT(FUL), STRAIGHT

blue .... LOYAL, STANCH

copy .... ESTREAT

level .... GEOID

love ...... LOVER, SWEETHEART, SPECIAL ONE

skin .... DERMIS

thing/happening .... FACT

up .... ALIGN, ALINE

True Grit is one .... OATER

Truffaut's ____ Kisses .... STOLEN

truffle .... FUNGUS, EARTHNUT, MUSHROOM, TUCKAHOE

Truk island .... TOL, MOEN

truism .... FACT, AXIOM, PLATITUDE, COMMONPLACE

trull .... TART, TROLLOP, STRUMPET, PROSTITUTE

truly .... QUITE, SOOTH, TIGHT, INDEED, IN FACT, REALLY, VERILY, ACTUALLY, FAITHFULLY

relevant .... GERMANE

Truman, birthplace of Harry S .... LAMAR

cabinet member .... SNYDER, ACHESON, KIMBALL, STIMSON

daughter of Harry S .... MARGARET

playwright .... CAPOTE

president .... HARRY

wife of Harry S .... BESS

trump .... EXCEL, OUTDO, SURPASS

in card game .... RUFF

Trump, businessman .... DONALD

trumpery .... TRASH, PALTRY, RUBBISH, NONSENSE

trumpet .... HORN, BUGLE, CORNET, CLARION, PROCLAIM

belt .... BALDRIC

blast .... BLARE, FANFARE

call .... TAPS, SENNET, REVEILLE

caller .... GABRIEL

flourish ..... TUCKET, FANFARE, TANTARA

muffler .... MUTE

muting device .... WAWA

shell .... CONCH, TRITON

signal .... CHAMADE, FLOURISH
sound .... TOOT, BLARE
trumpeter .... SWAN, AGAMI,
    BUGLER, HERALD, PIGEON,
    GABRIEL, ELEPHANT
Baker .... CHET
from New Orleans .... HIRT
trumps, five of .... PEDRO
truncate .... LOP, TRIM, STUMP,
    REDUCE, ABRIDGE, CURTAIL
truncheon .... CLUB, MACE,
    BATON, STAFF, CUDGEL
trundle ...... CART, ROLL, WHEEL,
    CASTER, ROTATE, REVOLVE
trunk .... BOX, STEM, CHEST,
    SNOUT, STOCK, CIRCUIT, MAIN
    LINE, PROBOSCIS,
    COMPARTMENT
animal's .... SOMA
human .... BODY, TORSO
insect's .... THORAX
knot .... BURL
tree .... BOLE, BURL
trunkfish .... TORO, CHAPIN,
    COWFISH
trunks .... SHORTS, BREECHES
trunnel .... TRE(E)NAIL
trunnion .... PIVOT, GUDGEON,
    JOURNAL
truss .... TIE, BIND, PACK, PROP,
    BRACE, STRAP, BUCKLE,
    BUNDLE, SKEWER
trust .... DUTY, HOPE, RELY,
    FAITH, BELIEF, CARTEL,
    CHARGE, CREDIT, CUSTODY,
    MONOPOLY, RELIANCE,
    CONFIDENCE
betrayal of .... PERFIDY
of/like a .... FIDUCIAL,
    FIDUCIARY
territory .... MANDATE
to the British .... TICK
trustee .... WARDEN, GUARDIAN,
    OVERSEER, CUSTODIAN,
    GARNISHEE
trustful .... CONFIDING
trustworthy .... SAFE, TRUE,
    LOYAL, TRIED, TESTED,
    STA(U)NCH, CONSTANT,
    CREDIBLE, RELIABLE,
    DEPENDABLE
trusty .... CONVICT, PRISONER
truth ...... FACT, VERITY, REALITY,
    VERITAS, VERACITY,
    ACTUALITY, CERTAINTY
accepted as .... GOSPEL
assumed in theology
    .... MYSTERY
drug .... PENTOTHAL
obvious .... AXIOM, MAXIM
personified .... UNA

self-evident .... AXIOM,
    TRUISM
stretcher .... LIAR
truthful .... PURE, HONEST,
    SINCERE, UP FRONT,
    VERACIOUS
boy .... (GEORGE) WASHINGTON
truthfulness .... HONESTY,
    ACCURACY, FIDELITY,
    VERACITY
try ...... MELT, STAB, TEST, ASSAY,
    ESSAY, PURIFY, REFINE,
    STRAIN, STRIVE, AFFLICT,
    ATTEMPT, ENDEAVOR,
    EXPERIMENT
again .... RETEST
cooked food .... SAMPLE
in court .... HEAR
to do .... TACKLE
to extract information
    .... PUMP
trygon .... RAY
trying .... DULL, BORING,
    IRKSOME, PAINFUL,
    ANNOYING, IRRITATING
experience .... ORDEAL,
    TRAUMA
time .... CRISIS
tryma .... NUT, HICKORY,
    DRUPELET
tryout .... TEST, TRIAL, AUDITION,
    EXPERIMENT
trypsin .... ENZYME
trysail .... SPENCER
tryst .... DATE, MEETING,
    RENDEZVOUS
Tsaritsyn .... STALINGRAD
tsaritza .... CZARINA, TSARINA
Tschaikowsky, composer
    .... PET(E)R
tsetse .... FLY, MAU, KIVU, MUSCID
caused disease .... NAGANA,
    SLEEPING SICKNESS
Tse-tung, Chinese leader
    .... MAO
tsine .... OX, BANTENG
Tuareg .... BERBER
tuatara .... REPTILE
tub ...... HOD, KEG, KID, KIT, POT,
    SOE, TUN, VAT, BOAT, CASK,
    KNOP, SHIP, TRAM, BARGE,
    BASIN, BATH(E), KEEVE,
    SKEEL, BUCKET, FIRKIN,
    KEELER, CAULDRON,
    HOGSHEAD
shaped like a .... TUBBY
slang ..... BLIMP, FATSO, ROLY-
    POLY
-thump .... ORATE
2-handled .... COWL
tuba .... HELICON, SAXHORN,

    BASSHORN, BOMBARDON
alcoholic drink source
    .... COCONUT-PALM
ancient Romans' .... WAR
    TRUMPET
instrument resembling
    .... EUPHONIUM
mouthpiece .... BOCAL
tubal ligation ...... STERILIZATION
tubby .... BULKY, SQUAT, ROLY-
    POLY
tube .... DUCT, HOSE, PIPE,
    CONDUIT, HUMIDOR,
    CYLINDER, TELESCOPE,
    (ELECTRIC)RAILROAD
cannon/gun .... BARREL
draining .... CATHETER
electric wires' .... CONDUIT
electron .... DIODE
for gas, smoke, etc. ...... FLUE
glass .... PIPET(TE)
graduated .... HYDROMETER
joint of .... ELL
slang .... TELEVISION
tapering .... BURETTE
underground .... SUBWAY,
    TUNNEL
vacuum .... DIODE
tuber .... OCA, YAM, BULB, CORM,
    EDDO, TARO, JALAP, ONION,
    MANIOC, POTATO, CASSAVA,
    RHIZOME
dried orchid .... SALEP
tubercle .... GROWTH, NODULE,
    PROCESS, PROJECTION
tubercular .... LUNGER,
    CONSUMPTIVE
tuberculosis .... PHTHISIS,
    CONSUMPTION, WHITE PLAGUE
bovine .... GRAPE
lymphatic gland .... SCROFULA
tuberculous .... PHTHISIC,
    CONSUMPTIVE
tuberous .... KNOBBY, BULBOUS
tubular .... TUBATE, FISTULOUS
tuck .... HEM, LAP, TAP, CRAM,
    FOLD, WRAP, COVER, PLEAT,
    RUCHE, SWORD, PUCKER
companion of .... NIP
tuckahoe .... PORIA, FUNGUS,
    TRUFFLE
tucker .... FAG, APRON, STUFF,
    WEARY, COLLAR, EXHAUST,
    TIRE(OUT), VITTLES,
    CHEMISETTE
companion of .... BIB
tuckered out .... SPENT, WORN-
    OUT
tucket .... TANTARA, FLOURISH
Tuesday, actress .... WELD
Shrove .... MARDIGRAS

tufa .... TUFF, TOPH(E), LIMESTONE
tuff .... ROCK, TUFA
tuft .... CLUMP, FLECK, FLOCK, CLUSTER
  having a .... COMOSE, CRESTED
  of feathers .... COP, CREST, PLUME, TOPKNOT
  feathers on helmet
  .... PANACHE
  grass ..... HASSOCK, TUSSOCK
  hair .... BEARD, GOATEE, MUTTON CHOPS
  seed hairs .... COMA
  threads, etc. .... TASSEL
  on woman's hat .... POMPON
tufted .... HAIRY, MOSSY, COMATE, COMOSE, SWARDY, CRESTED, C(A)ESPITOSE
tufthunter .... SNOB, TOADY, SYCOPHANT, SOCIAL CLIMBER
tug ...... DRAG, HAUL, PULL, TOIL, LABOR, DRUDGE, STRAIN, STRIVE, TOW(BOAT)
  boat pulled by .... SCOW, SHIP, BARGE
  -of-war ...... POWER-STRUGGLE, PULLING CONTEST
Tuileries .... PALACE
tuition .... BILL, COST, FEE(S), CHARGE, TUTELAGE, INSTRUCTION
tuitional .... EDUCATIONAL
tule .... BULRUSH
tulip .... BULB, FLOWER
  family .... LILY
  genus .... TULIPA
  shape .... CUP
  -shaped glass .... BRANDY SNIFTER
  tree .... POPLAR
tulle .... LACE, NET(TING), ILLUSION
tullibee .... WHITEFISH
Tully .... CICERO
tumble .... FALL, FLOP, LEAP, ROLL, TOSS, TRIP, PITCH, PLASH, SPILL, THROW, SPRING, OVERTURN, SOMERSAULT
  bug .... BEETLE
tumbler .... COG, DOVE, LEVER, PIGEON, TURNER, ACROBAT, GYMNAST, JUGGLER, TOPPLER, (DRINKING)GLASS
  dog .... GREYHOUND
  net of .... TRAMPOLIN(E)
tumbleweed .... THISTLE, AMARANTH
tumbling box .... DRUM, BARREL, RUMBLE(R)
tumbo fly-bite disease
  .... MYIASIS

tumbrel .... WAGON, CAISSON, (DUMP)CART
tumefy .... SWELL
tumescence .... SWELLING
tumid .... TURGID, BULGING, POMPOUS, SWOLLEN, TEEMING, ENLARGED, INFLATED, BOMBASTIC, DISTENDED
tummy .... STOMACH
  ache .... COLIC
tumor .... YAW, CYST, GUMMA, GROWTH, ANGIOMA, NEUROMA, HEMATOMA, MELANOMA, NEOPLASM, SCIRRHUS, SWELLING
  anal .... PILES, HEMORRHOID
  benign .... WEN, CORN, ADENOMA
  blood vessel .... ANGIOMA
  bony tissue .... OSTEOMA
  brain .... GLIOMA
  cartilaginous ...... CHONDROMA
  classification .... BENIGN, MALIGNANT
  combining form .... C(O)ELE
  epithelial .... CARCINOMA
  fat tissue .... LIPOMA
  fibrous .... KELOID, FIBROID, CHELOID, FIBROMA
  filled with blood
  .... HEMATOMA
  glandular .... ADENOMA
  liver .... HEPATOMA
  malignant .... CANCER, SARCOMA, TERATOMA, CARCINOMA
  not malignant .... BENIGN
  scar tissue .... KELOID, CHELOID
  secondary growth
  .... METASTASIS
  skin .... WEN, WART, MELANOMA, PAPILLOMA
  spinal cord .... GLIOMA
  tendon .... GANGLION
tumult .... DIN, RIOT, STIR, BABEL, NOISE, HUBBUB, UPROAR, TURMOIL, DISORDER, AGITATION, COMMOTION, CONFUSION
tumultuous .... AROAR, NOISY, RIOTOUS, VIOLENT, TURBULENT, BLUSTERING, BOISTEROUS
tumulus .... MOUND, BARROW
tun .... VAT, CASK
tuna .... PEAR, TUNNY, CACTUS, BLUEFIN, OPUNTIA, MACKEREL
  like fish .... BONITO, ALBACORE

tundra .... PLAIN, WASTELAND
  dweller .... LAPP
  like wasteland .... PAMPAS, STEPPE
tune .... AIR, ARIA, LILT, TONE, ADJUST, MELODY, CONCORD, HARMONY, MODULATE
tuneful .... MELODIC, MUSICAL, MELODIOUS
  in music .... ARIOSO
tuneless .... OFF-KEY, OUT-OF-TUNE
tunesmith .... COMPOSER, SONGWRITER
tungsten .... WOLFRAM, CARBOLOY
  mineral .... SCHEELITE, WOLFRAMITE
  part of bulb made of
  .... FILAMENT
tungstite .... OCHER
Tungus .... MANCHU, MONGOLIAN
tunic .... COAT, JAMA, ROBE, TOGA, VEST, FROCK, GIPON, JUPON, STOLE, WAIST, CHITON, KIRTLE
  of mail .... CHITON
  over armor ...... GIPON, JUPON, TABARD
  woman's tight-fitting
  .... BASQUE
tunicate .... SALPA, ASCIDIAN
  bulb .... ONION
tunicle .... VESTMENT
tuning fork .... DIAPASON
Tunisian Berber .... KABYLE
  cape .... BON, BLANC
  capital .... TUNIS
  city/town .... BEJA, GABES, GAFSA, MAHDIA, MSAKEN, NABEUL, SOUSSE, BIZERTE, KAIROUAN
  diplomat .... (MONGI) SLIM
  gulf .... GABES, TUNIS, HAMMAMET
  island .... DJERBA
  island group .... KERKENNAH
  measure .... SAA(H), UEBA, CAFIZ
  monetary unit .... DINAR
  mountain .... CHAMBI
  oasis .... GAFSA
  port ...... SFAX, GABES, SOUSSE
  president .... BOURGUIBA
  region .... JEFARA
  river .... MEDJERDA
  ruler .... BEY, DEY, PASHA
  weight .... UCKIA, KANTAR
tunnel ...... DIG, SAP, ADIT, CAVE, FLUE, LAIR, TUBE, BURROW, SUBWAY, CHANNEL,

PASSAGEWAY

disease .... BENDS,
CAISSON(DISEASE)
in the Alps .... SIMPLON
vision .... BLINDNESS
vision cause .... GLAUCOMA
tunneler .... ANT, DIGGER,
SAPPER, BURROWER
tunny .... AMIA, TUNA, ALBACORE,
MACKEREL
tup .... RAM, SHEEP
tupelo .... NYSSA, DOGWOOD,
LIME(TREE), WATER GUM,
PEPPERIDGE
Tupi .... INDIAN, GUARANI
tupik, e.g. .... TENT
tuque .... CAP
Turandot character .... PONG
composer .... (GIACOMO)
PUCCINI
turban .... HAT, MANDIL,
HEADDRESS
cloth .... LUNGI, LUNGEE
turbid .... ROILY, MUDDY,
CLOUDY, OPAQUE, ROILED,
CLOUDED, MUDDLED,
CONFUSED
turbine .... MOTOR, ROTOR,
ENGINE, PROPELLER
turbit .... PIGEON
turbot ...... BUTT, BRILL, FLATFISH
flatfish like .... SOLE, HALIBUT,
FLOUNDER
turbulence .... CHAOS, TUMULT,
UNREST, UPROAR, DISORDER,
VIOLENCE, COMMOTION
airplane .... BURBLE,
BUMP(INESS), AIR-POCKET
dizzying .... SWIRL
turbulent .... WILD, RAGING,
STORMY, UNRULY, CHAOTIC,
FURIOUS, RIOTOUS, AGITATED,
FRENZIED, TEMPESTUOUS
affair .... RIOT
turdine bird .... THRUSH
tureen .... (SOUP)DISH
adjunct .... LADLE
turf .... SOD, PEAT, SWARD,
DOMAIN, (RACE)TRACK,
TERRITORY
of/like .... CEPITOSE
piece of .... DIVOT
turfy .... GRASSY
Turgenev, novelist .... IVAN
heroine .... ELENA
turgid .... TUMID, TOROSE,
TOROUS, BLOATED, BULGING,
POMPOUS, SWOLLEN,
INFLATED, BOMBASTIC
Turin .... TORINO
Turk .... HORSE, TATAR, TURCO,

MOSLEM, TARTAR, OSMANLI,
OTTOMAN
Turkestan inhabitant .... SART
Moslem .... SALAR
mountain .... ALAI, PAMIRS
river ILI
tribe .... USBEG, KIRGHIZ
turkey, bird like .... CURASSOW
buzzard .... AURA, VULTURE
chin adornment of
.... WATTLE, CARUNCLE
cock .... TOM
male .... TOM, GOBBLER
slang ..... BUST, FLOP, FAILURE
sound .... GOBBLE
talk .... GOBBLE
trot .... DANCE
wild .... BUSTARD
young .... POULT
Turkey, Asiatic .... ANATOLIA
cape .... BABA, INCE, SINOP,
ANAMUR, HELLES, GELIDONYA
capital of .... ANKARA
capital, former name
.... ANGORA
city/town .... VAN, ICEL, PERA,
RIZE, URFA, USAK, ZARA, ZILE,
ADANA, AYDIN, BAFRA,
BURSA, HATAY, IZMIR, IZMIT,
TOKAT, ADALIA, BATMAN,
BEYKOZ, CEYHAN, EDESSA,
EDIRNE, EREGLI, MANISA,
MERSIN, SAMSUN, SMYRNA,
TARSUS, ANTALYA, ANTIOCH,
BEYOGLU, CANKAYA,
ERZURUM, ISPARTA, KADIKOY,
KARABUK, MALATYA,
SAKARYA, TRABZON,
USKUDAR, ALTINDAG,
BAKIRKOY, ISTANBUL,
BALIKESIR, ESKISEHIR,
GALLIPOLI, GAZIANTEP,
KARSIYAKA
gulf .... KERME, SAROS,
ANTALYA, CANDARLI,
MANDALYA, ALEXANDRETTA
island .... ADALAR, BURGAZ,
HEYBELI, MARMARA,
BOZCAADA, PRINKIPO
lake .... ACI, TUZ, VAN,
BEYSEHIR
mountain .... CILO, AKDAG,
ALADAG, ARARAT, KACKAR,
SUPHAN, ERCIYAS
mountains .... KURE, CANIK,
AMANOS, PONTIC, TAURUS,
KOROGLU
province ...... MUS, VAN, AGRI,
BOLU, ICEL, KARS, ORDU,
RIZE, URFA, ADANA, AYDIN,
BURSA, CORUM, HATAY, IZMIR,

KONYA, NIGDE, SIVAS, TOKAT,
ANKARA, BURDUR, MANISA,
SAMSUN, YOZGAT, DENIZLI,
ISPARTA, KAYSERI, TRABZON,
ISTANBUL, GAZIANTEP,
ZONGULDAK
red dye .... MADDER, ALIZARIN
region .... ANATOLIA,
KURDISTAN
river ...... ARPA, KOCA, ARAKS,
CORUH, DICLE, FIRAT, GEDIZ,
GOKSU, MERIC, MURAT,
SIMAV, CEYHAN, ERGENE,
KELKIT, PORSUK, SEYHAN,
TIGRIS, SAKARYA, MENDERES,
EUPHRATES
ruins .... TROY, ILIUM,
ABYDOS, EPHESUS
sea .... BLACK, AEGEAN,
MARMARA
seaport .... TRABZON,
TREBIZOND
strait .... BOSPORUS,
DARDANELLES
Turki .... OSMANLI, TURKOMAN
Turkic language .... TATAR
people .... UZBEG, UZBEK
Turkish bathhouse .... BAGNIO
cab/carriage .... ARABA
cap ...... FEZ, CALPAC, KALPAK
caravansary .... IMARET
cavalryman ..... SPAHI, SPAHEE
chamber .... ODA(H)
chieftain .... ZAIM
coin .... LIRA, PARA, ALTUN,
ASPER, YUZLUK, PIASTER,
PIASTRE
college/school .... ULEMA
commander .... SIRDAR
confection .... HALVAH
court .... PORTE
decree .... IRADE
delight .... CANDY
dialect .... JAGATAI
dispute with Greece
.... CYPRUS
district .... VILAYET
dulcimer .... CANUN
dynasty/tribe .... SELJUK
emblem .... CRESCENT
emissary .... CHIAUS
ensign .... CRESCENT,
HORSETAIL
father .... BABA
fig .... ELEME
flag .... ALEM, CRESCENT
float .... KALAK
foreign quarter .... PERA,
BEYOGLU
garment ...... CAFTAN, KAFTAN
general .... AGA, INONU,

KEMAL
government .... PORTE
governor .... BEY, MALI, WALI,
PASHA
harem resident .... KADEIN
hat .... FEZ
hell .... DAGH
hospice .... IMARET
house for men ...... SELAM LIK
inn .... KHAN, SERAI, IMARET
island .... TENEDOS
javelin ..... JER(R)ID, JER(R)EED
judge .... CADI, KADI
legendary leader .... SELCUK
liqueur .... RAKI
liquor .... MASTIC
magistrate .... CADI
major .... AGA
master .... EFFENDI
measure .... PIK, DRA(H),
HATT, KHAT, KILE, ZIRA,
ALMUD, BERRI, ARSHIN
messenger .... CHIAUS
military district .... ORDO
milk food .... YOG(H)URT
minister .... VIZI(E)R
mock battle .... JER(R)ID,
JER(R)EED
monetary unit .... LIRA
money .... PARA
money of account .... ASPER
monk .... DERVISH
non-Moslem .... RAIA, RAYAH,
GIAOUR
oak .... CERRIS
official .... EMIR, EMEER,
PACHA, PASHA, BASHAW
opium .... AFYON
oxcart .... ARABA
palace .... SERAI, SERAGLIO
parade .... ALAI
pasha's standard
.... HORSETAIL
pavilion .... KIOSK
peasant .... RAYA
peninsula .... GALLIPOLI
people .... KURD, TURKI,
OSMANLI
policeman .... ZAPTIAH
pound .... LIRA
prayer rug .... MELAS
premier .... DEMIREL
president .... BAYAR, SUNAY,
INONU, ATATURK
province .... VILAYET
regiment .... ALAI
rice dish .... PILAF, PILAU,
PILAW
robe .... DOLMAN, CAFTAN,
KAFTAN
royal court .... DIVAN

ruler .... KHAN, CALIPH,
SULTAN
saber .... YATAG(H)AN
scholar .... ULEMA
sergeant .... CHIAUS
sir .... EFFENDI
slave .... MAMELUKE
soldier .... NIZAM, JANIZARY,
JANISSARY
standard ..... ALEM, HORSETAIL
statesman .... INONU
sultan .... CALIF, SELIM,
CALIPH, PADISHAH
sultan's guard .... JANIZARY
sultan's palace .... SERAGLIO
sultan's visit to mosque
.... SELAM LIK
summerhouse .... KIOSK
sword .... SCIMITAR,
YATAGHAN
teacher .... MULLA(H)
title .... BEY, AG(H)A, EMIR,
EMEER, GHAZI, PACHA, PASHA,
EFFENDI
tobacco .... LATAKIA
tower ..... MANARAT, MENARET
tribesman .... TATAR
veil .... YASHMAC, YASHMAK
viceroy .... KHEDIVE
"victorious warrior"
.... GHAZI
vilayet. See **Turkey,** province
vilayet subdivision .... SANJAK
weight .... OKA, OKE, ROTL,
CEQUI, CHEKE, KERAT,
MAUND, DIRHAM, KANTAR,
MISKAL
whip .... KURBASH
zither .... CANUM
Turko .... ABO
-Tartar tribe .... BASHKIR
turmeric .... REA, GINGER,
CURCUMA
turmoil .... ADO, STOUR, HUBBUB,
TUMULT, UPROAR, WELTER,
AGITATION, COMMOTION,
CONFUSION
turn ...... BEND, CANT, COIL, REEL,
SPIN, AVERT, BLUNT, CURVE,
PIVOT, REPEL, SCREW, SHIFT,
TREND, TWIRL, TWIST,
DIVERT, ROTATE, SWITCH,
VOLUTE, DEVIATE, REVOLVE
a deaf ear to .... IGNORE
a new leaf .... CHANGE,
REFORM
about .... BY TURNS,
ALTERNATE
against .... CROSS, BETRAY
against one's benefactor
.... BITE THE HAND THAT

FEEDS ONE
around .... SLUE, PIVOT,
ROTATE, REVOLVE
aside ...... DAFF, VEER, BRUSH,
AVERT, DETER, SHUNT,
DEFLECT, DEVIATE, FEND(OFF)
away .... SHOO, AVERT,
REFUSE, REJECT, ESTRANGE
back .... PUSH, REPEL, REFLEX,
RETURN, REPULSE, RETREAT
combining form .... TROPO
complete .... LAP, CIRCLE
course/off course .... YAW
down ..... DENY, VETO, SPURN,
REFUSE, REJECT
equestrian/horsemanship
.... CARACOLE
in .... ENTER, BETRAY, REPORT,
DELIVER, HIT THE SACK
in music .... VOLTA
inside out ...... EVERT, INVERT,
RANSACK
into .... BECOME, CONVERT
into money .... (EN)CASH
left .... HAW
loose .... FREE, RELEASE,
LIBERATE
loose an inmate .... PAROLE
of mind .... CAPRICE
off .... REPEL, DAMPEN,
DISCOURAGE
on .... (A)ROUSE, AWAKEN,
EXCITE
on an axis .... ROLL
one side .... DEFLECT
one's back upon .... SNUB,
REBUFF
out .... ARRAY, EJECT, EVICT,
BECOME, OUTPUT, DISMISS,
EQUIPAGE, GATHERING
outward .... EVERT
over .... KEEL, CAPSIZE,
DELIVER, TRANSFER
over a new leaf .... MEND
ONE'S WAYS
over by tossing .... FLAP
over in the mind ...... PONDER,
REFLECT
page over .... LEAF
red .... BLUSH
right .... GEE, JEE
ship's .... YAW, TACK
single .... WINDING
-the-page dir. .... PTO
to .... BEGIN, DIVE IN,
EMBARK, CONSULT
topsy-turvy .... UPEND
toward .... FACE
unfriendly .... MADDEN,
ENVENOM, PROVOKE,
ALIENATE, EMBITTER,

ESTRANGE, ANTAGONIZE
up .... COME, SHOW, APPEAR,
ARRIVE, EXPOSE
up one's nose at .... SPURN,
FROWN AT, DISAPPROVE
upside down .... SUBVERT,
OVERTHROW
white .... PALE, BLANCH
turnabout .... SHIFT, REVERSAL,
VOLTE-FACE
turnaround .... FLIP-FLOP
contrivance .... CARROUSEL,
MERRY-GO-ROUND
turncoat .... RAT, BOLTER,
TRAITOR, APOSTATE,
DESERTER, RECREANT,
RENEGADE, RUNAGATE
turndown .... VETO, REBUFF,
BRUSH-OFF, REJECTION
turned back piece .... REVERSE
down page corners
.... DOGEARED
in mathematics .... VERSED
on .... ENTHUSIASTIC
traitor .... SOLD OUT
unfriendly .... ICY, COLD,
CHILLY, HOSTILE
up .... SNUB, ACOCK, TILTED
turner .... ACROBAT, GYMNAST,
TUMBLER
Turner, _____ .... IKE, NAT,
LANA, TINA
turning joint .... HINGE
machine .... LATHE, SPANNER
point .... CRUX, PIVOT,
CLIMAX, CRISIS, SOLSTICE
turnip .... NEEP, ROOT, SWEDE,
RUTABAGA
shaped .... NAPIFORM
turnip's lack .... BLOOD
turnix .... (GAME)BIRD
turnkey .... GAOLER, JAILER,
WARDER
turnout .... RIG, EQUIPAGE,
ATTENDANCE
turnover .... PIE, TART, SPILL,
UPSET, PASTRY
turnpike .... HIGHWAY, THRUWAY,
TOLLGATE, TOLLROAD
exit .... RAMP
turnsole .... DYE, SUNFLOWER,
HELIOTROPE
turnstile .... GATE
turnstone .... WADER, PLOVER,
(SHORE)BIRD
genus .... ARENARIA
relative .... CURLEW,
SANDPIPER
turntable operator .... DISC
JOCKEY
Turnverein member .... TURNER,

GYMNAST, TUMBLER
turpentine .... OIL, GAL(L)IPOT,
OLEORESIN
distillate .... ROSIN
substance like .... ELEMI
tree .... PINE, TARATA,
TEREBINTH
turpeth .... EMETIC, CATHARTIC
turpitude .... BASENESS,
VILENESS, DEPRAVITY
moral .... CORRUPTION
turquoise .... GEM, STONE,
GREENISH-BLUE
turret .... TOWER, BARBICAN
gun .... CUPOLA
open-roofed .... BELVEDERE
opening .... LOUVER
tower ..... BARTISAN, BARTIZAN
viewing .... GAZEBO
turtle ...... EMYD, ARRAU, JURARA,
REPTILE, SNAPPER, MOSSBACK,
CHELONIAN, TERRAPIN,
HAWK(S)BILL, LOGGERHEAD,
LEATHERBACK
descriptive of a
.... SLOW(FOOT)
enclosure for .... CRAWL
fresh-water .... TERRAPIN
genus .... EMYS, CARETTA
land .... TESTUDO, TORTOISE
largest living
.... LEATHERBACK
medium-sized ...... HAWKSBILL
of a/like a .... CHELONIAN
old .... MOSSBACK
protective covering .... MAIL
refuge of .... SHELL
shell .... PEE, CARAPACE,
PLASTRON
shell substance .... CALIPEE,
CALIPASH
turn .... CAPSIZE
Tuscany .... TOSCANA
city .... PISA, LUCCA, PRATO,
SIENA, AREZZO, FIRENZE,
LEGHORN, LIVORNO, FLORENCE
island .... ELBA
river .... ARNO, ORCIA,
OMBRONE
wine .... CHIANTI
tush .... CANINE-TOOTH
tusk .... FANG, HORN, IVORY,
TOOTH
small elephant's
.... SCRIVELLO
wound with a .... GORE
tusker .... BOAR, WALRUS,
NARWHAL, PECCARY,
WARTHOG, ELEPHANT
tussah .... SHANTUNG,
SILK(WORM)

tussis .... COUGH
tussle ...... FIGHT, SCRAP, BICKER,
CONTEND, GRAPPLE, SCUFFLE,
WRESTLE, STRUGGLE
tussock .... TUFT, CLUMP, THICKET
tut .... TSK
Tutankhamon's former name
.... TUTANKHATON
god .... ATON
kingdom .... AMARNA
predecessor .... AKHENATON,
AMENHOTEP
tutelage .... CARE, AEGIS,
AUSPICES, GUIDANCE,
TEACHING, WARDSHIP,
PROTECTION, INSTRUCTION
tutelary deity .... LAR(ES),
GENIUS, PENATES
tutor ...... COACH, GUIDE, MASTER,
MENTOR, TEACH(ER),
GUARDIAN, PEDAGOG(UE),
DISCIPLINE, INSTRUCT(OR)
tutto .... ALL, ENTIRE
Tutuila city .... PAGO PAGO
Tuvalu capital .... FUNAFUTI,
FONGAFALE
island/atoll .... NUI, NIUTAO,
NANUMEA
tuxedo .... TUX, BLACK TIE,
(DINNER)JACKET
tuyere .... TEW, PIPE, TUBE,
TEWEL, NOZZLE
TV. See **television**
TVA, part of .... TENNESSEE,
VALLEY, AUTHORITY
Tver .... KALININ
twaddle .... ROT, BUNK, PRATE,
DRIVEL, GABBLE, FUSTIAN,
PRATTLE, NONSENSE
twain .... TWO
Twain, humorist .... MARK
character .... SAWYER
invention .... SCRAPBOOK
twang .... TANG, PLUNK
twangy .... NASAL
tweak .... JERK, PINCH, PLUCK,
TWIST, TWITCH
Tweeddale .... PEEBLES
tweeg .... HELLBENDER
tweet .... PEEP, CHIRP
tweeter .... LOUDSPEAKER
tweeze .... PLUCK
tweezers .... PINCERS
Twelfth Night .... EPIPHANY
character .... FESTE, VIOLA,
ORSINO, MALVOLIO
composer .... AMRAM
twelve .... XII, DOZEN
Biblical .... APOSTLES,
DISCIPLES
by twelve .... GROSS

dozen .... GROSS
relating to .... DUODECIMAL
Twelve Apostles, one of the
.... JOHN, JUDE, JAMES, JUDAS,
PETER, SIMON, ANDREW,
PHILIP, THOMAS, MATTHEW,
BARTHOLOMEW
twelvemo .... DUODECIMO
Twelvetrees or Hayes ...... HELEN
twentieth .... VIGESIMAL
twenty .... XX, SCORE
combining form .... ICOS(A),
ICOSI, VIGINTI
dinars .... BISTI
-fifth anniversary ...... JUBILEE
-fifth wedding anniversary
.... SILVER(WEDDING)
five pounds .... PONY
four carat .... PURE
-minute walk .... MILE
of/based on .... VICENARY,
VIGESIMAL
one .... BLACK JACK
one merit badge wearer
.... EAGLE SCOUT
plane surfaces, figure with
.... ICOSAHEDRON
quires .... REAM
years, period of .... VICENNIAL
twerp .... CLOD, DOLT, LOUT,
CREEP, DULLARD
twibill .... MATTOCK, (BATTLE)AX
twice ..... BIS, DOUBLY, TWOFOLD,
TWO TIMES
halved .... ONCE
prefix .... BI, DI
-told .... REPEATED,
REITERATED
twiddle .... TOY, TWIRL, TRIFLE
one's _____ .... THUMBS
with .... PLAY
twig .... ROD, SLIP, LAYER,
(S)CION, SHOOT, SPRIG,
BRANCH, TENDRIL
abnormal enlargement of a
.... GALL
and branch angle .... AXIL
British: sl. .... NOTICE,
OBSERVE
broom .... BARSOM
dead .... STICK
flexible .... OSIER, WITHE,
SWITCH, WICKER, WILLOW
for grafting .... CION, SLIP
like a .... TWIGGY
willow .... SALLOW
young .... SHOOT
twiggy .... SLENDER, VIRGATE,
DELICATE
Twiggy, Britain's .... MODEL
twigs, bunch of .... FAGOT, WHISK

clump of .... TUSSOCK
having .... VIRGATE
of .... VIMINAL
twilight .... EVE, DUSK, SHADE,
EVENFALL, EVENTIDE,
GLOAM(ING), CREPUSCLE,
NIGHTFALL
like .... DIM
of the Gods .... RAGNAROK
poet .... EEN
sleep inducer ..... SCOPOLAMIN
twill .... PRUNELLA
twilled .... CORDED
fabric ...... REP, DENIM, SERGE,
CORDUROY
twin .... TWO, COPY, LIKE, GEMEL,
COUPLE, DOUBLE, PAIR(ED),
DIDYMOUS, IDENTICAL
artists Raphael and Moses
.... SOYERS
biblical .... ESAU, JACOB
bill .... DOUBLEHEADER
brother of Romulus .... REMUS
crystal .... MACLE
genetically identical
.... MONOVULAR,
MONOZYGOTIC
non-identical ...... BINOVULAR,
DIZYGOTIC
of Pollux, mortal ...... CASTOR
of sorts .... CLONE
sister of Apollo .... ARTEMIS
sons of Zeus, one of
.... CASTOR, POLLUX
Twin Cities, one of .... ST. PAUL,
MINNEAPOLIS
twinberry .... HONEYSUCKLE
twine .... CORD, LINE, SNARL,
TWIST, WEAVE, ENFOLD,
ENLACE, STRING, TANGLE,
THREAD, WREATHE, ENCIRCLE,
FILAMENT, INTERLACE
material .... HEMP, JUTE,
ABACA, OAKUM, MAGUEY
twinge .... ACHE, PAIN, PANG,
DOUBT, PINCH, SHOOT, THROB
of conscience .... QUALM,
SHAME, REMORSE, SCRUPLE,
COMPUNCTION
twining stem .... BINE
twinkle ...... WINK, BLINK, GLINT,
SHINE, FLICKER, GLIMMER,
SHIMMER, SPARKLE
twinkling .... INSTANT,
(SPLIT)SECOND
twins .... GEMINI
conjoined ..... SIAMESE(TWINS)
one of the Siamese .... ENG,
CHANG
twirl ...... COIL, SPIN, TURN, WIND,
TWIST, WHIRL, ROTATE,

FLOURISH
twist .... TIC, SKEW, TURN, WARP,
WIND, CURVE, SCREW, TWINE,
WRICK, WRING, SPRAIN,
SQUIRM, WRENCH, WRITHE,
CONTORT
a joint .... SPRAIN
and turn .... W(R)IGGLE
around .... COIL, CURL
around one's finger
.... DOMINATE, SPELLBIND
given to a ball .... SPIN
in a tree .... GNARL
into thread .... THROW
of fiction .... OLIVER
one's arm ...... URGE, COMPEL,
PERSUADE
out of shape .... DISTORT
the meaning of .... PERVERT,
MISINTERPRET
twisted .... WRY, AWRY, SKEW,
COMPLEX, TORTILE,
CONTORTED
cord .... TORSADE
doughnut .... CRULLER
inclination .... BIAS
mind, person with a
.... ODDBALL, SCREWBALL
roll of cotton .... SLUB
roll of tobacco .... PIGTAIL
rope/wire strands .... CABLE
thread .... LISLE
twister .... CYCLONE, TORNADO
twisting .... SPIRAL, TORSION
pinch/pluck .... TWEAK
twit .... RAG, RIB, GIBE, JEER,
JOSH, MOCK, CHAFF, SCOFF,
TAUNT, TEASE, BANTER,
DERIDE, UPBRAID, REPROACH,
RIDICULE
twitch .... TIC, TUG, JERK, PAIN,
PULL, PLUCK, SHAKE, SPASM,
TWEAK, FIDGET, SNATCH,
TWINGE, SQUEEZE, VELLICATE
of a muscle .... TIC,
FASCICULATION
twitter .... GIGGLE, TITTER,
CHATTER, CHIRRUP, FLUTTER,
CHIRP(ING)
twittering .... QUIVERING,
TREMBLING
''of the sparrows''
.... MAHJONG
twixt .... BETWEEN
ifs and buts .... ANDS
two ...... DUO, DUET, PAIR, BRACE,
TWAIN, COUPLE, LOWEST
CARD IN THE DECK
aces in dice .... CRABS, CRAPS,
SNAKE EYES

Americans who shared Nobel Prize for medicine, one of: 1992 .... (EDWIN) KREBS, (EDMOND) FISCHER

archaic .... TWAIN

at a time .... DOUBLY

-base hit .... DOUBLE, TWO-BAGGER

bells .... ONE O'CLOCK

bends or curves, having .... BIFLEX

-bit: sl. .... CHEAP, TAWDRY, SMALL-TIME, WORTHLESS

bits .... QUARTER

branches, having ...... FORKED, BIFURCATE

-by-four .... SMALL, LUMBER, NARROW, CRAMPED, LIMITED

by two .... BINAL

-celled .... BILOCULAR

-colored .... TWO-TONE, DICHROMATIC

-colored bird .... OWL, TERN, EAGLE, PARROT, PETREL, PENGUIN, SWALLOW

combining form .... BI, DI, BIS, DUO, DYO, TWI

consisting of .... DYAD(IC)

-continent nation .... RUSSIA

contrary states of the human soul, one of the (per Blake) .... INNOCENCE, EXPERIENCE

cups .... PINT

different focus, having .... BIFOCAL

divide by .... FIFTY-FIFTY

-edged .... ANCIPITAL, ANCIPITOUS

-element semiconductor .... DIODE

equal parts, divide into .... HALVE

-faced .... FALSE, BIFACIAL, DECEIVING, INSINCERE, DUPLICITOUS, HYPOCRITICAL

-faced being .... JANUS, HYPOCRITE

-fisted .... POTENT, VIRILE, VIGOROUS

-footed animal .... BIPED(AL)

for the price of one .... TWOFER

-forked .... BIFURCATE

groups/classes, division into .... DICHOTOMY

-handed .... BIMANOUS, AMBIDEXTROUS

-handed animal .... BIMANE

-headed .... BICEPHALOUS

-headed muscle .... BICEPS

heads, having .... DICEPHALOUS

-horned .... BICORN

-horse chariot .... BIGA

hundred milligrams .... CARAT

-leaf paper sheet .... FOLIO

-legged .... BIPED

legislative chambers, having .... BICAMERAL

magistrates, either of .... DUUMVIR

-masted squarerigger ..... BRIG

-month period .... BIMESTER

of .... DUAL

of a kind .... BRACE

of similar things ..... DOUBLET

-part mollusk .... CLAM, MUSSEL, BIVALVE

partners with joint authority .... DUUMVIRATE

people, conversation between .... DUOLOGUE, TETE-A-TETE

plus tid .... BITS

punches in quick succession .... ONE-TWO

-seater .... TANDEM, ROADSTER

shillings .... FLORIN

-sided .... BILATERAL

similar parts, having .... DUPLICATE

song for .... DUET

-spot .... DEUCE

-step .... DANCE

-striper .... CORPORAL

successive lines of verse .... COUPLET, DISTICH

-supplier controlled market .... DUOPOLY

-syllable foot .... TROCHEE

teeth, having .... BIDENTATE

the .... BOTH

thousand pounds .... NET TON, SHORT TON

-time .... DOUBLE-CROSS

-timer ...... SPY, CHEAT, JUDAS, INFIDEL, ADULTERER, ADULTERESS, DOUBLE-AGENT

-toed sloth .... UNAU

together .... DUAD, PAIR

-tusked animal .... WALRUS, ELEPHANT, (WILD)BOAR

units regarded as one .... DYAD, PAIR

vertical rows, arranged in .... DISTICHOUS

-way .... DUAL

-week period .... FORTNIGHT

-wheeled cab .... HANSOM

-wheeled carriage .... GIG, CART, CALASH, HANSOM, CALECHE, TILBURY

-wheeled vehicle .... TONGA, BICYCLE

-year old sheep .... TEG(G)

Two-Faced Woman star .... (GRETA) GARBO

Women star .... (SOPHIA) LOREN

Years Before the Mast author .... DANA

twofold .... DUAL, BINAL, BINARY, DOUBLE, DUPLE(X)

twosome .... COUPLE

Ty, baseball great .... COBB

Tyburn event .... HANGING, EXECUTION

Tyche .... FORTUNA, GODDESS

tycoon ...... TSAR, BARON, MOGUL, SHOGUN, MAGNATE, FINANCIER

Tydeus' son .... DIOMEDES

tyke .... CUR, DOG, LAD, BOOR, CHILD, MONGREL

Tyler, English rebel .... WAT

U.S. president .... JOHN

tympan .... DRUM

tympani .... KETTLEDRUMS

tympanic membrane .... EARDRUM

tympanist .... DRUMMER

tympanum .... MIDDLE EAR

tympany .... PRIDE, BOMBAST, CONCEIT, ARROGANCE

Tyndareus .... SPARTAN

wife of .... LEDA

Tyne river city .... JARROW

type .... KIND, SIGN, SORT, BREED, CLASS, GROUP, IDEAL, MODEL, TOKEN, EMBLEM, FIGURE, NATURE, VARIETY, CLASSIFY, (TYPE)WRITE

assortment of .... FO(U)NT

blank .... QUAD(RAT)

body measure .... POINT

break in .... BATTER

case .... LOWER, UPPER

disarrange .... SQUABBLE

face like writing ...... CURSIVE

face projection .... KERN

jumbled/mixed .... PI(E)

lead-in .... PROTO

line of .... SLUG

measure .... EM, EN

metal .... QUAD

mold .... MATRIX

of acid .... AMINO

button .... PANIC

clock .... ALARM, BANJO, GRANDFATHER

coat .... SPORT, DUFFEL,

TUXEDO, SWAGGER, SPIKETAIL, SWALLOWTAIL
diving board .... FLAT, SPRING
hands? .... DISHPAN
intelligence test .... IQ, BINET-SIMON, STANFORD-BINET
law .... DRY, GAG, BLUE, COMMON, UNWRITTEN
law enforcement agency .... SWAT
police operation .... STING
sleeve .... DOLMAN, LANTERN, LEG-OF-MUTTON
space .... AERO
surgeon .... HEART, NEURO, PLASTIC
trip .... EGO
ornamental line .... SERIF
part .... KERN
set .... COMPOSE
size ...., FONT, PICA, AGATE, RUBY, ELITE, ROMAN, MINION, BREVIER, DIAMOND, PARAGON, EXCELSIOR, NONPAREIL, LONG PRIMER
style .... ROMAN, BODONI, CASLON, GOTHIC, ITALIC, GARAMOND, GROTESQUE
tray .... GALLEY
type .... IONIC, ROMAN, ITALIC, SCRIPT, CURSIVE, BOLDFACE, OLD ENGLISH
typescript .... COPY
typesetter .... PRINTER,

COMPOSITOR, LINOTYPIST
typesetting .... COMPOSING
machine: colloq. .... LINO
typewriter, kind of .... TELEX, MANUAL, ELECTRIC, TELETYPE
part ..... KEY, PLATEN, ROLLER, SPACER, CARRIAGE, TABULATOR
type .... PICA, ELITE
typhlosis .... BLINDNESS
Typhoeus' killer .... ZEUS
typhoid fever bacterium .... SALMONELLA
drug treatment .... AMPICILLIN, ANTIBIOTICS
symptom ..... FEVER, MALAISE, HEADACHE
"Typhoid Mary" .... (MARY) MALLON
occupation of .... COOK
typhoon .... WIND, STORM, CYCLONE, TORNADO, HURRICANE
typhus carrier .... FLEA, LOUSE
cause of .... RICKETTSIA(E)
type of .... SCRUB, MURINE, ENDEMIC
typical .... IDEAL, MODEL, USUAL, NORMAL, GENERAL, REGULAR, SYMBOLIC, CHARACTERISTIC
typify .... EMBODY, EXEMPLIFY, SYMBOLIZE
typographer .... PRINTER
typographical error .... ERRATUM
Tyr .... TIU

father of .... ODIN
tyramine source .... ERGOT, MISTLETOE
tyrannical .... CRUEL, HARSH, UNJUST, DESPOTIC, OPPRESSIVE
tyrannize .... OPPRESS, DOMINEER
tyrannosaurus .... DINOSAUR
tyranny .... RIGOR, CRUELTY, SEVERITY, AUTOCRACY, DESPOTISM, OPPRESSION, TOTALITARIANISM
tyrant .... CZAR, TSAR, DESPOT, PHARAOH, USURPER, AUTOCRAT, DICTATOR, OPPRESSOR
Tyre, king of .... HIRAM
princess of .... DIDO
renowned export of .... PURPLE-DYE
tyro .... PUPIL, NOVICE, AMATEUR, LEARNER, BEGINNER, NEOPHYTE
Tyrol topography .... ALPS
Tyrolean city ...... ZAMS, PFUNDS, LANDECK, INNSBRUCK
hat wearer .... PINOCCHIO
mountains .... OTZTAL ALPS
pass .... BRENNER
patriot .... HOFER
refrain/song .... YODEL
river .... INN, ISAR(CO)
singer .... YOD(E)LER
tzar .... CZAR, TSAR, RULER, TYRANT
tzigane .... GYPSY

U

U-boat .... SUBMARINE
boat locator .... SONAR
Greek .... UPSILON
in chemistry .... URANIUM
in mathematics ...... UNIVERSE
letter .... EU
_____ of the U.N. .... THANT
-shaped bone .... HYOID
-shaped frame .... OXBOW
-turn, describing a .... HAIRPIN
Ubangi tributary .... UELE
Ubermensch .... OVERMAN, SUPERMAN
ubication .... LOCATION
ubiety .... LOCATION, POSITION, WHERENESS
ubique .... EVERYWHERE
ubiquitous .... PERVASIVE, INESCAPABLE, OMNIPRESENT

ubiquity .... OMNIPRESENCE
Ucayali tributary ...... APURIMAC
udder .... BAG, MAMMA
inflammation .... GARGET
product .... MILK
protuberance ..... TEAT, NIPPLE
udometer .... RAIN GAUGE
Uffizi Museum site .... FLORENCE
UFO, part of ...... UNIDENTIFIED, FLYING, OBJECT
Uganda capital .... KAMPALA
capital, former .... ENTEBBE
city/town .... ARUA, GULU, MOYO, JINJA, MBALE, MASAKA, MOROTI, SOROTI, TORORO
city on Lake Victoria .... ENTEBBE
dam .... OWEN FALLS

falls .... KABALEGA
islands .... SESE
kingdom .... BUGANDA
lake .... KIOGA, ALBERT, EDWARD, GEORGE, VICTORIA
language .... SOGA, TESO, NYORO, ACHOLI, SWAHILI
monetary unit .... SHILLING
mountain .... ELGON, MARGHERITA
president .... OBOTE, MUSEVENI
range .... VIRUNGA, RUWENZORI
religion .... ISLAM
ugly .... FOUL, VILE, CROSS, NASTY, PLAIN, GRISLY, HOMELY, HORRID, HIDEOUS, OMINOUS, DEFORMED,

GRUESOME, UNGAINLY, DANGEROUS, GROTESQUE, REPULSIVE, UNSIGHTLY

as _____ .... SIN

customer ..... CRANK, DRAGON, GROUCH, HOTHEAD, SOREHEAD

disposition, having
.... ORNERY

duckling once .... SWAN

face expression .... MOUE, POUT, FROWN, SCOWL, GLOWER, GRIMACE

figure in a field
.... SCARECROW

hopper .... TOAD

humpback/hunchback
.... QUASIMODO

make .... MAR, DEFACE, UGLIFY, DISFIGURE

object of fear .... SPECTER

ones .... HAGS, TOADS, WITCHES

savage creature .... CALIBAN

sight .... EYESORE

-tempered .... CROSS, HUFFY, TESTY, BITCHY, CRANKY, PEEVISH, IRRITABLE

Ugudai Khan's father
.... GENGHIS KHAN

nephew .... KUBLAI KHAN

uh-huh .... YES

uh-uh .... NOPE

uhlan .... GERMAN, SOLDIER, CAVALRYMAN

weapon of .... LANCE

uintaite ...... ASPHALT, GILSONITE

uitlander .... FOREIGNER

ukase .... DECREE

kin .... IRADE

Ukrainian capital .... KIEV

city/town .... KHARKOB, KHERSON

farmer .... KULAK

holy city .... KIEV

legislature .... RADA

money of account ..... GRIVNA

native .... COSSACK

port .... KHERSON

president
.... (LEONID)KRAVCHUK

sea .... BLACK

seaport .... ODESSA

ukulele, for short .... UKE

instrument like .... GUITAR

player .... HAWAIIAN

Ulalume poet .... POE

Ulan Bator .... URGA, KHOTO, KULUN

ulcer ...... SORE, ABSCESS, FISTULA

decubitus .... BEDSORE

discharge .... PUS, ICHOR,

SANIES

in the mouth .... APHTHOUS, CANKER-SORE

site, peptic .... STOMACH, DUODENUM

type of .... MOUTH, PEPTIC, CORNEAL, GASTRIC

venereal .... CHANCRE

ulcerate .... FESTER

ule .... CAUCHO

fluid .... LATEX

ulema .... MUFTI, SCHOLARS

Ullmann, actress LIV

ulmaceous tree .... ELM

ulmus .... ELM

ulna projection ...... OLECRANON

Ulster .... OVERCOAT

lake .... ERNE

ult. .... ULTIMO, ULTIMATE

ulterior .... BEYOND, HIDDEN, LATENT, REMOTE, FARTHER, CONCEALED

motive .... NISUS, DESIGNS

Ultima Thule .... ICELAND

ultimate .... LAST, FINAL, ENDALL, EXTREME, MAXIMUM, PRIMARY, EVENTUAL, FARTHEST

degree .... NTH

slang .... THE MOST

ultimatum .... DEMAND, WARNING, LAST OFFER

words .... OR ELSE

ultra .... EXTREME, RADICAL, EXCESSIVE, SUPERLATIVE

modern ...... FAR-OUT, AVANT-GARDE

nationalistic .... JINGO(ISTIC), CHAUVINIST(IC)

ultramarine .... (BLUE)PIGMENT

ultrasonic .... FASTER-THAN-SOUND

ulu .... KNIFE

ululant .... HOWLING

ululate .... BAY, CRY, HOWL, PULE, MEWL, WAIL, WEEP, LAMENT

Ulyanov, Vladimir .... LENIN

Ulysses .... ODYSSEUS

author of .... JOYCE

country/kingdom of
.... ITHACA

father of .... LAERTES

name given to Cyclops
.... NOMAN

son of .... TELEMACHUS

wife of .... PENELOPE

umbelliferous plant .... CARROT, PARSLEY

umber .... SHADE, SHADOW, PIGMENT, GRAYLING

bird .... UMBRETTE

umbilical cord .... FUNICULUS

umbilicus .... NAVEL

umbles .... ENTRAILS

umbo .... BEAK, BOSS, KNOB

umbra .... SHADE, SHADOW

umbrage .... HUFF, PIQUE, SHADOW, FOLIAGE, OFFENSE, RESENTMENT

umbrella .... GAMP, COVER, CHATTA, PARASOL, (SUN)SHADE

cloth for .... GLORIA

like flower .... UMBEL

like fungus .... MUSHROOM

of leaves .... TALIPOT

part .... RIB

style .... BUBBLE

thing like .... CANOPY, (PARA)CHUTE

tree .... MAGNOLIA

umbrette .... UMBER, HAMMERHEAD

Umbria town .... ASSISI

umiak .... CANOE, KAYAK

umlaut .... DIERESIS

in linguistics .... MUTATION

umpire .... UMP, JUDGE, ARBITER, DAYSMAN, REFEREE

UN adopted official language
.... ARABIC, FRENCH, CHINESE, ENGLISH, RUSSIAN, SPANISH

agency .... FAO, IDA, WHO, GATT, ICAO, UNRRA, UNESCO

goal .... PEACE

president .... ARCE, MAZA, SLIM, EVATT, MALIK, MUNRO, NERVO, SPAAK, ARANHA, PANDIT, ROMULO, MANESCU

secretary-general
.... (U)THANT, DE CUELLAR, (TRYGVE)LIE, BOUTROS-GHALI, (DAG)HAMMARSKJOLD

workers' org. .... ILO

una .... CATBOAT

unabashed .... COOL, BRAZEN

unable .... UNFIT, INCAPABLE

to act: sl. ...... OVER A BARREL

unaccented .... ATONIC, STRESSLESS

vowel sound .... SCHWA

unacceptable .... UNSUITABLE, INADMISSIBLE

unaccompanied .... SOLO, ALONE, SOLITARY, UNESCORTED

unaccustomed .... NEW, RARE

unadorned .... BALD, BARE, NAKED, PLAIN, STARK, SIMPLE

unadulterated .... NEAT, PURE, TRUE, GENUINE

unaffected .... NAIVE, PLAIN,

SIMPLE, ARTLESS, NATURAL, SINCERE, UNMOVED
unaided .... ALONE
Unalaskan .... ALEUT
unalloyed .... PURE
unanimity .... ACCORD, ONE-VOICE
unanimous .... SOLID
opinion .... CONSENSUS
unanimously .... AS ONE MAN
unapproachable .... COLD, ALOOF, DISTANT, INACCESSIBLE
unarmed .... WEAPONLESS, DEFENSELESS
unaspirated consonant .... LENE
unassuming .... SHY, MEEK, MODEST, NATURAL, RESERVED, RETIRING
unattached .... FREE, (A)LONE, LOOSE, SINGLE, VAGILE, INDEPENDENT
unau .... SLOTH
unauthorized .... ILLEGAL
departure .... FRENCH LEAVE
unavailing .... IDLE, VAIN, FUTILE, USELESS
unavoidable .... CERTAIN, INEVITABLE
unaware .... IGNORANT
unawares, take .... SURPRISE
unbalanced .... MAD, UNEVEN, DERANGED, LOPSIDED
unbearable .... ODIOUS
unbecoming .... UGLY, IMPROPER, ILL-SUITED, INDECOROUS
unbelievable .... FAR-FETCHED, INCREDIBLE
unbeliever .... PAGAN, ATHEIST, DOUBTER, HERETIC, INFIDEL, SKEPTIC, AGNOSTIC, MISCREANT
unbelieving .... INCREDULOUS
unbend .... THAW, RELAX, YIELD, RELENT, STRAIGHTEN
unbending ...... SET, FIRM, RIGID, ADAMANT, RESOLUTE
unbiased .... FAIR, JUST, IMPARTIAL, OBJECTIVE
unbleached .... ECRU
muslin .... MANTA
wool fabric .... BEIGE
unblemished .... CLEAN, FLAWLESS, SPOTLESS, STAINLESS
unblessed .... UNHAPPY, ACCURSED
unborn young in womb .... FETUS
unbosom .... TELL, REVEAL
unbounded .... INFINITE,

LIMITLESS
unbranded cow .... MAVERICK
unbreakable .... TOUGH, DURABLE
unbridled .... UNRULY, UNCONTROLLED
unbroken .... WILD, WHOLE, INTACT, UNTAMED, CONTINUOUS
unburden .... RID, REVEAL, UNLOAD, LIGHTEN, RELIEVE
unburnt brick .... ADOBE
uncalled-for .... UNDUE, ILL-TIMED, GRATUITOUS, IMPERTINENT, UNNECESSARY
uncanny ...... EERY, UNCO, EERIE, WEIRD, STRANGE, MYSTERIOUS
uncared-for .... NEGLECTED
Uncas' beloved .... CORA
unceasing .... ENDLESS, ETERNAL, PERPETUAL, CONTINUOUS
unceremonious .... CURT, ABRUPT, INFORMAL
uncertain ...... VAGUE, DOUBTFUL, UP IN THE AIR
uncertainty .... DOUBT, DUBIETY, QUESTION MARK
unchanged .... ORIGINAL, PRISTINE
uncharacteristic .... UNREALISTIC
of the upper class .... NONU
unchaste .... LEWD, WANTON
unchecked .... RIFE, LOOSE, RAMPANT
uncheerful .... DREAR
unchristian .... WICKED
unciform .... HOOK-SHAPED
uncinate .... HAMATE, HOOKED, HOOKLIKE
uncivil .... RUDE
uncivilized .... SAVAGE, BARBARIC, PRIMITIVE
unclad .... NUDE, NAKED
uncle ...... EAM, OOM, UNK, UNCS, NUNKS, NUNCLE
American .... SAM
cry .... YIELD, SURRENDER
of fiction .... REMUS
pertaining to ...... AVUNCULAR
Sandy's .... EME
slang .... PAWNBROKER
Uncle Fester's family ...... ADAMS
Remus' author .... HARRIS
Remus' rabbit .... BRE'R
Tom's _____ .... CABIN
Tom's Cabin author ...... (HARRIET BEECHER)STOWE
Tom's Cabin character .... ELIZA, TOPSY, LITTLE EVA, SIMON LEGREE
unclean .... BAD, FOUL, VILE,

DINGY, DIRTY, DUSTY, FETID, FUSTY, GRIMY, MOLDY, MUSTY, NASTY, SOOTY, FILTHY, FROWZY, IMPURE, SMUTTY, SOILED, UNTIDY, LEPROUS, OBSCENE, SQUALID, UNKEMPT
immoral dealings .... CORRUPTION
one: biblical .... LEPER
person .... SLOB
place .... DUMP, SEWER, PIGPEN, (PIG)STY, CESSPOOL
unclear .... DIM, VAGUE
uncloak .... EXPOSE, REVEAL
unclose .... OPE(N), REVEAL
unclothe .... STRIP, DIVEST, UNCOVER, UNDRESS
unclothed partially .... TOPLESS, DISHABILLE
uncluttered .... TIDY
unclouded .... CLEAR
unco .... VERY, NOVEL, WEIRD, NOTABLE, STRANGE, UNCANNY, UNKNOWN
uncoil .... UNWIND
uncoined metal .... BULLION
uncombed .... UNKEMPT
uncomely .... UGLY, PLAIN
uncomfortable .... UNEASY
feeling .... ACHE
uncommitted .... FREE, NEUTRAL, UNPLEDGED
uncommon .... ODD, RARE, EXOTIC, SCARCE, STRANGE, UNUSUAL, ORIGINAL, SINGULAR
thing .... RARITY
uncommunicative .... SILENT, RESERVE, RETICENT, TACITURN, SECRETIVE
uncompromising ...... SET, RIGID, STRICT, ADAMANT, AUSTERE, DETERMINED, INFLEXIBLE
unconcerned .... ALOOF, UNMOVED, DETACHED, INSOUCIANT, INDIFFERENT
unconditional .... FULL, TOTAL, ABSOLUTE, TERMLESS
unconfined .... FREE, LOOSE
unconfirmed news .... RUMOR, GOSSIP, REPORT, HEARSAY
unconformity .... ODDITY, ECCENTRICITY
unconnected .... DETACHED, DISCRETE, SEPARATE, UNRELATED
unconquerable .... INVINCIBLE
unconscionable .... WRONG, UNETHICAL
unconscious .... OUT, ASLEEP,

BLOTTO, UNAWARE, MINDLESS, UNWITTING

state .... COMA, SWOON, TRANCE, SYNCOPE, HYPNOSIS, NARCOSIS

unconstitutional .... UNFAIR, UNJUST, ILLEGAL

unconstrained ...... FREE, DEGAGE

uncontrolled .... WILD, UNRULY

unconventional .... OUTRE, UNUSUAL, BOHEMIAN, INFORMAL, OUT-OF-STEP

one .... REBEL

uncooked .... RAW

uncooperative .... CONTRARY, DIFFICULT, RELUCTANT

uncos .... NEWS

uncouth .... RUDE, CRUDE, GAWKY, CLUMSY, GAUCHE, SAVAGE, VULGAR, AWKWARD, BOORISH, AGRESTIC, UNREFINED

person .... CAD, OAF, BOOR, GAWK, LOUT, CHURL, YOKEL, CODGER, RUSTIC, BUM(P)KIN

variant .... UNCOS

uncover .... BARE, OPEN, DENUDE, EXPOSE, REVEAL

hat .... DOFF

uncovered .... BARE, NUDE, NAKED, EXPOSED, DISCOVERED

unction .... OIL, UNGUENT, OINTMENT

give extreme .... ANELE

unctuous .... OILY, BLAND, SLEEK, SOAPY, SUAVE, GREASY, SMOOTH, PINGUID, PLASTIC

as of soil .... RICH

substance .... CERATE, GREASE, LANOLIN, UNGUENT, OINTMENT

uncultivated .... WILD, COARSE, FALLOW, VIRGIN, UNTILLED, UNREFINED, ILLITERATE

uncultured .... RUDE, COARSE, BOORISH, ILL-BRED, UNCOUTH, UNREFINED, UNPOLISHED

uncurl .... STRAIGHTEN

und so weiter .... ETC, ET CETERA

undaunted ...... BOLD, FEARLESS, INTREPID, COURAGEOUS, UNDISMAYED

unde, in heraldry .... WAVY

undecided .... PENDENT, PENDING, DOUBTFUL, HESITANT, WAVERING, UNCERTAIN, IRRESOLUTE, UP IN THE AIR

undefeated .... CHAMPION, UNBEATEN

undefiled .... PURE, CHASTE

undemonstrative .... CALM, RESERVED

undeniable .... REAL, TRUE, FACTUAL, IRREFUTABLE

undeniably .... INDEED

under .... BELOW, LOWER, NETHER, (BE)NEATH

average .... INFERIOR

no circumstances ..... NOWAY, NOWISE

obligation ...... BOUND, OWING, INDEBTED

par .... ILL, SICK

poetic .... NEATH

prefix .... HYP, SUB

the influence .... STONED

the power of another .... SUBORDINATE

the Washington bridges .... POTOMAC RIVER

underage ...... MINOR, IMMATURE

underbrush .... BOSCAGE, THICKET

undercooked .... RARE

undercover ...... MASKED, SECRET, INCOGNITO

person .... SPY, SLEUTH, DETECTIVE

undercroft .... CRYPT

undercurrent .... INNUENDO

underdog .... LOSER, ALSO-RAN

victory of .... UPSET

underdone .... RARE

underestimate .... BELITTLE, MINIMIZE, DEPRECATE

undergarment .... SLIP, SHIRT, TEDDY, CHEMISE

man's .... SINGLET

undergo .... BEAR, STAND, ENDURE, SUFFER, EXPERIENCE

undergraduate .... FROSH, PLEBE, JUNIOR, FRESHMAN, SOPHOMORE

underground .... HIDDEN, SECRET

being .... DWARF, GNOME, TROLL

burial place .... CRYPT, CATACOMB

drain .... SEWER

fighter ..... EDES, ELAS, MAQUI, PARTISAN

foundation .... ROOTAGE

fungus .... TRUFFLE, EARTHNUT, TUCKAHOE

organization .... MAFIA

passage .... SAP, TUBE, BURROW, TUNNEL

railway .... TUBE, METRO, SUBWAY

resident .... DWARF, GNOME, TROLL

stem .... ONION, SALEP, STOCK, TUBER, MANIOC, POTATO, CASSAVA, RHIZOME

volunteer soldier .... GUER(R)ILLA

worker .... MINER, SANDHOG

underhand .... SLY, COVERT, SECRET, CLANDESTINE

underhanded .... SLY, TRICKY, DEVIOUS, FURTIVE, DECEITFUL, FRAUDULENT

underline .... MARK, STRESS, EMPHASIZE, UNDERSCORE

underling .... AIDE, SLAVE, FLUNKY, ASSISTANT, SUBALTERN, SUBORDINATE

underlying .... BASIC, ESSENTIAL, FUNDAMENTAL

principle .... ELIXIR

undermine .... SAP, ERODE, THWART, WEAKEN, SUBVERT, WEAR AWAY, FRUSTRATE

undernourish .... FAMISH, STARVE

undernourished .... UNFED, EMACIATED

underpin .... PROP

underpinning .... SUPPORT

colloquial .... LEGS

underrate .... BELITTLE

underscore ...... ACCENT, STRESS, EMPHASIZE, UNDERLINE

undersea craft .... UBOAT, SUBMARINE

explorer .... PICARD

undershirt .... VEST, JERSEY, SKIVVY, SINGLET

undersigned, the .... WRITER

undersized .... RUNTY, SMALL, SCRUBBY

being .... RUNT, DWARF, PIGMY

underskirt .... PETTICOAT

undersong .... REFRAIN

understand ...... KEN, SEE, KNOW, CATCH, GRASP, INFER, ASSUME, GATHER, DISCERN, REALIZE, CONSTRUE, PERCEIVE, APPREHEND, INTERPRET, APPRECIATE, COMPREHEND

colloquial .... DIG, GET, SAVVY

thoroughly .... FATHOM

understanding ...... CODE, NOUS, SENSE, ACCORD, INSIGHT, AGREEMENT, KNOWLEDGE, OPEN-MINDED

between nations, etc. .... ENTENTE

understate .... PLAY DOWN

understood .... TACIT, AGREED, SENSED, ASSUMED, IMPLIED,

IMPLICIT, PRESUMED

readily .... CLEAR, LUCID, LUCULENT

understrapper .... UNDERLING, SUBORDINATE

understudy .... STAND-IN, ALTERNATE, APPRENTICE, SUBSTITUTE

undertake .... TRY, OFFER, ASSUME, PLEDGE, TACKLE, ATTEMPT, PROMISE, CONTRACT, VOLUNTEER

undertaker .... EMBALMER, MORTICIAN

job of .... PALL-BEARING

undertaking .... JOB, TASK, CAPER, PROJECT, PROMISE, VENTURE, BUSINESS, ENDEAVOR, GUARANTEE, ENTERPRISE

undertow .... RIPTIDE

underwater .... SUNKEN, SUBMARINE, SUBMERGED

apparatus .... SCUBA, CAISSON, SNORKEL, BATHYSCAPH, BATHYSPHERE

craft .... UBOAT, PIGBOAT, SUBMARINE

eye of sort .... HYDROSCOPE

ledge .... REEF

plants .... BENTHOS

prefix .... HYP(O)

projectile .... TORPEDO

sound detection device .... SOFAR, SONAR

swimmer .... FROGMAN, (SKIN)DIVER, SNORK(E)LER

worker .... SANDHOG

underwear .... BRA, SLIP, PANTY, BRIEFS, CORSET, GIRDLE, SCANTY, SHORTS, UNDIES, DRAWERS, FLANNELS, LINGERIE, BRASSIERE

underworld .... HEL, EARTH, HADES, SHEOL, EREBUS, GANGLAND, ANTIPODES

character .... CRIMINAL, GANGSTER

king .... YAMA

queen .... HEL

underwrite ...... ASSUME, INSURE, AGREE(TO), FINANCE, SUBSCRIBE

slang .... BANKROLL

underwriter .... INSURER, SPONSOR, INSURANCE MAN

undeserving .... INDIGN, UNWORTHY

undesirable .... DISLIKED, UNWANTED, OBJECTIONABLE

person ..... BORE, BOOR, LOUT,

FELON, LEPER, PARIAH, OUTCAST, DERELICT

person: biblical .... HAGAR, ISHMAEL

undeveloped .... LATENT

quality .... POTENTIAL

undies .... PANTIES, LINGERIE, UNDERWEAR

undignified ...... MEAN, ILL-BRED, DEGRADING

undiluted .... NEAT, PURE, SHEER, STRAIGHT

undiminished .... WHOLE, UNABATED, UNSHAKEN, UNREDUCED

undine ...... NIX, GNOME, NYMPH, SYLPH, KELPIE, SEAMAID

undisciplined ...... WILD, SAVAGE, CHAOTIC, LAWLESS

undiscovered .... UNDETECTED

undisguised .... OPEN, TRUE, FRANK, OVERT, CANDID

undisputed .... ACCEPTED, UNCONTESTED, UNQUESTIONED

undisturbed .... CALM, COOL, QUIET

undivided .... ONE, WHOLE, ENTIRE, INTACT, SINGLE, UNITED

undo .... OPEN, UNTIE, CANCEL, UNFASTEN

a breach .... REUNIFY

undoer .... NEMESIS

undoing .... RUIN, DEFEAT, DOWNFALL

undomesticated .... WILD, FERAL, UNTAMED

undone ...... RUINED, ABANDONED, NEGLECTED, UNFINISHED

undoubtedly .... SURELY, CERTAINLY, ADMITTEDLY

undraped .... BARE, NUDE

undress .... STRIP, DISROBE, DISARRAY

slang .... PEEL

stage of .... DISHABILLE

undressed skin .... KIP, PELT

Undset, Norwegian novelist .... SIGRID

undue .... UNJUST, EXTREME, IMPROPER, EXCESSIVE, INORDINATE

undulant fever ...... BRUCELLOSIS

undulate .... RISE, ROLL, WAVE, SURGE, SWELL, BILLOW, RIPPLE

undulating .... WAVY

object .... WAVE, WORM, SNAKE, RIPPLE

undulation .... WAVE, HEAVE,

SURGE, RIPPLE, PULSATION

unduly .... UNJUSTLY, IMPROPERLY, EXCESSIVELY, UNREASONABLY

undyed .... PLAIN, TINTLESS

undying .... ABIDING, ETERNAL, IMMORTAL, UNENDING, EVERLASTING

unearth .... DIG UP, EXHUME, EXPOSE, UPROOT, DISCLOSE, DISCOVER

unearthly .... EERIE, WEIRD, GHOSTLY, UNCANNY, UNUSUAL

sight .... UFO

uneasiness .... FEAR, WORRY, UNREST, ANXIETY, MALAISE, DISCOMFORT

slang .... HEEBIE-JEEBIES

uneasy .... JUMPY, ANXIOUS, FEARFUL, FIDGETY, JITTERY, FRETFUL, NERVOUS, RESTIVE, RESTLESS, CONCERNED, DISTURBED, DISQUIETED

feeling .... MALAISE

uneducated .... IGNORANT, UNLEARNED, ILLITERATE, UNLETTERED

unemotional .... CALM, COOL, NUMB, APATHETIC, UNFEELING

unemployed .... FREE, IDLE, JOBLESS, AVAILABLE

unending .... ETERNAL, CEASELESS, PERPETUAL, CONTINUOUS

unenlightened .... BENIGHTED

unenthusiastic .... COLD, COOL, UNEAGER, LISTLESS, RELUCTANT, INDIFFERENT

unequal .... ROUGH, UNEVEN, UNFAIR, UNLIKE, IRREGULAR, INADEQUATE, UNBALANCED

angled .... SCALENE

combining form .... ANISO

unequalled .... SUPREME, PEERLESS, MATCHLESS, NONPAREIL

unequitable .... UNJUST

unequivocal .... CLEAR, PLAIN, CANDID, DEFINITE

unerring .... SURE, EXACT, CERTAIN, ACCURATE, CONSTANT

unescorted .... SOLO, ALONE

unessential .... NEEDLESS, DISPENSABLE

uneven .... ODD, EROSE, LUMPY, ROUGH, HUBBLY, RAGGED, RUGGED, SPOTTY, CROOKED, UNEQUAL, IRREGULAR

contest .... LOPSIDED

uneventful .... DULL, HUMDRUM
unexcited .... UNRUFFLED
unexciting .... DULL, TAME,
    VAPID, BORING, LIFELESS
unexpected .... ABRUPT, SUDDEN,
    UNFORESEEN
  astonishment .... SURPRISE
  attack .... AMBUSH
  candidate .... DARK HORSE
  defeat .... UPSET
  event .... ACCIDENT
  gain .... WINDFALL
  meeting .... ENCOUNTER
  source of delight .... TREAT
unexploded .... LIVE
unexpressive .... DULL, BLAND
unfading .... FAST
  flower .... AMARANTH,
  EVERLASTING
unfailing .... SURE, CERTAIN,
  REGULAR, CONSTANT,
  STEADFAST
unfair ...... FOUL, BIASED, UNJUST,
  PARTIAL, DISHONEST,
  PREJUDICED
unfaithful .... FICKLE, UNTRUE,
  CHEATING, DISLOYAL
unfamiliar .... NEW, STRANGE
unfasten .... OPEN, UNDO,
  DISCONNECT
  poetic .... OPE
unfavorable .... BAD, ILL,
  ADVERSE, CONTRARY,
  INIMICAL, NEGATIVE
  weather, describing
  .... INCLEMENT
unfeasible .... IMPRACTICAL
unfeeling .... NUMB, CRUEL,
  STONY, CALLOUS, HEARTLESS,
  INSENSATE, INSENSIBLE,
  HARD(-HEARTED)
unfeigned .... DIRECT, HONEST,
  UNDISGUISED
unfermented grape juice
  .... STUM
unfettered .... LOOSE, UNCHAINED
unfinished .... CRUDE, ROUGH,
  SKETCHY, INCOMPLETE
unfit .... INAPT, INEPT, UNABLE,
  UNSUITED
  to eat .... INEDIBLE
unfix .... DETACH, LOOSEN
unflappable .... CALM, FIRM
unflattering .... BLUNT, FRANK,
  CANDID, DEROGATORY
unflawed .... IDEAL
unfledged .... CALLOW
  bird .... EYAS, NESTLING
unflinching ...... FIRM, RESOLUTE,
  STEADFAST
unfold .... OPEN, EVOLVE, EXPOSE,

  REVEAL, SPREAD, UNFURL,
  UNROLL, DEVELOP, DISCLOSE
  in a verse .... OPE
unforeseen .... SUDDEN,
  UNEXPECTED, OUT-OF-THE-
  BLUE
unforgettable .... MEMORABLE
unforgiving .... VENGEFUL
unfortunate .... HAPLESS,
  UNLUCKY, ILL-STARRED
unfounded .... IDLE, BASELESS,
  GROUNDLESS
unfrequented .... LONELY,
  SOLITARY
unfriendly .... ILL, COLD,
  HOSTILE, INIMICAL,
  UNGENIAL, UNSOCIAL,
  ANTAGONISTIC
unfrock .... OUST, DEPOSE
unfruitful .... BARREN, STERILE,
  INFERTILE
unfulfilled .... UNATTAINED,
  UNSATISFIED
unfurl .... WAVE, SPREAD,
  UNFOLD, UNROLL, DISPLAY
ungainly .... UGLY, GAWKY,
  CLUMSY, AWKWARD
ungenerous .... STINGY
unglorified .... UNSUNG
unglued .... UPSET
ungodly .... BAD, PAGAN,
  UNHOLY, WICKED, IMPIOUS,
  PROFANE, SATANIC, DREADFUL
ungovernable ...... WILD, UNRULY,
  HEADSTRONG, REBELLIOUS
ungracious .... RUDE, UNCIVIL,
  IMPOLITE, UNFRIENDLY
ungrateful .... INGRATE
ungual growth ...... CLAW, HOOF,
  NAIL, TALON
unguarded .... CARELESS,
  UNDEFENDED, THOUGHTLESS
unguent .... BALM, SALVE,
  CHRISM, POMADE, OINTMENT
unguis .... CLAW, HOOF, NAIL,
  TALON, UNGULA
ungula .... CLAW, HOOF, NAIL,
  TALON, UNGUIS
ungulate ...... COW, HORSE, TAPIR,
  CATTLE, HOOFED
unhappy ...... SAD, BLUE, DISMAL,
  GLOOMY, MOROSE, JOYLESS,
  WRETCHED, MISERABLE
unharmed .... SAFE
unhealthy .... FRAIL, AILING,
  MORBID, SICKLY, OMINOUS
unheard-of .... UNBELIEVABLE
unhidden .... OPEN, FOUND,
  EXPOSED
unhinge .... DERANGE
unhinged .... DAFT, CRAZY

unhitch .... DETACH, RELEASE,
  UNFASTEN
unholy .... WICKED, IMPIOUS,
  PROFANE, UNGODLY
unhorse .... SPILL, UPSET,
  OVERTHROW
unhurried .... EASY
unicellular animal .... AM(O)EBA,
  PROTOZOAN
unicorn .... LIN, REEM,
  MONOCERO
  fish .... UNIE
  whale .... NARWHAL
unidentified flying object
  .... UFO
uniform .... EVEN, HABIT, OUTFIT,
  STABLE, STEADY, EQUABLE,
  STANDARD, UNVARYING,
  CONSISTENT
  servant's .... LIVERY
  shoulder ornament
  .... EPAULET(TE)
unify .... JOIN, WELD, UNITE,
  COMBINE, INTEGRATE,
  CONSOLIDATE
unilateral .... ONE-SIDED
unimpeachable .... CLEAN,
  INNOCENT, RELIABLE,
  BLAMELESS
unimportant .... PETTY, PUERILE,
  TRIVIAL, WORTHLESS,
  IMMATERIAL
  item .... NOTION
  slang .... PUNK
  things .... TRIVIA
uninformed .... IN-THE-DARK
uninhabited .... DESOLATE,
  TENANTLESS
uninhibited ...... FREE, NATURAL,
  UNRESERVED, UNSUPPRESSED
unintelligible .... MUMBLED,
  INCOHERENT, MEANINGLESS
  chatter .... GIBBER(ISH)
  handwriting ...... CACOGRAPHY
  language .... JARGON, PIDGIN
unintentional .... FORCED,
  UNPLANNED, UNWITTING,
  ACCIDENTAL, INADVERTENT
uninterested .... BORED
uninteresting .... DRY, DULL
uninterrupted .... CONSTANT,
  UNBROKEN, CONTINUOUS
unintimidated .... UNCOWED
uninvited .... UNASKED,
  UNWANTED, UNWELCOME
  person in a party .... GATE-
  CRASHER
uninvolved .... FREE, NEUTRAL
union .... UNITY, FUSION, LEAGUE,
  MERGER, CONCORD, LIAISON,
  ONE(NESS), ALLIANCE,

JUNCTION, MARRIAGE,
COALITION, CONNECTION,
COMBINATION
business .... CARTEL,
SYNDICATE
collection .... DUES
dues deduction ...... CHECKOFF
from birth .... CONNATION
jack .... FLAG
labor .... ARTEL
member .... FELLOW,
CARDHOLDER
merchants' .... HANSE
of nations, states ..... LEAGUE,
FEDERATION
of political intriguers
.... CABAL, JUNTA
of South Africa town
............................., MAFEKING
political ...... BLOC, COALITION
soldier .... YANKEE
trade .... GUILD
unionist .... TORY, JOINER,
FEDERALIST, CONSERVATIVE
unique .... LONE, ONLY, RARE,
SOLE, SINGLE, SPECIAL,
UNUSUAL, PECULIAR,
SINGULAR, MATCHLESS,
UNEQUALED
altogether .... SUIGENERIS
person .... ONER
unisexual .... DICLINOUS,
DIOECIOUS
unison ...... CONCORD, HARMONY,
AGREEMENT, UNANIMITY
utter in .... CHORUS
Unisphere, part of .... ASIA
unit .... ACE, ONE, ATOM, ITEM,
DIGIT, MONAD, PIECE,
MODULE, SINGLE, INTEGER,
STANDARD
Army Advance .... VAN
caloric .... THERM
capacitance .... FARAD
charge .... RATE
electrical .... REL, VOLT,
WATT, AMPERE
electro-magnetic .... FARAD
factor .... GENE
for measure of motor power
.... HORSEPOWER
for measure of
thermonuclear weapon
power .... KILOTON
in medicine .... DOSE, DOSAGE
of acceleration .... GAL
astronomical distance
.... PARSEC, SECPAR, LIGHT
YEAR
brightness, c g s
.... LAMBERT

capacity .... PINT, LITRE,
QUART, GALLON, KILOBYTE,
(KILO)LITER
conductance .... MHO
distance .... ROD, MILE,
SPAN, LEAGUE, FURLONG,
KILOMETER
dry measure ..... PECK, PINT,
QUART, BUSHEL
electric power .... KILOWATT
electrical resistance .... OHM
energy .... ERG, ERGON,
JOULE, KILERG
fluidity .... RHE
force .... OD, DENE, DYNE
heat .... THERM, CALORIE
illumination .... PHOT
instruction .... LESSON
length ..... FOOT, INCH, MILE,
YARD, CUBIT, DIGIT, METER,
METRE, MICRON, ANGSTROM,
KILOMETER
length of a stride .... PACE
light .... LUX, LUMEN
loudness .... SONE
luminous intensity .... NIT
magnetic intensity
.... OERSTED
magnetism .... GAUSS
measure for angles
.... DEGREE
metric measure .... ARE,
METER, HECTARE, CENTIARE
metrical time .... MORA
parliament follower
.... ARIAN
pressure .... TORR, BARAD,
BARYE, KILOBAR
quantity of electricity
.... FARADAY
radioactivity .... CURIE
reluctance .... REL
speed .... KNOT
value .... POINT
verse .... QUATRAIN
volume .... CUBIC-FEET,
CUBIC-INCH, CUBIC-YARD,
CUBIC-METER, CUBIC-
CENTIMETER
weight ..... KEG, TON, DRAM,
GRAM, KEEL, CARAT,
MAUND, OUNCE, POUND,
BUSHEL, KILO(GRAM),
MILLIGRAM
weight, smallest .... GRAIN
work .... ERG(ON), JOULE,
KILERG, KILOGRAMMETER
ultimate .... MONAD
wire .... MIL
unite .... MIX, ONE, WED, FUSE,
JOIN, WELD, BLEND, MARRY,

MERGE, PIECE, COMBINE,
COALESCE, FEDERATE
united .... ATONE
United Arab Republic country
.... EGYPT, SYRIA
Kingdom national flag
.... UNION JACK
Kingdom, part of
.... IRELAND, GREAT BRITAIN
Nations (see **UN**)
States (see **US/American**)
unity ...... PEACE, UNION, ACCORD,
FUSION, UNISON, CONCORD,
HARMONY, ONENESS,
COHERENCE, SOLIDARITY
univalent .... SINGLE, UNPAIRED
univalve .... SNAIL, MOLLUSK
shell's edge .... LABRUM
universal .... ASTRAL, COSMIC,
ENTIRE, GLOBAL, EARTHLY,
GENERAL, GENERIC,
CATHOLIC, PANDEMIC,
ECUMENIC(AL)
language .... IDO, VOLAPUK,
ESPERANTO
remedy .... AZOTH
ruler, 12th century
.... GENGHIS KHAN
universe .... EARTH, WORLD,
COSMOS, CREATION,
MACROCOSM
of the .... VAST, COSMIC
university .... ACADEMY,
INSTITUTE
business agent .... SYNDIC
composition of .... SCHOOLS,
COLLEGES
for clergy .... SEMINARY
grounds .... CAMPUS
group .... SORORITY,
FRAT(ERNITY)
lecturer .... PRELECTOR
official .... DEAN, BEADLE,
BURSAR, RECTOR, REGENT,
PROCTOR, PROVOST, TRUSTEE,
REGISTRAR
professorship .... CHAIR
program of studies
.... CURRICULUM
rank .... DEGREE
teacher .... PROFESSOR,
INSTRUCTOR
team .... VARSITY
unjust .... UNDUE, BIASED,
UNFAIR, PARTIAL
unjustly .... UNDULY
unkempt .... CRUDE, MESSY,
RATTY, ROUGH, SEEDY,
SHABBY, SHAGGY, UNTIDY,
SLOVENLY, UNCOMBED
unkind .... CRUEL, HARSH,

BRUTAL, SEVERE, INHUMAN

unknown .... UNCO, OBSCURE,
STRANGE, NAMELESS,
INCOGNITO
person .... ANONYM, JANE DOE,
JOHN DOE
writer, describing an
.... ANONYMOUS
**Unknown Soldier's Tomb
inscription ending: Known
But to _____** .... GOD
unlace .... UNTIE, LOOSEN,
UNFASTEN
unlatch .... OPEN
unlawful ...... CROOKED, ILLEGAL,
ILLICIT, CRIMINAL
act .... CRIME
goods/trade .... CONTRABAND
hunting .... POACHING
importation .... SMUGGLING
intrusion .... TRESPASS,
ENCROACHMENT
liquor .... BOOTLEG
seizure of power
.... USURPATION
unlearned .... IGNORANT,
ILLITERATE
unleash .... RELEASE, SET FREE,
(UN)LOOSE, UNSHACKLE
unleavened .... AZYMOUS
unless .... BUT, SAVE, EXCEPT,
BARRING
unlettered .... IGNORANT,
ILLITERATE, UNEDUCATED
unlike .... DISTINCT, DIFFERENT,
DISSIMILAR
unlikely .... FAR-FETCHED
unlimited .... FULL, VAST,
ABSOLUTE, INFINITE,
BOUNDLESS
limit .... SKY
unload .... RID, DUMP, EMPTY,
REMOVE, OFFLOAD,
UNBURDEN
unlock ...... OPEN, UNDO, REVEAL,
UNBOLT
unloose .... UNDO, UNTIE,
RELEASE, UNFASTEN
unlucky .... DOOMED, HAPLESS,
HOPELESS, ILL-FATED, ILL-
STARRED, UNFORTUNATE
fighters ...... POWS, PRISONERS-
OF-WAR
gem, believed to be ...... OPAL
unmake .... RUIN, DESTROY
unman .... WEAKEN, UNNERVE,
CASTRATE, ENERVATE
unmanageable .... UNRULY
unmanly .... EFFEMINATE
unmannerly ...... RUDE, CADDISH,
IMPOLITE, DISCOURTEOUS

unmarried .... UNWED, SINGLE,
DIVORCED
in law .... SOLE
man ...... BACHELOR, CELIBATE
state .... CELIBACY,
MAIDENHOOD
woman ...... MAIDEN, SPINSTER
unmask .... REVEAL, DISCLOSE
unmentionables ...... UNDERWEAR
unmerciful .... COLD-BLOODED,
HARD-HEARTED
unmistakable ...... CLEAR, OVERT,
PLAIN, EVIDENT, OBVIOUS,
APPARENT
unmitigated .... SHEER, UTTER,
ARRANT
unmixed drink .... NEAT
unmoved .... FIRM, INSENSATE,
UNAFFECTED, UNCONVINCED
unnatural .... STAGY, ABNORMAL,
AFFECTED, ARTIFICIAL
unnecessary .... NEEDLESS,
SUPERFLOUS
unnerve .... SHAKE, SHOCK,
UNMAN, RATTLE, UNHINGE
unobtrusive .... SHY, TIMID,
MODEST
unoccupied .... IDLE, EMPTY,
VACANT
unofficial .... TENTATIVE
unorganized .... DISORDERLY
unorthodox .... HERETICAL,
NONCONFORMIST
unowing .... SOLVENT
unpaid .... DUE, OWING
unpaired .... ODD, SINGLE,
UNIVALENT
unpalatable .... INSIPID, INEDIBLE,
UNSAVORY, TASTELESS
unperturbed .... SERENE
unpleasant .... BAD, MESSY,
NASTY, SURLY, NOISOME,
UNSAVORY, OFFENSIVE,
SICKENING, UNFRIENDLY,
DISAGREEABLE
unpleasantness .... SPAT,
QUARREL
unplowed ...... FALLOW, UNTILLED
unpolished .... RAW, CRUDE,
COARSE, AGRESTIC
unpopular .... DISLIKED
unprecedented ...... NEW, NOVEL
unpredictable .... CASUAL,
FICKLE, CAPRICIOUS
unprejudiced .... FAIR, UNBIASED,
IMPARTIAL
unpremeditated ...... IMPROMPTU,
IMPULSIVE, SPONTANEOUS
unprepared .... COLD, UNFIT,
UNREADY, HAPHAZARD,
SURPRISED

unpressed .... BAGGY, SEEDY,
RUMPLED
unpretentious .... MODEST
unprincipled .... EVIL, WICKED,
IMMORAL, UNSCRUPULOUS
unprintable usually .... OBSCENE,
OBSCENITY, VULGAR(ITY)
unproductive .... BARREN,
STERILE, IMPOTENT, INFERTILE
unprofessional ...... AMATEURISH
unprofitable ...... FUTILE, OTIOSE,
USELESS, BOOTLESS,
WORTHLESS
unpromising .... HOPELESS
unpropitious .... INOPPORTUNE
unqualified .... SHEER, UNFIT,
ABSOLUTE, COMPLETE,
OUTRIGHT
unquenchable .... ARID,
PARCHED, THIRSTY
unquestionable .... SURE,
CERTAIN
unravel .... FEAZE, SOLVE, TEASE,
UNFOLD, DEVELOP, UNTANGLE
unreadable .... ILLEGIBLE
unreal .... FALSE, FANCIED,
FANCIFUL, IMAGINARY,
FICTITIOUS
unreasonable ...... INANE, UNDUE,
ABSURD, STUBBORN,
ILLOGICAL, SENSELESS,
IRRATIONAL
unreasoning devotion .... FETISH
unredeemed territory
.... IRREDENTA
unreel .... UNWIND
unrefined .... RAW, RUDE, BRUTE,
CRASS, CRUDE, GROSS,
COARSE, COMMON, VULGAR,
NATURAL
unrelenting .... STERN, ADAMANT,
UNYIELDING
unreliable .... UNSURE, FALLIBLE,
UNCERTAIN
unremitting .... CHRONIC,
ENDLESS, NON-STOP,
INCESSANT, PERSISTENT
unrequited .... IGNORED,
SCORNED
unreserved .... OUTSPOKEN
unresolved .... UP-IN-THE-AIR
unrest .... FERMENT, DISQUIET,
AGITATION, INSURGENCE
unrestrained .... LAX, FREE,
LOOSE
unrestraint .... CANDOR
unrestricted .... WIDE-OPEN
unripe .... CRUDE, GREEN,
IMMATURE, PREMATURE
unrivaled .... PEERLESS,
MATCHLESS, NONPAREIL,

UNEQUALED

unroll .... OPEN, UNFURL, DISPLAY

unroot .... STUB, ERADICATE

unruffled .... CALM, COOL, POISED, SEDATE, SERENE, SMOOTH, UNFAZED

unruly .... WILD, BALKY, RESTIVE, FRACTIOUS, BOISTEROUS, DISORDERLY, INTRACTABLE

child .... BRAT

hair .... COWLICK

unsafe .... RISKY

unsatisfactory .... FAILING, WANTING, INADEQUATE

unsavory .... VILE, ACERB, ACRID, HARSH, NASTY, INSIPID, OFFENSIVE, REPULSIVE, TASTELESS, UNPLEASANT

unsay .... DENY, RETRACT, DISCLAIM

unscathed .... SAFE, UNHARMED

unschooled .... ILLITERATE, UNEDUCATED

unscientific .... UNTRUE, UNSOUND, UNPROVED

unscramble .... CRACK, SOLVE, DECODE, CLEAR UP, UNRAVEL, DECIPHER, UNTANGLE

unscrupulous .... DISHONEST, UNETHICAL, UNPRINCIPLED

person .... CHEAT(ER), SWINDLER

unseal .... OPEN

unseasonable .... UNTIMELY

unseasoned .... RAW, GREEN, UNVERSED, FLEDGLING

unseat .... OUST, DEPOSE, UNHORSE, DISLODGE, DISPLACE

unseemly ...... UNDUE, IMPROPER, UNFITTING, INDECOROUS, UNBECOMING

unseen .... INVISIBLE

unselfish .... LIBERAL, GENEROUS, SELFLESS, ALTRUISTIC

unselfishness .... ALTRUISM, FAIRNESS, GENEROSITY

unsettle .... UPSET, DISTURB, DISPLACE

unsettled .... MOOT, SHAKY, UNPAID, TROUBLED, UNSTABLE, UNCERTAIN

unsettling ...... JARRING, JOLTING, UPSETTING

unshaken .... TRUE, FIXED, STEELY

unshaven .... BEARDED, WHISKERED

unsheathe .... DRAW, DIVEST

unsightly .... UGLY, MESSY, UNGAINLY, UNATTRACTIVE

unskilled .... INAPT, INEPT, CLUMSY, AMATEUR, AWKWARD, HALF-BAKED

one .... KLUTZ

one at sports .... HACKER

unsmiling .... GRAVE, SOLEMN, SERIOUS

and grim .... DOUR

unsociable .... SHY, ALOOF, DISTANT

unsolicited .... VOLUNTARY

unsophisticated .... NAIVE, SIMPLE, SQUARE, ARTLESS, INNOCENT, INGENIOUS

unsound .... FAULTY, SICKLY, ILLOGICAL

unsounded .... MUM, MUTE, HUSHED

unsparing .... LAVISH, SEVERE, LIBERAL, PROFUSE

unspeakable .... VILE, WICKED, SHOCKING

unspoiled .... FRESH, WHOLE(SOME)

unspoken .... TACIT, SILENT, UNSAID, IMPLIED

unstable .... FICKLE, LABILE, ASTATIC, ERRATIC, VARIABLE, CHANGEABLE, INCONSTANT

unsteady .... SHAKY, INFIRM, ERRATIC, WOBBLY, UNSTABLE, WAVERING

unsubstantial .... FLIMSY, PAPERY, SLIGHT, UNREAL, IMMATERIAL, INTANGIBLE

unsuccessful .... LICKED, ABORTIVE, BOOTLESS

unsuitable .... INAPT, UNFIT(TING)

name .... MISNOMER

unsullied .... PURE, CHASTE, INNOCENT, VIRGIN(AL)

unsung .... IGNORED

unsure ...... DOUBTFUL, IGNORANT

unsurpassed ...... BEST, PEERLESS

unsusceptible .... CONSTANT, INFLEXIBLE

to disease .... IMMUNE

unsuspecting .... UNAWARE, TRUSTING

unswayable .... FIRM

unswayed .... UNBIASED, IMPARTIAL

unsweet .... SOUR, TART, ACERB

unsweetened .... DRY, SEC

unswerving .... FIRM, DIRECT, STEADY, STRAIGHT

unsymmetrical .... ALOP

unsympathetic ...... COLD, HARD, UNKIND, OBDURATE, HEARTLESS, UNCOMPASSIONED

untamed .... WILD, FERAL,

FERINE, SAVAGE, UNRULY

state .... FERITY

untangle .... COMB, (UN)RAVEL, STRAIGHTEN

untanned hide .... KIP, PELT, SHAGREEN

untenable .... INDEFENSIBLE

untenanted ...... EMPTY, VACANT, AVAILABLE

untended .... UNCARED, NEGLECTED

unterseeboot .... UBOAT, SUBMARINE

untested .... UNTRIED

unthinkable .... ABSURD, BEYOND BELIEF

untidy .... DOWDY, MESSY, MUSSY, SLOPPY, LITTERY, UNKEMPT, LITTERED, SLIPSHOD, SLOVENLY

animal .... PIG

person .... SLOB, SLOVEN, SLATTERN

place .... PIGPEN, (PIG)STY

untie ...... FREE, UNDO, LOOSE(N), UNBIND

until .... TILL, UNTO, (UP)TO, BEFORE, PENDING

now .... AS YET

untimely .... LATE, EARLY, PREMATURE, INOPPORTUNE

unto .... TO, TILL, UNTIL

untold .... LEGION, UNKNOWN, COUNTLESS, INNUMERABLE, UNDISCLOSED, INCALCULABLE

untouchable ...... LEPER, EXEMPT, BRAHMAN, SACRED COW

Untouchables' Eliot .... NESS

untouched .... PURE, VIRGIN, PRISTINE

untoward .... ADVERSE, PERVERSE, UNFAVORABLE, UNFORTUNATE

untrained ...... GREEN, UNTAMED, UNSKILLED

untreated .... RAW, UNPROCESSED

untrue .... FALSE, NOT SO, WRONG, DISLOYAL, FAITHLESS, FALSIFIED, UNFOUNDED, UNFAITHFUL

untruth .... FIB, LIE, FABLE, LYING, CANARD, FICTION, FALSEHOOD, MENDACITY

on the witness stand .... PERJURY

untwine .... (UN)RAVEL

untwist .... FEAZE, (UN)RAVEL, STRAIGHTEN

unusual .... ODD, RARE, NOVEL, OUTRE, QUEER, UNIQUE, ABNORMAL, PECULIAR, SINGULAR, UNCOMMON be .... TAKE THE CAKE

unvarnished .... PLAIN, SIMPLE, LITERAL

unvarying .... EVEN

sound .... DRONE, MONOTONE

unveil .... REVEAL, UNMASK, UNCOVER, DISCLOSE

unvoiced .... SURD, MUTED, ELIDED

unwanted fat .... FLAB

unwary .... RASH, UNWISE, CARELESS

unwed .... SINGLE

unwell .... ILL, SICK, AILING

unwholesome .... HARMFUL, NOXIOUS, NOISOME, PECCANT, DISEASED, STINKING, UNHEALTHY, DISTASTEFUL

unwieldy .... BULKY, CLUMSY, AWKWARD, UNGAINLY, PONDEROUS, CUMBERSOME

colloquial .... HULKING

ship .... ARK, HULK

unwilling .... BALKY, LOATH, AVERSE, FORCED, OPPOSED, GRUDGING, RELUCTANT

in days of yore .... NILL

to be photographed .... CAMERA-SHY

unwind .... RAVEL, RELAX, UNCOIL, UNREEL

unwise .... FOOLISH, UNSOUND, TACTLESS, IMPOLITIC, ILL-ADVISED

unwitting .... BLIND, UNAWARE, INNOCENT, UNCONSCIOUS

unwonted .... RARE, UNUSED, UNUSUAL, UNACCUSTOMED

unworldly .... ASTRAL, SPIRITUAL

unworthy .... INDIGN, WORTHLESS, UNDESERVED, UNDESERVING

of .... BENEATH

unwrinkled .... SMOOTH

unwritten .... BLANK, UNRECORDED

but understood .... TACIT

law .... CUSTOM, TRADITION

unyielding .... PAT, SET, FAST, FIRM, GRIM, HARD, IRON, RIGID, STEELY, ADAMANT, AUSTERE, OBDURATE, STUBBORN

up .... OVER, ABOVE, ALOFT, ARISEN, HIGHER

and about .... ASTIR

-and-coming .... PROMISING

front .... AHEAD

in _____ (aged) .... YEARS

in arms .... ANGRY, IRATE

prefix .... ANA

to _____ (in debt) .... OUR

EARS

-to-the-minute .... RED-HOT

up, _____ (impede) .... GUM

(wroth) .... HET

Upanishad .... ISHA

upas tree poison .... ANTIAR

upbeat ...... ARSIS, BRISK, LIVELY

upbraid ...... TWIT, CHIDE, SCOLD, SCORE, ACCUSE, BERATE, REBUKE, REVILE, CENSURE, REPROVE, ADMONISH, REPROACH

upbringing .... BREEDING, TRAINING

upcountry .... INLAND

update .... REVISE, MODERNIZE

Updike novel .... COUPLES, RABBIT REDUX

upend .... UPSET, TOPPLE, OVERTHROW

upgrade .... RAISE, BETTER, IMPROVE

upheaval .... STORM, REVOLT, UNREST, DEBACLE, AGITATION, CONVULSION

uphill .... RISING, DIFFICULT

uphold .... BACK, CONFIRM, SUPPORT, SUSTAIN, ADVOCATE, CHAMPION

upholstery ...... DOSSAL, DOSSEL, GOBELIN

material .... FRISE, SCRIM, LAMPAS, MOHAIR, MOREEN, VELURE, TABARET, VALANCE, VELOUR(S), MOQUETTE

stuffing .... FLOCK

upkeep .... CARE, REPAIR, PENSION, MAINTENANCE

upland .... MESA, PLATEAU

country .... TIBET

plover .... SANDPIPER

uplift .... RAISE, ELEVATE, BRASSIERE

Upolu town/seaport .... APIA

upon .... BY, ON, ATOP, OVER, ABOUT, ABOVE, UP AND ON, AGAINST, THROUGH, REGARDING

oxygen .... EPOXY

upper ...... VAMP, BERTH, HIGHER, SUPERIOR

air .... ETHER, OZONE

Amazon .... MARANON

case .... CAPITAL

class .... ELITE, MONEYED

classman .... JUNIOR, SENIOR

crust .... HIGH SOCIETY

hand .... LEAD, MASTERY, ADVANTAGE

house .... SENATE

limit .... CEILING

Upper Volta capital .... QUAGADOUGOU

city/town .... PO, LEO, KAYA, PAMA, YAKO, BANFORA, QUAHIGOUYA

language .... LOBI, SAMO, MOSSI, GOUROUNSI

monetary unit .... FRANC

president .... YAMEOGO, LAMIZAME

region .... SUDAN

river .... OTI, COMOE, RED VOLTA, BLACK VOLTA, WHITE VOLTA

uppermost .... FIRST

uppish/uppity .... PROUD, HAUGHTY, ARROGANT, SNOBBISH

one .... SNOOT

upright .... JUST, ERECT, ON END, HONEST, VERTICAL, HONORABLE

colloquial .... STRAIGHT

timber .... GATEPOST

uprise .... REBEL, SWELL, ASCEND

uprising .... COUP, RIOT, (E)MEUTE, MUTINY, PUTSCH, REVOLT, REBELLION

1794 tax .... WHISKY REBELLION

uproar .... ADO, DIN, RIOT, BABEL, NOISE, BEDLAM, BUSTLE, CLAMOR, HUBBUB, RACKET, RUCKUS, TUMULT, DISCORD, TURMOIL, BROUHAHA, COMMOTION, PANDEMONIUM

uproot ...... GRUB, STUB, ABOLISH, DESTROY, SUPPLANT, ERADICATE, DERACINATE

upset .... ADO, SPOIL, SWAGE, BOTHER, DEFEAT, TOPPLE, CAPSIZE, DISTURB, PERTURB, TOP OVER, DISORDER, DISTRESS, OVERTURN, REVERSAL

in one way .... DERAIL(ED)

upshot .... EFFECT, RESULT, OUTCOME

upside down .... UPENDED, INVERTED, TOPSY-TURVY

upsilon-shaped bone ...... HYOID

upstage ...... SNUB, ALOOF, SHOW UP, SNOOTY, CONCEITED

upstart .... SNOB, PARVENU, WHIPPERSNAPPER

upswing .... PICKUP

uptight .... TENSE

up-to-date .... NEW, FRESH, MODERN, MODISH, TIMELY, CURRENT energy .... SOLAR

slang .... HIP, MOD

upturned nose .... PUG, SNUB

upward .... MORE, ALOFT

movement .... LIFT, SCEND

Ur location .... MESOPOTAMIA

Royal Cemetery discoverer

.... (LEONARD) WOOLLEY

Uraeus .... ASP, COBRA

place of an .... HEADDRESS

symbol .... ASP

Ural Altaic branch .... TATAR

Urania .... MUSE, APHRODITE

sphere of .... ASTRONOMY

uranic .... CELESTIAL

Uranus' discoverer .... HERSCHEL

mother .... GAEA, GAIA

offspring .... RHEA, CRONUS,

FURIES, SATURN, TITANS,

CYCLOPES

satellite .... ARIEL

wife .... GAEA

urban ...... CITY, TOWN, OPPIDAN,

METROPOLITAN

blight .... SMOG

plague .... CRIME

urbane .... SUAVE, SMOOTH,

AFFABLE, DEBONAIR,

POLISHED

urbanize .... CITIFY, POLISH,

REFINE

urchin .... IMP, BRAT, CHILD,

GAMIN, MUDLARK,

HEDGEHOG, (STREET)ARAB

urd .... PYROL

urde .... CLECHE

Urdu .... HINDUSTANI

uredo .... HIVES, URTICARIA

urethane .... HYPNOTIC, SEDATIVE

uretic .... URINARY, DIURETIC

Urfa .... EDESSA

Urga .... ULAN BATOR

urge ...... EGG, YEN, COAX, GOAD,

PROD, PUSH, SPUR, PLEAD,

PRESS, ALLEGE, EXHORT,

INCITE, INDUCE, ENTREAT,

IMPULSE, SOLICIT, ADVOCATE,

IMPORTUNE

urgency .... EXIGENCY

urgent .... RUSH, GRAVE, EXIGENT,

PRESSING, INSISTENT

Uriah .... HEEP

wife of .... BATHSHEBA

urial .... SHA, CORIAL

Uriel .... ARCHANGEL

urinary .... URIC, URETIC,

URINOUS, DIURETIC

calculus .... STONE, UROLITH

diversion device .... CATHETER

duct .... URETER, URETHRA

funnel-shaped ducts .... RENAL

PELVES

inflammation .... CYSTITIS

tract, branch of medicine

concerning ..... UROLOGY

filtering units .... GLOMERULI

imaging of the

.... UROGRAPHY

infection .... URETHRITIS

part of .... BLADDER,

KIDNEYS, URETERS, URETHRA

specialist .... UROLOGIST

stone .... CALCULUS

tube .... URETHRA

urinate .... PEE, WET, PIDDLE,

MICTURATE

urination, difficult

.... STRANGURY

excessive .... POLYURIA

involuntary .... ENURESIS

painful .... DYSURIA

urine .... PEE, PISS, WATER

blood in the .... HEMATURIA

composition, part of .... SALT,

UREA, WATER

container for .... BEDPAN,

URINAL

high level of glucose in

.... DIABETES(MELLITUS)

inherited disorder

.... PORPHYRIA

lack of production by

kidneys .... ANURIA

low production of

.... OLIGURIA

passage of .... MICTURITION

substance giving yellow

color to ...... UROCHROME

substance giving orange

color to .... RIFAMPIN

suffix .... URIA

test .... URINALYSIS

thrombolytic drug prepared

from human

.... UROKINASE

unrestrained natural

discharge of

.... INCONTINENCE

waste product in .... UREA,

URIC ACID, CREATININE

Uris, author .... LEON

Urkel, for one .... NERD

urn .... JAR, KIST, VASE, STEEN,

VESSEL

figurative .... GRAVE

for bones .... OSSUARY

handle .... EAR

shaped .... URCEOLATE

uroxanthin .... INDICAN

Ursa .... BEAR

Major .... GREAT BEAR

Minor .... LITTLE BEAR

ursine animal .... BEAR

birthplace .... DEN

howler .... MONKEY,

ARAGUATO

Urth .... NORN

urticaria .... HIVES, UREDO

urticate .... STING

Uruguay cape .... POLONIO,

SANTA MARIA

capital .... MONTEVIDEO

city/town .... LA PAZ, MINAS,

ROCHA, SALTO, RIVERA,

ARTIGAS, CARMELO, DOLORES,

DURAZNO, MERCEDES,

PAYSANDU, TRINIDAD,

MALDONADO, LAS PIEDRAS

cowboy .... GAUCHO

dam .... BONETE

department .... ROCHA, SALTO,

RIVERA, COLONIA, FLORIDA,

SAN JOSE, SORIANO,

PAYSANDU, CANELONES,

MONTEVIDEO

discoverer .... DIAZ

falls .... SALTO GRANDE

first colony .... COLONIA

island .... LOBOS, TIGRE,

FLORES

lagoon .... MERIN, NEGRA,

ROCHA, SAUCE, GARZON,

CASTILLOS

language .... SPANISH

measure ...... CUADRA, SUERTE

monetary unit .... PESO

president .... GESTIDO

river .... YI, AIGUA, NEGRO,

PANDO, PARAO, DAYMAN,

ARAPEY, OLIMAR, ALFEREZ,

CUAREIM, LA PLATA,

QUEQUAY, SAN JOSE, TACUARI,

URUGUAY, CORDOBES,

YAGUARON, CARAGUATA,

CEBOLLATI

weight .... QUINTAL

urus .... OX, TUR, AUROCHS

US. See also **American**

.... AMERICA, NEW WORLD,

UNCLE SAM, UNITED STATES

Air Force mascot ...... FALCON

Army mascot .... MULE

capitalist, famous .... ASTOR

capitol lobbyist

.... RAINMAKER

chemist .... UREY

-China relations ..... PINGPONG

DIPLOMACY

consumer advocate ..... RALPH

NADER

educator .... NEILSON

expatriate in Paris .... STEIN

first aviatrix .... HARRIET

QUIMBY

black Supreme Court
Justice .... THURGOOD
MARSHALL

black woman elected to
Congress .... SHIRLEY
CHISHOLM

casualty of the Cold War
.... JOHN BIRCH

Catholic president .... JFK,
(JOHN FITZGERALD)
KENNEDY

city with cable cars ..... SAN
FRANCISCO

Navy veteran elected
president .... JOHN
KENNEDY

Secretary of Energy
.... SCHLESINGER

Supreme Court Chief
Justice .... JOHN JAY

flag .... OLD GLORY

foreign broadcasts: abbr.
.... VOA

General Eisenhower ...... IKE,
DWIGHT

M. Smith .... HOLLAND,
"HOWLIN' MAD"

MacArthur .... DOUGLAS

Schwarzkopf .... NORMAN,
"STORMIN' NORMAN"

Stilwell .... JOSEPH,
"VINEGAR JOE"

von _____ .... STEUBEN

of Vietnam War
.... WESTMORELAND

Gov't security .... E BOND

Great Lakes, largest of the
.... SUPERIOR

one of the ..... ERIE, HURON,
ONTARIO, MICHIGAN,
SUPERIOR

smallest of the ..... ONTARIO

lawyers' assn. .... ABA

Marine Corps emblem, part
of ..... EAGLE, GLOBE, ANCHOR

fighting knife .... KA-BAR

mascot .... BULLDOG

motto .... SEMPER FIDELIS,
ALWAYS FAITHFUL

remarkable airplane
.... (THE) HARRIER

Military branch .... ARMY,
NAVY, AIR FORCE, MARINE
CORPS, NATIONAL GUARD

missile ..... ABLE, ARGO, JUNO,
NIKE, THOR, AGENA

naturalist .... THOREAU

Navy mascot .... GOAT

or USSR .... SUPERPOWER

personified as a woman
.... COLUMBIA

president, first .... GEORGE
WASHINGTON

Washington's chef
.... HERCULES

who fathered 15 children
.... JOHN TYLER

who received the Pulitzer
Prize .... KENNEDY

who resigned .... NIXON

presidential retreat .... CAMP
DAVID

former name of
.... SHANGRI-LA

principal mountains,

highest of the .... MCKINLEY

one of the .... ELBERT,
SHASTA, RAINIER, WHITNEY,
MAUNA KEA, MAUNA LOA,
MCKINLEY, MITCHELL

railroad .... AMTRAK

reformer .... RIIS

region ..... MIDWEST, SUNBELT,
DIXIELAND, EAST(COAST),
WEST(COAST), NEW ENGLAND

river .... RED, OHIO, GREEN,
SNAKE, HUDSON, MOBILE,
PEEDEE, ALABAMA, POTOMAC,
ARKANSAS, COLORADO,
COLUMBIA, MISSOURI,
SAVANNAH, CUMBERLAND,
SACRAMENTO, MISSISSIPPI

**state admitted to the
Union:**

1787 .... DELAWARE, NEW
JERSEY, PENNSYLVANIA

1788 .... GEORGIA, NEW
YORK, MARYLAND, VIRGINIA,
CONNECTICUT, NEW
HAMPSHIRE,
MASSACHUSETTS, SOUTH
CAROLINA

1789 .... NORTH CAROLINA

1790 .... RHODE ISLAND

1791 .... VERMONT

1792 .... KENTUCKY

1796 .... TENNESSEE

1803 .... OHIO

1812 .... LOUISIANA

1816 .... INDIANA

1817 .... MISSISSIPPI

1818 .... ILLINOIS

1819 .... ALABAMA

1820 .... MAINE

1821 .... MISSOURI

1836 .... ARKANSAS

1837 .... MICHIGAN

1845 .... TEXAS, FLORIDA

1846 .... IOWA

1848 .... WISCONSIN

1850 .... CALIFORNIA

1858 .... MINNESOTA

1859 .... OREGON

1861 .... KANSAS

1863 .... WEST VIRGINIA

1864 .... NEVADA

1867 .... NEBRASKA

1876 .... COLORADO

1889 .... MONTANA,
WASHINGTON, NORTH
DAKOTA, SOUTH DAKOTA

1890 .... IDAHO, WYOMING

1896 .... UTAH

1907 .... OKLAHOMA

1912 .... ARIZONA, NEW
MEXICO

1959 .... ALASKA, HAWAII

state with one-syllable name
.... MAINE

Surgeon General .... KOOP,
NOVELLO, ELDERS

traditional data
.... AMERICANA

watchdog agency .... FDA

watchdog for animals
.... ASPCA

waterway .... RED, OHIO,
PECOS, YUKON, BRAZOS,
COLORADO, COLUMBIA,
MISSOURI, MISSISSIPPI

USA in France .... EUA

USAF Academy cadet
.... DOOLIE

USSR, official language of
.... RUSSIAN

usage .... USE, HABIT, CUSTOM,
MANNER, PRACTICE,
TREATMENT

usance .... USE, USAGE

use .... WEAR, AVAIL, ENJOY,
HABIT, TREAT, USAGE,
WORTH, EMPLOY, CONSUME,
PURPOSE, SERVICE, UTILITY,
UTILIZE, EXERCISE, FUNCTION

a dabber .... INK

davit .... HOIST

gripping device .... TONG

hammer .... NAIL

hose .... WATER

pawnshop .... HOCK

stiletto .... STAB

stopwatch .... TIME

strop .... HONE

stump .... ORATE

all one's energy for a
purpose .... DEVOTE

anti-freeze .... DE-ICE

art gum .... ERASE

as a remedy .... ADHIBIT

as example .... CITE

cosmetics .... PAINT
divining rod .... DOWSE
efforts .... EXERT, STRIVE
experimentally .... TRY OUT
galoshes .... SLOSH
litotes .... UNDERSTATE
of another's property
.... USUFRUCT
of extreme pressure,
     influence .... ARM-
                                    TWISTING
profanity .... SWEAR
salve on skin .... APPLY
the needle .... SEW
to make profit, unethical
.... EXPLOIT
up .... EAT, DRAIN, SPEND,
     EXPEND, CONSUME, EXHAUST
wastefully .... SQUANDER
with the hand(s) .... HANDLE
used .... SECONDHAND
at a Western necktie party
.... NOOSE
the PA system .... PAGED
to .... ACCUSTOMED
up .... EATEN, SPENT,
     DEPLETED, EXHAUSTED
useful .... UTILE, HELPFUL,
     PRACTICAL, BENEFICIAL,
     FUNCTIONAL, SERVICEABLE
for drivers .... MAP
for snapshots .... ALBUM
quality .... ASSET
useless .... IDLE, VAIN, FUTILE,
     OTIOSE, INUTILE, NEEDLESS,
     POINTLESS, WORTHLESS
user .... BUYER, CONSUMER,
     EMPLOYER, UTILIZER,
     EXPLOITER, PURCHASER
of exit .... GOER
usher .... ESCORT, INDUCT,
     DOORMAN, FORERUN,
     INTRODUCE, DOORKEEPER
in .... HERALD, ANNOUNCE
Uskudar .... SCUTARI
Usnach, son of .... NOISE
Uspallata Pass .... LA CUMBRE
location .... ANDES
usquebaugh .... WHISK(E)Y
ustulate .... BLACKENED,
     DISCOLORED
usual .... NORMAL, WONTED,
     REGULAR, TYPICAL,
     EVERYDAY, HABITUAL,
     ORDINARY, CUSTOMARY
openers .... PAIRS
usually .... AS A RULE,
     COMMONLY, NORMALLY,
     GENERALLY, ORDINARILY
usurer .... SHYLOCK, VAMPIRE,

LOAN-SHARK, MONEYLENDER
usurp .... SEIZE, ASSUME,
                                    ARROGATE
usurper .... TYRANT, ARROGATOR,
                                    OPPRESSOR
usury .... SHYLOCKING, LOAN-
                                    SHARKING
slang .... HIGHWAY ROBBERY
Utah asphalt .... GILSONITE,
                                    UINTA(H)ITE
canyon ..... GRAY, DESOLATION
capital .... SALT LAKE CITY
city/town .... LOA, ROY, OREM,
     DELTA, LOGAN, MAGNA,
     OGDEN, PRICE, PROVO,
     KEARNS, LAYTON, MURRAY,
     TOOELE, VERNAL, BRIGHAM,
     HOLLADAY, BOUNTIFUL,
     TAYLORSVILLE
county ...... IRON, JUAB, KANE,
     RICH, UTAH, CACHE, DAVIS,
     EMERY, GRAND, PIUTE, WEBER,
     CARBON, MORGAN, SEVIER,
     SUMMIT, TOOELE, UINTAH,
     SANPETE, SALT LAKE
desert ...... SEVIER, ESCALANTE
Indian .... NAVAHO, NAVAJO,
                                    P(A)IUTE
lake .... BEAR, FISH, SWAN,
     UTAH, CLEAR, NORTH,
     POWELL, SEVIER, GREAT SALT,
     LITTLE SALT
lily .... SEGO
mountain .... NEBO, WAAS,
     ELLEN, KINGS, PEALE,
     DUTTON, EMMONS, NAVAJO,
     AGASSIZ, HILGARD, HILLERS,
     MARVINE, PENNELL
mountain range .... ABAJO,
     CEDAR, HENRY, UINTA,
     BEAVER, PAVANT, WAHWAH,
     MINERAL
national park .... ZION,
     ARCHES, CANYONLANDS
natives .... MORMONS
peak .... BALDY, KINGS,
     PROVO, DELANO, MONROE
plateau .... AQUARIUS,
     TAVAPUTS
river .... BEAR, GREEN, MALAD,
     PARIA, PRICE, UINTA, WEBER,
     WHITE, BEAVER, JORDAN,
     SEVIER, VIRGIN, DOLORES,
     FREMONT, SAN JUAN,
     COLORADO, DUCHESNE, SAN
     PITCH, ESCALANTE
salt flats .... BONNEVILLE
speedway .... SALT FLATS
state bird .... SEA GULL
state flower .... SEGO LILY

state nickname .... BEEHIVE
state tree .... SPRUCE
university .... BRIGHAM YOUNG
utensil .... TOOL, IMPLEMENT
kitchen .... TONG, KNIFE,
     LADLE, SCOOP, SIEVE, BEATER,
     FUNNEL, GRATER, SIFTER,
     SKIMMER, STRAINER, CAN
     OPENER
maker .... COPPERSMITH
uterus .... WOMB, MATRIX
condition .... TIPPED
disorder .... PROLAPSE,
     MENORRHAGIA,
     DYSMENORRHEA
growth .... MOLE, TUMOR
infection/inflammation
.... ENDOMETRITIS
lining .... ENDOMETRIUM
pain .... METRALGIA
part .... CERVIX, MUSCLE,
     ENDOMETRIUM
swelling .... MOLE
tumor .... POLYP, FIBROID
Uther's son .... ARTHUR
utile .... PRACTICAL
doubly .... REVERSIBLE
utility .... AID, VALUE, WORTH,
     BENEFIT, SERVICE, FUNCTION
craft .... JOLLY BOAT
utilize .... USE, AVAIL, SERVE,
     EMPLOY, HARNESS
utmost .... BEST, FULL, FINAL,
     TOTAL, EXTREME, VERIEST,
     FARTHEST, GREATEST,
     MAXIMUM, REMOTEST
extent .... LIMIT
Uto Aztecan Indian .... YAQUI
utopia .... HEAVEN, ARCADIA,
     PARADISE
almost literally .... NOWHERE
imaginary .... SHANGRI-LA
Utopia author .... (THOMAS)MORE
Utopian .... ROSY, IDEAL, EDENIC,
     DREAMER, ARCADIAN,
     VISIONARY, IDEALIST(IC)
land of the Israelites
.... CANAAN, GOSHEN
place .... PROMISED LAND
scheme .... BUBBLE
visions .... IDEALS
utricle .... SAC, VESICLE
Uttar Pradesh capital
.... LUCKNOW
city .... AGRA, MEERUT
part of .... OUDH
utter .... SAY, EMIT, RANK, ISSUE,
     MOUTH, SHEER, SPEAK,
     STARK, TOTAL, VOICE,
     BROACH, ENTIRE, DIVULGE,

EXPRESS, ABSOLUTE,
COMPLETE, DOWNRIGHT,
PRONOUNCE
defeat .... ROUT
in unison .... CHORUS
lovingly .... COO
utterance .... DICTUM, REMARK,
EXPRESSION

uttered ...... ORAL, SAID, SPOKEN,
VERBAL, VOICED
utterly .... FULLY, STARK,
ENTIRELY, COMPLETELY
uttermost .... LAST, FINAL,
UTMOST
U-turn .... ABOUT-FACE
uvarovite .... GARNET

color .... GREEN
uvea, inflammation of the
.... IRITIS, UVEITIS, CYCLITIS
part of the ...... IRIS, CHOROID,
CILIARY BODY
uxorial .... WIFELY
Uzbek capital .... TASHKENT
city .... KHIVA

V .... VERSUS, VOLUME,
VOLT(AGE)
author of .... PYNCHON
formation flyers .... GEESE
Greek .... UPSILON
Hebrew .... VAV
in chemistry .... VANADIUM
in math .... VECTOR, VELOCITY
letter/shaped .... VEE
Roman numeral for ____
.... FIVE
shaped cut .... NOTCH
shaped piece .... PIE, WEDGE
symbol .... VICTORY
V.A., part of .... VETERANS,
ADMINISTRATION
vaca .... COW
vacancy .... GAP, VOID, BLANK,
BREAK, SPACE, VACUUM,
OPENING, VACUITY,
EMPTINESS
vacant .... FREE, IDLE, OPEN,
VOID, BLANK, EMPTY,
HOLLOW, VACUOUS,
UNOCCUPIED, UNTENANTED
vacate .... QUIT, VOID, ANNUL,
EMPTY, LEAVE, DEPART
a throne formally
.... ABDICATE
dangerous area ..... EVACUATE
out of necessity .... ABANDON,
RELINQUISH
quickly .... FLEE
suddenly .... DECAMP
vacation .... REST, LEAVE, RECESS,
HOLIDAY, RESPITE, TIME OFF
military personnel's
.... FURLOUGH
vacationer, short-stay
.... WEEKENDER
vaccinate ...... INJECT, IMMUNIZE,
INOCULATE
vaccination .... SHOT(S),
IMMUNIZATION
pioneer .... JENNER
vaccine .... SERO, VIRUS,
ANTIDOTE

developer, injected polio
.... (JONAS)SALK
developer, oral polio
.... (ALBERT)SABIN
discoverer .... (EDWARD)
JENNER
vaccinia .... COWPOX
vacillate .... WAVER, FALTER,
TEETER, WHIFFLE, HESITATE,
FLUCTUATE, BLOW HOT AND
COLD
vacuity .... VOID, VACUUM,
INANITY, EMPTINESS
vacuous .... DULL, IDLE, INANE,
STUPID, EMPTY(-HEADED)
vacuum ...... VOID, SPACE, SWEEP,
VACANCY, EMPTINESS
-packed .... AIRTIGHT
opposed to .... PLENUM
tube .... DIODE, OCTODE,
TRIODE, ELECTRODE
tube element .... GRID, ANODE,
PLATE, CATHODE
vade mecum .... MANUAL,
HANDBOOK
vagabond .... BUM, VAG, (HO)BO,
WAFFIE, LOREL, TRAMP,
BEGGAR, RASCAL, TRUANT,
DRIFTER, VAGRANT,
RUNAGATE, WANDERER,
WANDERING, LANDLO(U)PER
vagabondage .... VAGRANCY,
VAGRANTS, WANDERING
vagary .... WHIM, FANCY, FOIBLE,
NOTION, ODDITY, CAPRICE
vagrancy .... NOMADISM
vagrant .... BUM, HOBO, SPIV,
CAIRD, ROVER, STRAY,
TRAMP, BEGGAR, AIMLESS,
NOMAD(IC), WAYWARD,
VAGABOND, WANDERER
bedding carried by .... BINDLE
fortune-telling .... GYPSY
greeting of ..... HOBO, HOBEAU
jargon of .... SHELTA
place in city .... SKID ROW
slang .... BINDLE-STIFF

vague .... DIM, HAZY, LOOSE,
MISTY, BLURRY, BLURRED,
OBSCURE, SKETCHY,
UNCLEAR, NEBULOUS,
AMORPHOUS, UNCERTAIN,
INDEFINITE
become .... BLUR
vagus .... NERVE
nerve disorder .... MENINGITIS,
PEPTIC ULCER
nerve surgery ...... VAGOTOMY
vail .... TIP, DOFF, GRATUITY
vain .... IDLE, PERT, SMUG,
COCKY, EMPTY, PROUD,
FUTILE, OTIOSE, HAUGHTY,
USELESS, CONCEITED,
FRUITLESS
and affected .... FOPPISH
bird .... PEACOCK
colloquial .... STUCK-UP
manners .... AIRS
person ...... FOP, PRIG, DANDY,
EGOIST, COXCOMB, EGOTIST,
COCKSCOMB, CHAUVINIST
quest .... WILD-GOOSE-CHASE
vainglorious .... BOASTFUL,
CONCEITED, OVERPROUD
vainglory ...... AIRS, POMP, PRIDE,
VANITY, CONCEIT,
ARROGANCE
vair .... FUR
valance .... CURTAIN, DRAPERY
vale .... DALE, GLEN, ADIEU,
DINGLE, VALLEY, FAREWELL
valediction .... ADIEU, SPEECH,
GOODBY(E), FAREWELL
valedictory .... ADDRESS,
ORATION
Valence's river .... RHONE
valentine .... BELOVED,
SWEETHEART, (GREETING)
CARD
figure on a .... EROS, CUPID
Valera (Eamon de) nickname
.... DEV
valerian .... PLANT, BENNET,
ALLHEAL, HEMLOCK

valet .... DRESSER, MANSERVANT
valetudinarian .... INFIRM, SICKLY, INVALID, HYPOCHONDRIAC
Valetta native .... MALTESE
valgus .... KNOCK-KNEE(D)
Valhalla group .... AESIR
healer at .... EIR
maiden .... VALKYR(IE)
presider at .... ODIN
valiant .... BOLD, BRAVE, DARING, GALLANT, LIONHEARTED
valid .... JUST, LEGAL, SOUND, COGENT, LAWFUL, BINDING, IN FORCE, DEFENSIBLE
not .... NULL, VOID
validate .... SEAL, ATTEST, RATIFY, CONFIRM, LEGALIZE, SANCTION, AUTHORIZE
validity .... FORCE, WEIGHT, COGENCY, LEGALITY, SOUNDNESS
valise .... BAG, SATCHEL, SUITCASE, GRIP(SACK), PORTMANTEAU
Valjean, _____ (Hugo's) .... JEAN
pursuer of .... (DETECTIVE) JAVERT
what he stole .... LOAF
Valkyrie .... BRYNHILD, BRUN(N)HILD(E)
love of .... SIGURD
vallation .... WALL, TRENCH, RAMPART, EARTHWORK
valley .... DALE, DELL, GLEN, VALE, WADI, COMB(E), COOMB, GLADE, GULCH, KLOOF, SWALE, BOLSON, CANYON, DINGLE, GUTTER, HOLLOW, STRATH
a deep narrow .... GORGE, KLOOF, COULEE
a wide river .... STRATH
Apollo's .... TEMPE
Argolis .... NEMEA
between cliffs .... CAN(Y)ON
entrance of .... JAWS
moon .... RILL(E)
rich in coal .... SAAR
where David fought Goliath .... ELAH
valor .... VIRTUE, BRAVERY, COURAGE, HEROISM, BOLDNESS, CHIVALRY
valorous .... BOLD, BRAVE, HEROIC, GALLANT, VALIANT, STOUT(HEARTED)
valse .... WALTZ, TRISTE
valuable .... DEAR, COSTLY, PRIZED, USEFUL, WORTHY, PRECIOUS

discovery .... FIND
valuation .... ESTIMATE, APPRAISAL
value .... COST, RATE, MERIT, PRICE, PRIZE, WORTH, ADMIRE, ASSESS, ESTEEM, RATING, APPRAISE, TREASURE, APPRECIATE
beyond amount owed .... EQUITY
highly .... CHERISH
more .... PREFER
of little .... TRIFLE, TRIVIAL, FARTHING, TRIFLING
valued seashell .... CONCH
valueless .... CHEAP, PALTRY, WORTHLESS
valve .... COCK, CUSP, PLUG, CUTOFF, DAMPEN, POPPET, SPIGOT, PETCOCK, STOPCOCK, FLOODGATE
defect, heart .... STENOSIS
engine .... CHOKE, THROTTLE
heart .... MITRAL
reconstructive operation, heart .... VALVULOPLASTY
sliding .... PISTON
surgery, heart .... VALVOTOMY
vamo(o)se .... GO, LAM, BLOW, SCAT, LEAVE, SCRAM, BEAT IT, DECAMP, DEPART, BUZZ OFF, SKIDDOO, SKEDADDLE
vamp .... FLIRT, TEMPT, UPPER, REPAIR, SEDUCE, BEGUILE, BEWITCH, COQUETTE, PATCH(WORK)
in music .... DESCANT
name, silent .... POLA
vampire ...... BAT, FLIRT, GHOUL, HARPY, LAMIA, SIREN, LILITH, MONSTER, TEMPTER, PARASITE, TEMPTRESS, SEDUCTRESS, BLOODSUCKER
insect .... FLEA
kind of .... USURER, BLACKMAILER, EXTORTIONIST
Pericles' .... ASPASIA
Samson's .... DELILAH
singing .... LORELEI, PARTHENOPE
Transylvania's .... DRACULA
who leads men to ruin .... FEMME FATALE
who turned men into swine .... CIRCE
wicked, shameless .... JEZEBEL
worm .... LEECH
vampirism .... BLOODSUCKING
van .... FORE, LEAD, WING, FRONT, LORRY, TRUCK, WAGON, CARAVAN, TRAILER,

VANGUARD
kind of .... MAIL, MOVING
man .... MOVER
Van Buren, U.S. president .... MARTIN
Diemen's land ...... TASMANIA
Doren, critic ...... CARL, MARK
Druten character .... MAMA
Gogh, painter .... VINCENT
Vance, sleuth .... PHILO
vandal .... HUN, MARRER, RUINER
vandalism .... SAVAGERY, SPOLIATION, DESTRUCTIVENESS
vandalize .... MAR, WRECK, DAMAGE, DEFACE, SABOTAGE
Vanderbilt, industrialist .... CORNELIUS
of perfume fame .... GLORIA
Vandyke .... BEARD, COLLAR, GOATEE
forte of .... PORTRAITS
painter .... ANTHONY
vane .... WIND GAUGE, ANEMOMETER, (WEATHER)COCK
of arrow .... FEATHER
of feather .... VEXILLUM
of windmill .... TAIL, WINDSAIL
vanguard .... VAN, LEAD(ER), FRONT(LINE)
military forces .... MARINES
of the arts .... AVANT-GARDE
vanilla .... ORCHID, FLAVORING
vanish .... FADE, MELT, DISSOLVE, EVANESCE, DISAPPEAR
vanity ...... AIRS, PRIDE, CONCEIT, EGO(T)ISM, FUTILITY, SELF-LOVE, VAINGLORY, DRESSING TABLE
case .... ETUI, COMPACT
Vanity Fair author .... THACKERAY
ex-editor of .... TINA BROWN
vanquish .... BEAT, BEST, LICK, ROUT, QUELL, DEFEAT, MASTER, SUBDUE, THRASH, SILENCE, CONQUER, OVERCOME, SURMOUNT, OVERPOWER, SUBJUGATE
vantage point .... COIGN
Vanzetti's partner .... SACCO
vapid .... DULL, FLAT, PALL, TAME, INANE, STALE, BORING, INSIPID, LIFELESS, TASTELESS
vapor ...... AIR, GAS, BRAG, DAMP, FUME, MIST, REEK, BRUME, CLOUD, ETHER, SMOKE, STEAM, BLUSTER, HALITUS
aircraft's .... CONTRAIL

colorless .... NEON, ARGON
combining form .... ATMO
in air .... FOG, HAZE, MIST,
SMOG
in stomach .... FLATUS
mass of .... WRACK
pressure instrument
.... TONOMETER, TENSIMETER
pure, fresh .... OZONE
vaporize .... SPRAY, STEAM,
GASIFY, ATOMIZE, DISTILL
vaporizer .... ETNA, STILL,
SPRAYER, ATOMIZER
example of .... INHALER
vaporous .... FUMY, FOGGY,
GASSY, MISTY, CLOUDY,
STEAMY, GASEOUS, REEKING,
HALITOUS
vaquero .... COWBOY, HERDER
Varangian .... RO, SCANDINAVIAN
Vargas, Brazilian president
.... GETULIO
variable .... FICKLE, UNEVEN,
MUTABLE, PROTEAN,
ABERRANT, SHIFTING,
VOLATILE, CHANGEABLE
star .... CEPHEID
variance .... ODDS, DISCORD,
DISSENT, DIVISION,
DIFFERENCE
variation .... CHANGE, VARIETY,
DEVIATION, DIVERSITY
slight .... SHADE, NUANCE
varicella .... CHICKENPOX
varicolored .... MOTTLED,
POLYCHROME, MULTICOLORED
cloth .... MOTLEY
phenomenon .... RAINBOW
varicose .... VARIX, CIRSOID,
DILATED, SWOLLEN
veins in the anus
.... HEMORRHOIDS
in the esophagus
.... VARICES
in the scrotum
.... VARICOCELE
surgery .... VARICOTOMY
treatment
.... SCLEROTHERAPY
varied .... MIXED, D(A)EDAL,
DIVERSE, VARIOUS, ASSORTED,
MISCELLANEOUS
tunes, musical piece from
.... MEDLEY
variegate .... VARY, DIVERSIFY
variegated .... PIED, VARIED,
CHECKED, DAPPLED, DIVERSE,
MOTTLED, SPOTTED, STRIPED,
VARICOLORED,
MULTICOLORED
animal .... ZEBRA, LEOPARD

bed cover .... QUILT
bits of paper .... CONFETTI
cloth .... PLAID, CALICO,
MOTLEY
design .... MOSAIC
horse .... PINTO, PIEBALD
insect .... BUTTERFLY
instrument ...... KALEIDOSCOPE
variety .... KIND, SORT, BRAND,
CLASS, DIVERSITY
act .... TURN
show .... SKIT, VAUDEVILLE
word .... SOCKO
variola .... SMALLPOX
scar .... POCKMARK
vaccination .... VARIOLATION
various .... MANY, SUNDRY,
DIVERSE, SEVERAL, DIFFERENT
items .... SUNDRIES
varlet .... CUR, PAGE, KNAVE,
RASCAL, COISTREL,
SCOUNDREL
varmint .... BEAST, BRUTE,
VERMIN
varnish .... COLOR, GLOSS, JAPAN,
ENAMEL, LACQUER,
BRIGHTEN, SHELLAC(K),
EMBELLISH, WHITEWASH
and linseed oil mix
.... MEGILP
material .... COPAL, ELEMI,
RESIN, MASTIC, SHELLAC,
TUNG(OIL), OLEORESIN,
TURPENTINE
resin .... LAC
varsity .... TEAM, COLLEGIATE
varus .... BOWLEG(GED)
opposite of .... VALGUS
vary ...... ALTER, CHANGE, DIFFER,
MODIFY, DEVIATE, DIVERGE,
DIVERSIFY, FLUCTUATE
vas .... DUCT, VESSEL
vascular organ .... PLACENTA
vase .... CUP, JAR, JUG, URN,
TAZZA, AMPHORA, CHALICE,
POTICHE, LACRIMAL,
JARDINIERE
base .... STOOL
making material .... MURRHINE
support .... PEDESTAL
vasectomy .... STERILIZATION
Vaseline .... JELLY, OINTMENT,
LUBRICANT, PETROLATUM
Vashti's successor .... ESTHER
vassal .... SERF, SLAVE, BONDMAN,
SERVANT, SUBJECT,
LIEGE(MAN), (FEUDAL)TENANT
heritable land by a .... FIEF
loyalty/service required of a
.... FEALTY, VASSALAGE
of/like a .... SERVILE

tax paid by .... TRIBUTE
vassalage .... FIEF, FEALTY,
SERVITUDE
Vassar's pride .... MILLAY
vast .... HUGE, LARGE, COSMIC,
IMMENSE, MASSIVE, OCEANIC,
SIZ(E)ABLE, ENORMOUS,
INFINITE
chasm .... ABYSS
vat .... BAC, KEG, TUB, TUN, CASK,
DRUM, KIER, TANK, KEEVE,
BARREL, CALDRON, CISTERN
for beer/wine .... CASK,
PUNCHEON
used in making dairy
product .... CHESSEL
vatic .... PROPHETIC
Vatican .... PAPACY, POPEDOM
art gallery .... BELVEDERE
basilica .... ST. PETER'S
chapel .... SISTINE
guard's nationality .... SWISS
sculpture .... PIETA
vaticinate .... PREDICT, FORETELL,
PROPHESY
vaticinator .... SEER, ORACLE,
PROPHET
Vaud .... CANTON
capital of .... LAUSANNE
vaudeville .... BURLESQUE,
VARIETY(SHOW)
performer .... HOOFER
Vaughn role .... SOLO
vault .... ARCH, CELL, COPE,
DOME, JUMP, LEAP, SAFE,
BOUND, SPRING, CATACOMB
burial .... TOMB, CRYPT,
GRAVE, SEPULCHER
concave .... COVE
for bones .... OSSUARY
horse's .... CURVET
inside curve/surface
.... INTRADOS
of heaven .... SKY
underground .... DONJON,
DUNGEON
vaulted .... ARCHED
roof .... DOME
vaunt .... BRAG, CROW, BOAST,
VAPOR, BLUSTER
vaunty .... VAIN, PROUD
vavasor .... VASSAL
veal .... GIGOT
of/like .... VITULINE
neck .... SCRAG
sausage .... BOLOGNA
slice .... SCHNITZEL
stew .... GOULASH
Veda, Atharva- .... HYMNS
Rig- .... PSALMS
Sama- .... CHANTS

Yajur- .... SACRED FORMULAS
Vedas, language of the
.... VED(A)IC, SANSKRIT
one of the .... RIG, SAMA,
YAJUR, ATHARVA
vedette .... SENTINEL,
SCOUT(BOAT)
Vedic .... PALI, SANSKRIT
god .... AGNI, DYAUS
goddess .... USHAS
sky serpent .... AHI
vee .... FIN, FIVER
veer .... YAW, SLUE, TURN, SHEER,
SHIFT, SWERVE, DEVIATE
veery .... THRUSH
Vega constellation .... LYRA
for one .... STAR
Veganova .... FIXED STARS
vegetable .... PEA, POD, BEAN,
BEET, LEEK, OKRA, SASS,
PLANT, SAUCE, TUBER,
CARROT, ENDIVE, LEGUME,
POTATO, TOMATO, CABBAGE,
LETTUCE
basket .... SCUTTLE
boiled, buttered .... VICHY
decaying matter .... DUFF
farmer .... TRUCKER
garden ...... TRUCK, KAILYARD,
KALEYARD
gas .... METHANE
growing art .... HORTICULTURE
leafstalk .... CHARD
life .... FLORA, GREENERY,
VEGETATION
marrow .... SQUASH
oyster .... SALSIFY
poison .... PTOMAIN(E)
pulse .... PEAS, BEANS,
LEGUME, LENTILS
root ..... BULB, ONION, TURNIP,
PARSNIP
sponge .... LOOFA, LUFFA,
LOOFAH
vegetables, garden .... SASS
grown for sale .... TRUCK
vegetarian ...... VEGAN, MEATLESS
colloquial .... HEALTH NUT
sea mammal .... DUGONG,
SEACOW, MANATEE
vegetate .... EXIST, STAGNATE
vegetation, combining form
.... PHYTO
covered with green
.... VERDANT
green .... VERDURE
luxuriant .... LUSH
vegetative state .... COMA
vehemence .... FIRE, FURY, RAGE,
ZEAL, ARDOR, FORCE, VIGOR,
FERVOR, WARMTH, PASSION,

VIOLENCE
vehement .... HOT, LOUD, ANGRY,
FIERY, ARDENT, BITTER,
FERVID, FERVENT, IMPETUOUS,
PASSIONATE, IMPASSIONED
vehemently .... EAGERLY,
STRONGLY, EARNESTLY
vehicle .... BUS, CAB, CAR, VAN,
AUTO, CART, JEEP, BUGGY,
TRAIN, WAGON, CAMPER,
SLED(GE), TRAILER,
CARRIAGE, CONVEYANCE
air .... GLIDER, BALLOON,
AIRCRAFT, AIRPLANE,
DIRIGIBLE, HELICOPTER,
CONVERTIPLANE
air cushion .... HOVERCRAFT
armored .... TANK, HALF-
TRACK
baby's/infant's .... PRAM,
STROLLER, PERAMBULATOR
covered .... AUTO, COUPE,
SEDAN, CARAVAN, HARDTOP,
SCHOONER
decrepit .... SHANDRYDAN
farm .... TRACTOR
for Clydesdales .... DRAY
for handicapped
.... WHEELCHAIR
for sick, wounded ..... LITTER,
STRETCHER
funeral .... HEARSE
horse-drawn .... SULKY,
CALASH, CALESA, CHARIOT,
PHAETON
hospital .... AMBULANCE
"last ride" .... HURDLE,
TUMBREL, TUMBRIL
luxurious .... LIMO(USINE)
man-drawn .... (JIN)RICKSHA
of a kind ...... TRAM, SUBWAY,
TROLLEY, CABLE-CAR,
STREETCAR, TOURING CAR
old, ramshackle .... JALOPY
on runners .... SLED(GE),
SLEIGH, TOBOGGAN
open .... ROADSTER,
CONVERTIBLE
parade .... FLOAT
pedalled .... BIKE, MOPED,
BICYCLE, TRICYCLE
running on rails .... LORRY
sightseeing .... CHARABANC
slow-moving .... SLUG
space .... ROCKET, SHUTTLE,
SATELLITE
two-wheeled .... SULKY,
CHARIOT, BAROUCHE
with runners, water
.... SCOOTER, SAILBOAT

without wheels/runnered
.... PUNG, SLED, SLEIGH,
TRAVOIS, TOBOGGAN
veil ...... CAUL, HAZE, HIDE, MASK,
MESH, CLOAK, COVER,
SCREEN, SHROUD, WIMPLE,
CONCEAL, CURTAIN,
YAS(H)MAK, MANTILLA
having a .... VELATE
in botany .... VELUM
material .... TULLE, BAREGE,
ILLUSION
papal .... ORALE
veiled .... HIDDEN, VELATE,
COVERED, DISGUISED
veiling .... TULLE, CURTAIN
vein .... LODE, MOOD, VENA,
HUMOR, TENOR, INTIMA,
PHLEBO, STREAK, TEMPER,
BLOOD VESSEL
blood clotting in a
.... THROMBOPHLEBITIS
branch .... VENULE
diagnostic procedure on a
.... VENOGRAPHY,
PHLEBOGRAPHY
disorder .... SWELLING,
VARICOSE, DISTORTION
formation in a .... CLOT
heart .... VENA CAVA
inflammation .... PHLEBITIS
kind of .... RENAL, AZYGOS,
HEPATIC, JUGULAR,
SUBCLAVIAN
layer .... INNER, OUTER,
MIDDLE, MUSCULAR
leaf .... RIB
mine .... LODE, REEF, LEDGE
mineral .... LODE
of ore .... SEAM
process of withdrawing
blood from a
.... PHLEBOTOMY,
VENESECTION
rich ore .... BONANZA
swollen/varicose .... VARIX
veining, art of .... MARBLING
veinless .... AVENOUS
veins collectively .... VENATION
having .... VENOSE, VENOUS,
NERVATE
veinstone .... GANGUE
velamen .... MEMBRANE
velar .... GUTTURAL
veld(t) .... GRASSLAND
Velez, actress .... LUPE
velleity .... WISH, DESIRE,
VOLITION
vellicate .... PLUCK, TWITCH
vellication .... TIC, JERK,
TWITCH(ING)

vellum .... PARCHMENT, (SHEEP)SKIN
velocipcdc .... BICYCLE, HANDCAR, TRICYCLE
velocity .... RATE, SPEED, CELERITY, RAPIDITY, SWIFTNESS
measuring device .... TACHOMETER
velum .... VELAMEN, SOFT PALATE
velure .... PAD, VELVET
velutinous .... VELVETY
velvet .... SILK, PLUSH, PANNE, VELOUR
slang .... GAIN, PROFIT, WINNINGS
velveteen .... FUSTIAN
velvety .... MILD, SOFT, MOSSY, MELLOW, SMOOTH
vena .... VEIN
venal .... SORDID, CORRUPT, VENDIBLE, MERCENARY
vend .... SELL, ISSUE, PURVEY, PUBLISH
vendace .... WHITEFISH
vendee .... BUYER
vender .... SELLER, ALIENOR
vendetta .... FEUD, GRUDGE, VENGEANCE
vendible ...... VENAL, SAL(E)ABLE
vendition .... SALE
vendor .... HAWKER, SELLER, PEDDLER, HUCKSTER, SALESMAN
route of a .... WALK
vendue .... AUCTION
veneer .... BURL, LAYER, SHELL, ENAMEL, FACADE, FACING, COATING, OVERLAY, VARNISH
venerable .... OLD, AGED, HOARY, REVERED
man .... SAGE, PATRIARCH
monk .... BEDE
venerate .... ADORE, HALLOW, REVERE, RESPECT, WORSHIP
venerated .... HOLY, SACRED
veneration .... AWE, ESTEEM, HOMAGE, RESPECT, WORSHIP ADORATION, REVERENCE
venereal disease .... SYPHILIS, CHANCROID, GONORRHEA
infection .... HERPES
infection: sl. .... CLAP, DOSE
sore/ulcer .... CHANCRE
venery .... CHASE, HUNTING
venesection .... PHLEBOTOMY
Venetia .... VENETO
Venetian barge .... BUCENTAUR
boat .... GONDOLA
boatman .... GONDOLIER

bridge/business center .... RIALTO
canals .... RII
(chief) magistrate .... DOGE
gondolier's song .... BARCAROL(L)E
island .... RIALTO
nobleman .... MAGNIFICO
painter .... TITIAN, TIEPOLO, VERONESE, TINTORETTO
red .... SIEN(N)A
resort .... LIDO
ruler/official .... DOGE
song .... BARCAROL(L)E
street .... CANAL
traveler .... (MARCO) POLO
Venezia .... VENICE
Venezuela cape .... CODERA
capital .... CARACAS
city/town .... CORO, RUBIO, TOVAR, UPATA, CUMANA, MERIDA, TARIBA, VALERA, ZARAZA, BARINAS, CABIMAS, BOLIVAR, EL TIGRE, GUACARA, TURMERO, ACARIGUA, CALABOZO, CARUPANO, POZUELOS, TUCUPITA, TRUJILLO, VALENCIA, BARCELONA, MARACAIBO
city on the lake .... MARACAIBO
copper center .... AROA
dam .... GURI
discoverer of .... COLUMBUS
falls .... (SALTO)ANGEL
fish .... GUPPY
gulf .... PARIA, TRISTE
Indian .... CARIB, TIMOTE
island .... COCHE, CUBAGUA, LA ORCHILA, LA TORTUGA, MARGARITA
lake .... VALENCIA, MARACAIBO
language .... SPANISH
mining center .... AROA
minister .... IZAGUIRRE
monetary unit .... BOLIVAR
mountain ..... DUIDA, VENAMO, BOLIVAR, RORAIMA
mountain range .... IMERI, GUAMPI, PARIMA, IMATACA, TURAGUA, PACARAIMA
passage .... SERPENTS MOUTH
patriot .... BOLIVAR
peninsula .... PARIA, MACANAO, PARAGUANA
plain .... LLANO, GRAN SABANA
president ...... LEONI, CALDERA
river .... ARO, PAO, TUY, CUAO, META, APURE, BARIA,

CAURA, GUERE, NEGRO, OCAMO, SIAPA, TIGRE, UNARE, ZUATA, ZULIA, ARAUCA, CAPARO, CARONI, CARRAO, CURUTU, CUYUNI, SARARE, TOCUCO, TOCUYO, VENAMO, VOTAMO, AMACURO, CANAGUA, EREBATO, GUANARE, GUANIPA, GUARICO, ICABARU, ORINOCO, APONGUAO, CUQUENAN, VENTUARI
seaport .... MARACAIBO
snake .... LORA
state ..... LARA, APURE, SUCRE, ZULIA, ARAGUA, FALCON, MERIDA, BARINAS, BOLIVAR, GUERICO, MIRANDA, TACHIRA, CARABOBO, TRUJILLO
strait .... DRAGONS MOUTH
tree .... BALATA
Venezuelan god .... TSUMA
vengeance .... TALION, WANION, REVENGE, REPRISAL, REQUITAL, RETALIATION
vengeful .... SPITEFUL, VINDICTIVE
veni, vidi, _____ VICI
venial .... MINOR, TRIVIAL, EXCUSABLE, PARDONABLE
opposed to .... MORTAL
Venice famous district .... RIALTO
"Little" .... VENEZUELA
race in .... REGATTA
state barge .... BUCENTAUR
venireman .... JUROR
Venite .... PSALM, CANTICLE
venom .... BANE, GALL, SPITE, TOXIN, VIRUS, MALICE, POISON
antidote .... ANTIVENIN
venomous .... TOXIC, DEADLY, BANEFUL, NOXIOUS, SPITEFUL, VIPERINE, VIPERISH, VIRULENT, MALICIOUS, MALIGNANT, POISONOUS
arthropod .... SPIDER, CENTIPEDE, MILLIPEDE
fish ...... LION(FISH), SCORPION, STINGRAY, WEEVER(FISH)
reptile .... SNAKE, LIZARD
venous .... VEINY
vent .... EMIT, FLUE, HOLE, EXPEL, ISSUE, ESCAPE, FUNNEL, OUTLET, OPENING, ORIFICE, PASSAGE, APERTURE, UTTERANCE, EXPRESSION
in earth's crust .... GEYSER, VOLCANO
tailor's .... SLIT
whale's .... BLOWHOLE, SPIRACLE

ventage .... (FINGER)HOLE
venter ...... WAME, WOMB, BELLY,
ABDOMEN
ventilate .... FAN, AERATE,
AIR(OUT), EXPOSE, FRESHEN
ventilating shaft ...... DOWNCAST
ventilation .... AIRING
opening .... LOUVER
ventilator .... FAN, BLOWER
ventral ...... H(A)EMAD, STERNAL,
ABDOMINAL
ventriloquist .... BERGEN
Bergen's daughter
.... CANDICE
Bergen's dummy .... SNERD,
CHARLIE
medium of .... DUMMY,
PUPPET
venture ...... RISK, BRAVE, STAKE,
CHANCE, HAZARD, DARE(SAY),
SPECULATE, ENTERPRISE
venturesome one .... DARER
Venus .... PLANET, CYTHEREA,
PHOSPHOR, APHRODITE
as morning star .... LUCIFER
beloved of .... ADONIS
flytrap of .... DIONAEA
girdle .... CESTUS
in alchemy .... COPPER
island .... MELOS
Milo's .... STATUE
or Vesta .... DEA
planet .... VESPER
poetical .... LUCIFER,
HESPERUS
son of .... CUPID, AENEAS
tree sacred to .... MYRTLE
whence .... MILO
veracious .... TRUE, HONEST,
ACCURATE, TRUTHFUL
veracity .... TRUTH, HONESTY
veranda(h) .... STOA, LANAI,
PORCH, LOGGIA, PIAZZA,
BALCONY, PORTICO
in Dixie .... GALLERY
verb, biblical .... WAST
ending .... ATE, ESCE
expression of a .... ACTION,
EXISTENCE, OCCURRENCE
kind of .... AUXILIARY,
TRANSITIVE
verbal .... ORAL, VOCAL, SPOKEN,
UNWRITTEN
attack .... SERMON, TIRADE,
OBLOQUY, DIATRIBE,
HARANGUE, INVECTIVE
noun ...... GERUND, INFINITIVE,
PARTICIPLE
suffix .... ATE, ESCE
thrust .... DIG
verbalize .... EXPRESS

verbatim ...... EXACTLY, LITERAL,
WORD FOR WORD
verbenaceous plant .... LANTANA,
VERBENA, VERVAIN
tree .... TEAK
verbiage ...... DICTION, PROLIXITY,
WORDINESS
verbose .... WINDY, WORDY,
PROLIX, TALKATIVE, LONG-
WINDED
verboten .... TABU, TABOO,
FORBIDDEN, PROHIBITED
verbs, derived from
.... RHEMATIC
verd .... GREEN
antique .... MARBLE, PATINA,
VERDIGRIS
verdancy ...... NAIVETE, NAIVETY,
VIRIDITY, GREENNESS,
INEXPERIENCE
verdant .... FRESH, GREEN, NAIVE,
IMMATURE
Verdi, composer .... GIUSEPPE
opus .... OPERA
work .... AIDA, ERNANI,
OTELLO, NABUCCO, DON
CARLO, FALSTAFF,
(IL)TROVATORE
verdict .... DECREE, RULING,
FINDING, OPINION, DECISION,
JUDGMENT, SENTENCE
verdigris .... RUST, VERD, PATINA,
ANTIQUE
verdin .... BIRD, TITMOUSE
verditer .... BICE
Verdugo, actress .... ELENA
verdure .... GREENERY,
GREENNESS
verecund .... SHY, MODEST,
BASHFUL
Vereen .... BEN
verein .... SOCIETY
verge .... EVE, RIM, ROD, EDGE,
BRINK, MARGE, POINT, STAFF,
BORDER, MARGIN
Vergil's/Virgil's birthplace
.... MANTUA
family name .... MARO
hero .... (A)ENEAS
queen .... DIDO
word .... TIMEO
work .... (A)ENEID
veriest .... UTMOST, GREATEST
verify .... CHECK, PROVE, AFFIRM,
ATTEST, CONFIRM, IDENTIFY
verily ...... AMEN, TRULY, CERTES,
INDEED, IN FACT, REALLY
veritable .... REAL, VALID,
ACTUAL, GENUINE
veritas .... TRUTH
Verite author .... ZOLA

verity ...... FACT, TRUTH, REALITY
vermeil .... VERMILION
vermiform .... WORM-SHAPED
process .... APPENDIX
vermilion .... RED, MINIUM,
VERMEIL, PIGMENT, CINNABAR
vermin .... BUGS, LICE, MICE,
RATS, SCUM, FLIES, PESTS,
WEASEL, VARMENT, VARMINT,
RIFFRAFF
Vermont capital ...... MONTPELIER
city/town .... BARRE, DERBY,
ESSEX, JERICHO, NEWPORT,
RUTLAND, HARTFORD,
WOODSTOCK, BENNINGTON,
BURLINGTON, COLCHESTER,
MIDDLEBURY, SPRINGFIELD
college .... GODDARD
county .... ESSEX, ORANGE,
ADDISON, ORLEANS, RUTLAND,
WINDHAM, WINDSOR,
FRANKLIN, BENNINGTON,
CHITTENDEN, WASHINGTON
dam .... MOORE, WILDER,
COMERFORD
lake ..... ECHO, CARMI, SALEM,
GROTON, CASPIAN, CRYSTAL,
DUNMORE, HARVEYS,
SEYMOUR, BOMOSEEN,
HARDWICK, HORTONIA,
IROQUOIS, CHAMPLAIN,
MAIDSTONE
mountain .... BALD, GORE,
SNOW, BURKE, ELLEN, TABOR,
BOLTON, HUNGER, SPRUCE,
ABRAHAM, BROMLEY,
EQUINOX, ASCUTNEY,
HAYSTACK, STRATTON,
BELVIDERE, BLOODROOT,
MANSFIELD, CAMELS HUMP,
WHITE FACE
mountain range .... GREEN
river .... MAD, MILL, WEST,
BLACK, CLYDE, MOOSE,
TROUT, WAITS, WELLS, WHITE,
BARTON, HOOSIC, LITTLE,
LAMOILLE, NULHEGAN,
POULTNEY, WINOOSKI,
MISSISQUOI, PASSUMPSIC,
CONNECTICUT
state bird .... THRUSH
state flower .... RED CLOVER
state nickname .... GREEN
MOUNTAIN
state tree .... SUGAR MAPLE
university .... NORWICH
vermouth .... WINE
vernacular .... ARGOT, IDIOM,
JARGON, DIALECT
vernal .... GREEN, AESTIVAL,
YOUTHFUL, SPRINGLIKE

Verne, author .... JULES
   character .... NEMO
   submarine .... NAUTILUS
veronal .... BARBITAL
veronica .... SUDARY, FIGWORT,
       SUDARIUM, SPEEDWELL
verruca .... WART
verrucose .... WARTY
versant .... SLOPE
versatile ...... SKILLED, TALENTED,
     ADAPTABLE, MANY-SIDED
verse .... ALBA, EPIC, LINE, POEM,
    RIME, RUNE, SONG, CANTO,
    IONIC, RHYME, POETRY,
    STANZA, DIMETER, TRIPODY,
    TROCHEE
   accented .... ARSIS
   accented and unaccented
   .... TROCHEE
   analysis .... SCANSION
   book of .... GARLAND
   comic .... DOGGEREL
   form ...... ODE, IAMB, PANTUN,
     SONNET, ANAPEST, COUPLET,
    DIMETER, (DI)STICH, PANTOUM,
    SPONDEE, VIRELAY, MADRIGAL
   free .... VERS LIBRE
   group .... TERCET
   half line of .... HEMISTICH
   imaginative .... POESY
   inside ring .... POSY
   kind of .... EPIC, ELEGY,
     EPODE, JINGLE, DOGGEREL,
     LIMERICK, MADRIGAL
   measure .... MORA
   mournful .... ELEGY
   musical .... STAFF
   of a lyric sort .... STRAIN
   eight metrical feet
   .... OCTAMETER
   farewell .... ENVOI
   five lines .... PENTASTICH
   four lines .... QUATRAIN,
      TETRASTICH
   fourteen lines .... SONNET
   love .... MADRIGAL
   seven lines .... HEPTASTICH
   six lines .... HEXASTICH
   three metrical feet
   .... TRIPODY
   one-line .... MONOSTICH
   rhythm in .... METER,
      MEASURE
   satirical .... IAMBIC
   set to music .... LYRICS
   terse, witty .... EPIGRAM
   two-feet ...... DIPODY, SYZYGY,
      DIMETER
   two-line ..... COUPLET, DISTICH
   unit .... FOOT
   with nosegay .... POSY

versed .... ADEPT, TURNED,
   LEARNED, SKILLED, TRAINED,
   FAMILIAR, CONVERSANT,
   PROFICIENT, ACCOMPLISHED,
   KNOWLEDGEABLE
verses, set of .... STAVE, PANTUN,
     STANZA, STROPHE
versifier .... RIMER, RHYMER,
    POETESS, POET(ASTER),
    RHYMESTER
versify .... RHYME, METRIFY,
    POETIZE
version .... ACCOUNT, RECENSION,
    RENDITION, TRANSLATION
   of Bible .... DOUAY, VULGATE,
     APOCRYPHA, KING JAMES,
   SEPTUAGINT, NEW TESTAMENT,
     OLD TESTAMENT
verso, opposed to .... RECTO,
     OBVERSE
versus .... AGAINST
vertebra, body of .... CENTRUM
   combining form
   .... SPONDYL(O)
   top .... ATLAS
vertebral bone .... COCCYX,
     SACRUM
vertebrate .... AVIS, FISH,
    MAMMAL, REPTILE
vertex .... CAP, TOP, ACME, APEX,
    HEAD, CROWN, HEIGHT,
    SUMMIT, ZENITH, PINNACLE
vertical .... PLUMB, APLOMB,
    ERECT, UPRIGHT,
    PERPENDICULAR
vertically .... UP, APEAK
verticil .... WHORL
vertiginous .... DIZZY, GIDDY,
     SPINNING
vertigo .... GID, DINUS, MEGRIM,
    DIZZINESS, GIDDINESS
Vertigo actress ...... (KIM)NOVAK
Vertumnus' wife .... POMONA
verve .... PEP, DASH, ELAN,
    GUSTO, VIGOR, FERVOR,
    SPIRIT, VIVACITY,
    ENTHUSIASM
vervet .... MONKEY
   relative .... GRIVET
very .... EVEN, REAL, SAME, TRES,
    QUITE, TRULY, ACTUAL, EVER
    SO, HIGHLY, REALLY,
    GENUINE, EXTREMELY,
    EXCEEDINGLY
   accurate .... EXACT, PRECISE
   brave .... LION-HEARTED
   bright light .... FLARE,
     SPOTLIGHT
   bright star .... NOVA
   close .... NOSE-TO-NOSE
   colloquial .... AWFULLY,

     TERRIBLY
   dark .... INKY
   dry .... ARID
   dry champagne .... BRUT
   flamboyant pianist
   .... LIBERACE
   friendly .... PALSY-WALSY
   good reviews .... RAVES
   hard .... STONY, DIFFICULT
   important person .... STAR,
    BIGWIG, BIG WHEEL, TOP
   BRASS, CELEBRITY, DIGNITARY
   in English slang .... BALLY
   justifiable .... LEGAL,
     LEGITIMATE
   large .... DECUMAN
   little .... PETTY, MINUTE,
    PICAYUNE, MINIATURE
   lowest level ..... ROCK-BOTTOM
   neat .... TRIG
   new .... RED-HOT
   pleasing .... GROOVY
   powerful .... MIGHTY
   red .... BLOODY, CRIMSON
   red-complexioned ...... BURNT,
     SUNBURNED
   sharp .... QUICK-WITTED, AS
    HOT AS A PISTOL
   signal .... FLARE
   small .... WEE, TINY, DWARF,
    PIGMY, PYGMY, INSIGNIFICANT
   small cucumber .... GHERKIN
   small dog .... CHIHUAHUA
   small donkey .... BURRO
   tense .... TAUT, TIGHT
   true .... HONEST, VERACIOUS,
    UNMISTAKABLY SO
   well .... FINE, FIRST-RATE
vesica .... BLADDER
vesicant .... EPISPASTIC, MUSTARD
     GAS
vesicate .... BLISTER
vesicle .... SAC, BLEB, CYST,
    BULLA, CAVITY, BLISTER,
    UTRICLE
vespa .... WASP, YELLOWJACKET
vesper .... EVE, STAR, VENUS,
    EVENING, EVENTIDE,
    HESPERUS
vespers .... EVENSONG,
    CANONICAL HOUR
vespertilione .... BAT
vespiary inhabitant .... WASP,
    HORNET, VESPID
vespid .... WASP, HORNET,
    YELLOWJACKET
vespine insect .... WASP
Vespucci, explorer ...... AMERIGO
   friend of .... COLUMBUS
   nation named after
   .... AMERICA

vessel .... CAN, JUG, PAN, TUB, VAS, VAT, BOWL, CASK, DUCT, BOAT, SHIP, TUBE, BARGE, BASIN, CANAL, CRAFT, CRUSE, BARREL, GALLEY, LATEEN, LUGGER, AIRSHIP, CAR(R)ACK, CARRIER, (CAT)BOAT, FRIGATE, GALLEON, UTENSIL, CONTAINER
ancient .... TRIREME
anti-smuggling .... CUTTER
assayer's .... CUPEL
baptismal/holy water ..... FONT, PISCINA, SACRARIUM
body of a .... HULK, HULL
butter-making .... CHURN
cargo/commercial ...... BARGE, OILER, TANKER, STEAMER, FREIGHTER
carried on a warship .... DINGHY
Chinese .... JUNK, SAMPAN
clumsy .... ARK, HOOKER, DROGHER
combining form ...... VASO
cooking .... PAN, POT, FRYPAN, KETTLE, TEAPOT, CALDRON, SKILLET, STEAMER, CROCKPOT, STOCKPOT, RICE COOKER
cylindrical .... KEG, TUBE, BARREL
deck of a .... ORLOP
decorative .... VASE
deep-sea diving .... BATHYSCAPH(E)
drinking .... CUP, MUG, GLASS, GOBLET, TANKARD, TUMBLER
druggist's .... JAR, GALLIPOT
Ecclesiastical .... AMA, PYX
Eucharist .... CRUET
fishing .... SMACK, HOOKER, SEALER, WHALER, TRAWLER
for burning oil .... CRESSET
for coal .... HOD, SCUTTLE
for medicine .... VIAL, PHIAL
freight .... TRAMP, PACKET, FREIGHTER, WHALEBACK
funnel-shaped .... HOPPER
Holy Communion .... CHALICE
John Barleycorn's ..... BOTTLE
Levantine .... SAIC, KETCH
lightweight .... RAFT, BALSA, BATEAU
made of wicker .... BASKET, HAMPER, PANNIER
mail .... PACKET(BOAT)
Malay .... PRAU, PROA
merchant .... ARGOSY, GALLIOT
of the Vikings .... KNORR

part .... DECK, STERN
passenger .... FERRY, LINER, PACKET, AIRPLANE, STEAMSHIP
pleasure .... YACHT
racing .... SLOOP
sailing .... HOY, BARK, BRIG, SHIP, YAWL, KETCH, CARAVEL
single-decked .... GALLEY
single-masted .... GALLIOT
small .... JAR, TUBE, VIAL, CRUSE, PHIAL, CANISTER
small sailing ..... HOY, BARGE, PINNACE
supply .... COALER, TENDER
the Jumblies' .... SIEVE
thermos bottle .... DEWAR
three-masted .... BARK, ZEBEC, GALLEASS
trader .... GALLEON
transporting cars, people .... FERRY(BOAT)
two-masted ..... BRIG, HOOKER
type of .... BOX, PAN, POT, CASE, CADDY, TRAMP, BOTTLE, BASKET, BUSHEL, HOLDER, CONTAINER, RECEPTACLE
used in photometry .... CUVETTE
warship .... CRUISER, GALLEON, MONITOR, HYDROFOIL, SUBMARINE, ENTERPRISE, SUPERTANKER
water/liquid .... JUG, CASK, PAIL, FLASK, BOTTLE, BUCKET, CANTEEN, PITCHER, RUNDLET, PUNCHEON, KILDERKIN
vessels, having .... VASCULAR
vest .... ENDOW, BODICE, BOLERO, WESKIT, EMPOWER, FURNISH, WAISTCOAT, TATTERSALL
pocket .... SMALL
Vesta .... MATCH, HESTIA
vestal .... NUN, PURE, CHASTE, VIRGIN(AL)
virgin .... TUCCIA, AEMILIA, CLAUDIA, URBINIA, PRIESTESS
virgin Urbinia's burial place .... COLLINE GATE
Vestal Virgins .... ROMAN CULT
disciplinarian of the .... PONTIFEX-MAXIMUS
dwelling place .... ATRIUM-VESTAE
one of highly revered .... URBINIA
Roman goddess of the .... VESTA
who escaped, one of ..... TUCCIA, AEMILIA, CLAUDIA
vested .... FIXED, ROBED, ENDUED, GOWNED, SETTLED,

ABSOLUTE, RAIMENTED, ENTRENCHED
vestibule .... HALL, ENTRY, FOYER, LOBBY, ALCOVE, HALLWAY
vestige(s) .... BIT, MARK, SIGN, RELIC, SHRED, TRACE, TRACK, SHADOW, NARTHEX, REMAINS, EVIDENCE, REMAINDER
of burn .... ESCHAR
vestment .... GOWN, ROBE, FROCK, GARMENT, RAIMENT, TUNICLE
clerical ..... ALB, COPE, AMICE, TUNIC, TIPPET, CASSOCK, CHASUBLE, SURPLICE
English king's coronation .... DALMATIC
eucharistic .... MANIPLE
Jewish priest's .... EPHOD
papal .... FANON
place for .... AMBRY
vestments .... CANONICALS
vestry .... CHAPEL, SACRISTY
Vesuvian .... FUSEE, MATCH, VOLCANIC
vesuvianite .... EGERAN, IDOCRASE
vesuviate .... ERUPT
Vesuvius .... VOLCANO
city destroyed by ..... POMPEII, HERCULANEUM
site .... NAPLES
vetch .... ERS, AKRA, TARE, SATIVA
vet(eran) .... ELDER, STAGER, OLD HAND, OLDSTER, TROUPER, OLDTIMER, SEASONED, EX-SOLDIER, EXPERIENCED
of battles .... WAR HORSE
veterinarian .... LEECH, FARRIER, (ANIMAL)DOCTOR
colloquial .... VET
vetiver .... BENA, GRASS
veto .... NO, KILL, QUASH, TABOO, FORBID, KIBOSH, NEGATE, DISALLOW, PROHIBIT, DISAPPROVE
vetoer .... NOER
vex .... IRE, IRK, CARK, FASH, GALL, RILE, ROIL, ANNOY, CHAFE, PEEVE, PIQUE, TEASE, HARASS, NEEDLE, NETTLE, OFFEND, DISTURB, TORMENT, TROUBLE, ACERBATE, IRRITATE
vexation .... WOE, BANE, BOTHER, PLAGUE, ANXIETY, NUISANCE, AGITATION, ANNOYANCE
vexatious .... PESKY, IRKSOME, ANNOYING, IRRITABLE, PROVOKING, BOTHERSOME,

via ...... PER, ALONG, BY(WAY OF), TROUBLESOME, THROUGH

viable .... VITAL, ALIVE, CAPABLE, WORKABLE, PRACTICAL

viaduct .... BRIDGE, TRESTLE

vial .... PHIAL, BOTTLE, AMP(O)ULE

viand(s) .... DISH, FARE, FOOD, VICTUALS

viaticum .... EUCHARIST

viator ...... TRAVELER, WAYFARER

Viaud's pseudonym .... LOTI

vibes .... ECHO, VIBRATION

vibrant .... VITAL, ROBUST, DYNAMIC, HEALTHY, PULSING, RESONANT, ENERGETIC, QUIVERING

vibrate .... JAR, TIRL, THROB, DINDLE, QUIVER, SHIMMY, THRILL, FLUTTER, RESOUND, TREMBLE, RESONATE, OSCILLATE

vibration .... THROB, QUIVER, THRILL, SHAKING, TREMOLO, PULSATION

check .... DAMP

chest .... FREMITUS

vibrator .... OSCILLATOR

vibrissa .... WHISKERS

viburnum .... LIANA, LIANE, SHRUB, LANTANA, HONEYSUCKLE

vicar ...... AGENT, DEPUTY, PRIEST, MINISTER, VICEGERENT

assistant of .... CURATE

Christ's .... POPE

residence of .... VICARAGE

vicarious .... PROXY, DEPUTY, INDIRECT, DELEGATED, SUBSTITUTE

vice .... SIN, CRIME, ERROR, FAULT, STEAD, FRAILTY, INIQUITY, WEAKNESS, INSTEAD OF, ADDICTION

chairman, public dinner .... CROUPIER

companion of .... VERSA

president .... VEEP

versa .... CONVERSELY, OPPOSITELY

vicegerent .... VICAR, DEPUTY

vicenary number .... TWENTY

viceroy ...... REGENT, BUTTERFLY, VICEGERENT

of a .... VICEREGAL

wife of a .... VICEREINE

Vichy and others .... EAUX, SPAS, WATERS

vichyssoise .... SOUP

vicinage .... AREA, VICINITY, NEIGHBORHOOD

vicinal .... LOCAL

vicinity ...... ENVIRONS, LOCALITY, NEIGHBORHOOD

vicious ...... MEAN, VILE, WRONG, SINFUL, UNRULY, WICKED, CORRUPT, HEINOUS, IMMORAL, DEPRAVED, MALICIOUS

act .... CRIME, OUTRAGE

vicissitude .... CHANGE, UP AND DOWN

victim .... DUPE, GULL, LAMB, MARK, PREY, LOSER, QUARRY, WRETCH, SUFFERER

accident .... CASUALTY

blamed for others' mistakes .... SCAPEGOAT

Cain's .... ABEL

Corday's .... MARAT

easily cheated .... DUPE, GULL, SUCKER

left to face consequences .... FALL GUY

long-suffering .... MARTYR

of Bellerophon .... CHIMERA

of pranks .... STOOGE

used for dangerous work .... TOOL, CAT'S PAW

victimize ...... DUPE, FOOL, GULL, CHEAT, DECEIVE, SWINDLE, HOODWINK

victor .... MASTER, WINNER, CHAMPION, CONQUEROR

actor .... JORY, MATURE

character .... AXEL, LENA, HEYST

Victoria .... QUEEN, EMPRESS, CARRIAGE, WATERLILY, AUTO(MOBILE)

and Reichenbach .... FALLS

consort of Queen .... (PRINCE)ALBERT

goddess .... NIKE

manservant of Queen .... JOHN BROWN

Victoria (Australia) bay .... HOBSONS, WARATAH, PORTLAND, DISCOVERY, PORT PHILLIP

cape .... OTWAY, NELSON, BRIDGEWATER

capital .... MELBOURNE

city/town .... ALTONA, COBURG, ELTHAM, KEILOR, BENDIGO, CROYDON, GEELONG, PRAHRAN, PRESTON, BALLARAT, ESSENDON, SUNSHINE, WAVERLEY, BRUNSWICK, DANDENONG, LILLYDALE, MOORABBIN, CAMBERWELL

island .... FRENCH, PHILLIP

lake .... HUME, EILDON, TYRRELL, HINDMARSH, WELLINGTON, CORANGAMITE

mountain .... BOGONG, BULLER, DANDENONG, DIFFICULT

peninsula .... MORNINGTON

river .... AVOCA, OVENS, SNOWY, YARRA, LODDON, MURRAY, GLENEIG, HOPKINS, WIMMERA, CAMPASPE, MITCHELL

Victorian vice .... BIGOTRY, PRUDERY

victorious .... PALMARY, TRIUMPHAL, SUCCESSFUL, TRIUMPHANT

number .... ONE

victory .... MASTERY, SUCCESS, TRIUMPH, WINNING, CONQUEST

celebration .... SNAKE DANCE

costly .... PYRRHIC

crown of .... ANADEM, LAUREL

easy .... RUNAWAY, WALKAWAY

goddess of ...... NIKE, ATHENA

kind of .... ROUT, CADMEAN, PYRRHIC, LANDSLIDE

sign .... VEE

symbol .... VEE, PALM, LAUREL, TROPHY, CHAPLET

Victory, author of .... CONRAD

Victrola .... PHONOGRAPH

kin of .... GRAMOPHONE

victual(s) .... EAT, FEED, FOOD, VIAND, VITTLE, PROVISIONS

victualer .... SUTLER, CATERER, INNKEEPER

vicuna .... ALPACA

vide .... SEE

videlicet .... NAMELY

video .... TV, TELEVISION

meaning .... I SEE

vie .... BET, WAGER, STRIVE, COMPETE, CONTEND, EMULATE

vier .... RIVAL, ENTRANT

Vienna .... WIEN

park .... PRATER

Woods composer ..... STRAUSS

Viennese dress .... DIRNDL, LEDERHOSEN

Vientiane citizen .... LAO

money .... KIP

Vietnam bay .... VINH CAM RANH, VUNG CHON MAY

Buddhist sect .... HAO, HOA, CAO-DAI

cape .... MUI LAY, MUI DINH, MUI VARELLA, MUI NAM TRAM

capital .... HANOI
capital, former (South)
.... SAIGON
city/town .... HUE, VINH,
   DALAT, MYTHO, TAMKY,
   TANAN, DANANG, CANTHO,
   HONGAI, KONTUM, PLEIKU,
   SAIGON, BACLIEU, BIENHOA,
   CAMRANH, LACGIAO, PHUVINH,
   QUINHON, RACHGIA, TRAVINH,
   VUNGTAU, HAIPHONG,
   NHATRANG, PHANRANG,
   KHANH HUNG, LONG XUYEN,
   PHAN THIET, HO CHI MINH
economic reform program
.... DOI MOI
general (North) .... GIAP
guerrillas (South)
.... VIETCONG
gulf .... TONKIN
holiday/New Year .... TET
island .... PHU QUOC, DAO CAT
   BA, HON KHOAI, NIGHTINGALE
language .... MEO, YAO,
   KHMER, MUONG, FRENCH,
   CHINESE, VIETNAMESE
monetary unit .... DONG
monetary unit, former
   (South) .... PIASTRE
mountain .... RAOCO, NUI BA
   DEN, FAN SI PAN, CHU YANG
   SIN
native .... MEO
newspaper .... NHANDAN
offensive .... TET
plain .... JONCS
plateau .... KONTUM
premier (North) .... (PHAM
   VAN) DONG
premier (South) .... CAO KY,
   KHANH
president (North) .... (HO CHI)
   MINH
president, former (South)
.... DIEM, THIEU
river ...... RED, BLACK, SE SAN,
   SONG BA, SONG CA, IA DRANG,
   SONG CAI
Saigon's new name .... HO
   CHI MINH
section of .... ANNAM
view .... AIM, SEE, GOAL, SCAN,
   ANGLE, SCAPE, SCENE, SIGHT,
   VISTA, WATCH, ASPECT,
   BELIEF, NOTION, SURVEY,
   VISION, GLIMPSE, OPINION,
   PURPOSE, WITNESS,
   PANORAMA, PROSPECT
viewpoint .... ANGLE, OPINION,
   OUTLOOK, ATTITUDE
vigesimal .... TWENTIETH

vigil .... EVE, WAKE, WATCH,
   SURVEILLANCE
vigilance, in medicine
.... INSOMNIA
vigilant .... WARY, ALERT,
   CAREFUL, CAUTIOUS,
   WATCHFUL
vigilante .... NIGHTRIDER
vignette .... SQUIB, SKETCH,
   PICTURE, DEPICTION
vignettist .... ARTIST, AUTHOR,
   WRITER
vigor .... SAP, VIM, VIS, ZIP, DASH,
   SNAP, FORCE, MIGHT, POWER,
   VERVE, ENERGY, STAMINA,
   STRENGTH, VITALITY,
   INTENSITY
slang .... PEP
vigorous .... HALE, ALERT,
   HARDY, SOUND, STOUT,
   MIGHTY, POTENT, ROBUST,
   STRONG, STURDY, VIRILE,
   FORCEFUL, ENERGETIC
scuffle .... TUSSLE
Viking .... ROVER, PIRATE,
   SAILOR, NORSEMAN
famed .... ERIC, OLAF, ROLLO
hero .... RURIK
literature .... SAGAS
poet .... SKALD
**Vikings, name given by
Finnish to** .... RUS
vilayet .... EYALET, PROVINCE
subdivision of .... SANJAK
vile .... BAD, LOW, BASE, EVIL,
   FOUL, MEAN, NASTY, PALTRY,
   SCURVY, VULGAR, WICKED,
   OBSCENE, DEPRAVED,
   CONTEMPTIBLE
vilify .... SLUR, ABUSE, LIBEL,
   SMEAR, DEFAME, MALIGN,
   REVILE, ASPERSE, SLANDER,
   TRADUCE, CALUMNIATE
vilipend .... REVILE, VILIFY,
   BELITTLE, DISPARAGE
villa .... CHATEAU, MANSION
Villa, Mexican leader .... PANCHO
_____, near Rome .... DESTE
of Herod .... MASADA
village .... BURG, BURH, DORP,
   KAIK, STAD, TOWN, WICK,
   KRAAL, BARRIO, CASALE,
   HAMLET, THROP(E), CLACHAN,
   MUNICIPALITY
Biblical .... CANA
near castle .... BOURG
villain .... FELON, KNAVE, ROGUE,
   MEANIE, RASCAL, CRIMINAL,
   MISCREANT, SCOUNDREL
Dickens .... SIKES
expression of .... LEER

movie: sl. .... HEAVY, BAD
   GUY
of story .... LEGREE,
   RASSENDALE
"Star Wars" .... VADER
villainy .... CRIME
villatic .... RURAL, RUSTIC
villein .... ESNE, SERF, CARL(E),
   TENANT, PEASANT
Villon, Fr. poet .... FRANCOIS
Vilnius .... VILNA, WILNO
vim .... PEP, ZIP, ELAN, ZEST,
   VERVE, VIGOR, ENERGY,
   SPIRIT, STINGO
vimen .... SHOOT
vin .... WINE
vina .... ZITHER
vinaceous .... RED, VINOUS
fruit .... GRAPE
vinaigrette .... BOX, BOTTLE
Vincent's disease .... GINGIVITIS,
   TRENCH MOUTH
Vinci's patron .... SFORZA
vincible .... BEATABLE
vincit omnia _____ ...... VERITAS
vindicate .... CLEAR, ACQUIT,
   ABSOLVE, JUSTIFY
vindication .... APOLOGY,
   EXONERATION
vindicator .... AVENGER
vindictive .... BITTER, SPITEFUL,
   MALICIOUS, (RE)VENGEFUL
vine .... HOP, IVY, PEA, BINE,
   GRAPE, LIANA, LIANE,
   RUNNER, CLIMBER,
   COW(H)AGE, CREEPER,
   ANGLEPOD, WISTERIA
coil of .... TENDRIL
dresser .... PRUNER
gourd .... COLOCYNTH
support ..... LATTICE, TENDRIL,
   TRELLIS
tuberous .... TAMUS
type of .... GRAPE, JASMINE,
   CLEMATIS, WISTERIA, POISON
   IVY, MORNING GLORY
used in making leis .... MAILE
with twining stems .... BINE
woody .... SMILAX
young .... VINELET
vinegar .... EISEL, ACETUM,
   ALEGAR
bottle .... CRUET, CASTER,
   CASTOR
change to .... ACETIFY
dregs .... MOTHER
eel .... NEMATODE
formation in .... ROPE,
   MOTHER
from ale .... ALEGAR
kind of .... MALT, PALM, CIDER

like/of .... SOUR, ACETIC,
   ACETOSE, ACETOUS
pickling .... MARINADE
preserve in .... MARINATE
producing .... ACETOUS
spiced .... MARINADE
stringy substance ..... MOTHER
worm .... EEL
vinegarroon .... SCORPION
vinegary .... SOUR, ACETIC, ILL-
   HUMORED, ILL-TEMPERED
vinery ...... HOTHOUSE, VINEYARD,
   GREENHOUSE
vineyard ...... CRU, CLOS, VINERY,
   GRAPERY
vingt et un .... BLACKJACK,
   TWENTY ONE
vino .... WINE
vinous .... WINY, VINACEOUS
vinta .... CANOE
vintage .... AGE, CROP, TIME,
   WINE, YIELD, MODEL, CHOICE,
   PERIOD, HARVEST
autos, e.g. .... ANTIQUES
vintner's assistant ...... GOURMET
study .... (O)ENOLOGY
viol .... SARINDA
viola .... PANSY, PLANT, VIOLET
clef .... ALTO
violate ...... RAPE, ABUSE, BREAK,
   USURP, RAVISH, INFRACT,
   PROFANE, ENCROACH,
   INFRINGE, TRESPASS,
   DESECRATE
trust .... BETRAY
violation .... BREACH, OFFENSE,
   INFRACTION, DESECRATION
kind of law ...... RAPE, ARSON,
   MURDER, BURGLARY,
   KIDNAPING
of the law ...... CRIME, DELICT,
   FELONY, DELINQUENCY
violator .... LAWBREAKER
violence .... ROW, RIOT, FORCE,
   TURMOIL, SEVERITY
violent .... WILD, FIERY, ROUGH,
   FIERCE, RAGING, STORMY,
   STRONG, FURIOUS, TEARING,
   FORCEFUL
anger .... FURY
blow .... BASH
contact ..... IMPACT, COLLISION
disturbance ...... RIOT, RUMPUS
jar .... SHOCK
outburst/storm .... TEMPEST
stream .... TORRENT
struggle .... AGONY
temporary activity ...... SPASM
violently agitated .... TURBULENT
violet .... MAUVE, FLOWER,
   PURPLE

blue .... INDIGO
cousin of .... PANSY
violin ...... CELLO, VIOLA, FIDDLE,
   VIOL(ONCELLO)
bow .... ARCO, FIDDLESTICK
bow's knob .... NUT
companion of .... BOW
E-string .... QUINT
famous ...... AMATI, CREMONA,
   STRAD(IVARIUS)
forerunner of the .... REBEC(K)
inlaid border .... PURFLING
instrument resembling
.... REBEC(K)
maker ..... AMATI, STRADIVARI,
   GUARNERI(US)
maker Amati .... NICOLO
part of ..... NUT, NECK, WAIST,
   BRIDGE, BUTTON, PEG(BOX),
   SCROLL, CHINBOARD,
   TAILPIECE, FINGERBOARD
piano piece .... SONATA
player .... FIDDLER
rare .... KIT, AMATI, STRAD
small .... KIT
stroke .... UPBOW
violinist ...... AUER, ELMAN, STERN,
   YSAYE, HEIFETZ, MENUHIN,
   KREISLER
comedian .... BENNY
direction to .... SPICCATO
Elman .... MISCHA
Menuhin .... YEHUDI
Roman .... NERO
so-called .... (JACK) BENNY
violone .... CONTRABASS
VIP .... BIGWIG, BIGSHOT,
   MAGNATE, NOTABLE,
   TOPBRASS, CELEBRITY,
   DIGNITARY
bullring .... TORERO,
   MATADOR, TOREADOR
Easter .... BUNNY
June .... DAD
May .... MOM
part of .... VERY, PERSON,
   IMPORTANT
wheels for .... LIMO(USINE)
VIPs, assembly of .... GALAXY
viper .... ASP, BOA, ADDER,
   SNAKE, REPTILE, SERPENT,
   BUSHMASTER, COPPERHEAD,
   FER-DE-LANCE, RATTLESNAKE
horned .... CERASTES
viper's bugloss .... BLUEWEED
viperine .... VENOMOUS
viperous .... ASPISH, SPITEFUL,
   VENOMOUS, MALICIOUS
virago .... FURY, SCOLD, SHREW,
   VIXEN, AMAZON, MAENAD,
   HELLCAT, TERMAGANT

virelay .... POEM, VERSE
vireo .... RUDD, REDEYE,
   GREENLET, (SONG)BIRD
virescent .... GREENISH
virgate ...... TWIGGY, ROD-SHAPED
Virgil. See **Vergil**
virgin .... NUN, PURE, UNCUT,
   VIRGO, CHASTE, MAID(EN),
   VESTAL, INITIAL, MADONNA,
   PARTHENOS, UNTOUCHED
queen .... ELIZABETH
unblemished .... CAMILLA
woman .... OLD MAID,
   SPINSTER
Virgin Islands' discoverer
.... COLUMBUS
the .... MARY
Vestal .... RHEA, TUCCIA,
   CLAUDIA, URBINIA
virginal .... NEW, PURE, FRESH,
   SPINET, MAIDENLY,
   UNSULLIED, UNEXPLORED,
   HARPSICHORD
membrane .... HYMEN
Virginia bay .... BACK, MOBJACK,
   CHESAPEAKE
cape .... HENRY, CHARLES
capital .... RICHMOND
city/town .... SALEM,
   BEDFORD, BRISTOL, EMPORIA,
   FAIRFAX, HAMPTON, NORFOLK,
   ROANOKE, SUFFOLK,
   DANVILLE, GROVETON,
   HOPEWELL, MANASSAS,
   STAUNTON, ANNANDALE,
   ARLINGTON, LEXINGTON,
   LYNCHBURG, ALEXANDRIA,
   CHESAPEAKE, PORTSMOUTH,
   MOUNT VERNON, NEWPORT
   NEWS, SPRINGFIELD
college ..... AVERETT, HOLLINS,
   RADFORD, LONGWOOD,
   MARYMOUNT
county .... LEE, BATH, PAGE,
   WISE, YORK, BLAND, FLOYD,
   GILES, SCOTT, SMYTH, SURRY,
   WYTHE, AMELIA, ORANGE,
   AMHERST, AUGUSTA, FAIRFAX,
   HALIFAX, PULASKI, ROANOKE,
   RUSSELL, ACCOMACK,
   CAMPBELL, CULPEPER,
   POWHATAN, TAZEWELL,
   ARLINGTON, CHESTERFIELD
cowslip .... BLUEBELL
creeper .... IVY, VINE,
   WOODBINE
dance .... REEL
island ...... HOG, COBB, CEDAR,
   SMITH, TANGIER, WALLOPS,
   METOMPKIN, PARRAMORE,
   FISHERMANS

lake .... ANNA, GASTON, CLAYTOR, DRAMMOND, PHILPOTT, BLUESTONE, SOUTH HOLSTON, SMITH-MOUNTAIN

mount .... VERNON

mountain .... ROGERS, CUMBERLAND, SHENANDOAH, MASSANUTTEN

mountain range .... ALLEGHENY, BLUE RIDGE, APPALACHIAN

national cemetery .... ARLINGTON

pine .... LOBLOLLY

river .... NI, PO, DAN, NEW, HYCO, PIGG, YORK, JAMES, MAURY, SLATE, SMITH, CLINCH, LITTLE, POWELL, WILLIS, JACKSON, POTOMAC, RAPIDAN, RIVANNA, ROANOKE, TUG FORK, MEHERRIN, NOTTOWAY, PAMUNKEY, MATTAPONI

seaport .... NORFOLK

settlement .... JAMESTON

state bird .... CARDINAL

state flower .... DOGWOOD

state nickname .... OLD DOMINION

truffle .... TUCKAHOE

university .... OLD DOMINION

virginity .... PURITY, MAIDENHOOD, SPINSTERHOOD

virgin's-bower .... CLEMATIS

Virgo .... VIRGIN, CONSTELLATION

star .... SPICA

virgulate .... VIRGATE, ROD-SHAPED

viridian .... PIGMENT

viridity .... VERDANCY, GREENNESS

virile .... MACHO, MANLY, POTENT, VIGOROUS, MASCULINE

fellow .... HE-MAN

Virna, actress .... LISI

virtu ...... CURIO, RARITY, BIBELOT

virtual .... LITERAL, IMPLICIT, POTENTIAL

virtually .... ALMOST, NEARLY, LITERALLY

virtue .... MERIT, WORTH, QUALITY, CHASTITY, GOODNESS, MORALITY, EXCELLENCE

virtues, one of the .... HOPE, FAITH, CHARITY, JUSTICE, PRUDENCE

virtuous .... PURE, MORAL, NOBLE, RIGHT, WORTHY, LAUDABLE, DESERVING, EXCELLENT

virtuosity .... FLAIR, SKILL, KNOW-HOW, EXPERTISE

virtuoso .... ARTIST(E), MAESTRO, AESTHETE, CONNOISSEUR

virulence .... VENOM, DEADLINESS, MALIGNANCY

virulent .... RABID, TOXIC, DEADLY, CAUSTIC, NOXIOUS, VENOMOUS, MALIGNANT, POISONOUS, INFECTIOUS

virus ...... GERM, VENOM, POISON, VACCINE, PATHOGEN

disease .... FLU, AIDS, COLD, POLIO, GRIP(PE), HERPES, RABIES, MEASLES, VARIOLA, VIROSIS, SHINGLES, SMALLPOX, INFLUENZA, VARICELLA, CHICKEN POX

particle, single .... VIRION

type of .... POX, TOGA, ADENO, ARENA, RETRO, HERPES, CORONA, PAPOVA, PICOMA, RHABDO

vis ...... FORCE, POWER, STRENGTH

-a-vis .... FACE TO FACE

visa .... ENDORSEMENT

visage .... MAP, FACE, LOOK, GUISE, ASPECT, COUNTENANCE

viscera .... GUTS, VITALS, INNARDS, ENTRAILS, INTESTINES

viscid .... GUMMY, SYRUPY, STICKY, VISCOSE, VISCOUS

viscosity .... STICKINESS

viscount .... PEER, SHERIFF, NOBLE(MAN)

heir of .... MASTER

viscous .... ROPY, SIZY, GLUEY, MUCID, PASTY, SLIMY, STICKY, GREASY, VISCID, SYRUPY

product ..... GUM, GLUE, PASTE

substance .... TAR, PITCH, RESIN, SLIME, SYRUP, MOLASSES

vise .... CLAM, DIAL, CLAMP, CLINCH, GRIPPER

part of .... JAW

Vishinsky, Soviet diplomat .... ANDREI

Vishnu .... (THE) PRESERVER

avatar of .... KRISHNA

incarnation of .... RAMA, KRISHNA

wife of .... SRI

visible .... IN VIEW, VISUAL, EVIDENT, IN SIGHT, OBVIOUS, SEEABLE, DISCERNIBLE, PERCEPTIBLE

to naked eye .... MACROSCOPIC

Visigoth .... TEUTON

king/chief .... ALARIC

vision .... DREAM, FANCY, IMAGE, ESPIAL, OPTICS, IMAGINE, PICTURE, (EYE)SIGHT

blurred/distorted .... ASTIGMATISM

component of ...... EYE, BRAIN

deceptive, unreal ...... MIRAGE, ILLUSION

defect .... ANOPIA, MYOPIA, DIPLOPIA, HYPEROPIA, ASTIGMATISM

double .... DIPLOPIA, AMBLYOPIA

far-sighted .... PRESBYOPIA

focusing factor .... CORNEA

loss .... BLINDNESS

nearsightedness .... MYOPIA

night blindness .... NYCTALOPIA

pertaining to .... OCULAR, VISUAL, OPTIC(AL)

range .... KEN, EYESHOT, EYESIGHT

reduced in bright light .... HEMERALOPIA

scope .... SCAN

sharpness of .... VISUAL ACUITY

starting point .... RETINA

test, kind of ...... REFRACTION, VISUAL FIELD, VISUAL ACUITY, ACCOMMODATION

tri-dimensional .... STEREOPSIS

visionary .... FEY, DREAMER, FANTAST, UTOPIAN, IDEALIST, QUIXOTIC, THEORIST, IMAGINARY, STARRY-EYED, ILLUSIONIST, IMPRACTICAL

visit .... GO TO, STAY, TARRY, ASSAIL, CALL(ON), DROP IN, INFLICT, SOJOURN, STOPOVER

between whalers .... GAM(MING)

frequently .... HAUNT

kind of ...... SOCIAL, BUSINESS, OFFICIAL, PROFESSIONAL

short .... CALL, LOOK-IN

social .... GAM

visitant .... GUEST, VISITOR

visitation .... BLOW, CALAMITY, DISASTER, HARDSHIP, AFFLICTION

visitor .... GUEST, CALLER, COMPANY, VISITANT

seasonal .... SANTA(CLAUS)

supernatural .... GHOST

visor .... BRIM, MASK, VISARD, VIZARD, EYESHADE, SUNSHADE, EYESHIELD

site .... CAP, HELMET,

WINDSHIELD
vista ...... VIEW, SCENE, OUTLOOK,
PANORAMA, LANDSCAPE
Vistula River .... WISLA
city on .... TORUN
tributary .... SAN
visual .... OCULAR, OPTICAL,
VISIBLE
Acuity Test aid ..... SNELLEN'S
CHART
aids device .... CHART, GRAPH,
MOVIE, SLIDE
disorder .... SQUINT, SCOTOMA,
STRABISMUS
indication of a submerged
problem .... TIP OF THE
ICEBERG
perception area .... FIELD
purple .... RHODOPSIN
yellow .... RETINENE
visualize .... SEE, IMAGINE,
PICTURE, ENVISION
vita .... LIFE
Vita Nuova author .... DANTE
vital .... ALIVE, FATAL, DEADLY,
MORTAL, ESSENTIAL,
IMPORTANT
element .... GERM
fluid .... SAP, BLOOD
organ ..... LUNG, HEART, LIVER
principle .... SOUL
statistics of beauty contestant
.... MEASUREMENTS
vitality .... LIFE, ZEST, ZING,
POWER, VIGOR, ENERGY,
VIRILITY
vitalize .... LIVEN, ANIMATE,
ENERGIZE
vitamin A .... CAROTENE
deficiency disease
.... KWASHIORKOR
-like compounds
.... RETINOIDS
source .... EGGS, FISH, MILK,
LIVER, CARROT, APRICOT
vitamin B .... CHOLINE
B complex constituent
...... BIOTIN, NIACIN, THIAMINE,
FOLIC ACID, PYRIDOXINE
B component .... PABA
B deficiency disease
.... ECZEMA, BERIBERI,
PELLAGRA, CHLOROSIS,
(PERNICIOUS)ANEMIA
B_1 .... THIAMINE
B_2 .... RIBOFLAVIN
B_6 .... PYRIDOXINE
B_{12} .... CYANOCOBALAMIN
B_{12} deficiency patient
.... VEGAN
B_{12} source .... BEEF, BRAN,

EGGS, FISH, MILK, PEAS, PORK,
LIVER, YOGURT, PEANUTS,
POULTRY, SPINACH
B_{12} storage .... LIVER
vitamin C .... ASCORBIC ACID
deficiency disease ..... SCURVY
excessive intake result
.... NAUSEA, DIARRHEA,
KIDNEY STONE
source .... LIME, LEMON,
ORANGE, POTATO, TOMATO,
CANTALOUPE, STRAWBERRY
vitamin D .... CALCIFEROL
deficiency disease
.... RICKETS, OSTEOMALACIA
source ..... EGGS, TUNA, LIVER,
SALMON, HERRING, SARDINE,
ULTRAVIOLET RAYS
vitamin E .... TOCOPHEROL
deficiency disease ..... EDEMA,
ANEMIA
source ...... EGGS, MEAT, NUTS,
CEREALS, WHEAT GERM
vitamin H .... BIOTIN
vitelline .... EGG YOLK
vitellus .... YOLK
vitiate .... UNDO, VOID, SPOIL,
TAINT, DEBASE, IMPAIR,
WEAKEN, CORRUPT, PERVERT,
INVALIDATE
vitreous .... GLASSY, BRITTLE,
HYALINE, HYALOID,
TRANSPARENT
vitrics .... GLASSWARE
vitrify .... BAKE
vitrine .... SHOWCASE
vitriol .... SORY, SULFATE,
BLUEJACK, BLUESTONE
vitriolic .... SHARP, BITING,
CAUSTIC, SARCASTIC
vitta .... RIBBON, HEADBAND
vittle .... FOOD, VICTUAL
vituline animal .... CALF
vituperate .... RAIL, ABUSE,
SCOLD, BERATE, REBUKE,
REVILE, VILIFY, UPBRAID
vituperation ...... ABUSE, TIRADE,
INVECTIVE, TONGUE-LASHING
vituperative .... ABUSIVE,
SCOLDING
viva .... CHEER, ACCLAIM,
EXCLAMATION
voce .... ORAL(LY)
vivacious .... GAY, BREEZY,
LIVELY, ANIMATED,
CHEERFUL, SPIRITED,
SPORTIVE
vivacity .... PEP, BRIO, DASH,
ELAN, ARDOR, VERVE, VIGOR,
GAIETY, ANIMATION
vivandiere .... SUTLER

vivarium .... HOTHOUSE,
GREENHOUSE
vive le _____ .... ROI
vivid .... FRESH, BRIGHT, LIVE(LY),
GRAPHIC, ANIMATED,
STRIKING
vivify .... ANIMATE, ENLIVEN,
REFRESH
vixen .... FOX, HARPY, SCOLD,
SHREW, WITCH, VIRAGO,
HELLCAT, TERMAGANT
viz. .... NAMELY, VIDELICET
vizard .... MASK, VISOR
Vladimir Ilyich Ulyanov
.... LENIN
pianist .... HOROWITZ
vocabulary .... ARGOT, SLANG,
WORDS, JARGON, LEXICON,
GLOSSARY, WORDBOOK,
DICTIONARY
of a .... LEXICAL
vocal .... ORAL, SUNG, SONANT,
SPOKEN, VERBAL, VOICED,
UTTERED, ARTICULATE
composition .... SONG
cords inflammation
.... LARYNGITIS
cords site .... LARYNX
expression .... UTTERANCE
group .... CHOIR, OCTET
ornament .... ROULADE
solo .... ARIA, ARIOSO
vocalist .... SINGER, CROONER,
WARBLER
slang .... NIGHTINGALE
vocalize .... SAY, UTTER,
PHONATE, ENUNCIATE
vocally .... ALOUD
vocation .... WORK, CRAFT,
TRADE, CAREER, METIER,
CALLING, OCCUPATION,
PROFESSION
voce, _____ .... VIVA
voces .... VOX, VOICE
vociferation .... RANT, CLAMOR
vociferous .... LOUD, NOISY,
BLATANT, CLAMOROUS,
BOISTEROUS
vodka cocktail .... SCREWDRIVER
mixture .... ORANGE JUICE
vogue .... FAD, TON, MODE, RAGE,
STYLE, FASHION
voguish .... POPULAR,
FASHIONABLE
voice .... SAY, VOX, UTTER,
TONGUE, VOCALITY,
UTTER(ANCE), EXPRESS(ION),
ARTICULATION
between bass and tenor
.... BARITONE
box .... LARYNX

change in tone of
.... INFLECTION, MODULATION
colloquial .... SPOKESMAN,
MOUTHPIECE
female .... ALTO, SOPRANO,
CONTRALTO
highest female singing
.... SOPRANO
highest male singing .... ALTO
impairment .... DYSPHONIA
intonation .... TONE, PITCH
kind of .... ALTO, BASS(O),
TENOR, SOPRANO, BARITONE,
FALSETTO
loud, strident .... FOGHORN
lowest female singing
.... ALTO
male .... BASSO, TENOR
organ .... LARYNX
overused ...... HUSKY, HOARSE,
CROAKING
person with loud ..... STENTOR
pertaining to .... VOCAL,
PHONETIC
practice .... SOLFEGGIO
quality .... TIMBRE
range .... DIAPASON
range, artificial ...... FALSETTO
roaming .... VAGANS
temporary loss of
.... DYSPHONIA
total loss of .... APHONIA
voiced sound ...... SONG, SONANT,
SPEECH, VIBRANT, UTTERANCE
stop .... MEDIA
voiceful .... VOCAL
voiceless ...... MUM, DUMB, MUTE,
SILENT, APHONIC, SPIRATE,
SPEECHLESS, TONGUELESS
sound .... SURD, TENUIS
sound sign .... CEDILLA
voices, for all .... TUTTI
void .... NULL, ANNUL, BLANK,
EMPTY, CANCEL, HOLLOW,
NEGATE, VACANT, VACATE,
VACUUM, INVALID, LACKING,
NULLIFY, NULLITY
of infinite space .... INANE
voidance .... VETO, REPEAL,
VACANCY, ANNULMENT
voided escutcheon .... ORLE
voilà .... LO, SEE, BEHOLD
voile .... FABRIC
voiture .... WAGON, VEHICLE,
CARRIAGE
volant ...... AGILE, QUICK, FLYING,
NIMBLE
jumbo .... AIRLINER
Volapuk, inventor of
.... SCHLEYER
volar .... PALMAR

volatile .... AIRY, GIDDY, LIGHT,
FICKLE, BUOYANT, GASEOUS,
MUTABLE, MERCURIAL
liquid .... ETHER, ALCOHOL
volcanic .... FIERY, VESUVIAN,
EXPLOSIVE, EXTRUSIVE
activity .... BELCHING,
ERUPTION
ash .... TUFF
cinder .... SCORIA
crater .... MAAR
dust .... TUFF
earth .... TRASS
ejection .... LAVA, BELCH,
COULEE, PUMICE, SCORIA,
LAPILLUS
glass .... PUMICE, OBSIDIAN
island .... FAROE, LIPARI,
IWO(JIMA)
landform .... MAAR
mud .... SALSE
opening .... FUMAROLE
rock .... TUFF, WACK, TRASS,
BASALT, LATITE, PUMICE,
TAXITE, PERLITE, LAPILLUS,
OBSIDIAN, RHYOLITE,
TRACHYTE, TEPHRITE,
PROPYLITE, TALPATATE
rock cavity .... VESICLE
slag .... CINDER, SCORIA
soil .... TALPATATE
vent .... CRATER, SOLFATARA
volcano, cone of ...... MONTICULE
crater-like basin ...... CALDERA
island .... IWO JIMA
kind of ..... ACTIVE, DORMANT,
EXTINCT
molten rock .... LAVA, MAGMA
mouth of .... CRATER,
FUMAROLE
well known .... APO, ETNA,
FUJI, TAAL, ASAMA, MAYON,
PELEE, SHASTA, MAUNA LOA,
PINATUBO, VESUVIUS
vole .... RAT, SLAM, RODENT,
(FIELD)MOUSE
volery .... AVIARY
Volga figure .... BOATMAN
tributary .... OKA, KAMA
volitant .... FLYING, FLITTING
volitient .... WILLING
volition .... WILL, CHOICE, OPTION,
VELLEITY
volk .... NATION, PEOPLE
volley ...... BURST, ROUND, SALVO,
BROADSIDE, FUSILLADE
volplane .... COAST, GLIDE
Volstead Act dissenters .... WETS
supporters .... DRYS
Volsunga _____ .... SAGA
Saga dwarf .... NIBELUNG

Saga hero .... SIGURD,
SIEGFRIED
Saga king .... ATLI
volta, in music .... TIME, TURN
Voltaire .... AROUET
character .... PANGLOSS
novel by .... CANDIDE
volt-ampere .... WATT
volte-face ...... REVERSAL, ABOUT-
FACE
voluble .... GLIB, FLUENT,
VERBOSE, GARRULOUS,
TALKATIVE
volume .... BOOK, BULK, MASS,
SIZE, TOME, CUBAGE,
CAPACITY, CONTENTS,
CUBATURE, QUANTITY
of sound unit .... DECIBEL
voluminous .... BIG, AMPLE,
BULKY, LARGE, COPIOUS
dress .... MUMU, MUUMUU
voluntarily .... FREELY,
WILLINGLY
voluntary .... UNASKED, WILLFUL,
WILLING
volunteer .... OFFER, DONATE,
ENLIST, PROFFER
opposed to .... DRAFTEE,
CONSCRIPT
voluptuary .... HEDONIST,
SYBARITE, SENSUALIST
voluptuous ...... FLESHY, LYDIAN,
SENSUAL, WORLDLY,
SENSUOUS
slang .... SEXY
volute .... CURL, ROLL, TURN,
WHORL, SPIRAL(ED)
volution .... COIL, GYRE, HELIX,
SCROLL, ROLLING
vomica .... PUS
vomit .... PUKE, SPEW, BELCH,
EJECT, EMETIC, REJECT,
REGORGE, THROW UP,
DISGORGE
effort to .... RETCH
vomiting .... EMESIS
blood .... HEMATEMESIS
in pregnancy .... MORNING
SICKNESS
Vonnegut novel .... CAT'S
CRADLE
voodoo .... HEX, OBI, BEAH,
CHARM, HOODOO, FETISHISM,
BLACK MAGIC, WITCHCRAFT
deity .... ZOMBI(E)
spell .... MOJO
voracious ...... GREEDY, HUNGRY,
EDACIOUS, ESURIENT,
RAVENOUS, RAPACIOUS,
GLUTTONOUS, INSATIABLE
voracity .... GREED, EDACITY,

797

GLUTTONY, RAPACITY
Voroshilov, USSR president
.... KLEMENTI
vortex .... EDDY, GYRE,
WHIRLPOOL, WHIRLWIND
votary .... FAN, NUN, MONK,
DEVOTEE, BELIEVER,
CELIBATE, WORSHIPER,
ENTHUSIAST
vote .... BALLOT, SUFFRAGE
by gesture .... THUMBS UP,
THUMBS DOWN
counting .... POLL
in .... ELECT
in opposition .... CON
kind of .... CON, HAND,
PROXY, STRAW, SECRET
non-candidate's ...... WRITE-IN
of assent .... AYE, PLACET
presiding officer's .... CASTING
right to .... SUFFRAGE,
FRANCHISE
solicitation for a bill
.... LOBBY
survey .... POLL
voiced .... AYE, NAY, YEA
voter .... ELECTOR
voting amendment beneficiaries
as of 1971 ...... EIGHTEEN OR
OLDER
method .... VOICE, BALLOT
vouch .... BACK, AFFIRM, ASSURE,

ATTEST, CERTIFY, SPONSOR,
GUARANTEE
voucher .... CHIT, RECEIPT,
EVIDENCE, DEBENTURE
vouchsafe .... GIVE, DEIGN,
GRANT, BESTOW, CONCEDE,
GUARANTEE
vouge .... TON
vow .... OATH, SWEAR, PLEDGE,
PROMISE, DEDICATE
taker .... NUN, MONK, VOTARY,
WITNESS, CELIBATE, OFFICIAL,
DEFENDANT
to inflict harm .... THREATEN
vowel .... LETTER
change in sound ...... UMLAUT
contraction of .... SYNERESIS
gradation .... ABLAUT
mark .... BREVE, TILDE,
MACRON, UMLAUT,
DI(A)ERESIS, CIRCUMFLEX
slurring .... ELISION
vox .... VOICE
voyage .... SAIL, TRAVEL,
JOURNEY, PASSAGE, (SEA)TRIP
pleasure .... JAUNT, CRUISE
short .... EXCURSION
voyager .... SAILOR
voyageur .... BOATMAN,
TRAVELER
voyeur .... PEEPING TOM

vrouw .... LADY, WOMAN,
HOUSEWIFE
vs. .... VERSUS
Vulcan .... HEPHAESTUS,
HEPHAISTOS
Star Trek .... (MR) SPOCK
vulcanite .... RUBBER, EBONITE
vulgar ...... LOUD, CRASS, CRUDE,
GROSS, RANDY, COARSE,
COMMON, RIBALD, BOORISH,
LOW-BRED, OBSCENE,
UNCOUTH, PLEBEIAN
vulgarian .... CAD, LOUT, SLUT,
CHURL, BARBARIAN,
ROUGHNECK
vulgarity .... ILL-BREEDING
Vulgate, author of the
.... JEROME
vulnerable .... WEAK, ASSAILABLE
Vulpecula .... LITTLE FOX,
CONSTELLATION
vulpine ...... FOXY, WILY, CRAFTY,
TRICKY, CUNNING,
VULPECULAR
vulture .... URUBU, ATRATA,
CONDOR, BUZZARD, GRIFFON,
PREDATOR, SCAVENGER,
LAMMERGEI(E)R
food .... CARRION
hawk resembling
.... CARACARA

W, Arabic .... WAW
in chemistry .... TUNGSTEN
old English .... WEN
Waadt .... VAUD
Wabash Cannonball composer
.... (ROY)ACUFF
Wabash River City .... TERRE
HAUTE
tributary .... TIPPECANOE
wabble .... LARVA, WOBBLE
wacker .... QUAKER
wacky ...... ODD, QUEER, ERRATIC,
ECCENTRIC
person .... WACKO
wad .... BAT, PAD, CRAM, LUMP,
MASS, PLUG, BUNDLE, DOSSIL,
FILLING, STUFF(ING)
of paper money
.... (BANK)ROLL
used as wound dressing
.... PLEDGET
wadding material .... HEMP,
KAPOK, COTTON

waddle .... WAG, SWAY, LURCH,
TODDLE, WOBBLE
waddler ...... BABY, DUCK, GOOSE,
TODDLER
waddy ...... CANE, CLUB, COWBOY,
WALKING STICK
wade .... FORD, SLOG, SLOSH,
PADDLE, WALLOW
wader .... COOT, IBIS, RAIL,
CRANE, EGRET, HERON, SNIPE
waders .... BOOTS
wadi ...... OASIS, RAVINE, VALLEY,
CHANNEL, WATERCOURSE
wading bird. See also **bird**
.... IBIS
wadset .... MORTGAGE
wafer .... CAKE, DISK, SNAP,
CANDY, COOKIE, TABLET,
BISCUIT, CRACKER, LOZENGE
container .... PIX, PYX
of the Eucharist .... HOST
waff .... GUST, PUFF, WAVE,
GHOST, WHIFF, SOLITARY,

WORTHLESS
waffie .... VAGABOND
waffle .... PRATTLE, (BATTER)CAKE
like .... PANCAKE
waft .... BUOY, GUST, ROLL, WAIF,
WAVE, FLOAT, BREATH,
CONVEY, CARRY(OVER),
TRANSPORT
wag .... NOD, WIT, CARD, JERK,
SWAY, WAVE, JOKER, SHAKE,
JESTER, WAGGLE, WIGGLE,
FARCEUR, PUNSTER
wage .... PAY, HIRE, MAKE,
SALARY, CARRY ON,
CONDUCT, STIPEND,
ENGAGE(IN), EMOLUMENT
boost .... RAISE
deduct from .... DOCK
earner .... CARPENTER,
STEVEDORE, BRICKLAYER,
STONEMASON, LONGSHOREMAN
earners collectively .... LABOR
war .... LEVY

wager ...... BET, VIE, ANTE, GAGE, RISK, STAKE, GAMBLE, HAZARD, IMPONE, PARLAY

wages .... INCOME, REWARD, STIPEND, EARNINGS, EMOLUMENT, RECOMPENSE, COMPENSATION

after deductions .... TAKE-HOME

describing some .... LIVING, STARVATION

payment in kind .... TRUCK

wagged, thing that's .... FLAG, HEAD, TAIL, FINGER, TONGUE

wagger .... DOG, PIPIT

waggery .... WIT, JEST, JOKE, MERRIMENT

waggish .... DROLL, MERRY, JOCULAR, PLAYFUL, ROGUISH, SPORTIVE

waggle .... TOTTER

dancer .... BEE

Wagner, composer ...... RICHARD

father-in-law of .... LISZT

forte of .... OPERA

heroine of .... EVA, ELSA, ISOLDE

tetralogy of .... RING CYCLE

wife of .... COSIMA

work of .... LIEBESTOD, LOHENGRIN

Wagnerian earth goddess .... ERDA

heroine .... EVA, ELSA

music festival city .... BAYREUTH

opus .... RIENZI, PARSIFAL, LIEBESTOD, LOHENGRIN

role ...... ELSA, HAGEN, SENTA, WOTAN, ISOLDE, TRISTAN

soprano .... NILSSON

wagon .... CAR, VAN, DRAY, TRAM, WAIN, LORRY, (T)CART, TRUCK, CAMION, TRAILER, TUMBREL, TUMBRIL, VOITURE

ammunitions .... CAISSON

baggage .... FOURGON

battle .... DREADNAUGHT

box-like .... TRAM

builder .... WAINWRIGHT

Charlemagne's .... WAIN

driver .... CARTER, CHARIOTEER

for hauling .... DRAY

freight charge .... CARTAGE

horse .... POLER

horse-drawn .... CHARIOT

open four-wheeled .... T-CART, WAGONETTE

oriental .... ARABA

pin .... CLEVIS

police .... BLACK MARIA

prairie .... SCHOONER

repairer .... WAINWRIGHT

shaft .... THILL

tongue .... NEAP

track .... RUT

yoke .... INSPAN

Wagoner .... AURIGA, BIG DIPPER, CHARLES'S WAIN

wagons, convoy of .... WAGON TRAIN

wagtail .... BIRD, LARK, PIPIT, THRUSH

wahoo .... ELM, SHRUB, BASSWOOD, BURNING BUSH

fish .... ONO, PETO

waif .... WAFT, GAMIN, STRAY, SIGNAL, VAGRANT, MAVERICK, FOUNDLING, (STREET)ARAB

Waikiki .... BEACH

site .... HONOLULU

wall ...... CRY, SOB, HOWL, MOAN, WAWL, YOWL, MOURN, LAMENT, ULULATE, COMPLAIN, (CATER)WAUL

Wailing Wall chore ...... PRAYER, LAMENTATION

devotee .... JEW

site .... JERUSALEM

wain .... CART, WAGON

wainscot .... CEIL, LINING, PANEL(ING), WALLBOARD

waist ...... LOIN, BASQUE, BLOUSE, BODICE, MIDDLE, MIDRIFF

circumference .... GIRTH

garment .... SARONG, LOINCLOTH

molding garment .... GIRDLE

of dress .... TAILLE

wasters .... DIET

waistband .... OBI, BELT, SASH, GIRDLE, CINCTURE

waistcloth .... PAREUS, SARONG, LAVA-LAVA

waistcoat .... VEST, GILET, JACKET, WESKIT

waistline .... GIRTH

wait .... BIDE, STAY, DALLY, DELAY, SERVE, TARRY, ATTEND, LINGER, REMAIN

in ambush .... COUCH

lie in .... TRAP, AMBUSH

near at hand .... HOVER

on .... SERVE, VISIT, ATTEND

until a future time ..... POSTPONE, PROCRASTINATE

waiter .... TRAY, GARCON, POTMAN, SALVER, SERVER, STEWARD, ATTENDANT

drive-in .... CARHOP

female .... WAITRESS

portable .... DUMB

waiter's delight .... TIPPER

waiting line .... CUE, QUEUE

waitresses, chief of .... HOSTESS

waive .... DEFER, GIVE UP, FOR(E)GO, ABANDON, DISCLAIM, RENOUNCE, RELINQUISH

right or title .... QUITCLAIM

Wakashan people .... AHT, NOOTKA

wake .... PATH, STIR, TRACK, VIGIL, WATCH, AROUSE, EXCITE

periscope's .... FEATHER

robin .... ARUM, PLANT, SARAH, TRILLIUM, CUCKOOPINT, JACK-IN-THE-PULPIT

submarine's .... FEATHER

up from this .... COMA, DREAM, SLEEP, STUPOR, TRANCE, NIGHTMARE

wakeful .... ALERT, RESTLESS, INSOMNIAC, SLEEPLESS

Wake Island .... OTORI

waken .... STIR, AWAKE, (A)ROUSE, EXCITE, SHAKE UP

Waldheim, UN secretary-general .... KURT

nationality of .... AUSTRIAN

Waldorf .... SALAD

-Astoria .... HOTEL

-Astoria site .... NEW YORK

wale .... RIB, BLOW, WELT, W(H)EAL, WHELK, CHOICE, BLEMISH, TEXTURE, SELECT(ION)

on a fabric .... RIDGE

waled fabric .... CORDUROY

Waler .... HORSE

Wales bay .... CARDIGAN, TREMADOC, CARMARTHEN, SAINT BRIDES

capital .... CARDIFF

city/town .... BALA, RHYL, BARRY, CHIRK, FLINT, NEATH, NEFYN, BANGOR, HARLECH, MAESTEG, NEWPORT, PENARTH, SWANSEA, WREXHAM, ABERDARE, HAWARDEN, LLANELLI, RHONDDA, PEMBROKE, TREDEGAR

county .... CLWYD, DYFED, GWENT, POWYS, GWYNEDD, GLAMORGAN

dog .... (WELSH)CORGI, (WELSH)TERRIER

floral emblem .... LEEK

head .... CEMMAES

island .... HOLY, CALDY, BARDSEY, ANGLESEY
language .... CYMRIC, BRYTHONIC
mountain .... SNOWDON, PLYNLIMON
mountain range .... BLACK, BERWYN, PRESELI, CAMBRIAN
national park ...... SNOWDONIA
patron saint .... DAVID
peninsula .... GOWER, LLEYN
people of .... WELSH
poetic name .... CAMBRIA
port .... TALBOT
river ...... DEE, ELY, USK, WYE, TAFF, TOWY, DOVEY, TEIFI, SEVERN, RHYMNEY
seaport .... SWANSEA
strait .... MENAI

Walesa, Polish leader ...... LECH

walk .... GAIT, HIKE, HOOF, PLOD, STEP, STOA, TREK, ALLEY, AMBLE, MARCH, TRAMP, TREAD, RAMBLE, SPHERE, STROLL, TRAVEL
a beat .... PATROL
about .... AMBULATE
about idly .... STROLL, SAUNTER
about ostentatiously
.... PARADE
across a street carelessly
.... JAYWALK
aimlessly .... ROAM, ROVE, RAMBLE, WANDER
along .... MOSEY
around .... SKIRT
awkward, halting .... LIMP, HOBBLE
awkwardly .... SHAMBLE
baby's .... TODDLE, WADDLE
beach .... ESPLANADE
clumsily .... LUMBER, SHUFFLE
coating .... PARGET, PLASTER
covered .... STOA, ARCADE, PORTICO, CLOISTER
daintily .... MINCE
furtively .... STALK
kind of .... HIKE, LIMP, MINCE, STRUT, TRAMP, LUMBER, PRANCE, SASHAY, STRIDE, TODDLE, WADDLE, WOBBLE, LAMBETH, SWAGGER
leisurely .... AMBLE, STROLL, TRUDGE, SAUNTER, TRAIPSE, PROMENADE
like a crab .... SIDLE
long .... HIKE, MARCH
of life .... SPHERE
off .... LEAVE, DEPART
off with .... WIN, STEAL

on .... TREAD, TRAMPLE
on stilts .... TRAMPOLIO
out on .... LEAVE, DESERT, ABANDON
over .... BULLY, HENPECK, BULLDOZE
pompously .... STRUT
precariously .... TEETER
public .... PARADE, ESPLANADE, PROMENADE
self-importantly .... SASHAY
shaded .... MALL, ALAMEDA
slang .... HIT THE ROAD
softly .... PAD, TIPTOE
taken for one's health
.... CONSTITUTIONAL
this in Boston .... FREEDOM TRAIL
through mud .... SLOSH, WALLOW, SQUELCH
through water .... WADE
to and fro .... PACE
unsteadily .... TOTTER, STAGGER
vain .... STRUT, PEACOCK, SWAGGER
with a lame leg .... LIMP, HOBBLE
with heavy steps .... STAMP, STUMP, TRAMP, TRAMPLE

walkaway ...... TRIUMPH, VICTORY
walker .... HIKER, PACER, TREKKER, VAGRANT, AMBULANT, STROLLER, PEDESTRIAN
idle .... FLANEUR
walking .... HIKING, HOOFING, AMBULANT, FOOTWORK, GRADIENT, AMBULATORY, PEDESTRIAN
adapted for .... GRESSORIAL
aid .... CANE, WALKER, CRUTCHES
idle .... FLANERIE
miss one's step in
.... STUMBLE
on air .... ELATED
on all fours ...... PRONOGRADE
papers .... PINK SLIP, DISMISSAL
shoes .... RUBBERS, BALMORAL, SNEAKERS
stick .... CANE, POGO, STAFF, STILT, WADDY, MALAGA, RATTAN, MALACCA, SUPPLEJACK
vendor .... PEDDLER

walkout .... STRIKE
wall .... DIKE, SIDE, FENCE, LEVEE, PARIES, SEPTUM, BARRIER, PARAPET, PARTITION

aboard ship .... BULKHEAD
band .... CORDON
bench .... PODIUM
binder .... PERPEND
border .... DADO
bracket .... CORBEL, SCONCE
coating .... PAINT, PLASTER
column .... PILASTER
cover .... PAPER, MANTLE, LAG(GING), PANELING
dividing .... SEPTUM, PARTITION
end of .... ANTA
facing .... VENEER, REVETMENT
for defense .... RAMPART, PALISADE, VALLATION
fort .... RAMPART
garden .... HAHA
hanging cloth .... ARRAS, TAPESTRY
in .... CONFINE, ENCLOSE
indentation .... CRENEL(LE)
inscription .... GRAFFITO
kind of .... JETTY, STONE, RIPRAP
lining .... STEEN, WAINSCOT
lizard .... GECKO
loophole .... CRENEL(LE)
mine .... BRATTICE
molding .... CORNICE
opening .... BAY, SCUTTLE, CRENEL(LE), EMBRASURE
painter .... MURALIST
park .... HAHA
pertaining to .... MURAL
pier .... ANTA
protective .... PARAPET, RAMPART, PALISADE
recess .... BAY, NICHE
river ..... LEVEE, EMBANKMENT
rue .... FERN
sea .... DAM, DIKE, MOLE, PIER, BREAKWATER
section .... PANEL
step .... STILE
stone .... ASHLAR
tapestry .... ARRAS
top layer .... COPING
top slab .... CAPSTONE
water .... DAM, DIKE, PIER, WEIR, EMBANKMENT
wood lining .... WAINSCOT
wooden pin .... NOG
writing .... GRAFFITO

Wall Street ...... MONEY MARKET, STOCK EXCHANGE
operator .... BEAR, BULL, BROKER, SPECULATOR
transaction .... TRADE
watchdog .... SEC
Wall Streeter .... (STOCK)BROKER

wallaba ...... APA, TREE, ARAWAK
wallaby .... KANGAROO
Wallace, novelist .... LEW, IRVING
work ..... BEN HUR, THE WORD
Wallach, actor .... ELI
Wal(l)achian 15th century
ruler ...... VLAD TEPES, VLAD
DRACUL
wallaroo .... EURO, KANGAROO
wallboard .... WAINSCOT, GYPSUM
BOARD
walled .... ENCLOSED,
PARTITIONED
town .... BURG
wallet .... POUCH, PURSE, SCRIP,
BILLFOLD, (KNAP)SACK,
(MONEY)BAG, POCKETBOOK
walleye .... ALEWIFE, STRABISMUS
walleyed .... CROSSEYED
fish ..... PIKE, PERCH, ALEWIFE,
POLLACK
pike .... DORE, DORY
slang .... DRUNK
wallflower .... CUBA, HEARTSEASE
wallies .... FINERY
wallop .... HIT, BEAT, BELT,
PASTE, SMITE, THRASH
walloper .... WHOPPER
walloping .... STRONG, POWERFUL,
WHOPPING
wallow .... TOSS, REVEL, GROVEL,
PUDDLE, WELTER, MUDHOLE,
FLOUNDER, LUXURIATE,
ROLL(ABOUT)
walls, behind the .... IN PRISON
dividing .... SEPTA
wally .... TOY, FINE, GEWGAW,
PLEASING, FIRST-RATE
"Wally" .... DUCHESS OF
WINDSOR
walnut ...... TREE, WOOD, BROWN,
TRYMA, HICKORY, SHAGBARK
Walpurgis Night revelers
.... WITCHES
walrus .... BRUT, SEAL, MORSE,
SEACOW, TUSKER, PINNIPED,
SEAHORSE, ROSMARINE
herd .... POD
male .... BULL
tooth .... TUSK
tusk .... IVORY
weapon .... RUSK
Walton, basketball player
.... BILL
business tycoon .... SAM
fisherman .... IZAAK
waltz .... DANCE, MUSIC, VALSE,
WHIRL
a kind of .... BOSTON
dance like .... REDOWA
king .... STRAUSS

wamble .... REEL, STAGGER
wame ...... WOMB, BELLY, VENTER
wampum .... BEADS, MONEY,
PEAG(E), SE(A)WAN
wamus .... JACKET, CARDIGAN
wan .... ASHY, PALE, WAXY,
ASHEN, WAXEN, PALLID,
COLORLESS
wand .... ROD, MACE, BATON,
SHOOT STAFF, VERGE, WITHE,
SWITCH, WATTLE, SCEPTER
conductor's .... BATON
shaped like a .... VIRGATE
symbol of medical
profession ..... CADUCEUS
symbol of sovereignty
.... SCEPTER
wander .... GAD, ROAM, ROVE,
DRIFT, STRAY, RAMBLE,
STROLL, MEANDER, TRAIPSE,
DIVAGATE
about idly .... GAD
from main subject in talking
.... RAMBLE, DIGRESS,
DIVAGATE
over a wide area
.... STRAGGLE
predatorily .... PROWL
wanderer .... ARAB, HOBO,
GYPSY, NOMAD, ROVER,
TRAMP, BEDOUIN, VAGRANT,
VAGABOND, ITINERANT,
LANDLO(U)PER
wandering ...... ERRANT, ERRATIC,
NOMADIC, ODYSSEY,
VAGRANT, DEVIATING,
FOOTLOOSE
beggar .... FAKIR, ROGUE,
VAGABOND
caliph .... AL RASCHID
dervish .... CALENDER
extended .... ODYSSEY
from what is normal
.... ABERRANT
mental state .... DELIRIUM
minstrel/student .... GOLIARD
tribe .... GYPSY
wanderings .... ODYSSEY,
TRAVELS
wanderoo ...... LANGUR, MONKEY,
MACAQUE
wandle ...... AGILE, LITHE, SUPPLE
wane .... EBB, FADE, SINK, ABATE,
LESSEN, DECLINE, DWINDLE,
SLACKEN, SUBSIDE, DIMINISH
wangle .... GET, COAX, WRING,
OBTAIN, FALSIFY, FINAGLE,
JUGGLE, WHEEDLE,
W(R)IGGLE, CONTRIVE
wanigan .... ARK
want .... LACK, MISS, NEED, WISH,

CRAVE, DEARTH, DESIRE,
NEGLECT, POVERTY,
SCARCITY, SHORTAGE,
NECESSITY, DESTITUTION,
REQUIRE(MENT)
wanted man .... OUTLAW,
ESCAPEE, DESPERADO, PUBLIC
ENEMY
wanting .... MINUS, ABSENT,
WITHOUT
wanton .... LEWD, RASH, TART,
WILD, LOOSE, IMMORAL,
PLAYFUL, WAYWARD,
WILLFUL, HEEDLESS,
RECKLESS, UNCHASTE,
FROLICSOME
destroyer .... VANDAL
kittens make _____ ..... SOBER
CATS
man .... LIBERTINE
woman .... FLIRT, HUSSY,
TRAMP, TROLLOP
wapiti .... ELK, DEER
Wapner's bailiwick .... PEOPLE'S
COURT
wrap .... ROBE
war .... COMBAT, STRIFE,
CONFLICT, HOSTILITY,
BELLICOSITY, HOSTILITIES,
BELLIGERENCE
acquisition .... SPOILS
advocate for an all-out
.... HAWK, JINGO
against abuse .... CRUSADE
agency .... OSS
agreement .... TRUCE, CARTEL,
CEASEFIRE
ammo wagon .... CAISSON
arrange forces for battle in
.... MARSHAL
at .... BELLICOSE, BELLIGERENT
attack by military force
.... INVASION
between armed forces
.... BATTLE, COMBAT,
STRUGGLE
boat: abbr. .... LST
bonnet wearer .... INDIAN
casualty symbol .... GOLD
STAR
chariot .... ESSED
chief, name meaning
.... CEDRIC
cry ...... YELL, ALALA, AMORT,
WHOOP, BANZAI, SLOGAN
dance .... PYRRHIC
describing a mutually
destructive
.... INTERNECINE
drums .... TAM-TAM, TOM-TOM

engine, stone-throwing .... CATAPULT, TREBUCHET
event provoking .... CASUS BELLI
fleet .... ARMADA
foot soldiers .... INFANTRY
galley beak .... ROSTRUM
games .... MANEUVERS
gas .... MUSTARD, YPERITE, ADAMSITE
god .... TYR, ARES, IRRA, MARS, ODIN, WOTAN
goddess .... ENYO, ATHENA, BELLONA, MINERVA
holy .... JIHAD, CRUSADE
horse .... CHARGER, COURSER, VET(ERAN), DESTRIER
horse head armor .... CHAMFRON, CHAMFRAIN
long-continued, between families .... FEUD
maneuvering of military forces .... TACTICS
mounted troops .... CAVALRY
of words .... DEBATE
operation .... CAMPAIGN
paint: sl. .... REGALIA, COSMETICS
paint wearer .... INDIAN
participant .... GUNNER, MARINE, SAILOR, FIGHTER, SOLDIER, VETERAN, WARRIOR, COMBATANT, ANTAGONIST, BELLIGERENT
pertaining to .... MARTIAL
planning of large-scale operations .... STRATEGY
preparation .... MOBILIZATION
pretext for .... CASUS BELLI
religious .... CRUSADE
scheme to deceive enemy .... STRATAGEM
slogan of Marine Raiders .... GUNG-HO
symbol of .... MARS
-torn land .... IRAQ, IRAN, KUWAIT, CROATIA, LEBANON
troops' resurgence .... RALLY
troops' withdrawal .... RETREAT
vehicle .... JEEP, TANK, HALFTRACK
vessel .... U-BOAT, PT-BOAT, CRUISER, FLATTOP, TRIREME, CORVETTE, DESTROYER, SUB(MARINE), DREADNAUGHT, AIRCRAFT CARRIER
volunteer forces .... GUERRILLAS
weapon .... GAS, BOMB, GUNS, CANNON, ROCKET, MISSILE, TORPEDO, ARTILLERY
within nation .... CIVIL WAR, REVOLUTION

War and Peace author .... TOLSTOI
heroine .... NATASHA

warble .... SING, CAROL, LARVA, TRILL, TREMOR, YODEL, BABBLE, QUAVER

warbler. See also **songbird** .... SINGER, REDSTART, SONGSTER, BECCAFICO, TROCHILUS

warbling .... CHIRM, TWITTER

Warbucks .... DADDY

ward .... CARE, FEND, AVERT, GUARD, PARRY, WATCH, CHARGE, CUSTODY, DISTRICT, PROTEGE(E), DEPENDENT
heelers .... POLITICOS
kind of .... MINOR, INCOMPETENT
off .... AVERT, STAVE OFF
part of a .... PRECINCT
person (entrusted) with a .... PATRON, TRUSTEE, GUARDIAN
politician .... HEELER

warden .... PEAR, JAILER, JAILOR, ALCAIDE, TRUSTEE, KEEPER, GUARDIAN, CONSTABLE, CUSTODIAN, GATEKEEPER
famous .... LAWES
forest .... RANGER
kind of .... FIRE, GAME, FOREST, PRISON, AIR-RAID
of a minor .... CURATOR

warder .... ROD, GUARD, STAFF, TURNKEY, WATCHMAN, CUSTODIAN

wardrobe .... DUDS, ATTIRE, CLOSET, APPAREL, ARMOIRE, CLOTHES
bride's .... TROUSSEAU
room, clergy's .... VESTRY
servant's .... LIVERY, UNIFORMS
slang .... FINERY

wardship .... CUSTODY

ware .... WARY, WISE, AWARE, READY, DISHES, POTTERY, PRUDENT, CAUTIOUS, CONSCIOUS OF

warehouse .... HONG, DEPOT, ETAPE, STORE, BODEGA, GODOWN, CAMARIN, ELEVATOR, ENTREPOT, MAGAZINE
for candles .... CHANDLERY
items .... STORABLES
platform .... PALLET

public .... ETAPE
receipt .... QUEDAN, WARRANT
vehicle .... FORKLIFT
weapons .... ARSENAL

wares .... GOODS, MERCHANDISE

warfare .... CLASH, COMBAT, POLEMY, STRIFE, CONFLICT, FIGHTING, STRUGGLE, HOSTILITIES
kind of .... AIR, LAND, NAVAL, AERIAL, ATOMIC, MISSILE, CHEMICAL, AMPHIBIOUS, UNDERGROUND
temporary stoppage of .... TRUCE, ARMISTICE, CEASE-FIRE

Warfield, duchess .... WALLIS

warhead of missile .... PAYLOAD

Warhol .... ANDY

warlike .... ODINIC, HOSTILE, MARTIAL, MILITANT, TACTICAL, BELLICOSE, COMBATIVE, BELLIGERENT

warlock .... WIZARD, CONJURER, MAGICIAN, SORCERER

warm .... MILD, FRESH, MUGGY, SUNNY, ARDENT, FERVID, HEAT(ED), LIVELY, CORDIAL, THERMAL, ZEALOUS
and stuffy .... CLOSE
baths .... THERMAE
-blooded .... ARDENT, FERVENT, PASSIONATE
compress .... STUPE
-hearted .... KIND, LOVING, TENDER, CORDIAL
make moderately .... TEPEFY
moderately .... TEPID, WARMISH, LUKEWARM
springs .... THERMAE
state of being made .... CALEFACTION
very .... HOT, CANDENT

warmed-over .... (RE)HEATED

warmer .... STOVE, BURNER, HEATER, FURNACE

warmly lit .... AGLOW

warmonger .... HAWK, WARLORD, JINGO(IST), DEMAGOGUE, FIREBRAND, MILITARIST, RABBLEROUSER

warmth .... HEAT, ZEAL, ARDOR, ENTHUSIASM
increasing in .... CALESCENT
of emotion .... ARDOR, SPARK, VIVACITY, EAGERNESS
sensation of .... GLOW

warn .... FLAG, ALERT, ADVISE, DEMAND, EXHORT, NOTIFY, SIGNAL, CAUTION, PORTEND, ADMONISH, FOREBODE,

THREATEN

warning .... OMEN, ALARM, CHECK, AUGURY, LESSON, NOTICE, THREAT, TIP-OFF, PORTENT, PRESAGE, (AD)MONITION

from dermatologist .... SKIN-DONT(S)

in law .... CAVEAT

old style .... LARUM

signal ...... HISS, ALERT, SIREN, ALAR(U)M, BEACON, TOCSIN

signal device .... BELL, FLARE, SIREN, FOGHORN, RED FLAG

snake's .... HISS, RATTLE

system, for short .... DEWS

weather .... ADVISORY

word(s) of .... FORE, HALT, STOP, BEWARE, FREEZE, LOOK OUT, WATCH OUT, OFF LIMIT(S)

warp ...... MUD, BIAS, SILT, TWIST, DEFORM, CONTORT, DEVIATE, INCLINE, PERVERT, ABERRATION, DISTORT(ION), (BEND) OUT OF SHAPE

and woof .... WEAVE

thread ends .... THRUM

warped .... UNJUST, PREJUDICED

warplane .... SPAD, ZERO, STUKA, BOMBER, FIGHTER, SPITFIRE, FLYING FORTRESS

warplanes, fleet of
.... (AIR)ARMADA

warrant .... PASS, WRIT, MERIT, ORDER, STATE, ASSURE, CAVEAT, PERMIT, PLEDGE, PLEVIN, SURETY, TICKET, CERTIFY, JUSTIFY, PRECEPT, VOUCHER, GUARANTEE, AUTHORIZATION

convict's .... MITTIMUS

of arrest .... CAPIAS

officer .... BOSUN

one's ability, character .... AVOUCH, VOUCH FOR

royal .... BERAT, EDICT

to appear in court
.... SUMMONS, SUBPOENA

warranty .... PROMISE, ASSURANCE, GUARANTEE

warren .... HUTCH, SLUM(S), RABBITRY

inhabitant .... GAME, RABBIT

Warren, Chief Justice ...... EARL

warrigal .... DINGO

warring nations' agreement
...... TRUCE, CARTEL, TREATY, ARMISTICE

warrior .... JINGO, SINGH, FIGHTER, KURIPAN, SOLDIER,

COMBATANT, SERVICEMAN

arena .... GLADIATOR

Algerian .... SPAHI

female .... AMAZON

frenzied for battle
.... BERSERK(ER)

Indian .... BRAVE

Japanese .... SAMURAI

noted: poet. .... THANE

Philippine .... MAHARLIKA

warsaw .... FISH, GROUPER

warship .... RAZEE, GALLEY, CRUISER, FLATTOP, FRIGATE, GALLEON, MAN O'WAR, TRIREME, IRONCLAD, DESTROYER, BATTLEWAGON, DREADNAUGHT, DREADNOUGHT

armored .... MONITOR, IRONCLAD, MERRIMAC

boat on .... DINGHY, LAUNCH

convoy .... CORVET(TE)

deck, lowest .... ORLOP

eating quarters .... WARDROOM

gun emplacement ...... TURRET

gun shield .... CUPOLA

kitchen .... GALLEY

lookout .... CROW'S NEST

prison .... BRIG

ram .... BEAK

station for wounded
.... COCKPIT

tower .... TURRET

warships, fleet of .... ARMADA

involving .... NAVAL

wart .... BULGE, TUMOR, GROWTH, PAPULE, BLEMISH, VERRUCA, KERATOSIS, PAPILLOMA

on eyelids/armpit, describing
.... FILIFORM

on foot sole, describing
.... PLANTAR

type of .... FLAT, GENITAL, PLANTAR, DIGITATE, FILIFORM

Wartburg's important resident
.... LUTHER

wartime detainee .... INTERNEE

detention .... INTERNMENT

sea hazard .... MINE

warts, covered with
.... VERRUCOSE

wary .... SHY, ALERT, CAG(E)Y, CANNY, CHARY, LEERY, CAREFUL, GUARDED, PRUDENT, CAUTIOUS, DISCREET, SUSPICIOUS, CIRCUMSPECT

wash .... LAP, WET, LAVE, SLOP, BATHE, DRIFT, ELUTE, FLOOD, RINSE, SWILL, DRENCH, PURIFY, DETERGE, MOISTEN,

HOSE(DOWN)

away .... ERODE

and iron .... LAUNDER

basin/bowl .... LAVER, LAVABO, LABATORY

by rubbing hard .... SCOUR, SCRUB

hair/scalp .... SHAMPOO

in lye .... BUCK

kind of .... MOUTH, LOTION

lightly .... RINSE

one's hands of ...... ABANDON, GIVE UP, CAST OFF, DISCARD

out .... FADE, ELUTE

out with swift current of water .... FLUSH

to remove dirt, impurities
.... CLEAN(SE)

washbowl in church .... LAVABO

washed out .... FADED, BLEACHED

up ..... BEAT, BUSHED, POOPED, THROUGH, EXHAUSTED

washer .... GASKET, SCRUBBER

washerwoman .... LAUNDRESS

washing ...... ELUTION, FLUSHING, LAVATION, SCRUBBING, LAUNDERING

act/process of .... LAVATION

board .... DOLLY

body, in religious ceremony
.... ABLUTION

out of an organ .... ENEMA, LAVAGE

soapsuds .... LATHER

sound of .... SLOSH

water for .... LAVATION

Washington Air Force Base
.... MCCHORD, FAIRCHILD

airport .... DULLES

author .... IRVING

bay .... DABOB, PADILLA, WILLAPA, BOUNDARY

bills .... ONES

bloomer .... CHAT

cape .... ALAVA, FLATTERY, SHOALWATER, DISAPPOINTMENT

capital .... OLYMPIA

city/town ..... KELSO, AUBURN, BURIEN, RENTON, TACOMA, WAPATO, YAKIMA, EDMONDS, EVERETT, PULLMAN, REDMOND, SEATTLE, SPOKANE, ABERDEEN, BELLEVUE, LYNNWOOD, BREMERTON, KENNEWICK, VANCOUVER, BELLINGHAM, WALLA WALLA, MOUNT VERNON

college .... WHITMAN

county .... KING, ADAMS, CLARK, GRANT, LEWIS,

MASON, BENTON, CHELAN, ISLAND, KITSAP, PIERCE, SKAGIT, YAKIMA, COWLITZ, SPOKANE, WHATCOM, THURSTON, SNOHOMISH, WALLA WALLA

dam ..... ROSS, WELLS, ASOTIN, MCNARY, BOUNDARY, DRY FALLS, ICE HARBOR, O'SULLIVAN, THE DALLES, BONNEVILLE, GRAND COULEE

DC Air Force Base .... BOLLING

art gallery .... FREER

hostess .... HOWAR, MESTA

pressure group .... LOBBY(IST)

river .... ANACOSTIA

seeress .... DIXON

university ...... GEORGETOWN

educator .... BOOKER (T)

first U.S. president .... GEORGE

aide of .... (TOBIAS)LEAR

brother of .... LAWRENCE

chef of .... HERCULES

home of .... MOUNT VERNON

mother of ...... MARY (BALL)

physician of .... (JAMES)CRAIK

portrait painter .... (CHARLES)PEALE, (GILBERT)STUART

wife of .... MARTHA

football team .... REDSKINS

initials .... AID

Irving character .... RIP VAN WINKLE

island ..... LONG, SAND, LOPEZ, LUMMI, ORCAS, PUGET, SUCIA, CAMANO, BLALOCK, FIDALGO, TATOOSH, BAINBRIDGE, DESTRUCTION

lake .... BLUE, DEER, LONG, OMAK, ROCK, ROSS, SOAP, ALDER, BAKER, BANKS, MOSES, RIFLE, UNION, CELILO, CHELAN, CURLEW, DIABLO, ENTIAT, MERWIN, PALMER, SAMISH, SILVER, SPIRIT, SYLVAN, WALUPT, BUMPING, CUSHMAN, DIAMOND, OSOYOOS, PATEROS, SACHEEN, SPRAGUE, WALLULA, WANAPUM, CRESCENT, UMATILLA, QUINAULT, CAVANAUGH, VANCOUVER, WYNOOCHEE, BONNEVILLE

-Moscow telephone .... HOTLINE

mountain .... AIX, JACK,

ADAMS, LOGAN, DANIEL, REMMEL, STUART, GARDNER, OLYMPUS, RAINIER, SHUKSAN, SPOKANE, TIFFANY, BONAPARTE, SKOKOMISH, ABERCROMBIE, SAINT HELENS, TWIN SISTERS

mountain range .... BLUE, ROCKY, ENTIAT, CASCADE, OLYMPIC, WENATCHEE

national park .... OLYMPIC, SAN JUAN, MOUNT RAINIER

peak .... SNOW, BONANZA, SNOWFIELD

peninsula .... EDIZ HOOK

river .... HOH, SAUK, BAKER, CEDAR, GREEN, LEWIS, NORTH, SNAKE, TWISP, WHITE, CISPUS, ENTIAT, KALAMA, NACHES, SKAGIT, SULTAN, TIETON, TOUTLE, YAKIMA, CASCADE, CHIWAWA, COWLITZ, NASELLE, SANPOIL, SPOKANE, TOUCHET, CHEHALIS, COLUMBIA, COLVILLE, NOOKSACK, OKANOGAN, PASAYTEN, TUCANNON, DESCHUTES, NISQUALLY, SNOQUALMIE, WALLA WALLA

sound .... PUGET

state bird .... GOLDFINCH

state flower .... RHODODENDRON

state motto .... AL-KI

state nickname .... EVERGREEN

strait .... GEORGIA, ROSARIO, JUAN DE FUCA

university .... GONZAGA

washout .... FIASCO, FAILURE

washroom .... BATHROOM, LAVATORY, RESTROOM

washstand .... COMMODE

wasp .... WHAMP, DIGGER, HORNET, VESPID, STINGER, COW KILLER, MUDDAUBER, YELLOW JACKET

like a .... VESPINE, WASPISH

nest .... VESPIARY

prick of .... STING

waspish .... TESTY, SNAPPISH, IRASCIBLE, IRRITABLE, BAD-TEMPERED, SLIM-WAISTED, SLENDER-WAISTED

wassail .... SPREE, TOAST, GUZZLE, CAROUSE, REVEL(RY), CAROUSAL, CELEBRATION, DRINKING BOUT

Wasserman test subject .... SYPHILIS

waste .... EBB, LOSS, RUIN, CHAFF, DECAY, OCEAN, SPILL, SPOIL,

BARREN, DESERT, MISUSE, REFUSE, FRITTER, GARBAGE, RUBBISH, LEAK(AGE), LEFTOVER, (MIS)SPEND, SQUANDER, WEAR AWAY, EXCRETION, WILDERNESS

allowance .... TRET

arctic .... TUNDRA

away .... ROT, GNAW, PEAK, DECAY, MO(U)LDER, EMACIATE, MACERATE

cause of .... HASTE

colloquial .... BLOW

deposit .... SLUDGE

drain/duct .... SEWER

fiber .... NOIL, FLOSS

glass .... CULLET

lay .... RAZE, RAVAGE, DESTROY

maker .... HASTE

matter .... ASH, CULL, LEES, DREGS, FECES, SWEAT, REFUSE, GARBAGE, REJECTS

metal .... SLAG, DROSS

of time .... WILD-GOOSE-CHASE

piece of cloth .... RAG

pipe .... DRAIN, SEWER

product .... RUN-OFF

sugar cane/beets ..... BAGASSE, MEGASS(E)

time ...... IDLE, LOAF, DABBLE, DAWDLE, DIDDLE, FIDDLE, FRIVOL, LINGER, LOITER, PUTTER, FRIBBLE

wasted .... THIN, GAUNT, CONSUMED, EMACIATED

wasteful .... LAVISH, PRODIGAL, PROFLIGATE, CONSUMPTIVE, EXTRAVAGANT

wasteland .... MOOR, HEATH, DESERT, FOREST, STEPPE, TUNDRA, DUST BOWL, HINTERLAND, WILDERNESS

reclamation .... INNING

Waste Land author .... ELIOT

waster .... SPENDER, PRODIGAL, PROFLIGATE, SPENDTHRIFT

wasting .... DECAY, DEVASTATING

away .... TABID, ATROPHY, TABETIC, MARASMUS, TABESCENT, EMACIATION

disease .... TB, TABES, LEUKEMIA, CONSUMPTION, TUBERCULOSIS

disease, pertaining to .... HECTIC

wastrel .... BUM, WASTER, SPENDER, PRODIGAL, SPENDTHRIFT, GOOD-FOR-NOTHING

wat .... STEW, TEMPLE

watch .... EYE, LOOK, OGLE, TEND, VIEW, STARE, VIGIL, FOLLOW, SENTRY, SURVEY, LOOKOUT, OBSERVE, OVERSEE, GUARD(ING), HOROLOGE, TIMEPIECE
a person or thing .... MONITOR
act of keeping .... ESPIAL
bearing .... JEWEL
chain .... FOB
children .... BABYSIT
covering .... CRYSTAL
death .... WAKE, VIGIL
during exams .... INVIGILATE
duty .... VIGIL, PATROL
graveyard .... NIGHT SHIFT
kind of .... WRIST, POCKET, REPEATER
mounted .... VEDETTE
movement units .... LIGNES
night .... NEW YEAR'S EVE
over .... TEND, SUPERVISE
part .... BAND, CASE, DIAL, PAWL, STEM, STUD, CLICK, DETENT, PALLET, CRYSTAL, (HOUR)HAND, MINUTE HAND, SECOND HAND
pawl .... JUMPER
pocket .... FOB
secretly .... SPY, SHADOW
slang .... TICKER
soldier on .... SENTRY, SENTINEL
sound .... TICK
time .... HOROLOGE
undercover .... SPYING, ESPIONAGE
watchdog ...... BANDOG, MASTIFF, CERBERUS, GUARD(IAN), BLOODHOUND
kind of .... CHAPERON(E)
movie industry .... CENSOR
peace and order .... POLICE(MAN)
three-headed .... CERBERUS
warning .... GRR
watcher .... GUARD, LOOKOUT, SPOTTER, OBSERVER, OVERSEER
ballroom .... WALLFLOWER
secret ..... SPY, TAIL, SHADOW, DETECTIVE, PRIVATE EYE
watchful ...... ALERT, OPEN-EYED, VIGILANT, ATTENTIVE, OBSERVANT
man .... IRA
watchmaker .... HOROLOGIST
watchman .... GUARD, SCOUT, SENTRY, WARDEN, WARDER, LOOKOUT, VEDETTE, SENTINEL
mythological .... ARGUS,

TALOS, HEIMDALL
watchtower .... BEACON, LOOKOUT, MIRADOR, BARBICAN, LIGHTHOUSE
watchword .... CRY, MOTTO, SLOGAN, PASSWORD, BATTLECRY, CATCHWORD, SHIBBOLETH
person concerned with ...... GUARD, SENTRY, SENTINEL
water .... EAU, WET, AQUA, BATH, RAIN, DILUTE, DILUENT, IRRIGATE, SPRINKLE
animal .... HYDRA, POLYP, ROTIFER, BRYOZOAN, POLYZOAN, SEA ANEMONE
as source of power ..... WHITE COAL
baptismal .... LAVER
barely above .... AWASH
barrier ...... DAM, BOOM, DIKE, MOLE, WEIR, LEVEE, EMBANKMENT
bearer, in astronomy .... AQUARIUS
borne .... AFLOAT, FLOATING
bottle .... CARAFE, DECANTER
brash .... PYROSIS, HEARTBURN
buffalo .... ARNA, ARNEE, CARABAO
bug .... BEETLE, COCKROACH
capable of uniting with ..... HYDROPHILE, HYDROPHILIC
carrier .... CLOUD
carrier bird .... ALBATROSS
channel .... CANAL, DRAIN, FLUME, GULLY, GULLET, GUTTER, SLUICE, RACEWAY, AQUEDUCT
chestnut .... LING, CALTRAP, CALTROP
chinquapin .... LOTUS
clock .... CLEPSYDRA
closet .... STOOL, CLOACA, TOILET
cloud .... RAIN
color .... PAINTING, AQUARELLE
color painting .... FRESCO
coloring technique .... GOUACHE
combining form ...... HYDR(O)
conduit .... AQUEDUCT
container .... JUG, GOGLET, BREAKER, CANTEEN, CISTERN, GURGLET, PITCHER
containing .... HYDROUS
corral .... CRAWL
crake .... OUZEL
cress .... MUSTARD, POTHERB
cure .... TORTURE,

HYDROPATHY, HYDROTHERAPY
current .... RACE
deposit .... SILT, SEDIMENT
dog ..... SPANIEL, SALAMANDER
element .... OXYGEN, HYDROGEN
excursion .... CRUISE
exhibition .... AQUACADE
fairy .... NIX
fear of .... HYDROPHOBIA
floating on .... AWASH
foam on .... SUDS
gate .... SLUICE, WICKET
gauge .... UDOMETER
glass .... GOBLET, TUMBLER
gum .... TUPELO
heater .... SAMOVAR
hemlock .... COWBANE
hen .... COOT
hole .... POND, POOL
hunger for .... THIRST
ice .... SHERBET
in sheep's brain .... GID
jar .... EWER, OLLA, BANGA, HYDRIA
jet, revolving .... GIRANDOLE
journey .... CRUISE, VOYAGE, PASSAGE
jug/pitcher .... EWER, OLLA
keg .... BREAKER
kind of .... SEA, TAP, HOLY, RAIN, SALT, FRESH, SPRING, JAVELLE, MINERAL, DRINKING
like .... WET, AQUEOUS
lily ..... LOTOS, LOTUS, WOCAS, FANWORT, NELUMBO, VICTORIA
living in .... AQUATIC
logged .... SOGGY, SWAMPY
marker .... DANDY ROLL
mill .... CLOW
moccasin .... SNAKE, VIPER, COTTONMOUTH
move across a body of .... SWIM(MING)
movement .... EBB, TIDE, SEICHE
natural mineral .... SELTZER
not capable of absorbing .... HYDROPHOBIC
nymph .... NAIAD, NEREID, OCEANID
of .... AQUEOUS
on the brain .... HYDROCEPHALUS
opossum .... YAPOK
ouzel .... PIET, DIPPER, THRUSH
overflowing of .... FLOOD, DELUGE
parting .... DIVIDE
passage .... SLUICE, STRAIT,

CHANNEL
pepper .... SMARTWEED
pimpernel .... BROOKWEED
pipe .... HOSE, MAIN, DRAIN,
HOOKA(H), AQUEDUCT,
NARGHILE
plant .... LOTUS, BULRUSH,
CABOMBA, CALTROP, CATTAIL,
PAPYRUS, SEAWEED,
DUCKWEED, EELGRASS,
HYACINTH, PLANTAIN,
PONDWEED, WATERLILY,
CHINQUAPIN, WATERCRESS
plant leaf .... PAD
plant leaf walker .... JACANA
power .... HYDRAULIC
pump .... RAM
purify .... CHLORINATE
raising device .... RAM, NORIA,
TABUT
rat ...... VOLE, THIEF, MUSKRAT
rejection of .... OIL
rodent ...... NUTRIA, CAPYBARA
sapphire .... IOLITE
scented .... BAYRUM, COLOGNE
science of .... HYDROLOGY
scorpion .... NEPA
search for source of
.... DOWSE
shallow part of river/sea
.... SHOAL
snake .... MOCCASIN
soak in .... STEEP, IMMERSE,
SATURATE
soaked .... DRENCHED
soluble stuff .... HYDROGEN
sound .... (S)PLASH
sparkling mineral .... VICHY
spirit .... ARIEL, KELPY,
NIX(IE), KELPIE, UNDINE
sports .... AQUATICS
spout .... GUSH, SPATE,
GEYSER, GARGOYLE
spring .... LYMPH
sprite .... KELPY, NAIAD,
NIX(IE), NYMPH, KELPIE,
NEREID
standing .... PUDDLE
storage .... TANK, CISTERN,
RESERVOIR
stone .... HYDROLITE
surface .... RYME
surge of .... BILLOW
the garden .... HOSE
thin down with .... DILUTE
thrush .... OUZEL
transportation .... FERRY
trough, mining .... LAUNDER
tube .... HOSE
user .... BOAT, SHIP
vessel/pot .... LOTA(H)

washing .... LAVATION
wave .... BILLOW
wheel .... NORIA, TURBINE
witch .... GREBE, DOWSER
without .... DRY, ARID,
PARCHED, ANHYDROUS
worm .... NAID
Water Lilies painter ...... MONET
waterbuck .... KOB, ANTELOPE
watercourse .... DIKE, RACE,
BROOK, CANAL, FIORD,
GORGE, GULLY, NULLA,
CAN(Y)ON, RAVINE, RUNNEL,
CHANNEL
dry .... WADI
watercraft ...... BOAT, RAFT, SHIP
watercress .... POTHERB
watered ...... DILUTED, SPRINKLED,
ADULTERATED
down .... MILD, THIN, WEAK
fabric/silk .... MOIRE, TABBY
Wateree .... CAWTABA
waterfall .... FOSS, LIN(N), CHUTE,
FALLS, CASCADE, CHIGNON,
CATARACT
waterfinder .... DOWSER,
DOWSING ROD, DIVINING ROD
waterfront laborer
...... STEVEDORE, ROUSTABOUT
structure .... PIER
watergate .... FLOODGATE
Watergate scandal perpetrator
.... (RICHARD)NIXON
watering .... ADULTERATION
can .... SPRINKLER
eye .... EPIPHORA
place .... SPA, WELL, BATHS,
OASIS, SPRING(S)
waterless .... ARID, BARREN,
(BONE-)DRY, ANHYDROUS
Waterloo, victor of
.... WELLINGTON
waterproof .... SEALED,
HERMETIC, LEAKPROOF,
WATER-REPELLENT
covering .... PONCHO,
GOSSAMER, RAINCOAT,
TARP(AULIN)
garment .... WADER, RAINCOAT
material ...... RUBBER, PLASTIC
to .... PAY, CALK
Waters, ____ .... ETHEL
Waters of ____: Douay Bible
.... SILOE
watershed .... DIVIDE, RUNOFF,
RESERVOIR, CROSSROAD
waterside .... BEACH, COAST,
SHORE
watertight .... IRONCLAD
box .... CAISSON, COFFERDAM
make .... CA(U)LK

waterway .... RILL, CANAL,
CREEK, RIVER, CHANNEL,
CULVERT, STREAM, RIVULET,
AQUEDUCT, SHIP-ROUTE,
IRRIGATION DITCH
Antarctic .... ROSS SEA
waterworks: sl. .... TEARS
waterwort .... ELATINE
watery .... WET, THIN, RAINY,
SOGGY, WASHY, LIQUID,
SEROUS, AQUEOUS, HYDROUS
discharge .... RHEUM
grave .... SEA
wattle .... ROD, GILL, TWIG,
WAND, DEWLAP, LAPPET
birds' .... JOWL, GILL(S),
CARUNCLE
fish .... BARBEL
tree .... BOREE
Waugh, novelist .... EVELYN
waul .... HOWL, WAIL, SQUALL
waur .... WORSE
wave .... FLAP, SURF, SWAY, TIDE,
WAFF, CURVE, SURGE, SWELL,
BILLOW, COMBER, MOTION,
RIPPLE, ROLLER, SEESAW,
BREAKER, FLUTTER, GESTURE,
BRANDISH, FLOURISH,
UNDULATION
action .... LAP
back and forth .... WAG
channel .... BORE, EAGRE
controller .... HAIRNET
finger .... CURL
foam .... WHITECAP
hair .... PERMANENT
heave of a .... SCEND
hollow of .... VALLEY
large ..... SEA, SWELL, ROLLER,
DECUMAN
little .... RIPPLE
movement .... CHOP,
UNDULATION, CONVOLUTION
off .... SHOO
signaling .... WAFF
tidal .... BORE, EAGRE
to and fro .... WAG, FLAP
top of .... CREST
tossed .... AWASH
with foamy crest
.... WHITECAP
wavelet .... RIPPLE
Wavell, Earl .... ARCHIBALD
waver ...... SWAY, HOVER, FALTER,
QUAVER, TEETER, TOTTER,
FLUTTER, TREMBLE, HESITATE,
UNDULATE, FLUCTUATE,
VACILLATE
wavering .... FICKLE, UNSURE,
DOUBTFUL, UNSTEADY
sound .... TREMOLO

waves, breaking on shore
.... SURF
move in .... RIPPLE, UNDULATE
sound of .... ROAR
space between .... TROUGH
tidal .... EAGRE
tossing and tumbling
.... WELTER
wavy .... CURLY, SPIRAL, SINUATE,
SINUOUS, UNDULOUS
edged ...... REPAND, UNDULATE
form .... UNDULATION
in heraldry .... UNDE(E)
state .... UNDULANCY
wax .... CERA, CERE, GROW, PELA,
CERATE, GREASE, POLISH,
SEALER, CERESIN, CERUMEN,
PARAFFIN
and pitch mixture .... MALTHA
candle .... TAPER, CIERGE,
PARAFFIN
cloth treated with
.... CEREMENT, CERECLOTH
cobbler's .... CODE
combining form .... CER(O)
covered with .... CERATED
eloquent .... ORATE
figure .... CEROPLAST
like secretion .... CERUMEN
match .... VESTA
mineral .... OZOCERITE
modeled in .... CEROPLASTIC
myrtle .... BAYBERRY
ointment .... CERATE
palm .... CARNAUBA
producing .... CERIFEROUS
prolix .... SPOUT
source .... BEE, CARNAUBA
waxbill .... WEAVERBIRD
waxed runner .... SKI
waxen .... ASHY, PALE, ASHEN,
SALLOW
waxwing .... CEDARBIRD,
CHATTERER
waxwork artist .... TUSSAUD
waxy .... CERACEOUS
substance ...... CUTIN, SUBERIN
way .... LANE, MODE, PATH, PLAN,
ROAD, WONT, ROUTE, STYLE,
TREND, USAGE, AVENUE,
COURSE, CUSTOM, MANNER,
METHOD, STREET, PRACTICE
easy/direct .... STREET,
HIGHWAY, HIGHROAD
for people on foot .... PATH,
TRAIL
give .... YIELD
in the family .... PREGNANT,
PARTURIENT
of approaching .... ACCESS
of passage .... ALLEY,

CHANNEL
of walking/running .... GAIT
on the .... MOVING,
PROCEEDING
out .... AFAR, EXIT, EGRESS
station town .... WHISTLE STOP
train .... LOCAL
under .... MOVING, IN TRANSIT,
PROCEEDING, PROGRESSING
up .... STEP, ASCENT, STAIRS
usual .... HABIT, CUSTOM
waybill .... MANIFEST
wayfarer .... HIKER, VIATOR,
WALKER, PILGRIM, TRAVELER
shelter for .... INN, SPITAL
wayfaring tree .... VIBURNUM,
HOBBLEBUSH
waylay .... ACCOST, AMBUSH,
ATTACK, DETAIN, AMBUSCADE
Wayne, actor .... JOHN
nickname of .... DUKE
Wayne's The _____ .... GREEN
BERETS
wayward .... UNRULY, WANTON,
ERRATIC, VAGRANT, WILLFUL,
ACCIDENTAL, CAPRICIOUS,
HEADSTRONG, REBELLIOUS
WCTU bane .... ALCOHOL
We Are the World target
.... HUNGER
weak .... WAN, LAME, PUNY,
ANILE, FAINT, FRAIL, ANEMIC,
EFFETE, FEEBLE, FLABBY,
FLIMSY, INFIRM, POORLY,
SICKLY, FLACCID, FRAGILE,
DECREPIT, DELICATE,
HELPLESS, VULNERABLE,
INEFFECTIVE
drink .... TIFF
grow .... FLAG, DROOP,
COLLAPSE
-hearted .... AFRAID
-kneed .... SOFT, TIMID
-kneed: sl. .... CHICKEN
link .... ACHILLES' HEEL
-minded .... DAFT, FICKLE,
STUPID, FOOLISH, IDIOTIC,
MORONIC, WITLESS, IMBECILE,
INDECISIVE, WISHY-WASHY
morally .... FRAIL, CORRUPT
physically .... TIRED, WEARY,
PALSIED, FATIGUED, IMPOTENT
point .... FAULT, DEFECT,
FAILING
slang .... WOOZY
weaken .... EBB, SAP, BATE, FADE,
FLAG, WILT, ABATE, DAMAGE,
DILUTE, IMPAIR, CRIPPLE,
DEPLETE, EXHAUST, SLACKEN,
ENERVATE, ENFEEBLE,
ATTENUATE, UNDERMINE,

DEBILITATE
morally .... VITIATE
the spirit .... DEMORALIZE
weakened .... UNSOUND,
FATIGUED, UNHEALTHY
and disabled person
.... INVALID
body condition ...... CACHEXIA
weakener .... SAPPER, ENERVATOR
weakening .... SAPPING, DRAINING
weaker ones .... PREY
sex .... FEMALE,
WOMAN(HOOD)
weakfish .... ACOUPA, TOTUAVA
weakling .... SOP, WIMP, SISSY,
SOFTY, SOFTIE, WHINER,
CRYBABY, WALLYDRAG,
PANTYWAIST, MOLLYCODDLE
weakness .... FAULT, DEFECT,
FETISH, LIKING, FAILING,
FRAILTY, DEBILITY, DELICACY,
FONDNESS, IMPOTENCE,
INFIRMITY
bodily .... ATONY, ASTHENIA,
CACHEXIA
in behavior .... VICE
in character .... FOIBLE
moral .... FRAILTY
of an organ .... ATONY
small .... FOIBLE, FRAILTY
weal .... WALE, WELT, WHEAL,
STRIPE, WELFARE, WELL-
BEING
weald .... FOREST
wealth .... GOLD, MEANS, MONEY,
ASSET(S), RICHES, FORTUNE,
OPULENCE, PROPERTY,
ABUNDANCE, AFFLUENCE,
PLENITUDE
accumulated .... TREASURE
benefits/income from
.... USANCE
blind god of .... PLUTUS
ill-gotten .... PELF
personified .... MAMMON,
CROESUS
symbol of .... MONEYBAG
wealthy .... RICH, MONEYED,
OPULENT, WELL-OFF,
AFFLUENT, WELL-TO-DO,
PROSPEROUS
government by the
.... PLUTOCRACY
king .... MIDAS, CROESUS
person .... DIVES, NABOB,
MONEYBAGS, PLUTOCRAT,
CAPITALIST, BILLIONAIRE,
MILLIONAIRE
slang .... FILTHY RICH
wean ...... BABY, CHILD, DEPRIVE,
ESTRANGE, WITHDRAW

weapon .... ARM, GUN, CLUB, MACE, LANCE, SABER, SWORD, ARQUEBUS, CROSSBOW, SLINGSHOT
animal's .... HORN, TUSK
Australian aborigines'
.... WOMERA, BOOMERANG
bigot's .... STEREOTYPE
bird's ..... BEAK, CLAW, TALON
David's, that killed Goliath
.... STONE
duelist's .... PISTOL
for negotiation
.... BARGAINING CHIP
gaucho's .... BOLA(S)
"handy" .... FISTS
hood's .... SHIV
hoplite .... SPEAR
Indian .... TOMAHAWK
King Arthur's .... SWORD, EXCALIBUR
medieval ...... MACE, GISARME, HALBERD, ARBALEST, CATAPULT
old-time .... SNEE
pampas .... BOLAS
plant's .... SPINE
primitive .... SPEAR
Samson's .... JAWBONE
shafted .... SPONTOON
throwing stick
.... BOOMERANG
Vikings' .... AX, SWORD
war .... GUN, RIFLE, CANNON, BAYONET, REPEATER
weaponry .... ORDNANCE
weapons: colloq. ...... HARDWARE
wear ...... DON, USE, GARB, SHOW, CHAFE, ERODE, PUT ON, SPORT, CLOTHES, DISPLAY
away .... FRET, ERODE, ABRADE, CORRODE
down .... TIRE, ABRADE, DEPLETE, EXHAUST
on .... LINGER
out .... HACK, POOP
ragged .... FRAY, FRAZZLE
thin .... WEAKEN
to tatters .... FRAZZLE
well .... LAST, ENDURE
wearer, Arab headdress
.... VALENTINO
beret .... CHE GUEVARA
crash-helmet .... EVEL KNIEVEL
flier's helmet .... SNOOPY
hobo-hat .... EMMETT KELLY
peaked-cap .... JIM COURIER
plumed-hat .... CYRANO
Stetson .... JOHN WAYNE
top-hat .... FRED ASTAIRE

wearied .... ALL IN, BORED, JADED, TIRED, FAGGED
person .... JADED ONE
weariness .... ENNUI, TEDIUM, FATIGUE, LANGUOR, BOREDOM, MONOTONY, WEAKNESS, LASSITUDE
wearing apparel .... GARB, DRESS, ATTIRE, CLOTHES, RAIMENT, CLOTHING, GARMENTS
apparel at a masquerade
.... COSTUME
apparel, distinctive ...... HABIT
apparel: sl. .... RAGS
shoe gaiters .... SPATTED
shoes .... SHOD
wearisome ...... BORING, DREARY, TIRING, HUMDRUM, IRKSOME, TEDIOUS, TOILSOME, TIRESOME
grow .... BORE, PALL
person .... BORE, PEST
talker .... PROSER
weary .... BORE(D), FED-UP, JADE(D), SPENT, TIRE(D), FAG(GED), POOPED, IRKSOME, TEDIOUS, WORNOUT, FATIGUED, TUCKER(ED), CHAPFALLEN
weasand .... THROAT, TRACHEA, WINDPIPE, ESOPHAGUS
weasel ...... VARE, PEKAN, SNEAK, ERMINE, FERRET, HEDGER, VERMIN, ZORIL(A), SKULKER, MUSTELINE
family .... MUSTELA
like animal .... SABLE, MARTEN
relative .... MINK, OTTER, STOAT, FERRET, MARTEN
slang .... WELSH, PUSSYFOOT
words .... AMBIGUITIES, EQUIVOCATIONS
weather ...... SKY, CLIME, SEASON, CLIMATE, SURVIVE
-beaten .... WORN, FADED, INURED, SEASONED
become accustom to a
different .... ACCLIMATE
condition .... CLIMATE
indicator .... BAROMETER
indoors .... RAINY DAY
item ..... HUMIDITY, MOISTURE, TEMPERATURE
map line .... ISOBAR, ISALLOBAR
personified .... JACK FROST
phenomenon .... SMOG, SNOW, FLOOD, SLEET, SMAZE, STORM, CYCLONE, TORNADO, HAIL(STONE)

phrase .... HEAVY RAINS, SUNNY SKIES, CEILING ZERO, STRONG WINDS
prevailing .... CLIMATE
prolonged dry .... DROUT, DROUGHT
radar system .... SODAR
report .... ADVISORY
satellite .... TIROS
scientist .... METEOROLOGIST
season with heavy rains
.... MONSOON
study of .... METEOROLOGY
under the ..... ILL, SICK, TIPSY, AILING, UNWELL, INDISPOSED
warning .... ADVISORY
word .... FAIR, GALE, RAIN, SNOW, WARM, GUSTY, SLEET, FOGGY, SUNNY, WINDY, STORMY, SHOWER(S), THUNDER, TWISTER, HUMIDITY, TYPHOON, BLIZZARD, HURRICANE, LIGHTNING
weathercock .... FANE, VANE
weathered .... ENDURED, SURVIVED, OUTLASTED
weatherglass .... BAROMETER
weatherman .... FORECASTER, METEOROLOGIST
weathervane figure .... COCK
weave .... MAT, KNIT, SPIN, BRAID, PLAIT, PLEAT, TWIST, PLEACH, ENTWINE, CONTRIVE, INTERLACE, (INTER)TWINE
ornamental .... LACE
type of .... LENO, NETTING, NETWORK
weaver .... LOOM, WEBSTER, FABRICATOR
bobbin of .... PIRN
girl .... IRENE
material of/need of ...... REED, SLEY, YARN, FIBER, WICKER
twisted silk thread of
.... TRAM
weaverbird .... MAYA, TAHA, FINCH, WHIDAH, SPARROW, WAXBILL
weaving art .... LOOM
contestant .... ARACHNE
device ..... REED, REEL, SPOOL, SHUTTLE
machine/frame .... LOOM
occupation .... HANDICRAFT
reed .... SLEY
thread running horizontally
.... WOOF
thread running lengthwise
.... WARP
yarn .... WARP, WEFT, WOOF
web .... MESH, TRAP, SNARE,

TISSUE, NET(WORK), GOSSAMER

feather's .... VEXILLUM

footed/toed .... PALMATE

footed bird .... DUCK, SWAN, GOOSE, AVOCET

footed creature .... FROG, TOAD, OTTER, BEAVER, MUSKRAT

in anatomy .... TISSUE, MEMBRANE

kind of .... COB, SPIDER

like membrane .... TELA

pertaining to .... RETIARY

spinner .... SPIDER, ARACHNE

Webb, actor .... CLIFTON

webbed .... PALMATE

weber .... MAXWELL

weblike .... TELAR

wed ...... ONE, JOIN, WIVE, BLEND, MARRY, UNITE, ESPOUSE, TIE THE KNOT

wedding ...... BRIDAL, MARRIAGE, NUPTIALS

anniversary designation:
1st year .... PAPER
5th year .... WOOD
10th year .... TIN, ALUMINUM
15th year .... CRYSTAL
20th year .... CHINA
25th year .... SILVER
30th year .... PEARL
35th year .... JADE, CORAL
40th year .... RUBY
45th year .... SAPPHIRE
50th year .... GOLDEN
55th year .... EMERALD
75th year .... DIAMOND

announcement .... BAN(N)S

couple .... NEWLYWEDS

couple's holiday
.... HONEYMOON

March bride .... ELSA

party member .... MATRON, BESTMAN, RINGBOY, SPONSOR, BRIDESMAID, FLOWER GIRL, RING BEARER

place, biblical .... CANA

rite/sacrament ..... MATRIMONY

sight at a .... TRAIN

song .... AVE MARIA, HYMENEAL, OH PROMISE ME

word, one-time .... OBEY

wedge ...... JAM, KEY, SHIM, TRIG, BLOCK, CLEAT, QUOIN, COIGN(E), COTTER

driver .... MAUL, BEETLE

shaped ..... CUNEAL, CUNEATE, SPHENIC, SPHENOID, CUNEIFORM

shaped piece .... PIE, VEE, SHIM, CHOCK, QUOIN

shaped writing .... CUNEIFORM

to prevent rolling ...... CHOCK, QUOIN, SCOTCH

used in masonry .... SHIM

wedlock .... MARRIAGE, MATRIMONY

Wednesday .... MIDWEEK

Wednesday's child, lot of
.... WOE

god ..... ODIN, WODEN, WOTAN

wee .... TINY, SMALL, TEENY, LITTLE, MINUTE, TEENSY

hours .... DAWN

wee .... URINE, URINATE

weed .... BUR, RID, CULL, DOCK, BROME, COCKLE, NETTLE, QUITCH, REMOVE, SPURR(E)Y, CHARLOCK, PURSLANE, SANDBUR(R), TOADFLAX, DANDELION

biblical .... TARE

buckwheat .... DOCK

colloquial .... CIGAR, TOBACCO

digging tool .... SPUD

genus .... PORTULACA, TARAXACUM

killer .... HERBICIDE

Klamath .... EOLA

mourning ...... CRAPE, WEEPER

narcotic .... MARIHUANA, MARIJUANA

noxious/of grainfields
.... TARE

of mustard family
.... CHARLOCK

out .... UPROOT, EXTIRPATE

pickling .... DILL

poisonous ...... LOCO, DARNEL, JIMSON, HEMLOCK

roadside .... DOGFENNEL

weeding tool .... HOE, SPUD

weeds .... CRAPE, WRACK, WEEPER

wearer .... WIDOW

weedy .... SCRAWNY, GANGLING

plant ..... CELANDINE, BUTTER-AND-EGGS

week .... HEBDOMAD, SENNIGHT

weekday .... FERIA

weekly .... HEBDOMADAL, PERIODICAL

bonanza .... PAY

magazine .... TIME, PEOPLE, NEWSWEEK

portion .... DAY

weeks, 52 .... YEAR

two .... FORTNIGHT

Weems, bandleader .... TED

preacher .... PARSON

ween .... THINK, EXPECT, IMAGINE, SUPPOSE

weenie .... SAUSAGE, FRANKFURTER, WIENER(WURST)

weeny .... TINY, TEENY

weep ...... CRY, SOB, BAWL, WAIL, MOURN, BEWAIL, GRIEVE, LAMENT, BLUBBER, LAPWING

weeper output .... TEARDROP

weeping goddess .... NIOBE

philosopher .... HERACLITUS

weevil .... KIS, BOLL, BORER, BEETLE, CURCULIO

larva .... GRUGRU

wing cover .... SHARD

weft ...... WOOF, YARN, FILLING

Weiscsel .... VISTULA

weigh .... BEAR, HEFT, MULL, TELL, COUNT, HOIST, POISE, RAISE, BURDEN, PONDER, BALANCE, REFLECT, CONSIDER

anchor .... SAIL

down ...... DRAG, LOAD, PRESS, BURDEN, HAMPER

weighing device .... SCALE, TRONE, BALANCE, FAIRBANKS, STEELYARD, (WEIGH)BEAM

weight .... HEFT, LOAD, ROTL, OBOLE, POWER, VALUE, BURDEN, OBOLUS, STRESS, TON(NAGE), EMPHASIS, POUNDAGE, HEAVINESS, INFLUENCE, IMPORTANCE

allowance .... TARE, TRET

apothecaries .... DRAM, OUNCE, POUND, SCRUPLE

atomic .... MOLECULAR

avoirdupois .... TON, OUNCE, POUND

balance .... RIDER

balloon's .... BALLAST

boxer's .... HEAVY, LIGHT, BANTAM, MIDDLE, FEATHER

clock .... PEISE

coal .... KEEL

colloquial .... HEFT

deduction .... TARE

diamond .... CARAT

4,000-pound .... LAST

hundred pounds .... CENTAL, CENTNER

leaden .... PLUMB

lifting machine .... CRANE

measure .... TON, KILO, METAGE

metric .... TON, GRAM, KILO, CENTNER, QUINTAL, MYRIAGRAM

on animal's leg .... CLOG

pertaining to .... BARIC

problem .... OBESITY

stabilizer .... BALLAST

system .... TROY, METRIC, AVOIRDUPOIS, APOTHECARIES

3.086 grains .... (ONE)CARAT

troy .... CARAT, GRAIN, PENNYWEIGHT

200 milligrams .... CARAT

unit .... TON, GRAM, KILO, ROTL, CARAT, GRAIN, OUNCE, POUND, SHEKEL, QUINTAL

watcher .... BOXER, MODEL, DIETER, MILADY, ATHLETE

wool .... TOD

weightless .... LIGHT, FEATHERY

weights and measures, science of .... METROLOGY

weighty .... HEAVY, ONEROUS, SERIOUS, MOMENTOUS, PONDEROUS, BURDENSOME, OPPRESSIVE, INFLUENTIAL

weir .... TRAP, FENCE, GARTH, BARRIER, (MILL)DAM

weird .... ODD, EERY, UNCO, EERIE, QUEER, SPOOKY, BIZARRE, GHOSTLY, STRANGE, UNCANNY, ELDRITCH, SPECTRAL, UNEARTHLY, MYSTERIOUS

sister .... FATE, CLOTHO, ATROPOS, LACHESIS

weirdo .... NUT, KOOK, SCREWBALL

wejack .... PEKAN, WEASEL

weka .... RAIL

Welch, actress .... RAQUEL

welcome .... HAIL, SALUTE, EMBRACE, RECEIVE, GREET(ING), AGREEABLE, DESIRABLE, ACCEPT(ABLE)

benefit .... BOON

welcoming .... CORDIAL, RECEPTIVE, HOSPITABLE

weld .... FUSE, JOIN, UNITE, SOLDER, MIGNONETTE

Weld, actress .... TUESDAY

welding material .... SOLDER, THERMIT

welfare .... EASE, SAKE, COMFORT, WELL-BEING, (COMMON)WEAL, PROSPERITY

organization ...... CARE, YMCA, YWCA, RED CROSS, SALVATION ARMY

work .... SOCIAL SERVICE

Welfare Island's name change .... ROOSEVELT ISLAND

welkin .... SKY, HEAVEN, FIRMAMENT, ATMOSPHERE

well .... FIT, PIT, FLOW, GUSH, HALE, HOLE, SUMP, TRIG, SHAFT, HEARTY, PROPER, ROBUST, SPRING, STRONG, HEALTHY, EXPERTLY, FOUNT(AIN)

advised .... WISE

along .... FAR

balanced .... SANE, POISED, SENSIBLE

being .... WEAL, WELFARE, HAPPINESS

bred .... GENTEEL, EDUCATED

built .... STRONG

doer .... (BOY) SCOUT

done .... OVERCOOKED

done! .... BRAVO, HURRAH, RIGHT ON

dressed .... CHIC

earned .... WORTHY

favored .... PRETTY, HANDSOME

fed .... FAT, FULL, PLUMP

feeling .... EUPHORIA

groomed .... TRIG, SLEEK, SLICK, SOIGNE, SPRUCE

grounded .... SOUND, VALID, LOGICAL, INFORMED

heeled .... RICH, MONEYED, WEALTHY

kind of .... OIL, STAIR, ARTESIAN

known .... FAMOUS, FAMILIAR, RENOWNED, NOTORIOUS

beach .... LIDO

person .... CELEBRITY

ranger .... LONE

lining .... STEAN, STEEN

mannered .... POLITE, COURTEOUS

nigh .... ALMOST, NEARLY

off .... RICH, PROSPEROUS

ordered .... NEAT

pit .... SUMP

preserved .... GOOD AS NEW

proportioned .... TRIM

read person .... BOOKWORM

reported variable .... DOW JONES AVERAGE

set .... FIXED

settled .... ENSCONCED

suited .... CONVENIENT

supplied with money .... LOADED

thought of .... ESTEEMED, REPUTABLE

timed ...... TIMELY, EXPEDIENT, OPPORTUNE, AUSPICIOUS, SEASONABLE

to-do .... RICH, MONEYED, WEALTHY, AFFLUENT

versed .... INFORMED, SCHOOLED

watered .... IRRIGUOUS

worn .... TRITE, OVERUSED

Welland .... CANAL

wellaway .... ALAS, ALACK

Welle river .... UELE

Welles, actor .... ORSON

diplomat .... SUMNER

Wellington's soubriquet .... OLD NOSY, IRON DUKE

wellspring .... FOUNTAINHEAD

Welsh .... CYMRY, TAFFY, CELT(IC), CYMRIC, CAMBRIAN

astronomer .... MEE

boat .... CORACLE

buccaneer .... MORGAN

cheese dish .... RABBIT

dog .... CORGI, TERRIER

god of sea .... BRAN, DYLAN

onion .... CIBOL

poppy .... CAMBRICA

rabbit .... RAREBIT

slang .... CHEAT, SWINDLE

welsher .... CHEAT, SHIRKER, DEADBEAT, SWINDLER

Welshman .... CELT, CAMBRIAN

nickname for a .... TAFFY

welt .... BELT, LASH, WALE, RIDGE, W(H)EAL, LASH, STRIPE, THRASH

welter .... ROLL, RUCK, JUMBLE, SOAKED, WALLOW, FERMENT, TURMOIL, CONFUSION

wen .... CYST, MOLE, TALPA, TUMOR

wench .... LASS, MAID, HUSSY, WOMAN, WANTON, SERVANT

disreputable ..... BAWD, DOXY, SLUT, HARLOT, TROLLOP

wend .... GO (ON), TRAVEL, JOURNEY, PROCEED

Wendell, presidential candidate .... WILLKIE

Wendy's dog .... NANA

pal .... PETER PAN

went .... LEFT

out .... DIED

wer(e)gild .... CRO, BLOOD MONEY

werewolf .... LOUP-GAROU, LYCANTHROPE

wernard .... LIAR

wernerite .... SCAPOLITE

weskit .... VEST

Wesley (John) follower .... METHODIST

West .... OCCIDENT

English novelist ...... REBECCA

from the East .... MAE

newcomer to the .... TENDERFOOT

of Broadway .... MAE

wind .... ZEPHYR

wind, of the .... FAVONIAN

West African .... ASHANTI

baboon .... (MAN)DRILL
fetish .... JUJU
Gold Coast city .... ACCRA,
                       AKKRA
magic/taboo .... JUJU
secessionist state .... BIAFRA
tribe .... IBO
weaverbird .... WHIDAH
West Bengal capital
                      CALCUTTA
language .... HINDI, TAMIL,
                      BENGALI
West Flanders capital
                      BRUGES
West German capital .... BONN
chancellor .... BRANDT,
                      ADENAUER
president .... LUBKE
West Indian food plant
           RIMA(S), BREADFRUIT
rodent .... HUTIA
West Indies African ...... EBO(E),
                      MAROON
bird .... TODY, COURLAN,
                      LIMPKIN
capital:
    Barbados .... BRIDGETOWN
    Dominica .... ROSEAU
    Grenada .... ST. GEORGE'S
    Saint Kitts & Nevis
                   BASSETERRE
    Saint Lucia .... CASTRIES
    Saint Vincent
                   KINGSTOWN
coin .... PISTAREEN
egret .... GAULIN
fish .... BANG, BOGA, CERO,
    PEGA, SESI, TESTAR, BACALAO,
                   CABRILLA
flea .... CHIGOE, CHIGGER
grouper .... BONACI
heron .... GAULIN
hog plum .... AMRA, JOBO
Indian .... CARIB, TAINO,
                      ESTERON
island ..... CUBA, HAITI, NEVIS,
    CAICOS, TOBAGO, BAHAMA(S),
    CURACAO, GRENADA, JAMAICA,
      LEEWARD, ANTILLES,
      BARBADOS, DOMINICA,
    TRINIDAD, HISPANIOLA, SAINT
    KITTS, SAINT LUCIA, SAINT
                   VINCENT
liquor .... RUM, MOBBY
lizard ..... ARBALO, GALLIWASP
magic .... OBI, OBEAH
mahogany .... CAOBA
music .... CALYPSO
native .... CARIB, CREOLE
native chief .... CACIQUE
patois .... GUMBO

plant .... ANIL
rodent .... AGOUTI
rum .... TAF(F)IA
sailboat .... DROGHER
shark .... GATA
shrub .... ANIL, CASCARILLA
state .... ANTIGUA, GRENADA,
    DOMINICA, SAINT LUCIA, SAINT
                   VINCENT
talisman .... OBEAH
taro .... TANIA
tree .... ARALIE, BALATA,
    BONACE, CALABA, GENIP(AP),
                GREENHEART
vessel .... DROGHER
volcano .... PELEE
"white man" .... BUCKRA
witchcraft .... OBI, OBEAH
West Irian capital
         KOTABARU, HOLLANDIA
West Point motto, word in
officer candidates' .... DUTY,
        HONOR, COUNTRY
West Pointer .... CADET, PLEB(E),
                   YEARLING
West Virginia capital
                 CHARLESTON
city/town .... LOGAN, NITRO,
    WAYNE, WELCH, ELKINS,
    HINTON, KEYSER, RIPLEY,
    ROMNEY, SUTTON, VIENNA,
    WESTON, BECKLEY, GRAFTON,
    WEIRTON, FAIRMONT,
    WHEELING, BLUEFIELD,
    PRINCETON, CLARKSBURG,
    HUNTINGTON, MORGANTOWN,
    MARTINSBURG, PARKERSBURG
college .... SALEM, BETHANY,
    CONCORD, WESLEYAN
county ...... CLAY, OHIO, WIRT,
    WOOD, BOONE, GRANT,
    HARDY, LOGAN, MASON,
    WAYNE, CABELL, MARION,
    MERCER, PUTNAM, WETZEL,
    FAYETTE, HANCOCK,
    KANAWHA, PRESTON, RALEIGH,
    WYOMING, HARRISON,
               JEFFERSON
lake .... SUTTON, TYGART,
    EAST LYNN, BLUESTONE,
    MOUNT STORM, SUMMERSVILLE
mountain .... SPRUCE KNOB
river .... ELK, MUD, NEW,
    COAL, OHIO, CHEAT, STONY,
    CHERRY, GAULEY, HUGHES,
    MEADOW, CACAPON,
    KANAWHA, BUCKHANNON,
    GREENBRIER, GUYANDOTTE,
               POCATALICO
state bird .... CARDINAL
state flower .... ROSEBAY

          RHODODENDRON
state nickname .... MOUNTAIN,
                 PANHANDLE
state tree .... SUGAR MAPLE
university .... MORGANTOWN
western .... MOVIE, OATER,
    HESPERIAN, OCCIDENTAL
land .... HESPERIA
lawman .... MARSHAL, SHERIFF
movie character .... SCOUT,
    COWBOY, INDIAN, DESPERADO,
              FRONTIERSMAN
ocean .... ATLANTIC
soil .... GUMBO
Western Alliance .... NATO
Australia capital .... PERTH
Dvina .... RIVER
Islands .... HEBRIDES
Westerner .... PLAINSMAN
Westmacott, Mary ...... AGATHA
                 CHRISTIE
Westminster Abbey
                 PANTHEON
clock .... BIG BEN
landmark .... ABBEY
rite .... CORONATION
street .... WHITEHALL
wet .... DIP, RET, ASOP, DAMP,
    DANK, DEWY, (A)SOAK,
    BATHE, FOGGY, MISTY, MOIST,
    EMBRUE, SOAKED, DRENCHED
a line .... FISH
all .... WRONG, MISTAKEN
blanket .... KILLJOY,
    SPOILSPORT, PARTY POOPER
combining form .... HYGRO
lowland .... FEN
plaster painting .... FRESCO
with falling drops .... RAINY
wetback .... PEON, BRACERO
nationality of .... MEXICAN
wether .... SHEEP
wetland(s) .... SWAMPS, MARSHES
wetter .... BABY, CHILD
Weygand, French general
                 MAXIME
whack .... BEAT, BLOW, SLAP,
    SMACK, WHANG, THWACK
in .... IN LINE
out of .... DISORDERED
slang .... TRY, TRIAL, ATTEMPT
up .... SHARE, DIVIDE
whacked .... EXHAUSTED
whacky .... WILD, MADCAP,
    FOOLISH, ECCENTRIC
whale .... CETE, BEAT, FLOG,
    WHIP, SPERM, THRASH,
    BOWHEAD, FINBACK,
    CACHALOT, CETACEAN,
    BLACKFISH, LEVIATHAN
Arctic .... NARWHAL

baby .... CALF
biggest .... BLUE
blowhole .... SPIRACLE
carcass .... KRENG
colloquial .... WHOPPER
combining form .... CETO
cut blubber of .... FLENSE
dolphin .... ORCA
fat .... BLUBBER
female .... COW
finback .... RORQUAL,
PORPOISE
fishing .... WHALING
food .... BRIT, SHRIMP
food strainer .... BALEEN
grampus .... ORC(A)
growth on jaw .... BALEEN
herd .... GAM
hunter of fiction .... AHAB
killer .... ORC(A), DOLPHIN,
GRAMPUS
kind of ...... SEI, BLUE, SCRAG,
FIN(BACK), HUMPBACK
male .... BULL
mammal resembling
.... DUGONG, MANATEE
Melville's .... MOBY DICK
oil cask .... RIER
river .... DOLPHIN
shark .... MHOR
small .... DOLPHIN, HOGFISH,
PORPOISE, BLACKFISH
sound ...... MEW, BARK, CLICK,
WHINE, SQUEAL, CHIRRUP,
WHISTLE
sperm .... CACHALOT
tail part .... FLUKE
tusked .... NARWHAL
white .... HUSE, HUSO, BELUGA
young .... CALF
whaleback .... FREIGHTER
whalebone .... BALEEN
decorative article
.... SCRIMSHAW
whaleman .... HARPOONER
whaler's spear .... HARPOON
visit .... GAM
whales, pertaining to .... CETIC,
CETACEAN
school/herd of .... GAM, POD
skin .... SCULP
whaling ship .... PEQUOD
first to be sunk .... ESSEX
post .... LOGGERHEAD
whammy .... JINX, EVIL EYE
whang .... WHACK, STRIKE,
THRASH
whangee .... BAMBOO-(CANE),
WALKING-STICK
wharf .... DOCK, PIER, QUAI,
QUAY, JETTY, LANDING,

WATERFRONT
loafer .... RAT
Wharton, novelist .... EDITH
Wharton's Frome .... ETHAN
what .... HOW, WHICH, SORT OF
a CPA does .... AUDITS
a dentist can prettify
.... SMILE
a panhandle is
.... ELONGATION
a priest says .... MASS
a waiter waits for .... TIP,
ORDER
an accountant is .... BEAN
COUNTER
barflies do .... TIPPLE
Caesar's "Veni" means I
CAME
daily life is .... STRUGGLE
Don Juan wasn't
.... MISOGYNIC
for .... WHY
Godiva lacked .... HABIT
little shavers don't have
.... BEARDS
many heads make .... LIGHT
WORK
muses do .... INSPIRE
oneirocritics give
.... INTERPRETATIONS
questions do .... ARISE
setters do .... POINT
some do to a quarry
.... STALK
some say we all are
.... SINNERS
tempts a discount offer
.... CASH
the K.P. peel .... SPUDS
to pay a hero .... HOMAGE
tyros must learn .... ROPES
whatchamacallit
.... THINGAMAJIG
whatnot .... CABINET, ETAGERE,
WHATEVER
what's his name .... SO-AND-SO
left of fading hopes
.... GLIMMERING HOPES
what .... FACT, TRUTH
whaup .... CURLEW
wheal .... WALE, WELT, PIMPLE,
STRIPE, PUSTULE
wheat ...... CORN, DURRA, DURUM,
GRAIN, GRASS, SPELT, TRIGO,
CEREAL
beard .... AWN, ARISTA
beer .... WEISS
coat .... BRAN
cracked .... GROATS
disease .... BUNT, RUST, SMUT,
AECIA, ERGOT

flour foodstuff .... PASTA,
MACARONI, SPAGHETTI
flour substance .... GLUTEN
grass resembling .... CHEAT,
CHESS
ground .... MEAL, FLOUR
hard-grained .... DURUM,
SPELT
head .... EAR
hulled .... GROATS
liquor .... WHISK(E)Y
meal .... SEMOLINA
milling by-product .... SHORTS
stalk part .... AWN
wheatear .... CHAT, CHACK,
WHITETAIL
Wheatley, slave poetess
laureate .... PHILLIS
husband of .... (JOHN)PETERS
master of .... JOHN(WHEATLEY)
mistress of .... SUSANNAH
wheedle .... COAX, COURT,
HUMOR, CAJOLE, WANGLE,
BLARNEY, FLATTER
wheel .... DISK, HELM, SPIN, TURN,
CYCLE, PIVOT, TWIRL, WHIRL,
CIRCLE, PULLEY, ROLL(ER),
ROTATE, RUNDLE, REVOLVE
animalcule .... ROTIFER
band .... STRAKE
big: sl. .... VIP, BIGWIG,
(TOP)BRASS
block ..... TRIG, SPRAG, WEDGE
break .... DRAG, SKID, TRIG
center of .... HUB, NAVE
collar .... FLANGE
furniture .... CASTER
grooved .... SHEAVE
hoop .... TIRE
horse .... POLER
hub .... NAVE
like .... TROCHAL
little .... CASTER
motion .... ROLL, ROTATION
part ...... CAM, HOB, HUB, RIM,
AXLE, TIRE, FELLY, SPOKE
projection .... CAM
pulley .... SHEAVE
resembling a .... TROCHAL
rim .... FELLY, FELLOE,
FLANGE
shaft .... AXLE
shaped ..... ROTATE, ROTIFORM
small .... CASTER, TRUCKER,
TRUNDLE
spindle .... AXLE, ARBOR
spoke .... RUNG, RADIUS
spur .... ROWEL
swivel .... CASTER
tire .... STRAKE
tooth .... SPROCKET

toothed .... COG
turner in Hades .... IXION
turning around an axis
.... ROTARY
water .... NORIA
Wheel of Fortune host
.... (PAT)SAJAK
hostess .... (VANNA)WHITE
White's stint .... LETTER-
TURNER
wheeler .... PILOT, STEERSMAN
wheelman .... PILOT, CYCLIST
wheels, move on .... ROLL, DRIVE
of .... ROTAL
set of swiveled .... CASTER
shoe with .... SKATE
slang .... CAR, AUTO(MOBILE)
wheen .... FEW
wheeze .... GAG, GASP, JOKE,
PUFF, CHOKE
wheezy weather ...... ASTHMATIC
whelk .... MUREX, SNAIL, PAPULE,
PIMPLE, PUSTULE, GASTROPOD
whelm .... BURY, SINK, DROWN,
ENGULF, SUBMERGE
whelp .... CUR, LAD, PUP, BEAR,
HOUND, POOCH, PUPPY,
YOUTH, MONGREL
when ...... TIME, WHILE, MOMENT,
WHEREAS
both hands are up .... NOON,
MIDNIGHT
whenever .... ANYTIME
where .... WHITHER, WHAT PLACE,
WHEREABOUTS
a banner flies .... HEADLINE
a pest pains .... NECK
Aida premiered .... CAIRO
alligators are found
.... SWAMP
Bowie fell .... ALAMO
cappuccino is served
.... TRATTORIA
Charon labored .... STYX
Crockett fell .... ALAMO
Daniel was cast .... DEN OF
LIONS
David slew Goliath ...... ELAH
edelweiss bloom .... ALPS
Gideon defeated Midian
.... ENDOR
Ike commanded .... ETO
it rains mainly in the plain
.... SPAIN
Kipling's road leads
.... MANDALAY
loving couples get taken
.... ALTAR
lunettes sit .... NOSES
pants bag .... KNEE
Peter put his wife .... (IN

A)PUMPKIN SHELL
ships ply .... SEA LANES
some bettors to .... TO THE
DOGS
the action is .... ARENA,
CASINO
the buffalo roam .... RANGE
the Ganges flows .... INDIA
the heart is .... HOME
the Liffey flows .... ERIN
the tall corn grows
.... KANSAS, NEBRASKA,
OKLAHOMA
there is no opportunity to
advance .... BLIND ALLEY
there's ____, there's a way
.... A WILL
to read hidden meanings
.... BETWEEN THE LINES
to soul-search .... INWARD
Twain often summered
.... ELMIRA
wishes are fulfilled .... IN
DREAMS
whereabouts .... LOCATION
whereas .... WHILE
wherefore .... WHY, HENCE,
BECAUSE
wherefrom .... WHENCE
whereness .... UBIETY
whereupon .... WHEN, AFTER
WHICH
wherewithal .... CASH, FUNDS,
MEANS, MONEY, RESOURCES
wherry .... BARGE, SCULL,
LIGHTER, ROWBOAT
whet .... HONE, GRIND, EXCITE,
INSPIRE, SHARPEN, STIMULATE
the appetite .... TEASE, TEMPT,
TICKLE
whether .... IF, EITHER, IN CASE
whetstone .... BURR, HONE,
BUHR(STONE)
whey-faced .... PALE
of milk .... SERUM
which .... WHAT, WHATEVER
animal talked: biblical
.... DONKEY, SERPENT
whichever .... ANYONE, NO
MATTER WHAT
whidah .... WIDOW-BIRD,
WEAVERBIRD
whiff .... GUST, PUFF, WAFF,
WAFT, SMELL, SMOKE,
BREATH
whiffet .... DOG, PUFF
whiffle .... BLOW, VEER, SHIFT,
VACILLATE
Whig conspiracy, 1863
.... RYEHOUSE PLOT
opposed to .... TORY

whigmaleerie .... GEWGAW
while .... AS, YET, UNTIL, ALBEIT,
DURING, OCCUPY, WHEREAS
away .... KILL TIME
lead-in .... ERST, MEAN
whilom .... ONCE, QUONDAM,
FORMER(LY), ERST(WHILE)
whim .... KINK, CRANK, FANCY,
FREAK, QUIRK, DESIRE,
MAGGOT, NOTION, VAGARY,
CAPRICE, IMPULSE, CAPRICCIO
peculiar .... CROTCHET
wham ..... TRINKET, GIMCRACK
whimper .... CRY, MEWL, PULE,
WHINE, YAMMER
whimsical .... ODD, DROLL,
QUEER, QUAINT, CURIOUS,
FLIGHTY, WAGGISH, FANCIFUL,
FREAKISH, PECULIAR,
FANTASTIC, CAPRICIOUS
whimsicality .... ODDITY, CAPRICE
whimsy .... FANCY, HUMOR,
NOTION, CAPRICE
whin .... ROCK, TRAP, FURZE,
GORSE, GREENSTONE
whinchat .... SONGBIRD
whine .... CRY, MEWL, MOAN,
PULE, SNIVEL, YAMMER,
GRUMBLE, WHIMPER,
COMPLAIN
slang .... BELLYACHE
whiner .... PULER, GRIPER
whinny ...... FURZY, HINNY, NEIGH
whip ...... TAN, BEAT, BELT, FLAP,
FLAY, FLOG, LACE, LASH,
LICK, SNAP, WALE, FLAIL,
SWISH, WHALE, WHISK,
DEFEAT, LARRUP, SUBDUE,
THRASH, BELABOR, CONQUER,
PULLOUT, SCOURGE,
FLAGELLATE
Biblical .... SCORPION
blow .... FLICK
braided .... QUIRT, COWHIDE,
BLACKSNAKE
cream/egg whites .... WHISK
leather .... KNOUT, QUIRT,
COWHIDE, KURBASH
made of rhino hide
.... SJAMBOK
made of untanned hide
.... RAWHIDE
mark .... WALE, WELT,
W(H)EAL, STRIPE
riding .... CROP, QUIRT
severely .... TAN, FLOG,
THRASH, FLAGELLATE
stroke .... FLICK
to a froth .... MILL
up .... ROUSE, EXCITE

used by cattle drivers
.... BULLWHIP
whipcord .... CATGUT
whiplash .... FLOG, THONG,
INJURY, THRASH
snapper .... COSAQUE
sound .... WHISH
whippersnapper .... SQUIRT,
UPSTART, JACKANAPES
whippet .... DOG, GREYHOUND
whipping boy .... SCAPEGOAT
stick .... ROD, CANE, SWITCH
whippoorwill .... GOATSUCKER
feathers .... VIBRISSA
whir(r) ...... BIRR, BUZZ, VIBRATE
whirl .... EDDY, GYRE, REEL, SPIN,
STIR, TURN, DANCE, SWIRL,
TWIRL, CIRCLE, GYRATE,
ROTATE, UPROAR, REVOLVE,
PIROUETTE
whirler and howler ...... DERVISH
whirligig .... TOP, ROTOR, BEETLE,
CAROUSEL, MERRY-GO-ROUND
whirling _____ .... DERVISH
man .... DERVISH
motion .... SPIN, SWIRL
on toes .... PIROUETTE
wind .... CYCLONE, TORNADO
whirlpool .... EDDY, GULF, WEEL,
VORTEX, CHARYBDIS,
MAELSTROM
bath: trademark .... JACUZZI
whirlwind ...... ANE, EDDY, FAST,
SPEEDY, CYCLONE, TORNADO,
TWISTER, TYPHOON, DIZZYING,
HURRICANE, TOURBILLION
Faroes .... OES
whirlybird .... CHOPPER,
AUTOGYRO, HELICOPTER
whish .... WHIZ, SWISH
whisht .... QUIET, STILL,
HUSH(ED), WHISPER
whisk .... BEAT, WHIP, BROOM,
BRUSH, CARRY, FROTH, (EGG-
)BEATER
broom .... WISP
whiskers .... HAIR, BEARD,
BRISTLES, MUSTACHE,
BURNSIDES, SIDEBURNS
cat's .... VIBRISSA
chin .... GOATEE
closely trimmed, pointed
.... VANDYKE BEARD
insect's .... ANTENNA, FEELERS
short growth .... STUBBLE
side .... MUTTONCHOPS
whisk(e)y .... RYE, LIQUOR,
SCOTCH, ALCOHOL, BOURBON,
POT(H)EEN, SPIRITS
and soda .... HIGHBALL
colloquial .... BOOZE,

BOOTLEG, MOONSHINE
illegally distilled ...... POTEEN,
MOONSHINE, MOUNTAIN DEW
kind of .... BLENDED, PURE
MALT, SINGLE MALT
slang .... HOOCH, REDEYE,
ROTGUT
storeroom .... BUTTERY
to an Indian .... FIREWATER
whisper .... SIGH, MURMUR,
BREATH(E)
actor's .... ASIDE
whispered, something .... TIP,
HINT, RUMOR, GOSSIP,
SECRET, CONFIDENCE
whist ...... STILL, SILENT, SILENCE,
CARD GAME
game series .... RUBBER
game similar to .... RUFF,
BRIDGE
term .... MORT, SLAM, VOLE,
MISERI
whistle .... PIPE, TOOT, FLUTE,
SQUEAL, TOTTLE, FOGHORN,
TWEEDLE
blower .... SNITCH, INFORMER
holder .... LANYARD
stop .... STUMP, CAMPAIGN
time .... FIVE O'CLOCK
whistler .... OUSEL, MARMOT,
GOLDENEYE
whistling sound .... WHIZZ,
STRIDOR
in the ears .... TINNITUS
whit .... BIT, JOT, ATOM, DOIT,
IOTA, TITTLE, PARTICLE
white .... WAN, FAIR, PALE,
ASHEN, HOAR(Y), LIGHT,
MILKY, SNOWY, SILVER
admiral .... BUTTERFLY
alkali .... SODA ASH
and-pink-skinned .... BLOND
Anglo-Saxon Protestant
.... WASP
animal .... ALBINO
ant .... ANAY, TERMITE
bear .... POLAR
cabbage .... BACHOY
cedar .... ARBORVITAE
cliffs site .... DOVER
clouds .... CERRI
coal .... WATER
collar employee .... CLERK,
OFFICE WORKER
combining form .... ALBO,
LEUK(O)
creamy .... IVORY
earth .... GYPSUM, KAOLIN,
MAGNESIA, TERRA ALBA
egg's .... GLAIR, ALBUMEN
elephant: sl. .... LEMON

eye .... SONGBIRD
faced .... PALE, PALLID
flag signal .... TRUCE,
SURRENDER
gum .... EUCALYPTUS
gypsum .... ALABASTER
haired .... HOARY
hot .... INCANDESCENT
lead .... CERUSE, CERUSSITE
lie .... FIB
limestone .... CHALK
livered person .... COWARD
make .... BLANCH, BLEACH
mammary gland secretion
.... MILK
man .... BUCKRA
man's burden .... IMPERIALISM
meat .... VEAL, CHICKEN
men in .... DOCTORS
oak .... ROBLE
person .... PALEFACE,
CAUCASIAN
plague .... TUBERCULOSIS
poplar .... ABELE
race .... CAUCASIAN
-sale items .... LINENS
shade of off- .... BONE
slang .... FAIR, HONEST
smooth, hard gem .... PEARL
soap .... IVORY
spruce .... EPINETTE
thorn .... MAYFLOWER
tie .... DRESS
turning .... ALBESCENT
wax ...... CARNAUBA, PARAFFIN
whale .... BELUGA
women in .... NUNS, NURSES
yellowish .... CREAM,
EGGSHELL
White Friar .... ALSATIAN,
CARMELITE
Hart .... INN
House nickname .... ABE,
CAL, IKE, WOODY
office .... OVAL
resident .... PRESIDENT
room .... OVAL OFFICE
of "The Golden Girls"
.... BETTY
Rose house .... YORK
Sea gulf .... ARCHANGEL
whitebait .... BRIT, SMELT, SPRAT,
HERRING
whitecap .... WAVE
whitefish .... CISCO, ATINGA,
BELUGA, POLLAN, VENDACE,
MENHADEN, TULLIBEE
whitehead .... MILIA, BLEMISH
Whitelaw, American journalist
and diplomat .... REID
whiten .... BLANCH, BLEACH,

ETIOLATE

whitening .... CANESCENT

whitetail .... DEER, WHEATER

whitewall .... TIRE

whitewash .... FUDGE, PARGET, CONCEAL, PLASTER, VARNISH

whitewood .... TULIP, LINDEN

whither .... WHERE, WHEREVER

whiting .... COD, HAKE, CHALK, POLLACK, WALLEYE, DRUMFISH, MENHADEN, WEAKFISH

whitlow .... FELON, AGNAIL, ABSCESS

kind of .... HERPETIC

location .... TOE, FINGER

Whitman, poet .... WALT(ER)

Whitney, cotton gin inventor

.... ELI

Whitsunday .... PENTECOST

Whitsuntide .... PINKSTER

whittle .... CUT, DOCK, PARE, CARVE, ERODE, SHAVE, SLICE, DEDUCT, REDUCE

whittling refuse .... SHAVINGS

whiz(z) .... ZIP, HISS, WHIR(R), EXPERT, BARGAIN, SPEED BY

kid .... PRODIGY

kin .... LULU

whizzing sound .... PIRR

who a loaner likes .... PAYER

authorized Jesus of Nazareth's execution?

.... PILATE

claimed he shot John Wilkes Booth? .... "BOSTON" CORBETT

escaped with the Declaration of Independence?

.... DOLLEY MADISON

goes there? .... CHALLENGE

ordered John the Baptist's execution? .... ANTIPAS

refused to grow up, boy

.... PETER PAN

replaced Judas? ..... MATTHIAS

whoa .... STOP, HOLLA

whodunit .... MYSTERY

character .... DICK, BUTLER, SLEUTH, VICTIM, DETECTIVE

coiner of .... GORDON

movie ...... CHILLER, SUSPENSE

serial .... COLUMBO, PERRY MASON, HAWAII FIVE-O, MURDER SHE WROTE

staple .... CLUES, CRIME, MURDER

whoever .... ANYONE

whole .... BULK, LUMP, MASS, TOTO, UNCUT, INTACT, COMPLETE, ENTIRE(TY),

TOTAL(ITY), AGGREGATE, 100 PERCENT

as a .... ALTOGETHER

combining form .... HOLO

costume .... ENSEMBLE

note .... SEMIBREVE

number .... INTEGER

slang .... THE WORKS

wholehearted .... SINCERE

wholesale .... BULK, MASS, GROSS, CHEAPER, SWEEPING

house .... DISCOUNT STORE

opposed to .... RETAIL

wholesaler .... JOBBER, MIDDLEMAN, DISTRIBUTOR

wholesome ...... SOUND, HEALTHY, SALUTARY, HEALTHFUL, BENEFICIAL

wholly .... ALL, FULLY, PLUMB, IN TOTO, TOTALLY, ENTIRELY

whoooo cares? .... DON'T GIVE A HOOT

whoop .... CRY, CALL, HOOT, YELL, SHOUT, HOLLER

Hoople .... EGAD

it up .... CELEBRATE

whoopee ...... HOOPLA, FESTIVITY, MERRIMENT

whooper .... SWAN

whooping cough .... CHINCOUGH, PERTUSSIS

whop .... HIT, BEAT, FLOG, STRIKE, WALLOP, CLOBBER

whopper .... JUMBO, BIG (LIE)

whore ...... BAWD, HARLOT, CALL-GIRL, STRUMPET, PROSTITUTE

whorehouse .... BROTHEL

whorl .... VOLUTE, FLYWHEEL, VERTICIL, VOLUTION

fingerprint .... RIDGE

Who's station .... FIRST

why .... HOW COME

wick ...... TAPER, THORP, HAMLET, VILLAGE

kind of .... LAMP, CANDLE

lead-in .... BAILI

wicked .... BAD, EVIL, CRUEL, SINFUL, GODLESS, IMPIOUS, NAUGHTY, SATANIC, VICIOUS

act .... SIN, CRIME, MISDEED

city .... SODOM, BABYLON, GOMORRAH

colloquial .... NAUGHTY, MISCHIEVOUS

wickedness .... VICE

wicker .... BURI, TWIG, STRAW, WITHE, RAFFIA, RATTAN

basket ...... CORE, KISH, SKEP, CRATE, CREEL, HAMPER, KIPSEY, PANNIER

cradle .... BASSINET

tree .... OSIER, WILLOW

wickerwork material .... BURI, OSIER, STRAW, WITHE, RAFFIA, RAT(T)AN, WILLOW

wicket .... ARCH, DOOR, GATE, HOOP, WINDOW

in cricket .... INNING

in croquet .... ARCH, HOOP

part .... BAIL

wickiup .... TEPEE, WIGWAM

wicopy .... BASSWOOD

wide .... VAST, AMPLE, BROAD, LARGE, ROOMY, SPACIOUS

awake .... KEEN, ALERT, SLEEPLESS

eyed .... ASTARE

inlet .... BAY

open .... AGAPE, CLEAR

open break ..... ABYSS, CHASM

open space ..... PLAIN, DESERT

widely .... FAR-AND-NEAR, EXTENSIVELY

known .... FAMED

widen .... DILATE, SPREAD, BROADEN, ENLARGE, INCREASE

widespread .... RIFE, COMMON, GLOBAL, GENERAL, RAMPANT, REGNANT, PREVALENT, UNIVERSAL

disease .... EPIDEMIC

fear .... PANIC

widgeon ...... DUCK, SMEE, SMEW, GOOSE, ZUISIN, BALDPATE

genus .... MARECA

kin .... POCHARD, REDHEAD

widow .... MATRON, RELICT, SUTTEE, BEREAVE, FEME SOLE, SURVIVOR

bird .... WHIDAH

black .... SPIDER

grass .... DIVORCEE

Hindu .... SUTTEE

inheritance of .... DOWER

man .... WIDOWER

of a king .... QUEEN DOWAGER

titled, wealthy .... DOWAGER

widowhood .... VIDUAGE, VIDUITY

widow's dream cocktail

.... BENEDICTINE

mites .... LEPTA

mourning clothes .... WEEDS

third .... DOWER, DOWRY

width .... BEAM, SPAN, EXTENT, BREADTH, EXPANSE, LATITUDE, WIDENESS, BROADNESS

wield .... PLY, WAVE, EXERT, EMPLOY, HANDLE, MANAGE, CONTROL, BRANDISH, EXERCISE

wielder, authority .... BOSS, RULER, DICTATOR, GOVERNOR
blue pencil .... EDITOR, REDACTOR
wieldy .... PLIANT, DUCTILE, PLIABLE, FLEXIBLE, YIELDING
Wien .... VIENNA
wiener .... HOTDOG, FRANKFURTER
schnitzel .... VEAL
wurst .... SAUSAGE
wienie .... RED-HOT
Wiesbaden's location ...... HESSE
wife .... MRS., RIB, FEME, FERE, FRAU, FROW, BRIDE, MATRON, MISSIS, MISSUS, SPOUSE, HELPMATE, HELPMEET, YOKEFELLOW
beating .... ABUSE
bequest to .... DOS
common-law .... MISTRESS
domineering: sl. .... BATTLEAX
dowry of .... DOT
duke's, e.g. .... PEERESS
in law .... FEME
Indian .... SQUAW
killer .... UXORICIDE
king's .... QUEEN-CONSORT
knight's .... DAME
lord's .... LADY
man's prospective
.... INTENDED
of a .... UXORIAL
of Peter the Great
.... EUDOXIA
one .... MONOGAMY
rajah's .... RANI, RANEE
secondary .... CONCUBINE
slang .... OLD LADY, BETTER HALF, LITTLE WOMAN, BALL AND CHAIN
submissive to one's
.... UXORIOUS
take to .... WED, MARRY
wifely .... LOVING, UXORIAL
wig ...... TETE, PERUKE, TO(U)PEE, PERIWIG, POSTICHE, HAIRPIECE, HEADDRESS
gray .... GRIZZLE
small .... TOUPEE, WIGLET
used as part of coiffure
.... FALL, SWITCH, WIGLET
wigeon .... SMEE, WIDGEON
wigging .... REBUKE, SCOLDING
wiggle ...... WAG, SHAKE, SQUIRM, WANGLE, WOBBLE, WRIGGLE
wiggler .... LARVA, WRIGGLER
wigwag .... CODE, WAVE, SIGNAL, ALTERNATE
wigwam .... HUT, TENT, LODGE, TE(E)PEE, WICKIUP
wild .... GAGA, RANK, RASH,

FERAL, WASTE, DARING, FERINE, FIERCE, SAVAGE, STORMY, UNRULY, RIOTOUS, UNTAMED, VIOLENT, DESOLATE, RECKLESS, PHRENETIC, PRIMITIVE, UNBRIDLED, DISORDERLY, LICENTIOUS, HARUM-SCARUM
animal .... BEAST
apple .... CRAB, CREEPER
ass .... ONAGER
boar .... HOG
brier .... DOG ROSE
buffalo .... ARNA, ARNEE
cat .... EYRA, LYNX, BOBCAT, MARGAY, MARGOT, OCELOT, SERVAL
cattle .... GAUR, BANTENG
celery .... EELGRASS, SMALLAGE
country .... WEALD
cry .... EVOE, WHOOP, SCREAM, SHRIEK, SCREECH
dog .... CUON, DHOLE, DINGO
duck .... SCAUP, GADWALL, MALLARD, REDHEAD, GOLDENEYE, CANVASBACK
eyed .... HAGGARD
fowl .... DUCK, QUAIL, PHEASANT, PARTRIDGE
fowl flock .... SKEIN
goat .... IBEX, TAHR, TAIR
goose .... BRANT
goose's call .... HONK
guess .... STAB
hog ..... BENE, BOAR, PECCARY
honey source .... BEETREE
horse .... CAYUSE, TARPAN, BRONC(H)O, BRUMBIE, MUSTANG
hyacinth .... BLUEBELL
life .... GAME
life preserve .... WETLAND
madder .... BEDSTRAW
mint, e.g. .... POTHERB
mustard .... CHARLOCK
olive .... OLEASTER
ox ...... ANOA, REEM, BANTENG
ox hunter .... BUCCANEER
parsley .... LOVAGE
pig .... BOAR
plum .... SLOE
revelry .... ORGY
rose .... EGLANTINE, (SWEET)BRIER
sheep .... SHA, ARUI, UDAD, URIAL, AOUDAD, ARGALI, NAHOOR, BIGHORN, MOUFLON
sown .... OATS
state of being .... FERITY
swan .... ELKE

talker .... RAVER
the .... NATURE
time .... SPREE
try .... STAB
Wild Bill _____ .... HICKOK
Bill Hickok's burial place
.... MOUNT MORIAH
Bill Hickok's killer .... (JACK) MCCALL
Duck author .... IBSEN
Huntsman .... ODIN
West show .... RODEO
wildcat: colloq. .... RISKY, SPECULATIVE
grayish .... JAGUARUNDI
wildcatter's quest .... OIL
Wilde, actor .... CORNEL
dramatist .... OSCAR
ballad's subject .... GAOL
play .... SALOME
wildebeest .... GNU, ANTELOPE
country? .... GNUENGLAND
wilderness ...... WILD(S), DESERT, JUNGLE, STEPPE, TUNDRA, BOONDOCKS, WASTE(LAND)
biblical .... SIN
road traveler .... BOONE
wildfire .... LIGHTNING, ERYSIPELAS
wildlife preserve .... WETLAND, SANCTUARY
wildness .... FERITY
wile .... ART, LURE, DECEIT, BEGUILE, ARTIFICE, TRICK(ERY)
wiles .... CHARM
wilier .... ASTUTER, CRAFTIER
Wilkes, Antarctic explorer
.... CHARLES
ship of .... VINCENNES
will .... MIND, WISH, LEAVE, POWER, CHOICE, CHOOSE, DECREE, DESIRE, OPTION, BEQUEATH, PLEASURE, VOLITION
addition to a .... CODICIL
bequeathed by
.... TESTAMENTARY
convey by .... DEMISE
exercise of the .... VOLITION
handwritten .... HOLOGRAPH
having made a .... TESTATE
having no .... INTESTATE
in law .... TESTAMENT
maker ..... DEVISOR, TESTATOR
of one's free .... ACCORD
o'-the-wisp .... CHIMERA, WILDFIRE, IGNIS FATUUS
power .... SELF-CONTROL
power, loss of .... ABULIA

Willard, boxing champion
.... JESS
organization of Mrs. .... WCTU
temperance leader
.... FRANCES
willful .... WAYWARD, STUBBORN,
OBSTINATE, HEADSTRONG
William, actor .... HOLDEN
Howard ____, U.S.
president .... TAFT
in German .... WILHELM
Jefferson Blythe, born
.... BILL CLINTON
Williams, ballplayer .... TED
Williamson, Shakespearean
actor .... NICOL
Williamson, Texas judge
.... ROBERT
nickname of .... THREE-
LEGGED WILLIE
willies .... CREEPS, JITTERS,
NERVOUSNESS
willing .... BAIN, GAME, LIEF,
EAGER, READY, DOCILE,
MINDED, PLIANT, CONTENT,
DISPOSED, INCLINED,
UNFORCED, ASSENTING,
CONSENTING
reluctantly .... FAIN
variant: poet. .... FAINE
willingly .... LIEF, GLADLY,
READILY, VOLUNTARILY
archaic .... FAIN
willingness .... ASSENT, DESIRE,
ALACRITY, PENCHANT
Willkie, presidential candidate
.... WENDELL
utopian dream of .... ONE
WORLD
willow .... ITEA, OSIER, SALIX,
SALLOW
ament .... CHAT
bark, glucoside from
.... SALICIN
basket .... PRICKLE
catkin .... CHAT
herb .... ROSEBAY
of the .... SALICACEOUS
run product .... AUTO
shoot .... WAND
spike .... CHAT, AMENT,
CATKIN
twig .... OSIER, WITHE,
SALLOW
twigs, woven .... WICKER
willowy .... SLIM, LITHE, SVELT,
PLIANT, SUPPLE, SLENDER
Willy, bold peacemaker
.... BRANDT
Brandt's award: 1971
.... NOBEL PEACE PRIZE

birthplace .... LIBECK
bold policy .... OSTPOLITIK
real name .... HERBERT
FRAHM
willy-nilly .... PERFORCE,
INDECISIVE, IRRESOLUTE,
WHETHER OR NOT
Wilms' tumor
.... NEPHROBLASTOMA
locale .... KIDNEY
Wilson, U.S. president
.... WOODROW
nickname of .... WOODY
wife of .... EDITH
Wilson's thrush .... VEERY
wilt .... SAG, DROOP, WITHER,
SHRIVEL, COLLAPSE,
LANGUISH
Wilt of basketball fame
.... CHAMBERLAIN
the ____ .... STILT
wily .... SLY, FOXY, ARTFUL,
ASTUTE, CLEVER, CRAFTY,
SHIFTY, SUBTLE, TRICKY,
CROOKED, CUNNING,
INSIDIOUS
wimble .... AUGER, GIMLET
Wimbledon event .... TENNIS
wimp .... WEAKLING
wimple .... RIPPLE
wearer of .... NUN
win .... GET, HIT, BEAT, EARN,
GAIN, SWAY, REACH, MASTER,
OBTAIN, ACHIEVE, CONQUER,
PREVAIL, SUCCEED, TRIUMPH
a point .... ACE
acceptance .... SELL
all games .... SWEEP
all tricks .... SLAM, VOLE
overwhelming .... KNOCKOUT,
LANDSLIDE
wince .... SHY, REEL, QUAIL,
FLINCH, RECOIL, ROLLER,
SHRINK, GRIMACE
winch .... WHIM, CRANK, HOIST,
WINDLASS
Winchester .... RIFLE
wind .... AIR, AURA, BLOW, COIL,
GALE, GUST, HINT, PUFF,
REEL, BLAST, NOSER, SCENT,
STORM, WHIFF, BUSTER,
DUSTER, SAMIEL, SIMOOM,
ZEPHYR, PAMPERO, LEVANTER,
NONSENSE, CORKSCREW
away from .... ALEE
blowing down from the Alps
.... BISE
borne by the .... EOLIC
breath of .... WAFT, FLATUS
combining form .... ANEMO

coming across the mountains
.... TRAMONTANE
cone .... SLEEVE
crack in timber made by
.... ANEMOSIS
deposit .... LOESS, SEDIMENT
desert .... SAMIEL, SIMOOM,
SIROCCO
direction recorder
.... ANEMOGRAPH,
ANEMOSCOPE
driven clouds .... SCUD
dry .... FOEHN
east .... EURUS
equatorial .... TRADE
gauge .... ANEMOMETER
gentle .... AURA, BREEZE,
ZEPHYR
gust of .... PUFF, WAFT
high, strong .... GALE
Indian Ocean .... MONSOON
indicator .... CONE, SLEEVE,
(WIND)SOCK, (WEATHER)COCK,
(WEATHER)VANE
instrument .... HORN, OBOE,
PIPE, REED, TUBA, BUGLE,
FLUTE, SHAWM, CORNET,
BASSOON, OCARINA, SACKBUT,
CLARINET, TROMBONE,
HARMONICA
instrument finger hole
.... VENTAGE
instrument mouthpiece .... LIP
mythical .... SANSAR
north .... BISE, AQUILO,
BOREAS
northeast .... EURAQUILO,
EUROCLYDON
of the north .... BOREAL
puff .... FLATUS
Rocky Mountain .... CHINOOK
run before the .... SCUD
scale .... BEAUFORT
science of the .... ANEMOLOGY
shifting .... VARIABLE
side away from .... LEE
side toward .... WEATHER,
WINDWARD
sign of .... MARE'S TAIL
sound .... SOB, ROAR, SOUGH
south .... AUSTER
southeast .... EURUS
southwest .... AFER
strong .... GALE, STORM,
PAMPERO, TEMPEST, LEVANTER
sudden, brief .... FLAW,
FLURRY
sudden, violent .... SQUALL
up .... END, FINISH, CONCLUDE
warm, dry .... FOEHN
wave .... RIPPLE

west .... FAVONIAN,
ZEPHYR(US)
whirling .... CYCLONE,
TORNADO, TWISTER
with snow/rain .... FLAW
Wind in the Willows animal
.... OTTER
windbag .... GASBAG, BRAGGART,
CHATTERER
windblown dust .... STOUR
windbreaker .... JACKET
winded .... BREATHLESS
windfall .... BOON, FIND, VAIL,
BONUS, MANNA, PRIZE,
BONANZA, FORTUNE,
GODSEND
windflower .... ANEMONE
windhover ...... FALCON, KESTREL
windigo .... OGRE
winding .... MAZY, SNAKY,
SPIRAL, TURNING, TORTUOUS,
TWISTING, MEANDROUS,
LABYRINTHINE
gait of horse .... CARACOLE
line .... ZIGZAG
passages, structure with
.... LABYRINTH
pathway .... AMBAGE
sheet .... SHROUD, CEREMENT
structure .... SPIRAL STAIRCASE
windjammer .... SAILBOAT,
SAILING SHIP
slang .... WINDBAG
windlass .... REEL, CRANK, HOIST,
WINCH, LIFTER, PINION,
CAPSTAN
cylinder .... BARREL
windless .... CALM, STUFFY,
WINDED, AIRLESS, STIFLING
windmill fighter
.... (DON)QUIXOTE
part .... SAIL, VANE, SHAFT
pump .... GIN
Windmills of the Gods author
.... (SIDNEY)SHELDON
window bar .... MULLION
bay .... ORIEL
cleaned .... SQUEEGEED
door .... TRANSOM
dormer .... LUTHERN
drapery .... VALANCE,
LAMBREQUIN
dresser .... DECORATOR
dressing .... TRIM, FACADE,
DISPLAY, FALSE FRONT
fastener .... HASP, LATCH
frame .... CASEMENT
frame piece .... STILE
of a .... FENESTRAL
on a fort's wall .... LOOPHOLE,
EMBRASURE

part .... PANE, SASH, SILL,
FRAME, JAMB(E), GRILL(E),
LINTEL, GRATING
roof .... DORMER, SKYLIGHT
round .... ROUNDEL
sash sidepiece .... STILE
shade .... BLIND, SHUTTER
ship's .... PORTHOLE,
DEADLIGHT
shopping .... BROWSE,
LOOKING, BROWSING
small ..... WICKET, FENESTELLA
trellised .... LATTICE
with sloping slats ..... LOUVER
windpipe .... TRACHEA, WEASAND,
THROTTLE
part of .... LARYNX, THROAT
windrow .... SWATH, FURROW
winds, Alpine .... FOEHNS
annual .... ETESIAN
deviation caused by ..... DRIFT
god of .... AEOLUS
study of .... ANEMOLOGY
windshake .... ANEMOSIS
windshield .... WINDSCREEN
gadget .... WIPER, DEICER
Windsor's novel, 1944
.... FOREVER AMBER
windstorm .... BLOW, GALE,
BURAN, SQUALL, CYCLONE,
TORNADO, TWISTER, TYPHOON
of Central Asia .... BURA(N)
windup .... CLIMAX, END(ING),
FINALE, CLOSURE
Windward island ...... GRENADA,
DOMINICA, ST. LUCIA, ST.
VINCENT, MARTINIQUE
opposed to .... LEEWARD
windy ...... AIRY, BLOWY, GABBY,
GASSY, GUSTY, STORMY,
VERBOSE, BOASTFUL,
TALKATIVE, LONG-WINDED
city .... CHICAGO
spate .... GUST
wine .... PORT, DRINK, YQUEM,
CANARY, LIQUOR, NECTAR,
SHERRY, CATAWBA, MADEIRA,
VINTAGE, MUSCADEL,
MUSCATEL
addicted to .... VINOUS
addiction .... VINOSITY
age of .... VINTAGE
and dine .... TREAT,
ENTERTAIN
beverage ..... NEGUS, SILLABUB
bottle ..... MAGNUM, DECANTER
bottle indentation .... KICK
Burgundy .... CHABLIS
burning of .... USTULATION
cask .... TUN, BOSS, BUTT, PIPI,
PUNCHEON

cask deposit .... ARGAL,
ARGOL, TARTAR
choice .... VINTAGE
colored .... VINACEOUS
combining form .... OENO,
VINI
cup .... BEAKER
deposit .... LEES, GRIFFE
disorder .... CASSE
distillate .... BRANDY, COGNAC
drink, cold .... COBBLER,
SANGAREE, SILLABUB
dry .... SEC, BRUT, SACK,
CLARET, CHABLIS, CHIANTI,
TUSCANY, VERMOUTH
effervescent .... CHAMPAGNE
film on .... BEESWING
flavor .... MULL
flavoring .... DOSE, DOSAGE
formation in .... ROPE
fragrance of .... BOUQUET
glass .... RUMMER
god .... BACCHUS
grapes harvester .... VINTAGER
grower's patron .... VINCENT
indicating .... OENO
jug .... OLPE
kind of .... DRY, RED, PORT,
CIDER, PERRY, WHITE,
BRANDY, COOKING, CORDIAL,
MUSCATEL, SAUTERNE,
VERMOUTH, SPARKLING
like .... VINACEOUS
loss of color .... CASSE
measure .... ORNE
merchant .... VINTNER
mixture .... KIR, NEGUS
new .... MUST
of .... VINIC, VINOUS,
VINACEOUS
pitcher .... OLPE
prized .... VINTAGE
punch .... SANGRIA
receptacle .... AMA
red .... PORT, MEDOC, TINTA,
CLARET, CHIANTI, TUSCANY,
BURGUNDY, DUBONNET
refuse .... LEES, DREGS
revived .... STUM
Rhine .... HOCK, MOSELLE
sauterne .... YQUEM
seller .... VINTNER
sherry .... JEREZ, OLOROSO
shop .... BISTRO, TABERNA,
ESTAMINET
spiced .... NEGUS, BISHOP,
MARINADE, SANGAREE,
HIPPOCRAS
stock .... CELLAR
storage place .... CELLAR,
BUTTERY

strength .... SEVE
strengthen .... DOSE
sweet .... PORT, TOKAY,
CANARY, MADEIRA, MALMSEY,
ALICANTE, MUSCATEL,
SAUTERNE, VERMOUTH
sweeten .... MULL
taster .... GOURMET
term .... DRY, SEC, BODY,
BRUT, FLINTY, BOUQUET,
VINTAGE
unfermented .... MUST
vessel .... AMA, TUN, VAT,
BARREL, AMPULLA, CHALICE
white .... HOCK, SACK,
BARSAC, MALAGA, CHABLIS,
MADEIRA, MALMSEY,
MARSALA, MOSELLE,
BURGUNDY, SAUTERNE,
VERMOUTH
with honey .... MULSE
wines, study of .... OENOLOGY,
VINOLOGY
winesap .... (WINTER)APPLE
wing .... ALA, ARM, FLY, PINNA,
PENNON, PINION
bastard .... ALULA
bind the .... PINION
combining form .... PTERO
control .... AILERON
cover .... SHARD, ELYTRON,
ELYTRUM
feather .... REMEX, PINION
footed .... SWIFT, ALIPED
footed creature .... BAT,
LEMUR
furnish with .... IMP
having the form of a
.... PTERYGOID
in anatomy .... ALA
it, verbally .... AD LIB
length .... SPAN
movement .... BEAT, FLAP,
FLUTTER
of building .... BAY, ELL,
ANNEX, ALETTE, EXTENSION
protuberance .... CALCAR
shaped ...... ALAR(Y), ALIFORM
small .... ALULA
span of airplane .... SPREAD
support of airplane
.... CABANE
three-quilled .... ALULA
type of .... DELTA
winged .... ALAR, FLEW,
ALATE(D), PENNATE,
FEATHERED
being .... AMOR, ANGEL,
SERAPH(IM)
figure .... ICARUS, IDOLON,
IDOLUM

fruit .... SAMARA
goddess .... NIKE
hat .... PETASOS, PETASUS
hat wearer
.... HERMES(MERCURY)
horse .... PEGASUS
monster: myth. .... HARPY
sandals .... TALARIA
sandals wearer
.... MERCURY(HERMES)
staff .... CADUCEUS
two .... DIPTERAL, DIPTEROUS
wingless ...... APTERAL, APTEROUS
bird .... EMU, KIWI, APTERYX
winglet .... ALULA
winglike .... ALA(R), ALATE,
PTERYGOID
part .... FIN
wings, flap the .... WINNOW
furnish .... IMP
having .... ALATE(D)
having two .... BIPENNATE
wingspread .... SPAN
wink .... BAT, HINT, BLINK,
SIGNAL, SQUINT, INSTANT,
NICTATE, TWINKLE
at .... CONDONE, CONSENT
winker .... BLINDER, EYE(LASH)
winkle .... SNAIL
winks, forty .... NAP, DOZE
winner .... VICTOR, CHAMPION,
CONQUEROR
long shot/surprise
.... SLEEPER, DARK HORSE
Winnie _____ **Pu** .... ILLE
Winnie the Pooh author
.... MILNE
was his nickname
.... (WINSTON)CHURCHILL
winning .... AHEAD, TAKING,
CHARMING, DOMINANT,
ENGAGING, SPORTIVE,
ATTRACTIVE, CAPTIVATING
disposition .... SWEET,
PLEASANT
lottery combination ...... TERN
margin .... HAIR, NOSE
point .... ACE
winnings .... GAINS, RETURNS
slang .... VELVET
winnow .... FAN, SIFT, SCATTER,
SEPARATE
Winona, actress .... RYDER
winsome .... GAY, BONNY,
MERRY, LIVELY, LOVABLE,
WINNING, CHARMING,
ENGAGING
winter .... COLD, SEASON,
YULE(TIDE), HIBERNATE
apple .... ROME, RUSSET,
WINESAP, DELICIOUS

cap .... TUQUE
cover/blanket .... SNOW
cutter .... ICEBOAT
eave hanger .... ICICLE
festival .... POTLATCH
fodder .... SILAGE
glider .... SKI, SLED
hazard .... SKID, SLEET
melon .... CASABA
of/like .... BRUMAL, HIEMAL,
HIBERNAL
pear .... BOSC, WARDEN
precipitation ...... SNOW, SLEET
product .... SNOW, FROST
sleep .... HIBERNATION
solstice festival
.... SATURNALIA
spend the .... HIBERNATE
sport .... SKIING, SLALOM,
SKIJORING
squash .... CUSHAW
torpid in .... DORMANT
vehicle ...... SLED(GE), SLEIGH,
TOBOGGAN
wear .... GLOVES, MITTENS,
EARMUFFS, SNOWSHOES
weather .... SLEETY
winterberry .... HOLLY
wintergreen .... OIL, SHINLEAF,
TEABERRY
false .... PYROLA
Winters, actress .... SHELLEY
Winter's Tale shepherdess
.... MOPSA, DORCAS
wintertime creation
.... SNOWMAN
wintry .... COLD, SNOWY,
BRUMAL, HIEMAL, HIBERNAL
winze .... SHAFT
wipe ...... DRY, MOP, DUST, SWAB,
BRUSH, CLEAN, TOWEL,
EFFACE
out ...... KILL, ERASE, REMOVE,
ELIMINATE, ERADICATE,
LIQUIDATE, EXTERMINATE
wiper ...... CAM, TOWEL, DUSTER,
DISHRAG
finger/lip .... NAPKIN,
SERVIETTE
wire ...... CORD, LINE, TELEGRAM,
CABLE(GRAM), TELEGRAPH
brush .... CARD
coil .... SPRING
cutting tool .... PLIERS
drum's .... SNARE
insulated, electric .... FLEX
light bulb .... FILAMENT
measure .... MIL, STONE
nail .... BRAD
pen/enclosure .... CAGE
rope .... CABLE

service .... API, INS, UPI,
REUTERS
spiral of .... COIL
tapper .... TOUT, BUGGER
wiredancer .... AERIALIST
wirehair .... (FOX)TERRIER
wireless .... RADIO
adjunct ...... AERIAL, ANTENNA
devotee .... HAM
wirepuller .... PUPPETEER
wirework .... GRILLAGE
wireworm .... MILLIPEDE
wiry .... STIFF, TOUGH, SINEWY,
STRONG, MUSCULAR
Wisconsin bay .... GREEN,
CHEQUAMEGON
capital .... MADISON
city/town .... ALMA, ANTIGO,
BELOIT, JUNEAU, RACINE,
WAUSAU, ASHLAND, BARABOO,
ELKHORN, OSHKOSH,
APPLETON, KENOSHA, GREEN
BAY, LA CROSSE, SUPERIOR,
WAUKESHA, WEST BEND, EAU
CLAIRE, FOND DU LAC,
GREENDALE, MARINETTE,
MILWAUKEE, NEW BERLIN,
SHEBOYGAN, GREENFIELD,
JANESVILLE, INDEPENDENCE
college .... MILTON,
LAKELAND, NORTHLAND
county .... DANE, DOOR, DUNN,
IOWA, IRON, SAUK, BROWN,
CLARK, DODGE, GRANT,
BARRON, CALUMET, KENOSHA,
OZAUKEE, WAUPACA,
CHIPPEWA, COLUMBIA, LA
CROSSE, MARATHON,
MANITOWOC, MILWAUKEE,
OUTAGAMIE, SHEBOYGAN,
WINNEBAGO, WASHINGTON
football team .... GREEN BAY
PACKERS
Indian .... SAC, WINNEBAGO
island .... CAT, OAK, BEAR,
SAND, OUTER, CHAMBERS,
MADELINE, MICHIGAN,
STOCKTON, WASHINGTON
islands .... APOSTLE
lake .... CLAM, LONG, OWEN,
PINE, WIND, DU BAY, EAGLE,
MOOSE, NORTH, PEPIN, ROUND,
SHELL, TROUT, BARDON,
BEULAH, CHETAC, DENOON,
GENEVA, GOLDEN, POYGAN,
SPIDER, YELLOW, KEGONSA,
MENDOTA, METONGA, PELICAN,
PHANTOM, SHAWAMO,
THUNDER, CHIPPEWA,
MICHIGAN, SUPERIOR,
WINNEBAGO

mountain .... RIB, TIMMS HILL,
SUGARBUSH HILL
native .... BADGER
river .... FOX, CLAM, JUMP,
ROCK, WOLF, APPLE, BLACK,
SUGAR, OCONTO, YELLOW,
FLAMBEAU, KICKAPOO,
MONTREAL, PESHTIGO,
MENOMINEE, NAMEKAGON,
WISCONSIN, PECATONICA,
SAINT CROIX
state animal .... BADGER
state bird .... ROBIN
state fish .... MUSKY
state flower ..... WOOD VIOLET,
BUTTERFLY VIOLET
state nickname .... BADGER
strait .... PORTE DES MORTS
university .... LAWRENCE,
MARQUETTE
wisdom .... WIT, LORE, LEARNING,
SAGACITY, SAGENESS,
SAPIENCE, ERUDITION,
KNOWLEDGE
a love of .... PHILOSOPHY
Books of the Old Testament
.... JOB, PROVERBS,
ECCLESIASTES
goddess of .... ATHENA,
MINERVA
infinite .... OMNISCIENCE
source of .... LAMP
symbol of .... OWL
tooth .... MOLAR
universal .... PANSOPHY
words of ..... MAXIM, PROVERB
wise .... DEEP, SAGE, WITTY,
SHREWD, CUNNING, ERUDITE,
LEARNED, SAPIENT,
INFORMED, JUDICIOUS,
SAGACIOUS
adviser .... MENTOR
and pithy .... GNOMIC
guy .... SMART ALECK
lawmaker .... SOLON
leader .... STATESMAN
man .... SAGE, SOLON,
MASTER, MENTOR, NESTOR,
PUNDIT, SAVANT, MAHATMA,
SCHOLAR, SOLOMON
men, biblical .... MAGI
saying ..... SAW, REDE, ADAGE,
MAXIM, PROVERB
slang .... FRESH, SAVVY,
KNOWING, CONCEITED
wiseacre ...... QUACK, SMART ASS,
KNOW-IT-ALL, SMART ALECK
wisecrack .... GAG, GIBE, JEST,
JOKE, QUIP, RETORT
wisent .... BISON
wish ...... BID, HOPE, WANT, WILL,

CRAVE, DREAM, YEARN,
BEHEST, DESIRE
mere .... VELLEITY
undone .... RUE
wishbone .... FURCULA,
FURCULUM, FOURCHETTE
wishful .... HOPEFUL, LONGING
wishy-washy .... THIN, WEAK,
BLAND, FEEBLE, WATERY,
INSIPID, SLIPSHOD, SLOVENLY,
SPINELESS, NAMBY-PAMBY
Wisla .... VISTULA
wisp .... LOCK, TATE, TUFT,
BUNCH, SHRED, BUNDLE
wispy .... FRAIL, SLIGHT, SLENDER
wisteria .... PEA, SHRUB, FLOWER,
VIOLET
wistful .... EAGER, MUSING,
PENSIVE, YEARNING
wit .... WAG, MIND, IRONY, SENSE,
CUNNING, SARCASM,
HUMOR(IST)
bit of .... EPIGRAM
descriptive of .... QUICK,
NIMBLE
graceful, piercing .... ATTIC
SALT
lively .... ESPRIT
lowest form of .... PUN
sharp .... SALT
soul of .... BREVITY
sting of .... BARB
witch .... HAG, HEX, CRONE,
HARPY, LAMIA, SHREW, SIREN,
SYBIL, BELDAM(E), CARLINE,
CHARMER, HELLCAT,
WARLOCK, SORCERESS,
ENCHANTRESS
brew of .... HELLBROTH
city .... SALEM
doctor .... MEDICINE MAN
folklore .... LILITH
Homer's .... CIRCE
hunt .... PERSECUTION
in "Damn Yankees" .... LOLA
male equivalent of a
.... WARLOCK
means of transportation
.... BROOM
Shakespeare's .... DUESSA
who helped Jason ...... MEDEA
with snakes for hair
..... GORGON, MEDUSA, STHENO
witchcraft ...... MAGIC, SORCERY,
WIZARDRY, NECROMANCY
charm .... JUJU
talisman .... OBI, OBEAH
witchery .... CHARM, HOODOO,
VOODOO, SORCERY,
FASCINATION
witches' broom ...... HEXENBESEN

Sabbath .... ORGY, MEETING
witching .... MAGICAL,
      ENCHANTING
witchy words .... INCANTATION
wite .... BLAME, FAULT
with ...... BY, CUM, PLUS, AMONG,
      USING, THROUGH,
      ALONG(SIDE)
  bated breath .... TENSE,
        ANXIOUS
  child .... PREGNANT,
        EXPECTING
  competence .... ABLY
  cruel tendencies ...... SADISTIC
  finesse .... ADEPTLY
  force .... AMAIN
  great ineptness .... SADLY
  haste: poet. .... AMAIN
  humility .... MEEKLY
  it: sl. .... HEP, HIP
  more decibels .... LOUDER
  open arms .... WILLINGLY
  prefix .... SYN
  regard to .... AS FOR
  spirit, in music ...... CON BRIO
  the result .... SO AS
withal .... ALSO, STILL, BESIDES
withdraw .... QUIT, WEAN, LEAVE,
  DECAMP, DEPART, RECALL,
  RECANT, REMOVE, RESIGN,
  RETIRE, SECEDE, BACKOUT,
  PULLOUT, RETRACT, RETREAT,
  TAKE OUT, EVACUATE
withdrawn .... SHY, RESERVED,
     ISOLATED, RETIRING
withe .... OSIER, WICKER
wither .... BURN, FADE, SEAR,
  WILT, BLAST, DECAY, DROOP,
  DRY UP, WASTE, WIZEN,
  SCATHE, SCORCH, SHRIVEL
withered .... SERE
withering .... SARCASTIC
  away .... TABESCENT
  remark .... SARCASM
withershins .... COUNTER-
      CLOCKWISE
withhold .... DENY, CHECK,
  DETAIN, HINDER, REFUSE,
  HOLD BACK, KEEP(BACK),
  RESERVE, RESTRAIN
  approval .... DISSENT
  information .... CLAM UP
within .... BEN, INNER, INSIDE,
      INTERNAL
  audible frequencies ..... SONIC
  comb. form .... ESO, ENDO
  easy reach .... HANDY
without .... EX, SANS, SINE,
  MINUS, BEREFT, LACKING,
  OUTSIDE, DEVOID OF, NOT
  HAVING, EXTERNALLY

  a bit of light .... PITCH-DARK
  a mixer .... NEAT
  adequate help .... SHORT-
       HANDED
  charge .... FREE, GRATIS
  combining form .... ECTO
  delay ..... AT ONCE, PROMPTLY,
  FORTHWITH, IMMEDIATELY
  doubt .... POSITIVE(LY)
  embellishment .... PLAIN
  exception .... EXPRESS,
      UNQUALIFIED
  fail .... RELIGIOUSLY
  feet .... APOD
  fluid .... DRY, ANEROID,
      DEHYDRATED
  foundation .... FLIMSY
  gender .... NEUTER
  guile .... OPENLY
  legal force .... NULL
  life .... AZOIC
  modulation .... TONELESS
  ornamentation .... STARK
  passengers: colloq.
      .... DEADHEAD
  preparation .... EXTEMPORE,
      IMPROMPTU
  rhyme or reason
     .... SENSELESS, IRRATIONAL
  saddles, in geological
     parlance .... ASELLATE
  skill .... INEPT(LY)
  sound .... MUTE, SILENT
  teeth .... EDENTATE,
      EDENTULOUS
  warning .... ABRUPTLY,
  SUDDENLY, ALL OF A SUDDEN
  written records
     .... PRELITERATE
without a paddle, _____ ...... UP
      THE CREEK
withstand ...... BEAR, DEFY, FACE,
  ENDURE, OPPOSE, RESIST,
      CONFRONT
witless .... DULL, DUMB, SILLY,
  STUPID, FOOLISH, IDIOTIC
witness .... SEE, SIGN, PROOF,
  TASTE, ATTEST, TESTIFY,
  BEHOLD(ER), OBSERVE(R),
  ONLOOKER, TESTIFIER
  bear .... ATTEST, TESTIFY
  kind of .... EYE, HOSTILE
  perjured .... STRAWMAN
  place in court .... STAND
witticism .... GAG, PUN, JEST,
  JOKE, QUIP, SALLY,
  (BON)MOT, WISECRACK
Witt's planetoid .... EROS
witty .... DROLL, PITHY, SALTY,
  CLEVER, JOCOSE, AMUSING,
  JOCULAR, HUMOROUS,

      FACETIOUS
  exchange .... REPARTEE
  poem .... EPIGRAM
  remarks .... MOTS
  reply .... SALLY, RETORT,
      RIPOSTE
  sayings .... BONS MOTS
wive .... MARRY
wivern .... DRAGON
wizard ...... MAGE, SAGE, MAGIAN,
  PELLAR, SHAMAN, CONJURER,
  MAGICIAN, SORCERER,
      ARCHIMAGE
  Arthurian .... MERLIN
  colloquial .... EXPERT, MASTER
Wizard of Menlo Park
     .... EDISON
wizardry .... MAGIC, SORCERY
wizen .... BURN, SEAR, DRY UP,
      WITHER, SHRIVEL
wizened .... SERE
woad ...... DYE, PASTEL, MUSTARD
woald .... WELD
wobble .... REEL, ROCK, ROLL,
  SWAY, SHAKE, WAVER,
  SHIMMY, TEETER, TOTTER,
  WADDLE, STAGGER, TREMBLE,
      VACILLATE
"Wobblies" of 1905 .... IWW
wobbly .... ROCKY, SHAKY,
      GROGGY
Woden .... ODIN, OTHIN
woe .... BANE, BLUES, DOLOR,
  DUMPS, GRIEF, MISERY,
  SORROW, CHAGRIN, DESPAIR,
  TROUBLE, AFFLICTION
  is me! .... ALAS
  tale of .... JEREMIAD,
      LAMENTATION
woebegone .... SAD, DOLEFUL,
  PENSIVE, PITIFUL, TEARFUL,
  DESOLATE, LACHRYMOSE
woeful .... SAD, BLUE, GRAY,
     TRISTE, MELANCHOLY
wolaba .... KANGAROO
wold .... PLAIN, FLOWER,
      MIGNONETTE
wolf .... CANID, LARVA, LUPUS
  bound with magic rope
     .... FENRIR
  cry of .... HOWL
  female .... BITCH
  foot(print) .... PAD
  hunter .... WOLFER, WOLVER
  in sheep's clothing
     .... HYPOCRITE
  large .... LOBO, GRAYWOLF
  male .... DOG
  of a .... LUPINE
  pack leader .... AKELA

person changed into a .... WER(E)WOLF, LYCANTHROPE
prairie .... COYOTE
slang .... RAKE, ROUE, PHILANDERER
timber .... LOBO
up .... GULP, RAVEN, GOBBLE
young .... CUB, WHELP, WOLFKIN
Wolfe, fiction detective ...... NERO
victim of .... MONTCALM
Wolfert, writer .... IRA
wolfish .... GREEDY, RAVENOUS, RAPACIOUS
wolframite .... CAL TUNGSTEN
wolfhound .... ALAN, BORZOI
wolflike .... FIERCE, LUPINE, SAVAGE, RAVENOUS
animal .... HYENA
wolfsbane .... ACONITE, MONKSHOOD
Wollaston, physicist .... WILLIAM
mineral named after .... WOLLASTONITE
wolverine .... GLUTTON, CARCAJOU
relative .... BADGER, WEASEL
Wolverine State .... MICHIGAN
woman ...... MS, EVE, SHE, DAME, FRAU, GIRL, JILL, LADY, WIFE, MUJER, SQUAW, FEMALE, MULIER, DISTAFF
adviser .... EGERIA
annoyer .... OGLER, MASHER
attendant .... MATRON
bad-tempered .... SHREW, VIXEN, VIRAGO, HELLCAT, SPITFIRE, TERMAGANT
bearing second child .... MULTIPARA
beautiful .... BELLE, FREYA, HELEN, HOURI, SIREN, VENUS, VISION, STUNNER
birth control advocate .... SANGER
bold, brazen .... HUSSY, QUEAN
British: sl. .... BIRD
chaser ..... RAKE, ROUE, WOLF, CASANOVA, LOTHARIO, LADY-KILLER
chaste .... VESTAL, VIRGIN
colloquial .... HEN, BROAD, FILLY, FRAIL, PETTICOAT
combining form .... GYN(O)
companion .... CUMMER
conductor .... QUACH
country ...... GAFFER, GAMMER
deadly, alluring .... FEMME FATALE

dirty ..... DRAB, SLOB, MALKIN, SLOVEN, SLATTERN
domineering .... BATTLE-AX
dowdy .... FRUMP
elderly ...... GRANNY, MATRON, DOWAGER
escort of .... CHAPERON, (E)SQUIRE
evil .... HAG, HELLCAT, JEZEBEL
fairest .... HELEN
fascinating .... WITCH
flyer .... AVIATRIX
frenzied .... M(A)ENAD
graceful .... SYLPH
guard .... MATRON
half fish .... MERMAID
hater .... MISOGYNIST, MISANTHROPE
hideous .... WITCH, GORGON, MEDUSA, STHENO, BELDAME
homosexual .... LESBIAN
houseworker .... MARTHA
in the doll house .... NORA
in 30's song ..... LADY IN RED
in uniform .... WAC, WAF, SPAR, WAVE, WREN, NURSE
jungle .... SHEENA
kept .... DOXY, MISTRESS, PARAMOUR, CONCUBINE
killing .... FEMICIDE
little ...... JO, AMY, MEG, BETH, WIFE, SPOUSE
loose ..... BAWD, TART, HUSSY, QUEAN, TRULL, WENCH, WHORE, TROLLOP, STRUMPET
married .... MS, MRS., MADAM(E), MATRON, MISSUS
meek .... GRISELDA
member of U.S. Coast Guard .... SPAR
model .... MANNIKIN, MANNEQUIN
nagging .... SHREW
noble .... DUCHESS, BARONESS, COUNTESS, MARQUISE, PRINCESS
of Athens, influential .... ASPASIA
of poor repute .... DEMIREP, COURTESAN
of song .... AMY, MAMA, IRENE, LOUISE, ADELINE
old .... HAG, CRONE, WITCH, GAMMER, CARLINE, GRANDAM(E)
old, unmarried ..... OLD MAID, SPINSTER
opera comic .... BUFFA
patient .... GRISELDA
performer .... ACTRESS,

ARTISTE, DISEUSE, FARCEUSE, COMEDIENNE
pert .... MINX
pioneer aviatrix .... (AMELIA)EARHART
popular .... BELLE
pretty .... MODEL, PEACH, LOOKER, DAZZLER, STUNNER, KNOCKOUT
quarrelsome .... BITCH, SHREW, VIRAGO, HARRIDAN, TERMAGANT, XANTHIPPE
religious .... NUN, SISTER
repulsive .... GORGON
ruler .... QUEEN, REINE, EMPRESS, MATRIARCH
scolding .... NAG, SHREW, VIRAGO, FISHWIFE, HARRIDAN, TERMAGANT, XANTHIPPE
seducer .... SIREN, VAMPIRE, TEMPTRESS
sexually abnormal .... NYMPHO(MANIAC)
shameless .... JEZEBEL
shrewish .... HARRIDAN
singer .... SOPRANO, CHANTEUSE, CHANTRESS, CANTATRICE
slang .... HEN, BABE, DAME, BROAD, FRAIL, SKIRT, SQUAW, FLOSSY, HEIFER, TOOTS(Y), FLOSSIE, TOOTSIE
slave in a harem ..... ODALISK, ODALISQUE
soothsayer .... SEERESS, PYTHONESS
spiteful .... CAT
spy .... MATA HARI
stately .... JUNO
street .... WHORE, HOOKER, PROSTITUTE
suckling another's baby .... WET NURSE
treacherous .... DELILAH, SEDUCER, VAMPIRE, TEMPTRESS
ugly .... HAG, CRONE, WITCH, GORGON, BELDAM(E)
unattractive .... BAG, FRUMP
unfruitful, descriptively .... BARREN, JEJUNE, STERILE, CHILDLESS
untidy .... DRAB, SLOB, MALKIN, SLOVEN, SLATTERN
vagrant, homeless .... BAG LADY
violent .... FURY
warrior ..... AMAZON, CAMILLA
warrior of Israel: biblical .... DEBORAH

who advocates voting rights
.... SUFFRAGETTE
who rode horse naked
.... GODIVA
who rules a family
.... MATRIARCH
wicked .... JEZEBEL
yellow-haired .... BLONDE
young .... BABE, GIRL, LASS,
    MISS, NYMPH, DAMSEL,
    MAIDEN, DEMOISELLE
zodiac .... VIRGO
womanhood .... FEMININITY,
    MULIEBRITY
womanish .... WEAK, FEMININE,
    EFFEMINATE
womanizer .... RAKE, ROUE,
    LOTHARIO, LIBERTINE
woman's baggy trousers
.... BLOOMERS
blouse .... BASQUE
bonnet .... CAPOTE
cape .... MANTLE, MANTEAU,
    PELERINE
cloak ...... MANTUA, MANTEAU,
    PALETOT, CAPUCHIN,
    CARDINAL
coat .... MINK, MANDARIN,
    REDINGOTE, CHESTERFIELD
collar .... BERTHA
coronet .... TIARA
dowry .... DOT
drawers .... PANTALET(TES)
dressing gown .... FROCK,
    CAMISE, KIMONO
evening dress .... GOWN,
    FORMAL
hairstyle .... BOB, BANGS,
    CHIGNON, PAGEBOY, SHINGLE,
    UPSWEEP, POMPADOUR
hat .... TOQUE, BRETON,
    CLOCHE, TURBAN, PILLBOX
head and shoulder covering
.... NUBIA
headdress .... FRET, POUF,
    PINNER
jacket .... SACK, SIMAR,
    BLAZER, BOLERO, SACQUE,
    PALETOT, CAMISOLE
light housecoat .... DUSTER
mantle .... MANTEAU
masculine traits .... VIRILISM
neckwear .... STOLE, CHOKER
one-piece undergarment
.... TEDDY
origin .... RIB
pants .... CULOTTES, PEDAL-
    PUSHERS
riding costume .... HABIT,
    JOSEPH
robe .... SIMAR

scarf/veil .... MANTILLA
shoe .... PUMP, CHOPINE
shoe style ..... WEDGIE, CUBAN
    HEEL, SLING-BACK
short negligee .... CAMISOLE
short overskirt .... PEPLUM
skirt .... KIRTLE
skirt stretcher .... PANNIER
title ...... DONA, LADY, DONNA,
    MADAM, MADONNA
tongue, iron curb for
.... BRANKS
unacquainted annoyer
.... MASHER
undergarment .... BRA, SLIP,
    PANTY, TEDDY, CORSET,
    GIRDLE, UNDIES, STEP-IN,
    CHEMISE, BLOOMERS,
    KNICKERS, LINGERIE
vest .... JERKIN
weapon of yore .... HATPIN
work/concerns .... DISTAFF
wrap .... MANTA, NUBIA,
    DOLMAN
womb .... WAME, BELLY, MATRIX,
    UTERUS, VENTER
wombat ...... BADGER, MARSUPIAL
feature .... POUCH
like animal .... BEAR
women, club of .... SOROSIS,
    SORORITY
fondness for women
.... PHILOGYNY
government by
.... MATRIARCHY
in U.S. Army .... WACS
in U.S. Air Force .... WAFS
in U.S. Navy .... WAVES
lover of .... PHILOGYNIST
organization of .... NOW,
    NAFE, WCTU
preoccupation of .... DIET,
    STYLE, FIGURE, MAKE-UP,
    WEIGHT, FASHION
reformatory .... MAGDALENE
rights movement
.... FEMINISM, LIB(ERATION)
seclusion of .... PURDAH
with questionable ethics
.... DEMIMONDE
wonder .... AWE, MUSE, STUN,
    MARVEL, MIRACLE, SURPRISE,
    AMAZEMENT, ELECTRIFY
boy .... PRODIGY
world's .... PHAROS,
    PYRAMIDS, COLOSSUS, GRAND
    CANYON, CATACOMBS,
    STONEHENGE, HANGING
    GARDENS, GREAT WALL OF
    CHINA, LEANING TOWER OF
    PISA

wonderful .... COLOSSAL,
    TERRIFIC, OUT-OF-SIGHT
wonderwork .... MIRACLE
won't .... SHANT
wont .... USE, HABIT, CUSTOM,
    ROUTINE, ACCUSTOMED
wonted .... USUAL
woo .... COAX, LURE, SEEK, URGE,
    COURT, SPARK, PURSUE,
    ENTREAT, ROMANCE
musically .... SERENADE
wood .... LOG, BOARD, COPSE,
    GROVE, XYLEM, BOSQUE,
    FOREST, LUMBER, TIMBER
alcohol .... METHANOL
anemone .... THIMBLEWEED
aromatic .... LINALOA
ash oxide .... POTASH
ashes extract .... LYE
axe breaker .... QUEBRACHO
bar .... FID
batted for distance ..... TIPCAT
bend in .... SNY, WARP
betony .... LOUSEWORT
hits .... KINDLING
black .... TEAK, EBONY
block .... NOG, DOOR, TRIG,
    SPRAG, WEDGE
borer .... TEREDO
building .... TIMBER
burning piece .... FIREBRAND
charred .... BRAY
coal .... LIGNITE, CHARCOAL
combining form .... HYL(O),
    XYL(O), LIGNI, LIGN(O)
cutter .... RIPSAW
cutting .... HAG
destroying insect .... ANAY,
    TERMITE
destroying mollusk
.... TEREDO
dressed .... TIMBER
dresser/trimmer .... ADZ(E)
drug .... QUASSIA
dust .... COOM(B)
easily burned .... SPUNK
eater/wrecker .... ANAY,
    TERMITE
elastic .... YEW
engraving .... XYLOGRAPH
flat piece .... SPLAT
fluting .... CHAMFER
for bows .... YEW
for bridges/piles .... ALDER
for dagger hilt .... DUDGEON
for flooring .... MAPLE
for furniture .... OAK, TEAK,
    EBONY, NARRA, WALNUT,
    MAHOGANY, CALAMANDER
fragrant .... ALOES, CEDAR
groove .... CHAMFER

gum .... XYLAN
hard .... ASH, ELM, OAK,
ASPEN, BIRCH, EBONY, MAPLE,
NARRA, LOCUST, MOLAVE,
WALNUT, WILLOW, HICKORY,
MAHOGANY
hyacinth .... BLUEBELL,
HAREBELL
ibis .... STORK, JABIRU
inlaid .... BUHL
kind of .... DEAL
knot .... KNAR
layer .... VENEER
light .... BALSA
louse .... SLATER, SOW BUG
made of .... OAKEN, XYLOID
make into .... LIGNIFY
mark .... ROE
measure .... CORD, FOOT
nymph ..... MOTH, BUTTERFLY,
(HAMA)DRYAD, HUMMINGBIRD
of .... XYLOID, LIGNEOUS
oil .... TUNG
partially burned .... CINDER
piece of .... SLAT, BOARD,
PLANK, STAVE, BILLET
pigeon .... CULVER, CUSHAT,
RINGDOVE
pin .... FID, NOG, PEG
pin in boat .... THOLE
plug .... SPILE
preservative .... CREOSOTE
quantity .... CORDAGE
reddish .... CHERRY
reddish-brown ..... MAHOGANY
resinous .... SANDARAC,
LIGNALOES
small .... GROVE
soft .... FIR, PINE, CEDAR,
SPRUCE, HEMLOCK, REDWOOD
sorrel .... OCA, OXALIS
stand, top of .... CRISS
strip .... LATH, LIST, SLAT,
SLIP, SPLIT, STAVE, BATTEN,
SPLINT
striped .... TULIP, ARAROBA
tar distillate .... PITCH,
CREOSOTE
twist in .... WARP
type of .... HARD, SOFT
veneer .... BURL
warbler .... WAGTAIL
wheel brake .... NOG, TRIG,
SPRAG, WEDGE
worker .... SAWYER,
CARPENTER
worm .... THRIPS
wood, _____ (superstitious
statement) .... KNOCK ON
Wood, actress .... NATALIE
woodbine .... IVY, CREEPER,

PERIDOT, HONEYSUCKLE
woodchat .... SHRIKE
woodchuck .... MARMOT, WEJACK,
GROUNDHOG
woodcock relative .... PEWEE,
SNIPE, SANDPIPER
woodcraft .... HUNTING, TRAPPING
woodcutter .... LOGGER, SAWYER,
LUMBERJACK
wooded .... SYLVAN
area .... WEALD, BOONDOCKS
hill .... HOLT
wooden .... DULL, RIGID, STIFF,
TREEN, STOLID, XYLOID,
DEADPAN, LIFELESS,
LIGNEOUS, INFLEXIBLE,
INSENSITIVE
bar .... TREE
bench .... SETTEE
board for meat-carving
.... TRENCHER
bowl .... KITTY, MAZER,
MAZARD
brick .... DOOK
bucket .... CANNIKIN
club .... BILLET
collar .... CANGUE
hammer .... MALLET
horse giver .... TROJAN
Indian's place .... CIGAR
STORE
limb .... PEG LEG
nutmeg trick .... FRAUD
pail .... PIGGIN
peg/pin ...... FID, NOG, DOWEL,
SPILE, THOLE, TRE(E)NAIL
pole/post .... TREE
seat .... BENCH
shoe .... CLOG, SABOT, PATTEN
spool toy .... DIABOLO
stake .... TREE
strip .... LATH
time-beater .... CASTANETS
woodenware .... BOWLS, ROLLING
PIN
woodland .... GROVE, WOODS,
FOREST, SYLVAN
clearing .... GLADE
deity .... PAN, FAUN, SATYR,
SILENUS, SILVANUS
woodlark genus .... LULLULA
woodpecker .... CHAB, COLY,
FLICKER, REDHEAD, HIGH-
HOLE, POPINJAY, SAPSUCKER,
YELLOWHAMMER
cartoon creator
.... (WALTER)LANTZ
family .... PICIDAE
feature
.... (PROTRUSILE)TONGUE
genus .... SASIA, DINOPIUM,

PICOIDES, DENDROCOPOS
green .... COLY, ECCLE
green: genus ... PICUS VIRIDIS
lifestyle .... WOOD-BORING,
TREE-CLIMBING
specie .... ACORN, BLACK,
GREEN, WHITE, WRYNECK,
ARROWHEAD, RED-HEADED,
THREE-TOED, GOLDEN-NAPED,
IVORY-BILLED, RED-
COCKADED, GREAT SPOTTED
true .... PICINAE
wryneck .... JUNGINAE
woods ...... GROVE, SILVA, FOREST
attraction toward the
.... NEMOPHILA
out of the .... SAFE, CLEAR
woodsia .... FERN
wood(s)man .... HUNTER, LOGGER,
RANGER, TRAPPER, FORESTER,
VOYAGEUR, LUMBERJACK
woodsy .... SYLVAN
woodwaxen .... DYEWEED
woodwind .... OBOE, SAXE, FLUTE,
BASSOON, SAXHORN,
CLARINET, SAXOPHONE
woodwork .... DOORS, DIDOES,
FRAMES, MOLDING, PANELING
woody .... XYLOID, LIGNEOUS
fiber .... BAST
fiber substance .... LIGNIN
plant .... TREE, SHRUB
tissue .... XYLEM
vine .... LIANA, CLEMATIS,
WISTERIA, HONEYSUCKLE
vine bearing fruit .... GRAPE
Woody of the movies ...... ALLEN
Woody's boy .... ARLO
wooer .... SUITOR, PURSUER
woof .... ABB, BARK, WEFT,
CLOTH, FABRIC, FILLING,
TEXTURE
companion of .... WARP
woofer .... DOG, LOUDSPEAKER
wooing .... SUIT, COURTSHIP
wool .... HAIR, LANA, PILE,
ALPACA, ANGORA, FLEECE,
MERINO
and cashmere .... CASHA
and silk cloth .... CAMLET,
EOLIENNE
animal with .... RAM, GOAT,
LLAMA, SHEEP, ALPACA,
MERINO, VICUNA, GUANACO
bearing .... LANIFEROUS
blemish .... MOTE
cleaning machine
.... WILLOW(ER)
cluster .... NEP
coarse/matted .... SHAG
comb .... CARD

combed knot of .... NOIL
combining form .... LANI
covered with .... LANATE,
    FLOCCOSE
cuttings .... KERFS
fabric ..... REPP, REP(S), BEIGE,
    CASHA, BEAVER, TWEED,
    FRIEZE, HODDEN, TARTAN,
    CHALLIE, CHALLIS, DELAINE,
    ETAMINE, STAMMEL,
    VELOUR(S), LANDSDOWNE
fat .... LANOLIN(E)
felted .... CASHA, BEAVER
fiber .... NOIL, PILE, FLOCK,
    SLIVER
fiber, batted .... BATTING
gathering .... MOONING,
    STARGAZING, DAYDREAMING
goat's .... CASHMERE
grease .... SUINT
implement .... SHEARS,
    PICKLOCK
knitted .... JERSEY
knot .... BURL, NOIL
like .... DOWNY, HAIRY,
    FLEECY, FLUFFY
like fabric .... LANITAL
lock of .... TAG
matted .... SHAG, DAGLOCK
measure .... HEER
nemesis of .... LINT
oily substance .... GREASE
pack .... BALE
particles .... DOWN
piece of .... NOIL
produced one year .... CLIP
refuse .... COTT
roll of .... SLUB
rug fibers .... NAP, PILE
salvage .... MUNGO
seller .... STAPLER
sheared at one time ...... CLIP,
    FLEECE
sheep/fine .... MERINO
sheer .... VOILE
shreds of .... NOIL
spinning machine
    .... THROSTLE
still on animal ...... WOOLFELL
substitute .... ORLON
synthetic .... LANITAL
thread .... YARN, WORSTED
tuft .... LOCK, FLOCCUS,
    FLOCCULE
twisted .... ROVE
unbleached .... BEIGE
unravel .... CARD, TEASE
waste ..... FUD, FLOCK, MUNGO
watered .... MOREEN
weight .... TOD
yarn .... WORSTED

woolen blanket .... SERAPE,
    MACKINAW
cloth/fabric .... BAIZE, CASHA,
    LODEN, MUNGO, TWEED,
    CAMLET, DUFFEL, DUFFLE,
    FRIEZE, HODDEN, JERSEY,
    KERSEY, MELTON, MERINO,
    MOREEN, RATINE, SHODDY,
    TARTAN, DOESKIN, ETAMINE,
    RATTEEN, WORSTED,
    CAS(S)IMIRE, CALAMANCO,
    PETERSHAM, TRICOT(INE)
cheap .... MUNGO, SHODDY
coarse .... DUFFEL, DUFFLE
glossy .... CALAMANCO
loosely woven ...... FLANNEL
of silk and wool .... CAMLET
resembling gabardine
    .... TRICOTINE
ribbed .... KERSEY
silky .... MERINO
twilled .... SERGE, TWEED,
    RATINE, RATTEEN,
    CASHMERE, SHALLOON,
    CAS(S)IMIRE, TRICOTINE
undyed .... HODDEN
used for billiard tables
    .... BAIZE
jacket .... CARDIGAN
material .... CADDIS,
    CADDICE
shawl .... PAISLEY
sweater .... CARDIGAN,
    CASHMERE
woolly .... DOWNY, HAIRY,
    FLEECY, FLUFFY, LANATE,
    LANOSE, FLOCCULENT
bear .... CATERPILLAR
cud-chewing animal
    .... VICUNA
haired .... ULOTRICHOUS
haired people .... ULOTRICHI
Peruvian animal .... ALPACA
tuft .... FLOCCULUS
wild, reddish-brown animal
    .... GUANACO
woorali .... URARI, CURARE
woozy .... DOPEY, TIPSY, GROGGY,
    MUDDLED, CONFUSED,
    BEFUDDLED
word .... NEWS, TALK, TERM,
    ORDER, PAROL(E), PLEDGE,
    REMARK, SIGNAL, PROMISE,
    TIDINGS, LOCUTION,
    UTTERANCE, INFORMATION
action .... VERB
addition to beginning of
    .... PREFIX
addition to end of ..... SUFFIX,
    PARAGOGE
appropriate .... MOT JUSTE

auctioneer's .... GONE, SOLD,
    GOING
blindness .... ALEXIA
book .... LEXICON, LIBRETTO,
    THESAURUS, DICTIONARY
Captain Marvel's magic
    .... SHAZAM
change in a .... METAPLASM
coined and used for a single
    occasion .... NONCE
    WORD
derivation .... PARONYM
disapproving .... TUT
division .... INTO
dropping of middle sound of
    .... SYNCOPE
dropping of last sound/letter
    of .... APOCOPE
figurative .... TROPE, SIMILE,
    METAPHOR
final .... AMEN, ULTIMATUM
first of doxology .... GLORIA
for second base .... KEYSTONE
for word .... VERBAL, LITERAL,
    TEXTUAL, VERBATIM,
    METAPHRASE
formative ending
    .... DESINENCE
formed from another
    .... DERIVATIVE
four-letter .... TETRAGRAM
game .... RIDDLE, ANAGRAM,
    CHARADE, ACROSTIC,
    SCRABBLE, CONUNDRUM
hard to pronounce
    .... JAWBREAKER
in a .... BRIEFLY, IN SHORT
in an ultimatum .... ELSE
invented .... COINAGE
inventor .... NEOLOGIST
inversion .... ANASTROPHE
last .... AMEN
last syllable of .... ULTIMA
long: colloq. .... MOUTHFUL
Major Hoople's .... EGAD
meaning, study of
    ...... SEMANTICS, SEMASIOLOGY
misused .... BARBARITY
mystical, biblical .... SELAH
new or new meaning of
    .... NEOLOGY, NEOLOGISM
of admonition .... DON'T
agreement .... SURE
assent .... YEA, YES, AMEN
excitement .... WOW
honor .... PAROLE, PLEDGE,
    PROMISE
impatience .... PISH
inquiry .... HOW, WHO, WHY,
    WHAT, WHEN, WHICH,
    WHERE

lament .... ALAS
mouth .... ORAL, PAROL
only one .... MONOMIAL
opposite meaning
.... ANTONYM
rebuke .... TUT
similar meaning
.... SYNONYM
two or more base
   morphemes
.... COMPOUND
warning .... BEWARE,
   CAUTION
on the wall .... MENE
ordinary meaning ..... LITERAL
origin of a .... ETYMOLOGY
original form .... ETYMON
prisoner's .... PAROLE
puzzle .... REBUS, CHARADE,
   ACROSTIC, CROSSWORD,
   LOGOGRAPH
reading same backward
.... PALINDROME
roll-call .... HERE, PRESENT
ruer's .... ALAS
same pronunciation, different
   meaning .... HOMONYM,
   HOMOPHONE
same spelling, different
   meaning .... HETERONYM,
   HOMOGRAPH
shorten a .... SYNCOPE
sorority .... TAU
square .... PALINDROME
substitute .... METONYM
symbol .... LOGOGRAM
the .... BIBLE, LOGOS
ultimatum .... ELSE
unprintable, usually ..... FOUR-
   LETTER
vowel omission .... APHESIS
wedding announcement
.... NEE
with back or hands ...... BARE
   beat or stick .... DRUM
   Big or Gentle .... BEN
   bird or print .... BLUE
   Black or White .... SEA
   cake or change ...... SHORT
   car or maid .... PARLOR
   common or horse ..... SENSE
   cross .... ROADS
   deep or bitter .... END
   egg or pie .... PLANT
   fire or transit .... RAPID
   flower or fish .... STAR
   friend or fellow .... SHIP
   gas or ivy .... POISON
   golf or cuff .... LINK
   high or hole .... KNEE
   in or out .... TURN

Inchcape or Plymouth
.... ROCK
   jacket or lace .... STRAIT
   Lear or Kong .... KING
   lord or lady .... LAND
   maker or breaker .... LAW
   on or out .... TRY
   out or off .... RIP
   over or upon .... ONCE
   side or edge .... WISE
   sun or moon .... LIT
   tail .... BOB, CAT, HIGH
   term or time .... LONG
   to or through .... SEE
   up or down .... SHUT
   vegetable or victory
.... GARDEN
   view or fix .... PRE
   water or tea .... WAGON
   well or ill .... BRED
wordiest language .... ENGLISH
wordiness .... PLEONISM,
   VERBIAGE, PROLIXITY,
   VERBOSITY
wording .... TEXT, DICTION,
   PHRASING, PHRASEOLOGY
wordless .... MUM, MUTE, TACIT
comment .... SIGH
words .... TALK, TEXT, LYRICS,
   DISPUTE, ARGUMENT
argument about
.... LOGOMACHY
Almanac author .... ESPY
attack with ..... ABUSE, BASTE,
   SCOLD, CRITICIZE
author's .... TEXT
battle of .... DEBATE,
   LOGOMACHY
brush-off .... SOME OTHER
   TIME
choice of .... DICTION
clever exchange of
.... REPARTEE
doctrine of .... NEOLOGY
eat one's .... EAT CROW,
   RETRACT, SWALLOW, EAT
   HUMBLE PIE
for indefinite adjournment
.... SINE DIE
incorrect use of
.... CATACHRESIS
manner of expression
.... DICTION, ENUNCIATION
misuse of .... MALAPROPISM
of .... VERBAL
   approximation .... OR SO,
   MORE OR LESS
   determination .... I CAN
   few .... CURT, TERSE,
   LACONIC
   flattery .... PALAVER

understanding .... I SEE
   wisdom .... SAW, GNOME,
   MAXIM, SAYING
on airmail envelope .... PAR
   AVION
on the Tomb of the
   Unknown Soldier
.... KNOWN BUT TO GOD
play on .... PUN
prefix .... LOGO
preprandial .... GRACE
put into .... EXPRESS
ridiculous user of
.... (MRS.)MALAPROP
slang .... BULL SESSION
to a convalescent .... GET
   WELL
vengeful .... TIT FOR TAT
wordy .... WINDY, PROLIX,
   VERBOSE, REDUNDANT,
   TALKATIVE, LONG-WINDED
work .... DO, JOB, MOIL, OPUS,
   TASK, TOIL, CRAFT, ERGON,
   GRIND, LABOR, EFFORT,
   BUSINESS, EMPLOYMENT,
   OCCUPATION
against .... MILITATE
aimlessly ...... POTTER, PUTTER
amount of .... LOAD
arduously .... TOIL
artist's .... MASTER
assignment .... JOB, BEAT,
   TASK, SHIFT, STINT, TRICK
at .... PLY, PURSUE
avoid .... SHIRK, SKULK,
   MALINGER
clothes .... UNIFORM,
   COVERALL, OVERALLS
clothes cloth .... DENIM,
   DRILL, OSNABURG
crew .... GANG
delicate interlacing
.... TRACERY
energetically .... HUSTLE
evade .... MALINGER
for .... EARN
fussily .... NIGGLE
great .... MASTER(PIECE)
group .... BEE, CREW, GANG,
   TEAM, DETAIL
hard .... GRUB, PLUG, TOIL,
   LABOR, SWEAT, HUSTLE
house/farm .... CHORE
in .... INSERT
in a smokehouse .... CURE
incentive .... TIP, PERK,
   BONUS, RAISE, GRATUITY,
   PERQUISITE
life .... CAREER
measures .... MAN-HOURS,
   MAN-YEARS

of art .... OIL, OPUS, MUSIC, CARVING, ETCHING, PAINTING, SCULPTURE, COMPOSITION

of wonder .... MIRACLE

on antiques .... RESTORE

out .... SOLVE, TRAIN, EVOLVE, DEVELOP, EXERCISE, PRACTICE

pants .... LEVIS

parties .... BEES

patiently ..... PLY, PLOD, PLUG, TOIL

schedule .... STINT

second job .... MOONLIGHT

shift .... TRICK

shirker .... BUCK PASSER

shoes .... BROGAN

suitable .... METIER

tedious .... CHORE, GRIND, TRAVAIL, DRUDGERY

time-out from .... BREAK, RECESS, VACATION

trainee .... APPRENTICE

trousers .... DUNGAREES

together: slogan ...... GUNG HO

under compulsion .... SLAVE

unit of .... ERG(ON)

unskillfully .... DABBLE

with lead .... PLUMB

your fingers to the _____ (to the point of exhaustion) .... BONE

workable .... FEASIBLE, OPERABLE, PRACTICAL

workaday .... DRAB, USUAL, HUMDRUM, PROSAIC, ROUTINE, ORDINARY, QUOTIDIAN, COMMONPLACE

workaholic .... ERGOPHILE

workbag .... KIT

workbench adjunct .... VISE

workbook .... MANUAL

workbox .... ETUI, (TOOL)KIT

worked up .... AGOG, FIRED, RILED, EXCITED, INFLAMED

worker ...... DOER, HAND, MOILER, TOILER, ARTISAN, LABORER, EMPLOYE(E), WAGE-EARNER

agricultural ...... OKIE, FARMER

agricultural, illegal .... WETBACK

Atlantic City .... DEALER, CROUPIER

beginner .... NOVICE, APPRENTICE

coal mine .... COLLIER

dell ..... FARMER, AGRONOMIST

farm .... HIND, PEON

garage .... MECHANIC

gem .... JEWELER

hard .... SCRUB

hotel .... VALET, PORTER,

BELLBOY

in a caisson .... SANDHOG

in a royal household .... GROOM, YEOMAN, FOOTMAN

in a skilled trade .... ARTIST, WRITER, ARTISAN, MUSICIAN, ARTIFICER, CRAFTSMAN, MACHINIST, PROGRAMMER, TECHNICIAN

in accounting office .... ADDER, BOOKKEEPER

in oil fields .... RIGGER

iron .... SMELTER

itinerant .... BOOMER

kind of .... BREADWINNER

maintenance .... JANITOR

menial ..... DRUDGE, SERVANT, DOMESTIC

migratory .... HOBO, OKIE, PEON, BRACERO

non-union .... SCAB

of the working class .... PROLETARIAN

odd job ...... JACK, HANDYMAN

on strike, union .... PICKET

pavement .... BRICKLAYER

respite of .... VACATION

restless .... FLOATER

stone .... MASON, JEWELER

telephone .... OPERATOR

transient .... HOBO, OKIE, FLOATER, WETBACK

unskilled .... PEON, COOLIE, TINKER, COBBLER, LABORER

water system .... PLUMBER

waterfront .... STEVEDORE, LONGSHOREMAN

white collar .... CLERK

who had served apprenticeship .... JOURNEYMAN

who replaces striker ...... RAT, SCAB

workers .... STAFF, PERSONNEL, WORK FORCE

certain illicit .... MOONSHINERS

collectively .... LABOR

group: abbr. .... ILO

group, retired .... AARP

railroad track .... SPIKERS

working .... ACTIVE, RUNNING, OPERATING, FUNCTIONAL, FUNCTIONING

class .... PROLETARIAT

no longer .... RETIRED

not .... IDLE, UNEMPLOYED

workhorse .... HACK, SLAVE, DRUDGE, TOILER, PLODDER

workhouse .... ASYLUM, ALMSHOUSE

Workman, explorer .... FANNY

workmanlike .... EXPERT, SKILLED, SKILLFUL, PROFESSIONAL

workmanship .... FINISH, ARTIFICE, ARTISTRY, TECHNIQUE

workout ...... TEST, ESSAY, TRIAL, EXERCISE, PRACTICE, REHEARSAL

workroom .... DEN, STUDY

works, the .... OEUVRES, EVERYTHING

slang .... WHOLE SHEBANG

workshop ...... LAB, MILL, STORE, OFFICE, STUDIO, ATELIER

government department .... BUREAU

lumber .... SAWMILL

manufacturing .... PLANT, FACTORY

metal .... FOUNDRY

money .... MINT

remedial .... CLINIC

smelting .... IRONWORKS

with poor working conditions .... SWEATSHOP

world ...... EARTH, GLOBE, REALM, COSMOS, DOMAIN, NATURE, MANKIND, CREATION, UNIVERSE

bearer of the .... ATLAS

beater .... ONER

domain ..... ANIMAL, MINERAL, VEGETABLE

first national park in the .... YELLOWSTONE

largest clothing manufacturer of the .... LEVI STRAUSS

most populous nation of the .... CHINA

most populous democracy of the .... INDIA

nicknamed "oldest teenager" of the .... DICK CLARK

of the .... MUNDANE, SECULAR, TEMPORAL, TERRESTRIAL

out of this .... OUTRE

power .... RUSSIA, ENGLAND, UNITED STATES

-shaking .... GREAT, SIGNAL, BIG-TIME, MOMENTOUS

spinner .... LOVE

supporter .... ATLAS

trade agreement: abbr. .... RTA

workers group: abbr. .... ILO

World War I machine gun .... POMPOM

plane .... SPAD, TAUBE,

NIEUPORT
U.S. president .... WILSON
World War II. See **WW II**
worldly .... PROUD, CARNAL,
SORDID, EARTHLY, MUNDANE,
SECULAR, SELFISH, TERRENE,
TEMPORAL, MERCENARY,
TERRESTRIAL,
MATERIAL(ISTIC)
wise .... KNOWING,
EXPERIENCED, SOPHISTICATED
worldwide .... COMMON, GLOBAL,
GENERAL, CATHOLIC,
PANDEMIC, SWEEPING,
UNIVERSAL, ECUMENIC(AL),
ALL-EMBRACING
worm ...... ESS, LOA, NAID, TINEA,
INSECT, WRETCH, ANNELID,
ASCARID, CRAWLER,
HELMINTH, NEMATODE
bait .... LURG
bloodsucking .... LEECH
combining form .... VERMI
drug .... VERMICIDE
eaten ...... RAGGED, WORN-OUT
feeler of a .... PALP(US)
flat .... FLUKE, PLANARIAN,
TREMATODE
freshwater .... TUBIFEX
genus .... NEREIS, ASCARIS,
PLANARIA, LUMBRICUS
in .... EDGE IN, INTRUDE
in zoology .... LYTTA
infestation .... ASCARIASIS
larva .... GRUB, MAGGOT,
CERCARIA, CATERPILLAR
marine .... NEREIS, NEMERTEAN
measuring .... LOOPER
move like a .... CRAWL, CREEP
out (of) .... ELICIT, EXTRACT
out of trouble .... WRIGGLE
parasite of plants
.... PINWORM, HOOKWORM,
NEMATODE
parasitic ...... FLUKE, ASCARID,
CESTODE, CESTOID,
TAPEWORM, ROUNDWORM
round .... ASCARID
round, segmented .... LEECH,
ANNELID, EARTHWORM
sea .... ANNELID
segment .... SOMITE,
METAMERE
shaped .... VERMIFORM
ship .... CLAM, BORER,
TEREDO, COPPERWORM
silk .... ERIA, TUSSAH,
CATERPILLAR
slang .... PEST, INSECT
snail resembling .... SLUG
sucker .... LEECH

sucking organ of
.... PROBOSCIS
threadlike .... FILARIA
track .... NEREITE
used as fishing bait
.... ANGLEWORM, EARTHWORM,
HELLGRAMMITE
water .... LEECH, TEREDO,
TUBIFEX
worms, can of .... PROBLEM,
TROUBLE, HEADACHE
disease caused by parasitic
.... HELMINTHIASIS
medicine for intestinal
.... SANTONIN(E)
of the Nile .... ASPS
parasitic .... FILARIA,
HOOKWORM, TAPEWORM,
ROUNDWORM
wormseed .... SANTONICA
wormwood ...... MOXA, CHAGRIN,
ABSINTH(E), TARRAGON,
EMBARRASSMENT,
MORTIFICATION
wormy .... ROTTEN
worn .... OLD, USED, EROSE,
RAGGED, SHABBY, TATTERED
by friction .... ATTRITE
clothes .... RAGS
down .... TRODDEN
end .... FRAZZLE
look .... HAGGARD
out .... BEAT, SHOT, WEAK,
JADED, SEEDY, SPENT, TIRED,
WEARY, BUSHED, EFFETE,
FRAYED, POOPED, DECREPIT,
DOG-TIRED, EXHAUSTED
worried .... BESET, ANXIOUS,
CAREWORN, TROUBLED
worrier's crop .... ULCERS,
WRINKLES
worrisome .... IRKSOME,
ANNOYING
worry .... VEX, CARE, FEAR, FRET,
STEW, ANNOY, TEASE, UPSET,
HARASS, PESTER, ANXIETY,
DISTURB, GRIZZLE, DISTRESS
colloquial .... CONCERN,
LOOKOUT
worship .... PRAY, ADORE, DEIFY,
HOMAGE, REVERE, ADULATE,
IDOLIZE, RESPECT, DEVOTION,
ENSHRINE, VENERATE,
ADORATION
animal .... ZOOLATRY
bend the knee, as in
.... GENUFLECT
combining form .... LATRY
due to God alone ...... LATRIA
object of .... HERO, IDOL,
SWEETHEART

of all gods .... PANTHEISM
of idols .... IDOLISM,
IDOLATRY
of saints .... HAGIOLATRY
place of .... ALTAR, CHAPEL,
CHURCH, PAGODA, SHRINE,
TEMPLE, SYNAGOGUE
ritual .... LITURGY
system .... CULT, FETISH
worshiper .... DEIST, ADORER,
ADMIRER, DEIFIER, DEVOTEE,
VENERATOR
affected .... RELIGIONIST
devout .... VOTARY
exaggeratedly pious
.... PIETIST
of idols .... IDOLIST, IDOLATER
of the sun god .... INCA
of stars .... SABAIST
worshipful .... PIOUS, DEVOUT,
RELIGIOUS, REVERENTIAL
worst .... BEAT, BEST, DEFEAT,
CONQUER, POOREST
Worst Dressed Woman Awards
creator .... BLACKWELL
worsted .... BESTED
cloth .... WOOL, SERGE,
ETAMINE
ribbon/yarn .... CADDIS
wort .... HERB, PLANT
worth .... COST, MERIT, PRICE,
VALUE, ESTIMATION,
IMPORTANCE
having .... ASSET, DESIRABLE
of little .... TRIFLE, TRIFLING
person's character ...... CREDIT
worthless .... RIP, BASE, POOR,
VAIN, LOSEL, USELESS,
NUGATORY, GOOD-FOR-
NOTHING
almost .... PETTY, PALTRY,
PIDDLE
chap/fellow .... BUM, DOG,
IDLER, LOSER
horse .... NAG, RIP, JADE,
PLATER
ideas .... BILGE
remains .... DREGS, SCRAPS,
CARCASE, CARCASS
scrap .... ORT
slang .... LOUSY
thing .... RIP, CHIP, FICO, TRIPE
worthwhile .... GOOD, WORTHY,
GAINFUL, OF VALUE,
LUCRATIVE, BENEFICIAL
worthy .... HONEST, UPRIGHT,
VALUABLE, ADMIRABLE,
DESERVING, MERITORIOUS
Wouk, author .... HERMAN
ship .... CAINE
would be ...... HOPEFUL, ASPIRING

dialectical .... WOD
wound .... CUT, GASH, HURT,
 PAIN, SORE, STAB, INJURY,
 INSULT, LESION, OFFEND,
 PIERCE, TRAUMA, LACERATE
adhesion .... SCAR
blood shed from .... GORE,
 SANIES
discharge from a .... PUS,
 ICHOR, SANIES
dressing .... PATCH
edge of .... LIP
in a way .... SPOOLED
jagged .... LACERATION
mark .... SCAR
on a bobbin .... SPOOLED
plug .... TENT, DOSSIL
woven ...... KNIT, LACED, TWINED,
 WEBBED
double .... TWO-PLY
goods dealer .... HOSIER
material, netlike .... MESH
with raised design .... BROCHE
work made of sticks
 .... WATTLE
wow .... HIT, AMUSE,
 INTERJECTION
wowser .... PRUDE
wrack .... RUIN, CLOUDS,
 SEAWEED, WRECKAGE
wraith .... FETCH, GHOST,
 SPECTER, SPECTRE,
 APPARITION
wrangle .... ROW, SPAR, ARGUE,
 BRAWL, BICKER, DEBATE,
 HIGGLE, DISPUTE, QUARREL,
 SQUABBLE
wrangler ...... ARGUER, COWBOY,
 BRAWLER
wrap .... LAP, FOLD, HIDE, CLOAK,
 COVER, NUBIA, CLOTHE,
 SWATHE, ENCLOSE, CONCEAL,
 ENVELOP, SWADDLE
around .... SARONG,
 LOINCLOTH
in burial cloth .... CERE
shoulder .... CAPE, SHAWL
snugly .... TUCK
tightly: naut. .... FRAP
to deaden sound .... MUFFLE
up .... ENFOLD, FINISH,
 ENVELOP
woman's .... ROBE, SHAWL,
 DOLMAN, PELISSE
wrapped up .... COMPLETED
wrapper .... BINDER, VESTURE
book's .... JACKET
candy's .... TINFOIL
wrapping material .... LEAF,
 PAPER, KRAFT, MATTING,
 CELLOPHANE

wrasse .... CUNNER, FISHES,
 TAUTOG, HOGFISH
wrath .... IRE, FURY, RAGE,
 ANGER, CHOLER, VENGEANCE
wrathy .... ANGRY, INDIGNANT
wreak .... EXACT, PUNISH,
 INFLICT, OPPRESS
wreath .... LEI, ORLE, TORSE,
 ANADEM, CHAPLET, FESTOON,
 FLOWERS, GARLAND
bridal .... SPIREA
for achievement .... CORONA
for head .... ANADEM, LAUREL,
 CHAPLET
hanging .... FESTOON
heraldic .... ORLE
victor's .... CORONA, LAUREL
wreathe .... COIL, TWIST,
 ENTWINE, ENVELOP, ENCIRCLE
wreck .... RAZE, RUIN, CRASH,
 DAMAGE, DESTROY, CRACK-
 UP, SMASH(UP), UNDOING,
 ACCIDENT, DISASTER,
 COLLISION
building .... DEMOLISH, TEAR
 DOWN
wreckage .... (W)RACK, DEBRIS,
 JETSAM, FLOTSAM
wren .... JENNY, TOMTIT,
 SONGBIRD
wrench .... JERK, PULL, YANK,
 TWIST, WREST, WRICK,
 WRING, SPRAIN, SPANNER
kind of .... MONKEY, STILLSON
wrest .... GRAB, TURN, TWIST,
 WRING, EXTORT, SNATCH,
 STRAIN, USURP, WRENCH,
 EXTRACT
wrestle .... STRIVE, TUSSLE,
 CONTEND, GRAPPLE,
 STRUGGLE
wrestler .... MATMAN, MAULER,
 GRAPPLER, SCUFFLER
Hulk .... HOGAN
pad of .... MAT
wrestling champion Rowan
 .... CHAD
champion Rowan's name in
 Japan .... AKEBONO
down for the three-count in
 .... PINNED
highest rank in .... YOKUZUNA
hold .... SCISSORS, WRISTLOCK,
 (HEAD)LOCK, (HALF)NELSON
match division .... FALL
oriental .... SUMO
place/school ...... PAL(A)ESTRA
score .... FALL
sound .... THUD, GROAN,
 GRUNT
trick throw .... CHIP

wretch .... WORM, KNAVE, MISER,
 ROGUE, BEGGAR, PARIAH,
 RASCAL, CAITIFF, HILDING,
 OUTCAST, VILLAIN, SCULLION
wretched .... SAD, MEAN, ABJECT,
 DISMAL, PALTRY, SHABBY,
 WOEFUL, FORLORN, PITIFUL,
 UNHAPPY, MISERABLE
wriggle .... DODGE, SHAKE,
 SHIMMY, SQUIRM, WANGLE,
 WIGGLE
wriggler .... LARVA, TADPOLE,
 HULA DANCER
Wright, airplane inventor
 .... WILBUR, ORVILLE
wring .... PAIN, PRESS, TWIST,
 WREST, EXTORT, WRENCH,
 SQUEEZE, COMPRESS
neck of .... SCRAG
wrinkle .... FOLD, RUCK, RUGA,
 SEAM, ANGLE, CRIMP, RIDGE,
 TWIST, COCKLE, CREASE,
 FURROW, PUCKER, RIMPLE,
 RUMPLE, CRINKLE, CRUMPLE,
 NOVELTY, SHRIVEL
remover .... IRON
wrinkled .... LINED, RUGAL,
 RUGATE, RUGOSE
wrinkles around the eyes
 .... CROW'S FEET
wrist .... JOINT, CARPUS,
 CARPAL(E)
bone .... HAMATE, LUNATE,
 CAPITATE, PISIFORM,
 SCAPHOID, TRAPEZIUM,
 TRAPEZOID, TRIQUETRAL
bones, collectively .... CARPUS
guard .... BRACER
injury ..... SPRAIN, WRISTDROP,
 (COLLES')FRACTURE
number of bones in ..... EIGHT
wristband .... CUFF, BRACER
wristlet .... BRACELET, HANDCUFF
writ .... VENIRE, PRECEPT,
 PROCESS, SUMMONS,
 WARRANT, DOCUMENT,
 ALLOCATUR, OYER BREVE,
 INJUNCTION
Holy .... BIBLE
judicial .... TALES
of _____ .... RIGHT, VENIRE,
 MANDAMUS, EXECUTION,
 CERTIORARI, PROHIBITION
of execution .... ELEGIT
of right's issue .... MISE
order of arrest .... CAPIAS
to call up .... CERTIORARI
to serve in court .... VENIRE,
 SUMMONS, SUBPOENA
write .... PEN, COPY, INDITE,
 SCRAWL, SCRIVE, COMPOSE,

INSCRIBE, SCRIBBLE
a check .... DRAW
at length .... EXPATIATE
compose and .... INDITE
down .... JOT, LIST, RECORD
effusively .... GUSH
hurriedly .... SCRAWL,
DASH(OFF), SCRATCH
illegibly .... SCRIBBLE
in scholarly manner
.... LUCUBRATE
into law .... ENACT
on a surface .... INSCRIBE
on his own .... FREELANCE
one's name .... SIGN
out in large letters
.... ENGROSS
out in full (notes, speeches)
.... TRANSCRIBE
the screenplay for a book
.... ADAPT
up .... REPORT, SKETCH
writer ...... POET, CLERK, EDITOR,
PENMAN, SCRIBE, COPYIST,
AUTHOR(ESS), SCRIVENER,
AMANUENSIS, JOURNALIST
Dahl .... ROALD
Davis .... GWEN
for motion pictures
.... SCRIPTWRITER
"Fourth Estate"
.... JOURNALIST
inferior ..... HACK, POETASTER,
SCRIBBLER
kind of .... COPY, GHOST,
COPYIST, COMPILER,
REPORTER, COLUMNIST
of articles, speeches for
another ..... GHOSTWRITER
long fictional prose
.... NOVELIST
morals .... AESOP
news .... REPORTER
news from a distant place
.... CORRESPONDENT
plays .... DRAMATIST,
PLAYWRIGHT
research paper ..... ESSAYIST
text of an opera
.... LIBRETTIST
trilogies .... ASCH
unscrupulous .... PLAGIARIST
verse .... POET, RHYMER,
VERSIFIER
who indulges in faultfinding
and censure .... CRITIC
writer's bugaboo .... DEADLINE
cramp ..... SCRIVENER'S PALSY
own signature ..... AUTOGRAPH
writers' group .... PEN
writhe ...... WARP, TWIST, SQUIRM,

CONTORT, DISTORT
writing ...... BOOK, POEM, DIARY,
VERSE, LETTER, ARTICLE,
DOCUMENT, TREATISE,
MONOGRAPH, NARRATIVE
as a profession .... PEN
bad hand(writing)
.... CACOGRAPHY
beautiful hand(writing)
.... CALLIGRAPHY
characters .... ALPHABET
cipher .... CRYPTOGRAPHY
combining form .... LOG(UE)
desk ..... BUREAU, SECRETARY,
ESCRITOIRE
exalted to trivial .... BATHOS
expert .... GRAPHOLOGIST
flippant style of
.... PERSIFLAGE
flourish .... TAG, CURLICUE,
CURLYCUE
foolish .... HOGWASH,
TWADDLE
hand- .... PENMANSHIP,
CHIROGRAPHY
implement .... NIB, PEN,
BRUSH, CHALK, QUILL,
CRAYON, PENCIL, STYLUS,
BALLPOINT, (FOUNTAIN)PEN
instrument, ancient ...... STYLE
long tiresome piece of
.... SCREED
machine .... COMPUTER,
TELETYPE, STENOTYPE,
TYPEWRITER
mark .... CHARACTER
material .... STATIONERY
material, box for
.... PAPETERIE
mystic(al) .... RUNE
paper .... PAD, BOND, TABLET,
PAPYRUS, TALIPOT,
STATIONERY
roll of .... SCROLL
size .... DEMY, LEGAL,
LETTER, FOOLSCAP, IMPERIAL
specially treated
.... PARCHMENT
thin .... FLIMSY, ONIONSKIN
parchment .... VELLUM
pompous .... FUSTIAN
preliminary .... DRAFT
pretentious .... KITSCH
secret .... CODE, CIPHER
senseless .... BALDERDASH
sentimental .... SLUSH
stroke .... SERIF
style .... PROSE, POETRY
system of speed
.... SHORTHAND, STENOGRAPHY
table .... DESK, BUREAU,

ESCRITOIRE
tablet .... DIPTYCH
wall .... GRAFFITO
wedge-shaped
.... CUNEI(FORM)
writings .... LITERATURE,
COMPILATION, COMPOSITION
collection of .... PAPERS
sacred .... SCRIPTURE
unpublished .... REMAINS
written author's copy of work
.... MANUSCRIPT
copy .... TRANSCRIPT
copy by reporter .... FLIMSY
document, formal .... WRIT
in person's own handwriting
.... HOLOGRAPH(IC)
not .... ORAL, TACIT, VERBAL
off .... CANCELLED, CHARGED
OFF
order: law ...... WRIT, PRECEPT,
WARRANT, RESCRIPT
order issued by bank
.... CHECK, DRAFT
opposite of .... ORAL, TACIT,
SPOKEN, VERBAL, LINGUAL
plans, for short .... SKEDS
release .... QUITCLAIM
wrong .... BAD, EVIL, HARM,
ABUSE, AMISS, DAMAGE,
INJURE, OFFEND, SINFUL,
WICKED, IMMORAL, VICIOUS,
ERRONEOUS, INCORRECT
act .... CRIME, MISDEED,
VIOLATION, MISCONDUCT
civil/legal .... TORT
do .... SIN
do woman ..... ABUSE, SEDUCE
habit .... VICE
impression .... MISBELIEF
name .... MISNOMER
way, the .... AGAINST THE
GRAIN
"Wrong Way" Corrigan
.... DOUGLAS
wrongdoer .... CROOK, FELON,
THIEF, KILLER, OUTLAW,
RAPIST, SINNER, VANDAL,
CONVICT, HOODLUM,
MOBSTER, ARSONIST,
CRIMINAL, GANGSTER,
KIDNAPER, OFFENDER,
SCOFFLAW, SWINDLER,
TERRORIST, MALEFACTOR
wrongful .... UNFAIR, UNJUST,
HARMFUL, ILLEGAL, LAWLESS,
IMPROPER, UNLAWFUL
wrongheaded .... STUBBORN,
MISGUIDED
wrongly .... FALSELY,
MISTAKENLY

wroth .... MAD, SORE, ANGRY, CROSS, IRATE, INCENSED
wrought .... D(A)EDAL, SHAPED, DECORATED, FASHIONED
up .... AGOG, ANGRY, RILED, TENSE, EXCITED, DISTURBED
wry ...... ASKEW, IRONIC, WARPED, CROOKED, TWISTED, CONTRARY, PERVERSE, DISTORTED
wryneck .... WEET, LOXIA, (SNAKE)BIRD, TORTICOLLIS
genus .... JYNX
relative .... WOODPECKER
Wuthering Heights author
.... BRONTE
WW II Allies .... FRANCE, SOVIET UNION, GREAT BRITAIN, UNITED STATES
Axis power ...... ITALY, JAPAN, GERMANY
battle site .... GUAM, ST. LO, LEYTE, BATAAN, MIDWAY, SAIPAN, TARAWA, IWOJIMA, OKINAWA, NORMANDY, KWAJALEIN, CORREGIDOR, GUADALCANAL
beachhead .... ANZIO, NORMANDY
bomb site .... NORDEN, NAGASAKI, HIROSHIMA
British Prime Minister
.... (WINSTON) CHURCHILL
date .... D-DAY
Greek group .... EDES, ELAS
Japanese admiral .... ITO, OKA, OTA, TOGO, KIMURA, TAKAGI, TANAKA, TOYODA, YAMADA, YAMAMOTO, YAMAGUCHI
admiral, head of kamikaze units .... UGAKI
admiral, originator of kamikaze corps
.... ONISHI
Army Commander
.... HOMMA
battle cry .... BANZAI
battleship ...... FUSO, KONGO, HARUNA, MOGAMI, YAMATO, MUSASHI, YAMASHIRO
carrier .... AOBA, AKAGI, HOSHO, TAIHO, CHIYODA, ZUIKAKU
Commander of Pearl Harbor striking force
.... NAGUMO
cruiser .... YURA, NACHI, CHOKAI, HAGURO, FURUTAKA
death by suicide .... HARA-

KIRI
destroyer .... FUBUKI, AKIZUKI, SHIGURE
emperor .... HIROHITO
general .... CHO, NASU, SATO, TOJO, HOMMA, NAGAI, OSUGA, UMEZU, SUZUKI, TANAKA, NISHINO, MIYAZAKI, TOMINAGA, WATANABE, YAMASHITA
suicide pilot .... KAMIKAZE
warplane .... ZERO
"Little Tokyo" .... SAIPAN
Nazi dictator
.... (ADOLF)HITLER
org. .... OPA, OSS
powers .... AXIS
refugees, post .... DPS
Russian generalissimo
.... STALIN
sector/area: abbr. .... ETO
shouts .... HEILS
site of Japan's formal surrender .... MISSOURI
"The Big Three," one of the .... STALIN, CHURCHILL, ROOSEVELT
title .... SCAP
"Tokyo Rose" ..... IVA IKUKO TOGURI
WW II, U.S. admiral ...... HART, BLOCH, HALSEY, KIMMEL, NIMITZ, ROCKWELL, SPRUANCE
atomic bomb assembly place .... TINIAN
bomber .... ENOLA GAY, BOCK'S CAR
expert .... (WILLIAM)PARSONS
battleship ...... UTAH, NEVADA, ARIZONA, MARYLAND, MISSOURI, OKLAHOMA, SARATOGA, TENNESSEE, CALIFORNIA, WHITE PLAINS, PENNSYLVANIA, WEST VIRGINIA
"Bock's Car" bombardier
.... (KERMIT)BEAHAN
bomb site .... NAGASAKI
Commander
.... (CHARLES)SWEENEY
co-pilot .... ALBURY
cargo plane ..... C-FIFTY FOUR, C-FORTY SEVEN
carrier .... HORNET, YORKTOWN, LEXINGTON, ENTERPRISE
Commander-in-Chief who ordered use of atomic bomb on Japan
.... (HARRY)TRUMAN

cruiser .... BOISE, DENVER, DUNCAN, HELENA, AUGUSTA, HOUSTON, NASHVILLE, PENSACOLA, MINNEAPOLIS
D-Day top secret code word .... UTAH, OMAHA, NEPTUNE, MULBERRY, OVERLORD
destroyer ...... BLUE, FLETCHER
draft classification .... ONE-A
engineer .... SEABEE
"Enola Gay" bombardier
.... (THOMAS)FEREBEE
bomb site .... HIROSHIMA
Commander
.... (PAUL)TIBBETS
co-pilot .... (ROBERT)LEWIS
navigator ..... "DUTCH" VAN KIRK
general .... KING, SMITH, GROVES, PARKER, PATTON, PULLER, SPAATZ, FARRELL, MARSHALL, PERSHING, STILWELL, MACARTHUR, EISENHOWER, WAINWRIGHT
"Howlin' Mad" Smith's command ship
.... ELDORADO
in command of atomic bomb project
.... (THOMAS)FARRELL
of the Army ...... (DOUGLAS) MACARTHUR
landing craft .... LCI, LCV, LSD, LST, HIGGIN'S BOAT
last battleship sunk by enemy ...... INDIANAPOLIS
MacArthur-Halsey two-pronged drive
.... OPERATION CARTWHEEL
marine: nickname .... GYRENE, JARHEAD, LEATHERNECK
motor torpedo boat .... PT-BOAT
nickname of General Eisenhower .... IKE
Puller .... CHESTY
Smith .... HOWLIN' MAD
Spaatz .... TOOEY
Stilwell .... VINEGAR JOE
Wainwright .... SKINNY
Old ____ .... SARGE
president .... TRUMAN, ROOSEVELT
sailor: nickname
.... SWAB(BIE)
service woman ..... WAC, WAF, SPAR, WAVE
soldier: nickname
.... DOGFACE, DOUGHBOY
submarine .... CAVALLA,

war plan .... ORANGE-THREE
warplane .... B-SEVENTEEN,
P-FIFTY ONE, B-TWENTY FIVE,
B-TWENTY FOUR, B-TWENTY
NINE, P-THIRTY EIGHT,
GRUMMAN HELLCAT,
GRUMMAN WILDCAT
warplane's monicker
.... BOCK'S CAR, ENOLA GAY,
DINAH MIGHT, LONESOME
LADY, MEMPHIS BELLE,
DAUNTLESS DOTTY
Wolf pack unit .... U-BOAT
Wyandot .... HURON
Wycliffe, reformer .... JOHN
disciple .... LOLLARD
Wylie, novelist .... ELINOR
Wyoming basin .... BIGHORN,
SHIRLEY
capital .... CHEYENNE
cavern .... SHOSHONE
city/town .... CODY, CASPER,

ALBACORE, STINGRAY
LANDER, BUFFALO, DOUGLAS,
JACKSON, LARAMIE, RAWLINS,
WORLAND, EVANSTON,
GILLETTE, SHERIDAN,
SUNDANCE, WHEATLAND,
TORRINGTON
county .... PARK, CROOK,
TETON, UINTA, ALBANY,
GOSHEN, FREMONT, LARAMIE,
NATRONA, CAMPBELL,
SHERIDAN, SWEETWATER
dam .... BUFFALO BILL
lake .... LEWIS, BIGHORN,
FREMONT, JACKSON,
SHOSHONE, YELLOWSTONE
mountain .... HUNT, GREEN,
LEIDY, CROSBY, HOLMES,
ISABEL, NEEDLE, BURWELL,
DEADMAN, FORTRESS,
WASHBURN, INYAN KARA,
BONNEVILLE, TEAPOT DOME
mountain range .... ASPEN,
ROCKY, BIGHORN, GRANITE,

LARAMIE, SEMINOE
national monument .... DEVILS
TOWER
national park .... GRAND
TETON, YELLOWSTONE
peak .... CLOUD, EAGLE,
HOBACK, FREMONT, GANNETT,
LARAMIE, ATLANTIC
plateau .... MADISON
river .... BEAR, SALT, WIND,
WOOD, GREEN, GREYS, LAMAR,
SNAKE, HOBACK, POWDER,
BIGHORN, LARAMIE,
GREYBULL, MEDICINE BOW,
YELLOWSTONE, LITTLE
MISSOURI
state bird .... MEADOWLARK
state flower .... INDIAN
PAINTBRUSH
state nickname .... EQUALITY
state tree .... COTTONWOOD
Wystan Hugh .... AUDEN
wyvern .... DRAGON

X

X .... TEN, MARK, CROSS,
SIGNATURE
Greek XI
letter .... EX
marker, usually .... ILLITERATE
marks the _____ .... SPOT
shaped .... EX
word "dill" .... ANET
xanthic ...... TAWNY, YELLOW(ISH)
Xanthippe's husband
.... SOCRATES
prototype .... SHREW, NAGGER,
VIRAGO, TERMAGANT
xanthous .... FAIR, BLOND(E),
YELLOW(ISH)
Xavier, bandleader .... CUGAT
Saint .... FRANCIS

Xe, in chemistry .... XENON
xebec .... SHIP
common users .... CORSAIRS
xema .... GULL
xeno .... GUEST
as prefix .... FOREIGN,
STRANGE
xenophobe .... WARMONGER
Xeres .... JEREZ
xerophilous animal .... CAMEL
plant ...... CACTUS, XEROPHYTE
xerotic .... DRY
Xerxes I, father of .... DARIUS
wife .... ESTHER
xiphoid .... ENSIFORM, SWORD-
SHAPED
xiphosuran ...... ARACHNID, KING

CRAB
Xmas .... CHRISTMAS, YULE(TIDE)
X-rated feature .... NUDITY
X-ray ...... EXAMINE, PHOTOGRAPH
discoverer of ...... RO(E)NTGEN
Xtian .... CHRISTIAN
XV .... FIFTEEN
xylan .... PENTOSAN
xyloid .... WOOD(Y), LIGNEOUS
xylonite .... CELLULOID
xylophone-like instrument
.... SARON, MARIMBA
xylotomous insect .... ANAY,
TERMITE
xyst .... WALK, PORTICO
xyster .... (BONE)SCRAPER

Y

Y, Greek .... UPSILON
Hebrew .... YOD(H)
in mathematics ...... ORDINATE
letter .... WYE
men .... ELIS
yabber .... TALK, GIBBER, JABBER,
CHATTER
yacht .... SAIL, CUTTER,
CRUISE(R), KNOCKABOUT

club president
.... COMMODORE
flag .... BURGEE
haven of .... COVE
racing .... SONDERCLASS
racing champion ..... INTREPID
sail .... SPINNAKER
tender .... DINGHY
yachting center .... COWES

yachtsman .... LIPTON, YACHTER,
CORINTHIAN
Yadkin .... PEEDEE RIVER
yaffle .... WOODPECKER
yager .... RIFLEMAN
yahoo .... LOUT, BRUTE, KNAVE,
BUMPKIN
creator .... SWIFT
Yahwe(h) .... GOD, JEHOVAH

yak .... OX, SARLAK
   where found .... TIBET
yaki .... CAYMAN
Yakutsk river .... LENA
Yale .... ELI, LOCK, UNIVERSITY
   Bowl sound .... BOOLA
   elite secret society ..... SKULL
                  AND BONES
   clubhouse .... (THE)TOMB
   clubhouse member
                         BONESMAN
   Mr. .... (ELIHU)ROOT
Yalie .... ELI
Yalta conference member
            STALIN, CHURCHILL,
                    ROOSEVELT
   native .... CRIMEAN
yam .... HOI, UBE, UBI, ROOT,
                        POTATO
   bean .... KAMA, BONIATA
Yamashita, Japanese general
                    TOMOYUKI
   sobriquet .... TIGER
yamen resident .... MANDARIN
yammer .... CRY, HOWL, PULE,
     WAIL, YELL, GRIPE, WHINE,
   CLAMOR, WHIMPER, COMPLAIN
Yangtze River city .... WUHU,
                    NANKING
Yank .... JERK, PULL, TWIST,
                  AMERICAN
Yankee .... AMERICAN,
                 NORTHERNER
yap .... NAG, YIP, BARK, TALK,
     YAWP, YELP, JABBER,
                   SQUAWK
   slang .... MOUTH, ROWDY,
                    HOODLUM
Yaqui .... RIVER, INDIAN
yard .... AREA, SPAR, GROUNDS
   enclosed .... GARTH
   in law .... CURTILAGE
   kind of .... QUAD, COURT,
                         PATIO
   section .... FOOT
yards, 220 .... FURLONG
yardstick ...... RULE(R), MEASURE,
       STANDARD, CRITERION
yarn ...... FIB, SLUB, TALE, FABLE,
   FIBER, GEARN, INKLE, STORY,
   ANGORA, BOUCLE, SPINEL,
                    THREAD
   ball of .... CLEW, SKEIN
   count .... TYPP
   560 yards .... HANK
   flax .... LINEN
   knot .... BURL
   knitting .... SAXONY
   machine .... MULE
   measure .... COP, LEA, CLEW,
   CLUE, HANK, SKEIN, SPINDLE

mule .... SPINNING JENNY
   quantity .... SKEIN
   roll of .... COP
   skein of .... HASP
   teller .... ANGLER,
                MUNCHAUSEN
   twilled/twisted .... CREWEL
   warp .... ABB
   waste .... THRUM
   winder .... PIRNER
   with protruding pile
                    CHENILLE
   woolen, inferior .... SHODDY
   worsted .... CADDIS
yarrow .... HERB, MILFOIL
yashmak .... VEIL
yatag(h)an .... SABER
yaud .... JADE, MARE
yaupon .... ASSI, HOLLY,
         CASSENA, CASSINE
   use of .... TEA
yaw .... JIBE, TACK, VEER, TUMOR,
                    DEVIATE
yawl .... DANDY, KETCH,
   SAILBOAT, JOLLYBOAT
yawn .... GAPE, PART, CHASM,
           SPLIT, OSCITATE
   aloud .... YAUP, YAWP
   meaning of, usually
   .... ENNUI, BOREDOM, FATIGUE,
            DROWSINESS
yawner .... SLEEPYHEAD
yawning .... GAPING
   depth of .... ABYSS
   fit of .... GAPES
yawp ...... CRY, YAP, BAWL, GAPE,
   HOWL, WAIL, YAWN
yaws .... FRAMB(O)ESIA
   cause of .... SPIROCHETE
Yb, in chemistry .... YTTERBIUM
yclept .... NAMED, CALLED,
                KNOWN(AS)
ye .... THEE, THOU
yea(h) .... YES, TRULY, INDEED
yean .... REAR, BRING FORTH
yeanling .... KID, LAMB, NEWBORN
year .... AGE, ANNO, TIME,
            TWELVEMONTH
   continuing for a
   .... YEARLONG, YEAR-ROUND
   designating a .... LEAP,
   LUNAR, SOLAR, FISCAL,
   NATURAL, CALENDAR,
   SIDEREAL, TROPICAL,
           EQUINOCTIAL
   every .... ANNUALLY, PER
                    ANNUM
   good or bad .... VINTAGE
   half .... SEMESTER
   in the past .... IAD

   of plenary indulgence
                    JUBILEE
   with a bonus day .... LEAP
yearbook .... ANNAL, ANNUAL,
                   ALMANAC
yearling .... CUB, TEG, COLT,
   FILLY, WHELP, LEVERET
yearly .... ETESIAN, ANNUALLY
   calendar .... ALMANAC
yearn .... ACHE, HOPE, LONG,
   PINE, SIGH, CRAVE, MOURN,
                   HANKER
yearning ...... YEN, WISH, DESIRE,
         THIRST, LONGING
   for family .... HOMESICK
years, happening every eight
                  OCTENNIAL
   ten .... DECENNIAL
   two .... BIENNIAL
   old, 65 (usually) ...... RETIREE
   70 .... SEPTUAGENARIAN
   80 .... OCTOGENARIAN
   90 .... NONAGENARIAN
   100 .... CENTENNIAL
   period of 5 .... PENTAD
   10 .... DECADE, DECENARY,
             DECENNIUM
   100 .... CENTURY,
                CENTENARY
   1000 .... CHILIAD,
                MILLENIUM
   thousands and thousands of
                   (A)EON
yeast .... BARM, BEES, FOAM,
   FROTH, SPUME, FUNGUS,
   LEAVEN, ANAMITE, FERMENT
   disease-causing ...... CANDIDA-
                ALBICANS
   disease caused by
              CANDIDIASIS
   enzyme .... ZYMASE
yeasty .... BARMY, LIGHT, BUBBLY,
   BUBBLING, EBULLIENT
Yeats' _____ and the Swan
                    LEDA
yecchy .... ICKY, FILTHY
Yed(d)o .... EDO, TOKYO
yegg .... THIEF, ROBBER, BURGLAR,
            SAFECRACKER
yeld .... BARREN
yell ...... CRY, BAWL, ROAR, YELP,
   CHEER, SHOUT, BELLOW,
   HALLOO, HOLLER, OUTCRY,
   SCREAM, SHRIEK, YAMMER
   college .... RAH, CHEER
   ending cheers .... TIGER
yellow ...... DYE, AMBER, CHROME,
   GAMBOGE, LUTEOUS,
   PIGMENT, XANTHIC,
               XANTHOUS
   bird .... CANARY, MELINE,

ORIOLE, FLICKER, WARBLER,
GOLDFINCH
bright .... GOLDEN, GAMBOGE
brown ..... DUN, ECRU, SORREL
bugle .... IVA
calla .... AROID
clay .... OCHER, OCHRE
colloquial .... AFRAID,
CRAVEN, COWARDLY
color .... GOLD, ALOMA,
AMBER, LEMON, OCHER,
BUTTERY, SAFFRON, XANTHIC
colored fruit .... LEMON,
MANGO, BANANA, CITRON,
AZAROLE
combining form .... CHRYS(O),
LUTEO, XANTH(O)
compound .... LUTEOLIN
daisy .... BLACK-EYED SUSAN
dark .... OCHRE
deep .... GOLD
dull brownish .... TAN, BUFF,
ECRU, BEIGE
dye stuff .... MORIN, FLAVONE,
FLAVONOL, PHOSPHINE,
QUERCETIN
egg's .... YOLK
eyed .... ENVIOUS, JEALOUS,
JAUNDICED
fever .... VOMITO, INFECTION
fever carrier .... AEDES,
MOSQUITO
fever mosquito
.... STEGOMYIA, AEDES-
AEGYPTI
flag signal .... QUARANTINE
flower .... IRIS, CROCUS,
JASMINE, JONQUIL,
DANDELION, GOLDENROD,
SUNFLOWER, CHRYSANTHEMUM
gem .... TOPAZ
green .... NILE
greenish .... CHAMPAGNE
gum resin .... GAMBOGE,
CAMBOGIA
haired .... BLOND
jacket .... WASP, VESPA,
HORNET, VESPID
journalism
.... MELODRAMA(TICS)
journalism staple .... SCANDAL
lead ore .... WULFENITE
light .... CANARY, PRIMROSE
man .... MONGOLIAN
metal .... GOLD, BRASS
orange .... PEACH, CROCUS,
SAFFRON
pale ...... BUFF, MAIZE, STRAW,
FALLOW, FLAXEN
pigment .... SIL, OCHER,
OCHRE, FLAVIN, ETIOLIN,

GAMBOGE, ORPIMENT,
QUERCETIN
quartz .... CITRINE
race .... CHINESE,
MONGOL(IAN)
red .... CORAL
reddish .... SANDY
river .... HWANG HO
sickly, pale .... SALLOW
skin, cause of .... JAUNDICE
somewhat .... YELLOWISH
streak .... FEAR, FUNK,
COWARDICE
turning .... ICTERUS,
FLAVESCENT
Yellow Kid Weil .... JOSEPH
Pages .... DIRECTORY,
PHONEBOOK
Peril harbinger .... CHINESE,
MONGOLIANS
Sea .... HWANG HAI
Sea gulf .... POHAI
Sea port .... TSINGTAO
Sea, river into .... YALU
yellowhammer .... BIRD, YITE,
VERDIN, BUNTING, FLICKER,
WOODPECKER
Yellowhammer State
.... ALABAMA
yellowish brown .... DRAB, FAWN,
HAZEL, KHAKI, STRAW,
TAWNY, CHAMOIS, CINNAMON
green .... CHARTREUSE
orange .... PEACH, CADMIUM
pale complexion .... SALLOW
part of milk .... CREAM
red .... RUFOUS
semi-precious stone
.... CHRYSOBERYL
white .... CREAM
yellowlegs .... SANDPIPER
Yellowstone Park denizen
.... BEAR
Park employee .... RANGER
sight .... LAKE, PARK, FALLS
yellowtail .... MENHADEN,
ROCKFISH, CARANGOID
relative .... CAVALLA,
POMPANO
yellowthroat ...... BIRD, WARBLER
yellowweed .... RAGWORT,
CROWFOOT, GOLDENROD
yelp .... CRY, YAP, YIP, BARK,
YAWP, SQUAWK, SQUEAL
Yemen Arab Republic capital
.... SANA
city/town .... IBB, TAIZZ,
DHAMAR, HODEIDA
dynasty .... RASSITE
island .... ZUQAR, HANISH
king .... IMAM, (AL)BADR

language .... ARABIC
monetary unit .... RIYAL
mountain .... MANAR, SABIR
neighbor of .... OMAN
president/premier
.... (AL)SALAL
region .... TIHAMA
religion .... ISLAM
sea .... RED
seaport .... MOCHA
seat of government ...... TAIZZ
sect .... ZAIDI
strait .... MANDEB
Yemen, People's Democratic
Republic cape .... FARTAK
capital .... ADEN
city/town .... SELYUN,
MUKALLA
island .... PERIM, KAMARAN,
SOCATRA
language .... ARABIC
monetary unit .... DINAR
religion .... ISLAM
Yemenite .... ARAB(IAN), BEDOUIN
garment .... ABA
yen .... URGE, TASTE, DESIRE,
HUNGER, LIKING, CRAVING,
LONG(ING), PASSION,
YEARNING
is monetary unit of ____
.... JAPAN
yenite .... LIVAITE
yenta ...... BUSYBODY, GOSSIP(ER)
yeoman .... SQUIRE, DECKHAND,
MYRMIDON, ASSISTANT,
ATTENDANT, BODYGUARD,
FREEHOLDER, MANSERVANT,
SUBORDINATE
yeomanly .... BRAVE, LOYAL,
STURDY
yep .... YES
opposite of .... NOPE
yes .... AYE, YEP, YUP, SURE,
YEA(H), AGREEMENT,
AFFIRMATIVE
man .... TOADY, SYCOPHANT
yeshiva .... SEMINARY
yeso .... GYPSUM
yet .... NOW, ALSO, STILL,
BESIDES, HOWEVER,
NOTWITHSTANDING
to be published ...... UNEDITED
yeti ...... (ABOMINABLE) SNOWMAN
yew ...... TREE, CONIFER, HEMLOCK
fruit .... CONE, BERRY
genus .... TAXUS
Yezd is in ____ .... IRAN
Yezo .... HOKKAIDO
Yggdrasil .... ASH TREE
Yiddish .... JEWISH, LANGUAGE
noodles .... FARFEL, FERFEL

synagogue .... SHUL
thief .... GANEF, GANOF
yield .... OBEY, DEFER, GRANT,
COMPLY, GIVE(IN), GIVE UP,
RELENT, RETURN, SOFTEN,
SUBMIT, (CON)CEDE,
PRODUCT, SUCCUMB,
SURRENDER, CAPITULATE
a profit .... PAY
farm .... CROP, PRODUCE
gold .... PAN OUT
point .... CONCEDE
to Morpheus .... SLEEP
yielding .... SOFT, DOCILE, PLIANT,
FERTILE, PRODUCTIVE
yill .... ALE
yip .... CRY, YAP, BARK, YELP
Ymir .... GIANT
yo-heave-ho, for example
.... CHANT
yodel .... SING, WARBLE
yodeler .... SWISS, TYROLEAN
milieu of .... ALPS
yoga, form of .... HATHAYOGA
need .... CONCENTRATION
originator ...... HINDU, HINDOO
person who practices .... YOGI
posture/squat .... ASANA
yogi ...... SWAMI, MYSTIC, ASCETIC
Yogi, ballplayer .... BERRA
yoke .... TIE, BIND, BOND, LINK,
PAIR, CHAIN, CANGUE,
COUPLE, HALTER, INSPAN,
BONDAGE, ENSLAVE,
HARNESS, SLAVERY,
SERVITUDE, THRALLDOM
large, wooden .... CANGUE
part of .... OXBOW
yokefellow .... MATE, WIFE,
HUSBAND, PARTNER,
ASSOCIATE
yokel .... HICK, RUBE, YAHOO,
RUSTIC, BUMPKIN, PEASANT
Yoko .... ONO
Yokum's creator .... CAPP
yolk, egg ...... YELLOW, VITELLUS
of the egg .... VITELLINE
protein .... VITELLIN
yolked .... LECITHAL
yom .... DAY
Yom ____, Jewish holiday
.... KIPPUR
yon(der) .... THERE
yore .... ELD, LONG AGO, WAY
BACK, OLDEN TIMES
York, ____ .... SERGEANT
yorker, game associated with
.... CRICKET
Yorkshire native .... DALESMAN
port .... HULL, WHITBY

river .... AIRE
Yoruba native .... EGBA
Yosemite sight ...... PARK, FALLS,
CLIFFS, REDWOOD
Yoshihito's empire .... JAPAN
reign .... TAISHO
son .... HIROHITO
title .... EMPEROR
young .... NEW, RAW, FRESH,
GREEN, PUERILE, TEEN-AGE,
IMMATURE, JUVENILE,
YOUTHFUL, ADOLESCENT
animal .... CUB, KID, CALF,
TOTO, PUPPY, SLINK, WHELP,
SUCKLING
beef .... VEAL
bird .... CHICK, OWLET,
NESTLING, FLEDGLING
blood .... YOUTH
branch .... TWIG, SHOOT
bull .... CALF
cat .... KITTY, PUSSY, KITTEN
chicken .... FRYER
cod .... SCROD
cow .... CALF, HEIFER
deer .... DOE, FAWN
dog .... PUP(PY), WHELP
Duroc .... SHOAT
eagle .... AERIE, EYRIE
eel .... SNIG, ELVER
falcon .... EYAS
fish .... FRY, PARR, SMELT,
GRILSE, FINGERLING
fowl .... POULT
fox .... CUB
frog .... TADPOLE
girl .... LASS, MISS, MAIDEN,
MOPPET
goat .... KID
goose .... GOSLING
hare .... LEVERET
hawk .... EYAS, AERIE, EYRIE
hen .... CHICK, PULLET,
POULARD
herring .... BRIT, SPRAT,
SARDINE
hog .... GILT, SHOAT, SHOTE,
PORKER
hooter .... OWLET
horse .... COLT, FOAL, FILLY
kangaroo .... JOEY
lion .... CUB, WHELP, LIONET
male .... BUCK
man .... YOUTH, CHIEL(D),
MASTER
man of high birth ...... SQUIRE
man's fancy .... BEARD
moose .... CALF
oyster .... SPAT
ox .... STEER

pig .... FARROW
pigeon .... SQUAB
salmon .... PARR, SMOLT,
GRILSE
seal .... PUP
sheep .... LAMB
squab .... PIPER
swan .... CYGNET
tiger .... CUB, WHELP
turkey/pheasant .... POULT
whale .... CUB
with .... PREGNANT, ON THE
WAY
wolf .... WHELP
Young, actor .... GIG
actress .... LORETTA
Mormon church head
.... BRIGHAM
Turks, so-called .... REBELS
**young of animals born at one
time** .... LITTER
younger son .... CADET
youngster .... KID, LAD, TAD, TOT,
TIKE, TYKE, CHILD, MINOR,
YOUTH, SHAVER, URCHIN,
SAPLING, BUNTLING, SMALL
FRY, TEENAGER
colloquial .... BOBBY SOXER
with a sweet innocent face
.... CHERUB
yours truly .... ME, MYSELF
youth .... LAD, BABY, TEENS,
CHIEL(D), NONAGE, SHAVER,
BOY(HOOD), INFANCY,
PUBERTY, GIRL(HOOD),
MINORITY, TEENAGE(R),
CHILD(HOOD), PUERILITY,
STRIPLING, YOUNGSTER,
ADOLESCENCE
beautiful .... NARCISSUS
group: abbr. .... BSA, GSA
of a .... MINOR
who fell in love with his
image .... NARCISSUS
youthful ...... NEW, FRESH, GREEN,
YOUNG, ACTIVE, TENDER,
VERNAL, BUDDING, PUERILE,
IMMATURE, JUVENILE,
UNDERAGE
works .... JUVENALIA
yow .... OUCH
yowl .... CRY, WAIL, YELL
yperite .... MUSTARD GAS
where used in battle
.... YPRES
Yquem .... WINE, SAUTERNE(S)
Yseult .... ISOLDE
yuan .... TAEL, DYNASTY
is monetary unit of ____
.... CHINA

yuca .... MANIOC, CASSAVA
Yucatan capital .... MERIDA
   Indian/people .... MAYA
   leaf fiber .... SISAL
   Mayan city .... USMAL
   native .... MAYAN
yucca .... FLAT, LILY, PITA
   fiber .... ISTLE
   plant like .... SOTOL
Yuga .... AGE, ERA
   period .... KALI, KRITA, TRETA,
      DVAPARA
Yugoslavia cape .... KAMENJAK
   capital .... BEOGRAD,
      BELGRADE
   city/town .... BOR, NIS, PEC,
      POLA, STIP, ZARA, PIROT,
      SENTA, SPLIT, TUZLA, ZADAR,
      APATIN, OSIJEK, PRILEP,
      RIJEKA, SKOPJE, SOMBOR,
      ZAGREB, ZENICA, MARIBOR,
      NOVI SAD, SARAJEVO,
      SUBOTICA, TITOGRAD, BANJA
      LUKA, KRAGUJEVAC
   coin .... PARA, DINAR
   commune .... STIP
   division ...... BOSNIA, KOSOVO,
      SERBIA, CROATIA, SLOVENIA,
      MACEDONIA, MONTENEGRO,
      HERCEGOVINA
   guerrillas .... CHETNIKS,
      PARTISANS
   gulf .... KVARNER
   island ..... KRK, PAG, RAB, VIS,
      BRAC, CRES, HVAR, MLJET,
      SOLTA, ZIRJE, KORNAT,

      LASTOVO
lake .... OHRID, PRESPA,
      SCUTARI
language .... ALBANIAN,
   CROATIAN, SLOVENIAN,
   MACEDONIAN
measure .... OKA, RIF, AKOV,
   DONUM, KHVAT, LANAZ,
   PALAZ, STOPA
monetary unit .... DINAR
mountain .... KORAB, RUJEN,
   MIDZHUR, TRIGLAV, CVRSNICA
mountain range .... DINARIC
   ALPS
native .... SERB, CROAT,
   SLOVENE
news agency .... TANJUG
peninsula .... ISTRIA
port .... RIJEKA
premier .... PANIC, SPILJAK
president .... TITO (BROZ)
region .... DALMATIA,
   SLAVONIA
republic ...... SERBIA, CROATIA,
   SLOVENIA, MACEDONIA,
   MONTENEGRO
river .... LIM, MUR, UNA, IBAR,
   KUPA, SAVA, TARA, TISA,
   CAZMA, DRAVA, DRINA,
   TIMOK, VRBAS, BOSNIA,
   DANUBE, MORAVA, VARDAR,
   NERETVA
sea .... ADRIATIC
seaport ..... POLA, PULA, ZARA,
   RIJEKA, DUBROVNIK
weight .... TOVAR, WAGON,

   DRAMMA, SATLIJK
Yukon Territory capital
   .... WHITEHORSE
   city/town .... ELSA, FARO,
   MAYO, DAWSON, TESLIN, OLD
   CROW, CARCROSS
   flower .... FIREWEED
   island .... HERSCHEL
   lake .... MAYO, KLUANE,
   TESLIN, FRANCES
   mining town .... SKAGWAY
   mountain ...... LOGAN, SELOUS,
   CAMPBELL, SAINT ELIAS
   mountain range .... PELLY,
   ROCKY, SELWYN, BRITISH,
   CASSIAR, OGILVIE, MACKENZIE
   peak .... KEELE, LOGAN
   region .... KLONDIKE
   river .... HESS, PEEL, ALSEK,
   LIARD, PELLY, WHITE, YUKON,
   HYLAND, TESLIN, OGILVIE,
   STEWART, KLONDIKE,
   MACMILLAN, PORCUPINE
   tributary .... TANANA
yule .... CHRISTMAS
   short for .... XMAS
   symbol .... LOG, MISTLETOE
   tipple .... NOG
Yum Yum's friend .... KOKO
Yuma .... INDIAN, MOHAVE,
   MOJAVE
yummy .... TASTY, DELICIOUS,
   DELECTABLE
Yunnan capital .... KUNMING
yurt, e.g. .... TENT
Yutang, writer .... LIN

Z

Z, Arabic .... ZE
   English .... ZED
   Greek .... ZETA
   Hebrew .... ZAYIN
   in the UK .... ZED
   letter .... ZED, ZEE, IZZARD
   mark of _____ .... ZORRO
Zabrze is in _____ .... POLAND
zac .... IBEX
Zac Starr, father of .... RINGO
zacaton .... GRASS
Zaccur's father .... IMRI
Zaire capital .... KINSHASA
   city/town .... ABA, BENI,
   BOMA, BUTA, GOMA, KAMA,
   AKETI, BUMBA, BUNIA,
   DEMBA, ILEBO, ISIRO, WAMBA,
   WATSA, BUKAVU, KABALO,
   KALIMA, KAMINA, KIKWIT,

   MANONO, MATADI, BUTEMBO,
   KABINDA, KALEMIE, KANANGA,
   KASONGO, KOLWEZI, VIRUNGA,
   BANDUNDU, MBANDAKA,
   TSHIKAPA, YANGAMBI,
   KISANGANI, MWENE-DITU,
   LUBUMBASHI, PANDA-LIKASI
   falls .... BOYOMA, STANLEY,
   LIVINGSTONE
   lake .... KIVU, MWERU, TUMBA,
   ALBERT, EDWARD, MALEBO,
   UPEMBA, TANGANYIKA
   language .... MONGO, ZANDE,
   FRENCH, KIKONGO, LINGALI,
   SWAHILI
   monetary unit .... ZAIRE
   mountain .... KARISIMBI,
   MARGHERITA
   mountain range .... MURUNGU,

   VIRUNGA, RUWENZORI
   national park .... UPEMBA,
   GARAMBA, VIRUNGA
   president .... MOBUTO SESE
   SEKO
   province .... KIVU, KASAI,
   SHABA, BANDUNDU, BAS-
   ZAIRE, EQUATEUR, KINSHASA,
   HAUT-ZAIRE
   river .... KWA, LUA, BOMU,
   FIMI, GIRI, LOWA, UELE,
   CONGO, ELILA, KASAI, KWILU,
   LINDI, LULUA, LUVUA,
   KWANGO, LOANGE, LOKORO,
   LOMANI, LOMELA, LUFIRA,
   LUKUYA, RUZIZI, UBANGI,
   ULINDI, ARUWIMI, CHICAPA,
   LUALABA, LUAPULA, TSHUAPA,
   ITIMBIRI

Zambal .... MALAY
Zambezi tributary .... SHIRE
Zambia capital .... LUSAKA
   city/town .... KABWE, KITWE,
    MANSA, MONGU, NDOLA,
    KASAMA, ZAMBEZI, BANCROFT,
    CHINGOLA, LUANSHYA,
    MUFULIRA
   dam .... KARIBA
   falls .... KALAMBO, VICTORIA
   lake .... MWERU, KARIBA
   language .... LOZI, BEMBA,
    TONGA, LUVALE
   monetary unit .... KWACHA
   mountain .... SUNZU
   national park .... KAFUE
   president .... KAUNDA
   region .... BAROTSELAND
   river .... KAFUE, CUANDO,
    DONGWE, LUAPULA, ZAMBEZI
Zamenhof's invention
   .... ESPERANTO
Zane Grey locale .... MESA
zany .... DOLT, FOOL, CLOWN,
    COMIC, DUNCE, JESTER,
    MADCAP, NITWIT, BUFFOON,
    SIMPLETON
   Lucille .... BALL
Zanzibar island .... PEMBA
zap .... END, KAYO, KILL, BLAST
Zarathustra .... ZOROASTER
Zardari, Pakistan legislator
   .... ASIF ALI
   wife of ...... (BENAZIR)BHUTTO
zarf .... CUP
Zasu, comedienne .... PITTS
Zauberflote, _____ .... DIE
Zea .... KEOS, ISLAND
zeal .... ELAN, SOUL, ARDOR,
    VERVE, ENERGY, FERVOR,
    SPIRIT, PASSION, DEVOTION,
    ENTHUSIASM
Zealand city .... COPENHAGEN
   fiord .... ISSE
zealot .... FAN, BIGOT, ADDICT,
   DEVOTEE, DREAMER, FANATIC,
   PARTISAN, ENTHUSIAST,
   EAGER BEAVER
zealotry .... BIGOTRY, FANATICISM
Zealots' conqueror .... TITUS,
    VESPASIAN
zealous .... RABID, ARDENT,
   FERVID, FANATIC, FERVENT,
   INTENSE, HARD-CORE,
   SPIRITED
zebec(k) .... SHIP
Zebedee's son .... JOHN, JAMES
zebra and ass offspring
   .... ZEBRASS
   and horse offspring
   .... ZEBRULA

animal resembling .... ASS,
    HORSE, QUAGGA
   extinct .... QUAGGA
   of the .... ZEBRINE
   wood .... ARAROBA
   young .... COLT
zebu .... BRAHMA
   and yak offspring .... BO(H),
    ZOBO
   cousin of .... ANGONI
zebuder .... ZAC, IBEX
zecchin(o) .... COIN, SEQUIN
Zechariah's hymn .... (THE)
    BENEDICTUS
   son .... JOHN THE BAPTIST
   wife .... ELIZABETH
zed, equivalent of .... ZEE,
    IZZARD
zee .... IZZARD
Zeeland, capital of
   .... MIDDELBURG
   island .... WALCHEREN
Zeiger, talk show hosts' top
   banana .... LARRY KING
Zen .... CHAN
   Buddhism, central figure of
   .... SHAKA MUNI
zenana .... HAREM, SERAGLIO
   factotum .... EUNUCH
   resident .... ODALISK,
    CONCUBINE, ODALISQUE
   room .... ODA
zenith .... TOP, ACME, APEX,
   PEAK, APOGEE, CLIMAX,
   HEIGHT, SUMMIT, VERTEX,
   PINNACLE
   opposed to .... NADIR
   sun's .... NOON
Zeno follower .... CYNIC, STOIC
   of _____ .... ELEA, CITIUM
   philosophy .... STOICISM
Zenobia .... QUEEN
   domain of .... PALMYRA
zephyr ...... SOFT, WIND, BREATH,
    BREEZE, GENTLE
Zephyrus .... DEITY, FAVONIUS
zeppelin .... BLIMP, AIRSHIP,
    DIRIGIBLE
zero .... NIL, NONE, ZILCH, CIPHER,
    (N)AUGHT, (N)OUGHT,
    NOTHING, NULLITY
   colloquial .... ZIP
   in tennis .... LOVE
   on a compass .... NORTH
Zero Hour .... D-DAY
Zerulah's son .... ABISHAI
zest .... VIM, BRIO, TANG, ZEAL,
   ZING, GUSTO, TASTE, VIGOR,
   PEEL, FLAVOR, RELISH,
   STINGO, THRILL, APPETITE,

   PIQUANCY, VITALITY,
   VIVACITY, ANIMATION
   for life, with a .... LUSTY
zestful .... RACY, BRISK, SAPID,
   SPICY, ZIPPY, BREEZY,
   LIVELY, BRACING, PIQUANT
zeta .... ZED, ZEE, IZZARD
Zeus .... JUPITER
   attendant of .... NIKE
   beloved of .... IO, LEDA,
    EUROPA
   breastplate of .... (A)EGIS
   brother of .... HADES,
    POSEIDON
   changed her to stone
   .... NIOBE
   daughter of .... HEBE, IRENE,
    ATHENA
   disguise of .... SWAN
   Egyptian's .... AMMON
   epithet .... AMMON, SOTER
   father of .... CRONUS
   father of: var. .... KRONOS
   festival .... NEMEAN
   gift to Minos .... TALOS
   grandfather of .... URANUS
   messenger of .... IRIS
   monster killed by
   .... TYPHOEUS
   mother of .... RHEA
   mountain birthplace of
   .... IDA
   nurse of .... GOAT
   nymph loved by ..... CALLISTO
   oracle seat .... DODONA
   Phoenician princess loved by
   .... EUROPA
   punishment to mankind of
   .... PANDORA
   sacred tree of .... OAK
   shield of .... (A)EGIS
   sister of .... HERA, HESTIA,
    DEMETER
   son of .... ARES, ARCAS,
   ARGUS, MINOS, AEACUS,
   APOLLO, HERMES, AMPHION,
   PERSEUS, SARPEDON,
   TANTALUS, HEPHAESTUS
   surname of .... ALASTOR
   wife/lover of ...... HERA, JUNO,
   LEDA, LETO, MAIA, AEGLE,
   CERES, DANAE, DIONE, METIS,
   AEGINA, EUROPA, LATONA,
   SEMELE, THEMIS, ALCMENE,
   ANTIOPE, DEMETER, CALLISTO,
   EURYNOME
Zhivago's love .... LARA
Zhou _____ .... EN LAI
Zhukov, marshal .... GRIGORI
Zibeline .... (SABLE)FUR

Zibeon's son .... AIAH, ANAH
Ziegfeld show .... RIO RITA,
    SHOWGIRL
theatrical producer
    .... FLO(RENZ)
ziggurat .... PYRAMID
zigzag .... YAW, FORKED, JAGGED,
    CRANK(LE), CROOKED,
    STAGGER, SERRATED
course .... PLY, TACK
road .... SWITCHBACK
skiing race .... SLALOM
what it has plenty of
    .... ANGLES
zilch .... NIL, ZIP, NONE, ZERO,
    NAUGHT, NOTHING
courtwise .... LOVE
Zilpah's son .... GAD, ASHER
Zimbabwe .... STONE HOUSES
capital .... HARARE
capital, former ..... SALISBURY
city/town .... GWERU,
    HWANGA, KADOMA, KWEKWE,
    MUTARE, BINDURA,
    BULAWAYO, CHINHOYI
falls .... VICTORIA
former name of ..... RHODESIA
lake .... KARIBA
language .... BANTU, SHONA
monetary unit .... DOLLAR
mountain .... INYANGA(NI)
native .... BANTU, MBIRE
president .... MUGABE
river ...... SABI, LUNDI, MAZOE,
    SHASHE, SHANGAN, ZAMBEZI,
    MTILIKWE
tribe .... ILAS
Zimbalist, violinist .... EFREM
zinc .... SPELTER
alloy .... BIDRI, OROIDE,
    TOMBAK, TOMBAC(K)
aluminate .... GAHNITE
blende .... SPHALERITE
carbonate .... CALAMINE,
    SMITHSONITE
ingots .... SPELTER
oxide .... TUTTY
ore .... BLENDE
silicate .... CALAMINE
symbol .... ZN
zing .... PEP, VIM, DASH, ELAN,
    ZEST, FORCE, VIGOR, ENERGY,
    VITALITY
zingara/zingaro .... GYPSY
zingel .... PERCH
zinnia .... ASTER
Zion ...... JEW, HILL, HEAVEN
site of .... JERUSALEM
Zionism, founder of .... HERZL
Zionist leader .... WEIZMANN

revolutionary group .... IRGUN
zip .... PEP, VIM, ZEST, VIGOR,
    ENERGY, FASTEN
and _____ .... ZING
colloquial .... ZERO, ZILCH
slang .... HISS, SWISH, WHIZZ
up .... CLOSE
Zipangu .... JAPAN, CIPANGO
namer of .... (MARCO)POLO
zipper .... CLASP, TALON,
    (SLIDE)FASTENER
site .... FLY, BOOT, PLACKET,
    OVERSHOE
zippy ...... ZESTY, FRISKY, LIVELY,
    SNAPPY, ZESTFUL
zircon .... AZORITE, JACINTH
zither, instrument like ...... KOTO,
    LYRE, ROTA, VINA, CITHARA
of yore .... ASOR
zizany .... TARES, COCKLE
zizith .... TASSELS
zloty is money of _____
    .... POLAND
zoa, singular of .... ZOON
Zoan .... TANIS
zodiac .... CIRCLE, GIRDLE,
    CIRCUIT
sign, 1st .... ARIES
2nd .... TAURUS
3rd .... GEMINI
4th .... CANCER
5th .... LEO
6th .... VIRGO
7th .... LIBRA
8th .... SCORPIO
9th .... SAGITTARIUS
10th .... CAPRICORN
11th .... AQUARIUS
12th .... PISCES
starter .... ARIES
zodiacal archer ...... SAGITTARIUS
bull .... TAURUS
chart .... HOROSCOPE
crab .... CANCER
fish .... PISCES
goat .... CAPRICORN
lion .... LEO
ram .... ARIES
scale .... LIBRA
scorpion .... SCORPIO
twins .... GEMINI
virgin .... VIRGO
water carrier .... AQUARIUS
Zohar's son .... EPHRON
Zola, _____ .... EMILE
defender of .... DREYFUS
heroine .... NANA
novel .... NANA, VERITE,
    GERMINAL, THERESE RAQUIN
zombi(e) .... SNAKE, PYTHON,

    WEIRDO, COCKTAIL, WALKING
    DEAD
subject of .... CORPSE
zone .... AREA, BELT, WARD,
    CLIME, GIRDLE, REGION,
    SECTOR, CINCTURE, DISTRICT
designation .... FRIGID,
    TORRID, TEMPERATE
zoo .... VIVARIUM, MENAGERIE
animal ..... BEAR, LION, COATI,
    TIGER, MONKEY, ELEPHANT
attraction .... APE, GNU,
    MACAW, GORILLA, MACAQUE,
    SERPENT, WILDCAT
clean-up person .... POOPER-
    SCOOPER
equipment .... CAGE
floating .... ARK
sounds .... YIPS, ROARS, YELPS
zooid .... CORAL, HYDRANTH,
    POLYPITE
zoological region ...... NOTOGAEA
zoologist's concern
    .... ANIMAL(IA)
zoology branch on shells
    .... CONCHOLOGY
zoom .... FLY, SOAR
zoophyte .... ECTOPRACT
coral .... FUNGIA, ASTRANGIA
glass .... FARREA
horny .... CLIONA, GEODIA,
    SPONGILLA
sponge .... SCYPHA, GRANTIA
zoot _____ .... SUIT
Zorba the Greek composer
    .... THEODORAKIS
zoril(a) .... WEASEL, MARIPUT,
    POLECAT
animal like .... SKUNK
Zoroastrian .... YEMA, PARSI,
    PARSEE
bible .... AVESTA
demon .... DEVA
evil spirit .... AHRIMAN,
    ANGRA MAINYU
fire worshiper .... PARSI,
    CHEBER
god .... AHURA MAZDA
sacred writings
    .... (ZEND)AVESTA
supreme deity .... ORMAZD,
    ORMUZD
teaching .... HUMATA,
    HUKHATA, HUVARSHTA
Zoroastrianism, commentary
  on .... ZEND
zoster .... BELT, GIRDLE
zucetto .... SKULLCAP
zucchini .... SQUASH
Zug .... CANTON

Zuider _____ .... ZEE

zuisin .... WIDGEON

Zulu ...... BANTU, ISLAND, KAFFIR,
MATABELE

  band of warriors .... IMPI

  headman .... INDUNA

  language .... BANTU

  spear .... ASSAGAI, ASSEGAI

Zululand capital .... ESHOWE

Zuni .... PUEBLO

Zweig, novelist .... ARNOLD,
STEFAN

zwieback .... TOAST

zygodactyl bird .... PARROT

zygote .... OOSPERM, OOSPORE

zymase .... ENZYME

zymone .... GLUTEN

zythepsary .... BREWER

About the Author

Born in the Philippines, Edy Garcia Schaffer has studied at the Edison Technical School in Seattle and the American Institute of Banking in San Francisco, and has been a senior stenographer, secretary, liaison officer, and an executive administrator at trade firms and banking institutions in the Philippines, Guam, and California.

She migrated to the United States in 1969, following her marriage to Art Schaffer, her husband of twenty-six years. They have five children: Karl, Bobby, Lynn, Ruby, and Venus; and eleven grandchildren: Tanya, Liza, Jacquelyn, Eddie, Joel, Ricky, Eric, Robert, Jennifer Camille, Jade Benae, and Jon Benjamin.

Mrs. Schaffer is a member of the National Association of Female Executives (NAFE) and devotes her time to the pleasures of grannyhood and traveling with her husband all over America.